IN THE BEGINNING
WAS THE WORD, AND THE WORD WAS WITH GOD, AND THE WORD WAS GOD. THE SAME WAS IN THE BEGINNING WITH GOD. ALL THINGS WERE MADE BY HIM; AND WITHOUT HIM WAS NOT ANY THING MADE THAT WAS MADE. IN HIM WAS LIFE; AND THE LIFE WAS THE LIGHT OF MEN. AND THE LIGHT SHINETH IN DARKNESS; AND THE DARKNESS COMPREHENDED IT NOT.
SAINT JOHN 1:1-5
I0816641

To:
From:
Date:
Message:

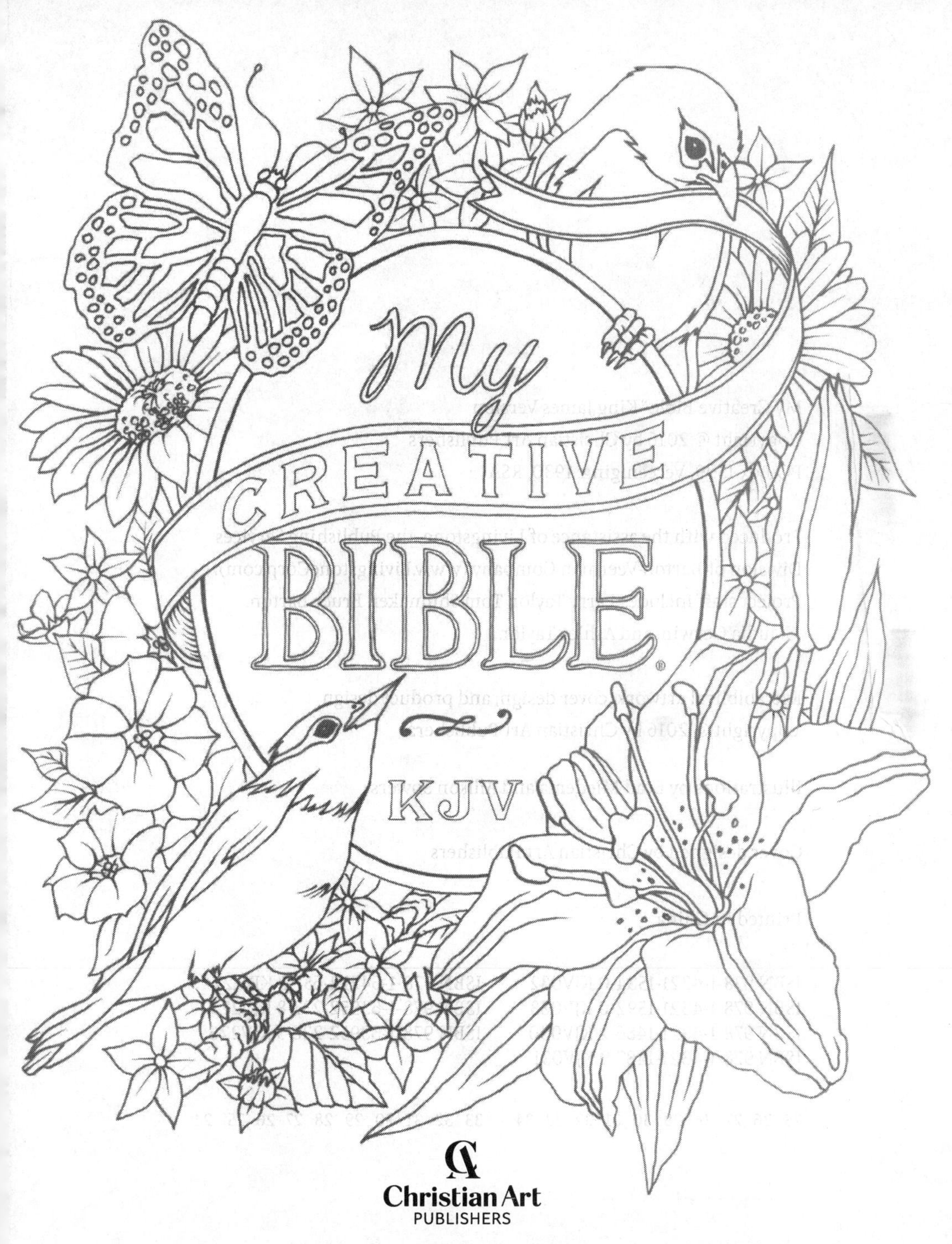
My
CREATIVE
BIBLE®
KJV
Christian Art
PUBLISHERS

PO Box 1599, Vereeniging, 1930, RSA

Produced with the assistance of Livingstone, the Publishing Services Division of Barton-Veerman Company (www.LivingstoneCorp.com). Project staff includes Larry Taylor, Tom Shumaker, Bruce Barton, Claudia Gerwin, and Ashley Taylor.

Illustrations by Brad Miedema and Allison Sowers

Cover designed by Christian Art Publishers

Printed in China

ISBN 978-1-4321-1534-0 KJV032
ISBN 978-1-4321-1592-0 KJV033
ISBN 978-1-4321-1486-2 KJV030
ISBN 978-1-4321-1487-9 KJV031
ISBN 978-1-64272-657-2 KJV124
ISBN 978-1-63952-237-8 KJV225
ISBN 978-1-63952-238-5 KJV226

25 26 27 28 29 30 31 32 33 34 – 33 32 31 30 29 28 27 26 25 24

THE NAMES AND CANONICAL ORDER

OF ALL THE

BOOKS OF THE OLD AND NEW TESTAMENTS

The Books of the Old Testament

Genesis ... 1
Exodus ... 67
Leviticus ... 122
Numbers ... 162
Deuteronomy ... 218
Joshua ... 264
Judges ... 296
Ruth ... 327
1 Samuel ... 332
2 Samuel ... 373
1 Kings ... 407
2 Kings ... 447
1 Chronicles ... 484
2 Chronicles ... 521
Ezra ... 565
Nehemiah ... 578
Esther ... 596
Job ... 606
Psalms ... 642
Proverbs ... 729
Ecclesiastes ... 759
The Song of Solomon ... 769
Isaiah ... 774
Jeremiah ... 835
Lamentations ... 903
Ezekiel ... 909
Daniel ... 972
Hosea ... 991
Joel ... 1000
Amos ... 1004
Obadiah ... 1012
Jonah ... 1014
Micah ... 1017
Nahum ... 1023
Habakkuk ... 1026
Zephaniah ... 1029
Haggai ... 1032
Zechariah ... 1034
Malachi ... 1045

The Books of the New Testament

Saint Matthew ... 1051
Saint Mark ... 1097
Saint Luke ... 1124
Saint John ... 1171
Acts ... 1205
Romans ... 1248
1 Corinthians ... 1265
2 Corinthians ... 1282
Galatians ... 1293
Ephesians ... 1300
Philippians ... 1307
Colossians ... 1312
1 Thessalonians ... 1316
2 Thessalonians ... 1320
1 Timothy ... 1322
2 Timothy ... 1327
Titus ... 1331
Philemon ... 1333
Hebrews ... 1334
James ... 1347
1 Peter ... 1352
2 Peter ... 1357
1 John ... 1360
2 John ... 1365
3 John ... 1366
Jude ... 1367
Revelation ... 1369

Index ... 1389

THE NAMES AND ALPHABETICAL ORDER

OF ALL THE

BOOKS OF THE OLD AND NEW TESTAMENTS

Acts 1205
Amos 1004
Chronicles, 1 484
Chronicles, 2 521
Colossians 1312
Corinthians, 1 1265
Corinthians, 2 1282
Daniel 972
Deuteronomy 218
Ecclesiastes 759
Ephesians 1300
Esther 596
Exodus 67
Ezekiel 909
Ezra 565
Galatians 1293
Genesis 1
Habakkuk 1026
Haggai 1032
Hebrews 1334
Hosea 991
Isaiah 774
James 1347
Jeremiah 835
Job 606
Joel 1000
John, Saint 1171
John, 1 1360
John, 2 1365
John, 3 1366
Jonah 1014
Joshua 264
Jude 1367
Judges 296
Kings, 1 407
Kings, 2 447
Lamentations 903
Leviticus 122
Luke, Saint 1124
Malachi 1045
Mark, Saint 1097
Matthew, Saint 1051
Micah 1017
Nahum 1023
Nehemiah 578
Numbers 162
Obadiah 1012
Peter, 1 1352
Peter, 2 1357
Philemon 1333
Philippians 1307
Proverbs 729
Psalms 642
Revelation 1369
Romans 1248
Ruth 327
Samuel, 1 332
Samuel, 2 373
The Song of Solomon 769
Thessalonians, 1 1316
Thessalonians, 2 1320
Timothy, 1 1322
Timothy, 2 1327
Titus 1331
Zechariah 1034
Zephaniah 1029

Old
Testament

Creation of Heaven and Earth

1 In the beginning God created the heaven and the earth.
2 And the earth was without form, and void; and darkness *was* upon the
face of the deep. And the Spirit of God moved upon the face of the waters.

Creation of the Light

3 And God said, Let there be light: and there was light.
4 And God saw the light, that *it was* good: and God divided the light from
the darkness.
5 And God called the light Day, and the darkness he called Night. And the
evening and the morning were the first day.

Creation of the Firmament

6 And God said, Let there be a firmament in the midst of the waters, and let
it divide the waters from the waters.
7 And God made the firmament, and divided the waters which *were* under
the firmament from the waters which *were* above the firmament: and it was so.
8 And God called the firmament Heaven. And the evening and the morning
were the second day.

The Earth Separated from the Waters

9 And God said, Let the waters under the heaven be gathered together unto
one place, and let the dry *land* appear: and it was so.
10 And God called the dry *land* Earth; and the gathering together of the
waters called he Seas: and God saw that *it was* good.
11 And God said, Let the earth bring forth grass, the herb yielding seed, *and*
the fruit tree yielding fruit after his kind, whose seed *is* in itself, upon the
earth: and it was so.
12 And the earth brought forth grass, *and* herb yielding seed after his kind,
and the tree yielding fruit, whose seed *was* in itself, after his kind: and God
saw that *it was* good.
13 And the evening and the morning were the third day.

Creation of the Sun, Moon, and Stars

14 And God said, Let there be lights in the firmament of the heaven to divide
the day from the night; and let them be for signs, and for seasons, and for days,
and years:
15 And let them be for lights in the firmament of the heaven to give light
upon the earth: and it was so.
16 And God made two great lights; the greater light to rule the day, and the
lesser light to rule the night: *he made* the stars also.
17 And God set them in the firmament of the heaven to give light upon the
earth,
18 And to rule over the day and over the night, and to divide the light from
the darkness: and God saw that *it was* good.
19 And the evening and the morning were the fourth day.

Creation of Fish, Fowl, Beasts, and Cattle

20 And God said, Let the waters bring forth abundantly the moving creature
that hath life, and fowl *that* may fly above the earth in the open firmament of
heaven.

21 And God created great whales, and every living creature that moveth,
which the waters brought forth abundantly, after their kind, and every winged
fowl after his kind: and God saw that *it was* good.
22 And God blessed them, saying, Be fruitful, and multiply, and fill the waters
in the seas, and let fowl multiply in the earth.
23 And the evening and the morning were the fifth day.
24 And God said, Let the earth bring forth the living creature after his kind,
cattle, and creeping thing, and beast of the earth after his kind: and it was so.
25 And God made the beast of the earth after his kind, and cattle after their
kind, and every thing that creepeth upon the earth after his kind: and God
saw that *it was* good.

Creation of Man in the Image of God

26 And God said, Let us make man in our image, after our likeness: and let
them have dominion over the fish of the sea, and over the fowl of the air, and
over the cattle, and over all the earth, and over every creeping thing that
creepeth upon the earth.
27 So God created man in his *own* image, in the image of God created he him;
male and female created he them.
28 And God blessed them, and God said unto them, Be fruitful, and multiply,
and replenish the earth, and subdue it: and have dominion over the fish of the
sea, and over the fowl of the air, and over every living thing that moveth upon
the earth.

Provision for Food

29 And God said, Behold, I have given you every herb bearing seed, which *is*
upon the face of all the earth, and every tree, in the which *is* the fruit of a tree
yielding seed; to you it shall be for meat.
30 And to every beast of the earth, and to every fowl of the air, and to every
thing that creepeth upon the earth, wherein *there is* life, *I have given* every
green herb for meat: and it was so.
31 And God saw every thing that he had made, and, behold, *it was* very good.
And the evening and the morning were the sixth day.

The First Sabbath

2 Thus the heavens and the earth were finished, and all the host of them.
2 And on the seventh day God ended his work which he had made; and
he rested on the seventh day from all his work which he had made.
3 And God blessed the seventh day, and sanctified it: because that in it he
had rested from all his work which God created and made.

The Manner of the Creation

4 These *are* the generations of the heavens and of the earth when they were
created, in the day that the LORD God made the earth and the heavens,
5 And every plant of the field before it was in the earth, and every herb of the
field before it grew: for the LORD God had not caused it to rain upon the earth,
and *there was* not a man to till the ground.
6 But there went up a mist from the earth, and watered the whole face of the
ground.
7 And the LORD God formed man *of* the dust of the ground, and breathed
into his nostrils the breath of life; and man became a living soul.

The Garden of Eden

8 And the LORD God planted a garden eastward in Eden; and there he put the
man whom he had formed.
9 And out of the ground made the LORD God to grow every tree that is pleasant
to the sight, and good for food; the tree of life also in the midst of the garden,
and the tree of knowledge of good and evil.

Creation
GENESIS 1·2
DAY 1
DAY NIGHT
DAY 2
DAY 3
DAY 4
DAY 5
DAY 6
DAY 7
REST
AND GOD BLESSED THE SEVENTH DAY, AND SANCTIFIED IT: BECAUSE THAT IN IT HE HAD RESTED FROM ALL HIS WORK WHICH GOD CREATED AND MADE.

10 And a river went out of Eden to water the garden; and from thence it was
parted, and became into four heads.
11 The name of the first *is* Pison: that *is* it which compasseth the whole land of
Havilah, where *there is* gold;
12 And the gold of that land *is* good: there *is* bdellium and the onyx stone.
13 And the name of the second river *is* Gihon: the same *is* it that compasseth
the whole land of Ethiopia.
14 And the name of the third river *is* Hiddekel: that *is* it which goeth toward
the east of Assyria. And the fourth river *is* Euphrates.
15 And the LORD God took the man, and put him into the garden of Eden to
dress it and to keep it.
16 And the LORD God commanded the man, saying, Of every tree of the garden
thou mayest freely eat:
17 But of the tree of the knowledge of good and evil, thou shalt not eat of it: for
in the day that thou eatest thereof thou shalt surely die.
18 And the LORD God said, *It is* not good that the man should be alone; I will
make him an help meet for him.
19 And out of the ground the LORD God formed every beast of the field, and
every fowl of the air; and brought *them* unto Adam to see what he would call
them: and whatsoever Adam called every living creature, that *was* the name
thereof.
20 And Adam gave names to all cattle, and to the fowl of the air, and to every
beast of the field; but for Adam there was not found an help meet for him.

God Creates Woman as a Helper for the Man

21 And the LORD God caused a deep sleep to fall upon Adam, and he slept: and
he took one of his ribs, and closed up the flesh instead thereof;
22 And the rib, which the LORD God had taken from man, made he a woman,
and brought her unto the man.
23 And Adam said, This *is* now bone of my bones, and flesh of my flesh: she shall
be called Woman, because she was taken out of Man.
24 Therefore shall a man leave his father and his mother, and shall cleave unto
his wife: and they shall be one flesh.
25 And they were both naked, the man and his wife, and were not ashamed.

The Serpent's Deception and Man's Shameful Fall

3 Now the serpent was more subtil than any beast of the field which the LORD
God had made. And he said unto the woman, Yea, hath God said, Ye shall not
eat of every tree of the garden?
2 And the woman said unto the serpent, We may eat of the fruit of the trees of
the garden:
3 But of the fruit of the tree which *is* in the midst of the garden, God hath said,
Ye shall not eat of it, neither shall ye touch it, lest ye die.
4 And the serpent said unto the woman, Ye shall not surely die:
5 For God doth know that in the day ye eat thereof, then your eyes shall be
opened, and ye shall be as gods, knowing good and evil.
6 And when the woman saw that the tree *was* good for food, and that it *was*
pleasant to the eyes, and a tree to be desired to make *one* wise, she took of the fruit
thereof, and did eat, and gave also unto her husband with her; and he did eat.
7 And the eyes of them both were opened, and they knew that they *were* naked;
and they sewed fig leaves together, and made themselves aprons.
8 And they heard the voice of the LORD God walking in the garden in the cool
of the day: and Adam and his wife hid themselves from the presence of the
LORD God amongst the trees of the garden.

God Questions Adam and Eve

9 And the LORD God called unto Adam, and said unto him, Where *art* thou?

10 And he said, I heard thy voice in the garden, and I was afraid, because I
was naked; and I hid myself.
11 And he said, Who told thee that thou *wast* naked? Hast thou eaten of the
tree, whereof I commanded thee that thou shouldest not eat?
12 And the man said, The woman whom thou gavest *to be* with me, she gave
me of the tree, and I did eat.
13 And the LORD God said unto the woman, What *is* this *that* thou hast done?
And the woman said, The serpent beguiled me, and I did eat.

The Serpent Is Cursed

14 And the LORD God said unto the serpent, Because thou hast done this, thou
art cursed above all cattle, and above every beast of the field; upon thy belly
shalt thou go, and dust shalt thou eat all the days of thy life:
15 And I will put enmity between thee and the woman, and between thy seed
and her seed; it shall bruise thy head, and thou shalt bruise his heel.

The Punishment God Promises for Mankind

16 Unto the woman he said, I will greatly multiply thy sorrow and thy con-
ception; in sorrow thou shalt bring forth children; and thy desire *shall be* to
thy husband, and he shall rule over thee.
17 And unto Adam he said, Because thou hast hearkened unto the voice of
thy wife, and hast eaten of the tree, of which I commanded thee, saying, Thou
shalt not eat of it: cursed *is* the ground for thy sake; in sorrow shalt thou eat
of it all the days of thy life;
18 Thorns also and thistles shall it bring forth to thee; and thou shalt eat the
herb of the field;
19 In the sweat of thy face shalt thou eat bread, till thou return unto the
ground; for out of it wast thou taken: for dust thou *art*, and unto dust shalt
thou return.
20 And Adam called his wife's name Eve; because she was the mother of all
living.
21 Unto Adam also and to his wife did the LORD God make coats of skins, and
clothed them.
22 And the LORD God said, Behold, the man is become as one of us, to know
good and evil: and now, lest he put forth his hand, and take also of the tree of
life, and eat, and live for ever:
23 Therefore the LORD God sent him forth from the garden of Eden, to till
the ground from whence he was taken.
24 So he drove out the man; and he placed at the east of the garden of Eden
Cherubims, and a flaming sword which turned every way, to keep the way of
the tree of life.

Cain and Abel

4 And Adam knew Eve his wife; and she conceived, and bare Cain, and said,
I have gotten a man from the LORD.
2 And she again bare his brother Abel. And Abel was a keeper of sheep, but
Cain was a tiller of the ground.
3 And in process of time it came to pass, that Cain brought of the fruit of the
ground an offering unto the LORD.
4 And Abel, he also brought of the firstlings of his flock and of the fat there-
of. And the LORD had respect unto Abel and to his offering:
5 But unto Cain and to his offering he had not respect. And Cain was very
wroth, and his countenance fell.
6 And the LORD said unto Cain, Why art thou wroth? and why is thy counte-
nance fallen?
7 If thou doest well, shalt thou not be accepted? and if thou doest not well,
sin lieth at the door. And unto thee *shall be* his desire, and thou shalt rule over
him.

Cain Murders Abel

8 And Cain talked with Abel his brother: and it came to pass, when they were in the field, that Cain rose up against Abel his brother, and slew him.

The Lord Places a Curse upon Cain

9 And the LORD said unto Cain, Where *is* Abel thy brother? And he said, I know not: *Am* I my brother's keeper?

10 And he said, What hast thou done? the voice of thy brother's blood crieth unto me from the ground.

11 And now *art* thou cursed from the earth, which hath opened her mouth to receive thy brother's blood from thy hand;

12 When thou tillest the ground, it shall not henceforth yield unto thee her strength; a fugitive and a vagabond shalt thou be in the earth.

13 And Cain said unto the LORD, My punishment *is* greater than I can bear.

14 Behold, thou hast driven me out this day from the face of the earth; and from thy face shall I be hid; and I shall be a fugitive and a vagabond in the earth; and it shall come to pass, *that* every one that findeth me shall slay me.

15 And the LORD said unto him, Therefore whosoever slayeth Cain, vengeance shall be taken on him sevenfold. And the LORD set a mark upon Cain, lest any finding him should kill him.

16 And Cain went out from the presence of the LORD, and dwelt in the land of Nod, on the east of Eden.

17 And Cain knew his wife; and she conceived, and bare Enoch: and he builded a city, and called the name of the city, after the name of his son, Enoch.

18 And unto Enoch was born Irad: and Irad begat Mehujael: and Mehujael begat Methusael: and Methusael begat Lamech.

Lamech and His Two Wives

19 And Lamech took unto him two wives: the name of the one *was* Adah, and the name of the other Zillah.

20 And Adah bare Jabal: he was the father of such as dwell in tents, and *of such as have* cattle.

21 And his brother's name *was* Jubal: he was the father of all such as handle the harp and organ.

22 And Zillah, she also bare Tubal-cain, an instructer of every artificer in brass and iron: and the sister of Tubal-cain *was* Naamah.

23 And Lamech said unto his wives, Adah and Zillah, Hear my voice; ye wives of Lamech, hearken unto my speech: for I have slain a man to my wounding, and a young man to my hurt.

24 If Cain shall be avenged sevenfold, truly Lamech seventy and sevenfold.

Births of Seth and Enos

25 And Adam knew his wife again; and she bare a son, and called his name Seth: For God, *said she*, hath appointed me another seed instead of Abel, whom Cain slew.

26 And to Seth, to him also there was born a son; and he called his name Enos: then began men to call upon the name of the LORD.

Genealogy of the Patriarchs

5 This *is* the book of the generations of Adam. In the day that God created man, in the likeness of God made he him;

2 Male and female created he them; and blessed them, and called their name Adam, in the day when they were created.

3 And Adam lived an hundred and thirty years, and begat *a son* in his own likeness, after his image; and called his name Seth:

4 And the days of Adam after he had begotten Seth were eight hundred years: and he begat sons and daughters:

5 And all the days that Adam lived were nine hundred and thirty years: and he
died.
6 And Seth lived an hundred and five years, and begat Enos:
7 And Seth lived after he begat Enos eight hundred and seven years, and begat
sons and daughters:
8 And all the days of Seth were nine hundred and twelve years: and he died.
9 And Enos lived ninety years, and begat Cainan:
10 And Enos lived after he begat Cainan eight hundred and fifteen years, and
begat sons and daughters:
11 And all the days of Enos were nine hundred and five years: and he died.
12 And Cainan lived seventy years, and begat Mahalaleel:
13 And Cainan lived after he begat Mahalaleel eight hundred and forty years,
and begat sons and daughters:
14 And all the days of Cainan were nine hundred and ten years: and he died.
15 And Mahalaleel lived sixty and five years, and begat Jared:
16 And Mahalaleel lived after he begat Jared eight hundred and thirty years,
and begat sons and daughters:
17 And all the days of Mahalaleel were eight hundred ninety and five years:
and he died.
18 And Jared lived an hundred sixty and two years, and he begat Enoch:
19 And Jared lived after he begat Enoch eight hundred years, and begat sons and
daughters:
20 And all the days of Jared were nine hundred sixty and two years: and he
died.
21 And Enoch lived sixty and five years, and begat Methuselah:
22 And Enoch walked with God after he begat Methuselah three hundred
years, and begat sons and daughters:
23 And all the days of Enoch were three hundred sixty and five years:
24 And Enoch walked with God: and he *was* not; for God took him.
25 And Methuselah lived an hundred eighty and seven years, and begat Lamech:
26 And Methuselah lived after he begat Lamech seven hundred eighty and
two years, and begat sons and daughters:
27 And all the days of Methuselah were nine hundred sixty and nine years:
and he died.
28 And Lamech lived an hundred eighty and two years, and begat a son:
29 And he called his name Noah, saying, This *same* shall comfort us concern-
ing our work and toil of our hands, because of the ground which the LORD
hath cursed.
30 And Lamech lived after he begat Noah five hundred ninety and five years,
and begat sons and daughters:
31 And all the days of Lamech were seven hundred seventy and seven years:
and he died.
32 And Noah was five hundred years old: and Noah begat Shem, Ham, and
Japheth.

The Wickedness of the World

6 And it came to pass, when men began to multiply on the face of the earth,
and daughters were born unto them,
2 That the sons of God saw the daughters of men that they *were* fair; and they
took them wives of all which they chose.
3 And the LORD said, My spirit shall not always strive with man, for that he
also *is* flesh: yet his days shall be an hundred and twenty years.
4 There were giants in the earth in those days; and also after that, when the
sons of God came in unto the daughters of men, and they bare *children* to
them, the same *became* mighty men which *were* of old, men of renown.

5 And God saw that the wickedness of man *was* great in the earth, and *that*
every imagination of the thoughts of his heart *was* only evil continually.
6 And it repented the LORD that he had made man on the earth, and it grieved
him at his heart.
7 And the LORD said, I will destroy man whom I have created from the face
of the earth; both man, and beast, and the creeping thing, and the fowls of the
air; for it repenteth me that I have made them.

Noah Finds Grace in God's Eyes

8 But Noah found grace in the eyes of the LORD.
9 These *are* the generations of Noah: Noah was a just man *and* perfect in his
generations, *and* Noah walked with God.
10 And Noah begat three sons, Shem, Ham, and Japheth.
11 The earth also was corrupt before God, and the earth was filled with violence.
12 And God looked upon the earth, and, behold, it was corrupt; for all flesh
had corrupted his way upon the earth.

Building the Ark

13 And God said unto Noah, The end of all flesh is come before me; for the
earth is filled with violence through them; and, behold, I will destroy them
with the earth.
14 Make thee an ark of gopher wood; rooms shalt thou make in the ark, and
shalt pitch it within and without with pitch.
15 And this *is the fashion* which thou shalt make it *of*: The length of the ark
shall be three hundred cubits, the breadth of it fifty cubits, and the height of
it thirty cubits.
16 A window shalt thou make to the ark, and in a cubit shalt thou finish it
above; and the door of the ark shalt thou set in the side thereof; *with* lower,
second, and third *stories* shalt thou make it.
17 And, behold, I, even I, do bring a flood of waters upon the earth, to destroy
all flesh, wherein *is* the breath of life, from under heaven; *and* every thing that
is in the earth shall die.
18 But with thee will I establish my covenant; and thou shalt come into the
ark, thou, and thy sons, and thy wife, and thy sons' wives with thee.
19 And of every living thing of all flesh, two of every *sort* shalt thou bring
into the ark, to keep *them* alive with thee; they shall be male and female.
20 Of fowls after their kind, and of cattle after their kind, of every creeping
thing of the earth after his kind, two of every *sort* shall come unto thee, to keep
them alive.
21 And take thou unto thee of all food that is eaten, and thou shalt gather *it*
to thee; and it shall be for food for thee, and for them.
22 Thus did Noah; according to all that God commanded him, so did he.

Noah, His Family, and the Creatures Enter the Ark

7 And the LORD said unto Noah, Come thou and all thy house into the ark;
for thee have I seen righteous before me in this generation.
2 Of every clean beast thou shalt take to thee by sevens, the male and his
female: and of beasts that *are* not clean by two, the male and his female.
3 Of fowls also of the air by sevens, the male and the female; to keep seed
alive upon the face of all the earth.
4 For yet seven days, and I will cause it to rain upon the earth forty days and
forty nights; and every living substance that I have made will I destroy from
off the face of the earth.
5 And Noah did according unto all that the LORD commanded him.
6 And Noah *was* six hundred years old when the flood of waters was upon
the earth.
7 And Noah went in, and his sons, and his wife, and his sons' wives with him,
into the ark, because of the waters of the flood.

8 Of clean beasts, and of beasts that *are* not clean, and of fowls, and of every
thing that creepeth upon the earth,
9 There went in two and two unto Noah into the ark, the male and the female,
as God had commanded Noah.
10 And it came to pass after seven days, that the waters of the flood were upon
the earth.
11 In the six hundredth year of Noah's life, in the second month, the seven-
teenth day of the month, the same day were all the fountains of the great deep
broken up, and the windows of heaven were opened.
12 And the rain was upon the earth forty days and forty nights.
13 In the selfsame day entered Noah, and Shem, and Ham, and Japheth, the
sons of Noah, and Noah's wife, and the three wives of his sons with them, into
the ark;
14 They, and every beast after his kind, and all the cattle after their kind, and
every creeping thing that creepeth upon the earth after his kind, and every
fowl after his kind, every bird of every sort.
15 And they went in unto Noah into the ark, two and two of all flesh, where-
in *is* the breath of life.
16 And they that went in, went in male and female of all flesh, as God had
commanded him: and the LORD shut him in.

The Flood

17 And the flood was forty days upon the earth; and the waters increased,
and bare up the ark, and it was lift up above the earth.
18 And the waters prevailed, and were increased greatly upon the earth; and
the ark went upon the face of the waters.
19 And the waters prevailed exceedingly upon the earth; and all the high
hills, that *were* under the whole heaven, were covered.
20 Fifteen cubits upward did the waters prevail; and the mountains were
covered.
21 And all flesh died that moved upon the earth, both of fowl, and of cattle,
and of beast, and of every creeping thing that creepeth upon the earth, and
every man:
22 All in whose nostrils *was* the breath of life, of all that *was* in the dry *land*,
died.
23 And every living substance was destroyed which was upon the face of the
ground, both man, and cattle, and the creeping things, and the fowl of the
heaven; and they were destroyed from the earth: and Noah only remained
alive, and they that *were* with him in the ark.
24 And the waters prevailed upon the earth an hundred and fifty days.

The Waters Subside

8 And God remembered Noah, and every living thing, and all the cattle that
was with him in the ark: and God made a wind to pass over the earth, and
the waters assuaged;
2 The fountains also of the deep and the windows of heaven were stopped,
and the rain from heaven was restrained;
3 And the waters returned from off the earth continually: and after the end
of the hundred and fifty days the waters were abated.

The Ark Rests on Ararat

4 And the ark rested in the seventh month, on the seventeenth day of the
month, upon the mountains of Ararat.
5 And the waters decreased continually until the tenth month: in the tenth
month, on the first *day* of the month, were the tops of the mountains seen.
6 And it came to pass at the end of forty days, that Noah opened the window
of the ark which he had made:

7 And he sent forth a raven, which went forth to and fro, until the waters
were dried up from off the earth.
8 Also he sent forth a dove from him, to see if the waters were abated from
off the face of the ground;
9 But the dove found no rest for the sole of her foot, and she returned unto
him into the ark, for the waters *were* on the face of the whole earth: then he
put forth his hand, and took her, and pulled her in unto him into the ark.
10 And he stayed yet other seven days; and again he sent forth the dove out
of the ark;
11 And the dove came in to him in the evening; and, lo, in her mouth *was* an
olive leaf pluckt off: so Noah knew that the waters were abated from off the
earth.
12 And he stayed yet other seven days; and sent forth the dove; which
returned not again unto him any more.
13 And it came to pass in the six hundredth and first year, in the first *month*,
the first *day* of the month, the waters were dried up from off the earth: and
Noah removed the covering of the ark, and looked, and, behold, the face of
the ground was dry.
14 And in the second month, on the seven and twentieth day of the month,
was the earth dried.

Noah Leaves the Ark

15 And God spake unto Noah, saying,
16 Go forth of the ark, thou, and thy wife, and thy sons, and thy sons' wives
with thee.
17 Bring forth with thee every living thing that *is* with thee, of all flesh, *both*
of fowl, and of cattle, and of every creeping thing that creepeth upon the earth;
that they may breed abundantly in the earth, and be fruitful, and multiply
upon the earth.
18 And Noah went forth, and his sons, and his wife, and his sons' wives with
him:
19 Every beast, every creeping thing, and every fowl, *and* whatsoever creepeth
upon the earth, after their kinds, went forth out of the ark.

Noah Builds an Altar and Offers Sacrifices

20 And Noah builded an altar unto the LORD; and took of every clean beast,
and of every clean fowl, and offered burnt offerings on the altar.
21 And the LORD smelled a sweet savour; and the LORD said in his heart, I will
not again curse the ground any more for man's sake; for the imagination of
man's heart *is* evil from his youth; neither will I again smite any more every
thing living, as I have done.
22 While the earth remaineth, seedtime and harvest, and cold and heat, and
summer and winter, and day and night shall not cease.

God Blesses Noah

9 And God blessed Noah and his sons, and said unto them, Be fruitful, and
multiply, and replenish the earth.
2 And the fear of you and the dread of you shall be upon every beast of the
earth, and upon every fowl of the air, upon all that moveth *upon* the earth,
and upon all the fishes of the sea; into your hand are they delivered.
3 Every moving thing that liveth shall be meat for you; even as the green herb
have I given you all things.
4 But flesh with the life thereof, *which is* the blood thereof, shall ye not eat.
5 And surely your blood of your lives will I require; at the hand of every beast
will I require it, and at the hand of man; at the hand of every man's brother
will I require the life of man.
6 Whoso sheddeth man's blood, by man shall his blood be shed: for in the
image of God made he man.

7 And you, be ye fruitful, and multiply; bring forth abundantly in the earth,
and multiply therein.
8 And God spake unto Noah, and to his sons with him, saying,
9 And I, behold, I establish my covenant with you, and with your seed after
you;
10 And with every living creature that *is* with you, of the fowl, of the cattle,
and of every beast of the earth with you; from all that go out of the ark, to every
beast of the earth.
11 And I will establish my covenant with you; neither shall all flesh be cut
off any more by the waters of a flood; neither shall there any more be a flood
to destroy the earth.
12 And God said, This *is* the token of the covenant which I make between me
and you and every living creature that *is* with you, for perpetual generations:
13 I do set my bow in the cloud, and it shall be for a token of a covenant
between me and the earth.
14 And it shall come to pass, when I bring a cloud over the earth, that the
bow shall be seen in the cloud:
15 And I will remember my covenant, which *is* between me and you and
every living creature of all flesh; and the waters shall no more become a flood
to destroy all flesh.
16 And the bow shall be in the cloud; and I will look upon it, that I may
remember the everlasting covenant between God and every living creature
of all flesh that *is* upon the earth.
17 And God said unto Noah, This *is* the token of the covenant, which I have
established between me and all flesh that *is* upon the earth.
18 And the sons of Noah, that went forth of the ark, were Shem, and Ham,
and Japheth: and Ham *is* the father of Canaan.
19 These *are* the three sons of Noah: and of them was the whole earth over-
spread.
20 And Noah began *to be* an husbandman, and he planted a vineyard:
21 And he drank of the wine, and was drunken; and he was uncovered with-
in his tent.
22 And Ham, the father of Canaan, saw the nakedness of his father, and told
his two brethren without.
23 And Shem and Japheth took a garment, and laid *it* upon both their shoul-
ders, and went backward, and covered the nakedness of their father; and their
faces *were* backward, and they saw not their father's nakedness.
24 And Noah awoke from his wine, and knew what his younger son had done
unto him.
25 And he said, Cursed *be* Canaan; a servant of servants shall he be unto his
brethren.
26 And he said, Blessed *be* the LORD God of Shem; and Canaan shall be his
servant.
27 God shall enlarge Japheth, and he shall dwell in the tents of Shem; and
Canaan shall be his servant.
28 And Noah lived after the flood three hundred and fifty years.
29 And all the days of Noah were nine hundred and fifty years: and he died.

The Generations of Noah

10 Now these *are* the generations of the sons of Noah, Shem, Ham, and
Japheth: and unto them were sons born after the flood.
2 The sons of Japheth; Gomer, and Magog, and Madai, and Javan, and Tubal,
and Meshech, and Tiras.
3 And the sons of Gomer; Ashkenaz, and Riphath, and Togarmah.
4 And the sons of Javan; Elishah, and Tarshish, Kittim, and Dodanim.

5 By these were the isles of the Gentiles divided in their lands; every one after
his tongue, after their families, in their nations.

The Sons of Ham

6 And the sons of Ham; Cush, and Mizraim, and Phut, and Canaan.
7 And the sons of Cush; Seba, and Havilah, and Sabtah, and Raamah, and
Sabtecha: and the sons of Raamah; Sheba, and Dedan.
8 And Cush begat Nimrod: he began to be a mighty one in the earth.
9 He was a mighty hunter before the LORD: wherefore it is said, Even as
Nimrod the mighty hunter before the LORD.
10 And the beginning of his kingdom was Babel, and Erech, and Accad, and
Calneh, in the land of Shinar.
11 Out of that land went forth Asshur, and builded Nineveh, and the city
Rehoboth, and Calah,
12 And Resen between Nineveh and Calah: the same *is* a great city.
13 And Mizraim begat Ludim, and Anamim, and Lehabim, and Naphtuhim,
14 And Pathrusim, and Casluhim, (out of whom came Philistim,) and
Caphtorim.
15 And Canaan begat Sidon his firstborn, and Heth,
16 And the Jebusite, and the Amorite, and the Girgasite,
17 And the Hivite, and the Arkite, and the Sinite,
18 And the Arvadite, and the Zemarite, and the Hamathite: and afterward
were the families of the Canaanites spread abroad.
19 And the border of the Canaanites was from Sidon, as thou comest to Gerar,
unto Gaza; as thou goest, unto Sodom, and Gomorrah, and Admah, and
Zeboim, even unto Lasha.
20 These *are* the sons of Ham, after their families, after their tongues, in their
countries, *and* in their nations.

The Sons of Shem

21 Unto Shem also, the father of all the children of Eber, the brother of
Japheth the elder, even to him were *children* born.
22 The children of Shem; Elam, and Asshur, and Arphaxad, and Lud, and
Aram.
23 And the children of Aram; Uz, and Hul, and Gether, and Mash.
24 And Arphaxad begat Salah; and Salah begat Eber.
25 And unto Eber were born two sons: the name of one *was* Peleg; for in his
days was the earth divided; and his brother's name *was* Joktan.
26 And Joktan begat Almodad, and Sheleph, and Hazar-maveth, and Jerah,
27 And Hadoram, and Uzal, and Diklah,
28 And Obal, and Abimael, and Sheba,
29 And Ophir, and Havilah, and Jobab: all these *were* the sons of Joktan.
30 And their dwelling was from Mesha, as thou goest unto Sephar a mount
of the east.
31 These *are* the sons of Shem, after their families, after their tongues, in
their lands, after their nations.
32 These *are* the families of the sons of Noah, after their generations, in their
nations: and by these were the nations divided in the earth after the flood.

One Language in the World

11 And the whole earth was of one language, and of one speech.
2 And it came to pass, as they journeyed from the east, that they found
a plain in the land of Shinar; and they dwelt there.
3 And they said one to another, Go to, let us make brick, and burn them
throughly. And they had brick for stone, and slime had they for morter.
4 And they said, Go to, let us build us a city and a tower, whose top *may reach*
unto heaven; and let us make us a name, lest we be scattered abroad upon the
face of the whole earth.

The Confusion of Languages

5 And the LORD came down to see the city and the tower, which the children
of men builded.
6 And the LORD said, Behold, the people *is* one, and they have all one language;
and this they begin to do: and now nothing will be restrained from them,
which they have imagined to do.
7 Go to, let us go down, and there confound their language, that they may
not understand one another's speech.
8 So the LORD scattered them abroad from thence upon the face of all the
earth: and they left off to build the city.
9 Therefore is the name of it called Babel; because the LORD did there con-
found the language of all the earth: and from thence did the LORD scatter them
abroad upon the face of all the earth.

The Generations of Shem, the Ancestor of Abram

10 These *are* the generations of Shem: Shem *was* an hundred years old, and
begat Arphaxad two years after the flood:
11 And Shem lived after he begat Arphaxad five hundred years, and begat
sons and daughters.
12 And Arphaxad lived five and thirty years, and begat Salah:
13 And Arphaxad lived after he begat Salah four hundred and three years,
and begat sons and daughters.
14 And Salah lived thirty years, and begat Eber:
15 And Salah lived after he begat Eber four hundred and three years, and
begat sons and daughters.
16 And Eber lived four and thirty years, and begat Peleg:
17 And Eber lived after he begat Peleg four hundred and thirty years, and
begat sons and daughters.
18 And Peleg lived thirty years, and begat Reu:
19 And Peleg lived after he begat Reu two hundred and nine years, and begat
sons and daughters.
20 And Reu lived two and thirty years, and begat Serug:
21 And Reu lived after he begat Serug two hundred and seven years, and begat
sons and daughters.
22 And Serug lived thirty years, and begat Nahor:
23 And Serug lived after he begat Nahor two hundred years, and begat sons
and daughters.
24 And Nahor lived nine and twenty years, and begat Terah:
25 And Nahor lived after he begat Terah an hundred and nineteen years, and
begat sons and daughters.
26 And Terah lived seventy years, and begat Abram, Nahor, and Haran.
27 Now these *are* the generations of Terah: Terah begat Abram, Nahor, and
Haran; and Haran begat Lot.
28 And Haran died before his father Terah in the land of his nativity, in Ur
of the Chaldees.
29 And Abram and Nahor took them wives: the name of Abram's wife *was*
Sarai; and the name of Nahor's wife, Milcah, the daughter of Haran, the father
of Milcah, and the father of Iscah.
30 But Sarai was barren; she *had* no child.
31 And Terah took Abram his son, and Lot the son of Haran his son's son,
and Sarai his daughter in law, his son Abram's wife; and they went forth with
them from Ur of the Chaldees, to go into the land of Canaan; and they came
unto Haran, and dwelt there.
32 And the days of Terah were two hundred and five years: and Terah died
in Haran.

God Calls Abram; Blesses Him with a Promise of Christ

12 Now the Lord had said unto Abram, Get thee out of thy country, and
from thy kindred, and from thy father's house, unto a land that I will
shew thee:
2 And I will make of thee a great nation, and I will bless thee, and make thy
name great; and thou shalt be a blessing:
3 And I will bless them that bless thee, and curse him that curseth thee: and
in thee shall all families of the earth be blessed.

Abram Departs with Lot from Haran

4 So Abram departed, as the Lord had spoken unto him; and Lot went with
him: and Abram *was* seventy and five years old when he departed out of Haran.
5 And Abram took Sarai his wife, and Lot his brother's son, and all their
substance that they had gathered, and the souls that they had gotten in Haran;
and they went forth to go into the land of Canaan; and into the land of Canaan
they came.

Abram Journeys through Canaan

6 And Abram passed through the land unto the place of Sichem, unto the
plain of Moreh. And the Canaanite *was* then in the land.
7 And the Lord appeared unto Abram, and said, Unto thy seed will I give
this land: and there builded he an altar unto the Lord, who appeared unto
him.
8 And he removed from thence unto a mountain on the east of Beth-el, and
pitched his tent, *having* Beth-el on the west, and Hai on the east: and there he
builded an altar unto the Lord, and called upon the name of the Lord.
9 And Abram journeyed, going on still toward the south.

Abram Is Driven by a Famine into Egypt

10 And there was a famine in the land: and Abram went down into Egypt to
sojourn there; for the famine *was* grievous in the land.
11 And it came to pass, when he was come near to enter into Egypt, that he
said unto Sarai his wife, Behold now, I know that thou *art* a fair woman to
look upon:
12 Therefore it shall come to pass, when the Egyptians shall see thee, that
they shall say, This *is* his wife: and they will kill me, but they will save thee alive.
13 Say, I pray thee, thou *art* my sister: that it may be well with me for thy sake;
and my soul shall live because of thee.

Sarai Is Taken by Pharaoh

14 And it came to pass, that, when Abram was come into Egypt, the Egyptians
beheld the woman that she *was* very fair.
15 The princes also of Pharaoh saw her, and commended her before Pharaoh:
and the woman was taken into Pharaoh's house.
16 And he entreated Abram well for her sake: and he had sheep, and oxen,
and he asses, and menservants, and maidservants, and she asses, and camels.
17 And the Lord plagued Pharaoh and his house with great plagues because
of Sarai Abram's wife.
18 And Pharaoh called Abram, and said, What *is* this *that* thou hast done
unto me? why didst thou not tell me that she *was* thy wife?
19 Why saidst thou, She *is* my sister? so I might have taken her to me to wife:
now therefore behold thy wife, take *her*, and go thy way.
20 And Pharaoh commanded *his* men concerning him: and they sent him
away, and his wife, and all that he had.

Abram and Lot Return out of Egypt and Agree to Separate

13 And Abram went up out of Egypt, he, and his wife, and all that he had,
and Lot with him, into the south.
2 And Abram *was* very rich in cattle, in silver, and in gold.

3 And he went on his journeys from the south even to Beth-el, unto the place
where his tent had been at the beginning, between Beth-el and Hai;
4 Unto the place of the altar, which he had made there at the first: and there
Abram called on the name of the LORD.
5 And Lot also, which went with Abram, had flocks, and herds, and tents.
6 And the land was not able to bear them, that they might dwell together: for
their substance was great, so that they could not dwell together.
7 And there was a strife between the herdmen of Abram's cattle and the herd-
men of Lot's cattle: and the Canaanite and the Perizzite dwelled then in the
land.
8 And Abram said unto Lot, Let there be no strife, I pray thee, between me
and thee, and between my herdmen and thy herdmen; for we *be* brethren.
9 *Is* not the whole land before thee? separate thyself, I pray thee, from me: if
thou wilt take the left hand, then I will go to the right; or if *thou depart* to the
right hand, then I will go to the left.

Lot Goes to Sodom

10 And Lot lifted up his eyes, and beheld all the plain of Jordan, that it *was*
well watered every where, before the LORD destroyed Sodom and Gomorrah,
even as the garden of the LORD, like the land of Egypt, as thou comest unto Zoar.
11 Then Lot chose him all the plain of Jordan; and Lot journeyed east: and
they separated themselves the one from the other.
12 Abram dwelled in the land of Canaan, and Lot dwelled in the cities of the
plain, and pitched *his* tent toward Sodom.
13 But the men of Sodom *were* wicked and sinners before the LORD exceedingly.

God Renews the Promise to Abram

14 And the LORD said unto Abram, after that Lot was separated from him, Lift
up now thine eyes, and look from the place where thou art northward, and
southward, and eastward, and westward:
15 For all the land which thou seest, to thee will I give it, and to thy seed for
ever.
16 And I will make thy seed as the dust of the earth: so that if a man can num-
ber the dust of the earth, *then* shall thy seed also be numbered.
17 Arise, walk through the land in the length of it and in the breadth of it; for
I will give it unto thee.
18 Then Abram removed *his* tent, and came and dwelt in the plain of Mamre,
which *is* in Hebron, and built there an altar unto the LORD.

The Battle of Four Kings against Five

14 And it came to pass in the days of Amraphel king of Shinar, Arioch king
of Ellasar, Chedorlaomer king of Elam, and Tidal king of nations;
2 *That these* made war with Bera king of Sodom, and with Birsha king of
Gomorrah, Shinab king of Admah, and Shemeber king of Zeboiim, and the
king of Bela, which is Zoar.
3 All these were joined together in the vale of Siddim, which is the salt sea.
4 Twelve years they served Chedorlaomer, and in the thirteenth year they
rebelled.
5 And in the fourteenth year came Chedorlaomer, and the kings that *were*
with him, and smote the Rephaims in Ashteroth Karnaim, and the Zuzims in
Ham, and the Emims in Shaveh Kiriathaim,
6 And the Horites in their mount Seir, unto El-paran, which *is* by the wilderness.
7 And they returned, and came to En-mishpat, which *is* Kadesh, and smote
all the country of the Amalekites, and also the Amorites, that dwelt in Hazezon-
tamar.
8 And there went out the king of Sodom, and the king of Gomorrah, and the
king of Admah, and the king of Zeboiim, and the king of Bela (the same *is* Zoar;)
and they joined battle with them in the vale of Siddim;

9 With Chedorlaomer the king of Elam, and with Tidal king of nations, and
Amraphel king of Shinar, and Arioch king of Ellasar; four kings with five.
10 And the vale of Siddim *was full of* slime-pits; and the kings of Sodom and
Gomorrah fled, and fell there; and they that remained fled to the mountain.
11 And they took all the goods of Sodom and Gomorrah, and all their victuals,
and went their way.
12 And they took Lot, Abram's brother's son, who dwelt in Sodom, and his
goods, and departed.
13 And there came one that had escaped, and told Abram the Hebrew; for
he dwelt in the plain of Mamre the Amorite, brother of Eshcol, and brother
of Aner: and these *were* confederate with Abram.
14 And when Abram heard that his brother was taken captive, he armed his
trained *servants*, born in his own house, three hundred and eighteen, and
pursued *them* unto Dan.
15 And he divided himself against them, he and his servants, by night, and
smote them, and pursued them unto Hobah, which *is* on the left hand of
Damascus.
16 And he brought back all the goods, and also brought again his brother
Lot, and his goods, and the women also, and the people.
17 And the king of Sodom went out to meet him after his return from the
slaughter of Chedorlaomer, and of the kings that *were* with him, at the valley
of Shaveh, which *is* the king's dale.
18 And Melchizedek king of Salem brought forth bread and wine: and he
was the priest of the most high God.
19 And he blessed him, and said, Blessed *be* Abram of the most high God,
possessor of heaven and earth:
20 And blessed be the most high God, which hath delivered thine enemies
into thy hand. And he gave him tithes of all.
21 And the king of Sodom said unto Abram, Give me the persons, and take
the goods to thyself.
22 And Abram said to the king of Sodom, I have lift up mine hand unto the
LORD, the most high God, the possessor of heaven and earth,
23 That I will not *take* from a thread even to a shoelatchet, and that I will not
take any thing that *is* thine, lest thou shouldest say, I have made Abram rich:
24 Save only that which the young men have eaten, and the portion of the
men which went with me, Aner, Eshcol, and Mamre; let them take their portion.

God Encourages Abram

15 After these things the word of the LORD came unto Abram in a vision,
saying, Fear not, Abram: I *am* thy shield, *and* thy exceeding great
reward.

Abram Complains for Lack of an Heir

2 And Abram said, Lord GOD, what wilt thou give me, seeing I go childless,
and the steward of my house *is* this Eliezer of Damascus?
3 And Abram said, Behold, to me thou hast given no seed: and, lo, one born
in my house is mine heir.
4 And, behold, the word of the LORD *came* unto him, saying, This shall not
be thine heir; but he that shall come forth out of thine own bowels shall be
thine heir.
5 And he brought him forth abroad, and said, Look now toward heaven, and
tell the stars, if thou be able to number them: and he said unto him, So shall
thy seed be.
6 And he believed in the LORD; and he counted it to him for righteousness.

Canaan Promised Again

7 And he said unto him, I *am* the LORD that brought thee out of Ur of the
Chaldees, to give thee this land to inherit it.

8 And he said, Lord GOD, whereby shall I know that I shall inherit it?

9 And he said unto him, Take me an heifer of three years old, and a she goat of three years old, and a ram of three years old, and a turtledove, and a young pigeon.

10 And he took unto him all these, and divided them in the midst, and laid each piece one against another: but the birds divided he not.

11 And when the fowls came down upon the carcases, Abram drove them away.

12 And when the sun was going down, a deep sleep fell upon Abram; and, lo, an horror of great darkness fell upon him.

13 And he said unto Abram, Know of a surety that thy seed shall be a stranger in a land *that is* not theirs, and shall serve them; and they shall afflict them four hundred years;

14 And also that nation, whom they shall serve, will I judge: and afterward shall they come out with great substance.

15 And thou shalt go to thy fathers in peace; thou shalt be buried in a good old age.

16 But in the fourth generation they shall come hither again: for the iniquity of the Amorites *is* not yet full.

17 And it came to pass, that, when the sun went down, and it was dark, behold a smoking furnace, and a burning lamp that passed between those pieces.

18 In the same day the LORD made a covenant with Abram, saying, Unto thy seed have I given this land, from the river of Egypt unto the great river, the river Euphrates:

19 The Kenites, and the Kenizzites, and the Kadmonites,

20 And the Hittites, and the Perizzites, and the Rephaims,

21 And the Amorites, and the Canaanites, and the Girgashites, and the Jebusites.

Sarai, Being Barren, Gives Hagar to Abram

16 Now Sarai Abram's wife bare him no children: and she had an handmaid, an Egyptian, whose name *was* Hagar.

2 And Sarai said unto Abram, Behold now, the LORD hath restrained me from bearing: I pray thee, go in unto my maid; it may be that I may obtain children by her. And Abram hearkened to the voice of Sarai.

3 And Sarai Abram's wife took Hagar her maid the Egyptian, after Abram had dwelt ten years in the land of Canaan, and gave her to her husband Abram to be his wife.

Hagar Runs Away

4 And he went in unto Hagar, and she conceived: and when she saw that she had conceived, her mistress was despised in her eyes.

5 And Sarai said unto Abram, My wrong *be* upon thee: I have given my maid into thy bosom; and when she saw that she had conceived, I was despised in her eyes: the LORD judge between me and thee.

6 But Abram said unto Sarai, Behold, thy maid *is* in thy hand; do to her as it pleaseth thee. And when Sarai dealt hardly with her, she fled from her face.

An Angel Sends Hagar Back, Telling Her She Will Bear a Child

7 And the angel of the LORD found her by a fountain of water in the wilderness, by the fountain in the way to Shur.

8 And he said, Hagar, Sarai's maid, whence camest thou? and whither wilt thou go? And she said, I flee from the face of my mistress Sarai.

9 And the angel of the LORD said unto her, Return to thy mistress, and submit thyself under her hands.

10 And the angel of the LORD said unto her, I will multiply thy seed exceedingly, that it shall not be numbered for multitude.

11 And the angel of the LORD said unto her, Behold, thou *art* with child, and shalt bear a son, and shalt call his name Ishmael; because the LORD hath heard thy affliction.

12 And he will be a wild man; his hand *will be* against every man, and every
man's hand against him; and he shall dwell in the presence of all his brethren.
13 And she called the name of the LORD that spake unto her, Thou God seest
me: for she said, Have I also here looked after him that seeth me?
14 Wherefore the well was called Beer-lahai-roi; behold, *it is* between Kadesh
and Bered.

Hagar Bears a Son Who Is Named Ishmael

15 And Hagar bare Abram a son: and Abram called his son's name, which
Hagar bare, Ishmael.
16 And Abram *was* fourscore and six years old, when Hagar bare Ishmael to
Abram.

God Renews the Covenant with Abram

17 And when Abram was ninety years old and nine, the LORD appeared
to Abram, and said unto him, I *am* the Almighty God; walk before me,
and be thou perfect.
2 And I will make my covenant between me and thee, and will multiply thee
exceedingly.
3 And Abram fell on his face: and God talked with him, saying,
4 As for me, behold, my covenant *is* with thee, and thou shalt be a father of
many nations.
5 Neither shall thy name any more be called Abram, but thy name shall be
Abraham; for a father of many nations have I made thee.
6 And I will make thee exceeding fruitful, and I will make nations of thee,
and kings shall come out of thee.
7 And I will establish my covenant between me and thee and thy seed after
thee in their generations for an everlasting covenant, to be a God unto thee,
and to thy seed after thee.
8 And I will give unto thee, and to thy seed after thee, the land wherein thou
art a stranger, all the land of Canaan, for an everlasting possession; and I will
be their God.
9 And God said unto Abraham, Thou shalt keep my covenant therefore, thou,
and thy seed after thee in their generations.
10 This *is* my covenant, which ye shall keep, between me and you and thy
seed after thee; Every man child among you shall be circumcised.
11 And ye shall circumcise the flesh of your foreskin; and it shall be a token
of the covenant betwixt me and you.
12 And he that is eight days old shall be circumcised among you, every man
child in your generations, he that is born in the house, or bought with money
of any stranger, which *is* not of thy seed.
13 He that is born in thy house, and he that is bought with thy money, must
needs be circumcised: and my covenant shall be in your flesh for an everlast-
ing covenant.
14 And the uncircumcised man child whose flesh of his foreskin is not circum-
cised, that soul shall be cut off from his people; he hath broken my covenant.

Sarai's Name Is Changed, and She Is Blessed

15 And God said unto Abraham, As for Sarai thy wife, thou shalt not call her
name Sarai, but Sarah *shall* her name *be*.
16 And I will bless her, and give thee a son also of her: yea, I will bless her, and
she shall be *a mother* of nations; kings of people shall be of her.
17 Then Abraham fell upon his face, and laughed, and said in his heart, Shall
a child be born unto him that is an hundred years old? and shall Sarah, that
is ninety years old, bear?
18 And Abraham said unto God, O that Ishmael might live before thee!

19 And God said, Sarah thy wife shall bear thee a son indeed; and thou shalt
call his name Isaac: and I will establish my covenant with him for an everlast-
ing covenant, *and* with his seed after him.
20 And as for Ishmael, I have heard thee: Behold, I have blessed him, and will
make him fruitful, and will multiply him exceedingly; twelve princes shall he
beget, and I will make him a great nation.
21 But my covenant will I establish with Isaac, which Sarah shall bear unto
thee at this set time in the next year.
22 And he left off talking with him, and God went up from Abraham.

Abraham and Ishmael Are Circumcised

23 And Abraham took Ishmael his son, and all that were born in his house,
and all that were bought with his money, every male among the men of
Abraham's house; and circumcised the flesh of their foreskin in the selfsame
day, as God had said unto him.
24 And Abraham *was* ninety years old and nine, when he was circumcised
in the flesh of his foreskin.
25 And Ishmael his son *was* thirteen years old, when he was circumcised in
the flesh of his foreskin.
26 In the selfsame day was Abraham circumcised, and Ishmael his son.
27 And all the men of his house, born in the house, and bought with money
of the stranger, were circumcised with him.

The Lord Appears to Abraham

18 And the LORD appeared unto him in the plains of Mamre: and he sat
in the tent door in the heat of the day;
2 And he lift up his eyes and looked, and, lo, three men stood by him: and
when he saw *them*, he ran to meet them from the tent door, and bowed him-
self toward the ground,
3 And said, My Lord, if now I have found favour in thy sight, pass not away,
I pray thee, from thy servant:
4 Let a little water, I pray you, be fetched, and wash your feet, and rest your-
selves under the tree:
5 And I will fetch a morsel of bread, and comfort ye your hearts; after that
ye shall pass on: for therefore are ye come to your servant. And they said, So
do, as thou hast said.
6 And Abraham hastened into the tent unto Sarah, and said, Make ready
quickly three measures of fine meal, knead *it*, and make cakes upon the hearth.
7 And Abraham ran unto the herd, and fetcht a calf tender and good, and
gave *it* unto a young man; and he hasted to dress it.
8 And he took butter, and milk, and the calf which he had dressed, and set *it*
before them; and he stood by them under the tree, and they did eat.

Sarah Is Reproved for Laughing at the Strange Promise

9 And they said unto him, Where *is* Sarah thy wife? And he said, Behold, in
the tent.
10 And he said, I will certainly return unto thee according to the time of life;
and, lo, Sarah thy wife shall have a son. And Sarah heard *it* in the tent door,
which *was* behind him.
11 Now Abraham and Sarah *were* old *and* well stricken in age; *and* it ceased
to be with Sarah after the manner of women.
12 Therefore Sarah laughed within herself, saying, After I am waxed old shall
I have pleasure, my lord being old also?
13 And the LORD said unto Abraham, Wherefore did Sarah laugh, saying,
Shall I of a surety bear a child, which am old?
14 Is any thing too hard for the LORD? At the time appointed I will return
unto thee, according to the time of life, and Sarah shall have a son.

15 Then Sarah denied, saying, I laughed not; for she was afraid. And he said,
Nay; but thou didst laugh.
16 And the men rose up from thence, and looked toward Sodom: and
Abraham went with them to bring them on the way.
17 And the LORD said, Shall I hide from Abraham that thing which I do;
18 Seeing that Abraham shall surely become a great and mighty nation, and
all the nations of the earth shall be blessed in him?
19 For I know him, that he will command his children and his household
after him, and they shall keep the way of the LORD, to do justice and judgment;
that the LORD may bring upon Abraham that which he hath spoken of him.
20 And the LORD said, Because the cry of Sodom and Gomorrah is great, and
because their sin is very grievous;
21 I will go down now, and see whether they have done altogether according
to the cry of it, which is come unto me; and if not, I will know.
22 And the men turned their faces from thence, and went toward Sodom:
but Abraham stood yet before the LORD.

Abraham Intercedes for the People of Sodom

23 And Abraham drew near, and said, Wilt thou also destroy the righteous
with the wicked?
24 Peradventure there be fifty righteous within the city: wilt thou also destroy
and not spare the place for the fifty righteous that *are* therein?
25 That be far from thee to do after this manner, to slay the righteous with
the wicked: and that the righteous should be as the wicked, that be far from
thee: Shall not the Judge of all the earth do right?
26 And the LORD said, If I find in Sodom fifty righteous within the city, then
I will spare all the place for their sakes.
27 And Abraham answered and said, Behold now, I have taken upon me to
speak unto the Lord, which *am but* dust and ashes:
28 Peradventure there shall lack five of the fifty righteous: wilt thou destroy
all the city for *lack of* five? And he said, If I find there forty and five, I will not
destroy *it*.
29 And he spake unto him yet again, and said, Peradventure there shall be
forty found there. And he said, I will not do *it* for forty's sake.
30 And he said *unto him*, Oh let not the Lord be angry, and I will speak:
Peradventure there shall thirty be found there. And he said, I will not do *it*, if
I find thirty there.
31 And he said, Behold now, I have taken upon me to speak unto the Lord:
Peradventure there shall be twenty found there. And he said, I will not destroy
it for twenty's sake.
32 And he said, Oh let not the Lord be angry, and I will speak yet but this once:
Peradventure ten shall be found there. And he said, I will not destroy *it* for
ten's sake.
33 And the LORD went his way, as soon as he had left communing with
Abraham: and Abraham returned unto his place.

Lot Entertains Two Angels

19 And there came two angels to Sodom at even; and Lot sat in the gate
of Sodom: and Lot seeing *them* rose up to meet them; and he bowed
himself with his face toward the ground;
2 And he said, Behold now, my lords, turn in, I pray you, into your servant's
house, and tarry all night, and wash your feet, and ye shall rise up early, and
go on your ways. And they said, Nay; but we will abide in the street all night.
3 And he pressed upon them greatly; and they turned in unto him, and
entered into his house; and he made them a feast, and did bake unleavened
bread, and they did eat.

The Vicious Sodomites Stricken with Blindness
4 But before they lay down, the men of the city, *even* the men of Sodom,
compassed the house round, both old and young, all the people from every
quarter:
5 And they called unto Lot, and said unto him, Where *are* the men which
came in to thee this night? bring them out unto us, that we may know them.
6 And Lot went out at the door unto them, and shut the door after him,
7 And said, I pray you, brethren, do not so wickedly.
8 Behold now, I have two daughters which have not known man; let me, I
pray you, bring them out unto you, and do ye to them as *is* good in your eyes:
only unto these men do nothing; for therefore came they under the shadow
of my roof.
9 And they said, Stand back. And they said *again*, This one *fellow* came in to
sojourn, and he will needs be a judge: now will we deal worse with thee, than
with them. And they pressed sore upon the man, *even* Lot, and came near to
break the door.
10 But the men put forth their hand, and pulled Lot into the house to them,
and shut to the door.
11 And they smote the men that *were* at the door of the house with blindness,
both small and great: so that they wearied themselves to find the door.

Lot Is Sent into the Mountains for Safety
12 And the men said unto Lot, Hast thou here any besides? son in law, and
thy sons, and thy daughters, and whatsoever thou hast in the city, bring *them*
out of this place:
13 For we will destroy this place, because the cry of them is waxen great
before the face of the LORD; and the LORD hath sent us to destroy it.
14 And Lot went out, and spake unto his sons in law, which married his
daughters, and said, Up, get you out of this place; for the LORD will destroy this
city. But he seemed as one that mocked unto his sons in law.
15 And when the morning arose, then the angels hastened Lot, saying, Arise,
take thy wife, and thy two daughters, which are here; lest thou be consumed
in the iniquity of the city.
16 And while he lingered, the men laid hold upon his hand, and upon the
hand of his wife, and upon the hand of his two daughters; the LORD being
merciful unto him: and they brought him forth, and set him without the city.
17 And it came to pass, when they had brought them forth abroad, that he
said, Escape for thy life; look not behind thee, neither stay thou in all the plain;
escape to the mountain, lest thou be consumed.
18 And Lot said unto them, Oh, not so, my Lord:
19 Behold now, thy servant hath found grace in thy sight, and thou hast mag-
nified thy mercy, which thou hast shewed unto me in saving my life; and I
cannot escape to the mountain, lest some evil take me, and I die:
20 Behold now, this city *is* near to flee unto, and it *is* a little one: Oh, let me
escape thither, (*is* it not a little one?) and my soul shall live.
21 And he said unto him, See, I have accepted thee concerning this thing also,
that I will not overthrow this city, for the which thou hast spoken.
22 Haste thee, escape thither; for I cannot do any thing till thou be come
thither. Therefore the name of the city was called Zoar.
23 The sun was risen upon the earth when Lot entered into Zoar.

Sodom and Gomorrah Are Destroyed
24 Then the LORD rained upon Sodom and upon Gomorrah brimstone and
fire from the LORD out of heaven;
25 And he overthrew those cities, and all the plain, and all the inhabitants of
the cities, and that which grew upon the ground.

Lot's Wife Becomes a Pillar of Salt

26 But his wife looked back from behind him, and she became a pillar of salt.
27 And Abraham gat up early in the morning to the place where he stood
before the LORD:
28 And he looked toward Sodom and Gomorrah, and toward all the land of
the plain, and beheld, and, lo, the smoke of the country went up as the smoke
of a furnace.
29 And it came to pass, when God destroyed the cities of the plain, that God
remembered Abraham, and sent Lot out of the midst of the overthrow, when
he overthrew the cities in the which Lot dwelt.

Beginnings of Moab and Ammon

30 And Lot went up out of Zoar, and dwelt in the mountain, and his two
daughters with him; for he feared to dwell in Zoar: and he dwelt in a cave, he
and his two daughters.
31 And the firstborn said unto the younger, Our father *is* old, and *there is*
not a man in the earth to come in unto us after the manner of all the earth:
32 Come, let us make our father drink wine, and we will lie with him, that
we may preserve seed of our father.
33 And they made their father drink wine that night: and the firstborn went
in, and lay with her father; and he perceived not when she lay down, nor when
she arose.
34 And it came to pass on the morrow, that the firstborn said unto the younger, Behold, I lay yesternight with my father: let us make him drink wine this
night also; and go thou in, *and* lie with him, that we may preserve seed of our
father.
35 And they made their father drink wine that night also: and the younger
arose, and lay with him; and he perceived not when she lay down, nor when
she arose.
36 Thus were both the daughters of Lot with child by their father.
37 And the firstborn bare a son, and called his name Moab: the same *is* the
father of the Moabites unto this day.
38 And the younger, she also bare a son, and called his name Ben-ammi: the
same *is* the father of the children of Ammon unto this day.

Abraham at Gerar

20 And Abraham journeyed from thence toward the south country, and
dwelled between Kadesh and Shur, and sojourned in Gerar.
2 And Abraham said of Sarah his wife, She *is* my sister: and Abimelech king
of Gerar sent, and took Sarah.

Abimelech Is Reproved by God for Taking Sarah

3 But God came to Abimelech in a dream by night, and said to him, Behold,
thou *art but* a dead man, for the woman which thou hast taken; for she *is* a
man's wife.
4 But Abimelech had not come near her: and he said, Lord, wilt thou slay also
a righteous nation?
5 Said he not unto me, She *is* my sister? and she, even she herself said, He *is*
my brother: in the integrity of my heart and innocency of my hands have I
done this.
6 And God said unto him in a dream, Yea, I know that thou didst this in the
integrity of thy heart; for I also withheld thee from sinning against me: therefore suffered I thee not to touch her.
7 Now therefore restore the man *his* wife; for he *is* a prophet, and he shall
pray for thee, and thou shalt live: and if thou restore *her* not, know thou that
thou shalt surely die, thou, and all that *are* thine.
8 Therefore Abimelech rose early in the morning, and called all his servants,
and told all these things in their ears: and the men were sore afraid.

9 Then Abimelech called Abraham, and said unto him, What hast thou done
unto us? and what have I offended thee, that thou hast brought on me and on
my kingdom a great sin? thou hast done deeds unto me that ought not to be
done.
10 And Abimelech said unto Abraham, What sawest thou, that thou hast
done this thing?
11 And Abraham said, Because I thought, Surely the fear of God *is* not in this
place; and they will slay me for my wife's sake.
12 And yet indeed *she is* my sister; she *is* the daughter of my father, but not
the daughter of my mother; and she became my wife.
13 And it came to pass, when God caused me to wander from my father's
house, that I said unto her, This *is* thy kindness which thou shalt shew unto
me; at every place whither we shall come, say of me, He *is* my brother.

Abimelech Restores Sarah

14 And Abimelech took sheep, and oxen, and menservants, and womenser-
vants, and gave *them* unto Abraham, and restored him Sarah his wife.
15 And Abimelech said, Behold, my land *is* before thee: dwell where it
pleaseth thee.
16 And unto Sarah he said, Behold, I have given thy brother a thousand *piec-
es* of silver: behold, he *is* to thee a covering of the eyes, unto all that *are* with
thee, and with all *other*: thus she was reproved.
17 So Abraham prayed unto God: and God healed Abimelech, and his wife,
and his maidservants; and they bare *children*.
18 For the LORD had fast closed up all the wombs of the house of Abimelech,
because of Sarah Abraham's wife.

Isaac Is Born

21 And the LORD visited Sarah as he had said, and the LORD did unto Sarah
as he had spoken.
2 For Sarah conceived, and bare Abraham a son in his old age, at the set time
of which God had spoken to him.
3 And Abraham called the name of his son that was born unto him, whom
Sarah bare to him, Isaac.
4 And Abraham circumcised his son Isaac being eight days old, as God had
commanded him.
5 And Abraham was an hundred years old, when his son Isaac was born unto
him.
6 And Sarah said, God hath made me to laugh, *so that* all that hear will laugh
with me.
7 And she said, Who would have said unto Abraham, that Sarah should have
given children suck? for I have born *him* a son in his old age.
8 And the child grew, and was weaned: and Abraham made a great feast the
same day that Isaac was weaned.

Hagar and Ishmael Are Expelled

9 And Sarah saw the son of Hagar the Egyptian, which she had born unto
Abraham, mocking.
10 Wherefore she said unto Abraham, Cast out this bondwoman and her
son: for the son of this bondwoman shall not be heir with my son, *even* with
Isaac.
11 And the thing was very grievous in Abraham's sight because of his son.
12 And God said unto Abraham, Let it not be grievous in thy sight because
of the lad, and because of thy bondwoman; in all that Sarah hath said unto
thee, hearken unto her voice; for in Isaac shall thy seed be called.
13 And also of the son of the bondwoman will I make a nation, because he
is thy seed.

14 And Abraham rose up early in the morning, and took bread, and a bottle
of water, and gave *it* unto Hagar, putting *it* on her shoulder, and the child, and
sent her away: and she departed, and wandered in the wilderness of Beer-sheba.
15 And the water was spent in the bottle, and she cast the child under one of
the shrubs.
16 And she went, and sat her down over against *him* a good way off, as it were
a bowshot: for she said, Let me not see the death of the child. And she sat over
against *him*, and lift up her voice, and wept.
17 And God heard the voice of the lad; and the angel of God called to Hagar
out of heaven, and said unto her, What aileth thee, Hagar? fear not; for God
hath heard the voice of the lad where he *is*.
18 Arise, lift up the lad, and hold him in thine hand; for I will make him a
great nation.
19 And God opened her eyes, and she saw a well of water; and she went, and
filled the bottle with water, and gave the lad drink.
20 And God was with the lad; and he grew, and dwelt in the wilderness, and
became an archer.
21 And he dwelt in the wilderness of Paran: and his mother took him a wife
out of the land of Egypt.

Abimelech and Abraham Make a Covenant

22 And it came to pass at that time, that Abimelech and Phichol the chief
captain of his host spake unto Abraham, saying, God *is* with thee in all that
thou doest:
23 Now therefore swear unto me here by God that thou wilt not deal falsely
with me, nor with my son, nor with my son's son: *but* according to the kindness
that I have done unto thee, thou shalt do unto me, and to the land wherein
thou hast sojourned.
24 And Abraham said, I will swear.
25 And Abraham reproved Abimelech because of a well of water, which
Abimelech's servants had violently taken away.
26 And Abimelech said, I wot not who hath done this thing: neither didst
thou tell me, neither yet heard I *of it*, but to day.
27 And Abraham took sheep and oxen, and gave them unto Abimelech; and
both of them made a covenant.
28 And Abraham set seven ewe lambs of the flock by themselves.
29 And Abimelech said unto Abraham, What *mean* these seven ewe lambs
which thou hast set by themselves?
30 And he said, For *these* seven ewe lambs shalt thou take of my hand, that
they may be a witness unto me, that I have digged this well.
31 Wherefore he called that place Beer-sheba; because there they sware both
of them.
32 Thus they made a covenant at Beer-sheba: then Abimelech rose up, and
Phichol the chief captain of his host, and they returned into the land of the
Philistines.
33 And *Abraham* planted a grove in Beer-sheba, and called there on the name
of the LORD, the everlasting God.
34 And Abraham sojourned in the Philistines' land many days.

God Asks Abraham to Sacrifice His Son

22 And it came to pass after these things, that God did tempt Abraham,
and said unto him, Abraham: and he said, Behold, *here* I *am*.
2 And he said, Take now thy son, thine only *son* Isaac, whom thou lovest, and
get thee into the land of Moriah; and offer him there for a burnt offering upon
one of the mountains which I will tell thee of.

Abraham Gives Proof of Faith and Obedience

3 And Abraham rose up early in the morning, and saddled his ass, and took
two of his young men with him, and Isaac his son, and clave the wood for the
burnt offering, and rose up, and went unto the place of which God had told
him.

4 Then on the third day Abraham lifted up his eyes, and saw the place afar off.

5 And Abraham said unto his young men, Abide ye here with the ass; and I
and the lad will go yonder and worship, and come again to you.

6 And Abraham took the wood of the burnt offering, and laid *it* upon Isaac
his son; and he took the fire in his hand, and a knife; and they went both of
them together.

7 And Isaac spake unto Abraham his father, and said, My father: and he said,
Here *am* I, my son. And he said, Behold the fire and the wood: but where *is*
the lamb for a burnt offering?

8 And Abraham said, My son, God will provide himself a lamb for a burnt
offering: so they went both of them together.

9 And they came to the place which God had told him of; and Abraham built
an altar there, and laid the wood in order, and bound Isaac his son, and laid
him on the altar upon the wood.

10 And Abraham stretched forth his hand, and took the knife to slay his son.

The Angel Stops Abraham

11 And the angel of the LORD called unto him out of heaven, and said,
Abraham, Abraham: and he said, Here *am* I.

12 And he said, Lay not thine hand upon the lad, neither do thou any thing
unto him: for now I know that thou fearest God, seeing thou hast not withheld
thy son, thine only *son* from me.

13 And Abraham lifted up his eyes, and looked, and behold behind *him* a
ram caught in a thicket by his horns: and Abraham went and took the ram,
and offered him up for a burnt offering in the stead of his son.

14 And Abraham called the name of that place Jehovah-jireh: as it is said *to*
this day, In the mount of the LORD it shall be seen.

Abraham Is Again Blessed

15 And the angel of the LORD called unto Abraham out of heaven the second
time,

16 And said, By myself have I sworn, saith the LORD, for because thou hast
done this thing, and hast not withheld thy son, thine only *son*:

17 That in blessing I will bless thee, and in multiplying I will multiply thy
seed as the stars of the heaven, and as the sand which *is* upon the sea shore;
and thy seed shall possess the gate of his enemies;

18 And in thy seed shall all the nations of the earth be blessed; because thou
hast obeyed my voice.

19 So Abraham returned unto his young men, and they rose up and went
together to Beer-sheba; and Abraham dwelt at Beer-sheba.

The Generations of Nahor to Rebekah

20 And it came to pass after these things, that it was told Abraham, saying,
Behold, Milcah, she hath also born children unto thy brother Nahor;

21 Huz his firstborn, and Buz his brother, and Kemuel the father of Aram,

22 And Chesed, and Hazo, and Pildash, and Jidlaph, and Bethuel.

23 And Bethuel begat Rebekah: these eight Milcah did bear to Nahor,
Abraham's brother.

24 And his concubine, whose name *was* Reumah, she bare also Tebah, and
Gaham, and Thahash, and Maachah.

The Age and Death of Sarah

23 And Sarah was an hundred and seven and twenty years old: *these were* the years of the life of Sarah.

2 And Sarah died in Kirjath-arba; the same *is* Hebron in the land of Canaan: and Abraham came to mourn for Sarah, and to weep for her.

The Purchase of Machpelah, Where Sarah Is Buried

3 And Abraham stood up from before his dead, and spake unto the sons of Heth, saying,

4 I *am* a stranger and a sojourner with you: give me a possession of a burying place with you, that I may bury my dead out of my sight.

5 And the children of Heth answered Abraham, saying unto him,

6 Hear us, my lord: thou *art* a mighty prince among us: in the choice of our sepulchres bury thy dead; none of us shall withhold from thee his sepulchre, but that thou mayest bury thy dead.

7 And Abraham stood up, and bowed himself to the people of the land, *even* to the children of Heth.

8 And he communed with them, saying, If it be your mind that I should bury my dead out of my sight; hear me, and intreat for me to Ephron the son of Zohar,

9 That he may give me the cave of Machpelah, which he hath, which *is* in the end of his field; for as much money as it is worth he shall give it me for a possession of a burying place amongst you.

10 And Ephron dwelt among the children of Heth: and Ephron the Hittite answered Abraham in the audience of the children of Heth, *even* of all that went in at the gate of his city, saying,

11 Nay, my lord, hear me: the field give I thee, and the cave that *is* therein, I give it thee; in the presence of the sons of my people give I it thee: bury thy dead.

12 And Abraham bowed down himself before the people of the land.

13 And he spake unto Ephron in the audience of the people of the land, saying, But if thou *wilt give it,* I pray thee, hear me: I will give thee money for the field; take *it* of me, and I will bury my dead there.

14 And Ephron answered Abraham, saying unto him,

15 My lord, hearken unto me: the land *is worth* four hundred shekels of silver; what *is* that betwixt me and thee? bury therefore thy dead.

16 And Abraham hearkened unto Ephron; and Abraham weighed to Ephron the silver, which he had named in the audience of the sons of Heth, four hundred shekels of silver, current *money* with the merchant.

17 And the field of Ephron, which *was* in Machpelah, which *was* before Mamre, the field, and the cave which *was* therein, and all the trees that *were* in the field, that *were* in all the borders round about, were made sure

18 Unto Abraham for a possession in the presence of the children of Heth, before all that went in at the gate of his city.

19 And after this, Abraham buried Sarah his wife in the cave of the field of Machpelah before Mamre: the same *is* Hebron in the land of Canaan.

20 And the field, and the cave that *is* therein, were made sure unto Abraham for a possession of a burying place by the sons of Heth.

Abraham's Servant Swears an Oath

24 And Abraham was old, *and* well stricken in age: and the LORD had blessed Abraham in all things.

2 And Abraham said unto his eldest servant of his house, that ruled over all that he had, Put, I pray thee, thy hand under my thigh:

3 And I will make thee swear by the LORD, the God of heaven, and the God of the earth, that thou shalt not take a wife unto my son of the daughters of the Canaanites, among whom I dwell:

4 But thou shalt go unto my country, and to my kindred, and take a wife unto
my son Isaac.
5 And the servant said unto him, Peradventure the woman will not be willing
to follow me unto this land: must I needs bring thy son again unto the land
from whence thou camest?
6 And Abraham said unto him, Beware thou that thou bring not my son
thither again.
7 The LORD God of heaven, which took me from my father's house, and from
the land of my kindred, and which spake unto me, and that sware unto me,
saying, Unto thy seed will I give this land; he shall send his angel before thee,
and thou shalt take a wife unto my son from thence.
8 And if the woman will not be willing to follow thee, then thou shalt be clear
from this my oath: only bring not my son thither again.
9 And the servant put his hand under the thigh of Abraham his master, and
sware to him concerning that matter.

The Servant's Journey

10 And the servant took ten camels of the camels of his master, and departed;
for all the goods of his master *were* in his hand: and he arose, and went to
Mesopotamia, unto the city of Nahor.
11 And he made his camels to kneel down without the city by a well of water
at the time of the evening, *even* the time that women go out to draw *water*.
12 And he said, O LORD God of my master Abraham, I pray thee, send me
good speed this day, and shew kindness unto my master Abraham.
13 Behold, I stand *here* by the well of water; and the daughters of the men of
the city come out to draw water:
14 And let it come to pass, that the damsel to whom I shall say, Let down thy
pitcher, I pray thee, that I may drink; and she shall say, Drink, and I will give
thy camels drink also: *let the same be* she *that* thou hast appointed for thy
servant Isaac; and thereby shall I know that thou hast shewed kindness unto
my master.
15 And it came to pass, before he had done speaking, that, behold, Rebekah
came out, who was born to Bethuel, son of Milcah, the wife of Nahor,
Abraham's brother, with her pitcher upon her shoulder.
16 And the damsel *was* very fair to look upon, a virgin, neither had any man
known her: and she went down to the well, and filled her pitcher, and came up.
17 And the servant ran to meet her, and said, Let me, I pray thee, drink a
little water of thy pitcher.
18 And she said, Drink, my lord: and she hasted, and let down her pitcher
upon her hand, and gave him drink.
19 And when she had done giving him drink, she said, I will draw *water* for
thy camels also, until they have done drinking.
20 And she hasted, and emptied her pitcher into the trough, and ran again
unto the well to draw *water*, and drew for all his camels.
21 And the man wondering at her held his peace, to wit whether the LORD
had made his journey prosperous or not.
22 And it came to pass, as the camels had done drinking, that the man took
a golden earring of half a shekel weight, and two bracelets for her hands of
ten *shekels* weight of gold;
23 And said, Whose daughter *art* thou? tell me, I pray thee: is there room *in*
thy father's house for us to lodge in?
24 And she said unto him, I *am* the daughter of Bethuel the son of Milcah,
which she bare unto Nahor.
25 She said moreover unto him, We have both straw and provender enough,
and room to lodge in.
26 And the man bowed down his head, and worshipped the LORD.

27 And he said, Blessed *be* the Lord God of my master Abraham, who hath
not left destitute my master of his mercy and his truth: I *being* in the way, the
Lord led me to the house of my master's brethren.
28 And the damsel ran, and told *them of* her mother's house these things.
29 And Rebekah had a brother, and his name *was* Laban: and Laban ran out
unto the man, unto the well.
30 And it came to pass, when he saw the earring and bracelets upon his sister's
hands, and when he heard the words of Rebekah his sister, saying, Thus spake
the man unto me; that he came unto the man; and, behold, he stood by the
camels at the well.
31 And he said, Come in, thou blessed of the Lord; wherefore standest thou
without? for I have prepared the house, and room for the camels.
32 And the man came into the house: and he ungirded his camels, and gave
straw and provender for the camels, and water to wash his feet, and the men's
feet that *were* with him.
33 And there was set *meat* before him to eat: but he said, I will not eat, until
I have told mine errand. And he said, Speak on.
34 And he said, I *am* Abraham's servant.
35 And the Lord hath blessed my master greatly; and he is become great: and
he hath given him flocks, and herds, and silver, and gold, and menservants,
and maidservants, and camels, and asses.
36 And Sarah my master's wife bare a son to my master when she was old:
and unto him hath he given all that he hath.
37 And my master made me swear, saying, Thou shalt not take a wife to my
son of the daughters of the Canaanites, in whose land I dwell:
38 But thou shalt go unto my father's house, and to my kindred, and take a
wife unto my son.
39 And I said unto my master, Peradventure the woman will not follow me.
40 And he said unto me, The Lord, before whom I walk, will send his angel
with thee, and prosper thy way; and thou shalt take a wife for my son of my
kindred, and of my father's house:
41 Then shalt thou be clear from *this* my oath, when thou comest to my
kindred; and if they give not thee *one*, thou shalt be clear from my oath.
42 And I came this day unto the well, and said, O Lord God of my master
Abraham, if now thou do prosper my way which I go:
43 Behold, I stand by the well of water; and it shall come to pass, that when
the virgin cometh forth to draw *water*, and I say to her, Give me, I pray thee,
a little water of thy pitcher to drink;
44 And she say to me, Both drink thou, and I will also draw for thy camels: *let*
the same *be* the woman whom the Lord hath appointed out for my master's son.
45 And before I had done speaking in mine heart, behold, Rebekah came
forth with her pitcher on her shoulder; and she went down unto the well, and
drew *water*: and I said unto her, Let me drink, I pray thee.
46 And she made haste, and let down her pitcher from her *shoulder*, and said,
Drink, and I will give thy camels drink also: so I drank, and she made the
camels drink also.
47 And I asked her, and said, Whose daughter *art* thou? And she said, The
daughter of Bethuel, Nahor's son, whom Milcah bare unto him: and I put the
earring upon her face, and the bracelets upon her hands.
48 And I bowed down my head, and worshipped the Lord, and blessed the
Lord God of my master Abraham, which had led me in the right way to take
my master's brother's daughter unto his son.
49 And now if ye will deal kindly and truly with my master, tell me: and if
not, tell me; that I may turn to the right hand, or to the left.
50 Then Laban and Bethuel answered and said, The thing proceedeth from
the Lord: we cannot speak unto thee bad or good.

51 Behold, Rebekah *is* before thee, take *her*, and go, and let her be thy master's
son's wife, as the LORD hath spoken.
52 And it came to pass, that, when Abraham's servant heard their words, he
worshipped the LORD, *bowing himself* to the earth.
53 And the servant brought forth jewels of silver, and jewels of gold, and
raiment, and gave *them* to Rebekah: he gave also to her brother and to her
mother precious things.
54 And they did eat and drink, he and the men that *were* with him, and tarried
all night; and they rose up in the morning, and he said, Send me away unto
my master.
55 And her brother and her mother said, Let the damsel abide with us *a few*
days, at the least ten; after that she shall go.
56 And he said unto them, Hinder me not, seeing the LORD hath prospered
my way; send me away that I may go to my master.
57 And they said, We will call the damsel, and enquire at her mouth.
58 And they called Rebekah, and said unto her, Wilt thou go with this man?
And she said, I will go.
59 And they sent away Rebekah their sister, and her nurse, and Abraham's
servant, and his men.
60 And they blessed Rebekah, and said unto her, Thou *art* our sister, be thou
the mother of thousands of millions, and let thy seed possess the gate of those
which hate them.
61 And Rebekah arose, and her damsels, and they rode upon the camels, and
followed the man: and the servant took Rebekah, and went his way.

The Meeting of Isaac and Rebekah

62 And Isaac came from the way of the well Lahai-roi; for he dwelt in the
south country.
63 And Isaac went out to meditate in the field at the eventide: and he lifted
up his eyes, and saw, and, behold, the camels *were* coming.
64 And Rebekah lifted up her eyes, and when she saw Isaac, she lighted off
the camel.
65 For she *had* said unto the servant, What man *is* this that walketh in the
field to meet us? And the servant *had* said, It *is* my master: therefore she took
a veil, and covered herself.
66 And the servant told Isaac all things that he had done.
67 And Isaac brought her into his mother Sarah's tent, and took Rebekah,
and she became his wife; and he loved her: and Isaac was comforted after his
mother's *death*.

The Sons of Abraham by Keturah

25 Then again Abraham took a wife, and her name *was* Keturah.
2 And she bare him Zimran, and Jokshan, and Medan, and Midian,
and Ishbak, and Shuah.
3 And Jokshan begat Sheba, and Dedan. And the sons of Dedan were
Asshurim, and Letushim, and Leummim.
4 And the sons of Midian; Ephah, and Epher, and Hanoch, and Abida, and
Eldaah. All these *were* the children of Keturah.
5 And Abraham gave all that he had unto Isaac.
6 But unto the sons of the concubines, which Abraham had, Abraham gave
gifts, and sent them away from Isaac his son, while he yet lived, eastward, unto
the east country.
7 And these *are* the days of the years of Abraham's life which he lived, an
hundred threescore and fifteen years.
8 Then Abraham gave up the ghost, and died in a good old age, an old man,
and full *of years*; and was gathered to his people.

9 And his sons Isaac and Ishmael buried him in the cave of Machpelah, in
the field of Ephron the son of Zohar the Hittite, which *is* before Mamre;
10 The field which Abraham purchased of the sons of Heth: there was
Abraham buried, and Sarah his wife.
11 And it came to pass after the death of Abraham, that God blessed his son
Isaac; and Isaac dwelt by the well Lahai-roi.
12 Now these *are* the generations of Ishmael, Abraham's son, whom Hagar
the Egyptian, Sarah's handmaid, bare unto Abraham:
13 And these *are* the names of the sons of Ishmael, by their names, according
to their generations: the firstborn of Ishmael, Nebajoth; and Kedar, and
Adbeel, and Mibsam,
14 And Mishma, and Dumah, and Massa,
15 Hadar, and Tema, Jetur, Naphish, and Kedemah:
16 These *are* the sons of Ishmael, and these *are* their names, by their towns,
and by their castles; twelve princes according to their nations.
17 And these *are* the years of the life of Ishmael, an hundred and thirty and
seven years: and he gave up the ghost and died; and was gathered unto his
people.
18 And they dwelt from Havilah unto Shur, that *is* before Egypt, as thou goest
toward Assyria: *and* he died in the presence of all his brethren.

Rebekah Gives Birth to Esau and Jacob

19 And these *are* the generations of Isaac, Abraham's son: Abraham begat
Isaac:
20 And Isaac was forty years old when he took Rebekah to wife, the daughter
of Bethuel the Syrian of Padan-aram, the sister to Laban the Syrian.
21 And Isaac intreated the LORD for his wife, because she *was* barren: and the
LORD was intreated of him, and Rebekah his wife conceived.
22 And the children struggled together within her; and she said, If *it be* so,
why *am* I thus? And she went to enquire of the LORD.
23 And the LORD said unto her, Two nations *are* in thy womb, and two man-
ner of people shall be separated from thy bowels; and *the one* people shall be
stronger than *the other* people; and the elder shall serve the younger.
24 And when her days to be delivered were fulfilled, behold, *there were* twins
in her womb.
25 And the first came out red, all over like an hairy garment; and they called
his name Esau.
26 And after that came his brother out, and his hand took hold on Esau's
heel; and his name was called Jacob: and Isaac *was* threescore years old when
she bare them.
27 And the boys grew: and Esau was a cunning hunter, a man of the field; and
Jacob *was* a plain man, dwelling in tents.
28 And Isaac loved Esau, because he did eat of *his* venison: but Rebekah loved
Jacob.

Esau Sells His Birthright

29 And Jacob sod pottage: and Esau came from the field, and he *was* faint:
30 And Esau said to Jacob, Feed me, I pray thee, with that same red *pottage*;
for I *am* faint: therefore was his name called Edom.
31 And Jacob said, Sell me this day thy birthright.
32 And Esau said, Behold, I *am* at the point to die: and what profit shall this
birthright do to me?
33 And Jacob said, Swear to me this day; and he sware unto him: and he sold
his birthright unto Jacob.
34 Then Jacob gave Esau bread and pottage of lentiles; and he did eat and
drink, and rose up, and went his way: thus Esau despised *his* birthright.

Isaac Goes to Gerar

26 And there was a famine in the land, beside the first famine that was in
the days of Abraham. And Isaac went unto Abimelech king of the
Philistines unto Gerar.
2 And the LORD appeared unto him, and said, Go not down into Egypt; dwell
in the land which I shall tell thee of:
3 Sojourn in this land, and I will be with thee, and will bless thee; for unto
thee, and unto thy seed, I will give all these countries, and I will perform the
oath which I sware unto Abraham thy father;
4 And I will make thy seed to multiply as the stars of heaven, and will give
unto thy seed all these countries; and in thy seed shall all the nations of the
earth be blessed;
5 Because that Abraham obeyed my voice, and kept my charge, my command-
ments, my statutes, and my laws.
6 And Isaac dwelt in Gerar:
7 And the men of the place asked *him* of his wife; and he said, She *is* my sister:
for he feared to say, *She is* my wife; lest, *said he*, the men of the place should
kill me for Rebekah; because she *was* fair to look upon.
8 And it came to pass, when he had been there a long time, that Abimelech
king of the Philistines looked out at a window, and saw, and, behold, Isaac *was*
sporting with Rebekah his wife.
9 And Abimelech called Isaac, and said, Behold, of a surety she *is* thy wife:
and how saidst thou, She *is* my sister? And Isaac said unto him, Because I said,
Lest I die for her.
10 And Abimelech said, What *is* this thou hast done unto us? one of the
people might lightly have lien with thy wife, and thou shouldest have brought
guiltiness upon us.
11 And Abimelech charged all *his* people, saying, He that toucheth this man
or his wife shall surely be put to death.

Isaac Grows Rich

12 Then Isaac sowed in that land, and received in the same year an hundred-
fold: and the LORD blessed him.
13 And the man waxed great, and went forward, and grew until he became
very great:
14 For he had possession of flocks, and possession of herds, and great store
of servants: and the Philistines envied him.
15 For all the wells which his father's servants had digged in the days of
Abraham his father, the Philistines had stopped them, and filled them with
earth.
16 And Abimelech said unto Isaac, Go from us; for thou art much mightier
than we.
17 And Isaac departed thence, and pitched his tent in the valley of Gerar, and
dwelt there.
18 And Isaac digged again the wells of water, which they had digged in the
days of Abraham his father; for the Philistines had stopped them after the
death of Abraham: and he called their names after the names by which his
father had called them.
19 And Isaac's servants digged in the valley, and found there a well of spring-
ing water.
20 And the herdmen of Gerar did strive with Isaac's herdmen, saying, The
water *is* ours: and he called the name of the well Esek; because they strove with
him.
21 And they digged another well, and strove for that also: and he called the
name of it Sitnah.

22 And he removed from thence, and digged another well; and for that they
strove not: and he called the name of it Rehoboth; and he said, For now the
LORD hath made room for us, and we shall be fruitful in the land.
23 And he went up from thence to Beer-sheba.
24 And the LORD appeared unto him the same night, and said, I *am* the God
of Abraham thy father: fear not, for I *am* with thee, and will bless thee, and
multiply thy seed for my servant Abraham's sake.
25 And he builded an altar there, and called upon the name of the LORD, and
pitched his tent there: and there Isaac's servants digged a well.
26 Then Abimelech went to him from Gerar, and Ahuzzath one of his friends,
and Phichol the chief captain of his army.
27 And Isaac said unto them, Wherefore come ye to me, seeing ye hate me,
and have sent me away from you?
28 And they said, We saw certainly that the LORD was with thee: and we said,
Let there be now an oath betwixt us, *even* betwixt us and thee, and let us make
a covenant with thee;
29 That thou wilt do us no hurt, as we have not touched thee, and as we have
done unto thee nothing but good, and have sent thee away in peace: thou *art*
now the blessed of the LORD.
30 And he made them a feast, and they did eat and drink.
31 And they rose up betimes in the morning, and sware one to another: and
Isaac sent them away, and they departed from him in peace.
32 And it came to pass the same day, that Isaac's servants came, and told him
concerning the well which they had digged, and said unto him, We have found
water.
33 And he called it Shebah: therefore the name of the city *is* Beer-sheba unto
this day.

Esau's Wives

34 And Esau was forty years old when he took to wife Judith the daughter of
Beeri the Hittite, and Bashemath the daughter of Elon the Hittite:
35 Which were a grief of mind unto Isaac and to Rebekah.

Isaac Sends Esau for Venison

27 And it came to pass, that when Isaac was old, and his eyes were dim,
so that he could not see, he called Esau his eldest son, and said unto
him, My son: and he said unto him, Behold, *here am* I.
2 And he said, Behold now, I am old, I know not the day of my death:
3 Now therefore take, I pray thee, thy weapons, thy quiver and thy bow, and
go out to the field, and take me *some* venison;
4 And make me savoury meat, such as I love, and bring *it* to me, that I may
eat; that my soul may bless thee before I die.
5 And Rebekah heard when Isaac spake to Esau his son. And Esau went to
the field to hunt *for* venison, *and* to bring *it*.

Rebekah and Jacob Conspire to Obtain Isaac's Blessing

6 And Rebekah spake unto Jacob her son, saying, Behold, I heard thy father
speak unto Esau thy brother, saying,
7 Bring me venison, and make me savoury meat, that I may eat, and bless
thee before the LORD before my death.
8 Now therefore, my son, obey my voice according to that which I command
thee.
9 Go now to the flock, and fetch me from thence two good kids of the goats;
and I will make them savoury meat for thy father, such as he loveth:
10 And thou shalt bring *it* to thy father, that he may eat, and that he may bless
thee before his death.
11 And Jacob said to Rebekah his mother, Behold, Esau my brother *is* a hairy
man, and I *am* a smooth man:

12 My father peradventure will feel me, and I shall seem to him as a deceiver;
and I shall bring a curse upon me, and not a blessing.

13 And his mother said unto him, Upon me *be* thy curse, my son: only obey
my voice, and go fetch me *them*.

14 And he went, and fetched, and brought *them* to his mother: and his moth-
er made savoury meat, such as his father loved.

15 And Rebekah took goodly raiment of her eldest son Esau, which *were* with
her in the house, and put them upon Jacob her younger son:

16 And she put the skins of the kids of the goats upon his hands, and upon
the smooth of his neck:

17 And she gave the savoury meat and the bread, which she had prepared,
into the hand of her son Jacob.

18 And he came unto his father, and said, My father: and he said, Here *am* I;
who *art* thou, my son?

19 And Jacob said unto his father, I *am* Esau thy firstborn; I have done accord-
ing as thou badest me: arise, I pray thee, sit and eat of my venison, that thy
soul may bless me.

20 And Isaac said unto his son, How *is it* that thou hast found *it* so quickly,
my son? And he said, Because the LORD thy God brought *it* to me.

21 And Isaac said unto Jacob, Come near, I pray thee, that I may feel thee, my
son, whether thou *be* my very son Esau or not.

22 And Jacob went near unto Isaac his father; and he felt him, and said, The
voice *is* Jacob's voice, but the hands *are* the hands of Esau.

23 And he discerned him not, because his hands were hairy, as his brother
Esau's hands: so he blessed him.

24 And he said, *Art* thou my very son Esau? And he said, I *am*.

25 And he said, Bring *it* near to me, and I will eat of my son's venison, that
my soul may bless thee. And he brought *it* near to him, and he did eat: and he
brought him wine, and he drank.

26 And his father Isaac said unto him, Come near now, and kiss me, my son.

27 And he came near, and kissed him: and he smelled the smell of his raiment,
and blessed him, and said, See, the smell of my son *is* as the smell of a field
which the LORD hath blessed:

28 Therefore God give thee of the dew of heaven, and the fatness of the earth,
and plenty of corn and wine:

29 Let people serve thee, and nations bow down to thee: be lord over thy
brethren, and let thy mother's sons bow down to thee: cursed *be* every one
that curseth thee, and blessed *be* he that blesseth thee.

Esau Brings Venison to His Father

30 And it came to pass, as soon as Isaac had made an end of blessing Jacob,
and Jacob was yet scarce gone out from the presence of Isaac his father, that
Esau his brother came in from his hunting.

31 And he also had made savoury meat, and brought it unto his father, and
said unto his father, Let my father arise, and eat of his son's venison, that thy
soul may bless me.

32 And Isaac his father said unto him, Who *art* thou? And he said, I *am* thy
son, thy firstborn Esau.

33 And Isaac trembled very exceedingly, and said, Who? where *is* he that
hath taken venison, and brought *it* me, and I have eaten of all before thou
camest, and have blessed him? yea, *and* he shall be blessed.

34 And when Esau heard the words of his father, he cried with a great and
exceeding bitter cry, and said unto his father, Bless me, *even* me also, O my
father.

35 And he said, Thy brother came with subtilty, and hath taken away thy
blessing.

36 And he said, Is not he rightly named Jacob? for he hath supplanted me
these two times: he took away my birthright; and, behold, now he hath taken
away my blessing. And he said, Hast thou not reserved a blessing for me?
37 And Isaac answered and said unto Esau, Behold, I have made him thy lord,
and all his brethren have I given to him for servants; and with corn and wine
have I sustained him: and what shall I do now unto thee, my son?
38 And Esau said unto his father, Hast thou but one blessing, my father? bless
me, *even* me also, O my father. And Esau lifted up his voice, and wept.
39 And Isaac his father answered and said unto him, Behold, thy dwelling
shall be the fatness of the earth, and of the dew of heaven from above;
40 And by thy sword shalt thou live, and shalt serve thy brother; and it shall
come to pass when thou shalt have the dominion, that thou shalt break his
yoke from off thy neck.

Esau Threatens to Kill Jacob

41 And Esau hated Jacob because of the blessing wherewith his father bless-
ed him: and Esau said in his heart, The days of mourning for my father are at
hand; then will I slay my brother Jacob.
42 And these words of Esau her elder son were told to Rebekah: and she sent
and called Jacob her younger son, and said unto him, Behold, thy brother Esau,
as touching thee, doth comfort himself, *purposing* to kill thee.
43 Now therefore, my son, obey my voice; and arise, flee thou to Laban my
brother to Haran;
44 And tarry with him a few days, until thy brother's fury turn away;
45 Until thy brother's anger turn away from thee, and he forget *that* which
thou hast done to him: then I will send, and fetch thee from thence: why should
I be deprived also of you both in one day?
46 And Rebekah said to Isaac, I am weary of my life because of the daughters
of Heth: if Jacob take a wife of the daughters of Heth, such as these *which are*
of the daughters of the land, what good shall my life do me?

Isaac Blesses Jacob and Sends Him to Padan-aram

28 And Isaac called Jacob, and blessed him, and charged him, and said
unto him, Thou shalt not take a wife of the daughters of Canaan.
2 Arise, go to Padan-aram, to the house of Bethuel thy mother's father; and
take thee a wife from thence of the daughters of Laban thy mother's brother.
3 And God Almighty bless thee, and make thee fruitful, and multiply thee,
that thou mayest be a multitude of people;
4 And give thee the blessing of Abraham, to thee, and to thy seed with thee;
that thou mayest inherit the land wherein thou art a stranger, which God gave
unto Abraham.
5 And Isaac sent away Jacob: and he went to Padan-aram unto Laban, son of
Bethuel the Syrian, the brother of Rebekah, Jacob's and Esau's mother.

Esau Marries Mahalath, Daughter of Ishmael

6 When Esau saw that Isaac had blessed Jacob, and sent him away to Padan-
aram, to take him a wife from thence; and that as he blessed him he gave him
a charge, saying, Thou shalt not take a wife of the daughters of Canaan;
7 And that Jacob obeyed his father and his mother, and was gone to Padan-aram;
8 And Esau seeing that the daughters of Canaan pleased not Isaac his father;
9 Then went Esau unto Ishmael, and took unto the wives which he had
Mahalath the daughter of Ishmael Abraham's son, the sister of Nebajoth, to
be his wife.

Jacob's Vision of a Ladder

10 And Jacob went out from Beer-sheba, and went toward Haran.
11 And he lighted upon a certain place, and tarried there all night, because
the sun was set; and he took of the stones of that place, and put *them for* his
pillows, and lay down in that place to sleep.

12 And he dreamed, and behold a ladder set up on the earth, and the top of
it reached to heaven: and behold the angels of God ascending and descending
on it.
13 And, behold, the LORD stood above it, and said, I *am* the LORD God of
Abraham thy father, and the God of Isaac: the land whereon thou liest, to thee
will I give it, and to thy seed;
14 And thy seed shall be as the dust of the earth, and thou shalt spread abroad
to the west, and to the east, and to the north, and to the south: and in thee and
in thy seed shall all the families of the earth be blessed.
15 And, behold, I *am* with thee, and will keep thee in all *places* whither thou
goest, and will bring thee again into this land; for I will not leave thee, until I
have done *that* which I have spoken to thee of.
16 And Jacob awaked out of his sleep, and he said, Surely the LORD is in this
place; and I knew *it* not.
17 And he was afraid, and said, How dreadful *is* this place! this *is* none other
but the house of God, and this *is* the gate of heaven.
18 And Jacob rose up early in the morning, and took the stone that he had
put *for* his pillows, and set it up *for* a pillar, and poured oil upon the top of it.
19 And he called the name of that place Beth-el: but the name of that city *was*
called Luz at the first.
20 And Jacob vowed a vow, saying, If God will be with me, and will keep me
in this way that I go, and will give me bread to eat, and raiment to put on,
21 So that I come again to my father's house in peace; then shall the LORD be
my God:
22 And this stone, which I have set *for* a pillar, shall be God's house: and of
all that thou shalt give me I will surely give the tenth unto thee.

Jacob Comes to the Well of Haran

29 Then Jacob went on his journey, and came into the land of the people
of the east.
2 And he looked, and behold a well in the field, and, lo, there *were* three flocks
of sheep lying by it; for out of that well they watered the flocks: and a great
stone *was* upon the well's mouth.
3 And thither were all the flocks gathered: and they rolled the stone from
the well's mouth, and watered the sheep, and put the stone again upon the
well's mouth in his place.
4 And Jacob said unto them, My brethren, whence *be* ye? And they said, Of
Haran *are* we.
5 And he said unto them, Know ye Laban the son of Nahor? And they said,
We know *him*.
6 And he said unto them, *Is* he well? And they said, *He is* well: and, behold,
Rachel his daughter cometh with the sheep.
7 And he said, Lo, *it is* yet high day, neither *is it* time that the cattle should
be gathered together: water ye the sheep, and go *and* feed *them*.
8 And they said, We cannot, until all the flocks be gathered together, and *till*
they roll the stone from the well's mouth; then we water the sheep.

Jacob Meets Rachel by the Well

9 And while he yet spake with them, Rachel came with her father's sheep: for
she kept them.
10 And it came to pass, when Jacob saw Rachel the daughter of Laban his
mother's brother, and the sheep of Laban his mother's brother, that Jacob
went near, and rolled the stone from the well's mouth, and watered the flock
of Laban his mother's brother.
11 And Jacob kissed Rachel, and lifted up his voice, and wept.
12 And Jacob told Rachel that he *was* her father's brother, and that he *was*
Rebekah's son: and she ran and told her father.

13 And it came to pass, when Laban heard the tidings of Jacob his sister's son, that he ran to meet him, and embraced him, and kissed him, and brought him to his house. And he told Laban all these things.

14 And Laban said to him, Surely thou *art* my bone and my flesh. And he abode with him the space of a month.

15 And Laban said unto Jacob, Because thou *art* my brother, shouldest thou therefore serve me for nought? tell me, what *shall* thy wages *be*?

16 And Laban had two daughters: the name of the elder *was* Leah, and the name of the younger *was* Rachel.

17 Leah *was* tender eyed; but Rachel was beautiful and well favoured.

18 And Jacob loved Rachel; and said, I will serve thee seven years for Rachel thy younger daughter.

19 And Laban said, *It is* better that I give her to thee, than that I should give her to another man: abide with me.

20 And Jacob served seven years for Rachel; and they seemed unto him *but* a few days, for the love he had to her.

21 And Jacob said unto Laban, Give *me* my wife, for my days are fulfilled, that I may go in unto her.

22 And Laban gathered together all the men of the place, and made a feast.

23 And it came to pass in the evening, that he took Leah his daughter, and brought her to him; and he went in unto her.

24 And Laban gave unto his daughter Leah Zilpah his maid *for* an handmaid.

25 And it came to pass, that in the morning, behold, it *was* Leah: and he said to Laban, What *is* this thou hast done unto me? did not I serve with thee for Rachel? wherefore then hast thou beguiled me?

26 And Laban said, It must not be so done in our country, to give the younger before the firstborn.

27 Fulfil her week, and we will give thee this also for the service which thou shalt serve with me yet seven other years.

28 And Jacob did so, and fulfilled her week: and he gave him Rachel his daughter to wife also.

29 And Laban gave to Rachel his daughter Bilhah his handmaid to be her maid.

30 And he went in also unto Rachel, and he loved also Rachel more than Leah, and served with him yet seven other years.

31 And when the LORD saw that Leah *was* hated, he opened her womb: but Rachel *was* barren.

32 And Leah conceived, and bare a son, and she called his name Reuben: for she said, Surely the LORD hath looked upon my affliction; now therefore my husband will love me.

33 And she conceived again, and bare a son; and said, Because the LORD hath heard that I *was* hated, he hath therefore given me this *son* also: and she called his name Simeon.

34 And she conceived again, and bare a son; and said, Now this time will my husband be joined unto me, because I have born him three sons: therefore was his name called Levi.

35 And she conceived again, and bare a son: and she said, Now will I praise the LORD: therefore she called his name Judah; and left bearing.

Rachel Gives Bilhah to Jacob

30 And when Rachel saw that she bare Jacob no children, Rachel envied her sister; and said unto Jacob, Give me children, or else I die.

2 And Jacob's anger was kindled against Rachel: and he said, *Am* I in God's stead, who hath withheld from thee the fruit of the womb?

3 And she said, Behold my maid Bilhah, go in unto her; and she shall bear upon my knees, that I may also have children by her.

4 And she gave him Bilhah her handmaid to wife: and Jacob went in unto
her.
5 And Bilhah conceived, and bare Jacob a son.
6 And Rachel said, God hath judged me, and hath also heard my voice, and
hath given me a son: therefore called she his name Dan.
7 And Bilhah Rachel's maid conceived again, and bare Jacob a second son.
8 And Rachel said, With great wrestlings have I wrestled with my sister, and
I have prevailed: and she called his name Naphtali.
9 When Leah saw that she had left bearing, she took Zilpah her maid, and
gave her Jacob to wife.
10 And Zilpah Leah's maid bare Jacob a son.
11 And Leah said, A troop cometh: and she called his name Gad.
12 And Zilpah Leah's maid bare Jacob a second son.
13 And Leah said, Happy am I, for the daughters will call me blessed: and she
called his name Asher.

Reuben Finds Mandrakes

14 And Reuben went in the days of wheat harvest, and found mandrakes in
the field, and brought them unto his mother Leah. Then Rachel said to Leah,
Give me, I pray thee, of thy son's mandrakes.
15 And she said unto her, *Is it* a small matter that thou hast taken my hus-
band? and wouldest thou take away my son's mandrakes also? And Rachel
said, Therefore he shall lie with thee to night for thy son's mandrakes.
16 And Jacob came out of the field in the evening, and Leah went out to meet
him, and said, Thou must come in unto me; for surely I have hired thee with
my son's mandrakes. And he lay with her that night.
17 And God hearkened unto Leah, and she conceived, and bare Jacob the
fifth son.
18 And Leah said, God hath given me my hire, because I have given my maid-
en to my husband: and she called his name Issachar.
19 And Leah conceived again, and bare Jacob the sixth son.
20 And Leah said, God hath endued me *with* a good dowry; now will my
husband dwell with me, because I have born him six sons: and she called his
name Zebulun.
21 And afterwards she bare a daughter, and called her name Dinah.
22 And God remembered Rachel, and God hearkened to her, and opened her
womb.
23 And she conceived, and bare a son; and said, God hath taken away my
reproach:
24 And she called his name Joseph; and said, The LORD shall add to me anoth-
er son.

Jacob Is Denied Permission to Depart

25 And it came to pass, when Rachel had born Joseph, that Jacob said unto
Laban, Send me away, that I may go unto mine own place, and to my country.
26 Give *me* my wives and my children, for whom I have served thee, and let
me go: for thou knowest my service which I have done thee.
27 And Laban said unto him, I pray thee, if I have found favour in thine eyes,
tarry: for I have learned by experience that the LORD hath blessed me for thy
sake.
28 And he said, Appoint me thy wages, and I will give *it*.
29 And he said unto him, Thou knowest how I have served thee, and how thy
cattle was with me.
30 For *it was* little which thou hadst before I *came*, and it is *now* increased
unto a multitude; and the LORD hath blessed thee since my coming: and now
when shall I provide for mine own house also?

31 And he said, What shall I give thee? And Jacob said, Thou shalt not give
me any thing: if thou wilt do this thing for me, I will again feed *and* keep thy
flock:
32 I will pass through all thy flock to day, removing from thence all the speck-
led and spotted cattle, and all the brown cattle among the sheep, and the
spotted and speckled among the goats: and *of such* shall be my hire.
33 So shall my righteousness answer for me in time to come, when it shall
come for my hire before thy face: every one that *is* not speckled and spotted
among the goats, and brown among the sheep, that shall be counted stolen
with me.
34 And Laban said, Behold, I would it might be according to thy word.
35 And he removed that day the he goats that were ringstraked and spotted,
and all the she goats that were speckled and spotted, *and* every one that had
some white in it, and all the brown among the sheep, and gave *them* into the
hand of his sons.
36 And he set three days' journey betwixt himself and Jacob: and Jacob fed
the rest of Laban's flocks.

Jacob's Policy, Whereby He Becomes Rich

37 And Jacob took him rods of green poplar, and of the hazel and chesnut
tree; and pilled white strakes in them, and made the white appear which *was*
in the rods.
38 And he set the rods which he had pilled before the flocks in the gutters in
the watering troughs when the flocks came to drink, that they should conceive
when they came to drink.
39 And the flocks conceived before the rods, and brought forth cattle ring-
straked, speckled, and spotted.
40 And Jacob did separate the lambs, and set the faces of the flocks toward
the ringstraked, and all the brown in the flock of Laban; and he put his own
flocks by themselves, and put them not unto Laban's cattle.
41 And it came to pass, whensoever the stronger cattle did conceive, that
Jacob laid the rods before the eyes of the cattle in the gutters, that they might
conceive among the rods.
42 But when the cattle were feeble, he put *them* not in: so the feebler were
Laban's, and the stronger Jacob's.
43 And the man increased exceedingly, and had much cattle, and maidser-
vants, and menservants, and camels, and asses.

Jacob Leaves Laban Secretly

31 And he heard the words of Laban's sons, saying, Jacob hath taken away
all that *was* our father's; and of *that* which *was* our father's hath he
gotten all this glory.
2 And Jacob beheld the countenance of Laban, and, behold, it *was* not toward
him as before.
3 And the LORD said unto Jacob, Return unto the land of thy fathers, and to
thy kindred; and I will be with thee.
4 And Jacob sent and called Rachel and Leah to the field unto his flock,
5 And said unto them, I see your father's countenance, that it *is* not toward
me as before; but the God of my father hath been with me.
6 And ye know that with all my power I have served your father.
7 And your father hath deceived me, and changed my wages ten times; but
God suffered him not to hurt me.
8 If he said thus, The speckled shall be thy wages; then all the cattle bare
speckled: and if he said thus, The ringstraked shall be thy hire; then bare all
the cattle ringstraked.
9 Thus God hath taken away the cattle of your father, and given *them* to me.

10 And it came to pass at the time that the cattle conceived, that I lifted up
mine eyes, and saw in a dream, and, behold, the rams which leaped upon the
cattle *were* ringstraked, speckled, and grisled.
11 And the angel of God spake unto me in a dream, *saying*, Jacob: And I said,
Here *am* I.
12 And he said, Lift up now thine eyes, and see, all the rams which leap upon
the cattle *are* ringstraked, speckled, and grisled: for I have seen all that Laban
doeth unto thee.
13 I *am* the God of Beth-el, where thou anointedst the pillar, *and* where thou
vowedst a vow unto me: now arise, get thee out from this land, and return
unto the land of thy kindred.
14 And Rachel and Leah answered and said unto him, *Is there* yet any portion
or inheritance for us in our father's house?
15 Are we not counted of him strangers? for he hath sold us, and hath quite
devoured also our money.
16 For all the riches which God hath taken from our father, that *is* ours, and
our children's: now then, whatsoever God hath said unto thee, do.
17 Then Jacob rose up, and set his sons and his wives upon camels;
18 And he carried away all his cattle, and all his goods which he had gotten,
the cattle of his getting, which he had gotten in Padan-aram, for to go to Isaac
his father in the land of Canaan.
19 And Laban went to shear his sheep: and Rachel had stolen the images that
were her father's.
20 And Jacob stole away unawares to Laban the Syrian, in that he told him
not that he fled.
21 So he fled with all that he had; and he rose up, and passed over the river,
and set his face *toward* the mount Gilead.
22 And it was told Laban on the third day that Jacob was fled.
23 And he took his brethren with him, and pursued after him seven days'
journey; and they overtook him in the mount Gilead.
24 And God came to Laban the Syrian in a dream by night, and said unto
him, Take heed that thou speak not to Jacob either good or bad.
25 Then Laban overtook Jacob. Now Jacob had pitched his tent in the mount:
and Laban with his brethren pitched in the mount of Gilead.
26 And Laban said to Jacob, What hast thou done, that thou hast stolen away
unawares to me, and carried away my daughters, as captives *taken* with the
sword?
27 Wherefore didst thou flee away secretly, and steal away from me; and didst
not tell me, that I might have sent thee away with mirth, and with songs, with
tabret, and with harp?
28 And hast not suffered me to kiss my sons and my daughters? thou hast
now done foolishly in *so* doing.
29 It is in the power of my hand to do you hurt: but the God of your father
spake unto me yesternight, saying, Take thou heed that thou speak not to Jacob
either good or bad.
30 And now, *though* thou wouldest needs be gone, because thou sore longedst
after thy father's house, *yet* wherefore hast thou stolen my gods?
31 And Jacob answered and said to Laban, Because I was afraid: for I said,
Peradventure thou wouldest take by force thy daughters from me.
32 With whomsoever thou findest thy gods, let him not live: before our breth-
ren discern thou what *is* thine with me, and take *it* to thee. For Jacob knew
not that Rachel had stolen them.
33 And Laban went into Jacob's tent, and into Leah's tent, and into the two
maidservants' tents; but he found *them* not. Then went he out of Leah's tent,
and entered into Rachel's tent.

34 Now Rachel had taken the images, and put them in the camel's furniture,
and sat upon them. And Laban searched all the tent, but found *them* not.
35 And she said to her father, Let it not displease my lord that I cannot rise
up before thee; for the custom of women *is* upon me. And he searched, but
found not the images.

Jacob's Complaint against Laban

36 And Jacob was wroth, and chode with Laban: and Jacob answered and
said to Laban, What *is* my trespass? what *is* my sin, that thou hast so hotly
pursued after me?
37 Whereas thou hast searched all my stuff, what hast thou found of all thy
household stuff? set *it* here before my brethren and thy brethren, that they
may judge betwixt us both.
38 This twenty years *have* I *been* with thee; thy ewes and thy she goats have
not cast their young, and the rams of thy flock have I not eaten.
39 That which was torn *of beasts* I brought not unto thee; I bare the loss of
it; of my hand didst thou require it, *whether* stolen by day, or stolen by night.
40 *Thus* I was; in the day the drought consumed me, and the frost by night;
and my sleep departed from mine eyes.
41 Thus have I been twenty years in thy house; I served thee fourteen years
for thy two daughters, and six years for thy cattle: and thou hast changed my
wages ten times.
42 Except the God of my father, the God of Abraham, and the fear of Isaac,
had been with me, surely thou hadst sent me away now empty. God hath seen
mine affliction and the labour of my hands, and rebuked *thee* yesternight.

Jacob and Laban Make a Covenant

43 And Laban answered and said unto Jacob, *These* daughters *are* my daugh-
ters, and *these* children *are* my children, and *these* cattle *are* my cattle, and all
that thou seest *is* mine: and what can I do this day unto these my daughters,
or unto their children which they have born?
44 Now therefore come thou, let us make a covenant, I and thou; and let it
be for a witness between me and thee.
45 And Jacob took a stone, and set it up *for* a pillar.
46 And Jacob said unto his brethren, Gather stones; and they took stones,
and made an heap: and they did eat there upon the heap.
47 And Laban called it Jegar-sahadutha: but Jacob called it Galeed.
48 And Laban said, This heap *is* a witness between me and thee this day.
Therefore was the name of it called Galeed;
49 And Mizpah; for he said, The LORD watch between me and thee, when we
are absent one from another.
50 If thou shalt afflict my daughters, or if thou shalt take *other* wives beside
my daughters, no man *is* with us; see, God *is* witness betwixt me and thee.
51 And Laban said to Jacob, Behold this heap, and behold *this* pillar, which
I have cast betwixt me and thee;
52 This heap *be* witness, and *this* pillar *be* witness, that I will not pass over
this heap to thee, and that thou shalt not pass over this heap and this pillar
unto me, for harm.
53 The God of Abraham, and the God of Nahor, the God of their father, judge
betwixt us. And Jacob sware by the fear of his father Isaac.
54 Then Jacob offered sacrifice upon the mount, and called his brethren to
eat bread: and they did eat bread, and tarried all night in the mount.
55 And early in the morning Laban rose up, and kissed his sons and his
daughters, and blessed them: and Laban departed, and returned unto his place.

Jacob Calls the Place of His Vision Mahanaim

32 And Jacob went on his way, and the angels of God met him.
2 And when Jacob saw them, he said, This *is* God's host: and he called the name of that place Mahanaim.

Jacob's Message to Esau

3 And Jacob sent messengers before him to Esau his brother unto the land of Seir, the country of Edom.

4 And he commanded them, saying, Thus shall ye speak unto my lord Esau; Thy servant Jacob saith thus, I have sojourned with Laban, and stayed there until now:

5 And I have oxen, and asses, flocks, and menservants, and womenservants: and I have sent to tell my lord, that I may find grace in thy sight.

6 And the messengers returned to Jacob, saying, We came to thy brother Esau, and also he cometh to meet thee, and four hundred men with him.

7 Then Jacob was greatly afraid and distressed: and he divided the people that *was* with him, and the flocks, and herds, and the camels, into two bands;

8 And said, If Esau come to the one company, and smite it, then the other company which is left shall escape.

Jacob Prays for Deliverance

9 And Jacob said, O God of my father Abraham, and God of my father Isaac, the LORD which saidst unto me, Return unto thy country, and to thy kindred, and I will deal well with thee:

10 I am not worthy of the least of all the mercies, and of all the truth, which thou hast shewed unto thy servant; for with my staff I passed over this Jordan; and now I am become two bands.

11 Deliver me, I pray thee, from the hand of my brother, from the hand of Esau: for I fear him, lest he will come and smite me, *and* the mother with the children.

12 And thou saidst, I will surely do thee good, and make thy seed as the sand of the sea, which cannot be numbered for multitude.

Jacob Sends a Present to Esau

13 And he lodged there that same night; and took of that which came to his hand a present for Esau his brother;

14 Two hundred she goats, and twenty he goats, two hundred ewes, and twenty rams,

15 Thirty milch camels with their colts, forty kine, and ten bulls, twenty she asses, and ten foals.

16 And he delivered *them* into the hand of his servants, every drove by themselves; and said unto his servants, Pass over before me, and put a space betwixt drove and drove.

17 And he commanded the foremost, saying, When Esau my brother meeteth thee, and asketh thee, saying, Whose *art* thou? and whither goest thou? and whose *are* these before thee?

18 Then thou shalt say, *They be* thy servant Jacob's; it *is* a present sent unto my lord Esau: and, behold, also he *is* behind us.

19 And so commanded he the second, and the third, and all that followed the droves, saying, On this manner shall ye speak unto Esau, when ye find him.

20 And say ye moreover, Behold, thy servant Jacob *is* behind us. For he said, I will appease him with the present that goeth before me, and afterward I will see his face; peradventure he will accept of me.

21 So went the present over before him: and himself lodged that night in the company.

22 And he rose up that night, and took his two wives, and his two womenservants, and his eleven sons, and passed over the ford Jabbok.

23 And he took them, and sent them over the brook, and sent over that he had.

Jacob's Name Is Changed to Israel

24 And Jacob was left alone; and there wrestled a man with him until the
breaking of the day.
25 And when he saw that he prevailed not against him, he touched the hollow
of his thigh; and the hollow of Jacob's thigh was out of joint, as he wrestled
with him.
26 And he said, Let me go, for the day breaketh. And he said, I will not let thee
go, except thou bless me.
27 And he said unto him, What *is* thy name? And he said, Jacob.
28 And he said, Thy name shall be called no more Jacob, but Israel: for as a
prince hast thou power with God and with men, and hast prevailed.
29 And Jacob asked *him*, and said, Tell *me*, I pray thee, thy name. And he said,
Wherefore *is* it *that* thou dost ask after my name? And he blessed him there.
30 And Jacob called the name of the place Peniel: for I have seen God face to
face, and my life is preserved.
31 And as he passed over Penuel the sun rose upon him, and he halted upon
his thigh.
32 Therefore the children of Israel eat not *of* the sinew which shrank, which
is upon the hollow of the thigh, unto this day: because he touched the hollow
of Jacob's thigh in the sinew that shrank.

Jacob and Esau Meet

33 And Jacob lifted up his eyes, and looked, and, behold, Esau came, and
with him four hundred men. And he divided the children unto Leah,
and unto Rachel, and unto the two handmaids.
2 And he put the handmaids and their children foremost, and Leah and her
children after, and Rachel and Joseph hindermost.
3 And he passed over before them, and bowed himself to the ground seven
times, until he came near to his brother.
4 And Esau ran to meet him, and embraced him, and fell on his neck, and
kissed him: and they wept.
5 And he lifted up his eyes, and saw the women and the children; and said,
Who *are* those with thee? And he said, The children which God hath gracious-
ly given thy servant.
6 Then the handmaidens came near, they and their children, and they bowed
themselves.
7 And Leah also with her children came near, and bowed themselves: and
after came Joseph near and Rachel, and they bowed themselves.
8 And he said, What *meanest* thou by all this drove which I met? And he said,
These are to find grace in the sight of my lord.
9 And Esau said, I have enough, my brother; keep that thou hast unto thyself.
10 And Jacob said, Nay, I pray thee, if now I have found grace in thy sight,
then receive my present at my hand: for therefore I have seen thy face, as
though I had seen the face of God, and thou wast pleased with me.
11 Take, I pray thee, my blessing that is brought to thee; because God hath
dealt graciously with me, and because I have enough. And he urged him, and
he took *it*.
12 And he said, Let us take our journey, and let us go, and I will go before thee.
13 And he said unto him, My lord knoweth that the children *are* tender, and
the flocks and herds with young *are* with me: and if men should overdrive
them one day, all the flock will die.
14 Let my lord, I pray thee, pass over before his servant: and I will lead on
softly, according as the cattle that goeth before me and the children be able
to endure, until I come unto my lord unto Seir.
15 And Esau said, Let me now leave with thee *some* of the folk that *are* with
me. And he said, What needeth it? let me find grace in the sight of my lord.

16 So Esau returned that day on his way unto Seir.
17 And Jacob journeyed to Succoth, and built him an house, and made booths
for his cattle: therefore the name of the place is called Succoth.
18 And Jacob came to Shalem, a city of Shechem, which *is* in the land of
Canaan, when he came from Padan-aram; and pitched his tent before the city.
19 And he bought a parcel of a field, where he had spread his tent, at the hand
of the children of Hamor, Shechem's father, for an hundred pieces of money.
20 And he erected there an altar, and called it El-elohe-Israel.

Dinah Is Ravished by Shechem

34 And Dinah the daughter of Leah, which she bare unto Jacob, went out
to see the daughters of the land.
2 And when Shechem the son of Hamor the Hivite, prince of the country,
saw her, he took her, and lay with her, and defiled her.
3 And his soul clave unto Dinah the daughter of Jacob, and he loved the
damsel, and spake kindly unto the damsel.
4 And Shechem spake unto his father Hamor, saying, Get me this damsel to
wife.
5 And Jacob heard that he had defiled Dinah his daughter: now his sons were
with his cattle in the field: and Jacob held his peace until they were come.
6 And Hamor the father of Shechem went out unto Jacob to commune with
him.
7 And the sons of Jacob came out of the field when they heard *it*: and the
men were grieved, and they were very wroth, because he had wrought folly in
Israel in lying with Jacob's daughter; which thing ought not to be done.
8 And Hamor communed with them, saying, The soul of my son Shechem
longeth for your daughter: I pray you give her him to wife.
9 And make ye marriages with us, *and* give your daughters unto us, and take
our daughters unto you.
10 And ye shall dwell with us: and the land shall be before you; dwell and
trade ye therein, and get you possessions therein.
11 And Shechem said unto her father and unto her brethren, Let me find
grace in your eyes, and what ye shall say unto me I will give.
12 Ask me never so much dowry and gift, and I will give according as ye shall
say unto me: but give me the damsel to wife.
13 And the sons of Jacob answered Shechem and Hamor his father deceit-
fully, and said, because he had defiled Dinah their sister:
14 And they said unto them, We cannot do this thing, to give our sister to one
that is uncircumcised; for that *were* a reproach unto us:
15 But in this will we consent unto you: If ye will be as we *be*, that every male
of you be circumcised;
16 Then will we give our daughters unto you, and we will take your daughters
to us, and we will dwell with you, and we will become one people.
17 But if ye will not hearken unto us, to be circumcised; then will we take our
daughter, and we will be gone.
18 And their words pleased Hamor, and Shechem Hamor's son.
19 And the young man deferred not to do the thing, because he had delight
in Jacob's daughter: and he *was* more honourable than all the house of his
father.
20 And Hamor and Shechem his son came unto the gate of their city, and
communed with the men of their city, saying,
21 These men *are* peaceable with us; therefore let them dwell in the land,
and trade therein; for the land, behold, *it is* large enough for them; let us take
their daughters to us for wives, and let us give them our daughters.
22 Only herein will the men consent unto us for to dwell with us, to be one
people, if every male among us be circumcised, as they *are* circumcised.

23 *Shall* not their cattle and their substance and every beast of theirs *be* ours?
only let us consent unto them, and they will dwell with us.
24 And unto Hamor and unto Shechem his son hearkened all that went out
of the gate of his city; and every male was circumcised, all that went out of the
gate of his city.

Jacob's Sons Kill the Men of Shechem

25 And it came to pass on the third day, when they were sore, that two of the
sons of Jacob, Simeon and Levi, Dinah's brethren, took each man his sword,
and came upon the city boldly, and slew all the males.
26 And they slew Hamor and Shechem his son with the edge of the sword,
and took Dinah out of Shechem's house, and went out.
27 The sons of Jacob came upon the slain, and spoiled the city, because they
had defiled their sister.
28 They took their sheep, and their oxen, and their asses, and that which *was*
in the city, and that which *was* in the field,
29 And all their wealth, and all their little ones, and their wives took they
captive, and spoiled even all that *was* in the house.
30 And Jacob said to Simeon and Levi, Ye have troubled me to make me to
stink among the inhabitants of the land, among the Canaanites and the
Perizzites: and I *being* few in number, they shall gather themselves together
against me, and slay me; and I shall be destroyed, I and my house.
31 And they said, Should he deal with our sister as with an harlot?

God Sends Jacob to Beth-el

35 And God said unto Jacob, Arise, go up to Beth-el, and dwell there: and
make there an altar unto God, that appeared unto thee when thou
fleddest from the face of Esau thy brother.
2 Then Jacob said unto his household, and to all that *were* with him, Put away
the strange gods that *are* among you, and be clean, and change your garments:
3 And let us arise, and go up to Beth-el; and I will make there an altar unto
God, who answered me in the day of my distress, and was with me in the way
which I went.
4 And they gave unto Jacob all the strange gods which *were* in their hand,
and *all their* earrings which *were* in their ears; and Jacob hid them under the
oak which *was* by Shechem.
5 And they journeyed: and the terror of God was upon the cities that *were*
round about them, and they did not pursue after the sons of Jacob.

Jacob Builds an Altar to God at Beth-el

6 So Jacob came to Luz, which *is* in the land of Canaan, that *is*, Beth-el, he
and all the people that *were* with him.
7 And he built there an altar, and called the place El-beth-el: because there
God appeared unto him, when he fled from the face of his brother.
8 But Deborah Rebekah's nurse died, and she was buried beneath Beth-el
under an oak: and the name of it was called Allon-bachuth.
9 And God appeared unto Jacob again, when he came out of Padan-aram,
and blessed him.
10 And God said unto him, Thy name *is* Jacob: thy name shall not be called
any more Jacob, but Israel shall be thy name: and he called his name Israel.
11 And God said unto him, I *am* God Almighty: be fruitful and multiply; a
nation and a company of nations shall be of thee, and kings shall come out of
thy loins;
12 And the land which I gave Abraham and Isaac, to thee I will give it, and to
thy seed after thee will I give the land.
13 And God went up from him in the place where he talked with him.

14 And Jacob set up a pillar in the place where he talked with him, *even* a
pillar of stone: and he poured a drink offering thereon, and he poured oil
thereon.
15 And Jacob called the name of the place where God spake with him, Beth-el.

Rachel Bears Benjamin and Dies

16 And they journeyed from Beth-el; and there was but a little way to come
to Ephrath: and Rachel travailed, and she had hard labour.
17 And it came to pass, when she was in hard labour, that the midwife said
unto her, Fear not; thou shalt have this son also.
18 And it came to pass, as her soul was in departing, (for she died) that she
called his name Ben-oni: but his father called him Benjamin.
19 And Rachel died, and was buried in the way to Ephrath, which *is* Beth-lehem.
20 And Jacob set a pillar upon her grave: that *is* the pillar of Rachel's grave
unto this day.
21 And Israel journeyed, and spread his tent beyond the tower of Edar.
22 And it came to pass, when Israel dwelt in that land, that Reuben went and
lay with Bilhah his father's concubine: and Israel heard *it*. Now the sons of
Jacob were twelve:
23 The sons of Leah; Reuben, Jacob's firstborn, and Simeon, and Levi, and
Judah, and Issachar, and Zebulun:
24 The sons of Rachel; Joseph, and Benjamin:
25 And the sons of Bilhah, Rachel's handmaid; Dan, and Naphtali:
26 And the sons of Zilpah, Leah's handmaid; Gad, and Asher: these *are* the
sons of Jacob, which were born to him in Padan-aram.
27 And Jacob came unto Isaac his father unto Mamre, unto the city of Arbah,
which *is* Hebron, where Abraham and Isaac sojourned.
28 And the days of Isaac were an hundred and fourscore years.
29 And Isaac gave up the ghost, and died, and was gathered unto his people,
being old and full of days: and his sons Esau and Jacob buried him.

Esau's Three Wives

36 Now these *are* the generations of Esau, who *is* Edom.
2 Esau took his wives of the daughters of Canaan; Adah the daughter
of Elon the Hittite, and Aholibamah the daughter of Anah the daughter of
Zibeon the Hivite;
3 And Bashemath Ishmael's daughter, sister of Nebajoth.
4 And Adah bare to Esau Eliphaz; and Bashemath bare Reuel;
5 And Aholibamah bare Jeush, and Jaalam, and Korah: these *are* the sons of
Esau, which were born unto him in the land of Canaan.
6 And Esau took his wives, and his sons, and his daughters, and all the persons
of his house, and his cattle, and all his beasts, and all his substance, which he
had got in the land of Canaan; and went into the country from the face of his
brother Jacob.
7 For their riches were more than that they might dwell together; and the
land wherein they were strangers could not bear them because of their cattle.
8 Thus dwelt Esau in mount Seir: Esau *is* Edom.

Esau's Sons

9 And these *are* the generations of Esau the father of the Edomites in mount
Seir:
10 These *are* the names of Esau's sons; Eliphaz the son of Adah the wife of
Esau, Reuel the son of Bashemath the wife of Esau.
11 And the sons of Eliphaz were Teman, Omar, Zepho, and Gatam, and Kenaz.
12 And Timna was concubine to Eliphaz Esau's son; and she bare to Eliphaz
Amalek: these *were* the sons of Adah Esau's wife.
13 And these *are* the sons of Reuel; Nahath, and Zerah, Shammah, and
Mizzah: these were the sons of Bashemath Esau's wife.

14 And these were the sons of Aholibamah, the daughter of Anah the daughter of Zibeon, Esau's wife: and she bare to Esau Jeush, and Jaalam, and Korah.
15 These *were* dukes of the sons of Esau: the sons of Eliphaz the firstborn *son* of Esau; duke Teman, duke Omar, duke Zepho, duke Kenaz,
16 Duke Korah, duke Gatam, *and* duke Amalek: these *are* the dukes *that came* of Eliphaz in the land of Edom; these *were* the sons of Adah.
17 And these *are* the sons of Reuel Esau's son; duke Nahath, duke Zerah, duke Shammah, duke Mizzah: these *are* the dukes *that came* of Reuel in the land of Edom; these *are* the sons of Bashemath Esau's wife.
18 And these *are* the sons of Aholibamah Esau's wife; duke Jeush, duke Jaalam, duke Korah: these *were* the dukes *that came* of Aholibamah the daughter of Anah, Esau's wife.
19 These *are* the sons of Esau, who *is* Edom, and these *are* their dukes.

The Children of Seir

20 These *are* the sons of Seir the Horite, who inhabited the land; Lotan, and Shobal, and Zibeon, and Anah,
21 And Dishon, and Ezer, and Dishan: these *are* the dukes of the Horites, the children of Seir in the land of Edom.
22 And the children of Lotan were Hori and Hemam; and Lotan's sister *was* Timna.
23 And the children of Shobal *were* these; Alvan, and Manahath, and Ebal, Shepho, and Onam.
24 And these *are* the children of Zibeon; both Ajah, and Anah: this *was that* Anah that found the mules in the wilderness, as he fed the asses of Zibeon his father.
25 And the children of Anah *were* these; Dishon, and Aholibamah the daughter of Anah.
26 And these *are* the children of Dishon; Hemdan, and Eshban, and Ithran, and Cheran.
27 The children of Ezer *are* these; Bilhan, and Zaavan, and Akan.
28 The children of Dishan *are* these; Uz, and Aran.
29 These *are* the dukes *that came* of the Horites; duke Lotan, duke Shobal, duke Zibeon, duke Anah,
30 Duke Dishon, duke Ezer, duke Dishan: these *are* the dukes *that came* of Hori, among their dukes in the land of Seir.

The Kings of Edom

31 And these *are* the kings that reigned in the land of Edom, before there reigned any king over the children of Israel.
32 And Bela the son of Beor reigned in Edom: and the name of his city *was* Dinhabah.
33 And Bela died, and Jobab the son of Zerah of Bozrah reigned in his stead.
34 And Jobab died, and Husham of the land of Temani reigned in his stead.
35 And Husham died, and Hadad the son of Bedad, who smote Midian in the field of Moab, reigned in his stead: and the name of his city *was* Avith.
36 And Hadad died, and Samlah of Masrekah reigned in his stead.
37 And Samlah died, and Saul of Rehoboth *by* the river reigned in his stead.
38 And Saul died, and Baal-hanan the son of Achbor reigned in his stead.
39 And Baal-hanan the son of Achbor died, and Hadar reigned in his stead: and the name of his city *was* Pau; and his wife's name *was* Mehetabel, the daughter of Matred, the daughter of Mezahab.
40 And these *are* the names of the dukes *that came* of Esau, according to their families, after their places, by their names; duke Timnah, duke Alvah, duke Jetheth,
41 Duke Aholibamah, duke Elah, duke Pinon,
42 Duke Kenaz, duke Teman, duke Mibzar,

43 Duke Magdiel, duke Iram: these *be* the dukes of Edom, according to their
habitations in the land of their possession: he *is* Esau the father of the
Edomites.

Jacob in Canaan

37 And Jacob dwelt in the land wherein his father was a stranger, in the
land of Canaan.
2 These *are* the generations of Jacob. Joseph, *being* seventeen years old, was
feeding the flock with his brethren; and the lad *was* with the sons of Bilhah,
and with the sons of Zilpah, his father's wives: and Joseph brought unto his
father their evil report.
3 Now Israel loved Joseph more than all his children, because he *was* the son
of his old age: and he made him a coat of *many* colours.
4 And when his brethren saw that their father loved him more than all his
brethren, they hated him, and could not speak peaceably unto him.

Joseph's Two Dreams

5 And Joseph dreamed a dream, and he told *it* his brethren: and they hated
him yet the more.
6 And he said unto them, Hear, I pray you, this dream which I have dreamed:
7 For, behold, we *were* binding sheaves in the field, and, lo, my sheaf arose,
and also stood upright; and, behold, your sheaves stood round about, and
made obeisance to my sheaf.
8 And his brethren said to him, Shalt thou indeed reign over us? or shalt
thou indeed have dominion over us? And they hated him yet the more for his
dreams, and for his words.
9 And he dreamed yet another dream, and told it his brethren, and said,
Behold, I have dreamed a dream more; and, behold, the sun and the moon
and the eleven stars made obeisance to me.
10 And he told *it* to his father, and to his brethren: and his father rebuked
him, and said unto him, What *is* this dream that thou hast dreamed? Shall I
and thy mother and thy brethren indeed come to bow down ourselves to thee
to the earth?
11 And his brethren envied him; but his father observed the saying.
12 And his brethren went to feed their father's flock in Shechem.
13 And Israel said unto Joseph, Do not thy brethren feed *the flock* in Shechem?
come, and I will send thee unto them. And he said to him, Here *am I*.
14 And he said to him, Go, I pray thee, see whether it be well with thy breth-
ren, and well with the flocks; and bring me word again. So he sent him out of
the vale of Hebron, and he came to Shechem.
15 And a certain man found him, and, behold, *he was* wandering in the field:
and the man asked him, saying, What seekest thou?
16 And he said, I seek my brethren: tell me, I pray thee, where they feed *their
flocks*.
17 And the man said, They are departed hence; for I heard them say, Let us
go to Dothan. And Joseph went after his brethren, and found them in Dothan.
18 And when they saw him afar off, even before he came near unto them,
they conspired against him to slay him.
19 And they said one to another, Behold, this dreamer cometh.
20 Come now therefore, and let us slay him, and cast him into some pit, and
we will say, Some evil beast hath devoured him: and we shall see what will
become of his dreams.
21 And Reuben heard *it*, and he delivered him out of their hands; and said,
Let us not kill him.
22 And Reuben said unto them, Shed no blood, *but* cast him into this pit that
is in the wilderness, and lay no hand upon him; that he might rid him out of
their hands, to deliver him to his father again.

23 And it came to pass, when Joseph was come unto his brethren, that they
stript Joseph out of his coat, *his* coat of *many* colours that *was* on him;
24 And they took him, and cast him into a pit: and the pit *was* empty, *there*
was no water in it.
25 And they sat down to eat bread: and they lifted up their eyes and looked,
and, behold, a company of Ishmeelites came from Gilead with their camels
bearing spicery and balm and myrrh, going to carry *it* down to Egypt.
26 And Judah said unto his brethren, What profit *is it* if we slay our brother,
and conceal his blood?
27 Come, and let us sell him to the Ishmeelites, and let not our hand be upon
him; for he *is* our brother *and* our flesh. And his brethren were content.
28 Then there passed by Midianites merchantmen; and they drew and lifted
up Joseph out of the pit, and sold Joseph to the Ishmeelites for twenty *pieces*
of silver: and they brought Joseph into Egypt.
29 And Reuben returned unto the pit; and, behold, Joseph *was* not in the pit;
and he rent his clothes.
30 And he returned unto his brethren, and said, The child *is* not; and I, whith-
er shall I go?

Jacob Deceived, Mourns for Joseph

31 And they took Joseph's coat, and killed a kid of the goats, and dipped the
coat in the blood;
32 And they sent the coat of *many* colours, and they brought *it* to their father;
and said, This have we found: know now whether it *be* thy son's coat or no.
33 And he knew it, and said, *It is* my son's coat; an evil beast hath devoured
him; Joseph is without doubt rent in pieces.
34 And Jacob rent his clothes, and put sackcloth upon his loins, and mourn-
ed for his son many days.
35 And all his sons and all his daughters rose up to comfort him; but he
refused to be comforted; and he said, For I will go down into the grave unto
my son mourning. Thus his father wept for him.
36 And the Midianites sold him into Egypt unto Potiphar, an officer of
Pharaoh's, *and* captain of the guard.

Judah Begets Er, Onan, and Shelah

38 And it came to pass at that time, that Judah went down from his breth-
ren, and turned in to a certain Adullamite, whose name *was* Hirah.
2 And Judah saw there a daughter of a certain Canaanite, whose name *was*
Shuah; and he took her, and went in unto her.
3 And she conceived, and bare a son; and he called his name Er.
4 And she conceived again, and bare a son; and she called his name Onan.
5 And she yet again conceived, and bare a son; and called his name Shelah:
and he was at Chezib, when she bare him.
6 And Judah took a wife for Er his firstborn, whose name *was* Tamar.
7 And Er, Judah's firstborn, was wicked in the sight of the LORD; and the LORD
slew him.
8 And Judah said unto Onan, Go in unto thy brother's wife, and marry her,
and raise up seed to thy brother.
9 And Onan knew that the seed should not be his; and it came to pass, when
he went in unto his brother's wife, that he spilled *it* on the ground, lest that
he should give seed to his brother.
10 And the thing which he did displeased the LORD: wherefore he slew him
also.
11 Then said Judah to Tamar his daughter in law, Remain a widow at thy
father's house, till Shelah my son be grown: for he said, Lest peradventure he
die also, as his brethren *did*. And Tamar went and dwelt in her father's house.

12 And in process of time the daughter of Shuah Judah's wife died; and Judah
was comforted, and went up unto his sheepshearers to Timnath, he and his
friend Hirah the Adullamite.
13 And it was told Tamar, saying, Behold thy father in law goeth up to Timnath
to shear his sheep.
14 And she put her widow's garments off from her, and covered her with a
veil, and wrapped herself, and sat in an open place, which *is* by the way to
Timnath; for she saw that Shelah was grown, and she was not given unto him
to wife.
15 When Judah saw her, he thought her *to be* an harlot; because she had
covered her face.
16 And he turned unto her by the way, and said, Go to, I pray thee, let me
come in unto thee; (for he knew not that she *was* his daughter in law.) And she
said, What wilt thou give me, that thou mayest come in unto me?
17 And he said, I will send *thee* a kid from the flock. And she said, Wilt thou
give *me* a pledge, till thou send *it*?
18 And he said, What pledge shall I give thee? And she said, Thy signet, and
thy bracelets, and thy staff that *is* in thine hand. And he gave *it* her, and came
in unto her, and she conceived by him.
19 And she arose, and went away, and laid by her veil from her, and put on
the garments of her widowhood.
20 And Judah sent the kid by the hand of his friend the Adullamite, to receive
his pledge from the woman's hand: but he found her not.
21 Then he asked the men of that place, saying, Where *is* the harlot, that *was*
openly by the way side? And they said, There was no harlot in this *place*.
22 And he returned to Judah, and said, I cannot find her; and also the men
of the place said, *that* there was no harlot in this *place*.
23 And Judah said, Let her take *it* to her, lest we be shamed: behold, I sent
this kid, and thou hast not found her.
24 And it came to pass about three months after, that it was told Judah, say-
ing, Tamar thy daughter in law hath played the harlot; and also, behold, she
is with child by whoredom. And Judah said, Bring her forth, and let her be
burnt.
25 When she *was* brought forth, she sent to her father in law, saying, By the
man, whose these *are*, *am* I with child: and she said, Discern, I pray thee, whose
are these, the signet, and bracelets, and staff.
26 And Judah acknowledged *them*, and said, She hath been more righteous
than I; because that I gave her not to Shelah my son. And he knew her again
no more.
27 And it came to pass in the time of her travail, that, behold, twins *were* in
her womb.
28 And it came to pass, when she travailed, that *the one* put out *his* hand: and
the midwife took and bound upon his hand a scarlet thread, saying, This came
out first.
29 And it came to pass, as he drew back his hand, that, behold, his brother
came out: and she said, How hast thou broken forth? *this* breach *be* upon thee:
therefore his name was called Pharez.
30 And afterward came out his brother, that had the scarlet thread upon his
hand: and his name was called Zarah.

Joseph Is Promoted in Potiphar's House

39 And Joseph was brought down to Egypt; and Potiphar, an officer of
Pharaoh, captain of the guard, an Egyptian, bought him of the hands
of the Ishmeelites, which had brought him down thither.
2 And the LORD was with Joseph, and he was a prosperous man; and he was
in the house of his master the Egyptian.

3 And his master saw that the LORD *was* with him, and that the LORD made
all that he did to prosper in his hand.
4 And Joseph found grace in his sight, and he served him: and he made him
overseer over his house, and all *that* he had he put into his hand.
5 And it came to pass from the time *that* he had made him overseer in his
house, and over all that he had, that the LORD blessed the Egyptian's house for
Joseph's sake; and the blessing of the LORD was upon all that he had in the
house, and in the field.
6 And he left all that he had in Joseph's hand; and he knew not ought he had,
save the bread which he did eat. And Joseph was *a* goodly *person*, and well
favoured.

Joseph Resists the Temptation of Potiphar's Wife

7 And it came to pass after these things, that his master's wife cast her eyes
upon Joseph; and she said, Lie with me.
8 But he refused, and said unto his master's wife, Behold, my master wotteth
not what *is* with me in the house, and he hath committed all that he hath to
my hand;
9 *There is* none greater in this house than I; neither hath he kept back any
thing from me but thee, because thou *art* his wife: how then can I do this great
wickedness, and sin against God?
10 And it came to pass, as she spake to Joseph day by day, that he hearkened
not unto her, to lie by her, *or* to be with her.
11 And it came to pass about this time, that *Joseph* went into the house to do
his business; and *there was* none of the men of the house there within.
12 And she caught him by his garment, saying, Lie with me: and he left his
garment in her hand, and fled, and got him out.

Joseph Is Falsely Accused

13 And it came to pass, when she saw that he had left his garment in her hand,
and was fled forth,
14 That she called unto the men of her house, and spake unto them, saying,
See, he hath brought in an Hebrew unto us to mock us; he came in unto me
to lie with me, and I cried with a loud voice:
15 And it came to pass, when he heard that I lifted up my voice and cried,
that he left his garment with me, and fled, and got him out.
16 And she laid up his garment by her, until his lord came home.
17 And she spake unto him according to these words, saying, The Hebrew
servant, which thou hast brought unto us, came in unto me to mock me:
18 And it came to pass, as I lifted up my voice and cried, that he left his gar-
ment with me, and fled out.

Joseph in Prison

19 And it came to pass, when his master heard the words of his wife, which
she spake unto him, saying, After this manner did thy servant to me; that his
wrath was kindled.
20 And Joseph's master took him, and put him into the prison, a place where
the king's prisoners *were* bound: and he was there in the prison.
21 But the LORD was with Joseph, and shewed him mercy, and gave him favour
in the sight of the keeper of the prison.
22 And the keeper of the prison committed to Joseph's hand all the prisoners
that *were* in the prison; and whatsoever they did there, he was the doer *of it*.
23 The keeper of the prison looked not to any thing *that was* under his hand;
because the LORD was with him, and *that* which he did, the LORD made *it* to
prosper.

The Butler and the Baker of Pharaoh Are with Joseph in Prison

40 And it came to pass after these things, *that* the butler of the king of
Egypt and *his* baker had offended their lord the king of Egypt.
2 And Pharaoh was wroth against two *of* his officers, against the chief of the
butlers, and against the chief of the bakers.
3 And he put them in ward in the house of the captain of the guard, into the
prison, the place where Joseph *was* bound.
4 And the captain of the guard charged Joseph with them, and he served
them: and they continued a season in ward.

Joseph Interprets the Prisoners' Dreams

5 And they dreamed a dream both of them, each man his dream in one night,
each man according to the interpretation of his dream, the butler and the
baker of the king of Egypt, which *were* bound in the prison.
6 And Joseph came in unto them in the morning, and looked upon them,
and, behold, they *were* sad.
7 And he asked Pharaoh's officers that *were* with him in the ward of his lord's
house, saying, Wherefore look ye *so* sadly to day?
8 And they said unto him, We have dreamed a dream, and *there is* no inter-
preter of it. And Joseph said unto them, *Do* not interpretations *belong* to God?
tell me *them*, I pray you.
9 And the chief butler told his dream to Joseph, and said to him, In my dream,
behold, a vine *was* before me;
10 And in the vine *were* three branches: and it *was* as though it budded, *and*
her blossoms shot forth; and the clusters thereof brought forth ripe grapes:
11 And Pharaoh's cup *was* in my hand: and I took the grapes, and pressed
them into Pharaoh's cup, and I gave the cup into Pharaoh's hand.
12 And Joseph said unto him, This *is* the interpretation of it: The three
branches *are* three days:
13 Yet within three days shall Pharaoh lift up thine head, and restore thee
unto thy place: and thou shalt deliver Pharaoh's cup into his hand, after the
former manner when thou wast his butler.
14 But think on me when it shall be well with thee, and shew kindness, I pray
thee, unto me, and make mention of me unto Pharaoh, and bring me out of
this house:
15 For indeed I was stolen away out of the land of the Hebrews: and here also
have I done nothing that they should put me into the dungeon.
16 When the chief baker saw that the interpretation was good, he said unto
Joseph, I also *was* in my dream, and, behold, *I had* three white baskets on my
head:
17 And in the uppermost basket *there was* of all manner of bakemeats for
Pharaoh; and the birds did eat them out of the basket upon my head.
18 And Joseph answered and said, This *is* the interpretation thereof: The
three baskets *are* three days:
19 Yet within three days shall Pharaoh lift up thy head from off thee, and
shall hang thee on a tree; and the birds shall eat thy flesh from off thee.

The Dreams Come to Pass According to Joseph's Interpretation

20 And it came to pass the third day, *which was* Pharaoh's birthday, that he
made a feast unto all his servants: and he lifted up the head of the chief butler
and of the chief baker among his servants.
21 And he restored the chief butler unto his butlership again; and he gave
the cup into Pharaoh's hand:
22 But he hanged the chief baker: as Joseph had interpreted to them.
23 Yet did not the chief butler remember Joseph, but forgat him.

Pharaoh's Dreams

41 And it came to pass at the end of two full years, that Pharaoh dreamed:
and, behold, he stood by the river.
2 And, behold, there came up out of the river seven well favoured kine and
fatfleshed; and they fed in a meadow.
3 And, behold, seven other kine came up after them out of the river, ill
favoured and leanfleshed; and stood by the *other* kine upon the brink of the
river.
4 And the ill favoured and leanfleshed kine did eat up the seven well favoured
and fat kine. So Pharaoh awoke.
5 And he slept and dreamed the second time: and, behold, seven ears of corn
came up upon one stalk, rank and good.
6 And, behold, seven thin ears and blasted with the east wind sprung up after
them.
7 And the seven thin ears devoured the seven rank and full ears. And Pharaoh
awoke, and, behold, *it was* a dream.
8 And it came to pass in the morning that his spirit was troubled; and he sent
and called for all the magicians of Egypt, and all the wise men thereof: and
Pharaoh told them his dream; but *there was* none that could interpret them
unto Pharaoh.

Joseph Interprets Pharaoh's Dreams

9 Then spake the chief butler unto Pharaoh, saying, I do remember my faults
this day:
10 Pharaoh was wroth with his servants, and put me in ward in the captain
of the guard's house, *both* me and the chief baker:
11 And we dreamed a dream in one night, I and he; we dreamed each man
according to the interpretation of his dream.
12 And *there was* there with us a young man, an Hebrew, servant to the cap-
tain of the guard; and we told him, and he interpreted to us our dreams; to
each man according to his dream he did interpret.
13 And it came to pass, as he interpreted to us, so it was; me he restored unto
mine office, and him he hanged.
14 Then Pharaoh sent and called Joseph, and they brought him hastily out
of the dungeon: and he shaved *himself*, and changed his raiment, and came
in unto Pharaoh.
15 And Pharaoh said unto Joseph, I have dreamed a dream, and *there is* none
that can interpret it: and I have heard say of thee, *that* thou canst understand
a dream to interpret it.
16 And Joseph answered Pharaoh, saying, *It is* not in me: God shall give
Pharaoh an answer of peace.
17 And Pharaoh said unto Joseph, In my dream, behold, I stood upon the
bank of the river:
18 And, behold, there came up out of the river seven kine, fatfleshed and well
favoured; and they fed in a meadow:
19 And, behold, seven other kine came up after them, poor and very ill
favoured and leanfleshed, such as I never saw in all the land of Egypt for bad-
ness:
20 And the lean and the ill favoured kine did eat up the first seven fat kine:
21 And when they had eaten them up, it could not be known that they had
eaten them; but they *were* still ill favoured, as at the beginning. So I awoke.
22 And I saw in my dream, and, behold, seven ears came up in one stalk, full
and good:
23 And, behold, seven ears, withered, thin, *and* blasted with the east wind,
sprung up after them:

24 And the thin ears devoured the seven good ears: and I told *this* unto the
magicians; but *there was* none that could declare *it* to me.
25 And Joseph said unto Pharaoh, The dream of Pharaoh *is* one: God hath
shewed Pharaoh what he *is* about to do.
26 The seven good kine *are* seven years; and the seven good ears *are* seven
years: the dream *is* one.
27 And the seven thin and ill favoured kine that came up after them *are* seven
years; and the seven empty ears blasted with the east wind shall be seven years
of famine.
28 This *is* the thing which I have spoken unto Pharaoh: What God *is* about
to do he sheweth unto Pharaoh.
29 Behold, there come seven years of great plenty throughout all the land of
Egypt:
30 And there shall arise after them seven years of famine; and all the plenty
shall be forgotten in the land of Egypt; and the famine shall consume the land;
31 And the plenty shall not be known in the land by reason of that famine
following; for it *shall be* very grievous.
32 And for that the dream was doubled unto Pharaoh twice; *it is* because the
thing *is* established by God, and God will shortly bring it to pass.

Joseph Gives Pharaoh Counsel

33 Now therefore let Pharaoh look out a man discreet and wise, and set him
over the land of Egypt.
34 Let Pharaoh do *this*, and let him appoint officers over the land, and take
up the fifth part of the land of Egypt in the seven plenteous years.
35 And let them gather all the food of those good years that come, and lay up
corn under the hand of Pharaoh, and let them keep food in the cities.
36 And that food shall be for store to the land against the seven years of
famine, which shall be in the land of Egypt; that the land perish not through
the famine.
37 And the thing was good in the eyes of Pharaoh, and in the eyes of all his
servants.
38 And Pharaoh said unto his servants, Can we find *such a one* as this *is*, a
man in whom the Spirit of God *is*?
39 And Pharaoh said unto Joseph, Forasmuch as God hath shewed thee all
this, *there is* none so discreet and wise as thou *art*:
40 Thou shalt be over my house, and according unto thy word shall all my
people be ruled: only in the throne will I be greater than thou.
41 And Pharaoh said unto Joseph, See, I have set thee over all the land of
Egypt.
42 And Pharaoh took off his ring from his hand, and put it upon Joseph's
hand, and arrayed him in vestures of fine linen, and put a gold chain about
his neck;
43 And he made him to ride in the second chariot which he had; and they
cried before him, Bow the knee: and he made him *ruler* over all the land of
Egypt.
44 And Pharaoh said unto Joseph, I *am* Pharaoh, and without thee shall no
man lift up his hand or foot in all the land of Egypt.
45 And Pharaoh called Joseph's name Zaphnath-paaneah; and he gave him
to wife Asenath the daughter of Poti-pherah priest of On. And Joseph went
out over *all* the land of Egypt.
46 And Joseph *was* thirty years old when he stood before Pharaoh king of
Egypt. And Joseph went out from the presence of Pharaoh, and went through-
out all the land of Egypt.
47 And in the seven plenteous years the earth brought forth by handfuls.

48 And he gathered up all the food of the seven years, which were in the land
of Egypt, and laid up the food in the cities: the food of the field, which *was*
round about every city, laid he up in the same.
49 And Joseph gathered corn as the sand of the sea, very much, until he left
numbering; for *it was* without number.
50 And unto Joseph were born two sons before the years of famine came,
which Asenath the daughter of Poti-pherah priest of On bare unto him.
51 And Joseph called the name of the firstborn Manasseh: For God, *said he*,
hath made me forget all my toil, and all my father's house.
52 And the name of the second called he Ephraim: For God hath caused me
to be fruitful in the land of my affliction.
53 And the seven years of plenteousness, that was in the land of Egypt, were
ended.
54 And the seven years of dearth began to come, according as Joseph had
said: and the dearth was in all lands; but in all the land of Egypt there was
bread.
55 And when all the land of Egypt was famished, the people cried to Pharaoh
for bread: and Pharaoh said unto all the Egyptians, Go unto Joseph; what he
saith to you, do.
56 And the famine was over all the face of the earth: And Joseph opened all
the storehouses, and sold unto the Egyptians; and the famine waxed sore in
the land of Egypt.
57 And all countries came into Egypt to Joseph for to buy *corn*; because that
the famine was *so* sore in all lands.

Jacob Sends His Ten Sons to Buy Corn in Egypt

42 Now when Jacob saw that there was corn in Egypt, Jacob said unto his
sons, Why do ye look one upon another?
2 And he said, Behold, I have heard that there is corn in Egypt: get you down
thither, and buy for us from thence; that we may live, and not die.
3 And Joseph's ten brethren went down to buy corn in Egypt.
4 But Benjamin, Joseph's brother, Jacob sent not with his brethren; for he
said, Lest peradventure mischief befall him.
5 And the sons of Israel came to buy *corn* among those that came: for the
famine was in the land of Canaan.
6 And Joseph *was* the governor over the land, *and* he *it was* that sold to all
the people of the land: and Joseph's brethren came, and bowed down them-
selves before him *with* their faces to the earth.
7 And Joseph saw his brethren, and he knew them, but made himself strange
unto them, and spake roughly unto them; and he said unto them, Whence
come ye? And they said, From the land of Canaan to buy food.
8 And Joseph knew his brethren, but they knew not him.
9 And Joseph remembered the dreams which he dreamed of them, and said
unto them, Ye *are* spies; to see the nakedness of the land ye are come.
10 And they said unto him, Nay, my lord, but to buy food are thy servants
come.
11 We *are* all one man's sons; we *are* true *men*, thy servants are no spies.
12 And he said unto them, Nay, but to see the nakedness of the land ye are
come.
13 And they said, Thy servants *are* twelve brethren, the sons of one man in
the land of Canaan; and, behold, the youngest *is* this day with our father, and
one *is* not.
14 And Joseph said unto them, That *is it* that I spake unto you, saying, Ye *are*
spies:
15 Hereby ye shall be proved: By the life of Pharaoh ye shall not go forth
hence, except your youngest brother come hither.

16 Send one of you, and let him fetch your brother, and ye shall be kept in
prison, that your words may be proved, whether *there be any* truth in you: or
else by the life of Pharaoh surely ye *are* spies.
17 And he put them all together into ward three days.
18 And Joseph said unto them the third day, This do, and live; *for* I fear God:
19 If ye *be* true *men*, let one of your brethren be bound in the house of your
prison: go ye, carry corn for the famine of your houses:
20 But bring your youngest brother unto me; so shall your words be verified,
and ye shall not die. And they did so.

The Sons Have Remorse for Joseph

21 And they said one to another, We *are* verily guilty concerning our broth-
er, in that we saw the anguish of his soul, when he besought us, and we would
not hear; therefore is this distress come upon us.
22 And Reuben answered them, saying, Spake I not unto you, saying, Do not
sin against the child; and ye would not hear? therefore, behold, also his blood
is required.
23 And they knew not that Joseph understood *them*; for he spake unto them
by an interpreter.
24 And he turned himself about from them, and wept; and returned to them
again, and communed with them, and took from them Simeon, and bound
him before their eyes.
25 Then Joseph commanded to fill their sacks with corn, and to restore every
man's money into his sack, and to give them provision for the way: and thus
did he unto them.
26 And they laded their asses with the corn, and departed thence.
27 And as one of them opened his sack to give his ass provender in the inn,
he espied his money; for, behold, it *was* in his sack's mouth.
28 And he said unto his brethren, My money is restored; and, lo, *it is* even in
my sack: and their heart failed *them*, and they were afraid, saying one to anoth-
er, What *is* this *that* God hath done unto us?
29 And they came unto Jacob their father unto the land of Canaan, and told
him all that befell unto them; saying,
30 The man, *who is* the lord of the land, spake roughly to us, and took us for
spies of the country.
31 And we said unto him, We *are* true *men*; we are no spies:
32 We *be* twelve brethren, sons of our father; one *is* not, and the youngest *is*
this day with our father in the land of Canaan.
33 And the man, the lord of the country, said unto us, Hereby shall I know
that ye *are* true *men*; leave one of your brethren *here* with me, and take *food*
for the famine of your households, and be gone:
34 And bring your youngest brother unto me: then shall I know that ye *are*
no spies, but *that* ye *are* true *men: so* will I deliver you your brother, and ye
shall traffick in the land.
35 And it came to pass as they emptied their sacks, that, behold, every man's
bundle of money *was* in his sack: and when *both* they and their father saw the
bundles of money, they were afraid.
36 And Jacob their father said unto them, Me have ye bereaved *of my children*:
Joseph *is* not, and Simeon *is* not, and ye will take Benjamin *away*: all these
things are against me.
37 And Reuben spake unto his father, saying, Slay my two sons, if I bring him
not to thee: deliver him into my hand, and I will bring him to thee again.
38 And he said, My son shall not go down with you; for his brother is dead,
and he is left alone: if mischief befall him by the way in the which ye go, then
shall ye bring down my gray hairs with sorrow to the grave.

Jacob Is Persuaded to Send Benjamin

43 And the famine *was* sore in the land.
2 And it came to pass, when they had eaten up the corn which they
had brought out of Egypt, their father said unto them, Go again, buy us a little
food.
3 And Judah spake unto him, saying, The man did solemnly protest unto us,
saying, Ye shall not see my face, except your brother *be* with you.
4 If thou wilt send our brother with us, we will go down and buy thee food:
5 But if thou wilt not send *him*, we will not go down: for the man said unto
us, Ye shall not see my face, except your brother *be* with you.
6 And Israel said, Wherefore dealt ye *so* ill with me, *as* to tell the man wheth-
er ye had yet a brother?
7 And they said, The man asked us straitly of our state, and of our kindred,
saying, *Is* your father yet alive? have ye *another* brother? and we told him
according to the tenor of these words: could we certainly know that he would
say, Bring your brother down?
8 And Judah said unto Israel his father, Send the lad with me, and we will
arise and go; that we may live, and not die, both we, and thou, *and* also our
little ones.
9 I will be surety for him; of my hand shalt thou require him: if I bring him
not unto thee, and set him before thee, then let me bear the blame for ever:
10 For except we had lingered, surely now we had returned this second time.
11 And their father Israel said unto them, If *it must be* so now, do this; take
of the best fruits in the land in your vessels, and carry down the man a present,
a little balm, and a little honey, spices, and myrrh, nuts, and almonds:
12 And take double money in your hand; and the money that was brought
again in the mouth of your sacks, carry *it* again in your hand; peradventure
it *was* an oversight:
13 Take also your brother, and arise, go again unto the man:
14 And God Almighty give you mercy before the man, that he may send away
your other brother, and Benjamin. If I be bereaved *of my children*, I am
bereaved.

Joseph Entertains His Brothers

15 And the men took that present, and they took double money in their hand,
and Benjamin; and rose up, and went down to Egypt, and stood before Joseph.
16 And when Joseph saw Benjamin with them, he said to the ruler of his
house, Bring *these* men home, and slay, and make ready; for *these* men shall
dine with me at noon.
17 And the man did as Joseph bade; and the man brought the men into
Joseph's house.
18 And the men were afraid, because they were brought into Joseph's house;
and they said, Because of the money that was returned in our sacks at the first
time are we brought in; that he may seek occasion against us, and fall upon
us, and take us for bondmen, and our asses.
19 And they came near to the steward of Joseph's house, and they communed
with him at the door of the house,
20 And said, O sir, we came indeed down at the first time to buy food:
21 And it came to pass, when we came to the inn, that we opened our sacks,
and, behold, *every* man's money *was* in the mouth of his sack, our money in
full weight: and we have brought it again in our hand.
22 And other money have we brought down in our hands to buy food: we
cannot tell who put our money in our sacks.
23 And he said, Peace *be* to you, fear not: your God, and the God of your father,
hath given you treasure in your sacks: I had your money. And he brought
Simeon out unto them.

24 And the man brought the men into Joseph's house, and gave *them* water,
and they washed their feet; and he gave their asses provender.
25 And they made ready the present against Joseph came at noon: for they
heard that they should eat bread there.
26 And when Joseph came home, they brought him the present which *was*
in their hand into the house, and bowed themselves to him to the earth.
27 And he asked them of *their* welfare, and said, *Is* your father well, the old
man of whom ye spake? *Is* he yet alive?
28 And they answered, Thy servant our father *is* in good health, he *is* yet alive.
And they bowed down their heads, and made obeisance.
29 And he lifted up his eyes, and saw his brother Benjamin, his mother's son,
and said, *Is* this your younger brother, of whom ye spake unto me? And he
said, God be gracious unto thee, my son.
30 And Joseph made haste; for his bowels did yearn upon his brother: and
he sought *where* to weep; and he entered into *his* chamber, and wept there.
31 And he washed his face, and went out, and refrained himself, and said,
Set on bread.
32 And they set on for him by himself, and for them by themselves, and for
the Egyptians, which did eat with him, by themselves: because the Egyptians
might not eat bread with the Hebrews; for that *is* an abomination unto the
Egyptians.
33 And they sat before him, the firstborn according to his birthright, and
the youngest according to his youth: and the men marvelled one at another.
34 And he took *and sent* messes unto them from before him: but Benjamin's
mess was five times so much as any of theirs. And they drank, and were merry
with him.

Joseph's Policy to Delay His Brothers

44 And he commanded the steward of his house, saying, Fill the men's
sacks *with* food, as much as they can carry, and put every man's money
in his sack's mouth.
2 And put my cup, the silver cup, in the sack's mouth of the youngest, and
his corn money. And he did according to the word that Joseph had spoken.
3 As soon as the morning was light, the men were sent away, they and their
asses.
4 *And* when they were gone out of the city, *and* not *yet* far off, Joseph said
unto his steward, Up, follow after the men; and when thou dost overtake them,
say unto them, Wherefore have ye rewarded evil for good?
5 *Is* not this *it* in which my lord drinketh, and whereby indeed he divineth?
ye have done evil in so doing.
6 And he overtook them, and he spake unto them these same words.
7 And they said unto him, Wherefore saith my lord these words? God forbid
that thy servants should do according to this thing:
8 Behold, the money, which we found in our sacks' mouths, we brought again
unto thee out of the land of Canaan: how then should we steal out of thy lord's
house silver or gold?
9 With whomsoever of thy servants it be found, both let him die, and we also
will be my lord's bondmen.
10 And he said, Now also *let* it *be* according unto your words: he with whom
it is found shall be my servant; and ye shall be blameless.
11 Then they speedily took down every man his sack to the ground, and
opened every man his sack.
12 And he searched, *and* began at the eldest, and left at the youngest: and the
cup was found in Benjamin's sack.
13 Then they rent their clothes, and laded every man his ass, and returned
to the city.

14 And Judah and his brethren came to Joseph's house; for he *was* yet there:
and they fell before him on the ground.
15 And Joseph said unto them, What deed *is* this that ye have done? wot ye
not that such a man as I can certainly divine?
16 And Judah said, What shall we say unto my lord? what shall we speak? or
how shall we clear ourselves? God hath found out the iniquity of thy servants:
behold, we *are* my lord's servants, both we, and *he* also with whom the cup is
found.
17 And he said, God forbid that I should do so: *but* the man in whose hand
the cup is found, he shall be my servant; and as for you, get you up in peace
unto your father.
18 Then Judah came near unto him, and said, Oh my lord, let thy servant, I
pray thee, speak a word in my lord's ears, and let not thine anger burn against
thy servant: for thou *art* even as Pharaoh.
19 My lord asked his servants, saying, Have ye a father, or a brother?
20 And we said unto my lord, We have a father, an old man, and a child of his
old age, a little one; and his brother is dead, and he alone is left of his mother,
and his father loveth him.
21 And thou saidst unto thy servants, Bring him down unto me, that I may
set mine eyes upon him.
22 And we said unto my lord, The lad cannot leave his father: for *if* he should
leave his father, *his father* would die.
23 And thou saidst unto thy servants, Except your youngest brother come
down with you, ye shall see my face no more.
24 And it came to pass when we came up unto thy servant my father, we told
him the words of my lord.
25 And our father said, Go again, *and* buy us a little food.
26 And we said, We cannot go down: if our youngest brother be with us, then
will we go down: for we may not see the man's face, except our youngest broth-
er *be* with us.
27 And thy servant my father said unto us, Ye know that my wife bare me two
sons:
28 And the one went out from me, and I said, Surely he is torn in pieces; and
I saw him not since:
29 And if ye take this also from me, and mischief befall him, ye shall bring
down my gray hairs with sorrow to the grave.
30 Now therefore when I come to thy servant my father, and the lad *be* not
with us; seeing that his life is bound up in the lad's life;
31 It shall come to pass, when he seeth that the lad *is* not *with us*, that he will
die: and thy servants shall bring down the gray hairs of thy servant our father
with sorrow to the grave.
32 For thy servant became surety for the lad unto my father, saying, If I bring
him not unto thee, then I shall bear the blame to my father for ever.
33 Now therefore, I pray thee, let thy servant abide instead of the lad a bond-
man to my lord; and let the lad go up with his brethren.
34 For how shall I go up to my father, and the lad *be* not with me? lest perad-
venture I see the evil that shall come on my father.

Joseph Makes Himself Known

45 Then Joseph could not refrain himself before all them that stood by him;
and he cried, Cause every man to go out from me. And there stood no
man with him, while Joseph made himself known unto his brethren.
2 And he wept aloud: and the Egyptians and the house of Pharaoh heard.
3 And Joseph said unto his brethren, I *am* Joseph; doth my father yet live?
And his brethren could not answer him; for they were troubled at his presence.

4 And Joseph said unto his brethren, Come near to me, I pray you. And they
came near. And he said, I *am* Joseph your brother, whom ye sold into Egypt.
5 Now therefore be not grieved, nor angry with yourselves, that ye sold me
hither: for God did send me before you to preserve life.
6 For these two years *hath* the famine *been* in the land: and yet *there are* five
years, in the which *there shall* neither *be* earing nor harvest.
7 And God sent me before you to preserve you a posterity in the earth, and
to save your lives by a great deliverance.
8 So now *it was* not you *that* sent me hither, but God: and he hath made me
a father to Pharaoh, and lord of all his house, and a ruler throughout all the
land of Egypt.
9 Haste ye, and go up to my father, and say unto him, Thus saith thy son
Joseph, God hath made me lord of all Egypt: come down unto me, tarry not:
10 And thou shalt dwell in the land of Goshen, and thou shalt be near unto
me, thou, and thy children, and thy children's children, and thy flocks, and
thy herds, and all that thou hast:
11 And there will I nourish thee; for yet *there are* five years of famine; lest
thou, and thy household, and all that thou hast, come to poverty.
12 And, behold, your eyes see, and the eyes of my brother Benjamin, that *it*
is my mouth that speaketh unto you.
13 And ye shall tell my father of all my glory in Egypt, and of all that ye have
seen; and ye shall haste and bring down my father hither.
14 And he fell upon his brother Benjamin's neck, and wept; and Benjamin
wept upon his neck.
15 Moreover he kissed all his brethren, and wept upon them: and after that
his brethren talked with him.

Pharaoh Is Pleased

16 And the fame thereof was heard in Pharaoh's house, saying, Joseph's breth-
ren are come: and it pleased Pharaoh well, and his servants.
17 And Pharaoh said unto Joseph, Say unto thy brethren, This do ye; lade your
beasts, and go, get you unto the land of Canaan;
18 And take your father and your households, and come unto me: and I will
give you the good of the land of Egypt, and ye shall eat the fat of the land.
19 Now thou art commanded, this do ye; take you wagons out of the land of
Egypt for your little ones, and for your wives, and bring your father, and come.
20 Also regard not your stuff; for the good of all the land of Egypt *is* yours.
21 And the children of Israel did so: and Joseph gave them wagons, according
to the commandment of Pharaoh, and gave them provision for the way.
22 To all of them he gave each man changes of raiment; but to Benjamin he
gave three hundred *pieces* of silver, and five changes of raiment.
23 And to his father he sent after this *manner*; ten asses laden with the good
things of Egypt, and ten she asses laden with corn and bread and meat for his
father by the way.
24 So he sent his brethren away, and they departed: and he said unto them,
See that ye fall not out by the way.

Jacob Learns That Joseph Is Alive

25 And they went up out of Egypt, and came into the land of Canaan unto
Jacob their father,
26 And told him, saying, Joseph *is* yet alive, and he *is* governor over all the
land of Egypt. And Jacob's heart fainted, for he believed them not.
27 And they told him all the words of Joseph, which he had said unto them:
and when he saw the wagons which Joseph had sent to carry him, the spirit
of Jacob their father revived:
28 And Israel said, *It is* enough; Joseph my son *is* yet alive: I will go and see
him before I die.

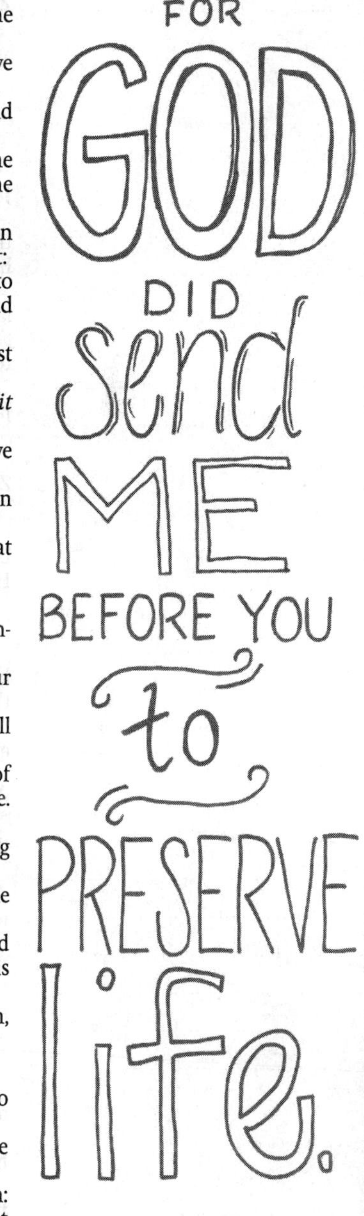

Jacob Is Comforted by God at Beer-sheba

46 And Israel took his journey with all that he had, and came to Beer-
sheba, and offered sacrifices unto the God of his father Isaac.
2 And God spake unto Israel in the visions of the night, and said, Jacob, Jacob.
And he said, Here *am* I.
3 And he said, I *am* God, the God of thy father: fear not to go down into Egypt;
for I will there make of thee a great nation:
4 I will go down with thee into Egypt; and I will also surely bring thee up
again: and Joseph shall put his hand upon thine eyes.

Jacob Journeys to Egypt

5 And Jacob rose up from Beer-sheba: and the sons of Israel carried Jacob
their father, and their little ones, and their wives, in the wagons which Pharaoh
had sent to carry him.
6 And they took their cattle, and their goods, which they had gotten in the
land of Canaan, and came into Egypt, Jacob, and all his seed with him:
7 His sons, and his sons' sons with him, his daughters, and his sons' daugh-
ters, and all his seed brought he with him into Egypt.
8 And these *are* the names of the children of Israel, which came into Egypt,
Jacob and his sons: Reuben, Jacob's firstborn.
9 And the sons of Reuben; Hanoch, and Phallu, and Hezron, and Carmi.
10 And the sons of Simeon; Jemuel, and Jamin, and Ohad, and Jachin, and
Zohar, and Shaul the son of a Canaanitish woman.
11 And the sons of Levi; Gershon, Kohath, and Merari.
12 And the sons of Judah; Er, and Onan, and Shelah, and Pharez, and Zerah:
but Er and Onan died in the land of Canaan. And the sons of Pharez were
Hezron and Hamul.
13 And the sons of Issachar; Tola, and Phuvah, and Job, and Shimron.
14 And the sons of Zebulun; Sered, and Elon, and Jahleel.
15 These *be* the sons of Leah, which she bare unto Jacob in Padan-aram, with
his daughter Dinah: all the souls of his sons and his daughters *were* thirty and
three.
16 And the sons of Gad; Ziphion, and Haggi, Shuni, and Ezbon, Eri, and Arodi,
and Areli.
17 And the sons of Asher; Jimnah, and Ishuah, and Isui, and Beriah, and Serah
their sister: and the sons of Beriah; Heber, and Malchiel.
18 These *are* the sons of Zilpah, whom Laban gave to Leah his daughter, and
these she bare unto Jacob, *even* sixteen souls.
19 The sons of Rachel Jacob's wife; Joseph, and Benjamin.
20 And unto Joseph in the land of Egypt were born Manasseh and Ephraim,
which Asenath the daughter of Poti-pherah priest of On bare unto him.
21 And the sons of Benjamin *were* Belah, and Becher, and Ashbel, Gera, and
Naaman, Ehi, and Rosh, Muppim, and Huppim, and Ard.
22 These *are* the sons of Rachel, which were born to Jacob: all the souls *were*
fourteen.
23 And the sons of Dan; Hushim.
24 And the sons of Naphtali; Jahzeel, and Guni, and Jezer, and Shillem.
25 These *are* the sons of Bilhah, which Laban gave unto Rachel his daughter,
and she bare these unto Jacob: all the souls *were* seven.
26 All the souls that came with Jacob into Egypt, which came out of his loins,
besides Jacob's sons' wives, all the souls *were* threescore and six;
27 And the sons of Joseph, which were born him in Egypt, *were* two souls: all
the souls of the house of Jacob, which came into Egypt, *were* threescore and ten.

Joseph Comes to Meet His Father

28 And he sent Judah before him unto Joseph, to direct his face unto Goshen;
and they came into the land of Goshen.

29 And Joseph made ready his chariot, and went up to meet Israel his father,
to Goshen, and presented himself unto him; and he fell on his neck, and wept
on his neck a good while.
30 And Israel said unto Joseph, Now let me die, since I have seen thy face,
because thou *art* yet alive.
31 And Joseph said unto his brethren, and unto his father's house, I will go
up, and shew Pharaoh, and say unto him, My brethren, and my father's house,
which *were* in the land of Canaan, are come unto me;
32 And the men *are* shepherds, for their trade hath been to feed cattle; and
they have brought their flocks, and their herds, and all that they have.
33 And it shall come to pass, when Pharaoh shall call you, and shall say, What
is your occupation?
34 That ye shall say, Thy servants' trade hath been about cattle from our youth
even until now, both we, *and* also our fathers: that ye may dwell in the land of
Goshen; for every shepherd *is* an abomination unto the Egyptians.

Joseph Presents Five of His Brothers

47 Then Joseph came and told Pharaoh, and said, My father and my breth-
ren, and their flocks, and their herds, and all that they have, are come
out of the land of Canaan; and, behold, they *are* in the land of Goshen.
2 And he took some of his brethren, *even* five men, and presented them unto
Pharaoh.
3 And Pharaoh said unto his brethren, What *is* your occupation? And they
said unto Pharaoh, Thy servants *are* shepherds, both we, *and* also our fathers.
4 They said moreover unto Pharaoh, For to sojourn in the land are we come;
for thy servants have no pasture for their flocks; for the famine *is* sore in the
land of Canaan: now therefore, we pray thee, let thy servants dwell in the land
of Goshen.
5 And Pharaoh spake unto Joseph, saying, Thy father and thy brethren are
come unto thee:
6 The land of Egypt *is* before thee; in the best of the land make thy father and
brethren to dwell; in the land of Goshen let them dwell: and if thou knowest
any men of activity among them, then make them rulers over my cattle.
7 And Joseph brought in Jacob his father, and set him before Pharaoh: and
Jacob blessed Pharaoh.
8 And Pharaoh said unto Jacob, How old *art* thou?
9 And Jacob said unto Pharaoh, The days of the years of my pilgrimage *are*
an hundred and thirty years: few and evil have the days of the years of my life
been, and have not attained unto the days of the years of the life of my fathers
in the days of their pilgrimage.
10 And Jacob blessed Pharaoh, and went out from before Pharaoh.
11 And Joseph placed his father and his brethren, and gave them a possession
in the land of Egypt, in the best of the land, in the land of Rameses, as Pharaoh
had commanded.
12 And Joseph nourished his father, and his brethren, and all his father's
household, with bread, according to *their* families.

Joseph Collects the Egyptians' Money

13 And *there was* no bread in all the land; for the famine *was* very sore, so
that the land of Egypt and *all* the land of Canaan fainted by reason of the
famine.
14 And Joseph gathered up all the money that was found in the land of Egypt,
and in the land of Canaan, for the corn which they bought: and Joseph brought
the money into Pharaoh's house.
15 And when money failed in the land of Egypt, and in the land of Canaan,
all the Egyptians came unto Joseph, and said, Give us bread: for why should
we die in thy presence? for the money faileth.

16 And Joseph said, Give your cattle; and I will give you for your cattle, if
money fail.
17 And they brought their cattle unto Joseph: and Joseph gave them bread
in exchange for horses, and for the flocks, and for the cattle of the herds, and
for the asses: and he fed them with bread for all their cattle for that year.
18 When that year was ended, they came unto him the second year, and said
unto him, We will not hide *it* from my lord, how that our money is spent; my
lord also hath our herds of cattle; there is not ought left in the sight of my lord,
but our bodies, and our lands:
19 Wherefore shall we die before thine eyes, both we and our land? buy us
and our land for bread, and we and our land will be servants unto Pharaoh:
and give *us* seed, that we may live, and not die, that the land be not desolate.
20 And Joseph bought all the land of Egypt for Pharaoh; for the Egyptians
sold every man his field, because the famine prevailed over them: so the land
became Pharaoh's.
21 And as for the people, he removed them to cities from *one* end of the
borders of Egypt even to the *other* end thereof.
22 Only the land of the priests bought he not; for the priests had a portion
assigned them of Pharaoh, and did eat their portion which Pharaoh gave them:
wherefore they sold not their lands.
23 Then Joseph said unto the people, Behold, I have bought you this day and
your land for Pharaoh: lo, *here is* seed for you, and ye shall sow the land.
24 And it shall come to pass in the increase, that ye shall give the fifth *part*
unto Pharaoh, and four parts shall be your own, for seed of the field, and for
your food, and for them of your households, and for food for your little ones.
25 And they said, Thou hast saved our lives: let us find grace in the sight of
my lord, and we will be Pharaoh's servants.
26 And Joseph made it a law over the land of Egypt unto this day, *that* Pharaoh
should have the fifth *part*; except the land of the priests only, *which* became
not Pharaoh's.
27 And Israel dwelt in the land of Egypt, in the country of Goshen; and they
had possessions therein, and grew, and multiplied exceedingly.
28 And Jacob lived in the land of Egypt seventeen years: so the whole age of
Jacob was an hundred forty and seven years.
29 And the time drew nigh that Israel must die: and he called his son Joseph,
and said unto him, If now I have found grace in thy sight, put, I pray thee, thy
hand under my thigh, and deal kindly and truly with me; bury me not, I pray
thee, in Egypt:
30 But I will lie with my fathers, and thou shalt carry me out of Egypt, and
bury me in their burying place. And he said, I will do as thou hast said.
31 And he said, Swear unto me. And he sware unto him. And Israel bowed
himself upon the bed's head.

Joseph Brings His Sons to Jacob

48 And it came to pass after these things, that *one* told Joseph, Behold, thy
father *is* sick: and he took with him his two sons, Manasseh and
Ephraim.
2 And *one* told Jacob, and said, Behold, thy son Joseph cometh unto thee: and
Israel strengthened himself, and sat upon the bed.
3 And Jacob said unto Joseph, God Almighty appeared unto me at Luz in the
land of Canaan, and blessed me,
4 And said unto me, Behold, I will make thee fruitful, and multiply thee, and
I will make of thee a multitude of people; and will give this land to thy seed
after thee *for* an everlasting possession.

5 And now thy two sons, Ephraim and Manasseh, which were born unto thee
in the land of Egypt before I came unto thee into Egypt, *are* mine; as Reuben
and Simeon, they shall be mine.
6 And thy issue, which thou begettest after them, shall be thine, *and* shall be
called after the name of their brethren in their inheritance.
7 And as for me, when I came from Padan, Rachel died by me in the land of
Canaan in the way, when yet *there was* but a little way to come unto Ephrath:
and I buried her there in the way of Ephrath; the same *is* Beth-lehem.
8 And Israel beheld Joseph's sons, and said, Who *are* these?
9 And Joseph said unto his father, They *are* my sons, whom God hath given
me in this *place*. And he said, Bring them, I pray thee, unto me, and I will bless
them.
10 Now the eyes of Israel were dim for age, *so that* he could not see. And he
brought them near unto him; and he kissed them, and embraced them.
11 And Israel said unto Joseph, I had not thought to see thy face: and, lo, God
hath shewed me also thy seed.
12 And Joseph brought them out from between his knees, and he bowed
himself with his face to the earth.
13 And Joseph took them both, Ephraim in his right hand toward Israel's left
hand, and Manasseh in his left hand toward Israel's right hand, and brought
them near unto him.
14 And Israel stretched out his right hand, and laid *it* upon Ephraim's head,
who *was* the younger, and his left hand upon Manasseh's head, guiding his
hands wittingly; for Manasseh *was* the firstborn.
15 And he blessed Joseph, and said, God, before whom my fathers Abraham
and Isaac did walk, the God which fed me all my life long unto this day,
16 The Angel which redeemed me from all evil, bless the lads; and let my
name be named on them, and the name of my fathers Abraham and Isaac; and
let them grow into a multitude in the midst of the earth.
17 And when Joseph saw that his father laid his right hand upon the head of
Ephraim, it displeased him: and he held up his father's hand, to remove it from
Ephraim's head unto Manasseh's head.
18 And Joseph said unto his father, Not so, my father: for this *is* the firstborn;
put thy right hand upon his head.
19 And his father refused, and said, I know *it*, my son, I know *it*: he also shall
become a people, and he also shall be great: but truly his younger brother shall
be greater than he, and his seed shall become a multitude of nations.
20 And he blessed them that day, saying, In thee shall Israel bless, saying, God
make thee as Ephraim and as Manasseh: and he set Ephraim before Manasseh.
21 And Israel said unto Joseph, Behold, I die: but God shall be with you, and
bring you again unto the land of your fathers.
22 Moreover I have given to thee one portion above thy brethren, which I
took out of the hand of the Amorite with my sword and with my bow.

Jacob Calls His Sons to Bless Them

49 And Jacob called unto his sons, and said, Gather yourselves together,
that I may tell you *that* which shall befall you in the last days.
2 Gather yourselves together, and hear, ye sons of Jacob; and hearken unto
Israel your father.
3 Reuben, thou *art* my firstborn, my might, and the beginning of my
strength, the excellency of dignity, and the excellency of power:
4 Unstable as water, thou shalt not excel; because thou wentest up to thy
father's bed; then defiledst thou *it*: he went up to my couch.
5 Simeon and Levi *are* brethren; instruments of cruelty *are in* their habitations.

GENESIS 49:18
I HAVE waited FOR THY Salvation, O LORD.

6 O my soul, come not thou into their secret; unto their assembly, mine hon-
our, be not thou united: for in their anger they slew a man, and in their selfwill
they digged down a wall.
7 Cursed *be* their anger, for *it was* fierce; and their wrath, for it was cruel: I
will divide them in Jacob, and scatter them in Israel.
8 Judah, thou *art he* whom thy brethren shall praise: thy hand *shall be* in the
neck of thine enemies; thy father's children shall bow down before thee.
9 Judah *is* a lion's whelp: from the prey, my son, thou art gone up: he stooped
down, he couched as a lion, and as an old lion; who shall rouse him up?
10 The sceptre shall not depart from Judah, nor a lawgiver from between his
feet, until Shiloh come; and unto him *shall* the gathering of the people *be*.
11 Binding his foal unto the vine, and his ass's colt unto the choice vine; he
washed his garments in wine, and his clothes in the blood of grapes:
12 His eyes *shall be* red with wine, and his teeth white with milk.
13 Zebulun shall dwell at the haven of the sea; and he *shall be* for an haven
of ships; and his border *shall be* unto Zidon.
14 Issachar *is* a strong ass couching down between two burdens:
15 And he saw that rest *was* good, and the land that *it was* pleasant; and
bowed his shoulder to bear, and became a servant unto tribute.
16 Dan shall judge his people, as one of the tribes of Israel.
17 Dan shall be a serpent by the way, an adder in the path, that biteth the
horse heels, so that his rider shall fall backward.
18 I have waited for thy salvation, O LORD.
19 Gad, a troop shall overcome him: but he shall overcome at the last.
20 Out of Asher his bread *shall be* fat, and he shall yield royal dainties.
21 Naphtali *is* a hind let loose: he giveth goodly words.
22 Joseph *is* a fruitful bough, *even* a fruitful bough by a well; *whose* branches
run over the wall:
23 The archers have sorely grieved him, and shot *at him*, and hated him:
24 But his bow abode in strength, and the arms of his hands were made
strong by the hands of the mighty *God* of Jacob; (from thence *is* the shepherd,
the stone of Israel:)
25 *Even* by the God of thy father, who shall help thee; and by the Almighty,
who shall bless thee with blessings of heaven above, blessings of the deep that
lieth under, blessings of the breasts, and of the womb:
26 The blessings of thy father have prevailed above the blessings of my pro-
genitors unto the utmost bound of the everlasting hills: they shall be on the
head of Joseph, and on the crown of the head of him that was separate from
his brethren.
27 Benjamin shall ravin *as* a wolf: in the morning he shall devour the prey,
and at night he shall divide the spoil.
28 All these *are* the twelve tribes of Israel: and this *is it* that their father spake
unto them, and blessed them; every one according to his blessing he blessed
them.
29 And he charged them, and said unto them, I am to be gathered unto my
people: bury me with my fathers in the cave that *is* in the field of Ephron the
Hittite,
30 In the cave that *is* in the field of Machpelah, which *is* before Mamre, in
the land of Canaan, which Abraham bought with the field of Ephron the
Hittite for a possession of a burying place.
31 There they buried Abraham and Sarah his wife; there they buried Isaac
and Rebekah his wife; and there I buried Leah.
32 The purchase of the field and of the cave that *is* therein *was* from the
children of Heth.

33 And when Jacob had made an end of commanding his sons, he gathered
up his feet into the bed, and yielded up the ghost, and was gathered unto his
people.

The Mourning for Jacob

50 And Joseph fell upon his father's face, and wept upon him, and kissed
him.
2 And Joseph commanded his servants the physicians to embalm his father:
and the physicians embalmed Israel.
3 And forty days were fulfilled for him; for so are fulfilled the days of those
which are embalmed: and the Egyptians mourned for him threescore and ten
days.
4 And when the days of his mourning were past, Joseph spake unto the house
of Pharaoh, saying, If now I have found grace in your eyes, speak, I pray you,
in the ears of Pharaoh, saying,
5 My father made me swear, saying, Lo, I die: in my grave which I have digged
for me in the land of Canaan, there shalt thou bury me. Now therefore let me
go up, I pray thee, and bury my father, and I will come again.
6 And Pharaoh said, Go up, and bury thy father, according as he made thee
swear.
7 And Joseph went up to bury his father: and with him went up all the ser-
vants of Pharaoh, the elders of his house, and all the elders of the land of Egypt,
8 And all the house of Joseph, and his brethren, and his father's house: only
their little ones, and their flocks, and their herds, they left in the land of
Goshen.
9 And there went up with him both chariots and horsemen: and it was a very
great company.
10 And they came to the threshingfloor of Atad, which *is* beyond Jordan, and
there they mourned with a great and very sore lamentation: and he made a
mourning for his father seven days.
11 And when the inhabitants of the land, the Canaanites, saw the mourning
in the floor of Atad, they said, This *is* a grievous mourning to the Egyptians:
wherefore the name of it was called Abel-mizraim, which *is* beyond Jordan.
12 And his sons did unto him according as he commanded them:
13 For his sons carried him into the land of Canaan, and buried him in the
cave of the field of Machpelah, which Abraham bought with the field for a
possession of a burying place of Ephron the Hittite, before Mamre.
14 And Joseph returned into Egypt, he, and his brethren, and all that went
up with him to bury his father, after he had buried his father.

Joseph Comforts His Brothers

15 And when Joseph's brethren saw that their father was dead, they said,
Joseph will peradventure hate us, and will certainly requite us all the evil which
we did unto him.
16 And they sent a messenger unto Joseph, saying, Thy father did command
before he died, saying,
17 So shall ye say unto Joseph, Forgive, I pray thee now, the trespass of thy
brethren, and their sin; for they did unto thee evil: and now, we pray thee,
forgive the trespass of the servants of the God of thy father. And Joseph wept
when they spake unto him.
18 And his brethren also went and fell down before his face; and they said,
Behold, we *be* thy servants.
19 And Joseph said unto them, Fear not: for *am* I in the place of God?
20 But as for you, ye thought evil against me; *but* God meant it unto good, to
bring to pass, as *it is* this day, to save much people alive.
21 Now therefore fear ye not: I will nourish you, and your little ones. And he
comforted them, and spake kindly unto them.

BUT AS FOR YOU,
ye thought
EVIL
AGAINST ME;
BUT
GOD
meant it unto
good,
to bring
to pass,
AS IT IS THIS DAY,
TO SAVE
MUCH PEOPLE
alive
GENESIS 50:20

Joseph's Age and Death
22 And Joseph dwelt in Egypt, he, and his father's house: and Joseph lived an
hundred and ten years.
23 And Joseph saw Ephraim's children of the third *generation*: the children
also of Machir the son of Manasseh were brought up upon Joseph's knees.
24 And Joseph said unto his brethren, I die: and God will surely visit you, and
bring you out of this land unto the land which he sware to Abraham, to Isaac,
and to Jacob.
25 And Joseph took an oath of the children of Israel, saying, God will surely
visit you, and ye shall carry up my bones from hence.
26 So Joseph died, *being* an hundred and ten years old: and they embalmed
him, and he was put in a coffin in Egypt.

The Israelites Increase

1 Now these *are* the names of the children of Israel, which came into Egypt; every man and his household came with Jacob.
2 Reuben, Simeon, Levi, and Judah,
3 Issachar, Zebulun, and Benjamin,
4 Dan, and Naphtali, Gad, and Asher.
5 And all the souls that came out of the loins of Jacob were seventy souls: for Joseph was in Egypt *already*.
6 And Joseph died, and all his brethren, and all that generation.
7 And the children of Israel were fruitful, and increased abundantly, and multiplied, and waxed exceeding mighty; and the land was filled with them.

A New King, Who Knew Not Joseph, Arises

8 Now there arose up a new king over Egypt, which knew not Joseph.
9 And he said unto his people, Behold, the people of the children of Israel *are* more and mightier than we:
10 Come on, let us deal wisely with them; lest they multiply, and it come to pass, that, when there falleth out any war, they join also unto our enemies, and fight against us, and *so* get them up out of the land.
11 Therefore they did set over them taskmasters to afflict them with their burdens. And they built for Pharaoh treasure cities, Pithom and Raamses.
12 But the more they afflicted them, the more they multiplied and grew. And they were grieved because of the children of Israel.
13 And the Egyptians made the children of Israel to serve with rigour:
14 And they made their lives bitter with hard bondage, in morter, and in brick, and in all manner of service in the field: all their service, wherein they made them serve, *was* with rigour.

The Midwives Save the Male Children

15 And the king of Egypt spake to the Hebrew midwives, of which the name of the one *was* Shiphrah, and the name of the other Puah:
16 And he said, When ye do the office of a midwife to the Hebrew women, and see *them* upon the stools; if it *be* a son, then ye shall kill him: but if it *be* a daughter, then she shall live.
17 But the midwives feared God, and did not as the king of Egypt commanded them, but saved the men children alive.
18 And the king of Egypt called for the midwives, and said unto them, Why have ye done this thing, and have saved the men children alive?
19 And the midwives said unto Pharaoh, Because the Hebrew women *are* not as the Egyptian women; for they *are* lively, and are delivered ere the midwives come in unto them.
20 Therefore God dealt well with the midwives: and the people multiplied, and waxed very mighty.
21 And it came to pass, because the midwives feared God, that he made them houses.
22 And Pharaoh charged all his people, saying, Every son that is born ye shall cast into the river, and every daughter ye shall save alive.

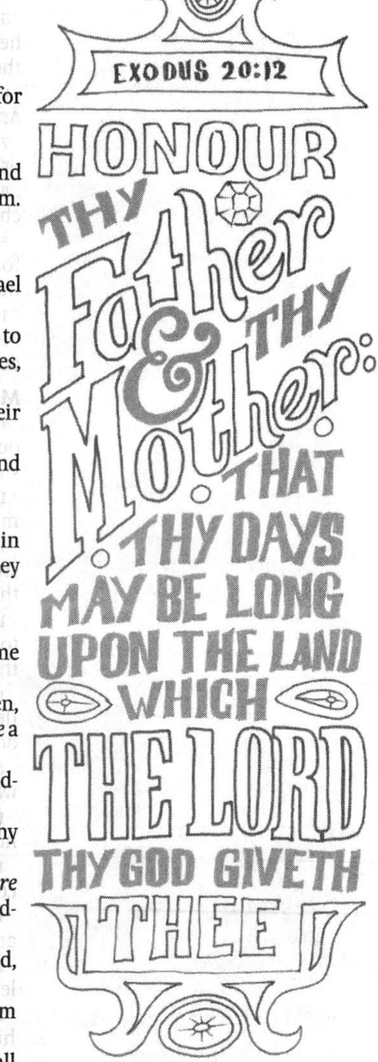

Moses Is Born

2 And there went a man of the house of Levi, and took *to wife* a daughter of
Levi.
2 And the woman conceived, and bare a son: and when she saw him that he
was a goodly *child*, she hid him three months.
3 And when she could not longer hide him, she took for him an ark of bul-
rushes, and daubed it with slime and with pitch, and put the child therein;
and she laid *it* in the flags by the river's brink.
4 And his sister stood afar off, to wit what would be done to him.

Moses Is Found, and Brought up by Pharaoh's Daughter

5 And the daughter of Pharaoh came down to wash *herself* at the river; and
her maidens walked along by the river's side; and when she saw the ark among
the flags, she sent her maid to fetch it.
6 And when she had opened *it*, she saw the child: and, behold, the babe wept.
And she had compassion on him, and said, This *is one* of the Hebrews' children.
7 Then said his sister to Pharaoh's daughter, Shall I go and call to thee a nurse
of the Hebrew women, that she may nurse the child for thee?
8 And Pharaoh's daughter said to her, Go. And the maid went and called the
child's mother.
9 And Pharaoh's daughter said unto her, Take this child away, and nurse it
for me, and I will give *thee* thy wages. And the woman took the child, and
nursed it.
10 And the child grew, and she brought him unto Pharaoh's daughter, and
he became her son. And she called his name Moses: and she said, Because I
drew him out of the water.

Moses Kills an Egyptian

11 And it came to pass in those days, when Moses was grown, that he went
out unto his brethren, and looked on their burdens: and he spied an Egyptian
smiting an Hebrew, one of his brethren.
12 And he looked this way and that way, and when he saw that *there was* no
man, he slew the Egyptian, and hid him in the sand.
13 And when he went out the second day, behold, two men of the Hebrews
strove together: and he said to him that did the wrong, Wherefore smitest
thou thy fellow?
14 And he said, Who made thee a prince and a judge over us? intendest thou
to kill me, as thou killedst the Egyptian? And Moses feared, and said, Surely
this thing is known.
15 Now when Pharaoh heard this thing, he sought to slay Moses. But Moses
fled from the face of Pharaoh, and dwelt in the land of Midian: and he sat
down by a well.
16 Now the priest of Midian had seven daughters: and they came and drew
water, and filled the troughs to water their father's flock.
17 And the shepherds came and drove them away: but Moses stood up and
helped them, and watered their flock.
18 And when they came to Reuel their father, he said, How *is it that* ye are
come so soon to day?
19 And they said, An Egyptian delivered us out of the hand of the shepherds,
and also drew *water* enough for us, and watered the flock.
20 And he said unto his daughters, And where *is* he? why *is* it *that* ye have
left the man? call him, that he may eat bread.
21 And Moses was content to dwell with the man: and he gave Moses Zipporah
his daughter.
22 And she bare *him* a son, and he called his name Gershom: for he said, I
have been a stranger in a strange land.

God Hears the Complaints of the Israelites

23 And it came to pass in process of time, that the king of Egypt died: and the
children of Israel sighed by reason of the bondage, and they cried, and their
cry came up unto God by reason of the bondage.
24 And God heard their groaning, and God remembered his covenant with
Abraham, with Isaac, and with Jacob.
25 And God looked upon the children of Israel, and God had respect unto
them.

Moses Keeps Jethro's Flock

3 Now Moses kept the flock of Jethro his father in law, the priest of Midian:
and he led the flock to the backside of the desert, and came to the mountain
of God, *even* to Horeb.
2 And the angel of the LORD appeared unto him in a flame of fire out of the
midst of a bush: and he looked, and, behold, the bush burned with fire, and
the bush *was* not consumed.
3 And Moses said, I will now turn aside, and see this great sight, why the bush
is not burnt.
4 And when the LORD saw that he turned aside to see, God called unto him
out of the midst of the bush, and said, Moses, Moses. And he said, Here *am* I.
5 And he said, Draw not nigh hither: put off thy shoes from off thy feet, for
the place whereon thou standest *is* holy ground.
6 Moreover he said, I *am* the God of thy father, the God of Abraham, the God
of Isaac, and the God of Jacob. And Moses hid his face; for he was afraid to look
upon God.
7 And the LORD said, I have surely seen the affliction of my people which *are*
in Egypt, and have heard their cry by reason of their taskmasters; for I know
their sorrows;
8 And I am come down to deliver them out of the hand of the Egyptians, and
to bring them up out of that land unto a good land and a large, unto a land
flowing with milk and honey; unto the place of the Canaanites, and the
Hittites, and the Amorites, and the Perizzites, and the Hivites, and the Jebusites.
9 Now therefore, behold, the cry of the children of Israel is come unto me:
and I have also seen the oppression wherewith the Egyptians oppress them.
10 Come now therefore, and I will send thee unto Pharaoh, that thou mayest
bring forth my people the children of Israel out of Egypt.
11 And Moses said unto God, Who *am* I, that I should go unto Pharaoh, and
that I should bring forth the children of Israel out of Egypt?
12 And he said, Certainly I will be with thee; and this *shall be* a token unto
thee, that I have sent thee: When thou hast brought forth the people out of
Egypt, ye shall serve God upon this mountain.
13 And Moses said unto God, Behold, *when* I come unto the children of Israel,
and shall say unto them, The God of your fathers hath sent me unto you; and
they shall say to me, What *is* his name? what shall I say unto them?
14 And God said unto Moses, I AM THAT I AM: and he said, Thus shalt thou
say unto the children of Israel, I AM hath sent me unto you.
15 And God said moreover unto Moses, Thus shalt thou say unto the children
of Israel, The LORD God of your fathers, the God of Abraham, the God of Isaac,
and the God of Jacob, hath sent me unto you: this *is* my name for ever, and this
is my memorial unto all generations.
16 Go, and gather the elders of Israel together, and say unto them, The LORD
God of your fathers, the God of Abraham, of Isaac, and of Jacob, appeared
unto me, saying, I have surely visited you, and *seen* that which is done to you
in Egypt:

17 And I have said, I will bring you up out of the affliction of Egypt unto the
land of the Canaanites, and the Hittites, and the Amorites, and the Perizzites,
and the Hivites, and the Jebusites, unto a land flowing with milk and honey.
18 And they shall hearken to thy voice: and thou shalt come, thou and the
elders of Israel, unto the king of Egypt, and ye shall say unto him, The LORD
God of the Hebrews hath met with us: and now let us go, we beseech thee,
three days' journey into the wilderness, that we may sacrifice to the LORD our
God.
19 And I am sure that the king of Egypt will not let you go, no, not by a mighty
hand.
20 And I will stretch out my hand, and smite Egypt with all my wonders which
I will do in the midst thereof: and after that he will let you go.
21 And I will give this people favour in the sight of the Egyptians: and it shall
come to pass, that, when ye go, ye shall not go empty:
22 But every woman shall borrow of her neighbour, and of her that sojour-
neth in her house, jewels of silver, and jewels of gold, and raiment: and ye shall
put *them* upon your sons, and upon your daughters; and ye shall spoil the
Egyptians.

Moses' Rod Is Turned into a Serpent as a Sign

4 And Moses answered and said, But, behold, they will not believe me, nor
hearken unto my voice: for they will say, The LORD hath not appeared unto
thee.
2 And the LORD said unto him, What *is* that in thine hand? And he said, A
rod.
3 And he said, Cast it on the ground. And he cast it on the ground, and it
became a serpent; and Moses fled from before it.
4 And the LORD said unto Moses, Put forth thine hand, and take it by the tail.
And he put forth his hand, and caught it, and it became a rod in his hand:
5 That they may believe that the LORD God of their fathers, the God of
Abraham, the God of Isaac, and the God of Jacob, hath appeared unto thee.
6 And the LORD said furthermore unto him, Put now thine hand into thy
bosom. And he put his hand into his bosom: and when he took it out, behold,
his hand *was* leprous as snow.
7 And he said, Put thine hand into thy bosom again. And he put his hand into
his bosom again; and plucked it out of his bosom, and, behold, it was turned
again as his *other* flesh.
8 And it shall come to pass, if they will not believe thee, neither hearken to
the voice of the first sign, that they will believe the voice of the latter sign.
9 And it shall come to pass, if they will not believe also these two signs, neither
hearken unto thy voice, that thou shalt take of the water of the river, and pour
it upon the dry *land*: and the water which thou takest out of the river shall
become blood upon the dry *land*.

Moses' Brother, Aaron, Joins Him

10 And Moses said unto the LORD, O my Lord, I *am* not eloquent, neither
heretofore, nor since thou hast spoken unto thy servant: but I *am* slow of
speech, and of a slow tongue.
11 And the LORD said unto him, Who hath made man's mouth? or who
maketh the dumb, or deaf, or the seeing, or the blind? have not I the LORD?
12 Now therefore go, and I will be with thy mouth, and teach thee what thou
shalt say.
13 And he said, O my Lord, send, I pray thee, by the hand *of him whom* thou
wilt send.
14 And the anger of the LORD was kindled against Moses, and he said, *Is* not
Aaron the Levite thy brother? I know that he can speak well. And also, behold,

he cometh forth to meet thee: and when he seeth thee, he will be glad in his
heart.
15 And thou shalt speak unto him, and put words in his mouth: and I will be
with thy mouth, and with his mouth, and will teach you what ye shall do.
16 And he shall be thy spokesman unto the people: and he shall be, *even* he
shall be to thee instead of a mouth, and thou shalt be to him instead of God.
17 And thou shalt take this rod in thine hand, wherewith thou shalt do signs.

Moses Departs from Jethro

18 And Moses went and returned to Jethro his father in law, and said unto
him, Let me go, I pray thee, and return unto my brethren which *are* in Egypt,
and see whether they be yet alive. And Jethro said to Moses, Go in peace.
19 And the LORD said unto Moses in Midian, Go, return into Egypt: for all the
men are dead which sought thy life.
20 And Moses took his wife and his sons, and set them upon an ass, and he
returned to the land of Egypt: and Moses took the rod of God in his hand.
21 And the LORD said unto Moses, When thou goest to return into Egypt, see
that thou do all those wonders before Pharaoh, which I have put in thine hand:
but I will harden his heart, that he shall not let the people go.
22 And thou shalt say unto Pharaoh, Thus saith the LORD, Israel *is* my son,
even my firstborn:
23 And I say unto thee, Let my son go, that he may serve me: and if thou refuse
to let him go, behold, I will slay thy son, *even* thy firstborn.

Zipporah Circumcises Her Son

24 And it came to pass by the way in the inn, that the LORD met him, and
sought to kill him.
25 Then Zipporah took a sharp stone, and cut off the foreskin of her son, and
cast *it* at his feet, and said, Surely a bloody husband *art* thou to me.
26 So he let him go: then she said, A bloody husband *thou art*, because of the
circumcision.
27 And the LORD said to Aaron, Go into the wilderness to meet Moses. And
he went, and met him in the mount of God, and kissed him.
28 And Moses told Aaron all the words of the LORD who had sent him, and
all the signs which he had commanded him.
29 And Moses and Aaron went and gathered together all the elders of the
children of Israel:
30 And Aaron spake all the words which the LORD had spoken unto Moses,
and did the signs in the sight of the people.
31 And the people believed: and when they heard that the LORD had visited
the children of Israel, and that he had looked upon their affliction, then they
bowed their heads and worshipped.

Pharaoh Chides Moses and Aaron for Their Message

5 And afterward Moses and Aaron went in, and told Pharaoh, Thus saith the
LORD God of Israel, Let my people go, that they may hold a feast unto me in
the wilderness.
2 And Pharaoh said, Who *is* the LORD, that I should obey his voice to let Israel
go? I know not the LORD, neither will I let Israel go.
3 And they said, The God of the Hebrews hath met with us: let us go, we pray
thee, three days' journey into the desert, and sacrifice unto the LORD our God;
lest he fall upon us with pestilence, or with the sword.
4 And the king of Egypt said unto them, Wherefore do ye, Moses and Aaron,
let the people from their works? get you unto your burdens.
5 And Pharaoh said, Behold, the people of the land now *are* many, and ye
make them rest from their burdens.
6 And Pharaoh commanded the same day the taskmasters of the people, and
their officers, saying,

7 Ye shall no more give the people straw to make brick, as heretofore: let them
go and gather straw for themselves.
8 And the tale of the bricks, which they did make heretofore, ye shall lay upon
them; ye shall not diminish *ought* thereof: for they *be* idle; therefore they cry,
saying, Let us go *and* sacrifice to our God.
9 Let there more work be laid upon the men, that they may labour therein;
and let them not regard vain words.
10 And the taskmasters of the people went out, and their officers, and they
spake to the people, saying, Thus saith Pharaoh, I will not give you straw.
11 Go ye, get you straw where ye can find it: yet not ought of your work shall
be diminished.
12 So the people were scattered abroad throughout all the land of Egypt to
gather stubble instead of straw.
13 And the taskmasters hasted *them*, saying, Fulfil your works, *your* daily
tasks, as when there was straw.
14 And the officers of the children of Israel, which Pharaoh's taskmasters
had set over them, were beaten, *and* demanded, Wherefore have ye not ful-
filled your task in making brick both yesterday and to day, as heretofore?

Pharaoh Opposes Their Complaints

15 Then the officers of the children of Israel came and cried unto Pharaoh,
saying, Wherefore dealest thou thus with thy servants?
16 There is no straw given unto thy servants, and they say to us, Make brick:
and, behold, thy servants *are* beaten; but the fault *is* in thine own people.
17 But he said, Ye *are* idle, *ye are* idle: therefore ye say, Let us go *and* do sac-
rifice to the LORD.
18 Go therefore now, *and* work; for there shall no straw be given you, yet
shall ye deliver the tale of bricks.
19 And the officers of the children of Israel did see *that* they *were* in evil *case*,
after it was said, Ye shall not minish *ought* from your bricks of your daily task.
20 And they met Moses and Aaron, who stood in the way, as they came forth
from Pharaoh:
21 And they said unto them, The LORD look upon you, and judge; because ye
have made our savour to be abhorred in the eyes of Pharaoh, and in the eyes
of his servants, to put a sword in their hand to slay us.
22 And Moses returned unto the LORD, and said, Lord, wherefore hast thou
so evil entreated this people? why *is* it *that* thou hast sent me?
23 For since I came to Pharaoh to speak in thy name, he hath done evil to this
people; neither hast thou delivered thy people at all.

God Renews His Promise by His Name Jehovah

6 Then the LORD said unto Moses, Now shalt thou see what I will do to
Pharaoh: for with a strong hand shall he let them go, and with a strong hand
shall he drive them out of his land.
2 And God spake unto Moses, and said unto him, I *am* the LORD:
3 And I appeared unto Abraham, unto Isaac, and unto Jacob, by *the name of*
God Almighty, but by my name JEHOVAH was I not known to them.
4 And I have also established my covenant with them, to give them the land
of Canaan, the land of their pilgrimage, wherein they were strangers.
5 And I have also heard the groaning of the children of Israel, whom the
Egyptians keep in bondage; and I have remembered my covenant.
6 Wherefore say unto the children of Israel, I *am* the LORD, and I will bring
you out from under the burdens of the Egyptians, and I will rid you out of
their bondage, and I will redeem you with a stretched out arm, and with great
judgments:

7 And I will take you to me for a people, and I will be to you a God: and ye
shall know that I *am* the LORD your God, which bringeth you out from under
the burdens of the Egyptians.
8 And I will bring you in unto the land, concerning the which I did swear to
give it to Abraham, to Isaac, and to Jacob; and I will give it you for an heritage:
I *am* the LORD.
9 And Moses spake so unto the children of Israel: but they hearkened not
unto Moses for anguish of spirit, and for cruel bondage.
10 And the LORD spake unto Moses, saying,
11 Go in, speak unto Pharaoh king of Egypt, that he let the children of Israel
go out of his land.
12 And Moses spake before the LORD, saying, Behold, the children of Israel
have not hearkened unto me; how then shall Pharaoh hear me, who *am* of
uncircumcised lips?
13 And the LORD spake unto Moses and unto Aaron, and gave them a charge
unto the children of Israel, and unto Pharaoh king of Egypt, to bring the chil-
dren of Israel out of the land of Egypt.

The Genealogy of Reuben

14 These *be* the heads of their fathers' houses: The sons of Reuben the first-
born of Israel; Hanoch, and Pallu, Hezron, and Carmi: these *be* the families
of Reuben.
15 And the sons of Simeon; Jemuel, and Jamin, and Ohad, and Jachin, and
Zohar, and Shaul the son of a Canaanitish woman: these *are* the families of
Simeon.
16 And these *are* the names of the sons of Levi according to their generations;
Gershon, and Kohath, and Merari: and the years of the life of Levi *were* an
hundred thirty and seven years.
17 The sons of Gershon; Libni, and Shimi, according to their families.
18 And the sons of Kohath; Amram, and Izhar, and Hebron, and Uzziel: and
the years of the life of Kohath *were* an hundred thirty and three years.
19 And the sons of Merari; Mahali and Mushi: these *are* the families of Levi
according to their generations.
20 And Amram took him Jochebed his father's sister to wife; and she bare
him Aaron and Moses: and the years of the life of Amram *were* an hundred
and thirty and seven years.
21 And the sons of Izhar; Korah, and Nepheg, and Zichri.
22 And the sons of Uzziel; Mishael, and Elzaphan, and Zithri.
23 And Aaron took him Elisheba, daughter of Amminadab, sister of Naashon,
to wife; and she bare him Nadab, and Abihu, Eleazar, and Ithamar.
24 And the sons of Korah; Assir, and Elkanah, and Abiasaph: these *are* the
families of the Korhites.
25 And Eleazar Aaron's son took him *one* of the daughters of Putiel to wife;
and she bare him Phinehas: these *are* the heads of the fathers of the Levites
according to their families.
26 These *are* that Aaron and Moses, to whom the LORD said, Bring out the
children of Israel from the land of Egypt according to their armies.
27 These *are* they which spake to Pharaoh king of Egypt, to bring out the
children of Israel from Egypt: these *are* that Moses and Aaron.
28 And it came to pass on the day *when* the LORD spake unto Moses in the
land of Egypt,
29 That the LORD spake unto Moses, saying, I *am* the LORD: speak thou unto
Pharaoh king of Egypt all that I say unto thee.
30 And Moses said before the LORD, Behold, I *am* of uncircumcised lips, and
how shall Pharaoh hearken unto me?

Moses Is Encouraged to Go to Pharaoh

7 And the LORD said unto Moses, See, I have made thee a god to Pharaoh: and Aaron thy brother shall be thy prophet.

2 Thou shalt speak all that I command thee: and Aaron thy brother shall speak unto Pharaoh, that he send the children of Israel out of his land.

3 And I will harden Pharaoh's heart, and multiply my signs and my wonders in the land of Egypt.

4 But Pharaoh shall not hearken unto you, that I may lay my hand upon Egypt, and bring forth mine armies, *and* my people the children of Israel, out of the land of Egypt by great judgments.

5 And the Egyptians shall know that I *am* the LORD, when I stretch forth mine hand upon Egypt, and bring out the children of Israel from among them.

6 And Moses and Aaron did as the LORD commanded them, so did they.

7 And Moses *was* fourscore years old, and Aaron fourscore and three years old, when they spake unto Pharaoh.

Moses' Rod Is Turned into a Serpent

8 And the LORD spake unto Moses and unto Aaron, saying,

9 When Pharaoh shall speak unto you, saying, Shew a miracle for you: then thou shalt say unto Aaron, Take thy rod, and cast *it* before Pharaoh, *and* it shall become a serpent.

10 And Moses and Aaron went in unto Pharaoh, and they did so as the LORD had commanded: and Aaron cast down his rod before Pharaoh, and before his servants, and it became a serpent.

11 Then Pharaoh also called the wise men and the sorcerers: now the magicians of Egypt, they also did in like manner with their enchantments.

12 For they cast down every man his rod, and they became serpents: but Aaron's rod swallowed up their rods.

13 And he hardened Pharaoh's heart, that he hearkened not unto them; as the LORD had said.

The Plague of Water Turned to Blood

14 And the LORD said unto Moses, Pharaoh's heart *is* hardened, he refuseth to let the people go.

15 Get thee unto Pharaoh in the morning; lo, he goeth out unto the water; and thou shalt stand by the river's brink against he come; and the rod which was turned to a serpent shalt thou take in thine hand.

16 And thou shalt say unto him, The LORD God of the Hebrews hath sent me unto thee, saying, Let my people go, that they may serve me in the wilderness: and, behold, hitherto thou wouldest not hear.

17 Thus saith the LORD, In this thou shalt know that I *am* the LORD: behold, I will smite with the rod that *is* in mine hand upon the waters which *are* in the river, and they shall be turned to blood.

18 And the fish that *is* in the river shall die, and the river shall stink; and the Egyptians shall lothe to drink of the water of the river.

19 And the LORD spake unto Moses, Say unto Aaron, Take thy rod, and stretch out thine hand upon the waters of Egypt, upon their streams, upon their rivers, and upon their ponds, and upon all their pools of water, that they may become blood; and *that* there may be blood throughout all the land of Egypt, both in *vessels of* wood, and in *vessels of* stone.

20 And Moses and Aaron did so, as the LORD commanded; and he lifted up the rod, and smote the waters that *were* in the river, in the sight of Pharaoh, and in the sight of his servants; and all the waters that *were* in the river were turned to blood.

21 And the fish that *was* in the river died; and the river stank, and the Egyptians could not drink of the water of the river; and there was blood throughout all the land of Egypt.

22 And the magicians of Egypt did so with their enchantments: and Pharaoh's
heart was hardened, neither did he hearken unto them; as the LORD had said.
23 And Pharaoh turned and went into his house, neither did he set his heart
to this also.
24 And all the Egyptians digged round about the river for water to drink; for
they could not drink of the water of the river.
25 And seven days were fulfilled, after that the LORD had smitten the river.

The Plague of Frogs

8 And the LORD spake unto Moses, Go unto Pharaoh, and say unto him, Thus
saith the LORD, Let my people go, that they may serve me.
2 And if thou refuse to let *them* go, behold, I will smite all thy borders with
frogs:
3 And the river shall bring forth frogs abundantly, which shall go up and
come into thine house, and into thy bedchamber, and upon thy bed, and into
the house of thy servants, and upon thy people, and into thine ovens, and into
thy kneadingtroughs:
4 And the frogs shall come up both on thee, and upon thy people, and upon
all thy servants.
5 And the LORD spake unto Moses, Say unto Aaron, Stretch forth thine hand
with thy rod over the streams, over the rivers, and over the ponds, and cause
frogs to come up upon the land of Egypt.
6 And Aaron stretched out his hand over the waters of Egypt; and the frogs
came up, and covered the land of Egypt.
7 And the magicians did so with their enchantments, and brought up frogs
upon the land of Egypt.
8 Then Pharaoh called for Moses and Aaron, and said, Intreat the LORD, that
he may take away the frogs from me, and from my people; and I will let the
people go, that they may do sacrifice unto the LORD.
9 And Moses said unto Pharaoh, Glory over me: when shall I intreat for thee,
and for thy servants, and for thy people, to destroy the frogs from thee and
thy houses, *that* they may remain in the river only?
10 And he said, To morrow. And he said, *Be it* according to thy word: that
thou mayest know that *there is* none like unto the LORD our God.
11 And the frogs shall depart from thee, and from thy houses, and from thy
servants, and from thy people; they shall remain in the river only.
12 And Moses and Aaron went out from Pharaoh: and Moses cried unto the
LORD because of the frogs which he had brought against Pharaoh.
13 And the LORD did according to the word of Moses; and the frogs died out
of the houses, out of the villages, and out of the fields.
14 And they gathered them together upon heaps: and the land stank.
15 But when Pharaoh saw that there was respite, he hardened his heart, and
hearkened not unto them; as the LORD had said.

The Plague of Lice

16 And the LORD said unto Moses, Say unto Aaron, Stretch out thy rod, and
smite the dust of the land, that it may become lice throughout all the land of
Egypt.
17 And they did so; for Aaron stretched out his hand with his rod, and smote
the dust of the earth, and it became lice in man, and in beast; all the dust of
the land became lice throughout all the land of Egypt.
18 And the magicians did so with their enchantments to bring forth lice, but
they could not: so there were lice upon man, and upon beast.
19 Then the magicians said unto Pharaoh, This *is* the finger of God: and
Pharaoh's heart was hardened, and he hearkened not unto them; as the LORD
had said.

The Plague of Swarms of Flies That Cover the Land

20 And the LORD said unto Moses, Rise up early in the morning, and stand
before Pharaoh; lo, he cometh forth to the water; and say unto him, Thus saith
the LORD, Let my people go, that they may serve me.
21 Else, if thou wilt not let my people go, behold, I will send swarms *of flies*
upon thee, and upon thy servants, and upon thy people, and into thy houses:
and the houses of the Egyptians shall be full of swarms *of flies*, and also the
ground whereon they *are*.
22 And I will sever in that day the land of Goshen, in which my people dwell,
that no swarms *of flies* shall be there; to the end thou mayest know that I *am*
the LORD in the midst of the earth.
23 And I will put a division between my people and thy people: to morrow
shall this sign be.
24 And the LORD did so; and there came a grievous swarm *of flies* into the
house of Pharaoh, and *into* his servants' houses, and into all the land of Egypt:
the land was corrupted by reason of the swarm *of flies*.
25 And Pharaoh called for Moses and for Aaron, and said, Go ye, sacrifice to
your God in the land.
26 And Moses said, It is not meet so to do; for we shall sacrifice the abomi-
nation of the Egyptians to the LORD our God: lo, shall we sacrifice the abomi-
nation of the Egyptians before their eyes, and will they not stone us?
27 We will go three days' journey into the wilderness, and sacrifice to the
LORD our God, as he shall command us.
28 And Pharaoh said, I will let you go, that ye may sacrifice to the LORD your
God in the wilderness; only ye shall not go very far away: intreat for me.
29 And Moses said, Behold, I go out from thee, and I will intreat the LORD
that the swarms *of flies* may depart from Pharaoh, from his servants, and from
his people, to morrow: but let not Pharaoh deal deceitfully any more in not
letting the people go to sacrifice to the LORD.
30 And Moses went out from Pharaoh, and intreated the LORD.
31 And the LORD did according to the word of Moses; and he removed the
swarms *of flies* from Pharaoh, from his servants, and from his people; there
remained not one.
32 And Pharaoh hardened his heart at this time also, neither would he let
the people go.

The Plague of Death on the Beasts

9 Then the LORD said unto Moses, Go in unto Pharaoh, and tell him, Thus
saith the LORD God of the Hebrews, Let my people go, that they may
serve me.
2 For if thou refuse to let *them* go, and wilt hold them still,
3 Behold, the hand of the LORD is upon thy cattle which *is* in the field, upon
the horses, upon the asses, upon the camels, upon the oxen, and upon the
sheep: *there shall be* a very grievous murrain.
4 And the LORD shall sever between the cattle of Israel and the cattle of Egypt:
and there shall nothing die of all *that is* the children's of Israel.
5 And the LORD appointed a set time, saying, To morrow the LORD shall do
this thing in the land.
6 And the LORD did that thing on the morrow, and all the cattle of Egypt died:
but of the cattle of the children of Israel died not one.
7 And Pharaoh sent, and, behold, there was not one of the cattle of the
Israelites dead. And the heart of Pharaoh was hardened, and he did not let the
people go.

The Plague of Boils and Blisters

8 And the LORD said unto Moses and unto Aaron, Take to you handfuls of
ashes of the furnace, and let Moses sprinkle it toward the heaven in the sight
of Pharaoh.
9 And it shall become small dust in all the land of Egypt, and shall be a boil
breaking forth *with* blains upon man, and upon beast, throughout all the land
of Egypt.
10 And they took ashes of the furnace, and stood before Pharaoh; and Moses
sprinkled it up toward heaven; and it became a boil breaking forth *with* blains
upon man, and upon beast.
11 And the magicians could not stand before Moses because of the boils; for
the boil was upon the magicians, and upon all the Egyptians.
12 And the LORD hardened the heart of Pharaoh, and he hearkened not unto
them; as the LORD had spoken unto Moses.

Moses Warns about the Coming Hail

13 And the LORD said unto Moses, Rise up early in the morning, and stand
before Pharaoh, and say unto him, Thus saith the LORD God of the Hebrews,
Let my people go, that they may serve me.
14 For I will at this time send all my plagues upon thine heart, and upon thy
servants, and upon thy people; that thou mayest know that *there is* none like
me in all the earth.
15 For now I will stretch out my hand, that I may smite thee and thy people
with pestilence; and thou shalt be cut off from the earth.
16 And in very deed for this *cause* have I raised thee up, for to shew *in* thee
my power; and that my name may be declared throughout all the earth.
17 As yet exaltest thou thyself against my people, that thou wilt not let them go?
18 Behold, to morrow about this time I will cause it to rain a very grievous
hail, such as hath not been in Egypt since the foundation thereof even until
now.
19 Send therefore now, *and* gather thy cattle, and all that thou hast in the field;
for upon every man and beast which shall be found in the field, and shall not
be brought home, the hail shall come down upon them, and they shall die.
20 He that feared the word of the LORD among the servants of Pharaoh made
his servants and his cattle flee into the houses:
21 And he that regarded not the word of the LORD left his servants and his
cattle in the field.

The Plague of Hail

22 And the LORD said unto Moses, Stretch forth thine hand toward heaven,
that there may be hail in all the land of Egypt, upon man, and upon beast, and
upon every herb of the field, throughout the land of Egypt.
23 And Moses stretched forth his rod toward heaven: and the LORD sent thun-
der and hail, and the fire ran along upon the ground; and the LORD rained hail
upon the land of Egypt.
24 So there was hail, and fire mingled with the hail, very grievous, such as
there was none like it in all the land of Egypt since it became a nation.
25 And the hail smote throughout all the land of Egypt all that *was* in the
field, both man and beast; and the hail smote every herb of the field, and brake
every tree of the field.
26 Only in the land of Goshen, where the children of Israel *were*, was there
no hail.
27 And Pharaoh sent, and called for Moses and Aaron, and said unto them,
I have sinned this time: the LORD *is* righteous, and I and my people *are* wicked.
28 Intreat the LORD (for *it is* enough) that there be no *more* mighty thunder-
ings and hail; and I will let you go, and ye shall stay no longer.

29 And Moses said unto him, As soon as I am gone out of the city, I will spread
abroad my hands unto the LORD; *and* the thunder shall cease, neither shall
there be any more hail; that thou mayest know how that the earth *is* the LORD's.
30 But as for thee and thy servants, I know that ye will not yet fear the LORD
God.
31 And the flax and the barley was smitten: for the barley *was* in the ear, and
the flax *was* bolled.
32 But the wheat and the rie were not smitten: for they *were* not grown up.
33 And Moses went out of the city from Pharaoh, and spread abroad his
hands unto the LORD: and the thunders and hail ceased, and the rain was not
poured upon the earth.
34 And when Pharaoh saw that the rain and the hail and the thunders were
ceased, he sinned yet more, and hardened his heart, he and his servants.
35 And the heart of Pharaoh was hardened, neither would he let the children
of Israel go; as the LORD had spoken by Moses.

God Threatens to Send Locusts

10 And the LORD said unto Moses, Go in unto Pharaoh: for I have hardened
his heart, and the heart of his servants, that I might shew these my
signs before him:
2 And that thou mayest tell in the ears of thy son, and of thy son's son, what
things I have wrought in Egypt, and my signs which I have done among them;
that ye may know how that I *am* the LORD.
3 And Moses and Aaron came in unto Pharaoh, and said unto him, Thus saith
the LORD God of the Hebrews, How long wilt thou refuse to humble thyself
before me? let my people go, that they may serve me.
4 Else, if thou refuse to let my people go, behold, to morrow will I bring the
locusts into thy coast:
5 And they shall cover the face of the earth, that one cannot be able to see
the earth: and they shall eat the residue of that which is escaped, which
remaineth unto you from the hail, and shall eat every tree which groweth for
you out of the field:
6 And they shall fill thy houses, and the houses of all thy servants, and the
houses of all the Egyptians; which neither thy fathers, nor thy fathers' fathers
have seen, since the day that they were upon the earth unto this day. And he
turned himself, and went out from Pharaoh.
7 And Pharaoh's servants said unto him, How long shall this man be a snare
unto us? let the men go, that they may serve the LORD their God: knowest thou
not yet that Egypt is destroyed?
8 And Moses and Aaron were brought again unto Pharaoh: and he said unto
them, Go, serve the LORD your God: *but* who *are* they that shall go?
9 And Moses said, We will go with our young and with our old, with our sons
and with our daughters, with our flocks and with our herds will we go; for we
must hold a feast unto the LORD.
10 And he said unto them, Let the LORD be so with you, as I will let you go,
and your little ones: look *to it*; for evil *is* before you.
11 Not so: go now ye *that are* men, and serve the LORD; for that ye did desire.
And they were driven out from Pharaoh's presence.

The Plague of Locusts

12 And the LORD said unto Moses, Stretch out thine hand over the land of
Egypt for the locusts, that they may come up upon the land of Egypt, and eat
every herb of the land, *even* all that the hail hath left.
13 And Moses stretched forth his rod over the land of Egypt, and the LORD
brought an east wind upon the land all that day, and all *that* night; *and* when
it was morning, the east wind brought the locusts.

14 And the locusts went up over all the land of Egypt, and rested in all the
coasts of Egypt: very grievous *were they*; before them there were no such locusts
as they, neither after them shall be such.
15 For they covered the face of the whole earth, so that the land was darkened;
and they did eat every herb of the land, and all the fruit of the trees which the
hail had left: and there remained not any green thing in the trees, or in the
herbs of the field, through all the land of Egypt.
16 Then Pharaoh called for Moses and Aaron in haste; and he said, I have
sinned against the LORD your God, and against you.
17 Now therefore forgive, I pray thee, my sin only this once, and intreat the
LORD your God, that he may take away from me this death only.
18 And he went out from Pharaoh, and intreated the LORD.
19 And the LORD turned a mighty strong west wind, which took away the
locusts, and cast them into the Red sea; there remained not one locust in all
the coasts of Egypt.
20 But the LORD hardened Pharaoh's heart, so that he would not let the chil-
dren of Israel go.

The Plague of Darkness

21 And the LORD said unto Moses, Stretch out thine hand toward heaven, that
there may be darkness over the land of Egypt, even darkness *which* may be
felt.
22 And Moses stretched forth his hand toward heaven; and there was a thick
darkness in all the land of Egypt three days:
23 They saw not one another, neither rose any from his place for three days:
but all the children of Israel had light in their dwellings.
24 And Pharaoh called unto Moses, and said, Go ye, serve the LORD; only let
your flocks and your herds be stayed: let your little ones also go with you.
25 And Moses said, Thou must give us also sacrifices and burnt offerings,
that we may sacrifice unto the LORD our God.
26 Our cattle also shall go with us; there shall not an hoof be left behind; for
thereof must we take to serve the LORD our God; and we know not with what
we must serve the LORD, until we come thither.
27 But the LORD hardened Pharaoh's heart, and he would not let them go.
28 And Pharaoh said unto him, Get thee from me, take heed to thyself, see
my face no more; for in *that* day thou seest my face thou shalt die.
29 And Moses said, Thou hast spoken well, I will see thy face again no more.

God's Message to the Israelites

11 And the LORD said unto Moses, Yet will I bring one plague *more* upon
Pharaoh, and upon Egypt; afterwards he will let you go hence: when
he shall let *you* go, he shall surely thrust you out hence altogether.
2 Speak now in the ears of the people, and let every man borrow of his neigh-
bour, and every woman of her neighbour, jewels of silver, and jewels of gold.
3 And the LORD gave the people favour in the sight of the Egyptians. Moreover
the man Moses *was* very great in the land of Egypt, in the sight of Pharaoh's
servants, and in the sight of the people.

Moses Threatens Pharaoh with the Death of the Firstborn

4 And Moses said, Thus saith the LORD, About midnight will I go out into the
midst of Egypt:
5 And all the firstborn in the land of Egypt shall die, from the firstborn of
Pharaoh that sitteth upon his throne, even unto the firstborn of the maidser-
vant that *is* behind the mill; and all the firstborn of beasts.
6 And there shall be a great cry throughout all the land of Egypt, such as there
was none like it, nor shall be like it any more.

7 But against any of the children of Israel shall not a dog move his tongue,
against man or beast: that ye may know how that the LORD doth put a differ-
ence between the Egyptians and Israel.
8 And all these thy servants shall come down unto me, and bow down them-
selves unto me, saying, Get thee out, and all the people that follow thee: and
after that I will go out. And he went out from Pharaoh in a great anger.
9 And the LORD said unto Moses, Pharaoh shall not hearken unto you; that
my wonders may be multiplied in the land of Egypt.
10 And Moses and Aaron did all these wonders before Pharaoh: and the LORD
hardened Pharaoh's heart, so that he would not let the children of Israel go
out of his land.

The Beginning of the Year Is Changed, and the Passover Is Instituted

12 And the LORD spake unto Moses and Aaron in the land of Egypt, saying,
2 This month *shall be* unto you the beginning of months: it *shall be*
the first month of the year to you.
3 Speak ye unto all the congregation of Israel, saying, In the tenth *day* of this
month they shall take to them every man a lamb, according to the house of
their fathers, a lamb for an house:
4 And if the household be too little for the lamb, let him and his neighbour
next unto his house take *it* according to the number of the souls; every man
according to his eating shall make your count for the lamb.
5 Your lamb shall be without blemish, a male of the first year: ye shall take
it out from the sheep, or from the goats:
6 And ye shall keep it up until the fourteenth day of the same month: and
the whole assembly of the congregation of Israel shall kill it in the evening.
7 And they shall take of the blood, and strike *it* on the two side posts and on
the upper door post of the houses, wherein they shall eat it.
8 And they shall eat the flesh in that night, roast with fire, and unleavened
bread; *and* with bitter *herbs* they shall eat it.
9 Eat not of it raw, nor sodden at all with water, but roast *with* fire; his head
with his legs, and with the purtenance thereof.
10 And ye shall let nothing of it remain until the morning; and that which
remaineth of it until the morning ye shall burn with fire.
11 And thus shall ye eat it; *with* your loins girded, your shoes on your feet,
and your staff in your hand; and ye shall eat it in haste: it *is* the LORD's passover.
12 For I will pass through the land of Egypt this night, and will smite all the
firstborn in the land of Egypt, both man and beast; and against all the gods of
Egypt I will execute judgment: I *am* the LORD.
13 And the blood shall be to you for a token upon the houses where ye *are*:
and when I see the blood, I will pass over you, and the plague shall not be upon
you to destroy *you*, when I smite the land of Egypt.
14 And this day shall be unto you for a memorial; and ye shall keep it a feast
to the LORD throughout your generations; ye shall keep it a feast by an ordi-
nance for ever.
15 Seven days shall ye eat unleavened bread; even the first day ye shall put
away leaven out of your houses: for whosoever eateth leavened bread from
the first day until the seventh day, that soul shall be cut off from Israel.
16 And in the first day *there shall be* an holy convocation, and in the seventh
day there shall be an holy convocation to you; no manner of work shall be
done in them, save *that* which every man must eat, that only may be done of
you.
17 And ye shall observe *the feast of* unleavened bread; for in this selfsame
day have I brought your armies out of the land of Egypt: therefore shall ye
observe this day in your generations by an ordinance for ever.

18 In the first *month*, on the fourteenth day of the month at even, ye shall
eat unleavened bread, until the one and twentieth day of the month at even.
19 Seven days shall there be no leaven found in your houses: for whosoever
eateth that which is leavened, even that soul shall be cut off from the congre-
gation of Israel, whether he be a stranger, or born in the land.
20 Ye shall eat nothing leavened; in all your habitations shall ye eat unleav-
ened bread.
21 Then Moses called for all the elders of Israel, and said unto them, Draw
out and take you a lamb according to your families, and kill the passover.
22 And ye shall take a bunch of hyssop, and dip *it* in the blood that *is* in the
bason, and strike the lintel and the two side posts with the blood that *is* in the
bason; and none of you shall go out at the door of his house until the morning.
23 For the LORD will pass through to smite the Egyptians; and when he seeth
the blood upon the lintel, and on the two side posts, the LORD will pass over
the door, and will not suffer the destroyer to come in unto your houses to
smite *you*.
24 And ye shall observe this thing for an ordinance to thee and to thy sons
for ever.
25 And it shall come to pass, when ye be come to the land which the LORD
will give you, according as he hath promised, that ye shall keep this service.
26 And it shall come to pass, when your children shall say unto you, What
mean ye by this service?
27 That ye shall say, It *is* the sacrifice of the LORD's passover, who passed over
the houses of the children of Israel in Egypt, when he smote the Egyptians,
and delivered our houses. And the people bowed the head and worshipped.
28 And the children of Israel went away, and did as the LORD had command-
ed Moses and Aaron, so did they.

The Firstborn Are Slain

29 And it came to pass, that at midnight the LORD smote all the firstborn in
the land of Egypt, from the firstborn of Pharaoh that sat on his throne unto
the firstborn of the captive that *was* in the dungeon; and all the firstborn of
cattle.
30 And Pharaoh rose up in the night, he, and all his servants, and all the
Egyptians; and there was a great cry in Egypt; for *there was* not a house where
there was not one dead.
31 And he called for Moses and Aaron by night, and said, Rise up, *and* get you
forth from among my people, both ye and the children of Israel; and go, serve
the LORD, as ye have said.
32 Also take your flocks and your herds, as ye have said, and be gone; and
bless me also.
33 And the Egyptians were urgent upon the people, that they might send
them out of the land in haste; for they said, We *be* all dead *men*.
34 And the people took their dough before it was leavened, their kneading-
troughs being bound up in their clothes upon their shoulders.
35 And the children of Israel did according to the word of Moses; and they
borrowed of the Egyptians jewels of silver, and jewels of gold, and raiment:
36 And the LORD gave the people favour in the sight of the Egyptians, so that
they lent unto them *such things as they required*. And they spoiled the
Egyptians.
37 And the children of Israel journeyed from Rameses to Succoth, about six
hundred thousand on foot *that were* men, beside children.
38 And a mixed multitude went up also with them; and flocks, and herds,
even very much cattle.

39 And they baked unleavened cakes of the dough which they brought forth
out of Egypt, for it was not leavened; because they were thrust out of Egypt,
and could not tarry, neither had they prepared for themselves any victual.
40 Now the sojourning of the children of Israel, who dwelt in Egypt, *was* four
hundred and thirty years.
41 And it came to pass at the end of the four hundred and thirty years, even
the selfsame day it came to pass, that all the hosts of the LORD went out from
the land of Egypt.
42 It *is* a night to be much observed unto the LORD for bringing them out
from the land of Egypt: this *is* that night of the LORD to be observed of all the
children of Israel in their generations.

The Ordinance of the Passover

43 And the LORD said unto Moses and Aaron, This *is* the ordinance of the
passover: There shall no stranger eat thereof:
44 But every man's servant that is bought for money, when thou hast circum-
cised him, then shall he eat thereof.
45 A foreigner and an hired servant shall not eat thereof.
46 In one house shall it be eaten; thou shalt not carry forth ought of the flesh
abroad out of the house; neither shall ye break a bone thereof.
47 All the congregation of Israel shall keep it.
48 And when a stranger shall sojourn with thee, and will keep the passover
to the LORD, let all his males be circumcised, and then let him come near and
keep it; and he shall be as one that is born in the land: for no uncircumcised
person shall eat thereof.
49 One law shall be to him that is homeborn, and unto the stranger that
sojourneth among you.
50 Thus did all the children of Israel; as the LORD commanded Moses and
Aaron, so did they.
51 And it came to pass the selfsame day, *that* the LORD did bring the children
of Israel out of the land of Egypt by their armies.

The Firstborn Are Sanctified to God

13 And the LORD spake unto Moses, saying,
2 Sanctify unto me all the firstborn, whatsoever openeth the womb
among the children of Israel, *both* of man and of beast: it *is* mine.
3 And Moses said unto the people, Remember this day, in which ye came out
from Egypt, out of the house of bondage; for by strength of hand the LORD
brought you out from this *place*: there shall no leavened bread be eaten.
4 This day came ye out in the month Abib.
5 And it shall be when the LORD shall bring thee into the land of the
Canaanites, and the Hittites, and the Amorites, and the Hivites, and the
Jebusites, which he sware unto thy fathers to give thee, a land flowing with
milk and honey, that thou shalt keep this service in this month.
6 Seven days thou shalt eat unleavened bread, and in the seventh day *shall
be* a feast to the LORD.
7 Unleavened bread shall be eaten seven days; and there shall no leavened
bread be seen with thee, neither shall there be leaven seen with thee in all thy
quarters.
8 And thou shalt shew thy son in that day, saying, *This is done* because of that
which the LORD did unto me when I came forth out of Egypt.
9 And it shall be for a sign unto thee upon thine hand, and for a memorial
between thine eyes, that the LORD's law may be in thy mouth: for with a strong
hand hath the LORD brought thee out of Egypt.
10 Thou shalt therefore keep this ordinance in his season from year to year.

The Firstborn of Beasts Are Set Apart

11 And it shall be when the LORD shall bring thee into the land of the
Canaanites, as he sware unto thee and to thy fathers, and shall give it thee,
12 That thou shalt set apart unto the LORD all that openeth the matrix, and
every firstling that cometh of a beast which thou hast; the males *shall be* the
LORD'S.
13 And every firstling of an ass thou shalt redeem with a lamb; and if thou
wilt not redeem it, then thou shalt break his neck: and all the firstborn of man
among thy children shalt thou redeem.
14 And it shall be when thy son asketh thee in time to come, saying, What *is*
this? that thou shalt say unto him, By strength of hand the LORD brought us
out from Egypt, from the house of bondage:
15 And it came to pass, when Pharaoh would hardly let us go, that the LORD
slew all the firstborn in the land of Egypt, both the firstborn of man, and the
firstborn of beast: therefore I sacrifice to the LORD all that openeth the matrix,
being males; but all the firstborn of my children I redeem.
16 And it shall be for a token upon thine hand, and for frontlets between
thine eyes: for by strength of hand the LORD brought us forth out of Egypt.

The Israelites Go out of Egypt, and Carry Joseph's Bones with Them

17 And it came to pass, when Pharaoh had let the people go, that God led
them not *through* the way of the land of the Philistines, although that *was*
near; for God said, Lest peradventure the people repent when they see war,
and they return to Egypt:
18 But God led the people about, *through* the way of the wilderness of the
Red sea: and the children of Israel went up harnessed out of the land of Egypt.
19 And Moses took the bones of Joseph with him: for he had straitly sworn
the children of Israel, saying, God will surely visit you; and ye shall carry up
my bones away hence with you.
20 And they took their journey from Succoth, and encamped in Etham, in
the edge of the wilderness.
21 And the LORD went before them by day in a pillar of a cloud, to lead them
the way; and by night in a pillar of fire, to give them light; to go by day and
night:
22 He took not away the pillar of the cloud by day, nor the pillar of fire by
night, *from* before the people.

God Instructs the Israelites in Their Journey

14 And the LORD spake unto Moses, saying,
2 Speak unto the children of Israel, that they turn and encamp before
Pi-hahiroth, between Migdol and the sea, over against Baal-zephon: before it
shall ye encamp by the sea.
3 For Pharaoh will say of the children of Israel, They *are* entangled in the
land, the wilderness hath shut them in.
4 And I will harden Pharaoh's heart, that he shall follow after them; and I
will be honoured upon Pharaoh, and upon all his host; that the Egyptians may
know that I *am* the LORD. And they did so.
5 And it was told the king of Egypt that the people fled: and the heart of
Pharaoh and of his servants was turned against the people, and they said, Why
have we done this, that we have let Israel go from serving us?
6 And he made ready his chariot, and took his people with him:
7 And he took six hundred chosen chariots, and all the chariots of Egypt, and
captains over every one of them.
8 And the LORD hardened the heart of Pharaoh king of Egypt, and he pursued
after the children of Israel: and the children of Israel went out with an high
hand.

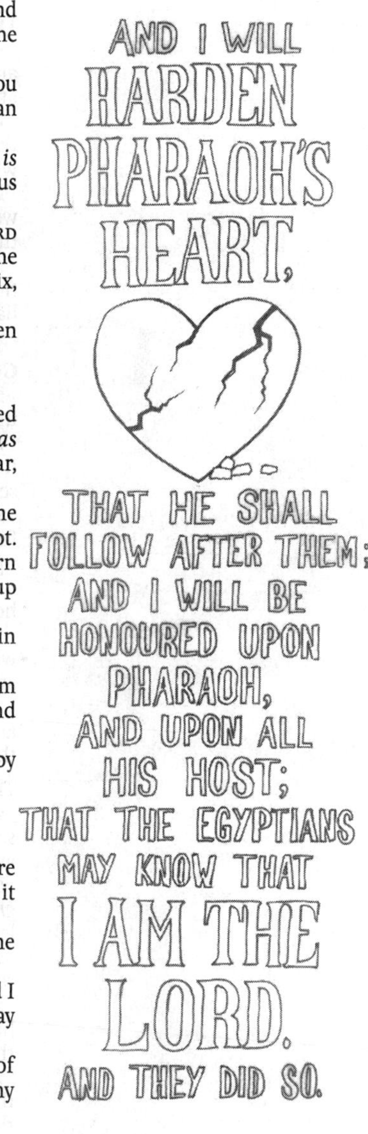

9 But the Egyptians pursued after them, all the horses *and* chariots of Pharaoh, and his horsemen, and his army, and overtook them encamping by the sea, beside Pi-hahiroth, before Baal-zephon.

The Israelites Murmur

10 And when Pharaoh drew nigh, the children of Israel lifted up their eyes, and, behold, the Egyptians marched after them; and they were sore afraid: and the children of Israel cried out unto the LORD.

11 And they said unto Moses, Because *there were* no graves in Egypt, hast thou taken us away to die in the wilderness? wherefore hast thou dealt thus with us, to carry us forth out of Egypt?

12 *Is* not this the word that we did tell thee in Egypt, saying, Let us alone, that we may serve the Egyptians? For *it had been* better for us to serve the Egyptians, than that we should die in the wilderness.

13 And Moses said unto the people, Fear ye not, stand still, and see the salvation of the LORD, which he will shew to you to day: for the Egyptians whom ye have seen to day, ye shall see them again no more for ever.

14 The LORD shall fight for you, and ye shall hold your peace.

God Instructs Moses

15 And the LORD said unto Moses, Wherefore criest thou unto me? speak unto the children of Israel, that they go forward:

16 But lift thou up thy rod, and stretch out thine hand over the sea, and divide it: and the children of Israel shall go on dry *ground* through the midst of the sea.

17 And I, behold, I will harden the hearts of the Egyptians, and they shall follow them: and I will get me honour upon Pharaoh, and upon all his host, upon his chariots, and upon his horsemen.

18 And the Egyptians shall know that I *am* the LORD, when I have gotten me honour upon Pharaoh, upon his chariots, and upon his horsemen.

19 And the angel of God, which went before the camp of Israel, removed and went behind them; and the pillar of the cloud went from before their face, and stood behind them:

20 And it came between the camp of the Egyptians and the camp of Israel; and it was a cloud and darkness *to them*, but it gave light by night *to these*: so that the one came not near the other all the night.

The Israelites Pass through the Red Sea

21 And Moses stretched out his hand over the sea; and the LORD caused the sea to go *back* by a strong east wind all that night, and made the sea dry *land*, and the waters were divided.

22 And the children of Israel went into the midst of the sea upon the dry *ground*: and the waters *were* a wall unto them on their right hand, and on their left.

23 And the Egyptians pursued, and went in after them to the midst of the sea, *even* all Pharaoh's horses, his chariots, and his horsemen.

24 And it came to pass, that in the morning watch the LORD looked unto the host of the Egyptians through the pillar of fire and of the cloud, and troubled the host of the Egyptians,

25 And took off their chariot wheels, that they drave them heavily: so that the Egyptians said, Let us flee from the face of Israel; for the LORD fighteth for them against the Egyptians.

26 And the LORD said unto Moses, Stretch out thine hand over the sea, that the waters may come again upon the Egyptians, upon their chariots, and upon their horsemen.

27 And Moses stretched forth his hand over the sea, and the sea returned to his strength when the morning appeared; and the Egyptians fled against it; and the LORD overthrew the Egyptians in the midst of the sea.

28 And the waters returned, and covered the chariots, and the horsemen,
and all the host of Pharaoh that came into the sea after them; there remained
not so much as one of them.
29 But the children of Israel walked upon dry *land* in the midst of the sea;
and the waters *were* a wall unto them on their right hand, and on their left.
30 Thus the LORD saved Israel that day out of the hand of the Egyptians; and
Israel saw the Egyptians dead upon the sea shore.
31 And Israel saw that great work which the LORD did upon the Egyptians:
and the people feared the LORD, and believed the LORD, and his servant Moses.

Moses' Song

15 Then sang Moses and the children of Israel this song unto the LORD,
and spake, saying, I will sing unto the LORD, for he hath triumphed
gloriously: the horse and his rider hath he thrown into the sea.
2 The LORD *is* my strength and song, and he is become my salvation: he *is* my
God, and I will prepare him an habitation; my father's God, and I will exalt
him.
3 The LORD *is* a man of war: the LORD *is* his name.
4 Pharaoh's chariots and his host hath he cast into the sea: his chosen cap-
tains also are drowned in the Red sea.
5 The depths have covered them: they sank into the bottom as a stone.
6 Thy right hand, O LORD, is become glorious in power: thy right hand, O
LORD, hath dashed in pieces the enemy.
7 And in the greatness of thine excellency thou hast overthrown them that
rose up against thee: thou sentest forth thy wrath, *which* consumed them as
stubble.
8 And with the blast of thy nostrils the waters were gathered together, the
floods stood upright as an heap, *and* the depths were congealed in the heart
of the sea.
9 The enemy said, I will pursue, I will overtake, I will divide the spoil; my lust
shall be satisfied upon them; I will draw my sword, my hand shall destroy
them.
10 Thou didst blow with thy wind, the sea covered them: they sank as lead in
the mighty waters.
11 Who *is* like unto thee, O LORD, among the gods? who *is* like thee, glorious
in holiness, fearful *in* praises, doing wonders?
12 Thou stretchedst out thy right hand, the earth swallowed them.
13 Thou in thy mercy hast led forth the people *which* thou hast redeemed:
thou hast guided *them* in thy strength unto thy holy habitation.
14 The people shall hear, *and* be afraid: sorrow shall take hold on the inhab-
itants of Palestina.
15 Then the dukes of Edom shall be amazed; the mighty men of Moab, trem-
bling shall take hold upon them; all the inhabitants of Canaan shall melt away.
16 Fear and dread shall fall upon them; by the greatness of thine arm they
shall be *as* still as a stone; till thy people pass over, O LORD, till the people pass
over, *which* thou hast purchased.
17 Thou shalt bring them in, and plant them in the mountain of thine inher-
itance, *in* the place, O LORD, *which* thou hast made for thee to dwell in, *in* the
Sanctuary, O Lord, *which* thy hands have established.
18 The LORD shall reign for ever and ever.
19 For the horse of Pharaoh went in with his chariots and with his horsemen
into the sea, and the LORD brought again the waters of the sea upon them; but
the children of Israel went on dry *land* in the midst of the sea.
20 And Miriam the prophetess, the sister of Aaron, took a timbrel in her
hand; and all the women went out after her with timbrels and with dances.

21 And Miriam answered them, Sing ye to the LORD, for he hath triumphed
gloriously; the horse and his rider hath he thrown into the sea.

The People Want Water, but the Waters at Marah Are Bitter

22 So Moses brought Israel from the Red sea, and they went out into the
wilderness of Shur; and they went three days in the wilderness, and found no
water.
23 And when they came to Marah, they could not drink of the waters of
Marah, for they *were* bitter: therefore the name of it was called Marah.
24 And the people murmured against Moses, saying, What shall we drink?
25 And he cried unto the LORD; and the LORD shewed him a tree, *which* when
he had cast into the waters, the waters were made sweet: there he made for
them a statute and an ordinance, and there he proved them,
26 And said, If thou wilt diligently hearken to the voice of the LORD thy God,
and wilt do that which is right in his sight, and wilt give ear to his command-
ments, and keep all his statutes, I will put none of these diseases upon thee,
which I have brought upon the Egyptians: for I *am* the LORD that healeth thee.
27 And they came to Elim, where *were* twelve wells of water, and threescore
and ten palm trees: and they encamped there by the waters.

God Sends Quail and Manna

16 And they took their journey from Elim, and all the congregation of the
children of Israel came unto the wilderness of Sin, which *is* between
Elim and Sinai, on the fifteenth day of the second month after their departing
out of the land of Egypt.
2 And the whole congregation of the children of Israel murmured against
Moses and Aaron in the wilderness:
3 And the children of Israel said unto them, Would to God we had died by
the hand of the LORD in the land of Egypt, when we sat by the flesh pots, *and*
when we did eat bread to the full; for ye have brought us forth into this wil-
derness, to kill this whole assembly with hunger.
4 Then said the LORD unto Moses, Behold, I will rain bread from heaven for
you; and the people shall go out and gather a certain rate every day, that I may
prove them, whether they will walk in my law, or no.
5 And it shall come to pass, that on the sixth day they shall prepare *that* which
they bring in; and it shall be twice as much as they gather daily.
6 And Moses and Aaron said unto all the children of Israel, At even, then ye
shall know that the LORD hath brought you out from the land of Egypt:
7 And in the morning, then ye shall see the glory of the LORD; for that he
heareth your murmurings against the LORD: and what *are* we, that ye murmur
against us?
8 And Moses said, *This shall be*, when the LORD shall give you in the evening
flesh to eat, and in the morning bread to the full; for that the LORD heareth
your murmurings which ye murmur against him: and what *are* we? your
murmurings *are* not against us, but against the LORD.
9 And Moses spake unto Aaron, Say unto all the congregation of the children
of Israel, Come near before the LORD: for he hath heard your murmurings.
10 And it came to pass, as Aaron spake unto the whole congregation of the
children of Israel, that they looked toward the wilderness, and, behold, the
glory of the LORD appeared in the cloud.
11 And the LORD spake unto Moses, saying,
12 I have heard the murmurings of the children of Israel: speak unto them,
saying, At even ye shall eat flesh, and in the morning ye shall be filled with
bread; and ye shall know that I *am* the LORD your God.
13 And it came to pass, that at even the quails came up, and covered the camp:
and in the morning the dew lay round about the host.

14 And when the dew that lay was gone up, behold, upon the face of the
wilderness *there lay* a small round thing, *as* small as the hoar frost on the
ground.
15 And when the children of Israel saw *it*, they said one to another, It *is*
manna: for they wist not what it *was*. And Moses said unto them, This *is* the
bread which the LORD hath given you to eat.
16 This *is* the thing which the LORD hath commanded, Gather of it every man
according to his eating, an omer for every man, *according to* the number of
your persons; take ye every man for *them* which *are* in his tents.
17 And the children of Israel did so, and gathered, some more, some less.
18 And when they did mete *it* with an omer, he that gathered much had
nothing over, and he that gathered little had no lack; they gathered every man
according to his eating.
19 And Moses said, Let no man leave of it till the morning.
20 Notwithstanding they hearkened not unto Moses; but some of them left
of it until the morning, and it bred worms, and stank: and Moses was wroth
with them.
21 And they gathered it every morning, every man according to his eating:
and when the sun waxed hot, it melted.
22 And it came to pass, *that* on the sixth day they gathered twice as much
bread, two omers for one *man*: and all the rulers of the congregation came
and told Moses.
23 And he said unto them, This *is that* which the LORD hath said, To morrow
is the rest of the holy sabbath unto the LORD: bake *that* which ye will bake *to
day*, and seethe that ye will seethe; and that which remaineth over lay up for
you to be kept until the morning.
24 And they laid it up till the morning, as Moses bade: and it did not stink,
neither was there any worm therein.
25 And Moses said, Eat that to day; for to day *is* a sabbath unto the LORD: to
day ye shall not find it in the field.
26 Six days ye shall gather it; but on the seventh day, *which is* the sabbath, in
it there shall be none.
27 And it came to pass, *that* there went out *some* of the people on the seventh
day for to gather, and they found none.
28 And the LORD said unto Moses, How long refuse ye to keep my command-
ments and my laws?
29 See, for that the LORD hath given you the sabbath, therefore he giveth you
on the sixth day the bread of two days; abide ye every man in his place, let no
man go out of his place on the seventh day.
30 So the people rested on the seventh day.
31 And the house of Israel called the name thereof Manna: and it *was* like
coriander seed, white; and the taste of it *was* like wafers *made* with honey.

An Omer of Manna Is Preserved

32 And Moses said, This *is* the thing which the LORD commandeth, Fill an
omer of it to be kept for your generations; that they may see the bread where-
with I have fed you in the wilderness, when I brought you forth from the land
of Egypt.
33 And Moses said unto Aaron, Take a pot, and put an omer full of manna
therein, and lay it up before the LORD, to be kept for your generations.
34 As the LORD commanded Moses, so Aaron laid it up before the Testimony,
to be kept.
35 And the children of Israel did eat manna forty years, until they came to a
land inhabited; they did eat manna, until they came unto the borders of the
land of Canaan.
36 Now an omer *is* the tenth *part* of an ephah.

The People Murmur for Water at Rephidim

17 And all the congregation of the children of Israel journeyed from the wilderness of Sin, after their journeys, according to the commandment of the LORD, and pitched in Rephidim: and *there was* no water for the people to drink.
2 Wherefore the people did chide with Moses, and said, Give us water that we may drink. And Moses said unto them, Why chide ye with me? wherefore do ye tempt the LORD?
3 And the people thirsted there for water; and the people murmured against Moses, and said, Wherefore *is* this *that* thou hast brought us up out of Egypt, to kill us and our children and our cattle with thirst?
4 And Moses cried unto the LORD, saying, What shall I do unto this people? they be almost ready to stone me.
5 And the LORD said unto Moses, Go on before the people, and take with thee of the elders of Israel; and thy rod, wherewith thou smotest the river, take in thine hand, and go.
6 Behold, I will stand before thee there upon the rock in Horeb; and thou shalt smite the rock, and there shall come water out of it, that the people may drink. And Moses did so in the sight of the elders of Israel.
7 And he called the name of the place Massah, and Meribah, because of the chiding of the children of Israel, and because they tempted the LORD, saying, Is the LORD among us, or not?

Amalek Is Conquered

8 Then came Amalek, and fought with Israel in Rephidim.
9 And Moses said unto Joshua, Choose us out men, and go out, fight with Amalek: to morrow I will stand on the top of the hill with the rod of God in mine hand.
10 So Joshua did as Moses had said to him, and fought with Amalek: and Moses, Aaron, and Hur went up to the top of the hill.
11 And it came to pass, when Moses held up his hand, that Israel prevailed: and when he let down his hand, Amalek prevailed.
12 But Moses' hands *were* heavy; and they took a stone, and put *it* under him, and he sat thereon; and Aaron and Hur stayed up his hands, the one on the one side, and the other on the other side; and his hands were steady until the going down of the sun.
13 And Joshua discomfited Amalek and his people with the edge of the sword.
14 And the LORD said unto Moses, Write this *for* a memorial in a book, and rehearse *it* in the ears of Joshua: for I will utterly put out the remembrance of Amalek from under heaven.
15 And Moses built an altar, and called the name of it Jehovah-nissi:
16 For he said, Because the LORD hath sworn *that* the LORD *will have* war with Amalek from generation to generation.

Jethro Brings to Moses His Wife and Two Sons

18 When Jethro, the priest of Midian, Moses' father in law, heard of all that God had done for Moses, and for Israel his people, *and* that the LORD had brought Israel out of Egypt;
2 Then Jethro, Moses' father in law, took Zipporah, Moses' wife, after he had sent her back,
3 And her two sons; of which the name of the one *was* Gershom; for he said, I have been an alien in a strange land:
4 And the name of the other *was* Eliezer; for the God of my father, *said he*, *was* mine help, and delivered me from the sword of Pharaoh:
5 And Jethro, Moses' father in law, came with his sons and his wife unto Moses into the wilderness, where he encamped at the mount of God:

6 And he said unto Moses, I thy father in law Jethro am come unto thee, and
thy wife, and her two sons with her.

Moses Entertains Jethro

7 And Moses went out to meet his father in law, and did obeisance, and kissed
him; and they asked each other of *their* welfare; and they came into the tent.
8 And Moses told his father in law all that the LORD had done unto Pharaoh
and to the Egyptians for Israel's sake, *and* all the travail that had come upon
them by the way, and *how* the LORD delivered them.
9 And Jethro rejoiced for all the goodness which the LORD had done to Israel,
whom he had delivered out of the hand of the Egyptians.
10 And Jethro said, Blessed *be* the LORD, who hath delivered you out of the
hand of the Egyptians, and out of the hand of Pharaoh, who hath delivered
the people from under the hand of the Egyptians.
11 Now I know that the LORD *is* greater than all gods: for in the thing where-
in they dealt proudly *he was* above them.
12 And Jethro, Moses' father in law, took a burnt offering and sacrifices for
God: and Aaron came, and all the elders of Israel, to eat bread with Moses'
father in law before God.

Moses Judges the People

13 And it came to pass on the morrow, that Moses sat to judge the people:
and the people stood by Moses from the morning unto the evening.
14 And when Moses' father in law saw all that he did to the people, he said,
What *is* this thing that thou doest to the people? why sittest thou thyself alone,
and all the people stand by thee from morning unto even?
15 And Moses said unto his father in law, Because the people come unto me
to enquire of God:
16 When they have a matter, they come unto me; and I judge between one
and another, and I do make *them* know the statutes of God, and his laws.
17 And Moses' father in law said unto him, The thing that thou doest *is* not
good.
18 Thou wilt surely wear away, both thou, and this people that *is* with thee:
for this thing *is* too heavy for thee; thou art not able to perform it thyself alone.
19 Hearken now unto my voice, I will give thee counsel, and God shall be
with thee: Be thou for the people to God-ward, that thou mayest bring the
causes unto God:
20 And thou shalt teach them ordinances and laws, and shalt shew them the
way wherein they must walk, and the work that they must do.
21 Moreover thou shalt provide out of all the people able men, such as fear
God, men of truth, hating covetousness; and place *such* over them, *to be* rulers
of thousands, *and* rulers of hundreds, rulers of fifties, and rulers of tens:
22 And let them judge the people at all seasons: and it shall be, *that* every
great matter they shall bring unto thee, but every small matter they shall judge:
so shall it be easier for thyself, and they shall bear *the burden* with thee.
23 If thou shalt do this thing, and God command thee *so*, then thou shalt be
able to endure, and all this people shall also go to their place in peace.
24 So Moses hearkened to the voice of his father in law, and did all that he
had said.
25 And Moses chose able men out of all Israel, and made them heads over
the people, rulers of thousands, rulers of hundreds, rulers of fifties, and rulers
of tens.
26 And they judged the people at all seasons: the hard causes they brought
unto Moses, but every small matter they judged themselves.
27 And Moses let his father in law depart; and he went his way into his own
land.

The People Come to Sinai

19 In the third month, when the children of Israel were gone forth out
of the land of Egypt, the same day came they *into* the wilderness of
Sinai.
2 For they were departed from Rephidim, and were come *to* the desert of
Sinai, and had pitched in the wilderness; and there Israel camped before the
mount.
3 And Moses went up unto God, and the LORD called unto him out of the
mountain, saying, Thus shalt thou say to the house of Jacob, and tell the chil-
dren of Israel;
4 Ye have seen what I did unto the Egyptians, and *how* I bare you on eagles'
wings, and brought you unto myself.
5 Now therefore, if ye will obey my voice indeed, and keep my covenant, then
ye shall be a peculiar treasure unto me above all people: for all the earth *is*
mine:
6 And ye shall be unto me a kingdom of priests, and an holy nation. These
are the words which thou shalt speak unto the children of Israel.
7 And Moses came and called for the elders of the people, and laid before
their faces all these words which the LORD commanded him.
8 And all the people answered together, and said, All that the LORD hath spo-
ken we will do. And Moses returned the words of the people unto the LORD.
9 And the LORD said unto Moses, Lo, I come unto thee in a thick cloud, that
the people may hear when I speak with thee, and believe thee for ever. And
Moses told the words of the people unto the LORD.
10 And the LORD said unto Moses, Go unto the people, and sanctify them to
day and to morrow, and let them wash their clothes,
11 And be ready against the third day: for the third day the LORD will come
down in the sight of all the people upon mount Sinai.
12 And thou shalt set bounds unto the people round about, saying, Take heed
to yourselves, *that ye* go *not* up into the mount, or touch the border of it:
whosoever toucheth the mount shall be surely put to death:
13 There shall not an hand touch it, but he shall surely be stoned, or shot
through; whether *it be* beast or man, it shall not live: when the trumpet soun-
deth long, they shall come up to the mount.
14 And Moses went down from the mount unto the people, and sanctified
the people; and they washed their clothes.
15 And he said unto the people, Be ready against the third day: come not at
your wives.

The Awe-inspiring Presence of God on Mount Sinai

16 And it came to pass on the third day in the morning, that there were thun-
ders and lightnings, and a thick cloud upon the mount, and the voice of the
trumpet exceeding loud; so that all the people that *was* in the camp trembled.
17 And Moses brought forth the people out of the camp to meet with God;
and they stood at the nether part of the mount.
18 And mount Sinai was altogether on a smoke, because the LORD descended
upon it in fire: and the smoke thereof ascended as the smoke of a furnace, and
the whole mount quaked greatly.
19 And when the voice of the trumpet sounded long, and waxed louder and
louder, Moses spake, and God answered him by a voice.
20 And the LORD came down upon mount Sinai, on the top of the mount: and
the LORD called Moses *up* to the top of the mount; and Moses went up.
21 And the LORD said unto Moses, Go down, charge the people, lest they break
through unto the LORD to gaze, and many of them perish.
22 And let the priests also, which come near to the LORD, sanctify themselves,
lest the LORD break forth upon them.

23 And Moses said unto the LORD, The people cannot come up to mount Sinai:
for thou chargedst us, saying, Set bounds about the mount, and sanctify it.
24 And the LORD said unto him, Away, get thee down, and thou shalt come
up, thou, and Aaron with thee: but let not the priests and the people break
through to come up unto the LORD, lest he break forth upon them.
25 So Moses went down unto the people, and spake unto them.

The Ten Commandments

20 And God spake all these words, saying,
2 I *am* the LORD thy God, which have brought thee out of the land of
Egypt, out of the house of bondage.
3 Thou shalt have no other gods before me.
4 Thou shalt not make unto thee any graven image, or any likeness *of any
thing* that *is* in heaven above, or that *is* in the earth beneath, or that *is* in the
water under the earth:
5 Thou shalt not bow down thyself to them, nor serve them: for I the LORD
thy God *am* a jealous God, visiting the iniquity of the fathers upon the children
unto the third and fourth *generation* of them that hate me;
6 And shewing mercy unto thousands of them that love me, and keep my
commandments.
7 Thou shalt not take the name of the LORD thy God in vain; for the LORD will
not hold him guiltless that taketh his name in vain.
8 Remember the sabbath day, to keep it holy.
9 Six days shalt thou labour, and do all thy work:
10 But the seventh day *is* the sabbath of the LORD thy God: *in it* thou shalt not
do any work, thou, nor thy son, nor thy daughter, thy manservant, nor thy
maidservant, nor thy cattle, nor thy stranger that *is* within thy gates:
11 For *in* six days the LORD made heaven and earth, the sea, and all that in
them *is*, and rested the seventh day: wherefore the LORD blessed the sabbath
day, and hallowed it.
12 Honour thy father and thy mother: that thy days may be long upon the
land which the LORD thy God giveth thee.
13 Thou shalt not kill.
14 Thou shalt not commit adultery.
15 Thou shalt not steal.
16 Thou shalt not bear false witness against thy neighbour.
17 Thou shalt not covet thy neighbour's house, thou shalt not covet thy neigh-
bour's wife, nor his manservant, nor his maidservant, nor his ox, nor his ass,
nor any thing that *is* thy neighbour's.

The People Are Afraid and Stand Far Away

18 And all the people saw the thunderings, and the lightnings, and the noise
of the trumpet, and the mountain smoking: and when the people saw *it*, they
removed, and stood afar off.
19 And they said unto Moses, Speak thou with us, and we will hear: but let
not God speak with us, lest we die.
20 And Moses said unto the people, Fear not: for God is come to prove you,
and that his fear may be before your faces, that ye sin not.
21 And the people stood afar off, and Moses drew near unto the thick dark-
ness where God *was*.

The People Are Forbidden to Make Images

22 And the LORD said unto Moses, Thus thou shalt say unto the children of
Israel, Ye have seen that I have talked with you from heaven.
23 Ye shall not make with me gods of silver, neither shall ye make unto you
gods of gold.

1. THOU SHALT HAVE NO OTHER GODS BEFORE ME.
2. THOU SHALT NOT MAKE UNTO THEE ANY GRAVEN IMAGE...
3. THOU SHALT NOT TAKE THE NAME OF THE LORD THY GOD IN VAIN...
4. REMEMBER THE SABBATH DAY, TO KEEP IT HOLY...
5. HONOUR THY FATHER AND THY MOTHER...
6. THOU SHALT NOT KILL.
7. THOU SHALT NOT COMMIT ADULTERY.
8. THOU SHALT NOT STEAL.
9. THOU SHALT NOT BEAR FALSE WITNESS AGAINST THY NEIGHBOUR.
10. THOU SHALT NOT COVET.
EXODUS 20
THE 10 COMMANDMENTS

24 An altar of earth thou shalt make unto me, and shalt sacrifice thereon thy
burnt offerings, and thy peace offerings, thy sheep, and thine oxen: in all plac-
es where I record my name I will come unto thee, and I will bless thee.
25 And if thou wilt make me an altar of stone, thou shalt not build it of hewn
stone: for if thou lift up thy tool upon it, thou hast polluted it.
26 Neither shalt thou go up by steps unto mine altar, that thy nakedness be
not discovered thereon.

Laws for Servants

21 Now these *are* the judgments which thou shalt set before them.
2 If thou buy an Hebrew servant, six years he shall serve: and in the
seventh he shall go out free for nothing.
3 If he came in by himself, he shall go out by himself: if he were married,
then his wife shall go out with him.
4 If his master have given him a wife, and she have born him sons or daugh-
ters; the wife and her children shall be her master's, and he shall go out by
himself.
5 And if the servant shall plainly say, I love my master, my wife, and my chil-
dren; I will not go out free:
6 Then his master shall bring him unto the judges; he shall also bring him
to the door, or unto the door post; and his master shall bore his ear through
with an aul; and he shall serve him for ever.
7 And if a man sell his daughter to be a maidservant, she shall not go out as
the menservants do.
8 If she please not her master, who hath betrothed her to himself, then shall
he let her be redeemed: to sell her unto a strange nation he shall have no power,
seeing he hath dealt deceitfully with her.
9 And if he have betrothed her unto his son, he shall deal with her after the
manner of daughters.
10 If he take him another *wife*; her food, her raiment, and her duty of mar-
riage, shall he not diminish.
11 And if he do not these three unto her, then shall she go out free without
money.

Laws about Manslaughter

12 He that smiteth a man, so that he die, shall be surely put to death.
13 And if a man lie not in wait, but God deliver *him* into his hand; then I will
appoint thee a place whither he shall flee.
14 But if a man come presumptuously upon his neighbour, to slay him with
guile; thou shalt take him from mine altar, that he may die.
15 And he that smiteth his father, or his mother, shall be surely put to death.
16 And he that stealeth a man, and selleth him, or if he be found in his hand,
he shall surely be put to death.
17 And he that curseth his father, or his mother, shall surely be put to death.
18 And if men strive together, and one smite another with a stone, or with
his fist, and he die not, but keepeth *his* bed:
19 If he rise again, and walk abroad upon his staff, then shall he that smote
him be quit: only he shall pay *for* the loss of his time, and shall cause *him* to
be thoroughly healed.
20 And if a man smite his servant, or his maid, with a rod, and he die under
his hand; he shall be surely punished.
21 Notwithstanding, if he continue a day or two, he shall not be punished:
for he *is* his money.

Laws about Those Hurt Accidentally

22 If men strive, and hurt a woman with child, so that her fruit depart *from
her*, and yet no mischief follow: he shall be surely punished, according as the
woman's husband will lay upon him; and he shall pay as the judges *determine*.

23 And if *any* mischief follow, then thou shalt give life for life,
24 Eye for eye, tooth for tooth, hand for hand, foot for foot,
25 Burning for burning, wound for wound, stripe for stripe.
26 And if a man smite the eye of his servant, or the eye of his maid, that it
perish; he shall let him go free for his eye's sake.
27 And if he smite out his manservant's tooth, or his maidservant's tooth; he
shall let him go free for his tooth's sake.
28 If an ox gore a man or a woman, that they die: then the ox shall be surely
stoned, and his flesh shall not be eaten; but the owner of the ox *shall be* quit.
29 But if the ox were wont to push with his horn in time past, and it hath
been testified to his owner, and he hath not kept him in, but that he hath killed
a man or a woman; the ox shall be stoned, and his owner also shall be put to
death.
30 If there be laid on him a sum of money, then he shall give for the ransom
of his life whatsoever is laid upon him.
31 Whether he have gored a son, or have gored a daughter, according to this
judgment shall it be done unto him.
32 If the ox shall push a manservant or a maidservant; he shall give unto their
master thirty shekels of silver, and the ox shall be stoned.
33 And if a man shall open a pit, or if a man shall dig a pit, and not cover it,
and an ox or an ass fall therein;
34 The owner of the pit shall make *it* good, *and* give money unto the owner
of them; and the dead *beast* shall be his.
35 And if one man's ox hurt another's, that he die; then they shall sell the live
ox, and divide the money of it; and the dead *ox* also they shall divide.
36 Or if it be known that the ox hath used to push in time past, and his owner
hath not kept him in; he shall surely pay ox for ox; and the dead shall be his
own.

Laws about Theft

22 If a man shall steal an ox, or a sheep, and kill it, or sell it; he shall restore
five oxen for an ox, and four sheep for a sheep.
2 If a thief be found breaking up, and be smitten that he die, *there shall* no
blood *be shed* for him.
3 If the sun be risen upon him, *there shall be* blood *shed* for him; *for* he
should make full restitution; if he have nothing, then he shall be sold for his
theft.
4 If the theft be certainly found in his hand alive, whether it be ox, or ass, or
sheep; he shall restore double.
5 If a man shall cause a field or vineyard to be eaten, and shall put in his beast,
and shall feed in another man's field; of the best of his own field, and of the
best of his own vineyard, shall he make restitution.
6 If fire break out, and catch in thorns, so that the stacks of corn, or the
standing corn, or the field, be consumed *therewith*; he that kindled the fire
shall surely make restitution.
7 If a man shall deliver unto his neighbour money or stuff to keep, and it be
stolen out of the man's house; if the thief be found, let him pay double.
8 If the thief be not found, then the master of the house shall be brought
unto the judges, *to see* whether he have put his hand unto his neighbour's
goods.
9 For all manner of trespass, *whether it be* for ox, for ass, for sheep, for rai-
ment, *or* for any manner of lost thing, which *another* challengeth to be his,
the cause of both parties shall come before the judges; *and* whom the judges
shall condemn, he shall pay double unto his neighbour.
10 If a man deliver unto his neighbour an ass, or an ox, or a sheep, or any
beast, to keep; and it die, or be hurt, or driven away, no man seeing *it*:

11 *Then* shall an oath of the LORD be between them both, that he hath not
put his hand unto his neighbour's goods; and the owner of it shall accept
thereof, and he shall not make *it* good.
12 And if it be stolen from him, he shall make restitution unto the owner
thereof.
13 If it be torn in pieces, *then* let him bring it *for* witness, *and* he shall not
make good that which was torn.
14 And if a man borrow *ought* of his neighbour, and it be hurt, or die, the
owner thereof *being* not with it, he shall surely make *it* good.
15 *But* if the owner thereof *be* with it, he shall not make *it* good: if it *be* an
hired *thing*, it came for his hire.

Laws about Fornication

16 And if a man entice a maid that is not betrothed, and lie with her, he shall
surely endow her to be his wife.
17 If her father utterly refuse to give her unto him, he shall pay money accord-
ing to the dowry of virgins.
18 Thou shalt not suffer a witch to live.
19 Whosoever lieth with a beast shall surely be put to death.
20 He that sacrificeth unto *any* god, save unto the LORD only, he shall be
utterly destroyed.
21 Thou shalt neither vex a stranger, nor oppress him: for ye were strangers
in the land of Egypt.
22 Ye shall not afflict any widow, or fatherless child.
23 If thou afflict them in any wise, and they cry at all unto me, I will surely
hear their cry;
24 And my wrath shall wax hot, and I will kill you with the sword; and your
wives shall be widows, and your children fatherless.

Laws about Usury

25 If thou lend money to *any of* my people *that is* poor by thee, thou shalt
not be to him as an usurer, neither shalt thou lay upon him usury.
26 If thou at all take thy neighbour's raiment to pledge, thou shalt deliver it
unto him by that the sun goeth down:
27 For that *is* his covering only, it *is* his raiment for his skin: wherein shall
he sleep? and it shall come to pass, when he crieth unto me, that I will hear;
for I *am* gracious.
28 Thou shalt not revile the gods, nor curse the ruler of thy people.
29 Thou shalt not delay *to offer* the first of thy ripe fruits, and of thy liquors:
the firstborn of thy sons shalt thou give unto me.
30 Likewise shalt thou do with thine oxen, *and* with thy sheep: seven days it
shall be with his dam; on the eighth day thou shalt give it me.
31 And ye shall be holy men unto me: neither shall ye eat *any* flesh *that is*
torn of beasts in the field; ye shall cast it to the dogs.

Laws about Slander and False Witness

23 Thou shalt not raise a false report: put not thine hand with the wicked
to be an unrighteous witness.
2 Thou shalt not follow a multitude to *do* evil; neither shalt thou speak in a
cause to decline after many to wrest *judgment*:
3 Neither shalt thou countenance a poor man in his cause.
4 If thou meet thine enemy's ox or his ass going astray, thou shalt surely bring
it back to him again.
5 If thou see the ass of him that hateth thee lying under his burden, and
wouldest forbear to help him, thou shalt surely help with him.
6 Thou shalt not wrest the judgment of thy poor in his cause.
7 Keep thee far from a false matter; and the innocent and righteous slay thou
not: for I will not justify the wicked.

8 And thou shalt take no gift: for the gift blindeth the wise, and perverteth
the words of the righteous.
9 Also thou shalt not oppress a stranger: for ye know the heart of a stranger,
seeing ye were strangers in the land of Egypt.

Laws about Rest for Land and People

10 And six years thou shalt sow thy land, and shalt gather in the fruits
thereof:
11 But the seventh *year* thou shalt let it rest and lie still; that the poor of thy
people may eat: and what they leave the beasts of the field shall eat. In like
manner thou shalt deal with thy vineyard, *and* with thy oliveyard.
12 Six days thou shalt do thy work, and on the seventh day thou shalt rest:
that thine ox and thine ass may rest, and the son of thy handmaid, and the
stranger, may be refreshed.
13 And in all *things* that I have said unto you be circumspect: and make no
mention of the name of other gods, neither let it be heard out of thy mouth.
14 Three times thou shalt keep a feast unto me in the year.
15 Thou shalt keep the feast of unleavened bread: (thou shalt eat unleavened
bread seven days, as I commanded thee, in the time appointed of the month
Abib; for in it thou camest out from Egypt: and none shall appear before me
empty:)
16 And the feast of harvest, the firstfruits of thy labours, which thou hast
sown in the field: and the feast of ingathering, *which is* in the end of the year,
when thou hast gathered in thy labours out of the field.
17 Three times in the year all thy males shall appear before the Lord God.
18 Thou shalt not offer the blood of my sacrifice with leavened bread; neither
shall the fat of my sacrifice remain until the morning.
19 The first of the firstfruits of thy land thou shalt bring into the house of
the Lord thy God. Thou shalt not seethe a kid in his mother's milk.

An Angel Is Promised

20 Behold, I send an Angel before thee, to keep thee in the way, and to bring
thee into the place which I have prepared.
21 Beware of him, and obey his voice, provoke him not; for he will not pardon
your transgressions: for my name *is* in him.
22 But if thou shalt indeed obey his voice, and do all that I speak; then I will
be an enemy unto thine enemies, and an adversary unto thine adversaries.
23 For mine Angel shall go before thee, and bring thee in unto the Amorites,
and the Hittites, and the Perizzites, and the Canaanites, the Hivites, and the
Jebusites: and I will cut them off.
24 Thou shalt not bow down to their gods, nor serve them, nor do after their
works: but thou shalt utterly overthrow them, and quite break down their
images.
25 And ye shall serve the Lord your God, and he shall bless thy bread, and
thy water; and I will take sickness away from the midst of thee.
26 There shall nothing cast their young, nor be barren, in thy land: the num-
ber of thy days I will fulfil.
27 I will send my fear before thee, and will destroy all the people to whom
thou shalt come, and I will make all thine enemies turn their backs unto thee.
28 And I will send hornets before thee, which shall drive out the Hivite, the
Canaanite, and the Hittite, from before thee.
29 I will not drive them out from before thee in one year; lest the land become
desolate, and the beast of the field multiply against thee.
30 By little and little I will drive them out from before thee, until thou be
increased, and inherit the land.

31 And I will set thy bounds from the Red sea even unto the sea of the
Philistines, and from the desert unto the river: for I will deliver the inhabitants
of the land into your hand; and thou shalt drive them out before thee.
32 Thou shalt make no covenant with them, nor with their gods.
33 They shall not dwell in thy land, lest they make thee sin against me: for if
thou serve their gods, it will surely be a snare unto thee.

Moses Is Called up into the Mountain

24 And he said unto Moses, Come up unto the LORD, thou, and Aaron,
Nadab, and Abihu, and seventy of the elders of Israel; and worship ye
afar off.
2 And Moses alone shall come near the LORD: but they shall not come nigh;
neither shall the people go up with him.
3 And Moses came and told the people all the words of the LORD, and all the
judgments: and all the people answered with one voice, and said, All the words
which the LORD hath said will we do.
4 And Moses wrote all the words of the LORD, and rose up early in the morn-
ing, and builded an altar under the hill, and twelve pillars, according to the
twelve tribes of Israel.
5 And he sent young men of the children of Israel, which offered burnt offer-
ings, and sacrificed peace offerings of oxen unto the LORD.
6 And Moses took half of the blood, and put *it* in basons; and half of the blood
he sprinkled on the altar.
7 And he took the book of the covenant, and read in the audience of the
people: and they said, All that the LORD hath said will we do, and be obedient.
8 And Moses took the blood, and sprinkled *it* on the people, and said, Behold
the blood of the covenant, which the LORD hath made with you concerning
all these words.

The Glory of God Appears

9 Then went up Moses, and Aaron, Nadab, and Abihu, and seventy of the
elders of Israel:
10 And they saw the God of Israel: and *there was* under his feet as it were a
paved work of a sapphire stone, and as it were the body of heaven in *his* clearness.
11 And upon the nobles of the children of Israel he laid not his hand: also
they saw God, and did eat and drink.
12 And the LORD said unto Moses, Come up to me into the mount, and be
there: and I will give thee tables of stone, and a law, and commandments which
I have written; that thou mayest teach them.
13 And Moses rose up, and his minister Joshua: and Moses went up into the
mount of God.
14 And he said unto the elders, Tarry ye here for us, until we come again unto
you: and, behold, Aaron and Hur *are* with you: if any man have any matters
to do, let him come unto them.
15 And Moses went up into the mount, and a cloud covered the mount.
16 And the glory of the LORD abode upon mount Sinai, and the cloud covered
it six days: and the seventh day he called unto Moses out of the midst of the
cloud.
17 And the sight of the glory of the LORD *was* like devouring fire on the top
of the mount in the eyes of the children of Israel.
18 And Moses went into the midst of the cloud, and gat him up into the
mount: and Moses was in the mount forty days and forty nights.

Offerings for the Tabernacle

25 And the LORD spake unto Moses, saying,
2 Speak unto the children of Israel, that they bring me an offering: of
every man that giveth it willingly with his heart ye shall take my offering.

3 And this *is* the offering which ye shall take of them; gold, and silver, and
brass,
4 And blue, and purple, and scarlet, and fine linen, and goats' *hair*,
5 And rams' skins dyed red, and badgers' skins, and shittim wood,
6 Oil for the light, spices for anointing oil, and for sweet incense,
7 Onyx stones, and stones to be set in the ephod, and in the breastplate.
8 And let them make me a sanctuary; that I may dwell among them.
9 According to all that I shew thee, *after* the pattern of the tabernacle, and
the pattern of all the instruments thereof, even so shall ye make *it*.

The Form of the Ark of the Testimony

10 And they shall make an ark *of* shittim wood: two cubits and a half *shall*
be the length thereof, and a cubit and a half the breadth thereof, and a cubit
and a half the height thereof.
11 And thou shalt overlay it with pure gold, within and without shalt thou
overlay it, and shalt make upon it a crown of gold round about.
12 And thou shalt cast four rings of gold for it, and put *them* in the four
corners thereof; and two rings *shall be* in the one side of it, and two rings in
the other side of it.
13 And thou shalt make staves *of* shittim wood, and overlay them with gold.
14 And thou shalt put the staves into the rings by the sides of the ark, that
the ark may be borne with them.
15 The staves shall be in the rings of the ark: they shall not be taken from it.
16 And thou shalt put into the ark the testimony which I shall give thee.
17 And thou shalt make a mercy seat *of* pure gold: two cubits and a half *shall*
be the length thereof, and a cubit and a half the breadth thereof.
18 And thou shalt make two cherubims *of* gold, *of* beaten work shalt thou
make them, in the two ends of the mercy seat.
19 And make one cherub on the one end, and the other cherub on the other
end: *even* of the mercy seat shall ye make the cherubims on the two ends
thereof.
20 And the cherubims shall stretch forth *their* wings on high, covering the
mercy seat with their wings, and their faces *shall look* one to another; toward
the mercy seat shall the faces of the cherubims be.
21 And thou shalt put the mercy seat above upon the ark; and in the ark thou
shalt put the testimony that I shall give thee.
22 And there I will meet with thee, and I will commune with thee from above
the mercy seat, from between the two cherubims which *are* upon the ark of
the testimony, of all *things* which I will give thee in commandment unto the
children of Israel.

The Table and Its Furniture

23 Thou shalt also make a table *of* shittim wood: two cubits *shall be* the length
thereof, and a cubit the breadth thereof, and a cubit and a half the height
thereof.
24 And thou shalt overlay it with pure gold, and make thereto a crown of
gold round about.
25 And thou shalt make unto it a border of an hand breadth round about,
and thou shalt make a golden crown to the border thereof round about.
26 And thou shalt make for it four rings of gold, and put the rings in the four
corners that *are* on the four feet thereof.
27 Over against the border shall the rings be for places of the staves to bear
the table.
28 And thou shalt make the staves *of* shittim wood, and overlay them with
gold, that the table may be borne with them.
29 And thou shalt make the dishes thereof, and spoons thereof, and covers
thereof, and bowls thereof, to cover withal: *of* pure gold shalt thou make them.

30 And thou shalt set upon the table shewbread before me alway.

The Candlestick and Its Instruments

31 And thou shalt make a candlestick *of* pure gold: *of* beaten work shall the
candlestick be made: his shaft, and his branches, his bowls, his knops, and his
flowers, shall be of the same.
32 And six branches shall come out of the sides of it; three branches of the
candlestick out of the one side, and three branches of the candlestick out of
the other side:
33 Three bowls made like unto almonds, *with* a knop and a flower in one
branch; and three bowls made like almonds in the other branch, *with* a knop
and a flower: so in the six branches that come out of the candlestick.
34 And in the candlestick *shall be* four bowls made like unto almonds, *with*
their knops and their flowers.
35 And *there shall be* a knop under two branches of the same, and a knop
under two branches of the same, and a knop under two branches of the same,
according to the six branches that proceed out of the candlestick.
36 Their knops and their branches shall be of the same: all it *shall be* one
beaten work *of* pure gold.
37 And thou shalt make the seven lamps thereof: and they shall light the
lamps thereof, that they may give light over against it.
38 And the tongs thereof, and the snuffdishes thereof, *shall be of* pure gold.
39 *Of* a talent of pure gold shall he make it, with all these vessels.
40 And look that thou make *them* after their pattern, which was shewed thee
in the mount.

The Ten Curtains of the Tabernacle

26 Moreover thou shalt make the tabernacle *with* ten curtains *of* fine
twined linen, and blue, and purple, and scarlet: *with* cherubims of
cunning work shalt thou make them.
2 The length of one curtain *shall be* eight and twenty cubits, and the breadth
of one curtain four cubits: and every one of the curtains shall have one mea-
sure.
3 The five curtains shall be coupled together one to another; and *other* five
curtains *shall be* coupled one to another.
4 And thou shalt make loops of blue upon the edge of the one curtain from
the selvedge in the coupling; and likewise shalt thou make in the uttermost
edge of *another* curtain, in the coupling of the second.
5 Fifty loops shalt thou make in the one curtain, and fifty loops shalt thou
make in the edge of the curtain that *is* in the coupling of the second; that the
loops may take hold one of another.
6 And thou shalt make fifty taches of gold, and couple the curtains together
with the taches: and it shall be one tabernacle.

The Eleven Curtains of Goats' Hair

7 And thou shalt make curtains *of* goats' *hair* to be a covering upon the tab-
ernacle: eleven curtains shalt thou make.
8 The length of one curtain *shall be* thirty cubits, and the breadth of one
curtain four cubits: and the eleven curtains *shall be all* of one measure.
9 And thou shalt couple five curtains by themselves, and six curtains by them-
selves, and shalt double the sixth curtain in the forefront of the tabernacle.
10 And thou shalt make fifty loops on the edge of the one curtain *that is*
outmost in the coupling, and fifty loops in the edge of the curtain which cou-
pleth the second.
11 And thou shalt make fifty taches of brass, and put the taches into the loops,
and couple the tent together, that it may be one.
12 And the remnant that remaineth of the curtains of the tent, the half cur-
tain that remaineth, shall hang over the backside of the tabernacle.

13 And a cubit on the one side, and a cubit on the other side of that which remaineth in the length of the curtains of the tent, it shall hang over the sides of the tabernacle on this side and on that side, to cover it.

14 And thou shalt make a covering for the tent *of* rams' skins dyed red, and a covering above *of* badgers' skins.

The Boards of the Tabernacle, with Their Sockets and Bars

15 And thou shalt make boards for the tabernacle *of* shittim wood standing up.

16 Ten cubits *shall be* the length of a board, and a cubit and a half *shall be* the breadth of one board.

17 Two tenons *shall there be* in one board, set in order one against another: thus shalt thou make for all the boards of the tabernacle.

18 And thou shalt make the boards for the tabernacle, twenty boards on the south side southward.

19 And thou shalt make forty sockets of silver under the twenty boards; two sockets under one board for his two tenons, and two sockets under another board for his two tenons.

20 And for the second side of the tabernacle on the north side *there shall be* twenty boards:

21 And their forty sockets *of* silver; two sockets under one board, and two sockets under another board.

22 And for the sides of the tabernacle westward thou shalt make six boards.

23 And two boards shalt thou make for the corners of the tabernacle in the two sides.

24 And they shall be coupled together beneath, and they shall be coupled together above the head of it unto one ring: thus shall it be for them both; they shall be for the two corners.

25 And they shall be eight boards, and their sockets *of* silver, sixteen sockets; two sockets under one board, and two sockets under another board.

26 And thou shalt make bars *of* shittim wood; five for the boards of the one side of the tabernacle,

27 And five bars for the boards of the other side of the tabernacle, and five bars for the boards of the side of the tabernacle, for the two sides westward.

28 And the middle bar in the midst of the boards shall reach from end to end.

29 And thou shalt overlay the boards with gold, and make their rings *of* gold *for* places for the bars: and thou shalt overlay the bars with gold.

30 And thou shalt rear up the tabernacle according to the fashion thereof which was shewed thee in the mount.

The Veil for the Ark

31 And thou shalt make a veil *of* blue, and purple, and scarlet, and fine twined linen of cunning work: with cherubims shall it be made:

32 And thou shalt hang it upon four pillars of shittim *wood* overlaid with gold: their hooks *shall be of* gold, upon the four sockets of silver.

33 And thou shalt hang up the veil under the taches, that thou mayest bring in thither within the veil the ark of the testimony: and the veil shall divide unto you between the holy *place* and the most holy.

34 And thou shalt put the mercy seat upon the ark of the testimony in the most holy *place*.

35 And thou shalt set the table without the veil, and the candlestick over against the table on the side of the tabernacle toward the south: and thou shalt put the table on the north side.

36 And thou shalt make an hanging for the door of the tent, *of* blue, and purple, and scarlet, and fine twined linen, wrought with needlework.

37 And thou shalt make for the hanging five pillars *of* shittim *wood*, and
overlay them with gold, *and* their hooks *shall be of* gold: and thou shalt cast
five sockets of brass for them.

The Altar of Burnt Offering with Its Vessels

27 And thou shalt make an altar *of* shittim wood, five cubits long, and five
cubits broad; the altar shall be foursquare: and the height thereof *shall*
be three cubits.
2 And thou shalt make the horns of it upon the four corners thereof: his
horns shall be of the same: and thou shalt overlay it with brass.
3 And thou shalt make his pans to receive his ashes, and his shovels, and his
basons, and his fleshhooks, and his firepans: all the vessels thereof thou shalt
make *of* brass.
4 And thou shalt make for it a grate of network *of* brass; and upon the net
shalt thou make four brasen rings in the four corners thereof.
5 And thou shalt put it under the compass of the altar beneath, that the net
may be even to the midst of the altar.
6 And thou shalt make staves for the altar, staves *of* shittim wood, and over-
lay them with brass.
7 And the staves shall be put into the rings, and the staves shall be upon the
two sides of the altar, to bear it.
8 Hollow with boards shalt thou make it: as it was shewed thee in the mount,
so shall they make *it*.

The Court of the Tabernacle

9 And thou shalt make the court of the tabernacle: for the south side south-
ward *there shall be* hangings for the court *of* fine twined linen of an hundred
cubits long for one side:
10 And the twenty pillars thereof and their twenty sockets *shall be of* brass;
the hooks of the pillars and their fillets *shall be of* silver.
11 And likewise for the north side in length *there shall be* hangings of an
hundred *cubits* long, and his twenty pillars and their twenty sockets *of* brass;
the hooks of the pillars and their fillets *of* silver.
12 And *for* the breadth of the court on the west side *shall be* hangings of fifty
cubits: their pillars ten, and their sockets ten.
13 And the breadth of the court on the east side eastward *shall be* fifty cubits.
14 The hangings of one side *of the gate shall be* fifteen cubits: their pillars
three, and their sockets three.
15 And on the other side *shall be* hangings fifteen *cubits*: their pillars three,
and their sockets three.
16 And for the gate of the court *shall be* an hanging of twenty cubits, *of* blue,
and purple, and scarlet, and fine twined linen, wrought with needlework: *and*
their pillars *shall be* four, and their sockets four.
17 All the pillars round about the court *shall be* filleted with silver; their
hooks *shall be of* silver, and their sockets *of* brass.
18 The length of the court *shall be* an hundred cubits, and the breadth fifty
every where, and the height five cubits *of* fine twined linen, and their sockets
of brass.
19 All the vessels of the tabernacle in all the service thereof, and all the pins
thereof, and all the pins of the court, *shall be of* brass.

The Oil for the Lamp

20 And thou shalt command the children of Israel, that they bring thee pure
oil olive beaten for the light, to cause the lamp to burn always.
21 In the tabernacle of the congregation without the veil, which *is* before
the testimony, Aaron and his sons shall order it from evening to morning
before the LORD: *it shall be* a statute for ever unto their generations on the
behalf of the children of Israel.

Aaron and His Sons Are Set Apart for the Priest's Office

28 And take thou unto thee Aaron thy brother, and his sons with him, from among the children of Israel, that he may minister unto me in the priest's office, *even* Aaron, Nadab and Abihu, Eleazar and Ithamar, Aaron's sons.

2 And thou shalt make holy garments for Aaron thy brother for glory and for beauty.

3 And thou shalt speak unto all *that are* wise hearted, whom I have filled with the spirit of wisdom, that they may make Aaron's garments to consecrate him, that he may minister unto me in the priest's office.

4 And these *are* the garments which they shall make; a breastplate, and an ephod, and a robe, and a broidered coat, a mitre, and a girdle: and they shall make holy garments for Aaron thy brother, and his sons, that he may minister unto me in the priest's office.

5 And they shall take gold, and blue, and purple, and scarlet, and fine linen.

The Ephod

6 And they shall make the ephod *of* gold, *of* blue, and *of* purple, *of* scarlet, and fine twined linen, with cunning work.

7 It shall have the two shoulderpieces thereof joined at the two edges thereof; and *so* it shall be joined together.

8 And the curious girdle of the ephod, which *is* upon it, shall be of the same, according to the work thereof; *even of* gold, *of* blue, and purple, and scarlet, and fine twined linen.

9 And thou shalt take two onyx stones, and grave on them the names of the children of Israel:

10 Six of their names on one stone, and *the other* six names of the rest on the other stone, according to their birth.

11 With the work of an engraver in stone, *like* the engravings of a signet, shalt thou engrave the two stones with the names of the children of Israel: thou shalt make them to be set in ouches of gold.

12 And thou shalt put the two stones upon the shoulders of the ephod *for* stones of memorial unto the children of Israel: and Aaron shall bear their names before the LORD upon his two shoulders for a memorial.

13 And thou shalt make ouches *of* gold;

14 And two chains *of* pure gold at the ends; *of* wreathen work shalt thou make them, and fasten the wreathen chains to the ouches.

The Breastplate, with Twelve Precious Stones

15 And thou shalt make the breastplate of judgment with cunning work; after the work of the ephod thou shalt make it; *of* gold, *of* blue, and *of* purple, and *of* scarlet, and *of* fine twined linen, shalt thou make it.

16 Foursquare it shall be *being* doubled; a span *shall be* the length thereof, and a span *shall be* the breadth thereof.

17 And thou shalt set in it settings of stones, *even* four rows of stones: *the first* row *shall be* a sardius, a topaz, and a carbuncle: *this shall be* the first row.

18 And the second row *shall be* an emerald, a sapphire, and a diamond.

19 And the third row a ligure, an agate, and an amethyst.

20 And the fourth row a beryl, and an onyx, and a jasper: they shall be set in gold in their inclosings.

21 And the stones shall be with the names of the children of Israel, twelve, according to their names, *like* the engravings of a signet; every one with his name shall they be according to the twelve tribes.

22 And thou shalt make upon the breastplate chains at the ends *of* wreathen work *of* pure gold.

23 And thou shalt make upon the breastplate two rings of gold, and shalt put the two rings on the two ends of the breastplate.

24 And thou shalt put the two wreathen *chains* of gold in the two rings *which*
are on the ends of the breastplate.
25 And *the other* two ends of the two wreathen *chains* thou shalt fasten in
the two ouches, and put *them* on the shoulderpieces of the ephod before it.
26 And thou shalt make two rings of gold, and thou shalt put them upon the
two ends of the breastplate in the border thereof, which *is* in the side of the
ephod inward.
27 And two *other* rings of gold thou shalt make, and shalt put them on the
two sides of the ephod underneath, toward the forepart thereof, over against
the *other* coupling thereof, above the curious girdle of the ephod.
28 And they shall bind the breastplate by the rings thereof unto the rings of
the ephod with a lace of blue, that *it* may be above the curious girdle of the
ephod, and that the breastplate be not loosed from the ephod.
29 And Aaron shall bear the names of the children of Israel in the breastplate
of judgment upon his heart, when he goeth in unto the holy *place*, for a memo-
rial before the LORD continually.
30 And thou shalt put in the breastplate of judgment the Urim and the
Thummim; and they shall be upon Aaron's heart, when he goeth in before the
LORD: and Aaron shall bear the judgment of the children of Israel upon his
heart before the LORD continually.

The Robe of the Ephod and the Plate of the Mitre

31 And thou shalt make the robe of the ephod all *of* blue.
32 And there shall be an hole in the top of it, in the midst thereof: it shall have
a binding of woven work round about the hole of it, as it were the hole of an
habergeon, that it be not rent.
33 And *beneath* upon the hem of it thou shalt make pomegranates *of* blue,
and *of* purple, and *of* scarlet, round about the hem thereof; and bells of gold
between them round about:
34 A golden bell and a pomegranate, a golden bell and a pomegranate, upon
the hem of the robe round about.
35 And it shall be upon Aaron to minister: and his sound shall be heard when
he goeth in unto the holy *place* before the LORD, and when he cometh out, that
he die not.
36 And thou shalt make a plate *of* pure gold, and grave upon it, *like* the engrav-
ings of a signet, HOLINESS TO THE LORD.
37 And thou shalt put it on a blue lace, that it may be upon the mitre; upon
the forefront of the mitre it shall be.
38 And it shall be upon Aaron's forehead, that Aaron may bear the iniquity
of the holy things, which the children of Israel shall hallow in all their holy
gifts; and it shall be always upon his forehead, that they may be accepted before
the LORD.
39 And thou shalt embroider the coat of fine linen, and thou shalt make the
mitre *of* fine linen, and thou shalt make the girdle *of* needlework.

The Garments for Aaron's Sons

40 And for Aaron's sons thou shalt make coats, and thou shalt make for them
girdles, and bonnets shalt thou make for them, for glory and for beauty.
41 And thou shalt put them upon Aaron thy brother, and his sons with him;
and shalt anoint them, and consecrate them, and sanctify them, that they may
minister unto me in the priest's office.
42 And thou shalt make them linen breeches to cover their nakedness; from
the loins even unto the thighs they shall reach:
43 And they shall be upon Aaron, and upon his sons, when they come in unto
the tabernacle of the congregation, or when they come near unto the altar to
minister in the holy *place*; that they bear not iniquity, and die: *it shall be* a
statute for ever unto him and his seed after him.

The Ceremonies of Consecrating the Priests

29 And this *is* the thing that thou shalt do unto them to hallow them, to
minister unto me in the priest's office: Take one young bullock, and
two rams without blemish,
2 And unleavened bread, and cakes unleavened tempered with oil, and wafers
unleavened anointed with oil: *of* wheaten flour shalt thou make them.
3 And thou shalt put them into one basket, and bring them in the basket,
with the bullock and the two rams.
4 And Aaron and his sons thou shalt bring unto the door of the tabernacle
of the congregation, and shalt wash them with water.
5 And thou shalt take the garments, and put upon Aaron the coat, and the
robe of the ephod, and the ephod, and the breastplate, and gird him with the
curious girdle of the ephod:
6 And thou shalt put the mitre upon his head, and put the holy crown upon
the mitre.
7 Then shalt thou take the anointing oil, and pour *it* upon his head, and
anoint him.
8 And thou shalt bring his sons, and put coats upon them.
9 And thou shalt gird them with girdles, Aaron and his sons, and put the
bonnets on them: and the priest's office shall be theirs for a perpetual statute:
and thou shalt consecrate Aaron and his sons.
10 And thou shalt cause a bullock to be brought before the tabernacle of the
congregation: and Aaron and his sons shall put their hands upon the head of
the bullock.
11 And thou shalt kill the bullock before the LORD, *by* the door of the taber-
nacle of the congregation.
12 And thou shalt take of the blood of the bullock, and put *it* upon the horns
of the altar with thy finger, and pour all the blood beside the bottom of the
altar.
13 And thou shalt take all the fat that covereth the inwards, and the caul *that*
is above the liver, and the two kidneys, and the fat that *is* upon them, and burn
them upon the altar.
14 But the flesh of the bullock, and his skin, and his dung, shalt thou burn
with fire without the camp: it *is* a sin offering.
15 Thou shalt also take one ram; and Aaron and his sons shall put their hands
upon the head of the ram.
16 And thou shalt slay the ram, and thou shalt take his blood, and sprinkle
it round about upon the altar.
17 And thou shalt cut the ram in pieces, and wash the inwards of him, and
his legs, and put *them* unto his pieces, and unto his head.
18 And thou shalt burn the whole ram upon the altar: it *is* a burnt offering
unto the LORD: it *is* a sweet savour, an offering made by fire unto the LORD.
19 And thou shalt take the other ram; and Aaron and his sons shall put their
hands upon the head of the ram.
20 Then shalt thou kill the ram, and take of his blood, and put *it* upon the
tip of the right ear of Aaron, and upon the tip of the right ear of his sons, and
upon the thumb of their right hand, and upon the great toe of their right foot,
and sprinkle the blood upon the altar round about.
21 And thou shalt take of the blood that *is* upon the altar, and of the anoint-
ing oil, and sprinkle *it* upon Aaron, and upon his garments, and upon his sons,
and upon the garments of his sons with him: and he shall be hallowed, and
his garments, and his sons, and his sons' garments with him.
22 Also thou shalt take of the ram the fat and the rump, and the fat that
covereth the inwards, and the caul *above* the liver, and the two kidneys, and
the fat that *is* upon them, and the right shoulder; for it *is* a ram of consecration:

23 And one loaf of bread, and one cake of oiled bread, and one wafer out of
the basket of the unleavened bread that *is* before the LORD:
24 And thou shalt put all in the hands of Aaron, and in the hands of his sons;
and shalt wave them *for* a wave offering before the LORD.
25 And thou shalt receive them of their hands, and burn *them* upon the altar
for a burnt offering, for a sweet savour before the LORD: it *is* an offering made
by fire unto the LORD.
26 And thou shalt take the breast of the ram of Aaron's consecration, and
wave it *for* a wave offering before the LORD: and it shall be thy part.
27 And thou shalt sanctify the breast of the wave offering, and the shoulder
of the heave offering, which is waved, and which is heaved up, of the ram of
the consecration, *even* of *that* which *is* for Aaron, and of *that* which is for his
sons:
28 And it shall be Aaron's and his sons' by a statute for ever from the children
of Israel: for it *is* an heave offering: and it shall be an heave offering from the
children of Israel of the sacrifice of their peace offerings, *even* their heave
offering unto the LORD.
29 And the holy garments of Aaron shall be his sons' after him, to be anoint-
ed therein, and to be consecrated in them.
30 *And* that son that is priest in his stead shall put them on seven days, when
he cometh into the tabernacle of the congregation to minister in the holy
place.
31 And thou shalt take the ram of the consecration, and seethe his flesh in
the holy place.
32 And Aaron and his sons shall eat the flesh of the ram, and the bread that
is in the basket, *by* the door of the tabernacle of the congregation.
33 And they shall eat those things wherewith the atonement was made, to
consecrate *and* to sanctify them: but a stranger shall not eat *thereof*, because
they *are* holy.
34 And if ought of the flesh of the consecrations, or of the bread, remain
unto the morning, then thou shalt burn the remainder with fire: it shall not
be eaten, because it *is* holy.
35 And thus shalt thou do unto Aaron, and to his sons, according to all *things*
which I have commanded thee: seven days shalt thou consecrate them.
36 And thou shalt offer every day a bullock *for* a sin offering for atonement:
and thou shalt cleanse the altar, when thou hast made an atonement for it,
and thou shalt anoint it, to sanctify it.
37 Seven days thou shalt make an atonement for the altar, and sanctify it;
and it shall be an altar most holy: whatsoever toucheth the altar shall be holy.

The Continual Burnt Offering

38 Now this *is that* which thou shalt offer upon the altar; two lambs of the
first year day by day continually.
39 The one lamb thou shalt offer in the morning; and the other lamb thou
shalt offer at even:
40 And with the one lamb a tenth deal of flour mingled with the fourth part
of an hin of beaten oil; and the fourth part of an hin of wine *for* a drink offering.
41 And the other lamb thou shalt offer at even, and shalt do thereto accord-
ing to the meat offering of the morning, and according to the drink offering
thereof, for a sweet savour, an offering made by fire unto the LORD.
42 *This shall be* a continual burnt offering throughout your generations *at*
the door of the tabernacle of the congregation before the LORD: where I will
meet you, to speak there unto thee.
43 And there I will meet with the children of Israel, and *the tabernacle* shall
be sanctified by my glory.

44 And I will sanctify the tabernacle of the congregation, and the altar: I will
sanctify also both Aaron and his sons, to minister to me in the priest's office.
45 And I will dwell among the children of Israel, and will be their God.
46 And they shall know that I *am* the LORD their God, that brought them
forth out of the land of Egypt, that I may dwell among them: I *am* the LORD
their God.

Directions for Making the Altar of Incense

30 And thou shalt make an altar to burn incense upon: *of* shittim wood
shalt thou make it.
2 A cubit *shall be* the length thereof, and a cubit the breadth thereof; four-
square shall it be: and two cubits *shall be* the height thereof: the horns there-
of *shall be* of the same.
3 And thou shalt overlay it with pure gold, the top thereof, and the sides
thereof round about, and the horns thereof; and thou shalt make unto it a
crown of gold round about.
4 And two golden rings shalt thou make to it under the crown of it, by the
two corners thereof, upon the two sides of it shalt thou make *it*; and they shall
be for places for the staves to bear it withal.
5 And thou shalt make the staves *of* shittim wood, and overlay them with
gold.
6 And thou shalt put it before the veil that *is* by the ark of the testimony,
before the mercy seat that *is* over the testimony, where I will meet with thee.
7 And Aaron shall burn thereon sweet incense every morning: when he dress-
eth the lamps, he shall burn incense upon it.
8 And when Aaron lighteth the lamps at even, he shall burn incense upon it,
a perpetual incense before the LORD throughout your generations.
9 Ye shall offer no strange incense thereon, nor burnt sacrifice, nor meat
offering; neither shall ye pour drink offering thereon.
10 And Aaron shall make an atonement upon the horns of it once in a year
with the blood of the sin offering of atonements: once in the year shall he
make atonement upon it throughout your generations: it *is* most holy unto
the LORD.

The Ransom of Souls

11 And the LORD spake unto Moses, saying,
12 When thou takest the sum of the children of Israel after their number,
then shall they give every man a ransom for his soul unto the LORD, when thou
numberest them; that there be no plague among them, when *thou* numberest
them.
13 This they shall give, every one that passeth among them that are num-
bered, half a shekel after the shekel of the sanctuary: (a shekel *is* twenty gerahs:)
an half shekel *shall be* the offering of the LORD.
14 Every one that passeth among them that are numbered, from twenty years
old and above, shall give an offering unto the LORD.
15 The rich shall not give more, and the poor shall not give less than half a
shekel, when *they* give an offering unto the LORD, to make an atonement for
your souls.
16 And thou shalt take the atonement money of the children of Israel, and
shalt appoint it for the service of the tabernacle of the congregation; that it
may be a memorial unto the children of Israel before the LORD, to make an
atonement for your souls.

The Brasen Laver

17 And the LORD spake unto Moses, saying,
18 Thou shalt also make a laver *of* brass, and his foot *also of* brass, to wash
withal: and thou shalt put it between the tabernacle of the congregation and
the altar, and thou shalt put water therein.

19 For Aaron and his sons shall wash their hands and their feet thereat:
20 When they go into the tabernacle of the congregation, they shall wash
with water, that they die not; or when they come near to the altar to minister,
to burn offering made by fire unto the LORD:
21 So they shall wash their hands and their feet, that they die not: and it shall
be a statute for ever to them, *even* to him and to his seed throughout their
generations.

The Holy Anointing Oil

22 Moreover the LORD spake unto Moses, saying,
23 Take thou also unto thee principal spices, of pure myrrh five hundred
shekels, and of sweet cinnamon half so much, *even* two hundred and fifty
shekels, and of sweet calamus two hundred and fifty *shekels*,
24 And of cassia five hundred *shekels*, after the shekel of the sanctuary, and
of oil olive an hin:
25 And thou shalt make it an oil of holy ointment, an ointment compound
after the art of the apothecary: it shall be an holy anointing oil.
26 And thou shalt anoint the tabernacle of the congregation therewith, and
the ark of the testimony,
27 And the table and all his vessels, and the candlestick and his vessels, and
the altar of incense,
28 And the altar of burnt offering with all his vessels, and the laver and his
foot.
29 And thou shalt sanctify them, that they may be most holy: whatsoever
toucheth them shall be holy.
30 And thou shalt anoint Aaron and his sons, and consecrate them, that *they*
may minister unto me in the priest's office.
31 And thou shalt speak unto the children of Israel, saying, This shall be an
holy anointing oil unto me throughout your generations.
32 Upon man's flesh shall it not be poured, neither shall ye make *any other*
like it, after the composition of it: it *is* holy, *and* it shall be holy unto you.
33 Whosoever compoundeth *any* like it, or whosoever putteth *any* of it upon
a stranger, shall even be cut off from his people.
34 And the LORD said unto Moses, Take unto thee sweet spices, stacte, and
onycha, and galbanum; *these* sweet spices with pure frankincense: of each
shall there be a like *weight*:
35 And thou shalt make it a perfume, a confection after the art of the apoth-
ecary, tempered together, pure *and* holy:
36 And thou shalt beat *some* of it very small, and put of it before the testimo-
ny in the tabernacle of the congregation, where I will meet with thee: it shall
be unto you most holy.
37 And *as for* the perfume which thou shalt make, ye shall not make to your-
selves according to the composition thereof: it shall be unto thee holy for the
LORD.
38 Whosoever shall make like unto that, to smell thereto, shall even be cut
off from his people.

Bezaleel and Aholiab Are Called for the Work of the Tabernacle

31 And the LORD spake unto Moses, saying,
2 See, I have called by name Bezaleel the son of Uri, the son of Hur, of
the tribe of Judah:
3 And I have filled him with the spirit of God, in wisdom, and in understand-
ing, and in knowledge, and in all manner of workmanship,
4 To devise cunning works, to work in gold, and in silver, and in brass,
5 And in cutting of stones, to set *them*, and in carving of timber, to work in
all manner of workmanship.

6 And I, behold, I have given with him Aholiab, the son of Ahisamach, of the
tribe of Dan: and in the hearts of all that are wise hearted I have put wisdom,
that they may make all that I have commanded thee;
7 The tabernacle of the congregation, and the ark of the testimony, and the
mercy seat that *is* thereupon, and all the furniture of the tabernacle,
8 And the table and his furniture, and the pure candlestick with all his fur-
niture, and the altar of incense,
9 And the altar of burnt offering with all his furniture, and the laver and his
foot,
10 And the cloths of service, and the holy garments for Aaron the priest, and
the garments of his sons, to minister in the priest's office,
11 And the anointing oil, and sweet incense for the holy *place*: according to
all that I have commanded thee shall they do.

The Observation of the Sabbath Is Commanded Again

12 And the LORD spake unto Moses, saying,
13 Speak thou also unto the children of Israel, saying, Verily my sabbaths ye
shall keep: for it *is* a sign between me and you throughout your generations;
that *ye* may know that I *am* the LORD that doth sanctify you.
14 Ye shall keep the sabbath therefore; for it *is* holy unto you: every one that
defileth it shall surely be put to death: for whosoever doeth *any* work therein,
that soul shall be cut off from among his people.
15 Six days may work be done; but in the seventh *is* the sabbath of rest, holy
to the LORD: whosoever doeth *any* work in the sabbath day, he shall surely be
put to death.
16 Wherefore the children of Israel shall keep the sabbath, to observe the
sabbath throughout their generations, *for* a perpetual covenant.
17 It *is* a sign between me and the children of Israel for ever: for *in* six days
the LORD made heaven and earth, and on the seventh day he rested, and was
refreshed.
18 And he gave unto Moses, when he had made an end of communing with
him upon mount Sinai, two tables of testimony, tables of stone, written with
the finger of God.

The Golden Calf

32 And when the people saw that Moses delayed to come down out of the
mount, the people gathered themselves together unto Aaron, and said
unto him, Up, make us gods, which shall go before us; for *as for* this Moses,
the man that brought us up out of the land of Egypt, we wot not what is become
of him.
2 And Aaron said unto them, Break off the golden earrings, which *are* in
the ears of your wives, of your sons, and of your daughters, and bring *them*
unto me.
3 And all the people brake off the golden earrings which *were* in their ears,
and brought *them* unto Aaron.
4 And he received *them* at their hand, and fashioned it with a graving tool,
after he had made it a molten calf: and they said, These *be* thy gods, O Israel,
which brought thee up out of the land of Egypt.
5 And when Aaron saw *it*, he built an altar before it; and Aaron made proc-
lamation, and said, To morrow *is* a feast to the LORD.
6 And they rose up early on the morrow, and offered burnt offerings, and
brought peace offerings; and the people sat down to eat and to drink, and rose
up to play.

God Is Angered

7 And the LORD said unto Moses, Go, get thee down; for thy people, which
thou broughtest out of the land of Egypt, have corrupted *themselves*:

8 They have turned aside quickly out of the way which I commanded them:
they have made them a molten calf, and have worshipped it, and have sacri-
ficed thereunto, and said, These *be* thy gods, O Israel, which have brought thee
up out of the land of Egypt.
9 And the LORD said unto Moses, I have seen this people, and, behold, it *is* a
stiffnecked people:
10 Now therefore let me alone, that my wrath may wax hot against them,
and that I may consume them: and I will make of thee a great nation.
11 And Moses besought the LORD his God, and said, LORD, why doth thy wrath
wax hot against thy people, which thou hast brought forth out of the land of
Egypt with great power, and with a mighty hand?
12 Wherefore should the Egyptians speak, and say, For mischief did he bring
them out, to slay them in the mountains, and to consume them from the face
of the earth? Turn from thy fierce wrath, and repent of this evil against thy
people.
13 Remember Abraham, Isaac, and Israel, thy servants, to whom thou swar-
est by thine own self, and saidst unto them, I will multiply your seed as the
stars of heaven, and all this land that I have spoken of will I give unto your
seed, and they shall inherit *it* for ever.
14 And the LORD repented of the evil which he thought to do unto his people.

Moses Comes down with the Tablets

15 And Moses turned, and went down from the mount, and the two tables
of the testimony *were* in his hand: the tables *were* written on both their sides;
on the one side and on the other *were* they written.
16 And the tables *were* the work of God, and the writing *was* the writing of
God, graven upon the tables.
17 And when Joshua heard the noise of the people as they shouted, he said
unto Moses, *There is* a noise of war in the camp.
18 And he said, *It is* not the voice of *them that* shout for mastery, neither *is*
it the voice of *them that* cry for being overcome: *but* the noise of *them that*
sing do I hear.
19 And it came to pass, as soon as he came nigh unto the camp, that he saw
the calf, and the dancing: and Moses' anger waxed hot, and he cast the tables
out of his hands, and brake them beneath the mount.
20 And he took the calf which they had made, and burnt *it* in the fire, and
ground *it* to powder, and strawed *it* upon the water, and made the children
of Israel drink *of it*.
21 And Moses said unto Aaron, What did this people unto thee, that thou
hast brought so great a sin upon them?
22 And Aaron said, Let not the anger of my lord wax hot: thou knowest the
people, that they *are set* on mischief.
23 For they said unto me, Make us gods, which shall go before us: for *as for*
this Moses, the man that brought us up out of the land of Egypt, we wot not
what is become of him.
24 And I said unto them, Whosoever hath any gold, let them break *it* off. So
they gave *it* me: then I cast it into the fire, and there came out this calf.
25 And when Moses saw that the people *were* naked; (for Aaron had made
them naked unto *their* shame among their enemies:)
26 Then Moses stood in the gate of the camp, and said, Who *is* on the LORD's
side? *let him come* unto me. And all the sons of Levi gathered themselves
together unto him.
27 And he said unto them, Thus saith the LORD God of Israel, Put every man
his sword by his side, *and* go in and out from gate to gate throughout the camp,
and slay every man his brother, and every man his companion, and every man
his neighbour.

28 And the children of Levi did according to the word of Moses: and there
fell of the people that day about three thousand men.
29 For Moses had said, Consecrate yourselves to day to the LORD, even every
man upon his son, and upon his brother; that he may bestow upon you a
blessing this day.

Moses Prays for the People

30 And it came to pass on the morrow, that Moses said unto the people, Ye
have sinned a great sin: and now I will go up unto the LORD; peradventure I
shall make an atonement for your sin.
31 And Moses returned unto the LORD, and said, Oh, this people have sinned
a great sin, and have made them gods of gold.
32 Yet now, if thou wilt forgive their sin—; and if not, blot me, I pray thee,
out of thy book which thou hast written.
33 And the LORD said unto Moses, Whosoever hath sinned against me, him
will I blot out of my book.
34 Therefore now go, lead the people unto *the place* of which I have spoken
unto thee: behold, mine Angel shall go before thee: nevertheless in the day
when I visit I will visit their sin upon them.
35 And the LORD plagued the people, because they made the calf, which Aaron
made.

The Lord Refuses to Go with the People

33 And the LORD said unto Moses, Depart, *and* go up hence, thou and the
people which thou hast brought up out of the land of Egypt, unto the
land which I sware unto Abraham, to Isaac, and to Jacob, saying, Unto thy seed
will I give it:
2 And I will send an angel before thee; and I will drive out the Canaanite, the
Amorite, and the Hittite, and the Perizzite, the Hivite, and the Jebusite:
3 Unto a land flowing with milk and honey: for I will not go up in the midst
of thee; for thou *art* a stiffnecked people: lest I consume thee in the way.
4 And when the people heard these evil tidings, they mourned: and no man
did put on him his ornaments.
5 For the LORD had said unto Moses, Say unto the children of Israel, Ye *are* a
stiffnecked people: I will come up into the midst of thee in a moment, and
consume thee: therefore now put off thy ornaments from thee, that I may
know what to do unto thee.
6 And the children of Israel stripped themselves of their ornaments by the
mount Horeb.

The Tabernacle Is Removed out of the Camp

7 And Moses took the tabernacle, and pitched it without the camp, afar off
from the camp, and called it the Tabernacle of the congregation. And it came
to pass, *that* every one which sought the LORD went out unto the tabernacle
of the congregation, which *was* without the camp.
8 And it came to pass, when Moses went out unto the tabernacle, *that* all the
people rose up, and stood every man *at* his tent door, and looked after Moses,
until he was gone into the tabernacle.
9 And it came to pass, as Moses entered into the tabernacle, the cloudy pillar
descended, and stood *at* the door of the tabernacle, and *the LORD* talked with
Moses.
10 And all the people saw the cloudy pillar stand *at* the tabernacle door: and
all the people rose up and worshipped, every man *in* his tent door.
11 And the LORD spake unto Moses face to face, as a man speaketh unto his
friend. And he turned again into the camp: but his servant Joshua, the son of
Nun, a young man, departed not out of the tabernacle.

Moses Desires to See the Glory of God

12 And Moses said unto the LORD, See, thou sayest unto me, Bring up this
people: and thou hast not let me know whom thou wilt send with me. Yet thou
hast said, I know thee by name, and thou hast also found grace in my sight.
13 Now therefore, I pray thee, if I have found grace in thy sight, shew me now
thy way, that I may know thee, that I may find grace in thy sight: and consider
that this nation *is* thy people.
14 And he said, My presence shall go *with thee*, and I will give thee rest.
15 And he said unto him, If thy presence go not *with me*, carry us not up
hence.
16 For wherein shall it be known here that I and thy people have found grace
in thy sight? *is it* not in that thou goest with us? so shall we be separated, I and
thy people, from all the people that *are* upon the face of the earth.
17 And the LORD said unto Moses, I will do this thing also that thou hast
spoken: for thou hast found grace in my sight, and I know thee by name.
18 And he said, I beseech thee, shew me thy glory.
19 And he said, I will make all my goodness pass before thee, and I will pro-
claim the name of the LORD before thee; and will be gracious to whom I will
be gracious, and will shew mercy on whom I will shew mercy.
20 And he said, Thou canst not see my face: for there shall no man see me,
and live.
21 And the LORD said, Behold, *there is* a place by me, and thou shalt stand
upon a rock:
22 And it shall come to pass, while my glory passeth by, that I will put thee
in a clift of the rock, and will cover thee with my hand while I pass by:
23 And I will take away mine hand, and thou shalt see my back parts: but my
face shall not be seen.

The Tablets Are Renewed

34 And the LORD said unto Moses, Hew thee two tables of stone like unto
the first: and I will write upon *these* tables the words that were in the
first tables, which thou brakest.
2 And be ready in the morning, and come up in the morning unto mount
Sinai, and present thyself there to me in the top of the mount.
3 And no man shall come up with thee, neither let any man be seen through-
out all the mount; neither let the flocks nor herds feed before that mount.
4 And he hewed two tables of stone like unto the first; and Moses rose up
early in the morning, and went up unto mount Sinai, as the LORD had com-
manded him, and took in his hand the two tables of stone.
5 And the LORD descended in the cloud, and stood with him there, and pro-
claimed the name of the LORD.
6 And the LORD passed by before him, and proclaimed, The LORD, The LORD
God, merciful and gracious, longsuffering, and abundant in goodness and
truth,
7 Keeping mercy for thousands, forgiving iniquity and transgression and
sin, and that will by no means clear *the guilty*; visiting the iniquity of the
fathers upon the children, and upon the children's children, unto the third
and to the fourth *generation*.
8 And Moses made haste, and bowed his head toward the earth, and wor-
shipped.
9 And he said, If now I have found grace in thy sight, O Lord, let my Lord, I
pray thee, go among us; for it *is* a stiffnecked people; and pardon our iniquity
and our sin, and take us for thine inheritance.

God Makes a Covenant with His People

10 And he said, Behold, I make a covenant: before all thy people I will do
marvels, such as have not been done in all the earth, nor in any nation: and all

the people among which thou *art* shall see the work of the LORD: for it *is* a
terrible thing that I will do with thee.
11 Observe thou that which I command thee this day: behold, I drive out
before thee the Amorite, and the Canaanite, and the Hittite, and the Perizzite,
and the Hivite, and the Jebusite.
12 Take heed to thyself, lest thou make a covenant with the inhabitants of
the land whither thou goest, lest it be for a snare in the midst of thee:
13 But ye shall destroy their altars, break their images, and cut down their
groves:
14 For thou shalt worship no other god: for the LORD, whose name *is* Jealous,
is a jealous God:
15 Lest thou make a covenant with the inhabitants of the land, and they go
a whoring after their gods, and do sacrifice unto their gods, and *one* call thee,
and thou eat of his sacrifice;
16 And thou take of their daughters unto thy sons, and their daughters go a
whoring after their gods, and make thy sons go a whoring after their gods.
17 Thou shalt make thee no molten gods.
18 The feast of unleavened bread shalt thou keep. Seven days thou shalt eat
unleavened bread, as I commanded thee, in the time of the month Abib: for
in the month Abib thou camest out from Egypt.
19 All that openeth the matrix *is* mine; and every firstling among thy cattle,
whether ox or sheep, *that is male.*
20 But the firstling of an ass thou shalt redeem with a lamb: and if thou
redeem *him* not, then shalt thou break his neck. All the firstborn of thy sons
thou shalt redeem. And none shall appear before me empty.
21 Six days thou shalt work, but on the seventh day thou shalt rest: in earing
time and in harvest thou shalt rest.
22 And thou shalt observe the feast of weeks, of the firstfruits of wheat harvest,
and the feast of ingathering at the year's end.
23 Thrice in the year shall all your men children appear before the Lord GOD,
the God of Israel.
24 For I will cast out the nations before thee, and enlarge thy borders: neither
shall any man desire thy land, when thou shalt go up to appear before the LORD
thy God thrice in the year.
25 Thou shalt not offer the blood of my sacrifice with leaven; neither shall
the sacrifice of the feast of the passover be left unto the morning.
26 The first of the firstfruits of thy land thou shalt bring unto the house of
the LORD thy God. Thou shalt not seethe a kid in his mother's milk.
27 And the LORD said unto Moses, Write thou these words: for after the tenor
of these words I have made a covenant with thee and with Israel.

Moses Returns from the Mountain

28 And he was there with the LORD forty days and forty nights; he did neither
eat bread, nor drink water. And he wrote upon the tables the words of the
covenant, the ten commandments.
29 And it came to pass, when Moses came down from mount Sinai with the
two tables of testimony in Moses' hand, when he came down from the mount,
that Moses wist not that the skin of his face shone while he talked with him.
30 And when Aaron and all the children of Israel saw Moses, behold, the skin
of his face shone; and they were afraid to come nigh him.
31 And Moses called unto them; and Aaron and all the rulers of the congregation
returned unto him: and Moses talked with them.
32 And afterward all the children of Israel came nigh: and he gave them in
commandment all that the LORD had spoken with him in mount Sinai.
33 And *till* Moses had done speaking with them, he put a veil on his face.

34 But when Moses went in before the LORD to speak with him, he took the
veil off, until he came out. And he came out, and spake unto the children of
Israel *that* which he was commanded.
35 And the children of Israel saw the face of Moses, that the skin of Moses'
face shone: and Moses put the veil upon his face again, until he went in to
speak with him.

The Sabbath

35 And Moses gathered all the congregation of the children of Israel
together, and said unto them, These *are* the words which the LORD hath
commanded, that *ye* should do them.
2 Six days shall work be done, but on the seventh day there shall be to you an
holy day, a sabbath of rest to the LORD: whosoever doeth work therein shall be
put to death.
3 Ye shall kindle no fire throughout your habitations upon the sabbath day.
4 And Moses spake unto all the congregation of the children of Israel, saying,
This *is* the thing which the LORD commanded, saying,
5 Take ye from among you an offering unto the LORD: whosoever *is* of a will-
ing heart, let him bring it, an offering of the LORD; gold, and silver, and brass,
6 And blue, and purple, and scarlet, and fine linen, and goats' *hair*,
7 And rams' skins dyed red, and badgers' skins, and shittim wood,
8 And oil for the light, and spices for anointing oil, and for the sweet incense,
9 And onyx stones, and stones to be set for the ephod, and for the breastplate.
10 And every wise hearted among you shall come, and make all that the LORD
hath commanded;
11 The tabernacle, his tent, and his covering, his taches, and his boards, his
bars, his pillars, and his sockets,
12 The ark, and the staves thereof, *with* the mercy seat, and the veil of the
covering,
13 The table, and his staves, and all his vessels, and the shewbread,
14 The candlestick also for the light, and his furniture, and his lamps, with
the oil for the light,
15 And the incense altar, and his staves, and the anointing oil, and the sweet
incense, and the hanging for the door at the entering in of the tabernacle,
16 The altar of burnt offering, with his brasen grate, his staves, and all his
vessels, the laver and his foot,
17 The hangings of the court, his pillars, and their sockets, and the hanging
for the door of the court,
18 The pins of the tabernacle, and the pins of the court, and their cords,
19 The cloths of service, to do service in the holy *place*, the holy garments for
Aaron the priest, and the garments of his sons, to minister in the priest's office.

The Readiness of the People to Make Offerings

20 And all the congregation of the children of Israel departed from the pres-
ence of Moses.
21 And they came, every one whose heart stirred him up, and every one whom
his spirit made willing, *and* they brought the LORD's offering to the work of
the tabernacle of the congregation, and for all his service, and for the holy
garments.
22 And they came, both men and women, as many as were willing hearted,
and brought bracelets, and earrings, and rings, and tablets, all jewels of gold:
and every man that offered *offered* an offering of gold unto the LORD.
23 And every man, with whom was found blue, and purple, and scarlet, and
fine linen, and goats' *hair*, and red skins of rams, and badgers' skins, brought
them.

24 Every one that did offer an offering of silver and brass brought the LORD's offering: and every man, with whom was found shittim wood for any work of the service, brought *it*.

25 And all the women that were wise hearted did spin with their hands, and brought that which they had spun, *both* of blue, and of purple, *and* of scarlet, and of fine linen.

26 And all the women whose heart stirred them up in wisdom spun goats' *hair*.

27 And the rulers brought onyx stones, and stones to be set, for the ephod, and for the breastplate;

28 And spice, and oil for the light, and for the anointing oil, and for the sweet incense.

29 The children of Israel brought a willing offering unto the LORD, every man and woman, whose heart made them willing to bring for all manner of work, which the LORD had commanded to be made by the hand of Moses.

Bezaleel and Aholiab Are Called to the Work

30 And Moses said unto the children of Israel, See, the LORD hath called by name Bezaleel the son of Uri, the son of Hur, of the tribe of Judah;

31 And he hath filled him with the spirit of God, in wisdom, in understanding, and in knowledge, and in all manner of workmanship;

32 And to devise curious works, to work in gold, and in silver, and in brass,

33 And in the cutting of stones, to set *them*, and in carving of wood, to make any manner of cunning work.

34 And he hath put in his heart that he may teach, *both* he, and Aholiab, the son of Ahisamach, of the tribe of Dan.

35 Them hath he filled with wisdom of heart, to work all manner of work, of the engraver, and of the cunning workman, and of the embroiderer, in blue, and in purple, in scarlet, and in fine linen, and of the weaver, *even* of them that do any work, and of those that devise cunning work.

The Offerings Are Delivered to the Workmen

36 Then wrought Bezaleel and Aholiab, and every wise hearted man, in whom the LORD put wisdom and understanding to know how to work all manner of work for the service of the sanctuary, according to all that the LORD had commanded.

2 And Moses called Bezaleel and Aholiab, and every wise hearted man, in whose heart the LORD had put wisdom, *even* every one whose heart stirred him up to come unto the work to do it:

3 And they received of Moses all the offering, which the children of Israel had brought for the work of the service of the sanctuary, to make it *withal*. And they brought yet unto him free offerings every morning.

4 And all the wise men, that wrought all the work of the sanctuary, came every man from his work which they made;

5 And they spake unto Moses, saying, The people bring much more than enough for the service of the work, which the LORD commanded to make.

6 And Moses gave commandment, and they caused it to be proclaimed throughout the camp, saying, Let neither man nor woman make any more work for the offering of the sanctuary. So the people were restrained from bringing.

7 For the stuff they had was sufficient for all the work to make it, and too much.

The Curtains of the Cherubim

8 And every wise hearted man among them that wrought the work of the tabernacle made ten curtains *of* fine twined linen, and blue, and purple, and scarlet: *with* cherubims of cunning work made he them.

9 The length of one curtain *was* twenty and eight cubits, and the breadth of
one curtain four cubits: the curtains *were* all of one size.
10 And he coupled the five curtains one unto another: and *the other* five
curtains he coupled one unto another.
11 And he made loops of blue on the edge of one curtain from the selvedge
in the coupling: likewise he made in the uttermost side of *another* curtain, in
the coupling of the second.
12 Fifty loops made he in one curtain, and fifty loops made he in the edge of
the curtain which *was* in the coupling of the second: the loops held one *curtain*
to another.
13 And he made fifty taches of gold, and coupled the curtains one unto
another with the taches: so it became one tabernacle.

The Curtains of Goats' Hair

14 And he made curtains *of* goats' *hair* for the tent over the tabernacle: eleven
curtains he made them.
15 The length of one curtain *was* thirty cubits, and four cubits *was* the
breadth of one curtain: the eleven curtains *were* of one size.
16 And he coupled five curtains by themselves, and six curtains by themselves.
17 And he made fifty loops upon the uttermost edge of the curtain in the
coupling, and fifty loops made he upon the edge of the curtain which coupleth
the second.
18 And he made fifty taches *of* brass to couple the tent together, that it might
be one.
19 And he made a covering for the tent *of* rams' skins dyed red, and a cover-
ing *of* badgers' skins above *that*.
20 And he made boards for the tabernacle *of* shittim wood, standing up.
21 The length of a board *was* ten cubits, and the breadth of a board one cubit
and a half.
22 One board had two tenons, equally distant one from another: thus did he
make for all the boards of the tabernacle.
23 And he made boards for the tabernacle; twenty boards for the south side
southward:
24 And forty sockets of silver he made under the twenty boards; two sockets
under one board for his two tenons, and two sockets under another board for
his two tenons.
25 And for the other side of the tabernacle, *which is* toward the north corner,
he made twenty boards,
26 And their forty sockets of silver; two sockets under one board, and two
sockets under another board.
27 And for the sides of the tabernacle westward he made six boards.
28 And two boards made he for the corners of the tabernacle in the two sides.
29 And they were coupled beneath, and coupled together at the head there-
of, to one ring: thus he did to both of them in both the corners.
30 And there were eight boards; and their sockets *were* sixteen sockets of
silver, under every board two sockets.
31 And he made bars of shittim wood; five for the boards of the one side of
the tabernacle,
32 And five bars for the boards of the other side of the tabernacle, and five
bars for the boards of the tabernacle for the sides westward.
33 And he made the middle bar to shoot through the boards from the one
end to the other.
34 And he overlaid the boards with gold, and made their rings *of* gold *to be*
places for the bars, and overlaid the bars with gold.

The Veil

35 And he made a veil *of* blue, and purple, and scarlet, and fine twined linen:
with cherubims made he it of cunning work.
36 And he made thereunto four pillars *of* shittim *wood*, and overlaid them
with gold: their hooks *were of* gold; and he cast for them four sockets of silver.
37 And he made an hanging for the tabernacle door *of* blue, and purple, and
scarlet, and fine twined linen, of needlework;
38 And the five pillars of it with their hooks: and he overlaid their chapiters
and their fillets with gold: but their five sockets *were of* brass.

The Ark

37 And Bezaleel made the ark *of* shittim wood: two cubits and a half *was*
the length of it, and a cubit and a half the breadth of it, and a cubit and
a half the height of it:
2 And he overlaid it with pure gold within and without, and made a crown
of gold to it round about.
3 And he cast for it four rings of gold, *to be set* by the four corners of it; even
two rings upon the one side of it, and two rings upon the other side of it.
4 And he made staves *of* shittim wood, and overlaid them with gold.
5 And he put the staves into the rings by the sides of the ark, to bear the ark.
6 And he made the mercy seat *of* pure gold: two cubits and a half *was* the
length thereof, and one cubit and a half the breadth thereof.
7 And he made two cherubims *of* gold, beaten out of one piece made he them,
on the two ends of the mercy seat;
8 One cherub on the end on this side, and another cherub on the *other* end
on that side: out of the mercy seat made he the cherubims on the two ends
thereof.
9 And the cherubims spread out *their* wings on high, *and* covered with their
wings over the mercy seat, with their faces one to another; *even* to the mercy
seatward were the faces of the cherubims.

The Table with Its Vessels

10 And he made the table *of* shittim wood: two cubits *was* the length thereof,
and a cubit the breadth thereof, and a cubit and a half the height thereof:
11 And he overlaid it with pure gold, and made thereunto a crown of gold
round about.
12 Also he made thereunto a border of an handbreadth round about; and
made a crown of gold for the border thereof round about.
13 And he cast for it four rings of gold, and put the rings upon the four cor-
ners that *were* in the four feet thereof.
14 Over against the border were the rings, the places for the staves to bear
the table.
15 And he made the staves *of* shittim wood, and overlaid them with gold, to
bear the table.
16 And he made the vessels which *were* upon the table, his dishes, and his
spoons, and his bowls, and his covers to cover withal, *of* pure gold.
17 And he made the candlestick *of* pure gold: *of* beaten work made he the
candlestick; his shaft, and his branch, his bowls, his knops, and his flowers,
were of the same:
18 And six branches going out of the sides thereof; three branches of the
candlestick out of the one side thereof, and three branches of the candlestick
out of the other side thereof:
19 Three bowls made after the fashion of almonds in one branch, a knop and
a flower; and three bowls made like almonds in another branch, a knop and a
flower: so throughout the six branches going out of the candlestick.
20 And in the candlestick *were* four bowls made like almonds, his knops, and
his flowers:

21 And a knop under two branches of the same, and a knop under two branches of the same, and a knop under two branches of the same, according to the six branches going out of it.

22 Their knops and their branches were of the same: all of it *was* one beaten work *of* pure gold.

23 And he made his seven lamps, and his snuffers, and his snuffdishes, *of* pure gold.

24 *Of* a talent of pure gold made he it, and all the vessels thereof.

The Altar of Incense

25 And he made the incense altar *of* shittim wood: the length of it *was* a cubit, and the breadth of it a cubit; *it was* foursquare; and two cubits *was* the height of it; the horns thereof were of the same.

26 And he overlaid it with pure gold, *both* the top of it, and the sides thereof round about, and the horns of it: also he made unto it a crown of gold round about.

27 And he made two rings of gold for it under the crown thereof, by the two corners of it, upon the two sides thereof, to be places for the staves to bear it withal.

28 And he made the staves *of* shittim wood, and overlaid them with gold.

29 And he made the holy anointing oil, and the pure incense of sweet spices, according to the work of the apothecary.

The Altar of Burnt Offering

38 And he made the altar of burnt offering *of* shittim wood: five cubits *was* the length thereof, and five cubits the breadth thereof; *it was* foursquare; and three cubits the height thereof.

2 And he made the horns thereof on the four corners of it; the horns thereof were of the same: and he overlaid it with brass.

3 And he made all the vessels of the altar, the pots, and the shovels, and the basons, *and* the fleshhooks, and the firepans: all the vessels thereof made he *of* brass.

4 And he made for the altar a brasen grate of network under the compass thereof beneath unto the midst of it.

5 And he cast four rings for the four ends of the grate of brass, *to be* places for the staves.

6 And he made the staves *of* shittim wood, and overlaid them with brass.

7 And he put the staves into the rings on the sides of the altar, to bear it withal; he made the altar hollow with boards.

8 And he made the laver *of* brass, and the foot of it *of* brass, of the lookingglasses of *the women* assembling, which assembled *at* the door of the tabernacle of the congregation.

The Court

9 And he made the court: on the south side southward the hangings of the court *were of* fine twined linen, an hundred cubits:

10 Their pillars *were* twenty, and their brasen sockets twenty; the hooks of the pillars and their fillets *were of* silver.

11 And for the north side *the hangings were* an hundred cubits, their pillars *were* twenty, and their sockets of brass twenty; the hooks of the pillars and their fillets *of* silver.

12 And for the west side *were* hangings of fifty cubits, their pillars ten, and their sockets ten; the hooks of the pillars and their fillets *of* silver.

13 And for the east side eastward fifty cubits.

14 The hangings of the one side *of the gate were* fifteen cubits; their pillars three, and their sockets three.

15 And for the other side of the court gate, on this hand and that hand, *were* hangings of fifteen cubits; their pillars three, and their sockets three.

16 All the hangings of the court round about *were* of fine twined linen.
17 And the sockets for the pillars *were of* brass; the hooks of the pillars and
their fillets *of* silver; and the overlaying of their chapiters *of* silver; and all the
pillars of the court *were* filleted with silver.
18 And the hanging for the gate of the court *was* needlework, *of* blue, and
purple, and scarlet, and fine twined linen: and twenty cubits *was* the length,
and the height in the breadth *was* five cubits, answerable to the hangings of
the court.
19 And their pillars *were* four, and their sockets *of* brass four; their hooks *of*
silver, and the overlaying of their chapiters and their fillets *of* silver.
20 And all the pins of the tabernacle, and of the court round about, *were of*
brass.

The People's Offering

21 This is the sum of the tabernacle, *even* of the tabernacle of testimony, as
it was counted, according to the commandment of Moses, *for* the service of
the Levites, by the hand of Ithamar, son to Aaron the priest.
22 And Bezaleel the son of Uri, the son of Hur, of the tribe of Judah, made all
that the LORD commanded Moses.
23 And with him *was* Aholiab, son of Ahisamach, of the tribe of Dan, an
engraver, and a cunning workman, and an embroiderer in blue, and in purple,
and in scarlet, and fine linen.
24 All the gold that was occupied for the work in all the work of the holy
place, even the gold of the offering, was twenty and nine talents, and seven
hundred and thirty shekels, after the shekel of the sanctuary.
25 And the silver of them that were numbered of the congregation *was* an
hundred talents, and a thousand seven hundred and threescore and fifteen
shekels, after the shekel of the sanctuary:
26 A bekah for every man, *that is*, half a shekel, after the shekel of the sanc-
tuary, for every one that went to be numbered, from twenty years old and
upward, for six hundred thousand and three thousand and five hundred and
fifty *men*.
27 And of the hundred talents of silver were cast the sockets of the sanctuary,
and the sockets of the veil; an hundred sockets of the hundred talents, a talent
for a socket.
28 And of the thousand seven hundred seventy and five shekels he made
hooks for the pillars, and overlaid their chapiters, and filleted them.
29 And the brass of the offering *was* seventy talents, and two thousand and
four hundred shekels.
30 And therewith he made the sockets to the door of the tabernacle of the
congregation, and the brasen altar, and the brasen grate for it, and all the
vessels of the altar,
31 And the sockets of the court round about, and the sockets of the court
gate, and all the pins of the tabernacle, and all the pins of the court round
about.

The Cloths of Service and Holy Garments

39 And of the blue, and purple, and scarlet, they made cloths of service,
to do service in the holy *place*, and made the holy garments for Aaron;
as the LORD commanded Moses.
2 And he made the ephod *of* gold, blue, and purple, and scarlet, and fine
twined linen.
3 And they did beat the gold into thin plates, and cut *it into* wires, to work
it in the blue, and in the purple, and in the scarlet, and in the fine linen, *with*
cunning work.
4 They made shoulderpieces for it, to couple *it* together: by the two edges
was it coupled together.

5 And the curious girdle of his ephod, that *was* upon it, *was* of the same,
according to the work thereof; *of* gold, blue, and purple, and scarlet, and fine
twined linen; as the LORD commanded Moses.
6 And they wrought onyx stones inclosed in ouches of gold, graven, as signets
are graven, with the names of the children of Israel.
7 And he put them on the shoulders of the ephod, *that they should be* stones
for a memorial to the children of Israel; as the LORD commanded Moses.
8 And he made the breastplate *of* cunning work, like the work of the ephod;
of gold, blue, and purple, and scarlet, and fine twined linen.
9 It was foursquare; they made the breastplate double: a span *was* the length
thereof, and a span the breadth thereof, *being* doubled.
10 And they set in it four rows of stones: *the first* row *was* a sardius, a topaz,
and a carbuncle: this *was* the first row.
11 And the second row, an emerald, a sapphire, and a diamond.
12 And the third row, a ligure, an agate, and an amethyst.
13 And the fourth row, a beryl, an onyx, and a jasper: *they were* inclosed in
ouches of gold in their inclosings.
14 And the stones *were* according to the names of the children of Israel,
twelve, according to their names, *like* the engravings of a signet, every one
with his name, according to the twelve tribes.
15 And they made upon the breastplate chains at the ends, *of* wreathen work
of pure gold.
16 And they made two ouches *of* gold, and two gold rings; and put the two
rings in the two ends of the breastplate.
17 And they put the two wreathen chains of gold in the two rings on the ends
of the breastplate.
18 And the two ends of the two wreathen chains they fastened in the two
ouches, and put them on the shoulderpieces of the ephod, before it.
19 And they made two rings of gold, and put *them* on the two ends of the
breastplate, upon the border of it, which *was* on the side of the ephod inward.
20 And they made two *other* golden rings, and put them on the two sides of
the ephod underneath, toward the forepart of it, over against the *other* cou-
pling thereof, above the curious girdle of the ephod.
21 And they did bind the breastplate by his rings unto the rings of the ephod
with a lace of blue, that it might be above the curious girdle of the ephod, and
that the breastplate might not be loosed from the ephod; as the LORD com-
manded Moses.
22 And he made the robe of the ephod *of* woven work, all *of* blue.
23 And *there was* an hole in the midst of the robe, as the hole of an habergeon,
with a band round about the hole, that it should not rend.
24 And they made upon the hems of the robe pomegranates *of* blue, and
purple, and scarlet, *and* twined *linen*.
25 And they made bells *of* pure gold, and put the bells between the pome-
granates upon the hem of the robe, round about between the pomegranates;
26 A bell and a pomegranate, a bell and a pomegranate, round about the hem
of the robe to minister *in*; as the LORD commanded Moses.
27 And they made coats *of* fine linen *of* woven work for Aaron, and for his
sons,
28 And a mitre *of* fine linen, and goodly bonnets *of* fine linen, and linen
breeches *of* fine twined linen,
29 And a girdle *of* fine twined linen, and blue, and purple, and scarlet, *of*
needlework; as the LORD commanded Moses.
30 And they made the plate of the holy crown *of* pure gold, and wrote upon
it a writing, *like to* the engravings of a signet, HOLINESS TO THE LORD.
31 And they tied unto it a lace of blue, to fasten *it* on high upon the mitre; as
the LORD commanded Moses.

All Is Viewed and Approved by Moses

32 Thus was all the work of the tabernacle of the tent of the congregation
finished: and the children of Israel did according to all that the LORD com-
manded Moses, so did they.
33 And they brought the tabernacle unto Moses, the tent, and all his furni-
ture, his taches, his boards, his bars, and his pillars, and his sockets,
34 And the covering of rams' skins dyed red, and the covering of badgers'
skins, and the veil of the covering,
35 The ark of the testimony, and the staves thereof, and the mercy seat,
36 The table, *and* all the vessels thereof, and the shewbread,
37 The pure candlestick, *with* the lamps thereof, *even with* the lamps to be
set in order, and all the vessels thereof, and the oil for light,
38 And the golden altar, and the anointing oil, and the sweet incense, and
the hanging for the tabernacle door,
39 The brasen altar, and his grate of brass, his staves, and all his vessels, the
laver and his foot,
40 The hangings of the court, his pillars, and his sockets, and the hanging for
the court gate, his cords, and his pins, and all the vessels of the service of the
tabernacle, for the tent of the congregation,
41 The cloths of service to do service in the holy *place*, and the holy garments
for Aaron the priest, and his sons' garments, to minister in the priest's office.
42 According to all that the LORD commanded Moses, so the children of Israel
made all the work.
43 And Moses did look upon all the work, and, behold, they had done it as
the LORD had commanded, even so had they done it: and Moses blessed them.

The Erection of the Tabernacle, with Its Anointing, Is Commanded

40 And the LORD spake unto Moses, saying,
2 On the first day of the first month shalt thou set up the tabernacle
of the tent of the congregation.
3 And thou shalt put therein the ark of the testimony, and cover the ark with
the veil.
4 And thou shalt bring in the table, and set in order the things that are to be
set in order upon it; and thou shalt bring in the candlestick, and light the
lamps thereof.
5 And thou shalt set the altar of gold for the incense before the ark of the
testimony, and put the hanging of the door to the tabernacle.
6 And thou shalt set the altar of the burnt offering before the door of the
tabernacle of the tent of the congregation.
7 And thou shalt set the laver between the tent of the congregation and the
altar, and shalt put water therein.
8 And thou shalt set up the court round about, and hang up the hanging at
the court gate.
9 And thou shalt take the anointing oil, and anoint the tabernacle, and all
that *is* therein, and shalt hallow it, and all the vessels thereof: and it shall be
holy.
10 And thou shalt anoint the altar of the burnt offering, and all his vessels,
and sanctify the altar: and it shall be an altar most holy.
11 And thou shalt anoint the laver and his foot, and sanctify it.
12 And thou shalt bring Aaron and his sons unto the door of the tabernacle
of the congregation, and wash them with water.
13 And thou shalt put upon Aaron the holy garments, and anoint him, and
sanctify him; that he may minister unto me in the priest's office.
14 And thou shalt bring his sons, and clothe them with coats:

15 And thou shalt anoint them, as thou didst anoint their father, that they
may minister unto me in the priest's office: for their anointing shall surely be
an everlasting priesthood throughout their generations.
16 Thus did Moses: according to all that the LORD commanded him, so did he.
17 And it came to pass in the first month in the second year, on the first *day*
of the month, *that* the tabernacle was reared up.
18 And Moses reared up the tabernacle, and fastened his sockets, and set up
the boards thereof, and put in the bars thereof, and reared up his pillars.
19 And he spread abroad the tent over the tabernacle, and put the covering
of the tent above upon it; as the LORD commanded Moses.
20 And he took and put the testimony into the ark, and set the staves on the
ark, and put the mercy seat above upon the ark:
21 And he brought the ark into the tabernacle, and set up the veil of the
covering, and covered the ark of the testimony; as the LORD commanded
Moses.
22 And he put the table in the tent of the congregation, upon the side of the
tabernacle northward, without the veil.
23 And he set the bread in order upon it before the LORD; as the LORD had
commanded Moses.
24 And he put the candlestick in the tent of the congregation, over against
the table, on the side of the tabernacle southward.
25 And he lighted the lamps before the LORD; as the LORD commanded Moses.
26 And he put the golden altar in the tent of the congregation before the veil:
27 And he burnt sweet incense thereon; as the LORD commanded Moses.
28 And he set up the hanging *at* the door of the tabernacle.
29 And he put the altar of burnt offering *by* the door of the tabernacle of the
tent of the congregation, and offered upon it the burnt offering and the meat
offering; as the LORD commanded Moses.
30 And he set the laver between the tent of the congregation and the altar,
and put water there, to wash *withal*.
31 And Moses and Aaron and his sons washed their hands and their feet
thereat:
32 When they went into the tent of the congregation, and when they came
near unto the altar, they washed; as the LORD commanded Moses.
33 And he reared up the court round about the tabernacle and the altar, and
set up the hanging of the court gate. So Moses finished the work.

A Cloud Covers the Tabernacle

34 Then a cloud covered the tent of the congregation, and the glory of the
LORD filled the tabernacle.
35 And Moses was not able to enter into the tent of the congregation, because
the cloud abode thereon, and the glory of the LORD filled the tabernacle.
36 And when the cloud was taken up from over the tabernacle, the children
of Israel went onward in all their journeys:
37 But if the cloud were not taken up, then they journeyed not till the day
that it was taken up.
38 For the cloud of the LORD *was* upon the tabernacle by day, and fire was on
it by night, in the sight of all the house of Israel, throughout all their journeys.

LEVITICUS

The Burnt Offerings

1 And the LORD called unto Moses, and spake unto him out of the tabernacle of the congregation, saying,

2 Speak unto the children of Israel, and say unto them, If any man of you bring an offering unto the LORD, ye shall bring your offering of the cattle, *even* of the herd, and of the flock.

The Burnt Offering of the Herd

3 If his offering *be* a burnt sacrifice of the herd, let him offer a male without blemish: he shall offer it of his own voluntary will at the door of the tabernacle of the congregation before the LORD.

4 And he shall put his hand upon the head of the burnt offering; and it shall be accepted for him to make atonement for him.

5 And he shall kill the bullock before the LORD: and the priests, Aaron's sons, shall bring the blood, and sprinkle the blood round about upon the altar that *is by* the door of the tabernacle of the congregation.

6 And he shall flay the burnt offering, and cut it into his pieces.

7 And the sons of Aaron the priest shall put fire upon the altar, and lay the wood in order upon the fire:

8 And the priests, Aaron's sons, shall lay the parts, the head, and the fat, in order upon the wood that *is* on the fire which *is* upon the altar:

9 But his inwards and his legs shall he wash in water: and the priest shall burn all on the altar, *to be* a burnt sacrifice, an offering made by fire, of a sweet savour unto the LORD.

The Burnt Offering of Flocks or Fowls

10 And if his offering *be* of the flocks, *namely*, of the sheep, or of the goats, for a burnt sacrifice; he shall bring it a male without blemish.

11 And he shall kill it on the side of the altar northward before the LORD: and the priests, Aaron's sons, shall sprinkle his blood round about upon the altar.

12 And he shall cut it into his pieces, with his head and his fat: and the priest shall lay them in order on the wood that *is* on the fire which *is* upon the altar:

13 But he shall wash the inwards and the legs with water: and the priest shall bring *it* all, and burn *it* upon the altar: it *is* a burnt sacrifice, an offering made by fire, of a sweet savour unto the LORD.

14 And if the burnt sacrifice for his offering to the LORD *be* of fowls, then he shall bring his offering of turtledoves, or of young pigeons.

15 And the priest shall bring it unto the altar, and wring off his head, and burn *it* on the altar; and the blood thereof shall be wrung out at the side of the altar:

16 And he shall pluck away his crop with his feathers, and cast it beside the altar on the east part, by the place of the ashes:

17 And he shall cleave it with the wings thereof, *but* shall not divide *it* asunder: and the priest shall burn it upon the altar, upon the wood that *is* upon the fire: it *is* a burnt sacrifice, an offering made by fire, of a sweet savour unto the LORD.

The Meat (Meal) Offering of Flour with Oil and Incense

2 And when any will offer a meat offering unto the LORD, his offering shall be *of* fine flour; and he shall pour oil upon it, and put frankincense thereon:

2 And he shall bring it to Aaron's sons the priests: and he shall take thereout his handful of the flour thereof, and of the oil thereof, with all the frankincense thereof; and the priest shall burn the memorial of it upon the altar, *to be* an offering made by fire, of a sweet savour unto the LORD:

3 And the remnant of the meat offering *shall be* Aaron's and his sons': *it is* a thing most holy of the offerings of the LORD made by fire.

4 And if thou bring an oblation of a meat offering baken in the oven, *it shall be* unleavened cakes of fine flour mingled with oil, or unleavened wafers anointed with oil.

5 And if thy oblation *be* a meat offering *baken* in a pan, it shall be *of* fine flour unleavened, mingled with oil.

6 Thou shalt part it in pieces, and pour oil thereon: it *is* a meat offering.

7 And if thy oblation *be* a meat offering *baken* in the fryingpan, it shall be made *of* fine flour with oil.

8 And thou shalt bring the meat offering that is made of these things unto the LORD: and when it is presented unto the priest, he shall bring it unto the altar.

9 And the priest shall take from the meat offering a memorial thereof, and shall burn *it* upon the altar: *it is* an offering made by fire, of a sweet savour unto the LORD.

10 And that which is left of the meat offering *shall be* Aaron's and his sons': *it is* a thing most holy of the offerings of the LORD made by fire.

11 No meat offering, which ye shall bring unto the LORD, shall be made with leaven: for ye shall burn no leaven, nor any honey, in any offering of the LORD made by fire.

12 As for the oblation of the firstfruits, ye shall offer them unto the LORD: but they shall not be burnt on thc altar for a sweet savour.

13 And every oblation of thy meat offering shalt thou season with salt; neither shalt thou suffer the salt of the covenant of thy God to be lacking from thy meat offering: with all thine offerings thou shalt offer salt.

14 And if thou offer a meat offering of thy firstfruits unto the LORD, thou shalt offer for the meat offering of thy firstfruits green ears of corn dried by the fire, *even* corn beaten out of full ears.

15 And thou shalt put oil upon it, and lay frankincense thereon: it *is* a meat offering.

16 And the priest shall burn the memorial of it, *part* of the beaten corn thereof, and *part* of the oil thereof, with all the frankincense thereof: *it is* an offering made by fire unto the LORD.

The Peace Offering of the Herd

3 And if his oblation *be* a sacrifice of peace offering, if he offer *it* of the herd; whether *it be* a male or female, he shall offer it without blemish before the LORD.

2 And he shall lay his hand upon the head of his offering, and kill it *at* the door of the tabernacle of the congregation: and Aaron's sons the priests shall sprinkle the blood upon the altar round about.

3 And he shall offer of the sacrifice of the peace offering an offering made by fire unto the LORD; the fat that covereth the inwards, and all the fat that *is* upon the inwards,

4 And the two kidneys, and the fat that *is* on them, which *is* by the flanks, and the caul above the liver, with the kidneys, it shall he take away.

5 And Aaron's sons shall burn it on the altar upon the burnt sacrifice, which
is upon the wood that *is* on the fire: *it is* an offering made by fire, of a sweet
savour unto the LORD.

The Peace Offering of the Flock

6 And if his offering for a sacrifice of peace offering unto the LORD *be* of the
flock; male or female, he shall offer it without blemish.
7 If he offer a lamb for his offering, then shall he offer it before the LORD.
8 And he shall lay his hand upon the head of his offering, and kill it before
the tabernacle of the congregation: and Aaron's sons shall sprinkle the blood
thereof round about upon the altar.
9 And he shall offer of the sacrifice of the peace offering an offering made
by fire unto the LORD; the fat thereof, *and* the whole rump, it shall he take off
hard by the backbone; and the fat that covereth the inwards, and all the fat
that *is* upon the inwards,
10 And the two kidneys, and the fat that *is* upon them, which *is* by the flanks,
and the caul above the liver, with the kidneys, it shall he take away.
11 And the priest shall burn it upon the altar: *it is* the food of the offering
made by fire unto the LORD.
12 And if his offering *be* a goat, then he shall offer it before the LORD.
13 And he shall lay his hand upon the head of it, and kill it before the taber-
nacle of the congregation: and the sons of Aaron shall sprinkle the blood
thereof upon the altar round about.
14 And he shall offer thereof his offering, *even* an offering made by fire unto
the LORD; the fat that covereth the inwards, and all the fat that *is* upon the
inwards,
15 And the two kidneys, and the fat that *is* upon them, which *is* by the flanks,
and the caul above the liver, with the kidneys, it shall he take away.
16 And the priest shall burn them upon the altar: *it is* the food of the offering
made by fire for a sweet savour: all the fat *is* the LORD'S.
17 *It shall be* a perpetual statute for your generations throughout all your
dwellings, that ye eat neither fat nor blood.

The Sin Offering of Ignorance

4 And the LORD spake unto Moses, saying,
2 Speak unto the children of Israel, saying, If a soul shall sin through
ignorance against any of the commandments of the LORD *concerning things*
which ought not to be done, and shall do against any of them:
3 If the priest that is anointed do sin according to the sin of the people; then
let him bring for his sin, which he hath sinned, a young bullock without blem-
ish unto the LORD for a sin offering.
4 And he shall bring the bullock unto the door of the tabernacle of the con-
gregation before the LORD; and shall lay his hand upon the bullock's head, and
kill the bullock before the LORD.
5 And the priest that is anointed shall take of the bullock's blood, and bring
it to the tabernacle of the congregation:
6 And the priest shall dip his finger in the blood, and sprinkle of the blood
seven times before the LORD, before the veil of the sanctuary.
7 And the priest shall put *some* of the blood upon the horns of the altar of
sweet incense before the LORD, which *is* in the tabernacle of the congregation;
and shall pour all the blood of the bullock at the bottom of the altar of the
burnt offering, which *is at* the door of the tabernacle of the congregation.
8 And he shall take off from it all the fat of the bullock for the sin offering;
the fat that covereth the inwards, and all the fat that *is* upon the inwards,
9 And the two kidneys, and the fat that *is* upon them, which *is* by the flanks,
and the caul above the liver, with the kidneys, it shall he take away,

10 As it was taken off from the bullock of the sacrifice of peace offerings: and
the priest shall burn them upon the altar of the burnt offering.
11 And the skin of the bullock, and all his flesh, with his head, and with his
legs, and his inwards, and his dung,
12 Even the whole bullock shall he carry forth without the camp unto a clean
place, where the ashes are poured out, and burn him on the wood with fire:
where the ashes are poured out shall he be burnt.

The Sin Offering for the Congregation

13 And if the whole congregation of Israel sin through ignorance, and the
thing be hid from the eyes of the assembly, and they have done *somewhat
against* any of the commandments of the LORD *concerning things* which
should not be done, and are guilty;
14 When the sin, which they have sinned against it, is known, then the con-
gregation shall offer a young bullock for the sin, and bring him before the
tabernacle of the congregation.
15 And the elders of the congregation shall lay their hands upon the head of
the bullock before the LORD: and the bullock shall be killed before the LORD.
16 And the priest that is anointed shall bring of the bullock's blood to the
tabernacle of the congregation:
17 And the priest shall dip his finger *in some* of the blood, and sprinkle *it*
seven times before the LORD, *even* before the veil.
18 And he shall put *some* of the blood upon the horns of the altar which *is*
before the LORD, that *is* in the tabernacle of the congregation, and shall pour
out all the blood at the bottom of the altar of the burnt offering, which *is at*
the door of the tabernacle of the congregation.
19 And he shall take all his fat from him, and burn *it* upon the altar.
20 And he shall do with the bullock as he did with the bullock for a sin offer-
ing, so shall he do with this: and the priest shall make an atonement for them,
and it shall be forgiven them.
21 And he shall carry forth the bullock without the camp, and burn him as
he burned the first bullock: it *is* a sin offering for the congregation.

The Sin Offering for the Ruler

22 When a ruler hath sinned, and done *somewhat* through ignorance *against*
any of the commandments of the LORD his God *concerning things* which
should not be done, and is guilty;
23 Or if his sin, wherein he hath sinned, come to his knowledge; he shall
bring his offering, a kid of the goats, a male without blemish:
24 And he shall lay his hand upon the head of the goat, and kill it in the place
where they kill the burnt offering before the LORD: it *is* a sin offering.
25 And the priest shall take of the blood of the sin offering with his finger,
and put *it* upon the horns of the altar of burnt offering, and shall pour out
his blood at the bottom of the altar of burnt offering.
26 And he shall burn all his fat upon the altar, as the fat of the sacrifice of
peace offerings: and the priest shall make an atonement for him as concerning
his sin, and it shall be forgiven him.

The Sin Offering for Other Individuals

27 And if any one of the common people sin through ignorance, while he
doeth *somewhat against* any of the commandments of the LORD *concerning
things* which ought not to be done, and be guilty;
28 Or if his sin, which he hath sinned, come to his knowledge: then he shall
bring his offering, a kid of the goats, a female without blemish, for his sin
which he hath sinned.
29 And he shall lay his hand upon the head of the sin offering, and slay the
sin offering in the place of the burnt offering.

30 And the priest shall take of the blood thereof with his finger, and put *it*
upon the horns of the altar of burnt offering, and shall pour out all the blood
thereof at the bottom of the altar.
31 And he shall take away all the fat thereof, as the fat is taken away from off
the sacrifice of peace offerings; and the priest shall burn *it* upon the altar for
a sweet savour unto the LORD; and the priest shall make an atonement for him,
and it shall be forgiven him.
32 And if he bring a lamb for a sin offering, he shall bring it a female without
blemish.
33 And he shall lay his hand upon the head of the sin offering, and slay it for
a sin offering in the place where they kill the burnt offering.
34 And the priest shall take of the blood of the sin offering with his finger,
and put *it* upon the horns of the altar of burnt offering, and shall pour out all
the blood thereof at the bottom of the altar:
35 And he shall take away all the fat thereof, as the fat of the lamb is taken
away from the sacrifice of the peace offerings; and the priest shall burn them
upon the altar, according to the offerings made by fire unto the LORD: and the
priest shall make an atonement for his sin that he hath committed, and it shall
be forgiven him.

The Sin of Concealing Knowledge of Guilt or of Unintended Transgression

5 And if a soul sin, and hear the voice of swearing, and *is* a witness, whether
he hath seen or known *of it*; if he do not utter *it*, then he shall bear his
iniquity.
2 Or if a soul touch any unclean thing, whether *it be* a carcase of an unclean
beast, or a carcase of unclean cattle, or the carcase of unclean creeping things,
and *if* it be hidden from him; he also shall be unclean, and guilty.
3 Or if he touch the uncleanness of man, whatsoever uncleanness *it be* that
a man shall be defiled withal, and it be hid from him; when he knoweth *of it*,
then he shall be guilty.
4 Or if a soul swear, pronouncing with *his* lips to do evil, or to do good,
whatsoever *it be* that a man shall pronounce with an oath, and it be hid from
him; when he knoweth *of it*, then he shall be guilty in one of these.
5 And it shall be, when he shall be guilty in one of these *things*, that he shall
confess that he hath sinned in that *thing*:
6 And he shall bring his trespass offering unto the LORD for his sin which he
hath sinned, a female from the flock, a lamb or a kid of the goats, for a sin
offering; and the priest shall make an atonement for him concerning his sin.

The Sin Offering of Fowls

7 And if he be not able to bring a lamb, then he shall bring for his trespass,
which he hath committed, two turtledoves, or two young pigeons, unto the
LORD; one for a sin offering, and the other for a burnt offering.
8 And he shall bring them unto the priest, who shall offer *that* which *is* for
the sin offering first, and wring off his head from his neck, but shall not divide
it asunder:
9 And he shall sprinkle of the blood of the sin offering upon the side of the
altar; and the rest of the blood shall be wrung out at the bottom of the altar:
it *is* a sin offering.
10 And he shall offer the second *for* a burnt offering, according to the man-
ner: and the priest shall make an atonement for him for his sin which he hath
sinned, and it shall be forgiven him.
11 But if he be not able to bring two turtledoves, or two young pigeons, then
he that sinned shall bring for his offering the tenth part of an ephah of fine

flour for a sin offering; he shall put no oil upon it, neither shall he put *any*
frankincense thereon: for it *is* a sin offering.
12 Then shall he bring it to the priest, and the priest shall take his handful
of it, *even* a memorial thereof, and burn *it* on the altar, according to the offer-
ings made by fire unto the LORD: it *is* a sin offering.
13 And the priest shall make an atonement for him as touching his sin that
he hath sinned in one of these, and it shall be forgiven him: and *the remnant*
shall be the priest's, as a meat offering.

The Trespass Offering

14 And the LORD spake unto Moses, saying,
15 If a soul commit a trespass, and sin through ignorance, in the holy things
of the LORD; then he shall bring for his trespass unto the LORD a ram without
blemish out of the flocks, with thy estimation by shekels of silver, after the
shekel of the sanctuary, for a trespass offering:
16 And he shall make amends for the harm that he hath done in the holy
thing, and shall add the fifth part thereto, and give it unto the priest: and the
priest shall make an atonement for him with the ram of the trespass offering,
and it shall be forgiven him.
17 And if a soul sin, and commit any of these things which are forbidden to
be done by the commandments of the LORD; though he wist *it* not, yet is he
guilty, and shall bear his iniquity.
18 And he shall bring a ram without blemish out of the flock, with thy esti-
mation, for a trespass offering, unto the priest: and the priest shall make an
atonement for him concerning his ignorance wherein he erred and wist *it*
not, and it shall be forgiven him.
19 It *is* a trespass offering: he hath certainly trespassed against the LORD.

The Trespass Offering for Sins Done Knowingly

6 And the LORD spake unto Moses, saying,
2 If a soul sin, and commit a trespass against the LORD, and lie unto his
neighbour in that which was delivered him to keep, or in fellowship, or in a
thing taken away by violence, or hath deceived his neighbour;
3 Or have found that which was lost, and lieth concerning it, and sweareth
falsely; in any of all these that a man doeth, sinning therein:
4 Then it shall be, because he hath sinned, and is guilty, that he shall restore
that which he took violently away, or the thing which he hath deceitfully got-
ten, or that which was delivered him to keep, or the lost thing which he found,
5 Or all that about which he hath sworn falsely; he shall even restore it in the
principal, and shall add the fifth part more thereto, *and* give it unto him to
whom it appertaineth, in the day of his trespass offering.
6 And he shall bring his trespass offering unto the LORD, a ram without blem-
ish out of the flock, with thy estimation, for a trespass offering, unto the priest:
7 And the priest shall make an atonement for him before the LORD: and it
shall be forgiven him for any thing of all that he hath done in trespassing
therein.

The Law of the Burnt Offering

8 And the LORD spake unto Moses, saying,
9 Command Aaron and his sons, saying, This *is* the law of the burnt offering:
It *is* the burnt offering, because of the burning upon the altar all night unto
the morning, and the fire of the altar shall be burning in it.
10 And the priest shall put on his linen garment, and his linen breeches shall
he put upon his flesh, and take up the ashes which the fire hath consumed
with the burnt offering on the altar, and he shall put them beside the altar.
11 And he shall put off his garments, and put on other garments, and carry
forth the ashes without the camp unto a clean place.

12 And the fire upon the altar shall be burning in it; it shall not be put out: and the priest shall burn wood on it every morning, and lay the burnt offering in order upon it; and he shall burn thereon the fat of the peace offerings.

13 The fire shall ever be burning upon the altar; it shall never go out.

The Law of the Meat (Meal) Offering

14 And this *is* the law of the meat offering: the sons of Aaron shall offer it before the LORD, before the altar.

15 And he shall take of it his handful, of the flour of the meat offering, and of the oil thereof, and all the frankincense which *is* upon the meat offering, and shall burn *it* upon the altar *for* a sweet savour, *even* the memorial of it, unto the LORD.

16 And the remainder thereof shall Aaron and his sons eat: with unleavened bread shall it be eaten in the holy place; in the court of the tabernacle of the congregation they shall eat it.

17 It shall not be baken with leaven. I have given it *unto them for* their portion of my offerings made by fire; it *is* most holy, as *is* the sin offering, and as the trespass offering.

18 All the males among the children of Aaron shall eat of it. *It shall be* a statute for ever in your generations concerning the offerings of the LORD made by fire: every one that toucheth them shall be holy.

19 And the LORD spake unto Moses, saying,

20 This *is* the offering of Aaron and of his sons, which they shall offer unto the LORD in the day when he is anointed; the tenth part of an ephah of fine flour for a meat offering perpetual, half of it in the morning, and half thereof at night.

21 In a pan it shall be made with oil; *and when it is* baken, thou shalt bring it in: *and* the baken pieces of the meat offering shalt thou offer *for* a sweet savour unto the LORD.

22 And the priest of his sons that is anointed in his stead shall offer it: *it is* a statute for ever unto the LORD; it shall be wholly burnt.

23 For every meat offering for the priest shall be wholly burnt: it shall not be eaten.

The Law of the Sin Offering

24 And the LORD spake unto Moses, saying,

25 Speak unto Aaron and to his sons, saying, This *is* the law of the sin offering: In the place where the burnt offering is killed shall the sin offering be killed before the LORD: it *is* most holy.

26 The priest that offereth it for sin shall eat it: in the holy place shall it be eaten, in the court of the tabernacle of the congregation.

27 Whatsoever shall touch the flesh thereof shall be holy: and when there is sprinkled of the blood thereof upon any garment, thou shalt wash that whereon it was sprinkled in the holy place.

28 But the earthen vessel wherein it is sodden shall be broken: and if it be sodden in a brasen pot, it shall be both scoured, and rinsed in water.

29 All the males among the priests shall eat thereof: it *is* most holy.

30 And no sin offering, whereof *any* of the blood is brought into the tabernacle of the congregation to reconcile *withal* in the holy *place*, shall be eaten: it shall be burnt in the fire.

The Laws of the Trespass Offering and of the Peace Offering

7 Likewise this *is* the law of the trespass offering: it *is* most holy.

2 In the place where they kill the burnt offering shall they kill the trespass offering: and the blood thereof shall he sprinkle round about upon the altar.

3 And he shall offer of it all the fat thereof; the rump, and the fat that covereth the inwards,

4 And the two kidneys, and the fat that *is* on them, which *is* by the flanks,
and the caul *that is* above the liver, with the kidneys, it shall he take away:
5 And the priest shall burn them upon the altar *for* an offering made by fire
unto the LORD: it *is* a trespass offering.
6 Every male among the priests shall eat thereof: it shall be eaten in the holy
place: it *is* most holy.
7 As the sin offering *is*, so *is* the trespass offering: *there is* one law for them:
the priest that maketh atonement therewith shall have *it*.
8 And the priest that offereth any man's burnt offering, *even* the priest shall
have to himself the skin of the burnt offering which he hath offered.
9 And all the meat offering that is baken in the oven, and all that is dressed
in the fryingpan, and in the pan, shall be the priest's that offereth it.
10 And every meat offering, mingled with oil, and dry, shall all the sons of
Aaron have, one *as much* as another.
11 And this *is* the law of the sacrifice of peace offerings, which he shall offer
unto the LORD.
12 If he offer it for a thanksgiving, then he shall offer with the sacrifice of
thanksgiving unleavened cakes mingled with oil, and unleavened wafers
anointed with oil, and cakes mingled with oil, of fine flour, fried.
13 Besides the cakes, he shall offer *for* his offering leavened bread with the
sacrifice of thanksgiving of his peace offerings.
14 And of it he shall offer one out of the whole oblation *for* an heave offering
unto the LORD, *and* it shall be the priest's that sprinkleth the blood of the peace
offerings.
15 And the flesh of the sacrifice of his peace offerings for thanksgiving shall
be eaten the same day that it is offered; he shall not leave any of it until the
morning.
16 But if the sacrifice of his offering *be* a vow, or a voluntary offering, it shall
be eaten the same day that he offereth his sacrifice: and on the morrow also
the remainder of it shall be eaten:
17 But the remainder of the flesh of the sacrifice on the third day shall be
burnt with fire.
18 And if *any* of the flesh of the sacrifice of his peace offerings be eaten at all
on the third day, it shall not be accepted, neither shall it be imputed unto him
that offereth it: it shall be an abomination, and the soul that eateth of it shall
bear his iniquity.
19 And the flesh that toucheth any unclean *thing* shall not be eaten; it shall
be burnt with fire: and as for the flesh, all that be clean shall eat thereof.
20 But the soul that eateth *of* the flesh of the sacrifice of peace offerings, that
pertain unto the LORD, having his uncleanness upon him, even that soul shall
be cut off from his people.
21 Moreover the soul that shall touch any unclean *thing, as* the uncleanness
of man, or *any* unclean beast, or any abominable unclean *thing*, and eat of
the flesh of the sacrifice of peace offerings, which *pertain* unto the LORD, even
that soul shall be cut off from his people.
22 And the LORD spake unto Moses, saying,
23 Speak unto the children of Israel, saying, Ye shall eat no manner of fat, of
ox, or of sheep, or of goat.
24 And the fat of the beast that dieth of itself, and the fat of that which is torn
with beasts, may be used in any other use: but ye shall in no wise eat of it.
25 For whosoever eateth the fat of the beast, of which men offer an offering
made by fire unto the LORD, even the soul that eateth *it* shall be cut off from
his people.
26 Moreover ye shall eat no manner of blood, *whether it be* of fowl or of beast,
in any of your dwellings.

27 Whatsoever soul *it be* that eateth any manner of blood, even that soul shall be cut off from his people.

28 And the LORD spake unto Moses, saying,

29 Speak unto the children of Israel, saying, He that offereth the sacrifice of his peace offerings unto the LORD shall bring his oblation unto the LORD of the sacrifice of his peace offerings.

30 His own hands shall bring the offerings of the LORD made by fire, the fat with the breast, it shall he bring, that the breast may be waved *for* a wave offering before the LORD.

31 And the priest shall burn the fat upon the altar: but the breast shall be Aaron's and his sons'.

32 And the right shoulder shall ye give unto the priest *for* an heave offering of the sacrifices of your peace offerings.

33 He among the sons of Aaron, that offereth the blood of the peace offerings, and the fat, shall have the right shoulder for *his* part.

34 For the wave breast and the heave shoulder have I taken of the children of Israel from off the sacrifices of their peace offerings, and have given them unto Aaron the priest and unto his sons by a statute for ever from among the children of Israel.

35 This *is the portion* of the anointing of Aaron, and of the anointing of his sons, out of the offerings of the LORD made by fire, in the day *when* he presented them to minister unto the LORD in the priest's office;

36 Which the LORD commanded to be given them of the children of Israel, in the day that he anointed them, *by* a statute for ever throughout their generations.

37 This *is* the law of the burnt offering, of the meat offering, and of the sin offering, and of the trespass offering, and of the consecrations, and of the sacrifice of the peace offerings;

38 Which the LORD commanded Moses in mount Sinai, in the day that he commanded the children of Israel to offer their oblations unto the LORD, in the wilderness of Sinai.

Moses Consecrates Aaron and His Sons

8 And the LORD spake unto Moses, saying,

2 Take Aaron and his sons with him, and the garments, and the anointing oil, and a bullock for the sin offering, and two rams, and a basket of unleavened bread;

3 And gather thou all the congregation together unto the door of the tabernacle of the congregation.

4 And Moses did as the LORD commanded him; and the assembly was gathered together unto the door of the tabernacle of the congregation.

5 And Moses said unto the congregation, This *is* the thing which the LORD commanded to be done.

6 And Moses brought Aaron and his sons, and washed them with water.

7 And he put upon him the coat, and girded him with the girdle, and clothed him with the robe, and put the ephod upon him, and he girded him with the curious girdle of the ephod, and bound *it* unto him therewith.

8 And he put the breastplate upon him: also he put in the breastplate the Urim and the Thummim.

9 And he put the mitre upon his head; also upon the mitre, *even* upon his forefront, did he put the golden plate, the holy crown; as the LORD commanded Moses.

10 And Moses took the anointing oil, and anointed the tabernacle and all that *was* therein, and sanctified them.

11 And he sprinkled thereof upon the altar seven times, and anointed the altar and all his vessels, both the laver and his foot, to sanctify them.

12 And he poured of the anointing oil upon Aaron's head, and anointed him, to sanctify him.

13 And Moses brought Aaron's sons, and put coats upon them, and girded them with girdles, and put bonnets upon them; as the LORD commanded Moses.

A Sin Offering for Aaron and His Sons

14 And he brought the bullock for the sin offering: and Aaron and his sons laid their hands upon the head of the bullock for the sin offering.

15 And he slew *it*; and Moses took the blood, and put *it* upon the horns of the altar round about with his finger, and purified the altar, and poured the blood at the bottom of the altar, and sanctified it, to make reconciliation upon it.

16 And he took all the fat that *was* upon the inwards, and the caul *above* the liver, and the two kidneys, and their fat, and Moses burned *it* upon the altar.

17 But the bullock, and his hide, his flesh, and his dung, he burnt with fire without the camp; as the LORD commanded Moses.

18 And he brought the ram for the burnt offering: and Aaron and his sons laid their hands upon the head of the ram.

19 And he killed *it*; and Moses sprinkled the blood upon the altar round about.

20 And he cut the ram into pieces; and Moses burnt the head, and the pieces, and the fat.

21 And he washed the inwards and the legs in water; and Moses burnt the whole ram upon the altar: it *was* a burnt sacrifice for a sweet savour, *and* an offering made by fire unto the LORD; as the LORD commanded Moses.

22 And he brought the other ram, the ram of consecration: and Aaron and his sons laid their hands upon the head of the ram.

23 And he slew *it*; and Moses took of the blood of it, and put *it* upon the tip of Aaron's right ear, and upon the thumb of his right hand, and upon the great toe of his right foot.

24 And he brought Aaron's sons, and Moses put of the blood upon the tip of their right ear, and upon the thumbs of their right hands, and upon the great toes of their right feet: and Moses sprinkled the blood upon the altar round about.

25 And he took the fat, and the rump, and all the fat that *was* upon the inwards, and the caul *above* the liver, and the two kidneys, and their fat, and the right shoulder:

26 And out of the basket of unleavened bread, that *was* before the LORD, he took one unleavened cake, and a cake of oiled bread, and one wafer, and put *them* on the fat, and upon the right shoulder:

27 And he put all upon Aaron's hands, and upon his sons' hands, and waved them *for* a wave offering before the LORD.

28 And Moses took them from off their hands, and burnt *them* on the altar upon the burnt offering: they *were* consecrations for a sweet savour: it *is* an offering made by fire unto the LORD.

29 And Moses took the breast, and waved it *for* a wave offering before the LORD: *for* of the ram of consecration it was Moses' part; as the LORD commanded Moses.

30 And Moses took of the anointing oil, and of the blood which *was* upon the altar, and sprinkled *it* upon Aaron, *and* upon his garments, and upon his sons, and upon his sons' garments with him; and sanctified Aaron, *and* his garments, and his sons, and his sons' garments with him.

The Place and Time of the Priests' Consecration

31 And Moses said unto Aaron and to his sons, Boil the flesh *at* the door of the tabernacle of the congregation: and there eat it with the bread that *is* in

the basket of consecrations, as I commanded, saying, Aaron and his sons shall
eat it.
32 And that which remaineth of the flesh and of the bread shall ye burn with
fire.
33 And ye shall not go out of the door of the tabernacle of the congregation
in seven days, until the days of your consecration be at an end: for seven days
shall he consecrate you.
34 As he hath done this day, *so* the LORD hath commanded to do, to make an
atonement for you.
35 Therefore shall ye abide *at* the door of the tabernacle of the congregation
day and night seven days, and keep the charge of the LORD, that ye die not: for
so I am commanded.
36 So Aaron and his sons did all things which the LORD commanded by the
hand of Moses.

Aaron's First Offerings

9 And it came to pass on the eighth day, *that* Moses called Aaron and his sons,
and the elders of Israel;
2 And he said unto Aaron, Take thee a young calf for a sin offering, and a ram
for a burnt offering, without blemish, and offer *them* before the LORD.
3 And unto the children of Israel thou shalt speak, saying, Take ye a kid of
the goats for a sin offering; and a calf and a lamb, *both* of the first year, without
blemish, for a burnt offering;
4 Also a bullock and a ram for peace offerings, to sacrifice before the LORD;
and a meat offering mingled with oil: for to day the LORD will appear unto you.
5 And they brought *that* which Moses commanded before the tabernacle of
the congregation: and all the congregation drew near and stood before the
LORD.
6 And Moses said, This *is* the thing which the LORD commanded that ye
should do: and the glory of the LORD shall appear unto you.
7 And Moses said unto Aaron, Go unto the altar, and offer thy sin offering,
and thy burnt offering, and make an atonement for thyself, and for the people:
and offer the offering of the people, and make an atonement for them; as the
LORD commanded.

Aaron's Sin Offering and Burnt Offering for Himself

8 Aaron therefore went unto the altar, and slew the calf of the sin offering,
which *was* for himself.
9 And the sons of Aaron brought the blood unto him: and he dipped his
finger in the blood, and put *it* upon the horns of the altar, and poured out the
blood at the bottom of the altar:
10 But the fat, and the kidneys, and the caul above the liver of the sin offering,
he burnt upon the altar; as the LORD commanded Moses.
11 And the flesh and the hide he burnt with fire without the camp.
12 And he slew the burnt offering; and Aaron's sons presented unto him the
blood, which he sprinkled round about upon the altar.
13 And they presented the burnt offering unto him, with the pieces thereof,
and the head: and he burnt *them* upon the altar.
14 And he did wash the inwards and the legs, and burnt *them* upon the burnt
offering on the altar.
15 And he brought the people's offering, and took the goat, which *was* the
sin offering for the people, and slew it, and offered it for sin, as the first.
16 And he brought the burnt offering, and offered it according to the manner.
17 And he brought the meat offering, and took an handful thereof, and burnt
it upon the altar, beside the burnt sacrifice of the morning.

18 He slew also the bullock and the ram *for* a sacrifice of peace offerings, which *was* for the people: and Aaron's sons presented unto him the blood, which he sprinkled upon the altar round about,

19 And the fat of the bullock and of the ram, the rump, and that which covereth *the inwards*, and the kidneys, and the caul *above* the liver:

20 And they put the fat upon the breasts, and he burnt the fat upon the altar:

21 And the breasts and the right shoulder Aaron waved *for* a wave offering before the LORD; as Moses commanded.

22 And Aaron lifted up his hand toward the people, and blessed them, and came down from offering of the sin offering, and the burnt offering, and peace offerings.

23 And Moses and Aaron went into the tabernacle of the congregation, and came out, and blessed the people: and the glory of the LORD appeared unto all the people.

24 And there came a fire out from before the LORD, and consumed upon the altar the burnt offering and the fat: *which* when all the people saw, they shouted, and fell on their faces.

Nadab and Abihu Are Killed

10 And Nadab and Abihu, the sons of Aaron, took either of them his censer, and put fire therein, and put incense thereon, and offered strange fire before the LORD, which he commanded them not.

2 And there went out fire from the LORD, and devoured them, and they died before the LORD.

3 Then Moses said unto Aaron, This *is it* that the LORD spake, saying, I will be sanctified in them that come nigh me, and before all the people I will be glorified. And Aaron held his peace.

4 And Moses called Mishael and Elzaphan, the sons of Uzziel the uncle of Aaron, and said unto them, Come near, carry your brethren from before the sanctuary out of the camp.

5 So they went near, and carried them in their coats out of the camp; as Moses had said.

6 And Moses said unto Aaron, and unto Eleazar and unto Ithamar, his sons, Uncover not your heads, neither rend your clothes; lest ye die, and lest wrath come upon all the people: but let your brethren, the whole house of Israel, bewail the burning which the LORD hath kindled.

7 And ye shall not go out from the door of the tabernacle of the congregation, lest ye die: for the anointing oil of the LORD *is* upon you. And they did according to the word of Moses.

The Priests Are Forbidden to Drink Wine before Serving in the Tabernacle

8 And the LORD spake unto Aaron, saying,

9 Do not drink wine nor strong drink, thou, nor thy sons with thee, when ye go into the tabernacle of the congregation, lest ye die: *it shall be* a statute for ever throughout your generations:

10 And that ye may put difference between holy and unholy, and between unclean and clean;

11 And that ye may teach the children of Israel all the statutes which the LORD hath spoken unto them by the hand of Moses.

The Law of Eating the Holy Things

12 And Moses spake unto Aaron, and unto Eleazar and unto Ithamar, his sons that were left, Take the meat offering that remaineth of the offerings of the LORD made by fire, and eat it without leaven beside the altar: for it *is* most holy:

13 And ye shall eat it in the holy place, because it *is* thy due, and thy sons' due,
of the sacrifices of the LORD made by fire: for so I am commanded.
14 And the wave breast and heave shoulder shall ye eat in a clean place; thou,
and thy sons, and thy daughters with thee: for *they be* thy due, and thy sons'
due, *which* are given out of the sacrifices of peace offerings of the children of
Israel.
15 The heave shoulder and the wave breast shall they bring with the offerings
made by fire of the fat, to wave *it for* a wave offering before the LORD; and it
shall be thine, and thy sons' with thee, by a statute for ever; as the LORD hath
commanded.
16 And Moses diligently sought the goat of the sin offering, and, behold, it
was burnt: and he was angry with Eleazar and Ithamar, the sons of Aaron
which were left *alive*, saying,
17 Wherefore have ye not eaten the sin offering in the holy place, seeing it *is*
most holy, and *God* hath given it you to bear the iniquity of the congregation,
to make atonement for them before the LORD?
18 Behold, the blood of it was not brought in within the holy *place*: ye should
indeed have eaten it in the holy *place*, as I commanded.
19 And Aaron said unto Moses, Behold, this day have they offered their sin
offering and their burnt offering before the LORD; and such things have befall-
en me: and *if* I had eaten the sin offering to day, should it have been accepted
in the sight of the LORD?
20 And when Moses heard *that*, he was content.

What Beasts May Be Eaten

11 And the LORD spake unto Moses and to Aaron, saying unto them,
2 Speak unto the children of Israel, saying, These *are* the beasts which
ye shall eat among all the beasts that *are* on the earth.
3 Whatsoever parteth the hoof, and is clovenfooted, *and* cheweth the cud,
among the beasts, that shall ye eat.
4 Nevertheless these shall ye not eat of them that chew the cud, or of them
that divide the hoof: *as* the camel, because he cheweth the cud, but divideth
not the hoof; he *is* unclean unto you.
5 And the coney, because he cheweth the cud, but divideth not the hoof; he
is unclean unto you.
6 And the hare, because he cheweth the cud, but divideth not the hoof; he *is*
unclean unto you.
7 And the swine, though he divide the hoof, and be clovenfooted, yet he
cheweth not the cud; he *is* unclean to you.
8 Of their flesh shall ye not eat, and their carcase shall ye not touch; they *are*
unclean to you.

What Fishes May Be Eaten

9 These shall ye eat of all that *are* in the waters: whatsoever hath fins and
scales in the waters, in the seas, and in the rivers, them shall ye eat.
10 And all that have not fins and scales in the seas, and in the rivers, of all
that move in the waters, and of any living thing which *is* in the waters, they
shall be an abomination unto you:
11 They shall be even an abomination unto you; ye shall not eat of their flesh,
but ye shall have their carcases in abomination.
12 Whatsoever hath no fins nor scales in the waters, that *shall be* an abom-
ination unto you.
13 And these *are they which* ye shall have in abomination among the fowls;
they shall not be eaten, they *are* an abomination: the eagle, and the ossifrage,
and the ospray,
14 And the vulture, and the kite after his kind;

15 Every raven after his kind;
16 And the owl, and the night hawk, and the cuckow, and the hawk after his
kind,
17 And the little owl, and the cormorant, and the great owl,
18 And the swan, and the pelican, and the gier eagle,
19 And the stork, the heron after her kind, and the lapwing, and the bat.
20 All fowls that creep, going upon *all* four, *shall be* an abomination unto
you.
21 Yet these may ye eat of every flying creeping thing that goeth upon *all*
four, which have legs above their feet, to leap withal upon the earth;
22 *Even* these of them ye may eat; the locust after his kind, and the bald locust
after his kind, and the beetle after his kind, and the grasshopper after his kind.
23 But all *other* flying creeping things, which have four feet, *shall be* an abom-
ination unto you.
24 And for these ye shall be unclean: whosoever toucheth the carcase of them
shall be unclean until the even.
25 And whosoever beareth *ought* of the carcase of them shall wash his
clothes, and be unclean until the even.
26 *The carcases* of every beast which divideth the hoof, and *is* not cloven-
footed, nor cheweth the cud, *are* unclean unto you: every one that toucheth
them shall be unclean.
27 And whatsoever goeth upon his paws, among all manner of beasts that
go on *all* four, those *are* unclean unto you: whoso toucheth their carcase shall
be unclean until the even.
28 And he that beareth the carcase of them shall wash his clothes, and be
unclean until the even: they *are* unclean unto you.
29 These also *shall be* unclean unto you among the creeping things that creep
upon the earth; the weasel, and the mouse, and the tortoise after his kind,
30 And the ferret, and the chameleon, and the lizard, and the snail, and the
mole.
31 These *are* unclean to you among all that creep: whosoever doth touch
them, when they be dead, shall be unclean until the even.
32 And upon whatsoever *any* of them, when they are dead, doth fall, it shall
be unclean; whether *it be* any vessel of wood, or raiment, or skin, or sack,
whatsoever vessel *it be*, wherein *any* work is done, it must be put into water,
and it shall be unclean until the even; so it shall be cleansed.
33 And every earthen vessel, whereinto *any* of them falleth, whatsoever *is* in
it shall be unclean; and ye shall break it.
34 Of all meat which may be eaten, *that* on which *such* water cometh shall
be unclean: and all drink that may be drunk in every *such* vessel shall be
unclean.
35 And every *thing* whereupon *any part* of their carcase falleth shall be
unclean; *whether it be* oven, or ranges for pots, they shall be broken down: *for*
they *are* unclean, and shall be unclean unto you.
36 Nevertheless a fountain or pit, *wherein there is* plenty of water, shall be
clean: but that which toucheth their carcase shall be unclean.
37 And if *any part* of their carcase fall upon any sowing seed which is to be
sown, it *shall be* clean.
38 But if *any* water be put upon the seed, and *any part* of their carcase fall
thereon, it *shall be* unclean unto you.
39 And if any beast, of which ye may eat, die; he that toucheth the carcase
thereof shall be unclean until the even.
40 And he that eateth of the carcase of it shall wash his clothes, and be
unclean until the even: he also that beareth the carcase of it shall wash his
clothes, and be unclean until the even.

41 And every creeping thing that creepeth upon the earth *shall be* an abomination; it shall not be eaten.

42 Whatsoever goeth upon the belly, and whatsoever goeth upon *all* four, or whatsoever hath more feet among all creeping things that creep upon the earth, them ye shall not eat; for they *are* an abomination.

43 Ye shall not make yourselves abominable with any creeping thing that creepeth, neither shall ye make yourselves unclean with them, that ye should be defiled thereby.

44 For I *am* the LORD your God: ye shall therefore sanctify yourselves, and ye shall be holy; for I *am* holy: neither shall ye defile yourselves with any manner of creeping thing that creepeth upon the earth.

45 For I *am* the LORD that bringeth you up out of the land of Egypt, to be your God: ye shall therefore be holy, for I *am* holy.

46 This *is* the law of the beasts, and of the fowl, and of every living creature that moveth in the waters, and of every creature that creepeth upon the earth:

47 To make a difference between the unclean and the clean, and between the beast that may be eaten and the beast that may not be eaten.

The Purification of Women after Childbirth

12 And the LORD spake unto Moses, saying,

2 Speak unto the children of Israel, saying, If a woman have conceived seed, and born a man child: then she shall be unclean seven days; according to the days of the separation for her infirmity shall she be unclean.

3 And in the eighth day the flesh of his foreskin shall be circumcised.

4 And she shall then continue in the blood of her purifying three and thirty days; she shall touch no hallowed thing, nor come into the sanctuary, until the days of her purifying be fulfilled.

5 But if she bear a maid child, then she shall be unclean two weeks, as in her separation: and she shall continue in the blood of her purifying threescore and six days.

A Woman's Purification Offerings

6 And when the days of her purifying are fulfilled, for a son, or for a daughter, she shall bring a lamb of the first year for a burnt offering, and a young pigeon, or a turtledove, for a sin offering, unto the door of the tabernacle of the congregation, unto the priest:

7 Who shall offer it before the LORD, and make an atonement for her; and she shall be cleansed from the issue of her blood. This *is* the law for her that hath born a male or a female.

8 And if she be not able to bring a lamb, then she shall bring two turtles, or two young pigeons; the one for the burnt offering, and the other for a sin offering: and the priest shall make an atonement for her, and she shall be clean.

Guidance for the Priests in Discerning Leprosy

13 And the LORD spake unto Moses and Aaron, saying,

2 When a man shall have in the skin of his flesh a rising, a scab, or bright spot, and it be in the skin of his flesh *like* the plague of leprosy; then he shall be brought unto Aaron the priest, or unto one of his sons the priests:

3 And the priest shall look on the plague in the skin of the flesh: and *when* the hair in the plague is turned white, and the plague in sight *be* deeper than the skin of his flesh, it *is* a plague of leprosy: and the priest shall look on him, and pronounce him unclean.

4 If the bright spot *be* white in the skin of his flesh, and in sight *be* not deeper than the skin, and the hair thereof be not turned white; then the priest shall shut up *him that hath* the plague seven days:

5 And the priest shall look on him the seventh day: and, behold, *if* the plague
in his sight be at a stay, *and* the plague spread not in the skin; then the priest
shall shut him up seven days more:
6 And the priest shall look on him again the seventh day: and, behold, *if* the
plague *be* somewhat dark, *and* the plague spread not in the skin, the priest
shall pronounce him clean: it *is but* a scab: and he shall wash his clothes, and
be clean.
7 But if the scab spread much abroad in the skin, after that he hath been seen
of the priest for his cleansing, he shall be seen of the priest again:
8 And *if* the priest see that, behold, the scab spreadeth in the skin, then the
priest shall pronounce him unclean: it *is* a leprosy.
9 When the plague of leprosy is in a man, then he shall be brought unto the
priest;
10 And the priest shall see *him*: and, behold, *if* the rising *be* white in the skin,
and it have turned the hair white, and *there be* quick raw flesh in the rising;
11 It *is* an old leprosy in the skin of his flesh, and the priest shall pronounce
him unclean, and shall not shut him up: for he *is* unclean.
12 And if a leprosy break out abroad in the skin, and the leprosy cover all the
skin of *him that hath* the plague from his head even to his foot, wheresoever
the priest looketh;
13 Then the priest shall consider: and, behold, *if* the leprosy have covered all
his flesh, he shall pronounce *him* clean *that hath* the plague: it is all turned
white: he *is* clean.
14 But when raw flesh appeareth in him, he shall be unclean.
15 And the priest shall see the raw flesh, and pronounce him to be unclean:
for the raw flesh *is* unclean: it *is* a leprosy.
16 Or if the raw flesh turn again, and be changed unto white, he shall come
unto the priest;
17 And the priest shall see him: and, behold, *if* the plague be turned into
white; then the priest shall pronounce *him* clean *that hath* the plague: he *is*
clean.
18 The flesh also, in which, *even* in the skin thereof, was a boil, and is healed,
19 And in the place of the boil there be a white rising, or a bright spot, white,
and somewhat reddish, and it be shewed to the priest;
20 And if, when the priest seeth it, behold, it *be* in sight lower than the skin,
and the hair thereof be turned white; the priest shall pronounce him unclean:
it *is* a plague of leprosy broken out of the boil.
21 But if the priest look on it, and, behold, *there be* no white hairs therein,
and *if* it *be* not lower than the skin, but *be* somewhat dark; then the priest shall
shut him up seven days:
22 And if it spread much abroad in the skin, then the priest shall pronounce
him unclean: it *is* a plague.
23 But if the bright spot stay in his place, *and* spread not, it *is* a burning boil;
and the priest shall pronounce him clean.
24 Or if there be *any* flesh, in the skin whereof *there is* a hot burning, and
the quick *flesh* that burneth have a white bright spot, somewhat reddish, or
white;
25 Then the priest shall look upon it: and, behold, *if* the hair in the bright
spot be turned white, and it *be in* sight deeper than the skin; it *is* a leprosy
broken out of the burning: wherefore the priest shall pronounce him unclean:
it *is* the plague of leprosy.
26 But if the priest look on it, and, behold, *there be* no white hair in the bright
spot, and it *be* no lower than the *other* skin, but *be* somewhat dark; then the
priest shall shut him up seven days:

27 And the priest shall look upon him the seventh day: *and* if it be spread much abroad in the skin, then the priest shall pronounce him unclean: it *is* the plague of leprosy.

28 And if the bright spot stay in his place, *and* spread not in the skin, but it *be* somewhat dark; it *is* a rising of the burning, and the priest shall pronounce him clean: for it *is* an inflammation of the burning.

29 If a man or woman have a plague upon the head or the beard;

30 Then the priest shall see the plague: and, behold, if it *be* in sight deeper than the skin; *and there be* in it a yellow thin hair; then the priest shall pronounce him unclean: it *is* a dry scall, *even* a leprosy upon the head or beard.

31 And if the priest look on the plague of the scall, and, behold, it *be* not in sight deeper than the skin, and *that there is* no black hair in it; then the priest shall shut up *him that hath* the plague of the scall seven days:

32 And in the seventh day the priest shall look on the plague: and, behold, *if* the scall spread not, and there be in it no yellow hair, and the scall *be* not in sight deeper than the skin;

33 He shall be shaven, but the scall shall he not shave; and the priest shall shut up *him that hath* the scall seven days more:

34 And in the seventh day the priest shall look on the scall: and, behold, *if* the scall be not spread in the skin, nor *be* in sight deeper than the skin; then the priest shall pronounce him clean: and he shall wash his clothes, and be clean.

35 But if the scall spread much in the skin after his cleansing;

36 Then the priest shall look on him: and, behold, if the scall be spread in the skin, the priest shall not seek for yellow hair; he *is* unclean.

37 But if the scall be in his sight at a stay, and *that* there is black hair grown up therein; the scall is healed, he *is* clean: and the priest shall pronounce him clean.

38 If a man also or a woman have in the skin of their flesh bright spots, *even* white bright spots;

39 Then the priest shall look: and, behold, *if* the bright spots in the skin of their flesh *be* darkish white; it *is* a freckled spot *that* groweth in the skin; he *is* clean.

40 And the man whose hair is fallen off his head, he *is* bald; *yet is* he clean.

41 And he that hath his hair fallen off from the part of his head toward his face, he *is* forehead bald: *yet is* he clean.

42 And if there be in the bald head, or bald forehead, a white reddish sore; it *is* a leprosy sprung up in his bald head, or his bald forehead.

43 Then the priest shall look upon it: and, behold, *if* the rising of the sore *be* white reddish in his bald head, or in his bald forehead, as the leprosy appeareth in the skin of the flesh;

44 He is a leprous man, he *is* unclean: the priest shall pronounce him utterly unclean; his plague *is* in his head.

45 And the leper in whom the plague *is*, his clothes shall be rent, and his head bare, and he shall put a covering upon his upper lip, and shall cry, Unclean, unclean.

46 All the days wherein the plague *shall be* in him he shall be defiled; he *is* unclean: he shall dwell alone; without the camp *shall* his habitation *be*.

47 The garment also that the plague of leprosy is in, *whether it be* a woollen garment, or a linen garment;

48 Whether *it be* in the warp, or woof; of linen, or of woollen; whether in a skin, or in any thing made of skin;

49 And if the plague be greenish or reddish in the garment, or in the skin, either in the warp, or in the woof, or in any thing of skin; it *is* a plague of leprosy, and shall be shewed unto the priest:

50 And the priest shall look upon the plague, and shut up *it that hath* the
plague seven days:
51 And he shall look on the plague on the seventh day: if the plague be spread
in the garment, either in the warp, or in the woof, or in a skin, *or* in any work
that is made of skin; the plague *is* a fretting leprosy; it *is* unclean.
52 He shall therefore burn that garment, whether warp or woof, in woollen
or in linen, or any thing of skin, wherein the plague is: for it *is* a fretting lep-
rosy; it shall be burnt in the fire.
53 And if the priest shall look, and, behold, the plague be not spread in the
garment, either in the warp, or in the woof, or in any thing of skin;
54 Then the priest shall command that they wash *the thing* wherein the
plague *is*, and he shall shut it up seven days more:
55 And the priest shall look on the plague, after that it is washed: and, behold,
if the plague have not changed his colour, and the plague be not spread; it *is*
unclean; thou shalt burn it in the fire; it *is* fret inward, *whether* it *be* bare
within or without.
56 And if the priest look, and, behold, the plague *be* somewhat dark after the
washing of it; then he shall rend it out of the garment, or out of the skin, or
out of the warp, or out of the woof:
57 And if it appear still in the garment, either in the warp, or in the woof, or
in any thing of skin; it *is* a spreading *plague*: thou shalt burn that wherein the
plague *is* with fire.
58 And the garment, either warp, or woof, or whatsoever thing of skin *it be*,
which thou shalt wash, if the plague be departed from them, then it shall be
washed the second time, and shall be clean.
59 This *is* the law of the plague of leprosy in a garment of woollen or linen,
either in the warp, or woof, or any thing of skins, to pronounce it clean, or to
pronounce it unclean.

The Rites and Sacrifices in Cleansing of a Leper

14 And the LORD spake unto Moses, saying,
2 This shall be the law of the leper in the day of his cleansing: He shall
be brought unto the priest:
3 And the priest shall go forth out of the camp; and the priest shall look, and,
behold, *if* the plague of leprosy be healed in the leper;
4 Then shall the priest command to take for him that is to be cleansed two
birds alive *and* clean, and cedar wood, and scarlet, and hyssop:
5 And the priest shall command that one of the birds be killed in an earthen
vessel over running water:
6 As for the living bird, he shall take it, and the cedar wood, and the scarlet,
and the hyssop, and shall dip them and the living bird in the blood of the bird
that was killed over the running water:
7 And he shall sprinkle upon him that is to be cleansed from the leprosy
seven times, and shall pronounce him clean, and shall let the living bird loose
into the open field.
8 And he that is to be cleansed shall wash his clothes, and shave off all his
hair, and wash himself in water, that he may be clean: and after that he shall
come into the camp, and shall tarry abroad out of his tent seven days.
9 But it shall be on the seventh day, that he shall shave all his hair off his head
and his beard and his eyebrows, even all his hair he shall shave off: and he shall
wash his clothes, also he shall wash his flesh in water, and he shall be clean.
10 And on the eighth day he shall take two he lambs without blemish, and
one ewe lamb of the first year without blemish, and three tenth deals of fine
flour *for* a meat offering, mingled with oil, and one log of oil.

11 And the priest that maketh *him* clean shall present the man that is to be
made clean, and those things, before the LORD, *at* the door of the tabernacle
of the congregation:
12 And the priest shall take one he lamb, and offer him for a trespass offering,
and the log of oil, and wave them *for* a wave offering before the LORD:
13 And he shall slay the lamb in the place where he shall kill the sin offering
and the burnt offering, in the holy place: for as the sin offering *is* the priest's,
so is the trespass offering: it *is* most holy:
14 And the priest shall take *some* of the blood of the trespass offering, and
the priest shall put *it* upon the tip of the right ear of him that is to be cleansed,
and upon the thumb of his right hand, and upon the great toe of his right foot:
15 And the priest shall take *some* of the log of oil, and pour *it* into the palm
of his own left hand:
16 And the priest shall dip his right finger in the oil that *is* in his left hand,
and shall sprinkle of the oil with his finger seven times before the LORD:
17 And of the rest of the oil that *is* in his hand shall the priest put upon the
tip of the right ear of him that is to be cleansed, and upon the thumb of his
right hand, and upon the great toe of his right foot, upon the blood of the
trespass offering:
18 And the remnant of the oil that *is* in the priest's hand he shall pour upon
the head of him that is to be cleansed: and the priest shall make an atonement
for him before the LORD.
19 And the priest shall offer the sin offering, and make an atonement for him
that is to be cleansed from his uncleanness; and afterward he shall kill the
burnt offering:
20 And the priest shall offer the burnt offering and the meat offering upon
the altar: and the priest shall make an atonement for him, and he shall be
clean.
21 And if he *be* poor, and cannot get so much; then he shall take one lamb
for a trespass offering to be waved, to make an atonement for him, and one
tenth deal of fine flour mingled with oil for a meat offering, and a log of oil;
22 And two turtledoves, or two young pigeons, such as he is able to get; and
the one shall be a sin offering, and the other a burnt offering.
23 And he shall bring them on the eighth day for his cleansing unto the priest,
unto the door of the tabernacle of the congregation, before the LORD.
24 And the priest shall take the lamb of the trespass offering, and the log of
oil, and the priest shall wave them *for* a wave offering before the LORD:
25 And he shall kill the lamb of the trespass offering, and the priest shall take
some of the blood of the trespass offering, and put *it* upon the tip of the right
ear of him that is to be cleansed, and upon the thumb of his right hand, and
upon the great toe of his right foot:
26 And the priest shall pour of the oil into the palm of his own left hand:
27 And the priest shall sprinkle with his right finger *some* of the oil that *is* in
his left hand seven times before the LORD:
28 And the priest shall put of the oil that *is* in his hand upon the tip of the
right ear of him that is to be cleansed, and upon the thumb of his right hand,
and upon the great toe of his right foot, upon the place of the blood of the
trespass offering:
29 And the rest of the oil that *is* in the priest's hand he shall put upon the
head of him that is to be cleansed, to make an atonement for him before the
LORD.
30 And he shall offer the one of the turtledoves, or of the young pigeons, such
as he can get;

31 *Even* such as he is able to get, the one *for* a sin offering, and the other *for*
a burnt offering, with the meat offering: and the priest shall make an atone-
ment for him that is to be cleansed before the LORD.
32 This *is* the law *of him* in whom *is* the plague of leprosy, whose hand is not
able to get *that which pertaineth* to his cleansing.

The Signs of Leprosy in a House, and the Cleansing Thereof

33 And the LORD spake unto Moses and unto Aaron, saying,
34 When ye be come into the land of Canaan, which I give to you for a posses-
sion, and I put the plague of leprosy in a house of the land of your possession;
35 And he that owneth the house shall come and tell the priest, saying, It
seemeth to me *there is* as it were a plague in the house:
36 Then the priest shall command that they empty the house, before the
priest go *into it* to see the plague, that all that *is* in the house be not made
unclean: and afterward the priest shall go in to see the house:
37 And he shall look on the plague, and, behold, *if* the plague *be* in the walls
of the house with hollow strakes, greenish or reddish, which in sight *are* lower
than the wall;
38 Then the priest shall go out of the house to the door of the house, and shut
up the house seven days:
39 And the priest shall come again the seventh day, and shall look: and,
behold, *if* the plague be spread in the walls of the house;
40 Then the priest shall command that they take away the stones in which
the plague *is*, and they shall cast them into an unclean place without the city:
41 And he shall cause the house to be scraped within round about, and they
shall pour out the dust that they scrape off without the city into an unclean
place:
42 And they shall take other stones, and put *them* in the place of those stones;
and he shall take other morter, and shall plaister the house.
43 And if the plague come again, and break out in the house, after that he
hath taken away the stones, and after he hath scraped the house, and after it
is plaistered;
44 Then the priest shall come and look, and, behold, *if* the plague be spread
in the house, it *is* a fretting leprosy in the house: it *is* unclean.
45 And he shall break down the house, the stones of it, and the timber there-
of, and all the morter of the house; and he shall carry *them* forth out of the
city into an unclean place.
46 Moreover he that goeth into the house all the while that it is shut up shall
be unclean until the even.
47 And he that lieth in the house shall wash his clothes; and he that eateth
in the house shall wash his clothes.
48 And if the priest shall come in, and look *upon it*, and, behold, the plague
hath not spread in the house, after the house was plaistered: then the priest
shall pronounce the house clean, because the plague is healed.
49 And he shall take to cleanse the house two birds, and cedar wood, and
scarlet, and hyssop:
50 And he shall kill the one of the birds in an earthen vessel over running
water:
51 And he shall take the cedar wood, and the hyssop, and the scarlet, and the
living bird, and dip them in the blood of the slain bird, and in the running
water, and sprinkle the house seven times:
52 And he shall cleanse the house with the blood of the bird, and with the
running water, and with the living bird, and with the cedar wood, and with
the hyssop, and with the scarlet:
53 But he shall let go the living bird out of the city into the open fields, and
make an atonement for the house: and it shall be clean.

54 This *is* the law for all manner of plague of leprosy, and scall,
55 And for the leprosy of a garment, and of a house,
56 And for a rising, and for a scab, and for a bright spot:
57 To teach when *it is* unclean, and when *it is* clean: this *is* the law of leprosy.

Discharges and Uncleanness

15 And the LORD spake unto Moses and to Aaron, saying,
2 Speak unto the children of Israel, and say unto them, When any man
hath a running issue out of his flesh, *because of* his issue he *is* unclean.
3 And this shall be his uncleanness in his issue: whether his flesh run with
his issue, or his flesh be stopped from his issue, it *is* his uncleanness.
4 Every bed, whereon he lieth that hath the issue, is unclean: and every thing,
whereon he sitteth, shall be unclean.
5 And whosoever toucheth his bed shall wash his clothes, and bathe *himself*
in water, and be unclean until the even.
6 And he that sitteth on *any* thing whereon he sat that hath the issue shall
wash his clothes, and bathe *himself* in water, and be unclean until the even.
7 And he that toucheth the flesh of him that hath the issue shall wash his
clothes, and bathe *himself* in water, and be unclean until the even.
8 And if he that hath the issue spit upon him that is clean; then he shall wash
his clothes, and bathe *himself* in water, and be unclean until the even.
9 And what saddle soever he rideth upon that hath the issue shall be unclean.
10 And whosoever toucheth any thing that was under him shall be unclean
until the even: and he that beareth *any of* those things shall wash his clothes,
and bathe *himself* in water, and be unclean until the even.
11 And whomsoever he toucheth that hath the issue, and hath not rinsed his
hands in water, he shall wash his clothes, and bathe *himself* in water, and be
unclean until the even.
12 And the vessel of earth, that he toucheth which hath the issue, shall be
broken: and every vessel of wood shall be rinsed in water.
13 And when he that hath an issue is cleansed of his issue; then he shall
number to himself seven days for his cleansing, and wash his clothes, and
bathe his flesh in running water, and shall be clean.
14 And on the eighth day he shall take to him two turtledoves, or two young
pigeons, and come before the LORD unto the door of the tabernacle of the
congregation, and give them unto the priest:
15 And the priest shall offer them, the one *for* a sin offering, and the other
for a burnt offering; and the priest shall make an atonement for him before
the LORD for his issue.
16 And if any man's seed of copulation go out from him, then he shall wash
all his flesh in water, and be unclean until the even.
17 And every garment, and every skin, whereon is the seed of copulation,
shall be washed with water, and be unclean until the even.
18 The woman also with whom man shall lie *with* seed of copulation, they
shall *both* bathe *themselves* in water, and be unclean until the even.
19 And if a woman have an issue, *and* her issue in her flesh be blood, she shall
be put apart seven days: and whosoever toucheth her shall be unclean until
the even.
20 And every thing that she lieth upon in her separation shall be unclean:
every thing also that she sitteth upon shall be unclean.
21 And whosoever toucheth her bed shall wash his clothes, and bathe *himself*
in water, and be unclean until the even.
22 And whosoever toucheth any thing that she sat upon shall wash his
clothes, and bathe *himself* in water, and be unclean until the even.
23 And if it *be* on *her* bed, or on any thing whereon she sitteth, when he
toucheth it, he shall be unclean until the even.

24 And if any man lie with her at all, and her flowers be upon him, he shall
be unclean seven days; and all the bed whereon he lieth shall be unclean.
25 And if a woman have an issue of her blood many days out of the time of
her separation, or if it run beyond the time of her separation; all the days of
the issue of her uncleanness shall be as the days of her separation: she *shall
be* unclean.
26 Every bed whereon she lieth all the days of her issue shall be unto her as
the bed of her separation: and whatsoever she sitteth upon shall be unclean,
as the uncleanness of her separation.
27 And whosoever toucheth those things shall be unclean, and shall wash
his clothes, and bathe *himself* in water, and be unclean until the even.
28 But if she be cleansed of her issue, then she shall number to herself seven
days, and after that she shall be clean.
29 And on the eighth day she shall take unto her two turtles, or two young
pigeons, and bring them unto the priest, to the door of the tabernacle of the
congregation.
30 And the priest shall offer the one *for* a sin offering, and the other *for* a
burnt offering; and the priest shall make an atonement for her before the
LORD for the issue of her uncleanness.
31 Thus shall ye separate the children of Israel from their uncleanness; that
they die not in their uncleanness, when they defile my tabernacle that *is*
among them.
32 This *is* the law of him that hath an issue, and *of him* whose seed goeth
from him, and is defiled therewith;
33 And of her that is sick of her flowers, and of him that hath an issue, of the
man, and of the woman, and of him that lieth with her that is unclean.

How the High Priest Must Enter into the Holy Place

16 And the LORD spake unto Moses after the death of the two sons of
Aaron, when they offered before the LORD, and died;
2 And the LORD said unto Moses, Speak unto Aaron thy brother, that he come
not at all times into the holy *place* within the veil before the mercy seat, which
is upon the ark; that he die not: for I will appear in the cloud upon the mercy
seat.
3 Thus shall Aaron come into the holy *place*: with a young bullock for a sin
offering, and a ram for a burnt offering.
4 He shall put on the holy linen coat, and he shall have the linen breeches
upon his flesh, and shall be girded with a linen girdle, and with the linen mitre
shall he be attired: these *are* holy garments; therefore shall he wash his flesh
in water, and *so* put them on.
5 And he shall take of the congregation of the children of Israel two kids of
the goats for a sin offering, and one ram for a burnt offering.
6 And Aaron shall offer his bullock of the sin offering, which *is* for himself,
and make an atonement for himself, and for his house.
7 And he shall take the two goats, and present them before the LORD *at* the
door of the tabernacle of the congregation.
8 And Aaron shall cast lots upon the two goats; one lot for the LORD, and the
other lot for the scapegoat.
9 And Aaron shall bring the goat upon which the LORD's lot fell, and offer
him *for* a sin offering.
10 But the goat, on which the lot fell to be the scapegoat, shall be presented
alive before the LORD, to make an atonement with him, *and* to let him go for
a scapegoat into the wilderness.
11 And Aaron shall bring the bullock of the sin offering, which *is* for himself,
and shall make an atonement for himself, and for his house, and shall kill the
bullock of the sin offering which *is* for himself:

12 And he shall take a censer full of burning coals of fire from off the altar
before the LORD, and his hands full of sweet incense beaten small, and bring
it within the veil:
13 And he shall put the incense upon the fire before the LORD, that the cloud
of the incense may cover the mercy seat that *is* upon the testimony, that he
die not:
14 And he shall take of the blood of the bullock, and sprinkle *it* with his
finger upon the mercy seat eastward; and before the mercy seat shall he sprin-
kle of the blood with his finger seven times.

The Sin Offering for the People

15 Then shall he kill the goat of the sin offering, that *is* for the people, and
bring his blood within the veil, and do with that blood as he did with the blood
of the bullock, and sprinkle it upon the mercy seat, and before the mercy seat:
16 And he shall make an atonement for the holy *place*, because of the unclean-
ness of the children of Israel, and because of their transgressions in all their
sins: and so shall he do for the tabernacle of the congregation, that remaineth
among them in the midst of their uncleanness.
17 And there shall be no man in the tabernacle of the congregation when he
goeth in to make an atonement in the holy *place*, until he come out, and have
made an atonement for himself, and for his household, and for all the con-
gregation of Israel.
18 And he shall go out unto the altar that *is* before the LORD, and make an
atonement for it; and shall take of the blood of the bullock, and of the blood
of the goat, and put *it* upon the horns of the altar round about.
19 And he shall sprinkle of the blood upon it with his finger seven times, and
cleanse it, and hallow it from the uncleanness of the children of Israel.
20 And when he hath made an end of reconciling the holy *place*, and the
tabernacle of the congregation, and the altar, he shall bring the live goat:
21 And Aaron shall lay both his hands upon the head of the live goat, and
confess over him all the iniquities of the children of Israel, and all their trans-
gressions in all their sins, putting them upon the head of the goat, and shall
send *him* away by the hand of a fit man into the wilderness:
22 And the goat shall bear upon him all their iniquities unto a land not inhab-
ited: and he shall let go the goat in the wilderness.
23 And Aaron shall come into the tabernacle of the congregation, and shall
put off the linen garments, which he put on when he went into the holy *place*,
and shall leave them there:
24 And he shall wash his flesh with water in the holy place, and put on his
garments, and come forth, and offer his burnt offering, and the burnt offering
of the people, and make an atonement for himself, and for the people.
25 And the fat of the sin offering shall he burn upon the altar.
26 And he that let go the goat for the scapegoat shall wash his clothes, and
bathe his flesh in water, and afterward come into the camp.
27 And the bullock *for* the sin offering, and the goat *for* the sin offering,
whose blood was brought in to make atonement in the holy *place*, shall *one*
carry forth without the camp; and they shall burn in the fire their skins, and
their flesh, and their dung.
28 And he that burneth them shall wash his clothes, and bathe his flesh in
water, and afterward he shall come into the camp.

The Annual Feast of Atonement

29 And *this* shall be a statute for ever unto you: *that* in the seventh month,
on the tenth *day* of the month, ye shall afflict your souls, and do no work at
all, *whether it be* one of your own country, or a stranger that sojourneth among
you:

30 For on that day shall *the priest* make an atonement for you, to cleanse you,
that ye may be clean from all your sins before the LORD.
31 It *shall be* a sabbath of rest unto you, and ye shall afflict your souls, by a
statute for ever.
32 And the priest, whom he shall anoint, and whom he shall consecrate to
minister in the priest's office in his father's stead, shall make the atonement,
and shall put on the linen clothes, *even* the holy garments:
33 And he shall make an atonement for the holy sanctuary, and he shall make
an atonement for the tabernacle of the congregation, and for the altar, and
he shall make an atonement for the priests, and for all the people of the con-
gregation.
34 And this shall be an everlasting statute unto you, to make an atonement
for the children of Israel for all their sins once a year. And he did as the LORD
commanded Moses.

Offering the Blood of Slain Beasts at the Door of the Tabernacle

17 And the LORD spake unto Moses, saying,
2 Speak unto Aaron, and unto his sons, and unto all the children of
Israel, and say unto them; This *is* the thing which the LORD hath commanded,
saying,
3 What man soever *there be* of the house of Israel, that killeth an ox, or lamb,
or goat, in the camp, or that killeth *it* out of the camp,
4 And bringeth it not unto the door of the tabernacle of the congregation,
to offer an offering unto the LORD before the tabernacle of the LORD; blood
shall be imputed unto that man; he hath shed blood; and that man shall be
cut off from among his people:
5 To the end that the children of Israel may bring their sacrifices, which they
offer in the open field, even that they may bring them unto the LORD, unto the
door of the tabernacle of the congregation, unto the priest, and offer them
for peace offerings unto the LORD.
6 And the priest shall sprinkle the blood upon the altar of the LORD *at* the
door of the tabernacle of the congregation, and burn the fat for a sweet savour
unto the LORD.
7 And they shall no more offer their sacrifices unto devils, after whom they
have gone a whoring. This shall be a statute for ever unto them throughout
their generations.
8 And thou shalt say unto them, Whatsoever man *there be* of the house of
Israel, or of the strangers which sojourn among you, that offereth a burnt
offering or sacrifice,
9 And bringeth it not unto the door of the tabernacle of the congregation,
to offer it unto the LORD; even that man shall be cut off from among his people.

All Eating of Blood Is Forbidden

10 And whatsoever man *there be* of the house of Israel, or of the strangers
that sojourn among you, that eateth any manner of blood; I will even set my
face against that soul that eateth blood, and will cut him off from among his
people.
11 For the life of the flesh *is* in the blood: and I have given it to you upon the
altar to make an atonement for your souls: for it *is* the blood *that* maketh an
atonement for the soul.
12 Therefore I said unto the children of Israel, No soul of you shall eat blood,
neither shall any stranger that sojourneth among you eat blood.
13 And whatsoever man *there be* of the children of Israel, or of the strangers
that sojourn among you, which hunteth and catcheth any beast or fowl that
may be eaten; he shall even pour out the blood thereof, and cover it with dust.

14 For *it is* the life of all flesh; the blood of it *is* for the life thereof: therefore
I said unto the children of Israel, Ye shall eat the blood of no manner of flesh:
for the life of all flesh *is* the blood thereof: whosoever eateth it shall be cut off.
15 And every soul that eateth that which died *of itself*, or that which was torn
with beasts, whether it be one of your own country, or a stranger, he shall both
wash his clothes, and bathe *himself* in water, and be unclean until the even:
then shall he be clean.
16 But if he wash *them* not, nor bathe his flesh; then he shall bear his iniquity.

Unlawful Marriages and Unlawful Lusts

18 And the LORD spake unto Moses, saying,
2 Speak unto the children of Israel, and say unto them, I am the LORD
your God.
3 After the doings of the land of Egypt, wherein ye dwelt, shall ye not do: and
after the doings of the land of Canaan, whither I bring you, shall ye not do:
neither shall ye walk in their ordinances.
4 Ye shall do my judgments, and keep mine ordinances, to walk therein: I *am*
the LORD your God.
5 Ye shall therefore keep my statutes, and my judgments: which if a man do,
he shall live in them: I *am* the LORD.
6 None of you shall approach to any that is near of kin to him, to uncover
their nakedness: I *am* the LORD.
7 The nakedness of thy father, or the nakedness of thy mother, shalt thou not
uncover: she *is* thy mother; thou shalt not uncover her nakedness.
8 The nakedness of thy father's wife shalt thou not uncover: it *is* thy father's
nakedness.
9 The nakedness of thy sister, the daughter of thy father, or daughter of thy
mother, *whether she be* born at home, or born abroad, *even* their nakedness
thou shalt not uncover.
10 The nakedness of thy son's daughter, or of thy daughter's daughter, *even*
their nakedness thou shalt not uncover: for theirs *is* thine own nakedness.
11 The nakedness of thy father's wife's daughter, begotten of thy father, she
is thy sister, thou shalt not uncover her nakedness.
12 Thou shalt not uncover the nakedness of thy father's sister: she *is* thy
father's near kinswoman.
13 Thou shalt not uncover the nakedness of thy mother's sister: for she *is* thy
mother's near kinswoman.
14 Thou shalt not uncover the nakedness of thy father's brother, thou shalt
not approach to his wife: she *is* thine aunt.
15 Thou shalt not uncover the nakedness of thy daughter in law: she *is* thy
son's wife; thou shalt not uncover her nakedness.
16 Thou shalt not uncover the nakedness of thy brother's wife: it *is* thy
brother's nakedness.
17 Thou shalt not uncover the nakedness of a woman and her daughter,
neither shalt thou take her son's daughter, or her daughter's daughter, to
uncover her nakedness; *for* they *are* her near kinswomen: it *is* wickedness.
18 Neither shalt thou take a wife to her sister, to vex *her*, to uncover her
nakedness, beside the other in her life *time*.
19 Also thou shalt not approach unto a woman to uncover her nakedness, as
long as she is put apart for her uncleanness.
20 Moreover thou shalt not lie carnally with thy neighbour's wife, to defile
thyself with her.
21 And thou shalt not let any of thy seed pass through *the fire* to Molech,
neither shalt thou profane the name of thy God: I *am* the LORD.
22 Thou shalt not lie with mankind, as with womankind: it *is* abomination.

23 Neither shalt thou lie with any beast to defile thyself therewith: neither
shall any woman stand before a beast to lie down thereto: it *is* confusion.
24 Defile not ye yourselves in any of these things: for in all these the nations
are defiled which I cast out before you:
25 And the land is defiled: therefore I do visit the iniquity thereof upon it,
and the land itself vomiteth out her inhabitants.
26 Ye shall therefore keep my statutes and my judgments, and shall not com-
mit *any* of these abominations; *neither* any of your own nation, nor any stran-
ger that sojourneth among you:
27 (For all these abominations have the men of the land done, which *were*
before you, and the land is defiled;)
28 That the land spue not you out also, when ye defile it, as it spued out the
nations that *were* before you.
29 For whosoever shall commit any of these abominations, even the souls
that commit *them* shall be cut off from among their people.
30 Therefore shall ye keep mine ordinance, that *ye* commit not *any one* of
these abominable customs, which were committed before you, and that ye
defile not yourselves therein: I *am* the LORD your God.

A Repetition of Various Laws

19 And the LORD spake unto Moses, saying,
2 Speak unto all the congregation of the children of Israel, and say
unto them, Ye shall be holy: for I the LORD your God *am* holy.
3 Ye shall fear every man his mother, and his father, and keep my sabbaths:
I *am* the LORD your God.
4 Turn ye not unto idols, nor make to yourselves molten gods: I *am* the LORD
your God.
5 And if ye offer a sacrifice of peace offerings unto the LORD, ye shall offer it
at your own will.
6 It shall be eaten the same day ye offer it, and on the morrow: and if ought
remain until the third day, it shall be burnt in the fire.
7 And if it be eaten at all on the third day, it *is* abominable; it shall not be
accepted.
8 Therefore *every one* that eateth it shall bear his iniquity, because he hath
profaned the hallowed thing of the LORD: and that soul shall be cut off from
among his people.
9 And when ye reap the harvest of your land, thou shalt not wholly reap the
corners of thy field, neither shalt thou gather the gleanings of thy harvest.
10 And thou shalt not glean thy vineyard, neither shalt thou gather *every*
grape of thy vineyard; thou shalt leave them for the poor and stranger: I *am*
the LORD your God.
11 Ye shall not steal, neither deal falsely, neither lie one to another.
12 And ye shall not swear by my name falsely, neither shalt thou profane the
name of thy God: I *am* the LORD.
13 Thou shalt not defraud thy neighbour, neither rob *him*: the wages of him
that is hired shall not abide with thee all night until the morning.
14 Thou shalt not curse the deaf, nor put a stumblingblock before the blind,
but shalt fear thy God: I *am* the LORD.
15 Ye shall do no unrighteousness in judgment: thou shalt not respect the
person of the poor, nor honour the person of the mighty: *but* in righteousness
shalt thou judge thy neighbour.
16 Thou shalt not go up and down *as* a talebearer among thy people: neither
shalt thou stand against the blood of thy neighbour: I *am* the LORD.
17 Thou shalt not hate thy brother in thine heart: thou shalt in any wise
rebuke thy neighbour, and not suffer sin upon him.

18 Thou shalt not avenge, nor bear any grudge against the children of thy
people, but thou shalt love thy neighbour as thyself: I *am* the LORD.
19 Ye shall keep my statutes. Thou shalt not let thy cattle gender with a diverse
kind: thou shalt not sow thy field with mingled seed: neither shall a garment
mingled of linen and woollen come upon thee.
20 And whosoever lieth carnally with a woman, that *is* a bondmaid, betrothed
to an husband, and not at all redeemed, nor freedom given her; she shall be
scourged; they shall not be put to death, because she was not free.
21 And he shall bring his trespass offering unto the LORD, unto the door of
the tabernacle of the congregation, *even* a ram for a trespass offering.
22 And the priest shall make an atonement for him with the ram of the tres-
pass offering before the LORD for his sin which he hath done: and the sin which
he hath done shall be forgiven him.
23 And when ye shall come into the land, and shall have planted all manner
of trees for food, then ye shall count the fruit thereof as uncircumcised: three
years shall it be as uncircumcised unto you: it shall not be eaten of.
24 But in the fourth year all the fruit thereof shall be holy to praise the LORD
withal.
25 And in the fifth year shall ye eat of the fruit thereof, that it may yield unto
you the increase thereof: I *am* the LORD your God.
26 Ye shall not eat *any thing* with the blood: neither shall ye use enchantment,
nor observe times.
27 Ye shall not round the corners of your heads, neither shalt thou mar the
corners of thy beard.
28 Ye shall not make any cuttings in your flesh for the dead, nor print any
marks upon you: I *am* the LORD.
29 Do not prostitute thy daughter, to cause her to be a whore; lest the land
fall to whoredom, and the land become full of wickedness.
30 Ye shall keep my sabbaths, and reverence my sanctuary: I *am* the LORD.
31 Regard not them that have familiar spirits, neither seek after wizards, to
be defiled by them: I *am* the LORD your God.
32 Thou shalt rise up before the hoary head, and honour the face of the old
man, and fear thy God: I *am* the LORD.
33 And if a stranger sojourn with thee in your land, ye shall not vex him.
34 *But* the stranger that dwelleth with you shall be unto you as one born
among you, and thou shalt love him as thyself; for ye were strangers in the
land of Egypt: I *am* the LORD your God.
35 Ye shall do no unrighteousness in judgment, in meteyard, in weight, or
in measure.
36 Just balances, just weights, a just ephah, and a just hin, shall ye have: I *am*
the LORD your God, which brought you out of the land of Egypt.
37 Therefore shall ye observe all my statutes, and all my judgments, and do
them: I *am* the LORD.

Punishment for Sacrificing Children to Molech

20 And the LORD spake unto Moses, saying,
2 Again, thou shalt say to the children of Israel, Whosoever *he be* of
the children of Israel, or of the strangers that sojourn in Israel, that giveth *any*
of his seed unto Molech; he shall surely be put to death: the people of the land
shall stone him with stones.
3 And I will set my face against that man, and will cut him off from among
his people; because he hath given of his seed unto Molech, to defile my sanc-
tuary, and to profane my holy name.
4 And if the people of the land do any ways hide their eyes from the man,
when he giveth of his seed unto Molech, and kill him not:

5 Then I will set my face against that man, and against his family, and will
cut him off, and all that go a whoring after him, to commit whoredom with
Molech, from among their people.
6 And the soul that turneth after such as have familiar spirits, and after wiz-
ards, to go a whoring after them, I will even set my face against that soul, and
will cut him off from among his people.
7 Sanctify yourselves therefore, and be ye holy: for I *am* the LORD your God.
8 And ye shall keep my statutes, and do them: I *am* the LORD which sanctify
you.
9 For every one that curseth his father or his mother shall be surely put to
death: he hath cursed his father or his mother; his blood *shall be* upon him.

Punishment for Adultery

10 And the man that committeth adultery with *another* man's wife, *even he*
that committeth adultery with his neighbour's wife, the adulterer and the
adulteress shall surely be put to death.
11 And the man that lieth with his father's wife hath uncovered his father's
nakedness: both of them shall surely be put to death; their blood *shall be* upon
them.
12 And if a man lie with his daughter in law, both of them shall surely be put
to death: they have wrought confusion; their blood *shall be* upon them.
13 If a man also lie with mankind, as he lieth with a woman, both of them
have committed an abomination: they shall surely be put to death; their blood
shall be upon them.
14 And if a man take a wife and her mother, it *is* wickedness: they shall be
burnt with fire, both he and they; that there be no wickedness among you.
15 And if a man lie with a beast, he shall surely be put to death: and ye shall
slay the beast.
16 And if a woman approach unto any beast, and lie down thereto, thou shalt
kill the woman, and the beast: they shall surely be put to death; their blood
shall be upon them.
17 And if a man shall take his sister, his father's daughter, or his mother's
daughter, and see her nakedness, and she see his nakedness; it *is* a wicked
thing; and they shall be cut off in the sight of their people: he hath uncovered
his sister's nakedness; he shall bear his iniquity.
18 And if a man shall lie with a woman having her sickness, and shall uncov-
er her nakedness; he hath discovered her fountain, and she hath uncovered
the fountain of her blood: and both of them shall be cut off from among their
people.
19 And thou shalt not uncover the nakedness of thy mother's sister, nor of
thy father's sister: for he uncovereth his near kin: they shall bear their iniquity.
20 And if a man shall lie with his uncle's wife, he hath uncovered his uncle's
nakedness: they shall bear their sin; they shall die childless.
21 And if a man shall take his brother's wife, it *is* an unclean thing: he hath
uncovered his brother's nakedness; they shall be childless.

Obedience Is Required with Holiness

22 Ye shall therefore keep all my statutes, and all my judgments, and do them:
that the land, whither I bring you to dwell therein, spue you not out.
23 And ye shall not walk in the manners of the nation, which I cast out before
you: for they committed all these things, and therefore I abhorred them.
24 But I have said unto you, Ye shall inherit their land, and I will give it unto
you to possess it, a land that floweth with milk and honey: I *am* the LORD your
God, which have separated you from *other* people.
25 Ye shall therefore put difference between clean beasts and unclean, and
between unclean fowls and clean: and ye shall not make your souls abomin-

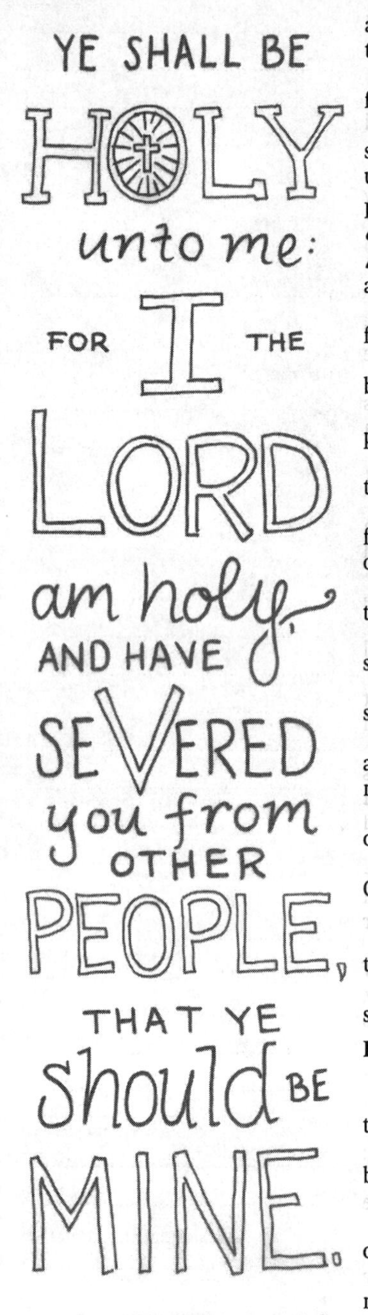

able by beast, or by fowl, or by any manner of living thing that creepeth on
the ground, which I have separated from you as unclean.
26 And ye shall be holy unto me: for I the LORD *am* holy, and have severed you
from *other* people, that ye should be mine.
27 A man also or woman that hath a familiar spirit, or that is a wizard, shall
surely be put to death: they shall stone them with stones: their blood *shall be*
upon them.

Rules for the Priests

21 And the LORD said unto Moses, Speak unto the priests the sons of
Aaron, and say unto them, There shall none be defiled for the dead
among his people:
2 But for his kin, that is near unto him, *that is*, for his mother, and for his
father, and for his son, and for his daughter, and for his brother,
3 And for his sister a virgin, that is nigh unto him, which hath had no hus-
band; for her may he be defiled.
4 *But* he shall not defile himself, *being* a chief man among his people, to
profane himself.
5 They shall not make baldness upon their head, neither shall they shave off
the corner of their beard, nor make any cuttings in their flesh.
6 They shall be holy unto their God, and not profane the name of their God:
for the offerings of the LORD made by fire, *and* the bread of their God, they do
offer: therefore they shall be holy.
7 They shall not take a wife *that is* a whore, or profane; neither shall they
take a woman put away from her husband: for he *is* holy unto his God.
8 Thou shalt sanctify him therefore; for he offereth the bread of thy God: he
shall be holy unto thee: for I the LORD, which sanctify you, *am* holy.
9 And the daughter of any priest, if she profane herself by playing the whore,
she profaneth her father: she shall be burnt with fire.
10 And *he that is* the high priest among his brethren, upon whose head the
anointing oil was poured, and that is consecrated to put on the garments, shall
not uncover his head, nor rend his clothes;
11 Neither shall he go in to any dead body, nor defile himself for his father,
or for his mother;
12 Neither shall he go out of the sanctuary, nor profane the sanctuary of his
God; for the crown of the anointing oil of his God *is* upon him: I *am* the LORD.
13 And he shall take a wife in her virginity.
14 A widow, or a divorced woman, or profane, *or* an harlot, these shall he not
take: but he shall take a virgin of his own people to wife.
15 Neither shall he profane his seed among his people: for I the LORD do
sanctify him.

Priests with Imperfections Are Not Allowed to Minister

16 And the LORD spake unto Moses, saying,
17 Speak unto Aaron, saying, Whosoever *he be* of thy seed in their generations
that hath *any* blemish, let him not approach to offer the bread of his God.
18 For whatsoever man *he be* that hath a blemish, he shall not approach: a
blind man, or a lame, or he that hath a flat nose, or any thing superfluous,
19 Or a man that is brokenfooted, or brokenhanded,
20 Or crookbackt, or a dwarf, or that hath a blemish in his eye, or be scurvy,
or scabbed, or hath his stones broken;
21 No man that hath a blemish of the seed of Aaron the priest shall come
nigh to offer the offerings of the LORD made by fire: he hath a blemish; he shall
not come nigh to offer the bread of his God.
22 He shall eat the bread of his God, *both* of the most holy, and of the holy.

23 Only he shall not go in unto the veil, nor come nigh unto the altar, because he hath a blemish; that he profane not my sanctuaries: for I the LORD do sanctify them.

24 And Moses told *it* unto Aaron, and to his sons, and unto all the children of Israel.

The Priests in Their Uncleanness Must Abstain from the Holy Things

22 And the LORD spake unto Moses, saying,

2 Speak unto Aaron and to his sons, that they separate themselves from the holy things of the children of Israel, and that they profane not my holy name *in those things* which they hallow unto me: I *am* the LORD.

3 Say unto them, Whosoever *he be* of all your seed among your generations, that goeth unto the holy things, which the children of Israel hallow unto the LORD, having his uncleanness upon him, that soul shall be cut off from my presence: I *am* the LORD.

4 What man soever of the seed of Aaron *is* a leper, or hath a running issue; he shall not eat of the holy things, until he be clean. And whoso toucheth any thing *that is* unclean *by* the dead, or a man whose seed goeth from him;

5 Or whosoever toucheth any creeping thing, whereby he may be made unclean, or a man of whom he may take uncleanness, whatsoever uncleanness he hath;

6 The soul which hath touched any such shall be unclean until even, and shall not eat of the holy things, unless he wash his flesh with water.

7 And when the sun is down, he shall be clean, and shall afterward eat of the holy things; because it *is* his food.

8 That which dieth of itself, or is torn *with beasts*, he shall not eat to defile himself therewith: I *am* the LORD.

9 They shall therefore keep mine ordinance, lest they bear sin for it, and die therefore, if they profane it: I the LORD do sanctify them.

Who of the Priest's House May Eat of the Holy Things

10 There shall no stranger eat *of* the holy thing: a sojourner of the priest, or an hired servant, shall not eat *of* the holy thing.

11 But if the priest buy *any* soul with his money, he shall eat of it, and he that is born in his house: they shall eat of his meat.

12 If the priest's daughter also be *married* unto a stranger, she may not eat of an offering of the holy things.

13 But if the priest's daughter be a widow, or divorced, and have no child, and is returned unto her father's house, as in her youth, she shall eat of her father's meat: but there shall no stranger eat thereof.

14 And if a man eat *of* the holy thing unwittingly, then he shall put the fifth *part* thereof unto it, and shall give *it* unto the priest with the holy thing.

15 And they shall not profane the holy things of the children of Israel, which they offer unto the LORD;

16 Or suffer them to bear the iniquity of trespass, when they eat their holy things: for I the LORD do sanctify them.

The Sacrifices Must Be without Blemish

17 And the LORD spake unto Moses, saying,

18 Speak unto Aaron, and to his sons, and unto all the children of Israel, and say unto them, Whatsoever *he be* of the house of Israel, or of the strangers in Israel, that will offer his oblation for all his vows, and for all his freewill offerings, which they will offer unto the LORD for a burnt offering;

19 *Ye shall offer* at your own will a male without blemish, of the beeves, of the sheep, or of the goats.

20 *But* whatsoever hath a blemish, *that* shall ye not offer: for it shall not be acceptable for you.

21 And whosoever offereth a sacrifice of peace offerings unto the LORD to accomplish *his* vow, or a freewill offering in beeves or sheep, it shall be perfect to be accepted; there shall be no blemish therein.
22 Blind, or broken, or maimed, or having a wen, or scurvy, or scabbed, ye shall not offer these unto the LORD, nor make an offering by fire of them upon the altar unto the LORD.
23 Either a bullock or a lamb that hath any thing superfluous or lacking in his parts, that mayest thou offer *for* a freewill offering; but for a vow it shall not be accepted.
24 Ye shall not offer unto the LORD that which is bruised, or crushed, or broken, or cut; neither shall ye make *any offering thereof* in your land.
25 Neither from a stranger's hand shall ye offer the bread of your God of any of these; because their corruption *is* in them, *and* blemishes *be* in them: they shall not be accepted for you.
26 And the LORD spake unto Moses, saying,
27 When a bullock, or a sheep, or a goat, is brought forth, then it shall be seven days under the dam; and from the eighth day and thenceforth it shall be accepted for an offering made by fire unto the LORD.
28 And *whether it be* cow or ewe, ye shall not kill it and her young both in one day.
29 And when ye will offer a sacrifice of thanksgiving unto the LORD, offer *it* at your own will.
30 On the same day it shall be eaten up; ye shall leave none of it until the morrow: I *am* the LORD.
31 Therefore shall ye keep my commandments, and do them: I *am* the LORD.
32 Neither shall ye profane my holy name; but I will be hallowed among the children of Israel: I *am* the LORD which hallow you,
33 That brought you out of the land of Egypt, to be your God: I *am* the LORD.

The Feasts of the Lord

23 And the LORD spake unto Moses, saying,
2 Speak unto the children of Israel, and say unto them, *Concerning* the feasts of the LORD, which ye shall proclaim *to be* holy convocations, *even* these *are* my feasts.
3 Six days shall work be done: but the seventh day *is* the sabbath of rest, an holy convocation; ye shall do no work *therein*: it *is* the sabbath of the LORD in all your dwellings.

The Passover

4 These *are* the feasts of the LORD, *even* holy convocations, which ye shall proclaim in their seasons.
5 In the fourteenth *day* of the first month at even *is* the LORD's passover.
6 And on the fifteenth day of the same month *is* the feast of unleavened bread unto the LORD: seven days ye must eat unleavened bread.
7 In the first day ye shall have an holy convocation: ye shall do no servile work therein.
8 But ye shall offer an offering made by fire unto the LORD seven days: in the seventh day *is* an holy convocation: ye shall do no servile work *therein*.
9 And the LORD spake unto Moses, saying,
10 Speak unto the children of Israel, and say unto them, When ye be come into the land which I give unto you, and shall reap the harvest thereof, then ye shall bring a sheaf of the firstfruits of your harvest unto the priest:
11 And he shall wave the sheaf before the LORD, to be accepted for you: on the morrow after the sabbath the priest shall wave it.
12 And ye shall offer that day when ye wave the sheaf an he lamb without blemish of the first year for a burnt offering unto the LORD.

13 And the meat offering thereof *shall be* two tenth deals of fine flour min-
gled with oil, an offering made by fire unto the LORD *for* a sweet savour: and
the drink offering thereof *shall be* of wine, the fourth *part* of an hin.
14 And ye shall eat neither bread, nor parched corn, nor green ears, until the
selfsame day that ye have brought an offering unto your God: *it shall be* a
statute for ever throughout your generations in all your dwellings.

The Feast of Pentecost

15 And ye shall count unto you from the morrow after the sabbath, from the
day that ye brought the sheaf of the wave offering; seven sabbaths shall be
complete:
16 Even unto the morrow after the seventh sabbath shall ye number fifty
days; and ye shall offer a new meat offering unto the LORD.
17 Ye shall bring out of your habitations two wave loaves of two tenth deals:
they shall be of fine flour; they shall be baken with leaven; *they are* the first-
fruits unto the LORD.
18 And ye shall offer with the bread seven lambs without blemish of the first
year, and one young bullock, and two rams: they shall be *for* a burnt offering
unto the LORD, with their meat offering, and their drink offerings, *even* an
offering made by fire, of sweet savour unto the LORD.
19 Then ye shall sacrifice one kid of the goats for a sin offering, and two lambs
of the first year for a sacrifice of peace offerings.
20 And the priest shall wave them with the bread of the firstfruits *for* a wave
offering before the LORD, with the two lambs: they shall be holy to the LORD
for the priest.
21 And ye shall proclaim on the selfsame day, *that* it may be an holy convo-
cation unto you: ye shall do no servile work *therein: it shall be* a statute for
ever in all your dwellings throughout your generations.
22 And when ye reap the harvest of your land, thou shalt not make clean
riddance of the corners of thy field when thou reapest, neither shalt thou
gather any gleaning of thy harvest: thou shalt leave them unto the poor, and
to the stranger: I *am* the LORD your God.

The Feast of Trumpets

23 And the LORD spake unto Moses, saying,
24 Speak unto the children of Israel, saying, In the seventh month, in the
first *day* of the month, shall ye have a sabbath, a memorial of blowing of
trumpets, an holy convocation.
25 Ye shall do no servile work *therein*: but ye shall offer an offering made by
fire unto the LORD.
26 And the LORD spake unto Moses, saying,
27 Also on the tenth *day* of this seventh month *there shall be* a day of atone-
ment: it shall be an holy convocation unto you; and ye shall afflict your souls,
and offer an offering made by fire unto the LORD.
28 And ye shall do no work in that same day: for it *is* a day of atonement, to
make an atonement for you before the LORD your God.
29 For whatsoever soul *it be* that shall not be afflicted in that same day, he
shall be cut off from among his people.
30 And whatsoever soul *it be* that doeth any work in that same day, the same
soul will I destroy from among his people.
31 Ye shall do no manner of work: *it shall be* a statute for ever throughout
your generations in all your dwellings.
32 It *shall be* unto you a sabbath of rest, and ye shall afflict your souls: in the
ninth *day* of the month at even, from even unto even, shall ye celebrate your
sabbath.

The Feast of Tabernacles

33 And the LORD spake unto Moses, saying,
34 Speak unto the children of Israel, saying, The fifteenth day of this seventh
month *shall be* the feast of tabernacles *for* seven days unto the LORD.
35 On the first day *shall be* an holy convocation: ye shall do no servile work
therein.
36 Seven days ye shall offer an offering made by fire unto the LORD: on the
eighth day shall be an holy convocation unto you; and ye shall offer an offer-
ing made by fire unto the LORD: it *is* a solemn assembly; *and* ye shall do no
servile work *therein.*
37 These *are* the feasts of the LORD, which ye shall proclaim *to be* holy con-
vocations, to offer an offering made by fire unto the LORD, a burnt offering,
and a meat offering, a sacrifice, and drink offerings, every thing upon his day:
38 Beside the sabbaths of the LORD, and beside your gifts, and beside all your
vows, and beside all your freewill offerings, which ye give unto the LORD.
39 Also in the fifteenth day of the seventh month, when ye have gathered in
the fruit of the land, ye shall keep a feast unto the LORD seven days: on the first
day *shall be* a sabbath, and on the eighth day *shall be* a sabbath.
40 And ye shall take you on the first day the boughs of goodly trees, branch-
es of palm trees, and the boughs of thick trees, and willows of the brook; and
ye shall rejoice before the LORD your God seven days.
41 And ye shall keep it a feast unto the LORD seven days in the year. *It shall be*
a statute for ever in your generations: ye shall celebrate it in the seventh month.
42 Ye shall dwell in booths seven days; all that are Israelites born shall dwell
in booths:
43 That your generations may know that I made the children of Israel to
dwell in booths, when I brought them out of the land of Egypt: I *am* the LORD
your God.
44 And Moses declared unto the children of Israel the feasts of the LORD.

The Oil for the Lamps That They May Burn Continually

24 And the LORD spake unto Moses, saying,
2 Command the children of Israel, that they bring unto thee pure oil
olive beaten for the light, to cause the lamps to burn continually.
3 Without the veil of the testimony, in the tabernacle of the congregation,
shall Aaron order it from the evening unto the morning before the LORD con-
tinually: *it shall be* a statute for ever in your generations.
4 He shall order the lamps upon the pure candlestick before the LORD con-
tinually.
5 And thou shalt take fine flour, and bake twelve cakes thereof: two tenth
deals shall be in one cake.
6 And thou shalt set them in two rows, six on a row, upon the pure table
before the LORD.
7 And thou shalt put pure frankincense upon *each* row, that it may be on the
bread for a memorial, *even* an offering made by fire unto the LORD.
8 Every sabbath he shall set it in order before the LORD continually, *being*
taken from the children of Israel by an everlasting covenant.
9 And it shall be Aaron's and his sons'; and they shall eat it in the holy place:
for it *is* most holy unto him of the offerings of the LORD made by fire by a
perpetual statute.

Shelomith's Son Blasphemes

10 And the son of an Israelitish woman, whose father *was* an Egyptian, went
out among the children of Israel: and this son of the Israelitish *woman* and a
man of Israel strove together in the camp;

11 And the Israelitish woman's son blasphemed the name *of the LORD*, and cursed. And they brought him unto Moses: (and his mother's name *was* Shelomith, the daughter of Dibri, of the tribe of Dan:)

12 And they put him in ward, that the mind of the LORD might be shewed them.

13 And the LORD spake unto Moses, saying,

14 Bring forth him that hath cursed without the camp; and let all that heard *him* lay their hands upon his head, and let all the congregation stone him.

15 And thou shalt speak unto the children of Israel, saying, Whosoever curseth his God shall bear his sin.

16 And he that blasphemeth the name of the LORD, he shall surely be put to death, *and* all the congregation shall certainly stone him: as well the stranger, as he that is born in the land, when he blasphemeth the name *of the LORD*, shall be put to death.

17 And he that killeth any man shall surely be put to death.

18 And he that killeth a beast shall make it good; beast for beast.

19 And if a man cause a blemish in his neighbour; as he hath done, so shall it be done to him;

20 Breach for breach, eye for eye, tooth for tooth: as he hath caused a blemish in a man, so shall it be done to him *again*.

21 And he that killeth a beast, he shall restore it: and he that killeth a man, he shall be put to death.

22 Ye shall have one manner of law, as well for the stranger, as for one of your own country: for I *am* the LORD your God.

23 And Moses spake to the children of Israel, that they should bring forth him that had cursed out of the camp, and stone him with stones. And the children of Israel did as the LORD commanded Moses.

The Sabbath of the Seventh Year and the Jubilee in the Fiftieth Year

25 And the LORD spake unto Moses in mount Sinai, saying,
2 Speak unto the children of Israel, and say unto them, When ye come into the land which I give you, then shall the land keep a sabbath unto the LORD.

3 Six years thou shalt sow thy field, and six years thou shalt prune thy vineyard, and gather in the fruit thereof;

4 But in the seventh year shall be a sabbath of rest unto the land, a sabbath for the LORD: thou shalt neither sow thy field, nor prune thy vineyard.

5 That which groweth of its own accord of thy harvest thou shalt not reap, neither gather the grapes of thy vine undressed: *for* it is a year of rest unto the land.

6 And the sabbath of the land shall be meat for you; for thee, and for thy servant, and for thy maid, and for thy hired servant, and for thy stranger that sojourneth with thee,

7 And for thy cattle, and for the beast that *are* in thy land, shall all the increase thereof be meat.

8 And thou shalt number seven sabbaths of years unto thee, seven times seven years; and the space of the seven sabbaths of years shall be unto thee forty and nine years.

9 Then shalt thou cause the trumpet of the jubile to sound on the tenth *day* of the seventh month, in the day of atonement shall ye make the trumpet sound throughout all your land.

10 And ye shall hallow the fiftieth year, and proclaim liberty throughout *all* the land unto all the inhabitants thereof: it shall be a jubile unto you; and ye shall return every man unto his possession, and ye shall return every man unto his family.

11 A jubile shall that fiftieth year be unto you: ye shall not sow, neither reap that which groweth of itself in it, nor gather *the grapes* in it of thy vine undressed.

12 For it *is* the jubile; it shall be holy unto you: ye shall eat the increase thereof out of the field.

13 In the year of this jubile ye shall return every man unto his possession.

14 And if thou sell ought unto thy neighbour, or buyest *ought* of thy neighbour's hand, ye shall not oppress one another:

15 According to the number of years after the jubile thou shalt buy of thy neighbour, *and* according unto the number of years of the fruits he shall sell unto thee:

16 According to the multitude of years thou shalt increase the price thereof, and according to the fewness of years thou shalt diminish the price of it: for *according* to the number *of the years* of the fruits doth he sell unto thee.

17 Ye shall not therefore oppress one another; but thou shalt fear thy God: for I *am* the LORD your God.

18 Wherefore ye shall do my statutes, and keep my judgments, and do them; and ye shall dwell in the land in safety.

19 And the land shall yield her fruit, and ye shall eat your fill, and dwell therein in safety.

20 And if ye shall say, What shall we eat the seventh year? behold, we shall not sow, nor gather in our increase:

21 Then I will command my blessing upon you in the sixth year, and it shall bring forth fruit for three years.

22 And ye shall sow the eighth year, and eat *yet* of old fruit until the ninth year; until her fruits come in ye shall eat *of* the old *store*.

The Redemption of Land

23 The land shall not be sold for ever: for the land *is* mine; for ye *are* strangers and sojourners with me.

24 And in all the land of your possession ye shall grant a redemption for the land.

25 If thy brother be waxen poor, and hath sold away *some* of his possession, and if any of his kin come to redeem it, then shall he redeem that which his brother sold.

26 And if the man have none to redeem it, and himself be able to redeem it;

27 Then let him count the years of the sale thereof, and restore the overplus unto the man to whom he sold it; that he may return unto his possession.

28 But if he be not able to restore *it* to him, then that which is sold shall remain in the hand of him that hath bought it until the year of jubile: and in the jubile it shall go out, and he shall return unto his possession.

29 And if a man sell a dwelling house in a walled city, then he may redeem it within a whole year after it is sold; *within* a full year may he redeem it.

30 And if it be not redeemed within the space of a full year, then the house that *is* in the walled city shall be established for ever to him that bought it throughout his generations: it shall not go out in the jubile.

31 But the houses of the villages which have no wall round about them shall be counted as the fields of the country: they may be redeemed, and they shall go out in the jubile.

32 Notwithstanding the cities of the Levites, *and* the houses of the cities of their possession, may the Levites redeem at any time.

33 And if a man purchase of the Levites, then the house that was sold, and the city of his possession, shall go out in *the year of* jubile: for the houses of the cities of the Levites *are* their possession among the children of Israel.

34 But the field of the suburbs of their cities may not be sold; for it *is* their perpetual possession.

35 And if thy brother be waxen poor, and fallen in decay with thee; then thou
shalt relieve him: *yea, though he be* a stranger, or a sojourner; that he may live
with thee.
36 Take thou no usury of him, or increase: but fear thy God; that thy brother
may live with thee.
37 Thou shalt not give him thy money upon usury, nor lend him thy victuals
for increase.
38 I *am* the LORD your God, which brought you forth out of the land of Egypt,
to give you the land of Canaan, *and* to be your God.

The Usage of Bondmen

39 And if thy brother *that dwelleth* by thee be waxen poor, and be sold unto
thee; thou shalt not compel him to serve as a bondservant:
40 *But* as an hired servant, *and* as a sojourner, he shall be with thee, *and* shall
serve thee unto the year of jubile:
41 And *then* shall he depart from thee, *both* he and his children with him,
and shall return unto his own family, and unto the possession of his fathers
shall he return.
42 For they *are* my servants, which I brought forth out of the land of Egypt:
they shall not be sold as bondmen.
43 Thou shalt not rule over him with rigour; but shalt fear thy God.
44 Both thy bondmen, and thy bondmaids, which thou shalt have, *shall be*
of the heathen that are round about you; of them shall ye buy bondmen and
bondmaids.
45 Moreover of the children of the strangers that do sojourn among you, of
them shall ye buy, and of their families that *are* with you, which they begat in
your land: and they shall be your possession.
46 And ye shall take them as an inheritance for your children after you, to
inherit *them for* a possession; they shall be your bondmen for ever: but over
your brethren the children of Israel, ye shall not rule one over another with
rigour.
47 And if a sojourner or stranger wax rich by thee, and thy brother *that*
dwelleth by him wax poor, and sell himself unto the stranger *or* sojourner by
thee, or to the stock of the stranger's family:
48 After that he is sold he may be redeemed again; one of his brethren may
redeem him:
49 Either his uncle, or his uncle's son, may redeem him, or *any* that is nigh
of kin unto him of his family may redeem him; or if he be able, he may redeem
himself.
50 And he shall reckon with him that bought him from the year that he was
sold to him unto the year of jubile: and the price of his sale shall be according
unto the number of years, according to the time of an hired servant shall it
be with him.
51 If *there be* yet many years *behind*, according unto them he shall give again
the price of his redemption out of the money that he was bought for.
52 And if there remain but few years unto the year of jubile, then he shall
count with him, *and* according unto his years shall he give him again the price
of his redemption.
53 *And* as a yearly hired servant shall he be with him: *and the other* shall not
rule with rigour over him in thy sight.
54 And if he be not redeemed in these *years*, then he shall go out in the year
of jubile, *both* he, and his children with him.
55 For unto me the children of Israel *are* servants; they *are* my servants whom
I brought forth out of the land of Egypt: I *am* the LORD your God.

Blessings for Obedience

26 Ye shall make you no idols nor graven image, neither rear you up
a standing image, neither shall ye set up *any* image of stone in your
land, to bow down unto it: for I *am* the LORD your God.
2 Ye shall keep my sabbaths, and reverence my sanctuary: I *am* the LORD.
3 If ye walk in my statutes, and keep my commandments, and do them;
4 Then I will give you rain in due season, and the land shall yield her increase,
and the trees of the field shall yield their fruit.
5 And your threshing shall reach unto the vintage, and the vintage shall reach
unto the sowing time: and ye shall eat your bread to the full, and dwell in your
land safely.
6 And I will give peace in the land, and ye shall lie down, and none shall make
you afraid: and I will rid evil beasts out of the land, neither shall the sword go
through your land.
7 And ye shall chase your enemies, and they shall fall before you by the sword.
8 And five of you shall chase an hundred, and an hundred of you shall put
ten thousand to flight: and your enemies shall fall before you by the sword.
9 For I will have respect unto you, and make you fruitful, and multiply you,
and establish my covenant with you.
10 And ye shall eat old store, and bring forth the old because of the new.
11 And I will set my tabernacle among you: and my soul shall not abhor you.
12 And I will walk among you, and will be your God, and ye shall be my
people.
13 I *am* the LORD your God, which brought you forth out of the land of Egypt,
that ye should not be their bondmen; and I have broken the bands of your
yoke, and made you go upright.

Curses for Disobedience

14 But if ye will not hearken unto me, and will not do all these command-
ments;
15 And if ye shall despise my statutes, or if your soul abhor my judgments,
so that ye will not do all my commandments, *but* that ye break my covenant:
16 I also will do this unto you; I will even appoint over you terror, consump-
tion, and the burning ague, that shall consume the eyes, and cause sorrow of
heart: and ye shall sow your seed in vain, for your enemies shall eat it.
17 And I will set my face against you, and ye shall be slain before your enemies:
they that hate you shall reign over you; and ye shall flee when none pursueth
you.
18 And if ye will not yet for all this hearken unto me, then I will punish you
seven times more for your sins.
19 And I will break the pride of your power; and I will make your heaven as
iron, and your earth as brass:
20 And your strength shall be spent in vain: for your land shall not yield her
increase, neither shall the trees of the land yield their fruits.
21 And if ye walk contrary unto me, and will not hearken unto me; I will
bring seven times more plagues upon you according to your sins.
22 I will also send wild beasts among you, which shall rob you of your chil-
dren, and destroy your cattle, and make you few in number; and your *high*
ways shall be desolate.
23 And if ye will not be reformed by me by these things, but will walk contrary
unto me;
24 Then will I also walk contrary unto you, and will punish you yet seven
times for your sins.
25 And I will bring a sword upon you, that shall avenge the quarrel of *my*
covenant: and when ye are gathered together within your cities, I will send
the pestilence among you; and ye shall be delivered into the hand of the enemy.

26 *And* when I have broken the staff of your bread, ten women shall bake
your bread in one oven, and they shall deliver *you* your bread again by weight:
and ye shall eat, and not be satisfied.
27 And if ye will not for all this hearken unto me, but walk contrary unto me;
28 Then I will walk contrary unto you also in fury; and I, even I, will chastise
you seven times for your sins.
29 And ye shall eat the flesh of your sons, and the flesh of your daughters
shall ye eat.
30 And I will destroy your high places, and cut down your images, and cast
your carcases upon the carcases of your idols, and my soul shall abhor you.
31 And I will make your cities waste, and bring your sanctuaries unto deso-
lation, and I will not smell the savour of your sweet odours.
32 And I will bring the land into desolation: and your enemies which dwell
therein shall be astonished at it.
33 And I will scatter you among the heathen, and will draw out a sword after
you: and your land shall be desolate, and your cities waste.
34 Then shall the land enjoy her sabbaths, as long as it lieth desolate, and ye
be in your enemies' land; *even* then shall the land rest, and enjoy her sabbaths.
35 As long as it lieth desolate it shall rest; because it did not rest in your
sabbaths, when ye dwelt upon it.
36 And upon them that are left *alive* of you I will send a faintness into their
hearts in the lands of their enemies; and the sound of a shaken leaf shall chase
them; and they shall flee, as fleeing from a sword; and they shall fall when
none pursueth.
37 And they shall fall one upon another, as it were before a sword, when none
pursueth: and ye shall have no power to stand before your enemies.
38 And ye shall perish among the heathen, and the land of your enemies shall
eat you up.
39 And they that are left of you shall pine away in their iniquity in your
enemies' lands; and also in the iniquities of their fathers shall they pine away
with them.

God Promises to Remember Those Who Repent

40 If they shall confess their iniquity, and the iniquity of their fathers, with
their trespass which they trespassed against me, and that also they have walked
contrary unto me;
41 And *that* I also have walked contrary unto them, and have brought them
into the land of their enemies; if then their uncircumcised hearts be humbled,
and they then accept of the punishment of their iniquity:
42 Then will I remember my covenant with Jacob, and also my covenant with
Isaac, and also my covenant with Abraham will I remember; and I will remem-
ber the land.
43 The land also shall be left of them, and shall enjoy her sabbaths, while she
lieth desolate without them: and they shall accept of the punishment of their
iniquity: because, even because they despised my judgments, and because
their soul abhorred my statutes.
44 And yet for all that, when they be in the land of their enemies, I will not
cast them away, neither will I abhor them, to destroy them utterly, and to break
my covenant with them: for I *am* the LORD their God.
45 But I will for their sakes remember the covenant of their ancestors, whom
I brought forth out of the land of Egypt in the sight of the heathen, that I might
be their God: I *am* the LORD.
46 These *are* the statutes and judgments and laws, which the LORD made
between him and the children of Israel in mount Sinai by the hand of Moses.

Gifts Pledged to the Lord

27 And the LORD spake unto Moses, saying,

2 Speak unto the children of Israel, and say unto them, When a man shall make a singular vow, the persons *shall be* for the LORD by thy estimation.

3 And thy estimation shall be of the male from twenty years old even unto sixty years old, even thy estimation shall be fifty shekels of silver, after the shekel of the sanctuary.

4 And if it *be* a female, then thy estimation shall be thirty shekels.

5 And if *it be* from five years old even unto twenty years old, then thy estimation shall be of the male twenty shekels, and for the female ten shekels.

6 And if *it be* from a month old even unto five years old, then thy estimation shall be of the male five shekels of silver, and for the female thy estimation *shall be* three shekels of silver.

7 And if *it be* from sixty years old and above; if *it be* a male, then thy estimation shall be fifteen shekels, and for the female ten shekels.

8 But if he be poorer than thy estimation, then he shall present himself before the priest, and the priest shall value him; according to his ability that vowed shall the priest value him.

9 And if *it be* a beast, whereof men bring an offering unto the LORD, all that *any man* giveth of such unto the LORD shall be holy.

10 He shall not alter it, nor change it, a good for a bad, or a bad for a good: and if he shall at all change beast for beast, then it and the exchange thereof shall be holy.

11 And if *it be* any unclean beast, of which they do not offer a sacrifice unto the LORD, then he shall present the beast before the priest:

12 And the priest shall value it, whether it be good or bad: as thou valuest it, *who art* the priest, so shall it be.

13 But if he will at all redeem it, then he shall add a fifth *part* thereof unto thy estimation.

Rules for Gifts Pledged to God

14 And when a man shall sanctify his house *to be* holy unto the LORD, then the priest shall estimate it, whether it be good or bad: as the priest shall estimate it, so shall it stand.

15 And if he that sanctified it will redeem his house, then he shall add the fifth *part* of the money of thy estimation unto it, and it shall be his.

16 And if a man shall sanctify unto the LORD *some part* of a field of his possession, then thy estimation shall be according to the seed thereof: an homer of barley seed *shall be valued* at fifty shekels of silver.

17 If he sanctify his field from the year of jubile, according to thy estimation it shall stand.

18 But if he sanctify his field after the jubile, then the priest shall reckon unto him the money according to the years that remain, even unto the year of the jubile, and it shall be abated from thy estimation.

19 And if he that sanctified the field will in any wise redeem it, then he shall add the fifth *part* of the money of thy estimation unto it, and it shall be assured to him.

20 And if he will not redeem the field, or if he have sold the field to another man, it shall not be redeemed any more.

21 But the field, when it goeth out in the jubile, shall be holy unto the LORD, as a field devoted; the possession thereof shall be the priest's.

22 And if *a man* sanctify unto the LORD a field which he hath bought, which *is* not of the fields of his possession;

23 Then the priest shall reckon unto him the worth of thy estimation, *even* unto the year of the jubile: and he shall give thine estimation in that day, *as* a holy thing unto the LORD.

24 In the year of the jubile the field shall return unto him of whom it was
bought, *even* to him to whom the possession of the land *did belong*.
25 And all thy estimations shall be according to the shekel of the sanctuary:
twenty gerahs shall be the shekel.
26 Only the firstling of the beasts, which should be the LORD's firstling, no
man shall sanctify it; whether *it be* ox, or sheep: it *is* the LORD's.
27 And if *it be* of an unclean beast, then he shall redeem *it* according to thine
estimation, and shall add a fifth *part* of it thereto: or if it be not redeemed,
then it shall be sold according to thy estimation.
28 Notwithstanding no devoted thing, that a man shall devote unto the LORD
of all that he hath, *both* of man and beast, and of the field of his possession,
shall be sold or redeemed: every devoted thing *is* most holy unto the LORD.
29 None devoted, which shall be devoted of men, shall be redeemed; *but* shall
surely be put to death.
30 And all the tithe of the land, *whether* of the seed of the land, *or* of the fruit
of the tree, *is* the LORD's: *it is* holy unto the LORD.
31 And if a man will at all redeem *ought* of his tithes, he shall add thereto the
fifth *part* thereof.
32 And concerning the tithe of the herd, or of the flock, *even* of whatsoever
passeth under the rod, the tenth shall be holy unto the LORD.
33 He shall not search whether it be good or bad, neither shall he change it:
and if he change it at all, then both it and the change thereof shall be holy; it
shall not be redeemed.
34 These *are* the commandments, which the LORD commanded Moses for
the children of Israel in mount Sinai.

NUMBERS

The LORD
Make
HIS
FACE
SHINE
UPON THEE,
AND BE
Gracious
UNTO THEE:
The LORD
LIFT UP HIS
Countenance
UPON THEE,
AND GIVE THEE
PEACE.
NUMBERS 6:25-26

God Commands Moses to Number the People

1 And the LORD spake unto Moses in the wilderness of Sinai, in the tabernacle
of the congregation, on the first *day* of the second month, in the second
year after they were come out of the land of Egypt, saying,
2 Take ye the sum of all the congregation of the children of Israel, after their
families, by the house of their fathers, with the number of *their* names, every
male by their polls;
3 From twenty years old and upward, all that are able to go forth to war in
Israel: thou and Aaron shall number them by their armies.
4 And with you there shall be a man of every tribe; every one head of the
house of his fathers.
5 And these *are* the names of the men that shall stand with you: of *the tribe
of* Reuben; Elizur the son of Shedeur.
6 Of Simeon; Shelumiel the son of Zurishaddai.
7 Of Judah; Nahshon the son of Amminadab.
8 Of Issachar; Nethaneel the son of Zuar.
9 Of Zebulun; Eliab the son of Helon.
10 Of the children of Joseph: of Ephraim; Elishama the son of Ammihud: of
Manasseh; Gamaliel the son of Pedahzur.
11 Of Benjamin; Abidan the son of Gideoni.
12 Of Dan; Ahiezer the son of Ammishaddai.
13 Of Asher; Pagiel the son of Ocran.
14 Of Gad; Eliasaph the son of Deuel.
15 Of Naphtali; Ahira the son of Enan.
16 These *were* the renowned of the congregation, princes of the tribes of
their fathers, heads of thousands in Israel.
17 And Moses and Aaron took these men which are expressed by *their* names:
18 And they assembled all the congregation together on the first *day* of the
second month, and they declared their pedigrees after their families, by the
house of their fathers, according to the number of the names, from twenty
years old and upward, by their polls.
19 As the LORD commanded Moses, so he numbered them in the wilderness
of Sinai.
20 And the children of Reuben, Israel's eldest son, by their generations, after
their families, by the house of their fathers, according to the number of the
names, by their polls, every male from twenty years old and upward, all that
were able to go forth to war;
21 Those that were numbered of them, *even* of the tribe of Reuben, *were* forty
and six thousand and five hundred.
22 Of the children of Simeon, by their generations, after their families, by
the house of their fathers, those that were numbered of them, according to
the number of the names, by their polls, every male from twenty years old and
upward, all that were able to go forth to war;
23 Those that were numbered of them, *even* of the tribe of Simeon, *were* fifty
and nine thousand and three hundred.
24 Of the children of Gad, by their generations, after their families, by the
house of their fathers, according to the number of the names, from twenty
years old and upward, all that were able to go forth to war;

25 Those that were numbered of them, *even* of the tribe of Gad, *were* forty
and five thousand six hundred and fifty.
26 Of the children of Judah, by their generations, after their families, by the
house of their fathers, according to the number of the names, from twenty
years old and upward, all that were able to go forth to war;
27 Those that were numbered of them, *even* of the tribe of Judah, *were* three-
score and fourteen thousand and six hundred.
28 Of the children of Issachar, by their generations, after their families, by
the house of their fathers, according to the number of the names, from twen-
ty years old and upward, all that were able to go forth to war;
29 Those that were numbered of them, *even* of the tribe of Issachar, *were* fifty
and four thousand and four hundred.
30 Of the children of Zebulun, by their generations, after their families, by
the house of their fathers, according to the number of the names, from twen-
ty years old and upward, all that were able to go forth to war;
31 Those that were numbered of them, *even* of the tribe of Zebulun, *were*
fifty and seven thousand and four hundred.
32 Of the children of Joseph, *namely*, of the children of Ephraim, by their
generations, after their families, by the house of their fathers, according to
the number of the names, from twenty years old and upward, all that were
able to go forth to war;
33 Those that were numbered of them, *even* of the tribe of Ephraim, *were*
forty thousand and five hundred.
34 Of the children of Manasseh, by their generations, after their families, by
the house of their fathers, according to the number of the names, from twen-
ty years old and upward, all that were able to go forth to war;
35 Those that were numbered of them, *even* of the tribe of Manasseh, *were*
thirty and two thousand and two hundred.
36 Of the children of Benjamin, by their generations, after their families, by
the house of their fathers, according to the number of the names, from twen-
ty years old and upward, all that were able to go forth to war;
37 Those that were numbered of them, *even* of the tribe of Benjamin, *were*
thirty and five thousand and four hundred.
38 Of the children of Dan, by their generations, after their families, by the
house of their fathers, according to the number of the names, from twenty
years old and upward, all that were able to go forth to war;
39 Those that were numbered of them, *even* of the tribe of Dan, *were* three-
score and two thousand and seven hundred.
40 Of the children of Asher, by their generations, after their families, by the
house of their fathers, according to the number of the names, from twenty
years old and upward, all that were able to go forth to war;
41 Those that were numbered of them, *even* of the tribe of Asher, *were* forty
and one thousand and five hundred.
42 Of the children of Naphtali, throughout their generations, after their
families, by the house of their fathers, according to the number of the names,
from twenty years old and upward, all that were able to go forth to war;
43 Those that were numbered of them, *even* of the tribe of Naphtali, *were*
fifty and three thousand and four hundred.
44 These *are* those that were numbered, which Moses and Aaron numbered,
and the princes of Israel, *being* twelve men: each one was for the house of his
fathers.
45 So were all those that were numbered of the children of Israel, by the
house of their fathers, from twenty years old and upward, all that were able
to go forth to war in Israel;
46 Even all they that were numbered were six hundred thousand and three
thousand and five hundred and fifty.

The Levites Are Exempted for the Service of the Lord

47 But the Levites after the tribe of their fathers were not numbered among them.

48 For the LORD had spoken unto Moses, saying,

49 Only thou shalt not number the tribe of Levi, neither take the sum of them among the children of Israel:

50 But thou shalt appoint the Levites over the tabernacle of testimony, and over all the vessels thereof, and over all things that *belong* to it: they shall bear the tabernacle, and all the vessels thereof; and they shall minister unto it, and shall encamp round about the tabernacle.

51 And when the tabernacle setteth forward, the Levites shall take it down: and when the tabernacle is to be pitched, the Levites shall set it up: and the stranger that cometh nigh shall be put to death.

52 And the children of Israel shall pitch their tents, every man by his own camp, and every man by his own standard, throughout their hosts.

53 But the Levites shall pitch round about the tabernacle of testimony, that there be no wrath upon the congregation of the children of Israel: and the Levites shall keep the charge of the tabernacle of testimony.

54 And the children of Israel did according to all that the LORD commanded Moses, so did they.

The Order of the Tribes in Their Tents

2 And the LORD spake unto Moses and unto Aaron, saying,

2 Every man of the children of Israel shall pitch by his own standard, with the ensign of their father's house: far off about the tabernacle of the congregation shall they pitch.

3 And on the east side toward the rising of the sun shall they of the standard of the camp of Judah pitch throughout their armies: and Nahshon the son of Amminadab *shall be* captain of the children of Judah.

4 And his host, and those that were numbered of them, *were* threescore and fourteen thousand and six hundred.

5 And those that do pitch next unto him *shall be* the tribe of Issachar: and Nethaneel the son of Zuar *shall be* captain of the children of Issachar.

6 And his host, and those that were numbered thereof, *were* fifty and four thousand and four hundred.

7 *Then* the tribe of Zebulun: and Eliab the son of Helon *shall be* captain of the children of Zebulun.

8 And his host, and those that were numbered thereof, *were* fifty and seven thousand and four hundred.

9 All that were numbered in the camp of Judah *were* an hundred thousand and fourscore thousand and six thousand and four hundred, throughout their armies. These shall first set forth.

10 On the south side *shall be* the standard of the camp of Reuben according to their armies: and the captain of the children of Reuben *shall be* Elizur the son of Shedeur.

11 And his host, and those that were numbered thereof, *were* forty and six thousand and five hundred.

12 And those which pitch by him *shall be* the tribe of Simeon: and the captain of the children of Simeon *shall be* Shelumiel the son of Zurishaddai.

13 And his host, and those that were numbered of them, *were* fifty and nine thousand and three hundred.

14 Then the tribe of Gad: and the captain of the sons of Gad *shall be* Eliasaph the son of Reuel.

15 And his host, and those that were numbered of them, *were* forty and five thousand and six hundred and fifty.

16 All that were numbered in the camp of Reuben *were* an hundred thousand
and fifty and one thousand and four hundred and fifty, throughout their
armies. And they shall set forth in the second rank.
17 Then the tabernacle of the congregation shall set forward with the camp
of the Levites in the midst of the camp: as they encamp, so shall they set for-
ward, every man in his place by their standards.
18 On the west side *shall be* the standard of the camp of Ephraim according
to their armies: and the captain of the sons of Ephraim *shall be* Elishama the
son of Ammihud.
19 And his host, and those that were numbered of them, *were* forty thousand
and five hundred.
20 And by him *shall be* the tribe of Manasseh: and the captain of the children
of Manasseh *shall be* Gamaliel the son of Pedahzur.
21 And his host, and those that were numbered of them, *were* thirty and two
thousand and two hundred.
22 Then the tribe of Benjamin: and the captain of the sons of Benjamin *shall
be* Abidan the son of Gideoni.
23 And his host, and those that were numbered of them, *were* thirty and five
thousand and four hundred.
24 All that were numbered of the camp of Ephraim *were* an hundred thou-
sand and eight thousand and an hundred, throughout their armies. And they
shall go forward in the third rank.
25 The standard of the camp of Dan *shall be* on the north side by their armies:
and the captain of the children of Dan *shall be* Ahiezer the son of Ammishaddai.
26 And his host, and those that were numbered of them, *were* threescore and
two thousand and seven hundred.
27 And those that encamp by him *shall be* the tribe of Asher: and the captain
of the children of Asher *shall be* Pagiel the son of Ocran.
28 And his host, and those that were numbered of them, *were* forty and one
thousand and five hundred.
29 Then the tribe of Naphtali: and the captain of the children of Naphtali
shall be Ahira the son of Enan.
30 And his host, and those that were numbered of them, *were* fifty and three
thousand and four hundred.
31 All they that were numbered in the camp of Dan *were* an hundred thou-
sand and fifty and seven thousand and six hundred. They shall go hindmost
with their standards.
32 These *are* those which were numbered of the children of Israel by the
house of their fathers: all those that were numbered of the camps throughout
their hosts *were* six hundred thousand and three thousand and five hundred
and fifty.
33 But the Levites were not numbered among the children of Israel; as the
LORD commanded Moses.
34 And the children of Israel did according to all that the LORD commanded
Moses: so they pitched by their standards, and so they set forward, every one
after their families, according to the house of their fathers.

The Sons of Aaron

3 These also *are* the generations of Aaron and Moses in the day *that* the LORD
spake with Moses in mount Sinai.
2 And these *are* the names of the sons of Aaron; Nadab the firstborn, and
Abihu, Eleazar, and Ithamar.
3 These *are* the names of the sons of Aaron, the priests which were anointed,
whom he consecrated to minister in the priest's office.
4 And Nadab and Abihu died before the LORD, when they offered strange fire
before the LORD, in the wilderness of Sinai, and they had no children: and

Eleazar and Ithamar ministered in the priest's office in the sight of Aaron
their father.
5 And the LORD spake unto Moses, saying,
6 Bring the tribe of Levi near, and present them before Aaron the priest, that
they may minister unto him.
7 And they shall keep his charge, and the charge of the whole congregation
before the tabernacle of the congregation, to do the service of the tabernacle.
8 And they shall keep all the instruments of the tabernacle of the congre-
gation, and the charge of the children of Israel, to do the service of the tab-
ernacle.
9 And thou shalt give the Levites unto Aaron and to his sons: they *are* whol-
ly given unto him out of the children of Israel.
10 And thou shalt appoint Aaron and his sons, and they shall wait on their
priest's office: and the stranger that cometh nigh shall be put to death.
11 And the LORD spake unto Moses, saying,
12 And I, behold, I have taken the Levites from among the children of Israel
instead of all the firstborn that openeth the matrix among the children of
Israel: therefore the Levites shall be mine;
13 Because all the firstborn *are* mine; *for* on the day that I smote all the
firstborn in the land of Egypt I hallowed unto me all the firstborn in Israel,
both man and beast: mine shall they be: I *am* the LORD.

The Levites Are Numbered by Their Families

14 And the LORD spake unto Moses in the wilderness of Sinai, saying,
15 Number the children of Levi after the house of their fathers, by their
families: every male from a month old and upward shalt thou number them.
16 And Moses numbered them according to the word of the LORD, as he was
commanded.
17 And these were the sons of Levi by their names; Gershon, and Kohath, and
Merari.
18 And these *are* the names of the sons of Gershon by their families; Libni,
and Shimei.
19 And the sons of Kohath by their families; Amram, and Izehar, Hebron,
and Uzziel.
20 And the sons of Merari by their families; Mahli, and Mushi. These *are* the
families of the Levites according to the house of their fathers.
21 Of Gershon *was* the family of the Libnites, and the family of the Shimites:
these *are* the families of the Gershonites.
22 Those that were numbered of them, according to the number of all the
males, from a month old and upward, *even* those that were numbered of them
were seven thousand and five hundred.
23 The families of the Gershonites shall pitch behind the tabernacle west-
ward.
24 And the chief of the house of the father of the Gershonites *shall be* Eliasaph
the son of Lael.
25 And the charge of the sons of Gershon in the tabernacle of the congrega-
tion *shall be* the tabernacle, and the tent, the covering thereof, and the hang-
ing for the door of the tabernacle of the congregation,
26 And the hangings of the court, and the curtain for the door of the court,
which *is* by the tabernacle, and by the altar round about, and the cords of it
for all the service thereof.
27 And of Kohath *was* the family of the Amramites, and the family of the
Izeharites, and the family of the Hebronites, and the family of the Uzzielites:
these *are* the families of the Kohathites.
28 In the number of all the males, from a month old and upward, *were* eight
thousand and six hundred, keeping the charge of the sanctuary.

29 The families of the sons of Kohath shall pitch on the side of the tabernacle
southward.
30 And the chief of the house of the father of the families of the Kohathites
shall be Elizaphan the son of Uzziel.
31 And their charge *shall be* the ark, and the table, and the candlestick, and
the altars, and the vessels of the sanctuary wherewith they minister, and the
hanging, and all the service thereof.
32 And Eleazar the son of Aaron the priest *shall be* chief over the chief of the
Levites, *and have* the oversight of them that keep the charge of the sanctuary.
33 Of Merari *was* the family of the Mahlites, and the family of the Mushites:
these *are* the families of Merari.
34 And those that were numbered of them, according to the number of all
the males, from a month old and upward, *were* six thousand and two hundred.
35 And the chief of the house of the father of the families of Merari *was* Zuriel
the son of Abihail: *these* shall pitch on the side of the tabernacle northward.
36 And *under* the custody and charge of the sons of Merari *shall be* the boards
of the tabernacle, and the bars thereof, and the pillars thereof, and the sockets
thereof, and all the vessels thereof, and all that serveth thereto,
37 And the pillars of the court round about, and their sockets, and their pins,
and their cords.
38 But those that encamp before the tabernacle toward the east, *even* before
the tabernacle of the congregation eastward, *shall be* Moses, and Aaron and
his sons, keeping the charge of the sanctuary for the charge of the children of
Israel; and the stranger that cometh nigh shall be put to death.
39 All that were numbered of the Levites, which Moses and Aaron numbered
at the commandment of the LORD, throughout their families, all the males
from a month old and upward, *were* twenty and two thousand.

The Firstborn Are Freed by the Levites

40 And the LORD said unto Moses, Number all the firstborn of the males of
the children of Israel from a month old and upward, and take the number of
their names.
41 And thou shalt take the Levites for me (I *am* the LORD) instead of all the
firstborn among the children of Israel; and the cattle of the Levites instead of
all the firstlings among the cattle of the children of Israel.
42 And Moses numbered, as the LORD commanded him, all the firstborn
among the children of Israel.
43 And all the firstborn males by the number of names, from a month old
and upward, of those that were numbered of them, were twenty and two
thousand two hundred and threescore and thirteen.
44 And the LORD spake unto Moses, saying,
45 Take the Levites instead of all the firstborn among the children of Israel,
and the cattle of the Levites instead of their cattle; and the Levites shall be
mine: I *am* the LORD.
46 And for those that are to be redeemed of the two hundred and threescore
and thirteen of the firstborn of the children of Israel, which are more than
the Levites;
47 Thou shalt even take five shekels apiece by the poll, after the shekel of the
sanctuary shalt thou take *them*: (the shekel *is* twenty gerahs:)
48 And thou shalt give the money, wherewith the odd number of them is to
be redeemed, unto Aaron and to his sons.
49 And Moses took the redemption money of them that were over and above
them that were redeemed by the Levites:
50 Of the firstborn of the children of Israel took he the money; a thousand
three hundred and threescore and five *shekels*, after the shekel of the sanctuary:

51 And Moses gave the money of them that were redeemed unto Aaron and
to his sons, according to the word of the LORD, as the LORD commanded Moses.

The Age and Time of the Levites' Service

4 And the LORD spake unto Moses and unto Aaron, saying,
2 Take the sum of the sons of Kohath from among the sons of Levi, after
their families, by the house of their fathers,
3 From thirty years old and upward even until fifty years old, all that enter
into the host, to do the work in the tabernacle of the congregation.
4 This *shall be* the service of the sons of Kohath in the tabernacle of the
congregation, *about* the most holy things:
5 And when the camp setteth forward, Aaron shall come, and his sons, and
they shall take down the covering veil, and cover the ark of testimony with it:
6 And shall put thereon the covering of badgers' skins, and shall spread over
it a cloth wholly of blue, and shall put in the staves thereof.
7 And upon the table of shewbread they shall spread a cloth of blue, and put
thereon the dishes, and the spoons, and the bowls, and covers to cover withal:
and the continual bread shall be thereon:
8 And they shall spread upon them a cloth of scarlet, and cover the same
with a covering of badgers' skins, and shall put in the staves thereof.
9 And they shall take a cloth of blue, and cover the candlestick of the light,
and his lamps, and his tongs, and his snuffdishes, and all the oil vessels there-
of, wherewith they minister unto it:
10 And they shall put it and all the vessels thereof within a covering of bad-
gers' skins, and shall put *it* upon a bar.
11 And upon the golden altar they shall spread a cloth of blue, and cover it
with a covering of badgers' skins, and shall put to the staves thereof:
12 And they shall take all the instruments of ministry, wherewith they min-
ister in the sanctuary, and put *them* in a cloth of blue, and cover them with a
covering of badgers' skins, and shall put *them* on a bar:
13 And they shall take away the ashes from the altar, and spread a purple
cloth thereon:
14 And they shall put upon it all the vessels thereof, wherewith they minister
about it, *even* the censers, the fleshhooks, and the shovels, and the basons, all
the vessels of the altar; and they shall spread upon it a covering of badgers'
skins, and put to the staves of it.
15 And when Aaron and his sons have made an end of covering the sanctuary,
and all the vessels of the sanctuary, as the camp is to set forward; after that,
the sons of Kohath shall come to bear *it*: but they shall not touch *any* holy
thing, lest they die. These *things are* the burden of the sons of Kohath in the
tabernacle of the congregation.
16 And to the office of Eleazar the son of Aaron the priest *pertaineth* the oil
for the light, and the sweet incense, and the daily meat offering, and the
anointing oil, *and* the oversight of all the tabernacle, and of all that therein
is, in the sanctuary, and in the vessels thereof.
17 And the LORD spake unto Moses and unto Aaron, saying,
18 Cut ye not off the tribe of the families of the Kohathites from among the
Levites:
19 But thus do unto them, that they may live, and not die, when they approach
unto the most holy things: Aaron and his sons shall go in, and appoint them
every one to his service and to his burden:
20 But they shall not go in to see when the holy things are covered, lest they die.

The Number of the Gershonites

21 And the LORD spake unto Moses, saying,
22 Take also the sum of the sons of Gershon, throughout the houses of their
fathers, by their families;

23 From thirty years old and upward until fifty years old shalt thou number
them; all that enter in to perform the service, to do the work in the tabernacle
of the congregation.
24 This *is* the service of the families of the Gershonites, to serve, and for
burdens:
25 And they shall bear the curtains of the tabernacle, and the tabernacle of
the congregation, his covering, and the covering of the badgers' skins that *is*
above upon it, and the hanging for the door of the tabernacle of the congre-
gation,
26 And the hangings of the court, and the hanging for the door of the gate
of the court, which *is* by the tabernacle and by the altar round about, and their
cords, and all the instruments of their service, and all that is made for them:
so shall they serve.
27 At the appointment of Aaron and his sons shall be all the service of the
sons of the Gershonites, in all their burdens, and in all their service: and ye
shall appoint unto them in charge all their burdens.
28 This *is* the service of the families of the sons of Gershon in the tabernacle
of the congregation: and their charge *shall be* under the hand of Ithamar the
son of Aaron the priest.
29 As for the sons of Merari, thou shalt number them after their families, by
the house of their fathers;
30 From thirty years old and upward even unto fifty years old shalt thou
number them, every one that entereth into the service, to do the work of the
tabernacle of the congregation.
31 And this *is* the charge of their burden, according to all their service in the
tabernacle of the congregation; the boards of the tabernacle, and the bars
thereof, and the pillars thereof, and sockets thereof,
32 And the pillars of the court round about, and their sockets, and their pins,
and their cords, with all their instruments, and with all their service: and by
name ye shall reckon the instruments of the charge of their burden.
33 This *is* the service of the families of the sons of Merari, according to all
their service, in the tabernacle of the congregation, under the hand of Ithamar
the son of Aaron the priest.

The Number of the Kohathites

34 And Moses and Aaron and the chief of the congregation numbered the
sons of the Kohathites after their families, and after the house of their fathers,
35 From thirty years old and upward even unto fifty years old, every one that
entereth into the service, for the work in the tabernacle of the congregation:
36 And those that were numbered of them by their families were two thou-
sand seven hundred and fifty.
37 These *were* they that were numbered of the families of the Kohathites, all
that might do service in the tabernacle of the congregation, which Moses and
Aaron did number according to the commandment of the LORD by the hand
of Moses.
38 And those that were numbered of the sons of Gershon, throughout their
families, and by the house of their fathers,
39 From thirty years old and upward even unto fifty years old, every one that
entereth into the service, for the work in the tabernacle of the congregation,
40 Even those that were numbered of them, throughout their families, by
the house of their fathers, were two thousand and six hundred and thirty.
41 These *are* they that were numbered of the families of the sons of Gershon,
of all that might do service in the tabernacle of the congregation, whom Moses
and Aaron did number according to the commandment of the LORD.
42 And those that were numbered of the families of the sons of Merari,
throughout their families, by the house of their fathers,

43 From thirty years old and upward even unto fifty years old, every one that
entereth into the service, for the work in the tabernacle of the congregation,
44 Even those that were numbered of them after their families, were three
thousand and two hundred.
45 These *be* those that were numbered of the families of the sons of Merari,
whom Moses and Aaron numbered according to the word of the LORD by the
hand of Moses.
46 All those that were numbered of the Levites, whom Moses and Aaron and
the chief of Israel numbered, after their families, and after the house of their
fathers,
47 From thirty years old and upward even unto fifty years old, every one that
came to do the service of the ministry, and the service of the burden in the
tabernacle of the congregation,
48 Even those that were numbered of them, were eight thousand and five
hundred and fourscore.
49 According to the commandment of the LORD they were numbered by the
hand of Moses, every one according to his service, and according to his burden:
thus were they numbered of him, as the LORD commanded Moses.

The Unclean Are Removed out of the Camp

5 And the LORD spake unto Moses, saying,
2 Command the children of Israel, that they put out of the camp every
leper, and every one that hath an issue, and whosoever is defiled by the dead:
3 Both male and female shall ye put out, without the camp shall ye put them;
that they defile not their camps, in the midst whereof I dwell.
4 And the children of Israel did so, and put them out without the camp: as
the LORD spake unto Moses, so did the children of Israel.
5 And the LORD spake unto Moses, saying,
6 Speak unto the children of Israel, When a man or woman shall commit
any sin that men commit, to do a trespass against the LORD, and that person
be guilty;
7 Then they shall confess their sin which they have done: and he shall rec-
ompense his trespass with the principal thereof, and add unto it the fifth *part*
thereof, and give *it* unto *him* against whom he hath trespassed.
8 But if the man have no kinsman to recompense the trespass unto, let the
trespass be recompensed unto the LORD, *even* to the priest; beside the ram of
the atonement, whereby an atonement shall be made for him.
9 And every offering of all the holy things of the children of Israel, which
they bring unto the priest, shall be his.
10 And every man's hallowed things shall be his: whatsoever any man giveth
the priest, it shall be his.

The Trial of Unfaithfulness

11 And the LORD spake unto Moses, saying,
12 Speak unto the children of Israel, and say unto them, If any man's wife go
aside, and commit a trespass against him,
13 And a man lie with her carnally, and it be hid from the eyes of her husband,
and be kept close, and she be defiled, and *there be* no witness against her,
neither she be taken *with the manner*;
14 And the spirit of jealousy come upon him, and he be jealous of his wife,
and she be defiled: or if the spirit of jealousy come upon him, and he be jealous
of his wife, and she be not defiled:
15 Then shall the man bring his wife unto the priest, and he shall bring her
offering for her, the tenth *part* of an ephah of barley meal; he shall pour no
oil upon it, nor put frankincense thereon; for it *is* an offering of jealousy, an
offering of memorial, bringing iniquity to remembrance.
16 And the priest shall bring her near, and set her before the LORD:

17 And the priest shall take holy water in an earthen vessel; and of the dust that is in the floor of the tabernacle the priest shall take, and put *it* into the water:

18 And the priest shall set the woman before the LORD, and uncover the woman's head, and put the offering of memorial in her hands, which *is* the jealousy offering: and the priest shall have in his hand the bitter water that causeth the curse:

19 And the priest shall charge her by an oath, and say unto the woman, If no man have lain with thee, and if thou hast not gone aside to uncleanness *with another* instead of thy husband, be thou free from this bitter water that causeth the curse:

20 But if thou hast gone aside *to another* instead of thy husband, and if thou be defiled, and some man have lain with thee beside thine husband:

21 Then the priest shall charge the woman with an oath of cursing, and the priest shall say unto the woman, The LORD make thee a curse and an oath among thy people, when the LORD doth make thy thigh to rot, and thy belly to swell;

22 And this water that causeth the curse shall go into thy bowels, to make *thy* belly to swell, and *thy* thigh to rot: And the woman shall say, Amen, amen.

23 And the priest shall write these curses in a book, and he shall blot *them* out with the bitter water:

24 And he shall cause the woman to drink the bitter water that causeth the curse: and the water that causeth the curse shall enter into her, *and become* bitter.

25 Then the priest shall take the jealousy offering out of the woman's hand, and shall wave the offering before the LORD, and offer it upon the altar:

26 And the priest shall take an handful of the offering, *even* the memorial thereof, and burn *it* upon the altar, and afterward shall cause the woman to drink the water.

27 And when he hath made her to drink the water, then it shall come to pass, *that*, if she be defiled, and have done trespass against her husband, that the water that causeth the curse shall enter into her, *and become* bitter, and her belly shall swell, and her thigh shall rot: and the woman shall be a curse among her people.

28 And if the woman be not defiled, but be clean; then she shall be free, and shall conceive seed.

29 This *is* the law of jealousies, when a wife goeth aside *to another* instead of her husband, and is defiled;

30 Or when the spirit of jealousy cometh upon him, and he be jealous over his wife, and shall set the woman before the LORD, and the priest shall execute upon her all this law.

31 Then shall the man be guiltless from iniquity, and this woman shall bear her iniquity.

The Law of the Nazarites

6 And the LORD spake unto Moses, saying,

2 Speak unto the children of Israel, and say unto them, When either man or woman shall separate *themselves* to vow a vow of a Nazarite, to separate *themselves* unto the LORD:

3 He shall separate *himself* from wine and strong drink, and shall drink no vinegar of wine, or vinegar of strong drink, neither shall he drink any liquor of grapes, nor eat moist grapes, or dried.

4 All the days of his separation shall he eat nothing that is made of the vine tree, from the kernels even to the husk.

5 All the days of the vow of his separation there shall no razor come upon
his head: until the days be fulfilled, in the which he separateth *himself* unto
the LORD, he shall be holy, *and* shall let the locks of the hair of his head grow.
6 All the days that he separateth *himself* unto the LORD he shall come at no
dead body.
7 He shall not make himself unclean for his father, or for his mother, for his
brother, or for his sister, when they die: because the consecration of his God
is upon his head.
8 All the days of his separation he *is* holy unto the LORD.
9 And if any man die very suddenly by him, and he hath defiled the head of
his consecration; then he shall shave his head in the day of his cleansing, on
the seventh day shall he shave it.
10 And on the eighth day he shall bring two turtles, or two young pigeons,
to the priest, to the door of the tabernacle of the congregation:
11 And the priest shall offer the one for a sin offering, and the other for a
burnt offering, and make an atonement for him, for that he sinned by the
dead, and shall hallow his head that same day.
12 And he shall consecrate unto the LORD the days of his separation, and shall
bring a lamb of the first year for a trespass offering: but the days that were
before shall be lost, because his separation was defiled.
13 And this *is* the law of the Nazarite, when the days of his separation are
fulfilled: he shall be brought unto the door of the tabernacle of the congrega-
tion:
14 And he shall offer his offering unto the LORD, one he lamb of the first year
without blemish for a burnt offering, and one ewe lamb of the first year with-
out blemish for a sin offering, and one ram without blemish for peace offer-
ings,
15 And a basket of unleavened bread, cakes of fine flour mingled with oil,
and wafers of unleavened bread anointed with oil, and their meat offering,
and their drink offerings.
16 And the priest shall bring *them* before the LORD, and shall offer his sin
offering, and his burnt offering:
17 And he shall offer the ram *for* a sacrifice of peace offerings unto the LORD,
with the basket of unleavened bread: the priest shall offer also his meat offer-
ing, and his drink offering.
18 And the Nazarite shall shave the head of his separation *at* the door of the
tabernacle of the congregation, and shall take the hair of the head of his sep-
aration, and put *it* in the fire which *is* under the sacrifice of the peace offerings.
19 And the priest shall take the sodden shoulder of the ram, and one unleav-
ened cake out of the basket, and one unleavened wafer, and shall put *them*
upon the hands of the Nazarite, after *the hair of* his separation is shaven:
20 And the priest shall wave them *for* a wave offering before the LORD: this
is holy for the priest, with the wave breast and heave shoulder: and after that
the Nazarite may drink wine.
21 This *is* the law of the Nazarite who hath vowed, *and of* his offering unto
the LORD for his separation, beside *that* that his hand shall get: according to
the vow which he vowed, so he must do after the law of his separation.

The Form of Blessing the People

22 And the LORD spake unto Moses, saying,
23 Speak unto Aaron and unto his sons, saying, On this wise ye shall bless the
children of Israel, saying unto them,
24 The LORD bless thee, and keep thee:
25 The LORD make his face shine upon thee, and be gracious unto thee:
26 The LORD lift up his countenance upon thee, and give thee peace.

27 And they shall put my name upon the children of Israel; and I will bless
them.

The Princes' Offering at the Dedication of the Tabernacle

7 And it came to pass on the day that Moses had fully set up the tabernacle,
and had anointed it, and sanctified it, and all the instruments thereof, both
the altar and all the vessels thereof, and had anointed them, and sanctified them;
2 That the princes of Israel, heads of the house of their fathers, who *were* the
princes of the tribes, and were over them that were numbered, offered:
3 And they brought their offering before the LORD, six covered wagons, and
twelve oxen; a wagon for two of the princes, and for each one an ox: and they
brought them before the tabernacle.
4 And the LORD spake unto Moses, saying,
5 Take *it* of them, that they may be to do the service of the tabernacle of the
congregation; and thou shalt give them unto the Levites, to every man accord-
ing to his service.
6 And Moses took the wagons and the oxen, and gave them unto the Levites.
7 Two wagons and four oxen he gave unto the sons of Gershon, according to
their service:
8 And four wagons and eight oxen he gave unto the sons of Merari, according
unto their service, under the hand of Ithamar the son of Aaron the priest.
9 But unto the sons of Kohath he gave none: because the service of the sanc-
tuary belonging unto them *was that* they should bear upon their shoulders.

The Princes' Offerings at the Dedication of the Altar

10 And the princes offered for dedicating of the altar in the day that it was
anointed, even the princes offered their offering before the altar.
11 And the LORD said unto Moses, They shall offer their offering, each prince
on his day, for the dedicating of the altar.
12 And he that offered his offering the first day was Nahshon the son of
Amminadab, of the tribe of Judah:
13 And his offering *was* one silver charger, the weight thereof *was* an hundred
and thirty *shekels*, one silver bowl of seventy shekels, after the shekel of the
sanctuary; both of them *were* full of fine flour mingled with oil for a meat
offering:
14 One spoon of ten *shekels* of gold, full of incense:
15 One young bullock, one ram, one lamb of the first year, for a burnt offering:
16 One kid of the goats for a sin offering:
17 And for a sacrifice of peace offerings, two oxen, five rams, five he goats,
five lambs of the first year: this *was* the offering of Nahshon the son of
Amminadab.
18 On the second day Nethaneel the son of Zuar, prince of Issachar, did offer:
19 He offered *for* his offering one silver charger, the weight whereof *was* an
hundred and thirty *shekels*, one silver bowl of seventy shekels, after the shek-
el of the sanctuary; both of them full of fine flour mingled with oil for a meat
offering:
20 One spoon of gold of ten *shekels*, full of incense:
21 One young bullock, one ram, one lamb of the first year, for a burnt offering:
22 One kid of the goats for a sin offering:
23 And for a sacrifice of peace offerings, two oxen, five rams, five he goats,
five lambs of the first year: this *was* the offering of Nethaneel the son of Zuar.
24 On the third day Eliab the son of Helon, prince of the children of Zebulun,
did offer:
25 His offering *was* one silver charger, the weight whereof *was* an hundred
and thirty *shekels*, one silver bowl of seventy shekels, after the shekel of the
sanctuary; both of them full of fine flour mingled with oil for a meat offering:
26 One golden spoon of ten *shekels*, full of incense:

27 One young bullock, one ram, one lamb of the first year, for a burnt offering:
28 One kid of the goats for a sin offering:
29 And for a sacrifice of peace offerings, two oxen, five rams, five he goats,
five lambs of the first year: this *was* the offering of Eliab the son of Helon.
30 On the fourth day Elizur the son of Shedeur, prince of the children of
Reuben, *did offer*:
31 His offering *was* one silver charger of the weight of an hundred and thirty
shekels, one silver bowl of seventy shekels, after the shekel of the sanctuary;
both of them full of fine flour mingled with oil for a meat offering:
32 One golden spoon of ten *shekels*, full of incense:
33 One young bullock, one ram, one lamb of the first year, for a burnt offering:
34 One kid of the goats for a sin offering:
35 And for a sacrifice of peace offerings, two oxen, five rams, five he goats,
five lambs of the first year: this *was* the offering of Elizur the son of Shedeur.
36 On the fifth day Shelumiel the son of Zurishaddai, prince of the children
of Simeon, *did offer*:
37 His offering *was* one silver charger, the weight whereof *was* an hundred
and thirty *shekels*, one silver bowl of seventy shekels, after the shekel of the
sanctuary; both of them full of fine flour mingled with oil for a meat offering:
38 One golden spoon of ten *shekels*, full of incense:
39 One young bullock, one ram, one lamb of the first year, for a burnt offering:
40 One kid of the goats for a sin offering:
41 And for a sacrifice of peace offerings, two oxen, five rams, five he goats,
five lambs of the first year: this *was* the offering of Shelumiel the son of
Zurishaddai.
42 On the sixth day Eliasaph the son of Deuel, prince of the children of Gad,
offered:
43 His offering *was* one silver charger of the weight of an hundred and thirty
shekels, a silver bowl of seventy shekels, after the shekel of the sanctuary; both
of them full of fine flour mingled with oil for a meat offering:
44 One golden spoon of ten *shekels*, full of incense:
45 One young bullock, one ram, one lamb of the first year, for a burnt offering:
46 One kid of the goats for a sin offering:
47 And for a sacrifice of peace offerings, two oxen, five rams, five he goats,
five lambs of the first year: this *was* the offering of Eliasaph the son of Deuel.
48 On the seventh day Elishama the son of Ammihud, prince of the children
of Ephraim, *offered*:
49 His offering *was* one silver charger, the weight whereof *was* an hundred
and thirty *shekels*, one silver bowl of seventy shekels, after the shekel of the
sanctuary; both of them full of fine flour mingled with oil for a meat offering:
50 One golden spoon of ten *shekels*, full of incense:
51 One young bullock, one ram, one lamb of the first year, for a burnt offering:
52 One kid of the goats for a sin offering:
53 And for a sacrifice of peace offerings, two oxen, five rams, five he goats,
five lambs of the first year: this *was* the offering of Elishama the son of
Ammihud.
54 On the eighth day *offered* Gamaliel the son of Pedahzur, prince of the
children of Manasseh:
55 His offering *was* one silver charger of the weight of an hundred and thirty
shekels, one silver bowl of seventy shekels, after the shekel of the sanctuary;
both of them full of fine flour mingled with oil for a meat offering:
56 One golden spoon of ten *shekels*, full of incense:
57 One young bullock, one ram, one lamb of the first year, for a burnt offering:
58 One kid of the goats for a sin offering:

59 And for a sacrifice of peace offerings, two oxen, five rams, five he goats,
five lambs of the first year: this *was* the offering of Gamaliel the son of
Pedahzur.
60 On the ninth day Abidan the son of Gideoni, prince of the children of
Benjamin, *offered*:
61 His offering *was* one silver charger, the weight whereof *was* an hundred
and thirty *shekels*, one silver bowl of seventy shekels, after the shekel of the
sanctuary; both of them full of fine flour mingled with oil for a meat offering:
62 One golden spoon of ten *shekels*, full of incense:
63 One young bullock, one ram, one lamb of the first year, for a burnt offering:
64 One kid of the goats for a sin offering:
65 And for a sacrifice of peace offerings, two oxen, five rams, five he goats,
five lambs of the first year: this *was* the offering of Abidan the son of Gideoni.
66 On the tenth day Ahiezer the son of Ammishaddai, prince of the children
of Dan, *offered*:
67 His offering *was* one silver charger, the weight whereof *was* an hundred
and thirty *shekels*, one silver bowl of seventy shekels, after the shekel of the
sanctuary; both of them full of fine flour mingled with oil for a meat offering:
68 One golden spoon of ten *shekels*, full of incense:
69 One young bullock, one ram, one lamb of the first year, for a burnt offering:
70 One kid of the goats for a sin offering:
71 And for a sacrifice of peace offerings, two oxen, five rams, five he goats,
five lambs of the first year: this *was* the offering of Ahiezer the son of
Ammishaddai.
72 On the eleventh day Pagiel the son of Ocran, prince of the children of
Asher, *offered*:
73 His offering *was* one silver charger, the weight whereof *was* an hundred
and thirty *shekels*, one silver bowl of seventy shekels, after the shekel of the
sanctuary; both of them full of fine flour mingled with oil for a meat offering:
74 One golden spoon of ten *shekels*, full of incense:
75 One young bullock, one ram, one lamb of the first year, for a burnt offering:
76 One kid of the goats for a sin offering:
77 And for a sacrifice of peace offerings, two oxen, five rams, five he goats,
five lambs of the first year: this *was* the offering of Pagiel the son of Ocran.
78 On the twelfth day Ahira the son of Enan, prince of the children of
Naphtali, *offered*:
79 His offering *was* one silver charger, the weight whereof *was* an hundred
and thirty *shekels*, one silver bowl of seventy shekels, after the shekel of the
sanctuary; both of them full of fine flour mingled with oil for a meat offering:
80 One golden spoon of ten *shekels*, full of incense:
81 One young bullock, one ram, one lamb of the first year, for a burnt offering:
82 One kid of the goats for a sin offering:
83 And for a sacrifice of peace offerings, two oxen, five rams, five he goats,
five lambs of the first year: this *was* the offering of Ahira the son of Enan.
84 This *was* the dedication of the altar, in the day when it was anointed, by
the princes of Israel: twelve chargers of silver, twelve silver bowls, twelve
spoons of gold:
85 Each charger of silver *weighing* an hundred and thirty *shekels*, each bowl
seventy: all the silver vessels *weighed* two thousand and four hundred *shekels*,
after the shekel of the sanctuary:
86 The golden spoons *were* twelve, full of incense, *weighing* ten *shekels* apiece,
after the shekel of the sanctuary: all the gold of the spoons *was* an hundred
and twenty *shekels*.
87 All the oxen for the burnt offering *were* twelve bullocks, the rams twelve,
the lambs of the first year twelve, with their meat offering: and the kids of the
goats for sin offering twelve.

88 And all the oxen for the sacrifice of the peace offerings *were* twenty and
four bullocks, the rams sixty, the he goats sixty, the lambs of the first year sixty.
This *was* the dedication of the altar, after that it was anointed.
89 And when Moses was gone into the tabernacle of the congregation to
speak with him, then he heard the voice of one speaking unto him from off
the mercy seat that *was* upon the ark of testimony, from between the two
cherubims: and he spake unto him.

How the Seven Lamps Are to Be Lighted

8 And the LORD spake unto Moses, saying,
2 Speak unto Aaron, and say unto him, When thou lightest the lamps, the
seven lamps shall give light over against the candlestick.
3 And Aaron did so; he lighted the lamps thereof over against the candlestick,
as the LORD commanded Moses.
4 And this work of the candlestick *was of* beaten gold, unto the shaft thereof,
unto the flowers thereof, *was* beaten work: according unto the pattern which
the LORD had shewed Moses, so he made the candlestick.

The Consecration of the Levites

5 And the LORD spake unto Moses, saying,
6 Take the Levites from among the children of Israel, and cleanse them.
7 And thus shalt thou do unto them, to cleanse them: Sprinkle water of puri-
fying upon them, and let them shave all their flesh, and let them wash their
clothes, and *so* make themselves clean.
8 Then let them take a young bullock with his meat offering, *even* fine flour
mingled with oil, and another young bullock shalt thou take for a sin offering.
9 And thou shalt bring the Levites before the tabernacle of the congregation:
and thou shalt gather the whole assembly of the children of Israel together:
10 And thou shalt bring the Levites before the LORD: and the children of Israel
shall put their hands upon the Levites:
11 And Aaron shall offer the Levites before the LORD *for* an offering of the
children of Israel, that they may execute the service of the LORD.
12 And the Levites shall lay their hands upon the heads of the bullocks: and
thou shalt offer the one *for* a sin offering, and the other *for* a burnt offering,
unto the LORD, to make an atonement for the Levites.
13 And thou shalt set the Levites before Aaron, and before his sons, and offer
them *for* an offering unto the LORD.
14 Thus shalt thou separate the Levites from among the children of Israel:
and the Levites shall be mine.
15 And after that shall the Levites go in to do the service of the tabernacle of
the congregation: and thou shalt cleanse them, and offer them *for* an offering.
16 For they *are* wholly given unto me from among the children of Israel;
instead of such as open every womb, *even instead of* the firstborn of all the
children of Israel, have I taken them unto me.
17 For all the firstborn of the children of Israel *are* mine, *both* man and beast:
on the day that I smote every firstborn in the land of Egypt I sanctified them
for myself.
18 And I have taken the Levites for all the firstborn of the children of Israel.
19 And I have given the Levites *as* a gift to Aaron and to his sons from among
the children of Israel, to do the service of the children of Israel in the taber-
nacle of the congregation, and to make an atonement for the children of Israel:
that there be no plague among the children of Israel, when the children of
Israel come nigh unto the sanctuary.
20 And Moses, and Aaron, and all the congregation of the children of Israel,
did to the Levites according unto all that the LORD commanded Moses con-
cerning the Levites, so did the children of Israel unto them.

21 And the Levites were purified, and they washed their clothes; and Aaron
offered them *as* an offering before the LORD; and Aaron made an atonement
for them to cleanse them.
22 And after that went the Levites in to do their service in the tabernacle of
the congregation before Aaron, and before his sons: as the LORD had com-
manded Moses concerning the Levites, so did they unto them.
23 And the LORD spake unto Moses, saying,
24 This *is it* that *belongeth* unto the Levites: from twenty and five years old
and upward they shall go in to wait upon the service of the tabernacle of the
congregation:
25 And from the age of fifty years they shall cease waiting upon the service
thereof, and shall serve no more:
26 But shall minister with their brethren in the tabernacle of the congrega-
tion, to keep the charge, and shall do no service. Thus shalt thou do unto the
Levites touching their charge.

The Passover Is Commanded Again

9 And the LORD spake unto Moses in the wilderness of Sinai, in the first month
of the second year after they were come out of the land of Egypt, saying,
2 Let the children of Israel also keep the passover at his appointed season.
3 In the fourteenth day of this month, at even, ye shall keep it in his appoint-
ed season: according to all the rites of it, and according to all the ceremonies
thereof, shall ye keep it.
4 And Moses spake unto the children of Israel, that they should keep the
passover.
5 And they kept the passover on the fourteenth day of the first month at even
in the wilderness of Sinai: according to all that the LORD commanded Moses,
so did the children of Israel.
6 And there were certain men, who were defiled by the dead body of a man,
that they could not keep the passover on that day: and they came before Moses
and before Aaron on that day:
7 And those men said unto him, We *are* defiled by the dead body of a man:
wherefore are we kept back, that we may not offer an offering of the LORD in
his appointed season among the children of Israel?
8 And Moses said unto them, Stand still, and I will hear what the LORD will
command concerning you.
9 And the LORD spake unto Moses, saying,
10 Speak unto the children of Israel, saying, If any man of you or of your
posterity shall be unclean by reason of a dead body, or *be* in a journey afar off,
yet he shall keep the passover unto the LORD.
11 The fourteenth day of the second month at even they shall keep it, *and*
eat it with unleavened bread and bitter *herbs*.
12 They shall leave none of it unto the morning, nor break any bone of it:
according to all the ordinances of the passover they shall keep it.
13 But the man that *is* clean, and is not in a journey, and forbeareth to keep
the passover, even the same soul shall be cut off from among his people:
because he brought not the offering of the LORD in his appointed season, that
man shall bear his sin.
14 And if a stranger shall sojourn among you, and will keep the passover unto
the LORD; according to the ordinance of the passover, and according to the
manner thereof, so shall he do: ye shall have one ordinance, both for the
stranger, and for him that was born in the land.

The Cloud Guides the Movements of the Camp

15 And on the day that the tabernacle was reared up the cloud covered the
tabernacle, *namely*, the tent of the testimony: and at even there was upon the
tabernacle as it were the appearance of fire, until the morning.

16 So it was alway: the cloud covered it *by day*, and the appearance of fire by
night.
17 And when the cloud was taken up from the tabernacle, then after that the
children of Israel journeyed: and in the place where the cloud abode, there
the children of Israel pitched their tents.
18 At the commandment of the LORD the children of Israel journeyed, and
at the commandment of the LORD they pitched: as long as the cloud abode
upon the tabernacle they rested in their tents.
19 And when the cloud tarried long upon the tabernacle many days, then
the children of Israel kept the charge of the LORD, and journeyed not.
20 And *so* it was, when the cloud was a few days upon the tabernacle; accord-
ing to the commandment of the LORD they abode in their tents, and according
to the commandment of the LORD they journeyed.
21 And *so* it was, when the cloud abode from even unto the morning, and
that the cloud was taken up in the morning, then they journeyed: whether *it
was* by day or by night that the cloud was taken up, they journeyed.
22 Or *whether it were* two days, or a month, or a year, that the cloud tarried
upon the tabernacle, remaining thereon, the children of Israel abode in their
tents, and journeyed not: but when it was taken up, they journeyed.
23 At the commandment of the LORD they rested in the tents, and at the
commandment of the LORD they journeyed: they kept the charge of the LORD,
at the commandment of the LORD by the hand of Moses.

The Use of the Silver Trumpets

10 And the LORD spake unto Moses, saying,
2 Make thee two trumpets of silver; of a whole piece shalt thou make
them: that thou mayest use them for the calling of the assembly, and for the
journeying of the camps.
3 And when they shall blow with them, all the assembly shall assemble them-
selves to thee at the door of the tabernacle of the congregation.
4 And if they blow *but* with one *trumpet*, then the princes, *which are* heads
of the thousands of Israel, shall gather themselves unto thee.
5 When ye blow an alarm, then the camps that lie on the east parts shall go
forward.
6 When ye blow an alarm the second time, then the camps that lie on the
south side shall take their journey: they shall blow an alarm for their journeys.
7 But when the congregation is to be gathered together, ye shall blow, but ye
shall not sound an alarm.
8 And the sons of Aaron, the priests, shall blow with the trumpets; and they
shall be to you for an ordinance for ever throughout your generations.
9 And if ye go to war in your land against the enemy that oppresseth you,
then ye shall blow an alarm with the trumpets; and ye shall be remembered
before the LORD your God, and ye shall be saved from your enemies.
10 Also in the day of your gladness, and in your solemn days, and in the
beginnings of your months, ye shall blow with the trumpets over your burnt
offerings, and over the sacrifices of your peace offerings; that they may be to
you for a memorial before your God: I *am* the LORD your God.

The Israelites Travel from Sinai to Paran

11 And it came to pass on the twentieth *day* of the second month, in the
second year, that the cloud was taken up from off the tabernacle of the testi-
mony.
12 And the children of Israel took their journeys out of the wilderness of
Sinai; and the cloud rested in the wilderness of Paran.
13 And they first took their journey according to the commandment of the
LORD by the hand of Moses.

14 In the first *place* went the standard of the camp of the children of Judah
according to their armies: and over his host *was* Nahshon the son of
Amminadab.
15 And over the host of the tribe of the children of Issachar *was* Nethaneel
the son of Zuar.
16 And over the host of the tribe of the children of Zebulun *was* Eliab the
son of Helon.
17 And the tabernacle was taken down; and the sons of Gershon and the sons
of Merari set forward, bearing the tabernacle.
18 And the standard of the camp of Reuben set forward according to their
armies: and over his host *was* Elizur the son of Shedeur.
19 And over the host of the tribe of the children of Simeon *was* Shelumiel
the son of Zurishaddai.
20 And over the host of the tribe of the children of Gad *was* Eliasaph the son
of Deuel.
21 And the Kohathites set forward, bearing the sanctuary: and *the other* did
set up the tabernacle against they came.
22 And the standard of the camp of the children of Ephraim set forward
according to their armies: and over his host *was* Elishama the son of Ammihud.
23 And over the host of the tribe of the children of Manasseh *was* Gamaliel
the son of Pedahzur.
24 And over the host of the tribe of the children of Benjamin *was* Abidan the
son of Gideoni.
25 And the standard of the camp of the children of Dan set forward, *which*
was the rereward of all the camps throughout their hosts: and over his host *was*
Ahiezer the son of Ammishaddai.
26 And over the host of the tribe of the children of Asher *was* Pagiel the son
of Ocran.
27 And over the host of the tribe of the children of Naphtali *was* Ahira the
son of Enan.
28 Thus *were* the journeyings of the children of Israel according to their
armies, when they set forward.

Hobab Is Entreated by Moses Not to Leave Them

29 And Moses said unto Hobab, the son of Raguel the Midianite, Moses' father
in law, We are journeying unto the place of which the LORD said, I will give it
you: come thou with us, and we will do thee good: for the LORD hath spoken
good concerning Israel.
30 And he said unto him, I will not go; but I will depart to mine own land,
and to my kindred.
31 And he said, Leave us not, I pray thee; forasmuch as thou knowest how we
are to encamp in the wilderness, and thou mayest be to us instead of eyes.
32 And it shall be, if thou go with us, yea, it shall be, that what goodness the
LORD shall do unto us, the same will we do unto thee.
33 And they departed from the mount of the LORD three days' journey: and
the ark of the covenant of the LORD went before them in the three days' jour-
ney, to search out a resting place for them.
34 And the cloud of the LORD *was* upon them by day, when they went out of
the camp.
35 And it came to pass, when the ark set forward, that Moses said, Rise up,
LORD, and let thine enemies be scattered; and let them that hate thee flee before
thee.
36 And when it rested, he said, Return, O LORD, unto the many thousands of
Israel.

Moses' Prayer Stops the Burning at Taberah

11 And *when* the people complained, it displeased the LORD: and the LORD
heard *it*; and his anger was kindled; and the fire of the LORD burnt
among them, and consumed *them that were* in the uttermost parts of the
camp.
2 And the people cried unto Moses; and when Moses prayed unto the LORD,
the fire was quenched.
3 And he called the name of the place Taberah: because the fire of the LORD
burnt among them.

The People Lust for Meat and Loathe Manna

4 And the mixt multitude that *was* among them fell a lusting: and the chil-
dren of Israel also wept again, and said, Who shall give us flesh to eat?
5 We remember the fish, which we did eat in Egypt freely; the cucumbers,
and the melons, and the leeks, and the onions, and the garlick:
6 But now our soul *is* dried away: *there is* nothing at all, beside this manna,
before our eyes.
7 And the manna *was* as coriander seed, and the colour thereof as the colour
of bdellium.
8 *And* the people went about, and gathered *it*, and ground *it* in mills, or beat
it in a mortar, and baked *it* in pans, and made cakes of it: and the taste of it
was as the taste of fresh oil.
9 And when the dew fell upon the camp in the night, the manna fell upon it.
10 Then Moses heard the people weep throughout their families, every man
in the door of his tent: and the anger of the LORD was kindled greatly; Moses
also was displeased.
11 And Moses said unto the LORD, Wherefore hast thou afflicted thy servant?
and wherefore have I not found favour in thy sight, that thou layest the burden
of all this people upon me?
12 Have I conceived all this people? have I begotten them, that thou shouldest
say unto me, Carry them in thy bosom, as a nursing father beareth the sucking
child, unto the land which thou swarest unto their fathers?
13 Whence should I have flesh to give unto all this people? for they weep
unto me, saying, Give us flesh, that we may eat.
14 I am not able to bear all this people alone, because *it is* too heavy for me.
15 And if thou deal thus with me, kill me, I pray thee, out of hand, if I have
found favour in thy sight; and let me not see my wretchedness.

God Divides Moses' Burden among Seventy Elders

16 And the LORD said unto Moses, Gather unto me seventy men of the elders
of Israel, whom thou knowest to be the elders of the people, and officers over
them; and bring them unto the tabernacle of the congregation, that they may
stand there with thee.
17 And I will come down and talk with thee there: and I will take of the
spirit which *is* upon thee, and will put *it* upon them; and they shall bear the
burden of the people with thee, that thou bear *it* not thyself alone.
18 And say thou unto the people, Sanctify yourselves against to morrow, and
ye shall eat flesh: for ye have wept in the ears of the LORD, saying, Who shall
give us flesh to eat? for *it was* well with us in Egypt: therefore the LORD will
give you flesh, and ye shall eat.
19 Ye shall not eat one day, nor two days, nor five days, neither ten days, nor
twenty days;
20 *But* even a whole month, until it come out at your nostrils, and it be loath-
some unto you: because that ye have despised the LORD which *is* among you,
and have wept before him, saying, Why came we forth out of Egypt?

21 And Moses said, The people, among whom I *am*, *are* six hundred thousand
footmen; and thou hast said, I will give them flesh, that they may eat a whole
month.
22 Shall the flocks and the herds be slain for them, to suffice them? or shall
all the fish of the sea be gathered together for them, to suffice them?
23 And the LORD said unto Moses, Is the LORD's hand waxed short? thou shalt
see now whether my word shall come to pass unto thee or not.
24 And Moses went out, and told the people the words of the LORD, and gath-
ered the seventy men of the elders of the people, and set them round about
the tabernacle.
25 And the LORD came down in a cloud, and spake unto him, and took of the
spirit that *was* upon him, and gave *it* unto the seventy elders: and it came to
pass, *that*, when the spirit rested upon them, they prophesied, and did not
cease.
26 But there remained two *of the* men in the camp, the name of the one *was*
Eldad, and the name of the other Medad: and the spirit rested upon them; and
they *were* of them that were written, but went not out unto the tabernacle:
and they prophesied in the camp.
27 And there ran a young man, and told Moses, and said, Eldad and Medad
do prophesy in the camp.
28 And Joshua the son of Nun, the servant of Moses, *one* of his young men,
answered and said, My lord Moses, forbid them.
29 And Moses said unto him, Enviest thou for my sake? would God that all
the LORD's people were prophets, *and* that the LORD would put his spirit upon
them!
30 And Moses gat him into the camp, he and the elders of Israel.

God Sends Quail

31 And there went forth a wind from the LORD, and brought quails from the
sea, and let *them* fall by the camp, as it were a day's journey on this side, and
as it were a day's journey on the other side, round about the camp, and as it
were two cubits *high* upon the face of the earth.
32 And the people stood up all that day, and all *that* night, and all the next
day, and they gathered the quails: he that gathered least gathered ten homers:
and they spread *them* all abroad for themselves round about the camp.
33 And while the flesh *was* yet between their teeth, ere it was chewed, the
wrath of the LORD was kindled against the people, and the LORD smote the
people with a very great plague.
34 And he called the name of that place Kibroth-hattaavah: because there
they buried the people that lusted.
35 *And* the people journeyed from Kibroth-hattaavah unto Hazeroth; and
abode at Hazeroth.

God Rebukes Aaron and Miriam

12 And Miriam and Aaron spake against Moses because of the Ethiopian
woman whom he had married: for he had married an Ethiopian
woman.
2 And they said, Hath the LORD indeed spoken only by Moses? hath he not
spoken also by us? And the LORD heard *it*.
3 (Now the man Moses *was* very meek, above all the men which *were* upon
the face of the earth.)
4 And the LORD spake suddenly unto Moses, and unto Aaron, and unto
Miriam, Come out ye three unto the tabernacle of the congregation. And they
three came out.
5 And the LORD came down in the pillar of the cloud, and stood *in* the door
of the tabernacle, and called Aaron and Miriam: and they both came forth.

6 And he said, Hear now my words: If there be a prophet among you, *I* the
LORD will make myself known unto him in a vision, *and* will speak unto him
in a dream.
7 My servant Moses *is* not so, who *is* faithful in all mine house.
8 With him will I speak mouth to mouth, even apparently, and not in dark
speeches; and the similitude of the LORD shall he behold: wherefore then were
ye not afraid to speak against my servant Moses?
9 And the anger of the LORD was kindled against them; and he departed.

God Gives Miriam Leprosy, She Is Sent Outside the Camp

10 And the cloud departed from off the tabernacle; and, behold, Miriam
became leprous, *white* as snow: and Aaron looked upon Miriam, and, behold,
she was leprous.
11 And Aaron said unto Moses, Alas, my lord, I beseech thee, lay not the sin
upon us, wherein we have done foolishly, and wherein we have sinned.
12 Let her not be as one dead, of whom the flesh is half consumed when he
cometh out of his mother's womb.
13 And Moses cried unto the LORD, saying, Heal her now, O God, I beseech
thee.
14 And the LORD said unto Moses, If her father had but spit in her face, should
she not be ashamed seven days? let her be shut out from the camp seven days,
and after that let her be received in *again*.
15 And Miriam was shut out from the camp seven days: and the people jour-
neyed not till Miriam was brought in *again*.
16 And afterward the people removed from Hazeroth, and pitched in the
wilderness of Paran.

Those Sent into Canaan

13 And the LORD spake unto Moses, saying,
2 Send thou men, that they may search the land of Canaan, which I
give unto the children of Israel: of every tribe of their fathers shall ye send a
man, every one a ruler among them.
3 And Moses by the commandment of the LORD sent them from the wilder-
ness of Paran: all those men *were* heads of the children of Israel.
4 And these *were* their names: of the tribe of Reuben, Shammua the son of
Zaccur.
5 Of the tribe of Simeon, Shaphat the son of Hori.
6 Of the tribe of Judah, Caleb the son of Jephunneh.
7 Of the tribe of Issachar, Igal the son of Joseph.
8 Of the tribe of Ephraim, Oshea the son of Nun.
9 Of the tribe of Benjamin, Palti the son of Raphu.
10 Of the tribe of Zebulun, Gaddiel the son of Sodi.
11 Of the tribe of Joseph, *namely*, of the tribe of Manasseh, Gaddi the son of
Susi.
12 Of the tribe of Dan, Ammiel the son of Gemalli.
13 Of the tribe of Asher, Sethur the son of Michael.
14 Of the tribe of Naphtali, Nahbi the son of Vophsi.
15 Of the tribe of Gad, Geuel the son of Machi.
16 These *are* the names of the men which Moses sent to spy out the land. And
Moses called Oshea the son of Nun Jehoshua.
17 And Moses sent them to spy out the land of Canaan, and said unto them,
Get you up this *way* southward, and go up into the mountain:
18 And see the land, what it *is*; and the people that dwelleth therein, wheth-
er they *be* strong or weak, few or many;
19 And what the land *is* that they dwell in, whether it *be* good or bad; and
what cities *they be* that they dwell in, whether in tents, or in strong holds;

20 And what the land *is*, whether it *be* fat or lean, whether there be wood
therein, or not. And be ye of good courage, and bring of the fruit of the land.
Now the time *was* the time of the firstripe grapes.

The Activities of the Spies

21 So they went up, and searched the land from the wilderness of Zin unto
Rehob, as men come to Hamath.
22 And they ascended by the south, and came unto Hebron; where Ahiman,
Sheshai, and Talmai, the children of Anak, *were*. (Now Hebron was built seven
years before Zoan in Egypt.)
23 And they came unto the brook of Eshcol, and cut down from thence a
branch with one cluster of grapes, and they bare it between two upon a staff;
and *they brought* of the pomegranates, and of the figs.
24 The place was called the brook Eshcol, because of the cluster of grapes
which the children of Israel cut down from thence.
25 And they returned from searching of the land after forty days.

The Spies Give an Unfavorable Report

26 And they went and came to Moses, and to Aaron, and to all the congrega-
tion of the children of Israel, unto the wilderness of Paran, to Kadesh; and
brought back word unto them, and unto all the congregation, and shewed
them the fruit of the land.
27 And they told him, and said, We came unto the land whither thou sentest
us, and surely it floweth with milk and honey; and this *is* the fruit of it.
28 Nevertheless the people *be* strong that dwell in the land, and the cities *are*
walled, *and* very great: and moreover we saw the children of Anak there.
29 The Amalekites dwell in the land of the south: and the Hittites, and the
Jebusites, and the Amorites, dwell in the mountains: and the Canaanites dwell
by the sea, and by the coast of Jordan.
30 And Caleb stilled the people before Moses, and said, Let us go up at once,
and possess it; for we are well able to overcome it.
31 But the men that went up with him said, We be not able to go up against
the people; for they *are* stronger than we.
32 And they brought up an evil report of the land which they had searched
unto the children of Israel, saying, The land, through which we have gone to
search it, *is* a land that eateth up the inhabitants thereof; and all the people
that we saw in it *are* men of a great stature.
33 And there we saw the giants, the sons of Anak, *which come* of the giants:
and we were in our own sight as grasshoppers, and so we were in their sight.

The People Murmur at the News

14 And all the congregation lifted up their voice, and cried; and the peo-
ple wept that night.
2 And all the children of Israel murmured against Moses and against Aaron:
and the whole congregation said unto them, Would God that we had died in
the land of Egypt! or would God we had died in this wilderness!
3 And wherefore hath the LORD brought us unto this land, to fall by the sword,
that our wives and our children should be a prey? were it not better for us to
return into Egypt?
4 And they said one to another, Let us make a captain, and let us return into
Egypt.
5 Then Moses and Aaron fell on their faces before all the assembly of the
congregation of the children of Israel.
6 And Joshua the son of Nun, and Caleb the son of Jephunneh, *which were*
of them that searched the land, rent their clothes:
7 And they spake unto all the company of the children of Israel, saying, The
land, which we passed through to search it, *is* an exceeding good land.

8 If the LORD delight in us, then he will bring us into this land, and give it us;
a land which floweth with milk and honey.
9 Only rebel not ye against the LORD, neither fear ye the people of the land;
for they *are* bread for us: their defence is departed from them, and the LORD
is with us: fear them not.
10 But all the congregation bade stone them with stones. And the glory of
the LORD appeared in the tabernacle of the congregation before all the children
of Israel.
11 And the LORD said unto Moses, How long will this people provoke me?
and how long will it be ere they believe me, for all the signs which I have
shewed among them?
12 I will smite them with the pestilence, and disinherit them, and will make
of thee a greater nation and mightier than they.
13 And Moses said unto the LORD, Then the Egyptians shall hear *it*, (for thou
broughtest up this people in thy might from among them;)
14 And they will tell *it* to the inhabitants of this land: *for* they have heard that
thou LORD *art* among this people, that thou LORD art seen face to face, and
that thy cloud standeth over them, and *that* thou goest before them, by day
time in a pillar of a cloud, and in a pillar of fire by night.
15 Now *if* thou shalt kill *all* this people as one man, then the nations which
have heard the fame of thee will speak, saying,
16 Because the LORD was not able to bring this people into the land which
he sware unto them, therefore he hath slain them in the wilderness.
17 And now, I beseech thee, let the power of my Lord be great, according as
thou hast spoken, saying,
18 The LORD *is* longsuffering, and of great mercy, forgiving iniquity and
transgression, and by no means clearing *the guilty*, visiting the iniquity of the
fathers upon the children unto the third and fourth *generation*.
19 Pardon, I beseech thee, the iniquity of this people according unto the
greatness of thy mercy, and as thou hast forgiven this people, from Egypt even
until now.
20 And the LORD said, I have pardoned according to thy word:
21 But *as* truly *as* I live, all the earth shall be filled with the glory of the LORD.
22 Because all those men which have seen my glory, and my miracles, which
I did in Egypt and in the wilderness, and have tempted me now these ten times,
and have not hearkened to my voice;
23 Surely they shall not see the land which I sware unto their fathers, neither
shall any of them that provoked me see it:
24 But my servant Caleb, because he had another spirit with him, and hath
followed me fully, him will I bring into the land whereinto he went; and his
seed shall possess it.
25 (Now the Amalekites and the Canaanites dwelt in the valley.) To morrow
turn you, and get you into the wilderness by the way of the Red sea.
26 And the LORD spake unto Moses and unto Aaron, saying,
27 How long *shall I bear with* this evil congregation, which murmur against
me? I have heard the murmurings of the children of Israel, which they mur-
mur against me.
28 Say unto them, *As truly as* I live, saith the LORD, as ye have spoken in mine
ears, so will I do to you:
29 Your carcases shall fall in this wilderness; and all that were numbered of
you, according to your whole number, from twenty years old and upward,
which have murmured against me,
30 Doubtless ye shall not come into the land, *concerning* which I sware to
make you dwell therein, save Caleb the son of Jephunneh, and Joshua the son
of Nun.

31 But your little ones, which ye said should be a prey, them will I bring in,
and they shall know the land which ye have despised.
32 But *as for* you, your carcases, they shall fall in this wilderness.
33 And your children shall wander in the wilderness forty years, and bear
your whoredoms, until your carcases be wasted in the wilderness.
34 After the number of the days in which ye searched the land, *even* forty
days, each day for a year, shall ye bear your iniquities, *even* forty years, and ye
shall know my breach of promise.
35 I the LORD have said, I will surely do it unto all this evil congregation, that
are gathered together against me: in this wilderness they shall be consumed,
and there they shall die.

The Men Who Brought the Unfavorable Report Die by a Plague

36 And the men, which Moses sent to search the land, who returned, and
made all the congregation to murmur against him, by bringing up a slander
upon the land,
37 Even those men that did bring up the evil report upon the land, died by
the plague before the LORD.
38 But Joshua the son of Nun, and Caleb the son of Jephunneh, *which were*
of the men that went to search the land, lived *still*.
39 And Moses told these sayings unto all the children of Israel: and the peo-
ple mourned greatly.
40 And they rose up early in the morning, and gat them up into the top of
the mountain, saying, Lo, we *be here*, and will go up unto the place which the
LORD hath promised: for we have sinned.
41 And Moses said, Wherefore now do ye transgress the commandment of
the LORD? but it shall not prosper.
42 Go not up, for the LORD *is* not among you; that ye be not smitten before
your enemies.
43 For the Amalekites and the Canaanites *are* there before you, and ye shall
fall by the sword: because ye are turned away from the LORD, therefore the
LORD will not be with you.
44 But they presumed to go up unto the hill top: nevertheless the ark of the
covenant of the LORD, and Moses, departed not out of the camp.
45 Then the Amalekites came down, and the Canaanites which dwelt in that
hill, and smote them, and discomfited them, *even* unto Hormah.

The Law of the Meal Offering and the Drink Offering

15 And the LORD spake unto Moses, saying,
2 Speak unto the children of Israel, and say unto them, When ye be
come into the land of your habitations, which I give unto you,
3 And will make an offering by fire unto the LORD, a burnt offering, or a
sacrifice in performing a vow, or in a freewill offering, or in your solemn feasts,
to make a sweet savour unto the LORD, of the herd, or of the flock:
4 Then shall he that offereth his offering unto the LORD bring a meat offering
of a tenth deal of flour mingled with the fourth *part* of an hin of oil.
5 And the fourth *part* of an hin of wine for a drink offering shalt thou prepare
with the burnt offering or sacrifice, for one lamb.
6 Or for a ram, thou shalt prepare *for* a meat offering two tenth deals of flour
mingled with the third *part* of an hin of oil.
7 And for a drink offering thou shalt offer the third *part* of an hin of wine,
for a sweet savour unto the LORD.
8 And when thou preparest a bullock *for* a burnt offering, or *for* a sacrifice
in performing a vow, or peace offerings unto the LORD:
9 Then shall he bring with a bullock a meat offering of three tenth deals of
flour mingled with half an hin of oil.

10 And thou shalt bring for a drink offering half an hin of wine, *for* an offer-
ing made by fire, of a sweet savour unto the LORD.

11 Thus shall it be done for one bullock, or for one ram, or for a lamb, or a
kid.

12 According to the number that ye shall prepare, so shall ye do to every one
according to their number.

13 All that are born of the country shall do these things after this manner,
in offering an offering made by fire, of a sweet savour unto the LORD.

14 And if a stranger sojourn with you, or whosoever *be* among you in your
generations, and will offer an offering made by fire, of a sweet savour unto
the LORD; as ye do, so he shall do.

15 One ordinance *shall be both* for you of the congregation, and also for the
stranger that sojourneth *with you*, an ordinance for ever in your generations:
as ye *are*, so shall the stranger be before the LORD.

16 One law and one manner shall be for you, and for the stranger that sojour-
neth with you.

17 And the LORD spake unto Moses, saying,

18 Speak unto the children of Israel, and say unto them, When ye come into
the land whither I bring you,

19 Then it shall be, that, when ye eat of the bread of the land, ye shall offer
up an heave offering unto the LORD.

20 Ye shall offer up a cake of the first of your dough *for* an heave offering: as
ye do the heave offering of the threshingfloor, so shall ye heave it.

21 Of the first of your dough ye shall give unto the LORD an heave offering in
your generations.

The Sacrifice for the Sin of Ignorance

22 And if ye have erred, and not observed all these commandments, which
the LORD hath spoken unto Moses,

23 *Even* all that the LORD hath commanded you by the hand of Moses, from
the day that the LORD commanded *Moses*, and henceforward among your
generations;

24 Then it shall be, if *ought* be committed by ignorance without the
knowledge of the congregation, that all the congregation shall offer one young
bullock for a burnt offering, for a sweet savour unto the LORD, with his meat
offering, and his drink offering, according to the manner, and one kid of the
goats for a sin offering.

25 And the priest shall make an atonement for all the congregation of the
children of Israel, and it shall be forgiven them; for it *is* ignorance: and they
shall bring their offering, a sacrifice made by fire unto the LORD, and their sin
offering before the LORD, for their ignorance:

26 And it shall be forgiven all the congregation of the children of Israel, and
the stranger that sojourneth among them; seeing all the people *were* in
ignorance.

27 And if any soul sin through ignorance, then he shall bring a she goat of
the first year for a sin offering.

28 And the priest shall make an atonement for the soul that sinneth
ignorantly, when he sinneth by ignorance before the LORD, to make an
atonement for him; and it shall be forgiven him.

29 Ye shall have one law for him that sinneth through ignorance, *both for*
him that is born among the children of Israel, and for the stranger that sojour-
neth among them.

The Punishment of the Presumptuous Person

30 But the soul that doeth *ought* presumptuously, *whether he be* born in the
land, or a stranger, the same reproacheth the LORD; and that soul shall be cut
off from among his people.

31 Because he hath despised the word of the LORD, and hath broken his com-
mandment, that soul shall utterly be cut off; his iniquity *shall be* upon him.
32 And while the children of Israel were in the wilderness, they found a man
that gathered sticks upon the sabbath day.
33 And they that found him gathering sticks brought him unto Moses and
Aaron, and unto all the congregation.
34 And they put him in ward, because it was not declared what should be
done to him.
35 And the LORD said unto Moses, The man shall be surely put to death: all
the congregation shall stone him with stones without the camp.
36 And all the congregation brought him without the camp, and stoned him
with stones, and he died; as the LORD commanded Moses.

The Law of Wearing Fringes as a Remembrance

37 And the LORD spake unto Moses, saying,
38 Speak unto the children of Israel, and bid them that they make them
fringes in the borders of their garments throughout their generations, and
that they put upon the fringe of the borders a ribband of blue:
39 And it shall be unto you for a fringe, that ye may look upon it, and remem-
ber all the commandments of the LORD, and do them; and that ye seek not
after your own heart and your own eyes, after which ye use to go a whoring:
40 That ye may remember, and do all my commandments, and be holy unto
your God.
41 I *am* the LORD your God, which brought you out of the land of Egypt, to
be your God: I *am* the LORD your God.

The Rebellion of Korah, Dathan, and Abiram

16 Now Korah, the son of Izhar, the son of Kohath, the son of Levi, and
Dathan and Abiram, the sons of Eliab, and On, the son of Peleth, sons
of Reuben, took *men*:
2 And they rose up before Moses, with certain of the children of Israel, two
hundred and fifty princes of the assembly, famous in the congregation, men
of renown:
3 And they gathered themselves together against Moses and against Aaron,
and said unto them, *Ye take* too much upon you, seeing all the congregation
are holy, every one of them, and the LORD *is* among them: wherefore then lift
ye up yourselves above the congregation of the LORD?
4 And when Moses heard *it*, he fell upon his face:
5 And he spake unto Korah and unto all his company, saying, Even to morrow
the LORD will shew who *are* his, and *who is* holy; and will cause *him* to come
near unto him: even *him* whom he hath chosen will he cause to come near
unto him.
6 This do; Take you censers, Korah, and all his company;
7 And put fire therein, and put incense in them before the LORD to morrow:
and it shall be *that* the man whom the LORD doth choose, he *shall be* holy: *ye*
take too much upon you, ye sons of Levi.
8 And Moses said unto Korah, Hear, I pray you, ye sons of Levi:
9 *Seemeth it but* a small thing unto you, that the God of Israel hath separ-
ated you from the congregation of Israel, to bring you near to himself to do
the service of the tabernacle of the LORD, and to stand before the congregation
to minister unto them?
10 And he hath brought thee near *to him*, and all thy brethren the sons of
Levi with thee: and seek ye the priesthood also?
11 For which cause *both* thou and all thy company *are* gathered together
against the LORD: and what *is* Aaron, that ye murmur against him?
12 And Moses sent to call Dathan and Abiram, the sons of Eliab: which said,
We will not come up:

13 *Is it* a small thing that thou hast brought us up out of a land that floweth
with milk and honey, to kill us in the wilderness, except thou make thyself
altogether a prince over us?
14 Moreover thou hast not brought us into a land that floweth with milk and
honey, or given us inheritance of fields and vineyards: wilt thou put out the
eyes of these men? we will not come up.
15 And Moses was very wroth, and said unto the LORD, Respect not thou their
offering: I have not taken one ass from them, neither have I hurt one of them.
16 And Moses said unto Korah, Be thou and all thy company before the LORD,
thou, and they, and Aaron, to morrow:
17 And take every man his censer, and put incense in them, and bring ye
before the LORD every man his censer, two hundred and fifty censers; thou
also, and Aaron, each *of you* his censer.
18 And they took every man his censer, and put fire in them, and laid incense
thereon, and stood in the door of the tabernacle of the congregation with
Moses and Aaron.
19 And Korah gathered all the congregation against them unto the door of
the tabernacle of the congregation: and the glory of the LORD appeared unto
all the congregation.
20 And the LORD spake unto Moses and unto Aaron, saying,
21 Separate yourselves from among this congregation, that I may consume
them in a moment.
22 And they fell upon their faces, and said, O God, the God of the spirits of
all flesh, shall one man sin, and wilt thou be wroth with all the congregation?

The Rebels and Their Families Are Swallowed by the Earth

23 And the LORD spake unto Moses, saying,
24 Speak unto the congregation, saying, Get you up from about the taber-
nacle of Korah, Dathan, and Abiram.
25 And Moses rose up and went unto Dathan and Abiram; and the elders of
Israel followed him.
26 And he spake unto the congregation, saying, Depart, I pray you, from the
tents of these wicked men, and touch nothing of theirs, lest ye be consumed
in all their sins.
27 So they gat up from the tabernacle of Korah, Dathan, and Abiram, on every
side: and Dathan and Abiram came out, and stood in the door of their tents,
and their wives, and their sons, and their little children.
28 And Moses said, Hereby ye shall know that the LORD hath sent me to do
all these works; for *I have* not *done them* of mine own mind.
29 If these men die the common death of all men, or if they be visited after
the visitation of all men; *then* the LORD hath not sent me.
30 But if the LORD make a new thing, and the earth open her mouth, and
swallow them up, with all that *appertain* unto them, and they go down quick
into the pit; then ye shall understand that these men have provoked the LORD.
31 And it came to pass, as he had made an end of speaking all these words,
that the ground clave asunder that *was* under them:
32 And the earth opened her mouth, and swallowed them up, and their
houses, and all the men that *appertained* unto Korah, and all *their* goods.
33 They, and all that *appertained* to them, went down alive into the pit, and
the earth closed upon them: and they perished from among the congregation.
34 And all Israel that *were* round about them fled at the cry of them: for they
said, Lest the earth swallow us up *also*.
35 And there came out a fire from the LORD, and consumed the two hundred
and fifty men that offered incense.
36 And the LORD spake unto Moses, saying,

37 Speak unto Eleazar the son of Aaron the priest, that he take up the censers
out of the burning, and scatter thou the fire yonder; for they are hallowed.
38 The censers of these sinners against their own souls, let them make them
broad plates *for* a covering of the altar: for they offered them before the LORD,
therefore they are hallowed: and they shall be a sign unto the children of Israel.
39 And Eleazar the priest took the brasen censers, wherewith they that were
burnt had offered; and they were made broad *plates for* a covering of the altar:
40 *To be* a memorial unto the children of Israel, that no stranger, which *is*
not of the seed of Aaron, come near to offer incense before the LORD; that he
be not as Korah, and as his company: as the LORD said to him by the hand of
Moses.

Many Are Slain for Murmuring against Moses and Aaron

41 But on the morrow all the congregation of the children of Israel mur-
mured against Moses and against Aaron, saying, Ye have killed the people of
the LORD.
42 And it came to pass, when the congregation was gathered against Moses
and against Aaron, that they looked toward the tabernacle of the congregation:
and, behold, the cloud covered it, and the glory of the LORD appeared.
43 And Moses and Aaron came before the tabernacle of the congregation.
44 And the LORD spake unto Moses, saying,
45 Get you up from among this congregation, that I may consume them as
in a moment. And they fell upon their faces.
46 And Moses said unto Aaron, Take a censer, and put fire therein from off
the altar, and put on incense, and go quickly unto the congregation, and make
an atonement for them: for there is wrath gone out from the LORD; the plague
is begun.
47 And Aaron took as Moses commanded, and ran into the midst of the con-
gregation; and, behold, the plague was begun among the people: and he put
on incense, and made an atonement for the people.
48 And he stood between the dead and the living; and the plague was stayed.
49 Now they that died in the plague were fourteen thousand and seven hun-
dred, beside them that died about the matter of Korah.
50 And Aaron returned unto Moses unto the door of the tabernacle of the
congregation: and the plague was stayed.

Aaron's Rod Blossoms

17 And the LORD spake unto Moses, saying,
2 Speak unto the children of Israel, and take of every one of them a
rod according to the house of *their* fathers, of all their princes according to
the house of their fathers twelve rods: write thou every man's name upon his
rod.
3 And thou shalt write Aaron's name upon the rod of Levi: for one rod *shall*
be for the head of the house of their fathers.
4 And thou shalt lay them up in the tabernacle of the congregation before
the testimony, where I will meet with you.
5 And it shall come to pass, *that* the man's rod, whom I shall choose, shall
blossom: and I will make to cease from me the murmurings of the children
of Israel, whereby they murmur against you.
6 And Moses spake unto the children of Israel, and every one of their princes
gave him a rod apiece, for each prince one, according to their fathers' houses,
even twelve rods: and the rod of Aaron *was* among their rods.
7 And Moses laid up the rods before the LORD in the tabernacle of witness.
8 And it came to pass, that on the morrow Moses went into the tabernacle
of witness; and, behold, the rod of Aaron for the house of Levi was budded,
and brought forth buds, and bloomed blossoms, and yielded almonds.

9 And Moses brought out all the rods from before the LORD unto all the
children of Israel: and they looked, and took every man his rod.
10 And the LORD said unto Moses, Bring Aaron's rod again before the testi-
mony, to be kept for a token against the rebels; and thou shalt quite take away
their murmurings from me, that they die not.
11 And Moses did *so*: as the LORD commanded him, so did he.
12 And the children of Israel spake unto Moses, saying, Behold, we die, we
perish, we all perish.
13 Whosoever cometh any thing near unto the tabernacle of the LORD shall
die: shall we be consumed with dying?

God's Charge to the Priests and Levites

18 And the LORD said unto Aaron, Thou and thy sons and thy father's house
with thee shall bear the iniquity of the sanctuary: and thou and thy
sons with thee shall bear the iniquity of your priesthood.
2 And thy brethren also of the tribe of Levi, the tribe of thy father, bring thou
with thee, that they may be joined unto thee, and minister unto thee: but thou
and thy sons with thee *shall minister* before the tabernacle of witness.
3 And they shall keep thy charge, and the charge of all the tabernacle: only
they shall not come nigh the vessels of the sanctuary and the altar, that neither
they, nor ye also, die.
4 And they shall be joined unto thee, and keep the charge of the tabernacle
of the congregation, for all the service of the tabernacle: and a stranger shall
not come nigh unto you.
5 And ye shall keep the charge of the sanctuary, and the charge of the altar:
that there be no wrath any more upon the children of Israel.
6 And I, behold, I have taken your brethren the Levites from among the chil-
dren of Israel: to you *they are* given *as* a gift for the LORD, to do the service of
the tabernacle of the congregation.
7 Therefore thou and thy sons with thee shall keep your priest's office for
every thing of the altar, and within the veil; and ye shall serve: I have given
your priest's office *unto you* as a service of gift: and the stranger that cometh
nigh shall be put to death.
8 And the LORD spake unto Aaron, Behold, I also have given thee the charge
of mine heave offerings of all the hallowed things of the children of Israel;
unto thee have I given them by reason of the anointing, and to thy sons, by an
ordinance for ever.
9 This shall be thine of the most holy things, *reserved* from the fire: every
oblation of theirs, every meat offering of theirs, and every sin offering of theirs,
and every trespass offering of theirs, which they shall render unto me, *shall
be* most holy for thee and for thy sons.
10 In the most holy *place* shalt thou eat it; every male shall eat it: it shall be
holy unto thee.
11 And this *is* thine; the heave offering of their gift, with all the wave offerings
of the children of Israel: I have given them unto thee, and to thy sons and to
thy daughters with thee, by a statute for ever: every one that is clean in thy
house shall eat of it.
12 All the best of the oil, and all the best of the wine, and of the wheat, the
firstfruits of them which they shall offer unto the LORD, them have I given
thee.
13 *And* whatsoever is first ripe in the land, which they shall bring unto the
LORD, shall be thine; every one that is clean in thine house shall eat *of* it.
14 Every thing devoted in Israel shall be thine.
15 Every thing that openeth the matrix in all flesh, which they bring unto
the LORD, *whether it be* of men or beasts, shall be thine: nevertheless the first-

born of man shalt thou surely redeem, and the firstling of unclean beasts shalt thou redeem.
16 And those that are to be redeemed from a month old shalt thou redeem, according to thine estimation, for the money of five shekels, after the shekel of the sanctuary, which *is* twenty gerahs.
17 But the firstling of a cow, or the firstling of a sheep, or the firstling of a goat, thou shalt not redeem; they *are* holy: thou shalt sprinkle their blood upon the altar, and shalt burn their fat *for* an offering made by fire, for a sweet savour unto the LORD.
18 And the flesh of them shall be thine, as the wave breast and as the right shoulder are thine.
19 All the heave offerings of the holy things, which the children of Israel offer unto the LORD, have I given thee, and thy sons and thy daughters with thee, by a statute for ever: it *is* a covenant of salt for ever before the LORD unto thee and to thy seed with thee.
20 And the LORD spake unto Aaron, Thou shalt have no inheritance in their land, neither shalt thou have any part among them: I *am* thy part and thine inheritance among the children of Israel.
21 And, behold, I have given the children of Levi all the tenth in Israel for an inheritance, for their service which they serve, *even* the service of the tabernacle of the congregation.
22 Neither must the children of Israel henceforth come nigh the tabernacle of the congregation, lest they bear sin, and die.
23 But the Levites shall do the service of the tabernacle of the congregation, and they shall bear their iniquity: *it shall be* a statute for ever throughout your generations, that among the children of Israel they have no inheritance.
24 But the tithes of the children of Israel, which they offer *as* an heave offering unto the LORD, I have given to the Levites to inherit: therefore I have said unto them, Among the children of Israel they shall have no inheritance.
25 And the LORD spake unto Moses, saying,
26 Thus speak unto the Levites, and say unto them, When ye take of the children of Israel the tithes which I have given you from them for your inheritance, then ye shall offer up an heave offering of it for the LORD, *even* a tenth *part* of the tithe.
27 And *this* your heave offering shall be reckoned unto you, as though *it were* the corn of the threshingfloor, and as the fulness of the winepress.
28 Thus ye also shall offer an heave offering unto the LORD of all your tithes, which ye receive of the children of Israel; and ye shall give thereof the LORD's heave offering to Aaron the priest.
29 Out of all your gifts ye shall offer every heave offering of the LORD, of all the best thereof, *even* the hallowed part thereof out of it.
30 Therefore thou shalt say unto them, When ye have heaved the best thereof from it, then it shall be counted unto the Levites as the increase of the threshingfloor, and as the increase of the winepress.
31 And ye shall eat it in every place, ye and your households: for it *is* your reward for your service in the tabernacle of the congregation.
32 And ye shall bear no sin by reason of it, when ye have heaved from it the best of it: neither shall ye pollute the holy things of the children of Israel, lest ye die.

The Water of Separation Made with the Ashes of a Red Heifer

19 And the LORD spake unto Moses and unto Aaron, saying,
2 This *is* the ordinance of the law which the LORD hath commanded, saying, Speak unto the children of Israel, that they bring thee a red heifer without spot, wherein *is* no blemish, *and* upon which never came yoke:

3 And ye shall give her unto Eleazar the priest, that he may bring her forth
without the camp, and *one* shall slay her before his face:
4 And Eleazar the priest shall take of her blood with his finger, and sprinkle
of her blood directly before the tabernacle of the congregation seven times:
5 And *one* shall burn the heifer in his sight; her skin, and her flesh, and her
blood, with her dung, shall he burn:
6 And the priest shall take cedar wood, and hyssop, and scarlet, and cast *it*
into the midst of the burning of the heifer.
7 Then the priest shall wash his clothes, and he shall bathe his flesh in water,
and afterward he shall come into the camp, and the priest shall be unclean
until the even.
8 And he that burneth her shall wash his clothes in water, and bathe his flesh
in water, and shall be unclean until the even.
9 And a man *that is* clean shall gather up the ashes of the heifer, and lay *them*
up without the camp in a clean place, and it shall be kept for the congregation
of the children of Israel for a water of separation: it *is* a purification for sin.
10 And he that gathereth the ashes of the heifer shall wash his clothes, and
be unclean until the even: and it shall be unto the children of Israel, and unto
the stranger that sojourneth among them, for a statute for ever.

The Law for the Use of the Water in Purification of the Unclean

11 He that toucheth the dead body of any man shall be unclean seven days.
12 He shall purify himself with it on the third day, and on the seventh day he
shall be clean: but if he purify not himself the third day, then the seventh day
he shall not be clean.
13 Whosoever toucheth the dead body of any man that is dead, and purifieth
not himself, defileth the tabernacle of the LORD; and that soul shall be cut off
from Israel: because the water of separation was not sprinkled upon him, he
shall be unclean; his uncleanness *is* yet upon him.
14 This *is* the law, when a man dieth in a tent: all that come into the tent, and
all that *is* in the tent, shall be unclean seven days.
15 And every open vessel, which hath no covering bound upon it, *is* unclean.
16 And whosoever toucheth one that is slain with a sword in the open fields,
or a dead body, or a bone of a man, or a grave, shall be unclean seven days.
17 And for an unclean *person* they shall take of the ashes of the burnt heifer
of purification for sin, and running water shall be put thereto in a vessel:
18 And a clean person shall take hyssop, and dip *it* in the water, and sprinkle
it upon the tent, and upon all the vessels, and upon the persons that were
there, and upon him that touched a bone, or one slain, or one dead, or a grave:
19 And the clean *person* shall sprinkle upon the unclean on the third day,
and on the seventh day: and on the seventh day he shall purify himself, and
wash his clothes, and bathe himself in water, and shall be clean at even.
20 But the man that shall be unclean, and shall not purify himself, that soul
shall be cut off from among the congregation, because he hath defiled the
sanctuary of the LORD: the water of separation hath not been sprinkled upon
him; he *is* unclean.
21 And it shall be a perpetual statute unto them, that he that sprinkleth the
water of separation shall wash his clothes; and he that toucheth the water of
separation shall be unclean until even.
22 And whatsoever the unclean *person* toucheth shall be unclean; and the
soul that toucheth *it* shall be unclean until even.

The Israelites Come to Zin, Where Miriam Dies

20 Then came the children of Israel, *even* the whole congregation, into
the desert of Zin in the first month: and the people abode in Kadesh;
and Miriam died there, and was buried there.
2 And there was no water for the congregation: and they gathered themselves
together against Moses and against Aaron.

3 And the people chode with Moses, and spake, saying, Would God that we
had died when our brethren died before the LORD!
4 And why have ye brought up the congregation of the LORD into this wil-
derness, that we and our cattle should die there?
5 And wherefore have ye made us to come up out of Egypt, to bring us in unto
this evil place? it *is* no place of seed, or of figs, or of vines, or of pomegranates;
neither *is* there any water to drink.
6 And Moses and Aaron went from the presence of the assembly unto the
door of the tabernacle of the congregation, and they fell upon their faces: and
the glory of the LORD appeared unto them.
7 And the LORD spake unto Moses, saying,
8 Take the rod, and gather thou the assembly together, thou, and Aaron thy
brother, and speak ye unto the rock before their eyes; and it shall give forth
his water, and thou shalt bring forth to them water out of the rock: so thou
shalt give the congregation and their beasts drink.
9 And Moses took the rod from before the LORD, as he commanded him.
10 And Moses and Aaron gathered the congregation together before the rock,
and he said unto them, Hear now, ye rebels; must we fetch you water out of
this rock?
11 And Moses lifted up his hand, and with his rod he smote the rock twice:
and the water came out abundantly, and the congregation drank, and their
beasts *also*.
12 And the LORD spake unto Moses and Aaron, Because ye believed me not,
to sanctify me in the eyes of the children of Israel, therefore ye shall not bring
this congregation into the land which I have given them.
13 This *is* the water of Meribah; because the children of Israel strove with
the LORD, and he was sanctified in them.

Edom Denies Moses' Request for Passage

14 And Moses sent messengers from Kadesh unto the king of Edom, Thus
saith thy brother Israel, Thou knowest all the travail that hath befallen us:
15 How our fathers went down into Egypt, and we have dwelt in Egypt a long
time; and the Egyptians vexed us, and our fathers:
16 And when we cried unto the LORD, he heard our voice, and sent an angel,
and hath brought us forth out of Egypt: and, behold, we *are* in Kadesh, a city
in the uttermost of thy border:
17 Let us pass, I pray thee, through thy country: we will not pass through the
fields, or through the vineyards, neither will we drink *of* the water of the wells:
we will go by the king's *high* way, we will not turn to the right hand nor to the
left, until we have passed thy borders.
18 And Edom said unto him, Thou shalt not pass by me, lest I come out against
thee with the sword.
19 And the children of Israel said unto him, We will go by the high way: and
if I and my cattle drink of thy water, then I will pay for it: I will only, without
doing any thing *else*, go through on my feet.
20 And he said, Thou shalt not go through. And Edom came out against him
with much people, and with a strong hand.
21 Thus Edom refused to give Israel passage through his border: wherefore
Israel turned away from him.

Before He Dies, Aaron Gives His Role as High Priest to Eleazar

22 And the children of Israel, *even* the whole congregation, journeyed from
Kadesh, and came unto mount Hor.
23 And the LORD spake unto Moses and Aaron in mount Hor, by the coast of
the land of Edom, saying,

24 Aaron shall be gathered unto his people: for he shall not enter into the
land which I have given unto the children of Israel, because ye rebelled against
my word at the water of Meribah.
25 Take Aaron and Eleazar his son, and bring them up unto mount Hor:
26 And strip Aaron of his garments, and put them upon Eleazar his son: and
Aaron shall be gathered *unto his people*, and shall die there.
27 And Moses did as the LORD commanded: and they went up into mount
Hor in the sight of all the congregation.
28 And Moses stripped Aaron of his garments, and put them upon Eleazar
his son; and Aaron died there in the top of the mount: and Moses and Eleazar
came down from the mount.
29 And when all the congregation saw that Aaron was dead, they mourned
for Aaron thirty days, *even* all the house of Israel.

The King of Arad Attacks

21 And *when* king Arad the Canaanite, which dwelt in the south, heard
tell that Israel came by the way of the spies; then he fought against
Israel, and took *some* of them prisoners.
2 And Israel vowed a vow unto the LORD, and said, If thou wilt indeed deliver
this people into my hand, then I will utterly destroy their cities.
3 And the LORD hearkened to the voice of Israel, and delivered up the
Canaanites; and they utterly destroyed them and their cities: and he called the
name of the place Hormah.

The Brass Serpent on a Pole Saves the People from Snake Bites

4 And they journeyed from mount Hor by the way of the Red sea, to compass
the land of Edom: and the soul of the people was much discouraged because
of the way.
5 And the people spake against God, and against Moses, Wherefore have ye
brought us up out of Egypt to die in the wilderness? for *there is* no bread,
neither *is there any* water; and our soul loatheth this light bread.
6 And the LORD sent fiery serpents among the people, and they bit the people;
and much people of Israel died.
7 Therefore the people came to Moses, and said, We have sinned, for we have
spoken against the LORD, and against thee; pray unto the LORD, that he take
away the serpents from us. And Moses prayed for the people.
8 And the LORD said unto Moses, Make thee a fiery serpent, and set it upon
a pole: and it shall come to pass, that every one that is bitten, when he looketh
upon it, shall live.
9 And Moses made a serpent of brass, and put it upon a pole, and it came to
pass, that if a serpent had bitten any man, when he beheld the serpent of brass,
he lived.

Various Journeys of the Israelites

10 And the children of Israel set forward, and pitched in Oboth.
11 And they journeyed from Oboth, and pitched at Ijeabarim, in the wilder-
ness which *is* before Moab, toward the sunrising.
12 From thence they removed, and pitched in the valley of Zared.
13 From thence they removed, and pitched on the other side of Arnon, which
is in the wilderness that cometh out of the coasts of the Amorites: for Arnon
is the border of Moab, between Moab and the Amorites.
14 Wherefore it is said in the book of the wars of the LORD, What he did in
the Red sea, and in the brooks of Arnon,
15 And at the stream of the brooks that goeth down to the dwelling of Ar,
and lieth upon the border of Moab.
16 And from thence *they went* to Beer: that *is* the well whereof the LORD spake
unto Moses, Gather the people together, and I will give them water.
17 Then Israel sang this song, Spring up, O well; sing ye unto it:

18 The princes digged the well, the nobles of the people digged it, by *the
direction of* the lawgiver, with their staves. And from the wilderness *they went*
to Mattanah:
19 And from Mattanah to Nahaliel: and from Nahaliel to Bamoth:
20 And from Bamoth *in* the valley, that *is* in the country of Moab, to the top
of Pisgah, which looketh toward Jeshimon.

The Amorite King Sihon Is Overcome

21 And Israel sent messengers unto Sihon king of the Amorites, saying,
22 Let me pass through thy land: we will not turn into the fields, or into the
vineyards; we will not drink *of* the waters of the well: *but* we will go along by
the king's *high* way, until we be past thy borders.
23 And Sihon would not suffer Israel to pass through his border: but Sihon
gathered all his people together, and went out against Israel into the wilder-
ness: and he came to Jahaz, and fought against Israel.
24 And Israel smote him with the edge of the sword, and possessed his land
from Arnon unto Jabbok, even unto the children of Ammon: for the border
of the children of Ammon *was* strong.
25 And Israel took all these cities: and Israel dwelt in all the cities of the
Amorites, in Heshbon, and in all the villages thereof.
26 For Heshbon *was* the city of Sihon the king of the Amorites, who had
fought against the former king of Moab, and taken all his land out of his hand,
even unto Arnon.
27 Wherefore they that speak in proverbs say, Come into Heshbon, let the
city of Sihon be built and prepared:
28 For there is a fire gone out of Heshbon, a flame from the city of Sihon: it
hath consumed Ar of Moab, *and* the lords of the high places of Arnon.
29 Woe to thee, Moab! thou art undone, O people of Chemosh: he hath given
his sons that escaped, and his daughters, into captivity unto Sihon king of the
Amorites.
30 We have shot at them; Heshbon is perished even unto Dibon, and we have
laid them waste even unto Nophah, which *reacheth* unto Medeba.
31 Thus Israel dwelt in the land of the Amorites.
32 And Moses sent to spy out Jaazer, and they took the villages thereof, and
drove out the Amorites that *were* there.
33 And they turned and went up by the way of Bashan: and Og the king of
Bashan went out against them, he, and all his people, to the battle at Edrei.
34 And the LORD said unto Moses, Fear him not: for I have delivered him into
thy hand, and all his people, and his land; and thou shalt do to him as thou
didst unto Sihon king of the Amorites, which dwelt at Heshbon.
35 So they smote him, and his sons, and all his people, until there was none
left him alive: and they possessed his land.

Balak's First Message for Balaam Is Refused

22 And the children of Israel set forward, and pitched in the plains of
Moab on this side Jordan *by* Jericho.
2 And Balak the son of Zippor saw all that Israel had done to the Amorites.
3 And Moab was sore afraid of the people, because they *were* many: and Moab
was distressed because of the children of Israel.
4 And Moab said unto the elders of Midian, Now shall this company lick up
all *that are* round about us, as the ox licketh up the grass of the field. And Balak
the son of Zippor *was* king of the Moabites at that time.
5 He sent messengers therefore unto Balaam the son of Beor to Pethor, which
is by the river of the land of the children of his people, to call him, saying,
Behold, there is a people come out from Egypt: behold, they cover the face of
the earth, and they abide over against me:

6 Come now therefore, I pray thee, curse me this people; for they *are* too mighty for me: peradventure I shall prevail, *that* we may smite them, and *that* I may drive them out of the land: for I wot that he whom thou blessest *is* blessed, and he whom thou cursest is cursed.

7 And the elders of Moab and the elders of Midian departed with the rewards of divination in their hand; and they came unto Balaam, and spake unto him the words of Balak.

8 And he said unto them, Lodge here this night, and I will bring you word again, as the LORD shall speak unto me: and the princes of Moab abode with Balaam.

9 And God came unto Balaam, and said, What men *are* these with thee?

10 And Balaam said unto God, Balak the son of Zippor, king of Moab, hath sent unto me, *saying*,

11 Behold, *there is* a people come out of Egypt, which covereth the face of the earth: come now, curse me them; peradventure I shall be able to overcome them, and drive them out.

12 And God said unto Balaam, Thou shalt not go with them; thou shalt not curse the people: for they *are* blessed.

13 And Balaam rose up in the morning, and said unto the princes of Balak, Get you into your land: for the LORD refuseth to give me leave to go with you.

14 And the princes of Moab rose up, and they went unto Balak, and said, Balaam refuseth to come with us.

Balaam Goes with the Messengers

15 And Balak sent yet again princes, more, and more honourable than they.

16 And they came to Balaam, and said to him, Thus saith Balak the son of Zippor, Let nothing, I pray thee, hinder thee from coming unto me:

17 For I will promote thee unto very great honour, and I will do whatsoever thou sayest unto me: come therefore, I pray thee, curse me this people.

18 And Balaam answered and said unto the servants of Balak, If Balak would give me his house full of silver and gold, I cannot go beyond the word of the LORD my God, to do less or more.

19 Now therefore, I pray you, tarry ye also here this night, that I may know what the LORD will say unto me more.

20 And God came unto Balaam at night, and said unto him, If the men come to call thee, rise up, *and* go with them; but yet the word which I shall say unto thee, that shalt thou do.

21 And Balaam rose up in the morning, and saddled his ass, and went with the princes of Moab.

Balaam's Donkey Speaks

22 And God's anger was kindled because he went: and the angel of the LORD stood in the way for an adversary against him. Now he was riding upon his ass, and his two servants *were* with him.

23 And the ass saw the angel of the LORD standing in the way, and his sword drawn in his hand: and the ass turned aside out of the way, and went into the field: and Balaam smote the ass, to turn her into the way.

24 But the angel of the LORD stood in a path of the vineyards, a wall *being* on this side, and a wall on that side.

25 And when the ass saw the angel of the LORD, she thrust herself unto the wall, and crushed Balaam's foot against the wall: and he smote her again.

26 And the angel of the LORD went further, and stood in a narrow place, where *was* no way to turn either to the right hand or to the left.

27 And when the ass saw the angel of the LORD, she fell down under Balaam: and Balaam's anger was kindled, and he smote the ass with a staff.

28 And the LORD opened the mouth of the ass, and she said unto Balaam, What have I done unto thee, that thou hast smitten me these three times?

29 And Balaam said unto the ass, Because thou hast mocked me: I would there
were a sword in mine hand, for now would I kill thee.
30 And the ass said unto Balaam, *Am* not I thine ass, upon which thou hast
ridden ever since *I was* thine unto this day? was I ever wont to do so unto thee?
And he said, Nay.
31 Then the LORD opened the eyes of Balaam, and he saw the angel of the
LORD standing in the way, and his sword drawn in his hand: and he bowed
down his head, and fell flat on his face.
32 And the angel of the LORD said unto him, Wherefore hast thou smitten
thine ass these three times? behold, I went out to withstand thee, because *thy*
way is perverse before me:
33 And the ass saw me, and turned from me these three times: unless she had
turned from me, surely now also I had slain thee, and saved her alive.
34 And Balaam said unto the angel of the LORD, I have sinned; for I knew not
that thou stoodest in the way against me: now therefore, if it displease thee, I
will get me back again.
35 And the angel of the LORD said unto Balaam, Go with the men: but only
the word that I shall speak unto thee, that thou shalt speak. So Balaam went
with the princes of Balak.

Balak Entertains Balaam

36 And when Balak heard that Balaam was come, he went out to meet him
unto a city of Moab, which *is* in the border of Arnon, which *is* in the utmost
coast.
37 And Balak said unto Balaam, Did I not earnestly send unto thee to call
thee? wherefore camest thou not unto me? am I not able indeed to promote
thee to honour?
38 And Balaam said unto Balak, Lo, I am come unto thee: have I now any
power at all to say any thing? the word that God putteth in my mouth, that
shall I speak.
39 And Balaam went with Balak, and they came unto Kirjath-huzoth.
40 And Balak offered oxen and sheep, and sent to Balaam, and to the princes
that *were* with him.
41 And it came to pass on the morrow, that Balak took Balaam, and brought
him up into the high places of Baal, that thence he might see the utmost *part*
of the people.

Balak's Sacrifice

23 And Balaam said unto Balak, Build me here seven altars, and prepare
me here seven oxen and seven rams.
2 And Balak did as Balaam had spoken; and Balak and Balaam offered on
every altar a bullock and a ram.
3 And Balaam said unto Balak, Stand by thy burnt offering, and I will go:
peradventure the LORD will come to meet me: and whatsoever he sheweth me
I will tell thee. And he went to an high place.
4 And God met Balaam: and he said unto him, I have prepared seven altars,
and I have offered upon *every* altar a bullock and a ram.
5 And the LORD put a word in Balaam's mouth, and said, Return unto Balak,
and thus thou shalt speak.
6 And he returned unto him, and, lo, he stood by his burnt sacrifice, he, and
all the princes of Moab.
7 And he took up his parable, and said, Balak the king of Moab hath brought
me from Aram, out of the mountains of the east, *saying*, Come, curse me Jacob,
and come, defy Israel.
8 How shall I curse, whom God hath not cursed? or how shall I defy, *whom*
the LORD hath not defied?

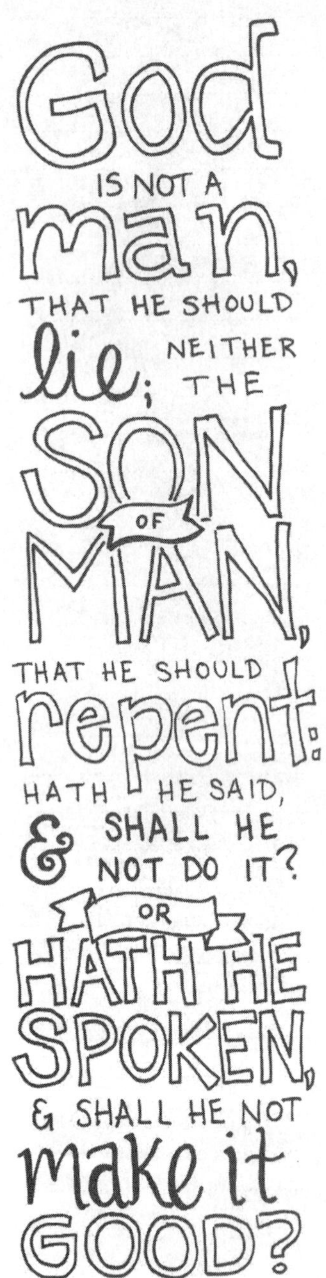

9 For from the top of the rocks I see him, and from the hills I behold him: lo,
the people shall dwell alone, and shall not be reckoned among the nations.
10 Who can count the dust of Jacob, and the number of the fourth *part* of
Israel? Let me die the death of the righteous, and let my last end be like his!
11 And Balak said unto Balaam, What hast thou done unto me? I took thee
to curse mine enemies, and, behold, thou hast blessed *them* altogether.
12 And he answered and said, Must I not take heed to speak that which the
LORD hath put in my mouth?
13 And Balak said unto him, Come, I pray thee, with me unto another place,
from whence thou mayest see them: thou shalt see but the utmost part of
them, and shalt not see them all: and curse me them from thence.
14 And he brought him into the field of Zophim, to the top of Pisgah, and
built seven altars, and offered a bullock and a ram on *every* altar.
15 And he said unto Balak, Stand here by thy burnt offering, while I meet *the*
LORD yonder.
16 And the LORD met Balaam, and put a word in his mouth, and said, Go again
unto Balak, and say thus.
17 And when he came to him, behold, he stood by his burnt offering, and the
princes of Moab with him. And Balak said unto him, What hath the LORD
spoken?
18 And he took up his parable, and said, Rise up, Balak, and hear; hearken
unto me, thou son of Zippor:
19 God *is* not a man, that he should lie; neither the son of man, that he should
repent: hath he said, and shall he not do *it*? or hath he spoken, and shall he
not make it good?
20 Behold, I have received *commandment* to bless: and he hath blessed; and
I cannot reverse it.
21 He hath not beheld iniquity in Jacob, neither hath he seen perverseness
in Israel: the LORD his God *is* with him, and the shout of a king *is* among them.
22 God brought them out of Egypt; he hath as it were the strength of an
unicorn.
23 Surely *there is* no enchantment against Jacob, neither *is there* any
divination against Israel: according to this time it shall be said of Jacob and
of Israel, What hath God wrought!
24 Behold, the people shall rise up as a great lion, and lift up himself as a
young lion: he shall not lie down until he eat *of* the prey, and drink the blood
of the slain.
25 And Balak said unto Balaam, Neither curse them at all, nor bless them at all.
26 But Balaam answered and said unto Balak, Told not I thee, saying, All that
the LORD speaketh, that I must do?
27 And Balak said unto Balaam, Come, I pray thee, I will bring thee unto
another place; peradventure it will please God that thou mayest curse me them
from thence.
28 And Balak brought Balaam unto the top of Peor, that looketh toward
Jeshimon.
29 And Balaam said unto Balak, Build me here seven altars, and prepare me
here seven bullocks and seven rams.
30 And Balak did as Balaam had said, and offered a bullock and a ram on
every altar.

Balaam, Leaving Divination, Prophesies the Happiness of Israel

24 And when Balaam saw that it pleased the LORD to bless Israel, he went
not, as at other times, to seek for enchantments, but he set his face
toward the wilderness.
2 And Balaam lifted up his eyes, and he saw Israel abiding *in his tents* accord-
ing to their tribes; and the spirit of God came upon him.

3 And he took up his parable, and said, Balaam the son of Beor hath said, and
the man whose eyes are open hath said:
4 He hath said, which heard the words of God, which saw the vision of the
Almighty, falling *into a trance*, but having his eyes open:
5 How goodly are thy tents, O Jacob, *and* thy tabernacles, O Israel!
6 As the valleys are they spread forth, as gardens by the river's side, as the
trees of lign aloes which the LORD hath planted, *and* as cedar trees beside the
waters.
7 He shall pour the water out of his buckets, and his seed *shall be* in many
waters, and his king shall be higher than Agag, and his kingdom shall be exalted.
8 God brought him forth out of Egypt; he hath as it were the strength of an
unicorn: he shall eat up the nations his enemies, and shall break their bones,
and pierce *them* through with his arrows.
9 He couched, he lay down as a lion, and as a great lion: who shall stir him
up? Blessed *is* he that blesseth thee, and cursed *is* he that curseth thee.

Balak Angrily Dismisses Balaam

10 And Balak's anger was kindled against Balaam, and he smote his hands
together: and Balak said unto Balaam, I called thee to curse mine enemies,
and, behold, thou hast altogether blessed *them* these three times.
11 Therefore now flee thou to thy place: I thought to promote thee unto great
honour; but, lo, the LORD hath kept thee back from honour.
12 And Balaam said unto Balak, Spake I not also to thy messengers which
thou sentest unto me, saying,
13 If Balak would give me his house full of silver and gold, I cannot go beyond
the commandment of the LORD, to do *either* good or bad of mine own mind;
but what the LORD saith, that will I speak?
14 And now, behold, I go unto my people: come *therefore, and* I will advertise
thee what this people shall do to thy people in the latter days.

Balaam Prophesies the Star of Jacob and the Destruction of Nations

15 And he took up his parable, and said, Balaam the son of Beor hath said,
and the man whose eyes are open hath said:
16 He hath said, which heard the words of God, and knew the knowledge of
the most High, *which* saw the vision of the Almighty, falling *into a trance*, but
having his eyes open:
17 I shall see him, but not now: I shall behold him, but not nigh: there shall
come a Star out of Jacob, and a Sceptre shall rise out of Israel, and shall smite
the corners of Moab, and destroy all the children of Sheth.
18 And Edom shall be a possession, Seir also shall be a possession for his
enemies; and Israel shall do valiantly.
19 Out of Jacob shall come he that shall have dominion, and shall destroy
him that remaineth of the city.
20 And when he looked on Amalek, he took up his parable, and said, Amalek
was the first of the nations; but his latter end *shall be* that he perish for ever.
21 And he looked on the Kenites, and took up his parable, and said, Strong
is thy dwellingplace, and thou puttest thy nest in a rock.
22 Nevertheless the Kenite shall be wasted, until Asshur shall carry thee away
captive.
23 And he took up his parable, and said, Alas, who shall live when God doeth
this!
24 And ships *shall come* from the coast of Chittim, and shall afflict Asshur,
and shall afflict Eber, and he also shall perish for ever.
25 And Balaam rose up, and went and returned to his place: and Balak also
went his way.

The Israelites Commit Idolatry at Shittim

25 And Israel abode in Shittim, and the people began to commit whore-
dom with the daughters of Moab.
2 And they called the people unto the sacrifices of their gods: and the people
did eat, and bowed down to their gods.
3 And Israel joined himself unto Baal-peor: and the anger of the LORD was
kindled against Israel.
4 And the LORD said unto Moses, Take all the heads of the people, and hang
them up before the LORD against the sun, that the fierce anger of the LORD may
be turned away from Israel.
5 And Moses said unto the judges of Israel, Slay ye every one his men that
were joined unto Baal-peor.

Phinehas Kills Zimri and Cozbi

6 And, behold, one of the children of Israel came and brought unto his breth-
ren a Midianitish woman in the sight of Moses, and in the sight of all the
congregation of the children of Israel, who *were* weeping *before* the door of
the tabernacle of the congregation.
7 And when Phinehas, the son of Eleazar, the son of Aaron the priest, saw *it*,
he rose up from among the congregation, and took a javelin in his hand;
8 And he went after the man of Israel into the tent, and thrust both of them
through, the man of Israel, and the woman through her belly. So the plague
was stayed from the children of Israel.
9 And those that died in the plague were twenty and four thousand.
10 And the LORD spake unto Moses, saying,
11 Phinehas, the son of Eleazar, the son of Aaron the priest, hath turned my
wrath away from the children of Israel, while he was zealous for my sake
among them, that I consumed not the children of Israel in my jealousy.
12 Wherefore say, Behold, I give unto him my covenant of peace:
13 And he shall have it, and his seed after him, *even* the covenant of an ever-
lasting priesthood; because he was zealous for his God, and made an atone-
ment for the children of Israel.
14 Now the name of the Israelite that was slain, *even* that was slain with the
Midianitish woman, *was* Zimri, the son of Salu, a prince of a chief house
among the Simeonites.
15 And the name of the Midianitish woman that was slain *was* Cozbi, the
daughter of Zur; he *was* head over a people, *and* of a chief house in Midian.

The Midianites Are to Be Killed

16 And the LORD spake unto Moses, saying,
17 Vex the Midianites, and smite them:
18 For they vex you with their wiles, wherewith they have beguiled you in
the matter of Peor, and in the matter of Cozbi, the daughter of a prince of
Midian, their sister, which was slain in the day of the plague for Peor's sake.

A Second Census of Israel

26 And it came to pass after the plague, that the LORD spake unto Moses
and unto Eleazar the son of Aaron the priest, saying,
2 Take the sum of all the congregation of the children of Israel, from twenty
years old and upward, throughout their fathers' house, all that are able to go
to war in Israel.
3 And Moses and Eleazar the priest spake with them in the plains of Moab
by Jordan *near* Jericho, saying,
4 *Take the sum of the people*, from twenty years old and upward; as the LORD
commanded Moses and the children of Israel, which went forth out of the
land of Egypt.
5 Reuben, the eldest son of Israel: the children of Reuben; Hanoch, *of whom
cometh* the family of the Hanochites: of Pallu, the family of the Palluites:

6 Of Hezron, the family of the Hezronites: of Carmi, the family of the
Carmites.
7 These *are* the families of the Reubenites: and they that were numbered of
them were forty and three thousand and seven hundred and thirty.
8 And the sons of Pallu; Eliab.
9 And the sons of Eliab; Nemuel, and Dathan, and Abiram. This *is that* Dathan
and Abiram, *which were* famous in the congregation, who strove against Moses
and against Aaron in the company of Korah, when they strove against the
LORD:
10 And the earth opened her mouth, and swallowed them up together with
Korah, when that company died, what time the fire devoured two hundred
and fifty men: and they became a sign.
11 Notwithstanding the children of Korah died not.
12 The sons of Simeon after their families: of Nemuel, the family of the
Nemuelites: of Jamin, the family of the Jaminites: of Jachin, the family of the
Jachinites:
13 Of Zerah, the family of the Zarhites: of Shaul, the family of the Shaulites.
14 These *are* the families of the Simeonites, twenty and two thousand and
two hundred.
15 The children of Gad after their families: of Zephon, the family of the
Zephonites: of Haggi, the family of the Haggites: of Shuni, the family of the
Shunites:
16 Of Ozni, the family of the Oznites: of Eri, the family of the Erites:
17 Of Arod, the family of the Arodites: of Areli, the family of the Arelites.
18 These *are* the families of the children of Gad according to those that were
numbered of them, forty thousand and five hundred.
19 The sons of Judah *were* Er and Onan: and Er and Onan died in the land of
Canaan.
20 And the sons of Judah after their families were; of Shelah, the family of
the Shelanites: of Pharez, the family of the Pharzites: of Zerah, the family of
the Zarhites.
21 And the sons of Pharez were; of Hezron, the family of the Hezronites: of
Hamul, the family of the Hamulites.
22 These *are* the families of Judah according to those that were numbered
of them, threescore and sixteen thousand and five hundred.
23 *Of* the sons of Issachar after their families: *of* Tola, the family of the
Tolaites: of Pua, the family of the Punites:
24 Of Jashub, the family of the Jashubites: of Shimron, the family of the
Shimronites.
25 These *are* the families of Issachar according to those that were numbered
of them, threescore and four thousand and three hundred.
26 *Of* the sons of Zebulun after their families: of Sered, the family of the
Sardites: of Elon, the family of the Elonites: of Jahleel, the family of the
Jahleelites.
27 These *are* the families of the Zebulunites according to those that were
numbered of them, threescore thousand and five hundred.
28 The sons of Joseph after their families *were* Manasseh and Ephraim.
29 Of the sons of Manasseh: of Machir, the family of the Machirites: and
Machir begat Gilead: of Gilead *come* the family of the Gileadites.
30 These *are* the sons of Gilead: *of* Jeezer, the family of the Jeezerites: of Helek,
the family of the Helekites:
31 And *of* Asriel, the family of the Asrielites: and *of* Shechem, the family of
the Shechemites:
32 And *of* Shemida, the family of the Shemidaites: and *of* Hepher, the family
of the Hepherites.

33 And Zelophehad the son of Hepher had no sons, but daughters: and the
names of the daughters of Zelophehad *were* Mahlah, and Noah, Hoglah,
Milcah, and Tirzah.
34 These *are* the families of Manasseh, and those that were numbered of
them, fifty and two thousand and seven hundred.
35 These *are* the sons of Ephraim after their families: of Shuthelah, the fam-
ily of the Shuthalhites: of Becher, the family of the Bachrites: of Tahan, the
family of the Tahanites.
36 And these *are* the sons of Shuthelah: of Eran, the family of the Eranites.
37 These *are* the families of the sons of Ephraim according to those that were
numbered of them, thirty and two thousand and five hundred. These *are* the
sons of Joseph after their families.
38 The sons of Benjamin after their families: of Bela, the family of the Belaites:
of Ashbel, the family of the Ashbelites: of Ahiram, the family of the Ahiramites:
39 Of Shupham, the family of the Shuphamites: of Hupham, the family of
the Huphamites.
40 And the sons of Bela were Ard and Naaman: *of Ard*, the family of the
Ardites: *and* of Naaman, the family of the Naamites.
41 These *are* the sons of Benjamin after their families: and they that were
numbered of them *were* forty and five thousand and six hundred.
42 These *are* the sons of Dan after their families: of Shuham, the family of
the Shuhamites. These *are* the families of Dan after their families.
43 All the families of the Shuhamites, according to those that were numbered
of them, *were* threescore and four thousand and four hundred.
44 *Of* the children of Asher after their families: of Jimna, the family of the
Jimnites: of Jesui, the family of the Jesuites: of Beriah, the family of the Beriites.
45 Of the sons of Beriah: of Heber, the family of the Heberites: of Malchiel,
the family of the Malchielites.
46 And the name of the daughter of Asher *was* Sarah.
47 These *are* the families of the sons of Asher according to those that were
numbered of them; *who were* fifty and three thousand and four hundred.
48 *Of* the sons of Naphtali after their families: of Jahzeel, the family of the
Jahzeelites: of Guni, the family of the Gunites:
49 Of Jezer, the family of the Jezerites: of Shillem, the family of the Shillemites.
50 These *are* the families of Naphtali according to their families: and they
that were numbered of them *were* forty and five thousand and four hundred.
51 These *were* the numbered of the children of Israel, six hundred thousand
and a thousand seven hundred and thirty.

God's Rules for Dividing the Land among the Tribes of Israel

52 And the LORD spake unto Moses, saying,
53 Unto these the land shall be divided for an inheritance according to the
number of names.
54 To many thou shalt give the more inheritance, and to few thou shalt give
the less inheritance: to every one shall his inheritance be given according to
those that were numbered of him.
55 Notwithstanding the land shall be divided by lot: according to the names
of the tribes of their fathers they shall inherit.
56 According to the lot shall the possession thereof be divided between many
and few.

The Families and Number of the Levites

57 And these *are* they that were numbered of the Levites after their families:
of Gershon, the family of the Gershonites: of Kohath, the family of the
Kohathites: of Merari, the family of the Merarites.

58 These *are* the families of the Levites: the family of the Libnites, the family of the Hebronites, the family of the Mahlites, the family of the Mushites, the family of the Korathites. And Kohath begat Amram.

59 And the name of Amram's wife *was* Jochebed, the daughter of Levi, whom *her mother* bare to Levi in Egypt: and she bare unto Amram Aaron and Moses, and Miriam their sister.

60 And unto Aaron was born Nadab, and Abihu, Eleazar, and Ithamar.

61 And Nadab and Abihu died, when they offered strange fire before the LORD.

62 And those that were numbered of them were twenty and three thousand, all males from a month old and upward: for they were not numbered among the children of Israel, because there was no inheritance given them among the children of Israel.

Caleb and Joshua Live to See the Land

63 These *are* they that were numbered by Moses and Eleazar the priest, who numbered the children of Israel in the plains of Moab by Jordan *near* Jericho.

64 But among these there was not a man of them whom Moses and Aaron the priest numbered, when they numbered the children of Israel in the wilderness of Sinai.

65 For the LORD had said of them, They shall surely die in the wilderness. And there was not left a man of them, save Caleb the son of Jephunneh, and Joshua the son of Nun.

The Daughters of Zelophehad Ask to Inherit Land

27 Then came the daughters of Zelophehad, the son of Hepher, the son of Gilead, the son of Machir, the son of Manasseh, of the families of Manasseh the son of Joseph: and these *are* the names of his daughters; Mahlah, Noah, and Hoglah, and Milcah, and Tirzah.

2 And they stood before Moses, and before Eleazar the priest, and before the princes and all the congregation, *by* the door of the tabernacle of the congregation, saying,

3 Our father died in the wilderness, and he was not in the company of them that gathered themselves together against the LORD in the company of Korah; but died in his own sin, and had no sons.

4 Why should the name of our father be done away from among his family, because he hath no son? Give unto us *therefore* a possession among the brethren of our father.

5 And Moses brought their cause before the LORD.

6 And the LORD spake unto Moses, saying,

7 The daughters of Zelophehad speak right: thou shalt surely give them a possession of an inheritance among their father's brethren; and thou shalt cause the inheritance of their father to pass unto them.

8 And thou shalt speak unto the children of Israel, saying, If a man die, and have no son, then ye shall cause his inheritance to pass unto his daughter.

9 And if he have no daughter, then ye shall give his inheritance unto his brethren.

10 And if he have no brethren, then ye shall give his inheritance unto his father's brethren.

11 And if his father have no brethren, then ye shall give his inheritance unto his kinsman that is next to him of his family, and he shall possess it: and it shall be unto the children of Israel a statute of judgment, as the LORD commanded Moses.

Moses Is Told of His Death

12 And the LORD said unto Moses, Get thee up into this mount Abarim, and see the land which I have given unto the children of Israel.

13 And when thou hast seen it, thou also shalt be gathered unto thy people, as Aaron thy brother was gathered.

14 For ye rebelled against my commandment in the desert of Zin, in the strife of the congregation, to sanctify me at the water before their eyes: that *is* the water of Meribah in Kadesh in the wilderness of Zin.

Moses Asks God to Appoint His Successor

15 And Moses spake unto the LORD, saying,

16 Let the LORD, the God of the spirits of all flesh, set a man over the congregation,

17 Which may go out before them, and which may go in before them, and which may lead them out, and which may bring them in; that the congregation of the LORD be not as sheep which have no shepherd.

18 And the LORD said unto Moses, Take thee Joshua the son of Nun, a man in whom *is* the spirit, and lay thine hand upon him;

19 And set him before Eleazar the priest, and before all the congregation; and give him a charge in their sight.

20 And thou shalt put *some* of thine honour upon him, that all the congregation of the children of Israel may be obedient.

21 And he shall stand before Eleazar the priest, who shall ask *counsel* for him after the judgment of Urim before the LORD: at his word shall they go out, and at his word they shall come in, *both* he, and all the children of Israel with him, even all the congregation.

22 And Moses did as the LORD commanded him: and he took Joshua, and set him before Eleazar the priest, and before all the congregation:

23 And he laid his hands upon him, and gave him a charge, as the LORD commanded by the hand of Moses.

Offerings Are to Be Observed

28 And the LORD spake unto Moses, saying,

2 Command the children of Israel, and say unto them, My offering, *and* my bread for my sacrifices made by fire, *for* a sweet savour unto me, shall ye observe to offer unto me in their due season.

3 And thou shalt say unto them, This *is* the offering made by fire which ye shall offer unto the LORD; two lambs of the first year without spot day by day, *for* a continual burnt offering.

4 The one lamb shalt thou offer in the morning, and the other lamb shalt thou offer at even;

5 And a tenth *part* of an ephah of flour for a meat offering, mingled with the fourth *part* of an hin of beaten oil.

6 *It is* a continual burnt offering, which was ordained in mount Sinai for a sweet savour, a sacrifice made by fire unto the LORD.

7 And the drink offering thereof *shall be* the fourth *part* of an hin for the one lamb: in the holy *place* shalt thou cause the strong wine to be poured unto the LORD *for* a drink offering.

8 And the other lamb shalt thou offer at even: as the meat offering of the morning, and as the drink offering thereof, thou shalt offer *it*, a sacrifice made by fire, of a sweet savour unto the LORD.

Various Offerings

9 And on the sabbath day two lambs of the first year without spot, and two tenth deals of flour *for* a meat offering, mingled with oil, and the drink offering thereof:

10 *This is* the burnt offering of every sabbath, beside the continual burnt offering, and his drink offering.

11 And in the beginnings of your months ye shall offer a burnt offering unto the LORD; two young bullocks, and one ram, seven lambs of the first year without spot;

12 And three tenth deals of flour *for* a meat offering, mingled with oil, for
one bullock; and two tenth deals of flour *for* a meat offering, mingled with
oil, for one ram;
13 And a several tenth deal of flour mingled with oil *for* a meat offering unto
one lamb; *for* a burnt offering of a sweet savour, a sacrifice made by fire unto
the LORD.
14 And their drink offerings shall be half an hin of wine unto a bullock, and
the third *part* of an hin unto a ram, and a fourth *part* of an hin unto a lamb:
this *is* the burnt offering of every month throughout the months of the year.
15 And one kid of the goats for a sin offering unto the LORD shall be offered,
beside the continual burnt offering, and his drink offering.

Observing Passover and Pentecost

16 And in the fourteenth day of the first month *is* the passover of the LORD.
17 And in the fifteenth day of this month *is* the feast: seven days shall unleav-
ened bread be eaten.
18 In the first day *shall be* an holy convocation; ye shall do no manner of
servile work *therein*:
19 But ye shall offer a sacrifice made by fire *for* a burnt offering unto the
LORD; two young bullocks, and one ram, and seven lambs of the first year: they
shall be unto you without blemish:
20 And their meat offering *shall be of* flour mingled with oil: three tenth
deals shall ye offer for a bullock, and two tenth deals for a ram;
21 A several tenth deal shalt thou offer for every lamb, throughout the seven
lambs:
22 And one goat *for* a sin offering, to make an atonement for you.
23 Ye shall offer these beside the burnt offering in the morning, which *is* for
a continual burnt offering.
24 After this manner ye shall offer daily, throughout the seven days, the meat
of the sacrifice made by fire, of a sweet savour unto the LORD: it shall be offered
beside the continual burnt offering, and his drink offering.
25 And on the seventh day ye shall have an holy convocation; ye shall do no
servile work.
26 Also in the day of the firstfruits, when ye bring a new meat offering unto
the LORD, after your weeks *be out*, ye shall have an holy convocation; ye shall
do no servile work:
27 But ye shall offer the burnt offering for a sweet savour unto the LORD; two
young bullocks, one ram, seven lambs of the first year;
28 And their meat offering of flour mingled with oil, three tenth deals unto
one bullock, two tenth deals unto one ram,
29 A several tenth deal unto one lamb, throughout the seven lambs;
30 *And* one kid of the goats, to make an atonement for you.
31 Ye shall offer *them* beside the continual burnt offering, and his meat offer-
ing, (they shall be unto you without blemish) and their drink offerings.

Observing Other Feasts

29 And in the seventh month, on the first *day* of the month, ye shall have
an holy convocation; ye shall do no servile work: it is a day of blowing
the trumpets unto you.
2 And ye shall offer a burnt offering for a sweet savour unto the LORD; one
young bullock, one ram, *and* seven lambs of the first year without blemish:
3 And their meat offering *shall be of* flour mingled with oil, three tenth deals
for a bullock, *and* two tenth deals for a ram,
4 And one tenth deal for one lamb, throughout the seven lambs:
5 And one kid of the goats *for* a sin offering, to make an atonement for you:

6 Beside the burnt offering of the month, and his meat offering, and the daily
burnt offering, and his meat offering, and their drink offerings, according
unto their manner, for a sweet savour, a sacrifice made by fire unto the LORD.
7 And ye shall have on the tenth *day* of this seventh month an holy convoca-
tion; and ye shall afflict your souls: ye shall not do any work *therein*:
8 But ye shall offer a burnt offering unto the LORD *for* a sweet savour; one
young bullock, one ram, *and* seven lambs of the first year; they shall be unto
you without blemish:
9 And their meat offering *shall be of* flour mingled with oil, three tenth deals
to a bullock, *and* two tenth deals to one ram,
10 A several tenth deal for one lamb, throughout the seven lambs:
11 One kid of the goats *for* a sin offering; beside the sin offering of atonement,
and the continual burnt offering, and the meat offering of it, and their drink
offerings.
12 And on the fifteenth day of the seventh month ye shall have an holy con-
vocation; ye shall do no servile work, and ye shall keep a feast unto the LORD
seven days:
13 And ye shall offer a burnt offering, a sacrifice made by fire, of a sweet
savour unto the LORD; thirteen young bullocks, two rams, *and* fourteen lambs
of the first year; they shall be without blemish:
14 And their meat offering *shall be of* flour mingled with oil, three tenth
deals unto every bullock of the thirteen bullocks, two tenth deals to each ram
of the two rams,
15 And a several tenth deal to each lamb of the fourteen lambs:
16 And one kid of the goats *for* a sin offering; beside the continual burnt
offering, his meat offering, and his drink offering.
17 And on the second day *ye shall offer* twelve young bullocks, two rams,
fourteen lambs of the first year without spot:
18 And their meat offering and their drink offerings for the bullocks, for the
rams, and for the lambs, *shall be* according to their number, after the manner:
19 And one kid of the goats *for* a sin offering; beside the continual burnt
offering, and the meat offering thereof, and their drink offerings.
20 And on the third day eleven bullocks, two rams, fourteen lambs of the first
year without blemish;
21 And their meat offering and their drink offerings for the bullocks, for the
rams, and for the lambs, *shall be* according to their number, after the manner:
22 And one goat *for* a sin offering; beside the continual burnt offering, and
his meat offering, and his drink offering.
23 And on the fourth day ten bullocks, two rams, *and* fourteen lambs of the
first year without blemish:
24 Their meat offering and their drink offerings for the bullocks, for the
rams, and for the lambs, *shall be* according to their number, after the manner:
25 And one kid of the goats *for* a sin offering; beside the continual burnt
offering, his meat offering, and his drink offering.
26 And on the fifth day nine bullocks, two rams, *and* fourteen lambs of the
first year without spot:
27 And their meat offering and their drink offerings for the bullocks, for the
rams, and for the lambs, *shall be* according to their number, after the manner:
28 And one goat *for* a sin offering; beside the continual burnt offering, and
his meat offering, and his drink offering.
29 And on the sixth day eight bullocks, two rams, *and* fourteen lambs of the
first year without blemish:
30 And their meat offering and their drink offerings for the bullocks, for the
rams, and for the lambs, *shall be* according to their number, after the manner:
31 And one goat *for* a sin offering; beside the continual burnt offering, his
meat offering, and his drink offering.

32 And on the seventh day seven bullocks, two rams, *and* fourteen lambs of
the first year without blemish:
33 And their meat offering and their drink offerings for the bullocks, for the
rams, and for the lambs, *shall be* according to their number, after the manner:
34 And one goat *for* a sin offering; beside the continual burnt offering, his
meat offering, and his drink offering.
35 On the eighth day ye shall have a solemn assembly: ye shall do no servile
work *therein*:
36 But ye shall offer a burnt offering, a sacrifice made by fire, of a sweet savour
unto the LORD: one bullock, one ram, seven lambs of the first year without
blemish:
37 Their meat offering and their drink offerings for the bullock, for the ram,
and for the lambs, *shall be* according to their number, after the manner:
38 And one goat *for* a sin offering; beside the continual burnt offering, and
his meat offering, and his drink offering.
39 These *things* ye shall do unto the LORD in your set feasts, beside your vows,
and your freewill offerings, for your burnt offerings, and for your meat offer-
ings, and for your drink offerings, and for your peace offerings.
40 And Moses told the children of Israel according to all that the LORD com-
manded Moses.

Vows Are Not to Be Broken

30 And Moses spake unto the heads of the tribes concerning the children
of Israel, saying, This *is* the thing which the LORD hath commanded.
2 If a man vow a vow unto the LORD, or swear an oath to bind his soul with
a bond; he shall not break his word, he shall do according to all that pro-
ceedeth out of his mouth.

The Exception of a Young Woman's Vow

3 If a woman also vow a vow unto the LORD, and bind herself by a bond, *being*
in her father's house in her youth;
4 And her father hear her vow, and her bond wherewith she hath bound her
soul, and her father shall hold his peace at her: then all her vows shall stand,
and every bond wherewith she hath bound her soul shall stand.
5 But if her father disallow her in the day that he heareth; not any of her
vows, or of her bonds wherewith she hath bound her soul, shall stand: and
the LORD shall forgive her, because her father disallowed her.
6 And if she had at all an husband, when she vowed, or uttered ought out of
her lips, wherewith she bound her soul;
7 And her husband heard *it*, and held his peace at her in the day that he heard
it: then her vows shall stand, and her bonds wherewith she bound her soul
shall stand.
8 But if her husband disallowed her on the day that he heard *it*; then he shall
make her vow which she vowed, and that which she uttered with her lips,
wherewith she bound her soul, of none effect: and the LORD shall forgive her.
9 But every vow of a widow, and of her that is divorced, wherewith they have
bound their souls, shall stand against her.
10 And if she vowed in her husband's house, or bound her soul by a bond
with an oath;
11 And her husband heard *it*, and held his peace at her, *and* disallowed her
not: then all her vows shall stand, and every bond wherewith she bound her
soul shall stand.
12 But if her husband hath utterly made them void on the day he heard *them*;
then whatsoever proceeded out of her lips concerning her vows, or concern-
ing the bond of her soul, shall not stand: her husband hath made them void;
and the LORD shall forgive her.

13 Every vow, and every binding oath to afflict the soul, her husband may
establish it, or her husband may make it void.
14 But if her husband altogether hold his peace at her from day to day; then
he establisheth all her vows, or all her bonds, which *are* upon her: he con-
firmeth them, because he held his peace at her in the day that he heard *them*.
15 But if he shall any ways make them void after that he hath heard *them*;
then he shall bear her iniquity.
16 These *are* the statutes, which the LORD commanded Moses, between a
man and his wife, between the father and his daughter, *being yet* in her youth
in her father's house.

The Israelites Defeat the Midianites and Kill Balaam

31 And the LORD spake unto Moses, saying,
2 Avenge the children of Israel of the Midianites: afterward shalt thou
be gathered unto thy people.
3 And Moses spake unto the people, saying, Arm some of yourselves unto the
war, and let them go against the Midianites, and avenge the LORD of Midian.
4 Of every tribe a thousand, throughout all the tribes of Israel, shall ye send
to the war.
5 So there were delivered out of the thousands of Israel, a thousand of *every*
tribe, twelve thousand armed for war.
6 And Moses sent them to the war, a thousand of *every* tribe, them and
Phinehas the son of Eleazar the priest, to the war, with the holy instruments,
and the trumpets to blow in his hand.
7 And they warred against the Midianites, as the LORD commanded Moses;
and they slew all the males.
8 And they slew the kings of Midian, beside the rest of them that were slain;
namely, Evi, and Rekem, and Zur, and Hur, and Reba, five kings of Midian:
Balaam also the son of Beor they slew with the sword.
9 And the children of Israel took *all* the women of Midian captives, and their
little ones, and took the spoil of all their cattle, and all their flocks, and all their
goods.
10 And they burnt all their cities wherein they dwelt, and all their goodly
castles, with fire.
11 And they took all the spoil, and all the prey, *both* of men and of beasts.
12 And they brought the captives, and the prey, and the spoil, unto Moses,
and Eleazar the priest, and unto the congregation of the children of Israel,
unto the camp at the plains of Moab, which *are* by Jordan *near* Jericho.

Moses Is Angry with the Officers

13 And Moses, and Eleazar the priest, and all the princes of the congregation,
went forth to meet them without the camp.
14 And Moses was wroth with the officers of the host, *with* the captains over
thousands, and captains over hundreds, which came from the battle.
15 And Moses said unto them, Have ye saved all the women alive?
16 Behold, these caused the children of Israel, through the counsel of Balaam,
to commit trespass against the LORD in the matter of Peor, and there was a
plague among the congregation of the LORD.
17 Now therefore kill every male among the little ones, and kill every woman
that hath known man by lying with him.
18 But all the women children, that have not known a man by lying with him,
keep alive for yourselves.
19 And do ye abide without the camp seven days: whosoever hath killed any
person, and whosoever hath touched any slain, purify *both* yourselves and
your captives on the third day, and on the seventh day.
20 And purify all *your* raiment, and all that is made of skins, and all work of
goats' *hair*, and all things made of wood.

21 And Eleazar the priest said unto the men of war which went to the battle,
This *is* the ordinance of the law which the LORD commanded Moses;
22 Only the gold, and the silver, the brass, the iron, the tin, and the lead,
23 Every thing that may abide the fire, ye shall make *it* go through the fire,
and it shall be clean: nevertheless it shall be purified with the water of separ-
ation: and all that abideth not the fire ye shall make go through the water.
24 And ye shall wash your clothes on the seventh day, and ye shall be clean,
and afterward ye shall come into the camp.

Proportions for Dividing the Spoils

25 And the LORD spake unto Moses, saying,
26 Take the sum of the prey that was taken, *both* of man and of beast, thou,
and Eleazar the priest, and the chief fathers of the congregation:
27 And divide the prey into two parts; between them that took the war upon
them, who went out to battle, and between all the congregation:
28 And levy a tribute unto the LORD of the men of war which went out to
battle: one soul of five hundred, *both* of the persons, and of the beeves, and of
the asses, and of the sheep:
29 Take *it* of their half, and give it unto Eleazar the priest, *for* an heave offer-
ing of the LORD.
30 And of the children of Israel's half, thou shalt take one portion of fifty, of
the persons, of the beeves, of the asses, and of the flocks, of all manner of
beasts, and give them unto the Levites, which keep the charge of the taber-
nacle of the LORD.
31 And Moses and Eleazar the priest did as the LORD commanded Moses.
32 And the booty, *being* the rest of the prey which the men of war had caught,
was six hundred thousand and seventy thousand and five thousand sheep,
33 And threescore and twelve thousand beeves,
34 And threescore and one thousand asses,
35 And thirty and two thousand persons in all, of women that had not known
man by lying with him.
36 And the half, *which was* the portion of them that went out to war, was in
number three hundred thousand and seven and thirty thousand and five
hundred sheep:
37 And the LORD's tribute of the sheep was six hundred and threescore and
fifteen.
38 And the beeves *were* thirty and six thousand; of which the LORD's tribute
was threescore and twelve.
39 And the asses *were* thirty thousand and five hundred; of which the LORD's
tribute *was* threescore and one.
40 And the persons *were* sixteen thousand; of which the LORD's tribute *was*
thirty and two persons.
41 And Moses gave the tribute, *which was* the LORD's heave offering, unto
Eleazar the priest, as the LORD commanded Moses.
42 And of the children of Israel's half, which Moses divided from the men
that warred,
43 (Now the half *that pertained unto* the congregation was three hundred
thousand and thirty thousand *and* seven thousand and five hundred sheep,
44 And thirty and six thousand beeves,
45 And thirty thousand asses and five hundred,
46 And sixteen thousand persons;)
47 Even of the children of Israel's half, Moses took one portion of fifty, *both*
of man and of beast, and gave them unto the Levites, which kept the charge
of the tabernacle of the LORD; as the LORD commanded Moses.

The Voluntary Offering

48 And the officers which *were* over thousands of the host, the captains of thousands, and captains of hundreds, came near unto Moses:

49 And they said unto Moses, Thy servants have taken the sum of the men of war which *are* under our charge, and there lacketh not one man of us.

50 We have therefore brought an oblation for the LORD, what every man hath gotten, of jewels of gold, chains, and bracelets, rings, earrings, and tablets, to make an atonement for our souls before the LORD.

51 And Moses and Eleazar the priest took the gold of them, *even* all wrought jewels.

52 And all the gold of the offering that they offered up to the LORD, of the captains of thousands, and of the captains of hundreds, was sixteen thousand seven hundred and fifty shekels.

53 (*For* the men of war had taken spoil, every man for himself.)

54 And Moses and Eleazar the priest took the gold of the captains of thousands and of hundreds, and brought it into the tabernacle of the congregation, *for* a memorial for the children of Israel before the LORD.

The Tribes of Reuben and Gad Request Land East of the Jordan

32 Now the children of Reuben and the children of Gad had a very great multitude of cattle: and when they saw the land of Jazer, and the land of Gilead, that, behold, the place *was* a place for cattle;

2 The children of Gad and the children of Reuben came and spake unto Moses, and to Eleazar the priest, and unto the princes of the congregation, saying,

3 Ataroth, and Dibon, and Jazer, and Nimrah, and Heshbon, and Elealeh, and Shebam, and Nebo, and Beon,

4 *Even* the country which the LORD smote before the congregation of Israel, *is* a land for cattle, and thy servants have cattle:

5 Wherefore, said they, if we have found grace in thy sight, let this land be given unto thy servants for a possession, *and* bring us not over Jordan.

6 And Moses said unto the children of Gad and to the children of Reuben, Shall your brethren go to war, and shall ye sit here?

7 And wherefore discourage ye the heart of the children of Israel from going over into the land which the LORD hath given them?

8 Thus did your fathers, when I sent them from Kadesh-barnea to see the land.

9 For when they went up unto the valley of Eshcol, and saw the land, they discouraged the heart of the children of Israel, that they should not go into the land which the LORD had given them.

10 And the LORD's anger was kindled the same time, and he sware, saying,

11 Surely none of the men that came up out of Egypt, from twenty years old and upward, shall see the land which I sware unto Abraham, unto Isaac, and unto Jacob; because they have not wholly followed me:

12 Save Caleb the son of Jephunneh the Kenezite, and Joshua the son of Nun: for they have wholly followed the LORD.

13 And the LORD's anger was kindled against Israel, and he made them wander in the wilderness forty years, until all the generation, that had done evil in the sight of the LORD, was consumed.

14 And, behold, ye are risen up in your fathers' stead, an increase of sinful men, to augment yet the fierce anger of the LORD toward Israel.

15 For if ye turn away from after him, he will yet again leave them in the wilderness; and ye shall destroy all this people.

The Tribes Offer Conditions That Are Satisfactory to Moses

16 And they came near unto him, and said, We will build sheepfolds here for our cattle, and cities for our little ones:

17 But we ourselves will go ready armed before the children of Israel, until
we have brought them unto their place: and our little ones shall dwell in the
fenced cities because of the inhabitants of the land.
18 We will not return unto our houses, until the children of Israel have in-
herited every man his inheritance.
19 For we will not inherit with them on yonder side Jordan, or forward;
because our inheritance is fallen to us on this side Jordan eastward.
20 And Moses said unto them, If ye will do this thing, if ye will go armed
before the LORD to war,
21 And will go all of you armed over Jordan before the LORD, until he hath
driven out his enemies from before him,
22 And the land be subdued before the LORD: then afterward ye shall return,
and be guiltless before the LORD, and before Israel; and this land shall be your
possession before the LORD.
23 But if ye will not do so, behold, ye have sinned against the LORD: and be
sure your sin will find you out.
24 Build you cities for your little ones, and folds for your sheep; and do that
which hath proceeded out of your mouth.
25 And the children of Gad and the children of Reuben spake unto Moses,
saying, Thy servants will do as my lord commandeth.
26 Our little ones, our wives, our flocks, and all our cattle, shall be there in
the cities of Gilead:
27 But thy servants will pass over, every man armed for war, before the LORD
to battle, as my lord saith.
28 So concerning them Moses commanded Eleazar the priest, and Joshua
the son of Nun, and the chief fathers of the tribes of the children of Israel:
29 And Moses said unto them, If the children of Gad and the children of
Reuben will pass with you over Jordan, every man armed to battle, before the
LORD, and the land shall be subdued before you; then ye shall give them the
land of Gilead for a possession:
30 But if they will not pass over with you armed, they shall have possessions
among you in the land of Canaan.
31 And the children of Gad and the children of Reuben answered, saying, As
the LORD hath said unto thy servants, so will we do.
32 We will pass over armed before the LORD into the land of Canaan, that the
possession of our inheritance on this side Jordan *may be* ours.
33 And Moses gave unto them, *even* to the children of Gad, and to the children
of Reuben, and unto half the tribe of Manasseh the son of Joseph, the kingdom
of Sihon king of the Amorites, and the kingdom of Og king of Bashan, the land,
with the cities thereof in the coasts, *even* the cities of the country round about.
34 And the children of Gad built Dibon, and Ataroth, and Aroer,
35 And Atroth, Shophan, and Jaazer, and Jogbehah,
36 And Beth-nimrah, and Beth-haran, fenced cities: and folds for sheep.
37 And the children of Reuben built Heshbon, and Elealeh, and Kirjathaim,
38 And Nebo, and Baal-meon, (their names being changed,) and Shibmah:
and gave other names unto the cities which they builded.
39 And the children of Machir the son of Manasseh went to Gilead, and took
it, and dispossessed the Amorite which *was* in it.
40 And Moses gave Gilead unto Machir the son of Manasseh; and he dwelt
therein.
41 And Jair the son of Manasseh went and took the small towns thereof, and
called them Havoth-jair.
42 And Nobah went and took Kenath, and the villages thereof, and called it
Nobah, after his own name.

Forty-Two Journeys of the Israelites

33 These *are* the journeys of the children of Israel, which went forth out
of the land of Egypt with their armies under the hand of Moses and
Aaron.
2 And Moses wrote their goings out according to their journeys by the com-
mandment of the LORD: and these *are* their journeys according to their goings
out.
3 And they departed from Rameses in the first month, on the fifteenth day
of the first month; on the morrow after the passover the children of Israel
went out with an high hand in the sight of all the Egyptians.
4 For the Egyptians buried all *their* firstborn, which the LORD had smitten
among them: upon their gods also the LORD executed judgments.
5 And the children of Israel removed from Rameses, and pitched in Succoth.
6 And they departed from Succoth, and pitched in Etham, which *is* in the
edge of the wilderness.
7 And they removed from Etham, and turned again unto Pi-hahiroth, which
is before Baal-zephon: and they pitched before Migdol.
8 And they departed from before Pi-hahiroth, and passed through the midst
of the sea into the wilderness, and went three days' journey in the wilderness
of Etham, and pitched in Marah.
9 And they removed from Marah, and came unto Elim: and in Elim *were*
twelve fountains of water, and threescore and ten palm trees; and they pitched
there.
10 And they removed from Elim, and encamped by the Red sea.
11 And they removed from the Red sea, and encamped in the wilderness of
Sin.
12 And they took their journey out of the wilderness of Sin, and encamped
in Dophkah.
13 And they departed from Dophkah, and encamped in Alush.
14 And they removed from Alush, and encamped at Rephidim, where was
no water for the people to drink.
15 And they departed from Rephidim, and pitched in the wilderness of Sinai.
16 And they removed from the desert of Sinai, and pitched at Kibroth-
hattaavah.
17 And they departed from Kibroth-hattaavah, and encamped at Hazeroth.
18 And they departed from Hazeroth, and pitched in Rithmah.
19 And they departed from Rithmah, and pitched at Rimmon-parez.
20 And they departed from Rimmon-parez, and pitched in Libnah.
21 And they removed from Libnah, and pitched at Rissah.
22 And they journeyed from Rissah, and pitched in Kehelathah.
23 And they went from Kehelathah, and pitched in mount Shapher.
24 And they removed from mount Shapher, and encamped in Haradah.
25 And they removed from Haradah, and pitched in Makheloth.
26 And they removed from Makheloth, and encamped at Tahath.
27 And they departed from Tahath, and pitched at Tarah.
28 And they removed from Tarah, and pitched in Mithcah.
29 And they went from Mithcah, and pitched in Hashmonah.
30 And they departed from Hashmonah, and encamped at Moseroth.
31 And they departed from Moseroth, and pitched in Bene-jaakan.
32 And they removed from Bene-jaakan, and encamped at Hor-hagidgad.
33 And they went from Hor-hagidgad, and pitched in Jotbathah.
34 And they removed from Jotbathah, and encamped at Ebronah.
35 And they departed from Ebronah, and encamped at Ezion-gaber.
36 And they removed from Ezion-gaber, and pitched in the wilderness of
Zin, which *is* Kadesh.

37 And they removed from Kadesh, and pitched in mount Hor, in the edge
of the land of Edom.
38 And Aaron the priest went up into mount Hor at the commandment of
the LORD, and died there, in the fortieth year after the children of Israel were
come out of the land of Egypt, in the first *day* of the fifth month.
39 And Aaron *was* an hundred and twenty and three years old when he died
in mount Hor.
40 And king Arad the Canaanite, which dwelt in the south in the land of
Canaan, heard of the coming of the children of Israel.
41 And they departed from mount Hor, and pitched in Zalmonah.
42 And they departed from Zalmonah, and pitched in Punon.
43 And they departed from Punon, and pitched in Oboth.
44 And they departed from Oboth, and pitched in Ijeabarim, in the border
of Moab.
45 And they departed from Iim, and pitched in Dibon-gad.
46 And they removed from Dibon-gad, and encamped in Almon-diblathaim.
47 And they removed from Almon-diblathaim, and pitched in the mountains
of Abarim, before Nebo.
48 And they departed from the mountains of Abarim, and pitched in the
plains of Moab by Jordan *near* Jericho.
49 And they pitched by Jordan, from Beth-jesimoth *even* unto Abel-shittim
in the plains of Moab.

The Canaanites Are to Be Destroyed

50 And the LORD spake unto Moses in the plains of Moab by Jordan *near*
Jericho, saying,
51 Speak unto the children of Israel, and say unto them, When ye are passed
over Jordan into the land of Canaan;
52 Then ye shall drive out all the inhabitants of the land from before you,
and destroy all their pictures, and destroy all their molten images, and quite
pluck down all their high places:
53 And ye shall dispossess *the inhabitants* of the land, and dwell therein: for
I have given you the land to possess it.
54 And ye shall divide the land by lot for an inheritance among your families:
and to the more ye shall give the more inheritance, and to the fewer ye shall
give the less inheritance: every man's *inheritance* shall be in the place where
his lot falleth; according to the tribes of your fathers ye shall inherit.
55 But if ye will not drive out the inhabitants of the land from before you;
then it shall come to pass, that those which ye let remain of them *shall be*
pricks in your eyes, and thorns in your sides, and shall vex you in the land
wherein ye dwell.
56 Moreover it shall come to pass, *that* I shall do unto you, as I thought to do
unto them.

The Borders of the Land

34 And the LORD spake unto Moses, saying,
2 Command the children of Israel, and say unto them, When ye come
into the land of Canaan; (this *is* the land that shall fall unto you for an inher-
itance, *even* the land of Canaan with the coasts thereof:)
3 Then your south quarter shall be from the wilderness of Zin along by the
coast of Edom, and your south border shall be the outmost coast of the salt
sea eastward:
4 And your border shall turn from the south to the ascent of Akrabbim, and
pass on to Zin: and the going forth thereof shall be from the south to Kadesh-
barnea, and shall go on to Hazar-addar, and pass on to Azmon:
5 And the border shall fetch a compass from Azmon unto the river of Egypt,
and the goings out of it shall be at the sea.

6 And *as for* the western border, ye shall even have the great sea for a border: this shall be your west border.
7 And this shall be your north border: from the great sea ye shall point out for you mount Hor:
8 From mount Hor ye shall point out *your border* unto the entrance of Hamath; and the goings forth of the border shall be to Zedad:
9 And the border shall go on to Ziphron, and the goings out of it shall be at Hazar-enan: this shall be your north border.
10 And ye shall point out your east border from Hazar-enan to Shepham:
11 And the coast shall go down from Shepham to Riblah, on the east side of Ain; and the border shall descend, and shall reach unto the side of the sea of Chinnereth eastward:
12 And the border shall go down to Jordan, and the goings out of it shall be at the salt sea: this shall be your land with the coasts thereof round about.
13 And Moses commanded the children of Israel, saying, This *is* the land which ye shall inherit by lot, which the LORD commanded to give unto the nine tribes, and to the half tribe:
14 For the tribe of the children of Reuben according to the house of their fathers, and the tribe of the children of Gad according to the house of their fathers, have received *their inheritance*; and half the tribe of Manasseh have received their inheritance:
15 The two tribes and the half tribe have received their inheritance on this side Jordan *near* Jericho eastward, toward the sunrising.

The Names of the Men Who Will Divide the Land

16 And the LORD spake unto Moses, saying,
17 These *are* the names of the men which shall divide the land unto you: Eleazar the priest, and Joshua the son of Nun.
18 And ye shall take one prince of every tribe, to divide the land by inheritance.
19 And the names of the men *are* these: Of the tribe of Judah, Caleb the son of Jephunneh.
20 And of the tribe of the children of Simeon, Shemuel the son of Ammihud.
21 Of the tribe of Benjamin, Elidad the son of Chislon.
22 And the prince of the tribe of the children of Dan, Bukki the son of Jogli.
23 The prince of the children of Joseph, for the tribe of the children of Manasseh, Hanniel the son of Ephod.
24 And the prince of the tribe of the children of Ephraim, Kemuel the son of Shiphtan.
25 And the prince of the tribe of the children of Zebulun, Elizaphan the son of Parnach.
26 And the prince of the tribe of the children of Issachar, Paltiel the son of Azzan.
27 And the prince of the tribe of the children of Asher, Ahihud the son of Shelomi.
28 And the prince of the tribe of the children of Naphtali, Pedahel the son of Ammihud.
29 These *are they* whom the LORD commanded to divide the inheritance unto the children of Israel in the land of Canaan.

Forty-Eight Levitical Cities

35 And the LORD spake unto Moses in the plains of Moab by Jordan *near* Jericho, saying,
2 Command the children of Israel, that they give unto the Levites of the inheritance of their possession cities to dwell in; and ye shall give *also* unto the Levites suburbs for the cities round about them.

3 And the cities shall they have to dwell in; and the suburbs of them shall be
for their cattle, and for their goods, and for all their beasts.
4 And the suburbs of the cities, which ye shall give unto the Levites, *shall*
reach from the wall of the city and outward a thousand cubits round about.
5 And ye shall measure from without the city on the east side two thousand
cubits, and on the south side two thousand cubits, and on the west side two
thousand cubits, and on the north side two thousand cubits; and the city *shall*
be in the midst: this shall be to them the suburbs of the cities.
6 And among the cities which ye shall give unto the Levites *there shall be* six
cities for refuge, which ye shall appoint for the manslayer, that he may flee
thither: and to them ye shall add forty and two cities.
7 *So* all the cities which ye shall give to the Levites *shall be* forty and eight
cities: them *shall ye give* with their suburbs.
8 And the cities which ye shall give *shall be* of the possession of the children
of Israel: from *them that have* many ye shall give many; but from *them that*
have few ye shall give few: every one shall give of his cities unto the Levites
according to his inheritance which he inheriteth.

Law of Murder and Cities of Refuge

9 And the LORD spake unto Moses, saying,
10 Speak unto the children of Israel, and say unto them, When ye be come
over Jordan into the land of Canaan;
11 Then ye shall appoint you cities to be cities of refuge for you; that the
slayer may flee thither, which killeth any person at unawares.
12 And they shall be unto you cities for refuge from the avenger; that the
manslayer die not, until he stand before the congregation in judgment.
13 And of these cities which ye shall give six cities shall ye have for refuge.
14 Ye shall give three cities on this side Jordan, and three cities shall ye give
in the land of Canaan, *which* shall be cities of refuge.
15 These six cities shall be a refuge, *both* for the children of Israel, and for
the stranger, and for the sojourner among them: that every one that killeth
any person unawares may flee thither.
16 And if he smite him with an instrument of iron, so that he die, he *is* a
murderer: the murderer shall surely be put to death.
17 And if he smite him with throwing a stone, wherewith he may die, and he
die, he *is* a murderer: the murderer shall surely be put to death.
18 Or *if* he smite him with an hand weapon of wood, wherewith he may die,
and he die, he *is* a murderer: the murderer shall surely be put to death.
19 The revenger of blood himself shall slay the murderer: when he meeteth
him, he shall slay him.
20 But if he thrust him of hatred, or hurl at him by laying of wait, that he die;
21 Or in enmity smite him with his hand, that he die: he that smote *him* shall
surely be put to death; *for* he *is* a murderer: the revenger of blood shall slay
the murderer, when he meeteth him.
22 But if he thrust him suddenly without enmity, or have cast upon him any
thing without laying of wait,
23 Or with any stone, wherewith a man may die, seeing *him* not, and cast *it*
upon him, that he die, and *was* not his enemy, neither sought his harm:
24 Then the congregation shall judge between the slayer and the revenger of
blood according to these judgments:
25 And the congregation shall deliver the slayer out of the hand of the
revenger of blood, and the congregation shall restore him to the city of his
refuge, whither he was fled: and he shall abide in it unto the death of the high
priest, which was anointed with the holy oil.
26 But if the slayer shall at any time come without the border of the city of
his refuge, whither he was fled;

27 And the revenger of blood find him without the borders of the city of his
refuge, and the revenger of blood kill the slayer; he shall not be guilty of blood:
28 Because he should have remained in the city of his refuge until the death
of the high priest: but after the death of the high priest the slayer shall return
into the land of his possession.
29 So these *things* shall be for a statute of judgment unto you throughout
your generations in all your dwellings.
30 Whoso killeth any person, the murderer shall be put to death by the mouth
of witnesses: but one witness shall not testify against any person *to cause him*
to die.
31 Moreover ye shall take no satisfaction for the life of a murderer, which *is*
guilty of death: but he shall be surely put to death.
32 And ye shall take no satisfaction for him that is fled to the city of his refuge,
that he should come again to dwell in the land, until the death of the priest.
33 So ye shall not pollute the land wherein ye *are*: for blood it defileth the
land: and the land cannot be cleansed of the blood that is shed therein, but
by the blood of him that shed it.
34 Defile not therefore the land which ye shall inhabit, wherein I dwell: for
I the LORD dwell among the children of Israel.

Expressions of Concern about Daughters Receiving Lands of Inheritance

36 And the chief fathers of the families of the children of Gilead, the son
of Machir, the son of Manasseh, of the families of the sons of Joseph,
came near, and spake before Moses, and before the princes, the chief fathers
of the children of Israel:
2 And they said, The LORD commanded my lord to give the land for an inher-
itance by lot to the children of Israel: and my lord was commanded by the
LORD to give the inheritance of Zelophehad our brother unto his daughters.
3 And if they be married to any of the sons of the *other* tribes of the children
of Israel, then shall their inheritance be taken from the inheritance of our
fathers, and shall be put to the inheritance of the tribe whereunto they are
received: so shall it be taken from the lot of our inheritance.
4 And when the jubile of the children of Israel shall be, then shall their inher-
itance be put unto the inheritance of the tribe whereunto they are received:
so shall their inheritance be taken away from the inheritance of the tribe of
our fathers.

Concern Is Answered by Requiring That Daughters Marry in Their Own Tribes

5 And Moses commanded the children of Israel according to the word of the
LORD, saying, The tribe of the sons of Joseph hath said well.
6 This *is* the thing which the LORD doth command concerning the daughters
of Zelophehad, saying, Let them marry to whom they think best; only to the
family of the tribe of their father shall they marry.
7 So shall not the inheritance of the children of Israel remove from tribe to
tribe: for every one of the children of Israel shall keep himself to the inher-
itance of the tribe of his fathers.
8 And every daughter, that possesseth an inheritance in any tribe of the chil-
dren of Israel, shall be wife unto one of the family of the tribe of her father,
that the children of Israel may enjoy every man the inheritance of his fathers.
9 Neither shall the inheritance remove from *one* tribe to another tribe; but
every one of the tribes of the children of Israel shall keep himself to his own
inheritance.
10 Even as the LORD commanded Moses, so did the daughters of Zelophehad:
11 For Mahlah, Tirzah, and Hoglah, and Milcah, and Noah, the daughters of
Zelophehad, were married unto their father's brothers' sons:

12 *And* they were married into the families of the sons of Manasseh the son
of Joseph, and their inheritance remained in the tribe of the family of their
father.
13 These *are* the commandments and the judgments, which the LORD com-
manded by the hand of Moses unto the children of Israel in the plains of Moab
by Jordan *near* Jericho.

DEUTERONOMY

Moses Speaks to the People

1 These *be* the words which Moses spake unto all Israel on this side Jordan in the wilderness, in the plain over against the Red *sea*, between Paran, and Tophel, and Laban, and Hazeroth, and Dizahab.

2 (*There are* eleven days' *journey* from Horeb by the way of mount Seir unto Kadesh-barnea.)

3 And it came to pass in the fortieth year, in the eleventh month, on the first *day* of the month, *that* Moses spake unto the children of Israel, according unto all that the LORD had given him in commandment unto them;

4 After he had slain Sihon the king of the Amorites, which dwelt in Heshbon, and Og the king of Bashan, which dwelt at Astaroth in Edrei:

5 On this side Jordan, in the land of Moab, began Moses to declare this law, saying,

6 The LORD our God spake unto us in Horeb, saying, Ye have dwelt long enough in this mount:

7 Turn you, and take your journey, and go to the mount of the Amorites, and unto all *the places* nigh thereunto, in the plain, in the hills, and in the vale, and in the south, and by the sea side, to the land of the Canaanites, and unto Lebanon, unto the great river, the river Euphrates.

8 Behold, I have set the land before you: go in and possess the land which the LORD sware unto your fathers, Abraham, Isaac, and Jacob, to give unto them and to their seed after them.

9 And I spake unto you at that time, saying, I am not able to bear you myself alone:

10 The LORD your God hath multiplied you, and, behold, ye *are* this day as the stars of heaven for multitude.

11 (The LORD God of your fathers make you a thousand times so many more as ye *are*, and bless you, as he hath promised you!)

12 How can I myself alone bear your cumbrance, and your burden, and your strife?

13 Take you wise men, and understanding, and known among your tribes, and I will make them rulers over you.

14 And ye answered me, and said, The thing which thou hast spoken *is* good *for us* to do.

15 So I took the chief of your tribes, wise men, and known, and made them heads over you, captains over thousands, and captains over hundreds, and captains over fifties, and captains over tens, and officers among your tribes.

16 And I charged your judges at that time, saying, Hear *the causes* between your brethren, and judge righteously between *every* man and his brother, and the stranger *that is* with him.

17 Ye shall not respect persons in judgment; *but* ye shall hear the small as well as the great; ye shall not be afraid of the face of man; for the judgment *is* God's: and the cause that is too hard for you, bring *it* unto me, and I will hear it.

18 And I commanded you at that time all the things which ye should do.

Moses Tells of Sending the Spies and the People's Rebellion

19 And when we departed from Horeb, we went through all that great and terrible wilderness, which ye saw by the way of the mountain of the Amorites, as the LORD our God commanded us; and we came to Kadesh-barnea.

20 And I said unto you, Ye are come unto the mountain of the Amorites,
which the LORD our God doth give unto us.
21 Behold, the LORD thy God hath set the land before thee: go up *and* possess
it, as the LORD God of thy fathers hath said unto thee; fear not, neither be
discouraged.
22 And ye came near unto me every one of you, and said, We will send men
before us, and they shall search us out the land, and bring us word again by
what way we must go up, and into what cities we shall come.
23 And the saying pleased me well: and I took twelve men of you, one of a
tribe:
24 And they turned and went up into the mountain, and came unto the val-
ley of Eshcol, and searched it out.
25 And they took of the fruit of the land in their hands, and brought *it* down
unto us, and brought us word again, and said, *It is* a good land which the LORD
our God doth give us.
26 Notwithstanding ye would not go up, but rebelled against the command-
ment of the LORD your God:
27 And ye murmured in your tents, and said, Because the LORD hated us, he
hath brought us forth out of the land of Egypt, to deliver us into the hand of
the Amorites, to destroy us.
28 Whither shall we go up? our brethren have discouraged our heart, saying,
The people *is* greater and taller than we; the cities *are* great and walled up to
heaven; and moreover we have seen the sons of the Anakims there.
29 Then I said unto you, Dread not, neither be afraid of them.
30 The LORD your God which goeth before you, he shall fight for you, accord-
ing to all that he did for you in Egypt before your eyes;
31 And in the wilderness, where thou hast seen how that the LORD thy God
bare thee, as a man doth bear his son, in all the way that ye went, until ye came
into this place.
32 Yet in this thing ye did not believe the LORD your God,
33 Who went in the way before you, to search you out a place to pitch your
tents *in*, in fire by night, to shew you by what way ye should go, and in a cloud
by day.
34 And the LORD heard the voice of your words, and was wroth, and sware,
saying,
35 Surely there shall not one of these men of this evil generation see that
good land, which I sware to give unto your fathers,
36 Save Caleb the son of Jephunneh; he shall see it, and to him will I give the
land that he hath trodden upon, and to his children, because he hath wholly
followed the LORD.
37 Also the LORD was angry with me for your sakes, saying, Thou also shalt
not go in thither.
38 *But* Joshua the son of Nun, which standeth before thee, he shall go in
thither: encourage him: for he shall cause Israel to inherit it.
39 Moreover your little ones, which ye said should be a prey, and your chil-
dren, which in that day had no knowledge between good and evil, they shall
go in thither, and unto them will I give it, and they shall possess it.
40 But *as for* you, turn you, and take your journey into the wilderness by the
way of the Red sea.
41 Then ye answered and said unto me, We have sinned against the LORD, we
will go up and fight, according to all that the LORD our God commanded us.
And when ye had girded on every man his weapons of war, ye were ready to
go up into the hill.
42 And the LORD said unto me, Say unto them, Go not up, neither fight; for I
am not among you; lest ye be smitten before your enemies.

43 So I spake unto you; and ye would not hear, but rebelled against the com-
mandment of the LORD, and went presumptuously up into the hill.
44 And the Amorites, which dwelt in that mountain, came out against you,
and chased you, as bees do, and destroyed you in Seir, *even* unto Hormah.
45 And ye returned and wept before the LORD; but the LORD would not
hearken to your voice, nor give ear unto you.
46 So ye abode in Kadesh many days, according unto the days that ye abode
there.

The Story of the Wilderness Wanderings

2 Then we turned, and took our journey into the wilderness by the way of the
Red sea, as the LORD spake unto me: and we compassed mount Seir many
days.
2 And the LORD spake unto me, saying,
3 Ye have compassed this mountain long enough: turn you northward.
4 And command thou the people, saying, Ye *are* to pass through the coast of
your brethren the children of Esau, which dwell in Seir; and they shall be
afraid of you: take ye good heed unto yourselves therefore:
5 Meddle not with them; for I will not give you of their land, no, not so much
as a foot breadth; because I have given mount Seir unto Esau *for* a possession.
6 Ye shall buy meat of them for money, that ye may eat; and ye shall also buy
water of them for money, that ye may drink.
7 For the LORD thy God hath blessed thee in all the works of thy hand: he
knoweth thy walking through this great wilderness: these forty years the LORD
thy God *hath been* with thee; thou hast lacked nothing.
8 And when we passed by from our brethren the children of Esau, which
dwelt in Seir, through the way of the plain from Elath, and from Ezion-gaber,
we turned and passed by the way of the wilderness of Moab.
9 And the LORD said unto me, Distress not the Moabites, neither contend
with them in battle: for I will not give thee of their land *for* a possession;
because I have given Ar unto the children of Lot *for* a possession.
10 The Emims dwelt therein in times past, a people great, and many, and tall,
as the Anakims;
11 Which also were accounted giants, as the Anakims; but the Moabites call
them Emims.
12 The Horims also dwelt in Seir beforetime; but the children of Esau suc-
ceeded them, when they had destroyed them from before them, and dwelt in
their stead; as Israel did unto the land of his possession, which the LORD gave
unto them.
13 Now rise up, *said I,* and get you over the brook Zered. And we went over
the brook Zered.
14 And the space in which we came from Kadesh-barnea, until we were come
over the brook Zered, *was* thirty and eight years; until all the generation of
the men of war were wasted out from among the host, as the LORD sware unto
them.
15 For indeed the hand of the LORD was against them, to destroy them from
among the host, until they were consumed.
16 So it came to pass, when all the men of war were consumed and dead from
among the people,
17 That the LORD spake unto me, saying,
18 Thou art to pass over through Ar, the coast of Moab, this day:
19 And *when* thou comest nigh over against the children of Ammon, distress
them not, nor meddle with them: for I will not give thee of the land of the
children of Ammon *any* possession; because I have given it unto the children
of Lot *for* a possession.

20 (That also was accounted a land of giants: giants dwelt therein in old time;
and the Ammonites call them Zamzummims;
21 A people great, and many, and tall, as the Anakims; but the LORD destroyed
them before them; and they succeeded them, and dwelt in their stead:
22 As he did to the children of Esau, which dwelt in Seir, when he destroyed
the Horims from before them; and they succeeded them, and dwelt in their
stead even unto this day:
23 And the Avims which dwelt in Hazerim, *even* unto Azzah, the Caphtorims,
which came forth out of Caphtor, destroyed them, and dwelt in their stead.)

The Story of the Conquest of Sihon the Amorite, King of Heshbon

24 Rise ye up, take your journey, and pass over the river Arnon: behold, I have
given into thine hand Sihon the Amorite, king of Heshbon, and his land: begin
to possess *it*, and contend with him in battle.
25 This day will I begin to put the dread of thee and the fear of thee upon the
nations *that are* under the whole heaven, who shall hear report of thee, and
shall tremble, and be in anguish because of thee.
26 And I sent messengers out of the wilderness of Kedemoth unto Sihon king
of Heshbon with words of peace, saying,
27 Let me pass through thy land: I will go along by the high way, I will neither
turn unto the right hand nor to the left.
28 Thou shalt sell me meat for money, that I may eat; and give me water for
money, that I may drink: only I will pass through on my feet;
29 (As the children of Esau which dwell in Seir, and the Moabites which dwell
in Ar, did unto me;) until I shall pass over Jordan into the land which the LORD
our God giveth us.
30 But Sihon king of Heshbon would not let us pass by him: for the LORD thy
God hardened his spirit, and made his heart obstinate, that he might deliver
him into thy hand, as *appeareth* this day.
31 And the LORD said unto me, Behold, I have begun to give Sihon and his
land before thee: begin to possess, that thou mayest inherit his land.
32 Then Sihon came out against us, he and all his people, to fight at Jahaz.
33 And the LORD our God delivered him before us; and we smote him, and
his sons, and all his people.
34 And we took all his cities at that time, and utterly destroyed the men, and
the women, and the little ones, of every city, we left none to remain:
35 Only the cattle we took for a prey unto ourselves, and the spoil of the
cities which we took.
36 From Aroer, which *is* by the brink of the river of Arnon, and *from* the city
that *is* by the river, even unto Gilead, there was not one city too strong for us:
the LORD our God delivered all unto us:
37 Only unto the land of the children of Ammon thou camest not, *nor* unto
any place of the river Jabbok, nor unto the cities in the mountains, nor unto
whatsoever the LORD our God forbad us.

The Story of the Conquest of Og, King of Bashan

3 Then we turned, and went up the way to Bashan: and Og the king of Bashan
came out against us, he and all his people, to battle at Edrei.
2 And the LORD said unto me, Fear him not: for I will deliver him, and all his
people, and his land, into thy hand; and thou shalt do unto him as thou didst
unto Sihon king of the Amorites, which dwelt at Heshbon.
3 So the LORD our God delivered into our hands Og also, the king of Bashan,
and all his people: and we smote him until none was left to him remaining.
4 And we took all his cities at that time, there was not a city which we took
not from them, threescore cities, all the region of Argob, the kingdom of Og
in Bashan.

5 All these cities *were* fenced with high walls, gates, and bars; beside unwalled
towns a great many.
6 And we utterly destroyed them, as we did unto Sihon king of Heshbon,
utterly destroying the men, women, and children, of every city.
7 But all the cattle, and the spoil of the cities, we took for a prey to ourselves.
8 And we took at that time out of the hand of the two kings of the Amorites
the land that *was* on this side Jordan, from the river of Arnon unto mount
Hermon;
9 (*Which* Hermon the Sidonians call Sirion; and the Amorites call it Shenir;)
10 All the cities of the plain, and all Gilead, and all Bashan, unto Salchah and
Edrei, cities of the kingdom of Og in Bashan.
11 For only Og king of Bashan remained of the remnant of giants; behold,
his bedstead *was* a bedstead of iron; *is* it not in Rabbath of the children of
Ammon? nine cubits *was* the length thereof, and four cubits the breadth of
it, after the cubit of a man.

The Distribution of Land to the Tribes East of the Jordan

12 And this land, *which* we possessed at that time, from Aroer, which *is* by
the river Arnon, and half mount Gilead, and the cities thereof, gave I unto the
Reubenites and to the Gadites.
13 And the rest of Gilead, and all Bashan, *being* the kingdom of Og, gave I
unto the half tribe of Manasseh; all the region of Argob, with all Bashan, which
was called the land of giants.
14 Jair the son of Manasseh took all the country of Argob unto the coasts of
Geshuri and Maachathi; and called them after his own name, Bashan-havoth-
jair, unto this day.
15 And I gave Gilead unto Machir.
16 And unto the Reubenites and unto the Gadites I gave from Gilead even
unto the river Arnon half the valley, and the border even unto the river Jabbok,
which is the border of the children of Ammon;
17 The plain also, and Jordan, and the coast *thereof*, from Chinnereth even
unto the sea of the plain, *even* the salt sea, under Ashdoth-pisgah eastward.
18 And I commanded you at that time, saying, The LORD your God hath given
you this land to possess it: ye shall pass over armed before your brethren the
children of Israel, all *that are* meet for the war.
19 But your wives, and your little ones, and your cattle, (*for* I know that ye
have much cattle,) shall abide in your cities which I have given you;
20 Until the LORD have given rest unto your brethren, as well as unto you,
and *until* they also possess the land which the LORD your God hath given them
beyond Jordan: and *then* shall ye return every man unto his possession, which
I have given you.
21 And I commanded Joshua at that time, saying, Thine eyes have seen all
that the LORD your God hath done unto these two kings: so shall the LORD do
unto all the kingdoms whither thou passest.
22 Ye shall not fear them: for the LORD your God he shall fight for you.
23 And I besought the LORD at that time, saying,
24 O Lord GOD, thou hast begun to shew thy servant thy greatness, and thy
mighty hand: for what God *is there* in heaven or in earth, that can do accord-
ing to thy works, and according to thy might?
25 I pray thee, let me go over, and see the good land that *is* beyond Jordan,
that goodly mountain, and Lebanon.
26 But the LORD was wroth with me for your sakes, and would not hear me:
and the LORD said unto me, Let it suffice thee; speak no more unto me of this
matter.

27 Get thee up into the top of Pisgah, and lift up thine eyes westward, and
northward, and southward, and eastward, and behold *it* with thine eyes: for
thou shalt not go over this Jordan.
28 But charge Joshua, and encourage him, and strengthen him: for he shall
go over before this people, and he shall cause them to inherit the land which
thou shalt see.
29 So we abode in the valley over against Beth-peor.

An Exhortation to Obedience

4 Now therefore hearken, O Israel, unto the statutes and unto the judgments,
which I teach you, for to do *them*, that ye may live, and go in and possess
the land which the LORD God of your fathers giveth you.
2 Ye shall not add unto the word which I command you, neither shall ye
diminish *ought* from it, that ye may keep the commandments of the LORD
your God which I command you.
3 Your eyes have seen what the LORD did because of Baal-peor: for all the men
that followed Baal-peor, the LORD thy God hath destroyed them from among
you.
4 But ye that did cleave unto the LORD your God *are* alive every one of you
this day.
5 Behold, I have taught you statutes and judgments, even as the LORD my God
commanded me, that ye should do so in the land whither ye go to possess it.
6 Keep therefore and do *them*; for this *is* your wisdom and your understand-
ing in the sight of the nations, which shall hear all these statutes, and say,
Surely this great nation *is* a wise and understanding people.
7 For what nation *is there so* great, who *hath* God *so* nigh unto them, as the
LORD our God *is* in all *things that* we call upon him *for*?
8 And what nation *is there so* great, that hath statutes and judgments *so*
righteous as all this law, which I set before you this day?
9 Only take heed to thyself, and keep thy soul diligently, lest thou forget the
things which thine eyes have seen, and lest they depart from thy heart all the
days of thy life: but teach them thy sons, and thy sons' sons;
10 *Specially* the day that thou stoodest before the LORD thy God in Horeb,
when the LORD said unto me, Gather me the people together, and I will make
them hear my words, that they may learn to fear me all the days that they shall
live upon the earth, and *that* they may teach their children.
11 And ye came near and stood under the mountain; and the mountain
burned with fire unto the midst of heaven, with darkness, clouds, and thick
darkness.
12 And the LORD spake unto you out of the midst of the fire: ye heard the
voice of the words, but saw no similitude; only *ye heard* a voice.
13 And he declared unto you his covenant, which he commanded you to
perform, *even* ten commandments; and he wrote them upon two tables of
stone.
14 And the LORD commanded me at that time to teach you statutes and judg-
ments, that ye might do them in the land whither ye go over to possess it.
15 Take ye therefore good heed unto yourselves; for ye saw no manner of
similitude on the day *that* the LORD spake unto you in Horeb out of the midst
of the fire:
16 Lest ye corrupt *yourselves*, and make you a graven image, the similitude
of any figure, the likeness of male or female,
17 The likeness of any beast that *is* on the earth, the likeness of any winged
fowl that flieth in the air,
18 The likeness of any thing that creepeth on the ground, the likeness of any
fish that *is* in the waters beneath the earth:

19 And lest thou lift up thine eyes unto heaven, and when thou seest the sun,
and the moon, and the stars, *even* all the host of heaven, shouldest be driven
to worship them, and serve them, which the LORD thy God hath divided unto
all nations under the whole heaven.
20 But the LORD hath taken you, and brought you forth out of the iron fur-
nace, *even* out of Egypt, to be unto him a people of inheritance, as *ye are* this
day.
21 Furthermore the LORD was angry with me for your sakes, and sware that
I should not go over Jordan, and that I should not go in unto that good land,
which the LORD thy God giveth thee *for* an inheritance:
22 But I must die in this land, I must not go over Jordan: but ye shall go over,
and possess that good land.
23 Take heed unto yourselves, lest ye forget the covenant of the LORD your
God, which he made with you, and make you a graven image, *or* the likeness
of any *thing*, which the LORD thy God hath forbidden thee.
24 For the LORD thy God *is* a consuming fire, *even* a jealous God.
25 When thou shalt beget children, and children's children, and ye shall have
remained long in the land, and shall corrupt *yourselves*, and make a graven
image, *or* the likeness of any *thing*, and shall do evil in the sight of the LORD
thy God, to provoke him to anger:
26 I call heaven and earth to witness against you this day, that ye shall soon
utterly perish from off the land whereunto ye go over Jordan to possess it; ye
shall not prolong *your* days upon it, but shall utterly be destroyed.
27 And the LORD shall scatter you among the nations, and ye shall be left few
in number among the heathen, whither the LORD shall lead you.
28 And there ye shall serve gods, the work of men's hands, wood and stone,
which neither see, nor hear, nor eat, nor smell.
29 But if from thence thou shalt seek the LORD thy God, thou shalt find *him*,
if thou seek him with all thy heart and with all thy soul.
30 When thou art in tribulation, and all these things are come upon thee,
even in the latter days, if thou turn to the LORD thy God, and shalt be obedient
unto his voice;
31 (For the LORD thy God *is* a merciful God;) he will not forsake thee, neither
destroy thee, nor forget the covenant of thy fathers which he sware unto them.
32 For ask now of the days that are past, which were before thee, since the
day that God created man upon the earth, and *ask* from the one side of heaven
unto the other, whether there hath been *any such thing* as this great thing *is*,
or hath been heard like it?
33 Did *ever* people hear the voice of God speaking out of the midst of the fire,
as thou hast heard, and live?
34 Or hath God assayed to go *and* take him a nation from the midst of
another nation, by temptations, by signs, and by wonders, and by war, and by
a mighty hand, and by a stretched out arm, and by great terrors, according to
all that the LORD your God did for you in Egypt before your eyes?
35 Unto thee it was shewed, that thou mightest know that the LORD he *is* God;
there is none else beside him.
36 Out of heaven he made thee to hear his voice, that he might instruct thee:
and upon earth he shewed thee his great fire; and thou heardest his words
out of the midst of the fire.
37 And because he loved thy fathers, therefore he chose their seed after them,
and brought thee out in his sight with his mighty power out of Egypt;
38 To drive out nations from before thee greater and mightier than thou *art*,
to bring thee in, to give thee their land *for* an inheritance, as *it is* this day.
39 Know therefore this day, and consider *it* in thine heart, that the LORD he
is God in heaven above, and upon the earth beneath: *there is* none else.

40 Thou shalt keep therefore his statutes, and his commandments, which I
command thee this day, that it may go well with thee, and with thy children
after thee, and that thou mayest prolong *thy* days upon the earth, which the
LORD thy God giveth thee, for ever.

Moses Appoints the Three Cities of Refuge beyond Jordan

41 Then Moses severed three cities on this side Jordan toward the sunrising;
42 That the slayer might flee thither, which should kill his neighbour
unawares, and hated him not in times past; and that fleeing unto one of these
cities he might live:
43 *Namely*, Bezer in the wilderness, in the plain country, of the Reubenites;
and Ramoth in Gilead, of the Gadites; and Golan in Bashan, of the Manassites.
44 And this *is* the law which Moses set before the children of Israel:
45 These *are* the testimonies, and the statutes, and the judgments, which
Moses spake unto the children of Israel, after they came forth out of Egypt,
46 On this side Jordan, in the valley over against Beth-peor, in the land of
Sihon king of the Amorites, who dwelt at Heshbon, whom Moses and the
children of Israel smote, after they were come forth out of Egypt:
47 And they possessed his land, and the land of Og king of Bashan, two kings
of the Amorites, which *were* on this side Jordan toward the sunrising;
48 From Aroer, which *is* by the bank of the river Arnon, even unto mount
Sion, which *is* Hermon,
49 And all the plain on this side Jordan eastward, even unto the sea of the
plain, under the springs of Pisgah.

The Covenant Made at Mount Horeb

5 And Moses called all Israel, and said unto them, Hear, O Israel, the statutes
and judgments which I speak in your ears this day, that ye may learn them,
and keep, and do them.
2 The LORD our God made a covenant with us in Horeb.
3 The LORD made not this covenant with our fathers, but with us, *even* us,
who *are* all of us here alive this day.
4 The LORD talked with you face to face in the mount out of the midst of the
fire,
5 (I stood between the LORD and you at that time, to shew you the word of
the LORD: for ye were afraid by reason of the fire, and went not up into the
mount;) saying,

The Ten Commandments

6 I *am* the LORD thy God, which brought thee out of the land of Egypt, from
the house of bondage.
7 Thou shalt have none other gods before me.
8 Thou shalt not make thee *any* graven image, *or* any likeness *of any thing*
that *is* in heaven above, or that *is* in the earth beneath, or that *is* in the waters
beneath the earth:
9 Thou shalt not bow down thyself unto them, nor serve them: for I the LORD
thy God *am* a jealous God, visiting the iniquity of the fathers upon the children
unto the third and fourth *generation* of them that hate me,
10 And shewing mercy unto thousands of them that love me and keep my
commandments.
11 Thou shalt not take the name of the LORD thy God in vain: for the LORD
will not hold *him* guiltless that taketh his name in vain.
12 Keep the sabbath day to sanctify it, as the LORD thy God hath commanded
thee.
13 Six days thou shalt labour, and do all thy work:
14 But the seventh day *is* the sabbath of the LORD thy God: *in it* thou shalt not
do any work, thou, nor thy son, nor thy daughter, nor thy manservant, nor thy
maidservant, nor thine ox, nor thine ass, nor any of thy cattle, nor thy stranger

that *is* within thy gates; that thy manservant and thy maidservant may rest as
well as thou.
15 And remember that thou wast a servant in the land of Egypt, and *that* the
LORD thy God brought thee out thence through a mighty hand and by a
stretched out arm: therefore the LORD thy God commanded thee to keep the
sabbath day.
16 Honour thy father and thy mother, as the LORD thy God hath command-
ed thee; that thy days may be prolonged, and that it may go well with thee, in
the land which the LORD thy God giveth thee.
17 Thou shalt not kill.
18 Neither shalt thou commit adultery.
19 Neither shalt thou steal.
20 Neither shalt thou bear false witness against thy neighbour.
21 Neither shalt thou desire thy neighbour's wife, neither shalt thou covet
thy neighbour's house, his field, or his manservant, or his maidservant, his
ox, or his ass, or any *thing* that *is* thy neighbour's.
22 These words the LORD spake unto all your assembly in the mount out of
the midst of the fire, of the cloud, and of the thick darkness, with a great voice:
and he added no more. And he wrote them in two tables of stone, and delivered
them unto me.
23 And it came to pass, when ye heard the voice out of the midst of the dark-
ness, (for the mountain did burn with fire,) that ye came near unto me, *even*
all the heads of your tribes, and your elders;
24 And ye said, Behold, the LORD our God hath shewed us his glory and his
greatness, and we have heard his voice out of the midst of the fire: we have
seen this day that God doth talk with man, and he liveth.
25 Now therefore why should we die? for this great fire will consume us: if
we hear the voice of the LORD our God any more, then we shall die.
26 For who *is there of* all flesh, that hath heard the voice of the living God
speaking out of the midst of the fire, as we *have*, and lived?
27 Go thou near, and hear all that the LORD our God shall say: and speak thou
unto us all that the LORD our God shall speak unto thee; and we will hear *it*,
and do *it*.
28 And the LORD heard the voice of your words, when ye spake unto me; and
the LORD said unto me, I have heard the voice of the words of this people, which
they have spoken unto thee: they have well said all that they have spoken.
29 O that there were such an heart in them, that they would fear me, and
keep all my commandments always, that it might be well with them, and with
their children for ever!
30 Go say to them, Get you into your tents again.
31 But as for thee, stand thou here by me, and I will speak unto thee all the
commandments, and the statutes, and the judgments, which thou shalt teach
them, that they may do *them* in the land which I give them to possess it.
32 Ye shall observe to do therefore as the LORD your God hath commanded
you: ye shall not turn aside to the right hand or to the left.
33 Ye shall walk in all the ways which the LORD your God hath commanded
you, that ye may live, and *that it may be* well with you, and *that* ye may prolong
your days in the land which ye shall possess.

The Purpose of the Law and an Exhortation to Obey It

6 Now these *are* the commandments, the statutes, and the judgments, which
the LORD your God commanded to teach you, that ye might do *them* in the
land whither ye go to possess it:
2 That thou mightest fear the LORD thy God, to keep all his statutes and his
commandments, which I command thee, thou, and thy son, and thy son's son,
all the days of thy life; and that thy days may be prolonged.

3 Hear therefore, O Israel, and observe to do *it*; that it may be well with thee,
and that ye may increase mightily, as the LORD God of thy fathers hath prom-
ised thee, in the land that floweth with milk and honey.
4 Hear, O Israel: The LORD our God *is* one LORD:
5 And thou shalt love the LORD thy God with all thine heart, and with all thy
soul, and with all thy might.
6 And these words, which I command thee this day, shall be in thine heart:
7 And thou shalt teach them diligently unto thy children, and shalt talk of
them when thou sittest in thine house, and when thou walkest by the way, and
when thou liest down, and when thou risest up.
8 And thou shalt bind them for a sign upon thine hand, and they shall be as
frontlets between thine eyes.
9 And thou shalt write them upon the posts of thy house, and on thy gates.
10 And it shall be, when the LORD thy God shall have brought thee into the
land which he sware unto thy fathers, to Abraham, to Isaac, and to Jacob, to
give thee great and goodly cities, which thou buildedst not,
11 And houses full of all good *things*, which thou filledst not, and wells
digged, which thou diggedest not, vineyards and olive trees, which thou plant-
edst not; when thou shalt have eaten and be full;
12 *Then* beware lest thou forget the LORD, which brought thee forth out of
the land of Egypt, from the house of bondage.
13 Thou shalt fear the LORD thy God, and serve him, and shalt swear by his
name.
14 Ye shall not go after other gods, of the gods of the people which *are* round
about you;
15 (For the LORD thy God *is* a jealous God among you) lest the anger of the
LORD thy God be kindled against thee, and destroy thee from off the face of
the earth.
16 Ye shall not tempt the LORD your God, as ye tempted *him* in Massah.
17 Ye shall diligently keep the commandments of the LORD your God, and
his testimonies, and his statutes, which he hath commanded thee.
18 And thou shalt do *that which is* right and good in the sight of the LORD:
that it may be well with thee, and that thou mayest go in and possess the good
land which the LORD sware unto thy fathers,
19 To cast out all thine enemies from before thee, as the LORD hath spoken.
20 *And* when thy son asketh thee in time to come, saying, What *mean* the
testimonies, and the statutes, and the judgments, which the LORD our God
hath commanded you?
21 Then thou shalt say unto thy son, We were Pharaoh's bondmen in Egypt;
and the LORD brought us out of Egypt with a mighty hand:
22 And the LORD shewed signs and wonders, great and sore, upon Egypt,
upon Pharaoh, and upon all his household, before our eyes:
23 And he brought us out from thence, that he might bring us in, to give us
the land which he sware unto our fathers.
24 And the LORD commanded us to do all these statutes, to fear the LORD our
God, for our good always, that he might preserve us alive, as *it is* at this day.
25 And it shall be our righteousness, if we observe to do all these command-
ments before the LORD our God, as he hath commanded us.

God Commands Israel to Destroy the Canaanites and Their Idols

7 When the LORD thy God shall bring thee into the land whither thou goest
to possess it, and hath cast out many nations before thee, the Hittites, and
the Girgashites, and the Amorites, and the Canaanites, and the Perizzites, and
the Hivites, and the Jebusites, seven nations greater and mightier than thou;

2 And when the LORD thy God shall deliver them before thee; thou shalt smite
them, *and* utterly destroy them; thou shalt make no covenant with them, nor
shew mercy unto them:
3 Neither shalt thou make marriages with them; thy daughter thou shalt not
give unto his son, nor his daughter shalt thou take unto thy son.
4 For they will turn away thy son from following me, that they may serve
other gods: so will the anger of the LORD be kindled against you, and destroy
thee suddenly.
5 But thus shall ye deal with them; ye shall destroy their altars, and break
down their images, and cut down their groves, and burn their graven images
with fire.
6 For thou *art* an holy people unto the LORD thy God: the LORD thy God hath
chosen thee to be a special people unto himself, above all people that *are* upon
the face of the earth.
7 The LORD did not set his love upon you, nor choose you, because ye were
more in number than any people; for ye *were* the fewest of all people:
8 But because the LORD loved you, and because he would keep the oath which
he had sworn unto your fathers, hath the LORD brought you out with a mighty
hand, and redeemed you out of the house of bondmen, from the hand of
Pharaoh king of Egypt.
9 Know therefore that the LORD thy God, he *is* God, the faithful God, which
keepeth covenant and mercy with them that love him and keep his command-
ments to a thousand generations;
10 And repayeth them that hate him to their face, to destroy them: he will
not be slack to him that hateth him, he will repay him to his face.
11 Thou shalt therefore keep the commandments, and the statutes, and the
judgments, which I command thee this day, to do them.
12 Wherefore it shall come to pass, if ye hearken to these judgments, and
keep, and do them, that the LORD thy God shall keep unto thee the covenant
and the mercy which he sware unto thy fathers:
13 And he will love thee, and bless thee, and multiply thee: he will also bless
the fruit of thy womb, and the fruit of thy land, thy corn, and thy wine, and
thine oil, the increase of thy kine, and the flocks of thy sheep, in the land which
he sware unto thy fathers to give thee.
14 Thou shalt be blessed above all people: there shall not be male or female
barren among you, or among your cattle.
15 And the LORD will take away from thee all sickness, and will put none of
the evil diseases of Egypt, which thou knowest, upon thee; but will lay them
upon all *them* that hate thee.
16 And thou shalt consume all the people which the LORD thy God shall
deliver thee; thine eye shall have no pity upon them: neither shalt thou serve
their gods; for that *will be* a snare unto thee.
17 If thou shalt say in thine heart, These nations *are* more than I; how can I
dispossess them?
18 Thou shalt not be afraid of them: *but* shalt well remember what the LORD
thy God did unto Pharaoh, and unto all Egypt;
19 The great temptations which thine eyes saw, and the signs, and the won-
ders, and the mighty hand, and the stretched out arm, whereby the LORD thy
God brought thee out: so shall the LORD thy God do unto all the people of
whom thou art afraid.
20 Moreover the LORD thy God will send the hornet among them, until they
that are left, and hide themselves from thee, be destroyed.
21 Thou shalt not be affrighted at them: for the LORD thy God *is* among you,
a mighty God and terrible.

22 And the LORD thy God will put out those nations before thee by little and
little: thou mayest not consume them at once, lest the beasts of the field
increase upon thee.
23 But the LORD thy God shall deliver them unto thee, and shall destroy them
with a mighty destruction, until they be destroyed.
24 And he shall deliver their kings into thine hand, and thou shalt destroy
their name from under heaven: there shall no man be able to stand before
thee, until thou have destroyed them.
25 The graven images of their gods shall ye burn with fire: thou shalt not
desire the silver or gold *that is* on them, nor take *it* unto thee, lest thou be
snared therein: for it *is* an abomination to the LORD thy God.
26 Neither shalt thou bring an abomination into thine house, lest thou be a
cursed thing like it: *but* thou shalt utterly detest it, and thou shalt utterly abhor
it; for it *is* a cursed thing.

An Exhortation to Obedience and Remembrance

8 All the commandments which I command thee this day shall ye observe to
do, that ye may live, and multiply, and go in and possess the land which the
LORD sware unto your fathers.
2 And thou shalt remember all the way which the LORD thy God led thee these
forty years in the wilderness, to humble thee, *and* to prove thee, to know what
was in thine heart, whether thou wouldest keep his commandments, or no.
3 And he humbled thee, and suffered thee to hunger, and fed thee with
manna, which thou knewest not, neither did thy fathers know; that he might
make thee know that man doth not live by bread only, but by every *word* that
proceedeth out of the mouth of the LORD doth man live.
4 Thy raiment waxed not old upon thee, neither did thy foot swell, these forty
years.
5 Thou shalt also consider in thine heart, that, as a man chasteneth his son,
so the LORD thy God chasteneth thee.
6 Therefore thou shalt keep the commandments of the LORD thy God, to walk
in his ways, and to fear him.
7 For the LORD thy God bringeth thee into a good land, a land of brooks of
water, of fountains and depths that spring out of valleys and hills;
8 A land of wheat, and barley, and vines, and fig trees, and pomegranates; a
land of oil olive, and honey;
9 A land wherein thou shalt eat bread without scarceness, thou shalt not lack
any *thing* in it; a land whose stones *are* iron, and out of whose hills thou
mayest dig brass.
10 When thou hast eaten and art full, then thou shalt bless the LORD thy God
for the good land which he hath given thee.
11 Beware that thou forget not the LORD thy God, in not keeping his com-
mandments, and his judgments, and his statutes, which I command thee this
day:
12 Lest *when* thou hast eaten and art full, and hast built goodly houses, and
dwelt *therein*;
13 And *when* thy herds and thy flocks multiply, and thy silver and thy gold is
multiplied, and all that thou hast is multiplied;
14 Then thine heart be lifted up, and thou forget the LORD thy God, which
brought thee forth out of the land of Egypt, from the house of bondage;
15 Who led thee through that great and terrible wilderness, *wherein were*
fiery serpents, and scorpions, and drought, where *there was* no water; who
brought thee forth water out of the rock of flint;
16 Who fed thee in the wilderness with manna, which thy fathers knew not,
that he might humble thee, and that he might prove thee, to do thee good at
thy latter end;

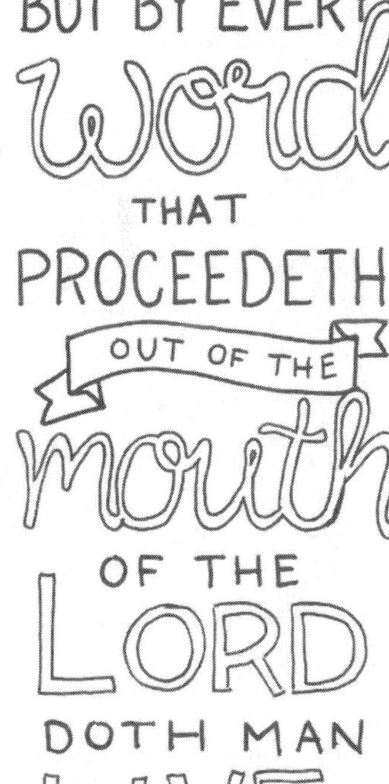

17 And thou say in thine heart, My power and the might of *mine* hand hath gotten me this wealth.

18 But thou shalt remember the LORD thy God: for *it is* he that giveth thee power to get wealth, that he may establish his covenant which he sware unto thy fathers, as *it is* this day.

19 And it shall be, if thou do at all forget the LORD thy God, and walk after other gods, and serve them, and worship them, I testify against you this day that ye shall surely perish.

20 As the nations which the LORD destroyeth before your face, so shall ye perish; because ye would not be obedient unto the voice of the LORD your God.

Moses Reminds the People of Their Many Rebellions

9 Hear, O Israel: Thou *art* to pass over Jordan this day, to go in to possess nations greater and mightier than thyself, cities great and fenced up to heaven,

2 A people great and tall, the children of the Anakims, whom thou knowest, and *of whom* thou hast heard *say*, Who can stand before the children of Anak!

3 Understand therefore this day, that the LORD thy God *is* he which goeth over before thee; *as* a consuming fire he shall destroy them, and he shall bring them down before thy face: so shalt thou drive them out, and destroy them quickly, as the LORD hath said unto thee.

4 Speak not thou in thine heart, after that the LORD thy God hath cast them out from before thee, saying, For my righteousness the LORD hath brought me in to possess this land: but for the wickedness of these nations the LORD doth drive them out from before thee.

5 Not for thy righteousness, or for the uprightness of thine heart, dost thou go to possess their land: but for the wickedness of these nations the LORD thy God doth drive them out from before thee, and that he may perform the word which the LORD sware unto thy fathers, Abraham, Isaac, and Jacob.

6 Understand therefore, that the LORD thy God giveth thee not this good land to possess it for thy righteousness; for thou *art* a stiffnecked people.

7 Remember, *and* forget not, how thou provokedst the LORD thy God to wrath in the wilderness: from the day that thou didst depart out of the land of Egypt, until ye came unto this place, ye have been rebellious against the LORD.

8 Also in Horeb ye provoked the LORD to wrath, so that the LORD was angry with you to have destroyed you.

9 When I was gone up into the mount to receive the tables of stone, *even* the tables of the covenant which the LORD made with you, then I abode in the mount forty days and forty nights, I neither did eat bread nor drink water:

10 And the LORD delivered unto me two tables of stone written with the finger of God; and on them *was written* according to all the words, which the LORD spake with you in the mount out of the midst of the fire in the day of the assembly.

11 And it came to pass at the end of forty days and forty nights, *that* the LORD gave me the two tables of stone, *even* the tables of the covenant.

12 And the LORD said unto me, Arise, get thee down quickly from hence; for thy people which thou hast brought forth out of Egypt have corrupted *themselves*; they are quickly turned aside out of the way which I commanded them; they have made them a molten image.

13 Furthermore the LORD spake unto me, saying, I have seen this people, and, behold, it *is* a stiffnecked people:

14 Let me alone, that I may destroy them, and blot out their name from under heaven: and I will make of thee a nation mightier and greater than they.

15 So I turned and came down from the mount, and the mount burned with fire: and the two tables of the covenant *were* in my two hands.

16 And I looked, and, behold, ye had sinned against the LORD your God, *and*
had made you a molten calf: ye had turned aside quickly out of the way which
the LORD had commanded you.
17 And I took the two tables, and cast them out of my two hands, and brake
them before your eyes.
18 And I fell down before the LORD, as at the first, forty days and forty nights:
I did neither eat bread, nor drink water, because of all your sins which ye
sinned, in doing wickedly in the sight of the LORD, to provoke him to anger.
19 For I was afraid of the anger and hot displeasure, wherewith the LORD was
wroth against you to destroy you. But the LORD hearkened unto me at that
time also.
20 And the LORD was very angry with Aaron to have destroyed him: and I
prayed for Aaron also the same time.
21 And I took your sin, the calf which ye had made, and burnt it with fire,
and stamped it, *and* ground *it* very small, *even* until it was as small as dust:
and I cast the dust thereof into the brook that descended out of the mount.
22 And at Taberah, and at Massah, and at Kibroth-hattaavah, ye provoked
the LORD to wrath.
23 Likewise when the LORD sent you from Kadesh-barnea, saying, Go up and
possess the land which I have given you; then ye rebelled against the com-
mandment of the LORD your God, and ye believed him not, nor hearkened to
his voice.
24 Ye have been rebellious against the LORD from the day that I knew you.
25 Thus I fell down before the LORD forty days and forty nights, as I fell down
at the first; because the LORD had said he would destroy you.
26 I prayed therefore unto the LORD, and said, O Lord GOD, destroy not thy
people and thine inheritance, which thou hast redeemed through thy great-
ness, which thou hast brought forth out of Egypt with a mighty hand.
27 Remember thy servants, Abraham, Isaac, and Jacob; look not unto the
stubbornness of this people, nor to their wickedness, nor to their sin:
28 Lest the land whence thou broughtest us out say, Because the LORD was
not able to bring them into the land which he promised them, and because
he hated them, he hath brought them out to slay them in the wilderness.
29 Yet they *are* thy people and thine inheritance, which thou broughtest out
by thy mighty power and by thy stretched out arm.

God's Mercy in Restoring the Two Tablets of the Ten Commandments

10 At that time the LORD said unto me, Hew thee two tables of stone like
unto the first, and come up unto me into the mount, and make thee
an ark of wood.
2 And I will write on the tables the words that were in the first tables which
thou brakest, and thou shalt put them in the ark.
3 And I made an ark *of* shittim wood, and hewed two tables of stone like unto
the first, and went up into the mount, having the two tables in mine hand.
4 And he wrote on the tables, according to the first writing, the ten com-
mandments, which the LORD spake unto you in the mount out of the midst of
the fire in the day of the assembly: and the LORD gave them unto me.
5 And I turned myself and came down from the mount, and put the tables
in the ark which I had made; and there they be, as the LORD commanded me.
6 And the children of Israel took their journey from Beeroth of the children
of Jaakan to Mosera: there Aaron died, and there he was buried; and Eleazar
his son ministered in the priest's office in his stead.
7 From thence they journeyed unto Gudgodah; and from Gudgodah to
Jotbath, a land of rivers of waters.

8 At that time the LORD separated the tribe of Levi, to bear the ark of the
covenant of the LORD, to stand before the LORD to minister unto him, and to
bless in his name, unto this day.
9 Wherefore Levi hath no part nor inheritance with his brethren; the LORD
is his inheritance, according as the LORD thy God promised him.
10 And I stayed in the mount, according to the first time, forty days and forty
nights; and the LORD hearkened unto me at that time also, *and* the LORD would
not destroy thee.
11 And the LORD said unto me, Arise, take *thy* journey before the people, that
they may go in and possess the land, which I sware unto their fathers to give
unto them.
12 And now, Israel, what doth the LORD thy God require of thee, but to fear
the LORD thy God, to walk in all his ways, and to love him, and to serve the LORD
thy God with all thy heart and with all thy soul,
13 To keep the commandments of the LORD, and his statutes, which I com-
mand thee this day for thy good?
14 Behold, the heaven and the heaven of heavens *is* the LORD's thy God, the
earth *also*, with all that therein *is*.
15 Only the LORD had a delight in thy fathers to love them, and he chose their
seed after them, *even* you above all people, as *it is* this day.
16 Circumcise therefore the foreskin of your heart, and be no more stiff-
necked.
17 For the LORD your God *is* God of gods, and Lord of lords, a great God, a
mighty, and a terrible, which regardeth not persons, nor taketh reward:
18 He doth execute the judgment of the fatherless and widow, and loveth the
stranger, in giving him food and raiment.
19 Love ye therefore the stranger: for ye were strangers in the land of Egypt.
20 Thou shalt fear the LORD thy God; him shalt thou serve, and to him shalt
thou cleave, and swear by his name.
21 He *is* thy praise, and he *is* thy God, that hath done for thee these great and
terrible things, which thine eyes have seen.
22 Thy fathers went down into Egypt with threescore and ten persons; and
now the LORD thy God hath made thee as the stars of heaven for multitude.

An Exhortation to Obey the Commandments

11 Therefore thou shalt love the LORD thy God, and keep his charge, and
his statutes, and his judgments, and his commandments, alway.
2 And know ye this day: for *I speak* not with your children which have not
known, and which have not seen the chastisement of the LORD your God, his
greatness, his mighty hand, and his stretched out arm,
3 And his miracles, and his acts, which he did in the midst of Egypt unto
Pharaoh the king of Egypt, and unto all his land;
4 And what he did unto the army of Egypt, unto their horses, and to their
chariots; how he made the water of the Red sea to overflow them as they
pursued after you, and *how* the LORD hath destroyed them unto this day;
5 And what he did unto you in the wilderness, until ye came into this place;
6 And what he did unto Dathan and Abiram, the sons of Eliab, the son of
Reuben: how the earth opened her mouth, and swallowed them up, and their
households, and their tents, and all the substance that *was* in their possession,
in the midst of all Israel:
7 But your eyes have seen all the great acts of the LORD which he did.

The Promise of God's Great Blessings

8 Therefore shall ye keep all the commandments which I command you this
day, that ye may be strong, and go in and possess the land, whither ye go to
possess it;

9 And that ye may prolong *your* days in the land, which the LORD sware unto
your fathers to give unto them and to their seed, a land that floweth with milk
and honey.
10 For the land, whither thou goest in to possess it, *is* not as the land of Egypt,
from whence ye came out, where thou sowedst thy seed, and wateredst *it* with
thy foot, as a garden of herbs:
11 But the land, whither ye go to possess it, *is* a land of hills and valleys, *and*
drinketh water of the rain of heaven:
12 A land which the LORD thy God careth for: the eyes of the LORD thy God
are always upon it, from the beginning of the year even unto the end of the
year.
13 And it shall come to pass, if ye shall hearken diligently unto my command-
ments which I command you this day, to love the LORD your God, and to serve
him with all your heart and with all your soul,
14 That I will give *you* the rain of your land in his due season, the first rain
and the latter rain, that thou mayest gather in thy corn, and thy wine, and
thine oil.
15 And I will send grass in thy fields for thy cattle, that thou mayest eat and
be full.
16 Take heed to yourselves, that your heart be not deceived, and ye turn aside,
and serve other gods, and worship them;
17 And *then* the LORD's wrath be kindled against you, and he shut up the
heaven, that there be no rain, and that the land yield not her fruit; and *lest* ye
perish quickly from off the good land which the LORD giveth you.

A Careful Study of God's Words Is Required

18 Therefore shall ye lay up these my words in your heart and in your soul,
and bind them for a sign upon your hand, that they may be as frontlets
between your eyes.
19 And ye shall teach them your children, speaking of them when thou sittest
in thine house, and when thou walkest by the way, when thou liest down, and
when thou risest up.
20 And thou shalt write them upon the door posts of thine house, and upon
thy gates:
21 That your days may be multiplied, and the days of your children, in the
land which the LORD sware unto your fathers to give them, as the days of heav-
en upon the earth.
22 For if ye shall diligently keep all these commandments which I command
you, to do them, to love the LORD your God, to walk in all his ways, and to cleave
unto him;
23 Then will the LORD drive out all these nations from before you, and ye shall
possess greater nations and mightier than yourselves.
24 Every place whereon the soles of your feet shall tread shall be yours: from
the wilderness and Lebanon, from the river, the river Euphrates, even unto
the uttermost sea shall your coast be.
25 There shall no man be able to stand before you: *for* the LORD your God
shall lay the fear of you and the dread of you upon all the land that ye shall
tread upon, as he hath said unto you.

A Blessing and a Curse Are Set before the People

26 Behold, I set before you this day a blessing and a curse;
27 A blessing, if ye obey the commandments of the LORD your God, which I
command you this day:
28 And a curse, if ye will not obey the commandments of the LORD your God,
but turn aside out of the way which I command you this day, to go after other
gods, which ye have not known.

29 And it shall come to pass, when the LORD thy God hath brought thee in
unto the land whither thou goest to possess it, that thou shalt put the blessing
upon mount Gerizim, and the curse upon mount Ebal.
30 *Are* they not on the other side Jordan, by the way where the sun goeth
down, in the land of the Canaanites, which dwell in the champaign over
against Gilgal, beside the plains of Moreh?
31 For ye shall pass over Jordan to go in to possess the land which the LORD
your God giveth you, and ye shall possess it, and dwell therein.
32 And ye shall observe to do all the statutes and judgments which I set before
you this day.

Monuments of Idolatry Are to Be Destroyed

12 These *are* the statutes and judgments, which ye shall observe to do in
the land, which the LORD God of thy fathers giveth thee to possess it,
all the days that ye live upon the earth.
2 Ye shall utterly destroy all the places, wherein the nations which ye shall
possess served their gods, upon the high mountains, and upon the hills, and
under every green tree:
3 And ye shall overthrow their altars, and break their pillars, and burn their
groves with fire; and ye shall hew down the graven images of their gods, and
destroy the names of them out of that place.
4 Ye shall not do so unto the LORD your God.

The Proper Place to Worship

5 But unto the place which the LORD your God shall choose out of all your
tribes to put his name there, *even* unto his habitation shall ye seek, and thither
thou shalt come:
6 And thither ye shall bring your burnt offerings, and your sacrifices, and
your tithes, and heave offerings of your hand, and your vows, and your freewill
offerings, and the firstlings of your herds and of your flocks:
7 And there ye shall eat before the LORD your God, and ye shall rejoice in all
that ye put your hand unto, ye and your households, wherein the LORD thy
God hath blessed thee.
8 Ye shall not do after all *the things* that we do here this day, every man what-
soever *is* right in his own eyes.
9 For ye are not as yet come to the rest and to the inheritance, which the LORD
your God giveth you.
10 But *when* ye go over Jordan, and dwell in the land which the LORD your
God giveth you to inherit, and *when* he giveth you rest from all your enemies
round about, so that ye dwell in safety;
11 Then there shall be a place which the LORD your God shall choose to cause
his name to dwell there; thither shall ye bring all that I command you; your
burnt offerings, and your sacrifices, your tithes, and the heave offering of your
hand, and all your choice vows which ye vow unto the LORD:
12 And ye shall rejoice before the LORD your God, ye, and your sons, and your
daughters, and your menservants, and your maidservants, and the Levite that
is within your gates; forasmuch as he hath no part nor inheritance with you.
13 Take heed to thyself that thou offer not thy burnt offerings in every place
that thou seest:
14 But in the place which the LORD shall choose in one of thy tribes, there
thou shalt offer thy burnt offerings, and there thou shalt do all that I command
thee.
15 Notwithstanding thou mayest kill and eat flesh in all thy gates, whatso-
ever thy soul lusteth after, according to the blessing of the LORD thy God which
he hath given thee: the unclean and the clean may eat thereof, as of the roe-
buck, and as of the hart.
16 Only ye shall not eat the blood; ye shall pour it upon the earth as water.

17 Thou mayest not eat within thy gates the tithe of thy corn, or of thy wine,
or of thy oil, or the firstlings of thy herds or of thy flock, nor any of thy vows
which thou vowest, nor thy freewill offerings, or heave offering of thine hand:
18 But thou must eat them before the LORD thy God in the place which the
LORD thy God shall choose, thou, and thy son, and thy daughter, and thy man-
servant, and thy maidservant, and the Levite that *is* within thy gates: and thou
shalt rejoice before the LORD thy God in all that thou puttest thine hands unto.
19 Take heed to thyself that thou forsake not the Levite as long as thou livest
upon the earth.
20 When the LORD thy God shall enlarge thy border, as he hath promised
thee, and thou shalt say, I will eat flesh, because thy soul longeth to eat flesh;
thou mayest eat flesh, whatsoever thy soul lusteth after.
21 If the place which the LORD thy God hath chosen to put his name there be
too far from thee, then thou shalt kill of thy herd and of thy flock, which the
LORD hath given thee, as I have commanded thee, and thou shalt eat in thy
gates whatsoever thy soul lusteth after.
22 Even as the roebuck and the hart is eaten, so thou shalt eat them: the
unclean and the clean shall eat *of* them alike.
23 Only be sure that thou eat not the blood: for the blood *is* the life; and thou
mayest not eat the life with the flesh.
24 Thou shalt not eat it; thou shalt pour it upon the earth as water.
25 Thou shalt not eat it; that it may go well with thee, and with thy children
after thee, when thou shalt do *that which is* right in the sight of the LORD.
26 Only thy holy things which thou hast, and thy vows, thou shalt take, and
go unto the place which the LORD shall choose:
27 And thou shalt offer thy burnt offerings, the flesh and the blood, upon
the altar of the LORD thy God: and the blood of thy sacrifices shall be poured
out upon the altar of the LORD thy God, and thou shalt eat the flesh.
28 Observe and hear all these words which I command thee, that it may go
well with thee, and with thy children after thee for ever, when thou doest *that
which is* good and right in the sight of the LORD thy God.
29 When the LORD thy God shall cut off the nations from before thee, whither
thou goest to possess them, and thou succeedest them, and dwellest in their
land;
30 Take heed to thyself that thou be not snared by following them, after that
they be destroyed from before thee; and that thou enquire not after their gods,
saying, How did these nations serve their gods? even so will I do likewise.
31 Thou shalt not do so unto the LORD thy God: for every abomination to the
LORD, which he hateth, have they done unto their gods; for even their sons and
their daughters they have burnt in the fire to their gods.
32 What thing soever I command you, observe to do it: thou shalt not add
thereto, nor diminish from it.

Dealing with False Prophets

13 If there arise among you a prophet, or a dreamer of dreams, and giveth
thee a sign or a wonder,
2 And the sign or the wonder come to pass, whereof he spake unto thee,
saying, Let us go after other gods, which thou hast not known, and let us serve
them;
3 Thou shalt not hearken unto the words of that prophet, or that dreamer
of dreams: for the LORD your God proveth you, to know whether ye love the
LORD your God with all your heart and with all your soul.
4 Ye shall walk after the LORD your God, and fear him, and keep his com-
mandments, and obey his voice, and ye shall serve him, and cleave unto him.
5 And that prophet, or that dreamer of dreams, shall be put to death; because
he hath spoken to turn *you* away from the LORD your God, which brought you

out of the land of Egypt, and redeemed you out of the house of bondage, to
thrust thee out of the way which the LORD thy God commanded thee to walk
in. So shalt thou put the evil away from the midst of thee.

Dealing with a Family Member's Idolatry

6 If thy brother, the son of thy mother, or thy son, or thy daughter, or the
wife of thy bosom, or thy friend, which *is* as thine own soul, entice thee secret-
ly, saying, Let us go and serve other gods, which thou hast not known, thou,
nor thy fathers;
7 *Namely*, of the gods of the people which *are* round about you, nigh unto
thee, or far off from thee, from the *one* end of the earth even unto the *other*
end of the earth;
8 Thou shalt not consent unto him, nor hearken unto him; neither shall
thine eye pity him, neither shalt thou spare, neither shalt thou conceal him:
9 But thou shalt surely kill him; thine hand shall be first upon him to put
him to death, and afterwards the hand of all the people.
10 And thou shalt stone him with stones, that he die; because he hath sought
to thrust thee away from the LORD thy God, which brought thee out of the
land of Egypt, from the house of bondage.
11 And all Israel shall hear, and fear, and shall do no more any such wicked-
ness as this is among you.

Dealing with Idolatrous Cities

12 If thou shalt hear *say* in one of thy cities, which the LORD thy God hath
given thee to dwell there, saying,
13 *Certain* men, the children of Belial, are gone out from among you, and
have withdrawn the inhabitants of their city, saying, Let us go and serve other
gods, which ye have not known;
14 Then shalt thou enquire, and make search, and ask diligently; and, behold,
if it be truth, *and* the thing certain, *that* such abomination is wrought among
you;
15 Thou shalt surely smite the inhabitants of that city with the edge of the
sword, destroying it utterly, and all that *is* therein, and the cattle thereof, with
the edge of the sword.
16 And thou shalt gather all the spoil of it into the midst of the street there-
of, and shalt burn with fire the city, and all the spoil thereof every whit, for
the LORD thy God: and it shall be an heap for ever; it shall not be built again.
17 And there shall cleave nought of the cursed thing to thine hand: that the
LORD may turn from the fierceness of his anger, and shew thee mercy, and
have compassion upon thee, and multiply thee, as he hath sworn unto thy
fathers;
18 When thou shalt hearken to the voice of the LORD thy God, to keep all his
commandments which I command thee this day, to do *that which is* right in
the eyes of the LORD thy God.

God's Children Are Not to Disfigure Themselves in Mourning

14 Ye *are* the children of the LORD your God: ye shall not cut yourselves,
nor make any baldness between your eyes for the dead.
2 For thou *art* an holy people unto the LORD thy God, and the LORD hath
chosen thee to be a peculiar people unto himself, above all the nations that
are upon the earth.
3 Thou shalt not eat any abominable thing.
4 These *are* the beasts which ye shall eat: the ox, the sheep, and the goat,
5 The hart, and the roebuck, and the fallow deer, and the wild goat, and the
pygarg, and the wild ox, and the chamois.
6 And every beast that parteth the hoof, and cleaveth the cleft into two claws,
and cheweth the cud among the beasts, that ye shall eat.

7 Nevertheless these ye shall not eat of them that chew the cud, or of them
that divide the cloven hoof; *as* the camel, and the hare, and the coney: for they
chew the cud, but divide not the hoof; *therefore* they *are* unclean unto you.
8 And the swine, because it divideth the hoof, yet cheweth not the cud, it *is*
unclean unto you: ye shall not eat of their flesh, nor touch their dead carcase.
9 These ye shall eat of all that *are* in the waters: all that have fins and scales
shall ye eat:
10 And whatsoever hath not fins and scales ye may not eat; it *is* unclean unto
you.
11 *Of* all clean birds ye shall eat.
12 But these *are they* of which ye shall not eat: the eagle, and the ossifrage,
and the ospray,
13 And the glede, and the kite, and the vulture after his kind,
14 And every raven after his kind,
15 And the owl, and the night hawk, and the cuckow, and the hawk after his
kind,
16 The little owl, and the great owl, and the swan,
17 And the pelican, and the gier eagle, and the cormorant,
18 And the stork, and the heron after her kind, and the lapwing, and the bat.
19 And every creeping thing that flieth *is* unclean unto you: they shall not be
eaten.
20 *But of* all clean fowls ye may eat.
21 Ye shall not eat *of* any thing that dieth of itself: thou shalt give it unto the
stranger that *is* in thy gates, that he may eat it; or thou mayest sell it unto an
alien: for thou *art* an holy people unto the LORD thy God. Thou shalt not seethe
a kid in his mother's milk.

Giving God One-Tenth of Everything

22 Thou shalt truly tithe all the increase of thy seed, that the field bringeth
forth year by year.
23 And thou shalt eat before the LORD thy God, in the place which he shall
choose to place his name there, the tithe of thy corn, of thy wine, and of thine
oil, and the firstlings of thy herds and of thy flocks; that thou mayest learn to
fear the LORD thy God always.
24 And if the way be too long for thee, so that thou art not able to carry it; *or*
if the place be too far from thee, which the LORD thy God shall choose to set
his name there, when the LORD thy God hath blessed thee:
25 Then shalt thou turn *it* into money, and bind up the money in thine hand,
and shalt go unto the place which the LORD thy God shall choose:
26 And thou shalt bestow that money for whatsoever thy soul lusteth after,
for oxen, or for sheep, or for wine, or for strong drink, or for whatsoever thy
soul desireth: and thou shalt eat there before the LORD thy God, and thou shalt
rejoice, thou, and thine household,
27 And the Levite that *is* within thy gates; thou shalt not forsake him; for he
hath no part nor inheritance with thee.
28 At the end of three years thou shalt bring forth all the tithe of thine
increase the same year, and shalt lay *it* up within thy gates:
29 And the Levite, (because he hath no part nor inheritance with thee,) and
the stranger, and the fatherless, and the widow, which *are* within thy gates,
shall come, and shall eat and be satisfied; that the LORD thy God may bless thee
in all the work of thine hand which thou doest.

Canceling Debts Every Seven Years

15 At the end of *every* seven years thou shalt make a release.
2 And this *is* the manner of the release: Every creditor that lendeth
ought unto his neighbour shall release *it*; he shall not exact *it* of his neighbour,
or of his brother; because it is called the LORD's release.

3 Of a foreigner thou mayest exact *it again*: but *that* which is thine with thy
brother thine hand shall release;
4 Save when there shall be no poor among you; for the Lord shall greatly
bless thee in the land which the Lord thy God giveth thee *for* an inheritance
to possess it:
5 Only if thou carefully hearken unto the voice of the Lord thy God, to
observe to do all these commandments which I command thee this day.
6 For the Lord thy God blesseth thee, as he promised thee: and thou shalt
lend unto many nations, but thou shalt not borrow; and thou shalt reign over
many nations, but they shall not reign over thee.
7 If there be among you a poor man of one of thy brethren within any of thy
gates in thy land which the Lord thy God giveth thee, thou shalt not harden
thine heart, nor shut thine hand from thy poor brother:
8 But thou shalt open thine hand wide unto him, and shalt surely lend him
sufficient for his need, *in that* which he wanteth.
9 Beware that there be not a thought in thy wicked heart, saying, The seventh
year, the year of release, is at hand; and thine eye be evil against thy poor
brother, and thou givest him nought; and he cry unto the Lord against thee,
and it be sin unto thee.
10 Thou shalt surely give him, and thine heart shall not be grieved when thou
givest unto him: because that for this thing the Lord thy God shall bless thee
in all thy works, and in all that thou puttest thine hand unto.
11 For the poor shall never cease out of the land: therefore I command thee,
saying, Thou shalt open thine hand wide unto thy brother, to thy poor, and to
thy needy, in thy land.

Laws Regarding Hebrew Slaves

12 *And* if thy brother, an Hebrew man, or an Hebrew woman, be sold unto
thee, and serve thee six years; then in the seventh year thou shalt let him go
free from thee.
13 And when thou sendest him out free from thee, thou shalt not let him go
away empty:
14 Thou shalt furnish him liberally out of thy flock, and out of thy floor, and
out of thy winepress: *of that* wherewith the Lord thy God hath blessed thee
thou shalt give unto him.
15 And thou shalt remember that thou wast a bondman in the land of Egypt,
and the Lord thy God redeemed thee: therefore I command thee this thing to
day.
16 And it shall be, if he say unto thee, I will not go away from thee; because
he loveth thee and thine house, because he is well with thee;
17 Then thou shalt take an aul, and thrust *it* through his ear unto the door,
and he shall be thy servant for ever. And also unto thy maidservant thou shalt
do likewise.
18 It shall not seem hard unto thee, when thou sendest him away free from
thee; for he hath been worth a double hired servant *to thee*, in serving thee
six years: and the Lord thy God shall bless thee in all that thou doest.
19 All the firstling males that come of thy herd and of thy flock thou shalt
sanctify unto the Lord thy God: thou shalt do no work with the firstling of thy
bullock, nor shear the firstling of thy sheep.
20 Thou shalt eat *it* before the Lord thy God year by year in the place which
the Lord shall choose, thou and thy household.
21 And if there be *any* blemish therein, *as if it be* lame, or blind, *or have* any
ill blemish, thou shalt not sacrifice it unto the Lord thy God.
22 Thou shalt eat it within thy gates: the unclean and the clean *person shall
eat it* alike, as the roebuck, and as the hart.

23 Only thou shalt not eat the blood thereof; thou shalt pour it upon the
ground as water.

The Three Major Festivals

16 Observe the month of Abib, and keep the passover unto the LORD thy
God: for in the month of Abib the LORD thy God brought thee forth
out of Egypt by night.
2 Thou shalt therefore sacrifice the passover unto the LORD thy God, of the
flock and the herd, in the place which the LORD shall choose to place his name
there.
3 Thou shalt eat no leavened bread with it; seven days shalt thou eat unleav-
ened bread therewith, *even* the bread of affliction; for thou camest forth out
of the land of Egypt in haste: that thou mayest remember the day when thou
camest forth out of the land of Egypt all the days of thy life.
4 And there shall be no leavened bread seen with thee in all thy coast seven
days; neither shall there *any thing* of the flesh, which thou sacrificedst the
first day at even, remain all night until the morning.
5 Thou mayest not sacrifice the passover within any of thy gates, which the
LORD thy God giveth thee:
6 But at the place which the LORD thy God shall choose to place his name in,
there thou shalt sacrifice the passover at even, at the going down of the sun,
at the season that thou camest forth out of Egypt.
7 And thou shalt roast and eat *it* in the place which the LORD thy God shall
choose: and thou shalt turn in the morning, and go unto thy tents.
8 Six days thou shalt eat unleavened bread: and on the seventh day *shall be*
a solemn assembly to the LORD thy God: thou shalt do no work *therein*.
9 Seven weeks shalt thou number unto thee: begin to number the seven weeks
from *such time as* thou beginnest *to put* the sickle to the corn.
10 And thou shalt keep the feast of weeks unto the LORD thy God with a trib-
ute of a freewill offering of thine hand, which thou shalt give *unto the LORD
thy God*, according as the LORD thy God hath blessed thee:
11 And thou shalt rejoice before the LORD thy God, thou, and thy son, and
thy daughter, and thy manservant, and thy maidservant, and the Levite that
is within thy gates, and the stranger, and the fatherless, and the widow, that
are among you, in the place which the LORD thy God hath chosen to place his
name there.
12 And thou shalt remember that thou wast a bondman in Egypt: and thou
shalt observe and do these statutes.
13 Thou shalt observe the feast of tabernacles seven days, after that thou hast
gathered in thy corn and thy wine:
14 And thou shalt rejoice in thy feast, thou, and thy son, and thy daughter,
and thy manservant, and thy maidservant, and the Levite, the stranger, and
the fatherless, and the widow, that *are* within thy gates.
15 Seven days shalt thou keep a solemn feast unto the LORD thy God in the
place which the LORD shall choose: because the LORD thy God shall bless thee
in all thine increase, and in all the works of thine hands, therefore thou shalt
surely rejoice.
16 Three times in a year shall all thy males appear before the LORD thy God
in the place which he shall choose; in the feast of unleavened bread, and in
the feast of weeks, and in the feast of tabernacles: and they shall not appear
before the LORD empty:
17 Every man *shall give* as he is able, according to the blessing of the LORD
thy God which he hath given thee.

Laws about Administering Justice

18 Judges and officers shalt thou make thee in all thy gates, which the LORD
thy God giveth thee, throughout thy tribes: and they shall judge the people
with just judgment.

19 Thou shalt not wrest judgment; thou shalt not respect persons, neither
take a gift: for a gift doth blind the eyes of the wise, and pervert the words of
the righteous.

20 That which is altogether just shalt thou follow, that thou mayest live, and
inherit the land which the LORD thy God giveth thee.

21 Thou shalt not plant thee a grove of any trees near unto the altar of the
LORD thy God, which thou shalt make thee.

22 Neither shalt thou set thee up *any* image; which the LORD thy God hateth.

Laws about the Sacrifices

17 Thou shalt not sacrifice unto the LORD thy God *any* bullock, or sheep,
wherein is blemish, *or* any evilfavouredness: for that *is* an abomination
unto the LORD thy God.

2 If there be found among you, within any of thy gates which the LORD thy
God giveth thee, man or woman, that hath wrought wickedness in the sight
of the LORD thy God, in transgressing his covenant,

3 And hath gone and served other gods, and worshipped them, either the
sun, or moon, or any of the host of heaven, which I have not commanded;

4 And it be told thee, and thou hast heard *of it*, and enquired diligently, and,
behold, *it be* true, *and* the thing certain, *that* such abomination is wrought
in Israel:

5 Then shalt thou bring forth that man or that woman, which have commit-
ted that wicked thing, unto thy gates, *even* that man or that woman, and shalt
stone them with stones, till they die.

6 At the mouth of two witnesses, or three witnesses, shall he that is worthy
of death be put to death; *but* at the mouth of one witness he shall not be put
to death.

7 The hands of the witnesses shall be first upon him to put him to death, and
afterward the hands of all the people. So thou shalt put the evil away from
among you.

Hard Controversies Ruled upon by the Priests and Judges

8 If there arise a matter too hard for thee in judgment, between blood and
blood, between plea and plea, and between stroke and stroke, *being* matters
of controversy within thy gates: then shalt thou arise, and get thee up into the
place which the LORD thy God shall choose;

9 And thou shalt come unto the priests the Levites, and unto the judge that
shall be in those days, and enquire; and they shall shew thee the sentence of
judgment:

10 And thou shalt do according to the sentence, which they of that place
which the LORD shall choose shall shew thee; and thou shalt observe to do
according to all that they inform thee:

11 According to the sentence of the law which they shall teach thee, and
according to the judgment which they shall tell thee, thou shalt do: thou shalt
not decline from the sentence which they shall shew thee, *to* the right hand,
nor *to* the left.

12 And the man that will do presumptuously, and will not hearken unto the
priest that standeth to minister there before the LORD thy God, or unto the
judge, even that man shall die: and thou shalt put away the evil from Israel.

13 And all the people shall hear, and fear, and do no more presumptuously.

The Duties of a King

14 When thou art come unto the land which the LORD thy God giveth thee,
and shalt possess it, and shalt dwell therein, and shalt say, I will set a king over
me, like as all the nations that *are* about me;
15 Thou shalt in any wise set *him* king over thee, whom the LORD thy God
shall choose: *one* from among thy brethren shalt thou set king over thee: thou
mayest not set a stranger over thee, which *is* not thy brother.
16 But he shall not multiply horses to himself, nor cause the people to return
to Egypt, to the end that he should multiply horses: forasmuch as the LORD
hath said unto you, Ye shall henceforth return no more that way.
17 Neither shall he multiply wives to himself, that his heart turn not away:
neither shall he greatly multiply to himself silver and gold.
18 And it shall be, when he sitteth upon the throne of his kingdom, that he
shall write him a copy of this law in a book out of *that which is* before the
priests the Levites:
19 And it shall be with him, and he shall read therein all the days of his life:
that he may learn to fear the LORD his God, to keep all the words of this law
and these statutes, to do them:
20 That his heart be not lifted up above his brethren, and that he turn not
aside from the commandment, *to* the right hand, or *to* the left: to the end that
he may prolong *his* days in his kingdom, he, and his children, in the midst of
Israel.

Laws about the Rightful Dues for the Priests and the Levites

18 The priests the Levites, *and* all the tribe of Levi, shall have no part nor
inheritance with Israel: they shall eat the offerings of the LORD made
by fire, and his inheritance.
2 Therefore shall they have no inheritance among their brethren: the LORD
is their inheritance, as he hath said unto them.
3 And this shall be the priest's due from the people, from them that offer a
sacrifice, whether *it be* ox or sheep; and they shall give unto the priest the
shoulder, and the two cheeks, and the maw.
4 The firstfruit *also* of thy corn, of thy wine, and of thine oil, and the first of
the fleece of thy sheep, shalt thou give him.
5 For the LORD thy God hath chosen him out of all thy tribes, to stand to
minister in the name of the LORD, him and his sons for ever.
6 And if a Levite come from any of thy gates out of all Israel, where he
sojourned, and come with all the desire of his mind unto the place which the
LORD shall choose;
7 Then he shall minister in the name of the LORD his God, as all his brethren
the Levites *do*, which stand there before the LORD.
8 They shall have like portions to eat, beside that which cometh of the sale
of his patrimony.

Laws about the Abominations of the Nations in the Land

9 When thou art come into the land which the LORD thy God giveth thee,
thou shalt not learn to do after the abominations of those nations.
10 There shall not be found among you *any one* that maketh his son or his
daughter to pass through the fire, *or* that useth divination, *or* an observer of
times, or an enchanter, or a witch,
11 Or a charmer, or a consulter with familiar spirits, or a wizard, or a necro-
mancer.
12 For all that do these things *are* an abomination unto the LORD: and because
of these abominations the LORD thy God doth drive them out from before
thee.
13 Thou shalt be perfect with the LORD thy God.

14 For these nations, which thou shalt possess, hearkened unto observers of
times, and unto diviners: but as for thee, the LORD thy God hath not suffered
thee so *to do*.

The Lord Will Raise up a Prophet

15 The LORD thy God will raise up unto thee a Prophet from the midst of thee,
of thy brethren, like unto me; unto him ye shall hearken;
16 According to all that thou desiredst of the LORD thy God in Horeb in the
day of the assembly, saying, Let me not hear again the voice of the LORD my
God, neither let me see this great fire any more, that I die not.
17 And the LORD said unto me, They have well *spoken that* which they have
spoken.
18 I will raise them up a Prophet from among their brethren, like unto thee,
and will put my words in his mouth; and he shall speak unto them all that I
shall command him.
19 And it shall come to pass, *that* whosoever will not hearken unto my words
which he shall speak in my name, I will require *it* of him.
20 But the prophet, which shall presume to speak a word in my name, which
I have not commanded him to speak, or that shall speak in the name of other
gods, even that prophet shall die.
21 And if thou say in thine heart, How shall we know the word which the
LORD hath not spoken?
22 When a prophet speaketh in the name of the LORD, if the thing follow not,
nor come to pass, that *is* the thing which the LORD hath not spoken, *but* the
prophet hath spoken it presumptuously: thou shalt not be afraid of him.

Laws about the Cities of Refuge

19 When the LORD thy God hath cut off the nations, whose land the LORD
thy God giveth thee, and thou succeedest them, and dwellest in their
cities, and in their houses;
2 Thou shalt separate three cities for thee in the midst of thy land, which the
LORD thy God giveth thee to possess it.
3 Thou shalt prepare thee a way, and divide the coasts of thy land, which the
LORD thy God giveth thee to inherit, into three parts, that every slayer may flee
thither.
4 And this *is* the case of the slayer, which shall flee thither, that he may live:
Whoso killeth his neighbour ignorantly, whom he hated not in time past;
5 As when a man goeth into the wood with his neighbour to hew wood, and
his hand fetcheth a stroke with the axe to cut down the tree, and the head
slippeth from the helve, and lighteth upon his neighbour, that he die; he shall
flee unto one of those cities, and live:
6 Lest the avenger of the blood pursue the slayer, while his heart is hot, and
overtake him, because the way is long, and slay him; whereas he *was* not
worthy of death, inasmuch as he hated him not in time past.
7 Wherefore I command thee, saying, Thou shalt separate three cities for
thee.
8 And if the LORD thy God enlarge thy coast, as he hath sworn unto thy fathers,
and give thee all the land which he promised to give unto thy fathers;
9 If thou shalt keep all these commandments to do them, which I command
thee this day, to love the LORD thy God, and to walk ever in his ways; then shalt
thou add three cities more for thee, beside these three:
10 That innocent blood be not shed in thy land, which the LORD thy God
giveth thee *for* an inheritance, and *so* blood be upon thee.
11 But if any man hate his neighbour, and lie in wait for him, and rise up
against him, and smite him mortally that he die, and fleeth into one of these
cities:

12 Then the elders of his city shall send and fetch him thence, and deliver
him into the hand of the avenger of blood, that he may die.
13 Thine eye shall not pity him, but thou shalt put away *the guilt of* innocent
blood from Israel, that it may go well with thee.

Laws about Land Boundaries and Witnesses at Trial

14 Thou shalt not remove thy neighbour's landmark, which they of old time
have set in thine inheritance, which thou shalt inherit in the land that the
LORD thy God giveth thee to possess it.
15 One witness shall not rise up against a man for any iniquity, or for any sin,
in any sin that he sinneth: at the mouth of two witnesses, or at the mouth of
three witnesses, shall the matter be established.
16 If a false witness rise up against any man to testify against him *that which
is* wrong;
17 Then both the men, between whom the controversy *is*, shall stand before
the LORD, before the priests and the judges, which shall be in those days;
18 And the judges shall make diligent inquisition: and, behold, *if* the witness
be a false witness, *and* hath testified falsely against his brother;
19 Then shall ye do unto him, as he had thought to have done unto his
brother: so shalt thou put the evil away from among you.
20 And those which remain shall hear, and fear, and shall henceforth commit
no more any such evil among you.
21 And thine eye shall not pity; *but* life *shall go* for life, eye for eye, tooth for
tooth, hand for hand, foot for foot.

Laws about Warfare and the Soldiers Sent into Battle

20 When thou goest out to battle against thine enemies, and seest horses,
and chariots, *and* a people more than thou, be not afraid of them: for
the LORD thy God *is* with thee, which brought thee up out of the land of Egypt.
2 And it shall be, when ye are come nigh unto the battle, that the priest shall
approach and speak unto the people,
3 And shall say unto them, Hear, O Israel, ye approach this day unto battle
against your enemies: let not your hearts faint, fear not, and do not tremble,
neither be ye terrified because of them;
4 For the LORD your God *is* he that goeth with you, to fight for you against
your enemies, to save you.
5 And the officers shall speak unto the people, saying, What man *is there* that
hath built a new house, and hath not dedicated it? let him go and return to
his house, lest he die in the battle, and another man dedicate it.
6 And what man *is he* that hath planted a vineyard, and hath not *yet* eaten
of it? let him *also* go and return unto his house, lest he die in the battle, and
another man eat of it.
7 And what man *is there* that hath betrothed a wife, and hath not taken her?
let him go and return unto his house, lest he die in the battle, and another
man take her.
8 And the officers shall speak further unto the people, and they shall say,
What man *is there that is* fearful and fainthearted? let him go and return unto
his house, lest his brethren's heart faint as well as his heart.
9 And it shall be, when the officers have made an end of speaking unto the
people, that they shall make captains of the armies to lead the people.

**What to Do to the Cities That Accept or Refuse
the Proclamation of Peace**

10 When thou comest nigh unto a city to fight against it, then proclaim peace
unto it.
11 And it shall be, if it make thee answer of peace, and open unto thee, then
it shall be, *that* all the people *that is* found therein shall be tributaries unto
thee, and they shall serve thee.

12 And if it will make no peace with thee, but will make war against thee,
then thou shalt besiege it:
13 And when the LORD thy God hath delivered it into thine hands, thou shalt
smite every male thereof with the edge of the sword:
14 But the women, and the little ones, and the cattle, and all that is in the city,
even all the spoil thereof, shalt thou take unto thyself; and thou shalt eat the
spoil of thine enemies, which the LORD thy God hath given thee.
15 Thus shalt thou do unto all the cities *which are* very far off from thee,
which *are* not of the cities of these nations.
16 But of the cities of these people, which the LORD thy God doth give thee
for an inheritance, thou shalt save alive nothing that breatheth:
17 But thou shalt utterly destroy them; *namely*, the Hittites, and the Amorites,
the Canaanites, and the Perizzites, the Hivites, and the Jebusites; as the LORD
thy God hath commanded thee:
18 That they teach you not to do after all their abominations, which they
have done unto their gods; so should ye sin against the LORD your God.
19 When thou shalt besiege a city a long time, in making war against it to
take it, thou shalt not destroy the trees thereof by forcing an axe against them:
for thou mayest eat of them, and thou shalt not cut them down (for the tree
of the field *is* man's *life*) to employ *them* in the siege:
20 Only the trees which thou knowest that they *be* not trees for meat, thou
shalt destroy and cut them down; and thou shalt build bulwarks against the
city that maketh war with thee, until it be subdued.

The Expiation of an Uncertain Murder

21 If *one* be found slain in the land which the LORD thy God giveth thee
to possess it, lying in the field, *and* it be not known who hath slain him:
2 Then thy elders and thy judges shall come forth, and they shall measure
unto the cities which *are* round about him that is slain:
3 And it shall be, *that* the city *which is* next unto the slain man, even the
elders of that city shall take an heifer, which hath not been wrought with, *and*
which hath not drawn in the yoke;
4 And the elders of that city shall bring down the heifer unto a rough valley,
which is neither eared nor sown, and shall strike off the heifer's neck there in
the valley:
5 And the priests the sons of Levi shall come near; for them the LORD thy God
hath chosen to minister unto him, and to bless in the name of the LORD; and
by their word shall every controversy and every stroke be *tried*:
6 And all the elders of that city, *that are* next unto the slain *man*, shall wash
their hands over the heifer that is beheaded in the valley:
7 And they shall answer and say, Our hands have not shed this blood, neither
have our eyes seen *it*.
8 Be merciful, O LORD, unto thy people Israel, whom thou hast redeemed,
and lay not innocent blood unto thy people of Israel's charge. And the blood
shall be forgiven them.
9 So shalt thou put away the *guilt of* innocent blood from among you, when
thou shalt do *that which is* right in the sight of the LORD.

The Treatment of a Captive Taken for a Wife

10 When thou goest forth to war against thine enemies, and the LORD thy
God hath delivered them into thine hands, and thou hast taken them captive,
11 And seest among the captives a beautiful woman, and hast a desire unto
her, that thou wouldest have her to thy wife;
12 Then thou shalt bring her home to thine house; and she shall shave her
head, and pare her nails;
13 And she shall put the raiment of her captivity from off her, and shall
remain in thine house, and bewail her father and her mother a full month:

and after that thou shalt go in unto her, and be her husband, and she shall be
thy wife.
14 And it shall be, if thou have no delight in her, then thou shalt let her go
whither she will; but thou shalt not sell her at all for money, thou shalt not
make merchandise of her, because thou hast humbled her.

The Firstborn Is Not to Be Disinherited on Private Preference

15 If a man have two wives, one beloved, and another hated, and they have
born him children, *both* the beloved and the hated; and *if* the firstborn son
be hers that was hated:
16 Then it shall be, when he maketh his sons to inherit *that* which he hath,
that he may not make the son of the beloved firstborn before the son of the
hated, *which is indeed* the firstborn:
17 But he shall acknowledge the son of the hated *for* the firstborn, by giving
him a double portion of all that he hath: for he *is* the beginning of his strength;
the right of the firstborn *is* his.

A Stubborn Son Shall Be Stoned to Death

18 If a man have a stubborn and rebellious son, which will not obey the voice
of his father, or the voice of his mother, and *that*, when they have chastened
him, will not hearken unto them:
19 Then shall his father and his mother lay hold on him, and bring him out
unto the elders of his city, and unto the gate of his place;
20 And they shall say unto the elders of his city, This our son *is* stubborn and
rebellious, he will not obey our voice; *he is* a glutton, and a drunkard.
21 And all the men of his city shall stone him with stones, that he die: so shalt
thou put evil away from among you; and all Israel shall hear, and fear.
22 And if a man have committed a sin worthy of death, and he be to be put
to death, and thou hang him on a tree:
23 His body shall not remain all night upon the tree, but thou shalt in any
wise bury him that day; (for he that is hanged *is* accursed of God;) that thy
land be not defiled, which the LORD thy God giveth thee *for* an inheritance.

Laws about Personal Property

22 Thou shalt not see thy brother's ox or his sheep go astray, and hide
thyself from them: thou shalt in any case bring them again unto thy
brother.
2 And if thy brother *be* not nigh unto thee, or if thou know him not, then
thou shalt bring it unto thine own house, and it shall be with thee until thy
brother seek after it, and thou shalt restore it to him again.
3 In like manner shalt thou do with his ass; and so shalt thou do with his
raiment; and with all lost thing of thy brother's, which he hath lost, and thou
hast found, shalt thou do likewise: thou mayest not hide thyself.
4 Thou shalt not see thy brother's ass or his ox fall down by the way, and hide
thyself from them: thou shalt surely help him to lift *them* up again.

Varied Laws

5 The woman shall not wear that which pertaineth unto a man, neither shall
a man put on a woman's garment: for all that do so *are* abomination unto the
LORD thy God.
6 If a bird's nest chance to be before thee in the way in any tree, or on the
ground, *whether they be* young ones, or eggs, and the dam sitting upon the
young, or upon the eggs, thou shalt not take the dam with the young:
7 *But* thou shalt in any wise let the dam go, and take the young to thee; that
it may be well with thee, and *that* thou mayest prolong *thy* days.
8 When thou buildest a new house, then thou shalt make a battlement for
thy roof, that thou bring not blood upon thine house, if any man fall from
thence.

9 Thou shalt not sow thy vineyard with divers seeds: lest the fruit of thy seed which thou hast sown, and the fruit of thy vineyard, be defiled.

10 Thou shalt not plow with an ox and an ass together.

11 Thou shalt not wear a garment of divers sorts, *as* of woollen and linen together.

12 Thou shalt make thee fringes upon the four quarters of thy vesture, wherewith thou coverest *thyself*.

Laws about Sex and Marriage

13 If any man take a wife, and go in unto her, and hate her,

14 And give occasions of speech against her, and bring up an evil name upon her, and say, I took this woman, and when I came to her, I found her not a maid:

15 Then shall the father of the damsel, and her mother, take and bring forth *the tokens of* the damsel's virginity unto the elders of the city in the gate:

16 And the damsel's father shall say unto the elders, I gave my daughter unto this man to wife, and he hateth her;

17 And, lo, he hath given occasions of speech *against her*, saying, I found not thy daughter a maid; and yet these *are the tokens of* my daughter's virginity. And they shall spread the cloth before the elders of the city.

18 And the elders of that city shall take that man and chastise him;

19 And they shall amerce him in an hundred *shekels* of silver, and give *them* unto the father of the damsel, because he hath brought up an evil name upon a virgin of Israel: and she shall be his wife; he may not put her away all his days.

20 But if this thing be true, *and the tokens of* virginity be not found for the damsel:

21 Then they shall bring out the damsel to the door of her father's house, and the men of her city shall stone her with stones that she die: because she hath wrought folly in Israel, to play the whore in her father's house: so shalt thou put evil away from among you.

22 If a man be found lying with a woman married to an husband, then they shall both of them die, *both* the man that lay with the woman, and the woman: so shalt thou put away evil from Israel.

23 If a damsel *that is* a virgin be betrothed unto an husband, and a man find her in the city, and lie with her;

24 Then ye shall bring them both out unto the gate of that city, and ye shall stone them with stones that they die; the damsel, because she cried not, *being* in the city; and the man, because he hath humbled his neighbour's wife: so thou shalt put away evil from among you.

25 But if a man find a betrothed damsel in the field, and the man force her, and lie with her: then the man only that lay with her shall die:

26 But unto the damsel thou shalt do nothing; *there is* in the damsel no sin *worthy* of death: for as when a man riseth against his neighbour, and slayeth him, even so *is* this matter:

27 For he found her in the field, *and* the betrothed damsel cried, and *there was* none to save her.

28 If a man find a damsel *that is* a virgin, which is not betrothed, and lay hold on her, and lie with her, and they be found;

29 Then the man that lay with her shall give unto the damsel's father fifty *shekels* of silver, and she shall be his wife; because he hath humbled her, he may not put her away all his days.

30 A man shall not take his father's wife, nor discover his father's skirt.

Who May or May Not Enter into the Congregation

23 He that is wounded in the stones, or hath his privy member cut off, shall not enter into the congregation of the LORD.

2 A bastard shall not enter into the congregation of the LORD; even to his tenth generation shall he not enter into the congregation of the LORD.

3 An Ammonite or Moabite shall not enter into the congregation of the LORD;
even to their tenth generation shall they not enter into the congregation of
the LORD for ever:
4 Because they met you not with bread and with water in the way, when ye
came forth out of Egypt; and because they hired against thee Balaam the son
of Beor of Pethor of Mesopotamia, to curse thee.
5 Nevertheless the LORD thy God would not hearken unto Balaam; but the
LORD thy God turned the curse into a blessing unto thee, because the LORD thy
God loved thee.
6 Thou shalt not seek their peace nor their prosperity all thy days for ever.
7 Thou shalt not abhor an Edomite; for he *is* thy brother: thou shalt not abhor
an Egyptian; because thou wast a stranger in his land.
8 The children that are begotten of them shall enter into the congregation
of the LORD in their third generation.

Uncleanness to Be Avoided in the Army

9 When the host goeth forth against thine enemies, then keep thee from
every wicked thing.
10 If there be among you any man, that is not clean by reason of uncleanness
that chanceth him by night, then shall he go abroad out of the camp, he shall
not come within the camp:
11 But it shall be, when evening cometh on, he shall wash *himself* with water:
and when the sun is down, he shall come into the camp *again*.
12 Thou shalt have a place also without the camp, whither thou shalt go forth
abroad:
13 And thou shalt have a paddle upon thy weapon; and it shall be, when thou
wilt ease thyself abroad, thou shalt dig therewith, and shalt turn back and
cover that which cometh from thee:
14 For the LORD thy God walketh in the midst of thy camp, to deliver thee,
and to give up thine enemies before thee; therefore shall thy camp be holy:
that he see no unclean thing in thee, and turn away from thee.

Varied Laws

15 Thou shalt not deliver unto his master the servant which is escaped from
his master unto thee:
16 He shall dwell with thee, *even* among you, in that place which he shall
choose in one of thy gates, where it liketh him best: thou shalt not oppress
him.
17 There shall be no whore of the daughters of Israel, nor a sodomite of the
sons of Israel.
18 Thou shalt not bring the hire of a whore, or the price of a dog, into the
house of the LORD thy God for any vow: for even both these *are* abomination
unto the LORD thy God.
19 Thou shalt not lend upon usury to thy brother; usury of money, usury of
victuals, usury of any thing that is lent upon usury:
20 Unto a stranger thou mayest lend upon usury; but unto thy brother thou
shalt not lend upon usury: that the LORD thy God may bless thee in all that
thou settest thine hand to in the land whither thou goest to possess it.
21 When thou shalt vow a vow unto the LORD thy God, thou shalt not slack
to pay it: for the LORD thy God will surely require it of thee; and it would be
sin in thee.
22 But if thou shalt forbear to vow, it shall be no sin in thee.
23 That which is gone out of thy lips thou shalt keep and perform; *even* a
freewill offering, according as thou hast vowed unto the LORD thy God, which
thou hast promised with thy mouth.
24 When thou comest into thy neighbour's vineyard, then thou mayest eat
grapes thy fill at thine own pleasure; but thou shalt not put *any* in thy vessel.

25 When thou comest into the standing corn of thy neighbour, then thou
mayest pluck the ears with thine hand; but thou shalt not move a sickle unto
thy neighbour's standing corn.

Laws about Divorce

24 When a man hath taken a wife, and married her, and it come to pass
that she find no favour in his eyes, because he hath found some
uncleanness in her: then let him write her a bill of divorcement, and give *it* in
her hand, and send her out of his house.
2 And when she is departed out of his house, she may go and be another
man's *wife*.
3 And *if* the latter husband hate her, and write her a bill of divorcement, and
giveth *it* in her hand, and sendeth her out of his house; or if the latter husband
die, which took her *to be* his wife;
4 Her former husband, which sent her away, may not take her again to be
his wife, after that she is defiled; for that *is* abomination before the LORD: and
thou shalt not cause the land to sin, which the LORD thy God giveth thee *for*
an inheritance.

Varied Laws

5 When a man hath taken a new wife, he shall not go out to war, neither shall
he be charged with any business: *but* he shall be free at home one year, and
shall cheer up his wife which he hath taken.
6 No man shall take the nether or the upper millstone to pledge: for he taketh
a man's life to pledge.
7 If a man be found stealing any of his brethren of the children of Israel, and
maketh merchandise of him, or selleth him; then that thief shall die; and thou
shalt put evil away from among you.
8 Take heed in the plague of leprosy, that thou observe diligently, and do
according to all that the priests the Levites shall teach you: as I commanded
them, *so* ye shall observe to do.
9 Remember what the LORD thy God did unto Miriam by the way, after that
ye were come forth out of Egypt.
10 When thou dost lend thy brother any thing, thou shalt not go into his
house to fetch his pledge.
11 Thou shalt stand abroad, and the man to whom thou dost lend shall bring
out the pledge abroad unto thee.
12 And if the man *be* poor, thou shalt not sleep with his pledge:
13 In any case thou shalt deliver him the pledge again when the sun goeth
down, that he may sleep in his own raiment, and bless thee: and it shall be
righteousness unto thee before the LORD thy God.

Varied Laws, Including Caring for the Poor, Widows, and Orphans

14 Thou shalt not oppress an hired servant *that is* poor and needy, *whether
he be* of thy brethren, or of thy strangers that *are* in thy land within thy gates:
15 At his day thou shalt give *him* his hire, neither shall the sun go down upon
it; for he *is* poor, and setteth his heart upon it: lest he cry against thee unto the
LORD, and it be sin unto thee.
16 The fathers shall not be put to death for the children, neither shall the
children be put to death for the fathers: every man shall be put to death for
his own sin.
17 Thou shalt not pervert the judgment of the stranger, *nor* of the fatherless;
nor take a widow's raiment to pledge:
18 But thou shalt remember that thou wast a bondman in Egypt, and the
LORD thy God redeemed thee thence: therefore I command thee to do this
thing.
19 When thou cuttest down thine harvest in thy field, and hast forgot a sheaf
in the field, thou shalt not go again to fetch it: it shall be for the stranger, for

the fatherless, and for the widow: that the LORD thy God may bless thee in all
the work of thine hands.
20 When thou beatest thine olive tree, thou shalt not go over the boughs
again: it shall be for the stranger, for the fatherless, and for the widow.
21 When thou gatherest the grapes of thy vineyard, thou shalt not glean *it*
afterward: it shall be for the stranger, for the fatherless, and for the widow.
22 And thou shalt remember that thou wast a bondman in the land of Egypt:
therefore I command thee to do this thing.

A Condemned Man Must Not Be Beaten with More Than Forty Stripes

25 If there be a controversy between men, and they come unto judgment,
that *the judges* may judge them; then they shall justify the righteous,
and condemn the wicked.
2 And it shall be, if the wicked man *be* worthy to be beaten, that the judge
shall cause him to lie down, and to be beaten before his face, according to his
fault, by a certain number.
3 Forty stripes he may give him, *and* not exceed: lest, *if* he should exceed, and
beat him above these with many stripes, then thy brother should seem vile
unto thee.
4 Thou shalt not muzzle the ox when he treadeth out *the corn*.

Laws about Keeping Family Lines

5 If brethren dwell together, and one of them die, and have no child, the wife
of the dead shall not marry without unto a stranger: her husband's brother
shall go in unto her, and take her to him to wife, and perform the duty of an
husband's brother unto her.
6 And it shall be, *that* the firstborn which she beareth shall succeed in the
name of his brother *which is* dead, that his name be not put out of Israel.
7 And if the man like not to take his brother's wife, then let his brother's wife
go up to the gate unto the elders, and say, My husband's brother refuseth to
raise up unto his brother a name in Israel, he will not perform the duty of my
husband's brother.
8 Then the elders of his city shall call him, and speak unto him: and *if* he
stand *to it*, and say, I like not to take her;
9 Then shall his brother's wife come unto him in the presence of the elders,
and loose his shoe from off his foot, and spit in his face, and shall answer and
say, So shall it be done unto that man that will not build up his brother's house.
10 And his name shall be called in Israel, The house of him that hath his shoe
loosed.
11 When men strive together one with another, and the wife of the one
draweth near for to deliver her husband out of the hand of him that smiteth
him, and putteth forth her hand, and taketh him by the secrets:
12 Then thou shalt cut off her hand, thine eye shall not pity *her*.

Varied Laws

13 Thou shalt not have in thy bag divers weights, a great and a small.
14 Thou shalt not have in thine house divers measures, a great and a small.
15 *But* thou shalt have a perfect and just weight, a perfect and just measure
shalt thou have: that thy days may be lengthened in the land which the LORD
thy God giveth thee.
16 For all that do such things, *and* all that do unrighteously, *are* an abomin-
ation unto the LORD thy God.
17 Remember what Amalek did unto thee by the way, when ye were come
forth out of Egypt;
18 How he met thee by the way, and smote the hindmost of thee, *even* all *that*
were feeble behind thee, when thou *wast* faint and weary; and he feared not
God.

19 Therefore it shall be, when the LORD thy God hath given thee rest from all
thine enemies round about, in the land which the LORD thy God giveth thee
for an inheritance to possess it, *that* thou shalt blot out the remembrance of
Amalek from under heaven; thou shalt not forget *it*.

Bringing the Firstfruits of the Land before the Lord in Thankfulness

26 And it shall be, when thou *art* come in unto the land which the LORD
thy God giveth thee *for* an inheritance, and possessest it, and dwellest
therein;

2 That thou shalt take of the first of all the fruit of the earth, which thou shalt
bring of thy land that the LORD thy God giveth thee, and shalt put *it* in a basket,
and shalt go unto the place which the LORD thy God shall choose to place his
name there.

3 And thou shalt go unto the priest that shall be in those days, and say unto
him, I profess this day unto the LORD thy God, that I am come unto the coun-
try which the LORD sware unto our fathers for to give us.

4 And the priest shall take the basket out of thine hand, and set it down before
the altar of the LORD thy God.

5 And thou shalt speak and say before the LORD thy God, A Syrian ready to
perish *was* my father, and he went down into Egypt, and sojourned there with
a few, and became there a nation, great, mighty, and populous:

6 And the Egyptians evil entreated us, and afflicted us, and laid upon us hard
bondage:

7 And when we cried unto the LORD God of our fathers, the LORD heard our
voice, and looked on our affliction, and our labour, and our oppression:

8 And the LORD brought us forth out of Egypt with a mighty hand, and with
an outstretched arm, and with great terribleness, and with signs, and with
wonders:

9 And he hath brought us into this place, and hath given us this land, *even* a
land that floweth with milk and honey.

10 And now, behold, I have brought the firstfruits of the land, which thou,
O LORD, hast given me. And thou shalt set it before the LORD thy God, and
worship before the LORD thy God:

11 And thou shalt rejoice in every good *thing* which the LORD thy God hath
given unto thee, and unto thine house, thou, and the Levite, and the stranger
that *is* among you.

The Prayer of Him That Gives His Third Year Tithes

12 When thou hast made an end of tithing all the tithes of thine increase the
third year, *which is* the year of tithing, and hast given *it* unto the Levite, the
stranger, the fatherless, and the widow, that they may eat within thy gates, and
be filled;

13 Then thou shalt say before the LORD thy God, I have brought away the
hallowed things out of *mine* house, and also have given them unto the Levite,
and unto the stranger, to the fatherless, and to the widow, according to all thy
commandments which thou hast commanded me: I have not transgressed
thy commandments, neither have I forgotten *them*:

14 I have not eaten thereof in my mourning, neither have I taken away *ought*
thereof for *any* unclean *use*, nor given *ought* thereof for the dead: *but* I have
hearkened to the voice of the LORD my God, *and* have done according to all
that thou hast commanded me.

15 Look down from thy holy habitation, from heaven, and bless thy people
Israel, and the land which thou hast given us, as thou swarest unto our fathers,
a land that floweth with milk and honey.

The Covenant between God and the People

16 This day the LORD thy God hath commanded thee to do these statutes and
judgments: thou shalt therefore keep and do them with all thine heart, and
with all thy soul.
17 Thou hast avouched the LORD this day to be thy God, and to walk in his
ways, and to keep his statutes, and his commandments, and his judgments,
and to hearken unto his voice:
18 And the LORD hath avouched thee this day to be his peculiar people, as he
hath promised thee, and that *thou* shouldest keep all his commandments;
19 And to make thee high above all nations which he hath made, in praise,
and in name, and in honour; and that thou mayest be an holy people unto the
LORD thy God, as he hath spoken.

The People Are Commanded to Write the Law upon Stones

27 And Moses with the elders of Israel commanded the people, saying,
Keep all the commandments which I command you this day.
2 And it shall be on the day when ye shall pass over Jordan unto the land
which the LORD thy God giveth thee, that thou shalt set thee up great stones,
and plaister them with plaister:
3 And thou shalt write upon them all the words of this law, when thou art
passed over, that thou mayest go in unto the land which the LORD thy God
giveth thee, a land that floweth with milk and honey; as the LORD God of thy
fathers hath promised thee.
4 Therefore it shall be when ye be gone over Jordan, *that* ye shall set up these
stones, which I command you this day, in mount Ebal, and thou shalt plaister
them with plaister.
5 And there shalt thou build an altar unto the LORD thy God, an altar of stones:
thou shalt not lift up *any* iron *tool* upon them.
6 Thou shalt build the altar of the LORD thy God of whole stones: and thou
shalt offer burnt offerings thereon unto the LORD thy God:
7 And thou shalt offer peace offerings, and shalt eat there, and rejoice before
the LORD thy God.
8 And thou shalt write upon the stones all the words of this law very plainly.
9 And Moses and the priests the Levites spake unto all Israel, saying, Take
heed, and hearken, O Israel; this day thou art become the people of the LORD
thy God.
10 Thou shalt therefore obey the voice of the LORD thy God, and do his com-
mandments and his statutes, which I command thee this day.

Reciting the Curses for Disobedience

11 And Moses charged the people the same day, saying,
12 These shall stand upon mount Gerizim to bless the people, when ye are
come over Jordan; Simeon, and Levi, and Judah, and Issachar, and Joseph, and
Benjamin:
13 And these shall stand upon mount Ebal to curse; Reuben, Gad, and Asher,
and Zebulun, Dan, and Naphtali.
14 And the Levites shall speak, and say unto all the men of Israel with a loud
voice,
15 Cursed *be* the man that maketh *any* graven or molten image, an abom-
ination unto the LORD, the work of the hands of the craftsman, and putteth *it*
in *a* secret *place*. And all the people shall answer and say, Amen.
16 Cursed *be* he that setteth light by his father or his mother. And all the
people shall say, Amen.
17 Cursed *be* he that removeth his neighbour's landmark. And all the people
shall say, Amen.
18 Cursed *be* he that maketh the blind to wander out of the way. And all the
people shall say, Amen.

19 Cursed *be* he that perverteth the judgment of the stranger, fatherless, and widow. And all the people shall say, Amen.

20 Cursed *be* he that lieth with his father's wife; because he uncovereth his father's skirt. And all the people shall say, Amen.

21 Cursed *be* he that lieth with any manner of beast. And all the people shall say, Amen.

22 Cursed *be* he that lieth with his sister, the daughter of his father, or the daughter of his mother. And all the people shall say, Amen.

23 Cursed *be* he that lieth with his mother in law. And all the people shall say, Amen.

24 Cursed *be* he that smiteth his neighbour secretly. And all the people shall say, Amen.

25 Cursed *be* he that taketh reward to slay an innocent person. And all the people shall say, Amen.

26 Cursed *be* he that confirmeth not *all* the words of this law to do them. And all the people shall say, Amen.

Reciting the Blessings for Obedience

28 And it shall come to pass, if thou shalt hearken diligently unto the voice of the Lord thy God, to observe *and* to do all his commandments which I command thee this day, that the Lord thy God will set thee on high above all nations of the earth:

2 And all these blessings shall come on thee, and overtake thee, if thou shalt hearken unto the voice of the Lord thy God.

3 Blessed *shalt* thou *be* in the city, and blessed *shalt* thou *be* in the field.

4 Blessed *shall be* the fruit of thy body, and the fruit of thy ground, and the fruit of thy cattle, the increase of thy kine, and the flocks of thy sheep.

5 Blessed *shall be* thy basket and thy store.

6 Blessed *shalt* thou *be* when thou comest in, and blessed *shalt* thou *be* when thou goest out.

7 The Lord shall cause thine enemies that rise up against thee to be smitten before thy face: they shall come out against thee one way, and flee before thee seven ways.

8 The Lord shall command the blessing upon thee in thy storehouses, and in all that thou settest thine hand unto; and he shall bless thee in the land which the Lord thy God giveth thee.

9 The Lord shall establish thee an holy people unto himself, as he hath sworn unto thee, if thou shalt keep the commandments of the Lord thy God, and walk in his ways.

10 And all people of the earth shall see that thou art called by the name of the Lord; and they shall be afraid of thee.

11 And the Lord shall make thee plenteous in goods, in the fruit of thy body, and in the fruit of thy cattle, and in the fruit of thy ground, in the land which the Lord sware unto thy fathers to give thee.

12 The Lord shall open unto thee his good treasure, the heaven to give the rain unto thy land in his season, and to bless all the work of thine hand: and thou shalt lend unto many nations, and thou shalt not borrow.

13 And the Lord shall make thee the head, and not the tail; and thou shalt be above only, and thou shalt not be beneath; if that thou hearken unto the commandments of the Lord thy God, which I command thee this day, to observe and to do *them*:

14 And thou shalt not go aside from any of the words which I command thee this day, *to* the right hand, or *to* the left, to go after other gods to serve them.

Curses from the Lord

15 But it shall come to pass, if thou wilt not hearken unto the voice of the Lord thy God, to observe to do all his commandments and his statutes which

I command thee this day; that all these curses shall come upon thee, and overtake thee:
16 Cursed *shalt* thou *be* in the city, and cursed *shalt* thou *be* in the field.
17 Cursed *shall be* thy basket and thy store.
18 Cursed *shall be* the fruit of thy body, and the fruit of thy land, the increase
of thy kine, and the flocks of thy sheep.
19 Cursed *shalt* thou *be* when thou comest in, and cursed *shalt* thou *be* when
thou goest out.
20 The LORD shall send upon thee cursing, vexation, and rebuke, in all that
thou settest thine hand unto for to do, until thou be destroyed, and until thou
perish quickly; because of the wickedness of thy doings, whereby thou hast
forsaken me.
21 The LORD shall make the pestilence cleave unto thee, until he have consumed thee from off the land, whither thou goest to possess it.
22 The LORD shall smite thee with a consumption, and with a fever, and with
an inflammation, and with an extreme burning, and with the sword, and with
blasting, and with mildew; and they shall pursue thee until thou perish.
23 And thy heaven that *is* over thy head shall be brass, and the earth that is
under thee *shall be* iron.
24 The LORD shall make the rain of thy land powder and dust: from heaven
shall it come down upon thee, until thou be destroyed.
25 The LORD shall cause thee to be smitten before thine enemies: thou shalt
go out one way against them, and flee seven ways before them: and shalt be
removed into all the kingdoms of the earth.
26 And thy carcase shall be meat unto all fowls of the air, and unto the beasts
of the earth, and no man shall fray *them* away.
27 The LORD will smite thee with the botch of Egypt, and with the emerods,
and with the scab, and with the itch, whereof thou canst not be healed.
28 The LORD shall smite thee with madness, and blindness, and astonishment
of heart:
29 And thou shalt grope at noonday, as the blind gropeth in darkness, and
thou shalt not prosper in thy ways: and thou shalt be only oppressed and
spoiled evermore, and no man shall save *thee*.
30 Thou shalt betroth a wife, and another man shall lie with her: thou shalt
build an house, and thou shalt not dwell therein: thou shalt plant a vineyard,
and shalt not gather the grapes thereof.
31 Thine ox *shall be* slain before thine eyes, and thou shalt not eat thereof:
thine ass *shall be* violently taken away from before thy face, and shall not be
restored to thee: thy sheep *shall be* given unto thine enemies, and thou shalt
have none to rescue *them*.
32 Thy sons and thy daughters *shall be* given unto another people, and thine
eyes shall look, and fail *with longing* for them all the day long: and *there shall
be* no might in thine hand.
33 The fruit of thy land, and all thy labours, shall a nation which thou knowest not eat up; and thou shalt be only oppressed and crushed alway:
34 So that thou shalt be mad for the sight of thine eyes which thou shalt see.
35 The LORD shall smite thee in the knees, and in the legs, with a sore botch
that cannot be healed, from the sole of thy foot unto the top of thy head.
36 The LORD shall bring thee, and thy king which thou shalt set over thee,
unto a nation which neither thou nor thy fathers have known; and there shalt
thou serve other gods, wood and stone.
37 And thou shalt become an astonishment, a proverb, and a byword, among
all nations whither the LORD shall lead thee.
38 Thou shalt carry much seed out into the field, and shalt gather *but* little
in; for the locust shall consume it.

39 Thou shalt plant vineyards, and dress *them*, but shalt neither drink *of* the
wine, nor gather *the grapes*; for the worms shall eat them.
40 Thou shalt have olive trees throughout all thy coasts, but thou shalt not
anoint *thyself* with the oil; for thine olive shall cast *his fruit*.
41 Thou shalt beget sons and daughters, but thou shalt not enjoy them; for
they shall go into captivity.
42 All thy trees and fruit of thy land shall the locust consume.
43 The stranger that *is* within thee shall get up above thee very high; and thou
shalt come down very low.
44 He shall lend to thee, and thou shalt not lend to him: he shall be the head,
and thou shalt be the tail.
45 Moreover all these curses shall come upon thee, and shall pursue thee,
and overtake thee, till thou be destroyed; because thou hearkenedst not unto
the voice of the LORD thy God, to keep his commandments and his statutes
which he commanded thee:
46 And they shall be upon thee for a sign and for a wonder, and upon thy
seed for ever.
47 Because thou servedst not the LORD thy God with joyfulness, and with
gladness of heart, for the abundance of all *things*;
48 Therefore shalt thou serve thine enemies which the LORD shall send
against thee, in hunger, and in thirst, and in nakedness, and in want of all
things: and he shall put a yoke of iron upon thy neck, until he have destroyed
thee.
49 The LORD shall bring a nation against thee from far, from the end of the
earth, *as swift* as the eagle flieth; a nation whose tongue thou shalt not under-
stand;
50 A nation of fierce countenance, which shall not regard the person of the
old, nor shew favour to the young:
51 And he shall eat the fruit of thy cattle, and the fruit of thy land, until thou
be destroyed: which *also* shall not leave thee *either* corn, wine, or oil, *or* the
increase of thy kine, or flocks of thy sheep, until he have destroyed thee.
52 And he shall besiege thee in all thy gates, until thy high and fenced walls
come down, wherein thou trustedst, throughout all thy land: and he shall
besiege thee in all thy gates throughout all thy land, which the LORD thy God
hath given thee.
53 And thou shalt eat the fruit of thine own body, the flesh of thy sons and
of thy daughters, which the LORD thy God hath given thee, in the siege, and in
the straitness, wherewith thine enemies shall distress thee:
54 *So that* the man *that is* tender among you, and very delicate, his eye shall
be evil toward his brother, and toward the wife of his bosom, and toward the
remnant of his children which he shall leave:
55 So that he will not give to any of them of the flesh of his children whom
he shall eat: because he hath nothing left him in the siege, and in the straitness,
wherewith thine enemies shall distress thee in all thy gates.
56 The tender and delicate woman among you, which would not adventure
to set the sole of her foot upon the ground for delicateness and tenderness,
her eye shall be evil toward the husband of her bosom, and toward her son,
and toward her daughter,
57 And toward her young one that cometh out from between her feet, and
toward her children which she shall bear: for she shall eat them for want of
all *things* secretly in the siege and straitness, wherewith thine enemy shall
distress thee in thy gates.
58 If thou wilt not observe to do all the words of this law that are written in
this book, that thou mayest fear this glorious and fearful name, THE LORD
THY GOD;

59 Then the LORD will make thy plagues wonderful, and the plagues of thy seed, *even* great plagues, and of long continuance, and sore sicknesses, and of long continuance.

60 Moreover he will bring upon thee all the diseases of Egypt, which thou wast afraid of; and they shall cleave unto thee.

61 Also every sickness, and every plague, which *is* not written in the book of this law, them will the LORD bring upon thee, until thou be destroyed.

62 And ye shall be left few in number, whereas ye were as the stars of heaven for multitude; because thou wouldest not obey the voice of the LORD thy God.

63 And it shall come to pass, *that* as the LORD rejoiced over you to do you good, and to multiply you; so the LORD will rejoice over you to destroy you, and to bring you to nought; and ye shall be plucked from off the land whither thou goest to possess it.

64 And the LORD shall scatter thee among all people, from the one end of the earth even unto the other; and there thou shalt serve other gods, which neither thou nor thy fathers have known, *even* wood and stone.

65 And among these nations shalt thou find no ease, neither shall the sole of thy foot have rest: but the LORD shall give thee there a trembling heart, and failing of eyes, and sorrow of mind:

66 And thy life shall hang in doubt before thee; and thou shalt fear day and night, and shalt have none assurance of thy life:

67 In the morning thou shalt say, Would God it were even! and at even thou shalt say, Would God it were morning! for the fear of thine heart wherewith thou shalt fear, and for the sight of thine eyes which thou shalt see.

68 And the LORD shall bring thee into Egypt again with ships, by the way whereof I spake unto thee, Thou shalt see it no more again: and there ye shall be sold unto your enemies for bondmen and bondwomen, and no man shall buy *you*.

Israel's Past, Present, and Future

29 These *are* the words of the covenant, which the LORD commanded Moses to make with the children of Israel in the land of Moab, beside the covenant which he made with them in Horeb.

2 And Moses called unto all Israel, and said unto them, Ye have seen all that the LORD did before your eyes in the land of Egypt unto Pharaoh, and unto all his servants, and unto all his land;

3 The great temptations which thine eyes have seen, the signs, and those great miracles:

4 Yet the LORD hath not given you an heart to perceive, and eyes to see, and ears to hear, unto this day.

5 And I have led you forty years in the wilderness: your clothes are not waxen old upon you, and thy shoe is not waxen old upon thy foot.

6 Ye have not eaten bread, neither have ye drunk wine or strong drink: that ye might know that I *am* the LORD your God.

7 And when ye came unto this place, Sihon the king of Heshbon, and Og the king of Bashan, came out against us unto battle, and we smote them:

8 And we took their land, and gave it for an inheritance unto the Reubenites, and to the Gadites, and to the half tribe of Manasseh.

9 Keep therefore the words of this covenant, and do them, that ye may prosper in all that ye do.

All Are Presented before the Lord to Enter into His Covenant

10 Ye stand this day all of you before the LORD your God; your captains of your tribes, your elders, and your officers, *with* all the men of Israel,

11 Your little ones, your wives, and thy stranger that *is* in thy camp, from the hewer of thy wood unto the drawer of thy water:

12 That thou shouldest enter into covenant with the LORD thy God, and into
his oath, which the LORD thy God maketh with thee this day:
13 That he may establish thee to day for a people unto himself, and *that* he
may be unto thee a God, as he hath said unto thee, and as he hath sworn unto
thy fathers, to Abraham, to Isaac, and to Jacob.
14 Neither with you only do I make this covenant and this oath;
15 But with *him* that standeth here with us this day before the LORD our God,
and also with *him* that *is* not here with us this day:
16 (For ye know how we have dwelt in the land of Egypt; and how we came
through the nations which ye passed by;
17 And ye have seen their abominations, and their idols, wood and stone,
silver and gold, which *were* among them:)
18 Lest there should be among you man, or woman, or family, or tribe, whose
heart turneth away this day from the LORD our God, to go *and* serve the gods
of these nations; lest there should be among you a root that beareth gall and
wormwood;
19 And it come to pass, when he heareth the words of this curse, that he bless
himself in his heart, saying, I shall have peace, though I walk in the imagin-
ation of mine heart, to add drunkenness to thirst:
20 The LORD will not spare him, but then the anger of the LORD and his jeal-
ousy shall smoke against that man, and all the curses that are written in this
book shall lie upon him, and the LORD shall blot out his name from under
heaven.
21 And the LORD shall separate him unto evil out of all the tribes of Israel,
according to all the curses of the covenant that are written in this book of the
law:
22 So that the generation to come of your children that shall rise up after
you, and the stranger that shall come from a far land, shall say, when they see
the plagues of that land, and the sicknesses which the LORD hath laid upon it;
23 *And that* the whole land thereof *is* brimstone, and salt, *and* burning, *that*
it is not sown, nor beareth, nor any grass groweth therein, like the overthrow
of Sodom, and Gomorrah, Admah, and Zeboim, which the LORD overthrew
in his anger, and in his wrath:
24 Even all nations shall say, Wherefore hath the LORD done thus unto this
land? what *meaneth* the heat of this great anger?
25 Then men shall say, Because they have forsaken the covenant of the LORD
God of their fathers, which he made with them when he brought them forth
out of the land of Egypt:
26 For they went and served other gods, and worshipped them, gods whom
they knew not, and *whom* he had not given unto them:
27 And the anger of the LORD was kindled against this land, to bring upon it
all the curses that are written in this book:
28 And the LORD rooted them out of their land in anger, and in wrath, and
in great indignation, and cast them into another land, as *it is* this day.
29 The secret *things belong* unto the LORD our God: but those *things which*
are revealed *belong* unto us and to our children for ever, that *we* may do all
the words of this law.

Great Mercies Promised to the Repentant

30 And it shall come to pass, when all these things are come upon thee,
the blessing and the curse, which I have set before thee, and thou shalt
call *them* to mind among all the nations, whither the LORD thy God hath driven
thee,
2 And shalt return unto the LORD thy God, and shalt obey his voice according
to all that I command thee this day, thou and thy children, with all thine heart,
and with all thy soul;

3 That then the LORD thy God will turn thy captivity, and have compassion
upon thee, and will return and gather thee from all the nations, whither the
LORD thy God hath scattered thee.
4 If *any* of thine be driven out unto the outmost *parts* of heaven, from thence
will the LORD thy God gather thee, and from thence will he fetch thee:
5 And the LORD thy God will bring thee into the land which thy fathers pos-
sessed, and thou shalt possess it; and he will do thee good, and multiply thee
above thy fathers.
6 And the LORD thy God will circumcise thine heart, and the heart of thy
seed, to love the LORD thy God with all thine heart, and with all thy soul, that
thou mayest live.
7 And the LORD thy God will put all these curses upon thine enemies, and on
them that hate thee, which persecuted thee.
8 And thou shalt return and obey the voice of the LORD, and do all his com-
mandments which I command thee this day.
9 And the LORD thy God will make thee plenteous in every work of thine
hand, in the fruit of thy body, and in the fruit of thy cattle, and in the fruit of
thy land, for good: for the LORD will again rejoice over thee for good, as he
rejoiced over thy fathers:
10 If thou shalt hearken unto the voice of the LORD thy God, to keep his
commandments and his statutes which are written in this book of the law,
and if thou turn unto the LORD thy God with all thine heart, and with all thy
soul.

The Commandment Is Not Hard

11 For this commandment which I command thee this day, it *is* not hidden
from thee, neither *is* it far off.
12 It *is* not in heaven, that thou shouldest say, Who shall go up for us to
heaven, and bring it unto us, that we may hear it, and do it?
13 Neither *is* it beyond the sea, that thou shouldest say, Who shall go over
the sea for us, and bring it unto us, that we may hear it, and do it?
14 But the word *is* very nigh unto thee, in thy mouth, and in thy heart, that
thou mayest do it.

The Choice between Death and Life

15 See, I have set before thee this day life and good, and death and evil;
16 In that I command thee this day to love the LORD thy God, to walk in his
ways, and to keep his commandments and his statutes and his judgments, that
thou mayest live and multiply: and the LORD thy God shall bless thee in the
land whither thou goest to possess it.
17 But if thine heart turn away, so that thou wilt not hear, but shalt be drawn
away, and worship other gods, and serve them;
18 I denounce unto you this day, that ye shall surely perish, *and that* ye shall
not prolong *your* days upon the land, whither thou passest over Jordan to go
to possess it.
19 I call heaven and earth to record this day against you, *that* I have set before
you life and death, blessing and cursing: therefore choose life, that both thou
and thy seed may live:
20 That thou mayest love the LORD thy God, *and* that thou mayest obey his
voice, and that thou mayest cleave unto him: for he *is* thy life, and the length
of thy days: that thou mayest dwell in the land which the LORD sware unto thy
fathers, to Abraham, to Isaac, and to Jacob, to give them.

Joshua Will Lead the People

31 And Moses went and spake these words unto all Israel.
2 And he said unto them, I *am* an hundred and twenty years old this
day; I can no more go out and come in: also the LORD hath said unto me, Thou
shalt not go over this Jordan.

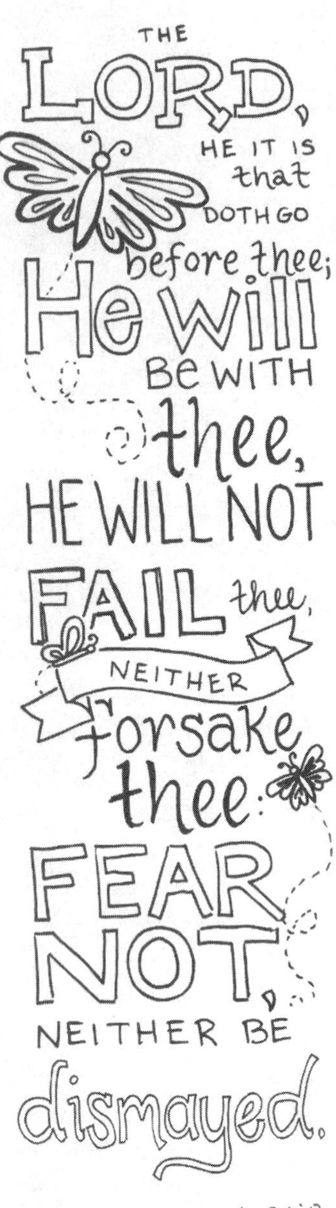

3 The LORD thy God, he will go over before thee, *and* he will destroy these
nations from before thee, and thou shalt possess them: *and* Joshua, he shall
go over before thee, as the LORD hath said.
4 And the LORD shall do unto them as he did to Sihon and to Og, kings of the
Amorites, and unto the land of them, whom he destroyed.
5 And the LORD shall give them up before your face, that ye may do unto them
according unto all the commandments which I have commanded you.
6 Be strong and of a good courage, fear not, nor be afraid of them: for the
LORD thy God, he *it is* that doth go with thee; he will not fail thee, nor forsake
thee.
7 And Moses called unto Joshua, and said unto him in the sight of all Israel,
Be strong and of a good courage: for thou must go with this people unto the
land which the LORD hath sworn unto their fathers to give them; and thou
shalt cause them to inherit it.
8 And the LORD, he *it is* that doth go before thee; he will be with thee, he will
not fail thee, neither forsake thee: fear not, neither be dismayed.

Moses Encourages Reading God's Law

9 And Moses wrote this law, and delivered it unto the priests the sons of Levi,
which bare the ark of the covenant of the LORD, and unto all the elders of Israel.
10 And Moses commanded them, saying, At the end of *every* seven years, in
the solemnity of the year of release, in the feast of tabernacles,
11 When all Israel is come to appear before the LORD thy God in the place
which he shall choose, thou shalt read this law before all Israel in their hearing.
12 Gather the people together, men, and women, and children, and thy
stranger that *is* within thy gates, that they may hear, and that they may learn,
and fear the LORD your God, and observe to do all the words of this law:
13 And *that* their children, which have not known *any thing*, may hear, and
learn to fear the LORD your God, as long as ye live in the land whither ye go
over Jordan to possess it.

God Gives a Charge to Joshua

14 And the LORD said unto Moses, Behold, thy days approach that thou must
die: call Joshua, and present yourselves in the tabernacle of the congregation,
that I may give him a charge. And Moses and Joshua went, and presented
themselves in the tabernacle of the congregation.
15 And the LORD appeared in the tabernacle in a pillar of a cloud: and the
pillar of the cloud stood over the door of the tabernacle.
16 And the LORD said unto Moses, Behold, thou shalt sleep with thy fathers;
and this people will rise up, and go a whoring after the gods of the strangers
of the land, whither they go *to be* among them, and will forsake me, and break
my covenant which I have made with them.
17 Then my anger shall be kindled against them in that day, and I will forsake
them, and I will hide my face from them, and they shall be devoured, and many
evils and troubles shall befall them; so that they will say in that day, Are not
these evils come upon us, because our God *is* not among us?
18 And I will surely hide my face in that day for all the evils which they shall
have wrought, in that they are turned unto other gods.
19 Now therefore write ye this song for you, and teach it the children of Israel:
put it in their mouths, that this song may be a witness for me against the
children of Israel.
20 For when I shall have brought them into the land which I sware unto their
fathers, that floweth with milk and honey; and they shall have eaten and filled
themselves, and waxen fat; then will they turn unto other gods, and serve
them, and provoke me, and break my covenant.
21 And it shall come to pass, when many evils and troubles are befallen them,
that this song shall testify against them as a witness; for it shall not be forgot-

ten out of the mouths of their seed: for I know their imagination which they
go about, even now, before I have brought them into the land which I sware.
22 Moses therefore wrote this song the same day, and taught it the children
of Israel.
23 And he gave Joshua the son of Nun a charge, and said, Be strong and of a
good courage: for thou shalt bring the children of Israel into the land which
I sware unto them: and I will be with thee.
24 And it came to pass, when Moses had made an end of writing the words
of this law in a book, until they were finished,
25 That Moses commanded the Levites, which bare the ark of the covenant
of the LORD, saying,
26 Take this book of the law, and put it in the side of the ark of the covenant
of the LORD your God, that it may be there for a witness against thee.
27 For I know thy rebellion, and thy stiff neck: behold, while I am yet alive
with you this day, ye have been rebellious against the LORD; and how much
more after my death?
28 Gather unto me all the elders of your tribes, and your officers, that I may
speak these words in their ears, and call heaven and earth to record against
them.
29 For I know that after my death ye will utterly corrupt *yourselves*, and turn
aside from the way which I have commanded you; and evil will befall you in
the latter days; because ye will do evil in the sight of the LORD, to provoke him
to anger through the work of your hands.
30 And Moses spake in the ears of all the congregation of Israel the words of
this song, until they were ended.

Moses' Song Which Sets Forth God's Mercy and Vengeance

32 Give ear, O ye heavens, and I will speak; and hear, O earth, the words
of my mouth.
2 My doctrine shall drop as the rain, my speech shall distil as the dew, as the
small rain upon the tender herb, and as the showers upon the grass:
3 Because I will publish the name of the LORD: ascribe ye greatness unto our
God.
4 *He is* the Rock, his work *is* perfect: for all his ways *are* judgment: a God of
truth and without iniquity, just and right *is* he.
5 They have corrupted themselves, their spot *is* not *the spot* of his children:
they are a perverse and crooked generation.
6 Do ye thus requite the LORD, O foolish people and unwise? *is* not he thy
father *that* hath bought thee? hath he not made thee, and established thee?
7 Remember the days of old, consider the years of many generations: ask thy
father, and he will shew thee; thy elders, and they will tell thee.
8 When the most High divided to the nations their inheritance, when he
separated the sons of Adam, he set the bounds of the people according to the
number of the children of Israel.
9 For the LORD's portion *is* his people; Jacob *is* the lot of his inheritance.
10 He found him in a desert land, and in the waste howling wilderness; he
led him about, he instructed him, he kept him as the apple of his eye.
11 As an eagle stirreth up her nest, fluttereth over her young, spreadeth
abroad her wings, taketh them, beareth them on her wings:
12 *So* the LORD alone did lead him, and *there was* no strange god with him.
13 He made him ride on the high places of the earth, that he might eat the
increase of the fields; and he made him to suck honey out of the rock, and oil
out of the flinty rock;
14 Butter of kine, and milk of sheep, with fat of lambs, and rams of the breed
of Bashan, and goats, with the fat of kidneys of wheat; and thou didst drink
the pure blood of the grape.

15 But Jeshurun waxed fat, and kicked: thou art waxen fat, thou art grown
thick, thou art covered *with fatness*; then he forsook God *which* made him,
and lightly esteemed the Rock of his salvation.
16 They provoked him to jealousy with strange *gods*, with abominations
provoked they him to anger.
17 They sacrificed unto devils, not to God; to gods whom they knew not, to
new *gods that* came newly up, whom your fathers feared not.
18 Of the Rock *that* begat thee thou art unmindful, and hast forgotten God
that formed thee.
19 And when the LORD saw *it*, he abhorred *them*, because of the provoking
of his sons, and of his daughters.
20 And he said, I will hide my face from them, I will see what their end *shall
be*: for they *are* a very froward generation, children in whom *is* no faith.
21 They have moved me to jealousy with *that which is* not God; they have
provoked me to anger with their vanities: and I will move them to jealousy
with *those which are* not a people; I will provoke them to anger with a foolish
nation.
22 For a fire is kindled in mine anger, and shall burn unto the lowest hell,
and shall consume the earth with her increase, and set on fire the foundations
of the mountains.
23 I will heap mischiefs upon them; I will spend mine arrows upon them.
24 *They shall be* burnt with hunger, and devoured with burning heat, and
with bitter destruction: I will also send the teeth of beasts upon them, with
the poison of serpents of the dust.
25 The sword without, and terror within, shall destroy both the young man
and the virgin, the suckling *also* with the man of gray hairs.
26 I said, I would scatter them into corners, I would make the remembrance
of them to cease from among men:
27 Were it not that I feared the wrath of the enemy, lest their adversaries
should behave themselves strangely, *and* lest they should say, Our hand *is* high,
and the LORD hath not done all this.
28 For they *are* a nation void of counsel, neither *is there any* understanding
in them.
29 O that they were wise, *that* they understood this, *that* they would consider
their latter end!
30 How should one chase a thousand, and two put ten thousand to flight,
except their Rock had sold them, and the LORD had shut them up?
31 For their rock *is* not as our Rock, even our enemies themselves *being* judges.
32 For their vine *is* of the vine of Sodom, and of the fields of Gomorrah: their
grapes *are* grapes of gall, their clusters *are* bitter:
33 Their wine *is* the poison of dragons, and the cruel venom of asps.
34 *Is* not this laid up in store with me, *and* sealed up among my treasures?
35 To me *belongeth* vengeance, and recompence; their foot shall slide in *due*
time: for the day of their calamity *is* at hand, and the things that shall come
upon them make haste.
36 For the LORD shall judge his people, and repent himself for his servants,
when he seeth that *their* power is gone, and *there is* none shut up, or left.
37 And he shall say, Where *are* their gods, *their* rock in whom they trusted,
38 Which did eat the fat of their sacrifices, *and* drank the wine of their drink
offerings? let them rise up and help you, *and* be your protection.
39 See now that I, *even* I, *am* he, and *there is* no god with me: I kill, and I make
alive; I wound, and I heal: neither *is there any* that can deliver out of my hand.
40 For I lift up my hand to heaven, and say, I live for ever.
41 If I whet my glittering sword, and mine hand take hold on judgment; I
will render vengeance to mine enemies, and will reward them that hate me.

42 I will make mine arrows drunk with blood, and my sword shall devour
flesh; *and that* with the blood of the slain and of the captives, from the begin-
ning of revenges upon the enemy.
43 Rejoice, O ye nations, *with* his people: for he will avenge the blood of his
servants, and will render vengeance to his adversaries, and will be merciful
unto his land, *and* to his people.
44 And Moses came and spake all the words of this song in the ears of the
people, he, and Hoshea the son of Nun.
45 And Moses made an end of speaking all these words to all Israel:
46 And he said unto them, Set your hearts unto all the words which I testify
among you this day, which ye shall command your children to observe to do,
all the words of this law.
47 For it *is* not a vain thing for you; because it *is* your life: and through this
thing ye shall prolong *your* days in the land, whither ye go over Jordan to
possess it.
48 And the LORD spake unto Moses that selfsame day, saying,
49 Get thee up into this mountain Abarim, *unto* mount Nebo, which *is* in
the land of Moab, that *is* over against Jericho; and behold the land of Canaan,
which I give unto the children of Israel for a possession:
50 And die in the mount whither thou goest up, and be gathered unto thy
people; as Aaron thy brother died in mount Hor, and was gathered unto his
people:
51 Because ye trespassed against me among the children of Israel at the
waters of Meribah-Kadesh, in the wilderness of Zin; because ye sanctified me
not in the midst of the children of Israel.
52 Yet thou shalt see the land before *thee*; but thou shalt not go thither unto
the land which I give the children of Israel.

The Blessings of the Twelve Tribes

33 And this *is* the blessing, wherewith Moses the man of God blessed the
children of Israel before his death.
2 And he said, The LORD came from Sinai, and rose up from Seir unto them;
he shined forth from mount Paran, and he came with ten thousands of saints:
from his right hand *went* a fiery law for them.
3 Yea, he loved the people; all his saints *are* in thy hand: and they sat down
at thy feet; *every one* shall receive of thy words.
4 Moses commanded us a law, *even* the inheritance of the congregation of
Jacob.
5 And he was king in Jeshurun, when the heads of the people *and* the tribes
of Israel were gathered together.
6 Let Reuben live, and not die; and let *not* his men be few.
7 And this *is the blessing* of Judah: and he said, Hear, LORD, the voice of Judah,
and bring him unto his people: let his hands be sufficient for him; and be thou
an help *to him* from his enemies.
8 And of Levi he said, *Let* thy Thummim and thy Urim *be* with thy holy one,
whom thou didst prove at Massah, *and with* whom thou didst strive at the
waters of Meribah;
9 Who said unto his father and to his mother, I have not seen him; neither
did he acknowledge his brethren, nor knew his own children: for they have
observed thy word, and kept thy covenant.
10 They shall teach Jacob thy judgments, and Israel thy law: they shall put
incense before thee, and whole burnt sacrifice upon thine altar.
11 Bless, LORD, his substance, and accept the work of his hands: smite through
the loins of them that rise against him, and of them that hate him, that they
rise not again.

12 *And* of Benjamin he said, The beloved of the LORD shall dwell in safety by him; *and the LORD* shall cover him all the day long, and he shall dwell between his shoulders.

13 And of Joseph he said, Blessed of the LORD *be* his land, for the precious things of heaven, for the dew, and for the deep that coucheth beneath,

14 And for the precious fruits *brought forth* by the sun, and for the precious things put forth by the moon,

15 And for the chief things of the ancient mountains, and for the precious things of the lasting hills,

16 And for the precious things of the earth and fulness thereof, and *for* the good will of him that dwelt in the bush: let *the blessing* come upon the head of Joseph, and upon the top of the head of him *that was* separated from his brethren.

17 His glory *is like* the firstling of his bullock, and his horns *are like* the horns of unicorns: with them he shall push the people together to the ends of the earth: and they *are* the ten thousands of Ephraim, and they *are* the thousands of Manasseh.

18 And of Zebulun he said, Rejoice, Zebulun, in thy going out; and, Issachar, in thy tents.

19 They shall call the people unto the mountain; there they shall offer sacrifices of righteousness: for they shall suck *of* the abundance of the seas, and *of* treasures hid in the sand.

20 And of Gad he said, Blessed *be* he that enlargeth Gad: he dwelleth as a lion, and teareth the arm with the crown of the head.

21 And he provided the first part for himself, because there, *in* a portion of the lawgiver, *was he* seated; and he came with the heads of the people, he executed the justice of the LORD, and his judgments with Israel.

22 And of Dan he said, Dan *is* a lion's whelp: he shall leap from Bashan.

23 And of Naphtali he said, O Naphtali, satisfied with favour, and full with the blessing of the LORD: possess thou the west and the south.

24 And of Asher he said, *Let* Asher *be* blessed with children; let him be acceptable to his brethren, and let him dip his foot in oil.

25 Thy shoes *shall be* iron and brass; and as thy days, *so shall* thy strength *be*.

The Everlasting Arms of the Eternal God

26 *There is* none like unto the God of Jeshurun, *who* rideth upon the heaven in thy help, and in his excellency on the sky.

27 The eternal God *is thy* refuge, and underneath *are* the everlasting arms: and he shall thrust out the enemy from before thee; and shall say, Destroy *them*.

28 Israel then shall dwell in safety alone: the fountain of Jacob *shall be* upon a land of corn and wine; also his heavens shall drop down dew.

29 Happy *art* thou, O Israel: who *is* like unto thee, O people saved by the LORD, the shield of thy help, and who *is* the sword of thy excellency! and thine enemies shall be found liars unto thee; and thou shalt tread upon their high places.

Moses Views the Land from Mount Nebo

34 And Moses went up from the plains of Moab unto the mountain of Nebo, to the top of Pisgah, that *is* over against Jericho. And the LORD shewed him all the land of Gilead, unto Dan,

2 And all Naphtali, and the land of Ephraim, and Manasseh, and all the land of Judah, unto the utmost sea,

3 And the south, and the plain of the valley of Jericho, the city of palm trees, unto Zoar.

4 And the LORD said unto him, This *is* the land which I sware unto Abraham,
unto Isaac, and unto Jacob, saying, I will give it unto thy seed: I have caused
thee to see *it* with thine eyes, but thou shalt not go over thither.

Moses Dies in the Land of Moab

5 So Moses the servant of the LORD died there in the land of Moab, according
to the word of the LORD.
6 And he buried him in a valley in the land of Moab, over against Beth-peor:
but no man knoweth of his sepulchre unto this day.
7 And Moses *was* an hundred and twenty years old when he died: his eye was
not dim, nor his natural force abated.
8 And the children of Israel wept for Moses in the plains of Moab thirty days:
so the days of weeping *and* mourning for Moses were ended.

Joshua Succeeds Moses

9 And Joshua the son of Nun was full of the spirit of wisdom; for Moses had
laid his hands upon him: and the children of Israel hearkened unto him, and
did as the LORD commanded Moses.
10 And there arose not a prophet since in Israel like unto Moses, whom the
LORD knew face to face,
11 In all the signs and the wonders, which the LORD sent him to do in the
land of Egypt to Pharaoh, and to all his servants, and to all his land,
12 And in all that mighty hand, and in all the great terror which Moses
shewed in the sight of all Israel.

The Lord Appoints Joshua to Succeed Moses

1 Now after the death of Moses the servant of the LORD it came to pass, that
the LORD spake unto Joshua the son of Nun, Moses' minister, saying,
2 Moses my servant is dead; now therefore arise, go over this Jordan, thou,
and all this people, unto the land which I do give to them, *even* to the children
of Israel.
3 Every place that the sole of your foot shall tread upon, that have I given
unto you, as I said unto Moses.
4 From the wilderness and this Lebanon even unto the great river, the river
Euphrates, all the land of the Hittites, and unto the great sea toward the going
down of the sun, shall be your coast.
5 There shall not any man be able to stand before thee all the days of thy life:
as I was with Moses, *so* I will be with thee: I will not fail thee, nor forsake thee.
6 Be strong and of a good courage: for unto this people shalt thou divide for
an inheritance the land, which I sware unto their fathers to give them.
7 Only be thou strong and very courageous, that thou mayest observe to do
according to all the law, which Moses my servant commanded thee: turn not
from it *to* the right hand or *to* the left, that thou mayest prosper whitherso-
ever thou goest.
8 This book of the law shall not depart out of thy mouth; but thou shalt
meditate therein day and night, that thou mayest observe to do according to
all that is written therein: for then thou shalt make thy way prosperous, and
then thou shalt have good success.
9 Have not I commanded thee? Be strong and of a good courage; be not
afraid, neither be thou dismayed: for the LORD thy God *is* with thee whither-
soever thou goest.

Joshua Prepares the People to Pass over Jordan

10 Then Joshua commanded the officers of the people, saying,
11 Pass through the host, and command the people, saying, Prepare you
victuals; for within three days ye shall pass over this Jordan, to go in to possess
the land, which the LORD your God giveth you to possess it.
12 And to the Reubenites, and to the Gadites, and to half the tribe of
Manasseh, spake Joshua, saying,
13 Remember the word which Moses the servant of the LORD commanded
you, saying, The LORD your God hath given you rest, and hath given you this
land.
14 Your wives, your little ones, and your cattle, shall remain in the land which
Moses gave you on this side Jordan; but ye shall pass before your brethren
armed, all the mighty men of valour, and help them;
15 Until the LORD have given your brethren rest, as *he hath given* you, and
they also have possessed the land which the LORD your God giveth them: then
ye shall return unto the land of your possession, and enjoy it, which Moses
the LORD's servant gave you on this side Jordan toward the sunrising.

The People Pledge Allegiance to Joshua

16 And they answered Joshua, saying, All that thou commandest us we will
do, and whithersoever thou sendest us, we will go.

17 According as we hearkened unto Moses in all things, so will we hearken unto thee: only the LORD thy God be with thee, as he was with Moses.

18 Whosoever *he be* that doth rebel against thy commandment, and will not hearken unto thy words in all that thou commandest him, he shall be put to death: only be strong and of a good courage.

Two Spies Are Sent from Shittim and Rahab Aids Them

2 And Joshua the son of Nun sent out of Shittim two men to spy secretly, saying, Go view the land, even Jericho. And they went, and came into an harlot's house, named Rahab, and lodged there.

2 And it was told the king of Jericho, saying, Behold, there came men in hither to night of the children of Israel to search out the country.

3 And the king of Jericho sent unto Rahab, saying, Bring forth the men that are come to thee, which are entered into thine house: for they be come to search out all the country.

4 And the woman took the two men, and hid them, and said thus, There came men unto me, but I wist not whence they *were*:

5 And it came to pass *about the time* of shutting of the gate, when it was dark, that the men went out: whither the men went I wot not: pursue after them quickly; for ye shall overtake them.

6 But she had brought them up to the roof of the house, and hid them with the stalks of flax, which she had laid in order upon the roof.

7 And the men pursued after them the way to Jordan unto the fords: and as soon as they which pursued after them were gone out, they shut the gate.

The Spies Make a Promise to Rahab

8 And before they were laid down, she came up unto them upon the roof;

9 And she said unto the men, I know that the LORD hath given you the land, and that your terror is fallen upon us, and that all the inhabitants of the land faint because of you.

10 For we have heard how the LORD dried up the water of the Red sea for you, when ye came out of Egypt; and what ye did unto the two kings of the Amorites, that *were* on the other side Jordan, Sihon and Og, whom ye utterly destroyed.

11 And as soon as we had heard *these things*, our hearts did melt, neither did there remain any more courage in any man, because of you: for the LORD your God, he *is* God in heaven above, and in earth beneath.

12 Now therefore, I pray you, swear unto me by the LORD, since I have shewed you kindness, that ye will also shew kindness unto my father's house, and give me a true token:

13 And *that* ye will save alive my father, and my mother, and my brethren, and my sisters, and all that they have, and deliver our lives from death.

14 And the men answered her, Our life for yours, if ye utter not this our business. And it shall be, when the LORD hath given us the land, that we will deal kindly and truly with thee.

15 Then she let them down by a cord through the window: for her house *was* upon the town wall, and she dwelt upon the wall.

16 And she said unto them, Get you to the mountain, lest the pursuers meet you; and hide yourselves there three days, until the pursuers be returned: and afterward may ye go your way.

17 And the men said unto her, We *will be* blameless of this thine oath which thou hast made us swear.

18 Behold, *when* we come into the land, thou shalt bind this line of scarlet thread in the window which thou didst let us down by: and thou shalt bring thy father, and thy mother, and thy brethren, and all thy father's household, home unto thee.

19 And it shall be, *that* whosoever shall go out of the doors of thy house into the street, his blood *shall be* upon his head, and we *will be* guiltless: and who-

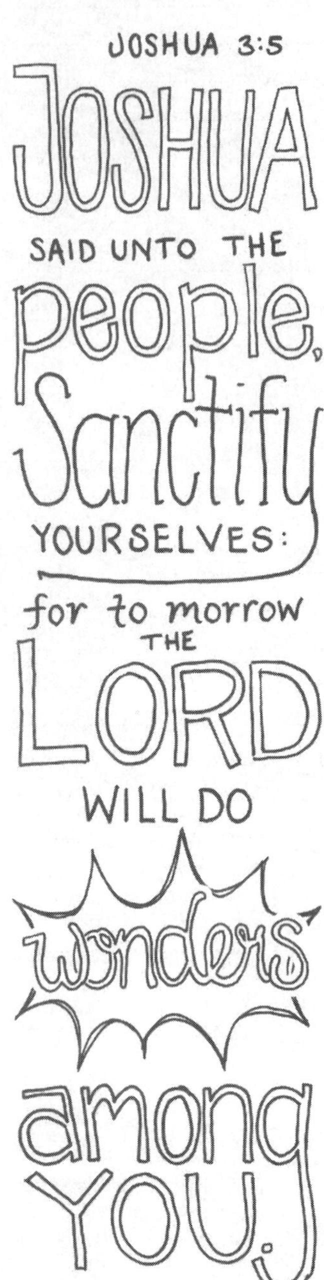

soever shall be with thee in the house, his blood *shall be* on our head, if *any*
hand be upon him.
20 And if thou utter this our business, then we will be quit of thine oath
which thou hast made us to swear.
21 And she said, According unto your words, so *be* it. And she sent them away,
and they departed: and she bound the scarlet line in the window.
22 And they went, and came unto the mountain, and abode there three days,
until the pursuers were returned: and the pursuers sought *them* throughout
all the way, but found *them* not.
23 So the two men returned, and descended from the mountain, and passed
over, and came to Joshua the son of Nun, and told him all *things* that befell
them:
24 And they said unto Joshua, Truly the LORD hath delivered into our hands
all the land; for even all the inhabitants of the country do faint because of us.

Crossing the Jordan River

3 And Joshua rose early in the morning; and they removed from Shittim, and
came to Jordan, he and all the children of Israel, and lodged there before
they passed over.
2 And it came to pass after three days, that the officers went through the
host;
3 And they commanded the people, saying, When ye see the ark of the cov-
enant of the LORD your God, and the priests the Levites bearing it, then ye shall
remove from your place, and go after it.
4 Yet there shall be a space between you and it, about two thousand cubits
by measure: come not near unto it, that ye may know the way by which ye
must go: for ye have not passed *this* way heretofore.
5 And Joshua said unto the people, Sanctify yourselves: for to morrow the
LORD will do wonders among you.
6 And Joshua spake unto the priests, saying, Take up the ark of the covenant,
and pass over before the people. And they took up the ark of the covenant, and
went before the people.

The Lord Encourages Joshua

7 And the LORD said unto Joshua, This day will I begin to magnify thee in the
sight of all Israel, that they may know that, as I was with Moses, *so* I will be
with thee.
8 And thou shalt command the priests that bear the ark of the covenant,
saying, When ye are come to the brink of the water of Jordan, ye shall stand
still in Jordan.
9 And Joshua said unto the children of Israel, Come hither, and hear the
words of the LORD your God.
10 And Joshua said, Hereby ye shall know that the living God *is* among you,
and *that* he will without fail drive out from before you the Canaanites, and
the Hittites, and the Hivites, and the Perizzites, and the Girgashites, and the
Amorites, and the Jebusites.
11 Behold, the ark of the covenant of the Lord of all the earth passeth over
before you into Jordan.
12 Now therefore take you twelve men out of the tribes of Israel, out of every
tribe a man.
13 And it shall come to pass, as soon as the soles of the feet of the priests that
bear the ark of the LORD, the Lord of all the earth, shall rest in the waters of
Jordan, *that* the waters of Jordan shall be cut off *from* the waters that come
down from above; and they shall stand upon an heap.

The Jordan River Is Divided

14 And it came to pass, when the people removed from their tents, to pass
over Jordan, and the priests bearing the ark of the covenant before the people;

15 And as they that bare the ark were come unto Jordan, and the feet of the
priests that bare the ark were dipped in the brim of the water, (for Jordan
overfloweth all his banks all the time of harvest,)
16 That the waters which came down from above stood *and* rose up upon
an heap very far from the city Adam, that *is* beside Zaretan: and those that
came down toward the sea of the plain, *even* the salt sea, failed, *and* were cut
off: and the people passed over right against Jericho.
17 And the priests that bare the ark of the covenant of the LORD stood firm
on dry ground in the midst of Jordan, and all the Israelites passed over on dry
ground, until all the people were passed clean over Jordan.

Twelve Stones Are Taken from the Jordan River for a Memorial

4 And it came to pass, when all the people were clean passed over Jordan, that
the LORD spake unto Joshua, saying,
2 Take you twelve men out of the people, out of every tribe a man,
3 And command ye them, saying, Take you hence out of the midst of Jordan,
out of the place where the priests' feet stood firm, twelve stones, and ye shall
carry them over with you, and leave them in the lodging place, where ye shall
lodge this night.
4 Then Joshua called the twelve men, whom he had prepared of the children
of Israel, out of every tribe a man:
5 And Joshua said unto them, Pass over before the ark of the LORD your God
into the midst of Jordan, and take ye up every man of you a stone upon his
shoulder, according unto the number of the tribes of the children of Israel:
6 That this may be a sign among you, *that* when your children ask *their
fathers* in time to come, saying, What *mean* ye by these stones?
7 Then ye shall answer them, That the waters of Jordan were cut off before
the ark of the covenant of the LORD; when it passed over Jordan, the waters of
Jordan were cut off: and these stones shall be for a memorial unto the children
of Israel for ever.
8 And the children of Israel did so as Joshua commanded, and took up twelve
stones out of the midst of Jordan, as the LORD spake unto Joshua, according
to the number of the tribes of the children of Israel, and carried them over
with them unto the place where they lodged, and laid them down there.
9 And Joshua set up twelve stones in the midst of Jordan, in the place where
the feet of the priests which bare the ark of the covenant stood: and they are
there unto this day.

The Jordan River's Water Returns

10 For the priests which bare the ark stood in the midst of Jordan, until every
thing was finished that the LORD commanded Joshua to speak unto the people,
according to all that Moses commanded Joshua: and the people hasted and
passed over.
11 And it came to pass, when all the people were clean passed over, that the
ark of the LORD passed over, and the priests, in the presence of the people.
12 And the children of Reuben, and the children of Gad, and half the tribe
of Manasseh, passed over armed before the children of Israel, as Moses spake
unto them:
13 About forty thousand prepared for war passed over before the LORD unto
battle, to the plains of Jericho.
14 On that day the LORD magnified Joshua in the sight of all Israel; and they
feared him, as they feared Moses, all the days of his life.
15 And the LORD spake unto Joshua, saying,
16 Command the priests that bear the ark of the testimony, that they come
up out of Jordan.
17 Joshua therefore commanded the priests, saying, Come ye up out of
Jordan.

18 And it came to pass, when the priests that bare the ark of the covenant of
the LORD were come up out of the midst of Jordan, *and* the soles of the priests'
feet were lifted up unto the dry land, that the waters of Jordan returned unto
their place, and flowed over all his banks, as *they did* before.
19 And the people came up out of Jordan on the tenth *day* of the first month,
and encamped in Gilgal, in the east border of Jericho.

The Twelve Stones Are Set up in Gilgal

20 And those twelve stones, which they took out of Jordan, did Joshua pitch
in Gilgal.
21 And he spake unto the children of Israel, saying, When your children shall
ask their fathers in time to come, saying, What *mean* these stones?
22 Then ye shall let your children know, saying, Israel came over this Jordan
on dry land.
23 For the LORD your God dried up the waters of Jordan from before you,
until ye were passed over, as the LORD your God did to the Red sea, which he
dried up from before us, until we were gone over:
24 That all the people of the earth might know the hand of the LORD, that it
is mighty: that ye might fear the LORD your God for ever.

Preparations for the Passover

5 And it came to pass, when all the kings of the Amorites, which *were* on the
side of Jordan westward, and all the kings of the Canaanites, which *were* by
the sea, heard that the LORD had dried up the waters of Jordan from before the
children of Israel, until we were passed over, that their heart melted, neither
was there spirit in them any more, because of the children of Israel.
2 At that time the LORD said unto Joshua, Make thee sharp knives, and cir-
cumcise again the children of Israel the second time.
3 And Joshua made him sharp knives, and circumcised the children of Israel
at the hill of the foreskins.
4 And this *is* the cause why Joshua did circumcise: All the people that came
out of Egypt, *that were* males, *even* all the men of war, died in the wilderness
by the way, after they came out of Egypt.
5 Now all the people that came out were circumcised: but all the people *that
were* born in the wilderness by the way as they came forth out of Egypt, *them*
they had not circumcised.
6 For the children of Israel walked forty years in the wilderness, till all the
people *that were* men of war, which came out of Egypt, were consumed,
because they obeyed not the voice of the LORD: unto whom the LORD sware
that he would not shew them the land, which the LORD sware unto their fathers
that he would give us, a land that floweth with milk and honey.
7 And their children, *whom* he raised up in their stead, them Joshua circum-
cised: for they were uncircumcised, because they had not circumcised them
by the way.
8 And it came to pass, when they had done circumcising all the people, that
they abode in their places in the camp, till they were whole.
9 And the LORD said unto Joshua, This day have I rolled away the reproach
of Egypt from off you. Wherefore the name of the place is called Gilgal unto
this day.

The Passover Is Kept at Gilgal

10 And the children of Israel encamped in Gilgal, and kept the passover on
the fourteenth day of the month at even in the plains of Jericho.
11 And they did eat of the old corn of the land on the morrow after the
passover, unleavened cakes, and parched *corn* in the selfsame day.
12 And the manna ceased on the morrow after they had eaten of the old corn
of the land; neither had the children of Israel manna any more; but they did
eat of the fruit of the land of Canaan that year.

13 And it came to pass, when Joshua was by Jericho, that he lifted up his eyes
and looked, and, behold, there stood a man over against him with his sword
drawn in his hand: and Joshua went unto him, and said unto him, *Art* thou
for us, or for our adversaries?
14 And he said, Nay; but *as* captain of the host of the LORD am I now come.
And Joshua fell on his face to the earth, and did worship, and said unto him,
What saith my lord unto his servant?
15 And the captain of the LORD's host said unto Joshua, Loose thy shoe from
off thy foot; for the place whereon thou standest *is* holy. And Joshua did so.

Jericho Is Destroyed

6 Now Jericho was straitly shut up because of the children of Israel: none
went out, and none came in.
2 And the LORD said unto Joshua, See, I have given into thine hand Jericho,
and the king thereof, *and* the mighty men of valour.
3 And ye shall compass the city, all *ye* men of war, *and* go round about the
city once. Thus shalt thou do six days.
4 And seven priests shall bear before the ark seven trumpets of rams' horns:
and the seventh day ye shall compass the city seven times, and the priests shall
blow with the trumpets.
5 And it shall come to pass, that when they make a long *blast* with the ram's
horn, *and* when ye hear the sound of the trumpet, all the people shall shout
with a great shout; and the wall of the city shall fall down flat, and the people
shall ascend up every man straight before him.
6 And Joshua the son of Nun called the priests, and said unto them, Take up
the ark of the covenant, and let seven priests bear seven trumpets of rams'
horns before the ark of the LORD.
7 And he said unto the people, Pass on, and compass the city, and let him that
is armed pass on before the ark of the LORD.
8 And it came to pass, when Joshua had spoken unto the people, that the
seven priests bearing the seven trumpets of rams' horns passed on before the
LORD, and blew with the trumpets: and the ark of the covenant of the LORD
followed them.
9 And the armed men went before the priests that blew with the trumpets,
and the rereward came after the ark, *the priests* going on, and blowing with
the trumpets.
10 And Joshua had commanded the people, saying, Ye shall not shout, nor
make any noise with your voice, neither shall *any* word proceed out of your
mouth, until the day I bid you shout; then shall ye shout.
11 So the ark of the LORD compassed the city, going about *it* once: and they
came into the camp, and lodged in the camp.
12 And Joshua rose early in the morning, and the priests took up the ark of
the LORD.
13 And seven priests bearing seven trumpets of rams' horns before the ark
of the LORD went on continually, and blew with the trumpets: and the armed
men went before them; but the rereward came after the ark of the LORD, *the
priests* going on, and blowing with the trumpets.
14 And the second day they compassed the city once, and returned into the
camp: so they did six days.
15 And it came to pass on the seventh day, that they rose early about the
dawning of the day, and compassed the city after the same manner seven times:
only on that day they compassed the city seven times.
16 And it came to pass at the seventh time, when the priests blew with the
trumpets, Joshua said unto the people, Shout; for the LORD hath given you the
city.

Jericho Must Be Destroyed, Except for Rahab

17 And the city shall be accursed, *even* it, and all that *are* therein, to the LORD: only Rahab the harlot shall live, she and all that *are* with her in the house, because she hid the messengers that we sent.

18 And ye, in any wise keep *yourselves* from the accursed thing, lest ye make *yourselves* accursed, when ye take of the accursed thing, and make the camp of Israel a curse, and trouble it.

19 But all the silver, and gold, and vessels of brass and iron, *are* consecrated unto the LORD: they shall come into the treasury of the LORD.

20 So the people shouted when *the priests* blew with the trumpets: and it came to pass, when the people heard the sound of the trumpet, and the people shouted with a great shout, that the wall fell down flat, so that the people went up into the city, every man straight before him, and they took the city.

21 And they utterly destroyed all that *was* in the city, both man and woman, young and old, and ox, and sheep, and ass, with the edge of the sword.

22 But Joshua had said unto the two men that had spied out the country, Go into the harlot's house, and bring out thence the woman, and all that she hath, as ye sware unto her.

23 And the young men that were spies went in, and brought out Rahab, and her father, and her mother, and her brethren, and all that she had; and they brought out all her kindred, and left them without the camp of Israel.

24 And they burnt the city with fire, and all that *was* therein: only the silver, and the gold, and the vessels of brass and of iron, they put into the treasury of the house of the LORD.

25 And Joshua saved Rahab the harlot alive, and her father's household, and all that she had; and she dwelleth in Israel *even* unto this day; because she hid the messengers, which Joshua sent to spy out Jericho.

26 And Joshua adjured *them* at that time, saying, Cursed *be* the man before the LORD, that riseth up and buildeth this city Jericho: he shall lay the foundation thereof in his firstborn, and in his youngest *son* shall he set up the gates of it.

27 So the LORD was with Joshua; and his fame was *noised* throughout all the country.

The Israelites Are Defeated at Ai

7 But the children of Israel committed a trespass in the accursed thing: for Achan, the son of Carmi, the son of Zabdi, the son of Zerah, of the tribe of Judah, took of the accursed thing: and the anger of the LORD was kindled against the children of Israel.

2 And Joshua sent men from Jericho to Ai, which *is* beside Beth-aven, on the east side of Beth-el, and spake unto them, saying, Go up and view the country. And the men went up and viewed Ai.

3 And they returned to Joshua, and said unto him, Let not all the people go up; but let about two or three thousand men go up and smite Ai; *and* make not all the people to labour thither; for they *are but* few.

4 So there went up thither of the people about three thousand men: and they fled before the men of Ai.

5 And the men of Ai smote of them about thirty and six men: for they chased them *from* before the gate *even* unto Shebarim, and smote them in the going down: wherefore the hearts of the people melted, and became as water.

Joshua's Complaint

6 And Joshua rent his clothes, and fell to the earth upon his face before the ark of the LORD until the eventide, he and the elders of Israel, and put dust upon their heads.

7 And Joshua said, Alas, O Lord GOD, wherefore hast thou at all brought this people over Jordan, to deliver us into the hand of the Amorites, to destroy us? would to God we had been content, and dwelt on the other side Jordan!

8 O Lord, what shall I say, when Israel turneth their backs before their enemies!

9 For the Canaanites and all the inhabitants of the land shall hear *of it*, and shall environ us round, and cut off our name from the earth: and what wilt thou do unto thy great name?

Joshua Must Deal with Sin in the Camp

10 And the LORD said unto Joshua, Get thee up; wherefore liest thou thus upon thy face?

11 Israel hath sinned, and they have also transgressed my covenant which I commanded them: for they have even taken of the accursed thing, and have also stolen, and dissembled also, and they have put *it* even among their own stuff.

12 Therefore the children of Israel could not stand before their enemies, *but* turned *their* backs before their enemies, because they were accursed: neither will I be with you any more, except ye destroy the accursed from among you.

13 Up, sanctify the people, and say, Sanctify yourselves against to morrow: for thus saith the LORD God of Israel, *There is* an accursed thing in the midst of thee, O Israel: thou canst not stand before thine enemies, until ye take away the accursed thing from among you.

14 In the morning therefore ye shall be brought according to your tribes: and it shall be, *that* the tribe which the LORD taketh shall come according to the families *thereof*; and the family which the LORD shall take shall come by households; and the household which the LORD shall take shall come man by man.

15 And it shall be, *that* he that is taken with the accursed thing shall be burnt with fire, he and all that he hath: because he hath transgressed the covenant of the LORD, and because he hath wrought folly in Israel.

Achan's Sin Destroys Him and His Family

16 So Joshua rose up early in the morning, and brought Israel by their tribes; and the tribe of Judah was taken:

17 And he brought the family of Judah; and he took the family of the Zarhites: and he brought the family of the Zarhites man by man; and Zabdi was taken:

18 And he brought his household man by man; and Achan, the son of Carmi, the son of Zabdi, the son of Zerah, of the tribe of Judah, was taken.

19 And Joshua said unto Achan, My son, give, I pray thee, glory to the LORD God of Israel, and make confession unto him; and tell me now what thou hast done; hide *it* not from me.

20 And Achan answered Joshua, and said, Indeed I have sinned against the LORD God of Israel, and thus and thus have I done:

21 When I saw among the spoils a goodly Babylonish garment, and two hundred shekels of silver, and a wedge of gold of fifty shekels weight, then I coveted them, and took them; and, behold, they *are* hid in the earth in the midst of my tent, and the silver under it.

22 So Joshua sent messengers, and they ran unto the tent; and, behold, *it was* hid in his tent, and the silver under it.

23 And they took them out of the midst of the tent, and brought them unto Joshua, and unto all the children of Israel, and laid them out before the LORD.

24 And Joshua, and all Israel with him, took Achan the son of Zerah, and the silver, and the garment, and the wedge of gold, and his sons, and his daughters, and his oxen, and his asses, and his sheep, and his tent, and all that he had: and they brought them unto the valley of Achor.

25 And Joshua said, Why hast thou troubled us? the LORD shall trouble thee
this day. And all Israel stoned him with stones, and burned them with fire,
after they had stoned them with stones.
26 And they raised over him a great heap of stones unto this day. So the LORD
turned from the fierceness of his anger. Wherefore the name of that place was
called, The valley of Achor, unto this day.

God Encourages Joshua

8 And the LORD said unto Joshua, Fear not, neither be thou dismayed: take all
the people of war with thee, and arise, go up to Ai: see, I have given into thy
hand the king of Ai, and his people, and his city, and his land:
2 And thou shalt do to Ai and her king as thou didst unto Jericho and her
king: only the spoil thereof, and the cattle thereof, shall ye take for a prey unto
yourselves: lay thee an ambush for the city behind it.

Israel's Victory at Ai

3 So Joshua arose, and all the people of war, to go up against Ai: and Joshua
chose out thirty thousand mighty men of valour, and sent them away by night.
4 And he commanded them, saying, Behold, ye shall lie in wait against the
city, *even* behind the city: go not very far from the city, but be ye all ready:
5 And I, and all the people that *are* with me, will approach unto the city: and
it shall come to pass, when they come out against us, as at the first, that we will
flee before them,
6 (For they will come out after us) till we have drawn them from the city; for
they will say, They flee before us, as at the first: therefore we will flee before
them.
7 Then ye shall rise up from the ambush, and seize upon the city: for the LORD
your God will deliver it into your hand.
8 And it shall be, when ye have taken the city, *that* ye shall set the city on fire:
according to the commandment of the LORD shall ye do. See, I have command-
ed you.
9 Joshua therefore sent them forth: and they went to lie in ambush, and
abode between Beth-el and Ai, on the west side of Ai: but Joshua lodged that
night among the people.
10 And Joshua rose up early in the morning, and numbered the people, and
went up, he and the elders of Israel, before the people to Ai.
11 And all the people, *even the people* of war that *were* with him, went up,
and drew nigh, and came before the city, and pitched on the north side of Ai:
now *there was* a valley between them and Ai.
12 And he took about five thousand men, and set them to lie in ambush
between Beth-el and Ai, on the west side of the city.
13 And when they had set the people, *even* all the host that *was* on the north
of the city, and their liers in wait on the west of the city, Joshua went that night
into the midst of the valley.
14 And it came to pass, when the king of Ai saw *it*, that they hasted and rose
up early, and the men of the city went out against Israel to battle, he and all
his people, at a time appointed, before the plain; but he wist not that *there*
were liers in ambush against him behind the city.
15 And Joshua and all Israel made as if they were beaten before them, and
fled by the way of the wilderness.
16 And all the people that *were* in Ai were called together to pursue after
them: and they pursued after Joshua, and were drawn away from the city.
17 And there was not a man left in Ai or Beth-el, that went not out after Israel:
and they left the city open, and pursued after Israel.
18 And the LORD said unto Joshua, Stretch out the spear that *is* in thy hand
toward Ai; for I will give it into thine hand. And Joshua stretched out the spear
that *he had* in his hand toward the city.

19 And the ambush arose quickly out of their place, and they ran as soon as
he had stretched out his hand: and they entered into the city, and took it, and
hasted and set the city on fire.
20 And when the men of Ai looked behind them, they saw, and, behold, the
smoke of the city ascended up to heaven, and they had no power to flee this
way or that way: and the people that fled to the wilderness turned back upon
the pursuers.
21 And when Joshua and all Israel saw that the ambush had taken the city,
and that the smoke of the city ascended, then they turned again, and slew the
men of Ai.
22 And the other issued out of the city against them; so they were in the midst
of Israel, some on this side, and some on that side: and they smote them, so
that they let none of them remain or escape.
23 And the king of Ai they took alive, and brought him to Joshua.
24 And it came to pass, when Israel had made an end of slaying all the inhab-
itants of Ai in the field, in the wilderness wherein they chased them, and when
they were all fallen on the edge of the sword, until they were consumed, that
all the Israelites returned unto Ai, and smote it with the edge of the sword.
25 And *so* it was, *that* all that fell that day, both of men and women, *were*
twelve thousand, *even* all the men of Ai.
26 For Joshua drew not his hand back, wherewith he stretched out the spear,
until he had utterly destroyed all the inhabitants of Ai.
27 Only the cattle and the spoil of that city Israel took for a prey unto them-
selves, according unto the word of the LORD which he commanded Joshua.
28 And Joshua burnt Ai, and made it an heap for ever, *even* a desolation unto
this day.
29 And the king of Ai he hanged on a tree until eventide: and as soon as the
sun was down, Joshua commanded that they should take his carcase down
from the tree, and cast it at the entering of the gate of the city, and raise there-
on a great heap of stones, *that remaineth* unto this day.

The Lord Renews His Promise

30 Then Joshua built an altar unto the LORD God of Israel in mount Ebal,
31 As Moses the servant of the LORD commanded the children of Israel, as it
is written in the book of the law of Moses, an altar of whole stones, over which
no man hath lift up *any* iron: and they offered thereon burnt offerings unto
the LORD, and sacrificed peace offerings.
32 And he wrote there upon the stones a copy of the law of Moses, which he
wrote in the presence of the children of Israel.
33 And all Israel, and their elders, and officers, and their judges, stood on
this side the ark and on that side before the priests the Levites, which bare the
ark of the covenant of the LORD, as well the stranger, as he that was born among
them; half of them over against mount Gerizim, and half of them over against
mount Ebal; as Moses the servant of the LORD had commanded before, that
they should bless the people of Israel.
34 And afterward he read all the words of the law, the blessings and cursings,
according to all that is written in the book of the law.
35 There was not a word of all that Moses commanded, which Joshua read
not before all the congregation of Israel, with the women, and the little ones,
and the strangers that were conversant among them.

The Kings Combine against Israel

9 And it came to pass, when all the kings which *were* on this side Jordan, in
the hills, and in the valleys, and in all the coasts of the great sea over against
Lebanon, the Hittite, and the Amorite, the Canaanite, the Perizzite, the Hivite,
and the Jebusite, heard *thereof*;

2 That they gathered themselves together, to fight with Joshua and with
Israel, with one accord.

The Gibeonites Obtain a Treaty through Deception

3 And when the inhabitants of Gibeon heard what Joshua had done unto
Jericho and to Ai,
4 They did work wilily, and went and made as if they had been ambassadors, and
took old sacks upon their asses, and wine bottles, old, and rent, and bound up;
5 And old shoes and clouted upon their feet, and old garments upon them;
and all the bread of their provision was dry *and* mouldy.
6 And they went to Joshua unto the camp at Gilgal, and said unto him, and
to the men of Israel, We be come from a far country: now therefore make ye
a league with us.
7 And the men of Israel said unto the Hivites, Peradventure ye dwell among
us; and how shall we make a league with you?
8 And they said unto Joshua, We *are* thy servants. And Joshua said unto them,
Who *are* ye? and from whence come ye?
9 And they said unto him, From a very far country thy servants are come
because of the name of the LORD thy God: for we have heard the fame of him,
and all that he did in Egypt,
10 And all that he did to the two kings of the Amorites, that *were* beyond
Jordan, to Sihon king of Heshbon, and to Og king of Bashan, which *was* at
Ashtaroth.
11 Wherefore our elders and all the inhabitants of our country spake to us,
saying, Take victuals with you for the journey, and go to meet them, and say
unto them, We *are* your servants: therefore now make ye a league with us.
12 This our bread we took hot *for* our provision out of our houses on the day
we came forth to go unto you; but now, behold, it is dry, and it is mouldy:
13 And these bottles of wine, which we filled, *were* new; and, behold, they be
rent: and these our garments and our shoes are become old by reason of the
very long journey.
14 And the men took of their victuals, and asked not *counsel* at the mouth of
the LORD.
15 And Joshua made peace with them, and made a league with them, to let
them live: and the princes of the congregation sware unto them.
16 And it came to pass at the end of three days after they had made a league
with them, that they heard that they *were* their neighbours, and *that* they
dwelt among them.
17 And the children of Israel journeyed, and came unto their cities on the
third day. Now their cities *were* Gibeon, and Chephirah, and Beeroth, and
Kirjath-jearim.
18 And the children of Israel smote them not, because the princes of the
congregation had sworn unto them by the LORD God of Israel. And all the
congregation murmured against the princes.
19 But all the princes said unto all the congregation, We have sworn unto
them by the LORD God of Israel: now therefore we may not touch them.
20 This we will do to them; we will even let them live, lest wrath be upon us,
because of the oath which we sware unto them.
21 And the princes said unto them, Let them live; but let them be hewers of
wood and drawers of water unto all the congregation; as the princes had prom-
ised them.

The Gibeonites Are Condemned to Perpetual Bondage

22 And Joshua called for them, and he spake unto them, saying, Wherefore
have ye beguiled us, saying, We *are* very far from you; when ye dwell among us?

23 Now therefore ye *are* cursed, and there shall none of you be freed from being bondmen, and hewers of wood and drawers of water for the house of my God.

24 And they answered Joshua, and said, Because it was certainly told thy servants, how that the Lord thy God commanded his servant Moses to give you all the land, and to destroy all the inhabitants of the land from before you, therefore we were sore afraid of our lives because of you, and have done this thing.

25 And now, behold, we *are* in thine hand: as it seemeth good and right unto thee to do unto us, do.

26 And so did he unto them, and delivered them out of the hand of the children of Israel, that they slew them not.

27 And Joshua made them that day hewers of wood and drawers of water for the congregation, and for the altar of the Lord, even unto this day, in the place which he should choose.

Five Kings War against Gibeon

10 Now it came to pass, when Adoni-zedek king of Jerusalem had heard how Joshua had taken Ai, and had utterly destroyed it; as he had done to Jericho and her king, so he had done to Ai and her king; and how the inhabitants of Gibeon had made peace with Israel, and were among them;

2 That they feared greatly, because Gibeon *was* a great city, as one of the royal cities, and because it *was* greater than Ai, and all the men thereof *were* mighty.

3 Wherefore Adoni-zedek king of Jerusalem sent unto Hoham king of Hebron, and unto Piram king of Jarmuth, and unto Japhia king of Lachish, and unto Debir king of Eglon, saying,

4 Come up unto me, and help me, that we may smite Gibeon: for it hath made peace with Joshua and with the children of Israel.

5 Therefore the five kings of the Amorites, the king of Jerusalem, the king of Hebron, the king of Jarmuth, the king of Lachish, the king of Eglon, gathered themselves together, and went up, they and all their hosts, and encamped before Gibeon, and made war against it.

6 And the men of Gibeon sent unto Joshua to the camp to Gilgal, saying, Slack not thy hand from thy servants; come up to us quickly, and save us, and help us: for all the kings of the Amorites that dwell in the mountains are gathered together against us.

7 So Joshua ascended from Gilgal, he, and all the people of war with him, and all the mighty men of valour.

8 And the Lord said unto Joshua, Fear them not: for I have delivered them into thine hand; there shall not a man of them stand before thee.

9 Joshua therefore came unto them suddenly, *and* went up from Gilgal all night.

10 And the Lord discomfited them before Israel, and slew them with a great slaughter at Gibeon, and chased them along the way that goeth up to Beth-horon, and smote them to Azekah, and unto Makkedah.

11 And it came to pass, as they fled from before Israel, *and* were in the going down to Beth-horon, that the Lord cast down great stones from heaven upon them unto Azekah, and they died: *they were* more which died with hailstones than *they* whom the children of Israel slew with the sword.

12 Then spake Joshua to the Lord in the day when the Lord delivered up the Amorites before the children of Israel, and he said in the sight of Israel, Sun, stand thou still upon Gibeon; and thou, Moon, in the valley of Ajalon.

13 And the sun stood still, and the moon stayed, until the people had avenged themselves upon their enemies. *Is* not this written in the book of Jasher? So the sun stood still in the midst of heaven, and hasted not to go down about a whole day.

14 And there was no day like that before it or after it, that the LORD hearkened
unto the voice of a man: for the LORD fought for Israel.

Joshua Defeats the Five Kings

15 And Joshua returned, and all Israel with him, unto the camp to Gilgal.
16 But these five kings fled, and hid themselves in a cave at Makkedah.
17 And it was told Joshua, saying, The five kings are found hid in a cave at
Makkedah.
18 And Joshua said, Roll great stones upon the mouth of the cave, and set
men by it for to keep them:
19 And stay ye not, *but* pursue after your enemies, and smite the hindmost
of them; suffer them not to enter into their cities: for the LORD your God hath
delivered them into your hand.
20 And it came to pass, when Joshua and the children of Israel had made an
end of slaying them with a very great slaughter, till they were consumed, that
the rest *which* remained of them entered into fenced cities.
21 And all the people returned to the camp to Joshua at Makkedah in peace:
none moved his tongue against any of the children of Israel.
22 Then said Joshua, Open the mouth of the cave, and bring out those five
kings unto me out of the cave.
23 And they did so, and brought forth those five kings unto him out of the
cave, the king of Jerusalem, the king of Hebron, the king of Jarmuth, the king
of Lachish, *and* the king of Eglon.
24 And it came to pass, when they brought out those kings unto Joshua, that
Joshua called for all the men of Israel, and said unto the captains of the men
of war which went with him, Come near, put your feet upon the necks of these
kings. And they came near, and put their feet upon the necks of them.
25 And Joshua said unto them, Fear not, nor be dismayed, be strong and of
good courage: for thus shall the LORD do to all your enemies against whom ye
fight.
26 And afterward Joshua smote them, and slew them, and hanged them on
five trees: and they were hanging upon the trees until the evening.
27 And it came to pass at the time of the going down of the sun, *that* Joshua
commanded, and they took them down off the trees, and cast them into the
cave wherein they had been hid, and laid great stones in the cave's mouth,
which remain until this very day.

Joshua Defeats the Southern Kings

28 And that day Joshua took Makkedah, and smote it with the edge of the
sword, and the king thereof he utterly destroyed, them, and all the souls that
were therein; he let none remain: and he did to the king of Makkedah as he
did unto the king of Jericho.
29 Then Joshua passed from Makkedah, and all Israel with him, unto Libnah,
and fought against Libnah:
30 And the LORD delivered it also, and the king thereof, into the hand of Israel;
and he smote it with the edge of the sword, and all the souls that *were* therein;
he let none remain in it; but did unto the king thereof as he did unto the king
of Jericho.
31 And Joshua passed from Libnah, and all Israel with him, unto Lachish,
and encamped against it, and fought against it:
32 And the LORD delivered Lachish into the hand of Israel, which took it on
the second day, and smote it with the edge of the sword, and all the souls that
were therein, according to all that he had done to Libnah.
33 Then Horam king of Gezer came up to help Lachish; and Joshua smote
him and his people, until he had left him none remaining.
34 And from Lachish Joshua passed unto Eglon, and all Israel with him; and
they encamped against it, and fought against it:

35 And they took it on that day, and smote it with the edge of the sword, and
all the souls that *were* therein he utterly destroyed that day, according to all
that he had done to Lachish.
36 And Joshua went up from Eglon, and all Israel with him, unto Hebron;
and they fought against it:
37 And they took it, and smote it with the edge of the sword, and the king
thereof, and all the cities thereof, and all the souls that *were* therein; he left
none remaining, according to all that he had done to Eglon; but destroyed it
utterly, and all the souls that *were* therein.
38 And Joshua returned, and all Israel with him, to Debir; and fought against it:
39 And he took it, and the king thereof, and all the cities thereof; and they
smote them with the edge of the sword, and utterly destroyed all the souls that
were therein; he left none remaining: as he had done to Hebron, so he did to
Debir, and to the king thereof; as he had done also to Libnah, and to her king.
40 So Joshua smote all the country of the hills, and of the south, and of the
vale, and of the springs, and all their kings: he left none remaining, but utter-
ly destroyed all that breathed, as the LORD God of Israel commanded.
41 And Joshua smote them from Kadesh-barnea even unto Gaza, and all the
country of Goshen, even unto Gibeon.
42 And all these kings and their land did Joshua take at one time, because the
LORD God of Israel fought for Israel.
43 And Joshua returned, and all Israel with him, unto the camp to Gilgal.

Joshua Defeats the Northern Kings at the Waters of Merom

11 And it came to pass, when Jabin king of Hazor had heard *those things*,
that he sent to Jobab king of Madon, and to the king of Shimron, and
to the king of Achshaph,
2 And to the kings that *were* on the north of the mountains, and of the plains
south of Chinneroth, and in the valley, and in the borders of Dor on the west,
3 *And to* the Canaanite on the east and on the west, and *to* the Amorite, and
the Hittite, and the Perizzite, and the Jebusite in the mountains, and *to* the
Hivite under Hermon in the land of Mizpeh.
4 And they went out, they and all their hosts with them, much people, even
as the sand that *is* upon the sea shore in multitude, with horses and chariots
very many.
5 And when all these kings were met together, they came and pitched togeth-
er at the waters of Merom, to fight against Israel.
6 And the LORD said unto Joshua, Be not afraid because of them: for to mor-
row about this time will I deliver them up all slain before Israel: thou shalt
hough their horses, and burn their chariots with fire.
7 So Joshua came, and all the people of war with him, against them by the
waters of Merom suddenly; and they fell upon them.
8 And the LORD delivered them into the hand of Israel, who smote them, and
chased them unto great Zidon, and unto Misrephoth-maim, and unto the
valley of Mizpeh eastward; and they smote them, until they left them none
remaining.
9 And Joshua did unto them as the LORD bade him: he houghed their horses,
and burnt their chariots with fire.

Joshua Captures the Whole Land

10 And Joshua at that time turned back, and took Hazor, and smote the king
thereof with the sword: for Hazor beforetime was the head of all those king-
doms.
11 And they smote all the souls that *were* therein with the edge of the sword,
utterly destroying *them*: there was not any left to breathe: and he burnt Hazor
with fire.

12 And all the cities of those kings, and all the kings of them, did Joshua take,
and smote them with the edge of the sword, *and* he utterly destroyed them,
as Moses the servant of the LORD commanded.
13 But *as for* the cities that stood still in their strength, Israel burned none
of them, save Hazor only; *that* did Joshua burn.
14 And all the spoil of these cities, and the cattle, the children of Israel took
for a prey unto themselves; but every man they smote with the edge of the
sword, until they had destroyed them, neither left they any to breathe.
15 As the LORD commanded Moses his servant, so did Moses command
Joshua, and so did Joshua; he left nothing undone of all that the LORD com-
manded Moses.
16 So Joshua took all that land, the hills, and all the south country, and all
the land of Goshen, and the valley, and the plain, and the mountain of Israel,
and the valley of the same;
17 *Even* from the mount Halak, that goeth up to Seir, even unto Baal-gad in
the valley of Lebanon under mount Hermon: and all their kings he took, and
smote them, and slew them.
18 Joshua made war a long time with all those kings.
19 There was not a city that made peace with the children of Israel, save the
Hivites the inhabitants of Gibeon: all *other* they took in battle.
20 For it was of the LORD to harden their hearts, that they should come against
Israel in battle, that he might destroy them utterly, *and* that they might have
no favour, but that he might destroy them, as the LORD commanded Moses.
21 And at that time came Joshua, and cut off the Anakims from the moun-
tains, from Hebron, from Debir, from Anab, and from all the mountains of
Judah, and from all the mountains of Israel: Joshua destroyed them utterly
with their cities.
22 There was none of the Anakims left in the land of the children of Israel:
only in Gaza, in Gath, and in Ashdod, there remained.
23 So Joshua took the whole land, according to all that the LORD said unto
Moses; and Joshua gave it for an inheritance unto Israel according to their
divisions by their tribes. And the land rested from war.

The Kings on the East and West of the Jordan River

12 Now these *are* the kings of the land, which the children of Israel smote,
and possessed their land on the other side Jordan toward the rising of
the sun, from the river Arnon unto mount Hermon, and all the plain on the
east:
2 Sihon king of the Amorites, who dwelt in Heshbon, *and* ruled from Aroer,
which *is* upon the bank of the river Arnon, and from the middle of the river,
and from half Gilead, even unto the river Jabbok, *which is* the border of the
children of Ammon;
3 And from the plain to the sea of Chinneroth on the east, and unto the sea
of the plain, *even* the salt sea on the east, the way to Beth-jeshimoth; and from
the south, under Ashdoth-pisgah:
4 And the coast of Og king of Bashan, *which was* of the remnant of the giants,
that dwelt at Ashtaroth and at Edrei,
5 And reigned in mount Hermon, and in Salcah, and in all Bashan, unto the
border of the Geshurites and the Maachathites, and half Gilead, the border
of Sihon king of Heshbon.
6 Them did Moses the servant of the LORD and the children of Israel smite:
and Moses the servant of the LORD gave it *for* a possession unto the Reubenites,
and the Gadites, and the half tribe of Manasseh.
7 And these *are* the kings of the country which Joshua and the children of
Israel smote on this side Jordan on the west, from Baal-gad in the valley of

Lebanon even unto the mount Halak, that goeth up to Seir; which Joshua gave
unto the tribes of Israel *for* a possession according to their divisions;
8 In the mountains, and in the valleys, and in the plains, and in the springs,
and in the wilderness, and in the south country; the Hittites, the Amorites,
and the Canaanites, the Perizzites, the Hivites, and the Jebusites:
9 The king of Jericho, one; the king of Ai, which *is* beside Beth-el, one;
10 The king of Jerusalem, one; the king of Hebron, one;
11 The king of Jarmuth, one; the king of Lachish, one;
12 The king of Eglon, one; the king of Gezer, one;
13 The king of Debir, one; the king of Geder, one;
14 The king of Hormah, one; the king of Arad, one;
15 The king of Libnah, one; the king of Adullam, one;
16 The king of Makkedah, one; the king of Beth-el, one;
17 The king of Tappuah, one; the king of Hepher, one;
18 The king of Aphek, one; the king of Lasharon, one;
19 The king of Madon, one; the king of Hazor, one;
20 The king of Shimron-meron, one; the king of Achshaph, one;
21 The king of Taanach, one; the king of Megiddo, one;
22 The king of Kedesh, one; the king of Jokneam of Carmel, one;
23 The king of Dor in the coast of Dor, one; the king of the nations of Gilgal,
one;
24 The king of Tirzah, one: all the kings thirty and one.

The Land Yet to Be Conquered and the Tribes East of the Jordan

13 Now Joshua was old *and* stricken in years; and the LORD said unto him,
Thou art old *and* stricken in years, and there remaineth yet very much
land to be possessed.
2 This *is* the land that yet remaineth: all the borders of the Philistines, and
all Geshuri,
3 From Sihor, which *is* before Egypt, even unto the borders of Ekron north-
ward, *which* is counted to the Canaanite: five lords of the Philistines; the
Gazathites, and the Ashdothites, the Eshkalonites, the Gittites, and the
Ekronites; also the Avites:
4 From the south, all the land of the Canaanites, and Mearah that *is* beside
the Sidonians, unto Aphek, to the borders of the Amorites:
5 And the land of the Giblites, and all Lebanon, toward the sunrising, from
Baal-gad under mount Hermon unto the entering into Hamath.
6 All the inhabitants of the hill country from Lebanon unto Misrephoth-
maim, *and* all the Sidonians, them will I drive out from before the children
of Israel: only divide thou it by lot unto the Israelites for an inheritance, as I
have commanded thee.
7 Now therefore divide this land for an inheritance unto the nine tribes, and
the half tribe of Manasseh,
8 With whom the Reubenites and the Gadites have received their inheritance,
which Moses gave them, beyond Jordan eastward, *even* as Moses the servant
of the LORD gave them;
9 From Aroer, that *is* upon the bank of the river Arnon, and the city that *is*
in the midst of the river, and all the plain of Medeba unto Dibon;
10 And all the cities of Sihon king of the Amorites, which reigned in Heshbon,
unto the border of the children of Ammon;
11 And Gilead, and the border of the Geshurites and Maachathites, and all
mount Hermon, and all Bashan unto Salcah;
12 All the kingdom of Og in Bashan, which reigned in Ashtaroth and in Edrei,
who remained of the remnant of the giants: for these did Moses smite, and
cast them out.

13 Nevertheless the children of Israel expelled not the Geshurites, nor the Maachathites: but the Geshurites and the Maachathites dwell among the Israelites until this day.
14 Only unto the tribe of Levi he gave none inheritance; the sacrifices of the LORD God of Israel made by fire *are* their inheritance, as he said unto them.
15 And Moses gave unto the tribe of the children of Reuben *inheritance* according to their families.
16 And their coast was from Aroer, that *is* on the bank of the river Arnon, and the city that *is* in the midst of the river, and all the plain by Medeba;
17 Heshbon, and all her cities that *are* in the plain; Dibon, and Bamoth-baal, and Beth-baal-meon,
18 And Jahazah, and Kedemoth, and Mephaath,
19 And Kirjathaim, and Sibmah, and Zarethshahar in the mount of the valley,
20 And Beth-peor, and Ashdoth-pisgah, and Beth-jeshimoth,
21 And all the cities of the plain, and all the kingdom of Sihon king of the Amorites, which reigned in Heshbon, whom Moses smote with the princes of Midian, Evi, and Rekem, and Zur, and Hur, and Reba, *which were* dukes of Sihon, dwelling in the country.
22 Balaam also the son of Beor, the soothsayer, did the children of Israel slay with the sword among them that were slain by them.
23 And the border of the children of Reuben was Jordan, and the border *thereof.* This *was* the inheritance of the children of Reuben after their families, the cities and the villages thereof.
24 And Moses gave *inheritance* unto the tribe of Gad, *even* unto the children of Gad according to their families.
25 And their coast was Jazer, and all the cities of Gilead, and half the land of the children of Ammon, unto Aroer that *is* before Rabbah;
26 And from Heshbon unto Ramath-mizpeh, and Betonim; and from Mahanaim unto the border of Debir;
27 And in the valley, Beth-aram, and Bethnimrah, and Succoth, and Zaphon, the rest of the kingdom of Sihon king of Heshbon, Jordan and *his* border, *even* unto the edge of the sea of Chinnereth on the other side Jordan eastward.
28 This *is* the inheritance of the children of Gad after their families, the cities, and their villages.
29 And Moses gave *inheritance* unto the half tribe of Manasseh: and *this* was *the possession* of the half tribe of the children of Manasseh by their families.
30 And their coast was from Mahanaim, all Bashan, all the kingdom of Og king of Bashan, and all the towns of Jair, which *are* in Bashan, threescore cities:
31 And half Gilead, and Ashtaroth, and Edrei, cities of the kingdom of Og in Bashan, *were pertaining* unto the children of Machir the son of Manasseh, *even* to the one half of the children of Machir by their families.
32 These *are the countries* which Moses did distribute for inheritance in the plains of Moab, on the other side Jordan, by Jericho, eastward.
33 But unto the tribe of Levi Moses gave not *any* inheritance: the LORD God of Israel *was* their inheritance, as he said unto them.

The Tribes West of the Jordan Receive Their Land by Lot

14 And these *are the countries* which the children of Israel inherited in the land of Canaan, which Eleazar the priest, and Joshua the son of Nun, and the heads of the fathers of the tribes of the children of Israel, distributed for inheritance to them.
2 By lot *was* their inheritance, as the LORD commanded by the hand of Moses, for the nine tribes, and *for* the half tribe.
3 For Moses had given the inheritance of two tribes and an half tribe on the other side Jordan: but unto the Levites he gave none inheritance among them.

4 For the children of Joseph were two tribes, Manasseh and Ephraim: there-
fore they gave no part unto the Levites in the land, save cities to dwell *in*, with
their suburbs for their cattle and for their substance.
5 As the LORD commanded Moses, so the children of Israel did, and they
divided the land.

Caleb Obtains Hebron

6 Then the children of Judah came unto Joshua in Gilgal: and Caleb the son
of Jephunneh the Kenezite said unto him, Thou knowest the thing that the
LORD said unto Moses the man of God concerning me and thee in Kadesh-
barnea.
7 Forty years old *was* I when Moses the servant of the LORD sent me from
Kadesh-barnea to espy out the land; and I brought him word again as *it was*
in mine heart.
8 Nevertheless my brethren that went up with me made the heart of the
people melt: but I wholly followed the LORD my God.
9 And Moses sware on that day, saying, Surely the land whereon thy feet have
trodden shall be thine inheritance, and thy children's for ever, because thou
hast wholly followed the LORD my God.
10 And now, behold, the LORD hath kept me alive, as he said, these forty and
five years, even since the LORD spake this word unto Moses, while *the children
of* Israel wandered in the wilderness: and now, lo, I *am* this day fourscore and
five years old.
11 As yet I *am as* strong this day as *I was* in the day that Moses sent me: as my
strength *was* then, even so *is* my strength now, for war, both to go out, and to
come in.
12 Now therefore give me this mountain, whereof the LORD spake in that
day; for thou heardest in that day how the Anakims *were* there, and *that* the
cities *were* great *and* fenced: if so be the LORD *will be* with me, then I shall be
able to drive them out, as the LORD said.
13 And Joshua blessed him, and gave unto Caleb the son of Jephunneh
Hebron for an inheritance.
14 Hebron therefore became the inheritance of Caleb the son of Jephunneh
the Kenezite unto this day, because that he wholly followed the LORD God of
Israel.
15 And the name of Hebron before *was* Kirjath-arba; *which Arba was* a great
man among the Anakims. And the land had rest from war.

Land for the Tribe of Judah

15 *This* then was the lot of the tribe of the children of Judah by their
families; *even* to the border of Edom the wilderness of Zin southward
was the uttermost part of the south coast.
2 And their south border was from the shore of the salt sea, from the bay
that looketh southward:
3 And it went out to the south side to Maaleh-acrabbim, and passed along to
Zin, and ascended up on the south side unto Kadesh-barnea, and passed along
to Hezron, and went up to Adar, and fetched a compass to Karkaa:
4 *From thence* it passed toward Azmon, and went out unto the river of Egypt;
and the goings out of that coast were at the sea: this shall be your south coast.
5 And the east border *was* the salt sea, *even* unto the end of Jordan. And *their*
border in the north quarter *was* from the bay of the sea at the uttermost part
of Jordan:
6 And the border went up to Beth-hogla, and passed along by the north of
Beth-arabah; and the border went up to the stone of Bohan the son of Reuben:
7 And the border went up toward Debir from the valley of Achor, and so
northward, looking toward Gilgal, that *is* before the going up to Adummim,

which *is* on the south side of the river: and the border passed toward the waters of Enshemesh, and the goings out thereof were at Enrogel:
8 And the border went up by the valley of the son of Hinnom unto the south side of the Jebusite; the same *is* Jerusalem: and the border went up to the top of the mountain that *lieth* before the valley of Hinnom westward, which *is* at the end of the valley of the giants northward:
9 And the border was drawn from the top of the hill unto the fountain of the water of Nephtoah, and went out to the cities of mount Ephron; and the border was drawn to Baalah, which *is* Kirjath-jearim:
10 And the border compassed from Baalah westward unto mount Seir, and passed along unto the side of mount Jearim, which *is* Chesalon, on the north side, and went down to Beth-shemesh, and passed on to Timnah:
11 And the border went out unto the side of Ekron northward: and the border was drawn to Shicron, and passed along to mount Baalah, and went out unto Jabneel; and the goings out of the border were at the sea.
12 And the west border *was* to the great sea, and the coast *thereof*. This *is* the coast of the children of Judah round about according to their families.
13 And unto Caleb the son of Jephunneh he gave a part among the children of Judah, according to the commandment of the LORD to Joshua, *even* the city of Arba the father of Anak, which *city is* Hebron.
14 And Caleb drove thence the three sons of Anak, Sheshai, and Ahiman, and Talmai, the children of Anak.
15 And he went up thence to the inhabitants of Debir: and the name of Debir before *was* Kirjath-sepher.
16 And Caleb said, He that smiteth Kirjath-sepher, and taketh it, to him will I give Achsah my daughter to wife.
17 And Othniel the son of Kenaz, the brother of Caleb, took it: and he gave him Achsah his daughter to wife.
18 And it came to pass, as she came *unto him*, that she moved him to ask of her father a field: and she lighted off *her* ass; and Caleb said unto her, What wouldest thou?
19 Who answered, Give me a blessing; for thou hast given me a south land; give me also springs of water. And he gave her the upper springs, and the nether springs.

The Cities of Judah

20 This *is* the inheritance of the tribe of the children of Judah according to their families.
21 And the uttermost cities of the tribe of the children of Judah toward the coast of Edom southward were Kabzeel, and Eder, and Jagur,
22 And Kinah, and Dimonah, and Adadah,
23 And Kedesh, and Hazor, and Ithnan,
24 Ziph, and Telem, and Bealoth,
25 And Hazor, Hadattah, and Kerioth, *and* Hezron, which *is* Hazor,
26 Amam, and Shema, and Moladah,
27 And Hazar-gaddah, and Heshmon, and Beth-palet,
28 And Hazar-shual, and Beer-sheba, and Bizjothjah,
29 Baalah, and Iim, and Azem,
30 And Eltolad, and Chesil, and Hormah,
31 And Ziklag, and Madmannah, and Sansannah,
32 And Lebaoth, and Shilhim, and Ain, and Rimmon: all the cities *are* twenty and nine, with their villages:
33 *And* in the valley, Eshtaol, and Zoreah, and Ashnah,
34 And Zanoah, and En-gannim, Tappuah, and Enam,
35 Jarmuth, and Adullam, Socoh, and Azekah,

36 And Sharaim, and Adithaim, and Gederah, and Gederothaim; fourteen
cities with their villages:
37 Zenan, and Hadashah, and Migdal-gad,
38 And Dilean, and Mizpeh, and Joktheel,
39 Lachish, and Bozkath, and Eglon,
40 And Cabbon, and Lahmam, and Kithlish,
41 And Gederoth, Beth-dagon, and Naamah, and Makkedah; sixteen cities
with their villages:
42 Libnah, and Ether, and Ashan,
43 And Jiphtah, and Ashnah, and Nezib,
44 And Keilah, and Achzib, and Mareshah; nine cities with their villages:
45 Ekron, with her towns and her villages:
46 From Ekron even unto the sea, all that *lay* near Ashdod, with their villages:
47 Ashdod with her towns and her villages, Gaza with her towns and her
villages, unto the river of Egypt, and the great sea, and the border *thereof*:
48 And in the mountains, Shamir, and Jattir, and Socoh,
49 And Dannah, and Kirjath-sannah, which *is* Debir,
50 And Anab, and Eshtemoh, and Anim,
51 And Goshen, and Holon, and Giloh; eleven cities with their villages:
52 Arab, and Dumah, and Eshean,
53 And Janum, and Beth-tappuah, and Aphekah,
54 And Humtah, and Kirjath-arba, which *is* Hebron, and Zior; nine cities
with their villages:
55 Maon, Carmel, and Ziph, and Juttah,
56 And Jezreel, and Jokdeam, and Zanoah,
57 Cain, Gibeah, and Timnah; ten cities with their villages:
58 Halhul, Beth-zur, and Gedor,
59 And Maarath, and Beth-anoth, and Eltekon; six cities with their villages:
60 Kirjath-baal, which *is* Kirjath-jearim, and Rabbah; two cities with their
villages:
61 In the wilderness, Beth-arabah, Middin, and Secacah,
62 And Nibshan, and the city of Salt, and Engedi; six cities with their villages.
63 As for the Jebusites the inhabitants of Jerusalem, the children of Judah
could not drive them out: but the Jebusites dwell with the children of Judah
at Jerusalem unto this day.

The Borders of the Land for the Sons of Joseph

16 And the lot of the children of Joseph fell from Jordan by Jericho, unto
the water of Jericho on the east, to the wilderness that goeth up from
Jericho throughout mount Beth-el,
2 And goeth out from Beth-el to Luz, and passeth along unto the borders of
Archi to Ataroth,
3 And goeth down westward to the coast of Japhleti, unto the coast of Beth-
horon the nether, and to Gezer: and the goings out thereof are at the sea.
4 So the children of Joseph, Manasseh and Ephraim, took their inheritance.

The Border of the Land for the Tribe of Ephraim

5 And the border of the children of Ephraim according to their families was
thus: even the border of their inheritance on the east side was Ataroth-addar,
unto Beth-horon the upper;
6 And the border went out toward the sea to Michmethah on the north side;
and the border went about eastward unto Taanathshiloh, and passed by it on
the east to Janohah;
7 And it went down from Janohah to Ataroth, and to Naarath, and came to
Jericho, and went out at Jordan.

8 The border went out from Tappuah westward unto the river Kanah; and the goings out thereof were at the sea. This *is* the inheritance of the tribe of the children of Ephraim by their families.

9 And the separate cities for the children of Ephraim *were* among the inheritance of the children of Manasseh, all the cities with their villages.

10 And they drave not out the Canaanites that dwelt in Gezer: but the Canaanites dwell among the Ephraimites unto this day, and serve under tribute.

Land for the Tribe of Manasseh

17 There was also a lot for the tribe of Manasseh; for he *was* the firstborn of Joseph; *to wit*, for Machir the firstborn of Manasseh, the father of Gilead: because he was a man of war, therefore he had Gilead and Bashan.

2 There was also *a lot* for the rest of the children of Manasseh by their families; for the children of Abiezer, and for the children of Helek, and for the children of Asriel, and for the children of Shechem, and for the children of Hepher, and for the children of Shemida: these *were* the male children of Manasseh the son of Joseph by their families.

3 But Zelophehad, the son of Hepher, the son of Gilead, the son of Machir, the son of Manasseh, had no sons, but daughters: and these *are* the names of his daughters, Mahlah, and Noah, Hoglah, Milcah, and Tirzah.

4 And they came near before Eleazar the priest, and before Joshua the son of Nun, and before the princes, saying, The LORD commanded Moses to give us an inheritance among our brethren. Therefore according to the commandment of the LORD he gave them an inheritance among the brethren of their father.

5 And there fell ten portions to Manasseh, beside the land of Gilead and Bashan, which *were* on the other side Jordan;

6 Because the daughters of Manasseh had an inheritance among his sons: and the rest of Manasseh's sons had the land of Gilead.

Manasseh's Boundaries

7 And the coast of Manasseh was from Asher to Michmethah, that *lieth* before Shechem; and the border went along on the right hand unto the inhabitants of En-tappuah.

8 *Now* Manasseh had the land of Tappuah: but Tappuah on the border of Manasseh *belonged* to the children of Ephraim;

9 And the coast descended unto the river Kanah, southward of the river: these cities of Ephraim *are* among the cities of Manasseh: the coast of Manasseh also *was* on the north side of the river, and the outgoings of it were at the sea:

10 Southward *it was* Ephraim's, and northward *it was* Manasseh's, and the sea is his border; and they met together in Asher on the north, and in Issachar on the east.

11 And Manasseh had in Issachar and in Asher Beth-shean and her towns, and Ibleam and her towns, and the inhabitants of Dor and her towns, and the inhabitants of En-dor and her towns, and the inhabitants of Taanach and her towns, and the inhabitants of Megiddo and her towns, *even* three countries.

12 Yet the children of Manasseh could not drive out *the inhabitants of* those cities; but the Canaanites would dwell in that land.

13 Yet it came to pass, when the children of Israel were waxen strong, that they put the Canaanites to tribute; but did not utterly drive them out.

The Children of Joseph Obtain Another Portion

14 And the children of Joseph spake unto Joshua, saying, Why hast thou given me *but* one lot and one portion to inherit, seeing I *am* a great people, forasmuch as the LORD hath blessed me hitherto?

15 And Joshua answered them, If thou *be* a great people, *then* get thee up to
the wood *country*, and cut down for thyself there in the land of the Perizzites
and of the giants, if mount Ephraim be too narrow for thee.
16 And the children of Joseph said, The hill is not enough for us: and all the
Canaanites that dwell in the land of the valley have chariots of iron, *both they*
who *are* of Beth-shean and her towns, and *they* who *are* of the valley of Jezreel.
17 And Joshua spake unto the house of Joseph, *even* to Ephraim and to
Manasseh, saying, Thou *art* a great people, and hast great power: thou shalt
not have one lot *only*:
18 But the mountain shall be thine; for it *is* a wood, and thou shalt cut it
down: and the outgoings of it shall be thine: for thou shalt drive out the
Canaanites, though they have iron chariots, *and* though they *be* strong.

The Tabernacle Is Set up at Shiloh

18 And the whole congregation of the children of Israel assembled togeth-
er at Shiloh, and set up the tabernacle of the congregation there. And
the land was subdued before them.

The Remainder of the Land Is Described and Divided

2 And there remained among the children of Israel seven tribes, which had
not yet received their inheritance.
3 And Joshua said unto the children of Israel, How long *are* ye slack to go to
possess the land, which the LORD God of your fathers hath given you?
4 Give out from among you three men for *each* tribe: and I will send them,
and they shall rise, and go through the land, and describe it according to the
inheritance of them; and they shall come *again* to me.
5 And they shall divide it into seven parts: Judah shall abide in their coast on
the south, and the house of Joseph shall abide in their coasts on the north.
6 Ye shall therefore describe the land *into* seven parts, and bring *the descrip-
tion* hither to me, that I may cast lots for you here before the LORD our God.
7 But the Levites have no part among you; for the priesthood of the LORD *is*
their inheritance: and Gad, and Reuben, and half the tribe of Manasseh, have
received their inheritance beyond Jordan on the east, which Moses the servant
of the LORD gave them.
8 And the men arose, and went away: and Joshua charged them that went to
describe the land, saying, Go and walk through the land, and describe it, and
come again to me, that I may here cast lots for you before the LORD in Shiloh.
9 And the men went and passed through the land, and described it by cities
into seven parts in a book, and came *again* to Joshua to the host at Shiloh.
10 And Joshua cast lots for them in Shiloh before the LORD: and there Joshua
divided the land unto the children of Israel according to their divisions.

Land for the Tribe of Benjamin

11 And the lot of the tribe of the children of Benjamin came up according
to their families: and the coast of their lot came forth between the children
of Judah and the children of Joseph.
12 And their border on the north side was from Jordan; and the border went
up to the side of Jericho on the north side, and went up through the mountains
westward; and the goings out thereof were at the wilderness of Beth-aven.
13 And the border went over from thence toward Luz, to the side of Luz,
which *is* Beth-el, southward; and the border descended to Ataroth-adar, near
the hill that *lieth* on the south side of the nether Beth-horon.
14 And the border was drawn *thence*, and compassed the corner of the sea
southward, from the hill that *lieth* before Beth-horon southward; and the
goings out thereof were at Kirjath-baal, which *is* Kirjath-jearim, a city of the
children of Judah: this *was* the west quarter.
15 And the south quarter *was* from the end of Kirjath-jearim, and the border
went out on the west, and went out to the well of waters of Nephtoah:

16 And the border came down to the end of the mountain that *lieth* before
the valley of the son of Hinnom, *and* which *is* in the valley of the giants on the
north, and descended to the valley of Hinnom, to the side of Jebusi on the
south, and descended to En-rogel,
17 And was drawn from the north, and went forth to En-shemesh, and went
forth toward Geliloth, which *is* over against the going up of Adummim, and
descended to the stone of Bohan the son of Reuben,
18 And passed along toward the side over against Arabah northward, and
went down unto Arabah:
19 And the border passed along to the side of Beth-hoglah northward: and
the outgoings of the border were at the north bay of the salt sea at the south
end of Jordan: this *was* the south coast.
20 And Jordan was the border of it on the east side. This *was* the inheritance
of the children of Benjamin, by the coasts thereof round about, according to
their families.
21 Now the cities of the tribe of the children of Benjamin according to their
families were Jericho, and Beth-hoglah, and the valley of Keziz,
22 And Beth-arabah, and Zemaraim, and Beth-el,
23 And Avim, and Parah, and Ophrah,
24 And Chephar-haammonai, and Ophni, and Gaba; twelve cities with their
villages:
25 Gibeon, and Ramah, and Beeroth,
26 And Mizpeh, and Chephirah, and Mozah,
27 And Rekem, and Irpeel, and Taralah,
28 And Zelah, Eleph, and Jebusi, which *is* Jerusalem, Gibeath, *and* Kirjath;
fourteen cities with their villages. This *is* the inheritance of the children of
Benjamin according to their families.

Land for the Tribe of Simeon

19 And the second lot came forth to Simeon, *even* for the tribe of the
children of Simeon according to their families: and their inheritance
was within the inheritance of the children of Judah.
2 And they had in their inheritance Beersheba, or Sheba, and Moladah,
3 And Hazar-shual, and Balah, and Azem,
4 And Eltolad, and Bethul, and Hormah,
5 And Ziklag, and Beth-marcaboth, and Hazar-susah,
6 And Beth-lebaoth, and Sharuhen; thirteen cities and their villages:
7 Ain, Remmon, and Ether, and Ashan; four cities and their villages:
8 And all the villages that *were* round about these cities to Baalath-beer,
Ramath of the south. This *is* the inheritance of the tribe of the children of
Simeon according to their families.
9 Out of the portion of the children of Judah *was* the inheritance of the
children of Simeon: for the part of the children of Judah was too much for
them: therefore the children of Simeon had their inheritance within the inher-
itance of them.

Land for the Tribe of Zebulun

10 And the third lot came up for the children of Zebulun according to their
families: and the border of their inheritance was unto Sarid:
11 And their border went up toward the sea, and Maralah, and reached to
Dabbasheth, and reached to the river that *is* before Jokneam;
12 And turned from Sarid eastward toward the sunrising unto the border of
Chislothtabor, and then goeth out to Daberath, and goeth up to Japhia,
13 And from thence passeth on along on the east to Gittah-hepher, to Ittah-
kazin, and goeth out to Remmon-methoar to Neah;
14 And the border compasseth it on the north side to Hannathon: and the
outgoings thereof are in the valley of Jiphthah-el:

15 And Kattath, and Nahallal, and Shimron, and Idalah, and Beth-lehem:
twelve cities with their villages.
16 This *is* the inheritance of the children of Zebulun according to their fam-
ilies, these cities with their villages.

Land for the Tribe of Issachar

17 *And* the fourth lot came out to Issachar, for the children of Issachar
according to their families.
18 And their border was toward Jezreel, and Chesulloth, and Shunem,
19 And Hapharaim, and Shion, and Anaharath,
20 And Rabbith, and Kishion, and Abez,
21 And Remeth, and En-gannim, and En-haddah, and Beth-pazzez;
22 And the coast reacheth to Tabor, and Shahazimah, and Beth-shemesh; and
the outgoings of their border were at Jordan: sixteen cities with their villages.
23 This *is* the inheritance of the tribe of the children of Issachar according
to their families, the cities and their villages.

Land for the Tribe of Asher

24 And the fifth lot came out for the tribe of the children of Asher according
to their families.
25 And their border was Helkath, and Hali, and Beten, and Achshaph,
26 And Alammelech, and Amad, and Misheal; and reacheth to Carmel west-
ward, and to Shihor-libnath;
27 And turneth toward the sunrising to Beth-dagon, and reacheth to Zebulun,
and to the valley of Jiphthah-el toward the north side of Beth-emek, and Neiel,
and goeth out to Cabul on the left hand,
28 And Hebron, and Rehob, and Hammon, and Kanah, *even* unto great Zidon;
29 And *then* the coast turneth to Ramah, and to the strong city Tyre; and the
coast turneth to Hosah; and the outgoings thereof are at the sea from the coast
to Achzib:
30 Ummah also, and Aphek, and Rehob: twenty and two cities with their
villages.
31 This *is* the inheritance of the tribe of the children of Asher according to
their families, these cities with their villages.

Land for the Tribe of Naphtali

32 The sixth lot came out to the children of Naphtali, *even* for the children
of Naphtali according to their families.
33 And their coast was from Heleph, from Allon to Zaanannim, and Adami,
Nekeb, and Jabneel, unto Lakum; and the outgoings thereof were at Jordan:
34 And *then* the coast turneth westward to Aznoth-tabor, and goeth out from
thence to Hukkok, and reacheth to Zebulun on the south side, and reacheth
to Asher on the west side, and to Judah upon Jordan toward the sunrising.
35 And the fenced cities *are* Ziddim, Zer, and Hammath, Rakkath, and
Chinnereth,
36 And Adamah, and Ramah, and Hazor,
37 And Kedesh, and Edrei, and En-hazor,
38 And Iron, and Migdalel, Horem, and Beth-anath, and Beth-shemesh; nine-
teen cities with their villages.
39 This *is* the inheritance of the tribe of the children of Naphtali according
to their families, the cities and their villages.

Land for the Tribe of Dan, and for Joshua

40 *And* the seventh lot came out for the tribe of the children of Dan accord-
ing to their families.
41 And the coast of their inheritance was Zorah, and Eshtaol, and Ir-shemesh,
42 And Shaalabbin, and Ajalon, and Jethlah,
43 And Elon, and Thimnathah, and Ekron,

44 And Eltekeh, and Gibbethon, and Baalath,

45 And Jehud, and Beneberak, and Gath-rimmon,

46 And Me-jarkon, and Rakkon, with the border before Japho.

47 And the coast of the children of Dan went out *too little* for them: therefore the children of Dan went up to fight against Leshem, and took it, and smote it with the edge of the sword, and possessed it, and dwelt therein, and called Leshem, Dan, after the name of Dan their father.

48 This *is* the inheritance of the tribe of the children of Dan according to their families, these cities with their villages.

49 When they had made an end of dividing the land for inheritance by their coasts, the children of Israel gave an inheritance to Joshua the son of Nun among them:

50 According to the word of the LORD they gave him the city which he asked, *even* Timnath-serah in mount Ephraim: and he built the city, and dwelt therein.

51 These *are* the inheritances, which Eleazar the priest, and Joshua the son of Nun, and the heads of the fathers of the tribes of the children of Israel, divided for an inheritance by lot in Shiloh before the LORD, at the door of the tabernacle of the congregation. So they made an end of dividing the country.

God Commands Cities of Refuge

20 The LORD also spake unto Joshua, saying,

2 Speak to the children of Israel, saying, Appoint out for you cities of refuge, whereof I spake unto you by the hand of Moses:

3 That the slayer that killeth *any* person unawares *and* unwittingly may flee thither: and they shall be your refuge from the avenger of blood.

4 And when he that doth flee unto one of those cities shall stand at the entering of the gate of the city, and shall declare his cause in the ears of the elders of that city, they shall take him into the city unto them, and give him a place, that he may dwell among them.

5 And if the avenger of blood pursue after him, then they shall not deliver the slayer up into his hand; because he smote his neighbour unwittingly, and hated him not beforetime.

6 And he shall dwell in that city, until he stand before the congregation for judgment, *and* until the death of the high priest that shall be in those days: then shall the slayer return, and come unto his own city, and unto his own house, unto the city from whence he fled.

The People Appoint the Six Cities of Refuge as God Commanded

7 And they appointed Kedesh in Galilee in mount Naphtali, and Shechem in mount Ephraim, and Kirjath-arba, which *is* Hebron, in the mountain of Judah.

8 And on the other side Jordan by Jericho eastward, they assigned Bezer in the wilderness upon the plain out of the tribe of Reuben, and Ramoth in Gilead out of the tribe of Gad, and Golan in Bashan out of the tribe of Manasseh.

9 These were the cities appointed for all the children of Israel, and for the stranger that sojourneth among them, that whosoever killeth *any* person at unawares might flee thither, and not die by the hand of the avenger of blood, until he stood before the congregation.

The Tribes Set Aside Forty-Eight Cities for the Levites

21 Then came near the heads of the fathers of the Levites unto Eleazar the priest, and unto Joshua the son of Nun, and unto the heads of the fathers of the tribes of the children of Israel;

2 And they spake unto them at Shiloh in the land of Canaan, saying, The LORD commanded by the hand of Moses to give us cities to dwell in, with the suburbs thereof for our cattle.

3 And the children of Israel gave unto the Levites out of their inheritance, at the commandment of the LORD, these cities and their suburbs.

4 And the lot came out for the families of the Kohathites: and the children
of Aaron the priest, *which were* of the Levites, had by lot out of the tribe of
Judah, and out of the tribe of Simeon, and out of the tribe of Benjamin, thirteen cities.
5 And the rest of the children of Kohath *had* by lot out of the families of the
tribe of Ephraim, and out of the tribe of Dan, and out of the half tribe of
Manasseh, ten cities.
6 And the children of Gershon *had* by lot out of the families of the tribe of
Issachar, and out of the tribe of Asher, and out of the tribe of Naphtali, and
out of the half tribe of Manasseh in Bashan, thirteen cities.
7 The children of Merari by their families *had* out of the tribe of Reuben,
and out of the tribe of Gad, and out of the tribe of Zebulun, twelve cities.
8 And the children of Israel gave by lot unto the Levites these cities with their
suburbs, as the LORD commanded by the hand of Moses.
9 And they gave out of the tribe of the children of Judah, and out of the tribe
of the children of Simeon, these cities which are *here* mentioned by name,
10 Which the children of Aaron, *being* of the families of the Kohathites, *who
were* of the children of Levi, had: for theirs was the first lot.
11 And they gave them the city of Arba the father of Anak, which *city is*
Hebron, in the hill *country* of Judah, with the suburbs thereof round about it.
12 But the fields of the city, and the villages thereof, gave they to Caleb the
son of Jephunneh for his possession.
13 Thus they gave to the children of Aaron the priest Hebron with her suburbs, *to be* a city of refuge for the slayer; and Libnah with her suburbs,
14 And Jattir with her suburbs, and Eshtemoa with her suburbs,
15 And Holon with her suburbs, and Debir with her suburbs,
16 And Ain with her suburbs, and Juttah with her suburbs, *and* Beth-shemesh
with her suburbs; nine cities out of those two tribes.
17 And out of the tribe of Benjamin, Gibeon with her suburbs, Geba with
her suburbs,
18 Anathoth with her suburbs, and Almon with her suburbs; four cities.
19 All the cities of the children of Aaron, the priests, *were* thirteen cities with
their suburbs.
20 And the families of the children of Kohath, the Levites which remained
of the children of Kohath, even they had the cities of their lot out of the tribe
of Ephraim.
21 For they gave them Shechem with her suburbs in mount Ephraim, *to be*
a city of refuge for the slayer; and Gezer with her suburbs,
22 And Kibzaim with her suburbs, and Beth-horon with her suburbs; four
cities.
23 And out of the tribe of Dan, Eltekeh with her suburbs, Gibbethon with
her suburbs,
24 Aijalon with her suburbs, Gath-rimmon with her suburbs; four cities.
25 And out of the half tribe of Manasseh, Tanach with her suburbs, and Gath-rimmon with her suburbs; two cities.
26 All the cities *were* ten with their suburbs for the families of the children
of Kohath that remained.
27 And unto the children of Gershon, of the families of the Levites, out of
the *other* half tribe of Manasseh *they gave* Golan in Bashan with her suburbs,
to be a city of refuge for the slayer; and Beeshterah with her suburbs; two
cities.
28 And out of the tribe of Issachar, Kishon with her suburbs, Dabareh with
her suburbs,
29 Jarmuth with her suburbs, En-gannim with her suburbs; four cities.
30 And out of the tribe of Asher, Mishal with her suburbs, Abdon with her
suburbs,

31 Helkath with her suburbs, and Rehob with her suburbs; four cities.
32 And out of the tribe of Naphtali, Kedesh in Galilee with her suburbs, *to*
be a city of refuge for the slayer; and Hammoth-dor with her suburbs, and
Kartan with her suburbs; three cities.
33 All the cities of the Gershonites according to their families *were* thirteen
cities with their suburbs.
34 And unto the families of the children of Merari, the rest of the Levites, out
of the tribe of Zebulun, Jokneam with her suburbs, and Kartah with her
suburbs,
35 Dimnah with her suburbs, Nahalal with her suburbs; four cities.
36 And out of the tribe of Reuben, Bezer with her suburbs, and Jahazah with
her suburbs,
37 Kedemoth with her suburbs, and Mephaath with her suburbs; four cities.
38 And out of the tribe of Gad, Ramoth in Gilead with her suburbs, *to be* a
city of refuge for the slayer; and Mahanaim with her suburbs,
39 Heshbon with her suburbs, Jazer with her suburbs; four cities in all.
40 So all the cities for the children of Merari by their families, which were
remaining of the families of the Levites, were *by* their lot twelve cities.
41 All the cities of the Levites within the possession of the children of Israel
were forty and eight cities with their suburbs.
42 These cities were every one with their suburbs round about them: thus
were all these cities.

God Gives the Land to the Israelites, Fulfilling His Promise

43 And the LORD gave unto Israel all the land which he sware to give unto
their fathers; and they possessed it, and dwelt therein.
44 And the LORD gave them rest round about, according to all that he sware
unto their fathers: and there stood not a man of all their enemies before them;
the LORD delivered all their enemies into their hand.
45 There failed not ought of any good thing which the LORD had spoken unto
the house of Israel; all came to pass.

Joshua Sends Home the Tribes East of the Jordan

22 Then Joshua called the Reubenites, and the Gadites, and the half tribe
of Manasseh,
2 And said unto them, Ye have kept all that Moses the servant of the LORD
commanded you, and have obeyed my voice in all that I commanded you:
3 Ye have not left your brethren these many days unto this day, but have kept
the charge of the commandment of the LORD your God.
4 And now the LORD your God hath given rest unto your brethren, as he
promised them: therefore now return ye, and get you unto your tents, *and*
unto the land of your possession, which Moses the servant of the LORD gave
you on the other side Jordan.
5 But take diligent heed to do the commandment and the law, which Moses
the servant of the LORD charged you, to love the LORD your God, and to walk
in all his ways, and to keep his commandments, and to cleave unto him, and
to serve him with all your heart and with all your soul.
6 So Joshua blessed them, and sent them away: and they went unto their
tents.
7 Now to the *one* half of the tribe of Manasseh Moses had given *possession*
in Bashan: but unto the *other* half thereof gave Joshua among their brethren
on this side Jordan westward. And when Joshua sent them away also unto their
tents, then he blessed them,
8 And he spake unto them, saying, Return with much riches unto your tents,
and with very much cattle, with silver, and with gold, and with brass, and with
iron, and with very much raiment: divide the spoil of your enemies with your
brethren.

9 And the children of Reuben and the children of Gad and the half tribe of Manasseh returned, and departed from the children of Israel out of Shiloh, which *is* in the land of Canaan, to go unto the country of Gilead, to the land of their possession, whereof they were possessed, according to the word of the LORD by the hand of Moses.

The Eastern Tribes Build an Altar for the Lord

10 And when they came unto the borders of Jordan, that *are* in the land of Canaan, the children of Reuben and the children of Gad and the half tribe of Manasseh built there an altar by Jordan, a great altar to see to.

11 And the children of Israel heard say, Behold, the children of Reuben and the children of Gad and the half tribe of Manasseh have built an altar over against the land of Canaan, in the borders of Jordan, at the passage of the children of Israel.

12 And when the children of Israel heard *of it*, the whole congregation of the children of Israel gathered themselves together at Shiloh, to go up to war against them.

13 And the children of Israel sent unto the children of Reuben, and to the children of Gad, and to the half tribe of Manasseh, into the land of Gilead, Phinehas the son of Eleazar the priest,

14 And with him ten princes, of each chief house a prince throughout all the tribes of Israel; and each one *was* an head of the house of their fathers among the thousands of Israel.

15 And they came unto the children of Reuben, and to the children of Gad, and to the half tribe of Manasseh, unto the land of Gilead, and they spake with them, saying,

16 Thus saith the whole congregation of the LORD, What trespass *is* this that ye have committed against the God of Israel, to turn away this day from following the LORD, in that ye have builded you an altar, that ye might rebel this day against the LORD?

17 *Is* the iniquity of Peor too little for us, from which we are not cleansed until this day, although there was a plague in the congregation of the LORD,

18 But that ye must turn away this day from following the LORD? and it will be, *seeing* ye rebel to day against the LORD, that to morrow he will be wroth with the whole congregation of Israel.

19 Notwithstanding, if the land of your possession *be* unclean, *then* pass ye over unto the land of the possession of the LORD, wherein the LORD's tabernacle dwelleth, and take possession among us: but rebel not against the LORD, nor rebel against us, in building you an altar beside the altar of the LORD our God.

20 Did not Achan the son of Zerah commit a trespass in the accursed thing, and wrath fell on all the congregation of Israel? and that man perished not alone in his iniquity.

The Altar Is Explained Satisfactorily

21 Then the children of Reuben and the children of Gad and the half tribe of Manasseh answered, and said unto the heads of the thousands of Israel,

22 The LORD God of gods, the LORD God of gods, he knoweth, and Israel he shall know; if *it be* in rebellion, or if in transgression against the LORD, (save us not this day,)

23 That we have built us an altar to turn from following the LORD, or if to offer thereon burnt offering or meat offering, or if to offer peace offerings thereon, let the LORD himself require *it*;

24 And if we have not *rather* done it for fear of *this* thing, saying, In time to come your children might speak unto our children, saying, What have ye to do with the LORD God of Israel?

25 For the LORD hath made Jordan a border between us and you, ye children of Reuben and children of Gad; ye have no part in the LORD: so shall your children make our children cease from fearing the LORD.

26 Therefore we said, Let us now prepare to build us an altar, not for burnt offering, nor for sacrifice:

27 But *that* it *may be* a witness between us, and you, and our generations after us, that we might do the service of the LORD before him with our burnt offerings, and with our sacrifices, and with our peace offerings; that your children may not say to our children in time to come, Ye have no part in the LORD.

28 Therefore said we, that it shall be, when they should *so* say to us or to our generations in time to come, that we may say *again*, Behold the pattern of the altar of the LORD, which our fathers made, not for burnt offerings, nor for sacrifices; but it *is* a witness between us and you.

29 God forbid that we should rebel against the LORD, and turn this day from following the LORD, to build an altar for burnt offerings, for meat offerings, or for sacrifices, beside the altar of the LORD our God that *is* before his tabernacle.

30 And when Phinehas the priest, and the princes of the congregation and heads of the thousands of Israel which *were* with him, heard the words that the children of Reuben and the children of Gad and the children of Manasseh spake, it pleased them.

31 And Phinehas the son of Eleazar the priest said unto the children of Reuben, and to the children of Gad, and to the children of Manasseh, This day we perceive that the LORD *is* among us, because ye have not committed this trespass against the LORD: now ye have delivered the children of Israel out of the hand of the LORD.

32 And Phinehas the son of Eleazar the priest, and the princes, returned from the children of Reuben, and from the children of Gad, out of the land of Gilead, unto the land of Canaan, to the children of Israel, and brought them word again.

33 And the thing pleased the children of Israel; and the children of Israel blessed God, and did not intend to go up against them in battle, to destroy the land wherein the children of Reuben and Gad dwelt.

34 And the children of Reuben and the children of Gad called the altar *Ed*: for it *shall be* a witness between us that the LORD *is* God.

Joshua's Exhortation before His Death

23 And it came to pass a long time after that the LORD had given rest unto Israel from all their enemies round about, that Joshua waxed old *and* stricken in age.

2 And Joshua called for all Israel, *and* for their elders, and for their heads, and for their judges, and for their officers, and said unto them, I am old *and* stricken in age:

3 And ye have seen all that the LORD your God hath done unto all these nations because of you; for the LORD your God *is* he that hath fought for you.

4 Behold, I have divided unto you by lot these nations that remain, to be an inheritance for your tribes, from Jordan, with all the nations that I have cut off, even unto the great sea westward.

5 And the LORD your God, he shall expel them from before you, and drive them from out of your sight; and ye shall possess their land, as the LORD your God hath promised unto you.

6 Be ye therefore very courageous to keep and to do all that is written in the book of the law of Moses, that ye turn not aside therefrom *to* the right hand or *to* the left;

7 That ye come not among these nations, these that remain among you; nei-
ther make mention of the name of their gods, nor cause to swear *by them*,
neither serve them, nor bow yourselves unto them:
8 But cleave unto the LORD your God, as ye have done unto this day.
9 For the LORD hath driven out from before you great nations and strong:
but *as for* you, no man hath been able to stand before you unto this day.
10 One man of you shall chase a thousand: for the LORD your God, he *it is*
that fighteth for you, as he hath promised you.

Warnings against Forsaking God

11 Take good heed therefore unto yourselves, that ye love the LORD your God.
12 Else if ye do in any wise go back, and cleave unto the remnant of these
nations, *even* these that remain among you, and shall make marriages with
them, and go in unto them, and they to you:
13 Know for a certainty that the LORD your God will no more drive out *any*
of these nations from before you; but they shall be snares and traps unto you,
and scourges in your sides, and thorns in your eyes, until ye perish from off
this good land which the LORD your God hath given you.
14 And, behold, this day I *am* going the way of all the earth: and ye know in
all your hearts and in all your souls, that not one thing hath failed of all the
good things which the LORD your God spake concerning you; all are come to
pass unto you, *and* not one thing hath failed thereof.
15 Therefore it shall come to pass, *that* as all good things are come upon you,
which the LORD your God promised you; so shall the LORD bring upon you all
evil things, until he have destroyed you from off this good land which the LORD
your God hath given you.
16 When ye have transgressed the covenant of the LORD your God, which he
commanded you, and have gone and served other gods, and bowed yourselves
to them; then shall the anger of the LORD be kindled against you, and ye shall
perish quickly from off the good land which he hath given unto you.

Joshua Assembles the Tribes at Shechem

24 And Joshua gathered all the tribes of Israel to Shechem, and called for
the elders of Israel, and for their heads, and for their judges, and for
their officers; and they presented themselves before God.
2 And Joshua said unto all the people, Thus saith the LORD God of Israel, Your
fathers dwelt on the other side of the flood in old time, *even* Terah, the father
of Abraham, and the father of Nachor: and they served other gods.
3 And I took your father Abraham from the other side of the flood, and led
him throughout all the land of Canaan, and multiplied his seed, and gave him
Isaac.
4 And I gave unto Isaac Jacob and Esau: and I gave unto Esau mount Seir, to
possess it; but Jacob and his children went down into Egypt.
5 I sent Moses also and Aaron, and I plagued Egypt, according to that which
I did among them: and afterward I brought you out.
6 And I brought your fathers out of Egypt: and ye came unto the sea; and the
Egyptians pursued after your fathers with chariots and horsemen unto the
Red sea.
7 And when they cried unto the LORD, he put darkness between you and the
Egyptians, and brought the sea upon them, and covered them; and your eyes
have seen what I have done in Egypt: and ye dwelt in the wilderness a long
season.
8 And I brought you into the land of the Amorites, which dwelt on the other
side Jordan; and they fought with you: and I gave them into your hand, that
ye might possess their land; and I destroyed them from before you.
9 Then Balak the son of Zippor, king of Moab, arose and warred against Israel,
and sent and called Balaam the son of Beor to curse you:

YE KNOW IN all your hearts & IN ALL YOUR Souls, THAT NOT ONE THING HATH FAILED OF ALL THE good things WHICH THE LORD your God SPAKE concerning YOU.

JOSHUA 23:14

— JOSHUA 24:15 —
CHOOSE YOU THIS DAY WHOM YE WILL SERVE... AS FOR ME & MY HOUSE WE WILL SERVE THE LORD.

10 But I would not hearken unto Balaam; therefore he blessed you still: so I
delivered you out of his hand.
11 And ye went over Jordan, and came unto Jericho: and the men of Jericho
fought against you, the Amorites, and the Perizzites, and the Canaanites, and
the Hittites, and the Girgashites, the Hivites, and the Jebusites; and I delivered
them into your hand.
12 And I sent the hornet before you, which drave them out from before you,
even the two kings of the Amorites; *but* not with thy sword, nor with thy bow.
13 And I have given you a land for which ye did not labour, and cities which
ye built not, and ye dwell in them; of the vineyards and oliveyards which ye
planted not do ye eat.
14 Now therefore fear the LORD, and serve him in sincerity and in truth: and
put away the gods which your fathers served on the other side of the flood,
and in Egypt; and serve ye the LORD.
15 And if it seem evil unto you to serve the LORD, choose you this day whom
ye will serve; whether the gods which your fathers served that *were* on the
other side of the flood, or the gods of the Amorites, in whose land ye dwell:
but as for me and my house, we will serve the LORD.
16 And the people answered and said, God forbid that we should forsake the
LORD, to serve other gods;
17 For the LORD our God, he *it is* that brought us up and our fathers out of
the land of Egypt, from the house of bondage, and which did those great signs
in our sight, and preserved us in all the way wherein we went, and among all
the people through whom we passed:
18 And the LORD drave out from before us all the people, even the Amorites
which dwelt in the land: *therefore* will we also serve the LORD; for he *is* our
God.
19 And Joshua said unto the people, Ye cannot serve the LORD: for he *is* an
holy God; he *is* a jealous God; he will not forgive your transgressions nor your
sins.
20 If ye forsake the LORD, and serve strange gods, then he will turn and do
you hurt, and consume you, after that he hath done you good.
21 And the people said unto Joshua, Nay; but we will serve the LORD.
22 And Joshua said unto the people, Ye *are* witnesses against yourselves that
ye have chosen you the LORD, to serve him. And they said, *We are* witnesses.
23 Now therefore put away, *said he,* the strange gods which *are* among you,
and incline your heart unto the LORD God of Israel.
24 And the people said unto Joshua, The LORD our God will we serve, and his
voice will we obey.
25 So Joshua made a covenant with the people that day, and set them a statute
and an ordinance in Shechem.
26 And Joshua wrote these words in the book of the law of God, and took a
great stone, and set it up there under an oak, that *was* by the sanctuary of the
LORD.
27 And Joshua said unto all the people, Behold, this stone shall be a witness
unto us; for it hath heard all the words of the LORD which he spake unto us: it
shall be therefore a witness unto you, lest ye deny your God.
28 So Joshua let the people depart, every man unto his inheritance.

Joshua's Age, Death and Burial

29 And it came to pass after these things, that Joshua the son of Nun, the
servant of the LORD, died, *being* an hundred and ten years old.
30 And they buried him in the border of his inheritance in Timnath-serah,
which *is* in mount Ephraim, on the north side of the hill of Gaash.

31 And Israel served the LORD all the days of Joshua, and all the days of the
elders that overlived Joshua, and which had known all the works of the LORD,
that he had done for Israel.
32 And the bones of Joseph, which the children of Israel brought up out of
Egypt, buried they in Shechem, in a parcel of ground which Jacob bought of
the sons of Hamor the father of Shechem for an hundred pieces of silver: and
it became the inheritance of the children of Joseph.
33 And Eleazar the son of Aaron died; and they buried him in a hill *that
pertained to* Phinehas his son, which was given him in mount Ephraim.

Israel's Battles in Canaan

1 Now after the death of Joshua it came to pass, that the children of Israel
asked the LORD, saying, Who shall go up for us against the Canaanites first,
to fight against them?
2 And the LORD said, Judah shall go up: behold, I have delivered the land into
his hand.
3 And Judah said unto Simeon his brother, Come up with me into my lot,
that we may fight against the Canaanites; and I likewise will go with thee into
thy lot. So Simeon went with him.
4 And Judah went up; and the LORD delivered the Canaanites and the
Perizzites into their hand: and they slew of them in Bezek ten thousand men.
5 And they found Adonibezek in Bezek: and they fought against him, and
they slew the Canaanites and the Perizzites.
6 But Adonibezek fled; and they pursued after him, and caught him, and cut
off his thumbs and his great toes.
7 And Adonibezek said, Threescore and ten kings, having their thumbs and
their great toes cut off, gathered *their meat* under my table: as I have done, so
God hath requited me. And they brought him to Jerusalem, and there he died.
8 Now the children of Judah had fought against Jerusalem, and had taken
it, and smitten it with the edge of the sword, and set the city on fire.
9 And afterward the children of Judah went down to fight against the
Canaanites, that dwelt in the mountain, and in the south, and in the valley.
10 And Judah went against the Canaanites that dwelt in Hebron: (now the
name of Hebron before *was* Kirjatharba:) and they slew Sheshai, and Ahiman,
and Talmai.
11 And from thence he went against the inhabitants of Debir: and the name
of Debir before *was* Kirjath-sepher:
12 And Caleb said, He that smiteth Kirjath-sepher, and taketh it, to him will
I give Achsah my daughter to wife.
13 And Othniel the son of Kenaz, Caleb's younger brother, took it: and he
gave him Achsah his daughter to wife.
14 And it came to pass, when she came *to him*, that she moved him to ask of
her father a field: and she lighted from off *her* ass; and Caleb said unto her,
What wilt thou?
15 And she said unto him, Give me a blessing: for thou hast given me a south
land; give me also springs of water. And Caleb gave her the upper springs and
the nether springs.
16 And the children of the Kenite, Moses' father in law, went up out of the
city of palm trees with the children of Judah into the wilderness of Judah,
which *lieth* in the south of Arad; and they went and dwelt among the people.
17 And Judah went with Simeon his brother, and they slew the Canaanites
that inhabited Zephath, and utterly destroyed it. And the name of the city was
called Hormah.
18 Also Judah took Gaza with the coast thereof, and Askelon with the coast
thereof, and Ekron with the coast thereof.
19 And the LORD was with Judah; and he drave out *the inhabitants of* the
mountain; but could not drive out the inhabitants of the valley, because they
had chariots of iron.

20 And they gave Hebron unto Caleb, as Moses said: and he expelled thence
the three sons of Anak.

Israel Fails to Conquer Canaan

21 And the children of Benjamin did not drive out the Jebusites that inhab-
ited Jerusalem; but the Jebusites dwell with the children of Benjamin in
Jerusalem unto this day.
22 And the house of Joseph, they also went up against Bethel: and the LORD
was with them.
23 And the house of Joseph sent to descry Bethel. (Now the name of the city
before *was* Luz.)
24 And the spies saw a man come forth out of the city, and they said unto
him, Shew us, we pray thee, the entrance into the city, and we will shew thee
mercy.
25 And when he shewed them the entrance into the city, they smote the city
with the edge of the sword; but they let go the man and all his family.
26 And the man went into the land of the Hittites, and built a city, and called
the name thereof Luz: which *is* the name thereof unto this day.
27 Neither did Manasseh drive out *the inhabitants of* Beth-shean and her
towns, nor Taanach and her towns, nor the inhabitants of Dor and her towns,
nor the inhabitants of Ibleam and her towns, nor the inhabitants of Megiddo
and her towns: but the Canaanites would dwell in that land.
28 And it came to pass, when Israel was strong, that they put the Canaanites
to tribute, and did not utterly drive them out.
29 Neither did Ephraim drive out the Canaanites that dwelt in Gezer; but
the Canaanites dwelt in Gezer among them.
30 Neither did Zebulun drive out the inhabitants of Kitron, nor the inhabi-
tants of Nahalol; but the Canaanites dwelt among them, and became tribu-
taries.
31 Neither did Asher drive out the inhabitants of Accho, nor the inhabitants
of Zidon, nor of Ahlab, nor of Achzib, nor of Helbah, nor of Aphik, nor of
Rehob:
32 But the Asherites dwelt among the Canaanites, the inhabitants of the land:
for they did not drive them out.
33 Neither did Naphtali drive out the inhabitants of Beth-shemesh, nor the
inhabitants of Beth-anath; but he dwelt among the Canaanites, the inhabitants
of the land: nevertheless the inhabitants of Beth-shemesh and of Beth-anath
became tributaries unto them.
34 And the Amorites forced the children of Dan into the mountain: for they
would not suffer them to come down to the valley:
35 But the Amorites would dwell in mount Heres in Aijalon, and in Shaalbim:
yet the hand of the house of Joseph prevailed, so that they became tributaries.
36 And the coast of the Amorites *was* from the going up to Akrabbim, from
the rock, and upward.

An Angel Rebukes the People

2 And an angel of the LORD came up from Gilgal to Bochim, and said, I made
you to go up out of Egypt, and have brought you unto the land which I sware
unto your fathers; and I said, I will never break my covenant with you.
2 And ye shall make no league with the inhabitants of this land; ye shall throw
down their altars: but ye have not obeyed my voice: why have ye done this?
3 Wherefore I also said, I will not drive them out from before you; but they
shall be *as thorns* in your sides, and their gods shall be a snare unto you.
4 And it came to pass, when the angel of the LORD spake these words unto all
the children of Israel, that the people lifted up their voice, and wept.
5 And they called the name of that place Bochim: and they sacrificed there
unto the LORD.

I WILL never BREAK my COVENANT with YOU.
JUDGES 2:1

The Wickedness of the New Generation after Joshua

6 And when Joshua had let the people go, the children of Israel went every man unto his inheritance to possess the land.

7 And the people served the LORD all the days of Joshua, and all the days of the elders that outlived Joshua, who had seen all the great works of the LORD, that he did for Israel.

8 And Joshua the son of Nun, the servant of the LORD, died, *being* an hundred and ten years old.

9 And they buried him in the border of his inheritance in Timnath-heres, in the mount of Ephraim, on the north side of the hill Gaash.

10 And also all that generation were gathered unto their fathers: and there arose another generation after them, which knew not the LORD, nor yet the works which he had done for Israel.

11 And the children of Israel did evil in the sight of the LORD, and served Baalim:

12 And they forsook the LORD God of their fathers, which brought them out of the land of Egypt, and followed other gods, of the gods of the people that *were* round about them, and bowed themselves unto them, and provoked the LORD to anger.

13 And they forsook the LORD, and served Baal and Ashtaroth.

14 And the anger of the LORD was hot against Israel, and he delivered them into the hands of spoilers that spoiled them, and he sold them into the hands of their enemies round about, so that they could not any longer stand before their enemies.

15 Whithersoever they went out, the hand of the LORD was against them for evil, as the LORD had said, and as the LORD had sworn unto them: and they were greatly distressed.

16 Nevertheless the LORD raised up judges, which delivered them out of the hand of those that spoiled them.

17 And yet they would not hearken unto their judges, but they went a whoring after other gods, and bowed themselves unto them: they turned quickly out of the way which their fathers walked in, obeying the commandments of the LORD; *but* they did not so.

18 And when the LORD raised them up judges, then the LORD was with the judge, and delivered them out of the hand of their enemies all the days of the judge: for it repented the LORD because of their groanings by reason of them that oppressed them and vexed them.

19 And it came to pass, when the judge was dead, *that* they returned, and corrupted *themselves* more than their fathers, in following other gods to serve them, and to bow down unto them; they ceased not from their own doings, nor from their stubborn way.

20 And the anger of the LORD was hot against Israel; and he said, Because that this people hath transgressed my covenant which I commanded their fathers, and have not hearkened unto my voice;

21 I also will not henceforth drive out any from before them of the nations which Joshua left when he died:

22 That through them I may prove Israel, whether they will keep the way of the LORD to walk therein, as their fathers did keep *it*, or not.

23 Therefore the LORD left those nations, without driving them out hastily; neither delivered he them into the hand of Joshua.

The Nations Which Were Left to Test Israel

3 Now these *are* the nations which the LORD left, to prove Israel by them, *even* as many *of Israel* as had not known all the wars of Canaan;

2 Only that the generations of the children of Israel might know, to teach them war, at the least such as before knew nothing thereof;

3 *Namely*, five lords of the Philistines, and all the Canaanites, and the
Sidonians, and the Hivites that dwelt in mount Lebanon, from mount Baal-
hermon unto the entering in of Hamath.
4 And they were to prove Israel by them, to know whether they would hear-
ken unto the commandments of the LORD, which he commanded their fathers
by the hand of Moses.
5 And the children of Israel dwelt among the Canaanites, Hittites, and
Amorites, and Perizzites, and Hivites, and Jebusites:
6 And they took their daughters to be their wives, and gave their daughters
to their sons, and served their gods.
7 And the children of Israel did evil in the sight of the LORD, and forgat the
LORD their God, and served Baalim and the groves.

Othniel Delivers Israel from Chushan-rishathaim

8 Therefore the anger of the LORD was hot against Israel, and he sold them
into the hand of Chushan-rishathaim king of Mesopotamia: and the children
of Israel served Chushan-rishathaim eight years.
9 And when the children of Israel cried unto the LORD, the LORD raised up a
deliverer to the children of Israel, who delivered them, *even* Othniel the son
of Kenaz, Caleb's younger brother.
10 And the Spirit of the LORD came upon him, and he judged Israel, and went
out to war: and the LORD delivered Chushan-rishathaim king of Mesopotamia
into his hand; and his hand prevailed against Chushan-rishathaim.
11 And the land had rest forty years. And Othniel the son of Kenaz died.

Ehud Frees Israel from Moab

12 And the children of Israel did evil again in the sight of the LORD: and the
LORD strengthened Eglon the king of Moab against Israel, because they had
done evil in the sight of the LORD.
13 And he gathered unto him the children of Ammon and Amalek, and went
and smote Israel, and possessed the city of palm trees.
14 So the children of Israel served Eglon the king of Moab eighteen years.
15 But when the children of Israel cried unto the LORD, the LORD raised them
up a deliverer, Ehud the son of Gera, a Benjamite, a man lefthanded: and by
him the children of Israel sent a present unto Eglon the king of Moab.
16 But Ehud made him a dagger which had two edges, of a cubit length; and
he did gird it under his raiment upon his right thigh.
17 And he brought the present unto Eglon king of Moab: and Eglon *was* a
very fat man.
18 And when he had made an end to offer the present, he sent away the
people that bare the present.
19 But he himself turned again from the quarries that *were* by Gilgal, and
said, I have a secret errand unto thee, O king: who said, Keep silence. And all
that stood by him went out from him.
20 And Ehud came unto him; and he was sitting in a summer parlour, which
he had for himself alone. And Ehud said, I have a message from God unto thee.
And he arose out of *his* seat.
21 And Ehud put forth his left hand, and took the dagger from his right thigh,
and thrust it into his belly:
22 And the haft also went in after the blade; and the fat closed upon the blade,
so that he could not draw the dagger out of his belly; and the dirt came out.
23 Then Ehud went forth through the porch, and shut the doors of the par-
lour upon him, and locked them.
24 When he was gone out, his servants came; and when they saw that, behold,
the doors of the parlour *were* locked, they said, Surely he covereth his feet in
his summer chamber.

25 And they tarried till they were ashamed: and, behold, he opened not the doors of the parlour; therefore they took a key, and opened *them*: and, behold, their lord *was* fallen down dead on the earth.

26 And Ehud escaped while they tarried, and passed beyond the quarries, and escaped unto Seirath.

27 And it came to pass, when he was come, that he blew a trumpet in the mountain of Ephraim, and the children of Israel went down with him from the mount, and he before them.

28 And he said unto them, Follow after me: for the LORD hath delivered your enemies the Moabites into your hand. And they went down after him, and took the fords of Jordan toward Moab, and suffered not a man to pass over.

29 And they slew of Moab at that time about ten thousand men, all lusty, and all men of valour; and there escaped not a man.

30 So Moab was subdued that day under the hand of Israel. And the land had rest fourscore years.

Shamgar Delivers Israel from the Philistines

31 And after him was Shamgar the son of Anath, which slew of the Philistines six hundred men with an ox goad: and he also delivered Israel.

Deborah and Barak Save Israel from Jabin and Sisera

4 And the children of Israel again did evil in the sight of the LORD, when Ehud was dead.

2 And the LORD sold them into the hand of Jabin king of Canaan, that reigned in Hazor; the captain of whose host *was* Sisera, which dwelt in Harosheth of the Gentiles.

3 And the children of Israel cried unto the LORD: for he had nine hundred chariots of iron; and twenty years he mightily oppressed the children of Israel.

4 And Deborah, a prophetess, the wife of Lapidoth, she judged Israel at that time.

5 And she dwelt under the palm tree of Deborah between Ramah and Bethel in mount Ephraim: and the children of Israel came up to her for judgment.

6 And she sent and called Barak the son of Abinoam out of Kedesh-naphtali, and said unto him, Hath not the LORD God of Israel commanded, *saying*, Go and draw toward mount Tabor, and take with thee ten thousand men of the children of Naphtali and of the children of Zebulun?

7 And I will draw unto thee to the river Kishon Sisera, the captain of Jabin's army, with his chariots and his multitude; and I will deliver him into thine hand.

8 And Barak said unto her, If thou wilt go with me, then I will go: but if thou wilt not go with me, *then* I will not go.

9 And she said, I will surely go with thee: notwithstanding the journey that thou takest shall not be for thine honour; for the LORD shall sell Sisera into the hand of a woman. And Deborah arose, and went with Barak to Kedesh.

10 And Barak called Zebulun and Naphtali to Kedesh; and he went up with ten thousand men at his feet: and Deborah went up with him.

11 Now Heber the Kenite, *which was* of the children of Hobab the father in law of Moses, had severed himself from the Kenites, and pitched his tent unto the plain of Zaanaim, which *is* by Kedesh.

12 And they shewed Sisera that Barak the son of Abinoam was gone up to mount Tabor.

13 And Sisera gathered together all his chariots, *even* nine hundred chariots of iron, and all the people that *were* with him, from Harosheth of the Gentiles unto the river of Kishon.

14 And Deborah said unto Barak, Up; for this *is* the day in which the LORD hath delivered Sisera into thine hand: is not the LORD gone out before thee? So Barak went down from mount Tabor, and ten thousand men after him.

15 And the LORD discomfited Sisera, and all *his* chariots, and all *his* host, with
the edge of the sword before Barak; so that Sisera lighted down off *his* chariot,
and fled away on his feet.
16 But Barak pursued after the chariots, and after the host, unto Harosheth
of the Gentiles: and all the host of Sisera fell upon the edge of the sword; *and*
there was not a man left.
17 Howbeit Sisera fled away on his feet to the tent of Jael the wife of Heber
the Kenite: for *there was* peace between Jabin the king of Hazor and the house
of Heber the Kenite.
18 And Jael went out to meet Sisera, and said unto him, Turn in, my lord, turn
in to me; fear not. And when he had turned in unto her into the tent, she
covered him with a mantle.
19 And he said unto her, Give me, I pray thee, a little water to drink; for I am
thirsty. And she opened a bottle of milk, and gave him drink, and covered him.
20 Again he said unto her, Stand in the door of the tent, and it shall be, when
any man doth come and enquire of thee, and say, Is there any man here? that
thou shalt say, No.
21 Then Jael Heber's wife took a nail of the tent, and took an hammer in her
hand, and went softly unto him, and smote the nail into his temples, and
fastened it into the ground: for he was fast asleep and weary. So he died.
22 And, behold, as Barak pursued Sisera, Jael came out to meet him, and said
unto him, Come, and I will shew thee the man whom thou seekest. And when
he came into her *tent*, behold, Sisera lay dead, and the nail *was* in his temples.
23 So God subdued on that day Jabin the king of Canaan before the children
of Israel.
24 And the hand of the children of Israel prospered, and prevailed against
Jabin the king of Canaan, until they had destroyed Jabin king of Canaan.

The Song of Deborah and Barak

5 Then sang Deborah and Barak the son of Abinoam on that day, saying,
2 Praise ye the LORD for the avenging of Israel, when the people willingly
offered themselves.
3 Hear, O ye kings; give ear, O ye princes; I, *even* I, will sing unto the LORD; I
will sing *praise* to the LORD God of Israel.
4 LORD, when thou wentest out of Seir, when thou marchedst out of the field
of Edom, the earth trembled, and the heavens dropped, the clouds also
dropped water.
5 The mountains melted from before the LORD, *even* that Sinai from before
the LORD God of Israel.
6 In the days of Shamgar the son of Anath, in the days of Jael, the highways
were unoccupied, and the travellers walked through byways.
7 *The inhabitants of* the villages ceased, they ceased in Israel, until that I
Deborah arose, that I arose a mother in Israel.
8 They chose new gods; then *was* war in the gates: was there a shield or spear
seen among forty thousand in Israel?
9 My heart *is* toward the governors of Israel, that offered themselves will-
ingly among the people. Bless ye the LORD.
10 Speak, ye that ride on white asses, ye that sit in judgment, and walk by the
way.
11 *They that are delivered* from the noise of archers in the places of drawing
water, there shall they rehearse the righteous acts of the LORD, *even* the righ-
teous acts *toward the inhabitants* of his villages in Israel: then shall the people
of the LORD go down to the gates.
12 Awake, awake, Deborah: awake, awake, utter a song: arise, Barak, and lead
thy captivity captive, thou son of Abinoam.
13 Then he made him that remaineth have dominion over the nobles among
the people: the LORD made me have dominion over the mighty.

14 Out of Ephraim *was there* a root of them against Amalek; after thee,
Benjamin, among thy people; out of Machir came down governors, and out
of Zebulun they that handle the pen of the writer.
15 And the princes of Issachar *were* with Deborah; even Issachar, and also
Barak: he was sent on foot into the valley. For the divisions of Reuben *there
were* great thoughts of heart.
16 Why abodest thou among the sheepfolds, to hear the bleatings of the
flocks? For the divisions of Reuben *there were* great searchings of heart.
17 Gilead abode beyond Jordan: and why did Dan remain in ships? Asher
continued on the sea shore, and abode in his breaches.
18 Zebulun and Naphtali *were* a people *that* jeoparded their lives unto the
death in the high places of the field.
19 The kings came *and* fought, then fought the kings of Canaan in Taanach
by the waters of Megiddo; they took no gain of money.
20 They fought from heaven; the stars in their courses fought against Sisera.
21 The river of Kishon swept them away, that ancient river, the river Kishon.
O my soul, thou hast trodden down strength.
22 Then were the horsehoofs broken by the means of the pransings, the
pransings of their mighty ones.
23 Curse ye Meroz, said the angel of the LORD, curse ye bitterly the inhabitants
thereof; because they came not to the help of the LORD, to the help of the LORD
against the mighty.
24 Blessed above women shall Jael the wife of Heber the Kenite be, blessed
shall she be above women in the tent.
25 He asked water, *and* she gave *him* milk; she brought forth butter in a
lordly dish.
26 She put her hand to the nail, and her right hand to the workmen's ham-
mer; and with the hammer she smote Sisera, she smote off his head, when she
had pierced and stricken through his temples.
27 At her feet he bowed, he fell, he lay down: at her feet he bowed, he fell:
where he bowed, there he fell down dead.
28 The mother of Sisera looked out at a window, and cried through the lattice,
Why is his chariot *so* long in coming? why tarry the wheels of his chariots?
29 Her wise ladies answered her, yea, she returned answer to herself,
30 Have they not sped? have they *not* divided the prey; to every man a dam-
sel *or* two; to Sisera a prey of divers colours, a prey of divers colours of needle-
work, of divers colours of needlework on both sides, *meet* for the necks of
them that take the spoil?
31 So let all thine enemies perish, O LORD: but *let* them that love him *be* as
the sun when he goeth forth in his might. And the land had rest forty years.

The Israelites Are Oppressed by Midian

6 And the children of Israel did evil in the sight of the LORD: and the LORD
delivered them into the hand of Midian seven years.
2 And the hand of Midian prevailed against Israel: *and* because of the
Midianites the children of Israel made them the dens which *are* in the moun-
tains, and caves, and strong holds.
3 And *so* it was, when Israel had sown, that the Midianites came up, and the
Amalekites, and the children of the east, even they came up against them;
4 And they encamped against them, and destroyed the increase of the earth,
till thou come unto Gaza, and left no sustenance for Israel, neither sheep, nor
ox, nor ass.
5 For they came up with their cattle and their tents, and they came as grass-
hoppers for multitude; *for* both they and their camels were without number:
and they entered into the land to destroy it.
6 And Israel was greatly impoverished because of the Midianites; and the
children of Israel cried unto the LORD.

7 And it came to pass, when the children of Israel cried unto the LORD because
of the Midianites,
8 That the LORD sent a prophet unto the children of Israel, which said unto
them, Thus saith the LORD God of Israel, I brought you up from Egypt, and
brought you forth out of the house of bondage;
9 And I delivered you out of the hand of the Egyptians, and out of the hand
of all that oppressed you, and drave them out from before you, and gave you
their land;
10 And I said unto you, I *am* the LORD your God; fear not the gods of the
Amorites, in whose land ye dwell: but ye have not obeyed my voice.

Gideon Is Chosen to Deliver Israel from Midian

11 And there came an angel of the LORD, and sat under an oak which *was* in
Ophrah, that *pertained* unto Joash the Abiezrite: and his son Gideon threshed
wheat by the winepress, to hide *it* from the Midianites.
12 And the angel of the LORD appeared unto him, and said unto him, The
LORD *is* with thee, thou mighty man of valour.
13 And Gideon said unto him, Oh my Lord, if the LORD be with us, why then
is all this befallen us? and where *be* all his miracles which our fathers told us
of, saying, Did not the LORD bring us up from Egypt? but now the LORD hath
forsaken us, and delivered us into the hands of the Midianites.
14 And the LORD looked upon him, and said, Go in this thy might, and thou
shalt save Israel from the hand of the Midianites: have not I sent thee?
15 And he said unto him, Oh my Lord, wherewith shall I save Israel? behold,
my family *is* poor in Manasseh, and I *am* the least in my father's house.
16 And the LORD said unto him, Surely I will be with thee, and thou shalt
smite the Midianites as one man.
17 And he said unto him, If now I have found grace in thy sight, then shew
me a sign that thou talkest with me.
18 Depart not hence, I pray thee, until I come unto thee, and bring forth my
present, and set *it* before thee. And he said, I will tarry until thou come again.
19 And Gideon went in, and made ready a kid, and unleavened cakes of an
ephah of flour: the flesh he put in a basket, and he put the broth in a pot, and
brought *it* out unto him under the oak, and presented *it*.
20 And the angel of God said unto him, Take the flesh and the unleavened
cakes, and lay *them* upon this rock, and pour out the broth. And he did so.
21 Then the angel of the LORD put forth the end of the staff that *was* in his
hand, and touched the flesh and the unleavened cakes; and there rose up fire
out of the rock, and consumed the flesh and the unleavened cakes. Then the
angel of the LORD departed out of his sight.
22 And when Gideon perceived that he *was* an angel of the LORD, Gideon
said, Alas, O Lord GOD! for because I have seen an angel of the LORD face to
face.
23 And the LORD said unto him, Peace *be* unto thee; fear not: thou shalt not
die.
24 Then Gideon built an altar there unto the LORD, and called it Jehovah-
shalom: unto this day it *is* yet in Ophrah of the Abiezrites.
25 And it came to pass the same night, that the LORD said unto him, Take thy
father's young bullock, even the second bullock of seven years old, and throw
down the altar of Baal that thy father hath, and cut down the grove that *is* by it:
26 And build an altar unto the LORD thy God upon the top of this rock, in the
ordered place, and take the second bullock, and offer a burnt sacrifice with
the wood of the grove which thou shalt cut down.
27 Then Gideon took ten men of his servants, and did as the LORD had said
unto him: and *so* it was, because he feared his father's household, and the men
of the city, that he could not do *it* by day, that he did *it* by night.

28 And when the men of the city arose early in the morning, behold, the altar
of Baal was cast down, and the grove was cut down that *was* by it, and the
second bullock was offered upon the altar *that was* built.
29 And they said one to another, Who hath done this thing? And when they
enquired and asked, they said, Gideon the son of Joash hath done this thing.
30 Then the men of the city said unto Joash, Bring out thy son, that he may
die: because he hath cast down the altar of Baal, and because he hath cut down
the grove that *was* by it.
31 And Joash said unto all that stood against him, Will ye plead for Baal? will
ye save him? he that will plead for him, let him be put to death whilst *it is yet*
morning: if he *be* a god, let him plead for himself, because *one* hath cast down
his altar.
32 Therefore on that day he called him Jerubbaal, saying, Let Baal plead
against him, because he hath thrown down his altar.

Gideon's Army

33 Then all the Midianites and the Amalekites and the children of the east
were gathered together, and went over, and pitched in the valley of Jezreel.
34 But the Spirit of the LORD came upon Gideon, and he blew a trumpet; and
Abiezer was gathered after him.
35 And he sent messengers throughout all Manasseh; who also was gathered
after him: and he sent messengers unto Asher, and unto Zebulun, and unto
Naphtali; and they came up to meet them.
36 And Gideon said unto God, If thou wilt save Israel by mine hand, as thou
hast said,
37 Behold, I will put a fleece of wool in the floor; *and* if the dew be on the
fleece only, and *it be* dry upon all the earth *beside*, then shall I know that thou
wilt save Israel by mine hand, as thou hast said.
38 And it was so: for he rose up early on the morrow, and thrust the fleece
together, and wringed the dew out of the fleece, a bowl full of water.
39 And Gideon said unto God, Let not thine anger be hot against me, and I
will speak but this once: let me prove, I pray thee, but this once with the fleece;
let it now be dry only upon the fleece, and upon all the ground let there be
dew.
40 And God did so that night: for it was dry upon the fleece only, and there
was dew on all the ground.

God Reduces Gideon's Army to Three Hundred Men

7 Then Jerubbaal, who *is* Gideon, and all the people that *were* with him, rose
up early, and pitched beside the well of Harod: so that the host of the
Midianites were on the north side of them, by the hill of Moreh, in the valley.
2 And the LORD said unto Gideon, The people that *are* with thee *are* too many
for me to give the Midianites into their hands, lest Israel vaunt themselves
against me, saying, Mine own hand hath saved me.
3 Now therefore go to, proclaim in the ears of the people, saying, Whosoever
is fearful and afraid, let him return and depart early from mount Gilead. And
there returned of the people twenty and two thousand; and there remained
ten thousand.
4 And the LORD said unto Gideon, The people *are* yet *too* many; bring them
down unto the water, and I will try them for thee there: and it shall be, *that*
of whom I say unto thee, This shall go with thee, the same shall go with thee;
and of whomsoever I say unto thee, This shall not go with thee, the same shall
not go.
5 So he brought down the people unto the water: and the LORD said unto
Gideon, Every one that lappeth of the water with his tongue, as a dog lappeth,
him shalt thou set by himself; likewise every one that boweth down upon his
knees to drink.

6 And the number of them that lapped, *putting* their hand to their mouth,
were three hundred men: but all the rest of the people bowed down upon
their knees to drink water.
7 And the LORD said unto Gideon, By the three hundred men that lapped will
I save you, and deliver the Midianites into thine hand: and let all the *other*
people go every man unto his place.
8 So the people took victuals in their hand, and their trumpets: and he sent
all *the rest of* Israel every man unto his tent, and retained those three hundred
men: and the host of Midian was beneath him in the valley.

The Lord Calls upon Gideon to Attack the Midianites

9 And it came to pass the same night, that the LORD said unto him, Arise, get
thee down unto the host; for I have delivered it into thine hand.
10 But if thou fear to go down, go thou with Phurah thy servant down to the
host:
11 And thou shalt hear what they say; and afterward shall thine hands be
strengthened to go down unto the host. Then went he down with Phurah his
servant unto the outside of the armed men that *were* in the host.
12 And the Midianites and the Amalekites and all the children of the east lay
along in the valley like grasshoppers for multitude; and their camels *were*
without number, as the sand by the sea side for multitude.
13 And when Gideon was come, behold, *there was* a man that told a dream
unto his fellow, and said, Behold, I dreamed a dream, and, lo, a cake of barley
bread tumbled into the host of Midian, and came unto a tent, and smote it
that it fell, and overturned it, that the tent lay along.
14 And his fellow answered and said, This *is* nothing else save the sword of
Gideon the son of Joash, a man of Israel: *for* into his hand hath God delivered
Midian, and all the host.
15 And it was *so*, when Gideon heard the telling of the dream, and the inter-
pretation thereof, that he worshipped, and returned into the host of Israel,
and said, Arise; for the LORD hath delivered into your hand the host of Midian.

Gideon's Unusual Battle Plan Delivers Israel from the Midianites

16 And he divided the three hundred men *into* three companies, and he put
a trumpet in every man's hand, with empty pitchers, and lamps within the
pitchers.
17 And he said unto them, Look on me, and do likewise: and, behold, when
I come to the outside of the camp, it shall be *that*, as I do, so shall ye do.
18 When I blow with a trumpet, I and all that *are* with me, then blow ye the
trumpets also on every side of all the camp, and say, *The sword* of the LORD,
and of Gideon.
19 So Gideon, and the hundred men that *were* with him, came unto the out-
side of the camp in the beginning of the middle watch; and they had but newly
set the watch: and they blew the trumpets, and brake the pitchers that *were*
in their hands.
20 And the three companies blew the trumpets, and brake the pitchers, and
held the lamps in their left hands, and the trumpets in their right hands to
blow *withal*: and they cried, The sword of the LORD, and of Gideon.
21 And they stood every man in his place round about the camp: and all the
host ran, and cried, and fled.
22 And the three hundred blew the trumpets, and the LORD set every man's
sword against his fellow, even throughout all the host: and the host fled to
Beth-shittah in Zererath, *and* to the border of Abelmeholah, unto Tabbath.
23 And the men of Israel gathered themselves together out of Naphtali, and
out of Asher, and out of all Manasseh, and pursued after the Midianites.
24 And Gideon sent messengers throughout all mount Ephraim, saying,
Come down against the Midianites, and take before them the waters unto

Beth-barah and Jordan. Then all the men of Ephraim gathered themselves
together, and took the waters unto Beth-barah and Jordan.
25 And they took two princes of the Midianites, Oreb and Zeeb; and they slew
Oreb upon the rock Oreb, and Zeeb they slew at the winepress of Zeeb, and
pursued Midian, and brought the heads of Oreb and Zeeb to Gideon on the
other side Jordan.

Gideon Pacifies the Ephraimites

8 And the men of Ephraim said unto him, Why hast thou served us thus, that
thou calledst us not, when thou wentest to fight with the Midianites? And
they did chide with him sharply.
2 And he said unto them, What have I done now in comparison of you? *Is*
not the gleaning of the grapes of Ephraim better than the vintage of Abiezer?
3 God hath delivered into your hands the princes of Midian, Oreb and Zeeb:
and what was I able to do in comparison of you? Then their anger was abated
toward him, when he had said that.
4 And Gideon came to Jordan, *and* passed over, he, and the three hundred
men that *were* with him, faint, yet pursuing *them*.
5 And he said unto the men of Succoth, Give, I pray you, loaves of bread unto
the people that follow me; for they *be* faint, and I am pursuing after Zebah
and Zalmunna, kings of Midian.
6 And the princes of Succoth said, *Are* the hands of Zebah and Zalmunna
now in thine hand, that we should give bread unto thine army?
7 And Gideon said, Therefore when the LORD hath delivered Zebah and
Zalmunna into mine hand, then I will tear your flesh with the thorns of the
wilderness and with briers.
8 And he went up thence to Penuel, and spake unto them likewise: and the
men of Penuel answered him as the men of Succoth had answered *him*.
9 And he spake also unto the men of Penuel, saying, When I come again in
peace, I will break down this tower.
10 Now Zebah and Zalmunna *were* in Karkor, and their hosts with them,
about fifteen thousand *men*, all that were left of all the hosts of the children
of the east: for there fell an hundred and twenty thousand men that drew
sword.
11 And Gideon went up by the way of them that dwelt in tents on the east of
Nobah and Jogbehah, and smote the host: for the host was secure.
12 And when Zebah and Zalmunna fled, he pursued after them, and took the
two kings of Midian, Zebah and Zalmunna, and discomfited all the host.
13 And Gideon the son of Joash returned from battle before the sun *was up*,
14 And caught a young man of the men of Succoth, and enquired of him: and
he described unto him the princes of Succoth, and the elders thereof, *even*
threescore and seventeen men.
15 And he came unto the men of Succoth, and said, Behold Zebah and
Zalmunna, with whom ye did upbraid me, saying, *Are* the hands of Zebah and
Zalmunna now in thine hand, that we should give bread unto thy men *that*
are weary?
16 And he took the elders of the city, and thorns of the wilderness and briers,
and with them he taught the men of Succoth.
17 And he beat down the tower of Penuel, and slew the men of the city.

Gideon Avenges His Brothers' Deaths by Killing Two Midianite Kings

18 Then said he unto Zebah and Zalmunna, What manner of men *were they*
whom ye slew at Tabor? And they answered, As thou *art*, so *were* they; each
one resembled the children of a king.
19 And he said, They *were* my brethren, *even* the sons of my mother: *as* the
LORD liveth, if ye had saved them alive, I would not slay you.
20 And he said unto Jether his firstborn, Up, *and* slay them. But the youth
drew not his sword: for he feared, because he *was* yet a youth.

21 Then Zebah and Zalmunna said, Rise thou, and fall upon us: for as the
man *is, so is* his strength. And Gideon arose, and slew Zebah and Zalmunna,
and took away the ornaments that *were* on their camels' necks.

Gideon Makes a Gold Idol

22 Then the men of Israel said unto Gideon, Rule thou over us, both thou,
and thy son, and thy son's son also: for thou hast delivered us from the hand
of Midian.
23 And Gideon said unto them, I will not rule over you, neither shall my son
rule over you: the LORD shall rule over you.
24 And Gideon said unto them, I would desire a request of you, that ye would
give me every man the earrings of his prey. (For they had golden earrings,
because they *were* Ishmaelites.)
25 And they answered, We will willingly give *them*. And they spread a gar-
ment, and did cast therein every man the earrings of his prey.
26 And the weight of the golden earrings that he requested was a thousand
and seven hundred *shekels* of gold; beside ornaments, and collars, and purple
raiment that *was* on the kings of Midian, and beside the chains that *were* about
their camels' necks.
27 And Gideon made an ephod thereof, and put it in his city, *even* in Ophrah:
and all Israel went thither a whoring after it: which thing became a snare unto
Gideon, and to his house.
28 Thus was Midian subdued before the children of Israel, so that they lifted
up their heads no more. And the country was in quietness forty years in the
days of Gideon.

Israel Returns to Idolatry

29 And Jerubbaal the son of Joash went and dwelt in his own house.
30 And Gideon had threescore and ten sons of his body begotten: for he had
many wives.
31 And his concubine that *was* in Shechem, she also bare him a son, whose
name he called Abimelech.
32 And Gideon the son of Joash died in a good old age, and was buried in the
sepulchre of Joash his father, in Ophrah of the Abiezrites.
33 And it came to pass, as soon as Gideon was dead, that the children of Israel
turned again, and went a whoring after Baalim, and made Baal-berith their
god.
34 And the children of Israel remembered not the LORD their God, who had
delivered them out of the hands of all their enemies on every side:
35 Neither shewed they kindness to the house of Jerubbaal, *namely*, Gideon,
according to all the goodness which he had shewed unto Israel.

Abimelech Kills His Brothers and Becomes King

9 And Abimelech the son of Jerubbaal went to Shechem unto his mother's
brethren, and communed with them, and with all the family of the house
of his mother's father, saying,
2 Speak, I pray you, in the ears of all the men of Shechem, Whether *is* better
for you, either that all the sons of Jerubbaal, *which are* threescore and ten
persons, reign over you, or that one reign over you? remember also that I *am*
your bone and your flesh.
3 And his mother's brethren spake of him in the ears of all the men of
Shechem all these words: and their hearts inclined to follow Abimelech; for
they said, He *is* our brother.
4 And they gave him threescore and ten *pieces* of silver out of the house of
Baal-berith, wherewith Abimelech hired vain and light persons, which fol-
lowed him.
5 And he went unto his father's house at Ophrah, and slew his brethren the
sons of Jerubbaal, *being* threescore and ten persons, upon one stone: notwith-
standing yet Jotham the youngest son of Jerubbaal was left; for he hid himself.

6 And all the men of Shechem gathered together, and all the house of Millo,
and went, and made Abimelech king, by the plain of the pillar that *was* in
Shechem.

Jotham Rebukes the Citizens of Shechem for Crowning Abimelech

7 And when they told *it* to Jotham, he went and stood in the top of mount
Gerizim, and lifted up his voice, and cried, and said unto them, Hearken unto
me, ye men of Shechem, that God may hearken unto you.
8 The trees went forth *on a time* to anoint a king over them; and they said
unto the olive tree, Reign thou over us.
9 But the olive tree said unto them, Should I leave my fatness, wherewith by
me they honour God and man, and go to be promoted over the trees?
10 And the trees said to the fig tree, Come thou, *and* reign over us.
11 But the fig tree said unto them, Should I forsake my sweetness, and my
good fruit, and go to be promoted over the trees?
12 Then said the trees unto the vine, Come thou, *and* reign over us.
13 And the vine said unto them, Should I leave my wine, which cheereth God
and man, and go to be promoted over the trees?
14 Then said all the trees unto the bramble, Come thou, *and* reign over us.
15 And the bramble said unto the trees, If in truth ye anoint me king over
you, *then* come *and* put your trust in my shadow: and if not, let fire come out
of the bramble, and devour the cedars of Lebanon.
16 Now therefore, if ye have done truly and sincerely, in that ye have made
Abimelech king, and if ye have dealt well with Jerubbaal and his house, and
have done unto him according to the deserving of his hands;
17 (For my father fought for you, and adventured his life far, and delivered
you out of the hand of Midian:
18 And ye are risen up against my father's house this day, and have slain his
sons, threescore and ten persons, upon one stone, and have made Abimelech,
the son of his maidservant, king over the men of Shechem, because he *is* your
brother;)
19 If ye then have dealt truly and sincerely with Jerubbaal and with his house
this day, *then* rejoice ye in Abimelech, and let him also rejoice in you:
20 But if not, let fire come out from Abimelech, and devour the men of
Shechem, and the house of Millo; and let fire come out from the men of
Shechem, and from the house of Millo, and devour Abimelech.
21 And Jotham ran away, and fled, and went to Beer, and dwelt there, for fear
of Abimelech his brother.

Gaal Conspires with the Shechemites against Abimelech

22 When Abimelech had reigned three years over Israel,
23 Then God sent an evil spirit between Abimelech and the men of Shechem;
and the men of Shechem dealt treacherously with Abimelech:
24 That the cruelty *done* to the threescore and ten sons of Jerubbaal might
come, and their blood be laid upon Abimelech their brother, which slew them;
and upon the men of Shechem, which aided him in the killing of his brethren.
25 And the men of Shechem set liers in wait for him in the top of the moun-
tains, and they robbed all that came along that way by them: and it was told
Abimelech.
26 And Gaal the son of Ebed came with his brethren, and went over to
Shechem: and the men of Shechem put their confidence in him.
27 And they went out into the fields, and gathered their vineyards, and trode
the grapes, and made merry, and went into the house of their god, and did eat
and drink, and cursed Abimelech.
28 And Gaal the son of Ebed said, Who *is* Abimelech, and who *is* Shechem,
that we should serve him? *is* not *he* the son of Jerubbaal? and Zebul his officer?
serve the men of Hamor the father of Shechem: for why should we serve him?

29 And would to God this people were under my hand! then would I remove
Abimelech. And he said to Abimelech, Increase thine army, and come out.
30 And when Zebul the ruler of the city heard the words of Gaal the son of
Ebed, his anger was kindled.
31 And he sent messengers unto Abimelech privily, saying, Behold, Gaal the
son of Ebed and his brethren be come to Shechem; and, behold, they fortify
the city against thee.
32 Now therefore up by night, thou and the people that *is* with thee, and lie
in wait in the field:
33 And it shall be, *that* in the morning, as soon as the sun is up, thou shalt
rise early, and set upon the city: and, behold, *when* he and the people that *is*
with him come out against thee, then mayest thou do to them as thou shalt
find occasion.
34 And Abimelech rose up, and all the people that *were* with him, by night,
and they laid wait against Shechem in four companies.
35 And Gaal the son of Ebed went out, and stood in the entering of the gate
of the city: and Abimelech rose up, and the people that *were* with him, from
lying in wait.
36 And when Gaal saw the people, he said to Zebul, Behold, there come peo-
ple down from the top of the mountains. And Zebul said unto him, Thou seest
the shadow of the mountains as *if they were* men.
37 And Gaal spake again and said, See there come people down by the middle
of the land, and another company come along by the plain of Meonenim.
38 Then said Zebul unto him, Where *is* now thy mouth, wherewith thou
saidst, Who *is* Abimelech, that we should serve him? *is* not this the people that
thou hast despised? go out, I pray now, and fight with them.
39 And Gaal went out before the men of Shechem, and fought with Abimelech.
40 And Abimelech chased him, and he fled before him, and many were over-
thrown *and* wounded, *even* unto the entering of the gate.
41 And Abimelech dwelt at Arumah: and Zebul thrust out Gaal and his breth-
ren, that they should not dwell in Shechem.
42 And it came to pass on the morrow, that the people went out into the field;
and they told Abimelech.
43 And he took the people, and divided them into three companies, and laid
wait in the field, and looked, and, behold, the people *were* come forth out of
the city; and he rose up against them, and smote them.
44 And Abimelech, and the company that *was* with him, rushed forward,
and stood in the entering of the gate of the city: and the two *other* companies
ran upon all *the people* that *were* in the fields, and slew them.
45 And Abimelech fought against the city all that day; and he took the city,
and slew the people that *was* therein, and beat down the city, and sowed it
with salt.
46 And when all the men of the tower of Shechem heard *that*, they entered
into an hold of the house of the god Berith.
47 And it was told Abimelech, that all the men of the tower of Shechem were
gathered together.
48 And Abimelech gat him up to mount Zalmon, he and all the people that
were with him; and Abimelech took an axe in his hand, and cut down a bough
from the trees, and took it, and laid *it* on his shoulder, and said unto the peo-
ple that *were* with him, What ye have seen me do, make haste, *and* do as I *have*
done.
49 And all the people likewise cut down every man his bough, and followed
Abimelech, and put *them* to the hold, and set the hold on fire upon them; so
that all the men of the tower of Shechem died also, about a thousand men and
women.

Abimelech Is Killed by a Millstone Dropped from the City Wall
50 Then went Abimelech to Thebez, and encamped against Thebez, and
took it.
51 But there was a strong tower within the city, and thither fled all the men
and women, and all they of the city, and shut *it* to them, and gat them up to
the top of the tower.
52 And Abimelech came unto the tower, and fought against it, and went hard
unto the door of the tower to burn it with fire.
53 And a certain woman cast a piece of a millstone upon Abimelech's head,
and all to brake his skull.
54 Then he called hastily unto the young man his armourbearer, and said
unto him, Draw thy sword, and slay me, that men say not of me, A woman slew
him. And his young man thrust him through, and he died.
55 And when the men of Israel saw that Abimelech was dead, they departed
every man unto his place.
56 Thus God rendered the wickedness of Abimelech, which he did unto his
father, in slaying his seventy brethren:
57 And all the evil of the men of Shechem did God render upon their heads:
and upon them came the curse of Jotham the son of Jerubbaal.

Tola and Jair Serve as Judges
10 And after Abimelech there arose to defend Israel Tola the son of Puah,
the son of Dodo, a man of Issachar; and he dwelt in Shamir in mount
Ephraim.
2 And he judged Israel twenty and three years, and died, and was buried in
Shamir.
3 And after him arose Jair, a Gileadite, and judged Israel twenty and two
years.
4 And he had thirty sons that rode on thirty ass colts, and they had thirty
cities, which are called Havothjair unto this day, which *are* in the land of
Gilead.
5 And Jair died, and was buried in Camon.

The Philistines and Ammonites Oppress Israel
6 And the children of Israel did evil again in the sight of the LORD, and served
Baalim, and Ashtaroth, and the gods of Syria, and the gods of Zidon, and the
gods of Moab, and the gods of the children of Ammon, and the gods of the
Philistines, and forsook the LORD, and served not him.
7 And the anger of the LORD was hot against Israel, and he sold them into the
hands of the Philistines, and into the hands of the children of Ammon.
8 And that year they vexed and oppressed the children of Israel: eighteen
years, all the children of Israel that *were* on the other side Jordan in the land
of the Amorites, which *is* in Gilead.
9 Moreover the children of Ammon passed over Jordan to fight also against
Judah, and against Benjamin, and against the house of Ephraim; so that Israel
was sore distressed.

God Chides the People for Their Trust in Idols
10 And the children of Israel cried unto the LORD, saying, We have sinned
against thee, both because we have forsaken our God, and also served Baalim.
11 And the LORD said unto the children of Israel, *Did* not *I deliver you* from
the Egyptians, and from the Amorites, from the children of Ammon, and from
the Philistines?
12 The Zidonians also, and the Amalekites, and the Maonites, did oppress
you; and ye cried to me, and I delivered you out of their hand.
13 Yet ye have forsaken me, and served other gods: wherefore I will deliver
you no more.
14 Go and cry unto the gods which ye have chosen; let them deliver you in
the time of your tribulation.

15 And the children of Israel said unto the LORD, We have sinned: do thou
unto us whatsoever seemeth good unto thee; deliver us only, we pray thee, this
day.
16 And they put away the strange gods from among them, and served the
LORD: and his soul was grieved for the misery of Israel.
17 Then the children of Ammon were gathered together, and encamped in
Gilead. And the children of Israel assembled themselves together, and encamp-
ed in Mizpeh.
18 And the people *and* princes of Gilead said one to another, What man *is*
he that will begin to fight against the children of Ammon? he shall be head
over all the inhabitants of Gilead.

The Covenant between Jephthah and Gilead

11 Now Jephthah the Gileadite was a mighty man of valour, and he *was*
the son of an harlot: and Gilead begat Jephthah.
2 And Gilead's wife bare him sons; and his wife's sons grew up, and they thrust
out Jephthah, and said unto him, Thou shalt not inherit in our father's house;
for thou *art* the son of a strange woman.
3 Then Jephthah fled from his brethren, and dwelt in the land of Tob: and
there were gathered vain men to Jephthah, and went out with him.
4 And it came to pass in process of time, that the children of Ammon made
war against Israel.
5 And it was so, that when the children of Ammon made war against Israel,
the elders of Gilead went to fetch Jephthah out of the land of Tob:
6 And they said unto Jephthah, Come, and be our captain, that we may fight
with the children of Ammon.
7 And Jephthah said unto the elders of Gilead, Did not ye hate me, and expel
me out of my father's house? and why are ye come unto me now when ye are
in distress?
8 And the elders of Gilead said unto Jephthah, Therefore we turn again to
thee now, that thou mayest go with us, and fight against the children of
Ammon, and be our head over all the inhabitants of Gilead.
9 And Jephthah said unto the elders of Gilead, If ye bring me home again to
fight against the children of Ammon, and the LORD deliver them before me,
shall I be your head?
10 And the elders of Gilead said unto Jephthah, The LORD be witness between
us, if we do not so according to thy words.
11 Then Jephthah went with the elders of Gilead, and the people made him
head and captain over them: and Jephthah uttered all his words before the
LORD in Mizpeh.

The Ammonites Reject Jephthah's Plea for Peace

12 And Jephthah sent messengers unto the king of the children of Ammon,
saying, What hast thou to do with me, that thou art come against me to fight
in my land?
13 And the king of the children of Ammon answered unto the messengers
of Jephthah, Because Israel took away my land, when they came up out of
Egypt, from Arnon even unto Jabbok, and unto Jordan: now therefore restore
those *lands* again peaceably.
14 And Jephthah sent messengers again unto the king of the children of
Ammon:
15 And said unto him, Thus saith Jephthah, Israel took not away the land of
Moab, nor the land of the children of Ammon:
16 But when Israel came up from Egypt, and walked through the wilderness
unto the Red sea, and came to Kadesh;
17 Then Israel sent messengers unto the king of Edom, saying, Let me, I pray
thee, pass through thy land: but the king of Edom would not hearken *thereto*.

And in like manner they sent unto the king of Moab: but he would not *consent*:
and Israel abode in Kadesh.
18 Then they went along through the wilderness, and compassed the land
of Edom, and the land of Moab, and came by the east side of the land of Moab,
and pitched on the other side of Arnon, but came not within the border of
Moab: for Arnon *was* the border of Moab.
19 And Israel sent messengers unto Sihon king of the Amorites, the king of
Heshbon; and Israel said unto him, Let us pass, we pray thee, through thy land
into my place.
20 But Sihon trusted not Israel to pass through his coast: but Sihon gathered
all his people together, and pitched in Jahaz, and fought against Israel.
21 And the Lord God of Israel delivered Sihon and all his people into the
hand of Israel, and they smote them: so Israel possessed all the land of the
Amorites, the inhabitants of that country.
22 And they possessed all the coasts of the Amorites, from Arnon even unto
Jabbok, and from the wilderness even unto Jordan.
23 So now the Lord God of Israel hath dispossessed the Amorites from before
his people Israel, and shouldest thou possess it?
24 Wilt not thou possess that which Chemosh thy god giveth thee to possess?
So whomsoever the Lord our God shall drive out from before us, them will
we possess.
25 And now *art* thou any thing better than Balak the son of Zippor, king of
Moab? did he ever strive against Israel, or did he ever fight against them,
26 While Israel dwelt in Heshbon and her towns, and in Aroer and her towns,
and in all the cities that *be* along by the coasts of Arnon, three hundred years?
why therefore did ye not recover *them* within that time?
27 Wherefore I have not sinned against thee, but thou doest me wrong to
war against me: the Lord the Judge be judge this day between the children of
Israel and the children of Ammon.
28 Howbeit the king of the children of Ammon hearkened not unto the
words of Jephthah which he sent him.

Jephthah's Vow and His Conquest of the Ammonites

29 Then the Spirit of the Lord came upon Jephthah, and he passed over
Gilead, and Manasseh, and passed over Mizpeh of Gilead, and from Mizpeh
of Gilead he passed over *unto* the children of Ammon.
30 And Jephthah vowed a vow unto the Lord, and said, If thou shalt without
fail deliver the children of Ammon into mine hands,
31 Then it shall be, that whatsoever cometh forth of the doors of my house
to meet me, when I return in peace from the children of Ammon, shall surely
be the Lord's, and I will offer it up for a burnt offering.
32 So Jephthah passed over unto the children of Ammon to fight against
them; and the Lord delivered them into his hands.
33 And he smote them from Aroer, even till thou come to Minnith, *even* twen-
ty cities, and unto the plain of the vineyards, with a very great slaughter. Thus
the children of Ammon were subdued before the children of Israel.
34 And Jephthah came to Mizpeh unto his house, and, behold, his daughter
came out to meet him with timbrels and with dances: and she *was his* only
child; beside her he had neither son nor daughter.
35 And it came to pass, when he saw her, that he rent his clothes, and said,
Alas, my daughter! thou hast brought me very low, and thou art one of them
that trouble me: for I have opened my mouth unto the Lord, and I cannot go
back.
36 And she said unto him, My father, *if* thou hast opened thy mouth unto the
Lord, do to me according to that which hath proceeded out of thy mouth;
forasmuch as the Lord hath taken vengeance for thee of thine enemies, *even*
of the children of Ammon.

37 And she said unto her father, Let this thing be done for me: let me alone
two months, that I may go up and down upon the mountains, and bewail my
virginity, I and my fellows.
38 And he said, Go. And he sent her away *for* two months: and she went with
her companions, and bewailed her virginity upon the mountains.
39 And it came to pass at the end of two months, that she returned unto her
father, who did with her *according* to his vow which he had vowed: and she
knew no man. And it was a custom in Israel,
40 *That* the daughters of Israel went yearly to lament the daughter of
Jephthah the Gileadite four days in a year.

The Ephraimites, Quarreling with Jephthah, Are Slain by the Gileadites

12 And the men of Ephraim gathered themselves together, and went
northward, and said unto Jephthah, Wherefore passedst thou over to
fight against the children of Ammon, and didst not call us to go with thee? we
will burn thine house upon thee with fire.
2 And Jephthah said unto them, I and my people were at great strife with the
children of Ammon; and when I called you, ye delivered me not out of their
hands.
3 And when I saw that ye delivered *me* not, I put my life in my hands, and
passed over against the children of Ammon, and the LORD delivered them into
my hand: wherefore then are ye come up unto me this day, to fight against
me?
4 Then Jephthah gathered together all the men of Gilead, and fought with
Ephraim: and the men of Gilead smote Ephraim, because they said, Ye
Gileadites *are* fugitives of Ephraim among the Ephraimites, *and* among the
Manassites.
5 And the Gileadites took the passages of Jordan before the Ephraimites: and
it was *so*, that when those Ephraimites which were escaped said, Let me go
over; that the men of Gilead said unto him, *Art* thou an Ephraimite? If he said,
Nay;
6 Then said they unto him, Say now Shibboleth: and he said Sibboleth: for
he could not frame to pronounce *it* right. Then they took him, and slew him
at the passages of Jordan: and there fell at that time of the Ephraimites forty
and two thousand.
7 And Jephthah judged Israel six years. Then died Jephthah the Gileadite,
and was buried in *one of* the cities of Gilead.

Ibzan, Elon, and Abdon Serve as Judges

8 And after him Ibzan of Beth-lehem judged Israel.
9 And he had thirty sons, and thirty daughters, *whom* he sent abroad, and
took in thirty daughters from abroad for his sons. And he judged Israel seven
years.
10 Then died Ibzan, and was buried at Beth-lehem.
11 And after him Elon, a Zebulonite, judged Israel; and he judged Israel ten
years.
12 And Elon the Zebulonite died, and was buried in Aijalon in the country
of Zebulun.
13 And after him Abdon the son of Hillel, a Pirathonite, judged Israel.
14 And he had forty sons and thirty nephews, that rode on threescore and
ten ass colts: and he judged Israel eight years.
15 And Abdon the son of Hillel the Pirathonite died, and was buried in
Pirathon in the land of Ephraim, in the mount of the Amalekites.

Israel Conquered by the Philistines

13 And the children of Israel did evil again in the sight of the LORD; and
the LORD delivered them into the hand of the Philistines forty years.
2 And there was a certain man of Zorah, of the family of the Danites, whose
name *was* Manoah; and his wife *was* barren, and bare not.

3 And the angel of the LORD appeared unto the woman, and said unto her,
Behold now, thou *art* barren, and bearest not: but thou shalt conceive, and
bear a son.
4 Now therefore beware, I pray thee, and drink not wine nor strong drink,
and eat not any unclean *thing*:
5 For, lo, thou shalt conceive, and bear a son; and no razor shall come on his
head: for the child shall be a Nazarite unto God from the womb: and he shall
begin to deliver Israel out of the hand of the Philistines.
6 Then the woman came and told her husband, saying, A man of God came
unto me, and his countenance *was* like the countenance of an angel of God,
very terrible: but I asked him not whence he *was*, neither told he me his name:
7 But he said unto me, Behold, thou shalt conceive, and bear a son; and now
drink no wine nor strong drink, neither eat any unclean *thing*: for the child
shall be a Nazarite to God from the womb to the day of his death.
8 Then Manoah intreated the LORD, and said, O my Lord, let the man of God
which thou didst send come again unto us, and teach us what we shall do unto
the child that shall be born.
9 And God hearkened to the voice of Manoah; and the angel of God came
again unto the woman as she sat in the field: but Manoah her husband *was*
not with her.
10 And the woman made haste, and ran, and shewed her husband, and said
unto him, Behold, the man hath appeared unto me, that came unto me the
other day.
11 And Manoah arose, and went after his wife, and came to the man, and said
unto him, *Art* thou the man that spakest unto the woman? And he said, I *am*.
12 And Manoah said, Now let thy words come to pass. How shall we order
the child, and *how* shall we do unto him?
13 And the angel of the LORD said unto Manoah, Of all that I said unto the
woman let her beware.
14 She may not eat of any *thing* that cometh of the vine, neither let her drink
wine or strong drink, nor eat any unclean *thing*: all that I commanded her let
her observe.

Manoah's Sacrifice Identifies the Angel

15 And Manoah said unto the angel of the LORD, I pray thee, let us detain
thee, until we shall have made ready a kid for thee.
16 And the angel of the LORD said unto Manoah, Though thou detain me, I
will not eat of thy bread: and if thou wilt offer a burnt offering, thou must
offer it unto the LORD. For Manoah knew not that he *was* an angel of the LORD.
17 And Manoah said unto the angel of the LORD, What *is* thy name, that when
thy sayings come to pass we may do thee honour?
18 And the angel of the LORD said unto him, Why askest thou thus after my
name, seeing it *is* secret?
19 So Manoah took a kid with a meat offering, and offered *it* upon a rock unto
the LORD: and *the angel* did wondrously; and Manoah and his wife looked on.
20 For it came to pass, when the flame went up toward heaven from off the
altar, that the angel of the LORD ascended in the flame of the altar. And Manoah
and his wife looked on *it*, and fell on their faces to the ground.
21 But the angel of the LORD did no more appear to Manoah and to his wife.
Then Manoah knew that he *was* an angel of the LORD.
22 And Manoah said unto his wife, We shall surely die, because we have seen
God.
23 But his wife said unto him, If the LORD were pleased to kill us, he would
not have received a burnt offering and a meat offering at our hands, neither
would he have shewed us all these *things*, nor would as at this time have told
us *such things* as these.

Samson Is Born

24 And the woman bare a son, and called his name Samson: and the child grew, and the LORD blessed him.

25 And the Spirit of the LORD began to move him at times in the camp of Dan between Zorah and Eshtaol.

Samson Desires a Wife of the Philistines

14 And Samson went down to Timnath, and saw a woman in Timnath of the daughters of the Philistines.

2 And he came up, and told his father and his mother, and said, I have seen a woman in Timnath of the daughters of the Philistines: now therefore get her for me to wife.

3 Then his father and his mother said unto him, *Is there* never a woman among the daughters of thy brethren, or among all my people, that thou goest to take a wife of the uncircumcised Philistines? And Samson said unto his father, Get her for me; for she pleaseth me well.

4 But his father and his mother knew not that it *was* of the LORD, that he sought an occasion against the Philistines: for at that time the Philistines had dominion over Israel.

5 Then went Samson down, and his father and his mother, to Timnath, and came to the vineyards of Timnath: and, behold, a young lion roared against him.

6 And the Spirit of the LORD came mightily upon him, and he rent him as he would have rent a kid, and *he had* nothing in his hand: but he told not his father or his mother what he had done.

7 And he went down, and talked with the woman; and she pleased Samson well.

8 And after a time he returned to take her, and he turned aside to see the carcase of the lion: and, behold, *there was* a swarm of bees and honey in the carcase of the lion.

9 And he took thereof in his hands, and went on eating, and came to his father and mother, and he gave them, and they did eat: but he told not them that he had taken the honey out of the carcase of the lion.

Samson's Marriage Feast

10 So his father went down unto the woman: and Samson made there a feast; for so used the young men to do.

11 And it came to pass, when they saw him, that they brought thirty companions to be with him.

12 And Samson said unto them, I will now put forth a riddle unto you: if ye can certainly declare it me within the seven days of the feast, and find *it* out, then I will give you thirty sheets and thirty change of garments:

13 But if ye cannot declare *it* me, then shall ye give me thirty sheets and thirty change of garments. And they said unto him, Put forth thy riddle, that we may hear it.

14 And he said unto them, Out of the eater came forth meat, and out of the strong came forth sweetness. And they could not in three days expound the riddle.

15 And it came to pass on the seventh day, that they said unto Samson's wife, Entice thy husband, that he may declare unto us the riddle, lest we burn thee and thy father's house with fire: have ye called us to take that we have? *is it* not *so*?

16 And Samson's wife wept before him, and said, Thou dost but hate me, and lovest me not: thou hast put forth a riddle unto the children of my people, and hast not told *it* me. And he said unto her, Behold, I have not told *it* my father nor my mother, and shall I tell *it* thee?

17 And she wept before him the seven days, while their feast lasted: and it
came to pass on the seventh day, that he told her, because she lay sore upon
him: and she told the riddle to the children of her people.
18 And the men of the city said unto him on the seventh day before the sun
went down, What *is* sweeter than honey? and what *is* stronger than a lion?
And he said unto them, If ye had not plowed with my heifer, ye had not found
out my riddle.
19 And the Spirit of the LORD came upon him, and he went down to Ashkelon,
and slew thirty men of them, and took their spoil, and gave change of garments
unto them which expounded the riddle. And his anger was kindled, and he
went up to his father's house.
20 But Samson's wife was *given* to his companion, whom he had used as his
friend.

Samson Serves as a Judge

15 But it came to pass within a while after, in the time of wheat harvest,
that Samson visited his wife with a kid; and he said, I will go in to my
wife into the chamber. But her father would not suffer him to go in.
2 And her father said, I verily thought that thou hadst utterly hated her;
therefore I gave her to thy companion: *is* not her younger sister fairer than
she? take her, I pray thee, instead of her.
3 And Samson said concerning them, Now shall I be more blameless than
the Philistines, though I do them a displeasure.
4 And Samson went and caught three hundred foxes, and took firebrands,
and turned tail to tail, and put a firebrand in the midst between two tails.
5 And when he had set the brands on fire, he let *them* go into the standing
corn of the Philistines, and burnt up both the shocks, and also the standing
corn, with the vineyards *and* olives.
6 Then the Philistines said, Who hath done this? And they answered, Samson,
the son in law of the Timnite, because he had taken his wife, and given her to
his companion. And the Philistines came up, and burnt her and her father
with fire.
7 And Samson said unto them, Though ye have done this, yet will I be avenged
of you, and after that I will cease.
8 And he smote them hip and thigh with a great slaughter: and he went down
and dwelt in the top of the rock Etam.

Samson Kills a Thousand Philistines with a Donkey's Jawbone

9 Then the Philistines went up, and pitched in Judah, and spread themselves
in Lehi.
10 And the men of Judah said, Why are ye come up against us? And they
answered, To bind Samson are we come up, to do to him as he hath done
to us.
11 Then three thousand men of Judah went to the top of the rock Etam, and
said to Samson, Knowest thou not that the Philistines *are* rulers over us? what
is this *that* thou hast done unto us? And he said unto them, As they did unto
me, so have I done unto them.
12 And they said unto him, We are come down to bind thee, that we may
deliver thee into the hand of the Philistines. And Samson said unto them,
Swear unto me, that ye will not fall upon me yourselves.
13 And they spake unto him, saying, No; but we will bind thee fast, and deliv-
er thee into their hand: but surely we will not kill thee. And they bound him
with two new cords, and brought him up from the rock.
14 *And* when he came unto Lehi, the Philistines shouted against him: and
the Spirit of the LORD came mightily upon him, and the cords that *were* upon
his arms became as flax that was burnt with fire, and his bands loosed from
off his hands.

15 And he found a new jawbone of an ass, and put forth his hand, and took
it, and slew a thousand men therewith.
16 And Samson said, With the jawbone of an ass, heaps upon heaps, with the
jaw of an ass have I slain a thousand men.
17 And it came to pass, when he had made an end of speaking, that he cast
away the jawbone out of his hand, and called that place Ramath-lehi.

God Provides a Fountain for Samson to Quench His Thirst

18 And he was sore athirst, and called on the LORD, and said, Thou hast given
this great deliverance into the hand of thy servant: and now shall I die for
thirst, and fall into the hand of the uncircumcised?
19 But God clave an hollow place that *was* in the jaw, and there came water
thereout; and when he had drunk, his spirit came again, and he revived: where-
fore he called the name thereof En-hakkore, which *is* in Lehi unto this day.
20 And he judged Israel in the days of the Philistines twenty years.

Samson Escapes from Gaza and Carries Away the City Gates

16 Then went Samson to Gaza, and saw there an harlot, and went in unto
her.
2 *And it was told* the Gazites, saying, Samson is come hither. And they com-
passed *him* in, and laid wait for him all night in the gate of the city, and were
quiet all the night, saying, In the morning, when it is day, we shall kill him.
3 And Samson lay till midnight, and arose at midnight, and took the doors
of the gate of the city, and the two posts, and went away with them, bar and
all, and put *them* upon his shoulders, and carried them up to the top of an hill
that *is* before Hebron.

Delilah Entices Samson to Tell Her the Secret of His Strength

4 And it came to pass afterward, that he loved a woman in the valley of Sorek,
whose name *was* Delilah.
5 And the lords of the Philistines came up unto her, and said unto her, Entice
him, and see wherein his great strength *lieth*, and by what *means* we may
prevail against him, that we may bind him to afflict him: and we will give thee
every one of us eleven hundred *pieces* of silver.
6 And Delilah said to Samson, Tell me, I pray thee, wherein thy great strength
lieth, and wherewith thou mightest be bound to afflict thee.
7 And Samson said unto her, If they bind me with seven green withs that
were never dried, then shall I be weak, and be as another man.
8 Then the lords of the Philistines brought up to her seven green withs which
had not been dried, and she bound him with them.
9 Now *there were* men lying in wait, abiding with her in the chamber. And
she said unto him, The Philistines *be* upon thee, Samson. And he brake the
withs, as a thread of tow is broken when it toucheth the fire. So his strength
was not known.
10 And Delilah said unto Samson, Behold, thou hast mocked me, and told
me lies: now tell me, I pray thee, wherewith thou mightest be bound.
11 And he said unto her, If they bind me fast with new ropes that never were
occupied, then shall I be weak, and be as another man.
12 Delilah therefore took new ropes, and bound him therewith, and said
unto him, The Philistines *be* upon thee, Samson. And *there were* liers in wait
abiding in the chamber. And he brake them from off his arms like a thread.
13 And Delilah said unto Samson, Hitherto thou hast mocked me, and told
me lies: tell me wherewith thou mightest be bound. And he said unto her, If
thou weavest the seven locks of my head with the web.
14 And she fastened *it* with the pin, and said unto him, The Philistines *be*
upon thee, Samson. And he awaked out of his sleep, and went away with the
pin of the beam, and with the web.

15 And she said unto him, How canst thou say, I love thee, when thine heart
is not with me? thou hast mocked me these three times, and hast not told me
wherein thy great strength *lieth*.
16 And it came to pass, when she pressed him daily with her words, and urged
him, *so* that his soul was vexed unto death;
17 That he told her all his heart, and said unto her, There hath not come a
razor upon mine head; for I *have been* a Nazarite unto God from my mother's
womb: if I be shaven, then my strength will go from me, and I shall become
weak, and be like any *other* man.
18 And when Delilah saw that he had told her all his heart, she sent and called
for the lords of the Philistines, saying, Come up this once, for he hath shewed
me all his heart. Then the lords of the Philistines came up unto her, and
brought money in their hand.
19 And she made him sleep upon her knees; and she called for a man, and
she caused him to shave off the seven locks of his head; and she began to afflict
him, and his strength went from him.
20 And she said, The Philistines *be* upon thee, Samson. And he awoke out of
his sleep, and said, I will go out as at other times before, and shake myself. And
he wist not that the LORD was departed from him.
21 But the Philistines took him, and put out his eyes, and brought him down
to Gaza, and bound him with fetters of brass; and he did grind in the prison
house.

Samson's Final Act Kills Many Philistines

22 Howbeit the hair of his head began to grow again after he was shaven.
23 Then the lords of the Philistines gathered them together for to offer a
great sacrifice unto Dagon their god, and to rejoice: for they said, Our god
hath delivered Samson our enemy into our hand.
24 And when the people saw him, they praised their god: for they said, Our
god hath delivered into our hands our enemy, and the destroyer of our country, which slew many of us.
25 And it came to pass, when their hearts were merry, that they said, Call for
Samson, that he may make us sport. And they called for Samson out of the
prison house; and he made them sport: and they set him between the pillars.
26 And Samson said unto the lad that held him by the hand, Suffer me that
I may feel the pillars whereupon the house standeth, that I may lean upon
them.
27 Now the house was full of men and women; and all the lords of the
Philistines *were* there; and *there were* upon the roof about three thousand
men and women, that beheld while Samson made sport.
28 And Samson called unto the LORD, and said, O Lord GOD, remember me,
I pray thee, and strengthen me, I pray thee, only this once, O God, that I may
be at once avenged of the Philistines for my two eyes.
29 And Samson took hold of the two middle pillars upon which the house
stood, and on which it was borne up, of the one with his right hand, and of
the other with his left.
30 And Samson said, Let me die with the Philistines. And he bowed himself
with *all his* might; and the house fell upon the lords, and upon all the people
that *were* therein. So the dead which he slew at his death were more than *they*
which he slew in his life.
31 Then his brethren and all the house of his father came down, and took
him, and brought *him* up, and buried him between Zorah and Eshtaol in the
buryingplace of Manoah his father. And he judged Israel twenty years.

Micah Builds an Idol and a Shrine for Worship

17 And there was a man of mount Ephraim, whose name *was* Micah.
2 And he said unto his mother, The eleven hundred *shekels* of silver
that were taken from thee, about which thou cursedst, and spakest of also in

mine ears, behold, the silver *is* with me; I took it. And his mother said, Blessed
be thou of the LORD, my son.
3 And when he had restored the eleven hundred *shekels* of silver to his moth-
er, his mother said, I had wholly dedicated the silver unto the LORD from my
hand for my son, to make a graven image and a molten image: now therefore
I will restore it unto thee.
4 Yet he restored the money unto his mother; and his mother took two hun-
dred *shekels* of silver, and gave them to the founder, who made thereof a grav-
en image and a molten image: and they were in the house of Micah.
5 And the man Micah had an house of gods, and made an ephod, and tera-
phim, and consecrated one of his sons, who became his priest.
6 In those days *there was* no king in Israel, *but* every man did *that which was*
right in his own eyes.

Micah Hires a Levite to Be Priest

7 And there was a young man out of Beth-lehem-judah of the family of Judah,
who *was* a Levite, and he sojourned there.
8 And the man departed out of the city from Beth-lehem-judah to sojourn
where he could find *a place*: and he came to mount Ephraim to the house of
Micah, as he journeyed.
9 And Micah said unto him, Whence comest thou? And he said unto him, I
am a Levite of Beth-lehem-judah, and I go to sojourn where I may find *a place*.
10 And Micah said unto him, Dwell with me, and be unto me a father and a
priest, and I will give thee ten *shekels* of silver by the year, and a suit of appar-
el, and thy victuals. So the Levite went in.
11 And the Levite was content to dwell with the man; and the young man was
unto him as one of his sons.
12 And Micah consecrated the Levite; and the young man became his priest,
and was in the house of Micah.
13 Then said Micah, Now know I that the LORD will do me good, seeing I have
a Levite to *my* priest.

The Tribe of Dan Looks for Land to Conquer

18 In those days *there was* no king in Israel: and in those days the tribe of
the Danites sought them an inheritance to dwell in; for unto that day
all their inheritance had not fallen unto them among the tribes of Israel.
2 And the children of Dan sent of their family five men from their coasts,
men of valour, from Zorah, and from Eshtaol, to spy out the land, and to search
it; and they said unto them, Go, search the land: who when they came to mount
Ephraim, to the house of Micah, they lodged there.
3 When they *were* by the house of Micah, they knew the voice of the young
man the Levite: and they turned in thither, and said unto him, Who brought
thee hither? and what makest thou in this *place*? and what hast thou here?
4 And he said unto them, Thus and thus dealeth Micah with me, and hath
hired me, and I am his priest.
5 And they said unto him, Ask counsel, we pray thee, of God, that we may
know whether our way which we go shall be prosperous.
6 And the priest said unto them, Go in peace: before the LORD *is* your way
wherein ye go.

The Tribe of Dan Decides to Attack the City of Laish

7 Then the five men departed, and came to Laish, and saw the people that
were therein, how they dwelt careless, after the manner of the Zidonians, quiet
and secure; and *there was* no magistrate in the land, that might put *them* to
shame in *any* thing; and they *were* far from the Zidonians, and had no business
with *any* man.
8 And they came unto their brethren to Zorah and Eshtaol: and their breth-
ren said unto them, What *say* ye?

9 And they said, Arise, that we may go up against them: for we have seen the
land, and, behold, it *is* very good: and *are* ye still? be not slothful to go, *and* to
enter to possess the land.
10 When ye go, ye shall come unto a people secure, and to a large land: for
God hath given it into your hands; a place where *there is* no want of any thing
that *is* in the earth.
11 And there went from thence of the family of the Danites, out of Zorah and
out of Eshtaol, six hundred men appointed with weapons of war.
12 And they went up, and pitched in Kirjath-jearim, in Judah: wherefore they
called that place Mahaneh-dan unto this day: behold, *it is* behind Kirjath-
jearim.
13 And they passed thence unto mount Ephraim, and came unto the house
of Micah.

The People of Dan Steal Micah's Idols and His Priest

14 Then answered the five men that went to spy out the country of Laish, and
said unto their brethren, Do ye know that there is in these houses an ephod,
and teraphim, and a graven image, and a molten image? now therefore con-
sider what ye have to do.
15 And they turned thitherward, and came to the house of the young man
the Levite, *even* unto the house of Micah, and saluted him.
16 And the six hundred men appointed with their weapons of war, which
were of the children of Dan, stood by the entering of the gate.
17 And the five men that went to spy out the land went up, *and* came in
thither, *and* took the graven image, and the ephod, and the teraphim, and the
molten image: and the priest stood in the entering of the gate with the six
hundred men *that were* appointed with weapons of war.
18 And these went into Micah's house, and fetched the carved image, the
ephod, and the teraphim, and the molten image. Then said the priest unto
them, What do ye?
19 And they said unto him, Hold thy peace, lay thine hand upon thy mouth,
and go with us, and be to us a father and a priest: *is it* better for thee to be a
priest unto the house of one man, or that thou be a priest unto a tribe and a
family in Israel?
20 And the priest's heart was glad, and he took the ephod, and the teraphim,
and the graven image, and went in the midst of the people.
21 So they turned and departed, and put the little ones and the cattle and the
carriage before them.
22 *And* when they were a good way from the house of Micah, the men that
were in the houses near to Micah's house were gathered together, and overtook
the children of Dan.
23 And they cried unto the children of Dan. And they turned their faces, and
said unto Micah, What aileth thee, that thou comest with such a company?
24 And he said, Ye have taken away my gods which I made, and the priest,
and ye are gone away: and what have I more? and what *is* this *that* ye say unto
me, What aileth thee?
25 And the children of Dan said unto him, Let not thy voice be heard among
us, lest angry fellows run upon thee, and thou lose thy life, with the lives of
thy household.
26 And the children of Dan went their way: and when Micah saw that they
were too strong for him, he turned and went back unto his house.

Laish Is Destroyed and Renamed Dan

27 And they took *the things* which Micah had made, and the priest which he
had, and came unto Laish, unto a people *that were* at quiet and secure: and
they smote them with the edge of the sword, and burnt the city with fire.

28 And *there was* no deliverer, because it *was* far from Zidon, and they had
no business with *any* man; and it was in the valley that *lieth* by Beth-rehob.
And they built a city, and dwelt therein.
29 And they called the name of the city Dan, after the name of Dan their
father, who was born unto Israel: howbeit the name of the city *was* Laish at
the first.
30 And the children of Dan set up the graven image: and Jonathan, the son
of Gershom, the son of Manasseh, he and his sons were priests to the tribe of
Dan until the day of the captivity of the land.
31 And they set them up Micah's graven image, which he made, all the time
that the house of God was in Shiloh.

A Levite Persuades His Unfaithful Wife to Return to Him

19 And it came to pass in those days, when *there was* no king in Israel,
that there was a certain Levite sojourning on the side of mount
Ephraim, who took to him a concubine out of Beth-lehem-judah.
2 And his concubine played the whore against him, and went away from him
unto her father's house to Beth-lehem-judah, and was there four whole
months.
3 And her husband arose, and went after her, to speak friendly unto her, *and*
to bring her again, having his servant with him, and a couple of asses: and she
brought him into her father's house: and when the father of the damsel saw
him, he rejoiced to meet him.
4 And his father in law, the damsel's father, retained him; and he abode with
him three days: so they did eat and drink, and lodged there.
5 And it came to pass on the fourth day, when they arose early in the morn-
ing, that he rose up to depart: and the damsel's father said unto his son in law,
Comfort thine heart with a morsel of bread, and afterward go your way.
6 And they sat down, and did eat and drink both of them together: for the
damsel's father had said unto the man, Be content, I pray thee, and tarry all
night, and let thine heart be merry.
7 And when the man rose up to depart, his father in law urged him: therefore
he lodged there again.
8 And he arose early in the morning on the fifth day to depart: and the dam-
sel's father said, Comfort thine heart, I pray thee. And they tarried until after-
noon, and they did eat both of them.
9 And when the man rose up to depart, he, and his concubine, and his ser-
vant, his father in law, the damsel's father, said unto him, Behold, now the day
draweth toward evening, I pray you tarry all night: behold, the day groweth
to an end, lodge here, that thine heart may be merry; and to morrow get you
early on your way, that thou mayest go home.
10 But the man would not tarry that night, but he rose up and departed, and
came over against Jebus, which *is* Jerusalem; and *there were* with him two
asses saddled, his concubine also *was* with him.
11 *And* when they *were* by Jebus, the day was far spent; and the servant said
unto his master, Come, I pray thee, and let us turn in into this city of the
Jebusites, and lodge in it.
12 And his master said unto him, We will not turn aside hither into the city
of a stranger, that *is* not of the children of Israel; we will pass over to Gibeah.
13 And he said unto his servant, Come, and let us draw near to one of these
places to lodge all night, in Gibeah, or in Ramah.
14 And they passed on and went their way; and the sun went down upon
them *when they were* by Gibeah, which *belongeth* to Benjamin.
15 And they turned aside thither, to go in *and* to lodge in Gibeah: and when
he went in, he sat him down in a street of the city: for *there was* no man that
took them into his house to lodging.

An Old Man Shows Hospitality

16 And, behold, there came an old man from his work out of the field at even, which *was* also of mount Ephraim; and he sojourned in Gibeah: but the men of the place *were* Benjamites.

17 And when he had lifted up his eyes, he saw a wayfaring man in the street of the city: and the old man said, Whither goest thou? and whence comest thou?

18 And he said unto him, We *are* passing from Beth-lehem-judah toward the side of mount Ephraim; from thence *am* I: and I went to Beth-lehem-judah, but I *am now* going to the house of the LORD; and there *is* no man that receiveth me to house.

19 Yet there is both straw and provender for our asses; and there is bread and wine also for me, and for thy handmaid, and for the young man *which is* with thy servants: *there is* no want of any thing.

20 And the old man said, Peace *be* with thee; howsoever *let* all thy wants *lie* upon me; only lodge not in the street.

21 So he brought him into his house, and gave provender unto the asses: and they washed their feet, and did eat and drink.

The Immoral Men of Gibeah Kill the Levite's Wife

22 *Now* as they were making their hearts merry, behold, the men of the city, certain sons of Belial, beset the house round about, *and* beat at the door, and spake to the master of the house, the old man, saying, Bring forth the man that came into thine house, that we may know him.

23 And the man, the master of the house, went out unto them, and said unto them, Nay, my brethren, *nay*, I pray you, do not *so* wickedly; seeing that this man is come into mine house, do not this folly.

24 Behold, *here is* my daughter a maiden, and his concubine; them I will bring out now, and humble ye them, and do with them what seemeth good unto you: but unto this man do not so vile a thing.

25 But the men would not hearken to him: so the man took his concubine, and brought her forth unto them; and they knew her, and abused her all the night until the morning: and when the day began to spring, they let her go.

26 Then came the woman in the dawning of the day, and fell down at the door of the man's house where her lord *was*, till it was light.

27 And her lord rose up in the morning, and opened the doors of the house, and went out to go his way: and, behold, the woman his concubine was fallen down *at* the door of the house, and her hands *were* upon the threshold.

28 And he said unto her, Up, and let us be going. But none answered. Then the man took her *up* upon an ass, and the man rose up, and gat him unto his place.

29 And when he was come into his house, he took a knife, and laid hold on his concubine, and divided her, *together* with her bones, into twelve pieces, and sent her into all the coasts of Israel.

30 And it was so, that all that saw it said, There was no such deed done nor seen from the day that the children of Israel came up out of the land of Egypt unto this day: consider of it, take advice, and speak *your minds.*

The Levite Explains His Desire for Revenge

20 Then all the children of Israel went out, and the congregation was gathered together as one man, from Dan even to Beer-sheba, with the land of Gilead, unto the LORD in Mizpeh.

2 And the chief of all the people, *even* of all the tribes of Israel, presented themselves in the assembly of the people of God, four hundred thousand footmen that drew sword.

3 (Now the children of Benjamin heard that the children of Israel were gone up to Mizpeh.) Then said the children of Israel, Tell *us*, how was this wickedness?

4 And the Levite, the husband of the woman that was slain, answered and
said, I came into Gibeah that *belongeth* to Benjamin, I and my concubine, to
lodge.
5 And the men of Gibeah rose against me, and beset the house round about
upon me by night, *and* thought to have slain me: and my concubine have they
forced, that she is dead.
6 And I took my concubine, and cut her in pieces, and sent her throughout
all the country of the inheritance of Israel: for they have committed lewdness
and folly in Israel.
7 Behold, ye *are* all children of Israel; give here your advice and counsel.
8 And all the people arose as one man, saying, We will not any *of us* go to his
tent, neither will we any *of us* turn into his house.
9 But now this *shall be* the thing which we will do to Gibeah; *we will go up*
by lot against it;
10 And we will take ten men of an hundred throughout all the tribes of Israel,
and an hundred of a thousand, and a thousand out of ten thousand, to fetch
victual for the people, that they may do, when they come to Gibeah of
Benjamin, according to all the folly that they have wrought in Israel.
11 So all the men of Israel were gathered against the city, knit together as one
man.
12 And the tribes of Israel sent men through all the tribe of Benjamin, saying,
What wickedness *is* this that is done among you?
13 Now therefore deliver *us* the men, the children of Belial, which *are* in
Gibeah, that we may put them to death, and put away evil from Israel. But the
children of Benjamin would not hearken to the voice of their brethren the
children of Israel:
14 But the children of Benjamin gathered themselves together out of the
cities unto Gibeah, to go out to battle against the children of Israel.
15 And the children of Benjamin were numbered at that time out of the
cities twenty and six thousand men that drew sword, beside the inhabitants
of Gibeah, which were numbered seven hundred chosen men.
16 Among all this people *there were* seven hundred chosen men lefthanded;
every one could sling stones at an hair *breadth*, and not miss.
17 And the men of Israel, beside Benjamin, were numbered four hundred
thousand men that drew sword: all these *were* men of war.

The Tribe of Benjamin Defends Itself against Two Attacks

18 And the children of Israel arose, and went up to the house of God, and
asked counsel of God, and said, Which of us shall go up first to the battle
against the children of Benjamin? And the LORD said, Judah *shall go up* first.
19 And the children of Israel rose up in the morning, and encamped against
Gibeah.
20 And the men of Israel went out to battle against Benjamin; and the men
of Israel put themselves in array to fight against them at Gibeah.
21 And the children of Benjamin came forth out of Gibeah, and destroyed
down to the ground of the Israelites that day twenty and two thousand men.
22 And the people the men of Israel encouraged themselves, and set their
battle again in array in the place where they put themselves in array the first
day.
23 (And the children of Israel went up and wept before the LORD until even,
and asked counsel of the LORD, saying, Shall I go up again to battle against the
children of Benjamin my brother? And the LORD said, Go up against him.)
24 And the children of Israel came near against the children of Benjamin the
second day.
25 And Benjamin went forth against them out of Gibeah the second day, and
destroyed down to the ground of the children of Israel again eighteen thou-
sand men; all these drew the sword.

The Tribe of Benjamin Is Finally Destroyed

26 Then all the children of Israel, and all the people, went up, and came unto
the house of God, and wept, and sat there before the LORD, and fasted that day
until even, and offered burnt offerings and peace offerings before the LORD.
27 And the children of Israel enquired of the LORD, (for the ark of the cove-
nant of God *was* there in those days,
28 And Phinehas, the son of Eleazar, the son of Aaron, stood before it in those
days,) saying, Shall I yet again go out to battle against the children of Benjamin
my brother, or shall I cease? And the LORD said, Go up; for to morrow I will
deliver them into thine hand.
29 And Israel set liers in wait round about Gibeah.
30 And the children of Israel went up against the children of Benjamin on
the third day, and put themselves in array against Gibeah, as at other times.
31 And the children of Benjamin went out against the people, *and* were
drawn away from the city; and they began to smite of the people, *and* kill, as
at other times, in the highways, of which one goeth up to the house of God,
and the other to Gibeah in the field, about thirty men of Israel.
32 And the children of Benjamin said, They *are* smitten down before us, as
at the first. But the children of Israel said, Let us flee, and draw them from the
city unto the highways.
33 And all the men of Israel rose up out of their place, and put themselves in
array at Baal-tamar: and the liers in wait of Israel came forth out of their
places, *even* out of the meadows of Gibeah.
34 And there came against Gibeah ten thousand chosen men out of all Israel,
and the battle was sore: but they knew not that evil *was* near them.
35 And the LORD smote Benjamin before Israel: and the children of Israel
destroyed of the Benjamites that day twenty and five thousand and an hundred
men: all these drew the sword.
36 So the children of Benjamin saw that they were smitten: for the men of
Israel gave place to the Benjamites, because they trusted unto the liers in wait
which they had set beside Gibeah.
37 And the liers in wait hasted, and rushed upon Gibeah; and the liers in wait
drew *themselves* along, and smote all the city with the edge of the sword.
38 Now there was an appointed sign between the men of Israel and the liers
in wait, that they should make a great flame with smoke rise up out of the city.
39 And when the men of Israel retired in the battle, Benjamin began to smite
and kill of the men of Israel about thirty persons: for they said, Surely they
are smitten down before us, as *in* the first battle.
40 But when the flame began to arise up out of the city with a pillar of smoke,
the Benjamites looked behind them, and, behold, the flame of the city ascend-
ed up to heaven.
41 And when the men of Israel turned again, the men of Benjamin were
amazed: for they saw that evil was come upon them.
42 Therefore they turned *their backs* before the men of Israel unto the way
of the wilderness; but the battle overtook them; and them which *came* out of
the cities they destroyed in the midst of them.
43 *Thus* they inclosed the Benjamites round about, *and* chased them, *and*
trode them down with ease over against Gibeah toward the sunrising.
44 And there fell of Benjamin eighteen thousand men; all these *were* men of
valour.
45 And they turned and fled toward the wilderness unto the rock of Rimmon:
and they gleaned of them in the highways five thousand men; and pursued
hard after them unto Gidom, and slew two thousand men of them.
46 So that all which fell that day of Benjamin were twenty and five thousand
men that drew the sword; all these *were* men of valour.
47 But six hundred men turned and fled to the wilderness unto the rock
Rimmon, and abode in the rock Rimmon four months.

48 And the men of Israel turned again upon the children of Benjamin, and
smote them with the edge of the sword, as well the men of *every* city, as the
beast, and all that came to hand: also they set on fire all the cities that they
came to.

The People Bewail the Desolation of Benjamin

21 Now the men of Israel had sworn in Mizpeh, saying, There shall not
any of us give his daughter unto Benjamin to wife.
2 And the people came to the house of God, and abode there till even before
God, and lifted up their voices, and wept sore;
3 And said, O LORD God of Israel, why is this come to pass in Israel, that there
should be to day one tribe lacking in Israel?
4 And it came to pass on the morrow, that the people rose early, and built
there an altar, and offered burnt offerings and peace offerings.
5 And the children of Israel said, Who *is there* among all the tribes of Israel
that came not up with the congregation unto the LORD? For they had made a
great oath concerning him that came not up to the LORD to Mizpeh, saying,
He shall surely be put to death.
6 And the children of Israel repented them for Benjamin their brother, and
said, There is one tribe cut off from Israel this day.
7 How shall we do for wives for them that remain, seeing we have sworn by
the LORD that we will not give them of our daughters to wives?
8 And they said, What one *is there* of the tribes of Israel that came not up to
Mizpeh to the LORD? And, behold, there came none to the camp from Jabesh-
gilead to the assembly.
9 For the people were numbered, and, behold, *there were* none of the inhab-
itants of Jabesh-gilead there.
10 And the congregation sent thither twelve thousand men of the valiantest,
and commanded them, saying, Go and smite the inhabitants of Jabesh-gilead
with the edge of the sword, with the women and the children.
11 And this *is* the thing that ye shall do, Ye shall utterly destroy every male,
and every woman that hath lain by man.
12 And they found among the inhabitants of Jabesh-gilead four hundred
young virgins, that had known no man by lying with any male: and they
brought them unto the camp to Shiloh, which *is* in the land of Canaan.
13 And the whole congregation sent *some* to speak to the children of
Benjamin that *were* in the rock Rimmon, and to call peaceably unto them.
14 And Benjamin came again at that time; and they gave them wives which
they had saved alive of the women of Jabesh-gilead: and yet so they sufficed
them not.
15 And the people repented them for Benjamin, because that the LORD had
made a breach in the tribes of Israel.

Israel Provides Wives for the Surviving Men of Benjamin

16 Then the elders of the congregation said, How shall we do for wives for
them that remain, seeing the women are destroyed out of Benjamin?
17 And they said, *There must be* an inheritance for them that be escaped of
Benjamin, that a tribe be not destroyed out of Israel.
18 Howbeit we may not give them wives of our daughters: for the children
of Israel have sworn, saying, Cursed *be* he that giveth a wife to Benjamin.
19 Then they said, Behold, *there is* a feast of the LORD in Shiloh yearly *in a
place* which *is* on the north side of Beth-el, on the east side of the highway that
goeth up from Beth-el to Shechem, and on the south of Lebonah.
20 Therefore they commanded the children of Benjamin, saying, Go and lie
in wait in the vineyards;
21 And see, and, behold, if the daughters of Shiloh come out to dance in
dances, then come ye out of the vineyards, and catch you every man his wife
of the daughters of Shiloh, and go to the land of Benjamin.

22 And it shall be, when their fathers or their brethren come unto us to
complain, that we will say unto them, Be favourable unto them for our sakes:
because we reserved not to each man his wife in the war: for ye did not give
unto them at this time, *that* ye should be guilty.
23 And the children of Benjamin did so, and took *them* wives, according to
their number, of them that danced, whom they caught: and they went and
returned unto their inheritance, and repaired the cities, and dwelt in them.
24 And the children of Israel departed thence at that time, every man to his
tribe and to his family, and they went out from thence every man to his inheritance.
25 In those days *there was* no king in Israel: every man did *that which was*
right in his own eyes.

The Move to Moab and Tragedy

1 Now it came to pass in the days when the judges ruled, that there was a famine in the land. And a certain man of Beth-lehem-judah went to sojourn in the country of Moab, he, and his wife, and his two sons.

2 And the name of the man *was* Elimelech, and the name of his wife Naomi, and the name of his two sons Mahlon and Chilion, Ephrathites of Beth-lehem-judah. And they came into the country of Moab, and continued there.

3 And Elimelech Naomi's husband died; and she was left, and her two sons.

4 And they took them wives of the women of Moab; the name of the one *was* Orpah, and the name of the other Ruth: and they dwelled there about ten years.

5 And Mahlon and Chilion died also both of them; and the woman was left of her two sons and her husband.

Naomi's Appeal to Her Daughters-in-Law

6 Then she arose with her daughters-in-law, that she might return from the country of Moab: for she had heard in the country of Moab how that the LORD had visited his people in giving them bread.

7 Wherefore she went forth out of the place where she was, and her two daughters in law with her; and they went on the way to return unto the land of Judah.

8 And Naomi said unto her two daughters in law, Go, return each to her mother's house: the LORD deal kindly with you, as ye have dealt with the dead, and with me.

9 The LORD grant you that ye may find rest, each *of you* in the house of her husband. Then she kissed them; and they lifted up their voice, and wept.

10 And they said unto her, Surely we will return with thee unto thy people.

11 And Naomi said, Turn again, my daughters: why will ye go with me? *are* there yet *any more* sons in my womb, that they may be your husbands?

12 Turn again, my daughters, go *your way*; for I am too old to have an husband. If I should say, I have hope, *if* I should have an husband also to night, and should also bear sons;

13 Would ye tarry for them till they were grown? would ye stay for them from having husbands? nay, my daughters; for it grieveth me much for your sakes that the hand of the LORD is gone out against me.

14 And they lifted up their voice, and wept again: and Orpah kissed her mother in law; but Ruth clave unto her.

15 And she said, Behold, thy sister in law is gone back unto her people, and unto her gods: return thou after thy sister in law.

16 And Ruth said, Intreat me not to leave thee, *or* to return from following after thee: for whither thou goest, I will go; and where thou lodgest, I will lodge: thy people *shall be* my people, and thy God my God:

17 Where thou diest, will I die, and there will I be buried: the LORD do so to me, and more also, *if ought* but death part thee and me.

18 When she saw that she was stedfastly minded to go with her, then she left speaking unto her.

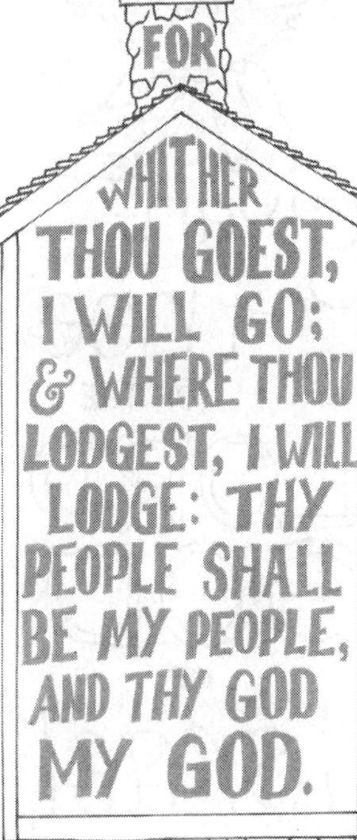

Naomi and Ruth Return Home, Where They Are Gladly Received

19 So they two went until they came to Beth-lehem. And it came to pass, when
they were come to Beth-lehem, that all the city was moved about them, and
they said, *Is* this Naomi?
20 And she said unto them, Call me not Naomi, call me Mara: for the Almighty
hath dealt very bitterly with me.
21 I went out full, and the LORD hath brought me home again empty: why
then call ye me Naomi, seeing the LORD hath testified against me, and the
Almighty hath afflicted me?
22 So Naomi returned, and Ruth the Moabitess, her daughter in law, with
her, which returned out of the country of Moab: and they came to Beth-lehem
in the beginning of barley harvest.

Ruth Gleans in the Fields of Boaz

2 And Naomi had a kinsman of her husband's, a mighty man of wealth, of
the family of Elimelech; and his name *was* Boaz.
2 And Ruth the Moabitess said unto Naomi, Let me now go to the field, and
glean ears of corn after *him* in whose sight I shall find grace. And she said unto
her, Go, my daughter.
3 And she went, and came, and gleaned in the field after the reapers: and her
hap was to light on a part of the field *belonging* unto Boaz, who *was* of the
kindred of Elimelech.

Boaz Speaks with Ruth and Shows Her Great Favor

4 And, behold, Boaz came from Beth-lehem, and said unto the reapers, The
LORD *be* with you. And they answered him, The LORD bless thee.
5 Then said Boaz unto his servant that was set over the reapers, Whose dam-
sel *is* this?
6 And the servant that was set over the reapers answered and said, It *is* the
Moabitish damsel that came back with Naomi out of the country of Moab:
7 And she said, I pray you, let me glean and gather after the reapers among
the sheaves: so she came, and hath continued even from the morning until
now, that she tarried a little in the house.
8 Then said Boaz unto Ruth, Hearest thou not, my daughter? Go not to glean
in another field, neither go from hence, but abide here fast by my maidens:
9 *Let* thine eyes *be* on the field that they do reap, and go thou after them: have
I not charged the young men that they shall not touch thee? and when thou
art athirst, go unto the vessels, and drink of *that* which the young men have
drawn.
10 Then she fell on her face, and bowed herself to the ground, and said unto
him, Why have I found grace in thine eyes, that thou shouldest take knowledge
of me, seeing I *am* a stranger?
11 And Boaz answered and said unto her, It hath fully been shewed me, all
that thou hast done unto thy mother in law since the death of thine husband:
and *how* thou hast left thy father and thy mother, and the land of thy nativity,
and art come unto a people which thou knewest not heretofore.
12 The LORD recompense thy work, and a full reward be given thee of the
LORD God of Israel, under whose wings thou art come to trust.
13 Then she said, Let me find favour in thy sight, my lord; for that thou hast
comforted me, and for that thou hast spoken friendly unto thine handmaid,
though I be not like unto one of thine handmaidens.
14 And Boaz said unto her, At mealtime come thou hither, and eat of the
bread, and dip thy morsel in the vinegar. And she sat beside the reapers: and
he reached her parched *corn*, and she did eat, and was sufficed, and left.
15 And when she was risen up to glean, Boaz commanded his young men,
saying, Let her glean even among the sheaves, and reproach her not:

16 And let fall also *some* of the handfuls of purpose for her, and leave *them*,
that she may glean *them*, and rebuke her not.
17 So she gleaned in the field until even, and beat out that she had gleaned:
and it was about an ephah of barley.
18 And she took *it* up, and went into the city: and her mother in law saw what
she had gleaned: and she brought forth, and gave to her that she had reserved
after she was sufficed.
19 And her mother in law said unto her, Where hast thou gleaned to day?
and where wroughtest thou? blessed be he that did take knowledge of thee.
And she shewed her mother in law with whom she had wrought, and said,
The man's name with whom I wrought to day *is* Boaz.
20 And Naomi said unto her daughter in law, Blessed *be* he of the LORD, who
hath not left off his kindness to the living and to the dead. And Naomi said
unto her, The man *is* near of kin unto us, one of our next kinsmen.
21 And Ruth the Moabitess said, He said unto me also, Thou shalt keep fast
by my young men, until they have ended all my harvest.
22 And Naomi said unto Ruth her daughter in law, *It is* good, my daughter,
that thou go out with his maidens, that they meet thee not in any other field.
23 So she kept fast by the maidens of Boaz to glean unto the end of barley
harvest and of wheat harvest; and dwelt with her mother in law.

Naomi's Plan for Ruth's Marriage

3 Then Naomi her mother in law said unto her, My daughter, shall I not seek
rest for thee, that it may be well with thee?
2 And now *is* not Boaz of our kindred, with whose maidens thou wast?
Behold, he winnoweth barley to night in the threshingfloor.
3 Wash thyself therefore, and anoint thee, and put thy raiment upon thee,
and get thee down to the floor: *but* make not thyself known unto the man,
until he shall have done eating and drinking.
4 And it shall be, when he lieth down, that thou shalt mark the place where
he shall lie, and thou shalt go in, and uncover his feet, and lay thee down; and
he will tell thee what thou shalt do.
5 And she said unto her, All that thou sayest unto me I will do.
6 And she went down unto the floor, and did according to all that her moth-
er in law bade her.
7 And when Boaz had eaten and drunk, and his heart was merry, he went to
lie down at the end of the heap of corn: and she came softly, and uncovered
his feet, and laid her down.
8 And it came to pass at midnight, that the man was afraid, and turned him-
self: and, behold, a woman lay at his feet.
9 And he said, Who *art* thou? And she answered, I *am* Ruth thine handmaid:
spread therefore thy skirt over thine handmaid; for thou *art* a near kinsman.
10 And he said, Blessed *be* thou of the LORD, my daughter: *for* thou hast
shewed more kindness in the latter end than at the beginning, inasmuch as
thou followedst not young men, whether poor or rich.
11 And now, my daughter, fear not; I will do to thee all that thou requirest:
for all the city of my people doth know that thou *art* a virtuous woman.
12 And now it is true that I *am thy* near kinsman: howbeit there is a kinsman
nearer than I.
13 Tarry this night, and it shall be in the morning, *that* if he will perform
unto thee the part of a kinsman, well; let him do the kinsman's part: but if he
will not do the part of a kinsman to thee, then will I do the part of a kinsman
to thee, *as* the LORD liveth: lie down until the morning.

RUTH 4:15
AND HE shall be UNTO THEE a Restorer OF THY LIFE, AND A nourisher OF THINE OLD AGE.

Boaz Sends Ruth Home with a Gift of Barley
14 And she lay at his feet until the morning: and she rose up before one could
know another. And he said, Let it not be known that a woman came into the
floor.
15 Also he said, Bring the veil that *thou hast* upon thee, and hold it. And when
she held it, he measured six *measures* of barley, and laid *it* on her: and she
went into the city.
16 And when she came to her mother in law, she said, Who *art* thou, my
daughter? And she told her all that the man had done to her.
17 And she said, These six *measures* of barley gave he me; for he said to me,
Go not empty unto thy mother in law.
18 Then said she, Sit still, my daughter, until thou know how the matter will
fall: for the man will not be in rest, until he have finished the thing this day.

Boaz Calls into Judgment the Next Kinsman
4 Then went Boaz up to the gate, and sat him down there: and, behold, the
kinsman of whom Boaz spake came by; unto whom he said, Ho, such a one!
turn aside, sit down here. And he turned aside, and sat down.
2 And he took ten men of the elders of the city, and said, Sit ye down here.
And they sat down.
3 And he said unto the kinsman, Naomi, that is come again out of the coun-
try of Moab, selleth a parcel of land, which *was* our brother Elimelech's:
4 And I thought to advertise thee, saying, Buy *it* before the inhabitants, and
before the elders of my people. If thou wilt redeem *it*, redeem *it*: but if thou
wilt not redeem *it, then* tell me, that I may know: for *there is* none to redeem
it beside thee; and I *am* after thee. And he said, I will redeem *it*.
5 Then said Boaz, What day thou buyest the field of the hand of Naomi, thou
must buy *it* also of Ruth the Moabitess, the wife of the dead, to raise up the
name of the dead upon his inheritance.
6 And the kinsman said, I cannot redeem *it* for myself, lest I mar mine own
inheritance: redeem thou my right to thyself; for I cannot redeem *it*.
7 Now this *was the manner* in former time in Israel concerning redeeming
and concerning changing, for to confirm all things; a man plucked off his
shoe, and gave *it* to his neighbour: and this *was* a testimony in Israel.
8 Therefore the kinsman said unto Boaz, Buy *it* for thee. So he drew off his
shoe.

Boaz Buys the Inheritance and Marries Ruth
9 And Boaz said unto the elders, and *unto* all the people, Ye *are* witnesses this
day, that I have bought all that *was* Elimelech's, and all that *was* Chilion's and
Mahlon's, of the hand of Naomi.
10 Moreover Ruth the Moabitess, the wife of Mahlon, have I purchased to be
my wife, to raise up the name of the dead upon his inheritance, that the name
of the dead be not cut off from among his brethren, and from the gate of his
place: ye *are* witnesses this day.
11 And all the people that *were* in the gate, and the elders, said, *We are* wit-
nesses. The LORD make the woman that is come into thine house like Rachel
and like Leah, which two did build the house of Israel: and do thou worthily
in Ephratah, and be famous in Beth-lehem:
12 And let thy house be like the house of Pharez, whom Tamar bare unto
Judah, of the seed which the LORD shall give thee of this young woman.

Ruth Bears Obed, the Grandfather of David
13 So Boaz took Ruth, and she was his wife: and when he went in unto her,
the LORD gave her conception, and she bare a son.
14 And the women said unto Naomi, Blessed *be* the LORD, which hath not left
thee this day without a kinsman, that his name may be famous in Israel.
15 And he shall be unto thee a restorer of *thy* life, and a nourisher of thine
old age: for thy daughter in law, which loveth thee, which is better to thee than
seven sons, hath born him.

16 And Naomi took the child, and laid it in her bosom, and became nurse
unto it.
17 And the women her neighbours gave it a name, saying, There is a son born
to Naomi; and they called his name Obed: he *is* the father of Jesse, the father
of David.
18 Now these *are* the generations of Pharez: Pharez begat Hezron,
19 And Hezron begat Ram, and Ram begat Amminadab,
20 And Amminadab begat Nahshon, and Nahshon begat Salmon,
21 And Salmon begat Boaz, and Boaz begat Obed,
22 And Obed begat Jesse, and Jesse begat David.

Elkanah and His Wives Go to Shiloh Every Year to Worship

1 Now there was a certain man of Ramathaim-zophim, of mount Ephraim,
and his name *was* Elkanah, the son of Jeroham, the son of Elihu, the son of
Tohu, the son of Zuph, an Ephrathite:
2 And he had two wives; the name of the one *was* Hannah, and the name of
the other Peninnah: and Peninnah had children, but Hannah had no children.
3 And this man went up out of his city yearly to worship and to sacrifice unto
the LORD of hosts in Shiloh. And the two sons of Eli, Hophni and Phinehas, the
priests of the LORD, *were* there.
4 And when the time was that Elkanah offered, he gave to Peninnah his wife,
and to all her sons and her daughters, portions:
5 But unto Hannah he gave a worthy portion; for he loved Hannah: but the
LORD had shut up her womb.
6 And her adversary also provoked her sore, for to make her fret, because
the LORD had shut up her womb.
7 And *as* he did so year by year, when she went up to the house of the LORD,
so she provoked her; therefore she wept, and did not eat.
8 Then said Elkanah her husband to her, Hannah, why weepest thou? and
why eatest thou not? and why is thy heart grieved? *am* not I better to thee
than ten sons?

Hannah Prays for a Child

9 So Hannah rose up after they had eaten in Shiloh, and after they had drunk.
Now Eli the priest sat upon a seat by a post of the temple of the LORD.
10 And she *was* in bitterness of soul, and prayed unto the LORD, and wept
sore.
11 And she vowed a vow, and said, O LORD of hosts, if thou wilt indeed look
on the affliction of thine handmaid, and remember me, and not forget thine
handmaid, but wilt give unto thine handmaid a man child, then I will give
him unto the LORD all the days of his life, and there shall no razor come upon
his head.
12 And it came to pass, as she continued praying before the LORD, that Eli
marked her mouth.
13 Now Hannah, she spake in her heart; only her lips moved, but her voice
was not heard: therefore Eli thought she had been drunken.
14 And Eli said unto her, How long wilt thou be drunken? put away thy wine
from thee.
15 And Hannah answered and said, No, my lord, I *am* a woman of a sorrow-
ful spirit: I have drunk neither wine nor strong drink, but have poured out
my soul before the LORD.
16 Count not thine handmaid for a daughter of Belial: for out of the abun-
dance of my complaint and grief have I spoken hitherto.
17 Then Eli answered and said, Go in peace: and the God of Israel grant *thee*
thy petition that thou hast asked of him.
18 And she said, Let thine handmaid find grace in thy sight. So the woman
went her way, and did eat, and her countenance was no more *sad*.

Hannah, Having Given Birth to Samuel, Stays at Home till He Is Weaned

19 And they rose up in the morning early, and worshipped before the LORD,
and returned, and came to their house to Ramah: and Elkanah knew Hannah
his wife; and the LORD remembered her.
20 Wherefore it came to pass, when the time was come about after Hannah
had conceived, that she bare a son, and called his name Samuel, *saying*, Because
I have asked him of the LORD.
21 And the man Elkanah, and all his house, went up to offer unto the LORD
the yearly sacrifice, and his vow.
22 But Hannah went not up; for she said unto her husband, *I will not go up*
until the child be weaned, and *then* I will bring him, that he may appear before
the LORD, and there abide for ever.
23 And Elkanah her husband said unto her, Do what seemeth thee good;
tarry until thou have weaned him; only the LORD establish his word. So the
woman abode, and gave her son suck until she weaned him.
24 And when she had weaned him, she took him up with her, with three
bullocks, and one ephah of flour, and a bottle of wine, and brought him unto
the house of the LORD in Shiloh: and the child *was* young.
25 And they slew a bullock, and brought the child to Eli.
26 And she said, Oh my lord, *as* thy soul liveth, my lord, I *am* the woman that
stood by thee here, praying unto the LORD.
27 For this child I prayed; and the LORD hath given me my petition which I
asked of him:
28 Therefore also I have lent him to the LORD; as long as he liveth he shall be
lent to the LORD. And he worshipped the LORD there.

Hannah's Song of Thankfulness

2 And Hannah prayed, and said, My heart rejoiceth in the LORD, mine horn
is exalted in the LORD: my mouth is enlarged over mine enemies; because I
rejoice in thy salvation.
2 *There is* none holy as the LORD: for *there is* none beside thee: neither *is there*
any rock like our God.
3 Talk no more so exceeding proudly; let *not* arrogancy come out of your
mouth: for the LORD *is* a God of knowledge, and by him actions are weighed.
4 The bows of the mighty men *are* broken, and they that stumbled are gird-
ed with strength.
5 *They that were* full have hired out themselves for bread; and *they that were*
hungry ceased: so that the barren hath born seven; and she that hath many
children is waxed feeble.
6 The LORD killeth, and maketh alive: he bringeth down to the grave, and
bringeth up.
7 The LORD maketh poor, and maketh rich: he bringeth low, and lifteth up.
8 He raiseth up the poor out of the dust, *and* lifteth up the beggar from the
dunghill, to set *them* among princes, and to make them inherit the throne of
glory: for the pillars of the earth *are* the LORD's, and he hath set the world upon
them.
9 He will keep the feet of his saints, and the wicked shall be silent in darkness;
for by strength shall no man prevail.
10 The adversaries of the LORD shall be broken to pieces; out of heaven shall
he thunder upon them: the LORD shall judge the ends of the earth; and he shall
give strength unto his king, and exalt the horn of his anointed.
11 And Elkanah went to Ramah to his house. And the child did minister unto
the LORD before Eli the priest.
12 Now the sons of Eli *were* sons of Belial; they knew not the LORD.

13 And the priests' custom with the people *was, that*, when any man offered
sacrifice, the priest's servant came, while the flesh was in seething, with a
fleshhook of three teeth in his hand;
14 And he struck *it* into the pan, or kettle, or caldron, or pot; all that the
fleshhook brought up the priest took for himself. So they did in Shiloh unto
all the Israelites that came thither.
15 Also before they burnt the fat, the priest's servant came, and said to the
man that sacrificed, Give flesh to roast for the priest; for he will not have
sodden flesh of thee, but raw.
16 And *if* any man said unto him, Let them not fail to burn the fat presently,
and *then* take *as much* as thy soul desireth; then he would answer him, *Nay*;
but thou shalt give *it me* now: and if not, I will take *it* by force.
17 Wherefore the sin of the young men was very great before the LORD: for
men abhorred the offering of the LORD.
18 But Samuel ministered before the LORD, *being* a child, girded with a linen
ephod.
19 Moreover his mother made him a little coat, and brought *it* to him from
year to year, when she came up with her husband to offer the yearly sacrifice.
20 And Eli blessed Elkanah and his wife, and said, The LORD give thee seed of
this woman for the loan which is lent to the LORD. And they went unto their
own home.
21 And the LORD visited Hannah, so that she conceived, and bare three sons
and two daughters. And the child Samuel grew before the LORD.
22 Now Eli was very old, and heard all that his sons did unto all Israel; and
how they lay with the women that assembled *at* the door of the tabernacle of
the congregation.
23 And he said unto them, Why do ye such things? for I hear of your evil
dealings by all this people.
24 Nay, my sons; for *it is* no good report that I hear: ye make the LORD's peo-
ple to transgress.
25 If one man sin against another, the judge shall judge him: but if a man sin
against the LORD, who shall intreat for him? Notwithstanding they hearkened
not unto the voice of their father, because the LORD would slay them.
26 And the child Samuel grew on, and was in favour both with the LORD, and
also with men.
27 And there came a man of God unto Eli, and said unto him, Thus saith the
LORD, Did I plainly appear unto the house of thy father, when they were in
Egypt in Pharaoh's house?
28 And did I choose him out of all the tribes of Israel *to be* my priest, to offer
upon mine altar, to burn incense, to wear an ephod before me? and did I give
unto the house of thy father all the offerings made by fire of the children of
Israel?
29 Wherefore kick ye at my sacrifice and at mine offering, which I have com-
manded *in my* habitation; and honourest thy sons above me, to make your-
selves fat with the chiefest of all the offerings of Israel my people?
30 Wherefore the LORD God of Israel saith, I said indeed *that* thy house, and
the house of thy father, should walk before me for ever: but now the LORD
saith, Be it far from me; for them that honour me I will honour, and they that
despise me shall be lightly esteemed.
31 Behold, the days come, that I will cut off thine arm, and the arm of thy
father's house, that there shall not be an old man in thine house.
32 And thou shalt see an enemy *in my* habitation, in all *the wealth* which *God*
shall give Israel: and there shall not be an old man in thine house for ever.
33 And the man of thine, *whom* I shall not cut off from mine altar, *shall be*
to consume thine eyes, and to grieve thine heart: and all the increase of thine
house shall die in the flower of their age.

34 And this *shall be* a sign unto thee, that shall come upon thy two sons, on
Hophni and Phinehas; in one day they shall die both of them.
35 And I will raise me up a faithful priest, *that* shall do according to *that*
which *is* in mine heart and in my mind: and I will build him a sure house; and
he shall walk before mine anointed for ever.
36 And it shall come to pass, *that* every one that is left in thine house shall
come *and* crouch to him for a piece of silver and a morsel of bread, and shall
say, Put me, I pray thee, into one of the priests' offices, that I may eat a piece
of bread.

How the Word of the Lord Was First Revealed to Samuel

3 And the child Samuel ministered unto the LORD before Eli. And the word
of the LORD was precious in those days; *there was* no open vision.
2 And it came to pass at that time, when Eli *was* laid down in his place, and
his eyes began to wax dim, *that* he could not see;
3 And ere the lamp of God went out in the temple of the LORD, where the ark
of God *was*, and Samuel was laid down *to sleep*;
4 That the LORD called Samuel: and he answered, Here *am* I.
5 And he ran unto Eli, and said, Here *am* I; for thou calledst me. And he said,
I called not; lie down again. And he went and lay down.
6 And the LORD called yet again, Samuel. And Samuel arose and went to Eli,
and said, Here *am* I; for thou didst call me. And he answered, I called not, my
son; lie down again.
7 Now Samuel did not yet know the LORD, neither was the word of the LORD
yet revealed unto him.
8 And the LORD called Samuel again the third time. And he arose and went
to Eli, and said, Here *am* I; for thou didst call me. And Eli perceived that the
LORD had called the child.
9 Therefore Eli said unto Samuel, Go, lie down: and it shall be, if he call thee,
that thou shalt say, Speak, LORD; for thy servant heareth. So Samuel went and
lay down in his place.
10 And the LORD came, and stood, and called as at other times, Samuel,
Samuel. Then Samuel answered, Speak; for thy servant heareth.
11 And the LORD said to Samuel, Behold, I will do a thing in Israel, at which
both the ears of every one that heareth it shall tingle.
12 In that day I will perform against Eli all *things* which I have spoken con-
cerning his house: when I begin, I will also make an end.
13 For I have told him that I will judge his house for ever for the iniquity
which he knoweth; because his sons made themselves vile, and he restrained
them not.
14 And therefore I have sworn unto the house of Eli, that the iniquity of Eli's
house shall not be purged with sacrifice nor offering for ever.
15 And Samuel lay until the morning, and opened the doors of the house of
the LORD. And Samuel feared to shew Eli the vision.
16 Then Eli called Samuel, and said, Samuel, my son. And he answered, Here
am I.
17 And he said, What *is* the thing that *the LORD* hath said unto thee? I pray
thee hide *it* not from me: God do so to thee, and more also, if thou hide *any*
thing from me of all the things that he said unto thee.
18 And Samuel told him every whit, and hid nothing from him. And he said,
It *is* the LORD: let him do what seemeth him good.

Samuel Grows in Favor

19 And Samuel grew, and the LORD was with him, and did let none of his
words fall to the ground.
20 And all Israel from Dan even to Beersheba knew that Samuel *was* estab-
lished *to be* a prophet of the LORD.

21 And the LORD appeared again in Shiloh: for the LORD revealed himself to
Samuel in Shiloh by the word of the LORD.

The Israelites Are Overcome by the Philistines

4 And the word of Samuel came to all Israel. Now Israel went out against the
Philistines to battle, and pitched beside Eben-ezer: and the Philistines
pitched in Aphek.
2 And the Philistines put themselves in array against Israel: and when they
joined battle, Israel was smitten before the Philistines: and they slew of the
army in the field about four thousand men.
3 And when the people were come into the camp, the elders of Israel said,
Wherefore hath the LORD smitten us to day before the Philistines? Let us fetch
the ark of the covenant of the LORD out of Shiloh unto us, that, when it cometh
among us, it may save us out of the hand of our enemies.
4 So the people sent to Shiloh, that they might bring from thence the ark of
the covenant of the LORD of hosts, which dwelleth *between* the cherubims: and
the two sons of Eli, Hophni and Phinehas, *were* there with the ark of the cov-
enant of God.
5 And when the ark of the covenant of the LORD came into the camp, all Israel
shouted with a great shout, so that the earth rang again.
6 And when the Philistines heard the noise of the shout, they said, What
meaneth the noise of this great shout in the camp of the Hebrews? And they
understood that the ark of the LORD was come into the camp.
7 And the Philistines were afraid, for they said, God is come into the camp.
And they said, Woe unto us! for there hath not been such a thing heretofore.
8 Woe unto us! who shall deliver us out of the hand of these mighty Gods?
these *are* the Gods that smote the Egyptians with all the plagues in the wilder-
ness.
9 Be strong, and quit yourselves like men, O ye Philistines, that ye be not
servants unto the Hebrews, as they have been to you: quit yourselves like men,
and fight.

Israel Is Defeated, the Ark Taken, Hophni and Phinehas Killed

10 And the Philistines fought, and Israel was smitten, and they fled every
man into his tent: and there was a very great slaughter; for there fell of Israel
thirty thousand footmen.
11 And the ark of God was taken; and the two sons of Eli, Hophni and
Phinehas, were slain.

Eli Falls Backward and Breaks His Neck

12 And there ran a man of Benjamin out of the army, and came to Shiloh the
same day with his clothes rent, and with earth upon his head.
13 And when he came, lo, Eli sat upon a seat by the wayside watching: for his
heart trembled for the ark of God. And when the man came into the city, and
told *it*, all the city cried out.
14 And when Eli heard the noise of the crying, he said, What *meaneth* the
noise of this tumult? And the man came in hastily, and told Eli.
15 Now Eli was ninety and eight years old; and his eyes were dim, that he
could not see.
16 And the man said unto Eli, I *am* he that came out of the army, and I fled
to day out of the army. And he said, What is there done, my son?
17 And the messenger answered and said, Israel is fled before the Philistines,
and there hath been also a great slaughter among the people, and thy two sons
also, Hophni and Phinehas, are dead, and the ark of God is taken.
18 And it came to pass, when he made mention of the ark of God, that he fell
from off the seat backward by the side of the gate, and his neck brake, and he
died: for he was an old man, and heavy. And he had judged Israel forty years.

Phinehas' Wife, Weakened by the News, Dies Giving Birth

19 And his daughter in law, Phinehas' wife, was with child, *near* to be deliv-
ered: and when she heard the tidings that the ark of God was taken, and that
her father in law and her husband were dead, she bowed herself and travailed;
for her pains came upon her.
20 And about the time of her death the women that stood by her said unto
her, Fear not; for thou hast born a son. But she answered not, neither did she
regard *it*.
21 And she named the child Ichabod, saying, The glory is departed from
Israel: because the ark of God was taken, and because of her father in law and
her husband.
22 And she said, The glory is departed from Israel: for the ark of God is taken.

The Philistines Place the Ark in the Temple of Dagon

5 And the Philistines took the ark of God, and brought it from Eben-ezer unto
Ashdod.
2 When the Philistines took the ark of God, they brought it into the house
of Dagon, and set it by Dagon.
3 And when they of Ashdod arose early on the morrow, behold, Dagon *was*
fallen upon his face to the earth before the ark of the LORD. And they took
Dagon, and set him in his place again.
4 And when they arose early on the morrow morning, behold, Dagon *was*
fallen upon his face to the ground before the ark of the LORD; and the head of
Dagon and both the palms of his hands *were* cut off upon the threshold; only
the stump of Dagon was left to him.
5 Therefore neither the priests of Dagon, nor any that come into Dagon's
house, tread on the threshold of Dagon in Ashdod unto this day.
6 But the hand of the LORD was heavy upon them of Ashdod, and he destroyed
them, and smote them with emerods, *even* Ashdod and the coasts thereof.
7 And when the men of Ashdod saw that *it was* so, they said, The ark of the
God of Israel shall not abide with us: for his hand is sore upon us, and upon
Dagon our god.
8 They sent therefore and gathered all the lords of the Philistines unto them,
and said, What shall we do with the ark of the God of Israel? And they
answered, Let the ark of the God of Israel be carried about unto Gath. And
they carried the ark of the God of Israel about *thither*.
9 And it was *so*, that, after they had carried it about, the hand of the LORD
was against the city with a very great destruction: and he smote the men of
the city, both small and great, and they had emerods in their secret parts.
10 Therefore they sent the ark of God to Ekron. And it came to pass, as the
ark of God came to Ekron, that the Ekronites cried out, saying, They have
brought about the ark of the God of Israel to us, to slay us and our people.
11 So they sent and gathered together all the lords of the Philistines, and said,
Send away the ark of the God of Israel, and let it go again to his own place, that
it slay us not, and our people: for there was a deadly destruction throughout
all the city; the hand of God was very heavy there.
12 And the men that died not were smitten with the emerods: and the cry of
the city went up to heaven.

The Philistines Take Counsel on How to Return the Ark to Israel

6 And the ark of the LORD was in the country of the Philistines seven months.
2 And the Philistines called for the priests and the diviners, saying, What
shall we do to the ark of the LORD? tell us wherewith we shall send it to his
place.
3 And they said, If ye send away the ark of the God of Israel, send it not empty;
but in any wise return him a trespass offering: then ye shall be healed, and it
shall be known to you why his hand is not removed from you.

4 Then said they, What *shall be* the trespass offering which we shall return
to him? They answered, Five golden emerods, and five golden mice, *according
to* the number of the lords of the Philistines: for one plague *was* on you all,
and on your lords.
5 Wherefore ye shall make images of your emerods, and images of your mice
that mar the land; and ye shall give glory unto the God of Israel: peradventure
he will lighten his hand from off you, and from off your gods, and from off
your land.
6 Wherefore then do ye harden your hearts, as the Egyptians and Pharaoh
hardened their hearts? when he had wrought wonderfully among them, did
they not let the people go, and they departed?
7 Now therefore make a new cart, and take two milch kine, on which there
hath come no yoke, and tie the kine to the cart, and bring their calves home
from them:
8 And take the ark of the LORD, and lay it upon the cart; and put the jewels of
gold, which ye return him *for* a trespass offering, in a coffer by the side there-
of; and send it away, that it may go.
9 And see, if it goeth up by the way of his own coast to Beth-shemesh, *then*
he hath done us this great evil: but if not, then we shall know that *it is* not his
hand *that* smote us: it *was* a chance *that* happened to us.

The Philistines Return the Ark to Israel on a New Cart

10 And the men did so; and took two milch kine, and tied them to the cart,
and shut up their calves at home:
11 And they laid the ark of the LORD upon the cart, and the coffer with the
mice of gold and the images of their emerods.
12 And the kine took the straight way to the way of Beth-shemesh, *and* went
along the highway, lowing as they went, and turned not aside *to* the right hand
or *to* the left; and the lords of the Philistines went after them unto the border
of Beth-shemesh.
13 And *they of* Beth-shemesh *were* reaping their wheat harvest in the valley:
and they lifted up their eyes, and saw the ark, and rejoiced to see *it*.
14 And the cart came into the field of Joshua, a Beth-shemite, and stood there,
where *there was* a great stone: and they clave the wood of the cart, and offered
the kine a burnt offering unto the LORD.
15 And the Levites took down the ark of the LORD, and the coffer that *was*
with it, wherein the jewels of gold *were*, and put *them* on the great stone: and
the men of Beth-shemesh offered burnt offerings and sacrificed sacrifices the
same day unto the LORD.
16 And when the five lords of the Philistines had seen *it*, they returned to
Ekron the same day.
17 And these *are* the golden emerods which the Philistines returned *for* a
trespass offering unto the LORD; for Ashdod one, for Gaza one, for Askelon
one, for Gath one, for Ekron one;
18 And the golden mice, *according to* the number of all the cities of the
Philistines *belonging* to the five lords, *both* of fenced cities, and of country
villages, even unto the great *stone of* Abel, whereon they set down the ark of
the LORD: *which stone remaineth* unto this day in the field of Joshua, the Beth-
shemite.

The People Are Killed for Looking into the Ark

19 And he smote the men of Beth-shemesh, because they had looked into the
ark of the LORD, even he smote of the people fifty thousand and threescore
and ten men: and the people lamented, because the LORD had smitten *many*
of the people with a great slaughter.
20 And the men of Beth-shemesh said, Who is able to stand before this holy
LORD God? and to whom shall he go up from us?

21 And they sent messengers to the inhabitants of Kirjath-jearim, saying, The
Philistines have brought again the ark of the LORD; come ye down, *and* fetch
it up to you.

The People of Kirjath-jearim Bring the Ark into the House of Abinadab

7 And the men of Kirjath-jearim came, and fetched up the ark of the LORD,
and brought it into the house of Abinadab in the hill, and sanctified Eleazar
his son to keep the ark of the LORD.
2 And it came to pass, while the ark abode in Kirjath-jearim, that the time
was long; for it was twenty years: and all the house of Israel lamented after the
LORD.

Through Samuel's Exhortation, the Israelites Repent of Their Sins

3 And Samuel spake unto all the house of Israel, saying, If ye do return unto
the LORD with all your hearts, *then* put away the strange gods and Ashtaroth
from among you, and prepare your hearts unto the LORD, and serve him only:
and he will deliver you out of the hand of the Philistines.
4 Then the children of Israel did put away Baalim and Ashtaroth, and served
the LORD only.
5 And Samuel said, Gather all Israel to Mizpeh, and I will pray for you unto
the LORD.
6 And they gathered together to Mizpeh, and drew water, and poured *it* out
before the LORD, and fasted on that day, and said there, We have sinned against
the LORD. And Samuel judged the children of Israel in Mizpeh.

While Samuel Prays and Sacrifices, the Lord Discomfits the Philistines

7 And when the Philistines heard that the children of Israel were gathered
together to Mizpeh, the lords of the Philistines went up against Israel. And
when the children of Israel heard *it*, they were afraid of the Philistines.
8 And the children of Israel said to Samuel, Cease not to cry unto the LORD
our God for us, that he will save us out of the hand of the Philistines.
9 And Samuel took a sucking lamb, and offered *it for* a burnt offering whol-
ly unto the LORD: and Samuel cried unto the LORD for Israel; and the LORD
heard him.
10 And as Samuel was offering up the burnt offering, the Philistines drew
near to battle against Israel: but the LORD thundered with a great thunder on
that day upon the Philistines, and discomfited them; and they were smitten
before Israel.
11 And the men of Israel went out of Mizpeh, and pursued the Philistines,
and smote them, until *they came* under Beth-car.
12 Then Samuel took a stone, and set *it* between Mizpeh and Shen, and called
the name of it Eben-ezer, saying, Hitherto hath the LORD helped us.

The Philistines Are Subdued

13 So the Philistines were subdued, and they came no more into the coast of
Israel: and the hand of the LORD was against the Philistines all the days of
Samuel.
14 And the cities which the Philistines had taken from Israel were restored
to Israel, from Ekron even unto Gath; and the coasts thereof did Israel deliver
out of the hands of the Philistines. And there was peace between Israel and
the Amorites.
15 And Samuel judged Israel all the days of his life.
16 And he went from year to year in circuit to Beth-el, and Gilgal, and Mizpeh,
and judged Israel in all those places.
17 And his return *was* to Ramah; for there *was* his house; and there he judged
Israel; and there he built an altar unto the LORD.

Samuel's Sons Are Evil Leaders, So Israel Asks for a King

8 And it came to pass, when Samuel was old, that he made his sons judges
over Israel.
2 Now the name of his firstborn was Joel; and the name of his second, Abiah:
they were judges in Beer-sheba.
3 And his sons walked not in his ways, but turned aside after lucre, and took
bribes, and perverted judgment.
4 Then all the elders of Israel gathered themselves together, and came to
Samuel unto Ramah,
5 And said unto him, Behold, thou art old, and thy sons walk not in thy ways:
now make us a king to judge us like all the nations.
6 But the thing displeased Samuel, when they said, Give us a king to judge
us. And Samuel prayed unto the LORD.
7 And the LORD said unto Samuel, Hearken unto the voice of the people in
all that they say unto thee: for they have not rejected thee, but they have reject-
ed me, that I should not reign over them.
8 According to all the works which they have done since the day that I
brought them up out of Egypt even unto this day, wherewith they have for-
saken me, and served other gods, so do they also unto thee.
9 Now therefore hearken unto their voice: howbeit yet protest solemnly unto
them, and shew them the manner of the king that shall reign over them.
10 And Samuel told all the words of the LORD unto the people that asked of
him a king.
11 And he said, This will be the manner of the king that shall reign over you:
He will take your sons, and appoint *them* for himself, for his chariots, and *to
be* his horsemen; and *some* shall run before his chariots.
12 And he will appoint him captains over thousands, and captains over fifties;
and *will set them* to ear his ground, and to reap his harvest, and to make his
instruments of war, and instruments of his chariots.
13 And he will take your daughters *to be* confectionaries, and *to be* cooks,
and *to be* bakers.
14 And he will take your fields, and your vineyards, and your oliveyards, *even*
the best *of them*, and give *them* to his servants.
15 And he will take the tenth of your seed, and of your vineyards, and give to
his officers, and to his servants.
16 And he will take your menservants, and your maidservants, and your
goodliest young men, and your asses, and put *them* to his work.
17 He will take the tenth of your sheep: and ye shall be his servants.
18 And ye shall cry out in that day because of your king which ye shall have
chosen you; and the LORD will not hear you in that day.
19 Nevertheless the people refused to obey the voice of Samuel; and they said,
Nay; but we will have a king over us;
20 That we also may be like all the nations; and that our king may judge us,
and go out before us, and fight our battles.
21 And Samuel heard all the words of the people, and he rehearsed them in
the ears of the LORD.
22 And the LORD said to Samuel, Hearken unto their voice, and make them
a king. And Samuel said unto the men of Israel, Go ye every man unto his city.

Saul Searches the Land for His Father's Donkeys

9 Now there was a man of Benjamin, whose name *was* Kish, the son of Abiel,
the son of Zeror, the son of Bechorath, the son of Aphiah, a Benjamite, a
mighty man of power.
2 And he had a son, whose name *was* Saul, a choice young man, and a good-
ly: and *there was* not among the children of Israel a goodlier person than he:
from his shoulders and upward *he was* higher than any of the people.

3 And the asses of Kish Saul's father were lost. And Kish said to Saul his son,
Take now one of the servants with thee, and arise, go seek the asses.
4 And he passed through mount Ephraim, and passed through the land of
Shalisha, but they found *them* not: then they passed through the land of
Shalim, and *there they were* not: and he passed through the land of the
Benjamites, but they found *them* not.
5 *And* when they were come to the land of Zuph, Saul said to his servant that
was with him, Come, and let us return; lest my father leave *caring* for the asses,
and take thought for us.
6 And he said unto him, Behold now, *there is* in this city a man of God, and
he is an honourable man; all that he saith cometh surely to pass: now let us go
thither; peradventure he can shew us our way that we should go.
7 Then said Saul to his servant, But, behold, *if* we go, what shall we bring the
man? for the bread is spent in our vessels, and *there is* not a present to bring
to the man of God: what have we?
8 And the servant answered Saul again, and said, Behold, I have here at hand
the fourth part of a shekel of silver: *that* will I give to the man of God, to tell
us our way.
9 (Beforetime in Israel, when a man went to enquire of God, thus he spake,
Come, and let us go to the seer: for *he that is* now *called* a Prophet was before-
time called a Seer.)
10 Then said Saul to his servant, Well said; come, let us go. So they went unto
the city where the man of God *was*.

Saul Seeks Samuel

11 *And* as they went up the hill to the city, they found young maidens going
out to draw water, and said unto them, Is the seer here?
12 And they answered them, and said, He is; behold, *he is* before you: make
haste now, for he came to day to the city; for *there is* a sacrifice of the people
to day in the high place:
13 As soon as ye be come into the city, ye shall straightway find him, before
he go up to the high place to eat: for the people will not eat until he come,
because he doth bless the sacrifice; *and* afterwards they eat that be bidden.
Now therefore get you up; for about this time ye shall find him.
14 And they went up into the city: *and* when they were come into the city,
behold, Samuel came out against them, for to go up to the high place.
15 Now the LORD had told Samuel in his ear a day before Saul came, saying,
16 To morrow about this time I will send thee a man out of the land of
Benjamin, and thou shalt anoint him *to be* captain over my people Israel, that
he may save my people out of the hand of the Philistines: for I have looked
upon my people, because their cry is come unto me.
17 And when Samuel saw Saul, the LORD said unto him, Behold the man
whom I spake to thee of! this same shall reign over my people.

Samuel Talks to Saul

18 Then Saul drew near to Samuel in the gate, and said, Tell me, I pray thee,
where the seer's house *is*.
19 And Samuel answered Saul, and said, I *am* the seer: go up before me unto
the high place; for ye shall eat with me to day, and to morrow I will let thee go,
and will tell thee all that *is* in thine heart.
20 And as for thine asses that were lost three days ago, set not thy mind on
them; for they are found. And on whom *is* all the desire of Israel? *Is it* not on
thee, and on all thy father's house?
21 And Saul answered and said, *Am* not I a Benjamite, of the smallest of the
tribes of Israel? and my family the least of all the families of the tribe of
Benjamin? wherefore then speakest thou so to me?

22 And Samuel took Saul and his servant, and brought them into the parlour, and made them sit in the chiefest place among them that were bidden, which *were* about thirty persons.

23 And Samuel said unto the cook, Bring the portion which I gave thee, of which I said unto thee, Set it by thee.

24 And the cook took up the shoulder, and *that* which *was* upon it, and set *it* before Saul. And *Samuel* said, Behold that which is left! set *it* before thee, *and* eat: for unto this time hath it been kept for thee since I said, I have invited the people. So Saul did eat with Samuel that day.

25 And when they were come down from the high place into the city, *Samuel* communed with Saul upon the top of the house.

26 And they arose early: and it came to pass about the spring of the day, that Samuel called Saul to the top of the house, saying, Up, that I may send thee away. And Saul arose, and they went out both of them, he and Samuel, abroad.

27 *And* as they were going down to the end of the city, Samuel said to Saul, Bid the servant pass on before us, (and he passed on,) but stand thou still a while, that I may shew thee the word of God.

Samuel Anoints Saul

10 Then Samuel took a vial of oil, and poured *it* upon his head, and kissed him, and said, *Is it* not because the LORD hath anointed thee *to be* captain over his inheritance?

2 When thou art departed from me to day, then thou shalt find two men by Rachel's sepulchre in the border of Benjamin at Zelzah; and they will say unto thee, The asses which thou wentest to seek are found: and, lo, thy father hath left the care of the asses, and sorroweth for you, saying, What shall I do for my son?

3 Then shalt thou go on forward from thence, and thou shalt come to the plain of Tabor, and there shall meet thee three men going up to God to Beth-el, one carrying three kids, and another carrying three loaves of bread, and another carrying a bottle of wine:

4 And they will salute thee, and give thee two *loaves* of bread; which thou shalt receive of their hands.

5 After that thou shalt come to the hill of God, where *is* the garrison of the Philistines: and it shall come to pass, when thou art come thither to the city, that thou shalt meet a company of prophets coming down from the high place with a psaltery, and a tabret, and a pipe, and a harp, before them; and they shall prophesy:

6 And the Spirit of the LORD will come upon thee, and thou shalt prophesy with them, and shalt be turned into another man.

7 And let it be, when these signs are come unto thee, *that* thou do as occasion serve thee; for God *is* with thee.

8 And thou shalt go down before me to Gilgal; and, behold, I will come down unto thee, to offer burnt offerings, *and* to sacrifice sacrifices of peace offerings: seven days shalt thou tarry, till I come to thee, and shew thee what thou shalt do.

Saul's Heart Is Changed, and He Prophesies

9 And it was *so*, that when he had turned his back to go from Samuel, God gave him another heart: and all those signs came to pass that day.

10 And when they came thither to the hill, behold, a company of prophets met him; and the Spirit of God came upon him, and he prophesied among them.

11 And it came to pass, when all that knew him beforetime saw that, behold, he prophesied among the prophets, then the people said one to another, What *is* this *that* is come unto the son of Kish? *Is* Saul also among the prophets?

12 And one of the same place answered and said, But who *is* their father? Therefore it became a proverb, *Is* Saul also among the prophets?

13 And when he had made an end of prophesying, he came to the high place.
14 And Saul's uncle said unto him and to his servant, Whither went ye? And
he said, To seek the asses: and when we saw that *they were* no where, we came
to Samuel.
15 And Saul's uncle said, Tell me, I pray thee, what Samuel said unto you.
16 And Saul said unto his uncle, He told us plainly that the asses were found.
But of the matter of the kingdom, whereof Samuel spake, he told him not.

The Lord Confirms His Choice of Saul

17 And Samuel called the people together unto the LORD to Mizpeh;
18 And said unto the children of Israel, Thus saith the LORD God of Israel, I
brought up Israel out of Egypt, and delivered you out of the hand of the
Egyptians, and out of the hand of all kingdoms, *and* of them that oppressed
you:
19 And ye have this day rejected your God, who himself saved you out of all
your adversities and your tribulations; and ye have said unto him, *Nay*, but
set a king over us. Now therefore present yourselves before the LORD by your
tribes, and by your thousands.
20 And when Samuel had caused all the tribes of Israel to come near, the tribe
of Benjamin was taken.
21 When he had caused the tribe of Benjamin to come near by their families,
the family of Matri was taken, and Saul the son of Kish was taken: and when
they sought him, he could not be found.
22 Therefore they enquired of the LORD further, if the man should yet come
thither. And the LORD answered, Behold, he hath hid himself among the stuff.
23 And they ran and fetched him thence: and when he stood among the
people, he was higher than any of the people from his shoulders and upward.
24 And Samuel said to all the people, See ye him whom the LORD hath chosen,
that *there is* none like him among all the people? And all the people shouted,
and said, God save the king.
25 Then Samuel told the people the manner of the kingdom, and wrote *it* in
a book, and laid *it* up before the LORD. And Samuel sent all the people away,
every man to his house.
26 And Saul also went home to Gibeah; and there went with him a band of
men, whose hearts God had touched.
27 But the children of Belial said, How shall this man save us? And they
despised him, and brought him no presents. But he held his peace.

Saul Defeats King Nahash of Ammon

11 Then Nahash the Ammonite came up, and encamped against Jabesh-
gilead: and all the men of Jabesh said unto Nahash, Make a covenant
with us, and we will serve thee.
2 And Nahash the Ammonite answered them, On this *condition* will I make
a covenant with you, that I may thrust out all your right eyes, and lay it *for* a
reproach upon all Israel.
3 And the elders of Jabesh said unto him, Give us seven days' respite, that we
may send messengers unto all the coasts of Israel: and then, if *there be* no man
to save us, we will come out to thee.
4 Then came the messengers to Gibeah of Saul, and told the tidings in the
ears of the people: and all the people lifted up their voices, and wept.
5 And, behold, Saul came after the herd out of the field; and Saul said, What
aileth the people that they weep? And they told him the tidings of the men of
Jabesh.
6 And the Spirit of God came upon Saul when he heard those tidings, and
his anger was kindled greatly.
7 And he took a yoke of oxen, and hewed them in pieces, and sent *them*
throughout all the coasts of Israel by the hands of messengers, saying,

1 SAMUEL 12:16
STAND & SEE THIS great THING, WHICH THE LORD WILL DO before your EYES.

Whosoever cometh not forth after Saul and after Samuel, so shall it be done
unto his oxen. And the fear of the LORD fell on the people, and they came out
with one consent.
8 And when he numbered them in Bezek, the children of Israel were three
hundred thousand, and the men of Judah thirty thousand.
9 And they said unto the messengers that came, Thus shall ye say unto the
men of Jabesh-gilead, To morrow, by *that time* the sun be hot, ye shall have
help. And the messengers came and shewed *it* to the men of Jabesh; and they
were glad.
10 Therefore the men of Jabesh said, To morrow we will come out unto you,
and ye shall do with us all that seemeth good unto you.
11 And it was *so* on the morrow, that Saul put the people in three companies;
and they came into the midst of the host in the morning watch, and slew the
Ammonites until the heat of the day: and it came to pass, that they which
remained were scattered, so that two of them were not left together.

Saul Is Confirmed in His Kingdom

12 And the people said unto Samuel, Who *is* he that said, Shall Saul reign over
us? bring the men, that we may put them to death.
13 And Saul said, There shall not a man be put to death this day: for to day
the LORD hath wrought salvation in Israel.
14 Then said Samuel to the people, Come, and let us go to Gilgal, and renew
the kingdom there.
15 And all the people went to Gilgal; and there they made Saul king before
the LORD in Gilgal; and there they sacrificed sacrifices of peace offerings before
the LORD; and there Saul and all the men of Israel rejoiced greatly.

Samuel Testifies to His Integrity

12 And Samuel said unto all Israel, Behold, I have hearkened unto your
voice in all that ye said unto me, and have made a king over you.
2 And now, behold, the king walketh before you: and I am old and grayhead-
ed; and, behold, my sons *are* with you: and I have walked before you from my
childhood unto this day.
3 Behold, here I *am*: witness against me before the LORD, and before his
anointed: whose ox have I taken? or whose ass have I taken? or whom have I
defrauded? whom have I oppressed? or of whose hand have I received *any*
bribe to blind mine eyes therewith? and I will restore it you.
4 And they said, Thou hast not defrauded us, nor oppressed us, neither hast
thou taken ought of any man's hand.
5 And he said unto them, The LORD *is* witness against you, and his anointed
is witness this day, that ye have not found ought in my hand. And they
answered, *He is* witness.

Samuel Reproves the People for Their Ingratitude

6 And Samuel said unto the people, *It is* the LORD that advanced Moses and
Aaron, and that brought your fathers up out of the land of Egypt.
7 Now therefore stand still, that I may reason with you before the LORD of
all the righteous acts of the LORD, which he did to you and to your fathers.
8 When Jacob was come into Egypt, and your fathers cried unto the LORD,
then the LORD sent Moses and Aaron, which brought forth your fathers out
of Egypt, and made them dwell in this place.
9 And when they forgat the LORD their God, he sold them into the hand of
Sisera, captain of the host of Hazor, and into the hand of the Philistines, and
into the hand of the king of Moab, and they fought against them.
10 And they cried unto the LORD, and said, We have sinned, because we have
forsaken the LORD, and have served Baalim and Ashtaroth: but now deliver us
out of the hand of our enemies, and we will serve thee.

11 And the LORD sent Jerubbaal, and Bedan, and Jephthah, and Samuel, and
delivered you out of the hand of your enemies on every side, and ye dwelled
safe.
12 And when ye saw that Nahash the king of the children of Ammon came
against you, ye said unto me, Nay; but a king shall reign over us: when the LORD
your God *was* your king.
13 Now therefore behold the king whom ye have chosen, *and* whom ye have
desired! and, behold, the LORD hath set a king over you.
14 If ye will fear the LORD, and serve him, and obey his voice, and not rebel
against the commandment of the LORD, then shall both ye and also the king
that reigneth over you continue following the LORD your God:
15 But if ye will not obey the voice of the LORD, but rebel against the com-
mandment of the LORD, then shall the hand of the LORD be against you, as *it
was* against your fathers.

Samuel Warns the People about Their Sin in Asking for a King

16 Now therefore stand and see this great thing, which the LORD will do
before your eyes.
17 *Is it* not wheat harvest to day? I will call unto the LORD, and he shall send
thunder and rain; that ye may perceive and see that your wickedness *is* great,
which ye have done in the sight of the LORD, in asking you a king.
18 So Samuel called unto the LORD; and the LORD sent thunder and rain that
day: and all the people greatly feared the LORD and Samuel.
19 And all the people said unto Samuel, Pray for thy servants unto the LORD
thy God, that we die not: for we have added unto all our sins *this* evil, to ask us
a king.
20 And Samuel said unto the people, Fear not: ye have done all this wicked-
ness: yet turn not aside from following the LORD, but serve the LORD with all
your heart;
21 And turn ye not aside: for *then should ye go* after vain *things*, which cannot
profit nor deliver; for they *are* vain.
22 For the LORD will not forsake his people for his great name's sake: because
it hath pleased the LORD to make you his people.
23 Moreover as for me, God forbid that I should sin against the LORD in ceas-
ing to pray for you: but I will teach you the good and the right way:
24 Only fear the LORD, and serve him in truth with all your heart: for consid-
er how great *things* he hath done for you.
25 But if ye shall still do wickedly, ye shall be consumed, both ye and your
king.

Saul's Select Band of Three Thousand Warriors

13 Saul reigned one year; and when he had reigned two years over Israel,
2 Saul chose him three thousand *men* of Israel; *whereof* two thousand
were with Saul in Michmash and in mount Beth-el, and a thousand were with
Jonathan in Gibeah of Benjamin: and the rest of the people he sent every man
to his tent.
3 And Jonathan smote the garrison of the Philistines that *was* in Geba, and
the Philistines heard *of it*. And Saul blew the trumpet throughout all the land,
saying, Let the Hebrews hear.
4 And all Israel heard say *that* Saul had smitten a garrison of the Philistines,
and *that* Israel also was had in abomination with the Philistines. And the
people were called together after Saul to Gilgal.
5 And the Philistines gathered themselves together to fight with Israel, thir-
ty thousand chariots, and six thousand horsemen, and people as the sand
which *is* on the sea shore in multitude: and they came up, and pitched in
Michmash, eastward from Beth-aven.

6 When the men of Israel saw that they were in a strait, (for the people were
distressed,) then the people did hide themselves in caves, and in thickets, and
in rocks, and in high places, and in pits.
7 And *some of* the Hebrews went over Jordan to the land of Gad and Gilead.
As for Saul, he *was* yet in Gilgal, and all the people followed him trembling.

Saul, Weary of Waiting for Samuel, Offers Sacrifice

8 And he tarried seven days, according to the set time that Samuel *had
appointed*: but Samuel came not to Gilgal; and the people were scattered from
him.
9 And Saul said, Bring hither a burnt offering to me, and peace offerings.
And he offered the burnt offering.
10 And it came to pass, that as soon as he had made an end of offering the
burnt offering, behold, Samuel came; and Saul went out to meet him, that he
might salute him.
11 And Samuel said, What hast thou done? And Saul said, Because I saw that
the people were scattered from me, and *that* thou camest not within the days
appointed, and *that* the Philistines gathered themselves together at
Michmash;
12 Therefore said I, The Philistines will come down now upon me to Gilgal,
and I have not made supplication unto the LORD: I forced myself therefore,
and offered a burnt offering.
13 And Samuel said to Saul, Thou hast done foolishly: thou hast not kept the
commandment of the LORD thy God, which he commanded thee: for now
would the LORD have established thy kingdom upon Israel for ever.
14 But now thy kingdom shall not continue: the LORD hath sought him a man
after his own heart, and the LORD hath commanded him *to be* captain over
his people, because thou hast not kept *that* which the LORD commanded thee.
15 And Samuel arose, and gat him up from Gilgal unto Gibeah of Benjamin.
And Saul numbered the people *that were* present with him, about six hundred
men.
16 And Saul, and Jonathan his son, and the people *that were* present with
them, abode in Gibeah of Benjamin: but the Philistines encamped in
Michmash.
17 And the spoilers came out of the camp of the Philistines in three compa-
nies: one company turned unto the way *that leadeth to* Ophrah, unto the land
of Shual:
18 And another company turned the way *to* Beth-horon: and another com-
pany turned *to* the way of the border that looketh to the valley of Zeboim
toward the wilderness.
19 Now there was no smith found throughout all the land of Israel: for the
Philistines said, Lest the Hebrews make *them* swords or spears:
20 But all the Israelites went down to the Philistines, to sharpen every man
his share, and his coulter, and his axe, and his mattock.
21 Yet they had a file for the mattocks, and for the coulters, and for the forks,
and for the axes, and to sharpen the goads.
22 So it came to pass in the day of battle, that there was neither sword nor
spear found in the hand of any of the people that *were* with Saul and Jonathan:
but with Saul and with Jonathan his son was there found.
23 And the garrison of the Philistines went out to the passage of Michmash.

Unknown to Saul, Jonathan Defeats the Philistines

14 Now it came to pass upon a day, that Jonathan the son of Saul said unto
the young man that bare his armour, Come, and let us go over to the
Philistines' garrison, that *is* on the other side. But he told not his father.

2 And Saul tarried in the uttermost part of Gibeah under a pomegranate tree
which *is* in Migron: and the people that *were* with him *were* about six hundred
men;
3 And Ahiah, the son of Ahitub, Ichabod's brother, the son of Phinehas, the
son of Eli, the LORD's priest in Shiloh, wearing an ephod. And the people knew
not that Jonathan was gone.
4 And between the passages, by which Jonathan sought to go over unto the
Philistines' garrison, *there was* a sharp rock on the one side, and a sharp rock
on the other side: and the name of the one *was* Bozez, and the name of the
other Seneh.
5 The forefront of the one *was* situate northward over against Michmash,
and the other southward over against Gibeah.
6 And Jonathan said to the young man that bare his armour, Come, and let
us go over unto the garrison of these uncircumcised: it may be that the LORD
will work for us: for *there is* no restraint to the LORD to save by many or by few.
7 And his armourbearer said unto him, Do all that *is* in thine heart: turn
thee; behold, I *am* with thee according to thy heart.
8 Then said Jonathan, Behold, we will pass over unto *these* men, and we will
discover ourselves unto them.
9 If they say thus unto us, Tarry until we come to you; then we will stand still
in our place, and will not go up unto them.
10 But if they say thus, Come up unto us; then we will go up: for the LORD
hath delivered them into our hand: and this *shall be* a sign unto us.
11 And both of them discovered themselves unto the garrison of the
Philistines: and the Philistines said, Behold, the Hebrews come forth out of
the holes where they had hid themselves.
12 And the men of the garrison answered Jonathan and his armourbearer,
and said, Come up to us, and we will shew you a thing. And Jonathan said unto
his armourbearer, Come up after me: for the LORD hath delivered them into
the hand of Israel.
13 And Jonathan climbed up upon his hands and upon his feet, and his
armourbearer after him: and they fell before Jonathan; and his armourbear-
er slew after him.
14 And that first slaughter, which Jonathan and his armourbearer made, was
about twenty men, within as it were an half acre of land, *which* a yoke *of oxen*
might plow.
15 And there was trembling in the host, in the field, and among all the people:
the garrison, and the spoilers, they also trembled, and the earth quaked: so it
was a very great trembling.
16 And the watchmen of Saul in Gibeah of Benjamin looked; and, behold,
the multitude melted away, and they went on beating down *one another*.
17 Then said Saul unto the people that *were* with him, Number now, and see
who is gone from us. And when they had numbered, behold, Jonathan and
his armourbearer *were* not *there*.
18 And Saul said unto Ahiah, Bring hither the ark of God. For the ark of God
was at that time with the children of Israel.
19 And it came to pass, while Saul talked unto the priest, that the noise that
was in the host of the Philistines went on and increased: and Saul said unto
the priest, Withdraw thine hand.
20 And Saul and all the people that *were* with him assembled themselves, and
they came to the battle: and, behold, every man's sword was against his fellow,
and there was a very great discomfiture.
21 Moreover the Hebrews *that* were with the Philistines before that time,
which went up with them into the camp *from the country* round about, even
they also *turned* to be with the Israelites that *were* with Saul and Jonathan.

22 Likewise all the men of Israel which had hid themselves in mount
Ephraim, *when* they heard that the Philistines fled, even they also followed
hard after them in the battle.
23 So the LORD saved Israel that day: and the battle passed over unto Beth-
aven.

Saul's Unadvised Command Hinders the Victory

24 And the men of Israel were distressed that day: for Saul had adjured the
people, saying, Cursed *be* the man that eateth *any* food until evening, that I
may be avenged on mine enemies. So none of the people tasted *any* food.
25 And all *they of* the land came to a wood; and there was honey upon the
ground.
26 And when the people were come into the wood, behold, the honey
dropped; but no man put his hand to his mouth: for the people feared the
oath.
27 But Jonathan heard not when his father charged the people with the oath:
wherefore he put forth the end of the rod that *was* in his hand, and dipped it
in an honeycomb, and put his hand to his mouth; and his eyes were enlight-
ened.
28 Then answered one of the people, and said, Thy father straitly charged
the people with an oath, saying, Cursed *be* the man that eateth *any* food this
day. And the people were faint.
29 Then said Jonathan, My father hath troubled the land: see, I pray you, how
mine eyes have been enlightened, because I tasted a little of this honey.
30 How much more, if haply the people had eaten freely to day of the spoil
of their enemies which they found? for had there not been now a much great-
er slaughter among the Philistines?
31 And they smote the Philistines that day from Michmash to Aijalon: and
the people were very faint.
32 And the people flew upon the spoil, and took sheep, and oxen, and calves,
and slew *them* on the ground: and the people did eat *them* with the blood.
33 Then they told Saul, saying, Behold, the people sin against the LORD, in
that they eat with the blood. And he said, Ye have transgressed: roll a great
stone unto me this day.
34 And Saul said, Disperse yourselves among the people, and say unto them,
Bring me hither every man his ox, and every man his sheep, and slay *them*
here, and eat; and sin not against the LORD in eating with the blood. And all
the people brought every man his ox with him that night, and slew *them* there.
35 And Saul built an altar unto the LORD: the same was the first altar that he
built unto the LORD.

Jonathan, Taken by Lot, Is Saved by the People

36 And Saul said, Let us go down after the Philistines by night, and spoil them
until the morning light, and let us not leave a man of them. And they said, Do
whatsoever seemeth good unto thee. Then said the priest, Let us draw near
hither unto God.
37 And Saul asked counsel of God, Shall I go down after the Philistines? wilt
thou deliver them into the hand of Israel? But he answered him not that day.
38 And Saul said, Draw ye near hither, all the chief of the people: and know
and see wherein this sin hath been this day.
39 For, *as* the LORD liveth, which saveth Israel, though it be in Jonathan my
son, he shall surely die. But *there was* not a man among all the people *that*
answered him.
40 Then said he unto all Israel, Be ye on one side, and I and Jonathan my son
will be on the other side. And the people said unto Saul, Do what seemeth good
unto thee.

41 Therefore Saul said unto the LORD God of Israel, Give a perfect *lot*. And
Saul and Jonathan were taken: but the people escaped.
42 And Saul said, Cast *lots* between me and Jonathan my son. And Jonathan
was taken.
43 Then Saul said to Jonathan, Tell me what thou hast done. And Jonathan
told him, and said, I did but taste a little honey with the end of the rod that
was in mine hand, *and*, lo, I must die.
44 And Saul answered, God do so and more also: for thou shalt surely die,
Jonathan.
45 And the people said unto Saul, Shall Jonathan die, who hath wrought this
great salvation in Israel? God forbid: *as* the LORD liveth, there shall not one
hair of his head fall to the ground; for he hath wrought with God this day. So
the people rescued Jonathan, that he died not.
46 Then Saul went up from following the Philistines: and the Philistines went
to their own place.

Saul's Strength and Family

47 So Saul took the kingdom over Israel, and fought against all his enemies
on every side, against Moab, and against the children of Ammon, and against
Edom, and against the kings of Zobah, and against the Philistines: and whith-
ersoever he turned himself, he vexed *them*.
48 And he gathered an host, and smote the Amalekites, and delivered Israel
out of the hands of them that spoiled them.
49 Now the sons of Saul were Jonathan, and Ishui, and Melchishua: and the
names of his two daughters *were these*; the name of the firstborn Merab, and
the name of the younger Michal:
50 And the name of Saul's wife *was* Ahinoam, the daughter of Ahimaaz: and
the name of the captain of his host *was* Abner, the son of Ner, Saul's uncle.
51 And Kish *was* the father of Saul; and Ner the father of Abner *was* the son
of Abiel.
52 And there was sore war against the Philistines all the days of Saul: and
when Saul saw any strong man, or any valiant man, he took him unto him.

Samuel Sends Saul to Destroy Amalek

15 Samuel also said unto Saul, The LORD sent me to anoint thee *to be* king
over his people, over Israel: now therefore hearken thou unto the voice
of the words of the LORD.
2 Thus saith the LORD of hosts, I remember *that* which Amalek did to Israel,
how he laid *wait* for him in the way, when he came up from Egypt.
3 Now go and smite Amalek, and utterly destroy all that they have, and spare
them not; but slay both man and woman, infant and suckling, ox and sheep,
camel and ass.
4 And Saul gathered the people together, and numbered them in Telaim, two
hundred thousand footmen, and ten thousand men of Judah.
5 And Saul came to a city of Amalek, and laid wait in the valley.
6 And Saul said unto the Kenites, Go, depart, get you down from among the
Amalekites, lest I destroy you with them: for ye shewed kindness to all the
children of Israel, when they came up out of Egypt. So the Kenites departed
from among the Amalekites.
7 And Saul smote the Amalekites from Havilah *until* thou comest to Shur,
that *is* over against Egypt.
8 And he took Agag the king of the Amalekites alive, and utterly destroyed
all the people with the edge of the sword.
9 But Saul and the people spared Agag, and the best of the sheep, and of the
oxen, and of the fatlings, and the lambs, and all *that was* good, and would not
utterly destroy them: but every thing *that was* vile and refuse, that they
destroyed utterly.

God Rejects Saul for His Disobedience

10 Then came the word of the LORD unto Samuel, saying,
11 It repenteth me that I have set up Saul *to be* king: for he is turned back
from following me, and hath not performed my commandments. And it
grieved Samuel; and he cried unto the LORD all night.
12 And when Samuel rose early to meet Saul in the morning, it was told
Samuel, saying, Saul came to Carmel, and, behold, he set him up a place, and
is gone about, and passed on, and gone down to Gilgal.
13 And Samuel came to Saul: and Saul said unto him, Blessed *be* thou of the
LORD: I have performed the commandment of the LORD.
14 And Samuel said, What *meaneth* then this bleating of the sheep in mine
ears, and the lowing of the oxen which I hear?
15 And Saul said, They have brought them from the Amalekites: for the peo-
ple spared the best of the sheep and of the oxen, to sacrifice unto the LORD thy
God; and the rest we have utterly destroyed.
16 Then Samuel said unto Saul, Stay, and I will tell thee what the LORD hath
said to me this night. And he said unto him, Say on.
17 And Samuel said, When thou *wast* little in thine own sight, *wast* thou not
made the head of the tribes of Israel, and the LORD anointed thee king over
Israel?
18 And the LORD sent thee on a journey, and said, Go and utterly destroy the
sinners the Amalekites, and fight against them until they be consumed.
19 Wherefore then didst thou not obey the voice of the LORD, but didst fly
upon the spoil, and didst evil in the sight of the LORD?
20 And Saul said unto Samuel, Yea, I have obeyed the voice of the LORD, and
have gone the way which the LORD sent me, and have brought Agag the king
of Amalek, and have utterly destroyed the Amalekites.
21 But the people took of the spoil, sheep and oxen, the chief of the things
which should have been utterly destroyed, to sacrifice unto the LORD thy God
in Gilgal.
22 And Samuel said, Hath the LORD *as great* delight in burnt offerings and
sacrifices, as in obeying the voice of the LORD? Behold, to obey *is* better than
sacrifice, *and* to hearken than the fat of rams.
23 For rebellion *is as* the sin of witchcraft, and stubbornness *is as* iniquity
and idolatry. Because thou hast rejected the word of the LORD, he hath also
rejected thee from *being* king.

Saul's Humiliation

24 And Saul said unto Samuel, I have sinned: for I have transgressed the com-
mandment of the LORD, and thy words: because I feared the people, and obeyed
their voice.
25 Now therefore, I pray thee, pardon my sin, and turn again with me, that
I may worship the LORD.
26 And Samuel said unto Saul, I will not return with thee: for thou hast reject-
ed the word of the LORD, and the LORD hath rejected thee from being king over
Israel.
27 And as Samuel turned about to go away, he laid hold upon the skirt of his
mantle, and it rent.
28 And Samuel said unto him, The LORD hath rent the kingdom of Israel from
thee this day, and hath given it to a neighbour of thine, *that is* better than
thou.
29 And also the Strength of Israel will not lie nor repent: for he *is* not a man,
that he should repent.
30 Then he said, I have sinned: *yet* honour me now, I pray thee, before the
elders of my people, and before Israel, and turn again with me, that I may
worship the LORD thy God.

31 So Samuel turned again after Saul; and Saul worshipped the LORD.

Samuel Kills Agag

32 Then said Samuel, Bring ye hither to me Agag the king of the Amalekites.
And Agag came unto him delicately. And Agag said, Surely the bitterness of
death is past.
33 And Samuel said, As thy sword hath made women childless, so shall thy
mother be childless among women. And Samuel hewed Agag in pieces before
the LORD in Gilgal.
34 Then Samuel went to Ramah; and Saul went up to his house to Gibeah of
Saul.
35 And Samuel came no more to see Saul until the day of his death: never-
theless Samuel mourned for Saul: and the LORD repented that he had made
Saul king over Israel.

Samuel Is Sent by God to Beth-lehem

16 And the LORD said unto Samuel, How long wilt thou mourn for Saul,
seeing I have rejected him from reigning over Israel? fill thine horn
with oil, and go, I will send thee to Jesse the Beth-lehemite: for I have provided
me a king among his sons.
2 And Samuel said, How can I go? if Saul hear *it*, he will kill me. And the LORD
said, Take an heifer with thee, and say, I am come to sacrifice to the LORD.
3 And call Jesse to the sacrifice, and I will shew thee what thou shalt do: and
thou shalt anoint unto me *him* whom I name unto thee.
4 And Samuel did that which the LORD spake, and came to Beth-lehem. And
the elders of the town trembled at his coming, and said, Comest thou peace-
ably?
5 And he said, Peaceably: I am come to sacrifice unto the LORD: sanctify your-
selves, and come with me to the sacrifice. And he sanctified Jesse and his sons,
and called them to the sacrifice.

David Is Chosen to Be King

6 And it came to pass, when they were come, that he looked on Eliab, and
said, Surely the LORD's anointed *is* before him.
7 But the LORD said unto Samuel, Look not on his countenance, or on the
height of his stature; because I have refused him: for *the LORD seeth* not as man
seeth; for man looketh on the outward appearance, but the LORD looketh on
the heart.
8 Then Jesse called Abinadab, and made him pass before Samuel. And he said,
Neither hath the LORD chosen this.
9 Then Jesse made Shammah to pass by. And he said, Neither hath the LORD
chosen this.
10 Again, Jesse made seven of his sons to pass before Samuel. And Samuel
said unto Jesse, The LORD hath not chosen these.
11 And Samuel said unto Jesse, Are here all *thy* children? And he said, There
remaineth yet the youngest, and, behold, he keepeth the sheep. And Samuel
said unto Jesse, Send and fetch him: for we will not sit down till he come
hither.
12 And he sent, and brought him in. Now he *was* ruddy, *and* withal of a
beautiful countenance, and goodly to look to. And the LORD said, Arise, anoint
him: for this *is* he.
13 Then Samuel took the horn of oil, and anointed him in the midst of his
brethren: and the Spirit of the LORD came upon David from that day forward.
So Samuel rose up, and went to Ramah.
14 But the Spirit of the LORD departed from Saul, and an evil spirit from the
LORD troubled him.
15 And Saul's servants said unto him, Behold now, an evil spirit from God
troubleth thee.

16 Let our lord now command thy servants, *which are* before thee, to seek out a man, *who is* a cunning player on an harp: and it shall come to pass, when the evil spirit from God is upon thee, that he shall play with his hand, and thou shalt be well.

17 And Saul said unto his servants, Provide me now a man that can play well, and bring *him* to me.

18 Then answered one of the servants, and said, Behold, I have seen a son of Jesse the Beth-lehemite, *that is* cunning in playing, and a mighty valiant man, and a man of war, and prudent in matters, and a comely person, and the LORD *is* with him.

19 Wherefore Saul sent messengers unto Jesse, and said, Send me David thy son, which *is* with the sheep.

20 And Jesse took an ass *laden* with bread, and a bottle of wine, and a kid, and sent *them* by David his son unto Saul.

21 And David came to Saul, and stood before him: and he loved him greatly; and he became his armourbearer.

22 And Saul sent to Jesse, saying, Let David, I pray thee, stand before me; for he hath found favour in my sight.

23 And it came to pass, when the *evil* spirit from God was upon Saul, that David took an harp, and played with his hand: so Saul was refreshed, and was well, and the evil spirit departed from him.

The Armies of the Israelites and Philistines Prepare to Fight

17 Now the Philistines gathered together their armies to battle, and were gathered together at Shochoh, which *belongeth* to Judah, and pitched between Shochoh and Azekah, in Ephes-dammim.

2 And Saul and the men of Israel were gathered together, and pitched by the valley of Elah, and set the battle in array against the Philistines.

3 And the Philistines stood on a mountain on the one side, and Israel stood on a mountain on the other side: and *there was* a valley between them.

4 And there went out a champion out of the camp of the Philistines, named Goliath, of Gath, whose height *was* six cubits and a span.

5 And *he had* an helmet of brass upon his head, and he *was* armed with a coat of mail; and the weight of the coat *was* five thousand shekels of brass.

6 And *he had* greaves of brass upon his legs, and a target of brass between his shoulders.

7 And the staff of his spear *was* like a weaver's beam; and his spear's head *weighed* six hundred shekels of iron: and one bearing a shield went before him.

8 And he stood and cried unto the armies of Israel, and said unto them, Why are ye come out to set *your* battle in array? *am* not I a Philistine, and ye servants to Saul? choose you a man for you, and let him come down to me.

9 If he be able to fight with me, and to kill me, then will we be your servants: but if I prevail against him, and kill him, then shall ye be our servants, and serve us.

10 And the Philistine said, I defy the armies of Israel this day; give me a man, that we may fight together.

11 When Saul and all Israel heard those words of the Philistine, they were dismayed, and greatly afraid.

David Defeats Goliath

12 Now David *was* the son of that Ephrathite of Beth-lehem-judah, whose name *was* Jesse; and he had eight sons: and the man went among men *for* an old man in the days of Saul.

13 And the three eldest sons of Jesse went *and* followed Saul to the battle: and the names of his three sons that went to the battle *were* Eliab the firstborn, and next unto him Abinadab, and the third Shammah.

14 And David *was* the youngest: and the three eldest followed Saul.
15 But David went and returned from Saul to feed his father's sheep at Beth-
lehem.
16 And the Philistine drew near morning and evening, and presented himself
forty days.
17 And Jesse said unto David his son, Take now for thy brethren an ephah of
this parched *corn*, and these ten loaves, and run to the camp to thy brethren;
18 And carry these ten cheeses unto the captain of *their* thousand, and look
how thy brethren fare, and take their pledge.
19 Now Saul, and they, and all the men of Israel, *were* in the valley of Elah,
fighting with the Philistines.
20 And David rose up early in the morning, and left the sheep with a keeper,
and took, and went, as Jesse had commanded him; and he came to the trench,
as the host was going forth to the fight, and shouted for the battle.
21 For Israel and the Philistines had put the battle in array, army against
army.
22 And David left his carriage in the hand of the keeper of the carriage, and
ran into the army, and came and saluted his brethren.
23 And as he talked with them, behold, there came up the champion, the
Philistine of Gath, Goliath by name, out of the armies of the Philistines, and
spake according to the same words: and David heard *them*.
24 And all the men of Israel, when they saw the man, fled from him, and were
sore afraid.
25 And the men of Israel said, Have ye seen this man that is come up? surely
to defy Israel is he come up: and it shall be, *that* the man who killeth him, the
king will enrich him with great riches, and will give him his daughter, and
make his father's house free in Israel.
26 And David spake to the men that stood by him, saying, What shall be done
to the man that killeth this Philistine, and taketh away the reproach from
Israel? for who *is* this uncircumcised Philistine, that he should defy the armies
of the living God?
27 And the people answered him after this manner, saying, So shall it be done
to the man that killeth him.
28 And Eliab his eldest brother heard when he spake unto the men; and
Eliab's anger was kindled against David, and he said, Why camest thou down
hither? and with whom hast thou left those few sheep in the wilderness? I
know thy pride, and the naughtiness of thine heart; for thou art come down
that thou mightest see the battle.
29 And David said, What have I now done? *Is there* not a cause?
30 And he turned from him toward another, and spake after the same man-
ner: and the people answered him again after the former manner.
31 And when the words were heard which David spake, they rehearsed *them*
before Saul: and he sent for him.
32 And David said to Saul, Let no man's heart fail because of him; thy servant
will go and fight with this Philistine.
33 And Saul said to David, Thou art not able to go against this Philistine to
fight with him: for thou *art but* a youth, and he a man of war from his youth.
34 And David said unto Saul, Thy servant kept his father's sheep, and there
came a lion, and a bear, and took a lamb out of the flock:
35 And I went out after him, and smote him, and delivered *it* out of his mouth:
and when he arose against me, I caught *him* by his beard, and smote him, and
slew him.
36 Thy servant slew both the lion and the bear: and this uncircumcised
Philistine shall be as one of them, seeing he hath defied the armies of the
living God.

37 David said moreover, The LORD that delivered me out of the paw of the
lion, and out of the paw of the bear, he will deliver me out of the hand of this
Philistine. And Saul said unto David, Go, and the LORD be with thee.
38 And Saul armed David with his armour, and he put an helmet of brass
upon his head; also he armed him with a coat of mail.
39 And David girded his sword upon his armour, and he assayed to go; for
he had not proved *it*. And David said unto Saul, I cannot go with these; for I
have not proved *them*. And David put them off him.
40 And he took his staff in his hand, and chose him five smooth stones out
of the brook, and put them in a shepherd's bag which he had, even in a scrip;
and his sling *was* in his hand: and he drew near to the Philistine.
41 And the Philistine came on and drew near unto David; and the man that
bare the shield *went* before him.
42 And when the Philistine looked about, and saw David, he disdained him:
for he was *but* a youth, and ruddy, and of a fair countenance.
43 And the Philistine said unto David, *Am* I a dog, that thou comest to me
with staves? And the Philistine cursed David by his gods.
44 And the Philistine said to David, Come to me, and I will give thy flesh unto
the fowls of the air, and to the beasts of the field.
45 Then said David to the Philistine, Thou comest to me with a sword, and
with a spear, and with a shield: but I come to thee in the name of the LORD of
hosts, the God of the armies of Israel, whom thou hast defied.
46 This day will the LORD deliver thee into mine hand; and I will smite thee,
and take thine head from thee; and I will give the carcases of the host of the
Philistines this day unto the fowls of the air, and to the wild beasts of the earth;
that all the earth may know that there is a God in Israel.
47 And all this assembly shall know that the LORD saveth not with sword and
spear: for the battle *is* the LORD'S, and he will give you into our hands.
48 And it came to pass, when the Philistine arose, and came and drew nigh
to meet David, that David hasted, and ran toward the army to meet the
Philistine.
49 And David put his hand in his bag, and took thence a stone, and slang *it*,
and smote the Philistine in his forehead, that the stone sunk into his forehead;
and he fell upon his face to the earth.
50 So David prevailed over the Philistine with a sling and with a stone, and
smote the Philistine, and slew him; but *there was* no sword in the hand of
David.
51 Therefore David ran, and stood upon the Philistine, and took his sword,
and drew it out of the sheath thereof, and slew him, and cut off his head
therewith. And when the Philistines saw their champion was dead, they fled.
52 And the men of Israel and of Judah arose, and shouted, and pursued the
Philistines, until thou come to the valley, and to the gates of Ekron. And the
wounded of the Philistines fell down by the way to Shaaraim, even unto Gath,
and unto Ekron.
53 And the children of Israel returned from chasing after the Philistines, and
they spoiled their tents.
54 And David took the head of the Philistine, and brought it to Jerusalem;
but he put his armour in his tent.
55 And when Saul saw David go forth against the Philistine, he said unto
Abner, the captain of the host, Abner, whose son *is* this youth? And Abner said,
As thy soul liveth, O king, I cannot tell.
56 And the king said, Enquire thou whose son the stripling *is*.
57 And as David returned from the slaughter of the Philistine, Abner took
him, and brought him before Saul with the head of the Philistine in his hand.
58 And Saul said to him, Whose son *art* thou, *thou* young man? And David
answered, I *am* the son of thy servant Jesse the Beth-lehemite.

The Friendship of Jonathan and David

18 And it came to pass, when he had made an end of speaking unto Saul,
that the soul of Jonathan was knit with the soul of David, and Jonathan
loved him as his own soul.
2 And Saul took him that day, and would let him go no more home to his
father's house.
3 Then Jonathan and David made a covenant, because he loved him as his
own soul.
4 And Jonathan stripped himself of the robe that *was* upon him, and gave it
to David, and his garments, even to his sword, and to his bow, and to his girdle.
5 And David went out whithersoever Saul sent him, *and* behaved himself
wisely: and Saul set him over the men of war, and he was accepted in the sight
of all the people, and also in the sight of Saul's servants.
6 And it came to pass as they came, when David was returned from the slaugh-
ter of the Philistine, that the women came out of all cities of Israel, singing
and dancing, to meet king Saul, with tabrets, with joy, and with instruments
of musick.
7 And the women answered *one another* as they played, and said, Saul hath
slain his thousands, and David his ten thousands.
8 And Saul was very wroth, and the saying displeased him; and he said, They
have ascribed unto David ten thousands, and to me they have ascribed *but*
thousands: and *what* can he have more but the kingdom?
9 And Saul eyed David from that day and forward.
10 And it came to pass on the morrow, that the evil spirit from God came
upon Saul, and he prophesied in the midst of the house: and David played with
his hand, as at other times: and *there was* a javelin in Saul's hand.
11 And Saul cast the javelin; for he said, I will smite David even to the wall
with it. And David avoided out of his presence twice.

Saul's Jealousy of David

12 And Saul was afraid of David, because the LORD was with him, and was
departed from Saul.
13 Therefore Saul removed him from him, and made him his captain over a
thousand; and he went out and came in before the people.
14 And David behaved himself wisely in all his ways; and the LORD *was* with
him.
15 Wherefore when Saul saw that he behaved himself very wisely, he was
afraid of him.
16 But all Israel and Judah loved David, because he went out and came in
before them.
17 And Saul said to David, Behold my elder daughter Merab, her will I give
thee to wife: only be thou valiant for me, and fight the LORD's battles. For Saul
said, Let not mine hand be upon him, but let the hand of the Philistines be
upon him.
18 And David said unto Saul, Who *am* I? and what *is* my life, *or* my father's
family in Israel, that I should be son in law to the king?
19 But it came to pass at the time when Merab Saul's daughter should have
been given to David, that she was given unto Adriel the Meholathite to wife.
20 And Michal Saul's daughter loved David: and they told Saul, and the thing
pleased him.
21 And Saul said, I will give him her, that she may be a snare to him, and that
the hand of the Philistines may be against him. Wherefore Saul said to David,
Thou shalt this day be my son in law in *the one of* the twain.
22 And Saul commanded his servants, *saying*, Commune with David secret-
ly, and say, Behold, the king hath delight in thee, and all his servants love thee:
now therefore be the king's son in law.

23 And Saul's servants spake those words in the ears of David. And David said,
Seemeth it to you *a* light *thing* to be a king's son in law, seeing that I *am* a poor
man, and lightly esteemed?
24 And the servants of Saul told him, saying, On this manner spake David.
25 And Saul said, Thus shall ye say to David, The king desireth not any dowry,
but an hundred foreskins of the Philistines, to be avenged of the king's ene-
mies. But Saul thought to make David fall by the hand of the Philistines.
26 And when his servants told David these words, it pleased David well to be
the king's son in law: and the days were not expired.
27 Wherefore David arose and went, he and his men, and slew of the
Philistines two hundred men; and David brought their foreskins, and they
gave them in full tale to the king, that he might be the king's son in law. And
Saul gave him Michal his daughter to wife.
28 And Saul saw and knew that the LORD *was* with David, and *that* Michal
Saul's daughter loved him.
29 And Saul was yet the more afraid of David; and Saul became David's enemy
continually.
30 Then the princes of the Philistines went forth: and it came to pass, after
they went forth, *that* David behaved himself more wisely than all the servants
of Saul; so that his name was much set by.

Saul Plans to Kill David, but Jonathan Intervenes

19 And Saul spake to Jonathan his son, and to all his servants, that they
should kill David.
2 But Jonathan Saul's son delighted much in David: and Jonathan told David,
saying, Saul my father seeketh to kill thee: now therefore, I pray thee, take heed
to thyself until the morning, and abide in a secret *place*, and hide thyself:
3 And I will go out and stand beside my father in the field where thou *art*,
and I will commune with my father of thee; and what I see, that I will tell thee.
4 And Jonathan spake good of David unto Saul his father, and said unto him,
Let not the king sin against his servant, against David; because he hath not
sinned against thee, and because his works *have been* to thee-ward very good:
5 For he did put his life in his hand, and slew the Philistine, and the LORD
wrought a great salvation for all Israel: thou sawest *it*, and didst rejoice: where-
fore then wilt thou sin against innocent blood, to slay David without a cause?
6 And Saul hearkened unto the voice of Jonathan: and Saul sware, *As* the LORD
liveth, he shall not be slain.
7 And Jonathan called David, and Jonathan shewed him all those things. And
Jonathan brought David to Saul, and he was in his presence, as in times past.

Saul Tries to Kill David, but Michal Intervenes

8 And there was war again: and David went out, and fought with the
Philistines, and slew them with a great slaughter; and they fled from him.
9 And the evil spirit from the LORD was upon Saul, as he sat in his house with
his javelin in his hand: and David played with *his* hand.
10 And Saul sought to smite David even to the wall with the javelin; but he
slipped away out of Saul's presence, and he smote the javelin into the wall: and
David fled, and escaped that night.
11 Saul also sent messengers unto David's house, to watch him, and to slay
him in the morning: and Michal David's wife told him, saying, If thou save not
thy life to night, to morrow thou shalt be slain.
12 So Michal let David down through a window: and he went, and fled, and
escaped.
13 And Michal took an image, and laid *it* in the bed, and put a pillow of goats'
hair for his bolster, and covered *it* with a cloth.
14 And when Saul sent messengers to take David, she said, He *is* sick.

15 And Saul sent the messengers *again* to see David, saying, Bring him up to
me in the bed, that I may slay him.
16 And when the messengers were come in, behold, *there was* an image in
the bed, with a pillow of goats' *hair* for his bolster.
17 And Saul said unto Michal, Why hast thou deceived me so, and sent away
mine enemy, that he is escaped? And Michal answered Saul, He said unto me,
Let me go; why should I kill thee?

David Escapes to Samuel

18 So David fled, and escaped, and came to Samuel to Ramah, and told him
all that Saul had done to him. And he and Samuel went and dwelt in Naioth.
19 And it was told Saul, saying, Behold, David *is* at Naioth in Ramah.
20 And Saul sent messengers to take David: and when they saw the company
of the prophets prophesying, and Samuel standing *as* appointed over them,
the Spirit of God was upon the messengers of Saul, and they also prophesied.
21 And when it was told Saul, he sent other messengers, and they prophesied
likewise. And Saul sent messengers again the third time, and they prophesied
also.
22 Then went he also to Ramah, and came to a great well that *is* in Sechu: and
he asked and said, Where *are* Samuel and David? And *one* said, Behold, *they*
be at Naioth in Ramah.
23 And he went thither to Naioth in Ramah: and the Spirit of God was upon
him also, and he went on, and prophesied, until he came to Naioth in Ramah.
24 And he stripped off his clothes also, and prophesied before Samuel in like
manner, and lay down naked all that day and all that night. Wherefore they
say, *Is* Saul also among the prophets?

David Makes a Promise to Jonathan

20 And David fled from Naioth in Ramah, and came and said before
Jonathan, What have I done? what *is* mine iniquity? and what *is* my
sin before thy father, that he seeketh my life?
2 And he said unto him, God forbid; thou shalt not die: behold, my father
will do nothing either great or small, but that he will shew it me: and why
should my father hide this thing from me? it *is* not *so*.
3 And David sware moreover, and said, Thy father certainly knoweth that I
have found grace in thine eyes; and he saith, Let not Jonathan know this, lest
he be grieved: but truly *as* the LORD liveth, and *as* thy soul liveth, *there is* but
a step between me and death.
4 Then said Jonathan unto David, Whatsoever thy soul desireth, I will even
do *it* for thee.
5 And David said unto Jonathan, Behold, to morrow *is* the new moon, and I
should not fail to sit with the king at meat: but let me go, that I may hide myself
in the field unto the third *day* at even.
6 If thy father at all miss me, then say, David earnestly asked *leave* of me that
he might run to Beth-lehem his city: for *there is* a yearly sacrifice there for all
the family.
7 If he say thus, *It is* well; thy servant shall have peace: but if he be very wroth,
then be sure that evil is determined by him.
8 Therefore thou shalt deal kindly with thy servant; for thou hast brought
thy servant into a covenant of the LORD with thee: notwithstanding, if there
be in me iniquity, slay me thyself; for why shouldest thou bring me to thy
father?
9 And Jonathan said, Far be it from thee: for if I knew certainly that evil were
determined by my father to come upon thee, then would not I tell it thee?
10 Then said David to Jonathan, Who shall tell me? or what *if* thy father
answer thee roughly?

11 And Jonathan said unto David, Come, and let us go out into the field. And
they went out both of them into the field.
12 And Jonathan said unto David, O LORD God of Israel, when I have sound-
ed my father about to morrow any time, *or* the third *day*, and, behold, *if there*
be good toward David, and I then send not unto thee, and shew it thee;
13 The LORD do so and much more to Jonathan: but if it please my father *to*
do thee evil, then I will shew it thee, and send thee away, that thou mayest go
in peace: and the LORD be with thee, as he hath been with my father.
14 And thou shalt not only while yet I live shew me the kindness of the LORD,
that I die not:
15 But *also* thou shalt not cut off thy kindness from my house for ever: no,
not when the LORD hath cut off the enemies of David every one from the face
of the earth.
16 So Jonathan made *a covenant* with the house of David, *saying*, Let the
LORD even require *it* at the hand of David's enemies.
17 And Jonathan caused David to swear again, because he loved him: for he
loved him as he loved his own soul.
18 Then Jonathan said to David, To morrow *is* the new moon: and thou shalt
be missed, because thy seat will be empty.
19 And *when* thou hast stayed three days, *then* thou shalt go down quickly,
and come to the place where thou didst hide thyself when the business was *in*
hand, and shalt remain by the stone Ezel.
20 And I will shoot three arrows on the side *thereof*, as though I shot at a
mark.
21 And, behold, I will send a lad, *saying*, Go, find out the arrows. If I express-
ly say unto the lad, Behold, the arrows *are* on this side of thee, take them; then
come thou: for *there is* peace to thee, and no hurt; *as* the LORD liveth.
22 But if I say thus unto the young man, Behold, the arrows *are* beyond thee;
go thy way: for the LORD hath sent thee away.
23 And *as touching* the matter which thou and I have spoken of, behold, the
LORD *be* between thee and me for ever.

Saul Seeks to Kill Jonathan out of Anger at David

24 So David hid himself in the field: and when the new moon was come, the
king sat him down to eat meat.
25 And the king sat upon his seat, as at other times, *even* upon a seat by the
wall: and Jonathan arose, and Abner sat by Saul's side, and David's place was
empty.
26 Nevertheless Saul spake not any thing that day: for he thought, Something
hath befallen him, he *is* not clean; surely he *is* not clean.
27 And it came to pass on the morrow, *which was* the second *day* of the
month, that David's place was empty: and Saul said unto Jonathan his son,
Wherefore cometh not the son of Jesse to meat, neither yesterday, nor to day?
28 And Jonathan answered Saul, David earnestly asked *leave* of me *to go* to
Beth-lehem:
29 And he said, Let me go, I pray thee; for our family hath a sacrifice in the
city; and my brother, he hath commanded me *to be there*: and now, if I have
found favour in thine eyes, let me get away, I pray thee, and see my brethren.
Therefore he cometh not unto the king's table.
30 Then Saul's anger was kindled against Jonathan, and he said unto him,
Thou son of the perverse rebellious *woman*, do not I know that thou hast
chosen the son of Jesse to thine own confusion, and unto the confusion of thy
mother's nakedness?
31 For as long as the son of Jesse liveth upon the ground, thou shalt not be
established, nor thy kingdom. Wherefore now send and fetch him unto me,
for he shall surely die.

32 And Jonathan answered Saul his father, and said unto him, Wherefore
shall he be slain? what hath he done?
33 And Saul cast a javelin at him to smite him: whereby Jonathan knew that
it was determined of his father to slay David.
34 So Jonathan arose from the table in fierce anger, and did eat no meat the
second day of the month: for he was grieved for David, because his father had
done him shame.

Jonathan and David Tearfully Part Ways

35 And it came to pass in the morning, that Jonathan went out into the field
at the time appointed with David, and a little lad with him.
36 And he said unto his lad, Run, find out now the arrows which I shoot. *And*
as the lad ran, he shot an arrow beyond him.
37 And when the lad was come to the place of the arrow which Jonathan had
shot, Jonathan cried after the lad, and said, *Is* not the arrow beyond thee?
38 And Jonathan cried after the lad, Make speed, haste, stay not. And
Jonathan's lad gathered up the arrows, and came to his master.
39 But the lad knew not any thing: only Jonathan and David knew the matter.
40 And Jonathan gave his artillery unto his lad, and said unto him, Go, carry
them to the city.
41 *And* as soon as the lad was gone, David arose out of *a place* toward the
south, and fell on his face to the ground, and bowed himself three times: and
they kissed one another, and wept one with another, until David exceeded.
42 And Jonathan said to David, Go in peace, forasmuch as we have sworn
both of us in the name of the LORD, saying, The LORD be between me and thee,
and between my seed and thy seed for ever. And he arose and departed: and
Jonathan went into the city.

David at Nob Requisitions the Hallowed Bread

21 Then came David to Nob to Ahimelech the priest: and Ahimelech was
afraid at the meeting of David, and said unto him, Why *art* thou alone,
and no man with thee?
2 And David said unto Ahimelech the priest, The king hath commanded me
a business, and hath said unto me, Let no man know any thing of the business
whereabout I send thee, and what I have commanded thee: and I have appoint-
ed *my* servants to such and such a place.
3 Now therefore what is under thine hand? give *me* five *loaves of* bread in
mine hand, or what there is present.
4 And the priest answered David, and said, *There is* no common bread under
mine hand, but there is hallowed bread; if the young men have kept themselves
at least from women.
5 And David answered the priest, and said unto him, Of a truth women *have
been* kept from us about these three days, since I came out, and the vessels of
the young men are holy, and *the bread is* in a manner common, yea, though
it were sanctified this day in the vessel.
6 So the priest gave him hallowed *bread*: for there was no bread there but
the shewbread, that was taken from before the LORD, to put hot bread in the
day when it was taken away.
7 Now a certain man of the servants of Saul *was* there that day, detained
before the LORD; and his name *was* Doeg, an Edomite, the chiefest of the herd-
men that *belonged* to Saul.
8 And David said unto Ahimelech, And is there not here under thine hand
spear or sword? for I have neither brought my sword nor my weapons with
me, because the king's business required haste.
9 And the priest said, The sword of Goliath the Philistine, whom thou slew-
est in the valley of Elah, behold, it *is here* wrapped in a cloth behind the ephod:

if thou wilt take that, take *it*: for *there is* no other save that here. And David said, *There is* none like that; give it me.

David at Gath Pretends to Be Mad

10 And David arose, and fled that day for fear of Saul, and went to Achish the king of Gath.

11 And the servants of Achish said unto him, *Is* not this David the king of the land? did they not sing one to another of him in dances, saying, Saul hath slain his thousands, and David his ten thousands?

12 And David laid up these words in his heart, and was sore afraid of Achish the king of Gath.

13 And he changed his behaviour before them, and feigned himself mad in their hands, and scrabbled on the doors of the gate, and let his spittle fall down upon his beard.

14 Then said Achish unto his servants, Lo, ye see the man is mad: wherefore *then* have ye brought him to me?

15 Have I need of mad men, that ye have brought this *fellow* to play the mad man in my presence? shall this *fellow* come into my house?

Many Gather around David as Their Commander

22 David therefore departed thence, and escaped to the cave Adullam: and when his brethren and all his father's house heard *it*, they went down thither to him.

2 And every one *that was* in distress, and every one that *was* in debt, and every one *that was* discontented, gathered themselves unto him; and he became a captain over them: and there were with him about four hundred men.

3 And David went thence to Mizpeh of Moab: and he said unto the king of Moab, Let my father and my mother, I pray thee, come forth, *and be* with you, till I know what God will do for me.

4 And he brought them before the king of Moab: and they dwelt with him all the while that David was in the hold.

5 And the prophet Gad said unto David, Abide not in the hold; depart, and get thee into the land of Judah. Then David departed, and came into the forest of Hareth.

Saul Massacres the Priests at Nob

6 When Saul heard that David was discovered, and the men that *were* with him, (now Saul abode in Gibeah under a tree in Ramah, having his spear in his hand, and all his servants *were* standing about him;)

7 Then Saul said unto his servants that stood about him, Hear now, ye Benjamites; will the son of Jesse give every one of you fields and vineyards, *and* make you all captains of thousands, and captains of hundreds;

8 That all of you have conspired against me, and *there is* none that sheweth me that my son hath made a league with the son of Jesse, and *there is* none of you that is sorry for me, or sheweth unto me that my son hath stirred up my servant against me, to lie in wait, as at this day?

9 Then answered Doeg the Edomite, which was set over the servants of Saul, and said, I saw the son of Jesse coming to Nob, to Ahimelech the son of Ahitub.

10 And he enquired of the LORD for him, and gave him victuals, and gave him the sword of Goliath the Philistine.

11 Then the king sent to call Ahimelech the priest, the son of Ahitub, and all his father's house, the priests that *were* in Nob: and they came all of them to the king.

12 And Saul said, Hear now, thou son of Ahitub. And he answered, Here I *am*, my lord.

13 And Saul said unto him, Why have ye conspired against me, thou and the
son of Jesse, in that thou hast given him bread, and a sword, and hast enquired
of God for him, that he should rise against me, to lie in wait, as at this day?
14 Then Ahimelech answered the king, and said, And who *is so* faithful
among all thy servants as David, which is the king's son in law, and goeth at
thy bidding, and is honourable in thine house?
15 Did I then begin to enquire of God for him? be it far from me: let not the
king impute *any* thing unto his servant, *nor* to all the house of my father: for
thy servant knew nothing of all this, less or more.
16 And the king said, Thou shalt surely die, Ahimelech, thou, and all thy
father's house.
17 And the king said unto the footmen that stood about him, Turn, and slay
the priests of the LORD; because their hand also *is* with David, and because
they knew when he fled, and did not shew it to me. But the servants of the king
would not put forth their hand to fall upon the priests of the LORD.
18 And the king said to Doeg, Turn thou, and fall upon the priests. And Doeg
the Edomite turned, and he fell upon the priests, and slew on that day four-
score and five persons that did wear a linen ephod.
19 And Nob, the city of the priests, smote he with the edge of the sword, both
men and women, children and sucklings, and oxen, and asses, and sheep, with
the edge of the sword.

Abiathar Escapes and Brings News to David

20 And one of the sons of Ahimelech the son of Ahitub, named Abiathar,
escaped, and fled after David.
21 And Abiathar shewed David that Saul had slain the LORD's priests.
22 And David said unto Abiathar, I knew *it* that day, when Doeg the Edomite
was there, that he would surely tell Saul: I have occasioned *the death* of all the
persons of thy father's house.
23 Abide thou with me, fear not: for he that seeketh my life seeketh thy life:
but with me thou *shalt be* in safeguard.

David, at the Word of the Lord, Rescues Keilah

23 Then they told David, saying, Behold, the Philistines fight against
Keilah, and they rob the threshingfloors.
2 Therefore David enquired of the LORD, saying, Shall I go and smite these
Philistines? And the LORD said unto David, Go, and smite the Philistines, and
save Keilah.
3 And David's men said unto him, Behold, we be afraid here in Judah: how
much more then if we come to Keilah against the armies of the Philistines?
4 Then David enquired of the LORD yet again. And the LORD answered him
and said, Arise, go down to Keilah; for I will deliver the Philistines into thine
hand.
5 So David and his men went to Keilah, and fought with the Philistines, and
brought away their cattle, and smote them with a great slaughter. So David
saved the inhabitants of Keilah.
6 And it came to pass, when Abiathar the son of Ahimelech fled to David to
Keilah, *that* he came down *with* an ephod in his hand.

God Helps David Escape Saul at Keilah

7 And it was told Saul that David was come to Keilah. And Saul said, God hath
delivered him into mine hand; for he is shut in, by entering into a town that
hath gates and bars.
8 And Saul called all the people together to war, to go down to Keilah, to
besiege David and his men.
9 And David knew that Saul secretly practised mischief against him; and he
said to Abiathar the priest, Bring hither the ephod.

10 Then said David, O LORD God of Israel, thy servant hath certainly heard
that Saul seeketh to come to Keilah, to destroy the city for my sake.
11 Will the men of Keilah deliver me up into his hand? will Saul come down,
as thy servant hath heard? O LORD God of Israel, I beseech thee, tell thy servant.
And the LORD said, He will come down.
12 Then said David, Will the men of Keilah deliver me and my men into the
hand of Saul? And the LORD said, They will deliver *thee* up.
13 Then David and his men, *which were* about six hundred, arose and depart-
ed out of Keilah, and went whithersoever they could go. And it was told Saul
that David was escaped from Keilah; and he forbare to go forth.

Jonathan Comforts David in the Wilderness

14 And David abode in the wilderness in strong holds, and remained in a
mountain in the wilderness of Ziph. And Saul sought him every day, but God
delivered him not into his hand.
15 And David saw that Saul was come out to seek his life: and David *was* in
the wilderness of Ziph in a wood.
16 And Jonathan Saul's son arose, and went to David into the wood, and
strengthened his hand in God.
17 And he said unto him, Fear not: for the hand of Saul my father shall not
find thee; and thou shalt be king over Israel, and I shall be next unto thee; and
that also Saul my father knoweth.
18 And they two made a covenant before the LORD: and David abode in the
wood, and Jonathan went to his house.

David in the Wilderness of Maon

19 Then came up the Ziphites to Saul to Gibeah, saying, Doth not David hide
himself with us in strong holds in the wood, in the hill of Hachilah, which *is*
on the south of Jeshimon?
20 Now therefore, O king, come down according to all the desire of thy soul
to come down; and our part *shall be* to deliver him into the king's hand.
21 And Saul said, Blessed *be* ye of the LORD; for ye have compassion on me.
22 Go, I pray you, prepare yet, and know and see his place where his haunt
is, *and* who hath seen him there: for it is told me *that* he dealeth very subtilly.
23 See therefore, and take knowledge of all the lurking places where he hideth
himself, and come ye again to me with the certainty, and I will go with you:
and it shall come to pass, if he be in the land, that I will search him out through-
out all the thousands of Judah.
24 And they arose, and went to Ziph before Saul: but David and his men *were*
in the wilderness of Maon, in the plain on the south of Jeshimon.
25 Saul also and his men went to seek *him*. And they told David: wherefore
he came down into a rock, and abode in the wilderness of Maon. And when
Saul heard *that*, he pursued after David in the wilderness of Maon.
26 And Saul went on this side of the mountain, and David and his men on
that side of the mountain: and David made haste to get away for fear of Saul;
for Saul and his men compassed David and his men round about to take them.
27 But there came a messenger unto Saul, saying, Haste thee, and come; for
the Philistines have invaded the land.
28 Wherefore Saul returned from pursuing after David, and went against
the Philistines: therefore they called that place Selahammahlekoth.
29 And David went up from thence, and dwelt in strong holds at En-gedi.

David Has a Chance to Kill Saul, but Spares Him

24 And it came to pass, when Saul was returned from following the
Philistines, that it was told him, saying, Behold, David *is* in the wilder-
ness of En-gedi.
2 Then Saul took three thousand chosen men out of all Israel, and went to
seek David and his men upon the rocks of the wild goats.

3 And he came to the sheepcotes by the way, where *was* a cave; and Saul went
in to cover his feet: and David and his men remained in the sides of the cave.
4 And the men of David said unto him, Behold the day of which the LORD
said unto thee, Behold, I will deliver thine enemy into thine hand, that thou
mayest do to him as it shall seem good unto thee. Then David arose, and cut
off the skirt of Saul's robe privily.
5 And it came to pass afterward, that David's heart smote him, because he
had cut off Saul's skirt.
6 And he said unto his men, The LORD forbid that I should do this thing unto
my master, the LORD's anointed, to stretch forth mine hand against him, seeing
he *is* the anointed of the LORD.
7 So David stayed his servants with these words, and suffered them not to
rise against Saul. But Saul rose up out of the cave, and went on *his* way.
8 David also arose afterward, and went out of the cave, and cried after Saul,
saying, My lord the king. And when Saul looked behind him, David stooped
with his face to the earth, and bowed himself.
9 And David said to Saul, Wherefore hearest thou men's words, saying,
Behold, David seeketh thy hurt?
10 Behold, this day thine eyes have seen how that the LORD had delivered thee
to day into mine hand in the cave: and *some* bade *me* kill thee: but *mine eye*
spared thee; and I said, I will not put forth mine hand against my lord; for he
is the LORD's anointed.
11 Moreover, my father, see, yea, see the skirt of thy robe in my hand: for in
that I cut off the skirt of thy robe, and killed thee not, know thou and see that
there is neither evil nor transgression in mine hand, and I have not sinned
against thee; yet thou huntest my soul to take it.
12 The LORD judge between me and thee, and the LORD avenge me of thee:
but mine hand shall not be upon thee.
13 As saith the proverb of the ancients, Wickedness proceedeth from the
wicked: but mine hand shall not be upon thee.
14 After whom is the king of Israel come out? after whom dost thou pursue?
after a dead dog, after a flea.
15 The LORD therefore be judge, and judge between me and thee, and see,
and plead my cause, and deliver me out of thine hand.

Saul Expresses Sorrow to David and Returns Home

16 And it came to pass, when David had made an end of speaking these words
unto Saul, that Saul said, *Is* this thy voice, my son David? And Saul lifted up his
voice, and wept.
17 And he said to David, Thou *art* more righteous than I: for thou hast
rewarded me good, whereas I have rewarded thee evil.
18 And thou hast shewed this day how that thou hast dealt well with me:
forasmuch as when the LORD had delivered me into thine hand, thou killedst
me not.
19 For if a man find his enemy, will he let him go well away? wherefore the
LORD reward thee good for that thou hast done unto me this day.
20 And now, behold, I know well that thou shalt surely be king, and that the
kingdom of Israel shall be established in thine hand.
21 Swear now therefore unto me by the LORD, that thou wilt not cut off my
seed after me, and that thou wilt not destroy my name out of my father's house.
22 And David sware unto Saul. And Saul went home; but David and his men
gat them up unto the hold.

Samuel Dies

25 And Samuel died; and all the Israelites were gathered together, and
lamented him, and buried him in his house at Ramah. And David arose,
and went down to the wilderness of Paran.

David, Nabal, and Abigail

2 And *there was* a man in Maon, whose possessions *were* in Carmel; and the
man *was* very great, and he had three thousand sheep, and a thousand goats:
and he was shearing his sheep in Carmel.
3 Now the name of the man *was* Nabal; and the name of his wife Abigail: and
she was a woman of good understanding, and of a beautiful countenance: but
the man *was* churlish and evil in his doings; and he *was* of the house of Caleb.
4 And David heard in the wilderness that Nabal did shear his sheep.
5 And David sent out ten young men, and David said unto the young men,
Get you up to Carmel, and go to Nabal, and greet him in my name:
6 And thus shall ye say to him that liveth *in prosperity*, Peace *be* both to thee,
and peace *be* to thine house, and peace *be* unto all that thou hast.
7 And now I have heard that thou hast shearers: now thy shepherds which
were with us, we hurt them not, neither was there ought missing unto them,
all the while they were in Carmel.
8 Ask thy young men, and they will shew thee. Wherefore let the young men
find favour in thine eyes: for we come in a good day: give, I pray thee, whatso-
ever cometh to thine hand unto thy servants, and to thy son David.
9 And when David's young men came, they spake to Nabal according to all
those words in the name of David, and ceased.
10 And Nabal answered David's servants, and said, Who *is* David? and who
is the son of Jesse? there be many servants now a days that break away every
man from his master.
11 Shall I then take my bread, and my water, and my flesh that I have killed
for my shearers, and give *it* unto men, whom I know not whence they *be*?
12 So David's young men turned their way, and went again, and came and
told him all those sayings.
13 And David said unto his men, Gird ye on every man his sword. And they
girded on every man his sword; and David also girded on his sword: and there
went up after David about four hundred men; and two hundred abode by the
stuff.
14 But one of the young men told Abigail, Nabal's wife, saying, Behold, David
sent messengers out of the wilderness to salute our master; and he railed on
them.
15 But the men *were* very good unto us, and we were not hurt, neither missed
we any thing, as long as we were conversant with them, when we were in the
fields:
16 They were a wall unto us both by night and day, all the while we were with
them keeping the sheep.
17 Now therefore know and consider what thou wilt do; for evil is deter-
mined against our master, and against all his household: for he *is such* a son
of Belial, that *a man* cannot speak to him.
18 Then Abigail made haste, and took two hundred loaves, and two bottles
of wine, and five sheep ready dressed, and five measures of parched *corn*, and
an hundred clusters of raisins, and two hundred cakes of figs, and laid *them*
on asses.
19 And she said unto her servants, Go on before me; behold, I come after you.
But she told not her husband Nabal.
20 And it was *so, as* she rode on the ass, that she came down by the covert of
the hill, and, behold, David and his men came down against her; and she met
them.
21 Now David had said, Surely in vain have I kept all that this *fellow* hath in
the wilderness, so that nothing was missed of all that *pertained* unto him: and
he hath requited me evil for good.
22 So and more also do God unto the enemies of David, if I leave of all that
pertain to him by the morning light any that pisseth against the wall.

23 And when Abigail saw David, she hasted, and lighted off the ass, and fell
before David on her face, and bowed herself to the ground,
24 And fell at his feet, and said, Upon me, my lord, *upon* me *let this* iniquity
be: and let thine handmaid, I pray thee, speak in thine audience, and hear the
words of thine handmaid.
25 Let not my lord, I pray thee, regard this man of Belial, *even* Nabal: for as
his name *is*, so *is* he; Nabal *is* his name, and folly *is* with him: but I thine
handmaid saw not the young men of my lord, whom thou didst send.
26 Now therefore, my lord, *as* the LORD liveth, and *as* thy soul liveth, seeing
the LORD hath withholden thee from coming to *shed* blood, and from aveng-
ing thyself with thine own hand, now let thine enemies, and they that seek
evil to my lord, be as Nabal.
27 And now this blessing which thine handmaid hath brought unto my lord,
let it even be given unto the young men that follow my lord.
28 I pray thee, forgive the trespass of thine handmaid: for the LORD will cer-
tainly make my lord a sure house; because my lord fighteth the battles of the
LORD, and evil hath not been found in thee *all* thy days.
29 Yet a man is risen to pursue thee, and to seek thy soul: but the soul of my
lord shall be bound in the bundle of life with the LORD thy God; and the souls
of thine enemies, them shall he sling out, *as out* of the middle of a sling.
30 And it shall come to pass, when the LORD shall have done to my lord accord-
ing to all the good that he hath spoken concerning thee, and shall have
appointed thee ruler over Israel;
31 That this shall be no grief unto thee, nor offence of heart unto my lord,
either that thou hast shed blood causeless, or that my lord hath avenged him-
self: but when the LORD shall have dealt well with my lord, then remember
thine handmaid.

Abigail Pacifies David

32 And David said to Abigail, Blessed *be* the LORD God of Israel, which sent
thee this day to meet me:
33 And blessed *be* thy advice, and blessed *be* thou, which hast kept me this
day from coming to *shed* blood, and from avenging myself with mine own
hand.
34 For in very deed, *as* the LORD God of Israel liveth, which hath kept me back
from hurting thee, except thou hadst hasted and come to meet me, surely
there had not been left unto Nabal by the morning light any that pisseth
against the wall.
35 So David received of her hand *that* which she had brought him, and said
unto her, Go up in peace to thine house; see, I have hearkened to thy voice,
and have accepted thy person.

Nabal Dies, and David Marries Abigail

36 And Abigail came to Nabal; and, behold, he held a feast in his house, like
the feast of a king; and Nabal's heart *was* merry within him, for he *was* very
drunken: wherefore she told him nothing, less or more, until the morning
light.
37 But it came to pass in the morning, when the wine was gone out of Nabal,
and his wife had told him these things, that his heart died within him, and he
became *as* a stone.
38 And it came to pass about ten days *after*, that the LORD smote Nabal, that
he died.
39 And when David heard that Nabal was dead, he said, Blessed *be* the LORD,
that hath pleaded the cause of my reproach from the hand of Nabal, and hath
kept his servant from evil: for the LORD hath returned the wickedness of Nabal
upon his own head. And David sent and communed with Abigail, to take her
to him to wife.

40 And when the servants of David were come to Abigail to Carmel, they
spake unto her, saying, David sent us unto thee, to take thee to him to wife.
41 And she arose, and bowed herself on *her* face to the earth, and said, Behold,
let thine handmaid *be* a servant to wash the feet of the servants of my lord.
42 And Abigail hasted, and arose, and rode upon an ass, with five damsels of
hers that went after her; and she went after the messengers of David, and
became his wife.
43 David also took Ahinoam of Jezreel; and they were also both of them his
wives.
44 But Saul had given Michal his daughter, David's wife, to Phalti the son of
Laish, which *was* of Gallim.

Saul's Final Pursuit of David

26 And the Ziphites came unto Saul to Gibeah, saying, Doth not David
hide himself in the hill of Hachilah, *which is* before Jeshimon?
2 Then Saul arose, and went down to the wilderness of Ziph, having three
thousand chosen men of Israel with him, to seek David in the wilderness of
Ziph.
3 And Saul pitched in the hill of Hachilah, which *is* before Jeshimon, by the
way. But David abode in the wilderness, and he saw that Saul came after him
into the wilderness.
4 David therefore sent out spies, and understood that Saul was come in very
deed.
5 And David arose, and came to the place where Saul had pitched: and David
beheld the place where Saul lay, and Abner the son of Ner, the captain of his
host: and Saul lay in the trench, and the people pitched round about him.
6 Then answered David and said to Ahimelech the Hittite, and to Abishai the
son of Zeruiah, brother to Joab, saying, Who will go down with me to Saul to
the camp? And Abishai said, I will go down with thee.
7 So David and Abishai came to the people by night: and, behold, Saul lay
sleeping within the trench, and his spear stuck in the ground at his bolster:
but Abner and the people lay round about him.
8 Then said Abishai to David, God hath delivered thine enemy into thine
hand this day: now therefore let me smite him, I pray thee, with the spear even
to the earth at once, and I will not *smite* him the second time.
9 And David said to Abishai, Destroy him not: for who can stretch forth his
hand against the LORD's anointed, and be guiltless?
10 David said furthermore, *As* the LORD liveth, the LORD shall smite him; or
his day shall come to die; or he shall descend into battle, and perish.
11 The LORD forbid that I should stretch forth mine hand against the LORD's
anointed: but, I pray thee, take thou now the spear that *is* at his bolster, and
the cruse of water, and let us go.
12 So David took the spear and the cruse of water from Saul's bolster; and
they gat them away, and no man saw *it*, nor knew *it*, neither awaked: for they
were all asleep; because a deep sleep from the LORD was fallen upon them.

David Reproves Abner and Pleads with Saul

13 Then David went over to the other side, and stood on the top of an hill
afar off; a great space *being* between them:
14 And David cried to the people, and to Abner the son of Ner, saying,
Answerest thou not, Abner? Then Abner answered and said, Who *art* thou
that criest to the king?
15 And David said to Abner, *Art* not thou a *valiant* man? and who *is* like to
thee in Israel? wherefore then hast thou not kept thy lord the king? for there
came one of the people in to destroy the king thy lord.

16 This thing *is* not good that thou hast done. *As* the LORD liveth, ye *are* wor-
thy to die, because ye have not kept your master, the LORD's anointed. And now
see where the king's spear *is*, and the cruse of water that *was* at his bolster.
17 And Saul knew David's voice, and said, *Is* this thy voice, my son David? And
David said, *It is* my voice, my lord, O king.
18 And he said, Wherefore doth my lord thus pursue after his servant? for
what have I done? or what evil *is* in mine hand?
19 Now therefore, I pray thee, let my lord the king hear the words of his
servant. If the LORD have stirred thee up against me, let him accept an offering:
but if *they be* the children of men, cursed *be* they before the LORD; for they
have driven me out this day from abiding in the inheritance of the LORD, say-
ing, Go, serve other gods.
20 Now therefore, let not my blood fall to the earth before the face of the
LORD: for the king of Israel is come out to seek a flea, as when one doth hunt
a partridge in the mountains.

Saul Acknowledges His Sin

21 Then said Saul, I have sinned: return, my son David: for I will no more do
thee harm, because my soul was precious in thine eyes this day: behold, I have
played the fool, and have erred exceedingly.
22 And David answered and said, Behold the king's spear! and let one of the
young men come over and fetch it.
23 The LORD render to every man his righteousness and his faithfulness: for
the LORD delivered thee into *my* hand to day, but I would not stretch forth
mine hand against the LORD's anointed.
24 And, behold, as thy life was much set by this day in mine eyes, so let my
life be much set by in the eyes of the LORD, and let him deliver me out of all
tribulation.
25 Then Saul said to David, Blessed *be* thou, my son David: thou shalt both
do great *things*, and also shalt still prevail. So David went on his way, and Saul
returned to his place.

David Escapes into Philistine Territory to Avoid Saul

27 And David said in his heart, I shall now perish one day by the hand of
Saul: *there is* nothing better for me than that I should speedily escape
into the land of the Philistines; and Saul shall despair of me, to seek me any
more in any coast of Israel: so shall I escape out of his hand.
2 And David arose, and he passed over with the six hundred men that *were*
with him unto Achish, the son of Maoch, king of Gath.
3 And David dwelt with Achish at Gath, he and his men, every man with his
household, *even* David with his two wives, Ahinoam the Jezreelitess, and
Abigail the Carmelitess, Nabal's wife.
4 And it was told Saul that David was fled to Gath: and he sought no more
again for him.
5 And David said unto Achish, If I have now found grace in thine eyes, let
them give me a place in some town in the country, that I may dwell there: for
why should thy servant dwell in the royal city with thee?
6 Then Achish gave him Ziklag that day: wherefore Ziklag pertaineth unto
the kings of Judah unto this day.
7 And the time that David dwelt in the country of the Philistines was a full
year and four months.

David Pretends to Serve King Achish of the Philistines

8 And David and his men went up, and invaded the Geshurites, and the
Gezrites, and the Amalekites: for those *nations were* of old the inhabitants of
the land, as thou goest to Shur, even unto the land of Egypt.

9 And David smote the land, and left neither man nor woman alive, and took
away the sheep, and the oxen, and the asses, and the camels, and the apparel,
and returned, and came to Achish.
10 And Achish said, Whither have ye made a road to day? And David said,
Against the south of Judah, and against the south of the Jerahmeelites, and
against the south of the Kenites.
11 And David saved neither man nor woman alive, to bring *tidings* to Gath,
saying, Lest they should tell on us, saying, So did David, and so *will be* his
manner all the while he dwelleth in the country of the Philistines.
12 And Achish believed David, saying, He hath made his people Israel utter-
ly to abhor him; therefore he shall be my servant for ever.

Achish Puts Confidence in David

28 And it came to pass in those days, that the Philistines gathered their
armies together for warfare, to fight with Israel. And Achish said unto
David, Know thou assuredly, that thou shalt go out with me to battle, thou and
thy men.
2 And David said to Achish, Surely thou shalt know what thy servant can do.
And Achish said to David, Therefore will I make thee keeper of mine head for
ever.
3 Now Samuel was dead, and all Israel had lamented him, and buried him
in Ramah, even in his own city. And Saul had put away those that had familiar
spirits, and the wizards, out of the land.
4 And the Philistines gathered themselves together, and came and pitched
in Shunem: and Saul gathered all Israel together, and they pitched in Gilboa.
5 And when Saul saw the host of the Philistines, he was afraid, and his heart
greatly trembled.
6 And when Saul enquired of the LORD, the LORD answered him not, neither
by dreams, nor by Urim, nor by prophets.

Saul Seeks for a Witch to Help Him

7 Then said Saul unto his servants, Seek me a woman that hath a familiar
spirit, that I may go to her, and enquire of her. And his servants said to him,
Behold, *there is* a woman that hath a familiar spirit at En-dor.
8 And Saul disguised himself, and put on other raiment, and he went, and
two men with him, and they came to the woman by night: and he said, I pray
thee, divine unto me by the familiar spirit, and bring me *him* up, whom I shall
name unto thee.
9 And the woman said unto him, Behold, thou knowest what Saul hath done,
how he hath cut off those that have familiar spirits, and the wizards, out of
the land: wherefore then layest thou a snare for my life, to cause me to die?
10 And Saul sware to her by the LORD, saying, *As* the LORD liveth, there shall
no punishment happen to thee for this thing.
11 Then said the woman, Whom shall I bring up unto thee? And he said,
Bring me up Samuel.
12 And when the woman saw Samuel, she cried with a loud voice: and the
woman spake to Saul, saying, Why hast thou deceived me? for thou *art* Saul.
13 And the king said unto her, Be not afraid: for what sawest thou? And the
woman said unto Saul, I saw gods ascending out of the earth.
14 And he said unto her, What form *is* he of? And she said, An old man com-
eth up; and he *is* covered with a mantle. And Saul perceived that it *was* Samuel,
and he stooped with *his* face to the ground, and bowed himself.

Saul Is Told His Fate

15 And Samuel said to Saul, Why hast thou disquieted me, to bring me up?
And Saul answered, I am sore distressed; for the Philistines make war against
me, and God is departed from me, and answereth me no more, neither by

prophets, nor by dreams: therefore I have called thee, that thou mayest make
known unto me what I shall do.
16 Then said Samuel, Wherefore then dost thou ask of me, seeing the LORD
is departed from thee, and is become thine enemy?
17 And the LORD hath done to him, as he spake by me: for the LORD hath rent
the kingdom out of thine hand, and given it to thy neighbour, *even* to David:
18 Because thou obeyedst not the voice of the LORD, nor executedst his fierce
wrath upon Amalek, therefore hath the LORD done this thing unto thee this
day.
19 Moreover the LORD will also deliver Israel with thee into the hand of the
Philistines: and to morrow *shalt* thou and thy sons *be* with me: the LORD also
shall deliver the host of Israel into the hand of the Philistines.
20 Then Saul fell straightway all along on the earth, and was sore afraid,
because of the words of Samuel: and there was no strength in him; for he had
eaten no bread all the day, nor all the night.
21 And the woman came unto Saul, and saw that he was sore troubled, and
said unto him, Behold, thine handmaid hath obeyed thy voice, and I have put
my life in my hand, and have hearkened unto thy words which thou spakest
unto me.
22 Now therefore, I pray thee, hearken thou also unto the voice of thine
handmaid, and let me set a morsel of bread before thee; and eat, that thou
mayest have strength, when thou goest on thy way.
23 But he refused, and said, I will not eat. But his servants, together with the
woman, compelled him; and he hearkened unto their voice. So he arose from
the earth, and sat upon the bed.
24 And the woman had a fat calf in the house; and she hasted, and killed it,
and took flour, and kneaded *it*, and did bake unleavened bread thereof:
25 And she brought *it* before Saul, and before his servants; and they did eat.
Then they rose up, and went away that night.

David Marches with the Philistines, but Is Rejected by Their Princes

29 Now the Philistines gathered together all their armies to Aphek: and
the Israelites pitched by a fountain which *is* in Jezreel.
2 And the lords of the Philistines passed on by hundreds, and by thousands:
but David and his men passed on in the rereward with Achish.
3 Then said the princes of the Philistines, What *do* these Hebrews *here*? And
Achish said unto the princes of the Philistines, *Is* not this David, the servant
of Saul the king of Israel, which hath been with me these days, or these years,
and I have found no fault in him since he fell *unto me* unto this day?
4 And the princes of the Philistines were wroth with him; and the princes
of the Philistines said unto him, Make this fellow return, that he may go again
to his place which thou hast appointed him, and let him not go down with us
to battle, lest in the battle he be an adversary to us: for wherewith should he
reconcile himself unto his master? *should it* not *be* with the heads of these
men?
5 *Is* not this David, of whom they sang one to another in dances, saying, Saul
slew his thousands, and David his ten thousands?

Achish Dismisses David, with Commendations

6 Then Achish called David, and said unto him, Surely, *as* the LORD liveth,
thou hast been upright, and thy going out and thy coming in with me in the
host *is* good in my sight: for I have not found evil in thee since the day of thy
coming unto me unto this day: nevertheless the lords favour thee not.
7 Wherefore now return, and go in peace, that thou displease not the lords
of the Philistines.

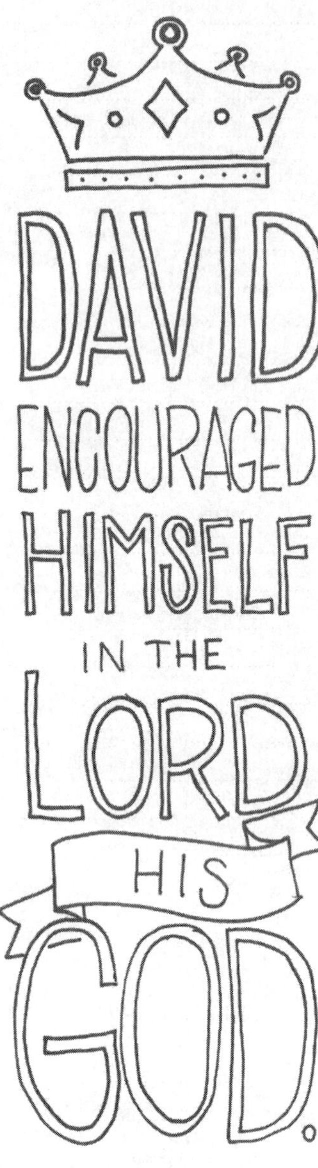

8 And David said unto Achish, But what have I done? and what hast thou
found in thy servant so long as I have been with thee unto this day, that I may
not go fight against the enemies of my lord the king?
9 And Achish answered and said to David, I know that thou *art* good in my
sight, as an angel of God: notwithstanding the princes of the Philistines have
said, He shall not go up with us to the battle.
10 Wherefore now rise up early in the morning with thy master's servants
that are come with thee: and as soon as ye be up early in the morning, and
have light, depart.
11 So David and his men rose up early to depart in the morning, to return
into the land of the Philistines. And the Philistines went up to Jezreel.

David Defeats the Amalekites

30 And it came to pass, when David and his men were come to Ziklag on
the third day, that the Amalekites had invaded the south, and Ziklag,
and smitten Ziklag, and burned it with fire;
2 And had taken the women captives, that *were* therein: they slew not any,
either great or small, but carried *them* away, and went on their way.
3 So David and his men came to the city, and, behold, *it was* burned with fire;
and their wives, and their sons, and their daughters, were taken captives.
4 Then David and the people that *were* with him lifted up their voice and
wept, until they had no more power to weep.
5 And David's two wives were taken captives, Ahinoam the Jezreelitess, and
Abigail the wife of Nabal the Carmelite.
6 And David was greatly distressed; for the people spake of stoning him,
because the soul of all the people was grieved, every man for his sons and for
his daughters: but David encouraged himself in the LORD his God.
7 And David said to Abiathar the priest, Ahimelech's son, I pray thee, bring
me hither the ephod. And Abiathar brought thither the ephod to David.
8 And David enquired at the LORD, saying, Shall I pursue after this troop?
shall I overtake them? And he answered him, Pursue: for thou shalt surely
overtake *them*, and without fail recover *all*.
9 So David went, he and the six hundred men that *were* with him, and came
to the brook Besor, where those that were left behind stayed.
10 But David pursued, he and four hundred men: for two hundred abode
behind, which were so faint that they could not go over the brook Besor.
11 And they found an Egyptian in the field, and brought him to David, and
gave him bread, and he did eat; and they made him drink water;
12 And they gave him a piece of a cake of figs, and two clusters of raisins: and
when he had eaten, his spirit came again to him: for he had eaten no bread,
nor drunk *any* water, three days and three nights.
13 And David said unto him, To whom *belongest* thou? and whence *art* thou?
And he said, I *am* a young man of Egypt, servant to an Amalekite; and my
master left me, because three days agone I fell sick.
14 We made an invasion *upon* the south of the Cherethites, and upon *the
coast* which *belongeth* to Judah, and upon the south of Caleb; and we burned
Ziklag with fire.
15 And David said to him, Canst thou bring me down to this company? And
he said, Swear unto me by God, that thou wilt neither kill me, nor deliver me
into the hands of my master, and I will bring thee down to this company.
16 And when he had brought him down, behold, *they were* spread abroad
upon all the earth, eating and drinking, and dancing, because of all the great
spoil that they had taken out of the land of the Philistines, and out of the land
of Judah.

17 And David smote them from the twilight even unto the evening of the
next day: and there escaped not a man of them, save four hundred young men,
which rode upon camels, and fled.
18 And David recovered all that the Amalekites had carried away: and David
rescued his two wives.
19 And there was nothing lacking to them, neither small nor great, neither
sons nor daughters, neither spoil, nor any *thing* that they had taken to them:
David recovered all.
20 And David took all the flocks and the herds, *which* they drave before those
other cattle, and said, This *is* David's spoil.
21 And David came to the two hundred men, which were so faint that they
could not follow David, whom they had made also to abide at the brook Besor:
and they went forth to meet David, and to meet the people that *were* with him:
and when David came near to the people, he saluted them.
22 Then answered all the wicked men and *men* of Belial, of those that went
with David, and said, Because they went not with us, we will not give them
ought of the spoil that we have recovered, save to every man his wife and his
children, that they may lead *them* away, and depart.
23 Then said David, Ye shall not do so, my brethren, with that which the LORD
hath given us, who hath preserved us, and delivered the company that came
against us into our hand.
24 For who will hearken unto you in this matter? but as his part *is* that goeth
down to the battle, so *shall* his part *be* that tarrieth by the stuff: they shall part
alike.
25 And it was *so* from that day forward, that he made it a statute and an
ordinance for Israel unto this day.
26 And when David came to Ziklag, he sent of the spoil unto the elders of
Judah, *even* to his friends, saying, Behold a present for you of the spoil of the
enemies of the LORD;
27 To *them* which *were* in Beth-el, and to *them* which *were* in south Ramoth,
and to *them* which *were* in Jattir,
28 And to *them* which *were* in Aroer, and to *them* which *were* in Siphmoth,
and to *them* which *were* in Eshtemoa,
29 And to *them* which *were* in Rachal, and to *them* which *were* in the cities
of the Jerahmeelites, and to *them* which *were* in the cities of the Kenites,
30 And to *them* which *were* in Hormah, and to *them* which *were* in Chorashan,
and to *them* which *were* in Athach,
31 And to *them* which *were* in Hebron, and to all the places where David
himself and his men were wont to haunt.

The Deaths of Saul and Jonathan

31 Now the Philistines fought against Israel: and the men of Israel fled
from before the Philistines, and fell down slain in mount Gilboa.
2 And the Philistines followed hard upon Saul and upon his sons; and the
Philistines slew Jonathan, and Abinadab, and Malchishua, Saul's sons.
3 And the battle went sore against Saul, and the archers hit him; and he was
sore wounded of the archers.
4 Then said Saul unto his armourbearer, Draw thy sword, and thrust me
through therewith; lest these uncircumcised come and thrust me through,
and abuse me. But his armourbearer would not; for he was sore afraid.
Therefore Saul took a sword, and fell upon it.
5 And when his armourbearer saw that Saul was dead, he fell likewise upon
his sword, and died with him.
6 So Saul died, and his three sons, and his armourbearer, and all his men,
that same day together.

7 And when the men of Israel that *were* on the other side of the valley, and
they that *were* on the other side Jordan, saw that the men of Israel fled, and
that Saul and his sons were dead, they forsook the cities, and fled; and the
Philistines came and dwelt in them.

The Philistines Triumph over Israel

8 And it came to pass on the morrow, when the Philistines came to strip the
slain, that they found Saul and his three sons fallen in mount Gilboa.
9 And they cut off his head, and stripped off his armour, and sent into the
land of the Philistines round about, to publish *it in* the house of their idols,
and among the people.
10 And they put his armour in the house of Ashtaroth: and they fastened his
body to the wall of Beth-shan.
11 And when the inhabitants of Jabesh-gilead heard of that which the
Philistines had done to Saul;
12 All the valiant men arose, and went all night, and took the body of Saul
and the bodies of his sons from the wall of Beth-shan, and came to Jabesh, and
burnt them there.
13 And they took their bones, and buried *them* under a tree at Jabesh, and
fasted seven days.

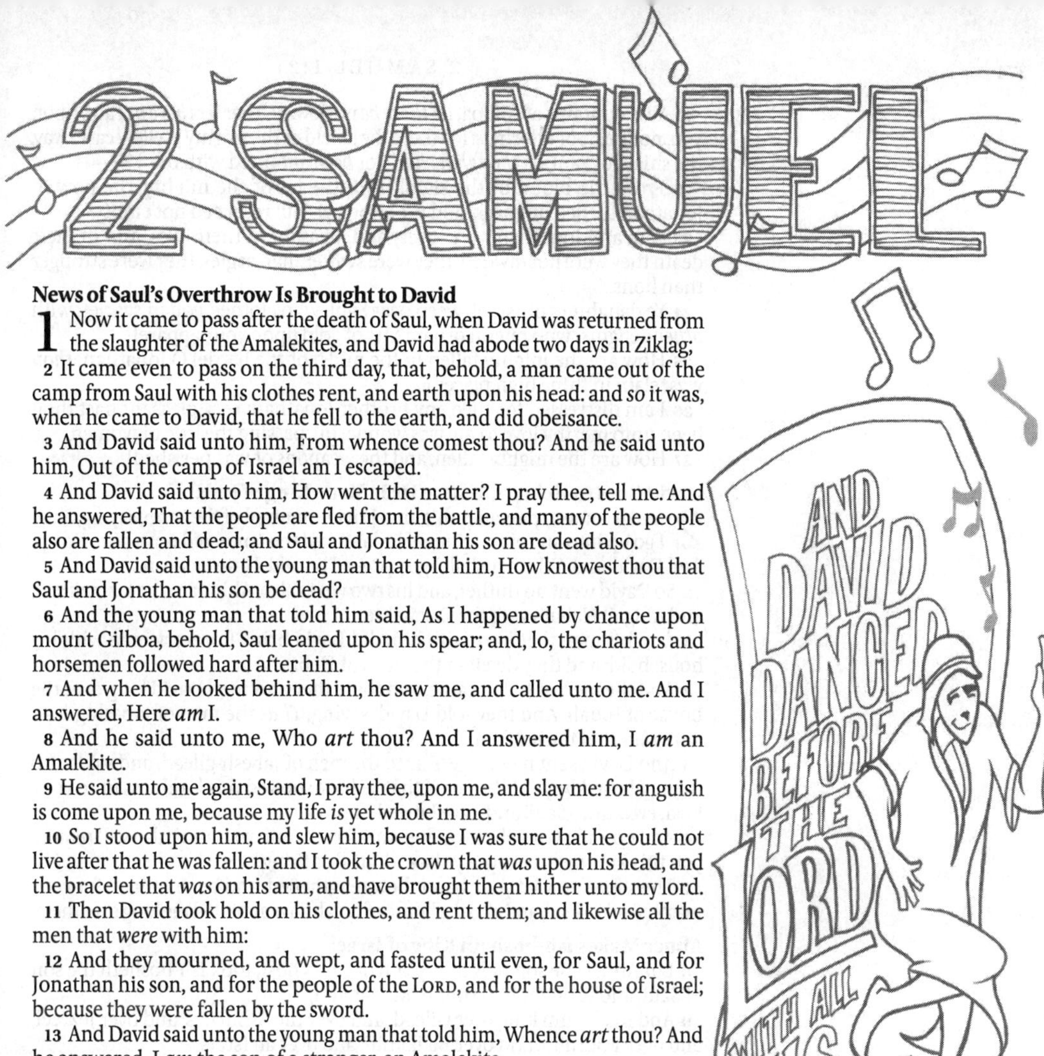

News of Saul's Overthrow Is Brought to David

1 Now it came to pass after the death of Saul, when David was returned from
the slaughter of the Amalekites, and David had abode two days in Ziklag;
2 It came even to pass on the third day, that, behold, a man came out of the
camp from Saul with his clothes rent, and earth upon his head: and *so* it was,
when he came to David, that he fell to the earth, and did obeisance.
3 And David said unto him, From whence comest thou? And he said unto
him, Out of the camp of Israel am I escaped.
4 And David said unto him, How went the matter? I pray thee, tell me. And
he answered, That the people are fled from the battle, and many of the people
also are fallen and dead; and Saul and Jonathan his son are dead also.
5 And David said unto the young man that told him, How knowest thou that
Saul and Jonathan his son be dead?
6 And the young man that told him said, As I happened by chance upon
mount Gilboa, behold, Saul leaned upon his spear; and, lo, the chariots and
horsemen followed hard after him.
7 And when he looked behind him, he saw me, and called unto me. And I
answered, Here *am* I.
8 And he said unto me, Who *art* thou? And I answered him, I *am* an
Amalekite.
9 He said unto me again, Stand, I pray thee, upon me, and slay me: for anguish
is come upon me, because my life *is* yet whole in me.
10 So I stood upon him, and slew him, because I was sure that he could not
live after that he was fallen: and I took the crown that *was* upon his head, and
the bracelet that *was* on his arm, and have brought them hither unto my lord.
11 Then David took hold on his clothes, and rent them; and likewise all the
men that *were* with him:
12 And they mourned, and wept, and fasted until even, for Saul, and for
Jonathan his son, and for the people of the LORD, and for the house of Israel;
because they were fallen by the sword.
13 And David said unto the young man that told him, Whence *art* thou? And
he answered, I *am* the son of a stranger, an Amalekite.
14 And David said unto him, How wast thou not afraid to stretch forth thine
hand to destroy the LORD's anointed?
15 And David called one of the young men, and said, Go near, *and* fall upon
him. And he smote him that he died.
16 And David said unto him, Thy blood *be* upon thy head; for thy mouth hath
testified against thee, saying, I have slain the LORD's anointed.

David Laments Saul and Jonathan with a Song

17 And David lamented with this lamentation over Saul and over Jonathan
his son:
18 (Also he bade them teach the children of Judah *the use of* the bow: behold,
it is written in the book of Jasher.)
19 The beauty of Israel is slain upon thy high places: how are the mighty
fallen!
20 Tell *it* not in Gath, publish *it* not in the streets of Askelon; lest the daughters
of the Philistines rejoice, lest the daughters of the uncircumcised triumph.

21 Ye mountains of Gilboa, *let there be* no dew, neither *let there be* rain, upon you, nor fields of offerings: for there the shield of the mighty is vilely cast away, the shield of Saul, *as though he had* not *been* anointed with oil.

22 From the blood of the slain, from the fat of the mighty, the bow of Jonathan turned not back, and the sword of Saul returned not empty.

23 Saul and Jonathan *were* lovely and pleasant in their lives, and in their death they were not divided: they were swifter than eagles, they were stronger than lions.

24 Ye daughters of Israel, weep over Saul, who clothed you in scarlet, with *other* delights, who put on ornaments of gold upon your apparel.

25 How are the mighty fallen in the midst of the battle! O Jonathan, *thou wast* slain in thine high places.

26 I am distressed for thee, my brother Jonathan: very pleasant hast thou been unto me: thy love to me was wonderful, passing the love of women.

27 How are the mighty fallen, and the weapons of war perished!

David Goes to Hebron, Where He Is Made King of Judah

2 And it came to pass after this, that David enquired of the LORD, saying, Shall I go up into any of the cities of Judah? And the LORD said unto him, Go up. And David said, Whither shall I go up? And he said, Unto Hebron.

2 So David went up thither, and his two wives also, Ahinoam the Jezreelitess, and Abigail Nabal's wife the Carmelite.

3 And his men that *were* with him did David bring up, every man with his household: and they dwelt in the cities of Hebron.

4 And the men of Judah came, and there they anointed David king over the house of Judah. And they told David, saying, *That* the men of Jabesh-gilead *were they* that buried Saul.

5 And David sent messengers unto the men of Jabesh-gilead, and said unto them, Blessed *be* ye of the LORD, that ye have shewed this kindness unto your lord, *even* unto Saul, and have buried him.

6 And now the LORD shew kindness and truth unto you: and I also will requite you this kindness, because ye have done this thing.

7 Therefore now let your hands be strengthened, and be ye valiant: for your master Saul is dead, and also the house of Judah have anointed me king over them.

Abner Makes Ish-bosheth King of Israel

8 But Abner the son of Ner, captain of Saul's host, took Ish-bosheth the son of Saul, and brought him over to Mahanaim;

9 And made him king over Gilead, and over the Ashurites, and over Jezreel, and over Ephraim, and over Benjamin, and over all Israel.

10 Ish-bosheth Saul's son *was* forty years old when he began to reign over Israel, and reigned two years. But the house of Judah followed David.

11 And the time that David was king in Hebron over the house of Judah was seven years and six months.

12 And Abner the son of Ner, and the servants of Ish-bosheth the son of Saul, went out from Mahanaim to Gibeon.

13 And Joab the son of Zeruiah, and the servants of David, went out, and met together by the pool of Gibeon: and they sat down, the one on the one side of the pool, and the other on the other side of the pool.

14 And Abner said to Joab, Let the young men now arise, and play before us. And Joab said, Let them arise.

15 Then there arose and went over by number twelve of Benjamin, which *pertained* to Ish-bosheth the son of Saul, and twelve of the servants of David.

16 And they caught every one his fellow by the head, and *thrust* his sword in his fellow's side; so they fell down together: wherefore that place was called Helkath-hazzurim, which *is* in Gibeon.

17 And there was a very sore battle that day; and Abner was beaten, and the
men of Israel, before the servants of David.

Conflicts between Abner and Joab

18 And there were three sons of Zeruiah there, Joab, and Abishai, and Asahel:
and Asahel *was as* light of foot as a wild roe.
19 And Asahel pursued after Abner; and in going he turned not to the right
hand nor to the left from following Abner.
20 Then Abner looked behind him, and said, *Art* thou Asahel? And he
answered, I *am*.
21 And Abner said to him, Turn thee aside to thy right hand or to thy left,
and lay thee hold on one of the young men, and take thee his armour. But
Asahel would not turn aside from following of him.
22 And Abner said again to Asahel, Turn thee aside from following me: where-
fore should I smite thee to the ground? how then should I hold up my face to
Joab thy brother?
23 Howbeit he refused to turn aside: wherefore Abner with the hinder end
of the spear smote him under the fifth *rib*, that the spear came out behind
him; and he fell down there, and died in the same place: and it came to pass,
that as many as came to the place where Asahel fell down and died stood still.
24 Joab also and Abishai pursued after Abner: and the sun went down when
they were come to the hill of Ammah, that *lieth* before Giah by the way of the
wilderness of Gibeon.

Abner Entreats Joab to End the Slaughter

25 And the children of Benjamin gathered themselves together after Abner,
and became one troop, and stood on the top of an hill.
26 Then Abner called to Joab, and said, Shall the sword devour for ever?
knowest thou not that it will be bitterness in the latter end? how long shall it
be then, ere thou bid the people return from following their brethren?
27 And Joab said, *As* God liveth, unless thou hadst spoken, surely then in the
morning the people had gone up every one from following his brother.
28 So Joab blew a trumpet, and all the people stood still, and pursued after
Israel no more, neither fought they any more.
29 And Abner and his men walked all that night through the plain, and passed
over Jordan, and went through all Bithron, and they came to Mahanaim.
30 And Joab returned from following Abner: and when he had gathered all
the people together, there lacked of David's servants nineteen men and Asahel.
31 But the servants of David had smitten of Benjamin, and of Abner's men,
so that three hundred and threescore men died.
32 And they took up Asahel, and buried him in the sepulchre of his father,
which *was in* Beth-lehem. And Joab and his men went all night, and they came
to Hebron at break of day.

During the War David Still Waxes Stronger

3 Now there was long war between the house of Saul and the house of David:
but David waxed stronger and stronger, and the house of Saul waxed weak-
er and weaker.
2 And unto David were sons born in Hebron: and his firstborn was Amnon,
of Ahinoam the Jezreelitess;
3 And his second, Chileab, of Abigail the wife of Nabal the Carmelite; and
the third, Absalom the son of Maacah the daughter of Talmai king of Geshur;
4 And the fourth, Adonijah the son of Haggith; and the fifth, Shephatiah the
son of Abital;
5 And the sixth, Ithream, by Eglah David's wife. These were born to David in
Hebron.
6 And it came to pass, while there was war between the house of Saul and
the house of David, that Abner made himself strong for the house of Saul.

7 And Saul had a concubine, whose name *was* Rizpah, the daughter of Aiah: and *Ish-bosheth* said to Abner, Wherefore hast thou gone in unto my father's concubine?

8 Then was Abner very wroth for the words of Ish-bosheth, and said, *Am* I a dog's head, which against Judah do shew kindness this day unto the house of Saul thy father, to his brethren, and to his friends, and have not delivered thee into the hand of David, that thou chargest me to day with a fault concerning this woman?

9 So do God to Abner, and more also, except, as the LORD hath sworn to David, even so I do to him;

10 To translate the kingdom from the house of Saul, and to set up the throne of David over Israel and over Judah, from Dan even to Beer-sheba.

11 And he could not answer Abner a word again, because he feared him.

12 And Abner sent messengers to David on his behalf, saying, Whose *is* the land? saying *also*, Make thy league with me, and, behold, my hand *shall be* with thee, to bring about all Israel unto thee.

13 And he said, Well; I will make a league with thee: but one thing I require of thee, that is, Thou shalt not see my face, except thou first bring Michal Saul's daughter, when thou comest to see my face.

14 And David sent messengers to Ish-bosheth Saul's son, saying, Deliver *me* my wife Michal, which I espoused to me for an hundred foreskins of the Philistines.

15 And Ish-bosheth sent, and took her from *her* husband, *even* from Phaltiel the son of Laish.

16 And her husband went with her along weeping behind her to Bahurim. Then said Abner unto him, Go, return. And he returned.

17 And Abner had communication with the elders of Israel, saying, Ye sought for David in times past *to be* king over you:

18 Now then do *it*: for the LORD hath spoken of David, saying, By the hand of my servant David I will save my people Israel out of the hand of the Philistines, and out of the hand of all their enemies.

19 And Abner also spake in the ears of Benjamin: and Abner went also to speak in the ears of David in Hebron all that seemed good to Israel, and that seemed good to the whole house of Benjamin.

20 So Abner came to David to Hebron, and twenty men with him. And David made Abner and the men that *were* with him a feast.

21 And Abner said unto David, I will arise and go, and will gather all Israel unto my lord the king, that they may make a league with thee, and that thou mayest reign over all that thine heart desireth. And David sent Abner away; and he went in peace.

Joab Is Displeased with David and Kills Abner Himself

22 And, behold, the servants of David and Joab came from *pursuing* a troop, and brought in a great spoil with them: but Abner *was* not with David in Hebron; for he had sent him away, and he was gone in peace.

23 When Joab and all the host that *was* with him were come, they told Joab, saying, Abner the son of Ner came to the king, and he hath sent him away, and he is gone in peace.

24 Then Joab came to the king, and said, What hast thou done? behold, Abner came unto thee; why *is* it *that* thou hast sent him away, and he is quite gone?

25 Thou knowest Abner the son of Ner, that he came to deceive thee, and to know thy going out and thy coming in, and to know all that thou doest.

26 And when Joab was come out from David, he sent messengers after Abner, which brought him again from the well of Sirah: but David knew *it* not.

27 And when Abner was returned to Hebron, Joab took him aside in the gate
to speak with him quietly, and smote him there under the fifth *rib*, that he
died, for the blood of Asahel his brother.
28 And afterward when David heard *it*, he said, I and my kingdom *are* guilt-
less before the LORD for ever from the blood of Abner the son of Ner:
29 Let it rest on the head of Joab, and on all his father's house; and let there
not fail from the house of Joab one that hath an issue, or that is a leper, or that
leaneth on a staff, or that falleth on the sword, or that lacketh bread.
30 So Joab and Abishai his brother slew Abner, because he had slain their
brother Asahel at Gibeon in the battle.
31 And David said to Joab, and to all the people that *were* with him, Rend
your clothes, and gird you with sackcloth, and mourn before Abner. And king
David *himself* followed the bier.
32 And they buried Abner in Hebron: and the king lifted up his voice, and
wept at the grave of Abner; and all the people wept.
33 And the king lamented over Abner, and said, Died Abner as a fool dieth?
34 Thy hands *were* not bound, nor thy feet put into fetters: as a man falleth
before wicked men, *so* fellest thou. And all the people wept again over him.
35 And when all the people came to cause David to eat meat while it was yet
day, David sware, saying, So do God to me, and more also, if I taste bread, or
ought else, till the sun be down.
36 And all the people took notice *of it*, and it pleased them: as whatsoever
the king did pleased all the people.
37 For all the people and all Israel understood that day that it was not of the
king to slay Abner the son of Ner.
38 And the king said unto his servants, Know ye not that there is a prince and
a great man fallen this day in Israel?
39 And I *am* this day weak, though anointed king; and these men the sons of
Zeruiah *be* too hard for me: the LORD shall reward the doer of evil according
to his wickedness.

Ish-bosheth Is Murdered and His Head Is Brought to David

4 And when Saul's son heard that Abner was dead in Hebron, his hands were
feeble, and all the Israelites were troubled.
2 And Saul's son had two men *that were* captains of bands: the name of the
one *was* Baanah, and the name of the other Rechab, the sons of Rimmon a
Beerothite, of the children of Benjamin: (for Beeroth also was reckoned to
Benjamin:
3 And the Beerothites fled to Gittaim, and were sojourners there until this
day.)
4 And Jonathan, Saul's son, had a son *that was* lame of *his* feet. He was five
years old when the tidings came of Saul and Jonathan out of Jezreel, and his
nurse took him up, and fled: and it came to pass, as she made haste to flee, that
he fell, and became lame. And his name *was* Mephibosheth.
5 And the sons of Rimmon the Beerothite, Rechab and Baanah, went, and
came about the heat of the day to the house of Ish-bosheth, who lay on a bed
at noon.
6 And they came thither into the midst of the house, *as though* they would
have fetched wheat; and they smote him under the fifth *rib*: and Rechab and
Baanah his brother escaped.
7 For when they came into the house, he lay on his bed in his bedchamber,
and they smote him, and slew him, and beheaded him, and took his head, and
gat them away through the plain all night.
8 And they brought the head of Ish-bosheth unto David to Hebron, and said
to the king, Behold the head of Ish-bosheth the son of Saul thine enemy, which
sought thy life; and the LORD hath avenged my lord the king this day of Saul,
and of his seed.

David Puts to Death the Men Who Murdered Ish-bosheth

9 And David answered Rechab and Baanah his brother, the sons of Rimmon
the Beerothite, and said unto them, *As* the LORD liveth, who hath redeemed
my soul out of all adversity,
10 When one told me, saying, Behold, Saul is dead, thinking to have brought
good tidings, I took hold of him, and slew him in Ziklag, who *thought* that I
would have given him a reward for his tidings:
11 How much more, when wicked men have slain a righteous person in his
own house upon his bed? shall I not therefore now require his blood of your
hand, and take you away from the earth?
12 And David commanded his young men, and they slew them, and cut off
their hands and their feet, and hanged *them* up over the pool in Hebron. But
they took the head of Ish-bosheth, and buried *it* in the sepulchre of Abner in
Hebron.

The Tribes Come to Hebron to Anoint David King over Israel

5 Then came all the tribes of Israel to David unto Hebron, and spake, saying,
Behold, we *are* thy bone and thy flesh.
2 Also in time past, when Saul was king over us, thou wast he that leddest out
and broughtest in Israel: and the LORD said to thee, Thou shalt feed my people
Israel, and thou shalt be a captain over Israel.
3 So all the elders of Israel came to the king to Hebron; and king David made
a league with them in Hebron before the LORD: and they anointed David king
over Israel.
4 David *was* thirty years old when he began to reign, *and* he reigned forty
years.
5 In Hebron he reigned over Judah seven years and six months: and in
Jerusalem he reigned thirty and three years over all Israel and Judah.

David Captures Jerusalem and Names It the City of David

6 And the king and his men went to Jerusalem unto the Jebusites, the inhab-
itants of the land: which spake unto David, saying, Except thou take away the
blind and the lame, thou shalt not come in hither: thinking, David cannot
come in hither.
7 Nevertheless David took the strong hold of Zion: the same *is* the city of
David.
8 And David said on that day, Whosoever getteth up to the gutter, and smiteth
the Jebusites, and the lame and the blind, *that are* hated of David's soul, *he
shall be chief and captain*. Wherefore they said, The blind and the lame shall
not come into the house.
9 So David dwelt in the fort, and called it the city of David. And David built
round about from Millo and inward.
10 And David went on, and grew great, and the LORD God of hosts *was* with him.

David's Palace, Wives, and Children

11 And Hiram king of Tyre sent messengers to David, and cedar trees, and
carpenters, and masons: and they built David an house.
12 And David perceived that the LORD had established him king over Israel,
and that he had exalted his kingdom for his people Israel's sake.
13 And David took *him* more concubines and wives out of Jerusalem, after
he was come from Hebron: and there were yet sons and daughters born to
David.
14 And these *be* the names of those that were born unto him in Jerusalem;
Shammua, and Shobab, and Nathan, and Solomon,
15 Ibhar also, and Elishua, and Nepheg, and Japhia,
16 And Elishama, and Eliada, and Eliphalet.

The Philistines Attack David, but He Defeats Them

17 But when the Philistines heard that they had anointed David king over Israel, all the Philistines came up to seek David; and David heard *of it*, and went down to the hold.

18 The Philistines also came and spread themselves in the valley of Rephaim.

19 And David enquired of the LORD, saying, Shall I go up to the Philistines? wilt thou deliver them into mine hand? And the LORD said unto David, Go up: for I will doubtless deliver the Philistines into thine hand.

20 And David came to Baal-perazim, and David smote them there, and said, The LORD hath broken forth upon mine enemies before me, as the breach of waters. Therefore he called the name of that place Baal-perazim.

21 And there they left their images, and David and his men burned them.

22 And the Philistines came up yet again, and spread themselves in the valley of Rephaim.

23 And when David enquired of the LORD, he said, Thou shalt not go up; *but* fetch a compass behind them, and come upon them over against the mulberry trees.

24 And let it be, when thou hearest the sound of a going in the tops of the mulberry trees, that then thou shalt bestir thyself: for then shall the LORD go out before thee, to smite the host of the Philistines.

25 And David did so, as the LORD had commanded him; and smote the Philistines from Geba until thou come to Gazer.

David Brings the Ark to Jerusalem on a New Cart

6 Again, David gathered together all *the* chosen *men* of Israel, thirty thousand.

2 And David arose, and went with all the people that *were* with him from Baale of Judah, to bring up from thence the ark of God, whose name is called by the name of the LORD of hosts that dwelleth *between* the cherubims.

3 And they set the ark of God upon a new cart, and brought it out of the house of Abinadab that *was* in Gibeah: and Uzzah and Ahio, the sons of Abinadab, drave the new cart.

4 And they brought it out of the house of Abinadab which *was* at Gibeah, accompanying the ark of God: and Ahio went before the ark.

5 And David and all the house of Israel played before the LORD on all manner of *instruments made of* fir wood, even on harps, and on psalteries, and on timbrels, and on cornets, and on cymbals.

Uzzah Is Killed for Touching the Ark

6 And when they came to Nachon's threshingfloor, Uzzah put forth *his hand* to the ark of God, and took hold of it; for the oxen shook *it*.

7 And the anger of the LORD was kindled against Uzzah; and God smote him there for *his* error; and there he died by the ark of God.

8 And David was displeased, because the LORD had made a breach upon Uzzah: and he called the name of the place Perez-uzzah to this day.

9 And David was afraid of the LORD that day, and said, How shall the ark of the LORD come to me?

10 So David would not remove the ark of the LORD unto him into the city of David: but David carried it aside into the house of Obed-edom the Gittite.

11 And the ark of the LORD continued in the house of Obed-edom the Gittite three months: and the LORD blessed Obed-edom, and all his household.

David Dances to Celebrate the Return of the Ark

12 And it was told king David, saying, The LORD hath blessed the house of Obed-edom, and all that *pertaineth* unto him, because of the ark of God. So David went and brought up the ark of God from the house of Obed-edom into the city of David with gladness.

13 And it was *so*, that when they that bare the ark of the LORD had gone six paces, he sacrificed oxen and fatlings.

14 And David danced before the LORD with all *his* might; and David *was* girded with a linen ephod.
15 So David and all the house of Israel brought up the ark of the LORD with shouting, and with the sound of the trumpet.
16 And as the ark of the LORD came into the city of David, Michal Saul's daughter looked through a window, and saw king David leaping and dancing before the LORD; and she despised him in her heart.
17 And they brought in the ark of the LORD, and set it in his place, in the midst of the tabernacle that David had pitched for it: and David offered burnt offerings and peace offerings before the LORD.
18 And as soon as David had made an end of offering burnt offerings and peace offerings, he blessed the people in the name of the LORD of hosts.
19 And he dealt among all the people, *even* among the whole multitude of Israel, as well to the women as men, to every one a cake of bread, and a good piece *of flesh*, and a flagon *of wine*. So all the people departed every one to his house.

Michal Despises David's Joy and Is Made Childless

20 Then David returned to bless his household. And Michal the daughter of Saul came out to meet David, and said, How glorious was the king of Israel to day, who uncovered himself to day in the eyes of the handmaids of his servants, as one of the vain fellows shamelessly uncovereth himself!
21 And David said unto Michal, *It was* before the LORD, which chose me before thy father, and before all his house, to appoint me ruler over the people of the LORD, over Israel: therefore will I play before the LORD.
22 And I will yet be more vile than thus, and will be base in mine own sight: and of the maidservants which thou hast spoken of, of them shall I be had in honour.
23 Therefore Michal the daughter of Saul had no child unto the day of her death.

David Desires to Build a Temple for God but Is Forbidden

7 And it came to pass, when the king sat in his house, and the LORD had given him rest round about from all his enemies;
2 That the king said unto Nathan the prophet, See now, I dwell in an house of cedar, but the ark of God dwelleth within curtains.
3 And Nathan said to the king, Go, do all that *is* in thine heart; for the LORD *is* with thee.
4 And it came to pass that night, that the word of the LORD came unto Nathan, saying,
5 Go and tell my servant David, Thus saith the LORD, Shalt thou build me an house for me to dwell in?
6 Whereas I have not dwelt in *any* house since the time that I brought up the children of Israel out of Egypt, even to this day, but have walked in a tent and in a tabernacle.
7 In all *the places* wherein I have walked with all the children of Israel spake I a word with any of the tribes of Israel, whom I commanded to feed my people Israel, saying, Why build ye not me an house of cedar?
8 Now therefore so shalt thou say unto my servant David, Thus saith the LORD of hosts, I took thee from the sheepcote, from following the sheep, to be ruler over my people, over Israel:
9 And I was with thee whithersoever thou wentest, and have cut off all thine enemies out of thy sight, and have made thee a great name, like unto the name of the great *men* that *are* in the earth.
10 Moreover I will appoint a place for my people Israel, and will plant them, that they may dwell in a place of their own, and move no more; neither shall the children of wickedness afflict them any more, as beforetime,

11 And as since the time that I commanded judges *to be* over my people Israel,
and have caused thee to rest from all thine enemies. Also the LORD telleth thee
that he will make thee an house.
12 And when thy days be fulfilled, and thou shalt sleep with thy fathers, I will
set up thy seed after thee, which shall proceed out of thy bowels, and I will
establish his kingdom.
13 He shall build an house for my name, and I will stablish the throne of his
kingdom for ever.
14 I will be his father, and he shall be my son. If he commit iniquity, I will
chasten him with the rod of men, and with the stripes of the children of men:
15 But my mercy shall not depart away from him, as I took *it* from Saul, whom
I put away before thee.
16 And thine house and thy kingdom shall be established for ever before
thee: thy throne shall be established for ever.
17 According to all these words, and according to all this vision, so did Nathan
speak unto David.

David's Prayer and Thanksgiving

18 Then went king David in, and sat before the LORD, and he said, Who *am*
I, O Lord GOD? and what *is* my house, that thou hast brought me hitherto?
19 And this was yet a small thing in thy sight, O Lord GOD; but thou hast
spoken also of thy servant's house for a great while to come. And *is* this the
manner of man, O Lord GOD?
20 And what can David say more unto thee? for thou, Lord GOD, knowest thy
servant.
21 For thy word's sake, and according to thine own heart, hast thou done all
these great things, to make thy servant know *them*.
22 Wherefore thou art great, O LORD God: for *there is* none like thee, neither
is there any God beside thee, according to all that we have heard with our ears.
23 And what one nation in the earth *is* like thy people, *even* like Israel, whom
God went to redeem for a people to himself, and to make him a name, and to
do for you great things and terrible, for thy land, before thy people, which
thou redeemedst to thee from Egypt, *from* the nations and their gods?
24 For thou hast confirmed to thyself thy people Israel *to be* a people unto
thee for ever: and thou, LORD, art become their God.
25 And now, O LORD God, the word that thou hast spoken concerning thy
servant, and concerning his house, establish *it* for ever, and do as thou hast
said.
26 And let thy name be magnified for ever, saying, The LORD of hosts *is* the
God over Israel: and let the house of thy servant David be established before
thee.
27 For thou, O LORD of hosts, God of Israel, hast revealed to thy servant,
saying, I will build thee an house: therefore hath thy servant found in his heart
to pray this prayer unto thee.
28 And now, O Lord GOD, thou *art* that God, and thy words be true, and thou
hast promised this goodness unto thy servant:
29 Therefore now let it please thee to bless the house of thy servant, that it
may continue for ever before thee: for thou, O Lord GOD, hast spoken *it*: and
with thy blessing let the house of thy servant be blessed for ever.

David's Successes over Various Kings and Nations

8 And after this it came to pass, that David smote the Philistines, and subdued
them: and David took Metheg-ammah out of the hand of the Philistines.
2 And he smote Moab, and measured them with a line, casting them down
to the ground; even with two lines measured he to put to death, and with one
full line to keep alive. And *so* the Moabites became David's servants, *and*
brought gifts.

3 David smote also Hadadezer, the son of Rehob, king of Zobah, as he went to recover his border at the river Euphrates.

4 And David took from him a thousand *chariots*, and seven hundred horsemen, and twenty thousand footmen: and David houghed all the chariot *horses*, but reserved of them *for* an hundred chariots.

5 And when the Syrians of Damascus came to succour Hadadezer king of Zobah, David slew of the Syrians two and twenty thousand men.

6 Then David put garrisons in Syria of Damascus: and the Syrians became servants to David, *and* brought gifts. And the LORD preserved David whithersoever he went.

7 And David took the shields of gold that were on the servants of Hadadezer, and brought them to Jerusalem.

8 And from Betah, and from Berothai, cities of Hadadezer, king David took exceeding much brass.

Toi Sends Joram with Presents to Bless David

9 When Toi king of Hamath heard that David had smitten all the host of Hadadezer,

10 Then Toi sent Joram his son unto king David, to salute him, and to bless him, because he had fought against Hadadezer, and smitten him: for Hadadezer had wars with Toi. And *Joram* brought with him vessels of silver, and vessels of gold, and vessels of brass:

11 Which also king David did dedicate unto the LORD, with the silver and gold that he had dedicated of all nations which he subdued;

12 Of Syria, and of Moab, and of the children of Ammon, and of the Philistines, and of Amalek, and of the spoil of Hadadezer, son of Rehob, king of Zobah.

13 And David gat *him* a name when he returned from smiting of the Syrians in the valley of salt, *being* eighteen thousand *men*.

14 And he put garrisons in Edom; throughout all Edom put he garrisons, and all they of Edom became David's servants. And the LORD preserved David whithersoever he went.

15 And David reigned over all Israel; and David executed judgment and justice unto all his people.

16 And Joab the son of Zeruiah *was* over the host; and Jehoshaphat the son of Ahilud *was* recorder;

17 And Zadok the son of Ahitub, and Ahimelech the son of Abiathar, *were* the priests; and Seraiah *was* the scribe;

18 And Benaiah the son of Jehoiada *was over* both the Cherethites and the Pelethites; and David's sons were chief rulers.

David Keeps His Promise to Jonathan

9 And David said, Is there yet any that is left of the house of Saul, that I may shew him kindness for Jonathan's sake?

2 And *there was* of the house of Saul a servant whose name *was* Ziba. And when they had called him unto David, the king said unto him, *Art* thou Ziba? And he said, Thy servant *is he*.

3 And the king said, *Is* there not yet any of the house of Saul, that I may shew the kindness of God unto him? And Ziba said unto the king, Jonathan hath yet a son, *which is* lame on *his* feet.

4 And the king said unto him, Where *is* he? And Ziba said unto the king, Behold, he *is* in the house of Machir, the son of Ammiel, in Lo-debar.

5 Then king David sent, and fetched him out of the house of Machir, the son of Ammiel, from Lo-debar.

6 Now when Mephibosheth, the son of Jonathan, the son of Saul, was come unto David, he fell on his face, and did reverence. And David said, Mephibosheth. And he answered, Behold thy servant!

7 And David said unto him, Fear not: for I will surely shew thee kindness for
Jonathan thy father's sake, and will restore thee all the land of Saul thy father;
and thou shalt eat bread at my table continually.
8 And he bowed himself, and said, What *is* thy servant, that thou shouldest
look upon such a dead dog as I *am*?

David Cares for Ziba, Saul's Servant

9 Then the king called to Ziba, Saul's servant, and said unto him, I have given
unto thy master's son all that pertained to Saul and to all his house.
10 Thou therefore, and thy sons, and thy servants, shall till the land for him,
and thou shalt bring in *the fruits*, that thy master's son may have food to eat:
but Mephibosheth thy master's son shall eat bread alway at my table. Now
Ziba had fifteen sons and twenty servants.
11 Then said Ziba unto the king, According to all that my lord the king hath
commanded his servant, so shall thy servant do. As for Mephibosheth, *said
the king*, he shall eat at my table, as one of the king's sons.
12 And Mephibosheth had a young son, whose name *was* Micha. And all that
dwelt in the house of Ziba *were* servants unto Mephibosheth.
13 So Mephibosheth dwelt in Jerusalem: for he did eat continually at the
king's table; and was lame on both his feet.

David's Messengers Are Treated Shamefully

10 And it came to pass after this, that the king of the children of Ammon
died, and Hanun his son reigned in his stead.
2 Then said David, I will shew kindness unto Hanun the son of Nahash, as
his father shewed kindness unto me. And David sent to comfort him by the
hand of his servants for his father. And David's servants came into the land of
the children of Ammon.
3 And the princes of the children of Ammon said unto Hanun their lord,
Thinkest thou that David doth honour thy father, that he hath sent comforters
unto thee? hath not David *rather* sent his servants unto thee, to search the
city, and to spy it out, and to overthrow it?
4 Wherefore Hanun took David's servants, and shaved off the one half of
their beards, and cut off their garments in the middle, *even* to their buttocks,
and sent them away.
5 When they told *it* unto David, he sent to meet them, because the men were
greatly ashamed: and the king said, Tarry at Jericho until your beards be
grown, and *then* return.

The Ammonites Are Overcome by Joab and Abishai

6 And when the children of Ammon saw that they stank before David, the
children of Ammon sent and hired the Syrians of Beth-rehob, and the Syrians
of Zoba, twenty thousand footmen, and of king Maacah a thousand men, and
of Ish-tob twelve thousand men.
7 And when David heard of *it*, he sent Joab, and all the host of the mighty
men.
8 And the children of Ammon came out, and put the battle in array at the
entering in of the gate: and the Syrians of Zoba, and of Rehob, and Ish-tob,
and Maacah, *were* by themselves in the field.
9 When Joab saw that the front of the battle was against him before and
behind, he chose of all the choice *men* of Israel, and put *them* in array against
the Syrians:
10 And the rest of the people he delivered into the hand of Abishai his brother,
that he might put *them* in array against the children of Ammon.
11 And he said, If the Syrians be too strong for me, then thou shalt help me:
but if the children of Ammon be too strong for thee, then I will come and help
thee.

12 Be of good courage, and let us play the men for our people, and for the cities of our God: and the LORD do that which seemeth him good.

13 And Joab drew nigh, and the people that *were* with him, unto the battle against the Syrians: and they fled before him.

14 And when the children of Ammon saw that the Syrians were fled, then fled they also before Abishai, and entered into the city. So Joab returned from the children of Ammon, and came to Jerusalem.

David Joins the Battle and Defeats the Syrians

15 And when the Syrians saw that they were smitten before Israel, they gathered themselves together.

16 And Hadarezer sent, and brought out the Syrians that *were* beyond the river: and they came to Helam; and Shobach the captain of the host of Hadarezer *went* before them.

17 And when it was told David, he gathered all Israel together, and passed over Jordan, and came to Helam. And the Syrians set themselves in array against David, and fought with him.

18 And the Syrians fled before Israel; and David slew *the men of* seven hundred chariots of the Syrians, and forty thousand horsemen, and smote Shobach the captain of their host, who died there.

19 And when all the kings *that were* servants to Hadarezer saw that they were smitten before Israel, they made peace with Israel, and served them. So the Syrians feared to help the children of Ammon any more.

David Commits Adultery with Bath-sheba

11 And it came to pass, after the year was expired, at the time when kings go forth *to battle*, that David sent Joab, and his servants with him, and all Israel; and they destroyed the children of Ammon, and besieged Rabbah. But David tarried still at Jerusalem.

2 And it came to pass in an eveningtide, that David arose from off his bed, and walked upon the roof of the king's house: and from the roof he saw a woman washing herself; and the woman *was* very beautiful to look upon.

3 And David sent and enquired after the woman. And *one* said, *Is* not this Bath-sheba, the daughter of Eliam, the wife of Uriah the Hittite?

4 And David sent messengers, and took her; and she came in unto him, and he lay with her; for she was purified from her uncleanness: and she returned unto her house.

5 And the woman conceived, and sent and told David, and said, I *am* with child.

David Brings Uriah Home to Conceal His Adultery

6 And David sent to Joab, *saying*, Send me Uriah the Hittite. And Joab sent Uriah to David.

7 And when Uriah was come unto him, David demanded *of him* how Joab did, and how the people did, and how the war prospered.

8 And David said to Uriah, Go down to thy house, and wash thy feet. And Uriah departed out of the king's house, and there followed him a mess *of meat* from the king.

9 But Uriah slept at the door of the king's house with all the servants of his lord, and went not down to his house.

10 And when they had told David, saying, Uriah went not down unto his house, David said unto Uriah, Camest thou not from *thy* journey? why *then* didst thou not go down unto thine house?

11 And Uriah said unto David, The ark, and Israel, and Judah, abide in tents; and my lord Joab, and the servants of my lord, are encamped in the open fields; shall I then go into mine house, to eat and to drink, and to lie with my wife? *as* thou livest, and *as* thy soul liveth, I will not do this thing.

12 And David said to Uriah, Tarry here to day also, and to morrow I will let
thee depart. So Uriah abode in Jerusalem that day, and the morrow.
13 And when David had called him, he did eat and drink before him; and he
made him drunk: and at even he went out to lie on his bed with the servants
of his lord, but went not down to his house.

David Orders Joab to Let Uriah Die in Battle

14 And it came to pass in the morning, that David wrote a letter to Joab, and
sent *it* by the hand of Uriah.
15 And he wrote in the letter, saying, Set ye Uriah in the forefront of the
hottest battle, and retire ye from him, that he may be smitten, and die.
16 And it came to pass, when Joab observed the city, that he assigned Uriah
unto a place where he knew that valiant men *were*.
17 And the men of the city went out, and fought with Joab: and there fell
some of the people of the servants of David; and Uriah the Hittite died also.
18 Then Joab sent and told David all the things concerning the war;
19 And charged the messenger, saying, When thou hast made an end of tell-
ing the matters of the war unto the king,
20 And if so be that the king's wrath arise, and he say unto thee, Wherefore
approached ye so nigh unto the city when ye did fight? knew ye not that they
would shoot from the wall?
21 Who smote Abimelech the son of Jerubbesheth? did not a woman cast a
piece of a millstone upon him from the wall, that he died in Thebez? why went
ye nigh the wall? then say thou, Thy servant Uriah the Hittite is dead also.
22 So the messenger went, and came and shewed David all that Joab had sent
him for.
23 And the messenger said unto David, Surely the men prevailed against us,
and came out unto us into the field, and we were upon them even unto the
entering of the gate.
24 And the shooters shot from off the wall upon thy servants; and *some* of
the king's servants be dead, and thy servant Uriah the Hittite is dead also.
25 Then David said unto the messenger, Thus shalt thou say unto Joab, Let
not this thing displease thee, for the sword devoureth one as well as another:
make thy battle more strong against the city, and overthrow it: and encourage
thou him.
26 And when the wife of Uriah heard that Uriah her husband was dead, she
mourned for her husband.
27 And when the mourning was past, David sent and fetched her to his house,
and she became his wife, and bare him a son. But the thing that David had
done displeased the LORD.

Nathan Reveals David's Sin with a Parable

12 And the LORD sent Nathan unto David. And he came unto him, and
said unto him, There were two men in one city; the one rich, and the
other poor.
2 The rich *man* had exceeding many flocks and herds:
3 But the poor *man* had nothing, save one little ewe lamb, which he had
bought and nourished up: and it grew up together with him, and with his
children; it did eat of his own meat, and drank of his own cup, and lay in his
bosom, and was unto him as a daughter.
4 And there came a traveller unto the rich man, and he spared to take of his
own flock and of his own herd, to dress for the wayfaring man that was come
unto him; but took the poor man's lamb, and dressed it for the man that was
come to him.
5 And David's anger was greatly kindled against the man; and he said to
Nathan, *As* the LORD liveth, the man that hath done this *thing* shall surely die:

6 And he shall restore the lamb fourfold, because he did this thing, and
because he had no pity.
7 And Nathan said to David, Thou *art* the man. Thus saith the LORD God of
Israel, I anointed thee king over Israel, and I delivered thee out of the hand of
Saul;
8 And I gave thee thy master's house, and thy master's wives into thy bosom,
and gave thee the house of Israel and of Judah; and if *that had been* too little,
I would moreover have given unto thee such and such things.
9 Wherefore hast thou despised the commandment of the LORD, to do evil
in his sight? thou hast killed Uriah the Hittite with the sword, and hast taken
his wife *to be* thy wife, and hast slain him with the sword of the children of
Ammon.
10 Now therefore the sword shall never depart from thine house; because
thou hast despised me, and hast taken the wife of Uriah the Hittite to be thy
wife.
11 Thus saith the LORD, Behold, I will raise up evil against thee out of thine
own house, and I will take thy wives before thine eyes, and give *them* unto thy
neighbour, and he shall lie with thy wives in the sight of this sun.
12 For thou didst *it* secretly: but I will do this thing before all Israel, and
before the sun.
13 And David said unto Nathan, I have sinned against the LORD. And Nathan
said unto David, The LORD also hath put away thy sin; thou shalt not die.
14 Howbeit, because by this deed thou hast given great occasion to the ene-
mies of the LORD to blaspheme, the child also *that is* born unto thee shall
surely die.

David Mourns and Prays for the Child

15 And Nathan departed unto his house. And the LORD struck the child that
Uriah's wife bare unto David, and it was very sick.
16 David therefore besought God for the child; and David fasted, and went
in, and lay all night upon the earth.
17 And the elders of his house arose, *and went* to him, to raise him up from
the earth: but he would not, neither did he eat bread with them.
18 And it came to pass on the seventh day, that the child died. And the servants
of David feared to tell him that the child was dead: for they said, Behold, while
the child was yet alive, we spake unto him, and he would not hearken unto
our voice: how will he then vex himself, if we tell him that the child is dead?
19 But when David saw that his servants whispered, David perceived that the
child was dead: therefore David said unto his servants, Is the child dead? And
they said, He is dead.
20 Then David arose from the earth, and washed, and anointed *himself*, and
changed his apparel, and came into the house of the LORD, and worshipped:
then he came to his own house; and when he required, they set bread before
him, and he did eat.
21 Then said his servants unto him, What thing *is* this that thou hast done?
thou didst fast and weep for the child, *while it was* alive; but when the child
was dead, thou didst rise and eat bread.
22 And he said, While the child was yet alive, I fasted and wept: for I said,
Who can tell *whether* GOD will be gracious to me, that the child may live?
23 But now he is dead, wherefore should I fast? can I bring him back again?
I shall go to him, but he shall not return to me.
24 And David comforted Bath-sheba his wife, and went in unto her, and lay
with her: and she bare a son, and he called his name Solomon: and the LORD
loved him.
25 And he sent by the hand of Nathan the prophet; and he called his name
Jedidiah, because of the LORD.

David Defeats the Ammonites and Plunders Their Cities

26 And Joab fought against Rabbah of the children of Ammon, and took the royal city.

27 And Joab sent messengers to David, and said, I have fought against Rabbah, and have taken the city of waters.

28 Now therefore gather the rest of the people together, and encamp against the city, and take it: lest I take the city, and it be called after my name.

29 And David gathered all the people together, and went to Rabbah, and fought against it, and took it.

30 And he took their king's crown from off his head, the weight whereof *was* a talent of gold with the precious stones: and it was *set* on David's head. And he brought forth the spoil of the city in great abundance.

31 And he brought forth the people that *were* therein, and put *them* under saws, and under harrows of iron, and under axes of iron, and made them pass through the brickkiln: and thus did he unto all the cities of the children of Ammon. So David and all the people returned unto Jerusalem.

Amnon Defiles Tamar

13 And it came to pass after this, that Absalom the son of David had a fair sister, whose name *was* Tamar; and Amnon the son of David loved her.

2 And Amnon was so vexed, that he fell sick for his sister Tamar; for she *was* a virgin; and Amnon thought it hard for him to do any thing to her.

3 But Amnon had a friend, whose name *was* Jonadab, the son of Shimeah David's brother: and Jonadab *was* a very subtil man.

4 And he said unto him, Why *art* thou, *being* the king's son, lean from day to day? wilt thou not tell me? And Amnon said unto him, I love Tamar, my brother Absalom's sister.

5 And Jonadab said unto him, Lay thee down on thy bed, and make thyself sick: and when thy father cometh to see thee, say unto him, I pray thee, let my sister Tamar come, and give me meat, and dress the meat in my sight, that I may see *it*, and eat *it* at her hand.

6 So Amnon lay down, and made himself sick: and when the king was come to see him, Amnon said unto the king, I pray thee, let Tamar my sister come, and make me a couple of cakes in my sight, that I may eat at her hand.

7 Then David sent home to Tamar, saying, Go now to thy brother Amnon's house, and dress him meat.

8 So Tamar went to her brother Amnon's house; and he was laid down. And she took flour, and kneaded *it*, and made cakes in his sight, and did bake the cakes.

9 And she took a pan, and poured *them* out before him; but he refused to eat. And Amnon said, Have out all men from me. And they went out every man from him.

10 And Amnon said unto Tamar, Bring the meat into the chamber, that I may eat of thine hand. And Tamar took the cakes which she had made, and brought *them* into the chamber to Amnon her brother.

11 And when she had brought *them* unto him to eat, he took hold of her, and said unto her, Come lie with me, my sister.

12 And she answered him, Nay, my brother, do not force me; for no such thing ought to be done in Israel: do not thou this folly.

13 And I, whither shall I cause my shame to go? and as for thee, thou shalt be as one of the fools in Israel. Now therefore, I pray thee, speak unto the king; for he will not withhold me from thee.

14 Howbeit he would not hearken unto her voice: but, being stronger than she, forced her, and lay with her.

15 Then Amnon hated her exceedingly; so that the hatred wherewith he hated her *was* greater than the love wherewith he had loved her. And Amnon said unto her, Arise, be gone.

16 And she said unto him, *There is* no cause: this evil in sending me away *is* greater than the other that thou didst unto me. But he would not hearken unto her.

17 Then he called his servant that ministered unto him, and said, Put now this *woman* out from me, and bolt the door after her.

18 And *she had* a garment of divers colours upon her: for with such robes were the king's daughters *that were* virgins apparelled. Then his servant brought her out, and bolted the door after her.

19 And Tamar put ashes on her head, and rent her garment of divers colours that *was* on her, and laid her hand on her head, and went on crying.

20 And Absalom her brother said unto her, Hath Amnon thy brother been with thee? but hold now thy peace, my sister: he *is* thy brother; regard not this thing. So Tamar remained desolate in her brother Absalom's house.

21 But when king David heard of all these things, he was very wroth.

22 And Absalom spake unto his brother Amnon neither good nor bad: for Absalom hated Amnon, because he had forced his sister Tamar.

23 And it came to pass after two full years, that Absalom had sheepshearers in Baalhazor, which *is* beside Ephraim: and Absalom invited all the king's sons.

24 And Absalom came to the king, and said, Behold now, thy servant hath sheepshearers; let the king, I beseech thee, and his servants go with thy servant.

25 And the king said to Absalom, Nay, my son, let us not all now go, lest we be chargeable unto thee. And he pressed him: howbeit he would not go, but blessed him.

26 Then said Absalom, If not, I pray thee, let my brother Amnon go with us. And the king said unto him, Why should he go with thee?

27 But Absalom pressed him, that he let Amnon and all the king's sons go with him.

28 Now Absalom had commanded his servants, saying, Mark ye now when Amnon's heart is merry with wine, and when I say unto you, Smite Amnon; then kill him, fear not: have not I commanded you? be courageous, and be valiant.

29 And the servants of Absalom did unto Amnon as Absalom had commanded. Then all the king's sons arose, and every man gat him up upon his mule, and fled.

David Grieves That Absalom Has Killed Amnon

30 And it came to pass, while they were in the way, that tidings came to David, saying, Absalom hath slain all the king's sons, and there is not one of them left.

31 Then the king arose, and tare his garments, and lay on the earth; and all his servants stood by with their clothes rent.

32 And Jonadab, the son of Shimeah David's brother, answered and said, Let not my lord suppose *that* they have slain all the young men the king's sons; for Amnon only is dead: for by the appointment of Absalom this hath been determined from the day that he forced his sister Tamar.

33 Now therefore let not my lord the king take the thing to his heart, to think that all the king's sons are dead: for Amnon only is dead.

34 But Absalom fled. And the young man that kept the watch lifted up his eyes, and looked, and, behold, there came much people by the way of the hill side behind him.

35 And Jonadab said unto the king, Behold, the king's sons come: as thy servant said, so it is.

36 And it came to pass, as soon as he had made an end of speaking, that,
behold, the king's sons came, and lifted up their voice and wept: and the king
also and all his servants wept very sore.
37 But Absalom fled, and went to Talmai, the son of Ammihud, king of
Geshur. And *David* mourned for his son every day.
38 So Absalom fled, and went to Geshur, and was there three years.
39 And *the soul of* king David longed to go forth unto Absalom: for he was
comforted concerning Amnon, seeing he was dead.

David Allows Absalom to Return to Jerusalem

14 Now Joab the son of Zeruiah perceived that the king's heart *was* toward
Absalom.
2 And Joab sent to Tekoah, and fetched thence a wise woman, and said unto
her, I pray thee, feign thyself to be a mourner, and put on now mourning
apparel, and anoint not thyself with oil, but be as a woman that had a long
time mourned for the dead:
3 And come to the king, and speak on this manner unto him. So Joab put the
words in her mouth.
4 And when the woman of Tekoah spake to the king, she fell on her face to
the ground, and did obeisance, and said, Help, O king.
5 And the king said unto her, What aileth thee? And she answered, I *am*
indeed a widow woman, and mine husband is dead.
6 And thy handmaid had two sons, and they two strove together in the field,
and *there was* none to part them, but the one smote the other, and slew him.
7 And, behold, the whole family is risen against thine handmaid, and they
said, Deliver him that smote his brother, that we may kill him, for the life of
his brother whom he slew; and we will destroy the heir also: and so they shall
quench my coal which is left, and shall not leave to my husband *neither* name
nor remainder upon the earth.
8 And the king said unto the woman, Go to thine house, and I will give charge
concerning thee.
9 And the woman of Tekoah said unto the king, My lord, O king, the iniqui-
ty *be* on me, and on my father's house: and the king and his throne *be* guiltless.
10 And the king said, Whosoever saith *ought* unto thee, bring him to me, and
he shall not touch thee any more.
11 Then said she, I pray thee, let the king remember the LORD thy God, that
thou wouldest not suffer the revengers of blood to destroy any more, lest they
destroy my son. And he said, *As* the LORD liveth, there shall not one hair of thy
son fall to the earth.
12 Then the woman said, Let thine handmaid, I pray thee, speak *one* word
unto my lord the king. And he said, Say on.
13 And the woman said, Wherefore then hast thou thought such a thing
against the people of God? for the king doth speak this thing as one which is
faulty, in that the king doth not fetch home again his banished.
14 For we must needs die, and *are* as water spilt on the ground, which cannot
be gathered up again; neither doth God respect *any* person: yet doth he devise
means, that his banished be not expelled from him.
15 Now therefore that I am come to speak of this thing unto my lord the king,
it is because the people have made me afraid: and thy handmaid said, I will
now speak unto the king; it may be that the king will perform the request of
his handmaid.
16 For the king will hear, to deliver his handmaid out of the hand of the man
that would destroy me and my son together out of the inheritance of God.
17 Then thine handmaid said, The word of my lord the king shall now be
comfortable: for as an angel of God, so *is* my lord the king to discern good and
bad: therefore the LORD thy God will be with thee.

18 Then the king answered and said unto the woman, Hide not from me, I
pray thee, the thing that I shall ask thee. And the woman said, Let my lord the
king now speak.
19 And the king said, *Is not* the hand of Joab with thee in all this? And the
woman answered and said, *As* thy soul liveth, my lord the king, none can turn
to the right hand or to the left from ought that my lord the king hath spoken:
for thy servant Joab, he bade me, and he put all these words in the mouth of
thine handmaid:
20 To fetch about this form of speech hath thy servant Joab done this thing:
and my lord *is* wise, according to the wisdom of an angel of God, to know all
things that *are* in the earth.
21 And the king said unto Joab, Behold now, I have done this thing: go there-
fore, bring the young man Absalom again.
22 And Joab fell to the ground on his face, and bowed himself, and thanked
the king: and Joab said, To day thy servant knoweth that I have found grace in
thy sight, my lord, O king, in that the king hath fulfilled the request of his
servant.
23 So Joab arose and went to Geshur, and brought Absalom to Jerusalem.
24 And the king said, Let him turn to his own house, and let him not see my
face. So Absalom returned to his own house, and saw not the king's face.
25 But in all Israel there was none to be so much praised as Absalom for his
beauty: from the sole of his foot even to the crown of his head there was no
blemish in him.
26 And when he polled his head, (for it was at every year's end that he polled
it: because *the hair* was heavy on him, therefore he polled it:) he weighed the
hair of his head at two hundred shekels after the king's weight.
27 And unto Absalom there were born three sons, and one daughter, whose
name *was* Tamar: she was a woman of a fair countenance.

Joab Brings Absalom into the King's Presence

28 So Absalom dwelt two full years in Jerusalem, and saw not the king's face.
29 Therefore Absalom sent for Joab, to have sent him to the king; but he would
not come to him: and when he sent again the second time, he would not come.
30 Therefore he said unto his servants, See, Joab's field is near mine, and he
hath barley there; go and set it on fire. And Absalom's servants set the field on
fire.
31 Then Joab arose, and came to Absalom unto *his* house, and said unto him,
Wherefore have thy servants set my field on fire?
32 And Absalom answered Joab, Behold, I sent unto thee, saying, Come hith-
er, that I may send thee to the king, to say, Wherefore am I come from Geshur?
it had been good for me *to have been* there still: now therefore let me see the
king's face; and if there be *any* iniquity in me, let him kill me.
33 So Joab came to the king, and told him: and when he had called for
Absalom, he came to the king, and bowed himself on his face to the ground
before the king: and the king kissed Absalom.

Absalom Wins the Affection of Israel

15 And it came to pass after this, that Absalom prepared him chariots and
horses, and fifty men to run before him.
2 And Absalom rose up early, and stood beside the way of the gate: and it was
so, that when any man that had a controversy came to the king for judgment,
then Absalom called unto him, and said, Of what city *art* thou? And he said,
Thy servant *is* of one of the tribes of Israel.
3 And Absalom said unto him, See, thy matters *are* good and right; but *there
is* no man *deputed* of the king to hear thee.

4 Absalom said moreover, Oh that I were made judge in the land, that every
man which hath any suit or cause might come unto me, and I would do him
justice!
5 And it was *so*, that when any man came nigh *to him* to do him obeisance,
he put forth his hand, and took him, and kissed him.
6 And on this manner did Absalom to all Israel that came to the king for
judgment: so Absalom stole the hearts of the men of Israel.

Absalom Instigates a Conspiracy to Overthrow His Father

7 And it came to pass after forty years, that Absalom said unto the king, I pray
thee, let me go and pay my vow, which I have vowed unto the LORD, in Hebron.
8 For thy servant vowed a vow while I abode at Geshur in Syria, saying, If the
LORD shall bring me again indeed to Jerusalem, then I will serve the LORD.
9 And the king said unto him, Go in peace. So he arose, and went to Hebron.
10 But Absalom sent spies throughout all the tribes of Israel, saying, As soon
as ye hear the sound of the trumpet, then ye shall say, Absalom reigneth in
Hebron.
11 And with Absalom went two hundred men out of Jerusalem, *that were*
called; and they went in their simplicity, and they knew not any thing.
12 And Absalom sent for Ahithophel the Gilonite, David's counsellor, from
his city, *even* from Giloh, while he offered sacrifices. And the conspiracy was
strong; for the people increased continually with Absalom.

David Flees from Jerusalem

13 And there came a messenger to David, saying, The hearts of the men of
Israel are after Absalom.
14 And David said unto all his servants that *were* with him at Jerusalem, Arise,
and let us flee; for we shall not *else* escape from Absalom: make speed to depart,
lest he overtake us suddenly, and bring evil upon us, and smite the city with
the edge of the sword.
15 And the king's servants said unto the king, Behold, thy servants *are ready
to do* whatsoever my lord the king shall appoint.
16 And the king went forth, and all his household after him. And the king
left ten women, *which were* concubines, to keep the house.
17 And the king went forth, and all the people after him, and tarried in a
place that was far off.
18 And all his servants passed on beside him; and all the Cherethites, and all
the Pelethites, and all the Gittites, six hundred men which came after him
from Gath, passed on before the king.
19 Then said the king to Ittai the Gittite, Wherefore goest thou also with us?
return to thy place, and abide with the king: for thou *art* a stranger, and also
an exile.
20 Whereas thou camest *but* yesterday, should I this day make thee go up and
down with us? seeing I go whither I may, return thou, and take back thy breth-
ren: mercy and truth *be* with thee.
21 And Ittai answered the king, and said, *As* the LORD liveth, and *as* my lord
the king liveth, surely in what place my lord the king shall be, whether in death
or life, even there also will thy servant be.
22 And David said to Ittai, Go and pass over. And Ittai the Gittite passed over,
and all his men, and all the little ones that *were* with him.
23 And all the country wept with a loud voice, and all the people passed over:
the king also himself passed over the brook Kidron, and all the people passed
over, toward the way of the wilderness.

Zadok and Abiathar Are Sent Back with the Ark

24 And lo Zadok also, and all the Levites *were* with him, bearing the ark of
the covenant of God: and they set down the ark of God; and Abiathar went up,
until all the people had done passing out of the city.

25 And the king said unto Zadok, Carry back the ark of God into the city: if
I shall find favour in the eyes of the LORD, he will bring me again, and shew
me *both* it, and his habitation:
26 But if he thus say, I have no delight in thee; behold, *here am* I, let him do
to me as seemeth good unto him.
27 The king said also unto Zadok the priest, *Art not* thou a seer? return into
the city in peace, and your two sons with you, Ahimaaz thy son, and Jonathan
the son of Abiathar.
28 See, I will tarry in the plain of the wilderness, until there come word from
you to certify me.
29 Zadok therefore and Abiathar carried the ark of God again to Jerusalem:
and they tarried there.
30 And David went up by the ascent of *mount* Olivet, and wept as he went up,
and had his head covered, and he went barefoot: and all the people that *was* with
him covered every man his head, and they went up, weeping as they went up.

David Prays against Ahithophel

31 And *one* told David, saying, Ahithophel *is* among the conspirators with
Absalom. And David said, O LORD, I pray thee, turn the counsel of Ahithophel
into foolishness.
32 And it came to pass, that *when* David was come to the top *of the mount*,
where he worshipped God, behold, Hushai the Archite came to meet him with
his coat rent, and earth upon his head:
33 Unto whom David said, If thou passest on with me, then thou shalt be a
burden unto me:
34 But if thou return to the city, and say unto Absalom, I will be thy servant,
O king; *as* I *have been* thy father's servant hitherto, so *will* I now also *be* thy
servant: then mayest thou for me defeat the counsel of Ahithophel.
35 And *hast thou* not there with thee Zadok and Abiathar the priests? there-
fore it shall be, *that* what thing soever thou shalt hear out of the king's house,
thou shalt tell *it* to Zadok and Abiathar the priests.
36 Behold, *they have* there with them their two sons, Ahimaaz Zadok's *son*,
and Jonathan Abiathar's *son*; and by them ye shall send unto me every thing
that ye can hear.
37 So Hushai David's friend came into the city, and Absalom came into
Jerusalem.

Ziba Brings Presents to David and Secures His Master's Inheritance

16 And when David was a little past the top *of the hill*, behold, Ziba the
servant of Mephibosheth met him, with a couple of asses saddled, and
upon them two hundred *loaves* of bread, and an hundred bunches of raisins,
and an hundred of summer fruits, and a bottle of wine.
2 And the king said unto Ziba, What meanest thou by these? And Ziba said,
The asses *be* for the king's household to ride on; and the bread and summer
fruit for the young men to eat; and the wine, that such as be faint in the wil-
derness may drink.
3 And the king said, And where *is* thy master's son? And Ziba said unto the
king, Behold, he abideth at Jerusalem: for he said, To day shall the house of
Israel restore me the kingdom of my father.
4 Then said the king to Ziba, Behold, thine *are* all that *pertained* unto
Mephibosheth. And Ziba said, I humbly beseech thee *that* I may find grace in
thy sight, my lord, O king.

Shimei Curses David

5 And when king David came to Bahurim, behold, thence came out a man
of the family of the house of Saul, whose name *was* Shimei, the son of Gera:
he came forth, and cursed still as he came.

6 And he cast stones at David, and at all the servants of king David: and all
the people and all the mighty men *were* on his right hand and on his left.
7 And thus said Shimei when he cursed, Come out, come out, thou bloody
man, and thou man of Belial:
8 The LORD hath returned upon thee all the blood of the house of Saul, in
whose stead thou hast reigned; and the LORD hath delivered the kingdom into
the hand of Absalom thy son: and, behold, thou *art taken* in thy mischief,
because thou *art* a bloody man.
9 Then said Abishai the son of Zeruiah unto the king, Why should this dead
dog curse my lord the king? let me go over, I pray thee, and take off his head.
10 And the king said, What have I to do with you, ye sons of Zeruiah? so let
him curse, because the LORD hath said unto him, Curse David. Who shall then
say, Wherefore hast thou done so?
11 And David said to Abishai, and to all his servants, Behold, my son, which
came forth of my bowels, seeketh my life: how much more now *may this*
Benjamite *do it*? let him alone, and let him curse; for the LORD hath bidden
him.
12 It may be that the LORD will look on mine affliction, and that the LORD will
requite me good for his cursing this day.
13 And as David and his men went by the way, Shimei went along on the hill's
side over against him, and cursed as he went, and threw stones at him, and
cast dust.
14 And the king, and all the people that *were* with him, came weary, and
refreshed themselves there.

Hushai Insinuates Himself into Absalom's Counsel

15 And Absalom, and all the people the men of Israel, came to Jerusalem, and
Ahithophel with him.
16 And it came to pass, when Hushai the Archite, David's friend, was come
unto Absalom, that Hushai said unto Absalom, God save the king, God save
the king.
17 And Absalom said to Hushai, *Is* this thy kindness to thy friend? why
wentest thou not with thy friend?
18 And Hushai said unto Absalom, Nay; but whom the LORD, and this people,
and all the men of Israel, choose, his will I be, and with him will I abide.
19 And again, whom should I serve? *should I* not *serve* in the presence of his
son? as I have served in thy father's presence, so will I be in thy presence.
20 Then said Absalom to Ahithophel, Give counsel among you what we shall do.
21 And Ahithophel said unto Absalom, Go in unto thy father's concubines,
which he hath left to keep the house; and all Israel shall hear that thou art
abhorred of thy father: then shall the hands of all that *are* with thee be strong.
22 So they spread Absalom a tent upon the top of the house; and Absalom
went in unto his father's concubines in the sight of all Israel.
23 And the counsel of Ahithophel, which he counselled in those days, *was* as
if a man had enquired at the oracle of God: so *was* all the counsel of Ahithophel
both with David and with Absalom.

Ahithophel's Counsel Is Overthrown by Hushai's

17 Moreover Ahithophel said unto Absalom, Let me now choose out
twelve thousand men, and I will arise and pursue after David this night:
2 And I will come upon him while he *is* weary and weak handed, and will
make him afraid: and all the people that *are* with him shall flee; and I will
smite the king only:
3 And I will bring back all the people unto thee: the man whom thou seekest
is as if all returned: *so* all the people shall be in peace.
4 And the saying pleased Absalom well, and all the elders of Israel.

5 Then said Absalom, Call now Hushai the Archite also, and let us hear likewise what he saith.

6 And when Hushai was come to Absalom, Absalom spake unto him, saying, Ahithophel hath spoken after this manner: shall we do *after* his saying? if not; speak thou.

7 And Hushai said unto Absalom, The counsel that Ahithophel hath given *is* not good at this time.

8 For, said Hushai, thou knowest thy father and his men, that they *be* mighty men, and they *be* chafed in their minds, as a bear robbed of her whelps in the field: and thy father *is* a man of war, and will not lodge with the people.

9 Behold, he is hid now in some pit, or in some *other* place: and it will come to pass, when some of them be overthrown at the first, that whosoever heareth it will say, There is a slaughter among the people that follow Absalom.

10 And he also *that is* valiant, whose heart *is* as the heart of a lion, shall utterly melt: for all Israel knoweth that thy father *is* a mighty man, and *they* which *be* with him *are* valiant men.

11 Therefore I counsel that all Israel be generally gathered unto thee, from Dan even to Beer-sheba, as the sand that *is* by the sea for multitude; and that thou go to battle in thine own person.

12 So shall we come upon him in some place where he shall be found, and we will light upon him as the dew falleth on the ground: and of him and of all the men that *are* with him there shall not be left so much as one.

13 Moreover, if he be gotten into a city, then shall all Israel bring ropes to that city, and we will draw it into the river, until there be not one small stone found there.

14 And Absalom and all the men of Israel said, The counsel of Hushai the Archite *is* better than the counsel of Ahithophel. For the Lord had appointed to defeat the good counsel of Ahithophel, to the intent that the Lord might bring evil upon Absalom.

David Receives Secret Intelligence

15 Then said Hushai unto Zadok and to Abiathar the priests, Thus and thus did Ahithophel counsel Absalom and the elders of Israel; and thus and thus have I counselled.

16 Now therefore send quickly, and tell David, saying, Lodge not this night in the plains of the wilderness, but speedily pass over; lest the king be swallowed up, and all the people that *are* with him.

17 Now Jonathan and Ahimaaz stayed by En-rogel; for they might not be seen to come into the city: and a wench went and told them; and they went and told king David.

18 Nevertheless a lad saw them, and told Absalom: but they went both of them away quickly, and came to a man's house in Bahurim, which had a well in his court; whither they went down.

19 And the woman took and spread a covering over the well's mouth, and spread ground corn thereon; and the thing was not known.

20 And when Absalom's servants came to the woman to the house, they said, Where *is* Ahimaaz and Jonathan? And the woman said unto them, They be gone over the brook of water. And when they had sought and could not find *them*, they returned to Jerusalem.

21 And it came to pass, after they were departed, that they came up out of the well, and went and told king David, and said unto David, Arise, and pass quickly over the water: for thus hath Ahithophel counselled against you.

22 Then David arose, and all the people that *were* with him, and they passed over Jordan: by the morning light there lacked not one of them that was not gone over Jordan.

23 And when Ahithophel saw that his counsel was not followed, he saddled
his ass, and arose, and gat him home to his house, to his city, and put his
household in order, and hanged himself, and died, and was buried in the
sepulchre of his father.
24 Then David came to Mahanaim. And Absalom passed over Jordan, he and
all the men of Israel with him.
25 And Absalom made Amasa captain of the host instead of Joab: which
Amasa *was* a man's son, whose name *was* Ithra an Israelite, that went in to
Abigail the daughter of Nahash, sister to Zeruiah Joab's mother.
26 So Israel and Absalom pitched in the land of Gilead.
27 And it came to pass, when David was come to Mahanaim, that Shobi the
son of Nahash of Rabbah of the children of Ammon, and Machir the son of
Ammiel of Lo-debar, and Barzillai the Gileadite of Rogelim,
28 Brought beds, and basons, and earthen vessels, and wheat, and barley, and
flour, and parched *corn*, and beans, and lentiles, and parched *pulse*,
29 And honey, and butter, and sheep, and cheese of kine, for David, and for
the people that *were* with him, to eat: for they said, The people *is* hungry, and
weary, and thirsty, in the wilderness.

David Sets out to Defeat Absalom, but Charges His Army to Be Kind

18 And David numbered the people that *were* with him, and set captains
of thousands and captains of hundreds over them.
2 And David sent forth a third part of the people under the hand of Joab, and
a third part under the hand of Abishai the son of Zeruiah, Joab's brother, and
a third part under the hand of Ittai the Gittite. And the king said unto the
people, I will surely go forth with you myself also.
3 But the people answered, Thou shalt not go forth: for if we flee away, they
will not care for us; neither if half of us die, will they care for us: but now *thou*
art worth ten thousand of us: therefore now *it is* better that thou succour us
out of the city.
4 And the king said unto them, What seemeth you best I will do. And the king
stood by the gate side, and all the people came out by hundreds and by thou-
sands.
5 And the king commanded Joab and Abish-ai and Ittai, saying, *Deal* gently
for my sake with the young man, *even* with Absalom. And all the people heard
when the king gave all the captains charge concerning Absalom.
6 So the people went out into the field against Israel: and the battle was in
the wood of Ephraim;
7 Where the people of Israel were slain before the servants of David, and
there was there a great slaughter that day of twenty thousand *men*.
8 For the battle was there scattered over the face of all the country: and the
wood devoured more people that day than the sword devoured.

Caught by His Hair in a Tree, Absalom Is Slain by Joab

9 And Absalom met the servants of David. And Absalom rode upon a mule,
and the mule went under the thick boughs of a great oak, and his head caught
hold of the oak, and he was taken up between the heaven and the earth; and
the mule that *was* under him went away.
10 And a certain man saw *it*, and told Joab, and said, Behold, I saw Absalom
hanged in an oak.
11 And Joab said unto the man that told him, And, behold, thou sawest *him*,
and why didst thou not smite him there to the ground? and I would have given
thee ten *shekels* of silver, and a girdle.
12 And the man said unto Joab, Though I should receive a thousand *shekels*
of silver in mine hand, *yet* would I not put forth mine hand against the king's
son: for in our hearing the king charged thee and Abishai and Ittai, saying,
Beware that none *touch* the young man Absalom.

13 Otherwise I should have wrought falsehood against mine own life: for there is no matter hid from the king, and thou thyself wouldest have set thyself against *me.*
14 Then said Joab, I may not tarry thus with thee. And he took three darts in his hand, and thrust them through the heart of Absalom, while he *was* yet alive in the midst of the oak.
15 And ten young men that bare Joab's armour compassed about and smote Absalom, and slew him.
16 And Joab blew the trumpet, and the people returned from pursuing after Israel: for Joab held back the people.
17 And they took Absalom, and cast him into a great pit in the wood, and laid a very great heap of stones upon him: and all Israel fled every one to his tent.
18 Now Absalom in his lifetime had taken and reared up for himself a pillar, which *is* in the king's dale: for he said, I have no son to keep my name in remembrance: and he called the pillar after his own name: and it is called unto this day, Absalom's place.

David Receives News of Absalom's Death

19 Then said Ahimaaz the son of Zadok, Let me now run, and bear the king tidings, how that the LORD hath avenged him of his enemies.
20 And Joab said unto him, Thou shalt not bear tidings this day, but thou shalt bear tidings another day: but this day thou shalt bear no tidings, because the king's son is dead.
21 Then said Joab to Cushi, Go tell the king what thou hast seen. And Cushi bowed himself unto Joab, and ran.
22 Then said Ahimaaz the son of Zadok yet again to Joab, But howsoever, let me, I pray thee, also run after Cushi. And Joab said, Wherefore wilt thou run, my son, seeing that thou hast no tidings ready?
23 But howsoever, *said he,* let me run. And he said unto him, Run. Then Ahimaaz ran by the way of the plain, and overran Cushi.
24 And David sat between the two gates: and the watchman went up to the roof over the gate unto the wall, and lifted up his eyes, and looked, and behold a man running alone.
25 And the watchman cried, and told the king. And the king said, If he *be* alone, *there is* tidings in his mouth. And he came apace, and drew near.
26 And the watchman saw another man running: and the watchman called unto the porter, and said, Behold *another* man running alone. And the king said, He also bringeth tidings.
27 And the watchman said, Me thinketh the running of the foremost is like the running of Ahimaaz the son of Zadok. And the king said, He *is* a good man, and cometh with good tidings.
28 And Ahimaaz called, and said unto the king, All is well. And he fell down to the earth upon his face before the king, and said, Blessed *be* the LORD thy God, which hath delivered up the men that lifted up their hand against my lord the king.
29 And the king said, Is the young man Absalom safe? And Ahimaaz answered, When Joab sent the king's servant, and *me* thy servant, I saw a great tumult, but I knew not what *it was.*
30 And the king said *unto him,* Turn aside, *and* stand here. And he turned aside, and stood still.
31 And, behold, Cushi came; and Cushi said, Tidings, my lord the king: for the LORD hath avenged thee this day of all them that rose up against thee.
32 And the king said unto Cushi, Is the young man Absalom safe? And Cushi answered, The enemies of my lord the king, and all that rise against thee to do *thee* hurt, be as *that* young man *is.*

33 And the king was much moved, and went up to the chamber over the gate,
and wept: and as he went, thus he said, O my son Absalom, my son, my son
Absalom! would God I had died for thee, O Absalom, my son, my son!

Joab Causes the King to Cease His Mourning

19 And it was told Joab, Behold, the king weepeth and mourneth for
Absalom.
2 And the victory that day was *turned* into mourning unto all the people: for
the people heard say that day how the king was grieved for his son.
3 And the people gat them by stealth that day into the city, as people being
ashamed steal away when they flee in battle.
4 But the king covered his face, and the king cried with a loud voice, O my
son Absalom, O Absalom, my son, my son!
5 And Joab came into the house to the king, and said, Thou hast shamed this
day the faces of all thy servants, which this day have saved thy life, and the lives
of thy sons and of thy daughters, and the lives of thy wives, and the lives of thy
concubines;
6 In that thou lovest thine enemies, and hatest thy friends. For thou hast
declared this day, that thou regardest neither princes nor servants: for this
day I perceive, that if Absalom had lived, and all we had died this day, then it
had pleased thee well.
7 Now therefore arise, go forth, and speak comfortably unto thy servants:
for I swear by the LORD, if thou go not forth, there will not tarry one with thee
this night: and that will be worse unto thee than all the evil that befell thee
from thy youth until now.
8 Then the king arose, and sat in the gate. And they told unto all the people,
saying, Behold, the king doth sit in the gate. And all the people came before
the king: for Israel had fled every man to his tent.

The Israelites Desire to Bring King David Back to Jerusalem

9 And all the people were at strife throughout all the tribes of Israel, saying,
The king saved us out of the hand of our enemies, and he delivered us out of
the hand of the Philistines; and now he is fled out of the land for Absalom.
10 And Absalom, whom we anointed over us, is dead in battle. Now therefore
why speak ye not a word of bringing the king back?
11 And king David sent to Zadok and to Abiathar the priests, saying, Speak
unto the elders of Judah, saying, Why are ye the last to bring the king back to
his house? seeing the speech of all Israel is come to the king, *even* to his house.
12 Ye *are* my brethren, ye *are* my bones and my flesh: wherefore then are ye
the last to bring back the king?
13 And say ye to Amasa, *Art* thou not of my bone, and of my flesh? God do so
to me, and more also, if thou be not captain of the host before me continual-
ly in the room of Joab.
14 And he bowed the heart of all the men of Judah, even as *the heart of* one
man; so that they sent *this word* unto the king, Return thou, and all thy servants.
15 So the king returned, and came to Jordan. And Judah came to Gilgal, to
go to meet the king, to conduct the king over Jordan.
16 And Shimei the son of Gera, a Benjamite, which *was* of Bahurim, hasted
and came down with the men of Judah to meet king David.
17 And *there were* a thousand men of Benjamin with him, and Ziba the ser-
vant of the house of Saul, and his fifteen sons and his twenty servants with
him; and they went over Jordan before the king.
18 And there went over a ferry boat to carry over the king's household, and
to do what he thought good. And Shimei the son of Gera fell down before the
king, as he was come over Jordan;

19 And said unto the king, Let not my lord impute iniquity unto me, neither
do thou remember that which thy servant did perversely the day that my lord
the king went out of Jerusalem, that the king should take it to his heart.
20 For thy servant doth know that I have sinned: therefore, behold, I am come
the first this day of all the house of Joseph to go down to meet my lord the king.
21 But Abishai the son of Zeruiah answered and said, Shall not Shimei be put
to death for this, because he cursed the LORD's anointed?
22 And David said, What have I to do with you, ye sons of Zeruiah, that ye
should this day be adversaries unto me? shall there any man be put to death
this day in Israel? for do not I know that I *am* this day king over Israel?
23 Therefore the king said unto Shimei, Thou shalt not die. And the king
sware unto him.

Mephibosheth Excused

24 And Mephibosheth the son of Saul came down to meet the king, and had
neither dressed his feet, nor trimmed his beard, nor washed his clothes, from
the day the king departed until the day he came *again* in peace.
25 And it came to pass, when he was come to Jerusalem to meet the king, that
the king said unto him, Wherefore wentest not thou with me, Mephibosheth?
26 And he answered, My lord, O king, my servant deceived me: for thy servant
said, I will saddle me an ass, that I may ride thereon, and go to the king; because
thy servant *is* lame.
27 And he hath slandered thy servant unto my lord the king; but my lord the
king *is* as an angel of God: do therefore *what is* good in thine eyes.
28 For all *of* my father's house were but dead men before my lord the king:
yet didst thou set thy servant among them that did eat at thine own table.
What right therefore have I yet to cry any more unto the king?
29 And the king said unto him, Why speakest thou any more of thy matters?
I have said, Thou and Ziba divide the land.
30 And Mephibosheth said unto the king, Yea, let him take all, forasmuch as
my lord the king is come again in peace unto his own house.
31 And Barzillai the Gileadite came down from Rogelim, and went over
Jordan with the king, to conduct him over Jordan.
32 Now Barzillai was a very aged man, *even* fourscore years old: and he had
provided the king of sustenance while he lay at Mahanaim; for he *was* a very
great man.
33 And the king said unto Barzillai, Come thou over with me, and I will feed
thee with me in Jerusalem.
34 And Barzillai said unto the king, How long have I to live, that I should go
up with the king unto Jerusalem?
35 I *am* this day fourscore years old: *and* can I discern between good and
evil? can thy servant taste what I eat or what I drink? can I hear any more the
voice of singing men and singing women? wherefore then should thy servant
be yet a burden unto my lord the king?
36 Thy servant will go a little way over Jordan with the king: and why should
the king recompense it me with such a reward?
37 Let thy servant, I pray thee, turn back again, that I may die in mine own
city, *and be buried* by the grave of my father and of my mother. But behold thy
servant Chimham; let him go over with my lord the king; and do to him what
shall seem good unto thee.
38 And the king answered, Chimham shall go over with me, and I will do to
him that which shall seem good unto thee: and whatsoever thou shalt require
of me, *that* will I do for thee.
39 And all the people went over Jordan. And when the king was come over,
the king kissed Barzillai, and blessed him; and he returned unto his own place.

40 Then the king went on to Gilgal, and Chimham went on with him: and all
the people of Judah conducted the king, and also half the people of Israel.
41 And, behold, all the men of Israel came to the king, and said unto the king,
Why have our brethren the men of Judah stolen thee away, and have brought
the king, and his household, and all David's men with him, over Jordan?
42 And all the men of Judah answered the men of Israel, Because the king *is*
near of kin to us: wherefore then be ye angry for this matter? have we eaten
at all of the king's *cost*? or hath he given us any gift?
43 And the men of Israel answered the men of Judah, and said, We have ten
parts in the king, and we have also more *right* in David than ye: why then did
ye despise us, that our advice should not be first had in bringing back our
king? And the words of the men of Judah were fiercer than the words of the
men of Israel.

Sheba Incites a Rebellion against King David

20 And there happened to be there a man of Belial, whose name *was*
Sheba, the son of Bichri, a Benjamite: and he blew a trumpet, and said,
We have no part in David, neither have we inheritance in the son of Jesse: every
man to his tents, O Israel.
2 So every man of Israel went up from after David, *and* followed Sheba the
son of Bichri: but the men of Judah clave unto their king, from Jordan even to
Jerusalem.
3 And David came to his house at Jerusalem; and the king took the ten women
his concubines, whom he had left to keep the house, and put them in ward,
and fed them, but went not in unto them. So they were shut up unto the day
of their death, living in widowhood.

Amasa, Made Captain over Judah, Is Slain by Joab

4 Then said the king to Amasa, Assemble me the men of Judah within three
days, and be thou here present.
5 So Amasa went to assemble *the men of* Judah: but he tarried longer than
the set time which he had appointed him.
6 And David said to Abishai, Now shall Sheba the son of Bichri do us more
harm than *did* Absalom: take thou thy lord's servants, and pursue after him,
lest he get him fenced cities, and escape us.
7 And there went out after him Joab's men, and the Cherethites, and the
Pelethites, and all the mighty men: and they went out of Jerusalem, to pursue
after Sheba the son of Bichri.
8 When they *were* at the great stone which *is* in Gibeon, Amasa went before
them. And Joab's garment that he had put on was girded unto him, and upon
it a girdle *with* a sword fastened upon his loins in the sheath thereof; and as
he went forth it fell out.
9 And Joab said to Amasa, *Art* thou in health, my brother? And Joab took
Amasa by the beard with the right hand to kiss him.
10 But Amasa took no heed to the sword that *was* in Joab's hand: so he smote
him therewith in the fifth *rib*, and shed out his bowels to the ground, and
struck him not again; and he died. So Joab and Abishai his brother pursued
after Sheba the son of Bichri.
11 And one of Joab's men stood by him, and said, He that favoureth Joab, and
he that *is* for David, *let him go* after Joab.
12 And Amasa wallowed in blood in the midst of the highway. And when the
man saw that all the people stood still, he removed Amasa out of the highway
into the field, and cast a cloth upon him, when he saw that every one that came
by him stood still.
13 When he was removed out of the highway, all the people went on after
Joab, to pursue after Sheba the son of Bichri.

Joab Pursues Sheba, Who Is Killed by the Citizens of Abel

14 And he went through all the tribes of Israel unto Abel, and to Beth-maachah, and all the Berites: and they were gathered together, and went also after him.

15 And they came and besieged him in Abel of Beth-maachah, and they cast up a bank against the city, and it stood in the trench: and all the people that *were* with Joab battered the wall, to throw it down.

16 Then cried a wise woman out of the city, Hear, hear; say, I pray you, unto Joab, Come near hither, that I may speak with thee.

17 And when he was come near unto her, the woman said, *Art* thou Joab? And he answered, I *am he.* Then she said unto him, Hear the words of thine handmaid. And he answered, I do hear.

18 Then she spake, saying, They were wont to speak in old time, saying, They shall surely ask *counsel* at Abel: and so they ended *the matter.*

19 I *am one of them that are* peaceable *and* faithful in Israel: thou seekest to destroy a city and a mother in Israel: why wilt thou swallow up the inheritance of the LORD?

20 And Joab answered and said, Far be it, far be it from me, that I should swallow up or destroy.

21 The matter *is* not so: but a man of mount Ephraim, Sheba the son of Bichri by name, hath lifted up his hand against the king, *even* against David: deliver him only, and I will depart from the city. And the woman said unto Joab, Behold, his head shall be thrown to thee over the wall.

22 Then the woman went unto all the people in her wisdom. And they cut off the head of Sheba the son of Bichri, and cast *it* out to Joab. And he blew a trumpet, and they retired from the city, every man to his tent. And Joab returned to Jerusalem unto the king.

David's Officers

23 Now Joab *was* over all the host of Israel: and Benaiah the son of Jehoiada *was* over the Cherethites and over the Pelethites:

24 And Adoram *was* over the tribute: and Jehoshaphat the son of Ahilud *was* recorder:

25 And Sheva *was* scribe: and Zadok and Abiathar *were* the priests:

26 And Ira also the Jairite was a chief ruler about David.

God Calls David to Avenge the People of Gibeon

21 Then there was a famine in the days of David three years, year after year; and David enquired of the LORD. And the LORD answered, *It is* for Saul, and for *his* bloody house, because he slew the Gibeonites.

2 And the king called the Gibeonites, and said unto them; (now the Gibeonites *were* not of the children of Israel, but of the remnant of the Amorites; and the children of Israel had sworn unto them: and Saul sought to slay them in his zeal to the children of Israel and Judah.)

3 Wherefore David said unto the Gibeonites, What shall I do for you? and wherewith shall I make the atonement, that ye may bless the inheritance of the LORD?

4 And the Gibeonites said unto him, We will have no silver nor gold of Saul, nor of his house; neither for us shalt thou kill any man in Israel. And he said, What ye shall say, *that* will I do for you.

5 And they answered the king, The man that consumed us, and that devised against us *that* we should be destroyed from remaining in any of the coasts of Israel,

6 Let seven men of his sons be delivered unto us, and we will hang them up unto the LORD in Gibeah of Saul, *whom* the LORD did choose. And the king said, I will give *them.*

7 But the king spared Mephibosheth, the son of Jonathan the son of Saul,
because of the LORD's oath that *was* between them, between David and
Jonathan the son of Saul.
8 But the king took the two sons of Rizpah the daughter of Aiah, whom she
bare unto Saul, Armoni and Mephibosheth; and the five sons of Michal the
daughter of Saul, whom she brought up for Adriel the son of Barzillai the
Meholathite:
9 And he delivered them into the hands of the Gibeonites, and they hanged
them in the hill before the LORD: and they fell *all* seven together, and were put
to death in the days of harvest, in the first *days*, in the beginning of barley
harvest.

Rizpah's Kindness to the Dead

10 And Rizpah the daughter of Aiah took sackcloth, and spread it for her
upon the rock, from the beginning of harvest until water dropped upon them
out of heaven, and suffered neither the birds of the air to rest on them by day,
nor the beasts of the field by night.
11 And it was told David what Rizpah the daughter of Aiah, the concubine
of Saul, had done.
12 And David went and took the bones of Saul and the bones of Jonathan his
son from the men of Jabesh-gilead, which had stolen them from the street of
Beth-shan, where the Philistines had hanged them, when the Philistines had
slain Saul in Gilboa:
13 And he brought up from thence the bones of Saul and the bones of
Jonathan his son; and they gathered the bones of them that were hanged.
14 And the bones of Saul and Jonathan his son buried they in the country of
Benjamin in Zelah, in the sepulchre of Kish his father: and they performed all
that the king commanded. And after that God was intreated for the land.

David Slays Four Giant Philistine Warriors

15 Moreover the Philistines had yet war again with Israel; and David went
down, and his servants with him, and fought against the Philistines: and David
waxed faint.
16 And Ishbi-benob, which *was* of the sons of the giant, the weight of whose
spear *weighed* three hundred *shekels* of brass in weight, he being girded with
a new *sword*, thought to have slain David.
17 But Abishai the son of Zeruiah succoured him, and smote the Philistine,
and killed him. Then the men of David sware unto him, saying, Thou shalt go
no more out with us to battle, that thou quench not the light of Israel.
18 And it came to pass after this, that there was again a battle with the
Philistines at Gob: then Sibbechai the Hushathite slew Saph, which *was* of the
sons of the giant.
19 And there was again a battle in Gob with the Philistines, where Elhanan
the son of Jaareoregim, a Beth-lehemite, slew *the brother of* Goliath the Gittite,
the staff of whose spear *was* like a weaver's beam.
20 And there was yet a battle in Gath, where was a man of *great* stature, that
had on every hand six fingers, and on every foot six toes, four and twenty in
number; and he also was born to the giant.
21 And when he defied Israel, Jonathan the son of Shimea the brother of
David slew him.
22 These four were born to the giant in Gath, and fell by the hand of David,
and by the hand of his servants.

A Psalm of Thanksgiving

22 And David spake unto the LORD the words of this song in the day *that*
the LORD had delivered him out of the hand of all his enemies, and out
of the hand of Saul:
2 And he said, The LORD *is* my rock, and my fortress, and my deliverer;

3 The God of my rock; in him will I trust: *he is* my shield, and the horn of my
salvation, my high tower, and my refuge, my saviour; thou savest me from
violence.
4 I will call on the LORD, *who is* worthy to be praised: so shall I be saved from
mine enemies.
5 When the waves of death compassed me, the floods of ungodly men made
me afraid;
6 The sorrows of hell compassed me about; the snares of death prevented me;
7 In my distress I called upon the LORD, and cried to my God: and he did hear
my voice out of his temple, and my cry *did enter* into his ears.
8 Then the earth shook and trembled; the foundations of heaven moved and
shook, because he was wroth.
9 There went up a smoke out of his nostrils, and fire out of his mouth
devoured: coals were kindled by it.
10 He bowed the heavens also, and came down; and darkness *was* under his feet.
11 And he rode upon a cherub, and did fly: and he was seen upon the wings
of the wind.
12 And he made darkness pavilions round about him, dark waters, *and* thick
clouds of the skies.
13 Through the brightness before him were coals of fire kindled.
14 The LORD thundered from heaven, and the most High uttered his voice.
15 And he sent out arrows, and scattered them; lightning, and discomfited them.
16 And the channels of the sea appeared, the foundations of the world were
discovered, at the rebuking of the LORD, at the blast of the breath of his nostrils.
17 He sent from above, he took me; he drew me out of many waters;
18 He delivered me from my strong enemy, *and* from them that hated me:
for they were too strong for me.
19 They prevented me in the day of my calamity: but the LORD was my stay.
20 He brought me forth also into a large place: he delivered me, because he
delighted in me.
21 The LORD rewarded me according to my righteousness: according to the
cleanness of my hands hath he recompensed me.
22 For I have kept the ways of the LORD, and have not wickedly departed from
my God.
23 For all his judgments *were* before me: and *as for* his statutes, I did not
depart from them.
24 I was also upright before him, and have kept myself from mine iniquity.
25 Therefore the LORD hath recompensed me according to my righteousness;
according to my cleanness in his eye sight.
26 With the merciful thou wilt shew thyself merciful, *and* with the upright
man thou wilt shew thyself upright.
27 With the pure thou wilt shew thyself pure; and with the froward thou wilt
shew thyself unsavoury.
28 And the afflicted people thou wilt save: but thine eyes *are* upon the haugh-
ty, *that* thou mayest bring *them* down.
29 For thou *art* my lamp, O LORD: and the LORD will lighten my darkness.
30 For by thee I have run through a troop: by my God have I leaped over a wall.
31 *As for* God, his way *is* perfect; the word of the LORD *is* tried: he *is* a buckler
to all them that trust in him.
32 For who *is* God, save the LORD? and who *is* a rock, save our God?
33 God *is* my strength *and* power: and he maketh my way perfect.
34 He maketh my feet like hinds' *feet*: and setteth me upon my high places.
35 He teacheth my hands to war; so that a bow of steel is broken by mine arms.
36 Thou hast also given me the shield of thy salvation: and thy gentleness
hath made me great.
37 Thou hast enlarged my steps under me; so that my feet did not slip.

38 I have pursued mine enemies, and destroyed them; and turned not again
until I had consumed them.
39 And I have consumed them, and wounded them, that they could not arise:
yea, they are fallen under my feet.
40 For thou hast girded me with strength to battle: them that rose up against
me hast thou subdued under me.
41 Thou hast also given me the necks of mine enemies, that I might destroy
them that hate me.
42 They looked, but *there was* none to save; *even* unto the LORD, but he
answered them not.
43 Then did I beat them as small as the dust of the earth, I did stamp them
as the mire of the street, *and* did spread them abroad.
44 Thou also hast delivered me from the strivings of my people, thou hast
kept me *to be* head of the heathen: a people *which* I knew not shall serve me.
45 Strangers shall submit themselves unto me: as soon as they hear, they shall
be obedient unto me.
46 Strangers shall fade away, and they shall be afraid out of their close places.
47 The LORD liveth; and blessed *be* my rock; and exalted be the God of the
rock of my salvation.
48 It *is* God that avengeth me, and that bringeth down the people under me,
49 And that bringeth me forth from mine enemies: thou also hast lifted me
up on high above them that rose up against me: thou hast delivered me from
the violent man.
50 Therefore I will give thanks unto thee, O LORD, among the heathen, and I
will sing praises unto thy name.
51 *He is* the tower of salvation for his king: and sheweth mercy to his anoint-
ed, unto David, and to his seed for evermore.

David Professes His Faith in God's Promises

23 Now these *be* the last words of David. David the son of Jesse said, and
the man *who was* raised up on high, the anointed of the God of Jacob,
and the sweet psalmist of Israel, said,
2 The Spirit of the LORD spake by me, and his word *was* in my tongue.
3 The God of Israel said, the Rock of Israel spake to me, He that ruleth over
men *must be* just, ruling in the fear of God.
4 And *he shall be* as the light of the morning, *when* the sun riseth, *even* a
morning without clouds; *as* the tender grass *springing* out of the earth by
clear shining after rain.
5 Although my house *be* not so with God; yet he hath made with me an ever-
lasting covenant, ordered in all *things*, and sure: for *this is* all my salvation,
and all *my* desire, although he make *it* not to grow.
6 But *the sons* of Belial *shall be* all of them as thorns thrust away, because
they cannot be taken with hands:
7 But the man *that* shall touch them must be fenced with iron and the staff
of a spear; and they shall be utterly burned with fire in the *same* place.

A Catalogue of David's Mighty Men

8 These *be* the names of the mighty men whom David had: The Tachmonite
that sat in the seat, chief among the captains; the same *was* Adino the Eznite:
he lift up his spear against eight hundred, whom he slew at one time.
9 And after him *was* Eleazar the son of Dodo the Ahohite, *one* of the three
mighty men with David, when they defied the Philistines *that* were there
gathered together to battle, and the men of Israel were gone away:
10 He arose, and smote the Philistines until his hand was weary, and his hand
clave unto the sword: and the LORD wrought a great victory that day; and the
people returned after him only to spoil.

11 And after him *was* Shammah the son of Agee the Hararite. And the
Philistines were gathered together into a troop, where was a piece of ground
full of lentiles: and the people fled from the Philistines.
12 But he stood in the midst of the ground, and defended it, and slew the
Philistines: and the LORD wrought a great victory.
13 And three of the thirty chief went down, and came to David in the harvest
time unto the cave of Adullam: and the troop of the Philistines pitched in the
valley of Rephaim.
14 And David *was* then in an hold, and the garrison of the Philistines *was*
then *in* Beth-lehem.
15 And David longed, and said, Oh that one would give me drink of the water
of the well of Beth-lehem, which *is* by the gate!
16 And the three mighty men brake through the host of the Philistines, and
drew water out of the well of Beth-lehem, that *was* by the gate, and took *it*,
and brought *it* to David: nevertheless he would not drink thereof, but poured
it out unto the LORD.
17 And he said, Be it far from me, O LORD, that I should do this: *is not this* the
blood of the men that went in jeopardy of their lives? therefore he would not
drink it. These things did these three mighty men.
18 And Abishai, the brother of Joab, the son of Zeruiah, was chief among
three. And he lifted up his spear against three hundred, *and* slew *them*, and
had the name among three.
19 Was he not most honourable of three? therefore he was their captain:
howbeit he attained not unto the *first* three.
20 And Benaiah the son of Jehoiada, the son of a valiant man, of Kabzeel, who
had done many acts, he slew two lionlike men of Moab: he went down also
and slew a lion in the midst of a pit in time of snow:
21 And he slew an Egyptian, a goodly man: and the Egyptian had a spear in
his hand; but he went down to him with a staff, and plucked the spear out of
the Egyptian's hand, and slew him with his own spear.
22 These *things* did Benaiah the son of Jehoiada, and had the name among
three mighty men.
23 He was more honourable than the thirty, but he attained not to the *first*
three. And David set him over his guard.
24 Asahel the brother of Joab *was* one of the thirty; Elhanan the son of Dodo
of Beth-lehem,
25 Shammah the Harodite, Elika the Harodite,
26 Helez the Paltite, Ira the son of Ikkesh the Tekoite,
27 Abiezer the Anethothite, Mebunnai the Hushathite,
28 Zalmon the Ahohite, Maharai the Netophathite,
29 Heleb the son of Baanah, a Netophathite, Ittai the son of Ribai out of
Gibeah of the children of Benjamin,
30 Benaiah the Pirathonite, Hiddai of the brooks of Gaash,
31 Abialbon the Arbathite, Azmaveth the Barhumite,
32 Eliahba the Shaalbonite, of the sons of Jashen, Jonathan,
33 Shammah the Hararite, Ahiam the son of Sharar the Hararite,
34 Eliphelet the son of Ahasbai, the son of the Maachathite, Eliam the son of
Ahithophel the Gilonite,
35 Hezrai the Carmelite, Paarai the Arbite,
36 Igal the son of Nathan of Zobah, Bani the Gadite,
37 Zelek the Ammonite, Naharai the Beerothite, armourbearer to Joab the
son of Zeruiah,
38 Ira an Ithrite, Gareb an Ithrite,
39 Uriah the Hittite: thirty and seven in all.

David Forces Joab to Number the People

24 And again the anger of the LORD was kindled against Israel, and he
moved David against them to say, Go, number Israel and Judah.
2 For the king said to Joab the captain of the host, which *was* with him, Go
now through all the tribes of Israel, from Dan even to Beer-sheba, and number
ye the people, that I may know the number of the people.
3 And Joab said unto the king, Now the LORD thy God add unto the people,
how many soever they be, an hundredfold, and that the eyes of my lord the
king may see *it*: but why doth my lord the king delight in this thing?
4 Notwithstanding the king's word prevailed against Joab, and against the
captains of the host. And Joab and the captains of the host went out from the
presence of the king, to number the people of Israel.
5 And they passed over Jordan, and pitched in Aroer, on the right side of the
city that *lieth* in the midst of the river of Gad, and toward Jazer:
6 Then they came to Gilead, and to the land of Tahtim-hodshi; and they came
to Dan-jaan, and about to Zidon,
7 And came to the strong hold of Tyre, and to all the cities of the Hivites, and
of the Canaanites: and they went out to the south of Judah, *even* to Beer-sheba.
8 So when they had gone through all the land, they came to Jerusalem at the
end of nine months and twenty days.
9 And Joab gave up the sum of the number of the people unto the king: and
there were in Israel eight hundred thousand valiant men that drew the sword;
and the men of Judah *were* five hundred thousand men.

Consequences of David's Sin

10 And David's heart smote him after that he had numbered the people. And
David said unto the LORD, I have sinned greatly in that I have done: and now,
I beseech thee, O LORD, take away the iniquity of thy servant; for I have done
very foolishly.
11 For when David was up in the morning, the word of the LORD came unto
the prophet Gad, David's seer, saying,
12 Go and say unto David, Thus saith the LORD, I offer thee three *things*;
choose thee one of them, that I may *do it* unto thee.
13 So Gad came to David, and told him, and said unto him, Shall seven years
of famine come unto thee in thy land? or wilt thou flee three months before
thine enemies, while they pursue thee? or that there be three days' pestilence
in thy land? now advise, and see what answer I shall return to him that sent
me.
14 And David said unto Gad, I am in a great strait: let us fall now into the
hand of the LORD; for his mercies *are* great: and let me not fall into the hand
of man.
15 So the LORD sent a pestilence upon Israel from the morning even to the
time appointed: and there died of the people from Dan even to Beer-sheba
seventy thousand men.
16 And when the angel stretched out his hand upon Jerusalem to destroy it,
the LORD repented him of the evil, and said to the angel that destroyed the
people, It is enough: stay now thine hand. And the angel of the LORD was by
the threshingplace of Araunah the Jebusite.
17 And David spake unto the LORD when he saw the angel that smote the
people, and said, Lo, I have sinned, and I have done wickedly: but these sheep,
what have they done? let thine hand, I pray thee, be against me, and against
my father's house.

David Purchases Araunah's Threshing Floor, Where the Plague Ends

18 And Gad came that day to David, and said unto him, Go up, rear an altar
unto the LORD in the threshingfloor of Araunah the Jebusite.
19 And David, according to the saying of Gad, went up as the LORD commanded.

20 And Araunah looked, and saw the king and his servants coming on toward
him: and Araunah went out, and bowed himself before the king on his face
upon the ground.
21 And Araunah said, Wherefore is my lord the king come to his servant?
And David said, To buy the threshingfloor of thee, to build an altar unto the
LORD, that the plague may be stayed from the people.
22 And Araunah said unto David, Let my lord the king take and offer up what
seemeth good unto him: behold, *here be* oxen for burnt sacrifice, and thresh-
ing instruments and *other* instruments of the oxen for wood.
23 All these *things* did Araunah, *as* a king, give unto the king. And Araunah
said unto the king, The LORD thy God accept thee.
24 And the king said unto Araunah, Nay; but I will surely buy *it* of thee at a
price: neither will I offer burnt offerings unto the LORD my God of that which
doth cost me nothing. So David bought the threshingfloor and the oxen for
fifty shekels of silver.
25 And David built there an altar unto the LORD, and offered burnt offerings
and peace offerings. So the LORD was intreated for the land, and the plague
was stayed from Israel.

Abishag Ministers to David

1 Now king David was old *and* stricken in years; and they covered him with
clothes, but he gat no heat.
2 Wherefore his servants said unto him, Let there be sought for my lord the
king a young virgin: and let her stand before the king, and let her cherish him,
and let her lie in thy bosom, that my lord the king may get heat.
3 So they sought for a fair damsel throughout all the coasts of Israel, and
found Abishag a Shunammite, and brought her to the king.
4 And the damsel *was* very fair, and cherished the king, and ministered to
him: but the king knew her not.

Adonijah, David's Favored Son, Usurps the Kingdom

5 Then Adonijah the son of Haggith exalted himself, saying, I will be king:
and he prepared him chariots and horsemen, and fifty men to run before him.
6 And his father had not displeased him at any time in saying, Why hast thou
done so? and he also *was a* very goodly *man*; and *his mother* bare him after
Absalom.
7 And he conferred with Joab the son of Zeruiah, and with Abiathar the
priest: and they following Adonijah helped *him*.
8 But Zadok the priest, and Benaiah the son of Jehoiada, and Nathan the
prophet, and Shimei, and Rei, and the mighty men which *belonged* to David,
were not with Adonijah.
9 And Adonijah slew sheep and oxen and fat cattle by the stone of Zoheleth,
which *is* by En-rogel, and called all his brethren the king's sons, and all the
men of Judah the king's servants:
10 But Nathan the prophet, and Benaiah, and the mighty men, and Solomon
his brother, he called not.

Nathan and Bath-sheba Tell David about Adonijah

11 Wherefore Nathan spake unto Bath-sheba the mother of Solomon, saying,
Hast thou not heard that Adonijah the son of Haggith doth reign, and David
our lord knoweth *it* not?
12 Now therefore come, let me, I pray thee, give thee counsel, that thou may-
est save thine own life, and the life of thy son Solomon.
13 Go and get thee in unto king David, and say unto him, Didst not thou, my
lord, O king, swear unto thine handmaid, saying, Assuredly Solomon thy son
shall reign after me, and he shall sit upon my throne? why then doth Adonijah
reign?
14 Behold, while thou yet talkest there with the king, I also will come in after
thee, and confirm thy words.
15 And Bath-sheba went in unto the king into the chamber: and the king was
very old; and Abishag the Shunammite ministered unto the king.
16 And Bath-sheba bowed, and did obeisance unto the king. And the king
said, What wouldest thou?
17 And she said unto him, My lord, thou swarest by the LORD thy God unto
thine handmaid, *saying*, Assuredly Solomon thy son shall reign after me, and
he shall sit upon my throne.
18 And now, behold, Adonijah reigneth; and now, my lord the king, thou
knowest *it* not:

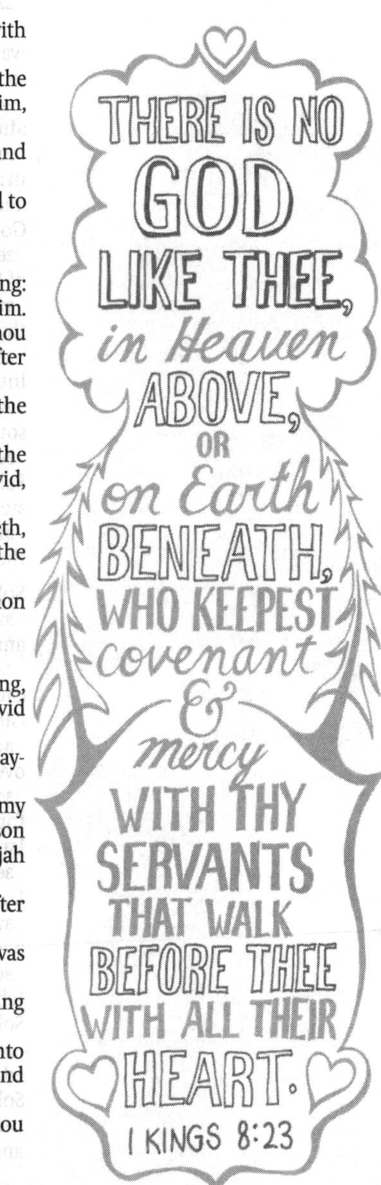

19 And he hath slain oxen and fat cattle and sheep in abundance, and hath
called all the sons of the king, and Abiathar the priest, and Joab the captain of
the host: but Solomon thy servant hath he not called.
20 And thou, my lord, O king, the eyes of all Israel *are* upon thee, that thou
shouldest tell them who shall sit on the throne of my lord the king after him.
21 Otherwise it shall come to pass, when my lord the king shall sleep with
his fathers, that I and my son Solomon shall be counted offenders.
22 And, lo, while she yet talked with the king, Nathan the prophet also came in.
23 And they told the king, saying, Behold Nathan the prophet. And when he
was come in before the king, he bowed himself before the king with his face
to the ground.
24 And Nathan said, My lord, O king, hast thou said, Adonijah shall reign
after me, and he shall sit upon my throne?
25 For he is gone down this day, and hath slain oxen and fat cattle and sheep
in abundance, and hath called all the king's sons, and the captains of the host,
and Abiathar the priest; and, behold, they eat and drink before him, and say,
God save king Adonijah.
26 But me, *even* me thy servant, and Zadok the priest, and Benaiah the son
of Jehoiada, and thy servant Solomon, hath he not called.
27 Is this thing done by my lord the king, and thou hast not shewed *it* unto
thy servant, who should sit on the throne of my lord the king after him?
28 Then king David answered and said, Call me Bath-sheba. And she came
into the king's presence, and stood before the king.
29 And the king sware, and said, *As* the LORD liveth, that hath redeemed my
soul out of all distress,
30 Even as I sware unto thee by the LORD God of Israel, saying, Assuredly
Solomon thy son shall reign after me, and he shall sit upon my throne in my
stead; even so will I certainly do this day.
31 Then Bath-sheba bowed with *her* face to the earth, and did reverence to
the king, and said, Let my lord king David live for ever.

Solomon Is Anointed King at David's Command

32 And king David said, Call me Zadok the priest, and Nathan the prophet,
and Benaiah the son of Jehoiada. And they came before the king.
33 The king also said unto them, Take with you the servants of your lord, and
cause Solomon my son to ride upon mine own mule, and bring him down to
Gihon:
34 And let Zadok the priest and Nathan the prophet anoint him there king
over Israel: and blow ye with the trumpet, and say, God save king Solomon.
35 Then ye shall come up after him, that he may come and sit upon my throne;
for he shall be king in my stead: and I have appointed him to be ruler over
Israel and over Judah.
36 And Benaiah the son of Jehoiada answered the king, and said, Amen: the
LORD God of my lord the king say so *too*.
37 As the LORD hath been with my lord the king, even so be he with Solomon,
and make his throne greater than the throne of my lord king David.
38 So Zadok the priest, and Nathan the prophet, and Benaiah the son of
Jehoiada, and the Cherethites, and the Pelethites, went down, and caused
Solomon to ride upon king David's mule, and brought him to Gihon.
39 And Zadok the priest took an horn of oil out of the tabernacle, and anoint-
ed Solomon. And they blew the trumpet; and all the people said, God save king
Solomon.
40 And all the people came up after him, and the people piped with pipes,
and rejoiced with great joy, so that the earth rent with the sound of them.

Adonijah Pleads for Mercy from Solomon

41 And Adonijah and all the guests that *were* with him heard *it* as they had
made an end of eating. And when Joab heard the sound of the trumpet, he
said, Wherefore *is this* noise of the city being in an uproar?
42 And while he yet spake, behold, Jonathan the son of Abiathar the priest
came: and Adonijah said unto him, Come in; for thou *art* a valiant man, and
bringest good tidings.
43 And Jonathan answered and said to Adonijah, Verily our lord king David
hath made Solomon king.
44 And the king hath sent with him Zadok the priest, and Nathan the proph-
et, and Benaiah the son of Jehoiada, and the Cherethites, and the Pelethites,
and they have caused him to ride upon the king's mule:
45 And Zadok the priest and Nathan the prophet have anointed him king in
Gihon: and they are come up from thence rejoicing, so that the city rang again.
This *is* the noise that ye have heard.
46 And also Solomon sitteth on the throne of the kingdom.
47 And moreover the king's servants came to bless our lord king David, say-
ing, God make the name of Solomon better than thy name, and make his
throne greater than thy throne. And the king bowed himself upon the bed.
48 And also thus said the king, Blessed *be* the LORD God of Israel, which hath
given *one* to sit on my throne this day, mine eyes even seeing *it*.
49 And all the guests that *were* with Adonijah were afraid, and rose up, and
went every man his way.
50 And Adonijah feared because of Solomon, and arose, and went, and caught
hold on the horns of the altar.
51 And it was told Solomon, saying, Behold, Adonijah feareth king Solomon:
for, lo, he hath caught hold on the horns of the altar, saying, Let king Solomon
swear unto me to day that he will not slay his servant with the sword.
52 And Solomon said, If he will shew himself a worthy man, there shall not
an hair of him fall to the earth: but if wickedness shall be found in him, he
shall die.
53 So king Solomon sent, and they brought him down from the altar. And he
came and bowed himself to king Solomon: and Solomon said unto him, Go
to thine house.

David Gives a Charge to Solomon

2 Now the days of David drew nigh that he should die; and he charged
Solomon his son, saying,
2 I go the way of all the earth: be thou strong therefore, and shew thyself a
man;
3 And keep the charge of the LORD thy God, to walk in his ways, to keep his
statutes, and his commandments, and his judgments, and his testimonies, as
it is written in the law of Moses, that thou mayest prosper in all that thou
doest, and whithersoever thou turnest thyself:
4 That the LORD may continue his word which he spake concerning me, say-
ing, If thy children take heed to their way, to walk before me in truth with all
their heart and with all their soul, there shall not fail thee (said he) a man on
the throne of Israel.
5 Moreover thou knowest also what Joab the son of Zeruiah did to me, *and*
what he did to the two captains of the hosts of Israel, unto Abner the son of
Ner, and unto Amasa the son of Jether, whom he slew, and shed the blood of
war in peace, and put the blood of war upon his girdle that *was* about his loins,
and in his shoes that *were* on his feet.
6 Do therefore according to thy wisdom, and let not his hoar head go down
to the grave in peace.

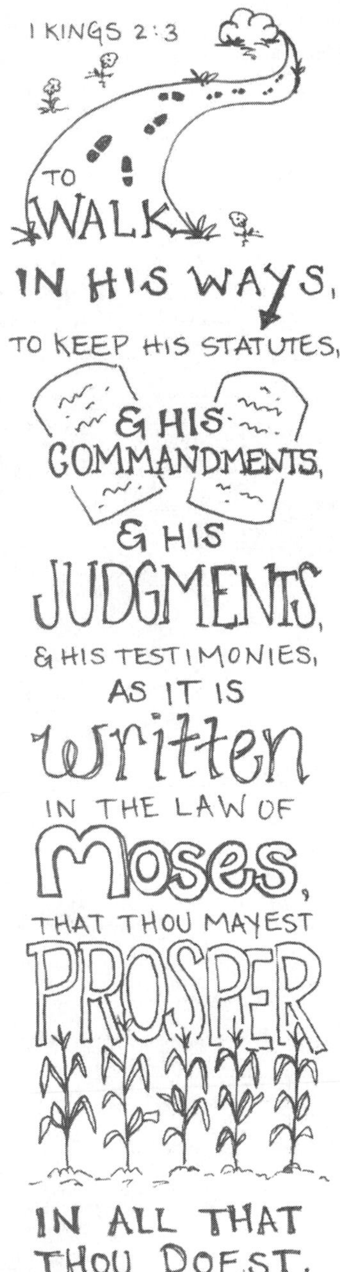

7 But shew kindness unto the sons of Barzillai the Gileadite, and let them be
of those that eat at thy table: for so they came to me when I fled because of
Absalom thy brother.
8 And, behold, *thou hast* with thee Shimei the son of Gera, a Benjamite of
Bahurim, which cursed me with a grievous curse in the day when I went to
Mahanaim: but he came down to meet me at Jordan, and I sware to him by
the LORD, saying, I will not put thee to death with the sword.
9 Now therefore hold him not guiltless: for thou *art* a wise man, and know-
est what thou oughtest to do unto him; but his hoar head bring thou down to
the grave with blood.
10 So David slept with his fathers, and was buried in the city of David.
11 And the days that David reigned over Israel *were* forty years: seven years
reigned he in Hebron, and thirty and three years reigned he in Jerusalem.

Solomon Succeeds David as King

12 Then sat Solomon upon the throne of David his father; and his kingdom
was established greatly.
13 And Adonijah the son of Haggith came to Bath-sheba the mother of
Solomon. And she said, Comest thou peaceably? And he said, Peaceably.
14 He said moreover, I have somewhat to say unto thee. And she said, Say on.
15 And he said, Thou knowest that the kingdom was mine, and *that* all Israel
set their faces on me, that I should reign: howbeit the kingdom is turned about,
and is become my brother's: for it was his from the LORD.
16 And now I ask one petition of thee, deny me not. And she said unto him,
Say on.
17 And he said, Speak, I pray thee, unto Solomon the king, (for he will not
say thee nay,) that he give me Abishag the Shunammite to wife.
18 And Bath-sheba said, Well; I will speak for thee unto the king.
19 Bath-sheba therefore went unto king Solomon, to speak unto him for
Adonijah. And the king rose up to meet her, and bowed himself unto her, and
sat down on his throne, and caused a seat to be set for the king's mother; and
she sat on his right hand.
20 Then she said, I desire one small petition of thee; *I pray thee*, say me not
nay. And the king said unto her, Ask on, my mother: for I will not say thee nay.
21 And she said, Let Abishag the Shunammite be given to Adonijah thy broth-
er to wife.
22 And king Solomon answered and said unto his mother, And why dost thou
ask Abishag the Shunammite for Adonijah? ask for him the kingdom also; for
he *is* mine elder brother; even for him, and for Abiathar the priest, and for
Joab the son of Zeruiah.
23 Then king Solomon sware by the LORD, saying, God do so to me, and more
also, if Adonijah have not spoken this word against his own life.
24 Now therefore, *as* the LORD liveth, which hath established me, and set me
on the throne of David my father, and who hath made me an house, as he
promised, Adonijah shall be put to death this day.
25 And king Solomon sent by the hand of Benaiah the son of Jehoiada; and
he fell upon him that he died.

Abiathar's Life Is Spared, but He Is Removed from the Priesthood

26 And unto Abiathar the priest said the king, Get thee to Anathoth, unto
thine own fields; for thou *art* worthy of death: but I will not at this time put
thee to death, because thou barest the ark of the Lord *GOD* before David my
father, and because thou hast been afflicted in all wherein my father was
afflicted.
27 So Solomon thrust out Abiathar from being priest unto the LORD; that he
might fulfil the word of the LORD, which he spake concerning the house of Eli
in Shiloh.

28 Then tidings came to Joab: for Joab had turned after Adonijah, though he
turned not after Absalom. And Joab fled unto the tabernacle of the LORD, and
caught hold on the horns of the altar.
29 And it was told king Solomon that Joab was fled unto the tabernacle of
the LORD; and, behold, *he is* by the altar. Then Solomon sent Benaiah the son
of Jehoiada, saying, Go, fall upon him.
30 And Benaiah came to the tabernacle of the LORD, and said unto him, Thus
saith the king, Come forth. And he said, Nay; but I will die here. And Benaiah
brought the king word again, saying, Thus said Joab, and thus he answered me.
31 And the king said unto him, Do as he hath said, and fall upon him, and
bury him; that thou mayest take away the innocent blood, which Joab shed,
from me, and from the house of my father.
32 And the LORD shall return his blood upon his own head, who fell upon
two men more righteous and better than he, and slew them with the sword,
my father David not knowing *thereof, to wit*, Abner the son of Ner, captain of
the host of Israel, and Amasa the son of Jether, captain of the host of Judah.
33 Their blood shall therefore return upon the head of Joab, and upon the
head of his seed for ever: but upon David, and upon his seed, and upon his
house, and upon his throne, shall there be peace for ever from the LORD.
34 So Benaiah the son of Jehoiada went up, and fell upon him, and slew him:
and he was buried in his own house in the wilderness.
35 And the king put Benaiah the son of Jehoiada in his room over the host:
and Zadok the priest did the king put in the room of Abiathar.
36 And the king sent and called for Shimei, and said unto him, Build thee an
house in Jerusalem, and dwell there, and go not forth thence any whither.
37 For it shall be, *that* on the day thou goest out, and passest over the brook
Kidron, thou shalt know for certain that thou shalt surely die: thy blood shall
be upon thine own head.
38 And Shimei said unto the king, The saying *is* good: as my lord the king
hath said, so will thy servant do. And Shimei dwelt in Jerusalem many days.
39 And it came to pass at the end of three years, that two of the servants of
Shimei ran away unto Achish son of Maachah king of Gath. And they told
Shimei, saying, Behold, thy servants *be* in Gath.
40 And Shimei arose, and saddled his ass, and went to Gath to Achish to seek
his servants: and Shimei went, and brought his servants from Gath.
41 And it was told Solomon that Shimei had gone from Jerusalem to Gath,
and was come again.
42 And the king sent and called for Shimei, and said unto him, Did I not make
thee to swear by the LORD, and protested unto thee, saying, Know for a certain,
on the day thou goest out, and walkest abroad any whither, that thou shalt
surely die? and thou saidst unto me, The word *that* I have heard *is* good.
43 Why then hast thou not kept the oath of the LORD, and the commandment
that I have charged thee with?
44 The king said moreover to Shimei, Thou knowest all the wickedness which
thine heart is privy to, that thou didst to David my father: therefore the LORD
shall return thy wickedness upon thine own head;
45 And king Solomon *shall be* blessed, and the throne of David shall be estab-
lished before the LORD for ever.
46 So the king commanded Benaiah the son of Jehoiada; which went out,
and fell upon him, that he died. And the kingdom was established in the hand
of Solomon.

Solomon Marries Pharaoh's Daughter

3 And Solomon made affinity with Pharaoh king of Egypt, and took Pharaoh's
daughter, and brought her into the city of David, until he had made an end
of building his own house, and the house of the LORD, and the wall of Jerusalem
round about.

2 Only the people sacrificed in high places, because there was no house built
unto the name of the LORD, until those days.
3 And Solomon loved the LORD, walking in the statutes of David his father:
only he sacrificed and burnt incense in high places.
4 And the king went to Gibeon to sacrifice there; for that *was* the great high
place: a thousand burnt offerings did Solomon offer upon that altar.

God Gives Solomon Wisdom, Riches, and Honor

5 In Gibeon the LORD appeared to Solomon in a dream by night: and God
said, Ask what I shall give thee.
6 And Solomon said, Thou hast shewed unto thy servant David my father
great mercy, according as he walked before thee in truth, and in righteousness,
and in uprightness of heart with thee; and thou hast kept for him this great
kindness, that thou hast given him a son to sit on his throne, as *it is* this day.
7 And now, O LORD my God, thou hast made thy servant king instead of David
my father: and I *am but* a little child: I know not *how* to go out or come in.
8 And thy servant *is* in the midst of thy people which thou hast chosen, a
great people, that cannot be numbered nor counted for multitude.
9 Give therefore thy servant an understanding heart to judge thy people, that
I may discern between good and bad: for who is able to judge this thy so great
a people?
10 And the speech pleased the Lord, that Solomon had asked this thing.
11 And God said unto him, Because thou hast asked this thing, and hast not
asked for thyself long life; neither hast asked riches for thyself, nor hast asked
the life of thine enemies; but hast asked for thyself understanding to discern
judgment;
12 Behold, I have done according to thy words: lo, I have given thee a wise
and an understanding heart; so that there was none like thee before thee,
neither after thee shall any arise like unto thee.
13 And I have also given thee that which thou hast not asked, both riches,
and honour: so that there shall not be any among the kings like unto thee all
thy days.
14 And if thou wilt walk in my ways, to keep my statutes and my command-
ments, as thy father David did walk, then I will lengthen thy days.
15 And Solomon awoke; and, behold, *it was* a dream. And he came to
Jerusalem, and stood before the ark of the covenant of the LORD, and offered
up burnt offerings, and offered peace offerings, and made a feast to all his
servants.

Solomon's Wise Judgment

16 Then came there two women, *that were* harlots, unto the king, and stood
before him.
17 And the one woman said, O my lord, I and this woman dwell in one house;
and I was delivered of a child with her in the house.
18 And it came to pass the third day after that I was delivered, that this woman
was delivered also: and we *were* together; *there was* no stranger with us in the
house, save we two in the house.
19 And this woman's child died in the night; because she overlaid it.
20 And she arose at midnight, and took my son from beside me, while thine
handmaid slept, and laid it in her bosom, and laid her dead child in my bosom.
21 And when I rose in the morning to give my child suck, behold, it was dead:
but when I had considered it in the morning, behold, it was not my son, which
I did bear.
22 And the other woman said, Nay; but the living *is* my son, and the dead *is*
thy son. And this said, No; but the dead *is* thy son, and the living *is* my son.
Thus they spake before the king.

23 Then said the king, The one saith, This *is* my son that liveth, and thy son
is the dead: and the other saith, Nay; but thy son *is* the dead, and my son *is* the
living.
24 And the king said, Bring me a sword. And they brought a sword before the
king.
25 And the king said, Divide the living child in two, and give half to the one,
and half to the other.
26 Then spake the woman whose the living child *was* unto the king, for her
bowels yearned upon her son, and she said, O my lord, give her the living child,
and in no wise slay it. But the other said, Let it be neither mine nor thine, *but*
divide *it*.
27 Then the king answered and said, Give her the living child, and in no wise
slay it: she *is* the mother thereof.
28 And all Israel heard of the judgment which the king had judged; and they
feared the king: for they saw that the wisdom of God *was* in him, to do judgment.

Solomon's Princes and Officers

4 So king Solomon was king over all Israel.
2 And these *were* the princes which he had; Azariah the son of Zadok the
priest,
3 Elihoreph and Ahiah, the sons of Shisha, scribes; Jehoshaphat the son of
Ahilud, the recorder.
4 And Benaiah the son of Jehoiada *was* over the host: and Zadok and Abiathar
were the priests:
5 And Azariah the son of Nathan *was* over the officers: and Zabud the son of
Nathan *was* principal officer, *and* the king's friend:
6 And Ahishar *was* over the household: and Adoniram the son of Abda *was*
over the tribute.
7 And Solomon had twelve officers over all Israel, which provided victuals
for the king and his household: each man his month in a year made provision.
8 And these *are* their names: The son of Hur, in mount Ephraim:
9 The son of Dekar, in Makaz, and in Shaalbim, and Beth-shemesh, and Elon-
beth-hanan:
10 The son of Hesed, in Aruboth; to him *pertained* Sochoh, and all the land
of Hepher:
11 The son of Abinadab, in all the region of Dor; which had Taphath the
daughter of Solomon to wife:
12 Baana the son of Ahilud; *to him pertained* Taanach and Megiddo, and all
Beth-shean, which *is* by Zartanah beneath Jezreel, from Beth-shean to Abel-
meholah, *even* unto *the place that is* beyond Jokneam:
13 The son of Geber, in Ramoth-gilead; to him *pertained* the towns of Jair
the son of Manasseh, which *are* in Gilead; to him *also pertained* the region of
Argob, which *is* in Bashan, threescore great cities with walls and brasen bars:
14 Ahinadab the son of Iddo *had* Mahanaim:
15 Ahimaaz *was* in Naphtali; he also took Basmath the daughter of Solomon
to wife:
16 Baanah the son of Hushai *was* in Asher and in Aloth:
17 Jehoshaphat the son of Paruah, in Issachar:
18 Shimei the son of Elah, in Benjamin:
19 Geber the son of Uri *was* in the country of Gilead, *in* the country of Sihon
king of the Amorites, and of Og king of Bashan; and *he was* the only officer
which *was* in the land.

The Peace of Solomon's Kingdom

20 Judah and Israel *were* many, as the sand which *is* by the sea in multitude,
eating and drinking, and making merry.

21 And Solomon reigned over all kingdoms from the river unto the land of
the Philistines, and unto the border of Egypt: they brought presents, and
served Solomon all the days of his life.
22 And Solomon's provision for one day was thirty measures of fine flour,
and threescore measures of meal,
23 Ten fat oxen, and twenty oxen out of the pastures, and an hundred sheep,
beside harts, and roebucks, and fallowdeer, and fatted fowl.
24 For he had dominion over all *the region* on this side the river, from Tiphsah
even to Azzah, over all the kings on this side the river: and he had peace on all
sides round about him.
25 And Judah and Israel dwelt safely, every man under his vine and under
his fig tree, from Dan even to Beer-sheba, all the days of Solomon.
26 And Solomon had forty thousand stalls of horses for his chariots, and
twelve thousand horsemen.
27 And those officers provided victual for king Solomon, and for all that came
unto king Solomon's table, every man in his month: they lacked nothing.
28 Barley also and straw for the horses and dromedaries brought they unto
the place where *the officers* were, every man according to his charge.

Solomon's Wisdom

29 And God gave Solomon wisdom and understanding exceeding much, and
largeness of heart, even as the sand that *is* on the sea shore.
30 And Solomon's wisdom excelled the wisdom of all the children of the east
country, and all the wisdom of Egypt.
31 For he was wiser than all men; than Ethan the Ezrahite, and Heman, and
Chalcol, and Darda, the sons of Mahol: and his fame was in all nations round
about.
32 And he spake three thousand proverbs: and his songs were a thousand
and five.
33 And he spake of trees, from the cedar tree that *is* in Lebanon even unto
the hyssop that springeth out of the wall: he spake also of beasts, and of fowl,
and of creeping things, and of fishes.
34 And there came of all people to hear the wisdom of Solomon, from all
kings of the earth, which had heard of his wisdom.

King Hiram of Tyre Supplies Timber for the Temple

5 And Hiram king of Tyre sent his servants unto Solomon; for he had heard
that they had anointed him king in the room of his father: for Hiram was
ever a lover of David.
2 And Solomon sent to Hiram, saying,
3 Thou knowest how that David my father could not build an house unto
the name of the LORD his God for the wars which were about him on every
side, until the LORD put them under the soles of his feet.
4 But now the LORD my God hath given me rest on every side, *so that there
is* neither adversary nor evil occurrent.
5 And, behold, I purpose to build an house unto the name of the LORD my
God, as the LORD spake unto David my father, saying, Thy son, whom I will set
upon thy throne in thy room, he shall build an house unto my name.
6 Now therefore command thou that they hew me cedar trees out of
Lebanon; and my servants shall be with thy servants: and unto thee will I give
hire for thy servants according to all that thou shalt appoint: for thou know-
est that *there is* not among us any that can skill to hew timber like unto the
Sidonians.
7 And it came to pass, when Hiram heard the words of Solomon, that he
rejoiced greatly, and said, Blessed *be* the LORD this day, which hath given unto
David a wise son over this great people.

8 And Hiram sent to Solomon, saying, I have considered the things which
thou sentest to me for: *and* I will do all thy desire concerning timber of cedar,
and concerning timber of fir.
9 My servants shall bring *them* down from Lebanon unto the sea: and I will
convey them by sea in floats unto the place that thou shalt appoint me, and
will cause them to be discharged there, and thou shalt receive *them*: and thou
shalt accomplish my desire, in giving food for my household.
10 So Hiram gave Solomon cedar trees and fir trees *according to* all his desire.
11 And Solomon gave Hiram twenty thousand measures of wheat *for* food
to his household, and twenty measures of pure oil: thus gave Solomon to
Hiram year by year.
12 And the LORD gave Solomon wisdom, as he promised him: and there was
peace between Hiram and Solomon; and they two made a league together.
13 And king Solomon raised a levy out of all Israel; and the levy was thirty
thousand men.
14 And he sent them to Lebanon, ten thousand a month by courses: a month
they were in Lebanon, *and* two months at home: and Adoniram *was* over the
levy.
15 And Solomon had threescore and ten thousand that bare burdens, and
fourscore thousand hewers in the mountains;
16 Beside the chief of Solomon's officers which *were* over the work, three
thousand and three hundred, which ruled over the people that wrought in
the work.
17 And the king commanded, and they brought great stones, costly stones,
and hewed stones, to lay the foundation of the house.
18 And Solomon's builders and Hiram's builders did hew *them*, and the ston-
esquarers: so they prepared timber and stones to build the house.

The Building of Solomon's Temple

6 And it came to pass in the four hundred and eightieth year after the children
of Israel were come out of the land of Egypt, in the fourth year of Solomon's
reign over Israel, in the month Zif, which *is* the second month, that he began to
build the house of the LORD.
2 And the house which king Solomon built for the LORD, the length thereof
was threescore cubits, and the breadth thereof twenty *cubits*, and the height
thereof thirty cubits.
3 And the porch before the temple of the house, twenty cubits *was* the length
thereof, according to the breadth of the house; *and* ten cubits *was* the breadth
thereof before the house.
4 And for the house he made windows of narrow lights.
5 And against the wall of the house he built chambers round about, *against*
the walls of the house round about, *both* of the temple and of the oracle: and
he made chambers round about:
6 The nethermost chamber *was* five cubits broad, and the middle *was* six
cubits broad, and the third *was* seven cubits broad: for without *in the wall* of
the house he made narrowed rests round about, that *the beams* should not be
fastened in the walls of the house.
7 And the house, when it was in building, was built of stone made ready
before it was brought thither: so that there was neither hammer nor axe *nor*
any tool of iron heard in the house, while it was in building.
8 The door for the middle chamber *was* in the right side of the house: and
they went up with winding stairs into the middle *chamber*, and out of the
middle into the third.
9 So he built the house, and finished it; and covered the house with beams
and boards of cedar.

10 And *then* he built chambers against all the house, five cubits high: and they rested on the house with timber of cedar.

God's Promise Concerning the Temple

11 And the word of the LORD came to Solomon, saying,

12 *Concerning* this house which thou art in building, if thou wilt walk in my statutes, and execute my judgments, and keep all my commandments to walk in them; then will I perform my word with thee, which I spake unto David thy father:

13 And I will dwell among the children of Israel, and will not forsake my people Israel.

14 So Solomon built the house, and finished it.

Details about the Temple's Interior Adornment

15 And he built the walls of the house within with boards of cedar, both the floor of the house, and the walls of the cieling: *and* he covered *them* on the inside with wood, and covered the floor of the house with planks of fir.

16 And he built twenty cubits on the sides of the house, both the floor and the walls with boards of cedar: he even built *them* for it within, *even* for the oracle, *even* for the most holy *place*.

17 And the house, that *is*, the temple before it, was forty cubits *long*.

18 And the cedar of the house within *was* carved with knops and open flowers: all *was* cedar; there was no stone seen.

19 And the oracle he prepared in the house within, to set there the ark of the covenant of the LORD.

20 And the oracle in the forepart *was* twenty cubits in length, and twenty cubits in breadth, and twenty cubits in the height thereof: and he overlaid it with pure gold; and *so* covered the altar *which was of* cedar.

21 So Solomon overlaid the house within with pure gold: and he made a partition by the chains of gold before the oracle; and he overlaid it with gold.

22 And the whole house he overlaid with gold, until he had finished all the house: also the whole altar that *was* by the oracle he overlaid with gold.

23 And within the oracle he made two cherubims *of* olive tree, *each* ten cubits high.

24 And five cubits *was* the one wing of the cherub, and five cubits the other wing of the cherub: from the uttermost part of the one wing unto the uttermost part of the other *were* ten cubits.

25 And the other cherub *was* ten cubits: both the cherubims *were* of one measure and one size.

26 The height of the one cherub *was* ten cubits, and so *was it* of the other cherub.

27 And he set the cherubims within the inner house: and they stretched forth the wings of the cherubims, so that the wing of the one touched the *one* wall, and the wing of the other cherub touched the other wall; and their wings touched one another in the midst of the house.

28 And he overlaid the cherubims with gold.

29 And he carved all the walls of the house round about with carved figures of cherubims and palm trees and open flowers, within and without.

30 And the floor of the house he overlaid with gold, within and without.

31 And for the entering of the oracle he made doors *of* olive tree: the lintel *and* side posts *were* a fifth part *of the wall*.

32 The two doors also *were of* olive tree; and he carved upon them carvings of cherubims and palm trees and open flowers, and overlaid *them* with gold, and spread gold upon the cherubims, and upon the palm trees.

33 So also made he for the door of the temple posts *of* olive tree, a fourth part *of the wall*.

34 And the two doors *were of* fir tree: the two leaves of the one door *were*
folding, and the two leaves of the other door *were* folding.
35 And he carved *thereon* cherubims and palm trees and open flowers: and
covered *them* with gold fitted upon the carved work.
36 And he built the inner court with three rows of hewed stone, and a row
of cedar beams.
37 In the fourth year was the foundation of the house of the LORD laid, in the
month Zif:
38 And in the eleventh year, in the month Bul, which *is* the eighth month,
was the house finished throughout all the parts thereof, and according to all
the fashion of it. So was he seven years in building it.

The Building of Solomon's House

7 But Solomon was building his own house thirteen years, and he finished
all his house.
2 He built also the house of the forest of Lebanon; the length thereof *was* an
hundred cubits, and the breadth thereof fifty cubits, and the height thereof
thirty cubits, upon four rows of cedar pillars, with cedar beams upon the
pillars.
3 And *it was* covered with cedar above upon the beams, that *lay* on forty five
pillars, fifteen *in* a row.
4 And *there were* windows *in* three rows, and light *was* against light *in* three
ranks.
5 And all the doors and posts *were* square, with the windows: and light *was*
against light *in* three ranks.
6 And he made a porch of pillars; the length thereof *was* fifty cubits, and the
breadth thereof thirty cubits: and the porch *was* before them: and the *other*
pillars and the thick beam *were* before them.
7 Then he made a porch for the throne where he might judge, *even* the porch
of judgment: and *it was* covered with cedar from one side of the floor to the
other.
8 And his house where he dwelt *had* another court within the porch, *which*
was of the like work. Solomon made also an house for Pharaoh's daughter,
whom he had taken *to wife*, like unto this porch.
9 All these *were of* costly stones, according to the measures of hewed stones,
sawed with saws, within and without, even from the foundation unto the
coping, and *so* on the outside toward the great court.
10 And the foundation *was of* costly stones, even great stones, stones of ten
cubits, and stones of eight cubits.
11 And above *were* costly stones, after the measures of hewed stones, and
cedars.
12 And the great court round about *was* with three rows of hewed stones,
and a row of cedar beams, both for the inner court of the house of the LORD,
and for the porch of the house.

Solomon Sends for Hiram to Do the Brass Work

13 And king Solomon sent and fetched Hiram out of Tyre.
14 He *was* a widow's son of the tribe of Naphtali, and his father *was* a man
of Tyre, a worker in brass: and he was filled with wisdom, and understanding,
and cunning to work all works in brass. And he came to king Solomon, and
wrought all his work.
15 For he cast two pillars of brass, of eighteen cubits high apiece: and a line
of twelve cubits did compass either of them about.
16 And he made two chapiters *of* molten brass, to set upon the tops of the
pillars: the height of the one chapiter *was* five cubits, and the height of the
other chapiter *was* five cubits:

17 *And* nets of checker work, and wreaths of chain work, for the chapiters
which *were* upon the top of the pillars; seven for the one chapiter, and seven
for the other chapiter.
18 And he made the pillars, and two rows round about upon the one network,
to cover the chapiters that *were* upon the top, with pomegranates: and so did
he for the other chapiter.
19 And the chapiters that *were* upon the top of the pillars *were* of lily work
in the porch, four cubits.
20 And the chapiters upon the two pillars *had pomegranates* also above, over
against the belly which *was* by the network: and the pomegranates *were* two
hundred in rows round about upon the other chapiter.
21 And he set up the pillars in the porch of the temple: and he set up the right
pillar, and called the name thereof Jachin: and he set up the left pillar, and
called the name thereof Boaz.
22 And upon the top of the pillars *was* lily work: so was the work of the pillars
finished.
23 And he made a molten sea, ten cubits from the one brim to the other: *it
was* round all about, and his height *was* five cubits: and a line of thirty cubits
did compass it round about.
24 And under the brim of it round about *there were* knops compassing it,
ten in a cubit, compassing the sea round about: the knops *were* cast in two
rows, when it was cast.
25 It stood upon twelve oxen, three looking toward the north, and three
looking toward the west, and three looking toward the south, and three look-
ing toward the east: and the sea *was set* above upon them, and all their hinder
parts *were* inward.
26 And it *was* an hand breadth thick, and the brim thereof was wrought like
the brim of a cup, with flowers of lilies: it contained two thousand baths.
27 And he made ten bases of brass; four cubits *was* the length of one base,
and four cubits the breadth thereof, and three cubits the height of it.
28 And the work of the bases *was* on this *manner*: they had borders, and the
borders *were* between the ledges:
29 And on the borders that *were* between the ledges *were* lions, oxen, and
cherubims: and upon the ledges *there was* a base above: and beneath the lions
and oxen *were* certain additions made of thin work.
30 And every base had four brasen wheels, and plates of brass: and the four
corners thereof had undersetters: under the laver *were* undersetters molten,
at the side of every addition.
31 And the mouth of it within the chapiter and above *was* a cubit: but the
mouth thereof *was* round *after* the work of the base, a cubit and an half: and
also upon the mouth of it *were* gravings with their borders, foursquare, not
round.
32 And under the borders *were* four wheels; and the axletrees of the wheels
were joined to the base: and the height of a wheel *was* a cubit and half a cubit.
33 And the work of the wheels *was* like the work of a chariot wheel: their
axletrees, and their naves, and their felloes, and their spokes, *were* all molten.
34 And *there were* four undersetters to the four corners of one base: *and* the
undersetters *were* of the very base itself.
35 And in the top of the base *was there* a round compass of half a cubit high:
and on the top of the base the ledges thereof and the borders thereof *were* of
the same.
36 For on the plates of the ledges thereof, and on the borders thereof, he
graved cherubims, lions, and palm trees, according to the proportion of every
one, and additions round about.
37 After this *manner* he made the ten bases: all of them had one casting, one
measure, *and* one size.

38 Then made he ten lavers of brass: one laver contained forty baths: *and*
every laver was four cubits: *and* upon every one of the ten bases one laver.
39 And he put five bases on the right side of the house, and five on the left
side of the house: and he set the sea on the right side of the house eastward
over against the south.
40 And Hiram made the lavers, and the shovels, and the basons. So Hiram
made an end of doing all the work that he made king Solomon for the house
of the LORD:
41 The two pillars, and the *two* bowls of the chapiters that *were* on the top of
the two pillars; and the two networks, to cover the two bowls of the chapiters
which *were* upon the top of the pillars;
42 And four hundred pomegranates for the two networks, *even* two rows of
pomegranates for one network, to cover the two bowls of the chapiters that
were upon the pillars;
43 And the ten bases, and ten lavers on the bases;
44 And one sea, and twelve oxen under the sea;
45 And the pots, and the shovels, and the basons: and all these vessels, which
Hiram made to king Solomon for the house of the LORD, *were of* bright brass.
46 In the plain of Jordan did the king cast them, in the clay ground between
Succoth and Zarthan.
47 And Solomon left all the vessels *unweighed*, because they were exceeding
many: neither was the weight of the brass found out.
48 And Solomon made all the vessels that *pertained* unto the house of the
LORD: the altar of gold, and the table of gold, whereupon the shewbread *was*,
49 And the candlesticks of pure gold, five on the right *side*, and five on the
left, before the oracle, with the flowers, and the lamps, and the tongs *of* gold,
50 And the bowls, and the snuffers, and the basons, and the spoons, and the
censers *of* pure gold; and the hinges *of* gold, *both* for the doors of the inner
house, the most holy *place, and* for the doors of the house, *to wit*, of the temple.
51 So was ended all the work that king Solomon made for the house of the
LORD. And Solomon brought in the things which David his father had dedi-
cated; *even* the silver, and the gold, and the vessels, did he put among the
treasures of the house of the LORD.

The Feast of the Dedication of the Temple

8 Then Solomon assembled the elders of Israel, and all the heads of the tribes,
the chief of the fathers of the children of Israel, unto king Solomon in
Jerusalem, that they might bring up the ark of the covenant of the LORD out of
the city of David, which *is* Zion.
2 And all the men of Israel assembled themselves unto king Solomon at the
feast in the month Ethanim, which *is* the seventh month.
3 And all the elders of Israel came, and the priests took up the ark.
4 And they brought up the ark of the LORD, and the tabernacle of the con-
gregation, and all the holy vessels that *were* in the tabernacle, even those did
the priests and the Levites bring up.
5 And king Solomon, and all the congregation of Israel, that were assembled
unto him, *were* with him before the ark, sacrificing sheep and oxen, that could
not be told nor numbered for multitude.
6 And the priests brought in the ark of the covenant of the LORD unto his
place, into the oracle of the house, to the most holy *place, even* under the wings
of the cherubims.
7 For the cherubims spread forth *their* two wings over the place of the ark,
and the cherubims covered the ark and the staves thereof above.
8 And they drew out the staves, that the ends of the staves were seen out in
the holy *place* before the oracle, and they were not seen without: and there
they are unto this day.

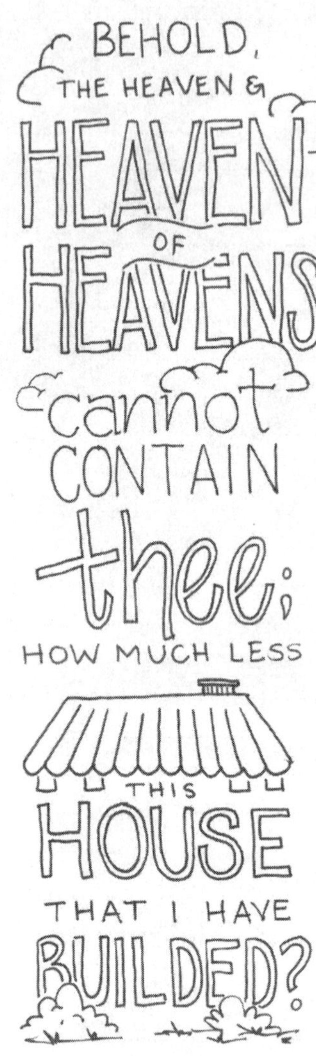

9 *There was* nothing in the ark save the two tables of stone, which Moses put
there at Horeb, when the LORD made *a covenant* with the children of Israel,
when they came out of the land of Egypt.
10 And it came to pass, when the priests were come out of the holy *place*, that
the cloud filled the house of the LORD,
11 So that the priests could not stand to minister because of the cloud: for
the glory of the LORD had filled the house of the LORD.

Solomon Blesses the Congregation of Israel

12 Then spake Solomon, The LORD said that he would dwell in the thick dark-
ness.
13 I have surely built thee an house to dwell in, a settled place for thee to
abide in for ever.
14 And the king turned his face about, and blessed all the congregation of
Israel: (and all the congregation of Israel stood;)
15 And he said, Blessed *be* the LORD God of Israel, which spake with his mouth
unto David my father, and hath with his hand fulfilled *it*, saying,
16 Since the day that I brought forth my people Israel out of Egypt, I chose
no city out of all the tribes of Israel to build an house, that my name might be
therein; but I chose David to be over my people Israel.
17 And it was in the heart of David my father to build an house for the name
of the LORD God of Israel.
18 And the LORD said unto David my father, Whereas it was in thine heart to
build an house unto my name, thou didst well that it was in thine heart.
19 Nevertheless thou shalt not build the house; but thy son that shall come
forth out of thy loins, he shall build the house unto my name.
20 And the LORD hath performed his word that he spake, and I am risen up
in the room of David my father, and sit on the throne of Israel, as the LORD
promised, and have built an house for the name of the LORD God of Israel.
21 And I have set there a place for the ark, wherein *is* the covenant of the
LORD, which he made with our fathers, when he brought them out of the land
of Egypt.

Solomon's Prayer of Dedication and Thanksgiving for the Temple

22 And Solomon stood before the altar of the LORD in the presence of all the
congregation of Israel, and spread forth his hands toward heaven:
23 And he said, LORD God of Israel, *there is* no God like thee, in heaven above,
or on earth beneath, who keepest covenant and mercy with thy servants that
walk before thee with all their heart:
24 Who hast kept with thy servant David my father that thou promisedst
him: thou spakest also with thy mouth, and hast fulfilled *it* with thine hand,
as *it is* this day.
25 Therefore now, LORD God of Israel, keep with thy servant David my father
that thou promisedst him, saying, There shall not fail thee a man in my sight
to sit on the throne of Israel; so that thy children take heed to their way, that
they walk before me as thou hast walked before me.
26 And now, O God of Israel, let thy word, I pray thee, be verified, which thou
spakest unto thy servant David my father.
27 But will God indeed dwell on the earth? behold, the heaven and heaven
of heavens cannot contain thee; how much less this house that I have builded?
28 Yet have thou respect unto the prayer of thy servant, and to his supplica-
tion, O LORD my God, to hearken unto the cry and to the prayer, which thy
servant prayeth before thee to day:
29 That thine eyes may be open toward this house night and day, *even* toward
the place of which thou hast said, My name shall be there: that thou mayest
hearken unto the prayer which thy servant shall make toward this place.

30 And hearken thou to the supplication of thy servant, and of thy people
Israel, when they shall pray toward this place: and hear thou in heaven thy
dwelling place: and when thou hearest, forgive.
31 If any man trespass against his neighbour, and an oath be laid upon him
to cause him to swear, and the oath come before thine altar in this house:
32 Then hear thou in heaven, and do, and judge thy servants, condemning
the wicked, to bring his way upon his head; and justifying the righteous, to
give him according to his righteousness.
33 When thy people Israel be smitten down before the enemy, because they
have sinned against thee, and shall turn again to thee, and confess thy name,
and pray, and make supplication unto thee in this house:
34 Then hear thou in heaven, and forgive the sin of thy people Israel, and
bring them again unto the land which thou gavest unto their fathers.
35 When heaven is shut up, and there is no rain, because they have sinned
against thee; if they pray toward this place, and confess thy name, and turn
from their sin, when thou afflictest them:
36 Then hear thou in heaven, and forgive the sin of thy servants, and of thy
people Israel, that thou teach them the good way wherein they should walk,
and give rain upon thy land, which thou hast given to thy people for an inher-
itance.
37 If there be in the land famine, if there be pestilence, blasting, mildew,
locust, *or* if there be caterpiller; if their enemy besiege them in the land of
their cities; whatsoever plague, whatsoever sickness *there be*;
38 What prayer and supplication soever be *made* by any man, *or* by all thy
people Israel, which shall know every man the plague of his own heart, and
spread forth his hands toward this house:
39 Then hear thou in heaven thy dwelling place, and forgive, and do, and give
to every man according to his ways, whose heart thou knowest; (for thou, *even*
thou only, knowest the hearts of all the children of men;)
40 That they may fear thee all the days that they live in the land which thou
gavest unto our fathers.
41 Moreover concerning a stranger, that *is* not of thy people Israel, but com-
eth out of a far country for thy name's sake;
42 (For they shall hear of thy great name, and of thy strong hand, and of thy
stretched out arm;) when he shall come and pray toward this house;
43 Hear thou in heaven thy dwelling place, and do according to all that the
stranger calleth to thee for: that all people of the earth may know thy name,
to fear thee, as *do* thy people Israel; and that they may know that this house,
which I have builded, is called by thy name.
44 If thy people go out to battle against their enemy, whithersoever thou
shalt send them, and shall pray unto the LORD toward the city which thou hast
chosen, and *toward* the house that I have built for thy name:
45 Then hear thou in heaven their prayer and their supplication, and main-
tain their cause.
46 If they sin against thee, (for *there is* no man that sinneth not,) and thou
be angry with them, and deliver them to the enemy, so that they carry them
away captives unto the land of the enemy, far or near;
47 *Yet* if they shall bethink themselves in the land whither they were carried
captives, and repent, and make supplication unto thee in the land of them
that carried them captives, saying, We have sinned, and have done perversely,
we have committed wickedness;
48 And *so* return unto thee with all their heart, and with all their soul, in the
land of their enemies, which led them away captive, and pray unto thee toward
their land, which thou gavest unto their fathers, the city which thou hast
chosen, and the house which I have built for thy name:

49 Then hear thou their prayer and their supplication in heaven thy dwelling
place, and maintain their cause,
50 And forgive thy people that have sinned against thee, and all their trans-
gressions wherein they have transgressed against thee, and give them com-
passion before them who carried them captive, that they may have compassion
on them:
51 For they *be* thy people, and thine inheritance, which thou broughtest
forth out of Egypt, from the midst of the furnace of iron:
52 That thine eyes may be open unto the supplication of thy servant, and
unto the supplication of thy people Israel, to hearken unto them in all that
they call for unto thee.
53 For thou didst separate them from among all the people of the earth, *to
be* thine inheritance, as thou spakest by the hand of Moses thy servant, when
thou broughtest our fathers out of Egypt, O Lord GOD.

Solomon's Blessing

54 And it was *so*, that when Solomon had made an end of praying all this
prayer and supplication unto the LORD, he arose from before the altar of the
LORD, from kneeling on his knees with his hands spread up to heaven.
55 And he stood, and blessed all the congregation of Israel with a loud voice,
saying,
56 Blessed *be* the LORD, that hath given rest unto his people Israel, according
to all that he promised: there hath not failed one word of all his good promise,
which he promised by the hand of Moses his servant.
57 The LORD our God be with us, as he was with our fathers: let him not leave
us, nor forsake us:
58 That he may incline our hearts unto him, to walk in all his ways, and to
keep his commandments, and his statutes, and his judgments, which he com-
manded our fathers.
59 And let these my words, wherewith I have made supplication before the
LORD, be nigh unto the LORD our God day and night, that he maintain the cause
of his servant, and the cause of his people Israel at all times, as the matter shall
require:
60 That all the people of the earth may know that the LORD *is* God, *and that
there is* none else.
61 Let your heart therefore be perfect with the LORD our God, to walk in his
statutes, and to keep his commandments, as at this day.

Solomon Sacrifices Peace Offerings

62 And the king, and all Israel with him, offered sacrifice before the LORD.
63 And Solomon offered a sacrifice of peace offerings, which he offered unto
the LORD, two and twenty thousand oxen, and an hundred and twenty thou-
sand sheep. So the king and all the children of Israel dedicated the house of
the LORD.
64 The same day did the king hallow the middle of the court that *was* before
the house of the LORD: for there he offered burnt offerings, and meat offerings,
and the fat of the peace offerings: because the brasen altar that *was* before the
LORD *was* too little to receive the burnt offerings, and meat offerings, and the
fat of the peace offerings.
65 And at that time Solomon held a feast, and all Israel with him, a great
congregation, from the entering in of Hamath unto the river of Egypt, before
the LORD our God, seven days and seven days, *even* fourteen days.
66 On the eighth day he sent the people away: and they blessed the king, and
went unto their tents joyful and glad of heart for all the goodness that the
LORD had done for David his servant, and for Israel his people.

God's Covenant, in a Vision, with Solomon

9 And it came to pass, when Solomon had finished the building of the house
of the LORD, and the king's house, and all Solomon's desire which he was
pleased to do,
2 That the LORD appeared to Solomon the second time, as he had appeared
unto him at Gibeon.
3 And the LORD said unto him, I have heard thy prayer and thy supplication,
that thou hast made before me: I have hallowed this house, which thou hast
built, to put my name there for ever; and mine eyes and mine heart shall be
there perpetually.
4 And if thou wilt walk before me, as David thy father walked, in integrity of
heart, and in uprightness, to do according to all that I have commanded thee,
and wilt keep my statutes and my judgments:
5 Then I will establish the throne of thy kingdom upon Israel for ever, as I
promised to David thy father, saying, There shall not fail thee a man upon the
throne of Israel.
6 *But* if ye shall at all turn from following me, ye or your children, and will
not keep my commandments *and* my statutes which I have set before you, but
go and serve other gods, and worship them:
7 Then will I cut off Israel out of the land which I have given them; and this
house, which I have hallowed for my name, will I cast out of my sight; and
Israel shall be a proverb and a byword among all people:
8 And at this house, *which* is high, every one that passeth by it shall be aston-
ished, and shall hiss; and they shall say, Why hath the LORD done thus unto
this land, and to this house?
9 And they shall answer, Because they forsook the LORD their God, who
brought forth their fathers out of the land of Egypt, and have taken hold upon
other gods, and have worshipped them, and served them: therefore hath the
LORD brought upon them all this evil.

Solomon and Hiram Give Each Other Gifts

10 And it came to pass at the end of twenty years, when Solomon had built
the two houses, the house of the LORD, and the king's house,
11 (*Now* Hiram the king of Tyre had furnished Solomon with cedar trees and
fir trees, and with gold, according to all his desire,) that then king Solomon
gave Hiram twenty cities in the land of Galilee.
12 And Hiram came out from Tyre to see the cities which Solomon had given
him; and they pleased him not.
13 And he said, What cities *are* these which thou hast given me, my brother?
And he called them the land of Cabul unto this day.
14 And Hiram sent to the king sixscore talents of gold.

Solomon's Workers

15 And this *is* the reason of the levy which king Solomon raised; for to build
the house of the LORD, and his own house, and Millo, and the wall of Jerusalem,
and Hazor, and Megiddo, and Gezer.
16 *For* Pharaoh king of Egypt had gone up, and taken Gezer, and burnt it
with fire, and slain the Canaanites that dwelt in the city, and given it *for* a
present unto his daughter, Solomon's wife.
17 And Solomon built Gezer, and Beth-horon the nether,
18 And Baalath, and Tadmor in the wilderness, in the land,
19 And all the cities of store that Solomon had, and cities for his chariots,
and cities for his horsemen, and that which Solomon desired to build in
Jerusalem, and in Lebanon, and in all the land of his dominion.
20 *And* all the people *that were* left of the Amorites, Hittites, Perizzites,
Hivites, and Jebusites, which *were* not of the children of Israel,

21 Their children that were left after them in the land, whom the children of Israel also were not able utterly to destroy, upon those did Solomon levy a tribute of bondservice unto this day.

22 But of the children of Israel did Solomon make no bondmen: but they *were* men of war, and his servants, and his princes, and his captains, and rulers of his chariots, and his horsemen.

23 These *were* the chief of the officers that *were* over Solomon's work, five hundred and fifty, which bare rule over the people that wrought in the work.

24 But Pharaoh's daughter came up out of the city of David unto her house which *Solomon* had built for her: then did he build Millo.

25 And three times in a year did Solomon offer burnt offerings and peace offerings upon the altar which he built unto the LORD, and he burnt incense upon the altar that *was* before the LORD. So he finished the house.

26 And king Solomon made a navy of ships in Ezion-geber, which *is* beside Eloth, on the shore of the Red sea, in the land of Edom.

27 And Hiram sent in the navy his servants, shipmen that had knowledge of the sea, with the servants of Solomon.

28 And they came to Ophir, and fetched from thence gold, four hundred and twenty talents, and brought *it* to king Solomon.

The Queen of Sheba Admires Solomon's Wisdom

10 And when the queen of Sheba heard of the fame of Solomon concerning the name of the LORD, she came to prove him with hard questions.

2 And she came to Jerusalem with a very great train, with camels that bare spices, and very much gold, and precious stones: and when she was come to Solomon, she communed with him of all that was in her heart.

3 And Solomon told her all her questions: there was not *any* thing hid from the king, which he told her not.

4 And when the queen of Sheba had seen all Solomon's wisdom, and the house that he had built,

5 And the meat of his table, and the sitting of his servants, and the attendance of his ministers, and their apparel, and his cupbearers, and his ascent by which he went up unto the house of the LORD; there was no more spirit in her.

6 And she said to the king, It was a true report that I heard in mine own land of thy acts and of thy wisdom.

7 Howbeit I believed not the words, until I came, and mine eyes had seen *it*: and, behold, the half was not told me: thy wisdom and prosperity exceedeth the fame which I heard.

8 Happy *are* thy men, happy *are* these thy servants, which stand continually before thee, *and* that hear thy wisdom.

9 Blessed be the LORD thy God, which delighted in thee, to set thee on the throne of Israel: because the LORD loved Israel for ever, therefore made he thee king, to do judgment and justice.

10 And she gave the king an hundred and twenty talents of gold, and of spices very great store, and precious stones: there came no more such abundance of spices as these which the queen of Sheba gave to king Solomon.

11 And the navy also of Hiram, that brought gold from Ophir, brought in from Ophir great plenty of almug trees, and precious stones.

12 And the king made of the almug trees pillars for the house of the LORD, and for the king's house, harps also and psalteries for singers: there came no such almug trees, nor were seen unto this day.

13 And king Solomon gave unto the queen of Sheba all her desire, whatsoever she asked, beside *that* which Solomon gave her of his royal bounty. So she turned and went to her own country, she and her servants.

Solomon's Gold

14 Now the weight of gold that came to Solomon in one year was six hundred
threescore and six talents of gold,
15 Beside *that he had* of the merchantmen, and of the traffick of the spice
merchants, and of all the kings of Arabia, and of the governors of the country.
16 And king Solomon made two hundred targets *of* beaten gold: six hundred
shekels of gold went to one target.
17 And *he made* three hundred shields *of* beaten gold; three pound of gold
went to one shield: and the king put them in the house of the forest of Lebanon.
18 Moreover the king made a great throne of ivory, and overlaid it with the
best gold.
19 The throne had six steps, and the top of the throne *was* round behind: and
there were stays on either side on the place of the seat, and two lions stood
beside the stays.
20 And twelve lions stood there on the one side and on the other upon the
six steps: there was not the like made in any kingdom.
21 And all king Solomon's drinking vessels *were of* gold, and all the vessels of
the house of the forest of Lebanon *were of* pure gold; none *were of* silver: it
was nothing accounted of in the days of Solomon.
22 For the king had at sea a navy of Tharshish with the navy of Hiram: once
in three years came the navy of Tharshish, bringing gold, and silver, ivory, and
apes, and peacocks.
23 So king Solomon exceeded all the kings of the earth for riches and for
wisdom.
24 And all the earth sought to Solomon, to hear his wisdom, which God had
put in his heart.
25 And they brought every man his present, vessels of silver, and vessels of
gold, and garments, and armour, and spices, horses, and mules, a rate year by
year.
26 And Solomon gathered together chariots and horsemen: and he had a
thousand and four hundred chariots, and twelve thousand horsemen, whom
he bestowed in the cities for chariots, and with the king at Jerusalem.
27 And the king made silver *to be* in Jerusalem as stones, and cedars made he
to be as the sycomore trees that *are* in the vale, for abundance.
28 And Solomon had horses brought out of Egypt, and linen yarn: the king's
merchants received the linen yarn at a price.
29 And a chariot came up and went out of Egypt for six hundred *shekels* of
silver, and an horse for an hundred and fifty: and so for all the kings of the
Hittites, and for the kings of Syria, did they bring *them* out by their means.

Solomon's Wives and Concubines Draw Him into Idolatry

11 But king Solomon loved many strange women, together with the
daughter of Pharaoh, women of the Moabites, Ammonites, Edomites,
Zidonians, *and* Hittites;
2 Of the nations *concerning* which the LORD said unto the children of Israel,
Ye shall not go in to them, neither shall they come in unto you: *for* surely they
will turn away your heart after their gods: Solomon clave unto these in love.
3 And he had seven hundred wives, princesses, and three hundred concu-
bines: and his wives turned away his heart.
4 For it came to pass, when Solomon was old, *that* his wives turned away his
heart after other gods: and his heart was not perfect with the LORD his God,
as *was* the heart of David his father.
5 For Solomon went after Ashtoreth the goddess of the Zidonians, and after
Milcom the abomination of the Ammonites.
6 And Solomon did evil in the sight of the LORD, and went not fully after the
LORD, as *did* David his father.

7 Then did Solomon build an high place for Chemosh, the abomination of
Moab, in the hill that *is* before Jerusalem, and for Molech, the abomination
of the children of Ammon.
8 And likewise did he for all his strange wives, which burnt incense and
sacrificed unto their gods.
9 And the LORD was angry with Solomon, because his heart was turned from
the LORD God of Israel, which had appeared unto him twice,
10 And had commanded him concerning this thing, that he should not go
after other gods: but he kept not that which the LORD commanded.
11 Wherefore the LORD said unto Solomon, Forasmuch as this is done of thee,
and thou hast not kept my covenant and my statutes, which I have command-
ed thee, I will surely rend the kingdom from thee, and will give it to thy servant.
12 Notwithstanding in thy days I will not do it for David thy father's sake:
but I will rend it out of the hand of thy son.
13 Howbeit I will not rend away all the kingdom; *but* will give one tribe to
thy son for David my servant's sake, and for Jerusalem's sake which I have
chosen.

Solomon's Adversaries: Hadad of Edom and Rezon of Syria

14 And the LORD stirred up an adversary unto Solomon, Hadad the Edomite:
he *was* of the king's seed in Edom.
15 For it came to pass, when David was in Edom, and Joab the captain of the
host was gone up to bury the slain, after he had smitten every male in Edom;
16 (For six months did Joab remain there with all Israel, until he had cut off
every male in Edom:)
17 That Hadad fled, he and certain Edomites of his father's servants with
him, to go into Egypt; Hadad *being* yet a little child.
18 And they arose out of Midian, and came to Paran: and they took men with
them out of Paran, and they came to Egypt, unto Pharaoh king of Egypt; which
gave him an house, and appointed him victuals, and gave him land.
19 And Hadad found great favour in the sight of Pharaoh, so that he gave
him to wife the sister of his own wife, the sister of Tahpenes the queen.
20 And the sister of Tahpenes bare him Genubath his son, whom Tahpenes
weaned in Pharaoh's house: and Genubath was in Pharaoh's household among
the sons of Pharaoh.
21 And when Hadad heard in Egypt that David slept with his fathers, and
that Joab the captain of the host was dead, Hadad said to Pharaoh, Let me
depart, that I may go to mine own country.
22 Then Pharaoh said unto him, But what hast thou lacked with me, that,
behold, thou seekest to go to thine own country? And he answered, Nothing:
howbeit let me go in any wise.
23 And God stirred him up *another* adversary, Rezon the son of Eliadah,
which fled from his lord Hadadezer king of Zobah:
24 And he gathered men unto him, and became captain over a band, when
David slew them *of Zobah*: and they went to Damascus, and dwelt therein, and
reigned in Damascus.
25 And he was an adversary to Israel all the days of Solomon, beside the mis-
chief that Hadad *did*: and he abhorred Israel, and reigned over Syria.

Solomon's Adversary: Jeroboam, One of His Officials

26 And Jeroboam the son of Nebat, an Ephrathite of Zereda, Solomon's serv-
ant, whose mother's name *was* Zeruah, a widow woman, even he lifted up *his*
hand against the king.
27 And this *was* the cause that he lifted up *his* hand against the king: Solomon
built Millo, *and* repaired the breaches of the city of David his father.

28 And the man Jeroboam *was* a mighty man of valour: and Solomon seeing
the young man that he was industrious, he made him ruler over all the charge
of the house of Joseph.
29 And it came to pass at that time when Jeroboam went out of Jerusalem,
that the prophet Ahijah the Shilonite found him in the way; and he had clad
himself with a new garment; and they two *were* alone in the field:
30 And Ahijah caught the new garment that *was* on him, and rent it *in* twelve
pieces:
31 And he said to Jeroboam, Take thee ten pieces: for thus saith the LORD, the
God of Israel, Behold, I will rend the kingdom out of the hand of Solomon,
and will give ten tribes to thee:
32 (But he shall have one tribe for my servant David's sake, and for Jerusalem's
sake, the city which I have chosen out of all the tribes of Israel:)
33 Because that they have forsaken me, and have worshipped Ashtoreth the
goddess of the Zidonians, Chemosh the god of the Moabites, and Milcom the
god of the children of Ammon, and have not walked in my ways, to do *that
which is* right in mine eyes, and *to keep* my statutes and my judgments, as *did*
David his father.
34 Howbeit I will not take the whole kingdom out of his hand: but I will make
him prince all the days of his life for David my servant's sake, whom I chose,
because he kept my commandments and my statutes:
35 But I will take the kingdom out of his son's hand, and will give it unto thee,
even ten tribes.
36 And unto his son will I give one tribe, that David my servant may have a
light alway before me in Jerusalem, the city which I have chosen me to put my
name there.
37 And I will take thee, and thou shalt reign according to all that thy soul
desireth, and shalt be king over Israel.
38 And it shall be, if thou wilt hearken unto all that I command thee, and
wilt walk in my ways, and do *that is* right in my sight, to keep my statutes and
my commandments, as David my servant did; that I will be with thee, and
build thee a sure house, as I built for David, and will give Israel unto thee.
39 And I will for this afflict the seed of David, but not for ever.
40 Solomon sought therefore to kill Jeroboam. And Jeroboam arose, and fled
into Egypt, unto Shishak king of Egypt, and was in Egypt until the death of
Solomon.

Solomon Is Succeeded by Rehoboam after a Forty-Year Reign

41 And the rest of the acts of Solomon, and all that he did, and his wisdom,
are they not written in the book of the acts of Solomon?
42 And the time that Solomon reigned in Jerusalem over all Israel *was* forty
years.
43 And Solomon slept with his fathers, and was buried in the city of David
his father: and Rehoboam his son reigned in his stead.

The Israelites Ask Rehoboam to Lighten Their Burdens

12 And Rehoboam went to Shechem: for all Israel were come to Shechem
to make him king.
2 And it came to pass, when Jeroboam the son of Nebat, who was yet in Egypt,
heard *of it*, (for he was fled from the presence of king Solomon, and Jeroboam
dwelt in Egypt;)
3 That they sent and called him. And Jeroboam and all the congregation of
Israel came, and spake unto Rehoboam, saying,
4 Thy father made our yoke grievous: now therefore make thou the grievous
service of thy father, and his heavy yoke which he put upon us, lighter, and we
will serve thee.

5 And he said unto them, Depart yet *for* three days, then come again to me.
And the people departed.
6 And king Rehoboam consulted with the old men, that stood before
Solomon his father while he yet lived, and said, How do ye advise that I may
answer this people?
7 And they spake unto him, saying, If thou wilt be a servant unto this people
this day, and wilt serve them, and answer them, and speak good words to them,
then they will be thy servants for ever.
8 But he forsook the counsel of the old men, which they had given him, and
consulted with the young men that were grown up with him, *and* which stood
before him:
9 And he said unto them, What counsel give ye that we may answer this
people, who have spoken to me, saying, Make the yoke which thy father did
put upon us lighter?
10 And the young men that were grown up with him spake unto him, saying,
Thus shalt thou speak unto this people that spake unto thee, saying, Thy father
made our yoke heavy, but make thou *it* lighter unto us; thus shalt thou say
unto them, My little *finger* shall be thicker than my father's loins.
11 And now whereas my father did lade you with a heavy yoke, I will add to
your yoke: my father hath chastised you with whips, but I will chastise you
with scorpions.
12 So Jeroboam and all the people came to Rehoboam the third day, as the
king had appointed, saying, Come to me again the third day.
13 And the king answered the people roughly, and forsook the old men's
counsel that they gave him;
14 And spake to them after the counsel of the young men, saying, My father
made your yoke heavy, and I will add to your yoke: my father *also* chastised
you with whips, but I will chastise you with scorpions.
15 Wherefore the king hearkened not unto the people; for the cause was
from the LORD, that he might perform his saying, which the LORD spake by
Ahijah the Shilonite unto Jeroboam the son of Nebat.

Ten Tribes Revolt against Rehoboam and Make Jeroboam Their King

16 So when all Israel saw that the king hearkened not unto them, the people
answered the king, saying, What portion have we in David? neither *have we*
inheritance in the son of Jesse: to your tents, O Israel: now see to thine own
house, David. So Israel departed unto their tents.
17 But *as for* the children of Israel which dwelt in the cities of Judah,
Rehoboam reigned over them.
18 Then king Rehoboam sent Adoram, who *was* over the tribute; and all Israel
stoned him with stones, that he died. Therefore king Rehoboam made speed
to get him up to his chariot, to flee to Jerusalem.
19 So Israel rebelled against the house of David unto this day.
20 And it came to pass, when all Israel heard that Jeroboam was come again,
that they sent and called him unto the congregation, and made him king over
all Israel: there was none that followed the house of David, but the tribe of
Judah only.
21 And when Rehoboam was come to Jerusalem, he assembled all the house
of Judah, with the tribe of Benjamin, an hundred and fourscore thousand
chosen men, which were warriors, to fight against the house of Israel, to bring
the kingdom again to Rehoboam the son of Solomon.
22 But the word of God came unto Shemaiah the man of God, saying,
23 Speak unto Rehoboam, the son of Solomon, king of Judah, and unto all
the house of Judah and Benjamin, and to the remnant of the people, saying,
24 Thus saith the LORD, Ye shall not go up, nor fight against your brethren
the children of Israel: return every man to his house; for this thing is from me.

They hearkened therefore to the word of the LORD, and returned to depart, according to the word of the LORD.

Jeroboam Sets Up Idol Worship in Israel at Beth-el and Dan

25 Then Jeroboam built Shechem in mount Ephraim, and dwelt therein; and
went out from thence, and built Penuel.
26 And Jeroboam said in his heart, Now shall the kingdom return to the
house of David:
27 If this people go up to do sacrifice in the house of the LORD at Jerusalem,
then shall the heart of this people turn again unto their lord, *even* unto
Rehoboam king of Judah, and they shall kill me, and go again to Rehoboam
king of Judah.
28 Whereupon the king took counsel, and made two calves *of* gold, and said
unto them, It is too much for you to go up to Jerusalem: behold thy gods, O
Israel, which brought thee up out of the land of Egypt.
29 And he set the one in Beth-el, and the other put he in Dan.
30 And this thing became a sin: for the people went *to worship* before the
one, *even* unto Dan.
31 And he made an house of high places, and made priests of the lowest of
the people, which were not of the sons of Levi.
32 And Jeroboam ordained a feast in the eighth month, on the fifteenth day
of the month, like unto the feast that *is* in Judah, and he offered upon the altar.
So did he in Beth-el, sacrificing unto the calves that he had made: and he placed
in Beth-el the priests of the high places which he had made.
33 So he offered upon the altar which he had made in Beth-el the fifteenth
day of the eighth month, *even* in the month which he had devised of his own
heart; and ordained a feast unto the children of Israel: and he offered upon
the altar, and burnt incense.

Jeroboam's Hand Withers and His Altar Splits Apart

13 And, behold, there came a man of God out of Judah by the word of the
LORD unto Beth-el: and Jeroboam stood by the altar to burn incense.
2 And he cried against the altar in the word of the LORD, and said, O altar,
altar, thus saith the LORD; Behold, a child shall be born unto the house of David,
Josiah by name; and upon thee shall he offer the priests of the high places that
burn incense upon thee, and men's bones shall be burnt upon thee.
3 And he gave a sign the same day, saying, This *is* the sign which the LORD
hath spoken; Behold, the altar shall be rent, and the ashes that *are* upon it
shall be poured out.
4 And it came to pass, when king Jeroboam heard the saying of the man of
God, which had cried against the altar in Beth-el, that he put forth his hand
from the altar, saying, Lay hold on him. And his hand, which he put forth
against him, dried up, so that he could not pull it in again to him.
5 The altar also was rent, and the ashes poured out from the altar, according
to the sign which the man of God had given by the word of the LORD.
6 And the king answered and said unto the man of God, Intreat now the face
of the LORD thy God, and pray for me, that my hand may be restored me again.
And the man of God besought the LORD, and the king's hand was restored him
again, and became as *it was* before.
7 And the king said unto the man of God, Come home with me, and refresh
thyself, and I will give thee a reward.
8 And the man of God said unto the king, If thou wilt give me half thine
house, I will not go in with thee, neither will I eat bread nor drink water in
this place:
9 For so was it charged me by the word of the LORD, saying, Eat no bread, nor
drink water, nor turn again by the same way that thou camest.

10 So he went another way, and returned not by the way that he came to
Beth-el.

The Man of God from Judah Is Enticed and Disobeys God

11 Now there dwelt an old prophet in Beth-el; and his sons came and told
him all the works that the man of God had done that day in Beth-el: the words
which he had spoken unto the king, them they told also to their father.
12 And their father said unto them, What way went he? For his sons had seen
what way the man of God went, which came from Judah.
13 And he said unto his sons, Saddle me the ass. So they saddled him the ass:
and he rode thereon,
14 And went after the man of God, and found him sitting under an oak: and
he said unto him, *Art* thou the man of God that camest from Judah? And he
said, I *am*.
15 Then he said unto him, Come home with me, and eat bread.
16 And he said, I may not return with thee, nor go in with thee: neither will
I eat bread nor drink water with thee in this place:
17 For it was said to me by the word of the LORD, Thou shalt eat no bread nor
drink water there, nor turn again to go by the way that thou camest.
18 He said unto him, I *am* a prophet also as thou *art*; and an angel spake unto
me by the word of the LORD, saying, Bring him back with thee into thine house,
that he may eat bread and drink water. *But* he lied unto him.
19 So he went back with him, and did eat bread in his house, and drank water.
20 And it came to pass, as they sat at the table, that the word of the LORD came
unto the prophet that brought him back:
21 And he cried unto the man of God that came from Judah, saying, Thus
saith the LORD, Forasmuch as thou hast disobeyed the mouth of the LORD, and
hast not kept the commandment which the LORD thy God commanded thee,
22 But camest back, and hast eaten bread and drunk water in the place, of
the which *the* LORD did say to thee, Eat no bread, and drink no water; thy carcase
shall not come unto the sepulchre of thy fathers.

The Man of God Is Slain by a Lion

23 And it came to pass, after he had eaten bread, and after he had drunk, that
he saddled for him the ass, *to wit*, for the prophet whom he had brought back.
24 And when he was gone, a lion met him by the way, and slew him: and his
carcase was cast in the way, and the ass stood by it, the lion also stood by the
carcase.
25 And, behold, men passed by, and saw the carcase cast in the way, and the
lion standing by the carcase: and they came and told *it* in the city where the
old prophet dwelt.
26 And when the prophet that brought him back from the way heard *there-
of*, he said, It *is* the man of God, who was disobedient unto the word of the
LORD: therefore the LORD hath delivered him unto the lion, which hath torn
him, and slain him, according to the word of the LORD, which he spake unto
him.
27 And he spake to his sons, saying, Saddle me the ass. And they saddled *him*.
28 And he went and found his carcase cast in the way, and the ass and the lion
standing by the carcase: the lion had not eaten the carcase, nor torn the ass.
29 And the prophet took up the carcase of the man of God, and laid it upon
the ass, and brought it back: and the old prophet came to the city, to mourn
and to bury him.
30 And he laid his carcase in his own grave; and they mourned over him,
saying, Alas, my brother!
31 And it came to pass, after he had buried him, that he spake to his sons,
saying, When I am dead, then bury me in the sepulchre wherein the man of
God *is* buried; lay my bones beside his bones:

32 For the saying which he cried by the word of the LORD against the altar in Bethel, and against all the houses of the high places which *are* in the cities of Samaria, shall surely come to pass.

33 After this thing Jeroboam returned not from his evil way, but made again of the lowest of the people priests of the high places: whosoever would, he consecrated him, and he became *one* of the priests of the high places.

34 And this thing became sin unto the house of Jeroboam, even to cut *it* off, and to destroy *it* from off the face of the earth.

Jeroboam Sends His Wife, Disguised, to the Prophet Ahijah

14 At that time Abijah the son of Jeroboam fell sick.

2 And Jeroboam said to his wife, Arise, I pray thee, and disguise thyself, that thou be not known to be the wife of Jeroboam; and get thee to Shiloh: behold, there *is* Ahijah the prophet, which told me that *I should be* king over this people.

3 And take with thee ten loaves, and cracknels, and a cruse of honey, and go to him: he shall tell thee what shall become of the child.

4 And Jeroboam's wife did so, and arose, and went to Shiloh, and came to the house of Ahijah. But Ahijah could not see; for his eyes were set by reason of his age.

5 And the LORD said unto Ahijah, Behold, the wife of Jeroboam cometh to ask a thing of thee for her son; for he *is* sick: thus and thus shalt thou say unto her: for it shall be, when she cometh in, that she shall feign herself *to be* another *woman*.

6 And it was *so*, when Ahijah heard the sound of her feet, as she came in at the door, that he said, Come in, thou wife of Jeroboam; why feignest thou thyself *to be* another? for I *am* sent to thee *with* heavy *tidings*.

7 Go, tell Jeroboam, Thus saith the LORD God of Israel, Forasmuch as I exalted thee from among the people, and made thee prince over my people Israel,

8 And rent the kingdom away from the house of David, and gave it thee: and *yet* thou hast not been as my servant David, who kept my commandments, and who followed me with all his heart, to do *that* only *which was* right in mine eyes;

9 But hast done evil above all that were before thee: for thou hast gone and made thee other gods, and molten images, to provoke me to anger, and hast cast me behind thy back:

10 Therefore, behold, I will bring evil upon the house of Jeroboam, and will cut off from Jeroboam him that pisseth against the wall, *and* him that is shut up and left in Israel, and will take away the remnant of the house of Jeroboam, as a man taketh away dung, till it be all gone.

11 Him that dieth of Jeroboam in the city shall the dogs eat; and him that dieth in the field shall the fowls of the air eat: for the LORD hath spoken *it*.

12 Arise thou therefore, get thee to thine own house: *and* when thy feet enter into the city, the child shall die.

13 And all Israel shall mourn for him, and bury him: for he only of Jeroboam shall come to the grave, because in him there is found *some* good thing toward the LORD God of Israel in the house of Jeroboam.

14 Moreover the LORD shall raise him up a king over Israel, who shall cut off the house of Jeroboam that day: but what? even now.

15 For the LORD shall smite Israel, as a reed is shaken in the water, and he shall root up Israel out of this good land, which he gave to their fathers, and shall scatter them beyond the river, because they have made their groves, provoking the LORD to anger.

16 And he shall give Israel up because of the sins of Jeroboam, who did sin, and who made Israel to sin.

17 And Jeroboam's wife arose, and departed, and came to Tirzah: *and* when
she came to the threshold of the door, the child died;
18 And they buried him; and all Israel mourned for him, according to the word
of the LORD, which he spake by the hand of his servant Ahijah the prophet.
19 And the rest of the acts of Jeroboam, how he warred, and how he reigned,
behold, they *are* written in the book of the chronicles of the kings of Israel.
20 And the days which Jeroboam reigned *were* two and twenty years: and he
slept with his fathers, and Nadab his son reigned in his stead.

Rehoboam's Evil Reign over the Southern Kingdom of Judah

21 And Rehoboam the son of Solomon reigned in Judah. Rehoboam *was* forty
and one years old when he began to reign, and he reigned seventeen years in
Jerusalem, the city which the LORD did choose out of all the tribes of Israel, to
put his name there. And his mother's name *was* Naamah an Ammonitess.
22 And Judah did evil in the sight of the LORD, and they provoked him to
jealousy with their sins which they had committed, above all that their fathers
had done.
23 For they also built them high places, and images, and groves, on every high
hill, and under every green tree.
24 And there were also sodomites in the land: *and* they did according to all
the abominations of the nations which the LORD cast out before the children
of Israel.
25 And it came to pass in the fifth year of king Rehoboam, *that* Shishak king
of Egypt came up against Jerusalem:
26 And he took away the treasures of the house of the LORD, and the treasures
of the king's house; he even took away all: and he took away all the shields of
gold which Solomon had made.
27 And king Rehoboam made in their stead brasen shields, and committed
them unto the hands of the chief of the guard, which kept the door of the king's
house.
28 And it was *so*, when the king went into the house of the LORD, that the
guard bare them, and brought them back into the guard chamber.
29 Now the rest of the acts of Rehoboam, and all that he did, *are* they not
written in the book of the chronicles of the kings of Judah?
30 And there was war between Rehoboam and Jeroboam all *their* days.
31 And Rehoboam slept with his fathers, and was buried with his fathers in
the city of David. And his mother's name *was* Naamah an Ammonitess. And
Abijam his son reigned in his stead.

Abijam's Evil Reign over Judah

15 Now in the eighteenth year of king Jeroboam the son of Nebat reigned
Abijam over Judah.
2 Three years reigned he in Jerusalem. And his mother's name *was* Maachah,
the daughter of Abishalom.
3 And he walked in all the sins of his father, which he had done before him:
and his heart was not perfect with the LORD his God, as the heart of David his
father.
4 Nevertheless for David's sake did the LORD his God give him a lamp in
Jerusalem, to set up his son after him, and to establish Jerusalem:
5 Because David did *that which was* right in the eyes of the LORD, and turned
not aside from any *thing* that he commanded him all the days of his life, save
only in the matter of Uriah the Hittite.
6 And there was war between Rehoboam and Jeroboam all the days of his
life.
7 Now the rest of the acts of Abijam, and all that he did, *are* they not written
in the book of the chronicles of the kings of Judah? And there was war between
Abijam and Jeroboam.

8 And Abijam slept with his fathers; and they buried him in the city of David:
and Asa his son reigned in his stead.

Asa's Good Reign over Judah

9 And in the twentieth year of Jeroboam king of Israel reigned Asa over Judah.
10 And forty and one years reigned he in Jerusalem. And his mother's name
was Maachah, the daughter of Abishalom.
11 And Asa did *that which was* right in the eyes of the LORD, as *did* David his
father.
12 And he took away the sodomites out of the land, and removed all the idols
that his fathers had made.
13 And also Maachah his mother, even her he removed from *being* queen,
because she had made an idol in a grove; and Asa destroyed her idol, and burnt
it by the brook Kidron.
14 But the high places were not removed: nevertheless Asa's heart was perfect
with the LORD all his days.
15 And he brought in the things which his father had dedicated, and the
things which himself had dedicated, into the house of the LORD, silver, and
gold, and vessels.
16 And there was war between Asa and Baasha king of Israel all their days.
17 And Baasha king of Israel went up against Judah, and built Ramah, that
he might not suffer any to go out or come in to Asa king of Judah.
18 Then Asa took all the silver and the gold *that were* left in the treasures of
the house of the LORD, and the treasures of the king's house, and delivered
them into the hand of his servants: and king Asa sent them to Ben-hadad, the
son of Tabrimon, the son of Hezion, king of Syria, that dwelt at Damascus,
saying,
19 *There is* a league between me and thee, *and* between my father and thy
father: behold, I have sent unto thee a present of silver and gold; come and
break thy league with Baasha king of Israel, that he may depart from me.
20 So Ben-hadad hearkened unto king Asa, and sent the captains of the hosts
which he had against the cities of Israel, and smote Ijon, and Dan, and Abel-
beth-maachah, and all Cinneroth, with all the land of Naphtali.
21 And it came to pass, when Baasha heard *thereof*, that he left off building
of Ramah, and dwelt in Tirzah.
22 Then king Asa made a proclamation throughout all Judah; none *was*
exempted: and they took away the stones of Ramah, and the timber thereof,
wherewith Baasha had builded; and king Asa built with them Geba of
Benjamin, and Mizpah.
23 The rest of all the acts of Asa, and all his might, and all that he did, and the
cities which he built, *are* they not written in the book of the chronicles of the
kings of Judah? Nevertheless in the time of his old age he was diseased in his
feet.
24 And Asa slept with his fathers, and was buried with his fathers in the city
of David his father: and Jehoshaphat his son reigned in his stead.

Nadab's Evil Reign over the Northern Kingdom of Israel

25 And Nadab the son of Jeroboam began to reign over Israel in the second
year of Asa king of Judah, and reigned over Israel two years.
26 And he did evil in the sight of the LORD, and walked in the way of his father,
and in his sin wherewith he made Israel to sin.
27 And Baasha the son of Ahijah, of the house of Issachar, conspired against
him; and Baasha smote him at Gibbethon, which *belonged* to the Philistines;
for Nadab and all Israel laid siege to Gibbethon.
28 Even in the third year of Asa king of Judah did Baasha slay him, and
reigned in his stead.

29 And it came to pass, when he reigned, *that* he smote all the house of Jeroboam; he left not to Jeroboam any that breathed, until he had destroyed him, according unto the saying of the LORD, which he spake by his servant Ahijah the Shilonite:

30 Because of the sins of Jeroboam which he sinned, and which he made Israel sin, by his provocation wherewith he provoked the LORD God of Israel to anger.

31 Now the rest of the acts of Nadab, and all that he did, *are* they not written in the book of the chronicles of the kings of Israel?

32 And there was war between Asa and Baasha king of Israel all their days.

33 In the third year of Asa king of Judah began Baasha the son of Ahijah to reign over all Israel in Tirzah, twenty and four years.

34 And he did evil in the sight of the LORD, and walked in the way of Jeroboam, and in his sin wherewith he made Israel to sin.

The Evil Reigns of Baasha and Elah over Israel

16 Then the word of the LORD came to Jehu the son of Hanani against Baasha, saying,

2 Forasmuch as I exalted thee out of the dust, and made thee prince over my people Israel; and thou hast walked in the way of Jeroboam, and hast made my people Israel to sin, to provoke me to anger with their sins;

3 Behold, I will take away the posterity of Baasha, and the posterity of his house; and will make thy house like the house of Jeroboam the son of Nebat.

4 Him that dieth of Baasha in the city shall the dogs eat; and him that dieth of his in the fields shall the fowls of the air eat.

5 Now the rest of the acts of Baasha, and what he did, and his might, *are* they not written in the book of the chronicles of the kings of Israel?

6 So Baasha slept with his fathers, and was buried in Tirzah: and Elah his son reigned in his stead.

7 And also by the hand of the prophet Jehu the son of Hanani came the word of the LORD against Baasha, and against his house, even for all the evil that he did in the sight of the LORD, in provoking him to anger with the work of his hands, in being like the house of Jeroboam; and because he killed him.

8 In the twenty and sixth year of Asa king of Judah began Elah the son of Baasha to reign over Israel in Tirzah, two years.

9 And his servant Zimri, captain of half *his* chariots, conspired against him, as he was in Tirzah, drinking himself drunk in the house of Arza steward of *his* house in Tirzah.

10 And Zimri went in and smote him, and killed him, in the twenty and seventh year of Asa king of Judah, and reigned in his stead.

11 And it came to pass, when he began to reign, as soon as he sat on his throne, *that* he slew all the house of Baasha: he left him not one that pisseth against a wall, neither of his kinsfolks, nor of his friends.

12 Thus did Zimri destroy all the house of Baasha, according to the word of the LORD, which he spake against Baasha by Jehu the prophet,

13 For all the sins of Baasha, and the sins of Elah his son, by which they sinned, and by which they made Israel to sin, in provoking the LORD God of Israel to anger with their vanities.

14 Now the rest of the acts of Elah, and all that he did, *are* they not written in the book of the chronicles of the kings of Israel?

The Evil Reigns of Zimri and Omri over Israel

15 In the twenty and seventh year of Asa king of Judah did Zimri reign seven days in Tirzah. And the people *were* encamped against Gibbethon, which *belonged* to the Philistines.

16 And the people *that were* encamped heard say, Zimri hath conspired, and hath also slain the king: wherefore all Israel made Omri, the captain of the host, king over Israel that day in the camp.
17 And Omri went up from Gibbethon, and all Israel with him, and they besieged Tirzah.
18 And it came to pass, when Zimri saw that the city was taken, that he went into the palace of the king's house, and burnt the king's house over him with fire, and died,
19 For his sins which he sinned in doing evil in the sight of the LORD, in walking in the way of Jeroboam, and in his sin which he did, to make Israel to sin.
20 Now the rest of the acts of Zimri, and his treason that he wrought, *are* they not written in the book of the chronicles of the kings of Israel?
21 Then were the people of Israel divided into two parts: half of the people followed Tibni the son of Ginath, to make him king; and half followed Omri.
22 But the people that followed Omri prevailed against the people that followed Tibni the son of Ginath: so Tibni died, and Omri reigned.
23 In the thirty and first year of Asa king of Judah began Omri to reign over Israel, twelve years: six years reigned he in Tirzah.
24 And he bought the hill Samaria of Shemer for two talents of silver, and built on the hill, and called the name of the city which he built, after the name of Shemer, owner of the hill, Samaria.
25 But Omri wrought evil in the eyes of the LORD, and did worse than all that *were* before him.
26 For he walked in all the way of Jeroboam the son of Nebat, and in his sin wherewith he made Israel to sin, to provoke the LORD God of Israel to anger with their vanities.
27 Now the rest of the acts of Omri which he did, and his might that he shewed, *are* they not written in the book of the chronicles of the kings of Israel?
28 So Omri slept with his fathers, and was buried in Samaria: and Ahab his son reigned in his stead.

Ahab's Most Wicked Reign over Israel

29 And in the thirty and eighth year of Asa king of Judah began Ahab the son of Omri to reign over Israel: and Ahab the son of Omri reigned over Israel in Samaria twenty and two years.
30 And Ahab the son of Omri did evil in the sight of the LORD above all that *were* before him.
31 And it came to pass, as if it had been a light thing for him to walk in the sins of Jeroboam the son of Nebat, that he took to wife Jezebel the daughter of Ethbaal king of the Zidonians, and went and served Baal, and worshipped him.
32 And he reared up an altar for Baal in the house of Baal, which he had built in Samaria.
33 And Ahab made a grove; and Ahab did more to provoke the LORD God of Israel to anger than all the kings of Israel that were before him.
34 In his days did Hiel the Bethelite build Jericho: he laid the foundation thereof in Abiram his firstborn, and set up the gates thereof in his youngest *son* Segub, according to the word of the LORD, which he spake by Joshua the son of Nun.

The Prophet Elijah Is Fed by Ravens

17 And Elijah the Tishbite, *who was* of the inhabitants of Gilead, said unto
Ahab, *As* the LORD God of Israel liveth, before whom I stand, there shall
not be dew nor rain these years, but according to my word.
2 And the word of the LORD came unto him, saying,

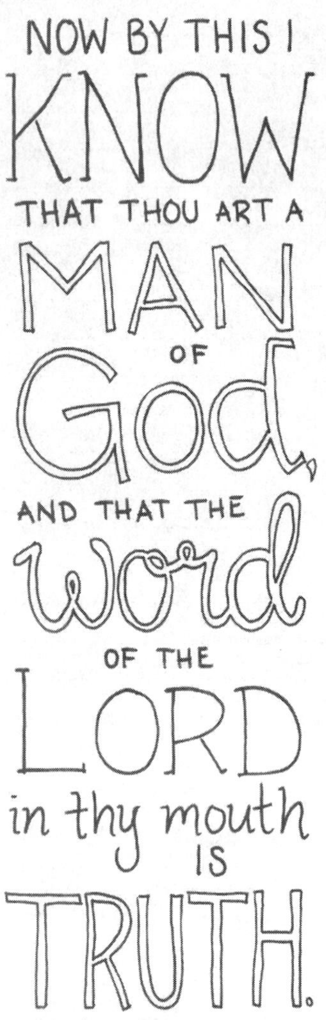

3 Get thee hence, and turn thee eastward, and hide thyself by the brook
Cherith, that *is* before Jordan.
4 And it shall be, *that* thou shalt drink of the brook; and I have commanded
the ravens to feed thee there.
5 So he went and did according unto the word of the LORD: for he went and
dwelt by the brook Cherith, that *is* before Jordan.
6 And the ravens brought him bread and flesh in the morning, and bread
and flesh in the evening; and he drank of the brook.
7 And it came to pass after a while, that the brook dried up, because there
had been no rain in the land.

Elijah Is Sent to the Widow of Zarephath

8 And the word of the LORD came unto him, saying,
9 Arise, get thee to Zarephath, which *belongeth* to Zidon, and dwell there:
behold, I have commanded a widow woman there to sustain thee.
10 So he arose and went to Zarephath. And when he came to the gate of the
city, behold, the widow woman *was* there gathering of sticks: and he called to
her, and said, Fetch me, I pray thee, a little water in a vessel, that I may drink.
11 And as she was going to fetch *it*, he called to her, and said, Bring me, I pray
thee, a morsel of bread in thine hand.
12 And she said, *As* the LORD thy God liveth, I have not a cake, but an handful of
meal in a barrel, and a little oil in a cruse: and, behold, I *am* gathering two sticks,
that I may go in and dress it for me and my son, that we may eat it, and die.
13 And Elijah said unto her, Fear not; go *and* do as thou hast said: but make
me thereof a little cake first, and bring *it* unto me, and after make for thee and
for thy son.
14 For thus saith the LORD God of Israel, The barrel of meal shall not waste,
neither shall the cruse of oil fail, until the day *that* the LORD sendeth rain upon
the earth.
15 And she went and did according to the saying of Elijah: and she, and he,
and her house, did eat *many* days.
16 *And* the barrel of meal wasted not, neither did the cruse of oil fail, accord-
ing to the word of the LORD, which he spake by Elijah.

Elijah Raises the Widow's Son from the Dead

17 And it came to pass after these things, *that* the son of the woman, the
mistress of the house, fell sick; and his sickness was so sore, that there was no
breath left in him.
18 And she said unto Elijah, What have I to do with thee, O thou man of God?
art thou come unto me to call my sin to remembrance, and to slay my son?
19 And he said unto her, Give me thy son. And he took him out of her bosom,
and carried him up into a loft, where he abode, and laid him upon his own
bed.
20 And he cried unto the LORD, and said, O LORD my God, hast thou also
brought evil upon the widow with whom I sojourn, by slaying her son?
21 And he stretched himself upon the child three times, and cried unto the
LORD, and said, O LORD my God, I pray thee, let this child's soul come into him
again.
22 And the LORD heard the voice of Elijah; and the soul of the child came into
him again, and he revived.
23 And Elijah took the child, and brought him down out of the chamber into
the house, and delivered him unto his mother: and Elijah said, See, thy son
liveth.
24 And the woman said to Elijah, Now by this I know that thou *art* a man of
God, *and* that the word of the LORD in thy mouth *is* truth.

The Lord's Faithful Servant Obadiah Meets Elijah

18 And it came to pass *after* many days, that the word of the LORD came
to Elijah in the third year, saying, Go, shew thyself unto Ahab; and I
will send rain upon the earth.
2 And Elijah went to shew himself unto Ahab. And *there was* a sore famine
in Samaria.
3 And Ahab called Obadiah, which *was* the governor of *his* house. (Now
Obadiah feared the LORD greatly:
4 For it was *so*, when Jezebel cut off the prophets of the LORD, that Obadiah
took an hundred prophets, and hid them by fifty in a cave, and fed them with
bread and water.)
5 And Ahab said unto Obadiah, Go into the land, unto all fountains of water,
and unto all brooks: peradventure we may find grass to save the horses and
mules alive, that we lose not all the beasts.
6 So they divided the land between them to pass throughout it: Ahab went
one way by himself, and Obadiah went another way by himself.
7 And as Obadiah was in the way, behold, Elijah met him: and he knew him,
and fell on his face, and said, *Art* thou that my lord Elijah?
8 And he answered him, I *am*: go, tell thy lord, Behold, Elijah *is here*.
9 And he said, What have I sinned, that thou wouldest deliver thy servant
into the hand of Ahab, to slay me?
10 *As* the LORD thy God liveth, there is no nation or kingdom, whither my
lord hath not sent to seek thee: and when they said, *He is* not *there*; he took an
oath of the kingdom and nation, that they found thee not.
11 And now thou sayest, Go, tell thy lord, Behold, Elijah *is here*.
12 And it shall come to pass, *as soon as* I am gone from thee, that the Spirit
of the LORD shall carry thee whither I know not; and *so* when I come and tell
Ahab, and he cannot find thee, he shall slay me: but I thy servant fear the LORD
from my youth.
13 Was it not told my lord what I did when Jezebel slew the prophets of the
LORD, how I hid an hundred men of the LORD's prophets by fifty in a cave, and
fed them with bread and water?
14 And now thou sayest, Go, tell thy lord, Behold, Elijah *is here*: and he shall
slay me.
15 And Elijah said, *As* the LORD of hosts liveth, before whom I stand, I will
surely shew myself unto him to day.
16 So Obadiah went to meet Ahab, and told him: and Ahab went to meet
Elijah.

Elijah Calls Down Fire from Heaven

17 And it came to pass, when Ahab saw Elijah, that Ahab said unto him, *Art*
thou he that troubleth Israel?
18 And he answered, I have not troubled Israel; but thou, and thy father's
house, in that ye have forsaken the commandments of the LORD, and thou hast
followed Baalim.
19 Now therefore send, *and* gather to me all Israel unto mount Carmel, and
the prophets of Baal four hundred and fifty, and the prophets of the groves
four hundred, which eat at Jezebel's table.
20 So Ahab sent unto all the children of Israel, and gathered the prophets
together unto mount Carmel.
21 And Elijah came unto all the people, and said, How long halt ye between
two opinions? if the LORD *be* God, follow him: but if Baal, *then* follow him.
And the people answered him not a word.
22 Then said Elijah unto the people, I, *even* I only, remain a prophet of the
LORD; but Baal's prophets *are* four hundred and fifty men.

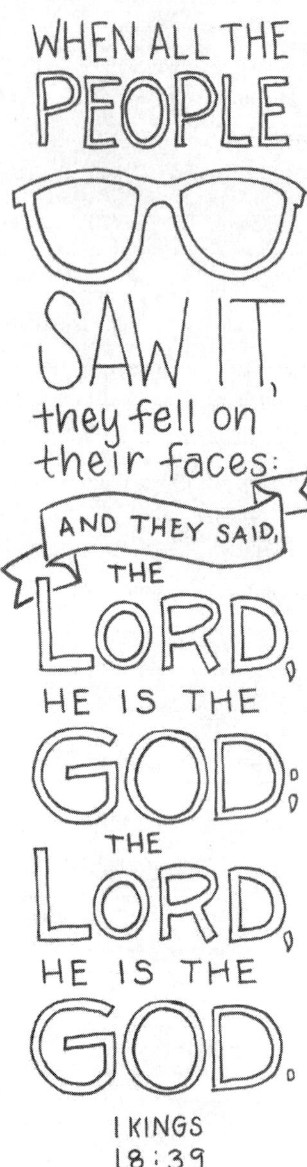

23 Let them therefore give us two bullocks; and let them choose one bullock
for themselves, and cut it in pieces, and lay *it* on wood, and put no fire *under*:
and I will dress the other bullock, and lay *it* on wood, and put no fire *under*.
24 And call ye on the name of your gods, and I will call on the name of the
LORD: and the God that answereth by fire, let him be God. And all the people
answered and said, It is well spoken.
25 And Elijah said unto the prophets of Baal, Choose you one bullock for
yourselves, and dress *it* first; for ye *are* many; and call on the name of your
gods, but put no fire *under*.
26 And they took the bullock which was given them, and they dressed *it*, and
called on the name of Baal from morning even until noon, saying, O Baal, hear
us. But *there was* no voice, nor any that answered. And they leaped upon the
altar which was made.
27 And it came to pass at noon, that Elijah mocked them, and said, Cry aloud:
for he *is* a god; either he is talking, or he is pursuing, or he is in a journey, *or*
peradventure he sleepeth, and must be awaked.
28 And they cried aloud, and cut themselves after their manner with knives
and lancets, till the blood gushed out upon them.
29 And it came to pass, when midday was past, and they prophesied until the
time of the offering of the *evening* sacrifice, that *there was* neither voice, nor
any to answer, nor any that regarded.
30 And Elijah said unto all the people, Come near unto me. And all the people
came near unto him. And he repaired the altar of the LORD *that was* broken
down.
31 And Elijah took twelve stones, according to the number of the tribes of
the sons of Jacob, unto whom the word of the LORD came, saying, Israel shall
be thy name:
32 And with the stones he built an altar in the name of the LORD: and he made
a trench about the altar, as great as would contain two measures of seed.
33 And he put the wood in order, and cut the bullock in pieces, and laid *him*
on the wood, and said, Fill four barrels with water, and pour *it* on the burnt
sacrifice, and on the wood.
34 And he said, Do *it* the second time. And they did *it* the second time. And
he said, Do *it* the third time. And they did *it* the third time.
35 And the water ran round about the altar; and he filled the trench also with
water.
36 And it came to pass at *the time of* the offering of the *evening* sacrifice, that
Elijah the prophet came near, and said, LORD God of Abraham, Isaac, and of
Israel, let it be known this day that thou *art* God in Israel, and *that* I *am* thy
servant, and *that* I have done all these things at thy word.
37 Hear me, O LORD, hear me, that this people may know that thou *art* the
LORD God, and *that* thou hast turned their heart back again.
38 Then the fire of the LORD fell, and consumed the burnt sacrifice, and the
wood, and the stones, and the dust, and licked up the water that *was* in the
trench.
39 And when all the people saw *it*, they fell on their faces: and they said, The
LORD, he *is* the God; the LORD, he *is* the God.
40 And Elijah said unto them, Take the prophets of Baal; let not one of them
escape. And they took them: and Elijah brought them down to the brook
Kishon, and slew them there.

Elijah Prays for Rain

41 And Elijah said unto Ahab, Get thee up, eat and drink; for *there is* a sound
of abundance of rain.

42 So Ahab went up to eat and to drink. And Elijah went up to the top of
Carmel; and he cast himself down upon the earth, and put his face between
his knees,
43 And said to his servant, Go up now, look toward the sea. And he went up,
and looked, and said, *There is* nothing. And he said, Go again seven times.
44 And it came to pass at the seventh time, that he said, Behold, there ariseth
a little cloud out of the sea, like a man's hand. And he said, Go up, say unto
Ahab, Prepare *thy chariot*, and get thee down, that the rain stop thee not.
45 And it came to pass in the mean while, that the heaven was black with
clouds and wind, and there was a great rain. And Ahab rode, and went to
Jezreel.
46 And the hand of the LORD was on Elijah; and he girded up his loins, and
ran before Ahab to the entrance of Jezreel.

Threatened by Jezebel, Elijah Flees to Beer-sheba, Then to Mount Horeb

19 And Ahab told Jezebel all that Elijah had done, and withal how he had
slain all the prophets with the sword.
2 Then Jezebel sent a messenger unto Elijah, saying, So let the gods do *to me*,
and more also, if I make not thy life as the life of one of them by to morrow
about this time.
3 And when he saw *that*, he arose, and went for his life, and came to Beer-
sheba, which *belongeth* to Judah, and left his servant there.
4 But he himself went a day's journey into the wilderness, and came and sat
down under a juniper tree: and he requested for himself that he might die;
and said, It is enough; now, O LORD, take away my life; for I *am* not better than
my fathers.
5 And as he lay and slept under a juniper tree, behold, then an angel touched
him, and said unto him, Arise *and* eat.
6 And he looked, and, behold, *there was* a cake baken on the coals, and a cruse
of water at his head. And he did eat and drink, and laid him down again.
7 And the angel of the LORD came again the second time, and touched him,
and said, Arise *and* eat; because the journey *is* too great for thee.
8 And he arose, and did eat and drink, and went in the strength of that meat
forty days and forty nights unto Horeb the mount of God.

God Sends Elijah to Anoint Hazael, Jehu, and Elisha

9 And he came thither unto a cave, and lodged there; and, behold, the word
of the LORD *came* to him, and he said unto him, What doest thou here, Elijah?
10 And he said, I have been very jealous for the LORD God of hosts: for the
children of Israel have forsaken thy covenant, thrown down thine altars, and
slain thy prophets with the sword; and I, *even* I only, am left; and they seek my
life, to take it away.
11 And he said, Go forth, and stand upon the mount before the LORD. And,
behold, the LORD passed by, and a great and strong wind rent the mountains,
and brake in pieces the rocks before the LORD; *but* the LORD *was* not in the
wind: and after the wind an earthquake; *but* the LORD *was* not in the earth-
quake:
12 And after the earthquake a fire; *but* the LORD *was* not in the fire: and after
the fire a still small voice.
13 And it was *so*, when Elijah heard *it*, that he wrapped his face in his mantle,
and went out, and stood in the entering in of the cave. And, behold, *there came*
a voice unto him, and said, What doest thou here, Elijah?
14 And he said, I have been very jealous for the LORD God of hosts: because
the children of Israel have forsaken thy covenant, thrown down thine altars,
and slain thy prophets with the sword; and I, *even* I only, am left; and they seek
my life, to take it away.

15 And the LORD said unto him, Go, return on thy way to the wilderness of Damascus: and when thou comest, anoint Hazael *to be* king over Syria:

16 And Jehu the son of Nimshi shalt thou anoint *to be* king over Israel: and Elisha the son of Shaphat of Abel-meholah shalt thou anoint *to be* prophet in thy room.

17 And it shall come to pass, *that* him that escapeth the sword of Hazael shall Jehu slay: and him that escapeth from the sword of Jehu shall Elisha slay.

18 Yet I have left *me* seven thousand in Israel, all the knees which have not bowed unto Baal, and every mouth which hath not kissed him.

Elisha Follows Elijah

19 So he departed thence, and found Elisha the son of Shaphat, who *was* plowing *with* twelve yoke *of oxen* before him, and he with the twelfth: and Elijah passed by him, and cast his mantle upon him.

20 And he left the oxen, and ran after Elijah, and said, Let me, I pray thee, kiss my father and my mother, and *then* I will follow thee. And he said unto him, Go back again: for what have I done to thee?

21 And he returned back from him, and took a yoke of oxen, and slew them, and boiled their flesh with the instruments of the oxen, and gave unto the people, and they did eat. Then he arose, and went after Elijah, and ministered unto him.

Ben-hadad of Syria Besieges Samaria, but Is Defeated by Ahab

20 And Ben-hadad the king of Syria gathered all his host together: and *there were* thirty and two kings with him, and horses, and chariots: and he went up and besieged Samaria, and warred against it.

2 And he sent messengers to Ahab king of Israel into the city, and said unto him, Thus saith Ben-hadad,

3 Thy silver and thy gold *is* mine; thy wives also and thy children, *even* the goodliest, *are* mine.

4 And the king of Israel answered and said, My lord, O king, according to thy saying, I *am* thine, and all that I have.

5 And the messengers came again, and said, Thus speaketh Ben-hadad, saying, Although I have sent unto thee, saying, Thou shalt deliver me thy silver, and thy gold, and thy wives, and thy children;

6 Yet I will send my servants unto thee to morrow about this time, and they shall search thine house, and the houses of thy servants; and it shall be, *that* whatsoever is pleasant in thine eyes, they shall put *it* in their hand, and take *it* away.

7 Then the king of Israel called all the elders of the land, and said, Mark, I pray you, and see how this *man* seeketh mischief: for he sent unto me for my wives, and for my children, and for my silver, and for my gold; and I denied him not.

8 And all the elders and all the people said unto him, Hearken not *unto him*, nor consent.

9 Wherefore he said unto the messengers of Ben-hadad, Tell my lord the king, All that thou didst send for to thy servant at the first I will do: but this thing I may not do. And the messengers departed, and brought him word again.

10 And Ben-hadad sent unto him, and said, The gods do so unto me, and more also, if the dust of Samaria shall suffice for handfuls for all the people that follow me.

11 And the king of Israel answered and said, Tell *him*, Let not him that girdeth on *his harness* boast himself as he that putteth it off.

12 And it came to pass, when *Ben-hadad* heard this message, as he *was* drinking, he and the kings in the pavilions, that he said unto his servants, Set *yourselves in array*. And they set *themselves in array* against the city.

13 And, behold, there came a prophet unto Ahab king of Israel, saying, Thus
saith the LORD, Hast thou seen all this great multitude? behold, I will deliver
it into thine hand this day; and thou shalt know that I *am* the LORD.
14 And Ahab said, By whom? And he said, Thus saith the LORD, *Even* by the
young men of the princes of the provinces. Then he said, Who shall order the
battle? And he answered, Thou.
15 Then he numbered the young men of the princes of the provinces, and
they were two hundred and thirty two: and after them he numbered all the
people, *even* all the children of Israel, *being* seven thousand.
16 And they went out at noon. But Ben-hadad *was* drinking himself drunk
in the pavilions, he and the kings, the thirty and two kings that helped him.
17 And the young men of the princes of the provinces went out first; and
Ben-hadad sent out, and they told him, saying, There are men come out of
Samaria.
18 And he said, Whether they be come out for peace, take them alive; or
whether they be come out for war, take them alive.
19 So these young men of the princes of the provinces came out of the city,
and the army which followed them.
20 And they slew every one his man: and the Syrians fled; and Israel pursued
them: and Ben-hadad the king of Syria escaped on an horse with the horsemen.
21 And the king of Israel went out, and smote the horses and chariots, and
slew the Syrians with a great slaughter.

As Ahab Was Forewarned, the Syrians Attack Again at Aphek

22 And the prophet came to the king of Israel, and said unto him, Go,
strengthen thyself, and mark, and see what thou doest: for at the return of the
year the king of Syria will come up against thee.
23 And the servants of the king of Syria said unto him, Their gods *are* gods
of the hills; therefore they were stronger than we; but let us fight against them
in the plain, and surely we shall be stronger than they.
24 And do this thing, Take the kings away, every man out of his place, and put
captains in their rooms:
25 And number thee an army, like the army that thou hast lost, horse for
horse, and chariot for chariot: and we will fight against them in the plain, *and*
surely we shall be stronger than they. And he hearkened unto their voice, and
did so.
26 And it came to pass at the return of the year, that Ben-hadad numbered
the Syrians, and went up to Aphek, to fight against Israel.
27 And the children of Israel were numbered, and were all present, and went
against them: and the children of Israel pitched before them like two little
flocks of kids; but the Syrians filled the country.
28 And there came a man of God, and spake unto the king of Israel, and said,
Thus saith the LORD, Because the Syrians have said, The LORD *is* God of the hills,
but he *is* not God of the valleys, therefore will I deliver all this great multitude
into thine hand, and ye shall know that I *am* the LORD.
29 And they pitched one over against the other seven days. And *so* it was, that
in the seventh day the battle was joined: and the children of Israel slew of the
Syrians an hundred thousand footmen in one day.
30 But the rest fled to Aphek, into the city; and *there* a wall fell upon twenty
and seven thousand of the men *that were* left. And Ben-hadad fled, and came
into the city, into an inner chamber.

A Prophet Condemns Ahab for Making a Covenant with Ben-hadad

31 And his servants said unto him, Behold now, we have heard that the kings
of the house of Israel *are* merciful kings: let us, I pray thee, put sackcloth on
our loins, and ropes upon our heads, and go out to the king of Israel: perad-
venture he will save thy life.

32 So they girded sackcloth on their loins, and *put* ropes on their heads, and
came to the king of Israel, and said, Thy servant Ben-hadad saith, I pray thee,
let me live. And he said, *Is* he yet alive? he *is* my brother.
33 Now the men did diligently observe whether *any thing would come* from
him, and did hastily catch *it*: and they said, Thy brother Ben-hadad. Then he
said, Go ye, bring him. Then Ben-hadad came forth to him; and he caused him
to come up into the chariot.
34 And *Ben-hadad* said unto him, The cities, which my father took from thy
father, I will restore; and thou shalt make streets for thee in Damascus, as my
father made in Samaria. Then *said Ahab*, I will send thee away with this cov-
enant. So he made a covenant with him, and sent him away.
35 And a certain man of the sons of the prophets said unto his neighbour in
the word of the LORD, Smite me, I pray thee. And the man refused to smite him.
36 Then said he unto him, Because thou hast not obeyed the voice of the
LORD, behold, as soon as thou art departed from me, a lion shall slay thee. And
as soon as he was departed from him, a lion found him, and slew him.
37 Then he found another man, and said, Smite me, I pray thee. And the man
smote him, so that in smiting he wounded *him*.
38 So the prophet departed, and waited for the king by the way, and disguised
himself with ashes upon his face.
39 And as the king passed by, he cried unto the king: and he said, Thy servant
went out into the midst of the battle; and, behold, a man turned aside, and
brought a man unto me, and said, Keep this man: if by any means he be miss-
ing, then shall thy life be for his life, or else thou shalt pay a talent of silver.
40 And as thy servant was busy here and there, he was gone. And the king of
Israel said unto him, So *shall* thy judgment *be*; thyself hast decided *it*.
41 And he hasted, and took the ashes away from his face; and the king of
Israel discerned him that he *was* of the prophets.
42 And he said unto him, Thus saith the LORD, Because thou hast let go out
of *thy* hand a man whom I appointed to utter destruction, therefore thy life
shall go for his life, and thy people for his people.
43 And the king of Israel went to his house heavy and displeased, and came
to Samaria.

Ahab Is Denied Naboth's Vineyard

21 And it came to pass after these things, *that* Naboth the Jezreelite had
a vineyard, which *was* in Jezreel, hard by the palace of Ahab king of
Samaria.
2 And Ahab spake unto Naboth, saying, Give me thy vineyard, that I may have
it for a garden of herbs, because it *is* near unto my house: and I will give thee
for it a better vineyard than it; *or*, if it seem good to thee, I will give thee the
worth of it in money.
3 And Naboth said to Ahab, The LORD forbid it me, that I should give the
inheritance of my fathers unto thee.
4 And Ahab came into his house heavy and displeased because of the word
which Naboth the Jezreelite had spoken to him: for he had said, I will not give
thee the inheritance of my fathers. And he laid him down upon his bed, and
turned away his face, and would eat no bread.

Jezebel Has Naboth Killed, and Elijah Condemns Both Ahab and Jezebel

5 But Jezebel his wife came to him, and said unto him, Why is thy spirit so
sad, that thou eatest no bread?
6 And he said unto her, Because I spake unto Naboth the Jezreelite, and said
unto him, Give me thy vineyard for money; or else, if it please thee, I will give
thee *another* vineyard for it: and he answered, I will not give thee my vineyard.

7 And Jezebel his wife said unto him, Dost thou now govern the kingdom of
Israel? arise, *and* eat bread, and let thine heart be merry: I will give thee the
vineyard of Naboth the Jezreelite.
8 So she wrote letters in Ahab's name, and sealed *them* with his seal, and sent
the letters unto the elders and to the nobles that *were* in his city, dwelling with
Naboth.
9 And she wrote in the letters, saying, Proclaim a fast, and set Naboth on high
among the people:
10 And set two men, sons of Belial, before him, to bear witness against him,
saying, Thou didst blaspheme God and the king. And *then* carry him out, and
stone him, that he may die.
11 And the men of his city, *even* the elders and the nobles who were the inhab-
itants in his city, did as Jezebel had sent unto them, *and* as it *was* written in
the letters which she had sent unto them.
12 They proclaimed a fast, and set Naboth on high among the people.
13 And there came in two men, children of Belial, and sat before him: and
the men of Belial witnessed against him, *even* against Naboth, in the presence
of the people, saying, Naboth did blaspheme God and the king. Then they
carried him forth out of the city, and stoned him with stones, that he died.
14 Then they sent to Jezebel, saying, Naboth is stoned, and is dead.
15 And it came to pass, when Jezebel heard that Naboth was stoned, and was
dead, that Jezebel said to Ahab, Arise, take possession of the vineyard of Naboth
the Jezreelite, which he refused to give thee for money: for Naboth is not alive,
but dead.
16 And it came to pass, when Ahab heard that Naboth was dead, that Ahab
rose up to go down to the vineyard of Naboth the Jezreelite, to take possession
of it.
17 And the word of the LORD came to Elijah the Tishbite, saying,
18 Arise, go down to meet Ahab king of Israel, which *is* in Samaria: behold,
he is in the vineyard of Naboth, whither he is gone down to possess it.
19 And thou shalt speak unto him, saying, Thus saith the LORD, Hast thou
killed, and also taken possession? And thou shalt speak unto him, saying, Thus
saith the LORD, In the place where dogs licked the blood of Naboth shall dogs
lick thy blood, even thine.
20 And Ahab said to Elijah, Hast thou found me, O mine enemy? And he
answered, I have found *thee*: because thou hast sold thyself to work evil in the
sight of the LORD.
21 Behold, I will bring evil upon thee, and will take away thy posterity, and
will cut off from Ahab him that pisseth against the wall, and him that is shut
up and left in Israel,
22 And will make thine house like the house of Jeroboam the son of Nebat,
and like the house of Baasha the son of Ahijah, for the provocation wherewith
thou hast provoked *me* to anger, and made Israel to sin.
23 And of Jezebel also spake the LORD, saying, The dogs shall eat Jezebel by
the wall of Jezreel.
24 Him that dieth of Ahab in the city the dogs shall eat; and him that dieth
in the field shall the fowls of the air eat.
25 But there was none like unto Ahab, which did sell himself to work wick-
edness in the sight of the LORD, whom Jezebel his wife stirred up.
26 And he did very abominably in following idols, according to all *things* as
did the Amorites, whom the LORD cast out before the children of Israel.
27 And it came to pass, when Ahab heard those words, that he rent his clothes,
and put sackcloth upon his flesh, and fasted, and lay in sackcloth, and went
softly.
28 And the word of the LORD came to Elijah the Tishbite, saying,

29 Seest thou how Ahab humbleth himself before me? because he humbleth himself before me, I will not bring the evil in his days: *but* in his son's days will I bring the evil upon his house.

Micaiah Prophesies That Ahab Will Be Slain at Ramoth-gilead

22 And they continued three years without war between Syria and Israel.
2 And it came to pass in the third year, that Jehoshaphat the king of Judah came down to the king of Israel.

3 And the king of Israel said unto his servants, Know ye that Ramoth in Gilead *is* ours, and we *be* still, *and* take it not out of the hand of the king of Syria?

4 And he said unto Jehoshaphat, Wilt thou go with me to battle to Ramoth-gilead? And Jehoshaphat said to the king of Israel, I *am* as thou *art*, my people as thy people, my horses as thy horses.

5 And Jehoshaphat said unto the king of Israel, Enquire, I pray thee, at the word of the Lord to day.

6 Then the king of Israel gathered the prophets together, about four hundred men, and said unto them, Shall I go against Ramoth-gilead to battle, or shall I forbear? And they said, Go up; for the Lord shall deliver *it* into the hand of the king.

7 And Jehoshaphat said, *Is there* not here a prophet of the Lord besides, that we might enquire of him?

8 And the king of Israel said unto Jehoshaphat, *There is* yet one man, Micaiah the son of Imlah, by whom we may enquire of the Lord: but I hate him; for he doth not prophesy good concerning me, but evil. And Jehoshaphat said, Let not the king say so.

9 Then the king of Israel called an officer, and said, Hasten *hither* Micaiah the son of Imlah.

10 And the king of Israel and Jehoshaphat the king of Judah sat each on his throne, having put on their robes, in a void place in the entrance of the gate of Samaria; and all the prophets prophesied before them.

11 And Zedekiah the son of Chenaanah made him horns of iron: and he said, Thus saith the Lord, With these shalt thou push the Syrians, until thou have consumed them.

12 And all the prophets prophesied so, saying, Go up to Ramoth-gilead, and prosper: for the Lord shall deliver *it* into the king's hand.

13 And the messenger that was gone to call Micaiah spake unto him, saying, Behold now, the words of the prophets *declare* good unto the king with one mouth: let thy word, I pray thee, be like the word of one of them, and speak *that which is* good.

14 And Micaiah said, *As* the Lord liveth, what the Lord saith unto me, that will I speak.

15 So he came to the king. And the king said unto him, Micaiah, shall we go against Ramoth-gilead to battle, or shall we forbear? And he answered him, Go, and prosper: for the Lord shall deliver *it* into the hand of the king.

16 And the king said unto him, How many times shall I adjure thee that thou tell me nothing but *that which is* true in the name of the Lord?

17 And he said, I saw all Israel scattered upon the hills, as sheep that have not a shepherd: and the Lord said, These have no master: let them return every man to his house in peace.

18 And the king of Israel said unto Jehoshaphat, Did I not tell thee that he would prophesy no good concerning me, but evil?

19 And he said, Hear thou therefore the word of the Lord: I saw the Lord sitting on his throne, and all the host of heaven standing by him on his right hand and on his left.

20 And the LORD said, Who shall persuade Ahab, that he may go up and fall
at Ramoth-gilead? And one said on this manner, and another said on that
manner.
21 And there came forth a spirit, and stood before the LORD, and said, I will
persuade him.
22 And the LORD said unto him, Wherewith? And he said, I will go forth, and
I will be a lying spirit in the mouth of all his prophets. And he said, Thou shalt
persuade *him*, and prevail also: go forth, and do so.
23 Now therefore, behold, the LORD hath put a lying spirit in the mouth of
all these thy prophets, and the LORD hath spoken evil concerning thee.
24 But Zedekiah the son of Chenaanah went near, and smote Micaiah on the
cheek, and said, Which way went the Spirit of the LORD from me to speak unto
thee?
25 And Micaiah said, Behold, thou shalt see in that day, when thou shalt go
into an inner chamber to hide thyself.
26 And the king of Israel said, Take Micaiah, and carry him back unto Amon
the governor of the city, and to Joash the king's son;
27 And say, Thus saith the king, Put this *fellow* in the prison, and feed him
with bread of affliction and with water of affliction, until I come in peace.
28 And Micaiah said, If thou return at all in peace, the LORD hath not spoken
by me. And he said, Hearken, O people, every one of you.
29 So the king of Israel and Jehoshaphat the king of Judah went up to Ramoth-
gilead.
30 And the king of Israel said unto Jehoshaphat, I will disguise myself, and
enter into the battle; but put thou on thy robes. And the king of Israel disguised
himself, and went into the battle.
31 But the king of Syria commanded his thirty and two captains that had
rule over his chariots, saying, Fight neither with small nor great, save only
with the king of Israel.
32 And it came to pass, when the captains of the chariots saw Jehoshaphat,
that they said, Surely it *is* the king of Israel. And they turned aside to fight
against him: and Jehoshaphat cried out.
33 And it came to pass, when the captains of the chariots perceived that it
was not the king of Israel, that they turned back from pursuing him.
34 And a *certain* man drew a bow at a venture, and smote the king of Israel
between the joints of the harness: wherefore he said unto the driver of his
chariot, Turn thine hand, and carry me out of the host; for I am wounded.
35 And the battle increased that day: and the king was stayed up in his char-
iot against the Syrians, and died at even: and the blood ran out of the wound
into the midst of the chariot.
36 And there went a proclamation throughout the host about the going down
of the sun, saying, Every man to his city, and every man to his own country.
37 So the king died, and was brought to Samaria; and they buried the king
in Samaria.
38 And *one* washed the chariot in the pool of Samaria; and the dogs licked
up his blood; and they washed his armour; according unto the word of the
LORD which he spake.
39 Now the rest of the acts of Ahab, and all that he did, and the ivory house
which he made, and all the cities that he built, *are* they not written in the book
of the chronicles of the kings of Israel?
40 So Ahab slept with his fathers; and Ahaziah his son reigned in his stead.

Jehoshaphat's Good Reign over Judah

41 And Jehoshaphat the son of Asa began to reign over Judah in the fourth
year of Ahab king of Israel.

42 Jehoshaphat *was* thirty and five years old when he began to reign; and he
reigned twenty and five years in Jerusalem. And his mother's name *was* Azubah
the daughter of Shilhi.
43 And he walked in all the ways of Asa his father; he turned not aside from
it, doing *that which was* right in the eyes of the LORD: nevertheless the high
places were not taken away; *for* the people offered and burnt incense yet in
the high places.
44 And Jehoshaphat made peace with the king of Israel.
45 Now the rest of the acts of Jehoshaphat, and his might that he shewed,
and how he warred, *are* they not written in the book of the chronicles of the
kings of Judah?
46 And the remnant of the sodomites, which remained in the days of his
father Asa, he took out of the land.
47 *There was* then no king in Edom: a deputy *was* king.
48 Jehoshaphat made ships of Tharshish to go to Ophir for gold: but they
went not; for the ships were broken at Ezion-geber.
49 Then said Ahaziah the son of Ahab unto Jehoshaphat, Let my servants go
with thy servants in the ships. But Jehoshaphat would not.
50 And Jehoshaphat slept with his fathers, and was buried with his fathers
in the city of David his father: and Jehoram his son reigned in his stead.
51 Ahaziah the son of Ahab began to reign over Israel in Samaria the seven-
teenth year of Jehoshaphat king of Judah, and reigned two years over Israel.
52 And he did evil in the sight of the LORD, and walked in the way of his father,
and in the way of his mother, and in the way of Jeroboam the son of Nebat,
who made Israel to sin:
53 For he served Baal, and worshipped him, and provoked to anger the LORD
God of Israel, according to all that his father had done.

Elijah Pronounces God's Judgment on Evil King Ahaziah of Israel

1 Then Moab rebelled against Israel after the death of Ahab.
2 And Ahaziah fell down through a lattice in his upper chamber that *was*
in Samaria, and was sick: and he sent messengers, and said unto them, Go,
enquire of Baal-zebub the god of Ekron whether I shall recover of this disease.
3 But the angel of the LORD said to Elijah the Tishbite, Arise, go up to meet
the messengers of the king of Samaria, and say unto them, *Is it* not because
there is not a God in Israel, *that* ye go to enquire of Baal-zebub the god of
Ekron?
4 Now therefore thus saith the LORD, Thou shalt not come down from that
bed on which thou art gone up, but shalt surely die. And Elijah departed.
5 And when the messengers turned back unto him, he said unto them, Why
are ye now turned back?
6 And they said unto him, There came a man up to meet us, and said unto
us, Go, turn again unto the king that sent you, and say unto him, Thus saith
the LORD, *Is it* not because *there is* not a God in Israel, *that* thou sendest to
enquire of Baal-zebub the god of Ekron? therefore thou shalt not come down
from that bed on which thou art gone up, but shalt surely die.
7 And he said unto them, What manner of man *was he* which came up to
meet you, and told you these words?
8 And they answered him, *He was* an hairy man, and girt with a girdle of
leather about his loins. And he said, It *is* Elijah the Tishbite.
9 Then the king sent unto him a captain of fifty with his fifty. And he went
up to him: and, behold, he sat on the top of an hill. And he spake unto him,
Thou man of God, the king hath said, Come down.
10 And Elijah answered and said to the captain of fifty, If I *be* a man of God,
then let fire come down from heaven, and consume thee and thy fifty. And
there came down fire from heaven, and consumed him and his fifty.
11 Again also he sent unto him another captain of fifty with his fifty. And he
answered and said unto him, O man of God, thus hath the king said, Come
down quickly.
12 And Elijah answered and said unto them, If I *be* a man of God, let fire come
down from heaven, and consume thee and thy fifty. And the fire of God came
down from heaven, and consumed him and his fifty.
13 And he sent again a captain of the third fifty with his fifty. And the third
captain of fifty went up, and came and fell on his knees before Elijah, and
besought him, and said unto him, O man of God, I pray thee, let my life, and
the life of these fifty thy servants, be precious in thy sight.
14 Behold, there came fire down from heaven, and burnt up the two captains
of the former fifties with their fifties: therefore let my life now be precious in
thy sight.
15 And the angel of the LORD said unto Elijah, Go down with him: be not
afraid of him. And he arose, and went down with him unto the king.
16 And he said unto him, Thus saith the LORD, Forasmuch as thou hast sent
messengers to enquire of Baal-zebub the god of Ekron, *is it* not because *there
is* no God in Israel to enquire of his word? therefore thou shalt not come down
off that bed on which thou art gone up, but shalt surely die.

17 So he died according to the word of the LORD which Elijah had spoken.
And Jehoram reigned in his stead in the second year of Jehoram the son of
Jehoshaphat king of Judah; because he had no son.
18 Now the rest of the acts of Ahaziah which he did, *are* they not written in
the book of the chronicles of the kings of Israel?

Elisha Knows That Elijah Will Be Taken from Him

2 And it came to pass, when the LORD would take up Elijah into heaven by a
whirlwind, that Elijah went with Elisha from Gilgal.
2 And Elijah said unto Elisha, Tarry here, I pray thee; for the LORD hath sent
me to Bethel. And Elisha said *unto him, As* the LORD liveth, and *as* thy soul
liveth, I will not leave thee. So they went down to Bethel.
3 And the sons of the prophets that *were* at Bethel came forth to Elisha, and
said unto him, Knowest thou that the LORD will take away thy master from thy
head to day? And he said, Yea, I know *it*; hold ye your peace.
4 And Elijah said unto him, Elisha, tarry here, I pray thee; for the LORD hath
sent me to Jericho. And he said, *As* the LORD liveth, and *as* thy soul liveth, I will
not leave thee. So they came to Jericho.
5 And the sons of the prophets that *were* at Jericho came to Elisha, and said
unto him, Knowest thou that the LORD will take away thy master from thy head
to day? And he answered, Yea, I know *it*; hold ye your peace.
6 And Elijah said unto him, Tarry, I pray thee, here; for the LORD hath sent
me to Jordan. And he said, *As* the LORD liveth, and *as* thy soul liveth, I will not
leave thee. And they two went on.
7 And fifty men of the sons of the prophets went, and stood to view afar off:
and they two stood by Jordan.
8 And Elijah took his mantle, and wrapped *it* together, and smote the waters,
and they were divided hither and thither, so that they two went over on dry
ground.

Elijah Is Taken to Heaven in a Chariot of Fire

9 And it came to pass, when they were gone over, that Elijah said unto Elisha,
Ask what I shall do for thee, before I be taken away from thee. And Elisha said,
I pray thee, let a double portion of thy spirit be upon me.
10 And he said, Thou hast asked a hard thing: *nevertheless*, if thou see me *when
I am* taken from thee, it shall be so unto thee; but if not, it shall not be *so*.
11 And it came to pass, as they still went on, and talked, that, behold, *there
appeared* a chariot of fire, and horses of fire, and parted them both asunder;
and Elijah went up by a whirlwind into heaven.
12 And Elisha saw *it*, and he cried, My father, my father, the chariot of Israel,
and the horsemen thereof. And he saw him no more: and he took hold of his
own clothes, and rent them in two pieces.
13 He took up also the mantle of Elijah that fell from him, and went back,
and stood by the bank of Jordan;
14 And he took the mantle of Elijah that fell from him, and smote the waters,
and said, Where *is* the LORD God of Elijah? and when he also had smitten the
waters, they parted hither and thither: and Elisha went over.
15 And when the sons of the prophets which *were* to view at Jericho saw him,
they said, The spirit of Elijah doth rest on Elisha. And they came to meet him,
and bowed themselves to the ground before him.
16 And they said unto him, Behold now, there be with thy servants fifty strong
men; let them go, we pray thee, and seek thy master: lest peradventure the
Spirit of the LORD hath taken him up, and cast him upon some mountain, or
into some valley. And he said, Ye shall not send.
17 And when they urged him till he was ashamed, he said, Send. They sent
therefore fifty men; and they sought three days, but found him not.

18 And when they came again to him, (for he tarried at Jericho,) he said unto
them, Did I not say unto you, Go not?

Elisha Heals the Water, Is Jeered by Some Youths

19 And the men of the city said unto Elisha, Behold, I pray thee, the situation
of this city *is* pleasant, as my lord seeth: but the water *is* naught, and the ground
barren.
20 And he said, Bring me a new cruse, and put salt therein. And they brought
it to him.
21 And he went forth unto the spring of the waters, and cast the salt in there,
and said, Thus saith the LORD, I have healed these waters; there shall not be
from thence any more death or barren *land*.
22 So the waters were healed unto this day, according to the saying of Elisha
which he spake.
23 And he went up from thence unto Bethel: and as he was going up by the
way, there came forth little children out of the city, and mocked him, and said
unto him, Go up, thou bald head; go up, thou bald head.
24 And he turned back, and looked on them, and cursed them in the name
of the LORD. And there came forth two she bears out of the wood, and tare
forty and two children of them.
25 And he went from thence to mount Carmel, and from thence he returned
to Samaria.

Jehoram's Evil Reign over Israel

3 Now Jehoram the son of Ahab began to reign over Israel in Samaria the
eighteenth year of Jehoshaphat king of Judah, and reigned twelve years.
2 And he wrought evil in the sight of the LORD; but not like his father, and
like his mother: for he put away the image of Baal that his father had made.
3 Nevertheless he cleaved unto the sins of Jeroboam the son of Nebat, which
made Israel to sin; he departed not therefrom.
4 And Mesha king of Moab was a sheepmaster, and rendered unto the king
of Israel an hundred thousand lambs, and an hundred thousand rams, with
the wool.
5 But it came to pass, when Ahab was dead, that the king of Moab rebelled
against the king of Israel.

Jehoram of Israel and Jehoshaphat of Judah Defeat the Moabites

6 And king Jehoram went out of Samaria the same time, and numbered all
Israel.
7 And he went and sent to Jehoshaphat the king of Judah, saying, The king
of Moab hath rebelled against me: wilt thou go with me against Moab to bat-
tle? And he said, I will go up: I *am* as thou *art*, my people as thy people, *and*
my horses as thy horses.
8 And he said, Which way shall we go up? And he answered, The way through
the wilderness of Edom.
9 So the king of Israel went, and the king of Judah, and the king of Edom:
and they fetched a compass of seven days' journey: and there was no water for
the host, and for the cattle that followed them.
10 And the king of Israel said, Alas! that the LORD hath called these three
kings together, to deliver them into the hand of Moab!
11 But Jehoshaphat said, *Is there* not here a prophet of the LORD, that we may
enquire of the LORD by him? And one of the king of Israel's servants answered
and said, Here *is* Elisha the son of Shaphat, which poured water on the hands
of Elijah.
12 And Jehoshaphat said, The word of the LORD is with him. So the king of
Israel and Jehoshaphat and the king of Edom went down to him.
13 And Elisha said unto the king of Israel, What have I to do with thee? get
thee to the prophets of thy father, and to the prophets of thy mother. And the

king of Israel said unto him, Nay: for the LORD hath called these three kings
together, to deliver them into the hand of Moab.
14 And Elisha said, *As* the LORD of hosts liveth, before whom I stand, surely,
were it not that I regard the presence of Jehoshaphat the king of Judah, I would
not look toward thee, nor see thee.
15 But now bring me a minstrel. And it came to pass, when the minstrel
played, that the hand of the LORD came upon him.
16 And he said, Thus saith the LORD, Make this valley full of ditches.
17 For thus saith the LORD, Ye shall not see wind, neither shall ye see rain; yet
that valley shall be filled with water, that ye may drink, both ye, and your
cattle, and your beasts.
18 And this is *but* a light thing in the sight of the LORD: he will deliver the
Moabites also into your hand.
19 And ye shall smite every fenced city, and every choice city, and shall fell
every good tree, and stop all wells of water, and mar every good piece of land
with stones.
20 And it came to pass in the morning, when the meat offering was offered,
that, behold, there came water by the way of Edom, and the country was filled
with water.
21 And when all the Moabites heard that the kings were come up to fight
against them, they gathered all that were able to put on armour, and upward,
and stood in the border.
22 And they rose up early in the morning, and the sun shone upon the water,
and the Moabites saw the water on the other side *as* red as blood:
23 And they said, This *is* blood: the kings are surely slain, and they have smit-
ten one another: now therefore, Moab, to the spoil.
24 And when they came to the camp of Israel, the Israelites rose up and smote
the Moabites, so that they fled before them: but they went forward smiting
the Moabites, even in *their* country.
25 And they beat down the cities, and on every good piece of land cast every
man his stone, and filled it; and they stopped all the wells of water, and felled
all the good trees: only in Kir-haraseth left they the stones thereof; howbeit
the slingers went about *it*, and smote it.
26 And when the king of Moab saw that the battle was too sore for him, he
took with him seven hundred men that drew swords, to break through *even*
unto the king of Edom: but they could not.
27 Then he took his eldest son that should have reigned in his stead, and
offered him *for* a burnt offering upon the wall. And there was great indigna-
tion against Israel: and they departed from him, and returned to *their own*
land.

Elisha Multiplies the Widow's Oil

4 Now there cried a certain woman of the wives of the sons of the prophets
unto Elisha, saying, Thy servant my husband is dead; and thou knowest that
thy servant did fear the LORD: and the creditor is come to take unto him my two
sons to be bondmen.
2 And Elisha said unto her, What shall I do for thee? tell me, what hast thou
in the house? And she said, Thine handmaid hath not any thing in the house,
save a pot of oil.
3 Then he said, Go, borrow thee vessels abroad of all thy neighbours, *even*
empty vessels; borrow not a few.
4 And when thou art come in, thou shalt shut the door upon thee and upon
thy sons, and shalt pour out into all those vessels, and thou shalt set aside that
which is full.
5 So she went from him, and shut the door upon her and upon her sons, who
brought *the vessels* to her; and she poured out.

6 And it came to pass, when the vessels were full, that she said unto her son,
Bring me yet a vessel. And he said unto her, *There is* not a vessel more. And the
oil stayed.
7 Then she came and told the man of God. And he said, Go, sell the oil, and
pay thy debt, and live thou and thy children of the rest.

Elisha Promises a Son to a Shunammite Woman

8 And it fell on a day, that Elisha passed to Shunem, where *was* a great woman;
and she constrained him to eat bread. And *so* it was, *that* as oft as he passed
by, he turned in thither to eat bread.
9 And she said unto her husband, Behold now, I perceive that this *is* an holy
man of God, which passeth by us continually.
10 Let us make a little chamber, I pray thee, on the wall; and let us set for him
there a bed, and a table, and a stool, and a candlestick: and it shall be, when
he cometh to us, that he shall turn in thither.
11 And it fell on a day, that he came thither, and he turned into the chamber,
and lay there.
12 And he said to Gehazi his servant, Call this Shunammite. And when he
had called her, she stood before him.
13 And he said unto him, Say now unto her, Behold, thou hast been careful
for us with all this care; what *is* to be done for thee? wouldest thou be spoken
for to the king, or to the captain of the host? And she answered, I dwell among
mine own people.
14 And he said, What then *is* to be done for her? And Gehazi answered, Verily
she hath no child, and her husband is old.
15 And he said, Call her. And when he had called her, she stood in the door.
16 And he said, About this season, according to the time of life, thou shalt
embrace a son. And she said, Nay, my lord, *thou* man of God, do not lie unto
thine handmaid.
17 And the woman conceived, and bare a son at that season that Elisha had
said unto her, according to the time of life.

Elisha Raises the Woman's Son from the Dead

18 And when the child was grown, it fell on a day, that he went out to his
father to the reapers.
19 And he said unto his father, My head, my head. And he said to a lad, Carry
him to his mother.
20 And when he had taken him, and brought him to his mother, he sat on
her knees till noon, and *then* died.
21 And she went up, and laid him on the bed of the man of God, and shut *the
door* upon him, and went out.
22 And she called unto her husband, and said, Send me, I pray thee, one of
the young men, and one of the asses, that I may run to the man of God, and
come again.
23 And he said, Wherefore wilt thou go to him to day? *it is* neither new moon,
nor sabbath. And she said, *It shall be* well.
24 Then she saddled an ass, and said to her servant, Drive, and go forward;
slack not *thy* riding for me, except I bid thee.
25 So she went and came unto the man of God to mount Carmel. And it came
to pass, when the man of God saw her afar off, that he said to Gehazi his serv-
ant, Behold, *yonder is* that Shunammite:
26 Run now, I pray thee, to meet her, and say unto her, *Is it* well with thee?
is it well with thy husband? *is it* well with the child? And she answered, *It is*
well.
27 And when she came to the man of God to the hill, she caught him by the
feet: but Gehazi came near to thrust her away. And the man of God said, Let

her alone; for her soul *is* vexed within her: and the LORD hath hid *it* from me,
and hath not told me.
28 Then she said, Did I desire a son of my lord? did I not say, Do not
deceive me?
29 Then he said to Gehazi, Gird up thy loins, and take my staff in thine hand,
and go thy way: if thou meet any man, salute him not; and if any salute thee,
answer him not again: and lay my staff upon the face of the child.
30 And the mother of the child said, *As* the LORD liveth, and *as* thy soul liveth,
I will not leave thee. And he arose, and followed her.
31 And Gehazi passed on before them, and laid the staff upon the face of the
child; but *there was* neither voice, nor hearing. Wherefore he went again to
meet him, and told him, saying, The child is not awaked.
32 And when Elisha was come into the house, behold, the child was dead,
and laid upon his bed.
33 He went in therefore, and shut the door upon them twain, and prayed
unto the LORD.
34 And he went up, and lay upon the child, and put his mouth upon his
mouth, and his eyes upon his eyes, and his hands upon his hands: and he
stretched himself upon the child; and the flesh of the child waxed warm.
35 Then he returned, and walked in the house to and fro; and went up, and
stretched himself upon him: and the child sneezed seven times, and the child
opened his eyes.
36 And he called Gehazi, and said, Call this Shunammite. So he called her.
And when she was come in unto him, he said, Take up thy son.
37 Then she went in, and fell at his feet, and bowed herself to the ground,
and took up her son, and went out.

Elisha Heals Poisoned Stew and Multiplies Bread

38 And Elisha came again to Gilgal: and *there was* a dearth in the land; and
the sons of the prophets *were* sitting before him: and he said unto his servant,
Set on the great pot, and seethe pottage for the sons of the prophets.
39 And one went out into the field to gather herbs, and found a wild vine,
and gathered thereof wild gourds his lap full, and came and shred *them* into
the pot of pottage: for they knew *them* not.
40 So they poured out for the men to eat. And it came to pass, as they were
eating of the pottage, that they cried out, and said, O *thou* man of God, *there*
is death in the pot. And they could not eat *thereof*.
41 But he said, Then bring meal. And he cast *it* into the pot; and he said, Pour
out for the people, that they may eat. And there was no harm in the pot.
42 And there came a man from Baal-shalisha, and brought the man of God
bread of the firstfruits, twenty loaves of barley, and full ears of corn in the
husk thereof. And he said, Give unto the people, that they may eat.
43 And his servitor said, What, should I set this before an hundred men? He
said again, Give the people, that they may eat: for thus saith the LORD, They
shall eat, and shall leave *thereof*.
44 So he set *it* before them, and they did eat, and left *thereof*, according to
the word of the LORD.

Naaman Goes to Samaria to Be Cured of His Leprosy

5 Now Naaman, captain of the host of the king of Syria, was a great man with
his master, and honourable, because by him the LORD had given deliverance
unto Syria: he was also a mighty man in valour, *but he was* a leper.
2 And the Syrians had gone out by companies, and had brought away captive
out of the land of Israel a little maid; and she waited on Naaman's wife.
3 And she said unto her mistress, Would God my lord *were* with the proph-
et that *is* in Samaria! for he would recover him of his leprosy.

4 And *one* went in, and told his lord, saying, Thus and thus said the maid that *is* of the land of Israel.

5 And the king of Syria said, Go to, go, and I will send a letter unto the king of Israel. And he departed, and took with him ten talents of silver, and six thousand *pieces* of gold, and ten changes of raiment.

6 And he brought the letter to the king of Israel, saying, Now when this letter is come unto thee, behold, I have *therewith* sent Naaman my servant to thee, that thou mayest recover him of his leprosy.

7 And it came to pass, when the king of Israel had read the letter, that he rent his clothes, and said, *Am* I God, to kill and to make alive, that this man doth send unto me to recover a man of his leprosy? wherefore consider, I pray you, and see how he seeketh a quarrel against me.

8 And it was *so*, when Elisha the man of God had heard that the king of Israel had rent his clothes, that he sent to the king, saying, Wherefore hast thou rent thy clothes? let him come now to me, and he shall know that there is a prophet in Israel.

9 So Naaman came with his horses and with his chariot, and stood at the door of the house of Elisha.

10 And Elisha sent a messenger unto him, saying, Go and wash in Jordan seven times, and thy flesh shall come again to thee, and thou shalt be clean.

11 But Naaman was wroth, and went away, and said, Behold, I thought, He will surely come out to me, and stand, and call on the name of the LORD his God, and strike his hand over the place, and recover the leper.

12 *Are* not Abana and Pharpar, rivers of Damascus, better than all the waters of Israel? may I not wash in them, and be clean? So he turned and went away in a rage.

13 And his servants came near, and spake unto him, and said, My father, *if* the prophet had bid thee *do some* great thing, wouldest thou not have done *it*? how much rather then, when he saith to thee, Wash, and be clean?

14 Then went he down, and dipped himself seven times in Jordan, according to the saying of the man of God: and his flesh came again like unto the flesh of a little child, and he was clean.

Elisha Declines Naaman's Gifts

15 And he returned to the man of God, he and all his company, and came, and stood before him: and he said, Behold, now I know that *there is* no God in all the earth, but in Israel: now therefore, I pray thee, take a blessing of thy servant.

16 But he said, *As* the LORD liveth, before whom I stand, I will receive none. And he urged him to take *it*; but he refused.

17 And Naaman said, Shall there not then, I pray thee, be given to thy servant two mules' burden of earth? for thy servant will henceforth offer neither burnt offering nor sacrifice unto other gods, but unto the LORD.

18 In this thing the LORD pardon thy servant, *that* when my master goeth into the house of Rimmon to worship there, and he leaneth on my hand, and I bow myself in the house of Rimmon: when I bow down myself in the house of Rimmon, the LORD pardon thy servant in this thing.

19 And he said unto him, Go in peace. So he departed from him a little way.

Gehazi, Lying to Naaman in Elisha's Name, Is Smitten with Leprosy

20 But Gehazi, the servant of Elisha the man of God, said, Behold, my master hath spared Naaman this Syrian, in not receiving at his hands that which he brought: but, *as* the LORD liveth, I will run after him, and take somewhat of him.

21 So Gehazi followed after Naaman. And when Naaman saw *him* running after him, he lighted down from the chariot to meet him, and said, *Is* all well?

22 And he said, All *is* well. My master hath sent me, saying, Behold, even now
there be come to me from mount Ephraim two young men of the sons of the
prophets: give them, I pray thee, a talent of silver, and two changes of garments.
23 And Naaman said, Be content, take two talents. And he urged him, and
bound two talents of silver in two bags, with two changes of garments, and
laid *them* upon two of his servants; and they bare *them* before him.
24 And when he came to the tower, he took *them* from their hand, and
bestowed *them* in the house: and he let the men go, and they departed.
25 But he went in, and stood before his master. And Elisha said unto him,
Whence *comest thou*, Gehazi? And he said, Thy servant went no whither.
26 And he said unto him, Went not mine heart *with thee*, when the man
turned again from his chariot to meet thee? *Is it* a time to receive money, and
to receive garments, and oliveyards, and vineyards, and sheep, and oxen, and
menservants, and maidservants?
27 The leprosy therefore of Naaman shall cleave unto thee, and unto thy seed
for ever. And he went out from his presence a leper *as white* as snow.

Elisha Makes an Axe Head Float

6 And the sons of the prophets said unto Elisha, Behold now, the place where
we dwell with thee is too strait for us.
2 Let us go, we pray thee, unto Jordan, and take thence every man a beam, and
let us make us a place there, where we may dwell. And he answered, Go ye.
3 And one said, Be content, I pray thee, and go with thy servants. And he
answered, I will go.
4 So he went with them. And when they came to Jordan, they cut down wood.
5 But as one was felling a beam, the axe head fell into the water: and he cried,
and said, Alas, master! for it was borrowed.
6 And the man of God said, Where fell it? And he shewed him the place. And
he cut down a stick, and cast *it* in thither; and the iron did swim.
7 Therefore said he, Take *it* up to thee. And he put out his hand, and took it.

Elisha Discloses Syria's Plans to the King of Israel

8 Then the king of Syria warred against Israel, and took counsel with his
servants, saying, In such and such a place *shall be* my camp.
9 And the man of God sent unto the king of Israel, saying, Beware that thou
pass not such a place; for thither the Syrians are come down.
10 And the king of Israel sent to the place which the man of God told him
and warned him of, and saved himself there, not once nor twice.
11 Therefore the heart of the king of Syria was sore troubled for this thing;
and he called his servants, and said unto them, Will ye not shew me which of
us *is* for the king of Israel?
12 And one of his servants said, None, my lord, O king: but Elisha, the proph-
et that *is* in Israel, telleth the king of Israel the words that thou speakest in thy
bedchamber.

The Syrian Army Goes to Dothan to Seize Elisha, but Is Blinded

13 And he said, Go and spy where he *is*, that I may send and fetch him. And
it was told him, saying, Behold, *he is* in Dothan.
14 Therefore sent he thither horses, and chariots, and a great host: and they
came by night, and compassed the city about.
15 And when the servant of the man of God was risen early, and gone forth,
behold, an host compassed the city both with horses and chariots. And his
servant said unto him, Alas, my master! how shall we do?
16 And he answered, Fear not: for they that *be* with us *are* more than they
that *be* with them.
17 And Elisha prayed, and said, LORD, I pray thee, open his eyes, that he may
see. And the LORD opened the eyes of the young man; and he saw: and, behold,
the mountain *was* full of horses and chariots of fire round about Elisha.

18 And when they came down to him, Elisha prayed unto the LORD, and said,
Smite this people, I pray thee, with blindness. And he smote them with blind-
ness according to the word of Elisha.
19 And Elisha said unto them, This *is* not the way, neither *is* this the city:
follow me, and I will bring you to the man whom ye seek. But he led them to
Samaria.
20 And it came to pass, when they were come into Samaria, that Elisha said,
LORD, open the eyes of these *men*, that they may see. And the LORD opened
their eyes, and they saw; and, behold, *they were* in the midst of Samaria.
21 And the king of Israel said unto Elisha, when he saw them, My father, shall
I smite *them*? shall I smite *them*?
22 And he answered, Thou shalt not smite *them*: wouldest thou smite those
whom thou hast taken captive with thy sword and with thy bow? set bread
and water before them, that they may eat and drink, and go to their master.
23 And he prepared great provision for them: and when they had eaten and
drunk, he sent them away, and they went to their master. So the bands of Syria
came no more into the land of Israel.

The Severity of the Famine in Besieged Samaria

24 And it came to pass after this, that Ben-hadad king of Syria gathered all
his host, and went up, and besieged Samaria.
25 And there was a great famine in Samaria: and, behold, they besieged it,
until an ass's head was *sold* for fourscore *pieces* of silver, and the fourth part
of a cab of dove's dung for five *pieces* of silver.
26 And as the king of Israel was passing by upon the wall, there cried a woman
unto him, saying, Help, my lord, O king.
27 And he said, If the LORD do not help thee, whence shall I help thee? out of
the barnfloor, or out of the winepress?
28 And the king said unto her, What aileth thee? And she answered, This
woman said unto me, Give thy son, that we may eat him to day, and we will eat
my son to morrow.
29 So we boiled my son, and did eat him: and I said unto her on the next day,
Give thy son, that we may eat him: and she hath hid her son.
30 And it came to pass, when the king heard the words of the woman, that
he rent his clothes; and he passed by upon the wall, and the people looked,
and, behold, *he had* sackcloth within upon his flesh.
31 Then he said, God do so and more also to me, if the head of Elisha the son
of Shaphat shall stand on him this day.
32 But Elisha sat in his house, and the elders sat with him; and *the king* sent
a man from before him: but ere the messenger came to him, he said to the
elders, See ye how this son of a murderer hath sent to take away mine head?
look, when the messenger cometh, shut the door, and hold him fast at the
door: *is* not the sound of his master's feet behind him?
33 And while he yet talked with them, behold, the messenger came down
unto him: and he said, Behold, this evil *is* of the LORD; what should I wait for
the LORD any longer?

Elisha Prophesies the End of the Famine in Samaria

7 Then Elisha said, Hear ye the word of the LORD; Thus saith the LORD, To
morrow about this time *shall* a measure of fine flour *be sold* for a shekel,
and two measures of barley for a shekel, in the gate of Samaria.
2 Then a lord on whose hand the king leaned answered the man of God, and
said, Behold, *if* the LORD would make windows in heaven, might this thing be?
And he said, Behold, thou shalt see *it* with thine eyes, but shalt not eat thereof.

Four Lepers Discover That the Syrian Army Has Fled

3 And there were four leprous men at the entering in of the gate: and they
said one to another, Why sit we here until we die?

4 If we say, We will enter into the city, then the famine *is* in the city, and we
shall die there: and if we sit still here, we die also. Now therefore come, and
let us fall unto the host of the Syrians: if they save us alive, we shall live; and if
they kill us, we shall but die.
5 And they rose up in the twilight, to go unto the camp of the Syrians: and
when they were come to the uttermost part of the camp of Syria, behold, *there*
was no man there.
6 For the Lord had made the host of the Syrians to hear a noise of chariots,
and a noise of horses, *even* the noise of a great host: and they said one to
another, Lo, the king of Israel hath hired against us the kings of the Hittites,
and the kings of the Egyptians, to come upon us.
7 Wherefore they arose and fled in the twilight, and left their tents, and their
horses, and their asses, even the camp as it *was*, and fled for their life.
8 And when these lepers came to the uttermost part of the camp, they went
into one tent, and did eat and drink, and carried thence silver, and gold, and
raiment, and went and hid *it*; and came again, and entered into another tent,
and carried thence *also*, and went and hid *it*.
9 Then they said one to another, We do not well: this day *is* a day of good
tidings, and we hold our peace: if we tarry till the morning light, some mischief
will come upon us: now therefore come, that we may go and tell the king's
household.
10 So they came and called unto the porter of the city: and they told them,
saying, We came to the camp of the Syrians, and, behold, *there was* no man
there, neither voice of man, but horses tied, and asses tied, and the tents as
they *were*.
11 And he called the porters; and they told *it* to the king's house within.

The King and the People Collect the Plunder

12 And the king arose in the night, and said unto his servants, I will now shew
you what the Syrians have done to us. They know that we *be* hungry; therefore
are they gone out of the camp to hide themselves in the field, saying, When
they come out of the city, we shall catch them alive, and get into the city.
13 And one of his servants answered and said, Let *some* take, I pray thee, five
of the horses that remain, which are left in the city, (behold, they *are* as all the
multitude of Israel that are left in it: behold, *I say*, they *are* even as all the
multitude of the Israelites that are consumed:) and let us send and see.
14 They took therefore two chariot horses; and the king sent after the host
of the Syrians, saying, Go and see.
15 And they went after them unto Jordan: and, lo, all the way *was* full of
garments and vessels, which the Syrians had cast away in their haste. And the
messengers returned, and told the king.
16 And the people went out, and spoiled the tents of the Syrians. So a measure
of fine flour was *sold* for a shekel, and two measures of barley for a shekel,
according to the word of the LORD.
17 And the king appointed the lord on whose hand he leaned to have the
charge of the gate: and the people trode upon him in the gate, and he died, as
the man of God had said, who spake when the king came down to him.
18 And it came to pass as the man of God had spoken to the king, saying, Two
measures of barley for a shekel, and a measure of fine flour for a shekel, shall
be to morrow about this time in the gate of Samaria:
19 And that lord answered the man of God, and said, Now, behold, *if* the LORD
should make windows in heaven, might such a thing be? And he said, Behold,
thou shalt see it with thine eyes, but shalt not eat thereof.
20 And so it fell out unto him: for the people trode upon him in the gate, and
he died.

The King Restores the Shunammite's Land

8 Then spake Elisha unto the woman, whose son he had restored to life, say-
ing, Arise, and go thou and thine household, and sojourn wheresoever thou
canst sojourn: for the LORD hath called for a famine; and it shall also come upon
the land seven years.
2 And the woman arose, and did after the saying of the man of God: and she
went with her household, and sojourned in the land of the Philistines seven
years.
3 And it came to pass at the seven years' end, that the woman returned out
of the land of the Philistines: and she went forth to cry unto the king for her
house and for her land.
4 And the king talked with Gehazi the servant of the man of God, saying, Tell
me, I pray thee, all the great things that Elisha hath done.
5 And it came to pass, as he was telling the king how he had restored a dead
body to life, that, behold, the woman, whose son he had restored to life, cried
to the king for her house and for her land. And Gehazi said, My lord, O king,
this *is* the woman, and this *is* her son, whom Elisha restored to life.
6 And when the king asked the woman, she told him. So the king appointed
unto her a certain officer, saying, Restore all that *was* hers, and all the fruits
of the field since the day that she left the land, even until now.

Hazael Murders Ben-hadad and Becomes King of Syria

7 And Elisha came to Damascus; and Ben-hadad the king of Syria was sick;
and it was told him, saying, The man of God is come hither.
8 And the king said unto Hazael, Take a present in thine hand, and go, meet
the man of God, and enquire of the LORD by him, saying, Shall I recover of this
disease?
9 So Hazael went to meet him, and took a present with him, even of every
good thing of Damascus, forty camels' burden, and came and stood before
him, and said, Thy son Ben-hadad king of Syria hath sent me to thee, saying,
Shall I recover of this disease?
10 And Elisha said unto him, Go, say unto him, Thou mayest certainly recov-
er: howbeit the LORD hath shewed me that he shall surely die.
11 And he settled his countenance stedfastly, until he was ashamed: and the
man of God wept.
12 And Hazael said, Why weepeth my lord? And he answered, Because I know
the evil that thou wilt do unto the children of Israel: their strong holds wilt
thou set on fire, and their young men wilt thou slay with the sword, and wilt
dash their children, and rip up their women with child.
13 And Hazael said, But what, *is* thy servant a dog, that he should do this great
thing? And Elisha answered, The LORD hath shewed me that thou *shalt be* king
over Syria.
14 So he departed from Elisha, and came to his master; who said to him, What
said Elisha to thee? And he answered, He told me *that* thou shouldest surely
recover.
15 And it came to pass on the morrow, that he took a thick cloth, and dipped
it in water, and spread *it* on his face, so that he died: and Hazael reigned in his
stead.

Jehoram's Evil Reign in Judah

16 And in the fifth year of Joram the son of Ahab king of Israel, Jehoshaphat
being then king of Judah, Jehoram the son of Jehoshaphat king of Judah began
to reign.
17 Thirty and two years old was he when he began to reign; and he reigned
eight years in Jerusalem.
18 And he walked in the way of the kings of Israel, as did the house of Ahab:
for the daughter of Ahab was his wife: and he did evil in the sight of the LORD.

19 Yet the LORD would not destroy Judah for David his servant's sake, as he promised him to give him alway a light, *and* to his children.
20 In his days Edom revolted from under the hand of Judah, and made a king over themselves.
21 So Joram went over to Zair, and all the chariots with him: and he rose by night, and smote the Edomites which compassed him about, and the captains of the chariots: and the people fled into their tents.
22 Yet Edom revolted from under the hand of Judah unto this day. Then Libnah revolted at the same time.
23 And the rest of the acts of Joram, and all that he did, *are* they not written in the book of the chronicles of the kings of Judah?
24 And Joram slept with his fathers, and was buried with his fathers in the city of David: and Ahaziah his son reigned in his stead.

Ahaziah's Evil Reign in Judah

25 In the twelfth year of Joram the son of Ahab king of Israel did Ahaziah the son of Jehoram king of Judah begin to reign.
26 Two and twenty years old *was* Ahaziah when he began to reign; and he reigned one year in Jerusalem. And his mother's name *was* Athaliah, the daughter of Omri king of Israel.
27 And he walked in the way of the house of Ahab, and did evil in the sight of the LORD, as *did* the house of Ahab: for he *was* the son in law of the house of Ahab.
28 And he went with Joram the son of Ahab to the war against Hazael king of Syria in Ramoth-gilead; and the Syrians wounded Joram.
29 And king Joram went back to be healed in Jezreel of the wounds which the Syrians had given him at Ramah, when he fought against Hazael king of Syria. And Ahaziah the son of Jehoram king of Judah went down to see Joram the son of Ahab in Jezreel, because he was sick.

Elisha Sends a Prophet to Anoint Jehu King of Israel

9 And Elisha the prophet called one of the children of the prophets, and said unto him, Gird up thy loins, and take this box of oil in thine hand, and go to Ramoth-gilead:
2 And when thou comest thither, look out there Jehu the son of Jehoshaphat the son of Nimshi, and go in, and make him arise up from among his brethren, and carry him to an inner chamber;
3 Then take the box of oil, and pour *it* on his head, and say, Thus saith the LORD, I have anointed thee king over Israel. Then open the door, and flee, and tarry not.
4 So the young man, *even* the young man the prophet, went to Ramoth-gilead.
5 And when he came, behold, the captains of the host *were* sitting; and he said, I have an errand to thee, O captain. And Jehu said, Unto which of all us? And he said, To thee, O captain.
6 And he arose, and went into the house; and he poured the oil on his head, and said unto him, Thus saith the LORD God of Israel, I have anointed thee king over the people of the LORD, *even* over Israel.
7 And thou shalt smite the house of Ahab thy master, that I may avenge the blood of my servants the prophets, and the blood of all the servants of the LORD, at the hand of Jezebel.
8 For the whole house of Ahab shall perish: and I will cut off from Ahab him that pisseth against the wall, and him that is shut up and left in Israel:
9 And I will make the house of Ahab like the house of Jeroboam the son of Nebat, and like the house of Baasha the son of Ahijah:
10 And the dogs shall eat Jezebel in the portion of Jezreel, and *there shall be* none to bury *her*. And he opened the door, and fled.

Jehu Kills Joram (Jehoram) of Israel and Ahaziah of Judah

11 Then Jehu came forth to the servants of his lord: and *one* said unto him,
Is all well? wherefore came this mad *fellow* to thee? And he said unto them,
Ye know the man, and his communication.
12 And they said, *It is* false; tell us now. And he said, Thus and thus spake he
to me, saying, Thus saith the LORD, I have anointed thee king over Israel.
13 Then they hasted, and took every man his garment, and put *it* under him
on the top of the stairs, and blew with trumpets, saying, Jehu is king.
14 So Jehu the son of Jehoshaphat the son of Nimshi conspired against Joram.
(Now Joram had kept Ramoth-gilead, he and all Israel, because of Hazael king
of Syria.
15 But king Joram was returned to be healed in Jezreel of the wounds which
the Syrians had given him, when he fought with Hazael king of Syria.) And
Jehu said, If it be your minds, *then* let none go forth *nor* escape out of the city
to go to tell *it* in Jezreel.
16 So Jehu rode in a chariot, and went to Jezreel; for Joram lay there. And
Ahaziah king of Judah was come down to see Joram.
17 And there stood a watchman on the tower in Jezreel, and he spied the
company of Jehu as he came, and said, I see a company. And Joram said, Take
an horseman, and send to meet them, and let him say, *Is it* peace?
18 So there went one on horseback to meet him, and said, Thus saith the king,
Is it peace? And Jehu said, What hast thou to do with peace? turn thee behind
me. And the watchman told, saying, The messenger came to them, but he
cometh not again.
19 Then he sent out a second on horseback, which came to them, and said,
Thus saith the king, *Is it* peace? And Jehu answered, What hast thou to do with
peace? turn thee behind me.
20 And the watchman told, saying, He came even unto them, and cometh
not again: and the driving *is* like the driving of Jehu the son of Nimshi; for he
driveth furiously.
21 And Joram said, Make ready. And his chariot was made ready. And Joram
king of Israel and Ahaziah king of Judah went out, each in his chariot, and
they went out against Jehu, and met him in the portion of Naboth the
Jezreelite.
22 And it came to pass, when Joram saw Jehu, that he said, *Is it* peace, Jehu?
And he answered, What peace, so long as the whoredoms of thy mother Jezebel
and her witchcrafts *are so* many?
23 And Joram turned his hands, and fled, and said to Ahaziah, *There is* treach-
ery, O Ahaziah.
24 And Jehu drew a bow with his full strength, and smote Jehoram between
his arms, and the arrow went out at his heart, and he sunk down in his chariot.
25 Then said *Jehu* to Bidkar his captain, Take up, *and* cast him in the portion
of the field of Naboth the Jezreelite: for remember how that, when I and thou
rode together after Ahab his father, the LORD laid this burden upon him;
26 Surely I have seen yesterday the blood of Naboth, and the blood of his
sons, saith the LORD; and I will requite thee in this plat, saith the LORD. Now
therefore take *and* cast him into the plat *of ground*, according to the word of
the LORD.
27 But when Ahaziah the king of Judah saw *this*, he fled by the way of the
garden house. And Jehu followed after him, and said, Smite him also in the
chariot. *And they did so* at the going up to Gur, which *is* by Ibleam. And he fled
to Megiddo, and died there.
28 And his servants carried him in a chariot to Jerusalem, and buried him
in his sepulchre with his fathers in the city of David.
29 And in the eleventh year of Joram the son of Ahab began Ahaziah to reign
over Judah.

Jezebel Dies Just as Elijah Had Predicted

30 And when Jehu was come to Jezreel, Jezebel heard *of it*; and she painted
her face, and tired her head, and looked out at a window.
31 And as Jehu entered in at the gate, she said, *Had* Zimri peace, who slew
his master?
32 And he lifted up his face to the window, and said, Who *is* on my side? who?
And there looked out to him two *or* three eunuchs.
33 And he said, Throw her down. So they threw her down: and *some* of her
blood was sprinkled on the wall, and on the horses: and he trode her under
foot.
34 And when he was come in, he did eat and drink, and said, Go, see now this
cursed *woman*, and bury her: for she *is* a king's daughter.
35 And they went to bury her: but they found no more of her than the skull,
and the feet, and the palms of *her* hands.
36 Wherefore they came again, and told him. And he said, This *is* the word
of the LORD, which he spake by his servant Elijah the Tishbite, saying, In the
portion of Jezreel shall dogs eat the flesh of Jezebel:
37 And the carcase of Jezebel shall be as dung upon the face of the field in
the portion of Jezreel; *so* that they shall not say, This *is* Jezebel.

Jehu Destroys Ahab's Family

10 And Ahab had seventy sons in Samaria. And Jehu wrote letters, and
sent to Samaria, unto the rulers of Jezreel, to the elders, and to them
that brought up Ahab's *children*, saying,
2 Now as soon as this letter cometh to you, seeing your master's sons *are* with
you, and *there are* with you chariots and horses, a fenced city also, and armour;
3 Look even out the best and meetest of your master's sons, and set *him* on
his father's throne, and fight for your master's house.
4 But they were exceedingly afraid, and said, Behold, two kings stood not
before him: how then shall we stand?
5 And he that *was* over the house, and he that *was* over the city, the elders
also, and the bringers up *of the children*, sent to Jehu, saying, We *are* thy ser-
vants, and will do all that thou shalt bid us; we will not make any king: do thou
that which is good in thine eyes.
6 Then he wrote a letter the second time to them, saying, If ye *be* mine, and
if ye will hearken unto my voice, take ye the heads of the men your master's
sons, and come to me to Jezreel by to morrow this time. Now the king's sons,
being seventy persons, *were* with the great men of the city, which brought
them up.
7 And it came to pass, when the letter came to them, that they took the king's
sons, and slew seventy persons, and put their heads in baskets, and sent him
them to Jezreel.
8 And there came a messenger, and told him, saying, They have brought the
heads of the king's sons. And he said, Lay ye them in two heaps at the entering
in of the gate until the morning.
9 And it came to pass in the morning, that he went out, and stood, and said
to all the people, Ye *be* righteous: behold, I conspired against my master, and
slew him: but who slew all these?
10 Know now that there shall fall unto the earth nothing of the word of the
LORD, which the LORD spake concerning the house of Ahab: for the LORD hath
done *that* which he spake by his servant Elijah.
11 So Jehu slew all that remained of the house of Ahab in Jezreel, and all his
great men, and his kinsfolks, and his priests, until he left him none remaining.
12 And he arose and departed, and came to Samaria. *And* as he *was* at the
shearing house in the way,

13 Jehu met with the brethren of Ahaziah king of Judah, and said, Who *are*
ye? And they answered, We *are* the brethren of Ahaziah; and we go down to
salute the children of the king and the children of the queen.
14 And he said, Take them alive. And they took them alive, and slew them at
the pit of the shearing house, *even* two and forty men; neither left he any of
them.

Jehu Destroys the Worshippers of Baal

15 And when he was departed thence, he lighted on Jehonadab the son of
Rechab *coming* to meet him: and he saluted him, and said to him, Is thine
heart right, as my heart *is* with thy heart? And Jehonadab answered, It is. If it
be, give *me* thine hand. And he gave *him* his hand; and he took him up to him
into the chariot.
16 And he said, Come with me, and see my zeal for the LORD. So they made
him ride in his chariot.
17 And when he came to Samaria, he slew all that remained unto Ahab in
Samaria, till he had destroyed him, according to the saying of the LORD, which
he spake to Elijah.
18 And Jehu gathered all the people together, and said unto them, Ahab
served Baal a little; *but* Jehu shall serve him much.
19 Now therefore call unto me all the prophets of Baal, all his servants, and
all his priests; let none be wanting: for I have a great sacrifice *to do* to Baal;
whosoever shall be wanting, he shall not live. But Jehu did *it* in subtilty, to the
intent that he might destroy the worshippers of Baal.
20 And Jehu said, Proclaim a solemn assembly for Baal. And they proclaimed *it*.
21 And Jehu sent through all Israel: and all the worshippers of Baal came, so
that there was not a man left that came not. And they came into the house of
Baal; and the house of Baal was full from one end to another.
22 And he said unto him that *was* over the vestry, Bring forth vestments for
all the worshippers of Baal. And he brought them forth vestments.
23 And Jehu went, and Jehonadab the son of Rechab, into the house of Baal,
and said unto the worshippers of Baal, Search, and look that there be here
with you none of the servants of the LORD, but the worshippers of Baal only.
24 And when they went in to offer sacrifices and burnt offerings, Jehu
appointed fourscore men without, and said, *If* any of the men whom I have
brought into your hands escape, *he that letteth him go*, his life *shall be* for the
life of him.
25 And it came to pass, as soon as he had made an end of offering the burnt
offering, that Jehu said to the guard and to the captains, Go in, *and* slay them;
let none come forth. And they smote them with the edge of the sword; and the
guard and the captains cast *them* out, and went to the city of the house of Baal.
26 And they brought forth the images out of the house of Baal, and burned
them.
27 And they brake down the image of Baal, and brake down the house of Baal,
and made it a draught house unto this day.
28 Thus Jehu destroyed Baal out of Israel.

Jehu Reigns in Israel, but Follows in Jeroboam's Sinful Path

29 Howbeit *from* the sins of Jeroboam the son of Nebat, who made Israel to
sin, Jehu departed not from after them, *to wit*, the golden calves that *were* in
Bethel, and that *were* in Dan.
30 And the LORD said unto Jehu, Because thou hast done well in executing
that which is right in mine eyes, *and* hast done unto the house of Ahab accord-
ing to all that *was* in mine heart, thy children of the fourth *generation* shall
sit on the throne of Israel.

31 But Jehu took no heed to walk in the law of the LORD God of Israel with
all his heart: for he departed not from the sins of Jeroboam, which made Israel
to sin.
32 In those days the LORD began to cut Israel short: and Hazael smote them
in all the coasts of Israel;
33 From Jordan eastward, all the land of Gilead, the Gadites, and the
Reubenites, and the Manassites, from Aroer, which *is* by the river Arnon, even
Gilead and Bashan.
34 Now the rest of the acts of Jehu, and all that he did, and all his might, *are*
they not written in the book of the chronicles of the kings of Israel?
35 And Jehu slept with his fathers: and they buried him in Samaria. And
Jehoahaz his son reigned in his stead.
36 And the time that Jehu reigned over Israel in Samaria *was* twenty and
eight years.

In Judah, Young Joash Is Saved from Queen Athaliah's Murderous Rage

11 And when Athaliah the mother of Ahaziah saw that her son was dead,
she arose and destroyed all the seed royal.
2 But Jehosheba, the daughter of king Joram, sister of Ahaziah, took Joash
the son of Ahaziah, and stole him from among the king's sons *which were* slain;
and they hid him, *even* him and his nurse, in the bedchamber from Athaliah,
so that he was not slain.
3 And he was with her hid in the house of the LORD six years. And Athaliah
did reign over the land.

Jehoiada Anoints Young Joash King over Judah

4 And the seventh year Jehoiada sent and fetched the rulers over hundreds,
with the captains and the guard, and brought them to him into the house of
the LORD, and made a covenant with them, and took an oath of them in the
house of the LORD, and shewed them the king's son.
5 And he commanded them, saying, This *is* the thing that ye shall do; A third
part of you that enter in on the sabbath shall even be keepers of the watch of
the king's house;
6 And a third part *shall be* at the gate of Sur; and a third part at the gate
behind the guard: so shall ye keep the watch of the house, that it be not broken
down.
7 And two parts of all you that go forth on the sabbath, even they shall keep
the watch of the house of the LORD about the king.
8 And ye shall compass the king round about, every man with his weapons
in his hand: and he that cometh within the ranges, let him be slain: and be ye
with the king as he goeth out and as he cometh in.
9 And the captains over the hundreds did according to all *things* that
Jehoiada the priest commanded: and they took every man his men that were
to come in on the sabbath, with them that should go out on the sabbath, and
came to Jehoiada the priest.
10 And to the captains over hundreds did the priest give king David's spears
and shields, that *were* in the temple of the LORD.
11 And the guard stood, every man with his weapons in his hand, round
about the king, from the right corner of the temple to the left corner of the
temple, *along* by the altar and the temple.
12 And he brought forth the king's son, and put the crown upon him, and
gave him the testimony; and they made him king, and anointed him; and they
clapped their hands, and said, God save the king.

Athaliah Is Slain

13 And when Athaliah heard the noise of the guard *and* of the people, she
came to the people into the temple of the LORD.

14 And when she looked, behold, the king stood by a pillar, as the manner
was, and the princes and the trumpeters by the king, and all the people of the
land rejoiced, and blew with trumpets: and Athaliah rent her clothes, and
cried, Treason, Treason.
15 But Jehoiada the priest commanded the captains of the hundreds, the
officers of the host, and said unto them, Have her forth without the ranges:
and him that followeth her kill with the sword. For the priest had said, Let her
not be slain in the house of the LORD.
16 And they laid hands on her; and she went by the way by the which the
horses came into the king's house: and there was she slain.

Jehoiada Restores the Worship of God

17 And Jehoiada made a covenant between the LORD and the king and the
people, that they should be the LORD's people; between the king also and the
people.
18 And all the people of the land went into the house of Baal, and brake it
down; his altars and his images brake they in pieces thoroughly, and slew
Mattan the priest of Baal before the altars. And the priest appointed officers
over the house of the LORD.
19 And he took the rulers over hundreds, and the captains, and the guard,
and all the people of the land; and they brought down the king from the house
of the LORD, and came by the way of the gate of the guard to the king's house.
And he sat on the throne of the kings.
20 And all the people of the land rejoiced, and the city was in quiet: and they
slew Athaliah with the sword *beside* the king's house.
21 Seven years old *was* Jehoash when he began to reign.

Jehoash (Joash) Gives Orders to Repair the Temple

12 In the seventh year of Jehu Jehoash began to reign; and forty years
reigned he in Jerusalem. And his mother's name *was* Zibiah of Beer-
sheba.
2 And Jehoash did *that which was* right in the sight of the LORD all his days
wherein Jehoiada the priest instructed him.
3 But the high places were not taken away: the people still sacrificed and
burnt incense in the high places.
4 And Jehoash said to the priests, All the money of the dedicated things that
is brought into the house of the LORD, *even* the money of every one that pass-
eth *the account*, the money that every man is set at, *and* all the money that
cometh into any man's heart to bring into the house of the LORD,
5 Let the priests take *it* to them, every man of his acquaintance: and let them
repair the breaches of the house, wheresoever any breach shall be found.
6 But it was *so, that* in the three and twentieth year of king Jehoash the priests
had not repaired the breaches of the house.
7 Then king Jehoash called for Jehoiada the priest, and the *other* priests, and
said unto them, Why repair ye not the breaches of the house? now therefore
receive no *more* money of your acquaintance, but deliver it for the breaches
of the house.
8 And the priests consented to receive no *more* money of the people, neither
to repair the breaches of the house.
9 But Jehoiada the priest took a chest, and bored a hole in the lid of it, and
set it beside the altar, on the right side as one cometh into the house of the
LORD: and the priests that kept the door put therein all the money *that was*
brought into the house of the LORD.
10 And it was *so*, when they saw that *there was* much money in the chest, that
the king's scribe and the high priest came up, and they put up in bags, and told
the money that was found in the house of the LORD.

11 And they gave the money, being told, into the hands of them that did the
work, that had the oversight of the house of the LORD: and they laid it out to
the carpenters and builders, that wrought upon the house of the LORD,
12 And to masons, and hewers of stone, and to buy timber and hewed stone
to repair the breaches of the house of the LORD, and for all that was laid out
for the house to repair *it*.
13 Howbeit there were not made for the house of the LORD bowls of silver,
snuffers, basons, trumpets, any vessels of gold, or vessels of silver, of the money
that was brought into the house of the LORD:
14 But they gave that to the workmen, and repaired therewith the house of
the LORD.
15 Moreover they reckoned not with the men, into whose hand they deliv-
ered the money to be bestowed on workmen: for they dealt faithfully.
16 The trespass money and sin money was not brought into the house of the
LORD: it was the priests'.

Hazael Is Diverted from Attacking Jerusalem by Gifts

17 Then Hazael king of Syria went up, and fought against Gath, and took it:
and Hazael set his face to go up to Jerusalem.
18 And Jehoash king of Judah took all the hallowed things that Jehoshaphat,
and Jehoram, and Ahaziah, his fathers, kings of Judah, had dedicated, and his
own hallowed things, and all the gold *that was* found in the treasures of the
house of the LORD, and in the king's house, and sent *it* to Hazael king of Syria:
and he went away from Jerusalem.
19 And the rest of the acts of Joash, and all that he did, *are* they not written
in the book of the chronicles of the kings of Judah?
20 And his servants arose, and made a conspiracy, and slew Joash in the house
of Millo, which goeth down to Silla.
21 For Jozachar the son of Shimeath, and Jehozabad the son of Shomer, his
servants, smote him, and he died; and they buried him with his fathers in the
city of David: and Amaziah his son reigned in his stead.

Jehoahaz's Evil Reign over Israel

13 In the three and twentieth year of Joash the son of Ahaziah king of
Judah Jehoahaz the son of Jehu began to reign over Israel in Samaria,
and reigned seventeen years.
2 And he did *that which was* evil in the sight of the LORD, and followed the
sins of Jeroboam the son of Nebat, which made Israel to sin; he departed not
therefrom.
3 And the anger of the LORD was kindled against Israel, and he delivered them
into the hand of Hazael king of Syria, and into the hand of Ben-hadad the son
of Hazael, all *their* days.
4 And Jehoahaz besought the LORD, and the LORD hearkened unto him: for
he saw the oppression of Israel, because the king of Syria oppressed them.
5 (And the LORD gave Israel a saviour, so that they went out from under the
hand of the Syrians: and the children of Israel dwelt in their tents, as before-
time.
6 Nevertheless they departed not from the sins of the house of Jeroboam,
who made Israel sin, *but* walked therein: and there remained the grove also
in Samaria.)
7 Neither did he leave of the people to Jehoahaz but fifty horsemen, and ten
chariots, and ten thousand footmen; for the king of Syria had destroyed them,
and had made them like the dust by threshing.
8 Now the rest of the acts of Jehoahaz, and all that he did, and his might, *are*
they not written in the book of the chronicles of the kings of Israel?
9 And Jehoahaz slept with his fathers; and they buried him in Samaria: and
Joash his son reigned in his stead.

Jehoash's Evil Reign over Israel

10 In the thirty and seventh year of Joash king of Judah began Jehoash the
son of Jehoahaz to reign over Israel in Samaria, *and reigned* sixteen years.
11 And he did *that which was* evil in the sight of the LORD; he departed not
from all the sins of Jeroboam the son of Nebat, who made Israel sin: *but* he
walked therein.
12 And the rest of the acts of Joash, and all that he did, and his might where-
with he fought against Amaziah king of Judah, *are* they not written in the
book of the chronicles of the kings of Israel?
13 And Joash slept with his fathers; and Jeroboam sat upon his throne: and
Joash was buried in Samaria with the kings of Israel.
14 Now Elisha was fallen sick of his sickness whereof he died. And Joash the
king of Israel came down unto him, and wept over his face, and said, O my
father, my father, the chariot of Israel, and the horsemen thereof.
15 And Elisha said unto him, Take bow and arrows. And he took unto him
bow and arrows.
16 And he said to the king of Israel, Put thine hand upon the bow. And he put
his hand *upon it*: and Elisha put his hands upon the king's hands.
17 And he said, Open the window eastward. And he opened *it*. Then Elisha
said, Shoot. And he shot. And he said, The arrow of the LORD's deliverance, and
the arrow of deliverance from Syria: for thou shalt smite the Syrians in Aphek,
till thou have consumed *them*.
18 And he said, Take the arrows. And he took *them*. And he said unto the king
of Israel, Smite upon the ground. And he smote thrice, and stayed.
19 And the man of God was wroth with him, and said, Thou shouldest have
smitten five or six times; then hadst thou smitten Syria till thou hadst con-
sumed *it*: whereas now thou shalt smite Syria *but* thrice.

Elisha's Bones Raise a Dead Man

20 And Elisha died, and they buried him. And the bands of the Moabites
invaded the land at the coming in of the year.
21 And it came to pass, as they were burying a man, that, behold, they spied
a band *of men*; and they cast the man into the sepulchre of Elisha: and when
the man was let down, and touched the bones of Elisha, he revived, and stood
up on his feet.
22 But Hazael king of Syria oppressed Israel all the days of Jehoahaz.
23 And the LORD was gracious unto them, and had compassion on them, and
had respect unto them, because of his covenant with Abraham, Isaac, and
Jacob, and would not destroy them, neither cast he them from his presence
as yet.
24 So Hazael king of Syria died; and Ben-hadad his son reigned in his stead.
25 And Jehoash the son of Jehoahaz took again out of the hand of Ben-hadad
the son of Hazael the cities, which he had taken out of the hand of Jehoahaz
his father by war. Three times did Joash beat him, and recovered the cities of
Israel.

Amaziah's Good Reign over Judah

14 In the second year of Joash son of Jehoahaz king of Israel reigned
Amaziah the son of Joash king of Judah.
2 He was twenty and five years old when he began to reign, and reigned
twenty and nine years in Jerusalem. And his mother's name *was* Jehoaddan
of Jerusalem.
3 And he did *that which was* right in the sight of the LORD, yet not like David
his father: he did according to all things as Joash his father did.
4 Howbeit the high places were not taken away: as yet the people did sacrifice
and burnt incense on the high places.

5 And it came to pass, as soon as the kingdom was confirmed in his hand,
that he slew his servants which had slain the king his father.
6 But the children of the murderers he slew not: according unto that which is
written in the book of the law of Moses, wherein the LORD commanded, saying,
The fathers shall not be put to death for the children, nor the children be put to
death for the fathers; but every man shall be put to death for his own sin.
7 He slew of Edom in the valley of salt ten thousand, and took Selah by war,
and called the name of it Joktheel unto this day.

Jehoash of Israel Attacks Amaziah and Spoils Jerusalem

8 Then Amaziah sent messengers to Jehoash, the son of Jehoahaz son of Jehu,
king of Israel, saying, Come, let us look one another in the face.
9 And Jehoash the king of Israel sent to Amaziah king of Judah, saying, The
thistle that *was* in Lebanon sent to the cedar that *was* in Lebanon, saying, Give
thy daughter to my son to wife: and there passed by a wild beast that *was* in
Lebanon, and trode down the thistle.
10 Thou hast indeed smitten Edom, and thine heart hath lifted thee up: glory
of this, and tarry at home: for why shouldest thou meddle to *thy* hurt, that
thou shouldest fall, *even* thou, and Judah with thee?
11 But Amaziah would not hear. Therefore Jehoash king of Israel went up;
and he and Amaziah king of Judah looked one another in the face at Beth-
shemesh, which *belongeth* to Judah.
12 And Judah was put to the worse before Israel; and they fled every man to
their tents.
13 And Jehoash king of Israel took Amaziah king of Judah, the son of Jehoash
the son of Ahaziah, at Beth-shemesh, and came to Jerusalem, and brake down
the wall of Jerusalem from the gate of Ephraim unto the corner gate, four
hundred cubits.
14 And he took all the gold and silver, and all the vessels that were found in
the house of the LORD, and in the treasures of the king's house, and hostages,
and returned to Samaria.

Jeroboam II Succeeds Jehoash in Israel

15 Now the rest of the acts of Jehoash which he did, and his might, and how
he fought with Amaziah king of Judah, *are* they not written in the book of the
chronicles of the kings of Israel?
16 And Jehoash slept with his fathers, and was buried in Samaria with the
kings of Israel; and Jeroboam his son reigned in his stead.
17 And Amaziah the son of Joash king of Judah lived after the death of
Jehoash son of Jehoahaz king of Israel fifteen years.
18 And the rest of the acts of Amaziah, *are* they not written in the book of
the chronicles of the kings of Judah?
19 Now they made a conspiracy against him in Jerusalem: and he fled to
Lachish; but they sent after him to Lachish, and slew him there.
20 And they brought him on horses: and he was buried at Jerusalem with his
fathers in the city of David.
21 And all the people of Judah took Azariah, which *was* sixteen years old, and
made him king instead of his father Amaziah.
22 He built Elath, and restored it to Judah, after that the king slept with his
fathers.

Jeroboam's Evil Reign in Israel

23 In the fifteenth year of Amaziah the son of Joash king of Judah Jeroboam
the son of Joash king of Israel began to reign in Samaria, *and reigned* forty
and one years.
24 And he did *that which was* evil in the sight of the LORD: he departed not
from all the sins of Jeroboam the son of Nebat, who made Israel to sin.

25 He restored the coast of Israel from the entering of Hamath unto the sea
of the plain, according to the word of the LORD God of Israel, which he spake
by the hand of his servant Jonah, the son of Amittai, the prophet, which *was*
of Gath-hepher.
26 For the LORD saw the affliction of Israel, *that it was* very bitter: for *there*
was not any shut up, nor any left, nor any helper for Israel.
27 And the LORD said not that he would blot out the name of Israel from
under heaven: but he saved them by the hand of Jeroboam the son of Joash.
28 Now the rest of the acts of Jeroboam, and all that he did, and his might,
how he warred, and how he recovered Damascus, and Hamath, *which belonged*
to Judah, for Israel, are they not written in the book of the chronicles of the
kings of Israel?
29 And Jeroboam slept with his fathers, *even* with the kings of Israel; and
Zachariah his son reigned in his stead.

Azariah's (Uzziah's) Good Reign over Judah

15 In the twenty and seventh year of Jeroboam king of Israel began
Azariah son of Amaziah king of Judah to reign.
2 Sixteen years old was he when he began to reign, and he reigned two and
fifty years in Jerusalem. And his mother's name *was* Jecholiah of Jerusalem.
3 And he did *that which was* right in the sight of the LORD, according to all
that his father Amaziah had done;
4 Save that the high places were not removed: the people sacrificed and burnt
incense still on the high places.
5 And the LORD smote the king, so that he was a leper unto the day of his
death, and dwelt in a several house. And Jotham the king's son *was* over the
house, judging the people of the land.
6 And the rest of the acts of Azariah, and all that he did, *are* they not written
in the book of the chronicles of the kings of Judah?
7 So Azariah slept with his fathers; and they buried him with his fathers in
the city of David: and Jotham his son reigned in his stead.

Zachariah, Shallum, and Others Reign Evilly over Israel

8 In the thirty and eighth year of Azariah king of Judah did Zachariah the
son of Jeroboam reign over Israel in Samaria six months.
9 And he did *that which was* evil in the sight of the LORD, as his fathers had
done: he departed not from the sins of Jeroboam the son of Nebat, who made
Israel to sin.
10 And Shallum the son of Jabesh conspired against him, and smote him
before the people, and slew him, and reigned in his stead.
11 And the rest of the acts of Zachariah, behold, they *are* written in the book
of the chronicles of the kings of Israel.
12 This *was* the word of the LORD which he spake unto Jehu, saying, Thy sons
shall sit on the throne of Israel unto the fourth *generation*. And so it came to
pass.
13 Shallum the son of Jabesh began to reign in the nine and thirtieth year of
Uzziah king of Judah; and he reigned a full month in Samaria.
14 For Menahem the son of Gadi went up from Tirzah, and came to Samaria,
and smote Shallum the son of Jabesh in Samaria, and slew him, and reigned
in his stead.
15 And the rest of the acts of Shallum, and his conspiracy which he made,
behold, they *are* written in the book of the chronicles of the kings of Israel.
16 Then Menahem smote Tiphsah, and all that *were* therein, and the coasts
thereof from Tirzah: because they opened not *to him*, therefore he smote *it;*
and all the women therein that were with child he ripped up.
17 In the nine and thirtieth year of Azariah king of Judah began Menahem
the son of Gadi to reign over Israel, *and reigned* ten years in Samaria.
18 And he did *that which was* evil in the sight of the LORD: he departed not all
his days from the sins of Jeroboam the son of Nebat, who made Israel to sin.

19 *And* Pul the king of Assyria came against the land: and Menahem gave Pul
a thousand talents of silver, that his hand might be with him to confirm the
kingdom in his hand.
20 And Menahem exacted the money of Israel, *even* of all the mighty men of
wealth, of each man fifty shekels of silver, to give to the king of Assyria. So the
king of Assyria turned back, and stayed not there in the land.
21 And the rest of the acts of Menahem, and all that he did, *are* they not
written in the book of the chronicles of the kings of Israel?
22 And Menahem slept with his fathers; and Pekahiah his son reigned in his
stead.
23 In the fiftieth year of Azariah king of Judah Pekahiah the son of Menahem
began to reign over Israel in Samaria, *and reigned* two years.
24 And he did *that which was* evil in the sight of the LORD: he departed not
from the sins of Jeroboam the son of Nebat, who made Israel to sin.
25 But Pekah the son of Remaliah, a captain of his, conspired against him,
and smote him in Samaria, in the palace of the king's house, with Argob and
Arieh, and with him fifty men of the Gileadites: and he killed him, and reigned
in his room.
26 And the rest of the acts of Pekahiah, and all that he did, behold, they *are*
written in the book of the chronicles of the kings of Israel.
27 In the two and fiftieth year of Azariah king of Judah Pekah the son of
Remaliah began to reign over Israel in Samaria, *and reigned* twenty years.
28 And he did *that which was* evil in the sight of the LORD: he departed not
from the sins of Jeroboam the son of Nebat, who made Israel to sin.
29 In the days of Pekah king of Israel came Tiglath-pileser king of Assyria,
and took Ijon, and Abel-beth-maachah, and Janoah, and Kedesh, and Hazor,
and Gilead, and Galilee, all the land of Naphtali, and carried them captive to
Assyria.
30 And Hoshea the son of Elah made a conspiracy against Pekah the son of
Remaliah, and smote him, and slew him, and reigned in his stead, in the twen-
tieth year of Jotham the son of Uzziah.
31 And the rest of the acts of Pekah, and all that he did, behold, they *are*
written in the book of the chronicles of the kings of Israel.

Jotham's Good Reign over Judah

32 In the second year of Pekah the son of Remaliah king of Israel began
Jotham the son of Uzziah king of Judah to reign.
33 Five and twenty years old was he when he began to reign, and he reigned
sixteen years in Jerusalem. And his mother's name *was* Jerusha, the daughter
of Zadok.
34 And he did *that which was* right in the sight of the LORD: he did according
to all that his father Uzziah had done.
35 Howbeit the high places were not removed: the people sacrificed and
burned incense still in the high places. He built the higher gate of the house
of the LORD.
36 Now the rest of the acts of Jotham, and all that he did, *are* they not written
in the book of the chronicles of the kings of Judah?
37 In those days the LORD began to send against Judah Rezin the king of Syria,
and Pekah the son of Remaliah.
38 And Jotham slept with his fathers, and was buried with his fathers in the
city of David his father: and Ahaz his son reigned in his stead.

Ahaz's Evil Reign over Judah

16 In the seventeenth year of Pekah the son of Remaliah Ahaz the son of
Jotham king of Judah began to reign.
2 Twenty years old *was* Ahaz when he began to reign, and reigned sixteen
years in Jerusalem, and did not *that which was* right in the sight of the LORD
his God, like David his father.

3 But he walked in the way of the kings of Israel, yea, and made his son to
pass through the fire, according to the abominations of the heathen, whom
the LORD cast out from before the children of Israel.
4 And he sacrificed and burnt incense in the high places, and on the hills,
and under every green tree.

Ahaz, Attacked by Rezin and Pekah, Hires Tiglath-pileser to Fight

5 Then Rezin king of Syria and Pekah son of Remaliah king of Israel came
up to Jerusalem to war: and they besieged Ahaz, but could not overcome *him*.
6 At that time Rezin king of Syria recovered Elath to Syria, and drave the Jews
from Elath: and the Syrians came to Elath, and dwelt there unto this day.
7 So Ahaz sent messengers to Tiglath-pileser king of Assyria, saying, I *am* thy
servant and thy son: come up, and save me out of the hand of the king of Syria,
and out of the hand of the king of Israel, which rise up against me.
8 And Ahaz took the silver and gold that was found in the house of the LORD,
and in the treasures of the king's house, and sent *it for* a present to the king
of Assyria.
9 And the king of Assyria hearkened unto him: for the king of Assyria went
up against Damascus, and took it, and carried *the people of* it captive to Kir,
and slew Rezin.

Ahaz Sends the Pattern of an Altar in Damascus to Urijah

10 And king Ahaz went to Damascus to meet Tiglath-pileser king of Assyria,
and saw an altar that *was* at Damascus: and king Ahaz sent to Urijah the priest
the fashion of the altar, and the pattern of it, according to all the workmanship
thereof.
11 And Urijah the priest built an altar according to all that king Ahaz had
sent from Damascus: so Urijah the priest made *it* against king Ahaz came from
Damascus.
12 And when the king was come from Damascus, the king saw the altar: and
the king approached to the altar, and offered thereon.
13 And he burnt his burnt offering and his meat offering, and poured his
drink offering, and sprinkled the blood of his peace offerings, upon the altar.
14 And he brought also the brasen altar, which *was* before the LORD, from
the forefront of the house, from between the altar and the house of the LORD,
and put it on the north side of the altar.
15 And king Ahaz commanded Urijah the priest, saying, Upon the great altar
burn the morning burnt offering, and the evening meat offering, and the
king's burnt sacrifice, and his meat offering, with the burnt offering of all the
people of the land, and their meat offering, and their drink offerings; and
sprinkle upon it all the blood of the burnt offering, and all the blood of the
sacrifice: and the brasen altar shall be for me to enquire *by*.
16 Thus did Urijah the priest, according to all that king Ahaz commanded.

Ahaz Spoils the Temple

17 And king Ahaz cut off the borders of the bases, and removed the laver
from off them; and took down the sea from off the brasen oxen that *were*
under it, and put it upon a pavement of stones.
18 And the covert for the sabbath that they had built in the house, and the
king's entry without, turned he from the house of the LORD for the king of
Assyria.
19 Now the rest of the acts of Ahaz which he did, *are* they not written in the
book of the chronicles of the kings of Judah?
20 And Ahaz slept with his fathers, and was buried with his fathers in the
city of David: and Hezekiah his son reigned in his stead.

During Hoshea's Evil Reign, Israel Is Conquered and Exiled

17 In the twelfth year of Ahaz king of Judah began Hoshea the son of Elah to reign in Samaria over Israel nine years.

2 And he did *that which was* evil in the sight of the LORD, but not as the kings of Israel that were before him.

3 Against him came up Shalmaneser king of Assyria; and Hoshea became his servant, and gave him presents.

4 And the king of Assyria found conspiracy in Hoshea: for he had sent messengers to So king of Egypt, and brought no present to the king of Assyria, as *he had done* year by year: therefore the king of Assyria shut him up, and bound him in prison.

5 Then the king of Assyria came up throughout all the land, and went up to Samaria, and besieged it three years.

6 In the ninth year of Hoshea the king of Assyria took Samaria, and carried Israel away into Assyria, and placed them in Halah and in Habor *by* the river of Gozan, and in the cities of the Medes.

7 For *so* it was, that the children of Israel had sinned against the LORD their God, which had brought them up out of the land of Egypt, from under the hand of Pharaoh king of Egypt, and had feared other gods,

8 And walked in the statutes of the heathen, whom the LORD cast out from before the children of Israel, and of the kings of Israel, which they had made.

9 And the children of Israel did secretly *those* things that *were* not right against the LORD their God, and they built them high places in all their cities, from the tower of the watchmen to the fenced city.

10 And they set them up images and groves in every high hill, and under every green tree:

11 And there they burnt incense in all the high places, as *did* the heathen whom the LORD carried away before them; and wrought wicked things to provoke the LORD to anger:

12 For they served idols, whereof the LORD had said unto them, Ye shall not do this thing.

13 Yet the LORD testified against Israel, and against Judah, by all the prophets, *and by* all the seers, saying, Turn ye from your evil ways, and keep my commandments *and* my statutes, according to all the law which I commanded your fathers, and which I sent to you by my servants the prophets.

14 Notwithstanding they would not hear, but hardened their necks, like to the neck of their fathers, that did not believe in the LORD their God.

15 And they rejected his statutes, and his covenant that he made with their fathers, and his testimonies which he testified against them; and they followed vanity, and became vain, and went after the heathen that *were* round about them, *concerning* whom the LORD had charged them, that they should not do like them.

16 And they left all the commandments of the LORD their God, and made them molten images, *even* two calves, and made a grove, and worshipped all the host of heaven, and served Baal.

17 And they caused their sons and their daughters to pass through the fire, and used divination and enchantments, and sold themselves to do evil in the sight of the LORD, to provoke him to anger.

18 Therefore the LORD was very angry with Israel, and removed them out of his sight: there was none left but the tribe of Judah only.

19 Also Judah kept not the commandments of the LORD their God, but walked in the statutes of Israel which they made.

20 And the LORD rejected all the seed of Israel, and afflicted them, and delivered them into the hand of spoilers, until he had cast them out of his sight.

21 For he rent Israel from the house of David; and they made Jeroboam the
son of Nebat king: and Jeroboam drave Israel from following the LORD, and
made them sin a great sin.
22 For the children of Israel walked in all the sins of Jeroboam which he did;
they departed not from them;
23 Until the LORD removed Israel out of his sight, as he had said by all his
servants the prophets. So was Israel carried away out of their own land to
Assyria unto this day.

The Foreign Nations, Transplanted in Samaria, Make a Mixture of Religions

24 And the king of Assyria brought *men* from Babylon, and from Cuthah,
and from Ava, and from Hamath, and from Sepharvaim, and placed *them* in
the cities of Samaria instead of the children of Israel: and they possessed
Samaria, and dwelt in the cities thereof.
25 And *so* it was at the beginning of their dwelling there, *that* they feared
not the LORD: therefore the LORD sent lions among them, which slew *some* of
them.
26 Wherefore they spake to the king of Assyria, saying, The nations which
thou hast removed, and placed in the cities of Samaria, know not the manner
of the God of the land: therefore he hath sent lions among them, and, behold,
they slay them, because they know not the manner of the God of the land.
27 Then the king of Assyria commanded, saying, Carry thither one of the
priests whom ye brought from thence; and let them go and dwell there, and
let him teach them the manner of the God of the land.
28 Then one of the priests whom they had carried away from Samaria came
and dwelt in Bethel, and taught them how they should fear the LORD.
29 Howbeit every nation made gods of their own, and put *them* in the houses of the high places which the Samaritans had made, every nation in their
cities wherein they dwelt.
30 And the men of Babylon made Succoth-benoth, and the men of Cuth made
Nergal, and the men of Hamath made Ashima,
31 And the Avites made Nibhaz and Tartak, and the Sepharvites burnt their
children in fire to Adrammelech and Anammelech, the gods of Sepharvaim.
32 So they feared the LORD, and made unto themselves of the lowest of them
priests of the high places, which sacrificed for them in the houses of the high
places.
33 They feared the LORD, and served their own gods, after the manner of the
nations whom they carried away from thence.
34 Unto this day they do after the former manners: they fear not the LORD,
neither do they after their statutes, or after their ordinances, or after the law
and commandment which the LORD commanded the children of Jacob, whom
he named Israel;
35 With whom the LORD had made a covenant, and charged them, saying, Ye
shall not fear other gods, nor bow yourselves to them, nor serve them, nor
sacrifice to them:
36 But the LORD, who brought you up out of the land of Egypt with great
power and a stretched out arm, him shall ye fear, and him shall ye worship,
and to him shall ye do sacrifice.
37 And the statutes, and the ordinances, and the law, and the commandment,
which he wrote for you, ye shall observe to do for evermore; and ye shall not
fear other gods.
38 And the covenant that I have made with you ye shall not forget; neither
shall ye fear other gods.
39 But the LORD your God ye shall fear; and he shall deliver you out of the
hand of all your enemies.

40 Howbeit they did not hearken, but they did after their former manner.
41 So these nations feared the LORD, and served their graven images, both
their children, and their children's children: as did their fathers, so do they
unto this day.

Hezekiah's Good Reign over Judah

18 Now it came to pass in the third year of Hoshea son of Elah king of
Israel, *that* Hezekiah the son of Ahaz king of Judah began to reign.
2 Twenty and five years old was he when he began to reign; and he reigned
twenty and nine years in Jerusalem. His mother's name also *was* Abi, the
daughter of Zachariah.
3 And he did *that which was* right in the sight of the LORD, according to all
that David his father did.
4 He removed the high places, and brake the images, and cut down the groves,
and brake in pieces the brasen serpent that Moses had made: for unto those
days the children of Israel did burn incense to it: and he called it Nehushtan.
5 He trusted in the LORD God of Israel; so that after him was none like him
among all the kings of Judah, nor *any* that were before him.
6 For he clave to the LORD, *and* departed not from following him, but kept
his commandments, which the LORD commanded Moses.
7 And the LORD was with him; *and* he prospered whithersoever he went forth:
and he rebelled against the king of Assyria, and served him not.
8 He smote the Philistines, *even* unto Gaza, and the borders thereof, from
the tower of the watchmen to the fenced city.

Assyria Destroys Israel and Later Attacks Judah

9 And it came to pass in the fourth year of king Hezekiah, which *was* the
seventh year of Hoshea son of Elah king of Israel, *that* Shalmaneser king of
Assyria came up against Samaria, and besieged it.
10 And at the end of three years they took it: *even* in the sixth year of Hezekiah,
that *is* the ninth year of Hoshea king of Israel, Samaria was taken.
11 And the king of Assyria did carry away Israel unto Assyria, and put them
in Halah and in Habor *by* the river of Gozan, and in the cities of the Medes:
12 Because they obeyed not the voice of the LORD their God, but transgressed
his covenant, *and* all that Moses the servant of the LORD commanded, and
would not hear *them*, nor do *them*.
13 Now in the fourteenth year of king Hezekiah did Sennacherib king of
Assyria come up against all the fenced cities of Judah, and took them.
14 And Hezekiah king of Judah sent to the king of Assyria to Lachish, saying,
I have offended; return from me: that which thou puttest on me will I bear.
And the king of Assyria appointed unto Hezekiah king of Judah three hundred
talents of silver and thirty talents of gold.
15 And Hezekiah gave *him* all the silver that was found in the house of the
LORD, and in the treasures of the king's house.
16 At that time did Hezekiah cut off *the gold from* the doors of the temple of
the LORD, and *from* the pillars which Hezekiah king of Judah had overlaid,
and gave it to the king of Assyria.

Sennacherib Threatens to Destroy Jerusalem

17 And the king of Assyria sent Tartan and Rab-saris and Rab-shakeh from
Lachish to king Hezekiah with a great host against Jerusalem. And they went
up and came to Jerusalem. And when they were come up, they came and stood
by the conduit of the upper pool, which *is* in the highway of the fuller's field.
18 And when they had called to the king, there came out to them Eliakim the
son of Hilkiah, which *was* over the household, and Shebna the scribe, and Joah
the son of Asaph the recorder.
19 And Rab-shakeh said unto them, Speak ye now to Hezekiah, Thus saith the
great king, the king of Assyria, What confidence *is* this wherein thou trustest?

20 Thou sayest, (but *they are but* vain words,) *I have* counsel and strength for the war. Now on whom dost thou trust, that thou rebellest against me?

21 Now, behold, thou trustest upon the staff of this bruised reed, *even* upon Egypt, on which if a man lean, it will go into his hand, and pierce it: so *is* Pharaoh king of Egypt unto all that trust on him.

22 But if ye say unto me, We trust in the LORD our God: *is* not that he, whose high places and whose altars Hezekiah hath taken away, and hath said to Judah and Jerusalem, Ye shall worship before this altar in Jerusalem?

23 Now therefore, I pray thee, give pledges to my lord the king of Assyria, and I will deliver thee two thousand horses, if thou be able on thy part to set riders upon them.

24 How then wilt thou turn away the face of one captain of the least of my master's servants, and put thy trust on Egypt for chariots and for horsemen?

25 Am I now come up without the LORD against this place to destroy it? The LORD said to me, Go up against this land, and destroy it.

26 Then said Eliakim the son of Hilkiah, and Shebna, and Joah, unto Rab-shakeh, Speak, I pray thee, to thy servants in the Syrian language; for we understand *it*: and talk not with us in the Jews' language in the ears of the people that *are* on the wall.

27 But Rab-shakeh said unto them, Hath my master sent me to thy master, and to thee, to speak these words? *hath he* not *sent me* to the men which sit on the wall, that they may eat their own dung, and drink their own piss with you?

28 Then Rab-shakeh stood and cried with a loud voice in the Jews' language, and spake, saying, Hear the word of the great king, the king of Assyria:

29 Thus saith the king, Let not Hezekiah deceive you: for he shall not be able to deliver you out of his hand:

30 Neither let Hezekiah make you trust in the LORD, saying, The LORD will surely deliver us, and this city shall not be delivered into the hand of the king of Assyria.

31 Hearken not to Hezekiah: for thus saith the king of Assyria, Make *an agreement* with me by a present, and come out to me, and *then* eat ye every man of his own vine, and every one of his fig tree, and drink ye every one the waters of his cistern:

32 Until I come and take you away to a land like your own land, a land of corn and wine, a land of bread and vineyards, a land of oil olive and of honey, that ye may live, and not die: and hearken not unto Hezekiah, when he persuadeth you, saying, The LORD will deliver us.

33 Hath any of the gods of the nations delivered at all his land out of the hand of the king of Assyria?

34 Where *are* the gods of Hamath, and of Arpad? where *are* the gods of Sepharvaim, Hena, and Ivah? have they delivered Samaria out of mine hand?

35 Who *are* they among all the gods of the countries, that have delivered their country out of mine hand, that the LORD should deliver Jerusalem out of mine hand?

36 But the people held their peace, and answered him not a word: for the king's commandment was, saying, Answer him not.

37 Then came Eliakim the son of Hilkiah, which *was* over the household, and Shebna the scribe, and Joah the son of Asaph the recorder, to Hezekiah with *their* clothes rent, and told him the words of Rab-shakeh.

Isaiah Prophesies Jerusalem's Deliverance from Sennacherib

19 And it came to pass, when king Hezekiah heard *it*, that he rent his clothes, and covered himself with sackcloth, and went into the house of the LORD.

2 And he sent Eliakim, which *was* over the household, and Shebna the scribe, and the elders of the priests, covered with sackcloth, to Isaiah the prophet the son of Amoz.

3 And they said unto him, Thus saith Hezekiah, This day *is* a day of trouble,
and of rebuke, and blasphemy: for the children are come to the birth, and
there is not strength to bring forth.
4 It may be the LORD thy God will hear all the words of Rab-shakeh, whom
the king of Assyria his master hath sent to reproach the living God; and will
reprove the words which the LORD thy God hath heard: wherefore lift up *thy*
prayer for the remnant that are left.
5 So the servants of king Hezekiah came to Isaiah.
6 And Isaiah said unto them, Thus shall ye say to your master, Thus saith the
LORD, Be not afraid of the words which thou hast heard, with which the ser-
vants of the king of Assyria have blasphemed me.
7 Behold, I will send a blast upon him, and he shall hear a rumour, and shall
return to his own land; and I will cause him to fall by the sword in his own
land.

Sennacherib Sends a Blasphemous Letter to Hezekiah

8 So Rab-shakeh returned, and found the king of Assyria warring against
Libnah: for he had heard that he was departed from Lachish.
9 And when he heard say of Tirhakah king of Ethiopia, Behold, he is come
out to fight against thee: he sent messengers again unto Hezekiah, saying,
10 Thus shall ye speak to Hezekiah king of Judah, saying, Let not thy God in
whom thou trustest deceive thee, saying, Jerusalem shall not be delivered into
the hand of the king of Assyria.
11 Behold, thou hast heard what the kings of Assyria have done to all lands,
by destroying them utterly: and shalt thou be delivered?
12 Have the gods of the nations delivered them which my fathers have
destroyed; *as* Gozan, and Haran, and Rezeph, and the children of Eden which
were in Thelasar?
13 Where *is* the king of Hamath, and the king of Arpad, and the king of the
city of Sepharvaim, of Hena, and Ivah?
14 And Hezekiah received the letter of the hand of the messengers, and read
it: and Hezekiah went up into the house of the LORD, and spread it before the
LORD.
15 And Hezekiah prayed before the LORD, and said, O LORD God of Israel,
which dwellest *between* the cherubims, thou art the God, *even* thou alone, of
all the kingdoms of the earth; thou hast made heaven and earth.
16 LORD, bow down thine ear, and hear: open, LORD, thine eyes, and see: and
hear the words of Sennacherib, which hath sent him to reproach the living
God.
17 Of a truth, LORD, the kings of Assyria have destroyed the nations and their
lands,
18 And have cast their gods into the fire: for they *were* no gods, but the work
of men's hands, wood and stone: therefore they have destroyed them.
19 Now therefore, O LORD our God, I beseech thee, save thou us out of his
hand, that all the kingdoms of the earth may know that thou *art* the LORD God,
even thou only.

Isaiah Prophesies the Destruction of Sennacherib

20 Then Isaiah the son of Amoz sent to Hezekiah, saying, Thus saith the LORD
God of Israel, *That* which thou hast prayed to me against Sennacherib king
of Assyria I have heard.
21 This *is* the word that the LORD hath spoken concerning him; The virgin
the daughter of Zion hath despised thee, *and* laughed thee to scorn; the daugh-
ter of Jerusalem hath shaken her head at thee.
22 Whom hast thou reproached and blasphemed? and against whom hast
thou exalted *thy* voice, and lifted up thine eyes on high? *even* against the Holy
One of Israel.

23 By thy messengers thou hast reproached the Lord, and hast said, With the multitude of my chariots I am come up to the height of the mountains, to the sides of Lebanon, and will cut down the tall cedar trees thereof, *and* the choice fir trees thereof: and I will enter into the lodgings of his borders, *and into* the forest of his Carmel.

24 I have digged and drunk strange waters, and with the sole of my feet have I dried up all the rivers of besieged places.

25 Hast thou not heard long ago *how* I have done it, *and* of ancient times that I have formed it? now have I brought it to pass, that thou shouldest be to lay waste fenced cities *into* ruinous heaps.

26 Therefore their inhabitants were of small power, they were dismayed and confounded; they were *as* the grass of the field, and *as* the green herb, *as* the grass on the housetops, and *as corn* blasted before it be grown up.

27 But I know thy abode, and thy going out, and thy coming in, and thy rage against me.

28 Because thy rage against me and thy tumult is come up into mine ears, therefore I will put my hook in thy nose, and my bridle in thy lips, and I will turn thee back by the way by which thou camest.

29 And this *shall be* a sign unto thee, Ye shall eat this year such things as grow of themselves, and in the second year that which springeth of the same; and in the third year sow ye, and reap, and plant vineyards, and eat the fruits thereof.

30 And the remnant that is escaped of the house of Judah shall yet again take root downward, and bear fruit upward.

31 For out of Jerusalem shall go forth a remnant, and they that escape out of mount Zion: the zeal of the LORD *of hosts* shall do this.

32 Therefore thus saith the LORD concerning the king of Assyria, He shall not come into this city, nor shoot an arrow there, nor come before it with shield, nor cast a bank against it.

33 By the way that he came, by the same shall he return, and shall not come into this city, saith the LORD.

34 For I will defend this city, to save it, for mine own sake, and for my servant David's sake.

The Angel of the Lord Slays the Assyrians

35 And it came to pass that night, that the angel of the LORD went out, and smote in the camp of the Assyrians an hundred fourscore and five thousand: and when they arose early in the morning, behold, they *were* all dead corpses.

36 So Sennacherib king of Assyria departed, and went and returned, and dwelt at Nineveh.

37 And it came to pass, as he was worshipping in the house of Nisroch his god, that Adrammelech and Sharezer his sons smote him with the sword: and they escaped into the land of Armenia. And Esar-haddon his son reigned in his stead.

Hezekiah Is Warned of His Death, but His Life Is Lengthened

20 In those days was Hezekiah sick unto death. And the prophet Isaiah the son of Amoz came to him, and said unto him, Thus saith the LORD, Set thine house in order; for thou shalt die, and not live.

2 Then he turned his face to the wall, and prayed unto the LORD, saying,

3 I beseech thee, O LORD, remember now how I have walked before thee in truth and with a perfect heart, and have done *that which is* good in thy sight. And Hezekiah wept sore.

4 And it came to pass, afore Isaiah was gone out into the middle court, that the word of the LORD came to him, saying,

5 Turn again, and tell Hezekiah the captain of my people, Thus saith the LORD, the God of David thy father, I have heard thy prayer, I have seen thy tears:

behold, I will heal thee: on the third day thou shalt go up unto the house of the LORD.

6 And I will add unto thy days fifteen years; and I will deliver thee and this city out of the hand of the king of Assyria; and I will defend this city for mine own sake, and for my servant David's sake.

7 And Isaiah said, Take a lump of figs. And they took and laid *it* on the boil, and he recovered.

8 And Hezekiah said unto Isaiah, What *shall be* the sign that the LORD will heal me, and that I shall go up into the house of the LORD the third day?

9 And Isaiah said, This sign shalt thou have of the LORD, that the LORD will do the thing that he hath spoken: shall the shadow go forward ten degrees, or go back ten degrees?

10 And Hezekiah answered, It is a light thing for the shadow to go down ten degrees: nay, but let the shadow return backward ten degrees.

11 And Isaiah the prophet cried unto the LORD: and he brought the shadow ten degrees backward, by which it had gone down in the dial of Ahaz.

Berodach-baladan Sends Visitors to Hezekiah

12 At that time Berodach-baladan, the son of Baladan, king of Babylon, sent letters and a present unto Hezekiah: for he had heard that Hezekiah had been sick.

13 And Hezekiah hearkened unto them, and shewed them all the house of his precious things, the silver, and the gold, and the spices, and the precious ointment, and *all* the house of his armour, and all that was found in his treasures: there was nothing in his house, nor in all his dominion, that Hezekiah shewed them not.

14 Then came Isaiah the prophet unto king Hezekiah, and said unto him, What said these men? and from whence came they unto thee? And Hezekiah said, They are come from a far country, *even* from Babylon.

15 And he said, What have they seen in thine house? And Hezekiah answered, All *the things* that *are* in mine house have they seen: there is nothing among my treasures that I have not shewed them.

16 And Isaiah said unto Hezekiah, Hear the word of the LORD.

17 Behold, the days come, that all that *is* in thine house, and that which thy fathers have laid up in store unto this day, shall be carried into Babylon: nothing shall be left, saith the LORD.

18 And of thy sons that shall issue from thee, which thou shalt beget, shall they take away; and they shall be eunuchs in the palace of the king of Babylon.

19 Then said Hezekiah unto Isaiah, Good *is* the word of the LORD which thou hast spoken. And he said, *Is it* not *good*, if peace and truth be in my days?

20 And the rest of the acts of Hezekiah, and all his might, and how he made a pool, and a conduit, and brought water into the city, *are* they not written in the book of the chronicles of the kings of Judah?

21 And Hezekiah slept with his fathers: and Manasseh his son reigned in his stead.

Manasseh's Evil Reign over Judah

21 Manasseh *was* twelve years old when he began to reign, and reigned fifty and five years in Jerusalem. And his mother's name *was* Hephzi-bah.

2 And he did *that which was* evil in the sight of the LORD, after the abominations of the heathen, whom the LORD cast out before the children of Israel.

3 For he built up again the high places which Hezekiah his father had destroyed; and he reared up altars for Baal, and made a grove, as did Ahab king of Israel; and worshipped all the host of heaven, and served them.

4 And he built altars in the house of the LORD, of which the LORD said, In Jerusalem will I put my name.

5 And he built altars for all the host of heaven in the two courts of the house
of the LORD.
6 And he made his son pass through the fire, and observed times, and used
enchantments, and dealt with familiar spirits and wizards: he wrought much
wickedness in the sight of the LORD, to provoke *him* to anger.
7 And he set a graven image of the grove that he had made in the house, of
which the LORD said to David, and to Solomon his son, In this house, and in
Jerusalem, which I have chosen out of all tribes of Israel, will I put my name
for ever:
8 Neither will I make the feet of Israel move any more out of the land which
I gave their fathers; only if they will observe to do according to all that I have
commanded them, and according to all the law that my servant Moses com-
manded them.
9 But they hearkened not: and Manasseh seduced them to do more evil than
did the nations whom the LORD destroyed before the children of Israel.

Manasseh's Wickedness Causes Prophecies against Judah

10 And the LORD spake by his servants the prophets, saying,
11 Because Manasseh king of Judah hath done these abominations, *and* hath
done wickedly above all that the Amorites did, which *were* before him, and
hath made Judah also to sin with his idols:
12 Therefore thus saith the LORD God of Israel, Behold, I *am* bringing *such*
evil upon Jerusalem and Judah, that whosoever heareth of it, both his ears
shall tingle.
13 And I will stretch over Jerusalem the line of Samaria, and the plummet of
the house of Ahab: and I will wipe Jerusalem as *a man* wipeth a dish, wiping
it, and turning *it* upside down.
14 And I will forsake the remnant of mine inheritance, and deliver them into
the hand of their enemies; and they shall become a prey and a spoil to all their
enemies;
15 Because they have done *that which was* evil in my sight, and have provoked
me to anger, since the day their fathers came forth out of Egypt, even unto this
day.
16 Moreover Manasseh shed innocent blood very much, till he had filled
Jerusalem from one end to another; beside his sin wherewith he made Judah
to sin, in doing *that which was* evil in the sight of the LORD.
17 Now the rest of the acts of Manasseh, and all that he did, and his sin that
he sinned, *are* they not written in the book of the chronicles of the kings of
Judah?
18 And Manasseh slept with his fathers, and was buried in the garden of his
own house, in the garden of Uzza: and Amon his son reigned in his stead.

Amon's Evil Reign over Judah

19 Amon *was* twenty and two years old when he began to reign, and he
reigned two years in Jerusalem. And his mother's name *was* Meshullemeth,
the daughter of Haruz of Jotbah.
20 And he did *that which was* evil in the sight of the LORD, as his father
Manasseh did.
21 And he walked in all the way that his father walked in, and served the idols
that his father served, and worshipped them:
22 And he forsook the LORD God of his fathers, and walked not in the way of
the LORD.
23 And the servants of Amon conspired against him, and slew the king in his
own house.
24 And the people of the land slew all them that had conspired against king
Amon; and the people of the land made Josiah his son king in his stead.

25 Now the rest of the acts of Amon which he did, *are* they not written in the book of the chronicles of the kings of Judah?

26 And he was buried in his sepulchre in the garden of Uzza: and Josiah his son reigned in his stead.

During Josiah's Good Reign over Judah, the Book of the Law Is Found

22 Josiah *was* eight years old when he began to reign, and he reigned thirty and one years in Jerusalem. And his mother's name *was* Jedidah, the daughter of Adaiah of Boscath.

2 And he did *that which was* right in the sight of the LORD, and walked in all the way of David his father, and turned not aside to the right hand or to the left.

3 And it came to pass in the eighteenth year of king Josiah, *that* the king sent Shaphan the son of Azaliah, the son of Meshullam, the scribe, to the house of the LORD, saying,

4 Go up to Hilkiah the high priest, that he may sum the silver which is brought into the house of the LORD, which the keepers of the door have gathered of the people:

5 And let them deliver it into the hand of the doers of the work, that have the oversight of the house of the LORD: and let them give it to the doers of the work which *is* in the house of the LORD, to repair the breaches of the house,

6 Unto carpenters, and builders, and masons, and to buy timber and hewn stone to repair the house.

7 Howbeit there was no reckoning made with them of the money that was delivered into their hand, because they dealt faithfully.

8 And Hilkiah the high priest said unto Shaphan the scribe, I have found the book of the law in the house of the LORD. And Hilkiah gave the book to Shaphan, and he read it.

9 And Shaphan the scribe came to the king, and brought the king word again, and said, Thy servants have gathered the money that was found in the house, and have delivered it into the hand of them that do the work, that have the oversight of the house of the LORD.

10 And Shaphan the scribe shewed the king, saying, Hilkiah the priest hath delivered me a book. And Shaphan read it before the king.

11 And it came to pass, when the king had heard the words of the book of the law, that he rent his clothes.

12 And the king commanded Hilkiah the priest, and Ahikam the son of Shaphan, and Achbor the son of Michaiah, and Shaphan the scribe, and Asahiah a servant of the king's, saying,

13 Go ye, enquire of the LORD for me, and for the people, and for all Judah, concerning the words of this book that is found: for great *is* the wrath of the LORD that is kindled against us, because our fathers have not hearkened unto the words of this book, to do according unto all that which is written concerning us.

14 So Hilkiah the priest, and Ahikam, and Achbor, and Shaphan, and Asahiah, went unto Huldah the prophetess, the wife of Shallum the son of Tikvah, the son of Harhas, keeper of the wardrobe; (now she dwelt in Jerusalem in the college;) and they communed with her.

15 And she said unto them, Thus saith the LORD God of Israel, Tell the man that sent you to me,

16 Thus saith the LORD, Behold, I will bring evil upon this place, and upon the inhabitants thereof, *even* all the words of the book which the king of Judah hath read:

17 Because they have forsaken me, and have burned incense unto other gods, that they might provoke me to anger with all the works of their hands; therefore my wrath shall be kindled against this place, and shall not be quenched.

18 But to the king of Judah which sent you to enquire of the LORD, thus shall
ye say to him, Thus saith the LORD God of Israel, *As touching* the words which
thou hast heard;
19 Because thine heart was tender, and thou hast humbled thyself before the
LORD, when thou heardest what I spake against this place, and against the inhab-
itants thereof, that they should become a desolation and a curse, and hast rent
thy clothes, and wept before me; I also have heard *thee*, saith the LORD.
20 Behold therefore, I will gather thee unto thy fathers, and thou shalt be
gathered into thy grave in peace; and thine eyes shall not see all the evil which
I will bring upon this place. And they brought the king word again.

Josiah Reads the Book of the Law in a Solemn Assembly

23 And the king sent, and they gathered unto him all the elders of Judah
and of Jerusalem.
2 And the king went up into the house of the LORD, and all the men of Judah
and all the inhabitants of Jerusalem with him, and the priests, and the proph-
ets, and all the people, both small and great: and he read in their ears all the
words of the book of the covenant which was found in the house of the LORD.
3 And the king stood by a pillar, and made a covenant before the LORD, to walk
after the LORD, and to keep his commandments and his testimonies and his
statutes with all *their* heart and all *their* soul, to perform the words of this cov-
enant that were written in this book. And all the people stood to the covenant.

Josiah Destroys Idolatry

4 And the king commanded Hilkiah the high priest, and the priests of the
second order, and the keepers of the door, to bring forth out of the temple of
the LORD all the vessels that were made for Baal, and for the grove, and for all
the host of heaven: and he burned them without Jerusalem in the fields of
Kidron, and carried the ashes of them unto Bethel.
5 And he put down the idolatrous priests, whom the kings of Judah had
ordained to burn incense in the high places in the cities of Judah, and in the
places round about Jerusalem; them also that burned incense unto Baal, to
the sun, and to the moon, and to the planets, and to all the host of heaven.
6 And he brought out the grove from the house of the LORD, without
Jerusalem, unto the brook Kidron, and burned it at the brook Kidron, and
stamped *it* small to powder, and cast the powder thereof upon the graves of
the children of the people.
7 And he brake down the houses of the sodomites, that *were* by the house of
the LORD, where the women wove hangings for the grove.
8 And he brought all the priests out of the cities of Judah, and defiled the
high places where the priests had burned incense, from Geba to Beer-sheba,
and brake down the high places of the gates that *were* in the entering in of the
gate of Joshua the governor of the city, which *were* on a man's left hand at the
gate of the city.
9 Nevertheless the priests of the high places came not up to the altar of the
LORD in Jerusalem, but they did eat of the unleavened bread among their
brethren.
10 And he defiled Topheth, which *is* in the valley of the children of Hinnom,
that no man might make his son or his daughter to pass through the fire to
Molech.
11 And he took away the horses that the kings of Judah had given to the sun,
at the entering in of the house of the LORD, by the chamber of Nathan-melech
the chamberlain, which *was* in the suburbs, and burned the chariots of the
sun with fire.
12 And the altars that *were* on the top of the upper chamber of Ahaz, which
the kings of Judah had made, and the altars which Manasseh had made in the

two courts of the house of the LORD, did the king beat down, and brake *them*
down from thence, and cast the dust of them into the brook Kidron.
13 And the high places that *were* before Jerusalem, which *were* on the right
hand of the mount of corruption, which Solomon the king of Israel had build-
ed for Ashtoreth the abomination of the Zidonians, and for Chemosh the
abomination of the Moabites, and for Milcom the abomination of the children
of Ammon, did the king defile.
14 And he brake in pieces the images, and cut down the groves, and filled
their places with the bones of men.
15 Moreover the altar that *was* at Bethel, *and* the high place which Jeroboam
the son of Nebat, who made Israel to sin, had made, both that altar and the
high place he brake down, and burned the high place, *and* stamped *it* small
to powder, and burned the grove.
16 And as Josiah turned himself, he spied the sepulchres that *were* there in
the mount, and sent, and took the bones out of the sepulchres, and burned
them upon the altar, and polluted it, according to the word of the LORD which
the man of God proclaimed, who proclaimed these words.
17 Then he said, What title *is* that that I see? And the men of the city told
him, *It is* the sepulchre of the man of God, which came from Judah, and pro-
claimed these things that thou hast done against the altar of Bethel.
18 And he said, Let him alone; let no man move his bones. So they let his
bones alone, with the bones of the prophet that came out of Samaria.
19 And all the houses also of the high places that *were* in the cities of Samaria,
which the kings of Israel had made to provoke *the LORD* to anger, Josiah took
away, and did to them according to all the acts that he had done in Bethel.
20 And he slew all the priests of the high places that *were* there upon the
altars, and burned men's bones upon them, and returned to Jerusalem.
21 And the king commanded all the people, saying, Keep the passover unto
the LORD your God, as *it is* written in the book of this covenant.
22 Surely there was not holden such a passover from the days of the judges
that judged Israel, nor in all the days of the kings of Israel, nor of the kings of
Judah;
23 But in the eighteenth year of king Josiah, *wherein* this passover was hold-
en to the LORD in Jerusalem.
24 Moreover the *workers with* familiar spirits, and the wizards, and the imag-
es, and the idols, and all the abominations that were spied in the land of Judah
and in Jerusalem, did Josiah put away, that he might perform the words of the
law which were written in the book that Hilkiah the priest found in the house
of the LORD.
25 And like unto him was there no king before him, that turned to the LORD
with all his heart, and with all his soul, and with all his might, according to all
the law of Moses; neither after him arose there *any* like him.
26 Notwithstanding the LORD turned not from the fierceness of his great
wrath, wherewith his anger was kindled against Judah, because of all the prov-
ocations that Manasseh had provoked him withal.
27 And the LORD said, I will remove Judah also out of my sight, as I have
removed Israel, and will cast off this city Jerusalem which I have chosen, and
the house of which I said, My name shall be there.
28 Now the rest of the acts of Josiah, and all that he did, *are* they not written
in the book of the chronicles of the kings of Judah?
29 In his days Pharaoh-nechoh king of Egypt went up against the king of
Assyria to the river Euphrates: and king Josiah went against him; and he slew
him at Megiddo, when he had seen him.
30 And his servants carried him in a chariot dead from Megiddo, and brought
him to Jerusalem, and buried him in his own sepulchre. And the people of the

land took Jehoahaz the son of Josiah, and anointed him, and made him king
in his father's stead.

The Evil Reigns of Jehoahaz and Jehoiakim over Judah

31 Jehoahaz *was* twenty and three years old when he began to reign; and he
reigned three months in Jerusalem. And his mother's name *was* Hamutal, the
daughter of Jeremiah of Libnah.
32 And he did *that which was* evil in the sight of the LORD, according to all
that his fathers had done.
33 And Pharaoh-nechoh put him in bands at Riblah in the land of Hamath,
that he might not reign in Jerusalem; and put the land to a tribute of an hun-
dred talents of silver, and a talent of gold.
34 And Pharaoh-nechoh made Eliakim the son of Josiah king in the room of
Josiah his father, and turned his name to Jehoiakim, and took Jehoahaz away:
and he came to Egypt, and died there.
35 And Jehoiakim gave the silver and the gold to Pharaoh; but he taxed the
land to give the money according to the commandment of Pharaoh: he exact-
ed the silver and the gold of the people of the land, of every one according to
his taxation, to give *it* unto Pharaoh-nechoh.
36 Jehoiakim *was* twenty and five years old when he began to reign; and he
reigned eleven years in Jerusalem. And his mother's name *was* Zebudah, the
daughter of Pedaiah of Rumah.
37 And he did *that which was* evil in the sight of the LORD, according to all
that his fathers had done.

Jehoiakim Is Subdued by Nebuchadnezzar of Babylon

24 In his days Nebuchadnezzar king of Babylon came up, and Jehoiakim
became his servant three years: then he turned and rebelled against
him.
2 And the LORD sent against him bands of the Chaldees, and bands of the
Syrians, and bands of the Moabites, and bands of the children of Ammon, and
sent them against Judah to destroy it, according to the word of the LORD, which
he spake by his servants the prophets.
3 Surely at the commandment of the LORD came *this* upon Judah, to remove
them out of his sight, for the sins of Manasseh, according to all that he did;
4 And also for the innocent blood that he shed: for he filled Jerusalem with
innocent blood; which the LORD would not pardon.
5 Now the rest of the acts of Jehoiakim, and all that he did, *are* they not
written in the book of the chronicles of the kings of Judah?
6 So Jehoiakim slept with his fathers: and Jehoiachin his son reigned in his
stead.
7 And the king of Egypt came not again any more out of his land: for the king
of Babylon had taken from the river of Egypt unto the river Euphrates all that
pertained to the king of Egypt.

During Jehoiachin's Evil Reign over Judah, Babylon Invades a Second Time

8 Jehoiachin *was* eighteen years old when he began to reign, and he reigned
in Jerusalem three months. And his mother's name *was* Nehushta, the daugh-
ter of Elnathan of Jerusalem.
9 And he did *that which was* evil in the sight of the LORD, according to all
that his father had done.
10 At that time the servants of Nebuchadnezzar king of Babylon came up
against Jerusalem, and the city was besieged.
11 And Nebuchadnezzar king of Babylon came against the city, and his
servants did besiege it.

12 And Jehoiachin the king of Judah went out to the king of Babylon, he, and
his mother, and his servants, and his princes, and his officers: and the king of
Babylon took him in the eighth year of his reign.
13 And he carried out thence all the treasures of the house of the LORD, and
the treasures of the king's house, and cut in pieces all the vessels of gold which
Solomon king of Israel had made in the temple of the LORD, as the LORD had said.
14 And he carried away all Jerusalem, and all the princes, and all the mighty
men of valour, *even* ten thousand captives, and all the craftsmen and smiths:
none remained, save the poorest sort of the people of the land.
15 And he carried away Jehoiachin to Babylon, and the king's mother, and
the king's wives, and his officers, and the mighty of the land, *those* carried he
into captivity from Jerusalem to Babylon.
16 And all the men of might, *even* seven thousand, and craftsmen and smiths
a thousand, all *that were* strong *and* apt for war, even them the king of Babylon
brought captive to Babylon.
17 And the king of Babylon made Mattaniah his father's brother king in his
stead, and changed his name to Zedekiah.
18 Zedekiah *was* twenty and one years old when he began to reign, and he
reigned eleven years in Jerusalem. And his mother's name *was* Hamutal, the
daughter of Jeremiah of Libnah.
19 And he did *that which was* evil in the sight of the LORD, according to all
that Jehoiakim had done.
20 For through the anger of the LORD it came to pass in Jerusalem and Judah,
until he had cast them out from his presence, that Zedekiah rebelled against
the king of Babylon.

Nebuchadnezzar Attacks Jerusalem the Third and Final Time

25 And it came to pass in the ninth year of his reign, in the tenth month,
in the tenth *day* of the month, *that* Nebuchadnezzar king of Babylon
came, he, and all his host, against Jerusalem, and pitched against it; and they
built forts against it round about.
2 And the city was besieged unto the eleventh year of king Zedekiah.
3 And on the ninth *day* of the *fourth* month the famine prevailed in the city,
and there was no bread for the people of the land.
4 And the city was broken up, and all the men of war *fled* by night by the way
of the gate between two walls, which *is* by the king's garden: (now the Chaldees
were against the city round about:) and *the king* went the way toward the plain.
5 And the army of the Chaldees pursued after the king, and overtook him in
the plains of Jericho: and all his army were scattered from him.
6 So they took the king, and brought him up to the king of Babylon to Riblah;
and they gave judgment upon him.
7 And they slew the sons of Zedekiah before his eyes, and put out the eyes of
Zedekiah, and bound him with fetters of brass, and carried him to Babylon.

The Babylonians Destroy Jerusalem and Take a Final Wave of Captives

8 And in the fifth month, on the seventh *day* of the month, which *is* the
nineteenth year of king Nebuchadnezzar king of Babylon, came Nebuzar-
adan, captain of the guard, a servant of the king of Babylon, unto Jerusalem:
9 And he burnt the house of the LORD, and the king's house, and all the hous-
es of Jerusalem, and every great *man's* house burnt he with fire.
10 And all the army of the Chaldees, that *were with* the captain of the guard,
brake down the walls of Jerusalem round about.
11 Now the rest of the people *that were* left in the city, and the fugitives that
fell away to the king of Babylon, with the remnant of the multitude, did
Nebuzar-adan the captain of the guard carry away.
12 But the captain of the guard left of the poor of the land *to be* vinedressers
and husbandmen.

13 And the pillars of brass that *were* in the house of the LORD, and the bases,
and the brasen sea that *was* in the house of the LORD, did the Chaldees break
in pieces, and carried the brass of them to Babylon.
14 And the pots, and the shovels, and the snuffers, and the spoons, and all
the vessels of brass wherewith they ministered, took they away.
15 And the firepans, and the bowls, *and* such things as *were* of gold, *in* gold,
and of silver, *in* silver, the captain of the guard took away.
16 The two pillars, one sea, and the bases which Solomon had made for the
house of the LORD; the brass of all these vessels was without weight.
17 The height of the one pillar *was* eighteen cubits, and the chapiter upon it
was brass: and the height of the chapiter three cubits; and the wreathen work,
and pomegranates upon the chapiter round about, all of brass: and like unto
these had the second pillar with wreathen work.
18 And the captain of the guard took Seraiah the chief priest, and Zephaniah
the second priest, and the three keepers of the door:
19 And out of the city he took an officer that was set over the men of war, and
five men of them that were in the king's presence, which were found in the
city, and the principal scribe of the host, which mustered the people of the
land, and threescore men of the people of the land *that were* found in the city:
20 And Nebuzar-adan captain of the guard took these, and brought them to
the king of Babylon to Riblah:
21 And the king of Babylon smote them, and slew them at Riblah in the land
of Hamath. So Judah was carried away out of their land.

Gedaliah Is Slain, and the Rest of Those Left Behind Flee to Egypt

22 And *as for* the people that remained in the land of Judah, whom
Nebuchadnezzar king of Babylon had left, even over them he made Gedaliah
the son of Ahikam, the son of Shaphan, ruler.
23 And when all the captains of the armies, they and their men, heard that
the king of Babylon had made Gedaliah governor, there came to Gedaliah to
Mizpah, even Ishmael the son of Nethaniah, and Johanan the son of Careah,
and Seraiah the son of Tanhumeth the Netophathite, and Jaazaniah the son
of a Maachathite, they and their men.
24 And Gedaliah sware to them, and to their men, and said unto them, Fear
not to be the servants of the Chaldees: dwell in the land, and serve the king of
Babylon; and it shall be well with you.
25 But it came to pass in the seventh month, that Ishmael the son of
Nethaniah, the son of Elishama, of the seed royal, came, and ten men with
him, and smote Gedaliah, that he died, and the Jews and the Chaldees that
were with him at Mizpah.
26 And all the people, both small and great, and the captains of the armies,
arose, and came to Egypt: for they were afraid of the Chaldees.
27 And it came to pass in the seven and thirtieth year of the captivity of
Jehoiachin king of Judah, in the twelfth month, on the seven and twentieth
day of the month, *that* Evil-merodach king of Babylon in the year that he
began to reign did lift up the head of Jehoiachin king of Judah out of prison;
28 And he spake kindly to him, and set his throne above the throne of the
kings that *were* with him in Babylon;
29 And changed his prison garments: and he did eat bread continually before
him all the days of his life.
30 And his allowance *was* a continual allowance given him of the king, a daily
rate for every day, all the days of his life.

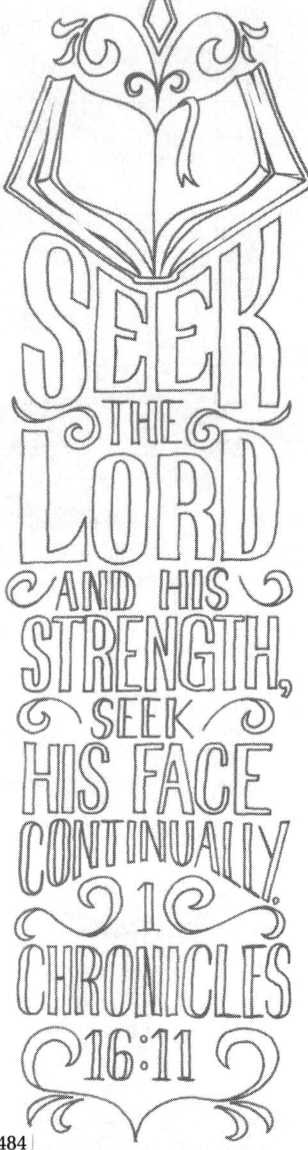

The Genealogy of Adam's Descendants

1 Adam, Sheth, Enosh,
2 Kenan, Mahalaleel, Jered,
3 Henoch, Methuselah, Lamech,
4 Noah, Shem, Ham, and Japheth.
5 The sons of Japheth; Gomer, and Magog, and Madai, and Javan, and Tubal,
and Meshech, and Tiras.
6 And the sons of Gomer; Ashchenaz, and Riphath, and Togarmah.
7 And the sons of Javan; Elishah, and Tarshish, Kittim, and Dodanim.
8 The sons of Ham; Cush, and Mizraim, Put, and Canaan.
9 And the sons of Cush; Seba, and Havilah, and Sabta, and Raamah, and
Sabtecha. And the sons of Raamah; Sheba, and Dedan.
10 And Cush begat Nimrod: he began to be mighty upon the earth.
11 And Mizraim begat Ludim, and Anamim, and Lehabim, and Naphtuhim,
12 And Pathrusim, and Casluhim, (of whom came the Philistines,) and
Caphthorim.
13 And Canaan begat Zidon his firstborn, and Heth,
14 The Jebusite also, and the Amorite, and the Girgashite,
15 And the Hivite, and the Arkite, and the Sinite,
16 And the Arvadite, and the Zemarite, and the Hamathite.
17 The sons of Shem; Elam, and Asshur, and Arphaxad, and Lud, and Aram,
and Uz, and Hul, and Gether, and Meshech.
18 And Arphaxad begat Shelah, and Shelah begat Eber.
19 And unto Eber were born two sons: the name of the one *was* Peleg; because
in his days the earth was divided: and his brother's name *was* Joktan.
20 And Joktan begat Almodad, and Sheleph, and Hazar-maveth, and Jerah,
21 Hadoram also, and Uzal, and Diklah,
22 And Ebal, and Abimael, and Sheba,
23 And Ophir, and Havilah, and Jobab. All these *were* the sons of Joktan.
24 Shem, Arphaxad, Shelah,
25 Eber, Peleg, Reu,
26 Serug, Nahor, Terah,
27 Abram; the same *is* Abraham.
28 The sons of Abraham; Isaac, and Ishmael.
29 These *are* their generations: The firstborn of Ishmael, Nebaioth; then
Kedar, and Adbeel, and Mibsam,
30 Mishma, and Dumah, Massa, Hadad, and Tema,
31 Jetur, Naphish, and Kedemah. These are the sons of Ishmael.
32 Now the sons of Keturah, Abraham's concubine: she bare Zimran, and
Jokshan, and Medan, and Midian, and Ishbak, and Shuah. And the sons of
Jokshan; Sheba, and Dedan.
33 And the sons of Midian; Ephah, and Epher, and Henoch, and Abida, and
Eldaah. All these *are* the sons of Keturah.
34 And Abraham begat Isaac. The sons of Isaac; Esau and Israel.
35 The sons of Esau; Eliphaz, Reuel, and Jeush, and Jaalam, and Korah.
36 The sons of Eliphaz; Teman, and Omar, Zephi, and Gatam, Kenaz, and
Timna, and Amalek.
37 The sons of Reuel; Nahath, Zerah, Shammah, and Mizzah.

38 And the sons of Seir; Lotan, and Shobal, and Zibeon, and Anah, and
Dishon, and Ezer, and Dishan.
39 And the sons of Lotan; Hori, and Homam: and Timna *was* Lotan's sister.
40 The sons of Shobal; Alian, and Manahath, and Ebal, Shephi, and Onam.
And the sons of Zibeon; Aiah, and Anah.
41 The sons of Anah; Dishon. And the sons of Dishon; Amram, and Eshban,
and Ithran, and Cheran.
42 The sons of Ezer; Bilhan, and Zavan, *and* Jakan. The sons of Dishan; Uz,
and Aran.
43 Now these *are* the kings that reigned in the land of Edom before *any* king
reigned over the children of Israel; Bela the son of Beor: and the name of his
city *was* Dinhabah.
44 And when Bela was dead, Jobab the son of Zerah of Bozrah reigned in his
stead.
45 And when Jobab was dead, Husham of the land of the Temanites reigned
in his stead.
46 And when Husham was dead, Hadad the son of Bedad, which smote
Midian in the field of Moab, reigned in his stead: and the name of his city *was*
Avith.
47 And when Hadad was dead, Samlah of Masrekah reigned in his stead.
48 And when Samlah was dead, Shaul of Rehoboth by the river reigned in
his stead.
49 And when Shaul was dead, Baal-hanan the son of Achbor reigned in his
stead.
50 And when Baal-hanan was dead, Hadad reigned in his stead: and the name
of his city *was* Pai; and his wife's name *was* Mehetabel, the daughter of Matred,
the daughter of Mezahab.
51 Hadad died also. And the dukes of Edom were; duke Timnah, duke Aliah,
duke Jetheth,
52 Duke Aholibamah, duke Elah, duke Pinon,
53 Duke Kenaz, duke Teman, duke Mibzar,
54 Duke Magdiel, duke Iram. These *are* the dukes of Edom.

Israel's Sons and Judah's Descendants

2 These *are* the sons of Israel; Reuben, Simeon, Levi, and Judah, Issachar, and
Zebulun,
2 Dan, Joseph, and Benjamin, Naphtali, Gad, and Asher.
3 The sons of Judah; Er, and Onan, and Shelah: *which* three were born unto
him of the daughter of Shua the Canaanitess. And Er, the firstborn of Judah,
was evil in the sight of the LORD; and he slew him.
4 And Tamar his daughter in law bare him Pharez and Zerah. All the sons of
Judah *were* five.
5 The sons of Pharez; Hezron, and Hamul.
6 And the sons of Zerah; Zimri, and Ethan, and Heman, and Calcol, and Dara:
five of them in all.
7 And the sons of Carmi; Achar, the troubler of Israel, who transgressed in
the thing accursed.
8 And the sons of Ethan; Azariah.
9 The sons also of Hezron, that were born unto him; Jerahmeel, and Ram,
and Chelubai.
10 And Ram begat Amminadab; and Amminadab begat Nahshon, prince of
the children of Judah;
11 And Nahshon begat Salma, and Salma begat Boaz,
12 And Boaz begat Obed, and Obed begat Jesse,
13 And Jesse begat his firstborn Eliab, and Abinadab the second, and Shimma
the third,

14 Nethaneel the fourth, Raddai the fifth,
15 Ozem the sixth, David the seventh:
16 Whose sisters *were* Zeruiah, and Abigail. And the sons of Zeruiah; Abishai,
and Joab, and Asahel, three.
17 And Abigail bare Amasa: and the father of Amasa *was* Jether the Ishmeelite.

Caleb's Descendants

18 And Caleb the son of Hezron begat *children* of Azubah *his* wife, and of
Jerioth: her sons *are* these; Jesher, and Shobab, and Ardon.
19 And when Azubah was dead, Caleb took unto him Ephrath, which bare
him Hur.
20 And Hur begat Uri, and Uri begat Bezaleel.
21 And afterward Hezron went in to the daughter of Machir the father of
Gilead, whom he married when he *was* threescore years old; and she bare him
Segub.
22 And Segub begat Jair, who had three and twenty cities in the land of Gilead.
23 And he took Geshur, and Aram, with the towns of Jair, from them, with
Kenath, and the towns thereof, *even* threescore cities. All these *belonged to* the
sons of Machir the father of Gilead.
24 And after that Hezron was dead in Caleb-ephratah, then Abiah Hezron's
wife bare him Ashur the father of Tekoa.
25 And the sons of Jerahmeel the firstborn of Hezron were, Ram the first-
born, and Bunah, and Oren, and Ozem, *and* Ahijah.
26 Jerahmeel had also another wife, whose name *was* Atarah; she *was* the
mother of Onam.
27 And the sons of Ram the firstborn of Jerahmeel were, Maaz, and Jamin,
and Eker.
28 And the sons of Onam were, Shammai, and Jada. And the sons of Shammai;
Nadab, and Abishur.
29 And the name of the wife of Abishur *was* Abihail, and she bare him Ahban,
and Molid.
30 And the sons of Nadab; Seled, and Appaim: but Seled died without chil-
dren.
31 And the sons of Appaim; Ishi. And the sons of Ishi; Sheshan. And the chil-
dren of Sheshan; Ahlai.
32 And the sons of Jada the brother of Shammai; Jether, and Jonathan: and
Jether died without children.
33 And the sons of Jonathan; Peleth, and Zaza. These were the sons of
Jerahmeel.
34 Now Sheshan had no sons, but daughters. And Sheshan had a servant, an
Egyptian, whose name *was* Jarha.
35 And Sheshan gave his daughter to Jarha his servant to wife; and she bare
him Attai.
36 And Attai begat Nathan, and Nathan begat Zabad,
37 And Zabad begat Ephlal, and Ephlal begat Obed,
38 And Obed begat Jehu, and Jehu begat Azariah,
39 And Azariah begat Helez, and Helez begat Eleasah,
40 And Eleasah begat Sisamai, and Sisamai begat Shallum,
41 And Shallum begat Jekamiah, and Jekamiah begat Elishama.
42 Now the sons of Caleb the brother of Jerahmeel *were*, Mesha his firstborn,
which was the father of Ziph; and the sons of Mareshah the father of Hebron.
43 And the sons of Hebron; Korah, and Tappuah, and Rekem, and Shema.
44 And Shema begat Raham, the father of Jorkoam: and Rekem begat
Shammai.
45 And the son of Shammai *was* Maon: and Maon *was* the father of Beth-zur.

46 And Ephah, Caleb's concubine, bare Haran, and Moza, and Gazez: and
Haran begat Gazez.
47 And the sons of Jahdai; Regem, and Jotham, and Geshan, and Pelet, and
Ephah, and Shaaph.
48 Maachah, Caleb's concubine, bare Sheber, and Tirhanah.
49 She bare also Shaaph the father of Madmannah, Sheva the father of
Machbenah, and the father of Gibea: and the daughter of Caleb *was* Achsah.
50 These were the sons of Caleb the son of Hur, the firstborn of Ephratah;
Shobal the father of Kirjath-jearim,
51 Salma the father of Beth-lehem, Hareph the father of Beth-gader.
52 And Shobal the father of Kirjath-jearim had sons; Haroeh, *and* half of the
Manahethites.
53 And the families of Kirjath-jearim; the Ithrites, and the Puhites, and the
Shumathites, and the Mishraites; of them came the Zareathites, and the
Eshtaulites.
54 The sons of Salma; Beth-lehem, and the Netophathites, Ataroth, the house
of Joab, and half of the Manahethites, the Zorites.
55 And the families of the scribes which dwelt at Jabez; the Tirathites, the
Shimeathites, *and* Suchathites. These *are* the Kenites that came of Hemath,
the father of the house of Rechab.

The Sons of David

3 Now these were the sons of David, which were born unto him in Hebron;
the firstborn Amnon, of Ahinoam the Jezreelitess; the second Daniel, of
Abigail the Carmelitess:
2 The third, Absalom the son of Maachah the daughter of Talmai king of
Geshur: the fourth, Adonijah the son of Haggith:
3 The fifth, Shephatiah of Abital: the sixth, Ithream by Eglah his wife.
4 *These* six were born unto him in Hebron; and there he reigned seven years
and six months: and in Jerusalem he reigned thirty and three years.
5 And these were born unto him in Jerusalem; Shimea, and Shobab, and
Nathan, and Solomon, four, of Bath-shua the daughter of Ammiel:
6 Ibhar also, and Elishama, and Eliphelet,
7 And Nogah, and Nepheg, and Japhia,
8 And Elishama, and Eliada, and Eliphelet, nine.
9 *These were* all the sons of David, beside the sons of the concubines, and
Tamar their sister.

David's Descendants

10 And Solomon's son *was* Rehoboam, Abia his son, Asa his son, Jehoshaphat
his son,
11 Joram his son, Ahaziah his son, Joash his son,
12 Amaziah his son, Azariah his son, Jotham his son,
13 Ahaz his son, Hezekiah his son, Manasseh his son,
14 Amon his son, Josiah his son.
15 And the sons of Josiah *were*, the firstborn Johanan, the second Jehoiakim,
the third Zedekiah, the fourth Shallum.
16 And the sons of Jehoiakim: Jeconiah his son, Zedekiah his son.
17 And the sons of Jeconiah; Assir, Salathiel his son,
18 Malchiram also, and Pedaiah, and Shenazar, Jecamiah, Hoshama, and
Nedabiah.
19 And the sons of Pedaiah *were*, Zerubbabel, and Shimei: and the sons of
Zerubbabel; Meshullam, and Hananiah, and Shelomith their sister:
20 And Hashubah, and Ohel, and Berechiah, and Hasadiah, Jushab-hesed,
five.
21 And the sons of Hananiah; Pelatiah, and Jesaiah: the sons of Rephaiah,
the sons of Arnan, the sons of Obadiah, the sons of Shechaniah.

GOD granted HIM THAT WHICH HE REQUESTED.

I CHRONICLES 4:10

22 And the sons of Shechaniah; Shemaiah: and the sons of Shemaiah; Hattush,
and Igeal, and Bariah, and Neariah, and Shaphat, six.
23 And the sons of Neariah; Elioenai, and Hezekiah, and Azrikam, three.
24 And the sons of Elioenai *were*, Hodaiah, and Eliashib, and Pelaiah, and
Akkub, and Johanan, and Dalaiah, and Anani, seven.

More of Judah's Descendants

4 The sons of Judah; Pharez, Hezron, and Carmi, and Hur, and Shobal.
2 And Reaiah the son of Shobal begat Jahath; and Jahath begat Ahumai,
and Lahad. These *are* the families of the Zorathites.
3 And these *were of* the father of Etam; Jezreel, and Ishma, and Idbash: and
the name of their sister *was* Hazelelponi:
4 And Penuel the father of Gedor, and Ezer the father of Hushah. These *are*
the sons of Hur, the firstborn of Ephratah, the father of Beth-lehem.
5 And Ashur the father of Tekoa had two wives, Helah and Naarah.
6 And Naarah bare him Ahuzam, and Hepher, and Temeni, and Haahashtari.
These *were* the sons of Naarah.
7 And the sons of Helah *were*, Zereth, and Jezoar, and Ethnan.
8 And Coz begat Anub, and Zobebah, and the families of Aharhel the son of
Harum.
9 And Jabez was more honourable than his brethren: and his mother called
his name Jabez, saying, Because I bare him with sorrow.
10 And Jabez called on the God of Israel, saying, Oh that thou wouldest bless
me indeed, and enlarge my coast, and that thine hand might be with me, and
that thou wouldest keep *me* from evil, that it may not grieve me! And God
granted him that which he requested.
11 And Chelub the brother of Shuah begat Mehir, which *was* the father of
Eshton.
12 And Eshton begat Beth-rapha, and Paseah, and Tehinnah the father of
Ir-nahash. These *are* the men of Rechah.
13 And the sons of Kenaz; Othniel, and Seraiah: and the sons of Othniel;
Hathath.
14 And Meonothai begat Ophrah: and Seraiah begat Joab, the father of the
valley of Charashim; for they were craftsmen.
15 And the sons of Caleb the son of Jephunneh; Iru, Elah, and Naam: and the
sons of Elah, even Kenaz.
16 And the sons of Jehaleleel; Ziph, and Ziphah, Tiria, and Asareel.
17 And the sons of Ezra *were*, Jether, and Mered, and Epher, and Jalon: and
she bare Miriam, and Shammai, and Ishbah the father of Eshtemoa.
18 And his wife Jehudijah bare Jered the father of Gedor, and Heber the father
of Socho, and Jekuthiel the father of Zanoah. And these *are* the sons of Bithiah
the daughter of Pharaoh, which Mered took.
19 And the sons of *his* wife Hodiah the sister of Naham, the father of Keilah
the Garmite, and Eshtemoa the Maachathite.
20 And the sons of Shimon *were*, Amnon, and Rinnah, Ben-hanan, and Tilon.
And the sons of Ishi *were*, Zoheth, and Ben-zoheth.
21 The sons of Shelah the son of Judah *were*, Er the father of Lecah, and
Laadah the father of Mareshah, and the families of the house of them that
wrought fine linen, of the house of Ashbea,
22 And Jokim, and the men of Chozeba, and Joash, and Saraph, who had the
dominion in Moab, and Jashubi-lehem. And *these are* ancient things.
23 These *were* the potters, and those that dwelt among plants and hedges:
there they dwelt with the king for his work.

Simeon's Descendants

24 The sons of Simeon *were*, Nemuel, and Jamin, Jarib, Zerah, *and* Shaul:
25 Shallum his son, Mibsam his son, Mishma his son.

26 And the sons of Mishma; Hamuel his son, Zacchur his son, Shimei his son.
27 And Shimei had sixteen sons and six daughters; but his brethren had not
many children, neither did all their family multiply, like to the children of
Judah.
28 And they dwelt at Beer-sheba, and Moladah, and Hazar-shual,
29 And at Bilhah, and at Ezem, and at Tolad,
30 And at Bethuel, and at Hormah, and at Ziklag,
31 And at Beth-marcaboth, and Hazar-susim, and at Beth-birei, and at
Shaaraim. These *were* their cities unto the reign of David.
32 And their villages *were*, Etam, and Ain, Rimmon, and Tochen, and Ashan,
five cities:
33 And all their villages that *were* round about the same cities, unto Baal.
These *were* their habitations, and their genealogy.
34 And Meshobab, and Jamlech, and Joshah the son of Amaziah,
35 And Joel, and Jehu the son of Josibiah, the son of Seraiah, the son of Asiel,
36 And Elioenai, and Jaakobah, and Jeshohaiah, and Asaiah, and Adiel, and
Jesimiel, and Benaiah,
37 And Ziza the son of Shiphi, the son of Allon, the son of Jedaiah, the son of
Shimri, the son of Shemaiah;
38 These mentioned by *their* names *were* princes in their families: and the
house of their fathers increased greatly.
39 And they went to the entrance of Gedor, *even* unto the east side of the
valley, to seek pasture for their flocks.
40 And they found fat pasture and good, and the land *was* wide, and quiet,
and peaceable; for *they* of Ham had dwelt there of old.
41 And these written by name came in the days of Hezekiah king of Judah,
and smote their tents, and the habitations that were found there, and
destroyed them utterly unto this day, and dwelt in their rooms: because *there*
was pasture there for their flocks.
42 And *some* of them, *even* of the sons of Simeon, five hundred men, went to
mount Seir, having for their captains Pelatiah, and Neariah, and Rephaiah,
and Uzziel, the sons of Ishi.
43 And they smote the rest of the Amalekites that were escaped, and dwelt
there unto this day.

Reuben's Descendants

5 Now the sons of Reuben the firstborn of Israel, (for he *was* the firstborn;
but, forasmuch as he defiled his father's bed, his birthright was given unto
the sons of Joseph the son of Israel: and the genealogy is not to be reckoned after
the birthright.
2 For Judah prevailed above his brethren, and of him *came* the chief ruler;
but the birthright *was* Joseph's:)
3 The sons, *I say*, of Reuben the firstborn of Israel *were*, Hanoch, and Pallu,
Hezron, and Carmi.
4 The sons of Joel; Shemaiah his son, Gog his son, Shimei his son,
5 Micah his son, Reaia his son, Baal his son,
6 Beerah his son, whom Tilgath-pilneser king of Assyria carried away *captive*:
he *was* prince of the Reubenites.
7 And his brethren by their families, when the genealogy of their generations
was reckoned, *were* the chief, Jeiel, and Zechariah,
8 And Bela the son of Azaz, the son of Shema, the son of Joel, who dwelt in
Aroer, even unto Nebo and Baal-meon:
9 And eastward he inhabited unto the entering in of the wilderness from the
river Euphrates: because their cattle were multiplied in the land of Gilead.
10 And in the days of Saul they made war with the Hagarites, who fell by their
hand: and they dwelt in their tents throughout all the east *land* of Gilead.

Gad's Descendants

11 And the children of Gad dwelt over against them, in the land of Bashan unto Salchah:

12 Joel the chief, and Shapham the next, and Jaanai, and Shaphat in Bashan.

13 And their brethren of the house of their fathers *were*, Michael, and Meshullam, and Sheba, and Jorai, and Jachan, and Zia, and Heber, seven.

14 These *are* the children of Abihail the son of Huri, the son of Jaroah, the son of Gilead, the son of Michael, the son of Jeshishai, the son of Jahdo, the son of Buz;

15 Ahi the son of Abdiel, the son of Guni, chief of the house of their fathers.

16 And they dwelt in Gilead in Bashan, and in her towns, and in all the suburbs of Sharon, upon their borders.

17 All these were reckoned by genealogies in the days of Jotham king of Judah, and in the days of Jeroboam king of Israel.

The Census and Conquests of Reuben, Gad, and the Half Tribe of Manasseh

18 The sons of Reuben, and the Gadites, and half the tribe of Manasseh, of valiant men, men able to bear buckler and sword, and to shoot with bow, and skilful in war, *were* four and forty thousand seven hundred and threescore, that went out to the war.

19 And they made war with the Hagarites, with Jetur, and Nephish, and Nodab.

20 And they were helped against them, and the Hagarites were delivered into their hand, and all that *were* with them: for they cried to God in the battle, and he was intreated of them; because they put their trust in him.

21 And they took away their cattle; of their camels fifty thousand, and of sheep two hundred and fifty thousand, and of asses two thousand, and of men an hundred thousand.

22 For there fell down many slain, because the war *was* of God. And they dwelt in their steads until the captivity.

23 And the children of the half tribe of Manasseh dwelt in the land: they increased from Bashan unto Baal-hermon and Senir, and unto mount Hermon.

24 And these *were* the heads of the house of their fathers, even Epher, and Ishi, and Eliel, and Azriel, and Jeremiah, and Hodaviah, and Jahdiel, mighty men of valour, famous men, *and* heads of the house of their fathers.

25 And they transgressed against the God of their fathers, and went a whoring after the gods of the people of the land, whom God destroyed before them.

26 And the God of Israel stirred up the spirit of Pul king of Assyria, and the spirit of Tilgath-pilneser king of Assyria, and he carried them away, even the Reubenites, and the Gadites, and the half tribe of Manasseh, and brought them unto Halah, and Habor, and Hara, and to the river Gozan, unto this day.

Levi's Descendants

6 The sons of Levi; Gershon, Kohath, and Merari.

2 And the sons of Kohath; Amram, Izhar, and Hebron, and Uzziel.

3 And the children of Amram; Aaron, and Moses, and Miriam. The sons also of Aaron; Nadab, and Abihu, Eleazar, and Ithamar.

4 Eleazar begat Phinehas, Phinehas begat Abishua,

5 And Abishua begat Bukki, and Bukki begat Uzzi,

6 And Uzzi begat Zerahiah, and Zerahiah begat Meraioth,

7 Meraioth begat Amariah, and Amariah begat Ahitub,

8 And Ahitub begat Zadok, and Zadok begat Ahimaaz,

9 And Ahimaaz begat Azariah, and Azariah begat Johanan,

10 And Johanan begat Azariah, (he *it is* that executed the priest's office in the temple that Solomon built in Jerusalem:)

11 And Azariah begat Amariah, and Amariah begat Ahitub,
12 And Ahitub begat Zadok, and Zadok begat Shallum,
13 And Shallum begat Hilkiah, and Hilkiah begat Azariah,
14 And Azariah begat Seraiah, and Seraiah begat Jehozadak,
15 And Jehozadak went *into captivity*, when the LORD carried away Judah
and Jerusalem by the hand of Nebuchadnezzar.
16 The sons of Levi; Gershom, Kohath, and Merari.
17 And these *be* the names of the sons of Gershom; Libni, and Shimei.
18 And the sons of Kohath *were*, Amram, and Izhar, and Hebron, and Uzziel.
19 The sons of Merari; Mahli, and Mushi. And these *are* the families of the
Levites according to their fathers.
20 Of Gershom; Libni his son, Jahath his son, Zimmah his son,
21 Joah his son, Iddo his son, Zerah his son, Jeaterai his son.
22 The sons of Kohath; Amminadab his son, Korah his son, Assir his son,
23 Elkanah his son, and Ebiasaph his son, and Assir his son,
24 Tahath his son, Uriel his son, Uzziah his son, and Shaul his son.
25 And the sons of Elkanah; Amasai, and Ahimoth.
26 *As for* Elkanah: the sons of Elkanah; Zophai his son, and Nahath his son,
27 Eliab his son, Jeroham his son, Elkanah his son.
28 And the sons of Samuel; the firstborn Vashni, and Abiah.
29 The sons of Merari; Mahli, Libni his son, Shimei his son, Uzza his son,
30 Shimea his son, Haggiah his son, Asaiah his son.
31 And these *are they* whom David set over the service of song in the house
of the LORD, after that the ark had rest.
32 And they ministered before the dwelling place of the tabernacle of the
congregation with singing, until Solomon had built the house of the LORD in
Jerusalem: and *then* they waited on their office according to their order.
33 And these *are* they that waited with their children. Of the sons of the
Kohathites: Heman a singer, the son of Joel, the son of Shemuel,
34 The son of Elkanah, the son of Jeroham, the son of Eliel, the son of Toah,
35 The son of Zuph, the son of Elkanah, the son of Mahath, the son of Amasai,
36 The son of Elkanah, the son of Joel, the son of Azariah, the son of
Zephaniah,
37 The son of Tahath, the son of Assir, the son of Ebiasaph, the son of Korah,
38 The son of Izhar, the son of Kohath, the son of Levi, the son of Israel.
39 And his brother Asaph, who stood on his right hand, *even* Asaph the son
of Berachiah, the son of Shimea,
40 The son of Michael, the son of Baaseiah, the son of Malchiah,
41 The son of Ethni, the son of Zerah, the son of Adaiah,
42 The son of Ethan, the son of Zimmah, the son of Shimei,
43 The son of Jahath, the son of Gershom, the son of Levi.
44 And their brethren the sons of Merari *stood* on the left hand: Ethan the
son of Kishi, the son of Abdi, the son of Malluch,
45 The son of Hashabiah, the son of Amaziah, the son of Hilkiah,
46 The son of Amzi, the son of Bani, the son of Shamer,
47 The son of Mahli, the son of Mushi, the son of Merari, the son of Levi.
48 Their brethren also the Levites *were* appointed unto all manner of service
of the tabernacle of the house of God.
49 But Aaron and his sons offered upon the altar of the burnt offering, and
on the altar of incense, *and were appointed* for all the work of the *place* most
holy, and to make an atonement for Israel, according to all that Moses the
servant of God had commanded.
50 And these *are* the sons of Aaron; Eleazar his son, Phinehas his son, Abishua
his son,
51 Bukki his son, Uzzi his son, Zerahiah his son,
52 Meraioth his son, Amariah his son, Ahitub his son,

53 Zadok his son, Ahimaaz his son.

The Cities of the Priests and Levites

54 Now these *are* their dwelling places throughout their castles in their
coasts, of the sons of Aaron, of the families of the Kohathites: for theirs was
the lot.
55 And they gave them Hebron in the land of Judah, and the suburbs there-
of round about it.
56 But the fields of the city, and the villages thereof, they gave to Caleb the
son of Jephunneh.
57 And to the sons of Aaron they gave the cities of Judah, *namely*, Hebron,
the city of refuge, and Libnah with her suburbs, and Jattir, and Eshtemoa, with
their suburbs,
58 And Hilen with her suburbs, Debir with her suburbs,
59 And Ashan with her suburbs, and Beth-shemesh with her suburbs:
60 And out of the tribe of Benjamin; Geba with her suburbs, and Alemeth
with her suburbs, and Anathoth with her suburbs. All their cities throughout
their families *were* thirteen cities.
61 And unto the sons of Kohath, *which were* left of the family of that tribe,
were cities given out of the half tribe, *namely, out of* the half *tribe* of Manasseh,
by lot, ten cities.
62 And to the sons of Gershom throughout their families out of the tribe of
Issachar, and out of the tribe of Asher, and out of the tribe of Naphtali, and
out of the tribe of Manasseh in Bashan, thirteen cities.
63 Unto the sons of Merari *were given* by lot, throughout their families, out
of the tribe of Reuben, and out of the tribe of Gad, and out of the tribe of
Zebulun, twelve cities.
64 And the children of Israel gave to the Levites *these* cities with their suburbs.
65 And they gave by lot out of the tribe of the children of Judah, and out of
the tribe of the children of Simeon, and out of the tribe of the children of
Benjamin, these cities, which are called by *their* names.
66 And *the residue* of the families of the sons of Kohath had cities of their
coasts out of the tribe of Ephraim.
67 And they gave unto them, *of* the cities of refuge, Shechem in mount
Ephraim with her suburbs; *they gave* also Gezer with her suburbs,
68 And Jokmeam with her suburbs, and Beth-horon with her suburbs,
69 And Aijalon with her suburbs, and Gath-rimmon with her suburbs:
70 And out of the half tribe of Manasseh; Aner with her suburbs, and Bileam
with her suburbs, for the family of the remnant of the sons of Kohath.
71 Unto the sons of Gershom *were given* out of the family of the half tribe of
Manasseh, Golan in Bashan with her suburbs, and Ashtaroth with her suburbs:
72 And out of the tribe of Issachar; Kedesh with her suburbs, Daberath with
her suburbs,
73 And Ramoth with her suburbs, and Anem with her suburbs:
74 And out of the tribe of Asher; Mashal with her suburbs, and Abdon with
her suburbs,
75 And Hukok with her suburbs, and Rehob with her suburbs:
76 And out of the tribe of Naphtali; Kedesh in Galilee with her suburbs, and
Hammon with her suburbs, and Kirjathaim with her suburbs.
77 Unto the rest of the children of Merari *were given* out of the tribe of
Zebulun, Rimmon with her suburbs, Tabor with her suburbs:
78 And on the other side Jordan by Jericho, on the east side of Jordan, *were
given them* out of the tribe of Reuben, Bezer in the wilderness with her sub-
urbs, and Jahzah with her suburbs,
79 Kedemoth also with her suburbs, and Mephaath with her suburbs:

80 And out of the tribe of Gad; Ramoth in Gilead with her suburbs, and
Mahanaim with her suburbs,
81 And Heshbon with her suburbs, and Jazer with her suburbs.

Issachar's Descendants

7 Now the sons of Issachar *were*, Tola, and Puah, Jashub, and Shimron, four.
2 And the sons of Tola; Uzzi, and Rephaiah, and Jeriel, and Jahmai, and
Jibsam, and Shemuel, heads of their father's house, *to wit*, of Tola: *they were*
valiant men of might in their generations; whose number *was* in the days of
David two and twenty thousand and six hundred.
3 And the sons of Uzzi; Izrahiah: and the sons of Izrahiah; Michael, and
Obadiah, and Joel, Ishiah, five: all of them chief men.
4 And with them, by their generations, after the house of their fathers, *were*
bands of soldiers for war, six and thirty thousand *men*: for they had many
wives and sons.
5 And their brethren among all the families of Issachar *were* valiant men of
might, reckoned in all by their genealogies fourscore and seven thousand.

Benjamin's Descendants

6 *The sons* of Benjamin; Bela, and Becher, and Jediael, three.
7 And the sons of Bela; Ezbon, and Uzzi, and Uzziel, and Jerimoth, and Iri,
five; heads of the house of *their* fathers, mighty men of valour; and were reck-
oned by their genealogies twenty and two thousand and thirty and four.
8 And the sons of Becher; Zemira, and Joash, and Eliezer, and Elioenai, and
Omri, and Jerimoth, and Abiah, and Anathoth, and Alameth. All these *are* the
sons of Becher.
9 And the number of them, after their genealogy by their generations, heads
of the house of their fathers, mighty men of valour, *was* twenty thousand and
two hundred.
10 The sons also of Jediael; Bilhan: and the sons of Bilhan; Jeush, and
Benjamin, and Ehud, and Chenaanah, and Zethan, and Tharshish, and
Ahishahar.
11 All these the sons of Jediael, by the heads of their fathers, mighty men of
valour, *were* seventeen thousand and two hundred *soldiers*, fit to go out for
war *and* battle.
12 Shuppim also, and Huppim, the children of Ir, *and* Hushim, the sons of
Aher.

Naphtali's Descendants

13 The sons of Naphtali; Jahziel, and Guni, and Jezer, and Shallum, the sons
of Bilhah.

Manasseh's Descendants Who Lived West of the Jordan

14 The sons of Manasseh; Ashriel, whom she bare: (*but* his concubine the
Aramitess bare Machir the father of Gilead:
15 And Machir took to wife *the sister* of Huppim and Shuppim, whose sister's
name *was* Maachah;) and the name of the second *was* Zelophehad: and
Zelophehad had daughters.
16 And Maachah the wife of Machir bare a son, and she called his name
Peresh; and the name of his brother *was* Sheresh; and his sons *were* Ulam and
Rakem.
17 And the sons of Ulam; Bedan. These *were* the sons of Gilead, the son of
Machir, the son of Manasseh.
18 And his sister Hammoleketh bare Ishod, and Abi-ezer, and Mahalah.
19 And the sons of Shemida were, Ahian, and Shechem, and Likhi, and Aniam.

Ephraim's Descendants

20 And the sons of Ephraim; Shuthelah, and Bered his son, and Tahath his
son, and Eladah his son, and Tahath his son,

21 And Zabad his son, and Shuthelah his son, and Ezer, and Elead, whom the
men of Gath *that were* born in *that* land slew, because they came down to take
away their cattle.
22 And Ephraim their father mourned many days, and his brethren came to
comfort him.
23 And when he went in to his wife, she conceived, and bare a son, and he
called his name Beriah, because it went evil with his house.
24 (And his daughter *was* Sherah, who built Beth-horon the nether, and the
upper, and Uzzen-sherah.)
25 And Rephah *was* his son, also Resheph, and Telah his son, and Tahan his
son,
26 Laadan his son, Ammihud his son, Elishama his son,
27 Non his son, Jehoshua his son.
28 And their possessions and habitations *were*, Beth-el and the towns there-
of, and eastward Naaran, and westward Gezer, with the towns thereof;
Shechem also and the towns thereof, unto Gaza and the towns thereof:
29 And by the borders of the children of Manasseh, Beth-shean and her
towns, Taanach and her towns, Megiddo and her towns, Dor and her towns.
In these dwelt the children of Joseph the son of Israel.

Asher's Descendants

30 The sons of Asher; Imnah, and Isuah, and Ishuai, and Beriah, and Serah
their sister.
31 And the sons of Beriah; Heber, and Malchiel, who *is* the father of Birzavith.
32 And Heber begat Japhlet, and Shomer, and Hotham, and Shua their sister.
33 And the sons of Japhlet; Pasach, and Bimhal, and Ashvath. These *are* the
children of Japhlet.
34 And the sons of Shamer; Ahi, and Rohgah, Jehubbah, and Aram.
35 And the sons of his brother Helem; Zophah, and Imna, and Shelesh, and
Amal.
36 The sons of Zophah; Suah, and Harnepher, and Shual, and Beri, and Imrah,
37 Bezer, and Hod, and Shamma, and Shilshah, and Ithran, and Beera.
38 And the sons of Jether; Jephunneh, and Pispah, and Ara.
39 And the sons of Ulla; Arah, and Haniel, and Rezia.
40 All these *were* the children of Asher, heads of *their* father's house, choice
and mighty men of valour, chief of the princes. And the number throughout
the genealogy of them that were apt to the war *and* to battle *was* twenty and
six thousand men.

More on Benjamin's Descendants

8 Now Benjamin begat Bela his firstborn, Ashbel the second, and Aharah the
third,
2 Nohah the fourth, and Rapha the fifth.
3 And the sons of Bela were, Addar, and Gera, and Abihud,
4 And Abishua, and Naaman, and Ahoah,
5 And Gera, and Shephuphan, and Huram.
6 And these *are* the sons of Ehud: these are the heads of the fathers of the
inhabitants of Geba, and they removed them to Manahath:
7 And Naaman, and Ahiah, and Gera, he removed them, and begat Uzza, and
Ahihud.
8 And Shaharaim begat *children* in the country of Moab, after he had sent
them away; Hushim and Baara *were* his wives.
9 And he begat of Hodesh his wife, Jobab, and Zibia, and Mesha, and
Malcham,
10 And Jeuz, and Shachia, and Mirma. These *were* his sons, heads of the
fathers.
11 And of Hushim he begat Abitub, and Elpaal.

12 The sons of Elpaal; Eber, and Misham, and Shamed, who built Ono, and
Lod, with the towns thereof:
13 Beriah also, and Shema, who *were* heads of the fathers of the inhabitants
of Aijalon, who drove away the inhabitants of Gath:
14 And Ahio, Shashak, and Jeremoth,
15 And Zebadiah, and Arad, and Ader,
16 And Michael, and Ispah, and Joha, the sons of Beriah;
17 And Zebadiah, and Meshullam, and Hezeki, and Heber,
18 Ishmerai also, and Jezliah, and Jobab, the sons of Elpaal;
19 And Jakim, and Zichri, and Zabdi,
20 And Elienai, and Zilthai, and Eliel,
21 And Adaiah, and Beraiah, and Shimrath, the sons of Shimhi;
22 And Ishpan, and Heber, and Eliel,
23 And Abdon, and Zichri, and Hanan,
24 And Hananiah, and Elam, and Antothijah,
25 And Iphedeiah, and Penuel, the sons of Shashak;
26 And Shamsherai, and Shehariah, and Athaliah,
27 And Jaresiah, and Eliah, and Zichri, the sons of Jeroham.
28 These *were* heads of the fathers, by their generations, chief *men*. These
dwelt in Jerusalem.
29 And at Gibeon dwelt the father of Gibeon; whose wife's name *was*
Maachah:
30 And his firstborn son Abdon, and Zur, and Kish, and Baal, and Nadab,
31 And Gedor, and Ahio, and Zacher.
32 And Mikloth begat Shimeah. And these also dwelt with their brethren in
Jerusalem, over against them.
33 And Ner begat Kish, and Kish begat Saul, and Saul begat Jonathan, and
Malchi-shua, and Abinadab, and Esh-baal.
34 And the son of Jonathan *was* Merib-baal; and Merib-baal begat Micah.
35 And the sons of Micah *were*, Pithon, and Melech, and Tarea, and Ahaz.
36 And Ahaz begat Jehoadah; and Jehoadah begat Alemeth, and Azmaveth,
and Zimri; and Zimri begat Moza,
37 And Moza begat Binea: Rapha *was* his son, Eleasah his son, Azel his son:
38 And Azel had six sons, whose names *are* these, Azrikam, Bocheru, and
Ishmael, and Sheariah, and Obadiah, and Hanan. All these *were* the sons of
Azel.
39 And the sons of Eshek his brother *were*, Ulam his firstborn, Jehush the
second, and Eliphelet the third.
40 And the sons of Ulam were mighty men of valour, archers, and had many
sons, and sons' sons, an hundred and fifty. All these *are* of the sons of Benjamin.

The People Who Lived in Jerusalem

9 So all Israel were reckoned by genealogies; and, behold, they *were* written
in the book of the kings of Israel and Judah, *who* were carried away to
Babylon for their transgression.
2 Now the first inhabitants that *dwelt* in their possessions in their cities *were*,
the Israelites, the priests, Levites, and the Nethinims.
3 And in Jerusalem dwelt of the children of Judah, and of the children of
Benjamin, and of the children of Ephraim, and Manasseh;
4 Uthai the son of Ammihud, the son of Omri, the son of Imri, the son of
Bani, of the children of Pharez the son of Judah.
5 And of the Shilonites; Asaiah the firstborn, and his sons.
6 And of the sons of Zerah; Jeuel, and their brethren, six hundred and ninety.
7 And of the sons of Benjamin; Sallu the son of Meshullam, the son of
Hodaviah, the son of Hasenuah,

8 And Ibneiah the son of Jeroham, and Elah the son of Uzzi, the son of Michri,
and Meshullam the son of Shephathiah, the son of Reuel, the son of Ibnijah;
9 And their brethren, according to their generations, nine hundred and fifty
and six. All these men *were* chief of the fathers in the house of their fathers.
10 And of the priests; Jedaiah, and Jehoiarib, and Jachin,
11 And Azariah the son of Hilkiah, the son of Meshullam, the son of Zadok,
the son of Meraioth, the son of Ahitub, the ruler of the house of God;
12 And Adaiah the son of Jeroham, the son of Pashur, the son of Malchijah,
and Maasiai the son of Adiel, the son of Jahzerah, the son of Meshullam, the
son of Meshillemith, the son of Immer;
13 And their brethren, heads of the house of their fathers, a thousand and
seven hundred and threescore; very able men for the work of the service of
the house of God.
14 And of the Levites; Shemaiah the son of Hasshub, the son of Azrikam, the
son of Hashabiah, of the sons of Merari;
15 And Bakbakkar, Heresh, and Galal, and Mattaniah the son of Micah, the
son of Zichri, the son of Asaph;
16 And Obadiah the son of Shemaiah, the son of Galal, the son of Jeduthun,
and Berechiah the son of Asa, the son of Elkanah, that dwelt in the villages of
the Netophathites.
17 And the porters *were*, Shallum, and Akkub, and Talmon, and Ahiman, and
their brethren: Shallum *was* the chief;
18 Who hitherto *waited* in the king's gate eastward: they *were* porters in the
companies of the children of Levi.
19 And Shallum the son of Kore, the son of Ebiasaph, the son of Korah, and
his brethren, of the house of his father, the Korahites, *were* over the work of
the service, keepers of the gates of the tabernacle: and their fathers, *being* over
the host of the LORD, *were* keepers of the entry.
20 And Phinehas the son of Eleazar was the ruler over them in time past, *and*
the LORD *was* with him.
21 *And* Zechariah the son of Meshelemiah *was* porter of the door of the
tabernacle of the congregation.
22 All these *which were* chosen to be porters in the gates *were* two hundred
and twelve. These were reckoned by their genealogy in their villages, whom
David and Samuel the seer did ordain in their set office.
23 So they and their children *had* the oversight of the gates of the house of
the LORD, *namely*, the house of the tabernacle, by wards.
24 In four quarters were the porters, toward the east, west, north, and south.
25 And their brethren, *which were* in their villages, *were* to come after seven
days from time to time with them.
26 For these Levites, the four chief porters, were in *their* set office, and were
over the chambers and treasuries of the house of God.
27 And they lodged round about the house of God, because the charge *was*
upon them, and the opening thereof every morning *pertained* to them.
28 And *certain* of them had the charge of the ministering vessels, that they
should bring them in and out by tale.
29 *Some* of them also *were* appointed to oversee the vessels, and all the instru-
ments of the sanctuary, and the fine flour, and the wine, and the oil, and the
frankincense, and the spices.
30 And *some* of the sons of the priests made the ointment of the spices.
31 And Mattithiah, *one* of the Levites, who *was* the firstborn of Shallum the
Korahite, had the set office over the things that were made in the pans.
32 And *other* of their brethren, of the sons of the Kohathites, *were* over the
shewbread, to prepare *it* every sabbath.

33 And these *are* the singers, chief of the fathers of the Levites, *who remaining* in the chambers *were* free: for they were employed in *that* work day and night.
34 These chief fathers of the Levites *were* chief throughout their generations; these dwelt at Jerusalem.

Saul's Descendants

35 And in Gibeon dwelt the father of Gibeon, Jehiel, whose wife's name *was* Maachah:
36 And his firstborn son Abdon, then Zur, and Kish, and Baal, and Ner, and Nadab,
37 And Gedor, and Ahio, and Zechariah, and Mikloth.
38 And Mikloth begat Shimeam. And they also dwelt with their brethren at Jerusalem, over against their brethren.
39 And Ner begat Kish; and Kish begat Saul; and Saul begat Jonathan, and Malchi-shua, and Abinadab, and Esh-baal.
40 And the son of Jonathan *was* Merib-baal: and Merib-baal begat Micah.
41 And the sons of Micah *were*, Pithon, and Melech, and Tahrea, *and Ahaz*.
42 And Ahaz begat Jarah; and Jarah begat Alemeth, and Azmaveth, and Zimri; and Zimri begat Moza;
43 And Moza begat Binea; and Rephaiah his son, Eleasah his son, Azel his son.
44 And Azel had six sons, whose names *are* these, Azrikam, Bocheru, and Ishmael, and Sheariah, and Obadiah, and Hanan: these *were* the sons of Azel.

Saul's Overthrow and Death

10 Now the Philistines fought against Israel; and the men of Israel fled from before the Philistines, and fell down slain in mount Gilboa.
2 And the Philistines followed hard after Saul, and after his sons; and the Philistines slew Jonathan, and Abinadab, and Malchi-shua, the sons of Saul.
3 And the battle went sore against Saul, and the archers hit him, and he was wounded of the archers.
4 Then said Saul to his armourbearer, Draw thy sword, and thrust me through therewith; lest these uncircumcised come and abuse me. But his armourbearer would not; for he was sore afraid. So Saul took a sword, and fell upon it.
5 And when his armourbearer saw that Saul was dead, he fell likewise on the sword, and died.
6 So Saul died, and his three sons, and all his house died together.
7 And when all the men of Israel that *were* in the valley saw that they fled, and that Saul and his sons were dead, then they forsook their cities, and fled: and the Philistines came and dwelt in them.
8 And it came to pass on the morrow, when the Philistines came to strip the slain, that they found Saul and his sons fallen in mount Gilboa.
9 And when they had stripped him, they took his head, and his armour, and sent into the land of the Philistines round about, to carry tidings unto their idols, and to the people.
10 And they put his armour in the house of their gods, and fastened his head in the temple of Dagon.
11 And when all Jabesh-gilead heard all that the Philistines had done to Saul,
12 They arose, all the valiant men, and took away the body of Saul, and the bodies of his sons, and brought them to Jabesh, and buried their bones under the oak in Jabesh, and fasted seven days.
13 So Saul died for his transgression which he committed against the LORD, *even* against the word of the LORD, which he kept not, and also for asking *counsel* of *one that had* a familiar spirit, to enquire *of it*;

14 And enquired not of the LORD: therefore he slew him, and turned the
kingdom unto David the son of Jesse.

David Is Anointed King of Israel and Captures Jerusalem

11 Then all Israel gathered themselves to David unto Hebron, saying,
Behold, we *are* thy bone and thy flesh.
2 And moreover in time past, even when Saul was king, thou *wast* he that
leddest out and broughtest in Israel: and the LORD thy God said unto thee,
Thou shalt feed my people Israel, and thou shalt be ruler over my people Israel.
3 Therefore came all the elders of Israel to the king to Hebron; and David
made a covenant with them in Hebron before the LORD; and they anointed
David king over Israel, according to the word of the LORD by Samuel.
4 And David and all Israel went to Jerusalem, which *is* Jebus; where the
Jebusites *were*, the inhabitants of the land.
5 And the inhabitants of Jebus said to David, Thou shalt not come hither.
Nevertheless David took the castle of Zion, which *is* the city of David.
6 And David said, Whosoever smiteth the Jebusites first shall be chief and
captain. So Joab the son of Zeruiah went first up, and was chief.
7 And David dwelt in the castle; therefore they called it the city of David.
8 And he built the city round about, even from Millo round about: and Joab
repaired the rest of the city.
9 So David waxed greater and greater: for the LORD of hosts *was* with him.

David's Mighty Men

10 These also *are* the chief of the mighty men whom David had, who strength-
ened themselves with him in his kingdom, *and* with all Israel, to make him
king, according to the word of the LORD concerning Israel.
11 And this *is* the number of the mighty men whom David had; Jashobeam,
an Hachmonite, the chief of the captains: he lifted up his spear against three
hundred slain *by him* at one time.
12 And after him *was* Eleazar the son of Dodo, the Ahohite, who *was one* of
the three mighties.
13 He was with David at Pas-dammim, and there the Philistines were gath-
ered together to battle, where was a parcel of ground full of barley; and the
people fled from before the Philistines.
14 And they set themselves in the midst of *that* parcel, and delivered it, and
slew the Philistines; and the LORD saved *them* by a great deliverance.
15 Now three of the thirty captains went down to the rock to David, into the
cave of Adullam; and the host of the Philistines encamped in the valley of
Rephaim.
16 And David *was* then in the hold, and the Philistines' garrison *was* then at
Beth-lehem.
17 And David longed, and said, Oh that one would give me drink of the water
of the well of Beth-lehem, that *is* at the gate!
18 And the three brake through the host of the Philistines, and drew water
out of the well of Beth-lehem, that *was* by the gate, and took *it*, and brought
it to David: but David would not drink *of* it, but poured it out to the LORD,
19 And said, My God forbid it me, that I should do this thing: shall I drink
the blood of these men that have put their lives in jeopardy? for with *the
jeopardy of* their lives they brought it. Therefore he would not drink it. These
things did these three mightiest.
20 And Abishai the brother of Joab, he was chief of the three: for lifting up
his spear against three hundred, he slew *them*, and had a name among the
three.
21 Of the three, he was more honourable than the two; for he was their cap-
tain: howbeit he attained not to the *first* three.

22 Benaiah the son of Jehoiada, the son of a valiant man of Kabzeel, who had
done many acts; he slew two lionlike men of Moab: also he went down and
slew a lion in a pit in a snowy day.
23 And he slew an Egyptian, a man of *great* stature, five cubits high; and in
the Egyptian's hand *was* a spear like a weaver's beam; and he went down to
him with a staff, and plucked the spear out of the Egyptian's hand, and slew
him with his own spear.
24 These *things* did Benaiah the son of Jehoiada, and had the name among
the three mighties.
25 Behold, he was honourable among the thirty, but attained not to the *first*
three: and David set him over his guard.
26 Also the valiant men of the armies *were*, Asahel the brother of Joab,
Elhanan the son of Dodo of Beth-lehem,
27 Shammoth the Harorite, Helez the Pelonite,
28 Ira the son of Ikkesh the Tekoite, Abi-ezer the Antothite,
29 Sibbecai the Hushathite, Ilai the Ahohite,
30 Maharai the Netophathite, Heled the son of Baanah the Netophathite,
31 Ithai the son of Ribai of Gibeah, *that pertained* to the children of
Benjamin, Benaiah the Pirathonite,
32 Hurai of the brooks of Gaash, Abiel the Arbathite,
33 Azmaveth the Baharumite, Eliahba the Shaalbonite,
34 The sons of Hashem the Gizonite, Jonathan the son of Shage the Hararite,
35 Ahiam the son of Sacar the Hararite, Eliphal the son of Ur,
36 Hepher the Mecherathite, Ahijah the Pelonite,
37 Hezro the Carmelite, Naarai the son of Ezbai,
38 Joel the brother of Nathan, Mibhar the son of Haggeri,
39 Zelek the Ammonite, Naharai the Berothite, the armourbearer of Joab
the son of Zeruiah,
40 Ira the Ithrite, Gareb the Ithrite,
41 Uriah the Hittite, Zabad the son of Ahlai,
42 Adina the son of Shiza the Reubenite, a captain of the Reubenites, and
thirty with him,
43 Hanan the son of Maachah, and Joshaphat the Mithnite,
44 Uzzia the Ashterathite, Shama and Jehiel the sons of Hothan the Aroerite,
45 Jediael the son of Shimri, and Joha his brother, the Tizite,
46 Eliel the Mahavite, and Jeribai, and Joshaviah, the sons of Elnaam, and
Ithmah the Moabite,
47 Eliel, and Obed, and Jasiel the Mesobaite.

The Men Who Helped David Become King

12 Now these *are* they that came to David to Ziklag, while he yet kept
himself close because of Saul the son of Kish: and they *were* among the
mighty men, helpers of the war.
2 *They were* armed with bows, and could use both the right hand and the left
in *hurling* stones and *shooting* arrows out of a bow, *even* of Saul's brethren of
Benjamin.
3 The chief *was* Ahiezer, then Joash, the sons of Shemaah the Gibeathite; and
Jeziel, and Pelet, the sons of Azmaveth; and Berachah, and Jehu the Antothite,
4 And Ismaiah the Gibeonite, a mighty man among the thirty, and over the
thirty; and Jeremiah, and Jahaziel, and Johanan, and Josabad the Gederathite,
5 Eluzai, and Jerimoth, and Bealiah, and Shemariah, and Shephatiah the
Haruphite,
6 Elkanah, and Jesiah, and Azareel, and Joezer, and Jashobeam, the Korhites,
7 And Joelah, and Zebadiah, the sons of Jeroham of Gedor.
8 And of the Gadites there separated themselves unto David into the hold to
the wilderness men of might, *and* men of war *fit* for the battle, that could

handle shield and buckler, whose faces *were like* the faces of lions, and *were*
as swift as the roes upon the mountains;
9 Ezer the first, Obadiah the second, Eliab the third,
10 Mishmannah the fourth, Jeremiah the fifth,
11 Attai the sixth, Eliel the seventh,
12 Johanan the eighth, Elzabad the ninth,
13 Jeremiah the tenth, Machbanai the eleventh.
14 These *were* of the sons of Gad, captains of the host: one of the least *was*
over an hundred, and the greatest over a thousand.
15 These *are* they that went over Jordan in the first month, when it had over-
flown all his banks; and they put to flight all *them* of the valleys, *both* toward
the east, and toward the west.
16 And there came of the children of Benjamin and Judah to the hold unto
David.
17 And David went out to meet them, and answered and said unto them, If
ye be come peaceably unto me to help me, mine heart shall be knit unto you:
but if *ye be come* to betray me to mine enemies, seeing *there is* no wrong in
mine hands, the God of our fathers look *thereon*, and rebuke *it*.
18 Then the spirit came upon Amasai, *who was* chief of the captains, *and he*
said, Thine *are we*, David, and on thy side, thou son of Jesse: peace, peace *be*
unto thee, and peace *be* to thine helpers; for thy God helpeth thee. Then David
received them, and made them captains of the band.
19 And there fell *some* of Manasseh to David, when he came with the
Philistines against Saul to battle: but they helped them not: for the lords of
the Philistines upon advisement sent him away, saying, He will fall to his mas-
ter Saul to *the jeopardy of* our heads.
20 As he went to Ziklag, there fell to him of Manasseh, Adnah, and Jozabad,
and Jediael, and Michael, and Jozabad, and Elihu, and Zilthai, captains of the
thousands that *were* of Manasseh.
21 And they helped David against the band *of the rovers*: for they *were* all
mighty men of valour, and were captains in the host.
22 For at *that* time day by day there came to David to help him, until *it was*
a great host, like the host of God.
23 And these *are* the numbers of the bands *that were* ready armed to the war,
and came to David to Hebron, to turn the kingdom of Saul to him, according
to the word of the LORD.
24 The children of Judah that bare shield and spear *were* six thousand and
eight hundred, ready armed to the war.
25 Of the children of Simeon, mighty men of valour for the war, seven thou-
sand and one hundred.
26 Of the children of Levi four thousand and six hundred.
27 And Jehoiada *was* the leader of the Aaronites, and with him *were* three
thousand and seven hundred;
28 And Zadok, a young man mighty of valour, and of his father's house twen-
ty and two captains.
29 And of the children of Benjamin, the kindred of Saul, three thousand: for
hitherto the greatest part of them had kept the ward of the house of Saul.
30 And of the children of Ephraim twenty thousand and eight hundred,
mighty men of valour, famous throughout the house of their fathers.
31 And of the half tribe of Manasseh eighteen thousand, which were
expressed by name, to come and make David king.
32 And of the children of Issachar, *which were men* that had understanding
of the times, to know what Israel ought to do; the heads of them *were* two
hundred; and all their brethren *were* at their commandment.

33 Of Zebulun, such as went forth to battle, expert in war, with all instruments of war, fifty thousand, which could keep rank: *they were* not of double heart.
34 And of Naphtali a thousand captains, and with them with shield and spear thirty and seven thousand.
35 And of the Danites expert in war twenty and eight thousand and six hundred.
36 And of Asher, such as went forth to battle, expert in war, forty thousand.
37 And on the other side of Jordan, of the Reubenites, and the Gadites, and of the half tribe of Manasseh, with all manner of instruments of war for the battle, an hundred and twenty thousand.
38 All these men of war, that could keep rank, came with a perfect heart to Hebron, to make David king over all Israel: and all the rest also of Israel *were* of one heart to make David king.
39 And there they were with David three days, eating and drinking: for their brethren had prepared for them.
40 Moreover they that were nigh them, *even* unto Issachar and Zebulun and Naphtali, brought bread on asses, and on camels, and on mules, and on oxen, *and* meat, meal, cakes of figs, and bunches of raisins, and wine, and oil, and oxen, and sheep abundantly: for *there was* joy in Israel.

David Brings the Ark from Kirjath-jearim

13 And David consulted with the captains of thousands and hundreds, *and* with every leader.
2 And David said unto all the congregation of Israel, If *it seem* good unto you, and *that it be* of the LORD our God, let us send abroad unto our brethren every where, *that are* left in all the land of Israel, and with them *also* to the priests and Levites *which are* in their cities *and* suburbs, that they may gather themselves unto us:
3 And let us bring again the ark of our God to us: for we enquired not at it in the days of Saul.
4 And all the congregation said that they would do so: for the thing was right in the eyes of all the people.
5 So David gathered all Israel together, from Shihor of Egypt even unto the entering of Hemath, to bring the ark of God from Kirjath-jearim.
6 And David went up, and all Israel, to Baalah, *that is*, to Kirjath-jearim, which *belonged* to Judah, to bring up thence the ark of God the LORD, that dwelleth *between* the cherubims, whose name is called *on it.*
7 And they carried the ark of God in a new cart out of the house of Abinadab: and Uzza and Ahio drave the cart.
8 And David and all Israel played before God with all *their* might, and with singing, and with harps, and with psalteries, and with timbrels, and with cymbals, and with trumpets.

Uzza Is Killed and the Ark Left at the House of Obed-edom

9 And when they came unto the threshingfloor of Chidon, Uzza put forth his hand to hold the ark; for the oxen stumbled.
10 And the anger of the LORD was kindled against Uzza, and he smote him, because he put his hand to the ark: and there he died before God.
11 And David was displeased, because the LORD had made a breach upon Uzza: wherefore that place is called Perez-uzza to this day.
12 And David was afraid of God that day, saying, How shall I bring the ark of God *home* to me?
13 So David brought not the ark *home* to himself to the city of David, but carried it aside into the house of Obed-edom the Gittite.

14 And the ark of God remained with the family of Obed-edom in his house
three months. And the LORD blessed the house of Obed-edom, and all that he
had.

Hiram's Kindness to David

14 Now Hiram king of Tyre sent messengers to David, and timber of
cedars, with masons and carpenters, to build him an house.
2 And David perceived that the LORD had confirmed him king over Israel,
for his kingdom was lifted up on high, because of his people Israel.
3 And David took more wives at Jerusalem: and David begat more sons and
daughters.
4 Now these *are* the names of *his* children which he had in Jerusalem;
Shammua, and Shobab, Nathan, and Solomon,
5 And Ibhar, and Elishua, and Elpalet,
6 And Nogah, and Nepheg, and Japhia,
7 And Elishama, and Beeliada, and Eliphalet.

David Defeats the Philistines

8 And when the Philistines heard that David was anointed king over all Israel,
all the Philistines went up to seek David. And David heard *of it*, and went out
against them.
9 And the Philistines came and spread themselves in the valley of Rephaim.
10 And David enquired of God, saying, Shall I go up against the Philistines?
and wilt thou deliver them into mine hand? And the LORD said unto him, Go
up; for I will deliver them into thine hand.
11 So they came up to Baal-perazim; and David smote them there. Then David
said, God hath broken in upon mine enemies by mine hand like the breaking
forth of waters: therefore they called the name of that place Baal-perazim.
12 And when they had left their gods there, David gave a commandment, and
they were burned with fire.
13 And the Philistines yet again spread themselves abroad in the valley.
14 Therefore David enquired again of God; and God said unto him, Go not
up after them; turn away from them, and come upon them over against the
mulberry trees.
15 And it shall be, when thou shalt hear a sound of going in the tops of the
mulberry trees, *that* then thou shalt go out to battle: for God is gone forth
before thee to smite the host of the Philistines.
16 David therefore did as God commanded him: and they smote the host of
the Philistines from Gibeon even to Gazer.
17 And the fame of David went out into all lands; and the LORD brought the
fear of him upon all nations.

David Joyfully Brings the Ark to Jerusalem

15 And *David* made him houses in the city of David, and prepared a place
for the ark of God, and pitched for it a tent.
2 Then David said, None ought to carry the ark of God but the Levites: for
them hath the LORD chosen to carry the ark of God, and to minister unto him
for ever.
3 And David gathered all Israel together to Jerusalem, to bring up the ark of
the LORD unto his place, which he had prepared for it.
4 And David assembled the children of Aaron, and the Levites:
5 Of the sons of Kohath; Uriel the chief, and his brethren an hundred and
twenty:
6 Of the sons of Merari; Asaiah the chief, and his brethren two hundred and
twenty:
7 Of the sons of Gershom; Joel the chief, and his brethren an hundred and
thirty:
8 Of the sons of Elizaphan; Shemaiah the chief, and his brethren two hundred:

9 Of the sons of Hebron; Eliel the chief, and his brethren fourscore:
10 Of the sons of Uzziel; Amminadab the chief, and his brethren an hundred
and twelve.
11 And David called for Zadok and Abiathar the priests, and for the Levites,
for Uriel, Asaiah, and Joel, Shemaiah, and Eliel, and Amminadab,
12 And said unto them, Ye *are* the chief of the fathers of the Levites: sanctify
yourselves, *both* ye and your brethren, that ye may bring up the ark of the LORD
God of Israel unto *the place that* I have prepared for it.
13 For because ye *did it* not at the first, the LORD our God made a breach upon
us, for that we sought him not after the due order.
14 So the priests and the Levites sanctified themselves to bring up the ark of
the LORD God of Israel.
15 And the children of the Levites bare the ark of God upon their shoulders
with the staves thereon, as Moses commanded according to the word of the
LORD.
16 And David spake to the chief of the Levites to appoint their brethren *to
be* the singers with instruments of musick, psalteries and harps and cymbals,
sounding, by lifting up the voice with joy.
17 So the Levites appointed Heman the son of Joel; and of his brethren, Asaph
the son of Berechiah; and of the sons of Merari their brethren, Ethan the son
of Kushaiah;
18 And with them their brethren of the second *degree*, Zechariah, Ben, and
Jaaziel, and Shemiramoth, and Jehiel, and Unni, Eliab, and Benaiah, and
Maaseiah, and Mattithiah, and Elipheleh, and Mikneiah, and Obed-edom, and
Jeiel, the porters.
19 So the singers, Heman, Asaph, and Ethan, *were appointed* to sound with
cymbals of brass;
20 And Zechariah, and Aziel, and Shemiramoth, and Jehiel, and Unni, and
Eliab, and Maaseiah, and Benaiah, with psalteries on Alamoth;
21 And Mattithiah, and Elipheleh, and Mikneiah, and Obed-edom, and Jeiel,
and Azaziah, with harps on the Sheminith to excel.
22 And Chenaniah, chief of the Levites, *was* for song: he instructed about the
song, because he *was* skilful.
23 And Berechiah and Elkanah *were* doorkeepers for the ark.
24 And Shebaniah, and Jehoshaphat, and Nethaneel, and Amasai, and
Zechariah, and Benaiah, and Eliezer, the priests, did blow with the trumpets
before the ark of God: and Obed-edom and Jehiah *were* doorkeepers for the
ark.
25 So David, and the elders of Israel, and the captains over thousands, went
to bring up the ark of the covenant of the LORD out of the house of Obed-edom
with joy.
26 And it came to pass, when God helped the Levites that bare the ark of the
covenant of the LORD, that they offered seven bullocks and seven rams.
27 And David *was* clothed with a robe of fine linen, and all the Levites that
bare the ark, and the singers, and Chenaniah the master of the song with the
singers: David also *had* upon him an ephod of linen.
28 Thus all Israel brought up the ark of the covenant of the LORD with shout-
ing, and with sound of the cornet, and with trumpets, and with cymbals,
making a noise with psalteries and harps.
29 And it came to pass, *as* the ark of the covenant of the LORD came to the
city of David, that Michal the daughter of Saul looking out at a window saw
king David dancing and playing: and she despised him in her heart.

David's Festival Sacrifice

16 So they brought the ark of God, and set it in the midst of the tent that
David had pitched for it: and they offered burnt sacrifices and peace
offerings before God.
2 And when David had made an end of offering the burnt offerings and the
peace offerings, he blessed the people in the name of the LORD.
3 And he dealt to every one of Israel, both man and woman, to every one a
loaf of bread, and a good piece of flesh, and a flagon *of wine*.
4 And he appointed *certain* of the Levites to minister before the ark of the
LORD, and to record, and to thank and praise the LORD God of Israel:
5 Asaph the chief, and next to him Zechariah, Jeiel, and Shemiramoth, and
Jehiel, and Mattithiah, and Eliab, and Benaiah, and Obed-edom: and Jeiel with
psalteries and with harps; but Asaph made a sound with cymbals;
6 Benaiah also and Jahaziel the priests with trumpets continually before the
ark of the covenant of God.

The Psalm of Thanksgiving

7 Then on that day David delivered first *this psalm* to thank the LORD into
the hand of Asaph and his brethren.
8 Give thanks unto the LORD, call upon his name, make known his deeds
among the people.
9 Sing unto him, sing psalms unto him, talk ye of all his wondrous works.
10 Glory ye in his holy name: let the heart of them rejoice that seek the LORD.
11 Seek the LORD and his strength, seek his face continually.
12 Remember his marvellous works that he hath done, his wonders, and the
judgments of his mouth;
13 O ye seed of Israel his servant, ye children of Jacob, his chosen ones.
14 He *is* the LORD our God; his judgments *are* in all the earth.
15 Be ye mindful always of his covenant; the word *which* he commanded to
a thousand generations;
16 *Even of the covenant* which he made with Abraham, and of his oath unto
Isaac;
17 And hath confirmed the same to Jacob for a law, *and* to Israel *for* an ever-
lasting covenant,
18 Saying, Unto thee will I give the land of Canaan, the lot of your inheritance;
19 When ye were but few, even a few, and strangers in it.
20 And *when* they went from nation to nation, and from *one* kingdom to
another people;
21 He suffered no man to do them wrong: yea, he reproved kings for their
sakes,
22 *Saying*, Touch not mine anointed, and do my prophets no harm.
23 Sing unto the LORD, all the earth; shew forth from day to day his salvation.
24 Declare his glory among the heathen; his marvellous works among all
nations.
25 For great *is* the LORD, and greatly to be praised: he also *is* to be feared above
all gods.
26 For all the gods of the people *are* idols: but the LORD made the heavens.
27 Glory and honour *are* in his presence; strength and gladness *are* in his
place.
28 Give unto the LORD, ye kindreds of the people, give unto the LORD glory
and strength.
29 Give unto the LORD the glory *due* unto his name: bring an offering, and
come before him: worship the LORD in the beauty of holiness.
30 Fear before him, all the earth: the world also shall be stable, that it be not
moved.

31 Let the heavens be glad, and let the earth rejoice: and let *men* say among
the nations, The LORD reigneth.
32 Let the sea roar, and the fulness thereof: let the fields rejoice, and all that
is therein.
33 Then shall the trees of the wood sing out at the presence of the LORD,
because he cometh to judge the earth.
34 O give thanks unto the LORD; for *he is* good; for his mercy *endureth* for
ever.
35 And say ye, Save us, O God of our salvation, and gather us together, and
deliver us from the heathen, that we may give thanks to thy holy name, *and*
glory in thy praise.
36 Blessed *be* the LORD God of Israel for ever and ever. And all the people said,
Amen, and praised the LORD.

David Appoints Many to Serve Continually before the Ark

37 So he left there before the ark of the covenant of the LORD Asaph and his
brethren, to minister before the ark continually, as every day's work required:
38 And Obed-edom with their brethren, threescore and eight; Obed-edom
also the son of Jeduthun and Hosah *to be* porters:
39 And Zadok the priest, and his brethren the priests, before the tabernacle
of the LORD in the high place that *was* at Gibeon,
40 To offer burnt offerings unto the LORD upon the altar of the burnt offering
continually morning and evening, and *to do* according to all that is written
in the law of the LORD, which he commanded Israel;
41 And with them Heman and Jeduthun, and the rest that were chosen, who
were expressed by name, to give thanks to the LORD, because his mercy
endureth for ever;
42 And with them Heman and Jeduthun with trumpets and cymbals for
those that should make a sound, and with musical instruments of God. And
the sons of Jeduthun *were* porters.
43 And all the people departed every man to his house: and David returned
to bless his house.

Though David Desires to Build God's House, God Says No

17 Now it came to pass, as David sat in his house, that David said to Nathan
the prophet, Lo, I dwell in an house of cedars, but the ark of the cove-
nant of the LORD *remaineth* under curtains.
2 Then Nathan said unto David, Do all that *is* in thine heart; for God *is* with
thee.
3 And it came to pass the same night, that the word of God came to Nathan,
saying,
4 Go and tell David my servant, Thus saith the LORD, Thou shalt not build me
an house to dwell in:
5 For I have not dwelt in an house since the day that I brought up Israel unto
this day; but have gone from tent to tent, and from *one* tabernacle *to another*.
6 Wheresoever I have walked with all Israel, spake I a word to any of the
judges of Israel, whom I commanded to feed my people, saying, Why have ye
not built me an house of cedars?
7 Now therefore thus shalt thou say unto my servant David, Thus saith the
LORD of hosts, I took thee from the sheepcote, *even* from following the sheep,
that thou shouldest be ruler over my people Israel:
8 And I have been with thee whithersoever thou hast walked, and have cut
off all thine enemies from before thee, and have made thee a name like the
name of the great men that *are* in the earth.
9 Also I will ordain a place for my people Israel, and will plant them, and
they shall dwell in their place, and shall be moved no more; neither shall the
children of wickedness waste them any more, as at the beginning,

O LORD, there is NONE LIKE THEE, NEITHER IS THERE ANY GOD BESIDE THEE.
1 CHRONICLES 17:20

10 And since the time that I commanded judges *to be* over my people Israel.
Moreover I will subdue all thine enemies. Furthermore I tell thee that the LORD
will build thee an house.
11 And it shall come to pass, when thy days be expired that thou must go *to*
be with thy fathers, that I will raise up thy seed after thee, which shall be of
thy sons; and I will establish his kingdom.
12 He shall build me an house, and I will stablish his throne for ever.
13 I will be his father, and he shall be my son: and I will not take my mercy
away from him, as I took *it* from *him* that was before thee:
14 But I will settle him in mine house and in my kingdom for ever: and his
throne shall be established for evermore.
15 According to all these words, and according to all this vision, so did Nathan
speak unto David.

David's Prayer and Thanksgiving

16 And David the king came and sat before the LORD, and said, Who *am* I, O
LORD God, and what *is* mine house, that thou hast brought me hitherto?
17 And *yet* this was a small thing in thine eyes, O God; for thou hast *also*
spoken of thy servant's house for a great while to come, and hast regarded me
according to the estate of a man of high degree, O LORD God.
18 What can David *speak* more to thee for the honour of thy servant? for
thou knowest thy servant.
19 O LORD, for thy servant's sake, and according to thine own heart, hast thou
done all this greatness, in making known all *these* great things.
20 O LORD, *there is* none like thee, neither *is there any* God beside thee,
according to all that we have heard with our ears.
21 And what one nation in the earth *is* like thy people Israel, whom God went
to redeem *to be* his own people, to make thee a name of greatness and terri-
bleness, by driving out nations from before thy people, whom thou hast
redeemed out of Egypt?
22 For thy people Israel didst thou make thine own people for ever; and thou,
LORD, becamest their God.
23 Therefore now, LORD, let the thing that thou hast spoken concerning thy
servant and concerning his house be established for ever, and do as thou hast
said.
24 Let it even be established, that thy name may be magnified for ever, saying,
The LORD of hosts *is* the God of Israel, *even* a God to Israel: and *let* the house
of David thy servant *be* established before thee.
25 For thou, O my God, hast told thy servant that thou wilt build him an
house: therefore thy servant hath found *in his heart* to pray before thee.
26 And now, LORD, thou art God, and hast promised this goodness unto thy
servant:
27 Now therefore let it please thee to bless the house of thy servant, that it
may be before thee for ever: for thou blessest, O LORD, and *it shall be* blessed
for ever.

David Subdues the Philistines and the Moabites

18 Now after this it came to pass, that David smote the Philistines, and
subdued them, and took Gath and her towns out of the hand of the
Philistines.
2 And he smote Moab; and the Moabites became David's servants, *and*
brought gifts.
3 And David smote Hadarezer king of Zobah unto Hamath, as he went to
stablish his dominion by the river Euphrates.
4 And David took from him a thousand chariots, and seven thousand horse-
men, and twenty thousand footmen: David also houghed all the chariot *hors-*
es, but reserved of them an hundred chariots.

5 And when the Syrians of Damascus came to help Hadarezer king of Zobah,
David slew of the Syrians two and twenty thousand men.
6 Then David put *garrisons* in Syria-damascus; and the Syrians became
David's servants, *and* brought gifts. Thus the LORD preserved David whither-
soever he went.
7 And David took the shields of gold that were on the servants of Hadarezer,
and brought them to Jerusalem.
8 Likewise from Tibhath, and from Chun, cities of Hadarezer, brought David
very much brass, wherewith Solomon made the brasen sea, and the pillars,
and the vessels of brass.

Tou Sends Hadoram with Presents to Congratulate David

9 Now when Tou king of Hamath heard how David had smitten all the host
of Hadarezer king of Zobah;
10 He sent Hadoram his son to king David, to enquire of his welfare, and to
congratulate him, because he had fought against Hadarezer, and smitten him;
(for Hadarezer had war with Tou;) and *with him* all manner of vessels of gold
and silver and brass.
11 Them also king David dedicated unto the LORD, with the silver and the
gold that he brought from all *these* nations; from Edom, and from Moab, and
from the children of Ammon, and from the Philistines, and from Amalek.
12 Moreover Abishai the son of Zeruiah slew of the Edomites in the valley of
salt eighteen thousand.
13 And he put garrisons in Edom; and all the Edomites became David's serv-
ants. Thus the LORD preserved David whithersoever he went.
14 So David reigned over all Israel, and executed judgment and justice among
all his people.
15 And Joab the son of Zeruiah *was* over the host; and Jehoshaphat the son
of Ahilud, recorder.
16 And Zadok the son of Ahitub, and Abimelech the son of Abiathar, *were* the
priests; and Shavsha was scribe;
17 And Benaiah the son of Jehoiada *was* over the Cherethites and the
Pelethites; and the sons of David *were* chief about the king.

David's Messengers Are Treated Shamefully

19 Now it came to pass after this, that Nahash the king of the children of
Ammon died, and his son reigned in his stead.
2 And David said, I will shew kindness unto Hanun the son of Nahash,
because his father shewed kindness to me. And David sent messengers to com-
fort him concerning his father. So the servants of David came into the land of
the children of Ammon to Hanun, to comfort him.
3 But the princes of the children of Ammon said to Hanun, Thinkest thou
that David doth honour thy father, that he hath sent comforters unto thee?
are not his servants come unto thee for to search, and to overthrow, and to
spy out the land?
4 Wherefore Hanun took David's servants, and shaved them, and cut off their
garments in the midst hard by their buttocks, and sent them away.
5 Then there went *certain*, and told David how the men were served. And he
sent to meet them: for the men were greatly ashamed. And the king said, Tarry
at Jericho until your beards be grown, and *then* return.

David Defeats Ammon and Syria

6 And when the children of Ammon saw that they had made themselves
odious to David, Hanun and the children of Ammon sent a thousand talents
of silver to hire them chariots and horsemen out of Mesopotamia, and out of
Syria-maachah, and out of Zobah.

7 So they hired thirty and two thousand chariots, and the king of Maachah and his people; who came and pitched before Medeba. And the children of Ammon gathered themselves together from their cities, and came to battle.

8 And when David heard *of it*, he sent Joab, and all the host of the mighty men.

9 And the children of Ammon came out, and put the battle in array before the gate of the city: and the kings that were come *were* by themselves in the field.

10 Now when Joab saw that the battle was set against him before and behind, he chose out of all the choice of Israel, and put *them* in array against the Syrians.

11 And the rest of the people he delivered unto the hand of Abishai his brother, and they set *themselves* in array against the children of Ammon.

12 And he said, If the Syrians be too strong for me, then thou shalt help me: but if the children of Ammon be too strong for thee, then I will help thee.

13 Be of good courage, and let us behave ourselves valiantly for our people, and for the cities of our God: and let the LORD do *that which is* good in his sight.

14 So Joab and the people that *were* with him drew nigh before the Syrians unto the battle; and they fled before him.

15 And when the children of Ammon saw that the Syrians were fled, they likewise fled before Abishai his brother, and entered into the city. Then Joab came to Jerusalem.

16 And when the Syrians saw that they were put to the worse before Israel, they sent messengers, and drew forth the Syrians that *were* beyond the river: and Shophach the captain of the host of Hadarezer *went* before them.

17 And it was told David; and he gathered all Israel, and passed over Jordan, and came upon them, and set *the battle* in array against them. So when David had put the battle in array against the Syrians, they fought with him.

18 But the Syrians fled before Israel; and David slew of the Syrians seven thousand *men which fought in* chariots, and forty thousand footmen, and killed Shophach the captain of the host.

19 And when the servants of Hadarezer saw that they were put to the worse before Israel, they made peace with David, and became his servants: neither would the Syrians help the children of Ammon any more.

David Defeats Rabbah

20 And it came to pass, that after the year was expired, at the time that kings go out *to battle*, Joab led forth the power of the army, and wasted the country of the children of Ammon, and came and besieged Rabbah. But David tarried at Jerusalem. And Joab smote Rabbah, and destroyed it.

2 And David took the crown of their king from off his head, and found it to weigh a talent of gold, and *there were* precious stones in it; and it was set upon David's head: and he brought also exceeding much spoil out of the city.

3 And he brought out the people that *were* in it, and cut *them* with saws, and with harrows of iron, and with axes. Even so dealt David with all the cities of the children of Ammon. And David and all the people returned to Jerusalem.

David's Victories over the Philistines

4 And it came to pass after this, that there arose war at Gezer with the Philistines; at which time Sibbechai the Hushathite slew Sippai, *that was* of the children of the giant: and they were subdued.

5 And there was war again with the Philistines; and Elhanan the son of Jair slew Lahmi the brother of Goliath the Gittite, whose spear staff *was* like a weaver's beam.

6 And yet again there was war at Gath, where was a man of *great* stature,
whose fingers and toes *were* four and twenty, six *on each hand*, and six *on each*
foot: and he also was the son of the giant.
7 But when he defied Israel, Jonathan the son of Shimea David's brother slew
him.
8 These were born unto the giant in Gath; and they fell by the hand of David,
and by the hand of his servants.

David, Tempted by Satan, Takes a Census

21 And Satan stood up against Israel, and provoked David to number
Israel.
2 And David said to Joab and to the rulers of the people, Go, number Israel
from Beer-sheba even to Dan; and bring the number of them to me, that I may
know *it*.
3 And Joab answered, The LORD make his people an hundred times so many
more as they *be*: but, my lord the king, *are* they not all my lord's servants? why
then doth my lord require this thing? why will he be a cause of trespass to
Israel?
4 Nevertheless the king's word prevailed against Joab. Wherefore Joab depart-
ed, and went throughout all Israel, and came to Jerusalem.
5 And Joab gave the sum of the number of the people unto David. And all
they of Israel were a thousand thousand and an hundred thousand men that
drew sword: and Judah *was* four hundred threescore and ten thousand men
that drew sword.
6 But Levi and Benjamin counted he not among them: for the king's word
was abominable to Joab.
7 And God was displeased with this thing; therefore he smote Israel.
8 And David said unto God, I have sinned greatly, because I have done this
thing: but now, I beseech thee, do away the iniquity of thy servant; for I have
done very foolishly.
9 And the LORD spake unto Gad, David's seer, saying,
10 Go and tell David, saying, Thus saith the LORD, I offer thee three *things*:
choose thee one of them, that I may do *it* unto thee.
11 So Gad came to David, and said unto him, Thus saith the LORD, Choose
thee
12 Either three years' famine; or three months to be destroyed before thy
foes, while that the sword of thine enemies overtaketh *thee*; or else three days
the sword of the LORD, even the pestilence, in the land, and the angel of the
LORD destroying throughout all the coasts of Israel. Now therefore advise thy-
self what word I shall bring again to him that sent me.
13 And David said unto Gad, I am in a great strait: let me fall now into the
hand of the LORD; for very great *are* his mercies: but let me not fall into the
hand of man.
14 So the LORD sent pestilence upon Israel: and there fell of Israel seventy
thousand men.
15 And God sent an angel unto Jerusalem to destroy it: and as he was destroy-
ing, the LORD beheld, and he repented him of the evil, and said to the angel
that destroyed, It is enough, stay now thine hand. And the angel of the LORD
stood by the threshingfloor of Ornan the Jebusite.
16 And David lifted up his eyes, and saw the angel of the LORD stand between
the earth and the heaven, having a drawn sword in his hand stretched out over
Jerusalem. Then David and the elders *of Israel, who were* clothed in sackcloth,
fell upon their faces.
17 And David said unto God, *Is it* not I *that* commanded the people to be
numbered? even I it is that have sinned and done evil indeed; but *as for* these
sheep, what have they done? let thine hand, I pray thee, O LORD my God, be

on me, and on my father's house; but not on thy people, that they should be plagued.

David Purchases Ornan's Threshingfloor

18 Then the angel of the LORD commanded Gad to say to David, that David should go up, and set up an altar unto the LORD in the threshingfloor of Ornan the Jebusite.

19 And David went up at the saying of Gad, which he spake in the name of the LORD.

20 And Ornan turned back, and saw the angel; and his four sons with him hid themselves. Now Ornan was threshing wheat.

21 And as David came to Ornan, Ornan looked and saw David, and went out of the threshingfloor, and bowed himself to David with *his* face to the ground.

22 Then David said to Ornan, Grant me the place of *this* threshingfloor, that I may build an altar therein unto the LORD: thou shalt grant it me for the full price: that the plague may be stayed from the people.

23 And Ornan said unto David, Take *it* to thee, and let my lord the king do *that which is* good in his eyes: lo, I give *thee* the oxen *also* for burnt offerings, and the threshing instruments for wood, and the wheat for the meat offering; I give it all.

24 And king David said to Ornan, Nay; but I will verily buy it for the full price: for I will not take *that* which *is* thine for the LORD, nor offer burnt offerings without cost.

25 So David gave to Ornan for the place six hundred shekels of gold by weight.

26 And David built there an altar unto the LORD, and offered burnt offerings and peace offerings, and called upon the LORD; and he answered him from heaven by fire upon the altar of burnt offering.

27 And the LORD commanded the angel; and he put up his sword again into the sheath thereof.

28 At that time when David saw that the LORD had answered him in the threshingfloor of Ornan the Jebusite, then he sacrificed there.

29 For the tabernacle of the LORD, which Moses made in the wilderness, and the altar of the burnt offering, *were* at that season in the high place at Gibeon.

30 But David could not go before it to enquire of God: for he was afraid because of the sword of the angel of the LORD.

David Helps Solomon Prepare for Building the Temple

22 Then David said, This *is* the house of the LORD God, and this *is* the altar of the burnt offering for Israel.

2 And David commanded to gather together the strangers that *were* in the land of Israel; and he set masons to hew wrought stones to build the house of God.

3 And David prepared iron in abundance for the nails for the doors of the gates, and for the joinings; and brass in abundance without weight;

4 Also cedar trees in abundance: for the Zidonians and they of Tyre brought much cedar wood to David.

5 And David said, Solomon my son *is* young and tender, and the house *that is* to be builded for the LORD *must be* exceeding magnifical, of fame and of glory throughout all countries: I will *therefore* now make preparation for it. So David prepared abundantly before his death.

David Instructs Solomon about Building God's Temple

6 Then he called for Solomon his son, and charged him to build an house for the LORD God of Israel.

7 And David said to Solomon, My son, as for me, it was in my mind to build an house unto the name of the LORD my God:

8 But the word of the LORD came to me, saying, Thou hast shed blood abun-
dantly, and hast made great wars: thou shalt not build an house unto my name,
because thou hast shed much blood upon the earth in my sight.
9 Behold, a son shall be born to thee, who shall be a man of rest; and I will
give him rest from all his enemies round about: for his name shall be Solomon,
and I will give peace and quietness unto Israel in his days.
10 He shall build an house for my name; and he shall be my son, and I *will
be* his father; and I will establish the throne of his kingdom over Israel for ever.
11 Now, my son, the LORD be with thee; and prosper thou, and build the house
of the LORD thy God, as he hath said of thee.
12 Only the LORD give thee wisdom and understanding, and give thee charge
concerning Israel, that thou mayest keep the law of the LORD thy God.
13 Then shalt thou prosper, if thou takest heed to fulfil the statutes and judg-
ments which the LORD charged Moses with concerning Israel: be strong, and
of good courage; dread not, nor be dismayed.
14 Now, behold, in my trouble I have prepared for the house of the LORD an
hundred thousand talents of gold, and a thousand thousand talents of silver;
and of brass and iron without weight; for it is in abundance: timber also and
stone have I prepared; and thou mayest add thereto.
15 Moreover *there are* workmen with thee in abundance, hewers and work-
ers of stone and timber, and all manner of cunning men for every manner of
work.
16 Of the gold, the silver, and the brass, and the iron, *there is* no number.
Arise *therefore*, and be doing, and the LORD be with thee.

David Commands the Princes to Assist His Son

17 David also commanded all the princes of Israel to help Solomon his son,
saying,
18 *Is* not the LORD your God with you? and hath he *not* given you rest on
every side? for he hath given the inhabitants of the land into mine hand; and
the land is subdued before the LORD, and before his people.
19 Now set your heart and your soul to seek the LORD your God; arise there-
fore, and build ye the sanctuary of the LORD God, to bring the ark of the cov-
enant of the LORD, and the holy vessels of God, into the house that is to be built
to the name of the LORD.

David Organizes the Levites to Serve in the Temple

23 So when David was old and full of days, he made Solomon his son king
over Israel.
2 And he gathered together all the princes of Israel, with the priests and the
Levites.
3 Now the Levites were numbered from the age of thirty years and upward:
and their number by their polls, man by man, was thirty and eight thousand.
4 Of which, twenty and four thousand *were* to set forward the work of the
house of the LORD; and six thousand *were* officers and judges:
5 Moreover four thousand *were* porters; and four thousand praised the LORD
with the instruments which I made, *said David*, to praise *therewith*.
6 And David divided them into courses among the sons of Levi, *namely*,
Gershon, Kohath, and Merari.
7 Of the Gershonites *were*, Laadan, and Shimei.
8 The sons of Laadan; the chief *was* Jehiel, and Zetham, and Joel, three.
9 The sons of Shimei; Shelomith, and Haziel, and Haran, three. These *were*
the chief of the fathers of Laadan.
10 And the sons of Shimei *were*, Jahath, Zina, and Jeush, and Beriah. These
four *were* the sons of Shimei.

11 And Jahath was the chief, and Zizah the second: but Jeush and Beriah had
not many sons; therefore they were in one reckoning, according to *their*
father's house.
12 The sons of Kohath; Amram, Izhar, Hebron, and Uzziel, four.
13 The sons of Amram; Aaron and Moses: and Aaron was separated, that he
should sanctify the most holy things, he and his sons for ever, to burn incense
before the LORD, to minister unto him, and to bless in his name for ever.
14 Now *concerning* Moses the man of God, his sons were named of the tribe
of Levi.
15 The sons of Moses *were*, Gershom, and Eliezer.
16 Of the sons of Gershom, Shebuel *was* the chief.
17 And the sons of Eliezer *were*, Rehabiah the chief. And Eliezer had none
other sons; but the sons of Rehabiah were very many.
18 Of the sons of Izhar; Shelomith the chief.
19 Of the sons of Hebron; Jeriah the first, Amariah the second, Jahaziel the
third, and Jekameam the fourth.
20 Of the sons of Uzziel; Michah the first, and Jesiah the second.
21 The sons of Merari; Mahli, and Mushi. The sons of Mahli; Eleazar, and Kish.
22 And Eleazar died, and had no sons, but daughters: and their brethren the
sons of Kish took them.
23 The sons of Mushi; Mahli, and Eder, and Jeremoth, three.
24 These *were* the sons of Levi after the house of their fathers; *even* the chief
of the fathers, as they were counted by number of names by their polls, that
did the work for the service of the house of the LORD, from the age of twenty
years and upward.
25 For David said, The LORD God of Israel hath given rest unto his people,
that they may dwell in Jerusalem for ever:
26 And also unto the Levites; they shall no *more* carry the tabernacle, nor any
vessels of it for the service thereof.
27 For by the last words of David the Levites *were* numbered from twenty
years old and above:
28 Because their office *was* to wait on the sons of Aaron for the service of the
house of the LORD, in the courts, and in the chambers, and in the purifying of
all holy things, and the work of the service of the house of God;
29 Both for the shewbread, and for the fine flour for meat offering, and for
the unleavened cakes, and for *that which is baked in* the pan, and for that
which is fried, and for all manner of measure and size;
30 And to stand every morning to thank and praise the LORD, and likewise at even;
31 And to offer all burnt sacrifices unto the LORD in the sabbaths, in the new
moons, and on the set feasts, by number, according to the order commanded
unto them, continually before the LORD:
32 And that they should keep the charge of the tabernacle of the congrega-
tion, and the charge of the holy *place*, and the charge of the sons of Aaron their
brethren, in the service of the house of the LORD.

The Organization of the Priests

24 Now *these are* the divisions of the sons of Aaron. The sons of Aaron;
Nadab, and Abihu, Eleazar, and Ithamar.
2 But Nadab and Abihu died before their father, and had no children: there-
fore Eleazar and Ithamar executed the priest's office.
3 And David distributed them, both Zadok of the sons of Eleazar, and
Ahimelech of the sons of Ithamar, according to their offices in their service.
4 And there were more chief men found of the sons of Eleazar than of the
sons of Ithamar; and *thus* were they divided. Among the sons of Eleazar *there*
were sixteen chief men of the house of *their* fathers, and eight among the sons
of Ithamar according to the house of their fathers.

5 Thus were they divided by lot, one sort with another; for the governors of
the sanctuary, and governors *of the house* of God, were of the sons of Eleazar,
and of the sons of Ithamar.
6 And Shemaiah the son of Nethaneel the scribe, *one* of the Levites, wrote
them before the king, and the princes, and Zadok the priest, and Ahimelech
the son of Abiathar, and *before* the chief of the fathers of the priests and Levites:
one principal household being taken for Eleazar, and *one* taken for Ithamar.
7 Now the first lot came forth to Jehoiarib, the second to Jedaiah,
8 The third to Harim, the fourth to Seorim,
9 The fifth to Malchijah, the sixth to Mijamin,
10 The seventh to Hakkoz, the eighth to Abijah,
11 The ninth to Jeshua, the tenth to Shecaniah,
12 The eleventh to Eliashib, the twelfth to Jakim,
13 The thirteenth to Huppah, the fourteenth to Jeshebeab,
14 The fifteenth to Bilgah, the sixteenth to Immer,
15 The seventeenth to Hezir, the eighteenth to Aphses,
16 The nineteenth to Pethahiah, the twentieth to Jehezekel,
17 The one and twentieth to Jachin, the two and twentieth to Gamul,
18 The three and twentieth to Delaiah, the four and twentieth to Maaziah.
19 These *were* the orderings of them in their service to come into the house
of the LORD, according to their manner, under Aaron their father, as the LORD
God of Israel had commanded him.

The Organization of the Levites

20 And the rest of the sons of Levi *were these*: Of the sons of Amram; Shubael:
of the sons of Shubael; Jehdeiah.
21 Concerning Rehabiah: of the sons of Rehabiah, the first *was* Isshiah.
22 Of the Izharites; Shelomoth: of the sons of Shelomoth; Jahath.
23 And the sons *of Hebron*; Jeriah *the first*, Amariah the second, Jahaziel the
third, Jekameam the fourth.
24 *Of* the sons of Uzziel; Michah: of the sons of Michah; Shamir.
25 The brother of Michah *was* Isshiah: of the sons of Isshiah; Zechariah.
26 The sons of Merari *were* Mahli and Mushi: the sons of Jaaziah; Beno.
27 The sons of Merari by Jaaziah; Beno, and Shoham, and Zaccur, and Ibri.
28 Of Mahli *came* Eleazar, who had no sons.
29 Concerning Kish: the son of Kish *was* Jerahmeel.
30 The sons also of Mushi; Mahli, and Eder, and Jerimoth. These *were* the
sons of the Levites after the house of their fathers.
31 These likewise cast lots over against their brethren the sons of Aaron in
the presence of David the king, and Zadok, and Ahimelech, and the chief of
the fathers of the priests and Levites, even the principal fathers over against
their younger brethren.

David Appoints Musicians for the Temple

25 Moreover David and the captains of the host separated to the service
of the sons of Asaph, and of Heman, and of Jeduthun, who should
prophesy with harps, with psalteries, and with cymbals: and the number of
the workmen according to their service was:
2 Of the sons of Asaph; Zaccur, and Joseph, and Nethaniah, and Asarelah,
the sons of Asaph under the hands of Asaph, which prophesied according to
the order of the king.
3 Of Jeduthun: the sons of Jeduthun; Gedaliah, and Zeri, and Jeshaiah,
Hashabiah, and Mattithiah, six, under the hands of their father Jeduthun,
who prophesied with a harp, to give thanks and to praise the LORD.
4 Of Heman: the sons of Heman; Bukkiah, Mattaniah, Uzziel, Shebuel, and
Jerimoth, Hananiah, Hanani, Eliathah, Giddalti, and Romamti-ezer,
Joshbekashah, Mallothi, Hothir, *and* Mahazioth:

5 All these *were* the sons of Heman the king's seer in the words of God, to lift
up the horn. And God gave to Heman fourteen sons and three daughters.
6 All these *were* under the hands of their father for song *in* the house of the
LORD, with cymbals, psalteries, and harps, for the service of the house of God,
according to the king's order to Asaph, Jeduthun, and Heman.
7 So the number of them, with their brethren that were instructed in the songs
of the LORD, *even* all that were cunning, was two hundred fourscore and eight.
8 And they cast lots, ward against *ward*, as well the small as the great, the
teacher as the scholar.
9 Now the first lot came forth for Asaph to Joseph: the second to Gedaliah,
who with his brethren and sons *were* twelve:
10 The third to Zaccur, *he*, his sons, and his brethren, *were* twelve:
11 The fourth to Izri, *he*, his sons, and his brethren, *were* twelve:
12 The fifth to Nethaniah, *he*, his sons, and his brethren, *were* twelve:
13 The sixth to Bukkiah, *he*, his sons, and his brethren, *were* twelve:
14 The seventh to Jesharelah, *he*, his sons, and his brethren, *were* twelve:
15 The eighth to Jeshaiah, *he*, his sons, and his brethren, *were* twelve:
16 The ninth to Mattaniah, *he*, his sons, and his brethren, *were* twelve:
17 The tenth to Shimei, *he*, his sons, and his brethren, *were* twelve:
18 The eleventh to Azareel, *he*, his sons, and his brethren, *were* twelve:
19 The twelfth to Hashabiah, *he*, his sons, and his brethren, *were* twelve:
20 The thirteenth to Shubael, *he*, his sons, and his brethren, *were* twelve:
21 The fourteenth to Mattithiah, *he*, his sons, and his brethren, *were* twelve:
22 The fifteenth to Jeremoth, *he*, his sons, and his brethren, *were* twelve:
23 The sixteenth to Hananiah, *he*, his sons, and his brethren, *were* twelve:
24 The seventeenth to Joshbekashah, *he*, his sons, and his brethren, *were* twelve:
25 The eighteenth to Hanani, *he*, his sons, and his brethren, *were* twelve:
26 The nineteenth to Mallothi, *he*, his sons, and his brethren, *were* twelve:
27 The twentieth to Eliathah, *he*, his sons, and his brethren, *were* twelve:
28 The one and twentieth to Hothir, *he*, his sons, and his brethren, *were* twelve:
29 The two and twentieth to Giddalti, *he*, his sons, and his brethren, *were* twelve:
30 The three and twentieth to Mahazioth, *he*, his sons, and his brethren, *were*
twelve:
31 The four and twentieth to Romamti-ezer, *he*, his sons, and his brethren,
were twelve.

David Appoints Porters for the Temple

26 Concerning the divisions of the porters: Of the Korhites *was*
Meshelemiah the son of Kore, of the sons of Asaph.
2 And the sons of Meshelemiah *were*, Zechariah the firstborn, Jediael the
second, Zebadiah the third, Jathniel the fourth,
3 Elam the fifth, Jehohanan the sixth, Elioenai the seventh.
4 Moreover the sons of Obed-edom *were*, Shemaiah the firstborn, Jehozabad
the second, Joah the third, and Sacar the fourth, and Nethaneel the fifth,
5 Ammiel the sixth, Issachar the seventh, Peulthai the eighth: for God bless-
ed him.
6 Also unto Shemaiah his son were sons born, that ruled throughout the
house of their father: for they *were* mighty men of valour.
7 The sons of Shemaiah; Othni, and Rephael, and Obed, Elzabad, whose
brethren *were* strong men, Elihu, and Semachiah.
8 All these of the sons of Obed-edom: they and their sons and their brethren,
able men for strength for the service, *were* threescore and two of Obed-edom.
9 And Meshelemiah had sons and brethren, strong men, eighteen.
10 Also Hosah, of the children of Merari, had sons; Simri the chief, (for
though he was not the firstborn, yet his father made him the chief;)

11 Hilkiah the second, Tebaliah the third, Zechariah the fourth: all the sons
and brethren of Hosah *were* thirteen.
12 Among these *were* the divisions of the porters, *even* among the chief men,
having wards one against another, to minister in the house of the LORD.
13 And they cast lots, as well the small as the great, according to the house of
their fathers, for every gate.
14 And the lot eastward fell to Shelemiah. Then for Zechariah his son, a wise
counsellor, they cast lots; and his lot came out northward.
15 To Obed-edom southward; and to his sons the house of Asuppim.
16 To Shuppim and Hosah *the lot came forth* westward, with the gate
Shallecheth, by the causeway of the going up, ward against ward.
17 Eastward *were* six Levites, northward four a day, southward four a day,
and toward Asuppim two *and* two.
18 At Parbar westward, four at the causeway, *and* two at Parbar.
19 These *are* the divisions of the porters among the sons of Kore, and among
the sons of Merari.

David Appoints Treasurers for the Temple

20 And of the Levites, Ahijah *was* over the treasures of the house of God, and
over the treasures of the dedicated things.
21 *As concerning* the sons of Laadan; the sons of the Gershonite Laadan, chief
fathers, *even* of Laadan the Gershonite, *were* Jehieli.
22 The sons of Jehieli; Zetham, and Joel his brother, *which were* over the
treasures of the house of the LORD.
23 Of the Amramites, *and* the Izharites, the Hebronites, *and* the Uzzielites:
24 And Shebuel the son of Gershom, the son of Moses, *was* ruler of the treasures.
25 And his brethren by Eliezer; Rehabiah his son, and Jeshaiah his son, and
Joram his son, and Zichri his son, and Shelomith his son.
26 Which Shelomith and his brethren *were* over all the treasures of the ded-
icated things, which David the king, and the chief fathers, the captains over
thousands and hundreds, and the captains of the host, had dedicated.
27 Out of the spoils won in battles did they dedicate to maintain the house
of the LORD.
28 And all that Samuel the seer, and Saul the son of Kish, and Abner the son
of Ner, and Joab the son of Zeruiah, had dedicated; *and* whosoever had dedi-
cated *any thing, it was* under the hand of Shelomith, and of his brethren.

David Appoints Levites to Oversee Israel's Worship

29 Of the Izharites, Chenaniah and his sons *were* for the outward business
over Israel, for officers and judges.
30 *And* of the Hebronites, Hashabiah and his brethren, men of valour, a
thousand and seven hundred, *were* officers among them of Israel on this side
Jordan westward in all the business of the LORD, and in the service of the king.
31 Among the Hebronites *was* Jerijah the chief, *even* among the Hebronites,
according to the generations of his fathers. In the fortieth year of the reign of
David they were sought for, and there were found among them mighty men
of valour at Jazer of Gilead.
32 And his brethren, men of valour, *were* two thousand and seven hundred
chief fathers, whom king David made rulers over the Reubenites, the Gadites,
and the half tribe of Manasseh, for every matter pertaining to God, and affairs
of the king.

The Twelve Captains, One for Each Month

27 Now the children of Israel after their number, *to wit*, the chief fathers
and captains of thousands and hundreds, and their officers that served
the king in any matter of the courses, which came in and went out month by
month throughout all the months of the year, of every course *were* twenty and
four thousand.

2 Over the first course for the first month *was* Jashobeam the son of Zabdiel:
and in his course *were* twenty and four thousand.
3 Of the children of Perez *was* the chief of all the captains of the host for the
first month.
4 And over the course of the second month *was* Dodai an Ahohite, and of his
course *was* Mikloth also the ruler: in his course likewise *were* twenty and four
thousand.
5 The third captain of the host for the third month *was* Benaiah the son of
Jehoiada, a chief priest: and in his course *were* twenty and four thousand.
6 This *is that* Benaiah, *who was* mighty *among* the thirty, and above the thir-
ty: and in his course *was* Ammizabad his son.
7 The fourth *captain* for the fourth month *was* Asahel the brother of Joab, and
Zebadiah his son after him: and in his course *were* twenty and four thousand.
8 The fifth captain for the fifth month *was* Shamhuth the Izrahite: and in
his course *were* twenty and four thousand.
9 The sixth *captain* for the sixth month *was* Ira the son of Ikkesh the Tekoite:
and in his course *were* twenty and four thousand.
10 The seventh *captain* for the seventh month *was* Helez the Pelonite, of the
children of Ephraim: and in his course *were* twenty and four thousand.
11 The eighth *captain* for the eighth month *was* Sibbecai the Hushathite, of
the Zarhites: and in his course *were* twenty and four thousand.
12 The ninth *captain* for the ninth month *was* Abi-ezer the Anetothite, of
the Benjamites: and in his course *were* twenty and four thousand.
13 The tenth *captain* for the tenth month *was* Maharai the Netophathite, of
the Zarhites: and in his course *were* twenty and four thousand.
14 The eleventh *captain* for the eleventh month *was* Benaiah the Pirathonite,
of the children of Ephraim: and in his course *were* twenty and four thousand.
15 The twelfth *captain* for the twelfth month *was* Heldai the Netophathite,
of Othniel: and in his course *were* twenty and four thousand.

The Princes of the Twelve Tribes

16 Furthermore over the tribes of Israel: the ruler of the Reubenites *was*
Eliezer the son of Zichri: of the Simeonites, Shephatiah the son of Maachah:
17 Of the Levites, Hashabiah the son of Kemuel: of the Aaronites, Zadok:
18 Of Judah, Elihu, *one* of the brethren of David: of Issachar, Omri the son
of Michael:
19 Of Zebulun, Ishmaiah the son of Obadiah: of Naphtali, Jerimoth the son
of Azriel:
20 Of the children of Ephraim, Hoshea the son of Azaziah: of the half tribe
of Manasseh, Joel the son of Pedaiah:
21 Of the half *tribe* of Manasseh in Gilead, Iddo the son of Zechariah: of
Benjamin, Jaasiel the son of Abner:
22 Of Dan, Azareel the son of Jeroham. These *were* the princes of the tribes
of Israel.
23 But David took not the number of them from twenty years old and under:
because the LORD had said he would increase Israel like to the stars of the
heavens.
24 Joab the son of Zeruiah began to number, but he finished not, because
there fell wrath for it against Israel; neither was the number put in the account
of the chronicles of king David.
25 And over the king's treasures *was* Azmaveth the son of Adiel: and over the
storehouses in the fields, in the cities, and in the villages, and in the castles,
was Jehonathan the son of Uzziah:
26 And over them that did the work of the field for tillage of the ground *was*
Ezri the son of Chelub:

27 And over the vineyards *was* Shimei the Ramathite: over the increase of
the vineyards for the wine cellars *was* Zabdi the Shiphmite:
28 And over the olive trees and the sycomore trees that *were* in the low plains
was Baal-hanan the Gederite: and over the cellars of oil *was* Joash:
29 And over the herds that fed in Sharon *was* Shitrai the Sharonite: and over
the herds *that were* in the valleys *was* Shaphat the son of Adlai:
30 Over the camels also *was* Obil the Ishmaelite: and over the asses *was*
Jehdeiah the Meronothite:
31 And over the flocks *was* Jaziz the Hagerite. All these *were* the rulers of the
substance which *was* king David's.
32 Also Jonathan David's uncle was a counsellor, a wise man, and a scribe:
and Jehiel the son of Hachmoni *was* with the king's sons:
33 And Ahithophel *was* the king's counsellor: and Hushai the Archite *was*
the king's companion:
34 And after Ahithophel *was* Jehoiada the son of Benaiah, and Abiathar: and
the general of the king's army *was* Joab.

David Exhorts the People to Fear God

28 And David assembled all the princes of Israel, the princes of the tribes,
and the captains of the companies that ministered to the king by
course, and the captains over the thousands, and captains over the hundreds,
and the stewards over all the substance and possession of the king, and of his
sons, with the officers, and with the mighty men, and with all the valiant men,
unto Jerusalem.
2 Then David the king stood up upon his feet, and said, Hear me, my breth-
ren, and my people: *As for me*, I *had* in mine heart to build an house of rest
for the ark of the covenant of the LORD, and for the footstool of our God, and
had made ready for the building:
3 But God said unto me, Thou shalt not build an house for my name, because
thou *hast been* a man of war, and hast shed blood.
4 Howbeit the LORD God of Israel chose me before all the house of my father
to be king over Israel for ever: for he hath chosen Judah *to be* the ruler; and of
the house of Judah, the house of my father; and among the sons of my father
he liked me to make *me* king over all Israel:
5 And of all my sons, (for the LORD hath given me many sons,) he hath chosen
Solomon my son to sit upon the throne of the kingdom of the LORD over Israel.
6 And he said unto me, Solomon thy son, he shall build my house and my
courts: for I have chosen him *to be* my son, and I will be his father.
7 Moreover I will establish his kingdom for ever, if he be constant to do my
commandments and my judgments, as at this day.
8 Now therefore in the sight of all Israel the congregation of the LORD, and
in the audience of our God, keep and seek for all the commandments of the
LORD your God: that ye may possess this good land, and leave *it* for an inheri-
tance for your children after you for ever.
9 And thou, Solomon my son, know thou the God of thy father, and serve
him with a perfect heart and with a willing mind: for the LORD searcheth all
hearts, and understandeth all the imaginations of the thoughts: if thou seek
him, he will be found of thee; but if thou forsake him, he will cast thee off for
ever.
10 Take heed now; for the LORD hath chosen thee to build an house for the
sanctuary: be strong, and do *it*.

David Gives Solomon Plans for the Temple and Its Vessels

11 Then David gave to Solomon his son the pattern of the porch, and of the
houses thereof, and of the treasuries thereof, and of the upper chambers there-
of, and of the inner parlours thereof, and of the place of the mercy seat,

IF THOU SEEK HIM, HE WILL BE FOUND OF THEE; BUT IF THOU forsake HIM, HE WILL cast THEE OFF FOR EVER.
1 CHRONICLES 28:9

12 And the pattern of all that he had by the spirit, of the courts of the house of the LORD, and of all the chambers round about, of the treasuries of the house of God, and of the treasuries of the dedicated things:

13 Also for the courses of the priests and the Levites, and for all the work of the service of the house of the LORD, and for all the vessels of service in the house of the LORD.

14 *He gave* of gold by weight for *things* of gold, for all instruments of all manner of service; *silver also* for all instruments of silver by weight, for all instruments of every kind of service:

15 Even the weight for the candlesticks of gold, and for their lamps of gold, by weight for every candlestick, and for the lamps thereof: and for the candlesticks of silver by weight, *both* for the candlestick, and *also* for the lamps thereof, according to the use of every candlestick.

16 And by weight *he gave* gold for the tables of shewbread, for every table; and *likewise* silver for the tables of silver:

17 Also pure gold for the fleshhooks, and the bowls, and the cups: and for the golden basons *he gave gold* by weight for every bason; and *likewise silver* by weight for every bason of silver:

18 And for the altar of incense refined gold by weight; and gold for the pattern of the chariot of the cherubims, that spread out *their wings*, and covered the ark of the covenant of the LORD.

19 All *this, said David*, the LORD made me understand in writing by *his* hand upon me, *even* all the works of this pattern.

20 And David said to Solomon his son, Be strong and of good courage, and do *it*: fear not, nor be dismayed: for the LORD God, *even* my God, *will be* with thee; he will not fail thee, nor forsake thee, until thou hast finished all the work for the service of the house of the LORD.

21 And, behold, the courses of the priests and the Levites, *even they shall be with thee* for all the service of the house of God: and *there shall be* with thee for all manner of workmanship every willing skilful man, for any manner of service: also the princes and all the people *will be* wholly at thy commandment.

David Gives to the Temple and Urges the People to Follow His Example

29 Furthermore David the king said unto all the congregation, Solomon my son, whom alone God hath chosen, *is yet* young and tender, and the work *is* great: for the palace *is* not for man, but for the LORD God.

2 Now I have prepared with all my might for the house of my God the gold for *things to be made* of gold, and the silver for *things* of silver, and the brass for *things* of brass, the iron for *things* of iron, and wood for *things* of wood; onyx stones, and *stones* to be set, glistering stones, and of divers colours, and all manner of precious stones, and marble stones in abundance.

3 Moreover, because I have set my affection to the house of my God, I have of mine own proper good, of gold and silver, *which* I have given to the house of my God, over and above all that I have prepared for the holy house,

4 *Even* three thousand talents of gold, of the gold of Ophir, and seven thousand talents of refined silver, to overlay the walls of the houses *withal*:

5 The gold for *things* of gold, and the silver for *things* of silver, and for all manner of work *to be made* by the hands of artificers. And who *then* is willing to consecrate his service this day unto the LORD?

6 Then the chief of the fathers and princes of the tribes of Israel, and the captains of thousands and of hundreds, with the rulers of the king's work, offered willingly,

7 And gave for the service of the house of God of gold five thousand talents and ten thousand drams, and of silver ten thousand talents, and of brass eighteen thousand talents, and one hundred thousand talents of iron.

8 And they with whom *precious* stones were found gave *them* to the treasure
of the house of the LORD, by the hand of Jehiel the Gershonite.
9 Then the people rejoiced, for that they offered willingly, because with per-
fect heart they offered willingly to the LORD: and David the king also rejoiced
with great joy.

David's Thanksgiving and Prayer

10 Wherefore David blessed the LORD before all the congregation: and David
said, Blessed *be* thou, LORD God of Israel our father, for ever and ever.
11 Thine, O LORD, *is* the greatness, and the power, and the glory, and the
victory, and the majesty: for all *that is* in the heaven and in the earth *is thine*;
thine *is* the kingdom, O LORD, and thou art exalted as head above all.
12 Both riches and honour *come* of thee, and thou reignest over all; and in
thine hand *is* power and might; and in thine hand *it is* to make great, and to
give strength unto all.
13 Now therefore, our God, we thank thee, and praise thy glorious name.
14 But who *am* I, and what *is* my people, that we should be able to offer so
willingly after this sort? for all things *come* of thee, and of thine own have we
given thee.
15 For we *are* strangers before thee, and sojourners, as *were* all our fathers:
our days on the earth *are* as a shadow, and *there is* none abiding.
16 O LORD our God, all this store that we have prepared to build thee an house
for thine holy name *cometh* of thine hand, and *is* all thine own.
17 I know also, my God, that thou triest the heart, and hast pleasure in
uprightness. As for me, in the uprightness of mine heart I have willingly
offered all these things: and now have I seen with joy thy people, which are
present here, to offer willingly unto thee.
18 O LORD God of Abraham, Isaac, and of Israel, our fathers, keep this for
ever in the imagination of the thoughts of the heart of thy people, and prepare
their heart unto thee:
19 And give unto Solomon my son a perfect heart, to keep thy command-
ments, thy testimonies, and thy statutes, and to do all *these things*, and to build
the palace, *for* the which I have made provision.
20 And David said to all the congregation, Now bless the LORD your God. And
all the congregation blessed the LORD God of their fathers, and bowed down
their heads, and worshipped the LORD, and the king.
21 And they sacrificed sacrifices unto the LORD, and offered burnt offerings
unto the LORD, on the morrow after that day, *even* a thousand bullocks, a thou-
sand rams, *and* a thousand lambs, with their drink offerings, and sacrifices
in abundance for all Israel:
22 And did eat and drink before the LORD on that day with great gladness.
And they made Solomon the son of David king the second time, and anointed
him unto the LORD *to be* the chief governor, and Zadok *to be* priest.

Solomon Takes the Throne

23 Then Solomon sat on the throne of the LORD as king instead of David his
father, and prospered; and all Israel obeyed him.
24 And all the princes, and the mighty men, and all the sons likewise of king
David, submitted themselves unto Solomon the king.
25 And the LORD magnified Solomon exceedingly in the sight of all Israel,
and bestowed upon him *such* royal majesty as had not been on any king before
him in Israel.
26 Thus David the son of Jesse reigned over all Israel.
27 And the time that he reigned over Israel *was* forty years; seven years
reigned he in Hebron, and thirty and three *years* reigned he in Jerusalem.
28 And he died in a good old age, full of days, riches, and honour: and
Solomon his son reigned in his stead.

29 Now the acts of David the king, first and last, behold, they *are* written in
the book of Samuel the seer, and in the book of Nathan the prophet, and in
the book of Gad the seer,
30 With all his reign and his might, and the times that went over him, and
over Israel, and over all the kingdoms of the countries.

2 CHRONICLES

God Appears to Solomon

1 And Solomon the son of David was strengthened in his kingdom, and the
LORD his God *was* with him, and magnified him exceedingly.
2 Then Solomon spake unto all Israel, to the captains of thousands and of
hundreds, and to the judges, and to every governor in all Israel, the chief of
the fathers.
3 So Solomon, and all the congregation with him, went to the high place that
was at Gibeon; for there was the tabernacle of the congregation of God, which
Moses the servant of the LORD had made in the wilderness.
4 But the ark of God had David brought up from Kirjath-jearim to *the place
which* David had prepared for it: for he had pitched a tent for it at Jerusalem.
5 Moreover the brasen altar, that Bezaleel the son of Uri, the son of Hur, had
made, he put before the tabernacle of the LORD: and Solomon and the congre-
gation sought unto it.
6 And Solomon went up thither to the brasen altar before the LORD, which
was at the tabernacle of the congregation, and offered a thousand burnt offer-
ings upon it.
7 In that night did God appear unto Solomon, and said unto him, Ask what
I shall give thee.
8 And Solomon said unto God, Thou hast shewed great mercy unto David
my father, and hast made me to reign in his stead.
9 Now, O LORD God, let thy promise unto David my father be established: for
thou hast made me king over a people like the dust of the earth in multitude.
10 Give me now wisdom and knowledge, that I may go out and come in before
this people: for who can judge this thy people, *that is so* great?
11 And God said to Solomon, Because this was in thine heart, and thou hast
not asked riches, wealth, or honour, nor the life of thine enemies, neither yet
hast asked long life; but hast asked wisdom and knowledge for thyself, that
thou mayest judge my people, over whom I have made thee king:
12 Wisdom and knowledge *is* granted unto thee; and I will give thee riches,
and wealth, and honour, such as none of the kings have had that *have been*
before thee, neither shall there any after thee have the like.

Solomon's Strength and Wealth

13 Then Solomon came *from his journey* to the high place that *was* at Gibeon
to Jerusalem, from before the tabernacle of the congregation, and reigned
over Israel.
14 And Solomon gathered chariots and horsemen: and he had a thousand
and four hundred chariots, and twelve thousand horsemen, which he placed
in the chariot cities, and with the king at Jerusalem.
15 And the king made silver and gold at Jerusalem *as plenteous* as stones, and
cedar trees made he as the sycomore trees that *are* in the vale for abundance.
16 And Solomon had horses brought out of Egypt, and linen yarn: the king's
merchants received the linen yarn at a price.
17 And they fetched up, and brought forth out of Egypt a chariot for six
hundred *shekels* of silver, and an horse for an hundred and fifty: and so
brought they out *horses* for all the kings of the Hittites, and for the kings of
Syria, by their means.

Solomon's Laborers for the Building of the Temple

2 And Solomon determined to build an house for the name of the LORD, and
an house for his kingdom.
2 And Solomon told out threescore and ten thousand men to bear burdens,
and fourscore thousand to hew in the mountain, and three thousand and six
hundred to oversee them.
3 And Solomon sent to Huram the king of Tyre, saying, As thou didst deal
with David my father, and didst send him cedars to build him an house to
dwell therein, *even so deal with me.*
4 Behold, I build an house to the name of the LORD my God, to dedicate *it* to
him, *and* to burn before him sweet incense, and for the continual shewbread,
and for the burnt offerings morning and evening, on the sabbaths, and on the
new moons, and on the solemn feasts of the LORD our God. This *is an ordinance*
for ever to Israel.
5 And the house which I build *is* great: for great *is* our God above all gods.
6 But who is able to build him an house, seeing the heaven and heaven of
heavens cannot contain him? who *am* I then, that I should build him an house,
save only to burn sacrifice before him?
7 Send me now therefore a man cunning to work in gold, and in silver, and
in brass, and in iron, and in purple, and crimson, and blue, and that can skill
to grave with the cunning men that *are* with me in Judah and in Jerusalem,
whom David my father did provide.
8 Send me also cedar trees, fir trees, and algum trees, out of Lebanon: for I
know that thy servants can skill to cut timber in Lebanon; and, behold, my
servants *shall be* with thy servants,
9 Even to prepare me timber in abundance: for the house which I am about
to build *shall be* wonderful great.
10 And, behold, I will give to thy servants, the hewers that cut timber, twen-
ty thousand measures of beaten wheat, and twenty thousand measures of
barley, and twenty thousand baths of wine, and twenty thousand baths of oil.
11 Then Huram the king of Tyre answered in writing, which he sent to
Solomon, Because the LORD hath loved his people, he hath made thee king
over them.
12 Huram said moreover, Blessed *be* the LORD God of Israel, that made heav-
en and earth, who hath given to David the king a wise son, endued with pru-
dence and understanding, that might build an house for the LORD, and an
house for his kingdom.
13 And now I have sent a cunning man, endued with understanding, of
Huram my father's,
14 The son of a woman of the daughters of Dan, and his father *was* a man of
Tyre, skilful to work in gold, and in silver, in brass, in iron, in stone, and in
timber, in purple, in blue, and in fine linen, and in crimson; also to grave any
manner of graving, and to find out every device which shall be put to him,
with thy cunning men, and with the cunning men of my lord David thy father.
15 Now therefore the wheat, and the barley, the oil, and the wine, which my
lord hath spoken of, let him send unto his servants:
16 And we will cut wood out of Lebanon, as much as thou shalt need: and we
will bring it to thee in floats by sea to Joppa; and thou shalt carry it up to
Jerusalem.
17 And Solomon numbered all the strangers that *were* in the land of Israel,
after the numbering wherewith David his father had numbered them; and
they were found an hundred and fifty thousand and three thousand and six
hundred.
18 And he set threescore and ten thousand of them *to be* bearers of burdens,
and fourscore thousand *to be* hewers in the mountain, and three thousand
and six hundred overseers to set the people a work.

The Temple Is Built

3 Then Solomon began to build the house of the LORD at Jerusalem in mount
Moriah, where *the LORD* appeared unto David his father, in the place that
David had prepared in the threshingfloor of Ornan the Jebusite.
2 And he began to build in the second *day* of the second month, in the fourth
year of his reign.
3 Now these *are the things wherein* Solomon was instructed for the building
of the house of God. The length by cubits after the first measure *was* threescore
cubits, and the breadth twenty cubits.
4 And the porch that *was* in the front *of the house*, the length *of it was* accord-
ing to the breadth of the house, twenty cubits, and the height *was* an hundred
and twenty: and he overlaid it within with pure gold.
5 And the greater house he cieled with fir tree, which he overlaid with fine
gold, and set thereon palm trees and chains.
6 And he garnished the house with precious stones for beauty: and the gold
was gold of Parvaim.
7 He overlaid also the house, the beams, the posts, and the walls thereof, and
the doors thereof, with gold; and graved cherubims on the walls.
8 And he made the most holy house, the length whereof *was* according to
the breadth of the house, twenty cubits, and the breadth thereof twenty cubits:
and he overlaid it with fine gold, *amounting* to six hundred talents.
9 And the weight of the nails *was* fifty shekels of gold. And he overlaid the
upper chambers with gold.
10 And in the most holy house he made two cherubims of image work, and
overlaid them with gold.
11 And the wings of the cherubims *were* twenty cubits long: one wing *of the
one cherub was* five cubits, reaching to the wall of the house: and the other
wing *was likewise* five cubits, reaching to the wing of the other cherub.
12 And *one* wing of the other cherub *was* five cubits, reaching to the wall of
the house: and the other wing *was* five cubits *also*, joining to the wing of the
other cherub.
13 The wings of these cherubims spread themselves forth twenty cubits: and
they stood on their feet, and their faces *were* inward.
14 And he made the veil *of* blue, and purple, and crimson, and fine linen, and
wrought cherubims thereon.
15 Also he made before the house two pillars of thirty and five cubits high,
and the chapiter that *was* on the top of each of them *was* five cubits.
16 And he made chains, *as* in the oracle, and put *them* on the heads of the
pillars; and made an hundred pomegranates, and put *them* on the chains.
17 And he reared up the pillars before the temple, one on the right hand, and
the other on the left; and called the name of that on the right hand Jachin, and
the name of that on the left Boaz.

The Furnishings for the Temple

4 Moreover he made an altar of brass, twenty cubits the length thereof, and
twenty cubits the breadth thereof, and ten cubits the height thereof.
2 Also he made a molten sea of ten cubits from brim to brim, round in com-
pass, and five cubits the height thereof; and a line of thirty cubits did compass
it round about.
3 And under it *was* the similitude of oxen, which did compass it round about:
ten in a cubit, compassing the sea round about. Two rows of oxen *were* cast,
when it was cast.
4 It stood upon twelve oxen, three looking toward the north, and three look-
ing toward the west, and three looking toward the south, and three looking
toward the east: and the sea *was set* above upon them, and all their hinder
parts *were* inward.

5 And the thickness of it *was* an handbreadth, and the brim of it like the work
of the brim of a cup, with flowers of lilies; *and* it received and held three
thousand baths.
6 He made also ten lavers, and put five on the right hand, and five on the left,
to wash in them: such things as they offered for the burnt offering they washed
in them; but the sea *was* for the priests to wash in.
7 And he made ten candlesticks of gold according to their form, and set *them*
in the temple, five on the right hand, and five on the left.
8 He made also ten tables, and placed *them* in the temple, five on the right
side, and five on the left. And he made an hundred basons of gold.
9 Furthermore he made the court of the priests, and the great court, and
doors for the court, and overlaid the doors of them with brass.
10 And he set the sea on the right side of the east end, over against the south.
11 And Huram made the pots, and the shovels, and the basons. And Huram
finished the work that he was to make for king Solomon for the house of God;
12 *To wit*, the two pillars, and the pommels, and the chapiters *which were* on
the top of the two pillars, and the two wreaths to cover the two pommels of
the chapiters which *were* on the top of the pillars;
13 And four hundred pomegranates on the two wreaths; two rows of pome-
granates on each wreath, to cover the two pommels of the chapiters which
were upon the pillars.
14 He made also bases, and lavers made he upon the bases;
15 One sea, and twelve oxen under it.
16 The pots also, and the shovels, and the fleshhooks, and all their instru-
ments, did Huram his father make to king Solomon for the house of the LORD
of bright brass.
17 In the plain of Jordan did the king cast them, in the clay ground between
Succoth and Zeredathah.
18 Thus Solomon made all these vessels in great abundance: for the weight
of the brass could not be found out.
19 And Solomon made all the vessels that *were for* the house of God, the
golden altar also, and the tables whereon the shewbread *was set*;
20 Moreover the candlesticks with their lamps, that they should burn after
the manner before the oracle, of pure gold;
21 And the flowers, and the lamps, and the tongs, *made he of* gold, *and* that
perfect gold;
22 And the snuffers, and the basons, and the spoons, and the censers, *of* pure
gold: and the entry of the house, the inner doors thereof for the most holy
place, and the doors of the house of the temple, *were of* gold.

The Lord's Glory Fills the Temple

5 Thus all the work that Solomon made for the house of the LORD was finished:
and Solomon brought in *all* the things that David his father had dedicated;
and the silver, and the gold, and all the instruments, put he among the treasures
of the house of God.
2 Then Solomon assembled the elders of Israel, and all the heads of the tribes,
the chief of the fathers of the children of Israel, unto Jerusalem, to bring up
the ark of the covenant of the LORD out of the city of David, which *is* Zion.
3 Wherefore all the men of Israel assembled themselves unto the king in the
feast which *was* in the seventh month.
4 And all the elders of Israel came; and the Levites took up the ark.
5 And they brought up the ark, and the tabernacle of the congregation, and
all the holy vessels that *were* in the tabernacle, these did the priests *and* the
Levites bring up.

6 Also king Solomon, and all the congregation of Israel that were assembled
unto him before the ark, sacrificed sheep and oxen, which could not be told
nor numbered for multitude.
7 And the priests brought in the ark of the covenant of the LORD unto his
place, to the oracle of the house, into the most holy *place, even* under the wings
of the cherubims:
8 For the cherubims spread forth *their* wings over the place of the ark, and
the cherubims covered the ark and the staves thereof above.
9 And they drew out the staves *of the ark*, that the ends of the staves were
seen from the ark before the oracle; but they were not seen without. And there
it is unto this day.
10 *There was* nothing in the ark save the two tables which Moses put *therein*
at Horeb, when the LORD made *a covenant* with the children of Israel, when
they came out of Egypt.
11 And it came to pass, when the priests were come out of the holy *place*: (for
all the priests *that were* present were sanctified, *and* did not *then* wait by
course:
12 Also the Levites *which were* the singers, all of them of Asaph, of Heman,
of Jeduthun, with their sons and their brethren, *being* arrayed in white linen,
having cymbals and psalteries and harps, stood at the east end of the altar, and
with them an hundred and twenty priests sounding with trumpets:)
13 It came even to pass, as the trumpeters and singers *were* as one, to make
one sound to be heard in praising and thanking the LORD; and when they
lifted up *their* voice with the trumpets and cymbals and instruments of
musick, and praised the LORD, *saying*, For *he is* good; for his mercy *endureth*
for ever: that *then* the house was filled with a cloud, *even* the house of the LORD;
14 So that the priests could not stand to minister by reason of the cloud: for
the glory of the LORD had filled the house of God.

Solomon Blesses the People and Praises God

6 Then said Solomon, The LORD hath said that he would dwell in the thick
darkness.
2 But I have built an house of habitation for thee, and a place for thy dwelling
for ever.
3 And the king turned his face, and blessed the whole congregation of Israel:
and all the congregation of Israel stood.
4 And he said, Blessed *be* the LORD God of Israel, who hath with his hands
fulfilled *that* which he spake with his mouth to my father David, saying,
5 Since the day that I brought forth my people out of the land of Egypt I chose
no city among all the tribes of Israel to build an house in, that my name might
be there; neither chose I any man to be a ruler over my people Israel:
6 But I have chosen Jerusalem, that my name might be there; and have cho-
sen David to be over my people Israel.
7 Now it was in the heart of David my father to build an house for the name
of the LORD God of Israel.
8 But the LORD said to David my father, Forasmuch as it was in thine heart
to build an house for my name, thou didst well in that it was in thine heart:
9 Notwithstanding thou shalt not build the house; but thy son which shall
come forth out of thy loins, he shall build the house for my name.
10 The LORD therefore hath performed his word that he hath spoken: for I
am risen up in the room of David my father, and am set on the throne of Israel,
as the LORD promised, and have built the house for the name of the LORD God
of Israel.
11 And in it have I put the ark, wherein *is* the covenant of the LORD, that he
made with the children of Israel.

Solomon's Prayer at the Dedication of the Temple

12 And he stood before the altar of the LORD in the presence of all the con-
gregation of Israel, and spread forth his hands:
13 For Solomon had made a brasen scaffold, of five cubits long, and five cubits
broad, and three cubits high, and had set it in the midst of the court: and upon
it he stood, and kneeled down upon his knees before all the congregation of
Israel, and spread forth his hands toward heaven,
14 And said, O LORD God of Israel, *there is* no God like thee in the heaven,
nor in the earth; which keepest covenant, and *shewest* mercy unto thy servants,
that walk before thee with all their hearts:
15 Thou which hast kept with thy servant David my father that which thou
hast promised him; and spakest with thy mouth, and hast fulfilled *it* with
thine hand, as *it is* this day.
16 Now therefore, O LORD God of Israel, keep with thy servant David my
father that which thou hast promised him, saying, There shall not fail thee a
man in my sight to sit upon the throne of Israel; yet so that thy children take
heed to their way to walk in my law, as thou hast walked before me.
17 Now then, O LORD God of Israel, let thy word be verified, which thou hast
spoken unto thy servant David.
18 But will God in very deed dwell with men on the earth? behold, heaven
and the heaven of heavens cannot contain thee; how much less this house
which I have built!
19 Have respect therefore to the prayer of thy servant, and to his supplication,
O LORD my God, to hearken unto the cry and the prayer which thy servant
prayeth before thee:
20 That thine eyes may be open upon this house day and night, upon the
place whereof thou hast said that thou wouldest put thy name there; to hear-
ken unto the prayer which thy servant prayeth toward this place.
21 Hearken therefore unto the supplications of thy servant, and of thy peo-
ple Israel, which they shall make toward this place: hear thou from thy dwell-
ing place, *even* from heaven; and when thou hearest, forgive.
22 If a man sin against his neighbour, and an oath be laid upon him to make
him swear, and the oath come before thine altar in this house;
23 Then hear thou from heaven, and do, and judge thy servants, by requiting
the wicked, by recompensing his way upon his own head; and by justifying
the righteous, by giving him according to his righteousness.
24 And if thy people Israel be put to the worse before the enemy, because
they have sinned against thee; and shall return and confess thy name, and pray
and make supplication before thee in this house;
25 Then hear thou from the heavens, and forgive the sin of thy people Israel,
and bring them again unto the land which thou gavest to them and to their
fathers.
26 When the heaven is shut up, and there is no rain, because they have sinned
against thee; *yet* if they pray toward this place, and confess thy name, and turn
from their sin, when thou dost afflict them;
27 Then hear thou from heaven, and forgive the sin of thy servants, and of
thy people Israel, when thou hast taught them the good way, wherein they
should walk; and send rain upon thy land, which thou hast given unto thy
people for an inheritance.
28 If there be dearth in the land, if there be pestilence, if there be blasting,
or mildew, locusts, or caterpillers; if their enemies besiege them in the cities
of their land; whatsoever sore or whatsoever sickness *there be*:
29 *Then* what prayer *or* what supplication soever shall be made of any man,
or of all thy people Israel, when every one shall know his own sore and his
own grief, and shall spread forth his hands in this house:

30 Then hear thou from heaven thy dwelling place, and forgive, and render
unto every man according unto all his ways, whose heart thou knowest; (for
thou only knowest the hearts of the children of men:)
31 That they may fear thee, to walk in thy ways, so long as they live in the land
which thou gavest unto our fathers.
32 Moreover concerning the stranger, which is not of thy people Israel, but
is come from a far country for thy great name's sake, and thy mighty hand,
and thy stretched out arm; if they come and pray in this house;
33 Then hear thou from the heavens, *even* from thy dwelling place, and do
according to all that the stranger calleth to thee for; that all people of the earth
may know thy name, and fear thee, as *doth* thy people Israel, and may know
that this house which I have built is called by thy name.
34 If thy people go out to war against their enemies by the way that thou shalt
send them, and they pray unto thee toward this city which thou hast chosen,
and the house which I have built for thy name;
35 Then hear thou from the heavens their prayer and their supplication, and
maintain their cause.
36 If they sin against thee, (for *there is* no man which sinneth not,) and thou
be angry with them, and deliver them over before *their* enemies, and they
carry them away captives unto a land far off or near;
37 Yet *if* they bethink themselves in the land whither they are carried captive,
and turn and pray unto thee in the land of their captivity, saying, We have
sinned, we have done amiss, and have dealt wickedly;
38 If they return to thee with all their heart and with all their soul in the land
of their captivity, whither they have carried them captives, and pray toward
their land, which thou gavest unto their fathers, and *toward* the city which
thou hast chosen, and toward the house which I have built for thy name:
39 Then hear thou from the heavens, *even* from thy dwelling place, their
prayer and their supplications, and maintain their cause, and forgive thy peo-
ple which have sinned against thee.
40 Now, my God, let, I beseech thee, thine eyes be open, and *let* thine ears *be*
attent unto the prayer *that is made* in this place.
41 Now therefore arise, O LORD God, into thy resting place, thou, and the ark
of thy strength: let thy priests, O LORD God, be clothed with salvation, and let
thy saints rejoice in goodness.
42 O LORD God, turn not away the face of thine anointed: remember the
mercies of David thy servant.

God Recognizes Solomon's Prayer by Fire from Heaven

7 Now when Solomon had made an end of praying, the fire came down from
heaven, and consumed the burnt offering and the sacrifices; and the glory
of the LORD filled the house.
2 And the priests could not enter into the house of the LORD, because the
glory of the LORD had filled the LORD's house.
3 And when all the children of Israel saw how the fire came down, and the
glory of the LORD upon the house, they bowed themselves with their faces to
the ground upon the pavement, and worshipped, and praised the LORD, *saying*,
For *he is* good; for his mercy *endureth* for ever.
4 Then the king and all the people offered sacrifices before the LORD.
5 And king Solomon offered a sacrifice of twenty and two thousand oxen,
and an hundred and twenty thousand sheep: so the king and all the people
dedicated the house of God.
6 And the priests waited on their offices: the Levites also with instruments
of musick of the LORD, which David the king had made to praise the LORD,
because his mercy *endureth* for ever, when David praised by their ministry;
and the priests sounded trumpets before them, and all Israel stood.

2 CHRONICLES 7:14
If my people, which are called by MY NAME, shall humble themselves, & PRAY, and seek my FACE, & TURN from their wicked ways; then will I hear from HEAVEN, and will FORGIVE their sin, & will HEAL their LAND.

7 Moreover Solomon hallowed the middle of the court that *was* before the
house of the LORD: for there he offered burnt offerings, and the fat of the peace offerings, because the brasen altar which Solomon had made was not able to receive the burnt offerings, and the meat offerings, and the fat.
8 Also at the same time Solomon kept the feast seven days, and all Israel with
him, a very great congregation, from the entering in of Hamath unto the river of Egypt.
9 And in the eighth day they made a solemn assembly: for they kept the ded-
ication of the altar seven days, and the feast seven days.
10 And on the three and twentieth day of the seventh month he sent the
people away into their tents, glad and merry in heart for the goodness that the LORD had shewed unto David, and to Solomon, and to Israel his people.
11 Thus Solomon finished the house of the LORD, and the king's house: and
all that came into Solomon's heart to make in the house of the LORD, and in his own house, he prosperously effected.

God Answers Solomon's Prayer

12 And the LORD appeared to Solomon by night, and said unto him, I have
heard thy prayer, and have chosen this place to myself for an house of sacrifice.
13 If I shut up heaven that there be no rain, or if I command the locusts to
devour the land, or if I send pestilence among my people;
14 If my people, which are called by my name, shall humble themselves, and
pray, and seek my face, and turn from their wicked ways; then will I hear from heaven, and will forgive their sin, and will heal their land.
15 Now mine eyes shall be open, and mine ears attent unto the prayer *that
is made* in this place.
16 For now have I chosen and sanctified this house, that my name may be
there for ever: and mine eyes and mine heart shall be there perpetually.
17 And as for thee, if thou wilt walk before me, as David thy father walked,
and do according to all that I have commanded thee, and shalt observe my statutes and my judgments;
18 Then will I stablish the throne of thy kingdom, according as I have cove-
nanted with David thy father, saying, There shall not fail thee a man *to be* ruler in Israel.
19 But if ye turn away, and forsake my statutes and my commandments,
which I have set before you, and shall go and serve other gods, and worship them;
20 Then will I pluck them up by the roots out of my land which I have given
them; and this house, which I have sanctified for my name, will I cast out of my sight, and will make it *to be* a proverb and a byword among all nations.
21 And this house, which is high, shall be an astonishment to every one that
passeth by it; so that he shall say, Why hath the LORD done thus unto this land, and unto this house?
22 And it shall be answered, Because they forsook the LORD God of their
fathers, which brought them forth out of the land of Egypt, and laid hold on other gods, and worshipped them, and served them: therefore hath he brought all this evil upon them.

Solomon's Construction Projects

8 And it came to pass at the end of twenty years, wherein Solomon had built
the house of the LORD, and his own house,
2 That the cities which Huram had restored to Solomon, Solomon built them,
and caused the children of Israel to dwell there.
3 And Solomon went to Hamath-zobah, and prevailed against it.
4 And he built Tadmor in the wilderness, and all the store cities, which he
built in Hamath.

IF MY PEOPLE, WHICH
ARE CALLED BY MY NAME,
SHALL HUMBLE THEMSELVES,
AND PRAY, AND SEEK MY
FACE, AND TURN FROM THEIR
WICKED WAYS; THEN WILL I
HEAR FROM HEAVEN, AND
WILL FORGIVE THEIR SIN,
AND WILL HEAL THEIR LAND.
2 CHRONICLES 7:14

5 Also he built Beth-horon the upper, and Beth-horon the nether, fenced cities, with walls, gates, and bars;

6 And Baalath, and all the store cities that Solomon had, and all the chariot cities, and the cities of the horsemen, and all that Solomon desired to build in Jerusalem, and in Lebanon, and throughout all the land of his dominion.

7 *As for* all the people *that were* left of the Hittites, and the Amorites, and the Perizzites, and the Hivites, and the Jebusites, which *were* not of Israel,

8 *But* of their children, who were left after them in the land, whom the children of Israel consumed not, them did Solomon make to pay tribute until this day.

9 But of the children of Israel did Solomon make no servants for his work; but they *were* men of war, and chief of his captains, and captains of his chariots and horsemen.

10 And these *were* the chief of king Solomon's officers, *even* two hundred and fifty, that bare rule over the people.

11 And Solomon brought up the daughter of Pharaoh out of the city of David unto the house that he had built for her: for he said, My wife shall not dwell in the house of David king of Israel, because *the places are* holy, whereunto the ark of the LORD hath come.

Solomon's Sacrifices

12 Then Solomon offered burnt offerings unto the LORD on the altar of the LORD, which he had built before the porch,

13 Even after a certain rate every day, offering according to the commandment of Moses, on the sabbaths, and on the new moons, and on the solemn feasts, three times in the year, *even* in the feast of unleavened bread, and in the feast of weeks, and in the feast of tabernacles.

14 And he appointed, according to the order of David his father, the courses of the priests to their service, and the Levites to their charges, to praise and minister before the priests, as the duty of every day required: the porters also by their courses at every gate: for so had David the man of God commanded.

15 And they departed not from the commandment of the king unto the priests and Levites concerning any matter, or concerning the treasures.

16 Now all the work of Solomon was prepared unto the day of the foundation of the house of the LORD, and until it was finished. *So* the house of the LORD was perfected.

17 Then went Solomon to Ezion-geber, and to Eloth, at the sea side in the land of Edom.

18 And Huram sent him by the hands of his servants ships, and servants that had knowledge of the sea; and they went with the servants of Solomon to Ophir, and took thence four hundred and fifty talents of gold, and brought *them* to king Solomon.

The Queen of Sheba Admires Solomon's Wisdom

9 And when the queen of Sheba heard of the fame of Solomon, she came to prove Solomon with hard questions at Jerusalem, with a very great company, and camels that bare spices, and gold in abundance, and precious stones: and when she was come to Solomon, she communed with him of all that was in her heart.

2 And Solomon told her all her questions: and there was nothing hid from Solomon which he told her not.

3 And when the queen of Sheba had seen the wisdom of Solomon, and the house that he had built,

4 And the meat of his table, and the sitting of his servants, and the attendance of his ministers, and their apparel; his cupbearers also, and their apparel; and his ascent by which he went up into the house of the LORD; there was no more spirit in her.

5 And she said to the king, *It was* a true report which I heard in mine own
land of thine acts, and of thy wisdom:
6 Howbeit I believed not their words, until I came, and mine eyes had seen
it: and, behold, the one half of the greatness of thy wisdom was not told me:
for thou exceedest the fame that I heard.
7 Happy *are* thy men, and happy *are* these thy servants, which stand contin-
ually before thee, and hear thy wisdom.
8 Blessed be the Lord thy God, which delighted in thee to set thee on his
throne, *to be* king for the Lord thy God: because thy God loved Israel, to estab-
lish them for ever, therefore made he thee king over them, to do judgment
and justice.
9 And she gave the king an hundred and twenty talents of gold, and of spic-
es great abundance, and precious stones: neither was there any such spice as
the queen of Sheba gave king Solomon.
10 And the servants also of Huram, and the servants of Solomon, which
brought gold from Ophir, brought algum trees and precious stones.
11 And the king made *of* the algum trees terraces to the house of the Lord,
and to the king's palace, and harps and psalteries for singers: and there were
none such seen before in the land of Judah.
12 And king Solomon gave to the queen of Sheba all her desire, whatsoever
she asked, beside *that* which she had brought unto the king. So she turned,
and went away to her own land, she and her servants.

Solomon's Wealth

13 Now the weight of gold that came to Solomon in one year was six hundred
and threescore and six talents of gold;
14 Beside *that which* chapmen and merchants brought. And all the kings of
Arabia and governors of the country brought gold and silver to Solomon.
15 And king Solomon made two hundred targets *of* beaten gold: six hundred
shekels of beaten gold went to one target.
16 And three hundred shields *made he of* beaten gold: three hundred *shekels*
of gold went to one shield. And the king put them in the house of the forest of
Lebanon.
17 Moreover the king made a great throne of ivory, and overlaid it with pure
gold.
18 And *there were* six steps to the throne, with a footstool of gold, *which were*
fastened to the throne, and stays on each side of the sitting place, and two lions
standing by the stays:
19 And twelve lions stood there on the one side and on the other upon the
six steps. There was not the like made in any kingdom.
20 And all the drinking vessels of king Solomon *were of* gold, and all the
vessels of the house of the forest of Lebanon *were of* pure gold: none *were of*
silver; it was *not* any thing accounted of in the days of Solomon.
21 For the king's ships went to Tarshish with the servants of Huram: every
three years once came the ships of Tarshish bringing gold, and silver, ivory,
and apes, and peacocks.
22 And king Solomon passed all the kings of the earth in riches and wisdom.
23 And all the kings of the earth sought the presence of Solomon, to hear his
wisdom, that God had put in his heart.
24 And they brought every man his present, vessels of silver, and vessels of
gold, and raiment, harness, and spices, horses, and mules, a rate year by year.
25 And Solomon had four thousand stalls for horses and chariots, and twelve
thousand horsemen; whom he bestowed in the chariot cities, and with the
king at Jerusalem.
26 And he reigned over all the kings from the river even unto the land of the
Philistines, and to the border of Egypt.

27 And the king made silver in Jerusalem as stones, and cedar trees made he
as the sycomore trees that *are* in the low plains in abundance.
28 And they brought unto Solomon horses out of Egypt, and out of all lands.

Solomon's Death

29 Now the rest of the acts of Solomon, first and last, *are* they not written in
the book of Nathan the prophet, and in the prophecy of Ahijah the Shilonite,
and in the visions of Iddo the seer against Jeroboam the son of Nebat?
30 And Solomon reigned in Jerusalem over all Israel forty years.
31 And Solomon slept with his fathers, and he was buried in the city of David
his father: and Rehoboam his son reigned in his stead.

Rehoboam Foolishly Rejects the People's Request

10 And Rehoboam went to Shechem: for to Shechem were all Israel come
to make him king.
2 And it came to pass, when Jeroboam the son of Nebat, who *was* in Egypt,
whither he had fled from the presence of Solomon the king, heard *it*, that
Jeroboam returned out of Egypt.
3 And they sent and called him. So Jeroboam and all Israel came and spake
to Rehoboam, saying,
4 Thy father made our yoke grievous: now therefore ease thou somewhat the
grievous servitude of thy father, and his heavy yoke that he put upon us, and
we will serve thee.
5 And he said unto them, Come again unto me after three days. And the
people departed.
6 And king Rehoboam took counsel with the old men that had stood before
Solomon his father while he yet lived, saying, What counsel give ye *me* to return
answer to this people?
7 And they spake unto him, saying, If thou be kind to this people, and please
them, and speak good words to them, they will be thy servants for ever.
8 But he forsook the counsel which the old men gave him, and took counsel
with the young men that were brought up with him, that stood before him.
9 And he said unto them, What advice give ye that we may return answer to
this people, which have spoken to me, saying, Ease somewhat the yoke that
thy father did put upon us?
10 And the young men that were brought up with him spake unto him, say-
ing, Thus shalt thou answer the people that spake unto thee, saying, Thy father
made our yoke heavy, but make thou *it* somewhat lighter for us; thus shalt
thou say unto them, My little *finger* shall be thicker than my father's loins.
11 For whereas my father put a heavy yoke upon you, I will put more to your
yoke: my father chastised you with whips, but I *will chastise you* with scorpions.
12 So Jeroboam and all the people came to Rehoboam on the third day, as
the king bade, saying, Come again to me on the third day.
13 And the king answered them roughly; and king Rehoboam forsook the
counsel of the old men,
14 And answered them after the advice of the young men, saying, My father
made your yoke heavy, but I will add thereto: my father chastised you with
whips, but I *will chastise you* with scorpions.
15 So the king hearkened not unto the people: for the cause was of God, that
the LORD might perform his word, which he spake by the hand of Ahijah the
Shilonite to Jeroboam the son of Nebat.
16 And when all Israel *saw* that the king would not hearken unto them, the
people answered the king, saying, What portion have we in David? and *we
have* none inheritance in the son of Jesse: every man to your tents, O Israel:
and now, David, see to thine own house. So all Israel went to their tents.
17 But *as for* the children of Israel that dwelt in the cities of Judah, Rehoboam
reigned over them.

18 Then king Rehoboam sent Hadoram that *was* over the tribute; and the
children of Israel stoned him with stones, that he died. But king Rehoboam
made speed to get him up to *his* chariot, to flee to Jerusalem.
19 And Israel rebelled against the house of David unto this day.

Rehoboam Raises an Army to Subdue the Rebellion

11 And when Rehoboam was come to Jerusalem, he gathered of the house
of Judah and Benjamin an hundred and fourscore thousand chosen
men, which were warriors, to fight against Israel, that he might bring the
kingdom again to Rehoboam.
2 But the word of the LORD came to Shemaiah the man of God, saying,
3 Speak unto Rehoboam the son of Solomon, king of Judah, and to all Israel
in Judah and Benjamin, saying,
4 Thus saith the LORD, Ye shall not go up, nor fight against your brethren:
return every man to his house: for this thing is done of me. And they obeyed
the words of the LORD, and returned from going against Jeroboam.
5 And Rehoboam dwelt in Jerusalem, and built cities for defence in Judah.
6 He built even Beth-lehem, and Etam, and Tekoa,
7 And Beth-zur, and Shoco, and Adullam,
8 And Gath, and Mareshah, and Ziph,
9 And Adoraim, and Lachish, and Azekah,
10 And Zorah, and Aijalon, and Hebron, which *are* in Judah and in Benjamin
fenced cities.
11 And he fortified the strong holds, and put captains in them, and store of
victual, and of oil and wine.
12 And in every several city *he put* shields and spears, and made them exceed-
ing strong, having Judah and Benjamin on his side.

The Priests and Levites Come to Judah

13 And the priests and the Levites that *were* in all Israel resorted to him out
of all their coasts.
14 For the Levites left their suburbs and their possession, and came to Judah
and Jerusalem: for Jeroboam and his sons had cast them off from executing
the priest's office unto the LORD:
15 And he ordained him priests for the high places, and for the devils, and
for the calves which he had made.
16 And after them out of all the tribes of Israel such as set their hearts to seek
the LORD God of Israel came to Jerusalem, to sacrifice unto the LORD God of
their fathers.
17 So they strengthened the kingdom of Judah, and made Rehoboam the son
of Solomon strong, three years: for three years they walked in the way of David
and Solomon.

Rehoboam's Family

18 And Rehoboam took him Mahalath the daughter of Jerimoth the son of
David to wife, *and* Abihail the daughter of Eliab the son of Jesse;
19 Which bare him children; Jeush, and Shamariah, and Zaham.
20 And after her he took Maachah the daughter of Absalom; which bare him
Abijah, and Attai, and Ziza, and Shelomith.
21 And Rehoboam loved Maachah the daughter of Absalom above all his
wives and his concubines: (for he took eighteen wives, and threescore concu-
bines; and begat twenty and eight sons, and threescore daughters.)
22 And Rehoboam made Abijah the son of Maachah the chief, *to be* ruler
among his brethren: for *he thought* to make him king.
23 And he dealt wisely, and dispersed of all his children throughout all the
countries of Judah and Benjamin, unto every fenced city: and he gave them
victual in abundance. And he desired many wives.

Shishak Takes the Temple Treasures

12 And it came to pass, when Rehoboam had established the kingdom, and had strengthened himself, he forsook the law of the LORD, and all Israel with him.

2 And it came to pass, *that* in the fifth year of king Rehoboam Shishak king of Egypt came up against Jerusalem, because they had transgressed against the LORD,

3 With twelve hundred chariots, and threescore thousand horsemen: and the people *were* without number that came with him out of Egypt; the Lubims, the Sukkiims, and the Ethiopians.

4 And he took the fenced cities which *pertained* to Judah, and came to Jerusalem.

5 Then came Shemaiah the prophet to Rehoboam, and *to* the princes of Judah, that were gathered together to Jerusalem because of Shishak, and said unto them, Thus saith the LORD, Ye have forsaken me, and therefore have I also left you in the hand of Shishak.

6 Whereupon the princes of Israel and the king humbled themselves; and they said, The LORD *is* righteous.

7 And when the LORD saw that they humbled themselves, the word of the LORD came to Shemaiah, saying, They have humbled themselves; *therefore* I will not destroy them, but I will grant them some deliverance; and my wrath shall not be poured out upon Jerusalem by the hand of Shishak.

8 Nevertheless they shall be his servants; that they may know my service, and the service of the kingdoms of the countries.

9 So Shishak king of Egypt came up against Jerusalem, and took away the treasures of the house of the LORD, and the treasures of the king's house; he took all: he carried away also the shields of gold which Solomon had made.

10 Instead of which king Rehoboam made shields of brass, and committed *them* to the hands of the chief of the guard, that kept the entrance of the king's house.

11 And when the king entered into the house of the LORD, the guard came and fetched them, and brought them again into the guard chamber.

12 And when he humbled himself, the wrath of the LORD turned from him, that he would not destroy *him* altogether: and also in Judah things went well.

Rehoboam's Death

13 So king Rehoboam strengthened himself in Jerusalem, and reigned: for Rehoboam *was* one and forty years old when he began to reign, and he reigned seventeen years in Jerusalem, the city which the LORD had chosen out of all the tribes of Israel, to put his name there. And his mother's name *was* Naamah an Ammonitess.

14 And he did evil, because he prepared not his heart to seek the LORD.

15 Now the acts of Rehoboam, first and last, *are* they not written in the book of Shemaiah the prophet, and of Iddo the seer concerning genealogies? And *there were* wars between Rehoboam and Jeroboam continually.

16 And Rehoboam slept with his fathers, and was buried in the city of David: and Abijah his son reigned in his stead.

Abijah Becomes King of Judah

13 Now in the eighteenth year of king Jeroboam began Abijah to reign over Judah.

2 He reigned three years in Jerusalem. His mother's name also *was* Michaiah the daughter of Uriel of Gibeah. And there was war between Abijah and Jeroboam.

3 And Abijah set the battle in array with an army of valiant men of war, *even* four hundred thousand chosen men: Jeroboam also set the battle in array

against him with eight hundred thousand chosen men, *being* mighty men of
valour.
4 And Abijah stood up upon mount Zemaraim, which *is* in mount Ephraim,
and said, Hear me, thou Jeroboam, and all Israel;
5 Ought ye not to know that the LORD God of Israel gave the kingdom over
Israel to David for ever, *even* to him and to his sons by a covenant of salt?
6 Yet Jeroboam the son of Nebat, the servant of Solomon the son of David,
is risen up, and hath rebelled against his lord.
7 And there are gathered unto him vain men, the children of Belial, and have
strengthened themselves against Rehoboam the son of Solomon, when
Rehoboam was young and tenderhearted, and could not withstand them.
8 And now ye think to withstand the kingdom of the LORD in the hand of the
sons of David; and ye *be* a great multitude, and *there are* with you golden calves,
which Jeroboam made you for gods.
9 Have ye not cast out the priests of the LORD, the sons of Aaron, and the
Levites, and have made you priests after the manner of the nations of *other*
lands? so that whosoever cometh to consecrate himself with a young bullock
and seven rams, *the same* may be a priest of *them that are* no gods.
10 But as for us, the LORD *is* our God, and we have not forsaken him; and the
priests, which minister unto the LORD, *are* the sons of Aaron, and the Levites
wait upon *their* business:
11 And they burn unto the LORD every morning and every evening burnt
sacrifices and sweet incense: the shewbread also *set they in order* upon the
pure table; and the candlestick of gold with the lamps thereof, to burn every
evening: for we keep the charge of the LORD our God; but ye have forsaken
him.
12 And, behold, God himself *is* with us for *our* captain, and his priests with
sounding trumpets to cry alarm against you. O children of Israel, fight ye not
against the LORD God of your fathers; for ye shall not prosper.

Trusting in God, Abijah Overcomes Jeroboam of Israel

13 But Jeroboam caused an ambushment to come about behind them: so
they were before Judah, and the ambushment *was* behind them.
14 And when Judah looked back, behold, the battle *was* before and behind:
and they cried unto the LORD, and the priests sounded with the trumpets.
15 Then the men of Judah gave a shout: and as the men of Judah shouted, it
came to pass, that God smote Jeroboam and all Israel before Abijah and Judah.
16 And the children of Israel fled before Judah: and God delivered them into
their hand.
17 And Abijah and his people slew them with a great slaughter: so there fell
down slain of Israel five hundred thousand chosen men.
18 Thus the children of Israel were brought under at that time, and the chil-
dren of Judah prevailed, because they relied upon the LORD God of their
fathers.
19 And Abijah pursued after Jeroboam, and took cities from him, Beth-el
with the towns thereof, and Jeshanah with the towns thereof, and Ephrain
with the towns thereof.
20 Neither did Jeroboam recover strength again in the days of Abijah: and
the LORD struck him, and he died.
21 But Abijah waxed mighty, and married fourteen wives, and begat twenty
and two sons, and sixteen daughters.
22 And the rest of the acts of Abijah, and his ways, and his sayings, *are* written
in the story of the prophet Iddo.

Asa Becomes King of Judah

14 So Abijah slept with his fathers, and they buried him in the city of
David: and Asa his son reigned in his stead. In his days the land was
quiet ten years.
2 And Asa did *that which was* good and right in the eyes of the LORD his God:
3 For he took away the altars of the strange *gods*, and the high places, and
brake down the images, and cut down the groves:
4 And commanded Judah to seek the LORD God of their fathers, and to do
the law and the commandment.
5 Also he took away out of all the cities of Judah the high places and the
images: and the kingdom was quiet before him.
6 And he built fenced cities in Judah: for the land had rest, and he had no
war in those years; because the LORD had given him rest.
7 Therefore he said unto Judah, Let us build these cities, and make about
them walls, and towers, gates, and bars, *while* the land *is* yet before us; because
we have sought the LORD our God, we have sought *him*, and he hath given us
rest on every side. So they built and prospered.
8 And Asa had an army *of men* that bare targets and spears, out of Judah three
hundred thousand; and out of Benjamin, that bare shields and drew bows,
two hundred and fourscore thousand: all these *were* mighty men of valour.

Asa Overthrows Zerah and Plunders the Ethiopians

9 And there came out against them Zerah the Ethiopian with an host of a
thousand thousand, and three hundred chariots; and came unto Mareshah.
10 Then Asa went out against him, and they set the battle in array in the
valley of Zephathah at Mareshah.
11 And Asa cried unto the LORD his God, and said, LORD, *it is* nothing with
thee to help, whether with many, or with them that have no power: help us, O
LORD our God; for we rest on thee, and in thy name we go against this multi-
tude. O LORD, thou *art* our God; let not man prevail against thee.
12 So the LORD smote the Ethiopians before Asa, and before Judah; and the
Ethiopians fled.
13 And Asa and the people that *were* with him pursued them unto Gerar: and
the Ethiopians were overthrown, that they could not recover themselves; for
they were destroyed before the LORD, and before his host; and they carried
away very much spoil.
14 And they smote all the cities round about Gerar; for the fear of the LORD
came upon them: and they spoiled all the cities; for there was exceeding much
spoil in them.
15 They smote also the tents of cattle, and carried away sheep and camels in
abundance, and returned to Jerusalem.

Asa, Judah, and Many of Israel Make a Covenant with God

15 And the Spirit of God came upon Azariah the son of Oded:
2 And he went out to meet Asa, and said unto him, Hear ye me, Asa,
and all Judah and Benjamin; The LORD *is* with you, while ye be with him; and
if ye seek him, he will be found of you; but if ye forsake him, he will forsake
you.
3 Now for a long season Israel *hath been* without the true God, and without
a teaching priest, and without law.
4 But when they in their trouble did turn unto the LORD God of Israel, and
sought him, he was found of them.
5 And in those times *there was* no peace to him that went out, nor to him
that came in, but great vexations *were* upon all the inhabitants of the countries.
6 And nation was destroyed of nation, and city of city: for God did vex them
with all adversity.

7 Be ye strong therefore, and let not your hands be weak: for your work shall
be rewarded.
8 And when Asa heard these words, and the prophecy of Oded the prophet,
he took courage, and put away the abominable idols out of all the land of Judah
and Benjamin, and out of the cities which he had taken from mount Ephraim,
and renewed the altar of the LORD, that *was* before the porch of the LORD.
9 And he gathered all Judah and Benjamin, and the strangers with them out
of Ephraim and Manasseh, and out of Simeon: for they fell to him out of Israel
in abundance, when they saw that the LORD his God *was* with him.
10 So they gathered themselves together at Jerusalem in the third month, in
the fifteenth year of the reign of Asa.
11 And they offered unto the LORD the same time, of the spoil *which* they had
brought, seven hundred oxen and seven thousand sheep.
12 And they entered into a covenant to seek the LORD God of their fathers
with all their heart and with all their soul;
13 That whosoever would not seek the LORD God of Israel should be put to
death, whether small or great, whether man or woman.
14 And they sware unto the LORD with a loud voice, and with shouting, and
with trumpets, and with cornets.
15 And all Judah rejoiced at the oath: for they had sworn with all their heart,
and sought him with their whole desire; and he was found of them: and the
LORD gave them rest round about.
16 And also *concerning* Maachah the mother of Asa the king, he removed
her from *being* queen, because she had made an idol in a grove: and Asa cut
down her idol, and stamped *it*, and burnt *it* at the brook Kidron.
17 But the high places were not taken away out of Israel: nevertheless the
heart of Asa was perfect all his days.
18 And he brought into the house of God the things that his father had dedicated,
and that he himself had dedicated, silver, and gold, and vessels.
19 And there was no *more* war unto the five and thirtieth year of the reign
of Asa.

Asa's War with Baasha of Israel

16 In the six and thirtieth year of the reign of Asa Baasha king of Israel
came up against Judah, and built Ramah, to the intent that he might
let none go out or come in to Asa king of Judah.
2 Then Asa brought out silver and gold out of the treasures of the house of
the LORD and of the king's house, and sent to Ben-hadad king of Syria, that
dwelt at Damascus, saying,
3 *There is* a league between me and thee, as *there was* between my father and
thy father: behold, I have sent thee silver and gold; go, break thy league with
Baasha king of Israel, that he may depart from me.
4 And Ben-hadad hearkened unto king Asa, and sent the captains of his
armies against the cities of Israel; and they smote Ijon, and Dan, and Abel-
maim, and all the store cities of Naphtali.
5 And it came to pass, when Baasha heard *it*, that he left off building of
Ramah, and let his work cease.
6 Then Asa the king took all Judah; and they carried away the stones of
Ramah, and the timber thereof, wherewith Baasha was building; and he built
therewith Geba and Mizpah.

Asa Is Reprimanded for Trusting in Syria and Not in the Lord

7 And at that time Hanani the seer came to Asa king of Judah, and said unto
him, Because thou hast relied on the king of Syria, and not relied on the LORD
thy God, therefore is the host of the king of Syria escaped out of thine hand.

8 Were not the Ethiopians and the Lubims a huge host, with very many chariots and horsemen? yet, because thou didst rely on the LORD, he delivered them into thine hand.
9 For the eyes of the LORD run to and fro throughout the whole earth, to shew himself strong in the behalf of *them* whose heart *is* perfect toward him. Herein thou hast done foolishly: therefore from henceforth thou shalt have wars.
10 Then Asa was wroth with the seer, and put him in a prison house; for *he was* in a rage with him because of this *thing*. And Asa oppressed *some* of the people the same time.
11 And, behold, the acts of Asa, first and last, lo, they *are* written in the book of the kings of Judah and Israel.
12 And Asa in the thirty and ninth year of his reign was diseased in his feet, until his disease *was* exceeding *great*: yet in his disease he sought not to the LORD, but to the physicians.
13 And Asa slept with his fathers, and died in the one and fortieth year of his reign.
14 And they buried him in his own sepulchres, which he had made for himself in the city of David, and laid him in the bed which was filled with sweet odours and divers kinds *of spices* prepared by the apothecaries' art: and they made a very great burning for him.

Jehoshaphat Becomes King of Judah

17 And Jehoshaphat his son reigned in his stead, and strengthened himself against Israel.
2 And he placed forces in all the fenced cities of Judah, and set garrisons in the land of Judah, and in the cities of Ephraim, which Asa his father had taken.
3 And the LORD was with Jehoshaphat, because he walked in the first ways of his father David, and sought not unto Baalim;
4 But sought to the *LORD* God of his father, and walked in his commandments, and not after the doings of Israel.
5 Therefore the LORD stablished the kingdom in his hand; and all Judah brought to Jehoshaphat presents; and he had riches and honour in abundance.
6 And his heart was lifted up in the ways of the LORD: moreover he took away the high places and groves out of Judah.
7 Also in the third year of his reign he sent to his princes, *even* to Ben-hail, and to Obadiah, and to Zechariah, and to Nethaneel, and to Michaiah, to teach in the cities of Judah.
8 And with them *he sent* Levites, *even* Shemaiah, and Nethaniah, and Zebadiah, and Asahel, and Shemiramoth, and Jehonathan, and Adonijah, and Tobijah, and Tob-adonijah, Levites; and with them Elishama and Jehoram, priests.
9 And they taught in Judah, and *had* the book of the law of the LORD with them, and went about throughout all the cities of Judah, and taught the people.

Some of Judah's Enemies, Being Afraid of God, Bring Presents and Tribute

10 And the fear of the LORD fell upon all the kingdoms of the lands that *were* round about Judah, so that they made no war against Jehoshaphat.
11 Also *some* of the Philistines brought Jehoshaphat presents, and tribute silver; and the Arabians brought him flocks, seven thousand and seven hundred rams, and seven thousand and seven hundred he goats.
12 And Jehoshaphat waxed great exceedingly; and he built in Judah castles, and cities of store.
13 And he had much business in the cities of Judah: and the men of war, mighty men of valour, *were* in Jerusalem.

14 And these *are* the numbers of them according to the house of their fathers:
Of Judah, the captains of thousands; Adnah the chief, and with him mighty
men of valour three hundred thousand.
15 And next to him *was* Jehohanan the captain, and with him two hundred
and fourscore thousand.
16 And next him *was* Amasiah the son of Zichri, who willingly offered him-
self unto the LORD; and with him two hundred thousand mighty men of valour.
17 And of Benjamin; Eliada a mighty man of valour, and with him armed
men with bow and shield two hundred thousand.
18 And next him *was* Jehozabad, and with him an hundred and fourscore
thousand ready prepared for the war.
19 These waited on the king, beside *those* whom the king put in the fenced
cities throughout all Judah.

Jehoshaphat Makes an Alliance with Ahab

18 Now Jehoshaphat had riches and honour in abundance, and joined
affinity with Ahab.
2 And after *certain* years he went down to Ahab to Samaria. And Ahab killed
sheep and oxen for him in abundance, and for the people that *he had* with
him, and persuaded him to go up *with him* to Ramoth-gilead.
3 And Ahab king of Israel said unto Jehoshaphat king of Judah, Wilt thou go
with me to Ramoth-gilead? And he answered him, I *am* as thou *art*, and my
people as thy people; and *we will be* with thee in the war.

Ahab Is Slain, According to the Word of Micaiah

4 And Jehoshaphat said unto the king of Israel, Enquire, I pray thee, at the
word of the LORD to day.
5 Therefore the king of Israel gathered together of prophets four hundred
men, and said unto them, Shall we go to Ramoth-gilead to battle, or shall I
forbear? And they said, Go up; for God will deliver *it* into the king's hand.
6 But Jehoshaphat said, *Is there* not here a prophet of the LORD besides, that
we might enquire of him?
7 And the king of Israel said unto Jehoshaphat, *There is* yet one man, by whom
we may enquire of the LORD: but I hate him; for he never prophesied good
unto me, but always evil: the same *is* Micaiah the son of Imla. And Jehoshaphat
said, Let not the king say so.
8 And the king of Israel called for one *of his* officers, and said, Fetch quickly
Micaiah the son of Imla.
9 And the king of Israel and Jehoshaphat king of Judah sat either of them on
his throne, clothed in *their* robes, and they sat in a void place at the entering
in of the gate of Samaria; and all the prophets prophesied before them.
10 And Zedekiah the son of Chenaanah had made him horns of iron, and
said, Thus saith the LORD, With these thou shalt push Syria until they be con-
sumed.
11 And all the prophets prophesied so, saying, Go up to Ramoth-gilead, and
prosper: for the LORD shall deliver *it* into the hand of the king.
12 And the messenger that went to call Micaiah spake to him, saying, Behold,
the words of the prophets *declare* good to the king with one assent; let thy
word therefore, I pray thee, be like one of theirs, and speak thou good.
13 And Micaiah said, *As* the LORD liveth, even what my God saith, that will I
speak.
14 And when he was come to the king, the king said unto him, Micaiah, shall
we go to Ramoth-gilead to battle, or shall I forbear? And he said, Go ye up, and
prosper, and they shall be delivered into your hand.
15 And the king said to him, How many times shall I adjure thee that thou
say nothing but the truth to me in the name of the LORD?

16 Then he said, I did see all Israel scattered upon the mountains, as sheep that have no shepherd: and the LORD said, These have no master; let them return *therefore* every man to his house in peace.
17 And the king of Israel said to Jehoshaphat, Did I not tell thee *that* he would not prophesy good unto me, but evil?
18 Again he said, Therefore hear the word of the LORD; I saw the LORD sitting upon his throne, and all the host of heaven standing on his right hand and *on* his left.
19 And the LORD said, Who shall entice Ahab king of Israel, that he may go up and fall at Ramoth-gilead? And one spake saying after this manner, and another saying after that manner.
20 Then there came out a spirit, and stood before the LORD, and said, I will entice him. And the LORD said unto him, Wherewith?
21 And he said, I will go out, and be a lying spirit in the mouth of all his prophets. And *the* LORD said, Thou shalt entice *him*, and thou shalt also prevail: go out, and do *even* so.
22 Now therefore, behold, the LORD hath put a lying spirit in the mouth of these thy prophets, and the LORD hath spoken evil against thee.
23 Then Zedekiah the son of Chenaanah came near, and smote Micaiah upon the cheek, and said, Which way went the Spirit of the LORD from me to speak unto thee?
24 And Micaiah said, Behold, thou shalt see on that day when thou shalt go into an inner chamber to hide thyself.
25 Then the king of Israel said, Take ye Micaiah, and carry him back to Amon the governor of the city, and to Joash the king's son;
26 And say, Thus saith the king, Put this *fellow* in the prison, and feed him with bread of affliction and with water of affliction, until I return in peace.
27 And Micaiah said, If thou certainly return in peace, *then* hath not the LORD spoken by me. And he said, Hearken, all ye people.
28 So the king of Israel and Jehoshaphat the king of Judah went up to Ramoth-gilead.
29 And the king of Israel said unto Jehoshaphat, I will disguise myself, and will go to the battle; but put thou on thy robes. So the king of Israel disguised himself; and they went to the battle.
30 Now the king of Syria had commanded the captains of the chariots that *were* with him, saying, Fight ye not with small or great, save only with the king of Israel.
31 And it came to pass, when the captains of the chariots saw Jehoshaphat, that they said, It *is* the king of Israel. Therefore they compassed about him to fight: but Jehoshaphat cried out, and the LORD helped him; and God moved them *to depart* from him.
32 For it came to pass, that, when the captains of the chariots perceived that it was not the king of Israel, they turned back again from pursuing him.
33 And a *certain* man drew a bow at a venture, and smote the king of Israel between the joints of the harness: therefore he said to his chariot man, Turn thine hand, that thou mayest carry me out of the host; for I am wounded.
34 And the battle increased that day: howbeit the king of Israel stayed *himself* up in *his* chariot against the Syrians until the even: and about the time of the sun going down he died.

Jehoshaphat's Religious Reforms

19 And Jehoshaphat the king of Judah returned to his house in peace to Jerusalem.
2 And Jehu the son of Hanani the seer went out to meet him, and said to king Jehoshaphat, Shouldest thou help the ungodly, and love them that hate the LORD? therefore *is* wrath upon thee from before the LORD.

3 Nevertheless there are good things found in thee, in that thou hast taken
away the groves out of the land, and hast prepared thine heart to seek God.
4 And Jehoshaphat dwelt at Jerusalem: and he went out again through the
people from Beer-sheba to mount Ephraim, and brought them back unto the
LORD God of their fathers.

Jehoshaphat's Instructions to the Judges

5 And he set judges in the land throughout all the fenced cities of Judah, city
by city,
6 And said to the judges, Take heed what ye do: for ye judge not for man, but
for the LORD, who *is* with you in the judgment.
7 Wherefore now let the fear of the LORD be upon you; take heed and do *it*:
for *there is* no iniquity with the LORD our God, nor respect of persons, nor
taking of gifts.
8 Moreover in Jerusalem did Jehoshaphat set of the Levites, and *of* the priests,
and of the chief of the fathers of Israel, for the judgment of the LORD, and for
controversies, when they returned to Jerusalem.
9 And he charged them, saying, Thus shall ye do in the fear of the LORD,
faithfully, and with a perfect heart.
10 And what cause soever shall come to you of your brethren that dwell in
their cities, between blood and blood, between law and commandment, stat-
utes and judgments, ye shall even warn them that they trespass not against
the LORD, and *so* wrath come upon you, and upon your brethren: this do, and
ye shall not trespass.
11 And, behold, Amariah the chief priest *is* over you in all matters of the LORD;
and Zebadiah the son of Ishmael, the ruler of the house of Judah, for all the
king's matters: also the Levites *shall be* officers before you. Deal courageously,
and the LORD shall be with the good.

Jehoshaphat Proclaims a Fast

20 It came to pass after this also, *that* the children of Moab, and the chil-
dren of Ammon, and with them *other* beside the Ammonites, came
against Jehoshaphat to battle.
2 Then there came some that told Jehoshaphat, saying, There cometh a great
multitude against thee from beyond the sea on this side Syria; and, behold,
they *be* in Hazazon-tamar, which *is* Engedi.
3 And Jehoshaphat feared, and set himself to seek the LORD, and proclaimed
a fast throughout all Judah.
4 And Judah gathered themselves together, to ask *help* of the LORD: even out
of all the cities of Judah they came to seek the LORD.
5 And Jehoshaphat stood in the congregation of Judah and Jerusalem, in the
house of the LORD, before the new court,
6 And said, O LORD God of our fathers, *art* not thou God in heaven? and
rulest *not* thou over all the kingdoms of the heathen? and in thine hand *is
there not* power and might, so that none is able to withstand thee?
7 *Art* not thou our God, *who* didst drive out the inhabitants of this land
before thy people Israel, and gavest it to the seed of Abraham thy friend for
ever?
8 And they dwelt therein, and have built thee a sanctuary therein for thy
name, saying,
9 If, *when* evil cometh upon us, *as* the sword, judgment, or pestilence, or
famine, we stand before this house, and in thy presence, (for thy name *is* in
this house,) and cry unto thee in our affliction, then thou wilt hear and help.
10 And now, behold, the children of Ammon and Moab and mount Seir,
whom thou wouldest not let Israel invade, when they came out of the land of
Egypt, but they turned from them, and destroyed them not;

11 Behold, *I say, how* they reward us, to come to cast us out of thy possession,
which thou hast given us to inherit.
12 O our God, wilt thou not judge them? for we have no might against this
great company that cometh against us; neither know we what to do: but our
eyes *are* upon thee.
13 And all Judah stood before the LORD, with their little ones, their wives,
and their children.

The Prophecy of Jahaziel

14 Then upon Jahaziel the son of Zechariah, the son of Benaiah, the son of
Jeiel, the son of Mattaniah, a Levite of the sons of Asaph, came the Spirit of the
LORD in the midst of the congregation;
15 And he said, Hearken ye, all Judah, and ye inhabitants of Jerusalem, and
thou king Jehoshaphat, Thus saith the LORD unto you, Be not afraid nor dis-
mayed by reason of this great multitude; for the battle *is* not yours, but God's.
16 To morrow go ye down against them: behold, they come up by the cliff of
Ziz; and ye shall find them at the end of the brook, before the wilderness of
Jeruel.
17 Ye shall not *need* to fight in this *battle*: set yourselves, stand ye *still*, and
see the salvation of the LORD with you, O Judah and Jerusalem: fear not, nor
be dismayed; to morrow go out against them: for the LORD *will be* with you.
18 And Jehoshaphat bowed his head with *his* face to the ground: and all Judah
and the inhabitants of Jerusalem fell before the LORD, worshipping the LORD.
19 And the Levites, of the children of the Kohathites, and of the children of
the Korhites, stood up to praise the LORD God of Israel with a loud voice on
high.

Jehoshaphat Defeats Judah's Enemies

20 And they rose early in the morning, and went forth into the wilderness
of Tekoa: and as they went forth, Jehoshaphat stood and said, Hear me, O
Judah, and ye inhabitants of Jerusalem; Believe in the LORD your God, so shall
ye be established; believe his prophets, so shall ye prosper.
21 And when he had consulted with the people, he appointed singers unto
the LORD, and that should praise the beauty of holiness, as they went out before
the army, and to say, Praise the LORD; for his mercy *endureth* for ever.
22 And when they began to sing and to praise, the LORD set ambushments
against the children of Ammon, Moab, and mount Seir, which were come
against Judah; and they were smitten.
23 For the children of Ammon and Moab stood up against the inhabitants
of mount Seir, utterly to slay and destroy *them*: and when they had made an
end of the inhabitants of Seir, every one helped to destroy another.
24 And when Judah came toward the watch tower in the wilderness, they
looked unto the multitude, and, behold, they *were* dead bodies fallen to the
earth, and none escaped.
25 And when Jehoshaphat and his people came to take away the spoil of them,
they found among them in abundance both riches with the dead bodies, and
precious jewels, which they stripped off for themselves, more than they could
carry away: and they were three days in gathering of the spoil, it was so much.
26 And on the fourth day they assembled themselves in the valley of Berachah;
for there they blessed the LORD: therefore the name of the same place was
called, The valley of Berachah, unto this day.
27 Then they returned, every man of Judah and Jerusalem, and Jehoshaphat
in the forefront of them, to go again to Jerusalem with joy; for the LORD had
made them to rejoice over their enemies.
28 And they came to Jerusalem with psalteries and harps and trumpets unto
the house of the LORD.

2 CHRON. 20:15
THUS SAITH THE LORD unto you, BE NOT AFRAID NOR DISMAYED BY REASON OF THIS GREAT multitude; FOR THE BATTLE IS NOT YOURS, - BUT - GOD'S.

29 And the fear of God was on all the kingdoms of *those* countries, when they
had heard that the LORD fought against the enemies of Israel.
30 So the realm of Jehoshaphat was quiet: for his God gave him rest round
about.

Jehoshaphat's Reign

31 And Jehoshaphat reigned over Judah: *he was* thirty and five years old when
he began to reign, and he reigned twenty and five years in Jerusalem. And his
mother's name *was* Azubah the daughter of Shilhi.
32 And he walked in the way of Asa his father, and departed not from it, doing
that which was right in the sight of the LORD.
33 Howbeit the high places were not taken away: for as yet the people had
not prepared their hearts unto the God of their fathers.
34 Now the rest of the acts of Jehoshaphat, first and last, behold, they *are*
written in the book of Jehu the son of Hanani, who *is* mentioned in the book
of the kings of Israel.
35 And after this did Jehoshaphat king of Judah join himself with Ahaziah
king of Israel, who did very wickedly:
36 And he joined himself with him to make ships to go to Tarshish: and they
made the ships in Ezion-geber.
37 Then Eliezer the son of Dodavah of Mareshah prophesied against
Jehoshaphat, saying, Because thou hast joined thyself with Ahaziah, the LORD
hath broken thy works. And the ships were broken, that they were not able to
go to Tarshish.

Jehoram Becomes King of Judah

21 Now Jehoshaphat slept with his fathers, and was buried with his fathers
in the city of David. And Jehoram his son reigned in his stead.
2 And he had brethren the sons of Jehoshaphat, Azariah, and Jehiel, and
Zechariah, and Azariah, and Michael, and Shephatiah: all these *were* the sons
of Jehoshaphat king of Israel.
3 And their father gave them great gifts of silver, and of gold, and of precious
things, with fenced cities in Judah: but the kingdom gave he to Jehoram;
because he *was* the firstborn.
4 Now when Jehoram was risen up to the kingdom of his father, he strength-
ened himself, and slew all his brethren with the sword, and *divers* also of the
princes of Israel.
5 Jehoram *was* thirty and two years old when he began to reign, and he
reigned eight years in Jerusalem.
6 And he walked in the way of the kings of Israel, like as did the house of
Ahab: for he had the daughter of Ahab to wife: and he wrought *that which was*
evil in the eyes of the LORD.
7 Howbeit the LORD would not destroy the house of David, because of the
covenant that he had made with David, and as he promised to give a light to
him and to his sons for ever.
8 In his days the Edomites revolted from under the dominion of Judah, and
made themselves a king.
9 Then Jehoram went forth with his princes, and all his chariots with him:
and he rose up by night, and smote the Edomites which compassed him in,
and the captains of the chariots.
10 So the Edomites revolted from under the hand of Judah unto this day. The
same time *also* did Libnah revolt from under his hand; because he had for-
saken the LORD God of his fathers.
11 Moreover he made high places in the mountains of Judah, and caused the
inhabitants of Jerusalem to commit fornication, and compelled Judah *thereto*.

Elijah Prophesies against Jehoram

12 And there came a writing to him from Elijah the prophet, saying, Thus
saith the LORD God of David thy father, Because thou hast not walked in the
ways of Jehoshaphat thy father, nor in the ways of Asa king of Judah,
13 But hast walked in the way of the kings of Israel, and hast made Judah and
the inhabitants of Jerusalem to go a whoring, like to the whoredoms of the
house of Ahab, and also hast slain thy brethren of thy father's house, *which
were* better than thyself:
14 Behold, with a great plague will the LORD smite thy people, and thy chil-
dren, and thy wives, and all thy goods:
15 And thou *shalt have* great sickness by disease of thy bowels, until thy
bowels fall out by reason of the sickness day by day.
16 Moreover the LORD stirred up against Jehoram the spirit of the Philistines,
and of the Arabians, that *were* near the Ethiopians:
17 And they came up into Judah, and brake into it, and carried away all the
substance that was found in the king's house, and his sons also, and his wives;
so that there was never a son left him, save Jehoahaz, the youngest of his sons.
18 And after all this the LORD smote him in his bowels with an incurable
disease.
19 And it came to pass, that in process of time, after the end of two years, his
bowels fell out by reason of his sickness: so he died of sore diseases. And his
people made no burning for him, like the burning of his fathers.
20 Thirty and two years old was he when he began to reign, and he reigned
in Jerusalem eight years, and departed without being desired. Howbeit they
buried him in the city of David, but not in the sepulchres of the kings.

Ahaziah Becomes King of Judah

22 And the inhabitants of Jerusalem made Ahaziah his youngest son king
in his stead: for the band of men that came with the Arabians to the
camp had slain all the eldest. So Ahaziah the son of Jehoram king of Judah
reigned.
2 Forty and two years old *was* Ahaziah when he began to reign, and he
reigned one year in Jerusalem. His mother's name also *was* Athaliah the daugh-
ter of Omri.
3 He also walked in the ways of the house of Ahab: for his mother was his
counsellor to do wickedly.
4 Wherefore he did evil in the sight of the LORD like the house of Ahab: for
they were his counsellors after the death of his father to his destruction.
5 He walked also after their counsel, and went with Jehoram the son of Ahab
king of Israel to war against Hazael king of Syria at Ramoth-gilead: and the
Syrians smote Joram.
6 And he returned to be healed in Jezreel because of the wounds which were
given him at Ramah, when he fought with Hazael king of Syria. And Azariah
the son of Jehoram king of Judah went down to see Jehoram the son of Ahab
at Jezreel, because he was sick.
7 And the destruction of Ahaziah was of God by coming to Joram: for when
he was come, he went out with Jehoram against Jehu the son of Nimshi, whom
the LORD had anointed to cut off the house of Ahab.
8 And it came to pass, that, when Jehu was executing judgment upon the
house of Ahab, and found the princes of Judah, and the sons of the brethren
of Ahaziah, that ministered to Ahaziah, he slew them.
9 And he sought Ahaziah: and they caught him, (for he was hid in Samaria,)
and brought him to Jehu: and when they had slain him, they buried him:
Because, said they, he *is* the son of Jehoshaphat, who sought the LORD with all
his heart. So the house of Ahaziah had no power to keep still the kingdom.

Athaliah Usurps the Throne of Judah

10 But when Athaliah the mother of Ahaziah saw that her son was dead, she arose and destroyed all the seed royal of the house of Judah.

11 But Jehoshabeath, the daughter of the king, took Joash the son of Ahaziah, and stole him from among the king's sons that were slain, and put him and his nurse in a bedchamber. So Jehoshabeath, the daughter of king Jehoram, the wife of Jehoiada the priest, (for she was the sister of Ahaziah,) hid him from Athaliah, so that she slew him not.

12 And he was with them hid in the house of God six years: and Athaliah reigned over the land.

Jehoiada Makes Joash King of Judah

23 And in the seventh year Jehoiada strengthened himself, and took the captains of hundreds, Azariah the son of Jeroham, and Ishmael the son of Jehohanan, and Azariah the son of Obed, and Maaseiah the son of Adaiah, and Elishaphat the son of Zichri, into covenant with him.

2 And they went about in Judah, and gathered the Levites out of all the cities of Judah, and the chief of the fathers of Israel, and they came to Jerusalem.

3 And all the congregation made a covenant with the king in the house of God. And he said unto them, Behold, the king's son shall reign, as the LORD hath said of the sons of David.

4 This *is* the thing that ye shall do; A third part of you entering on the sabbath, of the priests and of the Levites, *shall be* porters of the doors;

5 And a third part *shall be* at the king's house; and a third part at the gate of the foundation: and all the people *shall be* in the courts of the house of the LORD.

6 But let none come into the house of the LORD, save the priests, and they that minister of the Levites; they shall go in, for they *are* holy: but all the people shall keep the watch of the LORD.

7 And the Levites shall compass the king round about, every man with his weapons in his hand; and whosoever *else* cometh into the house, he shall be put to death: but be ye with the king when he cometh in, and when he goeth out.

8 So the Levites and all Judah did according to all things that Jehoiada the priest had commanded, and took every man his men that were to come in on the sabbath, with them that were to go *out* on the sabbath: for Jehoiada the priest dismissed not the courses.

9 Moreover Jehoiada the priest delivered to the captains of hundreds spears, and bucklers, and shields, that *had been* king David's, which *were* in the house of God.

10 And he set all the people, every man having his weapon in his hand, from the right side of the temple to the left side of the temple, along by the altar and the temple, by the king round about.

11 Then they brought out the king's son, and put upon him the crown, and *gave him* the testimony, and made him king. And Jehoiada and his sons anointed him, and said, God save the king.

Athaliah Is Slain

12 Now when Athaliah heard the noise of the people running and praising the king, she came to the people into the house of the LORD:

13 And she looked, and, behold, the king stood at his pillar at the entering in, and the princes and the trumpets by the king: and all the people of the land rejoiced, and sounded with trumpets, also the singers with instruments of musick, and such as taught to sing praise. Then Athaliah rent her clothes, and said, Treason, Treason.

14 Then Jehoiada the priest brought out the captains of hundreds that were set over the host, and said unto them, Have her forth of the ranges: and whoso

followeth her, let him be slain with the sword. For the priest said, Slay her not in the house of the LORD.

15 So they laid hands on her; and when she was come to the entering of the horse gate by the king's house, they slew her there.

16 And Jehoiada made a covenant between him, and between all the people, and between the king, that they should be the LORD's people.

17 Then all the people went to the house of Baal, and brake it down, and brake his altars and his images in pieces, and slew Mattan the priest of Baal before the altars.

18 Also Jehoiada appointed the offices of the house of the LORD by the hand of the priests the Levites, whom David had distributed in the house of the LORD, to offer the burnt offerings of the LORD, as *it is* written in the law of Moses, with rejoicing and with singing, *as it was ordained* by David.

19 And he set the porters at the gates of the house of the LORD, that none *which was* unclean in any thing should enter in.

20 And he took the captains of hundreds, and the nobles, and the governors of the people, and all the people of the land, and brought down the king from the house of the LORD: and they came through the high gate into the king's house, and set the king upon the throne of the kingdom.

21 And all the people of the land rejoiced: and the city was quiet, after that they had slain Athaliah with the sword.

Joash's Reign over Judah

24 Joash *was* seven years old when he began to reign, and he reigned forty years in Jerusalem. His mother's name also *was* Zibiah of Beer-sheba.

2 And Joash did *that which was* right in the sight of the LORD all the days of Jehoiada the priest.

3 And Jehoiada took for him two wives; and he begat sons and daughters.

4 And it came to pass after this, *that* Joash was minded to repair the house of the LORD.

5 And he gathered together the priests and the Levites, and said to them, Go out unto the cities of Judah, and gather of all Israel money to repair the house of your God from year to year, and see that ye hasten the matter. Howbeit the Levites hastened *it* not.

6 And the king called for Jehoiada the chief, and said unto him, Why hast thou not required of the Levites to bring in out of Judah and out of Jerusalem the collection, *according to the commandment* of Moses the servant of the LORD, and of the congregation of Israel, for the tabernacle of witness?

7 For the sons of Athaliah, that wicked woman, had broken up the house of God; and also all the dedicated things of the house of the LORD did they bestow upon Baalim.

8 And at the king's commandment they made a chest, and set it without at the gate of the house of the LORD.

9 And they made a proclamation through Judah and Jerusalem, to bring in to the LORD the collection *that* Moses the servant of God *laid* upon Israel in the wilderness.

10 And all the princes and all the people rejoiced, and brought in, and cast into the chest, until they had made an end.

11 Now it came to pass, that at what time the chest was brought unto the king's office by the hand of the Levites, and when they saw that *there was* much money, the king's scribe and the high priest's officer came and emptied the chest, and took it, and carried it to his place again. Thus they did day by day, and gathered money in abundance.

12 And the king and Jehoiada gave it to such as did the work of the service of the house of the LORD, and hired masons and carpenters to repair the house

of the LORD, and also such as wrought iron and brass to mend the house of the
LORD.
13 So the workmen wrought, and the work was perfected by them, and they
set the house of God in his state, and strengthened it.
14 And when they had finished *it*, they brought the rest of the money before
the king and Jehoiada, whereof were made vessels for the house of the LORD,
even vessels to minister, and to offer *withal*, and spoons, and vessels of gold
and silver. And they offered burnt offerings in the house of the LORD contin-
ually all the days of Jehoiada.

Joash's Sin Leads to His Assassination

15 But Jehoiada waxed old, and was full of days when he died; an hundred
and thirty years old *was he* when he died.
16 And they buried him in the city of David among the kings, because he had
done good in Israel, both toward God, and toward his house.
17 Now after the death of Jehoiada came the princes of Judah, and made
obeisance to the king. Then the king hearkened unto them.
18 And they left the house of the LORD God of their fathers, and served groves
and idols: and wrath came upon Judah and Jerusalem for this their trespass.
19 Yet he sent prophets to them, to bring them again unto the LORD; and they
testified against them: but they would not give ear.
20 And the Spirit of God came upon Zechariah the son of Jehoiada the priest,
which stood above the people, and said unto them, Thus saith God, Why trans-
gress ye the commandments of the LORD, that ye cannot prosper? because ye
have forsaken the LORD, he hath also forsaken you.
21 And they conspired against him, and stoned him with stones at the com-
mandment of the king in the court of the house of the LORD.
22 Thus Joash the king remembered not the kindness which Jehoiada his
father had done to him, but slew his son. And when he died, he said, The LORD
look upon *it*, and require *it*.
23 And it came to pass at the end of the year, *that* the host of Syria came up
against him: and they came to Judah and Jerusalem, and destroyed all the
princes of the people from among the people, and sent all the spoil of them
unto the king of Damascus.
24 For the army of the Syrians came with a small company of men, and the
LORD delivered a very great host into their hand, because they had forsaken
the LORD God of their fathers. So they executed judgment against Joash.
25 And when they were departed from him, (for they left him in great dis-
eases,) his own servants conspired against him for the blood of the sons of
Jehoiada the priest, and slew him on his bed, and he died: and they buried him
in the city of David, but they buried him not in the sepulchres of the kings.
26 And these are they that conspired against him; Zabad the son of Shimeath
an Ammonitess, and Jehozabad the son of Shimrith a Moabitess.
27 Now *concerning* his sons, and the greatness of the burdens *laid* upon him,
and the repairing of the house of God, behold, they *are* written in the story of
the book of the kings. And Amaziah his son reigned in his stead.

Amaziah Becomes King of Judah

25 Amaziah *was* twenty and five years old *when* he began to reign, and he
reigned twenty and nine years in Jerusalem. And his mother's name
was Jehoaddan of Jerusalem.
2 And he did *that which was* right in the sight of the LORD, but not with a
perfect heart.
3 Now it came to pass, when the kingdom was established to him, that he
slew his servants that had killed the king his father.
4 But he slew not their children, but *did* as *it is* written in the law in the book
of Moses, where the LORD commanded, saying, The fathers shall not die for

the children, neither shall the children die for the fathers, but every man shall
die for his own sin.
5 Moreover Amaziah gathered Judah together, and made them captains over
thousands, and captains over hundreds, according to the houses of *their*
fathers, throughout all Judah and Benjamin: and he numbered them from
twenty years old and above, and found them three hundred thousand choice
men, able to go forth to war, that could handle spear and shield.
6 He hired also an hundred thousand mighty men of valour out of Israel for
an hundred talents of silver.
7 But there came a man of God to him, saying, O king, let not the army of
Israel go with thee; for the LORD *is* not with Israel, *to wit, with* all the children
of Ephraim.
8 But if thou wilt go, do *it*, be strong for the battle: God shall make thee fall
before the enemy: for God hath power to help, and to cast down.
9 And Amaziah said to the man of God, But what shall we do for the hundred
talents which I have given to the army of Israel? And the man of God answered,
The LORD is able to give thee much more than this.
10 Then Amaziah separated them, *to wit*, the army that was come to him out
of Ephraim, to go home again: wherefore their anger was greatly kindled
against Judah, and they returned home in great anger.
11 And Amaziah strengthened himself, and led forth his people, and went
to the valley of salt, and smote of the children of Seir ten thousand.
12 And *other* ten thousand *left* alive did the children of Judah carry away
captive, and brought them unto the top of the rock, and cast them down from
the top of the rock, that they all were broken in pieces.
13 But the soldiers of the army which Amaziah sent back, that they should
not go with him to battle, fell upon the cities of Judah, from Samaria even unto
Beth-horon, and smote three thousand of them, and took much spoil.

Amaziah Serves the Gods of Edom

14 Now it came to pass, after that Amaziah was come from the slaughter of
the Edomites, that he brought the gods of the children of Seir, and set them
up *to be* his gods, and bowed down himself before them, and burned incense
unto them.
15 Wherefore the anger of the LORD was kindled against Amaziah, and he
sent unto him a prophet, which said unto him, Why hast thou sought after
the gods of the people, which could not deliver their own people out of thine
hand?
16 And it came to pass, as he talked with him, that *the king* said unto him,
Art thou made of the king's counsel? forbear; why shouldest thou be smitten?
Then the prophet forbare, and said, I know that God hath determined to
destroy thee, because thou hast done this, and hast not hearkened unto my
counsel.

Amaziah's Sin Leads to His Defeat

17 Then Amaziah king of Judah took advice, and sent to Joash, the son of
Jehoahaz, the son of Jehu, king of Israel, saying, Come, let us see one another
in the face.
18 And Joash king of Israel sent to Amaziah king of Judah, saying, The thistle
that *was* in Lebanon sent to the cedar that *was* in Lebanon, saying, Give thy
daughter to my son to wife: and there passed by a wild beast that *was* in
Lebanon, and trode down the thistle.
19 Thou sayest, Lo, thou hast smitten the Edomites; and thine heart lifteth
thee up to boast: abide now at home; why shouldest thou meddle to *thine* hurt,
that thou shouldest fall, *even* thou, and Judah with thee?

20 But Amaziah would not hear; for it *came* of God, that he might deliver
them into the hand *of their enemies*, because they sought after the gods of
Edom.
21 So Joash the king of Israel went up; and they saw one another in the face,
both he and Amaziah king of Judah, at Beth-shemesh, which *belongeth* to
Judah.
22 And Judah was put to the worse before Israel, and they fled every man to
his tent.
23 And Joash the king of Israel took Amaziah king of Judah, the son of Joash,
the son of Jehoahaz, at Beth-shemesh, and brought him to Jerusalem, and
brake down the wall of Jerusalem from the gate of Ephraim to the corner gate,
four hundred cubits.
24 And *he took* all the gold and the silver, and all the vessels that were found
in the house of God with Obededom, and the treasures of the king's house,
the hostages also, and returned to Samaria.
25 And Amaziah the son of Joash king of Judah lived after the death of Joash
son of Jehoahaz king of Israel fifteen years.
26 Now the rest of the acts of Amaziah, first and last, behold, *are* they not
written in the book of the kings of Judah and Israel?
27 Now after the time that Amaziah did turn away from following the LORD
they made a conspiracy against him in Jerusalem; and he fled to Lachish: but
they sent to Lachish after him, and slew him there.
28 And they brought him upon horses, and buried him with his fathers in
the city of Judah.

Uzziah Becomes King of Judah

26 Then all the people of Judah took Uzziah, who *was* sixteen years old,
and made him king in the room of his father Amaziah.
2 He built Eloth, and restored it to Judah, after that the king slept with his
fathers.
3 Sixteen years old *was* Uzziah when he began to reign, and he reigned fifty
and two years in Jerusalem. His mother's name also *was* Jecoliah of Jerusalem.
4 And he did *that which was* right in the sight of the LORD, according to all
that his father Amaziah did.
5 And he sought God in the days of Zechariah, who had understanding in the
visions of God: and as long as he sought the LORD, God made him to prosper.
6 And he went forth and warred against the Philistines, and brake down the
wall of Gath, and the wall of Jabneh, and the wall of Ashdod, and built cities
about Ashdod, and among the Philistines.
7 And God helped him against the Philistines, and against the Arabians that
dwelt in Gur-baal, and the Mehunims.
8 And the Ammonites gave gifts to Uzziah: and his name spread abroad *even*
to the entering in of Egypt; for he strengthened *himself* exceedingly.
9 Moreover Uzziah built towers in Jerusalem at the corner gate, and at the
valley gate, and at the turning *of the wall*, and fortified them.
10 Also he built towers in the desert, and digged many wells: for he had much
cattle, both in the low country, and in the plains: husbandmen *also*, and vine
dressers in the mountains, and in Carmel: for he loved husbandry.
11 Moreover Uzziah had an host of fighting men, that went out to war by
bands, according to the number of their account by the hand of Jeiel the scribe
and Maaseiah the ruler, under the hand of Hananiah, *one* of the king's captains.
12 The whole number of the chief of the fathers of the mighty men of valour
were two thousand and six hundred.
13 And under their hand *was* an army, three hundred thousand and seven
thousand and five hundred, that made war with mighty power, to help the
king against the enemy.

14 And Uzziah prepared for them throughout all the host shields, and spears,
and helmets, and habergeons, and bows, and slings *to cast* stones.
15 And he made in Jerusalem engines, invented by cunning men, to be on
the towers and upon the bulwarks, to shoot arrows and great stones withal.
And his name spread far abroad; for he was marvellously helped, till he was
strong.

Uzziah Is Smitten with Leprosy

16 But when he was strong, his heart was lifted up to *his* destruction: for he
transgressed against the LORD his God, and went into the temple of the LORD
to burn incense upon the altar of incense.
17 And Azariah the priest went in after him, and with him fourscore priests
of the LORD, *that were* valiant men:
18 And they withstood Uzziah the king, and said unto him, *It appertaineth*
not unto thee, Uzziah, to burn incense unto the LORD, but to the priests the
sons of Aaron, that are consecrated to burn incense: go out of the sanctuary;
for thou hast trespassed; neither *shall it be* for thine honour from the LORD
God.
19 Then Uzziah was wroth, and *had* a censer in his hand to burn incense:
and while he was wroth with the priests, the leprosy even rose up in his fore-
head before the priests in the house of the LORD, from beside the incense altar.
20 And Azariah the chief priest, and all the priests, looked upon him, and,
behold, he *was* leprous in his forehead, and they thrust him out from thence;
yea, himself hasted also to go out, because the LORD had smitten him.
21 And Uzziah the king was a leper unto the day of his death, and dwelt in a
several house, *being* a leper; for he was cut off from the house of the LORD: and
Jotham his son *was* over the king's house, judging the people of the land.
22 Now the rest of the acts of Uzziah, first and last, did Isaiah the prophet,
the son of Amoz, write.
23 So Uzziah slept with his fathers, and they buried him with his fathers in
the field of the burial which *belonged* to the kings; for they said, He *is* a leper:
and Jotham his son reigned in his stead.

Jotham Becomes King of Judah

27 Jotham *was* twenty and five years old when he began to reign, and he
reigned sixteen years in Jerusalem. His mother's name also *was*
Jerushah, the daughter of Zadok.
2 And he did *that which was* right in the sight of the LORD, according to all
that his father Uzziah did: howbeit he entered not into the temple of the LORD.
And the people did yet corruptly.
3 He built the high gate of the house of the LORD, and on the wall of Ophel
he built much.
4 Moreover he built cities in the mountains of Judah, and in the forests he
built castles and towers.
5 He fought also with the king of the Ammonites, and prevailed against them.
And the children of Ammon gave him the same year an hundred talents of
silver, and ten thousand measures of wheat, and ten thousand of barley. So
much did the children of Ammon pay unto him, both the second year, and
the third.
6 So Jotham became mighty, because he prepared his ways before the LORD
his God.
7 Now the rest of the acts of Jotham, and all his wars, and his ways, lo, they
are written in the book of the kings of Israel and Judah.
8 He was five and twenty years old when he began to reign, and reigned
sixteen years in Jerusalem.
9 And Jotham slept with his fathers, and they buried him in the city of David:
and Ahaz his son reigned in his stead.

Ahaz Becomes King of Judah

28 Ahaz *was* twenty years old when he began to reign, and he reigned
sixteen years in Jerusalem: but he did not *that which was* right in the
sight of the LORD, like David his father:
2 For he walked in the ways of the kings of Israel, and made also molten
images for Baalim.
3 Moreover he burnt incense in the valley of the son of Hinnom, and burnt
his children in the fire, after the abominations of the heathen whom the LORD
had cast out before the children of Israel.
4 He sacrificed also and burnt incense in the high places, and on the hills,
and under every green tree.
5 Wherefore the LORD his God delivered him into the hand of the king of
Syria; and they smote him, and carried away a great multitude of them cap-
tives, and brought *them* to Damascus. And he was also delivered into the hand
of the king of Israel, who smote him with a great slaughter.

Oded the Prophet Brings about Release of the Children of Judah

6 For Pekah the son of Remaliah slew in Judah an hundred and twenty thou-
sand in one day, *which were* all valiant men; because they had forsaken the
LORD God of their fathers.
7 And Zichri, a mighty man of Ephraim, slew Maaseiah the king's son, and
Azrikam the governor of the house, and Elkanah *that was* next to the king.
8 And the children of Israel carried away captive of their brethren two hun-
dred thousand, women, sons, and daughters, and took also away much spoil
from them, and brought the spoil to Samaria.
9 But a prophet of the LORD was there, whose name *was* Oded: and he went
out before the host that came to Samaria, and said unto them, Behold, because
the LORD God of your fathers was wroth with Judah, he hath delivered them
into your hand, and ye have slain them in a rage *that* reacheth up unto heaven.
10 And now ye purpose to keep under the children of Judah and Jerusalem
for bondmen and bondwomen unto you: *but are there* not with you, even with
you, sins against the LORD your God?
11 Now hear me therefore, and deliver the captives again, which ye have
taken captive of your brethren: for the fierce wrath of the LORD *is* upon you.
12 Then certain of the heads of the children of Ephraim, Azariah the son of
Johanan, Berechiah the son of Meshillemoth, and Jehizkiah the son of Shallum,
and Amasa the son of Hadlai, stood up against them that came from the war,
13 And said unto them, Ye shall not bring in the captives hither: for whereas
we have offended against the LORD *already*, ye intend to add *more* to our sins
and to our trespass: for our trespass is great, and *there is* fierce wrath against
Israel.
14 So the armed men left the captives and the spoil before the princes and
all the congregation.
15 And the men which were expressed by name rose up, and took the captives,
and with the spoil clothed all that were naked among them, and arrayed them,
and shod them, and gave them to eat and to drink, and anointed them, and
carried all the feeble of them upon asses, and brought them to Jericho, the
city of palm trees, to their brethren: then they returned to Samaria.

Ahaz Sends to Assyria for Aid but to No Avail

16 At that time did king Ahaz send unto the kings of Assyria to help him.
17 For again the Edomites had come and smitten Judah, and carried away
captives.
18 The Philistines also had invaded the cities of the low country, and of the
south of Judah, and had taken Beth-shemesh, and Ajalon, and Gederoth, and
Shocho with the villages thereof, and Timnah with the villages thereof, Gimzo
also and the villages thereof: and they dwelt there.

19 For the LORD brought Judah low because of Ahaz king of Israel; for he
made Judah naked, and transgressed sore against the LORD.
20 And Tilgath-pilneser king of Assyria came unto him, and distressed him,
but strengthened him not.
21 For Ahaz took away a portion *out* of the house of the LORD, and *out* of the
house of the king, and of the princes, and gave *it* unto the king of Assyria: but
he helped him not.
22 And in the time of his distress did he trespass yet more against the LORD:
this *is that* king Ahaz.
23 For he sacrificed unto the gods of Damascus, which smote him: and he
said, Because the gods of the kings of Syria help them, *therefore* will I sacrifice
to them, that they may help me. But they were the ruin of him, and of all Israel.
24 And Ahaz gathered together the vessels of the house of God, and cut in
pieces the vessels of the house of God, and shut up the doors of the house of
the LORD, and he made him altars in every corner of Jerusalem.
25 And in every several city of Judah he made high places to burn incense
unto other gods, and provoked to anger the LORD God of his fathers.
26 Now the rest of his acts and of all his ways, first and last, behold, they *are*
written in the book of the kings of Judah and Israel.
27 And Ahaz slept with his fathers, and they buried him in the city, *even* in
Jerusalem: but they brought him not into the sepulchres of the kings of Israel:
and Hezekiah his son reigned in his stead.

Hezekiah Becomes King of Judah

29 Hezekiah began to reign *when he was* five and twenty years old, and
he reigned nine and twenty years in Jerusalem. And his mother's name
was Abijah, the daughter of Zechariah.
2 And he did *that which was* right in the sight of the LORD, according to all
that David his father had done.
3 He in the first year of his reign, in the first month, opened the doors of the
house of the LORD, and repaired them.
4 And he brought in the priests and the Levites, and gathered them together
into the east street,
5 And said unto them, Hear me, ye Levites, sanctify now yourselves, and
sanctify the house of the LORD God of your fathers, and carry forth the filthi-
ness out of the holy *place*.
6 For our fathers have trespassed, and done *that which was* evil in the eyes
of the LORD our God, and have forsaken him, and have turned away their faces
from the habitation of the LORD, and turned *their* backs.
7 Also they have shut up the doors of the porch, and put out the lamps, and
have not burned incense nor offered burnt offerings in the holy *place* unto
the God of Israel.
8 Wherefore the wrath of the LORD was upon Judah and Jerusalem, and he
hath delivered them to trouble, to astonishment, and to hissing, as ye see with
your eyes.
9 For, lo, our fathers have fallen by the sword, and our sons and our daughters
and our wives *are* in captivity for this.
10 Now *it is* in mine heart to make a covenant with the LORD God of Israel,
that his fierce wrath may turn away from us.
11 My sons, be not now negligent: for the LORD hath chosen you to stand
before him, to serve him, and that ye should minister unto him, and burn
incense.

Priests and Levites Sanctify Themselves and Cleanse the Temple

12 Then the Levites arose, Mahath the son of Amasai, and Joel the son of
Azariah, of the sons of the Kohathites: and of the sons of Merari, Kish the son

of Abdi, and Azariah the son of Jehalelel: and of the Gershonites; Joah the son
of Zimmah, and Eden the son of Joah:
13 And of the sons of Elizaphan; Shimri, and Jeiel: and of the sons of Asaph;
Zechariah, and Mattaniah:
14 And of the sons of Heman; Jehiel, and Shimei: and of the sons of Jeduthun;
Shemaiah, and Uzziel.
15 And they gathered their brethren, and sanctified themselves, and came,
according to the commandment of the king, by the words of the LORD, to
cleanse the house of the LORD.
16 And the priests went into the inner part of the house of the LORD, to cleanse
it, and brought out all the uncleanness that they found in the temple of the
LORD into the court of the house of the LORD. And the Levites took *it*, to carry
it out abroad into the brook Kidron.
17 Now they began on the first *day* of the first month to sanctify, and on the
eighth day of the month came they to the porch of the LORD: so they sanctified
the house of the LORD in eight days; and in the sixteenth day of the first month
they made an end.
18 Then they went in to Hezekiah the king, and said, We have cleansed all
the house of the LORD, and the altar of burnt offering, with all the vessels
thereof, and the shewbread table, with all the vessels thereof.
19 Moreover all the vessels, which king Ahaz in his reign did cast away in his
transgression, have we prepared and sanctified, and, behold, they *are* before
the altar of the LORD.

Hezekiah Rededicates the Temple

20 Then Hezekiah the king rose early, and gathered the rulers of the city, and
went up to the house of the LORD.
21 And they brought seven bullocks, and seven rams, and seven lambs, and
seven he goats, for a sin offering for the kingdom, and for the sanctuary, and
for Judah. And he commanded the priests the sons of Aaron to offer *them* on
the altar of the LORD.
22 So they killed the bullocks, and the priests received the blood, and sprin-
kled *it* on the altar: likewise, when they had killed the rams, they sprinkled
the blood upon the altar: they killed also the lambs, and they sprinkled the
blood upon the altar.
23 And they brought forth the he goats *for* the sin offering before the king
and the congregation; and they laid their hands upon them:
24 And the priests killed them, and they made reconciliation with their blood
upon the altar, to make an atonement for all Israel: for the king commanded
that the burnt offering and the sin offering *should be made* for all Israel.
25 And he set the Levites in the house of the LORD with cymbals, with psal-
teries, and with harps, according to the commandment of David, and of Gad
the king's seer, and Nathan the prophet: for *so was* the commandment of the
LORD by his prophets.
26 And the Levites stood with the instruments of David, and the priests with
the trumpets.
27 And Hezekiah commanded to offer the burnt offering upon the altar. And
when the burnt offering began, the song of the LORD began *also* with the
trumpets, and with the instruments *ordained* by David king of Israel.
28 And all the congregation worshipped, and the singers sang, and the trum-
peters sounded: *and* all *this continued* until the burnt offering was finished.
29 And when they had made an end of offering, the king and all that were
present with him bowed themselves, and worshipped.
30 Moreover Hezekiah the king and the princes commanded the Levites to
sing praise unto the LORD with the words of David, and of Asaph the seer. And
they sang praises with gladness, and they bowed their heads and worshipped.

31 Then Hezekiah answered and said, Now ye have consecrated yourselves
unto the LORD, come near and bring sacrifices and thank offerings into the
house of the LORD. And the congregation brought in sacrifices and thank
offerings; and as many as were of a free heart burnt offerings.
32 And the number of the burnt offerings, which the congregation brought,
was threescore and ten bullocks, an hundred rams, *and* two hundred lambs:
all these *were* for a burnt offering to the LORD.
33 And the consecrated things *were* six hundred oxen and three thousand
sheep.
34 But the priests were too few, so that they could not flay all the burnt offer-
ings: wherefore their brethren the Levites did help them, till the work was
ended, and until the *other* priests had sanctified themselves: for the Levites
were more upright in heart to sanctify themselves than the priests.
35 And also the burnt offerings *were* in abundance, with the fat of the peace
offerings, and the drink offerings for *every* burnt offering. So the service of
the house of the LORD was set in order.
36 And Hezekiah rejoiced, and all the people, that God had prepared the
people: for the thing was *done* suddenly.

Hezekiah Celebrates Passover

30 And Hezekiah sent to all Israel and Judah, and wrote letters also to
Ephraim and Manasseh, that they should come to the house of the
LORD at Jerusalem, to keep the passover unto the LORD God of Israel.
2 For the king had taken counsel, and his princes, and all the congregation
in Jerusalem, to keep the passover in the second month.
3 For they could not keep it at that time, because the priests had not sancti-
fied themselves sufficiently, neither had the people gathered themselves
together to Jerusalem.
4 And the thing pleased the king and all the congregation.
5 So they established a decree to make proclamation throughout all Israel,
from Beersheba even to Dan, that they should come to keep the passover unto
the LORD God of Israel at Jerusalem: for they had not done *it* of a long *time in
such sort* as it was written.
6 So the posts went with the letters from the king and his princes throughout
all Israel and Judah, and according to the commandment of the king, saying,
Ye children of Israel, turn again unto the LORD God of Abraham, Isaac, and
Israel, and he will return to the remnant of you, that are escaped out of the
hand of the kings of Assyria.
7 And be not ye like your fathers, and like your brethren, which trespassed
against the LORD God of their fathers, *who* therefore gave them up to desola-
tion, as ye see.
8 Now be ye not stiffnecked, as your fathers *were, but* yield yourselves unto
the LORD, and enter into his sanctuary, which he hath sanctified for ever: and
serve the LORD your God, that the fierceness of his wrath may turn away from
you.
9 For if ye turn again unto the LORD, your brethren and your children *shall
find* compassion before them that lead them captive, so that they shall come
again into this land: for the LORD your God *is* gracious and merciful, and will
not turn away *his* face from you, if ye return unto him.
10 So the posts passed from city to city through the country of Ephraim and
Manasseh even unto Zebulun: but they laughed them to scorn, and mocked
them.
11 Nevertheless divers of Asher and Manasseh and of Zebulun humbled
themselves, and came to Jerusalem.
12 Also in Judah the hand of God was to give them one heart to do the com-
mandment of the king and of the princes, by the word of the LORD.

The People Celebrate the Feast of Unleavened Bread

13 And there assembled at Jerusalem much people to keep the feast of unleav-
ened bread in the second month, a very great congregation.
14 And they arose and took away the altars that *were* in Jerusalem, and all
the altars for incense took they away, and cast *them* into the brook Kidron.
15 Then they killed the passover on the fourteenth *day* of the second month:
and the priests and the Levites were ashamed, and sanctified themselves, and
brought in the burnt offerings into the house of the LORD.
16 And they stood in their place after their manner, according to the law of
Moses the man of God: the priests sprinkled the blood, *which they received* of
the hand of the Levites.
17 For *there were* many in the congregation that were not sanctified: there-
fore the Levites had the charge of the killing of the passovers for every one
that was not clean, to sanctify *them* unto the LORD.
18 For a multitude of the people, *even* many of Ephraim, and Manasseh,
Issachar, and Zebulun, had not cleansed themselves, yet did they eat the pass-
over otherwise than it was written. But Hezekiah prayed for them, saying, The
good LORD pardon every one
19 *That* prepareth his heart to seek God, the LORD God of his fathers, though
he be not *cleansed* according to the purification of the sanctuary.
20 And the LORD hearkened to Hezekiah, and healed the people.
21 And the children of Israel that were present at Jerusalem kept the feast of
unleavened bread seven days with great gladness: and the Levites and the
priests praised the LORD day by day, *singing* with loud instruments unto the
LORD.
22 And Hezekiah spake comfortably unto all the Levites that taught the good
knowledge of the LORD: and they did eat throughout the feast seven days, offer-
ing peace offerings, and making confession to the LORD God of their fathers.
23 And the whole assembly took counsel to keep other seven days: and they
kept *other* seven days with gladness.
24 For Hezekiah king of Judah did give to the congregation a thousand bull-
ocks and seven thousand sheep; and the princes gave to the congregation a
thousand bullocks and ten thousand sheep: and a great number of priests
sanctified themselves.
25 And all the congregation of Judah, with the priests and the Levites, and
all the congregation that came out of Israel, and the strangers that came out
of the land of Israel, and that dwelt in Judah, rejoiced.
26 So there was great joy in Jerusalem: for since the time of Solomon the son
of David king of Israel *there was* not the like in Jerusalem.
27 Then the priests the Levites arose and blessed the people: and their voice
was heard, and their prayer came *up* to his holy dwelling place, *even* unto
heaven.

Hezekiah Reforms Judah's Worship

31 Now when all this was finished, all Israel that were present went out
to the cities of Judah, and brake the images in pieces, and cut down
the groves, and threw down the high places and the altars out of all Judah and
Benjamin, in Ephraim also and Manasseh, until they had utterly destroyed
them all. Then all the children of Israel returned, every man to his possession,
into their own cities.
2 And Hezekiah appointed the courses of the priests and the Levites after
their courses, every man according to his service, the priests and Levites for
burnt offerings and for peace offerings, to minister, and to give thanks, and
to praise in the gates of the tents of the LORD.
3 *He appointed* also the king's portion of his substance for the burnt offer-
ings, *to wit*, for the morning and evening burnt offerings, and the burnt offer-

ings for the sabbaths, and for the new moons, and for the set feasts, as *it is*
written in the law of the LORD.
4 Moreover he commanded the people that dwelt in Jerusalem to give the
portion of the priests and the Levites, that they might be encouraged in the
law of the LORD.
5 And as soon as the commandment came abroad, the children of Israel
brought in abundance the firstfruits of corn, wine, and oil, and honey, and of
all the increase of the field; and the tithe of all *things* brought they in abun-
dantly.
6 And *concerning* the children of Israel and Judah, that dwelt in the cities of
Judah, they also brought in the tithe of oxen and sheep, and the tithe of holy
things which were consecrated unto the LORD their God, and laid *them* by
heaps.
7 In the third month they began to lay the foundation of the heaps, and
finished *them* in the seventh month.
8 And when Hezekiah and the princes came and saw the heaps, they blessed
the LORD, and his people Israel.
9 Then Hezekiah questioned with the priests and the Levites concerning the
heaps.
10 And Azariah the chief priest of the house of Zadok answered him, and
said, Since *the people* began to bring the offerings into the house of the LORD,
we have had enough to eat, and have left plenty: for the LORD hath blessed his
people; and that which is left *is* this great store.
11 Then Hezekiah commanded to prepare chambers in the house of the
LORD; and they prepared *them,*
12 And brought in the offerings and the tithes and the dedicated *things* faith-
fully: over which Cononiah the Levite *was* ruler, and Shimei his brother *was*
the next.
13 And Jehiel, and Azaziah, and Nahath, and Asahel, and Jerimoth, and
Jozabad, and Eliel, and Ismachiah, and Mahath, and Benaiah, *were* overseers
under the hand of Cononiah and Shimei his brother, at the commandment
of Hezekiah the king, and Azariah the ruler of the house of God.
14 And Kore the son of Imnah the Levite, the porter toward the east, *was* over
the freewill offerings of God, to distribute the oblations of the LORD, and the
most holy things.
15 And next him *were* Eden, and Miniamin, and Jeshua, and Shemaiah,
Amariah, and Shecaniah, in the cities of the priests, in *their* set office, to give
to their brethren by courses, as well to the great as to the small:
16 Beside their genealogy of males, from three years old and upward, *even*
unto every one that entereth into the house of the LORD, his daily portion for
their service in their charges according to their courses;
17 Both to the genealogy of the priests by the house of their fathers, and the
Levites from twenty years old and upward, in their charges by their courses;
18 And to the genealogy of all their little ones, their wives, and their sons,
and their daughters, through all the congregation: for in their set office they
sanctified themselves in holiness:
19 Also of the sons of Aaron the priests, *which were* in the fields of the suburbs
of their cities, in every several city, the men that were expressed by name, to
give portions to all the males among the priests, and to all that were reckoned
by genealogies among the Levites.
20 And thus did Hezekiah throughout all Judah, and wrought *that which*
was good and right and truth before the LORD his God.
21 And in every work that he began in the service of the house of God, and
in the law, and in the commandments, to seek his God, he did *it* with all his
heart, and prospered.

God Saves Judah from the Assyrians

32 After these things, and the establishment thereof, Sennacherib king
of Assyria came, and entered into Judah, and encamped against the
fenced cities, and thought to win them for himself.
2 And when Hezekiah saw that Sennacherib was come, and that he was pur-
posed to fight against Jerusalem,
3 He took counsel with his princes and his mighty men to stop the waters of
the fountains which *were* without the city: and they did help him.
4 So there was gathered much people together, who stopped all the fountains,
and the brook that ran through the midst of the land, saying, Why should the
kings of Assyria come, and find much water?
5 Also he strengthened himself, and built up all the wall that was broken,
and raised *it* up to the towers, and another wall without, and repaired Millo
in the city of David, and made darts and shields in abundance.
6 And he set captains of war over the people, and gathered them together to
him in the street of the gate of the city, and spake comfortably to them, saying,
7 Be strong and courageous, be not afraid nor dismayed for the king of
Assyria, nor for all the multitude that *is* with him: for *there be* more with us
than with him:
8 With him *is* an arm of flesh; but with us *is* the LORD our God to help us, and
to fight our battles. And the people rested themselves upon the words of
Hezekiah king of Judah.

Sennacherib's Blasphemous Messages

9 After this did Sennacherib king of Assyria send his servants to Jerusalem,
(but he *himself laid siege* against Lachish, and all his power with him,) unto
Hezekiah king of Judah, and unto all Judah that *were* at Jerusalem, saying,
10 Thus saith Sennacherib king of Assyria, Whereon do ye trust, that ye abide
in the siege in Jerusalem?
11 Doth not Hezekiah persuade you to give over yourselves to die by famine
and by thirst, saying, The LORD our God shall deliver us out of the hand of the
king of Assyria?
12 Hath not the same Hezekiah taken away his high places and his altars, and
commanded Judah and Jerusalem, saying, Ye shall worship before one altar,
and burn incense upon it?
13 Know ye not what I and my fathers have done unto all the people of *other*
lands? were the gods of the nations of those lands any ways able to deliver
their lands out of mine hand?
14 Who *was there* among all the gods of those nations that my fathers utter-
ly destroyed, that could deliver his people out of mine hand, that your God
should be able to deliver you out of mine hand?
15 Now therefore let not Hezekiah deceive you, nor persuade you on this
manner, neither yet believe him: for no god of any nation or kingdom was
able to deliver his people out of mine hand, and out of the hand of my fathers:
how much less shall your God deliver you out of mine hand?
16 And his servants spake yet *more* against the LORD God, and against his
servant Hezekiah.
17 He wrote also letters to rail on the LORD God of Israel, and to speak against
him, saying, As the gods of the nations of *other* lands have not delivered their
people out of mine hand, so shall not the God of Hezekiah deliver his people
out of mine hand.
18 Then they cried with a loud voice in the Jews' speech unto the people of
Jerusalem that *were* on the wall, to affright them, and to trouble them; that
they might take the city.
19 And they spake against the God of Jerusalem, as against the gods of the
people of the earth, *which were* the work of the hands of man.

20 And for this *cause* Hezekiah the king, and the prophet Isaiah the son of
Amoz, prayed and cried to heaven.
21 And the LORD sent an angel, which cut off all the mighty men of valour,
and the leaders and captains in the camp of the king of Assyria. So he returned
with shame of face to his own land. And when he was come into the house of
his god, they that came forth of his own bowels slew him there with the sword.
22 Thus the LORD saved Hezekiah and the inhabitants of Jerusalem from the
hand of Sennacherib the king of Assyria, and from the hand of all *other*, and
guided them on every side.
23 And many brought gifts unto the LORD to Jerusalem, and presents to
Hezekiah king of Judah: so that he was magnified in the sight of all nations
from thenceforth.

Other Events in Hezekiah's Life

24 In those days Hezekiah was sick to the death, and prayed unto the LORD:
and he spake unto him, and he gave him a sign.
25 But Hezekiah rendered not again according to the benefit *done* unto him;
for his heart was lifted up: therefore there was wrath upon him, and upon
Judah and Jerusalem.
26 Notwithstanding Hezekiah humbled himself for the pride of his heart,
both he and the inhabitants of Jerusalem, so that the wrath of the LORD came
not upon them in the days of Hezekiah.
27 And Hezekiah had exceeding much riches and honour: and he made him-
self treasuries for silver, and for gold, and for precious stones, and for spices,
and for shields, and for all manner of pleasant jewels;
28 Storehouses also for the increase of corn, and wine, and oil; and stalls for
all manner of beasts, and cotes for flocks.
29 Moreover he provided him cities, and possessions of flocks and herds in
abundance: for God had given him substance very much.
30 This same Hezekiah also stopped the upper watercourse of Gihon, and
brought it straight down to the west side of the city of David. And Hezekiah
prospered in all his works.
31 Howbeit in *the business of* the ambassadors of the princes of Babylon,
who sent unto him to enquire of the wonder that was *done* in the land, God
left him, to try him, that he might know all *that was* in his heart.
32 Now the rest of the acts of Hezekiah, and his goodness, behold, they *are*
written in the vision of Isaiah the prophet, the son of Amoz, *and* in the book
of the kings of Judah and Israel.
33 And Hezekiah slept with his fathers, and they buried him in the chiefest
of the sepulchres of the sons of David: and all Judah and the inhabitants of
Jerusalem did him honour at his death. And Manasseh his son reigned in his
stead.

Manasseh Becomes King of Judah

33 Manasseh *was* twelve years old when he began to reign, and he reigned
fifty and five years in Jerusalem:
2 But did *that which was* evil in the sight of the LORD, like unto the abomi-
nations of the heathen, whom the LORD had cast out before the children of
Israel.
3 For he built again the high places which Hezekiah his father had broken
down, and he reared up altars for Baalim, and made groves, and worshipped
all the host of heaven, and served them.
4 Also he built altars in the house of the LORD, whereof the LORD had said, In
Jerusalem shall my name be for ever.
5 And he built altars for all the host of heaven in the two courts of the house
of the LORD.

6 And he caused his children to pass through the fire in the valley of the son
of Hinnom: also he observed times, and used enchantments, and used witch-
craft, and dealt with a familiar spirit, and with wizards: he wrought much evil
in the sight of the LORD, to provoke him to anger.
7 And he set a carved image, the idol which he had made, in the house of
God, of which God had said to David and to Solomon his son, In this house,
and in Jerusalem, which I have chosen before all the tribes of Israel, will I put
my name for ever:
8 Neither will I any more remove the foot of Israel from out of the land which
I have appointed for your fathers; so that they will take heed to do all that I
have commanded them, according to the whole law and the statutes and the
ordinances by the hand of Moses.
9 So Manasseh made Judah and the inhabitants of Jerusalem to err, *and* to
do worse than the heathen, whom the LORD had destroyed before the children
of Israel.
10 And the LORD spake to Manasseh, and to his people: but they would not
hearken.

Manasseh Is Taken Captive to Babylon

11 Wherefore the LORD brought upon them the captains of the host of the
king of Assyria, which took Manasseh among the thorns, and bound him with
fetters, and carried him to Babylon.
12 And when he was in affliction, he besought the LORD his God, and humbled
himself greatly before the God of his fathers,
13 And prayed unto him: and he was intreated of him, and heard his suppli-
cation, and brought him again to Jerusalem into his kingdom. Then Manasseh
knew that the LORD he *was* God.
14 Now after this he built a wall without the city of David, on the west side
of Gihon, in the valley, even to the entering in at the fish gate, and compassed
about Ophel, and raised it up a very great height, and put captains of war in
all the fenced cities of Judah.
15 And he took away the strange gods, and the idol out of the house of the
LORD, and all the altars that he had built in the mount of the house of the LORD,
and in Jerusalem, and cast *them* out of the city.
16 And he repaired the altar of the LORD, and sacrificed thereon peace offer-
ings and thank offerings, and commanded Judah to serve the LORD God of
Israel.
17 Nevertheless the people did sacrifice still in the high places, *yet* unto the
LORD their God only.
18 Now the rest of the acts of Manasseh, and his prayer unto his God, and
the words of the seers that spake to him in the name of the LORD God of Israel,
behold, they *are written* in the book of the kings of Israel.
19 His prayer also, and *how God* was intreated of him, and all his sin, and his
trespass, and the places wherein he built high places, and set up groves and
graven images, before he was humbled: behold, they *are* written among the
sayings of the seers.
20 So Manasseh slept with his fathers, and they buried him in his own house:
and Amon his son reigned in his stead.

Amon Becomes King of Judah

21 Amon *was* two and twenty years old when he began to reign, and reigned
two years in Jerusalem.
22 But he did *that which was* evil in the sight of the LORD, as did Manasseh
his father: for Amon sacrificed unto all the carved images which Manasseh
his father had made, and served them;
23 And humbled not himself before the LORD, as Manasseh his father had
humbled himself; but Amon trespassed more and more.

24 And his servants conspired against him, and slew him in his own house.
25 But the people of the land slew all them that had conspired against king
Amon; and the people of the land made Josiah his son king in his stead.

Josiah Becomes King of Judah

34 Josiah *was* eight years old when he began to reign, and he reigned in
Jerusalem one and thirty years.
2 And he did *that which was* right in the sight of the LORD, and walked in the
ways of David his father, and declined *neither* to the right hand, nor to the
left.
3 For in the eighth year of his reign, while he was yet young, he began to seek
after the God of David his father: and in the twelfth year he began to purge
Judah and Jerusalem from the high places, and the groves, and the carved
images, and the molten images.
4 And they brake down the altars of Baalim in his presence; and the images,
that *were* on high above them, he cut down; and the groves, and the carved
images, and the molten images, he brake in pieces, and made dust *of them*,
and strowed *it* upon the graves of them that had sacrificed unto them.
5 And he burnt the bones of the priests upon their altars, and cleansed Judah
and Jerusalem.
6 And *so did he* in the cities of Manasseh, and Ephraim, and Simeon, even
unto Naphtali, with their mattocks round about.
7 And when he had broken down the altars and the groves, and had beaten
the graven images into powder, and cut down all the idols throughout all the
land of Israel, he returned to Jerusalem.

Josiah Repairs the Temple

8 Now in the eighteenth year of his reign, when he had purged the land, and
the house, he sent Shaphan the son of Azaliah, and Maaseiah the governor of
the city, and Joah the son of Joahaz the recorder, to repair the house of the
LORD his God.
9 And when they came to Hilkiah the high priest, they delivered the money
that was brought into the house of God, which the Levites that kept the doors
had gathered of the hand of Manasseh and Ephraim, and of all the remnant
of Israel, and of all Judah and Benjamin; and they returned to Jerusalem.
10 And they put *it* in the hand of the workmen that had the oversight of the
house of the LORD, and they gave it to the workmen that wrought in the house
of the LORD, to repair and amend the house:
11 Even to the artificers and builders gave they *it*, to buy hewn stone, and
timber for couplings, and to floor the houses which the kings of Judah had
destroyed.
12 And the men did the work faithfully: and the overseers of them *were* Jahath
and Obadiah, the Levites, of the sons of Merari; and Zechariah and Meshullam,
of the sons of the Kohathites, to set *it* forward; and *other of* the Levites, all that
could skill of instruments of musick.
13 Also *they were* over the bearers of burdens, and *were* overseers of all that
wrought the work in any manner of service: and of the Levites *there were*
scribes, and officers, and porters.
14 And when they brought out the money that was brought into the house
of the LORD, Hilkiah the priest found a book of the law of the LORD *given* by
Moses.
15 And Hilkiah answered and said to Shaphan the scribe, I have found the
book of the law in the house of the LORD. And Hilkiah delivered the book to
Shaphan.
16 And Shaphan carried the book to the king, and brought the king word
back again, saying, All that was committed to thy servants, they do *it*.

17 And they have gathered together the money that was found in the house
of the LORD, and have delivered it into the hand of the overseers, and to the
hand of the workmen.
18 Then Shaphan the scribe told the king, saying, Hilkiah the priest hath
given me a book. And Shaphan read it before the king.
19 And it came to pass, when the king had heard the words of the law, that
he rent his clothes.
20 And the king commanded Hilkiah, and Ahikam the son of Shaphan, and
Abdon the son of Micah, and Shaphan the scribe, and Asaiah a servant of the
king's, saying,
21 Go, enquire of the LORD for me, and for them that are left in Israel and in
Judah, concerning the words of the book that is found: for great *is* the wrath
of the LORD that is poured out upon us, because our fathers have not kept the
word of the LORD, to do after all that is written in this book.
22 And Hilkiah, and *they* that the king *had appointed*, went to Huldah the
prophetess, the wife of Shallum the son of Tikvath, the son of Hasrah, keeper
of the wardrobe; (now she dwelt in Jerusalem in the college:) and they spake
to her to that *effect*.
23 And she answered them, Thus saith the LORD God of Israel, Tell ye the man
that sent you to me,
24 Thus saith the LORD, Behold, I will bring evil upon this place, and upon
the inhabitants thereof, *even* all the curses that are written in the book which
they have read before the king of Judah:
25 Because they have forsaken me, and have burned incense unto other gods,
that they might provoke me to anger with all the works of their hands; there-
fore my wrath shall be poured out upon this place, and shall not be quenched.
26 And as for the king of Judah, who sent you to enquire of the LORD, so shall
ye say unto him, Thus saith the LORD God of Israel *concerning* the words which
thou hast heard;
27 Because thine heart was tender, and thou didst humble thyself before
God, when thou heardest his words against this place, and against the inhab-
itants thereof, and humbledst thyself before me, and didst rend thy clothes,
and weep before me; I have even heard *thee* also, saith the LORD.
28 Behold, I will gather thee to thy fathers, and thou shalt be gathered to thy
grave in peace, neither shall thine eyes see all the evil that I will bring upon
this place, and upon the inhabitants of the same. So they brought the king
word again.

The Book of the Covenant Is Read in a Solemn Assembly

29 Then the king sent and gathered together all the elders of Judah and
Jerusalem.
30 And the king went up into the house of the LORD, and all the men of Judah,
and the inhabitants of Jerusalem, and the priests, and the Levites, and all the
people, great and small: and he read in their ears all the words of the book of
the covenant that was found in the house of the LORD.
31 And the king stood in his place, and made a covenant before the LORD, to
walk after the LORD, and to keep his commandments, and his testimonies, and
his statutes, with all his heart, and with all his soul, to perform the words of
the covenant which are written in this book.
32 And he caused all that were present in Jerusalem and Benjamin to stand
to it. And the inhabitants of Jerusalem did according to the covenant of God,
the God of their fathers.
33 And Josiah took away all the abominations out of all the countries that
pertained to the children of Israel, and made all that were present in Israel to
serve, *even* to serve the LORD their God. *And* all his days they departed not from
following the LORD, the God of their fathers.

Josiah Celebrates Passover

35 Moreover Josiah kept a passover unto the LORD in Jerusalem: and they killed the passover on the fourteenth *day* of the first month.

2 And he set the priests in their charges, and encouraged them to the service of the house of the LORD,

3 And said unto the Levites that taught all Israel, which were holy unto the LORD, Put the holy ark in the house which Solomon the son of David king of Israel did build; *it shall* not *be* a burden upon *your* shoulders: serve now the LORD your God, and his people Israel,

4 And prepare *yourselves* by the houses of your fathers, after your courses, according to the writing of David king of Israel, and according to the writing of Solomon his son.

5 And stand in the holy *place* according to the divisions of the families of the fathers of your brethren the people, and *after* the division of the families of the Levites.

6 So kill the passover, and sanctify yourselves, and prepare your brethren, that *they* may do according to the word of the LORD by the hand of Moses.

7 And Josiah gave to the people, of the flock, lambs and kids, all for the passover offerings, for all that were present, to the number of thirty thousand, and three thousand bullocks: these *were* of the king's substance.

8 And his princes gave willingly unto the people, to the priests, and to the Levites: Hilkiah and Zechariah and Jehiel, rulers of the house of God, gave unto the priests for the passover offerings two thousand and six hundred *small cattle*, and three hundred oxen.

9 Conaniah also, and Shemaiah and Nethaneel, his brethren, and Hashabiah and Jeiel and Jozabad, chief of the Levites, gave unto the Levites for passover offerings five thousand *small cattle*, and five hundred oxen.

10 So the service was prepared, and the priests stood in their place, and the Levites in their courses, according to the king's commandment.

11 And they killed the passover, and the priests sprinkled *the blood* from their hands, and the Levites flayed *them*.

12 And they removed the burnt offerings, that they might give according to the divisions of the families of the people, to offer unto the LORD, as *it is* written in the book of Moses. And so *did they* with the oxen.

13 And they roasted the passover with fire according to the ordinance: but the *other* holy *offerings* sod they in pots, and in caldrons, and in pans, and divided *them* speedily among all the people.

14 And afterward they made ready for themselves, and for the priests: because the priests the sons of Aaron *were busied* in offering of burnt offerings and the fat until night; therefore the Levites prepared for themselves, and for the priests the sons of Aaron.

15 And the singers the sons of Asaph *were* in their place, according to the commandment of David, and Asaph, and Heman, and Jeduthun the king's seer; and the porters *waited* at every gate; they might not depart from their service; for their brethren the Levites prepared for them.

16 So all the service of the LORD was prepared the same day, to keep the passover, and to offer burnt offerings upon the altar of the LORD, according to the commandment of king Josiah.

17 And the children of Israel that were present kept the passover at that time, and the feast of unleavened bread seven days.

18 And there was no passover like to that kept in Israel from the days of Samuel the prophet; neither did all the kings of Israel keep such a passover as Josiah kept, and the priests, and the Levites, and all Judah and Israel that were present, and the inhabitants of Jerusalem.

19 In the eighteenth year of the reign of Josiah was this passover kept.

Josiah's Sin Leads to His Death

20 After all this, when Josiah had prepared the temple, Necho king of Egypt came
up to fight against Carchemish by Euphrates: and Josiah went out against him.
21 But he sent ambassadors to him, saying, What have I to do with thee, thou
king of Judah? *I come* not against thee this day, but against the house where-
with I have war: for God commanded me to make haste: forbear thee from
meddling with God, who *is* with me, that he destroy thee not.
22 Nevertheless Josiah would not turn his face from him, but disguised him-
self, that he might fight with him, and hearkened not unto the words of Necho
from the mouth of God, and came to fight in the valley of Megiddo.
23 And the archers shot at king Josiah; and the king said to his servants, Have
me away; for I am sore wounded.
24 His servants therefore took him out of that chariot, and put him in the
second chariot that he had; and they brought him to Jerusalem, and he died,
and was buried in *one of* the sepulchres of his fathers. And all Judah and
Jerusalem mourned for Josiah.
25 And Jeremiah lamented for Josiah: and all the singing men and the singing
women spake of Josiah in their lamentations to this day, and made them an
ordinance in Israel: and, behold, they *are* written in the lamentations.
26 Now the rest of the acts of Josiah, and his goodness, according to *that
which was* written in the law of the LORD,
27 And his deeds, first and last, behold, they *are* written in the book of the
kings of Israel and Judah.

Jehoahaz Becomes King of Judah

36 Then the people of the land took Jehoahaz the son of Josiah, and made
him king in his father's stead in Jerusalem.
2 Jehoahaz *was* twenty and three years old when he began to reign, and he
reigned three months in Jerusalem.
3 And the king of Egypt put him down at Jerusalem, and condemned the
land in an hundred talents of silver and a talent of gold.
4 And the king of Egypt made Eliakim his brother king over Judah and
Jerusalem, and turned his name to Jehoiakim. And Necho took Jehoahaz his
brother, and carried him to Egypt.

Jehoiakim Becomes King of Judah

5 Jehoiakim *was* twenty and five years old when he began to reign, and he
reigned eleven years in Jerusalem: and he did *that which was* evil in the sight
of the LORD his God.
6 Against him came up Nebuchadnezzar king of Babylon, and bound him
in fetters, to carry him to Babylon.
7 Nebuchadnezzar also carried of the vessels of the house of the LORD to
Babylon, and put them in his temple at Babylon.
8 Now the rest of the acts of Jehoiakim, and his abominations which he did,
and that which was found in him, behold, they *are* written in the book of the
kings of Israel and Judah: and Jehoiachin his son reigned in his stead.

Jehoiachin Becomes King of Judah

9 Jehoiachin *was* eight years old when he began to reign, and he reigned
three months and ten days in Jerusalem: and he did *that which was* evil in the
sight of the LORD.
10 And when the year was expired, king Nebuchadnezzar sent, and brought
him to Babylon, with the goodly vessels of the house of the LORD, and made
Zedekiah his brother king over Judah and Jerusalem.

Zedekiah Becomes King of Judah

11 Zedekiah *was* one and twenty years old when he began to reign, and
reigned eleven years in Jerusalem.

12 And he did *that which was* evil in the sight of the LORD his God, *and* hum-
bled not himself before Jeremiah the prophet *speaking* from the mouth of
the LORD.
13 And he also rebelled against king Nebuchadnezzar, who had made him
swear by God: but he stiffened his neck, and hardened his heart from turning
unto the LORD God of Israel.
14 Moreover all the chief of the priests, and the people, transgressed very
much after all the abominations of the heathen; and polluted the house of the
LORD which he had hallowed in Jerusalem.
15 And the LORD God of their fathers sent to them by his messengers, rising
up betimes, and sending; because he had compassion on his people, and on
his dwelling place:
16 But they mocked the messengers of God, and despised his words, and
misused his prophets, until the wrath of the LORD arose against his people, till
there was no remedy.
17 Therefore he brought upon them the king of the Chaldees, who slew their
young men with the sword in the house of their sanctuary, and had no com-
passion upon young man or maiden, old man, or him that stooped for age: he
gave *them* all into his hand.
18 And all the vessels of the house of God, great and small, and the treasures
of the house of the LORD, and the treasures of the king, and of his princes; all
these he brought to Babylon.
19 And they burnt the house of God, and brake down the wall of Jerusalem,
and burnt all the palaces thereof with fire, and destroyed all the goodly vessels
thereof.
20 And them that had escaped from the sword carried he away to Babylon;
where they were servants to him and his sons until the reign of the kingdom
of Persia:
21 To fulfil the word of the LORD by the mouth of Jeremiah, until the land
had enjoyed her sabbaths: *for* as long as she lay desolate she kept sabbath, to
fulfil threescore and ten years.

Cyrus of Persia Allows the Jews to Return to Their Land

22 Now in the first year of Cyrus king of Persia, that the word of the LORD
spoken by the mouth of Jeremiah might be accomplished, the LORD stirred up
the spirit of Cyrus king of Persia, that he made a proclamation throughout all
his kingdom, and *put it* also in writing, saying,
23 Thus saith Cyrus king of Persia, All the kingdoms of the earth hath the
LORD God of heaven given me; and he hath charged me to build him an house
in Jerusalem, which *is* in Judah. Who *is there* among you of all his people? The
LORD his God *be* with him, and let him go up.

EZRA

Cyrus Allows the Jews to Return from Babylon

1 Now in the first year of Cyrus king of Persia, that the word of the LORD by
the mouth of Jeremiah might be fulfilled, the LORD stirred up the spirit of
Cyrus king of Persia, that he made a proclamation throughout all his kingdom,
and *put it* also in writing, saying,
2 Thus saith Cyrus king of Persia, The LORD God of heaven hath given me all
the kingdoms of the earth; and he hath charged me to build him an house at
Jerusalem, which *is* in Judah.
3 Who *is there* among you of all his people? his God be with him, and let him
go up to Jerusalem, which *is* in Judah, and build the house of the LORD God of
Israel, (he *is* the God,) which *is* in Jerusalem.
4 And whosoever remaineth in any place where he sojourneth, let the men
of his place help him with silver, and with gold, and with goods, and with
beasts, beside the freewill offering for the house of God that *is* in Jerusalem.

The People Provide for the Rebuilding of the Temple

5 Then rose up the chief of the fathers of Judah and Benjamin, and the priests,
and the Levites, with all *them* whose spirit God had raised, to go up to build
the house of the LORD which *is* in Jerusalem.
6 And all they that *were* about them strengthened their hands with vessels
of silver, with gold, with goods, and with beasts, and with precious things,
beside all *that* was willingly offered.
7 Also Cyrus the king brought forth the vessels of the house of the LORD,
which Nebuchadnezzar had brought forth out of Jerusalem, and had put them
in the house of his gods;
8 Even those did Cyrus king of Persia bring forth by the hand of Mithredath
the treasurer, and numbered them unto Sheshbazzar, the prince of Judah.
9 And this *is* the number of them: thirty chargers of gold, a thousand chargers
of silver, nine and twenty knives,
10 Thirty basons of gold, silver basons of a second *sort* four hundred and
ten, *and* other vessels a thousand.
11 All the vessels of gold and of silver *were* five thousand and four hundred.
All *these* did Sheshbazzar bring up with *them of* the captivity that were brought
up from Babylon unto Jerusalem.

The Numbers of People Who Return with Zerubbabel

2 Now these *are* the children of the province that went up out of the captiv-
ity, of those which had been carried away, whom Nebuchadnezzar the king
of Babylon had carried away unto Babylon, and came again unto Jerusalem and
Judah, every one unto his city;
2 Which came with Zerubbabel: Jeshua, Nehemiah, Seraiah, Reelaiah,
Mordecai, Bilshan, Mispar, Bigvai, Rehum, Baanah. The number of the men
of the people of Israel:
3 The children of Parosh, two thousand an hundred seventy and two.
4 The children of Shephatiah, three hundred seventy and two.
5 The children of Arah, seven hundred seventy and five.
6 The children of Pahath-moab, of the children of Jeshua *and* Joab, two thou-
sand eight hundred and twelve.
7 The children of Elam, a thousand two hundred fifty and four.

8 The children of Zattu, nine hundred forty and five.
9 The children of Zaccai, seven hundred and threescore.
10 The children of Bani, six hundred forty and two.
11 The children of Bebai, six hundred twenty and three.
12 The children of Azgad, a thousand two hundred twenty and two.
13 The children of Adonikam, six hundred sixty and six.
14 The children of Bigvai, two thousand fifty and six.
15 The children of Adin, four hundred fifty and four.
16 The children of Ater of Hezekiah, ninety and eight.
17 The children of Bezai, three hundred twenty and three.
18 The children of Jorah, an hundred and twelve.
19 The children of Hashum, two hundred twenty and three.
20 The children of Gibbar, ninety and five.
21 The children of Beth-lehem, an hundred twenty and three.
22 The men of Netophah, fifty and six.
23 The men of Anathoth, an hundred twenty and eight.
24 The children of Azmaveth, forty and two.
25 The children of Kirjath-arim, Chephirah, and Beeroth, seven hundred and forty and three.
26 The children of Ramah and Gaba, six hundred twenty and one.
27 The men of Michmas, an hundred twenty and two.
28 The men of Bethel and Ai, two hundred twenty and three.
29 The children of Nebo, fifty and two.
30 The children of Magbish, an hundred fifty and six.
31 The children of the other Elam, a thousand two hundred fifty and four.
32 The children of Harim, three hundred and twenty.
33 The children of Lod, Hadid, and Ono, seven hundred twenty and five.
34 The children of Jericho, three hundred forty and five.
35 The children of Senaah, three thousand and six hundred and thirty.

The Numbers of Priests, Levites, and Others Who Return with Zerubbabel

36 The priests: the children of Jedaiah, of the house of Jeshua, nine hundred seventy and three.
37 The children of Immer, a thousand fifty and two.
38 The children of Pashur, a thousand two hundred forty and seven.
39 The children of Harim, a thousand and seventeen.
40 The Levites: the children of Jeshua and Kadmiel, of the children of Hodaviah, seventy and four.
41 The singers: the children of Asaph, an hundred twenty and eight.
42 The children of the porters: the children of Shallum, the children of Ater, the children of Talmon, the children of Akkub, the children of Hatita, the children of Shobai, *in* all an hundred thirty and nine.
43 The Nethinims: the children of Ziha, the children of Hasupha, the children of Tabbaoth,
44 The children of Keros, the children of Siaha, the children of Padon,
45 The children of Lebanah, the children of Hagabah, the children of Akkub,
46 The children of Hagab, the children of Shalmai, the children of Hanan,
47 The children of Giddel, the children of Gahar, the children of Reaiah,
48 The children of Rezin, the children of Nekoda, the children of Gazzam,
49 The children of Uzza, the children of Paseah, the children of Besai,
50 The children of Asnah, the children of Mehunim, the children of Nephusim,
51 The children of Bakbuk, the children of Hakupha, the children of Harhur,
52 The children of Bazluth, the children of Mehida, the children of Harsha,
53 The children of Barkos, the children of Sisera, the children of Thamah,

54 The children of Neziah, the children of Hatipha.
55 The children of Solomon's servants: the children of Sotai, the children of
Sophereth, the children of Peruda,
56 The children of Jaalah, the children of Darkon, the children of Giddel,
57 The children of Shephatiah, the children of Hattil, the children of
Pochereth of Zebaim, the children of Ami.
58 All the Nethinims, and the children of Solomon's servants, *were* three
hundred ninety and two.
59 And these *were* they which went up from Tel-melah, Tel-harsa, Cherub,
Addan, *and* Immer: but they could not shew their father's house, and their
seed, whether they *were* of Israel:
60 The children of Delaiah, the children of Tobiah, the children of Nekoda,
six hundred fifty and two.
61 And of the children of the priests: the children of Habaiah, the children
of Koz, the children of Barzillai; which took a wife of the daughters of Barzillai
the Gileadite, and was called after their name:
62 These sought their register *among* those that were reckoned by genealo-
gy, but they were not found: therefore were they, as polluted, put from the
priesthood.
63 And the Tirshatha said unto them, that they should not eat of the most
holy things, till there stood up a priest with Urim and with Thummim.

The Total Number of the People and Animals Returning from Exile

64 The whole congregation together *was* forty and two thousand three hun-
dred *and* threescore,
65 Beside their servants and their maids, of whom *there were* seven thousand
three hundred thirty and seven: and *there were* among them two hundred
singing men and singing women.
66 Their horses *were* seven hundred thirty and six; their mules, two hundred
forty and five;
67 Their camels, four hundred thirty and five; *their* asses, six thousand seven
hundred and twenty.
68 And *some* of the chief of the fathers, when they came to the house of the
LORD which *is* at Jerusalem, offered freely for the house of God to set it up in
his place:
69 They gave after their ability unto the treasure of the work threescore and
one thousand drams of gold, and five thousand pound of silver, and one hun-
dred priests' garments.
70 So the priests, and the Levites, and *some* of the people, and the singers, and
the porters, and the Nethinims, dwelt in their cities, and all Israel in their cities.

Worship at the Temple Site Begins Again

3 And when the seventh month was come, and the children of Israel *were* in
the cities, the people gathered themselves together as one man to Jerusalem.
2 Then stood up Jeshua the son of Jozadak, and his brethren the priests, and
Zerubbabel the son of Shealtiel, and his brethren, and builded the altar of the
God of Israel, to offer burnt offerings thereon, as *it is* written in the law of
Moses the man of God.
3 And they set the altar upon his bases; for fear *was* upon them because of
the people of those countries: and they offered burnt offerings thereon unto
the LORD, *even* burnt offerings morning and evening.
4 They kept also the feast of tabernacles, as *it is* written, and *offered* the daily
burnt offerings by number, according to the custom, as the duty of every day
required;
5 And afterward *offered* the continual burnt offering, both of the new moons,
and of all the set feasts of the LORD that were consecrated, and of every one
that willingly offered a freewill offering unto the LORD.

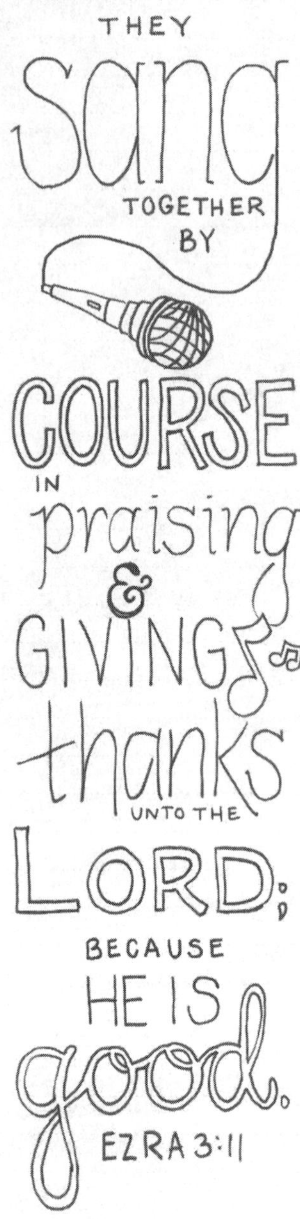

6 From the first day of the seventh month began they to offer burnt offerings unto the LORD. But the foundation of the temple of the LORD was not *yet* laid.

7 They gave money also unto the masons, and to the carpenters; and meat, and drink, and oil, unto them of Zidon, and to them of Tyre, to bring cedar trees from Lebanon to the sea of Joppa, according to the grant that they had of Cyrus king of Persia.

The Foundations of the Temple Are Laid, with Both Joy and Mourning

8 Now in the second year of their coming unto the house of God at Jerusalem, in the second month, began Zerubbabel the son of Shealtiel, and Jeshua the son of Jozadak, and the remnant of their brethren the priests and the Levites, and all they that were come out of the captivity unto Jerusalem; and appointed the Levites, from twenty years old and upward, to set forward the work of the house of the LORD.

9 Then stood Jeshua *with* his sons and his brethren, Kadmiel and his sons, the sons of Judah, together, to set forward the workmen in the house of God: the sons of Henadad, *with* their sons and their brethren the Levites.

10 And when the builders laid the foundation of the temple of the LORD, they set the priests in their apparel with trumpets, and the Levites the sons of Asaph with cymbals, to praise the LORD, after the ordinance of David king of Israel.

11 And they sang together by course in praising and giving thanks unto the LORD; because *he is* good, for his mercy *endureth* for ever toward Israel. And all the people shouted with a great shout, when they praised the LORD, because the foundation of the house of the LORD was laid.

12 But many of the priests and Levites and chief of the fathers, *who were* ancient men, that had seen the first house, when the foundation of this house was laid before their eyes, wept with a loud voice; and many shouted aloud for joy:

13 So that the people could not discern the noise of the shout of joy from the noise of the weeping of the people: for the people shouted with a loud shout, and the noise was heard afar off.

The People's Enemies Try to Hinder the Work

4 Now when the adversaries of Judah and Benjamin heard that the children of the captivity builded the temple unto the LORD God of Israel;

2 Then they came to Zerubbabel, and to the chief of the fathers, and said unto them, Let us build with you: for we seek your God, as ye *do*; and we do sacrifice unto him since the days of Esar-haddon king of Assur, which brought us up hither.

3 But Zerubbabel, and Jeshua, and the rest of the chief of the fathers of Israel, said unto them, Ye have nothing to do with us to build an house unto our God; but we ourselves together will build unto the LORD God of Israel, as king Cyrus the king of Persia hath commanded us.

4 Then the people of the land weakened the hands of the people of Judah, and troubled them in building,

5 And hired counsellors against them, to frustrate their purpose, all the days of Cyrus king of Persia, even until the reign of Darius king of Persia.

6 And in the reign of Ahasuerus, in the beginning of his reign, wrote they *unto him* an accusation against the inhabitants of Judah and Jerusalem.

7 And in the days of Artaxerxes wrote Bishlam, Mithredath, Tabeel, and the rest of their companions, unto Artaxerxes king of Persia; and the writing of the letter *was* written in the Syrian tongue, and interpreted in the Syrian tongue.

8 Rehum the chancellor and Shimshai the scribe wrote a letter against Jerusalem to Artaxerxes the king in this sort:

9 Then *wrote* Rehum the chancellor, and Shimshai the scribe, and the rest of their companions; the Dinaites, the Apharsathchites, the Tarpelites, the

Apharsites, the Archevites, the Babylonians, the Susanchites, the Dehavites,
and the Elamites,
10 And the rest of the nations whom the great and noble Asnappar brought
over, and set in the cities of Samaria, and the rest *that are* on this side the river,
and at such a time.
11 This *is* the copy of the letter that they sent unto him, *even* unto Artaxerxes
the king; Thy servants the men on this side the river, and at such a time.
12 Be it known unto the king, that the Jews which came up from thee to us
are come unto Jerusalem, building the rebellious and the bad city, and have
set up the walls *thereof*, and joined the foundations.
13 Be it known now unto the king, that, if this city be builded, and the walls
set up *again, then* will they not pay toll, tribute, and custom, and *so* thou shalt
endamage the revenue of the kings.
14 Now because we have maintenance from *the king's* palace, and it was not
meet for us to see the king's dishonour, therefore have we sent and certified
the king;
15 That search may be made in the book of the records of thy fathers: so shalt
thou find in the book of the records, and know that this city *is* a rebellious
city, and hurtful unto kings and provinces, and that they have moved sedition
within the same of old time: for which cause was this city destroyed.
16 We certify the king that, if this city be builded *again*, and the walls there-
of set up, by this means thou shalt have no portion on this side the river.

The Decree of Artaxerxes Stops Work on the Temple

17 *Then* sent the king an answer unto Rehum the chancellor, and *to* Shimshai
the scribe, and *to* the rest of their companions that dwell in Samaria, and *unto*
the rest beyond the river, Peace, and at such a time.
18 The letter which ye sent unto us hath been plainly read before me.
19 And I commanded, and search hath been made, and it is found that this
city of old time hath made insurrection against kings, and *that* rebellion and
sedition have been made therein.
20 There have been mighty kings also over Jerusalem, which have ruled over
all *countries* beyond the river; and toll, tribute, and custom, was paid unto them.
21 Give ye now commandment to cause these men to cease, and that this city
be not builded, until *another* commandment shall be given from me.
22 Take heed now that ye fail not to do this: why should damage grow to the
hurt of the kings?
23 Now when the copy of king Artaxerxes' letter *was* read before Rehum, and
Shimshai the scribe, and their companions, they went up in haste to Jerusalem
unto the Jews, and made them to cease by force and power.
24 Then ceased the work of the house of God which *is* at Jerusalem. So it
ceased unto the second year of the reign of Darius king of Persia.

Israel's Leaders and Prophets Continue Rebuilding of the Temple

5 Then the prophets, Haggai the prophet, and Zechariah the son of Iddo,
prophesied unto the Jews that *were* in Judah and Jerusalem in the name of
the God of Israel, *even* unto them.
2 Then rose up Zerubbabel the son of Shealtiel, and Jeshua the son of Jozadak,
and began to build the house of God which *is* at Jerusalem: and with them
were the prophets of God helping them.

Permission for Rebuilding Is Requested from Darius

3 At the same time came to them Tatnai, governor on this side the river, and
Shethar-boznai, and their companions, and said thus unto them, Who hath
commanded you to build this house, and to make up this wall?
4 Then said we unto them after this manner, What are the names of the men
that make this building?

5 But the eye of their God was upon the elders of the Jews, that they could
not cause them to cease, till the matter came to Darius: and then they returned
answer by letter concerning this *matter*.
6 The copy of the letter that Tatnai, governor on this side the river, and
Shethar-boznai, and his companions the Apharsachites, which *were* on this
side the river, sent unto Darius the king:
7 They sent a letter unto him, wherein was written thus; Unto Darius the
king, all peace.
8 Be it known unto the king, that we went into the province of Judea, to the
house of the great God, which is builded with great stones, and timber is laid
in the walls, and this work goeth fast on, and prospereth in their hands.
9 Then asked we those elders, *and* said unto them thus, Who commanded
you to build this house, and to make up these walls?
10 We asked their names also, to certify thee, that we might write the names
of the men that *were* the chief of them.
11 And thus they returned us answer, saying, We are the servants of the God
of heaven and earth, and build the house that was builded these many years
ago, which a great king of Israel builded and set up.
12 But after that our fathers had provoked the God of heaven unto wrath, he
gave them into the hand of Nebuchadnezzar the king of Babylon, the Chaldean,
who destroyed this house, and carried the people away into Babylon.
13 But in the first year of Cyrus the king of Babylon *the same* king Cyrus made
a decree to build this house of God.
14 And the vessels also of gold and silver of the house of God, which
Nebuchadnezzar took out of the temple that *was* in Jerusalem, and brought
them into the temple of Babylon, those did Cyrus the king take out of the
temple of Babylon, and they were delivered unto *one*, whose name *was*
Sheshbazzar, whom he had made governor;
15 And said unto him, Take these vessels, go, carry them into the temple that
is in Jerusalem, and let the house of God be builded in his place.
16 Then came the same Sheshbazzar, *and* laid the foundation of the house
of God which *is* in Jerusalem: and since that time even until now hath it been
in building, and *yet* it is not finished.
17 Now therefore, if *it seem* good to the king, let there be search made in the
king's treasure house, which *is* there at Babylon, whether it be *so*, that a decree
was made of Cyrus the king to build this house of God at Jerusalem, and let
the king send his pleasure to us concerning this matter.

Darius Decrees That the Building Can Continue

6 Then Darius the king made a decree, and search was made in the house of
the rolls, where the treasures were laid up in Babylon.
2 And there was found at Achmetha, in the palace that *is* in the province of
the Medes, a roll, and therein *was* a record thus written:
3 In the first year of Cyrus the king *the same* Cyrus the king made a decree
concerning the house of God at Jerusalem, Let the house be builded, the place
where they offered sacrifices, and let the foundations thereof be strongly laid;
the height thereof threescore cubits, *and* the breadth thereof threescore
cubits;
4 *With* three rows of great stones, and a row of new timber: and let the
expenses be given out of the king's house:
5 And also let the golden and silver vessels of the house of God, which
Nebuchadnezzar took forth out of the temple which *is* at Jerusalem, and
brought unto Babylon, be restored, and brought again unto the temple which
is at Jerusalem, *every one* to his place, and place *them* in the house of God.

6 Now *therefore*, Tatnai, governor beyond the river, Shethar-boznai, and your
companions the Apharsachites, which *are* beyond the river, be ye far from
thence:
7 Let the work of this house of God alone; let the governor of the Jews and
the elders of the Jews build this house of God in his place.
8 Moreover I make a decree what ye shall do to the elders of these Jews for
the building of this house of God: that of the king's goods, *even* of the tribute
beyond the river, forthwith expenses be given unto these men, that they be
not hindered.
9 And that which they have need of, both young bullocks, and rams, and
lambs, for the burnt offerings of the God of heaven, wheat, salt, wine, and oil,
according to the appointment of the priests which *are* at Jerusalem, let it be
given them day by day without fail:
10 That they may offer sacrifices of sweet savours unto the God of heaven,
and pray for the life of the king, and of his sons.
11 Also I have made a decree, that whosoever shall alter this word, let timber
be pulled down from his house, and being set up, let him be hanged thereon;
and let his house be made a dunghill for this.
12 And the God that hath caused his name to dwell there destroy all kings and
people, that shall put to their hand to alter *and* to destroy this house of God
which *is* at Jerusalem. I Darius have made a decree; let it be done with speed.

The Temple Is Finished and Passover Is Celebrated

13 Then Tatnai, governor on this side the river, Shethar-boznai, and their
companions, according to that which Darius the king had sent, so they did
speedily.
14 And the elders of the Jews builded, and they prospered through the proph-
esying of Haggai the prophet and Zechariah the son of Iddo. And they builded,
and finished *it*, according to the commandment of the God of Israel, and
according to the commandment of Cyrus, and Darius, and Artaxerxes king of
Persia.
15 And this house was finished on the third day of the month Adar, which
was in the sixth year of the reign of Darius the king.
16 And the children of Israel, the priests, and the Levites, and the rest of the
children of the captivity, kept the dedication of this house of God with joy,
17 And offered at the dedication of this house of God an hundred bullocks,
two hundred rams, four hundred lambs; and for a sin offering for all Israel,
twelve he goats, according to the number of the tribes of Israel.
18 And they set the priests in their divisions, and the Levites in their courses,
for the service of God, which *is* at Jerusalem; as it is written in the book of Moses.
19 And the children of the captivity kept the passover upon the fourteenth
day of the first month.
20 For the priests and the Levites were purified together, all of them *were*
pure, and killed the passover for all the children of the captivity, and for their
brethren the priests, and for themselves.
21 And the children of Israel, which were come again out of captivity, and
all such as had separated themselves unto them from the filthiness of the
heathen of the land, to seek the LORD God of Israel, did eat,
22 And kept the feast of unleavened bread seven days with joy: for the LORD
had made them joyful, and turned the heart of the king of Assyria unto them,
to strengthen their hands in the work of the house of God, the God of Israel.

Ezra Travels to Jerusalem from Babylon

7 Now after these things, in the reign of Artaxerxes king of Persia, Ezra the
son of Seraiah, the son of Azariah, the son of Hilkiah,
2 The son of Shallum, the son of Zadok, the son of Ahitub,
3 The son of Amariah, the son of Azariah, the son of Meraioth,
4 The son of Zerahiah, the son of Uzzi, the son of Bukki,

FOR EZRA HAD PREPARED HIS HEART TO SEEK THE LAW OF THE LORD, & TO DO IT.

EZRA 7:10

5 The son of Abishua, the son of Phinehas, the son of Eleazar, the son of Aaron
the chief priest:
6 This Ezra went up from Babylon; and he *was* a ready scribe in the law of
Moses, which the LORD God of Israel had given: and the king granted him all
his request, according to the hand of the LORD his God upon him.
7 And there went up *some* of the children of Israel, and of the priests, and
the Levites, and the singers, and the porters, and the Nethinims, unto
Jerusalem, in the seventh year of Artaxerxes the king.
8 And he came to Jerusalem in the fifth month, which *was* in the seventh
year of the king.
9 For upon the first *day* of the first month began he to go up from Babylon,
and on the first *day* of the fifth month came he to Jerusalem, according to the
good hand of his God upon him.
10 For Ezra had prepared his heart to seek the law of the LORD, and to do *it*,
and to teach in Israel statutes and judgments.

The Gracious Commission of Artaxerxes to Ezra

11 Now this *is* the copy of the letter that the king Artaxerxes gave unto Ezra
the priest, the scribe, *even* a scribe of the words of the commandments of the
LORD, and of his statutes to Israel.
12 Artaxerxes, king of kings, unto Ezra the priest, a scribe of the law of the
God of heaven, perfect *peace*, and at such a time.
13 I make a decree, that all they of the people of Israel, and *of* his priests and
Levites, in my realm, which are minded of their own freewill to go up to
Jerusalem, go with thee.
14 Forasmuch as thou art sent of the king, and of his seven counsellors, to
enquire concerning Judah and Jerusalem, according to the law of thy God
which *is* in thine hand;
15 And to carry the silver and gold, which the king and his counsellors have
freely offered unto the God of Israel, whose habitation *is* in Jerusalem,
16 And all the silver and gold that thou canst find in all the province of
Babylon, with the freewill offering of the people, and of the priests, offering
willingly for the house of their God which *is* in Jerusalem:
17 That thou mayest buy speedily with this money bullocks, rams, lambs,
with their meat offerings and their drink offerings, and offer them upon the
altar of the house of your God which *is* in Jerusalem.
18 And whatsoever shall seem good to thee, and to thy brethren, to do with
the rest of the silver and the gold, that do after the will of your God.
19 The vessels also that are given thee for the service of the house of thy God,
those deliver thou before the God of Jerusalem.
20 And whatsoever more shall be needful for the house of thy God, which
thou shalt have occasion to bestow, bestow *it* out of the king's treasure house.
21 And I, *even* I Artaxerxes the king, do make a decree to all the treasurers
which *are* beyond the river, that whatsoever Ezra the priest, the scribe of the
law of the God of heaven, shall require of you, it be done speedily,
22 Unto an hundred talents of silver, and to an hundred measures of wheat,
and to an hundred baths of wine, and to an hundred baths of oil, and salt
without prescribing *how much*.
23 Whatsoever is commanded by the God of heaven, let it be diligently done
for the house of the God of heaven: for why should there be wrath against the
realm of the king and his sons?
24 Also we certify you, that touching any of the priests and Levites, singers,
porters, Nethinims, or ministers of this house of God, it shall not be lawful to
impose toll, tribute, or custom, upon them.

25 And thou, Ezra, after the wisdom of thy God, that *is* in thine hand, set magistrates and judges, which may judge all the people that *are* beyond the river, all such as know the laws of thy God; and teach ye them that know *them* not.
26 And whosoever will not do the law of thy God, and the law of the king, let judgment be executed speedily upon him, whether *it be* unto death, or to banishment, or to confiscation of goods, or to imprisonment.

Ezra Praises God for His Favor

27 Blessed *be* the LORD God of our fathers, which hath put *such a thing* as this in the king's heart, to beautify the house of the LORD which *is* in Jerusalem:
28 And hath extended mercy unto me before the king, and his counsellors, and before all the king's mighty princes. And I was strengthened as the hand of the LORD my God *was* upon me, and I gathered together out of Israel chief men to go up with me.

The Numbers of People Who Returned from Babylon with Ezra

8 These *are* now the chief of their fathers, and *this is* the genealogy of them that went up with me from Babylon, in the reign of Artaxerxes the king.
2 Of the sons of Phinehas; Gershom: of the sons of Ithamar; Daniel: of the sons of David; Hattush.
3 Of the sons of Shechaniah, of the sons of Pharosh; Zechariah: and with him were reckoned by genealogy of the males an hundred and fifty.
4 Of the sons of Pahath-moab; Elihoenai the son of Zerahiah, and with him two hundred males.
5 Of the sons of Shechaniah; the son of Jahaziel, and with him three hundred males.
6 Of the sons also of Adin; Ebed the son of Jonathan, and with him fifty males.
7 And of the sons of Elam; Jeshaiah the son of Athaliah, and with him seventy males.
8 And of the sons of Shephatiah; Zebadiah the son of Michael, and with him fourscore males.
9 Of the sons of Joab; Obadiah the son of Jehiel, and with him two hundred and eighteen males.
10 And of the sons of Shelomith; the son of Josiphiah, and with him an hundred and threescore males.
11 And of the sons of Bebai; Zechariah the son of Bebai, and with him twenty and eight males.
12 And of the sons of Azgad; Johanan the son of Hakkatan, and with him an hundred and ten males.
13 And of the last sons of Adonikam, whose names *are* these, Eliphelet, Jeiel, and Shemaiah, and with them threescore males.
14 Of the sons also of Bigvai; Uthai, and Zabbud, and with them seventy males.
15 And I gathered them together to the river that runneth to Ahava; and there abode we in tents three days: and I viewed the people, and the priests, and found there none of the sons of Levi.
16 Then sent I for Eliezer, for Ariel, for Shemaiah, and for Elnathan, and for Jarib, and for Elnathan, and for Nathan, and for Zechariah, and for Meshullam, chief men; also for Joiarib, and for Elnathan, men of understanding.
17 And I sent them with commandment unto Iddo the chief at the place Casiphia, and I told them what they should say unto Iddo, *and* to his brethren the Nethinims, at the place Casiphia, that they should bring unto us ministers for the house of our God.
18 And by the good hand of our God upon us they brought us a man of understanding, of the sons of Mahli, the son of Levi, the son of Israel; and Sherebiah, with his sons and his brethren, eighteen;

19 And Hashabiah, and with him Jeshaiah of the sons of Merari, his brethren
and their sons, twenty;
20 Also of the Nethinims, whom David and the princes had appointed for
the service of the Levites, two hundred and twenty Nethinims: all of them
were expressed by name.
21 Then I proclaimed a fast there, at the river of Ahava, that we might afflict
ourselves before our God, to seek of him a right way for us, and for our little
ones, and for all our substance.
22 For I was ashamed to require of the king a band of soldiers and horsemen
to help us against the enemy in the way: because we had spoken unto the king,
saying, The hand of our God *is* upon all them for good that seek him; but his
power and his wrath *is* against all them that forsake him.
23 So we fasted and besought our God for this: and he was intreated of us.

Ezra Commits the Treasury to the Custody of the Priests

24 Then I separated twelve of the chief of the priests, Sherebiah, Hashabiah,
and ten of their brethren with them,
25 And weighed unto them the silver, and the gold, and the vessels, *even* the
offering of the house of our God, which the king, and his counsellors, and his
lords, and all Israel *there* present, had offered:
26 I even weighed unto their hand six hundred and fifty talents of silver, and
silver vessels an hundred talents, *and* of gold an hundred talents;
27 Also twenty basons of gold, of a thousand drams; and two vessels of fine
copper, precious as gold.
28 And I said unto them, Ye *are* holy unto the LORD; the vessels *are* holy also;
and the silver and the gold *are* a freewill offering unto the LORD God of your
fathers.
29 Watch ye, and keep *them*, until ye weigh *them* before the chief of the priests
and the Levites, and chief of the fathers of Israel, at Jerusalem, in the chambers
of the house of the LORD.
30 So took the priests and the Levites the weight of the silver, and the gold,
and the vessels, to bring *them* to Jerusalem unto the house of our God.

The People Leave Ahava and Arrive in Jerusalem

31 Then we departed from the river of Ahava on the twelfth *day* of the first
month, to go unto Jerusalem: and the hand of our God was upon us, and he
delivered us from the hand of the enemy, and of such as lay in wait by the way.
32 And we came to Jerusalem, and abode there three days.
33 Now on the fourth day was the silver and the gold and the vessels weighed
in the house of our God by the hand of Meremoth the son of Uriah the priest;
and with him *was* Eleazar the son of Phinehas; and with them *was* Jozabad
the son of Jeshua, and Noadiah the son of Binnui, Levites;
34 By number *and* by weight of every one: and all the weight was written at
that time.
35 *Also* the children of those that had been carried away, which were come
out of the captivity, offered burnt offerings unto the God of Israel, twelve
bullocks for all Israel, ninety and six rams, seventy and seven lambs, twelve he
goats *for* a sin offering: all *this was* a burnt offering unto the LORD.
36 And they delivered the king's commissions unto the king's lieutenants,
and to the governors on this side the river: and they furthered the people, and
the house of God.

Ezra Mourns Because of Israel's Apostasy

9 Now when these things were done, the princes came to me, saying, The
people of Israel, and the priests, and the Levites, have not separated them-
selves from the people of the lands, *doing* according to their abominations, *even*
of the Canaanites, the Hittites, the Perizzites, the Jebusites, the Ammonites, the
Moabites, the Egyptians, and the Amorites.

2 For they have taken of their daughters for themselves, and for their sons: so that the holy seed have mingled themselves with the people of *those* lands: yea, the hand of the princes and rulers hath been chief in this trespass.

3 And when I heard this thing, I rent my garment and my mantle, and plucked off the hair of my head and of my beard, and sat down astonied.

4 Then were assembled unto me every one that trembled at the words of the God of Israel, because of the transgression of those that had been carried away; and I sat astonied until the evening sacrifice.

Ezra Prays

5 And at the evening sacrifice I arose up from my heaviness; and having rent my garment and my mantle, I fell upon my knees, and spread out my hands unto the LORD my God,

6 And said, O my God, I am ashamed and blush to lift up my face to thee, my God: for our iniquities are increased over *our* head, and our trespass is grown up unto the heavens.

7 Since the days of our fathers *have* we *been* in a great trespass unto this day; and for our iniquities have we, our kings, *and* our priests, been delivered into the hand of the kings of the lands, to the sword, to captivity, and to a spoil, and to confusion of face, as *it is* this day.

8 And now for a little space grace hath been *shewed* from the LORD our God, to leave us a remnant to escape, and to give us a nail in his holy place, that our God may lighten our eyes, and give us a little reviving in our bondage.

9 For we *were* bondmen; yet our God hath not forsaken us in our bondage, but hath extended mercy unto us in the sight of the kings of Persia, to give us a reviving, to set up the house of our God, and to repair the desolations thereof, and to give us a wall in Judah and in Jerusalem.

10 And now, O our God, what shall we say after this? for we have forsaken thy commandments,

11 Which thou hast commanded by thy servants the prophets, saying, The land, unto which ye go to possess it, is an unclean land with the filthiness of the people of the lands, with their abominations, which have filled it from one end to another with their uncleanness.

12 Now therefore give not your daughters unto their sons, neither take their daughters unto your sons, nor seek their peace or their wealth for ever: that ye may be strong, and eat the good of the land, and leave *it* for an inheritance to your children for ever.

13 And after all that is come upon us for our evil deeds, and for our great trespass, seeing that thou our God hast punished us less than our iniquities *deserve*, and hast given us *such* deliverance as this;

14 Should we again break thy commandments, and join in affinity with the people of these abominations? wouldest not thou be angry with us till thou hadst consumed *us*, so that *there should be* no remnant nor escaping?

15 O LORD God of Israel, thou *art* righteous: for we remain yet escaped, as *it is* this day: behold, we *are* before thee in our trespasses: for we cannot stand before thee because of this.

Shechaniah Encourages Ezra to Reform the Foreign Marriages

10 Now when Ezra had prayed, and when he had confessed, weeping and casting himself down before the house of God, there assembled unto him out of Israel a very great congregation of men and women and children: for the people wept very sore.

2 And Shechaniah the son of Jehiel, *one* of the sons of Elam, answered and said unto Ezra, We have trespassed against our God, and have taken strange wives of the people of the land: yet now there is hope in Israel concerning this thing.

3 Now therefore let us make a covenant with our God to put away all the wives, and such as are born of them, according to the counsel of my lord, and

of those that tremble at the commandment of our God; and let it be done according to the law.

4 Arise; for *this* matter *belongeth* unto thee: we also *will be* with thee: be of good courage, and do *it*.

5 Then arose Ezra, and made the chief priests, the Levites, and all Israel, to swear that they should do according to this word. And they sware.

Ezra, Mourning, Assembles the People

6 Then Ezra rose up from before the house of God, and went into the chamber of Johanan the son of Eliashib: and *when* he came thither, he did eat no bread, nor drink water: for he mourned because of the transgression of them that had been carried away.

7 And they made proclamation throughout Judah and Jerusalem unto all the children of the captivity, that they should gather themselves together unto Jerusalem;

8 And that whosoever would not come within three days, according to the counsel of the princes and the elders, all his substance should be forfeited, and himself separated from the congregation of those that had been carried away.

9 Then all the men of Judah and Benjamin gathered themselves together unto Jerusalem within three days. It *was* the ninth month, on the twentieth *day* of the month; and all the people sat in the street of the house of God, trembling because of *this* matter, and for the great rain.

10 And Ezra the priest stood up, and said unto them, Ye have transgressed, and have taken strange wives, to increase the trespass of Israel.

11 Now therefore make confession unto the LORD God of your fathers, and do his pleasure: and separate yourselves from the people of the land, and from the strange wives.

12 Then all the congregation answered and said with a loud voice, As thou hast said, so must we do.

13 But the people *are* many, and *it is* a time of much rain, and we are not able to stand without, neither *is this* a work of one day or two: for we are many that have transgressed in this thing.

14 Let now our rulers of all the congregation stand, and let all them which have taken strange wives in our cities come at appointed times, and with them the elders of every city, and the judges thereof, until the fierce wrath of our God for this matter be turned from us.

Those Who Were Guilty of Marrying Foreign Women

15 Only Jonathan the son of Asahel and Jahaziah the son of Tikvah were employed about this *matter*: and Meshullam and Shabbethai the Levite helped them.

16 And the children of the captivity did so. And Ezra the priest, *with* certain chief of the fathers, after the house of their fathers, and all of them by *their* names, were separated, and sat down in the first day of the tenth month to examine the matter.

17 And they made an end with all the men that had taken strange wives by the first day of the first month.

18 And among the sons of the priests there were found that had taken strange wives: *namely*, of the sons of Jeshua the son of Jozadak, and his brethren; Maaseiah, and Eliezer, and Jarib, and Gedaliah.

19 And they gave their hands that they would put away their wives; and *being* guilty, *they offered* a ram of the flock for their trespass.

20 And of the sons of Immer; Hanani, and Zebadiah.

21 And of the sons of Harim; Maaseiah, and Elijah, and Shemaiah, and Jehiel, and Uzziah.

22 And of the sons of Pashur; Elioenai, Maaseiah, Ishmael, Nethaneel, Jozabad, and Elasah.

23 Also of the Levites; Jozabad, and Shimei, and Kelaiah, (the same *is* Kelita,)
Pethahiah, Judah, and Eliezer.
24 Of the singers also; Eliashib: and of the porters; Shallum, and Telem, and
Uri.
25 Moreover of Israel: of the sons of Parosh; Ramiah, and Jeziah, and
Malchiah, and Miamin, and Eleazar, and Malchijah, and Benaiah.
26 And of the sons of Elam; Mattaniah, Zechariah, and Jehiel, and Abdi, and
Jeremoth, and Eliah.
27 And of the sons of Zattu; Elioenai, Eliashib, Mattaniah, and Jeremoth, and
Zabad, and Aziza.
28 Of the sons also of Bebai; Jehohanan, Hananiah, Zabbai, *and* Athlai.
29 And of the sons of Bani; Meshullam, Malluch, and Adaiah, Jashub, and
Sheal, and Ramoth.
30 And of the sons of Pahath-moab; Adna, and Chelal, Benaiah, Maaseiah,
Mattaniah, Bezaleel, and Binnui, and Manasseh.
31 And *of* the sons of Harim; Eliezer, Ishijah, Malchiah, Shemaiah, Shimeon,
32 Benjamin, Malluch, *and* Shemariah.
33 Of the sons of Hashum; Mattenai, Mattathah, Zabad, Eliphelet, Jeremai,
Manasseh, *and* Shimei.
34 Of the sons of Bani; Maadai, Amram, and Uel,
35 Benaiah, Bedeiah, Chelluh,
36 Vaniah, Meremoth, Eliashib,
37 Mattaniah, Mattenai, and Jaasau,
38 And Bani, and Binnui, Shimei,
39 And Shelemiah, and Nathan, and Adaiah,
40 Machnadebai, Shashai, Sharai,
41 Azareel, and Shelemiah, Shemariah,
42 Shallum, Amariah, *and* Joseph.
43 Of the sons of Nebo; Jeiel, Mattithiah, Zabad, Zebina, Jadau, and Joel,
Benaiah.
44 All these had taken strange wives: and *some* of them had wives by whom
they had children.

Nehemiah Learns the Distressing News That Jerusalem's Wall Is Broken Down

1 The words of Nehemiah the son of Hachaliah. And it came to pass in the
month Chisleu, in the twentieth year, as I was in Shushan the palace,
2 That Hanani, one of my brethren, came, he and *certain* men of Judah; and
I asked them concerning the Jews that had escaped, which were left of the
captivity, and concerning Jerusalem.
3 And they said unto me, The remnant that are left of the captivity there in
the province *are* in great affliction and reproach: the wall of Jerusalem also *is*
broken down, and the gates thereof are burned with fire.
4 And it came to pass, when I heard these words, that I sat down and wept,
and mourned *certain* days, and fasted, and prayed before the God of heaven,

Nehemiah's Prayer

5 And said, I beseech thee, O LORD God of heaven, the great and terrible God,
that keepeth covenant and mercy for them that love him and observe his
commandments:
6 Let thine ear now be attentive, and thine eyes open, that thou mayest hear
the prayer of thy servant, which I pray before thee now, day and night, for the
children of Israel thy servants, and confess the sins of the children of Israel,
which we have sinned against thee: both I and my father's house have sinned.
7 We have dealt very corruptly against thee, and have not kept the command-
ments, nor the statutes, nor the judgments, which thou commandedst thy
servant Moses.
8 Remember, I beseech thee, the word that thou commandedst thy servant
Moses, saying, *If* ye transgress, I will scatter you abroad among the nations:
9 But *if* ye turn unto me, and keep my commandments, and do them; though
there were of you cast out unto the uttermost part of the heaven, *yet* will I
gather them from thence, and will bring them unto the place that I have cho-
sen to set my name there.
10 Now these *are* thy servants and thy people, whom thou hast redeemed by
thy great power, and by thy strong hand.
11 O Lord, I beseech thee, let now thine ear be attentive to the prayer of thy
servant, and to the prayer of thy servants, who desire to fear thy name: and
prosper, I pray thee, thy servant this day, and grant him mercy in the sight of
this man. For I was the king's cupbearer.

Artaxerxes Allows Nehemiah to Return to Jerusalem

2 And it came to pass in the month Nisan, in the twentieth year of Artaxerxes
the king, *that* wine *was* before him: and I took up the wine, and gave *it* unto
the king. Now I had not been *beforetime* sad in his presence.
2 Wherefore the king said unto me, Why *is* thy countenance sad, seeing thou
art not sick? this *is* nothing *else* but sorrow of heart. Then I was very sore
afraid,
3 And said unto the king, Let the king live for ever: why should not my coun-
tenance be sad, when the city, the place of my fathers' sepulchres, *lieth* waste,
and the gates thereof are consumed with fire?
4 Then the king said unto me, For what dost thou make request? So I prayed
to the God of heaven.

5 And I said unto the king, If it please the king, and if thy servant have found
favour in thy sight, that thou wouldest send me unto Judah, unto the city of
my fathers' sepulchres, that I may build it.
6 And the king said unto me, (the queen also sitting by him,) For how long
shall thy journey be? and when wilt thou return? So it pleased the king to send
me; and I set him a time.
7 Moreover I said unto the king, If it please the king, let letters be given me
to the governors beyond the river, that they may convey me over till I come
into Judah;
8 And a letter unto Asaph the keeper of the king's forest, that he may give me
timber to make beams for the gates of the palace which *appertained* to the
house, and for the wall of the city, and for the house that I shall enter into. And
the king granted me, according to the good hand of my God upon me.

Nehemiah Arrives in Jerusalem and Surveys the Damage to the Walls

9 Then I came to the governors beyond the river, and gave them the king's
letters. Now the king had sent captains of the army and horsemen with me.
10 When Sanballat the Horonite, and Tobiah the servant, the Ammonite,
heard *of it*, it grieved them exceedingly that there was come a man to seek the
welfare of the children of Israel.
11 So I came to Jerusalem, and was there three days.
12 And I arose in the night, I and some few men with me; neither told I *any*
man what my God had put in my heart to do at Jerusalem: neither *was there*
any beast with me, save the beast that I rode upon.
13 And I went out by night by the gate of the valley, even before the dragon
well, and to the dung port, and viewed the walls of Jerusalem, which were
broken down, and the gates thereof were consumed with fire.
14 Then I went on to the gate of the fountain, and to the king's pool: but *there*
was no place for the beast *that was* under me to pass.
15 Then went I up in the night by the brook, and viewed the wall, and turned
back, and entered by the gate of the valley, and *so* returned.
16 And the rulers knew not whither I went, or what I did; neither had I as yet
told *it* to the Jews, nor to the priests, nor to the nobles, nor to the rulers, nor
to the rest that did the work.
17 Then said I unto them, Ye see the distress that we *are* in, how Jerusalem
lieth waste, and the gates thereof are burned with fire: come, and let us build
up the wall of Jerusalem, that we be no more a reproach.
18 Then I told them of the hand of my God which was good upon me; as also
the king's words that he had spoken unto me. And they said, Let us rise up and
build. So they strengthened their hands for *this* good *work*.
19 But when Sanballat the Horonite, and Tobiah the servant, the Ammonite,
and Geshem the Arabian, heard *it*, they laughed us to scorn, and despised us,
and said, What *is* this thing that ye do? will ye rebel against the king?
20 Then answered I them, and said unto them, The God of heaven, he will
prosper us; therefore we his servants will arise and build: but ye have no por-
tion, nor right, nor memorial, in Jerusalem.

A List of the People Rebuilding Jerusalem's Walls

3 Then Eliashib the high priest rose up with his brethren the priests, and they
builded the sheep gate; they sanctified it, and set up the doors of it; even
unto the tower of Meah they sanctified it, unto the tower of Hananeel.
2 And next unto him builded the men of Jericho. And next to them builded
Zaccur the son of Imri.
3 But the fish gate did the sons of Hassenaah build, who *also* laid the beams
thereof, and set up the doors thereof, the locks thereof, and the bars thereof.

4 And next unto them repaired Meremoth the son of Urijah, the son of Koz.
And next unto them repaired Meshullam the son of Berechiah, the son of
Meshezabeel. And next unto them repaired Zadok the son of Baana.
5 And next unto them the Tekoites repaired; but their nobles put not their
necks to the work of their Lord.
6 Moreover the old gate repaired Jehoiada the son of Paseah, and Meshullam
the son of Besodeiah; they laid the beams thereof, and set up the doors there-
of, and the locks thereof, and the bars thereof.
7 And next unto them repaired Melatiah the Gibeonite, and Jadon the
Meronothite, the men of Gibeon, and of Mizpah, unto the throne of the gov-
ernor on this side the river.
8 Next unto him repaired Uzziel the son of Harhaiah, of the goldsmiths. Next
unto him also repaired Hananiah the son of *one of* the apothecaries, and they
fortified Jerusalem unto the broad wall.
9 And next unto them repaired Rephaiah the son of Hur, the ruler of the half
part of Jerusalem.
10 And next unto them repaired Jedaiah the son of Harumaph, even over
against his house. And next unto him repaired Hattush the son of Hashabniah.
11 Malchijah the son of Harim, and Hashub the son of Pahath-moab,
repaired the other piece, and the tower of the furnaces.
12 And next unto him repaired Shallum the son of Halohesh, the ruler of the
half part of Jerusalem, he and his daughters.
13 The valley gate repaired Hanun, and the inhabitants of Zanoah; they built
it, and set up the doors thereof, the locks thereof, and the bars thereof, and a
thousand cubits on the wall unto the dung gate.
14 But the dung gate repaired Malchiah the son of Rechab, the ruler of part
of Bethhaccerem; he built it, and set up the doors thereof, the locks thereof,
and the bars thereof.
15 But the gate of the fountain repaired Shallun the son of Colhozeh, the
ruler of part of Mizpah; he built it, and covered it, and set up the doors there-
of, the locks thereof, and the bars thereof, and the wall of the pool of Siloah
by the king's garden, and unto the stairs that go down from the city of David.
16 After him repaired Nehemiah the son of Azbuk, the ruler of the half part
of Beth-zur, unto *the place* over against the sepulchres of David, and to the
pool that was made, and unto the house of the mighty.
17 After him repaired the Levites, Rehum the son of Bani. Next unto him
repaired Hashabiah, the ruler of the half part of Keilah, in his part.
18 After him repaired their brethren, Bavai the son of Henadad, the ruler of
the half part of Keilah.
19 And next to him repaired Ezer the son of Jeshua, the ruler of Mizpah,
another piece over against the going up to the armoury at the turning *of the
wall*.
20 After him Baruch the son of Zabbai earnestly repaired the other piece,
from the turning *of the wall* unto the door of the house of Eliashib the high
priest.
21 After him repaired Meremoth the son of Urijah the son of Koz another
piece, from the door of the house of Eliashib even to the end of the house of
Eliashib.
22 And after him repaired the priests, the men of the plain.
23 After him repaired Benjamin and Hashub over against their house. After
him repaired Azariah the son of Maaseiah the son of Ananiah by his house.
24 After him repaired Binnui the son of Henadad another piece, from the
house of Azariah unto the turning *of the wall*, even unto the corner.
25 Palal the son of Uzai, over against the turning *of the wall*, and the tower
which lieth out from the king's high house, that *was* by the court of the prison.
After him Pedaiah the son of Parosh.

26 Moreover the Nethinims dwelt in Ophel, unto *the place* over against the
water gate toward the east, and the tower that lieth out.
27 After them the Tekoites repaired another piece, over against the great
tower that lieth out, even unto the wall of Ophel.
28 From above the horse gate repaired the priests, every one over against his
house.
29 After them repaired Zadok the son of Immer over against his house. After
him repaired also Shemaiah the son of Shechaniah, the keeper of the east gate.
30 After him repaired Hananiah the son of Shelemiah, and Hanun the sixth
son of Zalaph, another piece. After him repaired Meshullam the son of
Berechiah over against his chamber.
31 After him repaired Malchiah the goldsmith's son unto the place of the
Nethinims, and of the merchants, over against the gate Miphkad, and to the
going up of the corner.
32 And between the going up of the corner unto the sheep gate repaired the
goldsmiths and the merchants.

While the Enemies Scoff, Nehemiah Prays and Continues the Work

4 But it came to pass, that when Sanballat heard that we builded the wall, he
was wroth, and took great indignation, and mocked the Jews.
2 And he spake before his brethren and the army of Samaria, and said, What
do these feeble Jews? will they fortify themselves? will they sacrifice? will they
make an end in a day? will they revive the stones out of the heaps of the rubbish
which are burned?
3 Now Tobiah the Ammonite *was* by him, and he said, Even that which they
build, if a fox go up, he shall even break down their stone wall.
4 Hear, O our God; for we are despised: and turn their reproach upon their
own head, and give them for a prey in the land of captivity:
5 And cover not their iniquity, and let not their sin be blotted out from before
thee: for they have provoked *thee* to anger before the builders.
6 So built we the wall; and all the wall was joined together unto the half
thereof: for the people had a mind to work.

Nehemiah Overcomes Opposition from Sanballat

7 But it came to pass, *that* when Sanballat, and Tobiah, and the Arabians, and
the Ammonites, and the Ashdodites, heard that the walls of Jerusalem were
made up, *and* that the breaches began to be stopped, then they were very
wroth,
8 And conspired all of them together to come *and* to fight against Jerusalem,
and to hinder it.
9 Nevertheless we made our prayer unto our God, and set a watch against
them day and night, because of them.
10 And Judah said, The strength of the bearers of burdens is decayed, and
there is much rubbish; so that we are not able to build the wall.
11 And our adversaries said, They shall not know, neither see, till we come
in the midst among them, and slay them, and cause the work to cease.
12 And it came to pass, that when the Jews which dwelt by them came, they
said unto us ten times, From all places whence ye shall return unto us *they will
be upon you.*
13 Therefore set I in the lower places behind the wall, *and* on the higher
places, I even set the people after their families with their swords, their spears,
and their bows.
14 And I looked, and rose up, and said unto the nobles, and to the rulers, and
to the rest of the people, Be not ye afraid of them: remember the Lord, *which
is* great and terrible, and fight for your brethren, your sons, and your daugh-
ters, your wives, and your houses.

15 And it came to pass, when our enemies heard that it was known unto us, and God had brought their counsel to nought, that we returned all of us to the wall, every one unto his work.

16 And it came to pass from that time forth, *that* the half of my servants wrought in the work, and the other half of them held both the spears, the shields, and the bows, and the habergeons; and the rulers *were* behind all the house of Judah.

17 They which builded on the wall, and they that bare burdens, with those that laded, *every one* with one of his hands wrought in the work, and with the other *hand* held a weapon.

18 For the builders, every one had his sword girded by his side, and *so* builded. And he that sounded the trumpet *was* by me.

19 And I said unto the nobles, and to the rulers, and to the rest of the people, The work *is* great and large, and we are separated upon the wall, one far from another.

20 In what place *therefore* ye hear the sound of the trumpet, resort ye thither unto us: our God shall fight for us.

21 So we laboured in the work: and half of them held the spears from the rising of the morning till the stars appeared.

22 Likewise at the same time said I unto the people, Let every one with his servant lodge within Jerusalem, that in the night they may be a guard to us, and labour on the day.

23 So neither I, nor my brethren, nor my servants, nor the men of the guard which followed me, none of us put off our clothes, *saving that* every one put them off for washing.

The Poor Complain about Their Rich Relatives

5 And there was a great cry of the people and of their wives against their brethren the Jews.

2 For there were that said, We, our sons, and our daughters, *are* many: therefore we take up corn *for them*, that we may eat, and live.

3 *Some* also there were that said, We have mortgaged our lands, vineyards, and houses, that we might buy corn, because of the dearth.

4 There were also that said, We have borrowed money for the king's tribute, *and that upon* our lands and vineyards.

5 Yet now our flesh *is* as the flesh of our brethren, our children as their children: and, lo, we bring into bondage our sons and our daughters to be servants, and *some* of our daughters are brought unto bondage *already*: neither *is it* in our power *to redeem them*; for other men have our lands and vineyards.

Nehemiah Stops the Rich from Taking Advantage of the Poor

6 And I was very angry when I heard their cry and these words.

7 Then I consulted with myself, and I rebuked the nobles, and the rulers, and said unto them, Ye exact usury, every one of his brother. And I set a great assembly against them.

8 And I said unto them, We after our ability have redeemed our brethren the Jews, which were sold unto the heathen; and will ye even sell your brethren? or shall they be sold unto us? Then held they their peace, and found nothing *to answer*.

9 Also I said, It *is* not good that ye do: ought ye not to walk in the fear of our God because of the reproach of the heathen our enemies?

10 I likewise, *and* my brethren, and my servants, might exact of them money and corn: I pray you, let us leave off this usury.

11 Restore, I pray you, to them, even this day, their lands, their vineyards, their oliveyards, and their houses, also the hundredth *part* of the money, and of the corn, the wine, and the oil, that ye exact of them.

12 Then said they, We will restore *them*, and will require nothing of them;
so will we do as thou sayest. Then I called the priests, and took an oath of them,
that they should do according to this promise.
13 Also I shook my lap, and said, So God shake out every man from his house,
and from his labour, that performeth not this promise, even thus be he shak-
en out, and emptied. And all the congregation said, Amen, and praised the
LORD. And the people did according to this promise.

Nehemiah Never Takes What Is Rightfully His as Governor

14 Moreover from the time that I was appointed to be their governor in the
land of Judah, from the twentieth year even unto the two and thirtieth year
of Artaxerxes the king, *that is*, twelve years, I and my brethren have not eaten
the bread of the governor.
15 But the former governors that *had been* before me were chargeable unto
the people, and had taken of them bread and wine, beside forty shekels of
silver; yea, even their servants bare rule over the people: but so did not I,
because of the fear of God.
16 Yea, also I continued in the work of this wall, neither bought we any land:
and all my servants *were* gathered thither unto the work.
17 Moreover *there were* at my table an hundred and fifty of the Jews and rulers,
beside those that came unto us from among the heathen that *are* about us.
18 Now *that* which was prepared *for me* daily *was* one ox *and* six choice
sheep; also fowls were prepared for me, and once in ten days store of all sorts
of wine: yet for all this required not I the bread of the governor, because the
bondage was heavy upon this people.
19 Think upon me, my God, for good, *according* to all that I have done for
this people.

Sanballat Tries to Harm Nehemiah

6 Now it came to pass, when Sanballat, and Tobiah, and Geshem the Arabian,
and the rest of our enemies, heard that I had builded the wall, and *that*
there was no breach left therein; (though at that time I had not set up the doors
upon the gates;)
2 That Sanballat and Geshem sent unto me, saying, Come, let us meet togeth-
er in *some one of* the villages in the plain of Ono. But they thought to do me
mischief.
3 And I sent messengers unto them, saying, I *am* doing a great work, so that
I cannot come down: why should the work cease, whilst I leave it, and come
down to you?
4 Yet they sent unto me four times after this sort; and I answered them after
the same manner.
5 Then sent Sanballat his servant unto me in like manner the fifth time with
an open letter in his hand;
6 Wherein *was* written, It is reported among the heathen, and Gashmu saith
it, that thou and the Jews think to rebel: for which cause thou buildest the
wall, that thou mayest be their king, according to these words.
7 And thou hast also appointed prophets to preach of thee at Jerusalem,
saying, *There is* a king in Judah: and now shall it be reported to the king accord-
ing to these words. Come now therefore, and let us take counsel together.
8 Then I sent unto him, saying, There are no such things done as thou sayest,
but thou feignest them out of thine own heart.
9 For they all made us afraid, saying, Their hands shall be weakened from
the work, that it be not done. Now therefore, *O God*, strengthen my hands.
10 Afterward I came unto the house of Shemaiah the son of Delaiah the son
of Mehetabeel, who *was* shut up; and he said, Let us meet together in the house
of God, within the temple, and let us shut the doors of the temple: for they
will come to slay thee; yea, in the night will they come to slay thee.

11 And I said, Should such a man as I flee? and who *is there*, that, *being* as I *am*, would go into the temple to save his life? I will not go in.
12 And, lo, I perceived that God had not sent him; but that he pronounced this prophecy against me: for Tobiah and Sanballat had hired him.
13 Therefore *was* he hired, that I should be afraid, and do so, and sin, and *that* they might have *matter* for an evil report, that they might reproach me.
14 My God, think thou upon Tobiah and Sanballat according to these their works, and on the prophetess Noadiah, and the rest of the prophets, that would have put me in fear.

The Wall Is Rebuilt, in Spite of Opposition

15 So the wall was finished in the twenty and fifth *day* of *the month* Elul, in fifty and two days.
16 And it came to pass, that when all our enemies heard *thereof*, and all the heathen that *were* about us saw *these things*, they were much cast down in their own eyes: for they perceived that this work was wrought of our God.
17 Moreover in those days the nobles of Judah sent many letters unto Tobiah, and *the letters* of Tobiah came unto them.
18 For *there were* many in Judah sworn unto him, because he *was* the son in law of Shechaniah the son of Arah; and his son Johanan had taken the daughter of Meshullam the son of Berechiah.
19 Also they reported his good deeds before me, and uttered my words to him. *And* Tobiah sent letters to put me in fear.

Nehemiah Places Hanani and Hananiah in Charge of Guarding the City Gates

7 Now it came to pass, when the wall was built, and I had set up the doors, and the porters and the singers and the Levites were appointed,
2 That I gave my brother Hanani, and Hananiah the ruler of the palace, charge over Jerusalem: for he *was* a faithful man, and feared God above many.
3 And I said unto them, Let not the gates of Jerusalem be opened until the sun be hot; and while they stand by, let them shut the doors, and bar *them*: and appoint watches of the inhabitants of Jerusalem, every one in his watch, and every one *to be* over against his house.
4 Now the city *was* large and great: but the people *were* few therein, and the houses *were* not builded.

A Register of the Jewish Exiles Who First Returned to Jerusalem

5 And my God put into mine heart to gather together the nobles, and the rulers, and the people, that they might be reckoned by genealogy. And I found a register of the genealogy of them which came up at the first, and found written therein,
6 These *are* the children of the province, that went up out of the captivity, of those that had been carried away, whom Nebuchadnezzar the king of Babylon had carried away, and came again to Jerusalem and to Judah, every one unto his city;
7 Who came with Zerubbabel, Jeshua, Nehemiah, Azariah, Raamiah, Nahamani, Mordecai, Bilshan, Mispereth, Bigvai, Nehum, Baanah. The number, *I say*, of the men of the people of Israel *was this*;
8 The children of Parosh, two thousand an hundred seventy and two.
9 The children of Shephatiah, three hundred seventy and two.
10 The children of Arah, six hundred fifty and two.
11 The children of Pahath-moab, of the children of Jeshua and Joab, two thousand and eight hundred *and* eighteen.
12 The children of Elam, a thousand two hundred fifty and four.
13 The children of Zattu, eight hundred forty and five.
14 The children of Zaccai, seven hundred and threescore.
15 The children of Binnui, six hundred forty and eight.

16 The children of Bebai, six hundred twenty and eight.
17 The children of Azgad, two thousand three hundred twenty and two.
18 The children of Adonikam, six hundred threescore and seven.
19 The children of Bigvai, two thousand threescore and seven.
20 The children of Adin, six hundred fifty and five.
21 The children of Ater of Hezekiah, ninety and eight.
22 The children of Hashum, three hundred twenty and eight.
23 The children of Bezai, three hundred twenty and four.
24 The children of Hariph, an hundred and twelve.
25 The children of Gibeon, ninety and five.
26 The men of Beth-lehem and Netophah, an hundred fourscore and eight.
27 The men of Anathoth, an hundred twenty and eight.
28 The men of Beth-azmaveth, forty and two.
29 The men of Kirjath-jearim, Chephirah, and Beeroth, seven hundred forty
and three.
30 The men of Ramah and Geba, six hundred twenty and one.
31 The men of Michmas, an hundred and twenty and two.
32 The men of Beth-el and Ai, an hundred twenty and three.
33 The men of the other Nebo, fifty and two.
34 The children of the other Elam, a thousand two hundred fifty and four.
35 The children of Harim, three hundred and twenty.
36 The children of Jericho, three hundred forty and five.
37 The children of Lod, Hadid, and Ono, seven hundred twenty and one.
38 The children of Senaah, three thousand nine hundred and thirty.
39 The priests: the children of Jedaiah, of the house of Jeshua, nine hundred
seventy and three.
40 The children of Immer, a thousand fifty and two.
41 The children of Pashur, a thousand two hundred forty and seven.
42 The children of Harim, a thousand and seventeen.
43 The Levites: the children of Jeshua, of Kadmiel, *and* of the children of
Hodevah, seventy and four.
44 The singers: the children of Asaph, an hundred forty and eight.
45 The porters: the children of Shallum, the children of Ater, the children of
Talmon, the children of Akkub, the children of Hatita, the children of Shobai,
an hundred thirty and eight.
46 The Nethinims: the children of Ziha, the children of Hashupha, the chil-
dren of Tabbaoth,
47 The children of Keros, the children of Sia, the children of Padon,
48 The children of Lebana, the children of Hagaba, the children of Shalmai,
49 The children of Hanan, the children of Giddel, the children of Gahar,
50 The children of Reaiah, the children of Rezin, the children of Nekoda,
51 The children of Gazzam, the children of Uzza, the children of Phaseah,
52 The children of Besai, the children of Meunim, the children of
Nephishesim,
53 The children of Bakbuk, the children of Hakupha, the children of Harhur,
54 The children of Bazlith, the children of Mehida, the children of Harsha,
55 The children of Barkos, the children of Sisera, the children of Tamah,
56 The children of Neziah, the children of Hatipha.
57 The children of Solomon's servants: the children of Sotai, the children of
Sophereth, the children of Perida,
58 The children of Jaala, the children of Darkon, the children of Giddel,
59 The children of Shephatiah, the children of Hattil, the children of
Pochereth of Zebaim, the children of Amon.
60 All the Nethinims, and the children of Solomon's servants, *were* three
hundred ninety and two.

61 And these *were* they which went up *also* from Tel-melah, Tel-haresha,
Cherub, Addon, and Immer: but they could not shew their father's house, nor
their seed, whether they *were* of Israel.
62 The children of Delaiah, the children of Tobiah, the children of Nekoda,
six hundred forty and two.
63 And of the priests: the children of Habaiah, the children of Koz, the chil-
dren of Barzillai, which took *one* of the daughters of Barzillai the Gileadite to
wife, and was called after their name.
64 These sought their register *among* those that were reckoned by genealo-
gy, but it was not found: therefore were they, as polluted, put from the priest-
hood.
65 And the Tirshatha said unto them, that they should not eat of the most
holy things, till there stood *up* a priest with Urim and Thummim.
66 The whole congregation together *was* forty and two thousand three hun-
dred and threescore,
67 Beside their manservants and their maidservants, of whom *there were*
seven thousand three hundred thirty and seven: and they had two hundred
forty and five singing men and singing women.
68 Their horses, seven hundred thirty and six: their mules, two hundred forty
and five:
69 *Their* camels, four hundred thirty and five: six thousand seven hundred
and twenty asses.
70 And some of the chief of the fathers gave unto the work. The Tirshatha
gave to the treasure a thousand drams of gold, fifty basons, five hundred and
thirty priests' garments.
71 And *some* of the chief of the fathers gave to the treasure of the work twen-
ty thousand drams of gold, and two thousand and two hundred pound of
silver.
72 And *that* which the rest of the people gave *was* twenty thousand drams
of gold, and two thousand pound of silver, and threescore and seven priests'
garments.
73 So the priests, and the Levites, and the porters, and the singers, and *some*
of the people, and the Nethinims, and all Israel, dwelt in their cities; and when
the seventh month came, the children of Israel *were* in their cities.

The Public Reading of Moses' Law and Teachings

8 And all the people gathered themselves together as one man into the street
that *was* before the water gate; and they spake unto Ezra the scribe to bring
the book of the law of Moses, which the LORD had commanded to Israel.
2 And Ezra the priest brought the law before the congregation both of men
and women, and all that could hear with understanding, upon the first day
of the seventh month.
3 And he read therein before the street that *was* before the water gate from
the morning until midday, before the men and the women, and those that
could understand; and the ears of all the people *were attentive* unto the book
of the law.
4 And Ezra the scribe stood upon a pulpit of wood, which they had made for
the purpose; and beside him stood Mattithiah, and Shema, and Anaiah, and
Urijah, and Hilkiah, and Maaseiah, on his right hand; and on his left hand,
Pedaiah, and Mishael, and Malchiah, and Hashum, and Hashbadana,
Zechariah, *and* Meshullam.
5 And Ezra opened the book in the sight of all the people; (for he was above
all the people;) and when he opened it, all the people stood up:
6 And Ezra blessed the LORD, the great God. And all the people answered,
Amen, Amen, with lifting up their hands: and they bowed their heads, and
worshipped the LORD with *their* faces to the ground.

7 Also Jeshua, and Bani, and Sherebiah, Jamin, Akkub, Shabbethai, Hodijah,
Maaseiah, Kelita, Azariah, Jozabad, Hanan, Pelaiah, and the Levites, caused
the people to understand the law: and the people *stood* in their place.
8 So they read in the book in the law of God distinctly, and gave the sense,
and caused *them* to understand the reading.

Nehemiah, Ezra, and the Levites Comfort the People

9 And Nehemiah, which *is* the Tirshatha, and Ezra the priest the scribe, and
the Levites that taught the people, said unto all the people, This day *is* holy
unto the LORD your God; mourn not, nor weep. For all the people wept, when
they heard the words of the law.
10 Then he said unto them, Go your way, eat the fat, and drink the sweet, and
send portions unto them for whom nothing is prepared: for *this* day *is* holy
unto our Lord: neither be ye sorry; for the joy of the LORD is your strength.
11 So the Levites stilled all the people, saying, Hold your peace, for the day *is*
holy; neither be ye grieved.
12 And all the people went their way to eat, and to drink, and to send portions,
and to make great mirth, because they had understood the words that were
declared unto them.

The People Observe the Festival of Booths (Tabernacles)

13 And on the second day were gathered together the chief of the fathers of
all the people, the priests, and the Levites, unto Ezra the scribe, even to under-
stand the words of the law.
14 And they found written in the law which the LORD had commanded by
Moses, that the children of Israel should dwell in booths in the feast of the
seventh month:
15 And that they should publish and proclaim in all their cities, and in
Jerusalem, saying, Go forth unto the mount, and fetch olive branches, and
pine branches, and myrtle branches, and palm branches, and branches of
thick trees, to make booths, as *it is* written.
16 So the people went forth, and brought *them*, and made themselves booths,
every one upon the roof of his house, and in their courts, and in the courts of
the house of God, and in the street of the water gate, and in the street of the
gate of Ephraim.
17 And all the congregation of them that were come again out of the captiv-
ity made booths, and sat under the booths: for since the days of Jeshua the son
of Nun unto that day had not the children of Israel done so. And there was
very great gladness.
18 Also day by day, from the first day unto the last day, he read in the book of
the law of God. And they kept the feast seven days; and on the eighth day *was*
a solemn assembly, according unto the manner.

A Day of Fasting and Confession

9 Now in the twenty and fourth day of this month the children of Israel were
assembled with fasting, and with sackclothes, and earth upon them.
2 And the seed of Israel separated themselves from all strangers, and stood
and confessed their sins, and the iniquities of their fathers.
3 And they stood up in their place, and read in the book of the law of the
LORD their God *one* fourth part of the day; and *another* fourth part they con-
fessed, and worshipped the LORD their God.

A Day of Prayer

4 Then stood up upon the stairs, of the Levites, Jeshua, and Bani, Kadmiel,
Shebaniah, Bunni, Sherebiah, Bani, *and* Chenani, and cried with a loud voice
unto the LORD their God.
5 Then the Levites, Jeshua, and Kadmiel, Bani, Hashabniah, Sherebiah,
Hodijah, Shebaniah, *and* Pethahiah, said, Stand up *and* bless the LORD your

God for ever and ever: and blessed be thy glorious name, which is exalted above
all blessing and praise.
6 Thou, *even* thou, *art* LORD alone; thou hast made heaven, the heaven of
heavens, with all their host, the earth, and all *things* that *are* therein, the seas,
and all that *is* therein, and thou preservest them all; and the host of heaven
worshippeth thee.
7 Thou *art* the LORD the God, who didst choose Abram, and broughtest him
forth out of Ur of the Chaldees, and gavest him the name of Abraham;
8 And foundest his heart faithful before thee, and madest a covenant with
him to give the land of the Canaanites, the Hittites, the Amorites, and the
Perizzites, and the Jebusites, and the Girgashites, to give *it, I say*, to his seed,
and hast performed thy words; for thou *art* righteous:
9 And didst see the affliction of our fathers in Egypt, and heardest their cry
by the Red sea;
10 And shewedst signs and wonders upon Pharaoh, and on all his servants,
and on all the people of his land: for thou knewest that they dealt proudly
against them. So didst thou get thee a name, as *it is* this day.
11 And thou didst divide the sea before them, so that they went through the
midst of the sea on the dry land; and their persecutors thou threwest into the
deeps, as a stone into the mighty waters.
12 Moreover thou leddest them in the day by a cloudy pillar; and in the night
by a pillar of fire, to give them light in the way wherein they should go.
13 Thou camest down also upon mount Sinai, and spakest with them from
heaven, and gavest them right judgments, and true laws, good statutes and
commandments:
14 And madest known unto them thy holy sabbath, and commandedst them
precepts, statutes, and laws, by the hand of Moses thy servant:
15 And gavest them bread from heaven for their hunger, and broughtest
forth water for them out of the rock for their thirst, and promisedst them that
they should go in to possess the land which thou hadst sworn to give them.
16 But they and our fathers dealt proudly, and hardened their necks, and
hearkened not to thy commandments,
17 And refused to obey, neither were mindful of thy wonders that thou didst
among them; but hardened their necks, and in their rebellion appointed a
captain to return to their bondage: but thou *art* a God ready to pardon, gracious
and merciful, slow to anger, and of great kindness, and forsookest them not.
18 Yea, when they had made them a molten calf, and said, This *is* thy God
that brought thee up out of Egypt, and had wrought great provocations;
19 Yet thou in thy manifold mercies forsookest them not in the wilderness:
the pillar of the cloud departed not from them by day, to lead them in the way;
neither the pillar of fire by night, to shew them light, and the way wherein
they should go.
20 Thou gavest also thy good spirit to instruct them, and withheldest not thy
manna from their mouth, and gavest them water for their thirst.
21 Yea, forty years didst thou sustain them in the wilderness, *so that* they
lacked nothing; their clothes waxed not old, and their feet swelled not.
22 Moreover thou gavest them kingdoms and nations, and didst divide them
into corners: so they possessed the land of Sihon, and the land of the king of
Heshbon, and the land of Og king of Bashan.
23 Their children also multipliedst thou as the stars of heaven, and brough-
test them into the land, concerning which thou hadst promised to their
fathers, that they should go in to possess *it*.
24 So the children went in and possessed the land, and thou subduedst before
them the inhabitants of the land, the Canaanites, and gavest them into their
hands, with their kings, and the people of the land, that they might do with
them as they would.

25 And they took strong cities, and a fat land, and possessed houses full of
all goods, wells digged, vineyards, and oliveyards, and fruit trees in abundance:
so they did eat, and were filled, and became fat, and delighted themselves in
thy great goodness.
26 Nevertheless they were disobedient, and rebelled against thee, and cast
thy law behind their backs, and slew thy prophets which testified against them
to turn them to thee, and they wrought great provocations.
27 Therefore thou deliveredst them into the hand of their enemies, who
vexed them: and in the time of their trouble, when they cried unto thee, thou
heardest *them* from heaven; and according to thy manifold mercies thou gav-
est them saviours, who saved them out of the hand of their enemies.
28 But after they had rest, they did evil again before thee: therefore leftest
thou them in the hand of their enemies, so that they had the dominion over
them: yet when they returned, and cried unto thee, thou heardest *them* from
heaven; and many times didst thou deliver them according to thy mercies;
29 And testifiedst against them, that thou mightest bring them again unto
thy law: yet they dealt proudly, and hearkened not unto thy commandments,
but sinned against thy judgments, (which if a man do, he shall live in them;)
and withdrew the shoulder, and hardened their neck, and would not hear.
30 Yet many years didst thou forbear them, and testifiedst against them by
thy spirit in thy prophets: yet would they not give ear: therefore gavest thou
them into the hand of the people of the lands.
31 Nevertheless for thy great mercies' sake thou didst not utterly consume
them, nor forsake them; for thou *art* a gracious and merciful God.
32 Now therefore, our God, the great, the mighty, and the terrible God, who
keepest covenant and mercy, let not all the trouble seem little before thee, that
hath come upon us, on our kings, on our princes, and on our priests, and on
our prophets, and on our fathers, and on all thy people, since the time of the
kings of Assyria unto this day.
33 Howbeit thou *art* just in all that is brought upon us; for thou hast done
right, but we have done wickedly:
34 Neither have our kings, our princes, our priests, nor our fathers, kept thy
law, nor hearkened unto thy commandments and thy testimonies, wherewith
thou didst testify against them.
35 For they have not served thee in their kingdom, and in thy great goodness
that thou gavest them, and in the large and fat land which thou gavest before
them, neither turned they from their wicked works.
36 Behold, we *are* servants this day, and *for* the land that thou gavest unto
our fathers to eat the fruit thereof and the good thereof, behold, we *are* serv-
ants in it:
37 And it yieldeth much increase unto the kings whom thou hast set over us
because of our sins: also they have dominion over our bodies, and over our
cattle, at their pleasure, and we *are* in great distress.
38 And because of all this we make a sure *covenant*, and write *it*; and our
princes, Levites, *and* priests, seal *unto it.*

The Names of Those Who Sealed the Covenant

10 Now those that sealed *were*, Nehemiah, the Tirshatha, the son of
Hachaliah, and Zidkijah,
2 Seraiah, Azariah, Jeremiah,
3 Pashur, Amariah, Malchijah,
4 Hattush, Shebaniah, Malluch,
5 Harim, Meremoth, Obadiah,
6 Daniel, Ginnethon, Baruch,
7 Meshullam, Abijah, Mijamin,
8 Maaziah, Bilgai, Shemaiah: these *were* the priests.

9 And the Levites: both Jeshua the son of Azaniah, Binnui of the sons of
Henadad, Kadmiel;
10 And their brethren, Shebaniah, Hodijah, Kelita, Pelaiah, Hanan,
11 Micha, Rehob, Hashabiah,
12 Zaccur, Sherebiah, Shebaniah,
13 Hodijah, Bani, Beninu.
14 The chief of the people; Parosh, Pahathmoab, Elam, Zatthu, Bani,
15 Bunni, Azgad, Bebai,
16 Adonijah, Bigvai, Adin,
17 Ater, Hizkijah, Azzur,
18 Hodijah, Hashum, Bezai,
19 Hariph, Anathoth, Nebai,
20 Magpiash, Meshullam, Hezir,
21 Meshezabeel, Zadok, Jaddua,
22 Pelatiah, Hanan, Anaiah,
23 Hoshea, Hananiah, Hashub,
24 Hallohesh, Pileha, Shobek,
25 Rehum, Hashabnah, Maaseiah,
26 And Ahijah, Hanan, Anan,
27 Malluch, Harim, Baanah.
28 And the rest of the people, the priests, the Levites, the porters, the singers,
the Nethinims, and all they that had separated themselves from the people of
the lands unto the law of God, their wives, their sons, and their daughters,
every one having knowledge, and having understanding;
29 They clave to their brethren, their nobles, and entered into a curse, and
into an oath, to walk in God's law, which was given by Moses the servant of
God, and to observe and do all the commandments of the LORD our Lord, and
his judgments and his statutes;
30 And that we would not give our daughters unto the people of the land,
nor take their daughters for our sons:
31 And *if* the people of the land bring ware or any victuals on the sabbath
day to sell, *that* we would not buy it of them on the sabbath, or on the holy
day: and *that* we would leave the seventh year, and the exaction of every debt.
32 Also we made ordinances for us, to charge ourselves yearly with the third
part of a shekel for the service of the house of our God;
33 For the shewbread, and for the continual meat offering, and for the con-
tinual burnt offering, of the sabbaths, of the new moons, for the set feasts,
and for the holy *things*, and for the sin offerings to make an atonement for
Israel, and *for* all the work of the house of our God.
34 And we cast the lots among the priests, the Levites, and the people, for the
wood offering, to bring *it* into the house of our God, after the houses of our
fathers, at times appointed year by year, to burn upon the altar of the LORD
our God, as *it is* written in the law:
35 And to bring the firstfruits of our ground, and the firstfruits of all fruit
of all trees, year by year, unto the house of the LORD:
36 Also the firstborn of our sons, and of our cattle, as *it is* written in the law,
and the firstlings of our herds and of our flocks, to bring to the house of our
God, unto the priests that minister in the house of our God:
37 And *that* we should bring the firstfruits of our dough, and our offerings,
and the fruit of all manner of trees, of wine and of oil, unto the priests, to the
chambers of the house of our God; and the tithes of our ground unto the
Levites, that the same Levites might have the tithes in all the cities of our tillage.
38 And the priest the son of Aaron shall be with the Levites, when the Levites
take tithes: and the Levites shall bring up the tithe of the tithes unto the house
of our God, to the chambers, into the treasure house.

39 For the children of Israel and the children of Levi shall bring the offering
of the corn, of the new wine, and the oil, unto the chambers, where *are* the
vessels of the sanctuary, and the priests that minister, and the porters, and the
singers: and we will not forsake the house of our God.

New Residents for Jerusalem

11 And the rulers of the people dwelt at Jerusalem: the rest of the people
also cast lots, to bring one of ten to dwell in Jerusalem the holy city,
and nine parts *to dwell* in *other* cities.
2 And the people blessed all the men, that willingly offered themselves to
dwell at Jerusalem.
3 Now these *are* the chief of the province that dwelt in Jerusalem: but in the
cities of Judah dwelt every one in his possession in their cities, *to wit*, Israel,
the priests, and the Levites, and the Nethinims, and the children of Solomon's
servants.
4 And at Jerusalem dwelt *certain* of the children of Judah, and of the children
of Benjamin. Of the children of Judah; Athaiah the son of Uzziah, the son of
Zechariah, the son of Amariah, the son of Shephatiah, the son of Mahalaleel,
of the children of Perez;
5 And Maaseiah the son of Baruch, the son of Col-hozeh, the son of Hazaiah,
the son of Adaiah, the son of Joiarib, the son of Zechariah, the son of Shiloni.
6 All the sons of Perez that dwelt at Jerusalem *were* four hundred threescore
and eight valiant men.
7 And these *are* the sons of Benjamin; Sallu the son of Meshullam, the son
of Joed, the son of Pedaiah, the son of Kolaiah, the son of Maaseiah, the son
of Ithiel, the son of Jesaiah.
8 And after him Gabbai, Sallai, nine hundred twenty and eight.
9 And Joel the son of Zichri *was* their overseer: and Judah the son of Senuah
was second over the city.
10 Of the priests: Jedaiah the son of Joiarib, Jachin.
11 Seraiah the son of Hilkiah, the son of Meshullam, the son of Zadok, the
son of Meraioth, the son of Ahitub, *was* the ruler of the house of God.
12 And their brethren that did the work of the house *were* eight hundred
twenty and two: and Adaiah the son of Jeroham, the son of Pelaliah, the son
of Amzi, the son of Zechariah, the son of Pashur, the son of Malchiah,
13 And his brethren, chief of the fathers, two hundred forty and two: and
Amashai the son of Azareel, the son of Ahasai, the son of Meshillemoth, the
son of Immer,
14 And their brethren, mighty men of valour, an hundred twenty and eight:
and their overseer *was* Zabdiel, the son of *one of* the great men.
15 Also of the Levites: Shemaiah the son of Hashub, the son of Azrikam, the
son of Hashabiah, the son of Bunni;
16 And Shabbethai and Jozabad, of the chief of the Levites, *had* the oversight
of the outward business of the house of God.
17 And Mattaniah the son of Micha, the son of Zabdi, the son of Asaph, *was*
the principal to begin the thanksgiving in prayer: and Bakbukiah the second
among his brethren, and Abda the son of Shammua, the son of Galal, the son
of Jeduthun.
18 All the Levites in the holy city *were* two hundred fourscore and four.
19 Moreover the porters, Akkub, Talmon, and their brethren that kept the
gates, *were* an hundred seventy and two.

The Remainder Dwell in Other Cities

20 And the residue of Israel, of the priests, *and* the Levites, *were* in all the
cities of Judah, every one in his inheritance.
21 But the Nethinims dwelt in Ophel: and Ziha and Gispa *were* over the
Nethinims.

22 The overseer also of the Levites at Jerusalem *was* Uzzi the son of Bani, the
son of Hashabiah, the son of Mattaniah, the son of Micha. Of the sons of Asaph,
the singers *were* over the business of the house of God.
23 For *it was* the king's commandment concerning them, that a certain por-
tion should be for the singers, due for every day.
24 And Pethahiah the son of Meshezabeel, of the children of Zerah the son
of Judah, *was* at the king's hand in all matters concerning the people.
25 And for the villages, with their fields, *some* of the children of Judah dwelt
at Kirjath-arba, and *in* the villages thereof, and at Dibon, and *in* the villages
thereof, and at Jekabzeel, and *in* the villages thereof,
26 And at Jeshua, and at Moladah, and at Beth-phelet,
27 And at Hazar-shual, and at Beer-sheba, and *in* the villages thereof,
28 And at Ziklag, and at Mekonah, and in the villages thereof,
29 And at En-rimmon, and at Zareah, and at Jarmuth,
30 Zanoah, Adullam, and *in* their villages, at Lachish, and the fields thereof,
at Azekah, and *in* the villages thereof. And they dwelt from Beer-sheba unto
the valley of Hinnom.
31 The children also of Benjamin from Geba *dwelt* at Michmash, and Aija,
and Beth-el, and *in* their villages,
32 *And* at Anathoth, Nob, Ananiah,
33 Hazor, Ramah, Gittaim,
34 Hadid, Zeboim, Neballat,
35 Lod, and Ono, the valley of craftsmen.
36 And of the Levites *were* divisions *in* Judah, *and* in Benjamin.

The Priests

12 Now these *are* the priests and the Levites that went up with Zerubbabel
the son of Shealtiel, and Jeshua: Seraiah, Jeremiah, Ezra,
2 Amariah, Malluch, Hattush,
3 Shechaniah, Rehum, Meremoth,
4 Iddo, Ginnetho, Abijah,
5 Miamin, Maadiah, Bilgah,
6 Shemaiah, and Joiarib, Jedaiah,
7 Sallu, Amok, Hilkiah, Jedaiah. These *were* the chief of the priests and of
their brethren in the days of Jeshua.
8 Moreover the Levites: Jeshua, Binnui, Kadmiel, Sherebiah, Judah, *and*
Mattaniah, *which was* over the thanksgiving, he and his brethren.
9 Also Bakbukiah and Unni, their brethren, *were* over against them in the
watches.
10 And Jeshua begat Joiakim, Joiakim also begat Eliashib, and Eliashib begat
Joiada,
11 And Joiada begat Jonathan, and Jonathan begat Jaddua.
12 And in the days of Joiakim were priests, the chief of the fathers: of Seraiah,
Meraiah; of Jeremiah, Hananiah;
13 Of Ezra, Meshullam; of Amariah, Jehohanan;
14 Of Melicu, Jonathan; of Shebaniah, Joseph;
15 Of Harim, Adna; of Meraioth, Helkai;
16 Of Iddo, Zechariah; of Ginnethon, Meshullam;
17 Of Abijah, Zichri; of Miniamin, of Moadiah, Piltai;
18 Of Bilgah, Shammua; of Shemaiah, Jehonathan;
19 And of Joiarib, Mattenai; of Jedaiah, Uzzi;
20 Of Sallai, Kallai; of Amok, Eber;
21 Of Hilkiah, Hashabiah; of Jedaiah, Nethaneel.
22 The Levites in the days of Eliashib, Joiada, and Johanan, and Jaddua, *were*
recorded chief of the fathers: also the priests, to the reign of Darius the Persian.

23 The sons of Levi, the chief of the fathers, *were* written in the book of the
chronicles, even until the days of Johanan the son of Eliashib.
24 And the chief of the Levites: Hashabiah, Sherebiah, and Jeshua the son of
Kadmiel, with their brethren over against them, to praise *and* to give thanks,
according to the commandment of David the man of God, ward over against
ward.
25 Mattaniah, and Bakbukiah, Obadiah, Meshullam, Talmon, Akkub, *were*
porters keeping the ward at the thresholds of the gates.
26 These *were* in the days of Joiakim the son of Jeshua, the son of Jozadak,
and in the days of Nehemiah the governor, and of Ezra the priest, the scribe.

Jerusalem's Walls Are Dedicated to God

27 And at the dedication of the wall of Jerusalem they sought the Levites out
of all their places, to bring them to Jerusalem, to keep the dedication with
gladness, both with thanksgivings, and with singing, *with* cymbals, psalteries,
and with harps.
28 And the sons of the singers gathered themselves together, both out of the
plain country round about Jerusalem, and from the villages of Netophathi;
29 Also from the house of Gilgal, and out of the fields of Geba and Azmaveth:
for the singers had builded them villages round about Jerusalem.
30 And the priests and the Levites purified themselves, and purified the peo-
ple, and the gates, and the wall.
31 Then I brought up the princes of Judah upon the wall, and appointed two
great *companies of them that gave* thanks, *whereof one* went on the right hand
upon the wall toward the dung gate:
32 And after them went Hoshaiah, and half of the princes of Judah,
33 And Azariah, Ezra, and Meshullam,
34 Judah, and Benjamin, and Shemaiah, and Jeremiah,
35 And *certain* of the priests' sons with trumpets; *namely*, Zechariah the son
of Jonathan, the son of Shemaiah, the son of Mattaniah, the son of Michaiah,
the son of Zaccur, the son of Asaph:
36 And his brethren, Shemaiah, and Azarael, Milalai, Gilalai, Maai, Nethaneel,
and Judah, Hanani, with the musical instruments of David the man of God,
and Ezra the scribe before them.
37 And at the fountain gate, which was over against them, they went up by
the stairs of the city of David, at the going up of the wall, above the house of
David, even unto the water gate eastward.
38 And the other *company of them that gave* thanks went over against *them*,
and I after them, and the half of the people upon the wall, from beyond the
tower of the furnaces even unto the broad wall;
39 And from above the gate of Ephraim, and above the old gate, and above
the fish gate, and the tower of Hananeel, and the tower of Meah, even unto
the sheep gate: and they stood still in the prison gate.
40 So stood the two *companies of them that gave* thanks in the house of God,
and I, and the half of the rulers with me:
41 And the priests; Eliakim, Maaseiah, Miniamin, Michaiah, Elioenai,
Zechariah, *and* Hananiah, with trumpets;
42 And Maaseiah, and Shemaiah, and Eleazar, and Uzzi, and Jehohanan, and
Malchijah, and Elam, and Ezer. And the singers sang loud, with Jezrahiah *their*
overseer.
43 Also that day they offered great sacrifices, and rejoiced: for God had made
them rejoice with great joy: the wives also and the children rejoiced: so that
the joy of Jerusalem was heard even afar off.

The Duties of the Priests and Levites Appointed to Temple Service

44 And at that time were some appointed over the chambers for the treasures,
for the offerings, for the firstfruits, and for the tithes, to gather into them out

of the fields of the cities the portions of the law for the priests and Levites: for Judah rejoiced for the priests and for the Levites that waited.

45 And both the singers and the porters kept the ward of their God, and the ward of the purification, according to the commandment of David, *and* of Solomon his son.

46 For in the days of David and Asaph of old *there were* chief of the singers, and songs of praise and thanksgiving unto God.

47 And all Israel in the days of Zerubbabel, and in the days of Nehemiah, gave the portions of the singers and the porters, every day his portion: and they sanctified *holy things* unto the Levites; and the Levites sanctified *them* unto the children of Aaron.

The Israelites Are Separated from the Mixed Multitude

13 On that day they read in the book of Moses in the audience of the people; and therein was found written, that the Ammonite and the Moabite should not come into the congregation of God for ever;

2 Because they met not the children of Israel with bread and with water, but hired Balaam against them, that he should curse them: howbeit our God turned the curse into a blessing.

3 Now it came to pass, when they had heard the law, that they separated from Israel all the mixed multitude.

4 And before this, Eliashib the priest, having the oversight of the chamber of the house of our God, *was* allied unto Tobiah:

5 And he had prepared for him a great chamber, where aforetime they laid the meat offerings, the frankincense, and the vessels, and the tithes of the corn, the new wine, and the oil, which was commanded *to be given* to the Levites, and the singers, and the porters; and the offerings of the priests.

6 But in all this *time* was not I at Jerusalem: for in the two and thirtieth year of Artaxerxes king of Babylon came I unto the king, and after certain days obtained I leave of the king:

7 And I came to Jerusalem, and understood of the evil that Eliashib did for Tobiah, in preparing him a chamber in the courts of the house of God.

8 And it grieved me sore: therefore I cast forth all the household stuff of Tobiah out of the chamber.

9 Then I commanded, and they cleansed the chambers: and thither brought I again the vessels of the house of God, with the meat offering and the frankincense.

Nehemiah Ensures That the Levites Receive Their Portion

10 And I perceived that the portions of the Levites had not been given *them*: for the Levites and the singers, that did the work, were fled every one to his field.

11 Then contended I with the rulers, and said, Why is the house of God forsaken? And I gathered them together, and set them in their place.

12 Then brought all Judah the tithe of the corn and the new wine and the oil unto the treasuries.

13 And I made treasurers over the treasuries, Shelemiah the priest, and Zadok the scribe, and of the Levites, Pedaiah: and next to them *was* Hanan the son of Zaccur, the son of Mattaniah: for they were counted faithful, and their office *was* to distribute unto their brethren.

14 Remember me, O my God, concerning this, and wipe not out my good deeds that I have done for the house of my God, and for the offices thereof.

Nehemiah Ensures That No Work Is Done on the Sabbath

15 In those days saw I in Judah *some* treading wine presses on the sabbath, and bringing in sheaves, and lading asses; as also wine, grapes, and figs, and all *manner of* burdens, which they brought into Jerusalem on the sabbath day: and I testified *against them* in the day wherein they sold victuals.

16 There dwelt men of Tyre also therein, which brought fish, and all manner
of ware, and sold on the sabbath unto the children of Judah, and in Jerusalem.
17 Then I contended with the nobles of Judah, and said unto them, What evil
thing *is* this that ye do, and profane the sabbath day?
18 Did not your fathers thus, and did not our God bring all this evil upon us,
and upon this city? yet ye bring more wrath upon Israel by profaning the
sabbath.
19 And it came to pass, that when the gates of Jerusalem began to be dark
before the sabbath, I commanded that the gates should be shut, and charged
that they should not be opened till after the sabbath: and *some* of my servants
set I at the gates, *that* there should no burden be brought in on the sabbath day.
20 So the merchants and sellers of all kind of ware lodged without Jerusalem
once or twice.
21 Then I testified against them, and said unto them, Why lodge ye about the
wall? if ye do *so* again, I will lay hands on you. From that time forth came they
no *more* on the sabbath.
22 And I commanded the Levites that they should cleanse themselves, and
that they should come *and* keep the gates, to sanctify the sabbath day.
Remember me, O my God, *concerning* this also, and spare me according to
the greatness of thy mercy.

Nehemiah Dissolves Marriages to Foreigners

23 In those days also saw I Jews *that* had married wives of Ashdod, of Ammon,
and of Moab:
24 And their children spake half in the speech of Ashdod, and could not speak
in the Jews' language, but according to the language of each people.
25 And I contended with them, and cursed them, and smote certain of them,
and plucked off their hair, and made them swear by God, *saying*, Ye shall not
give your daughters unto their sons, nor take their daughters unto your sons,
or for yourselves.
26 Did not Solomon king of Israel sin by these things? yet among many
nations was there no king like him, who was beloved of his God, and God made
him king over all Israel: nevertheless even him did outlandish women cause
to sin.
27 Shall we then hearken unto you to do all this great evil, to transgress
against our God in marrying strange wives?
28 And *one* of the sons of Joiada, the son of Eliashib the high priest, *was* son
in law to Sanballat the Horonite: therefore I chased him from me.
29 Remember them, O my God, because they have defiled the priesthood,
and the covenant of the priesthood, and of the Levites.
30 Thus cleansed I them from all strangers, and appointed the wards of the
priests and the Levites, every one in his business;
31 And for the wood offering, at times appointed, and for the firstfruits.
Remember me, O my God, for good.

Esther

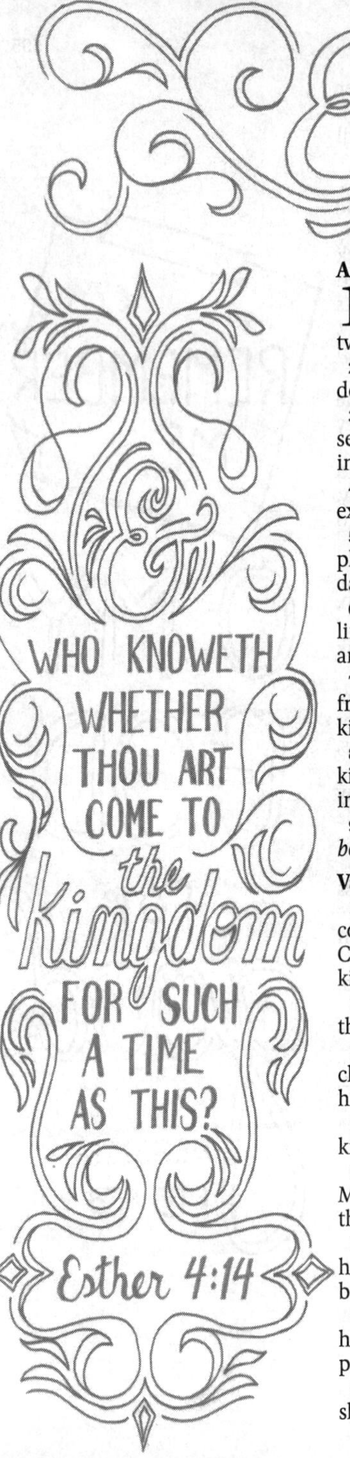

Ahasuerus Makes a Royal Feast

1 Now it came to pass in the days of Ahasuerus, (this *is* Ahasuerus which
reigned, from India even unto Ethiopia, *over* an hundred and seven and
twenty provinces:)
2 *That* in those days, when the king Ahasuerus sat on the throne of his king-
dom, which *was* in Shushan the palace,
3 In the third year of his reign, he made a feast unto all his princes and his
servants; the power of Persia and Media, the nobles and princes of the prov-
inces, *being* before him:
4 When he shewed the riches of his glorious kingdom and the honour of his
excellent majesty many days, *even* an hundred and fourscore days.
5 And when these days were expired, the king made a feast unto all the peo-
ple that were present in Shushan the palace, both unto great and small, seven
days, in the court of the garden of the king's palace;
6 *Where were* white, green, and blue, *hangings*, fastened with cords of fine
linen and purple to silver rings and pillars of marble: the beds *were of* gold
and silver, upon a pavement of red, and blue, and white, and black, marble.
7 And they gave *them* drink in vessels of gold, (the vessels being diverse one
from another,) and royal wine in abundance, according to the state of the
king.
8 And the drinking *was* according to the law; none did compel: for so the
king had appointed to all the officers of his house, that they should do accord-
ing to every man's pleasure.
9 Also Vashti the queen made a feast for the women *in* the royal house which
belonged to king Ahasuerus.

Vashti Disobeys the King's Command to Appear before Him

10 On the seventh day, when the heart of the king was merry with wine, he
commanded Mehuman, Biztha, Harbona, Bigtha, and Abagtha, Zethar, and
Carcas, the seven chamberlains that served in the presence of Ahasuerus the
king,
11 To bring Vashti the queen before the king with the crown royal, to shew
the people and the princes her beauty: for she *was* fair to look on.
12 But the queen Vashti refused to come at the king's commandment by *his*
chamberlains: therefore was the king very wroth, and his anger burned in
him.
13 Then the king said to the wise men, which knew the times, (for so *was* the
king's manner toward all that knew law and judgment:
14 And the next unto him *was* Carshena, Shethar, Admatha, Tarshish, Meres,
Marsena, *and* Memucan, the seven princes of Persia and Media, which saw
the king's face, *and* which sat the first in the kingdom;)
15 What shall we do unto the queen Vashti according to law, because she
hath not performed the commandment of the king Ahasuerus by the cham-
berlains?
16 And Memucan answered before the king and the princes, Vashti the queen
hath not done wrong to the king only, but also to all the princes, and to all the
people that *are* in all the provinces of the king Ahasuerus.
17 For *this* deed of the queen shall come abroad unto all women, so that they
shall despise their husbands in their eyes, when it shall be reported, The king

Ahasuerus commanded Vashti the queen to be brought in before him, but she
came not.
18 *Likewise* shall the ladies of Persia and Media say this day unto all the king's
princes, which have heard of the deed of the queen. Thus *shall there arise* too
much contempt and wrath.
19 If it please the king, let there go a royal commandment from him, and let
it be written among the laws of the Persians and the Medes, that it be not
altered, That Vashti come no more before king Ahasuerus; and let the king
give her royal estate unto another that is better than she.
20 And when the king's decree which he shall make shall be published
throughout all his empire, (for it is great,) all the wives shall give to their
husbands honour, both to great and small.
21 And the saying pleased the king and the princes; and the king did accord-
ing to the word of Memucan:
22 For he sent letters into all the king's provinces, into every province accord-
ing to the writing thereof, and to every people after their language, that every
man should bear rule in his own house, and that *it* should be published accord-
ing to the language of every people.

Esther Becomes Queen

2 After these things, when the wrath of king Ahasuerus was appeased, he
remembered Vashti, and what she had done, and what was decreed
against her.
2 Then said the king's servants that ministered unto him, Let there be fair
young virgins sought for the king:
3 And let the king appoint officers in all the provinces of his kingdom, that
they may gather together all the fair young virgins unto Shushan the palace,
to the house of the women, unto the custody of Hege the king's chamberlain,
keeper of the women; and let their things for purification be given *them*:
4 And let the maiden which pleaseth the king be queen instead of Vashti.
And the thing pleased the king; and he did so.
5 *Now* in Shushan the palace there was a certain Jew, whose name *was*
Mordecai, the son of Jair, the son of Shimei, the son of Kish, a Benjamite;
6 Who had been carried away from Jerusalem with the captivity which had
been carried away with Jeconiah king of Judah, whom Nebuchadnezzar the
king of Babylon had carried away.
7 And he brought up Hadassah, that *is*, Esther, his uncle's daughter: for she
had neither father nor mother, and the maid *was* fair and beautiful; whom
Mordecai, when her father and mother were dead, took for his own daughter.
8 So it came to pass, when the king's commandment and his decree was
heard, and when many maidens were gathered together unto Shushan the
palace, to the custody of Hegai, that Esther was brought also unto the king's
house, to the custody of Hegai, keeper of the women.
9 And the maiden pleased him, and she obtained kindness of him; and he
speedily gave her her things for purification, with such things as belonged to
her, and seven maidens, *which were* meet to be given her, out of the king's
house: and he preferred her and her maids unto the best *place* of the house
of the women.
10 Esther had not shewed her people nor her kindred: for Mordecai had
charged her that she should not shew *it*.
11 And Mordecai walked every day before the court of the women's house,
to know how Esther did, and what should become of her.
12 Now when every maid's turn was come to go in to king Ahasuerus, after
that she had been twelve months, according to the manner of the women, (for
so were the days of their purifications accomplished, *to wit*, six months with

oil of myrrh, and six months with sweet odours, and with *other* things for the
purifying of the women;)
13 Then thus came *every* maiden unto the king; whatsoever she desired was
given her to go with her out of the house of the women unto the king's house.
14 In the evening she went, and on the morrow she returned into the second
house of the women, to the custody of Shaashgaz, the king's chamberlain,
which kept the concubines: she came in unto the king no more, except the
king delighted in her, and that she were called by name.
15 Now when the turn of Esther, the daughter of Abihail the uncle of
Mordecai, who had taken her for his daughter, was come to go in unto the
king, she required nothing but what Hegai the king's chamberlain, the keep-
er of the women, appointed. And Esther obtained favour in the sight of all
them that looked upon her.
16 So Esther was taken unto king Ahasuerus into his house royal in the tenth
month, which *is* the month Tebeth, in the seventh year of his reign.
17 And the king loved Esther above all the women, and she obtained grace
and favour in his sight more than all the virgins; so that he set the royal crown
upon her head, and made her queen instead of Vashti.
18 Then the king made a great feast unto all his princes and his servants, *even*
Esther's feast; and he made a release to the provinces, and gave gifts, according
to the state of the king.
19 And when the virgins were gathered together the second time, then
Mordecai sat in the king's gate.
20 Esther had not *yet* shewed her kindred nor her people; as Mordecai had
charged her: for Esther did the commandment of Mordecai, like as when she
was brought up with him.

Mordecai's Loyalty Is Recorded in the Official Chronicles

21 In those days, while Mordecai sat in the king's gate, two of the king's cham-
berlains, Bigthan and Teresh, of those which kept the door, were wroth, and
sought to lay hand on the king Ahasuerus.
22 And the thing was known to Mordecai, who told *it* unto Esther the queen;
and Esther certified the king *thereof* in Mordecai's name.
23 And when inquisition was made of the matter, it was found out; therefore
they were both hanged on a tree: and it was written in the book of the chron-
icles before the king.

Mordecai Refuses to Bow to Haman

3 After these things did king Ahasuerus promote Haman the son of
Hammedatha the Agagite, and advanced him, and set his seat above all the
princes that *were* with him.
2 And all the king's servants, that *were* in the king's gate, bowed, and rever-
enced Haman: for the king had so commanded concerning him. But Mordecai
bowed not, nor did *him* reverence.
3 Then the king's servants, which *were* in the king's gate, said unto Mordecai,
Why transgressest thou the king's commandment?
4 Now it came to pass, when they spake daily unto him, and he hearkened
not unto them, that they told Haman, to see whether Mordecai's matters would
stand: for he had told them that he *was* a Jew.
5 And when Haman saw that Mordecai bowed not, nor did him reverence,
then was Haman full of wrath.
6 And he thought scorn to lay hands on Mordecai alone; for they had shewed
him the people of Mordecai: wherefore Haman sought to destroy all the Jews
that *were* throughout the whole kingdom of Ahasuerus, *even* the people of
Mordecai.

Haman's Plot against the Jews

7 In the first month, that *is*, the month Nisan, in the twelfth year of king Ahasuerus, they cast Pur, that *is*, the lot, before Haman from day to day, and from month to month, *to* the twelfth *month*, that *is*, the month Adar.

8 And Haman said unto king Ahasuerus, There is a certain people scattered abroad and dispersed among the people in all the provinces of thy kingdom; and their laws *are* diverse from all people; neither keep they the king's laws: therefore it *is* not for the king's profit to suffer them.

9 If it please the king, let it be written that they may be destroyed: and I will pay ten thousand talents of silver to the hands of those that have the charge of the business, to bring *it* into the king's treasuries.

10 And the king took his ring from his hand, and gave it unto Haman the son of Hammedatha the Agagite, the Jews' enemy.

11 And the king said unto Haman, The silver *is* given to thee, the people also, to do with them as it seemeth good to thee.

12 Then were the king's scribes called on the thirteenth day of the first month, and there was written according to all that Haman had commanded unto the king's lieutenants, and to the governors that *were* over every province, and to the rulers of every people of every province according to the writing thereof, and *to* every people after their language; in the name of king Ahasuerus was it written, and sealed with the king's ring.

13 And the letters were sent by posts into all the king's provinces, to destroy, to kill, and to cause to perish, all Jews, both young and old, little children and women, in one day, *even* upon the thirteenth *day* of the twelfth month, which is the month Adar, and *to take* the spoil of them for a prey.

14 The copy of the writing for a commandment to be given in every province was published unto all people, that they should be ready against that day.

15 The posts went out, being hastened by the king's commandment, and the decree was given in Shushan the palace. And the king and Haman sat down to drink; but the city Shushan was perplexed.

The Great Mourning of Mordecai and the Jews

4 When Mordecai perceived all that was done, Mordecai rent his clothes, and put on sackcloth with ashes, and went out into the midst of the city, and cried with a loud and a bitter cry;

2 And came even before the king's gate: for none *might* enter into the king's gate clothed with sackcloth.

3 And in every province, whithersoever the king's commandment and his decree came, *there was* great mourning among the Jews, and fasting, and weeping, and wailing; and many lay in sackcloth and ashes.

4 So Esther's maids and her chamberlains came and told *it* her. Then was the queen exceedingly grieved; and she sent raiment to clothe Mordecai, and to take away his sackcloth from him: but he received *it* not.

5 Then called Esther for Hatach, *one* of the king's chamberlains, whom he had appointed to attend upon her, and gave him a commandment to Mordecai, to know what it *was*, and why it *was*.

6 So Hatach went forth to Mordecai unto the street of the city, which *was* before the king's gate.

7 And Mordecai told him of all that had happened unto him, and of the sum of the money that Haman had promised to pay to the king's treasuries for the Jews, to destroy them.

8 Also he gave him the copy of the writing of the decree that was given at Shushan to destroy them, to shew *it* unto Esther, and to declare *it* unto her, and to charge her that she should go in unto the king, to make supplication unto him, and to make request before him for her people.

9 And Hatach came and told Esther the words of Mordecai.

10 Again Esther spake unto Hatach, and gave him commandment unto
Mordecai;
11 All the king's servants, and the people of the king's provinces, do know,
that whosoever, whether man or woman, shall come unto the king into the
inner court, who is not called, *there is* one law of his to put *him* to death, except
such to whom the king shall hold out the golden sceptre, that he may live: but
I have not been called to come in unto the king these thirty days.
12 And they told to Mordecai Esther's words.
13 Then Mordecai commanded to answer Esther, Think not with thyself that
thou shalt escape in the king's house, more than all the Jews.
14 For if thou altogether holdest thy peace at this time, *then* shall there
enlargement and deliverance arise to the Jews from another place; but thou
and thy father's house shall be destroyed: and who knoweth whether thou art
come to the kingdom for *such* a time as this?
15 Then Esther bade *them* return Mordecai *this answer*,
16 Go, gather together all the Jews that are present in Shushan, and fast ye
for me, and neither eat nor drink three days, night or day: I also and my maid-
ens will fast likewise; and so will I go in unto the king, which *is* not according
to the law: and if I perish, I perish.
17 So Mordecai went his way, and did according to all that Esther had com-
manded him.

Esther Risks the King's Disfavor to Bring Her Request to Him

5 Now it came to pass on the third day, that Esther put on *her* royal *apparel*,
and stood in the inner court of the king's house, over against the king's
house: and the king sat upon his royal throne in the royal house, over against
the gate of the house.
2 And it was so, when the king saw Esther the queen standing in the court,
that she obtained favour in his sight: and the king held out to Esther the gold-
en sceptre that *was* in his hand. So Esther drew near, and touched the top of
the sceptre.
3 Then said the king unto her, What wilt thou, queen Esther? and what *is*
thy request? it shall be even given thee to the half of the kingdom.
4 And Esther answered, If *it seem* good unto the king, let the king and Haman
come this day unto the banquet that I have prepared for him.
5 Then the king said, Cause Haman to make haste, that he may do as Esther
hath said. So the king and Haman came to the banquet that Esther had pre-
pared.
6 And the king said unto Esther at the banquet of wine, What *is* thy petition?
and it shall be granted thee: and what *is* thy request? even to the half of the
kingdom it shall be performed.
7 Then answered Esther, and said, My petition and my request *is*;
8 If I have found favour in the sight of the king, and if it please the king to
grant my petition, and to perform my request, let the king and Haman come
to the banquet that I shall prepare for them, and I will do to morrow as the
king hath said.

Haman Is Disgraced Because of Mordecai

9 Then went Haman forth that day joyful and with a glad heart: but when
Haman saw Mordecai in the king's gate, that he stood not up, nor moved for
him, he was full of indignation against Mordecai.
10 Nevertheless Haman refrained himself: and when he came home, he sent
and called for his friends, and Zeresh his wife.
11 And Haman told them of the glory of his riches, and the multitude of his
children, and all *the things* wherein the king had promoted him, and how he
had advanced him above the princes and servants of the king.

12 Haman said moreover, Yea, Esther the queen did let no man come in with
the king unto the banquet that she had prepared but myself; and to morrow
am I invited unto her also with the king.
13 Yet all this availeth me nothing, so long as I see Mordecai the Jew sitting
at the king's gate.
14 Then said Zeresh his wife and all his friends unto him, Let a gallows be
made of fifty cubits high, and to morrow speak thou unto the king that
Mordecai may be hanged thereon: then go thou in merrily with the king unto
the banquet. And the thing pleased Haman; and he caused the gallows to be
made.

Ahasuerus Reads of Mordecai's Good Service

6 On that night could not the king sleep, and he commanded to bring the
book of records of the chronicles; and they were read before the king.
2 And it was found written, that Mordecai had told of Bigthana and Teresh,
two of the king's chamberlains, the keepers of the door, who sought to lay
hand on the king Ahasuerus.
3 And the king said, What honour and dignity hath been done to Mordecai
for this? Then said the king's servants that ministered unto him, There is noth-
ing done for him.

Haman Unwittingly Gives Counsel on How to Honor Mordecai

4 And the king said, Who *is* in the court? Now Haman was come into the
outward court of the king's house, to speak unto the king to hang Mordecai
on the gallows that he had prepared for him.
5 And the king's servants said unto him, Behold, Haman standeth in the
court. And the king said, Let him come in.
6 So Haman came in. And the king said unto him, What shall be done unto
the man whom the king delighteth to honour? Now Haman thought in his
heart, To whom would the king delight to do honour more than to myself?
7 And Haman answered the king, For the man whom the king delighteth to
honour,
8 Let the royal apparel be brought which the king *useth* to wear, and the
horse that the king rideth upon, and the crown royal which is set upon his
head:
9 And let this apparel and horse be delivered to the hand of one of the king's
most noble princes, that they may array the man *withal* whom the king
delighteth to honour, and bring him on horseback through the street of the
city, and proclaim before him, Thus shall it be done to the man whom the king
delighteth to honour.
10 Then the king said to Haman, Make haste, *and* take the apparel and the
horse, as thou hast said, and do even so to Mordecai the Jew, that sitteth at the
king's gate: let nothing fail of all that thou hast spoken.
11 Then took Haman the apparel and the horse, and arrayed Mordecai, and
brought him on horseback through the street of the city, and proclaimed
before him, Thus shall it be done unto the man whom the king delighteth to
honour.

Haman Is Warned about Going against Mordecai

12 And Mordecai came again to the king's gate. But Haman hasted to his
house mourning, and having his head covered.
13 And Haman told Zeresh his wife and all his friends every *thing* that had
befallen him. Then said his wise men and Zeresh his wife unto him, If Mordecai
be of the seed of the Jews, before whom thou hast begun to fall, thou shalt not
prevail against him, but shalt surely fall before him.
14 And while they *were* yet talking with him, came the king's chamberlains,
and hasted to bring Haman unto the banquet that Esther had prepared.

Esther Pleads for Her Own Life and the Lives of Her People

7 So the king and Haman came to banquet with Esther the queen.
2 And the king said again unto Esther on the second day at the banquet
of wine, What *is* thy petition, queen Esther? and it shall be granted thee: and
what *is* thy request? and it shall be performed, *even* to the half of the kingdom.
3 Then Esther the queen answered and said, If I have found favour in thy
sight, O king, and if it please the king, let my life be given me at my petition,
and my people at my request:
4 For we are sold, I and my people, to be destroyed, to be slain, and to perish.
But if we had been sold for bondmen and bondwomen, I had held my tongue,
although the enemy could not countervail the king's damage.
5 Then the king Ahasuerus answered and said unto Esther the queen, Who
is he, and where is he, that durst presume in his heart to do so?
6 And Esther said, The adversary and enemy *is* this wicked Haman. Then
Haman was afraid before the king and the queen.

Haman Is Hanged upon the Gallows He Built for Mordecai

7 And the king arising from the banquet of wine in his wrath *went* into the
palace garden: and Haman stood up to make request for his life to Esther the
queen; for he saw that there was evil determined against him by the king.
8 Then the king returned out of the palace garden into the place of the banquet
of wine; and Haman was fallen upon the bed whereon Esther *was*. Then
said the king, Will he force the queen also before me in the house? As the word
went out of the king's mouth, they covered Haman's face.
9 And Harbonah, one of the chamberlains, said before the king, Behold also,
the gallows fifty cubits high, which Haman had made for Mordecai, who had
spoken good for the king, standeth in the house of Haman. Then the king said,
Hang him thereon.
10 So they hanged Haman on the gallows that he had prepared for Mordecai.
Then was the king's wrath pacified.

Mordecai Is Promoted

8 On that day did the king Ahasuerus give the house of Haman the Jews' enemy
unto Esther the queen. And Mordecai came before the king; for Esther had
told what he *was* unto her.
2 And the king took off his ring, which he had taken from Haman, and gave
it unto Mordecai. And Esther set Mordecai over the house of Haman.

Esther Makes a Plea to Reverse Haman's Letters

3 And Esther spake yet again before the king, and fell down at his feet, and
besought him with tears to put away the mischief of Haman the Agagite, and
his device that he had devised against the Jews.
4 Then the king held out the golden sceptre toward Esther. So Esther arose,
and stood before the king,
5 And said, If it please the king, and if I have found favour in his sight, and
the thing *seem* right before the king, and I *be* pleasing in his eyes, let it be
written to reverse the letters devised by Haman the son of Hammedatha the
Agagite, which he wrote to destroy the Jews which *are* in all the king's provinces:
6 For how can I endure to see the evil that shall come unto my people? or
how can I endure to see the destruction of my kindred?
7 Then the king Ahasuerus said unto Esther the queen and to Mordecai the
Jew, Behold, I have given Esther the house of Haman, and him they have
hanged upon the gallows, because he laid his hand upon the Jews.
8 Write ye also for the Jews, as it liketh you, in the king's name, and seal *it*
with the king's ring: for the writing which is written in the king's name, and
sealed with the king's ring, may no man reverse.
9 Then were the king's scribes called at that time in the third month, that *is*,
the month Sivan, on the three and twentieth *day* thereof; and it was written

according to all that Mordecai commanded unto the Jews, and to the lieuten-
ants, and the deputies and rulers of the provinces which *are* from India unto
Ethiopia, an hundred twenty and seven provinces, unto every province accord-
ing to the writing thereof, and unto every people after their language, and to
the Jews according to their writing, and according to their language.
10 And he wrote in the king Ahasuerus' name, and sealed *it* with the king's
ring, and sent letters by posts on horseback, *and* riders on mules, camels, *and*
young dromedaries:
11 Wherein the king granted the Jews which *were* in every city to gather
themselves together, and to stand for their life, to destroy, to slay, and to cause
to perish, all the power of the people and province that would assault them,
both little ones and women, and *to take* the spoil of them for a prey,
12 Upon one day in all the provinces of king Ahasuerus, *namely*, upon the
thirteenth *day* of the twelfth month, which *is* the month Adar.
13 The copy of the writing for a commandment to be given in every province
was published unto all people, and that the Jews should be ready against that
day to avenge themselves on their enemies.
14 *So* the posts that rode upon mules *and* camels went out, being hastened
and pressed on by the king's commandment. And the decree was given at
Shushan the palace.

Mordecai's Honor and the Joy of the Jews

15 And Mordecai went out from the presence of the king in royal apparel of
blue and white, and with a great crown of gold, and with a garment of fine
linen and purple: and the city of Shushan rejoiced and was glad.
16 The Jews had light, and gladness, and joy, and honour.
17 And in every province, and in every city, whithersoever the king's com-
mandment and his decree came, the Jews had joy and gladness, a feast and a
good day. And many of the people of the land became Jews; for the fear of the
Jews fell upon them.

The Jews Defend Themselves and Slay Their Enemies

9 Now in the twelfth month, that *is*, the month Adar, on the thirteenth day
of the same, when the king's commandment and his decree drew near to
be put in execution, in the day that the enemies of the Jews hoped to have power
over them, (though it was turned to the contrary, that the Jews had rule over
them that hated them;)
2 The Jews gathered themselves together in their cities throughout all the
provinces of the king Ahasuerus, to lay hand on such as sought their hurt: and
no man could withstand them; for the fear of them fell upon all people.
3 And all the rulers of the provinces, and the lieutenants, and the deputies,
and officers of the king, helped the Jews; because the fear of Mordecai fell
upon them.
4 For Mordecai *was* great in the king's house, and his fame went out through-
out all the provinces: for this man Mordecai waxed greater and greater.
5 Thus the Jews smote all their enemies with the stroke of the sword, and
slaughter, and destruction, and did what they would unto those that hated
them.
6 And in Shushan the palace the Jews slew and destroyed five hundred men.
7 And Parshandatha, and Dalphon, and Aspatha,
8 And Poratha, and Adalia, and Aridatha,
9 And Parmashta, and Arisai, and Aridai, and Vajezatha,
10 The ten sons of Haman the son of Hammedatha, the enemy of the Jews,
slew they; but on the spoil laid they not their hand.
11 On that day the number of those that were slain in Shushan the palace
was brought before the king.

12 And the king said unto Esther the queen, The Jews have slain and destroyed
five hundred men in Shushan the palace, and the ten sons of Haman; what
have they done in the rest of the king's provinces? now what *is* thy petition?
and it shall be granted thee: or what *is* thy request further? and it shall be
done.
13 Then said Esther, If it please the king, let it be granted to the Jews which
are in Shushan to do to morrow also according unto this day's decree, and let
Haman's ten sons be hanged upon the gallows.
14 And the king commanded it so to be done: and the decree was given at
Shushan; and they hanged Haman's ten sons.
15 For the Jews that *were* in Shushan gathered themselves together on the
fourteenth day also of the month Adar, and slew three hundred men at
Shushan; but on the prey they laid not their hand.
16 But the other Jews that *were* in the king's provinces gathered themselves
together, and stood for their lives, and had rest from their enemies, and slew
of their foes seventy and five thousand, but they laid not their hands on the
prey,
17 On the thirteenth day of the month Adar; and on the fourteenth day of
the same rested they, and made it a day of feasting and gladness.
18 But the Jews that *were* at Shushan assembled together on the thirteenth
day thereof, and on the fourteenth thereof; and on the fifteenth *day* of the
same they rested, and made it a day of feasting and gladness.
19 Therefore the Jews of the villages, that dwelt in the unwalled towns, made
the fourteenth day of the month Adar *a day of* gladness and feasting, and a
good day, and of sending portions one to another.

Mordecai and Esther Institute the Festival of Purim

20 And Mordecai wrote these things, and sent letters unto all the Jews that
were in all the provinces of the king Ahasuerus, *both* nigh and far,
21 To stablish *this* among them, that they should keep the fourteenth day of
the month Adar, and the fifteenth day of the same, yearly,
22 As the days wherein the Jews rested from their enemies, and the month
which was turned unto them from sorrow to joy, and from mourning into a
good day: that they should make them days of feasting and joy, and of sending
portions one to another, and gifts to the poor.
23 And the Jews undertook to do as they had begun, and as Mordecai had
written unto them;
24 Because Haman the son of Hammedatha, the Agagite, the enemy of all
the Jews, had devised against the Jews to destroy them, and had cast Pur, that
is, the lot, to consume them, and to destroy them;
25 But when *Esther* came before the king, he commanded by letters that his
wicked device, which he devised against the Jews, should return upon his own
head, and that he and his sons should be hanged on the gallows.
26 Wherefore they called these days Purim after the name of Pur. Therefore
for all the words of this letter, and *of that* which they had seen concerning
this matter, and which had come unto them,
27 The Jews ordained, and took upon them, and upon their seed, and upon
all such as joined themselves unto them, so as it should not fail, that they would
keep these two days according to their writing, and according to their *appoint-
ed* time every year;
28 And *that* these days *should be* remembered and kept throughout every
generation, every family, every province, and every city; and *that* these days
of Purim should not fail from among the Jews, nor the memorial of them
perish from their seed.
29 Then Esther the queen, the daughter of Abihail, and Mordecai the Jew,
wrote with all authority, to confirm this second letter of Purim.

30 And he sent the letters unto all the Jews, to the hundred twenty and seven
provinces of the kingdom of Ahasuerus, *with* words of peace and truth,
31 To confirm these days of Purim in their times *appointed*, according as
Mordecai the Jew and Esther the queen had enjoined them, and as they had
decreed for themselves and for their seed, the matters of the fastings and their
cry.
32 And the decree of Esther confirmed these matters of Purim; and it was
written in the book.

Mordecai's Greatness

10 And the king Ahasuerus laid a tribute upon the land, and *upon* the isles
of the sea.
2 And all the acts of his power and of his might, and the declaration of the
greatness of Mordecai, whereunto the king advanced him, *are* they not writ-
ten in the book of the chronicles of the kings of Media and Persia?
3 For Mordecai the Jew *was* next unto king Ahasuerus, and great among the
Jews, and accepted of the multitude of his brethren, seeking the wealth of his
people, and speaking peace to all his seed.

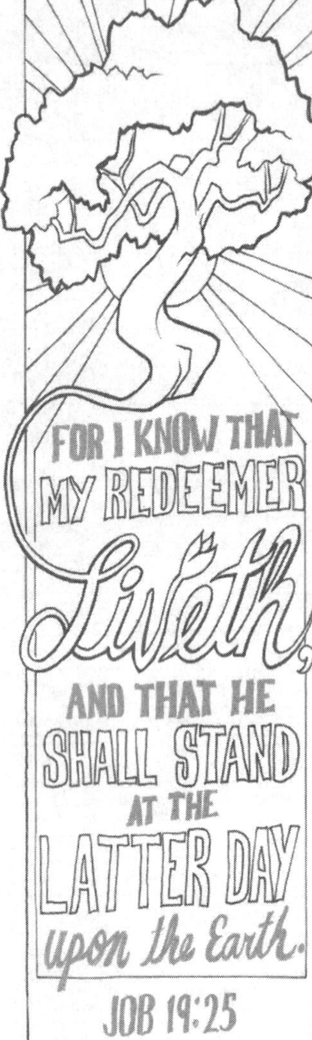

Job's Life, Family, and Faith

1 There was a man in the land of Uz, whose name *was* Job; and that man was
perfect and upright, and one that feared God, and eschewed evil.
2 And there were born unto him seven sons and three daughters.
3 His substance also was seven thousand sheep, and three thousand camels,
and five hundred yoke of oxen, and five hundred she asses, and a very great
household; so that this man was the greatest of all the men of the east.
4 And his sons went and feasted *in their* houses, every one his day; and sent
and called for their three sisters to eat and to drink with them.
5 And it was so, when the days of *their* feasting were gone about, that Job
sent and sanctified them, and rose up early in the morning, and offered burnt
offerings *according* to the number of them all: for Job said, It may be that my
sons have sinned, and cursed God in their hearts. Thus did Job continually.

Satan Asks to Test Job

6 Now there was a day when the sons of God came to present themselves
before the LORD, and Satan came also among them.
7 And the LORD said unto Satan, Whence comest thou? Then Satan answered
the LORD, and said, From going to and fro in the earth, and from walking up
and down in it.
8 And the LORD said unto Satan, Hast thou considered my servant Job, that
there is none like him in the earth, a perfect and an upright man, one that
feareth God, and escheweth evil?
9 Then Satan answered the LORD, and said, Doth Job fear God for nought?
10 Hast not thou made an hedge about him, and about his house, and about
all that he hath on every side? thou hast blessed the work of his hands, and
his substance is increased in the land.
11 But put forth thine hand now, and touch all that he hath, and he will curse
thee to thy face.
12 And the LORD said unto Satan, Behold, all that he hath *is* in thy power; only
upon himself put not forth thine hand. So Satan went forth from the presence
of the LORD.

Job Loses His Family and Wealth

13 And there was a day when his sons and his daughters *were* eating and
drinking wine in their eldest brother's house:
14 And there came a messenger unto Job, and said, The oxen were plowing,
and the asses feeding beside them:
15 And the Sabeans fell *upon them*, and took them away; yea, they have slain
the servants with the edge of the sword; and I only am escaped alone to tell
thee.
16 While he *was* yet speaking, there came also another, and said, The fire of
God is fallen from heaven, and hath burned up the sheep, and the servants,
and consumed them; and I only am escaped alone to tell thee.
17 While he *was* yet speaking, there came also another, and said, The
Chaldeans made out three bands, and fell upon the camels, and have carried
them away, yea, and slain the servants with the edge of the sword; and I only
am escaped alone to tell thee.

18 While he *was* yet speaking, there came also another, and said, Thy sons
and thy daughters *were* eating and drinking wine in their eldest brother's
house:
19 And, behold, there came a great wind from the wilderness, and smote the
four corners of the house, and it fell upon the young men, and they are dead;
and I only am escaped alone to tell thee.
20 Then Job arose, and rent his mantle, and shaved his head, and fell down
upon the ground, and worshipped,
21 And said, Naked came I out of my mother's womb, and naked shall I return
thither: the LORD gave, and the LORD hath taken away; blessed be the name of
the LORD.
22 In all this Job sinned not, nor charged God foolishly.

Satan Asks to Test Job Further

2 Again there was a day when the sons of God came to present themselves
before the LORD, and Satan came also among them to present himself before
the LORD.
2 And the LORD said unto Satan, From whence comest thou? And Satan
answered the LORD, and said, From going to and fro in the earth, and from
walking up and down in it.
3 And the LORD said unto Satan, Hast thou considered my servant Job, that
there is none like him in the earth, a perfect and an upright man, one that
feareth God, and escheweth evil? and still he holdeth fast his integrity,
although thou movedst me against him, to destroy him without cause.
4 And Satan answered the LORD, and said, Skin for skin, yea, all that a man
hath will he give for his life.
5 But put forth thine hand now, and touch his bone and his flesh, and he will
curse thee to thy face.
6 And the LORD said unto Satan, Behold, he *is* in thine hand; but save his life.

Job Loses His Health

7 So went Satan forth from the presence of the LORD, and smote Job with
sore boils from the sole of his foot unto his crown.
8 And he took him a potsherd to scrape himself withal; and he sat down
among the ashes.
9 Then said his wife unto him, Dost thou still retain thine integrity? curse
God, and die.
10 But he said unto her, Thou speakest as one of the foolish women speaketh.
What? shall we receive good at the hand of God, and shall we not receive evil?
In all this did not Job sin with his lips.

Three Friends Mourn with Him in Silence

11 Now when Job's three friends heard of all this evil that was come upon
him, they came every one from his own place; Eliphaz the Temanite, and Bildad
the Shuhite, and Zophar the Naamathite: for they had made an appointment
together to come to mourn with him and to comfort him.
12 And when they lifted up their eyes afar off, and knew him not, they lifted
up their voice, and wept; and they rent every one his mantle, and sprinkled
dust upon their heads toward heaven.
13 So they sat down with him upon the ground seven days and seven nights,
and none spake a word unto him: for they saw that *his* grief was very great.

Job Curses the Day He Was Born

3 After this opened Job his mouth, and cursed his day.
2 And Job spake, and said,
3 Let the day perish wherein I was born, and the night *in which* it was said,
There is a man child conceived.

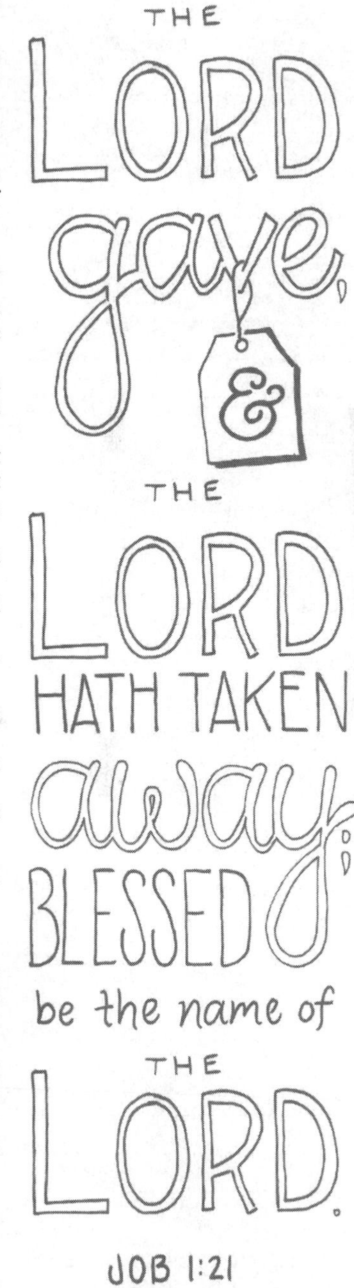

4 Let that day be darkness; let not God regard it from above, neither let the
light shine upon it.
5 Let darkness and the shadow of death stain it; let a cloud dwell upon it; let
the blackness of the day terrify it.
6 *As for* that night, let darkness seize upon it; let it not be joined unto the
days of the year, let it not come into the number of the months.
7 Lo, let that night be solitary, let no joyful voice come therein.
8 Let them curse it that curse the day, who are ready to raise up their mourn-
ing.
9 Let the stars of the twilight thereof be dark; let it look for light, but *have*
none; neither let it see the dawning of the day:
10 Because it shut not up the doors of my *mother's* womb, nor hid sorrow
from mine eyes.
11 Why died I not from the womb? *why* did I *not* give up the ghost when I
came out of the belly?
12 Why did the knees prevent me? or why the breasts that I should suck?
13 For now should I have lain still and been quiet, I should have slept: then
had I been at rest,
14 With kings and counsellors of the earth, which built desolate places for
themselves;
15 Or with princes that had gold, who filled their houses with silver:
16 Or as an hidden untimely birth I had not been; as infants *which* never saw
light.
17 There the wicked cease *from* troubling; and there the weary be at rest.
18 *There* the prisoners rest together; they hear not the voice of the oppressor.
19 The small and great are there; and the servant *is* free from his master.

Job: Why Live a Life of Anguish?

20 Wherefore is light given to him that is in misery, and life unto the bitter
in soul;
21 Which long for death, but it *cometh* not; and dig for it more than for hid
treasures;
22 Which rejoice exceedingly, *and* are glad, when they can find the grave?
23 *Why is light given* to a man whose way is hid, and whom God hath hedged
in?
24 For my sighing cometh before I eat, and my roarings are poured out like
the waters.
25 For the thing which I greatly feared is come upon me, and that which I
was afraid of is come unto me.
26 I was not in safety, neither had I rest, neither was I quiet; yet trouble came.

Eliphaz Tells Job to Be Patient

4 Then Eliphaz the Temanite answered and said,
2 *If* we assay to commune with thee, wilt thou be grieved? but who can
withhold himself from speaking?
3 Behold, thou hast instructed many, and thou hast strengthened the weak
hands.
4 Thy words have upholden him that was falling, and thou hast strengthened
the feeble knees.
5 But now it is come upon thee, and thou faintest; it toucheth thee, and thou
art troubled.
6 *Is* not *this* thy fear, thy confidence, thy hope, and the uprightness of thy
ways?

Eliphaz: Only Evil People Suffer

7 Remember, I pray thee, who *ever* perished, being innocent? or where were
the righteous cut off?

8 Even as I have seen, they that plow iniquity, and sow wickedness, reap the
same.
9 By the blast of God they perish, and by the breath of his nostrils are they
consumed.
10 The roaring of the lion, and the voice of the fierce lion, and the teeth of
the young lions, are broken.
11 The old lion perisheth for lack of prey, and the stout lion's whelps are
scattered abroad.

Eliphaz: Purity before God Is Impossible

12 Now a thing was secretly brought to me, and mine ear received a little
thereof.
13 In thoughts from the visions of the night, when deep sleep falleth on men,
14 Fear came upon me, and trembling, which made all my bones to shake.
15 Then a spirit passed before my face; the hair of my flesh stood up:
16 It stood still, but I could not discern the form thereof: an image *was* before
mine eyes, *there was* silence, and I heard a voice, *saying*,
17 Shall mortal man be more just than God? shall a man be more pure than
his maker?
18 Behold, he put no trust in his servants; and his angels he charged with
folly:
19 How much less *in* them that dwell in houses of clay, whose foundation *is*
in the dust, *which* are crushed before the moth?
20 They are destroyed from morning to evening: they perish for ever with-
out any regarding *it*.
21 Doth not their excellency *which is* in them go away? they die, even without
wisdom.

Eliphaz: Seek God's Help

5 Call now, if there be any that will answer thee; and to which of the saints
wilt thou turn?
2 For wrath killeth the foolish man, and envy slayeth the silly one.
3 I have seen the foolish taking root: but suddenly I cursed his habitation.
4 His children are far from safety, and they are crushed in the gate, neither
is there any to deliver *them*.
5 Whose harvest the hungry eateth up, and taketh it even out of the thorns,
and the robber swalloweth up their substance.
6 Although affliction cometh not forth of the dust, neither doth trouble
spring out of the ground;
7 Yet man is born unto trouble, as the sparks fly upward.
8 I would seek unto God, and unto God would I commit my cause:
9 Which doeth great things and unsearchable; marvellous things without
number:
10 Who giveth rain upon the earth, and sendeth waters upon the fields:
11 To set up on high those that be low; that those which mourn may be exalt-
ed to safety.
12 He disappointeth the devices of the crafty, so that their hands cannot
perform *their* enterprise.
13 He taketh the wise in their own craftiness: and the counsel of the froward
is carried headlong.
14 They meet with darkness in the daytime, and grope in the noonday as in
the night.
15 But he saveth the poor from the sword, from their mouth, and from the
hand of the mighty.
16 So the poor hath hope, and iniquity stoppeth her mouth.

Eliphaz: The Blessing of God's Correction

17 Behold, happy *is* the man whom God correcteth: therefore despise not thou the chastening of the Almighty:

18 For he maketh sore, and bindeth up: he woundeth, and his hands make whole.

19 He shall deliver thee in six troubles: yea, in seven there shall no evil touch thee.

20 In famine he shall redeem thee from death: and in war from the power of the sword.

21 Thou shalt be hid from the scourge of the tongue: neither shalt thou be afraid of destruction when it cometh.

22 At destruction and famine thou shalt laugh: neither shalt thou be afraid of the beasts of the earth.

23 For thou shalt be in league with the stones of the field: and the beasts of the field shall be at peace with thee.

24 And thou shalt know that thy tabernacle *shall be* in peace; and thou shalt visit thy habitation, and shalt not sin.

25 Thou shalt know also that thy seed *shall be* great, and thine offspring as the grass of the earth.

26 Thou shalt come to *thy* grave in a full age, like as a shock of corn cometh in in his season.

27 Lo this, we have searched it, so it *is*; hear it, and know thou *it* for thy good.

Job: God Has Attacked Me without Cause

6 But Job answered and said,
2 Oh that my grief were throughly weighed, and my calamity laid in the balances together!

3 For now it would be heavier than the sand of the sea: therefore my words are swallowed up.

4 For the arrows of the Almighty *are* within me, the poison whereof drinketh up my spirit: the terrors of God do set themselves in array against me.

5 Doth the wild ass bray when he hath grass? or loweth the ox over his fodder?

6 Can that which is unsavoury be eaten without salt? or is there *any* taste in the white of an egg?

7 The things *that* my soul refused to touch *are* as my sorrowful meat.

Job: I Desire the Comfort of Death

8 Oh that I might have my request; and that God would grant *me* the thing that I long for!

9 Even that it would please God to destroy me; that he would let loose his hand, and cut me off!

10 Then should I yet have comfort; yea, I would harden myself in sorrow: let him not spare; for I have not concealed the words of the Holy One.

11 What *is* my strength, that I should hope? and what *is* mine end, that I should prolong my life?

12 *Is* my strength the strength of stones? or *is* my flesh of brass?

13 *Is* not my help in me? and is wisdom driven quite from me?

Job: You Are Treating Me Unkindly

14 To him that is afflicted pity *should be shewed* from his friend; but he forsaketh the fear of the Almighty.

15 My brethren have dealt deceitfully as a brook, *and* as the stream of brooks they pass away;

16 Which are blackish by reason of the ice, *and* wherein the snow is hid:

17 What time they wax warm, they vanish: when it is hot, they are consumed out of their place.

18 The paths of their way are turned aside; they go to nothing, and perish.

19 The troops of Tema looked, the companies of Sheba waited for them.
20 They were confounded because they had hoped; they came thither, and
were ashamed.
21 For now ye are nothing; ye see *my* casting down, and are afraid.
22 Did I say, Bring unto me? or, Give a reward for me of your substance?
23 Or, Deliver me from the enemy's hand? or, Redeem me from the hand of
the mighty?
24 Teach me, and I will hold my tongue: and cause me to understand where-
in I have erred.
25 How forcible are right words! but what doth your arguing reprove?
26 Do ye imagine to reprove words, and the speeches of one that is desperate,
which are as wind?
27 Yea, ye overwhelm the fatherless, and ye dig *a pit* for your friend.
28 Now therefore be content, look upon me; for *it is* evident unto you if I lie.
29 Return, I pray you, let it not be iniquity; yea, return again, my righteous-
ness *is* in it.
30 Is there iniquity in my tongue? cannot my taste discern perverse things?

Job: Human Existence Is Futile

7 *Is there* not an appointed time to man upon earth? *are not* his days also
like the days of an hireling?
2 As a servant earnestly desireth the shadow, and as an hireling looketh for
the reward of his work:
3 So am I made to possess months of vanity, and wearisome nights are
appointed to me.
4 When I lie down, I say, When shall I arise, and the night be gone? and I am
full of tossings to and fro unto the dawning of the day.
5 My flesh is clothed with worms and clods of dust; my skin is broken, and
become loathsome.
6 My days are swifter than a weaver's shuttle, and are spent without hope.

Job: I Loathe My Life

7 O remember that my life *is* wind: mine eye shall no more see good.
8 The eye of him that hath seen me shall see me no *more*: thine eyes *are* upon
me, and I *am* not.
9 *As* the cloud is consumed and vanisheth away: so he that goeth down to
the grave shall come up no *more*.
10 He shall return no more to his house, neither shall his place know him
any more.
11 Therefore I will not refrain my mouth; I will speak in the anguish of my
spirit; I will complain in the bitterness of my soul.
12 *Am* I a sea, or a whale, that thou settest a watch over me?
13 When I say, My bed shall comfort me, my couch shall ease my complaint;
14 Then thou scarest me with dreams, and terrifiest me through visions:
15 So that my soul chooseth strangling, *and* death rather than my life.
16 I loathe *it*; I would not live alway: let me alone; for my days *are* vanity.
17 What *is* man, that thou shouldest magnify him? and that thou shouldest
set thine heart upon him?
18 And *that* thou shouldest visit him every morning, *and* try him every
moment?
19 How long wilt thou not depart from me, nor let me alone till I swallow
down my spittle?
20 I have sinned; what shall I do unto thee, O thou preserver of men? why
hast thou set me as a mark against thee, so that I am a burden to myself?
21 And why dost thou not pardon my transgression, and take away mine
iniquity? for now shall I sleep in the dust; and thou shalt seek me in the morn-
ing, but I *shall* not *be*.

TILL HE
fill
THY
MOUTH
WITH
laughing,
& THY LIPS
WITH
rejoicing.

JOB 8:21

Bildad: You Are Unjustly Accusing God

8 Then answered Bildad the Shuhite, and said,
2 How long wilt thou speak these *things*? and *how long shall* the words
of thy mouth *be like* a strong wind?
3 Doth God pervert judgment? or doth the Almighty pervert justice?
4 If thy children have sinned against him, and he have cast them away for
their transgression;
5 If thou wouldest seek unto God betimes, and make thy supplication to the
Almighty;
6 If thou *wert* pure and upright; surely now he would awake for thee, and
make the habitation of thy righteousness prosperous.
7 Though thy beginning was small, yet thy latter end should greatly increase.

Bildad: God Does Not Punish the Innocent

8 For enquire, I pray thee, of the former age, and prepare thyself to the search
of their fathers:
9 (For we *are but of* yesterday, and know nothing, because our days upon
earth *are* a shadow:)
10 Shall not they teach thee, *and* tell thee, and utter words out of their heart?
11 Can the rush grow up without mire? can the flag grow without water?
12 Whilst it *is* yet in his greenness, *and* not cut down, it withereth before any
other herb.
13 So *are* the paths of all that forget God; and the hypocrite's hope shall
perish:
14 Whose hope shall be cut off, and whose trust *shall be* a spider's web.
15 He shall lean upon his house, but it shall not stand: he shall hold it fast,
but it shall not endure.
16 He *is* green before the sun, and his branch shooteth forth in his garden.
17 His roots are wrapped about the heap, *and* seeth the place of stones.
18 If he destroy him from his place, then *it* shall deny him, *saying*, I have not
seen thee.
19 Behold, this *is* the joy of his way, and out of the earth shall others grow.
20 Behold, God will not cast away a perfect *man*, neither will he help the evil
doers:
21 Till he fill thy mouth with laughing, and thy lips with rejoicing.
22 They that hate thee shall be clothed with shame; and the dwelling place
of the wicked shall come to nought.

Job: It Is Futile to Argue with God

9 Then Job answered and said,
2 I know *it is* so of a truth: but how should man be just with God?
3 If he will contend with him, he cannot answer him one of a thousand.
4 *He is* wise in heart, and mighty in strength: who hath hardened *himself*
against him, and hath prospered?
5 Which removeth the mountains, and they know not: which overturneth
them in his anger.
6 Which shaketh the earth out of her place, and the pillars thereof tremble.
7 Which commandeth the sun, and it riseth not; and sealeth up the stars.
8 Which alone spreadeth out the heavens, and treadeth upon the waves of
the sea.
9 Which maketh Arcturus, Orion, and Pleiades, and the chambers of the
south.
10 Which doeth great things past finding out; yea, and wonders without
number.
11 Lo, he goeth by me, and I see *him* not: he passeth on also, but I perceive
him not.

12 Behold, he taketh away, who can hinder him? who will say unto him, What
dost thou?
13 *If* God will not withdraw his anger, the proud helpers do stoop under him.
14 How much less shall I answer him, *and* choose out my words *to reason*
with him?
15 Whom, though I were righteous, *yet* would I not answer, *but* I would make
supplication to my judge.
16 If I had called, and he had answered me; *yet* would I not believe that he
had hearkened unto my voice.
17 For he breaketh me with a tempest, and multiplieth my wounds without
cause.
18 He will not suffer me to take my breath, but filleth me with bitterness.
19 If *I speak* of strength, lo, *he is* strong: and if of judgment, who shall set me
a time *to plead*?
20 If I justify myself, mine own mouth shall condemn me: *if I say*, I *am* per-
fect, it shall also prove me perverse.
21 *Though* I *were* perfect, *yet* would I not know my soul: I would despise my
life.
22 This *is* one *thing*, therefore I said *it*, He destroyeth the perfect and the
wicked.
23 If the scourge slay suddenly, he will laugh at the trial of the innocent.
24 The earth is given into the hand of the wicked: he covereth the faces of the
judges thereof; if not, where, *and* who *is* he?
25 Now my days are swifter than a post: they flee away, they see no good.
26 They are passed away as the swift ships: as the eagle *that* hasteth to the
prey.
27 If I say, I will forget my complaint, I will leave off my heaviness, and com-
fort *myself*:
28 I am afraid of all my sorrows, I know that thou wilt not hold me innocent.
29 *If* I be wicked, why then labour I in vain?
30 If I wash myself with snow water, and make my hands never so clean;
31 Yet shalt thou plunge me in the ditch, and mine own clothes shall abhor
me.
32 For *he is* not a man, as I *am*, *that* I should answer him, *and* we should
come together in judgment.
33 Neither is there any daysman betwixt us, *that* might lay his hand upon us
both.
34 Let him take his rod away from me, and let not his fear terrify me:
35 *Then* would I speak, and not fear him; but *it is* not so with me.

Job: My Soul Is Weary of My Life

10 My soul is weary of my life; I will leave my complaint upon myself; I
will speak in the bitterness of my soul.
2 I will say unto God, Do not condemn me; shew me wherefore thou con-
tendest with me.
3 *Is it* good unto thee that thou shouldest oppress, that thou shouldest
despise the work of thine hands, and shine upon the counsel of the wicked?
4 Hast thou eyes of flesh? or seest thou as man seeth?
5 *Are* thy days as the days of man? *are* thy years as man's days,
6 That thou enquirest after mine iniquity, and searchest after my sin?
7 Thou knowest that I am not wicked; and *there is* none that can deliver out
of thine hand.
8 Thine hands have made me and fashioned me together round about; yet
thou dost destroy me.
9 Remember, I beseech thee, that thou hast made me as the clay; and wilt
thou bring me into dust again?

10 Hast thou not poured me out as milk, and curdled me like cheese?
11 Thou hast clothed me with skin and flesh, and hast fenced me with bones
and sinews.
12 Thou hast granted me life and favour, and thy visitation hath preserved
my spirit.
13 And these *things* hast thou hid in thine heart: I know that this *is* with thee.
14 If I sin, then thou markest me, and thou wilt not acquit me from mine
iniquity.
15 If I be wicked, woe unto me; and *if* I be righteous, *yet* will I not lift up my
head. *I am* full of confusion; therefore see thou mine affliction;
16 For it increaseth. Thou huntest me as a fierce lion: and again thou shewest
thyself marvellous upon me.
17 Thou renewest thy witnesses against me, and increasest thine indignation
upon me; changes and war *are* against me.
18 Wherefore then hast thou brought me forth out of the womb? Oh that I
had given up the ghost, and no eye had seen me!
19 I should have been as though I had not been; I should have been carried
from the womb to the grave.
20 *Are* not my days few? cease *then, and* let me alone, that I may take comfort
a little,
21 Before I go *whence* I shall not return, *even* to the land of darkness and the
shadow of death;
22 A land of darkness, as darkness *itself; and* of the shadow of death, without
any order, and *where* the light *is* as darkness.

Zophar: God Can Do as He Pleases

11 Then answered Zophar the Naamathite, and said,
2 Should not the multitude of words be answered? and should a man
full of talk be justified?
3 Should thy lies make men hold their peace? and when thou mockest, shall
no man make thee ashamed?
4 For thou hast said, My doctrine *is* pure, and I am clean in thine eyes.
5 But oh that God would speak, and open his lips against thee;
6 And that he would shew thee the secrets of wisdom, that *they are* double
to that which is! Know therefore that God exacteth of thee *less* than thine
iniquity *deserveth*.
7 Canst thou by searching find out God? canst thou find out the Almighty
unto perfection?
8 *It is* as high as heaven; what canst thou do? deeper than hell; what canst
thou know?
9 The measure thereof *is* longer than the earth, and broader than the sea.
10 If he cut off, and shut up, or gather together, then who can hinder him?
11 For he knoweth vain men: he seeth wickedness also; will he not then con-
sider *it*?
12 For vain man would be wise, though man be born *like* a wild ass's colt.

Zophar: Confess Your Sin and Be Forgiven

13 If thou prepare thine heart, and stretch out thine hands toward him;
14 If iniquity *be* in thine hand, put it far away, and let not wickedness dwell
in thy tabernacles.
15 For then shalt thou lift up thy face without spot; yea, thou shalt be stedfast,
and shalt not fear:
16 Because thou shalt forget *thy* misery, *and* remember *it* as waters *that* pass
away:
17 And *thine* age shall be clearer than the noonday; thou shalt shine forth,
thou shalt be as the morning.

THOU HAST
GRANTED
me life
& FAVOUR,

PRESERVED

18 And thou shalt be secure, because there is hope; yea, thou shalt dig *about*
thee, and thou shalt take thy rest in safety.
19 Also thou shalt lie down, and none shall make *thee* afraid; yea, many shall
make suit unto thee.
20 But the eyes of the wicked shall fail, and they shall not escape, and their
hope *shall be as* the giving up of the ghost.

Job: You Have No Wisdom

12 And Job answered and said,
2 No doubt but ye *are* the people, and wisdom shall die with you.
3 But I have understanding as well as you; I *am* not inferior to you: yea, who
knoweth not such things as these?
4 I am *as* one mocked of his neighbour, who calleth upon God, and he
answereth him: the just upright *man is* laughed to scorn.
5 He that is ready to slip with *his* feet *is as* a lamp despised in the thought of
him that is at ease.
6 The tabernacles of robbers prosper, and they that provoke God are secure;
into whose hand God bringeth *abundantly*.
7 But ask now the beasts, and they shall teach thee; and the fowls of the air,
and they shall tell thee:
8 Or speak to the earth, and it shall teach thee: and the fishes of the sea shall
declare unto thee.
9 Who knoweth not in all these that the hand of the LORD hath wrought this?
10 In whose hand *is* the soul of every living thing, and the breath of all man-
kind.
11 Doth not the ear try words? and the mouth taste his meat?

Job: Wisdom Comes from God

12 With the ancient *is* wisdom; and in length of days understanding.
13 With him *is* wisdom and strength, he hath counsel and understanding.
14 Behold, he breaketh down, and it cannot be built again: he shutteth up a
man, and there can be no opening.
15 Behold, he withholdeth the waters, and they dry up: also he sendeth them
out, and they overturn the earth.
16 With him *is* strength and wisdom: the deceived and the deceiver *are* his.
17 He leadeth counsellors away spoiled, and maketh the judges fools.
18 He looseth the bond of kings, and girdeth their loins with a girdle.
19 He leadeth princes away spoiled, and overthroweth the mighty.
20 He removeth away the speech of the trusty, and taketh away the under-
standing of the aged.
21 He poureth contempt upon princes, and weakeneth the strength of the
mighty.
22 He discovereth deep things out of darkness, and bringeth out to light the
shadow of death.
23 He increaseth the nations, and destroyeth them: he enlargeth the nations,
and straiteneth them *again*.
24 He taketh away the heart of the chief of the people of the earth, and
causeth them to wander in a wilderness *where there is* no way.
25 They grope in the dark without light, and he maketh them to stagger like
a drunken *man*.

Job: Though God Slay Me, I Will Trust Him

13 Lo, mine eye hath seen all *this*, mine ear hath heard and understood it.
2 What ye know, *the same* do I know also: I *am* not inferior unto you.
3 Surely I would speak to the Almighty, and I desire to reason with God.
4 But ye *are* forgers of lies, ye *are* all physicians of no value.
5 O that ye would altogether hold your peace! and it should be your wisdom.
6 Hear now my reasoning, and hearken to the pleadings of my lips.

7 Will ye speak wickedly for God? and talk deceitfully for him?
8 Will ye accept his person? will ye contend for God?
9 Is it good that he should search you out? or as one man mocketh another,
do ye *so* mock him?
10 He will surely reprove you, if ye do secretly accept persons.
11 Shall not his excellency make you afraid? and his dread fall upon you?
12 Your remembrances *are* like unto ashes, your bodies to bodies of clay.
13 Hold your peace, let me alone, that I may speak, and let come on me what
will.
14 Wherefore do I take my flesh in my teeth, and put my life in mine hand?
15 Though he slay me, yet will I trust in him: but I will maintain mine own
ways before him.
16 He also *shall be* my salvation: for an hypocrite shall not come before him.

Job: God, Please Hear Me

17 Hear diligently my speech, and my declaration with your ears.
18 Behold now, I have ordered *my* cause; I know that I shall be justified.
19 Who *is* he *that* will plead with me? for now, if I hold my tongue, I shall
give up the ghost.
20 Only do not two *things* unto me: then will I not hide myself from thee.
21 Withdraw thine hand far from me: and let not thy dread make me afraid.
22 Then call thou, and I will answer: or let me speak, and answer thou me.
23 How many *are* mine iniquities and sins? make me to know my transgres-
sion and my sin.
24 Wherefore hidest thou thy face, and holdest me for thine enemy?
25 Wilt thou break a leaf driven to and fro? and wilt thou pursue the dry
stubble?
26 For thou writest bitter things against me, and makest me to possess the
iniquities of my youth.
27 Thou puttest my feet also in the stocks, and lookest narrowly unto all my
paths; thou settest a print upon the heels of my feet.
28 And he, as a rotten thing, consumeth, as a garment that is moth eaten.

Job: God, Consider My Frail Human Nature

14 Man *that is* born of a woman *is* of few days, and full of trouble.
2 He cometh forth like a flower, and is cut down: he fleeth also as a
shadow, and continueth not.
3 And dost thou open thine eyes upon such an one, and bringest me into
judgment with thee?
4 Who can bring a clean *thing* out of an unclean? not one.
5 Seeing his days *are* determined, the number of his months *are* with thee,
thou hast appointed his bounds that he cannot pass;
6 Turn from him, that he may rest, till he shall accomplish, as an hireling,
his day.
7 For there is hope of a tree, if it be cut down, that it will sprout again, and
that the tender branch thereof will not cease.
8 Though the root thereof wax old in the earth, and the stock thereof die in
the ground;
9 *Yet* through the scent of water it will bud, and bring forth boughs like a
plant.
10 But man dieth, and wasteth away: yea, man giveth up the ghost, and where
is he?
11 *As* the waters fail from the sea, and the flood decayeth and drieth up:
12 So man lieth down, and riseth not: till the heavens *be* no more, they shall
not awake, nor be raised out of their sleep.

13 O that thou wouldest hide me in the grave, that thou wouldest keep me
secret, until thy wrath be past, that thou wouldest appoint me a set time, and
remember me!
14 If a man die, shall he live *again*? all the days of my appointed time will I
wait, till my change come.
15 Thou shalt call, and I will answer thee: thou wilt have a desire to the work
of thine hands.
16 For now thou numberest my steps: dost thou not watch over my sin?
17 My transgression *is* sealed up in a bag, and thou sewest up mine iniquity.
18 And surely the mountain falling cometh to nought, and the rock is
removed out of his place.
19 The waters wear the stones: thou washest away the things which grow *out*
of the dust of the earth; and thou destroyest the hope of man.
20 Thou prevailest for ever against him, and he passeth: thou changest his
countenance, and sendest him away.
21 His sons come to honour, and he knoweth *it* not; and they are brought
low, but he perceiveth *it* not of them.
22 But his flesh upon him shall have pain, and his soul within him shall
mourn.

Eliphaz: You Are Speaking Sinfully

15 Then answered Eliphaz the Temanite, and said,
2 Should a wise man utter vain knowledge, and fill his belly with the
east wind?
3 Should he reason with unprofitable talk? or with speeches wherewith he
can do no good?
4 Yea, thou castest off fear, and restrainest prayer before God.
5 For thy mouth uttereth thine iniquity, and thou choosest the tongue of the
crafty.
6 Thine own mouth condemneth thee, and not I: yea, thine own lips testify
against thee.
7 *Art* thou the first man *that* was born? or wast thou made before the hills?
8 Hast thou heard the secret of God? and dost thou restrain wisdom to thy-
self?
9 What knowest thou, that we know not? *what* understandest thou, which
is not in us?
10 With us *are* both the grayheaded and very aged men, much elder than thy
father.
11 *Are* the consolations of God small with thee? is there any secret thing with
thee?
12 Why doth thine heart carry thee away? and what do thy eyes wink at,
13 That thou turnest thy spirit against God, and lettest *such* words go out of
thy mouth?
14 What *is* man, that he should be clean? and *he which is* born of a woman,
that he should be righteous?
15 Behold, he putteth no trust in his saints; yea, the heavens are not clean in
his sight.
16 How much more abominable and filthy *is* man, which drinketh iniquity
like water?

Eliphaz: Wicked People Live Tortured Lives

17 I will shew thee, hear me; and that *which* I have seen I will declare;
18 Which wise men have told from their fathers, and have not hid *it*:
19 Unto whom alone the earth was given, and no stranger passed among
them.
20 The wicked man travaileth with pain all *his* days, and the number of years
is hidden to the oppressor.

21 A dreadful sound *is* in his ears: in prosperity the destroyer shall come
upon him.
22 He believeth not that he shall return out of darkness, and he is waited for
of the sword.
23 He wandereth abroad for bread, *saying*, Where *is it*? he knoweth that the
day of darkness is ready at his hand.
24 Trouble and anguish shall make him afraid; they shall prevail against him,
as a king ready to the battle.
25 For he stretcheth out his hand against God, and strengtheneth himself
against the Almighty.
26 He runneth upon him, *even* on *his* neck, upon the thick bosses of his
bucklers:
27 Because he covereth his face with his fatness, and maketh collops of fat
on *his* flanks.
28 And he dwelleth in desolate cities, *and* in houses which no man inhabiteth,
which are ready to become heaps.
29 He shall not be rich, neither shall his substance continue, neither shall
he prolong the perfection thereof upon the earth.
30 He shall not depart out of darkness; the flame shall dry up his branches,
and by the breath of his mouth shall he go away.
31 Let not him that is deceived trust in vanity: for vanity shall be his recom-
pence.
32 It shall be accomplished before his time, and his branch shall not be green.
33 He shall shake off his unripe grape as the vine, and shall cast off his flow-
er as the olive.
34 For the congregation of hypocrites *shall be* desolate, and fire shall con-
sume the tabernacles of bribery.
35 They conceive mischief, and bring forth vanity, and their belly prepareth
deceit.

Job: You, My Friends, Lack Mercy

16 Then Job answered and said,
2 I have heard many such things: miserable comforters *are* ye all.
3 Shall vain words have an end? or what emboldeneth thee that thou answer-
est?
4 I also could speak as ye *do*: if your soul were in my soul's stead, I could heap
up words against you, and shake mine head at you.
5 *But* I would strengthen you with my mouth, and the moving of my lips
should asswage *your grief*.
6 Though I speak, my grief is not asswaged: and *though* I forbear, what am I
eased?
7 But now he hath made me weary: thou hast made desolate all my company.
8 And thou hast filled me with wrinkles, *which* is a witness *against me*: and
my leanness rising up in me beareth witness to my face.

Job: My Eyes Pour out Tears to God

9 He teareth *me* in his wrath, who hateth me: he gnasheth upon me with his
teeth; mine enemy sharpeneth his eyes upon me.
10 They have gaped upon me with their mouth; they have smitten me upon
the cheek reproachfully; they have gathered themselves together against me.
11 God hath delivered me to the ungodly, and turned me over into the hands
of the wicked.
12 I was at ease, but he hath broken me asunder: he hath also taken *me* by
my neck, and shaken me to pieces, and set me up for his mark.
13 His archers compass me round about, he cleaveth my reins asunder, and
doth not spare; he poureth out my gall upon the ground.

14 He breaketh me with breach upon breach, he runneth upon me like a
giant.
15 I have sewed sackcloth upon my skin, and defiled my horn in the dust.
16 My face is foul with weeping, and on my eyelids *is* the shadow of death;
17 Not for *any* injustice in mine hands: also my prayer *is* pure.
18 O earth, cover not thou my blood, and let my cry have no place.
19 Also now, behold, my witness *is* in heaven, and my record *is* on high.
20 My friends scorn me: *but* mine eye poureth out *tears* unto God.
21 O that one might plead for a man with God, as a man *pleadeth* for his
neighbour!
22 When a few years are come, then I shall go the way *whence* I shall not
return.

Job: You, My Friends, Have No Wisdom

17 My breath is corrupt, my days are extinct, the graves *are ready* for me.
2 *Are there* not mockers with me? and doth not mine eye continue in
their provocation?
3 Lay down now, put me in a surety with thee; who *is* he *that* will strike hands
with me?
4 For thou hast hid their heart from understanding: therefore shalt thou not
exalt *them*.
5 He that speaketh flattery to *his* friends, even the eyes of his children shall
fail.
6 He hath made me also a byword of the people; and aforetime I was as a
tabret.
7 Mine eye also is dim by reason of sorrow, and all my members *are* as a
shadow.
8 Upright *men* shall be astonied at this, and the innocent shall stir up himself
against the hypocrite.
9 The righteous also shall hold on his way, and he that hath clean hands shall
be stronger and stronger.
10 But as for you all, do ye return, and come now: for I cannot find *one* wise
man among you.
11 My days are past, my purposes are broken off, *even* the thoughts of my
heart.
12 They change the night into day: the light *is* short because of darkness.
13 If I wait, the grave *is* mine house: I have made my bed in the darkness.
14 I have said to corruption, Thou *art* my father: to the worm, *Thou art* my
mother, and my sister.
15 And where *is* now my hope? as for my hope, who shall see it?
16 They shall go down to the bars of the pit, when *our* rest together *is* in the
dust.

Bildad: When Will You Stop Talking?

18 Then answered Bildad the Shuhite, and said,
2 How long *will it be ere* ye make an end of words? mark, and after-
wards we will speak.
3 Wherefore are we counted as beasts, *and* reputed vile in your sight?
4 He teareth himself in his anger: shall the earth be forsaken for thee? and
shall the rock be removed out of his place?

Bildad: The Wicked Live in Terror

5 Yea, the light of the wicked shall be put out, and the spark of his fire shall
not shine.
6 The light shall be dark in his tabernacle, and his candle shall be put out
with him.
7 The steps of his strength shall be straitened, and his own counsel shall cast
him down.

8 For he is cast into a net by his own feet, and he walketh upon a snare.
9 The gin shall take *him* by the heel, *and* the robber shall prevail against him.
10 The snare *is* laid for him in the ground, and a trap for him in the way.
11 Terrors shall make him afraid on every side, and shall drive him to his
feet.
12 His strength shall be hungerbitten, and destruction *shall be* ready at his
side.
13 It shall devour the strength of his skin: *even* the firstborn of death shall
devour his strength.
14 His confidence shall be rooted out of his tabernacle, and it shall bring
him to the king of terrors.
15 It shall dwell in his tabernacle, because *it is* none of his: brimstone shall
be scattered upon his habitation.
16 His roots shall be dried up beneath, and above shall his branch be cut off.
17 His remembrance shall perish from the earth, and he shall have no name
in the street.
18 He shall be driven from light into darkness, and chased out of the world.
19 He shall neither have son nor nephew among his people, nor any remain-
ing in his dwellings.
20 They that come after *him* shall be astonied at his day, as they that went
before were affrighted.
21 Surely such *are* the dwellings of the wicked, and this *is* the place *of him*
that knoweth not God.

Job: God Is Mistreating Me

19 Then Job answered and said,
2 How long will ye vex my soul, and break me in pieces with words?
3 These ten times have ye reproached me: ye are not ashamed *that* ye make
yourselves strange to me.
4 And be it indeed *that* I have erred, mine error remaineth with myself.
5 If indeed ye will magnify *yourselves* against me, and plead against me my
reproach:
6 Know now that God hath overthrown me, and hath compassed me with
his net.
7 Behold, I cry out of wrong, but I am not heard: I cry aloud, but *there is* no
judgment.
8 He hath fenced up my way that I cannot pass, and he hath set darkness in
my paths.
9 He hath stripped me of my glory, and taken the crown *from* my head.
10 He hath destroyed me on every side, and I am gone: and mine hope hath
he removed like a tree.
11 He hath also kindled his wrath against me, and he counteth me unto him
as *one of* his enemies.
12 His troops come together, and raise up their way against me, and encamp
round about my tabernacle.
13 He hath put my brethren far from me, and mine acquaintance are verily
estranged from me.
14 My kinsfolk have failed, and my familiar friends have forgotten me.
15 They that dwell in mine house, and my maids, count me for a stranger: I
am an alien in their sight.
16 I called my servant, and he gave *me* no answer; I intreated him with my
mouth.
17 My breath is strange to my wife, though I intreated for the children's *sake*
of mine own body.
18 Yea, young children despised me; I arose, and they spake against me.

19 All my inward friends abhorred me: and they whom I loved are turned
against me.
20 My bone cleaveth to my skin and to my flesh, and I am escaped with the
skin of my teeth.
21 Have pity upon me, have pity upon me, O ye my friends; for the hand of
God hath touched me.
22 Why do ye persecute me as God, and are not satisfied with my flesh?

Job: I Maintain Confidence in My God

23 Oh that my words were now written! oh that they were printed in a book!
24 That they were graven with an iron pen and lead in the rock for ever!
25 For I know *that* my redeemer liveth, and *that* he shall stand at the latter
day upon the earth:
26 And *though* after my skin *worms* destroy this *body*, yet in my flesh shall I
see God:
27 Whom I shall see for myself, and mine eyes shall behold, and not another;
though my reins be consumed within me.
28 But ye should say, Why persecute we him, seeing the root of the matter is
found in me?
29 Be ye afraid of the sword: for wrath *bringeth* the punishments of the
sword, that ye may know *there is* a judgment.

Zophar: The Wicked Have Little Joy, Much Pain

20 Then answered Zophar the Naamathite, and said,
2 Therefore do my thoughts cause me to answer, and for *this* I make
haste.
3 I have heard the check of my reproach, and the spirit of my understanding
causeth me to answer.
4 Knowest thou *not* this of old, since man was placed upon earth,
5 That the triumphing of the wicked *is* short, and the joy of the hypocrite
but for a moment?
6 Though his excellency mount up to the heavens, and his head reach unto
the clouds;
7 *Yet* he shall perish for ever like his own dung: they which have seen him
shall say, Where *is* he?
8 He shall fly away as a dream, and shall not be found: yea, he shall be chased
away as a vision of the night.
9 The eye also *which* saw him shall *see him* no more; neither shall his place
any more behold him.
10 His children shall seek to please the poor, and his hands shall restore their
goods.
11 His bones are full *of the sin* of his youth, which shall lie down with him
in the dust.
12 Though wickedness be sweet in his mouth, *though* he hide it under his
tongue;
13 *Though* he spare it, and forsake it not; but keep it still within his mouth:
14 *Yet* his meat in his bowels is turned, *it is* the gall of asps within him.
15 He hath swallowed down riches, and he shall vomit them up again: God
shall cast them out of his belly.
16 He shall suck the poison of asps: the viper's tongue shall slay him.
17 He shall not see the rivers, the floods, the brooks of honey and butter.
18 That which he laboured for shall he restore, and shall not swallow *it* down:
according to *his* substance *shall* the restitution *be*, and he shall not rejoice
therein.
19 Because he hath oppressed *and* hath forsaken the poor; *because* he hath
violently taken away an house which he builded not;

20 Surely he shall not feel quietness in his belly, he shall not save of that which
he desired.
21 There shall none of his meat be left; therefore shall no man look for his
goods.
22 In the fulness of his sufficiency he shall be in straits: every hand of the
wicked shall come upon him.
23 *When* he is about to fill his belly, *God* shall cast the fury of his wrath upon
him, and shall rain *it* upon him while he is eating.
24 He shall flee from the iron weapon, *and* the bow of steel shall strike him
through.
25 It is drawn, and cometh out of the body; yea, the glittering sword cometh
out of his gall: terrors *are* upon him.
26 All darkness *shall be* hid in his secret places: a fire not blown shall consume
him; it shall go ill with him that is left in his tabernacle.
27 The heaven shall reveal his iniquity; and the earth shall rise up against
him.
28 The increase of his house shall depart, *and his goods* shall flow away in
the day of his wrath.
29 This *is* the portion of a wicked man from God, and the heritage appoint-
ed unto him by God.

Job: Please Listen and Hear Me, My Friends

21 But Job answered and said,
2 Hear diligently my speech, and let this be your consolations.
3 Suffer me that I may speak; and after that I have spoken, mock on.
4 As for me, *is* my complaint to man? and if *it were so*, why should not my
spirit be troubled?
5 Mark me, and be astonished, and lay *your* hand upon *your* mouth.
6 Even when I remember I am afraid, and trembling taketh hold on my flesh.

Job: Sometimes the Wicked Do Prosper

7 Wherefore do the wicked live, become old, yea, are mighty in power?
8 Their seed is established in their sight with them, and their offspring before
their eyes.
9 Their houses *are* safe from fear, neither *is* the rod of God upon them.
10 Their bull gendereth, and faileth not; their cow calveth, and casteth not
her calf.
11 They send forth their little ones like a flock, and their children dance.
12 They take the timbrel and harp, and rejoice at the sound of the organ.
13 They spend their days in wealth, and in a moment go down to the grave.
14 Therefore they say unto God, Depart from us; for we desire not the knowl-
edge of thy ways.
15 What *is* the Almighty, that we should serve him? and what profit should
we have, if we pray unto him?
16 Lo, their good *is* not in their hand: the counsel of the wicked is far from me.
17 How oft is the candle of the wicked put out! and *how oft* cometh their
destruction upon them! *God* distributeth sorrows in his anger.
18 They are as stubble before the wind, and as chaff that the storm carrieth
away.
19 God layeth up his iniquity for his children: he rewardeth him, and he shall
know *it*.
20 His eyes shall see his destruction, and he shall drink of the wrath of the
Almighty.
21 For what pleasure *hath* he in his house after him, when the number of
his months is cut off in the midst?

Job: No One Understands God's Dealings

22 Shall *any* teach God knowledge? seeing he judgeth those that are high.
23 One dieth in his full strength, being wholly at ease and quiet.

24 His breasts are full of milk, and his bones are moistened with marrow.
25 And another dieth in the bitterness of his soul, and never eateth with
pleasure.
26 They shall lie down alike in the dust, and the worms shall cover them.
27 Behold, I know your thoughts, and the devices *which* ye wrongfully imagine
against me.
28 For ye say, Where *is* the house of the prince? and where *are* the dwelling
places of the wicked?
29 Have ye not asked them that go by the way? and do ye not know their
tokens,
30 That the wicked is reserved to the day of destruction? they shall be brought
forth to the day of wrath.
31 Who shall declare his way to his face? and who shall repay him *what* he
hath done?
32 Yet shall he be brought to the grave, and shall remain in the tomb.
33 The clods of the valley shall be sweet unto him, and every man shall draw
after him, as *there are* innumerable before him.
34 How then comfort ye me in vain, seeing in your answers there remaineth
falsehood?

Eliphaz: Man's Goodness Does Not Profit God

22 Then Eliphaz the Temanite answered and said,
2 Can a man be profitable unto God, as he that is wise may be profitable
unto himself?
3 *Is it* any pleasure to the Almighty, that thou art righteous? or *is it* gain *to*
him, that thou makest thy ways perfect?
4 Will he reprove thee for fear of thee? will he enter with thee into judgment?

Eliphaz: Admit You Are Wicked

5 *Is* not thy wickedness great? and thine iniquities infinite?
6 For thou hast taken a pledge from thy brother for nought, and stripped
the naked of their clothing.
7 Thou hast not given water to the weary to drink, and thou hast withholden
bread from the hungry.
8 But *as for* the mighty man, he had the earth; and the honourable man dwelt
in it.
9 Thou hast sent widows away empty, and the arms of the fatherless have
been broken.
10 Therefore snares *are* round about thee, and sudden fear troubleth thee;
11 Or darkness, *that* thou canst not see; and abundance of waters cover thee.
12 *Is* not God in the height of heaven? and behold the height of the stars,
how high they are!
13 And thou sayest, How doth God know? can he judge through the dark
cloud?
14 Thick clouds *are* a covering to him, that he seeth not; and he walketh in
the circuit of heaven.
15 Hast thou marked the old way which wicked men have trodden?
16 Which were cut down out of time, whose foundation was overflown with
a flood:
17 Which said unto God, Depart from us: and what can the Almighty do for
them?
18 Yet he filled their houses with good *things*: but the counsel of the wicked
is far from me.
19 The righteous see *it*, and are glad: and the innocent laugh them to scorn.
20 Whereas our substance is not cut down, but the remnant of them the fire
consumeth.

Eliphaz: Repent and Make Peace with God

21 Acquaint now thyself with him, and be at peace: thereby good shall come
unto thee.
22 Receive, I pray thee, the law from his mouth, and lay up his words in thine
heart.
23 If thou return to the Almighty, thou shalt be built up, thou shalt put away
iniquity far from thy tabernacles.
24 Then shalt thou lay up gold as dust, and the *gold* of Ophir as the stones of
the brooks.
25 Yea, the Almighty shall be thy defence, and thou shalt have plenty of silver.
26 For then shalt thou have thy delight in the Almighty, and shalt lift up thy
face unto God.
27 Thou shalt make thy prayer unto him, and he shall hear thee, and thou
shalt pay thy vows.
28 Thou shalt also decree a thing, and it shall be established unto thee: and
the light shall shine upon thy ways.
29 When *men* are cast down, then thou shalt say, *There is* lifting up; and he
shall save the humble person.
30 He shall deliver the island of the innocent: and it is delivered by the pure-
ness of thine hands.

Job: Where Can I Find God?

23 Then Job answered and said,
2 Even to day *is* my complaint bitter: my stroke is heavier than my
groaning.
3 Oh that I knew where I might find him! *that* I might come *even* to his seat!
4 I would order *my* cause before him, and fill my mouth with arguments.
5 I would know the words *which* he would answer me, and understand what
he would say unto me.
6 Will he plead against me with *his* great power? No; but he would put
strength in me.
7 There the righteous might dispute with him; so should I be delivered for
ever from my judge.
8 Behold, I go forward, but he *is* not *there*; and backward, but I cannot per-
ceive him:
9 On the left hand, where he doth work, but I cannot behold *him*: he hideth
himself on the right hand, that I cannot see *him*:
10 But he knoweth the way that I take: *when* he hath tried me, I shall come
forth as gold.
11 My foot hath held his steps, his way have I kept, and not declined.
12 Neither have I gone back from the commandment of his lips; I have
esteemed the words of his mouth more than my necessary *food*.

Job: God Will Not Change His Mind

13 But he *is* in one *mind*, and who can turn him? and *what* his soul desireth,
even *that* he doeth.
14 For he performeth *the thing that is* appointed for me: and many such
things are with him.
15 Therefore am I troubled at his presence: when I consider, I am afraid of
him.
16 For God maketh my heart soft, and the Almighty troubleth me:
17 Because I was not cut off before the darkness, *neither* hath he covered the
darkness from my face.

Job: Wickedness Often Goes Unpunished

24 Why, seeing times are not hidden from the Almighty, do they that know
him not see his days?
2 *Some* remove the landmarks; they violently take away flocks, and feed *thereof*.

3 They drive away the ass of the fatherless, they take the widow's ox for a
pledge.
4 They turn the needy out of the way: the poor of the earth hide themselves
together.
5 Behold, *as* wild asses in the desert, go they forth to their work; rising
betimes for a prey: the wilderness *yieldeth* food for them *and* for *their* chil-
dren.
6 They reap *every one* his corn in the field: and they gather the vintage of the
wicked.
7 They cause the naked to lodge without clothing, that *they have* no covering
in the cold.
8 They are wet with the showers of the mountains, and embrace the rock for
want of a shelter.
9 They pluck the fatherless from the breast, and take a pledge of the poor.
10 They cause *him* to go naked without clothing, and they take away the sheaf
from the hungry;
11 *Which* make oil within their walls, *and* tread *their* winepresses, and suffer
thirst.
12 Men groan from out of the city, and the soul of the wounded crieth out:
yet God layeth not folly *to them.*
13 They are of those that rebel against the light; they know not the ways
thereof, nor abide in the paths thereof.
14 The murderer rising with the light killeth the poor and needy, and in the
night is as a thief.
15 The eye also of the adulterer waiteth for the twilight, saying, No eye shall
see me: and disguiseth *his* face.
16 In the dark they dig through houses, *which* they had marked for them-
selves in the daytime: they know not the light.
17 For the morning *is* to them even as the shadow of death: if *one* know *them,*
they are in the terrors of the shadow of death.
18 He *is* swift as the waters; their portion is cursed in the earth: he beholdeth
not the way of the vineyards.
19 Drought and heat consume the snow waters: *so doth* the grave *those which*
have sinned.
20 The womb shall forget him; the worm shall feed sweetly on him; he shall
be no more remembered; and wickedness shall be broken as a tree.
21 He evil entreateth the barren *that* beareth not: and doeth not good to the
widow.
22 He draweth also the mighty with his power: he riseth up, and no *man* is
sure of life.
23 *Though* it be given him *to be* in safety, whereon he resteth; yet his eyes *are*
upon their ways.
24 They are exalted for a little while, but are gone and brought low; they are
taken out of the way as all *other,* and cut off as the tops of the ears of corn.
25 And if *it be* not *so* now, who will make me a liar, and make my speech
nothing worth?

Bildad: No One Is Justified before God

25 Then answered Bildad the Shuhite, and said,
2 Dominion and fear *are* with him, he maketh peace in his high places.
3 Is there any number of his armies? and upon whom doth not his light
arise?
4 How then can man be justified with God? or how can he be clean *that is*
born of a woman?
5 Behold even to the moon, and it shineth not; yea, the stars are not pure in
his sight.

6 How much less man, *that is* a worm? and the son of man, *which is* a worm?

Job: Your Advice Is Useless

26 But Job answered and said,
2 How hast thou helped *him that is* without power? *how* savest thou
the arm *that hath* no strength?
3 How hast thou counselled *him that hath* no wisdom? and *how* hast thou
plentifully declared the thing as it is?
4 To whom hast thou uttered words? and whose spirit came from thee?

Job: God's Power Is Infinite and Unsearchable

5 Dead *things* are formed from under the waters, and the inhabitants there-
of.
6 Hell *is* naked before him, and destruction hath no covering.
7 He stretcheth out the north over the empty place, *and* hangeth the earth
upon nothing.
8 He bindeth up the waters in his thick clouds; and the cloud is not rent
under them.
9 He holdeth back the face of his throne, *and* spreadeth his cloud upon it.
10 He hath compassed the waters with bounds, until the day and night come
to an end.
11 The pillars of heaven tremble and are astonished at his reproof.
12 He divideth the sea with his power, and by his understanding he smiteth
through the proud.
13 By his spirit he hath garnished the heavens; his hand hath formed the
crooked serpent.
14 Lo, these *are* parts of his ways: but how little a portion is heard of him?
but the thunder of his power who can understand?

Job: I Am Innocent

27 Moreover Job continued his parable, and said,
2 *As* God liveth, *who* hath taken away my judgment; and the Almighty,
who hath vexed my soul;
3 All the while my breath *is* in me, and the spirit of God *is* in my nostrils;
4 My lips shall not speak wickedness, nor my tongue utter deceit.
5 God forbid that I should justify you: till I die I will not remove mine integ-
rity from me.
6 My righteousness I hold fast, and will not let it go: my heart shall not
reproach *me* so long as I live.
7 Let mine enemy be as the wicked, and he that riseth up against me as the
unrighteous.
8 For what *is* the hope of the hypocrite, though he hath gained, when God
taketh away his soul?
9 Will God hear his cry when trouble cometh upon him?
10 Will he delight himself in the Almighty? will he always call upon God?

Job: The Wicked Will Face Punishment

11 I will teach you by the hand of God: *that* which *is* with the Almighty will
I not conceal.
12 Behold, all ye yourselves have seen *it*; why then are ye thus altogether vain?
13 This *is* the portion of a wicked man with God, and the heritage of oppres-
sors, *which* they shall receive of the Almighty.
14 If his children be multiplied, *it is* for the sword: and his offspring shall
not be satisfied with bread.
15 Those that remain of him shall be buried in death: and his widows shall
not weep.
16 Though he heap up silver as the dust, and prepare raiment as the clay;

17 He may prepare *it*, but the just shall put *it* on, and the innocent shall divide
the silver.
18 He buildeth his house as a moth, and as a booth *that* the keeper maketh.
19 The rich man shall lie down, but he shall not be gathered: he openeth his
eyes, and he *is* not.
20 Terrors take hold on him as waters, a tempest stealeth him away in the
night.
21 The east wind carrieth him away, and he departeth: and as a storm hurleth
him out of his place.
22 For *God* shall cast upon him, and not spare: he would fain flee out of his
hand.
23 *Men* shall clap their hands at him, and shall hiss him out of his place.

Job: True Wisdom Is God's Alone

28 Surely there is a vein for the silver, and a place for gold *where* they fine *it*.
2 Iron is taken out of the earth, and brass *is* molten *out of* the stone.
3 He setteth an end to darkness, and searcheth out all perfection: the stones
of darkness, and the shadow of death.
4 The flood breaketh out from the inhabitant; *even the waters* forgotten of
the foot: they are dried up, they are gone away from men.
5 *As for* the earth, out of it cometh bread: and under it is turned up as it were
fire.
6 The stones of it *are* the place of sapphires: and it hath dust of gold.
7 *There is* a path which no fowl knoweth, and which the vulture's eye hath
not seen:
8 The lion's whelps have not trodden it, nor the fierce lion passed by it.
9 He putteth forth his hand upon the rock; he overturneth the mountains
by the roots.
10 He cutteth out rivers among the rocks; and his eye seeth every precious
thing.
11 He bindeth the floods from overflowing; and *the thing that is* hid bringeth
he forth to light.
12 But where shall wisdom be found? and where *is* the place of understand-
ing?
13 Man knoweth not the price thereof; neither is it found in the land of the
living.
14 The depth saith, It *is* not in me: and the sea saith, *It is* not with me.
15 It cannot be gotten for gold, neither shall silver be weighed *for* the price
thereof.
16 It cannot be valued with the gold of Ophir, with the precious onyx, or the
sapphire.
17 The gold and the crystal cannot equal it: and the exchange of it *shall not
be for* jewels of fine gold.
18 No mention shall be made of coral, or of pearls: for the price of wisdom
is above rubies.
19 The topaz of Ethiopia shall not equal it, neither shall it be valued with
pure gold.
20 Whence then cometh wisdom? and where *is* the place of understanding?
21 Seeing it is hid from the eyes of all living, and kept close from the fowls of
the air.
22 Destruction and death say, We have heard the fame thereof with our ears.
23 God understandeth the way thereof, and he knoweth the place thereof.
24 For he looketh to the ends of the earth, *and* seeth under the whole heaven;
25 To make the weight for the winds; and he weigheth the waters by measure.
26 When he made a decree for the rain, and a way for the lightning of the
thunder:

27 Then did he see it, and declare it; he prepared it, yea, and searched it out.
28 And unto man he said, Behold, the fear of the Lord, that *is* wisdom; and to depart from evil *is* understanding.

Job: I Grieve for My Former Prosperity and Honor

29 Moreover Job continued his parable, and said,
2 Oh that I were as *in* months past, as *in* the days *when* God preserved me;
3 When his candle shined upon my head, *and when* by his light I walked *through* darkness;
4 As I was in the days of my youth, when the secret of God *was* upon my tabernacle;
5 When the Almighty *was* yet with me, *when* my children *were* about me;
6 When I washed my steps with butter, and the rock poured me out rivers of oil;
7 When I went out to the gate through the city, *when* I prepared my seat in the street!
8 The young men saw me, and hid themselves: and the aged arose, *and* stood up.
9 The princes refrained talking, and laid *their* hand on their mouth.
10 The nobles held their peace, and their tongue cleaved to the roof of their mouth.
11 When the ear heard *me*, then it blessed me; and when the eye saw *me*, it gave witness to me:
12 Because I delivered the poor that cried, and the fatherless, and *him that had* none to help him.
13 The blessing of him that was ready to perish came upon me: and I caused the widow's heart to sing for joy.
14 I put on righteousness, and it clothed me: my judgment *was* as a robe and a diadem.
15 I was eyes to the blind, and feet *was* I to the lame.
16 I *was* a father to the poor: and the cause *which* I knew not I searched out.
17 And I brake the jaws of the wicked, and plucked the spoil out of his teeth.
18 Then I said, I shall die in my nest, and I shall multiply *my* days as the sand.
19 My root *was* spread out by the waters, and the dew lay all night upon my branch.
20 My glory *was* fresh in me, and my bow was renewed in my hand.
21 Unto me *men* gave ear, and waited, and kept silence at my counsel.
22 After my words they spake not again; and my speech dropped upon them.
23 And they waited for me as for the rain; and they opened their mouth wide *as* for the latter rain.
24 *If* I laughed on them, they believed *it* not; and the light of my countenance they cast not down.
25 I chose out their way, and sat chief, and dwelt as a king in the army, as one *that* comforteth the mourners.

Job: I Am an Object of Ridicule

30 But now *they that are* younger than I have me in derision, whose fathers I would have disdained to have set with the dogs of my flock.
2 Yea, whereto *might* the strength of their hands *profit* me, in whom old age was perished?
3 For want and famine *they were* solitary; fleeing into the wilderness in former time desolate and waste.
4 Who cut up mallows by the bushes, and juniper roots *for* their meat.
5 They were driven forth from among *men*, (they cried after them as *after* a thief;)
6 To dwell in the clifts of the valleys, *in* caves of the earth, and *in* the rocks.

7 Among the bushes they brayed; under the nettles they were gathered
together.
8 *They were* children of fools, yea, children of base men: they were viler than
the earth.
9 And now am I their song, yea, I am their byword.
10 They abhor me, they flee far from me, and spare not to spit in my face.
11 Because he hath loosed my cord, and afflicted me, they have also let loose
the bridle before me.
12 Upon *my* right *hand* rise the youth; they push away my feet, and they raise
up against me the ways of their destruction.
13 They mar my path, they set forward my calamity, they have no helper.
14 They came *upon me* as a wide breaking in *of waters*: in the desolation they
rolled themselves *upon me.*

Job: I Am Being Punished by God

15 Terrors are turned upon me: they pursue my soul as the wind: and my
welfare passeth away as a cloud.
16 And now my soul is poured out upon me; the days of affliction have taken
hold upon me.
17 My bones are pierced in me in the night season: and my sinews take no
rest.
18 By the great force *of my disease* is my garment changed: it bindeth me
about as the collar of my coat.
19 He hath cast me into the mire, and I am become like dust and ashes.
20 I cry unto thee, and thou dost not hear me: I stand up, and thou regardest
me *not.*
21 Thou art become cruel to me: with thy strong hand thou opposest thyself
against me.
22 Thou liftest me up to the wind; thou causest me to ride *upon it,* and dis-
solvest my substance.
23 For I know *that* thou wilt bring me *to* death, and *to* the house appointed
for all living.
24 Howbeit he will not stretch out *his* hand to the grave, though they cry in
his destruction.
25 Did not I weep for him that was in trouble? was *not* my soul grieved for
the poor?
26 When I looked for good, then evil came *unto me*: and when I waited for
light, there came darkness.
27 My bowels boiled, and rested not: the days of affliction prevented me.
28 I went mourning without the sun: I stood up, *and* I cried in the congre-
gation.
29 I am a brother to dragons, and a companion to owls.
30 My skin is black upon me, and my bones are burned with heat.
31 My harp also is *turned* to mourning, and my organ into the voice of them
that weep.

Job: What Sin Have I Committed?

31 I made a covenant with mine eyes; why then should I think upon a
maid?
2 For what portion of God *is there* from above? and *what* inheritance of the
Almighty from on high?
3 *Is* not destruction to the wicked? and a strange *punishment* to the workers
of iniquity?
4 Doth not he see my ways, and count all my steps?
5 If I have walked with vanity, or if my foot hath hasted to deceit;
6 Let me be weighed in an even balance, that God may know mine integrity.

7 If my step hath turned out of the way, and mine heart walked after mine
eyes, and if any blot hath cleaved to mine hands;
8 *Then* let me sow, and let another eat; yea, let my offspring be rooted out.
9 If mine heart have been deceived by a woman, or *if* I have laid wait at my
neighbour's door;
10 *Then* let my wife grind unto another, and let others bow down upon her.
11 For this *is* an heinous crime; yea, it *is* an iniquity *to be punished by* the
judges.
12 For it *is* a fire *that* consumeth to destruction, and would root out all mine
increase.
13 If I did despise the cause of my manservant or of my maidservant, when
they contended with me;
14 What then shall I do when God riseth up? and when he visiteth, what shall
I answer him?
15 Did not he that made me in the womb make him? and did not one fashion
us in the womb?
16 If I have withheld the poor from *their* desire, or have caused the eyes of
the widow to fail;
17 Or have eaten my morsel myself alone, and the fatherless hath not eaten
thereof;
18 (For from my youth he was brought up with me, as *with* a father, and I
have guided her from my mother's womb;)
19 If I have seen any perish for want of clothing, or any poor without cover-
ing;
20 If his loins have not blessed me, and *if* he were *not* warmed with the fleece
of my sheep;
21 If I have lifted up my hand against the fatherless, when I saw my help in
the gate:
22 *Then* let mine arm fall from my shoulder blade, and mine arm be broken
from the bone.
23 For destruction *from* God *was* a terror to me, and by reason of his highness
I could not endure.
24 If I have made gold my hope, or have said to the fine gold, *Thou art* my
confidence;
25 If I rejoiced because my wealth *was* great, and because mine hand had
gotten much;
26 If I beheld the sun when it shined, or the moon walking *in* brightness;
27 And my heart hath been secretly enticed, or my mouth hath kissed my
hand:
28 This also *were* an iniquity *to be punished by* the judge: for I should have
denied the God *that is* above.
29 If I rejoiced at the destruction of him that hated me, or lifted up myself
when evil found him:
30 Neither have I suffered my mouth to sin by wishing a curse to his soul.
31 If the men of my tabernacle said not, Oh that we had of his flesh! we
cannot be satisfied.
32 The stranger did not lodge in the street: *but* I opened my doors to the
traveller.
33 If I covered my transgressions as Adam, by hiding mine iniquity in my
bosom:
34 Did I fear a great multitude, or did the contempt of families terrify me,
that I kept silence, *and* went not out of the door?
35 Oh that one would hear me! behold, my desire *is, that* the Almighty would
answer me, and *that* mine adversary had written a book.
36 Surely I would take it upon my shoulder, *and* bind it *as* a crown to me.

37 I would declare unto him the number of my steps; as a prince would I go
near unto him.
38 If my land cry against me, or that the furrows likewise thereof complain;
39 If I have eaten the fruits thereof without money, or have caused the own-
ers thereof to lose their life:
40 Let thistles grow instead of wheat, and cockle instead of barley. The words
of Job are ended.

A Fourth Friend, Elihu, Decides to Speak

32 So these three men ceased to answer Job, because he *was* righteous in
his own eyes.
2 Then was kindled the wrath of Elihu the son of Barachel the Buzite, of the
kindred of Ram: against Job was his wrath kindled, because he justified him-
self rather than God.
3 Also against his three friends was his wrath kindled, because they had
found no answer, and *yet* had condemned Job.
4 Now Elihu had waited till Job had spoken, because they *were* elder than he.
5 When Elihu saw that *there was* no answer in the mouth of *these* three men,
then his wrath was kindled.

Elihu: I Am Young, but Your Words Anger Me

6 And Elihu the son of Barachel the Buzite answered and said, I *am* young,
and ye *are* very old; wherefore I was afraid, and durst not shew you mine
opinion.
7 I said, Days should speak, and multitude of years should teach wisdom.
8 But *there is* a spirit in man: and the inspiration of the Almighty giveth them
understanding.
9 Great men are not *always* wise: neither do the aged understand judgment.
10 Therefore I said, Hearken to me; I also will shew mine opinion.
11 Behold, I waited for your words; I gave ear to your reasons, whilst ye
searched out what to say.
12 Yea, I attended unto you, and, behold, *there was* none of you that con-
vinced Job, *or* that answered his words:
13 Lest ye should say, We have found out wisdom: God thrusteth him down,
not man.
14 Now he hath not directed *his* words against me: neither will I answer him
with your speeches.
15 They were amazed, they answered no more: they left off speaking.
16 When I had waited, (for they spake not, but stood still, *and* answered no
more;)
17 *I said*, I will answer also my part, I also will shew mine opinion.
18 For I am full of matter, the spirit within me constraineth me.
19 Behold, my belly *is* as wine *which* hath no vent; it is ready to burst like new
bottles.
20 I will speak, that I may be refreshed: I will open my lips and answer.
21 Let me not, I pray you, accept any man's person, neither let me give flat-
tering titles unto man.
22 For I know not to give flattering titles; *in so doing* my maker would soon
take me away.

Elihu: I Want to Reason with You

33 Wherefore, Job, I pray thee, hear my speeches, and hearken to all my
words.
2 Behold, now I have opened my mouth, my tongue hath spoken in my
mouth.
3 My words *shall be of* the uprightness of my heart: and my lips shall utter
knowledge clearly.

4 The Spirit of God hath made me, and the breath of the Almighty hath given
me life.
5 If thou canst answer me, set *thy words* in order before me, stand up.
6 Behold, I *am* according to thy wish in God's stead: I also am formed out of
the clay.
7 Behold, my terror shall not make thee afraid, neither shall my hand be
heavy upon thee.

Elihu: God Does Not Have to Answer You

8 Surely thou hast spoken in mine hearing, and I have heard the voice of *thy*
words, *saying,*
9 I am clean without transgression, I *am* innocent; neither *is there* iniquity
in me.
10 Behold, he findeth occasions against me, he counteth me for his enemy,
11 He putteth my feet in the stocks, he marketh all my paths.
12 Behold, *in* this thou art not just: I will answer thee, that God is greater
than man.
13 Why dost thou strive against him? for he giveth not account of any of his
matters.

Elihu: God Calls Man to Repentance in Many Ways

14 For God speaketh once, yea twice, *yet man* perceiveth it not.
15 In a dream, in a vision of the night, when deep sleep falleth upon men, in
slumberings upon the bed;
16 Then he openeth the ears of men, and sealeth their instruction,
17 That he may withdraw man *from his* purpose, and hide pride from man.
18 He keepeth back his soul from the pit, and his life from perishing by the
sword.
19 He is chastened also with pain upon his bed, and the multitude of his
bones with strong *pain*:
20 So that his life abhorreth bread, and his soul dainty meat.
21 His flesh is consumed away, that it cannot be seen; and his bones *that*
were not seen stick out.
22 Yea, his soul draweth near unto the grave, and his life to the destroyers.
23 If there be a messenger with him, an interpreter, one among a thousand,
to shew unto man his uprightness:
24 Then he is gracious unto him, and saith, Deliver him from going down to
the pit: I have found a ransom.
25 His flesh shall be fresher than a child's: he shall return to the days of his
youth:
26 He shall pray unto God, and he will be favourable unto him: and he shall
see his face with joy: for he will render unto man his righteousness.
27 He looketh upon men, and *if any* say, I have sinned, and perverted *that
which was* right, and it profited me not;
28 He will deliver his soul from going into the pit, and his life shall see the
light.
29 Lo, all these *things* worketh God oftentimes with man,
30 To bring back his soul from the pit, to be enlightened with the light of the
living.
31 Mark well, O Job, hearken unto me: hold thy peace, and I will speak.
32 If thou hast any thing to say, answer me: speak, for I desire to justify thee.
33 If not, hearken unto me: hold thy peace, and I shall teach thee wisdom.

Elihu: Do Not Charge God with Injustice

34 Furthermore Elihu answered and said,
2 Hear my words, O ye wise *men*; and give ear unto me, ye that have
knowledge.
3 For the ear trieth words, as the mouth tasteth meat.

4 Let us choose to us judgment: let us know among ourselves what *is* good.
5 For Job hath said, I am righteous: and God hath taken away my judgment.
6 Should I lie against my right? my wound *is* incurable without transgression.
7 What man *is* like Job, *who* drinketh up scorning like water?
8 Which goeth in company with the workers of iniquity, and walketh with
wicked men.
9 For he hath said, It profiteth a man nothing that he should delight himself
with God.

Elihu: God Cannot Be Unjust

10 Therefore hearken unto me, ye men of understanding: far be it from God,
that he should do wickedness; and *from* the Almighty, *that he should commit*
iniquity.
11 For the work of a man shall he render unto him, and cause every man to
find according to *his* ways.
12 Yea, surely God will not do wickedly, neither will the Almighty pervert
judgment.
13 Who hath given him a charge over the earth? or who hath disposed the
whole world?
14 If he set his heart upon man, *if* he gather unto himself his spirit and his
breath;
15 All flesh shall perish together, and man shall turn again unto dust.
16 If now *thou hast* understanding, hear this: hearken to the voice of my
words.
17 Shall even he that hateth right govern? and wilt thou condemn him that
is most just?
18 *Is it fit* to say to a king, *Thou art* wicked? *and* to princes, *Ye are* ungodly?
19 *How much less to him* that accepteth not the persons of princes, nor
regardeth the rich more than the poor? for they all *are* the work of his hands.
20 In a moment shall they die, and the people shall be troubled at midnight,
and pass away: and the mighty shall be taken away without hand.
21 For his eyes *are* upon the ways of man, and he seeth all his goings.
22 *There is* no darkness, nor shadow of death, where the workers of iniquity
may hide themselves.
23 For he will not lay upon man more *than right*; that he should enter into
judgment with God.
24 He shall break in pieces mighty men without number, and set others in
their stead.
25 Therefore he knoweth their works, and he overturneth *them* in the night,
so that they are destroyed.
26 He striketh them as wicked men in the open sight of others;
27 Because they turned back from him, and would not consider any of his
ways:
28 So that they cause the cry of the poor to come unto him, and he heareth
the cry of the afflicted.
29 When he giveth quietness, who then can make trouble? and when he
hideth *his* face, who then can behold him? whether *it be done* against a nation,
or against a man only:
30 That the hypocrite reign not, lest the people be ensnared.

Elihu: Humble Yourself before God

31 Surely it is meet to be said unto God, I have borne *chastisement*, I will not
offend *any more*:
32 *That which* I see not teach thou me: if I have done iniquity, I will do no
more.
33 *Should it be* according to thy mind? he will recompense it, whether thou
refuse, or whether thou choose; and not I: therefore speak what thou knowest.

34 Let men of understanding tell me, and let a wise man hearken unto me.
35 Job hath spoken without knowledge, and his words *were* without wisdom.
36 My desire *is that* Job may be tried unto the end because of *his* answers for
wicked men.
37 For he addeth rebellion unto his sin, he clappeth *his hands* among us, and
multiplieth his words against God.

Elihu: Human Behavior Cannot Change God

35 Elihu spake moreover, and said,
2 Thinkest thou this to be right, *that* thou saidst, My righteousness *is*
more than God's?
3 For thou saidst, What advantage will it be unto thee? *and*, What profit shall
I have, *if I be cleansed* from my sin?
4 I will answer thee, and thy companions with thee.
5 Look unto the heavens, and see; and behold the clouds *which* are higher
than thou.
6 If thou sinnest, what doest thou against him? or *if* thy transgressions be
multiplied, what doest thou unto him?
7 If thou be righteous, what givest thou him? or what receiveth he of thine
hand?
8 Thy wickedness *may hurt* a man as thou *art*; and thy righteousness *may
profit* the son of man.
9 By reason of the multitude of oppressions they make *the oppressed* to cry:
they cry out by reason of the arm of the mighty.
10 But none saith, Where *is* God my maker, who giveth songs in the night;
11 Who teacheth us more than the beasts of the earth, and maketh us wiser
than the fowls of heaven?
12 There they cry, but none giveth answer, because of the pride of evil men.
13 Surely God will not hear vanity, neither will the Almighty regard it.
14 Although thou sayest thou shalt not see him, *yet* judgment *is* before him;
therefore trust thou in him.
15 But now, because *it is* not *so*, he hath visited in his anger; yet he knoweth
it not in great extremity:
16 Therefore doth Job open his mouth in vain; he multiplieth words without
knowledge.

Elihu: God Is Just in All His Ways

36 Elihu also proceeded, and said,
2 Suffer me a little, and I will shew thee that *I have* yet to speak on God's
behalf.
3 I will fetch my knowledge from afar, and will ascribe righteousness to my
Maker.
4 For truly my words *shall* not *be* false: he that is perfect in knowledge *is* with
thee.
5 Behold, God *is* mighty, and despiseth not *any: he is* mighty in strength *and*
wisdom.
6 He preserveth not the life of the wicked: but giveth right to the poor.
7 He withdraweth not his eyes from the righteous: but with kings *are they*
on the throne; yea, he doth establish them for ever, and they are exalted.
8 And if *they be* bound in fetters, *and* be holden in cords of affliction;
9 Then he sheweth them their work, and their transgressions that they have
exceeded.
10 He openeth also their ear to discipline, and commandeth that they return
from iniquity.
11 If they obey and serve *him*, they shall spend their days in prosperity, and
their years in pleasures.

12 But if they obey not, they shall perish by the sword, and they shall die
without knowledge.
13 But the hypocrites in heart heap up wrath: they cry not when he bindeth
them.
14 They die in youth, and their life *is* among the unclean.
15 He delivereth the poor in his affliction, and openeth their ears in oppres-
sion.
16 Even so would he have removed thee out of the strait *into* a broad place,
where *there is* no straitness; and that which should be set on thy table *should
be* full of fatness.
17 But thou hast fulfilled the judgment of the wicked: judgment and justice
take hold *on thee.*
18 Because *there is* wrath, *beware* lest he take thee away with *his* stroke: then
a great ransom cannot deliver thee.
19 Will he esteem thy riches? *no,* not gold, nor all the forces of strength.
20 Desire not the night, when people are cut off in their place.
21 Take heed, regard not iniquity: for this hast thou chosen rather than afflic-
tion.
22 Behold, God exalteth by his power: who teacheth like him?
23 Who hath enjoined him his way? or who can say, Thou hast wrought
iniquity?

Elihu: Magnify God's Works

24 Remember that thou magnify his work, which men behold.
25 Every man may see it; man may behold *it* afar off.
26 Behold, God *is* great, and we know *him* not, neither can the number of
his years be searched out.
27 For he maketh small the drops of water: they pour down rain according
to the vapour thereof:
28 Which the clouds do drop *and* distil upon man abundantly.
29 Also can *any* understand the spreadings of the clouds, *or* the noise of his
tabernacle?
30 Behold, he spreadeth his light upon it, and covereth the bottom of the sea.
31 For by them judgeth he the people; he giveth meat in abundance.
32 With clouds he covereth the light; and commandeth it *not to shine* by *the
cloud* that cometh betwixt.
33 The noise thereof sheweth concerning it, the cattle also concerning the
vapour.

Elihu: God Is to Be Feared

37 At this also my heart trembleth, and is moved out of his place.
2 Hear attentively the noise of his voice, and the sound *that* goeth out
of his mouth.
3 He directeth it under the whole heaven, and his lightning unto the ends
of the earth.
4 After it a voice roareth: he thundereth with the voice of his excellency; and
he will not stay them when his voice is heard.
5 God thundereth marvellously with his voice; great things doeth he, which
we cannot comprehend.
6 For he saith to the snow, Be thou *on* the earth; likewise to the small rain,
and to the great rain of his strength.
7 He sealeth up the hand of every man; that all men may know his work.
8 Then the beasts go into dens, and remain in their places.
9 Out of the south cometh the whirlwind: and cold out of the north.
10 By the breath of God frost is given: and the breadth of the waters is strait-
ened.

11 Also by watering he wearieth the thick cloud: he scattereth his bright
cloud:
12 And it is turned round about by his counsels: that they may do whatsoev-
er he commandeth them upon the face of the world in the earth.
13 He causeth it to come, whether for correction, or for his land, or for mercy.
14 Hearken unto this, O Job: stand still, and consider the wondrous works
of God.
15 Dost thou know when God disposed them, and caused the light of his
cloud to shine?
16 Dost thou know the balancings of the clouds, the wondrous works of him
which is perfect in knowledge?
17 How thy garments *are* warm, when he quieteth the earth by the south
wind?
18 Hast thou with him spread out the sky, *which is* strong, *and* as a molten
looking glass?
19 Teach us what we shall say unto him; *for* we cannot order *our speech* by
reason of darkness.
20 Shall it be told him that I speak? if a man speak, surely he shall be swal-
lowed up.
21 And now *men* see not the bright light which *is* in the clouds: but the wind
passeth, and cleanseth them.
22 Fair weather cometh out of the north: with God *is* terrible majesty.
23 *Touching* the Almighty, we cannot find him out: *he is* excellent in power,
and in judgment, and in plenty of justice: he will not afflict.
24 Men do therefore fear him: he respecteth not any *that are* wise of heart.

God: Who Is Able to Challenge Me?

38 Then the LORD answered Job out of the whirlwind, and said,
2 Who *is* this that darkeneth counsel by words without knowledge?
3 Gird up now thy loins like a man; for I will demand of thee, and answer
thou me.

God: Where Were You during Creation?

4 Where wast thou when I laid the foundations of the earth? declare, if thou
hast understanding.
5 Who hath laid the measures thereof, if thou knowest? or who hath
stretched the line upon it?
6 Whereupon are the foundations thereof fastened? or who laid the corner
stone thereof;
7 When the morning stars sang together, and all the sons of God shouted for joy?
8 Or *who* shut up the sea with doors, when it brake forth, *as if* it had issued
out of the womb?
9 When I made the cloud the garment thereof, and thick darkness a swad-
dlingband for it,
10 And brake up for it my decreed *place*, and set bars and doors,
11 And said, Hitherto shalt thou come, but no further: and here shall thy
proud waves be stayed?
12 Hast thou commanded the morning since thy days; *and* caused the day-
spring to know his place;
13 That it might take hold of the ends of the earth, that the wicked might be
shaken out of it?
14 It is turned as clay *to* the seal; and they stand as a garment.
15 And from the wicked their light is withholden, and the high arm shall be
broken.
16 Hast thou entered into the springs of the sea? or hast thou walked in the
search of the depth?

17 Have the gates of death been opened unto thee? or hast thou seen the
doors of the shadow of death?
18 Hast thou perceived the breadth of the earth? declare if thou knowest it
all.
19 Where *is* the way *where* light dwelleth? and *as for* darkness, where *is* the
place thereof,
20 That thou shouldest take it to the bound thereof, and that thou shouldest
know the paths *to* the house thereof?
21 Knowest thou *it*, because thou wast then born? or *because* the number
of thy days *is* great?
22 Hast thou entered into the treasures of the snow? or hast thou seen the
treasures of the hail,
23 Which I have reserved against the time of trouble, against the day of bat-
tle and war?
24 By what way is the light parted, *which* scattereth the east wind upon the
earth?
25 Who hath divided a watercourse for the overflowing of waters, or a way
for the lightning of thunder;
26 To cause it to rain on the earth, *where* no man *is; on* the wilderness, where-
in *there is* no man;
27 To satisfy the desolate and waste *ground*; and to cause the bud of the ten-
der herb to spring forth?
28 Hath the rain a father? or who hath begotten the drops of dew?
29 Out of whose womb came the ice? and the hoary frost of heaven, who
hath gendered it?
30 The waters are hid as *with* a stone, and the face of the deep is frozen.
31 Canst thou bind the sweet influences of Pleiades, or loose the bands of
Orion?
32 Canst thou bring forth Mazzaroth in his season? or canst thou guide
Arcturus with his sons?
33 Knowest thou the ordinances of heaven? canst thou set the dominion
thereof in the earth?
34 Canst thou lift up thy voice to the clouds, that abundance of waters may
cover thee?
35 Canst thou send lightnings, that they may go, and say unto thee, Here we
are?
36 Who hath put wisdom in the inward parts? or who hath given under-
standing to the heart?
37 Who can number the clouds in wisdom? or who can stay the bottles of
heaven,
38 When the dust groweth into hardness, and the clods cleave fast together?
39 Wilt thou hunt the prey for the lion? or fill the appetite of the young lions,
40 When they couch in *their* dens, *and* abide in the covert to lie in wait?
41 Who provideth for the raven his food? when his young ones cry unto God,
they wander for lack of meat.

God: Consider My Amazing Creation

39 Knowest thou the time when the wild goats of the rock bring forth?
or canst thou mark when the hinds do calve?
2 Canst thou number the months *that* they fulfil? or knowest thou the time
when they bring forth?
3 They bow themselves, they bring forth their young ones, they cast out their
sorrows.
4 Their young ones are in good liking, they grow up with corn; they go forth,
and return not unto them.
5 Who hath sent out the wild ass free? or who hath loosed the bands of the
wild ass?

6 Whose house I have made the wilderness, and the barren land his dwellings.
7 He scorneth the multitude of the city, neither regardeth he the crying of
the driver.
8 The range of the mountains *is* his pasture, and he searcheth after every
green thing.
9 Will the unicorn be willing to serve thee, or abide by thy crib?
10 Canst thou bind the unicorn with his band in the furrow? or will he har-
row the valleys after thee?
11 Wilt thou trust him, because his strength *is* great? or wilt thou leave thy
labour to him?
12 Wilt thou believe him, that he will bring home thy seed, and gather *it into*
thy barn?
13 *Gavest thou* the goodly wings unto the peacocks? or wings and feathers
unto the ostrich?
14 Which leaveth her eggs in the earth, and warmeth them in dust,
15 And forgetteth that the foot may crush them, or that the wild beast may
break them.
16 She is hardened against her young ones, as though *they were* not hers: her
labour is in vain without fear;
17 Because God hath deprived her of wisdom, neither hath he imparted to
her understanding.
18 What time she lifteth up herself on high, she scorneth the horse and his
rider.
19 Hast thou given the horse strength? hast thou clothed his neck with thun-
der?
20 Canst thou make him afraid as a grasshopper? the glory of his nostrils *is*
terrible.
21 He paweth in the valley, and rejoiceth in *his* strength: he goeth on to meet
the armed men.
22 He mocketh at fear, and is not affrighted; neither turneth he back from
the sword.
23 The quiver rattleth against him, the glittering spear and the shield.
24 He swalloweth the ground with fierceness and rage: neither believeth he
that *it is* the sound of the trumpet.
25 He saith among the trumpets, Ha, ha; and he smelleth the battle afar off,
the thunder of the captains, and the shouting.
26 Doth the hawk fly by thy wisdom, *and* stretch her wings toward the south?
27 Doth the eagle mount up at thy command, and make her nest on high?
28 She dwelleth and abideth on the rock, upon the crag of the rock, and the
strong place.
29 From thence she seeketh the prey, *and* her eyes behold afar off.
30 Her young ones also suck up blood: and where the slain *are*, there *is* she.

Job: God, I Humble Myself before You

40 Moreover the LORD answered Job, and said,
2 Shall he that contendeth with the Almighty instruct *him*? he that
reproveth God, let him answer it.
3 Then Job answered the LORD, and said,
4 Behold, I am vile; what shall I answer thee? I will lay mine hand upon my
mouth.
5 Once have I spoken; but I will not answer: yea, twice; but I will proceed no
further.

God: Can You Be like Me?

6 Then answered the LORD unto Job out of the whirlwind, and said,
7 Gird up thy loins now like a man: I will demand of thee, and declare thou
unto me.

8 Wilt thou also disannul my judgment? wilt thou condemn me, that thou
mayest be righteous?
9 Hast thou an arm like God? or canst thou thunder with a voice like him?
10 Deck thyself now *with* majesty and excellency; and array thyself with glory
and beauty.
11 Cast abroad the rage of thy wrath: and behold every one *that is* proud,
and abase him.
12 Look on every one *that is* proud, *and* bring him low; and tread down the
wicked in their place.
13 Hide them in the dust together; *and* bind their faces in secret.
14 Then will I also confess unto thee that thine own right hand can save thee.
15 Behold now behemoth, which I made with thee; he eateth grass as an ox.
16 Lo now, his strength *is* in his loins, and his force *is* in the navel of his belly.
17 He moveth his tail like a cedar: the sinews of his stones are wrapped together.
18 His bones *are as* strong pieces of brass; his bones *are* like bars of iron.
19 He *is* the chief of the ways of God: he that made him can make his sword
to approach *unto him.*
20 Surely the mountains bring him forth food, where all the beasts of the
field play.
21 He lieth under the shady trees, in the covert of the reed, and fens.
22 The shady trees cover him *with* their shadow; the willows of the brook
compass him about.
23 Behold, he drinketh up a river, *and* hasteth not: he trusteth that he can
draw up Jordan into his mouth.
24 He taketh it with his eyes: *his* nose pierceth through snares.

God: Can You Conquer Leviathan?

41 Canst thou draw out leviathan with an hook? or his tongue with a cord
which thou lettest down?
2 Canst thou put an hook into his nose? or bore his jaw through with a thorn?
3 Will he make many supplications unto thee? will he speak soft *words* unto
thee?
4 Will he make a covenant with thee? wilt thou take him for a servant for
ever?
5 Wilt thou play with him as *with* a bird? or wilt thou bind him for thy
maidens?
6 Shall the companions make a banquet of him? shall they part him among
the merchants?
7 Canst thou fill his skin with barbed irons? or his head with fish spears?
8 Lay thine hand upon him, remember the battle, do no more.
9 Behold, the hope of him is in vain: shall not *one* be cast down even at the
sight of him?
10 None *is so* fierce that dare stir him up: who then is able to stand before me?
11 Who hath prevented me, that I should repay *him? whatsoever is* under
the whole heaven is mine.
12 I will not conceal his parts, nor his power, nor his comely proportion.
13 Who can discover the face of his garment? *or* who can come *to him* with
his double bridle?
14 Who can open the doors of his face? his teeth *are* terrible round about.
15 *His* scales *are his* pride, shut up together *as with* a close seal.
16 One is so near to another, that no air can come between them.
17 They are joined one to another, they stick together, that they cannot be
sundered.
18 By his neesings a light doth shine, and his eyes *are* like the eyelids of the
morning.
19 Out of his mouth go burning lamps, *and* sparks of fire leap out.

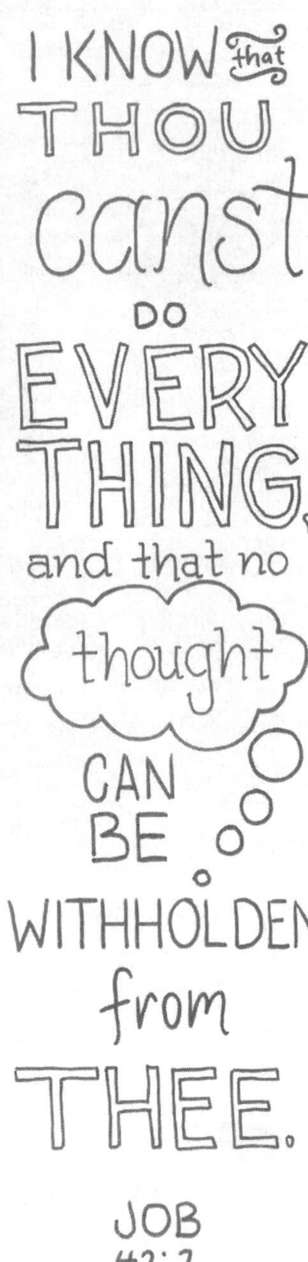

20 Out of his nostrils goeth smoke, as *out* of a seething pot or caldron.
21 His breath kindleth coals, and a flame goeth out of his mouth.
22 In his neck remaineth strength, and sorrow is turned into joy before him.
23 The flakes of his flesh are joined together: they are firm in themselves;
they cannot be moved.
24 His heart is as firm as a stone; yea, as hard as a piece of the nether *millstone*.
25 When he raiseth up himself, the mighty are afraid: by reason of breakings
they purify themselves.
26 The sword of him that layeth at him cannot hold: the spear, the dart, nor
the habergeon.
27 He esteemeth iron as straw, *and* brass as rotten wood.
28 The arrow cannot make him flee: slingstones are turned with him into
stubble.
29 Darts are counted as stubble: he laugheth at the shaking of a spear.
30 Sharp stones *are* under him: he spreadeth sharp pointed things upon the
mire.
31 He maketh the deep to boil like a pot: he maketh the sea like a pot of
ointment.
32 He maketh a path to shine after him; *one* would think the deep *to be* hoary.
33 Upon earth there is not his like, who is made without fear.
34 He beholdeth all high *things*: he *is* a king over all the children of pride.

Job Submits Himself to God

42 Then Job answered the LORD, and said,
2 I know that thou canst do every *thing*, and *that* no thought can be
withholden from thee.
3 Who *is* he that hideth counsel without knowledge? therefore have I uttered
that I understood not; things too wonderful for me, which I knew not.
4 Hear, I beseech thee, and I will speak: I will demand of thee, and declare
thou unto me.
5 I have heard of thee by the hearing of the ear: but now mine eye seeth thee.
6 Wherefore I abhor *myself*, and repent in dust and ashes.

God Disciplines Job's Friends

7 And it was *so*, that after the LORD had spoken these words unto Job, the
LORD said to Eliphaz the Temanite, My wrath is kindled against thee, and
against thy two friends: for ye have not spoken of me *the thing that is* right,
as my servant Job *hath*.
8 Therefore take unto you now seven bullocks and seven rams, and go to my
servant Job, and offer up for yourselves a burnt offering; and my servant Job
shall pray for you: for him will I accept: lest I deal with you *after your* folly, in
that ye have not spoken of me *the thing which is* right, like my servant Job.
9 So Eliphaz the Temanite and Bildad the Shuhite *and* Zophar the Naamathite
went, and did according as the LORD commanded them: the LORD also accept-
ed Job.

God Restores and Blesses Job

10 And the LORD turned the captivity of Job, when he prayed for his friends:
also the LORD gave Job twice as much as he had before.
11 Then came there unto him all his brethren, and all his sisters, and all they
that had been of his acquaintance before, and did eat bread with him in his
house: and they bemoaned him, and comforted him over all the evil that the
LORD had brought upon him: every man also gave him a piece of money, and
every one an earring of gold.
12 So the LORD blessed the latter end of Job more than his beginning: for he
had fourteen thousand sheep, and six thousand camels, and a thousand yoke
of oxen, and a thousand she asses.
13 He had also seven sons and three daughters.

14 And he called the name of the first, Jemima; and the name of the second,
Kezia; and the name of the third, Keren-happuch.
15 And in all the land were no women found *so* fair as the daughters of Job:
and their father gave them inheritance among their brethren.
16 After this lived Job an hundred and forty years, and saw his sons, and his
sons' sons, *even* four generations.
17 So Job died, *being* old and full of days.

PSALM 1
The Godly and the Ungodly

Blessed *is* the man that walketh not in the counsel of the ungodly, nor standeth in the way of sinners, nor sitteth in the seat of the scornful.
2 But his delight *is* in the law of the LORD; and in his law doth he meditate day and night.
3 And he shall be like a tree planted by the rivers of water, that bringeth forth his fruit in his season; his leaf also shall not wither; and whatsoever he doeth shall prosper.
4 The ungodly *are* not so: but *are* like the chaff which the wind driveth away.
5 Therefore the ungodly shall not stand in the judgment, nor sinners in the congregation of the righteous.
6 For the LORD knoweth the way of the righteous: but the way of the ungodly shall perish.

PSALM 2
The Kingdom of Christ

Why do the heathen rage, and the people imagine a vain thing?
2 The kings of the earth set themselves, and the rulers take counsel together, against the LORD, and against his anointed, *saying*,
3 Let us break their bands asunder, and cast away their cords from us.
4 He that sitteth in the heavens shall laugh: the Lord shall have them in derision.
5 Then shall he speak unto them in his wrath, and vex them in his sore displeasure.
6 Yet have I set my king upon my holy hill of Zion.
7 I will declare the decree: the LORD hath said unto me, Thou *art* my Son; this day have I begotten thee.
8 Ask of me, and I shall give *thee* the heathen *for* thine inheritance, and the uttermost parts of the earth *for* thy possession.
9 Thou shalt break them with a rod of iron; thou shalt dash them in pieces like a potter's vessel.
10 Be wise now therefore, O ye kings: be instructed, ye judges of the earth.
11 Serve the LORD with fear, and rejoice with trembling.
12 Kiss the Son, lest he be angry, and ye perish *from* the way, when his wrath is kindled but a little. Blessed *are* all they that put their trust in him.

PSALM 3
The Security of God's Protection

A Psalm of David, when he fled from Absalom his son.

LORD, how are they increased that trouble me! many *are* they that rise up against me.
2 Many *there be* which say of my soul, *There is* no help for him in God. Selah.
3 But thou, O LORD, *art* a shield for me; my glory, and the lifter up of mine head.
4 I cried unto the LORD with my voice, and he heard me out of his holy hill. Selah.
5 I laid me down and slept; I awaked; for the LORD sustained me.

6 I will not be afraid of ten thousands of people, that have set *themselves*
against me round about.
7 Arise, O LORD; save me, O my God: for thou hast smitten all mine enemies
upon the cheek bone; thou hast broken the teeth of the ungodly.
8 Salvation *belongeth* unto the LORD: thy blessing *is* upon thy people. Selah.

PSALM 4

David Prays for God to Hear Him

To the chief Musician on Neginoth, A Psalm of David.

Hear me when I call, O God of my righteousness: thou hast enlarged me
when I was in distress; have mercy upon me, and hear my prayer.
2 O ye sons of men, how long *will ye turn* my glory into shame? *how long* will
ye love vanity, *and* seek after leasing? Selah.
3 But know that the LORD hath set apart him that is godly for himself: the
LORD will hear when I call unto him.
4 Stand in awe, and sin not: commune with your own heart upon your bed,
and be still. Selah.
5 Offer the sacrifices of righteousness, and put your trust in the LORD.
6 *There be* many that say, Who will shew us *any* good? LORD, lift thou up the
light of thy countenance upon us.
7 Thou hast put gladness in my heart, more than in the time *that* their corn
and their wine increased.
8 I will both lay me down in peace, and sleep: for thou, LORD, only makest
me dwell in safety.

PSALM 5

David Prays That God Will Defend and Guide Him

To the chief Musician upon Nehiloth, A Psalm of David.

Give ear to my words, O LORD, consider my meditation.
2 Hearken unto the voice of my cry, my King, and my God: for unto
thee will I pray.
3 My voice shalt thou hear in the morning, O LORD; in the morning will I
direct *my prayer* unto thee, and will look up.
4 For thou *art* not a God that hath pleasure in wickedness: neither shall evil
dwell with thee.
5 The foolish shall not stand in thy sight: thou hatest all workers of iniquity.
6 Thou shalt destroy them that speak leasing: the LORD will abhor the bloody
and deceitful man.
7 But as for me, I will come *into* thy house in the multitude of thy mercy: *and*
in thy fear will I worship toward thy holy temple.
8 Lead me, O LORD, in thy righteousness because of mine enemies; make thy
way straight before my face.
9 For *there is* no faithfulness in their mouth; their inward part *is* very wick-
edness; their throat *is* an open sepulchre; they flatter with their tongue.
10 Destroy thou them, O God; let them fall by their own counsels; cast them
out in the multitude of their transgressions; for they have rebelled against
thee.
11 But let all those that put their trust in thee rejoice: let them ever shout for
joy, because thou defendest them: let them also that love thy name be joyful
in thee.
12 For thou, LORD, wilt bless the righteous; with favour wilt thou compass
him as *with* a shield.

PSALM 6

David Prays for Deliverance

To the chief Musician on Neginoth upon Sheminith, A Psalm of David.

O LORD, rebuke me not in thine anger, neither chasten me in thy hot dis-
pleasure.
2 Have mercy upon me, O LORD; for I *am* weak: O LORD, heal me; for my bones
are vexed.
3 My soul is also sore vexed: but thou, O LORD, how long?
4 Return, O LORD, deliver my soul: oh save me for thy mercies' sake.
5 For in death *there is* no remembrance of thee: in the grave who shall give
thee thanks?
6 I am weary with my groaning; all the night make I my bed to swim; I water
my couch with my tears.
7 Mine eye is consumed because of grief; it waxeth old because of all mine
enemies.
8 Depart from me, all ye workers of iniquity; for the LORD hath heard the
voice of my weeping.
9 The LORD hath heard my supplication; the LORD will receive my prayer.
10 Let all mine enemies be ashamed and sore vexed: let them return *and* be
ashamed suddenly.

PSALM 7

David Prays for Justice

Shiggaion of David, which he sang unto the LORD, concerning the words of Cush the Benjamite.

O LORD my God, in thee do I put my trust: save me from all them that per-
secute me, and deliver me:
2 Lest he tear my soul like a lion, rending *it* in pieces, while *there is* none to
deliver.
3 O LORD my God, if I have done this; if there be iniquity in my hands;
4 If I have rewarded evil unto him that was at peace with me; (yea, I have
delivered him that without cause is mine enemy:)
5 Let the enemy persecute my soul, and take *it*; yea, let him tread down my
life upon the earth, and lay mine honour in the dust. Selah.
6 Arise, O LORD, in thine anger, lift up thyself because of the rage of mine
enemies: and awake for me *to* the judgment *that* thou hast commanded.
7 So shall the congregation of the people compass thee about: for their sakes
therefore return thou on high.
8 The LORD shall judge the people: judge me, O LORD, according to my righ-
teousness, and according to mine integrity *that is* in me.
9 Oh let the wickedness of the wicked come to an end; but establish the just:
for the righteous God trieth the hearts and reins.
10 My defence *is* of God, which saveth the upright in heart.
11 God judgeth the righteous, and God is angry *with the wicked* every day.
12 If he turn not, he will whet his sword; he hath bent his bow, and made it
ready.
13 He hath also prepared for him the instruments of death; he ordaineth his
arrows against the persecutors.
14 Behold, he travaileth with iniquity, and hath conceived mischief, and
brought forth falsehood.
15 He made a pit, and digged it, and is fallen into the ditch *which* he made.
16 His mischief shall return upon his own head, and his violent dealing shall
come down upon his own pate.
17 I will praise the LORD according to his righteousness: and will sing praise
to the name of the LORD most high.

PSALM 8
Man Is God's Marvelous Creation
To the chief Musician upon Gittith, A Psalm of David.

O LORD our Lord, how excellent *is* thy name in all the earth! who hast set
thy glory above the heavens.
2 Out of the mouth of babes and sucklings hast thou ordained strength
because of thine enemies, that thou mightest still the enemy and the avenger.
3 When I consider thy heavens, the work of thy fingers, the moon and the
stars, which thou hast ordained;
4 What is man, that thou art mindful of him? and the son of man, that thou
visitest him?
5 For thou hast made him a little lower than the angels, and hast crowned
him with glory and honour.
6 Thou madest him to have dominion over the works of thy hands; thou hast
put all *things* under his feet:
7 All sheep and oxen, yea, and the beasts of the field;
8 The fowl of the air, and the fish of the sea, *and whatsoever* passeth through
the paths of the seas.
9 O LORD our Lord, how excellent *is* thy name in all the earth!

PSALM 9
David Praises God for Victory
To the chief Musician upon Muthlabben, A Psalm of David.

I will praise *thee*, O LORD, with my whole heart; I will shew forth all thy mar-
vellous works.
2 I will be glad and rejoice in thee: I will sing praise to thy name, O thou most
High.
3 When mine enemies are turned back, they shall fall and perish at thy pres-
ence.
4 For thou hast maintained my right and my cause; thou satest in the throne
judging right.
5 Thou hast rebuked the heathen, thou hast destroyed the wicked, thou hast
put out their name for ever and ever.
6 O thou enemy, destructions are come to a perpetual end: and thou hast
destroyed cities; their memorial is perished with them.
7 But the LORD shall endure for ever: he hath prepared his throne for judg-
ment.
8 And he shall judge the world in righteousness, he shall minister judgment
to the people in uprightness.
9 The LORD also will be a refuge for the oppressed, a refuge in times of trouble.
10 And they that know thy name will put their trust in thee: for thou, LORD,
hast not forsaken them that seek thee.
11 Sing praises to the LORD, which dwelleth in Zion: declare among the peo-
ple his doings.
12 When he maketh inquisition for blood, he remembereth them: he for-
getteth not the cry of the humble.
13 Have mercy upon me, O LORD; consider my trouble *which I suffer* of them
that hate me, thou that liftest me up from the gates of death:
14 That I may shew forth all thy praise in the gates of the daughter of Zion:
I will rejoice in thy salvation.
15 The heathen are sunk down in the pit *that* they made: in the net which
they hid is their own foot taken.
16 The LORD is known *by* the judgment *which* he executeth: the wicked is
snared in the work of his own hands. Higgaion. Selah.
17 The wicked shall be turned into hell, *and* all the nations that forget God.

18 For the needy shall not alway be forgotten: the expectation of the poor
shall *not* perish for ever.
19 Arise, O LORD; let not man prevail: let the heathen be judged in thy sight.
20 Put them in fear, O LORD: *that* the nations may know themselves *to be but*
men. Selah.

PSALM 10
David Complains to God about the Wicked

Why standest thou afar off, O LORD? *why* hidest thou *thyself* in times of
trouble?
2 The wicked in *his* pride doth persecute the poor: let them be taken in the
devices that they have imagined.
3 For the wicked boasteth of his heart's desire, and blesseth the covetous,
whom the LORD abhorreth.
4 The wicked, through the pride of his countenance, will not seek *after God*:
God *is* not in all his thoughts.
5 His ways are always grievous; thy judgments *are* far above out of his sight:
as for all his enemies, he puffeth at them.
6 He hath said in his heart, I shall not be moved: for *I shall* never *be* in
adversity.
7 His mouth is full of cursing and deceit and fraud: under his tongue *is* mis-
chief and vanity.
8 He sitteth in the lurking places of the villages: in the secret places doth he
murder the innocent: his eyes are privily set against the poor.
9 He lieth in wait secretly as a lion in his den: he lieth in wait to catch the
poor: he doth catch the poor, when he draweth him into his net.
10 He croucheth, *and* humbleth himself, that the poor may fall by his strong
ones.
11 He hath said in his heart, God hath forgotten: he hideth his face; he will
never see *it*.
12 Arise, O LORD; O God, lift up thine hand: forget not the humble.
13 Wherefore doth the wicked contemn God? he hath said in his heart, Thou
wilt not require *it*.
14 Thou hast seen *it*; for thou beholdest mischief and spite, to requite *it* with
thy hand: the poor committeth himself unto thee; thou art the helper of the
fatherless.
15 Break thou the arm of the wicked and the evil *man*: seek out his wickedness
till thou find none.
16 The LORD *is* King for ever and ever: the heathen are perished out of his
land.
17 LORD, thou hast heard the desire of the humble: thou wilt prepare their
heart, thou wilt cause thine ear to hear:
18 To judge the fatherless and the oppressed, that the man of the earth may
no more oppress.

PSALM 11
David Takes Refuge in God

To the chief Musician, A Psalm of David.

In the LORD put I my trust: how say ye to my soul, Flee *as* a bird to your moun-
tain?
2 For, lo, the wicked bend *their* bow, they make ready their arrow upon the
string, that they may privily shoot at the upright in heart.
3 If the foundations be destroyed, what can the righteous do?
4 The LORD *is* in his holy temple, the LORD's throne *is* in heaven: his eyes
behold, his eyelids try, the children of men.

5 The LORD trieth the righteous: but the wicked and him that loveth violence
his soul hateth.
6 Upon the wicked he shall rain snares, fire and brimstone, and an horrible
tempest: *this shall be* the portion of their cup.
7 For the righteous LORD loveth righteousness; his countenance doth behold
the upright.

PSALM 12
David Craves God's Protection

To the chief Musician upon Sheminith, A Psalm of David.

Help, LORD; for the godly man ceaseth; for the faithful fail from among the
children of men.
2 They speak vanity every one with his neighbour: *with* flattering lips *and*
with a double heart do they speak.
3 The LORD shall cut off all flattering lips, *and* the tongue that speaketh proud
things:
4 Who have said, With our tongue will we prevail; our lips *are* our own: who
is lord over us?
5 For the oppression of the poor, for the sighing of the needy, now will I arise,
saith the LORD; I will set *him* in safety *from him that* puffeth at him.
6 The words of the LORD *are* pure words: *as* silver tried in a furnace of earth,
purified seven times.
7 Thou shalt keep them, O LORD, thou shalt preserve them from this gener-
ation for ever.
8 The wicked walk on every side, when the vilest men are exalted.

PSALM 13
David Prays for Intervening Grace

To the chief Musician, A Psalm of David.

How long wilt thou forget me, O LORD? for ever? how long wilt thou hide
thy face from me?
2 How long shall I take counsel in my soul, *having* sorrow in my heart daily?
how long shall mine enemy be exalted over me?
3 Consider *and* hear me, O LORD my God: lighten mine eyes, lest I sleep the
sleep of death;
4 Lest mine enemy say, I have prevailed against him; *and* those that trouble
me rejoice when I am moved.
5 But I have trusted in thy mercy; my heart shall rejoice in thy salvation.
6 I will sing unto the LORD, because he hath dealt bountifully with me.

PSALM 14
David Describes Foolish People

To the chief Musician, *A Psalm* of David.

The fool hath said in his heart, *There is* no God. They are corrupt, they have
done abominable works, *there is* none that doeth good.
2 The LORD looked down from heaven upon the children of men, to see if
there were any that did understand, *and* seek God.
3 They are all gone aside, they are *all* together become filthy: *there is* none
that doeth good, no, not one.
4 Have all the workers of iniquity no knowledge? who eat up my people *as*
they eat bread, and call not upon the LORD.
5 There were they in great fear: for God *is* in the generation of the righteous.
6 Ye have shamed the counsel of the poor, because the LORD *is* his refuge.

7 Oh that the salvation of Israel *were come* out of Zion! when the LORD bringeth back the captivity of his people, Jacob shall rejoice, *and* Israel shall be glad.

PSALM 15
David Describes the Citizens of Zion

A Psalm of David.

LORD, who shall abide in thy tabernacle? who shall dwell in thy holy hill?
2 He that walketh uprightly, and worketh righteousness, and speaketh the truth in his heart.
3 *He that* backbiteth not with his tongue, nor doeth evil to his neighbour, nor taketh up a reproach against his neighbour.
4 In whose eyes a vile person is contemned; but he honoureth them that fear the LORD. *He that* sweareth to *his own* hurt, and changeth not.
5 *He that* putteth not out his money to usury, nor taketh reward against the innocent. He that doeth these *things* shall never be moved.

PSALM 16
David Flees to God for Safety

Michtam of David.

Preserve me, O God: for in thee do I put my trust.
2 *O my soul*, thou hast said unto the LORD, Thou *art* my Lord: my goodness *extendeth* not to thee;
3 *But* to the saints that *are* in the earth, and *to* the excellent, in whom *is* all my delight.
4 Their sorrows shall be multiplied *that* hasten *after* another *god*: their drink offerings of blood will I not offer, nor take up their names into my lips.
5 The LORD *is* the portion of mine inheritance and of my cup: thou maintainest my lot.
6 The lines are fallen unto me in pleasant *places*; yea, I have a goodly heritage.
7 I will bless the LORD, who hath given me counsel: my reins also instruct me in the night seasons.
8 I have set the LORD always before me: because *he is* at my right hand, I shall not be moved.
9 Therefore my heart is glad, and my glory rejoiceth: my flesh also shall rest in hope.
10 For thou wilt not leave my soul in hell; neither wilt thou suffer thine Holy One to see corruption.
11 Thou wilt shew me the path of life: in thy presence *is* fulness of joy; at thy right hand *there are* pleasures for evermore.

PSALM 17
David Pleas for Justice against His Enemies

A Prayer of David.

Hear the right, O LORD, attend unto my cry, give ear unto my prayer, *that goeth* not out of feigned lips.
2 Let my sentence come forth from thy presence; let thine eyes behold the things that are equal.
3 Thou hast proved mine heart; thou hast visited *me* in the night; thou hast tried me, *and* shalt find nothing; I am purposed *that* my mouth shall not transgress.
4 Concerning the works of men, by the word of thy lips I have kept *me from* the paths of the destroyer.
5 Hold up my goings in thy paths, *that* my footsteps slip not.

6 I have called upon thee, for thou wilt hear me, O God: incline thine ear
unto me, *and hear* my speech.
7 Shew thy marvellous lovingkindness, O thou that savest by thy right hand
them which put their trust *in thee* from those that rise up *against them*.
8 Keep me as the apple of the eye, hide me under the shadow of thy wings,
9 From the wicked that oppress me, *from* my deadly enemies, *who* compass
me about.
10 They are inclosed in their own fat: with their mouth they speak proudly.
11 They have now compassed us in our steps: they have set their eyes bowing
down to the earth;
12 Like as a lion *that* is greedy of his prey, and as it were a young lion lurking
in secret places.
13 Arise, O LORD, disappoint him, cast him down: deliver my soul from the
wicked, *which is* thy sword:
14 From men *which are* thy hand, O LORD, from men of the world, *which
have* their portion in *this* life, and whose belly thou fillest with thy hid *treasure*:
they are full of children, and leave the rest of their *substance* to their babes.
15 As for me, I will behold thy face in righteousness: I shall be satisfied, when
I awake, with thy likeness.

PSALM 18

David Praises God for His Marvelous Blessings

To the chief Musician, *A Psalm* of David, the servant of the LORD, who spake unto the LORD the words of this song in the day *that* the LORD delivered him from the hand of all his enemies, and from the hand of Saul: And he said,

I will love thee, O LORD, my strength.
2 The LORD *is* my rock, and my fortress, and my deliverer; my God, my
strength, in whom I will trust; my buckler, and the horn of my salvation, *and*
my high tower.
3 I will call upon the LORD, *who is worthy* to be praised: so shall I be saved
from mine enemies.
4 The sorrows of death compassed me, and the floods of ungodly men made
me afraid.
5 The sorrows of hell compassed me about: the snares of death prevented me.
6 In my distress I called upon the LORD, and cried unto my God: he heard my
voice out of his temple, and my cry came before him, *even* into his ears.
7 Then the earth shook and trembled; the foundations also of the hills moved
and were shaken, because he was wroth.
8 There went up a smoke out of his nostrils, and fire out of his mouth
devoured: coals were kindled by it.
9 He bowed the heavens also, and came down: and darkness *was* under his
feet.
10 And he rode upon a cherub, and did fly: yea, he did fly upon the wings of
the wind.
11 He made darkness his secret place; his pavilion round about him *were*
dark waters *and* thick clouds of the skies.
12 At the brightness *that was* before him his thick clouds passed, hail *stones*
and coals of fire.
13 The LORD also thundered in the heavens, and the Highest gave his voice;
hail *stones* and coals of fire.
14 Yea, he sent out his arrows, and scattered them; and he shot out lightnings,
and discomfited them.
15 Then the channels of waters were seen, and the foundations of the world
were discovered at thy rebuke, O LORD, at the blast of the breath of thy nostrils.
16 He sent from above, he took me, he drew me out of many waters.

THE LORD IS MY ROCK, AND MY FORTRESS, AND MY deliverer; MY GOD, MY STRENGTH, IN WHOM I WILL TRUST.

PSALM 18:2

17 He delivered me from my strong enemy, and from them which hated me:
for they were too strong for me.
18 They prevented me in the day of my calamity: but the LORD was my stay.
19 He brought me forth also into a large place; he delivered me, because he
delighted in me.
20 The LORD rewarded me according to my righteousness; according to the
cleanness of my hands hath he recompensed me.
21 For I have kept the ways of the LORD, and have not wickedly departed from
my God.
22 For all his judgments *were* before me, and I did not put away his statutes
from me.
23 I was also upright before him, and I kept myself from mine iniquity.
24 Therefore hath the LORD recompensed me according to my righteousness,
according to the cleanness of my hands in his eyesight.
25 With the merciful thou wilt shew thyself merciful; with an upright man
thou wilt shew thyself upright;
26 With the pure thou wilt shew thyself pure; and with the froward thou wilt
shew thyself froward.
27 For thou wilt save the afflicted people; but wilt bring down high looks.
28 For thou wilt light my candle: the LORD my God will enlighten my darkness.
29 For by thee I have run through a troop; and by my God have I leaped over
a wall.
30 *As for* God, his way *is* perfect: the word of the LORD is tried: he *is* a buckler
to all those that trust in him.
31 For who *is* God save the LORD? or who *is* a rock save our God?
32 *It is* God that girdeth me with strength, and maketh my way perfect.
33 He maketh my feet like hinds' *feet*, and setteth me upon my high places.
34 He teacheth my hands to war, so that a bow of steel is broken by mine
arms.
35 Thou hast also given me the shield of thy salvation: and thy right hand
hath holden me up, and thy gentleness hath made me great.
36 Thou hast enlarged my steps under me, that my feet did not slip.
37 I have pursued mine enemies, and overtaken them: neither did I turn
again till they were consumed.
38 I have wounded them that they were not able to rise: they are fallen under
my feet.
39 For thou hast girded me with strength unto the battle: thou hast subdued
under me those that rose up against me.
40 Thou hast also given me the necks of mine enemies; that I might destroy
them that hate me.
41 They cried, but *there was* none to save *them: even* unto the LORD, but he
answered them not.
42 Then did I beat them small as the dust before the wind: I did cast them
out as the dirt in the streets.
43 Thou hast delivered me from the strivings of the people; *and* thou hast made
me the head of the heathen: a people *whom* I have not known shall serve me.
44 As soon as they hear of me, they shall obey me: the strangers shall submit
themselves unto me.
45 The strangers shall fade away, and be afraid out of their close places.
46 The LORD liveth; and blessed *be* my rock; and let the God of my salvation
be exalted.
47 *It is* God that avengeth me, and subdueth the people under me.
48 He delivereth me from mine enemies: yea, thou liftest me up above those
that rise up against me: thou hast delivered me from the violent man.
49 Therefore will I give thanks unto thee, O LORD, among the heathen, and
sing praises unto thy name.
50 Great deliverance giveth he to his king; and sheweth mercy to his anoint-
ed, to David, and to his seed for evermore.

PSALM 19
God's Creation and Word Show His Glory

To the chief Musician, A Psalm of David.

The heavens declare the glory of God; and the firmament sheweth his handy-
work.
2 Day unto day uttereth speech, and night unto night sheweth knowledge.
3 *There is* no speech nor language, *where* their voice is not heard.
4 Their line is gone out through all the earth, and their words to the end of
the world. In them hath he set a tabernacle for the sun,
5 Which *is* as a bridegroom coming out of his chamber, *and* rejoiceth as a
strong man to run a race.
6 His going forth *is* from the end of the heaven, and his circuit unto the ends
of it: and there is nothing hid from the heat thereof.
7 The law of the LORD *is* perfect, converting the soul: the testimony of the
LORD *is* sure, making wise the simple.
8 The statutes of the LORD *are* right, rejoicing the heart: the commandment
of the LORD *is* pure, enlightening the eyes.
9 The fear of the LORD *is* clean, enduring for ever: the judgments of the LORD
are true *and* righteous altogether.
10 More to be desired *are they* than gold, yea, than much fine gold: sweeter
also than honey and the honeycomb.
11 Moreover by them is thy servant warned: *and* in keeping of them *there is*
great reward.
12 Who can understand *his* errors? cleanse thou me from secret *faults*.
13 Keep back thy servant also from presumptuous *sins*; let them not have
dominion over me: then shall I be upright, and I shall be innocent from the
great transgression.
14 Let the words of my mouth, and the meditation of my heart, be acceptable
in thy sight, O LORD, my strength, and my redeemer.

PSALM 20
David Prays for Victory in Battle

To the chief Musician, A Psalm of David.

The LORD hear thee in the day of trouble; the name of the God of Jacob defend
thee;
2 Send thee help from the sanctuary, and strengthen thee out of Zion;
3 Remember all thy offerings, and accept thy burnt sacrifice; Selah.
4 Grant thee according to thine own heart, and fulfil all thy counsel.
5 We will rejoice in thy salvation, and in the name of our God we will set up
our banners: the LORD fulfil all thy petitions.
6 Now know I that the LORD saveth his anointed; he will hear him from his
holy heaven with the saving strength of his right hand.
7 Some *trust* in chariots, and some in horses: but we will remember the name
of the LORD our God.
8 They are brought down and fallen: but we are risen, and stand upright.
9 Save, LORD: let the king hear us when we call.

PSALM 21
David Thanks God for Victory

To the chief Musician, A Psalm of David.

The king shall joy in thy strength, O LORD; and in thy salvation how greatly
shall he rejoice!
2 Thou hast given him his heart's desire, and hast not withholden the request
of his lips. Selah.
3 For thou preventest him with the blessings of goodness: thou settest a
crown of pure gold on his head.

4 He asked life of thee, *and* thou gavest *it* him, *even* length of days for ever
and ever.
5 His glory *is* great in thy salvation: honour and majesty hast thou laid upon him.
6 For thou hast made him most blessed for ever: thou hast made him exceed-
ing glad with thy countenance.
7 For the king trusteth in the LORD, and through the mercy of the most High
he shall not be moved.
8 Thine hand shall find out all thine enemies: thy right hand shall find out
those that hate thee.
9 Thou shalt make them as a fiery oven in the time of thine anger: the LORD
shall swallow them up in his wrath, and the fire shall devour them.
10 Their fruit shalt thou destroy from the earth, and their seed from among
the children of men.
11 For they intended evil against thee: they imagined a mischievous device,
which they are not able *to perform*.
12 Therefore shalt thou make them turn their back, *when* thou shalt make
ready *thine arrows* upon thy strings against the face of them.
13 Be thou exalted, LORD, in thine own strength: *so* will we sing and praise
thy power.

PSALM 22
In Great Suffering, David Prays

To the chief Musician upon Aijeleth Shahar, A Psalm of David.

My God, my God, why hast thou forsaken me? *why art thou so* far from
helping me, *and from* the words of my roaring?
2 O my God, I cry in the daytime, but thou hearest not; and in the night
season, and am not silent.
3 But thou *art* holy, *O thou* that inhabitest the praises of Israel.
4 Our fathers trusted in thee: they trusted, and thou didst deliver them.
5 They cried unto thee, and were delivered: they trusted in thee, and were
not confounded.
6 But I *am* a worm, and no man; a reproach of men, and despised of the
people.
7 All they that see me laugh me to scorn: they shoot out the lip, they shake
the head, *saying*,
8 He trusted on the LORD *that* he would deliver him: let him deliver him,
seeing he delighted in him.
9 But thou *art* he that took me out of the womb: thou didst make me hope
when I was upon my mother's breasts.
10 I was cast upon thee from the womb: thou *art* my God from my mother's
belly.
11 Be not far from me; for trouble *is* near; for *there is* none to help.
12 Many bulls have compassed me: strong *bulls* of Bashan have beset me
round.
13 They gaped upon me *with* their mouths, *as* a ravening and a roaring lion.
14 I am poured out like water, and all my bones are out of joint: my heart is
like wax; it is melted in the midst of my bowels.
15 My strength is dried up like a potsherd; and my tongue cleaveth to my
jaws; and thou hast brought me into the dust of death.
16 For dogs have compassed me: the assembly of the wicked have inclosed
me: they pierced my hands and my feet.
17 I may tell all my bones: they look *and* stare upon me.
18 They part my garments among them, and cast lots upon my vesture.
19 But be not thou far from me, O LORD: O my strength, haste thee to help me.
20 Deliver my soul from the sword; my darling from the power of the dog.

21 Save me from the lion's mouth: for thou hast heard me from the horns of
the unicorns.
22 I will declare thy name unto my brethren: in the midst of the congregation
will I praise thee.
23 Ye that fear the LORD, praise him; all ye the seed of Jacob, glorify him; and
fear him, all ye the seed of Israel.
24 For he hath not despised nor abhorred the affliction of the afflicted; nei-
ther hath he hid his face from him; but when he cried unto him, he heard.
25 My praise *shall be* of thee in the great congregation: I will pay my vows
before them that fear him.
26 The meek shall eat and be satisfied: they shall praise the LORD that seek
him: your heart shall live for ever.
27 All the ends of the world shall remember and turn unto the LORD: and all
the kindreds of the nations shall worship before thee.
28 For the kingdom *is* the LORD's: and he *is* the governor among the nations.
29 All *they that be* fat upon earth shall eat and worship: all they that go down
to the dust shall bow before him: and none can keep alive his own soul.
30 A seed shall serve him; it shall be accounted to the Lord for a generation.
31 They shall come, and shall declare his righteousness unto a people that
shall be born, that he hath done *this*.

PSALM 23

David's Confidence in God as His Shepherd

A Psalm of David.

The LORD *is* my shepherd; I shall not want.
2 He maketh me to lie down in green pastures: he leadeth me beside
the still waters.
3 He restoreth my soul: he leadeth me in the paths of righteousness for his
name's sake.
4 Yea, though I walk through the valley of the shadow of death, I will fear no
evil: for thou *art* with me; thy rod and thy staff they comfort me.
5 Thou preparest a table before me in the presence of mine enemies: thou
anointest my head with oil; my cup runneth over.
6 Surely goodness and mercy shall follow me all the days of my life: and I will
dwell in the house of the LORD for ever.

PSALM 24

David Calls All to Worship

A Psalm of David.

The earth *is* the LORD's, and the fulness thereof; the world, and they that dwell
therein.
2 For he hath founded it upon the seas, and established it upon the floods.
3 Who shall ascend into the hill of the LORD? or who shall stand in his holy
place?
4 He that hath clean hands, and a pure heart; who hath not lifted up his soul
unto vanity, nor sworn deceitfully.
5 He shall receive the blessing from the LORD, and righteousness from the
God of his salvation.
6 This *is* the generation of them that seek him, that seek thy face, O Jacob.
Selah.
7 Lift up your heads, O ye gates; and be ye lift up, ye everlasting doors; and
the King of glory shall come in.
8 Who *is* this King of glory? The LORD strong and mighty, the LORD mighty
in battle.
9 Lift up your heads, O ye gates; even lift *them* up, ye everlasting doors; and
the King of glory shall come in.
10 Who is this King of glory? The LORD of hosts, he *is* the King of glory. Selah.

The LORD is my Shepherd; I shall not want.
Psalm 23:1

PSALM 25
David's Confidence in Prayer

A Psalm of David.

Unto thee, O LORD, do I lift up my soul.
2 O my God, I trust in thee: let me not be ashamed, let not mine ene-
mies triumph over me.
3 Yea, let none that wait on thee be ashamed: let them be ashamed which
transgress without cause.
4 Shew me thy ways, O LORD; teach me thy paths.
5 Lead me in thy truth, and teach me: for thou *art* the God of my salvation;
on thee do I wait all the day.
6 Remember, O LORD, thy tender mercies and thy lovingkindnesses; for they
have been ever of old.
7 Remember not the sins of my youth, nor my transgressions: according to
thy mercy remember thou me for thy goodness' sake, O LORD.
8 Good and upright *is* the LORD: therefore will he teach sinners in the way.
9 The meek will he guide in judgment: and the meek will he teach his way.
10 All the paths of the LORD *are* mercy and truth unto such as keep his cove-
nant and his testimonies.
11 For thy name's sake, O LORD, pardon mine iniquity; for it *is* great.
12 What man *is* he that feareth the LORD? him shall he teach in the way *that*
he shall choose.
13 His soul shall dwell at ease; and his seed shall inherit the earth.
14 The secret of the LORD *is* with them that fear him; and he will shew them
his covenant.
15 Mine eyes *are* ever toward the LORD; for he shall pluck my feet out of the net.
16 Turn thee unto me, and have mercy upon me; for I *am* desolate and afflicted.
17 The troubles of my heart are enlarged: *O* bring thou me out of my distresses.
18 Look upon mine affliction and my pain; and forgive all my sins.
19 Consider mine enemies; for they are many; and they hate me with cruel
hatred.
20 O keep my soul, and deliver me: let me not be ashamed; for I put my trust
in thee.
21 Let integrity and uprightness preserve me; for I wait on thee.
22 Redeem Israel, O God, out of all his troubles.

PSALM 26
David Declares His Loyalty to God

A Psalm of David.

Judge me, O LORD; for I have walked in mine integrity: I have trusted also in
the LORD; *therefore* I shall not slide.
2 Examine me, O LORD, and prove me; try my reins and my heart.
3 For thy lovingkindness *is* before mine eyes: and I have walked in thy truth.
4 I have not sat with vain persons, neither will I go in with dissemblers.
5 I have hated the congregation of evil doers; and will not sit with the wicked.
6 I will wash mine hands in innocency: so will I compass thine altar, O LORD:
7 That I may publish with the voice of thanksgiving, and tell of all thy won-
drous works.
8 LORD, I have loved the habitation of thy house, and the place where thine
honour dwelleth.
9 Gather not my soul with sinners, nor my life with bloody men:
10 In whose hands *is* mischief, and their right hand is full of bribes.
11 But as for me, I will walk in mine integrity: redeem me, and be merciful
unto me.
12 My foot standeth in an even place: in the congregations will I bless the
LORD.

THE LORD IS MY light & my SALVATION; whom shall I fear?

PSALM 27:1

PSALM 27
David Is Confident in God's Power

A Psalm of David.

The LORD *is* my light and my salvation; whom shall I fear? the LORD *is* the
strength of my life; of whom shall I be afraid?
2 When the wicked, *even* mine enemies and my foes, came upon me to eat
up my flesh, they stumbled and fell.
3 Though an host should encamp against me, my heart shall not fear: though
war should rise against me, in this *will* I *be* confident.
4 One *thing* have I desired of the LORD, that will I seek after; that I may dwell
in the house of the LORD all the days of my life, to behold the beauty of the
LORD, and to enquire in his temple.
5 For in the time of trouble he shall hide me in his pavilion: in the secret of
his tabernacle shall he hide me; he shall set me up upon a rock.
6 And now shall mine head be lifted up above mine enemies round about
me: therefore will I offer in his tabernacle sacrifices of joy; I will sing, yea, I
will sing praises unto the LORD.
7 Hear, O LORD, *when* I cry with my voice: have mercy also upon me, and
answer me.
8 *When thou saidst*, Seek ye my face; my heart said unto thee, Thy face, LORD,
will I seek.
9 Hide not thy face *far* from me; put not thy servant away in anger: thou hast
been my help; leave me not, neither forsake me, O God of my salvation.
10 When my father and my mother forsake me, then the LORD will take me up.
11 Teach me thy way, O LORD, and lead me in a plain path, because of mine
enemies.
12 Deliver me not over unto the will of mine enemies: for false witnesses are
risen up against me, and such as breathe out cruelty.
13 *I had fainted*, unless I had believed to see the goodness of the LORD in the
land of the living.
14 Wait on the LORD: be of good courage, and he shall strengthen thine heart:
wait, I say, on the LORD.

PSALM 28
God Is David's Rock of Safety

A Psalm of David.

Unto thee will I cry, O LORD my rock; be not silent to me: lest, *if* thou be silent
to me, I become like them that go down into the pit.
2 Hear the voice of my supplications, when I cry unto thee, when I lift up my
hands toward thy holy oracle.
3 Draw me not away with the wicked, and with the workers of iniquity, which
speak peace to their neighbours, but mischief *is* in their hearts.
4 Give them according to their deeds, and according to the wickedness of
their endeavours: give them after the work of their hands; render to them
their desert.
5 Because they regard not the works of the LORD, nor the operation of his
hands, he shall destroy them, and not build them up.
6 Blessed *be* the LORD, because he hath heard the voice of my supplications.
7 The LORD *is* my strength and my shield; my heart trusted in him, and I am
helped: therefore my heart greatly rejoiceth; and with my song will I praise
him.
8 The LORD *is* their strength, and he *is* the saving strength of his anointed.
9 Save thy people, and bless thine inheritance: feed them also, and lift them
up for ever.

PSALM 29
David Ascribes All Glory to God

A Psalm of David.

Give unto the LORD, O ye mighty, give unto the LORD glory and strength.
2 Give unto the LORD the glory due unto his name; worship the LORD
in the beauty of holiness.
3 The voice of the LORD *is* upon the waters: the God of glory thundereth: the
LORD *is* upon many waters.
4 The voice of the LORD *is* powerful; the voice of the LORD *is* full of majesty.
5 The voice of the LORD breaketh the cedars; yea, the LORD breaketh the cedars
of Lebanon.
6 He maketh them also to skip like a calf; Lebanon and Sirion like a young
unicorn.
7 The voice of the LORD divideth the flames of fire.
8 The voice of the LORD shaketh the wilderness; the LORD shaketh the wilder-
ness of Kadesh.
9 The voice of the LORD maketh the hinds to calve, and discovereth the forests:
and in his temple doth every one speak of *his* glory.
10 The LORD sitteth upon the flood; yea, the LORD sitteth King for ever.
11 The LORD will give strength unto his people; the LORD will bless his people
with peace.

PSALM 30
David Praises God for His Deliverance

A Psalm *and* Song *at* the dedication of the house of David.

I will extol thee, O LORD; for thou hast lifted me up, and hast not made my foes
to rejoice over me.
2 O LORD my God, I cried unto thee, and thou hast healed me.
3 O LORD, thou hast brought up my soul from the grave: thou hast kept me
alive, that I should not go down to the pit.
4 Sing unto the LORD, O ye saints of his, and give thanks at the remembrance
of his holiness.
5 For his anger *endureth but* a moment; in his favour *is* life: weeping may
endure for a night, but joy *cometh* in the morning.
6 And in my prosperity I said, I shall never be moved.
7 LORD, by thy favour thou hast made my mountain to stand strong: thou
didst hide thy face, *and* I was troubled.
8 I cried to thee, O LORD; and unto the LORD I made supplication.
9 What profit *is there* in my blood, when I go down to the pit? Shall the dust
praise thee? shall it declare thy truth?
10 Hear, O LORD, and have mercy upon me: LORD, be thou my helper.
11 Thou hast turned for me my mourning into dancing: thou hast put off
my sackcloth, and girded me with gladness;
12 To the end that *my* glory may sing praise to thee, and not be silent. O LORD
my God, I will give thanks unto thee for ever.

PSALM 31
David Calls to God in Stress and Fear

To the chief Musician, A Psalm of David.

In thee, O LORD, do I put my trust; let me never be ashamed: deliver me in thy
righteousness.
2 Bow down thine ear to me; deliver me speedily: be thou my strong rock,
for an house of defence to save me.
3 For thou *art* my rock and my fortress; therefore for thy name's sake lead
me, and guide me.

4 Pull me out of the net that they have laid privily for me: for thou *art* my strength.
5 Into thine hand I commit my spirit: thou hast redeemed me, O Lord God of truth.
6 I have hated them that regard lying vanities: but I trust in the Lord.
7 I will be glad and rejoice in thy mercy: for thou hast considered my trouble; thou hast known my soul in adversities;
8 And hast not shut me up into the hand of the enemy: thou hast set my feet in a large room.
9 Have mercy upon me, O Lord, for I am in trouble: mine eye is consumed with grief, *yea*, my soul and my belly.
10 For my life is spent with grief, and my years with sighing: my strength faileth because of mine iniquity, and my bones are consumed.
11 I was a reproach among all mine enemies, but especially among my neighbours, and a fear to mine acquaintance: they that did see me without fled from me.
12 I am forgotten as a dead man out of mind: I am like a broken vessel.
13 For I have heard the slander of many: fear *was* on every side: while they took counsel together against me, they devised to take away my life.
14 But I trusted in thee, O Lord: I said, Thou *art* my God.
15 My times *are* in thy hand: deliver me from the hand of mine enemies, and from them that persecute me.
16 Make thy face to shine upon thy servant: save me for thy mercies' sake.
17 Let me not be ashamed, O Lord; for I have called upon thee: let the wicked be ashamed, *and* let them be silent in the grave.
18 Let the lying lips be put to silence; which speak grievous things proudly and contemptuously against the righteous.
19 *Oh* how great *is* thy goodness, which thou hast laid up for them that fear thee; *which* thou hast wrought for them that trust in thee before the sons of men!
20 Thou shalt hide them in the secret of thy presence from the pride of man: thou shalt keep them secretly in a pavilion from the strife of tongues.
21 Blessed *be* the Lord: for he hath shewed me his marvellous kindness in a strong city.
22 For I said in my haste, I am cut off from before thine eyes: nevertheless thou heardest the voice of my supplications when I cried unto thee.
23 O love the Lord, all ye his saints: *for* the Lord preserveth the faithful, and plentifully rewardeth the proud doer.
24 Be of good courage, and he shall strengthen your heart, all ye that hope in the Lord.

PSALM 32
David Sings of the Blessings of Forgiveness

A Psalm of David, Maschil.

Blessed *is he whose* transgression *is* forgiven, *whose* sin *is* covered.
2 Blessed *is* the man unto whom the Lord imputeth not iniquity, and in whose spirit *there is* no guile.
3 When I kept silence, my bones waxed old through my roaring all the day long.
4 For day and night thy hand was heavy upon me: my moisture is turned into the drought of summer. Selah.
5 I acknowledged my sin unto thee, and mine iniquity have I not hid. I said, I will confess my transgressions unto the Lord; and thou forgavest the iniquity of my sin. Selah.
6 For this shall every one that is godly pray unto thee in a time when thou mayest be found: surely in the floods of great waters they shall not come nigh unto him.

7 Thou *art* my hiding place; thou shalt preserve me from trouble; thou shalt
compass me about with songs of deliverance. Selah.
8 I will instruct thee and teach thee in the way which thou shalt go: I will
guide thee with mine eye.
9 Be ye not as the horse, *or* as the mule, *which* have no understanding: whose
mouth must be held in with bit and bridle, lest they come near unto thee.
10 Many sorrows *shall be* to the wicked: but he that trusteth in the LORD,
mercy shall compass him about.
11 Be glad in the LORD, and rejoice, ye righteous: and shout for joy, all *ye that*
are upright in heart.

PSALM 33

Praise God for His Goodness and Providence

Rejoice in the LORD, O ye righteous: *for* praise is comely for the upright.
2 Praise the LORD with harp: sing unto him with the psaltery *and* an
instrument of ten strings.
3 Sing unto him a new song; play skilfully with a loud noise.
4 For the word of the LORD *is* right; and all his works *are done* in truth.
5 He loveth righteousness and judgment: the earth is full of the goodness of
the LORD.
6 By the word of the LORD were the heavens made; and all the host of them
by the breath of his mouth.
7 He gathereth the waters of the sea together as an heap: he layeth up the
depth in storehouses.
8 Let all the earth fear the LORD: let all the inhabitants of the world stand in
awe of him.
9 For he spake, and it was *done*; he commanded, and it stood fast.
10 The LORD bringeth the counsel of the heathen to nought: he maketh the
devices of the people of none effect.
11 The counsel of the LORD standeth for ever, the thoughts of his heart to all
generations.
12 Blessed *is* the nation whose God *is* the LORD; *and* the people *whom* he hath
chosen for his own inheritance.
13 The LORD looketh from heaven; he beholdeth all the sons of men.
14 From the place of his habitation he looketh upon all the inhabitants of
the earth.
15 He fashioneth their hearts alike; he considereth all their works.
16 There is no king saved by the multitude of an host: a mighty man is not
delivered by much strength.
17 An horse *is* a vain thing for safety: neither shall he deliver *any* by his great
strength.
18 Behold, the eye of the LORD *is* upon them that fear him, upon them that
hope in his mercy;
19 To deliver their soul from death, and to keep them alive in famine.
20 Our soul waiteth for the LORD: he *is* our help and our shield.
21 For our heart shall rejoice in him, because we have trusted in his holy name.
22 Let thy mercy, O LORD, be upon us, according as we hope in thee.

PSALM 34

David Praises God at All Times

A Psalm of David, when he changed his behaviour before Abimelech; who drove him away, and he departed.

I will bless the LORD at all times: his praise *shall* continually *be* in my mouth.
2 My soul shall make her boast in the LORD: the humble shall hear *there-*
of, and be glad.
3 O magnify the LORD with me, and let us exalt his name together.

4 I sought the LORD, and he heard me, and delivered me from all my fears.
5 They looked unto him, and were lightened: and their faces were not
ashamed.
6 This poor man cried, and the LORD heard *him*, and saved him out of all his
troubles.
7 The angel of the LORD encampeth round about them that fear him, and
delivereth them.
8 O taste and see that the LORD *is* good: blessed *is* the man *that* trusteth in
him.
9 O fear the LORD, ye his saints: for *there is* no want to them that fear him.
10 The young lions do lack, and suffer hunger: but they that seek the LORD
shall not want any good *thing*.
11 Come, ye children, hearken unto me: I will teach you the fear of the LORD.
12 What man *is he that* desireth life, *and* loveth *many* days, that he may see
good?
13 Keep thy tongue from evil, and thy lips from speaking guile.
14 Depart from evil, and do good; seek peace, and pursue it.
15 The eyes of the LORD *are* upon the righteous, and his ears *are open* unto
their cry.
16 The face of the LORD *is* against them that do evil, to cut off the remem-
brance of them from the earth.
17 *The righteous* cry, and the LORD heareth, and delivereth them out of all
their troubles.
18 The LORD *is* nigh unto them that are of a broken heart; and saveth such as
be of a contrite spirit.
19 Many *are* the afflictions of the righteous: but the LORD delivereth him out
of them all.
20 He keepeth all his bones: not one of them is broken.
21 Evil shall slay the wicked: and they that hate the righteous shall be desolate.
22 The LORD redeemeth the soul of his servants: and none of them that trust
in him shall be desolate.

PSALM 35
David Appeals to God for Justice

A Psalm of David.

Plead *my cause*, O LORD, with them that strive with me: fight against them
that fight against me.
2 Take hold of shield and buckler, and stand up for mine help.
3 Draw out also the spear, and stop *the way* against them that persecute me:
say unto my soul, I *am* thy salvation.
4 Let them be confounded and put to shame that seek after my soul: let them
be turned back and brought to confusion that devise my hurt.
5 Let them be as chaff before the wind: and let the angel of the LORD chase
them.
6 Let their way be dark and slippery: and let the angel of the LORD persecute
them.
7 For without cause have they hid for me their net *in* a pit, *which* without
cause they have digged for my soul.
8 Let destruction come upon him at unawares; and let his net that he hath
hid catch himself: into that very destruction let him fall.
9 And my soul shall be joyful in the LORD: it shall rejoice in his salvation.
10 All my bones shall say, LORD, who *is* like unto thee, which deliverest the
poor from him that is too strong for him, yea, the poor and the needy from
him that spoileth him?
11 False witnesses did rise up; they laid to my charge *things* that I knew not.
12 They rewarded me evil for good *to* the spoiling of my soul.

13 But as for me, when they were sick, my clothing *was* sackcloth: I humbled
my soul with fasting; and my prayer returned into mine own bosom.
14 I behaved myself as though *he had been* my friend *or* brother: I bowed
down heavily, as one that mourneth *for his* mother.
15 But in mine adversity they rejoiced, and gathered themselves together:
yea, the abjects gathered themselves together against me, and I knew *it* not;
they did tear *me*, and ceased not:
16 With hypocritical mockers in feasts, they gnashed upon me with their
teeth.
17 Lord, how long wilt thou look on? rescue my soul from their destructions,
my darling from the lions.
18 I will give thee thanks in the great congregation: I will praise thee among
much people.
19 Let not them that are mine enemies wrongfully rejoice over me: *neither*
let them wink with the eye that hate me without a cause.
20 For they speak not peace: but they devise deceitful matters against *them*
that are quiet in the land.
21 Yea, they opened their mouth wide against me, *and* said, Aha, aha, our eye
hath seen *it*.
22 *This* thou hast seen, O LORD: keep not silence: O Lord, be not far from me.
23 Stir up thyself, and awake to my judgment, *even* unto my cause, my God
and my Lord.
24 Judge me, O LORD my God, according to thy righteousness; and let them
not rejoice over me.
25 Let them not say in their hearts, Ah, so would we have it: let them not say,
We have swallowed him up.
26 Let them be ashamed and brought to confusion together that rejoice at
mine hurt: let them be clothed with shame and dishonour that magnify *them-*
selves against me.
27 Let them shout for joy, and be glad, that favour my righteous cause: yea,
let them say continually, Let the LORD be magnified, which hath pleasure in
the prosperity of his servant.
28 And my tongue shall speak of thy righteousness *and* of thy praise all the
day long.

PSALM 36

David Proclaims God's Steadfast Love

To the chief Musician, *A Psalm* of David the servant of the LORD.

The transgression of the wicked saith within my heart, *that there is* no fear
of God before his eyes.
2 For he flattereth himself in his own eyes, until his iniquity be found to be
hateful.
3 The words of his mouth *are* iniquity and deceit: he hath left off to be wise,
and to do good.
4 He deviseth mischief upon his bed; he setteth himself in a way *that is* not
good; he abhorreth not evil.
5 Thy mercy, O LORD, *is* in the heavens; *and* thy faithfulness *reacheth* unto
the clouds.
6 Thy righteousness *is* like the great mountains; thy judgments *are* a great
deep: O LORD, thou preservest man and beast.
7 How excellent *is* thy lovingkindness, O God! therefore the children of men
put their trust under the shadow of thy wings.
8 They shall be abundantly satisfied with the fatness of thy house; and thou
shalt make them drink of the river of thy pleasures.
9 For with thee *is* the fountain of life: in thy light shall we see light.

PSALM 37:4-5
Delight
THYSELF ALSO IN
THE
LORD;
& HE SHALL
give thee
THE
desires
OF THINE
heart.
COMMIT
THY WAY UNTO
THE
LORD;
trust
ALSO IN HIM;
& HE SHALL
bring it to
pass.

10 O continue thy lovingkindness unto them that know thee; and thy righ-
teousness to the upright in heart.
11 Let not the foot of pride come against me, and let not the hand of the
wicked remove me.
12 There are the workers of iniquity fallen: they are cast down, and shall not
be able to rise.

PSALM 37
David Contrasts the Godly and the Wicked

A Psalm of David.

Fret not thyself because of evildoers, neither be thou envious against the
workers of iniquity.
2 For they shall soon be cut down like the grass, and wither as the green herb.
3 Trust in the LORD, and do good; *so* shalt thou dwell in the land, and verily
thou shalt be fed.
4 Delight thyself also in the LORD; and he shall give thee the desires of thine
heart.
5 Commit thy way unto the LORD; trust also in him; and he shall bring *it* to
pass.
6 And he shall bring forth thy righteousness as the light, and thy judgment
as the noonday.
7 Rest in the LORD, and wait patiently for him: fret not thyself because of him
who prospereth in his way, because of the man who bringeth wicked devices
to pass.
8 Cease from anger, and forsake wrath: fret not thyself in any wise to do evil.
9 For evildoers shall be cut off: but those that wait upon the LORD, they shall
inherit the earth.
10 For yet a little while, and the wicked *shall* not *be*: yea, thou shalt diligent-
ly consider his place, and it *shall* not *be*.
11 But the meek shall inherit the earth; and shall delight themselves in the
abundance of peace.
12 The wicked plotteth against the just, and gnasheth upon him with his teeth.
13 The Lord shall laugh at him: for he seeth that his day is coming.
14 The wicked have drawn out the sword, and have bent their bow, to cast
down the poor and needy, *and* to slay such as be of upright conversation.
15 Their sword shall enter into their own heart, and their bows shall be broken.
16 A little that a righteous man hath *is* better than the riches of many wicked.
17 For the arms of the wicked shall be broken: but the LORD upholdeth the
righteous.
18 The LORD knoweth the days of the upright: and their inheritance shall be
for ever.
19 They shall not be ashamed in the evil time: and in the days of famine they
shall be satisfied.
20 But the wicked shall perish, and the enemies of the LORD *shall be* as the
fat of lambs: they shall consume; into smoke shall they consume away.
21 The wicked borroweth, and payeth not again: but the righteous sheweth
mercy, and giveth.
22 For *such as be* blessed of him shall inherit the earth; and *they that be*
cursed of him shall be cut off.
23 The steps of a *good* man are ordered by the LORD: and he delighteth in his
way.
24 Though he fall, he shall not be utterly cast down: for the LORD upholdeth
him with his hand.
25 I have been young, and *now* am old; yet have I not seen the righteous
forsaken, nor his seed begging bread.
26 *He is* ever merciful, and lendeth; and his seed *is* blessed.

27 Depart from evil, and do good; and dwell for evermore.
28 For the LORD loveth judgment, and forsaketh not his saints; they are pre-
served for ever: but the seed of the wicked shall be cut off.
29 The righteous shall inherit the land, and dwell therein for ever.
30 The mouth of the righteous speaketh wisdom, and his tongue talketh of
judgment.
31 The law of his God *is* in his heart; none of his steps shall slide.
32 The wicked watcheth the righteous, and seeketh to slay him.
33 The LORD will not leave him in his hand, nor condemn him when he is
judged.
34 Wait on the LORD, and keep his way, and he shall exalt thee to inherit the
land: when the wicked are cut off, thou shalt see *it*.
35 I have seen the wicked in great power, and spreading himself like a green
bay tree.
36 Yet he passed away, and, lo, he *was* not: yea, I sought him, but he could not
be found.
37 Mark the perfect *man*, and behold the upright: for the end of *that* man *is*
peace.
38 But the transgressors shall be destroyed together: the end of the wicked
shall be cut off.
39 But the salvation of the righteous *is* of the LORD: *he is* their strength in the
time of trouble.
40 And the LORD shall help them, and deliver them: he shall deliver them
from the wicked, and save them, because they trust in him.

PSALM 38

David Appeals to God for Mercy

A Psalm of David, to bring to remembrance.

O LORD, rebuke me not in thy wrath: neither chasten me in thy hot displeasure.
2 For thine arrows stick fast in me, and thy hand presseth me sore.
3 *There is* no soundness in my flesh because of thine anger; neither *is there*
any rest in my bones because of my sin.
4 For mine iniquities are gone over mine head: as an heavy burden they are
too heavy for me.
5 My wounds stink *and* are corrupt because of my foolishness.
6 I am troubled; I am bowed down greatly; I go mourning all the day long.
7 For my loins are filled with a loathsome *disease*: and *there is* no soundness
in my flesh.
8 I am feeble and sore broken: I have roared by reason of the disquietness of
my heart.
9 Lord, all my desire *is* before thee; and my groaning is not hid from thee.
10 My heart panteth, my strength faileth me: as for the light of mine eyes, it
also is gone from me.
11 My lovers and my friends stand aloof from my sore; and my kinsmen stand
afar off.
12 They also that seek after my life lay snares *for me*: and they that seek my
hurt speak mischievous things, and imagine deceits all the day long.
13 But I, as a deaf *man*, heard not; and *I was* as a dumb man *that* openeth
not his mouth.
14 Thus I was as a man that heareth not, and in whose mouth *are* no reproofs.
15 For in thee, O LORD, do I hope: thou wilt hear, O Lord my God.
16 For I said, *Hear me*, lest *otherwise* they should rejoice over me: when my
foot slippeth, they magnify *themselves* against me.
17 For I *am* ready to halt, and my sorrow *is* continually before me.
18 For I will declare mine iniquity; I will be sorry for my sin.

19 But mine enemies *are* lively, *and* they are strong: and they that hate me
wrongfully are multiplied.
20 They also that render evil for good are mine adversaries; because I follow
the thing that good *is*.
21 Forsake me not, O LORD: O my God, be not far from me.
22 Make haste to help me, O Lord my salvation.

PSALM 39
David Places His Hope in God

To the chief Musician, *even* to Jeduthun, A Psalm of David.

I said, I will take heed to my ways, that I sin not with my tongue: I will keep
my mouth with a bridle, while the wicked is before me.
2 I was dumb with silence, I held my peace, *even* from good; and my sorrow
was stirred.
3 My heart was hot within me, while I was musing the fire burned: *then* spake
I with my tongue,
4 LORD, make me to know mine end, and the measure of my days, what it *is*;
that I may know how frail I *am*.
5 Behold, thou hast made my days *as* an handbreadth; and mine age *is* as
nothing before thee: verily every man at his best state *is* altogether vanity.
Selah.
6 Surely every man walketh in a vain shew: surely they are disquieted in vain:
he heapeth up *riches*, and knoweth not who shall gather them.
7 And now, Lord, what wait I for? my hope *is* in thee.
8 Deliver me from all my transgressions: make me not the reproach of the
foolish.
9 I was dumb, I opened not my mouth; because thou didst *it*.
10 Remove thy stroke away from me: I am consumed by the blow of thine
hand.
11 When thou with rebukes dost correct man for iniquity, thou makest his
beauty to consume away like a moth: surely every man *is* vanity. Selah.
12 Hear my prayer, O LORD, and give ear unto my cry; hold not thy peace at
my tears: for I *am* a stranger with thee, *and* a sojourner, as all my fathers *were*.
13 O spare me, that I may recover strength, before I go hence, and be no more.

PSALM 40
David Waits Patiently on God

To the chief Musician, A Psalm of David.

I waited patiently for the LORD; and he inclined unto me, and heard my cry.
2 He brought me up also out of an horrible pit, out of the miry clay, and
set my feet upon a rock, *and* established my goings.
3 And he hath put a new song in my mouth, *even* praise unto our God: many
shall see *it*, and fear, and shall trust in the LORD.
4 Blessed *is* that man that maketh the LORD his trust, and respecteth not the
proud, nor such as turn aside to lies.
5 Many, O LORD my God, *are* thy wonderful works *which* thou hast done, and
thy thoughts *which are* to us-ward: they cannot be reckoned up in order unto
thee: *if* I would declare and speak *of them*, they are more than can be num-
bered.
6 Sacrifice and offering thou didst not desire; mine ears hast thou opened:
burnt offering and sin offering hast thou not required.
7 Then said I, Lo, I come: in the volume of the book *it is* written of me,
8 I delight to do thy will, O my God: yea, thy law *is* within my heart.
9 I have preached righteousness in the great congregation: lo, I have not
refrained my lips, O LORD, thou knowest.

10 I have not hid thy righteousness within my heart; I have declared thy
faithfulness and thy salvation: I have not concealed thy lovingkindness and
thy truth from the great congregation.
11 Withhold not thou thy tender mercies from me, O LORD: let thy loving-
kindness and thy truth continually preserve me.
12 For innumerable evils have compassed me about: mine iniquities have
taken hold upon me, so that I am not able to look up; they are more than the
hairs of mine head: therefore my heart faileth me.
13 Be pleased, O LORD, to deliver me: O LORD, make haste to help me.
14 Let them be ashamed and confounded together that seek after my soul to
destroy it; let them be driven backward and put to shame that wish me evil.
15 Let them be desolate for a reward of their shame that say unto me, Aha, aha.
16 Let all those that seek thee rejoice and be glad in thee: let such as love thy
salvation say continually, The LORD be magnified.
17 But I *am* poor and needy; *yet* the Lord thinketh upon me: thou *art* my
help and my deliverer; make no tarrying, O my God.

PSALM 41

God's Care for the Poor

To the chief Musician, A Psalm of David.

Blessed *is* he that considereth the poor: the LORD will deliver him in time of
trouble.
2 The LORD will preserve him, and keep him alive; *and* he shall be blessed
upon the earth: and thou wilt not deliver him unto the will of his enemies.
3 The LORD will strengthen him upon the bed of languishing: thou wilt make
all his bed in his sickness.
4 I said, LORD, be merciful unto me: heal my soul; for I have sinned against
thee.
5 Mine enemies speak evil of me, When shall he die, and his name perish?
6 And if he come to see *me*, he speaketh vanity: his heart gathereth iniquity
to itself; *when* he goeth abroad, he telleth *it*.
7 All that hate me whisper together against me: against me do they devise
my hurt.
8 An evil disease, *say they*, cleaveth fast unto him: and *now* that he lieth he
shall rise up no more.
9 Yea, mine own familiar friend, in whom I trusted, which did eat of my
bread, hath lifted up *his* heel against me.
10 But thou, O LORD, be merciful unto me, and raise me up, that I may requite
them.
11 By this I know that thou favourest me, because mine enemy doth not
triumph over me.
12 And as for me, thou upholdest me in mine integrity, and settest me before
thy face for ever.
13 Blessed *be* the LORD God of Israel from everlasting, and to everlasting.
Amen, and Amen.

PSALM 42

Souls That Thirst after God Shall Be Quenched

To the chief Musician, Maschil, for the sons of Korah.

As the hart panteth after the water brooks, so panteth my soul after thee, O
God.
2 My soul thirsteth for God, for the living God: when shall I come and appear
before God?
3 My tears have been my meat day and night, while they continually say unto
me, Where *is* thy God?

4 When I remember these *things*, I pour out my soul in me: for I had gone
with the multitude, I went with them to the house of God, with the voice of
joy and praise, with a multitude that kept holyday.
5 Why art thou cast down, O my soul? and *why* art thou disquieted in me?
hope thou in God: for I shall yet praise him *for* the help of his countenance.
6 O my God, my soul is cast down within me: therefore will I remember thee
from the land of Jordan, and of the Hermonites, from the hill Mizar.
7 Deep calleth unto deep at the noise of thy waterspouts: all thy waves and
thy billows are gone over me.
8 *Yet* the LORD will command his lovingkindness in the daytime, and in the
night his song *shall be* with me, *and* my prayer unto the God of my life.
9 I will say unto God my rock, Why hast thou forgotten me? why go I mourn-
ing because of the oppression of the enemy?
10 *As* with a sword in my bones, mine enemies reproach me; while they say
daily unto me, Where *is* thy God?
11 Why art thou cast down, O my soul? and why art thou disquieted within
me? hope thou in God: for I shall yet praise him, *who is* the health of my
countenance, and my God.

PSALM 43

Downcast Souls Must Hope in God

Judge me, O God, and plead my cause against an ungodly nation: O deliver me
from the deceitful and unjust man.
2 For thou *art* the God of my strength: why dost thou cast me off? why go I
mourning because of the oppression of the enemy?
3 O send out thy light and thy truth: let them lead me; let them bring me
unto thy holy hill, and to thy tabernacles.
4 Then will I go unto the altar of God, unto God my exceeding joy: yea, upon
the harp will I praise thee, O God my God.
5 Why art thou cast down, O my soul? and why art thou disquieted within
me? hope in God: for I shall yet praise him, *who is* the health of my counte-
nance, and my God.

PSALM 44

A Reminder of Past Victories and a Plea for Help

To the chief Musician for the sons of Korah, Maschil.

We have heard with our ears, O God, our fathers have told us, *what* work
thou didst in their days, in the times of old.
2 *How* thou didst drive out the heathen with thy hand, and plantedst them;
how thou didst afflict the people, and cast them out.
3 For they got not the land in possession by their own sword, neither did
their own arm save them: but thy right hand, and thine arm, and the light of
thy countenance, because thou hadst a favour unto them.
4 Thou art my King, O God: command deliverances for Jacob.
5 Through thee will we push down our enemies: through thy name will we
tread them under that rise up against us.
6 For I will not trust in my bow, neither shall my sword save me.
7 But thou hast saved us from our enemies, and hast put them to shame that
hated us.
8 In God we boast all the day long, and praise thy name for ever. Selah.
9 But thou hast cast off, and put us to shame; and goest not forth with our
armies.
10 Thou makest us to turn back from the enemy: and they which hate us spoil
for themselves.
11 Thou hast given us like sheep *appointed* for meat; and hast scattered us
among the heathen.

12 Thou sellest thy people for nought, and dost not increase *thy wealth* by
their price.
13 Thou makest us a reproach to our neighbours, a scorn and a derision to
them that are round about us.
14 Thou makest us a byword among the heathen, a shaking of the head
among the people.
15 My confusion *is* continually before me, and the shame of my face hath
covered me,
16 For the voice of him that reproacheth and blasphemeth; by reason of the
enemy and avenger.
17 All this is come upon us; yet have we not forgotten thee, neither have we
dealt falsely in thy covenant.
18 Our heart is not turned back, neither have our steps declined from thy way;
19 Though thou hast sore broken us in the place of dragons, and covered us
with the shadow of death.
20 If we have forgotten the name of our God, or stretched out our hands to
a strange god;
21 Shall not God search this out? for he knoweth the secrets of the heart.
22 Yea, for thy sake are we killed all the day long; we are counted as sheep for
the slaughter.
23 Awake, why sleepest thou, O Lord? arise, cast *us* not off for ever.
24 Wherefore hidest thou thy face, *and* forgettest our affliction and our
oppression?
25 For our soul is bowed down to the dust: our belly cleaveth unto the earth.
26 Arise for our help, and redeem us for thy mercies' sake.

PSALM 45

The Majesty and Grace of Christ's Kingdom

To the chief Musician upon Shoshannim, for the sons of Korah, Maschil, A Song of loves.

My heart is inditing a good matter: I speak of the things which I have made
touching the king: my tongue *is* the pen of a ready writer.
2 Thou art fairer than the children of men: grace is poured into thy lips:
therefore God hath blessed thee for ever.
3 Gird thy sword upon *thy* thigh, O *most* mighty, with thy glory and thy
majesty.
4 And in thy majesty ride prosperously because of truth and meekness *and*
righteousness; and thy right hand shall teach thee terrible things.
5 Thine arrows *are* sharp in the heart of the king's enemies; *whereby* the
people fall under thee.
6 Thy throne, O God, *is* for ever and ever: the sceptre of thy kingdom *is* a right
sceptre.
7 Thou lovest righteousness, and hatest wickedness: therefore God, thy God,
hath anointed thee with the oil of gladness above thy fellows.
8 All thy garments *smell* of myrrh, and aloes, *and* cassia, out of the ivory
palaces, whereby they have made thee glad.
9 Kings' daughters *were* among thy honourable women: upon thy right hand
did stand the queen in gold of Ophir.
10 Hearken, O daughter, and consider, and incline thine ear; forget also thine
own people, and thy father's house;
11 So shall the king greatly desire thy beauty: for he *is* thy Lord; and worship
thou him.
12 And the daughter of Tyre *shall be there* with a gift; *even* the rich among
the people shall intreat thy favour.
13 The king's daughter *is* all glorious within: her clothing *is* of wrought gold.
14 She shall be brought unto the king in raiment of needlework: the virgins
her companions that follow her shall be brought unto thee.

15 With gladness and rejoicing shall they be brought: they shall enter into
the king's palace.
16 Instead of thy fathers shall be thy children, whom thou mayest make
princes in all the earth.
17 I will make thy name to be remembered in all generations: therefore shall
the people praise thee for ever and ever.

PSALM 46
God Is Our Refuge and Strength

To the chief Musician for the sons of Korah, A Song upon Alamoth.

God *is* our refuge and strength, a very present help in trouble.
2 Therefore will not we fear, though the earth be removed, and though
the mountains be carried into the midst of the sea;
3 *Though* the waters thereof roar *and* be troubled, *though* the mountains
shake with the swelling thereof. Selah.
4 *There is* a river, the streams whereof shall make glad the city of God, the
holy *place* of the tabernacles of the most High.
5 God *is* in the midst of her; she shall not be moved: God shall help her, *and*
that right early.
6 The heathen raged, the kingdoms were moved: he uttered his voice, the
earth melted.
7 The LORD of hosts *is* with us; the God of Jacob *is* our refuge. Selah.
8 Come, behold the works of the LORD, what desolations he hath made in
the earth.
9 He maketh wars to cease unto the end of the earth; he breaketh the bow,
and cutteth the spear in sunder; he burneth the chariot in the fire.
10 Be still, and know that I *am* God: I will be exalted among the heathen, I
will be exalted in the earth.
11 The LORD of hosts *is* with us; the God of Jacob *is* our refuge. Selah.

PSALM 47
God Is King over All the Earth

To the chief Musician, A Psalm for the sons of Korah.

O clap your hands, all ye people; shout unto God with the voice of triumph.
2 For the LORD most high *is* terrible; *he is* a great King over all the earth.
3 He shall subdue the people under us, and the nations under our feet.
4 He shall choose our inheritance for us, the excellency of Jacob whom he
loved. Selah.
5 God is gone up with a shout, the LORD with the sound of a trumpet.
6 Sing praises to God, sing praises: sing praises unto our King, sing praises.
7 For God *is* the King of all the earth: sing ye praises with understanding.
8 God reigneth over the heathen: God sitteth upon the throne of his holiness.
9 The princes of the people are gathered together, *even* the people of the God
of Abraham: for the shields of the earth *belong* unto God: he is greatly exalted.

PSALM 48
Great Is the LORD and Greatly to Be Praised

A Song *and* Psalm for the sons of Korah.

Great *is* the LORD, and greatly to be praised in the city of our God, *in* the
mountain of his holiness.
2 Beautiful for situation, the joy of the whole earth, *is* mount Zion, *on* the
sides of the north, the city of the great King.
3 God is known in her palaces for a refuge.
4 For, lo, the kings were assembled, they passed by together.
5 They saw *it, and* so they marvelled; they were troubled, *and* hasted away.
6 Fear took hold upon them there, *and* pain, as of a woman in travail.
7 Thou breakest the ships of Tarshish with an east wind.

Be still, & KNOW that I AM God: I WILL BE exalted AMONG THE HEATHEN, I WILL BE EXALTED IN THE EARTH.

PSALM 46:10

8 As we have heard, so have we seen in the city of the LORD of hosts, in the
city of our God: God will establish it for ever. Selah.
9 We have thought of thy lovingkindness, O God, in the midst of thy temple.
10 According to thy name, O God, so *is* thy praise unto the ends of the earth:
thy right hand is full of righteousness.
11 Let mount Zion rejoice, let the daughters of Judah be glad, because of thy
judgments.
12 Walk about Zion, and go round about her: tell the towers thereof.
13 Mark ye well her bulwarks, consider her palaces; that ye may tell *it* to the
generation following.
14 For this God *is* our God for ever and ever: he will be our guide *even* unto death.

PSALM 49
Earthly Riches Will Not Last

To the chief Musician, A Psalm for the sons of Korah.

Hear this, all *ye* people; give ear, all *ye* inhabitants of the world:
2 Both low and high, rich and poor, together.
3 My mouth shall speak of wisdom; and the meditation of my heart *shall be*
of understanding.
4 I will incline mine ear to a parable: I will open my dark saying upon the harp.
5 Wherefore should I fear in the days of evil, *when* the iniquity of my heels
shall compass me about?
6 They that trust in their wealth, and boast themselves in the multitude of
their riches;
7 None *of them* can by any means redeem his brother, nor give to God a
ransom for him:
8 (For the redemption of their soul *is* precious, and it ceaseth for ever:)
9 That he should still live for ever, *and* not see corruption.
10 For he seeth *that* wise men die, likewise the fool and the brutish person
perish, and leave their wealth to others.
11 Their inward thought *is, that* their houses *shall continue* for ever, *and*
their dwelling places to all generations; they call *their* lands after their own
names.
12 Nevertheless man *being* in honour abideth not: he is like the beasts *that*
perish.
13 This their way *is* their folly: yet their posterity approve their sayings. Selah.
14 Like sheep they are laid in the grave; death shall feed on them; and the
upright shall have dominion over them in the morning; and their beauty shall
consume in the grave from their dwelling.
15 But God will redeem my soul from the power of the grave: for he shall
receive me. Selah.
16 Be not thou afraid when one is made rich, when the glory of his house is
increased;
17 For when he dieth he shall carry nothing away: his glory shall not descend
after him.
18 Though while he lived he blessed his soul: and *men* will praise thee, when
thou doest well to thyself.
19 He shall go to the generation of his fathers; they shall never see light.
20 Man *that is* in honour, and understandeth not, is like the beasts *that* perish.

PSALM 50
God Desires Obedience More Than Sacrifices

A Psalm of Asaph.

The mighty God, *even* the LORD, hath spoken, and called the earth from the
rising of the sun unto the going down thereof.
2 Out of Zion, the perfection of beauty, God hath shined.

3 Our God shall come, and shall not keep silence: a fire shall devour before
him, and it shall be very tempestuous round about him.
4 He shall call to the heavens from above, and to the earth, that he may judge
his people.
5 Gather my saints together unto me; those that have made a covenant with
me by sacrifice.
6 And the heavens shall declare his righteousness: for God *is* judge himself.
Selah.
7 Hear, O my people, and I will speak; O Israel, and I will testify against thee:
I *am* God, *even* thy God.
8 I will not reprove thee for thy sacrifices or thy burnt offerings, *to have been*
continually before me.
9 I will take no bullock out of thy house, *nor* he goats out of thy folds.
10 For every beast of the forest *is* mine, *and* the cattle upon a thousand hills.
11 I know all the fowls of the mountains: and the wild beasts of the field *are*
mine.
12 If I were hungry, I would not tell thee: for the world *is* mine, and the fulness
thereof.
13 Will I eat the flesh of bulls, or drink the blood of goats?
14 Offer unto God thanksgiving; and pay thy vows unto the most High:
15 And call upon me in the day of trouble: I will deliver thee, and thou shalt
glorify me.
16 But unto the wicked God saith, What hast thou to do to declare my statutes,
or *that* thou shouldest take my covenant in thy mouth?
17 Seeing thou hatest instruction, and castest my words behind thee.
18 When thou sawest a thief, then thou consentedst with him, and hast been
partaker with adulterers.
19 Thou givest thy mouth to evil, and thy tongue frameth deceit.
20 Thou sittest *and* speakest against thy brother; thou slanderest thine own
mother's son.
21 These *things* hast thou done, and I kept silence; thou thoughtest that I was
altogether *such an one* as thyself: *but* I will reprove thee, and set *them* in order
before thine eyes.
22 Now consider this, ye that forget God, lest I tear *you* in pieces, and *there*
be none to deliver.
23 Whoso offereth praise glorifieth me: and to him that ordereth *his* con-
versation *aright* will I shew the salvation of God.

PSALM 51

David Confesses Sin and Prays for Forgiveness

To the chief Musician, A Psalm of David, when Nathan the prophet came unto him, after he had gone in to Bath-sheba.

Have mercy upon me, O God, according to thy lovingkindness: according
unto the multitude of thy tender mercies blot out my transgressions.
2 Wash me throughly from mine iniquity, and cleanse me from my sin.
3 For I acknowledge my transgressions: and my sin *is* ever before me.
4 Against thee, thee only, have I sinned, and done *this* evil in thy sight: that
thou mightest be justified when thou speakest, *and* be clear when thou judgest.
5 Behold, I was shapen in iniquity; and in sin did my mother conceive me.
6 Behold, thou desirest truth in the inward parts: and in the hidden *part*
thou shalt make me to know wisdom.
7 Purge me with hyssop, and I shall be clean: wash me, and I shall be whiter
than snow.
8 Make me to hear joy and gladness; *that* the bones *which* thou hast broken
may rejoice.
9 Hide thy face from my sins, and blot out all mine iniquities.

10 Create in me a clean heart, O God; and renew a right spirit within me.
11 Cast me not away from thy presence; and take not thy holy spirit from me.
12 Restore unto me the joy of thy salvation; and uphold me *with thy* free spirit.
13 *Then* will I teach transgressors thy ways; and sinners shall be converted
unto thee.
14 Deliver me from bloodguiltiness, O God, thou God of my salvation: *and*
my tongue shall sing aloud of thy righteousness.
15 O Lord, open thou my lips; and my mouth shall shew forth thy praise.
16 For thou desirest not sacrifice; else would I give *it*: thou delightest not in
burnt offering.
17 The sacrifices of God *are* a broken spirit: a broken and a contrite heart, O
God, thou wilt not despise.
18 Do good in thy good pleasure unto Zion: build thou the walls of Jerusalem.
19 Then shalt thou be pleased with the sacrifices of righteousness, with burnt
offering and whole burnt offering: then shall they offer bullocks upon thine
altar.

PSALM 52
David Prays against Evildoers

To the chief Musician, Maschil, *A Psalm* of David, when Doeg the Edomite came and told Saul, and said unto him, David is come to the house of Ahimelech.

Why boastest thou thyself in mischief, O mighty man? the goodness of God
endureth continually.
2 Thy tongue deviseth mischiefs; like a sharp razor, working deceitfully.
3 Thou lovest evil more than good; *and* lying rather than to speak righteous-
ness. Selah.
4 Thou lovest all devouring words, O *thou* deceitful tongue.
5 God shall likewise destroy thee for ever, he shall take thee away, and pluck
thee out of *thy* dwelling place, and root thee out of the land of the living. Selah.
6 The righteous also shall see, and fear, and shall laugh at him:
7 Lo, *this is* the man *that* made not God his strength; but trusted in the
abundance of his riches, *and* strengthened himself in his wickedness.
8 But I *am* like a green olive tree in the house of God: I trust in the mercy of
God for ever and ever.
9 I will praise thee for ever, because thou hast done *it*: and I will wait on thy
name; for *it is* good before thy saints.

PSALM 53
David Describes Man's Sinfulness

To the chief Musician upon Mahalath, Maschil, *A Psalm* of David.

The fool hath said in his heart, *There is* no God. Corrupt are they, and have
done abominable iniquity: *there is* none that doeth good.
2 God looked down from heaven upon the children of men, to see if there
were *any* that did understand, that did seek God.
3 Every one of them is gone back: they are altogether become filthy; *there is*
none that doeth good, no, not one.
4 Have the workers of iniquity no knowledge? who eat up my people *as* they
eat bread: they have not called upon God.
5 There were they in great fear, *where* no fear was: for God hath scattered the
bones of him that encampeth *against* thee: thou hast put *them* to shame,
because God hath despised them.
6 Oh that the salvation of Israel *were come* out of Zion! When God bringeth
back the captivity of his people, Jacob shall rejoice, *and* Israel shall be glad.

PSALM 54
David Trusts in God's Help

To the chief Musician on Neginoth, Maschil, *A Psalm* of David, when the Ziphims came and said to Saul, Doth not David hide himself with us?

Save me, O God, by thy name, and judge me by thy strength.
2 Hear my prayer, O God; give ear to the words of my mouth.
3 For strangers are risen up against me, and oppressors seek after my soul:
they have not set God before them. Selah.
4 Behold, God *is* mine helper: the Lord *is* with them that uphold my soul.
5 He shall reward evil unto mine enemies: cut them off in thy truth.
6 I will freely sacrifice unto thee: I will praise thy name, O LORD; for *it is* good.
7 For he hath delivered me out of all trouble: and mine eye hath seen *his*
desire upon mine enemies.

PSALM 55
David Is Hurt by a Close Friend

To the chief Musician on Neginoth, Maschil, *A Psalm* of David.

Give ear to my prayer, O God; and hide not thyself from my supplication.
2 Attend unto me, and hear me: I mourn in my complaint, and make a noise;
3 Because of the voice of the enemy, because of the oppression of the wicked:
for they cast iniquity upon me, and in wrath they hate me.
4 My heart is sore pained within me: and the terrors of death are fallen upon me.
5 Fearfulness and trembling are come upon me, and horror hath over-
whelmed me.
6 And I said, Oh that I had wings like a dove! *for then* would I fly away, and
be at rest.
7 Lo, *then* would I wander far off, *and* remain in the wilderness. Selah.
8 I would hasten my escape from the windy storm *and* tempest.
9 Destroy, O Lord, *and* divide their tongues: for I have seen violence and strife
in the city.
10 Day and night they go about it upon the walls thereof: mischief also and
sorrow *are* in the midst of it.
11 Wickedness *is* in the midst thereof: deceit and guile depart not from her
streets.
12 For *it was* not an enemy *that* reproached me; then I could have borne *it*:
neither *was it* he that hated me *that* did magnify *himself* against me; then I
would have hid myself from him:
13 But *it was* thou, a man mine equal, my guide, and mine acquaintance.
14 We took sweet counsel together, *and* walked unto the house of God in
company.
15 Let death seize upon them, *and* let them go down quick into hell: for
wickedness *is* in their dwellings, *and* among them.
16 As for me, I will call upon God; and the LORD shall save me.
17 Evening, and morning, and at noon, will I pray, and cry aloud: and he shall
hear my voice.
18 He hath delivered my soul in peace from the battle *that was* against me:
for there were many with me.
19 God shall hear, and afflict them, even he that abideth of old. Selah. Because
they have no changes, therefore they fear not God.
20 He hath put forth his hands against such as be at peace with him: he hath
broken his covenant.
21 *The words* of his mouth were smoother than butter, but war *was* in his
heart: his words were softer than oil, yet *were* they drawn swords.
22 Cast thy burden upon the LORD, and he shall sustain thee: he shall never
suffer the righteous to be moved.
23 But thou, O God, shalt bring them down into the pit of destruction: bloody
and deceitful men shall not live out half their days; but I will trust in thee.

PSALM 56

David Fears His Enemies, but Trusts God

To the chief Musician upon Jonathelem-rechokim, Michtam of David, when the Philistines took him in Gath.

Be merciful unto me, O God: for man would swallow me up; he fighting daily
oppresseth me.
2 Mine enemies would daily swallow *me* up: for *they be* many that fight
against me, O thou most High.
3 What time I am afraid, I will trust in thee.
4 In God I will praise his word, in God I have put my trust; I will not fear what
flesh can do unto me.
5 Every day they wrest my words: all their thoughts *are* against me for evil.
6 They gather themselves together, they hide themselves, they mark my steps,
when they wait for my soul.
7 Shall they escape by iniquity? in *thine* anger cast down the people, O God.
8 Thou tellest my wanderings: put thou my tears into thy bottle: *are they* not
in thy book?
9 When I cry *unto thee*, then shall mine enemies turn back: this I know; for
God *is* for me.
10 In God will I praise *his* word: in the LORD will I praise *his* word.
11 In God have I put my trust: I will not be afraid what man can do unto me.
12 Thy vows *are* upon me, O God: I will render praises unto thee.
13 For thou hast delivered my soul from death: *wilt* not *thou deliver* my feet
from falling, that I may walk before God in the light of the living?

PSALM 57

In Time of Trial, David Exalts God

To the chief Musician, Al-taschith, Michtam of David, when he fled from Saul in the cave.

Be merciful unto me, O God, be merciful unto me: for my soul trusteth in
thee: yea, in the shadow of thy wings will I make my refuge, until *these*
calamities be overpast.
2 I will cry unto God most high; unto God that performeth *all things* for me.
3 He shall send from heaven, and save me *from* the reproach of him that would
swallow me up. Selah. God shall send forth his mercy and his truth.
4 My soul *is* among lions: *and* I lie *even among* them that are set on fire, *even*
the sons of men, whose teeth *are* spears and arrows, and their tongue a sharp
sword.
5 Be thou exalted, O God, above the heavens; *let* thy glory *be* above all the earth.
6 They have prepared a net for my steps; my soul is bowed down: they have
digged a pit before me, into the midst whereof they are fallen *themselves*. Selah.
7 My heart is fixed, O God, my heart is fixed: I will sing and give praise.
8 Awake up, my glory; awake, psaltery and harp: I *myself* will awake early.
9 I will praise thee, O Lord, among the people: I will sing unto thee among the
nations.
10 For thy mercy *is* great unto the heavens, and thy truth unto the clouds.
11 Be thou exalted, O God, above the heavens: *let* thy glory *be* above all the earth.

PSALM 58

David Reproves Wicked Judges

To the chief Musician, Altaschith, Michtam of David.

Do ye indeed speak righteousness, O congregation? do ye judge uprightly,
O ye sons of men?
2 Yea, in heart ye work wickedness; ye weigh the violence of your hands in
the earth.
3 The wicked are estranged from the womb: they go astray as soon as they
be born, speaking lies.

4 Their poison *is* like the poison of a serpent: *they are* like the deaf adder *that*
stoppeth her ear;
5 Which will not hearken to the voice of charmers, charming never so wisely.
6 Break their teeth, O God, in their mouth: break out the great teeth of the
young lions, O LORD.
7 Let them melt away as waters *which* run continually: *when* he bendeth *his*
bow to shoot his arrows, let them be as cut in pieces.
8 As a snail *which* melteth, let *every one of them* pass away: *like* the untimely
birth of a woman, *that* they may not see the sun.
9 Before your pots can feel the thorns, he shall take them away as with a
whirlwind, both living, and in *his* wrath.
10 The righteous shall rejoice when he seeth the vengeance: he shall wash
his feet in the blood of the wicked.
11 So that a man shall say, Verily *there is* a reward for the righteous: verily he
is a God that judgeth in the earth.

PSALM 59

David Prays for Deliverance from Enemies

To the chief Musician, Al-taschith, Michtam of David; when Saul sent, and they watched the house to kill him.

Deliver me from mine enemies, O my God: defend me from them that rise
up against me.
2 Deliver me from the workers of iniquity, and save me from bloody men.
3 For, lo, they lie in wait for my soul: the mighty are gathered against me; not
for my transgression, nor *for* my sin, O LORD.
4 They run and prepare themselves without *my* fault: awake to help me, and
behold.
5 Thou therefore, O LORD God of hosts, the God of Israel, awake to visit all
the heathen: be not merciful to any wicked transgressors. Selah.
6 They return at evening: they make a noise like a dog, and go round about
the city.
7 Behold, they belch out with their mouth: swords *are* in their lips: for who,
say they, doth hear?
8 But thou, O LORD, shalt laugh at them; thou shalt have all the heathen in
derision.
9 *Because of* his strength will I wait upon thee: for God *is* my defence.
10 The God of my mercy shall prevent me: God shall let me see *my desire*
upon mine enemies.
11 Slay them not, lest my people forget: scatter them by thy power; and bring
them down, O Lord our shield.
12 *For* the sin of their mouth *and* the words of their lips let them even be
taken in their pride: and for cursing and lying *which* they speak.
13 Consume *them* in wrath, consume *them*, that they *may* not *be*: and let
them know that God ruleth in Jacob unto the ends of the earth. Selah.
14 And at evening let them return; *and* let them make a noise like a dog, and
go round about the city.
15 Let them wander up and down for meat, and grudge if they be not
satisfied.
16 But I will sing of thy power; yea, I will sing aloud of thy mercy in the
morning: for thou hast been my defence and refuge in the day of my trouble.
17 Unto thee, O my strength, will I sing: for God *is* my defence, *and* the God
of my mercy.

PSALM 60
David Prays for Israel's Deliverance

To the chief Musician upon Shushan-eduth, Michtam of David, to teach; when he strove with Aram-naharaim and with Aram-zobah, when Joab returned, and smote of Edom in the valley of salt twelve thousand.

O God, thou hast cast us off, thou hast scattered us, thou hast been dis-
pleased; O turn thyself to us again.
2 Thou hast made the earth to tremble; thou hast broken it: heal the breach-
es thereof; for it shaketh.
3 Thou hast shewed thy people hard things: thou hast made us to drink the
wine of astonishment.
4 Thou hast given a banner to them that fear thee, that it may be displayed
because of the truth. Selah.
5 That thy beloved may be delivered; save *with* thy right hand, and hear me.
6 God hath spoken in his holiness; I will rejoice, I will divide Shechem, and
mete out the valley of Succoth.
7 Gilead *is* mine, and Manasseh *is* mine; Ephraim also *is* the strength of mine
head; Judah *is* my lawgiver;
8 Moab *is* my washpot; over Edom will I cast out my shoe: Philistia, triumph
thou because of me.
9 Who will bring me *into* the strong city? who will lead me into Edom?
10 *Wilt* not thou, O God, *which* hadst cast us off? and *thou*, O God, *which*
didst not go out with our armies?
11 Give us help from trouble: for vain *is* the help of man.
12 Through God we shall do valiantly: for he *it is that* shall tread down our
enemies.

PSALM 61
David Takes Refuge in God

To the chief Musician upon Neginah, *A Psalm* of David.

Hear my cry, O God; attend unto my prayer.
2 From the end of the earth will I cry unto thee, when my heart is over-
whelmed: lead me to the rock *that* is higher than I.
3 For thou hast been a shelter for me, *and* a strong tower from the enemy.
4 I will abide in thy tabernacle for ever: I will trust in the covert of thy wings.
Selah.
5 For thou, O God, hast heard my vows: thou hast given *me* the heritage of
those that fear thy name.
6 Thou wilt prolong the king's life: *and* his years as many generations.
7 He shall abide before God for ever: O prepare mercy and truth, *which* may
preserve him.
8 So will I sing praise unto thy name for ever, that I may daily perform my
vows.

PSALM 62
David's Soul Rests in God

To the chief Musician, to Jeduthun, A Psalm of David.

Truly my soul waiteth upon God: from him *cometh* my salvation.
2 He only *is* my rock and my salvation; *he is* my defence; I shall not be
greatly moved.
3 How long will ye imagine mischief against a man? ye shall be slain all of
you: as a bowing wall *shall ye be, and as* a tottering fence.
4 They only consult to cast *him* down from his excellency: they delight in
lies: they bless with their mouth, but they curse inwardly. Selah.
5 My soul, wait thou only upon God; for my expectation *is* from him.

6 He only *is* my rock and my salvation: *he is* my defence; I shall not be moved.
7 In God *is* my salvation and my glory: the rock of my strength, *and* my refuge, *is* in God.
8 Trust in him at all times; *ye* people, pour out your heart before him: God *is* a refuge for us. Selah.
9 Surely men of low degree *are* vanity, *and* men of high degree *are* a lie: to be laid in the balance, they *are* altogether *lighter* than vanity.
10 Trust not in oppression, and become not vain in robbery: if riches increase, set not your heart *upon them.*
11 God hath spoken once; twice have I heard this; that power *belongeth* unto God.
12 Also unto thee, O Lord, *belongeth* mercy: for thou renderest to every man according to his work.

PSALM 63

David Thirsts for God

A Psalm of David, when he was in the wilderness of Judah.

O God, thou *art* my God; early will I seek thee: my soul thirsteth for thee, my flesh longeth for thee in a dry and thirsty land, where no water is;
2 To see thy power and thy glory, so *as* I have seen thee in the sanctuary.
3 Because thy lovingkindness *is* better than life, my lips shall praise thee.
4 Thus will I bless thee while I live: I will lift up my hands in thy name.
5 My soul shall be satisfied as *with* marrow and fatness; and my mouth shall praise *thee* with joyful lips:
6 When I remember thee upon my bed, *and* meditate on thee in the *night* watches.
7 Because thou hast been my help, therefore in the shadow of thy wings will I rejoice.
8 My soul followeth hard after thee: thy right hand upholdeth me.
9 But those *that* seek my soul, to destroy *it,* shall go into the lower parts of the earth.
10 They shall fall by the sword: they shall be a portion for foxes.
11 But the king shall rejoice in God; every one that sweareth by him shall glory: but the mouth of them that speak lies shall be stopped.

PSALM 64

David Prays against a Conspiracy

To the chief Musician, A Psalm of David.

Hear my voice, O God, in my prayer: preserve my life from fear of the enemy.
2 Hide me from the secret counsel of the wicked; from the insurrection of the workers of iniquity:
3 Who whet their tongue like a sword, *and* bend *their bows to shoot* their arrows, *even* bitter words:
4 That they may shoot in secret at the perfect: suddenly do they shoot at him, and fear not.
5 They encourage themselves *in* an evil matter: they commune of laying snares privily; they say, Who shall see them?
6 They search out iniquities; they accomplish a diligent search: both the inward *thought* of every one *of them,* and the heart, *is* deep.
7 But God shall shoot at them *with* an arrow; suddenly shall they be wounded.
8 So they shall make their own tongue to fall upon themselves: all that see them shall flee away.
9 And all men shall fear, and shall declare the work of God; for they shall wisely consider of his doing.
10 The righteous shall be glad in the LORD, and shall trust in him; and all the upright in heart shall glory.

PSALM 65
David Praises God for His Provision

To the chief Musician, A Psalm *and* Song of David.

Praise waiteth for thee, O God, in Sion: and unto thee shall the vow be per-
formed.
2 O thou that hearest prayer, unto thee shall all flesh come.
3 Iniquities prevail against me: *as for* our transgressions, thou shalt purge
them away.
4 Blessed *is the man whom* thou choosest, and causest to approach *unto thee,*
that he may dwell in thy courts: we shall be satisfied with the goodness of thy
house, *even* of thy holy temple.
5 *By* terrible things in righteousness wilt thou answer us, O God of our sal-
vation; *who art* the confidence of all the ends of the earth, and of them that
are afar off *upon* the sea:
6 Which by his strength setteth fast the mountains; *being* girded with power:
7 Which stilleth the noise of the seas, the noise of their waves, and the tumult
of the people.
8 They also that dwell in the uttermost parts are afraid at thy tokens: thou
makest the outgoings of the morning and evening to rejoice.
9 Thou visitest the earth, and waterest it: thou greatly enrichest it with the
river of God, *which* is full of water: thou preparest them corn, when thou hast
so provided for it.
10 Thou waterest the ridges thereof abundantly: thou settlest the furrows
thereof: thou makest it soft with showers: thou blessest the springing thereof.
11 Thou crownest the year with thy goodness; and thy paths drop fatness.
12 They drop *upon* the pastures of the wilderness: and the little hills rejoice
on every side.
13 The pastures are clothed with flocks; the valleys also are covered over with
corn; they shout for joy, they also sing.

PSALM 66
Come and See the Works of God

To the chief Musician, A Song *or* Psalm.

Make a joyful noise unto God, all ye lands:
2 Sing forth the honour of his name: make his praise glorious.
3 Say unto God, How terrible *art thou in* thy works! through the greatness
of thy power shall thine enemies submit themselves unto thee.
4 All the earth shall worship thee, and shall sing unto thee; they shall sing *to*
thy name. Selah.
5 Come and see the works of God: *he is* terrible *in his* doing toward the
children of men.
6 He turned the sea into dry *land*: they went through the flood on foot: there
did we rejoice in him.
7 He ruleth by his power for ever; his eyes behold the nations: let not the
rebellious exalt themselves. Selah.
8 O bless our God, ye people, and make the voice of his praise to be heard:
9 Which holdeth our soul in life, and suffereth not our feet to be moved.
10 For thou, O God, hast proved us: thou hast tried us, as silver is tried.
11 Thou broughtest us into the net; thou laidst affliction upon our loins.
12 Thou hast caused men to ride over our heads; we went through fire and
through water: but thou broughtest us out into a wealthy *place.*
13 I will go into thy house with burnt offerings: I will pay thee my vows,
14 Which my lips have uttered, and my mouth hath spoken, when I was in
trouble.

15 I will offer unto thee burnt sacrifices of fatlings, with the incense of rams;
I will offer bullocks with goats. Selah.
16 Come *and* hear, all ye that fear God, and I will declare what he hath done
for my soul.
17 I cried unto him with my mouth, and he was extolled with my tongue.
18 If I regard iniquity in my heart, the Lord will not hear *me*:
19 *But* verily God hath heard *me*; he hath attended to the voice of my prayer.
20 Blessed *be* God, which hath not turned away my prayer, nor his mercy
from me.

PSALM 67
May God's Face Shine upon His People

To the chief Musician on Neginoth, A Psalm *or* Song.

God be merciful unto us, and bless us; *and* cause his face to shine upon us;
Selah.
2 That thy way may be known upon earth, thy saving health among all
nations.
3 Let the people praise thee, O God; let all the people praise thee.
4 O let the nations be glad and sing for joy: for thou shalt judge the people
righteously, and govern the nations upon earth. Selah.
5 Let the people praise thee, O God; let all the people praise thee.
6 *Then* shall the earth yield her increase; *and* God, *even* our own God, shall
bless us.
7 God shall bless us; and all the ends of the earth shall fear him.

PSALM 68
David Honors God as Defender and Provider

To the chief Musician, A Psalm *or* Song of David.

Let God arise, let his enemies be scattered: let them also that hate him flee
before him.
2 As smoke is driven away, *so* drive *them* away: as wax melteth before the fire,
so let the wicked perish at the presence of God.
3 But let the righteous be glad; let them rejoice before God: yea, let them
exceedingly rejoice.
4 Sing unto God, sing praises to his name: extol him that rideth upon the
heavens by his name JAH, and rejoice before him.
5 A father of the fatherless, and a judge of the widows, *is* God in his holy
habitation.
6 God setteth the solitary in families: he bringeth out those which are bound
with chains: but the rebellious dwell in a dry *land*.
7 O God, when thou wentest forth before thy people, when thou didst march
through the wilderness; Selah:
8 The earth shook, the heavens also dropped at the presence of God: *even*
Sinai itself *was moved* at the presence of God, the God of Israel.
9 Thou, O God, didst send a plentiful rain, whereby thou didst confirm thine
inheritance, when it was weary.
10 Thy congregation hath dwelt therein: thou, O God, hast prepared of thy
goodness for the poor.
11 The Lord gave the word: great *was* the company of those that published *it*.
12 Kings of armies did flee apace: and she that tarried at home divided the
spoil.
13 Though ye have lien among the pots, *yet shall ye be as* the wings of a dove
covered with silver, and her feathers with yellow gold.
14 When the Almighty scattered kings in it, it was *white* as snow in Salmon.
15 The hill of God *is as* the hill of Bashan; an high hill *as* the hill of Bashan.

16 Why leap ye, ye high hills? *this is* the hill *which* God desireth to dwell in;
yea, the LORD will dwell *in it* for ever.
17 The chariots of God *are* twenty thousand, *even* thousands of angels: the
Lord *is* among them, *as in* Sinai, in the holy *place.*
18 Thou hast ascended on high, thou hast led captivity captive: thou hast
received gifts for men; yea, *for* the rebellious also, that the LORD God might
dwell *among them.*
19 Blessed *be* the Lord, *who* daily loadeth us *with benefits, even* the God of
our salvation. Selah.
20 *He that is* our God *is* the God of salvation; and unto GOD the Lord *belong*
the issues from death.
21 But God shall wound the head of his enemies, *and* the hairy scalp of such
an one as goeth on still in his trespasses.
22 The Lord said, I will bring again from Bashan, I will bring *my people* again
from the depths of the sea:
23 That thy foot may be dipped in the blood of *thine* enemies, *and* the tongue
of thy dogs in the same.
24 They have seen thy goings, O God; *even* the goings of my God, my King, in
the sanctuary.
25 The singers went before, the players on instruments *followed* after; among
them were the damsels playing with timbrels.
26 Bless ye God in the congregations, *even* the Lord, from the fountain of
Israel.
27 There *is* little Benjamin *with* their ruler, the princes of Judah *and* their
council, the princes of Zebulun, *and* the princes of Naphtali.
28 Thy God hath commanded thy strength: strengthen, O God, that which
thou hast wrought for us.
29 Because of thy temple at Jerusalem shall kings bring presents unto thee.
30 Rebuke the company of spearmen, the multitude of the bulls, with the
calves of the people, *till every one* submit himself with pieces of silver: scatter
thou the people *that* delight in war.
31 Princes shall come out of Egypt; Ethiopia shall soon stretch out her hands
unto God.
32 Sing unto God, ye kingdoms of the earth; O sing praises unto the Lord;
Selah:
33 To him that rideth upon the heavens of heavens, *which were* of old; lo, he
doth send out his voice, *and that* a mighty voice.
34 Ascribe ye strength unto God: his excellency *is* over Israel, and his strength
is in the clouds.
35 O God, *thou art* terrible out of thy holy places: the God of Israel *is* he that
giveth strength and power unto *his* people. Blessed *be* God.

PSALM 69

David Needs Rescue from His Enemies

To the chief Musician upon Shoshannim, *A Psalm* of David.

Save me, O God; for the waters are come in unto *my* soul.
2 I sink in deep mire, where *there is* no standing: I am come into deep
waters, where the floods overflow me.
3 I am weary of my crying: my throat is dried: mine eyes fail while I wait for
my God.
4 They that hate me without a cause are more than the hairs of mine head:
they that would destroy me, *being* mine enemies wrongfully, are mighty: then
I restored *that* which I took not away.
5 O God, thou knowest my foolishness; and my sins are not hid from thee.
6 Let not them that wait on thee, O Lord GOD of hosts, be ashamed for my
sake: let not those that seek thee be confounded for my sake, O God of Israel.

7 Because for thy sake I have borne reproach; shame hath covered my face.

8 I am become a stranger unto my brethren, and an alien unto my mother's children.

9 For the zeal of thine house hath eaten me up; and the reproaches of them that reproached thee are fallen upon me.

10 When I wept, *and chastened* my soul with fasting, that was to my reproach.

11 I made sackcloth also my garment; and I became a proverb to them.

12 They that sit in the gate speak against me; and I *was* the song of the drunkards.

13 But as for me, my prayer *is* unto thee, O LORD, *in* an acceptable time: O God, in the multitude of thy mercy hear me, in the truth of thy salvation.

14 Deliver me out of the mire, and let me not sink: let me be delivered from them that hate me, and out of the deep waters.

15 Let not the waterflood overflow me, neither let the deep swallow me up, and let not the pit shut her mouth upon me.

16 Hear me, O LORD; for thy lovingkindness *is* good: turn unto me according to the multitude of thy tender mercies.

17 And hide not thy face from thy servant; for I am in trouble: hear me speedily.

18 Draw nigh unto my soul, *and* redeem it: deliver me because of mine enemies.

19 Thou hast known my reproach, and my shame, and my dishonour: mine adversaries *are* all before thee.

20 Reproach hath broken my heart; and I am full of heaviness: and I looked *for some* to take pity, but *there was* none; and for comforters, but I found none.

21 They gave me also gall for my meat; and in my thirst they gave me vinegar to drink.

22 Let their table become a snare before them: and *that which should have been* for *their* welfare, *let it become* a trap.

23 Let their eyes be darkened, that they see not; and make their loins continually to shake.

24 Pour out thine indignation upon them, and let thy wrathful anger take hold of them.

25 Let their habitation be desolate; *and* let none dwell in their tents.

26 For they persecute *him* whom thou hast smitten; and they talk to the grief of those whom thou hast wounded.

27 Add iniquity unto their iniquity: and let them not come into thy righteousness.

28 Let them be blotted out of the book of the living, and not be written with the righteous.

29 But I *am* poor and sorrowful: let thy salvation, O God, set me up on high.

30 I will praise the name of God with a song, and will magnify him with thanksgiving.

31 *This* also shall please the LORD better than an ox *or* bullock that hath horns and hoofs.

32 The humble shall see *this, and* be glad: and your heart shall live that seek God.

33 For the LORD heareth the poor, and despiseth not his prisoners.

34 Let the heaven and earth praise him, the seas, and every thing that moveth therein.

35 For God will save Zion, and will build the cities of Judah: that they may dwell there, and have it in possession.

36 The seed also of his servants shall inherit it: and they that love his name shall dwell therein.

PSALM 70
David's Urgent Plea

To the chief Musician, *A Psalm* of David, to bring to remembrance.

Make haste, O God, to deliver me; make haste to help me, O LORD.
2 Let them be ashamed and confounded that seek after my soul: let
them be turned backward, and put to confusion, that desire my hurt.
3 Let them be turned back for a reward of their shame that say, Aha, aha.
4 Let all those that seek thee rejoice and be glad in thee: and let such as love
thy salvation say continually, Let God be magnified.
5 But I *am* poor and needy: make haste unto me, O God: thou *art* my help
and my deliverer; O LORD, make no tarrying.

PSALM 71
God's Constant Presence and Help

In thee, O LORD, do I put my trust: let me never be put to confusion.
2 Deliver me in thy righteousness, and cause me to escape: incline thine ear
unto me, and save me.
3 Be thou my strong habitation, whereunto I may continually resort: thou
hast given commandment to save me; for thou *art* my rock and my fortress.
4 Deliver me, O my God, out of the hand of the wicked, out of the hand of
the unrighteous and cruel man.
5 For thou *art* my hope, O Lord GOD: *thou art* my trust from my youth.
6 By thee have I been holden up from the womb: thou art he that took me
out of my mother's bowels: my praise *shall be* continually of thee.
7 I am as a wonder unto many; but thou *art* my strong refuge.
8 Let my mouth be filled *with* thy praise *and with* thy honour all the day.
9 Cast me not off in the time of old age; forsake me not when my strength
faileth.
10 For mine enemies speak against me; and they that lay wait for my soul
take counsel together,
11 Saying, God hath forsaken him: persecute and take him; for *there is* none
to deliver *him*.
12 O God, be not far from me: O my God, make haste for my help.
13 Let them be confounded *and* consumed that are adversaries to my soul;
let them be covered *with* reproach and dishonour that seek my hurt.
14 But I will hope continually, and will yet praise thee more and more.
15 My mouth shall shew forth thy righteousness *and* thy salvation all the
day; for I know not the numbers *thereof*.
16 I will go in the strength of the Lord GOD: I will make mention of thy righ-
teousness, *even* of thine only.
17 O God, thou hast taught me from my youth: and hitherto have I declared
thy wondrous works.
18 Now also when I am old and grayheaded, O God, forsake me not; until I
have shewed thy strength unto *this* generation, *and* thy power to every one
that is to come.
19 Thy righteousness also, O God, *is* very high, who hast done great things:
O God, who *is* like unto thee!
20 *Thou*, which hast shewed me great and sore troubles, shalt quicken me
again, and shalt bring me up again from the depths of the earth.
21 Thou shalt increase my greatness, and comfort me on every side.
22 I will also praise thee with the psaltery, *even* thy truth, O my God: unto
thee will I sing with the harp, O thou Holy One of Israel.
23 My lips shall greatly rejoice when I sing unto thee; and my soul, which
thou hast redeemed.
24 My tongue also shall talk of thy righteousness all the day long: for they are
confounded, for they are brought unto shame, that seek my hurt.

PSALM 72
A Prayer for Israel's King

***A Psalm* for Solomon.**

Give the king thy judgments, O God, and thy righteousness unto the king's
son.
2 He shall judge thy people with righteousness, and thy poor with judgment.
3 The mountains shall bring peace to the people, and the little hills, by righ-
teousness.
4 He shall judge the poor of the people, he shall save the children of the needy,
and shall break in pieces the oppressor.
5 They shall fear thee as long as the sun and moon endure, throughout all
generations.
6 He shall come down like rain upon the mown grass: as showers *that* water
the earth.
7 In his days shall the righteous flourish; and abundance of peace so long as
the moon endureth.
8 He shall have dominion also from sea to sea, and from the river unto the
ends of the earth.
9 They that dwell in the wilderness shall bow before him; and his enemies
shall lick the dust.
10 The kings of Tarshish and of the isles shall bring presents: the kings of
Sheba and Seba shall offer gifts.
11 Yea, all kings shall fall down before him: all nations shall serve him.
12 For he shall deliver the needy when he crieth; the poor also, and *him* that
hath no helper.
13 He shall spare the poor and needy, and shall save the souls of the needy.
14 He shall redeem their soul from deceit and violence: and precious shall
their blood be in his sight.
15 And he shall live, and to him shall be given of the gold of Sheba: prayer
also shall be made for him continually; *and* daily shall he be praised.
16 There shall be an handful of corn in the earth upon the top of the moun-
tains; the fruit thereof shall shake like Lebanon: and *they* of the city shall
flourish like grass of the earth.
17 His name shall endure for ever: his name shall be continued as long as the
sun: and *men* shall be blessed in him: all nations shall call him blessed.
18 Blessed *be* the LORD God, the God of Israel, who only doeth wondrous
things.
19 And blessed *be* his glorious name for ever: and let the whole earth be filled
with his glory; Amen, and Amen.
20 The prayers of David the son of Jesse are ended.

PSALM 73
Holy Living Will Bring Future Rewards

A Psalm of Asaph.

Truly God *is* good to Israel, *even* to such as are of a clean heart.
2 But as for me, my feet were almost gone; my steps had well nigh slipped.
3 For I was envious at the foolish, *when* I saw the prosperity of the wicked.
4 For *there are* no bands in their death: but their strength *is* firm.
5 They *are* not in trouble *as other* men; neither are they plagued like *other*
men.
6 Therefore pride compasseth them about as a chain; violence covereth them
as a garment.
7 Their eyes stand out with fatness: they have more than heart could wish.
8 They are corrupt, and speak wickedly *concerning* oppression: they speak
loftily.

9 They set their mouth against the heavens, and their tongue walketh
through the earth.
10 Therefore his people return hither: and waters of a full *cup* are wrung out
to them.
11 And they say, How doth God know? and is there knowledge in the most
High?
12 Behold, these *are* the ungodly, who prosper in the world; they increase *in*
riches.
13 Verily I have cleansed my heart *in* vain, and washed my hands in innocency.
14 For all the day long have I been plagued, and chastened every morning.
15 If I say, I will speak thus; behold, I should offend *against* the generation
of thy children.
16 When I thought to know this, it *was* too painful for me;
17 Until I went into the sanctuary of God; *then* understood I their end.
18 Surely thou didst set them in slippery places: thou castedst them down
into destruction.
19 How are they *brought* into desolation, as in a moment! they are utterly
consumed with terrors.
20 As a dream when *one* awaketh; *so*, O Lord, when thou awakest, thou shalt
despise their image.
21 Thus my heart was grieved, and I was pricked in my reins.
22 So foolish *was* I, and ignorant: I was *as* a beast before thee.
23 Nevertheless I *am* continually with thee: thou hast holden *me* by my right
hand.
24 Thou shalt guide me with thy counsel, and afterward receive me *to* glory.
25 Whom have I in heaven *but thee*? and *there is* none upon earth *that* I
desire beside thee.
26 My flesh and my heart faileth: *but* God *is* the strength of my heart, and
my portion for ever.
27 For, lo, they that are far from thee shall perish: thou hast destroyed all
them that go a whoring from thee.
28 But *it is* good for me to draw near to God: I have put my trust in the Lord
GOD, that I may declare all thy works.

PSALM 74

A Prayer for a Devastated People

Maschil of Asaph.

O God, why hast thou cast *us* off for ever? *why* doth thine anger smoke
against the sheep of thy pasture?
2 Remember thy congregation, *which* thou hast purchased of old; the rod
of thine inheritance, *which* thou hast redeemed; this mount Zion, wherein
thou hast dwelt.
3 Lift up thy feet unto the perpetual desolations; *even* all *that* the enemy hath
done wickedly in the sanctuary.
4 Thine enemies roar in the midst of thy congregations; they set up their
ensigns *for* signs.
5 *A man* was famous according as he had lifted up axes upon the thick trees.
6 But now they break down the carved work thereof at once with axes and
hammers.
7 They have cast fire into thy sanctuary, they have defiled *by casting down*
the dwelling place of thy name to the ground.
8 They said in their hearts, Let us destroy them together: they have burned
up all the synagogues of God in the land.
9 We see not our signs: *there is* no more any prophet: neither *is there* among
us any that knoweth how long.

10 O God, how long shall the adversary reproach? shall the enemy blaspheme
thy name for ever?
11 Why withdrawest thou thy hand, even thy right hand? pluck *it* out of thy
bosom.
12 For God *is* my King of old, working salvation in the midst of the earth.
13 Thou didst divide the sea by thy strength: thou brakest the heads of the
dragons in the waters.
14 Thou brakest the heads of leviathan in pieces, *and* gavest him *to be* meat
to the people inhabiting the wilderness.
15 Thou didst cleave the fountain and the flood: thou driedst up mighty
rivers.
16 The day *is* thine, the night also *is* thine: thou hast prepared the light and
the sun.
17 Thou hast set all the borders of the earth: thou hast made summer and
winter.
18 Remember this, *that* the enemy hath reproached, O LORD, and *that* the
foolish people have blasphemed thy name.
19 O deliver not the soul of thy turtledove unto the multitude *of the wicked*:
forget not the congregation of thy poor for ever.
20 Have respect unto the covenant: for the dark places of the earth are full
of the habitations of cruelty.
21 O let not the oppressed return ashamed: let the poor and needy praise thy
name.
22 Arise, O God, plead thine own cause: remember how the foolish man
reproacheth thee daily.
23 Forget not the voice of thine enemies: the tumult of those that rise up
against thee increaseth continually.

PSALM 75

God Will Judge Uprightly

To the chief Musician, Al-taschith, A Psalm *or* Song of Asaph.

Unto thee, O God, do we give thanks, *unto thee* do we give thanks: for *that*
thy name is near thy wondrous works declare.
2 When I shall receive the congregation I will judge uprightly.
3 The earth and all the inhabitants thereof are dissolved: I bear up the pillars
of it. Selah.
4 I said unto the fools, Deal not foolishly: and to the wicked, Lift not up the
horn:
5 Lift not up your horn on high: speak *not with* a stiff neck.
6 For promotion *cometh* neither from the east, nor from the west, nor from
the south.
7 But God *is* the judge: he putteth down one, and setteth up another.
8 For in the hand of the LORD *there is* a cup, and the wine is red; it is full of
mixture; and he poureth out of the same: but the dregs thereof, all the wicked
of the earth shall wring *them* out, *and* drink *them*.
9 But I will declare for ever; I will sing praises to the God of Jacob.
10 All the horns of the wicked also will I cut off; *but* the horns of the righteous
shall be exalted.

PSALM 76

God Alone Is to Be Feared

To the chief Musician on Neginoth, A Psalm *or* Song of Asaph.

In Judah *is* God known: his name *is* great in Israel.
2 In Salem also is his tabernacle, and his dwelling place in Zion.
3 There brake he the arrows of the bow, the shield, and the sword, and the
battle. Selah.

4 Thou *art* more glorious *and* excellent than the mountains of prey.
5 The stouthearted are spoiled, they have slept their sleep: and none of the
men of might have found their hands.
6 At thy rebuke, O God of Jacob, both the chariot and horse are cast into a
dead sleep.
7 Thou, *even* thou, *art* to be feared: and who may stand in thy sight when
once thou art angry?
8 Thou didst cause judgment to be heard from heaven; the earth feared, and
was still,
9 When God arose to judgment, to save all the meek of the earth. Selah.
10 Surely the wrath of man shall praise thee: the remainder of wrath shalt
thou restrain.
11 Vow, and pay unto the LORD your God: let all that be round about him
bring presents unto him that ought to be feared.
12 He shall cut off the spirit of princes: *he is* terrible to the kings of the earth.

PSALM 77
Remember God's Help in the Past

To the chief Musician, to Jeduthun, A Psalm of Asaph.

I cried unto God with my voice, *even* unto God with my voice; and he gave ear
unto me.
2 In the day of my trouble I sought the Lord: my sore ran in the night, and
ceased not: my soul refused to be comforted.
3 I remembered God, and was troubled: I complained, and my spirit was
overwhelmed. Selah.
4 Thou holdest mine eyes waking: I am so troubled that I cannot speak.
5 I have considered the days of old, the years of ancient times.
6 I call to remembrance my song in the night: I commune with mine own
heart: and my spirit made diligent search.
7 Will the Lord cast off for ever? and will he be favourable no more?
8 Is his mercy clean gone for ever? doth *his* promise fail for evermore?
9 Hath God forgotten to be gracious? hath he in anger shut up his tender
mercies? Selah.
10 And I said, This *is* my infirmity: *but I will remember* the years of the right
hand of the most High.
11 I will remember the works of the LORD: surely I will remember thy won-
ders of old.
12 I will meditate also of all thy work, and talk of thy doings.
13 Thy way, O God, *is* in the sanctuary: who *is so* great a God as *our* God?
14 Thou *art* the God that doest wonders: thou hast declared thy strength
among the people.
15 Thou hast with *thine* arm redeemed thy people, the sons of Jacob and
Joseph. Selah.
16 The waters saw thee, O God, the waters saw thee; they were afraid: the
depths also were troubled.
17 The clouds poured out water: the skies sent out a sound: thine arrows also
went abroad.
18 The voice of thy thunder *was* in the heaven: the lightnings lightened the
world: the earth trembled and shook.
19 Thy way *is* in the sea, and thy path in the great waters, and thy footsteps
are not known.
20 Thou leddest thy people like a flock by the hand of Moses and Aaron.

PSALM 78
Israel's Rich History

Maschil of Asaph.

Give ear, O my people, *to* my law: incline your ears to the words of my mouth.
2 I will open my mouth in a parable: I will utter dark sayings of old:
3 Which we have heard and known, and our fathers have told us.
4 We will not hide *them* from their children, shewing to the generation to
come the praises of the LORD, and his strength, and his wonderful works that
he hath done.
5 For he established a testimony in Jacob, and appointed a law in Israel, which
he commanded our fathers, that they should make them known to their chil-
dren:
6 That the generation to come might know *them, even* the children *which*
should be born; *who* should arise and declare *them* to their children:
7 That they might set their hope in God, and not forget the works of God,
but keep his commandments:
8 And might not be as their fathers, a stubborn and rebellious generation; a
generation *that* set not their heart aright, and whose spirit was not stedfast
with God.
9 The children of Ephraim, *being* armed, *and* carrying bows, turned back in
the day of battle.
10 They kept not the covenant of God, and refused to walk in his law;
11 And forgat his works, and his wonders that he had shewed them.
12 Marvellous things did he in the sight of their fathers, in the land of Egypt,
in the field of Zoan.
13 He divided the sea, and caused them to pass through; and he made the
waters to stand as an heap.
14 In the daytime also he led them with a cloud, and all the night with a light
of fire.
15 He clave the rocks in the wilderness, and gave *them* drink as *out of* the
great depths.
16 He brought streams also out of the rock, and caused waters to run down
like rivers.
17 And they sinned yet more against him by provoking the most High in the
wilderness.
18 And they tempted God in their heart by asking meat for their lust.
19 Yea, they spake against God; they said, Can God furnish a table in the
wilderness?
20 Behold, he smote the rock, that the waters gushed out, and the streams
overflowed; can he give bread also? can he provide flesh for his people?
21 Therefore the LORD heard *this*, and was wroth: so a fire was kindled against
Jacob, and anger also came up against Israel;
22 Because they believed not in God, and trusted not in his salvation:
23 Though he had commanded the clouds from above, and opened the doors
of heaven,
24 And had rained down manna upon them to eat, and had given them of
the corn of heaven.
25 Man did eat angels' food: he sent them meat to the full.
26 He caused an east wind to blow in the heaven: and by his power he brought
in the south wind.
27 He rained flesh also upon them as dust, and feathered fowls like as the
sand of the sea:
28 And he let *it* fall in the midst of their camp, round about their habitations.
29 So they did eat, and were well filled: for he gave them their own desire;
30 They were not estranged from their lust. But while their meat *was* yet in
their mouths,

31 The wrath of God came upon them, and slew the fattest of them, and smote
down the chosen *men* of Israel.
32 For all this they sinned still, and believed not for his wondrous works.
33 Therefore their days did he consume in vanity, and their years in trouble.
34 When he slew them, then they sought him: and they returned and
enquired early after God.
35 And they remembered that God *was* their rock, and the high God their
redeemer.
36 Nevertheless they did flatter him with their mouth, and they lied unto
him with their tongues.
37 For their heart was not right with him, neither were they stedfast in his
covenant.
38 But he, *being* full of compassion, forgave *their* iniquity, and destroyed
them not: yea, many a time turned he his anger away, and did not stir up all
his wrath.
39 For he remembered that they *were but* flesh; a wind that passeth away,
and cometh not again.
40 How oft did they provoke him in the wilderness, *and* grieve him in the
desert!
41 Yea, they turned back and tempted God, and limited the Holy One of Israel.
42 They remembered not his hand, *nor* the day when he delivered them from
the enemy.
43 How he had wrought his signs in Egypt, and his wonders in the field of
Zoan:
44 And had turned their rivers into blood; and their floods, that they could
not drink.
45 He sent divers sorts of flies among them, which devoured them; and frogs,
which destroyed them.
46 He gave also their increase unto the caterpiller, and their labour unto the
locust.
47 He destroyed their vines with hail, and their sycomore trees with frost.
48 He gave up their cattle also to the hail, and their flocks to hot thunderbolts.
49 He cast upon them the fierceness of his anger, wrath, and indignation,
and trouble, by sending evil angels *among them*.
50 He made a way to his anger; he spared not their soul from death, but gave
their life over to the pestilence;
51 And smote all the firstborn in Egypt; the chief of *their* strength in the
tabernacles of Ham:
52 But made his own people to go forth like sheep, and guided them in the
wilderness like a flock.
53 And he led them on safely, so that they feared not: but the sea overwhelmed
their enemies.
54 And he brought them to the border of his sanctuary, *even to* this mountain,
which his right hand had purchased.
55 He cast out the heathen also before them, and divided them an inheritance
by line, and made the tribes of Israel to dwell in their tents.
56 Yet they tempted and provoked the most high God, and kept not his tes-
timonies:
57 But turned back, and dealt unfaithfully like their fathers: they were turned
aside like a deceitful bow.
58 For they provoked him to anger with their high places, and moved him
to jealousy with their graven images.
59 When God heard *this*, he was wroth, and greatly abhorred Israel:
60 So that he forsook the tabernacle of Shiloh, the tent *which* he placed
among men;
61 And delivered his strength into captivity, and his glory into the enemy's
hand.

62 He gave his people over also unto the sword; and was wroth with his inher-
itance.
63 The fire consumed their young men; and their maidens were not given
to marriage.
64 Their priests fell by the sword; and their widows made no lamentation.
65 Then the Lord awaked as one out of sleep, *and* like a mighty man that
shouteth by reason of wine.
66 And he smote his enemies in the hinder parts: he put them to a perpetual
reproach.
67 Moreover he refused the tabernacle of Joseph, and chose not the tribe of
Ephraim:
68 But chose the tribe of Judah, the mount Zion which he loved.
69 And he built his sanctuary like high *palaces*, like the earth which he hath
established for ever.
70 He chose David also his servant, and took him from the sheepfolds:
71 From following the ewes great with young he brought him to feed Jacob
his people, and Israel his inheritance.
72 So he fed them according to the integrity of his heart; and guided them
by the skilfulness of his hands.

PSALM 79
A Cry to God after the Desolation of Jerusalem

A Psalm of Asaph.

O God, the heathen are come into thine inheritance; thy holy temple have
they defiled; they have laid Jerusalem on heaps.
2 The dead bodies of thy servants have they given *to be* meat unto the fowls
of the heaven, the flesh of thy saints unto the beasts of the earth.
3 Their blood have they shed like water round about Jerusalem; and *there*
was none to bury *them*.
4 We are become a reproach to our neighbours, a scorn and derision to them
that are round about us.
5 How long, LORD? wilt thou be angry for ever? shall thy jealousy burn like
fire?
6 Pour out thy wrath upon the heathen that have not known thee, and upon
the kingdoms that have not called upon thy name.
7 For they have devoured Jacob, and laid waste his dwelling place.
8 O remember not against us former iniquities: let thy tender mercies speed-
ily prevent us: for we are brought very low.
9 Help us, O God of our salvation, for the glory of thy name: and deliver us,
and purge away our sins, for thy name's sake.
10 Wherefore should the heathen say, Where *is* their God? let him be known
among the heathen in our sight *by* the revenging of the blood of thy servants
which is shed.
11 Let the sighing of the prisoner come before thee; according to the great-
ness of thy power preserve thou those that are appointed to die;
12 And render unto our neighbours sevenfold into their bosom their
reproach, wherewith they have reproached thee, O Lord.
13 So we thy people and sheep of thy pasture will give thee thanks for ever:
we will shew forth thy praise to all generations.

PSALM 80
A Prayer for Restoration

To the chief Musician upon Shoshannim-Eduth, A Psalm of Asaph.

Give ear, O Shepherd of Israel, thou that leadest Joseph like a flock; thou that
dwellest *between* the cherubims, shine forth.
2 Before Ephraim and Benjamin and Manasseh stir up thy strength, and
come *and* save us.

3 Turn us again, O God, and cause thy face to shine; and we shall be saved.
4 O LORD God of hosts, how long wilt thou be angry against the prayer of thy
people?
5 Thou feedest them with the bread of tears; and givest them tears to drink
in great measure.
6 Thou makest us a strife unto our neighbours: and our enemies laugh among
themselves.
7 Turn us again, O God of hosts, and cause thy face to shine; and we shall be
saved.
8 Thou hast brought a vine out of Egypt: thou hast cast out the heathen, and
planted it.
9 Thou preparedst *room* before it, and didst cause it to take deep root, and
it filled the land.
10 The hills were covered with the shadow of it, and the boughs thereof *were
like* the goodly cedars.
11 She sent out her boughs unto the sea, and her branches unto the river.
12 Why hast thou *then* broken down her hedges, so that all they which pass
by the way do pluck her?
13 The boar out of the wood doth waste it, and the wild beast of the field doth
devour it.
14 Return, we beseech thee, O God of hosts: look down from heaven, and
behold, and visit this vine;
15 And the vineyard which thy right hand hath planted, and the branch *that*
thou madest strong for thyself.
16 *It is* burned with fire, *it is* cut down: they perish at the rebuke of thy
countenance.
17 Let thy hand be upon the man of thy right hand, upon the son of man
whom thou madest strong for thyself.
18 So will not we go back from thee: quicken us, and we will call upon thy name.
19 Turn us again, O LORD God of hosts, cause thy face to shine; and we shall be saved.

PSALM 81

A Celebration of the Exodus from Egypt

To the chief Musician upon Gittith, *A Psalm* of Asaph.

Sing aloud unto God our strength: make a joyful noise unto the God of Jacob.
2 Take a psalm, and bring hither the timbrel, the pleasant harp with the
psaltery.
3 Blow up the trumpet in the new moon, in the time appointed, on our
solemn feast day.
4 For this *was* a statute for Israel, *and* a law of the God of Jacob.
5 This he ordained in Joseph *for* a testimony, when he went out through the
land of Egypt: *where* I heard a language *that* I understood not.
6 I removed his shoulder from the burden: his hands were delivered from
the pots.
7 Thou calledst in trouble, and I delivered thee; I answered thee in the secret
place of thunder: I proved thee at the waters of Meribah. Selah.
8 Hear, O my people, and I will testify unto thee: O Israel, if thou wilt hearken
unto me;
9 There shall no strange god be in thee; neither shalt thou worship any
strange god.
10 I *am* the LORD thy God, which brought thee out of the land of Egypt: open
thy mouth wide, and I will fill it.
11 But my people would not hearken to my voice; and Israel would none of me.
12 So I gave them up unto their own hearts' lust: *and* they walked in their
own counsels.
13 Oh that my people had hearkened unto me, *and* Israel had walked in my ways!

14 I should soon have subdued their enemies, and turned my hand against their adversaries.

15 The haters of the Lord should have submitted themselves unto him: but their time should have endured for ever.

16 He should have fed them also with the finest of the wheat: and with honey out of the rock should I have satisfied thee.

PSALM 82

God Will Judge the Wicked

A Psalm of Asaph.

God standeth in the congregation of the mighty; he judgeth among the gods.
2 How long will ye judge unjustly, and accept the persons of the wicked? Selah.

3 Defend the poor and fatherless: do justice to the afflicted and needy.

4 Deliver the poor and needy: rid *them* out of the hand of the wicked.

5 They know not, neither will they understand; they walk on in darkness: all the foundations of the earth are out of course.

6 I have said, Ye *are* gods; and all of you *are* children of the most High.

7 But ye shall die like men, and fall like one of the princes.

8 Arise, O God, judge the earth: for thou shalt inherit all nations.

PSALM 83

God Is Most High over All the Earth

A Song *or* Psalm of Asaph.

Keep not thou silence, O God: hold not thy peace, and be not still, O God.
2 For, lo, thine enemies make a tumult: and they that hate thee have lifted up the head.

3 They have taken crafty counsel against thy people, and consulted against thy hidden ones.

4 They have said, Come, and let us cut them off from *being* a nation; that the name of Israel may be no more in remembrance.

5 For they have consulted together with one consent: they are confederate against thee:

6 The tabernacles of Edom, and the Ishmaelites; of Moab, and the Hagarenes;

7 Gebal, and Ammon, and Amalek; the Philistines with the inhabitants of Tyre;

8 Assur also is joined with them: they have holpen the children of Lot. Selah.

9 Do unto them as *unto* the Midianites; as *to* Sisera, as *to* Jabin, at the brook of Kison:

10 *Which* perished at Endor: they became *as* dung for the earth.

11 Make their nobles like Oreb, and like Zeeb: yea, all their princes as Zebah, and as Zalmunna:

12 Who said, Let us take to ourselves the houses of God in possession.

13 O my God, make them like a wheel; as the stubble before the wind.

14 As the fire burneth a wood, and as the flame setteth the mountains on fire;

15 So persecute them with thy tempest, and make them afraid with thy storm.

16 Fill their faces with shame; that they may seek thy name, O Lord.

17 Let them be confounded and troubled for ever; yea, let them be put to shame, and perish:

18 That *men* may know that thou, whose name alone *is* JEHOVAH, *art* the most high over all the earth.

PSALM 84
The Joy of Fellowship in God's House

To the chief Musician upon Gittith, A Psalm for the sons of Korah.

How amiable *are* thy tabernacles, O LORD of hosts!
2 My soul longeth, yea, even fainteth for the courts of the LORD: my heart
and my flesh crieth out for the living God.
3 Yea, the sparrow hath found an house, and the swallow a nest for herself,
where she may lay her young, *even* thine altars, O LORD of hosts, my King, and
my God.
4 Blessed *are* they that dwell in thy house: they will be still praising thee.
Selah.
5 Blessed *is* the man whose strength *is* in thee; in whose heart *are* the ways
of them.
6 *Who* passing through the valley of Baca make it a well; the rain also filleth
the pools.
7 They go from strength to strength, *every one of them* in Zion appeareth
before God.
8 O LORD God of hosts, hear my prayer: give ear, O God of Jacob. Selah.
9 Behold, O God our shield, and look upon the face of thine anointed.
10 For a day in thy courts *is* better than a thousand. I had rather be a door-
keeper in the house of my God, than to dwell in the tents of wickedness.
11 For the LORD God *is* a sun and shield: the LORD will give grace and glory:
no good *thing* will he withhold from them that walk uprightly.
12 O LORD of hosts, blessed *is* the man that trusteth in thee.

PSALM 85
A Prayer for Mercy and Salvation

To the chief Musician, A Psalm for the sons of Korah.

LORD, thou hast been favourable unto thy land: thou hast brought back the
captivity of Jacob.
2 Thou hast forgiven the iniquity of thy people, thou hast covered all their
sin. Selah.
3 Thou hast taken away all thy wrath: thou hast turned *thyself* from the fierce-
ness of thine anger.
4 Turn us, O God of our salvation, and cause thine anger toward us to cease.
5 Wilt thou be angry with us for ever? wilt thou draw out thine anger to all
generations?
6 Wilt thou not revive us again: that thy people may rejoice in thee?
7 Shew us thy mercy, O LORD, and grant us thy salvation.
8 I will hear what God the LORD will speak: for he will speak peace unto his
people, and to his saints: but let them not turn again to folly.
9 Surely his salvation *is* nigh them that fear him; that glory may dwell in our land.
10 Mercy and truth are met together; righteousness and peace have kissed
each other.
11 Truth shall spring out of the earth; and righteousness shall look down
from heaven.
12 Yea, the LORD shall give *that which is* good; and our land shall yield her
increase.
13 Righteousness shall go before him; and shall set *us* in the way of his steps.

PSALM 86
David's Faith Is Firmly Rooted

A Prayer of David.

Bow down thine ear, O LORD, hear me: for I *am* poor and needy.
2 Preserve my soul; for I *am* holy: O thou my God, save thy servant that
trusteth in thee.

3 Be merciful unto me, O Lord: for I cry unto thee daily.
4 Rejoice the soul of thy servant: for unto thee, O Lord, do I lift up my soul.
5 For thou, Lord, *art* good, and ready to forgive; and plenteous in mercy unto
all them that call upon thee.
6 Give ear, O LORD, unto my prayer; and attend to the voice of my supplications.
7 In the day of my trouble I will call upon thee: for thou wilt answer me.
8 Among the gods *there is* none like unto thee, O Lord; neither *are there any*
works like unto thy works.
9 All nations whom thou hast made shall come and worship before thee, O
Lord; and shall glorify thy name.
10 For thou *art* great, and doest wondrous things: thou *art* God alone.
11 Teach me thy way, O LORD; I will walk in thy truth: unite my heart to fear
thy name.
12 I will praise thee, O Lord my God, with all my heart: and I will glorify thy
name for evermore.
13 For great *is* thy mercy toward me: and thou hast delivered my soul from
the lowest hell.
14 O God, the proud are risen against me, and the assemblies of violent *men*
have sought after my soul; and have not set thee before them.
15 But thou, O Lord, *art* a God full of compassion, and gracious, longsuffer-
ing, and plenteous in mercy and truth.
16 O turn unto me, and have mercy upon me; give thy strength unto thy
servant, and save the son of thine handmaid.
17 Shew me a token for good; that they which hate me may see *it*, and be
ashamed: because thou, LORD, hast holpen me, and comforted me.

PSALM 87
The Glorious City of God

A Psalm *or* Song for the sons of Korah.

His foundation *is* in the holy mountains.
2 The LORD loveth the gates of Zion more than all the dwellings of Jacob.
3 Glorious things are spoken of thee, O city of God. Selah.
4 I will make mention of Rahab and Babylon to them that know me: behold
Philistia, and Tyre, with Ethiopia; this *man* was born there.
5 And of Zion it shall be said, This and that man was born in her: and the
highest himself shall establish her.
6 The LORD shall count, when he writeth up the people, *that* this *man* was
born there. Selah.
7 As well the singers as the players on instruments *shall be there*: all my
springs *are* in thee.

PSALM 88
A Prayer from Deep Misery

A Song *or* Psalm for the sons of Korah, to the chief Musician upon Mahalath Leannoth, Maschil of Heman the Ezrahite.

O LORD God of my salvation, I have cried day *and* night before thee:
2 Let my prayer come before thee: incline thine ear unto my cry;
3 For my soul is full of troubles: and my life draweth nigh unto the grave.
4 I am counted with them that go down into the pit: I am as a man *that hath*
no strength:
5 Free among the dead, like the slain that lie in the grave, whom thou remem-
berest no more: and they are cut off from thy hand.
6 Thou hast laid me in the lowest pit, in darkness, in the deeps.
7 Thy wrath lieth hard upon me, and thou hast afflicted *me* with all thy waves.
Selah.

8 Thou hast put away mine acquaintance far from me; thou hast made me
an abomination unto them: *I am* shut up, and I cannot come forth.
9 Mine eye mourneth by reason of affliction: LORD, I have called daily upon
thee, I have stretched out my hands unto thee.
10 Wilt thou shew wonders to the dead? shall the dead arise *and* praise thee?
Selah.
11 Shall thy lovingkindness be declared in the grave? *or* thy faithfulness in
destruction?
12 Shall thy wonders be known in the dark? and thy righteousness in the
land of forgetfulness?
13 But unto thee have I cried, O LORD; and in the morning shall my prayer
prevent thee.
14 LORD, why castest thou off my soul? *why* hidest thou thy face from me?
15 I *am* afflicted and ready to die from *my* youth up: *while* I suffer thy terrors
I am distracted.
16 Thy fierce wrath goeth over me; thy terrors have cut me off.
17 They came round about me daily like water; they compassed me about
together.
18 Lover and friend hast thou put far from me, *and* mine acquaintance into
darkness.

PSALM 89

Praise to God for His Covenant Promises

Maschil of Ethan the Ezrahite.

I will sing of the mercies of the LORD for ever: with my mouth will I make
known thy faithfulness to all generations.
2 For I have said, Mercy shall be built up for ever: thy faithfulness shalt thou
establish in the very heavens.
3 I have made a covenant with my chosen, I have sworn unto David my serv-
ant,
4 Thy seed will I establish for ever, and build up thy throne to all generations.
Selah.
5 And the heavens shall praise thy wonders, O LORD: thy faithfulness also in
the congregation of the saints.
6 For who in the heaven can be compared unto the LORD? *who* among the
sons of the mighty can be likened unto the LORD?
7 God is greatly to be feared in the assembly of the saints, and to be had in
reverence of all *them that are* about him.
8 O LORD God of hosts, who *is* a strong LORD like unto thee? or to thy faith-
fulness round about thee?
9 Thou rulest the raging of the sea: when the waves thereof arise, thou still-
est them.
10 Thou hast broken Rahab in pieces, as one that is slain; thou hast scattered
thine enemies with thy strong arm.
11 The heavens *are* thine, the earth also *is* thine: *as for* the world and the
fulness thereof, thou hast founded them.
12 The north and the south thou hast created them: Tabor and Hermon shall
rejoice in thy name.
13 Thou hast a mighty arm: strong is thy hand, *and* high is thy right hand.
14 Justice and judgment *are* the habitation of thy throne: mercy and truth
shall go before thy face.
15 Blessed *is* the people that know the joyful sound: they shall walk, O LORD,
in the light of thy countenance.
16 In thy name shall they rejoice all the day: and in thy righteousness shall
they be exalted.

17 For thou *art* the glory of their strength: and in thy favour our horn shall
be exalted.
18 For the LORD *is* our defence; and the Holy One of Israel *is* our king.
19 Then thou spakest in vision to thy holy one, and saidst, I have laid help
upon *one that is* mighty; I have exalted *one* chosen out of the people.
20 I have found David my servant; with my holy oil have I anointed him:
21 With whom my hand shall be established: mine arm also shall strengthen
him.
22 The enemy shall not exact upon him; nor the son of wickedness afflict
him.
23 And I will beat down his foes before his face, and plague them that hate
him.
24 But my faithfulness and my mercy *shall be* with him: and in my name shall
his horn be exalted.
25 I will set his hand also in the sea, and his right hand in the rivers.
26 He shall cry unto me, Thou *art* my father, my God, and the rock of my
salvation.
27 Also I will make him *my* firstborn, higher than the kings of the earth.
28 My mercy will I keep for him for evermore, and my covenant shall stand
fast with him.
29 His seed also will I make *to endure* for ever, and his throne as the days of
heaven.
30 If his children forsake my law, and walk not in my judgments;
31 If they break my statutes, and keep not my commandments;
32 Then will I visit their transgression with the rod, and their iniquity with
stripes.
33 Nevertheless my lovingkindness will I not utterly take from him, nor suf-
fer my faithfulness to fail.
34 My covenant will I not break, nor alter the thing that is gone out of my lips.
35 Once have I sworn by my holiness that I will not lie unto David.
36 His seed shall endure for ever, and his throne as the sun before me.
37 It shall be established for ever as the moon, and *as* a faithful witness in
heaven. Selah.
38 But thou hast cast off and abhorred, thou hast been wroth with thine
anointed.
39 Thou hast made void the covenant of thy servant: thou hast profaned his
crown *by casting it* to the ground.
40 Thou hast broken down all his hedges; thou hast brought his strong holds
to ruin.
41 All that pass by the way spoil him: he is a reproach to his neighbours.
42 Thou hast set up the right hand of his adversaries; thou hast made all his
enemies to rejoice.
43 Thou hast also turned the edge of his sword, and hast not made him to
stand in the battle.
44 Thou hast made his glory to cease, and cast his throne down to the ground.
45 The days of his youth hast thou shortened: thou hast covered him with
shame. Selah.
46 How long, LORD? wilt thou hide thyself for ever? shall thy wrath burn like
fire?
47 Remember how short my time is: wherefore hast thou made all men in
vain?
48 What man *is he that* liveth, and shall not see death? shall he deliver his
soul from the hand of the grave? Selah.
49 Lord, where *are* thy former lovingkindnesses, *which* thou swarest unto
David in thy truth?

50 Remember, Lord, the reproach of thy servants; *how* I do bear in my bosom
the reproach of all the mighty people;
51 Wherewith thine enemies have reproached, O LORD; wherewith they have
reproached the footsteps of thine anointed.
52 Blessed *be* the LORD for evermore. Amen, and Amen.

PSALM 90

Moses Prays for the Nation

A Prayer of Moses the man of God.

Lord, thou hast been our dwelling place in all generations.
2 Before the mountains were brought forth, or ever thou hadst formed
the earth and the world, even from everlasting to everlasting, thou *art* God.
3 Thou turnest man to destruction; and sayest, Return, ye children of men.
4 For a thousand years in thy sight *are but* as yesterday when it is past, and
as a watch in the night.
5 Thou carriest them away as with a flood; they are *as* a sleep: in the morning
they are like grass *which* groweth up.
6 In the morning it flourisheth, and groweth up; in the evening it is cut down,
and withereth.
7 For we are consumed by thine anger, and by thy wrath are we troubled.
8 Thou hast set our iniquities before thee, our secret *sins* in the light of thy
countenance.
9 For all our days are passed away in thy wrath: we spend our years as a tale
that is told.
10 The days of our years *are* threescore years and ten; and if by reason of
strength *they be* fourscore years, yet *is* their strength labour and sorrow; for
it is soon cut off, and we fly away.
11 Who knoweth the power of thine anger? even according to thy fear, *so is*
thy wrath.
12 So teach *us* to number our days, that we may apply *our* hearts unto wis-
dom.
13 Return, O LORD, how long? and let it repent thee concerning thy servants.
14 O satisfy us early with thy mercy; that we may rejoice and be glad all our
days.
15 Make us glad according to the days *wherein* thou hast afflicted us, *and* the
years *wherein* we have seen evil.
16 Let thy work appear unto thy servants, and thy glory unto their children.
17 And let the beauty of the LORD our God be upon us: and establish thou the
work of our hands upon us; yea, the work of our hands establish thou it.

PSALM 91

God Will Protect and Rescue

He that dwelleth in the secret place of the most High shall abide under the
shadow of the Almighty.
2 I will say of the LORD, *He is* my refuge and my fortress: my God; in him will
I trust.
3 Surely he shall deliver thee from the snare of the fowler, *and* from the
noisome pestilence.
4 He shall cover thee with his feathers, and under his wings shalt thou trust:
his truth *shall be thy* shield and buckler.
5 Thou shalt not be afraid for the terror by night; *nor* for the arrow *that* flieth
by day;
6 *Nor* for the pestilence *that* walketh in darkness; *nor* for the destruction
that wasteth at noonday.
7 A thousand shall fall at thy side, and ten thousand at thy right hand; *but* it
shall not come nigh thee.

8 Only with thine eyes shalt thou behold and see the reward of the wicked.
9 Because thou hast made the Lord, *which is* my refuge, *even* the most High,
thy habitation;
10 There shall no evil befall thee, neither shall any plague come nigh thy
dwelling.
11 For he shall give his angels charge over thee, to keep thee in all thy ways.
12 They shall bear thee up in *their* hands, lest thou dash thy foot against a
stone.
13 Thou shalt tread upon the lion and adder: the young lion and the dragon
shalt thou trample under feet.
14 Because he hath set his love upon me, therefore will I deliver him: I will
set him on high, because he hath known my name.
15 He shall call upon me, and I will answer him: I *will be* with him in trouble;
I will deliver him, and honour him.
16 With long life will I satisfy him, and shew him my salvation.

PSALM 92
It Is a Good Thing to Praise God

A Psalm *or* Song for the sabbath day.

It is a good *thing* to give thanks unto the Lord, and to sing praises unto thy
name, O most High:
2 To shew forth thy lovingkindness in the morning, and thy faithfulness
every night,
3 Upon an instrument of ten strings, and upon the psaltery; upon the harp
with a solemn sound.
4 For thou, Lord, hast made me glad through thy work: I will triumph in the
works of thy hands.
5 O Lord, how great are thy works! *and* thy thoughts are very deep.
6 A brutish man knoweth not; neither doth a fool understand this.
7 When the wicked spring as the grass, and when all the workers of iniquity
do flourish; *it is* that they shall be destroyed for ever:
8 But thou, Lord, *art most* high for evermore.
9 For, lo, thine enemies, O Lord, for, lo, thine enemies shall perish; all the
workers of iniquity shall be scattered.
10 But my horn shalt thou exalt like *the horn of* an unicorn: I shall be anoint-
ed with fresh oil.
11 Mine eye also shall see *my desire* on mine enemies, *and* mine ears shall
hear *my desire* of the wicked that rise up against me.
12 The righteous shall flourish like the palm tree: he shall grow like a cedar
in Lebanon.
13 Those that be planted in the house of the Lord shall flourish in the courts
of our God.
14 They shall still bring forth fruit in old age; they shall be fat and flourishing;
15 To shew that the Lord *is* upright: *he is* my rock, and *there is* no unrigh-
teousness in him.

PSALM 93
The Lord Reigns

The Lord reigneth, he is clothed with majesty; the Lord is clothed with
strength, *wherewith* he hath girded himself: the world also is stablished,
that it cannot be moved.
2 Thy throne *is* established of old: thou *art* from everlasting.
3 The floods have lifted up, O Lord, the floods have lifted up their voice; the
floods lift up their waves.
4 The Lord on high *is* mightier than the noise of many waters, *yea, than* the
mighty waves of the sea.
5 Thy testimonies are very sure: holiness becometh thine house, O Lord, for ever.

PSALM 94
The Lord Will Avenge His People

O LORD God, to whom vengeance belongeth; O God, to whom vengeance
belongeth, shew thyself.
2 Lift up thyself, thou judge of the earth: render a reward to the proud.
3 LORD, how long shall the wicked, how long shall the wicked triumph?
4 *How long* shall they utter *and* speak hard things? *and* all the workers of
iniquity boast themselves?
5 They break in pieces thy people, O LORD, and afflict thine heritage.
6 They slay the widow and the stranger, and murder the fatherless.
7 Yet they say, The LORD shall not see, neither shall the God of Jacob regard *it*.
8 Understand, ye brutish among the people: and *ye* fools, when will ye be wise?
9 He that planted the ear, shall he not hear? he that formed the eye, shall he
not see?
10 He that chastiseth the heathen, shall not he correct? he that teacheth man
knowledge, *shall not he know*?
11 The LORD knoweth the thoughts of man, that they *are* vanity.
12 Blessed *is* the man whom thou chastenest, O LORD, and teachest him out
of thy law;
13 That thou mayest give him rest from the days of adversity, until the pit be
digged for the wicked.
14 For the LORD will not cast off his people, neither will he forsake his inher-
itance.
15 But judgment shall return unto righteousness: and all the upright in heart
shall follow it.
16 Who will rise up for me against the evildoers? *or* who will stand up for
me against the workers of iniquity?
17 Unless the LORD *had been* my help, my soul had almost dwelt in silence.
18 When I said, My foot slippeth; thy mercy, O LORD, held me up.
19 In the multitude of my thoughts within me thy comforts delight my soul.
20 Shall the throne of iniquity have fellowship with thee, which frameth
mischief by a law?
21 They gather themselves together against the soul of the righteous, and
condemn the innocent blood.
22 But the LORD is my defence; and my God *is* the rock of my refuge.
23 And he shall bring upon them their own iniquity, and shall cut them off
in their own wickedness; *yea*, the LORD our God shall cut them off.

PSALM 95
An Invitation to Praise God

O come, let us sing unto the LORD: let us make a joyful noise to the rock of
our salvation.
2 Let us come before his presence with thanksgiving, and make a joyful noise
unto him with psalms.
3 For the LORD *is* a great God, and a great King above all gods.
4 In his hand *are* the deep places of the earth: the strength of the hills *is* his
also.
5 The sea *is* his, and he made it: and his hands formed the dry *land*.
6 O come, let us worship and bow down: let us kneel before the LORD our
maker.
7 For he *is* our God; and we *are* the people of his pasture, and the sheep of
his hand. To day if ye will hear his voice,
8 Harden not your heart, as in the provocation, *and* as *in* the day of tempta-
tion in the wilderness:
9 When your fathers tempted me, proved me, and saw my work.

10 Forty years long was I grieved with *this* generation, and said, It *is* a people
that do err in their heart, and they have not known my ways:
11 Unto whom I sware in my wrath that they should not enter into my rest.

PSALM 96
Sing to the Lord a New Song

O sing unto the LORD a new song: sing unto the LORD, all the earth.
2 Sing unto the LORD, bless his name; shew forth his salvation from
day to day.
3 Declare his glory among the heathen, his wonders among all people.
4 For the LORD *is* great, and greatly to be praised: he *is* to be feared above all
gods.
5 For all the gods of the nations *are* idols: but the LORD made the heavens.
6 Honour and majesty *are* before him: strength and beauty *are* in his sanc-
tuary.
7 Give unto the LORD, O ye kindreds of the people, give unto the LORD glory
and strength.
8 Give unto the LORD the glory *due unto* his name: bring an offering, and
come into his courts.
9 O worship the LORD in the beauty of holiness: fear before him, all the earth.
10 Say among the heathen *that* the LORD reigneth: the world also shall be
established that it shall not be moved: he shall judge the people righteously.
11 Let the heavens rejoice, and let the earth be glad; let the sea roar, and the
fulness thereof.
12 Let the field be joyful, and all that *is* therein: then shall all the trees of the
wood rejoice
13 Before the LORD: for he cometh, for he cometh to judge the earth: he shall
judge the world with righteousness, and the people with his truth.

PSALM 97
The Majesty of God's Kingdom

The LORD reigneth; let the earth rejoice; let the multitude of isles be glad
thereof.
2 Clouds and darkness *are* round about him: righteousness and judgment
are the habitation of his throne.
3 A fire goeth before him, and burneth up his enemies round about.
4 His lightnings enlightened the world: the earth saw, and trembled.
5 The hills melted like wax at the presence of the LORD, at the presence of the
Lord of the whole earth.
6 The heavens declare his righteousness, and all the people see his glory.
7 Confounded be all they that serve graven images, that boast themselves of
idols: worship him, all *ye* gods.
8 Zion heard, and was glad; and the daughters of Judah rejoiced because of
thy judgments, O LORD.
9 For thou, LORD, *art* high above all the earth: thou art exalted far above all gods.
10 Ye that love the LORD, hate evil: he preserveth the souls of his saints; he
delivereth them out of the hand of the wicked.
11 Light is sown for the righteous, and gladness for the upright in heart.
12 Rejoice in the LORD, ye righteous; and give thanks at the remembrance of
his holiness.

O sing unto the LORD a new song: sing unto the LORD, all the EARTH.
PSALM 96:1

PSALM 98
Make a Joyful Noise unto the Lord

A Psalm.

O sing unto the Lord a new song; for he hath done marvellous things: his right hand, and his holy arm, hath gotten him the victory.
2 The Lord hath made known his salvation: his righteousness hath he openly shewed in the sight of the heathen.
3 He hath remembered his mercy and his truth toward the house of Israel: all the ends of the earth have seen the salvation of our God.
4 Make a joyful noise unto the Lord, all the earth: make a loud noise, and rejoice, and sing praise.
5 Sing unto the Lord with the harp; with the harp, and the voice of a psalm.
6 With trumpets and sound of cornet make a joyful noise before the Lord, the King.
7 Let the sea roar, and the fulness thereof; the world, and they that dwell therein.
8 Let the floods clap *their* hands: let the hills be joyful together
9 Before the Lord; for he cometh to judge the earth: with righteousness shall he judge the world, and the people with equity.

PSALM 99
The Lord Is Great in Zion

The Lord reigneth; let the people tremble: he sitteth *between* the cherubims; let the earth be moved.
2 The Lord *is* great in Zion; and he *is* high above all the people.
3 Let them praise thy great and terrible name; *for* it *is* holy.
4 The king's strength also loveth judgment; thou dost establish equity, thou executest judgment and righteousness in Jacob.
5 Exalt ye the Lord our God, and worship at his footstool; *for* he *is* holy.
6 Moses and Aaron among his priests, and Samuel among them that call upon his name; they called upon the Lord, and he answered them.
7 He spake unto them in the cloudy pillar: they kept his testimonies, and the ordinance *that* he gave them.
8 Thou answeredst them, O Lord our God: thou wast a God that forgavest them, though thou tookest vengeance of their inventions.
9 Exalt the Lord our God, and worship at his holy hill; for the Lord our God *is* holy.

PSALM 100
An Invitation to Praise God Cheerfully

A Psalm of praise.

Make a joyful noise unto the Lord, all ye lands.
2 Serve the Lord with gladness: come before his presence with singing.
3 Know ye that the Lord he *is* God: *it is* he *that* hath made us, and not we ourselves; *we are* his people, and the sheep of his pasture.
4 Enter into his gates with thanksgiving, *and* into his courts with praise: be thankful unto him, *and* bless his name.
5 For the Lord *is* good; his mercy *is* everlasting; and his truth *endureth* to all generations.

PSALM 101
David Prays to Live with Integrity

A Psalm of David.

I will sing of mercy and judgment: unto thee, O LORD, will I sing.
2 I will behave myself wisely in a perfect way. O when wilt thou come unto
me? I will walk within my house with a perfect heart.
3 I will set no wicked thing before mine eyes: I hate the work of them that
turn aside; *it* shall not cleave to me.
4 A froward heart shall depart from me: I will not know a wicked *person*.
5 Whoso privily slandereth his neighbour, him will I cut off: him that hath
an high look and a proud heart will not I suffer.
6 Mine eyes *shall be* upon the faithful of the land, that they may dwell with
me: he that walketh in a perfect way, he shall serve me.
7 He that worketh deceit shall not dwell within my house: he that telleth lies
shall not tarry in my sight.
8 I will early destroy all the wicked of the land; that I may cut off all wicked
doers from the city of the LORD.

PSALM 102
Comfort in the Mercy of God

A Prayer of the afflicted, when he is overwhelmed, and poureth out his complaint before the LORD.

Hear my prayer, O LORD, and let my cry come unto thee.
2 Hide not thy face from me in the day *when* I am in trouble; incline thine
ear unto me: in the day *when* I call answer me speedily.
3 For my days are consumed like smoke, and my bones are burned as an
hearth.
4 My heart is smitten, and withered like grass; so that I forget to eat my bread.
5 By reason of the voice of my groaning my bones cleave to my skin.
6 I am like a pelican of the wilderness: I am like an owl of the desert.
7 I watch, and am as a sparrow alone upon the house top.
8 Mine enemies reproach me all the day; *and* they that are mad against me
are sworn against me.
9 For I have eaten ashes like bread, and mingled my drink with weeping,
10 Because of thine indignation and thy wrath: for thou hast lifted me up,
and cast me down.
11 My days *are* like a shadow that declineth; and I am withered like grass.
12 But thou, O LORD, shalt endure for ever; and thy remembrance unto all
generations.
13 Thou shalt arise, *and* have mercy upon Zion: for the time to favour her,
yea, the set time, is come.
14 For thy servants take pleasure in her stones, and favour the dust thereof.
15 So the heathen shall fear the name of the LORD, and all the kings of the
earth thy glory.
16 When the LORD shall build up Zion, he shall appear in his glory.
17 He will regard the prayer of the destitute, and not despise their prayer.
18 This shall be written for the generation to come: and the people which
shall be created shall praise the LORD.
19 For he hath looked down from the height of his sanctuary; from heaven
did the LORD behold the earth;
20 To hear the groaning of the prisoner; to loose those that are appointed to
death;
21 To declare the name of the LORD in Zion, and his praise in Jerusalem;
22 When the people are gathered together, and the kingdoms, to serve the
LORD.
23 He weakened my strength in the way; he shortened my days.

24 I said, O my God, take me not away in the midst of my days: thy years *are*
throughout all generations.
25 Of old hast thou laid the foundation of the earth: and the heavens *are* the
work of thy hands.
26 They shall perish, but thou shalt endure: yea, all of them shall wax old like
a garment; as a vesture shalt thou change them, and they shall be changed:
27 But thou *art* the same, and thy years shall have no end.
28 The children of thy servants shall continue, and their seed shall be estab-
lished before thee.

PSALM 103
David Praises God's Great Love

A Psalm of David.

Bless the LORD, O my soul: and all that is within me, *bless* his holy name.
2 Bless the LORD, O my soul, and forget not all his benefits:
3 Who forgiveth all thine iniquities; who healeth all thy diseases;
4 Who redeemeth thy life from destruction; who crowneth thee with loving-
kindness and tender mercies;
5 Who satisfieth thy mouth with good *things; so that* thy youth is renewed
like the eagle's.
6 The LORD executeth righteousness and judgment for all that are oppressed.
7 He made known his ways unto Moses, his acts unto the children of Israel.
8 The LORD *is* merciful and gracious, slow to anger, and plenteous in mercy.
9 He will not always chide: neither will he keep *his anger* for ever.
10 He hath not dealt with us after our sins; nor rewarded us according to our
iniquities.
11 For as the heaven is high above the earth, *so* great is his mercy toward
them that fear him.
12 As far as the east is from the west, *so* far hath he removed our transgres-
sions from us.
13 Like as a father pitieth *his* children, *so* the LORD pitieth them that fear him.
14 For he knoweth our frame; he remembereth that we *are* dust.
15 *As for* man, his days *are* as grass: as a flower of the field, so he flourisheth.
16 For the wind passeth over it, and it is gone; and the place thereof shall
know it no more.
17 But the mercy of the LORD *is* from everlasting to everlasting upon them
that fear him, and his righteousness unto children's children;
18 To such as keep his covenant, and to those that remember his command-
ments to do them.
19 The LORD hath prepared his throne in the heavens; and his kingdom ruleth
over all.
20 Bless the LORD, ye his angels, that excel in strength, that do his command-
ments, hearkening unto the voice of his word.
21 Bless ye the LORD, all *ye* his hosts; *ye* ministers of his, that do his pleasure.
22 Bless the LORD, all his works in all places of his dominion: bless the LORD,
O my soul.

PSALM 104
A Meditation upon God's Mighty Creative Power

Bless the LORD, O my soul. O LORD my God, thou art very great; thou art
clothed with honour and majesty.
2 Who coverest *thyself* with light as *with* a garment: who stretchest out the
heavens like a curtain:
3 Who layeth the beams of his chambers in the waters: who maketh the
clouds his chariot: who walketh upon the wings of the wind:
4 Who maketh his angels spirits; his ministers a flaming fire:

5 *Who* laid the foundations of the earth, *that* it should not be removed for
ever.
6 Thou coveredst it with the deep as *with* a garment: the waters stood above
the mountains.
7 At thy rebuke they fled; at the voice of thy thunder they hasted away.
8 They go up by the mountains; they go down by the valleys unto the place
which thou hast founded for them.
9 Thou hast set a bound that they may not pass over; that they turn not again
to cover the earth.
10 He sendeth the springs into the valleys, *which* run among the hills.
11 They give drink to every beast of the field: the wild asses quench their
thirst.
12 By them shall the fowls of the heaven have their habitation, *which* sing
among the branches.
13 He watereth the hills from his chambers: the earth is satisfied with the
fruit of thy works.
14 He causeth the grass to grow for the cattle, and herb for the service of
man: that he may bring forth food out of the earth;
15 And wine *that* maketh glad the heart of man, *and* oil to make *his* face to
shine, and bread *which* strengtheneth man's heart.
16 The trees of the LORD are full *of sap*; the cedars of Lebanon, which he hath
planted;
17 Where the birds make their nests: *as for* the stork, the fir trees *are* her
house.
18 The high hills *are* a refuge for the wild goats; *and* the rocks for the conies.
19 He appointed the moon for seasons: the sun knoweth his going down.
20 Thou makest darkness, and it is night: wherein all the beasts of the forest
do creep *forth*.
21 The young lions roar after their prey, and seek their meat from God.
22 The sun ariseth, they gather themselves together, and lay them down in
their dens.
23 Man goeth forth unto his work and to his labour until the evening.
24 O LORD, how manifold are thy works! in wisdom hast thou made them
all: the earth is full of thy riches.
25 *So is* this great and wide sea, wherein *are* things creeping innumerable,
both small and great beasts.
26 There go the ships: *there is* that leviathan, *whom* thou hast made to play
therein.
27 These wait all upon thee; that thou mayest give *them* their meat in due
season.
28 *That* thou givest them they gather: thou openest thine hand, they are filled
with good.
29 Thou hidest thy face, they are troubled: thou takest away their breath, they
die, and return to their dust.
30 Thou sendest forth thy spirit, they are created: and thou renewest the face
of the earth.
31 The glory of the LORD shall endure for ever: the LORD shall rejoice in his
works.
32 He looketh on the earth, and it trembleth: he toucheth the hills, and they
smoke.
33 I will sing unto the LORD as long as I live: I will sing praise to my God while
I have my being.
34 My meditation of him shall be sweet: I will be glad in the LORD.
35 Let the sinners be consumed out of the earth, and let the wicked be no
more. Bless thou the LORD, O my soul. Praise ye the LORD.

PSALM 105
David Recalls God's Miracles for Israel

O give thanks unto the LORD; call upon his name: make known his deeds
among the people.
2 Sing unto him, sing psalms unto him: talk ye of all his wondrous works.
3 Glory ye in his holy name: let the heart of them rejoice that seek the LORD.
4 Seek the LORD, and his strength: seek his face evermore.
5 Remember his marvellous works that he hath done; his wonders, and the
judgments of his mouth;
6 O ye seed of Abraham his servant, ye children of Jacob his chosen.
7 He *is* the LORD our God: his judgments *are* in all the earth.
8 He hath remembered his covenant for ever, the word *which* he command-
ed to a thousand generations.
9 Which *covenant* he made with Abraham, and his oath unto Isaac;
10 And confirmed the same unto Jacob for a law, *and* to Israel *for* an ever-
lasting covenant:
11 Saying, Unto thee will I give the land of Canaan, the lot of your inheritance:
12 When they were *but* a few men in number; yea, very few, and strangers in it.
13 When they went from one nation to another, from *one* kingdom to anoth-
er people;
14 He suffered no man to do them wrong: yea, he reproved kings for their
sakes;
15 *Saying*, Touch not mine anointed, and do my prophets no harm.
16 Moreover he called for a famine upon the land: he brake the whole staff
of bread.
17 He sent a man before them, *even* Joseph, *who* was sold for a servant:
18 Whose feet they hurt with fetters: he was laid in iron:
19 Until the time that his word came: the word of the LORD tried him.
20 The king sent and loosed him; *even* the ruler of the people, and let him go
free.
21 He made him lord of his house, and ruler of all his substance:
22 To bind his princes at his pleasure; and teach his senators wisdom.
23 Israel also came into Egypt; and Jacob sojourned in the land of Ham.
24 And he increased his people greatly; and made them stronger than their
enemies.
25 He turned their heart to hate his people, to deal subtilly with his servants.
26 He sent Moses his servant; *and* Aaron whom he had chosen.
27 They shewed his signs among them, and wonders in the land of Ham.
28 He sent darkness, and made it dark; and they rebelled not against his word.
29 He turned their waters into blood, and slew their fish.
30 Their land brought forth frogs in abundance, in the chambers of their
kings.
31 He spake, and there came divers sorts of flies, *and* lice in all their coasts.
32 He gave them hail for rain, *and* flaming fire in their land.
33 He smote their vines also and their fig trees; and brake the trees of their
coasts.
34 He spake, and the locusts came, and caterpillers, and that without number,
35 And did eat up all the herbs in their land, and devoured the fruit of their
ground.
36 He smote also all the firstborn in their land, the chief of all their strength.
37 He brought them forth also with silver and gold: and *there was* not one
feeble *person* among their tribes.
38 Egypt was glad when they departed: for the fear of them fell upon them.
39 He spread a cloud for a covering; and fire to give light in the night.
40 *The people* asked, and he brought quails, and satisfied them with the bread
of heaven.

41 He opened the rock, and the waters gushed out; they ran in the dry places *like* a river.
42 For he remembered his holy promise, *and* Abraham his servant.
43 And he brought forth his people with joy, *and* his chosen with gladness:
44 And gave them the lands of the heathen: and they inherited the labour of the people;
45 That they might observe his statutes, and keep his laws. Praise ye the LORD.

PSALM 106

Israel Repents and Praises God

Praise ye the LORD. O give thanks unto the LORD; for *he is* good: for his mercy *endureth* for ever.
2 Who can utter the mighty acts of the LORD? *who* can shew forth all his praise?
3 Blessed *are* they that keep judgment, *and* he that doeth righteousness at all times.
4 Remember me, O LORD, with the favour *that thou bearest unto* thy people: O visit me with thy salvation;
5 That I may see the good of thy chosen, that I may rejoice in the gladness of thy nation, that I may glory with thine inheritance.
6 We have sinned with our fathers, we have committed iniquity, we have done wickedly.
7 Our fathers understood not thy wonders in Egypt; they remembered not the multitude of thy mercies; but provoked *him* at the sea, *even* at the Red sea.
8 Nevertheless he saved them for his name's sake, that he might make his mighty power to be known.
9 He rebuked the Red sea also, and it was dried up: so he led them through the depths, as through the wilderness.
10 And he saved them from the hand of him that hated *them*, and redeemed them from the hand of the enemy.
11 And the waters covered their enemies: there was not one of them left.
12 Then believed they his words; they sang his praise.
13 They soon forgat his works; they waited not for his counsel:
14 But lusted exceedingly in the wilderness, and tempted God in the desert.
15 And he gave them their request; but sent leanness into their soul.
16 They envied Moses also in the camp, *and* Aaron the saint of the LORD.
17 The earth opened and swallowed up Dathan, and covered the company of Abiram.
18 And a fire was kindled in their company; the flame burned up the wicked.
19 They made a calf in Horeb, and worshipped the molten image.
20 Thus they changed their glory into the similitude of an ox that eateth grass.
21 They forgat God their saviour, which had done great things in Egypt;
22 Wondrous works in the land of Ham, *and* terrible things by the Red sea.
23 Therefore he said that he would destroy them, had not Moses his chosen stood before him in the breach, to turn away his wrath, lest he should destroy *them*.
24 Yea, they despised the pleasant land, they believed not his word:
25 But murmured in their tents, *and* hearkened not unto the voice of the LORD.
26 Therefore he lifted up his hand against them, to overthrow them in the wilderness:
27 To overthrow their seed also among the nations, and to scatter them in the lands.
28 They joined themselves also unto Baal-peor, and ate the sacrifices of the dead.

29 Thus they provoked *him* to anger with their inventions: and the plague
brake in upon them.
30 Then stood up Phinehas, and executed judgment: and *so* the plague was
stayed.
31 And that was counted unto him for righteousness unto all generations
for evermore.
32 They angered *him* also at the waters of strife, so that it went ill with Moses
for their sakes:
33 Because they provoked his spirit, so that he spake unadvisedly with his
lips.
34 They did not destroy the nations, concerning whom the LORD command-
ed them:
35 But were mingled among the heathen, and learned their works.
36 And they served their idols: which were a snare unto them.
37 Yea, they sacrificed their sons and their daughters unto devils,
38 And shed innocent blood, *even* the blood of their sons and of their daugh-
ters, whom they sacrificed unto the idols of Canaan: and the land was pollut-
ed with blood.
39 Thus were they defiled with their own works, and went a whoring with
their own inventions.
40 Therefore was the wrath of the LORD kindled against his people, insomuch
that he abhorred his own inheritance.
41 And he gave them into the hand of the heathen; and they that hated them
ruled over them.
42 Their enemies also oppressed them, and they were brought into subjection
under their hand.
43 Many times did he deliver them; but they provoked *him* with their coun-
sel, and were brought low for their iniquity.
44 Nevertheless he regarded their affliction, when he heard their cry:
45 And he remembered for them his covenant, and repented according to
the multitude of his mercies.
46 He made them also to be pitied of all those that carried them captives.
47 Save us, O LORD our God, and gather us from among the heathen, to give
thanks unto thy holy name, *and* to triumph in thy praise.
48 Blessed *be* the LORD God of Israel from everlasting to everlasting: and let
all the people say, Amen. Praise ye the LORD.

PSALM 107

A Celebration of the Return from Exile

O give thanks unto the LORD, for *he is* good: for his mercy *endureth* for ever.
2 Let the redeemed of the LORD say *so,* whom he hath redeemed from
the hand of the enemy;
3 And gathered them out of the lands, from the east, and from the west, from
the north, and from the south.
4 They wandered in the wilderness in a solitary way; they found no city to
dwell in.
5 Hungry and thirsty, their soul fainted in them.
6 Then they cried unto the LORD in their trouble, *and* he delivered them out
of their distresses.
7 And he led them forth by the right way, that they might go to a city of
habitation.
8 Oh that *men* would praise the LORD *for* his goodness, and *for* his wonderful
works to the children of men!
9 For he satisfieth the longing soul, and filleth the hungry soul with goodness.
10 Such as sit in darkness and in the shadow of death, *being* bound in afflic-
tion and iron;

11 Because they rebelled against the words of God, and contemned the coun-
sel of the most High:
12 Therefore he brought down their heart with labour; they fell down, and
there was none to help.
13 Then they cried unto the LORD in their trouble, *and* he saved them out of
their distresses.
14 He brought them out of darkness and the shadow of death, and brake
their bands in sunder.
15 Oh that *men* would praise the LORD *for* his goodness, and *for* his wonder-
ful works to the children of men!
16 For he hath broken the gates of brass, and cut the bars of iron in sunder.
17 Fools because of their transgression, and because of their iniquities, are
afflicted.
18 Their soul abhorreth all manner of meat; and they draw near unto the
gates of death.
19 Then they cry unto the LORD in their trouble, *and* he saveth them out of
their distresses.
20 He sent his word, and healed them, and delivered *them* from their destruc-
tions.
21 Oh that *men* would praise the LORD *for* his goodness, and *for* his wonder-
ful works to the children of men!
22 And let them sacrifice the sacrifices of thanksgiving, and declare his works
with rejoicing.
23 They that go down to the sea in ships, that do business in great waters;
24 These see the works of the LORD, and his wonders in the deep.
25 For he commandeth, and raiseth the stormy wind, which lifteth up the
waves thereof.
26 They mount up to the heaven, they go down again to the depths: their soul
is melted because of trouble.
27 They reel to and fro, and stagger like a drunken man, and are at their wits'
end.
28 Then they cry unto the LORD in their trouble, and he bringeth them out
of their distresses.
29 He maketh the storm a calm, so that the waves thereof are still.
30 Then are they glad because they be quiet; so he bringeth them unto their
desired haven.
31 Oh that *men* would praise the LORD *for* his goodness, and *for* his wonder-
ful works to the children of men!
32 Let them exalt him also in the congregation of the people, and praise him
in the assembly of the elders.
33 He turneth rivers into a wilderness, and the watersprings into dry ground;
34 A fruitful land into barrenness, for the wickedness of them that dwell
therein.
35 He turneth the wilderness into a standing water, and dry ground into
watersprings.
36 And there he maketh the hungry to dwell, that they may prepare a city for
habitation;
37 And sow the fields, and plant vineyards, which may yield fruits of increase.
38 He blesseth them also, so that they are multiplied greatly; and suffereth
not their cattle to decrease.
39 Again, they are minished and brought low through oppression, affliction,
and sorrow.
40 He poureth contempt upon princes, and causeth them to wander in the
wilderness, *where there is* no way.
41 Yet setteth he the poor on high from affliction, and maketh *him* families
like a flock.

42 The righteous shall see *it*, and rejoice: and all iniquity shall stop her mouth.
43 Whoso *is* wise, and will observe these *things*, even they shall understand
the lovingkindness of the LORD.

PSALM 108

David Praises God's Faithfulness

A Song *or* Psalm of David.

O God, my heart is fixed; I will sing and give praise, even with my glory.
2 Awake, psaltery and harp: I *myself* will awake early.
3 I will praise thee, O LORD, among the people: and I will sing praises unto
thee among the nations.
4 For thy mercy *is* great above the heavens: and thy truth *reacheth* unto the
clouds.
5 Be thou exalted, O God, above the heavens: and thy glory above all the earth;
6 That thy beloved may be delivered: save *with* thy right hand, and answer me.
7 God hath spoken in his holiness; I will rejoice, I will divide Shechem, and
mete out the valley of Succoth.
8 Gilead *is* mine; Manasseh *is* mine; Ephraim also *is* the strength of mine
head; Judah *is* my lawgiver;
9 Moab *is* my washpot; over Edom will I cast out my shoe; over Philistia will
I triumph.
10 Who will bring me into the strong city? who will lead me into Edom?
11 *Wilt* not *thou*, O God, *who* hast cast us off? and wilt not thou, O God, go
forth with our hosts?
12 Give us help from trouble: for vain *is* the help of man.
13 Through God we shall do valiantly: for he *it is that* shall tread down our
enemies.

PSALM 109

David Prays against Slanderous Enemies

To the chief Musician, A Psalm of David.

Hold not thy peace, O God of my praise;
2 For the mouth of the wicked and the mouth of the deceitful are opened
against me: they have spoken against me with a lying tongue.
3 They compassed me about also with words of hatred; and fought against
me without a cause.
4 For my love they are my adversaries: but I *give myself unto* prayer.
5 And they have rewarded me evil for good, and hatred for my love.
6 Set thou a wicked man over him: and let Satan stand at his right hand.
7 When he shall be judged, let him be condemned: and let his prayer become sin.
8 Let his days be few; *and* let another take his office.
9 Let his children be fatherless, and his wife a widow.
10 Let his children be continually vagabonds, and beg: let them seek *their
bread* also out of their desolate places.
11 Let the extortioner catch all that he hath; and let the strangers spoil his
labour.
12 Let there be none to extend mercy unto him: neither let there be any to
favour his fatherless children.
13 Let his posterity be cut off; *and* in the generation following let their name
be blotted out.
14 Let the iniquity of his fathers be remembered with the LORD; and let not
the sin of his mother be blotted out.
15 Let them be before the LORD continually, that he may cut off the memory
of them from the earth.
16 Because that he remembered not to shew mercy, but persecuted the poor
and needy man, that he might even slay the broken in heart.

17 As he loved cursing, so let it come unto him: as he delighted not in blessing,
so let it be far from him.
18 As he clothed himself with cursing like as with his garment, so let it come
into his bowels like water, and like oil into his bones.
19 Let it be unto him as the garment *which* covereth him, and for a girdle
wherewith he is girded continually.
20 *Let* this *be* the reward of mine adversaries from the LORD, and of them
that speak evil against my soul.
21 But do thou for me, O GOD the Lord, for thy name's sake: because thy mercy
is good, deliver thou me.
22 For I *am* poor and needy, and my heart is wounded within me.
23 I am gone like the shadow when it declineth: I am tossed up and down as
the locust.
24 My knees are weak through fasting; and my flesh faileth of fatness.
25 I became also a reproach unto them: *when* they looked upon me they
shaked their heads.
26 Help me, O LORD my God: O save me according to thy mercy:
27 That they may know that this *is* thy hand; *that* thou, LORD, hast done it.
28 Let them curse, but bless thou: when they arise, let them be ashamed; but
let thy servant rejoice.
29 Let mine adversaries be clothed with shame, and let them cover them-
selves with their own confusion, as with a mantle.
30 I will greatly praise the LORD with my mouth; yea, I will praise him among
the multitude.
31 For he shall stand at the right hand of the poor, to save *him* from those
that condemn his soul.

PSALM 110

David Prophesies of the Coming Messiah

A Psalm of David.

The LORD said unto my Lord, Sit thou at my right hand, until I make thine
enemies thy footstool.
2 The LORD shall send the rod of thy strength out of Zion: rule thou in the
midst of thine enemies.
3 Thy people *shall be* willing in the day of thy power, in the beauties of holi-
ness from the womb of the morning: thou hast the dew of thy youth.
4 The LORD hath sworn, and will not repent, Thou *art* a priest for ever after
the order of Melchizedek.
5 The Lord at thy right hand shall strike through kings in the day of his wrath.
6 He shall judge among the heathen, he shall fill *the places* with the dead
bodies; he shall wound the heads over many countries.
7 He shall drink of the brook in the way: therefore shall he lift up the head.

PSALM 111

The Works of the Lord Are Great

Praise ye the LORD. I will praise the LORD with *my* whole heart, in the assem-
bly of the upright, and *in* the congregation.
2 The works of the LORD *are* great, sought out of all them that have pleasure
therein.
3 His work *is* honourable and glorious: and his righteousness endureth for
ever.
4 He hath made his wonderful works to be remembered: the LORD *is* gracious
and full of compassion.
5 He hath given meat unto them that fear him: he will ever be mindful of his
covenant.
6 He hath shewed his people the power of his works, that he may give them
the heritage of the heathen.

7 The works of his hands *are* verity and judgment; all his commandments
are sure.
8 They stand fast for ever and ever, *and are* done in truth and uprightness.
9 He sent redemption unto his people: he hath commanded his covenant
for ever: holy and reverend *is* his name.
10 The fear of the LORD *is* the beginning of wisdom: a good understanding
have all they that do *his commandments*: his praise endureth for ever.

PSALM 112

The Blessings of Godliness

Praise ye the LORD. Blessed *is* the man *that* feareth the LORD, *that* delighteth
greatly in his commandments.
2 His seed shall be mighty upon earth: the generation of the upright shall
be blessed.
3 Wealth and riches *shall be* in his house: and his righteousness endureth
for ever.
4 Unto the upright there ariseth light in the darkness: *he is* gracious, and full
of compassion, and righteous.
5 A good man sheweth favour, and lendeth: he will guide his affairs with
discretion.
6 Surely he shall not be moved for ever: the righteous shall be in everlasting
remembrance.
7 He shall not be afraid of evil tidings: his heart is fixed, trusting in the LORD.
8 His heart *is* established, he shall not be afraid, until he see *his desire* upon
his enemies.
9 He hath dispersed, he hath given to the poor; his righteousness endureth
for ever; his horn shall be exalted with honour.
10 The wicked shall see *it*, and be grieved; he shall gnash with his teeth, and
melt away: the desire of the wicked shall perish.

PSALM 113

Who Is like the Lord?

Praise ye the LORD. Praise, O ye servants of the LORD, praise the name of the
LORD.
2 Blessed be the name of the LORD from this time forth and for evermore.
3 From the rising of the sun unto the going down of the same the LORD's
name *is* to be praised.
4 The LORD *is* high above all nations, *and* his glory above the heavens.
5 Who *is* like unto the LORD our God, who dwelleth on high,
6 Who humbleth *himself* to behold *the things that are* in heaven, and in the
earth!
7 He raiseth up the poor out of the dust, *and* lifteth the needy out of the
dunghill;
8 That he may set *him* with princes, *even* with the princes of his people.
9 He maketh the barren woman to keep house, *and to be* a joyful mother of
children. Praise ye the LORD.

PSALM 114

Praise to God Who Delivered Israel out of Egypt

When Israel went out of Egypt, the house of Jacob from a people of strange
language;
2 Judah was his sanctuary, *and* Israel his dominion.
3 The sea saw *it*, and fled: Jordan was driven back.
4 The mountains skipped like rams, *and* the little hills like lambs.

5 What *ailed* thee, O thou sea, that thou fleddest? thou Jordan, *that* thou
wast driven back?
6 Ye mountains, *that* ye skipped like rams; *and* ye little hills, like lambs?
7 Tremble, thou earth, at the presence of the Lord, at the presence of the God
of Jacob;
8 Which turned the rock *into* a standing water, the flint into a fountain of
waters.

PSALM 115
God Is Truly Glorious

Not unto us, O LORD, not unto us, but unto thy name give glory, for thy mercy,
and for thy truth's sake.
2 Wherefore should the heathen say, Where *is* now their God?
3 But our God *is* in the heavens: he hath done whatsoever he hath pleased.
4 Their idols *are* silver and gold, the work of men's hands.
5 They have mouths, but they speak not: eyes have they, but they see not:
6 They have ears, but they hear not: noses have they, but they smell not:
7 They have hands, but they handle not: feet have they, but they walk not:
neither speak they through their throat.
8 They that make them are like unto them; *so is* every one that trusteth in
them.
9 O Israel, trust thou in the LORD: he *is* their help and their shield.
10 O house of Aaron, trust in the LORD: he *is* their help and their shield.
11 Ye that fear the LORD, trust in the LORD: he *is* their help and their shield.
12 The LORD hath been mindful of us: he will bless *us*; he will bless the house
of Israel; he will bless the house of Aaron.
13 He will bless them that fear the LORD, *both* small and great.
14 The LORD shall increase you more and more, you and your children.
15 Ye *are* blessed of the LORD which made heaven and earth.
16 The heaven, *even* the heavens, *are* the LORD's: but the earth hath he given
to the children of men.
17 The dead praise not the LORD, neither any that go down into silence.
18 But we will bless the LORD from this time forth and for evermore. Praise
the LORD.

PSALM 116
Gracious Is the Lord

I love the LORD, because he hath heard my voice *and* my supplications.
2 Because he hath inclined his ear unto me, therefore will I call upon
him as long as I live.
3 The sorrows of death compassed me, and the pains of hell gat hold upon
me: I found trouble and sorrow.
4 Then called I upon the name of the LORD; O LORD, I beseech thee, deliver
my soul.
5 Gracious *is* the LORD, and righteous; yea, our God *is* merciful.
6 The LORD preserveth the simple: I was brought low, and he helped me.
7 Return unto thy rest, O my soul; for the LORD hath dealt bountifully with
thee.
8 For thou hast delivered my soul from death, mine eyes from tears, *and* my
feet from falling.
9 I will walk before the LORD in the land of the living.
10 I believed, therefore have I spoken: I was greatly afflicted:
11 I said in my haste, All men *are* liars.
12 What shall I render unto the LORD *for* all his benefits toward me?
13 I will take the cup of salvation, and call upon the name of the LORD.
14 I will pay my vows unto the LORD now in the presence of all his people.

15 Precious in the sight of the LORD *is* the death of his saints.
16 O LORD, truly I *am* thy servant; I *am* thy servant, *and* the son of thine
handmaid: thou hast loosed my bonds.
17 I will offer to thee the sacrifice of thanksgiving, and will call upon the
name of the LORD.
18 I will pay my vows unto the LORD now in the presence of all his people,
19 In the courts of the LORD's house, in the midst of thee, O Jerusalem. Praise
ye the LORD.

PSALM 117

An Exhortation for All Nations to Praise the Lord

O praise the LORD, all ye nations: praise him, all ye people.
2 For his merciful kindness is great toward us: and the truth of the LORD
endureth for ever. Praise ye the LORD.

PSALM 118

God's Love Is Eternal

O give thanks unto the LORD; for *he is* good: because his mercy *endureth* for
ever.
2 Let Israel now say, that his mercy *endureth* for ever.
3 Let the house of Aaron now say, that his mercy *endureth* for ever.
4 Let them now that fear the LORD say, that his mercy *endureth* for ever.
5 I called upon the LORD in distress: the LORD answered me, *and set me* in a
large place.
6 The LORD *is* on my side; I will not fear: what can man do unto me?
7 The LORD taketh my part with them that help me: therefore shall I see *my
desire* upon them that hate me.
8 *It is* better to trust in the LORD than to put confidence in man.
9 *It is* better to trust in the LORD than to put confidence in princes.
10 All nations compassed me about: but in the name of the LORD will I destroy
them.
11 They compassed me about; yea, they compassed me about: but in the name
of the LORD I will destroy them.
12 They compassed me about like bees; they are quenched as the fire of
thorns: for in the name of the LORD I will destroy them.
13 Thou hast thrust sore at me that I might fall: but the LORD helped me.
14 The LORD *is* my strength and song, and is become my salvation.
15 The voice of rejoicing and salvation *is* in the tabernacles of the righteous:
the right hand of the LORD doeth valiantly.
16 The right hand of the LORD is exalted: the right hand of the LORD doeth
valiantly.
17 I shall not die, but live, and declare the works of the LORD.
18 The LORD hath chastened me sore: but he hath not given me over unto
death.
19 Open to me the gates of righteousness: I will go into them, *and* I will praise
the LORD:
20 This gate of the LORD, into which the righteous shall enter.
21 I will praise thee: for thou hast heard me, and art become my salvation.
22 The stone *which* the builders refused is become the head *stone* of the
corner.
23 This is the LORD's doing; it *is* marvellous in our eyes.
24 This *is* the day *which* the LORD hath made; we will rejoice and be glad in it.
25 Save now, I beseech thee, O LORD: O LORD, I beseech thee, send now pros-
perity.
26 Blessed *be* he that cometh in the name of the LORD: we have blessed you
out of the house of the LORD.

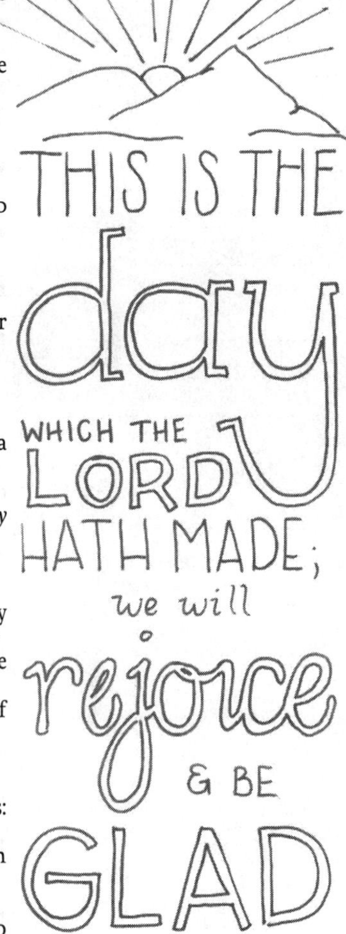

27 God *is* the LORD, which hath shewed us light: bind the sacrifice with cords,
even unto the horns of the altar.
28 Thou *art* my God, and I will praise thee: *thou art* my God, I will exalt thee.
29 O give thanks unto the LORD; for *he is* good: for his mercy *endureth* for ever.

PSALM 119
Praise for God's Wonderful Word

ALEPH

Blessed *are* the undefiled in the way, who walk in the law of the LORD.
2 Blessed *are* they that keep his testimonies, *and that* seek him with the
whole heart.
3 They also do no iniquity: they walk in his ways.
4 Thou hast commanded *us* to keep thy precepts diligently.
5 O that my ways were directed to keep thy statutes!
6 Then shall I not be ashamed, when I have respect unto all thy command-
ments.
7 I will praise thee with uprightness of heart, when I shall have learned thy
righteous judgments.
8 I will keep thy statutes: O forsake me not utterly.

BETH

9 Wherewithal shall a young man cleanse his way? by taking heed *thereto*
according to thy word.
10 With my whole heart have I sought thee: O let me not wander from thy
commandments.
11 Thy word have I hid in mine heart, that I might not sin against thee.
12 Blessed *art* thou, O LORD: teach me thy statutes.
13 With my lips have I declared all the judgments of thy mouth.
14 I have rejoiced in the way of thy testimonies, as *much as* in all riches.
15 I will meditate in thy precepts, and have respect unto thy ways.
16 I will delight myself in thy statutes: I will not forget thy word.

GIMEL

17 Deal bountifully with thy servant, *that* I may live, and keep thy word.
18 Open thou mine eyes, that I may behold wondrous things out of thy law.
19 I *am* a stranger in the earth: hide not thy commandments from me.
20 My soul breaketh for the longing *that it hath* unto thy judgments at all
times.
21 Thou hast rebuked the proud *that are* cursed, which do err from thy com-
mandments.
22 Remove from me reproach and contempt; for I have kept thy testimonies.
23 Princes also did sit *and* speak against me: *but* thy servant did meditate in
thy statutes.
24 Thy testimonies also *are* my delight *and* my counsellors.

DALETH

25 My soul cleaveth unto the dust: quicken thou me according to thy word.
26 I have declared my ways, and thou heardest me: teach me thy statutes.
27 Make me to understand the way of thy precepts: so shall I talk of thy won-
drous works.
28 My soul melteth for heaviness: strengthen thou me according unto thy
word.
29 Remove from me the way of lying: and grant me thy law graciously.
30 I have chosen the way of truth: thy judgments have I laid *before me*.
31 I have stuck unto thy testimonies: O LORD, put me not to shame.
32 I will run the way of thy commandments, when thou shalt enlarge my
heart.

HE

33 Teach me, O LORD, the way of thy statutes; and I shall keep it *unto* the end.
34 Give me understanding, and I shall keep thy law; yea, I shall observe it
with *my* whole heart.
35 Make me to go in the path of thy commandments; for therein do I delight.
36 Incline my heart unto thy testimonies, and not to covetousness.
37 Turn away mine eyes from beholding vanity; *and* quicken thou me in thy way.
38 Stablish thy word unto thy servant, who *is devoted* to thy fear.
39 Turn away my reproach which I fear: for thy judgments *are* good.
40 Behold, I have longed after thy precepts: quicken me in thy righteousness.

VAU

41 Let thy mercies come also unto me, O LORD, *even* thy salvation, according
to thy word.
42 So shall I have wherewith to answer him that reproacheth me: for I trust
in thy word.
43 And take not the word of truth utterly out of my mouth; for I have hoped
in thy judgments.
44 So shall I keep thy law continually for ever and ever.
45 And I will walk at liberty: for I seek thy precepts.
46 I will speak of thy testimonies also before kings, and will not be ashamed.
47 And I will delight myself in thy commandments, which I have loved.
48 My hands also will I lift up unto thy commandments, which I have loved;
and I will meditate in thy statutes.

ZAIN

49 Remember the word unto thy servant, upon which thou hast caused me
to hope.
50 This *is* my comfort in my affliction: for thy word hath quickened me.
51 The proud have had me greatly in derision: *yet* have I not declined from
thy law.
52 I remembered thy judgments of old, O LORD; and have comforted myself.
53 Horror hath taken hold upon me because of the wicked that forsake thy law.
54 Thy statutes have been my songs in the house of my pilgrimage.
55 I have remembered thy name, O LORD, in the night, and have kept thy law.
56 This I had, because I kept thy precepts.

CHETH

57 *Thou art* my portion, O LORD: I have said that I would keep thy words.
58 I intreated thy favour with *my* whole heart: be merciful unto me accord-
ing to thy word.
59 I thought on my ways, and turned my feet unto thy testimonies.
60 I made haste, and delayed not to keep thy commandments.
61 The bands of the wicked have robbed me: *but* I have not forgotten thy law.
62 At midnight I will rise to give thanks unto thee because of thy righteous
judgments.
63 I *am* a companion of all *them* that fear thee, and of them that keep thy
precepts.
64 The earth, O LORD, is full of thy mercy: teach me thy statutes.

TETH

65 Thou hast dealt well with thy servant, O LORD, according unto thy word.
66 Teach me good judgment and knowledge: for I have believed thy com-
mandments.
67 Before I was afflicted I went astray: but now have I kept thy word.
68 Thou *art* good, and doest good; teach me thy statutes.
69 The proud have forged a lie against me: *but* I will keep thy precepts with
my whole heart.
70 Their heart is as fat as grease; *but* I delight in thy law.

71 *It is* good for me that I have been afflicted; that I might learn thy statutes.
72 The law of thy mouth *is* better unto me than thousands of gold and silver.

JOD

73 Thy hands have made me and fashioned me: give me understanding, that I may learn thy commandments.
74 They that fear thee will be glad when they see me; because I have hoped in thy word.
75 I know, O LORD, that thy judgments *are* right, and *that* thou in faithfulness hast afflicted me.
76 Let, I pray thee, thy merciful kindness be for my comfort, according to thy word unto thy servant.
77 Let thy tender mercies come unto me, that I may live: for thy law *is* my delight.
78 Let the proud be ashamed; for they dealt perversely with me without a cause: *but* I will meditate in thy precepts.
79 Let those that fear thee turn unto me, and those that have known thy testimonies.
80 Let my heart be sound in thy statutes; that I be not ashamed.

CAPH

81 My soul fainteth for thy salvation: *but* I hope in thy word.
82 Mine eyes fail for thy word, saying, When wilt thou comfort me?
83 For I am become like a bottle in the smoke; *yet* do I not forget thy statutes.
84 How many *are* the days of thy servant? when wilt thou execute judgment on them that persecute me?
85 The proud have digged pits for me, which *are* not after thy law.
86 All thy commandments *are* faithful: they persecute me wrongfully; help thou me.
87 They had almost consumed me upon earth; but I forsook not thy precepts.
88 Quicken me after thy lovingkindness; so shall I keep the testimony of thy mouth.

LAMED

89 For ever, O LORD, thy word is settled in heaven.
90 Thy faithfulness *is* unto all generations: thou hast established the earth, and it abideth.
91 They continue this day according to thine ordinances: for all *are* thy servants.
92 Unless thy law *had been* my delights, I should then have perished in mine affliction.
93 I will never forget thy precepts: for with them thou hast quickened me.
94 I *am* thine, save me; for I have sought thy precepts.
95 The wicked have waited for me to destroy me: *but* I will consider thy testimonies.
96 I have seen an end of all perfection: *but* thy commandment *is* exceeding broad.

MEM

97 O how love I thy law! it *is* my meditation all the day.
98 Thou through thy commandments hast made me wiser than mine enemies: for they *are* ever with me.
99 I have more understanding than all my teachers: for thy testimonies *are* my meditation.
100 I understand more than the ancients, because I keep thy precepts.
101 I have refrained my feet from every evil way, that I might keep thy word.
102 I have not departed from thy judgments: for thou hast taught me.
103 How sweet are thy words unto my taste! *yea, sweeter* than honey to my mouth!
104 Through thy precepts I get understanding: therefore I hate every false way.

NUN

105 Thy word *is* a lamp unto my feet, and a light unto my path.
106 I have sworn, and I will perform *it*, that I will keep thy righteous judgments.
107 I am afflicted very much: quicken me, O LORD, according unto thy word.
108 Accept, I beseech thee, the freewill offerings of my mouth, O LORD, and teach me thy judgments.
109 My soul *is* continually in my hand: yet do I not forget thy law.
110 The wicked have laid a snare for me: yet I erred not from thy precepts.
111 Thy testimonies have I taken as an heritage for ever: for they *are* the rejoicing of my heart.
112 I have inclined mine heart to perform thy statutes alway, *even unto* the end.

SAMECH

113 I hate *vain* thoughts: but thy law do I love.
114 Thou *art* my hiding place and my shield: I hope in thy word.
115 Depart from me, ye evildoers: for I will keep the commandments of my God.
116 Uphold me according unto thy word, that I may live: and let me not be ashamed of my hope.
117 Hold thou me up, and I shall be safe: and I will have respect unto thy statutes continually.
118 Thou hast trodden down all them that err from thy statutes: for their deceit *is* falsehood.
119 Thou puttest away all the wicked of the earth *like* dross: therefore I love thy testimonies.
120 My flesh trembleth for fear of thee; and I am afraid of thy judgments.

AIN

121 I have done judgment and justice: leave me not to mine oppressors.
122 Be surety for thy servant for good: let not the proud oppress me.
123 Mine eyes fail for thy salvation, and for the word of thy righteousness.
124 Deal with thy servant according unto thy mercy, and teach me thy statutes.
125 I *am* thy servant; give me understanding, that I may know thy testimonies.
126 *It is* time for *thee*, LORD, to work: *for* they have made void thy law.
127 Therefore I love thy commandments above gold; yea, above fine gold.
128 Therefore I esteem all *thy* precepts *concerning* all *things to be* right; *and* I hate every false way.

PE

129 Thy testimonies *are* wonderful: therefore doth my soul keep them.
130 The entrance of thy words giveth light; it giveth understanding unto the simple.
131 I opened my mouth, and panted: for I longed for thy commandments.
132 Look thou upon me, and be merciful unto me, as thou usest to do unto those that love thy name.
133 Order my steps in thy word: and let not any iniquity have dominion over me.
134 Deliver me from the oppression of man: so will I keep thy precepts.
135 Make thy face to shine upon thy servant; and teach me thy statutes.
136 Rivers of waters run down mine eyes, because they keep not thy law.

TZADDI

137 Righteous *art* thou, O LORD, and upright *are* thy judgments.
138 Thy testimonies *that* thou hast commanded *are* righteous and very faithful.
139 My zeal hath consumed me, because mine enemies have forgotten thy words.
140 Thy word *is* very pure: therefore thy servant loveth it.
141 I *am* small and despised: *yet* do not I forget thy precepts.

142 Thy righteousness *is* an everlasting righteousness, and thy law *is* the truth.
143 Trouble and anguish have taken hold on me: *yet* thy commandments *are*
my delights.
144 The righteousness of thy testimonies *is* everlasting: give me understand-
ing, and I shall live.

KOPH

145 I cried with *my* whole heart; hear me, O LORD: I will keep thy statutes.
146 I cried unto thee; save me, and I shall keep thy testimonies.
147 I prevented the dawning of the morning, and cried: I hoped in thy word.
148 Mine eyes prevent the *night* watches, that I might meditate in thy word.
149 Hear my voice according unto thy lovingkindness: O LORD, quicken me
according to thy judgment.
150 They draw nigh that follow after mischief: they are far from thy law.
151 Thou *art* near, O LORD; and all thy commandments *are* truth.
152 Concerning thy testimonies, I have known of old that thou hast founded
them for ever.

RESH

153 Consider mine affliction, and deliver me: for I do not forget thy law.
154 Plead my cause, and deliver me: quicken me according to thy word.
155 Salvation *is* far from the wicked: for they seek not thy statutes.
156 Great *are* thy tender mercies, O LORD: quicken me according to thy judg-
ments.
157 Many *are* my persecutors and mine enemies; *yet* do I not decline from
thy testimonies.
158 I beheld the transgressors, and was grieved; because they kept not thy
word.
159 Consider how I love thy precepts: quicken me, O LORD, according to thy
lovingkindness.
160 Thy word *is* true *from* the beginning: and every one of thy righteous
judgments *endureth* for ever.

SCHIN

161 Princes have persecuted me without a cause: but my heart standeth in
awe of thy word.
162 I rejoice at thy word, as one that findeth great spoil.
163 I hate and abhor lying: *but* thy law do I love.
164 Seven times a day do I praise thee because of thy righteous judgments.
165 Great peace have they which love thy law: and nothing shall offend them.
166 LORD, I have hoped for thy salvation, and done thy commandments.
167 My soul hath kept thy testimonies; and I love them exceedingly.
168 I have kept thy precepts and thy testimonies: for all my ways *are* before
thee.

TAU

169 Let my cry come near before thee, O LORD: give me understanding accord-
ing to thy word.
170 Let my supplication come before thee: deliver me according to thy word.
171 My lips shall utter praise, when thou hast taught me thy statutes.
172 My tongue shall speak of thy word: for all thy commandments *are* righ-
teousness.
173 Let thine hand help me; for I have chosen thy precepts.
174 I have longed for thy salvation, O LORD; and thy law *is* my delight.
175 Let my soul live, and it shall praise thee; and let thy judgments help me.
176 I have gone astray like a lost sheep; seek thy servant; for I do not forget
thy commandments.

PSALM 120
A Prayer When in Distress

A Song of degrees.

In my distress I cried unto the LORD, and he heard me.
2 Deliver my soul, O LORD, from lying lips, *and* from a deceitful tongue.
3 What shall be given unto thee? or what shall be done unto thee, thou false
tongue?
4 Sharp arrows of the mighty, with coals of juniper.
5 Woe is me, that I sojourn in Mesech, *that* I dwell in the tents of Kedar!
6 My soul hath long dwelt with him that hateth peace.
7 I *am for* peace: but when I speak, they *are* for war.

PSALM 121
The Lord Will Preserve You from Evil

A Song of degrees.

I will lift up mine eyes unto the hills, from whence cometh my help.
2 My help *cometh* from the LORD, which made heaven and earth.
3 He will not suffer thy foot to be moved: he that keepeth thee will not slumber.
4 Behold, he that keepeth Israel shall neither slumber nor sleep.
5 The LORD *is* thy keeper: the LORD *is* thy shade upon thy right hand.
6 The sun shall not smite thee by day, nor the moon by night.
7 The LORD shall preserve thee from all evil: he shall preserve thy soul.
8 The LORD shall preserve thy going out and thy coming in from this time
forth, and even for evermore.

PSALM 122
David Prays for Peace in Jerusalem

A Song of degrees of David.

I was glad when they said unto me, Let us go into the house of the LORD.
2 Our feet shall stand within thy gates, O Jerusalem.
3 Jerusalem is builded as a city that is compact together:
4 Whither the tribes go up, the tribes of the LORD, unto the testimony of
Israel, to give thanks unto the name of the LORD.
5 For there are set thrones of judgment, the thrones of the house of David.
6 Pray for the peace of Jerusalem: they shall prosper that love thee.
7 Peace be within thy walls, *and* prosperity within thy palaces.
8 For my brethren and companions' sakes, I will now say, Peace *be* within thee.
9 Because of the house of the LORD our God I will seek thy good.

PSALM 123
The Godly Profess Their Confidence in God

A Song of degrees.

Unto thee lift I up mine eyes, O thou that dwellest in the heavens.
2 Behold, as the eyes of servants *look* unto the hand of their masters,
and as the eyes of a maiden unto the hand of her mistress; so our eyes *wait*
upon the LORD our God, until that he have mercy upon us.
3 Have mercy upon us, O LORD, have mercy upon us: for we are exceedingly
filled with contempt.
4 Our soul is exceedingly filled with the scorning of those that are at ease,
and with the contempt of the proud.

PSALM 124
God Delivers Those Who Trust Him

A Song of degrees of David.

If *it had not been* the LORD who was on our side, now may Israel say;
2 If *it had not been* the LORD who was on our side, when men rose up
against us:
3 Then they had swallowed us up quick, when their wrath was kindled
against us:
4 Then the waters had overwhelmed us, the stream had gone over our soul:
5 Then the proud waters had gone over our soul.
6 Blessed *be* the LORD, who hath not given us *as* a prey to their teeth.
7 Our soul is escaped as a bird out of the snare of the fowlers: the snare is
broken, and we are escaped.
8 Our help *is* in the name of the LORD, who made heaven and earth.

PSALM 125
The Safety of Those Who Trust God

A Song of degrees.

They that trust in the LORD *shall be* as mount Zion, *which* cannot be removed,
but abideth for ever.
2 As the mountains *are* round about Jerusalem, so the LORD *is* round about
his people from henceforth even for ever.
3 For the rod of the wicked shall not rest upon the lot of the righteous; lest
the righteous put forth their hands unto iniquity.
4 Do good, O LORD, unto *those that be* good, and *to them that are* upright in
their hearts.
5 As for such as turn aside unto their crooked ways, the LORD shall lead them
forth with the workers of iniquity: *but* peace *shall be* upon Israel.

PSALM 126
The Lord Has Done Great Things

A Song of degrees.

When the LORD turned again the captivity of Zion, we were like them that
dream.
2 Then was our mouth filled with laughter, and our tongue with singing:
then said they among the heathen, The LORD hath done great things for them.
3 The LORD hath done great things for us; *whereof* we are glad.
4 Turn again our captivity, O LORD, as the streams in the south.
5 They that sow in tears shall reap in joy.
6 He that goeth forth and weepeth, bearing precious seed, shall doubtless
come again with rejoicing, bringing his sheaves *with him.*

PSALM 127
The Virtue of God's Blessing

A Song of degrees for Solomon.

Except the LORD build the house, they labour in vain that build it: except the
LORD keep the city, the watchman waketh *but* in vain.
2 *It is* vain for you to rise up early, to sit up late, to eat the bread of sorrows:
for so he giveth his beloved sleep.
3 Lo, children *are* an heritage of the LORD: *and* the fruit of the womb *is his*
reward.
4 As arrows *are* in the hand of a mighty man; so *are* children of the youth.
5 Happy *is* the man that hath his quiver full of them: they shall not be
ashamed, but they shall speak with the enemies in the gate.

PSALM 128
Blessings for Those Who Fear God

A Song of degrees.

Blessed *is* every one that feareth the LORD; that walketh in his ways.
2 For thou shalt eat the labour of thine hands: happy *shalt* thou *be*,
and *it shall be* well with thee.
3 Thy wife *shall be* as a fruitful vine by the sides of thine house: thy children
like olive plants round about thy table.
4 Behold, that thus shall the man be blessed that feareth the LORD.
5 The LORD shall bless thee out of Zion: and thou shalt see the good of
Jerusalem all the days of thy life.
6 Yea, thou shalt see thy children's children, *and* peace upon Israel.

PSALM 129
Praise God for Deliverance from Affliction

A Song of degrees.

Many a time have they afflicted me from my youth, may Israel now say:
2 Many a time have they afflicted me from my youth: yet they have
not prevailed against me.
3 The plowers plowed upon my back: they made long their furrows.
4 The LORD *is* righteous: he hath cut asunder the cords of the wicked.
5 Let them all be confounded and turned back that hate Zion.
6 Let them be as the grass *upon* the housetops, which withereth afore it
groweth up:
7 Wherewith the mower filleth not his hand; nor he that bindeth sheaves
his bosom.
8 Neither do they which go by say, The blessing of the LORD *be* upon you: we
bless you in the name of the LORD.

PSALM 130
God Offers Forgiveness

A Song of degrees.

Out of the depths have I cried unto thee, O LORD.
2 Lord, hear my voice: let thine ears be attentive to the voice of my
supplications.
3 If thou, LORD, shouldest mark iniquities, O Lord, who shall stand?
4 But *there is* forgiveness with thee, that thou mayest be feared.
5 I wait for the LORD, my soul doth wait, and in his word do I hope.
6 My soul *waiteth* for the Lord more than they that watch for the morning:
I say, more than they that watch for the morning.
7 Let Israel hope in the LORD: for with the LORD *there is* mercy, and with him
is plenteous redemption.
8 And he shall redeem Israel from all his iniquities.

PSALM 131
David Professes Humility

A Song of degrees of David.

LORD, my heart is not haughty, nor mine eyes lofty: neither do I exercise myself
in great matters, or in things too high for me.
2 Surely I have behaved and quieted myself, as a child that is weaned of his
mother: my soul *is* even as a weaned child.
3 Let Israel hope in the LORD from henceforth and for ever.

PSALM 132
Praise for the Ark's Return to Jerusalem

A Song of degrees.

LORD, remember David, *and* all his afflictions:
2 How he sware unto the LORD, *and* vowed unto the mighty *God* of Jacob;
3 Surely I will not come into the tabernacle of my house, nor go up into my bed;
4 I will not give sleep to mine eyes, *or* slumber to mine eyelids,
5 Until I find out a place for the LORD, an habitation for the mighty *God* of Jacob.
6 Lo, we heard of it at Ephratah: we found it in the fields of the wood.
7 We will go into his tabernacles: we will worship at his footstool.
8 Arise, O LORD, into thy rest; thou, and the ark of thy strength.
9 Let thy priests be clothed with righteousness; and let thy saints shout for joy.
10 For thy servant David's sake turn not away the face of thine anointed.
11 The LORD hath sworn *in* truth unto David; he will not turn from it; Of the fruit of thy body will I set upon thy throne.
12 If thy children will keep my covenant and my testimony that I shall teach them, their children shall also sit upon thy throne for evermore.
13 For the LORD hath chosen Zion; he hath desired *it* for his habitation.
14 This *is* my rest for ever: here will I dwell; for I have desired it.
15 I will abundantly bless her provision: I will satisfy her poor with bread.
16 I will also clothe her priests with salvation: and her saints shall shout aloud for joy.
17 There will I make the horn of David to bud: I have ordained a lamp for mine anointed.
18 His enemies will I clothe with shame: but upon himself shall his crown flourish.

PSALM 133
Benefits from the Harmony of Believers

A Song of degrees of David.

Behold, how good and how pleasant *it is* for brethren to dwell together in unity!
2 *It is* like the precious ointment upon the head, that ran down upon the beard, *even* Aaron's beard: that went down to the skirts of his garments;
3 As the dew of Hermon, *and as the dew* that descended upon the mountains of Zion: for there the LORD commanded the blessing, *even* life for evermore.

PSALM 134
An Exhortation to Bless God

A Song of degrees.

Behold, bless ye the LORD, all *ye* servants of the LORD, which by night stand in the house of the LORD.
2 Lift up your hands *in* the sanctuary, and bless the LORD.
3 The LORD that made heaven and earth bless thee out of Zion.

PSALM 135
A Hymn of Praise

Praise ye the LORD. Praise ye the name of the LORD; praise *him*, O ye servants of the LORD.
2 Ye that stand in the house of the LORD, in the courts of the house of our God,

3 Praise the LORD; for the LORD *is* good: sing praises unto his name; for *it is*
pleasant.
4 For the LORD hath chosen Jacob unto himself, *and* Israel for his peculiar
treasure.
5 For I know that the LORD *is* great, and *that* our Lord *is* above all gods.
6 Whatsoever the LORD pleased, *that* did he in heaven, and in earth, in the
seas, and all deep places.
7 He causeth the vapours to ascend from the ends of the earth; he maketh
lightnings for the rain; he bringeth the wind out of his treasuries.
8 Who smote the firstborn of Egypt, both of man and beast.
9 *Who* sent tokens and wonders into the midst of thee, O Egypt, upon
Pharaoh, and upon all his servants.
10 Who smote great nations, and slew mighty kings;
11 Sihon king of the Amorites, and Og king of Bashan, and all the kingdoms
of Canaan:
12 And gave their land *for* an heritage, an heritage unto Israel his people.
13 Thy name, O LORD, *endureth* for ever; *and* thy memorial, O LORD, through-
out all generations.
14 For the LORD will judge his people, and he will repent himself concerning
his servants.
15 The idols of the heathen *are* silver and gold, the work of men's hands.
16 They have mouths, but they speak not; eyes have they, but they see not;
17 They have ears, but they hear not; neither is there *any* breath in their
mouths.
18 They that make them are like unto them: *so is* every one that trusteth in
them.
19 Bless the LORD, O house of Israel: bless the LORD, O house of Aaron:
20 Bless the LORD, O house of Levi: ye that fear the LORD, bless the LORD.
21 Blessed be the LORD out of Zion, which dwelleth at Jerusalem. Praise ye
the LORD.

PSALM 136
God's Mercy Endures Forever

O give thanks unto the LORD; for *he is* good: for his mercy *endureth* for ever.
2 O give thanks unto the God of gods: for his mercy *endureth* for ever.
3 O give thanks to the Lord of lords: for his mercy *endureth* for ever.
4 To him who alone doeth great wonders: for his mercy *endureth* for ever.
5 To him that by wisdom made the heavens: for his mercy *endureth* for ever.
6 To him that stretched out the earth above the waters: for his mercy *endureth*
for ever.
7 To him that made great lights: for his mercy *endureth* for ever:
8 The sun to rule by day: for his mercy *endureth* for ever:
9 The moon and stars to rule by night: for his mercy *endureth* for ever.
10 To him that smote Egypt in their firstborn: for his mercy *endureth* for
ever:
11 And brought out Israel from among them: for his mercy *endureth* for ever:
12 With a strong hand, and with a stretched out arm: for his mercy *endureth*
for ever.
13 To him which divided the Red sea into parts: for his mercy *endureth* for
ever:
14 And made Israel to pass through the midst of it: for his mercy *endureth*
for ever:
15 But overthrew Pharaoh and his host in the Red sea: for his mercy *endureth*
for ever.
16 To him which led his people through the wilderness: for his mercy
endureth for ever.

17 To him which smote great kings: for his mercy *endureth* for ever:
18 And slew famous kings: for his mercy *endureth* for ever:
19 Sihon king of the Amorites: for his mercy *endureth* for ever:
20 And Og the king of Bashan: for his mercy *endureth* for ever:
21 And gave their land for an heritage: for his mercy *endureth* for ever:
22 *Even* an heritage unto Israel his servant: for his mercy *endureth* for ever.
23 Who remembered us in our low estate: for his mercy *endureth* for ever:
24 And hath redeemed us from our enemies: for his mercy *endureth* for ever.
25 Who giveth food to all flesh: for his mercy *endureth* for ever.
26 O give thanks unto the God of heaven: for his mercy *endureth* for ever.

PSALM 137
The Bitterness of Exile

By the rivers of Babylon, there we sat down, yea, we wept, when we remem-
bered Zion.
2 We hanged our harps upon the willows in the midst thereof.
3 For there they that carried us away captive required of us a song; and they
that wasted us *required of us* mirth, *saying*, Sing us *one* of the songs of Zion.
4 How shall we sing the LORD's song in a strange land?
5 If I forget thee, O Jerusalem, let my right hand forget *her cunning*.
6 If I do not remember thee, let my tongue cleave to the roof of my mouth;
if I prefer not Jerusalem above my chief joy.
7 Remember, O LORD, the children of Edom in the day of Jerusalem; who
said, Rase *it*, rase *it*, *even* to the foundation thereof.
8 O daughter of Babylon, who art to be destroyed; happy *shall he be*, that
rewardeth thee as thou hast served us.
9 Happy *shall he be*, that taketh and dasheth thy little ones against the stones.

PSALM 138
David Praises God for Answered Prayer

A Psalm of David.

I will praise thee with my whole heart: before the gods will I sing praise unto
thee.
2 I will worship toward thy holy temple, and praise thy name for thy loving-
kindness and for thy truth: for thou hast magnified thy word above all thy
name.
3 In the day when I cried thou answeredst me, *and* strengthenedst me *with*
strength in my soul.
4 All the kings of the earth shall praise thee, O LORD, when they hear the
words of thy mouth.
5 Yea, they shall sing in the ways of the LORD: for great *is* the glory of the LORD.
6 Though the LORD *be* high, yet hath he respect unto the lowly: but the proud
he knoweth afar off.
7 Though I walk in the midst of trouble, thou wilt revive me: thou shalt
stretch forth thine hand against the wrath of mine enemies, and thy right
hand shall save me.
8 The LORD will perfect *that which* concerneth me: thy mercy, O LORD,
endureth for ever: forsake not the works of thine own hands.

PSALM 139
David Praises God for His All-Seeing Providence

To the chief Musician, A Psalm of David.

O LORD, thou hast searched me, and known *me*.
2 Thou knowest my downsitting and mine uprising, thou under-
standest my thought afar off.

3 Thou compassest my path and my lying down, and art acquainted *with* all
my ways.
4 For *there is* not a word in my tongue, *but*, lo, O LORD, thou knowest it alto-
gether.
5 Thou hast beset me behind and before, and laid thine hand upon me.
6 *Such* knowledge *is* too wonderful for me; it is high, I cannot *attain* unto it.
7 Whither shall I go from thy spirit? or whither shall I flee from thy presence?
8 If I ascend up into heaven, thou *art* there: if I make my bed in hell, behold,
thou *art there*.
9 *If* I take the wings of the morning, *and* dwell in the uttermost parts of the sea;
10 Even there shall thy hand lead me, and thy right hand shall hold me.
11 If I say, Surely the darkness shall cover me; even the night shall be light
about me.
12 Yea, the darkness hideth not from thee; but the night shineth as the day:
the darkness and the light *are* both alike *to thee*.
13 For thou hast possessed my reins: thou hast covered me in my mother's
womb.
14 I will praise thee; for I am fearfully *and* wonderfully made: marvellous
are thy works; and *that* my soul knoweth right well.
15 My substance was not hid from thee, when I was made in secret, *and*
curiously wrought in the lowest parts of the earth.
16 Thine eyes did see my substance, yet being unperfect; and in thy book all
my members were written, *which* in continuance were fashioned, when *as yet*
there was none of them.
17 How precious also are thy thoughts unto me, O God! how great is the sum
of them!
18 *If* I should count them, they are more in number than the sand: when I
awake, I am still with thee.
19 Surely thou wilt slay the wicked, O God: depart from me therefore, ye
bloody men.
20 For they speak against thee wickedly, *and* thine enemies take *thy name* in
vain.
21 Do not I hate them, O LORD, that hate thee? and am not I grieved with
those that rise up against thee?
22 I hate them with perfect hatred: I count them mine enemies.
23 Search me, O God, and know my heart: try me, and know my thoughts:
24 And see if *there be any* wicked way in me, and lead me in the way everlasting.

PSALM 140

David Prays for Deliverance from Evil Men

To the chief Musician, A Psalm of David.

Deliver me, O LORD, from the evil man: preserve me from the violent man;
2 Which imagine mischiefs in *their* heart; continually are they gath-
ered together *for* war.
3 They have sharpened their tongues like a serpent; adders' poison *is* under
their lips. Selah.
4 Keep me, O LORD, from the hands of the wicked; preserve me from the
violent man; who have purposed to overthrow my goings.
5 The proud have hid a snare for me, and cords; they have spread a net by the
wayside; they have set gins for me. Selah.
6 I said unto the LORD, Thou *art* my God: hear the voice of my supplications,
O LORD.
7 O GOD the Lord, the strength of my salvation, thou hast covered my head
in the day of battle.
8 Grant not, O LORD, the desires of the wicked: further not his wicked device;
lest they exalt themselves. Selah.

9 *As for* the head of those that compass me about, let the mischief of their own lips cover them.
10 Let burning coals fall upon them: let them be cast into the fire; into deep pits, that they rise not up again.
11 Let not an evil speaker be established in the earth: evil shall hunt the violent man to overthrow *him*.
12 I know that the LORD will maintain the cause of the afflicted, *and* the right of the poor.
13 Surely the righteous shall give thanks unto thy name: the upright shall dwell in thy presence.

PSALM 141

David Prays That His Plea May Be Acceptable

A Psalm of David.

LORD, I cry unto thee: make haste unto me; give ear unto my voice, when I cry unto thee.
2 Let my prayer be set forth before thee *as* incense; *and* the lifting up of my hands *as* the evening sacrifice.
3 Set a watch, O LORD, before my mouth; keep the door of my lips.
4 Incline not my heart to *any* evil thing, to practise wicked works with men that work iniquity: and let me not eat of their dainties.
5 Let the righteous smite me; *it shall be* a kindness: and let him reprove me; *it shall be* an excellent oil, *which* shall not break my head: for yet my prayer also *shall be* in their calamities.
6 When their judges are overthrown in stony places, they shall hear my words; for they are sweet.
7 Our bones are scattered at the grave's mouth, as when one cutteth and cleaveth *wood* upon the earth.
8 But mine eyes *are* unto thee, O GOD the Lord: in thee is my trust; leave not my soul destitute.
9 Keep me from the snares *which* they have laid for me, and the gins of the workers of iniquity.
10 Let the wicked fall into their own nets, whilst that I withal escape.

PSALM 142

David's Comfort in Prayer

Maschil of David; A Prayer when he was in the cave.

I cried unto the LORD with my voice; with my voice unto the LORD did I make my supplication.
2 I poured out my complaint before him; I shewed before him my trouble.
3 When my spirit was overwhelmed within me, then thou knewest my path. In the way wherein I walked have they privily laid a snare for me.
4 I looked on *my* right hand, and beheld, but *there was* no man that would know me: refuge failed me; no man cared for my soul.
5 I cried unto thee, O LORD: I said, Thou *art* my refuge *and* my portion in the land of the living.
6 Attend unto my cry; for I am brought very low: deliver me from my persecutors; for they are stronger than I.
7 Bring my soul out of prison, that I may praise thy name: the righteous shall compass me about; for thou shalt deal bountifully with me.

PSALM 143

David Prays for Favor in Judgment

A Psalm of David.

Hear my prayer, O LORD, give ear to my supplications: in thy faithfulness answer me, *and* in thy righteousness.

2 And enter not into judgment with thy servant: for in thy sight shall no man
living be justified.
3 For the enemy hath persecuted my soul; he hath smitten my life down to
the ground; he hath made me to dwell in darkness, as those that have been
long dead.
4 Therefore is my spirit overwhelmed within me; my heart within me is
desolate.
5 I remember the days of old; I meditate on all thy works; I muse on the work
of thy hands.
6 I stretch forth my hands unto thee: my soul *thirsteth* after thee, as a thirsty
land. Selah.
7 Hear me speedily, O LORD: my spirit faileth: hide not thy face from me, lest
I be like unto them that go down into the pit.
8 Cause me to hear thy lovingkindness in the morning; for in thee do I trust:
cause me to know the way wherein I should walk; for I lift up my soul unto thee.
9 Deliver me, O LORD, from mine enemies: I flee unto thee to hide me.
10 Teach me to do thy will; for thou *art* my God: thy spirit *is* good; lead me
into the land of uprightness.
11 Quicken me, O LORD, for thy name's sake: for thy righteousness' sake bring
my soul out of trouble.
12 And of thy mercy cut off mine enemies, and destroy all them that afflict
my soul: for I *am* thy servant.

PSALM 144

David Promises to Praise God

***A Psalm** of David.*

Blessed *be* the LORD my strength, which teacheth my hands to war, *and* my
fingers to fight:
2 My goodness, and my fortress; my high tower, and my deliverer; my shield,
and *he* in whom I trust; who subdueth my people under me.
3 LORD, what *is* man, that thou takest knowledge of him! *or* the son of man,
that thou makest account of him!
4 Man is like to vanity: his days *are* as a shadow that passeth away.
5 Bow thy heavens, O LORD, and come down: touch the mountains, and they
shall smoke.
6 Cast forth lightning, and scatter them: shoot out thine arrows, and destroy them.
7 Send thine hand from above; rid me, and deliver me out of great waters,
from the hand of strange children;
8 Whose mouth speaketh vanity, and their right hand *is* a right hand of falsehood.
9 I will sing a new song unto thee, O God: upon a psaltery *and* an instrument
of ten strings will I sing praises unto thee.
10 *It is he* that giveth salvation unto kings: who delivereth David his servant
from the hurtful sword.
11 Rid me, and deliver me from the hand of strange children, whose mouth
speaketh vanity, and their right hand *is* a right hand of falsehood:
12 That our sons *may be* as plants grown up in their youth; *that* our daughters
may be as corner stones, polished *after* the similitude of a palace:
13 *That* our garners *may be* full, affording all manner of store: *that* our sheep
may bring forth thousands and ten thousands in our streets:
14 *That* our oxen *may be* strong to labour; *that there be* no breaking in, nor
going out; that *there be* no complaining in our streets.
15 Happy *is that* people, that is in such a case: *yea*, happy *is that* people, whose
God *is* the LORD.

PSALM 145
David Praises God for His Fame

David's *Psalm* of praise.

I will extol thee, my God, O king; and I will bless thy name for ever and ever.
2 Every day will I bless thee; and I will praise thy name for ever and ever.
3 Great *is* the LORD, and greatly to be praised; and his greatness *is* unsearchable.
4 One generation shall praise thy works to another, and shall declare thy
mighty acts.
5 I will speak of the glorious honour of thy majesty, and of thy wondrous
works.
6 And *men* shall speak of the might of thy terrible acts: and I will declare thy
greatness.
7 They shall abundantly utter the memory of thy great goodness, and shall
sing of thy righteousness.
8 The LORD *is* gracious, and full of compassion; slow to anger, and of great mercy.
9 The LORD *is* good to all: and his tender mercies *are* over all his works.
10 All thy works shall praise thee, O LORD; and thy saints shall bless thee.
11 They shall speak of the glory of thy kingdom, and talk of thy power;
12 To make known to the sons of men his mighty acts, and the glorious maj-
esty of his kingdom.
13 Thy kingdom *is* an everlasting kingdom, and thy dominion *endureth*
throughout all generations.
14 The LORD upholdeth all that fall, and raiseth up all *those that be* bowed down.
15 The eyes of all wait upon thee; and thou givest them their meat in due
season.
16 Thou openest thine hand, and satisfiest the desire of every living thing.
17 The LORD *is* righteous in all his ways, and holy in all his works.
18 The LORD *is* nigh unto all them that call upon him, to all that call upon
him in truth.
19 He will fulfil the desire of them that fear him: he also will hear their cry,
and will save them.
20 The LORD preserveth all them that love him: but all the wicked will he
destroy.
21 My mouth shall speak the praise of the LORD: and let all flesh bless his holy
name for ever and ever.

PSALM 146
Trust in God Alone

Praise ye the LORD. Praise the LORD, O my soul.
2 While I live will I praise the LORD: I will sing praises unto my God
while I have any being.
3 Put not your trust in princes, *nor* in the son of man, in whom *there is* no help.
4 His breath goeth forth, he returneth to his earth; in that very day his
thoughts perish.
5 Happy *is he* that *hath* the God of Jacob for his help, whose hope *is* in the
LORD his God:
6 Which made heaven, and earth, the sea, and all that therein *is*: which keep-
eth truth for ever:
7 Which executeth judgment for the oppressed: which giveth food to the
hungry. The LORD looseth the prisoners:
8 The LORD openeth *the eyes of* the blind: the LORD raiseth them that are
bowed down: the LORD loveth the righteous:
9 The LORD preserveth the strangers; he relieveth the fatherless and widow:
but the way of the wicked he turneth upside down.
10 The LORD shall reign for ever, *even* thy God, O Zion, unto all generations.
Praise ye the LORD.

PSALM 147
Worship and Trust the Lord

Praise ye the LORD: for *it is* good to sing praises unto our God; for *it is* pleasant; *and* praise is comely.
2 The LORD doth build up Jerusalem: he gathereth together the outcasts of
Israel.
3 He healeth the broken in heart, and bindeth up their wounds.
4 He telleth the number of the stars; he calleth them all by *their* names.
5 Great *is* our Lord, and of great power: his understanding *is* infinite.
6 The LORD lifteth up the meek: he casteth the wicked down to the ground.
7 Sing unto the LORD with thanksgiving; sing praise upon the harp unto our God:
8 Who covereth the heaven with clouds, who prepareth rain for the earth,
who maketh grass to grow upon the mountains.
9 He giveth to the beast his food, *and* to the young ravens which cry.
10 He delighteth not in the strength of the horse: he taketh not pleasure in
the legs of a man.
11 The LORD taketh pleasure in them that fear him, in those that hope in his
mercy.
12 Praise the LORD, O Jerusalem; praise thy God, O Zion.
13 For he hath strengthened the bars of thy gates; he hath blessed thy children
within thee.
14 He maketh peace *in* thy borders, *and* filleth thee with the finest of the
wheat.
15 He sendeth forth his commandment *upon* earth: his word runneth very
swiftly.
16 He giveth snow like wool: he scattereth the hoarfrost like ashes.
17 He casteth forth his ice like morsels: who can stand before his cold?
18 He sendeth out his word, and melteth them: he causeth his wind to blow,
and the waters flow.
19 He sheweth his word unto Jacob, his statutes and his judgments unto
Israel.
20 He hath not dealt so with any nation: and *as for his* judgments, they have
not known them. Praise ye the LORD.

PSALM 148
Let All Creation Praise the Lord

Praise ye the LORD. Praise ye the LORD from the heavens: praise him in the heights.
2 Praise ye him, all his angels: praise ye him, all his hosts.
3 Praise ye him, sun and moon: praise him, all ye stars of light.
4 Praise him, ye heavens of heavens, and ye waters that *be* above the heavens.
5 Let them praise the name of the LORD: for he commanded, and they were
created.
6 He hath also stablished them for ever and ever: he hath made a decree
which shall not pass.
7 Praise the LORD from the earth, ye dragons, and all deeps:
8 Fire, and hail; snow, and vapour; stormy wind fulfilling his word:
9 Mountains, and all hills; fruitful trees, and all cedars:
10 Beasts, and all cattle; creeping things, and flying fowl:
11 Kings of the earth, and all people; princes, and all judges of the earth:
12 Both young men, and maidens; old men, and children:
13 Let them praise the name of the LORD: for his name alone is excellent; his
glory *is* above the earth and heaven.
14 He also exalteth the horn of his people, the praise of all his saints; *even* of
the children of Israel, a people near unto him. Praise ye the LORD.

PSALM 149
Let All the Saints Praise the Lord

Praise ye the Lord. Sing unto the Lord a new song, *and* his praise in the
congregation of saints.
2 Let Israel rejoice in him that made him: let the children of Zion be joyful
in their King.
3 Let them praise his name in the dance: let them sing praises unto him with
the timbrel and harp.
4 For the Lord taketh pleasure in his people: he will beautify the meek with
salvation.
5 Let the saints be joyful in glory: let them sing aloud upon their beds.
6 *Let* the high *praises* of God *be* in their mouth, and a twoedged sword in
their hand;
7 To execute vengeance upon the heathen, *and* punishments upon the people;
8 To bind their kings with chains, and their nobles with fetters of iron;
9 To execute upon them the judgment written: this honour have all his saints.
Praise ye the Lord.

PSALM 150
Praise the Lord

Praise ye the Lord. Praise God in his sanctuary: praise him in the firmament
of his power.
2 Praise him for his mighty acts: praise him according to his excellent greatness.
3 Praise him with the sound of the trumpet: praise him with the psaltery
and harp.
4 Praise him with the timbrel and dance: praise him with stringed instru-
ments and organs.
5 Praise him upon the loud cymbals: praise him upon the high sounding
cymbals.
6 Let every thing that hath breath praise the Lord. Praise ye the Lord.

PROVERBS

The Reasons for the Proverbs

1 The proverbs of Solomon the son of David, king of Israel;
2 To know wisdom and instruction; to perceive the words of understanding;
3 To receive the instruction of wisdom, justice, and judgment, and equity;
4 To give subtilty to the simple, to the young man knowledge and discretion.
5 A wise *man* will hear, and will increase learning; and a man of understand-
ing shall attain unto wise counsels:
6 To understand a proverb, and the interpretation; the words of the wise,
and their dark sayings.

Listen to Wisdom

7 The fear of the LORD *is* the beginning of knowledge: *but* fools despise wis-
dom and instruction.
8 My son, hear the instruction of thy father, and forsake not the law of thy
mother:
9 For they *shall be* an ornament of grace unto thy head, and chains about
thy neck.
10 My son, if sinners entice thee, consent thou not.
11 If they say, Come with us, let us lay wait for blood, let us lurk privily for
the innocent without cause:
12 Let us swallow them up alive as the grave; and whole, as those that go down
into the pit:
13 We shall find all precious substance, we shall fill our houses with spoil:
14 Cast in thy lot among us; let us all have one purse:
15 My son, walk not thou in the way with them; refrain thy foot from their
path:
16 For their feet run to evil, and make haste to shed blood.
17 Surely in vain the net is spread in the sight of any bird.
18 And they lay wait for their *own* blood; they lurk privily for their *own* lives.
19 So *are* the ways of every one that is greedy of gain; *which* taketh away the
life of the owners thereof.
20 Wisdom crieth without; she uttereth her voice in the streets:
21 She crieth in the chief place of concourse, in the openings of the gates: in
the city she uttereth her words, *saying*,
22 How long, ye simple ones, will ye love simplicity? and the scorners delight
in their scorning, and fools hate knowledge?
23 Turn you at my reproof: behold, I will pour out my spirit unto you, I will
make known my words unto you.
24 Because I have called, and ye refused; I have stretched out my hand, and
no man regarded;
25 But ye have set at nought all my counsel, and would none of my reproof:
26 I also will laugh at your calamity; I will mock when your fear cometh;
27 When your fear cometh as desolation, and your destruction cometh as a
whirlwind; when distress and anguish cometh upon you.
28 Then shall they call upon me, but I will not answer; they shall seek me
early, but they shall not find me:
29 For that they hated knowledge, and did not choose the fear of the LORD:
30 They would none of my counsel: they despised all my reproof.

31 Therefore shall they eat of the fruit of their own way, and be filled with
their own devices.
32 For the turning away of the simple shall slay them, and the prosperity of
fools shall destroy them.
33 But whoso hearkeneth unto me shall dwell safely, and shall be quiet from
fear of evil.

The Benefit of Wisdom

2 My son, if thou wilt receive my words, and hide my commandments with
thee;
2 So that thou incline thine ear unto wisdom, *and* apply thine heart to under-
standing;
3 Yea, if thou criest after knowledge, *and* liftest up thy voice for understand-
ing;
4 If thou seekest her as silver, and searchest for her as *for* hid treasures;
5 Then shalt thou understand the fear of the LORD, and find the knowledge
of God.
6 For the LORD giveth wisdom: out of his mouth *cometh* knowledge and
understanding.
7 He layeth up sound wisdom for the righteous: *he is* a buckler to them that
walk uprightly.
8 He keepeth the paths of judgment, and preserveth the way of his saints.
9 Then shalt thou understand righteousness, and judgment, and equity; *yea*,
every good path.
10 When wisdom entereth into thine heart, and knowledge is pleasant unto
thy soul;
11 Discretion shall preserve thee, understanding shall keep thee:
12 To deliver thee from the way of the evil *man*, from the man that speaketh
froward things;
13 Who leave the paths of uprightness, to walk in the ways of darkness;
14 Who rejoice to do evil, *and* delight in the frowardness of the wicked;
15 Whose ways *are* crooked, and *they* froward in their paths:
16 To deliver thee from the strange woman, *even* from the stranger *which*
flattereth with her words;
17 Which forsaketh the guide of her youth, and forgetteth the covenant of
her God.
18 For her house inclineth unto death, and her paths unto the dead.
19 None that go unto her return again, neither take they hold of the paths
of life.
20 That thou mayest walk in the way of good *men*, and keep the paths of the
righteous.
21 For the upright shall dwell in the land, and the perfect shall remain in it.
22 But the wicked shall be cut off from the earth, and the transgressors shall
be rooted out of it.

Using Wisdom

3 My son, forget not my law; but let thine heart keep my commandments:
2 For length of days, and long life, and peace, shall they add to thee.
3 Let not mercy and truth forsake thee: bind them about thy neck; write them
upon the table of thine heart:
4 So shalt thou find favour and good understanding in the sight of God and
man.
5 Trust in the LORD with all thine heart; and lean not unto thine own under-
standing.
6 In all thy ways acknowledge him, and he shall direct thy paths.
7 Be not wise in thine own eyes: fear the LORD, and depart from evil.
8 It shall be health to thy navel, and marrow to thy bones.

9 Honour the LORD with thy substance, and with the firstfruits of all thine
increase:
10 So shall thy barns be filled with plenty, and thy presses shall burst out with
new wine.
11 My son, despise not the chastening of the LORD; neither be weary of his
correction:
12 For whom the LORD loveth he correcteth; even as a father the son *in whom*
he delighteth.
13 Happy *is* the man *that* findeth wisdom, and the man *that* getteth under-
standing.
14 For the merchandise of it *is* better than the merchandise of silver, and the
gain thereof than fine gold.
15 She *is* more precious than rubies: and all the things thou canst desire are
not to be compared unto her.
16 Length of days *is* in her right hand; *and* in her left hand riches and honour.
17 Her ways *are* ways of pleasantness, and all her paths *are* peace.
18 She *is* a tree of life to them that lay hold upon her: and happy *is every one*
that retaineth her.
19 The LORD by wisdom hath founded the earth; by understanding hath he
established the heavens.
20 By his knowledge the depths are broken up, and the clouds drop down
the dew.
21 My son, let not them depart from thine eyes: keep sound wisdom and
discretion:
22 So shall they be life unto thy soul, and grace to thy neck.
23 Then shalt thou walk in thy way safely, and thy foot shall not stumble.
24 When thou liest down, thou shalt not be afraid: yea, thou shalt lie down,
and thy sleep shall be sweet.
25 Be not afraid of sudden fear, neither of the desolation of the wicked, when
it cometh.
26 For the LORD shall be thy confidence, and shall keep thy foot from being
taken.
27 Withhold not good from them to whom it is due, when it is in the power
of thine hand to do *it*.
28 Say not unto thy neighbour, Go, and come again, and to morrow I will
give; when thou hast it by thee.
29 Devise not evil against thy neighbour, seeing he dwelleth securely by thee.
30 Strive not with a man without cause, if he have done thee no harm.
31 Envy thou not the oppressor, and choose none of his ways.
32 For the froward *is* abomination to the LORD: but his secret *is* with the
righteous.
33 The curse of the LORD *is* in the house of the wicked: but he blesseth the
habitation of the just.
34 Surely he scorneth the scorners: but he giveth grace unto the lowly.
35 The wise shall inherit glory: but shame shall be the promotion of fools.

Cherish Wisdom

4 Hear, ye children, the instruction of a father, and attend to know under-
standing.
2 For I give you good doctrine, forsake ye not my law.
3 For I was my father's son, tender and only *beloved* in the sight of my mother.
4 He taught me also, and said unto me, Let thine heart retain my words: keep
my commandments, and live.
5 Get wisdom, get understanding: forget *it* not; neither decline from the
words of my mouth.

6 Forsake her not, and she shall preserve thee: love her, and she shall keep
thee.
7 Wisdom *is* the principal thing; *therefore* get wisdom: and with all thy get-
ting get understanding.
8 Exalt her, and she shall promote thee: she shall bring thee to honour, when
thou dost embrace her.
9 She shall give to thine head an ornament of grace: a crown of glory shall
she deliver to thee.
10 Hear, O my son, and receive my sayings; and the years of thy life shall be
many.
11 I have taught thee in the way of wisdom; I have led thee in right paths.
12 When thou goest, thy steps shall not be straitened; and when thou runnest,
thou shalt not stumble.
13 Take fast hold of instruction; let *her* not go: keep her; for she *is* thy life.

Stay on the Path of Wisdom

14 Enter not into the path of the wicked, and go not in the way of evil *men*.
15 Avoid it, pass not by it, turn from it, and pass away.
16 For they sleep not, except they have done mischief; and their sleep is taken
away, unless they cause *some* to fall.
17 For they eat the bread of wickedness, and drink the wine of violence.
18 But the path of the just *is* as the shining light, that shineth more and more
unto the perfect day.
19 The way of the wicked *is* as darkness: they know not at what they stumble.

Stay Focused on Wisdom

20 My son, attend to my words; incline thine ear unto my sayings.
21 Let them not depart from thine eyes; keep them in the midst of thine
heart.
22 For they *are* life unto those that find them, and health to all their flesh.
23 Keep thy heart with all diligence; for out of it *are* the issues of life.
24 Put away from thee a froward mouth, and perverse lips put far from thee.
25 Let thine eyes look right on, and let thine eyelids look straight before thee.
26 Ponder the path of thy feet, and let all thy ways be established.
27 Turn not to the right hand nor to the left: remove thy foot from evil.

Avoid Adultery

5 My son, attend unto my wisdom, *and* bow thine ear to my understanding:
2 That thou mayest regard discretion, and *that* thy lips may keep knowl-
edge.
3 For the lips of a strange woman drop *as* an honeycomb, and her mouth *is*
smoother than oil:
4 But her end is bitter as wormwood, sharp as a twoedged sword.
5 Her feet go down to death; her steps take hold on hell.
6 Lest thou shouldest ponder the path of life, her ways are moveable, *that*
thou canst not know *them*.
7 Hear me now therefore, O ye children, and depart not from the words of
my mouth.
8 Remove thy way far from her, and come not nigh the door of her house:
9 Lest thou give thine honour unto others, and thy years unto the cruel:
10 Lest strangers be filled with thy wealth; and thy labours *be* in the house
of a stranger;
11 And thou mourn at the last, when thy flesh and thy body are consumed,
12 And say, How have I hated instruction, and my heart despised reproof;
13 And have not obeyed the voice of my teachers, nor inclined mine ear to
them that instructed me!
14 I was almost in all evil in the midst of the congregation and assembly.

15 Drink waters out of thine own cistern, and running waters out of thine
own well.
16 Let thy fountains be dispersed abroad, *and* rivers of waters in the streets.
17 Let them be only thine own, and not strangers' with thee.
18 Let thy fountain be blessed: and rejoice with the wife of thy youth.
19 *Let her be as* the loving hind and pleasant roe; let her breasts satisfy thee
at all times; and be thou ravished always with her love.
20 And why wilt thou, my son, be ravished with a strange woman, and
embrace the bosom of a stranger?
21 For the ways of man *are* before the eyes of the LORD, and he pondereth all
his goings.
22 His own iniquities shall take the wicked himself, and he shall be holden
with the cords of his sins.
23 He shall die without instruction; and in the greatness of his folly he shall
go astray.

Avoid Disaster

6 My son, if thou be surety for thy friend, *if* thou hast stricken thy hand with
a stranger,
2 Thou art snared with the words of thy mouth, thou art taken with the words
of thy mouth.
3 Do this now, my son, and deliver thyself, when thou art come into the hand
of thy friend; go, humble thyself, and make sure thy friend.
4 Give not sleep to thine eyes, nor slumber to thine eyelids.
5 Deliver thyself as a roe from the hand *of the hunter*, and as a bird from the
hand of the fowler.
6 Go to the ant, thou sluggard; consider her ways, and be wise:
7 Which having no guide, overseer, or ruler,
8 Provideth her meat in the summer, *and* gathereth her food in the harvest.
9 How long wilt thou sleep, O sluggard? when wilt thou arise out of thy sleep?
10 *Yet* a little sleep, a little slumber, a little folding of the hands to sleep:
11 So shall thy poverty come as one that travelleth, and thy want as an armed
man.
12 A naughty person, a wicked man, walketh with a froward mouth.
13 He winketh with his eyes, he speaketh with his feet, he teacheth with his
fingers;
14 Frowardness *is* in his heart, he deviseth mischief continually; he soweth
discord.
15 Therefore shall his calamity come suddenly; suddenly shall he be broken
without remedy.
16 These six *things* doth the LORD hate: yea, seven *are* an abomination unto
him:
17 A proud look, a lying tongue, and hands that shed innocent blood,
18 An heart that deviseth wicked imaginations, feet that be swift in running
to mischief,
19 A false witness *that* speaketh lies, and he that soweth discord among
brethren.

More Advice about Avoiding Adultery

20 My son, keep thy father's commandment, and forsake not the law of thy
mother:
21 Bind them continually upon thine heart, *and* tie them about thy neck.
22 When thou goest, it shall lead thee; when thou sleepest, it shall keep thee;
and *when* thou awakest, it shall talk with thee.
23 For the commandment *is* a lamp; and the law *is* light; and reproofs of
instruction *are* the way of life:

24 To keep thee from the evil woman, from the flattery of the tongue of a
strange woman.
25 Lust not after her beauty in thine heart; neither let her take thee with her
eyelids.
26 For by means of a whorish woman *a man is brought* to a piece of bread:
and the adulteress will hunt for the precious life.
27 Can a man take fire in his bosom, and his clothes not be burned?
28 Can one go upon hot coals, and his feet not be burned?
29 So he that goeth in to his neighbour's wife; whosoever toucheth her shall
not be innocent.
30 *Men* do not despise a thief, if he steal to satisfy his soul when he is hungry;
31 But *if* he be found, he shall restore sevenfold; he shall give all the substance
of his house.
32 *But* whoso committeth adultery with a woman lacketh understanding:
he *that* doeth it destroyeth his own soul.
33 A wound and dishonour shall he get; and his reproach shall not be wiped
away.
34 For jealousy *is* the rage of a man: therefore he will not spare in the day of
vengeance.
35 He will not regard any ransom; neither will he rest content, though thou
givest many gifts.

Advice about Avoiding the Adulteress

7 My son, keep my words, and lay up my commandments with thee.
2 Keep my commandments, and live; and my law as the apple of thine eye.
3 Bind them upon thy fingers, write them upon the table of thine heart.
4 Say unto wisdom, Thou *art* my sister; and call understanding *thy* kinswoman:
5 That they may keep thee from the strange woman, from the stranger *which*
flattereth with her words.
6 For at the window of my house I looked through my casement,
7 And beheld among the simple ones, I discerned among the youths, a young
man void of understanding,
8 Passing through the street near her corner; and he went the way to her
house,
9 In the twilight, in the evening, in the black and dark night:
10 And, behold, there met him a woman *with* the attire of an harlot, and
subtil of heart.
11 (She *is* loud and stubborn; her feet abide not in her house:
12 Now *is she* without, now in the streets, and lieth in wait at every corner.)
13 So she caught him, and kissed him, *and* with an impudent face said unto
him,
14 *I have* peace offerings with me; this day have I payed my vows.
15 Therefore came I forth to meet thee, diligently to seek thy face, and I have
found thee.
16 I have decked my bed with coverings of tapestry, with carved *works*, with
fine linen of Egypt.
17 I have perfumed my bed with myrrh, aloes, and cinnamon.
18 Come, let us take our fill of love until the morning: let us solace ourselves
with loves.
19 For the goodman *is* not at home, he is gone a long journey:
20 He hath taken a bag of money with him, *and* will come home at the day
appointed.
21 With her much fair speech she caused him to yield, with the flattering of
her lips she forced him.
22 He goeth after her straightway, as an ox goeth to the slaughter, or as a fool
to the correction of the stocks;

23 Till a dart strike through his liver; as a bird hasteth to the snare, and
knoweth not that it *is* for his life.
24 Hearken unto me now therefore, O ye children, and attend to the words
of my mouth.
25 Let not thine heart decline to her ways, go not astray in her paths.
26 For she hath cast down many wounded: yea, many strong *men* have been
slain by her.
27 Her house *is* the way to hell, going down to the chambers of death.

Wisdom's Announcement

8 Doth not wisdom cry? and understanding put forth her voice?
2 She standeth in the top of high places, by the way in the places of the
paths.
3 She crieth at the gates, at the entry of the city, at the coming in at the doors.
4 Unto you, O men, I call; and my voice *is* to the sons of man.
5 O ye simple, understand wisdom: and, ye fools, be ye of an understanding
heart.
6 Hear; for I will speak of excellent things; and the opening of my lips *shall*
be right things.
7 For my mouth shall speak truth; and wickedness *is* an abomination to my
lips.
8 All the words of my mouth *are* in righteousness; *there is* nothing froward
or perverse in them.
9 They *are* all plain to him that understandeth, and right to them that find
knowledge.
10 Receive my instruction, and not silver; and knowledge rather than choice
gold.
11 For wisdom *is* better than rubies; and all the things that may be desired
are not to be compared to it.

Wisdom's Authority

12 I wisdom dwell with prudence, and find out knowledge of witty inven-
tions.
13 The fear of the LORD *is* to hate evil: pride, and arrogancy, and the evil way,
and the froward mouth, do I hate.
14 Counsel *is* mine, and sound wisdom: I *am* understanding; I have strength.
15 By me kings reign, and princes decree justice.
16 By me princes rule, and nobles, *even* all the judges of the earth.
17 I love them that love me; and those that seek me early shall find me.
18 Riches and honour *are* with me; *yea*, durable riches and righteousness.
19 My fruit *is* better than gold, yea, than fine gold; and my revenue than
choice silver.
20 I lead in the way of righteousness, in the midst of the paths of judgment:
21 That I may cause those that love me to inherit substance; and I will fill
their treasures.

Wisdom as Creator

22 The LORD possessed me in the beginning of his way, before his works of
old.
23 I was set up from everlasting, from the beginning, or ever the earth was.
24 When *there were* no depths, I was brought forth; when *there were* no foun-
tains abounding with water.
25 Before the mountains were settled, before the hills was I brought forth:
26 While as yet he had not made the earth, nor the fields, nor the highest
part of the dust of the world.
27 When he prepared the heavens, I *was* there: when he set a compass upon
the face of the depth:

28 When he established the clouds above: when he strengthened the fountains of the deep:
29 When he gave to the sea his decree, that the waters should not pass his commandment: when he appointed the foundations of the earth:
30 Then I was by him, *as* one brought up *with him*: and I was daily *his* delight, rejoicing always before him;
31 Rejoicing in the habitable part of his earth; and my delights *were* with the sons of men.

Wisdom as Lifegiver

32 Now therefore hearken unto me, O ye children: for blessed *are they that* keep my ways.
33 Hear instruction, and be wise, and refuse it not.
34 Blessed *is* the man that heareth me, watching daily at my gates, waiting at the posts of my doors.
35 For whoso findeth me findeth life, and shall obtain favour of the LORD.
36 But he that sinneth against me wrongeth his own soul: all they that hate me love death.

Wisdom Hosts a Banquet

9 Wisdom hath builded her house, she hath hewn out her seven pillars:
2 She hath killed her beasts; she hath mingled her wine; she hath also furnished her table.
3 She hath sent forth her maidens: she crieth upon the highest places of the city,
4 Whoso *is* simple, let him turn in hither: *as for* him that wanteth understanding, she saith to him,
5 Come, eat of my bread, and drink of the wine *which* I have mingled.
6 Forsake the foolish, and live; and go in the way of understanding.
7 He that reproveth a scorner getteth to himself shame: and he that rebuketh a wicked *man getteth* himself a blot.
8 Reprove not a scorner, lest he hate thee: rebuke a wise man, and he will love thee.
9 Give *instruction* to a wise *man*, and he will be yet wiser: teach a just *man*, and he will increase in learning.
10 The fear of the LORD *is* the beginning of wisdom: and the knowledge of the holy *is* understanding.
11 For by me thy days shall be multiplied, and the years of thy life shall be increased.
12 If thou be wise, thou shalt be wise for thyself: but *if* thou scornest, thou alone shalt bear *it*.

Stupidity Imitates Wisdom's Banquet

13 A foolish woman *is* clamorous: *she is* simple, and knoweth nothing.
14 For she sitteth at the door of her house, on a seat in the high places of the city,
15 To call passengers who go right on their ways:
16 Whoso *is* simple, let him turn in hither: and *as for* him that wanteth understanding, she saith to him,
17 Stolen waters are sweet, and bread *eaten* in secret is pleasant.
18 But he knoweth not that the dead *are* there; *and that* her guests *are* in the depths of hell.

A Wise Son Is Righteous

10 The proverbs of Solomon. A wise son maketh a glad father: but a foolish son *is* the heaviness of his mother.
2 Treasures of wickedness profit nothing: but righteousness delivereth from death.

3 The LORD will not suffer the soul of the righteous to famish: but he casteth
away the substance of the wicked.
4 He becometh poor that dealeth *with* a slack hand: but the hand of the
diligent maketh rich.
5 He that gathereth in summer *is* a wise son: *but* he that sleepeth in harvest
is a son that causeth shame.
6 Blessings *are* upon the head of the just: but violence covereth the mouth
of the wicked.
7 The memory of the just *is* blessed: but the name of the wicked shall rot.

Proverbs Concerning the Mouth

8 The wise in heart will receive commandments: but a prating fool shall fall.
9 He that walketh uprightly walketh surely: but he that perverteth his ways
shall be known.
10 He that winketh with the eye causeth sorrow: but a prating fool shall fall.
11 The mouth of a righteous *man is* a well of life: but violence covereth the
mouth of the wicked.
12 Hatred stirreth up strifes: but love covereth all sins.
13 In the lips of him that hath understanding wisdom is found: but a rod *is*
for the back of him that is void of understanding.
14 Wise *men* lay up knowledge: but the mouth of the foolish *is* near destruction.
15 The rich man's wealth *is* his strong city: the destruction of the poor *is* their
poverty.
16 The labour of the righteous *tendeth* to life: the fruit of the wicked to sin.
17 He *is in* the way of life that keepeth instruction: but he that refuseth
reproof erreth.
18 He that hideth hatred *with* lying lips, and he that uttereth a slander, *is* a
fool.
19 In the multitude of words there wanteth not sin: but he that refraineth
his lips *is* wise.
20 The tongue of the just *is as* choice silver: the heart of the wicked *is* little
worth.
21 The lips of the righteous feed many: but fools die for want of wisdom.
22 The blessing of the LORD, it maketh rich, and he addeth no sorrow with it.
23 *It is* as sport to a fool to do mischief: but a man of understanding hath
wisdom.

Contrast of Righteous and Wicked

24 The fear of the wicked, it shall come upon him: but the desire of the righ-
teous shall be granted.
25 As the whirlwind passeth, so *is* the wicked no *more*: but the righteous *is*
an everlasting foundation.
26 As vinegar to the teeth, and as smoke to the eyes, so *is* the sluggard to them
that send him.
27 The fear of the LORD prolongeth days: but the years of the wicked shall be
shortened.
28 The hope of the righteous *shall be* gladness: but the expectation of the
wicked shall perish.
29 The way of the LORD *is* strength to the upright: but destruction *shall be* to
the workers of iniquity.
30 The righteous shall never be removed: but the wicked shall not inhabit
the earth.
31 The mouth of the just bringeth forth wisdom: but the froward tongue
shall be cut out.
32 The lips of the righteous know what is acceptable: but the mouth of the
wicked *speaketh* frowardness.

The Value of Righteousness

11 A false balance *is* abomination to the LORD: but a just weight *is* his delight.

2 *When* pride cometh, then cometh shame: but with the lowly *is* wisdom.

3 The integrity of the upright shall guide them: but the perverseness of transgressors shall destroy them.

4 Riches profit not in the day of wrath: but righteousness delivereth from death.

5 The righteousness of the perfect shall direct his way: but the wicked shall fall by his own wickedness.

6 The righteousness of the upright shall deliver them: but transgressors shall be taken in *their own* naughtiness.

7 When a wicked man dieth, *his* expectation shall perish: and the hope of unjust *men* perisheth.

8 The righteous is delivered out of trouble, and the wicked cometh in his stead.

9 An hypocrite with *his* mouth destroyeth his neighbour: but through knowledge shall the just be delivered.

10 When it goeth well with the righteous, the city rejoiceth: and when the wicked perish, *there is* shouting.

11 By the blessing of the upright the city is exalted: but it is overthrown by the mouth of the wicked.

12 He that is void of wisdom despiseth his neighbour: but a man of understanding holdeth his peace.

13 A talebearer revealeth secrets: but he that is of a faithful spirit concealeth the matter.

14 Where no counsel *is*, the people fall: but in the multitude of counsellors *there is* safety.

15 He that is surety for a stranger shall smart *for it*: and he that hateth suretiship is sure.

16 A gracious woman retaineth honour: and strong *men* retain riches.

17 The merciful man doeth good to his own soul: but *he that is* cruel troubleth his own flesh.

18 The wicked worketh a deceitful work: but to him that soweth righteousness *shall be* a sure reward.

19 As righteousness *tendeth* to life: so he that pursueth evil *pursueth it* to his own death.

20 They that are of a froward heart *are* abomination to the LORD: but *such as are* upright in *their* way *are* his delight.

21 *Though* hand *join* in hand, the wicked shall not be unpunished: but the seed of the righteous shall be delivered.

22 *As* a jewel of gold in a swine's snout, *so is* a fair woman which is without discretion.

23 The desire of the righteous *is* only good: *but* the expectation of the wicked *is* wrath.

24 There is that scattereth, and yet increaseth; and *there is* that withholdeth more than is meet, but *it tendeth* to poverty.

25 The liberal soul shall be made fat: and he that watereth shall be watered also himself.

26 He that withholdeth corn, the people shall curse him: but blessing *shall be* upon the head of him that selleth *it*.

27 He that diligently seeketh good procureth favour: but he that seeketh mischief, it shall come unto him.

28 He that trusteth in his riches shall fall: but the righteous shall flourish as a branch.

29 He that troubleth his own house shall inherit the wind: and the fool *shall be* servant to the wise of heart.
30 The fruit of the righteous *is* a tree of life; and he that winneth souls *is* wise.
31 Behold, the righteous shall be recompensed in the earth: much more the wicked and the sinner.

Varied Observations on Virtues and Vices

12 Whoso loveth instruction loveth knowledge: but he that hateth reproof *is* brutish.
2 A good *man* obtaineth favour of the LORD: but a man of wicked devices will he condemn.
3 A man shall not be established by wickedness: but the root of the righteous shall not be moved.
4 A virtuous woman *is* a crown to her husband: but she that maketh ashamed *is* as rottenness in his bones.
5 The thoughts of the righteous *are* right: *but* the counsels of the wicked *are* deceit.
6 The words of the wicked *are* to lie in wait for blood: but the mouth of the upright shall deliver them.
7 The wicked are overthrown, and *are* not: but the house of the righteous shall stand.
8 A man shall be commended according to his wisdom: but he that is of a perverse heart shall be despised.
9 *He that is* despised, and hath a servant, *is* better than he that honoureth himself, and lacketh bread.
10 A righteous *man* regardeth the life of his beast: but the tender mercies of the wicked *are* cruel.
11 He that tilleth his land shall be satisfied with bread: but he that followeth vain *persons is* void of understanding.
12 The wicked desireth the net of evil *men*: but the root of the righteous yieldeth *fruit*.
13 The wicked is snared by the transgression of *his* lips: but the just shall come out of trouble.
14 A man shall be satisfied with good by the fruit of *his* mouth: and the recompence of a man's hands shall be rendered unto him.
15 The way of a fool *is* right in his own eyes: but he that hearkeneth unto counsel *is* wise.
16 A fool's wrath is presently known: but a prudent *man* covereth shame.
17 *He that* speaketh truth sheweth forth righteousness: but a false witness deceit.
18 There is that speaketh like the piercings of a sword: but the tongue of the wise *is* health.
19 The lip of truth shall be established for ever: but a lying tongue *is* but for a moment.
20 Deceit *is* in the heart of them that imagine evil: but to the counsellors of peace *is* joy.
21 There shall no evil happen to the just: but the wicked shall be filled with mischief.
22 Lying lips *are* abomination to the LORD: but they that deal truly *are* his delight.
23 A prudent man concealeth knowledge: but the heart of fools proclaimeth foolishness.
24 The hand of the diligent shall bear rule: but the slothful shall be under tribute.
25 Heaviness in the heart of man maketh it stoop: but a good word maketh it glad.

26 The righteous *is* more excellent than his neighbour: but the way of the wicked seduceth them.
27 The slothful *man* roasteth not that which he took in hunting: but the substance of a diligent man *is* precious.
28 In the way of righteousness *is* life; and *in* the pathway *thereof there is* no death.

A Wise Son Lives Righteously

13 A wise son *heareth* his father's instruction: but a scorner heareth not rebuke.
2 A man shall eat good by the fruit of *his* mouth: but the soul of the transgressors *shall eat* violence.
3 He that keepeth his mouth keepeth his life: *but* he that openeth wide his lips shall have destruction.
4 The soul of the sluggard desireth, and *hath* nothing: but the soul of the diligent shall be made fat.
5 A righteous *man* hateth lying: but a wicked *man* is loathsome, and cometh to shame.
6 Righteousness keepeth *him that is* upright in the way: but wickedness overthroweth the sinner.
7 There is that maketh himself rich, yet *hath* nothing: *there is* that maketh himself poor, yet *hath* great riches.
8 The ransom of a man's life *are* his riches: but the poor heareth not rebuke.
9 The light of the righteous rejoiceth: but the lamp of the wicked shall be put out.
10 Only by pride cometh contention: but with the well advised *is* wisdom.
11 Wealth *gotten* by vanity shall be diminished: but he that gathereth by labour shall increase.
12 Hope deferred maketh the heart sick: but *when* the desire cometh, *it is* a tree of life.
13 Whoso despiseth the word shall be destroyed: but he that feareth the commandment shall be rewarded.
14 The law of the wise *is* a fountain of life, to depart from the snares of death.
15 Good understanding giveth favour: but the way of transgressors *is* hard.
16 Every prudent *man* dealeth with knowledge: but a fool layeth open *his* folly.
17 A wicked messenger falleth into mischief: but a faithful ambassador *is* health.
18 Poverty and shame *shall be to* him that refuseth instruction: but he that regardeth reproof shall be honoured.
19 The desire accomplished is sweet to the soul: but *it is* abomination to fools to depart from evil.
20 He that walketh with wise *men* shall be wise: but a companion of fools shall be destroyed.
21 Evil pursueth sinners: but to the righteous good shall be repayed.
22 A good *man* leaveth an inheritance to his children's children: and the wealth of the sinner *is* laid up for the just.
23 Much food *is in* the tillage of the poor: but there is *that is* destroyed for want of judgment.
24 He that spareth his rod hateth his son: but he that loveth him chasteneth him betimes.
25 The righteous eateth to the satisfying of his soul: but the belly of the wicked shall want.

Wise People Live Righteously

14 Every wise woman buildeth her house: but the foolish plucketh it down with her hands.
2 He that walketh in his uprightness feareth the Lord: but *he that is* perverse in his ways despiseth him.

3 In the mouth of the foolish *is* a rod of pride: but the lips of the wise shall
preserve them.
4 Where no oxen *are*, the crib *is* clean: but much increase *is* by the strength
of the ox.
5 A faithful witness will not lie: but a false witness will utter lies.
6 A scorner seeketh wisdom, and *findeth it* not: but knowledge *is* easy unto
him that understandeth.
7 Go from the presence of a foolish man, when thou perceivest not *in him*
the lips of knowledge.
8 The wisdom of the prudent *is* to understand his way: but the folly of fools
is deceit.
9 Fools make a mock at sin: but among the righteous *there is* favour.
10 The heart knoweth his own bitterness; and a stranger doth not intermed-
dle with his joy.
11 The house of the wicked shall be overthrown: but the tabernacle of the
upright shall flourish.
12 There is a way which seemeth right unto a man, but the end thereof *are*
the ways of death.
13 Even in laughter the heart is sorrowful; and the end of that mirth *is* heaviness.
14 The backslider in heart shall be filled with his own ways: and a good man
shall be satisfied from himself.
15 The simple believeth every word: but the prudent *man* looketh well to his
going.
16 A wise *man* feareth, and departeth from evil: but the fool rageth, and is
confident.
17 *He that is* soon angry dealeth foolishly: and a man of wicked devices is
hated.
18 The simple inherit folly: but the prudent are crowned with knowledge.
19 The evil bow before the good; and the wicked at the gates of the righteous.
20 The poor is hated even of his own neighbour: but the rich *hath* many
friends.
21 He that despiseth his neighbour sinneth: but he that hath mercy on the
poor, happy *is* he.
22 Do they not err that devise evil? but mercy and truth *shall be* to them that
devise good.
23 In all labour there is profit: but the talk of the lips *tendeth* only to penury.
24 The crown of the wise *is* their riches: *but* the foolishness of fools *is* folly.
25 A true witness delivereth souls: but a deceitful *witness* speaketh lies.
26 In the fear of the Lord *is* strong confidence: and his children shall have a
place of refuge.
27 The fear of the Lord *is* a fountain of life, to depart from the snares of death.
28 In the multitude of people *is* the king's honour: but in the want of people
is the destruction of the prince.
29 *He that is* slow to wrath *is* of great understanding: but *he that is* hasty of
spirit exalteth folly.
30 A sound heart *is* the life of the flesh: but envy the rottenness of the bones.
31 He that oppresseth the poor reproacheth his Maker: but he that honoureth
him hath mercy on the poor.
32 The wicked is driven away in his wickedness: but the righteous hath hope
in his death.
33 Wisdom resteth in the heart of him that hath understanding: but *that
which is* in the midst of fools is made known.
34 Righteousness exalteth a nation: but sin *is* a reproach to any people.
35 The king's favour *is* toward a wise servant: but his wrath is *against* him
that causeth shame.

Wise Ways to Live

15 A soft answer turneth away wrath: but grievous words stir up anger.
2 The tongue of the wise useth knowledge aright: but the mouth of
fools poureth out foolishness.
3 The eyes of the LORD *are* in every place, beholding the evil and the good.
4 A wholesome tongue *is* a tree of life: but perverseness therein *is* a breach
in the spirit.
5 A fool despiseth his father's instruction: but he that regardeth reproof is
prudent.
6 In the house of the righteous *is* much treasure: but in the revenues of the
wicked is trouble.
7 The lips of the wise disperse knowledge: but the heart of the foolish *doeth*
not so.
8 The sacrifice of the wicked *is* an abomination to the LORD: but the prayer
of the upright *is* his delight.
9 The way of the wicked *is* an abomination unto the LORD: but he loveth him
that followeth after righteousness.
10 Correction *is* grievous unto him that forsaketh the way: *and* he that hateth
reproof shall die.
11 Hell and destruction *are* before the LORD: how much more then the hearts
of the children of men?
12 A scorner loveth not one that reproveth him: neither will he go unto the
wise.
13 A merry heart maketh a cheerful countenance: but by sorrow of the heart
the spirit is broken.
14 The heart of him that hath understanding seeketh knowledge: but the
mouth of fools feedeth on foolishness.
15 All the days of the afflicted *are* evil: but he that is of a merry heart *hath* a
continual feast.
16 Better *is* little with the fear of the LORD than great treasure and trouble
therewith.
17 Better *is* a dinner of herbs where love is, than a stalled ox and hatred
therewith.
18 A wrathful man stirreth up strife: but *he that is* slow to anger appeaseth
strife.
19 The way of the slothful *man is* as an hedge of thorns: but the way of the
righteous *is* made plain.
20 A wise son maketh a glad father: but a foolish man despiseth his mother.
21 Folly *is* joy to *him that is* destitute of wisdom: but a man of understanding
walketh uprightly.
22 Without counsel purposes are disappointed: but in the multitude of coun-
sellors they are established.
23 A man hath joy by the answer of his mouth: and a word *spoken* in due
season, how good *is it*!
24 The way of life *is* above to the wise, that he may depart from hell beneath.
25 The LORD will destroy the house of the proud: but he will establish the
border of the widow.
26 The thoughts of the wicked *are* an abomination to the LORD: but *the words*
of the pure *are* pleasant words.
27 He that is greedy of gain troubleth his own house; but he that hateth gifts
shall live.
28 The heart of the righteous studieth to answer: but the mouth of the wick-
ed poureth out evil things.
29 The LORD *is* far from the wicked: but he heareth the prayer of the righteous.
30 The light of the eyes rejoiceth the heart: *and* a good report maketh the
bones fat.

31 The ear that heareth the reproof of life abideth among the wise.
32 He that refuseth instruction despiseth his own soul: but he that heareth
reproof getteth understanding.
33 The fear of the LORD *is* the instruction of wisdom; and before honour *is*
humility.

Wisdom's Blessings Come from the Lord

16 The preparations of the heart in man, and the answer of the tongue,
is from the LORD.
2 All the ways of a man *are* clean in his own eyes; but the LORD weigheth the
spirits.
3 Commit thy works unto the LORD, and thy thoughts shall be established.
4 The LORD hath made all *things* for himself: yea, even the wicked for the day
of evil.
5 Every one *that is* proud in heart *is* an abomination to the LORD: *though*
hand *join* in hand, he shall not be unpunished.
6 By mercy and truth iniquity is purged: and by the fear of the LORD *men*
depart from evil.
7 When a man's ways please the LORD, he maketh even his enemies to be at
peace with him.
8 Better *is* a little with righteousness than great revenues without right.
9 A man's heart deviseth his way: but the LORD directeth his steps.
10 A divine sentence *is* in the lips of the king: his mouth transgresseth not
in judgment.
11 A just weight and balance *are* the LORD's: all the weights of the bag *are* his
work.
12 *It is* an abomination to kings to commit wickedness: for the throne is
established by righteousness.
13 Righteous lips *are* the delight of kings; and they love him that speaketh
right.
14 The wrath of a king *is as* messengers of death: but a wise man will pacify
it.
15 In the light of the king's countenance *is* life; and his favour *is* as a cloud
of the latter rain.
16 How much better *is it* to get wisdom than gold! and to get understanding
rather to be chosen than silver!
17 The highway of the upright *is* to depart from evil: he that keepeth his way
preserveth his soul.
18 Pride *goeth* before destruction, and an haughty spirit before a fall.
19 Better *it is to be* of an humble spirit with the lowly, than to divide the spoil
with the proud.
20 He that handleth a matter wisely shall find good: and whoso trusteth in
the LORD, happy *is* he.
21 The wise in heart shall be called prudent: and the sweetness of the lips
increaseth learning.
22 Understanding *is* a wellspring of life unto him that hath it: but the instruc-
tion of fools *is* folly.
23 The heart of the wise teacheth his mouth, and addeth learning to his lips.
24 Pleasant words *are as* an honeycomb, sweet to the soul, and health to the
bones.
25 There is a way that seemeth right unto a man, but the end thereof *are* the
ways of death.
26 He that laboureth laboureth for himself; for his mouth craveth it of him.
27 An ungodly man diggeth up evil: and in his lips *there is* as a burning fire.
28 A froward man soweth strife: and a whisperer separateth chief friends.

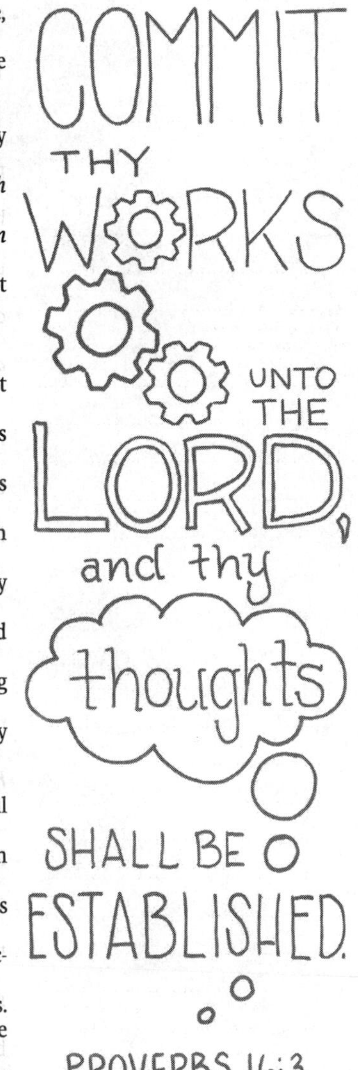

29 A violent man enticeth his neighbour, and leadeth him into the way *that is* not good.
30 He shutteth his eyes to devise froward things: moving his lips he bringeth evil to pass.
31 The hoary head *is* a crown of glory, *if* it be found in the way of righteousness.
32 *He that is* slow to anger *is* better than the mighty; and he that ruleth his spirit than he that taketh a city.
33 The lot is cast into the lap; but the whole disposing thereof *is* of the LORD.

The Consequences of Being a Fool

17 Better *is* a dry morsel, and quietness therewith, than an house full of sacrifices *with* strife.
2 A wise servant shall have rule over a son that causeth shame, and shall have part of the inheritance among the brethren.
3 The fining pot *is* for silver, and the furnace for gold: but the LORD trieth the hearts.
4 A wicked doer giveth heed to false lips; *and* a liar giveth ear to a naughty tongue.
5 Whoso mocketh the poor reproacheth his Maker: *and* he that is glad at calamities shall not be unpunished.
6 Children's children *are* the crown of old men; and the glory of children *are* their fathers.
7 Excellent speech becometh not a fool: much less do lying lips a prince.
8 A gift *is as* a precious stone in the eyes of him that hath it: whithersoever it turneth, it prospereth.
9 He that covereth a transgression seeketh love; but he that repeateth a matter separateth *very* friends.
10 A reproof entereth more into a wise man than an hundred stripes into a fool.
11 An evil *man* seeketh only rebellion: therefore a cruel messenger shall be sent against him.
12 Let a bear robbed of her whelps meet a man, rather than a fool in his folly.
13 Whoso rewardeth evil for good, evil shall not depart from his house.
14 The beginning of strife *is as* when one letteth out water: therefore leave off contention, before it be meddled with.
15 He that justifieth the wicked, and he that condemneth the just, even they both *are* abomination to the LORD.
16 Wherefore *is there* a price in the hand of a fool to get wisdom, seeing *he hath* no heart *to it*?
17 A friend loveth at all times, and a brother is born for adversity.
18 A man void of understanding striketh hands, *and* becometh surety in the presence of his friend.
19 He loveth transgression that loveth strife: *and* he that exalteth his gate seeketh destruction.
20 He that hath a froward heart findeth no good: and he that hath a perverse tongue falleth into mischief.
21 He that begetteth a fool *doeth it* to his sorrow: and the father of a fool hath no joy.
22 A merry heart doeth good *like* a medicine: but a broken spirit drieth the bones.
23 A wicked *man* taketh a gift out of the bosom to pervert the ways of judgment.
24 Wisdom *is* before him that hath understanding; but the eyes of a fool *are* in the ends of the earth.
25 A foolish son *is* a grief to his father, and bitterness to her that bare him.
26 Also to punish the just *is* not good, *nor* to strike princes for equity.

27 He that hath knowledge spareth his words: *and* a man of understanding
is of an excellent spirit.
28 Even a fool, when he holdeth his peace, is counted wise: *and* he that shut-
teth his lips *is esteemed* a man of understanding.

How Fools Live

18 Through desire a man, having separated himself, seeketh *and* inter-
meddleth with all wisdom.
2 A fool hath no delight in understanding, but that his heart may discover
itself.
3 When the wicked cometh, *then* cometh also contempt, and with ignominy
reproach.
4 The words of a man's mouth *are as* deep waters, *and* the wellspring of
wisdom *as* a flowing brook.
5 *It is* not good to accept the person of the wicked, to overthrow the righteous
in judgment.
6 A fool's lips enter into contention, and his mouth calleth for strokes.
7 A fool's mouth *is* his destruction, and his lips *are* the snare of his soul.
8 The words of a talebearer *are* as wounds, and they go down into the inner-
most parts of the belly.
9 He also that is slothful in his work is brother to him that is a great waster.
10 The name of the LORD *is* a strong tower: the righteous runneth into it, and
is safe.
11 The rich man's wealth *is* his strong city, and as an high wall in his own
conceit.
12 Before destruction the heart of man is haughty, and before honour *is*
humility.
13 He that answereth a matter before he heareth *it*, it *is* folly and shame unto
him.
14 The spirit of a man will sustain his infirmity; but a wounded spirit who
can bear?
15 The heart of the prudent getteth knowledge; and the ear of the wise
seeketh knowledge.
16 A man's gift maketh room for him, and bringeth him before great men.
17 *He that is* first in his own cause *seemeth* just; but his neighbour cometh
and searcheth him.
18 The lot causeth contentions to cease, and parteth between the mighty.
19 A brother offended *is harder to be won* than a strong city: and *their* con-
tentions *are* like the bars of a castle.
20 A man's belly shall be satisfied with the fruit of his mouth; *and* with the
increase of his lips shall he be filled.
21 Death and life *are* in the power of the tongue: and they that love it shall
eat the fruit thereof.
22 *Whoso* findeth a wife findeth a good *thing*, and obtaineth favour of the
LORD.
23 The poor useth intreaties; but the rich answereth roughly.
24 A man *that hath* friends must shew himself friendly: and there is a friend
that sticketh closer than a brother.

How to Avoid Fools and Foolishness

19 Better *is* the poor that walketh in his integrity, than *he that is* perverse
in his lips, and is a fool.
2 Also, *that* the soul *be* without knowledge, *it is* not good; and he that hasteth
with *his* feet sinneth.
3 The foolishness of man perverteth his way: and his heart fretteth against
the LORD.
4 Wealth maketh many friends; but the poor is separated from his neighbour.

5 A false witness shall not be unpunished, and *he that* speaketh lies shall not
escape.
6 Many will intreat the favour of the prince: and every man *is* a friend to him
that giveth gifts.
7 All the brethren of the poor do hate him: how much more do his friends
go far from him? he pursueth *them with* words, *yet* they *are* wanting *to him*.
8 He that getteth wisdom loveth his own soul: he that keepeth understanding
shall find good.
9 A false witness shall not be unpunished, and *he that* speaketh lies shall
perish.
10 Delight is not seemly for a fool; much less for a servant to have rule over
princes.
11 The discretion of a man deferreth his anger; and *it is* his glory to pass over
a transgression.
12 The king's wrath *is* as the roaring of a lion; but his favour *is* as dew upon
the grass.
13 A foolish son *is* the calamity of his father: and the contentions of a wife
are a continual dropping.
14 House and riches *are* the inheritance of fathers: and a prudent wife *is*
from the LORD.
15 Slothfulness casteth into a deep sleep; and an idle soul shall suffer hunger.
16 He that keepeth the commandment keepeth his own soul; *but* he that
despiseth his ways shall die.
17 He that hath pity upon the poor lendeth unto the LORD; and that which
he hath given will he pay him again.
18 Chasten thy son while there is hope, and let not thy soul spare for his
crying.
19 A man of great wrath shall suffer punishment: for if thou deliver *him*, yet
thou must do it again.
20 Hear counsel, and receive instruction, that thou mayest be wise in thy
latter end.
21 *There are* many devices in a man's heart; nevertheless the counsel of the
LORD, that shall stand.
22 The desire of a man *is* his kindness: and a poor man *is* better than a liar.
23 The fear of the LORD *tendeth* to life: and *he that hath it* shall abide satisfied;
he shall not be visited with evil.
24 A slothful *man* hideth his hand in *his* bosom, and will not so much as
bring it to his mouth again.
25 Smite a scorner, and the simple will beware: and reprove one that hath
understanding, *and* he will understand knowledge.
26 He that wasteth *his* father, *and* chaseth away *his* mother, *is* a son that
causeth shame, and bringeth reproach.
27 Cease, my son, to hear the instruction *that causeth* to err from the words
of knowledge.
28 An ungodly witness scorneth judgment: and the mouth of the wicked
devoureth iniquity.
29 Judgments are prepared for scorners, and stripes for the back of fools.

Foolproof Instructions

20 Wine *is* a mocker, strong drink *is* raging: and whosoever is deceived
thereby is not wise.
2 The fear of a king *is* as the roaring of a lion: *whoso* provoketh him to anger
sinneth *against* his own soul.
3 *It is* an honour for a man to cease from strife: but every fool will be meddling.
4 The sluggard will not plow by reason of the cold; *therefore* shall he beg in
harvest, and *have* nothing.

5 Counsel in the heart of man *is like* deep water; but a man of understanding
will draw it out.
6 Most men will proclaim every one his own goodness: but a faithful man
who can find?
7 The just *man* walketh in his integrity: his children *are* blessed after him.
8 A king that sitteth in the throne of judgment scattereth away all evil with
his eyes.
9 Who can say, I have made my heart clean, I am pure from my sin?
10 Divers weights, *and* divers measures, both of them *are* alike abomination
to the LORD.
11 Even a child is known by his doings, whether his work *be* pure, and wheth-
er *it be* right.
12 The hearing ear, and the seeing eye, the LORD hath made even both of
them.
13 Love not sleep, lest thou come to poverty; open thine eyes, *and* thou shalt
be satisfied with bread.
14 *It is* naught, *it is* naught, saith the buyer: but when he is gone his way, then
he boasteth.
15 There is gold, and a multitude of rubies: but the lips of knowledge *are* a
precious jewel.
16 Take his garment that is surety *for* a stranger: and take a pledge of him for
a strange woman.
17 Bread of deceit *is* sweet to a man; but afterwards his mouth shall be filled
with gravel.
18 *Every* purpose is established by counsel: and with good advice make war.
19 He that goeth about *as* a talebearer revealeth secrets: therefore meddle
not with him that flattereth with his lips.
20 Whoso curseth his father or his mother, his lamp shall be put out in
obscure darkness.
21 An inheritance *may be* gotten hastily at the beginning; but the end there-
of shall not be blessed.
22 Say not thou, I will recompense evil; *but* wait on the LORD, and he shall
save thee.
23 Divers weights *are* an abomination unto the LORD; and a false balance *is*
not good.
24 Man's goings *are* of the LORD; how can a man then understand his own
way?
25 *It is* a snare to the man *who* devoureth *that which is* holy, and after vows
to make enquiry.
26 A wise king scattereth the wicked, and bringeth the wheel over them.
27 The spirit of man *is* the candle of the LORD, searching all the inward parts
of the belly.
28 Mercy and truth preserve the king: and his throne is upholden by mercy.
29 The glory of young men *is* their strength: and the beauty of old men *is* the
gray head.
30 The blueness of a wound cleanseth away evil: so *do* stripes the inward parts
of the belly.

The Lord Controls Wise and Foolish People

21 The king's heart *is* in the hand of the LORD, *as* the rivers of water: he
turneth it whithersoever he will.
2 Every way of a man *is* right in his own eyes: but the LORD pondereth the
hearts.
3 To do justice and judgment *is* more acceptable to the LORD than sacrifice.
4 An high look, and a proud heart, *and* the plowing of the wicked, *is* sin.

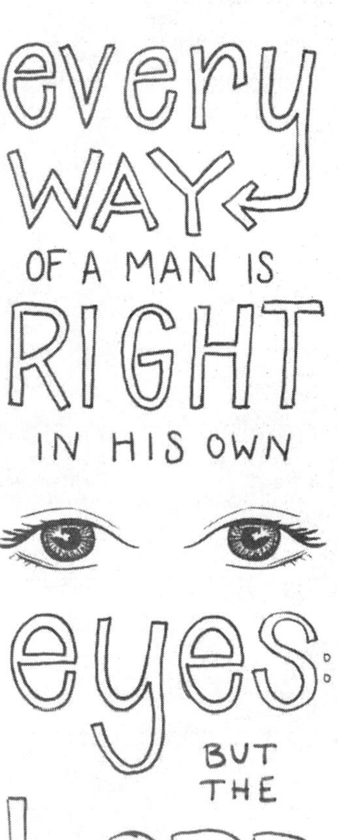

5 The thoughts of the diligent *tend* only to plenteousness; but of every one *that is* hasty only to want.

6 The getting of treasures by a lying tongue *is* a vanity tossed to and fro of them that seek death.

7 The robbery of the wicked shall destroy them; because they refuse to do judgment.

8 The way of man *is* froward and strange: but *as for* the pure, his work *is* right.

9 *It is* better to dwell in a corner of the housetop, than with a brawling woman in a wide house.

10 The soul of the wicked desireth evil: his neighbour findeth no favour in his eyes.

11 When the scorner is punished, the simple is made wise: and when the wise is instructed, he receiveth knowledge.

12 The righteous *man* wisely considereth the house of the wicked: *but God* overthroweth the wicked for *their* wickedness.

13 Whoso stoppeth his ears at the cry of the poor, he also shall cry himself, but shall not be heard.

14 A gift in secret pacifieth anger: and a reward in the bosom strong wrath.

15 *It is* joy to the just to do judgment: but destruction *shall be* to the workers of iniquity.

16 The man that wandereth out of the way of understanding shall remain in the congregation of the dead.

17 He that loveth pleasure *shall be* a poor man: he that loveth wine and oil shall not be rich.

18 The wicked *shall be* a ransom for the righteous, and the transgressor for the upright.

19 *It is* better to dwell in the wilderness, than with a contentious and an angry woman.

20 *There is* treasure to be desired and oil in the dwelling of the wise; but a foolish man spendeth it up.

21 He that followeth after righteousness and mercy findeth life, righteousness, and honour.

22 A wise *man* scaleth the city of the mighty, and casteth down the strength of the confidence thereof.

23 Whoso keepeth his mouth and his tongue keepeth his soul from troubles.

24 Proud *and* haughty scorner *is* his name, who dealeth in proud wrath.

25 The desire of the slothful killeth him; for his hands refuse to labour.

26 He coveteth greedily all the day long: but the righteous giveth and spareth not.

27 The sacrifice of the wicked *is* abomination: how much more, *when* he bringeth it with a wicked mind?

28 A false witness shall perish: but the man that heareth speaketh constantly.

29 A wicked man hardeneth his face: but *as for* the upright, he directeth his way.

30 *There is* no wisdom nor understanding nor counsel against the LORD.

31 The horse *is* prepared against the day of battle: but safety *is* of the LORD.

Wisdom Regarding Work and Being a Neighbor

22 A *good* name *is* rather to be chosen than great riches, *and* loving favour rather than silver and gold.

2 The rich and poor meet together: the LORD *is* the maker of them all.

3 A prudent *man* foreseeth the evil, and hideth himself: but the simple pass on, and are punished.

4 By humility *and* the fear of the LORD *are* riches, and honour, and life.

5 Thorns *and* snares *are* in the way of the froward: he that doth keep his soul
shall be far from them.
6 Train up a child in the way he should go: and when he is old, he will not
depart from it.
7 The rich ruleth over the poor, and the borrower *is* servant to the lender.
8 He that soweth iniquity shall reap vanity: and the rod of his anger shall
fail.
9 He that hath a bountiful eye shall be blessed; for he giveth of his bread to
the poor.
10 Cast out the scorner, and contention shall go out; yea, strife and reproach
shall cease.
11 He that loveth pureness of heart, *for* the grace of his lips the king *shall be*
his friend.
12 The eyes of the LORD preserve knowledge, and he overthroweth the words
of the transgressor.
13 The slothful *man* saith, *There is* a lion without, I shall be slain in the streets.
14 The mouth of strange women *is* a deep pit: he that is abhorred of the LORD
shall fall therein.
15 Foolishness *is* bound in the heart of a child; *but* the rod of correction shall
drive it far from him.
16 He that oppresseth the poor to increase his *riches, and* he that giveth to
the rich, *shall* surely *come* to want.
17 Bow down thine ear, and hear the words of the wise, and apply thine heart
unto my knowledge.
18 For *it is* a pleasant thing if thou keep them within thee; they shall withal
be fitted in thy lips.
19 That thy trust may be in the LORD, I have made known to thee this day,
even to thee.
20 Have not I written to thee excellent things in counsels and knowledge,
21 That I might make thee know the certainty of the words of truth; that
thou mightest answer the words of truth to them that send unto thee?
22 Rob not the poor, because he *is* poor: neither oppress the afflicted in the
gate:
23 For the LORD will plead their cause, and spoil the soul of those that spoiled
them.
24 Make no friendship with an angry man; and with a furious man thou shalt
not go:
25 Lest thou learn his ways, and get a snare to thy soul.
26 Be not thou *one* of them that strike hands, *or* of them that are sureties for
debts.
27 If thou hast nothing to pay, why should he take away thy bed from under
thee?
28 Remove not the ancient landmark, which thy fathers have set.
29 Seest thou a man diligent in his business? he shall stand before kings; he
shall not stand before mean *men*.

Live a Disciplined Life

23 When thou sittest to eat with a ruler, consider diligently what *is* before
thee:
2 And put a knife to thy throat, if thou *be* a man given to appetite.
3 Be not desirous of his dainties: for they *are* deceitful meat.
4 Labour not to be rich: cease from thine own wisdom.
5 Wilt thou set thine eyes upon that which is not? for *riches* certainly make
themselves wings; they fly away as an eagle toward heaven.
6 Eat thou not the bread of *him that hath* an evil eye, neither desire thou his
dainty meats:

7 For as he thinketh in his heart, so *is* he: Eat and drink, saith he to thee; but
his heart *is* not with thee.
8 The morsel *which* thou hast eaten shalt thou vomit up, and lose thy sweet
words.
9 Speak not in the ears of a fool: for he will despise the wisdom of thy words.
10 Remove not the old landmark; and enter not into the fields of the father-
less:
11 For their redeemer *is* mighty; he shall plead their cause with thee.
12 Apply thine heart unto instruction, and thine ears to the words of knowl-
edge.
13 Withhold not correction from the child: for *if* thou beatest him with the
rod, he shall not die.
14 Thou shalt beat him with the rod, and shalt deliver his soul from hell.
15 My son, if thine heart be wise, my heart shall rejoice, even mine.
16 Yea, my reins shall rejoice, when thy lips speak right things.
17 Let not thine heart envy sinners: but *be thou* in the fear of the LORD all the
day long.
18 For surely there is an end; and thine expectation shall not be cut off.
19 Hear thou, my son, and be wise, and guide thine heart in the way.
20 Be not among winebibbers; among riotous eaters of flesh:
21 For the drunkard and the glutton shall come to poverty: and drowsiness
shall clothe *a man* with rags.
22 Hearken unto thy father that begat thee, and despise not thy mother when
she is old.
23 Buy the truth, and sell *it* not; *also* wisdom, and instruction, and under-
standing.
24 The father of the righteous shall greatly rejoice: and he that begetteth a
wise *child* shall have joy of him.
25 Thy father and thy mother shall be glad, and she that bare thee shall
rejoice.
26 My son, give me thine heart, and let thine eyes observe my ways.
27 For a whore *is* a deep ditch; and a strange woman *is* a narrow pit.
28 She also lieth in wait as *for* a prey, and increaseth the transgressors among
men.
29 Who hath woe? who hath sorrow? who hath contentions? who hath bab-
bling? who hath wounds without cause? who hath redness of eyes?
30 They that tarry long at the wine; they that go to seek mixed wine.
31 Look not thou upon the wine when it is red, when it giveth his colour in
the cup, *when* it moveth itself aright.
32 At the last it biteth like a serpent, and stingeth like an adder.
33 Thine eyes shall behold strange women, and thine heart shall utter per-
verse things.
34 Yea, thou shalt be as he that lieth down in the midst of the sea, or as he
that lieth upon the top of a mast.
35 They have stricken me, *shalt thou say, and* I was not sick; they have beat-
en me, *and* I felt *it* not: when shall I awake? I will seek it yet again.

Fear the Lord

24 Be not thou envious against evil men, neither desire to be with them.
2 For their heart studieth destruction, and their lips talk of mischief.
3 Through wisdom is an house builded; and by understanding it is estab-
lished:
4 And by knowledge shall the chambers be filled with all precious and pleas-
ant riches.
5 A wise man *is* strong; yea, a man of knowledge increaseth strength.

6 For by wise counsel thou shalt make thy war: and in multitude of counsellors
there is safety.
7 Wisdom *is* too high for a fool: he openeth not his mouth in the gate.
8 He that deviseth to do evil shall be called a mischievous person.
9 The thought of foolishness *is* sin: and the scorner *is* an abomination to men.
10 *If* thou faint in the day of adversity, thy strength *is* small.
11 If thou forbear to deliver *them that are* drawn unto death, and *those that*
are ready to be slain;
12 If thou sayest, Behold, we knew it not; doth not he that pondereth the heart
consider *it*? and he that keepeth thy soul, doth *not* he know *it*? and shall *not*
he render to *every* man according to his works?
13 My son, eat thou honey, because *it is* good; and the honeycomb, *which is*
sweet to thy taste:
14 So *shall* the knowledge of wisdom *be* unto thy soul: when thou hast found
it, then there shall be a reward, and thy expectation shall not be cut off.
15 Lay not wait, O wicked *man*, against the dwelling of the righteous; spoil
not his resting place:
16 For a just *man* falleth seven times, and riseth up again: but the wicked shall
fall into mischief.
17 Rejoice not when thine enemy falleth, and let not thine heart be glad when
he stumbleth:
18 Lest the LORD see *it*, and it displease him, and he turn away his wrath from
him.
19 Fret not thyself because of evil *men*, neither be thou envious at the wicked;
20 For there shall be no reward to the evil *man*; the candle of the wicked shall
be put out.
21 My son, fear thou the LORD and the king: *and* meddle not with them that
are given to change:
22 For their calamity shall rise suddenly; and who knoweth the ruin of them
both?
23 These *things* also *belong* to the wise. *It is* not good to have respect of persons
in judgment.
24 He that saith unto the wicked, Thou *art* righteous; him shall the people
curse, nations shall abhor him:
25 But to them that rebuke *him* shall be delight, and a good blessing shall
come upon them.
26 *Every man* shall kiss *his* lips that giveth a right answer.
27 Prepare thy work without, and make it fit for thyself in the field; and after-
wards build thine house.
28 Be not a witness against thy neighbour without cause; and deceive *not* with
thy lips.
29 Say not, I will do so to him as he hath done to me: I will render to the man
according to his work.
30 I went by the field of the slothful, and by the vineyard of the man void of
understanding;
31 And, lo, it was all grown over with thorns, *and* nettles had covered the face
thereof, and the stone wall thereof was broken down.
32 Then I saw, *and* considered *it* well: I looked upon *it*, *and* received instruc-
tion.
33 *Yet* a little sleep, a little slumber, a little folding of the hands to sleep:
34 So shall thy poverty come *as* one that travelleth; and thy want as an armed
man.

Advice for Kings

25 These *are* also proverbs of Solomon, which the men of Hezekiah king
of Judah copied out.
2 *It is* the glory of God to conceal a thing: but the honour of kings *is* to search
out a matter.

3 The heaven for height, and the earth for depth, and the heart of kings *is*
unsearchable.
4 Take away the dross from the silver, and there shall come forth a vessel for
the finer.
5 Take away the wicked *from* before the king, and his throne shall be estab-
lished in righteousness.
6 Put not forth thyself in the presence of the king, and stand not in the place
of great *men*:
7 For better *it is* that it be said unto thee, Come up hither; than that thou
shouldest be put lower in the presence of the prince whom thine eyes have
seen.
8 Go not forth hastily to strive, lest *thou know not* what to do in the end
thereof, when thy neighbour hath put thee to shame.
9 Debate thy cause with thy neighbour *himself*; and discover not a secret to
another:
10 Lest he that heareth *it* put thee to shame, and thine infamy turn not away.
11 A word fitly spoken *is like* apples of gold in pictures of silver.
12 *As* an earring of gold, and an ornament of fine gold, *so is* a wise reprover
upon an obedient ear.
13 As the cold of snow in the time of harvest, *so is* a faithful messenger to
them that send him: for he refresheth the soul of his masters.
14 Whoso boasteth himself of a false gift *is like* clouds and wind without
rain.
15 By long forbearing is a prince persuaded, and a soft tongue breaketh the
bone.
16 Hast thou found honey? eat so much as is sufficient for thee, lest thou be
filled therewith, and vomit it.
17 Withdraw thy foot from thy neighbour's house; lest he be weary of thee,
and *so* hate thee.
18 A man that beareth false witness against his neighbour *is* a maul, and a
sword, and a sharp arrow.
19 Confidence in an unfaithful man in time of trouble *is like* a broken tooth,
and a foot out of joint.
20 *As* he that taketh away a garment in cold weather, *and as* vinegar upon
nitre, so *is* he that singeth songs to an heavy heart.
21 If thine enemy be hungry, give him bread to eat; and if he be thirsty, give
him water to drink:
22 For thou shalt heap coals of fire upon his head, and the LORD shall reward
thee.
23 The north wind driveth away rain: so *doth* an angry countenance a back-
biting tongue.
24 *It is* better to dwell in the corner of the housetop, than with a brawling
woman and in a wide house.
25 *As* cold waters to a thirsty soul, so *is* good news from a far country.
26 A righteous man falling down before the wicked *is as* a troubled fountain,
and a corrupt spring.
27 *It is* not good to eat much honey: so *for men* to search their own glory *is*
not glory.
28 He that *hath* no rule over his own spirit *is like* a city *that is* broken down,
and without walls.

Observations about Fools

26 As snow in summer, and as rain in harvest, so honour is not seemly
for a fool.
2 As the bird by wandering, as the swallow by flying, so the curse causeless
shall not come.

3 A whip for the horse, a bridle for the ass, and a rod for the fool's back.
4 Answer not a fool according to his folly, lest thou also be like unto him.
5 Answer a fool according to his folly, lest he be wise in his own conceit.
6 He that sendeth a message by the hand of a fool cutteth off the feet, *and*
drinketh damage.
7 The legs of the lame are not equal: so *is* a parable in the mouth of fools.
8 As he that bindeth a stone in a sling, so *is* he that giveth honour to a fool.
9 *As* a thorn goeth up into the hand of a drunkard, so *is* a parable in the
mouth of fools.
10 The great *God* that formed all *things* both rewardeth the fool, and
rewardeth transgressors.
11 As a dog returneth to his vomit, *so* a fool returneth to his folly.
12 Seest thou a man wise in his own conceit? *there is* more hope of a fool
than of him.
13 The slothful *man* saith, *There is* a lion in the way; a lion *is* in the streets.
14 *As* the door turneth upon his hinges, so *doth* the slothful upon his bed.
15 The slothful hideth his hand in *his* bosom; it grieveth him to bring it again
to his mouth.
16 The sluggard *is* wiser in his own conceit than seven men that can render
a reason.
17 He that passeth by, *and* meddleth with strife *belonging* not to him, *is like*
one that taketh a dog by the ears.
18 As a mad *man* who casteth firebrands, arrows, and death,
19 So *is* the man *that* deceiveth his neighbour, and saith, Am not I in sport?
20 Where no wood is, *there* the fire goeth out: so where *there is* no talebearer,
the strife ceaseth.
21 *As* coals *are* to burning coals, and wood to fire; so *is* a contentious man to
kindle strife.
22 The words of a talebearer *are* as wounds, and they go down into the inner-
most parts of the belly.
23 Burning lips and a wicked heart *are like* a potsherd covered with silver
dross.
24 He that hateth dissembleth with his lips, and layeth up deceit within him;
25 When he speaketh fair, believe him not: for *there are* seven abominations
in his heart.
26 *Whose* hatred is covered by deceit, his wickedness shall be shewed before
the *whole* congregation.
27 Whoso diggeth a pit shall fall therein: and he that rolleth a stone, it will
return upon him.
28 A lying tongue hateth *those that are* afflicted by it; and a flattering mouth
worketh ruin.

Observations about Life

27 Boast not thyself of to morrow; for thou knowest not what a day may
bring forth.
2 Let another man praise thee, and not thine own mouth; a stranger, and
not thine own lips.
3 A stone *is* heavy, and the sand weighty; but a fool's wrath *is* heavier than
them both.
4 Wrath *is* cruel, and anger *is* outrageous; but who *is* able to stand before
envy?
5 Open rebuke *is* better than secret love.
6 Faithful *are* the wounds of a friend; but the kisses of an enemy *are* deceit-
ful.
7 The full soul loatheth an honeycomb; but to the hungry soul every bitter
thing is sweet.

8 As a bird that wandereth from her nest, so *is* a man that wandereth from
his place.
9 Ointment and perfume rejoice the heart: so *doth* the sweetness of a man's
friend by hearty counsel.
10 Thine own friend, and thy father's friend, forsake not; neither go into thy
brother's house in the day of thy calamity: *for* better *is* a neighbour *that is*
near than a brother far off.
11 My son, be wise, and make my heart glad, that I may answer him that
reproacheth me.
12 A prudent *man* foreseeth the evil, *and* hideth himself; *but* the simple pass
on, *and* are punished.
13 Take his garment that is surety for a stranger, and take a pledge of him for
a strange woman.
14 He that blesseth his friend with a loud voice, rising early in the morning,
it shall be counted a curse to him.
15 A continual dropping in a very rainy day and a contentious woman are
alike.
16 Whosoever hideth her hideth the wind, and the ointment of his right
hand, *which* bewrayeth *itself.*
17 Iron sharpeneth iron; so a man sharpeneth the countenance of his friend.
18 Whoso keepeth the fig tree shall eat the fruit thereof: so he that waiteth
on his master shall be honoured.
19 As in water face *answereth* to face, so the heart of man to man.
20 Hell and destruction are never full; so the eyes of man are never satisfied.
21 *As* the fining pot for silver, and the furnace for gold; so *is* a man to his
praise.
22 Though thou shouldest bray a fool in a mortar among wheat with a pestle,
yet will not his foolishness depart from him.
23 Be thou diligent to know the state of thy flocks, *and* look well to thy herds.
24 For riches *are* not for ever: and doth the crown *endure* to every generation?
25 The hay appeareth, and the tender grass sheweth itself, and herbs of the
mountains are gathered.
26 The lambs *are* for thy clothing, and the goats *are* the price of the field.
27 And *thou shalt have* goats' milk enough for thy food, for the food of thy
household, and *for* the maintenance for thy maidens.

Observations on Impiety and Religious Integrity

28 The wicked flee when no man pursueth: but the righteous are bold as
a lion.
2 For the transgression of a land many *are* the princes thereof: but by a man
of understanding *and* knowledge the state *thereof* shall be prolonged.
3 A poor man that oppresseth the poor *is like* a sweeping rain which leaveth
no food.
4 They that forsake the law praise the wicked: but such as keep the law con-
tend with them.
5 Evil men understand not judgment: but they that seek the LORD understand
all *things.*
6 Better *is* the poor that walketh in his uprightness, than *he that is* perverse
in his ways, though he *be* rich.
7 Whoso keepeth the law *is* a wise son: but he that is a companion of riotous
men shameth his father.
8 He that by usury and unjust gain increaseth his substance, he shall gather
it for him that will pity the poor.
9 He that turneth away his ear from hearing the law, even his prayer *shall be*
abomination.

10 Whoso causeth the righteous to go astray in an evil way, he shall fall him-
self into his own pit: but the upright shall have good *things* in possession.
11 The rich man *is* wise in his own conceit; but the poor that hath under-
standing searcheth him out.
12 When righteous *men* do rejoice, *there is* great glory: but when the wicked
rise, a man is hidden.
13 He that covereth his sins shall not prosper: but whoso confesseth and
forsaketh *them* shall have mercy.
14 Happy *is* the man that feareth alway: but he that hardeneth his heart shall
fall into mischief.
15 *As* a roaring lion, and a ranging bear; *so is* a wicked ruler over the poor
people.
16 The prince that wanteth understanding *is* also a great oppressor: *but* he
that hateth covetousness shall prolong *his* days.
17 A man that doeth violence to the blood of *any* person shall flee to the pit;
let no man stay him.
18 Whoso walketh uprightly shall be saved: but *he that is* perverse *in his* ways
shall fall at once.

Observations on Wealth and Poverty

19 He that tilleth his land shall have plenty of bread: but he that followeth
after vain *persons* shall have poverty enough.
20 A faithful man shall abound with blessings: but he that maketh haste to
be rich shall not be innocent.
21 To have respect of persons *is* not good: for for a piece of bread *that* man
will transgress.
22 He that hasteth to be rich *hath* an evil eye, and considereth not that pov-
erty shall come upon him.
23 He that rebuketh a man afterwards shall find more favour than he that
flattereth with the tongue.
24 Whoso robbeth his father or his mother, and saith, *It is* no transgression;
the same *is* the companion of a destroyer.
25 He that is of a proud heart stirreth up strife: but he that putteth his trust
in the LORD shall be made fat.
26 He that trusteth in his own heart is a fool: but whoso walketh wisely, he
shall be delivered.
27 He that giveth unto the poor shall not lack: but he that hideth his eyes
shall have many a curse.
28 When the wicked rise, men hide themselves: but when they perish, the
righteous increase.

Observations on Living in Community

29 He, that being often reproved hardeneth *his* neck, shall suddenly be
destroyed, and that without remedy.
2 When the righteous are in authority, the people rejoice: but when the wick-
ed beareth rule, the people mourn.
3 Whoso loveth wisdom rejoiceth his father: but he that keepeth company
with harlots spendeth *his* substance.
4 The king by judgment establisheth the land: but he that receiveth gifts
overthroweth it.
5 A man that flattereth his neighbour spreadeth a net for his feet.
6 In the transgression of an evil man *there is* a snare: but the righteous doth
sing and rejoice.
7 The righteous considereth the cause of the poor: *but* the wicked regardeth
not to know *it*.
8 Scornful men bring a city into a snare: but wise *men* turn away wrath.

9 *If* a wise man contendeth with a foolish man, whether he rage or laugh,
there is no rest.
10 The bloodthirsty hate the upright: but the just seek his soul.
11 A fool uttereth all his mind: but a wise *man* keepeth it in till afterwards.
12 If a ruler hearken to lies, all his servants *are* wicked.
13 The poor and the deceitful man meet together: the LORD lighteneth both
their eyes.
14 The king that faithfully judgeth the poor, his throne shall be established
for ever.
15 The rod and reproof give wisdom: but a child left *to himself* bringeth his
mother to shame.
16 When the wicked are multiplied, transgression increaseth: but the righ-
teous shall see their fall.
17 Correct thy son, and he shall give thee rest; yea, he shall give delight unto
thy soul.
18 Where *there is* no vision, the people perish: but he that keepeth the law,
happy *is* he.
19 A servant will not be corrected by words: for though he understand he
will not answer.
20 Seest thou a man *that is* hasty in his words? *there is* more hope of a fool
than of him.
21 He that delicately bringeth up his servant from a child shall have him
become *his* son at the length.
22 An angry man stirreth up strife, and a furious man aboundeth in trans-
gression.
23 A man's pride shall bring him low: but honour shall uphold the humble
in spirit.
24 Whoso is partner with a thief hateth his own soul: he heareth cursing,
and bewrayeth *it* not.
25 The fear of man bringeth a snare: but whoso putteth his trust in the LORD
shall be safe.
26 Many seek the ruler's favour; but *every* man's judgment *cometh* from the
LORD.
27 An unjust man *is* an abomination to the just: and *he that is* upright in the
way *is* abomination to the wicked.

Agur's Confession of Faith

30 The words of Agur the son of Jakeh, *even* the prophecy: the man spake
unto Ithiel, even unto Ithiel and Ucal,
2 Surely I *am* more brutish than *any* man, and have not the understanding
of a man.
3 I neither learned wisdom, nor have the knowledge of the holy.
4 Who hath ascended up into heaven, or descended? who hath gathered the
wind in his fists? who hath bound the waters in a garment? who hath estab-
lished all the ends of the earth? what *is* his name, and what *is* his son's name,
if thou canst tell?
5 Every word of God *is* pure: he *is* a shield unto them that put their trust in
him.
6 Add thou not unto his words, lest he reprove thee, and thou be found a liar.
7 Two *things* have I required of thee; deny me *them* not before I die:
8 Remove far from me vanity and lies: give me neither poverty nor riches;
feed me with food convenient for me:
9 Lest I be full, and deny *thee*, and say, Who *is* the LORD? or lest I be poor, and
steal, and take the name of my God *in vain*.
10 Accuse not a servant unto his master, lest he curse thee, and thou be found
guilty.

11 *There is* a generation *that* curseth their father, and doth not bless their
mother.
12 *There is* a generation *that are* pure in their own eyes, and *yet* is not washed
from their filthiness.
13 *There is* a generation, O how lofty are their eyes! and their eyelids are
lifted up.
14 *There is* a generation, whose teeth *are as* swords, and their jaw teeth *as*
knives, to devour the poor from off the earth, and the needy from *among* men.
15 The horseleach hath two daughters, *crying*, Give, give. There are three
things that are never satisfied, *yea*, four *things* say not, *It is* enough:
16 The grave; and the barren womb; the earth *that* is not filled with water;
and the fire *that* saith not, *It is* enough.
17 The eye *that* mocketh at *his* father, and despiseth to obey *his* mother, the
ravens of the valley shall pick it out, and the young eagles shall eat it.
18 There be three *things which* are too wonderful for me, yea, four which I
know not:
19 The way of an eagle in the air; the way of a serpent upon a rock; the way
of a ship in the midst of the sea; and the way of a man with a maid.
20 Such *is* the way of an adulterous woman; she eateth, and wipeth her
mouth, and saith, I have done no wickedness.
21 For three *things* the earth is disquieted, and for four *which* it cannot bear:
22 For a servant when he reigneth; and a fool when he is filled with meat;
23 For an odious *woman* when she is married; and an handmaid that is heir
to her mistress.
24 There be four *things which are* little upon the earth, but they *are* exceed-
ing wise:
25 The ants *are* a people not strong, yet they prepare their meat in the summer;
26 The conies *are but* a feeble folk, yet make they their houses in the rocks;
27 The locusts have no king, yet go they forth all of them by bands;
28 The spider taketh hold with her hands, and is in kings' palaces.
29 There be three *things* which go well, yea, four are comely in going:
30 A lion *which is* strongest among beasts, and turneth not away for any;
31 A greyhound; an he goat also; and a king, against whom *there is* no rising up.
32 If thou hast done foolishly in lifting up thyself, or if thou hast thought
evil, *lay* thine hand upon thy mouth.
33 Surely the churning of milk bringeth forth butter, and the wringing of
the nose bringeth forth blood: so the forcing of wrath bringeth forth strife.

Lemuel's Lesson

31 The words of king Lemuel, the prophecy that his mother taught him.
2 What, my son? and what, the son of my womb? and what, the son
of my vows?
3 Give not thy strength unto women, nor thy ways to that which destroyeth
kings.
4 *It is* not for kings, O Lemuel, *it is* not for kings to drink wine; nor for princ-
es strong drink:
5 Lest they drink, and forget the law, and pervert the judgment of any of the
afflicted.
6 Give strong drink unto him that is ready to perish, and wine unto those
that be of heavy hearts.
7 Let him drink, and forget his poverty, and remember his misery no more.
8 Open thy mouth for the dumb in the cause of all such as are appointed to
destruction.
9 Open thy mouth, judge righteously, and plead the cause of the poor and
needy.

Praise for a Good Wife

10 Who can find a virtuous woman? for her price *is* far above rubies.
11 The heart of her husband doth safely trust in her, so that he shall have no
need of spoil.
12 She will do him good and not evil all the days of her life.
13 She seeketh wool, and flax, and worketh willingly with her hands.
14 She is like the merchants' ships; she bringeth her food from afar.
15 She riseth also while it is yet night, and giveth meat to her household, and
a portion to her maidens.
16 She considereth a field, and buyeth it: with the fruit of her hands she
planteth a vineyard.
17 She girdeth her loins with strength, and strengtheneth her arms.
18 She perceiveth that her merchandise *is* good: her candle goeth not out by
night.
19 She layeth her hands to the spindle, and her hands hold the distaff.
20 She stretcheth out her hand to the poor; yea, she reacheth forth her hands
to the needy.
21 She is not afraid of the snow for her household: for all her household *are*
clothed with scarlet.
22 She maketh herself coverings of tapestry; her clothing *is* silk and purple.
23 Her husband is known in the gates, when he sitteth among the elders of
the land.
24 She maketh fine linen, and selleth *it*; and delivereth girdles unto the mer-
chant.
25 Strength and honour *are* her clothing; and she shall rejoice in time to
come.
26 She openeth her mouth with wisdom; and in her tongue *is* the law of
kindness.
27 She looketh well to the ways of her household, and eateth not the bread
of idleness.
28 Her children arise up, and call her blessed; her husband *also*, and he
praiseth her.
29 Many daughters have done virtuously, but thou excellest them all.
30 Favour *is* deceitful, and beauty *is* vain: *but* a woman *that* feareth the LORD,
she shall be praised.
31 Give her of the fruit of her hands; and let her own works praise her in the
gates.

ECCLESIASTES

The Preacher Speaks of Vanity

1 The words of the Preacher, the son of David, king in Jerusalem.
2 Vanity of vanities, saith the Preacher, vanity of vanities; all *is* vanity.
3 What profit hath a man of all his labour which he taketh under the sun?

Life Is an Endless Circle

4 *One* generation passeth away, and *another* generation cometh: but the
earth abideth for ever.
5 The sun also ariseth, and the sun goeth down, and hasteth to his place where
he arose.
6 The wind goeth toward the south, and turneth about unto the north; it
whirleth about continually, and the wind returneth again according to his
circuits.
7 All the rivers run into the sea; yet the sea *is* not full; unto the place from
whence the rivers come, thither they return again.
8 All things *are* full of labour; man cannot utter *it*: the eye is not satisfied
with seeing, nor the ear filled with hearing.

Nothing New under the Sun

9 The thing that hath been, it *is that* which shall be; and that which is done
is that which shall be done: and *there is* no new *thing* under the sun.
10 Is there *any* thing whereof it may be said, See, this *is* new? it hath been
already of old time, which was before us.
11 *There is* no remembrance of former *things*; neither shall there be *any*
remembrance of *things* that are to come with *those* that shall come after.

The Preacher Undertakes His Study

12 I the Preacher was king over Israel in Jerusalem.
13 And I gave my heart to seek and search out by wisdom concerning all
things that are done under heaven: this sore travail hath God given to the sons
of man to be exercised therewith.
14 I have seen all the works that are done under the sun; and, behold, all *is*
vanity and vexation of spirit.
15 *That which is* crooked cannot be made straight: and that which is wanting
cannot be numbered.
16 I communed with mine own heart, saying, Lo, I am come to great estate,
and have gotten more wisdom than all *they* that have been before me in
Jerusalem: yea, my heart had great experience of wisdom and knowledge.
17 And I gave my heart to know wisdom, and to know madness and folly: I
perceived that this also is vexation of spirit.
18 For in much wisdom *is* much grief: and he that increaseth knowledge
increaseth sorrow.

The Vanity of Pleasure and Achievement

2 I said in mine heart, Go to now, I will prove thee with mirth, therefore enjoy
pleasure: and, behold, this also *is* vanity.
2 I said of laughter, *It is* mad: and of mirth, What doeth it?
3 I sought in mine heart to give myself unto wine, yet acquainting mine heart
with wisdom; and to lay hold on folly, till I might see what *was* that good for
the sons of men, which they should do under the heaven all the days of their
life.

4 I made me great works; I builded me houses; I planted me vineyards:

5 I made me gardens and orchards, and I planted trees in them of all *kind of* fruits:

6 I made me pools of water, to water therewith the wood that bringeth forth trees:

7 I got *me* servants and maidens, and had servants born in my house; also I had great possessions of great and small cattle above all that were in Jerusalem before me:

8 I gathered me also silver and gold, and the peculiar treasure of kings and of the provinces: I gat me men singers and women singers, and the delights of the sons of men, *as* musical instruments, and that of all sorts.

9 So I was great, and increased more than all that were before me in Jerusalem: also my wisdom remained with me.

10 And whatsoever mine eyes desired I kept not from them, I withheld not my heart from any joy; for my heart rejoiced in all my labour: and this was my portion of all my labour.

11 Then I looked on all the works that my hands had wrought, and on the labour that I had laboured to do: and, behold, all *was* vanity and vexation of spirit, and *there was* no profit under the sun.

Without God Everything Is Pointless

12 And I turned myself to behold wisdom, and madness, and folly: for what *can* the man *do* that cometh after the king? *even* that which hath been already done.

13 Then I saw that wisdom excelleth folly, as far as light excelleth darkness.

14 The wise man's eyes *are* in his head; but the fool walketh in darkness: and I myself perceived also that one event happeneth to them all.

15 Then said I in my heart, As it happeneth to the fool, so it happeneth even to me; and why was I then more wise? Then I said in my heart, that this also *is* vanity.

16 For *there is* no remembrance of the wise more than of the fool for ever; seeing that which now *is* in the days to come shall all be forgotten. And how dieth the wise *man*? as the fool.

17 Therefore I hated life; because the work that is wrought under the sun *is* grievous unto me: for all *is* vanity and vexation of spirit.

18 Yea, I hated all my labour which I had taken under the sun: because I should leave it unto the man that shall be after me.

19 And who knoweth whether he shall be a wise *man* or a fool? yet shall he have rule over all my labour wherein I have laboured, and wherein I have shewed myself wise under the sun. This *is* also vanity.

20 Therefore I went about to cause my heart to despair of all the labour which I took under the sun.

21 For there is a man whose labour *is* in wisdom, and in knowledge, and in equity; yet to a man that hath not laboured therein shall he leave it *for* his portion. This also *is* vanity and a great evil.

22 For what hath man of all his labour, and of the vexation of his heart, wherein he hath laboured under the sun?

23 For all his days *are* sorrows, and his travail grief; yea, his heart taketh not rest in the night. This is also vanity.

24 *There is* nothing better for a man, *than* that he should eat and drink, and *that* he should make his soul enjoy good in his labour. This also I saw, that it *was* from the hand of God.

25 For who can eat, or who else can hasten *hereunto*, more than I?

26 For *God* giveth to a man that *is* good in his sight wisdom, and knowledge, and joy: but to the sinner he giveth travail, to gather and to heap up, that he

may give to *him that is* good before God. This also *is* vanity and vexation of
spirit.

Everything in God's Own Time

3 To every *thing there is* a season, and a time to every purpose under the
heaven:
2 A time to be born, and a time to die; a time to plant, and a time to pluck up
that which is planted;
3 A time to kill, and a time to heal; a time to break down, and a time to build
up;
4 A time to weep, and a time to laugh; a time to mourn, and a time to dance;
5 A time to cast away stones, and a time to gather stones together; a time to
embrace, and a time to refrain from embracing;
6 A time to get, and a time to lose; a time to keep, and a time to cast away;
7 A time to rend, and a time to sew; a time to keep silence, and a time to speak;
8 A time to love, and a time to hate; a time of war, and a time of peace.
9 What profit hath he that worketh in that wherein he laboureth?
10 I have seen the travail, which God hath given to the sons of men to be
exercised in it.

The Excellency of God's Works

11 He hath made every *thing* beautiful in his time: also he hath set the world
in their heart, so that no man can find out the work that God maketh from
the beginning to the end.
12 I know that *there is* no good in them, but for *a man* to rejoice, and to do
good in his life.
13 And also that every man should eat and drink, and enjoy the good of all
his labour, it *is* the gift of God.
14 I know that, whatsoever God doeth, it shall be for ever: nothing can be
put to it, nor any thing taken from it: and God doeth *it*, that *men* should fear
before him.
15 That which hath been is now; and that which is to be hath already been;
and God requireth that which is past.

All Living Things Meet the Same End

16 And moreover I saw under the sun the place of judgment, *that* wickedness
was there; and the place of righteousness, *that* iniquity *was* there.
17 I said in mine heart, God shall judge the righteous and the wicked: for
there is a time there for every purpose and for every work.
18 I said in mine heart concerning the estate of the sons of men, that God
might manifest them, and that they might see that they themselves are beasts.
19 For that which befalleth the sons of men befalleth beasts; even one thing
befalleth them: as the one dieth, so dieth the other; yea, they have all one
breath; so that a man hath no preeminence above a beast: for all *is* vanity.
20 All go unto one place; all are of the dust, and all turn to dust again.
21 Who knoweth the spirit of man that goeth upward, and the spirit of the
beast that goeth downward to the earth?
22 Wherefore I perceive that *there is* nothing better, than that a man should
rejoice in his own works; for that *is* his portion: for who shall bring him to see
what shall be after him?

Acts of Oppression

4 So I returned, and considered all the oppressions that are done under the
sun: and behold the tears of *such as were* oppressed, and they had no com-
forter; and on the side of their oppressors *there was* power; but they had no
comforter.
2 Wherefore I praised the dead which are already dead more than the living
which are yet alive.

3 Yea, better *is he* than both they, which hath not yet been, who hath not seen
the evil work that is done under the sun.

Hard Work Versus Laziness

4 Again, I considered all travail, and every right work, that for this a man is
envied of his neighbour. This *is* also vanity and vexation of spirit.
5 The fool foldeth his hands together, and eateth his own flesh.
6 Better *is* an handful *with* quietness, than both the hands full *with* travail
and vexation of spirit.

Two Are Better Than One

7 Then I returned, and I saw vanity under the sun.
8 There is one *alone*, and *there is* not a second; yea, he hath neither child nor
brother: yet *is there* no end of all his labour; neither is his eye satisfied with
riches; neither *saith he*, For whom do I labour, and bereave my soul of good?
This *is* also vanity, yea, it *is* a sore travail.
9 Two *are* better than one; because they have a good reward for their labour.
10 For if they fall, the one will lift up his fellow: but woe to him *that is* alone
when he falleth; for *he hath* not another to help him up.
11 Again, if two lie together, then they have heat: but how can one be warm
alone?
12 And if one prevail against him, two shall withstand him; and a threefold
cord is not quickly broken.

Rulers and Fickle Citizens

13 Better *is* a poor and a wise child than an old and foolish king, who will no
more be admonished.
14 For out of prison he cometh to reign; whereas also *he that is* born in his
kingdom becometh poor.
15 I considered all the living which walk under the sun, with the second child
that shall stand up in his stead.
16 *There is* no end of all the people, *even* of all that have been before them:
they also that come after shall not rejoice in him. Surely this also *is* vanity and
vexation of spirit.

Vanities in Worship

5 Keep thy foot when thou goest to the house of God, and be more ready to
hear, than to give the sacrifice of fools: for they consider not that they do
evil.
2 Be not rash with thy mouth, and let not thine heart be hasty to utter *any*
thing before God: for God *is* in heaven, and thou upon earth: therefore let thy
words be few.
3 For a dream cometh through the multitude of business; and a fool's voice
is known by multitude of words.
4 When thou vowest a vow unto God, defer not to pay it; for *he hath* no
pleasure in fools: pay that which thou hast vowed.
5 Better *is it* that thou shouldest not vow, than that thou shouldest vow and
not pay.
6 Suffer not thy mouth to cause thy flesh to sin; neither say thou before the
angel, that it *was* an error: wherefore should God be angry at thy voice, and
destroy the work of thine hands?
7 For in the multitude of dreams and many words *there are* also *divers* van-
ities: but fear thou God.
8 If thou seest the oppression of the poor, and violent perverting of judgment
and justice in a province, marvel not at the matter: for *he that is* higher than
the highest regardeth; and *there be* higher than they.

Vanities in Riches

9 Moreover the profit of the earth is for all: the king *himself* is served by the
field.

10 He that loveth silver shall not be satisfied with silver; nor he that loveth
abundance with increase: this *is* also vanity.
11 When goods increase, they are increased that eat them: and what good *is*
there to the owners thereof, saving the beholding *of them* with their eyes?
12 The sleep of a labouring man *is* sweet, whether he eat little or much: but
the abundance of the rich will not suffer him to sleep.
13 There is a sore evil *which* I have seen under the sun, *namely*, riches kept
for the owners thereof to their hurt.
14 But those riches perish by evil travail: and he begetteth a son, and *there is*
nothing in his hand.
15 As he came forth of his mother's womb, naked shall he return to go as he
came, and shall take nothing of his labour, which he may carry away in his
hand.
16 And this also *is* a sore evil, *that* in all points as he came, so shall he go: and
what profit hath he that hath laboured for the wind?
17 All his days also he eateth in darkness, and *he hath* much sorrow and wrath
with his sickness.

God Alone Gives Contentment

18 Behold *that* which I have seen: *it is* good and comely *for one* to eat and to
drink, and to enjoy the good of all his labour that he taketh under the sun all
the days of his life, which God giveth him: for it *is* his portion.
19 Every man also to whom God hath given riches and wealth, and hath given
him power to eat thereof, and to take his portion, and to rejoice in his labour;
this *is* the gift of God.
20 For he shall not much remember the days of his life; because God answer-
eth *him* in the joy of his heart.

The Vanity of Riches without Use

6 There is an evil which I have seen under the sun, and it *is* common among
men:
2 A man to whom God hath given riches, wealth, and honour, so that he
wanteth nothing for his soul of all that he desireth, yet God giveth him not
power to eat thereof, but a stranger eateth it: this *is* vanity, and it *is* an evil
disease.
3 If a man beget an hundred *children*, and live many years, so that the days
of his years be many, and his soul be not filled with good, and also *that* he have
no burial; I say, *that* an untimely birth *is* better than he.
4 For he cometh in with vanity, and departeth in darkness, and his name
shall be covered with darkness.
5 Moreover he hath not seen the sun, nor known *any thing*: this hath more
rest than the other.
6 Yea, though he live a thousand years twice *told*, yet hath he seen no good:
do not all go to one place?
7 All the labour of man *is* for his mouth, and yet the appetite is not filled.
8 For what hath the wise more than the fool? what hath the poor, that
knoweth to walk before the living?
9 Better *is* the sight of the eyes than the wandering of the desire: this *is* also
vanity and vexation of spirit.
10 That which hath been is named already, and it is known that it *is* man:
neither may he contend with him that is mightier than he.

The Conclusion of Vanities

11 Seeing there be many things that increase vanity, what *is* man the better?
12 For who knoweth what *is* good for man in *this* life, all the days of his vain
life which he spendeth as a shadow? for who can tell a man what shall be after
him under the sun?

Remedies against Vanity

7 A good name *is* better than precious ointment; and the day of death than the day of one's birth.

2 *It is* better to go to the house of mourning, than to go to the house of feasting: for that *is* the end of all men; and the living will lay *it* to his heart.

3 Sorrow *is* better than laughter: for by the sadness of the countenance the heart is made better.

4 The heart of the wise *is* in the house of mourning; but the heart of fools *is* in the house of mirth.

5 *It is* better to hear the rebuke of the wise, than for a man to hear the song of fools.

6 For as the crackling of thorns under a pot, so *is* the laughter of the fool: this also *is* vanity.

7 Surely oppression maketh a wise man mad; and a gift destroyeth the heart.

8 Better *is* the end of a thing than the beginning thereof: *and* the patient in spirit *is* better than the proud in spirit.

9 Be not hasty in thy spirit to be angry: for anger resteth in the bosom of fools.

10 Say not thou, What is *the cause* that the former days were better than these? for thou dost not enquire wisely concerning this.

11 Wisdom *is* good with an inheritance: and *by it there is* profit to them that see the sun.

12 For wisdom *is* a defence, *and* money *is* a defence: but the excellency of knowledge *is, that* wisdom giveth life to them that have it.

13 Consider the work of God: for who can make *that* straight, which he hath made crooked?

14 In the day of prosperity be joyful, but in the day of adversity consider: God also hath set the one over against the other, to the end that man should find nothing after him.

15 All *things* have I seen in the days of my vanity: there is a just *man* that perisheth in his righteousness, and there is a wicked *man* that prolongeth *his life* in his wickedness.

16 Be not righteous over much; neither make thyself over wise: why shouldest thou destroy thyself?

17 Be not over much wicked, neither be thou foolish: why shouldest thou die before thy time?

18 *It is* good that thou shouldest take hold of this; yea, also from this withdraw not thine hand: for he that feareth God shall come forth of them all.

19 Wisdom strengtheneth the wise more than ten mighty *men* which are in the city.

20 For *there is* not a just man upon earth, that doeth good, and sinneth not.

21 Also take no heed unto all words that are spoken; lest thou hear thy servant curse thee:

22 For oftentimes also thine own heart knoweth that thou thyself likewise hast cursed others.

The Advantages of Wisdom

23 All this have I proved by wisdom: I said, I will be wise; but it *was* far from me.

24 That which is far off, and exceeding deep, who can find it out?

25 I applied mine heart to know, and to search, and to seek out wisdom, and the reason *of things*, and to know the wickedness of folly, even of foolishness *and* madness:

26 And I find more bitter than death the woman, whose heart *is* snares and nets, *and* her hands *as* bands: whoso pleaseth God shall escape from her; but the sinner shall be taken by her.

27 Behold, this have I found, saith the preacher, *counting* one by one, to find
out the account:
28 Which yet my soul seeketh, but I find not: one man among a thousand
have I found; but a woman among all those have I not found.
29 Lo, this only have I found, that God hath made man upright; but they have
sought out many inventions.

Enjoy Life

8 Who *is* as the wise *man*? and who knoweth the interpretation of a thing?
a man's wisdom maketh his face to shine, and the boldness of his face shall
be changed.
2 I *counsel thee* to keep the king's commandment, and *that* in regard of the
oath of God.
3 Be not hasty to go out of his sight: stand not in an evil thing; for he doeth
whatsoever pleaseth him.
4 Where the word of a king *is, there is* power: and who may say unto him,
What doest thou?
5 Whoso keepeth the commandment shall feel no evil thing: and a wise man's
heart discerneth both time and judgment.
6 Because to every purpose there is time and judgment, therefore the misery
of man *is* great upon him.
7 For he knoweth not that which shall be: for who can tell him when it shall be?
8 *There is* no man that hath power over the spirit to retain the spirit; neither
hath he power in the day of death: and *there is* no discharge in *that* war; nei-
ther shall wickedness deliver those that are given to it.
9 All this have I seen, and applied my heart unto every work that is done
under the sun: *there is* a time wherein one man ruleth over another to his own
hurt.
10 And so I saw the wicked buried, who had come and gone from the place
of the holy, and they were forgotten in the city where they had so done: this *is*
also vanity.
11 Because sentence against an evil work is not executed speedily, therefore
the heart of the sons of men is fully set in them to do evil.
12 Though a sinner do evil an hundred times, and his *days* be prolonged, yet
surely I know that it shall be well with them that fear God, which fear before
him:
13 But it shall not be well with the wicked, neither shall he prolong *his* days,
which are as a shadow; because he feareth not before God.
14 There is a vanity which is done upon the earth; that there be just *men*,
unto whom it happeneth according to the work of the wicked; again, there be
wicked *men*, to whom it happeneth according to the work of the righteous: I
said that this also *is* vanity.
15 Then I commended mirth, because a man hath no better thing under the
sun, than to eat, and to drink, and to be merry: for that shall abide with him
of his labour the days of his life, which God giveth him under the sun.
16 When I applied mine heart to know wisdom, and to see the business that
is done upon the earth: (for also *there is that* neither day nor night seeth sleep
with his eyes:)
17 Then I beheld all the work of God, that a man cannot find out the work
that is done under the sun: because though a man labour to seek *it* out, yet he
shall not find *it*; yea further; though a wise *man* think to know *it*, yet shall he
not be able to find *it*.

Everything Is in God's Hands

9 For all this I considered in my heart even to declare all this, that the righ-
teous, and the wise, and their works, *are* in the hand of God: no man
knoweth either love or hatred *by* all *that is* before them.

2 All *things come* alike to all: *there is* one event to the righteous, and to the wicked; to the good and to the clean, and to the unclean; to him that sacrificeth, and to him that sacrificeth not: as *is* the good, so *is* the sinner; *and* he that sweareth, as *he* that feareth an oath.

3 This *is* an evil among all *things* that are done under the sun, that *there is* one event unto all: yea, also the heart of the sons of men is full of evil, and madness *is* in their heart while they live, and after that *they go* to the dead.

4 For to him that is joined to all the living there is hope: for a living dog is better than a dead lion.

5 For the living know that they shall die: but the dead know not any thing, neither have they any more a reward; for the memory of them is forgotten.

6 Also their love, and their hatred, and their envy, is now perished; neither have they any more a portion for ever in any *thing* that is done under the sun.

7 Go thy way, eat thy bread with joy, and drink thy wine with a merry heart; for God now accepteth thy works.

8 Let thy garments be always white; and let thy head lack no ointment.

9 Live joyfully with the wife whom thou lovest all the days of the life of thy vanity, which he hath given thee under the sun, all the days of thy vanity: for that *is* thy portion in *this* life, and in thy labour which thou takest under the sun.

10 Whatsoever thy hand findeth to do, do *it* with thy might; for *there is* no work, nor device, nor knowledge, nor wisdom, in the grave, whither thou goest.

11 I returned, and saw under the sun, that the race *is* not to the swift, nor the battle to the strong, neither yet bread to the wise, nor yet riches to men of understanding, nor yet favour to men of skill; but time and chance happeneth to them all.

12 For man also knoweth not his time: as the fishes that are taken in an evil net, and as the birds that are caught in the snare; so *are* the sons of men snared in an evil time, when it falleth suddenly upon them.

13 This wisdom have I seen also under the sun, and it *seemed* great unto me:

14 *There was* a little city, and few men within it; and there came a great king against it, and besieged it, and built great bulwarks against it:

15 Now there was found in it a poor wise man, and he by his wisdom delivered the city; yet no man remembered that same poor man.

16 Then said I, Wisdom *is* better than strength: nevertheless the poor man's wisdom *is* despised, and his words are not heard.

17 The words of wise *men are* heard in quiet more than the cry of him that ruleth among fools.

18 Wisdom *is* better than weapons of war: but one sinner destroyeth much good.

Observations of Wisdom and Folly

10 Dead flies cause the ointment of the apothecary to send forth a stinking savour: *so doth* a little folly him that is in reputation for wisdom *and* honour.

2 A wise man's heart *is* at his right hand; but a fool's heart at his left.

3 Yea also, when he that is a fool walketh by the way, his wisdom faileth *him*, and he saith to every one *that* he *is* a fool.

4 If the spirit of the ruler rise up against thee, leave not thy place; for yielding pacifieth great offences.

5 There is an evil *which* I have seen under the sun, as an error *which* proceedeth from the ruler:

6 Folly is set in great dignity, and the rich sit in low place.

7 I have seen servants upon horses, and princes walking as servants upon the earth.

8 He that diggeth a pit shall fall into it; and whoso breaketh an hedge, a
serpent shall bite him.
9 Whoso removeth stones shall be hurt therewith; *and* he that cleaveth wood
shall be endangered thereby.
10 If the iron be blunt, and he do not whet the edge, then must he put to
more strength: but wisdom *is* profitable to direct.
11 Surely the serpent will bite without enchantment; and a babbler is no
better.
12 The words of a wise man's mouth *are* gracious; but the lips of a fool will
swallow up himself.
13 The beginning of the words of his mouth *is* foolishness: and the end of
his talk *is* mischievous madness.
14 A fool also is full of words: a man cannot tell what shall be; and what shall
be after him, who can tell him?
15 The labour of the foolish wearieth every one of them, because he knoweth
not how to go to the city.
16 Woe to thee, O land, when thy king *is* a child, and thy princes eat in the
morning!
17 Blessed *art* thou, O land, when thy king *is* the son of nobles, and thy princ-
es eat in due season, for strength, and not for drunkenness!
18 By much slothfulness the building decayeth; and through idleness of the
hands the house droppeth through.
19 A feast is made for laughter, and wine maketh merry: but money answer-
eth all *things*.
20 Curse not the king, no not in thy thought; and curse not the rich in thy
bedchamber: for a bird of the air shall carry the voice, and that which hath
wings shall tell the matter.

Directions for Charity

11 Cast thy bread upon the waters: for thou shalt find it after many days.
2 Give a portion to seven, and also to eight; for thou knowest not what
evil shall be upon the earth.
3 If the clouds be full of rain, they empty *themselves* upon the earth: and if
the tree fall toward the south, or toward the north, in the place where the tree
falleth, there it shall be.
4 He that observeth the wind shall not sow; and he that regardeth the clouds
shall not reap.
5 As thou knowest not what *is* the way of the spirit, *nor* how the bones *do*
grow in the womb of her that is with child: even so thou knowest not the works
of God who maketh all.
6 In the morning sow thy seed, and in the evening withhold not thine hand:
for thou knowest not whether shall prosper, either this or that, or whether
they both *shall be* alike good.

Enjoy Life

7 Truly the light *is* sweet, and a pleasant *thing it is* for the eyes to behold the
sun:
8 But if a man live many years, *and* rejoice in them all; yet let him remember
the days of darkness; for they shall be many. All that cometh *is* vanity.
9 Rejoice, O young man, in thy youth; and let thy heart cheer thee in the days
of thy youth, and walk in the ways of thine heart, and in the sight of thine eyes:
but know thou, that for all these *things* God will bring thee into judgment.
10 Therefore remove sorrow from thy heart, and put away evil from thy flesh:
for childhood and youth *are* vanity.

Remember Your Creator in Your Youth

12 Remember now thy Creator in the days of thy youth, while the evil
days come not, nor the years draw nigh, when thou shalt say, I have no
pleasure in them;
2 While the sun, or the light, or the moon, or the stars, be not darkened, nor
the clouds return after the rain:
3 In the day when the keepers of the house shall tremble, and the strong men
shall bow themselves, and the grinders cease because they are few, and those
that look out of the windows be darkened,
4 And the doors shall be shut in the streets, when the sound of the grinding
is low, and he shall rise up at the voice of the bird, and all the daughters of
musick shall be brought low;
5 Also *when* they shall be afraid of *that which is* high, and fears *shall be* in
the way, and the almond tree shall flourish, and the grasshopper shall be a
burden, and desire shall fail: because man goeth to his long home, and the
mourners go about the streets:
6 Or ever the silver cord be loosed, or the golden bowl be broken, or the
pitcher be broken at the fountain, or the wheel broken at the cistern.
7 Then shall the dust return to the earth as it was: and the spirit shall return
unto God who gave it.

Fear God and Keep His Commands

8 Vanity of vanities, saith the preacher; all *is* vanity.
9 And moreover, because the preacher was wise, he still taught the people
knowledge; yea, he gave good heed, and sought out, *and* set in order many
proverbs.
10 The preacher sought to find out acceptable words: and *that which was*
written *was* upright, *even* words of truth.
11 The words of the wise *are* as goads, and as nails fastened *by* the masters
of assemblies, *which* are given from one shepherd.
12 And further, by these, my son, be admonished: of making many books
there is no end; and much study *is* a weariness of the flesh.
13 Let us hear the conclusion of the whole matter: Fear God, and keep his
commandments: for this *is* the whole *duty* of man.
14 For God shall bring every work into judgment, with every secret thing,
whether *it be* good, or whether *it be* evil.

THE SONG OF SOLOMON

Solomon and the Young Woman

1 The song of songs, which *is* Solomon's.
2 Let him kiss me with the kisses of his mouth: for thy love *is* better than
wine.
3 Because of the savour of thy good ointments thy name *is as* ointment
poured forth, therefore do the virgins love thee.
4 Draw me, we will run after thee: the king hath brought me into his cham-
bers: we will be glad and rejoice in thee, we will remember thy love more than
wine: the upright love thee.
5 I *am* black, but comely, O ye daughters of Jerusalem, as the tents of Kedar,
as the curtains of Solomon.
6 Look not upon me, because I *am* black, because the sun hath looked upon
me: my mother's children were angry with me; they made me the keeper of
the vineyards; *but* mine own vineyard have I not kept.
7 Tell me, O thou whom my soul loveth, where thou feedest, where thou
makest *thy flock* to rest at noon: for why should I be as one that turneth aside
by the flocks of thy companions?
8 If thou know not, O thou fairest among women, go thy way forth by the
footsteps of the flock, and feed thy kids beside the shepherds' tents.

Solomon Desires the Young Woman's Love

9 I have compared thee, O my love, to a company of horses in Pharaoh's
chariots.
10 Thy cheeks are comely with rows *of jewels*, thy neck with chains *of gold*.
11 We will make thee borders of gold with studs of silver.
12 While the king *sitteth* at his table, my spikenard sendeth forth the smell
thereof.
13 A bundle of myrrh *is* my wellbeloved unto me; he shall lie all night betwixt
my breasts.
14 My beloved *is* unto me *as* a cluster of camphire in the vineyards of En-gedi.
15 Behold, thou *art* fair, my love; behold, thou *art* fair; thou *hast* doves' eyes.
16 Behold, thou *art* fair, my beloved, yea, pleasant: also our bed *is* green.
17 The beams of our house *are* cedar, *and* our rafters of fir.

Their Love Is Great

2 I *am* the rose of Sharon, *and* the lily of the valleys.
2 As the lily among thorns, so *is* my love among the daughters.
3 As the apple tree among the trees of the wood, so *is* my beloved among the
sons. I sat down under his shadow with great delight, and his fruit *was* sweet
to my taste.
4 He brought me to the banqueting house, and his banner over me *was* love.
5 Stay me with flagons, comfort me with apples: for I *am* sick of love.
6 His left hand *is* under my head, and his right hand doth embrace me.
7 I charge you, O ye daughters of Jerusalem, by the roes, and by the hinds of
the field, that ye stir not up, nor awake *my* love, till he please.

Remembering One Spring Day

8 The voice of my beloved! behold, he cometh leaping upon the mountains,
skipping upon the hills.

9 My beloved is like a roe or a young hart: behold, he standeth behind our
wall, he looketh forth at the windows, shewing himself through the lattice.
10 My beloved spake, and said unto me, Rise up, my love, my fair one, and
come away.
11 For, lo, the winter is past, the rain is over *and* gone;
12 The flowers appear on the earth; the time of the singing *of birds* is come,
and the voice of the turtle is heard in our land;
13 The fig tree putteth forth her green figs, and the vines *with* the tender
grape give a *good* smell. Arise, my love, my fair one, and come away.
14 O my dove, *that art* in the clefts of the rock, in the secret *places* of the
stairs, let me see thy countenance, let me hear thy voice; for sweet *is* thy voice,
and thy countenance *is* comely.
15 Take us the foxes, the little foxes, that spoil the vines: for our vines *have*
tender grapes.
16 My beloved *is* mine, and I *am* his: he feedeth among the lilies.
17 Until the day break, and the shadows flee away, turn, my beloved, and be
thou like a roe or a young hart upon the mountains of Bether.

Searching for the Beloved

3 By night on my bed I sought him whom my soul loveth: I sought him, but
I found him not.
2 I will rise now, and go about the city in the streets, and in the broad ways
I will seek him whom my soul loveth: I sought him, but I found him not.
3 The watchmen that go about the city found me: *to whom I said,* Saw ye him
whom my soul loveth?
4 *It was* but a little that I passed from them, but I found him whom my soul
loveth: I held him, and would not let him go, until I had brought him into my
mother's house, and into the chamber of her that conceived me.
5 I charge you, O ye daughters of Jerusalem, by the roes, and by the hinds of
the field, that ye stir not up, nor awake *my* love, till he please.

The Royal Procession

6 Who *is* this that cometh out of the wilderness like pillars of smoke, per-
fumed with myrrh and frankincense, with all powders of the merchant?
7 Behold his bed, which *is* Solomon's; threescore valiant men *are* about it,
of the valiant of Israel.
8 They all hold swords, *being* expert in war: every man *hath* his sword upon
his thigh because of fear in the night.
9 King Solomon made himself a chariot of the wood of Lebanon.
10 He made the pillars thereof *of* silver, the bottom thereof *of* gold, the cov-
ering of it *of* purple, the midst thereof being paved *with* love, for the daughters
of Jerusalem.
11 Go forth, O ye daughters of Zion, and behold king Solomon with the crown
wherewith his mother crowned him in the day of his espousals, and in the day
of the gladness of his heart.

Solomon Is Charmed by His Beloved

4 Behold, thou *art* fair, my love; behold, thou *art* fair; thou *hast* doves' eyes
within thy locks: thy hair *is* as a flock of goats, that appear from mount
Gilead.
2 Thy teeth *are* like a flock *of sheep that are even* shorn, which came up from
the washing; whereof every one bear twins, and none *is* barren among them.
3 Thy lips *are* like a thread of scarlet, and thy speech *is* comely: thy temples
are like a piece of a pomegranate within thy locks.
4 Thy neck *is* like the tower of David builded for an armoury, whereon there
hang a thousand bucklers, all shields of mighty men.
5 Thy two breasts *are* like two young roes that are twins, which feed among
the lilies.

6 Until the day break, and the shadows flee away, I will get me to the moun-
tain of myrrh, and to the hill of frankincense.
7 Thou *art* all fair, my love; *there is* no spot in thee.
8 Come with me from Lebanon, *my* spouse, with me from Lebanon: look
from the top of Amana, from the top of Shenir and Hermon, from the lions'
dens, from the mountains of the leopards.
9 Thou hast ravished my heart, my sister, *my* spouse; thou hast ravished my
heart with one of thine eyes, with one chain of thy neck.
10 How fair is thy love, my sister, *my* spouse! how much better is thy love
than wine! and the smell of thine ointments than all spices!
11 Thy lips, O *my* spouse, drop *as* the honeycomb: honey and milk *are* under
thy tongue; and the smell of thy garments *is* like the smell of Lebanon.
12 A garden inclosed *is* my sister, *my* spouse; a spring shut up, a fountain
sealed.
13 Thy plants *are* an orchard of pomegranates, with pleasant fruits; camphire,
with spikenard,
14 Spikenard and saffron; calamus and cinnamon, with all trees of frankin-
cense; myrrh and aloes, with all the chief spices:
15 A fountain of gardens, a well of living waters, and streams from Lebanon.
16 Awake, O north wind; and come, thou south; blow upon my garden, *that*
the spices thereof may flow out. Let my beloved come into his garden, and eat
his pleasant fruits.

The Young Woman Dreams of Marriage

5 I am come into my garden, my sister, *my* spouse: I have gathered my myrrh
with my spice; I have eaten my honeycomb with my honey; I have drunk
my wine with my milk: eat, O friends; drink, yea, drink abundantly, O beloved.
2 I sleep, but my heart waketh: *it is* the voice of my beloved that knocketh,
saying, Open to me, my sister, my love, my dove, my undefiled: for my head is
filled with dew, *and* my locks with the drops of the night.
3 I have put off my coat; how shall I put it on? I have washed my feet; how
shall I defile them?
4 My beloved put in his hand by the hole *of the door*, and my bowels were
moved for him.
5 I rose up to open to my beloved; and my hands dropped *with* myrrh, and
my fingers *with* sweet smelling myrrh, upon the handles of the lock.
6 I opened to my beloved; but my beloved had withdrawn himself, *and* was
gone: my soul failed when he spake: I sought him, but I could not find him; I
called him, but he gave me no answer.
7 The watchmen that went about the city found me, they smote me, they
wounded me; the keepers of the walls took away my veil from me.
8 I charge you, O daughters of Jerusalem, if ye find my beloved, that ye tell
him, that I *am* sick of love.
9 What *is* thy beloved more than *another* beloved, O thou fairest among
women? what *is* thy beloved more than *another* beloved, that thou dost so
charge us?
10 My beloved *is* white and ruddy, the chiefest among ten thousand.
11 His head *is as* the most fine gold, his locks *are* bushy, *and* black as a raven.
12 His eyes *are* as *the eyes* of doves by the rivers of waters, washed with milk,
and fitly set.
13 His cheeks *are* as a bed of spices, *as* sweet flowers: his lips *like* lilies, drop-
ping sweet smelling myrrh.
14 His hands *are as* gold rings set with the beryl: his belly *is as* bright ivory
overlaid *with* sapphires.
15 His legs *are as* pillars of marble, set upon sockets of fine gold: his counte-
nance *is* as Lebanon, excellent as the cedars.
16 His mouth *is* most sweet: yea, he *is* altogether lovely. This *is* my beloved,
and this *is* my friend, O daughters of Jerusalem.

Solomon Desires Her Love

6 Whither is thy beloved gone, O thou fairest among women? whither is thy
beloved turned aside? that we may seek him with thee.
2 My beloved is gone down into his garden, to the beds of spices, to feed in
the gardens, and to gather lilies.
3 I *am* my beloved's, and my beloved *is* mine: he feedeth among the lilies.
4 Thou *art* beautiful, O my love, as Tirzah, comely as Jerusalem, terrible as
an army with banners.
5 Turn away thine eyes from me, for they have overcome me: thy hair *is* as a
flock of goats that appear from Gilead.
6 Thy teeth *are* as a flock of sheep which go up from the washing, whereof
every one beareth twins, and *there is* not one barren among them.
7 As a piece of a pomegranate *are* thy temples within thy locks.
8 There are threescore queens, and fourscore concubines, and virgins with-
out number.
9 My dove, my undefiled is *but* one; she *is* the *only* one of her mother, she *is*
the choice *one* of her that bare her. The daughters saw her, and blessed her;
yea, the queens and the concubines, and they praised her.
10 Who *is* she *that* looketh forth as the morning, fair as the moon, clear as
the sun, *and* terrible as *an army* with banners?
11 I went down into the garden of nuts to see the fruits of the valley, *and* to
see whether the vine flourished, *and* the pomegranates budded.
12 Or ever I was aware, my soul made me *like* the chariots of Amminadib.
13 Return, return, O Shulamite; return, return, that we may look upon thee.
What will ye see in the Shulamite? As it were the company of two armies.

The Bride's Beauty

7 How beautiful are thy feet with shoes, O prince's daughter! the joints of thy
thighs *are* like jewels, the work of the hands of a cunning workman.
2 Thy navel *is like* a round goblet, *which* wanteth not liquor: thy belly *is like*
an heap of wheat set about with lilies.
3 Thy two breasts *are* like two young roes *that are* twins.
4 Thy neck *is* as a tower of ivory; thine eyes *like* the fishpools in Heshbon, by
the gate of Bath-rabbim: thy nose *is* as the tower of Lebanon which looketh
toward Damascus.
5 Thine head upon thee *is* like Carmel, and the hair of thine head like purple;
the king *is* held in the galleries.
6 How fair and how pleasant art thou, O love, for delights!
7 This thy stature is like to a palm tree, and thy breasts to clusters *of grapes*.
8 I said, I will go up to the palm tree, I will take hold of the boughs thereof:
now also thy breasts shall be as clusters of the vine, and the smell of thy nose
like apples;
9 And the roof of thy mouth like the best wine for my beloved, that goeth
down sweetly, causing the lips of those that are asleep to speak.
10 I *am* my beloved's, and his desire *is* toward me.
11 Come, my beloved, let us go forth into the field; let us lodge in the villages.
12 Let us get up early to the vineyards; let us see if the vine flourish, *whether*
the tender grape appear, *and* the pomegranates bud forth: there will I give
thee my loves.
13 The mandrakes give a smell, and at our gates *are* all manner of pleasant
fruits, new and old, *which* I have laid up for thee, O my beloved.

The Young Woman's Love

8 O that thou *wert* as my brother, that sucked the breasts of my mother! *when*
I should find thee without, I would kiss thee; yea, I should not be despised.
2 I would lead thee, *and* bring thee into my mother's house, *who* would
instruct me: I would cause thee to drink of spiced wine of the juice of my
pomegranate.

3 His left hand *should be* under my head, and his right hand should embrace
me.
4 I charge you, O daughters of Jerusalem, that ye stir not up, nor awake *my*
love, until he please.
5 Who *is* this that cometh up from the wilderness, leaning upon her beloved?
I raised thee up under the apple tree: there thy mother brought thee forth:
there she brought thee forth *that* bare thee.
6 Set me as a seal upon thine heart, as a seal upon thine arm: for love *is* strong
as death; jealousy *is* cruel as the grave: the coals thereof *are* coals of fire, *which*
hath a most vehement flame.
7 Many waters cannot quench love, neither can the floods drown it: if *a* man
would give all the substance of his house for love, it would utterly be con-
temned.
8 We have a little sister, and she hath no breasts: what shall we do for our
sister in the day when she shall be spoken for?
9 If she *be* a wall, we will build upon her a palace of silver: and if she *be* a door,
we will inclose her with boards of cedar.
10 I *am* a wall, and my breasts like towers: then was I in his eyes as one that
found favour.
11 Solomon had a vineyard at Baal-hamon; he let out the vineyard unto keep-
ers; every one for the fruit thereof was to bring a thousand *pieces* of silver.
12 My vineyard, which *is* mine, *is* before me: thou, O Solomon, *must have* a
thousand, and those that keep the fruit thereof two hundred.
13 Thou that dwellest in the gardens, the companions hearken to thy voice:
cause me to hear *it*.
14 Make haste, my beloved, and be thou like to a roe or to a young hart upon
the mountains of spices.

ISAIAH

Isaiah Describes Judah's Rebellion

1 The vision of Isaiah the son of Amoz, which he saw concerning Judah and
Jerusalem in the days of Uzziah, Jotham, Ahaz, *and* Hezekiah, kings of Judah.
2 Hear, O heavens, and give ear, O earth: for the LORD hath spoken, I have
nourished and brought up children, and they have rebelled against me.
3 The ox knoweth his owner, and the ass his master's crib: *but* Israel doth not
know, my people doth not consider.
4 Ah sinful nation, a people laden with iniquity, a seed of evildoers, children
that are corrupters: they have forsaken the LORD, they have provoked the Holy
One of Israel unto anger, they are gone away backward.
5 Why should ye be stricken any more? ye will revolt more and more: the
whole head is sick, and the whole heart faint.
6 From the sole of the foot even unto the head *there is* no soundness in it;
but wounds, and bruises, and putrifying sores: they have not been closed,
neither bound up, neither mollified with ointment.
7 Your country *is* desolate, your cities *are* burned with fire: your land, strang-
ers devour it in your presence, and *it is* desolate, as overthrown by strangers.
8 And the daughter of Zion is left as a cottage in a vineyard, as a lodge in a
garden of cucumbers, as a besieged city.
9 Except the LORD of hosts had left unto us a very small remnant, we should
have been as Sodom, *and* we should have been like unto Gomorrah.

Israel's Corrupt Religion

10 Hear the word of the LORD, ye rulers of Sodom; give ear unto the law of
our God, ye people of Gomorrah.
11 To what purpose *is* the multitude of your sacrifices unto me? saith the
LORD: I am full of the burnt offerings of rams, and the fat of fed beasts; and I
delight not in the blood of bullocks, or of lambs, or of he goats.
12 When ye come to appear before me, who hath required this at your hand,
to tread my courts?
13 Bring no more vain oblations; incense is an abomination unto me; the
new moons and sabbaths, the calling of assemblies, I cannot away with; *it is*
iniquity, even the solemn meeting.
14 Your new moons and your appointed feasts my soul hateth: they are a
trouble unto me; I am weary to bear *them*.
15 And when ye spread forth your hands, I will hide mine eyes from you: yea,
when ye make many prayers, I will not hear: your hands are full of blood.

Isaiah Exhorts Israel to Repentance

16 Wash you, make you clean; put away the evil of your doings from before
mine eyes; cease to do evil;
17 Learn to do well; seek judgment, relieve the oppressed, judge the fatherless,
plead for the widow.
18 Come now, and let us reason together, saith the LORD: though your sins
be as scarlet, they shall be as white as snow; though they be red like crimson,
they shall be as wool.
19 If ye be willing and obedient, ye shall eat the good of the land:
20 But if ye refuse and rebel, ye shall be devoured with the sword: for the
mouth of the LORD hath spoken *it*.

Jerusalem's Future

21 How is the faithful city become an harlot! it was full of judgment; righteousness lodged in it; but now murderers.
22 Thy silver is become dross, thy wine mixed with water:
23 Thy princes *are* rebellious, and companions of thieves: every one loveth gifts, and followeth after rewards: they judge not the fatherless, neither doth the cause of the widow come unto them.
24 Therefore saith the Lord, the LORD of hosts, the mighty One of Israel, Ah, I will ease me of mine adversaries, and avenge me of mine enemies:
25 And I will turn my hand upon thee, and purely purge away thy dross, and take away all thy tin:
26 And I will restore thy judges as at the first, and thy counsellors as at the beginning: afterward thou shalt be called, The city of righteousness, the faithful city.
27 Zion shall be redeemed with judgment, and her converts with righteousness.
28 And the destruction of the transgressors and of the sinners *shall be* together, and they that forsake the LORD shall be consumed.
29 For they shall be ashamed of the oaks which ye have desired, and ye shall be confounded for the gardens that ye have chosen.
30 For ye shall be as an oak whose leaf fadeth, and as a garden that hath no water.
31 And the strong shall be as tow, and the maker of it as a spark, and they shall both burn together, and none shall quench *them*.

Isaiah Prophesies the Coming of Christ's Kingdom

2 The word that Isaiah the son of Amoz saw concerning Judah and Jerusalem.
2 And it shall come to pass in the last days, *that* the mountain of the LORD's house shall be established in the top of the mountains, and shall be exalted above the hills; and all nations shall flow unto it.
3 And many people shall go and say, Come ye, and let us go up to the mountain of the LORD, to the house of the God of Jacob; and he will teach us of his ways, and we will walk in his paths: for out of Zion shall go forth the law, and the word of the LORD from Jerusalem.
4 And he shall judge among the nations, and shall rebuke many people: and they shall beat their swords into plowshares, and their spears into pruninghooks: nation shall not lift up sword against nation, neither shall they learn war any more.
5 O house of Jacob, come ye, and let us walk in the light of the LORD.

The People's Sins

6 Therefore thou hast forsaken thy people the house of Jacob, because they be replenished from the east, and *are* soothsayers like the Philistines, and they please themselves in the children of strangers.
7 Their land also is full of silver and gold, neither *is there any* end of their treasures; their land is also full of horses, neither *is there any* end of their chariots:
8 Their land also is full of idols; they worship the work of their own hands, that which their own fingers have made:
9 And the mean man boweth down, and the great man humbleth himself: therefore forgive them not.

Fear the Power of God's Majesty

10 Enter into the rock, and hide thee in the dust, for fear of the LORD, and for the glory of his majesty.
11 The lofty looks of man shall be humbled, and the haughtiness of men shall be bowed down, and the LORD alone shall be exalted in that day.

THOUGH YOUR SINS BE AS Scarlet, they shall be AS WHITE AS SNOW; THOUGH THEY BE red LIKE crimson, they shall be AS WOOL.

ISAIAH 1:18

12 For the day of the LORD of hosts *shall be* upon every *one that is* proud and
lofty, and upon every *one that is* lifted up; and he shall be brought low:
13 And upon all the cedars of Lebanon, *that are* high and lifted up, and upon
all the oaks of Bashan,
14 And upon all the high mountains, and upon all the hills *that are* lifted up,
15 And upon every high tower, and upon every fenced wall,
16 And upon all the ships of Tarshish, and upon all pleasant pictures.
17 And the loftiness of man shall be bowed down, and the haughtiness of
men shall be made low: and the LORD alone shall be exalted in that day.
18 And the idols he shall utterly abolish.
19 And they shall go into the holes of the rocks, and into the caves of the
earth, for fear of the LORD, and for the glory of his majesty, when he ariseth to
shake terribly the earth.
20 In that day a man shall cast his idols of silver, and his idols of gold, which
they made *each one* for himself to worship, to the moles and to the bats;
21 To go into the clefts of the rocks, and into the tops of the ragged rocks, for
fear of the LORD, and for the glory of his majesty, when he ariseth to shake
terribly the earth.
22 Cease ye from man, whose breath *is* in his nostrils: for wherein is he to be
accounted of?

The Lord's Judgment on Sin

3 For, behold, the Lord, the LORD of hosts, doth take away from Jerusalem and
from Judah the stay and the staff, the whole stay of bread, and the whole
stay of water,
2 The mighty man, and the man of war, the judge, and the prophet, and the
prudent, and the ancient,
3 The captain of fifty, and the honourable man, and the counsellor, and the
cunning artificer, and the eloquent orator.
4 And I will give children *to be* their princes, and babes shall rule over them.
5 And the people shall be oppressed, every one by another, and every one by
his neighbour: the child shall behave himself proudly against the ancient, and
the base against the honourable.
6 When a man shall take hold of his brother of the house of his father, *saying*,
Thou hast clothing, be thou our ruler, and *let* this ruin *be* under thy hand:
7 In that day shall he swear, saying, I will not be an healer; for in my house
is neither bread nor clothing: make me not a ruler of the people.
8 For Jerusalem is ruined, and Judah is fallen: because their tongue and their
doings *are* against the LORD, to provoke the eyes of his glory.

The Impudence of the People

9 The shew of their countenance doth witness against them; and they declare
their sin as Sodom, they hide *it* not. Woe unto their soul! for they have reward-
ed evil unto themselves.
10 Say ye to the righteous, that *it shall be* well *with him*: for they shall eat the
fruit of their doings.
11 Woe unto the wicked! *it shall be* ill *with him*: for the reward of his hands
shall be given him.
12 *As for* my people, children *are* their oppressors, and women rule over
them. O my people, they which lead thee cause *thee* to err, and destroy the way
of thy paths.
13 The LORD standeth up to plead, and standeth to judge the people.
14 The LORD will enter into judgment with the ancients of his people, and
the princes thereof: for ye have eaten up the vineyard; the spoil of the poor *is*
in your houses.
15 What mean ye *that* ye beat my people to pieces, and grind the faces of the
poor? saith the Lord GOD of hosts.

Judgments for the Women's Pride
16 Moreover the LORD saith, Because the daughters of Zion are haughty, and
walk with stretched forth necks and wanton eyes, walking and mincing *as*
they go, and making a tinkling with their feet:
17 Therefore the Lord will smite with a scab the crown of the head of the
daughters of Zion, and the LORD will discover their secret parts.
18 In that day the Lord will take away the bravery of *their* tinkling ornaments
about their feet, and *their* cauls, and *their* round tires like the moon,
19 The chains, and the bracelets, and the mufflers,
20 The bonnets, and the ornaments of the legs, and the headbands, and the
tablets, and the earrings,
21 The rings, and nose jewels,
22 The changeable suits of apparel, and the mantles, and the wimples, and
the crisping pins,
23 The glasses, and the fine linen, and the hoods, and the vails.
24 And it shall come to pass, *that* instead of sweet smell there shall be stink;
and instead of a girdle a rent; and instead of well set hair baldness; and instead
of a stomacher a girding of sackcloth; *and* burning instead of beauty.
25 Thy men shall fall by the sword, and thy mighty in the war.
26 And her gates shall lament and mourn; and she *being* desolate shall sit
upon the ground.

The Lord's New Glory for Jerusalem
4 And in that day seven women shall take hold of one man, saying, We will
eat our own bread, and wear our own apparel: only let us be called by thy
name, to take away our reproach.
2 In that day shall the branch of the LORD be beautiful and glorious, and the
fruit of the earth *shall be* excellent and comely for them that are escaped of
Israel.
3 And it shall come to pass, *that he that is* left in Zion, and *he that* remaineth
in Jerusalem, shall be called holy, *even* every one that is written among the
living in Jerusalem:
4 When the Lord shall have washed away the filth of the daughters of Zion,
and shall have purged the blood of Jerusalem from the midst thereof by the
spirit of judgment, and by the spirit of burning.
5 And the LORD will create upon every dwelling place of mount Zion, and
upon her assemblies, a cloud and smoke by day, and the shining of a flaming
fire by night: for upon all the glory *shall be* a defence.
6 And there shall be a tabernacle for a shadow in the daytime from the heat,
and for a place of refuge, and for a covert from storm and from rain.

The Parable of the Vineyard
5 Now will I sing to my wellbeloved a song of my beloved touching his vine-
yard. My wellbeloved hath a vineyard in a very fruitful hill:
2 And he fenced it, and gathered out the stones thereof, and planted it with
the choicest vine, and built a tower in the midst of it, and also made a winepress
therein: and he looked that it should bring forth grapes, and it brought forth
wild grapes.
3 And now, O inhabitants of Jerusalem, and men of Judah, judge, I pray you,
betwixt me and my vineyard.
4 What could have been done more to my vineyard, that I have not done in
it? wherefore, when I looked that it should bring forth grapes, brought it forth
wild grapes?
5 And now go to; I will tell you what I will do to my vineyard: I will take away
the hedge thereof, and it shall be eaten up; *and* break down the wall thereof,
and it shall be trodden down:

6 And I will lay it waste: it shall not be pruned, nor digged; but there shall
come up briers and thorns: I will also command the clouds that they rain no
rain upon it.
7 For the vineyard of the LORD of hosts *is* the house of Israel, and the men of
Judah his pleasant plant: and he looked for judgment, but behold oppression;
for righteousness, but behold a cry.

Six Sins Condemned

8 Woe unto them that join house to house, *that* lay field to field, till *there be*
no place, that they may be placed alone in the midst of the earth!
9 In mine ears *said* the LORD of hosts, Of a truth many houses shall be deso-
late, *even* great and fair, without inhabitant.
10 Yea, ten acres of vineyard shall yield one bath, and the seed of an homer
shall yield an ephah.
11 Woe unto them that rise up early in the morning, *that* they may follow
strong drink; that continue until night, *till* wine inflame them!
12 And the harp, and the viol, the tabret, and pipe, and wine, are in their
feasts: but they regard not the work of the LORD, neither consider the operation
of his hands.
13 Therefore my people are gone into captivity, because *they have* no knowl-
edge: and their honourable men *are* famished, and their multitude dried up
with thirst.
14 Therefore hell hath enlarged herself, and opened her mouth without
measure: and their glory, and their multitude, and their pomp, and he that
rejoiceth, shall descend into it.
15 And the mean man shall be brought down, and the mighty man shall be
humbled, and the eyes of the lofty shall be humbled:
16 But the LORD of hosts shall be exalted in judgment, and God that is holy
shall be sanctified in righteousness.
17 Then shall the lambs feed after their manner, and the waste places of the
fat ones shall strangers eat.
18 Woe unto them that draw iniquity with cords of vanity, and sin as it were
with a cart rope:
19 That say, Let him make speed, *and* hasten his work, that we may see *it*: and
let the counsel of the Holy One of Israel draw nigh and come, that we may
know *it*!
20 Woe unto them that call evil good, and good evil; that put darkness for
light, and light for darkness; that put bitter for sweet, and sweet for bitter!
21 Woe unto *them that are* wise in their own eyes, and prudent in their own
sight!
22 Woe unto *them that are* mighty to drink wine, and men of strength to
mingle strong drink:
23 Which justify the wicked for reward, and take away the righteousness of
the righteous from him!

Another Nation Will Punish Israel

24 Therefore as the fire devoureth the stubble, and the flame consumeth the
chaff, *so* their root shall be as rottenness, and their blossom shall go up as dust:
because they have cast away the law of the LORD of hosts, and despised the
word of the Holy One of Israel.
25 Therefore is the anger of the LORD kindled against his people, and he hath
stretched forth his hand against them, and hath smitten them: and the hills
did tremble, and their carcases *were* torn in the midst of the streets. For all
this his anger is not turned away, but his hand *is* stretched out still.
26 And he will lift up an ensign to the nations from far, and will hiss unto them
from the end of the earth: and, behold, they shall come with speed swiftly:

27 None shall be weary nor stumble among them; none shall slumber nor sleep; neither shall the girdle of their loins be loosed, nor the latchet of their shoes be broken:
28 Whose arrows *are* sharp, and all their bows bent, their horses' hoofs shall be counted like flint, and their wheels like a whirlwind:
29 Their roaring *shall be* like a lion, they shall roar like young lions: yea, they shall roar, and lay hold of the prey, and shall carry *it* away safe, and none shall deliver *it*.
30 And in that day they shall roar against them like the roaring of the sea: and if *one* look unto the land, behold darkness *and* sorrow, and the light is darkened in the heavens thereof.

Isaiah's Vision of the Lord's Glory

6 In the year that king Uzziah died I saw also the Lord sitting upon a throne, high and lifted up, and his train filled the temple.
2 Above it stood the seraphims: each one had six wings; with twain he covered his face, and with twain he covered his feet, and with twain he did fly.
3 And one cried unto another, and said, Holy, holy, holy, *is* the LORD of hosts: the whole earth *is* full of his glory.
4 And the posts of the door moved at the voice of him that cried, and the house was filled with smoke.
5 Then said I, Woe *is* me! for I am undone; because I *am* a man of unclean lips, and I dwell in the midst of a people of unclean lips: for mine eyes have seen the King, the LORD of hosts.
6 Then flew one of the seraphims unto me, having a live coal in his hand, *which* he had taken with the tongs from off the altar:
7 And he laid *it* upon my mouth, and said, Lo, this hath touched thy lips; and thine iniquity is taken away, and thy sin purged.
8 Also I heard the voice of the Lord, saying, Whom shall I send, and who will go for us? Then said I, Here *am* I; send me.

Isaiah's Message for Israel

9 And he said, Go, and tell this people, Hear ye indeed, but understand not; and see ye indeed, but perceive not.
10 Make the heart of this people fat, and make their ears heavy, and shut their eyes; lest they see with their eyes, and hear with their ears, and understand with their heart, and convert, and be healed.
11 Then said I, Lord, how long? And he answered, Until the cities be wasted without inhabitant, and the houses without man, and the land be utterly desolate,
12 And the LORD have removed men far away, and *there be* a great forsaking in the midst of the land.
13 But yet in it *shall be* a tenth, and *it* shall return, and shall be eaten: as a teil tree, and as an oak, whose substance *is* in them, when they cast *their leaves*: *so* the holy seed *shall be* the substance thereof.

The Virgin Will Have a Child

7 And it came to pass in the days of Ahaz the son of Jotham, the son of Uzziah, king of Judah, *that* Rezin the king of Syria, and Pekah the son of Remaliah, king of Israel, went up toward Jerusalem to war against it, but could not prevail against it.
2 And it was told the house of David, saying, Syria is confederate with Ephraim. And his heart was moved, and the heart of his people, as the trees of the wood are moved with the wind.
3 Then said the LORD unto Isaiah, Go forth now to meet Ahaz, thou, and Shear-jashub thy son, at the end of the conduit of the upper pool in the highway of the fuller's field;

4 And say unto him, Take heed, and be quiet; fear not, neither be faintheart-
ed for the two tails of these smoking firebrands, for the fierce anger of Rezin
with Syria, and of the son of Remaliah.

5 Because Syria, Ephraim, and the son of Remaliah, have taken evil counsel
against thee, saying,

6 Let us go up against Judah, and vex it, and let us make a breach therein for
us, and set a king in the midst of it, *even* the son of Tabeal:

7 Thus saith the Lord GOD, It shall not stand, neither shall it come to pass.

8 For the head of Syria *is* Damascus, and the head of Damascus *is* Rezin; and
within threescore and five years shall Ephraim be broken, that it be not a
people.

9 And the head of Ephraim *is* Samaria, and the head of Samaria *is* Remaliah's
son. If ye will not believe, surely ye shall not be established.

10 Moreover the LORD spake again unto Ahaz, saying,

11 Ask thee a sign of the LORD thy God; ask it either in the depth, or in the
height above.

12 But Ahaz said, I will not ask, neither will I tempt the LORD.

13 And he said, Hear ye now, O house of David; *Is it* a small thing for you to
weary men, but will ye weary my God also?

14 Therefore the Lord himself shall give you a sign; Behold, a virgin shall
conceive, and bear a son, and shall call his name Immanuel.

15 Butter and honey shall he eat, that he may know to refuse the evil, and
choose the good.

16 For before the child shall know to refuse the evil, and choose the good,
the land that thou abhorrest shall be forsaken of both her kings.

17 The LORD shall bring upon thee, and upon thy people, and upon thy
father's house, days that have not come, from the day that Ephraim departed
from Judah; *even* the king of Assyria.

18 And it shall come to pass in that day, *that* the LORD shall hiss for the fly
that *is* in the uttermost part of the rivers of Egypt, and for the bee that *is* in
the land of Assyria.

19 And they shall come, and shall rest all of them in the desolate valleys, and
in the holes of the rocks, and upon all thorns, and upon all bushes.

20 In the same day shall the Lord shave with a razor that is hired, *namely*, by
them beyond the river, by the king of Assyria, the head, and the hair of the
feet: and it shall also consume the beard.

21 And it shall come to pass in that day, *that* a man shall nourish a young
cow, and two sheep;

22 And it shall come to pass, for the abundance of milk *that* they shall give
he shall eat butter: for butter and honey shall every one eat that is left in the
land.

23 And it shall come to pass in that day, *that* every place shall be, where there
were a thousand vines at a thousand silverlings, it shall *even* be for briers and
thorns.

24 With arrows and with bows shall *men* come thither; because all the land
shall become briers and thorns.

25 And *on* all hills that shall be digged with the mattock, there shall not come
thither the fear of briers and thorns: but it shall be for the sending forth of
oxen, and for the treading of lesser cattle.

Isaiah's Child Is a Sign

8 Moreover the LORD said unto me, Take thee a great roll, and write in it with
a man's pen concerning Maher-shalal-hashbaz.

2 And I took unto me faithful witnesses to record, Uriah the priest, and
Zechariah the son of Jeberechiah.

3 And I went unto the prophetess; and she conceived, and bare a son. Then
said the LORD to me, Call his name Maher-shalal-hashbaz.
4 For before the child shall have knowledge to cry, My father, and my moth-
er, the riches of Damascus and the spoil of Samaria shall be taken away before
the king of Assyria.

Assyria Will Not Conquer Judah

5 The LORD spake also unto me again, saying,
6 Forasmuch as this people refuseth the waters of Shiloah that go softly, and
rejoice in Rezin and Remaliah's son;
7 Now therefore, behold, the Lord bringeth up upon them the waters of the
river, strong and many, *even* the king of Assyria, and all his glory: and he shall
come up over all his channels, and go over all his banks:
8 And he shall pass through Judah; he shall overflow and go over, he shall
reach *even* to the neck; and the stretching out of his wings shall fill the breadth
of thy land, O Immanuel.
9 Associate yourselves, O ye people, and ye shall be broken in pieces; and give
ear, all ye of far countries: gird yourselves, and ye shall be broken in pieces;
gird yourselves, and ye shall be broken in pieces.
10 Take counsel together, and it shall come to nought; speak the word, and
it shall not stand: for God *is* with us.

Some in Jerusalem Will Stumble

11 For the LORD spake thus to me with a strong hand, and instructed me that
I should not walk in the way of this people, saying,
12 Say ye not, A confederacy, to all *them to* whom this people shall say, A
confederacy; neither fear ye their fear, nor be afraid.
13 Sanctify the LORD of hosts himself; and *let* him *be* your fear, and *let* him
be your dread.
14 And he shall be for a sanctuary; but for a stone of stumbling and for a rock
of offence to both the houses of Israel, for a gin and for a snare to the inhabi-
tants of Jerusalem.
15 And many among them shall stumble, and fall, and be broken, and be
snared, and be taken.
16 Bind up the testimony, seal the law among my disciples.
17 And I will wait upon the LORD, that hideth his face from the house of Jacob,
and I will look for him.
18 Behold, I and the children whom the LORD hath given me *are* for signs
and for wonders in Israel from the LORD of hosts, which dwelleth in mount
Zion.
19 And when they shall say unto you, Seek unto them that have familiar spir-
its, and unto wizards that peep, and that mutter: should not a people seek unto
their God? for the living to the dead?
20 To the law and to the testimony: if they speak not according to this word,
it is because *there is* no light in them.
21 And they shall pass through it, hardly bestead and hungry: and it shall
come to pass, that when they shall be hungry, they shall fret themselves, and
curse their king and their God, and look upward.
22 And they shall look unto the earth; and behold trouble and darkness,
dimness of anguish; and *they shall be* driven to darkness.

The Coming Prince of Peace

9 Nevertheless the dimness *shall* not *be* such as *was* in her vexation, when at
the first he lightly afflicted the land of Zebulun and the land of Naphtali,
and afterward did more grievously afflict *her by* the way of the sea, beyond
Jordan, in Galilee of the nations.
2 The people that walked in darkness have seen a great light: they that dwell
in the land of the shadow of death, upon them hath the light shined.

HIS NAME SHALL BE CALLED
Wonderful,
COUNSELLOR,
THE MIGHTY GOD,
THE EVERLASTING Father,
THE PRINCE OF PEACE.
ISAIAH 9:6

3 Thou hast multiplied the nation, *and* not increased the joy: they joy before
thee according to the joy in harvest, *and* as *men* rejoice when they divide the
spoil.
4 For thou hast broken the yoke of his burden, and the staff of his shoulder,
the rod of his oppressor, as in the day of Midian.
5 For every battle of the warrior *is* with confused noise, and garments rolled
in blood; but *this* shall be with burning *and* fuel of fire.
6 For unto us a child is born, unto us a son is given: and the government shall
be upon his shoulder: and his name shall be called Wonderful, Counsellor,
The mighty God, The everlasting Father, The Prince of Peace.
7 Of the increase of *his* government and peace *there shall be* no end, upon
the throne of David, and upon his kingdom, to order it, and to establish it with
judgment and with justice from henceforth even for ever. The zeal of the Lord
of hosts will perform this.

Judgments upon the People for Pride

8 The Lord sent a word into Jacob, and it hath lighted upon Israel.
9 And all the people shall know, *even* Ephraim and the inhabitant of Samaria,
that say in the pride and stoutness of heart,
10 The bricks are fallen down, but we will build with hewn stones: the syco-
mores are cut down, but we will change *them into* cedars.
11 Therefore the Lord shall set up the adversaries of Rezin against him, and
join his enemies together;
12 The Syrians before, and the Philistines behind; and they shall devour Israel
with open mouth. For all this his anger is not turned away, but his hand *is*
stretched out still.
13 For the people turneth not unto him that smiteth them, neither do they
seek the Lord of hosts.
14 Therefore the Lord will cut off from Israel head and tail, branch and rush,
in one day.
15 The ancient and honourable, he *is* the head; and the prophet that teacheth
lies, he *is* the tail.
16 For the leaders of this people cause *them* to err; and *they that are* led of
them *are* destroyed.
17 Therefore the Lord shall have no joy in their young men, neither shall
have mercy on their fatherless and widows: for every one *is* an hypocrite and
an evildoer, and every mouth speaketh folly. For all this his anger is not turned
away, but his hand *is* stretched out still.
18 For wickedness burneth as the fire: it shall devour the briers and thorns,
and shall kindle in the thickets of the forest, and they shall mount up *like* the
lifting up of smoke.
19 Through the wrath of the Lord of hosts is the land darkened, and the
people shall be as the fuel of the fire: no man shall spare his brother.
20 And he shall snatch on the right hand, and be hungry; and he shall eat on
the left hand, and they shall not be satisfied: they shall eat every man the flesh
of his own arm:
21 Manasseh, Ephraim; and Ephraim, Manasseh: *and* they together *shall be*
against Judah. For all this his anger is not turned away, but his hand *is* stretched
out still.

Woe upon Tyrants

10 Woe unto them that decree unrighteous decrees, and that write griev-
ousness *which* they have prescribed;
2 To turn aside the needy from judgment, and to take away the right from
the poor of my people, that widows may be their prey, and *that* they may rob
the fatherless!

3 And what will ye do in the day of visitation, and in the desolation *which*
shall come from far? to whom will ye flee for help? and where will ye leave
your glory?
4 Without me they shall bow down under the prisoners, and they shall fall
under the slain. For all this his anger is not turned away, but his hand *is*
stretched out still.

Assyria Shall Be Broken

5 O Assyrian, the rod of mine anger, and the staff in their hand is mine indig-
nation.
6 I will send him against an hypocritical nation, and against the people of
my wrath will I give him a charge, to take the spoil, and to take the prey, and
to tread them down like the mire of the streets.
7 Howbeit he meaneth not so, neither doth his heart think so; but *it is* in his
heart to destroy and cut off nations not a few.
8 For he saith, *Are* not my princes altogether kings?
9 *Is* not Calno as Carchemish? *is* not Hamath as Arpad? *is* not Samaria as
Damascus?
10 As my hand hath found the kingdoms of the idols, and whose graven
images did excel them of Jerusalem and of Samaria;
11 Shall I not, as I have done unto Samaria and her idols, so do to Jerusalem
and her idols?
12 Wherefore it shall come to pass, *that* when the Lord hath performed his
whole work upon mount Zion and on Jerusalem, I will punish the fruit of the
stout heart of the king of Assyria, and the glory of his high looks.
13 For he saith, By the strength of my hand I have done *it*, and by my wisdom;
for I am prudent: and I have removed the bounds of the people, and have
robbed their treasures, and I have put down the inhabitants like a valiant *man*:
14 And my hand hath found as a nest the riches of the people: and as one
gathereth eggs *that are* left, have I gathered all the earth; and there was none
that moved the wing, or opened the mouth, or peeped.
15 Shall the axe boast itself against him that heweth therewith? *or* shall the
saw magnify itself against him that shaketh it? as if the rod should shake *itself*
against them that lift it up, *or* as if the staff should lift up *itself, as if it were* no
wood.
16 Therefore shall the Lord, the Lord of hosts, send among his fat ones lean-
ness; and under his glory he shall kindle a burning like the burning of a fire.
17 And the light of Israel shall be for a fire, and his Holy One for a flame: and
it shall burn and devour his thorns and his briers in one day;
18 And shall consume the glory of his forest, and of his fruitful field, both
soul and body: and they shall be as when a standardbearer fainteth.
19 And the rest of the trees of his forest shall be few, that a child may write
them.

A Remnant Shall Be Saved

20 And it shall come to pass in that day, *that* the remnant of Israel, and such
as are escaped of the house of Jacob, shall no more again stay upon him that
smote them; but shall stay upon the LORD, the Holy One of Israel, in truth.
21 The remnant shall return, *even* the remnant of Jacob, unto the mighty
God.
22 For though thy people Israel be as the sand of the sea, *yet* a remnant of
them shall return: the consumption decreed shall overflow with righteousness.
23 For the Lord GOD of hosts shall make a consumption, even determined,
in the midst of all the land.
24 Therefore thus saith the Lord GOD of hosts, O my people that dwellest in
Zion, be not afraid of the Assyrian: he shall smite thee with a rod, and shall lift
up his staff against thee, after the manner of Egypt.

25 For yet a very little while, and the indignation shall cease, and mine anger
in their destruction.
26 And the LORD of hosts shall stir up a scourge for him according to the
slaughter of Midian at the rock of Oreb: and *as* his rod *was* upon the sea, so
shall he lift it up after the manner of Egypt.
27 And it shall come to pass in that day, *that* his burden shall be taken away
from off thy shoulder, and his yoke from off thy neck, and the yoke shall be
destroyed because of the anointing.
28 He is come to Aiath, he is passed to Migron; at Michmash he hath laid up
his carriages:
29 They are gone over the passage: they have taken up their lodging at Geba;
Ramah is afraid; Gibeah of Saul is fled.
30 Lift up thy voice, O daughter of Gallim: cause it to be heard unto Laish, O
poor Anathoth.
31 Madmenah is removed; the inhabitants of Gebim gather themselves to
flee.
32 As yet shall he remain at Nob that day: he shall shake his hand *against* the
mount of the daughter of Zion, the hill of Jerusalem.
33 Behold, the Lord, the LORD of hosts, shall lop the bough with terror: and
the high ones of stature *shall be* hewn down, and the haughty shall be hum-
bled.
34 And he shall cut down the thickets of the forest with iron, and Lebanon
shall fall by a mighty one.

The Branch out of the Root of Jesse

11 And there shall come forth a rod out of the stem of Jesse, and a Branch
shall grow out of his roots:
2 And the spirit of the LORD shall rest upon him, the spirit of wisdom and
understanding, the spirit of counsel and might, the spirit of knowledge and
of the fear of the LORD;
3 And shall make him of quick understanding in the fear of the LORD: and
he shall not judge after the sight of his eyes, neither reprove after the hearing
of his ears:
4 But with righteousness shall he judge the poor, and reprove with equity
for the meek of the earth: and he shall smite the earth with the rod of his
mouth, and with the breath of his lips shall he slay the wicked.
5 And righteousness shall be the girdle of his loins, and faithfulness the gir-
dle of his reins.
6 The wolf also shall dwell with the lamb, and the leopard shall lie down with
the kid; and the calf and the young lion and the fatling together; and a little
child shall lead them.
7 And the cow and the bear shall feed; their young ones shall lie down togeth-
er: and the lion shall eat straw like the ox.
8 And the sucking child shall play on the hole of the asp, and the weaned
child shall put his hand on the cockatrice' den.
9 They shall not hurt nor destroy in all my holy mountain: for the earth shall
be full of the knowledge of the LORD, as the waters cover the sea.

The Restoration of Israel

10 And in that day there shall be a root of Jesse, which shall stand for an
ensign of the people; to it shall the Gentiles seek: and his rest shall be glorious.
11 And it shall come to pass in that day, *that* the Lord shall set his hand again
the second time to recover the remnant of his people, which shall be left, from
Assyria, and from Egypt, and from Pathros, and from Cush, and from Elam,
and from Shinar, and from Hamath, and from the islands of the sea.

12 And he shall set up an ensign for the nations, and shall assemble the out-
casts of Israel, and gather together the dispersed of Judah from the four cor-
ners of the earth.
13 The envy also of Ephraim shall depart, and the adversaries of Judah shall
be cut off: Ephraim shall not envy Judah, and Judah shall not vex Ephraim.
14 But they shall fly upon the shoulders of the Philistines toward the west;
they shall spoil them of the east together: they shall lay their hand upon Edom
and Moab; and the children of Ammon shall obey them.
15 And the LORD shall utterly destroy the tongue of the Egyptian sea; and
with his mighty wind shall he shake his hand over the river, and shall smite it
in the seven streams, and make *men* go over dryshod.
16 And there shall be an highway for the remnant of his people, which shall
be left, from Assyria; like as it was to Israel in the day that he came up out of
the land of Egypt.

A Hymn of Joyful Thanksgiving

12 And in that day thou shalt say, O LORD, I will praise thee: though thou
wast angry with me, thine anger is turned away, and thou comfortedst
me.
2 Behold, God *is* my salvation; I will trust, and not be afraid: for the LORD
JEHOVAH *is* my strength and *my* song; he also is become my salvation.
3 Therefore with joy shall ye draw water out of the wells of salvation.
4 And in that day shall ye say, Praise the LORD, call upon his name, declare
his doings among the people, make mention that his name is exalted.
5 Sing unto the LORD; for he hath done excellent things: this *is* known in all
the earth.
6 Cry out and shout, thou inhabitant of Zion: for great *is* the Holy One of
Israel in the midst of thee.

Babylon Will Be Punished

13 The burden of Babylon, which Isaiah the son of Amoz did see.
2 Lift ye up a banner upon the high mountain, exalt the voice unto
them, shake the hand, that they may go into the gates of the nobles.
3 I have commanded my sanctified ones, I have also called my mighty ones
for mine anger, *even* them that rejoice in my highness.
4 The noise of a multitude in the mountains, like as of a great people; a tumul-
tuous noise of the kingdoms of nations gathered together: the LORD of hosts
mustereth the host of the battle.
5 They come from a far country, from the end of heaven, *even* the LORD, and
the weapons of his indignation, to destroy the whole land.
6 Howl ye; for the day of the LORD *is* at hand; it shall come as a destruction
from the Almighty.
7 Therefore shall all hands be faint, and every man's heart shall melt:
8 And they shall be afraid: pangs and sorrows shall take hold of them; they
shall be in pain as a woman that travaileth: they shall be amazed one at anoth-
er; their faces *shall be as* flames.
9 Behold, the day of the LORD cometh, cruel both with wrath and fierce anger,
to lay the land desolate: and he shall destroy the sinners thereof out of it.
10 For the stars of heaven and the constellations thereof shall not give their
light: the sun shall be darkened in his going forth, and the moon shall not
cause her light to shine.
11 And I will punish the world for *their* evil, and the wicked for their iniqui-
ty; and I will cause the arrogancy of the proud to cease, and will lay low the
haughtiness of the terrible.
12 I will make a man more precious than fine gold; even a man than the
golden wedge of Ophir.

13 Therefore I will shake the heavens, and the earth shall remove out of her
place, in the wrath of the LORD of hosts, and in the day of his fierce anger.
14 And it shall be as the chased roe, and as a sheep that no man taketh up:
they shall every man turn to his own people, and flee every one into his own
land.
15 Every one that is found shall be thrust through; and every one that is joined
unto them shall fall by the sword.
16 Their children also shall be dashed to pieces before their eyes; their hous-
es shall be spoiled, and their wives ravished.
17 Behold, I will stir up the Medes against them, which shall not regard silver;
and *as for* gold, they shall not delight in it.
18 *Their* bows also shall dash the young men to pieces; and they shall have
no pity on the fruit of the womb; their eye shall not spare children.

The Desolation of Babylon

19 And Babylon, the glory of kingdoms, the beauty of the Chaldees' excellen-
cy, shall be as when God overthrew Sodom and Gomorrah.
20 It shall never be inhabited, neither shall it be dwelt in from generation to
generation: neither shall the Arabian pitch tent there; neither shall the shep-
herds make their fold there.
21 But wild beasts of the desert shall lie there; and their houses shall be full
of doleful creatures; and owls shall dwell there, and satyrs shall dance there.
22 And the wild beasts of the islands shall cry in their desolate houses, and
dragons in *their* pleasant palaces: and her time *is* near to come, and her days
shall not be prolonged.

God Will Rescue His People from Babylon

14 For the LORD will have mercy on Jacob, and will yet choose Israel, and
set them in their own land: and the strangers shall be joined with them,
and they shall cleave to the house of Jacob.
2 And the people shall take them, and bring them to their place: and the
house of Israel shall possess them in the land of the LORD for servants and
handmaids: and they shall take them captives, whose captives they were; and
they shall rule over their oppressors.
3 And it shall come to pass in the day that the LORD shall give thee rest from
thy sorrow, and from thy fear, and from the hard bondage wherein thou wast
made to serve,
4 That thou shalt take up this proverb against the king of Babylon, and say,
How hath the oppressor ceased! the golden city ceased!
5 The LORD hath broken the staff of the wicked, *and* the sceptre of the rulers.
6 He who smote the people in wrath with a continual stroke, he that ruled
the nations in anger, is persecuted, *and* none hindereth.
7 The whole earth is at rest, *and* is quiet: they break forth into singing.
8 Yea, the fir trees rejoice at thee, *and* the cedars of Lebanon, *saying*, Since
thou art laid down, no feller is come up against us.
9 Hell from beneath is moved for thee to meet *thee* at thy coming: it stirreth
up the dead for thee, *even* all the chief ones of the earth; it hath raised up from
their thrones all the kings of the nations.
10 All they shall speak and say unto thee, Art thou also become weak as we?
art thou become like unto us?
11 Thy pomp is brought down to the grave, *and* the noise of thy viols: the
worm is spread under thee, and the worms cover thee.
12 How art thou fallen from heaven, O Lucifer, son of the morning! *how* art
thou cut down to the ground, which didst weaken the nations!
13 For thou hast said in thine heart, I will ascend into heaven, I will exalt my
throne above the stars of God: I will sit also upon the mount of the congrega-
tion, in the sides of the north:

14 I will ascend above the heights of the clouds; I will be like the most High.
15 Yet thou shalt be brought down to hell, to the sides of the pit.
16 They that see thee shall narrowly look upon thee, *and* consider thee, *say-*
ing, Is this the man that made the earth to tremble, that did shake kingdoms;
17 *That* made the world as a wilderness, and destroyed the cities thereof;
that opened not the house of his prisoners?
18 All the kings of the nations, *even* all of them, lie in glory, every one in his
own house.
19 But thou art cast out of thy grave like an abominable branch, *and as* the
raiment of those that are slain, thrust through with a sword, that go down to
the stones of the pit; as a carcase trodden under feet.
20 Thou shalt not be joined with them in burial, because thou hast destroyed
thy land, *and* slain thy people: the seed of evildoers shall never be renowned.
21 Prepare slaughter for his children for the iniquity of their fathers; that
they do not rise, nor possess the land, nor fill the face of the world with cities.
22 For I will rise up against them, saith the LORD of hosts, and cut off from
Babylon the name, and remnant, and son, and nephew, saith the LORD.
23 I will also make it a possession for the bittern, and pools of water: and I
will sweep it with the besom of destruction, saith the LORD of hosts.

Assyria Will Be Punished

24 The LORD of hosts hath sworn, saying, Surely as I have thought, so shall it
come to pass; and as I have purposed, *so* shall it stand:
25 That I will break the Assyrian in my land, and upon my mountains tread
him under foot: then shall his yoke depart from off them, and his burden
depart from off their shoulders.
26 This *is* the purpose that is purposed upon the whole earth: and this *is* the
hand that is stretched out upon all the nations.
27 For the LORD of hosts hath purposed, and who shall disannul *it*? and his
hand *is* stretched out, and who shall turn it back?

The Philistines Will Be Punished

28 In the year that king Ahaz died was this burden.
29 Rejoice not thou, whole Palestina, because the rod of him that smote thee
is broken: for out of the serpent's root shall come forth a cockatrice, and his
fruit *shall be* a fiery flying serpent.
30 And the firstborn of the poor shall feed, and the needy shall lie down in
safety: and I will kill thy root with famine, and he shall slay thy remnant.
31 Howl, O gate; cry, O city; thou, whole Palestina, *art* dissolved: for there
shall come from the north a smoke, and none *shall be* alone in his appointed
times.
32 What shall *one* then answer the messengers of the nation? That the LORD
hath founded Zion, and the poor of his people shall trust in it.

Moab Will Be Punished

15 The burden of Moab. Because in the night Ar of Moab is laid waste,
and brought to silence; because in the night Kir of Moab is laid waste,
and brought to silence;
2 He is gone up to Bajith, and to Dibon, the high places, to weep: Moab shall
howl over Nebo, and over Medeba: on all their heads *shall be* baldness, *and*
every beard cut off.
3 In their streets they shall gird themselves with sackcloth: on the tops of
their houses, and in their streets, every one shall howl, weeping abundantly.
4 And Heshbon shall cry, and Elealeh: their voice shall be heard *even* unto
Jahaz: therefore the armed soldiers of Moab shall cry out; his life shall be
grievous unto him.

5 My heart shall cry out for Moab; his fugitives *shall flee* unto Zoar, an heif-
er of three years old: for by the mounting up of Luhith with weeping shall they
go it up; for in the way of Horonaim they shall raise up a cry of destruction.
6 For the waters of Nimrim shall be desolate: for the hay is withered away,
the grass faileth, there is no green thing.
7 Therefore the abundance they have gotten, and that which they have laid
up, shall they carry away to the brook of the willows.
8 For the cry is gone round about the borders of Moab; the howling thereof
unto Eglaim, and the howling thereof unto Beerelim.
9 For the waters of Dimon shall be full of blood: for I will bring more upon
Dimon, lions upon him that escapeth of Moab, and upon the remnant of the
land.

Judgment upon Moab

16 Send ye the lamb to the ruler of the land from Sela to the wilderness,
unto the mount of the daughter of Zion.
2 For it shall be, *that*, as a wandering bird cast out of the nest, *so* the daugh-
ters of Moab shall be at the fords of Arnon.
3 Take counsel, execute judgment; make thy shadow as the night in the midst
of the noonday; hide the outcasts; bewray not him that wandereth.
4 Let mine outcasts dwell with thee, Moab; be thou a covert to them from
the face of the spoiler: for the extortioner is at an end, the spoiler ceaseth, the
oppressors are consumed out of the land.
5 And in mercy shall the throne be established: and he shall sit upon it in
truth in the tabernacle of David, judging, and seeking judgment, and hasting
righteousness.
6 We have heard of the pride of Moab; *he is* very proud: *even* of his haughti-
ness, and his pride, and his wrath: *but* his lies *shall* not *be* so.
7 Therefore shall Moab howl for Moab, every one shall howl: for the foun-
dations of Kir-hareseth shall ye mourn; surely *they are* stricken.
8 For the fields of Heshbon languish, *and* the vine of Sibmah: the lords of
the heathen have broken down the principal plants thereof, they are come
even unto Jazer, they wandered *through* the wilderness: her branches are
stretched out, they are gone over the sea.
9 Therefore I will bewail with the weeping of Jazer the vine of Sibmah: I will
water thee with my tears, O Heshbon, and Elealeh: for the shouting for thy
summer fruits and for thy harvest is fallen.
10 And gladness is taken away, and joy out of the plentiful field; and in the
vineyards there shall be no singing, neither shall there be shouting: the tread-
ers shall tread out no wine in *their* presses; I have made *their vintage* shouting
to cease.
11 Wherefore my bowels shall sound like an harp for Moab, and mine inward
parts for Kir-haresh.
12 And it shall come to pass, when it is seen that Moab is weary on the high
place, that he shall come to his sanctuary to pray; but he shall not prevail.
13 This *is* the word that the LORD hath spoken concerning Moab since that
time.
14 But now the LORD hath spoken, saying, Within three years, as the years of
an hireling, and the glory of Moab shall be contemned, with all that great
multitude; and the remnant *shall be* very small *and* feeble.

Syria and Israel Will Be Punished

17 The burden of Damascus. Behold, Damascus is taken away from *being*
a city, and it shall be a ruinous heap.
2 The cities of Aroer *are* forsaken: they shall be for flocks, which shall lie
down, and none shall make *them* afraid.

3 The fortress also shall cease from Ephraim, and the kingdom from
Damascus, and the remnant of Syria: they shall be as the glory of the children
of Israel, saith the LORD of hosts.
4 And in that day it shall come to pass, *that* the glory of Jacob shall be made
thin, and the fatness of his flesh shall wax lean.
5 And it shall be as when the harvestman gathereth the corn, and reapeth
the ears with his arm; and it shall be as he that gathereth ears in the valley of
Rephaim.
6 Yet gleaning grapes shall be left in it, as the shaking of an olive tree, two *or*
three berries in the top of the uppermost bough, four *or* five in the outmost
fruitful branches thereof, saith the LORD God of Israel.
7 At that day shall a man look to his Maker, and his eyes shall have respect to
the Holy One of Israel.
8 And he shall not look to the altars, the work of his hands, neither shall
respect *that* which his fingers have made, either the groves, or the images.
9 In that day shall his strong cities be as a forsaken bough, and an uppermost
branch, which they left because of the children of Israel: and there shall be
desolation.
10 Because thou hast forgotten the God of thy salvation, and hast not been
mindful of the rock of thy strength, therefore shalt thou plant pleasant plants,
and shalt set it with strange slips:
11 In the day shalt thou make thy plant to grow, and in the morning shalt
thou make thy seed to flourish: *but* the harvest *shall be* a heap in the day of
grief and of desperate sorrow.
12 Woe to the multitude of many people, *which* make a noise like the noise
of the seas; and to the rushing of nations, *that* make a rushing like the rushing
of mighty waters!
13 The nations shall rush like the rushing of many waters: but *God* shall
rebuke them, and they shall flee far off, and shall be chased as the chaff of the
mountains before the wind, and like a rolling thing before the whirlwind.
14 And behold at eveningtide trouble; *and* before the morning he *is* not. This
is the portion of them that spoil us, and the lot of them that rob us.

Ethiopia Will Be Punished

18 Woe to the land shadowing with wings, which *is* beyond the rivers of
Ethiopia:
2 That sendeth ambassadors by the sea, even in vessels of bulrushes upon
the waters, *saying*, Go, ye swift messengers, to a nation scattered and peeled,
to a people terrible from their beginning hitherto; a nation meted out and
trodden down, whose land the rivers have spoiled!
3 All ye inhabitants of the world, and dwellers on the earth, see ye, when he
lifteth up an ensign on the mountains; and when he bloweth a trumpet, hear ye.
4 For so the LORD said unto me, I will take my rest, and I will consider in my
dwelling place like a clear heat upon herbs, *and* like a cloud of dew in the heat
of harvest.
5 For afore the harvest, when the bud is perfect, and the sour grape is ripen-
ing in the flower, he shall both cut off the sprigs with pruning hooks, and take
away *and* cut down the branches.
6 They shall be left together unto the fowls of the mountains, and to the
beasts of the earth: and the fowls shall summer upon them, and all the beasts
of the earth shall winter upon them.
7 In that time shall the present be brought unto the LORD of hosts of a people
scattered and peeled, and from a people terrible from their beginning hith-
erto; a nation meted out and trodden under foot, whose land the rivers have
spoiled, to the place of the name of the LORD of hosts, the mount Zion.

Egypt Will Be Punished

19 The burden of Egypt. Behold, the LORD rideth upon a swift cloud, and
shall come into Egypt: and the idols of Egypt shall be moved at his
presence, and the heart of Egypt shall melt in the midst of it.
2 And I will set the Egyptians against the Egyptians: and they shall fight every
one against his brother, and every one against his neighbour; city against city,
and kingdom against kingdom.
3 And the spirit of Egypt shall fail in the midst thereof; and I will destroy the
counsel thereof: and they shall seek to the idols, and to the charmers, and to
them that have familiar spirits, and to the wizards.
4 And the Egyptians will I give over into the hand of a cruel lord; and a fierce
king shall rule over them, saith the Lord, the LORD of hosts.
5 And the waters shall fail from the sea, and the river shall be wasted and
dried up.
6 And they shall turn the rivers far away; *and* the brooks of defence shall be
emptied and dried up: the reeds and flags shall wither.
7 The paper reeds by the brooks, by the mouth of the brooks, and every thing
sown by the brooks, shall wither, be driven away, and be no *more*.
8 The fishers also shall mourn, and all they that cast angle into the brooks
shall lament, and they that spread nets upon the waters shall languish.
9 Moreover they that work in fine flax, and they that weave networks, shall
be confounded.
10 And they shall be broken in the purposes thereof, all that make sluices
and ponds for fish.
11 Surely the princes of Zoan *are* fools, the counsel of the wise counsellors
of Pharaoh is become brutish: how say ye unto Pharaoh, I *am* the son of the
wise, the son of ancient kings?
12 Where *are* they? where *are* thy wise *men*? and let them tell thee now, and
let them know what the LORD of hosts hath purposed upon Egypt.
13 The princes of Zoan are become fools, the princes of Noph are deceived;
they have also seduced Egypt, *even they that are* the stay of the tribes thereof.
14 The LORD hath mingled a perverse spirit in the midst thereof: and they
have caused Egypt to err in every work thereof, as a drunken *man* staggereth
in his vomit.
15 Neither shall there be *any* work for Egypt, which the head or tail, branch
or rush, may do.
16 In that day shall Egypt be like unto women: and it shall be afraid and fear
because of the shaking of the hand of the LORD of hosts, which he shaketh over it.
17 And the land of Judah shall be a terror unto Egypt, every one that maketh
mention thereof shall be afraid in himself, because of the counsel of the LORD
of hosts, which he hath determined against it.
18 In that day shall five cities in the land of Egypt speak the language of
Canaan, and swear to the LORD of hosts; one shall be called, The city of destruc-
tion.
19 In that day shall there be an altar to the LORD in the midst of the land of
Egypt, and a pillar at the border thereof to the LORD.
20 And it shall be for a sign and for a witness unto the LORD of hosts in the
land of Egypt: for they shall cry unto the LORD because of the oppressors, and
he shall send them a saviour, and a great one, and he shall deliver them.
21 And the LORD shall be known to Egypt, and the Egyptians shall know the
LORD in that day, and shall do sacrifice and oblation; yea, they shall vow a vow
unto the LORD, and perform *it*.
22 And the LORD shall smite Egypt: he shall smite and heal *it*: and they shall
return *even* to the LORD, and he shall be intreated of them, and shall heal them.

23 In that day shall there be a highway out of Egypt to Assyria, and the
Assyrian shall come into Egypt, and the Egyptian into Assyria, and the
Egyptians shall serve with the Assyrians.
24 In that day shall Israel be the third with Egypt and with Assyria, *even* a
blessing in the midst of the land:
25 Whom the LORD of hosts shall bless, saying, Blessed *be* Egypt my people,
and Assyria the work of my hands, and Israel mine inheritance.

The Shame of Those Allied with Egypt

20 In the year that Tartan came unto Ashdod, (when Sargon the king of
Assyria sent him,) and fought against Ashdod, and took it;
2 At the same time spake the LORD by Isaiah the son of Amoz, saying, Go and
loose the sackcloth from off thy loins, and put off thy shoe from thy foot. And
he did so, walking naked and barefoot.
3 And the LORD said, Like as my servant Isaiah hath walked naked and bare-
foot three years *for* a sign and wonder upon Egypt and upon Ethiopia;
4 So shall the king of Assyria lead away the Egyptians prisoners, and the
Ethiopians captives, young and old, naked and barefoot, even with *their* but-
tocks uncovered, to the shame of Egypt.
5 And they shall be afraid and ashamed of Ethiopia their expectation, and
of Egypt their glory.
6 And the inhabitant of this isle shall say in that day, Behold, such *is* our
expectation, whither we flee for help to be delivered from the king of Assyria:
and how shall we escape?

The Fall of Babylon

21 The burden of the desert of the sea. As whirlwinds in the south pass
through; *so* it cometh from the desert, from a terrible land.
2 A grievous vision is declared unto me; the treacherous dealer dealeth
treacherously, and the spoiler spoileth. Go up, O Elam: besiege, O Media; all
the sighing thereof have I made to cease.
3 Therefore are my loins filled with pain: pangs have taken hold upon me,
as the pangs of a woman that travaileth: I was bowed down at the hearing *of*
it; I was dismayed at the seeing *of it*.
4 My heart panted, fearfulness affrighted me: the night of my pleasure hath
he turned into fear unto me.
5 Prepare the table, watch in the watchtower, eat, drink: arise, ye princes,
and anoint the shield.
6 For thus hath the Lord said unto me, Go, set a watchman, let him declare
what he seeth.
7 And he saw a chariot *with* a couple of horsemen, a chariot of asses, *and* a
chariot of camels; and he hearkened diligently with much heed:
8 And he cried, A lion: My lord, I stand continually upon the watchtower in
the daytime, and I am set in my ward whole nights:
9 And, behold, here cometh a chariot of men, *with* a couple of horsemen.
And he answered and said, Babylon is fallen, is fallen; and all the graven imag-
es of her gods he hath broken unto the ground.
10 O my threshing, and the corn of my floor: that which I have heard of the
LORD of hosts, the God of Israel, have I declared unto you.

Someone Calling from Seir

11 The burden of Dumah. He calleth to me out of Seir, Watchman, what of
the night? Watchman, what of the night?
12 The watchman said, The morning cometh, and also the night: if ye will
enquire, enquire ye: return, come.

Arabia Will Be Punished

13 The burden upon Arabia. In the forest in Arabia shall ye lodge, O ye trav-
elling companies of Dedanim.
14 The inhabitants of the land of Tema brought water to him that was thirsty,
they prevented with their bread him that fled.
15 For they fled from the swords, from the drawn sword, and from the bent
bow, and from the grievousness of war.
16 For thus hath the Lord said unto me, Within a year, according to the years
of an hireling, and all the glory of Kedar shall fail:
17 And the residue of the number of archers, the mighty men of the children
of Kedar, shall be diminished: for the LORD God of Israel hath spoken *it*.

Judah Will Be Punished

22 The burden of the valley of vision. What aileth thee now, that thou art
wholly gone up to the housetops?
2 Thou that art full of stirs, a tumultuous city, a joyous city: thy slain *men are*
not slain with the sword, nor dead in battle.
3 All thy rulers are fled together, they are bound by the archers: all that are
found in thee are bound together, *which* have fled from far.
4 Therefore said I, Look away from me; I will weep bitterly, labour not to
comfort me, because of the spoiling of the daughter of my people.
5 For *it is* a day of trouble, and of treading down, and of perplexity by the
Lord GOD of hosts in the valley of vision, breaking down the walls, and of
crying to the mountains.
6 And Elam bare the quiver with chariots of men *and* horsemen, and Kir
uncovered the shield.
7 And it shall come to pass, *that* thy choicest valleys shall be full of chariots,
and the horsemen shall set themselves in array at the gate.
8 And he discovered the covering of Judah, and thou didst look in that day
to the armour of the house of the forest.
9 Ye have seen also the breaches of the city of David, that they are many: and
ye gathered together the waters of the lower pool.
10 And ye have numbered the houses of Jerusalem, and the houses have ye
broken down to fortify the wall.
11 Ye made also a ditch between the two walls for the water of the old pool:
but ye have not looked unto the maker thereof, neither had respect unto him
that fashioned it long ago.
12 And in that day did the Lord GOD of hosts call to weeping, and to mourn-
ing, and to baldness, and to girding with sackcloth:
13 And behold joy and gladness, slaying oxen, and killing sheep, eating flesh,
and drinking wine: let us eat and drink; for to morrow we shall die.
14 And it was revealed in mine ears by the LORD of hosts, Surely this iniquity
shall not be purged from you till ye die, saith the Lord GOD of hosts.

Shebna's Dismissal from His Position

15 Thus saith the Lord GOD of hosts, Go, get thee unto this treasurer, *even*
unto Shebna, which *is* over the house, *and say*,
16 What hast thou here? and whom hast thou here, that thou hast hewed
thee out a sepulchre here, *as* he that heweth him out a sepulchre on high, *and*
that graveth an habitation for himself in a rock?
17 Behold, the LORD will carry thee away with a mighty captivity, and will
surely cover thee.
18 He will surely violently turn and toss thee *like* a ball into a large country:
there shalt thou die, and there the chariots of thy glory *shall be* the shame of
thy lord's house.
19 And I will drive thee from thy station, and from thy state shall he pull thee
down.

20 And it shall come to pass in that day, that I will call my servant Eliakim the
son of Hilkiah:
21 And I will clothe him with thy robe, and strengthen him with thy girdle,
and I will commit thy government into his hand: and he shall be a father to
the inhabitants of Jerusalem, and to the house of Judah.
22 And the key of the house of David will I lay upon his shoulder; so he shall
open, and none shall shut; and he shall shut, and none shall open.
23 And I will fasten him *as* a nail in a sure place; and he shall be for a glorious
throne to his father's house.
24 And they shall hang upon him all the glory of his father's house, the off-
spring and the issue, all vessels of small quantity, from the vessels of cups, even
to all the vessels of flagons.
25 In that day, saith the LORD of hosts, shall the nail that is fastened in the
sure place be removed, and be cut down, and fall; and the burden that *was*
upon it shall be cut off: for the LORD hath spoken *it*.

Tyre Will Be Punished

23 The burden of Tyre. Howl, ye ships of Tarshish; for it is laid waste, so
that there is no house, no entering in: from the land of Chittim it is
revealed to them.
2 Be still, ye inhabitants of the isle; thou whom the merchants of Zidon, that
pass over the sea, have replenished.
3 And by great waters the seed of Sihor, the harvest of the river, *is* her revenue;
and she is a mart of nations.
4 Be thou ashamed, O Zidon: for the sea hath spoken, *even* the strength of
the sea, saying, I travail not, nor bring forth children, neither do I nourish up
young men, *nor* bring up virgins.
5 As at the report concerning Egypt, *so* shall they be sorely pained at the
report of Tyre.
6 Pass ye over to Tarshish; howl, ye inhabitants of the isle.
7 *Is* this your joyous *city*, whose antiquity *is* of ancient days? her own feet
shall carry her afar off to sojourn.
8 Who hath taken this counsel against Tyre, the crowning *city*, whose mer-
chants *are* princes, whose traffickers *are* the honourable of the earth?
9 The LORD of hosts hath purposed it, to stain the pride of all glory, *and* to
bring into contempt all the honourable of the earth.
10 Pass through thy land as a river, O daughter of Tarshish: *there is* no more
strength.
11 He stretched out his hand over the sea, he shook the kingdoms: the LORD
hath given a commandment against the merchant *city*, to destroy the strong
holds thereof.
12 And he said, Thou shalt no more rejoice, O thou oppressed virgin, daugh-
ter of Zidon: arise, pass over to Chittim; there also shalt thou have no rest.
13 Behold the land of the Chaldeans; this people was not, *till* the Assyrian
founded it for them that dwell in the wilderness: they set up the towers there-
of, they raised up the palaces thereof; *and* he brought it to ruin.
14 Howl, ye ships of Tarshish: for your strength is laid waste.
15 And it shall come to pass in that day, that Tyre shall be forgotten seventy
years, according to the days of one king: after the end of seventy years shall
Tyre sing as an harlot.
16 Take an harp, go about the city, thou harlot that hast been forgotten; make
sweet melody, sing many songs, that thou mayest be remembered.
17 And it shall come to pass after the end of seventy years, that the LORD will
visit Tyre, and she shall turn to her hire, and shall commit fornication with
all the kingdoms of the world upon the face of the earth.

18 And her merchandise and her hire shall be holiness to the LORD: it shall
not be treasured nor laid up; for her merchandise shall be for them that dwell
before the LORD, to eat sufficiently, and for durable clothing.

God's Judgments upon the Land

24 Behold, the LORD maketh the earth empty, and maketh it waste, and
turneth it upside down, and scattereth abroad the inhabitants there-
of.
2 And it shall be, as with the people, so with the priest; as with the servant,
so with his master; as with the maid, so with her mistress; as with the buyer,
so with the seller; as with the lender, so with the borrower; as with the taker
of usury, so with the giver of usury to him.
3 The land shall be utterly emptied, and utterly spoiled: for the LORD hath
spoken this word.
4 The earth mourneth *and* fadeth away, the world languisheth *and* fadeth
away, the haughty people of the earth do languish.
5 The earth also is defiled under the inhabitants thereof; because they have
transgressed the laws, changed the ordinance, broken the everlasting cove-
nant.
6 Therefore hath the curse devoured the earth, and they that dwell therein
are desolate: therefore the inhabitants of the earth are burned, and few men
left.
7 The new wine mourneth, the vine languisheth, all the merryhearted do
sigh.
8 The mirth of tabrets ceaseth, the noise of them that rejoice endeth, the joy
of the harp ceaseth.
9 They shall not drink wine with a song; strong drink shall be bitter to them
that drink it.
10 The city of confusion is broken down: every house is shut up, that no man
may come in.
11 *There is* a crying for wine in the streets; all joy is darkened, the mirth of
the land is gone.
12 In the city is left desolation, and the gate is smitten with destruction.

A Remnant Shall Joyfully Praise God

13 When thus it shall be in the midst of the land among the people, *there
shall be* as the shaking of an olive tree, *and* as the gleaning grapes when the
vintage is done.
14 They shall lift up their voice, they shall sing for the majesty of the LORD,
they shall cry aloud from the sea.
15 Wherefore glorify ye the LORD in the fires, *even* the name of the LORD God
of Israel in the isles of the sea.

God Will Advance His Kingdom

16 From the uttermost part of the earth have we heard songs, *even* glory to
the righteous. But I said, My leanness, my leanness, woe unto me! the treach-
erous dealers have dealt treacherously; yea, the treacherous dealers have dealt
very treacherously.
17 Fear, and the pit, and the snare, *are* upon thee, O inhabitant of the earth.
18 And it shall come to pass, *that* he who fleeth from the noise of the fear
shall fall into the pit; and he that cometh up out of the midst of the pit shall
be taken in the snare: for the windows from on high are open, and the foun-
dations of the earth do shake.
19 The earth is utterly broken down, the earth is clean dissolved, the earth
is moved exceedingly.
20 The earth shall reel to and fro like a drunkard, and shall be removed like
a cottage; and the transgression thereof shall be heavy upon it; and it shall fall,
and not rise again.

21 And it shall come to pass in that day, *that* the LORD shall punish the host
of the high ones *that are* on high, and the kings of the earth upon the earth.
22 And they shall be gathered together, *as* prisoners are gathered in the pit,
and shall be shut up in the prison, and after many days shall they be visited.
23 Then the moon shall be confounded, and the sun ashamed, when the LORD
of hosts shall reign in mount Zion, and in Jerusalem, and before his ancients
gloriously.

Isaiah Praises God for His Judgments

25 O LORD, thou *art* my God; I will exalt thee, I will praise thy name; for
thou hast done wonderful *things; thy* counsels of old *are* faithfulness
and truth.
2 For thou hast made of a city an heap; *of* a defenced city a ruin: a palace of
strangers to be no city; it shall never be built.
3 Therefore shall the strong people glorify thee, the city of the terrible
nations shall fear thee.
4 For thou hast been a strength to the poor, a strength to the needy in his
distress, a refuge from the storm, a shadow from the heat, when the blast of
the terrible ones *is* as a storm *against* the wall.
5 Thou shalt bring down the noise of strangers, as the heat in a dry place;
even the heat with the shadow of a cloud: the branch of the terrible ones shall
be brought low.

Death Will Be Swallowed Up

6 And in this mountain shall the LORD of hosts make unto all people a feast
of fat things, a feast of wines on the lees, of fat things full of marrow, of wines
on the lees well refined.
7 And he will destroy in this mountain the face of the covering cast over all
people, and the vail that is spread over all nations.
8 He will swallow up death in victory; and the Lord GOD will wipe away tears
from off all faces; and the rebuke of his people shall he take away from off all
the earth: for the LORD hath spoken *it*.

God's Victorious Salvation

9 And it shall be said in that day, Lo, this *is* our God; we have waited for him,
and he will save us: this *is* the LORD; we have waited for him, we will be glad
and rejoice in his salvation.
10 For in this mountain shall the hand of the LORD rest, and Moab shall be
trodden down under him, even as straw is trodden down for the dunghill.
11 And he shall spread forth his hands in the midst of them, as he that swim-
meth spreadeth forth *his hands* to swim: and he shall bring down their pride
together with the spoils of their hands.
12 And the fortress of the high fort of thy walls shall he bring down, lay low,
and bring to the ground, *even* to the dust.

A Song of Confidence in God

26 In that day shall this song be sung in the land of Judah; We have a strong
city; salvation will *God* appoint *for* walls and bulwarks.
2 Open ye the gates, that the righteous nation which keepeth the truth may
enter in.
3 Thou wilt keep *him* in perfect peace, *whose* mind *is* stayed *on thee*: because
he trusteth in thee.
4 Trust ye in the LORD for ever: for in the LORD JEHOVAH *is* everlasting
strength:
5 For he bringeth down them that dwell on high; the lofty city, he layeth it
low; he layeth it low, *even* to the ground; he bringeth it *even* to the dust.
6 The foot shall tread it down, *even* the feet of the poor, *and* the steps of the
needy.

7 The way of the just *is* uprightness: thou, most upright, dost weigh the path
of the just.
8 Yea, in the way of thy judgments, O LORD, have we waited for thee; the desire
of *our* soul *is* to thy name, and to the remembrance of thee.
9 With my soul have I desired thee in the night; yea, with my spirit within
me will I seek thee early: for when thy judgments *are* in the earth, the inhab-
itants of the world will learn righteousness.
10 Let favour be shewed to the wicked, *yet* will he not learn righteousness:
in the land of uprightness will he deal unjustly, and will not behold the maj-
esty of the LORD.
11 LORD, *when* thy hand is lifted up, they will not see: *but* they shall see, and
be ashamed for *their* envy at the people; yea, the fire of thine enemies shall
devour them.
12 LORD, thou wilt ordain peace for us: for thou also hast wrought all our
works in us.
13 O LORD our God, *other* lords beside thee have had dominion over us: *but*
by thee only will we make mention of thy name.
14 *They are* dead, they shall not live; *they are* deceased, they shall not rise:
therefore hast thou visited and destroyed them, and made all their memory
to perish.
15 Thou hast increased the nation, O LORD, thou hast increased the nation:
thou art glorified: thou hadst removed *it* far *unto* all the ends of the earth.
16 LORD, in trouble have they visited thee, they poured out a prayer *when* thy
chastening *was* upon them.
17 Like as a woman with child, *that* draweth near the time of her delivery, is
in pain, *and* crieth out in her pangs; so have we been in thy sight, O LORD.
18 We have been with child, we have been in pain, we have as it were brought
forth wind; we have not wrought any deliverance in the earth; neither have
the inhabitants of the world fallen.
19 Thy dead *men* shall live, *together with* my dead body shall they arise. Awake
and sing, ye that dwell in dust: for thy dew *is as* the dew of herbs, and the earth
shall cast out the dead.
20 Come, my people, enter thou into thy chambers, and shut thy doors about
thee: hide thyself as it were for a little moment, until the indignation be over-
past.
21 For, behold, the LORD cometh out of his place to punish the inhabitants
of the earth for their iniquity: the earth also shall disclose her blood, and shall
no more cover her slain.

God's Care for His People

27 In that day the LORD with his sore and great and strong sword shall
punish leviathan the piercing serpent, even leviathan that crooked
serpent; and he shall slay the dragon that *is* in the sea.
2 In that day sing ye unto her, A vineyard of red wine.
3 I the LORD do keep it; I will water it every moment: lest *any* hurt it, I will
keep it night and day.
4 Fury *is* not in me: who would set the briers *and* thorns against me in battle?
I would go through them, I would burn them together.
5 Or let him take hold of my strength, *that* he may make peace with me; *and*
he shall make peace with me.
6 He shall cause them that come of Jacob to take root: Israel shall blossom
and bud, and fill the face of the world with fruit.
7 Hath he smitten him, as he smote those that smote him? *or* is he slain
according to the slaughter of them that are slain by him?
8 In measure, when it shooteth forth, thou wilt debate with it: he stayeth his
rough wind in the day of the east wind.

9 By this therefore shall the iniquity of Jacob be purged; and this *is* all the
fruit to take away his sin; when he maketh all the stones of the altar as chalk-
stones that are beaten in sunder, the groves and images shall not stand up.
10 Yet the defenced city *shall be* desolate, *and* the habitation forsaken, and
left like a wilderness: there shall the calf feed, and there shall he lie down, and
consume the branches thereof.
11 When the boughs thereof are withered, they shall be broken off: the
women come, *and* set them on fire: for it *is* a people of no understanding:
therefore he that made them will not have mercy on them, and he that formed
them will shew them no favour.
12 And it shall come to pass in that day, *that* the LORD shall beat off from the
channel of the river unto the stream of Egypt, and ye shall be gathered one by
one, O ye children of Israel.
13 And it shall come to pass in that day, *that* the great trumpet shall be blown,
and they shall come which were ready to perish in the land of Assyria, and the
outcasts in the land of Egypt, and shall worship the LORD in the holy mount
at Jerusalem.

Ephraim Will Fall

28 Woe to the crown of pride, to the drunkards of Ephraim, whose
glorious beauty *is* a fading flower, which *are* on the head of the fat
valleys of them that are overcome with wine!
2 Behold, the Lord hath a mighty and strong one, *which* as a tempest of hail
and a destroying storm, as a flood of mighty waters overflowing, shall cast
down to the earth with the hand.
3 The crown of pride, the drunkards of Ephraim, shall be trodden under
feet:
4 And the glorious beauty, which *is* on the head of the fat valley, shall be a
fading flower, *and* as the hasty fruit before the summer; which *when* he that
looketh upon it seeth, while it is yet in his hand he eateth it up.
5 In that day shall the LORD of hosts be for a crown of glory, and for a diadem
of beauty, unto the residue of his people,
6 And for a spirit of judgment to him that sitteth in judgment, and for
strength to them that turn the battle to the gate.
7 But they also have erred through wine, and through strong drink are out
of the way; the priest and the prophet have erred through strong drink, they
are swallowed up of wine, they are out of the way through strong drink; they
err in vision, they stumble *in* judgment.
8 For all tables are full of vomit *and* filthiness, *so that there is* no place *clean*.
9 Whom shall he teach knowledge? and whom shall he make to understand
doctrine? *them that are* weaned from the milk, *and* drawn from the breasts.
10 For precept *must be* upon precept, precept upon precept; line upon line,
line upon line; here a little, *and* there a little:
11 For with stammering lips and another tongue will he speak to this people.
12 To whom he said, This *is* the rest *wherewith* ye may cause the weary to rest;
and this *is* the refreshing: yet they would not hear.
13 But the word of the LORD was unto them precept upon precept, precept
upon precept; line upon line, line upon line; here a little, *and* there a little;
that they might go, and fall backward, and be broken, and snared, and taken.

A Message to Jerusalem

14 Wherefore hear the word of the LORD, ye scornful men, that rule this
people which *is* in Jerusalem.
15 Because ye have said, We have made a covenant with death, and with hell
are we at agreement; when the overflowing scourge shall pass through, it shall
not come unto us: for we have made lies our refuge, and under falsehood have
we hid ourselves:

16 Therefore thus saith the Lord God, Behold, I lay in Zion for a foundation
a stone, a tried stone, a precious corner *stone*, a sure foundation: he that
believeth shall not make haste.
17 Judgment also will I lay to the line, and righteousness to the plummet:
and the hail shall sweep away the refuge of lies, and the waters shall overflow
the hiding place.
18 And your covenant with death shall be disannulled, and your agreement
with hell shall not stand; when the overflowing scourge shall pass through,
then ye shall be trodden down by it.
19 From the time that it goeth forth it shall take you: for morning by morn-
ing shall it pass over, by day and by night: and it shall be a vexation only *to*
understand the report.
20 For the bed is shorter than that *a man* can stretch himself *on it*: and the
covering narrower than that he can wrap himself *in it*.
21 For the Lord shall rise up as *in* mount Perazim, he shall be wroth as *in* the
valley of Gibeon, that he may do his work, his strange work; and bring to pass
his act, his strange act.
22 Now therefore be ye not mockers, lest your bands be made strong: for I
have heard from the Lord God of hosts a consumption, even determined upon
the whole earth.
23 Give ye ear, and hear my voice; hearken, and hear my speech.
24 Doth the plowman plow all day to sow? doth he open and break the clods
of his ground?
25 When he hath made plain the face thereof, doth he not cast abroad the
fitches, and scatter the cummin, and cast in the principal wheat and the
appointed barley and the rie in their place?
26 For his God doth instruct him to discretion, *and* doth teach him.
27 For the fitches are not threshed with a threshing instrument, neither is a
cart wheel turned about upon the cummin; but the fitches are beaten out with
a staff, and the cummin with a rod.
28 Bread *corn* is bruised; because he will not ever be threshing it, nor break
it with the wheel of his cart, nor bruise it *with* his horsemen.
29 This also cometh forth from the Lord of hosts, *which* is wonderful in
counsel, *and* excellent in working.

God's Heavy Judgment upon Jerusalem

29 Woe to Ariel, to Ariel, the city *where* David dwelt! add ye year to year;
let them kill sacrifices.
2 Yet I will distress Ariel, and there shall be heaviness and sorrow: and it shall
be unto me as Ariel.
3 And I will camp against thee round about, and will lay siege against thee
with a mount, and I will raise forts against thee.
4 And thou shalt be brought down, *and* shalt speak out of the ground, and
thy speech shall be low out of the dust, and thy voice shall be, as of one that
hath a familiar spirit, out of the ground, and thy speech shall whisper out of
the dust.
5 Moreover the multitude of thy strangers shall be like small dust, and the
multitude of the terrible ones *shall be* as chaff that passeth away: yea, it shall
be at an instant suddenly.
6 Thou shalt be visited of the Lord of hosts with thunder, and with earth-
quake, and great noise, with storm and tempest, and the flame of devouring
fire.
7 And the multitude of all the nations that fight against Ariel, even all that
fight against her and her munition, and that distress her, shall be as a dream
of a night vision.

8 It shall even be as when an hungry *man* dreameth, and, behold, he eateth;
but he awaketh, and his soul is empty: or as when a thirsty man dreameth,
and, behold, he drinketh; but he awaketh, and, behold, *he is* faint, and his soul
hath appetite: so shall the multitude of all the nations be, that fight against
mount Zion.
9 Stay yourselves, and wonder; cry ye out, and cry: they are drunken, but not
with wine; they stagger, but not with strong drink.
10 For the LORD hath poured out upon you the spirit of deep sleep, and hath
closed your eyes: the prophets and your rulers, the seers hath he covered.
11 And the vision of all is become unto you as the words of a book that is
sealed, which *men* deliver to one that is learned, saying, Read this, I pray thee:
and he saith, I cannot; for it *is* sealed:
12 And the book is delivered to him that is not learned, saying, Read this, I
pray thee: and he saith, I am not learned.
13 Wherefore the Lord said, Forasmuch as this people draw near *me* with
their mouth, and with their lips do honour me, but have removed their heart
far from me, and their fear toward me is taught by the precept of men:
14 Therefore, behold, I will proceed to do a marvellous work among this
people, *even* a marvellous work and a wonder: for the wisdom of their wise
men shall perish, and the understanding of their prudent *men* shall be hid.
15 Woe unto them that seek deep to hide their counsel from the LORD, and
their works are in the dark, and they say, Who seeth us? and who knoweth us?
16 Surely your turning of things upside down shall be esteemed as the potter's
clay: for shall the work say of him that made it, He made me not? or shall the
thing framed say of him that framed it, He had no understanding?
17 *Is* it not yet a very little while, and Lebanon shall be turned into a fruitful
field, and the fruitful field shall be esteemed as a forest?
18 And in that day shall the deaf hear the words of the book, and the eyes of
the blind shall see out of obscurity, and out of darkness.
19 The meek also shall increase *their* joy in the LORD, and the poor among
men shall rejoice in the Holy One of Israel.
20 For the terrible one is brought to nought, and the scorner is consumed,
and all that watch for iniquity are cut off:
21 That make a man an offender for a word, and lay a snare for him that
reproveth in the gate, and turn aside the just for a thing of nought.
22 Therefore thus saith the LORD, who redeemed Abraham, concerning the
house of Jacob, Jacob shall not now be ashamed, neither shall his face now
wax pale.
23 But when he seeth his children, the work of mine hands, in the midst of
him, they shall sanctify my name, and sanctify the Holy One of Jacob, and shall
fear the God of Israel.
24 They also that erred in spirit shall come to understanding, and they that
murmured shall learn doctrine.

Trust the Lord, Not Egypt

30 Woe to the rebellious children, saith the LORD, that take counsel, but
not of me; and that cover with a covering, but not of my spirit, that
they may add sin to sin:
2 That walk to go down into Egypt, and have not asked at my mouth; to
strengthen themselves in the strength of Pharaoh, and to trust in the shadow
of Egypt!
3 Therefore shall the strength of Pharaoh be your shame, and the trust in
the shadow of Egypt *your* confusion.
4 For his princes were at Zoan, and his ambassadors came to Hanes.
5 They were all ashamed of a people *that* could not profit them, nor be an
help nor profit, but a shame, and also a reproach.

6 The burden of the beasts of the south: into the land of trouble and anguish,
from whence *come* the young and old lion, the viper and fiery flying serpent,
they will carry their riches upon the shoulders of young asses, and their
treasures upon the bunches of camels, to a people *that* shall not profit *them*.
7 For the Egyptians shall help in vain, and to no purpose: therefore have I
cried concerning this, Their strength *is* to sit still.
8 Now go, write it before them in a table, and note it in a book, that it may
be for the time to come for ever and ever:
9 That this *is* a rebellious people, lying children, children *that* will not hear
the law of the LORD:
10 Which say to the seers, See not; and to the prophets, Prophesy not unto
us right things, speak unto us smooth things, prophesy deceits:
11 Get you out of the way, turn aside out of the path, cause the Holy One of
Israel to cease from before us.
12 Wherefore thus saith the Holy One of Israel, Because ye despise this word,
and trust in oppression and perverseness, and stay thereon:
13 Therefore this iniquity shall be to you as a breach ready to fall, swelling
out in a high wall, whose breaking cometh suddenly at an instant.
14 And he shall break it as the breaking of the potters' vessel that is broken
in pieces; he shall not spare: so that there shall not be found in the bursting
of it a sherd to take fire from the hearth, or to take water *withal* out of the pit.
15 For thus saith the Lord GOD, the Holy One of Israel; In returning and rest
shall ye be saved; in quietness and in confidence shall be your strength: and
ye would not.
16 But ye said, No; for we will flee upon horses; therefore shall ye flee: and,
We will ride upon the swift; therefore shall they that pursue you be swift.
17 One thousand *shall flee* at the rebuke of one; at the rebuke of five shall ye
flee: till ye be left as a beacon upon the top of a mountain, and as an ensign on
an hill.

The Lord Will Heal His People

18 And therefore will the LORD wait, that he may be gracious unto you, and
therefore will he be exalted, that he may have mercy upon you: for the LORD
is a God of judgment: blessed *are* all they that wait for him.
19 For the people shall dwell in Zion at Jerusalem: thou shalt weep no more:
he will be very gracious unto thee at the voice of thy cry; when he shall hear
it, he will answer thee.
20 And *though* the Lord give you the bread of adversity, and the water of
affliction, yet shall not thy teachers be removed into a corner any more, but
thine eyes shall see thy teachers:
21 And thine ears shall hear a word behind thee, saying, This *is* the way, walk
ye in it, when ye turn to the right hand, and when ye turn to the left.
22 Ye shall defile also the covering of thy graven images of silver, and the
ornament of thy molten images of gold: thou shalt cast them away as a men-
struous cloth; thou shalt say unto it, Get thee hence.
23 Then shall he give the rain of thy seed, that thou shalt sow the ground
withal; and bread of the increase of the earth, and it shall be fat and plenteous:
in that day shall thy cattle feed in large pastures.
24 The oxen likewise and the young asses that ear the ground shall eat clean
provender, which hath been winnowed with the shovel and with the fan.
25 And there shall be upon every high mountain, and upon every high hill,
rivers *and* streams of waters in the day of the great slaughter, when the towers
fall.
26 Moreover the light of the moon shall be as the light of the sun, and the
light of the sun shall be sevenfold, as the light of seven days, in the day that the
LORD bindeth up the breach of his people, and healeth the stroke of their wound.

Joy over the Destruction of Assyria

27 Behold, the name of the LORD cometh from far, burning *with* his anger, and the burden *thereof is* heavy: his lips are full of indignation, and his tongue as a devouring fire:

28 And his breath, as an overflowing stream, shall reach to the midst of the neck, to sift the nations with the sieve of vanity: and *there shall be* a bridle in the jaws of the people, causing *them* to err.

29 Ye shall have a song, as in the night *when* a holy solemnity is kept; and gladness of heart, as when one goeth with a pipe to come into the mountain of the LORD, to the mighty One of Israel.

30 And the LORD shall cause his glorious voice to be heard, and shall shew the lighting down of his arm, with the indignation of *his* anger, and *with* the flame of a devouring fire, *with* scattering, and tempest, and hailstones.

31 For through the voice of the LORD shall the Assyrian be beaten down, *which* smote with a rod.

32 And *in* every place where the grounded staff shall pass, which the LORD shall lay upon him, *it* shall be with tabrets and harps: and in battles of shaking will he fight with it.

33 For Tophet *is* ordained of old; yea, for the king it is prepared; he hath made *it* deep *and* large: the pile thereof *is* fire and much wood; the breath of the LORD, like a stream of brimstone, doth kindle it.

The Lord Will Protect His People

31 Woe to them that go down to Egypt for help; and stay on horses, and trust in chariots, because *they are* many; and in horsemen, because they are very strong; but they look not unto the Holy One of Israel, neither seek the LORD!

2 Yet he also *is* wise, and will bring evil, and will not call back his words: but will arise against the house of the evildoers, and against the help of them that work iniquity.

3 Now the Egyptians *are* men, and not God; and their horses flesh, and not spirit. When the LORD shall stretch out his hand, both he that helpeth shall fall, and he that is holpen shall fall down, and they all shall fail together.

4 For thus hath the LORD spoken unto me, Like as the lion and the young lion roaring on his prey, when a multitude of shepherds is called forth against him, *he* will not be afraid of their voice, nor abase himself for the noise of them: so shall the LORD of hosts come down to fight for mount Zion, and for the hill thereof.

5 As birds flying, so will the LORD of hosts defend Jerusalem; defending also he will deliver *it; and* passing over he will preserve it.

6 Turn ye unto *him from* whom the children of Israel have deeply revolted.

7 For in that day every man shall cast away his idols of silver, and his idols of gold, which your own hands have made unto you *for* a sin.

8 Then shall the Assyrian fall with the sword, not of a mighty man; and the sword, not of a mean man, shall devour him: but he shall flee from the sword, and his young men shall be discomfited.

9 And he shall pass over to his strong hold for fear, and his princes shall be afraid of the ensign, saith the LORD, whose fire *is* in Zion, and his furnace in Jerusalem.

The Lord Will Pour out His Spirit

32 Behold, a king shall reign in righteousness, and princes shall rule in judgment.

2 And a man shall be as an hiding place from the wind, and a covert from the tempest; as rivers of water in a dry place, as the shadow of a great rock in a weary land.

3 And the eyes of them that see shall not be dim, and the ears of them that
hear shall hearken.
4 The heart also of the rash shall understand knowledge, and the tongue of
the stammerers shall be ready to speak plainly.
5 The vile person shall be no more called liberal, nor the churl said *to be*
bountiful.
6 For the vile person will speak villany, and his heart will work iniquity, to
practise hypocrisy, and to utter error against the LORD, to make empty the soul
of the hungry, and he will cause the drink of the thirsty to fail.
7 The instruments also of the churl *are* evil: he deviseth wicked devices to
destroy the poor with lying words, even when the needy speaketh right.
8 But the liberal deviseth liberal things; and by liberal things shall he stand.

Desolation Is Foretold

9 Rise up, ye women that are at ease; hear my voice, ye careless daughters;
give ear unto my speech.
10 Many days and years shall ye be troubled, ye careless women: for the vin-
tage shall fail, the gathering shall not come.
11 Tremble, ye women that are at ease; be troubled, ye careless ones: strip
you, and make you bare, and gird *sackcloth* upon *your* loins.
12 They shall lament for the teats, for the pleasant fields, for the fruitful vine.
13 Upon the land of my people shall come up thorns *and* briers; yea, upon
all the houses of joy *in* the joyous city:
14 Because the palaces shall be forsaken; the multitude of the city shall be
left; the forts and towers shall be for dens for ever, a joy of wild asses, a pasture
of flocks;
15 Until the spirit be poured upon us from on high, and the wilderness be a
fruitful field, and the fruitful field be counted for a forest.
16 Then judgment shall dwell in the wilderness, and righteousness remain
in the fruitful field.
17 And the work of righteousness shall be peace; and the effect of righteous-
ness quietness and assurance for ever.
18 And my people shall dwell in a peaceable habitation, and in sure dwellings,
and in quiet resting places;
19 When it shall hail, coming down on the forest; and the city shall be low
in a low place.
20 Blessed *are* ye that sow beside all waters, that send forth *thither* the feet
of the ox and the ass.

The Lord Will Rescue Jerusalem from Assyria

33 Woe to thee that spoilest, and thou *wast* not spoiled; and dealest treach-
erously, and they dealt not treacherously with thee! when thou shalt
cease to spoil, thou shalt be spoiled; *and* when thou shalt make an end to deal
treacherously, they shall deal treacherously with thee.
2 O LORD, be gracious unto us; we have waited for thee: be thou their arm
every morning, our salvation also in the time of trouble.
3 At the noise of the tumult the people fled; at the lifting up of thyself the
nations were scattered.
4 And your spoil shall be gathered *like* the gathering of the caterpiller: as the
running to and fro of locusts shall he run upon them.
5 The LORD is exalted; for he dwelleth on high: he hath filled Zion with judg-
ment and righteousness.
6 And wisdom and knowledge shall be the stability of thy times, *and* strength
of salvation: the fear of the LORD *is* his treasure.
7 Behold, their valiant ones shall cry without: the ambassadors of peace shall
weep bitterly.

8 The highways lie waste, the wayfaring man ceaseth: he hath broken the
covenant, he hath despised the cities, he regardeth no man.
9 The earth mourneth *and* languisheth: Lebanon is ashamed *and* hewn
down: Sharon is like a wilderness; and Bashan and Carmel shake off *their*
fruits.
10 Now will I rise, saith the LORD; now will I be exalted; now will I lift up
myself.
11 Ye shall conceive chaff, ye shall bring forth stubble: your breath, *as* fire,
shall devour you.
12 And the people shall be *as* the burnings of lime: *as* thorns cut up shall they
be burned in the fire.

The Privileges of the Godly

13 Hear, ye *that are* far off, what I have done; and, ye *that are* near, acknowl-
edge my might.
14 The sinners in Zion are afraid; fearfulness hath surprised the hypocrites.
Who among us shall dwell with the devouring fire? who among us shall dwell
with everlasting burnings?
15 He that walketh righteously, and speaketh uprightly; he that despiseth
the gain of oppressions, that shaketh his hands from holding of bribes, that
stoppeth his ears from hearing of blood, and shutteth his eyes from seeing
evil;
16 He shall dwell on high: his place of defence *shall be* the munitions of rocks:
bread shall be given him; his waters *shall be* sure.
17 Thine eyes shall see the king in his beauty: they shall behold the land that
is very far off.
18 Thine heart shall meditate terror. Where *is* the scribe? where *is* the receiv-
er? where *is* he that counted the towers?
19 Thou shalt not see a fierce people, a people of a deeper speech than thou
canst perceive; of a stammering tongue, *that thou canst* not understand.
20 Look upon Zion, the city of our solemnities: thine eyes shall see Jerusalem
a quiet habitation, a tabernacle *that* shall not be taken down; not one of the
stakes thereof shall ever be removed, neither shall any of the cords thereof be
broken.
21 But there the glorious LORD *will be* unto us a place of broad rivers *and*
streams; wherein shall go no galley with oars, neither shall gallant ship pass
thereby.
22 For the LORD *is* our judge, the LORD *is* our lawgiver, the LORD *is* our king;
he will save us.
23 Thy tacklings are loosed; they could not well strengthen their mast, they
could not spread the sail: then is the prey of a great spoil divided; the lame
take the prey.
24 And the inhabitant shall not say, I am sick: the people that dwell therein
shall be forgiven *their* iniquity.

Edom Will Fall

34 Come near, ye nations, to hear; and hearken, ye people: let the earth
hear, and all that is therein; the world, and all things that come forth
of it.
2 For the indignation of the LORD *is* upon all nations, and *his* fury upon all
their armies: he hath utterly destroyed them, he hath delivered them to the
slaughter.
3 Their slain also shall be cast out, and their stink shall come up out of their
carcases, and the mountains shall be melted with their blood.
4 And all the host of heaven shall be dissolved, and the heavens shall be rolled
together as a scroll: and all their host shall fall down, as the leaf falleth off from
the vine, and as a falling *fig* from the fig tree.

5 For my sword shall be bathed in heaven: behold, it shall come down upon Idumea, and upon the people of my curse, to judgment.
6 The sword of the LORD is filled with blood, it is made fat with fatness, *and* with the blood of lambs and goats, with the fat of the kidneys of rams: for the LORD hath a sacrifice in Bozrah, and a great slaughter in the land of Idumea.
7 And the unicorns shall come down with them, and the bullocks with the bulls; and their land shall be soaked with blood, and their dust made fat with fatness.
8 For *it is* the day of the LORD's vengeance, *and* the year of recompences for the controversy of Zion.
9 And the streams thereof shall be turned into pitch, and the dust thereof into brimstone, and the land thereof shall become burning pitch.
10 It shall not be quenched night nor day; the smoke thereof shall go up for ever: from generation to generation it shall lie waste; none shall pass through it for ever and ever.
11 But the cormorant and the bittern shall possess it; the owl also and the raven shall dwell in it: and he shall stretch out upon it the line of confusion, and the stones of emptiness.
12 They shall call the nobles thereof to the kingdom, but none *shall be* there, and all her princes shall be nothing.
13 And thorns shall come up in her palaces, nettles and brambles in the fortresses thereof: and it shall be an habitation of dragons, *and* a court for owls.
14 The wild beasts of the desert shall also meet with the wild beasts of the island, and the satyr shall cry to his fellow; the screech owl also shall rest there, and find for herself a place of rest.
15 There shall the great owl make her nest, and lay, and hatch, and gather under her shadow: there shall the vultures also be gathered, every one with her mate.
16 Seek ye out of the book of the LORD, and read: no one of these shall fail, none shall want her mate: for my mouth it hath commanded, and his spirit it hath gathered them.
17 And he hath cast the lot for them, and his hand hath divided it unto them by line: they shall possess it for ever, from generation to generation shall they dwell therein.

The Lord's People Will Have Joy

35 The wilderness and the solitary place shall be glad for them; and the desert shall rejoice, and blossom as the rose.
2 It shall blossom abundantly, and rejoice even with joy and singing: the glory of Lebanon shall be given unto it, the excellency of Carmel and Sharon, they shall see the glory of the LORD, *and* the excellency of our God.
3 Strengthen ye the weak hands, and confirm the feeble knees.
4 Say to them *that are* of a fearful heart, Be strong, fear not: behold, your God will come *with* vengeance, *even* God *with* a recompence; he will come and save you.
5 Then the eyes of the blind shall be opened, and the ears of the deaf shall be unstopped.
6 Then shall the lame *man* leap as an hart, and the tongue of the dumb sing: for in the wilderness shall waters break out, and streams in the desert.
7 And the parched ground shall become a pool, and the thirsty land springs of water: in the habitation of dragons, where each lay, *shall be* grass with reeds and rushes.
8 And an highway shall be there, and a way, and it shall be called The way of holiness; the unclean shall not pass over it; but it *shall be* for those: the wayfaring men, though fools, shall not err *therein*.

9 No lion shall be there, nor *any* ravenous beast shall go up thereon, it shall
not be found there; but the redeemed shall walk *there*:
10 And the ransomed of the LORD shall return, and come to Zion with songs
and everlasting joy upon their heads: they shall obtain joy and gladness, and
sorrow and sighing shall flee away.

Sennacherib of Assyria Invades Judah

36 Now it came to pass in the fourteenth year of king Hezekiah, *that*
Sennacherib king of Assyria came up against all the defenced cities of
Judah, and took them.
2 And the king of Assyria sent Rabshakeh from Lachish to Jerusalem unto
king Hezekiah with a great army. And he stood by the conduit of the upper
pool in the highway of the fuller's field.
3 Then came forth unto him Eliakim, Hilkiah's son, which was over the house,
and Shebna the scribe, and Joah, Asaph's son, the recorder.
4 And Rabshakeh said unto them, Say ye now to Hezekiah, Thus saith the
great king, the king of Assyria, What confidence *is* this wherein thou trustest?
5 I say, *sayest thou*, (but *they are but* vain words) *I have* counsel and strength
for war: now on whom dost thou trust, that thou rebellest against me?
6 Lo, thou trustest in the staff of this broken reed, on Egypt; whereon if a
man lean, it will go into his hand, and pierce it: so *is* Pharaoh king of Egypt to
all that trust in him.
7 But if thou say to me, We trust in the LORD our God: *is it* not he, whose high
places and whose altars Hezekiah hath taken away, and said to Judah and to
Jerusalem, Ye shall worship before this altar?
8 Now therefore give pledges, I pray thee, to my master the king of Assyria,
and I will give thee two thousand horses, if thou be able on thy part to set
riders upon them.
9 How then wilt thou turn away the face of one captain of the least of my
master's servants, and put thy trust on Egypt for chariots and for horsemen?
10 And am I now come up without the LORD against this land to destroy it?
the LORD said unto me, Go up against this land, and destroy it.
11 Then said Eliakim and Shebna and Joah unto Rabshakeh, Speak, I pray
thee, unto thy servants in the Syrian language; for we understand *it*: and speak
not to us in the Jews' language, in the ears of the people that *are* on the wall.
12 But Rabshakeh said, Hath my master sent me to thy master and to thee to
speak these words? *hath he* not *sent me* to the men that sit upon the wall, that
they may eat their own dung, and drink their own piss with you?
13 Then Rabshakeh stood, and cried with a loud voice in the Jews' language,
and said, Hear ye the words of the great king, the king of Assyria.
14 Thus saith the king, Let not Hezekiah deceive you: for he shall not be able
to deliver you.
15 Neither let Hezekiah make you trust in the LORD, saying, The LORD will
surely deliver us: this city shall not be delivered into the hand of the king of
Assyria.
16 Hearken not to Hezekiah: for thus saith the king of Assyria, Make *an agree-*
ment with me *by* a present, and come out to me: and eat ye every one of his
vine, and every one of his fig tree, and drink ye every one the waters of his own
cistern;
17 Until I come and take you away to a land like your own land, a land of corn
and wine, a land of bread and vineyards.
18 *Beware* lest Hezekiah persuade you, saying, The LORD will deliver us. Hath
any of the gods of the nations delivered his land out of the hand of the king
of Assyria?
19 Where *are* the gods of Hamath and Arphad? where *are* the gods of
Sepharvaim? and have they delivered Samaria out of my hand?

20 Who *are they* among all the gods of these lands, that have delivered their land out of my hand, that the LORD should deliver Jerusalem out of my hand?
21 But they held their peace, and answered him not a word: for the king's commandment was, saying, Answer him not.
22 Then came Eliakim, the son of Hilkiah, that *was* over the household, and Shebna the scribe, and Joah, the son of Asaph, the recorder, to Hezekiah with *their* clothes rent, and told him the words of Rabshakeh.

Hezekiah Asks Isaiah to Pray for the Nation

37 And it came to pass, when king Hezekiah heard *it*, that he rent his clothes, and covered himself with sackcloth, and went into the house of the LORD.
2 And he sent Eliakim, who *was* over the household, and Shebna the scribe, and the elders of the priests covered with sackcloth, unto Isaiah the prophet the son of Amoz.
3 And they said unto him, Thus saith Hezekiah, This day *is* a day of trouble, and of rebuke, and of blasphemy: for the children are come to the birth, and *there is* not strength to bring forth.
4 It may be the LORD thy God will hear the words of Rabshakeh, whom the king of Assyria his master hath sent to reproach the living God, and will reprove the words which the LORD thy God hath heard: wherefore lift up *thy* prayer for the remnant that is left.
5 So the servants of king Hezekiah came to Isaiah.
6 And Isaiah said unto them, Thus shall ye say unto your master, Thus saith the LORD, Be not afraid of the words that thou hast heard, wherewith the servants of the king of Assyria have blasphemed me.
7 Behold, I will send a blast upon him, and he shall hear a rumour, and return to his own land; and I will cause him to fall by the sword in his own land.

Sennacherib Sends a Blasphemous Letter to Hezekiah

8 So Rabshakeh returned, and found the king of Assyria warring against Libnah: for he had heard that he was departed from Lachish.
9 And he heard say concerning Tirhakah king of Ethiopia, He is come forth to make war with thee. And when he heard *it*, he sent messengers to Hezekiah, saying,
10 Thus shall ye speak to Hezekiah king of Judah, saying, Let not thy God, in whom thou trustest, deceive thee, saying, Jerusalem shall not be given into the hand of the king of Assyria.
11 Behold, thou hast heard what the kings of Assyria have done to all lands by destroying them utterly; and shalt thou be delivered?
12 Have the gods of the nations delivered them which my fathers have destroyed, *as* Gozan, and Haran, and Rezeph, and the children of Eden which *were* in Telassar?
13 Where *is* the king of Hamath, and the king of Arphad, and the king of the city of Sepharvaim, Hena, and Ivah?
14 And Hezekiah received the letter from the hand of the messengers, and read it: and Hezekiah went up unto the house of the LORD, and spread it before the LORD.
15 And Hezekiah prayed unto the LORD, saying,
16 O LORD of hosts, God of Israel, that dwellest *between* the cherubims, thou *art* the God, *even* thou alone, of all the kingdoms of the earth: thou hast made heaven and earth.
17 Incline thine ear, O LORD, and hear; open thine eyes, O LORD, and see: and hear all the words of Sennacherib, which hath sent to reproach the living God.
18 Of a truth, LORD, the kings of Assyria have laid waste all the nations, and their countries,

19 And have cast their gods into the fire: for they *were* no gods, but the work
of men's hands, wood and stone: therefore they have destroyed them.
20 Now therefore, O LORD our God, save us from his hand, that all the king-
doms of the earth may know that thou *art* the LORD, *even* thou only.

Isaiah's Prophecy against Sennacherib

21 Then Isaiah the son of Amoz sent unto Hezekiah, saying, Thus saith the
LORD God of Israel, Whereas thou hast prayed to me against Sennacherib king
of Assyria:
22 This *is* the word which the LORD hath spoken concerning him; The virgin,
the daughter of Zion, hath despised thee, *and* laughed thee to scorn; the daugh-
ter of Jerusalem hath shaken her head at thee.
23 Whom hast thou reproached and blasphemed? and against whom hast
thou exalted *thy* voice, and lifted up thine eyes on high? *even* against the Holy
One of Israel.
24 By thy servants hast thou reproached the Lord, and hast said, By the mul-
titude of my chariots am I come up to the height of the mountains, to the sides
of Lebanon; and I will cut down the tall cedars thereof, *and* the choice fir trees
thereof: and I will enter into the height of his border, *and* the forest of his
Carmel.
25 I have digged, and drunk water; and with the sole of my feet have I dried
up all the rivers of the besieged places.
26 Hast thou not heard long ago, *how* I have done it; *and* of ancient times,
that I have formed it? now have I brought it to pass, that thou shouldest be to
lay waste defenced cities *into* ruinous heaps.
27 Therefore their inhabitants *were* of small power, they were dismayed and
confounded: they were *as* the grass of the field, and *as* the green herb, *as* the
grass on the housetops, and *as corn* blasted before it be grown up.
28 But I know thy abode, and thy going out, and thy coming in, and thy rage
against me.
29 Because thy rage against me, and thy tumult, is come up into mine ears,
therefore will I put my hook in thy nose, and my bridle in thy lips, and I will
turn thee back by the way by which thou camest.
30 And this *shall be* a sign unto thee, Ye shall eat *this* year such as groweth of
itself; and the second year that which springeth of the same: and in the third
year sow ye, and reap, and plant vineyards, and eat the fruit thereof.
31 And the remnant that is escaped of the house of Judah shall again take
root downward, and bear fruit upward:
32 For out of Jerusalem shall go forth a remnant, and they that escape out of
mount Zion: the zeal of the LORD of hosts shall do this.
33 Therefore thus saith the LORD concerning the king of Assyria, He shall not
come into this city, nor shoot an arrow there, nor come before it with shields,
nor cast a bank against it.
34 By the way that he came, by the same shall he return, and shall not come
into this city, saith the LORD.
35 For I will *defend this city* to save it for mine own sake, and for my servant
David's sake.
36 Then the angel of the LORD went forth, and smote in the camp of the
Assyrians a hundred and fourscore and five thousand: and when they arose
early in the morning, behold, they *were* all dead corpses.
37 So Sennacherib king of Assyria departed, and went and returned, and
dwelt at Nineveh.
38 And it came to pass, as he was worshipping in the house of Nisroch his
god, that Adrammelech and Sharezer his sons smote him with the sword; and
they escaped into the land of Armenia: and Esar-haddon his son reigned in
his stead.

Hezekiah's Illness

38 In those days was Hezekiah sick unto death. And Isaiah the prophet the son of Amoz came unto him, and said unto him, Thus saith the LORD, Set thine house in order: for thou shalt die, and not live.

2 Then Hezekiah turned his face toward the wall, and prayed unto the LORD,
3 And said, Remember now, O LORD, I beseech thee, how I have walked before thee in truth and with a perfect heart, and have done *that which is* good in thy sight. And Hezekiah wept sore.
4 Then came the word of the LORD to Isaiah, saying,
5 Go, and say to Hezekiah, Thus saith the LORD, the God of David thy father, I have heard thy prayer, I have seen thy tears: behold, I will add unto thy days fifteen years.
6 And I will deliver thee and this city out of the hand of the king of Assyria: and I will defend this city.
7 And this *shall be* a sign unto thee from the LORD, that the LORD will do this thing that he hath spoken;
8 Behold, I will bring again the shadow of the degrees, which is gone down in the sun dial of Ahaz, ten degrees backward. So the sun returned ten degrees, by which degrees it was gone down.

Hezekiah's Song of Thanksgiving

9 The writing of Hezekiah king of Judah, when he had been sick, and was recovered of his sickness:
10 I said in the cutting off of my days, I shall go to the gates of the grave: I am deprived of the residue of my years.
11 I said, I shall not see the LORD, *even* the LORD, in the land of the living: I shall behold man no more with the inhabitants of the world.
12 Mine age is departed, and is removed from me as a shepherd's tent: I have cut off like a weaver my life: he will cut me off with pining sickness: from day *even* to night wilt thou make an end of me.
13 I reckoned till morning, *that,* as a lion, so will he break all my bones: from day *even* to night wilt thou make an end of me.
14 Like a crane *or* a swallow, so did I chatter: I did mourn as a dove: mine eyes fail *with looking* upward: O LORD, I am oppressed; undertake for me.
15 What shall I say? he hath both spoken unto me, and himself hath done *it*: I shall go softly all my years in the bitterness of my soul.
16 O Lord, by these *things men* live, and in all these *things is* the life of my spirit: so wilt thou recover me, and make me to live.
17 Behold, for peace I had great bitterness: but thou hast in love to my soul *delivered it* from the pit of corruption: for thou hast cast all my sins behind thy back.
18 For the grave cannot praise thee, death can *not* celebrate thee: they that go down into the pit cannot hope for thy truth.
19 The living, the living, he shall praise thee, as I *do* this day: the father to the children shall make known thy truth.
20 The LORD *was ready* to save me: therefore we will sing my songs to the stringed instruments all the days of our life in the house of the LORD.
21 For Isaiah had said, Let them take a lump of figs, and lay *it* for a plaister upon the boil, and he shall recover.
22 Hezekiah also had said, What is the sign that I shall go up to the house of the LORD?

Hezekiah Shows the Babylonians His Treasures

39 At that time Merodach-baladan, the son of Baladan, king of Babylon, sent letters and a present to Hezekiah: for he had heard that he had been sick, and was recovered.

2 And Hezekiah was glad of them, and shewed them the house of his precious
things, the silver, and the gold, and the spices, and the precious ointment, and
all the house of his armour, and all that was found in his treasures: there was
nothing in his house, nor in all his dominion, that Hezekiah shewed them
not.
3 Then came Isaiah the prophet unto king Hezekiah, and said unto him,
What said these men? and from whence came they unto thee? And Hezekiah
said, They are come from a far country unto me, *even* from Babylon.
4 Then said he, What have they seen in thine house? And Hezekiah answered,
All that *is* in mine house have they seen: there is nothing among my treasures
that I have not shewed them.
5 Then said Isaiah to Hezekiah, Hear the word of the LORD of hosts:
6 Behold, the days come, that all that *is* in thine house, and *that* which thy
fathers have laid up in store until this day, shall be carried to Babylon: nothing
shall be left, saith the LORD.
7 And of thy sons that shall issue from thee, which thou shalt beget, shall
they take away; and they shall be eunuchs in the palace of the king of Babylon.
8 Then said Hezekiah to Isaiah, Good *is* the word of the LORD which thou
hast spoken. He said moreover, For there shall be peace and truth in my days.

Comfort for the People

40 Comfort ye, comfort ye my people, saith your God.
2 Speak ye comfortably to Jerusalem, and cry unto her, that her warfare
is accomplished, that her iniquity is pardoned: for she hath received of the
LORD's hand double for all her sins.

Prophecy of John the Baptist

3 The voice of him that crieth in the wilderness, Prepare ye the way of the
LORD, make straight in the desert a highway for our God.
4 Every valley shall be exalted, and every mountain and hill shall be made
low: and the crooked shall be made straight, and the rough places plain:
5 And the glory of the LORD shall be revealed, and all flesh shall see *it* togeth-
er: for the mouth of the LORD hath spoken *it*.
6 The voice said, Cry. And he said, What shall I cry? All flesh *is* grass, and all
the goodliness thereof *is* as the flower of the field:
7 The grass withereth, the flower fadeth: because the spirit of the LORD
bloweth upon it: surely the people *is* grass.
8 The grass withereth, the flower fadeth: but the word of our God shall stand
for ever.
9 O Zion, that bringest good tidings, get thee up into the high mountain; O
Jerusalem, that bringest good tidings, lift up thy voice with strength; lift *it* up,
be not afraid; say unto the cities of Judah, Behold your God!
10 Behold, the Lord GOD will come with strong *hand*, and his arm shall rule
for him: behold, his reward *is* with him, and his work before him.
11 He shall feed his flock like a shepherd: he shall gather the lambs with his
arm, and carry *them* in his bosom, *and* shall gently lead those that are with
young.

The Omnipotence of God

12 Who hath measured the waters in the hollow of his hand, and meted out
heaven with the span, and comprehended the dust of the earth in a measure,
and weighed the mountains in scales, and the hills in a balance?
13 Who hath directed the Spirit of the LORD, or *being* his counsellor hath
taught him?
14 With whom took he counsel, and *who* instructed him, and taught him in
the path of judgment, and taught him knowledge, and shewed to him the way
of understanding?

15 Behold, the nations *are* as a drop of a bucket, and are counted as the small
dust of the balance: behold, he taketh up the isles as a very little thing.
16 And Lebanon *is* not sufficient to burn, nor the beasts thereof sufficient
for a burnt offering.
17 All nations before him *are* as nothing; and they are counted to him less
than nothing, and vanity.
18 To whom then will ye liken God? or what likeness will ye compare unto
him?
19 The workman melteth a graven image, and the goldsmith spreadeth it
over with gold, and casteth silver chains.
20 He that *is* so impoverished that he hath no oblation chooseth a tree *that*
will not rot; he seeketh unto him a cunning workman to prepare a graven
image, *that* shall not be moved.
21 Have ye not known? have ye not heard? hath it not been told you from
the beginning? have ye not understood from the foundations of the earth?
22 *It is* he that sitteth upon the circle of the earth, and the inhabitants thereof
are as grasshoppers; that stretcheth out the heavens as a curtain, and spreadeth
them out as a tent to dwell in:
23 That bringeth the princes to nothing; he maketh the judges of the earth
as vanity.
24 Yea, they shall not be planted; yea, they shall not be sown: yea, their stock
shall not take root in the earth: and he shall also blow upon them, and they
shall wither, and the whirlwind shall take them away as stubble.
25 To whom then will ye liken me, or shall I be equal? saith the Holy One.
26 Lift up your eyes on high, and behold who hath created these *things*, that
bringeth out their host by number: he calleth them all by names by the great-
ness of his might, for that *he is* strong in power; not one faileth.
27 Why sayest thou, O Jacob, and speakest, O Israel, My way is hid from the
LORD, and my judgment is passed over from my God?
28 Hast thou not known? hast thou not heard, *that* the everlasting God, the
LORD, the Creator of the ends of the earth, fainteth not, neither is weary? *there*
is no searching of his understanding.
29 He giveth power to the faint; and to *them that have* no might he increaseth
strength.
30 Even the youths shall faint and be weary, and the young men shall utterly
fall:
31 But they that wait upon the LORD shall renew *their* strength; they shall
mount up with wings as eagles; they shall run, and not be weary; *and* they
shall walk, and not faint.

God Reasons with His People

41 Keep silence before me, O islands; and let the people renew *their*
strength: let them come near; then let them speak: let us come near
together to judgment.
2 Who raised up the righteous *man* from the east, called him to his foot, gave
the nations before him, and made *him* rule over kings? he gave *them* as the
dust to his sword, *and* as driven stubble to his bow.
3 He pursued them, *and* passed safely; *even* by the way *that* he had not gone
with his feet.
4 Who hath wrought and done *it*, calling the generations from the begin-
ning? I the LORD, the first, and with the last; I *am* he.
5 The isles saw *it*, and feared; the ends of the earth were afraid, drew near,
and came.
6 They helped every one his neighbour; and *every one* said to his brother, Be
of good courage.

7 So the carpenter encouraged the goldsmith, *and* he that smootheth *with*
the hammer him that smote the anvil, saying, It *is* ready for the sodering: and
he fastened it with nails, *that* it should not be moved.
8 But thou, Israel, *art* my servant, Jacob whom I have chosen, the seed of
Abraham my friend.
9 *Thou* whom I have taken from the ends of the earth, and called thee from
the chief men thereof, and said unto thee, Thou *art* my servant; I have chosen
thee, and not cast thee away.

God Is with His People

10 Fear thou not; for I *am* with thee: be not dismayed; for I *am* thy God: I will
strengthen thee; yea, I will help thee; yea, I will uphold thee with the right
hand of my righteousness.
11 Behold, all they that were incensed against thee shall be ashamed and
confounded: they shall be as nothing; and they that strive with thee shall per-
ish.
12 Thou shalt seek them, and shalt not find them, *even* them that contended
with thee: they that war against thee shall be as nothing, and as a thing of
nought.
13 For I the LORD thy God will hold thy right hand, saying unto thee, Fear
not; I will help thee.
14 Fear not, thou worm Jacob, *and* ye men of Israel; I will help thee, saith the
LORD, and thy redeemer, the Holy One of Israel.
15 Behold, I will make thee a new sharp threshing instrument having teeth:
thou shalt thresh the mountains, and beat *them* small, and shalt make the hills
as chaff.
16 Thou shalt fan them, and the wind shall carry them away, and the whirl-
wind shall scatter them: and thou shalt rejoice in the LORD, *and* shalt glory in
the Holy One of Israel.
17 *When* the poor and needy seek water, and *there is* none, *and* their tongue
faileth for thirst, I the LORD will hear them, *I* the God of Israel will not forsake
them.
18 I will open rivers in high places, and fountains in the midst of the valleys:
I will make the wilderness a pool of water, and the dry land springs of water.
19 I will plant in the wilderness the cedar, the shittah tree, and the myrtle,
and the oil tree; I will set in the desert the fir tree, *and* the pine, and the box
tree together:
20 That they may see, and know, and consider, and understand together, that
the hand of the LORD hath done this, and the Holy One of Israel hath created it.

The Worthlessness of Idols

21 Produce your cause, saith the LORD; bring forth your strong *reasons*, saith
the King of Jacob.
22 Let them bring *them* forth, and shew us what shall happen: let them shew
the former things, what they *be*, that we may consider them, and know the
latter end of them; or declare us things for to come.
23 Shew the things that are to come hereafter, that we may know that ye *are*
gods: yea, do good, or do evil, that we may be dismayed, and behold *it* togeth-
er.
24 Behold, ye *are* of nothing, and your work of nought: an abomination *is*
he that chooseth you.
25 I have raised up *one* from the north, and he shall come: from the rising of
the sun shall he call upon my name: and he shall come upon princes as *upon*
morter, and as the potter treadeth clay.
26 Who hath declared from the beginning, that we may know? and before-
time, that we may say, *He is* righteous? yea, *there is* none that sheweth, yea,
there is none that declareth, yea, *there is* none that heareth your words.

27 The first *shall say* to Zion, Behold, behold them: and I will give to Jerusalem
one that bringeth good tidings.
28 For I beheld, and *there was* no man; even among them, and *there was* no
counsellor, that, when I asked of them, could answer a word.
29 Behold, they *are* all vanity; their works *are* nothing: their molten images
are wind and confusion.

The Work of Christ, the Servant

42 Behold my servant, whom I uphold; mine elect, *in whom* my soul
delighteth; I have put my spirit upon him: he shall bring forth judg-
ment to the Gentiles.
2 He shall not cry, nor lift up, nor cause his voice to be heard in the street.
3 A bruised reed shall he not break, and the smoking flax shall he not quench:
he shall bring forth judgment unto truth.
4 He shall not fail nor be discouraged, till he have set judgment in the earth:
and the isles shall wait for his law.

God's Promise to Christ

5 Thus saith God the LORD, he that created the heavens, and stretched them
out; he that spread forth the earth, and that which cometh out of it; he that
giveth breath unto the people upon it, and spirit to them that walk therein:
6 I the LORD have called thee in righteousness, and will hold thine hand, and
will keep thee, and give thee for a covenant of the people, for a light of the
Gentiles;
7 To open the blind eyes, to bring out the prisoners from the prison, *and*
them that sit in darkness out of the prison house.
8 I *am* the LORD: that *is* my name: and my glory will I not give to another,
neither my praise to graven images.
9 Behold, the former things are come to pass, and new things do I declare:
before they spring forth I tell you of them.

A Song about the Lord

10 Sing unto the LORD a new song, *and* his praise from the end of the earth,
ye that go down to the sea, and all that is therein; the isles, and the inhabitants
thereof.
11 Let the wilderness and the cities thereof lift up *their voice*, the villages *that*
Kedar doth inhabit: let the inhabitants of the rock sing, let them shout from
the top of the mountains.
12 Let them give glory unto the LORD, and declare his praise in the islands.
13 The LORD shall go forth as a mighty man, he shall stir up jealousy like a
man of war: he shall cry, yea, roar; he shall prevail against his enemies.
14 I have long time holden my peace; I have been still, *and* refrained myself:
now will I cry like a travailing woman; I will destroy and devour at once.
15 I will make waste mountains and hills, and dry up all their herbs; and I
will make the rivers islands, and I will dry up the pools.
16 And I will bring the blind by a way *that* they knew not; I will lead them in
paths *that* they have not known: I will make darkness light before them, and
crooked things straight. These things will I do unto them, and not forsake
them.
17 They shall be turned back, they shall be greatly ashamed, that trust in
graven images, that say to the molten images, Ye *are* our gods.

The Lord Will Bring His People Home

18 Hear, ye deaf; and look, ye blind, that ye may see.
19 Who *is* blind, but my servant? or deaf, as my messenger *that* I sent? who
is blind as *he that is* perfect, and blind as the LORD's servant?
20 Seeing many things, but thou observest not; opening the ears, but he
heareth not.

21 The LORD is well pleased for his righteousness' sake; he will magnify the
law, and make *it* honourable.
22 But this *is* a people robbed and spoiled; *they are* all of them snared in
holes, and they are hid in prison houses: they are for a prey, and none deliv-
ereth; for a spoil, and none saith, Restore.
23 Who among you will give ear to this? *who* will hearken and hear for the
time to come?
24 Who gave Jacob for a spoil, and Israel to the robbers? did not the LORD,
he against whom we have sinned? for they would not walk in his ways, neither
were they obedient unto his law.
25 Therefore he hath poured upon him the fury of his anger, and the strength
of battle: and it hath set him on fire round about, yet he knew not; and it
burned him, yet he laid *it* not to heart.

The Lord Comforts with His Promises

43 But now thus saith the LORD that created thee, O Jacob, and he that
formed thee, O Israel, Fear not: for I have redeemed thee, I have called
thee by thy name; thou *art* mine.
2 When thou passest through the waters, I *will be* with thee; and through
the rivers, they shall not overflow thee: when thou walkest through the fire,
thou shalt not be burned; neither shall the flame kindle upon thee.
3 For I *am* the LORD thy God, the Holy One of Israel, thy Saviour: I gave Egypt
for thy ransom, Ethiopia and Seba for thee.
4 Since thou wast precious in my sight, thou hast been honourable, and I
have loved thee: therefore will I give men for thee, and people for thy life.
5 Fear not: for I *am* with thee: I will bring thy seed from the east, and gather
thee from the west;
6 I will say to the north, Give up; and to the south, Keep not back: bring my
sons from far, and my daughters from the ends of the earth;
7 *Even* every one that is called by my name: for I have created him for my
glory, I have formed him; yea, I have made him.
8 Bring forth the blind people that have eyes, and the deaf that have ears.
9 Let all the nations be gathered together, and let the people be assembled:
who among them can declare this, and shew us former things? let them bring
forth their witnesses, that they may be justified: or let them hear, and say, *It
is* truth.
10 Ye *are* my witnesses, saith the LORD, and my servant whom I have chosen:
that ye may know and believe me, and understand that I *am* he: before me
there was no God formed, neither shall there be after me.
11 I, *even* I, *am* the LORD; and beside me *there is* no saviour.
12 I have declared, and have saved, and I have shewed, when *there was* no
strange *god* among you: therefore ye *are* my witnesses, saith the LORD, that I
am God.
13 Yea, before the day *was* I *am* he; and *there is* none that can deliver out of
my hand: I will work, and who shall let it?

The Destruction of Babylon

14 Thus saith the LORD, your redeemer, the Holy One of Israel; For your sake
I have sent to Babylon, and have brought down all their nobles, and the
Chaldeans, whose cry *is* in the ships.
15 I *am* the LORD, your Holy One, the creator of Israel, your King.
16 Thus saith the LORD, which maketh a way in the sea, and a path in the
mighty waters;
17 Which bringeth forth the chariot and horse, the army and the power; they
shall lie down together, they shall not rise: they are extinct, they are quenched
as tow.

The Lord Will Forgive

18 Remember ye not the former things, neither consider the things of old.
19 Behold, I will do a new thing; now it shall spring forth; shall ye not know
it? I will even make a way in the wilderness, *and* rivers in the desert.
20 The beast of the field shall honour me, the dragons and the owls: because
I give waters in the wilderness, *and* rivers in the desert, to give drink to my
people, my chosen.
21 This people have I formed for myself; they shall shew forth my praise.

The Lord Reproves the People

22 But thou hast not called upon me, O Jacob; but thou hast been weary of
me, O Israel.
23 Thou hast not brought me the small cattle of thy burnt offerings; neither
hast thou honoured me with thy sacrifices. I have not caused thee to serve
with an offering, nor wearied thee with incense.
24 Thou hast bought me no sweet cane with money, neither hast thou filled
me with the fat of thy sacrifices: but thou hast made me to serve with thy sins,
thou hast wearied me with thine iniquities.
25 I, *even* I, *am* he that blotteth out thy transgressions for mine own sake,
and will not remember thy sins.
26 Put me in remembrance: let us plead together: declare thou, that thou
mayest be justified.
27 Thy first father hath sinned, and thy teachers have transgressed against
me.
28 Therefore I have profaned the princes of the sanctuary, and have given
Jacob to the curse, and Israel to reproaches.

The Lord Will Help His People

44 Yet now hear, O Jacob my servant; and Israel, whom I have chosen:
2 Thus saith the LORD that made thee, and formed thee from the womb,
which will help thee; Fear not, O Jacob, my servant; and thou, Jesurun, whom
I have chosen.
3 For I will pour water upon him that is thirsty, and floods upon the dry
ground: I will pour my spirit upon thy seed, and my blessing upon thine off-
spring:
4 And they shall spring up *as* among the grass, as willows by the water cours-
es.
5 One shall say, I *am* the LORD's; and another shall call *himself* by the name
of Jacob; and another shall subscribe *with* his hand unto the LORD, and sur-
name *himself* by the name of Israel.
6 Thus saith the LORD the King of Israel, and his redeemer the LORD of hosts;
I *am* the first, and I *am* the last; and beside me *there is* no God.
7 And who, as I, shall call, and shall declare it, and set it in order for me, since
I appointed the ancient people? and the things that are coming, and shall
come, let them shew unto them.
8 Fear ye not, neither be afraid: have not I told thee from that time, and have
declared *it*? ye *are* even my witnesses. Is there a God beside me? yea, *there is*
no God; I know not *any*.
9 They that make a graven image *are* all of them vanity; and their delectable
things shall not profit; and they *are* their own witnesses; they see not, nor
know; that they may be ashamed.
10 Who hath formed a god, or molten a graven image *that* is profitable for
nothing?
11 Behold, all his fellows shall be ashamed: and the workmen, they *are* of
men: let them all be gathered together, let them stand up; *yet* they shall fear,
and they shall be ashamed together.

12 The smith with the tongs both worketh in the coals, and fashioneth it with
hammers, and worketh it with the strength of his arms: yea, he is hungry, and
his strength faileth: he drinketh no water, and is faint.
13 The carpenter stretcheth out *his* rule; he marketh it out with a line; he
fitteth it with planes, and he marketh it out with the compass, and maketh it
after the figure of a man, according to the beauty of a man; that it may remain
in the house.
14 He heweth him down cedars, and taketh the cypress and the oak, which
he strengtheneth for himself among the trees of the forest: he planteth an ash,
and the rain doth nourish *it*.
15 Then shall it be for a man to burn: for he will take thereof, and warm
himself; yea, he kindleth *it*, and baketh bread; yea, he maketh a god, and wor-
shippeth *it*; he maketh it a graven image, and falleth down thereto.
16 He burneth part thereof in the fire; with part thereof he eateth flesh; he
roasteth roast, and is satisfied: yea, he warmeth *himself*, and saith, Aha, I am
warm, I have seen the fire:
17 And the residue thereof he maketh a god, *even* his graven image: he falleth
down unto it, and worshippeth *it*, and prayeth unto it, and saith, Deliver me;
for thou *art* my god.
18 They have not known nor understood: for he hath shut their eyes, that
they cannot see; *and* their hearts, that they cannot understand.
19 And none considereth in his heart, neither *is there* knowledge nor under-
standing to say, I have burned part of it in the fire; yea, also I have baked bread
upon the coals thereof; I have roasted flesh, and eaten *it*: and shall I make the
residue thereof an abomination? shall I fall down to the stock of a tree?
20 He feedeth on ashes: a deceived heart hath turned him aside, that he can-
not deliver his soul, nor say, *Is there* not a lie in my right hand?

A Prophecy about Cyrus

21 Remember these, O Jacob and Israel; for thou *art* my servant: I have
formed thee; thou *art* my servant: O Israel, thou shalt not be forgotten of me.
22 I have blotted out, as a thick cloud, thy transgressions, and, as a cloud, thy
sins: return unto me; for I have redeemed thee.
23 Sing, O ye heavens; for the LORD hath done *it*: shout, ye lower parts of the
earth: break forth into singing, ye mountains, O forest, and every tree therein:
for the LORD hath redeemed Jacob, and glorified himself in Israel.
24 Thus saith the LORD, thy redeemer, and he that formed thee from the
womb, I *am* the LORD that maketh all *things*; that stretcheth forth the heavens
alone; that spreadeth abroad the earth by myself;
25 That frustrateth the tokens of the liars, and maketh diviners mad; that
turneth wise *men* backward, and maketh their knowledge foolish;
26 That confirmeth the word of his servant, and performeth the counsel of
his messengers; that saith to Jerusalem, Thou shalt be inhabited; and to the
cities of Judah, Ye shall be built, and I will raise up the decayed places thereof:
27 That saith to the deep, Be dry, and I will dry up thy rivers:
28 That saith of Cyrus, *He is* my shepherd, and shall perform all my pleasure:
even saying to Jerusalem, Thou shalt be built; and to the temple, Thy founda-
tion shall be laid.

God Calls Cyrus

45 Thus saith the LORD to his anointed, to Cyrus, whose right hand I have
holden, to subdue nations before him; and I will loose the loins of
kings, to open before him the two leaved gates; and the gates shall not be shut;
2 I will go before thee, and make the crooked places straight: I will break in
pieces the gates of brass, and cut in sunder the bars of iron:

3 And I will give thee the treasures of darkness, and hidden riches of secret
places, that thou mayest know that I, the LORD, which call *thee* by thy name,
am the God of Israel.
4 For Jacob my servant's sake, and Israel mine elect, I have even called thee
by thy name: I have surnamed thee, though thou hast not known me.

The Lord Alone Is God

5 I *am* the LORD, and *there is* none else, *there is* no God beside me: I girded
thee, though thou hast not known me:
6 That they may know from the rising of the sun, and from the west, that
there is none beside me. I *am* the LORD, and *there is* none else.
7 I form the light, and create darkness: I make peace, and create evil: I the
LORD do all these *things*.
8 Drop down, ye heavens, from above, and let the skies pour down righteous-
ness: let the earth open, and let them bring forth salvation, and let righteous-
ness spring up together; I the LORD have created it.
9 Woe unto him that striveth with his Maker! *Let* the potsherd *strive* with
the potsherds of the earth. Shall the clay say to him that fashioneth it, What
makest thou? or thy work, He hath no hands?
10 Woe unto him that saith unto *his* father, What begettest thou? or to the
woman, What hast thou brought forth?
11 Thus saith the LORD, the Holy One of Israel, and his Maker, Ask me of
things to come concerning my sons, and concerning the work of my hands
command ye me.
12 I have made the earth, and created man upon it: I, *even* my hands, have
stretched out the heavens, and all their host have I commanded.
13 I have raised him up in righteousness, and I will direct all his ways: he
shall build my city, and he shall let go my captives, not for price nor reward,
saith the LORD of hosts.
14 Thus saith the LORD, The labour of Egypt, and merchandise of Ethiopia
and of the Sabeans, men of stature, shall come over unto thee, and they shall
be thine: they shall come after thee; in chains they shall come over, and they
shall fall down unto thee, they shall make supplication unto thee, *saying*,
Surely God *is* in thee; and *there is* none else, *there is* no God.
15 Verily thou *art* a God that hidest thyself, O God of Israel, the Saviour.
16 They shall be ashamed, and also confounded, all of them: they shall go to
confusion together *that are* makers of idols.
17 *But* Israel shall be saved in the LORD with an everlasting salvation: ye shall
not be ashamed nor confounded world without end.
18 For thus saith the LORD that created the heavens; God himself that formed
the earth and made it; he hath established it, he created it not in vain, he
formed it to be inhabited: I *am* the LORD; and *there is* none else.
19 I have not spoken in secret, in a dark place of the earth: I said not unto the
seed of Jacob, Seek ye me in vain: I the LORD speak righteousness, I declare
things that are right.

God Shows the Worthlessness of Idols

20 Assemble yourselves and come; draw near together, ye *that are* escaped
of the nations: they have no knowledge that set up the wood of their graven
image, and pray unto a god *that* cannot save.
21 Tell ye, and bring *them* near; yea, let them take counsel together: who hath
declared this from ancient time? *who* hath told it from that time? *have* not I
the LORD? and *there is* no God else beside me; a just God and a Saviour; *there
is* none beside me.
22 Look unto me, and be ye saved, all the ends of the earth: for I *am* God, and
there is none else.

23 I have sworn by myself, the word is gone out of my mouth *in* righteousness,
and shall not return, That unto me every knee shall bow, every tongue shall
swear.
24 Surely, shall *one* say, in the LORD have I righteousness and strength: *even*
to him shall *men* come; and all that are incensed against him shall be ashamed.
25 In the LORD shall all the seed of Israel be justified, and shall glory.

Babylon's Idols Cannot Save Themselves

46 Bel boweth down, Nebo stoopeth, their idols were upon the beasts,
and upon the cattle: your carriages *were* heavy loaden; *they are* a bur-
den to the weary *beast*.
2 They stoop, they bow down together; they could not deliver the burden,
but themselves are gone into captivity.
3 Hearken unto me, O house of Jacob, and all the remnant of the house of
Israel, which are borne *by me* from the belly, which are carried from the womb:
4 And *even* to *your* old age I *am* he; and *even* to hoar hairs will I carry *you*: I
have made, and I will bear; even I will carry, and will deliver *you*.

Idols Are Powerless

5 To whom will ye liken me, and make *me* equal, and compare me, that we
may be like?
6 They lavish gold out of the bag, and weigh silver in the balance, *and* hire a
goldsmith; and he maketh it a god: they fall down, yea, they worship.
7 They bear him upon the shoulder, they carry him, and set him in his place,
and he standeth; from his place shall he not remove: yea, *one* shall cry unto
him, yet can he not answer, nor save him out of his trouble.
8 Remember this, and shew yourselves men: bring *it* again to mind, O ye
transgressors.
9 Remember the former things of old: for I *am* God, and *there is* none else;
I am God, and *there is* none like me,
10 Declaring the end from the beginning, and from ancient times *the things*
that are not *yet* done, saying, My counsel shall stand, and I will do all my
pleasure:
11 Calling a ravenous bird from the east, the man that executeth my counsel
from a far country: yea, I have spoken *it*, I will also bring it to pass; I have
purposed *it*, I will also do it.
12 Hearken unto me, ye stouthearted, that *are* far from righteousness:
13 I bring near my righteousness; it shall not be far off, and my salvation
shall not tarry: and I will place salvation in Zion for Israel my glory.

God's Judgment upon Babylon

47 Come down, and sit in the dust, O virgin daughter of Babylon, sit on
the ground: *there is* no throne, O daughter of the Chaldeans: for thou
shalt no more be called tender and delicate.
2 Take the millstones, and grind meal: uncover thy locks, make bare the leg,
uncover the thigh, pass over the rivers.
3 Thy nakedness shall be uncovered, yea, thy shame shall be seen: I will take
vengeance, and I will not meet *thee as* a man.
4 *As for* our redeemer, the LORD of hosts *is* his name, the Holy One of Israel.
5 Sit thou silent, and get thee into darkness, O daughter of the Chaldeans:
for thou shalt no more be called, The lady of kingdoms.
6 I was wroth with my people, I have polluted mine inheritance, and given
them into thine hand: thou didst shew them no mercy; upon the ancient hast
thou very heavily laid thy yoke.
7 And thou saidst, I shall be a lady for ever: *so* that thou didst not lay these
things to thy heart, neither didst remember the latter end of it.

8 Therefore hear now this, *thou that art* given to pleasures, that dwellest
carelessly, that sayest in thine heart, I *am*, and none else beside me; I shall not
sit *as* a widow, neither shall I know the loss of children:
9 But these two *things* shall come to thee in a moment in one day, the loss of
children, and widowhood: they shall come upon thee in their perfection for
the multitude of thy sorceries, *and* for the great abundance of thine enchant-
ments.
10 For thou hast trusted in thy wickedness: thou hast said, None seeth me.
Thy wisdom and thy knowledge, it hath perverted thee; and thou hast said in
thine heart, I *am*, and none else beside me.
11 Therefore shall evil come upon thee; thou shalt not know from whence
it riseth: and mischief shall fall upon thee; thou shalt not be able to put it off:
and desolation shall come upon thee suddenly, *which* thou shalt not know.
12 Stand now with thine enchantments, and with the multitude of thy sor-
ceries, wherein thou hast laboured from thy youth; if so be thou shalt be able
to profit, if so be thou mayest prevail.
13 Thou art wearied in the multitude of thy counsels. Let now the astrologers,
the stargazers, the monthly prognosticators, stand up, and save thee from
these things that shall come upon thee.
14 Behold, they shall be as stubble; the fire shall burn them; they shall not
deliver themselves from the power of the flame: *there shall* not *be* a coal to
warm at, *nor* fire to sit before it.
15 Thus shall they be unto thee with whom thou hast laboured, *even* thy
merchants, from thy youth: they shall wander every one to his quarter; none
shall save thee.

The Lord Will Refine and Rescue

48 Hear ye this, O house of Jacob, which are called by the name of Israel,
and are come forth out of the waters of Judah, which swear by the
name of the LORD, and make mention of the God of Israel, *but* not in truth,
nor in righteousness.
2 For they call themselves of the holy city, and stay themselves upon the God
of Israel; The LORD of hosts *is* his name.
3 I have declared the former things from the beginning; and they went forth
out of my mouth, and I shewed them; I did *them* suddenly, and they came to
pass.
4 Because I knew that thou *art* obstinate, and thy neck *is* an iron sinew, and
thy brow brass;
5 I have even from the beginning declared *it* to thee; before it came to pass
I shewed *it* thee: lest thou shouldest say, Mine idol hath done them, and my
graven image, and my molten image, hath commanded them.
6 Thou hast heard, see all this; and will not ye declare *it*? I have shewed thee
new things from this time, even hidden things, and thou didst not know them.
7 They are created now, and not from the beginning; even before the day
when thou heardest them not; lest thou shouldest say, Behold, I knew them.
8 Yea, thou heardest not; yea, thou knewest not; yea, from that time *that*
thine ear was not opened: for I knew that thou wouldest deal very treacher-
ously, and wast called a transgressor from the womb.

God Will Save His People for His Name's Sake

9 For my name's sake will I defer mine anger, and for my praise will I refrain
for thee, that I cut thee not off.
10 Behold, I have refined thee, but not with silver; I have chosen thee in the
furnace of affliction.
11 For mine own sake, *even* for mine own sake, will I do *it*: for how should
my name be polluted? and I will not give my glory unto another.

12 Hearken unto me, O Jacob and Israel, my called; I *am* he; I *am* the first, I also *am* the last.

13 Mine hand also hath laid the foundation of the earth, and my right hand hath spanned the heavens: *when* I call unto them, they stand up together.

14 All ye, assemble yourselves, and hear; which among them hath declared these *things*? The LORD hath loved him: he will do his pleasure on Babylon, and his arm *shall be on* the Chaldeans.

15 I, *even* I, have spoken; yea, I have called him: I have brought him, and he shall make his way prosperous.

God Calls His People to Listen

16 Come ye near unto me, hear ye this; I have not spoken in secret from the beginning; from the time that it was, there *am* I: and now the Lord GOD, and his Spirit, hath sent me.

17 Thus saith the LORD, thy Redeemer, the Holy One of Israel; I *am* the LORD thy God which teacheth thee to profit, which leadeth thee by the way *that* thou shouldest go.

18 O that thou hadst hearkened to my commandments! then had thy peace been as a river, and thy righteousness as the waves of the sea:

19 Thy seed also had been as the sand, and the offspring of thy bowels like the gravel thereof; his name should not have been cut off nor destroyed from before me.

20 Go ye forth of Babylon, flee ye from the Chaldeans, with a voice of singing declare ye, tell this, utter it *even* to the end of the earth; say ye, The LORD hath redeemed his servant Jacob.

21 And they thirsted not *when* he led them through the deserts: he caused the waters to flow out of the rock for them: he clave the rock also, and the waters gushed out.

22 *There is* no peace, saith the LORD, unto the wicked.

The Lord's Servant Will Bring Salvation

49 Listen, O isles, unto me; and hearken, ye people, from far; The LORD hath called me from the womb; from the bowels of my mother hath he made mention of my name.

2 And he hath made my mouth like a sharp sword; in the shadow of his hand hath he hid me, and made me a polished shaft; in his quiver hath he hid me;

3 And said unto me, Thou *art* my servant, O Israel, in whom I will be glorified.

4 Then I said, I have laboured in vain, I have spent my strength for nought, and in vain: *yet* surely my judgment *is* with the LORD, and my work with my God.

5 And now, saith the LORD that formed me from the womb *to be* his servant, to bring Jacob again to him, Though Israel be not gathered, yet shall I be glorious in the eyes of the LORD, and my God shall be my strength.

6 And he said, It is a light thing that thou shouldest be my servant to raise up the tribes of Jacob, and to restore the preserved of Israel: I will also give thee for a light to the Gentiles, that thou mayest be my salvation unto the end of the earth.

7 Thus saith the LORD, the Redeemer of Israel, *and* his Holy One, to him whom man despiseth, to him whom the nation abhorreth, to a servant of rulers, Kings shall see and arise, princes also shall worship, because of the LORD that is faithful, *and* the Holy One of Israel, and he shall choose thee.

8 Thus saith the LORD, In an acceptable time have I heard thee, and in a day of salvation have I helped thee: and I will preserve thee, and give thee for a covenant of the people, to establish the earth, to cause to inherit the desolate heritages;

9 That thou mayest say to the prisoners, Go forth; to them that *are* in dark-
ness, Shew yourselves. They shall feed in the ways, and their pastures *shall be*
in all high places.
10 They shall not hunger nor thirst; neither shall the heat nor sun smite them:
for he that hath mercy on them shall lead them, even by the springs of water
shall he guide them.
11 And I will make all my mountains a way, and my highways shall be exalted.
12 Behold, these shall come from far: and, lo, these from the north and from
the west; and these from the land of Sinim.

The Lord Has Not Forgotten His People

13 Sing, O heavens; and be joyful, O earth; and break forth into singing, O
mountains: for the LORD hath comforted his people, and will have mercy upon
his afflicted.
14 But Zion said, The LORD hath forsaken me, and my Lord hath forgotten
me.
15 Can a woman forget her sucking child, that she should not have compas-
sion on the son of her womb? yea, they may forget, yet will I not forget thee.
16 Behold, I have graven thee upon the palms of *my* hands; thy walls *are*
continually before me.
17 Thy children shall make haste; thy destroyers and they that made thee
waste shall go forth of thee.

The Restoration of the Church

18 Lift up thine eyes round about, and behold: all these gather themselves
together, *and* come to thee. *As* I live, saith the LORD, thou shalt surely clothe
thee with them all, as with an ornament, and bind them *on thee*, as a bride
doeth.
19 For thy waste and thy desolate places, and the land of thy destruction,
shall even now be too narrow by reason of the inhabitants, and they that
swallowed thee up shall be far away.
20 The children which thou shalt have, after thou hast lost the other, shall
say again in thine ears, The place *is* too strait for me: give place to me that I
may dwell.
21 Then shalt thou say in thine heart, Who hath begotten me these, seeing I
have lost my children, and am desolate, a captive, and removing to and fro?
and who hath brought up these? Behold, I was left alone; these, where *had*
they *been*?
22 Thus saith the Lord GOD, Behold, I will lift up mine hand to the Gentiles,
and set up my standard to the people: and they shall bring thy sons in *their*
arms, and thy daughters shall be carried upon *their* shoulders.
23 And kings shall be thy nursing fathers, and their queens thy nursing moth-
ers: they shall bow down to thee with *their* face toward the earth, and lick up
the dust of thy feet; and thou shalt know that I *am* the LORD: for they shall not
be ashamed that wait for me.
24 Shall the prey be taken from the mighty, or the lawful captive delivered?
25 But thus saith the LORD, Even the captives of the mighty shall be taken
away, and the prey of the terrible shall be delivered: for I will contend with
him that contendeth with thee, and I will save thy children.
26 And I will feed them that oppress thee with their own flesh; and they shall
be drunken with their own blood, as with sweet wine: and all flesh shall know
that I the LORD *am* thy Saviour and thy Redeemer, the mighty One of Jacob.

Punishment Because of Sin

50 Thus saith the LORD, Where *is* the bill of your mother's divorcement,
whom I have put away? or which of my creditors *is it* to whom I have
sold you? Behold, for your iniquities have ye sold yourselves, and for your
transgressions is your mother put away.

2 Wherefore, when I came, *was there* no man? when I called, *was there* none
to answer? Is my hand shortened at all, that it cannot redeem? or have I no
power to deliver? behold, at my rebuke I dry up the sea, I make the rivers a
wilderness: their fish stinketh, because *there is* no water, and dieth for thirst.
3 I clothe the heavens with blackness, and I make sackcloth their covering.

The Lord's Servant Trust in the Lord's Help

4 The Lord GOD hath given me the tongue of the learned, that I should know
how to speak a word in season to *him that is* weary: he wakeneth morning by
morning, he wakeneth mine ear to hear as the learned.
5 The Lord GOD hath opened mine ear, and I was not rebellious, neither
turned away back.
6 I gave my back to the smiters, and my cheeks to them that plucked off the
hair: I hid not my face from shame and spitting.
7 For the Lord GOD will help me; therefore shall I not be confounded: there-
fore have I set my face like a flint, and I know that I shall not be ashamed.
8 *He is* near that justifieth me; who will contend with me? let us stand togeth-
er: who *is* mine adversary? let him come near to me.
9 Behold, the Lord GOD will help me; who *is* he *that* shall condemn me? lo,
they all shall wax old as a garment; the moth shall eat them up.
10 Who *is* among you that feareth the LORD, that obeyeth the voice of his
servant, that walketh *in* darkness, and hath no light? let him trust in the name
of the LORD, and stay upon his God.
11 Behold, all ye that kindle a fire, that compass *yourselves* about with sparks:
walk in the light of your fire, and in the sparks *that* ye have kindled. This shall
ye have of mine hand; ye shall lie down in sorrow.

The Lord Will Save His People

51 Hearken to me, ye that follow after righteousness, ye that seek the LORD:
look unto the rock *whence* ye are hewn, and to the hole of the pit
whence ye are digged.
2 Look unto Abraham your father, and unto Sarah *that* bare you: for I called
him alone, and blessed him, and increased him.
3 For the LORD shall comfort Zion: he will comfort all her waste places; and
he will make her wilderness like Eden, and her desert like the garden of the
LORD; joy and gladness shall be found therein, thanksgiving, and the voice of
melody.

Listen to the Word of the Lord

4 Hearken unto me, my people; and give ear unto me, O my nation: for a law
shall proceed from me, and I will make my judgment to rest for a light of the
people.
5 My righteousness *is* near; my salvation is gone forth, and mine arms shall
judge the people; the isles shall wait upon me, and on mine arm shall they
trust.
6 Lift up your eyes to the heavens, and look upon the earth beneath: for the
heavens shall vanish away like smoke, and the earth shall wax old like a gar-
ment, and they that dwell therein shall die in like manner: but my salvation
shall be for ever, and my righteousness shall not be abolished.
7 Hearken unto me, ye that know righteousness, the people in whose heart
is my law; fear ye not the reproach of men, neither be ye afraid of their revil-
ings.
8 For the moth shall eat them up like a garment, and the worm shall eat them
like wool: but my righteousness shall be for ever, and my salvation from gen-
eration to generation.
9 Awake, awake, put on strength, O arm of the LORD; awake, as in the ancient
days, in the generations of old. *Art* thou not it that hath cut Rahab, *and* wound-
ed the dragon?

10 *Art* thou not it which hath dried the sea, the waters of the great deep; that hath made the depths of the sea a way for the ransomed to pass over?

11 Therefore the redeemed of the LORD shall return, and come with singing unto Zion; and everlasting joy *shall be* upon their head: they shall obtain gladness and joy; *and* sorrow and mourning shall flee away.

12 I, *even* I, *am* he that comforteth you: who *art* thou, that thou shouldest be afraid of a man *that* shall die, and of the son of man *which* shall be made *as* grass;

13 And forgettest the LORD thy maker, that hath stretched forth the heavens, and laid the foundations of the earth; and hast feared continually every day because of the fury of the oppressor, as if he were ready to destroy? and where *is* the fury of the oppressor?

14 The captive exile hasteneth that he may be loosed, and that he should not die in the pit, nor that his bread should fail.

15 But I *am* the LORD thy God, that divided the sea, whose waves roared: The LORD of hosts *is* his name.

16 And I have put my words in thy mouth, and I have covered thee in the shadow of mine hand, that I may plant the heavens, and lay the foundations of the earth, and say unto Zion, Thou *art* my people.

Awake, Jerusalem!

17 Awake, awake, stand up, O Jerusalem, which hast drunk at the hand of the LORD the cup of his fury; thou hast drunken the dregs of the cup of trembling, *and* wrung *them* out.

18 *There is* none to guide her among all the sons *whom* she hath brought forth; neither *is there any* that taketh her by the hand of all the sons *that* she hath brought up.

19 These two *things* are come unto thee; who shall be sorry for thee? desolation, and destruction, and the famine, and the sword: by whom shall I comfort thee?

20 Thy sons have fainted, they lie at the head of all the streets, as a wild bull in a net: they are full of the fury of the LORD, the rebuke of thy God.

21 Therefore hear now this, thou afflicted, and drunken, but not with wine:

22 Thus saith thy Lord the LORD, and thy God *that* pleadeth the cause of his people, Behold, I have taken out of thine hand the cup of trembling, *even* the dregs of the cup of my fury; thou shalt no more drink it again:

23 But I will put it into the hand of them that afflict thee; which have said to thy soul, Bow down, that we may go over: and thou hast laid thy body as the ground, and as the street, to them that went over.

The Lord Will Comfort His People

52 Awake, awake; put on thy strength, O Zion; put on thy beautiful garments, O Jerusalem, the holy city: for henceforth there shall no more come into thee the uncircumcised and the unclean.

2 Shake thyself from the dust; arise, *and* sit down, O Jerusalem: loose thyself from the bands of thy neck, O captive daughter of Zion.

3 For thus saith the LORD, Ye have sold yourselves for nought; and ye shall be redeemed without money.

4 For thus saith the Lord GOD, My people went down aforetime into Egypt to sojourn there; and the Assyrian oppressed them without cause.

5 Now therefore, what have I here, saith the LORD, that my people is taken away for nought? they that rule over them make them to howl, saith the LORD; and my name continually every day *is* blasphemed.

6 Therefore my people shall know my name: therefore *they shall know* in that day that I *am* he that doth speak: behold, *it is* I.

7 How beautiful upon the mountains are the feet of him that bringeth good
tidings, that publisheth peace; that bringeth good tidings of good, that pub-
lisheth salvation; that saith unto Zion, Thy God reigneth!
8 Thy watchmen shall lift up the voice; with the voice together shall they sing:
for they shall see eye to eye, when the LORD shall bring again Zion.
9 Break forth into joy, sing together, ye waste places of Jerusalem: for the
LORD hath comforted his people, he hath redeemed Jerusalem.
10 The LORD hath made bare his holy arm in the eyes of all the nations; and
all the ends of the earth shall see the salvation of our God.
11 Depart ye, depart ye, go ye out from thence, touch no unclean *thing*; go
ye out of the midst of her; be ye clean, that bear the vessels of the LORD.
12 For ye shall not go out with haste, nor go by flight: for the LORD will go
before you; and the God of Israel *will be* your rereward.

Christ's Kingdom Shall Be Exalted

13 Behold, my servant shall deal prudently, he shall be exalted and extolled,
and be very high.
14 As many were astonied at thee; his visage was so marred more than any
man, and his form more than the sons of men:
15 So shall he sprinkle many nations; the kings shall shut their mouths at
him: for *that* which had not been told them shall they see; and *that* which
they had not heard shall they consider.

The Suffering Servant

53 Who hath believed our report? and to whom is the arm of the LORD
revealed?
2 For he shall grow up before him as a tender plant, and as a root out of a dry
ground: he hath no form nor comeliness; and when we shall see him, *there is*
no beauty that we should desire him.
3 He is despised and rejected of men; a man of sorrows, and acquainted with
grief: and we hid as it were *our* faces from him; he was despised, and we
esteemed him not.

Christ's Passion Foretold

4 Surely he hath borne our griefs, and carried our sorrows: yet we did esteem
him stricken, smitten of God, and afflicted.
5 But he *was* wounded for our transgressions, *he was* bruised for our iniq-
uities: the chastisement of our peace *was* upon him; and with his stripes we
are healed.
6 All we like sheep have gone astray; we have turned every one to his own
way; and the LORD hath laid on him the iniquity of us all.
7 He was oppressed, and he was afflicted, yet he opened not his mouth: he
is brought as a lamb to the slaughter, and as a sheep before her shearers is
dumb, so he openeth not his mouth.
8 He was taken from prison and from judgment: and who shall declare his
generation? for he was cut off out of the land of the living: for the transgression
of my people was he stricken.
9 And he made his grave with the wicked, and with the rich in his death;
because he had done no violence, neither *was any* deceit in his mouth.

The Sacrifice of the Righteous Servant

10 Yet it pleased the LORD to bruise him; he hath put *him* to grief: when thou
shalt make his soul an offering for sin, he shall see *his* seed, he shall prolong
his days, and the pleasure of the LORD shall prosper in his hand.
11 He shall see of the travail of his soul, *and* shall be satisfied: by his knowl-
edge shall my righteous servant justify many; for he shall bear their iniquities.
12 Therefore will I divide him *a portion* with the great, and he shall divide
the spoil with the strong; because he hath poured out his soul unto death: and

he was numbered with the transgressors; and he bare the sin of many, and
made intercession for the transgressors.

The Lord's Compassion for the Childless

54 Sing, O barren, thou *that* didst not bear; break forth into singing, and
cry aloud, thou *that* didst not travail with child: for more *are* the chil-
dren of the desolate than the children of the married wife, saith the LORD.
2 Enlarge the place of thy tent, and let them stretch forth the curtains of
thine habitations: spare not, lengthen thy cords, and strengthen thy stakes;
3 For thou shalt break forth on the right hand and on the left; and thy seed
shall inherit the Gentiles, and make the desolate cities to be inhabited.
4 Fear not; for thou shalt not be ashamed: neither be thou confounded; for
thou shalt not be put to shame: for thou shalt forget the shame of thy youth,
and shalt not remember the reproach of thy widowhood any more.
5 For thy Maker *is* thine husband; the LORD of hosts *is* his name; and thy
Redeemer the Holy One of Israel; The God of the whole earth shall he be called.

Certain Deliverance from Affliction

6 For the LORD hath called thee as a woman forsaken and grieved in spirit,
and a wife of youth, when thou wast refused, saith thy God.
7 For a small moment have I forsaken thee; but with great mercies will I
gather thee.
8 In a little wrath I hid my face from thee for a moment; but with everlasting
kindness will I have mercy on thee, saith the LORD thy Redeemer.
9 For this *is as* the waters of Noah unto me: for *as* I have sworn that the waters
of Noah should no more go over the earth; so have I sworn that I would not
be wroth with thee, nor rebuke thee.
10 For the mountains shall depart, and the hills be removed; but my kindness
shall not depart from thee, neither shall the covenant of my peace be removed,
saith the LORD that hath mercy on thee.

God Will Restore

11 O thou afflicted, tossed with tempest, *and* not comforted, behold, I will
lay thy stones with fair colours, and lay thy foundations with sapphires.
12 And I will make thy windows of agates, and thy gates of carbuncles, and
all thy borders of pleasant stones.
13 And all thy children *shall be* taught of the LORD; and great *shall be* the
peace of thy children.
14 In righteousness shalt thou be established: thou shalt be far from oppres-
sion; for thou shalt not fear: and from terror; for it shall not come near thee.
15 Behold, they shall surely gather together, *but* not by me: whosoever shall
gather together against thee shall fall for thy sake.
16 Behold, I have created the smith that bloweth the coals in the fire, and
that bringeth forth an instrument for his work; and I have created the waster
to destroy.
17 No weapon that is formed against thee shall prosper; and every tongue
that shall rise against thee in judgment thou shalt condemn. This *is* the heri-
tage of the servants of the LORD, and their righteousness *is* of me, saith the
LORD.

Come to the Waters and Drink

55 Ho, every one that thirsteth, come ye to the waters, and he that hath
no money; come ye, buy, and eat; yea, come, buy wine and milk without
money and without price.
2 Wherefore do ye spend money for *that which is* not bread? and your labour
for *that which* satisfieth not? hearken diligently unto me, and eat ye *that which*
is good, and let your soul delight itself in fatness.

3 Incline your ear, and come unto me: hear, and your soul shall live; and I
will make an everlasting covenant with you, *even* the sure mercies of David.
4 Behold, I have given him *for* a witness to the people, a leader and com-
mander to the people.
5 Behold, thou shalt call a nation *that* thou knowest not, and nations *that*
knew not thee shall run unto thee because of the LORD thy God, and for the
Holy One of Israel; for he hath glorified thee.

Seek the Lord

6 Seek ye the LORD while he may be found, call ye upon him while he is near:
7 Let the wicked forsake his way, and the unrighteous man his thoughts: and
let him return unto the LORD, and he will have mercy upon him; and to our
God, for he will abundantly pardon.
8 For my thoughts *are* not your thoughts, neither *are* your ways my ways,
saith the LORD.
9 For *as* the heavens are higher than the earth, so are my ways higher than
your ways, and my thoughts than your thoughts.
10 For as the rain cometh down, and the snow from heaven, and returneth
not thither, but watereth the earth, and maketh it bring forth and bud, that
it may give seed to the sower, and bread to the eater:
11 So shall my word be that goeth forth out of my mouth: it shall not return
unto me void, but it shall accomplish that which I please, and it shall prosper
in the thing whereto I sent it.
12 For ye shall go out with joy, and be led forth with peace: the mountains
and the hills shall break forth before you into singing, and all the trees of the
field shall clap *their* hands.
13 Instead of the thorn shall come up the fir tree, and instead of the brier
shall come up the myrtle tree: and it shall be to the LORD for a name, for an
everlasting sign *that* shall not be cut off.

Salvation for All People

56 Thus saith the LORD, Keep ye judgment, and do justice: for my salvation
is near to come, and my righteousness to be revealed.
2 Blessed *is* the man *that* doeth this, and the son of man *that* layeth hold on
it; that keepeth the sabbath from polluting it, and keepeth his hand from
doing any evil.
3 Neither let the son of the stranger, that hath joined himself to the LORD,
speak, saying, The LORD hath utterly separated me from his people: neither let
the eunuch say, Behold, I *am* a dry tree.
4 For thus saith the LORD unto the eunuchs that keep my sabbaths, and
choose *the things* that please me, and take hold of my covenant;
5 Even unto them will I give in mine house and within my walls a place and
a name better than of sons and of daughters: I will give them an everlasting
name, that shall not be cut off.
6 Also the sons of the stranger, that join themselves to the LORD, to serve him,
and to love the name of the LORD, to be his servants, every one that keepeth
the sabbath from polluting it, and taketh hold of my covenant;
7 Even them will I bring to my holy mountain, and make them joyful in my
house of prayer: their burnt offerings and their sacrifices *shall be* accepted
upon mine altar; for mine house shall be called an house of prayer for all
people.
8 The Lord GOD which gathereth the outcasts of Israel saith, Yet will I gather
others to him, beside those that are gathered unto him.

God Denounces Blind Watchmen

9 All ye beasts of the field, come to devour, *yea*, all ye beasts in the forest.
10 His watchmen *are* blind: they are all ignorant, they *are* all dumb dogs,
they cannot bark; sleeping, lying down, loving to slumber.

11 Yea, *they are* greedy dogs *which* can never have enough, and they *are* shep-
herds *that* cannot understand: they all look to their own way, every one for
his gain, from his quarter.
12 Come ye, *say they*, I will fetch wine, and we will fill ourselves with strong
drink; and to morrow shall be as this day, *and* much more abundant.

The Blessed Death of the Righteous

57 The righteous perisheth, and no man layeth *it* to heart: and merciful
men *are* taken away, none considering that the righteous is taken away
from the evil *to come.*
2 He shall enter into peace: they shall rest in their beds, *each one* walking *in*
his uprightness.

God Reproves the People's Idolatry

3 But draw near hither, ye sons of the sorceress, the seed of the adulterer and
the whore.
4 Against whom do ye sport yourselves? against whom make ye a wide
mouth, *and* draw out the tongue? *are* ye not children of transgression, a seed
of falsehood,
5 Enflaming yourselves with idols under every green tree, slaying the chil-
dren in the valleys under the clifts of the rocks?
6 Among the smooth *stones* of the stream *is* thy portion; they, they *are* thy
lot: even to them hast thou poured a drink offering, thou hast offered a meat
offering. Should I receive comfort in these?
7 Upon a lofty and high mountain hast thou set thy bed: even thither wentest
thou up to offer sacrifice.
8 Behind the doors also and the posts hast thou set up thy remembrance: for
thou hast discovered *thyself to another* than me, and art gone up; thou hast
enlarged thy bed, and made thee *a covenant* with them; thou lovedst their bed
where thou sawest *it.*
9 And thou wentest to the king with ointment, and didst increase thy per-
fumes, and didst send thy messengers far off, and didst debase *thyself even*
unto hell.
10 Thou art wearied in the greatness of thy way; *yet* saidst thou not, There is
no hope: thou hast found the life of thine hand; therefore thou wast not
grieved.
11 And of whom hast thou been afraid or feared, that thou hast lied, and hast
not remembered me, nor laid *it* to thy heart? have not I held my peace even
of old, and thou fearest me not?
12 I will declare thy righteousness, and thy works; for they shall not profit
thee.

God Promises Forgiveness to the Penitent

13 When thou criest, let thy companies deliver thee; but the wind shall carry
them all away; vanity shall take *them*: but he that putteth his trust in me shall
possess the land, and shall inherit my holy mountain;
14 And shall say, Cast ye up, cast ye up, prepare the way, take up the stum-
blingblock out of the way of my people.
15 For thus saith the high and lofty One that inhabiteth eternity, whose name
is Holy; I dwell in the high and holy *place*, with him also *that is* of a contrite
and humble spirit, to revive the spirit of the humble, and to revive the heart
of the contrite ones.
16 For I will not contend for ever, neither will I be always wroth: for the
spirit should fail before me, and the souls *which* I have made.
17 For the iniquity of his covetousness was I wroth, and smote him: I hid me,
and was wroth, and he went on frowardly in the way of his heart.
18 I have seen his ways, and will heal him: I will lead him also, and restore
comforts unto him and to his mourners.

19 I create the fruit of the lips; Peace, peace to *him that is* far off, and to *him*
that is near, saith the LORD; and I will heal him.
20 But the wicked *are* like the troubled sea, when it cannot rest, whose waters
cast up mire and dirt.
21 *There is* no peace, saith my God, to the wicked.

Isaiah Reproves Hypocrisy

58 Cry aloud, spare not, lift up thy voice like a trumpet, and shew my
people their transgression, and the house of Jacob their sins.
2 Yet they seek me daily, and delight to know my ways, as a nation that did
righteousness, and forsook not the ordinance of their God: they ask of me the
ordinances of justice; they take delight in approaching to God.

True Fasting

3 Wherefore have we fasted, *say they*, and thou seest not? *wherefore* have we
afflicted our soul, and thou takest no knowledge? Behold, in the day of your
fast ye find pleasure, and exact all your labours.
4 Behold, ye fast for strife and debate, and to smite with the fist of wickedness:
ye shall not fast as *ye do this* day, to make your voice to be heard on high.
5 Is it such a fast that I have chosen? a day for a man to afflict his soul? *is it*
to bow down his head as a bulrush, and to spread sackcloth and ashes *under*
him? wilt thou call this a fast, and an acceptable day to the LORD?
6 *Is* not this the fast that I have chosen? to loose the bands of wickedness, to
undo the heavy burdens, and to let the oppressed go free, and that ye break
every yoke?
7 *Is it* not to deal thy bread to the hungry, and that thou bring the poor that
are cast out to thy house? when thou seest the naked, that thou cover him; and
that thou hide not thyself from thine own flesh?

The Rewards of Godliness

8 Then shall thy light break forth as the morning, and thine health shall
spring forth speedily: and thy righteousness shall go before thee; the glory of
the LORD shall be thy rereward.
9 Then shalt thou call, and the LORD shall answer; thou shalt cry, and he shall
say, Here I *am*. If thou take away from the midst of thee the yoke, the putting
forth of the finger, and speaking vanity;
10 And *if* thou draw out thy soul to the hungry, and satisfy the afflicted soul;
then shall thy light rise in obscurity, and thy darkness *be* as the noonday:
11 And the LORD shall guide thee continually, and satisfy thy soul in drought,
and make fat thy bones: and thou shalt be like a watered garden, and like a
spring of water, whose waters fail not.
12 And *they that shall be* of thee shall build the old waste places: thou shalt
raise up the foundations of many generations; and thou shalt be called, The
repairer of the breach, The restorer of paths to dwell in.

Keep the Sabbath

13 If thou turn away thy foot from the sabbath, *from* doing thy pleasure on
my holy day; and call the sabbath a delight, the holy of the LORD, honourable;
and shalt honour him, not doing thine own ways, nor finding thine own
pleasure, nor speaking *thine own* words:
14 Then shalt thou delight thyself in the LORD; and I will cause thee to ride
upon the high places of the earth, and feed thee with the heritage of Jacob thy
father: for the mouth of the LORD hath spoken *it*.

Sin Separates from God

59 Behold, the LORD's hand is not shortened, that it cannot save; neither
his ear heavy, that it cannot hear:
2 But your iniquities have separated between you and your God, and your
sins have hid *his* face from you, that he will not hear.

3 For your hands are defiled with blood, and your fingers with iniquity; your
lips have spoken lies, your tongue hath muttered perverseness.
4 None calleth for justice, nor *any* pleadeth for truth: they trust in vanity,
and speak lies; they conceive mischief, and bring forth iniquity.
5 They hatch cockatrice' eggs, and weave the spider's web: he that eateth of
their eggs dieth, and that which is crushed breaketh out into a viper.
6 Their webs shall not become garments, neither shall they cover themselves
with their works: their works *are* works of iniquity, and the act of violence *is*
in their hands.
7 Their feet run to evil, and they make haste to shed innocent blood: their
thoughts *are* thoughts of iniquity; wasting and destruction *are* in their paths.
8 The way of peace they know not; and *there is* no judgment in their goings:
they have made them crooked paths: whosoever goeth therein shall not know
peace.
9 Therefore is judgment far from us, neither doth justice overtake us: we wait
for light, but behold obscurity; for brightness, *but* we walk in darkness.
10 We grope for the wall like the blind, and we grope as if *we had* no eyes: we
stumble at noonday as in the night; *we are* in desolate places as dead *men*.
11 We roar all like bears, and mourn sore like doves: we look for judgment,
but *there is* none; for salvation, *but* it is far off from us.
12 For our transgressions are multiplied before thee, and our sins testify
against us: for our transgressions *are* with us; and *as for* our iniquities, we
know them;
13 In transgressing and lying against the LORD, and departing away from our
God, speaking oppression and revolt, conceiving and uttering from the heart
words of falsehood.
14 And judgment is turned away backward, and justice standeth afar off: for
truth is fallen in the street, and equity cannot enter.
15 Yea, truth faileth; and he *that* departeth from evil maketh himself a prey:
and the LORD saw *it*, and it displeased him that *there was* no judgment.
16 And he saw that *there was* no man, and wondered that *there was* no inter-
cessor: therefore his arm brought salvation unto him; and his righteousness,
it sustained him.
17 For he put on righteousness as a breastplate, and an helmet of salvation
upon his head; and he put on the garments of vengeance *for* clothing, and was
clad with zeal as a cloke.
18 According to *their* deeds, accordingly he will repay, fury to his adversaries,
recompence to his enemies; to the islands he will repay recompence.
19 So shall they fear the name of the LORD from the west, and his glory from
the rising of the sun. When the enemy shall come in like a flood, the Spirit of
the LORD shall lift up a standard against him.
20 And the Redeemer shall come to Zion, and unto them that turn from
transgression in Jacob, saith the LORD.
21 As for me, this *is* my covenant with them, saith the LORD; My spirit that *is*
upon thee, and my words which I have put in thy mouth, shall not depart out
of thy mouth, nor out of the mouth of thy seed, nor out of the mouth of thy
seed's seed, saith the LORD, from henceforth and for ever.

The Lord Will Be Jerusalem's Glory

60 Arise, shine; for thy light is come, and the glory of the LORD is risen
upon thee.
2 For, behold, the darkness shall cover the earth, and gross darkness the
people: but the LORD shall arise upon thee, and his glory shall be seen upon
thee.
3 And the Gentiles shall come to thy light, and kings to the brightness of thy
rising.

4 Lift up thine eyes round about, and see: all they gather themselves togeth-
er, they come to thee: thy sons shall come from far, and thy daughters shall be
nursed at *thy* side.
5 Then thou shalt see, and flow together, and thine heart shall fear, and be
enlarged; because the abundance of the sea shall be converted unto thee, the
forces of the Gentiles shall come unto thee.
6 The multitude of camels shall cover thee, the dromedaries of Midian and
Ephah; all they from Sheba shall come: they shall bring gold and incense; and
they shall shew forth the praises of the LORD.
7 All the flocks of Kedar shall be gathered together unto thee, the rams of
Nebaioth shall minister unto thee: they shall come up with acceptance on
mine altar, and I will glorify the house of my glory.
8 Who *are* these *that* fly as a cloud, and as the doves to their windows?
9 Surely the isles shall wait for me, and the ships of Tarshish first, to bring
thy sons from far, their silver and their gold with them, unto the name of the
LORD thy God, and to the Holy One of Israel, because he hath glorified thee.
10 And the sons of strangers shall build up thy walls, and their kings shall
minister unto thee: for in my wrath I smote thee, but in my favour have I had
mercy on thee.
11 Therefore thy gates shall be open continually; they shall not be shut day
nor night; that *men* may bring unto thee the forces of the Gentiles, and *that*
their kings *may be* brought.
12 For the nation and kingdom that will not serve thee shall perish; yea, *those*
nations shall be utterly wasted.
13 The glory of Lebanon shall come unto thee, the fir tree, the pine tree, and
the box together, to beautify the place of my sanctuary; and I will make the
place of my feet glorious.
14 The sons also of them that afflicted thee shall come bending unto thee;
and all they that despised thee shall bow themselves down at the soles of thy
feet; and they shall call thee, The city of the LORD, The Zion of the Holy One of
Israel.
15 Whereas thou hast been forsaken and hated, so that no man went through
thee, I will make thee an eternal excellency, a joy of many generations.
16 Thou shalt also suck the milk of the Gentiles, and shalt suck the breast of
kings: and thou shalt know that I the LORD *am* thy Saviour and thy Redeemer,
the mighty One of Jacob.
17 For brass I will bring gold, and for iron I will bring silver, and for wood
brass, and for stones iron: I will also make thy officers peace, and thine exac-
tors righteousness.
18 Violence shall no more be heard in thy land, wasting nor destruction
within thy borders; but thou shalt call thy walls Salvation, and thy gates Praise.
19 The sun shall be no more thy light by day; neither for brightness shall the
moon give light unto thee: but the LORD shall be unto thee an everlasting light,
and thy God thy glory.
20 Thy sun shall no more go down; neither shall thy moon withdraw itself:
for the LORD shall be thine everlasting light, and the days of thy mourning
shall be ended.
21 Thy people also *shall be* all righteous: they shall inherit the land for ever,
the branch of my planting, the work of my hands, that I may be glorified.
22 A little one shall become a thousand, and a small one a strong nation: I
the LORD will hasten it in his time.

The Work of Christ

61 The Spirit of the Lord GOD *is* upon me; because the LORD hath anoint-
ed me to preach good tidings unto the meek; he hath sent me to bind
up the brokenhearted, to proclaim liberty to the captives, and the opening of
the prison to *them that are* bound;

2 To proclaim the acceptable year of the LORD, and the day of vengeance of
our God; to comfort all that mourn;
3 To appoint unto them that mourn in Zion, to give unto them beauty for
ashes, the oil of joy for mourning, the garment of praise for the spirit of heavi-
ness; that they might be called trees of righteousness, the planting of the LORD,
that he might be glorified.
4 And they shall build the old wastes, they shall raise up the former desola-
tions, and they shall repair the waste cities, the desolations of many genera-
tions.
5 And strangers shall stand and feed your flocks, and the sons of the alien
shall be your plowmen and your vinedressers.
6 But ye shall be named the Priests of the LORD: *men* shall call you the
Ministers of our God: ye shall eat the riches of the Gentiles, and in their glory
shall ye boast yourselves.
7 For your shame *ye shall have* double; and *for* confusion they shall rejoice
in their portion: therefore in their land they shall possess the double: everlast-
ing joy shall be unto them.
8 For I the LORD love judgment, I hate robbery for burnt offering; and I will
direct their work in truth, and I will make an everlasting covenant with them.
9 And their seed shall be known among the Gentiles, and their offspring
among the people: all that see them shall acknowledge them, that they *are* the
seed *which* the LORD hath blessed.
10 I will greatly rejoice in the LORD, my soul shall be joyful in my God; for he
hath clothed me with the garments of salvation, he hath covered me with the
robe of righteousness, as a bridegroom decketh *himself* with ornaments, and
as a bride adorneth *herself* with her jewels.
11 For as the earth bringeth forth her bud, and as the garden causeth the
things that are sown in it to spring forth; so the Lord GOD will cause righteous-
ness and praise to spring forth before all the nations.

Jerusalem's Salvation Is Coming

62 For Zion's sake will I not hold my peace, and for Jerusalem's sake I will
not rest, until the righteousness thereof go forth as brightness, and
the salvation thereof as a lamp *that* burneth.
2 And the Gentiles shall see thy righteousness, and all kings thy glory: and
thou shalt be called by a new name, which the mouth of the LORD shall name.
3 Thou shalt also be a crown of glory in the hand of the LORD, and a royal
diadem in the hand of thy God.
4 Thou shalt no more be termed Forsaken; neither shall thy land any more
be termed Desolate: but thou shalt be called Hephzibah, and thy land Beulah:
for the LORD delighteth in thee, and thy land shall be married.
5 For *as* a young man marrieth a virgin, *so* shall thy sons marry thee: and *as*
the bridegroom rejoiceth over the bride, *so* shall thy God rejoice over thee.
6 I have set watchmen upon thy walls, O Jerusalem, *which* shall never hold
their peace day nor night: ye that make mention of the LORD, keep not silence,
7 And give him no rest, till he establish, and till he make Jerusalem a praise
in the earth.
8 The LORD hath sworn by his right hand, and by the arm of his strength,
Surely I will no more give thy corn *to be* meat for thine enemies; and the sons
of the stranger shall not drink thy wine, for the which thou hast laboured:
9 But they that have gathered it shall eat it, and praise the LORD; and they
that have brought it together shall drink it in the courts of my holiness.

The Savior Is Coming

10 Go through, go through the gates; prepare ye the way of the people; cast
up, cast up the highway; gather out the stones; lift up a standard for the people.

11 Behold, the LORD hath proclaimed unto the end of the world, Say ye to the
daughter of Zion, Behold, thy salvation cometh; behold, his reward *is* with
him, and his work before him.
12 And they shall call them, The holy people, The redeemed of the LORD: and
thou shalt be called, Sought out, A city not forsaken.

The Lord Will Be Victorious

63 Who *is* this that cometh from Edom, with dyed garments from Bozrah?
this *that is* glorious in his apparel, travelling in the greatness of his
strength? I that speak in righteousness, mighty to save.
2 Wherefore *art thou* red in thine apparel, and thy garments like him that
treadeth in the winefat?
3 I have trodden the winepress alone; and of the people *there was* none with
me: for I will tread them in mine anger, and trample them in my fury; and
their blood shall be sprinkled upon my garments, and I will stain all my rai-
ment.
4 For the day of vengeance *is* in mine heart, and the year of my redeemed is
come.
5 And I looked, and *there was* none to help; and I wondered that *there was*
none to uphold: therefore mine own arm brought salvation unto me; and my
fury, it upheld me.
6 And I will tread down the people in mine anger, and make them drunk in
my fury, and I will bring down their strength to the earth.

The Lord's People Pray

7 I will mention the lovingkindnesses of the LORD, *and* the praises of the
LORD, according to all that the LORD hath bestowed on us, and the great good-
ness toward the house of Israel, which he hath bestowed on them according
to his mercies, and according to the multitude of his lovingkindnesses.
8 For he said, Surely they *are* my people, children *that* will not lie: so he was
their Saviour.
9 In all their affliction he was afflicted, and the angel of his presence saved
them: in his love and in his pity he redeemed them; and he bare them, and
carried them all the days of old.
10 But they rebelled, and vexed his holy Spirit: therefore he was turned to be
their enemy, *and* he fought against them.
11 Then he remembered the days of old, Moses, *and* his people, *saying*, Where
is he that brought them up out of the sea with the shepherd of his flock? where
is he that put his holy Spirit within him?
12 That led *them* by the right hand of Moses with his glorious arm, dividing
the water before them, to make himself an everlasting name?
13 That led them through the deep, as an horse in the wilderness, *that* they
should not stumble?
14 As a beast goeth down into the valley, the Spirit of the LORD caused him
to rest: so didst thou lead thy people, to make thyself a glorious name.
15 Look down from heaven, and behold from the habitation of thy holiness
and of thy glory: where *is* thy zeal and thy strength, the sounding of thy bow-
els and of thy mercies toward me? are they restrained?
16 Doubtless thou *art* our father, though Abraham be ignorant of us, and
Israel acknowledge us not: thou, O LORD, *art* our father, our redeemer; thy
name *is* from everlasting.
17 O LORD, why hast thou made us to err from thy ways, *and* hardened our
heart from thy fear? Return for thy servants' sake, the tribes of thine inheri-
tance.
18 The people of thy holiness have possessed *it* but a little while: our adver-
saries have trodden down thy sanctuary.
19 We are *thine*: thou never barest rule over them; they were not called by
thy name.

Prayer for a Sign of God's Power

64 Oh that thou wouldest rend the heavens, that thou wouldest come
down, that the mountains might flow down at thy presence,
2 As *when* the melting fire burneth, the fire causeth the waters to boil, to
make thy name known to thine adversaries, *that* the nations may tremble at
thy presence!
3 When thou didst terrible things *which* we looked not for, thou camest
down, the mountains flowed down at thy presence.
4 For since the beginning of the world *men* have not heard, nor perceived
by the ear, neither hath the eye seen, O God, beside thee, *what* he hath prepared
for him that waiteth for him.
5 Thou meetest him that rejoiceth and worketh righteousness, *those that*
remember thee in thy ways: behold, thou art wroth; for we have sinned: in
those is continuance, and we shall be saved.
6 But we are all as an unclean *thing*, and all our righteousnesses *are* as filthy
rags; and we all do fade as a leaf; and our iniquities, like the wind, have taken
us away.
7 And *there is* none that calleth upon thy name, that stirreth up himself to
take hold of thee: for thou hast hid thy face from us, and hast consumed us,
because of our iniquities.
8 But now, O Lord, thou *art* our father; we *are* the clay, and thou our potter;
and we all *are* the work of thy hand.
9 Be not wroth very sore, O Lord, neither remember iniquity for ever: behold,
see, we beseech thee, we *are* all thy people.
10 Thy holy cities are a wilderness, Zion is a wilderness, Jerusalem a desola-
tion.
11 Our holy and our beautiful house, where our fathers praised thee, is
burned up with fire: and all our pleasant things are laid waste.
12 Wilt thou refrain thyself for these *things*, O Lord? wilt thou hold thy peace,
and afflict us very sore?

The Calling of the Gentiles

65 I am sought of *them that* asked not *for me*; I am found of *them that*
sought me not: I said, Behold me, behold me, unto a nation *that* was
not called by my name.
2 I have spread out my hands all the day unto a rebellious people, which
walketh in a way *that was* not good, after their own thoughts;
3 A people that provoketh me to anger continually to my face; that sacrificeth
in gardens, and burneth incense upon altars of brick;
4 Which remain among the graves, and lodge in the monuments, which eat
swine's flesh, and broth of abominable *things is in* their vessels;
5 Which say, Stand by thyself, come not near to me; for I am holier than thou.
These *are* a smoke in my nose, a fire that burneth all the day.
6 Behold, *it is* written before me: I will not keep silence, but will recompense,
even recompense into their bosom,
7 Your iniquities, and the iniquities of your fathers together, saith the Lord,
which have burned incense upon the mountains, and blasphemed me upon
the hills: therefore will I measure their former work into their bosom.

A Remnant Shall Be Saved

8 Thus saith the Lord, As the new wine is found in the cluster, and *one* saith,
Destroy it not; for a blessing *is* in it: so will I do for my servants' sakes, that I
may not destroy them all.
9 And I will bring forth a seed out of Jacob, and out of Judah an inheritor of
my mountains: and mine elect shall inherit it, and my servants shall dwell
there.

10 And Sharon shall be a fold of flocks, and the valley of Achor a place for the
herds to lie down in, for my people that have sought me.

Judgments of the Wicked, and Blessings on the Godly

11 But ye *are* they that forsake the LORD, that forget my holy mountain, that
prepare a table for that troop, and that furnish the drink offering unto that
number.
12 Therefore will I number you to the sword, and ye shall all bow down to
the slaughter: because when I called, ye did not answer; when I spake, ye did
not hear; but did evil before mine eyes, and did choose *that* wherein I delight-
ed not.
13 Therefore thus saith the Lord GOD, Behold, my servants shall eat, but ye
shall be hungry: behold, my servants shall drink, but ye shall be thirsty: behold,
my servants shall rejoice, but ye shall be ashamed:
14 Behold, my servants shall sing for joy of heart, but ye shall cry for sorrow
of heart, and shall howl for vexation of spirit.
15 And ye shall leave your name for a curse unto my chosen: for the Lord GOD
shall slay thee, and call his servants by another name:
16 That he who blesseth himself in the earth shall bless himself in the God
of truth; and he that sweareth in the earth shall swear by the God of truth;
because the former troubles are forgotten, and because they are hid from
mine eyes.

New Heavens and a New Earth

17 For, behold, I create new heavens and a new earth: and the former shall
not be remembered, nor come into mind.
18 But be ye glad and rejoice for ever *in that* which I create: for, behold, I
create Jerusalem a rejoicing, and her people a joy.
19 And I will rejoice in Jerusalem, and joy in my people: and the voice of
weeping shall be no more heard in her, nor the voice of crying.
20 There shall be no more thence an infant of days, nor an old man that hath
not filled his days: for the child shall die an hundred years old; but the sinner
being an hundred years old shall be accursed.
21 And they shall build houses, and inhabit *them*; and they shall plant vine-
yards, and eat the fruit of them.
22 They shall not build, and another inhabit; they shall not plant, and anoth-
er eat: for as the days of a tree *are* the days of my people, and mine elect shall
long enjoy the work of their hands.
23 They shall not labour in vain, nor bring forth for trouble; for they *are* the
seed of the blessed of the LORD, and their offspring with them.
24 And it shall come to pass, that before they call, I will answer; and while
they are yet speaking, I will hear.
25 The wolf and the lamb shall feed together, and the lion shall eat straw like
the bullock: and dust *shall be* the serpent's meat. They shall not hurt nor
destroy in all my holy mountain, saith the LORD.

God Will Be Served in Humble Sincerity

66 Thus saith the LORD, The heaven *is* my throne, and the earth *is* my
footstool: where *is* the house that ye build unto me? and where *is* the
place of my rest?
2 For all those *things* hath mine hand made, and all those *things* have been,
saith the LORD: but to this *man* will I look, *even* to *him that is* poor and of a
contrite spirit, and trembleth at my word.
3 He that killeth an ox *is as if* he slew a man; he that sacrificeth a lamb, *as if*
he cut off a dog's neck; he that offereth an oblation, *as if he offered* swine's
blood; he that burneth incense, *as if* he blessed an idol. Yea, they have chosen
their own ways, and their soul delighteth in their abominations.

4 I also will choose their delusions, and will bring their fears upon them;
because when I called, none did answer; when I spake, they did not hear: but
they did evil before mine eyes, and chose *that* in which I delighted not.

God Comforts the Humble with Marvels

5 Hear the word of the LORD, ye that tremble at his word; Your brethren that
hated you, that cast you out for my name's sake, said, Let the LORD be glorified:
but he shall appear to your joy, and they shall be ashamed.
6 A voice of noise from the city, a voice from the temple, a voice of the LORD
that rendereth recompence to his enemies.
7 Before she travailed, she brought forth; before her pain came, she was
delivered of a man child.
8 Who hath heard such a thing? who hath seen such things? Shall the earth
be made to bring forth in one day? *or* shall a nation be born at once? for as
soon as Zion travailed, she brought forth her children.
9 Shall I bring to the birth, and not cause to bring forth? saith the LORD: shall
I cause to bring forth, and shut *the womb*? saith thy God.
10 Rejoice ye with Jerusalem, and be glad with her, all ye that love her: rejoice
for joy with her, all ye that mourn for her:
11 That ye may suck, and be satisfied with the breasts of her consolations;
that ye may milk out, and be delighted with the abundance of her glory.
12 For thus saith the LORD, Behold, I will extend peace to her like a river, and
the glory of the Gentiles like a flowing stream: then shall ye suck, ye shall be
borne upon *her* sides, and be dandled upon *her* knees.
13 As one whom his mother comforteth, so will I comfort you; and ye shall
be comforted in Jerusalem.
14 And when ye see *this*, your heart shall rejoice, and your bones shall flour-
ish like an herb: and the hand of the LORD shall be known toward his servants,
and *his* indignation toward his enemies.

The New Creation

15 For, behold, the LORD will come with fire, and with his chariots like a
whirlwind, to render his anger with fury, and his rebuke with flames of fire.
16 For by fire and by his sword will the LORD plead with all flesh: and the slain
of the LORD shall be many.
17 They that sanctify themselves, and purify themselves in the gardens
behind one *tree* in the midst, eating swine's flesh, and the abomination, and
the mouse, shall be consumed together, saith the LORD.
18 For I *know* their works and their thoughts: it shall come, that I will gath-
er all nations and tongues; and they shall come, and see my glory.
19 And I will set a sign among them, and I will send those that escape of them
unto the nations, *to* Tarshish, Pul, and Lud, that draw the bow, *to* Tubal, and
Javan, *to* the isles afar off, that have not heard my fame, neither have seen my
glory; and they shall declare my glory among the Gentiles.
20 And they shall bring all your brethren *for* an offering unto the LORD out
of all nations upon horses, and in chariots, and in litters, and upon mules, and
upon swift beasts, to my holy mountain Jerusalem, saith the LORD, as the chil-
dren of Israel bring an offering in a clean vessel into the house of the LORD.
21 And I will also take of them for priests *and* for Levites, saith the LORD.
22 For as the new heavens and the new earth, which I will make, shall remain
before me, saith the LORD, so shall your seed and your name remain.
23 And it shall come to pass, *that* from one new moon to another, and from
one sabbath to another, shall all flesh come to worship before me, saith the
LORD.
24 And they shall go forth, and look upon the carcases of the men that have
transgressed against me: for their worm shall not die, neither shall their fire
be quenched; and they shall be an abhorring unto all flesh.

The Prophet Jeremiah

1 The words of Jeremiah the son of Hilkiah, of the priests that *were* in
Anathoth in the land of Benjamin:
2 To whom the word of the LORD came in the days of Josiah the son of Amon
king of Judah, in the thirteenth year of his reign.
3 It came also in the days of Jehoiakim the son of Josiah king of Judah, unto
the end of the eleventh year of Zedekiah the son of Josiah king of Judah, unto
the carrying away of Jerusalem captive in the fifth month.

The Calling of Jeremiah

4 Then the word of the LORD came unto me, saying,
5 Before I formed thee in the belly I knew thee; and before thou camest forth
out of the womb I sanctified thee, *and* I ordained thee a prophet unto the
nations.
6 Then said I, Ah, Lord GOD! behold, I cannot speak: for I *am* a child.
7 But the LORD said unto me, Say not, I *am* a child: for thou shalt go to all that
I shall send thee, and whatsoever I command thee thou shalt speak.
8 Be not afraid of their faces: for I *am* with thee to deliver thee, saith the LORD.
9 Then the LORD put forth his hand, and touched my mouth. And the LORD
said unto me, Behold, I have put my words in thy mouth.
10 See, I have this day set thee over the nations and over the kingdoms, to
root out, and to pull down, and to destroy, and to throw down, to build, and
to plant.

Visions of an Almond Rod and a Boiling Pot

11 Moreover the word of the LORD came unto me, saying, Jeremiah, what
seest thou? And I said, I see a rod of an almond tree.
12 Then said the LORD unto me, Thou hast well seen: for I will hasten my word
to perform it.
13 And the word of the LORD came unto me the second time, saying, What
seest thou? And I said, I see a seething pot; and the face thereof *is* toward the
north.
14 Then the LORD said unto me, Out of the north an evil shall break forth
upon all the inhabitants of the land.
15 For, lo, I will call all the families of the kingdoms of the north, saith the
LORD; and they shall come, and they shall set every one his throne at the enter-
ing of the gates of Jerusalem, and against all the walls thereof round about,
and against all the cities of Judah.
16 And I will utter my judgments against them touching all their wickedness,
who have forsaken me, and have burned incense unto other gods, and wor-
shipped the works of their own hands.
17 Thou therefore gird up thy loins, and arise, and speak unto them all that
I command thee: be not dismayed at their faces, lest I confound thee before
them.
18 For, behold, I have made thee this day a defenced city, and an iron pillar,
and brasen walls against the whole land, against the kings of Judah, against
the princes thereof, against the priests thereof, and against the people of the
land.

19 And they shall fight against thee; but they shall not prevail against thee;
for I *am* with thee, saith the LORD, to deliver thee.

God's People Continue to Reject Him

2 Moreover the word of the LORD came to me, saying,
2 Go and cry in the ears of Jerusalem, saying, Thus saith the LORD; I
remember thee, the kindness of thy youth, the love of thine espousals, when
thou wentest after me in the wilderness, in a land *that was* not sown.
3 Israel *was* holiness unto the LORD, *and* the firstfruits of his increase: all
that devour him shall offend; evil shall come upon them, saith the LORD.
4 Hear ye the word of the LORD, O house of Jacob, and all the families of the
house of Israel:
5 Thus saith the LORD, What iniquity have your fathers found in me, that
they are gone far from me, and have walked after vanity, and are become vain?
6 Neither said they, Where *is* the LORD that brought us up out of the land of
Egypt, that led us through the wilderness, through a land of deserts and of
pits, through a land of drought, and of the shadow of death, through a land
that no man passed through, and where no man dwelt?
7 And I brought you into a plentiful country, to eat the fruit thereof and the
goodness thereof; but when ye entered, ye defiled my land, and made mine
heritage an abomination.
8 The priests said not, Where *is* the LORD? and they that handle the law knew
me not: the pastors also transgressed against me, and the prophets prophesied
by Baal, and walked after *things that* do not profit.

God's People Exchanged Him for Idols

9 Wherefore I will yet plead with you, saith the LORD, and with your children's
children will I plead.
10 For pass over the isles of Chittim, and see; and send unto Kedar, and con-
sider diligently, and see if there be such a thing.
11 Hath a nation changed *their* gods, which *are* yet no gods? but my people
have changed their glory for *that which* doth not profit.
12 Be astonished, O ye heavens, at this, and be horribly afraid, be ye very
desolate, saith the LORD.
13 For my people have committed two evils; they have forsaken me the foun-
tain of living waters, *and* hewed them out cisterns, broken cisterns, that can
hold no water.

How Bitter It Is to Abandon God

14 *Is* Israel a servant? *is* he a homeborn *slave*? why is he spoiled?
15 The young lions roared upon him, *and* yelled, and they made his land
waste: his cities are burned without inhabitant.
16 Also the children of Noph and Tahapanes have broken the crown of thy
head.
17 Hast thou not procured this unto thyself, in that thou hast forsaken the
LORD thy God, when he led thee by the way?
18 And now what hast thou to do in the way of Egypt, to drink the waters of
Sihor? or what hast thou to do in the way of Assyria, to drink the waters of the
river?
19 Thine own wickedness shall correct thee, and thy backslidings shall
reprove thee: know therefore and see that *it is* an evil *thing* and bitter, that
thou hast forsaken the LORD thy God, and that my fear *is* not in thee, saith the
Lord GOD of hosts.

The Sins of Judah

20 For of old time I have broken thy yoke, *and* burst thy bands; and thou
saidst, I will not transgress; when upon every high hill and under every green
tree thou wanderest, playing the harlot.

21 Yet I had planted thee a noble vine, wholly a right seed: how then art thou
turned into the degenerate plant of a strange vine unto me?
22 For though thou wash thee with nitre, and take thee much soap, *yet* thine
iniquity is marked before me, saith the Lord GOD.
23 How canst thou say, I am not polluted, I have not gone after Baalim? see
thy way in the valley, know what thou hast done: *thou art* a swift dromedary
traversing her ways;
24 A wild ass used to the wilderness, *that* snuffeth up the wind at her pleasure;
in her occasion who can turn her away? all they that seek her will not weary
themselves; in her month they shall find her.
25 Withhold thy foot from being unshod, and thy throat from thirst: but
thou saidst, There is no hope: no; for I have loved strangers, and after them
will I go.
26 As the thief is ashamed when he is found, so is the house of Israel ashamed;
they, their kings, their princes, and their priests, and their prophets,
27 Saying to a stock, Thou *art* my father; and to a stone, Thou hast brought
me forth: for they have turned *their* back unto me, and not *their* face: but in
the time of their trouble they will say, Arise, and save us.
28 But where *are* thy gods that thou hast made thee? let them arise, if they
can save thee in the time of thy trouble: for *according to* the number of thy
cities are thy gods, O Judah.
29 Wherefore will ye plead with me? ye all have transgressed against me,
saith the LORD.
30 In vain have I smitten your children; they received no correction: your
own sword hath devoured your prophets, like a destroying lion.
31 O generation, see ye the word of the LORD. Have I been a wilderness unto
Israel? a land of darkness? wherefore say my people, We are lords; we will
come no more unto thee?
32 Can a maid forget her ornaments, *or* a bride her attire? yet my people
have forgotten me days without number.
33 Why trimmest thou thy way to seek love? therefore hast thou also taught
the wicked ones thy ways.
34 Also in thy skirts is found the blood of the souls of the poor innocents: I
have not found it by secret search, but upon all these.
35 Yet thou sayest, Because I am innocent, surely his anger shall turn from
me. Behold, I will plead with thee, because thou sayest, I have not sinned.
36 Why gaddest thou about so much to change thy way? thou also shalt be
ashamed of Egypt, as thou wast ashamed of Assyria.
37 Yea, thou shalt go forth from him, and thine hands upon thine head: for
the LORD hath rejected thy confidences, and thou shalt not prosper in them.

The People Act Shamelessly

3 They say, If a man put away his wife, and she go from him, and become
another man's, shall he return unto her again? shall not that land be great-
ly polluted? but thou hast played the harlot with many lovers; yet return again
to me, saith the LORD.
2 Lift up thine eyes unto the high places, and see where thou hast not been
lien with. In the ways hast thou sat for them, as the Arabian in the wilderness;
and thou hast polluted the land with thy whoredoms and with thy wickedness.
3 Therefore the showers have been withholden, and there hath been no lat-
ter rain; and thou hadst a whore's forehead, thou refusedst to be ashamed.
4 Wilt thou not from this time cry unto me, My father, thou *art* the guide of
my youth?
5 Will he reserve *his anger* for ever? will he keep *it* to the end? Behold, thou
hast spoken and done evil things as thou couldest.

Judah Is Worse Than Israel

6 The LORD said also unto me in the days of Josiah the king, Hast thou seen
that which backsliding Israel hath done? she is gone up upon every high
mountain and under every green tree, and there hath played the harlot.
7 And I said after she had done all these *things*, Turn thou unto me. But she
returned not. And her treacherous sister Judah saw *it*.
8 And I saw, when for all the causes whereby backsliding Israel committed
adultery I had put her away, and given her a bill of divorce; yet her treacherous
sister Judah feared not, but went and played the harlot also.
9 And it came to pass through the lightness of her whoredom, that she defiled
the land, and committed adultery with stones and with stocks.
10 And yet for all this her treacherous sister Judah hath not turned unto me
with her whole heart, but feignedly, saith the LORD.
11 And the LORD said unto me, The backsliding Israel hath justified herself
more than treacherous Judah.

The Promises of God to the Penitent

12 Go and proclaim these words toward the north, and say, Return, thou
backsliding Israel, saith the LORD; *and* I will not cause mine anger to fall upon
you: for I *am* merciful, saith the LORD, *and* I will not keep *anger* for ever.
13 Only acknowledge thine iniquity, that thou hast transgressed against the
LORD thy God, and hast scattered thy ways to the strangers under every green
tree, and ye have not obeyed my voice, saith the LORD.
14 Turn, O backsliding children, saith the LORD; for I am married unto you:
and I will take you one of a city, and two of a family, and I will bring you to
Zion:
15 And I will give you pastors according to mine heart, which shall feed you
with knowledge and understanding.
16 And it shall come to pass, when ye be multiplied and increased in the land,
in those days, saith the LORD, they shall say no more, The ark of the covenant
of the LORD: neither shall it come to mind: neither shall they remember it;
neither shall they visit *it*; neither shall *that* be done any more.
17 At that time they shall call Jerusalem the throne of the LORD; and all the
nations shall be gathered unto it, to the name of the LORD, to Jerusalem: neither
shall they walk any more after the imagination of their evil heart.
18 In those days the house of Judah shall walk with the house of Israel, and
they shall come together out of the land of the north to the land that I have
given for an inheritance unto your fathers.
19 But I said, How shall I put thee among the children, and give thee a pleas-
ant land, a goodly heritage of the hosts of nations? and I said, Thou shalt call
me, My father; and shalt not turn away from me.
20 Surely *as* a wife treacherously departeth from her husband, so have ye
dealt treacherously with me, O house of Israel, saith the LORD.
21 A voice was heard upon the high places, weeping *and* supplications of the
children of Israel: for they have perverted their way, *and* they have forgotten
the LORD their God.
22 Return, ye backsliding children, *and* I will heal your backslidings. Behold,
we come unto thee; for thou *art* the LORD our God.
23 Truly in vain *is salvation hoped for* from the hills, *and from* the multitude
of mountains: truly in the LORD our God *is* the salvation of Israel.
24 For shame hath devoured the labour of our fathers from our youth; their
flocks and their herds, their sons and their daughters.
25 We lie down in our shame, and our confusion covereth us: for we have
sinned against the LORD our God, we and our fathers, from our youth even
unto this day, and have not obeyed the voice of the LORD our God.

God Calls Israel by His Promise

4 If thou wilt return, O Israel, saith the LORD, return unto me: and if thou wilt
put away thine abominations out of my sight, then shalt thou not remove.
2 And thou shalt swear, The LORD liveth, in truth, in judgment, and in righ-
teousness; and the nations shall bless themselves in him, and in him shall they
glory.

Destruction from the North

3 For thus saith the LORD to the men of Judah and Jerusalem, Break up your
fallow ground, and sow not among thorns.
4 Circumcise yourselves to the LORD, and take away the foreskins of your
heart, ye men of Judah and inhabitants of Jerusalem: lest my fury come forth
like fire, and burn that none can quench *it*, because of the evil of your doings.
5 Declare ye in Judah, and publish in Jerusalem; and say, Blow ye the trumpet
in the land: cry, gather together, and say, Assemble yourselves, and let us go
into the defenced cities.
6 Set up the standard toward Zion: retire, stay not: for I will bring evil from
the north, and a great destruction.
7 The lion is come up from his thicket, and the destroyer of the Gentiles is
on his way; he is gone forth from his place to make thy land desolate; *and* thy
cities shall be laid waste, without an inhabitant.
8 For this gird you with sackcloth, lament and howl: for the fierce anger of
the LORD is not turned back from us.
9 And it shall come to pass at that day, saith the LORD, *that* the heart of the
king shall perish, and the heart of the princes; and the priests shall be aston-
ished, and the prophets shall wonder.
10 Then said I, Ah, Lord GOD! surely thou hast greatly deceived this people
and Jerusalem, saying, Ye shall have peace; whereas the sword reacheth unto
the soul.
11 At that time shall it be said to this people and to Jerusalem, A dry wind of
the high places in the wilderness toward the daughter of my people, not to
fan, nor to cleanse,
12 *Even* a full wind from those *places* shall come unto me: now also will I give
sentence against them.
13 Behold, he shall come up as clouds, and his chariots *shall be* as a whirl-
wind: his horses are swifter than eagles. Woe unto us! for we are spoiled.
14 O Jerusalem, wash thine heart from wickedness, that thou mayest be saved.
How long shall thy vain thoughts lodge within thee?
15 For a voice declareth from Dan, and publisheth affliction from mount
Ephraim.
16 Make ye mention to the nations; behold, publish against Jerusalem, *that*
watchers come from a far country, and give out their voice against the cities
of Judah.
17 As keepers of a field, are they against her round about; because she hath
been rebellious against me, saith the LORD.
18 Thy way and thy doings have procured these *things* unto thee; this *is* thy
wickedness, because it is bitter, because it reacheth unto thine heart.

A Lament for the Miseries of Judah

19 My bowels, my bowels! I am pained at my very heart; my heart maketh a
noise in me; I cannot hold my peace, because thou hast heard, O my soul, the
sound of the trumpet, the alarm of war.
20 Destruction upon destruction is cried; for the whole land is spoiled: sud-
denly are my tents spoiled, *and* my curtains in a moment.
21 How long shall I see the standard, *and* hear the sound of the trumpet?

22 For my people *is* foolish, they have not known me; they *are* sottish chil-
dren, and they have none understanding: they *are* wise to do evil, but to do
good they have no knowledge.
23 I beheld the earth, and, lo, *it was* without form, and void; and the heavens,
and they *had* no light.
24 I beheld the mountains, and, lo, they trembled, and all the hills moved
lightly.
25 I beheld, and, lo, *there was* no man, and all the birds of the heavens were
fled.
26 I beheld, and, lo, the fruitful place *was* a wilderness, and all the cities
thereof were broken down at the presence of the LORD, *and* by his fierce anger.
27 For thus hath the LORD said, The whole land shall be desolate; yet will I
not make a full end.
28 For this shall the earth mourn, and the heavens above be black: because
I have spoken *it*, I have purposed *it*, and will not repent, neither will I turn
back from it.
29 The whole city shall flee for the noise of the horsemen and bowmen; they
shall go into thickets, and climb up upon the rocks: every city *shall be* forsak-
en, and not a man dwell therein.
30 And *when* thou *art* spoiled, what wilt thou do? Though thou clothest
thyself with crimson, though thou deckest thee with ornaments of gold,
though thou rentest thy face with painting, in vain shalt thou make thyself
fair; *thy* lovers will despise thee, they will seek thy life.
31 For I have heard a voice as of a woman in travail, *and* the anguish as of
her that bringeth forth her first child, the voice of the daughter of Zion, *that*
bewaileth herself, *that* spreadeth her hands, *saying*, Woe *is* me now! for my
soul is wearied because of murderers.

Judah's Complete Rejection of the Lord

5 Run ye to and fro through the streets of Jerusalem, and see now, and know,
and seek in the broad places thereof, if ye can find a man, if there be *any*
that executeth judgment, that seeketh the truth; and I will pardon it.
2 And though they say, The LORD liveth; surely they swear falsely.
3 O LORD, *are* not thine eyes upon the truth? thou hast stricken them, but
they have not grieved; thou hast consumed them, *but* they have refused to
receive correction: they have made their faces harder than a rock; they have
refused to return.
4 Therefore I said, Surely these *are* poor; they are foolish: for they know not
the way of the LORD, *nor* the judgment of their God.
5 I will get me unto the great men, and will speak unto them; for they have
known the way of the LORD, *and* the judgment of their God: but these have
altogether broken the yoke, *and* burst the bonds.
6 Wherefore a lion out of the forest shall slay them, *and* a wolf of the evenings
shall spoil them, a leopard shall watch over their cities: every one that goeth
out thence shall be torn in pieces: because their transgressions are many, *and*
their backslidings are increased.
7 How shall I pardon thee for this? thy children have forsaken me, and sworn
by *them that are* no gods: when I had fed them to the full, they then commit-
ted adultery, and assembled themselves by troops in the harlots' houses.
8 They were *as* fed horses in the morning: every one neighed after his neigh-
bour's wife.
9 Shall I not visit for these *things*? saith the LORD: and shall not my soul be
avenged on such a nation as this?
10 Go ye up upon her walls, and destroy; but make not a full end: take away
her battlements; for they *are* not the LORD's.

11 For the house of Israel and the house of Judah have dealt very treacher-
ously against me, saith the LORD.
12 They have belied the LORD, and said, *It is* not he; neither shall evil come
upon us; neither shall we see sword nor famine:
13 And the prophets shall become wind, and the word *is* not in them: thus
shall it be done unto them.
14 Wherefore thus saith the LORD God of hosts, Because ye speak this word,
behold, I will make my words in thy mouth fire, and this people wood, and it
shall devour them.
15 Lo, I will bring a nation upon you from far, O house of Israel, saith the
LORD: it *is* a mighty nation, it *is* an ancient nation, a nation whose language
thou knowest not, neither understandest what they say.
16 Their quiver *is* as an open sepulchre, they *are* all mighty men.
17 And they shall eat up thine harvest, and thy bread, *which* thy sons and thy
daughters should eat: they shall eat up thy flocks and thine herds: they shall
eat up thy vines and thy fig trees: they shall impoverish thy fenced cities, where-
in thou trustedst, with the sword.
18 Nevertheless in those days, saith the LORD, I will not make a full end with
you.
19 And it shall come to pass, when ye shall say, Wherefore doeth the LORD
our God all these *things* unto us? then shalt thou answer them, Like as ye have
forsaken me, and served strange gods in your land, so shall ye serve strangers
in a land *that is* not yours.
20 Declare this in the house of Jacob, and publish it in Judah, saying,
21 Hear now this, O foolish people, and without understanding; which have
eyes, and see not; which have ears, and hear not:
22 Fear ye not me? saith the LORD: will ye not tremble at my presence, which
have placed the sand *for* the bound of the sea by a perpetual decree, that it
cannot pass it: and though the waves thereof toss themselves, yet can they not
prevail; though they roar, yet can they not pass over it?
23 But this people hath a revolting and a rebellious heart; they are revolted
and gone.
24 Neither say they in their heart, Let us now fear the LORD our God, that
giveth rain, both the former and the latter, in his season: he reserveth unto us
the appointed weeks of the harvest.
25 Your iniquities have turned away these *things*, and your sins have with-
holden good *things* from you.
26 For among my people are found wicked *men*: they lay wait, as he that
setteth snares; they set a trap, they catch men.
27 As a cage is full of birds, so *are* their houses full of deceit: therefore they
are become great, and waxen rich.
28 They are waxen fat, they shine: yea, they overpass the deeds of the wicked:
they judge not the cause, the cause of the fatherless, yet they prosper; and the
right of the needy do they not judge.
29 Shall I not visit for these *things*? saith the LORD: shall not my soul be
avenged on such a nation as this?
30 A wonderful and horrible thing is committed in the land;
31 The prophets prophesy falsely, and the priests bear rule by their means;
and my people love *to have it* so: and what will ye do in the end thereof?

The Lord's Rejection of Judah

6 O ye children of Benjamin, gather yourselves to flee out of the midst of
Jerusalem, and blow the trumpet in Tekoa, and set up a sign of fire in Beth-
haccerem: for evil appeareth out of the north, and great destruction.
2 I have likened the daughter of Zion to a comely and delicate *woman*.

3 The shepherds with their flocks shall come unto her; they shall pitch *their*
tents against her round about; they shall feed every one in his place.
4 Prepare ye war against her; arise, and let us go up at noon. Woe unto us!
for the day goeth away, for the shadows of the evening are stretched out.
5 Arise, and let us go by night, and let us destroy her palaces.
6 For thus hath the LORD of hosts said, Hew ye down trees, and cast a mount
against Jerusalem: this *is* the city to be visited; she *is* wholly oppression in the
midst of her.
7 As a fountain casteth out her waters, so she casteth out her wickedness:
violence and spoil is heard in her; before me continually *is* grief and wounds.
8 Be thou instructed, O Jerusalem, lest my soul depart from thee; lest I make
thee desolate, a land not inhabited.
9 Thus saith the LORD of hosts, They shall throughly glean the remnant of
Israel as a vine: turn back thine hand as a grapegatherer into the baskets.
10 To whom shall I speak, and give warning, that they may hear? behold,
their ear *is* uncircumcised, and they cannot hearken: behold, the word of the
LORD is unto them a reproach; they have no delight in it.
11 Therefore I am full of the fury of the LORD; I am weary with holding in: I
will pour it out upon the children abroad, and upon the assembly of young
men together: for even the husband with the wife shall be taken, the aged with
him that is full of days.
12 And their houses shall be turned unto others, *with their* fields and wives
together: for I will stretch out my hand upon the inhabitants of the land, saith
the LORD.
13 For from the least of them even unto the greatest of them every one *is*
given to covetousness; and from the prophet even unto the priest every one
dealeth falsely.
14 They have healed also the hurt *of the daughter* of my people slightly, say-
ing, Peace, peace; when *there is* no peace.
15 Were they ashamed when they had committed abomination? nay, they
were not at all ashamed, neither could they blush: therefore they shall fall
among them that fall: at the time *that* I visit them they shall be cast down,
saith the LORD.
16 Thus saith the LORD, Stand ye in the ways, and see, and ask for the old paths,
where *is* the good way, and walk therein, and ye shall find rest for your souls.
But they said, We will not walk *therein*.
17 Also I set watchmen over you, *saying*, Hearken to the sound of the trum-
pet. But they said, We will not hearken.
18 Therefore hear, ye nations, and know, O congregation, what *is* among
them.
19 Hear, O earth: behold, I will bring evil upon this people, *even* the fruit of
their thoughts, because they have not hearkened unto my words, nor to my
law, but rejected it.
20 To what purpose cometh there to me incense from Sheba, and the sweet
cane from a far country? your burnt offerings *are* not acceptable, nor your
sacrifices sweet unto me.
21 Therefore thus saith the LORD, Behold, I will lay stumblingblocks before
this people, and the fathers and the sons together shall fall upon them; the
neighbour and his friend shall perish.
22 Thus saith the LORD, Behold, a people cometh from the north country,
and a great nation shall be raised from the sides of the earth.
23 They shall lay hold on bow and spear; they *are* cruel, and have no mercy;
their voice roareth like the sea; and they ride upon horses, set in array as men
for war against thee, O daughter of Zion.
24 We have heard the fame thereof: our hands wax feeble: anguish hath taken
hold of us, *and* pain, as of a woman in travail.

25 Go not forth into the field, nor walk by the way; for the sword of the enemy
and fear *is* on every side.
26 O daughter of my people, gird *thee* with sackcloth, and wallow thyself in
ashes: make thee mourning, *as for* an only son, most bitter lamentation: for
the spoiler shall suddenly come upon us.
27 I have set thee *for* a tower *and* a fortress among my people, that thou
mayest know and try their way.
28 They *are* all grievous revolters, walking with slanders: *they are* brass and
iron; they *are* all corrupters.
29 The bellows are burned, the lead is consumed of the fire; the founder
melteth in vain: for the wicked are not plucked away.
30 Reprobate silver shall *men* call them, because the LORD hath rejected them.

Judah Trusts the Wrong Things

7 The word that came to Jeremiah from the LORD, saying,
2 Stand in the gate of the LORD's house, and proclaim there this word, and
say, Hear the word of the LORD, all *ye of* Judah, that enter in at these gates to
worship the LORD.
3 Thus saith the LORD of hosts, the God of Israel, Amend your ways and your
doings, and I will cause you to dwell in this place.
4 Trust ye not in lying words, saying, The temple of the LORD, The temple of
the LORD, The temple of the LORD, *are* these.
5 For if ye throughly amend your ways and your doings; if ye throughly exe-
cute judgment between a man and his neighbour;
6 *If* ye oppress not the stranger, the fatherless, and the widow, and shed not
innocent blood in this place, neither walk after other gods to your hurt:
7 Then will I cause you to dwell in this place, in the land that I gave to your
fathers, for ever and ever.
8 Behold, ye trust in lying words, that cannot profit.
9 Will ye steal, murder, and commit adultery, and swear falsely, and burn
incense unto Baal, and walk after other gods whom ye know not;
10 And come and stand before me in this house, which is called by my name,
and say, We are delivered to do all these abominations?
11 Is this house, which is called by my name, become a den of robbers in your
eyes? Behold, even I have seen *it*, saith the LORD.
12 But go ye now unto my place which *was* in Shiloh, where I set my name
at the first, and see what I did to it for the wickedness of my people Israel.
13 And now, because ye have done all these works, saith the LORD, and I spake
unto you, rising up early and speaking, but ye heard not; and I called you, but
ye answered not;
14 Therefore will I do unto *this* house, which is called by my name, wherein
ye trust, and unto the place which I gave to you and to your fathers, as I have
done to Shiloh.
15 And I will cast you out of my sight, as I have cast out all your brethren,
even the whole seed of Ephraim.
16 Therefore pray not thou for this people, neither lift up cry nor prayer for
them, neither make intercession to me: for I will not hear thee.
17 Seest thou not what they do in the cities of Judah and in the streets of
Jerusalem?
18 The children gather wood, and the fathers kindle the fire, and the women
knead *their* dough, to make cakes to the queen of heaven, and to pour out
drink offerings unto other gods, that they may provoke me to anger.
19 Do they provoke me to anger? saith the LORD: *do they* not *provoke* them-
selves to the confusion of their own faces?
20 Therefore thus saith the Lord GOD; Behold, mine anger and my fury shall
be poured out upon this place, upon man, and upon beast, and upon the trees

of the field, and upon the fruit of the ground; and it shall burn, and shall not be quenched.

The Lord Rejects the Sacrifices of the Disobedient

21 Thus saith the LORD of hosts, the God of Israel; Put your burnt offerings unto your sacrifices, and eat flesh.

22 For I spake not unto your fathers, nor commanded them in the day that I brought them out of the land of Egypt, concerning burnt offerings or sacrifices:

23 But this thing commanded I them, saying, Obey my voice, and I will be your God, and ye shall be my people: and walk ye in all the ways that I have commanded you, that it may be well unto you.

24 But they hearkened not, nor inclined their ear, but walked in the counsels *and* in the imagination of their evil heart, and went backward, and not forward.

25 Since the day that your fathers came forth out of the land of Egypt unto this day I have even sent unto you all my servants the prophets, daily rising up early and sending *them*:

26 Yet they hearkened not unto me, nor inclined their ear, but hardened their neck: they did worse than their fathers.

27 Therefore thou shalt speak all these words unto them; but they will not hearken to thee: thou shalt also call unto them; but they will not answer thee.

28 But thou shalt say unto them, This *is* a nation that obeyeth not the voice of the LORD their God, nor receiveth correction: truth is perished, and is cut off from their mouth.

Jeremiah Tells the People to Mourn

29 Cut off thine hair, *O Jerusalem*, and cast *it* away, and take up a lamentation on high places; for the LORD hath rejected and forsaken the generation of his wrath.

30 For the children of Judah have done evil in my sight, saith the LORD: they have set their abominations in the house which is called by my name, to pollute it.

31 And they have built the high places of Tophet, which *is* in the valley of the son of Hinnom, to burn their sons and their daughters in the fire; which I commanded *them* not, neither came it into my heart.

32 Therefore, behold, the days come, saith the LORD, that it shall no more be called Tophet, nor the valley of the son of Hinnom, but the valley of slaughter: for they shall bury in Tophet, till there be no place.

33 And the carcases of this people shall be meat for the fowls of the heaven, and for the beasts of the earth; and none shall fray *them* away.

34 Then will I cause to cease from the cities of Judah, and from the streets of Jerusalem, the voice of mirth, and the voice of gladness, the voice of the bridegroom, and the voice of the bride: for the land shall be desolate.

The Calamity Visited upon the People

8 At that time, saith the LORD, they shall bring out the bones of the kings of Judah, and the bones of his princes, and the bones of the priests, and the bones of the prophets, and the bones of the inhabitants of Jerusalem, out of their graves:

2 And they shall spread them before the sun, and the moon, and all the host of heaven, whom they have loved, and whom they have served, and after whom they have walked, and whom they have sought, and whom they have worshipped: they shall not be gathered, nor be buried; they shall be for dung upon the face of the earth.

3 And death shall be chosen rather than life by all the residue of them that remain of this evil family, which remain in all the places whither I have driven them, saith the LORD of hosts.

Judgment on False Religion

4 Moreover thou shalt say unto them, Thus saith the LORD; Shall they fall,
and not arise? shall he turn away, and not return?
5 Why *then* is this people of Jerusalem slidden back by a perpetual backslid-
ing? they hold fast deceit, they refuse to return.
6 I hearkened and heard, *but* they spake not aright: no man repented him
of his wickedness, saying, What have I done? every one turned to his course,
as the horse rusheth into the battle.
7 Yea, the stork in the heaven knoweth her appointed times; and the turtle
and the crane and the swallow observe the time of their coming; but my peo-
ple know not the judgment of the LORD.
8 How do ye say, We *are* wise, and the law of the LORD *is* with us? Lo, certain-
ly in vain made he *it*; the pen of the scribes *is* in vain.
9 The wise *men* are ashamed, they are dismayed and taken: lo, they have
rejected the word of the LORD; and what wisdom *is* in them?
10 Therefore will I give their wives unto others, *and* their fields to them that
shall inherit *them*: for every one from the least even unto the greatest is given to
covetousness, from the prophet even unto the priest every one dealeth falsely.
11 For they have healed the hurt of the daughter of my people slightly, saying,
Peace, peace; when *there is* no peace.
12 Were they ashamed when they had committed abomination? nay, they
were not at all ashamed, neither could they blush: therefore shall they fall
among them that fall: in the time of their visitation they shall be cast down,
saith the LORD.
13 I will surely consume them, saith the LORD: *there shall be* no grapes on the
vine, nor figs on the fig tree, and the leaf shall fade; and *the things that* I have
given them shall pass away from them.
14 Why do we sit still? assemble yourselves, and let us enter into the defenced
cities, and let us be silent there: for the LORD our God hath put us to silence,
and given us water of gall to drink, because we have sinned against the LORD.
15 We looked for peace, but no good *came; and* for a time of health, and
behold trouble!
16 The snorting of his horses was heard from Dan: the whole land trembled
at the sound of the neighing of his strong ones; for they are come, and have
devoured the land, and all that is in it; the city, and those that dwell therein.
17 For, behold, I will send serpents, cockatrices, among you, which *will* not
be charmed, and they shall bite you, saith the LORD.

Jeremiah's Grief over His People's Sin

18 *When* I would comfort myself against sorrow, my heart *is* faint in me.
19 Behold the voice of the cry of the daughter of my people because of them
that dwell in a far country: *Is* not the LORD in Zion? *is* not her king in her? Why
have they provoked me to anger with their graven images, *and* with strange
vanities?
20 The harvest is past, the summer is ended, and we are not saved.
21 For the hurt of the daughter of my people am I hurt; I am black; astonish-
ment hath taken hold on me.
22 *Is there* no balm in Gilead; *is there* no physician there? why then is not
the health of the daughter of my people recovered?

Jeremiah Laments the Coming Judgment

9 Oh that my head were waters, and mine eyes a fountain of tears, that I might
weep day and night for the slain of the daughter of my people!
2 Oh that I had in the wilderness a lodging place of wayfaring men; that I
might leave my people, and go from them! for they *be* all adulterers, an assem-
bly of treacherous men.

3 And they bend their tongues *like* their bow *for* lies: but they are not valiant
for the truth upon the earth; for they proceed from evil to evil, and they know
not me, saith the LORD.
4 Take ye heed every one of his neighbour, and trust ye not in any brother:
for every brother will utterly supplant, and every neighbour will walk with
slanders.
5 And they will deceive every one his neighbour, and will not speak the truth:
they have taught their tongue to speak lies, *and* weary themselves to commit
iniquity.
6 Thine habitation *is* in the midst of deceit; through deceit they refuse to
know me, saith the LORD.
7 Therefore thus saith the LORD of hosts, Behold, I will melt them, and try
them; for how shall I do for the daughter of my people?
8 Their tongue *is as* an arrow shot out; it speaketh deceit: *one* speaketh peace-
ably to his neighbour with his mouth, but in heart he layeth his wait.
9 Shall I not visit them for these *things*? saith the LORD: shall not my soul be
avenged on such a nation as this?
10 For the mountains will I take up a weeping and wailing, and for the hab-
itations of the wilderness a lamentation, because they are burned up, so that
none can pass through *them*; neither can *men* hear the voice of the cattle; both
the fowl of the heavens and the beast are fled; they are gone.
11 And I will make Jerusalem heaps, *and* a den of dragons; and I will make
the cities of Judah desolate, without an inhabitant.
12 Who *is* the wise man, that may understand this? and *who is he* to whom
the mouth of the LORD hath spoken, that he may declare it, for what the land
perisheth *and* is burned up like a wilderness, that none passeth through?
13 And the LORD saith, Because they have forsaken my law which I set before
them, and have not obeyed my voice, neither walked therein;
14 But have walked after the imagination of their own heart, and after
Baalim, which their fathers taught them:
15 Therefore thus saith the LORD of hosts, the God of Israel; Behold, I will
feed them, *even* this people, with wormwood, and give them water of gall to
drink.
16 I will scatter them also among the heathen, whom neither they nor their
fathers have known: and I will send a sword after them, till I have consumed
them.
17 Thus saith the LORD of hosts, Consider ye, and call for the mourning
women, that they may come; and send for cunning *women*, that they may
come:
18 And let them make haste, and take up a wailing for us, that our eyes may
run down with tears, and our eyelids gush out with waters.
19 For a voice of wailing is heard out of Zion, How are we spoiled! we are
greatly confounded, because we have forsaken the land, because our dwellings
have cast *us* out.
20 Yet hear the word of the LORD, O ye women, and let your ear receive the
word of his mouth, and teach your daughters wailing, and every one her neigh-
bour lamentation.
21 For death is come up into our windows, *and* is entered into our palaces,
to cut off the children from without, *and* the young men from the streets.
22 Speak, Thus saith the LORD, Even the carcases of men shall fall as dung
upon the open field, and as the handful after the harvestman, and none shall
gather *them*.

The Lord Will Bring Justice

23 Thus saith the LORD, Let not the wise *man* glory in his wisdom, neither let
the mighty *man* glory in his might, let not the rich *man* glory in his riches:

24 But let him that glorieth glory in this, that he understandeth and knoweth
me, that I *am* the LORD which exercise lovingkindness, judgment, and righ-
teousness, in the earth: for in these *things* I delight, saith the LORD.
25 Behold, the days come, saith the LORD, that I will punish all *them which*
are circumcised with the uncircumcised;
26 Egypt, and Judah, and Edom, and the children of Ammon, and Moab, and
all *that are* in the utmost corners, that dwell in the wilderness: for all *these*
nations *are* uncircumcised, and all the house of Israel *are* uncircumcised in
the heart.

The Lord Is the Only True God

10 Hear ye the word which the LORD speaketh unto you, O house of Israel:
2 Thus saith the LORD, Learn not the way of the heathen, and be not
dismayed at the signs of heaven; for the heathen are dismayed at them.
3 For the customs of the people *are* vain: for *one* cutteth a tree out of the
forest, the work of the hands of the workman, with the axe.
4 They deck it with silver and with gold; they fasten it with nails and with
hammers, that it move not.
5 They *are* upright as the palm tree, but speak not: they must needs be borne,
because they cannot go. Be not afraid of them; for they cannot do evil, neither
also *is it* in them to do good.
6 Forasmuch as *there is* none like unto thee, O LORD; thou *art* great, and thy
name *is* great in might.
7 Who would not fear thee, O King of nations? for to thee doth it appertain:
forasmuch as among all the wise *men* of the nations, and in all their kingdoms,
there is none like unto thee.
8 But they are altogether brutish and foolish: the stock *is* a doctrine of van-
ities.
9 Silver spread into plates is brought from Tarshish, and gold from Uphaz,
the work of the workman, and of the hands of the founder: blue and purple
is their clothing: they *are* all the work of cunning *men*.
10 But the LORD *is* the true God, he *is* the living God, and an everlasting king:
at his wrath the earth shall tremble, and the nations shall not be able to abide
his indignation.
11 Thus shall ye say unto them, The gods that have not made the heavens and
the earth, *even* they shall perish from the earth, and from under these heavens.
12 He hath made the earth by his power, he hath established the world by
his wisdom, and hath stretched out the heavens by his discretion.
13 When he uttereth his voice, *there is* a multitude of waters in the heavens,
and he causeth the vapours to ascend from the ends of the earth; he maketh
lightnings with rain, and bringeth forth the wind out of his treasures.
14 Every man is brutish in *his* knowledge: every founder is confounded by
the graven image: for his molten image *is* falsehood, and *there is* no breath in
them.
15 They *are* vanity, *and* the work of errors: in the time of their visitation they
shall perish.
16 The portion of Jacob *is* not like them: for he *is* the former of all *things*;
and Israel *is* the rod of his inheritance: The LORD of hosts *is* his name.
17 Gather up thy wares out of the land, O inhabitant of the fortress.
18 For thus saith the LORD, Behold, I will sling out the inhabitants of the land
at this once, and will distress them, that they may find *it so*.
19 Woe is me for my hurt! my wound is grievous: but I said, Truly this *is* a
grief, and I must bear it.
20 My tabernacle is spoiled, and all my cords are broken: my children are
gone forth of me, and they *are* not: *there is* none to stretch forth my tent any
more, and to set up my curtains.

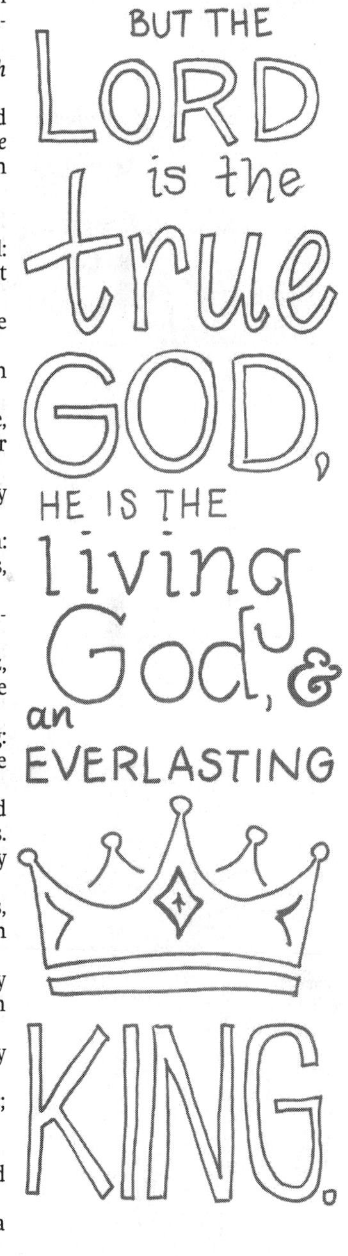

21 For the pastors are become brutish, and have not sought the LORD: therefore they shall not prosper, and all their flocks shall be scattered.

22 Behold, the noise of the bruit is come, and a great commotion out of the north country, to make the cities of Judah desolate, *and* a den of dragons.

23 O LORD, I know that the way of man *is* not in himself: *it is* not in man that walketh to direct his steps.

24 O LORD, correct me, but with judgment; not in thine anger, lest thou bring me to nothing.

25 Pour out thy fury upon the heathen that know thee not, and upon the families that call not on thy name: for they have eaten up Jacob, and devoured him, and consumed him, and have made his habitation desolate.

Judah Has Disobeyed God's Covenant

11 The word that came to Jeremiah from the LORD, saying,
2 Hear ye the words of this covenant, and speak unto the men of Judah, and to the inhabitants of Jerusalem;

3 And say thou unto them, Thus saith the LORD God of Israel; Cursed *be* the man that obeyeth not the words of this covenant,

4 Which I commanded your fathers in the day *that* I brought them forth out of the land of Egypt, from the iron furnace, saying, Obey my voice, and do them, according to all which I command you: so shall ye be my people, and I will be your God:

5 That I may perform the oath which I have sworn unto your fathers, to give them a land flowing with milk and honey, as *it is* this day. Then answered I, and said, So be it, O LORD.

6 Then the LORD said unto me, Proclaim all these words in the cities of Judah, and in the streets of Jerusalem, saying, Hear ye the words of this covenant, and do them.

7 For I earnestly protested unto your fathers in the day *that* I brought them up out of the land of Egypt, *even* unto this day, rising early and protesting, saying, Obey my voice.

8 Yet they obeyed not, nor inclined their ear, but walked every one in the imagination of their evil heart: therefore I will bring upon them all the words of this covenant, which I commanded *them* to do; but they did *them* not.

9 And the LORD said unto me, A conspiracy is found among the men of Judah, and among the inhabitants of Jerusalem.

10 They are turned back to the iniquities of their forefathers, which refused to hear my words; and they went after other gods to serve them: the house of Israel and the house of Judah have broken my covenant which I made with their fathers.

11 Therefore thus saith the LORD, Behold, I will bring evil upon them, which they shall not be able to escape; and though they shall cry unto me, I will not hearken unto them.

12 Then shall the cities of Judah and inhabitants of Jerusalem go, and cry unto the gods unto whom they offer incense: but they shall not save them at all in the time of their trouble.

13 For *according to* the number of thy cities were thy gods, O Judah; and *according to* the number of the streets of Jerusalem have ye set up altars to *that* shameful thing, *even* altars to burn incense unto Baal.

14 Therefore pray not thou for this people, neither lift up a cry or prayer for them: for I will not hear *them* in the time that they cry unto me for their trouble.

15 What hath my beloved to do in mine house, *seeing* she hath wrought lewdness with many, and the holy flesh is passed from thee? when thou dost evil, then thou rejoicest.

16 The LORD called thy name, A green olive tree, fair, *and* of goodly fruit: with
the noise of a great tumult he hath kindled fire upon it, and the branches of
it are broken.
17 For the LORD of hosts, that planted thee, hath pronounced evil against
thee, for the evil of the house of Israel and of the house of Judah, which they
have done against themselves to provoke me to anger in offering incense unto
Baal.

Jeremiah's Life Is Threatened

18 And the LORD hath given me knowledge *of it*, and I know *it*: then thou
shewedst me their doings.
19 But I *was* like a lamb *or* an ox *that* is brought to the slaughter; and I knew
not that they had devised devices against me, *saying*, Let us destroy the tree
with the fruit thereof, and let us cut him off from the land of the living, that
his name may be no more remembered.
20 But, O LORD of hosts, that judgest righteously, that triest the reins and the
heart, let me see thy vengeance on them: for unto thee have I revealed my
cause.
21 Therefore thus saith the LORD of the men of Anathoth, that seek thy life,
saying, Prophesy not in the name of the LORD, that thou die not by our hand:
22 Therefore thus saith the LORD of hosts, Behold, I will punish them: the
young men shall die by the sword; their sons and their daughters shall die by
famine:
23 And there shall be no remnant of them: for I will bring evil upon the men
of Anathoth, *even* the year of their visitation.

Jeremiah's Question

12 Righteous *art* thou, O LORD, when I plead with thee: yet let me talk
with thee of *thy* judgments: Wherefore doth the way of the wicked
prosper? *wherefore* are all they happy that deal very treacherously?
2 Thou hast planted them, yea, they have taken root: they grow, yea, they
bring forth fruit: thou *art* near in their mouth, and far from their reins.
3 But thou, O LORD, knowest me: thou hast seen me, and tried mine heart
toward thee: pull them out like sheep for the slaughter, and prepare them for
the day of slaughter.
4 How long shall the land mourn, and the herbs of every field wither, for the
wickedness of them that dwell therein? the beasts are consumed, and the
birds; because they said, He shall not see our last end.

The Lord's Reply

5 If thou hast run with the footmen, and they have wearied thee, then how
canst thou contend with horses? and *if* in the land of peace, *wherein* thou
trustedst, *they wearied thee*, then how wilt thou do in the swelling of Jordan?
6 For even thy brethren, and the house of thy father, even they have dealt
treacherously with thee; yea, they have called a multitude after thee: believe
them not, though they speak fair words unto thee.
7 I have forsaken mine house, I have left mine heritage; I have given the
dearly beloved of my soul into the hand of her enemies.
8 Mine heritage is unto me as a lion in the forest; it crieth out against me:
therefore have I hated it.
9 Mine heritage *is* unto me *as* a speckled bird, the birds round about *are*
against her; come ye, assemble all the beasts of the field, come to devour.
10 Many pastors have destroyed my vineyard, they have trodden my portion
under foot, they have made my pleasant portion a desolate wilderness.
11 They have made it desolate, *and being* desolate it mourneth unto me; the
whole land is made desolate, because no man layeth *it* to heart.

12 The spoilers are come upon all high places through the wilderness: for
the sword of the LORD shall devour from the *one* end of the land even to the
other end of the land: no flesh shall have peace.

13 They have sown wheat, but shall reap thorns: they have put themselves to
pain, *but* shall not profit: and they shall be ashamed of your revenues because
of the fierce anger of the LORD.

God Promises the Penitent They Will Return

14 Thus saith the LORD against all mine evil neighbours, that touch the inher-
itance which I have caused my people Israel to inherit; Behold, I will pluck
them out of their land, and pluck out the house of Judah from among them.

15 And it shall come to pass, after that I have plucked them out I will return,
and have compassion on them, and will bring them again, every man to his
heritage, and every man to his land.

16 And it shall come to pass, if they will diligently learn the ways of my peo-
ple, to swear by my name, The LORD liveth; as they taught my people to swear
by Baal; then shall they be built in the midst of my people.

17 But if they will not obey, I will utterly pluck up and destroy that nation,
saith the LORD.

Jeremiah's Linen Belt

13 Thus saith the LORD unto me, Go and get thee a linen girdle, and put
it upon thy loins, and put it not in water.

2 So I got a girdle according to the word of the LORD, and put *it* on my loins.

3 And the word of the LORD came unto me the second time, saying,

4 Take the girdle that thou hast got, which *is* upon thy loins, and arise, go to
Euphrates, and hide it there in a hole of the rock.

5 So I went, and hid it by Euphrates, as the LORD commanded me.

6 And it came to pass after many days, that the LORD said unto me, Arise, go
to Euphrates, and take the girdle from thence, which I commanded thee to
hide there.

7 Then I went to Euphrates, and digged, and took the girdle from the place
where I had hid it: and, behold, the girdle was marred, it was profitable for
nothing.

8 Then the word of the LORD came unto me, saying,

9 Thus saith the LORD, After this manner will I mar the pride of Judah, and
the great pride of Jerusalem.

10 This evil people, which refuse to hear my words, which walk in the imag-
ination of their heart, and walk after other gods, to serve them, and to worship
them, shall even be as this girdle, which is good for nothing.

11 For as the girdle cleaveth to the loins of a man, so have I caused to cleave
unto me the whole house of Israel and the whole house of Judah, saith the
LORD; that they might be unto me for a people, and for a name, and for a praise,
and for a glory: but they would not hear.

12 Therefore thou shalt speak unto them this word; Thus saith the LORD God
of Israel, Every bottle shall be filled with wine: and they shall say unto thee,
Do we not certainly know that every bottle shall be filled with wine?

13 Then shalt thou say unto them, Thus saith the LORD, Behold, I will fill all
the inhabitants of this land, even the kings that sit upon David's throne, and
the priests, and the prophets, and all the inhabitants of Jerusalem, with drunk-
enness.

14 And I will dash them one against another, even the fathers and the sons
together, saith the LORD: I will not pity, nor spare, nor have mercy, but destroy
them.

15 Hear ye, and give ear; be not proud: for the LORD hath spoken.

16 Give glory to the LORD your God, before he cause darkness, and before
your feet stumble upon the dark mountains, and, while ye look for light, he
turn it into the shadow of death, *and* make *it* gross darkness.
17 But if ye will not hear it, my soul shall weep in secret places for *your* pride;
and mine eye shall weep sore, and run down with tears, because the LORD's
flock is carried away captive.
18 Say unto the king and to the queen, Humble yourselves, sit down: for your
principalities shall come down, *even* the crown of your glory.
19 The cities of the south shall be shut up, and none shall open *them*: Judah
shall be carried away captive all of it, it shall be wholly carried away captive.
20 Lift up your eyes, and behold them that come from the north: where *is*
the flock *that* was given thee, thy beautiful flock?
21 What wilt thou say when he shall punish thee? for thou hast taught them
to be captains, *and* as chief over thee: shall not sorrows take thee, as a woman
in travail?
22 And if thou say in thine heart, Wherefore come these things upon me?
For the greatness of thine iniquity are thy skirts discovered, *and* thy heels
made bare.
23 Can the Ethiopian change his skin, or the leopard his spots? *then* may ye
also do good, that are accustomed to do evil.
24 Therefore will I scatter them as the stubble that passeth away by the wind
of the wilderness.
25 This *is* thy lot, the portion of thy measures from me, saith the LORD;
because thou hast forgotten me, and trusted in falsehood.
26 Therefore will I discover thy skirts upon thy face, that thy shame may
appear.
27 I have seen thine adulteries, and thy neighings, the lewdness of thy whore-
dom, *and* thine abominations on the hills in the fields. Woe unto thee, O
Jerusalem! wilt thou not be made clean? when *shall it* once *be*?

The Grievous Famine

14 The word of the LORD that came to Jeremiah concerning the dearth.
2 Judah mourneth, and the gates thereof languish; they are black unto
the ground; and the cry of Jerusalem is gone up.
3 And their nobles have sent their little ones to the waters: they came to the
pits, *and* found no water; they returned with their vessels empty; they were
ashamed and confounded, and covered their heads.
4 Because the ground is chapt, for there was no rain in the earth, the plow-
men were ashamed, they covered their heads.
5 Yea, the hind also calved in the field, and forsook *it*, because there was no
grass.
6 And the wild asses did stand in the high places, they snuffed up the wind
like dragons; their eyes did fail, because *there was* no grass.
7 O LORD, though our iniquities testify against us, do thou *it* for thy name's
sake: for our backslidings are many; we have sinned against thee.
8 O the hope of Israel, the saviour thereof in time of trouble, why shouldest
thou be as a stranger in the land, and as a wayfaring man *that* turneth aside
to tarry for a night?
9 Why shouldest thou be as a man astonied, as a mighty man *that* cannot
save? yet thou, O LORD, *art* in the midst of us, and we are called by thy name;
leave us not.

The Lord Refuses to Hear

10 Thus saith the LORD unto this people, Thus have they loved to wander, they
have not refrained their feet, therefore the LORD doth not accept them; he will
now remember their iniquity, and visit their sins.
11 Then said the LORD unto me, Pray not for this people for *their* good.

12 When they fast, I will not hear their cry; and when they offer burnt offering and an oblation, I will not accept them: but I will consume them by the sword, and by the famine, and by the pestilence.

13 Then said I, Ah, Lord GOD! behold, the prophets say unto them, Ye shall not see the sword, neither shall ye have famine; but I will give you assured peace in this place.

14 Then the LORD said unto me, The prophets prophesy lies in my name: I sent them not, neither have I commanded them, neither spake unto them: they prophesy unto you a false vision and divination, and a thing of nought, and the deceit of their heart.

15 Therefore thus saith the LORD concerning the prophets that prophesy in my name, and I sent them not, yet they say, Sword and famine shall not be in this land; By sword and famine shall those prophets be consumed.

16 And the people to whom they prophesy shall be cast out in the streets of Jerusalem because of the famine and the sword; and they shall have none to bury them, them, their wives, nor their sons, nor their daughters: for I will pour their wickedness upon them.

Jeremiah Voices Their Complaint

17 Therefore thou shalt say this word unto them; Let mine eyes run down with tears night and day, and let them not cease: for the virgin daughter of my people is broken with a great breach, with a very grievous blow.

18 If I go forth into the field, then behold the slain with the sword! and if I enter into the city, then behold them that are sick with famine! yea, both the prophet and the priest go about into a land that they know not.

19 Hast thou utterly rejected Judah? hath thy soul lothed Zion? why hast thou smitten us, and *there is* no healing for us? we looked for peace, and *there is* no good; and for the time of healing, and behold trouble!

20 We acknowledge, O LORD, our wickedness, *and* the iniquity of our fathers: for we have sinned against thee.

21 Do not abhor *us*, for thy name's sake, do not disgrace the throne of thy glory: remember, break not thy covenant with us.

22 Are there *any* among the vanities of the Gentiles that can cause rain? or can the heavens give showers? *art* not thou he, O LORD our God? therefore we will wait upon thee: for thou hast made all these *things*.

God's Rejection of His People

15 Then said the LORD unto me, Though Moses and Samuel stood before me, *yet* my mind *could* not *be* toward this people: cast *them* out of my sight, and let them go forth.

2 And it shall come to pass, if they say unto thee, Whither shall we go forth? then thou shalt tell them, Thus saith the LORD; Such as *are* for death, to death; and such as *are* for the sword, to the sword; and such as *are* for the famine, to the famine; and such as *are* for the captivity, to the captivity.

3 And I will appoint over them four kinds, saith the LORD: the sword to slay, and the dogs to tear, and the fowls of the heaven, and the beasts of the earth, to devour and destroy.

4 And I will cause them to be removed into all kingdoms of the earth, because of Manasseh the son of Hezekiah king of Judah, for *that* which he did in Jerusalem.

5 For who shall have pity upon thee, O Jerusalem? or who shall bemoan thee? or who shall go aside to ask how thou doest?

6 Thou hast forsaken me, saith the LORD, thou art gone backward: therefore will I stretch out my hand against thee, and destroy thee; I am weary with repenting.

7 And I will fan them with a fan in the gates of the land; I will bereave *them* of children, I will destroy my people, *since* they return not from their ways.

8 Their widows are increased to me above the sand of the seas: I have brought
upon them against the mother of the young men a spoiler at noonday: I have
caused *him* to fall upon it suddenly, and terrors upon the city.
9 She that hath borne seven languisheth: she hath given up the ghost; her
sun is gone down while *it was* yet day: she hath been ashamed and confound-
ed: and the residue of them will I deliver to the sword before their enemies,
saith the LORD.

Jeremiah Complains Bitterly

10 Woe is me, my mother, that thou hast borne me a man of strife and a man
of contention to the whole earth! I have neither lent on usury, nor men have
lent to me on usury; *yet* every one of them doth curse me.
11 The LORD said, Verily it shall be well with thy remnant; verily I will cause
the enemy to entreat thee *well* in the time of evil and in the time of affliction.
12 Shall iron break the northern iron and the steel?
13 Thy substance and thy treasures will I give to the spoil without price, and
that for all thy sins, even in all thy borders.
14 And I will make *thee* to pass with thine enemies into a land *which* thou
knowest not: for a fire is kindled in mine anger, *which* shall burn upon you.

Jeremiah Prays

15 O LORD, thou knowest: remember me, and visit me, and revenge me of my
persecutors; take me not away in thy longsuffering: know that for thy sake I
have suffered rebuke.
16 Thy words were found, and I did eat them; and thy word was unto me the
joy and rejoicing of mine heart: for I am called by thy name, O LORD God of
hosts.
17 I sat not in the assembly of the mockers, nor rejoiced; I sat alone because
of thy hand: for thou hast filled me with indignation.
18 Why is my pain perpetual, and my wound incurable, *which* refuseth to be
healed? wilt thou be altogether unto me as a liar, *and as* waters *that* fail?
19 Therefore thus saith the LORD, If thou return, then will I bring thee again,
and thou shalt stand before me: and if thou take forth the precious from the
vile, thou shalt be as my mouth: let them return unto thee; but return not thou
unto them.
20 And I will make thee unto this people a fenced brasen wall: and they shall
fight against thee, but they shall not prevail against thee: for I *am* with thee
to save thee and to deliver thee, saith the LORD.
21 And I will deliver thee out of the hand of the wicked, and I will redeem
thee out of the hand of the terrible.

Jeremiah Must Not Marry

16 The word of the LORD came also unto me, saying,
2 Thou shalt not take thee a wife, neither shalt thou have sons or
daughters in this place.
3 For thus saith the LORD concerning the sons and concerning the daughters
that are born in this place, and concerning their mothers that bare them, and
concerning their fathers that begat them in this land;
4 They shall die of grievous deaths; they shall not be lamented; neither shall
they be buried; *but* they shall be as dung upon the face of the earth: and they
shall be consumed by the sword, and by famine; and their carcases shall be
meat for the fowls of heaven, and for the beasts of the earth.
5 For thus saith the LORD, Enter not into the house of mourning, neither go
to lament nor bemoan them: for I have taken away my peace from this people,
saith the LORD, *even* lovingkindness and mercies.
6 Both the great and the small shall die in this land: they shall not be buried,
neither shall *men* lament for them, nor cut themselves, nor make themselves
bald for them:

7 Neither shall *men* tear *themselves* for them in mourning, to comfort them
for the dead; neither shall *men* give them the cup of consolation to drink for
their father or for their mother.
8 Thou shalt not also go into the house of feasting, to sit with them to eat and
to drink.
9 For thus saith the LORD of hosts, the God of Israel; Behold, I will cause to
cease out of this place in your eyes, and in your days, the voice of mirth, and
the voice of gladness, the voice of the bridegroom, and the voice of the bride.

Answers to Why

10 And it shall come to pass, when thou shalt shew this people all these words,
and they shall say unto thee, Wherefore hath the LORD pronounced all this
great evil against us? or what *is* our iniquity? or what *is* our sin that we have
committed against the LORD our God?
11 Then shalt thou say unto them, Because your fathers have forsaken me,
saith the LORD, and have walked after other gods, and have served them, and
have worshipped them, and have forsaken me, and have not kept my law;
12 And ye have done worse than your fathers; for, behold, ye walk every one
after the imagination of his evil heart, that they may not hearken unto me:
13 Therefore will I cast you out of this land into a land that ye know not,
neither ye nor your fathers; and there shall ye serve other gods day and night;
where I will not shew you favour.
14 Therefore, behold, the days come, saith the LORD, that it shall no more be
said, The LORD liveth, that brought up the children of Israel out of the land of
Egypt;
15 But, The LORD liveth, that brought up the children of Israel from the land
of the north, and from all the lands whither he had driven them: and I will
bring them again into their land that I gave unto their fathers.
16 Behold, I will send for many fishers, saith the LORD, and they shall fish
them; and after will I send for many hunters, and they shall hunt them from
every mountain, and from every hill, and out of the holes of the rocks.
17 For mine eyes *are* upon all their ways: they are not hid from my face,
neither is their iniquity hid from mine eyes.
18 And first I will recompense their iniquity and their sin double; because
they have defiled my land, they have filled mine inheritance with the carcases
of their detestable and abominable things.
19 O LORD, my strength, and my fortress, and my refuge in the day of afflic-
tion, the Gentiles shall come unto thee from the ends of the earth, and shall
say, Surely our fathers have inherited lies, vanity, and *things* wherein *there is*
no profit.
20 Shall a man make gods unto himself, and they *are* no gods?
21 Therefore, behold, I will this once cause them to know, I will cause them
to know mine hand and my might; and they shall know that my name *is* The
LORD.

The Captivity of Judah

17 The sin of Judah *is* written with a pen of iron, *and* with the point of a
diamond: *it is* graven upon the table of their heart, and upon the horns
of your altars;
2 Whilst their children remember their altars and their groves by the green
trees upon the high hills.
3 O my mountain in the field, I will give thy substance *and* all thy treasures
to the spoil, *and* thy high places for sin, throughout all thy borders.
4 And thou, even thyself, shalt discontinue from thine heritage that I gave
thee; and I will cause thee to serve thine enemies in the land which thou know-
est not: for ye have kindled a fire in mine anger, *which* shall burn for ever.

Do Not Trust in Humans

5 Thus saith the LORD; Cursed *be* the man that trusteth in man, and maketh
flesh his arm, and whose heart departeth from the LORD.
6 For he shall be like the heath in the desert, and shall not see when good
cometh; but shall inhabit the parched places in the wilderness, *in* a salt land
and not inhabited.
7 Blessed *is* the man that trusteth in the LORD, and whose hope the LORD is.
8 For he shall be as a tree planted by the waters, and *that* spreadeth out her
roots by the river, and shall not see when heat cometh, but her leaf shall be
green; and shall not be careful in the year of drought, neither shall cease from
yielding fruit.
9 The heart *is* deceitful above all *things*, and desperately wicked: who can
know it?
10 I the LORD search the heart, *I* try the reins, even to give every man accord-
ing to his ways, *and* according to the fruit of his doings.
11 *As* the partridge sitteth *on eggs*, and hatcheth *them* not; *so* he that getteth
riches, and not by right, shall leave them in the midst of his days, and at his
end shall be a fool.

Hope and Salvation Are to Be Found in God

12 A glorious high throne from the beginning *is* the place of our sanctuary.
13 O LORD, the hope of Israel, all that forsake thee shall be ashamed, *and* they
that depart from me shall be written in the earth, because they have forsaken
the LORD, the fountain of living waters.
14 Heal me, O LORD, and I shall be healed; save me, and I shall be saved: for
thou *art* my praise.
15 Behold, they say unto me, Where *is* the word of the LORD? let it come now.
16 As for me, I have not hastened from *being* a pastor to follow thee: neither
have I desired the woeful day; thou knowest: that which came out of my lips
was *right* before thee.
17 Be not a terror unto me: thou *art* my hope in the day of evil.
18 Let them be confounded that persecute me, but let not me be confound-
ed: let them be dismayed, but let not me be dismayed: bring upon them the
day of evil, and destroy them with double destruction.

Remember the Sabbath

19 Thus said the LORD unto me; Go and stand in the gate of the children of
the people, whereby the kings of Judah come in, and by the which they go out,
and in all the gates of Jerusalem;
20 And say unto them, Hear ye the word of the LORD, ye kings of Judah, and
all Judah, and all the inhabitants of Jerusalem, that enter in by these gates:
21 Thus saith the LORD; Take heed to yourselves, and bear no burden on the
sabbath day, nor bring *it* in by the gates of Jerusalem;
22 Neither carry forth a burden out of your houses on the sabbath day, nei-
ther do ye any work, but hallow ye the sabbath day, as I commanded your
fathers.
23 But they obeyed not, neither inclined their ear, but made their neck stiff,
that they might not hear, nor receive instruction.
24 And it shall come to pass, if ye diligently hearken unto me, saith the LORD,
to bring in no burden through the gates of this city on the sabbath day, but
hallow the sabbath day, to do no work therein;
25 Then shall there enter into the gates of this city kings and princes sitting
upon the throne of David, riding in chariots and on horses, they, and their
princes, the men of Judah, and the inhabitants of Jerusalem: and this city shall
remain for ever.
26 And they shall come from the cities of Judah, and from the places about
Jerusalem, and from the land of Benjamin, and from the plain, and from the

mountains, and from the south, bringing burnt offerings, and sacrifices, and meat offerings, and incense, and bringing sacrifices of praise, unto the house of the LORD.

27 But if ye will not hearken unto me to hallow the sabbath day, and not to bear a burden, even entering in at the gates of Jerusalem on the sabbath day; then will I kindle a fire in the gates thereof, and it shall devour the palaces of Jerusalem, and it shall not be quenched.

The Clay and the Potter

18 The word which came to Jeremiah from the LORD, saying,
2 Arise, and go down to the potter's house, and there I will cause thee
to hear my words.

3 Then I went down to the potter's house, and, behold, he wrought a work on the wheels.

4 And the vessel that he made of clay was marred in the hand of the potter: so he made it again another vessel, as seemed good to the potter to make *it*.

5 Then the word of the LORD came to me, saying,

6 O house of Israel, cannot I do with you as this potter? saith the LORD. Behold, as the clay *is* in the potter's hand, so *are* ye in mine hand, O house of Israel.

7 *At what* instant I shall speak concerning a nation, and concerning a kingdom, to pluck up, and to pull down, and to destroy *it*;

8 If that nation, against whom I have pronounced, turn from their evil, I will repent of the evil that I thought to do unto them.

9 And *at what* instant I shall speak concerning a nation, and concerning a kingdom, to build and to plant *it*;

10 If it do evil in my sight, that it obey not my voice, then I will repent of the good, wherewith I said I would benefit them.

Judgments Threatened to Judah

11 Now therefore go to, speak to the men of Judah, and to the inhabitants of Jerusalem, saying, Thus saith the LORD; Behold, I frame evil against you, and devise a device against you: return ye now every one from his evil way, and make your ways and your doings good.

12 And they said, There is no hope: but we will walk after our own devices, and we will every one do the imagination of his evil heart.

13 Therefore thus saith the LORD; Ask ye now among the heathen, who hath heard such things: the virgin of Israel hath done a very horrible thing.

14 Will *a man* leave the snow of Lebanon *which cometh* from the rock of the field? *or* shall the cold flowing waters that come from another place be forsaken?

15 Because my people hath forgotten me, they have burned incense to vanity, and they have caused them to stumble in their ways *from* the ancient paths, to walk in paths, *in* a way not cast up;

16 To make their land desolate, *and* a perpetual hissing; every one that passeth thereby shall be astonished, and wag his head.

17 I will scatter them as with an east wind before the enemy; I will shew them the back, and not the face, in the day of their calamity.

Jeremiah Prays

18 Then said they, Come, and let us devise devices against Jeremiah; for the law shall not perish from the priest, nor counsel from the wise, nor the word from the prophet. Come, and let us smite him with the tongue, and let us not give heed to any of his words.

19 Give heed to me, O LORD, and hearken to the voice of them that contend with me.

20 Shall evil be recompensed for good? for they have digged a pit for my soul.
Remember that I stood before thee to speak good for them, *and* to turn away
thy wrath from them.
21 Therefore deliver up their children to the famine, and pour out their *blood*
by the force of the sword; and let their wives be bereaved of their children,
and *be* widows; and let their men be put to death; *let* their young men *be* slain
by the sword in battle.
22 Let a cry be heard from their houses, when thou shalt bring a troop sud-
denly upon them: for they have digged a pit to take me, and hid snares for my
feet.
23 Yet, LORD, thou knowest all their counsel against me to slay *me*: forgive
not their iniquity, neither blot out their sin from thy sight, but let them be
overthrown before thee; deal *thus* with them in the time of thine anger.

Israel Will Be Destroyed

19 Thus saith the LORD, Go and get a potter's earthen bottle, and *take* of
the ancients of the people, and of the ancients of the priests;
2 And go forth unto the valley of the son of Hinnom, which *is* by the entry
of the east gate, and proclaim there the words that I shall tell thee,
3 And say, Hear ye the word of the LORD, O kings of Judah, and inhabitants
of Jerusalem; Thus saith the LORD of hosts, the God of Israel; Behold, I will
bring evil upon this place, the which whosoever heareth, his ears shall tingle.
4 Because they have forsaken me, and have estranged this place, and have
burned incense in it unto other gods, whom neither they nor their fathers
have known, nor the kings of Judah, and have filled this place with the blood
of innocents;
5 They have built also the high places of Baal, to burn their sons with fire *for*
burnt offerings unto Baal, which I commanded not, nor spake *it*, neither came
it into my mind:
6 Therefore, behold, the days come, saith the LORD, that this place shall no
more be called Tophet, nor The valley of the son of Hinnom, but The valley of
slaughter.
7 And I will make void the counsel of Judah and Jerusalem in this place; and
I will cause them to fall by the sword before their enemies, and by the hands
of them that seek their lives: and their carcases will I give to be meat for the
fowls of the heaven, and for the beasts of the earth.
8 And I will make this city desolate, and an hissing; every one that passeth
thereby shall be astonished and hiss because of all the plagues thereof.
9 And I will cause them to eat the flesh of their sons and the flesh of their
daughters, and they shall eat every one the flesh of his friend in the siege and
straitness, wherewith their enemies, and they that seek their lives, shall strait-
en them.
10 Then shalt thou break the bottle in the sight of the men that go with thee,
11 And shalt say unto them, Thus saith the LORD of hosts; Even so will I break
this people and this city, as *one* breaketh a potter's vessel, that cannot be made
whole again: and they shall bury *them* in Tophet, till *there be* no place to bury.
12 Thus will I do unto this place, saith the LORD, and to the inhabitants there-
of, and *even* make this city as Tophet:
13 And the houses of Jerusalem, and the houses of the kings of Judah, shall
be defiled as the place of Tophet, because of all the houses upon whose roofs
they have burned incense unto all the host of heaven, and have poured out
drink offerings unto other gods.
14 Then came Jeremiah from Tophet, whither the LORD had sent him to
prophesy; and he stood in the court of the LORD's house; and said to all the
people,

BUT HIS
WORD
WAS IN MINE
HEART
AS A
BURNING
FIRE.
JEREMIAH 20:9

15 Thus saith the LORD of hosts, the God of Israel; Behold, I will bring upon
this city and upon all her towns all the evil that I have pronounced against it,
because they have hardened their necks, that they might not hear my words.

Pashur Imprisons Jeremiah

20 Now Pashur the son of Immer the priest, who *was* also chief governor
in the house of the LORD, heard that Jeremiah prophesied these things.
2 Then Pashur smote Jeremiah the prophet, and put him in the stocks that
were in the high gate of Benjamin, which *was* by the house of the LORD.
3 And it came to pass on the morrow, that Pashur brought forth Jeremiah
out of the stocks. Then said Jeremiah unto him, The LORD hath not called thy
name Pashur, but Magor-missabib.
4 For thus saith the LORD, Behold, I will make thee a terror to thyself, and to
all thy friends: and they shall fall by the sword of their enemies, and thine eyes
shall behold *it*: and I will give all Judah into the hand of the king of Babylon,
and he shall carry them captive into Babylon, and shall slay them with the
sword.
5 Moreover I will deliver all the strength of this city, and all the labours
thereof, and all the precious things thereof, and all the treasures of the kings
of Judah will I give into the hand of their enemies, which shall spoil them, and
take them, and carry them to Babylon.
6 And thou, Pashur, and all that dwell in thine house shall go into captivity:
and thou shalt come to Babylon, and there thou shalt die, and shalt be buried
there, thou, and all thy friends, to whom thou hast prophesied lies.

Jeremiah Prays to the Lord

7 O LORD, thou hast deceived me, and I was deceived: thou art stronger than
I, and hast prevailed: I am in derision daily, every one mocketh me.
8 For since I spake, I cried out, I cried violence and spoil; because the word
of the LORD was made a reproach unto me, and a derision, daily.
9 Then I said, I will not make mention of him, nor speak any more in his
name. But *his word* was in mine heart as a burning fire shut up in my bones,
and I was weary with forbearing, and I could not *stay*.
10 For I heard the defaming of many, fear on every side. Report, *say they*, and
we will report it. All my familiars watched for my halting, *saying*, Peradventure
he will be enticed, and we shall prevail against him, and we shall take our
revenge on him.
11 But the LORD *is* with me as a mighty terrible one: therefore my persecutors
shall stumble, and they shall not prevail: they shall be greatly ashamed; for
they shall not prosper: *their* everlasting confusion shall never be forgotten.
12 But, O LORD of hosts, that triest the righteous, *and* seest the reins and the
heart, let me see thy vengeance on them: for unto thee have I opened my cause.
13 Sing unto the LORD, praise ye the LORD: for he hath delivered the soul of
the poor from the hand of evildoers.
14 Cursed *be* the day wherein I was born: let not the day wherein my moth-
er bare me be blessed.
15 Cursed *be* the man who brought tidings to my father, saying, A man child
is born unto thee; making him very glad.
16 And let that man be as the cities which the LORD overthrew, and repented
not: and let him hear the cry in the morning, and the shouting at noontide;
17 Because he slew me not from the womb; or that my mother might have
been my grave, and her womb *to be* always great *with me*.
18 Wherefore came I forth out of the womb to see labour and sorrow, that
my days should be consumed with shame?

Jerusalem Will Be Captured by the Babylonians

21 The word which came unto Jeremiah from the LORD, when king Zedekiah sent unto him Pashur the son of Melchiah, and Zephaniah the son of Maaseiah the priest, saying,
2 Enquire, I pray thee, of the LORD for us; for Nebuchadrezzar king of Babylon maketh war against us; if so be that the LORD will deal with us according to all his wondrous works, that he may go up from us.
3 Then said Jeremiah unto them, Thus shall ye say to Zedekiah:
4 Thus saith the LORD God of Israel; Behold, I will turn back the weapons of war that *are* in your hands, wherewith ye fight against the king of Babylon, and *against* the Chaldeans, which besiege you without the walls, and I will assemble them into the midst of this city.
5 And I myself will fight against you with an outstretched hand and with a strong arm, even in anger, and in fury, and in great wrath.
6 And I will smite the inhabitants of this city, both man and beast: they shall die of a great pestilence.
7 And afterward, saith the LORD, I will deliver Zedekiah king of Judah, and his servants, and the people, and such as are left in this city from the pestilence, from the sword, and from the famine, into the hand of Nebuchadrezzar king of Babylon, and into the hand of their enemies, and into the hand of those that seek their life: and he shall smite them with the edge of the sword; he shall not spare them, neither have pity, nor have mercy.

Jeremiah Counsels Surrender

8 And unto this people thou shalt say, Thus saith the LORD; Behold, I set before you the way of life, and the way of death.
9 He that abideth in this city shall die by the sword, and by the famine, and by the pestilence: but he that goeth out, and falleth to the Chaldeans that besiege you, he shall live, and his life shall be unto him for a prey.
10 For I have set my face against this city for evil, and not for good, saith the LORD: it shall be given into the hand of the king of Babylon, and he shall burn it with fire.
11 And touching the house of the king of Judah, *say*, Hear ye the word of the LORD;
12 O house of David, thus saith the LORD; Execute judgment in the morning, and deliver *him that is* spoiled out of the hand of the oppressor, lest my fury go out like fire, and burn that none can quench *it*, because of the evil of your doings.
13 Behold, I *am* against thee, O inhabitant of the valley, *and* rock of the plain, saith the LORD; which say, Who shall come down against us? or who shall enter into our habitations?
14 But I will punish you according to the fruit of your doings, saith the LORD: and I will kindle a fire in the forest thereof, and it shall devour all things round about it.

Warnings to the Wicked Kings

22 Thus saith the LORD; Go down to the house of the king of Judah, and speak there this word,
2 And say, Hear the word of the LORD, O king of Judah, that sittest upon the throne of David, thou, and thy servants, and thy people that enter in by these gates:
3 Thus saith the LORD; Execute ye judgment and righteousness, and deliver the spoiled out of the hand of the oppressor: and do no wrong, do no violence to the stranger, the fatherless, nor the widow, neither shed innocent blood in this place.

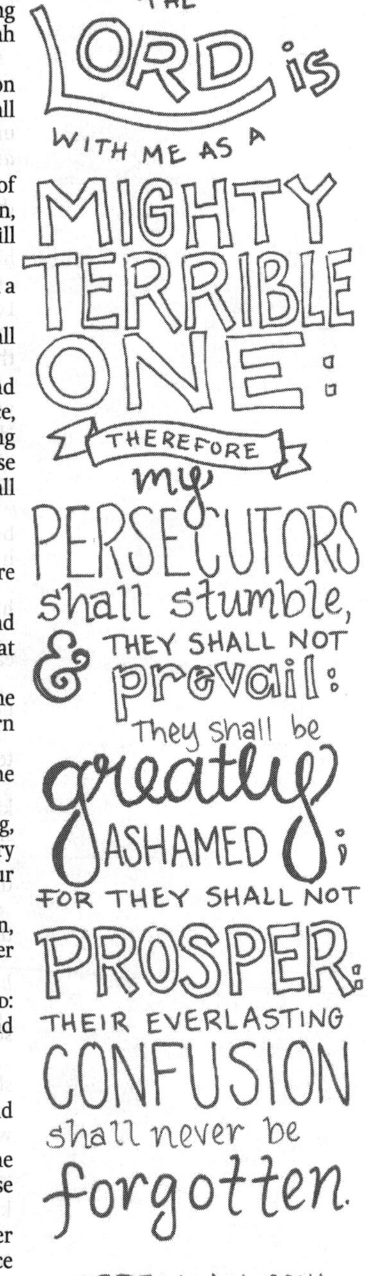

4 For if ye do this thing indeed, then shall there enter in by the gates of this
house kings sitting upon the throne of David, riding in chariots and on horses, he, and his servants, and his people.
5 But if ye will not hear these words, I swear by myself, saith the LORD, that
this house shall become a desolation.
6 For thus saith the LORD unto the king's house of Judah; Thou *art* Gilead
unto me, *and* the head of Lebanon: *yet* surely I will make thee a wilderness, *and* cities *which* are not inhabited.
7 And I will prepare destroyers against thee, every one with his weapons: and
they shall cut down thy choice cedars, and cast *them* into the fire.
8 And many nations shall pass by this city, and they shall say every man to
his neighbour, Wherefore hath the LORD done thus unto this great city?
9 Then they shall answer, Because they have forsaken the covenant of the
LORD their God, and worshipped other gods, and served them.
10 Weep ye not for the dead, neither bemoan him: *but* weep sore for him
that goeth away: for he shall return no more, nor see his native country.
11 For thus saith the LORD touching Shallum the son of Josiah king of Judah,
which reigned instead of Josiah his father, which went forth out of this place; He shall not return thither any more:
12 But he shall die in the place whither they have led him captive, and shall
see this land no more.
13 Woe unto him that buildeth his house by unrighteousness, and his cham-
bers by wrong; *that* useth his neighbour's service without wages, and giveth him not for his work;
14 That saith, I will build me a wide house and large chambers, and cutteth
him out windows; and *it is* cieled with cedar, and painted with vermilion.
15 Shalt thou reign, because thou closest *thyself* in cedar? did not thy father
eat and drink, and do judgment and justice, *and* then *it was* well with him?
16 He judged the cause of the poor and needy; then *it was* well *with him: was*
not this to know me? saith the LORD.
17 But thine eyes and thine heart *are* not but for thy covetousness, and for
to shed innocent blood, and for oppression, and for violence, to do *it*.
18 Therefore thus saith the LORD concerning Jehoiakim the son of Josiah
king of Judah; They shall not lament for him, *saying*, Ah my brother! or, Ah sister! they shall not lament for him, *saying*, Ah lord! or, Ah his glory!
19 He shall be buried with the burial of an ass, drawn and cast forth beyond
the gates of Jerusalem.
20 Go up to Lebanon, and cry; and lift up thy voice in Bashan, and cry from
the passages: for all thy lovers are destroyed.
21 I spake unto thee in thy prosperity; *but* thou saidst, I will not hear. This
hath been thy manner from thy youth, that thou obeyedst not my voice.
22 The wind shall eat up all thy pastors, and thy lovers shall go into captivity:
surely then shalt thou be ashamed and confounded for all thy wickedness.
23 O inhabitant of Lebanon, that makest thy nest in the cedars, how gracious
shalt thou be when pangs come upon thee, the pain as of a woman in travail!
24 *As* I live, saith the LORD, though Coniah the son of Jehoiakim king of Judah
were the signet upon my right hand, yet would I pluck thee thence;
25 And I will give thee into the hand of them that seek thy life, and into the
hand *of them* whose face thou fearest, even into the hand of Nebuchadrezzar king of Babylon, and into the hand of the Chaldeans.
26 And I will cast thee out, and thy mother that bare thee, into another coun-
try, where ye were not born; and there shall ye die.
27 But to the land whereunto they desire to return, thither shall they not
return.

28 *Is* this man Coniah a despised broken idol? *is he* a vessel wherein *is* no
pleasure? wherefore are they cast out, he and his seed, and are cast into a land
which they know not?
29 O earth, earth, earth, hear the word of the LORD.
30 Thus saith the LORD, Write ye this man childless, a man *that* shall not
prosper in his days: for no man of his seed shall prosper, sitting upon the
throne of David, and ruling any more in Judah.

The Righteous Branch

23 Woe be unto the pastors that destroy and scatter the sheep of my pas-
ture! saith the LORD.
2 Therefore thus saith the LORD God of Israel against the pastors that feed
my people; Ye have scattered my flock, and driven them away, and have not
visited them: behold, I will visit upon you the evil of your doings, saith the
LORD.
3 And I will gather the remnant of my flock out of all countries whither I
have driven them, and will bring them again to their folds; and they shall be
fruitful and increase.
4 And I will set up shepherds over them which shall feed them: and they shall
fear no more, nor be dismayed, neither shall they be lacking, saith the LORD.
5 Behold, the days come, saith the LORD, that I will raise unto David a righ-
teous Branch, and a King shall reign and prosper, and shall execute judgment
and justice in the earth.
6 In his days Judah shall be saved, and Israel shall dwell safely: and this *is* his
name whereby he shall be called, THE LORD OUR RIGHTEOUSNESS.
7 Therefore, behold, the days come, saith the LORD, that they shall no more
say, The LORD liveth, which brought up the children of Israel out of the land
of Egypt;
8 But, The LORD liveth, which brought up and which led the seed of the house
of Israel out of the north country, and from all countries whither I had driven
them; and they shall dwell in their own land.

Warnings to the False Prophets

9 Mine heart within me is broken because of the prophets; all my bones
shake; I am like a drunken man, and like a man whom wine hath overcome,
because of the LORD, and because of the words of his holiness.
10 For the land is full of adulterers; for because of swearing the land
mourneth; the pleasant places of the wilderness are dried up, and their course
is evil, and their force *is* not right.
11 For both prophet and priest are profane; yea, in my house have I found
their wickedness, saith the LORD.
12 Wherefore their way shall be unto them as slippery *ways* in the darkness:
they shall be driven on, and fall therein: for I will bring evil upon them, *even*
the year of their visitation, saith the LORD.
13 And I have seen folly in the prophets of Samaria; they prophesied in Baal,
and caused my people Israel to err.
14 I have seen also in the prophets of Jerusalem an horrible thing: they com-
mit adultery, and walk in lies: they strengthen also the hands of evildoers, that
none doth return from his wickedness: they are all of them unto me as Sodom,
and the inhabitants thereof as Gomorrah.
15 Therefore thus saith the LORD of hosts concerning the prophets; Behold,
I will feed them with wormwood, and make them drink the water of gall: for
from the prophets of Jerusalem is profaneness gone forth into all the land.
16 Thus saith the LORD of hosts, Hearken not unto the words of the prophets
that prophesy unto you: they make you vain: they speak a vision of their own
heart, *and* not out of the mouth of the LORD.

17 They say still unto them that despise me, The LORD hath said, Ye shall have
peace; and they say unto every one that walketh after the imagination of his
own heart, No evil shall come upon you.
18 For who hath stood in the counsel of the LORD, and hath perceived and
heard his word? who hath marked his word, and heard *it*?
19 Behold, a whirlwind of the LORD is gone forth in fury, even a grievous
whirlwind: it shall fall grievously upon the head of the wicked.
20 The anger of the LORD shall not return, until he have executed, and till he
have performed the thoughts of his heart: in the latter days ye shall consider
it perfectly.
21 I have not sent these prophets, yet they ran: I have not spoken to them, yet
they prophesied.
22 But if they had stood in my counsel, and had caused my people to hear
my words, then they should have turned them from their evil way, and from
the evil of their doings.
23 *Am* I a God at hand, saith the LORD, and not a God afar off?
24 Can any hide himself in secret places that I shall not see him? saith the
LORD. Do not I fill heaven and earth? saith the LORD.
25 I have heard what the prophets said, that prophesy lies in my name, saying,
I have dreamed, I have dreamed.
26 How long shall *this* be in the heart of the prophets that prophesy lies? yea,
they are prophets of the deceit of their own heart;
27 Which think to cause my people to forget my name by their dreams which
they tell every man to his neighbour, as their fathers have forgotten my name
for Baal.
28 The prophet that hath a dream, let him tell a dream; and he that hath my
word, let him speak my word faithfully. What *is* the chaff to the wheat? saith
the LORD.
29 *Is* not my word like as a fire? saith the LORD; and like a hammer *that*
breaketh the rock in pieces?
30 Therefore, behold, I *am* against the prophets, saith the LORD, that steal my
words every one from his neighbour.
31 Behold, I *am* against the prophets, saith the LORD, that use their tongues,
and say, He saith.
32 Behold, I *am* against them that prophesy false dreams, saith the LORD, and
do tell them, and cause my people to err by their lies, and by their lightness;
yet I sent them not, nor commanded them: therefore they shall not profit this
people at all, saith the LORD.
33 And when this people, or the prophet, or a priest, shall ask thee, saying,
What *is* the burden of the LORD? thou shalt then say unto them, What burden?
I will even forsake you, saith the LORD.
34 And *as for* the prophet, and the priest, and the people, that shall say, The
burden of the LORD, I will even punish that man and his house.
35 Thus shall ye say every one to his neighbour, and every one to his brother,
What hath the LORD answered? and, What hath the LORD spoken?
36 And the burden of the LORD shall ye mention no more: for every man's
word shall be his burden; for ye have perverted the words of the living God,
of the LORD of hosts our God.
37 Thus shalt thou say to the prophet, What hath the LORD answered thee?
and, What hath the LORD spoken?
38 But since ye say, The burden of the LORD; therefore thus saith the LORD;
Because ye say this word, The burden of the LORD, and I have sent unto you,
saying, Ye shall not say, The burden of the LORD;
39 Therefore, behold, I, even I, will utterly forget you, and I will forsake you,
and the city that I gave you and your fathers, *and cast you* out of my presence:
40 And I will bring an everlasting reproach upon you, and a perpetual shame,
which shall not be forgotten.

Good and Bad Figs

24 The LORD shewed me, and, behold, two baskets of figs *were* set before
the temple of the LORD, after that Nebuchadrezzar king of Babylon
had carried away captive Jeconiah the son of Jehoiakim king of Judah, and the
princes of Judah, with the carpenters and smiths, from Jerusalem, and had
brought them to Babylon.
2 One basket *had* very good figs, *even* like the figs *that are* first ripe: and the
other basket *had* very naughty figs, which could not be eaten, they were so
bad.
3 Then said the LORD unto me, What seest thou, Jeremiah? And I said, Figs;
the good figs, very good; and the evil, very evil, that cannot be eaten, they are
so evil.
4 Again the word of the LORD came unto me, saying,
5 Thus saith the LORD, the God of Israel; Like these good figs, so will I acknowl-
edge them that are carried away captive of Judah, whom I have sent out of this
place into the land of the Chaldeans for *their* good.
6 For I will set mine eyes upon them for good, and I will bring them again to
this land: and I will build them, and not pull *them* down; and I will plant them,
and not pluck *them* up.
7 And I will give them an heart to know me, that I *am* the LORD: and they
shall be my people, and I will be their God: for they shall return unto me with
their whole heart.
8 And as the evil figs, which cannot be eaten, they are so evil; surely thus saith
the LORD, So will I give Zedekiah the king of Judah, and his princes, and the
residue of Jerusalem, that remain in this land, and them that dwell in the land
of Egypt:
9 And I will deliver them to be removed into all the kingdoms of the earth
for *their* hurt, *to be* a reproach and a proverb, a taunt and a curse, in all places
whither I shall drive them.
10 And I will send the sword, the famine, and the pestilence, among them,
till they be consumed from off the land that I gave unto them and to their
fathers.

Judgment on Judah and the Nations

25 The word that came to Jeremiah concerning all the people of Judah in
the fourth year of Jehoiakim the son of Josiah king of Judah, that *was*
the first year of Nebuchadrezzar king of Babylon;
2 The which Jeremiah the prophet spake unto all the people of Judah, and
to all the inhabitants of Jerusalem, saying,
3 From the thirteenth year of Josiah the son of Amon king of Judah, even
unto this day, that *is* the three and twentieth year, the word of the LORD hath
come unto me, and I have spoken unto you, rising early and speaking; but ye
have not hearkened.
4 And the LORD hath sent unto you all his servants the prophets, rising early
and sending *them*; but ye have not hearkened, nor inclined your ear to hear.
5 They said, Turn ye again now every one from his evil way, and from the evil
of your doings, and dwell in the land that the LORD hath given unto you and
to your fathers for ever and ever:
6 And go not after other gods to serve them, and to worship them, and pro-
voke me not to anger with the works of your hands; and I will do you no hurt.
7 Yet ye have not hearkened unto me, saith the LORD; that ye might provoke
me to anger with the works of your hands to your own hurt.

Jeremiah Foretells the Seventy Years' Captivity

8 Therefore thus saith the LORD of hosts; Because ye have not heard my words,
9 Behold, I will send and take all the families of the north, saith the LORD,
and Nebuchadrezzar the king of Babylon, my servant, and will bring them
against this land, and against the inhabitants thereof, and against all these

nations round about, and will utterly destroy them, and make them an astonishment, and an hissing, and perpetual desolations.

10 Moreover I will take from them the voice of mirth, and the voice of gladness, the voice of the bridegroom, and the voice of the bride, the sound of the millstones, and the light of the candle.

11 And this whole land shall be a desolation, *and* an astonishment; and these nations shall serve the king of Babylon seventy years.

12 And it shall come to pass, when seventy years are accomplished, *that* I will punish the king of Babylon, and that nation, saith the LORD, for their iniquity, and the land of the Chaldeans, and will make it perpetual desolations.

13 And I will bring upon that land all my words which I have pronounced against it, *even* all that is written in this book, which Jeremiah hath prophesied against all the nations.

14 For many nations and great kings shall serve themselves of them also: and I will recompense them according to their deeds, and according to the works of their own hands.

The Coming Destruction of the Nations

15 For thus saith the LORD God of Israel unto me; Take the wine cup of this fury at my hand, and cause all the nations, to whom I send thee, to drink it.

16 And they shall drink, and be moved, and be mad, because of the sword that I will send among them.

17 Then took I the cup at the LORD's hand, and made all the nations to drink, unto whom the LORD had sent me:

18 *To wit*, Jerusalem, and the cities of Judah, and the kings thereof, and the princes thereof, to make them a desolation, an astonishment, an hissing, and a curse; as *it is* this day;

19 Pharaoh king of Egypt, and his servants, and his princes, and all his people;

20 And all the mingled people, and all the kings of the land of Uz, and all the kings of the land of the Philistines, and Ashkelon, and Azzah, and Ekron, and the remnant of Ashdod,

21 Edom, and Moab, and the children of Ammon,

22 And all the kings of Tyrus, and all the kings of Zidon, and the kings of the isles which *are* beyond the sea,

23 Dedan, and Tema, and Buz, and all *that are* in the utmost corners,

24 And all the kings of Arabia, and all the kings of the mingled people that dwell in the desert,

25 And all the kings of Zimri, and all the kings of Elam, and all the kings of the Medes,

26 And all the kings of the north, far and near, one with another, and all the kingdoms of the world, which *are* upon the face of the earth: and the king of Sheshach shall drink after them.

27 Therefore thou shalt say unto them, Thus saith the LORD of hosts, the God of Israel; Drink ye, and be drunken, and spue, and fall, and rise no more, because of the sword which I will send among you.

28 And it shall be, if they refuse to take the cup at thine hand to drink, then shalt thou say unto them, Thus saith the LORD of hosts; Ye shall certainly drink.

29 For, lo, I begin to bring evil on the city which is called by my name, and should ye be utterly unpunished? Ye shall not be unpunished: for I will call for a sword upon all the inhabitants of the earth, saith the LORD of hosts.

30 Therefore prophesy thou against them all these words, and say unto them, The LORD shall roar from on high, and utter his voice from his holy habitation; he shall mightily roar upon his habitation; he shall give a shout, as they that tread *the grapes*, against all the inhabitants of the earth.

31 A noise shall come *even* to the ends of the earth; for the LORD hath a con-
troversy with the nations, he will plead with all flesh; he will give them *that*
are wicked to the sword, saith the LORD.
32 Thus saith the LORD of hosts, Behold, evil shall go forth from nation to
nation, and a great whirlwind shall be raised up from the coasts of the earth.
33 And the slain of the LORD shall be at that day from *one* end of the earth
even unto the *other* end of the earth: they shall not be lamented, neither gath-
ered, nor buried; they shall be dung upon the ground.
34 Howl, ye shepherds, and cry; and wallow yourselves *in the ashes*, ye prin-
cipal of the flock: for the days of your slaughter and of your dispersions are
accomplished; and ye shall fall like a pleasant vessel.
35 And the shepherds shall have no way to flee, nor the principal of the flock
to escape.
36 A voice of the cry of the shepherds, and an howling of the principal of the
flock, *shall be heard*: for the LORD hath spoiled their pasture.
37 And the peaceable habitations are cut down because of the fierce anger
of the LORD.
38 He hath forsaken his covert, as the lion: for their land is desolate because
of the fierceness of the oppressor, and because of his fierce anger.

Jeremiah Is Arrested

26 In the beginning of the reign of Jehoiakim the son of Josiah king of
Judah came this word from the LORD, saying,
2 Thus saith the LORD; Stand in the court of the LORD's house, and speak unto
all the cities of Judah, which come to worship in the LORD's house, all the words
that I command thee to speak unto them; diminish not a word:
3 If so be they will hearken, and turn every man from his evil way, that I may
repent me of the evil, which I purpose to do unto them because of the evil of
their doings.
4 And thou shalt say unto them, Thus saith the LORD; If ye will not hearken
to me, to walk in my law, which I have set before you,
5 To hearken to the words of my servants the prophets, whom I sent unto
you, both rising up early, and sending *them*, but ye have not hearkened;
6 Then will I make this house like Shiloh, and will make this city a curse to
all the nations of the earth.
7 So the priests and the prophets and all the people heard Jeremiah speaking
these words in the house of the LORD.
8 Now it came to pass, when Jeremiah had made an end of speaking all that
the LORD had commanded *him* to speak unto all the people, that the priests
and the prophets and all the people took him, saying, Thou shalt surely die.
9 Why hast thou prophesied in the name of the LORD, saying, This house shall
be like Shiloh, and this city shall be desolate without an inhabitant? And all
the people were gathered against Jeremiah in the house of the LORD.
10 When the princes of Judah heard these things, then they came up from
the king's house unto the house of the LORD, and sat down in the entry of the
new gate of the LORD's *house*.
11 Then spake the priests and the prophets unto the princes and to all the
people, saying, This man *is* worthy to die; for he hath prophesied against this
city, as ye have heard with your ears.
12 Then spake Jeremiah unto all the princes and to all the people, saying, The
LORD sent me to prophesy against this house and against this city all the words
that ye have heard.
13 Therefore now amend your ways and your doings, and obey the voice of
the LORD your God; and the LORD will repent him of the evil that he hath
pronounced against you.

14 As for me, behold, I *am* in your hand: do with me as seemeth good and meet unto you.

15 But know ye for certain, that if ye put me to death, ye shall surely bring innocent blood upon yourselves, and upon this city, and upon the inhabitants thereof: for of a truth the LORD hath sent me unto you to speak all these words in your ears.

Jeremiah Is Acquitted

16 Then said the princes and all the people unto the priests and to the prophets; This man *is* not worthy to die: for he hath spoken to us in the name of the LORD our God.

17 Then rose up certain of the elders of the land, and spake to all the assembly of the people, saying,

18 Micah the Morasthite prophesied in the days of Hezekiah king of Judah, and spake to all the people of Judah, saying, Thus saith the LORD of hosts; Zion shall be plowed *like* a field, and Jerusalem shall become heaps, and the mountain of the house as the high places of a forest.

19 Did Hezekiah king of Judah and all Judah put him at all to death? did he not fear the LORD, and besought the LORD, and the LORD repented him of the evil which he had pronounced against them? Thus might we procure great evil against our souls.

20 And there was also a man that prophesied in the name of the LORD, Urijah the son of Shemaiah of Kirjath-jearim, who prophesied against this city and against this land according to all the words of Jeremiah:

21 And when Jehoiakim the king, with all his mighty men, and all the princes, heard his words, the king sought to put him to death: but when Urijah heard it, he was afraid, and fled, and went into Egypt;

22 And Jehoiakim the king sent men into Egypt, *namely*, Elnathan the son of Achbor, and *certain* men with him into Egypt.

23 And they fetched forth Urijah out of Egypt, and brought him unto Jehoiakim the king; who slew him with the sword, and cast his dead body into the graves of the common people.

24 Nevertheless the hand of Ahikam the son of Shaphan was with Jeremiah, that they should not give him into the hand of the people to put him to death.

The Yoke of Babylon

27 In the beginning of the reign of Jehoiakim the son of Josiah king of Judah came this word unto Jeremiah from the LORD, saying,

2 Thus saith the LORD to me; Make thee bonds and yokes, and put them upon thy neck,

3 And send them to the king of Edom, and to the king of Moab, and to the king of the Ammonites, and to the king of Tyrus, and to the king of Zidon, by the hand of the messengers which come to Jerusalem unto Zedekiah king of Judah;

4 And command them to say unto their masters, Thus saith the LORD of hosts, the God of Israel; Thus shall ye say unto your masters;

5 I have made the earth, the man and the beast that *are* upon the ground, by my great power and by my outstretched arm, and have given it unto whom it seemed meet unto me.

6 And now have I given all these lands into the hand of Nebuchadnezzar the king of Babylon, my servant; and the beasts of the field have I given him also to serve him.

7 And all nations shall serve him, and his son, and his son's son, until the very time of his land come: and then many nations and great kings shall serve themselves of him.

8 And it shall come to pass, *that* the nation and kingdom which will not serve the same Nebuchadnezzar the king of Babylon, and that will not put their

neck under the yoke of the king of Babylon, that nation will I punish, saith the LORD, with the sword, and with the famine, and with the pestilence, until I have consumed them by his hand.

9 Therefore hearken not ye to your prophets, nor to your diviners, nor to your dreamers, nor to your enchanters, nor to your sorcerers, which speak unto you, saying, Ye shall not serve the king of Babylon:

10 For they prophesy a lie unto you, to remove you far from your land; and that I should drive you out, and ye should perish.

11 But the nations that bring their neck under the yoke of the king of Babylon, and serve him, those will I let remain still in their own land, saith the LORD; and they shall till it, and dwell therein.

12 I spake also to Zedekiah king of Judah according to all these words, saying, Bring your necks under the yoke of the king of Babylon, and serve him and his people, and live.

13 Why will ye die, thou and thy people, by the sword, by the famine, and by the pestilence, as the LORD hath spoken against the nation that will not serve the king of Babylon?

14 Therefore hearken not unto the words of the prophets that speak unto you, saying, Ye shall not serve the king of Babylon: for they prophesy a lie unto you.

15 For I have not sent them, saith the LORD, yet they prophesy a lie in my name; that I might drive you out, and that ye might perish, ye, and the prophets that prophesy unto you.

16 Also I spake to the priests and to all this people, saying, Thus saith the LORD; Hearken not to the words of your prophets that prophesy unto you, saying, Behold, the vessels of the LORD's house shall now shortly be brought again from Babylon: for they prophesy a lie unto you.

17 Hearken not unto them; serve the king of Babylon, and live: wherefore should this city be laid waste?

18 But if they *be* prophets, and if the word of the LORD be with them, let them now make intercession to the LORD of hosts, that the vessels which are left in the house of the LORD, and *in* the house of the king of Judah, and at Jerusalem, go not to Babylon.

19 For thus saith the LORD of hosts concerning the pillars, and concerning the sea, and concerning the bases, and concerning the residue of the vessels that remain in this city,

20 Which Nebuchadnezzar king of Babylon took not, when he carried away captive Jeconiah the son of Jehoiakim king of Judah from Jerusalem to Babylon, and all the nobles of Judah and Jerusalem;

21 Yea, thus saith the LORD of hosts, the God of Israel, concerning the vessels that remain *in* the house of the LORD, and *in* the house of the king of Judah and of Jerusalem;

22 They shall be carried to Babylon, and there shall they be until the day that I visit them, saith the LORD; then will I bring them up, and restore them to this place.

Hananiah Prophesies Falsely

28 And it came to pass the same year, in the beginning of the reign of Zedekiah king of Judah, in the fourth year, *and* in the fifth month, *that* Hananiah the son of Azur the prophet, which *was* of Gibeon, spake unto me in the house of the LORD, in the presence of the priests and of all the people, saying,

2 Thus speaketh the LORD of hosts, the God of Israel, saying, I have broken the yoke of the king of Babylon.

3 Within two full years will I bring again into this place all the vessels of the
LORD's house, that Nebuchadnezzar king of Babylon took away from this place,
and carried them to Babylon:
4 And I will bring again to this place Jeconiah the son of Jehoiakim king of
Judah, with all the captives of Judah, that went into Babylon, saith the LORD:
for I will break the yoke of the king of Babylon.
5 Then the prophet Jeremiah said unto the prophet Hananiah in the presence
of the priests, and in the presence of all the people that stood in the house of
the LORD,
6 Even the prophet Jeremiah said, Amen: the LORD do so: the LORD perform
thy words which thou hast prophesied, to bring again the vessels of the LORD's
house, and all that is carried away captive, from Babylon into this place.
7 Nevertheless hear thou now this word that I speak in thine ears, and in the
ears of all the people;
8 The prophets that have been before me and before thee of old prophesied
both against many countries, and against great kingdoms, of war, and of evil,
and of pestilence.
9 The prophet which prophesieth of peace, when the word of the prophet
shall come to pass, *then* shall the prophet be known, that the LORD hath truly
sent him.

Hananiah Breaks Jeremiah's Yoke

10 Then Hananiah the prophet took the yoke from off the prophet Jeremiah's
neck, and brake it.
11 And Hananiah spake in the presence of all the people, saying, Thus saith
the LORD; Even so will I break the yoke of Nebuchadnezzar king of Babylon
from the neck of all nations within the space of two full years. And the proph-
et Jeremiah went his way.
12 Then the word of the LORD came unto Jeremiah *the prophet*, after that
Hananiah the prophet had broken the yoke from off the neck of the prophet
Jeremiah, saying,
13 Go and tell Hananiah, saying, Thus saith the LORD; Thou hast broken the
yokes of wood; but thou shalt make for them yokes of iron.
14 For thus saith the LORD of hosts, the God of Israel; I have put a yoke of iron
upon the neck of all these nations, that they may serve Nebuchadnezzar king
of Babylon; and they shall serve him: and I have given him the beasts of the
field also.
15 Then said the prophet Jeremiah unto Hananiah the prophet, Hear now,
Hananiah; The LORD hath not sent thee; but thou makest this people to trust
in a lie.
16 Therefore thus saith the LORD; Behold, I will cast thee from off the face of
the earth: this year thou shalt die, because thou hast taught rebellion against
the LORD.
17 So Hananiah the prophet died the same year in the seventh month.

Jeremiah Writes to the Captives in Babylon

29 Now these *are* the words of the letter that Jeremiah the prophet sent
from Jerusalem unto the residue of the elders which were carried away
captives, and to the priests, and to the prophets, and to all the people whom
Nebuchadnezzar had carried away captive from Jerusalem to Babylon;
2 (After that Jeconiah the king, and the queen, and the eunuchs, the princes
of Judah and Jerusalem, and the carpenters, and the smiths, were departed
from Jerusalem;)
3 By the hand of Elasah the son of Shaphan, and Gemariah the son of Hilkiah,
(whom Zedekiah king of Judah sent unto Babylon to Nebuchadnezzar king
of Babylon) saying,

4 Thus saith the LORD of hosts, the God of Israel, unto all that are carried
away captives, whom I have caused to be carried away from Jerusalem unto
Babylon;
5 Build ye houses, and dwell *in them*; and plant gardens, and eat the fruit of
them;
6 Take ye wives, and beget sons and daughters; and take wives for your sons,
and give your daughters to husbands, that they may bear sons and daughters;
that ye may be increased there, and not diminished.
7 And seek the peace of the city whither I have caused you to be carried away
captives, and pray unto the LORD for it: for in the peace thereof shall ye have
peace.
8 For thus saith the LORD of hosts, the God of Israel; Let not your prophets
and your diviners, that *be* in the midst of you, deceive you, neither hearken to
your dreams which ye cause to be dreamed.
9 For they prophesy falsely unto you in my name: I have not sent them, saith
the LORD.
10 For thus saith the LORD, That after seventy years be accomplished at
Babylon I will visit you, and perform my good word toward you, in causing
you to return to this place.
11 For I know the thoughts that I think toward you, saith the LORD, thoughts
of peace, and not of evil, to give you an expected end.
12 Then shall ye call upon me, and ye shall go and pray unto me, and I will
hearken unto you.
13 And ye shall seek me, and find *me*, when ye shall search for me with all
your heart.
14 And I will be found of you, saith the LORD: and I will turn away your cap-
tivity, and I will gather you from all the nations, and from all the places whith-
er I have driven you, saith the LORD; and I will bring you again into the place
whence I caused you to be carried away captive.
15 Because ye have said, The LORD hath raised us up prophets in Babylon;
16 *Know* that thus saith the LORD of the king that sitteth upon the throne of
David, and of all the people that dwelleth in this city, *and* of your brethren
that are not gone forth with you into captivity;
17 Thus saith the LORD of hosts; Behold, I will send upon them the sword,
the famine, and the pestilence, and will make them like vile figs, that cannot
be eaten, they are so evil.
18 And I will persecute them with the sword, with the famine, and with the
pestilence, and will deliver them to be removed to all the kingdoms of the
earth, to be a curse, and an astonishment, and an hissing, and a reproach,
among all the nations whither I have driven them:
19 Because they have not hearkened to my words, saith the LORD, which I
sent unto them by my servants the prophets, rising up early and sending *them*;
but ye would not hear, saith the LORD.
20 Hear ye therefore the word of the LORD, all ye of the captivity, whom I have
sent from Jerusalem to Babylon:
21 Thus saith the LORD of hosts, the God of Israel, of Ahab the son of Kolaiah,
and of Zedekiah the son of Maaseiah, which prophesy a lie unto you in my
name; Behold, I will deliver them into the hand of Nebuchadrezzar king of
Babylon; and he shall slay them before your eyes;
22 And of them shall be taken up a curse by all the captivity of Judah which
are in Babylon, saying, The LORD make thee like Zedekiah and like Ahab, whom
the king of Babylon roasted in the fire;
23 Because they have committed villany in Israel, and have committed adul-
tery with their neighbours' wives, and have spoken lying words in my name,
which I have not commanded them; even I know, and *am* a witness, saith the
LORD.

Shemaiah Writes a Letter against Jeremiah

24 *Thus* shalt thou also speak to Shemaiah the Nehelamite, saying,

25 Thus speaketh the LORD of hosts, the God of Israel, saying, Because thou hast sent letters in thy name unto all the people that *are* at Jerusalem, and to Zephaniah the son of Maaseiah the priest, and to all the priests, saying,

26 The LORD hath made thee priest in the stead of Jehoiada the priest, that ye should be officers in the house of the LORD, for every man *that is* mad, and maketh himself a prophet, that thou shouldest put him in prison, and in the stocks.

27 Now therefore why hast thou not reproved Jeremiah of Anathoth, which maketh himself a prophet to you?

28 For therefore he sent unto us *in* Babylon, saying, This *captivity is* long: build ye houses, and dwell *in them*; and plant gardens, and eat the fruit of them.

29 And Zephaniah the priest read this letter in the ears of Jeremiah the prophet.

30 Then came the word of the LORD unto Jeremiah, saying,

31 Send to all them of the captivity, saying, Thus saith the LORD concerning Shemaiah the Nehelamite; Because that Shemaiah hath prophesied unto you, and I sent him not, and he caused you to trust in a lie:

32 Therefore thus saith the LORD; Behold, I will punish Shemaiah the Nehelamite, and his seed: he shall not have a man to dwell among this people; neither shall he behold the good that I will do for my people, saith the LORD; because he hath taught rebellion against the LORD.

The Future Glorious Return of the Jews

30 The word that came to Jeremiah from the LORD, saying,

2 Thus speaketh the LORD God of Israel, saying, Write thee all the words that I have spoken unto thee in a book.

3 For, lo, the days come, saith the LORD, that I will bring again the captivity of my people Israel and Judah, saith the LORD: and I will cause them to return to the land that I gave to their fathers, and they shall possess it.

4 And these *are* the words that the LORD spake concerning Israel and concerning Judah.

5 For thus saith the LORD; We have heard a voice of trembling, of fear, and not of peace.

6 Ask ye now, and see whether a man doth travail with child? wherefore do I see every man with his hands on his loins, as a woman in travail, and all faces are turned into paleness?

7 Alas! for that day *is* great, so that none *is* like it: it *is* even the time of Jacob's trouble; but he shall be saved out of it.

8 For it shall come to pass in that day, saith the LORD of hosts, *that* I will break his yoke from off thy neck, and will burst thy bonds, and strangers shall no more serve themselves of him:

9 But they shall serve the LORD their God, and David their king, whom I will raise up unto them.

10 Therefore fear thou not, O my servant Jacob, saith the LORD; neither be dismayed, O Israel: for, lo, I will save thee from afar, and thy seed from the land of their captivity; and Jacob shall return, and shall be in rest, and be quiet, and none shall make *him* afraid.

11 For I *am* with thee, saith the LORD, to save thee: though I make a full end of all nations whither I have scattered thee, yet will I not make a full end of thee: but I will correct thee in measure, and will not leave thee altogether unpunished.

12 For thus saith the LORD, Thy bruise *is* incurable, *and* thy wound *is* grievous.

13 *There is* none to plead thy cause, that thou mayest be bound up: thou hast
no healing medicines.
14 All thy lovers have forgotten thee; they seek thee not; for I have wounded
thee with the wound of an enemy, with the chastisement of a cruel one, for
the multitude of thine iniquity; *because* thy sins were increased.
15 Why criest thou for thine affliction? thy sorrow *is* incurable for the mul-
titude of thine iniquity: *because* thy sins were increased, I have done these
things unto thee.
16 Therefore all they that devour thee shall be devoured; and all thine adver-
saries, every one of them, shall go into captivity; and they that spoil thee shall
be a spoil, and all that prey upon thee will I give for a prey.
17 For I will restore health unto thee, and I will heal thee of thy wounds, saith
the LORD; because they called thee an Outcast, *saying*, This *is* Zion, whom no
man seeketh after.
18 Thus saith the LORD; Behold, I will bring again the captivity of Jacob's tents,
and have mercy on his dwellingplaces; and the city shall be builded upon her
own heap, and the palace shall remain after the manner thereof.
19 And out of them shall proceed thanksgiving and the voice of them that
make merry: and I will multiply them, and they shall not be few; I will also
glorify them, and they shall not be small.
20 Their children also shall be as aforetime, and their congregation shall be
established before me, and I will punish all that oppress them.
21 And their nobles shall be of themselves, and their governor shall proceed
from the midst of them; and I will cause him to draw near, and he shall
approach unto me: for who *is* this that engaged his heart to approach unto
me? saith the LORD.
22 And ye shall be my people, and I will be your God.
23 Behold, the whirlwind of the LORD goeth forth with fury, a continuing
whirlwind: it shall fall with pain upon the head of the wicked.
24 The fierce anger of the LORD shall not return, until he have done *it*, and
until he have performed the intents of his heart: in the latter days ye shall
consider it.

The Restoration of Israel and Judah

31 At the same time, saith the LORD, will I be the God of all the families of
Israel, and they shall be my people.
2 Thus saith the LORD, The people *which were* left of the sword found grace
in the wilderness; *even* Israel, when I went to cause him to rest.
3 The LORD hath appeared of old unto me, *saying*, Yea, I have loved thee with
an everlasting love: therefore with lovingkindness have I drawn thee.
4 Again I will build thee, and thou shalt be built, O virgin of Israel: thou shalt
again be adorned with thy tabrets, and shalt go forth in the dances of them
that make merry.
5 Thou shalt yet plant vines upon the mountains of Samaria: the planters
shall plant, and shall eat *them* as common things.
6 For there shall be a day, *that* the watchmen upon the mount Ephraim shall
cry, Arise ye, and let us go up to Zion unto the LORD our God.
7 For thus saith the LORD; Sing with gladness for Jacob, and shout among the
chief of the nations: publish ye, praise ye, and say, O LORD, save thy people, the
remnant of Israel.
8 Behold, I will bring them from the north country, and gather them from
the coasts of the earth, *and* with them the blind and the lame, the woman with
child and her that travaileth with child together: a great company shall return
thither.

9 They shall come with weeping, and with supplications will I lead them: I will cause them to walk by the rivers of waters in a straight way, wherein they shall not stumble: for I am a father to Israel, and Ephraim *is* my firstborn.

10 Hear the word of the LORD, O ye nations, and declare *it* in the isles afar off, and say, He that scattered Israel will gather him, and keep him, as a shepherd *doth* his flock.

11 For the LORD hath redeemed Jacob, and ransomed him from the hand of *him that was* stronger than he.

12 Therefore they shall come and sing in the height of Zion, and shall flow together to the goodness of the LORD, for wheat, and for wine, and for oil, and for the young of the flock and of the herd: and their soul shall be as a watered garden; and they shall not sorrow any more at all.

13 Then shall the virgin rejoice in the dance, both young men and old together: for I will turn their mourning into joy, and will comfort them, and make them rejoice from their sorrow.

14 And I will satiate the soul of the priests with fatness, and my people shall be satisfied with my goodness, saith the LORD.

15 Thus saith the LORD; A voice was heard in Ramah, lamentation, *and* bitter weeping; Rahel weeping for her children refused to be comforted for her children, because they *were* not.

16 Thus saith the LORD; Refrain thy voice from weeping, and thine eyes from tears: for thy work shall be rewarded, saith the LORD; and they shall come again from the land of the enemy.

17 And there is hope in thine end, saith the LORD, that thy children shall come again to their own border.

18 I have surely heard Ephraim bemoaning himself *thus*; Thou hast chastised me, and I was chastised, as a bullock unaccustomed *to the yoke*: turn thou me, and I shall be turned; for thou *art* the LORD my God.

19 Surely after that I was turned, I repented; and after that I was instructed, I smote upon *my* thigh: I was ashamed, yea, even confounded, because I did bear the reproach of my youth.

20 *Is* Ephraim my dear son? *is he* a pleasant child? for since I spake against him, I do earnestly remember him still: therefore my bowels are troubled for him; I will surely have mercy upon him, saith the LORD.

21 Set thee up waymarks, make thee high heaps: set thine heart toward the highway, *even* the way *which* thou wentest: turn again, O virgin of Israel, turn again to these thy cities.

22 How long wilt thou go about, O thou backsliding daughter? for the LORD hath created a new thing in the earth, A woman shall compass a man.

23 Thus saith the LORD of hosts, the God of Israel; As yet they shall use this speech in the land of Judah and in the cities thereof, when I shall bring again their captivity; The LORD bless thee, O habitation of justice, *and* mountain of holiness.

24 And there shall dwell in Judah itself, and in all the cities thereof together, husbandmen, and they *that* go forth with flocks.

25 For I have satiated the weary soul, and I have replenished every sorrowful soul.

26 Upon this I awaked, and beheld; and my sleep was sweet unto me.

27 Behold, the days come, saith the LORD, that I will sow the house of Israel and the house of Judah with the seed of man, and with the seed of beast.

28 And it shall come to pass, *that* like as I have watched over them, to pluck up, and to break down, and to throw down, and to destroy, and to afflict; so will I watch over them, to build, and to plant, saith the LORD.

29 In those days they shall say no more, The fathers have eaten a sour grape, and the children's teeth are set on edge.

30 But every one shall die for his own iniquity: every man that eateth the sour
grape, his teeth shall be set on edge.

The New Promise

31 Behold, the days come, saith the LORD, that I will make a new covenant
with the house of Israel, and with the house of Judah:
32 Not according to the covenant that I made with their fathers in the day
that I took them by the hand to bring them out of the land of Egypt; which
my covenant they brake, although I was an husband unto them, saith the LORD:
33 But this *shall be* the covenant that I will make with the house of Israel;
After those days, saith the LORD, I will put my law in their inward parts, and
write it in their hearts; and will be their God, and they shall be my people.
34 And they shall teach no more every man his neighbour, and every man
his brother, saying, Know the LORD: for they shall all know me, from the least
of them unto the greatest of them, saith the LORD: for I will forgive their iniq-
uity, and I will remember their sin no more.
35 Thus saith the LORD, which giveth the sun for a light by day, *and* the ordi-
nances of the moon and of the stars for a light by night, which divideth the
sea when the waves thereof roar; The LORD of hosts *is* his name:
36 If those ordinances depart from before me, saith the LORD, *then* the seed
of Israel also shall cease from being a nation before me for ever.
37 Thus saith the LORD; If heaven above can be measured, and the founda-
tions of the earth searched out beneath, I will also cast off all the seed of Israel
for all that they have done, saith the LORD.
38 Behold, the days come, saith the LORD, that the city shall be built to the
LORD from the tower of Hananeel unto the gate of the corner.
39 And the measuring line shall yet go forth over against it upon the hill
Gareb, and shall compass about to Goath.
40 And the whole valley of the dead bodies, and of the ashes, and all the fields
unto the brook of Kidron, unto the corner of the horse gate toward the east,
shall be holy unto the LORD; it shall not be plucked up, nor thrown down any
more for ever.

Jeremiah Buys a Field

32 The word that came to Jeremiah from the LORD in the tenth year of
Zedekiah king of Judah, which *was* the eighteenth year of
Nebuchadrezzar.
2 For then the king of Babylon's army besieged Jerusalem: and Jeremiah the
prophet was shut up in the court of the prison, which *was* in the king of Judah's
house.
3 For Zedekiah king of Judah had shut him up, saying, Wherefore dost thou
prophesy, and say, Thus saith the LORD, Behold, I will give this city into the
hand of the king of Babylon, and he shall take it;
4 And Zedekiah king of Judah shall not escape out of the hand of the
Chaldeans, but shall surely be delivered into the hand of the king of Babylon,
and shall speak with him mouth to mouth, and his eyes shall behold his eyes;
5 And he shall lead Zedekiah to Babylon, and there shall he be until I visit
him, saith the LORD: though ye fight with the Chaldeans, ye shall not prosper.
6 And Jeremiah said, The word of the LORD came unto me, saying,
7 Behold, Hanameel the son of Shallum thine uncle shall come unto thee,
saying, Buy thee my field that *is* in Anathoth: for the right of redemption *is*
thine to buy *it*.
8 So Hanameel mine uncle's son came to me in the court of the prison accord-
ing to the word of the LORD, and said unto me, Buy my field, I pray thee, that
is in Anathoth, which *is* in the country of Benjamin: for the right of inheri-
tance *is* thine, and the redemption *is* thine; buy *it* for thyself. Then I knew that
this *was* the word of the LORD.

9 And I bought the field of Hanameel my uncle's son, that *was* in Anathoth,
and weighed him the money, *even* seventeen shekels of silver.
10 And I subscribed the evidence, and sealed *it*, and took witnesses, and
weighed *him* the money in the balances.
11 So I took the evidence of the purchase, *both* that which was sealed *according*
to the law and custom, and that which was open:
12 And I gave the evidence of the purchase unto Baruch the son of Neriah,
the son of Maaseiah, in the sight of Hanameel mine uncle's *son*, and in the
presence of the witnesses that subscribed the book of the purchase, before all
the Jews that sat in the court of the prison.
13 And I charged Baruch before them, saying,
14 Thus saith the LORD of hosts, the God of Israel; Take these evidences, this
evidence of the purchase, both which is sealed, and this evidence which is
open; and put them in an earthen vessel, that they may continue many days.
15 For thus saith the LORD of hosts, the God of Israel; Houses and fields and
vineyards shall be possessed again in this land.

Jeremiah's Prayer

16 Now when I had delivered the evidence of the purchase unto Baruch the
son of Neriah, I prayed unto the LORD, saying,
17 Ah Lord GOD! behold, thou hast made the heaven and the earth by thy
great power and stretched out arm, *and* there is nothing too hard for thee:
18 Thou shewest lovingkindness unto thousands, and recompensest the
iniquity of the fathers into the bosom of their children after them: the Great,
the Mighty God, the LORD of hosts, *is* his name,
19 Great in counsel, and mighty in work: for thine eyes *are* open upon all the
ways of the sons of men: to give every one according to his ways, and according
to the fruit of his doings:
20 Which hast set signs and wonders in the land of Egypt, *even* unto this day,
and in Israel, and among *other* men; and hast made thee a name, as at this day;
21 And hast brought forth thy people Israel out of the land of Egypt with
signs, and with wonders, and with a strong hand, and with a stretched out
arm, and with great terror;
22 And hast given them this land, which thou didst swear to their fathers to
give them, a land flowing with milk and honey;
23 And they came in, and possessed it; but they obeyed not thy voice, neither
walked in thy law; they have done nothing of all that thou commandedst them
to do: therefore thou hast caused all this evil to come upon them:
24 Behold the mounts, they are come unto the city to take it; and the city is
given into the hand of the Chaldeans, that fight against it, because of the
sword, and of the famine, and of the pestilence: and what thou hast spoken is
come to pass; and, behold, thou seest *it*.
25 And thou hast said unto me, O Lord GOD, Buy thee the field for money,
and take witnesses; for the city is given into the hand of the Chaldeans.

Nothing Is Too Hard for the Lord

26 Then came the word of the LORD unto Jeremiah, saying,
27 Behold, I *am* the LORD, the God of all flesh: is there any thing too hard for me?
28 Therefore thus saith the LORD; Behold, I will give this city into the hand
of the Chaldeans, and into the hand of Nebuchadrezzar king of Babylon, and
he shall take it:
29 And the Chaldeans, that fight against this city, shall come and set fire on
this city, and burn it with the houses, upon whose roofs they have offered
incense unto Baal, and poured out drink offerings unto other gods, to provoke
me to anger.

30 For the children of Israel and the children of Judah have only done evil
before me from their youth: for the children of Israel have only provoked me
to anger with the work of their hands, saith the LORD.
31 For this city hath been to me *as* a provocation of mine anger and of my
fury from the day that they built it even unto this day; that I should remove it
from before my face,
32 Because of all the evil of the children of Israel and of the children of Judah,
which they have done to provoke me to anger, they, their kings, their princes,
their priests, and their prophets, and the men of Judah, and the inhabitants
of Jerusalem.
33 And they have turned unto me the back, and not the face: though I taught
them, rising up early and teaching *them*, yet they have not hearkened to receive
instruction.
34 But they set their abominations in the house, which is called by my name,
to defile it.
35 And they built the high places of Baal, which *are* in the valley of the son
of Hinnom, to cause their sons and their daughters to pass through *the fire*
unto Molech; which I commanded them not, neither came it into my mind,
that they should do this abomination, to cause Judah to sin.
36 And now therefore thus saith the LORD, the God of Israel, concerning this
city, whereof ye say, It shall be delivered into the hand of the king of Babylon
by the sword, and by the famine, and by the pestilence;
37 Behold, I will gather them out of all countries, whither I have driven them
in mine anger, and in my fury, and in great wrath; and I will bring them again
unto this place, and I will cause them to dwell safely:
38 And they shall be my people, and I will be their God:
39 And I will give them one heart, and one way, that they may fear me for
ever, for the good of them, and of their children after them:
40 And I will make an everlasting covenant with them, that I will not turn
away from them, to do them good; but I will put my fear in their hearts, that
they shall not depart from me.
41 Yea, I will rejoice over them to do them good, and I will plant them in this
land assuredly with my whole heart and with my whole soul.
42 For thus saith the LORD; Like as I have brought all this great evil upon this
people, so will I bring upon them all the good that I have promised them.
43 And fields shall be bought in this land, whereof ye say, *It is* desolate with-
out man or beast; it is given into the hand of the Chaldeans.
44 Men shall buy fields for money, and subscribe evidences, and seal *them*,
and take witnesses in the land of Benjamin, and in the places about Jerusalem,
and in the cities of Judah, and in the cities of the mountains, and in the cities
of the valley, and in the cities of the south: for I will cause their captivity to
return, saith the LORD.

God Promises to End the Captivity

33 Moreover the word of the LORD came unto Jeremiah the second time,
while he was yet shut up in the court of the prison, saying,
2 Thus saith the LORD the maker thereof, the LORD that formed it, to establish
it; the LORD *is* his name;
3 Call unto me, and I will answer thee, and shew thee great and mighty
things, which thou knowest not.
4 For thus saith the LORD, the God of Israel, concerning the houses of this
city, and concerning the houses of the kings of Judah, which are thrown down
by the mounts, and by the sword;
5 They come to fight with the Chaldeans, but *it is* to fill them with the dead
bodies of men, whom I have slain in mine anger and in my fury, and for all
whose wickedness I have hid my face from this city.

6 Behold, I will bring it health and cure, and I will cure them, and will reveal
unto them the abundance of peace and truth.
7 And I will cause the captivity of Judah and the captivity of Israel to return,
and will build them, as at the first.
8 And I will cleanse them from all their iniquity, whereby they have sinned
against me; and I will pardon all their iniquities, whereby they have sinned,
and whereby they have transgressed against me.
9 And it shall be to me a name of joy, a praise and an honour before all the
nations of the earth, which shall hear all the good that I do unto them: and
they shall fear and tremble for all the goodness and for all the prosperity that
I procure unto it.
10 Thus saith the LORD; Again there shall be heard in this place, which ye say
shall be desolate without man and without beast, *even* in the cities of Judah,
and in the streets of Jerusalem, that are desolate, without man, and without
inhabitant, and without beast,
11 The voice of joy, and the voice of gladness, the voice of the bridegroom,
and the voice of the bride, the voice of them that shall say, Praise the LORD of
hosts: for the LORD *is* good; for his mercy *endureth* for ever: *and* of them that
shall bring the sacrifice of praise into the house of the LORD. For I will cause
to return the captivity of the land, as at the first, saith the LORD.
12 Thus saith the LORD of hosts; Again in this place, which is desolate without
man and without beast, and in all the cities thereof, shall be an habitation of
shepherds causing *their* flocks to lie down.
13 In the cities of the mountains, in the cities of the vale, and in the cities of
the south, and in the land of Benjamin, and in the places about Jerusalem, and
in the cities of Judah, shall the flocks pass again under the hands of him that
telleth *them*, saith the LORD.
14 Behold, the days come, saith the LORD, that I will perform that good thing
which I have promised unto the house of Israel and to the house of Judah.
15 In those days, and at that time, will I cause the Branch of righteousness
to grow up unto David; and he shall execute judgment and righteousness in
the land.
16 In those days shall Judah be saved, and Jerusalem shall dwell safely: and
this *is the name* wherewith she shall be called, The LORD our righteousness.
17 For thus saith the LORD; David shall never want a man to sit upon the
throne of the house of Israel;
18 Neither shall the priests the Levites want a man before me to offer burnt
offerings, and to kindle meat offerings, and to do sacrifice continually.
19 And the word of the LORD came unto Jeremiah, saying,
20 Thus saith the LORD; If ye can break my covenant of the day, and my cov-
enant of the night, and that there should not be day and night in their season;
21 *Then* may also my covenant be broken with David my servant, that he
should not have a son to reign upon his throne; and with the Levites the priests,
my ministers.
22 As the host of heaven cannot be numbered, neither the sand of the sea
measured: so will I multiply the seed of David my servant, and the Levites that
minister unto me.
23 Moreover the word of the LORD came to Jeremiah, saying,
24 Considerest thou not what this people have spoken, saying, The two fam-
ilies which the LORD hath chosen, he hath even cast them off? thus they have
despised my people, that they should be no more a nation before them.
25 Thus saith the LORD; If my covenant *be* not with day and night, *and if* I
have not appointed the ordinances of heaven and earth;
26 Then will I cast away the seed of Jacob, and David my servant, *so* that I will
not take *any* of his seed *to be* rulers over the seed of Abraham, Isaac, and Jacob:
for I will cause their captivity to return, and have mercy on them.

Jeremiah Prophesies the Captivity of Zedekiah and the City

34 The word which came unto Jeremiah from the LORD, when
Nebuchadnezzar king of Babylon, and all his army, and all the king-
doms of the earth of his dominion, and all the people, fought against
Jerusalem, and against all the cities thereof, saying,
2 Thus saith the LORD, the God of Israel; Go and speak to Zedekiah king of
Judah, and tell him, Thus saith the LORD; Behold, I will give this city into the
hand of the king of Babylon, and he shall burn it with fire:
3 And thou shalt not escape out of his hand, but shalt surely be taken, and
delivered into his hand; and thine eyes shall behold the eyes of the king of
Babylon, and he shall speak with thee mouth to mouth, and thou shalt go to
Babylon.
4 Yet hear the word of the LORD, O Zedekiah king of Judah; Thus saith the
LORD of thee, Thou shalt not die by the sword:
5 *But* thou shalt die in peace: and with the burnings of thy fathers, the former
kings which were before thee, so shall they burn *odours* for thee; and they will
lament thee, *saying*, Ah lord! for I have pronounced the word, saith the LORD.
6 Then Jeremiah the prophet spake all these words unto Zedekiah king of
Judah in Jerusalem,
7 When the king of Babylon's army fought against Jerusalem, and against all
the cities of Judah that were left, against Lachish, and against Azekah: for these
defenced cities remained of the cities of Judah.
8 *This is* the word that came unto Jeremiah from the LORD, after that the king
Zedekiah had made a covenant with all the people which *were* at Jerusalem,
to proclaim liberty unto them;
9 That every man should let his manservant, and every man his maidservant,
being an Hebrew or an Hebrewess, go free; that none should serve himself of
them, *to wit*, of a Jew his brother.
10 Now when all the princes, and all the people, which had entered into the
covenant, heard that every one should let his manservant, and every one his
maidservant, go free, that none should serve themselves of them any more,
then they obeyed, and let *them* go.
11 But afterward they turned, and caused the servants and the handmaids,
whom they had let go free, to return, and brought them into subjection for
servants and for handmaids.
12 Therefore the word of the LORD came to Jeremiah from the LORD, saying,
13 Thus saith the LORD, the God of Israel; I made a covenant with your fathers
in the day that I brought them forth out of the land of Egypt, out of the house
of bondmen, saying,
14 At the end of seven years let ye go every man his brother an Hebrew, which
hath been sold unto thee; and when he hath served thee six years, thou shalt
let him go free from thee: but your fathers hearkened not unto me, neither
inclined their ear.
15 And ye were now turned, and had done right in my sight, in proclaiming
liberty every man to his neighbour; and ye had made a covenant before me in
the house which is called by my name:
16 But ye turned and polluted my name, and caused every man his servant,
and every man his handmaid, whom ye had set at liberty at their pleasure, to
return, and brought them into subjection, to be unto you for servants and for
handmaids.
17 Therefore thus saith the LORD; Ye have not hearkened unto me, in pro-
claiming liberty, every one to his brother, and every man to his neighbour:
behold, I proclaim a liberty for you, saith the LORD, to the sword, to the pesti-
lence, and to the famine; and I will make you to be removed into all the king-
doms of the earth.

18 And I will give the men that have transgressed my covenant, which have
not performed the words of the covenant which they had made before me,
when they cut the calf in twain, and passed between the parts thereof,
19 The princes of Judah, and the princes of Jerusalem, the eunuchs, and the
priests, and all the people of the land, which passed between the parts of the
calf;
20 I will even give them into the hand of their enemies, and into the hand of
them that seek their life: and their dead bodies shall be for meat unto the fowls
of the heaven, and to the beasts of the earth.
21 And Zedekiah king of Judah and his princes will I give into the hand of
their enemies, and into the hand of them that seek their life, and into the hand
of the king of Babylon's army, which are gone up from you.
22 Behold, I will command, saith the LORD, and cause them to return to this
city; and they shall fight against it, and take it, and burn it with fire: and I will
make the cities of Judah a desolation without an inhabitant.

The Obedience of the Rechabites

35 The word which came unto Jeremiah from the LORD in the days of
Jehoiakim the son of Josiah king of Judah, saying,
2 Go unto the house of the Rechabites, and speak unto them, and bring them
into the house of the LORD, into one of the chambers, and give them wine to
drink.
3 Then I took Jaazaniah the son of Jeremiah, the son of Habaziniah, and his
brethren, and all his sons, and the whole house of the Rechabites;
4 And I brought them into the house of the LORD, into the chamber of the
sons of Hanan, the son of Igdaliah, a man of God, which *was* by the chamber
of the princes, which *was* above the chamber of Maaseiah the son of Shallum,
the keeper of the door:
5 And I set before the sons of the house of the Rechabites pots full of wine,
and cups, and I said unto them, Drink ye wine.
6 But they said, We will drink no wine: for Jonadab the son of Rechab our
father commanded us, saying, Ye shall drink no wine, *neither ye*, nor your sons
for ever:
7 Neither shall ye build house, nor sow seed, nor plant vineyard, nor have
any: but all your days ye shall dwell in tents; that ye may live many days in the
land where ye *be* strangers.
8 Thus have we obeyed the voice of Jonadab the son of Rechab our father in
all that he hath charged us, to drink no wine all our days, we, our wives, our
sons, nor our daughters;
9 Nor to build houses for us to dwell in: neither have we vineyard, nor field,
nor seed:
10 But we have dwelt in tents, and have obeyed, and done according to all
that Jonadab our father commanded us.
11 But it came to pass, when Nebuchadrezzar king of Babylon came up into
the land, that we said, Come, and let us go to Jerusalem for fear of the army of
the Chaldeans, and for fear of the army of the Syrians: so we dwell at Jerusalem.

Jeremiah Condemns the Disobedience of the Jews

12 Then came the word of the LORD unto Jeremiah, saying,
13 Thus saith the LORD of hosts, the God of Israel; Go and tell the men of
Judah and the inhabitants of Jerusalem, Will ye not receive instruction to
hearken to my words? saith the LORD.
14 The words of Jonadab the son of Rechab, that he commanded his sons not
to drink wine, are performed; for unto this day they drink none, but obey their
father's commandment: notwithstanding I have spoken unto you, rising early
and speaking; but ye hearkened not unto me.

15 I have sent also unto you all my servants the prophets, rising up early and
sending *them*, saying, Return ye now every man from his evil way, and amend
your doings, and go not after other gods to serve them, and ye shall dwell in
the land which I have given to you and to your fathers: but ye have not inclined
your ear, nor hearkened unto me.
16 Because the sons of Jonadab the son of Rechab have performed the com-
mandment of their father, which he commanded them; but this people hath
not hearkened unto me:
17 Therefore thus saith the LORD God of hosts, the God of Israel; Behold, I
will bring upon Judah and upon all the inhabitants of Jerusalem all the evil
that I have pronounced against them: because I have spoken unto them, but
they have not heard; and I have called unto them, but they have not answered.
18 And Jeremiah said unto the house of the Rechabites, Thus saith the LORD
of hosts, the God of Israel; Because ye have obeyed the commandment of
Jonadab your father, and kept all his precepts, and done according unto all
that he hath commanded you:
19 Therefore thus saith the LORD of hosts, the God of Israel; Jonadab the son
of Rechab shall not want a man to stand before me for ever.

The Prophecies Are Read and Burned

36 And it came to pass in the fourth year of Jehoiakim the son of Josiah
king of Judah, *that* this word came unto Jeremiah from the LORD, say-
ing,
2 Take thee a roll of a book, and write therein all the words that I have spoken
unto thee against Israel, and against Judah, and against all the nations, from
the day I spake unto thee, from the days of Josiah, even unto this day.
3 It may be that the house of Judah will hear all the evil which I purpose to
do unto them; that they may return every man from his evil way; that I may
forgive their iniquity and their sin.
4 Then Jeremiah called Baruch the son of Neriah: and Baruch wrote from
the mouth of Jeremiah all the words of the LORD, which he had spoken unto
him, upon a roll of a book.
5 And Jeremiah commanded Baruch, saying, I *am* shut up; I cannot go into
the house of the LORD:
6 Therefore go thou, and read in the roll, which thou hast written from my
mouth, the words of the LORD in the ears of the people in the LORD's house
upon the fasting day: and also thou shalt read them in the ears of all Judah
that come out of their cities.
7 It may be they will present their supplication before the LORD, and will
return every one from his evil way: for great *is* the anger and the fury that the
LORD hath pronounced against this people.
8 And Baruch the son of Neriah did according to all that Jeremiah the proph-
et commanded him, reading in the book the words of the LORD in the LORD's
house.
9 And it came to pass in the fifth year of Jehoiakim the son of Josiah king of
Judah, in the ninth month, *that* they proclaimed a fast before the LORD to all
the people in Jerusalem, and to all the people that came from the cities of
Judah unto Jerusalem.
10 Then read Baruch in the book the words of Jeremiah in the house of the
LORD, in the chamber of Gemariah the son of Shaphan the scribe, in the high-
er court, at the entry of the new gate of the LORD's house, in the ears of all the
people.
11 When Michaiah the son of Gemariah, the son of Shaphan, had heard out
of the book all the words of the LORD,
12 Then he went down into the king's house, into the scribe's chamber: and,
lo, all the princes sat there, *even* Elishama the scribe, and Delaiah the son of

Shemaiah, and Elnathan the son of Achbor, and Gemariah the son of Shaphan,
and Zedekiah the son of Hananiah, and all the princes.
13 Then Michaiah declared unto them all the words that he had heard, when
Baruch read the book in the ears of the people.
14 Therefore all the princes sent Jehudi the son of Nethaniah, the son of
Shelemiah, the son of Cushi, unto Baruch, saying, Take in thine hand the roll
wherein thou hast read in the ears of the people, and come. So Baruch the son
of Neriah took the roll in his hand, and came unto them.
15 And they said unto him, Sit down now, and read it in our ears. So Baruch
read *it* in their ears.
16 Now it came to pass, when they had heard all the words, they were afraid
both one and other, and said unto Baruch, We will surely tell the king of all
these words.
17 And they asked Baruch, saying, Tell us now, How didst thou write all these
words at his mouth?
18 Then Baruch answered them, He pronounced all these words unto me
with his mouth, and I wrote *them* with ink in the book.
19 Then said the princes unto Baruch, Go, hide thee, thou and Jeremiah; and
let no man know where ye be.
20 And they went in to the king into the court, but they laid up the roll in the
chamber of Elishama the scribe, and told all the words in the ears of the king.
21 So the king sent Jehudi to fetch the roll: and he took it out of Elishama the
scribe's chamber. And Jehudi read it in the ears of the king, and in the ears of
all the princes which stood beside the king.
22 Now the king sat in the winterhouse in the ninth month: and *there was
a fire* on the hearth burning before him.
23 And it came to pass, *that* when Jehudi had read three or four leaves, he
cut it with the penknife, and cast *it* into the fire that *was* on the hearth, until
all the roll was consumed in the fire that *was* on the hearth.
24 Yet they were not afraid, nor rent their garments, *neither* the king, nor
any of his servants that heard all these words.
25 Nevertheless Elnathan and Delaiah and Gemariah had made intercession
to the king that he would not burn the roll: but he would not hear them.
26 But the king commanded Jerahmeel the son of Hammelech, and Seraiah
the son of Azriel, and Shelemiah the son of Abdeel, to take Baruch the scribe
and Jeremiah the prophet: but the LORD hid them.
27 Then the word of the LORD came to Jeremiah, after that the king had
burned the roll, and the words which Baruch wrote at the mouth of Jeremiah,
saying,
28 Take thee again another roll, and write in it all the former words that were
in the first roll, which Jehoiakim the king of Judah hath burned.
29 And thou shalt say to Jehoiakim king of Judah, Thus saith the LORD; Thou
hast burned this roll, saying, Why hast thou written therein, saying, The king
of Babylon shall certainly come and destroy this land, and shall cause to cease
from thence man and beast?
30 Therefore thus saith the LORD of Jehoiakim king of Judah; He shall have
none to sit upon the throne of David: and his dead body shall be cast out in
the day to the heat, and in the night to the frost.
31 And I will punish him and his seed and his servants for their iniquity; and
I will bring upon them, and upon the inhabitants of Jerusalem, and upon the
men of Judah, all the evil that I have pronounced against them; but they hear-
kened not.
32 Then took Jeremiah another roll, and gave it to Baruch the scribe, the son
of Neriah; who wrote therein from the mouth of Jeremiah all the words of
the book which Jehoiakim king of Judah had burned in the fire: and there
were added besides unto them many like words.

Jeremiah Advises Zedekiah

37 And king Zedekiah the son of Josiah reigned instead of Coniah the son
of Jehoiakim, whom Nebuchadrezzar king of Babylon made king in
the land of Judah.
2 But neither he, nor his servants, nor the people of the land, did hearken
unto the words of the LORD, which he spake by the prophet Jeremiah.
3 And Zedekiah the king sent Jehucal the son of Shelemiah and Zephaniah
the son of Maaseiah the priest to the prophet Jeremiah, saying, Pray now unto
the LORD our God for us.
4 Now Jeremiah came in and went out among the people: for they had not
put him into prison.
5 Then Pharaoh's army was come forth out of Egypt: and when the Chaldeans
that besieged Jerusalem heard tidings of them, they departed from Jerusalem.
6 Then came the word of the LORD unto the prophet Jeremiah, saying,
7 Thus saith the LORD, the God of Israel; Thus shall ye say to the king of Judah,
that sent you unto me to enquire of me; Behold, Pharaoh's army, which is come
forth to help you, shall return to Egypt into their own land.
8 And the Chaldeans shall come again, and fight against this city, and take
it, and burn it with fire.
9 Thus saith the LORD; Deceive not yourselves, saying, The Chaldeans shall
surely depart from us: for they shall not depart.
10 For though ye had smitten the whole army of the Chaldeans that fight
against you, and there remained *but* wounded men among them, *yet* should
they rise up every man in his tent, and burn this city with fire.

Jeremiah Is Taken for a Traitor

11 And it came to pass, that when the army of the Chaldeans was broken up
from Jerusalem for fear of Pharaoh's army,
12 Then Jeremiah went forth out of Jerusalem to go into the land of Benjamin,
to separate himself thence in the midst of the people.
13 And when he was in the gate of Benjamin, a captain of the ward *was* there,
whose name *was* Irijah, the son of Shelemiah, the son of Hananiah; and he
took Jeremiah the prophet, saying, Thou fallest away to the Chaldeans.
14 Then said Jeremiah, *It is* false; I fall not away to the Chaldeans. But he hear-
kened not to him: so Irijah took Jeremiah, and brought him to the princes.
15 Wherefore the princes were wroth with Jeremiah, and smote him, and
put him in prison in the house of Jonathan the scribe: for they had made that
the prison.
16 When Jeremiah was entered into the dungeon, and into the cabins, and
Jeremiah had remained there many days;
17 Then Zedekiah the king sent, and took him out: and the king asked him
secretly in his house, and said, Is there *any* word from the LORD? And Jeremiah
said, There is: for, said he, thou shalt be delivered into the hand of the king of
Babylon.
18 Moreover Jeremiah said unto king Zedekiah, What have I offended against
thee, or against thy servants, or against this people, that ye have put me in
prison?
19 Where *are* now your prophets which prophesied unto you, saying, The
king of Babylon shall not come against you, nor against this land?
20 Therefore hear now, I pray thee, O my lord the king: let my supplication,
I pray thee, be accepted before thee; that thou cause me not to return to the
house of Jonathan the scribe, lest I die there.
21 Then Zedekiah the king commanded that they should commit Jeremiah
into the court of the prison, and that they should give him daily a piece of
bread out of the bakers' street, until all the bread in the city were spent. Thus
Jeremiah remained in the court of the prison.

Jeremiah Is Thrown into a Dungeon

38 Then Shephatiah the son of Mattan, and Gedaliah the son of Pashur, and Jucal the son of Shelemiah, and Pashur the son of Malchiah, heard the words that Jeremiah had spoken unto all the people, saying,

2 Thus saith the LORD, He that remaineth in this city shall die by the sword, by the famine, and by the pestilence: but he that goeth forth to the Chaldeans shall live; for he shall have his life for a prey, and shall live.

3 Thus saith the LORD, This city shall surely be given into the hand of the king of Babylon's army, which shall take it.

4 Therefore the princes said unto the king, We beseech thee, let this man be put to death: for thus he weakeneth the hands of the men of war that remain in this city, and the hands of all the people, in speaking such words unto them: for this man seeketh not the welfare of this people, but the hurt.

5 Then Zedekiah the king said, Behold, he *is* in your hand: for the king *is* not *he that* can do *any* thing against you.

6 Then took they Jeremiah, and cast him into the dungeon of Malchiah the son of Hammelech, that *was* in the court of the prison: and they let down Jeremiah with cords. And in the dungeon *there was* no water, but mire: so Jeremiah sunk in the mire.

7 Now when Ebedmelech the Ethiopian, one of the eunuchs which was in the king's house, heard that they had put Jeremiah in the dungeon; the king then sitting in the gate of Benjamin;

8 Ebedmelech went forth out of the king's house, and spake to the king, saying,

9 My lord the king, these men have done evil in all that they have done to Jeremiah the prophet, whom they have cast into the dungeon; and he is like to die for hunger in the place where he is: for *there is* no more bread in the city.

10 Then the king commanded Ebed-melech the Ethiopian, saying, Take from hence thirty men with thee, and take up Jeremiah the prophet out of the dungeon, before he die.

11 So Ebed-melech took the men with him, and went into the house of the king under the treasury, and took thence old cast clouts and old rotten rags, and let them down by cords into the dungeon to Jeremiah.

12 And Ebed-melech the Ethiopian said unto Jeremiah, Put now *these* old cast clouts and rotten rags under thine armholes under the cords. And Jeremiah did so.

13 So they drew up Jeremiah with cords, and took him up out of the dungeon: and Jeremiah remained in the court of the prison.

14 Then Zedekiah the king sent, and took Jeremiah the prophet unto him into the third entry that *is* in the house of the LORD: and the king said unto Jeremiah, I will ask thee a thing; hide nothing from me.

15 Then Jeremiah said unto Zedekiah, If I declare *it* unto thee, wilt thou not surely put me to death? and if I give thee counsel, wilt thou not hearken unto me?

16 So Zedekiah the king sware secretly unto Jeremiah, saying, *As* the LORD liveth, that made us this soul, I will not put thee to death, neither will I give thee into the hand of these men that seek thy life.

17 Then said Jeremiah unto Zedekiah, Thus saith the LORD, the God of hosts, the God of Israel; If thou wilt assuredly go forth unto the king of Babylon's princes, then thy soul shall live, and this city shall not be burned with fire; and thou shalt live, and thine house:

18 But if thou wilt not go forth to the king of Babylon's princes, then shall this city be given into the hand of the Chaldeans, and they shall burn it with fire, and thou shalt not escape out of their hand.

19 And Zedekiah the king said unto Jeremiah, I am afraid of the Jews that are
fallen to the Chaldeans, lest they deliver me into their hand, and they mock
me.
20 But Jeremiah said, They shall not deliver *thee*. Obey, I beseech thee, the
voice of the LORD, which I speak unto thee: so it shall be well unto thee, and
thy soul shall live.
21 But if thou refuse to go forth, this *is* the word that the LORD hath shewed
me:
22 And, behold, all the women that are left in the king of Judah's house *shall
be* brought forth to the king of Babylon's princes, and those *women* shall say,
Thy friends have set thee on, and have prevailed against thee: thy feet are sunk
in the mire, *and* they are turned away back.
23 So they shall bring out all thy wives and thy children to the Chaldeans:
and thou shalt not escape out of their hand, but shalt be taken by the hand of
the king of Babylon: and thou shalt cause this city to be burned with fire.

Jeremiah and Zedekiah Make an Agreement

24 Then said Zedekiah unto Jeremiah, Let no man know of these words, and
thou shalt not die.
25 But if the princes hear that I have talked with thee, and they come unto
thee, and say unto thee, Declare unto us now what thou hast said unto the
king, hide it not from us, and we will not put thee to death; also what the king
said unto thee:
26 Then thou shalt say unto them, I presented my supplication before the
king, that he would not cause me to return to Jonathan's house, to die there.
27 Then came all the princes unto Jeremiah, and asked him: and he told them
according to all these words that the king had commanded. So they left off
speaking with him; for the matter was not perceived.
28 So Jeremiah abode in the court of the prison until the day that Jerusalem
was taken: and he was *there* when Jerusalem was taken.

Jerusalem Is Captured

39 In the ninth year of Zedekiah king of Judah, in the tenth month, came
Nebuchadrezzar king of Babylon and all his army against Jerusalem,
and they besieged it.
2 *And* in the eleventh year of Zedekiah, in the fourth month, the ninth *day*
of the month, the city was broken up.
3 And all the princes of the king of Babylon came in, and sat in the middle
gate, *even* Nergal-sharezer, Samgar-nebo, Sarsechim, Rab-saris, Nergal-
sharezer, Rab-mag, with all the residue of the princes of the king of Babylon.
4 And it came to pass, *that* when Zedekiah the king of Judah saw them, and
all the men of war, then they fled, and went forth out of the city by night, by
the way of the king's garden, by the gate betwixt the two walls: and he went
out the way of the plain.
5 But the Chaldeans' army pursued after them, and overtook Zedekiah in
the plains of Jericho: and when they had taken him, they brought him up to
Nebuchadnezzar king of Babylon to Riblah in the land of Hamath, where he
gave judgment upon him.
6 Then the king of Babylon slew the sons of Zedekiah in Riblah before his
eyes: also the king of Babylon slew all the nobles of Judah.
7 Moreover he put out Zedekiah's eyes, and bound him with chains, to carry
him to Babylon.
8 And the Chaldeans burned the king's house, and the houses of the people,
with fire, and brake down the walls of Jerusalem.
9 Then Nebuzar-adan the captain of the guard carried away captive into
Babylon the remnant of the people that remained in the city, and those that
fell away, that fell to him, with the rest of the people that remained.

10 But Nebuzar-adan the captain of the guard left of the poor of the people, which had nothing, in the land of Judah, and gave them vineyards and fields at the same time.

Nebuchadrezzar Commands Good Treatment for Jeremiah

11 Now Nebuchadrezzar king of Babylon gave charge concerning Jeremiah to Nebuzar-adan the captain of the guard, saying,

12 Take him, and look well to him, and do him no harm; but do unto him even as he shall say unto thee.

13 So Nebuzar-adan the captain of the guard sent, and Nebushasban, Rab-saris, and Nergal-sharezer, Rab-mag, and all the king of Babylon's princes;

14 Even they sent, and took Jeremiah out of the court of the prison, and committed him unto Gedaliah the son of Ahikam the son of Shaphan, that he should carry him home: so he dwelt among the people.

15 Now the word of the LORD came unto Jeremiah, while he was shut up in the court of the prison, saying,

16 Go and speak to Ebedmelech the Ethiopian, saying, Thus saith the LORD of hosts, the God of Israel; Behold, I will bring my words upon this city for evil, and not for good; and they shall be *accomplished* in that day before thee.

17 But I will deliver thee in that day, saith the LORD: and thou shalt not be given into the hand of the men of whom thou *art* afraid.

18 For I will surely deliver thee, and thou shalt not fall by the sword, but thy life shall be for a prey unto thee: because thou hast put thy trust in me, saith the LORD.

Jeremiah Is Freed

40 The word that came to Jeremiah from the LORD, after that Nebuzar-adan the captain of the guard had let him go from Ramah, when he had taken him being bound in chains among all that were carried away captive of Jerusalem and Judah, which were carried away captive unto Babylon.

2 And the captain of the guard took Jeremiah, and said unto him, The LORD thy God hath pronounced this evil upon this place.

3 Now the LORD hath brought *it*, and done according as he hath said: because ye have sinned against the LORD, and have not obeyed his voice, therefore this thing is come upon you.

4 And now, behold, I loose thee this day from the chains which *were* upon thine hand. If it seem good unto thee to come with me into Babylon, come; and I will look well unto thee: but if it seem ill unto thee to come with me into Babylon, forbear: behold, all the land *is* before thee: whither it seemeth good and convenient for thee to go, thither go.

5 Now while he was not yet gone back, *he said*, Go back also to Gedaliah the son of Ahikam the son of Shaphan, whom the king of Babylon hath made governor over the cities of Judah, and dwell with him among the people: or go wheresoever it seemeth convenient unto thee to go. So the captain of the guard gave him victuals and a reward, and let him go.

6 Then went Jeremiah unto Gedaliah the son of Ahikam to Mizpah; and dwelt with him among the people that were left in the land.

The Dispersed Jews Rally around Gedaliah

7 Now when all the captains of the forces which *were* in the fields, *even* they and their men, heard that the king of Babylon had made Gedaliah the son of Ahikam governor in the land, and had committed unto him men, and women, and children, and of the poor of the land, of them that were not carried away captive to Babylon;

8 Then they came to Gedaliah to Mizpah, even Ishmael the son of Nethaniah, and Johanan and Jonathan the sons of Kareah, and Seraiah the son of Tanhumeth, and the sons of Ephai the Netophathite, and Jezaniah the son of a Maachathite, they and their men.

9 And Gedaliah the son of Ahikam the son of Shaphan sware unto them and
to their men, saying, Fear not to serve the Chaldeans: dwell in the land, and
serve the king of Babylon, and it shall be well with you.
10 As for me, behold, I will dwell at Mizpah to serve the Chaldeans, which
will come unto us: but ye, gather ye wine, and summer fruits, and oil, and put
them in your vessels, and dwell in your cities that ye have taken.
11 Likewise when all the Jews that *were* in Moab, and among the Ammonites,
and in Edom, and that *were* in all the countries, heard that the king of Babylon
had left a remnant of Judah, and that he had set over them Gedaliah the son
of Ahikam the son of Shaphan;
12 Even all the Jews returned out of all places whither they were driven, and
came to the land of Judah, to Gedaliah, unto Mizpah, and gathered wine and
summer fruits very much.
13 Moreover Johanan the son of Kareah, and all the captains of the forces
that *were* in the fields, came to Gedaliah to Mizpah,
14 And said unto him, Dost thou certainly know that Baalis the king of the
Ammonites hath sent Ishmael the son of Nethaniah to slay thee? But Gedaliah
the son of Ahikam believed them not.
15 Then Johanan the son of Kareah spake to Gedaliah in Mizpah secretly,
saying, Let me go, I pray thee, and I will slay Ishmael the son of Nethaniah,
and no man shall know *it*: wherefore should he slay thee, that all the Jews
which are gathered unto thee should be scattered, and the remnant in Judah
perish?
16 But Gedaliah the son of Ahikam said unto Johanan the son of Kareah,
Thou shalt not do this thing: for thou speakest falsely of Ishmael.

Ishamel Slays Gedaliah

41 Now it came to pass in the seventh month, *that* Ishmael the son of
Nethaniah the son of Elishama, of the seed royal, and the princes of
the king, even ten men with him, came unto Gedaliah the son of Ahikam to
Mizpah; and there they did eat bread together in Mizpah.
2 Then arose Ishmael the son of Nethaniah, and the ten men that were with
him, and smote Gedaliah the son of Ahikam the son of Shaphan with the
sword, and slew him, whom the king of Babylon had made governor over the
land.
3 Ishmael also slew all the Jews that were with him, *even* with Gedaliah, at
Mizpah, and the Chaldeans that were found there, *and* the men of war.
4 And it came to pass the second day after he had slain Gedaliah, and no man
knew *it*,
5 That there came certain from Shechem, from Shiloh, and from Samaria,
even fourscore men, having their beards shaven, and their clothes rent, and
having cut themselves, with offerings and incense in their hand, to bring *them*
to the house of the LORD.
6 And Ishmael the son of Nethaniah went forth from Mizpah to meet them,
weeping all along as he went: and it came to pass, as he met them, he said unto
them, Come to Gedaliah the son of Ahikam.
7 And it was *so*, when they came into the midst of the city, that Ishmael the
son of Nethaniah slew them, *and cast them* into the midst of the pit, he, and
the men that *were* with him.
8 But ten men were found among them that said unto Ishmael, Slay us not:
for we have treasures in the field, of wheat, and of barley, and of oil, and of
honey. So he forbare, and slew them not among their brethren.
9 Now the pit wherein Ishmael had cast all the dead bodies of the men, whom
he had slain because of Gedaliah, *was* it which Asa the king had made for fear
of Baasha king of Israel: *and* Ishmael the son of Nethaniah filled it with *them
that were* slain.

10 Then Ishmael carried away captive all the residue of the people that *were*
in Mizpah, *even* the king's daughters, and all the people that remained in
Mizpah, whom Nebuzar-adan the captain of the guard had committed to
Gedaliah the son of Ahikam: and Ishmael the son of Nethaniah carried them
away captive, and departed to go over to the Ammonites.

Plans to Flee into Egypt

11 But when Johanan the son of Kareah, and all the captains of the forces
that *were* with him, heard of all the evil that Ishmael the son of Nethaniah
had done,
12 Then they took all the men, and went to fight with Ishmael the son of
Nethaniah, and found him by the great waters that *are* in Gibeon.
13 Now it came to pass, *that* when all the people which *were* with Ishmael
saw Johanan the son of Kareah, and all the captains of the forces that *were*
with him, then they were glad.
14 So all the people that Ishmael had carried away captive from Mizpah cast
about and returned, and went unto Johanan the son of Kareah.
15 But Ishmael the son of Nethaniah escaped from Johanan with eight men,
and went to the Ammonites.
16 Then took Johanan the son of Kareah, and all the captains of the forces
that *were* with him, all the remnant of the people whom he had recovered
from Ishmael the son of Nethaniah, from Mizpah, after *that* he had slain
Gedaliah the son of Ahikam, *even* mighty men of war, and the women, and
the children, and the eunuchs, whom he had brought again from Gibeon:
17 And they departed, and dwelt in the habitation of Chimham, which is by
Bethlehem, to go to enter into Egypt,
18 Because of the Chaldeans: for they were afraid of them, because Ishmael
the son of Nethaniah had slain Gedaliah the son of Ahikam, whom the king
of Babylon made governor in the land.

Jeremiah Warns the People Not to Go to Egypt

42 Then all the captains of the forces, and Johanan the son of Kareah, and
Jezaniah the son of Hoshaiah, and all the people from the least even
unto the greatest, came near,
2 And said unto Jeremiah the prophet, Let, we beseech thee, our supplication
be accepted before thee, and pray for us unto the LORD thy God, *even* for all
this remnant; (for we are left *but* a few of many, as thine eyes do behold us:)
3 That the LORD thy God may shew us the way wherein we may walk, and the
thing that we may do.
4 Then Jeremiah the prophet said unto them, I have heard *you*; behold, I will
pray unto the LORD your God according to your words; and it shall come to
pass, *that* whatsoever thing the LORD shall answer you, I will declare *it* unto
you; I will keep nothing back from you.
5 Then they said to Jeremiah, The LORD be a true and faithful witness between
us, if we do not even according to all things for the which the LORD thy God
shall send thee to us.
6 Whether *it be* good, or whether *it be* evil, we will obey the voice of the LORD
our God, to whom we send thee; that it may be well with us, when we obey the
voice of the LORD our God.
7 And it came to pass after ten days, that the word of the LORD came unto
Jeremiah.
8 Then called he Johanan the son of Kareah, and all the captains of the forc-
es which *were* with him, and all the people from the least even to the greatest,
9 And said unto them, Thus saith the LORD, the God of Israel, unto whom ye
sent me to present your supplication before him;

10 If ye will still abide in this land, then will I build you, and not pull *you*
down, and I will plant you, and not pluck *you* up: for I repent me of the evil
that I have done unto you.
11 Be not afraid of the king of Babylon, of whom ye are afraid; be not afraid
of him, saith the LORD: for I *am* with you to save you, and to deliver you from
his hand.
12 And I will shew mercies unto you, that he may have mercy upon you, and
cause you to return to your own land.
13 But if ye say, We will not dwell in this land, neither obey the voice of the
LORD your God,
14 Saying, No; but we will go into the land of Egypt, where we shall see no
war, nor hear the sound of the trumpet, nor have hunger of bread; and there
will we dwell:
15 And now therefore hear the word of the LORD, ye remnant of Judah; Thus
saith the LORD of hosts, the God of Israel; If ye wholly set your faces to enter
into Egypt, and go to sojourn there;
16 Then it shall come to pass, *that* the sword, which ye feared, shall overtake
you there in the land of Egypt, and the famine, whereof ye were afraid, shall
follow close after you there in Egypt; and there ye shall die.
17 So shall it be with all the men that set their faces to go into Egypt to sojourn
there; they shall die by the sword, by the famine, and by the pestilence: and
none of them shall remain or escape from the evil that I will bring upon them.
18 For thus saith the LORD of hosts, the God of Israel; As mine anger and my
fury hath been poured forth upon the inhabitants of Jerusalem; so shall my
fury be poured forth upon you, when ye shall enter into Egypt: and ye shall be
an execration, and an astonishment, and a curse, and a reproach; and ye shall
see this place no more.
19 The LORD hath said concerning you, O ye remnant of Judah; Go ye not into
Egypt: know certainly that I have admonished you this day.
20 For ye dissembled in your hearts, when ye sent me unto the LORD your
God, saying, Pray for us unto the LORD our God; and according unto all that
the LORD our God shall say, so declare unto us, and we will do *it*.
21 And *now* I have this day declared *it* to you; but ye have not obeyed the voice
of the LORD your God, nor any *thing* for the which he hath sent me unto you.
22 Now therefore know certainly that ye shall die by the sword, by the famine,
and by the pestilence, in the place whither ye desire to go *and* to sojourn.

Jeremiah Is Forced to Go to Egypt

43 And it came to pass, *that* when Jeremiah had made an end of speaking
unto all the people all the words of the LORD their God, for which the
LORD their God had sent him to them, *even* all these words,
2 Then spake Azariah the son of Hoshaiah, and Johanan the son of Kareah,
and all the proud men, saying unto Jeremiah, Thou speakest falsely: the LORD
our God hath not sent thee to say, Go not into Egypt to sojourn there:
3 But Baruch the son of Neriah setteth thee on against us, for to deliver us
into the hand of the Chaldeans, that they might put us to death, and carry us
away captives into Babylon.
4 So Johanan the son of Kareah, and all the captains of the forces, and all the
people, obeyed not the voice of the LORD, to dwell in the land of Judah.
5 But Johanan the son of Kareah, and all the captains of the forces, took all
the remnant of Judah, that were returned from all nations, whither they had
been driven, to dwell in the land of Judah;
6 *Even* men, and women, and children, and the king's daughters, and every
person that Nebuzar-adan the captain of the guard had left with Gedaliah the
son of Ahikam the son of Shaphan, and Jeremiah the prophet, and Baruch the
son of Neriah.

7 So they came into the land of Egypt: for they obeyed not the voice of the
LORD: thus came they *even* to Tahpanhes.

Jeremiah Prophesies the Conquest of Egypt by Babylon

8 Then came the word of the LORD unto Jeremiah in Tahpanhes, saying,
9 Take great stones in thine hand, and hide them in the clay in the brickkiln,
which *is* at the entry of Pharaoh's house in Tahpanhes, in the sight of the men
of Judah;
10 And say unto them, Thus saith the LORD of hosts, the God of Israel; Behold,
I will send and take Nebuchadrezzar the king of Babylon, my servant, and will
set his throne upon these stones that I have hid; and he shall spread his royal
pavilion over them.
11 And when he cometh, he shall smite the land of Egypt, *and deliver* such
as are for death to death; and such *as are* for captivity to captivity; and such
as are for the sword to the sword.
12 And I will kindle a fire in the houses of the gods of Egypt; and he shall
burn them, and carry them away captives: and he shall array himself with the
land of Egypt, as a shepherd putteth on his garment; and he shall go forth from
thence in peace.
13 He shall break also the images of Bethshemesh, that *is* in the land of Egypt;
and the houses of the gods of the Egyptians shall he burn with fire.

Punishment for Idolatry

44 The word that came to Jeremiah concerning all the Jews which dwell
in the land of Egypt, which dwell at Migdol, and at Tahpanhes, and at
Noph, and in the country of Pathros, saying,
2 Thus saith the LORD of hosts, the God of Israel; Ye have seen all the evil that
I have brought upon Jerusalem, and upon all the cities of Judah; and, behold,
this day they *are* a desolation, and no man dwelleth therein,
3 Because of their wickedness which they have committed to provoke me to
anger, in that they went to burn incense, *and* to serve other gods, whom they
knew not, *neither* they, ye, nor your fathers.
4 Howbeit I sent unto you all my servants the prophets, rising early and
sending *them*, saying, Oh, do not this abominable thing that I hate.
5 But they hearkened not, nor inclined their ear to turn from their wicked-
ness, to burn no incense unto other gods.
6 Wherefore my fury and mine anger was poured forth, and was kindled in
the cities of Judah and in the streets of Jerusalem; and they are wasted *and*
desolate, as at this day.
7 Therefore now thus saith the LORD, the God of hosts, the God of Israel;
Wherefore commit ye *this* great evil against your souls, to cut off from you
man and woman, child and suckling, out of Judah, to leave you none to remain;
8 In that ye provoke me unto wrath with the works of your hands, burning
incense unto other gods in the land of Egypt, whither ye be gone to dwell, that
ye might cut yourselves off, and that ye might be a curse and a reproach among
all the nations of the earth?
9 Have ye forgotten the wickedness of your fathers, and the wickedness of
the kings of Judah, and the wickedness of their wives, and your own wicked-
ness, and the wickedness of your wives, which they have committed in the
land of Judah, and in the streets of Jerusalem?
10 They are not humbled *even* unto this day, neither have they feared, nor
walked in my law, nor in my statutes, that I set before you and before your
fathers.
11 Therefore thus saith the LORD of hosts, the God of Israel; Behold, I will set
my face against you for evil, and to cut off all Judah.
12 And I will take the remnant of Judah, that have set their faces to go into
the land of Egypt to sojourn there, and they shall all be consumed, *and* fall in

the land of Egypt; they shall *even* be consumed by the sword *and* by the famine:
they shall die, from the least even unto the greatest, by the sword and by the
famine: and they shall be an execration, *and* an astonishment, and a curse,
and a reproach.
13 For I will punish them that dwell in the land of Egypt, as I have punished
Jerusalem, by the sword, by the famine, and by the pestilence:
14 So that none of the remnant of Judah, which are gone into the land of
Egypt to sojourn there, shall escape or remain, that they should return into
the land of Judah, to the which they have a desire to return to dwell there: for
none shall return but such as shall escape.

The Obstinacy of the Jews

15 Then all the men which knew that their wives had burned incense unto
other gods, and all the women that stood by, a great multitude, even all the
people that dwelt in the land of Egypt, in Pathros, answered Jeremiah, saying,
16 *As for* the word that thou hast spoken unto us in the name of the LORD,
we will not hearken unto thee.
17 But we will certainly do whatsoever thing goeth forth out of our own
mouth, to burn incense unto the queen of heaven, and to pour out drink
offerings unto her, as we have done, we, and our fathers, our kings, and our
princes, in the cities of Judah, and in the streets of Jerusalem: for *then* had we
plenty of victuals, and were well, and saw no evil.
18 But since we left off to burn incense to the queen of heaven, and to pour
out drink offerings unto her, we have wanted all *things*, and have been con-
sumed by the sword and by the famine.
19 And when we burned incense to the queen of heaven, and poured out
drink offerings unto her, did we make her cakes to worship her, and pour out
drink offerings unto her, without our men?

Jeremiah Threatens Destruction

20 Then Jeremiah said unto all the people, to the men, and to the women,
and to all the people which had given him *that* answer, saying,
21 The incense that ye burned in the cities of Judah, and in the streets of
Jerusalem, ye, and your fathers, your kings, and your princes, and the people
of the land, did not the LORD remember them, and came it *not* into his mind?
22 So that the LORD could no longer bear, because of the evil of your doings,
and because of the abominations which ye have committed; therefore is your
land a desolation, and an astonishment, and a curse, without an inhabitant,
as at this day.
23 Because ye have burned incense, and because ye have sinned against the
LORD, and have not obeyed the voice of the LORD, nor walked in his law, nor in
his statutes, nor in his testimonies; therefore this evil is happened unto you,
as at this day.
24 Moreover Jeremiah said unto all the people, and to all the women, Hear
the word of the LORD, all Judah that *are* in the land of Egypt:
25 Thus saith the LORD of hosts, the God of Israel, saying; Ye and your wives
have both spoken with your mouths, and fulfilled with your hand, saying, We
will surely perform our vows that we have vowed, to burn incense to the queen
of heaven, and to pour out drink offerings unto her: ye will surely accomplish
your vows, and surely perform your vows.
26 Therefore hear ye the word of the LORD, all Judah that dwell in the land
of Egypt; Behold, I have sworn by my great name, saith the LORD, that my name
shall no more be named in the mouth of any man of Judah in all the land of
Egypt, saying, The Lord GOD liveth.
27 Behold, I will watch over them for evil, and not for good: and all the men
of Judah that *are* in the land of Egypt shall be consumed by the sword and by
the famine, until there be an end of them.

28 Yet a small number that escape the sword shall return out of the land of
Egypt into the land of Judah, and all the remnant of Judah, that are gone into
the land of Egypt to sojourn there, shall know whose words shall stand, mine,
or theirs.
29 And this *shall be* a sign unto you, saith the LORD, that I will punish you in
this place, that ye may know that my words shall surely stand against you for
evil:
30 Thus saith the LORD; Behold, I will give Pharaoh-hophra king of Egypt into
the hand of his enemies, and into the hand of them that seek his life; as I gave
Zedekiah king of Judah into the hand of Nebuchadrezzar king of Babylon, his
enemy, and that sought his life.

The Lord's Promise to Baruch

45 The word that Jeremiah the prophet spake unto Baruch the son of
Neriah, when he had written these words in a book at the mouth of
Jeremiah, in the fourth year of Jehoiakim the son of Josiah king of Judah,
saying,
2 Thus saith the LORD, the God of Israel, unto thee, O Baruch;
3 Thou didst say, Woe is me now! for the LORD hath added grief to my sorrow;
I fainted in my sighing, and I find no rest.
4 Thus shalt thou say unto him, The LORD saith thus; Behold, *that* which I
have built will I break down, and that which I have planted I will pluck up,
even this whole land.
5 And seekest thou great things for thyself? seek *them* not: for, behold, I will
bring evil upon all flesh, saith the LORD: but thy life will I give unto thee for a
prey in all places whither thou goest.

A Prophecy against Egypt

46 The word of the LORD which came to Jeremiah the prophet against the
Gentiles;
2 Against Egypt, against the army of Pharaoh-necho king of Egypt, which
was by the river Euphrates in Carchemish, which Nebuchadrezzar king of
Babylon smote in the fourth year of Jehoiakim the son of Josiah king of Judah.
3 Order ye the buckler and shield, and draw near to battle.
4 Harness the horses; and get up, ye horsemen, and stand forth with *your*
helmets; furbish the spears, *and* put on the brigandines.
5 Wherefore have I seen them dismayed *and* turned away back? and their
mighty ones are beaten down, and are fled apace, and look not back: *for* fear
was round about, saith the LORD.
6 Let not the swift flee away, nor the mighty man escape; they shall stumble,
and fall toward the north by the river Euphrates.
7 Who *is* this *that* cometh up as a flood, whose waters are moved as the
rivers?
8 Egypt riseth up like a flood, and *his* waters are moved like the rivers; and
he saith, I will go up, *and* will cover the earth; I will destroy the city and the
inhabitants thereof.
9 Come up, ye horses; and rage, ye chariots; and let the mighty men come
forth; the Ethiopians and the Libyans, that handle the shield; and the Lydians,
that handle *and* bend the bow.
10 For this *is* the day of the Lord GOD of hosts, a day of vengeance, that he
may avenge him of his adversaries: and the sword shall devour, and it shall be
satiate and made drunk with their blood: for the Lord GOD of hosts hath a
sacrifice in the north country by the river Euphrates.
11 Go up into Gilead, and take balm, O virgin, the daughter of Egypt: in vain
shalt thou use many medicines; *for* thou shalt not be cured.

12 The nations have heard of thy shame, and thy cry hath filled the land: for the mighty man hath stumbled against the mighty, *and* they are fallen both together.

13 The word that the LORD spake to Jeremiah the prophet, how Nebuchadrezzar king of Babylon should come *and* smite the land of Egypt.

14 Declare ye in Egypt, and publish in Migdol, and publish in Noph and in Tahpanhes: say ye, Stand fast, and prepare thee; for the sword shall devour round about thee.

15 Why are thy valiant *men* swept away? they stood not, because the LORD did drive them.

16 He made many to fall, yea, one fell upon another: and they said, Arise, and let us go again to our own people, and to the land of our nativity, from the oppressing sword.

17 They did cry there, Pharaoh king of Egypt *is but* a noise; he hath passed the time appointed.

18 *As* I live, saith the King, whose name *is* the LORD of hosts, Surely as Tabor *is* among the mountains, and as Carmel by the sea, *so* shall he come.

19 O thou daughter dwelling in Egypt, furnish thyself to go into captivity: for Noph shall be waste and desolate without an inhabitant.

20 Egypt *is like* a very fair heifer, *but* destruction cometh; it cometh out of the north.

21 Also her hired men *are* in the midst of her like fatted bullocks; for they also are turned back, *and* are fled away together: they did not stand, because the day of their calamity was come upon them, *and* the time of their visitation.

22 The voice thereof shall go like a serpent; for they shall march with an army, and come against her with axes, as hewers of wood.

23 They shall cut down her forest, saith the LORD, though it cannot be searched; because they are more than the grasshoppers, and *are* innumerable.

24 The daughter of Egypt shall be confounded; she shall be delivered into the hand of the people of the north.

25 The LORD of hosts, the God of Israel, saith; Behold, I will punish the multitude of No, and Pharaoh, and Egypt, with their gods, and their kings; even Pharaoh, and *all* them that trust in him:

26 And I will deliver them into the hand of those that seek their lives, and into the hand of Nebuchadrezzar king of Babylon, and into the hand of his servants: and afterward it shall be inhabited, as in the days of old, saith the LORD.

27 But fear not thou, O my servant Jacob, and be not dismayed, O Israel: for, behold, I will save thee from afar off, and thy seed from the land of their captivity; and Jacob shall return, and be in rest and at ease, and none shall make *him* afraid.

28 Fear thou not, O Jacob my servant, saith the LORD: for I *am* with thee; for I will make a full end of all the nations whither I have driven thee: but I will not make a full end of thee, but correct thee in measure; yet will I not leave thee wholly unpunished.

A Prophecy against Philistia

47 The word of the LORD that came to Jeremiah the prophet against the Philistines, before that Pharaoh smote Gaza.

2 Thus saith the LORD; Behold, waters rise up out of the north, and shall be an overflowing flood, and shall overflow the land, and all that is therein; the city, and them that dwell therein: then the men shall cry, and all the inhabitants of the land shall howl.

3 At the noise of the stamping of the hoofs of his strong *horses*, at the rushing of his chariots, *and at* the rumbling of his wheels, the fathers shall not look back to *their* children for feebleness of hands;

4 Because of the day that cometh to spoil all the Philistines, *and* to cut off
from Tyrus and Zidon every helper that remaineth: for the LORD will spoil the
Philistines, the remnant of the country of Caphtor.
5 Baldness is come upon Gaza; Ashkelon is cut off *with* the remnant of their
valley: how long wilt thou cut thyself?
6 O thou sword of the LORD, how long *will it be* ere thou be quiet? put up
thyself into thy scabbard, rest, and be still.
7 How can it be quiet, seeing the LORD hath given it a charge against Ashkelon,
and against the sea shore? there hath he appointed it.

A Prophecy against Moab

48 Against Moab thus saith the LORD of hosts, the God of Israel; Woe unto
Nebo! for it is spoiled: Kiriathaim is confounded *and* taken: Misgab is
confounded and dismayed.
2 *There shall be* no more praise of Moab: in Heshbon they have devised evil
against it; come, and let us cut it off from *being* a nation. Also thou shalt be
cut down, O Madmen; the sword shall pursue thee.
3 A voice of crying *shall be* from Horonaim, spoiling and great destruction.
4 Moab is destroyed; her little ones have caused a cry to be heard.
5 For in the going up of Luhith continual weeping shall go up; for in the
going down of Horonaim the enemies have heard a cry of destruction.
6 Flee, save your lives, and be like the heath in the wilderness.
7 For because thou hast trusted in thy works and in thy treasures, thou shalt
also be taken: and Chemosh shall go forth into captivity *with* his priests and
his princes together.
8 And the spoiler shall come upon every city, and no city shall escape: the
valley also shall perish, and the plain shall be destroyed, as the LORD hath
spoken.
9 Give wings unto Moab, that it may flee and get away: for the cities thereof
shall be desolate, without any to dwell therein.
10 Cursed *be* he that doeth the work of the LORD deceitfully, and cursed *be*
he that keepeth back his sword from blood.
11 Moab hath been at ease from his youth, and he hath settled on his lees,
and hath not been emptied from vessel to vessel, neither hath he gone into
captivity: therefore his taste remained in him, and his scent is not changed.
12 Therefore, behold, the days come, saith the LORD, that I will send unto him
wanderers, that shall cause him to wander, and shall empty his vessels, and
break their bottles.
13 And Moab shall be ashamed of Chemosh, as the house of Israel was
ashamed of Beth-el their confidence.
14 How say ye, We *are* mighty and strong men for the war?
15 Moab is spoiled, and gone up *out of* her cities, and his chosen young men
are gone down to the slaughter, saith the King, whose name *is* the LORD of
hosts.
16 The calamity of Moab *is* near to come, and his affliction hasteth fast.
17 All ye that are about him, bemoan him; and all ye that know his name, say,
How is the strong staff broken, *and* the beautiful rod!
18 Thou daughter that dost inhabit Dibon, come down from *thy* glory, and
sit in thirst; for the spoiler of Moab shall come upon thee, *and* he shall destroy
thy strong holds.
19 O inhabitant of Aroer, stand by the way, and espy; ask him that fleeth, and
her that escapeth, *and* say, What is done?
20 Moab is confounded; for it is broken down: howl and cry; tell ye it in
Arnon, that Moab is spoiled,
21 And judgment is come upon the plain country; upon Holon, and upon
Jahazah, and upon Mephaath,

22 And upon Dibon, and upon Nebo, and upon Beth-diblathaim,
23 And upon Kiriathaim, and upon Bethgamul, and upon Beth-meon,
24 And upon Kerioth, and upon Bozrah, and upon all the cities of the land
of Moab, far or near.
25 The horn of Moab is cut off, and his arm is broken, saith the LORD.
26 Make ye him drunken: for he magnified *himself* against the LORD: Moab
also shall wallow in his vomit, and he also shall be in derision.
27 For was not Israel a derision unto thee? was he found among thieves? for
since thou spakest of him, thou skippedst for joy.
28 O ye that dwell in Moab, leave the cities, and dwell in the rock, and be like
the dove *that* maketh her nest in the sides of the hole's mouth.
29 We have heard the pride of Moab, (he is exceeding proud) his loftiness,
and his arrogancy, and his pride, and the haughtiness of his heart.
30 I know his wrath, saith the LORD; but *it shall* not *be* so; his lies shall not so
effect *it*.
31 Therefore will I howl for Moab, and I will cry out for all Moab; *mine heart*
shall mourn for the men of Kir-heres.
32 O vine of Sibmah, I will weep for thee with the weeping of Jazer: thy plants
are gone over the sea, they reach *even* to the sea of Jazer: the spoiler is fallen
upon thy summer fruits and upon thy vintage.
33 And joy and gladness is taken from the plentiful field, and from the land
of Moab; and I have caused wine to fail from the winepresses: none shall tread
with shouting; *their* shouting *shall be* no shouting.
34 From the cry of Heshbon *even* unto Elealeh, *and even* unto Jahaz, have
they uttered their voice, from Zoar *even* unto Horonaim, *as* an heifer of three
years old: for the waters also of Nimrim shall be desolate.
35 Moreover I will cause to cease in Moab, saith the LORD, him that offereth
in the high places, and him that burneth incense to his gods.
36 Therefore mine heart shall sound for Moab like pipes, and mine heart
shall sound like pipes for the men of Kir-heres: because the riches *that* he hath
gotten are perished.
37 For every head *shall be* bald, and every beard clipped: upon all the hands
shall be cuttings, and upon the loins sackcloth.
38 *There shall be* lamentation generally upon all the housetops of Moab, and
in the streets thereof: for I have broken Moab like a vessel wherein *is* no
pleasure, saith the LORD.
39 They shall howl, *saying*, How is it broken down! how hath Moab turned
the back with shame! so shall Moab be a derision and a dismaying to all them
about him.
40 For thus saith the LORD; Behold, he shall fly as an eagle, and shall spread
his wings over Moab.
41 Kerioth is taken, and the strong holds are surprised, and the mighty men's
hearts in Moab at that day shall be as the heart of a woman in her pangs.
42 And Moab shall be destroyed from *being* a people, because he hath mag-
nified *himself* against the LORD.
43 Fear, and the pit, and the snare, *shall be* upon thee, O inhabitant of Moab,
saith the LORD.
44 He that fleeth from the fear shall fall into the pit; and he that getteth up
out of the pit shall be taken in the snare: for I will bring upon it, *even* upon
Moab, the year of their visitation, saith the LORD.
45 They that fled stood under the shadow of Heshbon because of the force:
but a fire shall come forth out of Heshbon, and a flame from the midst of
Sihon, and shall devour the corner of Moab, and the crown of the head of the
tumultuous ones.
46 Woe be unto thee, O Moab! the people of Chemosh perisheth: for thy sons
are taken captives, and thy daughters captives.

47 Yet will I bring again the captivity of Moab in the latter days, saith the
LORD. Thus far *is* the judgment of Moab.

A Prophecy against Ammon

49 Concerning the Ammonites, thus saith the LORD; Hath Israel no sons?
hath he no heir? why *then* doth their king inherit Gad, and his people
dwell in his cities?
2 Therefore, behold, the days come, saith the LORD, that I will cause an alarm
of war to be heard in Rabbah of the Ammonites; and it shall be a desolate heap,
and her daughters shall be burned with fire: then shall Israel be heir unto
them that were his heirs, saith the LORD.
3 Howl, O Heshbon, for Ai is spoiled: cry, ye daughters of Rabbah, gird you
with sackcloth; lament, and run to and fro by the hedges; for their king shall
go into captivity, *and* his priests and his princes together.
4 Wherefore gloriest thou in the valleys, thy flowing valley, O backsliding
daughter? that trusted in her treasures, *saying*, Who shall come unto me?
5 Behold, I will bring a fear upon thee, saith the Lord GOD of hosts, from all
those that be about thee; and ye shall be driven out every man right forth; and
none shall gather up him that wandereth.
6 And afterward I will bring again the captivity of the children of Ammon,
saith the LORD.

A Prophecy against Edom

7 Concerning Edom, thus saith the LORD of hosts; *Is* wisdom no more in
Teman? is counsel perished from the prudent? is their wisdom vanished?
8 Flee ye, turn back, dwell deep, O inhabitants of Dedan; for I will bring the
calamity of Esau upon him, the time *that* I will visit him.
9 If grapegatherers come to thee, would they not leave *some* gleaning grapes?
if thieves by night, they will destroy till they have enough.
10 But I have made Esau bare, I have uncovered his secret places, and he shall
not be able to hide himself: his seed is spoiled, and his brethren, and his neigh-
bours, and he *is* not.
11 Leave thy fatherless children, I will preserve *them* alive; and let thy widows
trust in me.
12 For thus saith the LORD; Behold, they whose judgment *was* not to drink
of the cup have assuredly drunken; and *art* thou he *that* shall altogether go
unpunished? thou shalt not go unpunished, but thou shalt surely drink *of it*.
13 For I have sworn by myself, saith the LORD, that Bozrah shall become a
desolation, a reproach, a waste, and a curse; and all the cities thereof shall be
perpetual wastes.
14 I have heard a rumour from the LORD, and an ambassador is sent unto the
heathen, *saying*, Gather ye together, and come against her, and rise up to the
battle.
15 For, lo, I will make thee small among the heathen, *and* despised among
men.
16 Thy terribleness hath deceived thee, *and* the pride of thine heart, O thou
that dwellest in the clefts of the rock, that holdest the height of the hill: though
thou shouldest make thy nest as high as the eagle, I will bring thee down from
thence, saith the LORD.
17 Also Edom shall be a desolation: every one that goeth by it shall be aston-
ished, and shall hiss at all the plagues thereof.
18 As in the overthrow of Sodom and Gomorrah and the neighbour *cities*
thereof, saith the LORD, no man shall abide there, neither shall a son of man
dwell in it.
19 Behold, he shall come up like a lion from the swelling of Jordan against
the habitation of the strong: but I will suddenly make him run away from her:
and who *is* a chosen *man, that* I may appoint over her? for who *is* like me?

and who will appoint me the time? and who *is* that shepherd that will stand
before me?
20 Therefore hear the counsel of the LORD, that he hath taken against Edom;
and his purposes, that he hath purposed against the inhabitants of Teman:
Surely the least of the flock shall draw them out: surely he shall make their
habitations desolate with them.
21 The earth is moved at the noise of their fall, at the cry the noise thereof
was heard in the Red sea.
22 Behold, he shall come up and fly as the eagle, and spread his wings over
Bozrah: and at that day shall the heart of the mighty men of Edom be as the
heart of a woman in her pangs.

A Prophecy against Damascus

23 Concerning Damascus. Hamath is confounded, and Arpad: for they have
heard evil tidings: they are fainthearted; *there is* sorrow on the sea; it cannot
be quiet.
24 Damascus is waxed feeble, *and* turneth herself to flee, and fear hath seized
on *her*: anguish and sorrows have taken her, as a woman in travail.
25 How is the city of praise not left, the city of my joy!
26 Therefore her young men shall fall in her streets, and all the men of war
shall be cut off in that day, saith the LORD of hosts.
27 And I will kindle a fire in the wall of Damascus, and it shall consume the
palaces of Ben-hadad.

A Prophecy against Kedar and Hazor

28 Concerning Kedar, and concerning the kingdoms of Hazor, which
Nebuchadrezzar king of Babylon shall smite, thus saith the LORD; Arise ye, go
up to Kedar, and spoil the men of the east.
29 Their tents and their flocks shall they take away: they shall take to them-
selves their curtains, and all their vessels, and their camels; and they shall cry
unto them, Fear *is* on every side.
30 Flee, get you far off, dwell deep, O ye inhabitants of Hazor, saith the LORD;
for Nebuchadrezzar king of Babylon hath taken counsel against you, and hath
conceived a purpose against you.
31 Arise, get you up unto the wealthy nation, that dwelleth without care,
saith the LORD, which have neither gates nor bars, *which* dwell alone.
32 And their camels shall be a booty, and the multitude of their cattle a spoil:
and I will scatter into all winds them *that are* in the utmost corners; and I will
bring their calamity from all sides thereof, saith the LORD.
33 And Hazor shall be a dwelling for dragons, *and* a desolation for ever: there
shall no man abide there, nor *any* son of man dwell in it.

A Prophecy against Elam

34 The word of the LORD that came to Jeremiah the prophet against Elam in
the beginning of the reign of Zedekiah king of Judah, saying,
35 Thus saith the LORD of hosts; Behold, I will break the bow of Elam, the
chief of their might.
36 And upon Elam will I bring the four winds from the four quarters of
heaven, and will scatter them toward all those winds; and there shall be no
nation whither the outcasts of Elam shall not come.
37 For I will cause Elam to be dismayed before their enemies, and before
them that seek their life: and I will bring evil upon them, *even* my fierce anger,
saith the LORD; and I will send the sword after them, till I have consumed them:
38 And I will set my throne in Elam, and will destroy from thence the king
and the princes, saith the LORD.
39 But it shall come to pass in the latter days, *that* I will bring again the
captivity of Elam, saith the LORD.

A Prophecy against Babylon

50 The word that the LORD spake against Babylon *and* against the land of
the Chaldeans by Jeremiah the prophet.
2 Declare ye among the nations, and publish, and set up a standard; publish,
and conceal not: say, Babylon is taken, Bel is confounded, Merodach is broken
in pieces; her idols are confounded, her images are broken in pieces.
3 For out of the north there cometh up a nation against her, which shall make
her land desolate, and none shall dwell therein: they shall remove, they shall
depart, both man and beast.
4 In those days, and in that time, saith the LORD, the children of Israel shall
come, they and the children of Judah together, going and weeping: they shall
go, and seek the LORD their God.
5 They shall ask the way to Zion with their faces thitherward, *saying*, Come,
and let us join ourselves to the LORD in a perpetual covenant *that* shall not be
forgotten.
6 My people hath been lost sheep: their shepherds have caused them to go
astray, they have turned them away *on* the mountains: they have gone from
mountain to hill, they have forgotten their restingplace.
7 All that found them have devoured them: and their adversaries said, We
offend not, because they have sinned against the LORD, the habitation of jus-
tice, even the LORD, the hope of their fathers.
8 Remove out of the midst of Babylon, and go forth out of the land of the
Chaldeans, and be as the he goats before the flocks.
9 For, lo, I will raise and cause to come up against Babylon an assembly of
great nations from the north country: and they shall set themselves in array
against her; from thence she shall be taken: their arrows *shall be* as of a mighty
expert man; none shall return in vain.
10 And Chaldea shall be a spoil: all that spoil her shall be satisfied, saith the
LORD.
11 Because ye were glad, because ye rejoiced, O ye destroyers of mine heritage,
because ye are grown fat as the heifer at grass, and bellow as bulls;
12 Your mother shall be sore confounded; she that bare you shall be ashamed:
behold, the hindermost of the nations *shall be* a wilderness, a dry land, and a
desert.
13 Because of the wrath of the LORD it shall not be inhabited, but it shall be
wholly desolate: every one that goeth by Babylon shall be astonished, and hiss
at all her plagues.
14 Put yourselves in array against Babylon round about: all ye that bend the
bow, shoot at her, spare no arrows: for she hath sinned against the LORD.
15 Shout against her round about: she hath given her hand: her foundations
are fallen, her walls are thrown down: for it *is* the vengeance of the LORD: take
vengeance upon her; as she hath done, do unto her.
16 Cut off the sower from Babylon, and him that handleth the sickle in the
time of harvest: for fear of the oppressing sword they shall turn every one to
his people, and they shall flee every one to his own land.
17 Israel *is* a scattered sheep; the lions have driven *him* away: first the king
of Assyria hath devoured him; and last this Nebuchadrezzar king of Babylon
hath broken his bones.
18 Therefore thus saith the LORD of hosts, the God of Israel; Behold, I will
punish the king of Babylon and his land, as I have punished the king of Assyria.
19 And I will bring Israel again to his habitation, and he shall feed on Carmel
and Bashan, and his soul shall be satisfied upon mount Ephraim and Gilead.
20 In those days, and in that time, saith the LORD, the iniquity of Israel shall
be sought for, and *there shall be* none; and the sins of Judah, and they shall
not be found: for I will pardon them whom I reserve.

21 Go up against the land of Merathaim, *even* against it, and against the
inhabitants of Pekod: waste and utterly destroy after them, saith the LORD,
and do according to all that I have commanded thee.
22 A sound of battle *is* in the land, and of great destruction.
23 How is the hammer of the whole earth cut asunder and broken! how is
Babylon become a desolation among the nations!
24 I have laid a snare for thee, and thou art also taken, O Babylon, and thou
wast not aware: thou art found, and also caught, because thou hast striven
against the LORD.
25 The LORD hath opened his armoury, and hath brought forth the weapons
of his indignation: for this *is* the work of the Lord GOD of hosts in the land of
the Chaldeans.
26 Come against her from the utmost border, open her storehouses: cast her
up as heaps, and destroy her utterly: let nothing of her be left.
27 Slay all her bullocks; let them go down to the slaughter: woe unto them!
for their day is come, the time of their visitation.
28 The voice of them that flee and escape out of the land of Babylon, to declare
in Zion the vengeance of the LORD our God, the vengeance of his temple.
29 Call together the archers against Babylon: all ye that bend the bow, camp
against it round about; let none thereof escape: recompense her according to
her work; according to all that she hath done, do unto her: for she hath been
proud against the LORD, against the Holy One of Israel.
30 Therefore shall her young men fall in the streets, and all her men of war
shall be cut off in that day, saith the LORD.
31 Behold, I *am* against thee, *O thou* most proud, saith the Lord GOD of hosts:
for thy day is come, the time *that* I will visit thee.
32 And the most proud shall stumble and fall, and none shall raise him up:
and I will kindle a fire in his cities, and it shall devour all round about him.
33 Thus saith the LORD of hosts; The children of Israel and the children of
Judah *were* oppressed together: and all that took them captives held them fast;
they refused to let them go.
34 Their Redeemer *is* strong; the LORD of hosts *is* his name: he shall through-
ly plead their cause, that he may give rest to the land, and disquiet the inhab-
itants of Babylon.
35 A sword *is* upon the Chaldeans, saith the LORD, and upon the inhabitants
of Babylon, and upon her princes, and upon her wise *men*.
36 A sword *is* upon the liars; and they shall dote: a sword *is* upon her mighty
men; and they shall be dismayed.
37 A sword *is* upon their horses, and upon their chariots, and upon all the
mingled people that *are* in the midst of her; and they shall become as women:
a sword *is* upon her treasures; and they shall be robbed.
38 A drought *is* upon her waters; and they shall be dried up: for it *is* the land
of graven images, and they are mad upon *their* idols.
39 Therefore the wild beasts of the desert with the wild beasts of the islands
shall dwell *there*, and the owls shall dwell therein: and it shall be no more
inhabited for ever; neither shall it be dwelt in from generation to generation.
40 As God overthrew Sodom and Gomorrah and the neighbour *cities* there-
of, saith the LORD; *so* shall no man abide there, neither shall any son of man
dwell therein.
41 Behold, a people shall come from the north, and a great nation, and many
kings shall be raised up from the coasts of the earth.
42 They shall hold the bow and the lance: they *are* cruel, and will not shew
mercy: their voice shall roar like the sea, and they shall ride upon horses, *every
one* put in array, like a man to the battle, against thee, O daughter of Babylon.
43 The king of Babylon hath heard the report of them, and his hands waxed
feeble: anguish took hold of him, *and* pangs as of a woman in travail.

44 Behold, he shall come up like a lion from the swelling of Jordan unto the
habitation of the strong: but I will make them suddenly run away from her:
and who *is* a chosen *man, that* I may appoint over her? for who *is* like me?
and who will appoint me the time? and who *is* that shepherd that will stand
before me?
45 Therefore hear ye the counsel of the LORD, that he hath taken against
Babylon; and his purposes, that he hath purposed against the land of the
Chaldeans: Surely the least of the flock shall draw them out: surely he shall
make *their* habitation desolate with them.
46 At the noise of the taking of Babylon the earth is moved, and the cry is
heard among the nations.

The Severe Judgment of God on Babylon

51 Thus saith the LORD; Behold, I will raise up against Babylon, and against
them that dwell in the midst of them that rise up against me, a destroy-
ing wind;
2 And will send unto Babylon fanners, that shall fan her, and shall empty her
land: for in the day of trouble they shall be against her round about.
3 Against *him that* bendeth let the archer bend his bow, and against *him that*
lifteth himself up in his brigandine: and spare ye not her young men; destroy
ye utterly all her host.
4 Thus the slain shall fall in the land of the Chaldeans, and *they that are*
thrust through in her streets.
5 For Israel *hath* not *been* forsaken, nor Judah of his God, of the LORD of
hosts; though their land was filled with sin against the Holy One of Israel.
6 Flee out of the midst of Babylon, and deliver every man his soul: be not cut
off in her iniquity; for this *is* the time of the LORD's vengeance; he will render
unto her a recompence.
7 Babylon *hath been* a golden cup in the LORD's hand, that made all the earth
drunken: the nations have drunken of her wine; therefore the nations are
mad.
8 Babylon is suddenly fallen and destroyed: howl for her; take balm for her
pain, if so be she may be healed.
9 We would have healed Babylon, but she is not healed: forsake her, and let
us go every one into his own country: for her judgment reacheth unto heaven,
and is lifted up *even* to the skies.
10 The LORD hath brought forth our righteousness: come, and let us declare
in Zion the work of the LORD our God.
11 Make bright the arrows; gather the shields: the LORD hath raised up the
spirit of the kings of the Medes: for his device *is* against Babylon, to destroy
it; because it *is* the vengeance of the LORD, the vengeance of his temple.
12 Set up the standard upon the walls of Babylon, make the watch strong, set
up the watchmen, prepare the ambushes: for the LORD hath both devised and
done that which he spake against the inhabitants of Babylon.
13 O thou that dwellest upon many waters, abundant in treasures, thine end
is come, *and* the measure of thy covetousness.
14 The LORD of hosts hath sworn by himself, *saying*, Surely I will fill thee with
men, as with caterpillers; and they shall lift up a shout against thee.
15 He hath made the earth by his power, he hath established the world by
his wisdom, and hath stretched out the heaven by his understanding.
16 When he uttereth *his* voice, *there is* a multitude of waters in the heavens;
and he causeth the vapours to ascend from the ends of the earth: he maketh
lightnings with rain, and bringeth forth the wind out of his treasures.
17 Every man is brutish by *his* knowledge; every founder is confounded by
the graven image: for his molten image *is* falsehood, and *there is* no breath in
them.

18 They *are* vanity, the work of errors: in the time of their visitation they shall
perish.
19 The portion of Jacob *is* not like them; for he *is* the former of all things:
and *Israel is* the rod of his inheritance: the LORD of hosts *is* his name.
20 Thou *art* my battle axe *and* weapons of war: for with thee will I break in
pieces the nations, and with thee will I destroy kingdoms;
21 And with thee will I break in pieces the horse and his rider; and with thee
will I break in pieces the chariot and his rider;
22 With thee also will I break in pieces man and woman; and with thee will
I break in pieces old and young; and with thee will I break in pieces the young
man and the maid;
23 I will also break in pieces with thee the shepherd and his flock; and with
thee will I break in pieces the husbandman and his yoke of oxen; and with
thee will I break in pieces captains and rulers.
24 And I will render unto Babylon and to all the inhabitants of Chaldea all
their evil that they have done in Zion in your sight, saith the LORD.
25 Behold, I *am* against thee, O destroying mountain, saith the LORD, which
destroyest all the earth: and I will stretch out mine hand upon thee, and roll
thee down from the rocks, and will make thee a burnt mountain.
26 And they shall not take of thee a stone for a corner, nor a stone for foun-
dations; but thou shalt be desolate for ever, saith the LORD.
27 Set ye up a standard in the land, blow the trumpet among the nations,
prepare the nations against her, call together against her the kingdoms of
Ararat, Minni, and Ashchenaz; appoint a captain against her; cause the hors-
es to come up as the rough caterpillers.
28 Prepare against her the nations with the kings of the Medes, the captains
thereof, and all the rulers thereof, and all the land of his dominion.
29 And the land shall tremble and sorrow: for every purpose of the LORD shall
be performed against Babylon, to make the land of Babylon a desolation with-
out an inhabitant.
30 The mighty men of Babylon have forborn to fight, they have remained in
their holds: their might hath failed; they became as women: they have burned
her dwellingplaces; her bars are broken.
31 One post shall run to meet another, and one messenger to meet another,
to shew the king of Babylon that his city is taken at *one* end,
32 And that the passages are stopped, and the reeds they have burned with
fire, and the men of war are affrighted.
33 For thus saith the LORD of hosts, the God of Israel; The daughter of Babylon
is like a threshingfloor, *it is* time to thresh her: yet a little while, and the time
of her harvest shall come.
34 Nebuchadrezzar the king of Babylon hath devoured me, he hath crushed
me, he hath made me an empty vessel, he hath swallowed me up like a dragon,
he hath filled his belly with my delicates, he hath cast me out.
35 The violence done to me and to my flesh *be* upon Babylon, shall the inhab-
itant of Zion say; and my blood upon the inhabitants of Chaldea, shall
Jerusalem say.
36 Therefore thus saith the LORD; Behold, I will plead thy cause, and take
vengeance for thee; and I will dry up her sea, and make her springs dry.
37 And Babylon shall become heaps, a dwellingplace for dragons, an aston-
ishment, and an hissing, without an inhabitant.
38 They shall roar together like lions: they shall yell as lions' whelps.
39 In their heat I will make their feasts, and I will make them drunken, that
they may rejoice, and sleep a perpetual sleep, and not wake, saith the LORD.
40 I will bring them down like lambs to the slaughter, like rams with he goats.
41 How is Sheshach taken! and how is the praise of the whole earth surprised!
how is Babylon become an astonishment among the nations!

42 The sea is come up upon Babylon: she is covered with the multitude of the
waves thereof.
43 Her cities are a desolation, a dry land, and a wilderness, a land wherein
no man dwelleth, neither doth *any* son of man pass thereby.
44 And I will punish Bel in Babylon, and I will bring forth out of his mouth
that which he hath swallowed up: and the nations shall not flow together any
more unto him: yea, the wall of Babylon shall fall.
45 My people, go ye out of the midst of her, and deliver ye every man his soul
from the fierce anger of the LORD.
46 And lest your heart faint, and ye fear for the rumour that shall be heard
in the land; a rumour shall both come *one* year, and after that in *another* year
shall come a rumour, and violence in the land, ruler against ruler.
47 Therefore, behold, the days come, that I will do judgment upon the grav-
en images of Babylon: and her whole land shall be confounded, and all her
slain shall fall in the midst of her.
48 Then the heaven and the earth, and all that *is* therein, shall sing for
Babylon: for the spoilers shall come unto her from the north, saith the LORD.
49 As Babylon *hath caused* the slain of Israel to fall, so at Babylon shall fall
the slain of all the earth.
50 Ye that have escaped the sword, go away, stand not still: remember the
LORD afar off, and let Jerusalem come into your mind.
51 We are confounded, because we have heard reproach: shame hath covered
our faces: for strangers are come into the sanctuaries of the LORD's house.
52 Wherefore, behold, the days come, saith the LORD, that I will do judgment
upon her graven images: and through all her land the wounded shall groan.
53 Though Babylon should mount up to heaven, and though she should for-
tify the height of her strength, *yet* from me shall spoilers come unto her, saith
the LORD.
54 A sound of a cry *cometh* from Babylon, and great destruction from the
land of the Chaldeans:
55 Because the LORD hath spoiled Babylon, and destroyed out of her the great
voice; when her waves do roar like great waters, a noise of their voice is uttered:
56 Because the spoiler is come upon her, *even* upon Babylon, and her mighty
men are taken, every one of their bows is broken: for the LORD God of recom-
pences shall surely requite.
57 And I will make drunk her princes, and her wise *men*, her captains, and
her rulers, and her mighty men: and they shall sleep a perpetual sleep, and
not wake, saith the King, whose name *is* the LORD of hosts.
58 Thus saith the LORD of hosts; The broad walls of Babylon shall be utterly
broken, and her high gates shall be burned with fire; and the people shall
labour in vain, and the folk in the fire, and they shall be weary.
59 The word which Jeremiah the prophet commanded Seraiah the son of
Neriah, the son of Maaseiah, when he went with Zedekiah the king of Judah
into Babylon in the fourth year of his reign. And *this* Seraiah *was* a quiet prince.
60 So Jeremiah wrote in a book all the evil that should come upon Babylon,
even all these words that are written against Babylon.
61 And Jeremiah said to Seraiah, When thou comest to Babylon, and shalt
see, and shalt read all these words;
62 Then shalt thou say, O LORD, thou hast spoken against this place, to cut it
off, that none shall remain in it, neither man nor beast, but that it shall be
desolate for ever.
63 And it shall be, when thou hast made an end of reading this book, *that*
thou shalt bind a stone to it, and cast it into the midst of Euphrates:
64 And thou shalt say, Thus shall Babylon sink, and shall not rise from the
evil that I will bring upon her: and they shall be weary. Thus far *are* the words
of Jeremiah.

The Fall of Jerusalem

52 Zedekiah *was* one and twenty years old when he began to reign, and
he reigned eleven years in Jerusalem. And his mother's name *was*
Hamutal the daughter of Jeremiah of Libnah.
2 And he did *that which was* evil in the eyes of the LORD, according to all that
Jehoiakim had done.
3 For through the anger of the LORD it came to pass in Jerusalem and Judah,
till he had cast them out from his presence, that Zedekiah rebelled against the
king of Babylon.
4 And it came to pass in the ninth year of his reign, in the tenth month, in
the tenth *day* of the month, *that* Nebuchadrezzar king of Babylon came, he
and all his army, against Jerusalem, and pitched against it, and built forts
against it round about.
5 So the city was besieged unto the eleventh year of king Zedekiah.
6 And in the fourth month, in the ninth *day* of the month, the famine was
sore in the city, so that there was no bread for the people of the land.
7 Then the city was broken up, and all the men of war fled, and went forth
out of the city by night by the way of the gate between the two walls, which
was by the king's garden; (now the Chaldeans *were* by the city round about:)
and they went by the way of the plain.
8 But the army of the Chaldeans pursued after the king, and overtook
Zedekiah in the plains of Jericho; and all his army was scattered from him.
9 Then they took the king, and carried him up unto the king of Babylon to
Riblah in the land of Hamath; where he gave judgment upon him.
10 And the king of Babylon slew the sons of Zedekiah before his eyes: he slew
also all the princes of Judah in Riblah.
11 Then he put out the eyes of Zedekiah; and the king of Babylon bound him
in chains, and carried him to Babylon, and put him in prison till the day of
his death.
12 Now in the fifth month, in the tenth *day* of the month, which *was* the
nineteenth year of Nebuchadrezzar king of Babylon, came Nebuzar-adan,
captain of the guard, *which* served the king of Babylon, into Jerusalem,
13 And burned the house of the LORD, and the king's house; and all the hous-
es of Jerusalem, and all the houses of the great *men*, burned he with fire:
14 And all the army of the Chaldeans, that *were* with the captain of the guard,
brake down all the walls of Jerusalem round about.
15 Then Nebuzar-adan the captain of the guard carried away captive *certain*
of the poor of the people, and the residue of the people that remained in the
city, and those that fell away, that fell to the king of Babylon, and the rest of
the multitude.
16 But Nebuzar-adan the captain of the guard left *certain* of the poor of the
land for vinedressers and for husbandmen.
17 Also the pillars of brass that *were* in the house of the LORD, and the bases,
and the brasen sea that *was* in the house of the LORD, the Chaldeans brake,
and carried all the brass of them to Babylon.
18 The caldrons also, and the shovels, and the snuffers, and the bowls, and
the spoons, and all the vessels of brass wherewith they ministered, took they
away.
19 And the basons, and the firepans, and the bowls, and the caldrons, and
the candlesticks, and the spoons, and the cups; *that* which *was* of gold *in* gold,
and *that* which *was* of silver *in* silver, took the captain of the guard away.
20 The two pillars, one sea, and twelve brasen bulls that *were* under the bases,
which king Solomon had made in the house of the LORD: the brass of all these
vessels was without weight.
21 And *concerning* the pillars, the height of one pillar *was* eighteen cubits;
and a fillet of twelve cubits did compass it; and the thickness thereof *was* four
fingers: *it was* hollow.

22 And a chapiter of brass *was* upon it; and the height of one chapiter *was*
five cubits, with network and pomegranates upon the chapiters round about,
all *of* brass. The second pillar also and the pomegranates *were* like unto these.
23 And there were ninety and six pomegranates on a side; *and* all the pome-
granates upon the network *were* an hundred round about.
24 And the captain of the guard took Seraiah the chief priest, and Zephaniah
the second priest, and the three keepers of the door:
25 He took also out of the city an eunuch, which had the charge of the men
of war; and seven men of them that were near the king's person, which were
found in the city; and the principal scribe of the host, who mustered the peo-
ple of the land; and threescore men of the people of the land, that were found
in the midst of the city.
26 So Nebuzar-adan the captain of the guard took them, and brought them
to the king of Babylon to Riblah.
27 And the king of Babylon smote them, and put them to death in Riblah in
the land of Hamath. Thus Judah was carried away captive out of his own land.
28 This *is* the people whom Nebuchadrezzar carried away captive: in the
seventh year three thousand Jews and three and twenty:
29 In the eighteenth year of Nebuchadrezzar he carried away captive from
Jerusalem eight hundred thirty and two persons:
30 In the three and twentieth year of Nebuchadrezzar Nebuzar-adan the
captain of the guard carried away captive of the Jews seven hundred forty and
five persons: all the persons *were* four thousand and six hundred.

Jehoiachin Is Released from Prison

31 And it came to pass in the seven and thirtieth year of the captivity of
Jehoiachin king of Judah, in the twelfth month, in the five and twentieth *day*
of the month, *that* Evilmerodach king of Babylon in the *first* year of his reign
lifted up the head of Jehoiachin king of Judah, and brought him forth out of
prison,
32 And spake kindly unto him, and set his throne above the throne of the
kings that *were* with him in Babylon,
33 And changed his prison garments: and he did continually eat bread before
him all the days of his life.
34 And *for* his diet, there was a continual diet given him of the king of
Babylon, every day a portion until the day of his death, all the days of his life.

LAMENTATIONS

The Misery of Jerusalem Because of Her Sin

1 How doth the city sit solitary, *that was* full of people! *how* is she become as
a widow! she *that was* great among the nations, *and* princess among the
provinces, *how* is she become tributary!
2 She weepeth sore in the night, and her tears *are* on her cheeks: among all
her lovers she hath none to comfort *her*: all her friends have dealt treacher-
ously with her, they are become her enemies.
3 Judah is gone into captivity because of affliction, and because of great
servitude: she dwelleth among the heathen, she findeth no rest: all her perse-
cutors overtook her between the straits.
4 The ways of Zion do mourn, because none come to the solemn feasts: all
her gates are desolate: her priests sigh, her virgins are afflicted, and she *is* in
bitterness.
5 Her adversaries are the chief, her enemies prosper; for the LORD hath afflict-
ed her for the multitude of her transgressions: her children are gone into
captivity before the enemy.
6 And from the daughter of Zion all her beauty is departed: her princes are
become like harts *that* find no pasture, and they are gone without strength
before the pursuer.
7 Jerusalem remembered in the days of her affliction and of her miseries all
her pleasant things that she had in the days of old, when her people fell into
the hand of the enemy, and none did help her: the adversaries saw her, *and*
did mock at her sabbaths.
8 Jerusalem hath grievously sinned; therefore she is removed: all that hon-
oured her despise her, because they have seen her nakedness: yea, she sigheth,
and turneth backward.
9 Her filthiness *is* in her skirts; she remembereth not her last end; therefore
she came down wonderfully: she had no comforter. O LORD, behold my afflic-
tion: for the enemy hath magnified *himself*.
10 The adversary hath spread out his hand upon all her pleasant things: for
she hath seen *that* the heathen entered into her sanctuary, whom thou didst
command *that* they should not enter into thy congregation.
11 All her people sigh, they seek bread; they have given their pleasant things
for meat to relieve the soul: see, O LORD, and consider; for I am become vile.

Jerusalem Complains of Her Grief

12 *Is it* nothing to you, all ye that pass by? behold, and see if there be any
sorrow like unto my sorrow, which is done unto me, wherewith the LORD hath
afflicted *me* in the day of his fierce anger.
13 From above hath he sent fire into my bones, and it prevaileth against them:
he hath spread a net for my feet, he hath turned me back: he hath made me
desolate *and* faint all the day.
14 The yoke of my transgressions is bound by his hand: they are wreathed,
and come up upon my neck: he hath made my strength to fall, the Lord hath
delivered me into *their* hands, *from whom* I am not able to rise up.
15 The Lord hath trodden under foot all my mighty *men* in the midst of me:
he hath called an assembly against me to crush my young men: the Lord hath
trodden the virgin, the daughter of Judah, *as* in a winepress.

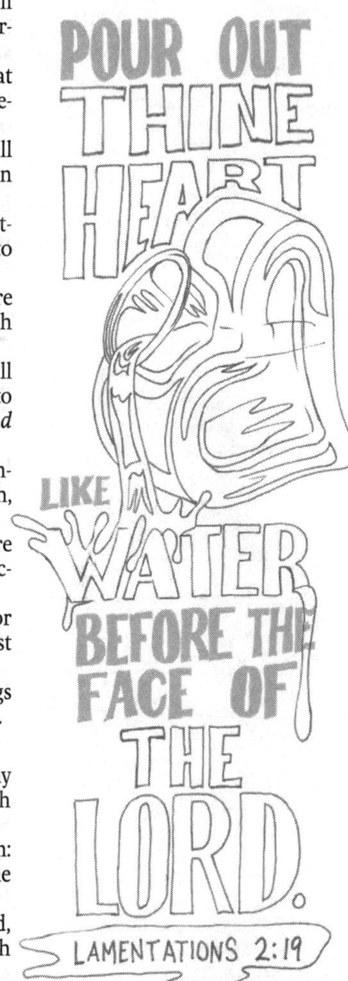

16 For these *things* I weep; mine eye, mine eye runneth down with water, because the comforter that should relieve my soul is far from me: my children are desolate, because the enemy prevailed.

17 Zion spreadeth forth her hands, *and there is* none to comfort her: the LORD hath commanded concerning Jacob, *that* his adversaries *should be* round about him: Jerusalem is as a menstruous woman among them.

18 The LORD is righteous; for I have rebelled against his commandment: hear, I pray you, all people, and behold my sorrow: my virgins and my young men are gone into captivity.

19 I called for my lovers, *but* they deceived me: my priests and mine elders gave up the ghost in the city, while they sought their meat to relieve their souls.

20 Behold, O LORD; for I *am* in distress: my bowels are troubled; mine heart is turned within me; for I have grievously rebelled: abroad the sword bereaveth, at home *there is* as death.

21 They have heard that I sigh: *there is* none to comfort me: all mine enemies have heard of my trouble; they are glad that thou hast done *it*: thou wilt bring the day *that* thou hast called, and they shall be like unto me.

22 Let all their wickedness come before thee; and do unto them, as thou hast done unto me for all my transgressions: for my sighs *are* many, and my heart *is* faint.

Jeremiah Laments the Misery of Jerusalem

2 How hath the Lord covered the daughter of Zion with a cloud in his anger, *and* cast down from heaven unto the earth the beauty of Israel, and remembered not his footstool in the day of his anger!

2 The Lord hath swallowed up all the habitations of Jacob, and hath not pitied: he hath thrown down in his wrath the strong holds of the daughter of Judah; he hath brought *them* down to the ground: he hath polluted the kingdom and the princes thereof.

3 He hath cut off in *his* fierce anger all the horn of Israel: he hath drawn back his right hand from before the enemy, and he burned against Jacob like a flaming fire, *which* devoureth round about.

4 He hath bent his bow like an enemy: he stood with his right hand as an adversary, and slew all *that were* pleasant to the eye in the tabernacle of the daughter of Zion: he poured out his fury like fire.

5 The Lord was as an enemy: he hath swallowed up Israel, he hath swallowed up all her palaces: he hath destroyed his strong holds, and hath increased in the daughter of Judah mourning and lamentation.

6 And he hath violently taken away his tabernacle, as *if it were of* a garden: he hath destroyed his places of the assembly: the LORD hath caused the solemn feasts and sabbaths to be forgotten in Zion, and hath despised in the indignation of his anger the king and the priest.

7 The Lord hath cast off his altar, he hath abhorred his sanctuary, he hath given up into the hand of the enemy the walls of her palaces; they have made a noise in the house of the LORD, as in the day of a solemn feast.

8 The LORD hath purposed to destroy the wall of the daughter of Zion: he hath stretched out a line, he hath not withdrawn his hand from destroying: therefore he made the rampart and the wall to lament; they languished together.

9 Her gates are sunk into the ground; he hath destroyed and broken her bars: her king and her princes *are* among the Gentiles: the law *is* no *more*; her prophets also find no vision from the LORD.

10 The elders of the daughter of Zion sit upon the ground, *and* keep silence: they have cast up dust upon their heads; they have girded themselves with sackcloth: the virgins of Jerusalem hang down their heads to the ground.

11 Mine eyes do fail with tears, my bowels are troubled, my liver is poured
upon the earth, for the destruction of the daughter of my people; because the
children and the sucklings swoon in the streets of the city.
12 They say to their mothers, Where *is* corn and wine? when they swooned
as the wounded in the streets of the city, when their soul was poured out into
their mothers' bosom.
13 What thing shall I take to witness for thee? what thing shall I liken to thee,
O daughter of Jerusalem? what shall I equal to thee, that I may comfort thee,
O virgin daughter of Zion? for thy breach *is* great like the sea: who can heal
thee?
14 Thy prophets have seen vain and foolish things for thee: and they have
not discovered thine iniquity, to turn away thy captivity; but have seen for thee
false burdens and causes of banishment.
15 All that pass by clap *their* hands at thee; they hiss and wag their head at
the daughter of Jerusalem, *saying*, *Is* this the city that *men* call The perfection
of beauty, The joy of the whole earth?
16 All thine enemies have opened their mouth against thee: they hiss and
gnash the teeth: they say, We have swallowed *her* up: certainly this *is* the day
that we looked for; we have found, we have seen *it*.
17 The LORD hath done *that* which he had devised; he hath fulfilled his word
that he had commanded in the days of old: he hath thrown down, and hath
not pitied: and he hath caused *thine* enemy to rejoice over thee, he hath set
up the horn of thine adversaries.
18 Their heart cried unto the Lord, O wall of the daughter of Zion, let tears
run down like a river day and night: give thyself no rest; let not the apple of
thine eye cease.
19 Arise, cry out in the night: in the beginning of the watches pour out thine
heart like water before the face of the Lord: lift up thy hands toward him for
the life of thy young children, that faint for hunger in the top of every street.
20 Behold, O LORD, and consider to whom thou hast done this. Shall the
women eat their fruit, *and* children of a span long? shall the priest and the
prophet be slain in the sanctuary of the Lord?
21 The young and the old lie on the ground in the streets: my virgins and my
young men are fallen by the sword; thou hast slain *them* in the day of thine
anger; thou hast killed, *and* not pitied.
22 Thou hast called as in a solemn day my terrors round about, so that in the
day of the LORD's anger none escaped nor remained: those that I have swaddled
and brought up hath mine enemy consumed.

Jeremiah Despairs, Yet Hopes

3 I *am* the man *that* hath seen affliction by the rod of his wrath.
2 He hath led me, and brought *me into* darkness, but not *into* light.
3 Surely against me is he turned; he turneth his hand *against me* all the day.
4 My flesh and my skin hath he made old; he hath broken my bones.
5 He hath builded against me, and compassed *me* with gall and travail.
6 He hath set me in dark places, as *they that be* dead of old.
7 He hath hedged me about, that I cannot get out: he hath made my chain
heavy.
8 Also when I cry and shout, he shutteth out my prayer.
9 He hath inclosed my ways with hewn stone, he hath made my paths crooked.
10 He *was* unto me *as* a bear lying in wait, *and as* a lion in secret places.
11 He hath turned aside my ways, and pulled me in pieces: he hath made me
desolate.
12 He hath bent his bow, and set me as a mark for the arrow.
13 He hath caused the arrows of his quiver to enter into my reins.
14 I was a derision to all my people; *and* their song all the day.

THE
LORD
IS MY
PORTION,
saith
my
Soul;
Therefore
WILL I
HOPE
in
HIM

LAMENTATIONS 3:24

15 He hath filled me with bitterness, he hath made me drunken with worm-
wood.
16 He hath also broken my teeth with gravel stones, he hath covered me with
ashes.
17 And thou hast removed my soul far off from peace: I forgat prosperity.
18 And I said, My strength and my hope is perished from the LORD:
19 Remembering mine affliction and my misery, the wormwood and the
gall.
20 My soul hath *them* still in remembrance, and is humbled in me.
21 This I recall to my mind, therefore have I hope.
22 *It is of* the LORD's mercies that we are not consumed, because his compas-
sions fail not.
23 *They are* new every morning: great *is* thy faithfulness.
24 The LORD *is* my portion, saith my soul; therefore will I hope in him.
25 The LORD *is* good unto them that wait for him, to the soul *that* seeketh
him.
26 *It is* good that *a man* should both hope and quietly wait for the salvation
of the LORD.
27 *It is* good for a man that he bear the yoke in his youth.
28 He sitteth alone and keepeth silence, because he hath borne *it* upon him.
29 He putteth his mouth in the dust; if so be there may be hope.
30 He giveth *his* cheek to him that smiteth him: he is filled full with reproach.
31 For the Lord will not cast off for ever:
32 But though he cause grief, yet will he have compassion according to the
multitude of his mercies.
33 For he doth not afflict willingly nor grieve the children of men.
34 To crush under his feet all the prisoners of the earth,
35 To turn aside the right of a man before the face of the most High,
36 To subvert a man in his cause, the Lord approveth not.
37 Who *is* he *that* saith, and it cometh to pass, *when* the Lord commandeth
it not?
38 Out of the mouth of the most High proceedeth not evil and good?
39 Wherefore doth a living man complain, a man for the punishment of his
sins?
40 Let us search and try our ways, and turn again to the LORD.
41 Let us lift up our heart with *our* hands unto God in the heavens.
42 We have transgressed and have rebelled: thou hast not pardoned.
43 Thou hast covered with anger, and persecuted us: thou hast slain, thou
hast not pitied.
44 Thou hast covered thyself with a cloud, that *our* prayer should not pass
through.
45 Thou hast made us *as* the offscouring and refuse in the midst of the people.
46 All our enemies have opened their mouths against us.
47 Fear and a snare is come upon us, desolation and destruction.
48 Mine eye runneth down with rivers of water for the destruction of the
daughter of my people.
49 Mine eye trickleth down, and ceaseth not, without any intermission,
50 Till the LORD look down, and behold from heaven.
51 Mine eye affecteth mine heart because of all the daughters of my city.
52 Mine enemies chased me sore, like a bird, without cause.
53 They have cut off my life in the dungeon, and cast a stone upon me.
54 Waters flowed over mine head; *then* I said, I am cut off.
55 I called upon thy name, O LORD, out of the low dungeon.
56 Thou hast heard my voice: hide not thine ear at my breathing, at my cry.
57 Thou drewest near in the day *that* I called upon thee: thou saidst, Fear
not.

58 O Lord, thou hast pleaded the causes of my soul; thou hast redeemed my
life.
59 O LORD, thou hast seen my wrong: judge thou my cause.
60 Thou hast seen all their vengeance *and* all their imaginations against me.
61 Thou hast heard their reproach, O LORD, *and* all their imaginations
against me;
62 The lips of those that rose up against me, and their device against me all
the day.
63 Behold their sitting down, and their rising up; I *am* their musick.
64 Render unto them a recompence, O LORD, according to the work of their
hands.
65 Give them sorrow of heart, thy curse unto them.
66 Persecute and destroy them in anger from under the heavens of the LORD.

Zion Bewails Her Pitiful State

4 How is the gold become dim! *how* is the most fine gold changed! the stones
of the sanctuary are poured out in the top of every street.
2 The precious sons of Zion, comparable to fine gold, how are they esteemed
as earthen pitchers, the work of the hands of the potter!
3 Even the sea monsters draw out the breast, they give suck to their young
ones: the daughter of my people *is become* cruel, like the ostriches in the wil-
derness.
4 The tongue of the sucking child cleaveth to the roof of his mouth for thirst:
the young children ask bread, *and* no man breaketh *it* unto them.
5 They that did feed delicately are desolate in the streets: they that were
brought up in scarlet embrace dunghills.
6 For the punishment of the iniquity of the daughter of my people is greater
than the punishment of the sin of Sodom, that was overthrown as in a
moment, and no hands stayed on her.
7 Her Nazarites were purer than snow, they were whiter than milk, they were
more ruddy in body than rubies, their polishing *was* of sapphire:
8 Their visage is blacker than a coal; they are not known in the streets: their
skin cleaveth to their bones; it is withered, it is become like a stick.
9 *They that be* slain with the sword are better than *they that be* slain with
hunger: for these pine away, stricken through for *want of* the fruits of the field.
10 The hands of the pitiful women have sodden their own children: they
were their meat in the destruction of the daughter of my people.
11 The LORD hath accomplished his fury; he hath poured out his fierce anger,
and hath kindled a fire in Zion, and it hath devoured the foundations thereof.
12 The kings of the earth, and all the inhabitants of the world, would not
have believed that the adversary and the enemy should have entered into the
gates of Jerusalem.
13 For the sins of her prophets, *and* the iniquities of her priests, that have
shed the blood of the just in the midst of her,
14 They have wandered *as* blind *men* in the streets, they have polluted them-
selves with blood, so that men could not touch their garments.
15 They cried unto them, Depart ye; *it is* unclean; depart, depart, touch not:
when they fled away and wandered, they said among the heathen, They shall
no more sojourn *there*.
16 The anger of the LORD hath divided them; he will no more regard them:
they respected not the persons of the priests, they favoured not the elders.
17 As for us, our eyes as yet failed for our vain help: in our watching we have
watched for a nation *that* could not save *us*.
18 They hunt our steps, that we cannot go in our streets: our end is near, our
days are fulfilled; for our end is come.

19 Our persecutors are swifter than the eagles of the heaven: they pursued
us upon the mountains, they laid wait for us in the wilderness.
20 The breath of our nostrils, the anointed of the LORD, was taken in their
pits, of whom we said, Under his shadow we shall live among the heathen.

Edom's Impending Doom

21 Rejoice and be glad, O daughter of Edom, that dwellest in the land of Uz;
the cup also shall pass through unto thee: thou shalt be drunken, and shalt
make thyself naked.
22 The punishment of thine iniquity is accomplished, O daughter of Zion;
he will no more carry thee away into captivity: he will visit thine iniquity, O
daughter of Edom; he will discover thy sins.

Jeremiah's Prayer

5 Remember, O LORD, what is come upon us: consider, and behold our
reproach.
2 Our inheritance is turned to strangers, our houses to aliens.
3 We are orphans and fatherless, our mothers *are* as widows.
4 We have drunken our water for money; our wood is sold unto us.
5 Our necks *are* under persecution: we labour, *and* have no rest.
6 We have given the hand *to* the Egyptians, *and to* the Assyrians, to be satis-
fied with bread.
7 Our fathers have sinned, *and are* not; and we have borne their iniquities.
8 Servants have ruled over us: *there is* none that doth deliver *us* out of their
hand.
9 We gat our bread with *the peril of* our lives because of the sword of the
wilderness.
10 Our skin was black like an oven because of the terrible famine.
11 They ravished the women in Zion, *and* the maids in the cities of Judah.
12 Princes are hanged up by their hand: the faces of elders were not honoured.
13 They took the young men to grind, and the children fell under the wood.
14 The elders have ceased from the gate, the young men from their musick.
15 The joy of our heart is ceased; our dance is turned into mourning.
16 The crown is fallen *from* our head: woe unto us, that we have sinned!
17 For this our heart is faint; for these *things* our eyes are dim.
18 Because of the mountain of Zion, which is desolate, the foxes walk upon it.
19 Thou, O LORD, remainest for ever; thy throne from generation to generation.
20 Wherefore dost thou forget us for ever, *and* forsake us so long time?
21 Turn thou us unto thee, O LORD, and we shall be turned; renew our days
as of old.
22 But thou hast utterly rejected us; thou art very wroth against us.

LAMENTATIONS 5:21

The Time of Ezekiel's Prophecy at Chebar

1 Now it came to pass in the thirtieth year, in the fourth *month*, in the fifth
day of the month, as I *was* among the captives by the river of Chebar, *that*
the heavens were opened, and I saw visions of God.
2 In the fifth *day* of the month, which *was* the fifth year of king Jehoiachin's
captivity,
3 The word of the LORD came expressly unto Ezekiel the priest, the son of
Buzi, in the land of the Chaldeans by the river Chebar; and the hand of the
LORD was there upon him.

Ezekiel's Vision of Four Living Creatures

4 And I looked, and, behold, a whirlwind came out of the north, a great cloud,
and a fire infolding itself, and a brightness *was* about it, and out of the midst
thereof as the colour of amber, out of the midst of the fire.
5 Also out of the midst thereof *came* the likeness of four living creatures.
And this *was* their appearance; they had the likeness of a man.
6 And every one had four faces, and every one had four wings.
7 And their feet *were* straight feet; and the sole of their feet *was* like the sole
of a calf's foot: and they sparkled like the colour of burnished brass.
8 And *they had* the hands of a man under their wings on their four sides; and
they four had their faces and their wings.
9 Their wings *were* joined one to another; they turned not when they went;
they went every one straight forward.
10 As for the likeness of their faces, they four had the face of a man, and the
face of a lion, on the right side: and they four had the face of an ox on the left
side; they four also had the face of an eagle.
11 Thus *were* their faces: and their wings *were* stretched upward; two *wings*
of every one *were* joined one to another, and two covered their bodies.
12 And they went every one straight forward: whither the spirit was to go,
they went; *and* they turned not when they went.
13 As for the likeness of the living creatures, their appearance *was* like burn-
ing coals of fire, *and* like the appearance of lamps: it went up and down among
the living creatures; and the fire was bright, and out of the fire went forth
lightning.
14 And the living creatures ran and returned as the appearance of a flash of
lightning.

Ezekiel's Vision of Four Wheels

15 Now as I beheld the living creatures, behold one wheel upon the earth by
the living creatures, with his four faces.
16 The appearance of the wheels and their work *was* like unto the colour of
a beryl: and they four had one likeness: and their appearance and their work
was as it were a wheel in the middle of a wheel.
17 When they went, they went upon their four sides: *and* they turned not
when they went.
18 As for their rings, they were so high that they were dreadful; and their
rings *were* full of eyes round about them four.
19 And when the living creatures went, the wheels went by them: and when
the living creatures were lifted up from the earth, the wheels were lifted up.

20 Whithersoever the spirit was to go, they went, thither *was their* spirit to go; and the wheels were lifted up over against them: for the spirit of the living creature *was* in the wheels.
21 When those went, *these* went; and when those stood, *these* stood; and when those were lifted up from the earth, the wheels were lifted up over against them: for the spirit of the living creature *was* in the wheels.
22 And the likeness of the firmament upon the heads of the living creature *was* as the colour of the terrible crystal, stretched forth over their heads above.
23 And under the firmament *were* their wings straight, the one toward the other: every one had two, which covered on this side, and every one had two, which covered on that side, their bodies.
24 And when they went, I heard the noise of their wings, like the noise of great waters, as the voice of the Almighty, the voice of speech, as the noise of an host: when they stood, they let down their wings.
25 And there was a voice from the firmament that *was* over their heads, when they stood, *and* had let down their wings.

Ezekiel Sees the Glory of God

26 And above the firmament that *was* over their heads *was* the likeness of a throne, as the appearance of a sapphire stone: and upon the likeness of the throne *was* the likeness as the appearance of a man above upon it.
27 And I saw as the colour of amber, as the appearance of fire round about within it, from the appearance of his loins even upward, and from the appearance of his loins even downward, I saw as it were the appearance of fire, and it had brightness round about.
28 As the appearance of the bow that is in the cloud in the day of rain, so *was* the appearance of the brightness round about. This *was* the appearance of the likeness of the glory of the LORD. And when I saw *it*, I fell upon my face, and I heard a voice of one that spake.

Ezekiel's Commission

2 And he said unto me, Son of man, stand upon thy feet, and I will speak unto thee.
2 And the spirit entered into me when he spake unto me, and set me upon my feet, that I heard him that spake unto me.
3 And he said unto me, Son of man, I send thee to the children of Israel, to a rebellious nation that hath rebelled against me: they and their fathers have transgressed against me, *even* unto this very day.
4 For *they are* impudent children and stiffhearted. I do send thee unto them; and thou shalt say unto them, Thus saith the Lord GOD.
5 And they, whether they will hear, or whether they will forbear, (for they *are* a rebellious house,) yet shall know that there hath been a prophet among them.
6 And thou, son of man, be not afraid of them, neither be afraid of their words, though briers and thorns *be* with thee, and thou dost dwell among scorpions: be not afraid of their words, nor be dismayed at their looks, though they *be* a rebellious house.
7 And thou shalt speak my words unto them, whether they will hear, or whether they will forbear: for they *are* most rebellious.
8 But thou, son of man, hear what I say unto thee; Be not thou rebellious like that rebellious house: open thy mouth, and eat that I give thee.
9 And when I looked, behold, an hand *was* sent unto me; and, lo, a roll of a book *was* therein;
10 And he spread it before me; and it *was* written within and without: and *there was* written therein lamentations, and mourning, and woe.

Ezekiel's Vision of a Scroll

3 Moreover he said unto me, Son of man, eat that thou findest; eat this roll,
and go speak unto the house of Israel.
2 So I opened my mouth, and he caused me to eat that roll.
3 And he said unto me, Son of man, cause thy belly to eat, and fill thy bowels
with this roll that I give thee. Then did I eat *it*; and it was in my mouth as honey
for sweetness.
4 And he said unto me, Son of man, go, get thee unto the house of Israel, and
speak with my words unto them.
5 For thou *art* not sent to a people of a strange speech and of an hard lan-
guage, *but* to the house of Israel;
6 Not to many people of a strange speech and of an hard language, whose
words thou canst not understand. Surely, had I sent thee to them, they would
have hearkened unto thee.
7 But the house of Israel will not hearken unto thee; for they will not hearken
unto me: for all the house of Israel *are* impudent and hardhearted.
8 Behold, I have made thy face strong against their faces, and thy forehead
strong against their foreheads.
9 As an adamant harder than flint have I made thy forehead: fear them not,
neither be dismayed at their looks, though they *be* a rebellious house.
10 Moreover he said unto me, Son of man, all my words that I shall speak
unto thee receive in thine heart, and hear with thine ears.
11 And go, get thee to them of the captivity, unto the children of thy people,
and speak unto them, and tell them, Thus saith the Lord GOD; whether they
will hear, or whether they will forbear.
12 Then the spirit took me up, and I heard behind me a voice of a great
rushing, *saying*, Blessed *be* the glory of the LORD from his place.
13 *I heard* also the noise of the wings of the living creatures that touched one
another, and the noise of the wheels over against them, and a noise of a great
rushing.
14 So the spirit lifted me up, and took me away, and I went in bitterness, in
the heat of my spirit; but the hand of the LORD was strong upon me.
15 Then I came to them of the captivity at Telabib, that dwelt by the river of
Chebar, and I sat where they sat, and remained there astonished among them
seven days.

Ezekiel Is Appointed to Be a Watchman

16 And it came to pass at the end of seven days, that the word of the LORD
came unto me, saying,
17 Son of man, I have made thee a watchman unto the house of Israel: there-
fore hear the word at my mouth, and give them warning from me.
18 When I say unto the wicked, Thou shalt surely die; and thou givest him
not warning, nor speakest to warn the wicked from his wicked way, to save
his life; the same wicked *man* shall die in his iniquity; but his blood will I
require at thine hand.
19 Yet if thou warn the wicked, and he turn not from his wickedness, nor
from his wicked way, he shall die in his iniquity; but thou hast delivered thy
soul.
20 Again, When a righteous *man* doth turn from his righteousness, and com-
mit iniquity, and I lay a stumblingblock before him, he shall die: because thou
hast not given him warning, he shall die in his sin, and his righteousness which
he hath done shall not be remembered; but his blood will I require at thine
hand.
21 Nevertheless if thou warn the righteous *man*, that the righteous sin not,
and he doth not sin, he shall surely live, because he is warned; also thou hast
delivered thy soul.

The Lord Instructs Ezekiel

22 And the hand of the LORD was there upon me; and he said unto me, Arise,
go forth into the plain, and I will there talk with thee.
23 Then I arose, and went forth into the plain: and, behold, the glory of the
LORD stood there, as the glory which I saw by the river of Chebar: and I fell on
my face.
24 Then the spirit entered into me, and set me upon my feet, and spake with
me, and said unto me, Go, shut thyself within thine house.
25 But thou, O son of man, behold, they shall put bands upon thee, and shall
bind thee with them, and thou shalt not go out among them:
26 And I will make thy tongue cleave to the roof of thy mouth, that thou shalt
be dumb, and shalt not be to them a reprover: for they *are* a rebellious house.
27 But when I speak with thee, I will open thy mouth, and thou shalt say unto
them, Thus saith the Lord GOD; He that heareth, let him hear; and he that
forbeareth, let him forbear: for they *are* a rebellious house.

Ezekiel Foretells the Siege of Jerusalem

4 Thou also, son of man, take thee a tile, and lay it before thee, and pourtray
upon it the city, *even* Jerusalem:
2 And lay siege against it, and build a fort against it, and cast a mount against
it; set the camp also against it, and set *battering* rams against it round about.
3 Moreover take thou unto thee an iron pan, and set it *for* a wall of iron
between thee and the city: and set thy face against it, and it shall be besieged,
and thou shalt lay siege against it. This *shall be* a sign to the house of Israel.
4 Lie thou also upon thy left side, and lay the iniquity of the house of Israel
upon it: *according* to the number of the days that thou shalt lie upon it thou
shalt bear their iniquity.
5 For I have laid upon thee the years of their iniquity, according to the num-
ber of the days, three hundred and ninety days: so shalt thou bear the iniqui-
ty of the house of Israel.
6 And when thou hast accomplished them, lie again on thy right side, and
thou shalt bear the iniquity of the house of Judah forty days: I have appointed
thee each day for a year.
7 Therefore thou shalt set thy face toward the siege of Jerusalem, and thine
arm *shall be* uncovered, and thou shalt prophesy against it.
8 And, behold, I will lay bands upon thee, and thou shalt not turn thee from
one side to another, till thou hast ended the days of thy siege.
9 Take thou also unto thee wheat, and barley, and beans, and lentiles, and
millet, and fitches, and put them in one vessel, and make thee bread thereof,
according to the number of the days that thou shalt lie upon thy side, three
hundred and ninety days shalt thou eat thereof.
10 And thy meat which thou shalt eat *shall be* by weight, twenty shekels a
day: from time to time shalt thou eat it.
11 Thou shalt drink also water by measure, the sixth part of an hin: from
time to time shalt thou drink.
12 And thou shalt eat it *as* barley cakes, and thou shalt bake it with dung that
cometh out of man, in their sight.
13 And the LORD said, Even thus shall the children of Israel eat their defiled
bread among the Gentiles, whither I will drive them.
14 Then said I, Ah Lord GOD! behold, my soul hath not been polluted: for
from my youth up even till now have I not eaten of that which dieth of itself,
or is torn in pieces; neither came there abominable flesh into my mouth.
15 Then he said unto me, Lo, I have given thee cow's dung for man's dung,
and thou shalt prepare thy bread therewith.

16 Moreover he said unto me, Son of man, behold, I will break the staff of
bread in Jerusalem: and they shall eat bread by weight, and with care; and they
shall drink water by measure, and with astonishment:
17 That they may want bread and water, and be astonied one with another,
and consume away for their iniquity.

The Coming Fall of Jerusalem

5 And thou, son of man, take thee a sharp knife, take thee a barber's razor,
and cause *it* to pass upon thine head and upon thy beard: then take thee
balances to weigh, and divide the *hair*.
2 Thou shalt burn with fire a third part in the midst of the city, when the
days of the siege are fulfilled: and thou shalt take a third part, *and* smite about
it with a knife: and a third part thou shalt scatter in the wind; and I will draw
out a sword after them.
3 Thou shalt also take thereof a few in number, and bind them in thy skirts.
4 Then take of them again, and cast them into the midst of the fire, and burn
them in the fire; *for* thereof shall a fire come forth into all the house of Israel.
5 Thus saith the Lord GOD; This *is* Jerusalem: I have set it in the midst of the
nations and countries *that are* round about her.
6 And she hath changed my judgments into wickedness more than the
nations, and my statutes more than the countries that *are* round about her:
for they have refused my judgments and my statutes, they have not walked in
them.
7 Therefore thus saith the Lord GOD; Because ye multiplied more than the
nations that *are* round about you, *and* have not walked in my statutes, neither
have kept my judgments, neither have done according to the judgments of the
nations that *are* round about you;
8 Therefore thus saith the Lord GOD; Behold, I, even I, *am* against thee, and
will execute judgments in the midst of thee in the sight of the nations.
9 And I will do in thee that which I have not done, and whereunto I will not
do any more the like, because of all thine abominations.
10 Therefore the fathers shall eat the sons in the midst of thee, and the sons
shall eat their fathers; and I will execute judgments in thee, and the whole
remnant of thee will I scatter into all the winds.
11 Wherefore, *as* I live, saith the Lord GOD; Surely, because thou hast defiled
my sanctuary with all thy detestable things, and with all thine abominations,
therefore will I also diminish *thee*; neither shall mine eye spare, neither will
I have any pity.
12 A third part of thee shall die with the pestilence, and with famine shall
they be consumed in the midst of thee: and a third part shall fall by the sword
round about thee; and I will scatter a third part into all the winds, and I will
draw out a sword after them.
13 Thus shall mine anger be accomplished, and I will cause my fury to rest
upon them, and I will be comforted: and they shall know that I the LORD have
spoken *it* in my zeal, when I have accomplished my fury in them.
14 Moreover I will make thee waste, and a reproach among the nations that
are round about thee, in the sight of all that pass by.
15 So it shall be a reproach and a taunt, an instruction and an astonishment
unto the nations that *are* round about thee, when I shall execute judgments
in thee in anger and in fury and in furious rebukes. I the LORD have spoken *it*.
16 When I shall send upon them the evil arrows of famine, which shall be
for *their* destruction, *and* which I will send to destroy you: and I will increase
the famine upon you, and will break your staff of bread:
17 So will I send upon you famine and evil beasts, and they shall bereave thee;
and pestilence and blood shall pass through thee; and I will bring the sword
upon thee. I the LORD have spoken *it*.

The Judgment of Israel for Idolatry

6 And the word of the LORD came unto me, saying,
2 Son of man, set thy face toward the mountains of Israel, and prophesy
against them,
3 And say, Ye mountains of Israel, hear the word of the Lord GOD; Thus saith
the Lord GOD to the mountains, and to the hills, to the rivers, and to the valleys;
Behold, I, *even* I, will bring a sword upon you, and I will destroy your high
places.
4 And your altars shall be desolate, and your images shall be broken: and I
will cast down your slain *men* before your idols.
5 And I will lay the dead carcases of the children of Israel before their idols;
and I will scatter your bones round about your altars.
6 In all your dwellingplaces the cities shall be laid waste, and the high places
shall be desolate; that your altars may be laid waste and made desolate, and
your idols may be broken and cease, and your images may be cut down, and
your works may be abolished.
7 And the slain shall fall in the midst of you, and ye shall know that I *am* the
LORD.

A Remnant Shall Be Blessed

8 Yet will I leave a remnant, that ye may have *some* that shall escape the sword
among the nations, when ye shall be scattered through the countries.
9 And they that escape of you shall remember me among the nations whith-
er they shall be carried captives, because I am broken with their whorish heart,
which hath departed from me, and with their eyes, which go a whoring after
their idols: and they shall lothe themselves for the evils which they have com-
mitted in all their abominations.
10 And they shall know that I *am* the LORD, *and that* I have not said in vain
that I would do this evil unto them.

The Faithful Are Exhorted to Lament

11 Thus saith the Lord GOD; Smite with thine hand, and stamp with thy foot,
and say, Alas for all the evil abominations of the house of Israel! for they shall
fall by the sword, by the famine, and by the pestilence.
12 He that is far off shall die of the pestilence; and he that is near shall fall by
the sword; and he that remaineth and is besieged shall die by the famine: thus
will I accomplish my fury upon them.
13 Then shall ye know that I *am* the LORD, when their slain *men* shall be
among their idols round about their altars, upon every high hill, in all the tops
of the mountains, and under every green tree, and under every thick oak, the
place where they did offer sweet savour to all their idols.
14 So will I stretch out my hand upon them, and make the land desolate, yea,
more desolate than the wilderness toward Diblath, in all their habitations:
and they shall know that I *am* the LORD.

The Final Desolation of Israel

7 Moreover the word of the LORD came unto me, saying,
2 Also, thou son of man, thus saith the Lord GOD unto the land of Israel;
An end, the end is come upon the four corners of the land.
3 Now *is* the end *come* upon thee, and I will send mine anger upon thee, and
will judge thee according to thy ways, and will recompense upon thee all thine
abominations.
4 And mine eye shall not spare thee, neither will I have pity: but I will rec-
ompense thy ways upon thee, and thine abominations shall be in the midst
of thee: and ye shall know that I *am* the LORD.
5 Thus saith the Lord GOD; An evil, an only evil, behold, is come.
6 An end is come, the end is come: it watcheth for thee; behold, it is come.

7 The morning is come unto thee, O thou that dwellest in the land: the time
is come, the day of trouble *is* near, and not the sounding again of the mountains.
8 Now will I shortly pour out my fury upon thee, and accomplish mine anger
upon thee: and I will judge thee according to thy ways, and will recompense
thee for all thine abominations.
9 And mine eye shall not spare, neither will I have pity: I will recompense
thee according to thy ways and thine abominations *that* are in the midst of
thee; and ye shall know that I *am* the LORD that smiteth.
10 Behold the day, behold, it is come: the morning is gone forth; the rod hath
blossomed, pride hath budded.
11 Violence is risen up into a rod of wickedness: none of them *shall remain*,
nor of their multitude, nor of any of theirs: neither *shall there be* wailing for
them.
12 The time is come, the day draweth near: let not the buyer rejoice, nor the
seller mourn: for wrath *is* upon all the multitude thereof.
13 For the seller shall not return to that which is sold, although they were
yet alive: for the vision *is* touching the whole multitude thereof, *which* shall
not return; neither shall any strengthen himself in the iniquity of his life.
14 They have blown the trumpet, even to make all ready; but none goeth to
the battle: for my wrath *is* upon all the multitude thereof.
15 The sword *is* without, and the pestilence and the famine within: he that
is in the field shall die with the sword; and he that *is* in the city, famine and
pestilence shall devour him.

The Repentance of Those Who Escape

16 But they that escape of them shall escape, and shall be on the mountains
like doves of the valleys, all of them mourning, every one for his iniquity.
17 All hands shall be feeble, and all knees shall be weak *as* water.
18 They shall also gird *themselves* with sackcloth, and horror shall cover
them; and shame *shall be* upon all faces, and baldness upon all their heads.
19 They shall cast their silver in the streets, and their gold shall be removed:
their silver and their gold shall not be able to deliver them in the day of the
wrath of the LORD: they shall not satisfy their souls, neither fill their bowels:
because it is the stumblingblock of their iniquity.
20 As for the beauty of his ornament, he set it in majesty: but they made the
images of their abominations *and* of their detestable things therein: therefore
have I set it far from them.
21 And I will give it into the hands of the strangers for a prey, and to the
wicked of the earth for a spoil; and they shall pollute it.
22 My face will I turn also from them, and they shall pollute my secret *place*:
for the robbers shall enter into it, and defile it.

The Figure of a Chain

23 Make a chain: for the land is full of bloody crimes, and the city is full of
violence.
24 Wherefore I will bring the worst of the heathen, and they shall possess
their houses: I will also make the pomp of the strong to cease; and their holy
places shall be defiled.
25 Destruction cometh; and they shall seek peace, and *there shall be* none.
26 Mischief shall come upon mischief, and rumour shall be upon rumour;
then shall they seek a vision of the prophet; but the law shall perish from the
priest, and counsel from the ancients.
27 The king shall mourn, and the prince shall be clothed with desolation,
and the hands of the people of the land shall be troubled: I will do unto them
after their way, and according to their deserts will I judge them; and they shall
know that I *am* the LORD.

Idolatry in Jerusalem

8 And it came to pass in the sixth year, in the sixth *month*, in the fifth *day* of the month, *as* I sat in mine house, and the elders of Judah sat before me, that the hand of the Lord GOD fell there upon me.

2 Then I beheld, and lo a likeness as the appearance of fire: from the appearance of his loins even downward, fire; and from his loins even upward, as the appearance of brightness, as the colour of amber.

3 And he put forth the form of an hand, and took me by a lock of mine head; and the spirit lifted me up between the earth and the heaven, and brought me in the visions of God to Jerusalem, to the door of the inner gate that looketh toward the north; where *was* the seat of the image of jealousy, which provoketh to jealousy.

4 And, behold, the glory of the God of Israel *was* there, according to the vision that I saw in the plain.

5 Then said he unto me, Son of man, lift up thine eyes now the way toward the north. So I lifted up mine eyes the way toward the north, and behold northward at the gate of the altar this image of jealousy in the entry.

6 He said furthermore unto me, Son of man, seest thou what they do? *even* the great abominations that the house of Israel committeth here, that I should go far off from my sanctuary? but turn thee yet again, *and* thou shalt see greater abominations.

The Chambers of Idolatry

7 And he brought me to the door of the court; and when I looked, behold a hole in the wall.

8 Then said he unto me, Son of man, dig now in the wall: and when I had digged in the wall, behold a door.

9 And he said unto me, Go in, and behold the wicked abominations that they do here.

10 So I went in and saw; and behold every form of creeping things, and abominable beasts, and all the idols of the house of Israel, pourtrayed upon the wall round about.

11 And there stood before them seventy men of the ancients of the house of Israel, and in the midst of them stood Jaazaniah the son of Shaphan, with every man his censer in his hand; and a thick cloud of incense went up.

12 Then said he unto me, Son of man, hast thou seen what the ancients of the house of Israel do in the dark, every man in the chambers of his imagery? for they say, The LORD seeth us not; the LORD hath forsaken the earth.

The Mourners for Tammuz

13 He said also unto me, Turn thee yet again, *and* thou shalt see greater abominations that they do.

14 Then he brought me to the door of the gate of the LORD's house which *was* toward the north; and, behold, there sat women weeping for Tammuz.

15 Then said he unto me, Hast thou seen *this*, O son of man? turn thee yet again, *and* thou shalt see greater abominations than these.

16 And he brought me into the inner court of the LORD's house, and, behold, at the door of the temple of the LORD, between the porch and the altar, *were* about five and twenty men, with their backs toward the temple of the LORD, and their faces toward the east; and they worshipped the sun toward the east.

17 Then he said unto me, Hast thou seen *this*, O son of man? Is it a light thing to the house of Judah that they commit the abominations which they commit here? for they have filled the land with violence, and have returned to provoke me to anger: and, lo, they put the branch to their nose.

18 Therefore will I also deal in fury: mine eye shall not spare, neither will I have pity: and though they cry in mine ears with a loud voice, *yet* will I not hear them.

The Coming Destruction of the Temple

9 He cried also in mine ears with a loud voice, saying, Cause them that have
charge over the city to draw near, even every man *with* his destroying weap-
on in his hand.
2 And, behold, six men came from the way of the higher gate, which lieth
toward the north, and every man a slaughter weapon in his hand; and one
man among them *was* clothed with linen, with a writer's inkhorn by his side:
and they went in, and stood beside the brasen altar.
3 And the glory of the God of Israel was gone up from the cherub, whereup-
on he was, to the threshold of the house. And he called to the man clothed
with linen, which *had* the writer's inkhorn by his side;
4 And the LORD said unto him, Go through the midst of the city, through the
midst of Jerusalem, and set a mark upon the foreheads of the men that sigh
and that cry for all the abominations that be done in the midst thereof.
5 And to the others he said in mine hearing, Go ye after him through the city,
and smite: let not your eye spare, neither have ye pity:
6 Slay utterly old *and* young, both maids, and little children, and women:
but come not near any man upon whom *is* the mark; and begin at my sanctu-
ary. Then they began at the ancient men which *were* before the house.
7 And he said unto them, Defile the house, and fill the courts with the slain:
go ye forth. And they went forth, and slew in the city.
8 And it came to pass, while they were slaying them, and I was left, that I fell
upon my face, and cried, and said, Ah Lord GOD! wilt thou destroy all the
residue of Israel in thy pouring out of thy fury upon Jerusalem?
9 Then said he unto me, The iniquity of the house of Israel and Judah *is*
exceeding great, and the land is full of blood, and the city full of perverseness:
for they say, The LORD hath forsaken the earth, and the LORD seeth not.
10 And as for me also, mine eye shall not spare, neither will I have pity, *but* I
will recompense their way upon their head.
11 And, behold, the man clothed with linen, which *had* the inkhorn by his
side, reported the matter, saying, I have done as thou hast commanded me.

The Lord's Glory Leaves the Temple

10 Then I looked, and, behold, in the firmament that was above the head
of the cherubims there appeared over them as it were a sapphire stone,
as the appearance of the likeness of a throne.
2 And he spake unto the man clothed with linen, and said, Go in between
the wheels, *even* under the cherub, and fill thine hand with coals of fire from
between the cherubims, and scatter *them* over the city. And he went in in my
sight.
3 Now the cherubims stood on the right side of the house, when the man
went in; and the cloud filled the inner court.
4 Then the glory of the LORD went up from the cherub, *and stood* over the
threshold of the house; and the house was filled with the cloud, and the court
was full of the brightness of the LORD's glory.
5 And the sound of the cherubims' wings was heard *even* to the outer court,
as the voice of the Almighty God when he speaketh.
6 And it came to pass, *that* when he had commanded the man clothed with
linen, saying, Take fire from between the wheels, from between the cherubims;
then he went in, and stood beside the wheels.
7 And *one* cherub stretched forth his hand from between the cherubims
unto the fire that *was* between the cherubims, and took *thereof*, and put *it*
into the hands of *him that was* clothed with linen: who took *it*, and went out.
8 And there appeared in the cherubims the form of a man's hand under their
wings.

9 And when I looked, behold the four wheels by the cherubims, one wheel
by one cherub, and another wheel by another cherub: and the appearance of
the wheels *was* as the colour of a beryl stone.
10 And *as for* their appearances, they four had one likeness, as if a wheel had
been in the midst of a wheel.
11 When they went, they went upon their four sides; they turned not as they
went, but to the place whither the head looked they followed it; they turned
not as they went.
12 And their whole body, and their backs, and their hands, and their wings,
and the wheels, *were* full of eyes round about, *even* the wheels that they four
had.
13 As for the wheels, it was cried unto them in my hearing, O wheel.
14 And every one had four faces: the first face *was* the face of a cherub, and
the second face *was* the face of a man, and the third the face of a lion, and the
fourth the face of an eagle.
15 And the cherubims were lifted up. This *is* the living creature that I saw by
the river of Chebar.
16 And when the cherubims went, the wheels went by them: and when the
cherubims lifted up their wings to mount up from the earth, the same wheels
also turned not from beside them.
17 When they stood, *these* stood; and when they were lifted up, *these* lifted
up themselves *also*: for the spirit of the living creature *was* in them.
18 Then the glory of the LORD departed from off the threshold of the house,
and stood over the cherubims.
19 And the cherubims lifted up their wings, and mounted up from the earth
in my sight: when they went out, the wheels also *were* beside them, and *every
one* stood at the door of the east gate of the LORD's house; and the glory of the
God of Israel *was* over them above.
20 This *is* the living creature that I saw under the God of Israel by the river
of Chebar; and I knew that they *were* the cherubims.
21 Every one had four faces apiece, and every one four wings; and the likeness
of the hands of a man *was* under their wings.
22 And the likeness of their faces *was* the same faces which I saw by the river
of Chebar, their appearances and themselves: they went every one straight
forward.

Judgment on Israel's Rulers

11 Moreover the spirit lifted me up, and brought me unto the east gate
of the LORD's house, which looketh eastward: and behold at the door
of the gate five and twenty men; among whom I saw Jaazaniah the son of Azur,
and Pelatiah the son of Benaiah, princes of the people.
2 Then said he unto me, Son of man, these *are* the men that devise mischief,
and give wicked counsel in this city:
3 Which say, *It is* not near; let us build houses: this *city is* the caldron, and
we *be* the flesh.
4 Therefore prophesy against them, prophesy, O son of man.
5 And the Spirit of the LORD fell upon me, and said unto me, Speak; Thus saith
the LORD; Thus have ye said, O house of Israel: for I know the things that come
into your mind, *every one of* them.
6 Ye have multiplied your slain in this city, and ye have filled the streets there-
of with the slain.
7 Therefore thus saith the Lord GOD; Your slain whom ye have laid in the
midst of it, they *are* the flesh, and this *city is* the caldron: but I will bring you
forth out of the midst of it.
8 Ye have feared the sword; and I will bring a sword upon you, saith the Lord
GOD.

9 And I will bring you out of the midst thereof, and deliver you into the hands
of strangers, and will execute judgments among you.
10 Ye shall fall by the sword; I will judge you in the border of Israel; and ye
shall know that I *am* the LORD.
11 This *city* shall not be your caldron, neither shall ye be the flesh in the midst
thereof; *but* I will judge you in the border of Israel:
12 And ye shall know that I *am* the LORD: for ye have not walked in my statutes,
neither executed my judgments, but have done after the manners of the heathen that *are* round about you.
13 And it came to pass, when I prophesied, that Pelatiah the son of Benaiah
died. Then fell I down upon my face, and cried with a loud voice, and said, Ah
Lord GOD! wilt thou make a full end of the remnant of Israel?

God Will Gather Israel

14 Again the word of the LORD came unto me, saying,
15 Son of man, thy brethren, *even* thy brethren, the men of thy kindred, and
all the house of Israel wholly, *are* they unto whom the inhabitants of Jerusalem
have said, Get you far from the LORD: unto us is this land given in possession.
16 Therefore say, Thus saith the Lord GOD; Although I have cast them far off
among the heathen, and although I have scattered them among the countries,
yet will I be to them as a little sanctuary in the countries where they shall come.
17 Therefore say, Thus saith the Lord GOD; I will even gather you from the
people, and assemble you out of the countries where ye have been scattered,
and I will give you the land of Israel.
18 And they shall come thither, and they shall take away all the detestable
things thereof and all the abominations thereof from thence.
19 And I will give them one heart, and I will put a new spirit within you; and
I will take the stony heart out of their flesh, and will give them an heart of
flesh:
20 That they may walk in my statutes, and keep mine ordinances, and do
them: and they shall be my people, and I will be their God.
21 But *as for them* whose heart walketh after the heart of their detestable
things and their abominations, I will recompense their way upon their own
heads, saith the Lord GOD.

The Lord's Glory Leaves Jerusalem

22 Then did the cherubims lift up their wings, and the wheels beside them;
and the glory of the God of Israel *was* over them above.
23 And the glory of the LORD went up from the midst of the city, and stood
upon the mountain which *is* on the east side of the city.
24 Afterwards the spirit took me up, and brought me in a vision by the Spirit
of God into Chaldea, to them of the captivity. So the vision that I had seen went
up from me.
25 Then I spake unto them of the captivity all the things that the LORD had
shewed me.

Ezekiel Foretells Israel's Exile

12 The word of the LORD also came unto me, saying,
2 Son of man, thou dwellest in the midst of a rebellious house, which
have eyes to see, and see not; they have ears to hear, and hear not: for they *are*
a rebellious house.
3 Therefore, thou son of man, prepare thee stuff for removing, and remove
by day in their sight; and thou shalt remove from thy place to another place
in their sight: it may be they will consider, though they *be* a rebellious house.
4 Then shalt thou bring forth thy stuff by day in their sight, as stuff for removing: and thou shalt go forth at even in their sight, as they that go forth into
captivity.
5 Dig thou through the wall in their sight, and carry out thereby.

6 In their sight shalt thou bear *it* upon *thy* shoulders, *and* carry *it* forth in
the twilight: thou shalt cover thy face, that thou see not the ground: for I have
set thee *for* a sign unto the house of Israel.
7 And I did so as I was commanded: I brought forth my stuff by day, as stuff
for captivity, and in the even I digged through the wall with mine hand; I
brought *it* forth in the twilight, *and* I bare *it* upon *my* shoulder in their sight.
8 And in the morning came the word of the LORD unto me, saying,
9 Son of man, hath not the house of Israel, the rebellious house, said unto
thee, What doest thou?
10 Say thou unto them, Thus saith the Lord GOD; This burden *concerneth* the
prince in Jerusalem, and all the house of Israel that *are* among them.
11 Say, I *am* your sign: like as I have done, so shall it be done unto them: they
shall remove *and* go into captivity.
12 And the prince that *is* among them shall bear upon *his* shoulder in the
twilight, and shall go forth: they shall dig through the wall to carry out there-
by: he shall cover his face, that he see not the ground with *his* eyes.
13 My net also will I spread upon him, and he shall be taken in my snare: and
I will bring him to Babylon *to* the land of the Chaldeans; yet shall he not see
it, though he shall die there.
14 And I will scatter toward every wind all that *are* about him to help him,
and all his bands; and I will draw out the sword after them.
15 And they shall know that I *am* the LORD, when I shall scatter them among
the nations, and disperse them in the countries.
16 But I will leave a few men of them from the sword, from the famine, and
from the pestilence; that they may declare all their abominations among the
heathen whither they come; and they shall know that I *am* the LORD.

The Coming Desolation

17 Moreover the word of the LORD came to me, saying,
18 Son of man, eat thy bread with quaking, and drink thy water with trem-
bling and with carefulness;
19 And say unto the people of the land, Thus saith the Lord GOD of the inhab-
itants of Jerusalem, *and* of the land of Israel; They shall eat their bread with
carefulness, and drink their water with astonishment, that her land may be
desolate from all that is therein, because of the violence of all them that dwell
therein.
20 And the cities that are inhabited shall be laid waste, and the land shall be
desolate; and ye shall know that I *am* the LORD.

Every Vision Will Come True

21 And the word of the LORD came unto me, saying,
22 Son of man, what *is* that proverb *that* ye have in the land of Israel, saying,
The days are prolonged, and every vision faileth?
23 Tell them therefore, Thus saith the Lord GOD; I will make this proverb to
cease, and they shall no more use it as a proverb in Israel; but say unto them,
The days are at hand, and the effect of every vision.
24 For there shall be no more any vain vision nor flattering divination with-
in the house of Israel.
25 For I *am* the LORD: I will speak, and the word that I shall speak shall come
to pass; it shall be no more prolonged: for in your days, O rebellious house,
will I say the word, and will perform it, saith the Lord GOD.
26 Again the word of the LORD came to me, saying,
27 Son of man, behold, *they of* the house of Israel say, The vision that he seeth
is for many days *to come*, and he prophesieth of the times *that are* far off.
28 Therefore say unto them, Thus saith the Lord GOD; There shall none of my
words be prolonged any more, but the word which I have spoken shall be
done, saith the Lord GOD.

False Prophets Are Condemned

13 And the word of the LORD came unto me, saying,
2 Son of man, prophesy against the prophets of Israel that prophesy,
and say thou unto them that prophesy out of their own hearts, Hear ye the
word of the LORD;
3 Thus saith the Lord GOD; Woe unto the foolish prophets, that follow their
own spirit, and have seen nothing!
4 O Israel, thy prophets are like the foxes in the deserts.
5 Ye have not gone up into the gaps, neither made up the hedge for the house
of Israel to stand in the battle in the day of the LORD.
6 They have seen vanity and lying divination, saying, The LORD saith: and the
LORD hath not sent them: and they have made *others* to hope that they would
confirm the word.
7 Have ye not seen a vain vision, and have ye not spoken a lying divination,
whereas ye say, The LORD saith *it*; albeit I have not spoken?
8 Therefore thus saith the Lord GOD; Because ye have spoken vanity, and seen
lies, therefore, behold, I *am* against you, saith the Lord GOD.
9 And mine hand shall be upon the prophets that see vanity, and that divine
lies: they shall not be in the assembly of my people, neither shall they be writ-
ten in the writing of the house of Israel, neither shall they enter into the land
of Israel; and ye shall know that I *am* the Lord GOD.
10 Because, even because they have seduced my people, saying, Peace; and
there was no peace; and one built up a wall, and, lo, others daubed it with
untempered *morter*:
11 Say unto them which daub *it* with untempered *morter*, that it shall fall:
there shall be an overflowing shower; and ye, O great hailstones, shall fall; and
a stormy wind shall rend *it*.
12 Lo, when the wall is fallen, shall it not be said unto you, Where *is* the
daubing wherewith ye have daubed *it*?
13 Therefore thus saith the Lord GOD; I will even rend *it* with a stormy wind
in my fury; and there shall be an overflowing shower in mine anger, and great
hailstones in *my* fury to consume *it*.
14 So will I break down the wall that ye have daubed with untempered *mort-
er*, and bring it down to the ground, so that the foundation thereof shall be
discovered, and it shall fall, and ye shall be consumed in the midst thereof:
and ye shall know that I *am* the LORD.
15 Thus will I accomplish my wrath upon the wall, and upon them that have
daubed it with untempered *morter*, and will say unto you, The wall *is* no *more*,
neither they that daubed it;
16 *To wit*, the prophets of Israel which prophesy concerning Jerusalem, and
which see visions of peace for her, and *there is* no peace, saith the Lord GOD.
17 Likewise, thou son of man, set thy face against the daughters of thy people,
which prophesy out of their own heart; and prophesy thou against them,
18 And say, Thus saith the Lord GOD; Woe to the *women* that sew pillows to
all armholes, and make kerchiefs upon the head of every stature to hunt souls!
Will ye hunt the souls of my people, and will ye save the souls alive *that come*
unto you?
19 And will ye pollute me among my people for handfuls of barley and for
pieces of bread, to slay the souls that should not die, and to save the souls alive
that should not live, by your lying to my people that hear *your* lies?
20 Wherefore thus saith the Lord GOD; Behold, I *am* against your pillows,
wherewith ye there hunt the souls to make *them* fly, and I will tear them from
your arms, and will let the souls go, *even* the souls that ye hunt to make *them* fly.
21 Your kerchiefs also will I tear, and deliver my people out of your hand,
and they shall be no more in your hand to be hunted; and ye shall know that
I *am* the LORD.

22 Because with lies ye have made the heart of the righteous sad, whom I
have not made sad; and strengthened the hands of the wicked, that he should
not return from his wicked way, by promising him life:
23 Therefore ye shall see no more vanity, nor divine divinations: for I will
deliver my people out of your hand: and ye shall know that I *am* the LORD.

Idolaters Are Condemned

14 Then came certain of the elders of Israel unto me, and sat before me.
2 And the word of the LORD came unto me, saying,
3 Son of man, these men have set up their idols in their heart, and put the
stumblingblock of their iniquity before their face: should I be enquired of at
all by them?
4 Therefore speak unto them, and say unto them, Thus saith the Lord GOD;
Every man of the house of Israel that setteth up his idols in his heart, and
putteth the stumblingblock of his iniquity before his face, and cometh to the
prophet; I the LORD will answer him that cometh according to the multitude
of his idols;
5 That I may take the house of Israel in their own heart, because they are all
estranged from me through their idols.
6 Therefore say unto the house of Israel, Thus saith the Lord GOD; Repent,
and turn *yourselves* from your idols; and turn away your faces from all your
abominations.
7 For every one of the house of Israel, or of the stranger that sojourneth in
Israel, which separateth himself from me, and setteth up his idols in his heart,
and putteth the stumblingblock of his iniquity before his face, and cometh to
a prophet to enquire of him concerning me; I the LORD will answer him by
myself:
8 And I will set my face against that man, and will make him a sign and a
proverb, and I will cut him off from the midst of my people; and ye shall know
that I *am* the LORD.
9 And if the prophet be deceived when he hath spoken a thing, I the LORD
have deceived that prophet, and I will stretch out my hand upon him, and will
destroy him from the midst of my people Israel.
10 And they shall bear the punishment of their iniquity: the punishment of
the prophet shall be even as the punishment of him that seeketh *unto him*;
11 That the house of Israel may go no more astray from me, neither be pol-
luted any more with all their transgressions; but that they may be my people,
and I may be their God, saith the Lord GOD.
12 The word of the LORD came again to me, saying,
13 Son of man, when the land sinneth against me by trespassing grievously,
then will I stretch out mine hand upon it, and will break the staff of the bread
thereof, and will send famine upon it, and will cut off man and beast from it:
14 Though these three men, Noah, Daniel, and Job, were in it, they should
deliver *but* their own souls by their righteousness, saith the Lord GOD.
15 If I cause noisome beasts to pass through the land, and they spoil it, so
that it be desolate, that no man may pass through because of the beasts:
16 *Though* these three men *were* in it, *as* I live, saith the Lord GOD, they shall
deliver neither sons nor daughters; they only shall be delivered, but the land
shall be desolate.
17 Or *if* I bring a sword upon that land, and say, Sword, go through the land;
so that I cut off man and beast from it:
18 Though these three men *were* in it, *as* I live, saith the Lord GOD, they shall
deliver neither sons nor daughters, but they only shall be delivered themselves.
19 Or *if* I send a pestilence into that land, and pour out my fury upon it in
blood, to cut off from it man and beast:

20 Though Noah, Daniel, and Job, *were* in it, *as* I live, saith the Lord GOD, they
shall deliver neither son nor daughter; they shall *but* deliver their own souls
by their righteousness.
21 For thus saith the Lord GOD; How much more when I send my four sore
judgments upon Jerusalem, the sword, and the famine, and the noisome beast,
and the pestilence, to cut off from it man and beast?
22 Yet, behold, therein shall be left a remnant that shall be brought forth,
both sons and daughters: behold, they shall come forth unto you, and ye shall
see their way and their doings: and ye shall be comforted concerning the evil
that I have brought upon Jerusalem, *even* concerning all that I have brought
upon it.
23 And they shall comfort you, when ye see their ways and their doings: and
ye shall know that I have not done without cause all that I have done in it, saith
the Lord GOD.

Jerusalem Is a Worthless Vine

15 And the word of the LORD came unto me, saying,
2 Son of man, What is the vine tree more than any tree, *or than* a
branch which is among the trees of the forest?
3 Shall wood be taken thereof to do any work? or will *men* take a pin of it to
hang any vessel thereon?
4 Behold, it is cast into the fire for fuel; the fire devoureth both the ends of
it, and the midst of it is burned. Is it meet for *any* work?
5 Behold, when it was whole, it was meet for no work: how much less shall
it be meet yet for *any* work, when the fire hath devoured it, and it is burned?
6 Therefore thus saith the Lord GOD; As the vine tree among the trees of the
forest, which I have given to the fire for fuel, so will I give the inhabitants of
Jerusalem.
7 And I will set my face against them; they shall go out from *one* fire, and
another fire shall devour them; and ye shall know that I *am* the LORD, when I
set my face against them.
8 And I will make the land desolate, because they have committed a trespass,
saith the Lord GOD.

A Description of Jerusalem's Sins

16 Again the word of the LORD came unto me, saying,
2 Son of man, cause Jerusalem to know her abominations,
3 And say, Thus saith the Lord GOD unto Jerusalem; Thy birth and thy nativ-
ity *is* of the land of Canaan; thy father *was* an Amorite, and thy mother an
Hittite.
4 And *as for* thy nativity, in the day thou wast born thy navel was not cut,
neither wast thou washed in water to supple *thee*; thou wast not salted at all,
nor swaddled at all.
5 None eye pitied thee, to do any of these unto thee, to have compassion upon
thee; but thou wast cast out in the open field, to the lothing of thy person, in
the day that thou wast born.

God's Extraordinary Love

6 And when I passed by thee, and saw thee polluted in thine own blood, I
said unto thee *when thou wast* in thy blood, Live; yea, I said unto thee *when
thou wast* in thy blood, Live.
7 I have caused thee to multiply as the bud of the field, and thou hast
increased and waxen great, and thou art come to excellent ornaments: *thy*
breasts are fashioned, and thine hair is grown, whereas thou *wast* naked and
bare.
8 Now when I passed by thee, and looked upon thee, behold, thy time *was*
the time of love; and I spread my skirt over thee, and covered thy nakedness:

yea, I sware unto thee, and entered into a covenant with thee, saith the Lord
GOD, and thou becamest mine.
9 Then washed I thee with water; yea, I throughly washed away thy blood
from thee, and I anointed thee with oil.
10 I clothed thee also with broidered work, and shod thee with badgers' skin,
and I girded thee about with fine linen, and I covered thee with silk.
11 I decked thee also with ornaments, and I put bracelets upon thy hands,
and a chain on thy neck.
12 And I put a jewel on thy forehead, and earrings in thine ears, and a beau-
tiful crown upon thine head.
13 Thus wast thou decked with gold and silver; and thy raiment *was of* fine
linen, and silk, and broidered work; thou didst eat fine flour, and honey, and
oil: and thou wast exceeding beautiful, and thou didst prosper into a kingdom.
14 And thy renown went forth among the heathen for thy beauty: for it *was*
perfect through my comeliness, which I had put upon thee, saith the Lord
GOD.

Jerusalem's Lewdness

15 But thou didst trust in thine own beauty, and playedst the harlot because
of thy renown, and pouredst out thy fornications on every one that passed by;
his it was.
16 And of thy garments thou didst take, and deckedst thy high places with
divers colours, and playedst the harlot thereupon: *the like things* shall not
come, neither shall it be *so*.
17 Thou hast also taken thy fair jewels of my gold and of my silver, which I
had given thee, and madest to thyself images of men, and didst commit whore-
dom with them,
18 And tookest thy broidered garments, and coveredst them: and thou hast
set mine oil and mine incense before them.
19 My meat also which I gave thee, fine flour, and oil, and honey, *wherewith*
I fed thee, thou hast even set it before them for a sweet savour: and *thus* it was,
saith the Lord GOD.
20 Moreover thou hast taken thy sons and thy daughters, whom thou hast
borne unto me, and these hast thou sacrificed unto them to be devoured. *Is
this* of thy whoredoms a small matter,
21 That thou hast slain my children, and delivered them to cause them to
pass through *the fire* for them?
22 And in all thine abominations and thy whoredoms thou hast not remem-
bered the days of thy youth, when thou wast naked and bare, *and* wast pollut-
ed in thy blood.
23 And it came to pass after all thy wickedness, (woe, woe unto thee! saith
the Lord GOD;)
24 *That* thou hast also built unto thee an eminent place, and hast made thee
an high place in every street.
25 Thou hast built thy high place at every head of the way, and hast made thy
beauty to be abhorred, and hast opened thy feet to every one that passed by,
and multiplied thy whoredoms.
26 Thou hast also committed fornication with the Egyptians thy neighbours,
great of flesh; and hast increased thy whoredoms, to provoke me to anger.
27 Behold, therefore I have stretched out my hand over thee, and have dimin-
ished thine ordinary *food*, and delivered thee unto the will of them that hate
thee, the daughters of the Philistines, which are ashamed of thy lewd way.
28 Thou hast played the whore also with the Assyrians, because thou wast
unsatiable; yea, thou hast played the harlot with them, and yet couldest not
be satisfied.

29 Thou hast moreover multiplied thy fornication in the land of Canaan
unto Chaldea; and yet thou wast not satisfied herewith.
30 How weak is thine heart, saith the Lord GOD, seeing thou doest all these
things, the work of an imperious whorish woman;
31 In that thou buildest thine eminent place in the head of every way, and
makest thine high place in every street; and hast not been as an harlot, in that
thou scornest hire;
32 *But as* a wife that committeth adultery, *which* taketh strangers instead of
her husband!
33 They give gifts to all whores: but thou givest thy gifts to all thy lovers, and
hirest them, that they may come unto thee on every side for thy whoredom.
34 And the contrary is in thee from *other* women in thy whoredoms, where-
as none followeth thee to commit whoredoms: and in that thou givest a
reward, and no reward is given unto thee, therefore thou art contrary.

Jerusalem's Punishment

35 Wherefore, O harlot, hear the word of the LORD:
36 Thus saith the Lord GOD; Because thy filthiness was poured out, and thy
nakedness discovered through thy whoredoms with thy lovers, and with all
the idols of thy abominations, and by the blood of thy children, which thou
didst give unto them;
37 Behold, therefore I will gather all thy lovers, with whom thou hast taken
pleasure, and all *them* that thou hast loved, with all *them* that thou hast hated;
I will even gather them round about against thee, and will discover thy naked-
ness unto them, that they may see all thy nakedness.
38 And I will judge thee, as women that break wedlock and shed blood are
judged; and I will give thee blood in fury and jealousy.
39 And I will also give thee into their hand, and they shall throw down thine
eminent place, and shall break down thy high places: they shall strip thee also
of thy clothes, and shall take thy fair jewels, and leave thee naked and bare.
40 They shall also bring up a company against thee, and they shall stone thee
with stones, and thrust thee through with their swords.
41 And they shall burn thine houses with fire, and execute judgments upon
thee in the sight of many women: and I will cause thee to cease from playing
the harlot, and thou also shalt give no hire any more.
42 So will I make my fury toward thee to rest, and my jealousy shall depart
from thee, and I will be quiet, and will be no more angry.
43 Because thou hast not remembered the days of thy youth, but hast fretted
me in all these *things*; behold, therefore I also will recompense thy way upon
thine head, saith the Lord GOD: and thou shalt not commit this lewdness above
all thine abominations.
44 Behold, every one that useth proverbs shall use *this* proverb against thee,
saying, As *is* the mother, *so is* her daughter.
45 Thou *art* thy mother's daughter, that lotheth her husband and her chil-
dren; and thou *art* the sister of thy sisters, which lothed their husbands and
their children: your mother *was* an Hittite, and your father an Amorite.
46 And thine elder sister *is* Samaria, she and her daughters that dwell at thy
left hand: and thy younger sister, that dwelleth at thy right hand, *is* Sodom
and her daughters.
47 Yet hast thou not walked after their ways, nor done after their abomina-
tions: but, as *if that were* a very little *thing*, thou wast corrupted more than
they in all thy ways.
48 *As* I live, saith the Lord GOD, Sodom thy sister hath not done, she nor her
daughters, as thou hast done, thou and thy daughters.

49 Behold, this was the iniquity of thy sister Sodom, pride, fulness of bread,
and abundance of idleness was in her and in her daughters, neither did she
strengthen the hand of the poor and needy.
50 And they were haughty, and committed abomination before me: therefore
I took them away as I saw *good*.
51 Neither hath Samaria committed half of thy sins; but thou hast multiplied
thine abominations more than they, and hast justified thy sisters in all thine
abominations which thou hast done.
52 Thou also, which hast judged thy sisters, bear thine own shame for thy
sins that thou hast committed more abominable than they: they are more
righteous than thou: yea, be thou confounded also, and bear thy shame, in
that thou hast justified thy sisters.
53 When I shall bring again their captivity, the captivity of Sodom and her
daughters, and the captivity of Samaria and her daughters, then *will I bring
again* the captivity of thy captives in the midst of them:
54 That thou mayest bear thine own shame, and mayest be confounded in
all that thou hast done, in that thou art a comfort unto them.
55 When thy sisters, Sodom and her daughters, shall return to their former
estate, and Samaria and her daughters shall return to their former estate, then
thou and thy daughters shall return to your former estate.
56 For thy sister Sodom was not mentioned by thy mouth in the day of thy
pride,
57 Before thy wickedness was discovered, as at the time of *thy* reproach of
the daughters of Syria, and all *that are* round about her, the daughters of the
Philistines, which despise thee round about.
58 Thou hast borne thy lewdness and thine abominations, saith the LORD.
59 For thus saith the Lord GOD; I will even deal with thee as thou hast done,
which hast despised the oath in breaking the covenant.
60 Nevertheless I will remember my covenant with thee in the days of thy
youth, and I will establish unto thee an everlasting covenant.
61 Then thou shalt remember thy ways, and be ashamed, when thou shalt
receive thy sisters, thine elder and thy younger: and I will give them unto thee
for daughters, but not by thy covenant.
62 And I will establish my covenant with thee; and thou shalt know that I *am*
the LORD:
63 That thou mayest remember, and be confounded, and never open thy
mouth any more because of thy shame, when I am pacified toward thee for
all that thou hast done, saith the Lord GOD.

Judah Is Compared to a Tree

17 And the word of the LORD came unto me, saying,
2 Son of man, put forth a riddle, and speak a parable unto the house
of Israel;
3 And say, Thus saith the Lord GOD; A great eagle with great wings, long-
winged, full of feathers, which had divers colours, came unto Lebanon, and
took the highest branch of the cedar:
4 He cropped off the top of his young twigs, and carried it into a land of
traffick; he set it in a city of merchants.
5 He took also of the seed of the land, and planted it in a fruitful field; he
placed *it* by great waters, *and* set it *as* a willow tree.
6 And it grew, and became a spreading vine of low stature, whose branches
turned toward him, and the roots thereof were under him: so it became a vine,
and brought forth branches, and shot forth sprigs.
7 There was also another great eagle with great wings and many feathers:
and, behold, this vine did bend her roots toward him, and shot forth her
branches toward him, that he might water it by the furrows of her plantation.

8 It was planted in a good soil by great waters, that it might bring forth
branches, and that it might bear fruit, that it might be a goodly vine.
9 Say thou, Thus saith the Lord GOD; Shall it prosper? shall he not pull up the
roots thereof, and cut off the fruit thereof, that it wither? it shall wither in all
the leaves of her spring, even without great power or many people to pluck it
up by the roots thereof.
10 Yea, behold, *being* planted, shall it prosper? shall it not utterly wither,
when the east wind toucheth it? it shall wither in the furrows where it grew.
11 Moreover the word of the LORD came unto me, saying,
12 Say now to the rebellious house, Know ye not what these *things mean*?
tell *them*, Behold, the king of Babylon is come to Jerusalem, and hath taken
the king thereof, and the princes thereof, and led them with him to Babylon;
13 And hath taken of the king's seed, and made a covenant with him, and
hath taken an oath of him: he hath also taken the mighty of the land:
14 That the kingdom might be base, that it might not lift itself up, *but* that
by keeping of his covenant it might stand.
15 But he rebelled against him in sending his ambassadors into Egypt, that
they might give him horses and much people. Shall he prosper? shall he escape
that doeth such *things*? or shall he break the covenant, and be delivered?
16 *As* I live, saith the Lord GOD, surely in the place *where* the king *dwelleth*
that made him king, whose oath he despised, and whose covenant he brake,
even with him in the midst of Babylon he shall die.
17 Neither shall Pharaoh with *his* mighty army and great company make for
him in the war, by casting up mounts, and building forts, to cut off many
persons:
18 Seeing he despised the oath by breaking the covenant, when, lo, he had
given his hand, and hath done all these *things*, he shall not escape.
19 Therefore thus saith the Lord GOD; *As* I live, surely mine oath that he hath
despised, and my covenant that he hath broken, even it will I recompense
upon his own head.
20 And I will spread my net upon him, and he shall be taken in my snare, and
I will bring him to Babylon, and will plead with him there for his trespass that
he hath trespassed against me.
21 And all his fugitives with all his bands shall fall by the sword, and they that
remain shall be scattered toward all winds: and ye shall know that I the LORD
have spoken *it*.

God Promises to Plant the Cedar

22 Thus saith the Lord GOD; I will also take of the highest branch of the high
cedar, and will set *it*; I will crop off from the top of his young twigs a tender
one, and will plant *it* upon an high mountain and eminent:
23 In the mountain of the height of Israel will I plant it: and it shall bring
forth boughs, and bear fruit, and be a goodly cedar: and under it shall dwell
all fowl of every wing; in the shadow of the branches thereof shall they dwell.
24 And all the trees of the field shall know that I the LORD have brought down
the high tree, have exalted the low tree, have dried up the green tree, and have
made the dry tree to flourish: I the LORD have spoken and have done *it*.

Everyone Will Suffer for His Own Sins

18 The word of the LORD came unto me again, saying,
2 What mean ye, that ye use this proverb concerning the land of Israel,
saying, The fathers have eaten sour grapes, and the children's teeth are set on
edge?
3 *As* I live, saith the Lord GOD, ye shall not have *occasion* any more to use this
proverb in Israel.
4 Behold, all souls are mine; as the soul of the father, so also the soul of the
son is mine: the soul that sinneth, it shall die.

5 But if a man be just, and do that which is lawful and right,
6 *And* hath not eaten upon the mountains, neither hath lifted up his eyes to
the idols of the house of Israel, neither hath defiled his neighbour's wife,
neither hath come near to a menstruous woman,
7 And hath not oppressed any, *but* hath restored to the debtor his pledge,
hath spoiled none by violence, hath given his bread to the hungry, and hath
covered the naked with a garment;
8 He *that* hath not given forth upon usury, neither hath taken any increase,
that hath withdrawn his hand from iniquity, hath executed true judgment
between man and man,
9 Hath walked in my statutes, and hath kept my judgments, to deal truly; he
is just, he shall surely live, saith the Lord God.
10 If he beget a son *that is* a robber, a shedder of blood, and *that* doeth the
like to *any* one of these *things*,
11 And that doeth not any of those *duties*, but even hath eaten upon the
mountains, and defiled his neighbour's wife,
12 Hath oppressed the poor and needy, hath spoiled by violence, hath not
restored the pledge, and hath lifted up his eyes to the idols, hath committed
abomination,
13 Hath given forth upon usury, and hath taken increase: shall he then live?
he shall not live: he hath done all these abominations; he shall surely die; his
blood shall be upon him.
14 Now, lo, *if* he beget a son, that seeth all his father's sins which he hath
done, and considereth, and doeth not such like,
15 *That* hath not eaten upon the mountains, neither hath lifted up his eyes
to the idols of the house of Israel, hath not defiled his neighbour's wife,
16 Neither hath oppressed any, hath not withholden the pledge, neither hath
spoiled by violence, *but* hath given his bread to the hungry, and hath covered
the naked with a garment,
17 *That* hath taken off his hand from the poor, *that* hath not received usury
nor increase, hath executed my judgments, hath walked in my statutes; he
shall not die for the iniquity of his father, he shall surely live.
18 *As for* his father, because he cruelly oppressed, spoiled his brother by
violence, and did *that* which *is* not good among his people, lo, even he shall
die in his iniquity.
19 Yet say ye, Why? doth not the son bear the iniquity of the father? When
the son hath done that which is lawful and right, *and* hath kept all my statutes,
and hath done them, he shall surely live.
20 The soul that sinneth, it shall die. The son shall not bear the iniquity of
the father, neither shall the father bear the iniquity of the son: the righteous-
ness of the righteous shall be upon him, and the wickedness of the wicked
shall be upon him.
21 But if the wicked will turn from all his sins that he hath committed, and
keep all my statutes, and do that which is lawful and right, he shall surely live,
he shall not die.
22 All his transgressions that he hath committed, they shall not be mentioned
unto him: in his righteousness that he hath done he shall live.
23 Have I any pleasure at all that the wicked should die? saith the Lord God:
and not that he should return from his ways, and live?
24 But when the righteous turneth away from his righteousness, and com-
mitteth iniquity, *and* doeth according to all the abominations that the wicked
man doeth, shall he live? All his righteousness that he hath done shall not be
mentioned: in his trespass that he hath trespassed, and in his sin that he hath
sinned, in them shall he die.
25 Yet ye say, The way of the Lord is not equal. Hear now, O house of Israel;
Is not my way equal? are not your ways unequal?

26 When a righteous *man* turneth away from his righteousness, and com-
mitteth iniquity, and dieth in them; for his iniquity that he hath done shall he
die.
27 Again, when the wicked *man* turneth away from his wickedness that he
hath committed, and doeth that which is lawful and right, he shall save his
soul alive.
28 Because he considereth, and turneth away from all his transgressions that
he hath committed, he shall surely live, he shall not die.
29 Yet saith the house of Israel, The way of the Lord is not equal. O house of
Israel, are not my ways equal? are not your ways unequal?
30 Therefore I will judge you, O house of Israel, every one according to his
ways, saith the Lord GOD. Repent, and turn *yourselves* from all your transgres-
sions; so iniquity shall not be your ruin.
31 Cast away from you all your transgressions, whereby ye have transgressed;
and make you a new heart and a new spirit: for why will ye die, O house of
Israel?
32 For I have no pleasure in the death of him that dieth, saith the Lord GOD:
wherefore turn *yourselves*, and live ye.

A Lamentation for Israel's Princes

19 Moreover take thou up a lamentation for the princes of Israel,
2 And say, What *is* thy mother? A lioness: she lay down among lions,
she nourished her whelps among young lions.
3 And she brought up one of her whelps: it became a young lion, and it
learned to catch the prey; it devoured men.
4 The nations also heard of him; he was taken in their pit, and they brought
him with chains unto the land of Egypt.
5 Now when she saw that she had waited, *and* her hope was lost, then she
took another of her whelps, *and* made him a young lion.
6 And he went up and down among the lions, he became a young lion, and
learned to catch the prey, *and* devoured men.
7 And he knew their desolate palaces, and he laid waste their cities; and the
land was desolate, and the fulness thereof, by the noise of his roaring.
8 Then the nations set against him on every side from the provinces, and
spread their net over him: he was taken in their pit.
9 And they put him in ward in chains, and brought him to the king of
Babylon: they brought him into holds, that his voice should no more be heard
upon the mountains of Israel.

A Lamentation for Jerusalem

10 Thy mother *is* like a vine in thy blood, planted by the waters: she was
fruitful and full of branches by reason of many waters.
11 And she had strong rods for the sceptres of them that bare rule, and her
stature was exalted among the thick branches, and she appeared in her height
with the multitude of her branches.
12 But she was plucked up in fury, she was cast down to the ground, and the
east wind dried up her fruit: her strong rods were broken and withered; the
fire consumed them.
13 And now she *is* planted in the wilderness, in a dry and thirsty ground.
14 And fire is gone out of a rod of her branches, *which* hath devoured her
fruit, so that she hath no strong rod *to be* a sceptre to rule. This *is* a lamentation,
and shall be for a lamentation.

Israel's Past and Present Sins

20 And it came to pass in the seventh year, in the fifth *month*, the tenth
day of the month, *that* certain of the elders of Israel came to enquire
of the LORD, and sat before me.
2 Then came the word of the LORD unto me, saying,

3 Son of man, speak unto the elders of Israel, and say unto them, Thus saith
the Lord God; Are ye come to enquire of me? *As* I live, saith the Lord God, I
will not be enquired of by you.
4 Wilt thou judge them, son of man, wilt thou judge *them*? cause them to
know the abominations of their fathers:

Israel's Rebellions in Egypt

5 And say unto them, Thus saith the Lord God; In the day when I chose Israel,
and lifted up mine hand unto the seed of the house of Jacob, and made myself
known unto them in the land of Egypt, when I lifted up mine hand unto them,
saying, I *am* the Lord your God;
6 In the day *that* I lifted up mine hand unto them, to bring them forth of the
land of Egypt into a land that I had espied for them, flowing with milk and
honey, which *is* the glory of all lands:
7 Then said I unto them, Cast ye away every man the abominations of his
eyes, and defile not yourselves with the idols of Egypt: I *am* the Lord your God.
8 But they rebelled against me, and would not hearken unto me: they did
not every man cast away the abominations of their eyes, neither did they for-
sake the idols of Egypt: then I said, I will pour out my fury upon them, to
accomplish my anger against them in the midst of the land of Egypt.
9 But I wrought for my name's sake, that it should not be polluted before the
heathen, among whom they *were*, in whose sight I made myself known unto
them, in bringing them forth out of the land of Egypt.

Israel's Rebellions in the Wilderness

10 Wherefore I caused them to go forth out of the land of Egypt, and brought
them into the wilderness.
11 And I gave them my statutes, and shewed them my judgments, which *if* a
man do, he shall even live in them.
12 Moreover also I gave them my sabbaths, to be a sign between me and them,
that they might know that I *am* the Lord that sanctify them.
13 But the house of Israel rebelled against me in the wilderness: they walked
not in my statutes, and they despised my judgments, which *if* a man do, he
shall even live in them; and my sabbaths they greatly polluted: then I said, I
would pour out my fury upon them in the wilderness, to consume them.
14 But I wrought for my name's sake, that it should not be polluted before
the heathen, in whose sight I brought them out.
15 Yet also I lifted up my hand unto them in the wilderness, that I would not
bring them into the land which I had given *them*, flowing with milk and honey,
which *is* the glory of all lands;
16 Because they despised my judgments, and walked not in my statutes, but
polluted my sabbaths: for their heart went after their idols.
17 Nevertheless mine eye spared them from destroying them, neither did I
make an end of them in the wilderness.
18 But I said unto their children in the wilderness, Walk ye not in the statutes
of your fathers, neither observe their judgments, nor defile yourselves with
their idols:
19 I *am* the Lord your God; walk in my statutes, and keep my judgments, and
do them;
20 And hallow my sabbaths; and they shall be a sign between me and you,
that ye may know that I *am* the Lord your God.
21 Notwithstanding the children rebelled against me: they walked not in my
statutes, neither kept my judgments to do them, which *if* a man do, he shall
even live in them; they polluted my sabbaths: then I said, I would pour out my
fury upon them, to accomplish my anger against them in the wilderness.

22 Nevertheless I withdrew mine hand, and wrought for my name's sake,
that it should not be polluted in the sight of the heathen, in whose sight I
brought them forth.
23 I lifted up mine hand unto them also in the wilderness, that I would scat-
ter them among the heathen, and disperse them through the countries;
24 Because they had not executed my judgments, but had despised my stat-
utes, and had polluted my sabbaths, and their eyes were after their fathers'
idols.
25 Wherefore I gave them also statutes *that were* not good, and judgments
whereby they should not live;
26 And I polluted them in their own gifts, in that they caused to pass through
the fire all that openeth the womb, that I might make them desolate, to the
end that they might know that I *am* the LORD.

Israel's Rebellion in the Promised Land

27 Therefore, son of man, speak unto the house of Israel, and say unto them,
Thus saith the Lord GOD; Yet in this your fathers have blasphemed me, in that
they have committed a trespass against me.
28 *For* when I had brought them into the land, *for* the which I lifted up mine
hand to give it to them, then they saw every high hill, and all the thick trees,
and they offered there their sacrifices, and there they presented the provoca-
tion of their offering: there also they made their sweet savour, and poured out
there their drink offerings.
29 Then I said unto them, What *is* the high place whereunto ye go? And the
name thereof is called Bamah unto this day.
30 Wherefore say unto the house of Israel, Thus saith the Lord GOD; Are ye
polluted after the manner of your fathers? and commit ye whoredom after
their abominations?
31 For when ye offer your gifts, when ye make your sons to pass through the
fire, ye pollute yourselves with all your idols, even unto this day: and shall I be
enquired of by you, O house of Israel? *As* I live, saith the Lord GOD, I will not
be enquired of by you.
32 And that which cometh into your mind shall not be at all, that ye say, We
will be as the heathen, as the families of the countries, to serve wood and stone.
33 *As* I live, saith the Lord GOD, surely with a mighty hand, and with a
stretched out arm, and with fury poured out, will I rule over you:
34 And I will bring you out from the people, and will gather you out of the
countries wherein ye are scattered, with a mighty hand, and with a stretched
out arm, and with fury poured out.

Israel's Future

35 And I will bring you into the wilderness of the people, and there will I
plead with you face to face.
36 Like as I pleaded with your fathers in the wilderness of the land of Egypt,
so will I plead with you, saith the Lord GOD.
37 And I will cause you to pass under the rod, and I will bring you into the
bond of the covenant:
38 And I will purge out from among you the rebels, and them that transgress
against me: I will bring them forth out of the country where they sojourn, and
they shall not enter into the land of Israel: and ye shall know that I *am* the
LORD.
39 As for you, O house of Israel, thus saith the Lord GOD; Go ye, serve ye every
one his idols, and hereafter *also*, if ye will not hearken unto me: but pollute
ye my holy name no more with your gifts, and with your idols.
40 For in mine holy mountain, in the mountain of the height of Israel, saith
the Lord GOD, there shall all the house of Israel, all of them in the land, serve

me: there will I accept them, and there will I require your offerings, and the
firstfruits of your oblations, with all your holy things.
41 I will accept you with your sweet savour, when I bring you out from the
people, and gather you out of the countries wherein ye have been scattered;
and I will be sanctified in you before the heathen.
42 And ye shall know that I *am* the LORD, when I shall bring you into the land
of Israel, into the country *for* the which I lifted up mine hand to give it to your
fathers.
43 And there shall ye remember your ways, and all your doings, wherein ye
have been defiled; and ye shall lothe yourselves in your own sight for all your
evils that ye have committed.
44 And ye shall know that I *am* the LORD, when I have wrought with you for
my name's sake, not according to your wicked ways, nor according to your
corrupt doings, O ye house of Israel, saith the Lord GOD.

The Burning Forest

45 Moreover the word of the LORD came unto me, saying,
46 Son of man, set thy face toward the south, and drop *thy word* toward the
south, and prophesy against the forest of the south field;
47 And say to the forest of the south, Hear the word of the LORD; Thus saith
the Lord GOD; Behold, I will kindle a fire in thee, and it shall devour every green
tree in thee, and every dry tree: the flaming flame shall not be quenched, and
all faces from the south to the north shall be burned therein.
48 And all flesh shall see that I the LORD have kindled it: it shall not be
quenched.
49 Then said I, Ah Lord GOD! they say of me, Doth he not speak parables?

The Sword of the Lord

21 And the word of the LORD came unto me, saying,
2 Son of man, set thy face toward Jerusalem, and drop *thy word* toward
the holy places, and prophesy against the land of Israel,
3 And say to the land of Israel, Thus saith the LORD; Behold, I *am* against thee,
and will draw forth my sword out of his sheath, and will cut off from thee the
righteous and the wicked.
4 Seeing then that I will cut off from thee the righteous and the wicked,
therefore shall my sword go forth out of his sheath against all flesh from the
south to the north:
5 That all flesh may know that I the LORD have drawn forth my sword out of
his sheath: it shall not return any more.
6 Sigh therefore, thou son of man, with the breaking of *thy* loins; and with
bitterness sigh before their eyes.
7 And it shall be, when they say unto thee, Wherefore sighest thou? that thou
shalt answer, For the tidings; because it cometh: and every heart shall melt,
and all hands shall be feeble, and every spirit shall faint, and all knees shall be
weak *as* water: behold, it cometh, and shall be brought to pass, saith the Lord
GOD.
8 Again the word of the LORD came unto me, saying,
9 Son of man, prophesy, and say, Thus saith the LORD; Say, A sword, a sword
is sharpened, and also furbished:
10 It is sharpened to make a sore slaughter; it is furbished that it may glitter:
should we then make mirth? it contemneth the rod of my son, *as* every tree.
11 And he hath given it to be furbished, that it may be handled: this sword
is sharpened, and it is furbished, to give it into the hand of the slayer.
12 Cry and howl, son of man: for it shall be upon my people, it *shall be* upon
all the princes of Israel: terrors by reason of the sword shall be upon my people:
smite therefore upon *thy* thigh.

13 Because *it is* a trial, and what if *the sword* contemn even the rod? it shall
be no *more*, saith the Lord GOD.
14 Thou therefore, son of man, prophesy, and smite *thine* hands together,
and let the sword be doubled the third time, the sword of the slain: it *is* the
sword of the great *men that are* slain, which entereth into their privy cham-
bers.
15 I have set the point of the sword against all their gates, that *their* heart
may faint, and *their* ruins be multiplied: ah! *it is* made bright, *it is* wrapped
up for the slaughter.
16 Go thee one way or other, *either* on the right hand, *or* on the left, whith-
ersoever thy face *is* set.
17 I will also smite mine hands together, and I will cause my fury to rest: I
the LORD have said *it*.

The Sword of Babylon's King

18 The word of the LORD came unto me again, saying,
19 Also, thou son of man, appoint thee two ways, that the sword of the king
of Babylon may come: both twain shall come forth out of one land: and choose
thou a place, choose *it* at the head of the way to the city.
20 Appoint a way, that the sword may come to Rabbath of the Ammonites,
and to Judah in Jerusalem the defenced.
21 For the king of Babylon stood at the parting of the way, at the head of the
two ways, to use divination: he made *his* arrows bright, he consulted with
images, he looked in the liver.
22 At his right hand was the divination for Jerusalem, to appoint captains,
to open the mouth in the slaughter, to lift up the voice with shouting, to
appoint *battering* rams against the gates, to cast a mount, *and* to build a fort.
23 And it shall be unto them as a false divination in their sight, to them that
have sworn oaths: but he will call to remembrance the iniquity, that they may
be taken.
24 Therefore thus saith the Lord GOD; Because ye have made your iniquity
to be remembered, in that your transgressions are discovered, so that in all
your doings your sins do appear; because, *I say*, that ye are come to remem-
brance, ye shall be taken with the hand.
25 And thou, profane wicked prince of Israel, whose day is come, when iniq-
uity *shall have* an end,
26 Thus saith the Lord GOD; Remove the diadem, and take off the crown: this
shall not *be* the same: exalt *him that is* low, and abase *him that is* high.
27 I will overturn, overturn, overturn, it: and it shall be no *more*, until he
come whose right it is; and I will give it *him*.

A Prophecy against the Ammonites

28 And thou, son of man, prophesy and say, Thus saith the Lord GOD con-
cerning the Ammonites, and concerning their reproach; even say thou, The
sword, the sword *is* drawn: for the slaughter *it is* furbished, to consume
because of the glittering:
29 Whiles they see vanity unto thee, whiles they divine a lie unto thee, to
bring thee upon the necks of *them that are* slain, of the wicked, whose day is
come, when their iniquity *shall have* an end.
30 Shall I cause *it* to return into his sheath? I will judge thee in the place
where thou wast created, in the land of thy nativity.
31 And I will pour out mine indignation upon thee, I will blow against thee
in the fire of my wrath, and deliver thee into the hand of brutish men, *and*
skilful to destroy.
32 Thou shalt be for fuel to the fire; thy blood shall be in the midst of the
land; thou shalt be no *more* remembered: for I the LORD have spoken *it*.

The Sins of Jerusalem

22 Moreover the word of the LORD came unto me, saying,

2 Now, thou son of man, wilt thou judge, wilt thou judge the bloody city? yea, thou shalt shew her all her abominations.

3 Then say thou, Thus saith the Lord GOD, The city sheddeth blood in the midst of it, that her time may come, and maketh idols against herself to defile herself.

4 Thou art become guilty in thy blood that thou hast shed; and hast defiled thyself in thine idols which thou hast made; and thou hast caused thy days to draw near, and art come *even* unto thy years: therefore have I made thee a reproach unto the heathen, and a mocking to all countries.

5 *Those that be* near, and *those that be* far from thee, shall mock thee, *which art* infamous *and* much vexed.

6 Behold, the princes of Israel, every one were in thee to their power to shed blood.

7 In thee have they set light by father and mother: in the midst of thee have they dealt by oppression with the stranger: in thee have they vexed the fatherless and the widow.

8 Thou hast despised mine holy things, and hast profaned my sabbaths.

9 In thee are men that carry tales to shed blood: and in thee they eat upon the mountains: in the midst of thee they commit lewdness.

10 In thee have they discovered their fathers' nakedness: in thee have they humbled her that was set apart for pollution.

11 And one hath committed abomination with his neighbour's wife; and another hath lewdly defiled his daughter in law; and another in thee hath humbled his sister, his father's daughter.

12 In thee have they taken gifts to shed blood; thou hast taken usury and increase, and thou hast greedily gained of thy neighbours by extortion, and hast forgotten me, saith the Lord GOD.

13 Behold, therefore I have smitten mine hand at thy dishonest gain which thou hast made, and at thy blood which hath been in the midst of thee.

14 Can thine heart endure, or can thine hands be strong, in the days that I shall deal with thee? I the LORD have spoken *it*, and will do *it*.

15 And I will scatter thee among the heathen, and disperse thee in the countries, and will consume thy filthiness out of thee.

16 And thou shalt take thine inheritance in thyself in the sight of the heathen, and thou shalt know that I *am* the LORD.

17 And the word of the LORD came unto me, saying,

18 Son of man, the house of Israel is to me become dross: all they *are* brass, and tin, and iron, and lead, in the midst of the furnace; they are *even* the dross of silver.

19 Therefore thus saith the Lord GOD; Because ye are all become dross, behold, therefore I will gather you into the midst of Jerusalem.

20 *As* they gather silver, and brass, and iron, and lead, and tin, into the midst of the furnace, to blow the fire upon it, to melt *it*; so will I gather *you* in mine anger and in my fury, and I will leave *you there*, and melt you.

21 Yea, I will gather you, and blow upon you in the fire of my wrath, and ye shall be melted in the midst thereof.

22 As silver is melted in the midst of the furnace, so shall ye be melted in the midst thereof; and ye shall know that I the LORD have poured out my fury upon you.

The People's Corruption

23 And the word of the LORD came unto me, saying,

24 Son of man, say unto her, Thou *art* the land that is not cleansed, nor rained upon in the day of indignation.

25 *There is* a conspiracy of her prophets in the midst thereof, like a roaring
lion ravening the prey; they have devoured souls; they have taken the treasure
and precious things; they have made her many widows in the midst thereof.
26 Her priests have violated my law, and have profaned mine holy things:
they have put no difference between the holy and profane, neither have they
shewed *difference* between the unclean and the clean, and have hid their eyes
from my sabbaths, and I am profaned among them.
27 Her princes in the midst thereof *are* like wolves ravening the prey, to shed
blood, *and* to destroy souls, to get dishonest gain.
28 And her prophets have daubed them with untempered *morter*, seeing
vanity, and divining lies unto them, saying, Thus saith the Lord GOD, when the
LORD hath not spoken.
29 The people of the land have used oppression, and exercised robbery, and
have vexed the poor and needy: yea, they have oppressed the stranger wrong-
fully.
30 And I sought for a man among them, that should make up the hedge, and
stand in the gap before me for the land, that I should not destroy it: but I found
none.
31 Therefore have I poured out mine indignation upon them; I have con-
sumed them with the fire of my wrath: their own way have I recompensed
upon their heads, saith the Lord GOD.

The Lewdness of Jerusalem and Samaria

23 The word of the LORD came again unto me, saying,
2 Son of man, there were two women, the daughters of one mother:
3 And they committed whoredoms in Egypt; they committed whoredoms
in their youth: there were their breasts pressed, and there they bruised the
teats of their virginity.
4 And the names of them *were* Aholah the elder, and Aholibah her sister: and
they were mine, and they bare sons and daughters. Thus *were* their names;
Samaria *is* Aholah, and Jerusalem Aholibah.
5 And Aholah played the harlot when she was mine; and she doted on her
lovers, on the Assyrians *her* neighbours,
6 *Which were* clothed with blue, captains and rulers, all of them desirable
young men, horsemen riding upon horses.
7 Thus she committed her whoredoms with them, with all them *that were*
the chosen men of Assyria, and with all on whom she doted: with all their idols
she defiled herself.
8 Neither left she her whoredoms *brought* from Egypt: for in her youth they
lay with her, and they bruised the breasts of her virginity, and poured their
whoredom upon her.
9 Wherefore I have delivered her into the hand of her lovers, into the hand
of the Assyrians, upon whom she doted.
10 These discovered her nakedness: they took her sons and her daughters,
and slew her with the sword: and she became famous among women; for they
had executed judgment upon her.
11 And when her sister Aholibah saw *this*, she was more corrupt in her inor-
dinate love than she, and in her whoredoms more than her sister in *her* whore-
doms.
12 She doted upon the Assyrians *her* neighbours, captains and rulers clothed
most gorgeously, horsemen riding upon horses, all of them desirable young
men.
13 Then I saw that she was defiled, *that* they *took* both one way,
14 And *that* she increased her whoredoms: for when she saw men pourtrayed
upon the wall, the images of the Chaldeans pourtrayed with vermilion,

15 Girded with girdles upon their loins, exceeding in dyed attire upon their
heads, all of them princes to look to, after the manner of the Babylonians of
Chaldea, the land of their nativity:
16 And as soon as she saw them with her eyes, she doted upon them, and sent
messengers unto them into Chaldea.
17 And the Babylonians came to her into the bed of love, and they defiled
her with their whoredom, and she was polluted with them, and her mind was
alienated from them.
18 So she discovered her whoredoms, and discovered her nakedness: then
my mind was alienated from her, like as my mind was alienated from her
sister.
19 Yet she multiplied her whoredoms, in calling to remembrance the days
of her youth, wherein she had played the harlot in the land of Egypt.
20 For she doted upon their paramours, whose flesh *is as* the flesh of asses,
and whose issue *is like* the issue of horses.
21 Thus thou calledst to remembrance the lewdness of thy youth, in bruising
thy teats by the Egyptians for the paps of thy youth.
22 Therefore, O Aholibah, thus saith the Lord God; Behold, I will raise up thy
lovers against thee, from whom thy mind is alienated, and I will bring them
against thee on every side;
23 The Babylonians, and all the Chaldeans, Pekod, and Shoa, and Koa, *and*
all the Assyrians with them: all of them desirable young men, captains and
rulers, great lords and renowned, all of them riding upon horses.
24 And they shall come against thee with chariots, wagons, and wheels, and
with an assembly of people, *which* shall set against thee buckler and shield
and helmet round about: and I will set judgment before them, and they shall
judge thee according to their judgments.
25 And I will set my jealousy against thee, and they shall deal furiously with
thee: they shall take away thy nose and thine ears; and thy remnant shall fall
by the sword: they shall take thy sons and thy daughters; and thy residue shall
be devoured by the fire.
26 They shall also strip thee out of thy clothes, and take away thy fair jewels.
27 Thus will I make thy lewdness to cease from thee, and thy whoredom
brought from the land of Egypt: so that thou shalt not lift up thine eyes unto
them, nor remember Egypt any more.
28 For thus saith the Lord God; Behold, I will deliver thee into the hand *of*
them whom thou hatest, into the hand *of them* from whom thy mind is alien-
ated:
29 And they shall deal with thee hatefully, and shall take away all thy labour,
and shall leave thee naked and bare: and the nakedness of thy whoredoms
shall be discovered, both thy lewdness and thy whoredoms.
30 I will do these *things* unto thee, because thou hast gone a whoring after
the heathen, *and* because thou art polluted with their idols.
31 Thou hast walked in the way of thy sister; therefore will I give her cup into
thine hand.
32 Thus saith the Lord God; Thou shalt drink of thy sister's cup deep and
large: thou shalt be laughed to scorn and had in derision; it containeth much.
33 Thou shalt be filled with drunkenness and sorrow, with the cup of aston-
ishment and desolation, with the cup of thy sister Samaria.
34 Thou shalt even drink it and suck *it* out, and thou shalt break the sherds
thereof, and pluck off thine own breasts: for I have spoken *it*, saith the Lord
God.
35 Therefore thus saith the Lord God; Because thou hast forgotten me, and
cast me behind thy back, therefore bear thou also thy lewdness and thy
whoredoms.

36 The LORD said moreover unto me; Son of man, wilt thou judge Aholah and
Aholibah? yea, declare unto them their abominations;
37 That they have committed adultery, and blood *is* in their hands, and with
their idols have they committed adultery, and have also caused their sons,
whom they bare unto me, to pass for them through *the fire*, to devour *them*.
38 Moreover this they have done unto me: they have defiled my sanctuary in
the same day, and have profaned my sabbaths.
39 For when they had slain their children to their idols, then they came the
same day into my sanctuary to profane it; and, lo, thus have they done in the
midst of mine house.
40 And furthermore, that ye have sent for men to come from far, unto whom
a messenger *was* sent; and, lo, they came: for whom thou didst wash thyself,
paintedst thy eyes, and deckedst thyself with ornaments,
41 And satest upon a stately bed, and a table prepared before it, whereupon
thou hast set mine incense and mine oil.
42 And a voice of a multitude being at ease *was* with her: and with the men
of the common sort *were* brought Sabeans from the wilderness, which put
bracelets upon their hands, and beautiful crowns upon their heads.
43 Then said I unto *her that was* old in adulteries, Will they now commit
whoredoms with her, and she *with them*?
44 Yet they went in unto her, as they go in unto a woman that playeth the
harlot: so went they in unto Aholah and unto Aholibah, the lewd women.
45 And the righteous men, they shall judge them after the manner of adul-
teresses, and after the manner of women that shed blood; because they *are*
adulteresses, and blood *is* in their hands.
46 For thus saith the Lord GOD; I will bring up a company upon them, and
will give them to be removed and spoiled.
47 And the company shall stone them with stones, and dispatch them with
their swords; they shall slay their sons and their daughters, and burn up their
houses with fire.
48 Thus will I cause lewdness to cease out of the land, that all women may be
taught not to do after your lewdness.
49 And they shall recompense your lewdness upon you, and ye shall bear the
sins of your idols: and ye shall know that I *am* the Lord GOD.

Judah Is a Boiling Pot

24 Again in the ninth year, in the tenth month, in the tenth *day* of the
month, the word of the LORD came unto me, saying,
2 Son of man, write thee the name of the day, *even* of this same day: the king
of Babylon set himself against Jerusalem this same day.
3 And utter a parable unto the rebellious house, and say unto them, Thus
saith the Lord GOD; Set on a pot, set *it* on, and also pour water into it:
4 Gather the pieces thereof into it, *even* every good piece, the thigh, and the
shoulder; fill *it* with the choice bones.
5 Take the choice of the flock, and burn also the bones under it, *and* make it
boil well, and let them seethe the bones of it therein.
6 Wherefore thus saith the Lord GOD; Woe to the bloody city, to the pot whose
scum *is* therein, and whose scum is not gone out of it! bring it out piece by
piece; let no lot fall upon it.
7 For her blood is in the midst of her; she set it upon the top of a rock; she
poured it not upon the ground, to cover it with dust;
8 That it might cause fury to come up to take vengeance; I have set her blood
upon the top of a rock, that it should not be covered.
9 Therefore thus saith the Lord GOD; Woe to the bloody city! I will even make
the pile for fire great.
10 Heap on wood, kindle the fire, consume the flesh, and spice it well, and
let the bones be burned.

11 Then set it empty upon the coals thereof, that the brass of it may be hot,
and may burn, and *that* the filthiness of it may be molten in it, *that* the scum
of it may be consumed.
12 She hath wearied *herself* with lies, and her great scum went not forth out
of her: her scum *shall be* in the fire.
13 In thy filthiness *is* lewdness: because I have purged thee, and thou wast
not purged, thou shalt not be purged from thy filthiness any more, till I have
caused my fury to rest upon thee.
14 I the LORD have spoken *it*: it shall come to pass, and I will do *it*; I will not
go back, neither will I spare, neither will I repent; according to thy ways, and
according to thy doings, shall they judge thee, saith the Lord GOD.

Ezekiel Silently Mourns

15 Also the word of the LORD came unto me, saying,
16 Son of man, behold, I take away from thee the desire of thine eyes with a
stroke: yet neither shalt thou mourn nor weep, neither shall thy tears run
down.
17 Forbear to cry, make no mourning for the dead, bind the tire of thine head
upon thee, and put on thy shoes upon thy feet, and cover not *thy* lips, and eat
not the bread of men.
18 So I spake unto the people in the morning: and at even my wife died; and
I did in the morning as I was commanded.
19 And the people said unto me, Wilt thou not tell us what these *things are*
to us, that thou doest *so*?
20 Then I answered them, The word of the LORD came unto me, saying,
21 Speak unto the house of Israel, Thus saith the Lord GOD; Behold, I will
profane my sanctuary, the excellency of your strength, the desire of your eyes,
and that which your soul pitieth; and your sons and your daughters whom ye
have left shall fall by the sword.
22 And ye shall do as I have done: ye shall not cover *your* lips, nor eat the
bread of men.
23 And your tires *shall be* upon your heads, and your shoes upon your feet:
ye shall not mourn nor weep; but ye shall pine away for your iniquities, and
mourn one toward another.
24 Thus Ezekiel is unto you a sign: according to all that he hath done shall ye
do: and when this cometh, ye shall know that I *am* the Lord GOD.
25 Also, thou son of man, *shall it* not *be* in the day when I take from them
their strength, the joy of their glory, the desire of their eyes, and that where-
upon they set their minds, their sons and their daughters,
26 *That* he that escapeth in that day shall come unto thee, to cause *thee* to
hear *it* with *thine* ears?
27 In that day shall thy mouth be opened to him which is escaped, and thou
shalt speak, and be no more dumb: and thou shalt be a sign unto them; and
they shall know that I *am* the LORD.

Judgment on Ammon

25 The word of the LORD came again unto me, saying,
2 Son of man, set thy face against the Ammonites, and prophesy against
them;
3 And say unto the Ammonites, Hear the word of the Lord GOD; Thus saith
the Lord GOD; Because thou saidst, Aha, against my sanctuary, when it was
profaned; and against the land of Israel, when it was desolate; and against the
house of Judah, when they went into captivity;
4 Behold, therefore I will deliver thee to the men of the east for a possession,
and they shall set their palaces in thee, and make their dwellings in thee: they
shall eat thy fruit, and they shall drink thy milk.
5 And I will make Rabbah a stable for camels, and the Ammonites a couch-
ingplace for flocks: and ye shall know that I *am* the LORD.

6 For thus saith the Lord GOD; Because thou hast clapped *thine* hands, and
stamped with the feet, and rejoiced in heart with all thy despite against the
land of Israel;
7 Behold, therefore I will stretch out mine hand upon thee, and will deliver
thee for a spoil to the heathen; and I will cut thee off from the people, and I
will cause thee to perish out of the countries: I will destroy thee; and thou
shalt know that I *am* the LORD.

Judgment on Moab

8 Thus saith the Lord GOD; Because that Moab and Seir do say, Behold, the
house of Judah *is* like unto all the heathen;
9 Therefore, behold, I will open the side of Moab from the cities, from his
cities *which are* on his frontiers, the glory of the country, Beth-jeshimoth,
Baal-meon, and Kiriathaim,
10 Unto the men of the east with the Ammonites, and will give them in pos-
session, that the Ammonites may not be remembered among the nations.
11 And I will execute judgments upon Moab; and they shall know that I *am*
the LORD.

Judgment on Edom

12 Thus saith the Lord GOD; Because that Edom hath dealt against the house
of Judah by taking vengeance, and hath greatly offended, and revenged him-
self upon them;
13 Therefore thus saith the Lord GOD; I will also stretch out mine hand upon
Edom, and will cut off man and beast from it; and I will make it desolate from
Teman; and they of Dedan shall fall by the sword.
14 And I will lay my vengeance upon Edom by the hand of my people Israel:
and they shall do in Edom according to mine anger and according to my fury;
and they shall know my vengeance, saith the Lord GOD.

Judgment on Philistia

15 Thus saith the Lord GOD; Because the Philistines have dealt by revenge,
and have taken vengeance with a despiteful heart, to destroy *it* for the old
hatred;
16 Therefore thus saith the Lord GOD; Behold, I will stretch out mine hand
upon the Philistines, and I will cut off the Cherethims, and destroy the rem-
nant of the sea coast.
17 And I will execute great vengeance upon them with furious rebukes; and
they shall know that I *am* the LORD, when I shall lay my vengeance upon them.

Judgment on Tyrus (Tyre)

26 And it came to pass in the eleventh year, in the first *day* of the month,
that the word of the LORD came unto me, saying,
2 Son of man, because that Tyrus hath said against Jerusalem, Aha, she is
broken *that was* the gates of the people: she is turned unto me: I shall be
replenished, *now* she is laid waste:
3 Therefore thus saith the Lord GOD; Behold, I *am* against thee, O Tyrus, and
will cause many nations to come up against thee, as the sea causeth his waves
to come up.
4 And they shall destroy the walls of Tyrus, and break down her towers: I will
also scrape her dust from her, and make her like the top of a rock.
5 It shall be *a place for* the spreading of nets in the midst of the sea: for I have
spoken *it*, saith the Lord GOD: and it shall become a spoil to the nations.
6 And her daughters which *are* in the field shall be slain by the sword; and
they shall know that I *am* the LORD.
7 For thus saith the Lord GOD; Behold, I will bring upon Tyrus Nebuchadrezzar
king of Babylon, a king of kings, from the north, with horses, and with char-
iots, and with horsemen, and companies, and much people.

8 He shall slay with the sword thy daughters in the field: and he shall make a fort against thee, and cast a mount against thee, and lift up the buckler against thee.

9 And he shall set engines of war against thy walls, and with his axes he shall break down thy towers.

10 By reason of the abundance of his horses their dust shall cover thee: thy walls shall shake at the noise of the horsemen, and of the wheels, and of the chariots, when he shall enter into thy gates, as men enter into a city wherein is made a breach.

11 With the hoofs of his horses shall he tread down all thy streets: he shall slay thy people by the sword, and thy strong garrisons shall go down to the ground.

12 And they shall make a spoil of thy riches, and make a prey of thy merchandise: and they shall break down thy walls, and destroy thy pleasant houses: and they shall lay thy stones and thy timber and thy dust in the midst of the water.

13 And I will cause the noise of thy songs to cease; and the sound of thy harps shall be no more heard.

14 And I will make thee like the top of a rock: thou shalt be *a place* to spread nets upon; thou shalt be built no more: for I the LORD have spoken *it*, saith the Lord GOD.

The Coming Fall of Tyrus (Tyre)

15 Thus saith the Lord GOD to Tyrus; Shall not the isles shake at the sound of thy fall, when the wounded cry, when the slaughter is made in the midst of thee?

16 Then all the princes of the sea shall come down from their thrones, and lay away their robes, and put off their broidered garments: they shall clothe themselves with trembling; they shall sit upon the ground, and shall tremble at *every* moment, and be astonished at thee.

17 And they shall take up a lamentation for thee, and say to thee, How art thou destroyed, *that wast* inhabited of seafaring men, the renowned city, which wast strong in the sea, she and her inhabitants, which cause their terror *to be* on all that haunt it!

18 Now shall the isles tremble in the day of thy fall; yea, the isles that *are* in the sea shall be troubled at thy departure.

19 For thus saith the Lord GOD; When I shall make thee a desolate city, like the cities that are not inhabited; when I shall bring up the deep upon thee, and great waters shall cover thee;

20 When I shall bring thee down with them that descend into the pit, with the people of old time, and shall set thee in the low parts of the earth, in places desolate of old, with them that go down to the pit, that thou be not inhabited; and I shall set glory in the land of the living;

21 I will make thee a terror, and thou *shalt be* no *more*: though thou be sought for, yet shalt thou never be found again, saith the Lord GOD.

A Funeral Song for Tyrus (Tyre)

27 The word of the LORD came again unto me, saying,
2 Now, thou son of man, take up a lamentation for Tyrus;

3 And say unto Tyrus, O thou that art situate at the entry of the sea, *which art* a merchant of the people for many isles, Thus saith the Lord GOD; O Tyrus, thou hast said, I *am* of perfect beauty.

4 Thy borders *are* in the midst of the seas, thy builders have perfected thy beauty.

5 They have made all thy *ship* boards of fir trees of Senir: they have taken cedars from Lebanon to make masts for thee.

6 *Of* the oaks of Bashan have they made thine oars; the company of the
Ashurites have made thy benches *of* ivory, *brought* out of the isles of Chittim.
7 Fine linen with broidered work from Egypt was that which thou spreadest
forth to be thy sail; blue and purple from the isles of Elishah was that which
covered thee.
8 The inhabitants of Zidon and Arvad were thy mariners: thy wise *men*, O
Tyrus, *that* were in thee, were thy pilots.
9 The ancients of Gebal and the wise *men* thereof were in thee thy calkers:
all the ships of the sea with their mariners were in thee to occupy thy mer-
chandise.
10 They of Persia and of Lud and of Phut were in thine army, thy men of war:
they hanged the shield and helmet in thee; they set forth thy comeliness.
11 The men of Arvad with thine army *were* upon thy walls round about, and
the Gammadims were in thy towers: they hanged their shields upon thy walls
round about; they have made thy beauty perfect.
12 Tarshish *was* thy merchant by reason of the multitude of all *kind of* rich-
es; with silver, iron, tin, and lead, they traded in thy fairs.
13 Javan, Tubal, and Meshech, they *were* thy merchants: they traded the per-
sons of men and vessels of brass in thy market.
14 They of the house of Togarmah traded in thy fairs with horses and horse-
men and mules.
15 The men of Dedan *were* thy merchants; many isles *were* the merchandise
of thine hand: they brought thee *for* a present horns of ivory and ebony.
16 Syria *was* thy merchant by reason of the multitude of the wares of thy
making: they occupied in thy fairs with emeralds, purple, and broidered work,
and fine linen, and coral, and agate.
17 Judah, and the land of Israel, they *were* thy merchants: they traded in thy
market wheat of Minnith, and Pannag, and honey, and oil, and balm.
18 Damascus *was* thy merchant in the multitude of the wares of thy making,
for the multitude of all riches; in the wine of Helbon, and white wool.
19 Dan also and Javan going to and fro occupied in thy fairs: bright iron,
cassia, and calamus, were in thy market.
20 Dedan *was* thy merchant in precious clothes for chariots.
21 Arabia, and all the princes of Kedar, they occupied with thee in lambs,
and rams, and goats: in these *were they* thy merchants.
22 The merchants of Sheba and Raamah, they *were* thy merchants: they occu-
pied in thy fairs with chief of all spices, and with all precious stones, and gold.
23 Haran, and Canneh, and Eden, the merchants of Sheba, Asshur, *and*
Chilmad, *were* thy merchants.
24 These *were* thy merchants in all sorts *of things*, in blue clothes, and broi-
dered work, and in chests of rich apparel, bound with cords, and made of
cedar, among thy merchandise.
25 The ships of Tarshish did sing of thee in thy market: and thou wast replen-
ished, and made very glorious in the midst of the seas.
26 Thy rowers have brought thee into great waters: the east wind hath broken
thee in the midst of the seas.
27 Thy riches, and thy fairs, thy merchandise, thy mariners, and thy pilots,
thy calkers, and the occupiers of thy merchandise, and all thy men of war, that
are in thee, and in all thy company which *is* in the midst of thee, shall fall into
the midst of the seas in the day of thy ruin.
28 The suburbs shall shake at the sound of the cry of thy pilots.
29 And all that handle the oar, the mariners, *and* all the pilots of the sea, shall
come down from their ships, they shall stand upon the land;
30 And shall cause their voice to be heard against thee, and shall cry bitterly,
and shall cast up dust upon their heads, they shall wallow themselves in the
ashes:

31 And they shall make themselves utterly bald for thee, and gird them with
sackcloth, and they shall weep for thee with bitterness of heart *and* bitter
wailing.
32 And in their wailing they shall take up a lamentation for thee, and lament
over thee, *saying*, What *city is* like Tyrus, like the destroyed in the midst of the
sea?
33 When thy wares went forth out of the seas, thou filledst many people;
thou didst enrich the kings of the earth with the multitude of thy riches and
of thy merchandise.
34 In the time *when* thou shalt be broken by the seas in the depths of the
waters thy merchandise and all thy company in the midst of thee shall fall.
35 All the inhabitants of the isles shall be astonished at thee, and their kings
shall be sore afraid, they shall be troubled in *their* countenance.
36 The merchants among the people shall hiss at thee; thou shalt be a terror,
and never *shalt be* any more.

God's Judgment on the Prince of Tyrus (Tyre)

28 The word of the LORD came again unto me, saying,
2 Son of man, say unto the prince of Tyrus, Thus saith the Lord GOD;
Because thine heart *is* lifted up, and thou hast said, I *am* a God, I sit *in* the seat
of God, in the midst of the seas; yet thou *art* a man, and not God, though thou
set thine heart as the heart of God:
3 Behold, thou *art* wiser than Daniel; there is no secret that they can hide
from thee:
4 With thy wisdom and with thine understanding thou hast gotten thee
riches, and hast gotten gold and silver into thy treasures:
5 By thy great wisdom *and* by thy traffick hast thou increased thy riches, and
thine heart is lifted up because of thy riches:
6 Therefore thus saith the Lord GOD; Because thou hast set thine heart as the
heart of God;
7 Behold, therefore I will bring strangers upon thee, the terrible of the
nations: and they shall draw their swords against the beauty of thy wisdom,
and they shall defile thy brightness.
8 They shall bring thee down to the pit, and thou shalt die the deaths of *them*
that are slain in the midst of the seas.
9 Wilt thou yet say before him that slayeth thee, I *am* God? but thou *shalt be*
a man, and no God, in the hand of him that slayeth thee.
10 Thou shalt die the deaths of the uncircumcised by the hand of strangers:
for I have spoken *it*, saith the Lord GOD.

A Lamentation for the King

11 Moreover the word of the LORD came unto me, saying,
12 Son of man, take up a lamentation upon the king of Tyrus, and say unto
him, Thus saith the Lord GOD; Thou sealest up the sum, full of wisdom, and
perfect in beauty.
13 Thou hast been in Eden the garden of God; every precious stone *was* thy
covering, the sardius, topaz, and the diamond, the beryl, the onyx, and the
jasper, the sapphire, the emerald, and the carbuncle, and gold: the workman-
ship of thy tabrets and of thy pipes was prepared in thee in the day that thou
wast created.
14 Thou *art* the anointed cherub that covereth; and I have set thee *so*: thou
wast upon the holy mountain of God; thou hast walked up and down in the
midst of the stones of fire.
15 Thou *wast* perfect in thy ways from the day that thou wast created, till
iniquity was found in thee.
16 By the multitude of thy merchandise they have filled the midst of thee
with violence, and thou hast sinned: therefore I will cast thee as profane out

of the mountain of God: and I will destroy thee, O covering cherub, from the
midst of the stones of fire.
17 Thine heart was lifted up because of thy beauty, thou hast corrupted thy
wisdom by reason of thy brightness: I will cast thee to the ground, I will lay
thee before kings, that they may behold thee.
18 Thou hast defiled thy sanctuaries by the multitude of thine iniquities, by
the iniquity of thy traffick; therefore will I bring forth a fire from the midst
of thee, it shall devour thee, and I will bring thee to ashes upon the earth in
the sight of all them that behold thee.
19 All they that know thee among the people shall be astonished at thee: thou
shalt be a terror, and never *shalt* thou *be* any more.

Judgment on Zidon (Sidon)

20 Again the word of the LORD came unto me, saying,
21 Son of man, set thy face against Zidon, and prophesy against it,
22 And say, Thus saith the Lord GOD; Behold, I *am* against thee, O Zidon; and
I will be glorified in the midst of thee: and they shall know that I *am* the LORD,
when I shall have executed judgments in her, and shall be sanctified in her.
23 For I will send into her pestilence, and blood into her streets; and the
wounded shall be judged in the midst of her by the sword upon her on every
side; and they shall know that I *am* the LORD.
24 And there shall be no more a pricking brier unto the house of Israel, nor
any grieving thorn of all *that are* round about them, that despised them; and
they shall know that I *am* the Lord GOD.
25 Thus saith the Lord GOD; When I shall have gathered the house of Israel
from the people among whom they are scattered, and shall be sanctified in
them in the sight of the heathen, then shall they dwell in their land that I have
given to my servant Jacob.
26 And they shall dwell safely therein, and shall build houses, and plant vine-
yards; yea, they shall dwell with confidence, when I have executed judgments
upon all those that despise them round about them; and they shall know that
I *am* the LORD their God.

Judgment on Egypt

29 In the tenth year, in the tenth *month*, in the twelfth *day* of the month,
the word of the LORD came unto me, saying,
2 Son of man, set thy face against Pharaoh king of Egypt, and prophesy
against him, and against all Egypt:
3 Speak, and say, Thus saith the Lord GOD; Behold, I *am* against thee, Pharaoh
king of Egypt, the great dragon that lieth in the midst of his rivers, which hath
said, My river *is* mine own, and I have made *it* for myself.
4 But I will put hooks in thy jaws, and I will cause the fish of thy rivers to stick
unto thy scales, and I will bring thee up out of the midst of thy rivers, and all
the fish of thy rivers shall stick unto thy scales.
5 And I will leave thee *thrown* into the wilderness, thee and all the fish of thy
rivers: thou shalt fall upon the open fields; thou shalt not be brought togeth-
er, nor gathered: I have given thee for meat to the beasts of the field and to the
fowls of the heaven.
6 And all the inhabitants of Egypt shall know that I *am* the LORD, because
they have been a staff of reed to the house of Israel.
7 When they took hold of thee by thy hand, thou didst break, and rend all
their shoulder: and when they leaned upon thee, thou brakest, and madest all
their loins to be at a stand.

The Desolation of Egypt

8 Therefore thus saith the Lord GOD; Behold, I will bring a sword upon thee,
and cut off man and beast out of thee.

9 And the land of Egypt shall be desolate and waste; and they shall know that
I *am* the LORD: because he hath said, The river *is* mine, and I have made *it*.
10 Behold, therefore I *am* against thee, and against thy rivers, and I will make
the land of Egypt utterly waste *and* desolate, from the tower of Syene even
unto the border of Ethiopia.
11 No foot of man shall pass through it, nor foot of beast shall pass through
it, neither shall it be inhabited forty years.
12 And I will make the land of Egypt desolate in the midst of the countries
that are desolate, and her cities among the cities *that are* laid waste shall be
desolate forty years: and I will scatter the Egyptians among the nations, and
will disperse them through the countries.
13 Yet thus saith the Lord GOD; At the end of forty years will I gather the
Egyptians from the people whither they were scattered:
14 And I will bring again the captivity of Egypt, and will cause them to return
into the land of Pathros, into the land of their habitation; and they shall be
there a base kingdom.
15 It shall be the basest of the kingdoms; neither shall it exalt itself any more
above the nations: for I will diminish them, that they shall no more rule over
the nations.
16 And it shall be no more the confidence of the house of Israel, which
bringeth *their* iniquity to remembrance, when they shall look after them: but
they shall know that I *am* the Lord GOD.

Egypt to Be Conquered by Babylon

17 And it came to pass in the seven and twentieth year, in the first *month*, in
the first *day* of the month, the word of the LORD came unto me, saying,
18 Son of man, Nebuchadrezzar king of Babylon caused his army to serve a
great service against Tyrus: every head *was* made bald, and every shoulder *was*
peeled: yet had he no wages, nor his army, for Tyrus, for the service that he
had served against it:
19 Therefore thus saith the Lord GOD; Behold, I will give the land of Egypt
unto Nebuchadrezzar king of Babylon; and he shall take her multitude, and
take her spoil, and take her prey; and it shall be the wages for his army.
20 I have given him the land of Egypt *for* his labour wherewith he served
against it, because they wrought for me, saith the Lord GOD.
21 In that day will I cause the horn of the house of Israel to bud forth, and I
will give thee the opening of the mouth in the midst of them; and they shall
know that I *am* the LORD.

The Desolation of Egypt and Her Helpers

30 The word of the LORD came again unto me, saying,
2 Son of man, prophesy and say, Thus saith the Lord GOD; Howl ye,
Woe worth the day!
3 For the day *is* near, even the day of the LORD *is* near, a cloudy day; it shall be
the time of the heathen.
4 And the sword shall come upon Egypt, and great pain shall be in Ethiopia,
when the slain shall fall in Egypt, and they shall take away her multitude, and
her foundations shall be broken down.
5 Ethiopia, and Libya, and Lydia, and all the mingled people, and Chub, and
the men of the land that is in league, shall fall with them by the sword.
6 Thus saith the LORD; They also that uphold Egypt shall fall; and the pride
of her power shall come down: from the tower of Syene shall they fall in it by
the sword, saith the Lord GOD.
7 And they shall be desolate in the midst of the countries *that are* desolate,
and her cities shall be in the midst of the cities *that are* wasted.
8 And they shall know that I *am* the LORD, when I have set a fire in Egypt, and
when all her helpers shall be destroyed.

9 In that day shall messengers go forth from me in ships to make the careless
Ethiopians afraid, and great pain shall come upon them, as in the day of Egypt:
for, lo, it cometh.
10 Thus saith the Lord GOD; I will also make the multitude of Egypt to cease
by the hand of Nebuchadrezzar king of Babylon.
11 He and his people with him, the terrible of the nations, shall be brought
to destroy the land: and they shall draw their swords against Egypt, and fill
the land with the slain.
12 And I will make the rivers dry, and sell the land into the hand of the wick-
ed: and I will make the land waste, and all that is therein, by the hand of
strangers: I the LORD have spoken *it*.
13 Thus saith the Lord GOD; I will also destroy the idols, and I will cause *their*
images to cease out of Noph; and there shall be no more a prince of the land
of Egypt: and I will put a fear in the land of Egypt.
14 And I will make Pathros desolate, and will set fire in Zoan, and will execute
judgments in No.
15 And I will pour my fury upon Sin, the strength of Egypt; and I will cut off
the multitude of No.
16 And I will set fire in Egypt: Sin shall have great pain, and No shall be rent
asunder, and Noph *shall have* distresses daily.
17 The young men of Aven and of Pi-beseth shall fall by the sword: and these
cities shall go into captivity.
18 At Tehaphnehes also the day shall be darkened, when I shall break there
the yokes of Egypt: and the pomp of her strength shall cease in her: as for her,
a cloud shall cover her, and her daughters shall go into captivity.
19 Thus will I execute judgments in Egypt: and they shall know that I *am* the
LORD.

The Arm of Egypt Will Be Broken

20 And it came to pass in the eleventh year, in the first *month*, in the seventh
day of the month, *that* the word of the LORD came unto me, saying,
21 Son of man, I have broken the arm of Pharaoh king of Egypt; and, lo, it
shall not be bound up to be healed, to put a roller to bind it, to make it strong
to hold the sword.
22 Therefore thus saith the Lord GOD; Behold, I *am* against Pharaoh king of
Egypt, and will break his arms, the strong, and that which was broken; and I
will cause the sword to fall out of his hand.
23 And I will scatter the Egyptians among the nations, and will disperse them
through the countries.
24 And I will strengthen the arms of the king of Babylon, and put my sword
in his hand: but I will break Pharaoh's arms, and he shall groan before him
with the groanings of a deadly wounded *man*.
25 But I will strengthen the arms of the king of Babylon, and the arms of
Pharaoh shall fall down; and they shall know that I *am* the LORD, when I shall
put my sword into the hand of the king of Babylon, and he shall stretch it out
upon the land of Egypt.
26 And I will scatter the Egyptians among the nations, and disperse them
among the countries; and they shall know that I *am* the LORD.

Egypt Will Be Conquered

31 And it came to pass in the eleventh year, in the third *month*, in the first
day of the month, *that* the word of the LORD came unto me, saying,
2 Son of man, speak unto Pharaoh king of Egypt, and to his multitude; Whom
art thou like in thy greatness?
3 Behold, the Assyrian *was* a cedar in Lebanon with fair branches, and with
a shadowing shroud, and of an high stature; and his top was among the thick
boughs.

4 The waters made him great, the deep set him up on high with her rivers
running round about his plants, and sent out her little rivers unto all the trees
of the field.
5 Therefore his height was exalted above all the trees of the field, and his
boughs were multiplied, and his branches became long because of the mul-
titude of waters, when he shot forth.
6 All the fowls of heaven made their nests in his boughs, and under his
branches did all the beasts of the field bring forth their young, and under his
shadow dwelt all great nations.
7 Thus was he fair in his greatness, in the length of his branches: for his root
was by great waters.
8 The cedars in the garden of God could not hide him: the fir trees were not
like his boughs, and the chesnut trees were not like his branches; nor any tree
in the garden of God was like unto him in his beauty.
9 I have made him fair by the multitude of his branches: so that all the trees
of Eden, that *were* in the garden of God, envied him.

Egypt's Pride

10 Therefore thus saith the Lord GOD; Because thou hast lifted up thyself in
height, and he hath shot up his top among the thick boughs, and his heart is
lifted up in his height;
11 I have therefore delivered him into the hand of the mighty one of the
heathen; he shall surely deal with him: I have driven him out for his wicked-
ness.
12 And strangers, the terrible of the nations, have cut him off, and have left
him: upon the mountains and in all the valleys his branches are fallen, and
his boughs are broken by all the rivers of the land; and all the people of the
earth are gone down from his shadow, and have left him.
13 Upon his ruin shall all the fowls of the heaven remain, and all the beasts
of the field shall be upon his branches:
14 To the end that none of all the trees by the waters exalt themselves for
their height, neither shoot up their top among the thick boughs, neither their
trees stand up in their height, all that drink water: for they are all delivered
unto death, to the nether parts of the earth, in the midst of the children of
men, with them that go down to the pit.
15 Thus saith the Lord GOD; In the day when he went down to the grave I
caused a mourning: I covered the deep for him, and I restrained the floods
thereof, and the great waters were stayed: and I caused Lebanon to mourn for
him, and all the trees of the field fainted for him.
16 I made the nations to shake at the sound of his fall, when I cast him down
to hell with them that descend into the pit: and all the trees of Eden, the choice
and best of Lebanon, all that drink water, shall be comforted in the nether
parts of the earth.
17 They also went down into hell with him unto *them that be* slain with the
sword; and *they that were* his arm, *that* dwelt under his shadow in the midst
of the heathen.
18 To whom art thou thus like in glory and in greatness among the trees of
Eden? yet shalt thou be brought down with the trees of Eden unto the nether
parts of the earth: thou shalt lie in the midst of the uncircumcised with *them
that be* slain by the sword. This *is* Pharaoh and all his multitude, saith the Lord
GOD.

A Lamentation for Pharaoh

32 And it came to pass in the twelfth year, in the twelfth month, in the
first *day* of the month, *that* the word of the LORD came unto me, saying,
2 Son of man, take up a lamentation for Pharaoh king of Egypt, and say unto
him, Thou art like a young lion of the nations, and thou *art* as a whale in the

seas: and thou camest forth with thy rivers, and troubledst the waters with
thy feet, and fouledst their rivers.
3 Thus saith the Lord God; I will therefore spread out my net over thee with
a company of many people; and they shall bring thee up in my net.
4 Then will I leave thee upon the land, I will cast thee forth upon the open
field, and will cause all the fowls of the heaven to remain upon thee, and I will
fill the beasts of the whole earth with thee.
5 And I will lay thy flesh upon the mountains, and fill the valleys with thy
height.
6 I will also water with thy blood the land wherein thou swimmest, *even* to
the mountains; and the rivers shall be full of thee.
7 And when I shall put thee out, I will cover the heaven, and make the stars
thereof dark; I will cover the sun with a cloud, and the moon shall not give
her light.
8 All the bright lights of heaven will I make dark over thee, and set darkness
upon thy land, saith the Lord God.
9 I will also vex the hearts of many people, when I shall bring thy destruction
among the nations, into the countries which thou hast not known.
10 Yea, I will make many people amazed at thee, and their kings shall be
horribly afraid for thee, when I shall brandish my sword before them; and
they shall tremble at *every* moment, every man for his own life, in the day of
thy fall.
11 For thus saith the Lord God; The sword of the king of Babylon shall come
upon thee.
12 By the swords of the mighty will I cause thy multitude to fall, the terrible
of the nations, all of them: and they shall spoil the pomp of Egypt, and all the
multitude thereof shall be destroyed.
13 I will destroy also all the beasts thereof from beside the great waters;
neither shall the foot of man trouble them any more, nor the hoofs of beasts
trouble them.
14 Then will I make their waters deep, and cause their rivers to run like oil,
saith the Lord God.
15 When I shall make the land of Egypt desolate, and the country shall be
destitute of that whereof it was full, when I shall smite all them that dwell
therein, then shall they know that I *am* the Lord.
16 This *is* the lamentation wherewith they shall lament her: the daughters
of the nations shall lament her: they shall lament for her, *even* for Egypt, and
for all her multitude, saith the Lord God.

Egypt Will Be Brought Down
17 It came to pass also in the twelfth year, in the fifteenth *day* of the month,
that the word of the Lord came unto me, saying,
18 Son of man, wail for the multitude of Egypt, and cast them down, *even*
her, and the daughters of the famous nations, unto the nether parts of the
earth, with them that go down into the pit.
19 Whom dost thou pass in beauty? go down, and be thou laid with the
uncircumcised.
20 They shall fall in the midst of *them that are* slain by the sword: she is
delivered to the sword: draw her and all her multitudes.
21 The strong among the mighty shall speak to him out of the midst of hell
with them that help him: they are gone down, they lie uncircumcised, slain
by the sword.
22 Asshur *is* there and all her company: his graves *are* about him: all of them
slain, fallen by the sword:

23 Whose graves are set in the sides of the pit, and her company is round
about her grave: all of them slain, fallen by the sword, which caused terror in
the land of the living.
24 There *is* Elam and all her multitude round about her grave, all of them
slain, fallen by the sword, which are gone down uncircumcised into the neth-
er parts of the earth, which caused their terror in the land of the living; yet
have they borne their shame with them that go down to the pit.
25 They have set her a bed in the midst of the slain with all her multitude:
her graves *are* round about him: all of them uncircumcised, slain by the sword:
though their terror was caused in the land of the living, yet have they borne
their shame with them that go down to the pit: he is put in the midst of *them
that be* slain.
26 There *is* Meshech, Tubal, and all her multitude: her graves *are* round about
him: all of them uncircumcised, slain by the sword, though they caused their
terror in the land of the living.
27 And they shall not lie with the mighty *that are* fallen of the uncircumcised,
which are gone down to hell with their weapons of war: and they have laid
their swords under their heads, but their iniquities shall be upon their bones,
though *they were* the terror of the mighty in the land of the living.
28 Yea, thou shalt be broken in the midst of the uncircumcised, and shalt lie
with *them that are* slain with the sword.
29 There *is* Edom, her kings, and all her princes, which with their might are
laid by *them that were* slain by the sword: they shall lie with the uncircumcised,
and with them that go down to the pit.
30 There *be* the princes of the north, all of them, and all the Zidonians, which
are gone down with the slain; with their terror they are ashamed of their
might; and they lie uncircumcised with *them that be* slain by the sword, and
bear their shame with them that go down to the pit.
31 Pharaoh shall see them, and shall be comforted over all his multitude,
even Pharaoh and all his army slain by the sword, saith the Lord GOD.
32 For I have caused my terror in the land of the living: and he shall be laid
in the midst of the uncircumcised with *them that are* slain with the sword,
even Pharaoh and all his multitude, saith the Lord GOD.

Ezekiel Is a Watchman

33 Again the word of the LORD came unto me, saying,
2 Son of man, speak to the children of thy people, and say unto them,
When I bring the sword upon a land, if the people of the land take a man of
their coasts, and set him for their watchman:
3 If when he seeth the sword come upon the land, he blow the trumpet, and
warn the people;
4 Then whosoever heareth the sound of the trumpet, and taketh not warning;
if the sword come, and take him away, his blood shall be upon his own head.
5 He heard the sound of the trumpet, and took not warning; his blood shall
be upon him. But he that taketh warning shall deliver his soul.
6 But if the watchman see the sword come, and blow not the trumpet, and
the people be not warned; if the sword come, and take *any* person from among
them, he is taken away in his iniquity; but his blood will I require at the watch-
man's hand.
7 So thou, O son of man, I have set thee a watchman unto the house of Israel;
therefore thou shalt hear the word at my mouth, and warn them from me.
8 When I say unto the wicked, O wicked *man*, thou shalt surely die; if thou
dost not speak to warn the wicked from his way, that wicked *man* shall die in
his iniquity; but his blood will I require at thine hand.

9 Nevertheless, if thou warn the wicked of his way to turn from it; if he do
not turn from his way, he shall die in his iniquity; but thou hast delivered thy
soul.

God Shows His Justice

10 Therefore, O thou son of man, speak unto the house of Israel; Thus ye
speak, saying, If our transgressions and our sins *be* upon us, and we pine away
in them, how should we then live?
11 Say unto them, *As* I live, saith the Lord GOD, I have no pleasure in the death
of the wicked; but that the wicked turn from his way and live: turn ye, turn ye
from your evil ways; for why will ye die, O house of Israel?
12 Therefore, thou son of man, say unto the children of thy people, The righ-
teousness of the righteous shall not deliver him in the day of his transgression:
as for the wickedness of the wicked, he shall not fall thereby in the day that he
turneth from his wickedness; neither shall the righteous be able to live for his
righteousness in the day that he sinneth.
13 When I shall say to the righteous, *that* he shall surely live; if he trust to his
own righteousness, and commit iniquity, all his righteousnesses shall not be
remembered; but for his iniquity that he hath committed, he shall die for it.
14 Again, when I say unto the wicked, Thou shalt surely die; if he turn from
his sin, and do that which is lawful and right;
15 *If* the wicked restore the pledge, give again that he had robbed, walk in
the statutes of life, without committing iniquity; he shall surely live, he shall
not die.
16 None of his sins that he hath committed shall be mentioned unto him:
he hath done that which is lawful and right; he shall surely live.
17 Yet the children of thy people say, The way of the Lord is not equal: but as
for them, their way is not equal.
18 When the righteous turneth from his righteousness, and committeth
iniquity, he shall even die thereby.
19 But if the wicked turn from his wickedness, and do that which is lawful
and right, he shall live thereby.
20 Yet ye say, The way of the Lord is not equal. O ye house of Israel, I will judge
you every one after his ways.

Ezekiel Receives News of Jerusalem's Fall

21 And it came to pass in the twelfth year of our captivity, in the tenth *month*,
in the fifth *day* of the month, *that* one that had escaped out of Jerusalem came
unto me, saying, The city is smitten.
22 Now the hand of the LORD was upon me in the evening, afore he that was
escaped came; and had opened my mouth, until he came to me in the morn-
ing; and my mouth was opened, and I was no more dumb.
23 Then the word of the LORD came unto me, saying,
24 Son of man, they that inhabit those wastes of the land of Israel speak,
saying, Abraham was one, and he inherited the land: but we *are* many; the
land is given us for inheritance.
25 Wherefore say unto them, Thus saith the Lord GOD; Ye eat with the blood,
and lift up your eyes toward your idols, and shed blood: and shall ye possess
the land?
26 Ye stand upon your sword, ye work abomination, and ye defile every one
his neighbour's wife: and shall ye possess the land?
27 Say thou thus unto them, Thus saith the Lord GOD; *As* I live, surely they
that *are* in the wastes shall fall by the sword, and him that *is* in the open field
will I give to the beasts to be devoured, and they that *be* in the forts and in the
caves shall die of the pestilence.

28 For I will lay the land most desolate, and the pomp of her strength shall cease; and the mountains of Israel shall be desolate, that none shall pass through.

29 Then shall they know that I *am* the LORD, when I have laid the land most desolate because of all their abominations which they have committed.

God's Judgment on the Mockers

30 Also, thou son of man, the children of thy people still are talking against thee by the walls and in the doors of the houses, and speak one to another, every one to his brother, saying, Come, I pray you, and hear what is the word that cometh forth from the LORD.

31 And they come unto thee as the people cometh, and they sit before thee *as* my people, and they hear thy words, but they will not do them: for with their mouth they shew much love, *but* their heart goeth after their covetousness.

32 And, lo, thou *art* unto them as a very lovely song of one that hath a pleasant voice, and can play well on an instrument: for they hear thy words, but they do them not.

33 And when this cometh to pass, (lo, it will come,) then shall they know that a prophet hath been among them.

The Promise of a New Shepherd

34 And the word of the LORD came unto me, saying,

2 Son of man, prophesy against the shepherds of Israel, prophesy, and say unto them, Thus saith the Lord GOD unto the shepherds; Woe *be* to the shepherds of Israel that do feed themselves! should not the shepherds feed the flocks?

3 Ye eat the fat, and ye clothe you with the wool, ye kill them that are fed: *but* ye feed not the flock.

4 The diseased have ye not strengthened, neither have ye healed that which was sick, neither have ye bound up *that which was* broken, neither have ye brought again that which was driven away, neither have ye sought that which was lost; but with force and with cruelty have ye ruled them.

5 And they were scattered, because *there is* no shepherd: and they became meat to all the beasts of the field, when they were scattered.

6 My sheep wandered through all the mountains, and upon every high hill: yea, my flock was scattered upon all the face of the earth, and none did search or seek *after them*.

7 Therefore, ye shepherds, hear the word of the LORD;

8 *As* I live, saith the Lord GOD, surely because my flock became a prey, and my flock became meat to every beast of the field, because *there was* no shepherd, neither did my shepherds search for my flock, but the shepherds fed themselves, and fed not my flock;

9 Therefore, O ye shepherds, hear the word of the LORD;

10 Thus saith the Lord GOD; Behold, I *am* against the shepherds; and I will require my flock at their hand, and cause them to cease from feeding the flock; neither shall the shepherds feed themselves any more; for I will deliver my flock from their mouth, that they may not be meat for them.

11 For thus saith the Lord GOD; Behold, I, *even* I, will both search my sheep, and seek them out.

12 As a shepherd seeketh out his flock in the day that he is among his sheep *that are* scattered; so will I seek out my sheep, and will deliver them out of all places where they have been scattered in the cloudy and dark day.

13 And I will bring them out from the people, and gather them from the countries, and will bring them to their own land, and feed them upon the mountains of Israel by the rivers, and in all the inhabited places of the country.

14 I will feed them in a good pasture, and upon the high mountains of Israel
shall their fold be: there shall they lie in a good fold, and *in* a fat pasture shall
they feed upon the mountains of Israel.
15 I will feed my flock, and I will cause them to lie down, saith the Lord GOD.
16 I will seek that which was lost, and bring again that which was driven
away, and will bind up *that which was* broken, and will strengthen that which
was sick: but I will destroy the fat and the strong; I will feed them with judg-
ment.
17 And *as for* you, O my flock, thus saith the Lord GOD; Behold, I judge
between cattle and cattle, between the rams and the he goats.
18 *Seemeth it* a small thing unto you to have eaten up the good pasture, but
ye must tread down with your feet the residue of your pastures? and to have
drunk of the deep waters, but ye must foul the residue with your feet?
19 And *as for* my flock, they eat that which ye have trodden with your feet;
and they drink that which ye have fouled with your feet.
20 Therefore thus saith the Lord GOD unto them; Behold, I, *even* I, will judge
between the fat cattle and between the lean cattle.
21 Because ye have thrust with side and with shoulder, and pushed all the
diseased with your horns, till ye have scattered them abroad;
22 Therefore will I save my flock, and they shall no more be a prey; and I will
judge between cattle and cattle.
23 And I will set up one shepherd over them, and he shall feed them, *even* my
servant David; he shall feed them, and he shall be their shepherd.
24 And I the LORD will be their God, and my servant David a prince among
them; I the LORD have spoken *it*.
25 And I will make with them a covenant of peace, and will cause the evil
beasts to cease out of the land: and they shall dwell safely in the wilderness,
and sleep in the woods.
26 And I will make them and the places round about my hill a blessing; and
I will cause the shower to come down in his season; there shall be showers of
blessing.
27 And the tree of the field shall yield her fruit, and the earth shall yield her
increase, and they shall be safe in their land, and shall know that I *am* the
LORD, when I have broken the bands of their yoke, and delivered them out of
the hand of those that served themselves of them.
28 And they shall no more be a prey to the heathen, neither shall the beast
of the land devour them; but they shall dwell safely, and none shall make *them*
afraid.
29 And I will raise up for them a plant of renown, and they shall be no more
consumed with hunger in the land, neither bear the shame of the heathen
any more.
30 Thus shall they know that I the LORD their God *am* with them, and *that*
they, *even* the house of Israel, *are* my people, saith the Lord GOD.
31 And ye my flock, the flock of my pasture, *are* men, *and* I *am* your God,
saith the Lord GOD.

Judgment on Edom

35 Moreover the word of the LORD came unto me, saying,
2 Son of man, set thy face against mount Seir, and prophesy against it,
3 And say unto it, Thus saith the Lord GOD; Behold, O mount Seir, I *am* against
thee, and I will stretch out mine hand against thee, and I will make thee most
desolate.
4 I will lay thy cities waste, and thou shalt be desolate, and thou shalt know
that I *am* the LORD.

5 Because thou hast had a perpetual hatred, and hast shed *the blood of* the
children of Israel by the force of the sword in the time of their calamity, in the
time *that their* iniquity *had* an end:
6 Therefore, *as* I live, saith the Lord GOD, I will prepare thee unto blood, and
blood shall pursue thee: sith thou hast not hated blood, even blood shall pur-
sue thee.
7 Thus will I make mount Seir most desolate, and cut off from it him that
passeth out and him that returneth.
8 And I will fill his mountains with his slain *men*: in thy hills, and in thy
valleys, and in all thy rivers, shall they fall that are slain with the sword.
9 I will make thee perpetual desolations, and thy cities shall not return: and
ye shall know that I *am* the LORD.
10 Because thou hast said, These two nations and these two countries shall
be mine, and we will possess it; whereas the LORD was there:
11 Therefore, *as* I live, saith the Lord GOD, I will even do according to thine
anger, and according to thine envy which thou hast used out of thy hatred
against them; and I will make myself known among them, when I have judged
thee.
12 And thou shalt know that I *am* the LORD, *and that* I have heard all thy
blasphemies which thou hast spoken against the mountains of Israel, saying,
They are laid desolate, they are given us to consume.
13 Thus with your mouth ye have boasted against me, and have multiplied
your words against me: I have heard *them*.
14 Thus saith the Lord GOD; When the whole earth rejoiceth, I will make thee
desolate.
15 As thou didst rejoice at the inheritance of the house of Israel, because it
was desolate, so will I do unto thee: thou shalt be desolate, O mount Seir, and
all Idumea, *even* all of it: and they shall know that I *am* the LORD.

Blessings for Israel

36 Also, thou son of man, prophesy unto the mountains of Israel, and say,
Ye mountains of Israel, hear the word of the LORD:
2 Thus saith the Lord GOD; Because the enemy hath said against you, Aha,
even the ancient high places are ours in possession:
3 Therefore prophesy and say, Thus saith the Lord GOD; Because they have
made *you* desolate, and swallowed you up on every side, that ye might be a
possession unto the residue of the heathen, and ye are taken up in the lips of
talkers, and *are* an infamy of the people:
4 Therefore, ye mountains of Israel, hear the word of the Lord GOD; Thus
saith the Lord GOD to the mountains, and to the hills, to the rivers, and to the
valleys, to the desolate wastes, and to the cities that are forsaken, which became
a prey and derision to the residue of the heathen that *are* round about;
5 Therefore thus saith the Lord GOD; Surely in the fire of my jealousy have I
spoken against the residue of the heathen, and against all Idumea, which have
appointed my land into their possession with the joy of all *their* heart, with
despiteful minds, to cast it out for a prey.
6 Prophesy therefore concerning the land of Israel, and say unto the moun-
tains, and to the hills, to the rivers, and to the valleys, Thus saith the Lord GOD;
Behold, I have spoken in my jealousy and in my fury, because ye have borne
the shame of the heathen:
7 Therefore thus saith the Lord GOD; I have lifted up mine hand, Surely the
heathen that *are* about you, they shall bear their shame.
8 But ye, O mountains of Israel, ye shall shoot forth your branches, and yield
your fruit to my people of Israel; for they are at hand to come.
9 For, behold, I *am* for you, and I will turn unto you, and ye shall be tilled
and sown:

10 And I will multiply men upon you, all the house of Israel, *even* all of it: and
the cities shall be inhabited, and the wastes shall be builded:
11 And I will multiply upon you man and beast; and they shall increase and
bring fruit: and I will settle you after your old estates, and will do better *unto
you* than at your beginnings: and ye shall know that I *am* the LORD.
12 Yea, I will cause men to walk upon you, *even* my people Israel; and they
shall possess thee, and thou shalt be their inheritance, and thou shalt no more
henceforth bereave them *of men*.
13 Thus saith the Lord GOD; Because they say unto you, Thou *land* devourest
up men, and hast bereaved thy nations;
14 Therefore thou shalt devour men no more, neither bereave thy nations
any more, saith the Lord GOD.
15 Neither will I cause *men* to hear in thee the shame of the heathen any
more, neither shalt thou bear the reproach of the people any more, neither
shalt thou cause thy nations to fall any more, saith the Lord GOD.

Israel Was Rejected Because of Sin

16 Moreover the word of the LORD came unto me, saying,
17 Son of man, when the house of Israel dwelt in their own land, they defiled
it by their own way and by their doings: their way was before me as the
uncleanness of a removed woman.
18 Wherefore I poured my fury upon them for the blood that they had shed
upon the land, and for their idols *wherewith* they had polluted it:
19 And I scattered them among the heathen, and they were dispersed
through the countries: according to their way and according to their doings
I judged them.
20 And when they entered unto the heathen, whither they went, they pro-
faned my holy name, when they said to them, These *are* the people of the LORD,
and are gone forth out of his land.
21 But I had pity for mine holy name, which the house of Israel had profaned
among the heathen, whither they went.
22 Therefore say unto the house of Israel, Thus saith the Lord GOD; I do not
this for your sakes, O house of Israel, but for mine holy name's sake, which ye
have profaned among the heathen, whither ye went.
23 And I will sanctify my great name, which was profaned among the hea-
then, which ye have profaned in the midst of them; and the heathen shall
know that I *am* the LORD, saith the Lord GOD, when I shall be sanctified in you
before their eyes.
24 For I will take you from among the heathen, and gather you out of all
countries, and will bring you into your own land.
25 Then will I sprinkle clean water upon you, and ye shall be clean: from all
your filthiness, and from all your idols, will I cleanse you.
26 A new heart also will I give you, and a new spirit will I put within you: and
I will take away the stony heart out of your flesh, and I will give you an heart
of flesh.
27 And I will put my spirit within you, and cause you to walk in my statutes,
and ye shall keep my judgments, and do *them*.
28 And ye shall dwell in the land that I gave to your fathers; and ye shall be
my people, and I will be your God.
29 I will also save you from all your uncleannesses: and I will call for the corn,
and will increase it, and lay no famine upon you.
30 And I will multiply the fruit of the tree, and the increase of the field, that
ye shall receive no more reproach of famine among the heathen.
31 Then shall ye remember your own evil ways, and your doings that *were*
not good, and shall lothe yourselves in your own sight for your iniquities and
for your abominations.

32 Not for your sakes do I *this*, saith the Lord GOD, be it known unto you: be
ashamed and confounded for your own ways, O house of Israel.
33 Thus saith the Lord GOD; In the day that I shall have cleansed you from all
your iniquities I will also cause *you* to dwell in the cities, and the wastes shall
be builded.
34 And the desolate land shall be tilled, whereas it lay desolate in the sight of
all that passed by.
35 And they shall say, This land that was desolate is become like the garden
of Eden; and the waste and desolate and ruined cities *are become* fenced, *and*
are inhabited.
36 Then the heathen that are left round about you shall know that I the LORD
build the ruined *places, and* plant that that was desolate: I the LORD have
spoken *it*, and I will do *it*.
37 Thus saith the Lord GOD; I will yet *for* this be enquired of by the house of
Israel, to do *it* for them; I will increase them with men like a flock.
38 As the holy flock, as the flock of Jerusalem in her solemn feasts; so shall
the waste cities be filled with flocks of men: and they shall know that I *am* the
LORD.

The Valley of Dry Bones

37 The hand of the LORD was upon me, and carried me out in the spirit of
the LORD, and set me down in the midst of the valley which *was* full of
bones,
2 And caused me to pass by them round about: and, behold, *there were* very
many in the open valley; and, lo, *they were* very dry.
3 And he said unto me, Son of man, can these bones live? And I answered, O
Lord GOD, thou knowest.
4 Again he said unto me, Prophesy upon these bones, and say unto them, O
ye dry bones, hear the word of the LORD.
5 Thus saith the Lord GOD unto these bones; Behold, I will cause breath to
enter into you, and ye shall live:
6 And I will lay sinews upon you, and will bring up flesh upon you, and cover
you with skin, and put breath in you, and ye shall live; and ye shall know that
I *am* the LORD.
7 So I prophesied as I was commanded: and as I prophesied, there was a noise,
and behold a shaking, and the bones came together, bone to his bone.
8 And when I beheld, lo, the sinews and the flesh came up upon them, and
the skin covered them above: but *there was* no breath in them.
9 Then said he unto me, Prophesy unto the wind, prophesy, son of man, and
say to the wind, Thus saith the Lord GOD; Come from the four winds, O breath,
and breathe upon these slain, that they may live.
10 So I prophesied as he commanded me, and the breath came into them,
and they lived, and stood up upon their feet, an exceeding great army.
11 Then he said unto me, Son of man, these bones are the whole house of
Israel: behold, they say, Our bones are dried, and our hope is lost: we are cut
off for our parts.
12 Therefore prophesy and say unto them, Thus saith the Lord GOD; Behold,
O my people, I will open your graves, and cause you to come up out of your
graves, and bring you into the land of Israel.
13 And ye shall know that I *am* the LORD, when I have opened your graves, O
my people, and brought you up out of your graves,
14 And shall put my spirit in you, and ye shall live, and I shall place you in
your own land: then shall ye know that I the LORD have spoken *it*, and per-
formed *it*, saith the LORD.

Uniting the Two Sticks

15 The word of the LORD came again unto me, saying,
16 Moreover, thou son of man, take thee one stick, and write upon it, For
Judah, and for the children of Israel his companions: then take another stick,

and write upon it, For Joseph, the stick of Ephraim, and *for* all the house of
Israel his companions:
17 And join them one to another into one stick; and they shall become one
in thine hand.
18 And when the children of thy people shall speak unto thee, saying, Wilt
thou not shew us what thou *meanest* by these?
19 Say unto them, Thus saith the Lord GOD; Behold, I will take the stick of
Joseph, which *is* in the hand of Ephraim, and the tribes of Israel his fellows,
and will put them with him, *even* with the stick of Judah, and make them one
stick, and they shall be one in mine hand.
20 And the sticks whereon thou writest shall be in thine hand before their
eyes.
21 And say unto them, Thus saith the Lord GOD; Behold, I will take the chil-
dren of Israel from among the heathen, whither they be gone, and will gather
them on every side, and bring them into their own land:
22 And I will make them one nation in the land upon the mountains of Israel;
and one king shall be king to them all: and they shall be no more two nations,
neither shall they be divided into two kingdoms any more at all:
23 Neither shall they defile themselves any more with their idols, nor with
their detestable things, nor with any of their transgressions: but I will save
them out of all their dwellingplaces, wherein they have sinned, and will cleanse
them: so shall they be my people, and I will be their God.
24 And David my servant *shall be* king over them; and they all shall have one
shepherd: they shall also walk in my judgments, and observe my statutes, and
do them.
25 And they shall dwell in the land that I have given unto Jacob my servant,
wherein your fathers have dwelt; and they shall dwell therein, *even* they, and
their children, and their children's children for ever: and my servant David
shall be their prince for ever.
26 Moreover I will make a covenant of peace with them; it shall be an ever-
lasting covenant with them: and I will place them, and multiply them, and
will set my sanctuary in the midst of them for evermore.
27 My tabernacle also shall be with them: yea, I will be their God, and they
shall be my people.
28 And the heathen shall know that I the LORD do sanctify Israel, when my
sanctuary shall be in the midst of them for evermore.

The Destruction of Gog

38 And the word of the LORD came unto me, saying,
2 Son of man, set thy face against Gog, the land of Magog, the chief
prince of Meshech and Tubal, and prophesy against him,
3 And say, Thus saith the Lord GOD; Behold, I *am* against thee, O Gog, the
chief prince of Meshech and Tubal:
4 And I will turn thee back, and put hooks into thy jaws, and I will bring thee
forth, and all thine army, horses and horsemen, all of them clothed with all
sorts *of armour, even* a great company *with* bucklers and shields, all of them
handling swords:
5 Persia, Ethiopia, and Libya with them; all of them with shield and helmet:
6 Gomer, and all his bands; the house of Togarmah of the north quarters,
and all his bands: *and* many people with thee.
7 Be thou prepared, and prepare for thyself, thou, and all thy company that
are assembled unto thee, and be thou a guard unto them.
8 After many days thou shalt be visited: in the latter years thou shalt come
into the land *that is* brought back from the sword, *and is* gathered out of many
people, against the mountains of Israel, which have been always waste: but it
is brought forth out of the nations, and they shall dwell safely all of them.

9 Thou shalt ascend and come like a storm, thou shalt be like a cloud to cover
the land, thou, and all thy bands, and many people with thee.
10 Thus saith the Lord GOD; It shall also come to pass, *that* at the same time
shall things come into thy mind, and thou shalt think an evil thought:
11 And thou shalt say, I will go up to the land of unwalled villages; I will go
to them that are at rest, that dwell safely, all of them dwelling without walls,
and having neither bars nor gates,
12 To take a spoil, and to take a prey; to turn thine hand upon the desolate
places *that are now* inhabited, and upon the people *that are* gathered out of
the nations, which have gotten cattle and goods, that dwell in the midst of the
land.
13 Sheba, and Dedan, and the merchants of Tarshish, with all the young lions
thereof, shall say unto thee, Art thou come to take a spoil? hast thou gathered
thy company to take a prey? to carry away silver and gold, to take away cattle
and goods, to take a great spoil?

God's Judgment against Gog

14 Therefore, son of man, prophesy and say unto Gog, Thus saith the Lord GOD;
In that day when my people of Israel dwelleth safely, shalt thou not know *it*?
15 And thou shalt come from thy place out of the north parts, thou, and many
people with thee, all of them riding upon horses, a great company, and a
mighty army:
16 And thou shalt come up against my people of Israel, as a cloud to cover
the land; it shall be in the latter days, and I will bring thee against my land,
that the heathen may know me, when I shall be sanctified in thee, O Gog,
before their eyes.
17 Thus saith the Lord GOD; *Art* thou he of whom I have spoken in old time
by my servants the prophets of Israel, which prophesied in those days *many*
years that I would bring thee against them?
18 And it shall come to pass at the same time when Gog shall come against
the land of Israel, saith the Lord GOD, *that* my fury shall come up in my face.
19 For in my jealousy *and* in the fire of my wrath have I spoken, Surely in
that day there shall be a great shaking in the land of Israel;
20 So that the fishes of the sea, and the fowls of the heaven, and the beasts of
the field, and all creeping things that creep upon the earth, and all the men
that *are* upon the face of the earth, shall shake at my presence, and the moun-
tains shall be thrown down, and the steep places shall fall, and every wall shall
fall to the ground.
21 And I will call for a sword against him throughout all my mountains, saith
the Lord GOD: every man's sword shall be against his brother.
22 And I will plead against him with pestilence and with blood; and I will
rain upon him, and upon his bands, and upon the many people that *are* with
him, an overflowing rain, and great hailstones, fire, and brimstone.
23 Thus will I magnify myself, and sanctify myself; and I will be known in
the eyes of many nations, and they shall know that I *am* the LORD.

Gog Shall Be Destroyed

39 Therefore, thou son of man, prophesy against Gog, and say, Thus saith
the Lord GOD; Behold, I *am* against thee, O Gog, the chief prince of
Meshech and Tubal:
2 And I will turn thee back, and leave but the sixth part of thee, and will cause
thee to come up from the north parts, and will bring thee upon the mountains
of Israel:
3 And I will smite thy bow out of thy left hand, and will cause thine arrows
to fall out of thy right hand.

4 Thou shalt fall upon the mountains of Israel, thou, and all thy bands, and
the people that *is* with thee: I will give thee unto the ravenous birds of every
sort, and *to* the beasts of the field to be devoured.
5 Thou shalt fall upon the open field: for I have spoken *it*, saith the Lord God.
6 And I will send a fire on Magog, and among them that dwell carelessly in
the isles: and they shall know that I *am* the Lord.
7 So will I make my holy name known in the midst of my people Israel; and
I will not *let them* pollute my holy name any more: and the heathen shall know
that I *am* the Lord, the Holy One in Israel.

Israel's Victory

8 Behold, it is come, and it is done, saith the Lord God; this *is* the day where-
of I have spoken.
9 And they that dwell in the cities of Israel shall go forth, and shall set on fire
and burn the weapons, both the shields and the bucklers, the bows and the
arrows, and the handstaves, and the spears, and they shall burn them with
fire seven years:
10 So that they shall take no wood out of the field, neither cut down *any* out
of the forests; for they shall burn the weapons with fire: and they shall spoil
those that spoiled them, and rob those that robbed them, saith the Lord God.
11 And it shall come to pass in that day, *that* I will give unto Gog a place there
of graves in Israel, the valley of the passengers on the east of the sea: and it
shall stop the *noses* of the passengers: and there shall they bury Gog and all
his multitude: and they shall call *it* The valley of Hamon-gog.
12 And seven months shall the house of Israel be burying of them, that they
may cleanse the land.
13 Yea, all the people of the land shall bury *them*; and it shall be to them a
renown the day that I shall be glorified, saith the Lord God.
14 And they shall sever out men of continual employment, passing through
the land to bury with the passengers those that remain upon the face of the
earth, to cleanse it: after the end of seven months shall they search.
15 And the passengers *that* pass through the land, when *any* seeth a man's
bone, then shall he set up a sign by it, till the buriers have buried it in the
valley of Hamon-gog.
16 And also the name of the city *shall be* Hamonah. Thus shall they cleanse
the land.
17 And, thou son of man, thus saith the Lord God; Speak unto every feathered
fowl, and to every beast of the field, Assemble yourselves, and come; gather
yourselves on every side to my sacrifice that I do sacrifice for you, *even* a great
sacrifice upon the mountains of Israel, that ye may eat flesh, and drink blood.
18 Ye shall eat the flesh of the mighty, and drink the blood of the princes of
the earth, of rams, of lambs, and of goats, of bullocks, all of them fatlings of
Bashan.
19 And ye shall eat fat till ye be full, and drink blood till ye be drunken, of my
sacrifice which I have sacrificed for you.
20 Thus ye shall be filled at my table with horses and chariots, with mighty
men, and with all men of war, saith the Lord God.
21 And I will set my glory among the heathen, and all the heathen shall see
my judgment that I have executed, and my hand that I have laid upon them.
22 So the house of Israel shall know that I *am* the Lord their God from that
day and forward.
23 And the heathen shall know that the house of Israel went into captivity
for their iniquity: because they trespassed against me, therefore hid I my face
from them, and gave them into the hand of their enemies: so fell they all by
the sword.

24 According to their uncleanness and according to their transgressions
have I done unto them, and hid my face from them.

Israel Shall Be Restored

25 Therefore thus saith the Lord GOD; Now will I bring again the captivity of
Jacob, and have mercy upon the whole house of Israel, and will be jealous for
my holy name;
26 After that they have borne their shame, and all their trespasses whereby
they have trespassed against me, when they dwelt safely in their land, and
none made *them* afraid.
27 When I have brought them again from the people, and gathered them out
of their enemies' lands, and am sanctified in them in the sight of many nations;
28 Then shall they know that I *am* the LORD their God, which caused them
to be led into captivity among the heathen: but I have gathered them unto
their own land, and have left none of them any more there.
29 Neither will I hide my face any more from them: for I have poured out my
spirit upon the house of Israel, saith the Lord GOD.

The New Temple of God

40 In the five and twentieth year of our captivity, in the beginning of the
year, in the tenth *day* of the month, in the fourteenth year after that
the city was smitten, in the selfsame day the hand of the LORD was upon me,
and brought me thither.
2 In the visions of God brought he me into the land of Israel, and set me upon
a very high mountain, by which *was* as the frame of a city on the south.
3 And he brought me thither, and, behold, *there was* a man, whose appear-
ance *was* like the appearance of brass, with a line of flax in his hand, and a
measuring reed; and he stood in the gate.
4 And the man said unto me, Son of man, behold with thine eyes, and hear
with thine ears, and set thine heart upon all that I shall shew thee; for to the
intent that I might shew *them* unto thee *art* thou brought hither: declare all
that thou seest to the house of Israel.
5 And behold a wall on the outside of the house round about, and in the
man's hand a measuring reed of six cubits *long* by the cubit and an hand
breadth: so he measured the breadth of the building, one reed; and the height,
one reed.
6 Then came he unto the gate which looketh toward the east, and went up
the stairs thereof, and measured the threshold of the gate, *which was* one reed
broad; and the other threshold *of the gate, which was* one reed broad.
7 And *every* little chamber *was* one reed long, and one reed broad; and
between the little chambers *were* five cubits; and the threshold of the gate by
the porch of the gate within *was* one reed.
8 He measured also the porch of the gate within, one reed.
9 Then measured he the porch of the gate, eight cubits; and the posts there-
of, two cubits; and the porch of the gate *was* inward.
10 And the little chambers of the gate eastward *were* three on this side, and
three on that side; they three *were* of one measure: and the posts had one
measure on this side and on that side.
11 And he measured the breadth of the entry of the gate, ten cubits; *and* the
length of the gate, thirteen cubits.
12 The space also before the little chambers *was* one cubit *on this side*, and
the space *was* one cubit on that side: and the little chambers *were* six cubits
on this side, and six cubits on that side.
13 He measured then the gate from the roof of *one* little chamber to the roof
of another: the breadth *was* five and twenty cubits, door against door.
14 He made also posts of threescore cubits, even unto the post of the court
round about the gate.

15 And from the face of the gate of the entrance unto the face of the porch
of the inner gate *were* fifty cubits.
16 And *there were* narrow windows to the little chambers, and to their posts
within the gate round about, and likewise to the arches: and windows *were*
round about inward: and upon *each* post *were* palm trees.
17 Then brought he me into the outward court, and, lo, *there were* chambers,
and a pavement made for the court round about: thirty chambers *were* upon
the pavement.
18 And the pavement by the side of the gates over against the length of the
gates *was* the lower pavement.
19 Then he measured the breadth from the forefront of the lower gate unto
the forefront of the inner court without, an hundred cubits eastward and
northward.
20 And the gate of the outward court that looked toward the north, he
measured the length thereof, and the breadth thereof.
21 And the little chambers thereof *were* three on this side and three on that
side; and the posts thereof and the arches thereof were after the measure of
the first gate: the length thereof *was* fifty cubits, and the breadth five and
twenty cubits.
22 And their windows, and their arches, and their palm trees, *were* after the
measure of the gate that looketh toward the east; and they went up unto it by
seven steps; and the arches thereof *were* before them.
23 And the gate of the inner court *was* over against the gate toward the north,
and toward the east; and he measured from gate to gate an hundred cubits.
24 After that he brought me toward the south, and behold a gate toward the
south: and he measured the posts thereof and the arches thereof according
to these measures.
25 And *there were* windows in it and in the arches thereof round about, like
those windows: the length *was* fifty cubits, and the breadth five and twenty
cubits.
26 And *there were* seven steps to go up to it, and the arches thereof *were* before
them: and it had palm trees, one on this side, and another on that side, upon
the posts thereof.
27 And *there was* a gate in the inner court toward the south: and he measured
from gate to gate toward the south an hundred cubits.
28 And he brought me to the inner court by the south gate: and he measured
the south gate according to these measures;
29 And the little chambers thereof, and the posts thereof, and the arches
thereof, according to these measures: and *there were* windows in it and in the
arches thereof round about: *it was* fifty cubits long, and five and twenty cubits
broad.
30 And the arches round about *were* five and twenty cubits long, and five
cubits broad.
31 And the arches thereof *were* toward the utter court; and palm trees *were*
upon the posts thereof: and the going up to it *had* eight steps.
32 And he brought me into the inner court toward the east: and he measured
the gate according to these measures.
33 And the little chambers thereof, and the posts thereof, and the arches
thereof, *were* according to these measures: and *there were* windows therein
and in the arches thereof round about: *it was* fifty cubits long, and five and
twenty cubits broad.
34 And the arches thereof *were* toward the outward court; and palm trees
were upon the posts thereof, on this side, and on that side: and the going up
to it *had* eight steps.
35 And he brought me to the north gate, and measured *it* according to these
measures;

36 The little chambers thereof, the posts thereof, and the arches thereof, and
the windows to it round about: the length *was* fifty cubits, and the breadth
five and twenty cubits.
37 And the posts thereof *were* toward the utter court; and palm trees *were*
upon the posts thereof, on this side, and on that side: and the going up to it
had eight steps.
38 And the chambers and the entries thereof *were* by the posts of the gates,
where they washed the burnt offering.
39 And in the porch of the gate *were* two tables on this side, and two tables
on that side, to slay thereon the burnt offering and the sin offering and the
trespass offering.
40 And at the side without, as one goeth up to the entry of the north gate,
were two tables; and on the other side, which *was* at the porch of the gate, *were*
two tables.
41 Four tables *were* on this side, and four tables on that side, by the side of
the gate; eight tables, whereupon they slew *their sacrifices*.
42 And the four tables *were* of hewn stone for the burnt offering, of a cubit
and an half long, and a cubit and an half broad, and one cubit high: whereup-
on also they laid the instruments wherewith they slew the burnt offering and
the sacrifice.
43 And within *were* hooks, an hand broad, fastened round about: and upon
the tables *was* the flesh of the offering.
44 And without the inner gate *were* the chambers of the singers in the inner
court, which *was* at the side of the north gate; and their prospect *was* toward
the south: one at the side of the east gate *having* the prospect toward the north.
45 And he said unto me, This chamber, whose prospect *is* toward the south,
is for the priests, the keepers of the charge of the house.
46 And the chamber whose prospect *is* toward the north *is* for the priests,
the keepers of the charge of the altar: these *are* the sons of Zadok among the
sons of Levi, which come near to the LORD to minister unto him.
47 So he measured the court, an hundred cubits long, and an hundred cubits
broad, foursquare; and the altar *that was* before the house.
48 And he brought me to the porch of the house, and measured *each* post of
the porch, five cubits on this side, and five cubits on that side: and the breadth
of the gate *was* three cubits on this side, and three cubits on that side.
49 The length of the porch *was* twenty cubits, and the breadth eleven cubits;
and *he brought me* by the steps whereby they went up to it: and *there were*
pillars by the posts, one on this side, and another on that side.

The Holy Place in the Temple

41 Afterward he brought me to the temple, and measured the posts, six
cubits broad on the one side, and six cubits broad on the other side,
which was the breadth of the tabernacle.
2 And the breadth of the door *was* ten cubits; and the sides of the door *were*
five cubits on the one side, and five cubits on the other side: and he measured
the length thereof, forty cubits: and the breadth, twenty cubits.
3 Then went he inward, and measured the post of the door, two cubits; and
the door, six cubits; and the breadth of the door, seven cubits.
4 So he measured the length thereof, twenty cubits; and the breadth, twenty
cubits, before the temple: and he said unto me, This *is* the most holy *place*.
5 After he measured the wall of the house, six cubits; and the breadth of *every*
side chamber, four cubits, round about the house on every side.
6 And the side chambers *were* three, one over another, and thirty in order;
and they entered into the wall which *was* of the house for the side chambers
round about, that they might have hold, but they had not hold in the wall of
the house.

7 And *there was* an enlarging, and a winding about still upward to the side
chambers: for the winding about of the house went still upward round about
the house: therefore the breadth of the house *was still* upward, and so
increased *from* the lowest *chamber* to the highest by the midst.
8 I saw also the height of the house round about: the foundations of the side
chambers *were* a full reed of six great cubits.
9 The thickness of the wall, which *was* for the side chamber without, *was*
five cubits: and *that* which *was* left *was* the place of the side chambers that
were within.
10 And between the chambers *was* the wideness of twenty cubits round about
the house on every side.
11 And the doors of the side chambers *were* toward *the place that was* left,
one door toward the north, and another door toward the south: and the
breadth of the place that was left *was* five cubits round about.
12 Now the building that *was* before the separate place at the end toward the
west *was* seventy cubits broad; and the wall of the building *was* five cubits
thick round about, and the length thereof ninety cubits.
13 So he measured the house, an hundred cubits long; and the separate place,
and the building, with the walls thereof, an hundred cubits long;
14 Also the breadth of the face of the house, and of the separate place toward
the east, an hundred cubits.
15 And he measured the length of the building over against the separate place
which *was* behind it, and the galleries thereof on the one side and on the other
side, an hundred cubits, with the inner temple, and the porches of the court;
16 The door posts, and the narrow windows, and the galleries round about
on their three stories, over against the door, cieled with wood round about,
and from the ground up to the windows, and the windows *were* covered;
17 To that above the door, even unto the inner house, and without, and by
all the wall round about within and without, by measure.
18 And *it was* made with cherubims and palm trees, so that a palm tree *was*
between a cherub and a cherub; and *every* cherub had two faces;
19 So that the face of a man *was* toward the palm tree on the one side, and
the face of a young lion toward the palm tree on the other side: *it was* made
through all the house round about.
20 From the ground unto above the door *were* cherubims and palm trees
made, and *on* the wall of the temple.
21 The posts of the temple *were* squared, *and* the face of the sanctuary; the
appearance *of the one* as the appearance *of the other*.
22 The altar of wood *was* three cubits high, and the length thereof two cubits;
and the corners thereof, and the length thereof, and the walls thereof, *were* of
wood: and he said unto me, This *is* the table that *is* before the LORD.
23 And the temple and the sanctuary had two doors.
24 And the doors had two leaves *apiece*, two turning leaves; two *leaves* for
the one door, and two leaves for the other *door*.
25 And *there were* made on them, on the doors of the temple, cherubims and
palm trees, like as *were* made upon the walls; and *there were* thick planks upon
the face of the porch without.
26 And *there were* narrow windows and palm trees on the one side and on
the other side, on the sides of the porch, and *upon* the side chambers of the
house, and thick planks.

The Courtyards of the Temple

42 Then he brought me forth into the utter court, the way toward the
north: and he brought me into the chamber that *was* over against the
separate place, and which *was* before the building toward the north.

2 Before the length of an hundred cubits *was* the north door, and the breadth
was fifty cubits.
3 Over against the twenty *cubits* which *were* for the inner court, and over
against the pavement which *was* for the utter court, *was* gallery against gallery
in three *stories*.
4 And before the chambers *was* a walk of ten cubits breadth inward, a way
of one cubit; and their doors toward the north.
5 Now the upper chambers *were* shorter: for the galleries were higher than
these, than the lower, and than the middlemost of the building.
6 For they *were* in three *stories*, but had not pillars as the pillars of the courts:
therefore *the building* was straitened more than the lowest and the middle-
most from the ground.
7 And the wall that *was* without over against the chambers, toward the utter
court on the forepart of the chambers, the length thereof *was* fifty cubits.
8 For the length of the chambers that *were* in the utter court *was* fifty cubits:
and, lo, before the temple *were* an hundred cubits.
9 And from under these chambers *was* the entry on the east side, as one goeth
into them from the utter court.
10 The chambers *were* in the thickness of the wall of the court toward the
east, over against the separate place, and over against the building.
11 And the way before them *was* like the appearance of the chambers which
were toward the north, as long as they, *and* as broad as they: and all their goings
out *were* both according to their fashions, and according to their doors.
12 And according to the doors of the chambers that *were* toward the south
was a door in the head of the way, *even* the way directly before the wall toward
the east, as one entereth into them.
13 Then said he unto me, The north chambers *and* the south chambers,
which *are* before the separate place, they *be* holy chambers, where the priests
that approach unto the LORD shall eat the most holy things: there shall they
lay the most holy things, and the meat offering, and the sin offering, and the
trespass offering; for the place *is* holy.
14 When the priests enter therein, then shall they not go out of the holy *place*
into the utter court, but there they shall lay their garments wherein they min-
ister; for they *are* holy; and shall put on other garments, and shall approach
to *those things* which *are* for the people.
15 Now when he had made an end of measuring the inner house, he brought
me forth toward the gate whose prospect *is* toward the east, and measured it
round about.
16 He measured the east side with the measuring reed, five hundred reeds,
with the measuring reed round about.
17 He measured the north side, five hundred reeds, with the measuring reed
round about.
18 He measured the south side, five hundred reeds, with the measuring reed.
19 He turned about to the west side, *and* measured five hundred reeds with
the measuring reed.
20 He measured it by the four sides: it had a wall round about, five hundred
reeds long, and five hundred broad, to make a separation between the sanc-
tuary and the profane place.

God's Glory Again Fills the Temple

43 Afterward he brought me to the gate, *even* the gate that looketh toward
the east:
2 And, behold, the glory of the God of Israel came from the way of the east:
and his voice *was* like a noise of many waters: and the earth shined with his
glory.

3 And *it was* according to the appearance of the vision which I saw, *even*
according to the vision that I saw when I came to destroy the city: and the
visions *were* like the vision that I saw by the river Chebar; and I fell upon my
face.
4 And the glory of the LORD came into the house by the way of the gate whose
prospect *is* toward the east.
5 So the spirit took me up, and brought me into the inner court; and, behold,
the glory of the LORD filled the house.
6 And I heard *him* speaking unto me out of the house; and the man stood by
me.

The Sin of Israel Had Prevented God's Presence

7 And he said unto me, Son of man, the place of my throne, and the place of
the soles of my feet, where I will dwell in the midst of the children of Israel
for ever, and my holy name, shall the house of Israel no more defile, *neither*
they, nor their kings, by their whoredom, nor by the carcases of their kings in
their high places.
8 In their setting of their threshold by my thresholds, and their post by my
posts, and the wall between me and them, they have even defiled my holy name
by their abominations that they have committed: wherefore I have consumed
them in mine anger.
9 Now let them put away their whoredom, and the carcases of their kings,
far from me, and I will dwell in the midst of them for ever.
10 Thou son of man, shew the house to the house of Israel, that they may be
ashamed of their iniquities: and let them measure the pattern.
11 And if they be ashamed of all that they have done, shew them the form of
the house, and the fashion thereof, and the goings out thereof, and the comings
in thereof, and all the forms thereof, and all the ordinances thereof, and all
the forms thereof, and all the laws thereof: and write *it* in their sight, that they
may keep the whole form thereof, and all the ordinances thereof, and do them.
12 This *is* the law of the house; Upon the top of the mountain the whole limit
thereof round about *shall be* most holy. Behold, this *is* the law of the house.

The Altar in the Temple

13 And these *are* the measures of the altar after the cubits: The cubit *is* a cubit
and an hand breadth; even the bottom *shall be* a cubit, and the breadth a cubit,
and the border thereof by the edge thereof round about *shall be* a span: and
this *shall be* the higher place of the altar.
14 And from the bottom *upon* the ground *even* to the lower settle *shall be*
two cubits, and the breadth one cubit; and from the lesser settle *even* to the
greater settle *shall be* four cubits, and the breadth *one* cubit.
15 So the altar *shall be* four cubits; and from the altar and upward *shall be*
four horns.
16 And the altar *shall be* twelve *cubits* long, twelve broad, square in the four
squares thereof.
17 And the settle *shall be* fourteen *cubits* long and fourteen broad in the four
squares thereof; and the border about it *shall be* half a cubit; and the bottom
thereof *shall be* a cubit about; and his stairs shall look toward the east.
18 And he said unto me, Son of man, thus saith the Lord GOD; These *are* the
ordinances of the altar in the day when they shall make it, to offer burnt
offerings thereon, and to sprinkle blood thereon.
19 And thou shalt give to the priests the Levites that be of the seed of Zadok,
which approach unto me, to minister unto me, saith the Lord GOD, a young
bullock for a sin offering.
20 And thou shalt take of the blood thereof, and put *it* on the four horns of
it, and on the four corners of the settle, and upon the border round about:
thus shalt thou cleanse and purge it.

21 Thou shalt take the bullock also of the sin offering, and he shall burn it in
the appointed place of the house, without the sanctuary.
22 And on the second day thou shalt offer a kid of the goats without blemish
for a sin offering; and they shall cleanse the altar, as they did cleanse *it* with
the bullock.
23 When thou hast made an end of cleansing *it*, thou shalt offer a young
bullock without blemish, and a ram out of the flock without blemish.
24 And thou shalt offer them before the LORD, and the priests shall cast salt
upon them, and they shall offer them up *for* a burnt offering unto the LORD.
25 Seven days shalt thou prepare every day a goat *for* a sin offering: they shall
also prepare a young bullock, and a ram out of the flock, without blemish.
26 Seven days shall they purge the altar and purify it; and they shall conse-
crate themselves.
27 And when these days are expired, it shall be, *that* upon the eighth day, and
so forward, the priests shall make your burnt offerings upon the altar, and
your peace offerings; and I will accept you, saith the Lord GOD.

The East Gate Is Sealed Shut

44 Then he brought me back the way of the gate of the outward sanctuary
which looketh toward the east; and it *was* shut.
2 Then said the LORD unto me; This gate shall be shut, it shall not be opened,
and no man shall enter in by it; because the LORD, the God of Israel, hath
entered in by it, therefore it shall be shut.
3 *It is* for the prince; the prince, he shall sit in it to eat bread before the LORD;
he shall enter by the way of the porch of *that* gate, and shall go out by the way
of the same.

Those Serving in the Temple

4 Then brought he me the way of the north gate before the house: and I
looked, and, behold, the glory of the LORD filled the house of the LORD: and I
fell upon my face.
5 And the LORD said unto me, Son of man, mark well, and behold with thine
eyes, and hear with thine ears all that I say unto thee concerning all the ordi-
nances of the house of the LORD, and all the laws thereof; and mark well the
entering in of the house, with every going forth of the sanctuary.
6 And thou shalt say to the rebellious, *even* to the house of Israel, Thus saith
the Lord GOD; O ye house of Israel, let it suffice you of all your abominations,
7 In that ye have brought *into my sanctuary* strangers, uncircumcised in
heart, and uncircumcised in flesh, to be in my sanctuary, to pollute it, *even* my
house, when ye offer my bread, the fat and the blood, and they have broken
my covenant because of all your abominations.
8 And ye have not kept the charge of mine holy things: but ye have set keep-
ers of my charge in my sanctuary for yourselves.
9 Thus saith the Lord GOD; No stranger, uncircumcised in heart, nor uncir-
cumcised in flesh, shall enter into my sanctuary, of any stranger that *is* among
the children of Israel.
10 And the Levites that are gone away far from me, when Israel went astray,
which went astray away from me after their idols; they shall even bear their
iniquity.
11 Yet they shall be ministers in my sanctuary, *having* charge at the gates of
the house, and ministering to the house: they shall slay the burnt offering and
the sacrifice for the people, and they shall stand before them to minister unto
them.
12 Because they ministered unto them before their idols, and caused the
house of Israel to fall into iniquity; therefore have I lifted up mine hand against
them, saith the Lord GOD, and they shall bear their iniquity.

13 And they shall not come near unto me, to do the office of a priest unto
me, nor to come near to any of my holy things, in the most holy *place*: but they
shall bear their shame, and their abominations which they have committed.
14 But I will make them keepers of the charge of the house, for all the service
thereof, and for all that shall be done therein.
15 But the priests the Levites, the sons of Zadok, that kept the charge of my
sanctuary when the children of Israel went astray from me, they shall come
near to me to minister unto me, and they shall stand before me to offer unto
me the fat and the blood, saith the Lord GOD:
16 They shall enter into my sanctuary, and they shall come near to my table,
to minister unto me, and they shall keep my charge.

Ordinances for the Priests

17 And it shall come to pass, *that* when they enter in at the gates of the inner
court, they shall be clothed with linen garments; and no wool shall come upon
them, whiles they minister in the gates of the inner court, and within.
18 They shall have linen bonnets upon their heads, and shall have linen
breeches upon their loins; they shall not gird *themselves* with any thing that
causeth sweat.
19 And when they go forth into the utter court, *even* into the utter court to
the people, they shall put off their garments wherein they ministered, and lay
them in the holy chambers, and they shall put on other garments; and they
shall not sanctify the people with their garments.
20 Neither shall they shave their heads, nor suffer their locks to grow long;
they shall only poll their heads.
21 Neither shall any priest drink wine, when they enter into the inner court.
22 Neither shall they take for their wives a widow, nor her that is put away:
but they shall take maidens of the seed of the house of Israel, or a widow that
had a priest before.
23 And they shall teach my people *the difference* between the holy and pro-
fane, and cause them to discern between the unclean and the clean.
24 And in controversy they shall stand in judgment; *and* they shall judge it
according to my judgments: and they shall keep my laws and my statutes in
all mine assemblies; and they shall hallow my sabbaths.
25 And they shall come at no dead person to defile themselves: but for father,
or for mother, or for son, or for daughter, for brother, or for sister that hath
had no husband, they may defile themselves.
26 And after he is cleansed, they shall reckon unto him seven days.
27 And in the day that he goeth into the sanctuary, unto the inner court, to
minister in the sanctuary, he shall offer his sin offering, saith the Lord GOD.
28 And it shall be unto them for an inheritance: I *am* their inheritance: and
ye shall give them no possession in Israel: I *am* their possession.
29 They shall eat the meat offering, and the sin offering, and the trespass
offering; and every dedicated thing in Israel shall be theirs.
30 And the first of all the firstfruits of all *things*, and every oblation of all, of
every *sort* of your oblations, shall be the priest's: ye shall also give unto the
priest the first of your dough, that he may cause the blessing to rest in thine
house.
31 The priests shall not eat of any thing that is dead of itself, or torn, wheth-
er it be fowl or beast.

The Portions of Land

45 Moreover, when ye shall divide by lot the land for inheritance, ye shall
offer an oblation unto the LORD, an holy portion of the land: the length
shall be the length of five and twenty thousand *reeds*, and the breadth *shall
be* ten thousand. This *shall be* holy in all the borders thereof round about.

2 Of this there shall be for the sanctuary five hundred *in length*, with five
hundred *in breadth*, square round about; and fifty cubits round about for the
suburbs thereof.
3 And of this measure shalt thou measure the length of five and twenty thou-
sand, and the breadth of ten thousand: and in it shall be the sanctuary *and*
the most holy *place*.
4 The holy *portion* of the land shall be for the priests the ministers of the
sanctuary, which shall come near to minister unto the LORD: and it shall be a
place for their houses, and an holy place for the sanctuary.
5 And the five and twenty thousand of length, and the ten thousand of
breadth, shall also the Levites, the ministers of the house, have for themselves,
for a possession for twenty chambers.
6 And ye shall appoint the possession of the city five thousand broad, and
five and twenty thousand long, over against the oblation of the holy *portion*:
it shall be for the whole house of Israel.
7 And a *portion shall be* for the prince on the one side and on the other side
of the oblation of the holy *portion*, and of the possession of the city, before
the oblation of the holy *portion*, and before the possession of the city, from
the west side westward, and from the east side eastward: and the length *shall
be* over against one of the portions, from the west border unto the east border.
8 In the land shall be his possession in Israel: and my princes shall no more
oppress my people; and *the rest of* the land shall they give to the house of Israel
according to their tribes.

Honest Weights and Measures

9 Thus saith the Lord GOD; Let it suffice you, O princes of Israel: remove
violence and spoil, and execute judgment and justice, take away your exactions
from my people, saith the Lord GOD.
10 Ye shall have just balances, and a just ephah, and a just bath.
11 The ephah and the bath shall be of one measure, that the bath may contain
the tenth part of an homer, and the ephah the tenth part of an homer: the
measure thereof shall be after the homer.
12 And the shekel *shall be* twenty gerahs: twenty shekels, five and twenty
shekels, fifteen shekels, shall be your maneh.

Rules for Worship

13 This *is* the oblation that ye shall offer; the sixth part of an ephah of an
homer of wheat, and ye shall give the sixth part of an ephah of an homer of
barley:
14 Concerning the ordinance of oil, the bath of oil, *ye shall offer* the tenth
part of a bath out of the cor, *which is* an homer of ten baths; for ten baths *are*
an homer:
15 And one lamb out of the flock, out of two hundred, out of the fat pastures
of Israel; for a meat offering, and for a burnt offering, and for peace offerings,
to make reconciliation for them, saith the Lord GOD.
16 All the people of the land shall give this oblation for the prince in Israel.
17 And it shall be the prince's part *to give* burnt offerings, and meat offerings,
and drink offerings, in the feasts, and in the new moons, and in the sabbaths,
in all solemnities of the house of Israel: he shall prepare the sin offering, and
the meat offering, and the burnt offering, and the peace offerings, to make
reconciliation for the house of Israel.
18 Thus saith the Lord GOD; In the first *month*, in the first *day* of the month,
thou shalt take a young bullock without blemish, and cleanse the sanctuary:
19 And the priest shall take of the blood of the sin offering, and put *it* upon
the posts of the house, and upon the four corners of the settle of the altar, and
upon the posts of the gate of the inner court.

20 And so thou shalt do the seventh *day* of the month for every one that
erreth, and for *him that is* simple: so shall ye reconcile the house.
21 In the first *month*, in the fourteenth day of the month, ye shall have the
passover, a feast of seven days; unleavened bread shall be eaten.
22 And upon that day shall the prince prepare for himself and for all the
people of the land a bullock *for* a sin offering.
23 And seven days of the feast he shall prepare a burnt offering to the LORD,
seven bullocks and seven rams without blemish daily the seven days; and a kid
of the goats daily *for* a sin offering.
24 And he shall prepare a meat offering of an ephah for a bullock, and an
ephah for a ram, and an hin of oil for an ephah.
25 In the seventh *month*, in the fifteenth day of the month, shall he do the like
in the feast of the seven days, according to the sin offering, according to the
burnt offering, and according to the meat offering, and according to the oil.

More Regulations for Worship

46 Thus saith the Lord GOD; The gate of the inner court that looketh
toward the east shall be shut the six working days; but on the sabbath
it shall be opened, and in the day of the new moon it shall be opened.
2 And the prince shall enter by the way of the porch of *that* gate without,
and shall stand by the post of the gate, and the priests shall prepare his burnt
offering and his peace offerings, and he shall worship at the threshold of the
gate: then he shall go forth; but the gate shall not be shut until the evening.
3 Likewise the people of the land shall worship at the door of this gate before
the LORD in the sabbaths and in the new moons.
4 And the burnt offering that the prince shall offer unto the LORD in the
sabbath day *shall be* six lambs without blemish, and a ram without blemish.
5 And the meat offering *shall be* an ephah for a ram, and the meat offering
for the lambs as he shall be able to give, and an hin of oil to an ephah.
6 And in the day of the new moon *it shall be* a young bullock without blem-
ish, and six lambs, and a ram: they shall be without blemish.
7 And he shall prepare a meat offering, an ephah for a bullock, and an ephah
for a ram, and for the lambs according as his hand shall attain unto, and an
hin of oil to an ephah.
8 And when the prince shall enter, he shall go in by the way of the porch of
that gate, and he shall go forth by the way thereof.
9 But when the people of the land shall come before the LORD in the solemn
feasts, he that entereth in by the way of the north gate to worship shall go out
by the way of the south gate; and he that entereth by the way of the south gate
shall go forth by the way of the north gate: he shall not return by the way of
the gate whereby he came in, but shall go forth over against it.
10 And the prince in the midst of them, when they go in, shall go in; and
when they go forth, shall go forth.
11 And in the feasts and in the solemnities the meat offering shall be an ephah
to a bullock, and an ephah to a ram, and to the lambs as he is able to give, and
an hin of oil to an ephah.
12 Now when the prince shall prepare a voluntary burnt offering or peace
offerings voluntarily unto the LORD, *one* shall then open him the gate that
looketh toward the east, and he shall prepare his burnt offering and his peace
offerings, as he did on the sabbath day: then he shall go forth; and after his
going forth *one* shall shut the gate.
13 Thou shalt daily prepare a burnt offering unto the LORD *of* a lamb of the
first year without blemish: thou shalt prepare it every morning.
14 And thou shalt prepare a meat offering for it every morning, the sixth
part of an ephah, and the third part of an hin of oil, to temper with the fine
flour; a meat offering continually by a perpetual ordinance unto the LORD.

15 Thus shall they prepare the lamb, and the meat offering, and the oil, every morning *for* a continual burnt offering.

An Order for the Prince's Inheritance

16 Thus saith the Lord GOD; If the prince give a gift unto any of his sons, the inheritance thereof shall be his sons'; it *shall be* their possession by inheritance.

17 But if he give a gift of his inheritance to one of his servants, then it shall be his to the year of liberty; after it shall return to the prince: but his inheritance shall be his sons' for them.

18 Moreover the prince shall not take of the people's inheritance by oppression, to thrust them out of their possession; *but* he shall give his sons inheritance out of his own possession: that my people be not scattered every man from his possession.

The Courts for Boiling and Baking

19 After he brought me through the entry, which *was* at the side of the gate, into the holy chambers of the priests, which looked toward the north: and, behold, there *was* a place on the two sides westward.

20 Then said he unto me, This *is* the place where the priests shall boil the trespass offering and the sin offering, where they shall bake the meat offering; that they bear *them* not out into the utter court, to sanctify the people.

21 Then he brought me forth into the utter court, and caused me to pass by the four corners of the court; and, behold, in every corner of the court *there was* a court.

22 In the four corners of the court *there were* courts joined of forty *cubits* long and thirty broad: these four corners *were* of one measure.

23 And *there was* a row *of building* round about in them, round about them four, and *it was* made with boiling places under the rows round about.

24 Then said he unto me, These *are* the places of them that boil, where the ministers of the house shall boil the sacrifice of the people.

Water Flowing from the Temple

47 Afterward he brought me again unto the door of the house; and, behold, waters issued out from under the threshold of the house eastward: for the forefront of the house *stood toward* the east, and the waters came down from under from the right side of the house, at the south *side* of the altar.

2 Then brought he me out of the way of the gate northward, and led me about the way without unto the utter gate by the way that looketh eastward; and, behold, there ran out waters on the right side.

3 And when the man that had the line in his hand went forth eastward, he measured a thousand cubits, and he brought me through the waters; the waters *were* to the ankles.

4 Again he measured a thousand, and brought me through the waters; the waters *were* to the knees. Again he measured a thousand, and brought me through; the waters *were* to the loins.

5 Afterward he measured a thousand; *and it was* a river that I could not pass over: for the waters were risen, waters to swim in, a river that could not be passed over.

6 And he said unto me, Son of man, hast thou seen *this*? Then he brought me, and caused me to return to the brink of the river.

7 Now when I had returned, behold, at the bank of the river *were* very many trees on the one side and on the other.

8 Then said he unto me, These waters issue out toward the east country, and go down into the desert, and go into the sea: *which being* brought forth into the sea, the waters shall be healed.

9 And it shall come to pass, *that* every thing that liveth, which moveth, whith-
ersoever the rivers shall come, shall live: and there shall be a very great mul-
titude of fish, because these waters shall come thither: for they shall be healed;
and every thing shall live whither the river cometh.
10 And it shall come to pass, *that* the fishers shall stand upon it from En-gedi
even unto En-eglaim; they shall be a *place* to spread forth nets; their fish shall
be according to their kinds, as the fish of the great sea, exceeding many.
11 But the miry places thereof and the marishes thereof shall not be healed;
they shall be given to salt.
12 And by the river upon the bank thereof, on this side and on that side, shall
grow all trees for meat, whose leaf shall not fade, neither shall the fruit there-
of be consumed: it shall bring forth new fruit according to his months, because
their waters they issued out of the sanctuary: and the fruit thereof shall be for
meat, and the leaf thereof for medicine.

Dividing the Land

13 Thus saith the Lord GOD; This *shall be* the border, whereby ye shall inher-
it the land according to the twelve tribes of Israel: Joseph *shall have two* por-
tions.
14 And ye shall inherit it, one as well as another: *concerning* the which I
lifted up mine hand to give it unto your fathers: and this land shall fall unto
you for inheritance.
15 And this *shall be* the border of the land toward the north side, from the
great sea, the way of Hethlon, as men go to Zedad;
16 Hamath, Berothah, Sibraim, which *is* between the border of Damascus
and the border of Hamath; Hazar-hatticon, which *is* by the coast of Hauran.
17 And the border from the sea shall be Hazar-enan, the border of Damascus,
and the north northward, and the border of Hamath. And *this is* the north
side.
18 And the east side ye shall measure from Hauran, and from Damascus, and
from Gilead, and from the land of Israel *by* Jordan, from the border unto the
east sea. And *this is* the east side.
19 And the south side southward, from Tamar *even* to the waters of strife *in*
Kadesh, the river to the great sea. And *this is* the south side southward.
20 The west side also *shall be* the great sea from the border, till a man come
over against Hamath. This *is* the west side.
21 So shall ye divide this land unto you according to the tribes of Israel.
22 And it shall come to pass, *that* ye shall divide it by lot for an inheritance
unto you, and to the strangers that sojourn among you, which shall beget
children among you: and they shall be unto you as born in the country among
the children of Israel; they shall have inheritance with you among the tribes
of Israel.
23 And it shall come to pass, *that* in what tribe the stranger sojourneth, there
shall ye give *him* his inheritance, saith the Lord GOD.

Portions for the Tribes

48 Now these *are* the names of the tribes. From the north end to the coast
of the way of Hethlon, as one goeth to Hamath, Hazar-enan, the border
of Damascus northward, to the coast of Hamath; for these are his sides east
and west; a *portion for* Dan.
2 And by the border of Dan, from the east side unto the west side, a *portion*
for Asher.
3 And by the border of Asher, from the east side even unto the west side, a
portion for Naphtali.
4 And by the border of Naphtali, from the east side unto the west side, a
portion for Manasseh.

5 And by the border of Manasseh, from the east side unto the west side, a
portion for Ephraim.
6 And by the border of Ephraim, from the east side even unto the west side,
a *portion for* Reuben.
7 And by the border of Reuben, from the east side unto the west side, a *por-*
tion for Judah.
8 And by the border of Judah, from the east side unto the west side, shall be
the offering which ye shall offer of five and twenty thousand *reeds in* breadth,
and *in* length as one of the *other* parts, from the east side unto the west side:
and the sanctuary shall be in the midst of it.
9 The oblation that ye shall offer unto the LORD *shall be* of five and twenty
thousand in length, and of ten thousand in breadth.
10 And for them, *even* for the priests, shall be *this* holy oblation; toward the
north five and twenty thousand *in length*, and toward the west ten thousand
in breadth, and toward the east ten thousand in breadth, and toward the south
five and twenty thousand in length: and the sanctuary of the LORD shall be in
the midst thereof.
11 *It shall be* for the priests that are sanctified of the sons of Zadok; which
have kept my charge, which went not astray when the children of Israel went
astray, as the Levites went astray.
12 And *this* oblation of the land that is offered shall be unto them a thing
most holy by the border of the Levites.
13 And over against the border of the priests the Levites *shall have* five and
twenty thousand in length, and ten thousand in breadth: all the length *shall*
be five and twenty thousand, and the breadth ten thousand.
14 And they shall not sell of it, neither exchange, nor alienate the firstfruits
of the land: for *it is* holy unto the LORD.
15 And the five thousand, that are left in the breadth over against the five
and twenty thousand, shall be a profane *place* for the city, for dwelling, and
for suburbs: and the city shall be in the midst thereof.
16 And these *shall be* the measures thereof; the north side four thousand and
five hundred, and the south side four thousand and five hundred, and on the
east side four thousand and five hundred, and the west side four thousand
and five hundred.
17 And the suburbs of the city shall be toward the north two hundred and
fifty, and toward the south two hundred and fifty, and toward the east two
hundred and fifty, and toward the west two hundred and fifty.
18 And the residue in length over against the oblation of the holy *portion*
shall be ten thousand eastward, and ten thousand westward: and it shall be
over against the oblation of the holy *portion*; and the increase thereof shall
be for food unto them that serve the city.
19 And they that serve the city shall serve it out of all the tribes of Israel.
20 All the oblation *shall be* five and twenty thousand by five and twenty thou-
sand: ye shall offer the holy oblation foursquare, with the possession of the
city.
21 And the residue *shall be* for the prince, on the one side and on the other
of the holy oblation, and of the possession of the city, over against the five and
twenty thousand of the oblation toward the east border, and westward over
against the five and twenty thousand toward the west border, over against the
portions for the prince: and it shall be the holy oblation; and the sanctuary of
the house *shall be* in the midst thereof.
22 Moreover from the possession of the Levites, and from the possession of
the city, *being* in the midst *of that* which is the prince's, between the border
of Judah and the border of Benjamin, shall be for the prince.
23 As for the rest of the tribes, from the east side unto the west side, Benjamin
shall have a *portion*.

24 And by the border of Benjamin, from the east side unto the west side,
Simeon *shall have* a *portion.*
25 And by the border of Simeon, from the east side unto the west side,
Issachar a *portion.*
26 And by the border of Issachar, from the east side unto the west side,
Zebulun a *portion.*
27 And by the border of Zebulun, from the east side unto the west side, Gad
a *portion.*
28 And by the border of Gad, at the south side southward, the border shall
be even from Tamar *unto* the waters of strife *in* Kadesh, *and* to the river toward
the great sea.
29 This *is* the land which ye shall divide by lot unto the tribes of Israel for
inheritance, and these *are* their portions, saith the Lord God.

The New City of God

30 And these *are* the goings out of the city on the north side, four thousand
and five hundred measures.
31 And the gates of the city *shall be* after the names of the tribes of Israel:
three gates northward; one gate of Reuben, one gate of Judah, one gate of Levi.
32 And at the east side four thousand and five hundred: and three gates; and
one gate of Joseph, one gate of Benjamin, one gate of Dan.
33 And at the south side four thousand and five hundred measures: and three
gates; one gate of Simeon, one gate of Issachar, one gate of Zebulun.
34 At the west side four thousand and five hundred, *with* their three gates;
one gate of Gad, one gate of Asher, one gate of Naphtali.
35 *It was* round about eighteen thousand *measures*: and the name of the city
from *that* day *shall be*, The Lord *is* there.

DANIEL

Daniel and His Friends Remain Faithful to God

1 In the third year of the reign of Jehoiakim king of Judah came
Nebuchadnezzar king of Babylon unto Jerusalem, and besieged it.
2 And the Lord gave Jehoiakim king of Judah into his hand, with part of the
vessels of the house of God: which he carried into the land of Shinar to the
house of his god; and he brought the vessels into the treasure house of his god.
3 And the king spake unto Ashpenaz the master of his eunuchs, that he
should bring *certain* of the children of Israel, and of the king's seed, and of
the princes;
4 Children in whom *was* no blemish, but well favoured, and skilful in all
wisdom, and cunning in knowledge, and understanding science, and such as
had ability in them to stand in the king's palace, and whom they might teach
the learning and the tongue of the Chaldeans.
5 And the king appointed them a daily provision of the king's meat, and of
the wine which he drank: so nourishing them three years, that at the end
thereof they might stand before the king.
6 Now among these were of the children of Judah, Daniel, Hananiah,
Mishael, and Azariah:
7 Unto whom the prince of the eunuchs gave names: for he gave unto Daniel
the name of Belteshazzar; and to Hananiah, of Shadrach; and to Mishael, of
Meshach; and to Azariah, of Abed-nego.
8 But Daniel purposed in his heart that he would not defile himself with the
portion of the king's meat, nor with the wine which he drank: therefore he
requested of the prince of the eunuchs that he might not defile himself.
9 Now God had brought Daniel into favour and tender love with the prince
of the eunuchs.
10 And the prince of the eunuchs said unto Daniel, I fear my lord the king,
who hath appointed your meat and your drink: for why should he see your
faces worse liking than the children which *are* of your sort? then shall ye make
me endanger my head to the king.
11 Then said Daniel to Melzar, whom the prince of the eunuchs had set over
Daniel, Hananiah, Mishael, and Azariah,
12 Prove thy servants, I beseech thee, ten days; and let them give us pulse to
eat, and water to drink.
13 Then let our countenances be looked upon before thee, and the counte-
nance of the children that eat of the portion of the king's meat: and as thou
seest, deal with thy servants.
14 So he consented to them in this matter, and proved them ten days.
15 And at the end of ten days their countenances appeared fairer and fatter
in flesh than all the children which did eat the portion of the king's meat.
16 Thus Melzar took away the portion of their meat, and the wine that they
should drink; and gave them pulse.
17 As for these four children, God gave them knowledge and skill in all learn-
ing and wisdom: and Daniel had understanding in all visions and dreams.
18 Now at the end of the days that the king had said he should bring them
in, then the prince of the eunuchs brought them in before Nebuchadnezzar.

19 And the king communed with them; and among them all was found none
like Daniel, Hananiah, Mishael, and Azariah: therefore stood they before the
king.
20 And in all matters of wisdom *and* understanding, that the king enquired
of them, he found them ten times better than all the magicians *and* astrologers
that *were* in all his realm.
21 And Daniel continued *even* unto the first year of king Cyrus.

Nebuchadnezzar Dreams

2 And in the second year of the reign of Nebuchadnezzar Nebuchadnezzar
dreamed dreams, wherewith his spirit was troubled, and his sleep brake
from him.
2 Then the king commanded to call the magicians, and the astrologers, and
the sorcerers, and the Chaldeans, for to shew the king his dreams. So they
came and stood before the king.
3 And the king said unto them, I have dreamed a dream, and my spirit was
troubled to know the dream.
4 Then spake the Chaldeans to the king in Syriack, O king, live for ever: tell
thy servants the dream, and we will shew the interpretation.
5 The king answered and said to the Chaldeans, The thing is gone from me:
if ye will not make known unto me the dream, with the interpretation there-
of, ye shall be cut in pieces, and your houses shall be made a dunghill.
6 But if ye shew the dream, and the interpretation thereof, ye shall receive
of me gifts and rewards and great honour: therefore shew me the dream, and
the interpretation thereof.
7 They answered again and said, Let the king tell his servants the dream, and
we will shew the interpretation of it.
8 The king answered and said, I know of certainty that ye would gain the
time, because ye see the thing is gone from me.
9 But if ye will not make known unto me the dream, *there is but* one decree
for you: for ye have prepared lying and corrupt words to speak before me, till
the time be changed: therefore tell me the dream, and I shall know that ye can
shew me the interpretation thereof.
10 The Chaldeans answered before the king, and said, There is not a man
upon the earth that can shew the king's matter: therefore *there is* no king, lord,
nor ruler, *that* asked such things at any magician, or astrologer, or Chaldean.
11 And *it is* a rare thing that the king requireth, and there is none other that
can shew it before the king, except the gods, whose dwelling is not with flesh.
12 For this cause the king was angry and very furious, and commanded to
destroy all the wise *men* of Babylon.
13 And the decree went forth that the wise *men* should be slain; and they
sought Daniel and his fellows to be slain.

The Dream Is Revealed to Daniel

14 Then Daniel answered with counsel and wisdom to Arioch the captain of
the king's guard, which was gone forth to slay the wise *men* of Babylon:
15 He answered and said to Arioch the king's captain, Why *is* the decree *so*
hasty from the king? Then Arioch made the thing known to Daniel.
16 Then Daniel went in, and desired of the king that he would give him time,
and that he would shew the king the interpretation.
17 Then Daniel went to his house, and made the thing known to Hananiah,
Mishael, and Azariah, his companions:
18 That they would desire mercies of the God of heaven concerning this
secret; that Daniel and his fellows should not perish with the rest of the wise
men of Babylon.
19 Then was the secret revealed unto Daniel in a night vision. Then Daniel
blessed the God of heaven.

20 Daniel answered and said, Blessed be the name of God for ever and ever: for wisdom and might are his:
21 And he changeth the times and the seasons: he removeth kings, and setteth up kings: he giveth wisdom unto the wise, and knowledge to them that know understanding:
22 He revealeth the deep and secret things: he knoweth what *is* in the darkness, and the light dwelleth with him.
23 I thank thee, and praise thee, O thou God of my fathers, who hast given me wisdom and might, and hast made known unto me now what we desired of thee: for thou hast *now* made known unto us the king's matter.
24 Therefore Daniel went in unto Arioch, whom the king had ordained to destroy the wise *men* of Babylon: he went and said thus unto him; Destroy not the wise *men* of Babylon: bring me in before the king, and I will shew unto the king the interpretation.
25 Then Arioch brought in Daniel before the king in haste, and said thus unto him, I have found a man of the captives of Judah, that will make known unto the king the interpretation.
26 The king answered and said to Daniel, whose name *was* Belteshazzar, Art thou able to make known unto me the dream which I have seen, and the interpretation thereof?
27 Daniel answered in the presence of the king, and said, The secret which the king hath demanded cannot the wise *men*, the astrologers, the magicians, the soothsayers, shew unto the king;
28 But there is a God in heaven that reveal-eth secrets, and maketh known to the king Nebuchadnezzar what shall be in the latter days. Thy dream, and the visions of thy head upon thy bed, are these;
29 As for thee, O king, thy thoughts came *into thy mind* upon thy bed, what should come to pass hereafter: and he that revealeth secrets maketh known to thee what shall come to pass.
30 But as for me, this secret is not revealed to me for *any* wisdom that I have more than any living, but for *their* sakes that shall make known the interpretation to the king, and that thou mightest know the thoughts of thy heart.

The Dream

31 Thou, O king, sawest, and behold a great image. This great image, whose brightness *was* excellent, stood before thee; and the form thereof *was* terrible.
32 This image's head *was* of fine gold, his breast and his arms of silver, his belly and his thighs of brass,
33 His legs of iron, his feet part of iron and part of clay.
34 Thou sawest till that a stone was cut out without hands, which smote the image upon his feet *that were* of iron and clay, and brake them to pieces.
35 Then was the iron, the clay, the brass, the silver, and the gold, broken to pieces together, and became like the chaff of the summer threshingfloors; and the wind carried them away, that no place was found for them: and the stone that smote the image became a great mountain, and filled the whole earth.
36 This *is* the dream; and we will tell the interpretation thereof before the king.
37 Thou, O king, *art* a king of kings: for the God of heaven hath given thee a kingdom, power, and strength, and glory.
38 And wheresoever the children of men dwell, the beasts of the field and the fowls of the heaven hath he given into thine hand, and hath made thee ruler over them all. Thou *art* this head of gold.
39 And after thee shall arise another kingdom inferior to thee, and another third kingdom of brass, which shall bear rule over all the earth.

40 And the fourth kingdom shall be strong as iron: forasmuch as iron
breaketh in pieces and subdueth all *things*: and as iron that breaketh all these,
shall it break in pieces and bruise.
41 And whereas thou sawest the feet and toes, part of potters' clay, and part
of iron, the kingdom shall be divided; but there shall be in it of the strength
of the iron, forasmuch as thou sawest the iron mixed with miry clay.
42 And *as* the toes of the feet *were* part of iron, and part of clay, *so* the king-
dom shall be partly strong, and partly broken.
43 And whereas thou sawest iron mixed with miry clay, they shall mingle
themselves with the seed of men: but they shall not cleave one to another, even
as iron is not mixed with clay.
44 And in the days of these kings shall the God of heaven set up a kingdom,
which shall never be destroyed: and the kingdom shall not be left to other
people, *but* it shall break in pieces and consume all these kingdoms, and it
shall stand for ever.
45 Forasmuch as thou sawest that the stone was cut out of the mountain
without hands, and that it brake in pieces the iron, the brass, the clay, the
silver, and the gold; the great God hath made known to the king what shall
come to pass hereafter: and the dream *is* certain, and the interpretation there-
of sure.

Daniel's Advancement

46 Then the king Nebuchadnezzar fell upon his face, and worshipped Daniel,
and commanded that they should offer an oblation and sweet odours unto
him.
47 The king answered unto Daniel, and said, Of a truth *it is*, that your God *is*
a God of gods, and a Lord of kings, and a revealer of secrets, seeing thou
couldest reveal this secret.
48 Then the king made Daniel a great man, and gave him many great gifts,
and made him ruler over the whole province of Babylon, and chief of the
governors over all the wise *men* of Babylon.
49 Then Daniel requested of the king, and he set Shadrach, Meshach, and
Abed-nego, over the affairs of the province of Babylon: but Daniel *sat* in the
gate of the king.

Nebuchadnezzar Dedicates a Golden Image

3 Nebuchadnezzar the king made an image of gold, whose height *was* three-
score cubits, *and* the breadth thereof six cubits: he set it up in the plain of
Dura, in the province of Babylon.
2 Then Nebuchadnezzar the king sent to gather together the princes, the
governors, and the captains, the judges, the treasurers, the counsellors, the
sheriffs, and all the rulers of the provinces, to come to the dedication of the
image which Nebuchadnezzar the king had set up.
3 Then the princes, the governors, and captains, the judges, the treasurers,
the counsellors, the sheriffs, and all the rulers of the provinces, were gathered
together unto the dedication of the image that Nebuchadnezzar the king had
set up; and they stood before the image that Nebuchadnezzar had set up.
4 Then an herald cried aloud, To you it is commanded, O people, nations,
and languages,
5 *That* at what time ye hear the sound of the cornet, flute, harp, sackbut,
psaltery, dulcimer, and all kinds of musick, ye fall down and worship the gold-
en image that Nebuchadnezzar the king hath set up:
6 And whoso falleth not down and worshippeth shall the same hour be cast
into the midst of a burning fiery furnace.
7 Therefore at that time, when all the people heard the sound of the cornet,
flute, harp, sackbut, psaltery, and all kinds of musick, all the people, the

BE IT known UNTO THEE, O KING, THAT WE WILL NOT Serve thy gods, NOR WORSHIP THE GOLDEN IMAGE WHICH THOU HAST set up.

DANIEL 3:18

nations, and the languages, fell down *and* worshipped the golden image that
Nebuchadnezzar the king had set up.

The Fiery Furnace

8 Wherefore at that time certain Chaldeans came near, and accused the Jews.
9 They spake and said to the king Nebuchadnezzar, O king, live for ever.
10 Thou, O king, hast made a decree, that every man that shall hear the sound
of the cornet, flute, harp, sackbut, psaltery, and dulcimer, and all kinds of
musick, shall fall down and worship the golden image:
11 And whoso falleth not down and worshippeth, *that* he should be cast into
the midst of a burning fiery furnace.
12 There are certain Jews whom thou hast set over the affairs of the province
of Babylon, Shadrach, Meshach, and Abed-nego; these men, O king, have not
regarded thee: they serve not thy gods, nor worship the golden image which
thou hast set up.
13 Then Nebuchadnezzar in *his* rage and fury commanded to bring Shadrach,
Meshach, and Abed-nego. Then they brought these men before the king.
14 Nebuchadnezzar spake and said unto them, *Is it* true, O Shadrach,
Meshach, and Abed-nego, do not ye serve my gods, nor worship the golden
image which I have set up?
15 Now if ye be ready that at what time ye hear the sound of the cornet, flute,
harp, sackbut, psaltery, and dulcimer, and all kinds of musick, ye fall down
and worship the image which I have made; *well*: but if ye worship not, ye shall
be cast the same hour into the midst of a burning fiery furnace; and who *is*
that God that shall deliver you out of my hands?
16 Shadrach, Meshach, and Abed-nego, answered and said to the king, O
Nebuchadnezzar, we *are* not careful to answer thee in this matter.
17 If it be *so*, our God whom we serve is able to deliver us from the burning
fiery furnace, and he will deliver *us* out of thine hand, O king.
18 But if not, be it known unto thee, O king, that we will not serve thy gods,
nor worship the golden image which thou hast set up.
19 Then was Nebuchadnezzar full of fury, and the form of his visage was
changed against Shadrach, Meshach, and Abed-nego: *therefore* he spake, and
commanded that they should heat the furnace one seven times more than it
was wont to be heated.
20 And he commanded the most mighty men that *were* in his army to bind
Shadrach, Meshach, and Abed-nego, *and* to cast *them* into the burning fiery
furnace.
21 Then these men were bound in their coats, their hosen, and their hats,
and their *other* garments, and were cast into the midst of the burning fiery
furnace.
22 Therefore because the king's commandment was urgent, and the furnace
exceeding hot, the flame of the fire slew those men that took up Shadrach,
Meshach, and Abed-nego.
23 And these three men, Shadrach, Meshach, and Abed-nego, fell down
bound into the midst of the burning fiery furnace.
24 Then Nebuchadnezzar the king was astonied, and rose up in haste, *and*
spake, and said unto his counsellors, Did not we cast three men bound into
the midst of the fire? They answered and said unto the king, True, O king.
25 He answered and said, Lo, I see four men loose, walking in the midst of
the fire, and they have no hurt; and the form of the fourth is like the Son of
God.
26 Then Nebuchadnezzar came near to the mouth of the burning fiery fur-
nace, *and* spake, and said, Shadrach, Meshach, and Abed-nego, ye servants of
the most high God, come forth, and come *hither*. Then Shadrach, Meshach,
and Abed-nego, came forth of the midst of the fire.

27 And the princes, governors, and captains, and the king's counsellors, being
gathered together, saw these men, upon whose bodies the fire had no power,
nor was an hair of their head singed, neither were their coats changed, nor
the smell of fire had passed on them.
28 *Then* Nebuchadnezzar spake, and said, Blessed *be* the God of Shadrach,
Meshach, and Abed-nego, who hath sent his angel, and delivered his servants
that trusted in him, and have changed the king's word, and yielded their bod-
ies, that they might not serve nor worship any god, except their own God.
29 Therefore I make a decree, That every people, nation, and language, which
speak any thing amiss against the God of Shadrach, Meshach, and Abed-nego,
shall be cut in pieces, and their houses shall be made a dunghill: because there
is no other God that can deliver after this sort.
30 Then the king promoted Shadrach, Meshach, and Abed-nego, in the prov-
ince of Babylon.

Nebuchadnezzar Praises God

4 Nebuchadnezzar the king, unto all people, nations, and languages, that
dwell in all the earth; Peace be multiplied unto you.
2 I thought it good to shew the signs and wonders that the high God hath
wrought toward me.
3 How great *are* his signs! and how mighty *are* his wonders! his kingdom *is*
an everlasting kingdom, and his dominion *is* from generation to generation.

Nebuchadnezzar Has Another Dream

4 I Nebuchadnezzar was at rest in mine house, and flourishing in my palace:
5 I saw a dream which made me afraid, and the thoughts upon my bed and
the visions of my head troubled me.
6 Therefore made I a decree to bring in all the wise *men* of Babylon before
me, that they might make known unto me the interpretation of the dream.
7 Then came in the magicians, the astrologers, the Chaldeans, and the sooth-
sayers: and I told the dream before them; but they did not make known unto
me the interpretation thereof.
8 But at the last Daniel came in before me, whose name *was* Belteshazzar,
according to the name of my god, and in whom *is* the spirit of the holy gods:
and before him I told the dream, *saying*,
9 O Belteshazzar, master of the magicians, because I know that the spirit of
the holy gods *is* in thee, and no secret troubleth thee, tell me the visions of my
dream that I have seen, and the interpretation thereof.
10 Thus *were* the visions of mine head in my bed; I saw, and behold a tree in
the midst of the earth, and the height thereof *was* great.
11 The tree grew, and was strong, and the height thereof reached unto heav-
en, and the sight thereof to the end of all the earth:
12 The leaves thereof *were* fair, and the fruit thereof much, and in it *was* meat
for all: the beasts of the field had shadow under it, and the fowls of the heaven
dwelt in the boughs thereof, and all flesh was fed of it.
13 I saw in the visions of my head upon my bed, and, behold, a watcher and
an holy one came down from heaven;
14 He cried aloud, and said thus, Hew down the tree, and cut off his branch-
es, shake off his leaves, and scatter his fruit: let the beasts get away from under
it, and the fowls from his branches:
15 Nevertheless leave the stump of his roots in the earth, even with a band
of iron and brass, in the tender grass of the field; and let it be wet with the dew
of heaven, and *let* his portion *be* with the beasts in the grass of the earth:
16 Let his heart be changed from man's, and let a beast's heart be given unto
him; and let seven times pass over him.
17 This matter *is* by the decree of the watchers, and the demand by the word
of the holy ones: to the intent that the living may know that the most High

ruleth in the kingdom of men, and giveth it to whomsoever he will, and setteth
up over it the basest of men.
18 This dream I king Nebuchadnezzar have seen. Now thou, O Belteshazzar,
declare the interpretation thereof, forasmuch as all the wise *men* of my king-
dom are not able to make known unto me the interpretation: but thou *art*
able; for the spirit of the holy gods *is* in thee.

Daniel Interprets the Dream

19 Then Daniel, whose name *was* Belteshazzar, was astonied for one hour,
and his thoughts troubled him. The king spake, and said, Belteshazzar, let not
the dream, or the interpretation thereof, trouble thee. Belteshazzar answered
and said, My lord, the dream *be* to them that hate thee, and the interpretation
thereof to thine enemies.
20 The tree that thou sawest, which grew, and was strong, whose height
reached unto the heaven, and the sight thereof to all the earth;
21 Whose leaves *were* fair, and the fruit thereof much, and in it *was* meat for
all; under which the beasts of the field dwelt, and upon whose branches the
fowls of the heaven had their habitation:
22 It *is* thou, O king, that art grown and become strong: for thy greatness is
grown, and reacheth unto heaven, and thy dominion to the end of the earth.
23 And whereas the king saw a watcher and an holy one coming down from
heaven, and saying, Hew the tree down, and destroy it; yet leave the stump of
the roots thereof in the earth, even with a band of iron and brass, in the tender
grass of the field; and let it be wet with the dew of heaven, and *let* his portion
be with the beasts of the field, till seven times pass over him;
24 This *is* the interpretation, O king, and this *is* the decree of the most High,
which is come upon my lord the king:
25 That they shall drive thee from men, and thy dwelling shall be with the
beasts of the field, and they shall make thee to eat grass as oxen, and they shall
wet thee with the dew of heaven, and seven times shall pass over thee, till thou
know that the most High ruleth in the kingdom of men, and giveth it to whom-
soever he will.
26 And whereas they commanded to leave the stump of the tree roots; thy
kingdom shall be sure unto thee, after that thou shalt have known that the
heavens do rule.
27 Wherefore, O king, let my counsel be acceptable unto thee, and break off
thy sins by righteousness, and thine iniquities by shewing mercy to the poor;
if it may be a lengthening of thy tranquillity.

Nebuchadnezzar's Temporary Insanity

28 All this came upon the king Nebuchadnezzar.
29 At the end of twelve months he walked in the palace of the kingdom of
Babylon.
30 The king spake, and said, Is not this great Babylon, that I have built for the
house of the kingdom by the might of my power, and for the honour of my
majesty?
31 While the word *was* in the king's mouth, there fell a voice from heaven,
saying, O king Nebuchadnezzar, to thee it is spoken; The kingdom is departed
from thee.
32 And they shall drive thee from men, and thy dwelling *shall be* with the
beasts of the field: they shall make thee to eat grass as oxen, and seven times
shall pass over thee, until thou know that the most High ruleth in the kingdom
of men, and giveth it to whomsoever he will.
33 The same hour was the thing fulfilled upon Nebuchadnezzar: and he was
driven from men, and did eat grass as oxen, and his body was wet with the
dew of heaven, till his hairs were grown like eagles' *feathers*, and his nails like
birds' *claws*.

Nebuchadnezzar Praises God

34 And at the end of the days I Nebuchadnezzar lifted up mine eyes unto heaven, and mine understanding returned unto me, and I blessed the most High, and I praised and honoured him that liveth for ever, whose dominion *is* an everlasting dominion, and his kingdom *is* from generation to generation:

35 And all the inhabitants of the earth *are* reputed as nothing: and he doeth according to his will in the army of heaven, and *among* the inhabitants of the earth: and none can stay his hand, or say unto him, What doest thou?

36 At the same time my reason returned unto me; and for the glory of my kingdom, mine honour and brightness returned unto me; and my counsellors and my lords sought unto me; and I was established in my kingdom, and excellent majesty was added unto me.

37 Now I Nebuchadnezzar praise and extol and honour the King of heaven, all whose works *are* truth, and his ways judgment: and those that walk in pride he is able to abase.

Belshazzar's Impious Feast

5 Belshazzar the king made a great feast to a thousand of his lords, and drank wine before the thousand.

2 Belshazzar, whiles he tasted the wine, commanded to bring the golden and silver vessels which his father Nebuchadnezzar had taken out of the temple which *was* in Jerusalem; that the king, and his princes, his wives, and his concubines, might drink therein.

3 Then they brought the golden vessels that were taken out of the temple of the house of God which *was* at Jerusalem; and the king, and his princes, his wives, and his concubines, drank in them.

4 They drank wine, and praised the gods of gold, and of silver, of brass, of iron, of wood, and of stone.

The Handwriting on the Wall

5 In the same hour came forth fingers of a man's hand, and wrote over against the candlestick upon the plaister of the wall of the king's palace: and the king saw the part of the hand that wrote.

6 Then the king's countenance was changed, and his thoughts troubled him, so that the joints of his loins were loosed, and his knees smote one against another.

7 The king cried aloud to bring in the astrologers, the Chaldeans, and the soothsayers. *And* the king spake, and said to the wise *men* of Babylon, Whosoever shall read this writing, and shew me the interpretation thereof, shall be clothed with scarlet, and *have* a chain of gold about his neck, and shall be the third ruler in the kingdom.

8 Then came in all the king's wise *men*: but they could not read the writing, nor make known to the king the interpretation thereof.

9 Then was king Belshazzar greatly troubled, and his countenance was changed in him, and his lords were astonied.

The End of Babylon

10 *Now* the queen, by reason of the words of the king and his lords, came into the banquet house: *and* the queen spake and said, O king, live for ever: let not thy thoughts trouble thee, nor let thy countenance be changed:

11 There is a man in thy kingdom, in whom *is* the spirit of the holy gods; and in the days of thy father light and understanding and wisdom, like the wisdom of the gods, was found in him; whom the king Nebuchadnezzar thy father, the king, *I say*, thy father, made master of the magicians, astrologers, Chaldeans, *and* soothsayers;

12 Forasmuch as an excellent spirit, and knowledge, and understanding, interpreting of dreams, and shewing of hard sentences, and dissolving of

doubts, were found in the same Daniel, whom the king named Belteshazzar:
now let Daniel be called, and he will shew the interpretation.
13 Then was Daniel brought in before the king. *And* the king spake and said
unto Daniel, *Art* thou that Daniel, which *art* of the children of the captivity
of Judah, whom the king my father brought out of Jewry?
14 I have even heard of thee, that the spirit of the gods *is* in thee, and *that*
light and understanding and excellent wisdom is found in thee.
15 And now the wise *men*, the astrologers, have been brought in before me,
that they should read this writing, and make known unto me the interpreta-
tion thereof: but they could not shew the interpretation of the thing:
16 And I have heard of thee, that thou canst make interpretations, and dis-
solve doubts: now if thou canst read the writing, and make known to me the
interpretation thereof, thou shalt be clothed with scarlet, and *have* a chain of
gold about thy neck, and shalt be the third ruler in the kingdom.
17 Then Daniel answered and said before the king, Let thy gifts be to thyself,
and give thy rewards to another; yet I will read the writing unto the king, and
make known to him the interpretation.
18 O thou king, the most high God gave Nebuchadnezzar thy father a king-
dom, and majesty, and glory, and honour:
19 And for the majesty that he gave him, all people, nations, and languages,
trembled and feared before him: whom he would he slew; and whom he would
he kept alive; and whom he would he set up; and whom he would he put down.
20 But when his heart was lifted up, and his mind hardened in pride, he was
deposed from his kingly throne, and they took his glory from him:
21 And he was driven from the sons of men; and his heart was made like the
beasts, and his dwelling *was* with the wild asses: they fed him with grass like
oxen, and his body was wet with the dew of heaven; till he knew that the most
high God ruled in the kingdom of men, and *that* he appointeth over it whom-
soever he will.
22 And thou his son, O Belshazzar, hast not humbled thine heart, though
thou knewest all this;
23 But hast lifted up thyself against the Lord of heaven; and they have brought
the vessels of his house before thee, and thou, and thy lords, thy wives, and
thy concubines, have drunk wine in them; and thou hast praised the gods of
silver, and gold, of brass, iron, wood, and stone, which see not, nor hear, nor
know: and the God in whose hand thy breath *is*, and whose *are* all thy ways,
hast thou not glorified:
24 Then was the part of the hand sent from him; and this writing was written.
25 And this *is* the writing that was written, MENE, MENE, TEKEL, UPHARSIN.
26 This *is* the interpretation of the thing: MENE; God hath numbered thy
kingdom, and finished it.
27 TEKEL; Thou art weighed in the balances, and art found wanting.
28 PERES; Thy kingdom is divided, and given to the Medes and Persians.
29 Then commanded Belshazzar, and they clothed Daniel with scarlet, and
put a chain of gold about his neck, and made a proclamation concerning him,
that he should be the third ruler in the kingdom.
30 In that night was Belshazzar the king of the Chaldeans slain.
31 And Darius the Median took the kingdom, *being* about threescore and
two years old.

Daniel in the Lions' Den

6 It pleased Darius to set over the kingdom an hundred and twenty princes,
which should be over the whole kingdom;
2 And over these three presidents; of whom Daniel *was* first: that the princ-
es might give accounts unto them, and the king should have no damage.

3 Then this Daniel was preferred above the presidents and princes, because
an excellent spirit *was* in him; and the king thought to set him over the whole
realm.
4 Then the presidents and princes sought to find occasion against Daniel
concerning the kingdom; but they could find none occasion nor fault; foras-
much as he *was* faithful, neither was there any error or fault found in him.
5 Then said these men, We shall not find any occasion against this Daniel,
except we find *it* against him concerning the law of his God.
6 Then these presidents and princes assembled together to the king, and said
thus unto him, King Darius, live for ever.
7 All the presidents of the kingdom, the governors, and the princes, the coun-
sellors, and the captains, have consulted together to establish a royal statute,
and to make a firm decree, that whosoever shall ask a petition of any God or
man for thirty days, save of thee, O king, he shall be cast into the den of lions.
8 Now, O king, establish the decree, and sign the writing, that it be not
changed, according to the law of the Medes and Persians, which altereth not.
9 Wherefore king Darius signed the writing and the decree.
10 Now when Daniel knew that the writing was signed, he went into his
house; and his windows being open in his chamber toward Jerusalem, he
kneeled upon his knees three times a day, and prayed, and gave thanks before
his God, as he did aforetime.
11 Then these men assembled, and found Daniel praying and making sup-
plication before his God.
12 Then they came near, and spake before the king concerning the king's
decree; Hast thou not signed a decree, that every man that shall ask *a petition*
of any God or man within thirty days, save of thee, O king, shall be cast into
the den of lions? The king answered and said, The thing *is* true, according to
the law of the Medes and Persians, which altereth not.
13 Then answered they and said before the king, That Daniel, which *is* of the
children of the captivity of Judah, regardeth not thee, O king, nor the decree
that thou hast signed, but maketh his petition three times a day.
14 Then the king, when he heard *these* words, was sore displeased with him-
self, and set *his* heart on Daniel to deliver him: and he laboured till the going
down of the sun to deliver him.
15 Then these men assembled unto the king, and said unto the king, Know,
O king, that the law of the Medes and Persians *is*, That no decree nor statute
which the king establisheth may be changed.
16 Then the king commanded, and they brought Daniel, and cast *him* into
the den of lions. *Now* the king spake and said unto Daniel, Thy God whom
thou servest continually, he will deliver thee.
17 And a stone was brought, and laid upon the mouth of the den; and the
king sealed it with his own signet, and with the signet of his lords; that the
purpose might not be changed concerning Daniel.
18 Then the king went to his palace, and passed the night fasting: neither
were instruments of musick brought before him: and his sleep went from
him.
19 Then the king arose very early in the morning, and went in haste unto the
den of lions.
20 And when he came to the den, he cried with a lamentable voice unto
Daniel: *and* the king spake and said to Daniel, O Daniel, servant of the living
God, is thy God, whom thou servest continually, able to deliver thee from the
lions?
21 Then said Daniel unto the king, O king, live for ever.
22 My God hath sent his angel, and hath shut the lions' mouths, that they
have not hurt me: forasmuch as before him innocency was found in me; and
also before thee, O king, have I done no hurt.

23 Then was the king exceeding glad for him, and commanded that they
should take Daniel up out of the den. So Daniel was taken up out of the den,
and no manner of hurt was found upon him, because he believed in his God.
24 And the king commanded, and they brought those men which had
accused Daniel, and they cast *them* into the den of lions, them, their children,
and their wives; and the lions had the mastery of them, and brake all their
bones in pieces or ever they came at the bottom of the den.
25 Then king Darius wrote unto all people, nations, and languages, that dwell
in all the earth; Peace be multiplied unto you.
26 I make a decree, That in every dominion of my kingdom men tremble and
fear before the God of Daniel: for he *is* the living God, and stedfast for ever,
and his kingdom *that* which shall not be destroyed, and his dominion *shall
be even* unto the end.
27 He delivereth and rescueth, and he worketh signs and wonders in heaven
and in earth, who hath delivered Daniel from the power of the lions.
28 So this Daniel prospered in the reign of Darius, and in the reign of Cyrus
the Persian.

Daniel's Vision of Four Beasts

7 In the first year of Belshazzar king of Babylon Daniel had a dream and
visions of his head upon his bed: then he wrote the dream, *and* told the
sum of the matters.
2 Daniel spake and said, I saw in my vision by night, and, behold, the four
winds of the heaven strove upon the great sea.
3 And four great beasts came up from the sea, diverse one from another.
4 The first *was* like a lion, and had eagle's wings: I beheld till the wings there-
of were plucked, and it was lifted up from the earth, and made stand upon the
feet as a man, and a man's heart was given to it.
5 And behold another beast, a second, like to a bear, and it raised up itself
on one side, and *it had* three ribs in the mouth of it between the teeth of it:
and they said thus unto it, Arise, devour much flesh.
6 After this I beheld, and lo another, like a leopard, which had upon the back
of it four wings of a fowl; the beast had also four heads; and dominion was
given to it.
7 After this I saw in the night visions, and behold a fourth beast, dreadful
and terrible, and strong exceedingly; and it had great iron teeth: it devoured
and brake in pieces, and stamped the residue with the feet of it: and it *was*
diverse from all the beasts that *were* before it; and it had ten horns.
8 I considered the horns, and, behold, there came up among them another
little horn, before whom there were three of the first horns plucked up by the
roots: and, behold, in this horn *were* eyes like the eyes of man, and a mouth
speaking great things.
9 I beheld till the thrones were cast down, and the Ancient of days did sit,
whose garment *was* white as snow, and the hair of his head like the pure wool:
his throne *was like* the fiery flame, *and* his wheels *as* burning fire.
10 A fiery stream issued and came forth from before him: thousand thou-
sands ministered unto him, and ten thousand times ten thousand stood before
him: the judgment was set, and the books were opened.
11 I beheld then because of the voice of the great words which the horn spake:
I beheld *even* till the beast was slain, and his body destroyed, and given to the
burning flame.
12 As concerning the rest of the beasts, they had their dominion taken away:
yet their lives were prolonged for a season and time.
13 I saw in the night visions, and, behold, *one* like the Son of man came with
the clouds of heaven, and came to the Ancient of days, and they brought him
near before him.

14 And there was given him dominion, and glory, and a kingdom, that all
people, nations, and languages, should serve him: his dominion *is* an everlast-
ing dominion, which shall not pass away, and his kingdom *that* which shall
not be destroyed.

The Interpretation of the Vision

15 I Daniel was grieved in my spirit in the midst of *my* body, and the visions
of my head troubled me.
16 I came near unto one of them that stood by, and asked him the truth of
all this. So he told me, and made me know the interpretation of the things.
17 These great beasts, which are four, *are* four kings, *which* shall arise out of
the earth.
18 But the saints of the most High shall take the kingdom, and possess the
kingdom for ever, even for ever and ever.
19 Then I would know the truth of the fourth beast, which was diverse from
all the others, exceeding dreadful, whose teeth *were of* iron, and his nails *of*
brass; *which* devoured, brake in pieces, and stamped the residue with his feet;
20 And of the ten horns that *were* in his head, and *of* the other which came
up, and before whom three fell; even *of* that horn that had eyes, and a mouth
that spake very great things, whose look *was* more stout than his fellows.
21 I beheld, and the same horn made war with the saints, and prevailed
against them;
22 Until the Ancient of days came, and judgment was given to the saints of
the most High; and the time came that the saints possessed the kingdom.
23 Thus he said, The fourth beast shall be the fourth kingdom upon earth,
which shall be diverse from all kingdoms, and shall devour the whole earth,
and shall tread it down, and break it in pieces.
24 And the ten horns out of this kingdom *are* ten kings *that* shall arise: and
another shall rise after them; and he shall be diverse from the first, and he
shall subdue three kings.
25 And he shall speak *great* words against the most High, and shall wear out
the saints of the most High, and think to change times and laws: and they shall
be given into his hand until a time and times and the dividing of time.
26 But the judgment shall sit, and they shall take away his dominion, to con-
sume and to destroy *it* unto the end.
27 And the kingdom and dominion, and the greatness of the kingdom under
the whole heaven, shall be given to the people of the saints of the most High,
whose kingdom *is* an everlasting kingdom, and all dominions shall serve and
obey him.
28 Hitherto *is* the end of the matter. As for me Daniel, my cogitations much
troubled me, and my countenance changed in me: but I kept the matter in my
heart.

Daniel's Vision of the Ram and the Goat

8 In the third year of the reign of king Belshazzar a vision appeared unto me,
even unto me Daniel, after that which appeared unto me at the first.
2 And I saw in a vision; and it came to pass, when I saw, that I *was* at Shushan
in the palace, which *is* in the province of Elam; and I saw in a vision, and I was
by the river of Ulai.
3 Then I lifted up mine eyes, and saw, and, behold, there stood before the
river a ram which had *two* horns: and the *two* horns *were* high; but one *was*
higher than the other, and the higher came up last.
4 I saw the ram pushing westward, and northward, and southward; so that
no beasts might stand before him, neither *was there any* that could deliver
out of his hand; but he did according to his will, and became great.

5 And as I was considering, behold, an he goat came from the west on the
face of the whole earth, and touched not the ground: and the goat *had* a nota-
ble horn between his eyes.
6 And he came to the ram that had *two* horns, which I had seen standing
before the river, and ran unto him in the fury of his power.
7 And I saw him come close unto the ram, and he was moved with choler
against him, and smote the ram, and brake his two horns: and there was no
power in the ram to stand before him, but he cast him down to the ground,
and stamped upon him: and there was none that could deliver the ram out of
his hand.
8 Therefore the he goat waxed very great: and when he was strong, the great
horn was broken; and for it came up four notable ones toward the four winds
of heaven.
9 And out of one of them came forth a little horn, which waxed exceeding
great, toward the south, and toward the east, and toward the pleasant *land*.
10 And it waxed great, *even* to the host of heaven; and it cast down *some* of
the host and of the stars to the ground, and stamped upon them.
11 Yea, he magnified *himself* even to the prince of the host, and by him the
daily *sacrifice* was taken away, and the place of his sanctuary was cast down.
12 And an host was given *him* against the daily *sacrifice* by reason of transgres-
sion, and it cast down the truth to the ground; and it practised, and prospered.
13 Then I heard one saint speaking, and another saint said unto that certain
saint which spake, How long *shall be* the vision *concerning* the daily *sacrifice*,
and the transgression of desolation, to give both the sanctuary and the host
to be trodden under foot?
14 And he said unto me, Unto two thousand and three hundred days; then
shall the sanctuary be cleansed.

Gabriel Comforts Daniel

15 And it came to pass, when I, *even* I Daniel, had seen the vision, and sought
for the meaning, then, behold, there stood before me as the appearance of a
man.
16 And I heard a man's voice between *the banks of* Ulai, which called, and
said, Gabriel, make this *man* to understand the vision.
17 So he came near where I stood: and when he came, I was afraid, and fell
upon my face: but he said unto me, Understand, O son of man: for at the time
of the end *shall be* the vision.
18 Now as he was speaking with me, I was in a deep sleep on my face toward
the ground: but he touched me, and set me upright.
19 And he said, Behold, I will make thee know what shall be in the last end
of the indignation: for at the time appointed the end *shall be*.
20 The ram which thou sawest having *two* horns *are* the kings of Media and
Persia.
21 And the rough goat *is* the king of Grecia: and the great horn that *is* between
his eyes *is* the first king.
22 Now that being broken, whereas four stood up for it, four kingdoms shall
stand up out of the nation, but not in his power.
23 And in the latter time of their kingdom, when the transgressors are come
to the full, a king of fierce countenance, and understanding dark sentences,
shall stand up.
24 And his power shall be mighty, but not by his own power: and he shall
destroy wonderfully, and shall prosper, and practise, and shall destroy the
mighty and the holy people.
25 And through his policy also he shall cause craft to prosper in his hand;
and he shall magnify *himself* in his heart, and by peace shall destroy many: he

shall also stand up against the Prince of princes; but he shall be broken without hand.
26 And the vision of the evening and the morning which was told *is* true:
wherefore shut thou up the vision; for it *shall be* for many days.
27 And I Daniel fainted, and was sick *certain* days; afterward I rose up, and did
the king's business; and I was astonished at the vision, but none understood *it*.

Daniel's Prayer Is Answered

9 In the first year of Darius the son of Ahasuerus, of the seed of the Medes,
which was made king over the realm of the Chaldeans;
2 In the first year of his reign I Daniel understood by books the number of
the years, whereof the word of the LORD came to Jeremiah the prophet, that
he would accomplish seventy years in the desolations of Jerusalem.
3 And I set my face unto the Lord God, to seek by prayer and supplications,
with fasting, and sackcloth, and ashes:
4 And I prayed unto the LORD my God, and made my confession, and said, O
Lord, the great and dreadful God, keeping the covenant and mercy to them
that love him, and to them that keep his commandments;
5 We have sinned, and have committed iniquity, and have done wickedly, and
have rebelled, even by departing from thy precepts and from thy judgments:
6 Neither have we hearkened unto thy servants the prophets, which spake
in thy name to our kings, our princes, and our fathers, and to all the people
of the land.
7 O Lord, righteousness *belongeth* unto thee, but unto us confusion of faces,
as at this day; to the men of Judah, and to the inhabitants of Jerusalem, and
unto all Israel, *that are* near, and *that are* far off, through all the countries
whither thou hast driven them, because of their trespass that they have trespassed against thee.
8 O Lord, to us *belongeth* confusion of face, to our kings, to our princes, and
to our fathers, because we have sinned against thee.
9 To the Lord our God *belong* mercies and forgivenesses, though we have
rebelled against him;
10 Neither have we obeyed the voice of the LORD our God, to walk in his laws,
which he set before us by his servants the prophets.
11 Yea, all Israel have transgressed thy law, even by departing, that they might
not obey thy voice; therefore the curse is poured upon us, and the oath that *is*
written in the law of Moses the servant of God, because we have sinned against
him.
12 And he hath confirmed his words, which he spake against us, and against
our judges that judged us, by bringing upon us a great evil: for under the whole
heaven hath not been done as hath been done upon Jerusalem.
13 As *it is* written in the law of Moses, all this evil is come upon us: yet made
we not our prayer before the LORD our God, that we might turn from our
iniquities, and understand thy truth.
14 Therefore hath the LORD watched upon the evil, and brought it upon us:
for the LORD our God *is* righteous in all his works which he doeth: for we
obeyed not his voice.
15 And now, O Lord our God, that hast brought thy people forth out of the
land of Egypt with a mighty hand, and hast gotten thee renown, as at this day;
we have sinned, we have done wickedly.
16 O Lord, according to all thy righteousness, I beseech thee, let thine anger
and thy fury be turned away from thy city Jerusalem, thy holy mountain:
because for our sins, and for the iniquities of our fathers, Jerusalem and thy
people *are become* a reproach to all *that are* about us.

17 Now therefore, O our God, hear the prayer of thy servant, and his suppli-
cations, and cause thy face to shine upon thy sanctuary that is desolate, for
the Lord's sake.
18 O my God, incline thine ear, and hear; open thine eyes, and behold our
desolations, and the city which is called by thy name: for we do not present
our supplications before thee for our righteousnesses, but for thy great mer-
cies.
19 O Lord, hear; O Lord, forgive; O Lord, hearken and do; defer not, for thine
own sake, O my God: for thy city and thy people are called by thy name.

The Seventy Weeks

20 And whiles I *was* speaking, and praying, and confessing my sin and the
sin of my people Israel, and presenting my supplication before the LORD my
God for the holy mountain of my God;
21 Yea, whiles I *was* speaking in prayer, even the man Gabriel, whom I had
seen in the vision at the beginning, being caused to fly swiftly, touched me
about the time of the evening oblation.
22 And he informed *me*, and talked with me, and said, O Daniel, I am now
come forth to give thee skill and understanding.
23 At the beginning of thy supplications the commandment came forth, and
I am come to shew *thee*; for thou *art* greatly beloved: therefore understand
the matter, and consider the vision.
24 Seventy weeks are determined upon thy people and upon thy holy city, to
finish the transgression, and to make an end of sins, and to make reconcilia-
tion for iniquity, and to bring in everlasting righteousness, and to seal up the
vision and prophecy, and to anoint the most Holy.
25 Know therefore and understand, *that* from the going forth of the com-
mandment to restore and to build Jerusalem unto the Messiah the Prince *shall*
be seven weeks, and threescore and two weeks: the street shall be built again,
and the wall, even in troublous times.
26 And after threescore and two weeks shall Messiah be cut off, but not for
himself: and the people of the prince that shall come shall destroy the city and
the sanctuary; and the end thereof *shall be* with a flood, and unto the end of
the war desolations are determined.
27 And he shall confirm the covenant with many for one week: and in the
midst of the week he shall cause the sacrifice and the oblation to cease, and
for the overspreading of abominations he shall make *it* desolate, even until
the consummation, and that determined shall be poured upon the desolate.

An Angel Brings a Message

10 In the third year of Cyrus king of Persia a thing was revealed unto
Daniel, whose name was called Belteshazzar; and the thing *was* true,
but the time appointed *was* long: and he understood the thing, and had under-
standing of the vision.
2 In those days I Daniel was mourning three full weeks.
3 I ate no pleasant bread, neither came flesh nor wine in my mouth, neither
did I anoint myself at all, till three whole weeks were fulfilled.
4 And in the four and twentieth day of the first month, as I was by the side
of the great river, which *is* Hiddekel;
5 Then I lifted up mine eyes, and looked, and behold a certain man clothed
in linen, whose loins *were* girded with fine gold of Uphaz:
6 His body also *was* like the beryl, and his face as the appearance of lightning,
and his eyes as lamps of fire, and his arms and his feet like in colour to polished
brass, and the voice of his words like the voice of a multitude.
7 And I Daniel alone saw the vision: for the men that were with me saw not the
vision; but a great quaking fell upon them, so that they fled to hide themselves.

8 Therefore I was left alone, and saw this great vision, and there remained
no strength in me: for my comeliness was turned in me into corruption, and
I retained no strength.
9 Yet heard I the voice of his words: and when I heard the voice of his words,
then was I in a deep sleep on my face, and my face toward the ground.
10 And, behold, an hand touched me, which set me upon my knees and *upon*
the palms of my hands.
11 And he said unto me, O Daniel, a man greatly beloved, understand the
words that I speak unto thee, and stand upright: for unto thee am I now sent.
And when he had spoken this word unto me, I stood trembling.
12 Then said he unto me, Fear not, Daniel: for from the first day that thou
didst set thine heart to understand, and to chasten thyself before thy God, thy
words were heard, and I am come for thy words.
13 But the prince of the kingdom of Persia withstood me one and twenty
days: but, lo, Michael, one of the chief princes, came to help me; and I remained
there with the kings of Persia.
14 Now I am come to make thee understand what shall befall thy people in
the latter days: for yet the vision *is* for *many* days.
15 And when he had spoken such words unto me, I set my face toward the
ground, and I became dumb.
16 And, behold, *one* like the similitude of the sons of men touched my lips:
then I opened my mouth, and spake, and said unto him that stood before me,
O my lord, by the vision my sorrows are turned upon me, and I have retained
no strength.
17 For how can the servant of this my lord talk with this my lord? for as for
me, straightway there remained no strength in me, neither is there breath left
in me.
18 Then there came again and touched me *one* like the appearance of a man,
and he strengthened me,
19 And said, O man greatly beloved, fear not: peace *be* unto thee, be strong,
yea, be strong. And when he had spoken unto me, I was strengthened, and
said, Let my lord speak; for thou hast strengthened me.
20 Then said he, Knowest thou wherefore I come unto thee? and now will I
return to fight with the prince of Persia: and when I am gone forth, lo, the
prince of Grecia shall come.
21 But I will shew thee that which is noted in the scripture of truth: and *there*
is none that holdeth with me in these things, but Michael your prince.

Greece Will Conquer Persia

11 Also I in the first year of Darius the Mede, *even* I, stood to confirm and
to strengthen him.
2 And now will I shew thee the truth. Behold, there shall stand up yet three
kings in Persia; and the fourth shall be far richer than *they* all: and by his
strength through his riches he shall stir up all against the realm of Grecia.
3 And a mighty king shall stand up, that shall rule with great dominion, and
do according to his will.
4 And when he shall stand up, his kingdom shall be broken, and shall be
divided toward the four winds of heaven; and not to his posterity, nor accord-
ing to his dominion which he ruled: for his kingdom shall be plucked up, even
for others beside those.

The Northern and Southern Kings

5 And the king of the south shall be strong, and *one* of his princes; and he
shall be strong above him, and have dominion; his dominion *shall be* a great
dominion.
6 And in the end of years they shall join themselves together; for the king's
daughter of the south shall come to the king of the north to make an agree-

ment: but she shall not retain the power of the arm; neither shall he stand,
nor his arm: but she shall be given up, and they that brought her, and he that
begat her, and he that strengthened her in *these* times.
7 But out of a branch of her roots shall *one* stand up in his estate, which shall
come with an army, and shall enter into the fortress of the king of the north,
and shall deal against them, and shall prevail:
8 And shall also carry captives into Egypt their gods, with their princes, *and*
with their precious vessels of silver and of gold; and he shall continue *more*
years than the king of the north.
9 So the king of the south shall come into *his* kingdom, and shall return into
his own land.
10 But his sons shall be stirred up, and shall assemble a multitude of great
forces: and *one* shall certainly come, and overflow, and pass through: then
shall he return, and be stirred up, *even* to his fortress.
11 And the king of the south shall be moved with choler, and shall come forth
and fight with him, *even* with the king of the north: and he shall set forth a
great multitude; but the multitude shall be given into his hand.
12 *And* when he hath taken away the multitude, his heart shall be lifted up;
and he shall cast down *many* ten thousands: but he shall not be strengthened
by it.
13 For the king of the north shall return, and shall set forth a multitude
greater than the former, and shall certainly come after certain years with a
great army and with much riches.
14 And in those times there shall many stand up against the king of the south:
also the robbers of thy people shall exalt themselves to establish the vision;
but they shall fall.
15 So the king of the north shall come, and cast up a mount, and take the
most fenced cities: and the arms of the south shall not withstand, neither his
chosen people, neither *shall there be any* strength to withstand.
16 But he that cometh against him shall do according to his own will, and
none shall stand before him: and he shall stand in the glorious land, which by
his hand shall be consumed.
17 He shall also set his face to enter with the strength of his whole kingdom,
and upright ones with him; thus shall he do: and he shall give him the daugh-
ter of women, corrupting her: but she shall not stand *on his side*, neither be
for him.
18 After this shall he turn his face unto the isles, and shall take many: but a
prince for his own behalf shall cause the reproach offered by him to cease;
without his own reproach he shall cause *it* to turn upon him.
19 Then he shall turn his face toward the fort of his own land: but he shall
stumble and fall, and not be found.
20 Then shall stand up in his estate a raiser of taxes *in* the glory of the king-
dom: but within few days he shall be destroyed, neither in anger, nor in battle.
21 And in his estate shall stand up a vile person, to whom they shall not give
the honour of the kingdom: but he shall come in peaceably, and obtain the
kingdom by flatteries.
22 And with the arms of a flood shall they be overflown from before him,
and shall be broken; yea, also the prince of the covenant.
23 And after the league *made* with him he shall work deceitfully: for he shall
come up, and shall become strong with a small people.
24 He shall enter peaceably even upon the fattest places of the province; and
he shall do *that* which his fathers have not done, nor his fathers' fathers; he
shall scatter among them the prey, and spoil, and riches: *yea*, and he shall
forecast his devices against the strong holds, even for a time.
25 And he shall stir up his power and his courage against the king of the south
with a great army; and the king of the south shall be stirred up to battle with

a very great and mighty army; but he shall not stand: for they shall forecast
devices against him.
26 Yea, they that feed of the portion of his meat shall destroy him, and his
army shall overflow: and many shall fall down slain.
27 And both these kings' hearts *shall be* to do mischief, and they shall speak
lies at one table; but it shall not prosper: for yet the end *shall be* at the time
appointed.
28 Then shall he return into his land with great riches; and his heart *shall be*
against the holy covenant; and he shall do *exploits*, and return to his own land.
29 At the time appointed he shall return, and come toward the south; but it
shall not be as the former, or as the latter.
30 For the ships of Chittim shall come against him: therefore he shall be
grieved, and return, and have indignation against the holy covenant: so shall
he do; he shall even return, and have intelligence with them that forsake the
holy covenant.
31 And arms shall stand on his part, and they shall pollute the sanctuary of
strength, and shall take away the daily *sacrifice*, and they shall place the abom-
ination that maketh desolate.
32 And such as do wickedly against the covenant shall he corrupt by flatter-
ies: but the people that do know their God shall be strong, and do *exploits*.
33 And they that understand among the people shall instruct many: yet they
shall fall by the sword, and by flame, by captivity, and by spoil, *many* days.
34 Now when they shall fall, they shall be holpen with a little help: but many
shall cleave to them with flatteries.
35 And *some* of them of understanding shall fall, to try them, and to purge,
and to make *them* white, *even* to the time of the end: because *it is* yet for a time
appointed.
36 And the king shall do according to his will; and he shall exalt himself, and
magnify himself above every god, and shall speak marvellous things against
the God of gods, and shall prosper till the indignation be accomplished: for
that that is determined shall be done.
37 Neither shall he regard the God of his fathers, nor the desire of women,
nor regard any god: for he shall magnify himself above all.
38 But in his estate shall he honour the God of forces: and a god whom his
fathers knew not shall he honour with gold, and silver, and with precious
stones, and pleasant things.
39 Thus shall he do in the most strong holds with a strange god, whom he
shall acknowledge *and* increase with glory: and he shall cause them to rule
over many, and shall divide the land for gain.
40 And at the time of the end shall the king of the south push at him: and the
king of the north shall come against him like a whirlwind, with chariots, and
with horsemen, and with many ships; and he shall enter into the countries,
and shall overflow and pass over.
41 He shall enter also into the glorious land, and many *countries* shall be
overthrown: but these shall escape out of his hand, *even* Edom, and Moab, and
the chief of the children of Ammon.
42 He shall stretch forth his hand also upon the countries: and the land of
Egypt shall not escape.
43 But he shall have power over the treasures of gold and of silver, and over
all the precious things of Egypt: and the Libyans and the Ethiopians *shall be*
at his steps.
44 But tidings out of the east and out of the north shall trouble him: therefore
he shall go forth with great fury to destroy, and utterly to make away many.
45 And he shall plant the tabernacles of his palace between the seas in the
glorious holy mountain; yet he shall come to his end, and none shall help him.

The Words Are Sealed

12 And at that time shall Michael stand up, the great prince which
standeth for the children of thy people: and there shall be a time of
trouble, such as never was since there was a nation *even* to that same time: and
at that time thy people shall be delivered, every one that shall be found written
in the book.
2 And many of them that sleep in the dust of the earth shall awake, some to
everlasting life, and some to shame *and* everlasting contempt.
3 And they that be wise shall shine as the brightness of the firmament; and
they that turn many to righteousness as the stars for ever and ever.
4 But thou, O Daniel, shut up the words, and seal the book, *even* to the time
of the end: many shall run to and fro, and knowledge shall be increased.
5 Then I Daniel looked, and, behold, there stood other two, the one on this
side of the bank of the river, and the other on that side of the bank of the river.
6 And *one* said to the man clothed in linen, which *was* upon the waters of
the river, How long *shall it be to* the end of these wonders?
7 And I heard the man clothed in linen, which *was* upon the waters of the
river, when he held up his right hand and his left hand unto heaven, and sware
by him that liveth for ever that *it shall be* for a time, times, and an half; and
when he shall have accomplished to scatter the power of the holy people, all
these *things* shall be finished.
8 And I heard, but I understood not: then said I, O my Lord, what *shall be*
the end of these *things*?
9 And he said, Go thy way, Daniel: for the words *are* closed up and sealed till
the time of the end.
10 Many shall be purified, and made white, and tried; but the wicked shall
do wickedly: and none of the wicked shall understand; but the wise shall
understand.
11 And from the time *that* the daily *sacrifice* shall be taken away, and the
abomination that maketh desolate set up, *there shall be* a thousand two hun-
dred and ninety days.
12 Blessed *is* he that waiteth, and cometh to the thousand three hundred and
five and thirty days.
13 But go thou thy way till the end *be*: for thou shalt rest, and stand in thy lot
at the end of the days.

Hosea Marries a Prostitute

1 The word of the LORD that came unto Hosea, the son of Beeri, in the days
of Uzziah, Jotham, Ahaz, *and* Hezekiah, kings of Judah, and in the days of
Jeroboam the son of Joash, king of Israel.
2 The beginning of the word of the LORD by Hosea. And the LORD said to
Hosea, Go, take unto thee a wife of whoredoms and children of whoredoms:
for the land hath committed great whoredom, *departing* from the LORD.
3 So he went and took Gomer the daughter of Diblaim; which conceived,
and bare him a son.
4 And the LORD said unto him, Call his name Jezreel; for yet a little *while*, and
I will avenge the blood of Jezreel upon the house of Jehu, and will cause to
cease the kingdom of the house of Israel.
5 And it shall come to pass at that day, that I will break the bow of Israel in
the valley of Jezreel.
6 And she conceived again, and bare a daughter. And *God* said unto him, Call
her name Lo-ruhamah: for I will no more have mercy upon the house of Israel;
but I will utterly take them away.
7 But I will have mercy upon the house of Judah, and will save them by the
LORD their God, and will not save them by bow, nor by sword, nor by battle,
by horses, nor by horsemen.
8 Now when she had weaned Lo-ruhamah, she conceived, and bare a son.
9 Then said *God*, Call his name Lo-ammi: for ye *are* not my people, and I will
not be your *God*.
10 Yet the number of the children of Israel shall be as the sand of the sea,
which cannot be measured nor numbered; and it shall come to pass, *that* in
the place where it was said unto them, Ye *are* not my people, *there* it shall be
said unto them, *Ye are* the sons of the living God.
11 Then shall the children of Judah and the children of Israel be gathered
together, and appoint themselves one head, and they shall come up out of the
land: for great *shall be* the day of Jezreel.

Israel Is the Lord's Unfaithful Wife

2 Say ye unto your brethren, Ammi; and to your sisters, Ruhamah.
2 Plead with your mother, plead: for she *is* not my wife, neither *am* I her
husband: let her therefore put away her whoredoms out of her sight, and her
adulteries from between her breasts;
3 Lest I strip her naked, and set her as in the day that she was born, and make
her as a wilderness, and set her like a dry land, and slay her with thirst.
4 And I will not have mercy upon her children; for they *be* the children of
whoredoms.
5 For their mother hath played the harlot: she that conceived them hath
done shamefully: for she said, I will go after my lovers, that give *me* my bread
and my water, my wool and my flax, mine oil and my drink.

God's Judgments against Israel

6 Therefore, behold, I will hedge up thy way with thorns, and make a wall,
that she shall not find her paths.

THOU ART MY *people*; and they shall SAY, THOU ART MY *God*.

HOSEA 2:23

7 And she shall follow after her lovers, but she shall not overtake them; and
she shall seek them, but shall not find *them*: then shall she say, I will go and
return to my first husband; for then *was it* better with me than now.
8 For she did not know that I gave her corn, and wine, and oil, and multiplied
her silver and gold, *which* they prepared for Baal.
9 Therefore will I return, and take away my corn in the time thereof, and my
wine in the season thereof, and will recover my wool and my flax *given* to cover
her nakedness.
10 And now will I discover her lewdness in the sight of her lovers, and none
shall deliver her out of mine hand.
11 I will also cause all her mirth to cease, her feast days, her new moons, and
her sabbaths, and all her solemn feasts.
12 And I will destroy her vines and her fig trees, whereof she hath said, These
are my rewards that my lovers have given me: and I will make them a forest,
and the beasts of the field shall eat them.
13 And I will visit upon her the days of Baalim, wherein she burned incense
to them, and she decked herself with her earrings and her jewels, and she went
after her lovers, and forgat me, saith the LORD.

God's Promises of Reconciliation

14 Therefore, behold, I will allure her, and bring her into the wilderness, and
speak comfortably unto her.
15 And I will give her her vineyards from thence, and the valley of Achor for
a door of hope: and she shall sing there, as in the days of her youth, and as in
the day when she came up out of the land of Egypt.
16 And it shall be at that day, saith the LORD, *that* thou shalt call me Ishi; and
shalt call me no more Baali.
17 For I will take away the names of Baalim out of her mouth, and they shall
no more be remembered by their name.
18 And in that day will I make a covenant for them with the beasts of the
field, and with the fowls of heaven, and *with* the creeping things of the ground:
and I will break the bow and the sword and the battle out of the earth, and
will make them to lie down safely.
19 And I will betroth thee unto me for ever; yea, I will betroth thee unto me
in righteousness, and in judgment, and in lovingkindness, and in mercies.
20 I will even betroth thee unto me in faithfulness: and thou shalt know the
LORD.
21 And it shall come to pass in that day, I will hear, saith the LORD, I will hear
the heavens, and they shall hear the earth;
22 And the earth shall hear the corn, and the wine, and the oil; and they shall
hear Jezreel.
23 And I will sow her unto me in the earth; and I will have mercy upon her
that had not obtained mercy; and I will say to *them which were* not my people,
Thou *art* my people; and they shall say, *Thou art* my God.

Hosea's Adulterous Wife

3 Then said the LORD unto me, Go yet, love a woman beloved of *her* friend,
yet an adulteress, according to the love of the LORD toward the children of
Israel, who look to other gods, and love flagons of wine.
2 So I bought her to me for fifteen *pieces* of silver, and *for* an homer of barley,
and an half homer of barley:
3 And I said unto her, Thou shalt abide for me many days; thou shalt not play
the harlot, and thou shalt not be for *another* man: so *will* I also *be* for thee.
4 For the children of Israel shall abide many days without a king, and with-
out a prince, and without a sacrifice, and without an image, and without an
ephod, and *without* teraphim:

5 Afterward shall the children of Israel return, and seek the LORD their God,
and David their king; and shall fear the LORD and his goodness in the latter
days.

God's Judgments on the Sins of the People

4 Hear the word of the LORD, ye children of Israel: for the LORD hath a con-
troversy with the inhabitants of the land, because *there is* no truth, nor
mercy, nor knowledge of God in the land.
2 By swearing, and lying, and killing, and stealing, and committing adultery,
they break out, and blood toucheth blood.
3 Therefore shall the land mourn, and every one that dwelleth therein shall
languish, with the beasts of the field, and with the fowls of heaven; yea, the
fishes of the sea also shall be taken away.
4 Yet let no man strive, nor reprove another: for thy people *are* as they that
strive with the priest.
5 Therefore shalt thou fall in the day, and the prophet also shall fall with thee
in the night, and I will destroy thy mother.
6 My people are destroyed for lack of knowledge: because thou hast rejected
knowledge, I will also reject thee, that thou shalt be no priest to me: seeing
thou hast forgotten the law of thy God, I will also forget thy children.
7 As they were increased, so they sinned against me: *therefore* will I change
their glory into shame.
8 They eat up the sin of my people, and they set their heart on their iniquity.
9 And there shall be, like people, like priest: and I will punish them for their
ways, and reward them their doings.
10 For they shall eat, and not have enough: they shall commit whoredom,
and shall not increase: because they have left off to take heed to the LORD.
11 Whoredom and wine and new wine take away the heart.
12 My people ask counsel at their stocks, and their staff declareth unto them:
for the spirit of whoredoms hath caused *them* to err, and they have gone a
whoring from under their God.
13 They sacrifice upon the tops of the mountains, and burn incense upon
the hills, under oaks and poplars and elms, because the shadow thereof *is*
good: therefore your daughters shall commit whoredom, and your spouses
shall commit adultery.
14 I will not punish your daughters when they commit whoredom, nor your
spouses when they commit adultery: for themselves are separated with
whores, and they sacrifice with harlots: therefore the people *that* doth not
understand shall fall.
15 Though thou, Israel, play the harlot, *yet* let not Judah offend; and come
not ye unto Gilgal, neither go ye up to Bethaven, nor swear, The LORD liveth.
16 For Israel slideth back as a backsliding heifer: now the LORD will feed them
as a lamb in a large place.
17 Ephraim *is* joined to idols: let him alone.
18 Their drink is sour: they have committed whoredom continually: her
rulers *with* shame do love, Give ye.
19 The wind hath bound her up in her wings, and they shall be ashamed
because of their sacrifices.

The Lord's Verdict against Israel

5 Hear ye this, O priests; and hearken, ye house of Israel; and give ye ear, O
house of the king; for judgment *is* toward you, because ye have been a snare
on Mizpah, and a net spread upon Tabor.
2 And the revolters are profound to make slaughter, though I *have been* a
rebuker of them all.
3 I know Ephraim, and Israel is not hid from me: for now, O Ephraim, thou
committest whoredom, *and* Israel is defiled.

4 They will not frame their doings to turn unto their God: for the spirit of whoredoms *is* in the midst of them, and they have not known the LORD.

5 And the pride of Israel doth testify to his face: therefore shall Israel and Ephraim fall in their iniquity; Judah also shall fall with them.

6 They shall go with their flocks and with their herds to seek the LORD; but they shall not find *him*; he hath withdrawn himself from them.

7 They have dealt treacherously against the LORD: for they have begotten strange children: now shall a month devour them with their portions.

8 Blow ye the cornet in Gibeah, *and* the trumpet in Ramah: cry aloud *at* Bethaven, after thee, O Benjamin.

9 Ephraim shall be desolate in the day of rebuke: among the tribes of Israel have I made known that which shall surely be.

10 The princes of Judah were like them that remove the bound: *therefore* I will pour out my wrath upon them like water.

11 Ephraim *is* oppressed *and* broken in judgment, because he willingly walked after the commandment.

12 Therefore *will* I *be* unto Ephraim as a moth, and to the house of Judah as rottenness.

13 When Ephraim saw his sickness, and Judah *saw* his wound, then went Ephraim to the Assyrian, and sent to king Jareb: yet could he not heal you, nor cure you of your wound.

14 For I *will be* unto Ephraim as a lion, and as a young lion to the house of Judah: I, *even* I, will tear and go away; I will take away, and none shall rescue *him*.

15 I will go *and* return to my place, till they acknowledge their offence, and seek my face: in their affliction they will seek me early.

Israel Rejected the Lord's Promise

6 Come, and let us return unto the LORD: for he hath torn, and he will heal us; he hath smitten, and he will bind us up.

2 After two days will he revive us: in the third day he will raise us up, and we shall live in his sight.

3 Then shall we know, *if* we follow on to know the LORD: his going forth is prepared as the morning; and he shall come unto us as the rain, as the latter *and* former rain unto the earth.

4 O Ephraim, what shall I do unto thee? O Judah, what shall I do unto thee? for your goodness *is* as a morning cloud, and as the early dew it goeth away.

5 Therefore have I hewed *them* by the prophets; I have slain them by the words of my mouth: and thy judgments *are as* the light *that* goeth forth.

6 For I desired mercy, and not sacrifice; and the knowledge of God more than burnt offerings.

7 But they like men have transgressed the covenant: there have they dealt treacherously against me.

8 Gilead *is* a city of them that work iniquity, *and is* polluted with blood.

9 And as troops of robbers wait for a man, *so* the company of priests murder in the way by consent: for they commit lewdness.

10 I have seen an horrible thing in the house of Israel: there *is* the whoredom of Ephraim, Israel is defiled.

11 Also, O Judah, he hath set an harvest for thee, when I returned the captivity of my people.

God Reproves Israel for Many Sins

7 When I would have healed Israel, then the iniquity of Ephraim was discovered, and the wickedness of Samaria: for they commit falsehood; and the thief cometh in, *and* the troop of robbers spoileth without.

2 And they consider not in their hearts *that* I remember all their wickedness: now their own doings have beset them about; they are before my face.

3 They make the king glad with their wickedness, and the princes with their
lies.
4 They *are* all adulterers, as an oven heated by the baker, *who* ceaseth from
raising after he hath kneaded the dough, until it be leavened.
5 In the day of our king the princes have made *him* sick with bottles of wine;
he stretched out his hand with scorners.
6 For they have made ready their heart like an oven, whiles they lie in wait:
their baker sleepeth all the night; in the morning it burneth as a flaming fire.
7 They are all hot as an oven, and have devoured their judges; all their kings
are fallen: *there is* none among them that calleth unto me.
8 Ephraim, he hath mixed himself among the people; Ephraim is a cake not
turned.
9 Strangers have devoured his strength, and he knoweth *it* not: yea, gray hairs
are here and there upon him, yet he knoweth not.
10 And the pride of Israel testifieth to his face: and they do not return to the
LORD their God, nor seek him for all this.
11 Ephraim also is like a silly dove without heart: they call to Egypt, they go
to Assyria.
12 When they shall go, I will spread my net upon them; I will bring them
down as the fowls of the heaven; I will chastise them, as their congregation
hath heard.
13 Woe unto them! for they have fled from me: destruction unto them!
because they have transgressed against me: though I have redeemed them, yet
they have spoken lies against me.
14 And they have not cried unto me with their heart, when they howled
upon their beds: they assemble themselves for corn and wine, *and* they rebel
against me.
15 Though I have bound *and* strengthened their arms, yet do they imagine
mischief against me.
16 They return, *but* not to the most High: they are like a deceitful bow: their
princes shall fall by the sword for the rage of their tongue: this *shall be* their
derision in the land of Egypt.

Destruction Is Threatened

8 *Set* the trumpet to thy mouth. *He shall come* as an eagle against the house
of the LORD, because they have transgressed my covenant, and trespassed
against my law.
2 Israel shall cry unto me, My God, we know thee.
3 Israel hath cast off *the thing that is* good: the enemy shall pursue him.
4 They have set up kings, but not by me: they have made princes, and I knew
it not: of their silver and their gold have they made them idols, that they may
be cut off.
5 Thy calf, O Samaria, hath cast *thee* off; mine anger is kindled against them:
how long *will it be* ere they attain to innocency?
6 For from Israel *was* it also: the workman made it; therefore it *is* not God:
but the calf of Samaria shall be broken in pieces.
7 For they have sown the wind, and they shall reap the whirlwind: it hath no
stalk: the bud shall yield no meal: if so be it yield, the strangers shall swallow
it up.
8 Israel is swallowed up: now shall they be among the Gentiles as a vessel
wherein *is* no pleasure.
9 For they are gone up to Assyria, a wild ass alone by himself: Ephraim hath
hired lovers.
10 Yea, though they have hired among the nations, now will I gather them,
and they shall sorrow a little for the burden of the king of princes.

11 Because Ephraim hath made many altars to sin, altars shall be unto him
to sin.
12 I have written to him the great things of my law, *but* they were counted
as a strange thing.
13 They sacrifice flesh *for* the sacrifices of mine offerings, and eat *it; but* the
LORD accepteth them not; now will he remember their iniquity, and visit their
sins: they shall return to Egypt.
14 For Israel hath forgotten his Maker, and buildeth temples; and Judah hath
multiplied fenced cities: but I will send a fire upon his cities, and it shall devour
the palaces thereof.

Distress and Captivity for Sins and Idolatry

9 Rejoice not, O Israel, for joy, as *other* people: for thou hast gone a whoring
from thy God, thou hast loved a reward upon every cornfloor.
2 The floor and the winepress shall not feed them, and the new wine shall
fail in her.
3 They shall not dwell in the LORD's land; but Ephraim shall return to Egypt,
and they shall eat unclean *things* in Assyria.
4 They shall not offer wine *offerings* to the LORD, neither shall they be pleas-
ing unto him: their sacrifices *shall be* unto them as the bread of mourners; all
that eat thereof shall be polluted: for their bread for their soul shall not come
into the house of the LORD.
5 What will ye do in the solemn day, and in the day of the feast of the LORD?
6 For, lo, they are gone because of destruction: Egypt shall gather them up,
Memphis shall bury them: the pleasant *places* for their silver, nettles shall
possess them: thorns *shall be* in their tabernacles.
7 The days of visitation are come, the days of recompence are come; Israel
shall know *it*: the prophet *is* a fool, the spiritual man *is* mad, for the multitude
of thine iniquity, and the great hatred.
8 The watchman of Ephraim *was* with my God: *but* the prophet *is* a snare of
a fowler in all his ways, *and* hatred in the house of his God.
9 They have deeply corrupted *themselves*, as in the days of Gibeah: *therefore*
he will remember their iniquity, he will visit their sins.

Israel Is like Rotten Grapes or Figs

10 I found Israel like grapes in the wilderness; I saw your fathers as the
firstripe in the fig tree at her first time: *but* they went to Baal-peor, and
separated themselves unto *that* shame; and *their* abominations were
according as they loved.
11 *As for* Ephraim, their glory shall fly away like a bird, from the birth, and
from the womb, and from the conception.
12 Though they bring up their children, yet will I bereave them, *that there
shall* not *be* a man *left*: yea, woe also to them when I depart from them!
13 Ephraim, as I saw Tyrus, *is* planted in a pleasant place: but Ephraim shall
bring forth his children to the murderer.
14 Give them, O LORD: what wilt thou give? give them a miscarrying womb
and dry breasts.
15 All their wickedness *is* in Gilgal: for there I hated them: for the wickedness
of their doings I will drive them out of mine house, I will love them no more:
all their princes *are* revolters.
16 Ephraim is smitten, their root is dried up, they shall bear no fruit: yea,
though they bring forth, yet will I slay *even* the beloved *fruit* of their womb.
17 My God will cast them away, because they did not hearken unto him: and
they shall be wanderers among the nations.

Israel Is like a Rotten Vine

10 Israel *is* an empty vine, he bringeth forth fruit unto himself:
according to the multitude of his fruit he hath increased the altars;
according to the goodness of his land they have made goodly images.
2 Their heart is divided; now shall they be found faulty: he shall break down
their altars, he shall spoil their images.
3 For now they shall say, We have no king, because we feared not the LORD;
what then should a king do to us?
4 They have spoken words, swearing falsely in making a covenant: thus judg-
ment springeth up as hemlock in the furrows of the field.
5 The inhabitants of Samaria shall fear because of the calves of Beth-aven:
for the people thereof shall mourn over it, and the priests thereof *that* rejoiced
on it, for the glory thereof, because it is departed from it.
6 It shall be also carried unto Assyria *for* a present to king Jareb: Ephraim
shall receive shame, and Israel shall be ashamed of his own counsel.
7 *As for* Samaria, her king is cut off as the foam upon the water.
8 The high places also of Aven, the sin of Israel, shall be destroyed: the thorn
and the thistle shall come up on their altars; and they shall say to the moun-
tains, Cover us; and to the hills, Fall on us.
9 O Israel, thou hast sinned from the days of Gibeah: there they stood: the
battle in Gibeah against the children of iniquity did not overtake them.
10 *It is* in my desire that I should chastise them; and the people shall be
gathered against them, when they shall bind themselves in their two furrows.

Israel Is like a Heifer

11 And Ephraim *is as* an heifer *that is* taught, *and* loveth to tread out *the*
corn; but I passed over upon her fair neck: I will make Ephraim to ride; Judah
shall plow, *and* Jacob shall break his clods.
12 Sow to yourselves in righteousness, reap in mercy; break up your fallow
ground: for *it is* time to seek the LORD, till he come and rain righteousness
upon you.
13 Ye have plowed wickedness, ye have reaped iniquity; ye have eaten the
fruit of lies: because thou didst trust in thy way, in the multitude of thy mighty
men.
14 Therefore shall a tumult arise among thy people, and all thy fortresses
shall be spoiled, as Shalman spoiled Beth-arbel in the day of battle: the moth-
er was dashed in pieces upon *her* children.
15 So shall Beth-el do unto you because of your great wickedness: in a morn-
ing shall the king of Israel utterly be cut off.

Israel Is like a Bad Son

11 When Israel *was* a child, then I loved him, and called my son out
of Egypt.
2 *As* they called them, so they went from them: they sacrificed unto Baalim,
and burned incense to graven images.
3 I taught Ephraim also to go, taking them by their arms; but they knew not
that I healed them.
4 I drew them with cords of a man, with bands of love: and I was to them as
they that take off the yoke on their jaws, and I laid meat unto them.
5 He shall not return into the land of Egypt, but the Assyrian shall be his
king, because they refused to return.
6 And the sword shall abide on his cities, and shall consume his branches,
and devour *them*, because of their own counsels.
7 And my people are bent to backsliding from me: though they called them
to the most High, none at all would exalt *him*.

—HOSEA 12:6—
Therefore TURN THOU TO thy God: KEEP mercy & JUDGMENT & wait on thy GOD CONTINUALLY.

God's Mercy toward His People

8 How shall I give thee up, Ephraim? *how* shall I deliver thee, Israel? how
shall I make thee as Admah? *how* shall I set thee as Zeboim? mine heart is
turned within me, my repentings are kindled together.
9 I will not execute the fierceness of mine anger, I will not return to destroy
Ephraim: for I *am* God, and not man; the Holy One in the midst of thee: and
I will not enter into the city.
10 They shall walk after the LORD: he shall roar like a lion: when he shall roar,
then the children shall tremble from the west.
11 They shall tremble as a bird out of Egypt, and as a dove out of the land of
Assyria: and I will place them in their houses, saith the LORD.
12 Ephraim compasseth me about with lies, and the house of Israel with
deceit: but Judah yet ruleth with God, and is faithful with the saints.

The People Ignored God's Mighty Works

12 Ephraim feedeth on wind, and followeth after the east wind: he
daily increaseth lies and desolation; and they do make a covenant
with the Assyrians, and oil is carried into Egypt.
2 The LORD hath also a controversy with Judah, and will punish Jacob accord-
ing to his ways; according to his doings will he recompense him.
3 He took his brother by the heel in the womb, and by his strength he had
power with God:
4 Yea, he had power over the angel, and prevailed: he wept, and made sup-
plication unto him: he found him *in* Beth-el, and there he spake with us;
5 Even the LORD God of hosts; the LORD *is* his memorial.
6 Therefore turn thou to thy God: keep mercy and judgment, and wait on
thy God continually.

The People's Sins Provoke God

7 *He is* a merchant, the balances of deceit *are* in his hand: he loveth to
oppress.
8 And Ephraim said, Yet I am become rich, I have found me out substance:
in all my labours they shall find none iniquity in me that *were* sin.
9 And I *that am* the LORD thy God from the land of Egypt will yet make thee
to dwell in tabernacles, as in the days of the solemn feast.
10 I have also spoken by the prophets, and I have multiplied visions, and used
similitudes, by the ministry of the prophets.
11 *Is there* iniquity *in* Gilead? surely they are vanity: they sacrifice bullocks
in Gilgal; yea, their altars *are* as heaps in the furrows of the fields.
12 And Jacob fled into the country of Syria, and Israel served for a wife, and
for a wife he kept *sheep*.
13 And by a prophet the LORD brought Israel out of Egypt, and by a prophet
was he preserved.
14 Ephraim provoked *him* to anger most bitterly: therefore shall he leave his
blood upon him, and his reproach shall his Lord return unto him.

Idolatry Will Be Punished

13 When Ephraim spake trembling, he exalted himself in Israel; but
when he offended in Baal, he died.
2 And now they sin more and more, and have made them molten images of
their silver, *and* idols according to their own understanding, all of it the work
of the craftsmen: they say of them, Let the men that sacrifice kiss the calves.
3 Therefore they shall be as the morning cloud, and as the early dew that
passeth away, as the chaff *that* is driven with the whirlwind out of the floor,
and as the smoke out of the chimney.
4 Yet I *am* the LORD thy God from the land of Egypt, and thou shalt know no
god but me: for *there is* no saviour beside me.
5 I did know thee in the wilderness, in the land of great drought.

6 According to their pasture, so were they filled; they were filled, and their
heart was exalted; therefore have they forgotten me.
7 Therefore I will be unto them as a lion: as a leopard by the way will I observe
them:
8 I will meet them as a bear *that is* bereaved *of her whelps*, and will rend the
caul of their heart, and there will I devour them like a lion: the wild beast shall
tear them.
9 O Israel, thou hast destroyed thyself; but in me *is* thine help.
10 I will be thy king: where *is any other* that may save thee in all thy cities?
and thy judges of whom thou saidst, Give me a king and princes?
11 I gave thee a king in mine anger, and took *him* away in my wrath.
12 The iniquity of Ephraim *is* bound up; his sin *is* hid.
13 The sorrows of a travailing woman shall come upon him: he *is* an unwise
son; for he should not stay long in *the place of* the breaking forth of children.
14 I will ransom them from the power of the grave; I will redeem them from
death: O death, I will be thy plagues; O grave, I will be thy destruction:
repentance shall be hid from mine eyes.
15 Though he be fruitful among *his* brethren, an east wind shall come, the
wind of the LORD shall come up from the wilderness, and his spring shall
become dry, and his fountain shall be dried up: he shall spoil the treasure of
all pleasant vessels.
16 Samaria shall become desolate; for she hath rebelled against her God:
they shall fall by the sword: their infants shall be dashed in pieces, and their
women with child shall be ripped up.

The Lord Offers to Forgive

14 O Israel, return unto the LORD thy God; for thou hast fallen by thine
iniquity.
2 Take with you words, and turn to the LORD: say unto him, Take away all
iniquity, and receive *us* graciously: so will we render the calves of our lips.
3 Asshur shall not save us; we will not ride upon horses: neither will we say
any more to the work of our hands, *Ye are* our gods: for in thee the fatherless
findeth mercy.
4 I will heal their backsliding, I will love them freely: for mine anger is turned
away from him.
5 I will be as the dew unto Israel: he shall grow as the lily, and cast forth his
roots as Lebanon.
6 His branches shall spread, and his beauty shall be as the olive tree, and his
smell as Lebanon.
7 They that dwell under his shadow shall return; they shall revive *as* the corn,
and grow as the vine: the scent thereof *shall be* as the wine of Lebanon.
8 Ephraim *shall say*, What have I to do any more with idols? I have heard
him, and observed him: I *am* like a green fir tree. From me is thy fruit found.
9 Who *is* wise, and he shall understand these *things*? prudent, and he shall
know them? for the ways of the LORD *are* right, and the just shall walk in them:
but the transgressors shall fall therein.

Judah Is Plagued with Locusts and Famine

1 The word of the LORD that came to Joel the son of Pethuel.
2 Hear this, ye old men, and give ear, all ye inhabitants of the land. Hath
this been in your days, or even in the days of your fathers?
3 Tell ye your children of it, and *let* your children *tell* their children, and
their children another generation.
4 That which the palmerworm hath left hath the locust eaten; and that which
the locust hath left hath the cankerworm eaten; and that which the canker-
worm hath left hath the caterpiller eaten.
5 Awake, ye drunkards, and weep; and howl, all ye drinkers of wine, because
of the new wine; for it is cut off from your mouth.
6 For a nation is come up upon my land, strong, and without number, whose
teeth *are* the teeth of a lion, and he hath the cheek teeth of a great lion.
7 He hath laid my vine waste, and barked my fig tree: he hath made it clean
bare, and cast *it* away; the branches thereof are made white.

Judah Told to Mourn

8 Lament like a virgin girded with sackcloth for the husband of her youth.
9 The meat offering and the drink offering is cut off from the house of the
LORD; the priests, the LORD's ministers, mourn.
10 The field is wasted, the land mourneth; for the corn is wasted: the new
wine is dried up, the oil languisheth.
11 Be ye ashamed, O ye husbandmen; howl, O ye vinedressers, for the wheat
and for the barley; because the harvest of the field is perished.
12 The vine is dried up, and the fig tree languisheth; the pomegranate tree,
the palm tree also, and the apple tree, *even* all the trees of the field, are with-
ered: because joy is withered away from the sons of men.
13 Gird yourselves, and lament, ye priests: howl, ye ministers of the altar:
come, lie all night in sackcloth, ye ministers of my God: for the meat offering
and the drink offering is withholden from the house of your God.
14 Sanctify ye a fast, call a solemn assembly, gather the elders *and* all the
inhabitants of the land *into* the house of the LORD your God, and cry unto the
LORD,
15 Alas for the day! for the day of the LORD *is* at hand, and as a destruction
from the Almighty shall it come.
16 Is not the meat cut off before our eyes, *yea*, joy and gladness from the
house of our God?
17 The seed is rotten under their clods, the garners are laid desolate, the barns
are broken down; for the corn is withered.
18 How do the beasts groan! the herds of cattle are perplexed, because they
have no pasture; yea, the flocks of sheep are made desolate.
19 O LORD, to thee will I cry: for the fire hath devoured the pastures of the
wilderness, and the flame hath burned all the trees of the field.
20 The beasts of the field cry also unto thee: for the rivers of waters are dried
up, and the fire hath devoured the pastures of the wilderness.

The Day of the Lord

2 Blow ye the trumpet in Zion, and sound an alarm in my holy mountain: let
all the inhabitants of the land tremble: for the day of the LORD cometh, for
it is nigh at hand;
2 A day of darkness and of gloominess, a day of clouds and of thick darkness,
as the morning spread upon the mountains: a great people and a strong; there
hath not been ever the like, neither shall be any more after it, *even* to the years
of many generations.
3 A fire devoureth before them; and behind them a flame burneth: the land
is as the garden of Eden before them, and behind them a desolate wilderness;
yea, and nothing shall escape them.
4 The appearance of them *is* as the appearance of horses; and as horsemen,
so shall they run.
5 Like the noise of chariots on the tops of mountains shall they leap, like the
noise of a flame of fire that devoureth the stubble, as a strong people set in
battle array.
6 Before their face the people shall be much pained: all faces shall gather
blackness.
7 They shall run like mighty men; they shall climb the wall like men of war;
and they shall march every one on his ways, and they shall not break their
ranks:
8 Neither shall one thrust another; they shall walk every one in his path: and
when they fall upon the sword, they shall not be wounded.
9 They shall run to and fro in the city; they shall run upon the wall, they shall
climb up upon the houses; they shall enter in at the windows like a thief.
10 The earth shall quake before them; the heavens shall tremble: the sun and
the moon shall be dark, and the stars shall withdraw their shining:
11 And the LORD shall utter his voice before his army: for his camp *is* very
great: for *he is* strong that executeth his word: for the day of the LORD *is* great
and very terrible; and who can abide it?

The Lord Invites His People Back

12 Therefore also now, saith the LORD, turn ye *even* to me with all your heart,
and with fasting, and with weeping, and with mourning:
13 And rend your heart, and not your garments, and turn unto the LORD your
God: for he *is* gracious and merciful, slow to anger, and of great kindness, and
repenteth him of the evil.
14 Who knoweth *if* he will return and repent, and leave a blessing behind
him; *even* a meat offering and a drink offering unto the LORD your God?
15 Blow the trumpet in Zion, sanctify a fast, call a solemn assembly:
16 Gather the people, sanctify the congregation, assemble the elders, gather
the children, and those that suck the breasts: let the bridegroom go forth of
his chamber, and the bride out of her closet.
17 Let the priests, the ministers of the LORD, weep between the porch and
the altar, and let them say, Spare thy people, O LORD, and give not thine heritage
to reproach, that the heathen should rule over them: wherefore should they
say among the people, Where *is* their God?

The Lord Promises Blessings

18 Then will the LORD be jealous for his land, and pity his people.
19 Yea, the LORD will answer and say unto his people, Behold, I will send you
corn, and wine, and oil, and ye shall be satisfied therewith: and I will no more
make you a reproach among the heathen:
20 But I will remove far off from you the northern *army*, and will drive him
into a land barren and desolate, with his face toward the east sea, and his
hinder part toward the utmost sea, and his stink shall come up, and his ill
savour shall come up, because he hath done great things.

21 Fear not, O land; be glad and rejoice: for the LORD will do great things.
22 Be not afraid, ye beasts of the field: for the pastures of the wilderness do
spring, for the tree beareth her fruit, the fig tree and the vine do yield their
strength.
23 Be glad then, ye children of Zion, and rejoice in the LORD your God: for he
hath given you the former rain moderately, and he will cause to come down
for you the rain, the former rain, and the latter rain in the first *month*.
24 And the floors shall be full of wheat, and the fats shall overflow with wine
and oil.
25 And I will restore to you the years that the locust hath eaten, the canker-
worm, and the caterpiller, and the palmerworm, my great army which I sent
among you.
26 And ye shall eat in plenty, and be satisfied, and praise the name of the LORD
your God, that hath dealt wondrously with you: and my people shall never be
ashamed.
27 And ye shall know that I *am* in the midst of Israel, and *that* I *am* the LORD
your God, and none else: and my people shall never be ashamed.

The Lord Will Pour out His Spirit

28 And it shall come to pass afterward, *that* I will pour out my spirit upon
all flesh; and your sons and your daughters shall prophesy, your old men shall
dream dreams, your young men shall see visions:
29 And also upon the servants and upon the handmaids in those days will I
pour out my spirit.
30 And I will shew wonders in the heavens and in the earth, blood, and fire,
and pillars of smoke.
31 The sun shall be turned into darkness, and the moon into blood, before
the great and the terrible day of the LORD come.
32 And it shall come to pass, *that* whosoever shall call on the name of the
LORD shall be delivered: for in mount Zion and in Jerusalem shall be deliver-
ance, as the LORD hath said, and in the remnant whom the LORD shall call.

The Lord Will Rescue His People

3 For, behold, in those days, and in that time, when I shall bring again the
captivity of Judah and Jerusalem,
2 I will also gather all nations, and will bring them down into the valley of
Jehoshaphat, and will plead with them there for my people and *for* my heritage
Israel, whom they have scattered among the nations, and parted my land.
3 And they have cast lots for my people; and have given a boy for an harlot,
and sold a girl for wine, that they might drink.
4 Yea, and what have ye to do with me, O Tyre, and Zidon, and all the coasts
of Palestine? will ye render me a recompence? and if ye recompense me, swift-
ly *and* speedily will I return your recompence upon your own head;
5 Because ye have taken my silver and my gold, and have carried into your
temples my goodly pleasant things:
6 The children also of Judah and the children of Jerusalem have ye sold unto
the Grecians, that ye might remove them far from their border.
7 Behold, I will raise them out of the place whither ye have sold them, and
will return your recompence upon your own head:
8 And I will sell your sons and your daughters into the hand of the children
of Judah, and they shall sell them to the Sabeans, to a people far off: for the
LORD hath spoken *it*.
9 Proclaim ye this among the Gentiles; Prepare war, wake up the mighty men,
let all the men of war draw near; let them come up:
10 Beat your plowshares into swords, and your pruninghooks into spears:
let the weak say, I *am* strong.

JOEL 2:28
I WILL POUR OUT my Spirit UPON ALL FLESH; AND YOUR SONS & YOUR daughters SHALL PROPHESY, YOUR OLD MEN SHALL dream dreams, your young men shall see VISIONS.

11 Assemble yourselves, and come, all ye heathen, and gather yourselves
together round about: thither cause thy mighty ones to come down, O LORD.
12 Let the heathen be wakened, and come up to the valley of Jehoshaphat:
for there will I sit to judge all the heathen round about.
13 Put ye in the sickle, for the harvest is ripe: come, get you down; for the
press is full, the fats overflow; for their wickedness *is* great.
14 Multitudes, multitudes in the valley of decision: for the day of the LORD
is near in the valley of decision.
15 The sun and the moon shall be darkened, and the stars shall withdraw
their shining.
16 The LORD also shall roar out of Zion, and utter his voice from Jerusalem;
and the heavens and the earth shall shake: but the LORD *will be* the hope of his
people, and the strength of the children of Israel.
17 So shall ye know that I *am* the LORD your God dwelling in Zion, my holy
mountain: then shall Jerusalem be holy, and there shall no strangers pass
through her any more.
18 And it shall come to pass in that day, *that* the mountains shall drop down
new wine, and the hills shall flow with milk, and all the rivers of Judah shall
flow with waters, and a fountain shall come forth of the house of the LORD,
and shall water the valley of Shittim.
19 Egypt shall be a desolation, and Edom shall be a desolate wilderness, for
the violence *against* the children of Judah, because they have shed innocent
blood in their land.
20 But Judah shall dwell for ever, and Jerusalem from generation to genera-
tion.
21 For I will cleanse their blood *that* I have not cleansed: for the LORD dwel-
leth in Zion.

God's Judgment upon Damascus

1 The words of Amos, who was among the herdmen of Tekoa, which he saw
concerning Israel in the days of Uzziah king of Judah, and in the days of
Jeroboam the son of Joash king of Israel, two years before the earthquake.
2 And he said, The LORD will roar from Zion, and utter his voice from
Jerusalem; and the habitations of the shepherds shall mourn, and the top of
Carmel shall wither.
3 Thus saith the LORD; For three transgressions of Damascus, and for four, I
will not turn away *the punishment* thereof; because they have threshed Gilead
with threshing instruments of iron:
4 But I will send a fire into the house of Hazael, which shall devour the pal-
aces of Ben-hadad.
5 I will break also the bar of Damascus, and cut off the inhabitant from the
plain of Aven, and him that holdeth the sceptre from the house of Eden: and
the people of Syria shall go into captivity unto Kir, saith the LORD.

God's Judgment upon Gaza

6 Thus saith the LORD; For three transgressions of Gaza, and for four, I will
not turn away *the punishment* thereof; because they carried away captive the
whole captivity, to deliver *them* up to Edom:
7 But I will send a fire on the wall of Gaza, which shall devour the palaces
thereof:
8 And I will cut off the inhabitant from Ashdod, and him that holdeth the
sceptre from Ashkelon, and I will turn mine hand against Ekron: and the
remnant of the Philistines shall perish, saith the Lord GOD.

God's Judgment upon Tyre

9 Thus saith the LORD; For three transgressions of Tyrus, and for four, I will
not turn away *the punishment* thereof; because they delivered up the whole
captivity to Edom, and remembered not the brotherly covenant:
10 But I will send a fire on the wall of Tyrus, which shall devour the palaces
thereof.

God's Judgment upon Edom

11 Thus saith the LORD; For three transgressions of Edom, and for four, I will
not turn away *the punishment* thereof; because he did pursue his brother with
the sword, and did cast off all pity, and his anger did tear perpetually, and he
kept his wrath for ever:
12 But I will send a fire upon Teman, which shall devour the palaces of
Bozrah.

God's Judgment upon Ammon

13 Thus saith the LORD; For three transgressions of the children of Ammon,
and for four, I will not turn away *the punishment* thereof; because they have
ripped up the women with child of Gilead, that they might enlarge their border:
14 But I will kindle a fire in the wall of Rabbah, and it shall devour the pal-
aces thereof, with shouting in the day of battle, with a tempest in the day of
the whirlwind:
15 And their king shall go into captivity, he and his princes together, saith
the LORD.

God's Judgment upon Moab

2 Thus saith the LORD; For three transgressions of Moab, and for four, I will
not turn away *the punishment* thereof; because he burned the bones of the
king of Edom into lime:
2 But I will send a fire upon Moab, and it shall devour the palaces of Kerioth:
and Moab shall die with tumult, with shouting, *and* with the sound of the
trumpet:
3 And I will cut off the judge from the midst thereof, and will slay all the
princes thereof with him, saith the LORD.

God's Judgment upon Judah

4 Thus saith the LORD; For three transgressions of Judah, and for four, I will
not turn away *the punishment* thereof; because they have despised the law of
the LORD, and have not kept his commandments, and their lies caused them
to err, after the which their fathers have walked:
5 But I will send a fire upon Judah, and it shall devour the palaces of
Jerusalem.

God's Judgment upon Israel

6 Thus saith the LORD; For three transgressions of Israel, and for four, I will
not turn away *the punishment* thereof; because they sold the righteous for
silver, and the poor for a pair of shoes;
7 That pant after the dust of the earth on the head of the poor, and turn aside
the way of the meek: and a man and his father will go in unto the *same* maid,
to profane my holy name:
8 And they lay *themselves* down upon clothes laid to pledge by every altar,
and they drink the wine of the condemned *in* the house of their god.
9 Yet destroyed I the Amorite before them, whose height *was* like the height
of the cedars, and he *was* strong as the oaks; yet I destroyed his fruit from
above, and his roots from beneath.
10 Also I brought you up from the land of Egypt, and led you forty years
through the wilderness, to possess the land of the Amorite.
11 And I raised up of your sons for prophets, and of your young men for
Nazarites. *Is it* not even thus, O ye children of Israel? saith the LORD.
12 But ye gave the Nazarites wine to drink; and commanded the prophets,
saying, Prophesy not.
13 Behold, I am pressed under you, as a cart is pressed *that is* full of sheaves.
14 Therefore the flight shall perish from the swift, and the strong shall not
strengthen his force, neither shall the mighty deliver himself:
15 Neither shall he stand that handleth the bow; and *he that is* swift of foot
shall not deliver *himself*: neither shall he that rideth the horse deliver himself.
16 And *he that is* courageous among the mighty shall flee away naked in that
day, saith the LORD.

The Necessity of God's Judgment against Israel

3 Hear this word that the LORD hath spoken against you, O children of Israel,
against the whole family which I brought up from the land of Egypt, saying,
2 You only have I known of all the families of the earth: therefore I will pun-
ish you for all your iniquities.
3 Can two walk together, except they be agreed?
4 Will a lion roar in the forest, when he hath no prey? will a young lion cry
out of his den, if he have taken nothing?
5 Can a bird fall in a snare upon the earth, where no gin *is* for him? shall *one*
take up a snare from the earth, and have taken nothing at all?
6 Shall a trumpet be blown in the city, and the people not be afraid? shall
there be evil in a city, and the LORD hath not done *it*?
7 Surely the Lord GOD will do nothing, but he revealeth his secret unto his
servants the prophets.

8 The lion hath roared, who will not fear? the Lord God hath spoken, who
can but prophesy?
9 Publish in the palaces at Ashdod, and in the palaces in the land of Egypt,
and say, Assemble yourselves upon the mountains of Samaria, and behold the
great tumults in the midst thereof, and the oppressed in the midst thereof.
10 For they know not to do right, saith the Lord, who store up violence and
robbery in their palaces.
11 Therefore thus saith the Lord God; An adversary *there shall be* even round
about the land; and he shall bring down thy strength from thee, and thy pal-
aces shall be spoiled.
12 Thus saith the Lord; As the shepherd taketh out of the mouth of the lion
two legs, or a piece of an ear; so shall the children of Israel be taken out that
dwell in Samaria in the corner of a bed, and in Damascus *in* a couch.
13 Hear ye, and testify in the house of Jacob, saith the Lord God, the God of
hosts,
14 That in the day that I shall visit the transgressions of Israel upon him I
will also visit the altars of Beth-el: and the horns of the altar shall be cut off,
and fall to the ground.
15 And I will smite the winter house with the summer house; and the hous-
es of ivory shall perish, and the great houses shall have an end, saith the Lord.

Punishment for the Women of Samaria

4 Hear this word, ye kine of Bashan, that *are* in the mountain of Samaria,
which oppress the poor, which crush the needy, which say to their masters,
Bring, and let us drink.
2 The Lord God hath sworn by his holiness, that, lo, the days shall come upon
you, that he will take you away with hooks, and your posterity with fishhooks.
3 And ye shall go out at the breaches, every *cow at that which is* before her;
and ye shall cast *them* into the palace, saith the Lord.
4 Come to Beth-el, and transgress; at Gilgal multiply transgression; and bring
your sacrifices every morning, *and* your tithes after three years:
5 And offer a sacrifice of thanksgiving with leaven, and proclaim *and* publish
the free offerings: for this liketh you, O ye children of Israel, saith the Lord
God.
6 And I also have given you cleanness of teeth in all your cities, and want of
bread in all your places: yet have ye not returned unto me, saith the Lord.
7 And also I have withholden the rain from you, when *there were* yet three
months to the harvest: and I caused it to rain upon one city, and caused it not
to rain upon another city: one piece was rained upon, and the piece where-
upon it rained not withered.
8 So two *or* three cities wandered unto one city, to drink water; but they were
not satisfied: yet have ye not returned unto me, saith the Lord.
9 I have smitten you with blasting and mildew: when your gardens and your
vineyards and your fig trees and your olive trees increased, the palmerworm
devoured *them*: yet have ye not returned unto me, saith the Lord.
10 I have sent among you the pestilence after the manner of Egypt: your
young men have I slain with the sword, and have taken away your horses; and
I have made the stink of your camps to come up unto your nostrils: yet have
ye not returned unto me, saith the Lord.
11 I have overthrown *some* of you, as God overthrew Sodom and Gomorrah,
and ye were as a firebrand plucked out of the burning: yet have ye not returned
unto me, saith the Lord.
12 Therefore thus will I do unto thee, O Israel: *and* because I will do this unto
thee, prepare to meet thy God, O Israel.
13 For, lo, he that formeth the mountains, and createth the wind, and declar-
eth unto man what *is* his thought, that maketh the morning darkness, and

treadeth upon the high places of the earth, The LORD, The God of hosts, *is* his
name.

A Lamentation for Israel

5 Hear ye this word which I take up against you, *even* a lamentation, O house
of Israel.
2 The virgin of Israel is fallen; she shall no more rise: she is forsaken upon
her land; *there is* none to raise her up.
3 For thus saith the Lord GOD; The city that went out *by* a thousand shall leave
an hundred, and that which went forth *by* an hundred shall leave ten, to the
house of Israel.

An Exhortation to Repentance

4 For thus saith the LORD unto the house of Israel, Seek ye me, and ye shall
live:
5 But seek not Beth-el, nor enter into Gilgal, and pass not to Beer-sheba: for
Gilgal shall surely go into captivity, and Beth-el shall come to nought.
6 Seek the LORD, and ye shall live; lest he break out like fire in the house of
Joseph, and devour *it*, and *there be* none to quench *it* in Beth-el.
7 Ye who turn judgment to wormwood, and leave off righteousness in the
earth,
8 *Seek him* that maketh the seven stars and Orion, and turneth the shadow
of death into the morning, and maketh the day dark with night: that calleth
for the waters of the sea, and poureth them out upon the face of the earth: The
LORD *is* his name:
9 That strengtheneth the spoiled against the strong, so that the spoiled shall
come against the fortress.
10 They hate him that rebuketh in the gate, and they abhor him that speaketh
uprightly.
11 Forasmuch therefore as your treading *is* upon the poor, and ye take from
him burdens of wheat: ye have built houses of hewn stone, but ye shall not
dwell in them; ye have planted pleasant vineyards, but ye shall not drink wine
of them.
12 For I know your manifold transgressions and your mighty sins: they afflict
the just, they take a bribe, and they turn aside the poor in the gate *from their
right.*
13 Therefore the prudent shall keep silence in that time; for it *is* an evil time.
14 Seek good, and not evil, that ye may live: and so the LORD, the God of hosts,
shall be with you, as ye have spoken.
15 Hate the evil, and love the good, and establish judgment in the gate: it may
be that the LORD God of hosts will be gracious unto the remnant of Joseph.
16 Therefore the LORD, the God of hosts, the Lord, saith thus; Wailing *shall
be* in all streets; and they shall say in all the highways, Alas! alas! and they shall
call the husbandman to mourning, and such as are skilful of lamentation to
wailing.
17 And in all vineyards *shall be* wailing: for I will pass through thee, saith the
LORD.
18 Woe unto you that desire the day of the LORD! to what end *is* it for you?
the day of the LORD *is* darkness, and not light.
19 As if a man did flee from a lion, and a bear met him; or went into the house,
and leaned his hand on the wall, and a serpent bit him.
20 *Shall* not the day of the LORD *be* darkness, and not light? even very dark,
and no brightness in it?

God Rejects Their Hypocritical Worship

21 I hate, I despise your feast days, and I will not smell in your solemn assemblies.
22 Though ye offer me burnt offerings and your meat offerings, I will not
accept *them*: neither will I regard the peace offerings of your fat beasts.

23 Take thou away from me the noise of thy songs; for I will not hear the
melody of thy viols.
24 But let judgment run down as waters, and righteousness as a mighty
stream.
25 Have ye offered unto me sacrifices and offerings in the wilderness forty
years, O house of Israel?
26 But ye have borne the tabernacle of your Moloch and Chiun your images,
the star of your god, which ye made to yourselves.
27 Therefore will I cause you to go into captivity beyond Damascus, saith the
LORD, whose name *is* The God of hosts.

The Fall of Samaria

6 Woe to them *that are* at ease in Zion, and trust in the mountain of Samaria,
which are named chief of the nations, to whom the house of Israel came!
2 Pass ye unto Calneh, and see; and from thence go ye to Hamath the great:
then go down to Gath of the Philistines: *be they* better than these kingdoms?
or their border greater than your border?
3 Ye that put far away the evil day, and cause the seat of violence to come near;
4 That lie upon beds of ivory, and stretch themselves upon their couches,
and eat the lambs out of the flock, and the calves out of the midst of the stall;
5 That chant to the sound of the viol, *and* invent to themselves instruments
of musick, like David;
6 That drink wine in bowls, and anoint themselves with the chief ointments:
but they are not grieved for the affliction of Joseph.
7 Therefore now shall they go captive with the first that go captive, and the
banquet of them that stretched themselves shall be removed.
8 The Lord GOD hath sworn by himself, saith the LORD the God of hosts, I
abhor the excellency of Jacob, and hate his palaces: therefore will I deliver up
the city with all that is therein.
9 And it shall come to pass, if there remain ten men in one house, that they
shall die.
10 And a man's uncle shall take him up, and he that burneth him, to bring
out the bones out of the house, and shall say unto him that *is* by the sides of
the house, *Is there* yet *any* with thee? and he shall say, No. Then shall he say,
Hold thy tongue: for we may not make mention of the name of the LORD.
11 For, behold, the LORD commandeth, and he will smite the great house with
breaches, and the little house with clefts.
12 Shall horses run upon the rock? will *one* plow *there* with oxen? for ye have
turned judgment into gall, and the fruit of righteousness into hemlock:
13 Ye which rejoice in a thing of nought, which say, Have we not taken to us
horns by our own strength?
14 But, behold, I will raise up against you a nation, O house of Israel, saith
the LORD the God of hosts; and they shall afflict you from the entering in of
Hemath unto the river of the wilderness.

Famine by Grasshoppers (Locusts)

7 Thus hath the Lord GOD shewed unto me; and, behold, he formed grass-
hoppers in the beginning of the shooting up of the latter growth; and, lo,
it was the latter growth after the king's mowings.
2 And it came to pass, *that* when they had made an end of eating the grass
of the land, then I said, O Lord GOD, forgive, I beseech thee: by whom shall
Jacob arise? for he *is* small.
3 The LORD repented for this: It shall not be, saith the LORD.

Drought by Fire

4 Thus hath the Lord GOD shewed unto me: and, behold, the Lord GOD called
to contend by fire, and it devoured the great deep, and did eat up a part.

5 Then said I, O Lord God, cease, I beseech thee: by whom shall Jacob arise?
for he *is* small.
6 The Lord repented for this: This also shall not be, saith the Lord God.

The Plumbline

7 Thus he shewed me: and, behold, the Lord stood upon a wall *made* by a
plumbline, with a plumbline in his hand.
8 And the Lord said unto me, Amos, what seest thou? And I said, A plumbline.
Then said the Lord, Behold, I will set a plumbline in the midst of my people
Israel: I will not again pass by them any more:
9 And the high places of Isaac shall be desolate, and the sanctuaries of Israel
shall be laid waste; and I will rise against the house of Jeroboam with the
sword.

Amaziah Opposes Amos

10 Then Amaziah the priest of Beth-el sent to Jeroboam king of Israel, saying,
Amos hath conspired against thee in the midst of the house of Israel: the land
is not able to bear all his words.
11 For thus Amos saith, Jeroboam shall die by the sword, and Israel shall
surely be led away captive out of their own land.
12 Also Amaziah said unto Amos, O thou seer, go, flee thee away into the land
of Judah, and there eat bread, and prophesy there:
13 But prophesy not again any more at Beth-el: for it *is* the king's chapel, and
it *is* the king's court.
14 Then answered Amos, and said to Amaziah, I *was* no prophet, neither *was*
I a prophet's son; but I *was* an herdman, and a gatherer of sycomore fruit:
15 And the Lord took me as I followed the flock, and the Lord said unto me,
Go, prophesy unto my people Israel.
16 Now therefore hear thou the word of the Lord: Thou sayest, Prophesy not
against Israel, and drop not *thy word* against the house of Isaac.
17 Therefore thus saith the Lord; Thy wife shall be an harlot in the city, and
thy sons and thy daughters shall fall by the sword, and thy land shall be divid-
ed by line; and thou shalt die in a polluted land: and Israel shall surely go into
captivity forth of his land.

A Basket of Summer Fruit

8 Thus hath the Lord God shewed unto me: and behold a basket of summer
fruit.
2 And he said, Amos, what seest thou? And I said, A basket of summer fruit.
Then said the Lord unto me, The end is come upon my people of Israel; I will
not again pass by them any more.
3 And the songs of the temple shall be howlings in that day, saith the Lord
God: *there shall be* many dead bodies in every place; they shall cast *them* forth
with silence.

Oppression Is Reproved

4 Hear this, O ye that swallow up the needy, even to make the poor of the
land to fail,
5 Saying, When will the new moon be gone, that we may sell corn? and the
sabbath, that we may set forth wheat, making the ephah small, and the shek-
el great, and falsifying the balances by deceit?
6 That we may buy the poor for silver, and the needy for a pair of shoes; *yea*,
and sell the refuse of the wheat?
7 The Lord hath sworn by the excellency of Jacob, Surely I will never forget
any of their works.
8 Shall not the land tremble for this, and every one mourn that dwelleth
therein? and it shall rise up wholly as a flood; and it shall be cast out and
drowned, as *by* the flood of Egypt.

9 And it shall come to pass in that day, saith the Lord GOD, that I will cause
the sun to go down at noon, and I will darken the earth in the clear day:
10 And I will turn your feasts into mourning, and all your songs into lamen-
tation; and I will bring up sackcloth upon all loins, and baldness upon every
head; and I will make it as the mourning of an only *son*, and the end thereof
as a bitter day.

A Famine of God's Word

11 Behold, the days come, saith the Lord GOD, that I will send a famine in the
land, not a famine of bread, nor a thirst for water, but of hearing the words
of the LORD:
12 And they shall wander from sea to sea, and from the north even to the east,
they shall run to and fro to seek the word of the LORD, and shall not find *it*.
13 In that day shall the fair virgins and young men faint for thirst.
14 They that swear by the sin of Samaria, and say, Thy god, O Dan, liveth; and,
The manner of Beer-sheba liveth; even they shall fall, and never rise up again.

The Certainty of the Desolation

9 I saw the Lord standing upon the altar: and he said, Smite the lintel of the
door, that the posts may shake: and cut them in the head, all of them; and
I will slay the last of them with the sword: he that fleeth of them shall not flee
away, and he that escapeth of them shall not be delivered.
2 Though they dig into hell, thence shall mine hand take them; though they
climb up to heaven, thence will I bring them down:
3 And though they hide themselves in the top of Carmel, I will search and
take them out thence; and though they be hid from my sight in the bottom of
the sea, thence will I command the serpent, and he shall bite them:
4 And though they go into captivity before their enemies, thence will I com-
mand the sword, and it shall slay them: and I will set mine eyes upon them for
evil, and not for good.
5 And the Lord GOD of hosts *is* he that toucheth the land, and it shall melt,
and all that dwell therein shall mourn: and it shall rise up wholly like a flood;
and shall be drowned, as *by* the flood of Egypt.
6 *It is* he that buildeth his stories in the heaven, and hath founded his troop
in the earth; he that calleth for the waters of the sea, and poureth them out
upon the face of the earth: The LORD *is* his name.
7 *Are* ye not as children of the Ethiopians unto me, O children of Israel? saith
the LORD. Have not I brought up Israel out of the land of Egypt? and the
Philistines from Caphtor, and the Syrians from Kir?
8 Behold, the eyes of the Lord GOD *are* upon the sinful kingdom, and I will
destroy it from off the face of the earth; saving that I will not utterly destroy
the house of Jacob, saith the LORD.
9 For, lo, I will command, and I will sift the house of Israel among all nations,
like as *corn* is sifted in a sieve, yet shall not the least grain fall upon the earth.
10 All the sinners of my people shall die by the sword, which say, The evil
shall not overtake nor prevent us.

Restoration Promised

11 In that day will I raise up the tabernacle of David that is fallen, and close
up the breaches thereof; and I will raise up his ruins, and I will build it as in
the days of old:
12 That they may possess the remnant of Edom, and of all the heathen, which
are called by my name, saith the LORD that doeth this.
13 Behold, the days come, saith the LORD, that the plowman shall overtake
the reaper, and the treader of grapes him that soweth seed; and the mountains
shall drop sweet wine, and all the hills shall melt.

14 And I will bring again the captivity of my people of Israel, and they shall
build the waste cities, and inhabit *them*; and they shall plant vineyards, and
drink the wine thereof; they shall also make gardens, and eat the fruit of them.
15 And I will plant them upon their land, and they shall no more be pulled
up out of their land which I have given them, saith the LORD thy God.

OBADIAH

The Destruction of Edom

1 The vision of Obadiah. Thus saith the Lord God concerning Edom; We have heard a rumour from the Lord, and an ambassador is sent among the heathen, Arise ye, and let us rise up against her in battle.

2 Behold, I have made thee small among the heathen: thou art greatly despised.

3 The pride of thine heart hath deceived thee, thou that dwellest in the clefts of the rock, whose habitation *is* high; that saith in his heart, Who shall bring me down to the ground?

4 Though thou exalt *thyself* as the eagle, and though thou set thy nest among the stars, thence will I bring thee down, saith the Lord.

5 If thieves came to thee, if robbers by night, (how art thou cut off!) would they not have stolen till they had enough? if the grapegatherers came to thee, would they not leave *some* grapes?

6 How are *the things* of Esau searched out! *how* are his hidden things sought up!

7 All the men of thy confederacy have brought thee *even* to the border: the men that were at peace with thee have deceived thee, *and* prevailed against thee; *they that eat* thy bread have laid a wound under thee: *there is* none understanding in him.

8 Shall I not in that day, saith the Lord, even destroy the wise *men* out of Edom, and understanding out of the mount of Esau?

9 And thy mighty *men*, O Teman, shall be dismayed, to the end that every one of the mount of Esau may be cut off by slaughter.

Why Edom Will Be Destroyed

10 For *thy* violence against thy brother Jacob shame shall cover thee, and thou shalt be cut off for ever.

11 In the day that thou stoodest on the other side, in the day that the strangers carried away captive his forces, and foreigners entered into his gates, and cast lots upon Jerusalem, even thou *wast* as one of them.

12 But thou shouldest not have looked on the day of thy brother in the day that he became a stranger; neither shouldest thou have rejoiced over the children of Judah in the day of their destruction; neither shouldest thou have spoken proudly in the day of distress.

13 Thou shouldest not have entered into the gate of my people in the day of their calamity; yea, thou shouldest not have looked on their affliction in the day of their calamity, nor have laid *hands* on their substance in the day of their calamity;

14 Neither shouldest thou have stood in the crossway, to cut off those of his that did escape; neither shouldest thou have delivered up those of his that did remain in the day of distress.

15 For the day of the Lord *is* near upon all the heathen: as thou hast done, it shall be done unto thee: thy reward shall return upon thine own head.

16 For as ye have drunk upon my holy mountain, *so* shall all the heathen drink continually, yea, they shall drink, and they shall swallow down, and they shall be as though they had not been.

The Salvation and Victory of Jacob

17 But upon mount Zion shall be deliverance, and there shall be holiness;
and the house of Jacob shall possess their possessions.
18 And the house of Jacob shall be a fire, and the house of Joseph a flame,
and the house of Esau for stubble, and they shall kindle in them, and devour
them; and there shall not be *any* remaining of the house of Esau; for the LORD
hath spoken *it*.
19 And *they of* the south shall possess the mount of Esau; and *they of* the plain
the Philistines: and they shall possess the fields of Ephraim, and the fields of
Samaria: and Benjamin *shall possess* Gilead.
20 And the captivity of this host of the children of Israel *shall possess* that of
the Canaanites, *even* unto Zarephath; and the captivity of Jerusalem, which *is*
in Sepharad, shall possess the cities of the south.
21 And saviours shall come up on mount Zion to judge the mount of Esau;
and the kingdom shall be the LORD's.

Jonah Tries to Run from God

1 Now the word of the LORD came unto Jonah the son of Amittai, saying,

2 Arise, go to Nineveh, that great city, and cry against it; for their wickedness is come up before me.

3 But Jonah rose up to flee unto Tarshish from the presence of the LORD, and went down to Joppa; and he found a ship going to Tarshish: so he paid the fare thereof, and went down into it, to go with them unto Tarshish from the presence of the LORD.

The Storm at Sea

4 But the LORD sent out a great wind into the sea, and there was a mighty tempest in the sea, so that the ship was like to be broken.

5 Then the mariners were afraid, and cried every man unto his god, and cast forth the wares that *were* in the ship into the sea, to lighten *it* of them. But Jonah was gone down into the sides of the ship; and he lay, and was fast asleep.

6 So the shipmaster came to him, and said unto him, What meanest thou, O sleeper? arise, call upon thy God, if so be that God will think upon us, that we perish not.

7 And they said every one to his fellow, Come, and let us cast lots, that we may know for whose cause this evil *is* upon us. So they cast lots, and the lot fell upon Jonah.

8 Then said they unto him, Tell us, we pray thee, for whose cause this evil *is* upon us; What *is* thine occupation? and whence comest thou? what *is* thy country? and of what people *art* thou?

9 And he said unto them, I *am* an Hebrew; and I fear the LORD, the God of heaven, which hath made the sea and the dry *land*.

10 Then were the men exceedingly afraid, and said unto him, Why hast thou done this? For the men knew that he fled from the presence of the LORD, because he had told them.

A Great Fish Swallows Jonah

11 Then said they unto him, What shall we do unto thee, that the sea may be calm unto us? for the sea wrought, and was tempestuous.

12 And he said unto them, Take me up, and cast me forth into the sea; so shall the sea be calm unto you: for I know that for my sake this great tempest *is* upon you.

13 Nevertheless the men rowed hard to bring *it* to the land; but they could not: for the sea wrought, and was tempestuous against them.

14 Wherefore they cried unto the LORD, and said, We beseech thee, O LORD, we beseech thee, let us not perish for this man's life, and lay not upon us innocent blood: for thou, O LORD, hast done as it pleased thee.

15 So they took up Jonah, and cast him forth into the sea: and the sea ceased from her raging.

16 Then the men feared the LORD exceedingly, and offered a sacrifice unto the LORD, and made vows.

17 Now the LORD had prepared a great fish to swallow up Jonah. And Jonah was in the belly of the fish three days and three nights.

The Prayer of Jonah

2 Then Jonah prayed unto the LORD his God out of the fish's belly,
2 And said, I cried by reason of mine affliction unto the LORD, and he
heard me; out of the belly of hell cried I, *and* thou heardest my voice.
3 For thou hadst cast me into the deep, in the midst of the seas; and the floods
compassed me about: all thy billows and thy waves passed over me.
4 Then I said, I am cast out of thy sight; yet I will look again toward thy holy
temple.
5 The waters compassed me about, *even* to the soul: the depth closed me
round about, the weeds were wrapped about my head.
6 I went down to the bottoms of the mountains; the earth with her bars *was*
about me for ever: yet hast thou brought up my life from corruption, O LORD
my God.
7 When my soul fainted within me I remembered the LORD: and my prayer
came in unto thee, into thine holy temple.
8 They that observe lying vanities forsake their own mercy.
9 But I will sacrifice unto thee with the voice of thanksgiving; I will pay *that*
that I have vowed. Salvation *is* of the LORD.
10 And the LORD spake unto the fish, and it vomited out Jonah upon the dry
land.

The People of Nineveh Repent

3 And the word of the LORD came unto Jonah the second time, saying,
2 Arise, go unto Nineveh, that great city, and preach unto it the preaching
that I bid thee.
3 So Jonah arose, and went unto Nineveh, according to the word of the LORD.
Now Nineveh was an exceeding great city of three days' journey.
4 And Jonah began to enter into the city a day's journey, and he cried, and
said, Yet forty days, and Nineveh shall be overthrown.
5 So the people of Nineveh believed God, and proclaimed a fast, and put on
sackcloth, from the greatest of them even to the least of them.
6 For word came unto the king of Nineveh, and he arose from his throne,
and he laid his robe from him, and covered *him* with sackcloth, and sat in
ashes.
7 And he caused *it* to be proclaimed and published through Nineveh by the
decree of the king and his nobles, saying, Let neither man nor beast, herd nor
flock, taste any thing: let them not feed, nor drink water:
8 But let man and beast be covered with sackcloth, and cry mightily unto
God: yea, let them turn every one from his evil way, and from the violence that
is in their hands.
9 Who can tell *if* God will turn and repent, and turn away from his fierce
anger, that we perish not?
10 And God saw their works, that they turned from their evil way; and God
repented of the evil, that he had said that he would do unto them; and he did
it not.

Jonah's Anger at God's Mercy

4 But it displeased Jonah exceedingly, and he was very angry.
2 And he prayed unto the LORD, and said, I pray thee, O LORD, *was* not this
my saying, when I was yet in my country? Therefore I fled before unto Tarshish:
for I knew that thou *art* a gracious God, and merciful, slow to anger, and of
great kindness, and repentest thee of the evil.
3 Therefore now, O LORD, take, I beseech thee, my life from me; for *it is* bet-
ter for me to die than to live.
4 Then said the LORD, Doest thou well to be angry?

5 So Jonah went out of the city, and sat on the east side of the city, and there
made him a booth, and sat under it in the shadow, till he might see what would
become of the city.
6 And the LORD God prepared a gourd, and made *it* to come up over Jonah,
that it might be a shadow over his head, to deliver him from his grief. So Jonah
was exceeding glad of the gourd.
7 But God prepared a worm when the morning rose the next day, and it smote
the gourd that it withered.
8 And it came to pass, when the sun did arise, that God prepared a vehement
east wind; and the sun beat upon the head of Jonah, that he fainted, and wished
in himself to die, and said, *It is* better for me to die than to live.
9 And God said to Jonah, Doest thou well to be angry for the gourd? And he
said, I do well to be angry, *even* unto death.
10 Then said the LORD, Thou hast had pity on the gourd, for the which thou
hast not laboured, neither madest it grow; which came up in a night, and
perished in a night:
11 And should not I spare Nineveh, that great city, wherein are more than
sixscore thousand persons that cannot discern between their right hand and
their left hand; and *also* much cattle?

Capital Cities of Israel and Judah to Be Destroyed

1 The word of the LORD that came to Micah the Morasthite in the days of
Jotham, Ahaz, *and* Hezekiah, kings of Judah, which he saw concerning
Samaria and Jerusalem.
2 Hear, all ye people; hearken, O earth, and all that therein is: and let the Lord
GOD be witness against you, the Lord from his holy temple.
3 For, behold, the LORD cometh forth out of his place, and will come down,
and tread upon the high places of the earth.
4 And the mountains shall be molten under him, and the valleys shall be
cleft, as wax before the fire, *and* as the waters *that are* poured down a steep
place.
5 For the transgression of Jacob *is* all this, and for the sins of the house of
Israel. What *is* the transgression of Jacob? *is it* not Samaria? and what *are* the
high places of Judah? *are they* not Jerusalem?
6 Therefore I will make Samaria as an heap of the field, *and* as plantings of
a vineyard: and I will pour down the stones thereof into the valley, and I will
discover the foundations thereof.
7 And all the graven images thereof shall be beaten to pieces, and all the hires
thereof shall be burned with the fire, and all the idols thereof will I lay desolate:
for she gathered *it* of the hire of an harlot, and they shall return to the hire of
an harlot.
8 Therefore I will wail and howl, I will go stripped and naked: I will make a
wailing like the dragons, and mourning as the owls.
9 For her wound *is* incurable; for it is come unto Judah; he is come unto the
gate of my people, *even* to Jerusalem.
10 Declare ye *it* not at Gath, weep ye not at all: in the house of Aphrah roll
thyself in the dust.
11 Pass ye away, thou inhabitant of Saphir, having thy shame naked: the
inhabitant of Zaanan came not forth in the mourning of Beth-ezel; he shall
receive of you his standing.
12 For the inhabitant of Maroth waited carefully for good: but evil came
down from the LORD unto the gate of Jerusalem.
13 O thou inhabitant of Lachish, bind the chariot to the swift beast: she *is*
the beginning of the sin to the daughter of Zion: for the transgressions of
Israel were found in thee.
14 Therefore shalt thou give presents to Moresheth-gath: the houses of
Achzib *shall be* a lie to the kings of Israel.
15 Yet will I bring an heir unto thee, O inhabitant of Mareshah: he shall come
unto Adullam the glory of Israel.
16 Make thee bald, and poll thee for thy delicate children; enlarge thy bald-
ness as the eagle; for they are gone into captivity from thee.

Israel's Sins Are Condemned

2 Woe to them that devise iniquity, and work evil upon their beds! when the
morning is light, they practise it, because it is in the power of their hand.
2 And they covet fields, and take *them* by violence; and houses, and take *them*
away: so they oppress a man and his house, even a man and his heritage.

3 Therefore thus saith the LORD; Behold, against this family do I devise an
evil, from which ye shall not remove your necks; neither shall ye go haughtily:
for this time *is* evil.
4 In that day shall *one* take up a parable against you, and lament with a dole-
ful lamentation, *and* say, We be utterly spoiled: he hath changed the portion
of my people: how hath he removed *it* from me! turning away he hath divided
our fields.
5 Therefore thou shalt have none that shall cast a cord by lot in the congre-
gation of the LORD.
6 Prophesy ye not, *say they to them that* prophesy: they shall not prophesy
to them, *that* they shall not take shame.
7 O *thou that art* named the house of Jacob, is the spirit of the LORD strait-
ened? *are* these his doings? do not my words do good to him that walketh
uprightly?
8 Even of late my people is risen up as an enemy: ye pull off the robe with the
garment from them that pass by securely as men averse from war.
9 The women of my people have ye cast out from their pleasant houses; from
their children have ye taken away my glory for ever.
10 Arise ye, and depart; for this *is* not *your* rest: because it is polluted, it shall
destroy *you*, even with a sore destruction.
11 If a man walking in the spirit and falsehood do lie, *saying*, I will prophesy
unto thee of wine and of strong drink; he shall even be the prophet of this
people.

Israel Will Be Gathered Again

12 I will surely assemble, O Jacob, all of thee; I will surely gather the remnant
of Israel; I will put them together as the sheep of Bozrah, as the flock in the
midst of their fold: they shall make great noise by reason of *the multitude of*
men.
13 The breaker is come up before them: they have broken up, and have passed
through the gate, and are gone out by it: and their king shall pass before them,
and the LORD on the head of them.

Israel's Sinful Leaders

3 And I said, Hear, I pray you, O heads of Jacob, and ye princes of the house
of Israel; *Is it* not for you to know judgment?
2 Who hate the good, and love the evil; who pluck off their skin from off
them, and their flesh from off their bones;
3 Who also eat the flesh of my people, and flay their skin from off them; and
they break their bones, and chop them in pieces, as for the pot, and as flesh
within the caldron.
4 Then shall they cry unto the LORD, but he will not hear them: he will even
hide his face from them at that time, as they have behaved themselves ill in
their doings.
5 Thus saith the LORD concerning the prophets that make my people err, that
bite with their teeth, and cry, Peace; and he that putteth not into their mouths,
they even prepare war against him.
6 Therefore night *shall be* unto you, that ye shall not have a vision; and it
shall be dark unto you, that ye shall not divine; and the sun shall go down over
the prophets, and the day shall be dark over them.
7 Then shall the seers be ashamed, and the diviners confounded: yea, they
shall all cover their lips; for *there is* no answer of God.
8 But truly I am full of power by the spirit of the LORD, and of judgment, and
of might, to declare unto Jacob his transgression, and to Israel his sin.
9 Hear this, I pray you, ye heads of the house of Jacob, and princes of the
house of Israel, that abhor judgment, and pervert all equity.
10 They build up Zion with blood, and Jerusalem with iniquity.

11 The heads thereof judge for reward, and the priests thereof teach for hire, and the prophets thereof divine for money: yet will they lean upon the LORD, and say, *Is* not the LORD among us? none evil can come upon us.

12 Therefore shall Zion for your sake be plowed *as* a field, and Jerusalem shall become heaps, and the mountain of the house as the high places of the forest.

The Lord Will Teach the Nations

4 But in the last days it shall come to pass, *that* the mountain of the house of the LORD shall be established in the top of the mountains, and it shall be exalted above the hills; and people shall flow unto it.

2 And many nations shall come, and say, Come, and let us go up to the mountain of the LORD, and to the house of the God of Jacob; and he will teach us of his ways, and we will walk in his paths: for the law shall go forth of Zion, and the word of the LORD from Jerusalem.

3 And he shall judge among many people, and rebuke strong nations afar off; and they shall beat their swords into plowshares, and their spears into pruninghooks: nation shall not lift up a sword against nation, neither shall they learn war any more.

4 But they shall sit every man under his vine and under his fig tree; and none shall make *them* afraid: for the mouth of the LORD of hosts hath spoken *it*.

5 For all people will walk every one in the name of his god, and we will walk in the name of the LORD our God for ever and ever.

6 In that day, saith the LORD, will I assemble her that halteth, and I will gather her that is driven out, and her that I have afflicted;

7 And I will make her that halted a remnant, and her that was cast far off a strong nation: and the LORD shall reign over them in mount Zion from henceforth, even for ever.

8 And thou, O tower of the flock, the strong hold of the daughter of Zion, unto thee shall it come, even the first dominion; the kingdom shall come to the daughter of Jerusalem.

9 Now why dost thou cry out aloud? *is there* no king in thee? is thy counsellor perished? for pangs have taken thee as a woman in travail.

10 Be in pain, and labour to bring forth, O daughter of Zion, like a woman in travail: for now shalt thou go forth out of the city, and thou shalt dwell in the field, and thou shalt go *even* to Babylon; there shalt thou be delivered; there the LORD shall redeem thee from the hand of thine enemies.

11 Now also many nations are gathered against thee, that say, Let her be defiled, and let our eye look upon Zion.

12 But they know not the thoughts of the LORD, neither understand they his counsel: for he shall gather them as the sheaves into the floor.

13 Arise and thresh, O daughter of Zion: for I will make thine horn iron, and I will make thy hoofs brass: and thou shalt beat in pieces many people: and I will consecrate their gain unto the LORD, and their substance unto the Lord of the whole earth.

The Birth of Christ

5 Now gather thyself in troops, O daughter of troops: he hath laid siege against us: they shall smite the judge of Israel with a rod upon the cheek.

2 But thou, Beth-lehem Ephratah, *though* thou be little among the thousands of Judah, *yet* out of thee shall he come forth unto me *that is* to be ruler in Israel; whose goings forth *have been* from of old, from everlasting.

3 Therefore will he give them up, until the time *that* she which travaileth hath brought forth: then the remnant of his brethren shall return unto the children of Israel.

4 And he shall stand and feed in the strength of the LORD, in the majesty of the name of the LORD his God; and they shall abide: for now shall he be great unto the ends of the earth.

5 And this *man* shall be the peace, when the Assyrian shall come into our
land: and when he shall tread in our palaces, then shall we raise against him
seven shepherds, and eight principal men.
6 And they shall waste the land of Assyria with the sword, and the land of
Nimrod in the entrances thereof: thus shall he deliver *us* from the Assyrian,
when he cometh into our land, and when he treadeth within our borders.
7 And the remnant of Jacob shall be in the midst of many people as a dew
from the Lord, as the showers upon the grass, that tarrieth not for man, nor
waiteth for the sons of men.
8 And the remnant of Jacob shall be among the Gentiles in the midst of many
people as a lion among the beasts of the forest, as a young lion among the
flocks of sheep: who, if he go through, both treadeth down, and teareth in
pieces, and none can deliver.
9 Thine hand shall be lifted up upon thine adversaries, and all thine enemies
shall be cut off.
10 And it shall come to pass in that day, saith the Lord, that I will cut off thy
horses out of the midst of thee, and I will destroy thy chariots:
11 And I will cut off the cities of thy land, and throw down all thy strong
holds:
12 And I will cut off witchcrafts out of thine hand; and thou shalt have no
more soothsayers:
13 Thy graven images also will I cut off, and thy standing images out of the
midst of thee; and thou shalt no more worship the work of thine hands.
14 And I will pluck up thy groves out of the midst of thee: so will I destroy
thy cities.
15 And I will execute vengeance in anger and fury upon the heathen, such
as they have not heard.

God's Lawsuit against His People

6 Hear ye now what the Lord saith; Arise, contend thou before the mountains,
and let the hills hear thy voice.
2 Hear ye, O mountains, the Lord's controversy, and ye strong foundations
of the earth: for the Lord hath a controversy with his people, and he will plead
with Israel.
3 O my people, what have I done unto thee? and wherein have I wearied
thee? testify against me.
4 For I brought thee up out of the land of Egypt, and redeemed thee out of
the house of servants; and I sent before thee Moses, Aaron, and Miriam.
5 O my people, remember now what Balak king of Moab consulted, and what
Balaam the son of Beor answered him from Shittim unto Gilgal; that ye may
know the righteousness of the Lord.
6 Wherewith shall I come before the Lord, *and* bow myself before the high
God? shall I come before him with burnt offerings, with calves of a year old?
7 Will the Lord be pleased with thousands of rams, *or* with ten thousands
of rivers of oil? shall I give my firstborn *for* my transgression, the fruit of my
body *for* the sin of my soul?
8 He hath shewed thee, O man, what *is* good; and what doth the Lord require
of thee, but to do justly, and to love mercy, and to walk humbly with thy God?
9 The Lord's voice crieth unto the city, and *the man of* wisdom shall see thy
name: hear ye the rod, and who hath appointed it.
10 Are there yet the treasures of wickedness in the house of the wicked, and
the scant measure *that is* abominable?
11 Shall I count *them* pure with the wicked balances, and with the bag of
deceitful weights?
12 For the rich men thereof are full of violence, and the inhabitants thereof
have spoken lies, and their tongue *is* deceitful in their mouth.

13 Therefore also will I make *thee* sick in smiting thee, in making *thee* deso-
late because of thy sins.
14 Thou shalt eat, but not be satisfied; and thy casting down *shall be* in the
midst of thee; and thou shalt take hold, but shalt not deliver; and *that* which
thou deliverest will I give up to the sword.
15 Thou shalt sow, but thou shalt not reap; thou shalt tread the olives, but
thou shalt not anoint thee with oil; and sweet wine, but shalt not drink wine.
16 For the statutes of Omri are kept, and all the works of the house of Ahab,
and ye walk in their counsels; that I should make thee a desolation, and the
inhabitants thereof an hissing: therefore ye shall bear the reproach of my
people.

The People Confess Their Sin

7 Woe is me! for I am as when they have gathered the summer fruits, as the
grapegleanings of the vintage: *there is* no cluster to eat: my soul desired the
firstripe fruit.
2 The good *man* is perished out of the earth: and *there is* none upright among
men: they all lie in wait for blood; they hunt every man his brother with a net.
3 That they may do evil with both hands earnestly, the prince asketh, and the
judge *asketh* for a reward; and the great *man*, he uttereth his mischievous
desire: so they wrap it up.
4 The best of them *is* as a brier: the most upright *is sharper* than a thorn
hedge: the day of thy watchmen *and* thy visitation cometh; now shall be their
perplexity.
5 Trust ye not in a friend, put ye not confidence in a guide: keep the doors of
thy mouth from her that lieth in thy bosom.
6 For the son dishonoureth the father, the daughter riseth up against her
mother, the daughter in law against her mother in law; a man's enemies *are*
the men of his own house.
7 Therefore I will look unto the LORD; I will wait for the God of my salvation:
my God will hear me.
8 Rejoice not against me, O mine enemy: when I fall, I shall arise; when I sit
in darkness, the LORD *shall be* a light unto me.
9 I will bear the indignation of the LORD, because I have sinned against him,
until he plead my cause, and execute judgment for me: he will bring me forth
to the light, *and* I shall behold his righteousness.
10 Then *she that is* mine enemy shall see *it*, and shame shall cover her which
said unto me, Where is the LORD thy God? mine eyes shall behold her: now
shall she be trodden down as the mire of the streets.
11 *In* the day that thy walls are to be built, *in* that day shall the decree be far
removed.
12 *In* that day *also* he shall come even to thee from Assyria, and *from* the
fortified cities, and from the fortress even to the river, and from sea to sea, and
from mountain to mountain.
13 Notwithstanding the land shall be desolate because of them that dwell
therein, for the fruit of their doings.

God Comforts His People

14 Feed thy people with thy rod, the flock of thine heritage, which dwell
solitarily *in* the wood, in the midst of Carmel: let them feed *in* Bashan and
Gilead, as in the days of old.
15 According to the days of thy coming out of the land of Egypt will I shew
unto him marvellous *things*.
16 The nations shall see and be confounded at all their might: they shall lay
their hand upon *their* mouth, their ears shall be deaf.

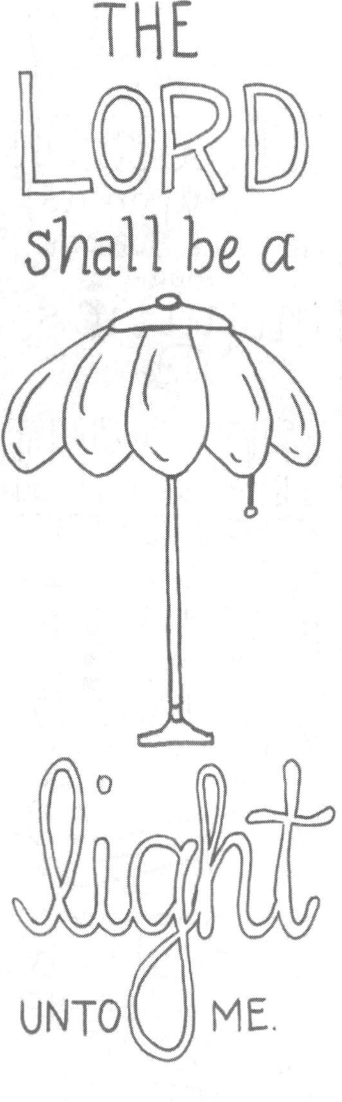

17 They shall lick the dust like a serpent, they shall move out of their holes
like worms of the earth: they shall be afraid of the LORD our God, and shall
fear because of thee.
18 Who *is* a God like unto thee, that pardoneth iniquity, and passeth by the
transgression of the remnant of his heritage? he retaineth not his anger for
ever, because he delighteth *in* mercy.
19 He will turn again, he will have compassion upon us; he will subdue our
iniquities; and thou wilt cast all their sins into the depths of the sea.
20 Thou wilt perform the truth to Jacob, *and* the mercy to Abraham, which
thou hast sworn unto our fathers from the days of old.

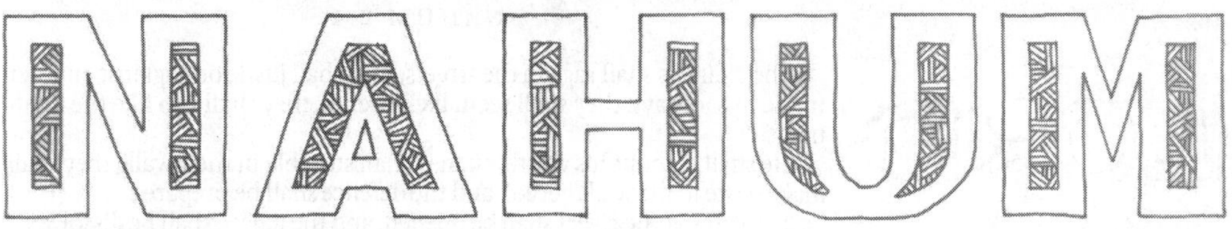

Who Can Withstand the Lord's Anger?

1 The burden of Nineveh. The book of the vision of Nahum the Elkoshite.
2 God *is* jealous, and the LORD revengeth; the LORD revengeth, and *is* furi-
ous; the LORD will take vengeance on his adversaries, and he reserveth *wrath*
for his enemies.
3 The LORD *is* slow to anger, and great in power, and will not at all acquit *the*
wicked: the LORD hath his way in the whirlwind and in the storm, and the
clouds *are* the dust of his feet.
4 He rebuketh the sea, and maketh it dry, and drieth up all the rivers: Bashan
languisheth, and Carmel, and the flower of Lebanon languisheth.
5 The mountains quake at him, and the hills melt, and the earth is burned
at his presence, yea, the world, and all that dwell therein.
6 Who can stand before his indignation? and who can abide in the fierceness
of his anger? his fury is poured out like fire, and the rocks are thrown down
by him.

Why Does Nineveh Oppose the Lord?

7 The LORD *is* good, a strong hold in the day of trouble; and he knoweth them
that trust in him.
8 But with an overrunning flood he will make an utter end of the place there-
of, and darkness shall pursue his enemies.
9 What do ye imagine against the LORD? he will make an utter end: affliction
shall not rise up the second time.
10 For while *they be* folden together *as* thorns, and while they are drunken
as drunkards, they shall be devoured as stubble fully dry.
11 There is *one* come out of thee, that imagineth evil against the LORD, a
wicked counsellor.

Nineveh Will Fall

12 Thus saith the LORD; Though *they be* quiet, and likewise many, yet thus
shall they be cut down, when he shall pass through. Though I have afflicted
thee, I will afflict thee no more.
13 For now will I break his yoke from off thee, and will burst thy bonds in
sunder.
14 And the LORD hath given a commandment concerning thee, *that* no more
of thy name be sown: out of the house of thy gods will I cut off the graven
image and the molten image: I will make thy grave; for thou art vile.
15 Behold upon the mountains the feet of him that bringeth good tidings,
that publisheth peace! O Judah, keep thy solemn feasts, perform thy vows: for
the wicked shall no more pass through thee; he is utterly cut off.

An Army Will Conquer Nineveh

2 He that dasheth in pieces is come up before thy face: keep the munition,
watch the way, make *thy* loins strong, fortify *thy* power mightily.
2 For the LORD hath turned away the excellency of Jacob, as the excellency of
Israel: for the emptiers have emptied them out, and marred their vine
branches.
3 The shield of his mighty men is made red, the valiant men *are* in scarlet:
the chariots *shall be* with flaming torches in the day of his preparation, and
the fir trees shall be terribly shaken.

4 The chariots shall rage in the streets, they shall justle one against another
in the broad ways: they shall seem like torches, they shall run like the light-
nings.
5 He shall recount his worthies: they shall stumble in their walk; they shall
make haste to the wall thereof, and the defence shall be prepared.
6 The gates of the rivers shall be opened, and the palace shall be dissolved.
7 And Huzzab shall be led away captive, she shall be brought up, and her
maids shall lead *her* as with the voice of doves, tabering upon their breasts.
8 But Nineveh *is* of old like a pool of water: yet they shall flee away. Stand,
stand, *shall they cry*; but none shall look back.
9 Take ye the spoil of silver, take the spoil of gold: for *there is* none end of the
store *and* glory out of all the pleasant furniture.
10 She is empty, and void, and waste: and the heart melteth, and the knees
smite together, and much pain *is* in all loins, and the faces of them all gather
blackness.
11 Where *is* the dwelling of the lions, and the feedingplace of the young lions,
where the lion, *even* the old lion, walked, *and* the lion's whelp, and none made
them afraid?
12 The lion did tear in pieces enough for his whelps, and strangled for his
lionesses, and filled his holes with prey, and his dens with ravin.
13 Behold, I *am* against thee, saith the LORD of hosts, and I will burn her
chariots in the smoke, and the sword shall devour thy young lions: and I will
cut off thy prey from the earth, and the voice of thy messengers shall no more
be heard.

The Miserable Ruin of Nineveh

3 Woe to the bloody city! it *is* all full of lies *and* robbery; the prey departeth
not;
2 The noise of a whip, and the noise of the rattling of the wheels, and of the
pransing horses, and of the jumping chariots.
3 The horseman lifteth up both the bright sword and the glittering spear:
and *there is* a multitude of slain, and a great number of carcases; and *there is*
none end of *their* corpses; they stumble upon their corpses:
4 Because of the multitude of the whoredoms of the wellfavoured harlot,
the mistress of witchcrafts, that selleth nations through her whoredoms, and
families through her witchcrafts.
5 Behold, I *am* against thee, saith the LORD of hosts; and I will discover thy
skirts upon thy face, and I will shew the nations thy nakedness, and the king-
doms thy shame.
6 And I will cast abominable filth upon thee, and make thee vile, and will set
thee as a gazingstock.
7 And it shall come to pass, *that* all they that look upon thee shall flee from
thee, and say, Nineveh is laid waste: who will bemoan her? whence shall I seek
comforters for thee?
8 Art thou better than populous No, that was situate among the rivers, *that
had* the waters round about it, whose rampart *was* the sea, *and* her wall *was*
from the sea?
9 Ethiopia and Egypt *were* her strength, and *it was* infinite; Put and Lubim
were thy helpers.
10 Yet *was* she carried away, she went into captivity: her young children also
were dashed in pieces at the top of all the streets: and they cast lots for her
honourable men, and all her great men were bound in chains.
11 Thou also shalt be drunken: thou shalt be hid, thou also shalt seek strength
because of the enemy.
12 All thy strong holds *shall be like* fig trees with the firstripe figs: if they be
shaken, they shall even fall into the mouth of the eater.

13 Behold, thy people in the midst of thee *are* women: the gates of thy land
shall be set wide open unto thine enemies: the fire shall devour thy bars.
14 Draw thee waters for the siege, fortify thy strong holds: go into clay, and
tread the morter, make strong the brickkiln.
15 There shall the fire devour thee; the sword shall cut thee off, it shall eat
thee up like the cankerworm: make thyself many as the cankerworm, make
thyself many as the locusts.
16 Thou hast multiplied thy merchants above the stars of heaven: the can-
kerworm spoileth, and flieth away.
17 Thy crowned *are* as the locusts, and thy captains as the great grasshoppers,
which camp in the hedges in the cold day, *but* when the sun ariseth they flee
away, and their place is not known where they *are*.
18 Thy shepherds slumber, O king of Assyria: thy nobles shall dwell *in the
dust*: thy people is scattered upon the mountains, and no man gathereth *them*.
19 *There is* no healing of thy bruise; thy wound is grievous: all that hear the
bruit of thee shall clap the hands over thee: for upon whom hath not thy
wickedness passed continually?

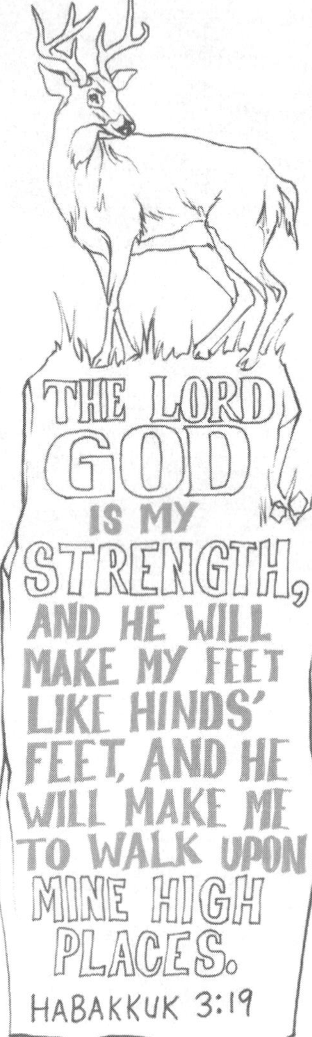

Habakkuk's Question

1 The burden which Habakkuk the prophet did see.
2 O LORD, how long shall I cry, and thou wilt not hear! *even* cry out unto
thee *of* violence, and thou wilt not save!
3 Why dost thou shew me iniquity, and cause *me* to behold grievance? for
spoiling and violence *are* before me: and there are *that* raise up strife and
contention.
4 Therefore the law is slacked, and judgment doth never go forth: for the
wicked doth compass about the righteous; therefore wrong judgment pro-
ceedeth.

The Lord's Answer

5 Behold ye among the heathen, and regard, and wonder marvellously: for
I will work a work in your days, *which* ye will not believe, though it be told *you*.
6 For, lo, I raise up the Chaldeans, *that* bitter and hasty nation, which shall
march through the breadth of the land, to possess the dwellingplaces *that are*
not theirs.
7 They *are* terrible and dreadful: their judgment and their dignity shall pro-
ceed of themselves.
8 Their horses also are swifter than the leopards, and are more fierce than
the evening wolves: and their horsemen shall spread themselves, and their
horsemen shall come from far; they shall fly as the eagle *that* hasteth to eat.
9 They shall come all for violence: their faces shall sup up *as* the east wind,
and they shall gather the captivity as the sand.
10 And they shall scoff at the kings, and the princes shall be a scorn unto
them: they shall deride every strong hold; for they shall heap dust, and take it.
11 Then shall *his* mind change, and he shall pass over, and offend, *imputing*
this his power unto his god.

Another Question from Habakkuk

12 *Art* thou not from everlasting, O LORD my God, mine Holy One? we shall
not die. O LORD, thou hast ordained them for judgment; and, O mighty God,
thou hast established them for correction.
13 *Thou art* of purer eyes than to behold evil, and canst not look on iniquity:
wherefore lookest thou upon them that deal treacherously, *and* holdest thy
tongue when the wicked devoureth *the man that is* more righteous than he?
14 And makest men as the fishes of the sea, as the creeping things, *that have*
no ruler over them?
15 They take up all of them with the angle, they catch them in their net, and
gather them in their drag: therefore they rejoice and are glad.
16 Therefore they sacrifice unto their net, and burn incense unto their drag;
because by them their portion *is* fat, and their meat plenteous.
17 Shall they therefore empty their net, and not spare continually to slay the
nations?

Habakkuk Awaits the Lord's Answer

2 I will stand upon my watch, and set me upon the tower, and will watch to
see what he will say unto me, and what I shall answer when I am reproved.

The Lord's Answer

2 And the LORD answered me, and said, Write the vision, and make *it* plain
upon tables, that he may run that readeth it.

3 For the vision *is* yet for an appointed time, but at the end it shall speak, and
not lie: though it tarry, wait for it; because it will surely come, it will not tarry.
4 Behold, his soul *which* is lifted up is not upright in him: but the just shall
live by his faith.
5 Yea also, because he transgresseth by wine, *he is* a proud man, neither
keepeth at home, who enlargeth his desire as hell, and *is* as death, and cannot
be satisfied, but gathereth unto him all nations, and heapeth unto him all
people:
6 Shall not all these take up a parable against him, and a taunting proverb
against him, and say, Woe to him that increaseth *that which is* not his! how
long? and to him that ladeth himself with thick clay!
7 Shall they not rise up suddenly that shall bite thee, and awake that shall
vex thee, and thou shalt be for booties unto them?
8 Because thou hast spoiled many nations, all the remnant of the people shall
spoil thee; because of men's blood, and *for* the violence of the land, of the city,
and of all that dwell therein.
9 Woe to him that coveteth an evil covetousness to his house, that he may set
his nest on high, that he may be delivered from the power of evil!
10 Thou hast consulted shame to thy house by cutting off many people, and
hast sinned *against* thy soul.
11 For the stone shall cry out of the wall, and the beam out of the timber shall
answer it.
12 Woe to him that buildeth a town with blood, and stablisheth a city by
iniquity!
13 Behold, *is it* not of the LORD of hosts that the people shall labour in the
very fire, and the people shall weary themselves for very vanity?
14 For the earth shall be filled with the knowledge of the glory of the LORD,
as the waters cover the sea.
15 Woe unto him that giveth his neighbour drink, that puttest thy bottle to
him, and makest *him* drunken also, that thou mayest look on their nakedness!
16 Thou art filled with shame for glory: drink thou also, and let thy foreskin
be uncovered: the cup of the LORD's right hand shall be turned unto thee, and
shameful spewing *shall be* on thy glory.
17 For the violence of Lebanon shall cover thee, and the spoil of beasts, *which*
made them afraid, because of men's blood, and for the violence of the land,
of the city, and of all that dwell therein.
18 What profiteth the graven image that the maker thereof hath graven it;
the molten image, and a teacher of lies, that the maker of his work trusteth
therein, to make dumb idols?
19 Woe unto him that saith to the wood, Awake; to the dumb stone, Arise, it
shall teach! Behold, it *is* laid over with gold and silver, and *there is* no breath
at all in the midst of it.
20 But the LORD *is* in his holy temple: let all the earth keep silence before him.

Habakkuk's Prayer

3 A prayer of Habakkuk the prophet upon Shigionoth.
2 O LORD, I have heard thy speech, *and* was afraid: O LORD, revive thy work
in the midst of the years, in the midst of the years make known; in wrath
remember mercy.
3 God came from Teman, and the Holy One from mount Paran. Selah. His
glory covered the heavens, and the earth was full of his praise.
4 And *his* brightness was as the light; he had horns *coming* out of his hand:
and there *was* the hiding of his power.
5 Before him went the pestilence, and burning coals went forth at his feet.

6 He stood, and measured the earth: he beheld, and drove asunder the
nations; and the everlasting mountains were scattered, the perpetual hills did
bow: his ways *are* everlasting.
7 I saw the tents of Cushan in affliction: *and* the curtains of the land of
Midian did tremble.
8 Was the LORD displeased against the rivers? *was* thine anger against the
rivers? *was* thy wrath against the sea, that thou didst ride upon thine horses
and thy chariots of salvation?
9 Thy bow was made quite naked, *according* to the oaths of the tribes, *even*
thy word. Selah. Thou didst cleave the earth with rivers.
10 The mountains saw thee, *and* they trembled: the overflowing of the water
passed by: the deep uttered his voice, *and* lifted up his hands on high.
11 The sun *and* moon stood still in their habitation: at the light of thine
arrows they went, *and* at the shining of thy glittering spear.
12 Thou didst march through the land in indignation, thou didst thresh the
heathen in anger.
13 Thou wentest forth for the salvation of thy people, *even* for salvation with
thine anointed; thou woundedst the head out of the house of the wicked, by
discovering the foundation unto the neck. Selah.
14 Thou didst strike through with his staves the head of his villages: they
came out as a whirlwind to scatter me: their rejoicing *was* as to devour the
poor secretly.
15 Thou didst walk through the sea with thine horses, *through* the heap of
great waters.
16 When I heard, my belly trembled; my lips quivered at the voice: rottenness
entered into my bones, and I trembled in myself, that I might rest in the day
of trouble: when he cometh up unto the people, he will invade them with his
troops.
17 Although the fig tree shall not blossom, neither *shall* fruit *be* in the vines;
the labour of the olive shall fail, and the fields shall yield no meat; the flock
shall be cut off from the fold, and *there shall be* no herd in the stalls:
18 Yet I will rejoice in the LORD, I will joy in the God of my salvation.
19 The LORD God *is* my strength, and he will make my feet like hinds' *feet*,
and he will make me to walk upon mine high places. To the chief singer on
my stringed instruments.

The Lord Will Judge the Earth

1 The word of the LORD which came unto Zephaniah the son of Cushi, the
son of Gedaliah, the son of Amariah, the son of Hizkiah, in the days of Josiah
the son of Amon, king of Judah.
2 I will utterly consume all *things* from off the land, saith the LORD.
3 I will consume man and beast; I will consume the fowls of the heaven, and
the fishes of the sea, and the stumblingblocks with the wicked; and I will cut
off man from off the land, saith the LORD.

The Lord Will Judge Judah

4 I will also stretch out mine hand upon Judah, and upon all the inhabitants
of Jerusalem; and I will cut off the remnant of Baal from this place, *and* the
name of the Chemarims with the priests;
5 And them that worship the host of heaven upon the housetops; and them
that worship *and* that swear by the LORD, and that swear by Malcham;
6 And them that are turned back from the LORD; and *those* that have not
sought the LORD, nor enquired for him.
7 Hold thy peace at the presence of the Lord GOD: for the day of the LORD *is*
at hand: for the LORD hath prepared a sacrifice, he hath bid his guests.
8 And it shall come to pass in the day of the LORD's sacrifice, that I will punish
the princes, and the king's children, and all such as are clothed with strange
apparel.
9 In the same day also will I punish all those that leap on the threshold, which
fill their masters' houses with violence and deceit.
10 And it shall come to pass in that day, saith the LORD, *that there shall be* the
noise of a cry from the fish gate, and an howling from the second, and a great
crashing from the hills.
11 Howl, ye inhabitants of Maktesh, for all the merchant people are cut down;
all they that bear silver are cut off.
12 And it shall come to pass at that time, *that* I will search Jerusalem with
candles, and punish the men that are settled on their lees: that say in their
heart, The LORD will not do good, neither will he do evil.
13 Therefore their goods shall become a booty, and their houses a desolation:
they shall also build houses, but not inhabit *them*; and they shall plant vine-
yards, but not drink the wine thereof.

The Day of the Lord

14 The great day of the LORD *is* near, *it is* near, and hasteth greatly, *even* the
voice of the day of the LORD: the mighty man shall cry there bitterly.
15 That day *is* a day of wrath, a day of trouble and distress, a day of wasteness
and desolation, a day of darkness and gloominess, a day of clouds and thick
darkness,
16 A day of the trumpet and alarm against the fenced cities, and against the
high towers.
17 And I will bring distress upon men, that they shall walk like blind men,
because they have sinned against the LORD: and their blood shall be poured
out as dust, and their flesh as the dung.
18 Neither their silver nor their gold shall be able to deliver them in the day
of the LORD's wrath; but the whole land shall be devoured by the fire of his

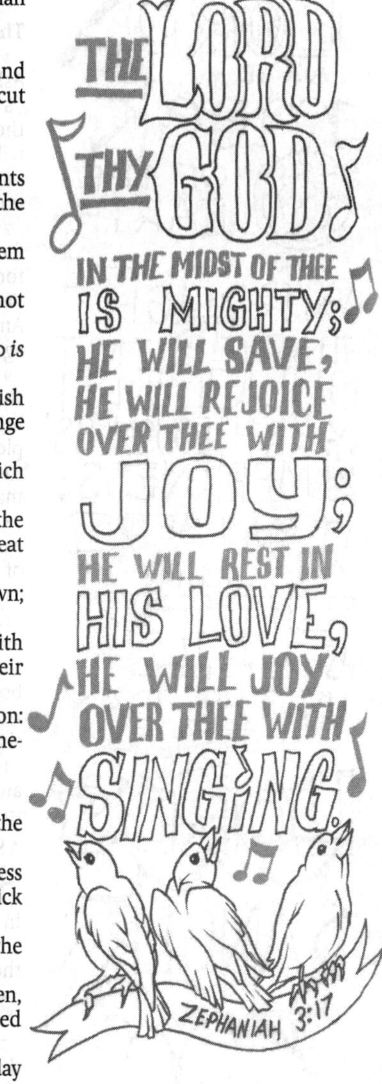

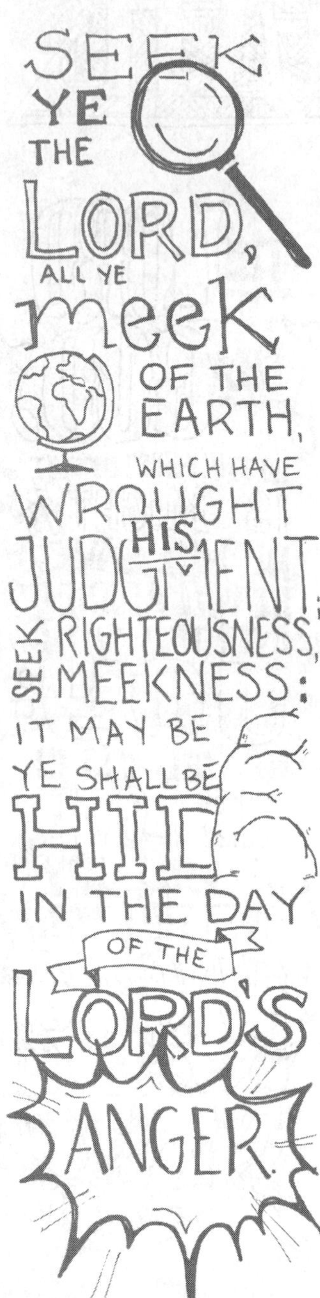

jealousy: for he shall make even a speedy riddance of all them that dwell in
the land.

An Exhortation to Repentance

2 Gather yourselves together, yea, gather together, O nation not desired;
2 Before the decree bring forth, *before* the day pass as the chaff, before
the fierce anger of the Lord come upon you, before the day of the Lord's anger
come upon you.
3 Seek ye the Lord, all ye meek of the earth, which have wrought his judg-
ment; seek righteousness, seek meekness: it may be ye shall be hid in the day
of the Lord's anger.

The Lord Will Judge His People's Enemies

4 For Gaza shall be forsaken, and Ashkelon a desolation: they shall drive out
Ashdod at the noon day, and Ekron shall be rooted up.
5 Woe unto the inhabitants of the sea coast, the nation of the Cherethites!
the word of the Lord *is* against you; O Canaan, the land of the Philistines, I
will even destroy thee, that there shall be no inhabitant.
6 And the sea coast shall be dwellings *and* cottages for shepherds, and folds
for flocks.
7 And the coast shall be for the remnant of the house of Judah; they shall
feed thereupon: in the houses of Ashkelon shall they lie down in the evening:
for the Lord their God shall visit them, and turn away their captivity.
8 I have heard the reproach of Moab, and the revilings of the children of
Ammon, whereby they have reproached my people, and magnified *themselves*
against their border.
9 Therefore *as* I live, saith the Lord of hosts, the God of Israel, Surely Moab
shall be as Sodom, and the children of Ammon as Gomorrah, *even* the breed-
ing of nettles, and saltpits, and a perpetual desolation: the residue of my peo-
ple shall spoil them, and the remnant of my people shall possess them.
10 This shall they have for their pride, because they have reproached and
magnified *themselves* against the people of the Lord of hosts.
11 The Lord *will be* terrible unto them: for he will famish all the gods of the
earth; and *men* shall worship him, every one from his place, *even* all the isles
of the heathen.
12 Ye Ethiopians also, ye *shall be* slain by my sword.
13 And he will stretch out his hand against the north, and destroy Assyria;
and will make Nineveh a desolation, *and* dry like a wilderness.
14 And flocks shall lie down in the midst of her, all the beasts of the nations:
both the cormorant and the bittern shall lodge in the upper lintels of it; *their*
voice shall sing in the windows; desolation *shall be* in the thresholds: for he
shall uncover the cedar work.
15 This *is* the rejoicing city that dwelt carelessly, that said in her heart, I *am*,
and *there is* none beside me: how is she become a desolation, a place for beasts
to lie down in! every one that passeth by her shall hiss, *and* wag his hand.

A Sharp Reproof for Jerusalem

3 Woe to her that is filthy and polluted, to the oppressing city!
2 She obeyed not the voice; she received not correction; she trusted not
in the Lord; she drew not near to her God.
3 Her princes within her *are* roaring lions; her judges *are* evening wolves;
they gnaw not the bones till the morrow.
4 Her prophets *are* light *and* treacherous persons: her priests have polluted
the sanctuary, they have done violence to the law.
5 The just Lord *is* in the midst thereof; he will not do iniquity: every morning
doth he bring his judgment to light, he faileth not; but the unjust knoweth no
shame.

6 I have cut off the nations: their towers are desolate; I made their streets
waste, that none passeth by: their cities are destroyed, so that there is no man,
that there is none inhabitant.
7 I said, Surely thou wilt fear me, thou wilt receive instruction; so their dwell-
ing should not be cut off, howsoever I punished them: but they rose early, *and*
corrupted all their doings.

Wait for Israel's Restoration

8 Therefore wait ye upon me, saith the LORD, until the day that I rise up to
the prey: for my determination *is* to gather the nations, that I may assemble
the kingdoms, to pour upon them mine indignation, *even* all my fierce anger:
for all the earth shall be devoured with the fire of my jealousy.
9 For then will I turn to the people a pure language, that they may all call
upon the name of the LORD, to serve him with one consent.
10 From beyond the rivers of Ethiopia my suppliants, *even* the daughter of
my dispersed, shall bring mine offering.
11 In that day shalt thou not be ashamed for all thy doings, wherein thou
hast transgressed against me: for then I will take away out of the midst of thee
them that rejoice in thy pride, and thou shalt no more be haughty because of
my holy mountain.
12 I will also leave in the midst of thee an afflicted and poor people, and they
shall trust in the name of the LORD.
13 The remnant of Israel shall not do iniquity, nor speak lies; neither shall a
deceitful tongue be found in their mouth: for they shall feed and lie down,
and none shall make *them* afraid.

Rejoice at the People's Salvation

14 Sing, O daughter of Zion; shout, O Israel; be glad and rejoice with all the
heart, O daughter of Jerusalem.
15 The LORD hath taken away thy judgments, he hath cast out thine enemy:
the king of Israel, *even* the LORD, *is* in the midst of thee: thou shalt not see evil
any more.
16 In that day it shall be said to Jerusalem, Fear thou not: *and to* Zion, Let not
thine hands be slack.
17 The LORD thy God in the midst of thee *is* mighty; he will save, he will rejoice
over thee with joy; he will rest in his love, he will joy over thee with singing.
18 I will gather *them that are* sorrowful for the solemn assembly, *who* are of
thee, *to whom* the reproach of it *was* a burden.
19 Behold, at that time I will undo all that afflict thee: and I will save her that
halteth, and gather her that was driven out; and I will get them praise and
fame in every land where they have been put to shame.
20 At that time will I bring you *again*, even in the time that I gather you: for
I will make you a name and a praise among all people of the earth, when I turn
back your captivity before your eyes, saith the LORD.

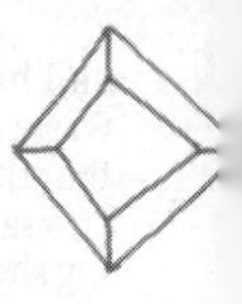

A Call to Rebuild the Lord's House

1 In the second year of Darius the king, in the sixth month, in the first day of the month, came the word of the LORD by Haggai the prophet unto Zerubbabel the son of Shealtiel, governor of Judah, and to Joshua the son of Josedech, the high priest, saying,

2 Thus speaketh the LORD of hosts, saying, This people say, The time is not come, the time that the LORD's house should be built.

3 Then came the word of the LORD by Haggai the prophet, saying,

4 *Is it* time for you, O ye, to dwell in your cieled houses, and this house *lie* waste?

5 Now therefore thus saith the LORD of hosts; Consider your ways.

6 Ye have sown much, and bring in little; ye eat, but ye have not enough; ye drink, but ye are not filled with drink; ye clothe you, but there is none warm; and he that earneth wages earneth wages *to put it* into a bag with holes.

7 Thus saith the LORD of hosts; Consider your ways.

8 Go up to the mountain, and bring wood, and build the house; and I will take pleasure in it, and I will be glorified, saith the LORD.

9 Ye looked for much, and, lo, *it came* to little; and when ye brought *it* home, I did blow upon it. Why? saith the LORD of hosts. Because of mine house that *is* waste, and ye run every man unto his own house.

10 Therefore the heaven over you is stayed from dew, and the earth is stayed *from* her fruit.

11 And I called for a drought upon the land, and upon the mountains, and upon the corn, and upon the new wine, and upon the oil, and upon *that* which the ground bringeth forth, and upon men, and upon cattle, and upon all the labour of the hands.

The Work on God's House Resumes

12 Then Zerubbabel the son of Shealtiel, and Joshua the son of Josedech, the high priest, with all the remnant of the people, obeyed the voice of the LORD their God, and the words of Haggai the prophet, as the LORD their God had sent him, and the people did fear before the LORD.

13 Then spake Haggai the LORD's messenger in the LORD's message unto the people, saying, I *am* with you, saith the LORD.

14 And the LORD stirred up the spirit of Zerubbabel the son of Shealtiel, governor of Judah, and the spirit of Joshua the son of Josedech, the high priest, and the spirit of all the remnant of the people; and they came and did work in the house of the LORD of hosts, their God,

15 In the four and twentieth day of the sixth month, in the second year of Darius the king.

Greater Glory for the Second Temple

2 In the seventh *month*, in the one and twentieth *day* of the month, came the word of the LORD by the prophet Haggai, saying,

2 Speak now to Zerubbabel the son of Shealtiel, governor of Judah, and to Joshua the son of Josedech, the high priest, and to the residue of the people, saying,

3 Who *is* left among you that saw this house in her first glory? and how do ye see it now? *is it* not in your eyes in comparison of it as nothing?

4 Yet now be strong, O Zerubbabel, saith the LORD; and be strong, O Joshua,
son of Josedech, the high priest; and be strong, all ye people of the land, saith
the LORD, and work: for I *am* with you, saith the LORD of hosts:
5 *According to* the word that I covenanted with you when ye came out of
Egypt, so my spirit remaineth among you: fear ye not.
6 For thus saith the LORD of hosts; Yet once, it *is* a little while, and I will shake
the heavens, and the earth, and the sea, and the dry *land*;
7 And I will shake all nations, and the desire of all nations shall come: and I
will fill this house with glory, saith the LORD of hosts.
8 The silver *is* mine, and the gold *is* mine, saith the LORD of hosts.
9 The glory of this latter house shall be greater than of the former, saith the
LORD of hosts: and in this place will I give peace, saith the LORD of hosts.

The Lord Will Bless

10 In the four and twentieth *day* of the ninth *month*, in the second year of
Darius, came the word of the LORD by Haggai the prophet, saying,
11 Thus saith the LORD of hosts; Ask now the priests *concerning* the law, saying,
12 If one bear holy flesh in the skirt of his garment, and with his skirt do
touch bread, or pottage, or wine, or oil, or any meat, shall it be holy? And the
priests answered and said, No.
13 Then said Haggai, If *one that is* unclean by a dead body touch any of these,
shall it be unclean? And the priests answered and said, It shall be unclean.
14 Then answered Haggai, and said, So *is* this people, and so *is* this nation
before me, saith the LORD; and so *is* every work of their hands; and that which
they offer there *is* unclean.
15 And now, I pray you, consider from this day and upward, from before a
stone was laid upon a stone in the temple of the LORD:
16 Since those *days* were, when *one* came to an heap of twenty *measures*,
there were *but* ten: when *one* came to the pressfat for to draw out fifty *vessels*
out of the press, there were *but* twenty.
17 I smote you with blasting and with mildew and with hail in all the labours
of your hands; yet ye *turned* not to me, saith the LORD.
18 Consider now from this day and upward, from the four and twentieth
day of the ninth *month, even* from the day that the foundation of the LORD's
temple was laid, consider *it*.
19 Is the seed yet in the barn? yea, as yet the vine, and the fig tree, and the
pomegranate, and the olive tree, hath not brought forth: from this day will I
bless *you*.

God's Promise to Zerubbabel

20 And again the word of the LORD came unto Haggai in the four and twen-
tieth *day* of the month, saying,
21 Speak to Zerubbabel, governor of Judah, saying, I will shake the heavens
and the earth;
22 And I will overthrow the throne of kingdoms, and I will destroy the
strength of the kingdoms of the heathen; and I will overthrow the chariots,
and those that ride in them; and the horses and their riders shall come down,
every one by the sword of his brother.
23 In that day, saith the LORD of hosts, will I take thee, O Zerubbabel, my
servant, the son of Shealtiel, saith the LORD, and will make thee as a signet: for
I have chosen thee, saith the LORD of hosts.

Zechariah Exhorts the Jews to Repent

1 In the eighth month, in the second year of Darius, came the word of the
LORD unto Zechariah, the son of Berechiah, the son of Iddo the prophet,
saying,
2 The LORD hath been sore displeased with your fathers.
3 Therefore say thou unto them, Thus saith the LORD of hosts; Turn ye unto
me, saith the LORD of hosts, and I will turn unto you, saith the LORD of hosts.
4 Be ye not as your fathers, unto whom the former prophets have cried,
saying, Thus saith the LORD of hosts; Turn ye now from your evil ways, and
from your evil doings: but they did not hear, nor hearken unto me, saith the
LORD.
5 Your fathers, where *are* they? and the prophets, do they live for ever?
6 But my words and my statutes, which I commanded my servants the proph-
ets, did they not take hold of your fathers? and they returned and said, Like
as the LORD of hosts thought to do unto us, according to our ways, and accord-
ing to our doings, so hath he dealt with us.

The Vision of the Horses

7 Upon the four and twentieth day of the eleventh month, which *is* the
month Sebat, in the second year of Darius, came the word of the LORD unto
Zechariah, the son of Berechiah, the son of Iddo the prophet, saying,
8 I saw by night, and behold a man riding upon a red horse, and he stood
among the myrtle trees that *were* in the bottom; and behind him *were there*
red horses, speckled, and white.
9 Then said I, O my lord, what *are* these? And the angel that talked with me
said unto me, I will shew thee what these *be*.
10 And the man that stood among the myrtle trees answered and said, These
are they whom the LORD hath sent to walk to and fro through the earth.
11 And they answered the angel of the LORD that stood among the myrtle
trees, and said, We have walked to and fro through the earth, and, behold, all
the earth sitteth still, and is at rest.
12 Then the angel of the LORD answered and said, O LORD of hosts, how long
wilt thou not have mercy on Jerusalem and on the cities of Judah, against
which thou hast had indignation these threescore and ten years?
13 And the LORD answered the angel that talked with me *with* good words
and comfortable words.
14 So the angel that communed with me said unto me, Cry thou, saying, Thus
saith the LORD of hosts; I am jealous for Jerusalem and for Zion with a great
jealousy.
15 And I am very sore displeased with the heathen *that are* at ease: for I was
but a little displeased, and they helped forward the affliction.
16 Therefore thus saith the LORD; I am returned to Jerusalem with mercies:
my house shall be built in it, saith the LORD of hosts, and a line shall be
stretched forth upon Jerusalem.
17 Cry yet, saying, Thus saith the LORD of hosts; My cities through prosperi-
ty shall yet be spread abroad; and the LORD shall yet comfort Zion, and shall
yet choose Jerusalem.

The Vision of the Four Horns and the Four Smiths

18 Then lifted I up mine eyes, and saw, and behold four horns.
19 And I said unto the angel that talked with me, What *be* these? And he
answered me, These *are* the horns which have scattered Judah, Israel, and
Jerusalem.
20 And the LORD shewed me four carpenters.
21 Then said I, What come these to do? And he spake, saying, These *are* the
horns which have scattered Judah, so that no man did lift up his head: but
these are come to fray them, to cast out the horns of the Gentiles, which lifted
up *their* horn over the land of Judah to scatter it.

The Lord Will Choose Jerusalem

2 I lifted up mine eyes again, and looked, and behold a man with a measuring
line in his hand.
2 Then said I, Whither goest thou? And he said unto me, To measure
Jerusalem, to see what *is* the breadth thereof, and what *is* the length thereof.
3 And, behold, the angel that talked with me went forth, and another angel
went out to meet him,
4 And said unto him, Run, speak to this young man, saying, Jerusalem shall
be inhabited *as* towns without walls for the multitude of men and cattle
therein:
5 For I, saith the LORD, will be unto her a wall of fire round about, and will
be the glory in the midst of her.
6 Ho, ho, *come forth*, and flee from the land of the north, saith the LORD: for
I have spread you abroad as the four winds of the heaven, saith the LORD.
7 Deliver thyself, O Zion, that dwellest *with* the daughter of Babylon.
8 For thus saith the LORD of hosts; After the glory hath he sent me unto the
nations which spoiled you: for he that toucheth you toucheth the apple of his
eye.
9 For, behold, I will shake mine hand upon them, and they shall be a spoil to
their servants: and ye shall know that the LORD of hosts hath sent me.
10 Sing and rejoice, O daughter of Zion: for, lo, I come, and I will dwell in the
midst of thee, saith the LORD.
11 And many nations shall be joined to the LORD in that day, and shall be my
people: and I will dwell in the midst of thee, and thou shalt know that the LORD
of hosts hath sent me unto thee.
12 And the LORD shall inherit Judah his portion in the holy land, and shall
choose Jerusalem again.
13 Be silent, O all flesh, before the LORD: for he is raised up out of his holy
habitation.

The Lord Will Send His Servant

3 And he shewed me Joshua the high priest standing before the angel of the
LORD, and Satan standing at his right hand to resist him.
2 And the LORD said unto Satan, The LORD rebuke thee, O Satan; even the LORD
that hath chosen Jerusalem rebuke thee: *is* not this a brand plucked out of the
fire?
3 Now Joshua was clothed with filthy garments, and stood before the angel.
4 And he answered and spake unto those that stood before him, saying, Take
away the filthy garments from him. And unto him he said, Behold, I have
caused thine iniquity to pass from thee, and I will clothe thee with change of
raiment.
5 And I said, Let them set a fair mitre upon his head. So they set a fair mitre
upon his head, and clothed him with garments. And the angel of the LORD
stood by.
6 And the angel of the LORD protested unto Joshua, saying,

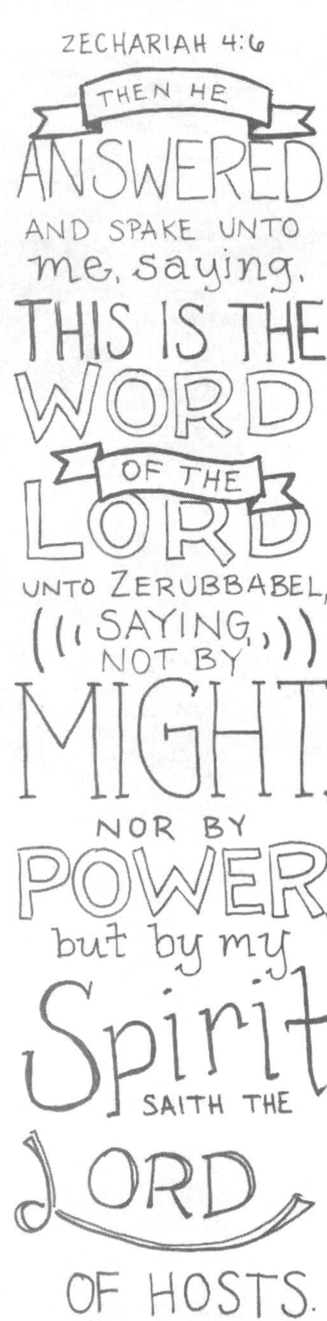

7 Thus saith the LORD of hosts; If thou wilt walk in my ways, and if thou wilt
keep my charge, then thou shalt also judge my house, and shalt also keep my
courts, and I will give thee places to walk among these that stand by.
8 Hear now, O Joshua the high priest, thou, and thy fellows that sit before
thee: for they *are* men wondered at: for, behold, I will bring forth my servant
the BRANCH.
9 For behold the stone that I have laid before Joshua; upon one stone *shall
be* seven eyes: behold, I will engrave the graving thereof, saith the LORD of hosts,
and I will remove the iniquity of that land in one day.
10 In that day, saith the LORD of hosts, shall ye call every man his neighbour
under the vine and under the fig tree.

The Lord's House Will Be Rebuilt

4 And the angel that talked with me came again, and waked me, as a man that
is wakened out of his sleep,
2 And said unto me, What seest thou? And I said, I have looked, and behold
a candlestick all *of* gold, with a bowl upon the top of it, and his seven lamps
thereon, and seven pipes to the seven lamps, which *are* upon the top thereof:
3 And two olive trees by it, one upon the right *side* of the bowl, and the other
upon the left *side* thereof.
4 So I answered and spake to the angel that talked with me, saying, What *are*
these, my lord?
5 Then the angel that talked with me answered and said unto me, Knowest
thou not what these be? And I said, No, my lord.
6 Then he answered and spake unto me, saying, This *is* the word of the LORD
unto Zerubbabel, saying, Not by might, nor by power, but by my spirit, saith
the LORD of hosts.
7 Who *art* thou, O great mountain? before Zerubbabel *thou shalt become* a
plain: and he shall bring forth the headstone *thereof with* shoutings, *crying*,
Grace, grace unto it.
8 Moreover the word of the LORD came unto me, saying,
9 The hands of Zerubbabel have laid the foundation of this house; his hands
shall also finish it; and thou shalt know that the LORD of hosts hath sent me
unto you.
10 For who hath despised the day of small things? for they shall rejoice, and
shall see the plummet in the hand of Zerubbabel *with* those seven; they *are*
the eyes of the LORD, which run to and fro through the whole earth.
11 Then answered I, and said unto him, What *are* these two olive trees upon
the right *side* of the candlestick and upon the left *side* thereof?
12 And I answered again, and said unto him, What *be these* two olive branch-
es which through the two golden pipes empty the golden *oil* out of themselves?
13 And he answered me and said, Knowest thou not what these *be*? And I
said, No, my lord.
14 Then said he, These *are* the two anointed ones, that stand by the Lord of
the whole earth.

Visions of a Flying Scroll

5 Then I turned, and lifted up mine eyes, and looked, and behold a flying roll.
2 And he said unto me, What seest thou? And I answered, I see a flying
roll; the length thereof *is* twenty cubits, and the breadth thereof ten cubits.
3 Then said he unto me, This *is* the curse that goeth forth over the face of the
whole earth: for every one that stealeth shall be cut off *as* on this side accord-
ing to it; and every one that sweareth shall be cut off *as* on that side according
to it.
4 I will bring it forth, saith the LORD of hosts, and it shall enter into the house
of the thief, and into the house of him that sweareth falsely by my name: and

it shall remain in the midst of his house, and shall consume it with the timber
thereof and the stones thereof.

Vision of a Woman in a Basket

5 Then the angel that talked with me went forth, and said unto me, Lift up
now thine eyes, and see what *is* this that goeth forth.
6 And I said, What *is* it? And he said, This *is* an ephah that goeth forth. He
said moreover, This *is* their resemblance through all the earth.
7 And, behold, there was lifted up a talent of lead: and this *is* a woman that
sitteth in the midst of the ephah.
8 And he said, This *is* wickedness. And he cast it into the midst of the ephah;
and he cast the weight of lead upon the mouth thereof.
9 Then lifted I up mine eyes, and looked, and, behold, there came out two
women, and the wind *was* in their wings; for they had wings like the wings of
a stork: and they lifted up the ephah between the earth and the heaven.
10 Then said I to the angel that talked with me, Whither do these bear the
ephah?
11 And he said unto me, To build it an house in the land of Shinar: and it shall
be established, and set there upon her own base.

The Vision of the Four Chariots

6 And I turned, and lifted up mine eyes, and looked, and, behold, there came
four chariots out from between two mountains; and the mountains *were*
mountains of brass.
2 In the first chariot *were* red horses; and in the second chariot black horses;
3 And in the third chariot white horses; and in the fourth chariot grisled and
bay horses.
4 Then I answered and said unto the angel that talked with me, What *are*
these, my lord?
5 And the angel answered and said unto me, These *are* the four spirits of the
heavens, which go forth from standing before the Lord of all the earth.
6 The black horses which *are* therein go forth into the north country; and
the white go forth after them; and the grisled go forth toward the south
country.
7 And the bay went forth, and sought to go that they might walk to and fro
through the earth: and he said, Get you hence, walk to and fro through the
earth. So they walked to and fro through the earth.
8 Then cried he upon me, and spake unto me, saying, Behold, these that go
toward the north country have quieted my spirit in the north country.

Priest and King

9 And the word of the LORD came unto me, saying,
10 Take of *them of* the captivity, *even* of Heldai, of Tobijah, and of Jedaiah,
which are come from Babylon, and come thou the same day, and go into the
house of Josiah the son of Zephaniah;
11 Then take silver and gold, and make crowns, and set *them* upon the head
of Joshua the son of Josedech, the high priest;
12 And speak unto him, saying, Thus speaketh the LORD of hosts, saying,
Behold the man whose name *is* The BRANCH; and he shall grow up out of his
place, and he shall build the temple of the LORD:
13 Even he shall build the temple of the LORD; and he shall bear the glory,
and shall sit and rule upon his throne; and he shall be a priest upon his throne:
and the counsel of peace shall be between them both.
14 And the crowns shall be to Helem, and to Tobijah, and to Jedaiah, and to
Hen the son of Zephaniah, for a memorial in the temple of the LORD.
15 And they *that are* far off shall come and build in the temple of the LORD,
and ye shall know that the LORD of hosts hath sent me unto you. And *this* shall
come to pass, if ye will diligently obey the voice of the LORD your God.

SHEW
mercy
&
compassions
every
MAN
TO HIS
brother.

ZECHARIAH 7:9

The Words of the Lord's Prophets

7 And it came to pass in the fourth year of king Darius, *that* the word of the LORD came unto Zechariah in the fourth *day* of the ninth month, *even* in Chisleu;

2 When they had sent unto the house of God Sherezer and Regemmelech, and their men, to pray before the LORD,

3 *And* to speak unto the priests which *were* in the house of the LORD of hosts, and to the prophets, saying, Should I weep in the fifth month, separating myself, as I have done these so many years?

4 Then came the word of the LORD of hosts unto me, saying,

5 Speak unto all the people of the land, and to the priests, saying, When ye fasted and mourned in the fifth and seventh *month*, even those seventy years, did ye at all fast unto me, *even* to me?

6 And when ye did eat, and when ye did drink, did not ye eat *for yourselves*, and drink *for yourselves*?

7 *Should ye* not *hear* the words which the LORD hath cried by the former prophets, when Jerusalem was inhabited and in prosperity, and the cities thereof round about her, when *men* inhabited the south and the plain?

The Cause of Captivity

8 And the word of the LORD came unto Zechariah, saying,

9 Thus speaketh the LORD of hosts, saying, Execute true judgment, and shew mercy and compassions every man to his brother:

10 And oppress not the widow, nor the fatherless, the stranger, nor the poor; and let none of you imagine evil against his brother in your heart.

11 But they refused to hearken, and pulled away the shoulder, and stopped their ears, that they should not hear.

12 Yea, they made their hearts *as* an adamant stone, lest they should hear the law, and the words which the LORD of hosts hath sent in his spirit by the former prophets: therefore came a great wrath from the LORD of hosts.

13 Therefore it is come to pass, *that* as he cried, and they would not hear; so they cried, and I would not hear, saith the LORD of hosts:

14 But I scattered them with a whirlwind among all the nations whom they knew not. Thus the land was desolate after them, that no man passed through nor returned: for they laid the pleasant land desolate.

The Restoration of Jerusalem

8 Again the word of the LORD of hosts came *to me*, saying,

2 Thus saith the LORD of hosts; I was jealous for Zion with great jealousy, and I was jealous for her with great fury.

3 Thus saith the LORD; I am returned unto Zion, and will dwell in the midst of Jerusalem: and Jerusalem shall be called a city of truth; and the mountain of the LORD of hosts the holy mountain.

4 Thus saith the LORD of hosts; There shall yet old men and old women dwell in the streets of Jerusalem, and every man with his staff in his hand for very age.

5 And the streets of the city shall be full of boys and girls playing in the streets thereof.

6 Thus saith the LORD of hosts; If it be marvellous in the eyes of the remnant of this people in these days, should it also be marvellous in mine eyes? saith the LORD of hosts.

7 Thus saith the LORD of hosts; Behold, I will save my people from the east country, and from the west country;

8 And I will bring them, and they shall dwell in the midst of Jerusalem: and they shall be my people, and I will be their God, in truth and in righteousness.

The Jews Are Encouraged to Build

9 Thus saith the LORD of hosts; Let your hands be strong, ye that hear in these
days these words by the mouth of the prophets, which *were* in the day *that* the
foundation of the house of the LORD of hosts was laid, that the temple might
be built.
10 For before these days there was no hire for man, nor any hire for beast;
neither *was there any* peace to him that went out or came in because of the
affliction: for I set all men every one against his neighbour.
11 But now I *will* not *be* unto the residue of this people as in the former days,
saith the LORD of hosts.
12 For the seed *shall be* prosperous; the vine shall give her fruit, and the
ground shall give her increase, and the heavens shall give their dew; and I will
cause the remnant of this people to possess all these *things*.
13 And it shall come to pass, *that* as ye were a curse among the heathen, O
house of Judah, and house of Israel; so will I save you, and ye shall be a blessing:
fear not, *but* let your hands be strong.
14 For thus saith the LORD of hosts; As I thought to punish you, when your
fathers provoked me to wrath, saith the LORD of hosts, and I repented not:
15 So again have I thought in these days to do well unto Jerusalem and to the
house of Judah: fear ye not.
16 These *are* the things that ye shall do; Speak ye every man the truth to his
neighbour; execute the judgment of truth and peace in your gates:
17 And let none of you imagine evil in your hearts against his neighbour; and
love no false oath: for all these *are things* that I hate, saith the LORD.

Many Nations Will Come

18 And the word of the LORD of hosts came unto me, saying,
19 Thus saith the LORD of hosts; The fast of the fourth *month*, and the fast of
the fifth, and the fast of the seventh, and the fast of the tenth, shall be to the
house of Judah joy and gladness, and cheerful feasts; therefore love the truth
and peace.
20 Thus saith the LORD of hosts; *It shall* yet *come to pass*, that there shall come
people, and the inhabitants of many cities:
21 And the inhabitants of one *city* shall go to another, saying, Let us go speed-
ily to pray before the LORD, and to seek the LORD of hosts: I will go also.
22 Yea, many people and strong nations shall come to seek the LORD of hosts
in Jerusalem, and to pray before the LORD.
23 Thus saith the LORD of hosts; In those days *it shall come to pass*, that ten
men shall take hold out of all languages of the nations, even shall take hold of
the skirt of him that is a Jew, saying, We will go with you: for we have heard
that God *is* with you.

The Lord Protects His House

9 The burden of the word of the LORD in the land of Hadrach, and Damascus
shall be the rest thereof: when the eyes of man, as of all the tribes of Israel,
shall be toward the LORD.
2 And Hamath also shall border thereby; Tyrus, and Zidon, though it be very
wise.
3 And Tyrus did build herself a strong hold, and heaped up silver as the dust,
and fine gold as the mire of the streets.
4 Behold, the Lord will cast her out, and he will smite her power in the sea;
and she shall be devoured with fire.
5 Ashkelon shall see *it*, and fear; Gaza also *shall see it*, and be very sorrowful,
and Ekron; for her expectation shall be ashamed; and the king shall perish
from Gaza, and Ashkelon shall not be inhabited.
6 And a bastard shall dwell in Ashdod, and I will cut off the pride of the
Philistines.

7 And I will take away his blood out of his mouth, and his abominations from
between his teeth: but he that remaineth, even he, *shall be* for our God, and
he shall be as a governor in Judah, and Ekron as a Jebusite.
8 And I will encamp about mine house because of the army, because of him
that passeth by, and because of him that returneth: and no oppressor shall
pass through them any more: for now have I seen with mine eyes.

The Lord Sends His King

9 Rejoice greatly, O daughter of Zion; shout, O daughter of Jerusalem: behold,
thy King cometh unto thee: he *is* just, and having salvation; lowly, and riding
upon an ass, and upon a colt the foal of an ass.
10 And I will cut off the chariot from Ephraim, and the horse from Jerusalem,
and the battle bow shall be cut off: and he shall speak peace unto the heathen:
and his dominion *shall be* from sea *even* to sea, and from the river *even* to the
ends of the earth.
11 As for thee also, by the blood of thy covenant I have sent forth thy prison-
ers out of the pit wherein *is* no water.

God Promises Victory and Defense

12 Turn you to the strong hold, ye prisoners of hope: even to day do I declare
that I will render double unto thee;
13 When I have bent Judah for me, filled the bow with Ephraim, and raised
up thy sons, O Zion, against thy sons, O Greece, and made thee as the sword
of a mighty man.
14 And the LORD shall be seen over them, and his arrow shall go forth as the
lightning: and the Lord GOD shall blow the trumpet, and shall go with whirl-
winds of the south.
15 The LORD of hosts shall defend them; and they shall devour, and subdue
with sling stones; and they shall drink, *and* make a noise as through wine; and
they shall be filled like bowls, *and* as the corners of the altar.
16 And the LORD their God shall save them in that day as the flock of his
people: for *they shall be as* the stones of a crown, lifted up as an ensign upon
his land.
17 For how great *is* his goodness, and how great *is* his beauty! corn shall make
the young men cheerful, and new wine the maids.

The Lord's People Will Be Victorious

10 Ask ye of the LORD rain in the time of the latter rain; *so* the LORD shall
make bright clouds, and give them showers of rain, to every one grass
in the field.
2 For the idols have spoken vanity, and the diviners have seen a lie, and have
told false dreams; they comfort in vain: therefore they went their way as a
flock, they were troubled, because *there was* no shepherd.
3 Mine anger was kindled against the shepherds, and I punished the goats:
for the LORD of hosts hath visited his flock the house of Judah, and hath made
them as his goodly horse in the battle.
4 Out of him came forth the corner, out of him the nail, out of him the
battle bow, out of him every oppressor together.
5 And they shall be as mighty *men*, which tread down *their enemies* in the
mire of the streets in the battle: and they shall fight, because the LORD *is* with
them, and the riders on horses shall be confounded.
6 And I will strengthen the house of Judah, and I will save the house of Joseph,
and I will bring them again to place them; for I have mercy upon them: and
they shall be as though I had not cast them off: for I *am* the LORD their God,
and will hear them.
7 And *they of* Ephraim shall be like a mighty *man*, and their heart shall rejoice
as through wine: yea, their children shall see *it*, and be glad; their heart shall
rejoice in the LORD.

8 I will hiss for them, and gather them; for I have redeemed them: and they
shall increase as they have increased.
9 And I will sow them among the people: and they shall remember me in far
countries; and they shall live with their children, and turn again.
10 I will bring them again also out of the land of Egypt, and gather them out
of Assyria; and I will bring them into the land of Gilead and Lebanon; and
place shall not be found for them.
11 And he shall pass through the sea with affliction, and shall smite the waves
in the sea, and all the deeps of the river shall dry up: and the pride of Assyria
shall be brought down, and the sceptre of Egypt shall depart away.
12 And I will strengthen them in the LORD; and they shall walk up and down
in his name, saith the LORD.

Zechariah to Care for the Sheep

11 Open thy doors, O Lebanon, that the fire may devour thy cedars.
2 Howl, fir tree; for the cedar is fallen; because the mighty are spoiled:
howl, O ye oaks of Bashan; for the forest of the vintage is come down.
3 *There is* a voice of the howling of the shepherds; for their glory is spoiled:
a voice of the roaring of young lions; for the pride of Jordan is spoiled.
4 Thus saith the LORD my God; Feed the flock of the slaughter;
5 Whose possessors slay them, and hold themselves not guilty: and they that
sell them say, Blessed *be* the LORD; for I am rich: and their own shepherds pity
them not.
6 For I will no more pity the inhabitants of the land, saith the LORD: but, lo,
I will deliver the men every one into his neighbour's hand, and into the hand
of his king: and they shall smite the land, and out of their hand I will not
deliver *them*.
7 And I will feed the flock of slaughter, *even* you, O poor of the flock. And I
took unto me two staves; the one I called Beauty, and the other I called Bands;
and I fed the flock.
8 Three shepherds also I cut off in one month; and my soul lothed them, and
their soul also abhorred me.
9 Then said I, I will not feed you: that that dieth, let it die; and that that is to
be cut off, let it be cut off; and let the rest eat every one the flesh of another.
10 And I took my staff, *even* Beauty, and cut it asunder, that I might break my
covenant which I had made with all the people.
11 And it was broken in that day: and so the poor of the flock that waited
upon me knew that it *was* the word of the LORD.
12 And I said unto them, If ye think good, give *me* my price; and if not, forbear.
So they weighed for my price thirty *pieces* of silver.
13 And the LORD said unto me, Cast it unto the potter: a goodly price that I
was prised at of them. And I took the thirty *pieces* of silver, and cast them to
the potter in the house of the LORD.
14 Then I cut asunder mine other staff, *even* Bands, that I might break the
brotherhood between Judah and Israel.

The Example and Curse of a Foolish Shepherd

15 And the LORD said unto me, Take unto thee yet the instruments of a fool-
ish shepherd.
16 For, lo, I will raise up a shepherd in the land, *which* shall not visit those
that be cut off, neither shall seek the young one, nor heal that that is broken,
nor feed that that standeth still: but he shall eat the flesh of the fat, and tear
their claws in pieces.
17 Woe to the idol shepherd that leaveth the flock! the sword *shall be* upon
his arm, and upon his right eye: his arm shall be clean dried up, and his right
eye shall be utterly darkened.

The Cup of Trembling

12 The burden of the word of the LORD for Israel, saith the LORD, which
stretcheth forth the heavens, and layeth the foundation of the earth,
and formeth the spirit of man within him.
2 Behold, I will make Jerusalem a cup of trembling unto all the people round
about, when they shall be in the siege both against Judah *and* against
Jerusalem.
3 And in that day will I make Jerusalem a burdensome stone for all people:
all that burden themselves with it shall be cut in pieces, though all the people
of the earth be gathered together against it.
4 In that day, saith the LORD, I will smite every horse with astonishment, and
his rider with madness: and I will open mine eyes upon the house of Judah,
and will smite every horse of the people with blindness.
5 And the governors of Judah shall say in their heart, The inhabitants of
Jerusalem *shall be* my strength in the LORD of hosts their God.
6 In that day will I make the governors of Judah like an hearth of fire among
the wood, and like a torch of fire in a sheaf; and they shall devour all the peo-
ple round about, on the right hand and on the left: and Jerusalem shall be
inhabited again in her own place, *even* in Jerusalem.
7 The LORD also shall save the tents of Judah first, that the glory of the house
of David and the glory of the inhabitants of Jerusalem do not magnify *them-
selves* against Judah.
8 In that day shall the LORD defend the inhabitants of Jerusalem; and he that
is feeble among them at that day shall be as David; and the house of David *shall
be* as God, as the angel of the LORD before them.

The Repentance of Jerusalem

9 And it shall come to pass in that day, *that* I will seek to destroy all the nations
that come against Jerusalem.
10 And I will pour upon the house of David, and upon the inhabitants of
Jerusalem, the spirit of grace and of supplications: and they shall look upon
me whom they have pierced, and they shall mourn for him, as one mourneth
for *his* only *son*, and shall be in bitterness for him, as one that is in bitterness
for *his* firstborn.
11 In that day shall there be a great mourning in Jerusalem, as the mourning
of Hadadrimmon in the valley of Megiddon.
12 And the land shall mourn, every family apart; the family of the house of
David apart, and their wives apart; the family of the house of Nathan apart,
and their wives apart;
13 The family of the house of Levi apart, and their wives apart; the family of
Shimei apart, and their wives apart;
14 All the families that remain, every family apart, and their wives apart.

False Prophets Will Be Judged

13 In that day there shall be a fountain opened to the house of David and
to the inhabitants of Jerusalem for sin and for uncleanness.
2 And it shall come to pass in that day, saith the LORD of hosts, *that* I will cut
off the names of the idols out of the land, and they shall no more be remem-
bered: and also I will cause the prophets and the unclean spirit to pass out of
the land.
3 And it shall come to pass, *that* when any shall yet prophesy, then his father
and his mother that begat him shall say unto him, Thou shalt not live; for thou
speakest lies in the name of the LORD: and his father and his mother that begat
him shall thrust him through when he prophesieth.
4 And it shall come to pass in that day, *that* the prophets shall be ashamed
every one of his vision, when he hath prophesied; neither shall they wear a
rough garment to deceive:

5 But he shall say, I *am* no prophet, I *am* an husbandman; for man taught
me to keep cattle from my youth.
6 And *one* shall say unto him, What *are* these wounds in thine hands? Then
he shall answer, *Those* with which I was wounded *in* the house of my friends.

The Death of Christ Foretold

7 Awake, O sword, against my shepherd, and against the man *that is* my
fellow, saith the LORD of hosts: smite the shepherd, and the sheep shall be
scattered: and I will turn mine hand upon the little ones.
8 And it shall come to pass, *that* in all the land, saith the LORD, two parts
therein shall be cut off *and* die; but the third shall be left therein.
9 And I will bring the third part through the fire, and will refine them as
silver is refined, and will try them as gold is tried: they shall call on my name,
and I will hear them: I will say, It *is* my people: and they shall say, The LORD *is*
my God.

The Destroyers Will Be Destroyed

14 Behold, the day of the LORD cometh, and thy spoil shall be divided in
the midst of thee.
2 For I will gather all nations against Jerusalem to battle; and the city shall
be taken, and the houses rifled, and the women ravished; and half of the city
shall go forth into captivity, and the residue of the people shall not be cut off
from the city.
3 Then shall the LORD go forth, and fight against those nations, as when he
fought in the day of battle.
4 And his feet shall stand in that day upon the mount of Olives, which *is*
before Jerusalem on the east, and the mount of Olives shall cleave in the midst
thereof toward the east and toward the west, *and there shall be* a very great
valley; and half of the mountain shall remove toward the north, and half of it
toward the south.
5 And ye shall flee *to* the valley of the mountains; for the valley of the moun-
tains shall reach unto Azal: yea, ye shall flee, like as ye fled from before the
earthquake in the days of Uzziah king of Judah: and the LORD my God shall
come, *and* all the saints with thee.
6 And it shall come to pass in that day, *that* the light shall not be clear, *nor*
dark:
7 But it shall be one day which shall be known to the LORD, not day, nor night:
but it shall come to pass, *that* at evening time it shall be light.

Living Waters

8 And it shall be in that day, *that* living waters shall go out from Jerusalem;
half of them toward the former sea, and half of them toward the hinder sea:
in summer and in winter shall it be.
9 And the LORD shall be king over all the earth: in that day shall there be one
LORD, and his name one.
10 All the land shall be turned as a plain from Geba to Rimmon south of
Jerusalem: and it shall be lifted up, and inhabited in her place, from Benjamin's
gate unto the place of the first gate, unto the corner gate, and *from* the tower
of Hananeel unto the king's winepresses.
11 And *men* shall dwell in it, and there shall be no more utter destruction;
but Jerusalem shall be safely inhabited.
12 And this shall be the plague wherewith the LORD will smite all the people
that have fought against Jerusalem; Their flesh shall consume away while they
stand upon their feet, and their eyes shall consume away in their holes, and
their tongue shall consume away in their mouth.
13 And it shall come to pass in that day, *that* a great tumult from the LORD
shall be among them; and they shall lay hold every one on the hand of his
neighbour, and his hand shall rise up against the hand of his neighbour.

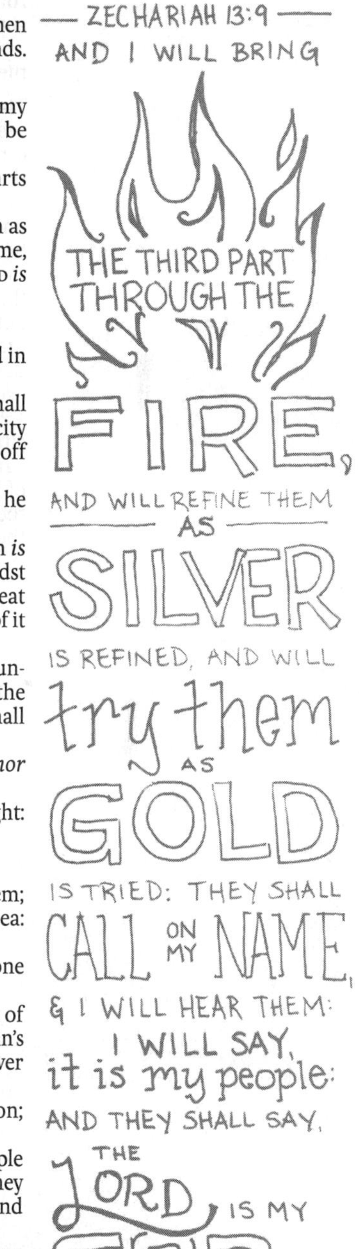

14 And Judah also shall fight at Jerusalem; and the wealth of all the heathen
round about shall be gathered together, gold, and silver, and apparel, in great
abundance.
15 And so shall be the plague of the horse, of the mule, of the camel, and of
the ass, and of all the beasts that shall be in these tents, as this plague.

The Remnant Shall Turn to the Lord

16 And it shall come to pass, *that* every one that is left of all the nations which
came against Jerusalem shall even go up from year to year to worship the King,
the LORD of hosts, and to keep the feast of tabernacles.
17 And it shall be, *that* whoso will not come up of *all* the families of the earth
unto Jerusalem to worship the King, the LORD of hosts, even upon them shall
be no rain.
18 And if the family of Egypt go not up, and come not, that *have* no *rain*;
there shall be the plague, wherewith the LORD will smite the heathen that come
not up to keep the feast of tabernacles.
19 This shall be the punishment of Egypt, and the punishment of all nations
that come not up to keep the feast of tabernacles.
20 In that day shall there be upon the bells of the horses, HOLINESS UNTO
THE LORD; and the pots in the LORD's house shall be like the bowls before the
altar.
21 Yea, every pot in Jerusalem and in Judah shall be holiness unto the LORD
of hosts: and all they that sacrifice shall come and take of them, and seethe
therein: and in that day there shall be no more the Canaanite in the house of
the LORD of hosts.

God's Complaint against Israel

1 The burden of the word of the LORD to Israel by Malachi.
2 I have loved you, saith the LORD. Yet ye say, Wherein hast thou loved us?
Was not Esau Jacob's brother? saith the LORD: yet I loved Jacob,
3 And I hated Esau, and laid his mountains and his heritage waste for the
dragons of the wilderness.
4 Whereas Edom saith, We are impoverished, but we will return and build
the desolate places; thus saith the LORD of hosts, They shall build, but I will
throw down; and they shall call them, The border of wickedness, and, The
people against whom the LORD hath indignation for ever.
5 And your eyes shall see, and ye shall say, The LORD will be magnified from
the border of Israel.

Unacceptable Sacrifices

6 A son honoureth *his* father, and a servant his master: if then I *be* a father,
where *is* mine honour? and if I *be* a master, where *is* my fear? saith the LORD
of hosts unto you, O priests, that despise my name. And ye say, Wherein have
we despised thy name?
7 Ye offer polluted bread upon mine altar; and ye say, Wherein have we pol-
luted thee? In that ye say, The table of the LORD *is* contemptible.
8 And if ye offer the blind for sacrifice, *is it* not evil? and if ye offer the lame
and sick, *is it* not evil? offer it now unto thy governor; will he be pleased with
thee, or accept thy person? saith the LORD of hosts.
9 And now, I pray you, beseech God that he will be gracious unto us: this hath
been by your means: will he regard your persons? saith the LORD of hosts.
10 Who *is there* even among you that would shut the doors *for nought*? nei-
ther do ye kindle *fire* on mine altar for nought. I have no pleasure in you, saith
the LORD of hosts, neither will I accept an offering at your hand.
11 For from the rising of the sun even unto the going down of the same my
name *shall be* great among the Gentiles; and in every place incense *shall be*
offered unto my name, and a pure offering: for my name *shall be* great among
the heathen, saith the LORD of hosts.
12 But ye have profaned it, in that ye say, The table of the LORD *is* polluted;
and the fruit thereof, *even* his meat, *is* contemptible.
13 Ye said also, Behold, what a weariness *is it*! and ye have snuffed at it, saith
the LORD of hosts; and ye brought *that which was* torn, and the lame, and the
sick; thus ye brought an offering: should I accept this of your hand? saith the
LORD.
14 But cursed *be* the deceiver, which hath in his flock a male, and voweth,
and sacrificeth unto the Lord a corrupt thing: for I *am* a great King, saith the
LORD of hosts, and my name *is* dreadful among the heathen.

The Priests Neglect Their Covenant

2 And now, O ye priests, this commandment *is* for you.
2 If ye will not hear, and if ye will not lay *it* to heart, to give glory unto my
name, saith the LORD of hosts, I will even send a curse upon you, and I will
curse your blessings: yea, I have cursed them already, because ye do not lay *it*
to heart.

3 Behold, I will corrupt your seed, and spread dung upon your faces, *even*
the dung of your solemn feasts; and *one* shall take you away with it.
4 And ye shall know that I have sent this commandment unto you, that my
covenant might be with Levi, saith the LORD of hosts.
5 My covenant was with him of life and peace; and I gave them to him *for*
the fear wherewith he feared me, and was afraid before my name.
6 The law of truth was in his mouth, and iniquity was not found in his lips:
he walked with me in peace and equity, and did turn many away from iniquity.
7 For the priest's lips should keep knowledge, and they should seek the law
at his mouth: for he *is* the messenger of the LORD of hosts.
8 But ye are departed out of the way; ye have caused many to stumble at the
law; ye have corrupted the covenant of Levi, saith the LORD of hosts.
9 Therefore have I also made you contemptible and base before all the peo-
ple, according as ye have not kept my ways, but have been partial in the law.

The People Break Marriage Vows

10 Have we not all one father? hath not one God created us? why do we deal
treacherously every man against his brother, by profaning the covenant of
our fathers?
11 Judah hath dealt treacherously, and an abomination is committed in Israel
and in Jerusalem; for Judah hath profaned the holiness of the LORD which he
loved, and hath married the daughter of a strange god.
12 The LORD will cut off the man that doeth this, the master and the scholar,
out of the tabernacles of Jacob, and him that offereth an offering unto the
LORD of hosts.
13 And this have ye done again, covering the altar of the LORD with tears, with
weeping, and with crying out, insomuch that he regardeth not the offering
any more, or receiveth *it* with good will at your hand.
14 Yet ye say, Wherefore? Because the LORD hath been witness between thee
and the wife of thy youth, against whom thou hast dealt treacherously: yet *is*
she thy companion, and the wife of thy covenant.
15 And did not he make one? Yet had he the residue of the spirit. And where-
fore one? That he might seek a godly seed. Therefore take heed to your spirit,
and let none deal treacherously against the wife of his youth.
16 For the LORD, the God of Israel, saith that he hateth putting away: for *one*
covereth violence with his garment, saith the LORD of hosts: therefore take
heed to your spirit, that ye deal not treacherously.
17 Ye have wearied the LORD with your words. Yet ye say, Wherein have we
wearied *him*? When ye say, Every one that doeth evil *is* good in the sight of the
LORD, and he delighteth in them; or, Where *is* the God of judgment?

The Coming Messenger

3 Behold, I will send my messenger, and he shall prepare the way before me:
and the Lord, whom ye seek, shall suddenly come to his temple, even the
messenger of the covenant, whom ye delight in: behold, he shall come, saith the
LORD of hosts.
2 But who may abide the day of his coming? and who shall stand when he
appeareth? for he *is* like a refiner's fire, and like fullers' soap:
3 And he shall sit *as* a refiner and purifier of silver: and he shall purify the
sons of Levi, and purge them as gold and silver, that they may offer unto the
LORD an offering in righteousness.
4 Then shall the offering of Judah and Jerusalem be pleasant unto the LORD,
as in the days of old, and as in former years.
5 And I will come near to you to judgment; and I will be a swift witness against
the sorcerers, and against the adulterers, and against false swearers, and
against those that oppress the hireling in *his* wages, the widow, and the father-

less, and that turn aside the stranger *from his right*, and fear not me, saith the LORD of hosts.

6 For I *am* the LORD, I change not; therefore ye sons of Jacob are not consumed.

The Importance of Tithing

7 Even from the days of your fathers ye are gone away from mine ordinances, and have not kept *them*. Return unto me, and I will return unto you, saith the LORD of hosts. But ye said, Wherein shall we return?

8 Will a man rob God? Yet ye have robbed me. But ye say, Wherein have we robbed thee? In tithes and offerings.

9 Ye *are* cursed with a curse: for ye have robbed me, *even* this whole nation.

10 Bring ye all the tithes into the storehouse, that there may be meat in mine house, and prove me now herewith, saith the LORD of hosts, if I will not open you the windows of heaven, and pour you out a blessing, that *there shall* not *be room* enough *to receive it*.

11 And I will rebuke the devourer for your sakes, and he shall not destroy the fruits of your ground; neither shall your vine cast her fruit before the time in the field, saith the LORD of hosts.

12 And all nations shall call you blessed: for ye shall be a delightsome land, saith the LORD of hosts.

13 Your words have been stout against me, saith the LORD. Yet ye say, What have we spoken *so much* against thee?

14 Ye have said, It *is* vain to serve God: and what profit *is it* that we have kept his ordinance, and that we have walked mournfully before the LORD of hosts?

15 And now we call the proud happy; yea, they that work wickedness are set up; yea, *they that* tempt God are even delivered.

16 Then they that feared the LORD spake often one to another: and the LORD hearkened, and heard *it*, and a book of remembrance was written before him for them that feared the LORD, and that thought upon his name.

17 And they shall be mine, saith the LORD of hosts, in that day when I make up my jewels; and I will spare them, as a man spareth his own son that serveth him.

18 Then shall ye return, and discern between the righteous and the wicked, between him that serveth God and him that serveth him not.

God's Judgment on the Wicked

4 For, behold, the day cometh, that shall burn as an oven; and all the proud, yea, and all that do wickedly, shall be stubble: and the day that cometh shall burn them up, saith the LORD of hosts, that it shall leave them neither root nor branch.

2 But unto you that fear my name shall the Sun of righteousness arise with healing in his wings; and ye shall go forth, and grow up as calves of the stall.

3 And ye shall tread down the wicked; for they shall be ashes under the soles of your feet in the day that I shall do *this*, saith the LORD of hosts.

Remember What God Has Done

4 Remember ye the law of Moses my servant, which I commanded unto him in Horeb for all Israel, *with* the statutes and judgments.

5 Behold, I will send you Elijah the prophet before the coming of the great and dreadful day of the LORD:

6 And he shall turn the heart of the fathers to the children, and the heart of the children to their fathers, lest I come and smite the earth with a curse.

I AM THE
LORD,
I
change
NOT;
THEREFORE YE
SONS
OF
JACOB
ARE NOT
CONSUMED.

MALACHI 3:6

less, and that turn aside the stranger *from his right*, and fear not me, saith the
LORD of hosts.
6 For I *am* the LORD, I change not; therefore ye sons of Jacob are not
consumed.

The Importance of Tithing

7 Even from the days of your fathers ye are gone away from mine ordinances,
and have not kept *them*. Return unto me, and I will return unto you, saith the
LORD of hosts. But ye said, Wherein shall we return?
8 Will a man rob God? Yet ye have robbed me. But ye say, Wherein have we
robbed thee? In tithes and offerings.
9 Ye *are* cursed with a curse: for ye have robbed me, *even* this whole nation.
10 Bring ye all the tithes into the storehouse, that there may be meat in mine
house, and prove me now herewith, saith the LORD of hosts, if I will not open
you the windows of heaven, and pour you out a blessing, that *there shall* not
be room enough *to receive it*.
11 And I will rebuke the devourer for your sakes, and he shall not destroy the
fruits of your ground; neither shall your vine cast her fruit before the time in
the field, saith the LORD of hosts.
12 And all nations shall call you blessed: for ye shall be a delightsome land,
saith the LORD of hosts.
13 Your words have been stout against me, saith the LORD. Yet ye say, What
have we spoken so *much* against thee?
14 Ye have said, It *is* vain to serve God: and what profit *is it* that we have kept
his ordinance, and that we have walked mournfully before the LORD of hosts?
15 And now we call the proud happy; yea, they that work wickedness are set
up; yea, *they that* tempt God are even delivered.
16 Then they that feared the LORD spake often one to another: and the LORD
hearkened, and heard *it*, and a book of remembrance was written before him
for them that feared the LORD, and that thought upon his name.
17 And they shall be mine, saith the LORD of hosts, in that day when I make
up my jewels; and I will spare them, as a man spareth his own son that serveth
him.
18 Then shall ye return, and discern between the righteous and the wicked,
between him that serveth God and him that serveth him not.

God's Judgment on the Wicked

4 For, behold, the day cometh, that shall burn as an oven; and all the proud,
yea, and all that do wickedly, shall be stubble: and the day that cometh shall
burn them up, saith the LORD of hosts, that it shall leave them neither root nor
branch.
2 But unto you that fear my name shall the Sun of righteousness arise with
healing in his wings; and ye shall go forth, and grow up as calves of the stall.
3 And ye shall tread down the wicked; for they shall be ashes under the soles
of your feet in the day that I shall do *this*, saith the LORD of hosts.

Remember What God Has Done

4 Remember ye the law of Moses my servant, which I commanded unto him
in Horeb for all Israel, *with* the statutes and judgments.
5 Behold, I will send you Elijah the prophet before the coming of the great
and dreadful day of the LORD:
6 And he shall turn the heart of the fathers to the children, and the heart of
the children to their fathers, lest I come and smite the earth with a curse.

New Testament

INRI

SAINT MATTHEW

The Genealogy of Christ from Abraham to Joseph

1 The book of the generation of Jesus Christ, the son of David, the son of
Abraham.
2 Abraham begat Isaac; and Isaac begat Jacob; and Jacob begat Judas and his
brethren;
3 And Judas begat Phares and Zara of Thamar; and Phares begat Esrom; and
Esrom begat Aram;
4 And Aram begat Aminadab; and Aminadab begat Naasson; and Naasson
begat Salmon;
5 And Salmon begat Booz of Rachab; and Booz begat Obed of Ruth; and Obed
begat Jesse;
6 And Jesse begat David the king; and David the king begat Solomon of her
that had been the wife of Urias;
7 And Solomon begat Roboam; and Roboam begat Abia; and Abia begat Asa;
8 And Asa begat Josaphat; and Josaphat begat Joram; and Joram begat Ozias;
9 And Ozias begat Joatham; and Joatham begat Achaz; and Achaz begat
Ezekias;
10 And Ezekias begat Manasses; and Manasses begat Amon; and Amon begat
Josias;
11 And Josias begat Jechonias and his brethren, about the time they were
carried away to Babylon:
12 And after they were brought to Babylon, Jechonias begat Salathiel; and
Salathiel begat Zorobabel;
13 And Zorobabel begat Abiud; and Abiud begat Eliakim; and Eliakim begat
Azor;
14 And Azor begat Sadoc; and Sadoc begat Achim; and Achim begat Eliud;
15 And Eliud begat Eleazar; and Eleazar begat Matthan; and Matthan begat
Jacob;
16 And Jacob begat Joseph the husband of Mary, of whom was born Jesus,
who is called Christ.
17 So all the generations from Abraham to David *are* fourteen generations;
and from David until the carrying away into Babylon *are* fourteen generations;
and from the carrying away into Babylon unto Christ *are* fourteen generations.

The Story of Jesus' Birth

18 Now the birth of Jesus Christ was on this wise: When as his mother Mary
was espoused to Joseph, before they came together, she was found with child
of the Holy Ghost.
19 Then Joseph her husband, being a just *man*, and not willing to make her
a publick example, was minded to put her away privily.
20 But while he thought on these things, behold, the angel of the Lord
appeared unto him in a dream, saying, Joseph, thou son of David, fear not to
take unto thee Mary thy wife: for that which is conceived in her is of the Holy
Ghost.
21 And she shall bring forth a son, and thou shalt call his name JESUS: for he
shall save his people from their sins.
22 Now all this was done, that it might be fulfilled which was spoken of the
Lord by the prophet, saying,

23 Behold, a virgin shall be with child, and shall bring forth a son, and they
shall call his name Emmanuel, which being interpreted is, God with us.
24 Then Joseph being raised from sleep did as the angel of the Lord had
bidden him, and took unto him his wife:
25 And knew her not till she had brought forth her firstborn son: and he
called his name JESUS.

The Wise Men Visit

2 Now when Jesus was born in Beth-lehem of Judaea in the days of Herod the
king, behold, there came wise men from the east to Jerusalem,
2 Saying, Where is he that is born King of the Jews? for we have seen his star
in the east, and are come to worship him.
3 When Herod the king had heard *these things*, he was troubled, and all
Jerusalem with him.
4 And when he had gathered all the chief priests and scribes of the people
together, he demanded of them where Christ should be born.
5 And they said unto him, In Beth-lehem of Judaea: for thus it is written by
the prophet,
6 And thou Beth-lehem, *in* the land of Juda, art not the least among the
princes of Juda: for out of thee shall come a Governor, that shall rule my people
Israel.
7 Then Herod, when he had privily called the wise men, enquired of them
diligently what time the star appeared.
8 And he sent them to Beth-lehem, and said, Go and search diligently for the
young child; and when ye have found *him*, bring me word again, that I may
come and worship him also.
9 When they had heard the king, they departed; and, lo, the star, which they
saw in the east, went before them, till it came and stood over where the young
child was.
10 When they saw the star, they rejoiced with exceeding great joy.
11 And when they were come into the house, they saw the young child with
Mary his mother, and fell down, and worshipped him: and when they had
opened their treasures, they presented unto him gifts; gold, and frankincense,
and myrrh.
12 And being warned of God in a dream that they should not return to Herod,
they departed into their own country another way.

Escape to Egypt

13 And when they were departed, behold, the angel of the Lord appeareth
to Joseph in a dream, saying, Arise, and take the young child and his mother,
and flee into Egypt, and be thou there until I bring thee word: for Herod will
seek the young child to destroy him.
14 When he arose, he took the young child and his mother by night, and
departed into Egypt:
15 And was there until the death of Herod: that it might be fulfilled which was
spoken of the Lord by the prophet, saying, Out of Egypt have I called my son.

Herod Slays the Children

16 Then Herod, when he saw that he was mocked of the wise men, was
exceeding wroth, and sent forth, and slew all the children that were in Beth-
lehem, and in all the coasts thereof, from two years old and under, according
to the time which he had diligently enquired of the wise men.
17 Then was fulfilled that which was spoken by Jeremy the prophet, saying,
18 In Rama was there a voice heard, lamentation, and weeping, and great
mourning, Rachel weeping *for* her children, and would not be comforted,
because they are not.

From Egypt to Nazareth
19 But when Herod was dead, behold, an angel of the Lord appeareth in a
dream to Joseph in Egypt,
20 Saying, Arise, and take the young child and his mother, and go into the
land of Israel: for they are dead which sought the young child's life.
21 And he arose, and took the young child and his mother, and came into the
land of Israel.
22 But when he heard that Archelaus did reign in Judaea in the room of his
father Herod, he was afraid to go thither: notwithstanding, being warned of
God in a dream, he turned aside into the parts of Galilee:
23 And he came and dwelt in a city called Nazareth: that it might be fulfilled
which was spoken by the prophets, He shall be called a Nazarene.

John Prepares the Way for Jesus
3 In those days came John the Baptist, preaching in the wilderness of Judaea,
2 And saying, Repent ye: for the kingdom of heaven is at hand.
3 For this is he that was spoken of by the prophet Esaias, saying, The voice of
one crying in the wilderness, Prepare ye the way of the Lord, make his paths
straight.
4 And the same John had his raiment of camel's hair, and a leathern girdle
about his loins; and his meat was locusts and wild honey.
5 Then went out to him Jerusalem, and all Judaea, and all the region round
about Jordan,
6 And were baptized of him in Jordan, confessing their sins.
7 But when he saw many of the Pharisees and Sadducees come to his baptism,
he said unto them, O generation of vipers, who hath warned you to flee from
the wrath to come?
8 Bring forth therefore fruits meet for repentance:
9 And think not to say within yourselves, We have Abraham to *our* father:
for I say unto you, that God is able of these stones to raise up children unto
Abraham.
10 And now also the axe is laid unto the root of the trees: therefore every tree
which bringeth not forth good fruit is hewn down, and cast into the fire.
11 I indeed baptize you with water unto repentance: but he that cometh after
me is mightier than I, whose shoes I am not worthy to bear: he shall baptize
you with the Holy Ghost, and *with* fire:
12 Whose fan *is* in his hand, and he will throughly purge his floor, and gath-
er his wheat into the garner; but he will burn up the chaff with unquenchable
fire.

John Baptizes Jesus
13 Then cometh Jesus from Galilee to Jordan unto John, to be baptized of
him.
14 But John forbad him, saying, I have need to be baptized of thee, and comest
thou to me?
15 And Jesus answering said unto him, Suffer *it to be so* now: for thus it
becometh us to fulfil all righteousness. Then he suffered him.
16 And Jesus, when he was baptized, went up straightway out of the water:
and, lo, the heavens were opened unto him, and he saw the Spirit of God
descending like a dove, and lighting upon him:
17 And lo a voice from heaven, saying, This is my beloved Son, in whom I am
well pleased.

The Temptation of Jesus
4 Then was Jesus led up of the Spirit into the wilderness to be tempted of the
devil.
2 And when he had fasted forty days and forty nights, he was afterward an
hungred.

3 And when the tempter came to him, he said, If thou be the Son of God,
command that these stones be made bread.
4 But he answered and said, It is written, Man shall not live by bread alone,
but by every word that proceedeth out of the mouth of God.
5 Then the devil taketh him up into the holy city, and setteth him on a pin-
nacle of the temple,
6 And saith unto him, If thou be the Son of God, cast thyself down: for it is
written, He shall give his angels charge concerning thee: and in *their* hands
they shall bear thee up, lest at any time thou dash thy foot against a stone.
7 Jesus said unto him, It is written again, Thou shalt not tempt the Lord thy
God.
8 Again, the devil taketh him up into an exceeding high mountain, and
sheweth him all the kingdoms of the world, and the glory of them;
9 And saith unto him, All these things will I give thee, if thou wilt fall down
and worship me.
10 Then saith Jesus unto him, Get thee hence, Satan: for it is written, Thou
shalt worship the Lord thy God, and him only shalt thou serve.
11 Then the devil leaveth him, and, behold, angels came and ministered unto
him.

A Light Has Risen

12 Now when Jesus had heard that John was cast into prison, he departed
into Galilee;
13 And leaving Nazareth, he came and dwelt in Capernaum, which is upon
the sea coast, in the borders of Zabulon and Nephthalim:
14 That it might be fulfilled which was spoken by Esaias the prophet, saying,
15 The land of Zabulon, and the land of Nephthalim, *by* the way of the sea,
beyond Jordan, Galilee of the Gentiles;
16 The people which sat in darkness saw great light; and to them which sat
in the region and shadow of death light is sprung up.
17 From that time Jesus began to preach, and to say, Repent: for the kingdom
of heaven is at hand.

Jesus Calls the First Disciples

18 And Jesus, walking by the sea of Galilee, saw two brethren, Simon called
Peter, and Andrew his brother, casting a net into the sea: for they were fishers.
19 And he saith unto them, Follow me, and I will make you fishers of men.
20 And they straightway left *their* nets, and followed him.
21 And going on from thence, he saw other two brethren, James *the son* of
Zebedee, and John his brother, in a ship with Zebedee their father, mending
their nets; and he called them.
22 And they immediately left the ship and their father, and followed him.

Spreading the Good News in Galilee

23 And Jesus went about all Galilee, teaching in their synagogues, and preach-
ing the gospel of the kingdom, and healing all manner of sickness and all
manner of disease among the people.
24 And his fame went throughout all Syria: and they brought unto him all
sick people that were taken with divers diseases and torments, and those which
were possessed with devils, and those which were lunatick, and those that had
the palsy; and he healed them.
25 And there followed him great multitudes of people from Galilee, and *from*
Decapolis, and *from* Jerusalem, and *from* Judaea, and *from* beyond Jordan.

The Sermon on the Mount

5 And seeing the multitudes, he went up into a mountain: and when he was
set, his disciples came unto him:
2 And he opened his mouth, and taught them, saying,

FOLLOW me, AND I WILL MAKE YOU fishers OF MEN.

SAINT MATTHEW 4:19

The Beatitudes

3 Blessed *are* the poor in spirit: for theirs is the kingdom of heaven.
4 Blessed *are* they that mourn: for they shall be comforted.
5 Blessed *are* the meek: for they shall inherit the earth.
6 Blessed *are* they which do hunger and thirst after righteousness: for they
shall be filled.
7 Blessed *are* the merciful: for they shall obtain mercy.
8 Blessed *are* the pure in heart: for they shall see God.
9 Blessed *are* the peacemakers: for they shall be called the children of God.
10 Blessed *are* they which are persecuted for righteousness' sake: for theirs
is the kingdom of heaven.
11 Blessed are ye, when *men* shall revile you, and persecute *you*, and shall say
all manner of evil against you falsely, for my sake.
12 Rejoice, and be exceeding glad: for great *is* your reward in heaven: for so
persecuted they the prophets which were before you.

God's People Make a Difference

13 Ye are the salt of the earth: but if the salt have lost his savour, wherewith
shall it be salted? it is thenceforth good for nothing, but to be cast out, and to
be trodden under foot of men.
14 Ye are the light of the world. A city that is set on an hill cannot be hid.
15 Neither do men light a candle, and put it under a bushel, but on a candle-
stick; and it giveth light unto all that are in the house.
16 Let your light so shine before men, that they may see your good works,
and glorify your Father which is in heaven.

Jesus Came to Fulfill the Law

17 Think not that I am come to destroy the law, or the prophets: I am not
come to destroy, but to fulfil.
18 For verily I say unto you, Till heaven and earth pass, one jot or one tittle
shall in no wise pass from the law, till all be fulfilled.
19 Whosoever therefore shall break one of these least commandments, and
shall teach men so, he shall be called the least in the kingdom of heaven: but
whosoever shall do and teach *them*, the same shall be called great in the king-
dom of heaven.
20 For I say unto you, That except your righteousness shall exceed *the righ-
teousness* of the scribes and Pharisees, ye shall in no case enter into the king-
dom of heaven.

Jesus Talks about Anger

21 Ye have heard that it was said by them of old time, Thou shalt not kill; and
whosoever shall kill shall be in danger of the judgment:
22 But I say unto you, That whosoever is angry with his brother without a
cause shall be in danger of the judgment: and whosoever shall say to his broth-
er, Raca, shall be in danger of the council: but whosoever shall say, Thou fool,
shall be in danger of hell fire.
23 Therefore if thou bring thy gift to the altar, and there rememberest that
thy brother hath ought against thee;
24 Leave there thy gift before the altar, and go thy way; first be reconciled to
thy brother, and then come and offer thy gift.
25 Agree with thine adversary quickly, whiles thou art in the way with him;
lest at any time the adversary deliver thee to the judge, and the judge deliver
thee to the officer, and thou be cast into prison.
26 Verily I say unto thee, Thou shalt by no means come out thence, till thou
hast paid the uttermost farthing.

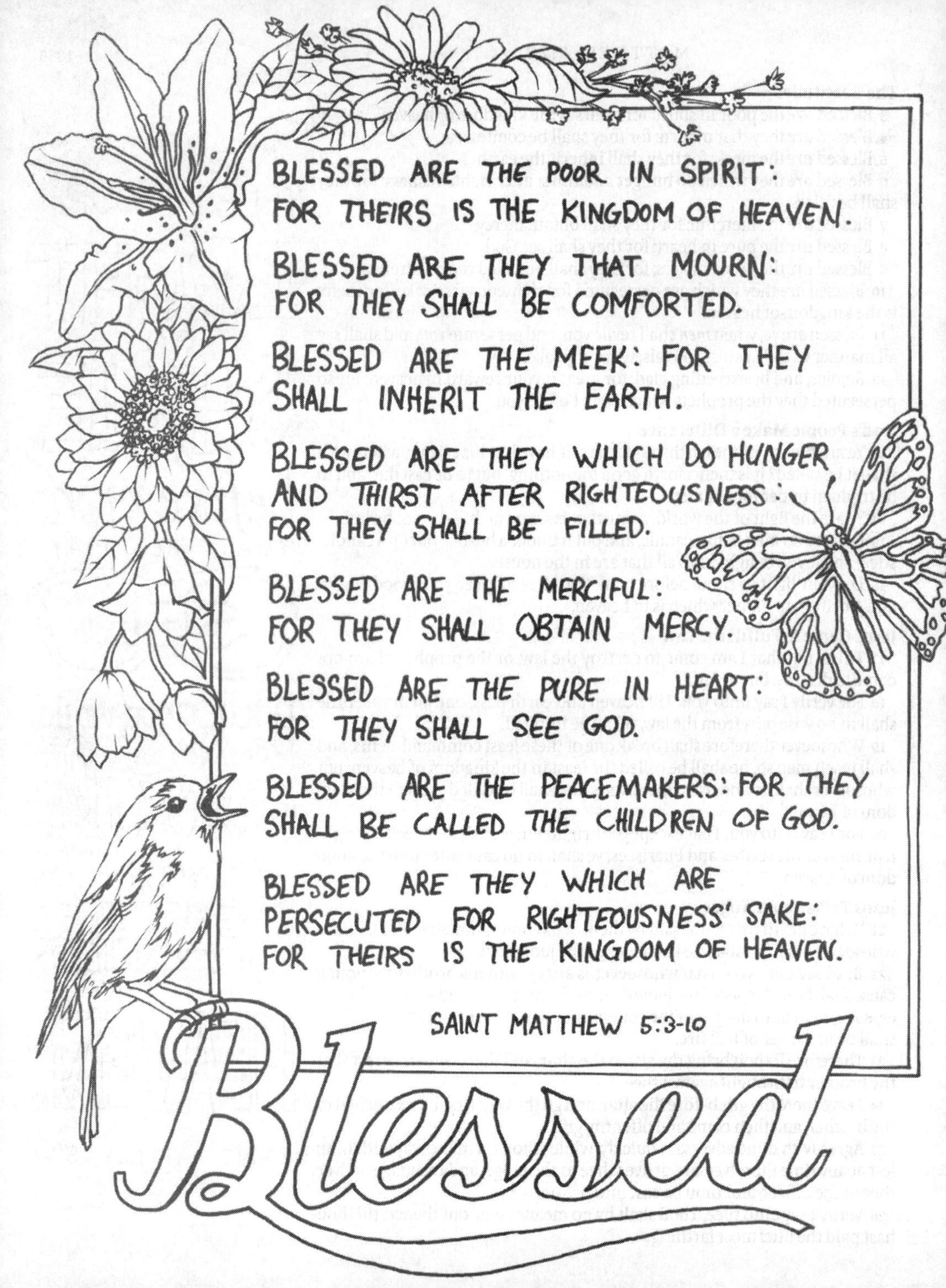
BLESSED ARE THE POOR IN SPIRIT: FOR THEIRS IS THE KINGDOM OF HEAVEN.
BLESSED ARE THEY THAT MOURN: FOR THEY SHALL BE COMFORTED.
BLESSED ARE THE MEEK: FOR THEY SHALL INHERIT THE EARTH.
BLESSED ARE THEY WHICH DO HUNGER AND THIRST AFTER RIGHTEOUSNESS: FOR THEY SHALL BE FILLED.
BLESSED ARE THE MERCIFUL: FOR THEY SHALL OBTAIN MERCY.
BLESSED ARE THE PURE IN HEART: FOR THEY SHALL SEE GOD.
BLESSED ARE THE PEACEMAKERS: FOR THEY SHALL BE CALLED THE CHILDREN OF GOD.
BLESSED ARE THEY WHICH ARE PERSECUTED FOR RIGHTEOUSNESS' SAKE: FOR THEIRS IS THE KINGDOM OF HEAVEN.
SAINT MATTHEW 5:3-10
Blessed

Jesus Talks about Sexual Sin
27 Ye have heard that it was said by them of old time, Thou shalt not commit
adultery:
28 But I say unto you, That whosoever looketh on a woman to lust after her
hath committed adultery with her already in his heart.
29 And if thy right eye offend thee, pluck it out, and cast *it* from thee: for it
is profitable for thee that one of thy members should perish, and not *that* thy
whole body should be cast into hell.
30 And if thy right hand offend thee, cut it off, and cast *it* from thee: for it is
profitable for thee that one of thy members should perish, and not *that* thy
whole body should be cast into hell.
31 It hath been said, Whosoever shall put away his wife, let him give her a
writing of divorcement:
32 But I say unto you, That whosoever shall put away his wife, saving for the
cause of fornication, causeth her to commit adultery: and whosoever shall
marry her that is divorced committeth adultery.

Jesus Talks about Oaths
33 Again, ye have heard that it hath been said by them of old time, Thou shalt
not forswear thyself, but shalt perform unto the Lord thine oaths:
34 But I say unto you, Swear not at all; neither by heaven; for it is God's throne:
35 Nor by the earth; for it is his footstool: neither by Jerusalem; for it is the
city of the great King.
36 Neither shalt thou swear by thy head, because thou canst not make one
hair white or black.
37 But let your communication be, Yea, yea; Nay, nay: for whatsoever is more
than these cometh of evil.

Love Your Enemies
38 Ye have heard that it hath been said, An eye for an eye, and a tooth for a
tooth:
39 But I say unto you, That ye resist not evil: but whosoever shall smite thee
on thy right cheek, turn to him the other also.
40 And if any man will sue thee at the law, and take away thy coat, let him
have *thy* cloke also.
41 And whosoever shall compel thee to go a mile, go with him twain.
42 Give to him that asketh thee, and from him that would borrow of thee
turn not thou away.
43 Ye have heard that it hath been said, Thou shalt love thy neighbour, and
hate thine enemy.
44 But I say unto you, Love your enemies, bless them that curse you, do good
to them that hate you, and pray for them which despitefully use you, and
persecute you;
45 That ye may be the children of your Father which is in heaven: for he
maketh his sun to rise on the evil and on the good, and sendeth rain on the
just and on the unjust.
46 For if ye love them which love you, what reward have ye? do not even the
publicans the same?
47 And if ye salute your brethren only, what do ye more *than others*? do not
even the publicans so?
48 Be ye therefore perfect, even as your Father which is in heaven is perfect.

Don't Do Good Works for Praise
6 Take heed that ye do not your alms before men, to be seen of them: otherwise
ye have no reward of your Father which is in heaven.
2 Therefore when thou doest *thine* alms, do not sound a trumpet before thee,
as the hypocrites do in the synagogues and in the streets, that they may have
glory of men. Verily I say unto you, They have their reward.

3 But when thou doest alms, let not thy left hand know what thy right hand
doeth:
4 That thine alms may be in secret: and thy Father which seeth in secret
himself shall reward thee openly.

The Lord's Prayer

5 And when thou prayest, thou shalt not be as the hypocrites *are*: for they
love to pray standing in the synagogues and in the corners of the streets, that
they may be seen of men. Verily I say unto you, They have their reward.
6 But thou, when thou prayest, enter into thy closet, and when thou hast shut
thy door, pray to thy Father which is in secret; and thy Father which seeth in
secret shall reward thee openly.
7 But when ye pray, use not vain repetitions, as the heathen *do*: for they think
that they shall be heard for their much speaking.
8 Be not ye therefore like unto them: for your Father knoweth what things
ye have need of, before ye ask him.
9 After this manner therefore pray ye: Our Father which art in heaven,
Hallowed be thy name.
10 Thy kingdom come. Thy will be done in earth, as *it is* in heaven.
11 Give us this day our daily bread.
12 And forgive us our debts, as we forgive our debtors.
13 And lead us not into temptation, but deliver us from evil: For thine is the
kingdom, and the power, and the glory, for ever. Amen.
14 For if ye forgive men their trespasses, your heavenly Father will also forgive
you:
15 But if ye forgive not men their trespasses, neither will your Father forgive
your trespasses.

Fasting

16 Moreover when ye fast, be not, as the hypocrites, of a sad countenance:
for they disfigure their faces, that they may appear unto men to fast. Verily I
say unto you, They have their reward.
17 But thou, when thou fastest, anoint thine head, and wash thy face;
18 That thou appear not unto men to fast, but unto thy Father which is in
secret: and thy Father, which seeth in secret, shall reward thee openly.

True Riches

19 Lay not up for yourselves treasures upon earth, where moth and rust doth
corrupt, and where thieves break through and steal:
20 But lay up for yourselves treasures in heaven, where neither moth nor
rust doth corrupt, and where thieves do not break through nor steal:
21 For where your treasure is, there will your heart be also.
22 The light of the body is the eye: if therefore thine eye be single, thy whole
body shall be full of light.
23 But if thine eye be evil, thy whole body shall be full of darkness. If therefore
the light that is in thee be darkness, how great *is* that darkness!
24 No man can serve two masters: for either he will hate the one, and love
the other; or else he will hold to the one, and despise the other. Ye cannot serve
God and mammon.

Worry

25 Therefore I say unto you, Take no thought for your life, what ye shall eat,
or what ye shall drink; nor yet for your body, what ye shall put on. Is not the
life more than meat, and the body than raiment?
26 Behold the fowls of the air: for they sow not, neither do they reap, nor
gather into barns; yet your heavenly Father feedeth them. Are ye not much
better than they?
27 Which of you by taking thought can add one cubit unto his stature?

THE LORD'S PRAYER
OUR FATHER WHICH ART IN HEAVEN, HALLOWED BE THY NAME. THY KINGDOM COME. THY WILL BE DONE IN EARTH, AS IT IS IN HEAVEN. GIVE US THIS DAY OUR DAILY BREAD. AND FORGIVE US OUR DEBTS, AS WE FORGIVE OUR DEBTORS. AND LEAD US NOT INTO TEMPTATION, BUT DELIVER US FROM EVIL: FOR THINE IS THE KINGDOM, AND THE POWER, AND THE GLORY. FOR EVER. AMEN.
SAINT MATTHEW 6:9-13

SEEK YE first THE Kingdom OF God, & HIS righteousness; AND ALL THESE THINGS SHALL BE ADDED UNTO YOU.

SAINT MATTHEW 6:33

28 And why take ye thought for raiment? Consider the lilies of the field, how
they grow; they toil not, neither do they spin:
29 And yet I say unto you, That even Solomon in all his glory was not arrayed
like one of these.
30 Wherefore, if God so clothe the grass of the field, which to day is, and to
morrow is cast into the oven, *shall he* not much more *clothe* you, O ye of little
faith?
31 Therefore take no thought, saying, What shall we eat? or, What shall we
drink? or, Wherewithal shall we be clothed?
32 (For after all these things do the Gentiles seek:) for your heavenly Father
knoweth that ye have need of all these things.
33 But seek ye first the kingdom of God, and his righteousness; and all these
things shall be added unto you.
34 Take therefore no thought for the morrow: for the morrow shall take
thought for the things of itself. Sufficient unto the day *is* the evil thereof.

Making Judgments

7 Judge not, that ye be not judged.
2 For with what judgment ye judge, ye shall be judged: and with what
measure ye mete, it shall be measured to you again.
3 And why beholdest thou the mote that is in thy brother's eye, but consid-
erest not the beam that is in thine own eye?
4 Or how wilt thou say to thy brother, Let me pull out the mote out of thine
eye; and, behold, a beam *is* in thine own eye?
5 Thou hypocrite, first cast out the beam out of thine own eye; and then shalt
thou see clearly to cast out the mote out of thy brother's eye.
6 Give not that which is holy unto the dogs, neither cast ye your pearls before
swine, lest they trample them under their feet, and turn again and rend you.

Prayer and Good Actions

7 Ask, and it shall be given you; seek, and ye shall find; knock, and it shall be
opened unto you:
8 For every one that asketh receiveth; and he that seeketh findeth; and to
him that knocketh it shall be opened.
9 Or what man is there of you, whom if his son ask bread, will he give him a
stone?
10 Or if he ask a fish, will he give him a serpent?
11 If ye then, being evil, know how to give good gifts unto your children, how
much more shall your Father which is in heaven give good things to them that
ask him?
12 Therefore all things whatsoever ye would that men should do to you, do
ye even so to them: for this is the law and the prophets.
13 Enter ye in at the strait gate: for wide *is* the gate, and broad *is* the way, that
leadeth to destruction, and many there be which go in thereat:
14 Because strait *is* the gate, and narrow *is* the way, which leadeth unto life,
and few there be that find it.

Beware of False Prophets

15 Beware of false prophets, which come to you in sheep's clothing, but
inwardly they are ravening wolves.
16 Ye shall know them by their fruits. Do men gather grapes of thorns, or
figs of thistles?
17 Even so every good tree bringeth forth good fruit; but a corrupt tree
bringeth forth evil fruit.
18 A good tree cannot bring forth evil fruit, neither *can* a corrupt tree bring
forth good fruit.
19 Every tree that bringeth not forth good fruit is hewn down, and cast into
the fire.
20 Wherefore by their fruits ye shall know them.

Be Doers of the Word

21 Not every one that saith unto me, Lord, Lord, shall enter into the kingdom
of heaven; but he that doeth the will of my Father which is in heaven.
22 Many will say to me in that day, Lord, Lord, have we not prophesied in thy
name? and in thy name have cast out devils? and in thy name done many
wonderful works?
23 And then will I profess unto them, I never knew you: depart from me, ye
that work iniquity.
24 Therefore whosoever heareth these sayings of mine, and doeth them, I
will liken him unto a wise man, which built his house upon a rock:
25 And the rain descended, and the floods came, and the winds blew, and
beat upon that house; and it fell not: for it was founded upon a rock.
26 And every one that heareth these sayings of mine, and doeth them not,
shall be likened unto a foolish man, which built his house upon the sand:
27 And the rain descended, and the floods came, and the winds blew, and
beat upon that house; and it fell: and great was the fall of it.
28 And it came to pass, when Jesus had ended these sayings, the people were
astonished at his doctrine:
29 For he taught them as *one* having authority, and not as the scribes.

Jesus Cleanses the Leper

8 When he was come down from the mountain, great multitudes followed
him.
2 And, behold, there came a leper and worshipped him, saying, Lord, if thou
wilt, thou canst make me clean.
3 And Jesus put forth *his* hand, and touched him, saying, I will; be thou clean.
And immediately his leprosy was cleansed.
4 And Jesus saith unto him, See thou tell no man; but go thy way, shew thyself
to the priest, and offer the gift that Moses commanded, for a testimony unto
them.

Jesus Heals the Centurion's Servant

5 And when Jesus was entered into Capernaum, there came unto him a cen-
turion, beseeching him,
6 And saying, Lord, my servant lieth at home sick of the palsy, grievously
tormented.
7 And Jesus saith unto him, I will come and heal him.
8 The centurion answered and said, Lord, I am not worthy that thou
shouldest come under my roof: but speak the word only, and my servant shall
be healed.
9 For I am a man under authority, having soldiers under me: and I say to this
man, Go, and he goeth; and to another, Come, and he cometh; and to my
servant, Do this, and he doeth *it*.
10 When Jesus heard *it*, he marvelled, and said to them that followed, Verily
I say unto you, I have not found so great faith, no, not in Israel.
11 And I say unto you, That many shall come from the east and west, and
shall sit down with Abraham, and Isaac, and Jacob, in the kingdom of heaven.
12 But the children of the kingdom shall be cast out into outer darkness:
there shall be weeping and gnashing of teeth.
13 And Jesus said unto the centurion, Go thy way; and as thou hast believed,
so be it done unto thee. And his servant was healed in the selfsame hour.

Jesus Heals Peter's Mother-in-law and Others

14 And when Jesus was come into Peter's house, he saw his wife's mother laid,
and sick of a fever.
15 And he touched her hand, and the fever left her: and she arose, and min-
istered unto them.

16 When the even was come, they brought unto him many that were pos-
sessed with devils: and he cast out the spirits with *his* word, and healed all that
were sick:
17 That it might be fulfilled which was spoken by Esaias the prophet, saying,
Himself took our infirmities, and bare *our* sicknesses.

What It Takes to Be a Disciple

18 Now when Jesus saw great multitudes about him, he gave commandment
to depart unto the other side.
19 And a certain scribe came, and said unto him, Master, I will follow thee
whithersoever thou goest.
20 And Jesus saith unto him, The foxes have holes, and the birds of the air
have nests; but the Son of man hath not where to lay *his* head.
21 And another of his disciples said unto him, Lord, suffer me first to go and
bury my father.
22 But Jesus said unto him, Follow me; and let the dead bury their dead.

Jesus Calms the Sea

23 And when he was entered into a ship, his disciples followed him.
24 And, behold, there arose a great tempest in the sea, insomuch that the
ship was covered with the waves: but he was asleep.
25 And his disciples came to *him*, and awoke him, saying, Lord, save us: we
perish.
26 And he saith unto them, Why are ye fearful, O ye of little faith? Then he
arose, and rebuked the winds and the sea; and there was a great calm.
27 But the men marvelled, saying, What manner of man is this, that even the
winds and the sea obey him!

Jesus Cures Two Demoniacs

28 And when he was come to the other side into the country of the Gergesenes,
there met him two possessed with devils, coming out of the tombs, exceeding
fierce, so that no man might pass by that way.
29 And, behold, they cried out, saying, What have we to do with thee, Jesus,
thou Son of God? art thou come hither to torment us before the time?
30 And there was a good way off from them an herd of many swine feeding.
31 So the devils besought him, saying, If thou cast us out, suffer us to go away
into the herd of swine.
32 And he said unto them, Go. And when they were come out, they went into
the herd of swine: and, behold, the whole herd of swine ran violently down a
steep place into the sea, and perished in the waters.
33 And they that kept them fled, and went their ways into the city, and told
every thing, and what was befallen to the possessed of the devils.
34 And, behold, the whole city came out to meet Jesus: and when they saw
him, they besought *him* that he would depart out of their coasts.

Jesus Cures a Paralytic

9 And he entered into a ship, and passed over, and came into his own city.
2 And, behold, they brought to him a man sick of the palsy, lying on a bed:
and Jesus seeing their faith said unto the sick of the palsy; Son, be of good
cheer; thy sins be forgiven thee.
3 And, behold, certain of the scribes said within themselves, This *man* blas-
phemeth.
4 And Jesus knowing their thoughts said, Wherefore think ye evil in your
hearts?
5 For whether is easier, to say, *Thy* sins be forgiven thee; or to say, Arise, and
walk?

6 But that ye may know that the Son of man hath power on earth to forgive
sins, (then saith he to the sick of the palsy,) Arise, take up thy bed, and go unto
thine house.
7 And he arose, and departed to his house.
8 But when the multitudes saw *it*, they marvelled, and glorified God, which
had given such power unto men.

Jesus Calls Matthew to Be a Disciple

9 And as Jesus passed forth from thence, he saw a man, named Matthew,
sitting at the receipt of custom: and he saith unto him, Follow me. And he
arose, and followed him.
10 And it came to pass, as Jesus sat at meat in the house, behold, many pub-
licans and sinners came and sat down with him and his disciples.
11 And when the Pharisees saw *it*, they said unto his disciples, Why eateth
your Master with publicans and sinners?
12 But when Jesus heard *that*, he said unto them, They that be whole need
not a physician, but they that are sick.
13 But go ye and learn what *that* meaneth, I will have mercy, and not sacrifice:
for I am not come to call the righteous, but sinners to repentance.

Jesus Is Questioned about Fasting

14 Then came to him the disciples of John, saying, Why do we and the
Pharisees fast oft, but thy disciples fast not?
15 And Jesus said unto them, Can the children of the bridechamber mourn,
as long as the bridegroom is with them? but the days will come, when the
bridegroom shall be taken from them, and then shall they fast.
16 No man putteth a piece of new cloth unto an old garment, for that which
is put in to fill it up taketh from the garment, and the rent is made worse.
17 Neither do men put new wine into old bottles: else the bottles break, and
the wine runneth out, and the bottles perish: but they put new wine into new
bottles, and both are preserved.

Jesus Raises a Dead Girl and Heals a Bleeding Woman

18 While he spake these things unto them, behold, there came a certain ruler,
and worshipped him, saying, My daughter is even now dead: but come and
lay thy hand upon her, and she shall live.
19 And Jesus arose, and followed him, and *so did* his disciples.
20 And, behold, a woman, which was diseased with an issue of blood twelve
years, came behind *him*, and touched the hem of his garment:
21 For she said within herself, If I may but touch his garment, I shall be whole.
22 But Jesus turned him about, and when he saw her, he said, Daughter, be
of good comfort; thy faith hath made thee whole. And the woman was made
whole from that hour.
23 And when Jesus came into the ruler's house, and saw the minstrels and
the people making a noise,
24 He said unto them, Give place: for the maid is not dead, but sleepeth. And
they laughed him to scorn.
25 But when the people were put forth, he went in, and took her by the hand,
and the maid arose.
26 And the fame hereof went abroad into all that land.

Jesus Heals Two Blind Men

27 And when Jesus departed thence, two blind men followed him, crying,
and saying, *Thou* Son of David, have mercy on us.
28 And when he was come into the house, the blind men came to him: and
Jesus saith unto them, Believe ye that I am able to do this? They said unto him,
Yea, Lord.
29 Then touched he their eyes, saying, According to your faith be it unto you.

30 And their eyes were opened; and Jesus straitly charged them, saying, See
that no man know *it*.
31 But they, when they were departed, spread abroad his fame in all that
country.

Jesus Sends a Demon out of a Man

32 As they went out, behold, they brought to him a dumb man possessed
with a devil.
33 And when the devil was cast out, the dumb spake: and the multitudes
marvelled, saying, It was never so seen in Israel.
34 But the Pharisees said, He casteth out devils through the prince of the
devils.

Jesus' Compassion

35 And Jesus went about all the cities and villages, teaching in their syna-
gogues, and preaching the gospel of the kingdom, and healing every sickness
and every disease among the people.
36 But when he saw the multitudes, he was moved with compassion on them,
because they fainted, and were scattered abroad, as sheep having no shepherd.
37 Then saith he unto his disciples, The harvest truly *is* plenteous, but the
labourers *are* few;
38 Pray ye therefore the Lord of the harvest, that he will send forth labourers
into his harvest.

Jesus Appoints Twelve Disciples

10 And when he had called unto *him* his twelve disciples, he gave them
power *against* unclean spirits, to cast them out, and to heal all man-
ner of sickness and all manner of disease.
2 Now the names of the twelve apostles are these; The first, Simon, who is
called Peter, and Andrew his brother; James *the son* of Zebedee, and John his
brother;
3 Philip, and Bartholomew; Thomas, and Matthew the publican; James *the
son* of Alphaeus, and Lebbaeus, whose surname was Thaddaeus;
4 Simon the Canaanite, and Judas Iscariot, who also betrayed him.

Jesus Sends out the Twelve

5 These twelve Jesus sent forth, and commanded them, saying, Go not into
the way of the Gentiles, and into *any* city of the Samaritans enter ye not:
6 But go rather to the lost sheep of the house of Israel.
7 And as ye go, preach, saying, The kingdom of heaven is at hand.
8 Heal the sick, cleanse the lepers, raise the dead, cast out devils: freely ye
have received, freely give.
9 Provide neither gold, nor silver, nor brass in your purses,
10 Nor scrip for *your* journey, neither two coats, neither shoes, nor yet staves:
for the workman is worthy of his meat.
11 And into whatsoever city or town ye shall enter, enquire who in it is wor-
thy; and there abide till ye go thence.
12 And when ye come into an house, salute it.
13 And if the house be worthy, let your peace come upon it: but if it be not
worthy, let your peace return to you.
14 And whosoever shall not receive you, nor hear your words, when ye depart
out of that house or city, shake off the dust of your feet.
15 Verily I say unto you, It shall be more tolerable for the land of Sodom and
Gomorrha in the day of judgment, than for that city.
16 Behold, I send you forth as sheep in the midst of wolves: be ye therefore
wise as serpents, and harmless as doves.
17 But beware of men: for they will deliver you up to the councils, and they
will scourge you in their synagogues;

18 And ye shall be brought before governors and kings for my sake, for a
testimony against them and the Gentiles.
19 But when they deliver you up, take no thought how or what ye shall speak:
for it shall be given you in that same hour what ye shall speak.
20 For it is not ye that speak, but the Spirit of your Father which speaketh in
you.
21 And the brother shall deliver up the brother to death, and the father the
child: and the children shall rise up against *their* parents, and cause them to
be put to death.
22 And ye shall be hated of all *men* for my name's sake: but he that endureth
to the end shall be saved.
23 But when they persecute you in this city, flee ye into another: for verily I
say unto you, Ye shall not have gone over the cities of Israel, till the Son of man
be come.
24 The disciple is not above *his* master, nor the servant above his lord.
25 It is enough for the disciple that he be as his master, and the servant as his
lord. If they have called the master of the house Beelzebub, how much more
shall they call them of his household?
26 Fear them not therefore: for there is nothing covered, that shall not be
revealed; and hid, that shall not be known.
27 What I tell you in darkness, *that* speak ye in light: and what ye hear in the
ear, *that* preach ye upon the housetops.
28 And fear not them which kill the body, but are not able to kill the soul: but
rather fear him which is able to destroy both soul and body in hell.
29 Are not two sparrows sold for a farthing? and one of them shall not fall
on the ground without your Father.
30 But the very hairs of your head are all numbered.
31 Fear ye not therefore, ye are of more value than many sparrows.
32 Whosoever therefore shall confess me before men, him will I confess also
before my Father which is in heaven.
33 But whosoever shall deny me before men, him will I also deny before my
Father which is in heaven.
34 Think not that I am come to send peace on earth: I came not to send peace,
but a sword.
35 For I am come to set a man at variance against his father, and the daugh-
ter against her mother, and the daughter in law against her mother in law.
36 And a man's foes *shall be* they of his own household.
37 He that loveth father or mother more than me is not worthy of me: and
he that loveth son or daughter more than me is not worthy of me.
38 And he that taketh not his cross, and followeth after me, is not worthy of me.
39 He that findeth his life shall lose it: and he that loseth his life for my sake
shall find it.
40 He that receiveth you receiveth me, and he that receiveth me receiveth
him that sent me.
41 He that receiveth a prophet in the name of a prophet shall receive a proph-
et's reward; and he that receiveth a righteous man in the name of a righteous
man shall receive a righteous man's reward.
42 And whosoever shall give to drink unto one of these little ones a cup of
cold *water* only in the name of a disciple, verily I say unto you, he shall in no
wise lose his reward.

Jesus Reassures John

11 And it came to pass, when Jesus had made an end of commanding
his twelve disciples, he departed thence to teach and to preach in
their cities.
2 Now when John had heard in the prison the works of Christ, he sent two
of his disciples,
3 And said unto him, Art thou he that should come, or do we look for another?

4 Jesus answered and said unto them, Go and shew John again those things
which ye do hear and see:
5 The blind receive their sight, and the lame walk, the lepers are cleansed,
and the deaf hear, the dead are raised up, and the poor have the gospel
preached to them.
6 And blessed is *he*, whosoever shall not be offended in me.

Jesus Speaks about John

7 And as they departed, Jesus began to say unto the multitudes concerning
John, What went ye out into the wilderness to see? A reed shaken with the
wind?
8 But what went ye out for to see? A man clothed in soft raiment? behold,
they that wear soft *clothing* are in kings' houses.
9 But what went ye out for to see? A prophet? yea, I say unto you, and more
than a prophet.
10 For this is *he*, of whom it is written, Behold, I send my messenger before
thy face, which shall prepare thy way before thee.
11 Verily I say unto you, Among them that are born of women there hath not
risen a greater than John the Baptist: notwithstanding he that is least in the
kingdom of heaven is greater than he.
12 And from the days of John the Baptist until now the kingdom of heaven
suffereth violence, and the violent take it by force.
13 For all the prophets and the law prophesied until John.
14 And if ye will receive *it*, this is Elias, which was for to come.
15 He that hath ears to hear, let him hear.
16 But whereunto shall I liken this generation? It is like unto children sitting
in the markets, and calling unto their fellows,
17 And saying, We have piped unto you, and ye have not danced; we have
mourned unto you, and ye have not lamented.
18 For John came neither eating nor drinking, and they say, He hath a devil.
19 The Son of man came eating and drinking, and they say, Behold a man
gluttonous, and a winebibber, a friend of publicans and sinners. But wisdom
is justified of her children.

Jesus Warns Some Cities

20 Then began he to upbraid the cities wherein most of his mighty works
were done, because they repented not:
21 Woe unto thee, Chorazin! woe unto thee, Bethsaida! for if the mighty
works, which were done in you, had been done in Tyre and Sidon, they would
have repented long ago in sackcloth and ashes.
22 But I say unto you, It shall be more tolerable for Tyre and Sidon at the day
of judgment, than for you.
23 And thou, Capernaum, which art exalted unto heaven, shalt be brought
down to hell: for if the mighty works, which have been done in thee, had been
done in Sodom, it would have remained until this day.
24 But I say unto you, That it shall be more tolerable for the land of Sodom
in the day of judgment, than for thee.

Jesus Calls the Weary to Come

25 At that time Jesus answered and said, I thank thee, O Father, Lord of heav-
en and earth, because thou hast hid these things from the wise and prudent,
and hast revealed them unto babes.
26 Even so, Father: for so it seemed good in thy sight.
27 All things are delivered unto me of my Father: and no man knoweth the
Son, but the Father; neither knoweth any man the Father, save the Son, and *he*
to whomsoever the Son will reveal *him*.
28 Come unto me, all *ye* that labour and are heavy laden, and I will give you
rest.

29 Take my yoke upon you, and learn of me; for I am meek and lowly in heart:
and ye shall find rest unto your souls.
30 For my yoke *is* easy, and my burden is light.

Jesus Has Authority over the Sabbath

12 At that time Jesus went on the sabbath day through the corn; and
his disciples were an hungred, and began to pluck the ears of corn,
and to eat.
2 But when the Pharisees saw *it*, they said unto him, Behold, thy disciples do
that which is not lawful to do upon the sabbath day.
3 But he said unto them, Have ye not read what David did, when he was an
hungred, and they that were with him;
4 How he entered into the house of God, and did eat the shewbread, which
was not lawful for him to eat, neither for them which were with him, but only
for the priests?
5 Or have ye not read in the law, how that on the sabbath days the priests in
the temple profane the sabbath, and are blameless?
6 But I say unto you, That in this place is *one* greater than the temple.
7 But if ye had known what *this* meaneth, I will have mercy, and not sacrifice,
ye would not have condemned the guiltless.
8 For the Son of man is Lord even of the sabbath day.
9 And when he was departed thence, he went into their synagogue:
10 And, behold, there was a man which had *his* hand withered. And they
asked him, saying, Is it lawful to heal on the sabbath days? that they might
accuse him.
11 And he said unto them, What man shall there be among you, that shall
have one sheep, and if it fall into a pit on the sabbath day, will he not lay hold
on it, and lift *it* out?
12 How much then is a man better than a sheep? Wherefore it is lawful to
do well on the sabbath days.
13 Then saith he to the man, Stretch forth thine hand. And he stretched *it*
forth; and it was restored whole, like as the other.
14 Then the Pharisees went out, and held a council against him, how they
might destroy him.
15 But when Jesus knew *it*, he withdrew himself from thence: and great mul-
titudes followed him, and he healed them all;

Jesus Is God's Servant

16 And charged them that they should not make him known:
17 That it might be fulfilled which was spoken by Esaias the prophet, saying,
18 Behold my servant, whom I have chosen; my beloved, in whom my soul
is well pleased: I will put my spirit upon him, and he shall shew judgment to
the Gentiles.
19 He shall not strive, nor cry; neither shall any man hear his voice in the
streets.
20 A bruised reed shall he not break, and smoking flax shall he not quench,
till he send forth judgment unto victory.
21 And in his name shall the Gentiles trust.

Jesus Is Accused of Working with Beelzebub

22 Then was brought unto him one possessed with a devil, blind, and dumb:
and he healed him, insomuch that the blind and dumb both spake and saw.
23 And all the people were amazed, and said, Is not this the son of David?
24 But when the Pharisees heard *it*, they said, This *fellow* doth not cast out
devils, but by Beelzebub the prince of the devils.
25 And Jesus knew their thoughts, and said unto them, Every kingdom
divided against itself is brought to desolation; and every city or house divided
against itself shall not stand:

26 And if Satan cast out Satan, he is divided against himself; how shall then
his kingdom stand?
27 And if I by Beelzebub cast out devils, by whom do your children cast *them*
out? therefore they shall be your judges.
28 But if I cast out devils by the Spirit of God, then the kingdom of God is
come unto you.
29 Or else how can one enter into a strong man's house, and spoil his goods,
except he first bind the strong man? and then he will spoil his house.
30 He that is not with me is against me; and he that gathereth not with me
scattereth abroad.
31 Wherefore I say unto you, All manner of sin and blasphemy shall be
forgiven unto men: but the blasphemy *against* the *Holy* Ghost shall not be
forgiven unto men.
32 And whosoever speaketh a word against the Son of man, it shall be
forgiven him: but whosoever speaketh against the Holy Ghost, it shall not be
forgiven him, neither in this world, neither in the *world* to come.
33 Either make the tree good, and his fruit good; or else make the tree
corrupt, and his fruit corrupt: for the tree is known by *his* fruit.
34 O generation of vipers, how can ye, being evil, speak good things? for out
of the abundance of the heart the mouth speaketh.
35 A good man out of the good treasure of the heart bringeth forth good
things: and an evil man out of the evil treasure bringeth forth evil things.
36 But I say unto you, That every idle word that men shall speak, they shall
give account thereof in the day of judgment.
37 For by thy words thou shalt be justified, and by thy words thou shalt be
condemned.

The Sign of Jonah

38 Then certain of the scribes and of the Pharisees answered, saying, Master,
we would see a sign from thee.
39 But he answered and said unto them, An evil and adulterous generation
seeketh after a sign; and there shall no sign be given to it, but the sign of the
prophet Jonas:
40 For as Jonas was three days and three nights in the whale's belly; so shall
the Son of man be three days and three nights in the heart of the earth.
41 The men of Nineveh shall rise in judgment with this generation, and shall
condemn it: because they repented at the preaching of Jonas; and, behold, a
greater than Jonas *is* here.
42 The queen of the south shall rise up in the judgment with this generation,
and shall condemn it: for she came from the uttermost parts of the earth to
hear the wisdom of Solomon; and, behold, a greater than Solomon *is* here.
43 When the unclean spirit is gone out of a man, he walketh through dry
places, seeking rest, and findeth none.
44 Then he saith, I will return into my house from whence I came out; and
when he is come, he findeth *it* empty, swept, and garnished.
45 Then goeth he, and taketh with himself seven other spirits more wicked
than himself, and they enter in and dwell there: and the last *state* of that man
is worse than the first. Even so shall it be also unto this wicked generation.

The True Family of Jesus

46 While he yet talked to the people, behold, *his* mother and his brethren
stood without, desiring to speak with him.
47 Then one said unto him, Behold, thy mother and thy brethren stand with-
out, desiring to speak with thee.
48 But he answered and said unto him that told him, Who is my mother?
and who are my brethren?

49 And he stretched forth his hand toward his disciples, and said, Behold my
mother and my brethren!
50 For whosoever shall do the will of my Father which is in heaven, the same
is my brother, and sister, and mother.

The Parable of the Sower and the Seed

13 The same day went Jesus out of the house, and sat by the sea side.
2 And great multitudes were gathered together unto him, so that he
went into a ship, and sat; and the whole multitude stood on the shore.
3 And he spake many things unto them in parables, saying, Behold, a sower
went forth to sow;
4 And when he sowed, some *seeds* fell by the way side, and the fowls came
and devoured them up:
5 Some fell upon stony places, where they had not much earth: and forthwith
they sprung up, because they had no deepness of earth:
6 And when the sun was up, they were scorched; and because they had no
root, they withered away.
7 And some fell among thorns; and the thorns sprung up, and choked them:
8 But other fell into good ground, and brought forth fruit, some an hundred-
fold, some sixtyfold, some thirtyfold.
9 Who hath ears to hear, let him hear.
10 And the disciples came, and said unto him, Why speakest thou unto them
in parables?
11 He answered and said unto them, Because it is given unto you to know
the mysteries of the kingdom of heaven, but to them it is not given.
12 For whosoever hath, to him shall be given, and he shall have more abun-
dance: but whosoever hath not, from him shall be taken away even that he
hath.
13 Therefore speak I to them in parables: because they seeing see not; and
hearing they hear not, neither do they understand.
14 And in them is fulfilled the prophecy of Esaias, which saith, By hearing
ye shall hear, and shall not understand; and seeing ye shall see, and shall not
perceive:
15 For this people's heart is waxed gross, and *their* ears are dull of hearing,
and their eyes they have closed; lest at any time they should see with *their* eyes,
and hear with *their* ears, and should understand with *their* heart, and should
be converted, and I should heal them.
16 But blessed *are* your eyes, for they see: and your ears, for they hear.
17 For verily I say unto you, That many prophets and righteous *men* have
desired to see *those things* which ye see, and have not seen *them*; and to hear
those things which ye hear, and have not heard *them*.
18 Hear ye therefore the parable of the sower.
19 When any one heareth the word of the kingdom, and understandeth *it*
not, then cometh the wicked *one*, and catcheth away that which was sown in
his heart. This is he which received seed by the way side.
20 But he that received the seed into stony places, the same is he that heareth
the word, and anon with joy receiveth it;
21 Yet hath he not root in himself, but dureth for a while: for when tribula-
tion or persecution ariseth because of the word, by and by he is offended.
22 He also that received seed among the thorns is he that heareth the word;
and the care of this world, and the deceitfulness of riches, choke the word,
and he becometh unfruitful.
23 But he that received seed into the good ground is he that heareth the word,
and understandeth *it*; which also beareth fruit, and bringeth forth, some an
hundredfold, some sixty, some thirty.

The Parable of the Tares
24 Another parable put he forth unto them, saying, The kingdom of heaven
is likened unto a man which sowed good seed in his field:
25 But while men slept, his enemy came and sowed tares among the wheat,
and went his way.
26 But when the blade was sprung up, and brought forth fruit, then appeared
the tares also.
27 So the servants of the householder came and said unto him, Sir, didst not
thou sow good seed in thy field? from whence then hath it tares?
28 He said unto them, An enemy hath done this. The servants said unto him,
Wilt thou then that we go and gather them up?
29 But he said, Nay; lest while ye gather up the tares, ye root up also the wheat
with them.
30 Let both grow together until the harvest: and in the time of harvest I will
say to the reapers, Gather ye together first the tares, and bind them in bundles
to burn them: but gather the wheat into my barn.

Descriptions of the Kingdom of Heaven
31 Another parable put he forth unto them, saying, The kingdom of heaven
is like to a grain of mustard seed, which a man took, and sowed in his field:
32 Which indeed is the least of all seeds: but when it is grown, it is the great-
est among herbs, and becometh a tree, so that the birds of the air come and
lodge in the branches thereof.
33 Another parable spake he unto them; The kingdom of heaven is like unto
leaven, which a woman took, and hid in three measures of meal, till the whole
was leavened.
34 All these things spake Jesus unto the multitude in parables; and without
a parable spake he not unto them:
35 That it might be fulfilled which was spoken by the prophet, saying, I will
open my mouth in parables; I will utter things which have been kept secret
from the foundation of the world.

The Meaning of the Tares
36 Then Jesus sent the multitude away, and went into the house: and his
disciples came unto him, saying, Declare unto us the parable of the tares of
the field.
37 He answered and said unto them, He that soweth the good seed is the Son
of man;
38 The field is the world; the good seed are the children of the kingdom; but
the tares are the children of the wicked *one*;
39 The enemy that sowed them is the devil; the harvest is the end of the world;
and the reapers are the angels.
40 As therefore the tares are gathered and burned in the fire; so shall it be in
the end of this world.
41 The Son of man shall send forth his angels, and they shall gather out of
his kingdom all things that offend, and them which do iniquity;
42 And shall cast them into a furnace of fire: there shall be wailing and gnash-
ing of teeth.
43 Then shall the righteous shine forth as the sun in the kingdom of their
Father. Who hath ears to hear, let him hear.

More Descriptions of the Kingdom
44 Again, the kingdom of heaven is like unto treasure hid in a field; the which
when a man hath found, he hideth, and for joy thereof goeth and selleth all
that he hath, and buyeth that field.
45 Again, the kingdom of heaven is like unto a merchant man, seeking good-
ly pearls:

46 Who, when he had found one pearl of great price, went and sold all that
he had, and bought it.
47 Again, the kingdom of heaven is like unto a net, that was cast into the sea,
and gathered of every kind:
48 Which, when it was full, they drew to shore, and sat down, and gathered
the good into vessels, but cast the bad away.
49 So shall it be at the end of the world: the angels shall come forth, and sever
the wicked from among the just,
50 And shall cast them into the furnace of fire: there shall be wailing and
gnashing of teeth.
51 Jesus saith unto them, Have ye understood all these things? They say unto
him, Yea, Lord.
52 Then said he unto them, Therefore every scribe *which is* instructed unto
the kingdom of heaven is like unto a man *that is* an householder, which
bringeth forth out of his treasure *things* new and old.

Christ Is Rejected by His Own Countrymen

53 And it came to pass, *that* when Jesus had finished these parables, he
departed thence.
54 And when he was come into his own country, he taught them in their
synagogue, insomuch that they were astonished, and said, Whence hath this
man this wisdom, and *these* mighty works?
55 Is not this the carpenter's son? is not his mother called Mary? and his
brethren, James, and Joses, and Simon, and Judas?
56 And his sisters, are they not all with us? Whence then hath this *man* all
these things?
57 And they were offended in him. But Jesus said unto them, A prophet is not
without honour, save in his own country, and in his own house.
58 And he did not many mighty works there because of their unbelief.

The Death of John the Baptist

14 At that time Herod the tetrarch heard of the fame of Jesus,
2 And said unto his servants, This is John the Baptist; he is risen from
the dead; and therefore mighty works do shew forth themselves in him.
3 For Herod had laid hold on John, and bound him, and put *him* in prison
for Herodias' sake, his brother Philip's wife.
4 For John said unto him, It is not lawful for thee to have her.
5 And when he would have put him to death, he feared the multitude, because
they counted him as a prophet.
6 But when Herod's birthday was kept, the daughter of Herodias danced
before them, and pleased Herod.
7 Whereupon he promised with an oath to give her whatsoever she would
ask.
8 And she, being before instructed of her mother, said, Give me here John
Baptist's head in a charger.
9 And the king was sorry: nevertheless for the oath's sake, and them which
sat with him at meat, he commanded *it* to be given *her*.
10 And he sent, and beheaded John in the prison.
11 And his head was brought in a charger, and given to the damsel: and she
brought *it* to her mother.
12 And his disciples came, and took up the body, and buried it, and went and
told Jesus.

Jesus Feeds More Than Five Thousand

13 When Jesus heard *of it*, he departed thence by ship into a desert place
apart: and when the people had heard *thereof*, they followed him on foot out
of the cities.

14 And Jesus went forth, and saw a great multitude, and was moved with compassion toward them, and he healed their sick.

15 And when it was evening, his disciples came to him, saying, This is a desert place, and the time is now past; send the multitude away, that they may go into the villages, and buy themselves victuals.

16 But Jesus said unto them, They need not depart; give ye them to eat.

17 And they say unto him, We have here but five loaves, and two fishes.

18 He said, Bring them hither to me.

19 And he commanded the multitude to sit down on the grass, and took the five loaves, and the two fishes, and looking up to heaven, he blessed, and brake, and gave the loaves to *his* disciples, and the disciples to the multitude.

20 And they did all eat, and were filled: and they took up of the fragments that remained twelve baskets full.

21 And they that had eaten were about five thousand men, beside women and children.

Jesus Walks on the Sea

22 And straightway Jesus constrained his disciples to get into a ship, and to go before him unto the other side, while he sent the multitudes away.

23 And when he had sent the multitudes away, he went up into a mountain apart to pray: and when the evening was come, he was there alone.

24 But the ship was now in the midst of the sea, tossed with waves: for the wind was contrary.

25 And in the fourth watch of the night Jesus went unto them, walking on the sea.

26 And when the disciples saw him walking on the sea, they were troubled, saying, It is a spirit; and they cried out for fear.

27 But straightway Jesus spake unto them, saying, Be of good cheer; it is I; be not afraid.

28 And Peter answered him and said, Lord, if it be thou, bid me come unto thee on the water.

29 And he said, Come. And when Peter was come down out of the ship, he walked on the water, to go to Jesus.

30 But when he saw the wind boisterous, he was afraid; and beginning to sink, he cried, saying, Lord, save me.

31 And immediately Jesus stretched forth *his* hand, and caught him, and said unto him, O thou of little faith, wherefore didst thou doubt?

32 And when they were come into the ship, the wind ceased.

33 Then they that were in the ship came and worshipped him, saying, Of a truth thou art the Son of God.

Jesus Heals the Sick

34 And when they were gone over, they came into the land of Gennesaret.

35 And when the men of that place had knowledge of him, they sent out into all that country round about, and brought unto him all that were diseased;

36 And besought him that they might only touch the hem of his garment: and as many as touched were made perfectly whole.

The Religious Leaders Criticize the Disciples

15 Then came to Jesus scribes and Pharisees, which were of Jerusalem, saying,

2 Why do thy disciples transgress the tradition of the elders? for they wash not their hands when they eat bread.

3 But he answered and said unto them, Why do ye also transgress the commandment of God by your tradition?

4 For God commanded, saying, Honour thy father and mother: and, He that curseth father or mother, let him die the death.

5 But ye say, Whosoever shall say to *his* father or *his* mother, *It is* a gift, by whatsoever thou mightest be profited by me;

6 And honour not his father or his mother, *he shall be free*. Thus have ye made
the commandment of God of none effect by your tradition.
7 *Ye* hypocrites, well did Esaias prophesy of you, saying,
8 This people draweth nigh unto me with their mouth, and honoureth me
with *their* lips; but their heart is far from me.
9 But in vain they do worship me, teaching *for* doctrines the commandments
of men.
10 And he called the multitude, and said unto them, Hear, and understand:
11 Not that which goeth into the mouth defileth a man; but that which com-
eth out of the mouth, this defileth a man.
12 Then came his disciples, and said unto him, Knowest thou that the
Pharisees were offended, after they heard this saying?
13 But he answered and said, Every plant, which my heavenly Father hath
not planted, shall be rooted up.
14 Let them alone: they be blind leaders of the blind. And if the blind lead
the blind, both shall fall into the ditch.
15 Then answered Peter and said unto him, Declare unto us this parable.
16 And Jesus said, Are ye also yet without understanding?
17 Do not ye yet understand, that whatsoever entereth in at the mouth goeth
into the belly, and is cast out into the draught?
18 But those things which proceed out of the mouth come forth from the
heart; and they defile the man.
19 For out of the heart proceed evil thoughts, murders, adulteries, fornica-
tions, thefts, false witness, blasphemies:
20 These are *the things* which defile a man: but to eat with unwashen hands
defileth not a man.

The Faith of a Canaanite Woman

21 Then Jesus went thence, and departed into the coasts of Tyre and Sidon.
22 And, behold, a woman of Canaan came out of the same coasts, and cried
unto him, saying, Have mercy on me, O Lord, *thou* Son of David; my daughter
is grievously vexed with a devil.
23 But he answered her not a word. And his disciples came and besought
him, saying, Send her away; for she crieth after us.
24 But he answered and said, I am not sent but unto the lost sheep of the
house of Israel.
25 Then came she and worshipped him, saying, Lord, help me.
26 But he answered and said, It is not meet to take the children's bread, and
to cast *it* to dogs.
27 And she said, Truth, Lord: yet the dogs eat of the crumbs which fall from
their masters' table.
28 Then Jesus answered and said unto her, O woman, great *is* thy faith: be it
unto thee even as thou wilt. And her daughter was made whole from that very
hour.
29 And Jesus departed from thence, and came nigh unto the sea of Galilee;
and went up into a mountain, and sat down there.
30 And great multitudes came unto him, having with them *those that were*
lame, blind, dumb, maimed, and many others, and cast them down at Jesus'
feet; and he healed them:
31 Insomuch that the multitude wondered, when they saw the dumb to
speak, the maimed to be whole, the lame to walk, and the blind to see: and
they glorified the God of Israel.

Jesus Feeds More Than Four Thousand

32 Then Jesus called his disciples *unto him*, and said, I have compassion on
the multitude, because they continue with me now three days, and have noth-
ing to eat: and I will not send them away fasting, lest they faint in the way.

33 And his disciples say unto him, Whence should we have so much bread
in the wilderness, as to fill so great a multitude?
34 And Jesus saith unto them, How many loaves have ye? And they said, Seven,
and a few little fishes.
35 And he commanded the multitude to sit down on the ground.
36 And he took the seven loaves and the fishes, and gave thanks, and brake
them, and gave to his disciples, and the disciples to the multitude.
37 And they did all eat, and were filled: and they took up of the broken *meat*
that was left seven baskets full.
38 And they that did eat were four thousand men, beside women and children.
39 And he sent away the multitude, and took ship, and came into the coasts
of Magdala.

The Pharisees Demand a Sign

16 The Pharisees also with the Sadducees came, and tempting desired
him that he would shew them a sign from heaven.
2 He answered and said unto them, When it is evening, ye say, *It will be* fair
weather: for the sky is red.
3 And in the morning, *It will be* foul weather to day: for the sky is red and
lowring. O *ye* hypocrites, ye can discern the face of the sky; but can ye not
discern the signs of the times?
4 A wicked and adulterous generation seeketh after a sign; and there shall
no sign be given unto it, but the sign of the prophet Jonas. And he left them,
and departed.
5 And when his disciples were come to the other side, they had forgotten to
take bread.
6 Then Jesus said unto them, Take heed and beware of the leaven of the
Pharisees and of the Sadducees.
7 And they reasoned among themselves, saying, *It is* because we have taken
no bread.
8 *Which* when Jesus perceived, he said unto them, O ye of little faith, why
reason ye among yourselves, because ye have brought no bread?
9 Do ye not yet understand, neither remember the five loaves of the five
thousand, and how many baskets ye took up?
10 Neither the seven loaves of the four thousand, and how many baskets ye
took up?
11 How is it that ye do not understand that I spake *it* not to you concerning
bread, that ye should beware of the leaven of the Pharisees and of the
Sadducees?
12 Then understood they how that he bade *them* not beware of the leaven of
bread, but of the doctrine of the Pharisees and of the Sadducees.

Peter Declares His Faith

13 When Jesus came into the coasts of Caesarea Philippi, he asked his
disciples, saying, Whom do men say that I the Son of man am?
14 And they said, Some *say that thou art* John the Baptist: some, Elias; and
others, Jeremias, or one of the prophets.
15 He saith unto them, But whom say ye that I am?
16 And Simon Peter answered and said, Thou art the Christ, the Son of the
living God.
17 And Jesus answered and said unto him, Blessed art thou, Simon Bar-jona:
for flesh and blood hath not revealed *it* unto thee, but my Father which is in
heaven.
18 And I say also unto thee, That thou art Peter, and upon this rock I will
build my church; and the gates of hell shall not prevail against it.

19 And I will give unto thee the keys of the kingdom of heaven: and whatso-
ever thou shalt bind on earth shall be bound in heaven: and whatsoever thou
shalt loose on earth shall be loosed in heaven.
20 Then charged he his disciples that they should tell no man that he was
Jesus the Christ.

Jesus Foretells His Death and Resurrection

21 From that time forth began Jesus to shew unto his disciples, how that he
must go unto Jerusalem, and suffer many things of the elders and chief priests
and scribes, and be killed, and be raised again the third day.
22 Then Peter took him, and began to rebuke him, saying, Be it far from thee,
Lord: this shall not be unto thee.
23 But he turned, and said unto Peter, Get thee behind me, Satan: thou art
an offence unto me: for thou savourest not the things that be of God, but those
that be of men.

What It Means to Follow Jesus

24 Then said Jesus unto his disciples, If any *man* will come after me, let him
deny himself, and take up his cross, and follow me.
25 For whosoever will save his life shall lose it: and whosoever will lose his
life for my sake shall find it.
26 For what is a man profited, if he shall gain the whole world, and lose his
own soul? or what shall a man give in exchange for his soul?
27 For the Son of man shall come in the glory of his Father with his angels;
and then he shall reward every man according to his works.
28 Verily I say unto you, There be some standing here, which shall not taste
of death, till they see the Son of man coming in his kingdom.

The Transfiguration

17 And after six days Jesus taketh Peter, James, and John his brother,
and bringeth them up into an high mountain apart,
2 And was transfigured before them: and his face did shine as the sun, and
his raiment was white as the light.
3 And, behold, there appeared unto them Moses and Elias talking with him.
4 Then answered Peter, and said unto Jesus, Lord, it is good for us to be here:
if thou wilt, let us make here three tabernacles; one for thee, and one for Moses,
and one for Elias.
5 While he yet spake, behold, a bright cloud overshadowed them: and behold
a voice out of the cloud, which said, This is my beloved Son, in whom I am well
pleased; hear ye him.
6 And when the disciples heard *it*, they fell on their face, and were sore afraid.
7 And Jesus came and touched them, and said, Arise, and be not afraid.
8 And when they had lifted up their eyes, they saw no man, save Jesus only.
9 And as they came down from the mountain, Jesus charged them, saying,
Tell the vision to no man, until the Son of man be risen again from the dead.
10 And his disciples asked him, saying, Why then say the scribes that Elias
must first come?
11 And Jesus answered and said unto them, Elias truly shall first come, and
restore all things.
12 But I say unto you, That Elias is come already, and they knew him not, but
have done unto him whatsoever they listed. Likewise shall also the Son of man
suffer of them.
13 Then the disciples understood that he spake unto them of John the Baptist.

Jesus Heals a Demon-Possessed Boy

14 And when they were come to the multitude, there came to him a *certain*
man, kneeling down to him, and saying,

15 Lord, have mercy on my son: for he is lunatick, and sore vexed: for ofttimes
he falleth into the fire, and oft into the water.
16 And I brought him to thy disciples, and they could not cure him.
17 Then Jesus answered and said, O faithless and perverse generation, how
long shall I be with you? how long shall I suffer you? bring him hither to me.
18 And Jesus rebuked the devil; and he departed out of him: and the child
was cured from that very hour.
19 Then came the disciples to Jesus apart, and said, Why could not we cast
him out?
20 And Jesus said unto them, Because of your unbelief: for verily I say unto
you, If ye have faith as a grain of mustard seed, ye shall say unto this mountain,
Remove hence to yonder place; and it shall remove; and nothing shall be
impossible unto you.
21 Howbeit this kind goeth not out but by prayer and fasting.

Jesus Again Foretells His Death and Resurrection

22 And while they abode in Galilee, Jesus said unto them, The Son of man
shall be betrayed into the hands of men:
23 And they shall kill him, and the third day he shall be raised again. And
they were exceeding sorry.

Paying the Temple Tax

24 And when they were come to Capernaum, they that received tribute *money*
came to Peter, and said, Doth not your master pay tribute?
25 He saith, Yes. And when he was come into the house, Jesus prevented him,
saying, What thinkest thou, Simon? of whom do the kings of the earth take
custom or tribute? of their own children, or of strangers?
26 Peter saith unto him, Of strangers. Jesus saith unto him, Then are the
children free.
27 Notwithstanding, lest we should offend them, go thou to the sea, and cast
an hook, and take up the fish that first cometh up; and when thou hast opened
his mouth, thou shalt find a piece of money: that take, and give unto them for
me and thee.

Greatness in the Kingdom

18 At the same time came the disciples unto Jesus, saying, Who is the
greatest in the kingdom of heaven?
2 And Jesus called a little child unto him, and set him in the midst of them,
3 And said, Verily I say unto you, Except ye be converted, and become as little
children, ye shall not enter into the kingdom of heaven.
4 Whosoever therefore shall humble himself as this little child, the same is
greatest in the kingdom of heaven.
5 And whoso shall receive one such little child in my name receiveth me.

Causing Others to Sin

6 But whoso shall offend one of these little ones which believe in me, it were
better for him that a millstone were hanged about his neck, and *that* he were
drowned in the depth of the sea.
7 Woe unto the world because of offences! for it must needs be that offences
come; but woe to that man by whom the offence cometh!
8 Wherefore if thy hand or thy foot offend thee, cut them off, and cast *them*
from thee: it is better for thee to enter into life halt or maimed, rather than
having two hands or two feet to be cast into everlasting fire.
9 And if thine eye offend thee, pluck it out, and cast *it* from thee: it is better
for thee to enter into life with one eye, rather than having two eyes to be cast
into hell fire.

10 Take heed that ye despise not one of these little ones; for I say unto you,
That in heaven their angels do always behold the face of my Father which is
in heaven.
11 For the Son of man is come to save that which was lost.

The Lost Sheep

12 How think ye? if a man have an hundred sheep, and one of them be gone
astray, doth he not leave the ninety and nine, and goeth into the mountains,
and seeketh that which is gone astray?
13 And if so be that he find it, verily I say unto you, he rejoiceth more of that
sheep, than of the ninety and nine which went not astray.
14 Even so it is not the will of your Father which is in heaven, that one of
these little ones should perish.

Dealing with Believers Who Do Wrong

15 Moreover if thy brother shall trespass against thee, go and tell him his
fault between thee and him alone: if he shall hear thee, thou hast gained thy
brother.
16 But if he will not hear *thee, then* take with thee one or two more, that in
the mouth of two or three witnesses every word may be established.
17 And if he shall neglect to hear them, tell *it* unto the church: but if he
neglect to hear the church, let him be unto thee as an heathen man and a
publican.
18 Verily I say unto you, Whatsoever ye shall bind on earth shall be bound
in heaven: and whatsoever ye shall loose on earth shall be loosed in heaven.
19 Again I say unto you, That if two of you shall agree on earth as touching
any thing that they shall ask, it shall be done for them of my Father which is
in heaven.
20 For where two or three are gathered together in my name, there am I in
the midst of them.

Forgiving Others

21 Then came Peter to him, and said, Lord, how oft shall my brother sin
against me, and I forgive him? till seven times?
22 Jesus saith unto him, I say not unto thee, Until seven times: but, Until
seventy times seven.
23 Therefore is the kingdom of heaven likened unto a certain king, which
would take account of his servants.
24 And when he had begun to reckon, one was brought unto him, which
owed him ten thousand talents.
25 But forasmuch as he had not to pay, his lord commanded him to be sold,
and his wife, and children, and all that he had, and payment to be made.
26 The servant therefore fell down, and worshipped him, saying, Lord, have
patience with me, and I will pay thee all.
27 Then the lord of that servant was moved with compassion, and loosed
him, and forgave him the debt.
28 But the same servant went out, and found one of his fellowservants, which
owed him an hundred pence: and he laid hands on him, and took *him* by the
throat, saying, Pay me that thou owest.
29 And his fellowservant fell down at his feet, and besought him, saying, Have
patience with me, and I will pay thee all.
30 And he would not: but went and cast him into prison, till he should pay
the debt.
31 So when his fellowservants saw what was done, they were very sorry, and
came and told unto their lord all that was done.
32 Then his lord, after that he had called him, said unto him, O thou wicked
servant, I forgave thee all that debt, because thou desiredst me:

33 Shouldest not thou also have had compassion on thy fellowservant, even
as I had pity on thee?
34 And his lord was wroth, and delivered him to the tormentors, till he should
pay all that was due unto him.
35 So likewise shall my heavenly Father do also unto you, if ye from your
hearts forgive not every one his brother their trespasses.

Jesus Heals Many

19 And it came to pass, *that* when Jesus had finished these sayings, he
departed from Galilee, and came into the coasts of Judaea beyond
Jordan;
2 And great multitudes followed him; and he healed them there.

A Discussion about Divorce

3 The Pharisees also came unto him, tempting him, and saying unto him, Is
it lawful for a man to put away his wife for every cause?
4 And he answered and said unto them, Have ye not read, that he which made
them at the beginning made them male and female,
5 And said, For this cause shall a man leave father and mother, and shall
cleave to his wife: and they twain shall be one flesh?
6 Wherefore they are no more twain, but one flesh. What therefore God hath
joined together, let not man put asunder.
7 They say unto him, Why did Moses then command to give a writing of
divorcement, and to put her away?
8 He saith unto them, Moses because of the hardness of your hearts suffered
you to put away your wives: but from the beginning it was not so.
9 And I say unto you, Whosoever shall put away his wife, except *it be* for
fornication, and shall marry another, committeth adultery: and whoso mar-
rieth her which is put away doth commit adultery.
10 His disciples say unto him, If the case of the man be so with *his* wife, it is
not good to marry.
11 But he said unto them, All *men* cannot receive this saying, save *they* to
whom it is given.
12 For there are some eunuchs, which were so born from *their* mother's
womb: and there are some eunuchs, which were made eunuchs of men: and
there be eunuchs, which have made themselves eunuchs for the kingdom of
heaven's sake. He that is able to receive *it*, let him receive *it*.

Jesus Blesses Little Children

13 Then were there brought unto him little children, that he should put *his*
hands on them, and pray: and the disciples rebuked them.
14 But Jesus said, Suffer little children, and forbid them not, to come unto
me: for of such is the kingdom of heaven.
15 And he laid *his* hands on them, and departed thence.

Jesus and the Rich Young Man

16 And, behold, one came and said unto him, Good Master, what good thing
shall I do, that I may have eternal life?
17 And he said unto him, Why callest thou me good? *there is* none good but
one, *that is*, God: but if thou wilt enter into life, keep the commandments.
18 He saith unto him, Which? Jesus said, Thou shalt do no murder, Thou shalt
not commit adultery, Thou shalt not steal, Thou shalt not bear false witness,
19 Honour thy father and *thy* mother: and, Thou shalt love thy neighbour as
thyself.
20 The young man saith unto him, All these things have I kept from my youth
up: what lack I yet?
21 Jesus said unto him, If thou wilt be perfect, go *and* sell that thou hast, and
give to the poor, and thou shalt have treasure in heaven: and come *and* follow me.

22 But when the young man heard that saying, he went away sorrowful: for
he had great possessions.

It Is Difficult for the Rich to Enter the Kingdom

23 Then said Jesus unto his disciples, Verily I say unto you, That a rich man
shall hardly enter into the kingdom of heaven.
24 And again I say unto you, It is easier for a camel to go through the eye of
a needle, than for a rich man to enter into the kingdom of God.
25 When his disciples heard *it*, they were exceedingly amazed, saying, Who
then can be saved?
26 But Jesus beheld *them*, and said unto them, With men this is impossible;
but with God all things are possible.
27 Then answered Peter and said unto him, Behold, we have forsaken all, and
followed thee; what shall we have therefore?
28 And Jesus said unto them, Verily I say unto you, That ye which have fol-
lowed me, in the regeneration when the Son of man shall sit in the throne of
his glory, ye also shall sit upon twelve thrones, judging the twelve tribes of
Israel.
29 And every one that hath forsaken houses, or brethren, or sisters, or father,
or mother, or wife, or children, or lands, for my name's sake, shall receive an
hundredfold, and shall inherit everlasting life.
30 But many *that are* first shall be last; and the last *shall be* first.

The Parable of the Vineyard Workers

20 For the kingdom of heaven is like unto a man *that is* an household-
er, which went out early in the morning to hire labourers into his
vineyard.
2 And when he had agreed with the labourers for a penny a day, he sent them
into his vineyard.
3 And he went out about the third hour, and saw others standing idle in the
marketplace,
4 And said unto them; Go ye also into the vineyard, and whatsoever is right
I will give you. And they went their way.
5 Again he went out about the sixth and ninth hour, and did likewise.
6 And about the eleventh hour he went out, and found others standing idle,
and saith unto them, Why stand ye here all the day idle?
7 They say unto him, Because no man hath hired us. He saith unto them, Go
ye also into the vineyard; and whatsoever is right, *that* shall ye receive.
8 So when even was come, the lord of the vineyard saith unto his steward,
Call the labourers, and give them *their* hire, beginning from the last unto the
first.
9 And when they came that *were hired* about the eleventh hour, they received
every man a penny.
10 But when the first came, they supposed that they should have received
more; and they likewise received every man a penny.
11 And when they had received *it*, they murmured against the goodman of
the house,
12 Saying, These last have wrought *but* one hour, and thou hast made them
equal unto us, which have borne the burden and heat of the day.
13 But he answered one of them, and said, Friend, I do thee no wrong: didst
not thou agree with me for a penny?
14 Take *that* thine *is*, and go thy way: I will give unto this last, even as unto
thee.
15 Is it not lawful for me to do what I will with mine own? Is thine eye evil,
because I am good?
16 So the last shall be first, and the first last: for many be called, but few
chosen.

Jesus Again Foretells His Death and Resurrection

17 And Jesus going up to Jerusalem took the twelve disciples apart in the way,
and said unto them,
18 Behold, we go up to Jerusalem; and the Son of man shall be betrayed unto
the chief priests and unto the scribes, and they shall condemn him to death,
19 And shall deliver him to the Gentiles to mock, and to scourge, and to
crucify *him*: and the third day he shall rise again.

A Mother's Request

20 Then came to him the mother of Zebedee's children with her sons, wor-
shipping *him*, and desiring a certain thing of him.
21 And he said unto her, What wilt thou? She saith unto him, Grant that these
my two sons may sit, the one on thy right hand, and the other on the left, in
thy kingdom.
22 But Jesus answered and said, Ye know not what ye ask. Are ye able to drink
of the cup that I shall drink of, and to be baptized with the baptism that I am
baptized with? They say unto him, We are able.
23 And he saith unto them, Ye shall drink indeed of my cup, and be baptized
with the baptism that I am baptized with: but to sit on my right hand, and on
my left, is not mine to give, but *it shall be given to them* for whom it is prepared
of my Father.
24 And when the ten heard *it*, they were moved with indignation against the
two brethren.
25 But Jesus called them *unto him*, and said, Ye know that the princes of the
Gentiles exercise dominion over them, and they that are great exercise author-
ity upon them.
26 But it shall not be so among you: but whosoever will be great among you,
let him be your minister;
27 And whosoever will be chief among you, let him be your servant:
28 Even as the Son of man came not to be ministered unto, but to minister,
and to give his life a ransom for many.

Jesus Heals Two Blind Men

29 And as they departed from Jericho, a great multitude followed him.
30 And, behold, two blind men sitting by the way side, when they heard that
Jesus passed by, cried out, saying, Have mercy on us, O Lord, *thou* Son of David.
31 And the multitude rebuked them, because they should hold their peace:
but they cried the more, saying, Have mercy on us, O Lord, *thou* Son of David.
32 And Jesus stood still, and called them, and said, What will ye that I shall
do unto you?
33 They say unto him, Lord, that our eyes may be opened.
34 So Jesus had compassion *on them*, and touched their eyes: and immedi-
ately their eyes received sight, and they followed him.

Jesus Rides into Jerusalem

21 And when they drew nigh unto Jerusalem, and were come to
Bethphage, unto the mount of Olives, then sent Jesus two disciples,
2 Saying unto them, Go into the village over against you, and straightway ye
shall find an ass tied, and a colt with her: loose *them*, and bring *them* unto me.
3 And if any *man* say ought unto you, ye shall say, The Lord hath need of
them; and straightway he will send them.
4 All this was done, that it might be fulfilled which was spoken by the proph-
et, saying,
5 Tell ye the daughter of Sion, Behold, thy King cometh unto thee, meek, and
sitting upon an ass, and a colt the foal of an ass.
6 And the disciples went, and did as Jesus commanded them,
7 And brought the ass, and the colt, and put on them their clothes, and they
set *him* thereon.

8 And a very great multitude spread their garments in the way; others cut
down branches from the trees, and strawed *them* in the way.
9 And the multitudes that went before, and that followed, cried, saying,
Hosanna to the Son of David: Blessed *is* he that cometh in the name of the
Lord; Hosanna in the highest.
10 And when he was come into Jerusalem, all the city was moved, saying,
Who is this?
11 And the multitude said, This is Jesus the prophet of Nazareth of Galilee.

Jesus Drives the Moneychangers out of the Temple

12 And Jesus went into the temple of God, and cast out all them that sold and
bought in the temple, and overthrew the tables of the moneychangers, and
the seats of them that sold doves,
13 And said unto them, It is written, My house shall be called the house of
prayer; but ye have made it a den of thieves.
14 And the blind and the lame came to him in the temple; and he healed
them.
15 And when the chief priests and scribes saw the wonderful things that he
did, and the children crying in the temple, and saying, Hosanna to the Son of
David; they were sore displeased,
16 And said unto him, Hearest thou what these say? And Jesus saith unto
them, Yea; have ye never read, Out of the mouth of babes and sucklings thou
hast perfected praise?
17 And he left them, and went out of the city into Bethany; and he lodged
there.

Jesus Curses the Fig Tree

18 Now in the morning as he returned into the city, he hungered.
19 And when he saw a fig tree in the way, he came to it, and found nothing
thereon, but leaves only, and said unto it, Let no fruit grow on thee hence-
forward for ever. And presently the fig tree withered away.
20 And when the disciples saw *it*, they marvelled, saying, How soon is the fig
tree withered away!
21 Jesus answered and said unto them, Verily I say unto you, If ye have faith,
and doubt not, ye shall not only do this *which is done* to the fig tree, but also
if ye shall say unto this mountain, Be thou removed, and be thou cast into the
sea; it shall be done.
22 And all things, whatsoever ye shall ask in prayer, believing, ye shall receive.

Jesus' Authority Is Challenged

23 And when he was come into the temple, the chief priests and the elders
of the people came unto him as he was teaching, and said, By what authority
doest thou these things? and who gave thee this authority?
24 And Jesus answered and said unto them, I also will ask you one thing,
which if ye tell me, I in like wise will tell you by what authority I do these things.
25 The baptism of John, whence was it? from heaven, or of men? And they
reasoned with themselves, saying, If we shall say, From heaven; he will say unto
us, Why did ye not then believe him?
26 But if we shall say, Of men; we fear the people; for all hold John as a prophet.
27 And they answered Jesus, and said, We cannot tell. And he said unto them,
Neither tell I you by what authority I do these things.

The Parable of the Prodigal Son

28 But what think ye? A *certain* man had two sons; and he came to the first,
and said, Son, go work to day in my vineyard.
29 He answered and said, I will not: but afterward he repented, and went.
30 And he came to the second, and said likewise. And he answered and said,
I *go*, sir: and went not.

31 Whether of them twain did the will of *his* father? They say unto him, The
first. Jesus saith unto them, Verily I say unto you, That the publicans and the
harlots go into the kingdom of God before you.
32 For John came unto you in the way of righteousness, and ye believed him
not: but the publicans and the harlots believed him: and ye, when ye had seen
it, repented not afterward, that ye might believe him.

The Parable of the Wicked Husbandmen

33 Hear another parable: There was a certain householder, which planted a
vineyard, and hedged it round about, and digged a winepress in it, and built
a tower, and let it out to husbandmen, and went into a far country:
34 And when the time of the fruit drew near, he sent his servants to the
husbandmen, that they might receive the fruits of it.
35 And the husbandmen took his servants, and beat one, and killed another,
and stoned another.
36 Again, he sent other servants more than the first: and they did unto them
likewise.
37 But last of all he sent unto them his son, saying, They will reverence my son.
38 But when the husbandmen saw the son, they said among themselves, This
is the heir; come, let us kill him, and let us seize on his inheritance.
39 And they caught him, and cast *him* out of the vineyard, and slew *him*.
40 When the lord therefore of the vineyard cometh, what will he do unto
those husbandmen?
41 They say unto him, He will miserably destroy those wicked men, and will
let out *his* vineyard unto other husbandmen, which shall render him the fruits
in their seasons.
42 Jesus saith unto them, Did ye never read in the scriptures, The stone which
the builders rejected, the same is become the head of the corner: this is the
Lord's doing, and it is marvellous in our eyes?
43 Therefore say I unto you, The kingdom of God shall be taken from you,
and given to a nation bringing forth the fruits thereof.
44 And whosoever shall fall on this stone shall be broken: but on whomso-
ever it shall fall, it will grind him to powder.
45 And when the chief priests and Pharisees had heard his parables, they
perceived that he spake of them.
46 But when they sought to lay hands on him, they feared the multitude,
because they took him for a prophet.

The Parable of the Marriage of the King's Son

22 And Jesus answered and spake unto them again by parables, and
said,
2 The kingdom of heaven is like unto a certain king, which made a marriage
for his son,
3 And sent forth his servants to call them that were bidden to the wedding:
and they would not come.
4 Again, he sent forth other servants, saying, Tell them which are bidden,
Behold, I have prepared my dinner: my oxen and *my* fatlings *are* killed, and
all things *are* ready: come unto the marriage.
5 But they made light of *it*, and went their ways, one to his farm, another to
his merchandise:
6 And the remnant took his servants, and entreated *them* spitefully, and slew
them.
7 But when the king heard *thereof*, he was wroth: and he sent forth his
armies, and destroyed those murderers, and burned up their city.
8 Then saith he to his servants, The wedding is ready, but they which were
bidden were not worthy.

9 Go ye therefore into the highways, and as many as ye shall find, bid to the
marriage.
10 So those servants went out into the highways, and gathered together all
as many as they found, both bad and good: and the wedding was furnished
with guests.
11 And when the king came in to see the guests, he saw there a man which
had not on a wedding garment:
12 And he saith unto him, Friend, how camest thou in hither not having a
wedding garment? And he was speechless.
13 Then said the king to the servants, Bind him hand and foot, and take him
away, and cast *him* into outer darkness; there shall be weeping and gnashing
of teeth.
14 For many are called, but few *are* chosen.

A Question about Taxes

15 Then went the Pharisees, and took counsel how they might entangle him
in *his* talk.
16 And they sent out unto him their disciples with the Herodians, saying,
Master, we know that thou art true, and teachest the way of God in truth,
neither carest thou for any *man*: for thou regardest not the person of men.
17 Tell us therefore, What thinkest thou? Is it lawful to give tribute unto
Caesar, or not?
18 But Jesus perceived their wickedness, and said, Why tempt ye me, *ye*
hypocrites?
19 Shew me the tribute money. And they brought unto him a penny.
20 And he saith unto them, Whose *is* this image and superscription?
21 They say unto him, Caesar's. Then saith he unto them, Render therefore
unto Caesar the things which are Caesar's; and unto God the things that are
God's.
22 When they had heard *these words*, they marvelled, and left him, and went
their way.

Christ Refutes the Sadducees about the Resurrection

23 The same day came to him the Sadducees, which say that there is no res-
urrection, and asked him,
24 Saying, Master, Moses said, If a man die, having no children, his brother
shall marry his wife, and raise up seed unto his brother.
25 Now there were with us seven brethren: and the first, when he had mar-
ried a wife, deceased, and, having no issue, left his wife unto his brother:
26 Likewise the second also, and the third, unto the seventh.
27 And last of all the woman died also.
28 Therefore in the resurrection whose wife shall she be of the seven? for
they all had her.
29 Jesus answered and said unto them, Ye do err, not knowing the scriptures,
nor the power of God.
30 For in the resurrection they neither marry, nor are given in marriage, but
are as the angels of God in heaven.
31 But as touching the resurrection of the dead, have ye not read that which
was spoken unto you by God, saying,
32 I am the God of Abraham, and the God of Isaac, and the God of Jacob?
God is not the God of the dead, but of the living.
33 And when the multitude heard *this*, they were astonished at his doctrine.

The Greatest Commandment

34 But when the Pharisees had heard that he had put the Sadducees to silence,
they were gathered together.
35 Then one of them, *which was* a lawyer, asked *him a question*, tempting
him, and saying,

36 Master, which *is* the great commandment in the law?
37 Jesus said unto him, Thou shalt love the Lord thy God with all thy heart,
and with all thy soul, and with all thy mind.
38 This is the first and great commandment.
39 And the second *is* like unto it, Thou shalt love thy neighbour as thyself.
40 On these two commandments hang all the law and the prophets.

Jesus Silences the Pharisees about the Messiah

41 While the Pharisees were gathered together, Jesus asked them,
42 Saying, What think ye of Christ? whose son is he? They say unto him, *The*
Son of David.
43 He saith unto them, How then doth David in spirit call him Lord, saying,
44 The LORD said unto my Lord, Sit thou on my right hand, till I make thine
enemies thy footstool?
45 If David then call him Lord, how is he his son?
46 And no man was able to answer him a word, neither durst any *man* from
that day forth ask him any more *questions*.

Jesus Warns about the Scribes and Pharisees

23 Then spake Jesus to the multitude, and to his disciples,
2 Saying, The scribes and the Pharisees sit in Moses' seat:
3 All therefore whatsoever they bid you observe, *that* observe and do; but do
not ye after their works: for they say, and do not.
4 For they bind heavy burdens and grievous to be borne, and lay *them* on
men's shoulders; but they *themselves* will not move them with one of their
fingers.
5 But all their works they do for to be seen of men: they make broad their
phylacteries, and enlarge the borders of their garments,
6 And love the uppermost rooms at feasts, and the chief seats in the syna-
gogues,
7 And greetings in the markets, and to be called of men, Rabbi, Rabbi.
8 But be not ye called Rabbi: for one is your Master, *even* Christ; and all ye
are brethren.
9 And call no *man* your father upon the earth: for one is your Father, which
is in heaven.
10 Neither be ye called masters: for one is your Master, *even* Christ.
11 But he that is greatest among you shall be your servant.
12 And whosoever shall exalt himself shall be abased; and he that shall hum-
ble himself shall be exalted.

The Hypocrisy of the Scribes and Pharisees

13 But woe unto you, scribes and Pharisees, hypocrites! for ye shut up the
kingdom of heaven against men: for ye neither go in *yourselves*, neither suffer
ye them that are entering to go in.
14 Woe unto you, scribes and Pharisees, hypocrites! for ye devour widows'
houses, and for a pretence make long prayer: therefore ye shall receive the
greater damnation.
15 Woe unto you, scribes and Pharisees, hypocrites! for ye compass sea and
land to make one proselyte, and when he is made, ye make him twofold more
the child of hell than yourselves.
16 Woe unto you, *ye* blind guides, which say, Whosoever shall swear by the
temple, it is nothing; but whosoever shall swear by the gold of the temple, he
is a debtor!
17 *Ye* fools and blind: for whether is greater, the gold, or the temple that
sanctifieth the gold?
18 And, Whosoever shall swear by the altar, it is nothing; but whosoever
sweareth by the gift that is upon it, he is guilty.

19 *Ye* fools and blind: for whether *is* greater, the gift, or the altar that sancti-
fieth the gift?
20 Whoso therefore shall swear by the altar, sweareth by it, and by all things
thereon.
21 And whoso shall swear by the temple, sweareth by it, and by him that
dwelleth therein.
22 And he that shall swear by heaven, sweareth by the throne of God, and by
him that sitteth thereon.
23 Woe unto you, scribes and Pharisees, hypocrites! for ye pay tithe of mint
and anise and cummin, and have omitted the weightier *matters* of the law,
judgment, mercy, and faith: these ought ye to have done, and not to leave the
other undone.
24 *Ye* blind guides, which strain at a gnat, and swallow a camel.
25 Woe unto you, scribes and Pharisees, hypocrites! for ye make clean the
outside of the cup and of the platter, but within they are full of extortion and
excess.
26 *Thou* blind Pharisee, cleanse first that *which is* within the cup and platter,
that the outside of them may be clean also.
27 Woe unto you, scribes and Pharisees, hypocrites! for ye are like unto
whited sepulchres, which indeed appear beautiful outward, but are within
full of dead *men's* bones, and of all uncleanness.
28 Even so ye also outwardly appear righteous unto men, but within ye are
full of hypocrisy and iniquity.
29 Woe unto you, scribes and Pharisees, hypocrites! because ye build the
tombs of the prophets, and garnish the sepulchres of the righteous,
30 And say, If we had been in the days of our fathers, we would not have been
partakers with them in the blood of the prophets.
31 Wherefore ye be witnesses unto yourselves, that ye are the children of
them which killed the prophets.
32 Fill ye up then the measure of your fathers.
33 *Ye* serpents, *ye* generation of vipers, how can ye escape the damnation of
hell?

Jesus Prophesies the Destruction of Jerusalem

34 Wherefore, behold, I send unto you prophets, and wise men, and scribes:
and *some* of them ye shall kill and crucify; and *some* of them shall ye scourge
in your synagogues, and persecute *them* from city to city:
35 That upon you may come all the righteous blood shed upon the earth,
from the blood of righteous Abel unto the blood of Zacharias son of Barachias,
whom ye slew between the temple and the altar.
36 Verily I say unto you, All these things shall come upon this generation.
37 O Jerusalem, Jerusalem, *thou* that killest the prophets, and stonest them
which are sent unto thee, how often would I have gathered thy children togeth-
er, even as a hen gathereth her chickens under *her* wings, and ye would not!
38 Behold, your house is left unto you desolate.
39 For I say unto you, Ye shall not see me henceforth, till ye shall say, Blessed
is he that cometh in the name of the Lord.

Jesus Tells about the Future

24 And Jesus went out, and departed from the temple: and his disciples
came to *him* for to shew him the buildings of the temple.
2 And Jesus said unto them, See ye not all these things? verily I say unto you,
There shall not be left here one stone upon another, that shall not be thrown
down.
3 And as he sat upon the mount of Olives, the disciples came unto him pri-
vately, saying, Tell us, when shall these things be? and what *shall be* the sign
of thy coming, and of the end of the world?

4 And Jesus answered and said unto them, Take heed that no man deceive you.
5 For many shall come in my name, saying, I am Christ; and shall deceive
many.
6 And ye shall hear of wars and rumours of wars: see that ye be not troubled:
for all *these things* must come to pass, but the end is not yet.
7 For nation shall rise against nation, and kingdom against kingdom: and
there shall be famines, and pestilences, and earthquakes, in divers places.
8 All these *are* the beginning of sorrows.
9 Then shall they deliver you up to be afflicted, and shall kill you: and ye shall
be hated of all nations for my name's sake.
10 And then shall many be offended, and shall betray one another, and shall
hate one another.
11 And many false prophets shall rise, and shall deceive many.
12 And because iniquity shall abound, the love of many shall wax cold.
13 But he that shall endure unto the end, the same shall be saved.
14 And this gospel of the kingdom shall be preached in all the world for a
witness unto all nations; and then shall the end come.
15 When ye therefore shall see the abomination of desolation, spoken of by
Daniel the prophet, stand in the holy place, (whoso readeth, let him under-
stand:)
16 Then let them which be in Judaea flee into the mountains:
17 Let him which is on the housetop not come down to take any thing out
of his house:
18 Neither let him which is in the field return back to take his clothes.
19 And woe unto them that are with child, and to them that give suck in those
days!
20 But pray ye that your flight be not in the winter, neither on the sabbath
day:
21 For then shall be great tribulation, such as was not since the beginning of
the world to this time, no, nor ever shall be.
22 And except those days should be shortened, there should no flesh be saved:
but for the elect's sake those days shall be shortened.
23 Then if any man shall say unto you, Lo, here *is* Christ, or there; believe *it*
not.
24 For there shall arise false Christs, and false prophets, and shall shew great
signs and wonders; insomuch that, if *it were* possible, they shall deceive the
very elect.
25 Behold, I have told you before.
26 Wherefore if they shall say unto you, Behold, he is in the desert; go not
forth: behold, *he is* in the secret chambers; believe *it* not.
27 For as the lightning cometh out of the east, and shineth even unto the
west; so shall also the coming of the Son of man be.
28 For wheresoever the carcase is, there will the eagles be gathered together.
29 Immediately after the tribulation of those days shall the sun be darkened,
and the moon shall not give her light, and the stars shall fall from heaven, and
the powers of the heavens shall be shaken:
30 And then shall appear the sign of the Son of man in heaven: and then shall
all the tribes of the earth mourn, and they shall see the Son of man coming in
the clouds of heaven with power and great glory.
31 And he shall send his angels with a great sound of a trumpet, and they
shall gather together his elect from the four winds, from one end of heaven
to the other.
32 Now learn a parable of the fig tree; When his branch is yet tender, and
putteth forth leaves, ye know that summer *is* nigh:
33 So likewise ye, when ye shall see all these things, know that it is near, *even*
at the doors.

34 Verily I say unto you, This generation shall not pass, till all these things be
fulfilled.
35 Heaven and earth shall pass away, but my words shall not pass away.

No One Knows When Jesus Will Return

36 But of that day and hour knoweth no *man*, no, not the angels of heaven,
but my Father only.
37 But as the days of Noe *were*, so shall also the coming of the Son of man be.
38 For as in the days that were before the flood they were eating and drinking,
marrying and giving in marriage, until the day that Noe entered into the ark,
39 And knew not until the flood came, and took them all away; so shall also
the coming of the Son of man be.
40 Then shall two be in the field; the one shall be taken, and the other left.
41 Two *women shall be* grinding at the mill; the one shall be taken, and the
other left.
42 Watch therefore: for ye know not what hour your Lord doth come.
43 But know this, that if the goodman of the house had known in what watch
the thief would come, he would have watched, and would not have suffered
his house to be broken up.
44 Therefore be ye also ready: for in such an hour as ye think not the Son of
man cometh.
45 Who then is a faithful and wise servant, whom his lord hath made ruler
over his household, to give them meat in due season?
46 Blessed *is* that servant, whom his lord when he cometh shall find so doing.
47 Verily I say unto you, That he shall make him ruler over all his goods.
48 But and if that evil servant shall say in his heart, My lord delayeth his
coming;
49 And shall begin to smite *his* fellowservants, and to eat and drink with the
drunken;
50 The lord of that servant shall come in a day when he looketh not for *him*,
and in an hour that he is not aware of,
51 And shall cut him asunder, and appoint *him* his portion with the hypo-
crites: there shall be weeping and gnashing of teeth.

The Parable of the Ten Virgins

25 Then shall the kingdom of heaven be likened unto ten virgins,
which took their lamps, and went forth to meet the bridegroom.
2 And five of them were wise, and five *were* foolish.
3 They that *were* foolish took their lamps, and took no oil with them:
4 But the wise took oil in their vessels with their lamps.
5 While the bridegroom tarried, they all slumbered and slept.
6 And at midnight there was a cry made, Behold, the bridegroom cometh;
go ye out to meet him.
7 Then all those virgins arose, and trimmed their lamps.
8 And the foolish said unto the wise, Give us of your oil; for our lamps are
gone out.
9 But the wise answered, saying, *Not so*; lest there be not enough for us and
you: but go ye rather to them that sell, and buy for yourselves.
10 And while they went to buy, the bridegroom came; and they that were
ready went in with him to the marriage: and the door was shut.
11 Afterward came also the other virgins, saying, Lord, Lord, open to us.
12 But he answered and said, Verily I say unto you, I know you not.
13 Watch therefore, for ye know neither the day nor the hour wherein the
Son of man cometh.

The Parable of the Talents

14 For *the kingdom of heaven is* as a man travelling into a far country, *who*
called his own servants, and delivered unto them his goods.

15 And unto one he gave five talents, to another two, and to another one; to
every man according to his several ability; and straightway took his journey.
16 Then he that had received the five talents went and traded with the same,
and made *them* other five talents.
17 And likewise he that *had received* two, he also gained other two.
18 But he that had received one went and digged in the earth, and hid his
lord's money.
19 After a long time the lord of those servants cometh, and reckoneth with
them.
20 And so he that had received five talents came and brought other five tal-
ents, saying, Lord, thou deliveredst unto me five talents: behold, I have gained
beside them five talents more.
21 His lord said unto him, Well done, *thou* good and faithful servant: thou
hast been faithful over a few things, I will make thee ruler over many things:
enter thou into the joy of thy lord.
22 He also that had received two talents came and said, Lord, thou deliveredst
unto me two talents: behold, I have gained two other talents beside them.
23 His lord said unto him, Well done, good and faithful servant; thou hast
been faithful over a few things, I will make thee ruler over many things: enter
thou into the joy of thy lord.
24 Then he which had received the one talent came and said, Lord, I knew
thee that thou art an hard man, reaping where thou hast not sown, and gath-
ering where thou hast not strawed:
25 And I was afraid, and went and hid thy talent in the earth: lo, *there* thou
hast *that is* thine.
26 His lord answered and said unto him, *Thou* wicked and slothful servant,
thou knewest that I reap where I sowed not, and gather where I have not
strawed:
27 Thou oughtest therefore to have put my money to the exchangers, and
then at my coming I should have received mine own with usury.
28 Take therefore the talent from him, and give *it* unto him which hath ten
talents.
29 For unto every one that hath shall be given, and he shall have abundance:
but from him that hath not shall be taken away even that which he hath.
30 And cast ye the unprofitable servant into outer darkness: there shall be
weeping and gnashing of teeth.

The Description of the Last Judgment

31 When the Son of man shall come in his glory, and all the holy angels with
him, then shall he sit upon the throne of his glory:
32 And before him shall be gathered all nations: and he shall separate them
one from another, as a shepherd divideth *his* sheep from the goats:
33 And he shall set the sheep on his right hand, but the goats on the left.
34 Then shall the King say unto them on his right hand, Come, ye blessed of
my Father, inherit the kingdom prepared for you from the foundation of the
world:
35 For I was an hungred, and ye gave me meat: I was thirsty, and ye gave me
drink: I was a stranger, and ye took me in:
36 Naked, and ye clothed me: I was sick, and ye visited me: I was in prison,
and ye came unto me.
37 Then shall the righteous answer him, saying, Lord, when saw we thee an
hungred, and fed *thee*? or thirsty, and gave *thee* drink?
38 When saw we thee a stranger, and took *thee* in? or naked, and clothed
thee?
39 Or when saw we thee sick, or in prison, and came unto thee?

40 And the King shall answer and say unto them, Verily I say unto you,
Inasmuch as ye have done *it* unto one of the least of these my brethren, ye have
done *it* unto me.
41 Then shall he say also unto them on the left hand, Depart from me, ye
cursed, into everlasting fire, prepared for the devil and his angels:
42 For I was an hungred, and ye gave me no meat: I was thirsty, and ye gave
me no drink:
43 I was a stranger, and ye took me not in: naked, and ye clothed me not: sick,
and in prison, and ye visited me not.
44 Then shall they also answer him, saying, Lord, when saw we thee an hun-
gred, or athirst, or a stranger, or naked, or sick, or in prison, and did not
minister unto thee?
45 Then shall he answer them, saying, Verily I say unto you, Inasmuch as ye
did *it* not to one of the least of these, ye did *it* not to me.
46 And these shall go away into everlasting punishment: but the righteous
into life eternal.

The Plot to Kill Jesus

26 And it came to pass, when Jesus had finished all these sayings, he
said unto his disciples,
2 Ye know that after two days is *the feast of* the passover, and the Son of man
is betrayed to be crucified.
3 Then assembled together the chief priests, and the scribes, and the elders
of the people, unto the palace of the high priest, who was called Caiaphas,
4 And consulted that they might take Jesus by subtilty, and kill *him*.
5 But they said, Not on the feast *day*, lest there be an uproar among the
people.

A Woman Anoints Jesus with Precious Ointment

6 Now when Jesus was in Bethany, in the house of Simon the leper,
7 There came unto him a woman having an alabaster box of very precious
ointment, and poured it on his head, as he sat *at meat*.
8 But when his disciples saw *it*, they had indignation, saying, To what purpose
is this waste?
9 For this ointment might have been sold for much, and given to the poor.
10 When Jesus understood *it*, he said unto them, Why trouble ye the woman?
for she hath wrought a good work upon me.
11 For ye have the poor always with you; but me ye have not always.
12 For in that she hath poured this ointment on my body, she did *it* for my
burial.
13 Verily I say unto you, Wheresoever this gospel shall be preached in the
whole world, *there* shall also this, that this woman hath done, be told for a
memorial of her.

Judas Betrays Jesus

14 Then one of the twelve, called Judas Iscariot, went unto the chief priests,
15 And said *unto them*, What will ye give me, and I will deliver him unto you?
And they covenanted with him for thirty pieces of silver.
16 And from that time he sought opportunity to betray him.

Jesus and the Disciples Eat the Passover

17 Now the first *day* of the *feast of* unleavened bread the disciples came to
Jesus, saying unto him, Where wilt thou that we prepare for thee to eat the
passover?
18 And he said, Go into the city to such a man, and say unto him, The Master
saith, My time is at hand; I will keep the passover at thy house with my disciples.
19 And the disciples did as Jesus had appointed them; and they made ready
the passover.

20 Now when the even was come, he sat down with the twelve.
21 And as they did eat, he said, Verily I say unto you, that one of you shall
betray me.
22 And they were exceeding sorrowful, and began every one of them to say
unto him, Lord, is it I?
23 And he answered and said, He that dippeth *his* hand with me in the dish,
the same shall betray me.
24 The Son of man goeth as it is written of him: but woe unto that man by
whom the Son of man is betrayed! it had been good for that man if he had not
been born.
25 Then Judas, which betrayed him, answered and said, Master, is it I? He
said unto him, Thou hast said.

Jesus Institutes His Holy Supper

26 And as they were eating, Jesus took bread, and blessed *it*, and brake *it*, and
gave *it* to the disciples, and said, Take, eat; this is my body.
27 And he took the cup, and gave thanks, and gave *it* to them, saying, Drink
ye all of it;
28 For this is my blood of the new testament, which is shed for many for the
remission of sins.
29 But I say unto you, I will not drink henceforth of this fruit of the vine,
until that day when I drink it new with you in my Father's kingdom.
30 And when they had sung an hymn, they went out into the mount of Olives.

Jesus Predicts Peter's Denial

31 Then saith Jesus unto them, All ye shall be offended because of me this
night: for it is written, I will smite the shepherd, and the sheep of the flock
shall be scattered abroad.
32 But after I am risen again, I will go before you into Galilee.
33 Peter answered and said unto him, Though all *men* shall be offended
because of thee, *yet* will I never be offended.
34 Jesus said unto him, Verily I say unto thee, That this night, before the cock
crow, thou shalt deny me thrice.
35 Peter said unto him, Though I should die with thee, yet will I not deny
thee. Likewise also said all the disciples.

Jesus Prays in Gethsemane

36 Then cometh Jesus with them unto a place called Gethsemane, and saith
unto the disciples, Sit ye here, while I go and pray yonder.
37 And he took with him Peter and the two sons of Zebedee, and began to be
sorrowful and very heavy.
38 Then saith he unto them, My soul is exceeding sorrowful, even unto death:
tarry ye here, and watch with me.
39 And he went a little further, and fell on his face, and prayed, saying, O my
Father, if it be possible, let this cup pass from me: nevertheless not as I will,
but as thou *wilt*.
40 And he cometh unto the disciples, and findeth them asleep, and saith unto
Peter, What, could ye not watch with me one hour?
41 Watch and pray, that ye enter not into temptation: the spirit indeed *is*
willing, but the flesh *is* weak.
42 He went away again the second time, and prayed, saying, O my Father, if
this cup may not pass away from me, except I drink it, thy will be done.
43 And he came and found them asleep again: for their eyes were heavy.
44 And he left them, and went away again, and prayed the third time, saying
the same words.
45 Then cometh he to his disciples, and saith unto them, Sleep on now, and
take *your* rest: behold, the hour is at hand, and the Son of man is betrayed into
the hands of sinners.
46 Rise, let us be going: behold, he is at hand that doth betray me.

Jesus Is Betrayed with a Kiss
47 And while he yet spake, lo, Judas, one of the twelve, came, and with him a
great multitude with swords and staves, from the chief priests and elders of
the people.
48 Now he that betrayed him gave them a sign, saying, Whomsoever I shall
kiss, that same is he: hold him fast.
49 And forthwith he came to Jesus, and said, Hail, master; and kissed him.
50 And Jesus said unto him, Friend, wherefore art thou come? Then came
they, and laid hands on Jesus, and took him.
51 And, behold, one of them which were with Jesus stretched out *his* hand,
and drew his sword, and struck a servant of the high priest's, and smote off
his ear.
52 Then said Jesus unto him, Put up again thy sword into his place: for all
they that take the sword shall perish with the sword.
53 Thinkest thou that I cannot now pray to my Father, and he shall present-
ly give me more than twelve legions of angels?
54 But how then shall the scriptures be fulfilled, that thus it must be?
55 In that same hour said Jesus to the multitudes, Are ye come out as against
a thief with swords and staves for to take me? I sat daily with you teaching in
the temple, and ye laid no hold on me.
56 But all this was done, that the scriptures of the prophets might be fulfilled.
Then all the disciples forsook him, and fled.

Jesus Is Tried before the Jewish Council
57 And they that had laid hold on Jesus led *him* away to Caiaphas the high
priest, where the scribes and the elders were assembled.
58 But Peter followed him afar off unto the high priest's palace, and went in,
and sat with the servants, to see the end.
59 Now the chief priests, and elders, and all the council, sought false witness
against Jesus, to put him to death;
60 But found none: yea, though many false witnesses came, *yet* found they
none. At the last came two false witnesses,
61 And said, This *fellow* said, I am able to destroy the temple of God, and to
build it in three days.
62 And the high priest arose, and said unto him, Answerest thou nothing?
what *is it which* these witness against thee?
63 But Jesus held his peace. And the high priest answered and said unto him,
I adjure thee by the living God, that thou tell us whether thou be the Christ,
the Son of God.
64 Jesus saith unto him, Thou hast said: nevertheless I say unto you, Hereafter
shall ye see the Son of man sitting on the right hand of power, and coming in
the clouds of heaven.
65 Then the high priest rent his clothes, saying, He hath spoken blasphemy;
what further need have we of witnesses? behold, now ye have heard his blas-
phemy.
66 What think ye? They answered and said, He is guilty of death.
67 Then did they spit in his face, and buffeted him; and others smote *him*
with the palms of their hands,
68 Saying, Prophesy unto us, thou Christ, Who is he that smote thee?

Peter Denies Jesus
69 Now Peter sat without in the palace: and a damsel came unto him, saying,
Thou also wast with Jesus of Galilee.
70 But he denied before *them* all, saying, I know not what thou sayest.
71 And when he was gone out into the porch, another *maid* saw him, and
said unto them that were there, This *fellow* was also with Jesus of Nazareth.
72 And again he denied with an oath, I do not know the man.

73 And after a while came unto *him* they that stood by, and said to Peter,
Surely thou also art *one* of them; for thy speech bewrayeth thee.
74 Then began he to curse and to swear, *saying*, I know not the man. And
immediately the cock crew.
75 And Peter remembered the word of Jesus, which said unto him, Before
the cock crow, thou shalt deny me thrice. And he went out, and wept bitterly.

The Death of Judas

27 When the morning was come, all the chief priests and elders of the
people took counsel against Jesus to put him to death:
2 And when they had bound him, they led *him* away, and delivered him to
Pontius Pilate the governor.
3 Then Judas, which had betrayed him, when he saw that he was condemned,
repented himself, and brought again the thirty pieces of silver to the chief
priests and elders,
4 Saying, I have sinned in that I have betrayed the innocent blood. And they
said, What *is that* to us? see thou *to that*.
5 And he cast down the pieces of silver in the temple, and departed, and went
and hanged himself.
6 And the chief priests took the silver pieces, and said, It is not lawful for to
put them into the treasury, because it is the price of blood.
7 And they took counsel, and bought with them the potter's field, to bury
strangers in.
8 Wherefore that field was called, The field of blood, unto this day.
9 Then was fulfilled that which was spoken by Jeremy the prophet, saying,
And they took the thirty pieces of silver, the price of him that was valued,
whom they of the children of Israel did value;
10 And gave them for the potter's field, as the Lord appointed me.

The Trial before Pilate

11 And Jesus stood before the governor: and the governor asked him, saying,
Art thou the King of the Jews? And Jesus said unto him, Thou sayest.
12 And when he was accused of the chief priests and elders, he answered
nothing.
13 Then said Pilate unto him, Hearest thou not how many things they witness
against thee?
14 And he answered him to never a word; insomuch that the governor mar-
velled greatly.
15 Now at *that* feast the governor was wont to release unto the people a
prisoner, whom they would.
16 And they had then a notable prisoner, called Barabbas.
17 Therefore when they were gathered together, Pilate said unto them, Whom
will ye that I release unto you? Barabbas, or Jesus which is called Christ?
18 For he knew that for envy they had delivered him.
19 When he was set down on the judgment seat, his wife sent unto him,
saying, Have thou nothing to do with that just man: for I have suffered many
things this day in a dream because of him.
20 But the chief priests and elders persuaded the multitude that they should
ask Barabbas, and destroy Jesus.
21 The governor answered and said unto them, Whether of the twain will ye
that I release unto you? They said, Barabbas.
22 Pilate saith unto them, What shall I do then with Jesus which is called
Christ? *They* all say unto him, Let him be crucified.
23 And the governor said, Why, what evil hath he done? But they cried out
the more, saying, Let him be crucified.

24 When Pilate saw that he could prevail nothing, but *that* rather a tumult
was made, he took water, and washed *his* hands before the multitude, saying,
I am innocent of the blood of this just person: see ye *to it.*
25 Then answered all the people, and said, His blood *be* on us, and on our
children.

Jesus Is Mocked and Crucified

26 Then released he Barabbas unto them: and when he had scourged Jesus,
he delivered *him* to be crucified.
27 Then the soldiers of the governor took Jesus into the common hall, and
gathered unto him the whole band *of soldiers.*
28 And they stripped him, and put on him a scarlet robe.
29 And when they had platted a crown of thorns, they put *it* upon his head,
and a reed in his right hand: and they bowed the knee before him, and mocked
him, saying, Hail, King of the Jews!
30 And they spit upon him, and took the reed, and smote him on the head.
31 And after that they had mocked him, they took the robe off from him,
and put his own raiment on him, and led him away to crucify *him.*
32 And as they came out, they found a man of Cyrene, Simon by name: him
they compelled to bear his cross.
33 And when they were come unto a place called Golgotha, that is to say, a
place of a skull,
34 They gave him vinegar to drink mingled with gall: and when he had tast-
ed *thereof,* he would not drink.
35 And they crucified him, and parted his garments, casting lots: that it might
be fulfilled which was spoken by the prophet, They parted my garments among
them, and upon my vesture did they cast lots.
36 And sitting down they watched him there;
37 And set up over his head his accusation written, THIS IS JESUS THE KING
OF THE JEWS.
38 Then were there two thieves crucified with him, one on the right hand,
and another on the left.
39 And they that passed by reviled him, wagging their heads,
40 And saying, Thou that destroyest the temple, and buildest *it* in three days,
save thyself. If thou be the Son of God, come down from the cross.
41 Likewise also the chief priests mocking *him,* with the scribes and elders,
said,
42 He saved others; himself he cannot save. If he be the King of Israel, let him
now come down from the cross, and we will believe him.
43 He trusted in God; let him deliver him now, if he will have him: for he said,
I am the Son of God.
44 The thieves also, which were crucified with him, cast the same in his teeth.
45 Now from the sixth hour there was darkness over all the land unto the
ninth hour.
46 And about the ninth hour Jesus cried with a loud voice, saying, Eli, Eli, lama
sabachthani? that is to say, My God, my God, why hast thou forsaken me?
47 Some of them that stood there, when they heard *that,* said, This *man*
calleth for Elias.
48 And straightway one of them ran, and took a spunge, and filled *it* with
vinegar, and put *it* on a reed, and gave him to drink.
49 The rest said, Let be, let us see whether Elias will come to save him.

Jesus Dies and Is Buried

50 Jesus, when he had cried again with a loud voice, yielded up the ghost.
51 And, behold, the veil of the temple was rent in twain from the top to the
bottom; and the earth did quake, and the rocks rent;

52 And the graves were opened; and many bodies of the saints which slept
arose,
53 And came out of the graves after his resurrection, and went into the holy
city, and appeared unto many.
54 Now when the centurion, and they that were with him, watching Jesus,
saw the earthquake, and those things that were done, they feared greatly, say-
ing, Truly this was the Son of God.
55 And many women were there beholding afar off, which followed Jesus
from Galilee, ministering unto him:
56 Among which was Mary Magdalene, and Mary the mother of James and
Joses, and the mother of Zebedee's children.
57 When the even was come, there came a rich man of Arimathaea, named
Joseph, who also himself was Jesus' disciple:
58 He went to Pilate, and begged the body of Jesus. Then Pilate commanded
the body to be delivered.
59 And when Joseph had taken the body, he wrapped it in a clean linen cloth,
60 And laid it in his own new tomb, which he had hewn out in the rock: and
he rolled a great stone to the door of the sepulchre, and departed.
61 And there was Mary Magdalene, and the other Mary, sitting over against
the sepulchre.
62 Now the next day, that followed the day of the preparation, the chief
priests and Pharisees came together unto Pilate,
63 Saying, Sir, we remember that that deceiver said, while he was yet alive,
After three days I will rise again.
64 Command therefore that the sepulchre be made sure until the third day,
lest his disciples come by night, and steal him away, and say unto the people,
He is risen from the dead: so the last error shall be worse than the first.
65 Pilate said unto them, Ye have a watch: go your way, make *it* as sure as ye
can.
66 So they went, and made the sepulchre sure, sealing the stone, and setting
a watch.

Jesus' Resurrection

28 In the end of the sabbath, as it began to dawn toward the first *day*
of the week, came Mary Magdalene and the other Mary to see the
sepulchre.
2 And, behold, there was a great earthquake: for the angel of the Lord
descended from heaven, and came and rolled back the stone from the door,
and sat upon it.
3 His countenance was like lightning, and his raiment white as snow:
4 And for fear of him the keepers did shake, and became as dead *men*.
5 And the angel answered and said unto the women, Fear not ye: for I know
that ye seek Jesus, which was crucified.
6 He is not here: for he is risen, as he said. Come, see the place where the Lord
lay.
7 And go quickly, and tell his disciples that he is risen from the dead; and,
behold, he goeth before you into Galilee; there shall ye see him: lo, I have told
you.
8 And they departed quickly from the sepulchre with fear and great joy; and
did run to bring his disciples word.
9 And as they went to tell his disciples, behold, Jesus met them, saying, All
hail. And they came and held him by the feet, and worshipped him.
10 Then said Jesus unto them, Be not afraid: go tell my brethren that they go
into Galilee, and there shall they see me.

He is
Risen
SAINT MATTHEW 28:6

GO YE THEREFORE,
& teach
ALL NATIONS,
baptizing
them
IN THE NAME
of the
FATHER,
& OF THE
Son,
& OF THE
Holy
Ghost.
SAINT MATTHEW 28:19

The Soldiers Are Bribed

11 Now when they were going, behold, some of the watch came into the city,
and shewed unto the chief priests all the things that were done.
12 And when they were assembled with the elders, and had taken counsel,
they gave large money unto the soldiers,
13 Saying, Say ye, His disciples came by night, and stole him *away* while we
slept.
14 And if this come to the governor's ears, we will persuade him, and secure
you.
15 So they took the money, and did as they were taught: and this saying is
commonly reported among the Jews until this day.

Jesus Gives the Great Commission

16 Then the eleven disciples went away into Galilee, into a mountain where
Jesus had appointed them.
17 And when they saw him, they worshipped him: but some doubted.
18 And Jesus came and spake unto them, saying, All power is given unto me
in heaven and in earth.
19 Go ye therefore, and teach all nations, baptizing them in the name of the
Father, and of the Son, and of the Holy Ghost:
20 Teaching them to observe all things whatsoever I have commanded you:
and, lo, I am with you alway, *even* unto the end of the world. Amen.

The Mission of John the Baptist

1 The beginning of the gospel of Jesus Christ, the Son of God;

2 As it is written in the prophets, Behold, I send my messenger before thy face, which shall prepare thy way before thee.

3 The voice of one crying in the wilderness, Prepare ye the way of the Lord, make his paths straight.

4 John did baptize in the wilderness, and preach the baptism of repentance for the remission of sins.

5 And there went out unto him all the land of Judaea, and they of Jerusalem, and were all baptized of him in the river of Jordan, confessing their sins.

6 And John was clothed with camel's hair, and with a girdle of a skin about his loins; and he did eat locusts and wild honey;

7 And preached, saying, There cometh one mightier than I after me, the latchet of whose shoes I am not worthy to stoop down and unloose.

8 I indeed have baptized you with water: but he shall baptize you with the Holy Ghost.

John Baptizes Jesus

9 And it came to pass in those days, that Jesus came from Nazareth of Galilee, and was baptized of John in Jordan.

10 And straightway coming up out of the water, he saw the heavens opened, and the Spirit like a dove descending upon him:

11 And there came a voice from heaven, *saying*, Thou art my beloved Son, in whom I am well pleased.

Satan Tempts Jesus

12 And immediately the Spirit driveth him into the wilderness.

13 And he was there in the wilderness forty days, tempted of Satan; and was with the wild beasts; and the angels ministered unto him.

Calling the First Disciples

14 Now after that John was put in prison, Jesus came into Galilee, preaching the gospel of the kingdom of God,

15 And saying, The time is fulfilled, and the kingdom of God is at hand: repent ye, and believe the gospel.

16 Now as he walked by the sea of Galilee, he saw Simon and Andrew his brother casting a net into the sea: for they were fishers.

17 And Jesus said unto them, Come ye after me, and I will make you to become fishers of men.

18 And straightway they forsook their nets, and followed him.

19 And when he had gone a little further thence, he saw James the *son* of Zebedee, and John his brother, who also were in the ship mending their nets.

20 And straightway he called them: and they left their father Zebedee in the ship with the hired servants, and went after him.

21 And they went into Capernaum; and straightway on the sabbath day he entered into the synagogue, and taught.

22 And they were astonished at his doctrine: for he taught them as one that had authority, and not as the scribes.

AND HE SAID UNTO THEM, Go Ye INTO ALL THE WORLD, & Preach THE Gospel TO EVERY CREATURE.

SAINT MARK 16:15

Jesus Sends out an Unclean Spirit

23 And there was in their synagogue a man with an unclean spirit; and he
cried out,
24 Saying, Let *us* alone; what have we to do with thee, thou Jesus of Nazareth?
art thou come to destroy us? I know thee who thou art, the Holy One of God.
25 And Jesus rebuked him, saying, Hold thy peace, and come out of him.
26 And when the unclean spirit had torn him, and cried with a loud voice,
he came out of him.
27 And they were all amazed, insomuch that they questioned among them-
selves, saying, What thing is this? what new doctrine *is* this? for with author-
ity commandeth he even the unclean spirits, and they do obey him.
28 And immediately his fame spread abroad throughout all the region round
about Galilee.

Jesus Heals Peter's Mother-in-Law and Many Others

29 And forthwith, when they were come out of the synagogue, they entered
into the house of Simon and Andrew, with James and John.
30 But Simon's wife's mother lay sick of a fever, and anon they tell him of her.
31 And he came and took her by the hand, and lifted her up; and immediate-
ly the fever left her, and she ministered unto them.
32 And at even, when the sun did set, they brought unto him all that were
diseased, and them that were possessed with devils.
33 And all the city was gathered together at the door.
34 And he healed many that were sick of divers diseases, and cast out many
devils; and suffered not the devils to speak, because they knew him.
35 And in the morning, rising up a great while before day, he went out, and
departed into a solitary place, and there prayed.
36 And Simon and they that were with him followed after him.
37 And when they had found him, they said unto him, All *men* seek for thee.
38 And he said unto them, Let us go into the next towns, that I may preach
there also: for therefore came I forth.
39 And he preached in their synagogues throughout all Galilee, and cast out
devils.

Jesus Cleanses a Leper

40 And there came a leper to him, beseeching him, and kneeling down to
him, and saying unto him, If thou wilt, thou canst make me clean.
41 And Jesus, moved with compassion, put forth *his* hand, and touched him,
and saith unto him, I will; be thou clean.
42 And as soon as he had spoken, immediately the leprosy departed from
him, and he was cleansed.
43 And he straitly charged him, and forthwith sent him away;
44 And saith unto him, See thou say nothing to any man: but go thy way, shew
thyself to the priest, and offer for thy cleansing those things which Moses
commanded, for a testimony unto them.
45 But he went out, and began to publish *it* much, and to blaze abroad the
matter, insomuch that Jesus could no more openly enter into the city, but was
without in desert places: and they came to him from every quarter.

Jesus Heals and Forgives

2 And again he entered into Capernaum after *some* days; and it was noised
that he was in the house.
2 And straightway many were gathered together, insomuch that there was
no room to receive *them*, no, not so much as about the door: and he preached
the word unto them.
3 And they come unto him, bringing one sick of the palsy, which was borne
of four.

4 And when they could not come nigh unto him for the press, they uncovered
the roof where he was: and when they had broken *it* up, they let down the bed
wherein the sick of the palsy lay.
5 When Jesus saw their faith, he said unto the sick of the palsy, Son, thy sins
be forgiven thee.
6 But there were certain of the scribes sitting there, and reasoning in their
hearts,
7 Why doth this *man* thus speak blasphemies? who can forgive sins but God
only?
8 And immediately when Jesus perceived in his spirit that they so reasoned
within themselves, he said unto them, Why reason ye these things in your
hearts?
9 Whether is it easier to say to the sick of the palsy, *Thy* sins be forgiven thee;
or to say, Arise, and take up thy bed, and walk?
10 But that ye may know that the Son of man hath power on earth to forgive
sins, (he saith to the sick of the palsy,)
11 I say unto thee, Arise, and take up thy bed, and go thy way into thine house.
12 And immediately he arose, took up the bed, and went forth before them
all; insomuch that they were all amazed, and glorified God, saying, We never
saw it on this fashion.

Jesus Chooses Levi (Matthew)

13 And he went forth again by the sea side; and all the multitude resorted
unto him, and he taught them.
14 And as he passed by, he saw Levi the *son* of Alphaeus sitting at the receipt
of custom, and said unto him, Follow me. And he arose and followed him.
15 And it came to pass, that, as Jesus sat at meat in his house, many publicans
and sinners sat also together with Jesus and his disciples: for there were many,
and they followed him.
16 And when the scribes and Pharisees saw him eat with publicans and sin-
ners, they said unto his disciples, How is it that he eateth and drinketh with
publicans and sinners?
17 When Jesus heard *it*, he saith unto them, They that are whole have no need
of the physician, but they that are sick: I came not to call the righteous, but
sinners to repentance.

Questions about Fasting

18 And the disciples of John and of the Pharisees used to fast: and they come
and say unto him, Why do the disciples of John and of the Pharisees fast, but
thy disciples fast not?
19 And Jesus said unto them, Can the children of the bridechamber fast,
while the bridegroom is with them? as long as they have the bridegroom with
them, they cannot fast.
20 But the days will come, when the bridegroom shall be taken away from
them, and then shall they fast in those days.
21 No man also seweth a piece of new cloth on an old garment: else the new
piece that filled it up taketh away from the old, and the rent is made worse.
22 And no man putteth new wine into old bottles: else the new wine doth
burst the bottles, and the wine is spilled, and the bottles will be marred: but
new wine must be put into new bottles.

Jesus Has Authority over the Sabbath

23 And it came to pass, that he went through the corn fields on the sabbath
day; and his disciples began, as they went, to pluck the ears of corn.
24 And the Pharisees said unto him, Behold, why do they on the sabbath day
that which is not lawful?
25 And he said unto them, Have ye never read what David did, when he had
need, and was an hungred, he, and they that were with him?

26 How he went into the house of God in the days of Abiathar the high priest,
and did eat the shewbread, which is not lawful to eat but for the priests, and
gave also to them which were with him?
27 And he said unto them, The sabbath was made for man, and not man for
the sabbath:
28 Therefore the Son of man is Lord also of the sabbath.

Jesus Heals on the Sabbath

3 And he entered again into the synagogue; and there was a man there which
had a withered hand.
2 And they watched him, whether he would heal him on the sabbath day;
that they might accuse him.
3 And he saith unto the man which had the withered hand, Stand forth.
4 And he saith unto them, Is it lawful to do good on the sabbath days, or to
do evil? to save life, or to kill? But they held their peace.
5 And when he had looked round about on them with anger, being grieved
for the hardness of their hearts, he saith unto the man, Stretch forth thine
hand. And he stretched *it* out: and his hand was restored whole as the other.
6 And the Pharisees went forth, and straightway took counsel with the
Herodians against him, how they might destroy him.
7 But Jesus withdrew himself with his disciples to the sea: and a great mul-
titude from Galilee followed him, and from Judaea,
8 And from Jerusalem, and from Idumaea, and *from* beyond Jordan; and
they about Tyre and Sidon, a great multitude, when they had heard what great
things he did, came unto him.
9 And he spake to his disciples, that a small ship should wait on him because
of the multitude, lest they should throng him.
10 For he had healed many; insomuch that they pressed upon him for to
touch him, as many as had plagues.
11 And unclean spirits, when they saw him, fell down before him, and cried,
saying, Thou art the Son of God.
12 And he straitly charged them that they should not make him known.

Jesus Chooses Twelve Apostles

13 And he goeth up into a mountain, and calleth *unto him* whom he would:
and they came unto him.
14 And he ordained twelve, that they should be with him, and that he might
send them forth to preach,
15 And to have power to heal sicknesses, and to cast out devils:
16 And Simon he surnamed Peter;
17 And James the *son* of Zebedee, and John the brother of James; and he
surnamed them Boanerges, which is, The sons of thunder:
18 And Andrew, and Philip, and Bartholomew, and Matthew, and Thomas,
and James the *son* of Alphaeus, and Thaddaeus, and Simon the Canaanite,
19 And Judas Iscariot, which also betrayed him: and they went into an house.
20 And the multitude cometh together again, so that they could not so much
as eat bread.
21 And when his friends heard *of it*, they went out to lay hold on him: for
they said, He is beside himself.

Jesus Is Accused of Working with Satan

22 And the scribes which came down from Jerusalem said, He hath Beelzebub,
and by the prince of the devils casteth he out devils.
23 And he called them *unto him*, and said unto them in parables, How can
Satan cast out Satan?
24 And if a kingdom be divided against itself, that kingdom cannot stand.
25 And if a house be divided against itself, that house cannot stand.

26 And if Satan rise up against himself, and be divided, he cannot stand, but
hath an end.
27 No man can enter into a strong man's house, and spoil his goods, except
he will first bind the strong man; and then he will spoil his house.
28 Verily I say unto you, All sins shall be forgiven unto the sons of men, and
blasphemies wherewith soever they shall blaspheme:
29 But he that shall blaspheme against the Holy Ghost hath never forgiveness,
but is in danger of eternal damnation:
30 Because they said, He hath an unclean spirit.

Jesus Describes His True Family

31 There came then his brethren and his mother, and, standing without, sent
unto him, calling him.
32 And the multitude sat about him, and they said unto him, Behold, thy
mother and thy brethren without seek for thee.
33 And he answered them, saying, Who is my mother, or my brethren?
34 And he looked round about on them which sat about him, and said, Behold
my mother and my brethren!
35 For whosoever shall do the will of God, the same is my brother, and my
sister, and mother.

The Parable of the Sower

4 And he began again to teach by the sea side: and there was gathered unto
him a great multitude, so that he entered into a ship, and sat in the sea; and
the whole multitude was by the sea on the land.
2 And he taught them many things by parables, and said unto them in his
doctrine,
3 Hearken; Behold, there went out a sower to sow:
4 And it came to pass, as he sowed, some fell by the way side, and the fowls
of the air came and devoured it up.
5 And some fell on stony ground, where it had not much earth; and imme-
diately it sprang up, because it had no depth of earth:
6 But when the sun was up, it was scorched; and because it had no root, it
withered away.
7 And some fell among thorns, and the thorns grew up, and choked it, and
it yielded no fruit.
8 And other fell on good ground, and did yield fruit that sprang up and
increased; and brought forth, some thirty, and some sixty, and some an hun-
dred.
9 And he said unto them, He that hath ears to hear, let him hear.
10 And when he was alone, they that were about him with the twelve asked
of him the parable.
11 And he said unto them, Unto you it is given to know the mystery of the
kingdom of God: but unto them that are without, all *these* things are done in
parables:
12 That seeing they may see, and not perceive; and hearing they may hear,
and not understand; lest at any time they should be converted, and *their* sins
should be forgiven them.
13 And he said unto them, Know ye not this parable? and how then will ye
know all parables?
14 The sower soweth the word.
15 And these are they by the way side, where the word is sown; but when they
have heard, Satan cometh immediately, and taketh away the word that was
sown in their hearts.
16 And these are they likewise which are sown on stony ground; who, when
they have heard the word, immediately receive it with gladness;

17 And have no root in themselves, and so endure but for a time: afterward,
when affliction or persecution ariseth for the word's sake, immediately they
are offended.
18 And these are they which are sown among thorns; such as hear the word,
19 And the cares of this world, and the deceitfulness of riches, and the lusts
of other things entering in, choke the word, and it becometh unfruitful.
20 And these are they which are sown on good ground; such as hear the word,
and receive *it*, and bring forth fruit, some thirtyfold, some sixty, and some an
hundred.

A Parable about a Light

21 And he said unto them, Is a candle brought to be put under a bushel, or
under a bed? and not to be set on a candlestick?
22 For there is nothing hid, which shall not be manifested; neither was any
thing kept secret, but that it should come abroad.
23 If any man have ears to hear, let him hear.
24 And he said unto them, Take heed what ye hear: with what measure ye
mete, it shall be measured to you: and unto you that hear shall more be given.
25 For he that hath, to him shall be given: and he that hath not, from him
shall be taken even that which he hath.

A Parable about Seeds

26 And he said, So is the kingdom of God, as if a man should cast seed into
the ground;
27 And should sleep, and rise night and day, and the seed should spring and
grow up, he knoweth not how.
28 For the earth bringeth forth fruit of herself; first the blade, then the ear,
after that the full corn in the ear.
29 But when the fruit is brought forth, immediately he putteth in the sickle,
because the harvest is come.

Describing the Kingdom of Heaven

30 And he said, Whereunto shall we liken the kingdom of God? or with what
comparison shall we compare it?
31 *It is* like a grain of mustard seed, which, when it is sown in the earth, is
less than all the seeds that be in the earth:
32 But when it is sown, it groweth up, and becometh greater than all herbs,
and shooteth out great branches; so that the fowls of the air may lodge under
the shadow of it.
33 And with many such parables spake he the word unto them, as they were
able to hear *it*.
34 But without a parable spake he not unto them: and when they were alone,
he expounded all things to his disciples.

Jesus Calms the Sea

35 And the same day, when the even was come, he saith unto them, Let us
pass over unto the other side.
36 And when they had sent away the multitude, they took him even as he was
in the ship. And there were also with him other little ships.
37 And there arose a great storm of wind, and the waves beat into the ship,
so that it was now full.
38 And he was in the hinder part of the ship, asleep on a pillow: and they
awake him, and say unto him, Master, carest thou not that we perish?
39 And he arose, and rebuked the wind, and said unto the sea, Peace, be still.
And the wind ceased, and there was a great calm.
40 And he said unto them, Why are ye so fearful? how is it that ye have no
faith?

41 And they feared exceedingly, and said one to another, What manner of
man is this, that even the wind and the sea obey him?

Jesus Heals a Man Possessed by Many Demons

5 And they came over unto the other side of the sea, into the country of the
Gadarenes.
2 And when he was come out of the ship, immediately there met him out of
the tombs a man with an unclean spirit,
3 Who had *his* dwelling among the tombs; and no man could bind him, no,
not with chains:
4 Because that he had been often bound with fetters and chains, and the
chains had been plucked asunder by him, and the fetters broken in pieces:
neither could any *man* tame him.
5 And always, night and day, he was in the mountains, and in the tombs,
crying, and cutting himself with stones.
6 But when he saw Jesus afar off, he ran and worshipped him,
7 And cried with a loud voice, and said, What have I to do with thee, Jesus,
thou Son of the most high God? I adjure thee by God, that thou torment me
not.
8 For he said unto him, Come out of the man, *thou* unclean spirit.
9 And he asked him, What *is* thy name? And he answered, saying, My name
is Legion: for we are many.
10 And he besought him much that he would not send them away out of the
country.
11 Now there was there nigh unto the mountains a great herd of swine feeding.
12 And all the devils besought him, saying, Send us into the swine, that we
may enter into them.
13 And forthwith Jesus gave them leave. And the unclean spirits went out,
and entered into the swine: and the herd ran violently down a steep place into
the sea, (they were about two thousand;) and were choked in the sea.
14 And they that fed the swine fled, and told *it* in the city, and in the country.
And they went out to see what it was that was done.
15 And they come to Jesus, and see him that was possessed with the devil,
and had the legion, sitting, and clothed, and in his right mind: and they were
afraid.
16 And they that saw *it* told them how it befell to him that was possessed
with the devil, and *also* concerning the swine.
17 And they began to pray him to depart out of their coasts.
18 And when he was come into the ship, he that had been possessed with the
devil prayed him that he might be with him.
19 Howbeit Jesus suffered him not, but saith unto him, Go home to thy
friends, and tell them how great things the Lord hath done for thee, and hath
had compassion on thee.
20 And he departed, and began to publish in Decapolis how great things Jesus
had done for him: and all *men* did marvel.

Jesus Raises a Girl from the Dead and Heals a Bleeding Woman

21 And when Jesus was passed over again by ship unto the other side, much
people gathered unto him: and he was nigh unto the sea.
22 And, behold, there cometh one of the rulers of the synagogue, Jairus by
name; and when he saw him, he fell at his feet,
23 And besought him greatly, saying, My little daughter lieth at the point of
death: *I pray thee*, come and lay thy hands on her, that she may be healed; and
she shall live.
24 And *Jesus* went with him; and much people followed him, and thronged
him.
25 And a certain woman, which had an issue of blood twelve years,

26 And had suffered many things of many physicians, and had spent all that
she had, and was nothing bettered, but rather grew worse,
27 When she had heard of Jesus, came in the press behind, and touched his
garment.
28 For she said, If I may touch but his clothes, I shall be whole.
29 And straightway the fountain of her blood was dried up; and she felt in
her body that she was healed of that plague.
30 And Jesus, immediately knowing in himself that virtue had gone out of
him, turned him about in the press, and said, Who touched my clothes?
31 And his disciples said unto him, Thou seest the multitude thronging thee,
and sayest thou, Who touched me?
32 And he looked round about to see her that had done this thing.
33 But the woman fearing and trembling, knowing what was done in her,
came and fell down before him, and told him all the truth.
34 And he said unto her, Daughter, thy faith hath made thee whole; go in
peace, and be whole of thy plague.
35 While he yet spake, there came from the ruler of the synagogue's *house*
certain which said, Thy daughter is dead: why troublest thou the Master any
further?
36 As soon as Jesus heard the word that was spoken, he saith unto the ruler
of the synagogue, Be not afraid, only believe.
37 And he suffered no man to follow him, save Peter, and James, and John
the brother of James.
38 And he cometh to the house of the ruler of the synagogue, and seeth the
tumult, and them that wept and wailed greatly.
39 And when he was come in, he saith unto them, Why make ye this ado, and
weep? the damsel is not dead, but sleepeth.
40 And they laughed him to scorn. But when he had put them all out, he
taketh the father and the mother of the damsel, and them that were with him,
and entereth in where the damsel was lying.
41 And he took the damsel by the hand, and said unto her, Talitha cumi;
which is, being interpreted, Damsel, I say unto thee, arise.
42 And straightway the damsel arose, and walked; for she was *of the age* of
twelve years. And they were astonished with a great astonishment.
43 And he charged them straitly that no man should know it; and command-
ed that something should be given her to eat.

Jesus Is Rejected by His Countrymen

6 And he went out from thence, and came into his own country; and his
disciples follow him.
2 And when the sabbath day was come, he began to teach in the synagogue:
and many hearing *him* were astonished, saying, From whence hath this *man*
these things? and what wisdom *is* this which is given unto him, that even such
mighty works are wrought by his hands?
3 Is not this the carpenter, the son of Mary, the brother of James, and Joses,
and of Juda, and Simon? and are not his sisters here with us? And they were
offended at him.
4 But Jesus said unto them, A prophet is not without honour, but in his own
country, and among his own kin, and in his own house.
5 And he could there do no mighty work, save that he laid his hands upon a
few sick folk, and healed *them*.
6 And he marvelled because of their unbelief. And he went round about the
villages, teaching.

Jesus Sends Out the Twelve

7 And he called *unto him* the twelve, and began to send them forth by two
and two; and gave them power over unclean spirits;

8 And commanded them that they should take nothing for *their* journey,
save a staff only; no scrip, no bread, no money in *their* purse:
9 But *be* shod with sandals; and not put on two coats.
10 And he said unto them, In what place soever ye enter into an house, there
abide till ye depart from that place.
11 And whosoever shall not receive you, nor hear you, when ye depart thence,
shake off the dust under your feet for a testimony against them. Verily I say
unto you, It shall be more tolerable for Sodom and Gomorrha in the day of
judgment, than for that city.
12 And they went out, and preached that men should repent.
13 And they cast out many devils, and anointed with oil many that were sick,
and healed *them*.

The Death of John the Baptist

14 And king Herod heard *of him*; (for his name was spread abroad:) and he
said, That John the Baptist was risen from the dead, and therefore mighty
works do shew forth themselves in him.
15 Others said, That it is Elias. And others said, That it is a prophet, or as one
of the prophets.
16 But when Herod heard *thereof*, he said, It is John, whom I beheaded: he
is risen from the dead.
17 For Herod himself had sent forth and laid hold upon John, and bound
him in prison for Herodias' sake, his brother Philip's wife: for he had married
her.
18 For John had said unto Herod, It is not lawful for thee to have thy brother's
wife.
19 Therefore Herodias had a quarrel against him, and would have killed him;
but she could not:
20 For Herod feared John, knowing that he was a just man and an holy, and
observed him; and when he heard him, he did many things, and heard him
gladly.
21 And when a convenient day was come, that Herod on his birthday made
a supper to his lords, high captains, and chief *estates* of Galilee;
22 And when the daughter of the said Herodias came in, and danced, and
pleased Herod and them that sat with him, the king said unto the damsel, Ask
of me whatsoever thou wilt, and I will give *it* thee.
23 And he sware unto her, Whatsoever thou shalt ask of me, I will give *it* thee,
unto the half of my kingdom.
24 And she went forth, and said unto her mother, What shall I ask? And she
said, The head of John the Baptist.
25 And she came in straightway with haste unto the king, and asked, saying,
I will that thou give me by and by in a charger the head of John the Baptist.
26 And the king was exceeding sorry; *yet* for his oath's sake, and for their
sakes which sat with him, he would not reject her.
27 And immediately the king sent an executioner, and commanded his head
to be brought: and he went and beheaded him in the prison,
28 And brought his head in a charger, and gave it to the damsel: and the
damsel gave it to her mother.
29 And when his disciples heard *of it*, they came and took up his corpse, and
laid it in a tomb.

Jesus Feeds More Than Five Thousand

30 And the apostles gathered themselves together unto Jesus, and told him
all things, both what they had done, and what they had taught.
31 And he said unto them, Come ye yourselves apart into a desert place, and
rest a while: for there were many coming and going, and they had no leisure
so much as to eat.

32 And they departed into a desert place by ship privately.
33 And the people saw them departing, and many knew him, and ran afoot
thither out of all cities, and outwent them, and came together unto him.
34 And Jesus, when he came out, saw much people, and was moved with
compassion toward them, because they were as sheep not having a shepherd:
and he began to teach them many things.
35 And when the day was now far spent, his disciples came unto him, and
said, This is a desert place, and now the time *is* far passed:
36 Send them away, that they may go into the country round about, and into
the villages, and buy themselves bread: for they have nothing to eat.
37 He answered and said unto them, Give ye them to eat. And they say unto
him, Shall we go and buy two hundred pennyworth of bread, and give them
to eat?
38 He saith unto them, How many loaves have ye? go and see. And when they
knew, they say, Five, and two fishes.
39 And he commanded them to make all sit down by companies upon the
green grass.
40 And they sat down in ranks, by hundreds, and by fifties.
41 And when he had taken the five loaves and the two fishes, he looked up to
heaven, and blessed, and brake the loaves, and gave *them* to his disciples to set
before them; and the two fishes divided he among them all.
42 And they did all eat, and were filled.
43 And they took up twelve baskets full of the fragments, and of the fishes.
44 And they that did eat of the loaves were about five thousand men.

Jesus Walks on the Sea

45 And straightway he constrained his disciples to get into the ship, and to
go to the other side before unto Bethsaida, while he sent away the people.
46 And when he had sent them away, he departed into a mountain to pray.
47 And when even was come, the ship was in the midst of the sea, and he
alone on the land.
48 And he saw them toiling in rowing; for the wind was contrary unto them:
and about the fourth watch of the night he cometh unto them, walking upon
the sea, and would have passed by them.
49 But when they saw him walking upon the sea, they supposed it had been
a spirit, and cried out:
50 For they all saw him, and were troubled. And immediately he talked with
them, and saith unto them, Be of good cheer: it is I; be not afraid.
51 And he went up unto them into the ship; and the wind ceased: and they
were sore amazed in themselves beyond measure, and wondered.
52 For they considered not *the miracle* of the loaves: for their heart was hard-
ened.
53 And when they had passed over, they came into the land of Gennesaret,
and drew to the shore.
54 And when they were come out of the ship, straightway they knew him,
55 And ran through that whole region round about, and began to carry about
in beds those that were sick, where they heard he was.
56 And whithersoever he entered, into villages, or cities, or country, they laid
the sick in the streets, and besought him that they might touch if it were but
the border of his garment: and as many as touched him were made whole.

Jesus Challenges the Pharisees' Traditions

7 Then came together unto him the Pharisees, and certain of the scribes,
which came from Jerusalem.
2 And when they saw some of his disciples eat bread with defiled, that is to
say, with unwashen, hands, they found fault.
3 For the Pharisees, and all the Jews, except they wash *their* hands oft, eat
not, holding the tradition of the elders.

4 And *when they come* from the market, except they wash, they eat not. And
many other things there be, which they have received to hold, *as* the washing
of cups, and pots, brasen vessels, and of tables.
5 Then the Pharisees and scribes asked him, Why walk not thy disciples
according to the tradition of the elders, but eat bread with unwashen hands?
6 He answered and said unto them, Well hath Esaias prophesied of you hyp-
ocrites, as it is written, This people honoureth me with *their* lips, but their
heart is far from me.
7 Howbeit in vain do they worship me, teaching *for* doctrines the command-
ments of men.
8 For laying aside the commandment of God, ye hold the tradition of men,
as the washing of pots and cups: and many other such like things ye do.
9 And he said unto them, Full well ye reject the commandment of God, that
ye may keep your own tradition.
10 For Moses said, Honour thy father and thy mother; and, Whoso curseth
father or mother, let him die the death:
11 But ye say, If a man shall say to his father or mother, *It is* Corban, that is
to say, a gift, by whatsoever thou mightest be profited by me; *he shall be free.*
12 And ye suffer him no more to do ought for his father or his mother;
13 Making the word of God of none effect through your tradition, which ye
have delivered: and many such like things do ye.
14 And when he had called all the people *unto him*, he said unto them,
Hearken unto me every one *of you*, and understand:
15 There is nothing from without a man, that entering into him can defile
him: but the things which come out of him, those are they that defile the man.
16 If any man have ears to hear, let him hear.
17 And when he was entered into the house from the people, his disciples
asked him concerning the parable.
18 And he saith unto them, Are ye so without understanding also? Do ye not
perceive, that whatsoever thing from without entereth into the man, *it* cannot
defile him;
19 Because it entereth not into his heart, but into the belly, and goeth out
into the draught, purging all meats?
20 And he said, That which cometh out of the man, that defileth the man.
21 For from within, out of the heart of men, proceed evil thoughts, adulter-
ies, fornications, murders,
22 Thefts, covetousness, wickedness, deceit, lasciviousness, an evil eye, blas-
phemy, pride, foolishness:
23 All these evil things come from within, and defile the man.

Jesus Heals the Syrophenician Woman's Daughter

24 And from thence he arose, and went into the borders of Tyre and Sidon,
and entered into an house, and would have no man know *it*: but he could not
be hid.
25 For a *certain* woman, whose young daughter had an unclean spirit, heard
of him, and came and fell at his feet:
26 The woman was a Greek, a Syrophenician by nation; and she besought
him that he would cast forth the devil out of her daughter.
27 But Jesus said unto her, Let the children first be filled: for it is not meet to
take the children's bread, and to cast *it* unto the dogs.
28 And she answered and said unto him, Yes, Lord: yet the dogs under the
table eat of the children's crumbs.
29 And he said unto her, For this saying go thy way; the devil is gone out of
thy daughter.
30 And when she was come to her house, she found the devil gone out, and
her daughter laid upon the bed.

Jesus Heals a Deaf Man

31 And again, departing from the coasts of Tyre and Sidon, he came unto the
sea of Galilee, through the midst of the coasts of Decapolis.
32 And they bring unto him one that was deaf, and had an impediment in
his speech; and they beseech him to put his hand upon him.
33 And he took him aside from the multitude, and put his fingers into his
ears, and he spit, and touched his tongue;
34 And looking up to heaven, he sighed, and saith unto him, Ephphatha, that
is, Be opened.
35 And straightway his ears were opened, and the string of his tongue was
loosed, and he spake plain.
36 And he charged them that they should tell no man: but the more he
charged them, so much the more a great deal they published *it*;
37 And were beyond measure astonished, saying, He hath done all things
well: he maketh both the deaf to hear, and the dumb to speak.

Jesus Feeds More Than Four Thousand

8 In those days the multitude being very great, and having nothing to eat,
Jesus called his disciples *unto him*, and saith unto them,
2 I have compassion on the multitude, because they have now been with me
three days, and have nothing to eat:
3 And if I send them away fasting to their own houses, they will faint by the
way: for divers of them came from far.
4 And his disciples answered him, From whence can a man satisfy these *men*
with bread here in the wilderness?
5 And he asked them, How many loaves have ye? And they said, Seven.
6 And he commanded the people to sit down on the ground: and he took the
seven loaves, and gave thanks, and brake, and gave to his disciples to set before
them; and they did set *them* before the people.
7 And they had a few small fishes: and he blessed, and commanded to set
them also before *them*.
8 So they did eat, and were filled: and they took up of the broken *meat* that
was left seven baskets.
9 And they that had eaten were about four thousand: and he sent them away.

Jesus Warns about the Pharisees

10 And straightway he entered into a ship with his disciples, and came into
the parts of Dalmanutha.
11 And the Pharisees came forth, and began to question with him, seeking
of him a sign from heaven, tempting him.
12 And he sighed deeply in his spirit, and saith, Why doth this generation
seek after a sign? verily I say unto you, There shall no sign be given unto this
generation.
13 And he left them, and entering into the ship again departed to the other
side.
14 Now *the disciples* had forgotten to take bread, neither had they in the ship
with them more than one loaf.
15 And he charged them, saying, Take heed, beware of the leaven of the
Pharisees, and *of* the leaven of Herod.
16 And they reasoned among themselves, saying, *It is* because we have no
bread.
17 And when Jesus knew *it*, he saith unto them, Why reason ye, because ye
have no bread? perceive ye not yet, neither understand? have ye your heart
yet hardened?
18 Having eyes, see ye not? and having ears, hear ye not? and do ye not
remember?

19 When I brake the five loaves among five thousand, how many baskets full
of fragments took ye up? They say unto him, Twelve.
20 And when the seven among four thousand, how many baskets full of frag-
ments took ye up? And they said, Seven.
21 And he said unto them, How is it that ye do not understand?

Jesus Heals a Blind Man

22 And he cometh to Bethsaida; and they bring a blind man unto him, and
besought him to touch him.
23 And he took the blind man by the hand, and led him out of the town; and
when he had spit on his eyes, and put his hands upon him, he asked him if he
saw ought.
24 And he looked up, and said, I see men as trees, walking.
25 After that he put *his* hands again upon his eyes, and made him look up:
and he was restored, and saw every man clearly.
26 And he sent him away to his house, saying, Neither go into the town, nor
tell *it* to any in the town.

Peter Declares His Faith

27 And Jesus went out, and his disciples, into the towns of Caesarea Philippi:
and by the way he asked his disciples, saying unto them, Whom do men say
that I am?
28 And they answered, John the Baptist: but some *say*, Elias; and others, One
of the prophets.
29 And he saith unto them, But whom say ye that I am? And Peter answereth
and saith unto him, Thou art the Christ.
30 And he charged them that they should tell no man of him.

Jesus Says He Will Die and Rise Again

31 And he began to teach them, that the Son of man must suffer many things,
and be rejected of the elders, and *of* the chief priests, and scribes, and be killed,
and after three days rise again.
32 And he spake that saying openly. And Peter took him, and began to rebuke
him.
33 But when he had turned about and looked on his disciples, he rebuked
Peter, saying, Get thee behind me, Satan: for thou savourest not the things that
be of God, but the things that be of men.

What It Means to Follow Jesus

34 And when he had called the people *unto him* with his disciples also, he
said unto them, Whosoever will come after me, let him deny himself, and take
up his cross, and follow me.
35 For whosoever will save his life shall lose it; but whosoever shall lose his
life for my sake and the gospel's, the same shall save it.
36 For what shall it profit a man, if he shall gain the whole world, and lose
his own soul?
37 Or what shall a man give in exchange for his soul?
38 Whosoever therefore shall be ashamed of me and of my words in this
adulterous and sinful generation; of him also shall the Son of man be ashamed,
when he cometh in the glory of his Father with the holy angels.

The Transfiguration

9 And he said unto them, Verily I say unto you, That there be some of them
that stand here, which shall not taste of death, till they have seen the king-
dom of God come with power.
2 And after six days Jesus taketh *with him* Peter, and James, and John, and
leadeth them up into an high mountain apart by themselves: and he was trans-
figured before them.

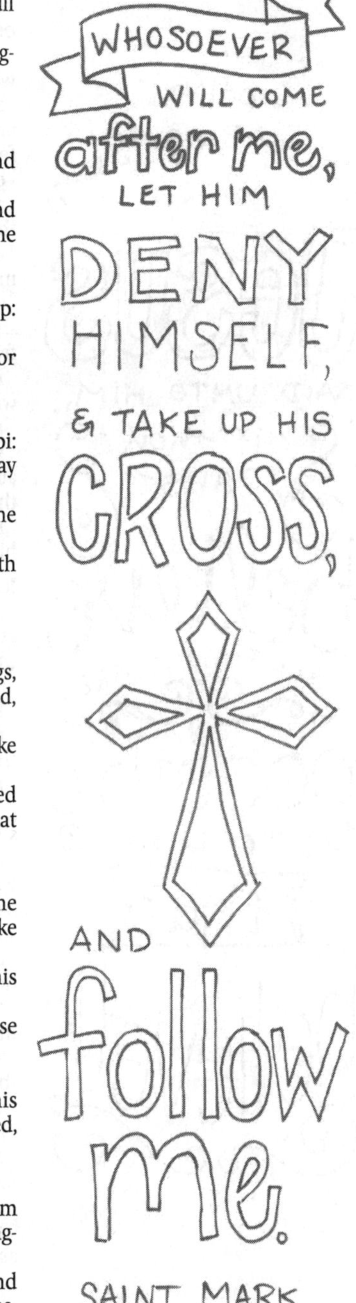

3 And his raiment became shining, exceeding white as snow; so as no fuller
on earth can white them.
4 And there appeared unto them Elias with Moses: and they were talking
with Jesus.
5 And Peter answered and said to Jesus, Master, it is good for us to be here:
and let us make three tabernacles; one for thee, and one for Moses, and one
for Elias.
6 For he wist not what to say; for they were sore afraid.
7 And there was a cloud that overshadowed them: and a voice came out of
the cloud, saying, This is my beloved Son: hear him.
8 And suddenly, when they had looked round about, they saw no man any
more, save Jesus only with themselves.
9 And as they came down from the mountain, he charged them that they
should tell no man what things they had seen, till the Son of man were risen
from the dead.
10 And they kept that saying with themselves, questioning one with another
what the rising from the dead should mean.
11 And they asked him, saying, Why say the scribes that Elias must first come?
12 And he answered and told them, Elias verily cometh first, and restoreth
all things; and how it is written of the Son of man, that he must suffer many
things, and be set at nought.
13 But I say unto you, That Elias is indeed come, and they have done unto
him whatsoever they listed, as it is written of him.

Jesus Heals a Demon-Possessed Boy

14 And when he came to *his* disciples, he saw a great multitude about them,
and the scribes questioning with them.
15 And straightway all the people, when they beheld him, were greatly
amazed, and running to *him* saluted him.
16 And he asked the scribes, What question ye with them?
17 And one of the multitude answered and said, Master, I have brought unto
thee my son, which hath a dumb spirit;
18 And wheresoever he taketh him, he teareth him: and he foameth, and
gnasheth with his teeth, and pineth away: and I spake to thy disciples that they
should cast him out; and they could not.
19 He answereth him, and saith, O faithless generation, how long shall I be
with you? how long shall I suffer you? bring him unto me.
20 And they brought him unto him: and when he saw him, straightway the
spirit tare him; and he fell on the ground, and wallowed foaming.
21 And he asked his father, How long is it ago since this came unto him? And
he said, Of a child.
22 And ofttimes it hath cast him into the fire, and into the waters, to destroy
him: but if thou canst do any thing, have compassion on us, and help us.
23 Jesus said unto him, If thou canst believe, all things *are* possible to him
that believeth.
24 And straightway the father of the child cried out, and said with tears, Lord,
I believe; help thou mine unbelief.
25 When Jesus saw that the people came running together, he rebuked the
foul spirit, saying unto him, *Thou* dumb and deaf spirit, I charge thee, come
out of him, and enter no more into him.
26 And *the spirit* cried, and rent him sore, and came out of him: and he was
as one dead; insomuch that many said, He is dead.
27 But Jesus took him by the hand, and lifted him up; and he arose.
28 And when he was come into the house, his disciples asked him privately,
Why could not we cast him out?

29 And he said unto them, This kind can come forth by nothing, but by prayer
and fasting.

Jesus Again Foretells His Death and Resurrection

30 And they departed thence, and passed through Galilee; and he would not
that any man should know *it*.
31 For he taught his disciples, and said unto them, The Son of man is delivered
into the hands of men, and they shall kill him; and after that he is killed, he
shall rise the third day.
32 But they understood not that saying, and were afraid to ask him.

Greatness in the Kingdom

33 And he came to Capernaum: and being in the house he asked them, What
was it that ye disputed among yourselves by the way?
34 But they held their peace: for by the way they had disputed among them-
selves, who *should be* the greatest.
35 And he sat down, and called the twelve, and saith unto them, If any man
desire to be first, *the same* shall be last of all, and servant of all.
36 And he took a child, and set him in the midst of them: and when he had
taken him in his arms, he said unto them,
37 Whosoever shall receive one of such children in my name, receiveth me:
and whosoever shall receive me, receiveth not me, but him that sent me.

Using the Name of Jesus

38 And John answered him, saying, Master, we saw one casting out devils in
thy name, and he followeth not us: and we forbad him, because he followeth
not us.
39 But Jesus said, Forbid him not: for there is no man which shall do a mir-
acle in my name, that can lightly speak evil of me.
40 For he that is not against us is on our part.
41 For whosoever shall give you a cup of water to drink in my name, because
ye belong to Christ, verily I say unto you, he shall not lose his reward.

Causing Others to Lose Faith

42 And whosoever shall offend one of *these* little ones that believe in me, it
is better for him that a millstone were hanged about his neck, and he were
cast into the sea.
43 And if thy hand offend thee, cut it off: it is better for thee to enter into life
maimed, than having two hands to go into hell, into the fire that never shall
be quenched:
44 Where their worm dieth not, and the fire is not quenched.
45 And if thy foot offend thee, cut it off: it is better for thee to enter halt into
life, than having two feet to be cast into hell, into the fire that never shall be
quenched:
46 Where their worm dieth not, and the fire is not quenched.
47 And if thine eye offend thee, pluck it out: it is better for thee to enter into
the kingdom of God with one eye, than having two eyes to be cast into hell
fire:
48 Where their worm dieth not, and the fire is not quenched.
49 For every one shall be salted with fire, and every sacrifice shall be salted
with salt.
50 Salt *is* good: but if the salt have lost his saltness, wherewith will ye season
it? Have salt in yourselves, and have peace one with another.

A Discussion about Divorce

10 And he arose from thence, and cometh into the coasts of Judaea by
the farther side of Jordan: and the people resort unto him again;
and, as he was wont, he taught them again.

2 And the Pharisees came to him, and asked him, Is it lawful for a man to put
away *his* wife? tempting him.
3 And he answered and said unto them, What did Moses command you?
4 And they said, Moses suffered to write a bill of divorcement, and to put *her*
away.
5 And Jesus answered and said unto them, For the hardness of your heart he
wrote you this precept.
6 But from the beginning of the creation God made them male and female.
7 For this cause shall a man leave his father and mother, and cleave to his
wife;
8 And they twain shall be one flesh: so then they are no more twain, but one
flesh.
9 What therefore God hath joined together, let not man put asunder.
10 And in the house his disciples asked him again of the same *matter*.
11 And he saith unto them, Whosoever shall put away his wife, and marry
another, committeth adultery against her.
12 And if a woman shall put away her husband, and be married to another,
she committeth adultery.

Jesus Blesses the Children

13 And they brought young children to him, that he should touch them: and
his disciples rebuked those that brought *them*.
14 But when Jesus saw *it*, he was much displeased, and said unto them, Suffer
the little children to come unto me, and forbid them not: for of such is the
kingdom of God.
15 Verily I say unto you, Whosoever shall not receive the kingdom of God as
a little child, he shall not enter therein.
16 And he took them up in his arms, put *his* hands upon them, and blessed
them.

The Danger of Riches

17 And when he was gone forth into the way, there came one running, and
kneeled to him, and asked him, Good Master, what shall I do that I may inher-
it eternal life?
18 And Jesus said unto him, Why callest thou me good? *there is* none good
but one, *that is*, God.
19 Thou knowest the commandments, Do not commit adultery, Do not kill,
Do not steal, Do not bear false witness, Defraud not, Honour thy father and
mother.
20 And he answered and said unto him, Master, all these have I observed from
my youth.
21 Then Jesus beholding him loved him, and said unto him, One thing thou
lackest: go thy way, sell whatsoever thou hast, and give to the poor, and thou
shalt have treasure in heaven: and come, take up the cross, and follow me.
22 And he was sad at that saying, and went away grieved: for he had great
possessions.
23 And Jesus looked round about, and saith unto his disciples, How hardly
shall they that have riches enter into the kingdom of God!
24 And the disciples were astonished at his words. But Jesus answereth again,
and saith unto them, Children, how hard is it for them that trust in riches to
enter into the kingdom of God!
25 It is easier for a camel to go through the eye of a needle, than for a rich
man to enter into the kingdom of God.
26 And they were astonished out of measure, saying among themselves, Who
then can be saved?
27 And Jesus looking upon them saith, With men *it is* impossible, but not
with God: for with God all things are possible.

28 Then Peter began to say unto him, Lo, we have left all, and have followed
thee.
29 And Jesus answered and said, Verily I say unto you, There is no man that
hath left house, or brethren, or sisters, or father, or mother, or wife, or chil-
dren, or lands, for my sake, and the gospel's,
30 But he shall receive an hundredfold now in this time, houses, and breth-
ren, and sisters, and mothers, and children, and lands, with persecutions; and
in the world to come eternal life.
31 But many *that are* first shall be last; and the last first.

Jesus Again Foretells His Death and Resurrection

32 And they were in the way going up to Jerusalem; and Jesus went before
them: and they were amazed; and as they followed, they were afraid. And he
took again the twelve, and began to tell them what things should happen unto
him,
33 *Saying*, Behold, we go up to Jerusalem; and the Son of man shall be deliv-
ered unto the chief priests, and unto the scribes; and they shall condemn him
to death, and shall deliver him to the Gentiles:
34 And they shall mock him, and shall scourge him, and shall spit upon him,
and shall kill him: and the third day he shall rise again.

Two Disciples Make a Request

35 And James and John, the sons of Zebedee, come unto him, saying, Master,
we would that thou shouldest do for us whatsoever we shall desire.
36 And he said unto them, What would ye that I should do for you?
37 They said unto him, Grant unto us that we may sit, one on thy right hand,
and the other on thy left hand, in thy glory.
38 But Jesus said unto them, Ye know not what ye ask: can ye drink of the cup
that I drink of? and be baptized with the baptism that I am baptized with?
39 And they said unto him, We can. And Jesus said unto them, Ye shall indeed
drink of the cup that I drink of; and with the baptism that I am baptized
withal shall ye be baptized:
40 But to sit on my right hand and on my left hand is not mine to give; but *it*
shall be given to them for whom it is prepared.
41 And when the ten heard *it*, they began to be much displeased with James
and John.
42 But Jesus called them *to him*, and saith unto them, Ye know that they which
are accounted to rule over the Gentiles exercise lordship over them; and their
great ones exercise authority upon them.
43 But so shall it not be among you: but whosoever will be great among you,
shall be your minister:
44 And whosoever of you will be the chiefest, shall be servant of all.
45 For even the Son of man came not to be ministered unto, but to minister,
and to give his life a ransom for many.

Jesus Restores Sight to Bartimaeus

46 And they came to Jericho: and as he went out of Jericho with his disciples
and a great number of people, blind Bartimaeus, the son of Timaeus, sat by
the highway side begging.
47 And when he heard that it was Jesus of Nazareth, he began to cry out, and
say, Jesus, *thou* Son of David, have mercy on me.
48 And many charged him that he should hold his peace: but he cried the
more a great deal, *Thou* Son of David, have mercy on me.
49 And Jesus stood still, and commanded him to be called. And they call the
blind man, saying unto him, Be of good comfort, rise; he calleth thee.
50 And he, casting away his garment, rose, and came to Jesus.
51 And Jesus answered and said unto him, What wilt thou that I should do
unto thee? The blind man said unto him, Lord, that I might receive my sight.

52 And Jesus said unto him, Go thy way; thy faith hath made thee whole. And
immediately he received his sight, and followed Jesus in the way.

Jesus Rides in Triumph into Jerusalem

11 And when they came nigh to Jerusalem, unto Bethphage and Bethany,
at the mount of Olives, he sendeth forth two of his disciples,
2 And saith unto them, Go your way into the village over against you: and as
soon as ye be entered into it, ye shall find a colt tied, whereon never man sat;
loose him, and bring *him*.
3 And if any man say unto you, Why do ye this? say ye that the Lord hath need
of him; and straightway he will send him hither.
4 And they went their way, and found the colt tied by the door without in a
place where two ways met; and they loose him.
5 And certain of them that stood there said unto them, What do ye, loosing
the colt?
6 And they said unto them even as Jesus had commanded: and they let them go.
7 And they brought the colt to Jesus, and cast their garments on him; and he
sat upon him.
8 And many spread their garments in the way: and others cut down branch-
es off the trees, and strawed *them* in the way.
9 And they that went before, and they that followed, cried, saying, Hosanna;
Blessed *is* he that cometh in the name of the Lord:
10 Blessed *be* the kingdom of our father David, that cometh in the name of
the Lord: Hosanna in the highest.
11 And Jesus entered into Jerusalem, and into the temple: and when he had
looked round about upon all things, and now the eventide was come, he went
out unto Bethany with the twelve.

Jesus Curses the Fig Tree

12 And on the morrow, when they were come from Bethany, he was hungry:
13 And seeing a fig tree afar off having leaves, he came, if haply he might find
any thing thereon: and when he came to it, he found nothing but leaves; for
the time of figs was not *yet*.
14 And Jesus answered and said unto it, No man eat fruit of thee hereafter
for ever. And his disciples heard *it*.

Jesus Throws the Moneychangers out of the Temple

15 And they come to Jerusalem: and Jesus went into the temple, and began
to cast out them that sold and bought in the temple, and overthrew the tables
of the moneychangers, and the seats of them that sold doves;
16 And would not suffer that any man should carry *any* vessel through the
temple.
17 And he taught, saying unto them, Is it not written, My house shall be called
of all nations the house of prayer? but ye have made it a den of thieves.
18 And the scribes and chief priests heard *it*, and sought how they might
destroy him: for they feared him, because all the people was astonished at his
doctrine.
19 And when even was come, he went out of the city.

The Fig Tree Dries Up

20 And in the morning, as they passed by, they saw the fig tree dried up from
the roots.
21 And Peter calling to remembrance saith unto him, Master, behold, the fig
tree which thou cursedst is withered away.
22 And Jesus answering saith unto them, Have faith in God.
23 For verily I say unto you, That whosoever shall say unto this mountain, Be
thou removed, and be thou cast into the sea; and shall not doubt in his heart,

but shall believe that those things which he saith shall come to pass; he shall
have whatsoever he saith.
24 Therefore I say unto you, What things soever ye desire, when ye pray,
believe that ye receive *them*, and ye shall have *them*.
25 And when ye stand praying, forgive, if ye have ought against any: that your
Father also which is in heaven may forgive you your trespasses.
26 But if ye do not forgive, neither will your Father which is in heaven forgive
your trespasses.

Jesus' Authority Is Challenged

27 And they come again to Jerusalem: and as he was walking in the temple,
there come to him the chief priests, and the scribes, and the elders,
28 And say unto him, By what authority doest thou these things? and who
gave thee this authority to do these things?
29 And Jesus answered and said unto them, I will also ask of you one question,
and answer me, and I will tell you by what authority I do these things.
30 The baptism of John, was *it* from heaven, or of men? answer me.
31 And they reasoned with themselves, saying, If we shall say, From heaven;
he will say, Why then did ye not believe him?
32 But if we shall say, Of men; they feared the people: for all *men* counted
John, that he was a prophet indeed.
33 And they answered and said unto Jesus, We cannot tell. And Jesus answer-
ing saith unto them, Neither do I tell you by what authority I do these things.

A Parable about a Vineyard

12 And he began to speak unto them by parables. A *certain* man plant-
ed a vineyard, and set an hedge about *it*, and digged *a place for* the
winefat, and built a tower, and let it out to husbandmen, and went into a
far country.
2 And at the season he sent to the husbandmen a servant, that he might
receive from the husbandmen of the fruit of the vineyard.
3 And they caught *him*, and beat him, and sent *him* away empty.
4 And again he sent unto them another servant; and at him they cast stones,
and wounded *him* in the head, and sent *him* away shamefully handled.
5 And again he sent another; and him they killed, and many others; beating
some, and killing some.
6 Having yet therefore one son, his wellbeloved, he sent him also last unto
them, saying, They will reverence my son.
7 But those husbandmen said among themselves, This is the heir; come, let
us kill him, and the inheritance shall be ours.
8 And they took him, and killed *him*, and cast *him* out of the vineyard.
9 What shall therefore the lord of the vineyard do? he will come and destroy
the husbandmen, and will give the vineyard unto others.
10 And have ye not read this scripture; The stone which the builders rejected
is become the head of the corner:
11 This was the Lord's doing, and it is marvellous in our eyes?
12 And they sought to lay hold on him, but feared the people: for they knew
that he had spoken the parable against them: and they left him, and went their
way.

A Question about Paying Tribute to Caesar

13 And they send unto him certain of the Pharisees and of the Herodians, to
catch him in *his* words.
14 And when they were come, they say unto him, Master, we know that thou
art true, and carest for no man: for thou regardest not the person of men, but
teachest the way of God in truth: Is it lawful to give tribute to Caesar, or not?
15 Shall we give, or shall we not give? But he, knowing their hypocrisy, said
unto them, Why tempt ye me? bring me a penny, that I may see *it*.

16 And they brought *it*. And he saith unto them, Whose *is* this image and
superscription? And they said unto him, Caesar's.
17 And Jesus answering said unto them, Render to Caesar the things that are
Caesar's, and to God the things that are God's. And they marvelled at him.

A Question about the Resurrection

18 Then come unto him the Sadducees, which say there is no resurrection;
and they asked him, saying,
19 Master, Moses wrote unto us, If a man's brother die, and leave *his* wife
behind him, and leave no children, that his brother should take his wife, and
raise up seed unto his brother.
20 Now there were seven brethren: and the first took a wife, and dying left
no seed.
21 And the second took her, and died, neither left he any seed: and the third
likewise.
22 And the seven had her, and left no seed: last of all the woman died also.
23 In the resurrection therefore, when they shall rise, whose wife shall she
be of them? for the seven had her to wife.
24 And Jesus answering said unto them, Do ye not therefore err, because ye
know not the scriptures, neither the power of God?
25 For when they shall rise from the dead, they neither marry, nor are given
in marriage; but are as the angels which are in heaven.
26 And as touching the dead, that they rise: have ye not read in the book of
Moses, how in the bush God spake unto him, saying, I *am* the God of Abraham,
and the God of Isaac, and the God of Jacob?
27 He is not the God of the dead, but the God of the living: ye therefore do
greatly err.

The Greatest Commandment

28 And one of the scribes came, and having heard them reasoning together,
and perceiving that he had answered them well, asked him, Which is the first
commandment of all?
29 And Jesus answered him, The first of all the commandments *is*, Hear, O
Israel; The Lord our God is one Lord:
30 And thou shalt love the Lord thy God with all thy heart, and with all thy
soul, and with all thy mind, and with all thy strength: this *is* the first com-
mandment.
31 And the second *is* like, *namely* this, Thou shalt love thy neighbour as thy-
self. There is none other commandment greater than these.
32 And the scribe said unto him, Well, Master, thou hast said the truth: for
there is one God; and there is none other but he:
33 And to love him with all the heart, and with all the understanding, and
with all the soul, and with all the strength, and to love *his* neighbour as himself,
is more than all whole burnt offerings and sacrifices.
34 And when Jesus saw that he answered discreetly, he said unto him, Thou
art not far from the kingdom of God. And no man after that durst ask him *any*
question.

David's Son Is David's Lord

35 And Jesus answered and said, while he taught in the temple, How say the
scribes that Christ is the Son of David?
36 For David himself said by the Holy Ghost, The LORD said to my Lord, Sit
thou on my right hand, till I make thine enemies thy footstool.
37 David therefore himself calleth him Lord; and whence is he *then* his son?
And the common people heard him gladly.
38 And he said unto them in his doctrine, Beware of the scribes, which love
to go in long clothing, and *love* salutations in the marketplaces,
39 And the chief seats in the synagogues, and the uppermost rooms at feasts:

40 Which devour widows' houses, and for a pretence make long prayers: these
shall receive greater damnation.

Jesus Commends a Poor Widow

41 And Jesus sat over against the treasury, and beheld how the people cast
money into the treasury: and many that were rich cast in much.
42 And there came a certain poor widow, and she threw in two mites, which
make a farthing.
43 And he called *unto him* his disciples, and saith unto them, Verily I say unto
you, That this poor widow hath cast more in, than all they which have cast
into the treasury:
44 For all *they* did cast in of their abundance; but she of her want did cast in
all that she had, *even* all her living.

Jesus Foretells Future Destruction

13 And as he went out of the temple, one of his disciples saith unto
him, Master, see what manner of stones and what buildings *are*
here!
2 And Jesus answering said unto him, Seest thou these great buildings? there
shall not be left one stone upon another, that shall not be thrown down.
3 And as he sat upon the mount of Olives over against the temple, Peter and
James and John and Andrew asked him privately,
4 Tell us, when shall these things be? and what *shall be* the sign when all
these things shall be fulfilled?
5 And Jesus answering them began to say, Take heed lest any *man* deceive
you:
6 For many shall come in my name, saying, I am *Christ*; and shall deceive
many.
7 And when ye shall hear of wars and rumours of wars, be ye not troubled:
for *such things* must needs be; but the end *shall* not *be* yet.
8 For nation shall rise against nation, and kingdom against kingdom: and
there shall be earthquakes in divers places, and there shall be famines and
troubles: these *are* the beginnings of sorrows.
9 But take heed to yourselves: for they shall deliver you up to councils; and in
the synagogues ye shall be beaten: and ye shall be brought before rulers and
kings for my sake, for a testimony against them.
10 And the gospel must first be published among all nations.
11 But when they shall lead *you*, and deliver you up, take no thought before-
hand what ye shall speak, neither do ye premeditate: but whatsoever shall be
given you in that hour, that speak ye: for it is not ye that speak, but the Holy
Ghost.
12 Now the brother shall betray the brother to death, and the father the son;
and children shall rise up against *their* parents, and shall cause them to be put
to death.
13 And ye shall be hated of all *men* for my name's sake: but he that shall
endure unto the end, the same shall be saved.

Great Calamities Shall Befall the Jews

14 But when ye shall see the abomination of desolation, spoken of by Daniel
the prophet, standing where it ought not, (let him that readeth understand,)
then let them that be in Judaea flee to the mountains:
15 And let him that is on the housetop not go down into the house, neither
enter *therein*, to take any thing out of his house:
16 And let him that is in the field not turn back again for to take up his gar-
ment.
17 But woe to them that are with child, and to them that give suck in those
days!
18 And pray ye that your flight be not in the winter.

19 For *in* those days shall be affliction, such as was not from the beginning
of the creation which God created unto this time, neither shall be.
20 And except that the Lord had shortened those days, no flesh should be
saved: but for the elect's sake, whom he hath chosen, he hath shortened the
days.
21 And then if any man shall say to you, Lo, here *is* Christ; or, lo, *he is* there;
believe *him* not:
22 For false Christs and false prophets shall rise, and shall shew signs and
wonders, to seduce, if *it were* possible, even the elect.
23 But take ye heed: behold, I have foretold you all things.

Jesus Foretells the Manner of His Coming

24 But in those days, after that tribulation, the sun shall be darkened, and
the moon shall not give her light,
25 And the stars of heaven shall fall, and the powers that are in heaven shall
be shaken.
26 And then shall they see the Son of man coming in the clouds with great
power and glory.
27 And then shall he send his angels, and shall gather together his elect from
the four winds, from the uttermost part of the earth to the uttermost part of
heaven.
28 Now learn a parable of the fig tree; When her branch is yet tender, and
putteth forth leaves, ye know that summer is near:
29 So ye in like manner, when ye shall see these things come to pass, know
that it is nigh, *even* at the doors.
30 Verily I say unto you, that this generation shall not pass, till all these things
be done.
31 Heaven and earth shall pass away: but my words shall not pass away.
32 But of that day and *that* hour knoweth no man, no, not the angels which
are in heaven, neither the Son, but the Father.
33 Take ye heed, watch and pray: for ye know not when the time is.
34 *For the Son of man is* as a man taking a far journey, who left his house,
and gave authority to his servants, and to every man his work, and command-
ed the porter to watch.
35 Watch ye therefore: for ye know not when the master of the house cometh,
at even, or at midnight, or at the cockcrowing, or in the morning:
36 Lest coming suddenly he find you sleeping.
37 And what I say unto you I say unto all, Watch.

The Plot to Kill Jesus

14 After two days was *the feast of* the passover, and of unleavened
bread: and the chief priests and the scribes sought how they might
take him by craft, and put *him* to death.
2 But they said, Not on the feast *day*, lest there be an uproar of the people.

A Woman Anoints Jesus' Body

3 And being in Bethany in the house of Simon the leper, as he sat at meat,
there came a woman having an alabaster box of ointment of spikenard very
precious; and she brake the box, and poured *it* on his head.
4 And there were some that had indignation within themselves, and said,
Why was this waste of the ointment made?
5 For it might have been sold for more than three hundred pence, and have
been given to the poor. And they murmured against her.
6 And Jesus said, Let her alone; why trouble ye her? she hath wrought a good
work on me.
7 For ye have the poor with you always, and whensoever ye will ye may do
them good: but me ye have not always.

8 She hath done what she could: she is come aforehand to anoint my body
to the burying.
9 Verily I say unto you, Wheresoever this gospel shall be preached through-
out the whole world, *this* also that she hath done shall be spoken of for a
memorial of her.

Judas Plans to Betray Jesus

10 And Judas Iscariot, one of the twelve, went unto the chief priests, to betray
him unto them.
11 And when they heard *it*, they were glad, and promised to give him money.
And he sought how he might conveniently betray him.

Preparations for the Passover

12 And the first day of unleavened bread, when they killed the passover, his
disciples said unto him, Where wilt thou that we go and prepare that thou
mayest eat the passover?
13 And he sendeth forth two of his disciples, and saith unto them, Go ye into
the city, and there shall meet you a man bearing a pitcher of water: follow him.
14 And wheresoever he shall go in, say ye to the goodman of the house, The
Master saith, Where is the guestchamber, where I shall eat the passover with
my disciples?
15 And he will shew you a large upper room furnished *and* prepared: there
make ready for us.
16 And his disciples went forth, and came into the city, and found as he had
said unto them: and they made ready the passover.
17 And in the evening he cometh with the twelve.

Jesus Knows Who Will Betray Him

18 And as they sat and did eat, Jesus said, Verily I say unto you, One of you
which eateth with me shall betray me.
19 And they began to be sorrowful, and to say unto him one by one, *Is* it I?
and another *said*, *Is* it I?
20 And he answered and said unto them, *It is* one of the twelve, that dippeth
with me in the dish.
21 The Son of man indeed goeth, as it is written of him: but woe to that man
by whom the Son of man is betrayed! good were it for that man if he had never
been born.

The Lord's Supper

22 And as they did eat, Jesus took bread, and blessed, and brake *it*, and gave
to them, and said, Take, eat: this is my body.
23 And he took the cup, and when he had given thanks, he gave *it* to them:
and they all drank of it.
24 And he said unto them, This is my blood of the new testament, which is
shed for many.
25 Verily I say unto you, I will drink no more of the fruit of the vine, until
that day that I drink it new in the kingdom of God.
26 And when they had sung an hymn, they went out into the mount of Olives.

Jesus Predicts Peter's Denial

27 And Jesus saith unto them, All ye shall be offended because of me this
night: for it is written, I will smite the shepherd, and the sheep shall be scat-
tered.
28 But after that I am risen, I will go before you into Galilee.
29 But Peter said unto him, Although all shall be offended, yet *will* not I.
30 And Jesus saith unto him, Verily I say unto thee, That this day, *even* in this
night, before the cock crow twice, thou shalt deny me thrice.
31 But he spake the more vehemently, If I should die with thee, I will not deny
thee in any wise. Likewise also said they all.

Jesus Prays in Gethsemane

32 And they came to a place which was named Gethsemane: and he saith to
his disciples, Sit ye here, while I shall pray.
33 And he taketh with him Peter and James and John, and began to be sore
amazed, and to be very heavy;
34 And saith unto them, My soul is exceeding sorrowful unto death: tarry ye
here, and watch.
35 And he went forward a little, and fell on the ground, and prayed that, if it
were possible, the hour might pass from him.
36 And he said, Abba, Father, all things *are* possible unto thee; take away this
cup from me: nevertheless not what I will, but what thou wilt.
37 And he cometh, and findeth them sleeping, and saith unto Peter, Simon,
sleepest thou? couldest not thou watch one hour?
38 Watch ye and pray, lest ye enter into temptation. The spirit truly *is* ready,
but the flesh *is* weak.
39 And again he went away, and prayed, and spake the same words.
40 And when he returned, he found them asleep again, (for their eyes were
heavy,) neither wist they what to answer him.
41 And he cometh the third time, and saith unto them, Sleep on now, and
take *your* rest: it is enough, the hour is come; behold, the Son of man is betrayed
into the hands of sinners.
42 Rise up, let us go; lo, he that betrayeth me is at hand.

Judas Betrays Jesus with a Kiss

43 And immediately, while he yet spake, cometh Judas, one of the twelve, and
with him a great multitude with swords and staves, from the chief priests and
the scribes and the elders.
44 And he that betrayed him had given them a token, saying, Whomsoever
I shall kiss, that same is he; take him, and lead *him* away safely.
45 And as soon as he was come, he goeth straightway to him, and saith,
Master, master; and kissed him.
46 And they laid their hands on him, and took him.
47 And one of them that stood by drew a sword, and smote a servant of the
high priest, and cut off his ear.
48 And Jesus answered and said unto them, Are ye come out, as against a thief,
with swords and *with* staves to take me?
49 I was daily with you in the temple teaching, and ye took me not: but the
scriptures must be fulfilled.
50 And they all forsook him, and fled.
51 And there followed him a certain young man, having a linen cloth cast
about *his* naked *body*; and the young men laid hold on him:
52 And he left the linen cloth, and fled from them naked.

The Trial by the Jewish Council

53 And they led Jesus away to the high priest: and with him were assembled
all the chief priests and the elders and the scribes.
54 And Peter followed him afar off, even into the palace of the high priest:
and he sat with the servants, and warmed himself at the fire.
55 And the chief priests and all the council sought for witness against Jesus
to put him to death; and found none.
56 For many bare false witness against him, but their witness agreed not
together.
57 And there arose certain, and bare false witness against him, saying,
58 We heard him say, I will destroy this temple that is made with hands, and
within three days I will build another made without hands.
59 But neither so did their witness agree together.

60 And the high priest stood up in the midst, and asked Jesus, saying,
Answerest thou nothing? what *is it which* these witness against thee?
61 But he held his peace, and answered nothing. Again the high priest asked
him, and said unto him, Art thou the Christ, the Son of the Blessed?
62 And Jesus said, I am: and ye shall see the Son of man sitting on the right
hand of power, and coming in the clouds of heaven.
63 Then the high priest rent his clothes, and saith, What need we any further
witnesses?
64 Ye have heard the blasphemy: what think ye? And they all condemned
him to be guilty of death.
65 And some began to spit on him, and to cover his face, and to buffet him,
and to say unto him, Prophesy: and the servants did strike him with the palms
of their hands.

Peter Denies Jesus

66 And as Peter was beneath in the palace, there cometh one of the maids of
the high priest:
67 And when she saw Peter warming himself, she looked upon him, and said,
And thou also wast with Jesus of Nazareth.
68 But he denied, saying, I know not, neither understand I what thou sayest.
And he went out into the porch; and the cock crew.
69 And a maid saw him again, and began to say to them that stood by, This is
one of them.
70 And he denied it again. And a little after, they that stood by said again to
Peter, Surely thou art *one* of them: for thou art a Galilaean, and thy speech
agreeth *thereto*.
71 But he began to curse and to swear, *saying*, I know not this man of whom
ye speak.
72 And the second time the cock crew. And Peter called to mind the word
that Jesus said unto him, Before the cock crow twice, thou shalt deny me thrice.
And when he thought thereon, he wept.

The Trial before Pilate

15 And straightway in the morning the chief priests held a consulta-
tion with the elders and scribes and the whole council, and bound
Jesus, and carried *him* away, and delivered *him* to Pilate.
2 And Pilate asked him, Art thou the King of the Jews? And he answering said
unto him, Thou sayest *it*.
3 And the chief priests accused him of many things: but he answered nothing.
4 And Pilate asked him again, saying, Answerest thou nothing? behold how
many things they witness against thee.
5 But Jesus yet answered nothing; so that Pilate marvelled.
6 Now at *that* feast he released unto them one prisoner, whomsoever they
desired.
7 And there was *one* named Barabbas, *which lay* bound with them that had
made insurrection with him, who had committed murder in the insurrection.
8 And the multitude crying aloud began to desire *him to do* as he had ever
done unto them.
9 But Pilate answered them, saying, Will ye that I release unto you the King
of the Jews?
10 For he knew that the chief priests had delivered him for envy.
11 But the chief priests moved the people, that he should rather release
Barabbas unto them.
12 And Pilate answered and said again unto them, What will ye then that I
shall do *unto him* whom ye call the King of the Jews?
13 And they cried out again, Crucify him.

TRULY THIS man WAS THE Son OF GOD.

SAINT MARK 15:39

14 Then Pilate said unto them, Why, what evil hath he done? And they cried
out the more exceedingly, Crucify him.

Jesus Is Mocked and Crucified

15 And *so* Pilate, willing to content the people, released Barabbas unto them,
and delivered Jesus, when he had scourged *him*, to be crucified.
16 And the soldiers led him away into the hall, called Praetorium; and they
call together the whole band.
17 And they clothed him with purple, and platted a crown of thorns, and put
it about his *head*,
18 And began to salute him, Hail, King of the Jews!
19 And they smote him on the head with a reed, and did spit upon him, and
bowing *their* knees worshipped him.
20 And when they had mocked him, they took off the purple from him, and
put his own clothes on him, and led him out to crucify him.
21 And they compel one Simon a Cyrenian, who passed by, coming out of
the country, the father of Alexander and Rufus, to bear his cross.
22 And they bring him unto the place Golgotha, which is, being interpreted,
The place of a skull.
23 And they gave him to drink wine mingled with myrrh: but he received *it*
not.
24 And when they had crucified him, they parted his garments, casting lots
upon them, what every man should take.
25 And it was the third hour, and they crucified him.
26 And the superscription of his accusation was written over, THE KING OF
THE JEWS.
27 And with him they crucify two thieves; the one on his right hand, and the
other on his left.
28 And the scripture was fulfilled, which saith, And he was numbered with
the transgressors.
29 And they that passed by railed on him, wagging their heads, and saying,
Ah, thou that destroyest the temple, and buildest *it* in three days,
30 Save thyself, and come down from the cross.
31 Likewise also the chief priests mocking said among themselves with the
scribes, He saved others; himself he cannot save.
32 Let Christ the King of Israel descend now from the cross, that we may see
and believe. And they that were crucified with him reviled him.

Jesus Dies

33 And when the sixth hour was come, there was darkness over the whole
land until the ninth hour.
34 And at the ninth hour Jesus cried with a loud voice, saying, Eloi, Eloi, lama
sabachthani? which is, being interpreted, My God, my God, why hast thou
forsaken me?
35 And some of them that stood by, when they heard *it*, said, Behold, he
calleth Elias.
36 And one ran and filled a spunge full of vinegar, and put *it* on a reed, and
gave him to drink, saying, Let alone; let us see whether Elias will come to take
him down.
37 And Jesus cried with a loud voice, and gave up the ghost.
38 And the veil of the temple was rent in twain from the top to the bottom.
39 And when the centurion, which stood over against him, saw that he so
cried out, and gave up the ghost, he said, Truly this man was the Son of God.
40 There were also women looking on afar off: among whom was Mary
Magdalene, and Mary the mother of James the less and of Joses, and Salome;
41 (Who also, when he was in Galilee, followed him, and ministered unto
him;) and many other women which came up with him unto Jerusalem.

Jesus Is Buried

42 And now when the even was come, because it was the preparation, that
is, the day before the sabbath,
43 Joseph of Arimathaea, an honourable counsellor, which also waited for
the kingdom of God, came, and went in boldly unto Pilate, and craved the
body of Jesus.
44 And Pilate marvelled if he were already dead: and calling *unto him* the
centurion, he asked him whether he had been any while dead.
45 And when he knew *it* of the centurion, he gave the body to Joseph.
46 And he bought fine linen, and took him down, and wrapped him in the
linen, and laid him in a sepulchre which was hewn out of a rock, and rolled a
stone unto the door of the sepulchre.
47 And Mary Magdalene and Mary *the mother* of Joses beheld where he was
laid.

Jesus' Resurrection

16 And when the sabbath was past, Mary Magdalene, and Mary the
mother of James, and Salome, had bought sweet spices, that they
might come and anoint him.
2 And very early in the morning the first *day* of the week, they came unto
the sepulchre at the rising of the sun.
3 And they said among themselves, Who shall roll us away the stone from
the door of the sepulchre?
4 And when they looked, they saw that the stone was rolled away: for it was
very great.
5 And entering into the sepulchre, they saw a young man sitting on the right
side, clothed in a long white garment; and they were affrighted.
6 And he saith unto them, Be not affrighted: Ye seek Jesus of Nazareth, which
was crucified: he is risen; he is not here: behold the place where they laid him.
7 But go your way, tell his disciples and Peter that he goeth before you into
Galilee: there shall ye see him, as he said unto you.
8 And they went out quickly, and fled from the sepulchre; for they trembled
and were amazed: neither said they any thing to any *man*; for they were afraid.
9 Now when *Jesus* was risen early the first *day* of the week, he appeared first
to Mary Magdalene, out of whom he had cast seven devils.
10 *And* she went and told them that had been with him, as they mourned
and wept.
11 And they, when they had heard that he was alive, and had been seen of
her, believed not.
12 After that he appeared in another form unto two of them, as they walked,
and went into the country.
13 And they went and told *it* unto the residue: neither believed they them.
14 Afterward he appeared unto the eleven as they sat at meat, and upbraided
them with their unbelief and hardness of heart, because they believed not
them which had seen him after he was risen.
15 And he said unto them, Go ye into all the world, and preach the gospel to
every creature.
16 He that believeth and is baptized shall be saved; but he that believeth not
shall be damned.
17 And these signs shall follow them that believe; In my name shall they cast
out devils; they shall speak with new tongues;
18 They shall take up serpents; and if they drink any deadly thing, it shall not
hurt them; they shall lay hands on the sick, and they shall recover.
19 So then after the Lord had spoken unto them, he was received up into
heaven, and sat on the right hand of God.
20 And they went forth, and preached every where, the Lord working with
them, and confirming the word with signs following. Amen.

Luke's Preface

1 Forasmuch as many have taken in hand to set forth in order a declaration of those things which are most surely believed among us,
2 Even as they delivered them unto us, which from the beginning were eyewitnesses, and ministers of the word;
3 It seemed good to me also, having had perfect understanding of all things from the very first, to write unto thee in order, most excellent Theophilus,
4 That thou mightest know the certainty of those things, wherein thou hast been instructed.

The Angel Gabriel Appears to Zacharias

5 There was in the days of Herod, the king of Judaea, a certain priest named Zacharias, of the course of Abia: and his wife *was* of the daughters of Aaron, and her name *was* Elisabeth.
6 And they were both righteous before God, walking in all the commandments and ordinances of the Lord blameless.
7 And they had no child, because that Elisabeth was barren, and they both were *now* well stricken in years.
8 And it came to pass, that while he executed the priest's office before God in the order of his course,
9 According to the custom of the priest's office, his lot was to burn incense when he went into the temple of the Lord.
10 And the whole multitude of the people were praying without at the time of incense.
11 And there appeared unto him an angel of the Lord standing on the right side of the altar of incense.
12 And when Zacharias saw *him*, he was troubled, and fear fell upon him.
13 But the angel said unto him, Fear not, Zacharias: for thy prayer is heard; and thy wife Elisabeth shall bear thee a son, and thou shalt call his name John.
14 And thou shalt have joy and gladness; and many shall rejoice at his birth.
15 For he shall be great in the sight of the Lord, and shall drink neither wine nor strong drink; and he shall be filled with the Holy Ghost, even from his mother's womb.
16 And many of the children of Israel shall he turn to the Lord their God.
17 And he shall go before him in the spirit and power of Elias, to turn the hearts of the fathers to the children, and the disobedient to the wisdom of the just; to make ready a people prepared for the Lord.
18 And Zacharias said unto the angel, Whereby shall I know this? for I am an old man, and my wife well stricken in years.
19 And the angel answering said unto him, I am Gabriel, that stand in the presence of God; and am sent to speak unto thee, and to shew thee these glad tidings.
20 And, behold, thou shalt be dumb, and not able to speak, until the day that these things shall be performed, because thou believest not my words, which shall be fulfilled in their season.
21 And the people waited for Zacharias, and marvelled that he tarried so long in the temple.

22 And when he came out, he could not speak unto them: and they perceived
that he had seen a vision in the temple: for he beckoned unto them, and
remained speechless.
23 And it came to pass, that, as soon as the days of his ministration were
accomplished, he departed to his own house.
24 And after those days his wife Elisabeth conceived, and hid herself five
months, saying,
25 Thus hath the Lord dealt with me in the days wherein he looked on *me*,
to take away my reproach among men.

The Angel Gabriel Appears to Mary

26 And in the sixth month the angel Gabriel was sent from God unto a city
of Galilee, named Nazareth,
27 To a virgin espoused to a man whose name was Joseph, of the house of
David; and the virgin's name *was* Mary.
28 And the angel came in unto her, and said, Hail, *thou that art* highly
favoured, the Lord *is* with thee: blessed *art* thou among women.
29 And when she saw *him*, she was troubled at his saying, and cast in her
mind what manner of salutation this should be.
30 And the angel said unto her, Fear not, Mary: for thou hast found favour
with God.
31 And, behold, thou shalt conceive in thy womb, and bring forth a son, and
shalt call his name JESUS.
32 He shall be great, and shall be called the Son of the Highest: and the Lord
God shall give unto him the throne of his father David:
33 And he shall reign over the house of Jacob for ever; and of his kingdom
there shall be no end.
34 Then said Mary unto the angel, How shall this be, seeing I know not a
man?
35 And the angel answered and said unto her, The Holy Ghost shall come
upon thee, and the power of the Highest shall overshadow thee: therefore also
that holy thing which shall be born of thee shall be called the Son of God.
36 And, behold, thy cousin Elisabeth, she hath also conceived a son in her
old age: and this is the sixth month with her, who was called barren.
37 For with God nothing shall be impossible.
38 And Mary said, Behold the handmaid of the Lord; be it unto me according
to thy word. And the angel departed from her.

Mary Visits Elisabeth

39 And Mary arose in those days, and went into the hill country with haste,
into a city of Juda;
40 And entered into the house of Zacharias, and saluted Elisabeth.
41 And it came to pass, that, when Elisabeth heard the salutation of Mary,
the babe leaped in her womb; and Elisabeth was filled with the Holy Ghost:
42 And she spake out with a loud voice, and said, Blessed *art* thou among
women, and blessed *is* the fruit of thy womb.
43 And whence *is* this to me, that the mother of my Lord should come to me?
44 For, lo, as soon as the voice of thy salutation sounded in mine ears, the
babe leaped in my womb for joy.
45 And blessed *is* she that believed: for there shall be a performance of those
things which were told her from the Lord.

Mary Praises God

46 And Mary said, My soul doth magnify the Lord,
47 And my spirit hath rejoiced in God my Saviour.
48 For he hath regarded the low estate of his handmaiden: for, behold, from
henceforth all generations shall call me blessed.
49 For he that is mighty hath done to me great things; and holy *is* his name.

50 And his mercy *is* on them that fear him from generation to generation.
51 He hath shewed strength with his arm; he hath scattered the proud in the
imagination of their hearts.
52 He hath put down the mighty from *their* seats, and exalted them of low
degree.
53 He hath filled the hungry with good things; and the rich he hath sent
empty away.
54 He hath holpen his servant Israel, in remembrance of *his* mercy;
55 As he spake to our fathers, to Abraham, and to his seed for ever.
56 And Mary abode with her about three months, and returned to her own
house.

The Birth of John

57 Now Elisabeth's full time came that she should be delivered; and she
brought forth a son.
58 And her neighbours and her cousins heard how the Lord had shewed
great mercy upon her; and they rejoiced with her.
59 And it came to pass, that on the eighth day they came to circumcise the
child; and they called him Zacharias, after the name of his father.
60 And his mother answered and said, Not *so*; but he shall be called John.
61 And they said unto her, There is none of thy kindred that is called by this
name.
62 And they made signs to his father, how he would have him called.
63 And he asked for a writing table, and wrote, saying, His name is John. And
they marvelled all.
64 And his mouth was opened immediately, and his tongue *loosed*, and he
spake, and praised God.
65 And fear came on all that dwelt round about them: and all these sayings
were noised abroad throughout all the hill country of Judaea.
66 And all they that heard *them* laid *them* up in their hearts, saying, What
manner of child shall this be! And the hand of the Lord was with him.

The Prophecy of Zacharias

67 And his father Zacharias was filled with the Holy Ghost, and prophesied,
saying,
68 Blessed *be* the Lord God of Israel; for he hath visited and redeemed his
people,
69 And hath raised up an horn of salvation for us in the house of his servant
David;
70 As he spake by the mouth of his holy prophets, which have been since the
world began:
71 That we should be saved from our enemies, and from the hand of all that
hate us;
72 To perform the mercy *promised* to our fathers, and to remember his holy
covenant;
73 The oath which he sware to our father Abraham,
74 That he would grant unto us, that we being delivered out of the hand of
our enemies might serve him without fear,
75 In holiness and righteousness before him, all the days of our life.
76 And thou, child, shalt be called the prophet of the Highest: for thou shalt
go before the face of the Lord to prepare his ways;
77 To give knowledge of salvation unto his people by the remission of their
sins,
78 Through the tender mercy of our God; whereby the dayspring from on
high hath visited us,
79 To give light to them that sit in darkness and *in* the shadow of death, to
guide our feet into the way of peace.

80 And the child grew, and waxed strong in spirit, and was in the deserts till
the day of his shewing unto Israel.

Jesus Is Born

2 And it came to pass in those days, that there went out a decree from Caesar
Augustus, that all the world should be taxed.
2 (*And* this taxing was first made when Cyrenius was governor of Syria.)
3 And all went to be taxed, every one into his own city.
4 And Joseph also went up from Galilee, out of the city of Nazareth, into
Judaea, unto the city of David, which is called Beth-lehem; (because he was of
the house and lineage of David:)
5 To be taxed with Mary his espoused wife, being great with child.
6 And so it was, that, while they were there, the days were accomplished that
she should be delivered.
7 And she brought forth her firstborn son, and wrapped him in swaddling
clothes, and laid him in a manger; because there was no room for them in the
inn.

Angels Announce Jesus' Birth

8 And there were in the same country shepherds abiding in the field, keeping
watch over their flock by night.
9 And, lo, the angel of the Lord came upon them, and the glory of the Lord
shone round about them: and they were sore afraid.
10 And the angel said unto them, Fear not: for, behold, I bring you good
tidings of great joy, which shall be to all people.
11 For unto you is born this day in the city of David a Saviour, which is Christ
the Lord.
12 And this *shall be* a sign unto you; Ye shall find the babe wrapped in swad-
dling clothes, lying in a manger.
13 And suddenly there was with the angel a multitude of the heavenly host
praising God, and saying,
14 Glory to God in the highest, and on earth peace, good will toward men.
15 And it came to pass, as the angels were gone away from them into heaven,
the shepherds said one to another, Let us now go even unto Beth-lehem, and see
this thing which is come to pass, which the Lord hath made known unto us.
16 And they came with haste, and found Mary, and Joseph, and the babe lying
in a manger.
17 And when they had seen *it*, they made known abroad the saying which
was told them concerning this child.
18 And all they that heard *it* wondered at those things which were told them
by the shepherds.
19 But Mary kept all these things, and pondered *them* in her heart.
20 And the shepherds returned, glorifying and praising God for all the things
that they had heard and seen, as it was told unto them.

Jesus' Parents Obey the Law of Moses

21 And when eight days were accomplished for the circumcising of the child,
his name was called JESUS, which was so named of the angel before he was
conceived in the womb.
22 And when the days of her purification according to the law of Moses were
accomplished, they brought him to Jerusalem, to present *him* to the Lord;
23 (As it is written in the law of the Lord, Every male that openeth the womb
shall be called holy to the Lord;)
24 And to offer a sacrifice according to that which is said in the law of the
Lord, A pair of turtledoves, or two young pigeons.

Saint Luke 2:14
Glory to God
in the highest,
and on earth
peace, good will
toward men.

Simeon and Anna Prophesy of Jesus

25 And, behold, there was a man in Jerusalem, whose name *was* Simeon; and
the same man *was* just and devout, waiting for the consolation of Israel: and
the Holy Ghost was upon him.
26 And it was revealed unto him by the Holy Ghost, that he should not see
death, before he had seen the Lord's Christ.
27 And he came by the Spirit into the temple: and when the parents brought
in the child Jesus, to do for him after the custom of the law,
28 Then took he him up in his arms, and blessed God, and said,
29 Lord, now lettest thou thy servant depart in peace, according to thy word:
30 For mine eyes have seen thy salvation,
31 Which thou hast prepared before the face of all people;
32 A light to lighten the Gentiles, and the glory of thy people Israel.
33 And Joseph and his mother marvelled at those things which were spoken
of him.
34 And Simeon blessed them, and said unto Mary his mother, Behold, this
child is set for the fall and rising again of many in Israel; and for a sign which
shall be spoken against;
35 (Yea, a sword shall pierce through thy own soul also,) that the thoughts
of many hearts may be revealed.
36 And there was one Anna, a prophetess, the daughter of Phanuel, of the
tribe of Aser: she was of a great age, and had lived with an husband seven years
from her virginity;
37 And she *was* a widow of about fourscore and four years, which departed
not from the temple, but served *God* with fastings and prayers night and day.
38 And she coming in that instant gave thanks likewise unto the Lord, and
spake of him to all them that looked for redemption in Jerusalem.
39 And when they had performed all things according to the law of the Lord,
they returned into Galilee, to their own city Nazareth.
40 And the child grew, and waxed strong in spirit, filled with wisdom: and
the grace of God was upon him.

Jesus Grows Up

41 Now his parents went to Jerusalem every year at the feast of the passover.
42 And when he was twelve years old, they went up to Jerusalem after the
custom of the feast.
43 And when they had fulfilled the days, as they returned, the child Jesus
tarried behind in Jerusalem; and Joseph and his mother knew not *of it*.
44 But they, supposing him to have been in the company, went a day's journey;
and they sought him among *their* kinsfolk and acquaintance.
45 And when they found him not, they turned back again to Jerusalem, seek-
ing him.
46 And it came to pass, that after three days they found him in the temple,
sitting in the midst of the doctors, both hearing them, and asking them ques-
tions.
47 And all that heard him were astonished at his understanding and answers.
48 And when they saw him, they were amazed: and his mother said unto him,
Son, why hast thou thus dealt with us? behold, thy father and I have sought
thee sorrowing.
49 And he said unto them, How is it that ye sought me? wist ye not that I must
be about my Father's business?
50 And they understood not the saying which he spake unto them.
51 And he went down with them, and came to Nazareth, and was subject
unto them: but his mother kept all these sayings in her heart.
52 And Jesus increased in wisdom and stature, and in favour with God and
man.

The Preaching and Baptism of John

3 Now in the fifteenth year of the reign of Tiberius Caesar, Pontius Pilate
being governor of Judaea, and Herod being tetrarch of Galilee, and his
brother Philip tetrarch of Ituraea and of the region of Trachonitis, and Lysanias
the tetrarch of Abilene,
2 Annas and Caiaphas being the high priests, the word of God came unto
John the son of Zacharias in the wilderness.
3 And he came into all the country about Jordan, preaching the baptism of
repentance for the remission of sins;
4 As it is written in the book of the words of Esaias the prophet, saying, The
voice of one crying in the wilderness, Prepare ye the way of the Lord, make
his paths straight.
5 Every valley shall be filled, and every mountain and hill shall be brought
low; and the crooked shall be made straight, and the rough ways *shall be* made
smooth;
6 And all flesh shall see the salvation of God.
7 Then said he to the multitude that came forth to be baptized of him, O
generation of vipers, who hath warned you to flee from the wrath to come?
8 Bring forth therefore fruits worthy of repentance, and begin not to say
within yourselves, We have Abraham to *our* father: for I say unto you, That
God is able of these stones to raise up children unto Abraham.
9 And now also the axe is laid unto the root of the trees: every tree therefore
which bringeth not forth good fruit is hewn down, and cast into the fire.
10 And the people asked him, saying, What shall we do then?
11 He answereth and saith unto them, He that hath two coats, let him impart
to him that hath none; and he that hath meat, let him do likewise.
12 Then came also publicans to be baptized, and said unto him, Master, what
shall we do?
13 And he said unto them, Exact no more than that which is appointed you.
14 And the soldiers likewise demanded of him, saying, And what shall we
do? And he said unto them, Do violence to no man, neither accuse *any* falsely;
and be content with your wages.

John's Testimony Concerning Christ

15 And as the people were in expectation, and all men mused in their hearts
of John, whether he were the Christ, or not;
16 John answered, saying unto *them* all, I indeed baptize you with water; but
one mightier than I cometh, the latchet of whose shoes I am not worthy to
unloose: he shall baptize you with the Holy Ghost and with fire:
17 Whose fan *is* in his hand, and he will throughly purge his floor, and will
gather the wheat into his garner; but the chaff he will burn with fire unquench-
able.
18 And many other things in his exhortation preached he unto the people.
19 But Herod the tetrarch, being reproved by him for Herodias his brother
Philip's wife, and for all the evils which Herod had done,
20 Added yet this above all, that he shut up John in prison.

The Baptism of Jesus

21 Now when all the people were baptized, it came to pass, that Jesus also
being baptized, and praying, the heaven was opened,
22 And the Holy Ghost descended in a bodily shape like a dove upon him,
and a voice came from heaven, which said, Thou art my beloved Son; in thee
I am well pleased.

The Ancestors of Jesus

23 And Jesus himself began to be about thirty years of age, being (as was
supposed) the son of Joseph, which was *the son* of Heli,

24 Which was *the son* of Matthat, which was *the son* of Levi, which was *the*
son of Melchi, which was *the son* of Janna, which was *the son* of Joseph,
25 Which was *the son* of Mattathias, which was *the son* of Amos, which was
the son of Naum, which was *the son* of Esli, which was *the son* of Nagge,
26 Which was *the son* of Maath, which was *the son* of Mattathias, which was
the son of Semei, which was *the son* of Joseph, which was *the son* of Juda,
27 Which was *the son* of Joanna, which was *the son* of Rhesa, which was *the*
son of Zorobabel, which was *the son* of Salathiel, which was *the son* of Neri,
28 Which was *the son* of Melchi, which was *the son* of Addi, which was *the*
son of Cosam, which was *the son* of Elmodam, which was *the son* of Er,
29 Which was *the son* of Jose, which was *the son* of Eliezer, which was *the son*
of Jorim, which was *the son* of Matthat, which was *the son* of Levi,
30 Which was *the son* of Simeon, which was *the son* of Juda, which was *the*
son of Joseph, which was *the son* of Jonan, which was *the son* of Eliakim,
31 Which was *the son* of Melea, which was *the son* of Menan, which was *the*
son of Mattatha, which was *the son* of Nathan, which was *the son* of David,
32 Which was *the son* of Jesse, which was *the son* of Obed, which was *the son*
of Booz, which was *the son* of Salmon, which was *the son* of Naasson,
33 Which was *the son* of Aminadab, which was *the son* of Aram, which was
the son of Esrom, which was *the son* of Phares, which was *the son* of Juda,
34 Which was *the son* of Jacob, which was *the son* of Isaac, which was *the son*
of Abraham, which was *the son* of Thara, which was *the son* of Nachor,
35 Which was *the son* of Saruch, which was *the son* of Ragau, which was *the*
son of Phalec, which was *the son* of Heber, which was *the son* of Sala,
36 Which was *the son* of Cainan, which was *the son* of Arphaxad, which was
the son of Sem, which was *the son* of Noe, which was *the son* of Lamech,
37 Which was *the son* of Mathusala, which was *the son* of Enoch, which was
the son of Jared, which was *the son* of Maleleel, which was *the son* of Cainan,
38 Which was *the son* of Enos, which was *the son* of Seth, which was *the son*
of Adam, which was *the son* of God.

The Temptation of Jesus

4 And Jesus being full of the Holy Ghost returned from Jordan, and was led
by the Spirit into the wilderness,
2 Being forty days tempted of the devil. And in those days he did eat nothing:
and when they were ended, he afterward hungered.
3 And the devil said unto him, If thou be the Son of God, command this stone
that it be made bread.
4 And Jesus answered him, saying, It is written, That man shall not live by
bread alone, but by every word of God.
5 And the devil, taking him up into an high mountain, shewed unto him all
the kingdoms of the world in a moment of time.
6 And the devil said unto him, All this power will I give thee, and the glory
of them: for that is delivered unto me; and to whomsoever I will I give it.
7 If thou therefore wilt worship me, all shall be thine.
8 And Jesus answered and said unto him, Get thee behind me, Satan: for it
is written, Thou shalt worship the Lord thy God, and him only shalt thou serve.
9 And he brought him to Jerusalem, and set him on a pinnacle of the temple,
and said unto him, If thou be the Son of God, cast thyself down from hence:
10 For it is written, He shall give his angels charge over thee, to keep thee:
11 And in *their* hands they shall bear thee up, lest at any time thou dash thy
foot against a stone.
12 And Jesus answering said unto him, It is said, Thou shalt not tempt the
Lord thy God.
13 And when the devil had ended all the temptation, he departed from him
for a season.

Jesus Teaches and Is Rejected in His Hometown

14 And Jesus returned in the power of the Spirit into Galilee: and there went
out a fame of him through all the region round about.
15 And he taught in their synagogues, being glorified of all.
16 And he came to Nazareth, where he had been brought up: and, as his
custom was, he went into the synagogue on the sabbath day, and stood up for
to read.
17 And there was delivered unto him the book of the prophet Esaias. And
when he had opened the book, he found the place where it was written,
18 The Spirit of the Lord *is* upon me, because he hath anointed me to preach
the gospel to the poor; he hath sent me to heal the brokenhearted, to preach
deliverance to the captives, and recovering of sight to the blind, to set at lib-
erty them that are bruised,
19 To preach the acceptable year of the Lord.
20 And he closed the book, and he gave *it* again to the minister, and sat down.
And the eyes of all them that were in the synagogue were fastened on him.
21 And he began to say unto them, This day is this scripture fulfilled in your
ears.
22 And all bare him witness, and wondered at the gracious words which
proceeded out of his mouth. And they said, Is not this Joseph's son?
23 And he said unto them, Ye will surely say unto me this proverb, Physician,
heal thyself: whatsoever we have heard done in Capernaum, do also here in
thy country.
24 And he said, Verily I say unto you, No prophet is accepted in his own
country.
25 But I tell you of a truth, many widows were in Israel in the days of Elias,
when the heaven was shut up three years and six months, when great famine
was throughout all the land;
26 But unto none of them was Elias sent, save unto Sarepta, *a city* of Sidon,
unto a woman *that was* a widow.
27 And many lepers were in Israel in the time of Eliseus the prophet; and
none of them was cleansed, saving Naaman the Syrian.
28 And all they in the synagogue, when they heard these things, were filled
with wrath,
29 And rose up, and thrust him out of the city, and led him unto the brow of
the hill whereon their city was built, that they might cast him down headlong.
30 But he passing through the midst of them went his way,

Jesus Sends out an Evil Spirit

31 And came down to Capernaum, a city of Galilee, and taught them on the
sabbath days.
32 And they were astonished at his doctrine: for his word was with power.
33 And in the synagogue there was a man, which had a spirit of an unclean
devil, and cried out with a loud voice,
34 Saying, Let *us* alone; what have we to do with thee, *thou* Jesus of Nazareth?
art thou come to destroy us? I know thee who thou art; the Holy One of God.
35 And Jesus rebuked him, saying, Hold thy peace, and come out of him. And
when the devil had thrown him in the midst, he came out of him, and hurt
him not.
36 And they were all amazed, and spake among themselves, saying, What a
word *is* this! for with authority and power he commandeth the unclean spir-
its, and they come out.
37 And the fame of him went out into every place of the country round about.

Jesus Cures Peter's Mother-in-Law and Many Others

38 And he arose out of the synagogue, and entered into Simon's house. And
Simon's wife's mother was taken with a great fever; and they besought him for
her.
39 And he stood over her, and rebuked the fever; and it left her: and imme-
diately she arose and ministered unto them.
40 Now when the sun was setting, all they that had any sick with divers dis-
eases brought them unto him; and he laid his hands on every one of them,
and healed them.
41 And devils also came out of many, crying out, and saying, Thou art Christ
the Son of God. And he rebuking *them* suffered them not to speak: for they
knew that he was Christ.

Spreading the Good News

42 And when it was day, he departed and went into a desert place: and the
people sought him, and came unto him, and stayed him, that he should not
depart from them.
43 And he said unto them, I must preach the kingdom of God to other cities
also: for therefore am I sent.
44 And he preached in the synagogues of Galilee.

A Miraculous Catch of Fish

5 And it came to pass, that, as the people pressed upon him to hear the word
of God, he stood by the lake of Gennesaret,
2 And saw two ships standing by the lake: but the fishermen were gone out
of them, and were washing *their* nets.
3 And he entered into one of the ships, which was Simon's, and prayed him
that he would thrust out a little from the land. And he sat down, and taught
the people out of the ship.
4 Now when he had left speaking, he said unto Simon, Launch out into the
deep, and let down your nets for a draught.
5 And Simon answering said unto him, Master, we have toiled all the night,
and have taken nothing: nevertheless at thy word I will let down the net.
6 And when they had this done, they inclosed a great multitude of fishes:
and their net brake.
7 And they beckoned unto *their* partners, which were in the other ship, that
they should come and help them. And they came, and filled both the ships, so
that they began to sink.
8 When Simon Peter saw *it*, he fell down at Jesus' knees, saying, Depart from
me; for I am a sinful man, O Lord.
9 For he was astonished, and all that were with him, at the draught of the
fishes which they had taken:
10 And so *was* also James, and John, the sons of Zebedee, which were partners
with Simon. And Jesus said unto Simon, Fear not; from henceforth thou shalt
catch men.
11 And when they had brought their ships to land, they forsook all, and fol-
lowed him.

Christ Cleanses the Leper

12 And it came to pass, when he was in a certain city, behold a man full of
leprosy: who seeing Jesus fell on *his* face, and besought him, saying, Lord, if
thou wilt, thou canst make me clean.
13 And he put forth *his* hand, and touched him, saying, I will: be thou clean.
And immediately the leprosy departed from him.
14 And he charged him to tell no man: but go, and shew thyself to the priest,
and offer for thy cleansing, according as Moses commanded, for a testimony
unto them.

15 But so much the more went there a fame abroad of him: and great mul-
titudes came together to hear, and to be healed by him of their infirmities.
16 And he withdrew himself into the wilderness, and prayed.

Jesus Heals the Paralyzed Man

17 And it came to pass on a certain day, as he was teaching, that there were
Pharisees and doctors of the law sitting by, which were come out of every town
of Galilee, and Judaea, and Jerusalem: and the power of the Lord was *present*
to heal them.
18 And, behold, men brought in a bed a man which was taken with a palsy:
and they sought *means* to bring him in, and to lay *him* before him.
19 And when they could not find by what *way* they might bring him in
because of the multitude, they went upon the housetop, and let him down
through the tiling with *his* couch into the midst before Jesus.
20 And when he saw their faith, he said unto him, Man, thy sins are forgiven
thee.
21 And the scribes and the Pharisees began to reason, saying, Who is this
which speaketh blasphemies? Who can forgive sins, but God alone?
22 But when Jesus perceived their thoughts, he answering said unto them,
What reason ye in your hearts?
23 Whether is easier, to say, Thy sins be forgiven thee; or to say, Rise up and
walk?
24 But that ye may know that the Son of man hath power upon earth to
forgive sins, (he said unto the sick of the palsy,) I say unto thee, Arise, and take
up thy couch, and go into thine house.
25 And immediately he rose up before them, and took up that whereon he
lay, and departed to his own house, glorifying God.
26 And they were all amazed, and they glorified God, and were filled with
fear, saying, We have seen strange things to day.

Jesus Calls Levi (Matthew)

27 And after these things he went forth, and saw a publican, named Levi,
sitting at the receipt of custom: and he said unto him, Follow me.
28 And he left all, rose up, and followed him.
29 And Levi made him a great feast in his own house: and there was a great
company of publicans and of others that sat down with them.
30 But their scribes and Pharisees murmured against his disciples, saying,
Why do ye eat and drink with publicans and sinners?
31 And Jesus answering said unto them, They that are whole need not a phy-
sician; but they that are sick.
32 I came not to call the righteous, but sinners to repentance.

New Wine Needs New Wineskins

33 And they said unto him, Why do the disciples of John fast often, and make
prayers, and likewise *the disciples* of the Pharisees; but thine eat and drink?
34 And he said unto them, Can ye make the children of the bridechamber
fast, while the bridegroom is with them?
35 But the days will come, when the bridegroom shall be taken away from
them, and then shall they fast in those days.
36 And he spake also a parable unto them; No man putteth a piece of a new
garment upon an old; if otherwise, then both the new maketh a rent, and the
piece that was *taken* out of the new agreeth not with the old.
37 And no man putteth new wine into old bottles; else the new wine will
burst the bottles, and be spilled, and the bottles shall perish.
38 But new wine must be put into new bottles; and both are preserved.
39 No man also having drunk old *wine* straightway desireth new: for he saith,
The old is better.

Jesus Has Authority over the Sabbath

6 And it came to pass on the second sabbath after the first, that he went
through the corn fields; and his disciples plucked the ears of corn, and did
eat, rubbing *them* in *their* hands.
2 And certain of the Pharisees said unto them, Why do ye that which is not
lawful to do on the sabbath days?
3 And Jesus answering them said, Have ye not read so much as this, what
David did, when himself was an hungred, and they which were with him;
4 How he went into the house of God, and did take and eat the shewbread,
and gave also to them that were with him; which it is not lawful to eat but for
the priests alone?
5 And he said unto them, That the Son of man is Lord also of the sabbath.

Jesus Heals on the Sabbath

6 And it came to pass also on another sabbath, that he entered into the syn-
agogue and taught: and there was a man whose right hand was withered.
7 And the scribes and Pharisees watched him, whether he would heal on the
sabbath day; that they might find an accusation against him.
8 But he knew their thoughts, and said to the man which had the withered
hand, Rise up, and stand forth in the midst. And he arose and stood forth.
9 Then said Jesus unto them, I will ask you one thing; Is it lawful on the
sabbath days to do good, or to do evil? to save life, or to destroy *it*?
10 And looking round about upon them all, he said unto the man, Stretch
forth thy hand. And he did so: and his hand was restored whole as the other.
11 And they were filled with madness; and communed one with another
what they might do to Jesus.

Jesus Chooses Twelve Disciples

12 And it came to pass in those days, that he went out into a mountain to
pray, and continued all night in prayer to God.
13 And when it was day, he called *unto him* his disciples: and of them he chose
twelve, whom also he named apostles;
14 Simon, (whom he also named Peter,) and Andrew his brother, James and
John, Philip and Bartholomew,
15 Matthew and Thomas, James the *son* of Alphaeus, and Simon called
Zelotes,
16 And Judas *the brother* of James, and Judas Iscariot, which also was the
traitor.

Jesus Heals Many

17 And he came down with them, and stood in the plain, and the company
of his disciples, and a great multitude of people out of all Judaea and Jerusalem,
and from the sea coast of Tyre and Sidon, which came to hear him, and to be
healed of their diseases;
18 And they that were vexed with unclean spirits: and they were healed.
19 And the whole multitude sought to touch him: for there went virtue out
of him, and healed *them* all.

Jesus Teaches about Blessings and Curses

20 And he lifted up his eyes on his disciples, and said, Blessed *be ye* poor: for
yours is the kingdom of God.
21 Blessed *are ye* that hunger now: for ye shall be filled. Blessed *are ye* that
weep now: for ye shall laugh.
22 Blessed are ye, when men shall hate you, and when they shall separate you
from their company, and shall reproach *you*, and cast out your name as evil,
for the Son of man's sake.
23 Rejoice ye in that day, and leap for joy: for, behold, your reward *is* great in
heaven: for in the like manner did their fathers unto the prophets.

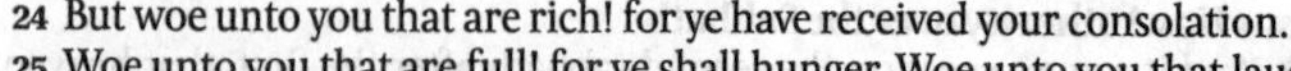

24 But woe unto you that are rich! for ye have received your consolation.
25 Woe unto you that are full! for ye shall hunger. Woe unto you that laugh
now! for ye shall mourn and weep.
26 Woe unto you, when all men shall speak well of you! for so did their fathers
to the false prophets.

Love Your Enemies

27 But I say unto you which hear, Love your enemies, do good to them which
hate you,
28 Bless them that curse you, and pray for them which despitefully use you.
29 And unto him that smiteth thee on the *one* cheek offer also the other; and
him that taketh away thy cloke forbid not *to take thy* coat also.
30 Give to every man that asketh of thee; and of him that taketh away thy
goods ask *them* not again.
31 And as ye would that men should do to you, do ye also to them likewise.
32 For if ye love them which love you, what thank have ye? for sinners also
love those that love them.
33 And if ye do good to them which do good to you, what thank have ye? for
sinners also do even the same.
34 And if ye lend *to them* of whom ye hope to receive, what thank have ye?
for sinners also lend to sinners, to receive as much again.
35 But love ye your enemies, and do good, and lend, hoping for nothing again;
and your reward shall be great, and ye shall be the children of the Highest: for
he is kind unto the unthankful and *to* the evil.
36 Be ye therefore merciful, as your Father also is merciful.

Do Not Judge Others

37 Judge not, and ye shall not be judged: condemn not, and ye shall not be
condemned: forgive, and ye shall be forgiven:
38 Give, and it shall be given unto you; good measure, pressed down, and
shaken together, and running over, shall men give into your bosom. For with
the same measure that ye mete withal it shall be measured to you again.
39 And he spake a parable unto them, Can the blind lead the blind? shall they
not both fall into the ditch?
40 The disciple is not above his master: but every one that is perfect shall be
as his master.
41 And why beholdest thou the mote that is in thy brother's eye, but per-
ceivest not the beam that is in thine own eye?
42 Either how canst thou say to thy brother, Brother, let me pull out the mote
that is in thine eye, when thou thyself beholdest not the beam that is in thine
own eye? Thou hypocrite, cast out first the beam out of thine own eye, and
then shalt thou see clearly to pull out the mote that is in thy brother's eye.

An Illustration of Trees and Their Fruit

43 For a good tree bringeth not forth corrupt fruit; neither doth a corrupt
tree bring forth good fruit.
44 For every tree is known by his own fruit. For of thorns men do not gather
figs, nor of a bramble bush gather they grapes.
45 A good man out of the good treasure of his heart bringeth forth that which
is good; and an evil man out of the evil treasure of his heart bringeth forth
that which is evil: for of the abundance of the heart his mouth speaketh.

Build on the Rock

46 And why call ye me, Lord, Lord, and do not the things which I say?
47 Whosoever cometh to me, and heareth my sayings, and doeth them, I will
shew you to whom he is like:

48 He is like a man which built an house, and digged deep, and laid the foun-
dation on a rock: and when the flood arose, the stream beat vehemently upon
that house, and could not shake it: for it was founded upon a rock.
49 But he that heareth, and doeth not, is like a man that without a foundation
built an house upon the earth; against which the stream did beat vehemently,
and immediately it fell; and the ruin of that house was great.

The Centurion's Faith

7 Now when he had ended all his sayings in the audience of the people, he
entered into Capernaum.
2 And a certain centurion's servant, who was dear unto him, was sick, and
ready to die.
3 And when he heard of Jesus, he sent unto him the elders of the Jews,
beseeching him that he would come and heal his servant.
4 And when they came to Jesus, they besought him instantly, saying, That he
was worthy for whom he should do this:
5 For he loveth our nation, and he hath built us a synagogue.
6 Then Jesus went with them. And when he was now not far from the house,
the centurion sent friends to him, saying unto him, Lord, trouble not thyself:
for I am not worthy that thou shouldest enter under my roof:
7 Wherefore neither thought I myself worthy to come unto thee: but say in
a word, and my servant shall be healed.
8 For I also am a man set under authority, having under me soldiers, and I
say unto one, Go, and he goeth; and to another, Come, and he cometh; and to
my servant, Do this, and he doeth *it*.
9 When Jesus heard these things, he marvelled at him, and turned him about,
and said unto the people that followed him, I say unto you, I have not found
so great faith, no, not in Israel.
10 And they that were sent, returning to the house, found the servant whole
that had been sick.

Jesus Raises the Widow's Son from the Dead

11 And it came to pass the day after, that he went into a city called Nain; and
many of his disciples went with him, and much people.
12 Now when he came nigh to the gate of the city, behold, there was a dead
man carried out, the only son of his mother, and she was a widow: and much
people of the city was with her.
13 And when the Lord saw her, he had compassion on her, and said unto her,
Weep not.
14 And he came and touched the bier: and they that bare *him* stood still. And
he said, Young man, I say unto thee, Arise.
15 And he that was dead sat up, and began to speak. And he delivered him to
his mother.
16 And there came a fear on all: and they glorified God, saying, That a great
prophet is risen up among us; and, That God hath visited his people.
17 And this rumour of him went forth throughout all Judaea, and through-
out all the region round about.

Jesus Reassures John the Baptist

18 And the disciples of John shewed him of all these things.
19 And John calling *unto him* two of his disciples sent *them* to Jesus, saying,
Art thou he that should come? or look we for another?
20 When the men were come unto him, they said, John Baptist hath sent us
unto thee, saying, Art thou he that should come? or look we for another?
21 And in that same hour he cured many of *their* infirmities and plagues,
and of evil spirits; and unto many *that were* blind he gave sight.
22 Then Jesus answering said unto them, Go your way, and tell John what
things ye have seen and heard; how that the blind see, the lame walk, the

lepers are cleansed, the deaf hear, the dead are raised, to the poor the gospel
is preached.
23 And blessed is *he*, whosoever shall not be offended in me.
24 And when the messengers of John were departed, he began to speak unto
the people concerning John, What went ye out into the wilderness for to see?
A reed shaken with the wind?
25 But what went ye out for to see? A man clothed in soft raiment? Behold,
they which are gorgeously apparelled, and live delicately, are in kings' courts.
26 But what went ye out for to see? A prophet? Yea, I say unto you, and much
more than a prophet.
27 This is *he*, of whom it is written, Behold, I send my messenger before thy
face, which shall prepare thy way before thee.
28 For I say unto you, Among those that are born of women there is not a
greater prophet than John the Baptist: but he that is least in the kingdom of
God is greater than he.
29 And all the people that heard *him*, and the publicans, justified God, being
baptized with the baptism of John.
30 But the Pharisees and lawyers rejected the counsel of God against them-
selves, being not baptized of him.
31 And the Lord said, Whereunto then shall I liken the men of this genera-
tion? and to what are they like?
32 They are like unto children sitting in the marketplace, and calling one to
another, and saying, We have piped unto you, and ye have not danced; we have
mourned to you, and ye have not wept.
33 For John the Baptist came neither eating bread nor drinking wine; and
ye say, He hath a devil.
34 The Son of man is come eating and drinking; and ye say, Behold a glutton-
ous man, and a winebibber, a friend of publicans and sinners!
35 But wisdom is justified of all her children.

A Sinful Woman Receives Forgiveness

36 And one of the Pharisees desired him that he would eat with him. And he
went into the Pharisee's house, and sat down to meat.
37 And, behold, a woman in the city, which was a sinner, when she knew that
Jesus sat at meat in the Pharisee's house, brought an alabaster box of ointment,
38 And stood at his feet behind *him* weeping, and began to wash his feet with
tears, and did wipe *them* with the hairs of her head, and kissed his feet, and
anointed *them* with the ointment.
39 Now when the Pharisee which had bidden him saw *it*, he spake within
himself, saying, This man, if he were a prophet, would have known who and
what manner of woman *this is* that toucheth him: for she is a sinner.
40 And Jesus answering said unto him, Simon, I have somewhat to say unto
thee. And he saith, Master, say on.
41 There was a certain creditor which had two debtors: the one owed five
hundred pence, and the other fifty.
42 And when they had nothing to pay, he frankly forgave them both. Tell me
therefore, which of them will love him most?
43 Simon answered and said, I suppose that *he*, to whom he forgave most.
And he said unto him, Thou hast rightly judged.
44 And he turned to the woman, and said unto Simon, Seest thou this
woman? I entered into thine house, thou gavest me no water for my feet: but
she hath washed my feet with tears, and wiped *them* with the hairs of her head.
45 Thou gavest me no kiss: but this woman since the time I came in hath not
ceased to kiss my feet.
46 My head with oil thou didst not anoint: but this woman hath anointed
my feet with ointment.

47 Wherefore I say unto thee, Her sins, which are many, are forgiven; for she
loved much: but to whom little is forgiven, *the same* loveth little.
48 And he said unto her, Thy sins are forgiven.
49 And they that sat at meat with him began to say within themselves, Who
is this that forgiveth sins also?
50 And he said to the woman, Thy faith hath saved thee; go in peace.

Women Who Supported Jesus

8 And it came to pass afterward, that he went throughout every city and vil-
lage, preaching and shewing the glad tidings of the kingdom of God: and
the twelve *were* with him,
2 And certain women, which had been healed of evil spirits and infirmities,
Mary called Magdalene, out of whom went seven devils,
3 And Joanna the wife of Chuza Herod's steward, and Susanna, and many
others, which ministered unto him of their substance.

The Parable of the Sower

4 And when much people were gathered together, and were come to him
out of every city, he spake by a parable:
5 A sower went out to sow his seed: and as he sowed, some fell by the way
side; and it was trodden down, and the fowls of the air devoured it.
6 And some fell upon a rock; and as soon as it was sprung up, it withered
away, because it lacked moisture.
7 And some fell among thorns; and the thorns sprang up with it, and choked it.
8 And other fell on good ground, and sprang up, and bare fruit an hundred-
fold. And when he had said these things, he cried, He that hath ears to hear,
let him hear.
9 And his disciples asked him, saying, What might this parable be?
10 And he said, Unto you it is given to know the mysteries of the kingdom of
God: but to others in parables; that seeing they might not see, and hearing
they might not understand.
11 Now the parable is this: The seed is the word of God.
12 Those by the way side are they that hear; then cometh the devil, and taketh
away the word out of their hearts, lest they should believe and be saved.
13 They on the rock *are they*, which, when they hear, receive the word with
joy; and these have no root, which for a while believe, and in time of tempta-
tion fall away.
14 And that which fell among thorns are they, which, when they have heard,
go forth, and are choked with cares and riches and pleasures of *this* life, and
bring no fruit to perfection.
15 But that on the good ground are they, which in an honest and good heart,
having heard the word, keep *it*, and bring forth fruit with patience.
16 No man, when he hath lighted a candle, covereth it with a vessel, or putteth
it under a bed; but setteth *it* on a candlestick, that they which enter in may
see the light.
17 For nothing is secret, that shall not be made manifest; neither *any thing*
hid, that shall not be known and come abroad.
18 Take heed therefore how ye hear: for whosoever hath, to him shall be
given; and whosoever hath not, from him shall be taken even that which he
seemeth to have.

Jesus Describes His True Family

19 Then came to him *his* mother and his brethren, and could not come at
him for the press.
20 And it was told him *by certain* which said, Thy mother and thy brethren
stand without, desiring to see thee.
21 And he answered and said unto them, My mother and my brethren are
these which hear the word of God, and do it.

Jesus Calms the Sea

22 Now it came to pass on a certain day, that he went into a ship with his
disciples: and he said unto them, Let us go over unto the other side of the lake.
And they launched forth.
23 But as they sailed he fell asleep: and there came down a storm of wind on
the lake; and they were filled *with water*, and were in jeopardy.
24 And they came to him, and awoke him, saying, Master, master, we perish.
Then he arose, and rebuked the wind and the raging of the water: and they
ceased, and there was a calm.
25 And he said unto them, Where is your faith? And they being afraid won-
dered, saying one to another, What manner of man is this! for he commandeth
even the winds and water, and they obey him.

Jesus Heals a Demon-Possessed Man

26 And they arrived at the country of the Gadarenes, which is over against
Galilee.
27 And when he went forth to land, there met him out of the city a certain
man, which had devils long time, and ware no clothes, neither abode in *any*
house, but in the tombs.
28 When he saw Jesus, he cried out, and fell down before him, and with a
loud voice said, What have I to do with thee, Jesus, *thou* Son of God most high?
I beseech thee, torment me not.
29 (For he had commanded the unclean spirit to come out of the man. For
oftentimes it had caught him: and he was kept bound with chains and in
fetters; and he brake the bands, and was driven of the devil into the wilder-
ness.)
30 And Jesus asked him, saying, What is thy name? And he said, Legion:
because many devils were entered into him.
31 And they besought him that he would not command them to go out into
the deep.
32 And there was there an herd of many swine feeding on the mountain: and
they besought him that he would suffer them to enter into them. And he
suffered them.
33 Then went the devils out of the man, and entered into the swine: and the
herd ran violently down a steep place into the lake, and were choked.
34 When they that fed *them* saw what was done, they fled, and went and told
it in the city and in the country.
35 Then they went out to see what was done; and came to Jesus, and found
the man, out of whom the devils were departed, sitting at the feet of Jesus,
clothed, and in his right mind: and they were afraid.
36 They also which saw *it* told them by what means he that was possessed of
the devils was healed.
37 Then the whole multitude of the country of the Gadarenes round about
besought him to depart from them; for they were taken with great fear: and
he went up into the ship, and returned back again.
38 Now the man out of whom the devils were departed besought him that
he might be with him: but Jesus sent him away, saying,
39 Return to thine own house, and shew how great things God hath done
unto thee. And he went his way, and published throughout the whole city how
great things Jesus had done unto him.

Jesus Raises a Dead Girl and Cures a Bleeding Woman

40 And it came to pass, that, when Jesus was returned, the people *gladly*
received him: for they were all waiting for him.
41 And, behold, there came a man named Jairus, and he was a ruler of the
synagogue: and he fell down at Jesus' feet, and besought him that he would
come into his house:

42 For he had one only daughter, about twelve years of age, and she lay a
dying. But as he went the people thronged him.
43 And a woman having an issue of blood twelve years, which had spent all
her living upon physicians, neither could be healed of any,
44 Came behind *him*, and touched the border of his garment: and immedi-
ately her issue of blood stanched.
45 And Jesus said, Who touched me? When all denied, Peter and they that
were with him said, Master, the multitude throng thee and press *thee*, and
sayest thou, Who touched me?
46 And Jesus said, Somebody hath touched me: for I perceive that virtue is
gone out of me.
47 And when the woman saw that she was not hid, she came trembling, and
falling down before him, she declared unto him before all the people for what
cause she had touched him, and how she was healed immediately.
48 And he said unto her, Daughter, be of good comfort: thy faith hath made
thee whole; go in peace.
49 While he yet spake, there cometh one from the ruler of the synagogue's
house, saying to him, Thy daughter is dead; trouble not the Master.
50 But when Jesus heard *it*, he answered him, saying, Fear not: believe only,
and she shall be made whole.
51 And when he came into the house, he suffered no man to go in, save Peter,
and James, and John, and the father and the mother of the maiden.
52 And all wept, and bewailed her: but he said, Weep not; she is not dead, but
sleepeth.
53 And they laughed him to scorn, knowing that she was dead.
54 And he put them all out, and took her by the hand, and called, saying,
Maid, arise.
55 And her spirit came again, and she arose straightway: and he command-
ed to give her meat.
56 And her parents were astonished: but he charged them that they should
tell no man what was done.

Jesus Sends out the Twelve

9 Then he called his twelve disciples together, and gave them power and
authority over all devils, and to cure diseases.
2 And he sent them to preach the kingdom of God, and to heal the sick.
3 And he said unto them, Take nothing for *your* journey, neither staves, nor
scrip, neither bread, neither money; neither have two coats apiece.
4 And whatsoever house ye enter into, there abide, and thence depart.
5 And whosoever will not receive you, when ye go out of that city, shake off
the very dust from your feet for a testimony against them.
6 And they departed, and went through the towns, preaching the gospel, and
healing every where.

Herod Wants to Meet Jesus

7 Now Herod the tetrarch heard of all that was done by him: and he was
perplexed, because that it was said of some, that John was risen from the dead;
8 And of some, that Elias had appeared; and of others, that one of the old
prophets was risen again.
9 And Herod said, John have I beheaded: but who is this, of whom I hear
such things? And he desired to see him.

Jesus Feeds More Than Five Thousand

10 And the apostles, when they were returned, told him all that they had
done. And he took them, and went aside privately into a desert place belonging
to the city called Bethsaida.

11 And the people, when they knew *it*, followed him: and he received them,
and spake unto them of the kingdom of God, and healed them that had need
of healing.
12 And when the day began to wear away, then came the twelve, and said
unto him, Send the multitude away, that they may go into the towns and coun-
try round about, and lodge, and get victuals: for we are here in a desert place.
13 But he said unto them, Give ye them to eat. And they said, We have no
more but five loaves and two fishes; except we should go and buy meat for all
this people.
14 For they were about five thousand men. And he said to his disciples, Make
them sit down by fifties in a company.
15 And they did so, and made them all sit down.
16 Then he took the five loaves and the two fishes, and looking up to heaven,
he blessed them, and brake, and gave to the disciples to set before the multi-
tude.
17 And they did eat, and were all filled: and there was taken up of fragments
that remained to them twelve baskets.

Peter Declares His Faith

18 And it came to pass, as he was alone praying, his disciples were with him:
and he asked them, saying, Whom say the people that I am?
19 They answering said, John the Baptist; but some *say*, Elias; and others *say*,
that one of the old prophets is risen again.
20 He said unto them, But whom say ye that I am? Peter answering said, The
Christ of God.
21 And he straitly charged them, and commanded *them* to tell no man that
thing;

Jesus Foretells His Death and Resurrection

22 Saying, The Son of man must suffer many things, and be rejected of the
elders and chief priests and scribes, and be slain, and be raised the third day.

Take up Your Cross Daily

23 And he said to *them* all, If any *man* will come after me, let him deny him-
self, and take up his cross daily, and follow me.
24 For whosoever will save his life shall lose it: but whosoever will lose his
life for my sake, the same shall save it.
25 For what is a man advantaged, if he gain the whole world, and lose himself,
or be cast away?
26 For whosoever shall be ashamed of me and of my words, of him shall the
Son of man be ashamed, when he shall come in his own glory, and *in his*
Father's, and of the holy angels.
27 But I tell you of a truth, there be some standing here, which shall not taste
of death, till they see the kingdom of God.

The Transfiguration

28 And it came to pass about an eight days after these sayings, he took Peter
and John and James, and went up into a mountain to pray.
29 And as he prayed, the fashion of his countenance was altered, and his
raiment *was* white *and* glistering.
30 And, behold, there talked with him two men, which were Moses and Elias:
31 Who appeared in glory, and spake of his decease which he should accom-
plish at Jerusalem.
32 But Peter and they that were with him were heavy with sleep: and when
they were awake, they saw his glory, and the two men that stood with him.
33 And it came to pass, as they departed from him, Peter said unto Jesus,
Master, it is good for us to be here: and let us make three tabernacles; one for
thee, and one for Moses, and one for Elias: not knowing what he said.

34 While he thus spake, there came a cloud, and overshadowed them: and
they feared as they entered into the cloud.
35 And there came a voice out of the cloud, saying, This is my beloved Son:
hear him.
36 And when the voice was past, Jesus was found alone. And they kept *it* close,
and told no man in those days any of those things which they had seen.

Jesus Heals a Demon-Possessed Boy

37 And it came to pass, that on the next day, when they were come down from
the hill, much people met him.
38 And, behold, a man of the company cried out, saying, Master, I beseech
thee, look upon my son: for he is mine only child.
39 And, lo, a spirit taketh him, and he suddenly crieth out; and it teareth him
that he foameth again, and bruising him hardly departeth from him.
40 And I besought thy disciples to cast him out; and they could not.
41 And Jesus answering said, O faithless and perverse generation, how long
shall I be with you, and suffer you? Bring thy son hither.
42 And as he was yet a coming, the devil threw him down, and tare *him*. And
Jesus rebuked the unclean spirit, and healed the child, and delivered him again
to his father.

Jesus Again Foretells His Betrayal, Death, and Resurrection

43 And they were all amazed at the mighty power of God. But while they
wondered every one at all things which Jesus did, he said unto his disciples,
44 Let these sayings sink down into your ears: for the Son of man shall be
delivered into the hands of men.
45 But they understood not this saying, and it was hid from them, that they
perceived it not: and they feared to ask him of that saying.

Greatness in the Kingdom

46 Then there arose a reasoning among them, which of them should be greatest.
47 And Jesus, perceiving the thought of their heart, took a child, and set him
by him,
48 And said unto them, Whosoever shall receive this child in my name
receiveth me: and whosoever shall receive me receiveth him that sent me: for
he that is least among you all, the same shall be great.

Using the Name of Jesus

49 And John answered and said, Master, we saw one casting out devils in thy
name; and we forbad him, because he followeth not with us.
50 And Jesus said unto him, Forbid *him* not: for he that is not against us is
for us.

A Samaritan Village Rejects Jesus

51 And it came to pass, when the time was come that he should be received
up, he stedfastly set his face to go to Jerusalem,
52 And sent messengers before his face: and they went, and entered into a
village of the Samaritans, to make ready for him.
53 And they did not receive him, because his face was as though he would go
to Jerusalem.
54 And when his disciples James and John saw *this*, they said, Lord, wilt thou
that we command fire to come down from heaven, and consume them, even
as Elias did?
55 But he turned, and rebuked them, and said, Ye know not what manner of
spirit ye are of.
56 For the Son of man is not come to destroy men's lives, but to save *them*.
And they went to another village.

What It Takes to Follow Jesus

57 And it came to pass, that, as they went in the way, a certain *man* said unto
him, Lord, I will follow thee whithersoever thou goest.

58 And Jesus said unto him, Foxes have holes, and birds of the air *have* nests;
but the Son of man hath not where to lay *his* head.

59 And he said unto another, Follow me. But he said, Lord, suffer me first to
go and bury my father.

60 Jesus said unto him, Let the dead bury their dead: but go thou and preach
the kingdom of God.

61 And another also said, Lord, I will follow thee; but let me first go bid them
farewell, which are at home at my house.

62 And Jesus said unto him, No man, having put his hand to the plough, and
looking back, is fit for the kingdom of God.

Jesus Sends out Seventy Disciples

10 After these things the Lord appointed other seventy also, and sent
them two and two before his face into every city and place, whith-
er he himself would come.

2 Therefore said he unto them, The harvest truly *is* great, but the labourers
are few: pray ye therefore the Lord of the harvest, that he would send forth
labourers into his harvest.

3 Go your ways: behold, I send you forth as lambs among wolves.

4 Carry neither purse, nor scrip, nor shoes: and salute no man by the way.

5 And into whatsoever house ye enter, first say, Peace *be* to this house.

6 And if the son of peace be there, your peace shall rest upon it: if not, it shall
turn to you again.

7 And in the same house remain, eating and drinking such things as they
give: for the labourer is worthy of his hire. Go not from house to house.

8 And into whatsoever city ye enter, and they receive you, eat such things as
are set before you:

9 And heal the sick that are therein, and say unto them, The kingdom of God
is come nigh unto you.

10 But into whatsoever city ye enter, and they receive you not, go your ways
out into the streets of the same, and say,

11 Even the very dust of your city, which cleaveth on us, we do wipe off against
you: notwithstanding be ye sure of this, that the kingdom of God is come nigh
unto you.

12 But I say unto you, that it shall be more tolerable in that day for Sodom,
than for that city.

13 Woe unto thee, Chorazin! woe unto thee, Bethsaida! for if the mighty
works had been done in Tyre and Sidon, which have been done in you, they
had a great while ago repented, sitting in sackcloth and ashes.

14 But it shall be more tolerable for Tyre and Sidon at the judgment, than for
you.

15 And thou, Capernaum, which art exalted to heaven, shalt be thrust down
to hell.

16 He that heareth you heareth me; and he that despiseth you despiseth me;
and he that despiseth me despiseth him that sent me.

17 And the seventy returned again with joy, saying, Lord, even the devils are
subject unto us through thy name.

18 And he said unto them, I beheld Satan as lightning fall from heaven.

19 Behold, I give unto you power to tread on serpents and scorpions, and
over all the power of the enemy: and nothing shall by any means hurt you.

20 Notwithstanding in this rejoice not, that the spirits are subject unto you;
but rather rejoice, because your names are written in heaven.

21 In that hour Jesus rejoiced in spirit, and said, I thank thee, O Father, Lord
of heaven and earth, that thou hast hid these things from the wise and prudent,
and hast revealed them unto babes: even so, Father; for so it seemed good in
thy sight.
22 All things are delivered to me of my Father: and no man knoweth who the
Son is, but the Father; and who the Father is, but the Son, and *he* to whom the
Son will reveal *him*.
23 And he turned him unto *his* disciples, and said privately, Blessed *are* the
eyes which see the things that ye see:
24 For I tell you, that many prophets and kings have desired to see those
things which ye see, and have not seen *them*; and to hear those things which
ye hear, and have not heard *them*.

The Good Samaritan

25 And, behold, a certain lawyer stood up, and tempted him, saying, Master,
what shall I do to inherit eternal life?
26 He said unto him, What is written in the law? how readest thou?
27 And he answering said, Thou shalt love the Lord thy God with all thy heart,
and with all thy soul, and with all thy strength, and with all thy mind; and thy
neighbour as thyself.
28 And he said unto him, Thou hast answered right: this do, and thou shalt
live.
29 But he, willing to justify himself, said unto Jesus, And who is my neigh-
bour?
30 And Jesus answering said, A certain *man* went down from Jerusalem to
Jericho, and fell among thieves, which stripped him of his raiment, and
wounded *him*, and departed, leaving *him* half dead.
31 And by chance there came down a certain priest that way: and when he
saw him, he passed by on the other side.
32 And likewise a Levite, when he was at the place, came and looked *on him*,
and passed by on the other side.
33 But a certain Samaritan, as he journeyed, came where he was: and when
he saw him, he had compassion *on him*,
34 And went to *him*, and bound up his wounds, pouring in oil and wine, and
set him on his own beast, and brought him to an inn, and took care of him.
35 And on the morrow when he departed, he took out two pence, and gave
them to the host, and said unto him, Take care of him; and whatsoever thou
spendest more, when I come again, I will repay thee.
36 Which now of these three, thinkest thou, was neighbour unto him that
fell among the thieves?
37 And he said, He that shewed mercy on him. Then said Jesus unto him, Go,
and do thou likewise.

Mary and Martha

38 Now it came to pass, as they went, that he entered into a certain village:
and a certain woman named Martha received him into her house.
39 And she had a sister called Mary, which also sat at Jesus' feet, and heard
his word.
40 But Martha was cumbered about much serving, and came to him, and
said, Lord, dost thou not care that my sister hath left me to serve alone? bid
her therefore that she help me.
41 And Jesus answered and said unto her, Martha, Martha, thou art careful
and troubled about many things:
42 But one thing is needful: and Mary hath chosen that good part, which
shall not be taken away from her.

Jesus Teaches How to Pray

11 And it came to pass, that, as he was praying in a certain place, when he ceased, one of his disciples said unto him, Lord, teach us to pray, as John also taught his disciples.

2 And he said unto them, When ye pray, say, Our Father which art in heaven, Hallowed be thy name. Thy kingdom come. Thy will be done, as in heaven, so in earth.

3 Give us day by day our daily bread.

4 And forgive us our sins; for we also forgive every one that is indebted to us. And lead us not into temptation; but deliver us from evil.

5 And he said unto them, Which of you shall have a friend, and shall go unto him at midnight, and say unto him, Friend, lend me three loaves;

6 For a friend of mine in his journey is come to me, and I have nothing to set before him?

7 And he from within shall answer and say, Trouble me not: the door is now shut, and my children are with me in bed; I cannot rise and give thee.

8 I say unto you, Though he will not rise and give him, because he is his friend, yet because of his importunity he will rise and give him as many as he needeth.

9 And I say unto you, Ask, and it shall be given you; seek, and ye shall find; knock, and it shall be opened unto you.

10 For every one that asketh receiveth; and he that seeketh findeth; and to him that knocketh it shall be opened.

11 If a son shall ask bread of any of you that is a father, will he give him a stone? or if *he ask* a fish, will he for a fish give him a serpent?

12 Or if he shall ask an egg, will he offer him a scorpion?

13 If ye then, being evil, know how to give good gifts unto your children: how much more shall *your* heavenly Father give the Holy Spirit to them that ask him?

Jesus Is Accused of Working with Beelzebub

14 And he was casting out a devil, and it was dumb. And it came to pass, when the devil was gone out, the dumb spake; and the people wondered.

15 But some of them said, He casteth out devils through Beelzebub the chief of the devils.

16 And others, tempting *him*, sought of him a sign from heaven.

17 But he, knowing their thoughts, said unto them, Every kingdom divided against itself is brought to desolation; and a house *divided* against a house falleth.

18 If Satan also be divided against himself, how shall his kingdom stand? because ye say that I cast out devils through Beelzebub.

19 And if I by Beelzebub cast out devils, by whom do your sons cast *them* out? therefore shall they be your judges.

20 But if I with the finger of God cast out devils, no doubt the kingdom of God is come upon you.

21 When a strong man armed keepeth his palace, his goods are in peace:

22 But when a stronger than he shall come upon him, and overcome him, he taketh from him all his armour wherein he trusted, and divideth his spoils.

23 He that is not with me is against me: and he that gathereth not with me scattereth.

24 When the unclean spirit is gone out of a man, he walketh through dry places, seeking rest; and finding none, he saith, I will return unto my house whence I came out.

25 And when he cometh, he findeth *it* swept and garnished.

26 Then goeth he, and taketh *to him* seven other spirits more wicked than himself; and they enter in, and dwell there: and the last *state* of that man is worse than the first.

27 And it came to pass, as he spake these things, a certain woman of the
company lifted up her voice, and said unto him, Blessed *is* the womb that bare
thee, and the paps which thou hast sucked.
28 But he said, Yea rather, blessed *are* they that hear the word of God, and
keep it.

The Sign of Jonah

29 And when the people were gathered thick together, he began to say, This
is an evil generation: they seek a sign; and there shall no sign be given it, but
the sign of Jonas the prophet.
30 For as Jonas was a sign unto the Ninevites, so shall also the Son of man be
to this generation.
31 The queen of the south shall rise up in the judgment with the men of this
generation, and condemn them: for she came from the utmost parts of the
earth to hear the wisdom of Solomon; and, behold, a greater than Solomon *is*
here.
32 The men of Nineve shall rise up in the judgment with this generation, and
shall condemn it: for they repented at the preaching of Jonas; and, behold, a
greater than Jonas *is* here.

Jesus Talks about Light

33 No man, when he hath lighted a candle, putteth *it* in a secret place, neither
under a bushel, but on a candlestick, that they which come in may see the
light.
34 The light of the body is the eye: therefore when thine eye is single, thy
whole body also is full of light; but when *thine eye* is evil, thy body also *is* full
of darkness.
35 Take heed therefore that the light which is in thee be not darkness.
36 If thy whole body therefore *be* full of light, having no part dark, the whole
shall be full of light, as when the bright shining of a candle doth give thee light.

Jesus Rebukes the Hypocrisy of the Religious Leaders

37 And as he spake, a certain Pharisee besought him to dine with him: and
he went in, and sat down to meat.
38 And when the Pharisee saw *it*, he marvelled that he had not first washed
before dinner.
39 And the Lord said unto him, Now do ye Pharisees make clean the outside
of the cup and the platter; but your inward part is full of ravening and wick-
edness.
40 *Ye* fools, did not he that made that which is without make that which is
within also?
41 But rather give alms of such things as ye have; and, behold, all things are
clean unto you.
42 But woe unto you, Pharisees! for ye tithe mint and rue and all manner of
herbs, and pass over judgment and the love of God: these ought ye to have
done, and not to leave the other undone.
43 Woe unto you, Pharisees! for ye love the uppermost seats in the syna-
gogues, and greetings in the markets.
44 Woe unto you, scribes and Pharisees, hypocrites! for ye are as graves which
appear not, and the men that walk over *them* are not aware *of them*.
45 Then answered one of the lawyers, and said unto him, Master, thus saying
thou reproachest us also.
46 And he said, Woe unto you also, *ye* lawyers! for ye lade men with burdens
grievous to be borne, and ye yourselves touch not the burdens with one of
your fingers.
47 Woe unto you! for ye build the sepulchres of the prophets, and your fathers
killed them.

48 Truly ye bear witness that ye allow the deeds of your fathers: for they
indeed killed them, and ye build their sepulchres.
49 Therefore also said the wisdom of God, I will send them prophets and
apostles, and *some* of them they shall slay and persecute:
50 That the blood of all the prophets, which was shed from the foundation
of the world, may be required of this generation;
51 From the blood of Abel unto the blood of Zacharias, which perished
between the altar and the temple: verily I say unto you, It shall be required of
this generation.
52 Woe unto you, lawyers! for ye have taken away the key of knowledge: ye
entered not in yourselves, and them that were entering in ye hindered.
53 And as he said these things unto them, the scribes and the Pharisees began
to urge *him* vehemently, and to provoke him to speak of many things:
54 Laying wait for him, and seeking to catch something out of his mouth,
that they might accuse him.

Jesus Encourages His Disciples

12 In the mean time, when there were gathered together an innumer-
able multitude of people, insomuch that they trode one upon
another, he began to say unto his disciples first of all, Beware ye of the
leaven of the Pharisees, which is hypocrisy.
2 For there is nothing covered, that shall not be revealed; neither hid, that
shall not be known.
3 Therefore whatsoever ye have spoken in darkness shall be heard in the
light; and that which ye have spoken in the ear in closets shall be proclaimed
upon the housetops.
4 And I say unto you my friends, Be not afraid of them that kill the body, and
after that have no more that they can do.
5 But I will forewarn you whom ye shall fear: Fear him, which after he hath
killed hath power to cast into hell; yea, I say unto you, Fear him.
6 Are not five sparrows sold for two farthings, and not one of them is forgot-
ten before God?
7 But even the very hairs of your head are all numbered. Fear not therefore:
ye are of more value than many sparrows.
8 Also I say unto you, Whosoever shall confess me before men, him shall the
Son of man also confess before the angels of God:
9 But he that denieth me before men shall be denied before the angels of
God.
10 And whosoever shall speak a word against the Son of man, it shall be
forgiven him: but unto him that blasphemeth against the Holy Ghost it shall
not be forgiven.
11 And when they bring you unto the synagogues, and *unto* magistrates, and
powers, take ye no thought how or what thing ye shall answer, or what ye shall
say:
12 For the Holy Ghost shall teach you in the same hour what ye ought to say.

A Parable about Greed

13 And one of the company said unto him, Master, speak to my brother, that
he divide the inheritance with me.
14 And he said unto him, Man, who made me a judge or a divider over you?
15 And he said unto them, Take heed, and beware of covetousness: for a man's
life consisteth not in the abundance of the things which he possesseth.
16 And he spake a parable unto them, saying, The ground of a certain rich
man brought forth plentifully:
17 And he thought within himself, saying, What shall I do, because I have no
room where to bestow my fruits?

18 And he said, This will I do: I will pull down my barns, and build greater;
and there will I bestow all my fruits and my goods.
19 And I will say to my soul, Soul, thou hast much goods laid up for many
years; take thine ease, eat, drink, *and* be merry.
20 But God said unto him, *Thou* fool, this night thy soul shall be required of
thee: then whose shall those things be, which thou hast provided?
21 So *is* he that layeth up treasure for himself, and is not rich toward God.

Do Not Be Anxious

22 And he said unto his disciples, Therefore I say unto you, Take no thought
for your life, what ye shall eat; neither for the body, what ye shall put on.
23 The life is more than meat, and the body *is more* than raiment.
24 Consider the ravens: for they neither sow nor reap; which neither have
storehouse nor barn; and God feedeth them: how much more are ye better
than the fowls?
25 And which of you with taking thought can add to his stature one cubit?
26 If ye then be not able to do that thing which is least, why take ye thought
for the rest?
27 Consider the lilies how they grow: they toil not, they spin not; and yet I
say unto you, that Solomon in all his glory was not arrayed like one of these.
28 If then God so clothe the grass, which is to day in the field, and to morrow
is cast into the oven; how much more *will he clothe* you, O ye of little faith?
29 And seek not ye what ye shall eat, or what ye shall drink, neither be ye of
doubtful mind.
30 For all these things do the nations of the world seek after: and your Father
knoweth that ye have need of these things.
31 But rather seek ye the kingdom of God; and all these things shall be added
unto you.
32 Fear not, little flock; for it is your Father's good pleasure to give you the
kingdom.
33 Sell that ye have, and give alms; provide yourselves bags which wax not
old, a treasure in the heavens that faileth not, where no thief approacheth,
neither moth corrupteth.
34 For where your treasure is, there will your heart be also.

Jesus Will Return Unexpectedly

35 Let your loins be girded about, and *your* lights burning;
36 And ye yourselves like unto men that wait for their lord, when he will
return from the wedding; that when he cometh and knocketh, they may open
unto him immediately.
37 Blessed *are* those servants, whom the lord when he cometh shall find
watching: verily I say unto you, that he shall gird himself, and make them to
sit down to meat, and will come forth and serve them.
38 And if he shall come in the second watch, or come in the third watch, and
find *them* so, blessed are those servants.
39 And this know, that if the goodman of the house had known what hour
the thief would come, he would have watched, and not have suffered his house
to be broken through.
40 Be ye therefore ready also: for the Son of man cometh at an hour when ye
think not.
41 Then Peter said unto him, Lord, speakest thou this parable unto us, or
even to all?
42 And the Lord said, Who then is that faithful and wise steward, whom *his*
lord shall make ruler over his household, to give *them their* portion of meat
in due season?
43 Blessed *is* that servant, whom his lord when he cometh shall find so doing.
44 Of a truth I say unto you, that he will make him ruler over all that he hath.

45 But and if that servant say in his heart, My lord delayeth his coming; and
shall begin to beat the menservants and maidens, and to eat and drink, and
to be drunken;
46 The lord of that servant will come in a day when he looketh not for *him*,
and at an hour when he is not aware, and will cut him in sunder, and will
appoint him his portion with the unbelievers.
47 And that servant, which knew his lord's will, and prepared not *himself*,
neither did according to his will, shall be beaten with many *stripes*.
48 But he that knew not, and did commit things worthy of stripes, shall be
beaten with few *stripes*. For unto whomsoever much is given, of him shall be
much required: and to whom men have committed much, of him they will
ask the more.
49 I am come to send fire on the earth; and what will I, if it be already kin-
dled?
50 But I have a baptism to be baptized with; and how am I straitened till it
be accomplished!
51 Suppose ye that I am come to give peace on earth? I tell you, Nay; but
rather division:
52 For from henceforth there shall be five in one house divided, three against
two, and two against three.
53 The father shall be divided against the son, and the son against the father;
the mother against the daughter, and the daughter against the mother; the
mother in law against her daughter in law, and the daughter in law against
her mother in law.

Use Good Judgment

54 And he said also to the people, When ye see a cloud rise out of the west,
straightway ye say, There cometh a shower; and so it is.
55 And when *ye see* the south wind blow, ye say, There will be heat; and it
cometh to pass.
56 *Ye* hypocrites, ye can discern the face of the sky and of the earth; but how
is it that ye do not discern this time?
57 Yea, and why even of yourselves judge ye not what is right?
58 When thou goest with thine adversary to the magistrate, *as thou art* in
the way, give diligence that thou mayest be delivered from him; lest he hale
thee to the judge, and the judge deliver thee to the officer, and the officer cast
thee into prison.
59 I tell thee, thou shalt not depart thence, till thou hast paid the very last
mite.

Jesus Preaches Repentance

13 There were present at that season some that told him of the
Galilaeans, whose blood Pilate had mingled with their sacrifices.
2 And Jesus answering said unto them, Suppose ye that these Galilaeans were
sinners above all the Galilaeans, because they suffered such things?
3 I tell you, Nay: but, except ye repent, ye shall all likewise perish.
4 Or those eighteen, upon whom the tower in Siloam fell, and slew them,
think ye that they were sinners above all men that dwelt in Jerusalem?
5 I tell you, Nay: but, except ye repent, ye shall all likewise perish.

The Fruitless Fig Tree

6 He spake also this parable; A certain *man* had a fig tree planted in his
vineyard; and he came and sought fruit thereon, and found none.
7 Then said he unto the dresser of his vineyard, Behold, these three years I
come seeking fruit on this fig tree, and find none: cut it down; why cumbereth
it the ground?
8 And he answering said unto him, Lord, let it alone this year also, till I shall
dig about it, and dung *it*:
9 And if it bear fruit, *well*: and if not, *then* after that thou shalt cut it down.

Jesus Heals on the Sabbath

10 And he was teaching in one of the synagogues on the sabbath.
11 And, behold, there was a woman which had a spirit of infirmity eighteen
years, and was bowed together, and could in no wise lift up *herself*.
12 And when Jesus saw her, he called *her to him*, and said unto her, Woman,
thou art loosed from thine infirmity.
13 And he laid *his* hands on her: and immediately she was made straight, and
glorified God.
14 And the ruler of the synagogue answered with indignation, because that
Jesus had healed on the sabbath day, and said unto the people, There are six
days in which men ought to work: in them therefore come and be healed, and
not on the sabbath day.
15 The Lord then answered him, and said, *Thou* hypocrite, doth not each one
of you on the sabbath loose his ox or *his* ass from the stall, and lead *him* away
to watering?
16 And ought not this woman, being a daughter of Abraham, whom Satan
hath bound, lo, these eighteen years, be loosed from this bond on the sabbath
day?
17 And when he had said these things, all his adversaries were ashamed: and
all the people rejoiced for all the glorious things that were done by him.

Parables of Seed and Leaven

18 Then said he, Unto what is the kingdom of God like? and whereunto shall
I resemble it?
19 It is like a grain of mustard seed, which a man took, and cast into his
garden; and it grew, and waxed a great tree; and the fowls of the air lodged in
the branches of it.
20 And again he said, Whereunto shall I liken the kingdom of God?
21 It is like leaven, which a woman took and hid in three measures of meal,
till the whole was leavened.

The Narrow Gate

22 And he went through the cities and villages, teaching, and journeying
toward Jerusalem.
23 Then said one unto him, Lord, are there few that be saved? And he said
unto them,
24 Strive to enter in at the strait gate: for many, I say unto you, will seek to
enter in, and shall not be able.
25 When once the master of the house is risen up, and hath shut to the door,
and ye begin to stand without, and to knock at the door, saying, Lord, Lord,
open unto us; and he shall answer and say unto you, I know you not whence
ye are:
26 Then shall ye begin to say, We have eaten and drunk in thy presence, and
thou hast taught in our streets.
27 But he shall say, I tell you, I know you not whence ye are; depart from me,
all *ye* workers of iniquity.
28 There shall be weeping and gnashing of teeth, when ye shall see Abraham,
and Isaac, and Jacob, and all the prophets, in the kingdom of God, and you
yourselves thrust out.
29 And they shall come from the east, and *from* the west, and from the north,
and *from* the south, and shall sit down in the kingdom of God.
30 And, behold, there are last which shall be first, and there are first which
shall be last.

Jesus Warns Jerusalem

31 The same day there came certain of the Pharisees, saying unto him, Get
thee out, and depart hence: for Herod will kill thee.

32 And he said unto them, Go ye, and tell that fox, Behold, I cast out devils,
and I do cures to day and to morrow, and the third *day* I shall be perfected.
33 Nevertheless I must walk to day, and to morrow, and the *day* following:
for it cannot be that a prophet perish out of Jerusalem.
34 O Jerusalem, Jerusalem, which killest the prophets, and stonest them that
are sent unto thee; how often would I have gathered thy children together, as
a hen *doth gather* her brood under *her* wings, and ye would not!
35 Behold, your house is left unto you desolate: and verily I say unto you, Ye
shall not see me, until *the time* come when ye shall say, Blessed *is* he that
cometh in the name of the Lord.

Jesus Heals a Man on the Sabbath

14 And it came to pass, as he went into the house of one of the chief
Pharisees to eat bread on the sabbath day, that they watched him.
2 And, behold, there was a certain man before him which had the dropsy.
3 And Jesus answering spake unto the lawyers and Pharisees, saying, Is it
lawful to heal on the sabbath day?
4 And they held their peace. And he took *him*, and healed him, and let him go;
5 And answered them, saying, Which of you shall have an ass or an ox fallen
into a pit, and will not straightway pull him out on the sabbath day?
6 And they could not answer him again to these things.

Jesus Attends a Banquet

7 And he put forth a parable to those which were bidden, when he marked
how they chose out the chief rooms; saying unto them,
8 When thou art bidden of any *man* to a wedding, sit not down in the high-
est room; lest a more honourable man than thou be bidden of him;
9 And he that bade thee and him come and say to thee, Give this man place;
and thou begin with shame to take the lowest room.
10 But when thou art bidden, go and sit down in the lowest room; that when
he that bade thee cometh, he may say unto thee, Friend, go up higher: then
shalt thou have worship in the presence of them that sit at meat with thee.
11 For whosoever exalteth himself shall be abased; and he that humbleth
himself shall be exalted.
12 Then said he also to him that bade him, When thou makest a dinner or a
supper, call not thy friends, nor thy brethren, neither thy kinsmen, nor *thy*
rich neighbours; lest they also bid thee again, and a recompence be made thee.
13 But when thou makest a feast, call the poor, the maimed, the lame, the
blind:
14 And thou shalt be blessed; for they cannot recompense thee: for thou shalt
be recompensed at the resurrection of the just.

A Parable about Heaven's Banquet

15 And when one of them that sat at meat with him heard these things, he
said unto him, Blessed *is* he that shall eat bread in the kingdom of God.
16 Then said he unto him, A certain man made a great supper, and bade many:
17 And sent his servant at supper time to say to them that were bidden, Come;
for all things are now ready.
18 And they all with one *consent* began to make excuse. The first said unto
him, I have bought a piece of ground, and I must needs go and see it: I pray
thee have me excused.
19 And another said, I have bought five yoke of oxen, and I go to prove them:
I pray thee have me excused.
20 And another said, I have married a wife, and therefore I cannot come.
21 So that servant came, and shewed his lord these things. Then the master
of the house being angry said to his servant, Go out quickly into the streets
and lanes of the city, and bring in hither the poor, and the maimed, and the
halt, and the blind.

22 And the servant said, Lord, it is done as thou hast commanded, and yet
there is room.
23 And the lord said unto the servant, Go out into the highways and hedges,
and compel *them* to come in, that my house may be filled.
24 For I say unto you, That none of those men which were bidden shall taste
of my supper.

The Cost of Being a Disciple

25 And there went great multitudes with him: and he turned, and said unto
them,
26 If any *man* come to me, and hate not his father, and mother, and wife, and
children, and brethren, and sisters, yea, and his own life also, he cannot be my
disciple.
27 And whosoever doth not bear his cross, and come after me, cannot be my
disciple.
28 For which of you, intending to build a tower, sitteth not down first, and
counteth the cost, whether he have *sufficient* to finish *it*?
29 Lest haply, after he hath laid the foundation, and is not able to finish *it*,
all that behold *it* begin to mock him,
30 Saying, This man began to build, and was not able to finish.
31 Or what king, going to make war against another king, sitteth not down
first, and consulteth whether he be able with ten thousand to meet him that
cometh against him with twenty thousand?
32 Or else, while the other is yet a great way off, he sendeth an ambassage,
and desireth conditions of peace.
33 So likewise, whosoever he be of you that forsaketh not all that he hath, he
cannot be my disciple.
34 Salt *is* good: but if the salt have lost his savour, wherewith shall it be sea-
soned?
35 It is neither fit for the land, nor yet for the dunghill; *but* men cast it out.
He that hath ears to hear, let him hear.

The Lost Sheep

15 Then drew near unto him all the publicans and sinners for to hear
him.
2 And the Pharisees and scribes murmured, saying, This man receiveth sin-
ners, and eateth with them.
3 And he spake this parable unto them, saying,
4 What man of you, having an hundred sheep, if he lose one of them, doth
not leave the ninety and nine in the wilderness, and go after that which is lost,
until he find it?
5 And when he hath found *it*, he layeth *it* on his shoulders, rejoicing.
6 And when he cometh home, he calleth together *his* friends and neighbours,
saying unto them, Rejoice with me; for I have found my sheep which was lost.
7 I say unto you, that likewise joy shall be in heaven over one sinner that repent-
eth, more than over ninety and nine just persons, which need no repentance.

The Lost Coin

8 Either what woman having ten pieces of silver, if she lose one piece, doth
not light a candle, and sweep the house, and seek diligently till she find *it*?
9 And when she hath found *it*, she calleth *her* friends and *her* neighbours
together, saying, Rejoice with me; for I have found the piece which I had lost.
10 Likewise, I say unto you, there is joy in the presence of the angels of God
over one sinner that repenteth.

The Prodigal Son

11 And he said, A certain man had two sons:

12 And the younger of them said to *his* father, Father, give me the portion of
goods that falleth *to me*. And he divided unto them *his* living.
13 And not many days after the younger son gathered all together, and took
his journey into a far country, and there wasted his substance with riotous
living.
14 And when he had spent all, there arose a mighty famine in that land; and
he began to be in want.
15 And he went and joined himself to a citizen of that country; and he sent
him into his fields to feed swine.
16 And he would fain have filled his belly with the husks that the swine did
eat: and no man gave unto him.
17 And when he came to himself, he said, How many hired servants of my
father's have bread enough and to spare, and I perish with hunger!
18 I will arise and go to my father, and will say unto him, Father, I have sinned
against heaven, and before thee,
19 And am no more worthy to be called thy son: make me as one of thy hired
servants.
20 And he arose, and came to his father. But when he was yet a great way off,
his father saw him, and had compassion, and ran, and fell on his neck, and
kissed him.
21 And the son said unto him, Father, I have sinned against heaven, and in
thy sight, and am no more worthy to be called thy son.
22 But the father said to his servants, Bring forth the best robe, and put *it* on
him; and put a ring on his hand, and shoes on *his* feet:
23 And bring hither the fatted calf, and kill *it*; and let us eat, and be merry:
24 For this my son was dead, and is alive again; he was lost, and is found. And
they began to be merry.
25 Now his elder son was in the field: and as he came and drew nigh to the
house, he heard musick and dancing.
26 And he called one of the servants, and asked what these things meant.
27 And he said unto him, Thy brother is come; and thy father hath killed the
fatted calf, because he hath received him safe and sound.
28 And he was angry, and would not go in: therefore came his father out, and
intreated him.
29 And he answering said to *his* father, Lo, these many years do I serve thee,
neither transgressed I at any time thy commandment: and yet thou never
gavest me a kid, that I might make merry with my friends:
30 But as soon as this thy son was come, which hath devoured thy living with
harlots, thou hast killed for him the fatted calf.
31 And he said unto him, Son, thou art ever with me, and all that I have is
thine.
32 It was meet that we should make merry, and be glad: for this thy brother
was dead, and is alive again; and was lost, and is found.

The Parable of the Unfaithful Steward

16 And he said also unto his disciples, There was a certain rich man,
which had a steward; and the same was accused unto him that he
had wasted his goods.
2 And he called him, and said unto him, How is it that I hear this of thee?
give an account of thy stewardship; for thou mayest be no longer steward.
3 Then the steward said within himself, What shall I do? for my lord taketh
away from me the stewardship: I cannot dig; to beg I am ashamed.
4 I am resolved what to do, that, when I am put out of the stewardship, they
may receive me into their houses.
5 So he called every one of his lord's debtors *unto him*, and said unto the first,
How much owest thou unto my lord?

6 And he said, An hundred measures of oil. And he said unto him, Take thy
bill, and sit down quickly, and write fifty.
7 Then said he to another, And how much owest thou? And he said, An hun-
dred measures of wheat. And he said unto him, Take thy bill, and write four-
score.
8 And the lord commended the unjust steward, because he had done wisely:
for the children of this world are in their generation wiser than the children
of light.
9 And I say unto you, Make to yourselves friends of the mammon of unrigh-
teousness; that, when ye fail, they may receive you into everlasting habitations.
10 He that is faithful in that which is least is faithful also in much: and he
that is unjust in the least is unjust also in much.
11 If therefore ye have not been faithful in the unrighteous mammon, who
will commit to your trust the true *riches*?
12 And if ye have not been faithful in that which is another man's, who shall
give you that which is your own?
13 No servant can serve two masters: for either he will hate the one, and love
the other; or else he will hold to the one, and despise the other. Ye cannot serve
God and mammon.
14 And the Pharisees also, who were covetous, heard all these things: and
they derided him.
15 And he said unto them, Ye are they which justify yourselves before men;
but God knoweth your hearts: for that which is highly esteemed among men
is abomination in the sight of God.
16 The law and the prophets *were* until John: since that time the kingdom of
God is preached, and every man presseth into it.
17 And it is easier for heaven and earth to pass, than one tittle of the law to
fail.
18 Whosoever putteth away his wife, and marrieth another, committeth
adultery: and whosoever marrieth her that is put away from *her* husband
committeth adultery.

The Rich Man and Lazarus

19 There was a certain rich man, which was clothed in purple and fine linen,
and fared sumptuously every day:
20 And there was a certain beggar named Lazarus, which was laid at his gate,
full of sores,
21 And desiring to be fed with the crumbs which fell from the rich man's
table: moreover the dogs came and licked his sores.
22 And it came to pass, that the beggar died, and was carried by the angels
into Abraham's bosom: the rich man also died, and was buried;
23 And in hell he lift up his eyes, being in torments, and seeth Abraham afar
off, and Lazarus in his bosom.
24 And he cried and said, Father Abraham, have mercy on me, and send
Lazarus, that he may dip the tip of his finger in water, and cool my tongue; for
I am tormented in this flame.
25 But Abraham said, Son, remember that thou in thy lifetime receivedst thy
good things, and likewise Lazarus evil things: but now he is comforted, and
thou art tormented.
26 And beside all this, between us and you there is a great gulf fixed: so that
they which would pass from hence to you cannot; neither can they pass to us,
that *would come* from thence.
27 Then he said, I pray thee therefore, father, that thou wouldest send him
to my father's house:
28 For I have five brethren; that he may testify unto them, lest they also come
into this place of torment.

29 Abraham saith unto him, They have Moses and the prophets; let them
hear them.
30 And he said, Nay, father Abraham: but if one went unto them from the
dead, they will repent.
31 And he said unto him, If they hear not Moses and the prophets, neither
will they be persuaded, though one rose from the dead.

Dealing with Others

17 Then said he unto the disciples, It is impossible but that offences
will come: but woe *unto him*, through whom they come!
2 It were better for him that a millstone were hanged about his neck, and he
cast into the sea, than that he should offend one of these little ones.
3 Take heed to yourselves: If thy brother trespass against thee, rebuke him;
and if he repent, forgive him.
4 And if he trespass against thee seven times in a day, and seven times in a
day turn again to thee, saying, I repent; thou shalt forgive him.
5 And the apostles said unto the Lord, Increase our faith.
6 And the Lord said, If ye had faith as a grain of mustard seed, ye might say
unto this sycamine tree, Be thou plucked up by the root, and be thou planted
in the sea; and it should obey you.
7 But which of you, having a servant plowing or feeding cattle, will say unto
him by and by, when he is come from the field, Go and sit down to meat?
8 And will not rather say unto him, Make ready wherewith I may sup, and
gird thyself, and serve me, till I have eaten and drunken; and afterward thou
shalt eat and drink?
9 Doth he thank that servant because he did the things that were command-
ed him? I trow not.
10 So likewise ye, when ye shall have done all those things which are com-
manded you, say, We are unprofitable servants: we have done that which was
our duty to do.

Jesus Heals Ten Lepers

11 And it came to pass, as he went to Jerusalem, that he passed through the
midst of Samaria and Galilee.
12 And as he entered into a certain village, there met him ten men that were
lepers, which stood afar off:
13 And they lifted up *their* voices, and said, Jesus, Master, have mercy on us.
14 And when he saw *them*, he said unto them, Go shew yourselves unto the
priests. And it came to pass, that, as they went, they were cleansed.
15 And one of them, when he saw that he was healed, turned back, and with
a loud voice glorified God,
16 And fell down on *his* face at his feet, giving him thanks: and he was a
Samaritan.
17 And Jesus answering said, Were there not ten cleansed? but where *are* the
nine?
18 There are not found that returned to give glory to God, save this stranger.
19 And he said unto him, Arise, go thy way: thy faith hath made thee whole.

The Kingdom of God

20 And when he was demanded of the Pharisees, when the kingdom of God
should come, he answered them and said, The kingdom of God cometh not
with observation:
21 Neither shall they say, Lo here! or, lo there! for, behold, the kingdom of
God is within you.
22 And he said unto the disciples, The days will come, when ye shall desire
to see one of the days of the Son of man, and ye shall not see *it*.
23 And they shall say to you, See here; or, see there: go not after *them*, nor
follow *them*.

24 For as the lightning, that lighteneth out of the one *part* under heaven,
shineth unto the other *part* under heaven; so shall also the Son of man be in
his day.
25 But first must he suffer many things, and be rejected of this generation.
26 And as it was in the days of Noe, so shall it be also in the days of the Son
of man.
27 They did eat, they drank, they married wives, they were given in marriage,
until the day that Noe entered into the ark, and the flood came, and destroyed
them all.
28 Likewise also as it was in the days of Lot; they did eat, they drank, they
bought, they sold, they planted, they builded;
29 But the same day that Lot went out of Sodom it rained fire and brimstone
from heaven, and destroyed *them* all.
30 Even thus shall it be in the day when the Son of man is revealed.
31 In that day, he which shall be upon the housetop, and his stuff in the house,
let him not come down to take it away: and he that is in the field, let him
likewise not return back.
32 Remember Lot's wife.
33 Whosoever shall seek to save his life shall lose it; and whosoever shall lose
his life shall preserve it.
34 I tell you, in that night there shall be two *men* in one bed; the one shall be
taken, and the other shall be left.
35 Two *women* shall be grinding together; the one shall be taken, and the
other left.
36 Two *men* shall be in the field; the one shall be taken, and the other left.
37 And they answered and said unto him, Where, Lord? And he said unto
them, Wheresoever the body *is*, thither will the eagles be gathered together.

God Will Help His People

18 And he spake a parable unto them *to this end*, that men ought always
to pray, and not to faint;
2 Saying, There was in a city a judge, which feared not God, neither regarded
man:
3 And there was a widow in that city; and she came unto him, saying, Avenge
me of mine adversary.
4 And he would not for a while: but afterward he said within himself, Though
I fear not God, nor regard man;
5 Yet because this widow troubleth me, I will avenge her, lest by her contin-
ual coming she weary me.
6 And the Lord said, Hear what the unjust judge saith.
7 And shall not God avenge his own elect, which cry day and night unto him,
though he bear long with them?
8 I tell you that he will avenge them speedily. Nevertheless when the Son of
man cometh, shall he find faith on the earth?

The Pharisee and the Tax Collector

9 And he spake this parable unto certain which trusted in themselves that
they were righteous, and despised others:
10 Two men went up into the temple to pray; the one a Pharisee, and the
other a publican.
11 The Pharisee stood and prayed thus with himself, God, I thank thee, that
I am not as other men *are*, extortioners, unjust, adulterers, or even as this
publican.
12 I fast twice in the week, I give tithes of all that I possess.
13 And the publican, standing afar off, would not lift up so much as *his* eyes
unto heaven, but smote upon his breast, saying, God be merciful to me a sinner.

14 I tell you, this man went down to his house justified *rather* than the other:
for every one that exalteth himself shall be abased; and he that humbleth
himself shall be exalted.

Jesus Blesses the Children

15 And they brought unto him also infants, that he would touch them: but
when *his* disciples saw *it*, they rebuked them.
16 But Jesus called them *unto him*, and said, Suffer little children to come
unto me, and forbid them not: for of such is the kingdom of God.
17 Verily I say unto you, Whosoever shall not receive the kingdom of God as
a little child shall in no wise enter therein.

A Rich Young Ruler

18 And a certain ruler asked him, saying, Good Master, what shall I do to
inherit eternal life?
19 And Jesus said unto him, Why callest thou me good? none *is* good, save
one, *that is*, God.
20 Thou knowest the commandments, Do not commit adultery, Do not kill,
Do not steal, Do not bear false witness, Honour thy father and thy mother.
21 And he said, All these have I kept from my youth up.
22 Now when Jesus heard these things, he said unto him, Yet lackest thou
one thing: sell all that thou hast, and distribute unto the poor, and thou shalt
have treasure in heaven: and come, follow me.
23 And when he heard this, he was very sorrowful: for he was very rich.
24 And when Jesus saw that he was very sorrowful, he said, How hardly shall
they that have riches enter into the kingdom of God!
25 For it is easier for a camel to go through a needle's eye, than for a rich man
to enter into the kingdom of God.
26 And they that heard *it* said, Who then can be saved?
27 And he said, The things which are impossible with men are possible with
God.
28 Then Peter said, Lo, we have left all, and followed thee.
29 And he said unto them, Verily I say unto you, There is no man that hath
left house, or parents, or brethren, or wife, or children, for the kingdom of
God's sake,
30 Who shall not receive manifold more in this present time, and in the world
to come life everlasting.

Jesus Again Foretells His Death and Resurrection

31 Then he took *unto him* the twelve, and said unto them, Behold, we go up
to Jerusalem, and all things that are written by the prophets concerning the
Son of man shall be accomplished.
32 For he shall be delivered unto the Gentiles, and shall be mocked, and
spitefully entreated, and spitted on:
33 And they shall scourge *him*, and put him to death: and the third day he
shall rise again.
34 And they understood none of these things: and this saying was hid from
them, neither knew they the things which were spoken.

Jesus Heals a Blind Man

35 And it came to pass, that as he was come nigh unto Jericho, a certain blind
man sat by the way side begging:
36 And hearing the multitude pass by, he asked what it meant.
37 And they told him, that Jesus of Nazareth passeth by.
38 And he cried, saying, Jesus, *thou* Son of David, have mercy on me.
39 And they which went before rebuked him, that he should hold his peace:
but he cried so much the more, *Thou* Son of David, have mercy on me.

40 And Jesus stood, and commanded him to be brought unto him: and when
he was come near, he asked him,
41 Saying, What wilt thou that I shall do unto thee? And he said, Lord, that
I may receive my sight.
42 And Jesus said unto him, Receive thy sight: thy faith hath saved thee.
43 And immediately he received his sight, and followed him, glorifying God:
and all the people, when they saw *it*, gave praise unto God.

Zacchaeus Meets Jesus

19 And *Jesus* entered and passed through Jericho.
2 And, behold, *there was* a man named Zacchaeus, which was the chief
among the publicans, and he was rich.
3 And he sought to see Jesus who he was; and could not for the press, because
he was little of stature.
4 And he ran before, and climbed up into a sycomore tree to see him: for he
was to pass that *way*.
5 And when Jesus came to the place, he looked up, and saw him, and said
unto him, Zacchaeus, make haste, and come down; for to day I must abide at
thy house.
6 And he made haste, and came down, and received him joyfully.
7 And when they saw *it*, they all murmured, saying, That he was gone to be
guest with a man that is a sinner.
8 And Zacchaeus stood, and said unto the Lord; Behold, Lord, the half of my
goods I give to the poor; and if I have taken any thing from any man by false
accusation, I restore *him* fourfold.
9 And Jesus said unto him, This day is salvation come to this house, forso-
much as he also is a son of Abraham.
10 For the Son of man is come to seek and to save that which was lost.

The Parable of the Pounds

11 And as they heard these things, he added and spake a parable, because he
was nigh to Jerusalem, and because they thought that the kingdom of God
should immediately appear.
12 He said therefore, A certain nobleman went into a far country to receive
for himself a kingdom, and to return.
13 And he called his ten servants, and delivered them ten pounds, and said
unto them, Occupy till I come.
14 But his citizens hated him, and sent a message after him, saying, We will
not have this *man* to reign over us.
15 And it came to pass, that when he was returned, having received the king-
dom, then he commanded these servants to be called unto him, to whom he
had given the money, that he might know how much every man had gained
by trading.
16 Then came the first, saying, Lord, thy pound hath gained ten pounds.
17 And he said unto him, Well, thou good servant: because thou hast been
faithful in a very little, have thou authority over ten cities.
18 And the second came, saying, Lord, thy pound hath gained five pounds.
19 And he said likewise to him, Be thou also over five cities.
20 And another came, saying, Lord, behold, *here is* thy pound, which I have
kept laid up in a napkin:
21 For I feared thee, because thou art an austere man: thou takest up that
thou layedst not down, and reapest that thou didst not sow.
22 And he saith unto him, Out of thine own mouth will I judge thee, *thou*
wicked servant. Thou knewest that I was an austere man, taking up that I laid
not down, and reaping that I did not sow:
23 Wherefore then gavest not thou my money into the bank, that at my com-
ing I might have required mine own with usury?

24 And he said unto them that stood by, Take from him the pound, and give
it to him that hath ten pounds.
25 (And they said unto him, Lord, he hath ten pounds.)
26 For I say unto you, That unto every one which hath shall be given; and
from him that hath not, even that he hath shall be taken away from him.
27 But those mine enemies, which would not that I should reign over them,
bring hither, and slay *them* before me.

Jesus Enters Jerusalem in Triumph

28 And when he had thus spoken, he went before, ascending up to Jerusalem.
29 And it came to pass, when he was come nigh to Bethphage and Bethany,
at the mount called *the mount* of Olives, he sent two of his disciples,
30 Saying, Go ye into the village over against *you*; in the which at your enter-
ing ye shall find a colt tied, whereon yet never man sat: loose him, and bring
him hither.
31 And if any man ask you, Why do ye loose *him*? thus shall ye say unto him,
Because the Lord hath need of him.
32 And they that were sent went their way, and found even as he had said
unto them.
33 And as they were loosing the colt, the owners thereof said unto them, Why
loose ye the colt?
34 And they said, The Lord hath need of him.
35 And they brought him to Jesus: and they cast their garments upon the
colt, and they set Jesus thereon.
36 And as he went, they spread their clothes in the way.
37 And when he was come nigh, even now at the descent of the mount of
Olives, the whole multitude of the disciples began to rejoice and praise God
with a loud voice for all the mighty works that they had seen;
38 Saying, Blessed *be* the King that cometh in the name of the Lord: peace in
heaven, and glory in the highest.
39 And some of the Pharisees from among the multitude said unto him,
Master, rebuke thy disciples.
40 And he answered and said unto them, I tell you that, if these should hold
their peace, the stones would immediately cry out.

Jesus Weeps over Jerusalem

41 And when he was come near, he beheld the city, and wept over it,
42 Saying, If thou hadst known, even thou, at least in this thy day, the things
which belong unto thy peace! but now they are hid from thine eyes.
43 For the days shall come upon thee, that thine enemies shall cast a trench
about thee, and compass thee round, and keep thee in on every side,
44 And shall lay thee even with the ground, and thy children within thee;
and they shall not leave in thee one stone upon another; because thou knew-
est not the time of thy visitation.

Jesus Throws Moneychangers from the Temple

45 And he went into the temple, and began to cast out them that sold there-
in, and them that bought;
46 Saying unto them, It is written, My house is the house of prayer: but ye
have made it a den of thieves.
47 And he taught daily in the temple. But the chief priests and the scribes
and the chief of the people sought to destroy him,
48 And could not find what they might do: for all the people were very atten-
tive to hear him.

Jesus' Authority Is Challenged

20 And it came to pass, *that* on one of those days, as he taught the
people in the temple, and preached the gospel, the chief priests
and the scribes came upon *him* with the elders,
2 And spake unto him, saying, Tell us, by what authority doest thou these
things? or who is he that gave thee this authority?
3 And he answered and said unto them, I will also ask you one thing; and
answer me:
4 The baptism of John, was it from heaven, or of men?
5 And they reasoned with themselves, saying, If we shall say, From heaven;
he will say, Why then believed ye him not?
6 But and if we say, Of men; all the people will stone us: for they be persuad-
ed that John was a prophet.
7 And they answered, that they could not tell whence *it was*.
8 And Jesus said unto them, Neither tell I you by what authority I do these
things.

The Parable of the Vineyard

9 Then began he to speak to the people this parable; A certain man planted
a vineyard, and let it forth to husbandmen, and went into a far country for a
long time.
10 And at the season he sent a servant to the husbandmen, that they should
give him of the fruit of the vineyard: but the husbandmen beat him, and sent
him away empty.
11 And again he sent another servant: and they beat him also, and entreated
him shamefully, and sent *him* away empty.
12 And again he sent a third: and they wounded him also, and cast *him* out.
13 Then said the lord of the vineyard, What shall I do? I will send my beloved
son: it may be they will reverence *him* when they see him.
14 But when the husbandmen saw him, they reasoned among themselves,
saying, This is the heir: come, let us kill him, that the inheritance may be ours.
15 So they cast him out of the vineyard, and killed *him*. What therefore shall
the lord of the vineyard do unto them?
16 He shall come and destroy these husbandmen, and shall give the vineyard
to others. And when they heard *it*, they said, God forbid.
17 And he beheld them, and said, What is this then that is written, The stone
which the builders rejected, the same is become the head of the corner?
18 Whosoever shall fall upon that stone shall be broken; but on whomsoev-
er it shall fall, it will grind him to powder.
19 And the chief priests and the scribes the same hour sought to lay hands
on him; and they feared the people: for they perceived that he had spoken this
parable against them.

A Question about Taxes

20 And they watched *him*, and sent forth spies, which should feign them-
selves just men, that they might take hold of his words, that so they might
deliver him unto the power and authority of the governor.
21 And they asked him, saying, Master, we know that thou sayest and teachest
rightly, neither acceptest thou the person *of any*, but teachest the way of God
truly:
22 Is it lawful for us to give tribute unto Caesar, or no?
23 But he perceived their craftiness, and said unto them, Why tempt ye me?
24 Shew me a penny. Whose image and superscription hath it? They answered
and said, Caesar's.
25 And he said unto them, Render therefore unto Caesar the things which
be Caesar's, and unto God the things which be God's.

26 And they could not take hold of his words before the people: and they
marvelled at his answer, and held their peace.

A Question about the Resurrection

27 Then came to *him* certain of the Sadducees, which deny that there is any
resurrection; and they asked him,
28 Saying, Master, Moses wrote unto us, If any man's brother die, having a
wife, and he die without children, that his brother should take his wife, and
raise up seed unto his brother.
29 There were therefore seven brethren: and the first took a wife, and died
without children.
30 And the second took her to wife, and he died childless.
31 And the third took her; and in like manner the seven also: and they left
no children, and died.
32 Last of all the woman died also.
33 Therefore in the resurrection whose wife of them is she? for seven had
her to wife.
34 And Jesus answering said unto them, The children of this world marry,
and are given in marriage:
35 But they which shall be accounted worthy to obtain that world, and the
resurrection from the dead, neither marry, nor are given in marriage:
36 Neither can they die any more: for they are equal unto the angels; and are
the children of God, being the children of the resurrection.
37 Now that the dead are raised, even Moses shewed at the bush, when he
calleth the Lord the God of Abraham, and the God of Isaac, and the God of
Jacob.
38 For he is not a God of the dead, but of the living: for all live unto him.
39 Then certain of the scribes answering said, Master, thou hast well said.
40 And after that they durst not ask him any *question at all*.

David's Son, David's Lord

41 And he said unto them, How say they that Christ is David's son?
42 And David himself saith in the book of Psalms, The LORD said unto my
Lord, Sit thou on my right hand,
43 Till I make thine enemies thy footstool.
44 David therefore calleth him Lord, how is he then his son?

Beware of the Scribes

45 Then in the audience of all the people he said unto his disciples,
46 Beware of the scribes, which desire to walk in long robes, and love greet-
ings in the markets, and the highest seats in the synagogues, and the chief
rooms at feasts;
47 Which devour widows' houses, and for a shew make long prayers: the same
shall receive greater damnation.

The Poor Widow's Gift

21 And he looked up, and saw the rich men casting their gifts into the
treasury.
2 And he saw also a certain poor widow casting in thither two mites.
3 And he said, Of a truth I say unto you, that this poor widow hath cast in
more than they all:
4 For all these have of their abundance cast in unto the offerings of God: but
she of her penury hath cast in all the living that she had.

Jesus Discusses the Future

5 And as some spake of the temple, how it was adorned with goodly stones
and gifts, he said,
6 *As for* these things which ye behold, the days will come, in the which there
shall not be left one stone upon another, that shall not be thrown down.

7 And they asked him, saying, Master, but when shall these things be? and
what sign *will there be* when these things shall come to pass?
8 And he said, Take heed that ye be not deceived: for many shall come in my
name, saying, I am *Christ*; and the time draweth near: go ye not therefore after
them.
9 But when ye shall hear of wars and commotions, be not terrified: for these
things must first come to pass; but the end *is* not by and by.
10 Then said he unto them, Nation shall rise against nation, and kingdom
against kingdom:
11 And great earthquakes shall be in divers places, and famines, and pesti-
lences; and fearful sights and great signs shall there be from heaven.
12 But before all these, they shall lay their hands on you, and persecute *you*,
delivering *you* up to the synagogues, and into prisons, being brought before
kings and rulers for my name's sake.
13 And it shall turn to you for a testimony.
14 Settle *it* therefore in your hearts, not to meditate before what ye shall
answer:
15 For I will give you a mouth and wisdom, which all your adversaries shall
not be able to gainsay nor resist.
16 And ye shall be betrayed both by parents, and brethren, and kinsfolks,
and friends; and *some* of you shall they cause to be put to death.
17 And ye shall be hated of all *men* for my name's sake.
18 But there shall not an hair of your head perish.
19 In your patience possess ye your souls.
20 And when ye shall see Jerusalem compassed with armies, then know that
the desolation thereof is nigh.
21 Then let them which are in Judaea flee to the mountains; and let them
which are in the midst of it depart out; and let not them that are in the coun-
tries enter thereinto.
22 For these be the days of vengeance, that all things which are written may
be fulfilled.
23 But woe unto them that are with child, and to them that give suck, in those
days! for there shall be great distress in the land, and wrath upon this people.
24 And they shall fall by the edge of the sword, and shall be led away captive
into all nations: and Jerusalem shall be trodden down of the Gentiles, until
the times of the Gentiles be fulfilled.
25 And there shall be signs in the sun, and in the moon, and in the stars; and
upon the earth distress of nations, with perplexity; the sea and the waves
roaring;
26 Men's hearts failing them for fear, and for looking after those things which
are coming on the earth: for the powers of heaven shall be shaken.
27 And then shall they see the Son of man coming in a cloud with power and
great glory.
28 And when these things begin to come to pass, then look up, and lift up
your heads; for your redemption draweth nigh.
29 And he spake to them a parable; Behold the fig tree, and all the trees;
30 When they now shoot forth, ye see and know of your own selves that
summer is now nigh at hand.
31 So likewise ye, when ye see these things come to pass, know ye that the
kingdom of God is nigh at hand.
32 Verily I say unto you, This generation shall not pass away, till all be fulfilled.
33 Heaven and earth shall pass away: but my words shall not pass away.
34 And take heed to yourselves, lest at any time your hearts be overcharged
with surfeiting, and drunkenness, and cares of this life, and *so* that day come
upon you unawares.

35 For as a snare shall it come on all them that dwell on the face of the whole
earth.
36 Watch ye therefore, and pray always, that ye may be accounted worthy to
escape all these things that shall come to pass, and to stand before the Son of
man.
37 And in the day time he was teaching in the temple; and at night he went
out, and abode in the mount that is called *the mount* of Olives.
38 And all the people came early in the morning to him in the temple, for to
hear him.

The Jews Conspire against Jesus

22 Now the feast of unleavened bread drew nigh, which is called the
Passover.
2 And the chief priests and scribes sought how they might kill him; for they
feared the people.
3 Then entered Satan into Judas surnamed Iscariot, being of the number of
the twelve.
4 And he went his way, and communed with the chief priests and captains,
how he might betray him unto them.
5 And they were glad, and covenanted to give him money.
6 And he promised, and sought opportunity to betray him unto them in the
absence of the multitude.

The Apostles Prepare the Passover

7 Then came the day of unleavened bread, when the passover must be killed.
8 And he sent Peter and John, saying, Go and prepare us the passover, that
we may eat.
9 And they said unto him, Where wilt thou that we prepare?
10 And he said unto them, Behold, when ye are entered into the city, there
shall a man meet you, bearing a pitcher of water; follow him into the house
where he entereth in.
11 And ye shall say unto the goodman of the house, The Master saith unto thee,
Where is the guestchamber, where I shall eat the passover with my disciples?
12 And he shall shew you a large upper room furnished: there make ready.
13 And they went, and found as he had said unto them: and they made ready
the passover.
14 And when the hour was come, he sat down, and the twelve apostles with
him.
15 And he said unto them, With desire I have desired to eat this passover with
you before I suffer:
16 For I say unto you, I will not any more eat thereof, until it be fulfilled in
the kingdom of God.
17 And he took the cup, and gave thanks, and said, Take this, and divide *it*
among yourselves:
18 For I say unto you, I will not drink of the fruit of the vine, until the king-
dom of God shall come.
19 And he took bread, and gave thanks, and brake *it*, and gave unto them,
saying, This is my body which is given for you: this do in remembrance of me.
20 Likewise also the cup after supper, saying, This cup *is* the new testament
in my blood, which is shed for you.

Jesus Knows His Traitor

21 But, behold, the hand of him that betrayeth me *is* with me on the table.
22 And truly the Son of man goeth, as it was determined: but woe unto that
man by whom he is betrayed!
23 And they began to enquire among themselves, which of them it was that
should do this thing.

An Argument about Greatness

24 And there was also a strife among them, which of them should be account-
ed the greatest.
25 And he said unto them, The kings of the Gentiles exercise lordship over
them; and they that exercise authority upon them are called benefactors.
26 But ye *shall* not *be* so: but he that is greatest among you, let him be as the
younger; and he that is chief, as he that doth serve.
27 For whether *is* greater, he that sitteth at meat, or he that serveth? *is* not
he that sitteth at meat? but I am among you as he that serveth.
28 Ye are they which have continued with me in my temptations.
29 And I appoint unto you a kingdom, as my Father hath appointed unto me;
30 That ye may eat and drink at my table in my kingdom, and sit on thrones
judging the twelve tribes of Israel.

Jesus Predicts Peter's Denial

31 And the Lord said, Simon, Simon, behold, Satan hath desired *to have* you,
that he may sift *you* as wheat:
32 But I have prayed for thee, that thy faith fail not: and when thou art con-
verted, strengthen thy brethren.
33 And he said unto him, Lord, I am ready to go with thee, both into prison,
and to death.
34 And he said, I tell thee, Peter, the cock shall not crow this day, before that
thou shalt thrice deny that thou knowest me.
35 And he said unto them, When I sent you without purse, and scrip, and
shoes, lacked ye any thing? And they said, Nothing.
36 Then said he unto them, But now, he that hath a purse, let him take *it*, and
likewise *his* scrip: and he that hath no sword, let him sell his garment, and buy
one.
37 For I say unto you, that this that is written must yet be accomplished in
me, And he was reckoned among the transgressors: for the things concerning
me have an end.
38 And they said, Lord, behold, here *are* two swords. And he said unto them,
It is enough.

Jesus Prays in Gethsemane

39 And he came out, and went, as he was wont, to the mount of Olives; and
his disciples also followed him.
40 And when he was at the place, he said unto them, Pray that ye enter not
into temptation.
41 And he was withdrawn from them about a stone's cast, and kneeled down,
and prayed,
42 Saying, Father, if thou be willing, remove this cup from me: nevertheless
not my will, but thine, be done.
43 And there appeared an angel unto him from heaven, strengthening him.
44 And being in an agony he prayed more earnestly: and his sweat was as it
were great drops of blood falling down to the ground.
45 And when he rose up from prayer, and was come to his disciples, he found
them sleeping for sorrow,
46 And said unto them, Why sleep ye? rise and pray, lest ye enter into temp-
tation.

Jesus Is Betrayed with a Kiss

47 And while he yet spake, behold a multitude, and he that was called Judas,
one of the twelve, went before them, and drew near unto Jesus to kiss him.
48 But Jesus said unto him, Judas, betrayest thou the Son of man with a kiss?
49 When they which were about him saw what would follow, they said unto
him, Lord, shall we smite with the sword?

50 And one of them smote the servant of the high priest, and cut off his right
ear.
51 And Jesus answered and said, Suffer ye thus far. And he touched his ear,
and healed him.
52 Then Jesus said unto the chief priests, and captains of the temple, and the
elders, which were come to him, Be ye come out, as against a thief, with swords
and staves?
53 When I was daily with you in the temple, ye stretched forth no hands
against me: but this is your hour, and the power of darkness.

Jesus Is Denied by Peter

54 Then took they him, and led *him*, and brought him into the high priest's
house. And Peter followed afar off.
55 And when they had kindled a fire in the midst of the hall, and were set
down together, Peter sat down among them.
56 But a certain maid beheld him as he sat by the fire, and earnestly looked
upon him, and said, This man was also with him.
57 And he denied him, saying, Woman, I know him not.
58 And after a little while another saw him, and said, Thou art also of them.
And Peter said, Man, I am not.
59 And about the space of one hour after another confidently affirmed, say-
ing, Of a truth this *fellow* also was with him: for he is a Galilaean.
60 And Peter said, Man, I know not what thou sayest. And immediately, while
he yet spake, the cock crew.
61 And the Lord turned, and looked upon Peter. And Peter remembered the
word of the Lord, how he had said unto him, Before the cock crow, thou shalt
deny me thrice.
62 And Peter went out, and wept bitterly.

The Trial by the Jewish Council

63 And the men that held Jesus mocked him, and smote *him*.
64 And when they had blindfolded him, they struck him on the face, and
asked him, saying, Prophesy, who is it that smote thee?
65 And many other things blasphemously spake they against him.
66 And as soon as it was day, the elders of the people and the chief priests and
the scribes came together, and led him into their council, saying,
67 Art thou the Christ? tell us. And he said unto them, If I tell you, ye will not
believe:
68 And if I also ask *you*, ye will not answer me, nor let *me* go.
69 Hereafter shall the Son of man sit on the right hand of the power of God.
70 Then said they all, Art thou then the Son of God? And he said unto them,
Ye say that I am.
71 And they said, What need we any further witness? for we ourselves have
heard of his own mouth.

Pilate Questions Jesus

23 And the whole multitude of them arose, and led him unto Pilate.
2 And they began to accuse him, saying, We found this *fellow* pervert-
ing the nation, and forbidding to give tribute to Caesar, saying that he himself
is Christ a King.
3 And Pilate asked him, saying, Art thou the King of the Jews? And he
answered him and said, Thou sayest *it*.
4 Then said Pilate to the chief priests and *to* the people, I find no fault in this
man.

Jesus before Herod

5 And they were the more fierce, saying, He stirreth up the people, teaching
throughout all Jewry, beginning from Galilee to this place.

6 When Pilate heard of Galilee, he asked whether the man were a Galilaean.
7 And as soon as he knew that he belonged unto Herod's jurisdiction, he sent
him to Herod, who himself also was at Jerusalem at that time.
8 And when Herod saw Jesus, he was exceeding glad: for he was desirous to
see him of a long *season*, because he had heard many things of him; and he
hoped to have seen some miracle done by him.
9 Then he questioned with him in many words; but he answered him nothing.
10 And the chief priests and scribes stood and vehemently accused him.
11 And Herod with his men of war set him at nought, and mocked *him*, and
arrayed him in a gorgeous robe, and sent him again to Pilate.
12 And the same day Pilate and Herod were made friends together: for before
they were at enmity between themselves.

The Crowd Rejects Jesus

13 And Pilate, when he had called together the chief priests and the rulers
and the people,
14 Said unto them, Ye have brought this man unto me, as one that perverteth
the people: and, behold, I, having examined *him* before you, have found no
fault in this man touching those things whereof ye accuse him:
15 No, nor yet Herod: for I sent you to him; and, lo, nothing worthy of death
is done unto him.
16 I will therefore chastise him, and release *him*.
17 (For of necessity he must release one unto them at the feast.)
18 And they cried out all at once, saying, Away with this *man*, and release
unto us Barabbas:
19 (Who for a certain sedition made in the city, and for murder, was cast into
prison.)
20 Pilate therefore, willing to release Jesus, spake again to them.
21 But they cried, saying, Crucify *him*, crucify him.
22 And he said unto them the third time, Why, what evil hath he done? I have
found no cause of death in him: I will therefore chastise him, and let *him* go.
23 And they were instant with loud voices, requiring that he might be cru-
cified. And the voices of them and of the chief priests prevailed.
24 And Pilate gave sentence that it should be as they required.
25 And he released unto them him that for sedition and murder was cast
into prison, whom they had desired; but he delivered Jesus to their will.

Jesus Is Led Away to be Crucified

26 And as they led him away, they laid hold upon one Simon, a Cyrenian,
coming out of the country, and on him they laid the cross, that he might bear
it after Jesus.
27 And there followed him a great company of people, and of women, which
also bewailed and lamented him.
28 But Jesus turning unto them said, Daughters of Jerusalem, weep not for
me, but weep for yourselves, and for your children.
29 For, behold, the days are coming, in the which they shall say, Blessed *are* the
barren, and the wombs that never bare, and the paps which never gave suck.
30 Then shall they begin to say to the mountains, Fall on us; and to the hills,
Cover us.
31 For if they do these things in a green tree, what shall be done in the dry?
32 And there were also two other, malefactors, led with him to be put to death.
33 And when they were come to the place, which is called Calvary, there they
crucified him, and the malefactors, one on the right hand, and the other on
the left.
34 Then said Jesus, Father, forgive them; for they know not what they do. And
they parted his raiment, and cast lots.

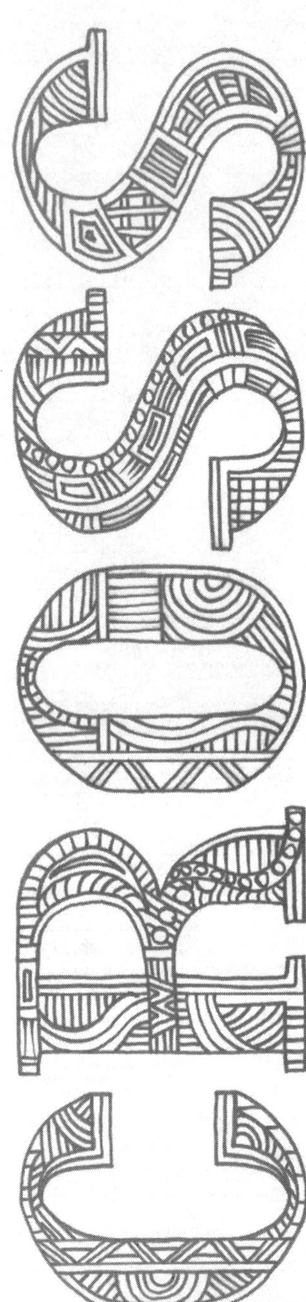

35 And the people stood beholding. And the rulers also with them derided
him, saying, He saved others; let him save himself, if he be Christ, the chosen
of God.
36 And the soldiers also mocked him, coming to him, and offering him vin-
egar,
37 And saying, If thou be the king of the Jews, save thyself.
38 And a superscription also was written over him in letters of Greek, and
Latin, and Hebrew, THIS IS THE KING OF THE JEWS.

The Criminal Believes

39 And one of the malefactors which were hanged railed on him, saying, If
thou be Christ, save thyself and us.
40 But the other answering rebuked him, saying, Dost not thou fear God,
seeing thou art in the same condemnation?
41 And we indeed justly; for we receive the due reward of our deeds: but this
man hath done nothing amiss.
42 And he said unto Jesus, Lord, remember me when thou comest into thy
kingdom.
43 And Jesus said unto him, Verily I say unto thee, To day shalt thou be with
me in paradise.

Jesus Dies on the Cross

44 And it was about the sixth hour, and there was a darkness over all the earth
until the ninth hour.
45 And the sun was darkened, and the veil of the temple was rent in the midst.
46 And when Jesus had cried with a loud voice, he said, Father, into thy hands
I commend my spirit: and having said thus, he gave up the ghost.
47 Now when the centurion saw what was done, he glorified God, saying,
Certainly this was a righteous man.
48 And all the people that came together to that sight, beholding the things
which were done, smote their breasts, and returned.
49 And all his acquaintance, and the women that followed him from Galilee,
stood afar off, beholding these things.

Jesus Is Buried

50 And, behold, *there was* a man named Joseph, a counsellor; *and he was* a
good man, and a just:
51 (The same had not consented to the counsel and deed of them;) *he was* of
Arimathaea, a city of the Jews: who also himself waited for the kingdom of
God.
52 This *man* went unto Pilate, and begged the body of Jesus.
53 And he took it down, and wrapped it in linen, and laid it in a sepulchre
that was hewn in stone, wherein never man before was laid.
54 And that day was the preparation, and the sabbath drew on.
55 And the women also, which came with him from Galilee, followed after,
and beheld the sepulchre, and how his body was laid.
56 And they returned, and prepared spices and ointments; and rested the
sabbath day according to the commandment.

Jesus' Resurrection

24 Now upon the first *day* of the week, very early in the morning, they
came unto the sepulchre, bringing the spices which they had pre-
pared, and certain *others* with them.
2 And they found the stone rolled away from the sepulchre.
3 And they entered in, and found not the body of the Lord Jesus.
4 And it came to pass, as they were much perplexed thereabout, behold, two
men stood by them in shining garments:
5 And as they were afraid, and bowed down *their* faces to the earth, they said
unto them, Why seek ye the living among the dead?

6 He is not here, but is risen: remember how he spake unto you when he was
yet in Galilee,
7 Saying, The Son of man must be delivered into the hands of sinful men,
and be crucified, and the third day rise again.
8 And they remembered his words,
9 And returned from the sepulchre, and told all these things unto the eleven,
and to all the rest.
10 It was Mary Magdalene, and Joanna, and Mary *the mother* of James, and
other *women that were* with them, which told these things unto the apostles.
11 And their words seemed to them as idle tales, and they believed them not.
12 Then arose Peter, and ran unto the sepulchre; and stooping down, he
beheld the linen clothes laid by themselves, and departed, wondering in him-
self at that which was come to pass.

Jesus Appears on the Road to Emmaus

13 And, behold, two of them went that same day to a village called Emmaus,
which was from Jerusalem *about* threescore furlongs.
14 And they talked together of all these things which had happened.
15 And it came to pass, that, while they communed *together* and reasoned,
Jesus himself drew near, and went with them.
16 But their eyes were holden that they should not know him.
17 And he said unto them, What manner of communications *are* these that
ye have one to another, as ye walk, and are sad?
18 And the one of them, whose name was Cleopas, answering said unto him,
Art thou only a stranger in Jerusalem, and hast not known the things which
are come to pass there in these days?
19 And he said unto them, What things? And they said unto him, Concerning
Jesus of Nazareth, which was a prophet mighty in deed and word before God
and all the people:
20 And how the chief priests and our rulers delivered him to be condemned
to death, and have crucified him.
21 But we trusted that it had been he which should have redeemed Israel:
and beside all this, to day is the third day since these things were done.
22 Yea, and certain women also of our company made us astonished, which
were early at the sepulchre;
23 And when they found not his body, they came, saying, that they had also
seen a vision of angels, which said that he was alive.
24 And certain of them which were with us went to the sepulchre, and found
it even so as the women had said: but him they saw not.
25 Then he said unto them, O fools, and slow of heart to believe all that the
prophets have spoken:
26 Ought not Christ to have suffered these things, and to enter into his glory?
27 And beginning at Moses and all the prophets, he expounded unto them
in all the scriptures the things concerning himself.
28 And they drew nigh unto the village, whither they went: and he made as
though he would have gone further.
29 But they constrained him, saying, Abide with us: for it is toward evening,
and the day is far spent. And he went in to tarry with them.
30 And it came to pass, as he sat at meat with them, he took bread, and bless-
ed *it*, and brake, and gave to them.
31 And their eyes were opened, and they knew him; and he vanished out of
their sight.
32 And they said one to another, Did not our heart burn within us, while he
talked with us by the way, and while he opened to us the scriptures?
33 And they rose up the same hour, and returned to Jerusalem, and found
the eleven gathered together, and them that were with them,

34 Saying, The Lord is risen indeed, and hath appeared to Simon.
35 And they told what things *were done* in the way, and how he was known
of them in breaking of bread.

Jesus Appears to the Apostles

36 And as they thus spake, Jesus himself stood in the midst of them, and saith
unto them, Peace *be* unto you.
37 But they were terrified and affrighted, and supposed that they had seen
a spirit.
38 And he said unto them, Why are ye troubled? and why do thoughts arise
in your hearts?
39 Behold my hands and my feet, that it is I myself: handle me, and see; for a
spirit hath not flesh and bones, as ye see me have.
40 And when he had thus spoken, he shewed them *his* hands and *his* feet.
41 And while they yet believed not for joy, and wondered, he said unto them,
Have ye here any meat?
42 And they gave him a piece of a broiled fish, and of an honeycomb.
43 And he took *it*, and did eat before them.
44 And he said unto them, These *are* the words which I spake unto you, while
I was yet with you, that all things must be fulfilled, which were written in the
law of Moses, and *in* the prophets, and *in* the psalms, concerning me.
45 Then opened he their understanding, that they might understand the
scriptures,
46 And said unto them, Thus it is written, and thus it behoved Christ to suf-
fer, and to rise from the dead the third day:
47 And that repentance and remission of sins should be preached in his name
among all nations, beginning at Jerusalem.
48 And ye are witnesses of these things.
49 And, behold, I send the promise of my Father upon you: but tarry ye in
the city of Jerusalem, until ye be endued with power from on high.
50 And he led them out as far as to Bethany, and he lifted up his hands, and
blessed them.
51 And it came to pass, while he blessed them, he was parted from them, and
carried up into heaven.
52 And they worshipped him, and returned to Jerusalem with great joy:
53 And were continually in the temple, praising and blessing God. Amen.

SAINT JOHN

The Word Becomes Human

1 In the beginning was the Word, and the Word was with God, and the Word was God.
2 The same was in the beginning with God.
3 All things were made by him; and without him was not any thing made that was made.
4 In him was life; and the life was the light of men.
5 And the light shineth in darkness; and the darkness comprehended it not.
6 There was a man sent from God, whose name *was* John.
7 The same came for a witness, to bear witness of the Light, that all *men* through him might believe.
8 He was not that Light, but *was sent* to bear witness of that Light.
9 *That* was the true Light, which lighteth every man that cometh into the world.
10 He was in the world, and the world was made by him, and the world knew him not.
11 He came unto his own, and his own received him not.
12 But as many as received him, to them gave he power to become the sons of God, *even* to them that believe on his name:
13 Which were born, not of blood, nor of the will of the flesh, nor of the will of man, but of God.
14 And the Word was made flesh, and dwelt among us, (and we beheld his glory, the glory as of the only begotten of the Father,) full of grace and truth.

John's Testimony Concerning Christ

15 John bare witness of him, and cried, saying, This was he of whom I spake, He that cometh after me is preferred before me: for he was before me.
16 And of his fulness have all we received, and grace for grace.
17 For the law was given by Moses, *but* grace and truth came by Jesus Christ.
18 No man hath seen God at any time; the only begotten Son, which is in the bosom of the Father, he hath declared *him*.
19 And this is the record of John, when the Jews sent priests and Levites from Jerusalem to ask him, Who art thou?
20 And he confessed, and denied not; but confessed, I am not the Christ.
21 And they asked him, What then? Art thou Elias? And he saith, I am not. Art thou that prophet? And he answered, No.
22 Then said they unto him, Who art thou? that we may give an answer to them that sent us. What sayest thou of thyself?
23 He said, I *am* the voice of one crying in the wilderness, Make straight the way of the Lord, as said the prophet Esaias.
24 And they which were sent were of the Pharisees.
25 And they asked him, and said unto him, Why baptizest thou then, if thou be not that Christ, nor Elias, neither that prophet?
26 John answered them, saying, I baptize with water: but there standeth one among you, whom ye know not;
27 He it is, who coming after me is preferred before me, whose shoe's latchet I am not worthy to unloose.
28 These things were done in Bethabara beyond Jordan, where John was baptizing.

29 The next day John seeth Jesus coming unto him, and saith, Behold the
Lamb of God, which taketh away the sin of the world.
30 This is he of whom I said, After me cometh a man which is preferred before
me: for he was before me.
31 And I knew him not: but that he should be made manifest to Israel, there-
fore am I come baptizing with water.
32 And John bare record, saying, I saw the Spirit descending from heaven
like a dove, and it abode upon him.
33 And I knew him not: but he that sent me to baptize with water, the same
said unto me, Upon whom thou shalt see the Spirit descending, and remaining
on him, the same is he which baptizeth with the Holy Ghost.
34 And I saw, and bare record that this is the Son of God.

The First Disciples

35 Again the next day after John stood, and two of his disciples;
36 And looking upon Jesus as he walked, he saith, Behold the Lamb of God!
37 And the two disciples heard him speak, and they followed Jesus.
38 Then Jesus turned, and saw them following, and saith unto them, What
seek ye? They said unto him, Rabbi, (which is to say, being interpreted, Master,)
where dwellest thou?
39 He saith unto them, Come and see. They came and saw where he dwelt,
and abode with him that day: for it was about the tenth hour.
40 One of the two which heard John *speak*, and followed him, was Andrew,
Simon Peter's brother.
41 He first findeth his own brother Simon, and saith unto him, We have
found the Messias, which is, being interpreted, the Christ.
42 And he brought him to Jesus. And when Jesus beheld him, he said, Thou
art Simon the son of Jona: thou shalt be called Cephas, which is by interpre-
tation, A stone.
43 The day following Jesus would go forth into Galilee, and findeth Philip,
and saith unto him, Follow me.
44 Now Philip was of Bethsaida, the city of Andrew and Peter.
45 Philip findeth Nathanael, and saith unto him, We have found him, of
whom Moses in the law, and the prophets, did write, Jesus of Nazareth, the
son of Joseph.
46 And Nathanael said unto him, Can there any good thing come out of
Nazareth? Philip saith unto him, Come and see.
47 Jesus saw Nathanael coming to him, and saith of him, Behold an Israelite
indeed, in whom is no guile!
48 Nathanael saith unto him, Whence knowest thou me? Jesus answered
and said unto him, Before that Philip called thee, when thou wast under the
fig tree, I saw thee.
49 Nathanael answered and saith unto him, Rabbi, thou art the Son of God;
thou art the King of Israel.
50 Jesus answered and said unto him, Because I said unto thee, I saw thee
under the fig tree, believest thou? thou shalt see greater things than these.
51 And he saith unto him, Verily, verily, I say unto you, Hereafter ye shall see
heaven open, and the angels of God ascending and descending upon the Son
of man.

Jesus Turns Water into Wine

2 And the third day there was a marriage in Cana of Galilee; and the mother
of Jesus was there:
2 And both Jesus was called, and his disciples, to the marriage.
3 And when they wanted wine, the mother of Jesus saith unto him, They have
no wine.

4 Jesus saith unto her, Woman, what have I to do with thee? mine hour is
not yet come.
5 His mother saith unto the servants, Whatsoever he saith unto you, do *it*.
6 And there were set there six waterpots of stone, after the manner of the
purifying of the Jews, containing two or three firkins apiece.
7 Jesus saith unto them, Fill the waterpots with water. And they filled them
up to the brim.
8 And he saith unto them, Draw out now, and bear unto the governor of the
feast. And they bare *it*.
9 When the ruler of the feast had tasted the water that was made wine, and
knew not whence it was: (but the servants which drew the water knew;) the
governor of the feast called the bridegroom,
10 And saith unto him, Every man at the beginning doth set forth good wine;
and when men have well drunk, then that which is worse: *but* thou hast kept
the good wine until now.
11 This beginning of miracles did Jesus in Cana of Galilee, and manifested
forth his glory; and his disciples believed on him.

Jesus Throws Moneychangers out of the Temple

12 After this he went down to Capernaum, he, and his mother, and his breth-
ren, and his disciples: and they continued there not many days.
13 And the Jews' passover was at hand, and Jesus went up to Jerusalem,
14 And found in the temple those that sold oxen and sheep and doves, and
the changers of money sitting:
15 And when he had made a scourge of small cords, he drove them all out of
the temple, and the sheep, and the oxen; and poured out the changers' money,
and overthrew the tables;
16 And said unto them that sold doves, Take these things hence; make not
my Father's house an house of merchandise.
17 And his disciples remembered that it was written, The zeal of thine house
hath eaten me up.
18 Then answered the Jews and said unto him, What sign shewest thou unto
us, seeing that thou doest these things?
19 Jesus answered and said unto them, Destroy this temple, and in three days
I will raise it up.
20 Then said the Jews, Forty and six years was this temple in building, and
wilt thou rear it up in three days?
21 But he spake of the temple of his body.
22 When therefore he was risen from the dead, his disciples remembered
that he had said this unto them; and they believed the scripture, and the word
which Jesus had said.
23 Now when he was in Jerusalem at the passover, in the feast *day*, many
believed in his name, when they saw the miracles which he did.
24 But Jesus did not commit himself unto them, because he knew all *men*,
25 And needed not that any should testify of man: for he knew what was in
man.

Jesus and Nicodemus

3 There was a man of the Pharisees, named Nicodemus, a ruler of the Jews:
2 The same came to Jesus by night, and said unto him, Rabbi, we know
that thou art a teacher come from God: for no man can do these miracles that
thou doest, except God be with him.
3 Jesus answered and said unto him, Verily, verily, I say unto thee, Except a
man be born again, he cannot see the kingdom of God.
4 Nicodemus saith unto him, How can a man be born when he is old? can
he enter the second time into his mother's womb, and be born?

5 Jesus answered, Verily, verily, I say unto thee, Except a man be born of water
and *of* the Spirit, he cannot enter into the kingdom of God.
6 That which is born of the flesh is flesh; and that which is born of the Spirit
is spirit.
7 Marvel not that I said unto thee, Ye must be born again.
8 The wind bloweth where it listeth, and thou hearest the sound thereof, but
canst not tell whence it cometh, and whither it goeth: so is every one that is
born of the Spirit.
9 Nicodemus answered and said unto him, How can these things be?
10 Jesus answered and said unto him, Art thou a master of Israel, and know-
est not these things?
11 Verily, verily, I say unto thee, We speak that we do know, and testify that
we have seen; and ye receive not our witness.
12 If I have told you earthly things, and ye believe not, how shall ye believe,
if I tell you *of* heavenly things?
13 And no man hath ascended up to heaven, but he that came down from
heaven, *even* the Son of man which is in heaven.
14 And as Moses lifted up the serpent in the wilderness, even so must the Son
of man be lifted up:
15 That whosoever believeth in him should not perish, but have eternal life.
16 For God so loved the world, that he gave his only begotten Son, that who-
soever believeth in him should not perish, but have everlasting life.
17 For God sent not his Son into the world to condemn the world; but that
the world through him might be saved.
18 He that believeth on him is not condemned: but he that believeth not is
condemned already, because he hath not believed in the name of the only
begotten Son of God.
19 And this is the condemnation, that light is come into the world, and men
loved darkness rather than light, because their deeds were evil.
20 For every one that doeth evil hateth the light, neither cometh to the light,
lest his deeds should be reproved.
21 But he that doeth truth cometh to the light, that his deeds may be made
manifest, that they are wrought in God.

John the Baptist and Jesus

22 After these things came Jesus and his disciples into the land of Judaea; and
there he tarried with them, and baptized.
23 And John also was baptizing in Aenon near to Salim, because there was
much water there: and they came, and were baptized.
24 For John was not yet cast into prison.
25 Then there arose a question between *some* of John's disciples and the Jews
about purifying.
26 And they came unto John, and said unto him, Rabbi, he that was with thee
beyond Jordan, to whom thou barest witness, behold, the same baptizeth, and
all *men* come to him.
27 John answered and said, A man can receive nothing, except it be given
him from heaven.
28 Ye yourselves bear me witness, that I said, I am not the Christ, but that I
am sent before him.
29 He that hath the bride is the bridegroom: but the friend of the bride-
groom, which standeth and heareth him, rejoiceth greatly because of the
bridegroom's voice: this my joy therefore is fulfilled.
30 He must increase, but I *must* decrease.
31 He that cometh from above is above all: he that is of the earth is earthly,
and speaketh of the earth: he that cometh from heaven is above all.

INRI
FOR GOD SO LOVED THE WORLD, THAT HE GAVE HIS ONLY BEGOTTEN SON, THAT WHOSOEVER BELIEVETH IN HIM SHOULD NOT PERISH, BUT HAVE EVERLASTING LIFE.
SAINT JOHN 3:16

32 And what he hath seen and heard, that he testifieth; and no man receiveth
his testimony.
33 He that hath received his testimony hath set to his seal that God is true.
34 For he whom God hath sent speaketh the words of God: for God giveth
not the Spirit by measure *unto him*.
35 The Father loveth the Son, and hath given all things into his hand.
36 He that believeth on the Son hath everlasting life: and he that believeth
not the Son shall not see life; but the wrath of God abideth on him.

Jesus Talks with a Samaritan Woman

4 When therefore the Lord knew how the Pharisees had heard that Jesus
made and baptized more disciples than John,
2 (Though Jesus himself baptized not, but his disciples,)
3 He left Judaea, and departed again into Galilee.
4 And he must needs go through Samaria.
5 Then cometh he to a city of Samaria, which is called Sychar, near to the
parcel of ground that Jacob gave to his son Joseph.
6 Now Jacob's well was there. Jesus therefore, being wearied with *his* journey,
sat thus on the well: *and* it was about the sixth hour.
7 There cometh a woman of Samaria to draw water: Jesus saith unto her, Give
me to drink.
8 (For his disciples were gone away unto the city to buy meat.)
9 Then saith the woman of Samaria unto him, How is it that thou, being a
Jew, askest drink of me, which am a woman of Samaria? for the Jews have no
dealings with the Samaritans.
10 Jesus answered and said unto her, If thou knewest the gift of God, and
who it is that saith to thee, Give me to drink; thou wouldest have asked of him,
and he would have given thee living water.
11 The woman saith unto him, Sir, thou hast nothing to draw with, and the
well is deep: from whence then hast thou that living water?
12 Art thou greater than our father Jacob, which gave us the well, and drank
thereof himself, and his children, and his cattle?
13 Jesus answered and said unto her, Whosoever drinketh of this water shall
thirst again:
14 But whosoever drinketh of the water that I shall give him shall never thirst;
but the water that I shall give him shall be in him a well of water springing up
into everlasting life.
15 The woman saith unto him, Sir, give me this water, that I thirst not, neither
come hither to draw.
16 Jesus saith unto her, Go, call thy husband, and come hither.
17 The woman answered and said, I have no husband. Jesus said unto her,
Thou hast well said, I have no husband:
18 For thou hast had five husbands; and he whom thou now hast is not thy
husband: in that saidst thou truly.
19 The woman saith unto him, Sir, I perceive that thou art a prophet.
20 Our fathers worshipped in this mountain; and ye say, that in Jerusalem
is the place where men ought to worship.
21 Jesus saith unto her, Woman, believe me, the hour cometh, when ye shall
neither in this mountain, nor yet at Jerusalem, worship the Father.
22 Ye worship ye know not what: we know what we worship: for salvation is
of the Jews.
23 But the hour cometh, and now is, when the true worshippers shall worship
the Father in spirit and in truth: for the Father seeketh such to worship him.
24 God *is* a Spirit: and they that worship him must worship *him* in spirit and
in truth.

25 The woman saith unto him, I know that Messias cometh, which is called
Christ: when he is come, he will tell us all things.
26 Jesus saith unto her, I that speak unto thee am *he*.
27 And upon this came his disciples, and marvelled that he talked with the
woman: yet no man said, What seekest thou? or, Why talkest thou with her?
28 The woman then left her waterpot, and went her way into the city, and
saith to the men,
29 Come, see a man, which told me all things that ever I did: is not this the
Christ?
30 Then they went out of the city, and came unto him.
31 In the mean while his disciples prayed him, saying, Master, eat.
32 But he said unto them, I have meat to eat that ye know not of.
33 Therefore said the disciples one to another, Hath any man brought him
ought to eat?
34 Jesus saith unto them, My meat is to do the will of him that sent me, and
to finish his work.
35 Say not ye, There are yet four months, and *then* cometh harvest? behold,
I say unto you, Lift up your eyes, and look on the fields; for they are white
already to harvest.
36 And he that reapeth receiveth wages, and gathereth fruit unto life eternal:
that both he that soweth and he that reapeth may rejoice together.
37 And herein is that saying true, One soweth, and another reapeth.
38 I sent you to reap that whereon ye bestowed no labour: other men
laboured, and ye are entered into their labours.
39 And many of the Samaritans of that city believed on him for the saying of
the woman, which testified, He told me all that ever I did.
40 So when the Samaritans were come unto him, they besought him that he
would tarry with them: and he abode there two days.
41 And many more believed because of his own word;
42 And said unto the woman, Now we believe, not because of thy saying: for
we have heard *him* ourselves, and know that this is indeed the Christ, the
Saviour of the world.

Jesus Heals a Nobleman's Son

43 Now after two days he departed thence, and went into Galilee.
44 For Jesus himself testified, that a prophet hath no honour in his own
country.
45 Then when he was come into Galilee, the Galilaeans received him, having
seen all the things that he did at Jerusalem at the feast: for they also went unto
the feast.
46 So Jesus came again into Cana of Galilee, where he made the water wine.
And there was a certain nobleman, whose son was sick at Capernaum.
47 When he heard that Jesus was come out of Judaea into Galilee, he went
unto him, and besought him that he would come down, and heal his son: for
he was at the point of death.
48 Then said Jesus unto him, Except ye see signs and wonders, ye will not
believe.
49 The nobleman saith unto him, Sir, come down ere my child die.
50 Jesus saith unto him, Go thy way; thy son liveth. And the man believed the
word that Jesus had spoken unto him, and he went his way.
51 And as he was now going down, his servants met him, and told *him*, saying,
Thy son liveth.
52 Then enquired he of them the hour when he began to amend. And they
said unto him, Yesterday at the seventh hour the fever left him.
53 So the father knew that *it was* at the same hour, in the which Jesus said
unto him, Thy son liveth: and himself believed, and his whole house.

54 This *is* again the second miracle *that* Jesus did, when he was come out of
Judaea into Galilee.

Jesus Heals a Lame Man at Bethesda Pool

5 After this there was a feast of the Jews; and Jesus went up to Jerusalem.
2 Now there is at Jerusalem by the sheep *market* a pool, which is called
in the Hebrew tongue Bethesda, having five porches.
3 In these lay a great multitude of impotent folk, of blind, halt, withered,
waiting for the moving of the water.
4 For an angel went down at a certain season into the pool, and troubled the
water: whosoever then first after the troubling of the water stepped in was
made whole of whatsoever disease he had.
5 And a certain man was there, which had an infirmity thirty and eight years.
6 When Jesus saw him lie, and knew that he had been now a long time *in
that case*, he saith unto him, Wilt thou be made whole?
7 The impotent man answered him, Sir, I have no man, when the water is
troubled, to put me into the pool: but while I am coming, another steppeth
down before me.
8 Jesus saith unto him, Rise, take up thy bed, and walk.
9 And immediately the man was made whole, and took up his bed, and
walked: and on the same day was the sabbath.
10 The Jews therefore said unto him that was cured, It is the sabbath day: it
is not lawful for thee to carry *thy* bed.
11 He answered them, He that made me whole, the same said unto me, Take
up thy bed, and walk.
12 Then asked they him, What man is that which said unto thee, Take up thy
bed, and walk?
13 And he that was healed wist not who it was: for Jesus had conveyed himself
away, a multitude being in *that* place.
14 Afterward Jesus findeth him in the temple, and said unto him, Behold,
thou art made whole: sin no more, lest a worse thing come unto thee.
15 The man departed, and told the Jews that it was Jesus, which had made
him whole.
16 And therefore did the Jews persecute Jesus, and sought to slay him, because
he had done these things on the sabbath day.

Jesus Is One with the Father

17 But Jesus answered them, My Father worketh hitherto, and I work.
18 Therefore the Jews sought the more to kill him, because he not only had
broken the sabbath, but said also that God was his Father, making himself
equal with God.
19 Then answered Jesus and said unto them, Verily, verily, I say unto you, The
Son can do nothing of himself, but what he seeth the Father do: for what things
soever he doeth, these also doeth the Son likewise.
20 For the Father loveth the Son, and sheweth him all things that himself
doeth: and he will shew him greater works than these, that ye may marvel.
21 For as the Father raiseth up the dead, and quickeneth *them*; even so the
Son quickeneth whom he will.
22 For the Father judgeth no man, but hath committed all judgment unto
the Son:
23 That all *men* should honour the Son, even as they honour the Father. He
that honoureth not the Son honoureth not the Father which hath sent him.
24 Verily, verily, I say unto you, He that heareth my word, and believeth on
him that sent me, hath everlasting life, and shall not come into condemnation;
but is passed from death unto life.
25 Verily, verily, I say unto you, The hour is coming, and now is, when the
dead shall hear the voice of the Son of God: and they that hear shall live.

26 For as the Father hath life in himself; so hath he given to the Son to have
life in himself;
27 And hath given him authority to execute judgment also, because he is the
Son of man.
28 Marvel not at this: for the hour is coming, in the which all that are in the
graves shall hear his voice,
29 And shall come forth; they that have done good, unto the resurrection of
life; and they that have done evil, unto the resurrection of damnation.
30 I can of mine own self do nothing: as I hear, I judge: and my judgment is
just; because I seek not mine own will, but the will of the Father which hath
sent me.
31 If I bear witness of myself, my witness is not true.
32 There is another that beareth witness of me; and I know that the witness
which he witnesseth of me is true.
33 Ye sent unto John, and he bare witness unto the truth.
34 But I receive not testimony from man: but these things I say, that ye might
be saved.
35 He was a burning and a shining light: and ye were willing for a season to
rejoice in his light.
36 But I have greater witness than *that* of John: for the works which the
Father hath given me to finish, the same works that I do, bear witness of me,
that the Father hath sent me.
37 And the Father himself, which hath sent me, hath borne witness of me.
Ye have neither heard his voice at any time, nor seen his shape.
38 And ye have not his word abiding in you: for whom he hath sent, him ye
believe not.
39 Search the scriptures; for in them ye think ye have eternal life: and they
are they which testify of me.
40 And ye will not come to me, that ye might have life.
41 I receive not honour from men.
42 But I know you, that ye have not the love of God in you.
43 I am come in my Father's name, and ye receive me not: if another shall
come in his own name, him ye will receive.
44 How can ye believe, which receive honour one of another, and seek not
the honour that *cometh* from God only?
45 Do not think that I will accuse you to the Father: there is *one* that accuseth
you, *even* Moses, in whom ye trust.
46 For had ye believed Moses, ye would have believed me: for he wrote of me.
47 But if ye believe not his writings, how shall ye believe my words?

Jesus Feeds More Than Five Thousand

6 After these things Jesus went over the sea of Galilee, which is *the sea* of
Tiberias.
2 And a great multitude followed him, because they saw his miracles which
he did on them that were diseased.
3 And Jesus went up into a mountain, and there he sat with his disciples.
4 And the passover, a feast of the Jews, was nigh.
5 When Jesus then lifted up *his* eyes, and saw a great company come unto
him, he saith unto Philip, Whence shall we buy bread, that these may eat?
6 And this he said to prove him: for he himself knew what he would do.
7 Philip answered him, Two hundred pennyworth of bread is not sufficient
for them, that every one of them may take a little.
8 One of his disciples, Andrew, Simon Peter's brother, saith unto him,
9 There is a lad here, which hath five barley loaves, and two small fishes: but
what are they among so many?

10 And Jesus said, Make the men sit down. Now there was much grass in the
place. So the men sat down, in number about five thousand.
11 And Jesus took the loaves; and when he had given thanks, he distributed
to the disciples, and the disciples to them that were set down; and likewise of
the fishes as much as they would.
12 When they were filled, he said unto his disciples, Gather up the fragments
that remain, that nothing be lost.
13 Therefore they gathered *them* together, and filled twelve baskets with the
fragments of the five barley loaves, which remained over and above unto them
that had eaten.
14 Then those men, when they had seen the miracle that Jesus did, said, This
is of a truth that prophet that should come into the world.
15 When Jesus therefore perceived that they would come and take him by
force, to make him a king, he departed again into a mountain himself alone.

Jesus Walks on the Sea

16 And when even was *now* come, his disciples went down unto the sea,
17 And entered into a ship, and went over the sea toward Capernaum. And
it was now dark, and Jesus was not come to them.
18 And the sea arose by reason of a great wind that blew.
19 So when they had rowed about five and twenty or thirty furlongs, they
see Jesus walking on the sea, and drawing nigh unto the ship: and they were
afraid.
20 But he saith unto them, It is I; be not afraid.
21 Then they willingly received him into the ship: and immediately the ship
was at the land whither they went.

Jesus Is the Bread of Life

22 The day following, when the people which stood on the other side of the
sea saw that there was none other boat there, save that one whereinto his
disciples were entered, and that Jesus went not with his disciples into the boat,
but *that* his disciples were gone away alone;
23 (Howbeit there came other boats from Tiberias nigh unto the place where
they did eat bread, after that the Lord had given thanks:)
24 When the people therefore saw that Jesus was not there, neither his dis-
ciples, they also took shipping, and came to Capernaum, seeking for Jesus.
25 And when they had found him on the other side of the sea, they said unto
him, Rabbi, when camest thou hither?
26 Jesus answered them and said, Verily, verily, I say unto you, Ye seek me,
not because ye saw the miracles, but because ye did eat of the loaves, and were
filled.
27 Labour not for the meat which perisheth, but for that meat which
endureth unto everlasting life, which the Son of man shall give unto you: for
him hath God the Father sealed.
28 Then said they unto him, What shall we do, that we might work the works
of God?
29 Jesus answered and said unto them, This is the work of God, that ye believe
on him whom he hath sent.
30 They said therefore unto him, What sign shewest thou then, that we may
see, and believe thee? what dost thou work?
31 Our fathers did eat manna in the desert; as it is written, He gave them
bread from heaven to eat.
32 Then Jesus said unto them, Verily, verily, I say unto you, Moses gave you
not that bread from heaven; but my Father giveth you the true bread from
heaven.
33 For the bread of God is he which cometh down from heaven, and giveth
life unto the world.

34 Then said they unto him, Lord, evermore give us this bread.
35 And Jesus said unto them, I am the bread of life: he that cometh to me
shall never hunger; and he that believeth on me shall never thirst.
36 But I said unto you, That ye also have seen me, and believe not.
37 All that the Father giveth me shall come to me; and him that cometh to
me I will in no wise cast out.
38 For I came down from heaven, not to do mine own will, but the will of
him that sent me.
39 And this is the Father's will which hath sent me, that of all which he hath
given me I should lose nothing, but should raise it up again at the last day.
40 And this is the will of him that sent me, that every one which seeth the
Son, and believeth on him, may have everlasting life: and I will raise him up
at the last day.
41 The Jews then murmured at him, because he said, I am the bread which
came down from heaven.
42 And they said, Is not this Jesus, the son of Joseph, whose father and moth-
er we know? how is it then that he saith, I came down from heaven?
43 Jesus therefore answered and said unto them, Murmur not among your-
selves.
44 No man can come to me, except the Father which hath sent me draw him:
and I will raise him up at the last day.
45 It is written in the prophets, And they shall be all taught of God. Every man
therefore that hath heard, and hath learned of the Father, cometh unto me.
46 Not that any man hath seen the Father, save he which is of God, he hath
seen the Father.
47 Verily, verily, I say unto you, He that believeth on me hath everlasting life.
48 I am that bread of life.
49 Your fathers did eat manna in the wilderness, and are dead.
50 This is the bread which cometh down from heaven, that a man may eat
thereof, and not die.
51 I am the living bread which came down from heaven: if any man eat of
this bread, he shall live for ever: and the bread that I will give is my flesh, which
I will give for the life of the world.
52 The Jews therefore strove among themselves, saying, How can this man
give us *his* flesh to eat?
53 Then Jesus said unto them, Verily, verily, I say unto you, Except ye eat the
flesh of the Son of man, and drink his blood, ye have no life in you.
54 Whoso eateth my flesh, and drinketh my blood, hath eternal life; and I
will raise him up at the last day.
55 For my flesh is meat indeed, and my blood is drink indeed.
56 He that eateth my flesh, and drinketh my blood, dwelleth in me, and I in
him.
57 As the living Father hath sent me, and I live by the Father: so he that eateth
me, even he shall live by me.
58 This is that bread which came down from heaven: not as your fathers did
eat manna, and are dead: he that eateth of this bread shall live for ever.
59 These things said he in the synagogue, as he taught in Capernaum.
60 Many therefore of his disciples, when they had heard *this*, said, This is an
hard saying; who can hear it?
61 When Jesus knew in himself that his disciples murmured at it, he said
unto them, Doth this offend you?
62 *What* and if ye shall see the Son of man ascend up where he was before?
63 It is the spirit that quickeneth; the flesh profiteth nothing: the words that
I speak unto you, *they* are spirit, and *they* are life.
64 But there are some of you that believe not. For Jesus knew from the begin-
ning who they were that believed not, and who should betray him.

65 And he said, Therefore said I unto you, that no man can come unto me,
except it were given unto him of my Father.
66 From that *time* many of his disciples went back, and walked no more with
him.
67 Then said Jesus unto the twelve, Will ye also go away?
68 Then Simon Peter answered him, Lord, to whom shall we go? thou hast
the words of eternal life.
69 And we believe and are sure that thou art that Christ, the Son of the living
God.
70 Jesus answered them, Have not I chosen you twelve, and one of you is a
devil?
71 He spake of Judas Iscariot *the son* of Simon: for he it was that should betray
him, being one of the twelve.

Jesus Teaches at the Feast of Tabernacles

7 After these things Jesus walked in Galilee: for he would not walk in Jewry,
because the Jews sought to kill him.
2 Now the Jews' feast of tabernacles was at hand.
3 His brethren therefore said unto him, Depart hence, and go into Judaea,
that thy disciples also may see the works that thou doest.
4 For *there is* no man *that* doeth any thing in secret, and he himself seeketh
to be known openly. If thou do these things, shew thyself to the world.
5 For neither did his brethren believe in him.
6 Then Jesus said unto them, My time is not yet come: but your time is alway
ready.
7 The world cannot hate you; but me it hateth, because I testify of it, that the
works thereof are evil.
8 Go ye up unto this feast: I go not up yet unto this feast; for my time is not
yet full come.
9 When he had said these words unto them, he abode *still* in Galilee.
10 But when his brethren were gone up, then went he also up unto the feast,
not openly, but as it were in secret.
11 Then the Jews sought him at the feast, and said, Where is he?
12 And there was much murmuring among the people concerning him: for
some said, He is a good man: others said, Nay; but he deceiveth the people.
13 Howbeit no man spake openly of him for fear of the Jews.
14 Now about the midst of the feast Jesus went up into the temple, and taught.
15 And the Jews marvelled, saying, How knoweth this man letters, having
never learned?
16 Jesus answered them, and said, My doctrine is not mine, but his that sent me.
17 If any man will do his will, he shall know of the doctrine, whether it be of
God, or *whether* I speak of myself.
18 He that speaketh of himself seeketh his own glory: but he that seeketh his
glory that sent him, the same is true, and no unrighteousness is in him.
19 Did not Moses give you the law, and *yet* none of you keepeth the law? Why
go ye about to kill me?
20 The people answered and said, Thou hast a devil: who goeth about to kill
thee?
21 Jesus answered and said unto them, I have done one work, and ye all marvel.
22 Moses therefore gave unto you circumcision; (not because it is of Moses,
but of the fathers;) and ye on the sabbath day circumcise a man.
23 If a man on the sabbath day receive circumcision, that the law of Moses
should not be broken; are ye angry at me, because I have made a man every
whit whole on the sabbath day?
24 Judge not according to the appearance, but judge righteous judgment.

25 Then said some of them of Jerusalem, Is not this he, whom they seek to
kill?
26 But, lo, he speaketh boldly, and they say nothing unto him. Do the rulers
know indeed that this is the very Christ?
27 Howbeit we know this man whence he is: but when Christ cometh, no
man knoweth whence he is.
28 Then cried Jesus in the temple as he taught, saying, Ye both know me, and
ye know whence I am: and I am not come of myself, but he that sent me is true,
whom ye know not.
29 But I know him: for I am from him, and he hath sent me.
30 Then they sought to take him: but no man laid hands on him, because his
hour was not yet come.
31 And many of the people believed on him, and said, When Christ cometh,
will he do more miracles than these which this *man* hath done?
32 The Pharisees heard that the people murmured such things concerning
him; and the Pharisees and the chief priests sent officers to take him.
33 Then said Jesus unto them, Yet a little while am I with you, and *then* I go
unto him that sent me.
34 Ye shall seek me, and shall not find *me*: and where I am, *thither* ye cannot
come.
35 Then said the Jews among themselves, Whither will he go, that we shall
not find him? will he go unto the dispersed among the Gentiles, and teach the
Gentiles?
36 What *manner of* saying is this that he said, Ye shall seek me, and shall not
find *me*: and where I am, *thither* ye cannot come?
37 In the last day, that great *day* of the feast, Jesus stood and cried, saying, If
any man thirst, let him come unto me, and drink.
38 He that believeth on me, as the scripture hath said, out of his belly shall
flow rivers of living water.
39 (But this spake he of the Spirit, which they that believe on him should
receive: for the Holy Ghost was not yet *given*; because that Jesus was not yet
glorified.)
40 Many of the people therefore, when they heard this saying, said, Of a truth
this is the Prophet.
41 Others said, This is the Christ. But some said, Shall Christ come out of
Galilee?
42 Hath not the scripture said, That Christ cometh of the seed of David, and
out of the town of Beth-lehem, where David was?
43 So there was a division among the people because of him.
44 And some of them would have taken him; but no man laid hands on him.

The Pharisees Are Angry and Rebuke Nicodemus

45 Then came the officers to the chief priests and Pharisees; and they said
unto them, Why have ye not brought him?
46 The officers answered, Never man spake like this man.
47 Then answered them the Pharisees, Are ye also deceived?
48 Have any of the rulers or of the Pharisees believed on him?
49 But this people who knoweth not the law are cursed.
50 Nicodemus saith unto them, (he that came to Jesus by night, being one of
them,)
51 Doth our law judge *any* man, before it hear him, and know what he doeth?
52 They answered and said unto him, Art thou also of Galilee? Search, and
look: for out of Galilee ariseth no prophet.
53 And every man went unto his own house.

Christ Frees the Woman Taken in Adultery

8 Jesus went unto the mount of Olives.
2 And early in the morning he came again into the temple, and all the
people came unto him; and he sat down, and taught them.
3 And the scribes and Pharisees brought unto him a woman taken in adul-
tery; and when they had set her in the midst,
4 They say unto him, Master, this woman was taken in adultery, in the very
act.
5 Now Moses in the law commanded us, that such should be stoned: but
what sayest thou?
6 This they said, tempting him, that they might have to accuse him. But Jesus
stooped down, and with *his* finger wrote on the ground, *as though he heard
them not.*
7 So when they continued asking him, he lifted up himself, and said unto
them, He that is without sin among you, let him first cast a stone at her.
8 And again he stooped down, and wrote on the ground.
9 And they which heard *it*, being convicted by *their own* conscience, went
out one by one, beginning at the eldest, *even* unto the last: and Jesus was left
alone, and the woman standing in the midst.
10 When Jesus had lifted up himself, and saw none but the woman, he said
unto her, Woman, where are those thine accusers? hath no man condemned
thee?
11 She said, No man, Lord. And Jesus said unto her, Neither do I condemn
thee: go, and sin no more.

Jesus Is the Light of the World

12 Then spake Jesus again unto them, saying, I am the light of the world: he
that followeth me shall not walk in darkness, but shall have the light of life.
13 The Pharisees therefore said unto him, Thou bearest record of thyself; thy
record is not true.
14 Jesus answered and said unto them, Though I bear record of myself, *yet*
my record is true: for I know whence I came, and whither I go; but ye cannot
tell whence I come, and whither I go.
15 Ye judge after the flesh; I judge no man.
16 And yet if I judge, my judgment is true: for I am not alone, but I and the
Father that sent me.
17 It is also written in your law, that the testimony of two men is true.
18 I am one that bear witness of myself, and the Father that sent me beareth
witness of me.
19 Then said they unto him, Where is thy Father? Jesus answered, Ye neither
know me, nor my Father: if ye had known me, ye should have known my Father
also.
20 These words spake Jesus in the treasury, as he taught in the temple: and
no man laid hands on him; for his hour was not yet come.
21 Then said Jesus again unto them, I go my way, and ye shall seek me, and
shall die in your sins: whither I go, ye cannot come.
22 Then said the Jews, Will he kill himself? because he saith, Whither I go,
ye cannot come.
23 And he said unto them, Ye are from beneath; I am from above: ye are of
this world; I am not of this world.
24 I said therefore unto you, that ye shall die in your sins: for if ye believe not
that I am *he*, ye shall die in your sins.
25 Then said they unto him, Who art thou? And Jesus saith unto them, Even
the same that I said unto you from the beginning.
26 I have many things to say and to judge of you: but he that sent me is true;
and I speak to the world those things which I have heard of him.

27 They understood not that he spake to them of the Father.
28 Then said Jesus unto them, When ye have lifted up the Son of man, then
shall ye know that I am *he*, and *that* I do nothing of myself; but as my Father
hath taught me, I speak these things.
29 And he that sent me is with me: the Father hath not left me alone; for I do
always those things that please him.
30 As he spake these words, many believed on him.
31 Then said Jesus to those Jews which believed on him, If ye continue in my
word, *then* are ye my disciples indeed;
32 And ye shall know the truth, and the truth shall make you free.
33 They answered him, We be Abraham's seed, and were never in bondage
to any man: how sayest thou, Ye shall be made free?
34 Jesus answered them, Verily, verily, I say unto you, Whosoever committeth
sin is the servant of sin.
35 And the servant abideth not in the house for ever: *but* the Son abideth
ever.
36 If the Son therefore shall make you free, ye shall be free indeed.
37 I know that ye are Abraham's seed; but ye seek to kill me, because my word
hath no place in you.
38 I speak that which I have seen with my Father: and ye do that which ye
have seen with your father.
39 They answered and said unto him, Abraham is our father. Jesus saith unto
them, If ye were Abraham's children, ye would do the works of Abraham.
40 But now ye seek to kill me, a man that hath told you the truth, which I
have heard of God: this did not Abraham.
41 Ye do the deeds of your father. Then said they to him, We be not born of
fornication; we have one Father, *even* God.
42 Jesus said unto them, If God were your Father, ye would love me: for I
proceeded forth and came from God; neither came I of myself, but he sent me.
43 Why do ye not understand my speech? *even* because ye cannot hear my
word.
44 Ye are of *your* father the devil, and the lusts of your father ye will do. He
was a murderer from the beginning, and abode not in the truth, because there
is no truth in him. When he speaketh a lie, he speaketh of his own: for he is a
liar, and the father of it.
45 And because I tell *you* the truth, ye believe me not.
46 Which of you convinceth me of sin? And if I say the truth, why do ye not
believe me?
47 He that is of God heareth God's words: ye therefore hear *them* not, because
ye are not of God.
48 Then answered the Jews, and said unto him, Say we not well that thou art
a Samaritan, and hast a devil?
49 Jesus answered, I have not a devil; but I honour my Father, and ye do
dishonour me.
50 And I seek not mine own glory: there is one that seeketh and judgeth.
51 Verily, verily, I say unto you, If a man keep my saying, he shall never see
death.
52 Then said the Jews unto him, Now we know that thou hast a devil. Abraham
is dead, and the prophets; and thou sayest, If a man keep my saying, he shall
never taste of death.
53 Art thou greater than our father Abraham, which is dead? and the proph-
ets are dead: whom makest thou thyself?
54 Jesus answered, If I honour myself, my honour is nothing: it is my Father
that honoureth me; of whom ye say, that he is your God:
55 Yet ye have not known him; but I know him: and if I should say, I know
him not, I shall be a liar like unto you: but I know him, and keep his saying.

56 Your father Abraham rejoiced to see my day: and he saw *it*, and was glad.
57 Then said the Jews unto him, Thou art not yet fifty years old, and hast thou
seen Abraham?
58 Jesus said unto them, Verily, verily, I say unto you, Before Abraham was, I am.
59 Then took they up stones to cast at him: but Jesus hid himself, and went
out of the temple, going through the midst of them, and so passed by.

Jesus Heals a Blind Man

9 And as *Jesus* passed by, he saw a man which was blind from *his* birth.
2 And his disciples asked him, saying, Master, who did sin, this man, or
his parents, that he was born blind?
3 Jesus answered, Neither hath this man sinned, nor his parents: but that
the works of God should be made manifest in him.
4 I must work the works of him that sent me, while it is day: the night com-
eth, when no man can work.
5 As long as I am in the world, I am the light of the world.
6 When he had thus spoken, he spat on the ground, and made clay of the
spittle, and he anointed the eyes of the blind man with the clay,
7 And said unto him, Go, wash in the pool of Siloam, (which is by interpre-
tation, Sent.) He went his way therefore, and washed, and came seeing.
8 The neighbours therefore, and they which before had seen him that he was
blind, said, Is not this he that sat and begged?
9 Some said, This is he: others *said*, He is like him: *but* he said, I am *he*.
10 Therefore said they unto him, How were thine eyes opened?
11 He answered and said, A man that is called Jesus made clay, and anointed
mine eyes, and said unto me, Go to the pool of Siloam, and wash: and I went
and washed, and I received sight.
12 Then said they unto him, Where is he? He said, I know not.
13 They brought to the Pharisees him that aforetime was blind.
14 And it was the sabbath day when Jesus made the clay, and opened his eyes.
15 Then again the Pharisees also asked him how he had received his sight.
He said unto them, He put clay upon mine eyes, and I washed, and do see.
16 Therefore said some of the Pharisees, This man is not of God, because he
keepeth not the sabbath day. Others said, How can a man that is a sinner do
such miracles? And there was a division among them.
17 They say unto the blind man again, What sayest thou of him, that he hath
opened thine eyes? He said, He is a prophet.
18 But the Jews did not believe concerning him, that he had been blind, and
received his sight, until they called the parents of him that had received his
sight.
19 And they asked them, saying, Is this your son, who ye say was born blind?
how then doth he now see?
20 His parents answered them and said, We know that this is our son, and
that he was born blind:
21 But by what means he now seeth, we know not; or who hath opened his
eyes, we know not: he is of age; ask him: he shall speak for himself.
22 These *words* spake his parents, because they feared the Jews: for the Jews
had agreed already, that if any man did confess that he was Christ, he should
be put out of the synagogue.
23 Therefore said his parents, He is of age; ask him.
24 Then again called they the man that was blind, and said unto him, Give
God the praise: we know that this man is a sinner.
25 He answered and said, Whether he be a sinner *or no*, I know not: one thing
I know, that, whereas I was blind, now I see.
26 Then said they to him again, What did he to thee? how opened he thine
eyes?

27 He answered them, I have told you already, and ye did not hear: wherefore
would ye hear *it* again? will ye also be his disciples?
28 Then they reviled him, and said, Thou art his disciple; but we are Moses'
disciples.
29 We know that God spake unto Moses: *as for* this *fellow*, we know not from
whence he is.
30 The man answered and said unto them, Why herein is a marvellous thing,
that ye know not from whence he is, and *yet* he hath opened mine eyes.
31 Now we know that God heareth not sinners: but if any man be a worship-
per of God, and doeth his will, him he heareth.
32 Since the world began was it not heard that any man opened the eyes of
one that was born blind.
33 If this man were not of God, he could do nothing.
34 They answered and said unto him, Thou wast altogether born in sins, and
dost thou teach us? And they cast him out.
35 Jesus heard that they had cast him out; and when he had found him, he
said unto him, Dost thou believe on the Son of God?
36 He answered and said, Who is he, Lord, that I might believe on him?
37 And Jesus said unto him, Thou hast both seen him, and it is he that talketh
with thee.
38 And he said, Lord, I believe. And he worshipped him.
39 And Jesus said, For judgment I am come into this world, that they which
see not might see; and that they which see might be made blind.
40 And *some* of the Pharisees which were with him heard these words, and
said unto him, Are we blind also?
41 Jesus said unto them, If ye were blind, ye should have no sin: but now ye
say, We see; therefore your sin remaineth.

Jesus Is the Good Shepherd

10 Verily, verily, I say unto you, He that entereth not by the door into
the sheepfold, but climbeth up some other way, the same is a thief
and a robber.
2 But he that entereth in by the door is the shepherd of the sheep.
3 To him the porter openeth; and the sheep hear his voice: and he calleth his
own sheep by name, and leadeth them out.
4 And when he putteth forth his own sheep, he goeth before them, and the
sheep follow him: for they know his voice.
5 And a stranger will they not follow, but will flee from him: for they know
not the voice of strangers.
6 This parable spake Jesus unto them: but they understood not what things
they were which he spake unto them.
7 Then said Jesus unto them again, Verily, verily, I say unto you, I am the door
of the sheep.
8 All that ever came before me are thieves and robbers: but the sheep did not
hear them.
9 I am the door: by me if any man enter in, he shall be saved, and shall go in
and out, and find pasture.
10 The thief cometh not, but for to steal, and to kill, and to destroy: I am come
that they might have life, and that they might have *it* more abundantly.
11 I am the good shepherd: the good shepherd giveth his life for the sheep.
12 But he that is an hireling, and not the shepherd, whose own the sheep are
not, seeth the wolf coming, and leaveth the sheep, and fleeth: and the wolf
catcheth them, and scattereth the sheep.
13 The hireling fleeth, because he is an hireling, and careth not for the sheep.
14 I am the good shepherd, and know my *sheep*, and am known of mine.
15 As the Father knoweth me, even so know I the Father: and I lay down my
life for the sheep.

16 And other sheep I have, which are not of this fold: them also I must bring,
and they shall hear my voice; and there shall be one fold, *and* one shepherd.
17 Therefore doth my Father love me, because I lay down my life, that I might
take it again.
18 No man taketh it from me, but I lay it down of myself. I have power to lay
it down, and I have power to take it again. This commandment have I received
of my Father.
19 There was a division therefore again among the Jews for these sayings.
20 And many of them said, He hath a devil, and is mad; why hear ye him?
21 Others said, These are not the words of him that hath a devil. Can a devil
open the eyes of the blind?

Many Jews Reject Jesus

22 And it was at Jerusalem the feast of the dedication, and it was winter.
23 And Jesus walked in the temple in Solomon's porch.
24 Then came the Jews round about him, and said unto him, How long dost
thou make us to doubt? If thou be the Christ, tell us plainly.
25 Jesus answered them, I told you, and ye believed not: the works that I do
in my Father's name, they bear witness of me.
26 But ye believe not, because ye are not of my sheep, as I said unto you.
27 My sheep hear my voice, and I know them, and they follow me:
28 And I give unto them eternal life; and they shall never perish, neither shall
any *man* pluck them out of my hand.
29 My Father, which gave *them* me, is greater than all; and no *man* is able to
pluck *them* out of my Father's hand.
30 I and *my* Father are one.
31 Then the Jews took up stones again to stone him.
32 Jesus answered them, Many good works have I shewed you from my
Father; for which of those works do ye stone me?
33 The Jews answered him, saying, For a good work we stone thee not; but
for blasphemy; and because that thou, being a man, makest thyself God.
34 Jesus answered them, Is it not written in your law, I said, Ye are gods?
35 If he called them gods, unto whom the word of God came, and the scrip-
ture cannot be broken;
36 Say ye of him, whom the Father hath sanctified, and sent into the world,
Thou blasphemest; because I said, I am the Son of God?
37 If I do not the works of my Father, believe me not.
38 But if I do, though ye believe not me, believe the works: that ye may know,
and believe, that the Father *is* in me, and I in him.
39 Therefore they sought again to take him: but he escaped out of their hand,
40 And went away again beyond Jordan into the place where John at first
baptized; and there he abode.
41 And many resorted unto him, and said, John did no miracle: but all things
that John spake of this man were true.
42 And many believed on him there.

Jesus Raises Lazarus from the Dead

11 Now a certain *man* was sick, *named* Lazarus, of Bethany, the town
of Mary and her sister Martha.
2 (It was *that* Mary which anointed the Lord with ointment, and wiped his
feet with her hair, whose brother Lazarus was sick.)
3 Therefore his sisters sent unto him, saying, Lord, behold, he whom thou
lovest is sick.
4 When Jesus heard *that*, he said, This sickness is not unto death, but for the
glory of God, that the Son of God might be glorified thereby.
5 Now Jesus loved Martha, and her sister, and Lazarus.
6 When he had heard therefore that he was sick, he abode two days still in
the same place where he was.

7 Then after that saith he to *his* disciples, Let us go into Judaea again.
8 *His* disciples say unto him, Master, the Jews of late sought to stone thee;
and goest thou thither again?
9 Jesus answered, Are there not twelve hours in the day? If any man walk in
the day, he stumbleth not, because he seeth the light of this world.
10 But if a man walk in the night, he stumbleth, because there is no light in
him.
11 These things said he: and after that he saith unto them, Our friend Lazarus
sleepeth; but I go, that I may awake him out of sleep.
12 Then said his disciples, Lord, if he sleep, he shall do well.
13 Howbeit Jesus spake of his death: but they thought that he had spoken of
taking of rest in sleep.
14 Then said Jesus unto them plainly, Lazarus is dead.
15 And I am glad for your sakes that I was not there, to the intent ye may
believe; nevertheless let us go unto him.
16 Then said Thomas, which is called Didymus, unto his fellowdisciples, Let
us also go, that we may die with him.
17 Then when Jesus came, he found that he had *lain* in the grave four days
already.
18 Now Bethany was nigh unto Jerusalem, about fifteen furlongs off:
19 And many of the Jews came to Martha and Mary, to comfort them con-
cerning their brother.
20 Then Martha, as soon as she heard that Jesus was coming, went and met
him: but Mary sat *still* in the house.
21 Then said Martha unto Jesus, Lord, if thou hadst been here, my brother
had not died.
22 But I know, that even now, whatsoever thou wilt ask of God, God will give
it thee.
23 Jesus saith unto her, Thy brother shall rise again.
24 Martha saith unto him, I know that he shall rise again in the resurrection
at the last day.
25 Jesus said unto her, I am the resurrection, and the life: he that believeth
in me, though he were dead, yet shall he live:
26 And whosoever liveth and believeth in me shall never die. Believest thou
this?
27 She saith unto him, Yea, Lord: I believe that thou art the Christ, the Son
of God, which should come into the world.
28 And when she had so said, she went her way, and called Mary her sister
secretly, saying, The Master is come, and calleth for thee.
29 As soon as she heard *that*, she arose quickly, and came unto him.
30 Now Jesus was not yet come into the town, but was in that place where
Martha met him.
31 The Jews then which were with her in the house, and comforted her, when
they saw Mary, that she rose up hastily and went out, followed her, saying, She
goeth unto the grave to weep there.
32 Then when Mary was come where Jesus was, and saw him, she fell down
at his feet, saying unto him, Lord, if thou hadst been here, my brother had not
died.
33 When Jesus therefore saw her weeping, and the Jews also weeping which
came with her, he groaned in the spirit, and was troubled,
34 And said, Where have ye laid him? They said unto him, Lord, come and
see.
35 Jesus wept.
36 Then said the Jews, Behold how he loved him!
37 And some of them said, Could not this man, which opened the eyes of the
blind, have caused that even this man should not have died?

38 Jesus therefore again groaning in himself cometh to the grave. It was a
cave, and a stone lay upon it.
39 Jesus said, Take ye away the stone. Martha, the sister of him that was dead,
saith unto him, Lord, by this time he stinketh: for he hath been *dead* four days.
40 Jesus saith unto her, Said I not unto thee, that, if thou wouldest believe,
thou shouldest see the glory of God?
41 Then they took away the stone *from the place* where the dead was laid. And
Jesus lifted up *his* eyes, and said, Father, I thank thee that thou hast heard me.
42 And I knew that thou hearest me always: but because of the people which
stand by I said *it*, that they may believe that thou hast sent me.
43 And when he thus had spoken, he cried with a loud voice, Lazarus, come
forth.
44 And he that was dead came forth, bound hand and foot with graveclothes:
and his face was bound about with a napkin. Jesus saith unto them, Loose him,
and let him go.

The Jewish Council Plots to Kill Jesus

45 Then many of the Jews which came to Mary, and had seen the things which
Jesus did, believed on him.
46 But some of them went their ways to the Pharisees, and told them what
things Jesus had done.
47 Then gathered the chief priests and the Pharisees a council, and said, What
do we? for this man doeth many miracles.
48 If we let him thus alone, all *men* will believe on him: and the Romans shall
come and take away both our place and nation.
49 And one of them, *named* Caiaphas, being the high priest that same year,
said unto them, Ye know nothing at all,
50 Nor consider that it is expedient for us, that one man should die for the
people, and that the whole nation perish not.
51 And this spake he not of himself: but being high priest that year, he proph-
esied that Jesus should die for that nation;
52 And not for that nation only, but that also he should gather together in
one the children of God that were scattered abroad.
53 Then from that day forth they took counsel together for to put him to
death.
54 Jesus therefore walked no more openly among the Jews; but went thence
unto a country near to the wilderness, into a city called Ephraim, and there
continued with his disciples.
55 And the Jews' passover was nigh at hand: and many went out of the coun-
try up to Jerusalem before the passover, to purify themselves.
56 Then sought they for Jesus, and spake among themselves, as they stood in
the temple, What think ye, that he will not come to the feast?
57 Now both the chief priests and the Pharisees had given a commandment,
that, if any man knew where he were, he should shew *it*, that they might take
him.

Mary Anoints Jesus

12 Then Jesus six days before the passover came to Bethany, where
Lazarus was which had been dead, whom he raised from the dead.
2 There they made him a supper; and Martha served: but Lazarus was one
of them that sat at the table with him.
3 Then took Mary a pound of ointment of spikenard, very costly, and anoint-
ed the feet of Jesus, and wiped his feet with her hair: and the house was filled
with the odour of the ointment.
4 Then saith one of his disciples, Judas Iscariot, Simon's *son*, which should
betray him,

5 Why was not this ointment sold for three hundred pence, and given to the
poor?
6 This he said, not that he cared for the poor; but because he was a thief, and
had the bag, and bare what was put therein.
7 Then said Jesus, Let her alone: against the day of my burying hath she kept
this.
8 For the poor always ye have with you; but me ye have not always.
9 Much people of the Jews therefore knew that he was there: and they came
not for Jesus' sake only, but that they might see Lazarus also, whom he had
raised from the dead.
10 But the chief priests consulted that they might put Lazarus also to death;
11 Because that by reason of him many of the Jews went away, and believed
on Jesus.

Jesus Rides into Jerusalem

12 On the next day much people that were come to the feast, when they heard
that Jesus was coming to Jerusalem,
13 Took branches of palm trees, and went forth to meet him, and cried,
Hosanna: Blessed *is* the King of Israel that cometh in the name of the Lord.
14 And Jesus, when he had found a young ass, sat thereon; as it is written,
15 Fear not, daughter of Sion: behold, thy King cometh, sitting on an ass's
colt.
16 These things understood not his disciples at the first: but when Jesus was
glorified, then remembered they that these things were written of him, and
that they had done these things unto him.
17 The people therefore that was with him when he called Lazarus out of his
grave, and raised him from the dead, bare record.
18 For this cause the people also met him, for that they heard that he had
done this miracle.
19 The Pharisees therefore said among themselves, Perceive ye how ye prevail
nothing? behold, the world is gone after him.

Some Greeks Desire to See Jesus

20 And there were certain Greeks among them that came up to worship at
the feast:
21 The same came therefore to Philip, which was of Bethsaida of Galilee, and
desired him, saying, Sir, we would see Jesus.
22 Philip cometh and telleth Andrew: and again Andrew and Philip tell Jesus.
23 And Jesus answered them, saying, The hour is come, that the Son of man
should be glorified.
24 Verily, verily, I say unto you, Except a corn of wheat fall into the ground
and die, it abideth alone: but if it die, it bringeth forth much fruit.
25 He that loveth his life shall lose it; and he that hateth his life in this world
shall keep it unto life eternal.
26 If any man serve me, let him follow me; and where I am, there shall also
my servant be: if any man serve me, him will *my* Father honour.
27 Now is my soul troubled; and what shall I say? Father, save me from this
hour: but for this cause came I unto this hour.
28 Father, glorify thy name. Then came there a voice from heaven, *saying*, I
have both glorified *it*, and will glorify *it* again.
29 The people therefore, that stood by, and heard *it*, said that it thundered:
others said, An angel spake to him.
30 Jesus answered and said, This voice came not because of me, but for your
sakes.
31 Now is the judgment of this world: now shall the prince of this world be
cast out.
32 And I, if I be lifted up from the earth, will draw all *men* unto me.

33 This he said, signifying what death he should die.
34 The people answered him, We have heard out of the law that Christ
abideth for ever: and how sayest thou, The Son of man must be lifted up? who
is this Son of man?
35 Then Jesus said unto them, Yet a little while is the light with you. Walk
while ye have the light, lest darkness come upon you: for he that walketh in
darkness knoweth not whither he goeth.
36 While ye have light, believe in the light, that ye may be the children of
light. These things spake Jesus, and departed, and did hide himself from them.

The Jews Are Generally Blinded

37 But though he had done so many miracles before them, yet they believed
not on him:
38 That the saying of Esaias the prophet might be fulfilled, which he spake,
Lord, who hath believed our report? and to whom hath the arm of the Lord
been revealed?
39 Therefore they could not believe, because that Esaias said again,
40 He hath blinded their eyes, and hardened their heart; that they should
not see with *their* eyes, nor understand with *their* heart, and be converted,
and I should heal them.
41 These things said Esaias, when he saw his glory, and spake of him.

Many Chief Rulers Believe, but Do Not Confess Him

42 Nevertheless among the chief rulers also many believed on him; but
because of the Pharisees they did not confess *him*, lest they should be put out
of the synagogue:
43 For they loved the praise of men more than the praise of God.

Jesus Calls All to Believe

44 Jesus cried and said, He that believeth on me, believeth not on me, but on
him that sent me.
45 And he that seeth me seeth him that sent me.
46 I am come a light into the world, that whosoever believeth on me should
not abide in darkness.
47 And if any man hear my words, and believe not, I judge him not: for I came
not to judge the world, but to save the world.
48 He that rejecteth me, and receiveth not my words, hath one that judgeth
him: the word that I have spoken, the same shall judge him in the last day.
49 For I have not spoken of myself; but the Father which sent me, he gave me
a commandment, what I should say, and what I should speak.
50 And I know that his commandment is life everlasting: whatsoever I speak
therefore, even as the Father said unto me, so I speak.

Jesus Washes the Disciples' Feet

13 Now before the feast of the passover, when Jesus knew that his hour
was come that he should depart out of this world unto the Father,
having loved his own which were in the world, he loved them unto the
end.
2 And supper being ended, the devil having now put into the heart of Judas
Iscariot, Simon's *son*, to betray him;
3 Jesus knowing that the Father had given all things into his hands, and that
he was come from God, and went to God;
4 He riseth from supper, and laid aside his garments; and took a towel, and
girded himself.
5 After that he poureth water into a bason, and began to wash the disciples'
feet, and to wipe *them* with the towel wherewith he was girded.
6 Then cometh he to Simon Peter: and Peter saith unto him, Lord, dost thou
wash my feet?

7 Jesus answered and said unto him, What I do thou knowest not now; but
thou shalt know hereafter.
8 Peter saith unto him, Thou shalt never wash my feet. Jesus answered him,
If I wash thee not, thou hast no part with me.
9 Simon Peter saith unto him, Lord, not my feet only, but also *my* hands and
my head.
10 Jesus saith to him, He that is washed needeth not save to wash *his* feet, but
is clean every whit: and ye are clean, but not all.
11 For he knew who should betray him; therefore said he, Ye are not all clean.
12 So after he had washed their feet, and had taken his garments, and was
set down again, he said unto them, Know ye what I have done to you?
13 Ye call me Master and Lord: and ye say well; for *so* I am.
14 If I then, *your* Lord and Master, have washed your feet; ye also ought to
wash one another's feet.
15 For I have given you an example, that ye should do as I have done to you.
16 Verily, verily, I say unto you, The servant is not greater than his lord; neither
he that is sent greater than he that sent him.
17 If ye know these things, happy are ye if ye do them.

Jesus Foretells His Betrayal

18 I speak not of you all: I know whom I have chosen: but that the scripture may
be fulfilled, He that eateth bread with me hath lifted up his heel against me.
19 Now I tell you before it come, that, when it is come to pass, ye may believe
that I am *he*.
20 Verily, verily, I say unto you, He that receiveth whomsoever I send receiveth
me; and he that receiveth me receiveth him that sent me.
21 When Jesus had thus said, he was troubled in spirit, and testified, and said,
Verily, verily, I say unto you, that one of you shall betray me.
22 Then the disciples looked one on another, doubting of whom he spake.
23 Now there was leaning on Jesus' bosom one of his disciples, whom Jesus
loved.
24 Simon Peter therefore beckoned to him, that he should ask who it should
be of whom he spake.
25 He then lying on Jesus' breast saith unto him, Lord, who is it?
26 Jesus answered, He it is, to whom I shall give a sop, when I have dipped *it*.
And when he had dipped the sop, he gave *it* to Judas Iscariot, *the son* of Simon.
27 And after the sop Satan entered into him. Then said Jesus unto him, That
thou doest, do quickly.
28 Now no man at the table knew for what intent he spake this unto him.
29 For some *of them* thought, because Judas had the bag, that Jesus had said
unto him, Buy *those things* that we have need of against the feast; or, that he
should give something to the poor.
30 He then having received the sop went immediately out: and it was night.

Jesus Commands the Disciples to Love

31 Therefore, when he was gone out, Jesus said, Now is the Son of man glo-
rified, and God is glorified in him.
32 If God be glorified in him, God shall also glorify him in himself, and shall
straightway glorify him.
33 Little children, yet a little while I am with you. Ye shall seek me: and as I
said unto the Jews, Whither I go, ye cannot come; so now I say to you.
34 A new commandment I give unto you, That ye love one another; as I have
loved you, that ye also love one another.
35 By this shall all *men* know that ye are my disciples, if ye have love one to
another.

LET NOT your heart be TROUBLED: YE believe IN God, BELIEVE ALSO IN me.

SAINT JOHN 14:1

Jesus Forewarns Peter of His Denial

36 Simon Peter said unto him, Lord, whither goest thou? Jesus answered
him, Whither I go, thou canst not follow me now; but thou shalt follow me
afterwards.
37 Peter said unto him, Lord, why cannot I follow thee now? I will lay down
my life for thy sake.
38 Jesus answered him, Wilt thou lay down thy life for my sake? Verily, veri-
ly, I say unto thee, The cock shall not crow, till thou hast denied me thrice.

Jesus Promises to Send the Holy Spirit

14 Let not your heart be troubled: ye believe in God, believe also in me.
2 In my Father's house are many mansions: if *it were* not *so*, I would
have told you. I go to prepare a place for you.
3 And if I go and prepare a place for you, I will come again, and receive you
unto myself; that where I am, *there* ye may be also.
4 And whither I go ye know, and the way ye know.
5 Thomas saith unto him, Lord, we know not whither thou goest; and how
can we know the way?
6 Jesus saith unto him, I am the way, the truth, and the life: no man cometh
unto the Father, but by me.
7 If ye had known me, ye should have known my Father also: and from hence-
forth ye know him, and have seen him.
8 Philip saith unto him, Lord, shew us the Father, and it sufficeth us.
9 Jesus saith unto him, Have I been so long time with you, and yet hast thou
not known me, Philip? he that hath seen me hath seen the Father; and how
sayest thou *then*, Shew us the Father?
10 Believest thou not that I am in the Father, and the Father in me? the words
that I speak unto you I speak not of myself: but the Father that dwelleth in me,
he doeth the works.
11 Believe me that I *am* in the Father, and the Father in me: or else believe
me for the very works' sake.
12 Verily, verily, I say unto you, He that believeth on me, the works that I do
shall he do also; and greater *works* than these shall he do; because I go unto
my Father.
13 And whatsoever ye shall ask in my name, that will I do, that the Father
may be glorified in the Son.
14 If ye shall ask any thing in my name, I will do *it*.
15 If ye love me, keep my commandments.
16 And I will pray the Father, and he shall give you another Comforter, that
he may abide with you for ever;
17 *Even* the Spirit of truth; whom the world cannot receive, because it seeth
him not, neither knoweth him: but ye know him; for he dwelleth with you,
and shall be in you.
18 I will not leave you comfortless: I will come to you.
19 Yet a little while, and the world seeth me no more; but ye see me: because
I live, ye shall live also.
20 At that day ye shall know that I *am* in my Father, and ye in me, and I in
you.
21 He that hath my commandments, and keepeth them, he it is that loveth
me: and he that loveth me shall be loved of my Father, and I will love him, and
will manifest myself to him.
22 Judas saith unto him, not Iscariot, Lord, how is it that thou wilt manifest
thyself unto us, and not unto the world?
23 Jesus answered and said unto him, If a man love me, he will keep my words:
and my Father will love him, and we will come unto him, and make our abode
with him.

24 He that loveth me not keepeth not my sayings: and the word which ye hear is not mine, but the Father's which sent me.

25 These things have I spoken unto you, being *yet* present with you.

26 But the Comforter, *which is* the Holy Ghost, whom the Father will send in my name, he shall teach you all things, and bring all things to your remembrance, whatsoever I have said unto you.

27 Peace I leave with you, my peace I give unto you: not as the world giveth, give I unto you. Let not your heart be troubled, neither let it be afraid.

28 Ye have heard how I said unto you, I go away, and come *again* unto you. If ye loved me, ye would rejoice, because I said, I go unto the Father: for my Father is greater than I.

29 And now I have told you before it come to pass, that, when it is come to pass, ye might believe.

30 Hereafter I will not talk much with you: for the prince of this world cometh, and hath nothing in me.

31 But that the world may know that I love the Father; and as the Father gave me commandment, even so I do. Arise, let us go hence.

Jesus Is the Vine

15 I am the true vine, and my Father is the husbandman.

2 Every branch in me that beareth not fruit he taketh away: and every *branch* that beareth fruit, he purgeth it, that it may bring forth more fruit.

3 Now ye are clean through the word which I have spoken unto you.

4 Abide in me, and I in you. As the branch cannot bear fruit of itself, except it abide in the vine; no more can ye, except ye abide in me.

5 I am the vine, ye *are* the branches: He that abideth in me, and I in him, the same bringeth forth much fruit: for without me ye can do nothing.

6 If a man abide not in me, he is cast forth as a branch, and is withered; and men gather them, and cast *them* into the fire, and they are burned.

7 If ye abide in me, and my words abide in you, ye shall ask what ye will, and it shall be done unto you.

8 Herein is my Father glorified, that ye bear much fruit; so shall ye be my disciples.

9 As the Father hath loved me, so have I loved you: continue ye in my love.

10 If ye keep my commandments, ye shall abide in my love; even as I have kept my Father's commandments, and abide in his love.

11 These things have I spoken unto you, that my joy might remain in you, and *that* your joy might be full.

12 This is my commandment, That ye love one another, as I have loved you.

13 Greater love hath no man than this, that a man lay down his life for his friends.

14 Ye are my friends, if ye do whatsoever I command you.

15 Henceforth I call you not servants; for the servant knoweth not what his lord doeth: but I have called you friends; for all things that I have heard of my Father I have made known unto you.

16 Ye have not chosen me, but I have chosen you, and ordained you, that ye should go and bring forth fruit, and *that* your fruit should remain: that whatsoever ye shall ask of the Father in my name, he may give it you.

17 These things I command you, that ye love one another.

Comfort in Persecution

18 If the world hate you, ye know that it hated me before *it hated* you.

19 If ye were of the world, the world would love his own: but because ye are not of the world, but I have chosen you out of the world, therefore the world hateth you.

20 Remember the word that I said unto you, The servant is not greater than
his lord. If they have persecuted me, they will also persecute you; if they have
kept my saying, they will keep yours also.
21 But all these things will they do unto you for my name's sake, because they
know not him that sent me.
22 If I had not come and spoken unto them, they had not had sin: but now
they have no cloke for their sin.
23 He that hateth me hateth my Father also.
24 If I had not done among them the works which none other man did, they
had not had sin: but now have they both seen and hated both me and my
Father.
25 But *this cometh to pass*, that the word might be fulfilled that is written in
their law, They hated me without a cause.

The Work of the Holy Spirit

26 But when the Comforter is come, whom I will send unto you from the
Father, *even* the Spirit of truth, which proceedeth from the Father, he shall
testify of me:
27 And ye also shall bear witness, because ye have been with me from the
beginning.

Sadness Will Turn to Joy

16 These things have I spoken unto you, that ye should not be offended.
2 They shall put you out of the synagogues: yea, the time cometh, that
whosoever killeth you will think that he doeth God service.
3 And these things will they do unto you, because they have not known the
Father, nor me.
4 But these things have I told you, that when the time shall come, ye may
remember that I told you of them. And these things I said not unto you at the
beginning, because I was with you.
5 But now I go my way to him that sent me; and none of you asketh me,
Whither goest thou?
6 But because I have said these things unto you, sorrow hath filled your heart.
7 Nevertheless I tell you the truth; It is expedient for you that I go away: for
if I go not away, the Comforter will not come unto you; but if I depart, I will
send him unto you.
8 And when he is come, he will reprove the world of sin, and of righteousness,
and of judgment:
9 Of sin, because they believe not on me;
10 Of righteousness, because I go to my Father, and ye see me no more;
11 Of judgment, because the prince of this world is judged.
12 I have yet many things to say unto you, but ye cannot bear them now.
13 Howbeit when he, the Spirit of truth, is come, he will guide you into all
truth: for he shall not speak of himself; but whatsoever he shall hear, *that* shall
he speak: and he will shew you things to come.
14 He shall glorify me: for he shall receive of mine, and shall shew *it* unto
you.
15 All things that the Father hath are mine: therefore said I, that he shall take
of mine, and shall shew *it* unto you.
16 A little while, and ye shall not see me: and again, a little while, and ye shall
see me, because I go to the Father.
17 Then said *some* of his disciples among themselves, What is this that he
saith unto us, A little while, and ye shall not see me: and again, a little while,
and ye shall see me: and, Because I go to the Father?
18 They said therefore, What is this that he saith, A little while? we cannot
tell what he saith.

19 Now Jesus knew that they were desirous to ask him, and said unto them,
Do ye enquire among yourselves of that I said, A little while, and ye shall not
see me: and again, a little while, and ye shall see me?
20 Verily, verily, I say unto you, That ye shall weep and lament, but the world
shall rejoice: and ye shall be sorrowful, but your sorrow shall be turned into
joy.
21 A woman when she is in travail hath sorrow, because her hour is come:
but as soon as she is delivered of the child, she remembereth no more the
anguish, for joy that a man is born into the world.
22 And ye now therefore have sorrow: but I will see you again, and your heart
shall rejoice, and your joy no man taketh from you.

Assurance of Answered Prayer

23 And in that day ye shall ask me nothing. Verily, verily, I say unto you,
Whatsoever ye shall ask the Father in my name, he will give *it* you.
24 Hitherto have ye asked nothing in my name: ask, and ye shall receive, that
your joy may be full.
25 These things have I spoken unto you in proverbs: but the time cometh,
when I shall no more speak unto you in proverbs, but I shall shew you plainly
of the Father.
26 At that day ye shall ask in my name: and I say not unto you, that I will pray
the Father for you:
27 For the Father himself loveth you, because ye have loved me, and have
believed that I came out from God.
28 I came forth from the Father, and am come into the world: again, I leave
the world, and go to the Father.
29 His disciples said unto him, Lo, now speakest thou plainly, and speakest
no proverb.
30 Now are we sure that thou knowest all things, and needest not that any
man should ask thee: by this we believe that thou camest forth from God.
31 Jesus answered them, Do ye now believe?
32 Behold, the hour cometh, yea, is now come, that ye shall be scattered, every
man to his own, and shall leave me alone: and yet I am not alone, because the
Father is with me.
33 These things I have spoken unto you, that in me ye might have peace. In
the world ye shall have tribulation: but be of good cheer; I have overcome the
world.

Jesus Prays for Himself, His Disciples, and His Church

17 These words spake Jesus, and lifted up his eyes to heaven, and said,
Father, the hour is come; glorify thy Son, that thy Son also may
glorify thee:
2 As thou hast given him power over all flesh, that he should give eternal life
to as many as thou hast given him.
3 And this is life eternal, that they might know thee the only true God, and
Jesus Christ, whom thou hast sent.
4 I have glorified thee on the earth: I have finished the work which thou
gavest me to do.
5 And now, O Father, glorify thou me with thine own self with the glory which
I had with thee before the world was.
6 I have manifested thy name unto the men which thou gavest me out of the
world: thine they were, and thou gavest them me; and they have kept thy word.
7 Now they have known that all things whatsoever thou hast given me are
of thee.
8 For I have given unto them the words which thou gavest me; and they have
received *them*, and have known surely that I came out from thee, and they
have believed that thou didst send me.
9 I pray for them: I pray not for the world, but for them which thou hast
given me; for they are thine.

IN THE WORLD YE SHALL HAVE tribulation: BUT BE OF good cheer; I HAVE OVERCOME the WORLD.

SAINT JOHN 16:33

10 And all mine are thine, and thine are mine; and I am glorified in them.
11 And now I am no more in the world, but these are in the world, and I come
to thee. Holy Father, keep through thine own name those whom thou hast
given me, that they may be one, as we *are*.
12 While I was with them in the world, I kept them in thy name: those that
thou gavest me I have kept, and none of them is lost, but the son of perdition;
that the scripture might be fulfilled.
13 And now come I to thee; and these things I speak in the world, that they
might have my joy fulfilled in themselves.
14 I have given them thy word; and the world hath hated them, because they
are not of the world, even as I am not of the world.
15 I pray not that thou shouldest take them out of the world, but that thou
shouldest keep them from the evil.
16 They are not of the world, even as I am not of the world.
17 Sanctify them through thy truth: thy word is truth.
18 As thou hast sent me into the world, even so have I also sent them into the
world.
19 And for their sakes I sanctify myself, that they also might be sanctified
through the truth.
20 Neither pray I for these alone, but for them also which shall believe on
me through their word;
21 That they all may be one; as thou, Father, *art* in me, and I in thee, that they
also may be one in us: that the world may believe that thou hast sent me.
22 And the glory which thou gavest me I have given them; that they may be
one, even as we are one:
23 I in them, and thou in me, that they may be made perfect in one; and that
the world may know that thou hast sent me, and hast loved them, as thou hast
loved me.
24 Father, I will that they also, whom thou hast given me, be with me where
I am; that they may behold my glory, which thou hast given me: for thou
lovedst me before the foundation of the world.
25 O righteous Father, the world hath not known thee: but I have known
thee, and these have known that thou hast sent me.
26 And I have declared unto them thy name, and will declare *it*: that the love
wherewith thou hast loved me may be in them, and I in them.

Jesus Is Arrested

18 When Jesus had spoken these words, he went forth with his disci-
ples over the brook Cedron, where was a garden, into the which he
entered, and his disciples.
2 And Judas also, which betrayed him, knew the place: for Jesus ofttimes
resorted thither with his disciples.
3 Judas then, having received a band *of men* and officers from the chief
priests and Pharisees, cometh thither with lanterns and torches and weapons.
4 Jesus therefore, knowing all things that should come upon him, went forth,
and said unto them, Whom seek ye?
5 They answered him, Jesus of Nazareth. Jesus saith unto them, I am *he*. And
Judas also, which betrayed him, stood with them.
6 As soon then as he had said unto them, I am *he*, they went backward, and
fell to the ground.
7 Then asked he them again, Whom seek ye? And they said, Jesus of Nazareth.
8 Jesus answered, I have told you that I am *he*: if therefore ye seek me, let
these go their way:
9 That the saying might be fulfilled, which he spake, Of them which thou
gavest me have I lost none.
10 Then Simon Peter having a sword drew it, and smote the high priest's
servant, and cut off his right ear. The servant's name was Malchus.

11 Then said Jesus unto Peter, Put up thy sword into the sheath: the cup which
my Father hath given me, shall I not drink it?
12 Then the band and the captain and officers of the Jews took Jesus, and
bound him,
13 And led him away to Annas first; for he was father in law to Caiaphas,
which was the high priest that same year.
14 Now Caiaphas was he, which gave counsel to the Jews, that it was expedi-
ent that one man should die for the people.

Peter Denies Jesus

15 And Simon Peter followed Jesus, and *so did* another disciple: that disciple
was known unto the high priest, and went in with Jesus into the palace of the
high priest.
16 But Peter stood at the door without. Then went out that other disciple,
which was known unto the high priest, and spake unto her that kept the door,
and brought in Peter.
17 Then saith the damsel that kept the door unto Peter, Art not thou also *one*
of this man's disciples? He saith, I am not.
18 And the servants and officers stood there, who had made a fire of coals;
for it was cold: and they warmed themselves: and Peter stood with them, and
warmed himself.

The High Priest Questions Jesus

19 The high priest then asked Jesus of his disciples, and of his doctrine.
20 Jesus answered him, I spake openly to the world; I ever taught in the syn-
agogue, and in the temple, whither the Jews always resort; and in secret have
I said nothing.
21 Why askest thou me? ask them which heard me, what I have said unto
them: behold, they know what I said.
22 And when he had thus spoken, one of the officers which stood by struck
Jesus with the palm of his hand, saying, Answerest thou the high priest so?
23 Jesus answered him, If I have spoken evil, bear witness of the evil: but if
well, why smitest thou me?
24 Now Annas had sent him bound unto Caiaphas the high priest.

Peter Denies Jesus Again

25 And Simon Peter stood and warmed himself. They said therefore unto
him, Art not thou also *one* of his disciples? He denied *it*, and said, I am not.
26 One of the servants of the high priest, being *his* kinsman whose ear Peter
cut off, saith, Did not I see thee in the garden with him?
27 Peter then denied again: and immediately the cock crew.

Pilate Questions Jesus

28 Then led they Jesus from Caiaphas unto the hall of judgment: and it was
early; and they themselves went not into the judgment hall, lest they should
be defiled; but that they might eat the passover.
29 Pilate then went out unto them, and said, What accusation bring ye against
this man?
30 They answered and said unto him, If he were not a malefactor, we would
not have delivered him up unto thee.
31 Then said Pilate unto them, Take ye him, and judge him according to your
law. The Jews therefore said unto him, It is not lawful for us to put any man to
death:
32 That the saying of Jesus might be fulfilled, which he spake, signifying what
death he should die.
33 Then Pilate entered into the judgment hall again, and called Jesus, and
said unto him, Art thou the King of the Jews?

34 Jesus answered him, Sayest thou this thing of thyself, or did others tell it
thee of me?
35 Pilate answered, Am I a Jew? Thine own nation and the chief priests have
delivered thee unto me: what hast thou done?
36 Jesus answered, My kingdom is not of this world: if my kingdom were of
this world, then would my servants fight, that I should not be delivered to the
Jews: but now is my kingdom not from hence.
37 Pilate therefore said unto him, Art thou a king then? Jesus answered, Thou
sayest that I am a king. To this end was I born, and for this cause came I into
the world, that I should bear witness unto the truth. Every one that is of the
truth heareth my voice.
38 Pilate saith unto him, What is truth? And when he had said this, he went
out again unto the Jews, and saith unto them, I find in him no fault *at all*.
39 But ye have a custom, that I should release unto you one at the passover:
will ye therefore that I release unto you the King of the Jews?
40 Then cried they all again, saying, Not this man, but Barabbas. Now
Barabbas was a robber.

Christ Is Mocked and Rejected

19 Then Pilate therefore took Jesus, and scourged *him*.
2 And the soldiers platted a crown of thorns, and put *it* on his head,
and they put on him a purple robe,
3 And said, Hail, King of the Jews! and they smote him with their hands.
4 Pilate therefore went forth again, and saith unto them, Behold, I bring him
forth to you, that ye may know that I find no fault in him.
5 Then came Jesus forth, wearing the crown of thorns, and the purple robe.
And *Pilate* saith unto them, Behold the man!
6 When the chief priests therefore and officers saw him, they cried out, say-
ing, Crucify *him*, crucify *him*. Pilate saith unto them, Take ye him, and cruci-
fy *him*: for I find no fault in him.
7 The Jews answered him, We have a law, and by our law he ought to die,
because he made himself the Son of God.
8 When Pilate therefore heard that saying, he was the more afraid;
9 And went again into the judgment hall, and saith unto Jesus, Whence art
thou? But Jesus gave him no answer.
10 Then saith Pilate unto him, Speakest thou not unto me? knowest thou not
that I have power to crucify thee, and have power to release thee?
11 Jesus answered, Thou couldest have no power *at all* against me, except it
were given thee from above: therefore he that delivered me unto thee hath
the greater sin.
12 And from thenceforth Pilate sought to release him: but the Jews cried out,
saying, If thou let this man go, thou art not Caesar's friend: whosoever maketh
himself a king speaketh against Caesar.
13 When Pilate therefore heard that saying, he brought Jesus forth, and sat
down in the judgment seat in a place that is called the Pavement, but in the
Hebrew, Gabbatha.
14 And it was the preparation of the passover, and about the sixth hour: and
he saith unto the Jews, Behold your King!
15 But they cried out, Away with *him*, away with *him*, crucify him. Pilate saith
unto them, Shall I crucify your King? The chief priests answered, We have no
king but Caesar.
16 Then delivered he him therefore unto them to be crucified. And they took
Jesus, and led *him* away.

Jesus Is Crucified

17 And he bearing his cross went forth into a place called *the place* of a skull,
which is called in the Hebrew Golgotha:

18 Where they crucified him, and two other with him, on either side one,
and Jesus in the midst.
19 And Pilate wrote a title, and put *it* on the cross. And the writing was, JESUS
OF NAZARETH THE KING OF THE JEWS.
20 This title then read many of the Jews: for the place where Jesus was cruci-
fied was nigh to the city: and it was written in Hebrew, *and* Greek, *and* Latin.
21 Then said the chief priests of the Jews to Pilate, Write not, The King of the
Jews; but that he said, I am King of the Jews.
22 Pilate answered, What I have written I have written.
23 Then the soldiers, when they had crucified Jesus, took his garments, and
made four parts, to every soldier a part; and also *his* coat: now the coat was
without seam, woven from the top throughout.
24 They said therefore among themselves, Let us not rend it, but cast lots for
it, whose it shall be: that the scripture might be fulfilled, which saith, They
parted my raiment among them, and for my vesture they did cast lots. These
things therefore the soldiers did.
25 Now there stood by the cross of Jesus his mother, and his mother's sister,
Mary the *wife* of Cleophas, and Mary Magdalene.
26 When Jesus therefore saw his mother, and the disciple standing by, whom
he loved, he saith unto his mother, Woman, behold thy son!
27 Then saith he to the disciple, Behold thy mother! And from that hour that
disciple took her unto his own *home*.

Jesus Dies on the Cross

28 After this, Jesus knowing that all things were now accomplished, that the
scripture might be fulfilled, saith, I thirst.
29 Now there was set a vessel full of vinegar: and they filled a spunge with
vinegar, and put *it* upon hyssop, and put *it* to his mouth.
30 When Jesus therefore had received the vinegar, he said, It is finished: and
he bowed his head, and gave up the ghost.
31 The Jews therefore, because it was the preparation, that the bodies should
not remain upon the cross on the sabbath day, (for that sabbath day was an
high day,) besought Pilate that their legs might be broken, and *that* they might
be taken away.
32 Then came the soldiers, and brake the legs of the first, and of the other
which was crucified with him.
33 But when they came to Jesus, and saw that he was dead already, they brake
not his legs:
34 But one of the soldiers with a spear pierced his side, and forthwith came
there out blood and water.
35 And he that saw *it* bare record, and his record is true: and he knoweth
that he saith true, that ye might believe.
36 For these things were done, that the scripture should be fulfilled, A bone
of him shall not be broken.
37 And again another scripture saith, They shall look on him whom they
pierced.

Jesus Is Buried by Joseph and Nicodemus

38 And after this Joseph of Arimathaea, being a disciple of Jesus, but secret-
ly for fear of the Jews, besought Pilate that he might take away the body of
Jesus: and Pilate gave *him* leave. He came therefore, and took the body of Jesus.
39 And there came also Nicodemus, which at the first came to Jesus by night,
and brought a mixture of myrrh and aloes, about an hundred pound *weight*.
40 Then took they the body of Jesus, and wound it in linen clothes with the
spices, as the manner of the Jews is to bury.
41 Now in the place where he was crucified there was a garden; and in the
garden a new sepulchre, wherein was never man yet laid.

42 There laid they Jesus therefore because of the Jews' preparation *day*; for the sepulchre was nigh at hand.

Jesus Is Resurrected

20 The first *day* of the week cometh Mary Magdalene early, when it was yet dark, unto the sepulchre, and seeth the stone taken away from the sepulchre.

2 Then she runneth, and cometh to Simon Peter, and to the other disciple, whom Jesus loved, and saith unto them, They have taken away the Lord out of the sepulchre, and we know not where they have laid him.

3 Peter therefore went forth, and that other disciple, and came to the sepulchre.

4 So they ran both together: and the other disciple did outrun Peter, and came first to the sepulchre.

5 And he stooping down, *and looking in*, saw the linen clothes lying; yet went he not in.

6 Then cometh Simon Peter following him, and went into the sepulchre, and seeth the linen clothes lie,

7 And the napkin, that was about his head, not lying with the linen clothes, but wrapped together in a place by itself.

8 Then went in also that other disciple, which came first to the sepulchre, and he saw, and believed.

9 For as yet they knew not the scripture, that he must rise again from the dead.

10 Then the disciples went away again unto their own home.

Jesus Appears to Mary Magdalene

11 But Mary stood without at the sepulchre weeping: and as she wept, she stooped down, *and looked* into the sepulchre,

12 And seeth two angels in white sitting, the one at the head, and the other at the feet, where the body of Jesus had lain.

13 And they say unto her, Woman, why weepest thou? She saith unto them, Because they have taken away my Lord, and I know not where they have laid him.

14 And when she had thus said, she turned herself back, and saw Jesus standing, and knew not that it was Jesus.

15 Jesus saith unto her, Woman, why weepest thou? whom seekest thou? She, supposing him to be the gardener, saith unto him, Sir, if thou have borne him hence, tell me where thou hast laid him, and I will take him away.

16 Jesus saith unto her, Mary. She turned herself, and saith unto him, Rabboni; which is to say, Master.

17 Jesus saith unto her, Touch me not; for I am not yet ascended to my Father: but go to my brethren, and say unto them, I ascend unto my Father, and your Father; and *to* my God, and your God.

18 Mary Magdalene came and told the disciples that she had seen the Lord, and *that* he had spoken these things unto her.

Jesus Appears to His Disciples

19 Then the same day at evening, being the first *day* of the week, when the doors were shut where the disciples were assembled for fear of the Jews, came Jesus and stood in the midst, and saith unto them, Peace *be* unto you.

20 And when he had so said, he shewed unto them *his* hands and his side. Then were the disciples glad, when they saw the Lord.

21 Then said Jesus to them again, Peace *be* unto you: as *my* Father hath sent me, even so send I you.

22 And when he had said this, he breathed on *them*, and saith unto them, Receive ye the Holy Ghost:

23 Whose soever sins ye remit, they are remitted unto them; *and* whose soev-
er *sins* ye retain, they are retained.

Jesus Appears to Thomas

24 But Thomas, one of the twelve, called Didymus, was not with them when
Jesus came.
25 The other disciples therefore said unto him, We have seen the Lord. But
he said unto them, Except I shall see in his hands the print of the nails, and
put my finger into the print of the nails, and thrust my hand into his side, I
will not believe.
26 And after eight days again his disciples were within, and Thomas with
them: *then* came Jesus, the doors being shut, and stood in the midst, and said,
Peace *be* unto you.
27 Then saith he to Thomas, Reach hither thy finger, and behold my hands;
and reach hither thy hand, and thrust *it* into my side: and be not faithless, but
believing.
28 And Thomas answered and said unto him, My Lord and my God.
29 Jesus saith unto him, Thomas, because thou hast seen me, thou hast
believed: blessed *are* they that have not seen, and *yet* have believed.
30 And many other signs truly did Jesus in the presence of his disciples, which
are not written in this book:
31 But these are written, that ye might believe that Jesus is the Christ, the Son
of God; and that believing ye might have life through his name.

Another Miraculous Catch of Fish

21 After these things Jesus shewed himself again to the disciples at the
sea of Tiberias; and on this wise shewed he *himself*.
2 There were together Simon Peter, and Thomas called Didymus, and
Nathanael of Cana in Galilee, and the *sons* of Zebedee, and two other of his
disciples.
3 Simon Peter saith unto them, I go a fishing. They say unto him, We also go
with thee. They went forth, and entered into a ship immediately; and that
night they caught nothing.
4 But when the morning was now come, Jesus stood on the shore: but the
disciples knew not that it was Jesus.
5 Then Jesus saith unto them, Children, have ye any meat? They answered
him, No.
6 And he said unto them, Cast the net on the right side of the ship, and ye
shall find. They cast therefore, and now they were not able to draw it for the
multitude of fishes.
7 Therefore that disciple whom Jesus loved saith unto Peter, It is the Lord.
Now when Simon Peter heard that it was the Lord, he girt *his* fisher's coat *unto*
him, (for he was naked,) and did cast himself into the sea.
8 And the other disciples came in a little ship; (for they were not far from
land, but as it were two hundred cubits,) dragging the net with fishes.
9 As soon then as they were come to land, they saw a fire of coals there, and
fish laid thereon, and bread.
10 Jesus saith unto them, Bring of the fish which ye have now caught.
11 Simon Peter went up, and drew the net to land full of great fishes, an
hundred and fifty and three: and for all there were so many, yet was not the
net broken.
12 Jesus saith unto them, Come *and* dine. And none of the disciples durst
ask him, Who art thou? knowing that it was the Lord.
13 Jesus then cometh, and taketh bread, and giveth them, and fish likewise.
14 This is now the third time that Jesus shewed himself to his disciples, after
that he was risen from the dead.

Jesus Speaks with Peter

15 So when they had dined, Jesus saith to Simon Peter, Simon, *son* of Jonas,
lovest thou me more than these? He saith unto him, Yea, Lord; thou knowest
that I love thee. He saith unto him, Feed my lambs.
16 He saith to him again the second time, Simon, *son* of Jonas, lovest thou
me? He saith unto him, Yea, Lord; thou knowest that I love thee. He saith unto
him, Feed my sheep.
17 He saith unto him the third time, Simon, *son* of Jonas, lovest thou me?
Peter was grieved because he said unto him the third time, Lovest thou me?
And he said unto him, Lord, thou knowest all things; thou knowest that I love
thee. Jesus saith unto him, Feed my sheep.
18 Verily, verily, I say unto thee, When thou wast young, thou girdedst thyself,
and walkedst whither thou wouldest: but when thou shalt be old, thou shalt
stretch forth thy hands, and another shall gird thee, and carry *thee* whither
thou wouldest not.
19 This spake he, signifying by what death he should glorify God. And when
he had spoken this, he saith unto him, Follow me.
20 Then Peter, turning about, seeth the disciple whom Jesus loved following;
which also leaned on his breast at supper, and said, Lord, which is he that
betrayeth thee?
21 Peter seeing him saith to Jesus, Lord, and what *shall* this man *do*?
22 Jesus saith unto him, If I will that he tarry till I come, what *is that* to thee?
follow thou me.
23 Then went this saying abroad among the brethren, that that disciple
should not die: yet Jesus said not unto him, He shall not die; but, If I will that
he tarry till I come, what *is that* to thee?
24 This is the disciple which testifieth of these things, and wrote these things:
and we know that his testimony is true.
25 And there are also many other things which Jesus did, the which, if they
should be written every one, I suppose that even the world itself could not
contain the books that should be written. Amen.

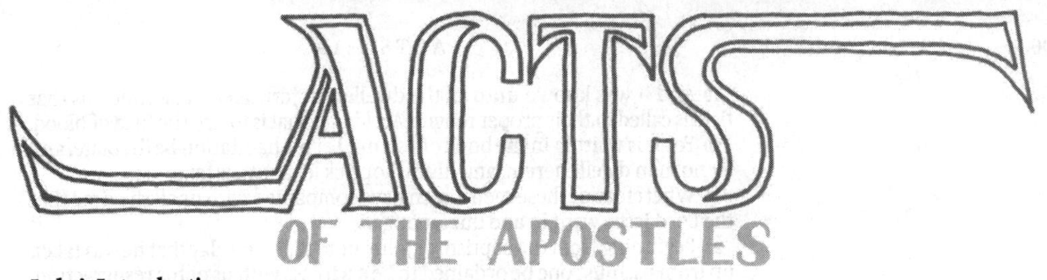

Luke's Introduction

1 The former treatise have I made, O Theophilus, of all that Jesus began both
to do and teach,
2 Until the day in which he was taken up, after that he through the Holy
Ghost had given commandments unto the apostles whom he had chosen:

Jesus Ascends to Heaven

3 To whom also he shewed himself alive after his passion by many infallible
proofs, being seen of them forty days, and speaking of the things pertaining
to the kingdom of God:
4 And, being assembled together with *them*, commanded them that they
should not depart from Jerusalem, but wait for the promise of the Father,
which, *saith he*, ye have heard of me.
5 For John truly baptized with water; but ye shall be baptized with the Holy
Ghost not many days hence.
6 When they therefore were come together, they asked of him, saying, Lord,
wilt thou at this time restore again the kingdom to Israel?
7 And he said unto them, It is not for you to know the times or the seasons,
which the Father hath put in his own power.
8 But ye shall receive power, after that the Holy Ghost is come upon you: and
ye shall be witnesses unto me both in Jerusalem, and in all Judaea, and in
Samaria, and unto the uttermost part of the earth.
9 And when he had spoken these things, while they beheld, he was taken up;
and a cloud received him out of their sight.
10 And while they looked stedfastly toward heaven as he went up, behold,
two men stood by them in white apparel;
11 Which also said, Ye men of Galilee, why stand ye gazing up into heaven?
this same Jesus, which is taken up from you into heaven, shall so come in like
manner as ye have seen him go into heaven.

The Apostles Devote Themselves to Prayer

12 Then returned they unto Jerusalem from the mount called Olivet, which
is from Jerusalem a sabbath day's journey.
13 And when they were come in, they went up into an upper room, where
abode both Peter, and James, and John, and Andrew, Philip, and Thomas,
Bartholomew, and Matthew, James *the son* of Alphaeus, and Simon Zelotes,
and Judas *the brother* of James.
14 These all continued with one accord in prayer and supplication, with the
women, and Mary the mother of Jesus, and with his brethren.

Matthias Replaces Judas

15 And in those days Peter stood up in the midst of the disciples, and said,
(the number of names together were about an hundred and twenty,)
16 Men *and* brethren, this scripture must needs have been fulfilled, which
the Holy Ghost by the mouth of David spake before concerning Judas, which
was guide to them that took Jesus.
17 For he was numbered with us, and had obtained part of this ministry.
18 Now this man purchased a field with the reward of iniquity; and falling
headlong, he burst asunder in the midst, and all his bowels gushed out.

19 And it was known unto all the dwellers at Jerusalem; insomuch as that
field is called in their proper tongue, Aceldama, that is to say, The field of blood.
20 For it is written in the book of Psalms, Let his habitation be desolate, and
let no man dwell therein: and his bishoprick let another take.
21 Wherefore of these men which have companied with us all the time that
the Lord Jesus went in and out among us,
22 Beginning from the baptism of John, unto that same day that he was taken
up from us, must one be ordained to be a witness with us of his resurrection.
23 And they appointed two, Joseph called Barsabas, who was surnamed
Justus, and Matthias.
24 And they prayed, and said, Thou, Lord, which knowest the hearts of all
men, shew whether of these two thou hast chosen,
25 That he may take part of this ministry and apostleship, from which Judas
by transgression fell, that he might go to his own place.
26 And they gave forth their lots; and the lot fell upon Matthias; and he was
numbered with the eleven apostles.

The Apostles Are Filled with the Holy Spirit

2 And when the day of Pentecost was fully come, they were all with one accord
in one place.
2 And suddenly there came a sound from heaven as of a rushing mighty wind,
and it filled all the house where they were sitting.
3 And there appeared unto them cloven tongues like as of fire, and it sat upon
each of them.
4 And they were all filled with the Holy Ghost, and began to speak with other
tongues, as the Spirit gave them utterance.
5 And there were dwelling at Jerusalem Jews, devout men, out of every nation
under heaven.
6 Now when this was noised abroad, the multitude came together, and were
confounded, because that every man heard them speak in his own language.
7 And they were all amazed and marvelled, saying one to another, Behold,
are not all these which speak Galilaeans?
8 And how hear we every man in our own tongue, wherein we were born?
9 Parthians, and Medes, and Elamites, and the dwellers in Mesopotamia,
and in Judaea, and Cappadocia, in Pontus, and Asia,
10 Phrygia, and Pamphylia, in Egypt, and in the parts of Libya about Cyrene,
and strangers of Rome, Jews and proselytes,
11 Cretes and Arabians, we do hear them speak in our tongues the wonder-
ful works of God.
12 And they were all amazed, and were in doubt, saying one to another, What
meaneth this?
13 Others mocking said, These men are full of new wine.

Peter Preaches to the Crowd

14 But Peter, standing up with the eleven, lifted up his voice, and said unto
them, Ye men of Judaea, and all *ye* that dwell at Jerusalem, be this known unto
you, and hearken to my words:
15 For these are not drunken, as ye suppose, seeing it is *but* the third hour of
the day.
16 But this is that which was spoken by the prophet Joel;
17 And it shall come to pass in the last days, saith God, I will pour out of my
Spirit upon all flesh: and your sons and your daughters shall prophesy, and
your young men shall see visions, and your old men shall dream dreams:
18 And on my servants and on my handmaidens I will pour out in those days
of my Spirit; and they shall prophesy:
19 And I will shew wonders in heaven above, and signs in the earth beneath;
blood, and fire, and vapour of smoke:

20 The sun shall be turned into darkness, and the moon into blood, before
that great and notable day of the Lord come:
21 And it shall come to pass, *that* whosoever shall call on the name of the
Lord shall be saved.
22 Ye men of Israel, hear these words; Jesus of Nazareth, a man approved of
God among you by miracles and wonders and signs, which God did by him
in the midst of you, as ye yourselves also know:
23 Him, being delivered by the determinate counsel and foreknowledge of
God, ye have taken, and by wicked hands have crucified and slain:
24 Whom God hath raised up, having loosed the pains of death: because it
was not possible that he should be holden of it.
25 For David speaketh concerning him, I foresaw the Lord always before my
face, for he is on my right hand, that I should not be moved:
26 Therefore did my heart rejoice, and my tongue was glad; moreover also
my flesh shall rest in hope:
27 Because thou wilt not leave my soul in hell, neither wilt thou suffer thine
Holy One to see corruption.
28 Thou hast made known to me the ways of life; thou shalt make me full of
joy with thy countenance.
29 Men *and* brethren, let me freely speak unto you of the patriarch David,
that he is both dead and buried, and his sepulchre is with us unto this day.
30 Therefore being a prophet, and knowing that God had sworn with an oath
to him, that of the fruit of his loins, according to the flesh, he would raise up
Christ to sit on his throne;
31 He seeing this before spake of the resurrection of Christ, that his soul was
not left in hell, neither his flesh did see corruption.
32 This Jesus hath God raised up, whereof we all are witnesses.
33 Therefore being by the right hand of God exalted, and having received of
the Father the promise of the Holy Ghost, he hath shed forth this, which ye
now see and hear.
34 For David is not ascended into the heavens: but he saith himself, The LORD
said unto my Lord, Sit thou on my right hand,
35 Until I make thy foes thy footstool.
36 Therefore let all the house of Israel know assuredly, that God hath made
that same Jesus, whom ye have crucified, both Lord and Christ.

Three Thousand Are Converted

37 Now when they heard *this*, they were pricked in their heart, and said unto
Peter and to the rest of the apostles, Men *and* brethren, what shall we do?
38 Then Peter said unto them, Repent, and be baptized every one of you in
the name of Jesus Christ for the remission of sins, and ye shall receive the gift
of the Holy Ghost.
39 For the promise is unto you, and to your children, and to all that are afar
off, *even* as many as the Lord our God shall call.
40 And with many other words did he testify and exhort, saying, Save your-
selves from this untoward generation.
41 Then they that gladly received his word were baptized: and the same day
there were added *unto them* about three thousand souls.

The Apostles Work Miracles

42 And they continued stedfastly in the apostles' doctrine and fellowship,
and in breaking of bread, and in prayers.
43 And fear came upon every soul: and many wonders and signs were done
by the apostles.
44 And all that believed were together, and had all things common;
45 And sold their possessions and goods, and parted them to all *men*, as every
man had need.

ACTS 2:38
Repent,
& BE
BAPTIZED
every one
OF YOU
IN THE NAME OF
Jesus
Christ
FOR THE
remission
OF
SINS,
& YE SHALL RECEIVE
THE GIFT OF THE
Holy
Ghost.

46 And they, continuing daily with one accord in the temple, and breaking
bread from house to house, did eat their meat with gladness and singleness
of heart,
47 Praising God, and having favour with all the people. And the Lord added
to the church daily such as should be saved.

A Lame Man Is Healed

3 Now Peter and John went up together into the temple at the hour of prayer,
being the ninth *hour*.
2 And a certain man lame from his mother's womb was carried, whom they
laid daily at the gate of the temple which is called Beautiful, to ask alms of
them that entered into the temple;
3 Who seeing Peter and John about to go into the temple asked an alms.
4 And Peter, fastening his eyes upon him with John, said, Look on us.
5 And he gave heed unto them, expecting to receive something of them.
6 Then Peter said, Silver and gold have I none; but such as I have give I thee:
In the name of Jesus Christ of Nazareth rise up and walk.
7 And he took him by the right hand, and lifted *him* up: and immediately his
feet and ankle bones received strength.
8 And he leaping up stood, and walked, and entered with them into the tem-
ple, walking, and leaping, and praising God.
9 And all the people saw him walking and praising God:
10 And they knew that it was he which sat for alms at the Beautiful gate of
the temple: and they were filled with wonder and amazement at that which
had happened unto him.
11 And as the lame man which was healed held Peter and John, all the people
ran together unto them in the porch that is called Solomon's, greatly wondering.

Peter Speaks to the People

12 And when Peter saw *it*, he answered unto the people, Ye men of Israel,
why marvel ye at this? or why look ye so earnestly on us, as though by our own
power or holiness we had made this man to walk?
13 The God of Abraham, and of Isaac, and of Jacob, the God of our fathers,
hath glorified his Son Jesus; whom ye delivered up, and denied him in the
presence of Pilate, when he was determined to let *him* go.
14 But ye denied the Holy One and the Just, and desired a murderer to be
granted unto you;
15 And killed the Prince of life, whom God hath raised from the dead; where-
of we are witnesses.
16 And his name through faith in his name hath made this man strong,
whom ye see and know: yea, the faith which is by him hath given him this
perfect soundness in the presence of you all.
17 And now, brethren, I wot that through ignorance ye did *it*, as *did* also your
rulers.
18 But those things, which God before had shewed by the mouth of all his
prophets, that Christ should suffer, he hath so fulfilled.
19 Repent ye therefore, and be converted, that your sins may be blotted out,
when the times of refreshing shall come from the presence of the Lord;
20 And he shall send Jesus Christ, which before was preached unto you:
21 Whom the heaven must receive until the times of restitution of all things,
which God hath spoken by the mouth of all his holy prophets since the world
began.
22 For Moses truly said unto the fathers, A prophet shall the Lord your God
raise up unto you of your brethren, like unto me; him shall ye hear in all things
whatsoever he shall say unto you.
23 And it shall come to pass, *that* every soul, which will not hear that proph-
et, shall be destroyed from among the people.

24 Yea, and all the prophets from Samuel and those that follow after, as many
as have spoken, have likewise foretold of these days.
25 Ye are the children of the prophets, and of the covenant which God made
with our fathers, saying unto Abraham, And in thy seed shall all the kindreds
of the earth be blessed.
26 Unto you first God, having raised up his Son Jesus, sent him to bless you,
in turning away every one of you from his iniquities.

Peter and John Are Arrested and Tried

4 And as they spake unto the people, the priests, and the captain of the temple,
and the Sadducees, came upon them,
2 Being grieved that they taught the people, and preached through Jesus the
resurrection from the dead.
3 And they laid hands on them, and put *them* in hold unto the next day: for
it was now eventide.
4 Howbeit many of them which heard the word believed; and the number
of the men was about five thousand.
5 And it came to pass on the morrow, that their rulers, and elders, and scribes,
6 And Annas the high priest, and Caiaphas, and John, and Alexander, and as
many as were of the kindred of the high priest, were gathered together at
Jerusalem.
7 And when they had set them in the midst, they asked, By what power, or
by what name, have ye done this?
8 Then Peter, filled with the Holy Ghost, said unto them, Ye rulers of the
people, and elders of Israel,
9 If we this day be examined of the good deed done to the impotent man, by
what means he is made whole;
10 Be it known unto you all, and to all the people of Israel, that by the name
of Jesus Christ of Nazareth, whom ye crucified, whom God raised from the
dead, *even* by him doth this man stand here before you whole.
11 This is the stone which was set at nought of you builders, which is become
the head of the corner.
12 Neither is there salvation in any other: for there is none other name under
heaven given among men, whereby we must be saved.
13 Now when they saw the boldness of Peter and John, and perceived that
they were unlearned and ignorant men, they marvelled; and they took knowl-
edge of them, that they had been with Jesus.
14 And beholding the man which was healed standing with them, they could
say nothing against it.
15 But when they had commanded them to go aside out of the council, they
conferred among themselves,
16 Saying, What shall we do to these men? for that indeed a notable miracle
hath been done by them *is* manifest to all them that dwell in Jerusalem; and
we cannot deny *it*.
17 But that it spread no further among the people, let us straitly threaten
them, that they speak henceforth to no man in this name.
18 And they called them, and commanded them not to speak at all nor teach
in the name of Jesus.
19 But Peter and John answered and said unto them, Whether it be right in
the sight of God to hearken unto you more than unto God, judge ye.
20 For we cannot but speak the things which we have seen and heard.
21 So when they had further threatened them, they let them go, finding noth-
ing how they might punish them, because of the people: for all *men* glorified
God for that which was done.
22 For the man was above forty years old, on whom this miracle of healing
was shewed.

The Church Prays for God's Help

23 And being let go, they went to their own company, and reported all that
the chief priests and elders had said unto them.
24 And when they heard that, they lifted up their voice to God with one
accord, and said, Lord, thou *art* God, which hast made heaven, and earth, and
the sea, and all that in them is:
25 Who by the mouth of thy servant David hast said, Why did the heathen
rage, and the people imagine vain things?
26 The kings of the earth stood up, and the rulers were gathered together
against the Lord, and against his Christ.
27 For of a truth against thy holy child Jesus, whom thou hast anointed, both
Herod, and Pontius Pilate, with the Gentiles, and the people of Israel, were
gathered together,
28 For to do whatsoever thy hand and thy counsel determined before to be
done.
29 And now, Lord, behold their threatenings: and grant unto thy servants,
that with all boldness they may speak thy word,
30 By stretching forth thine hand to heal; and that signs and wonders may
be done by the name of thy holy child Jesus.
31 And when they had prayed, the place was shaken where they were assem-
bled together; and they were all filled with the Holy Ghost, and they spake the
word of God with boldness.

The Believers Share Their Property

32 And the multitude of them that believed were of one heart and of one
soul: neither said any *of them* that ought of the things which he possessed was
his own; but they had all things common.
33 And with great power gave the apostles witness of the resurrection of the
Lord Jesus: and great grace was upon them all.
34 Neither was there any among them that lacked: for as many as were pos-
sessors of lands or houses sold them, and brought the prices of the things that
were sold,
35 And laid *them* down at the apostles' feet: and distribution was made unto
every man according as he had need.
36 And Joses, who by the apostles was surnamed Barnabas, (which is, being
interpreted, The son of consolation,) a Levite, *and* of the country of Cyprus,
37 Having land, sold *it*, and brought the money, and laid *it* at the apostles'
feet.

Ananias and Sapphira

5 But a certain man named Ananias, with Sapphira his wife, sold a possession,
2 And kept back *part* of the price, his wife also being privy *to it*, and
brought a certain part, and laid *it* at the apostles' feet.
3 But Peter said, Ananias, why hath Satan filled thine heart to lie to the Holy
Ghost, and to keep back *part* of the price of the land?
4 Whiles it remained, was it not thine own? and after it was sold, was it not
in thine own power? why hast thou conceived this thing in thine heart? thou
hast not lied unto men, but unto God.
5 And Ananias hearing these words fell down, and gave up the ghost: and
great fear came on all them that heard these things.
6 And the young men arose, wound him up, and carried *him* out, and buried
him.
7 And it was about the space of three hours after, when his wife, not knowing
what was done, came in.
8 And Peter answered unto her, Tell me whether ye sold the land for so much?
And she said, Yea, for so much.

9 Then Peter said unto her, How is it that ye have agreed together to tempt
the Spirit of the Lord? behold, the feet of them which have buried thy husband
are at the door, and shall carry thee out.
10 Then fell she down straightway at his feet, and yielded up the ghost: and
the young men came in, and found her dead, and, carrying *her* forth, buried
her by her husband.
11 And great fear came upon all the church, and upon as many as heard these
things.

The Apostles Work Many Miracles

12 And by the hands of the apostles were many signs and wonders wrought
among the people; (and they were all with one accord in Solomon's porch.
13 And of the rest durst no man join himself to them: but the people magnified them.
14 And believers were the more added to the Lord, multitudes both of men
and women.)
15 Insomuch that they brought forth the sick into the streets, and laid *them*
on beds and couches, that at the least the shadow of Peter passing by might
overshadow some of them.
16 There came also a multitude *out* of the cities round about unto Jerusalem,
bringing sick folks, and them which were vexed with unclean spirits: and they
were healed every one.

The Apostles Are Again Imprisoned

17 Then the high priest rose up, and all they that were with him, (which is
the sect of the Sadducees,) and were filled with indignation,
18 And laid their hands on the apostles, and put them in the common prison.
19 But the angel of the Lord by night opened the prison doors, and brought
them forth, and said,
20 Go, stand and speak in the temple to the people all the words of this life.
21 And when they heard *that*, they entered into the temple early in the morning, and taught. But the high priest came, and they that were with him, and
called the council together, and all the senate of the children of Israel, and
sent to the prison to have them brought.
22 But when the officers came, and found them not in the prison, they
returned, and told,
23 Saying, The prison truly found we shut with all safety, and the keepers
standing without before the doors: but when we had opened, we found no
man within.
24 Now when the high priest and the captain of the temple and the chief
priests heard these things, they doubted of them whereunto this would grow.
25 Then came one and told them, saying, Behold, the men whom ye put in
prison are standing in the temple, and teaching the people.
26 Then went the captain with the officers, and brought them without violence: for they feared the people, lest they should have been stoned.
27 And when they had brought them, they set *them* before the council: and
the high priest asked them,
28 Saying, Did not we straitly command you that ye should not teach in this
name? and, behold, ye have filled Jerusalem with your doctrine, and intend
to bring this man's blood upon us.
29 Then Peter and the *other* apostles answered and said, We ought to obey
God rather than men.
30 The God of our fathers raised up Jesus, whom ye slew and hanged on a
tree.
31 Him hath God exalted with his right hand *to be* a Prince and a Saviour,
for to give repentance to Israel, and forgiveness of sins.

32 And we are his witnesses of these things; and *so is* also the Holy Ghost,
whom God hath given to them that obey him.
33 When they heard *that*, they were cut *to the heart*, and took counsel to slay
them.
34 Then stood there up one in the council, a Pharisee, named Gamaliel, a
doctor of the law, had in reputation among all the people, and commanded
to put the apostles forth a little space;
35 And said unto them, Ye men of Israel, take heed to yourselves what ye
intend to do as touching these men.
36 For before these days rose up Theudas, boasting himself to be somebody;
to whom a number of men, about four hundred, joined themselves: who was
slain; and all, as many as obeyed him, were scattered, and brought to nought.
37 After this man rose up Judas of Galilee in the days of the taxing, and drew
away much people after him: he also perished; and all, *even* as many as obeyed
him, were dispersed.
38 And now I say unto you, Refrain from these men, and let them alone: for
if this counsel or this work be of men, it will come to nought:
39 But if it be of God, ye cannot overthrow it; lest haply ye be found even to
fight against God.
40 And to him they agreed: and when they had called the apostles, and beat-
en *them*, they commanded that they should not speak in the name of Jesus,
and let them go.
41 And they departed from the presence of the council, rejoicing that they
were counted worthy to suffer shame for his name.
42 And daily in the temple, and in every house, they ceased not to teach and
preach Jesus Christ.

The Apostles Choose Seven Helpers

6 And in those days, when the number of the disciples was multiplied, there
arose a murmuring of the Grecians against the Hebrews, because their
widows were neglected in the daily ministration.
2 Then the twelve called the multitude of the disciples *unto them*, and said,
It is not reason that we should leave the word of God, and serve tables.
3 Wherefore, brethren, look ye out among you seven men of honest report,
full of the Holy Ghost and wisdom, whom we may appoint over this business.
4 But we will give ourselves continually to prayer, and to the ministry of the
word.
5 And the saying pleased the whole multitude: and they chose Stephen, a
man full of faith and of the Holy Ghost, and Philip, and Prochorus, and
Nicanor, and Timon, and Parmenas, and Nicolas a proselyte of Antioch:
6 Whom they set before the apostles: and when they had prayed, they laid
their hands on them.
7 And the word of God increased; and the number of the disciples multiplied
in Jerusalem greatly; and a great company of the priests were obedient to the
faith.

Stephen Is Arrested

8 And Stephen, full of faith and power, did great wonders and miracles
among the people.
9 Then there arose certain of the synagogue, which is called *the synagogue*
of the Libertines, and Cyrenians, and Alexandrians, and of them of Cilicia and
of Asia, disputing with Stephen.
10 And they were not able to resist the wisdom and the spirit by which he
spake.
11 Then they suborned men, which said, We have heard him speak blasphe-
mous words against Moses, and *against* God.

12 And they stirred up the people, and the elders, and the scribes, and came
upon *him*, and caught him, and brought *him* to the council,
13 And set up false witnesses, which said, This man ceaseth not to speak
blasphemous words against this holy place, and the law:
14 For we have heard him say, that this Jesus of Nazareth shall destroy this
place, and shall change the customs which Moses delivered us.
15 And all that sat in the council, looking stedfastly on him, saw his face as
it had been the face of an angel.

Stephen Speaks in His Own Defense

7 Then said the high priest, Are these things so?
2 And he said, Men, brethren, and fathers, hearken; The God of glory
appeared unto our father Abraham, when he was in Mesopotamia, before he
dwelt in Charran,
3 And said unto him, Get thee out of thy country, and from thy kindred, and
come into the land which I shall shew thee.
4 Then came he out of the land of the Chaldaeans, and dwelt in Charran: and
from thence, when his father was dead, he removed him into this land, where-
in ye now dwell.
5 And he gave him none inheritance in it, no, not *so much as* to set his foot
on: yet he promised that he would give it to him for a possession, and to his
seed after him, when *as yet* he had no child.
6 And God spake on this wise, That his seed should sojourn in a strange land;
and that they should bring them into bondage, and entreat *them* evil four
hundred years.
7 And the nation to whom they shall be in bondage will I judge, said God:
and after that shall they come forth, and serve me in this place.
8 And he gave him the covenant of circumcision: and so *Abraham* begat
Isaac, and circumcised him the eighth day; and Isaac *begat* Jacob; and Jacob
begat the twelve patriarchs.
9 And the patriarchs, moved with envy, sold Joseph into Egypt: but God was
with him,
10 And delivered him out of all his afflictions, and gave him favour and wis-
dom in the sight of Pharaoh king of Egypt; and he made him governor over
Egypt and all his house.
11 Now there came a dearth over all the land of Egypt and Chanaan, and
great affliction: and our fathers found no sustenance.
12 But when Jacob heard that there was corn in Egypt, he sent out our fathers
first.
13 And at the second *time* Joseph was made known to his brethren; and
Joseph's kindred was made known unto Pharaoh.
14 Then sent Joseph, and called his father Jacob to *him*, and all his kindred,
threescore and fifteen souls.
15 So Jacob went down into Egypt, and died, he, and our fathers,
16 And were carried over into Sychem, and laid in the sepulchre that
Abraham bought for a sum of money of the sons of Emmor *the father* of
Sychem.
17 But when the time of the promise drew nigh, which God had sworn to
Abraham, the people grew and multiplied in Egypt,
18 Till another king arose, which knew not Joseph.
19 The same dealt subtilly with our kindred, and evil entreated our fathers,
so that they cast out their young children, to the end they might not live.
20 In which time Moses was born, and was exceeding fair, and nourished up
in his father's house three months:
21 And when he was cast out, Pharaoh's daughter took him up, and nourished
him for her own son.

22 And Moses was learned in all the wisdom of the Egyptians, and was mighty
in words and in deeds.
23 And when he was full forty years old, it came into his heart to visit his
brethren the children of Israel.
24 And seeing one *of them* suffer wrong, he defended *him*, and avenged him
that was oppressed, and smote the Egyptian:
25 For he supposed his brethren would have understood how that God by
his hand would deliver them: but they understood not.
26 And the next day he shewed himself unto them as they strove, and would
have set them at one again, saying, Sirs, ye are brethren; why do ye wrong one
to another?
27 But he that did his neighbour wrong thrust him away, saying, Who made
thee a ruler and a judge over us?
28 Wilt thou kill me, as thou diddest the Egyptian yesterday?
29 Then fled Moses at this saying, and was a stranger in the land of Madian,
where he begat two sons.
30 And when forty years were expired, there appeared to him in the wilder-
ness of mount Sina an angel of the Lord in a flame of fire in a bush.
31 When Moses saw *it*, he wondered at the sight: and as he drew near to
behold *it*, the voice of the Lord came unto him,
32 *Saying*, I *am* the God of thy fathers, the God of Abraham, and the God of
Isaac, and the God of Jacob. Then Moses trembled, and durst not behold.
33 Then said the Lord to him, Put off thy shoes from thy feet: for the place
where thou standest is holy ground.
34 I have seen, I have seen the affliction of my people which is in Egypt, and
I have heard their groaning, and am come down to deliver them. And now
come, I will send thee into Egypt.
35 This Moses whom they refused, saying, Who made thee a ruler and a
judge? the same did God send *to be* a ruler and a deliverer by the hand of the
angel which appeared to him in the bush.
36 He brought them out, after that he had shewed wonders and signs in the
land of Egypt, and in the Red sea, and in the wilderness forty years.
37 This is that Moses, which said unto the children of Israel, A prophet shall
the Lord your God raise up unto you of your brethren, like unto me; him shall
ye hear.
38 This is he, that was in the church in the wilderness with the angel which
spake to him in the mount Sina, and *with* our fathers: who received the lively
oracles to give unto us:
39 To whom our fathers would not obey, but thrust *him* from them, and in
their hearts turned back again into Egypt,
40 Saying unto Aaron, Make us gods to go before us: for *as for* this Moses,
which brought us out of the land of Egypt, we wot not what is become of him.
41 And they made a calf in those days, and offered sacrifice unto the idol,
and rejoiced in the works of their own hands.
42 Then God turned, and gave them up to worship the host of heaven; as it
is written in the book of the prophets, O ye house of Israel, have ye offered to
me slain beasts and sacrifices *by the space of* forty years in the wilderness?
43 Yea, ye took up the tabernacle of Moloch, and the star of your god
Remphan, figures which ye made to worship them: and I will carry you away
beyond Babylon.
44 Our fathers had the tabernacle of witness in the wilderness, as he had
appointed, speaking unto Moses, that he should make it according to the fash-
ion that he had seen.
45 Which also our fathers that came after brought in with Jesus into the
possession of the Gentiles, whom God drave out before the face of our fathers,
unto the days of David;

46 Who found favour before God, and desired to find a tabernacle for the
God of Jacob.
47 But Solomon built him an house.
48 Howbeit the most High dwelleth not in temples made with hands; as saith
the prophet,
49 Heaven *is* my throne, and earth *is* my footstool: what house will ye build
me? saith the Lord: or what *is* the place of my rest?
50 Hath not my hand made all these things?
51 Ye stiffnecked and uncircumcised in heart and ears, ye do always resist
the Holy Ghost: as your fathers *did*, so *do* ye.
52 Which of the prophets have not your fathers persecuted? and they have
slain them which shewed before of the coming of the Just One; of whom ye
have been now the betrayers and murderers:
53 Who have received the law by the disposition of angels, and have not kept
it.

Stephen Is Executed

54 When they heard these things, they were cut to the heart, and they gnashed
on him with *their* teeth.
55 But he, being full of the Holy Ghost, looked up stedfastly into heaven, and
saw the glory of God, and Jesus standing on the right hand of God,
56 And said, Behold, I see the heavens opened, and the Son of man standing
on the right hand of God.
57 Then they cried out with a loud voice, and stopped their ears, and ran
upon him with one accord,
58 And cast *him* out of the city, and stoned *him*: and the witnesses laid down
their clothes at a young man's feet, whose name was Saul.
59 And they stoned Stephen, calling upon *God*, and saying, Lord Jesus, receive
my spirit.
60 And he kneeled down, and cried with a loud voice, Lord, lay not this sin
to their charge. And when he had said this, he fell asleep.

Saul Persecutes the Believers

8 And Saul was consenting unto his death. And at that time there was a great
persecution against the church which was at Jerusalem; and they were all
scattered abroad throughout the regions of Judaea and Samaria, except the
apostles.
2 And devout men carried Stephen *to his burial*, and made great lamentation
over him.
3 As for Saul, he made havock of the church, entering into every house, and
haling men and women committed *them* to prison.

Some Samaritans Become Believers

4 Therefore they that were scattered abroad went every where preaching the
word.
5 Then Philip went down to the city of Samaria, and preached Christ unto
them.
6 And the people with one accord gave heed unto those things which Philip
spake, hearing and seeing the miracles which he did.
7 For unclean spirits, crying with loud voice, came out of many that were
possessed *with them*: and many taken with palsies, and that were lame, were
healed.
8 And there was great joy in that city.
9 But there was a certain man, called Simon, which beforetime in the same
city used sorcery, and bewitched the people of Samaria, giving out that himself
was some great one:
10 To whom they all gave heed, from the least to the greatest, saying, This
man is the great power of God.

11 And to him they had regard, because that of long time he had bewitched
them with sorceries.
12 But when they believed Philip preaching the things concerning the king-
dom of God, and the name of Jesus Christ, they were baptized, both men and
women.
13 Then Simon himself believed also: and when he was baptized, he contin-
ued with Philip, and wondered, beholding the miracles and signs which were
done.
14 Now when the apostles which were at Jerusalem heard that Samaria had
received the word of God, they sent unto them Peter and John:
15 Who, when they were come down, prayed for them, that they might
receive the Holy Ghost:
16 (For as yet he was fallen upon none of them: only they were baptized in
the name of the Lord Jesus.)
17 Then laid they *their* hands on them, and they received the Holy Ghost.
18 And when Simon saw that through laying on of the apostles' hands the
Holy Ghost was given, he offered them money,
19 Saying, Give me also this power, that on whomsoever I lay hands, he may
receive the Holy Ghost.
20 But Peter said unto him, Thy money perish with thee, because thou hast
thought that the gift of God may be purchased with money.
21 Thou hast neither part nor lot in this matter: for thy heart is not right in
the sight of God.
22 Repent therefore of this thy wickedness, and pray God, if perhaps the
thought of thine heart may be forgiven thee.
23 For I perceive that thou art in the gall of bitterness, and *in* the bond of
iniquity.
24 Then answered Simon, and said, Pray ye to the Lord for me, that none of
these things which ye have spoken come upon me.
25 And they, when they had testified and preached the word of the Lord,
returned to Jerusalem, and preached the gospel in many villages of the
Samaritans.

The Ethiopian Eunuch

26 And the angel of the Lord spake unto Philip, saying, Arise, and go toward
the south unto the way that goeth down from Jerusalem unto Gaza, which is
desert.
27 And he arose and went: and, behold, a man of Ethiopia, an eunuch of great
authority under Candace queen of the Ethiopians, who had the charge of all
her treasure, and had come to Jerusalem for to worship,
28 Was returning, and sitting in his chariot read Esaias the prophet.
29 Then the Spirit said unto Philip, Go near, and join thyself to this chariot.
30 And Philip ran thither to *him*, and heard him read the prophet Esaias,
and said, Understandest thou what thou readest?
31 And he said, How can I, except some man should guide me? And he desired
Philip that he would come up and sit with him.
32 The place of the scripture which he read was this, He was led as a sheep
to the slaughter; and like a lamb dumb before his shearer, so opened he not
his mouth:
33 In his humiliation his judgment was taken away: and who shall declare
his generation? for his life is taken from the earth.
34 And the eunuch answered Philip, and said, I pray thee, of whom speaketh
the prophet this? of himself, or of some other man?
35 Then Philip opened his mouth, and began at the same scripture, and
preached unto him Jesus.

36 And as they went on *their* way, they came unto a certain water: and the
eunuch said, See, *here is* water; what doth hinder me to be baptized?
37 And Philip said, If thou believest with all thine heart, thou mayest. And
he answered and said, I believe that Jesus Christ is the Son of God.
38 And he commanded the chariot to stand still: and they went down both
into the water, both Philip and the eunuch; and he baptized him.
39 And when they were come up out of the water, the Spirit of the Lord caught
away Philip, that the eunuch saw him no more: and he went on his way rejoic-
ing.
40 But Philip was found at Azotus: and passing through he preached in all
the cities, till he came to Caesarea.

Saul Becomes a Christian

9 And Saul, yet breathing out threatenings and slaughter against the disciples
of the Lord, went unto the high priest,
2 And desired of him letters to Damascus to the synagogues, that if he found
any of this way, whether they were men or women, he might bring them bound
unto Jerusalem.
3 And as he journeyed, he came near Damascus: and suddenly there shined
round about him a light from heaven:
4 And he fell to the earth, and heard a voice saying unto him, Saul, Saul, why
persecutest thou me?
5 And he said, Who art thou, Lord? And the Lord said, I am Jesus whom thou
persecutest: *it is* hard for thee to kick against the pricks.
6 And he trembling and astonished said, Lord, what wilt thou have me to
do? And the Lord *said* unto him, Arise, and go into the city, and it shall be told
thee what thou must do.
7 And the men which journeyed with him stood speechless, hearing a voice,
but seeing no man.
8 And Saul arose from the earth; and when his eyes were opened, he saw no
man: but they led him by the hand, and brought *him* into Damascus.
9 And he was three days without sight, and neither did eat nor drink.

Saul Is Called to the Gentiles

10 And there was a certain disciple at Damascus, named Ananias; and to him
said the Lord in a vision, Ananias. And he said, Behold, I *am here*, Lord.
11 And the Lord *said* unto him, Arise, and go into the street which is called
Straight, and enquire in the house of Judas for *one* called Saul, of Tarsus: for,
behold, he prayeth,
12 And hath seen in a vision a man named Ananias coming in, and putting
his hand on him, that he might receive his sight.
13 Then Ananias answered, Lord, I have heard by many of this man, how
much evil he hath done to thy saints at Jerusalem:
14 And here he hath authority from the chief priests to bind all that call on
thy name.
15 But the Lord said unto him, Go thy way: for he is a chosen vessel unto me,
to bear my name before the Gentiles, and kings, and the children of Israel:
16 For I will shew him how great things he must suffer for my name's sake.
17 And Ananias went his way, and entered into the house; and putting his
hands on him said, Brother Saul, the Lord, *even* Jesus, that appeared unto thee
in the way as thou camest, hath sent me, that thou mightest receive thy sight,
and be filled with the Holy Ghost.
18 And immediately there fell from his eyes as it had been scales: and he
received sight forthwith, and arose, and was baptized.
19 And when he had received meat, he was strengthened. Then was Saul
certain days with the disciples which were at Damascus.

20 And straightway he preached Christ in the synagogues, that he is the Son
of God.
21 But all that heard *him* were amazed, and said; Is not this he that destroyed
them which called on this name in Jerusalem, and came hither for that intent,
that he might bring them bound unto the chief priests?
22 But Saul increased the more in strength, and confounded the Jews which
dwelt at Damascus, proving that this is very Christ.

The Jews Lay Wait to Kill Saul

23 And after that many days were fulfilled, the Jews took counsel to kill him:
24 But their laying await was known of Saul. And they watched the gates day
and night to kill him.
25 Then the disciples took him by night, and let *him* down by the wall in a
basket.
26 And when Saul was come to Jerusalem, he assayed to join himself to the
disciples: but they were all afraid of him, and believed not that he was a disci-
ple.
27 But Barnabas took him, and brought *him* to the apostles, and declared
unto them how he had seen the Lord in the way, and that he had spoken to
him, and how he had preached boldly at Damascus in the name of Jesus.
28 And he was with them coming in and going out at Jerusalem.
29 And he spake boldly in the name of the Lord Jesus, and disputed against
the Grecians: but they went about to slay him.
30 *Which* when the brethren knew, they brought him down to Caesarea, and
sent him forth to Tarsus.
31 Then had the churches rest throughout all Judaea and Galilee and Samaria,
and were edified; and walking in the fear of the Lord, and in the comfort of
the Holy Ghost, were multiplied.

Peter Heals Aeneas

32 And it came to pass, as Peter passed throughout all *quarters*, he came down
also to the saints which dwelt at Lydda.
33 And there he found a certain man named Aeneas, which had kept his bed
eight years, and was sick of the palsy.
34 And Peter said unto him, Aeneas, Jesus Christ maketh thee whole: arise,
and make thy bed. And he arose immediately.
35 And all that dwelt at Lydda and Saron saw him, and turned to the Lord.

Peter Restores Tabitha to Life

36 Now there was at Joppa a certain disciple named Tabitha, which by inter-
pretation is called Dorcas: this woman was full of good works and almsdeeds
which she did.
37 And it came to pass in those days, that she was sick, and died: whom when
they had washed, they laid *her* in an upper chamber.
38 And forasmuch as Lydda was nigh to Joppa, and the disciples had heard
that Peter was there, they sent unto him two men, desiring *him* that he would
not delay to come to them.
39 Then Peter arose and went with them. When he was come, they brought
him into the upper chamber: and all the widows stood by him weeping, and
shewing the coats and garments which Dorcas made, while she was with them.
40 But Peter put them all forth, and kneeled down, and prayed; and turning
him to the body said, Tabitha, arise. And she opened her eyes: and when she
saw Peter, she sat up.
41 And he gave her *his* hand, and lifted her up, and when he had called the
saints and widows, presented her alive.
42 And it was known throughout all Joppa; and many believed in the Lord.
43 And it came to pass, that he tarried many days in Joppa with one Simon a
tanner.

Cornelius Has a Vision

10 There was a certain man in Caesarea called Cornelius, a centurion of the band called the Italian *band*,
2 *A* devout *man*, and one that feared God with all his house, which gave much
alms to the people, and prayed to God alway.
3 He saw in a vision evidently about the ninth hour of the day an angel of
God coming in to him, and saying unto him, Cornelius.
4 And when he looked on him, he was afraid, and said, What is it, Lord? And
he said unto him, Thy prayers and thine alms are come up for a memorial
before God.
5 And now send men to Joppa, and call for *one* Simon, whose surname is
Peter:
6 He lodgeth with one Simon a tanner, whose house is by the sea side: he
shall tell thee what thou oughtest to do.
7 And when the angel which spake unto Cornelius was departed, he called
two of his household servants, and a devout soldier of them that waited on
him continually;
8 And when he had declared all *these* things unto them, he sent them to
Joppa.

Peter Has a Vision

9 On the morrow, as they went on their journey, and drew nigh unto the city,
Peter went up upon the housetop to pray about the sixth hour:
10 And he became very hungry, and would have eaten: but while they made
ready, he fell into a trance,
11 And saw heaven opened, and a certain vessel descending unto him, as it
had been a great sheet knit at the four corners, and let down to the earth:
12 Wherein were all manner of fourfooted beasts of the earth, and wild
beasts, and creeping things, and fowls of the air.
13 And there came a voice to him, Rise, Peter; kill, and eat.
14 But Peter said, Not so, Lord; for I have never eaten any thing that is com-
mon or unclean.
15 And the voice *spake* unto him again the second time, What God hath
cleansed, *that* call not thou common.
16 This was done thrice: and the vessel was received up again into heaven.
17 Now while Peter doubted in himself what this vision which he had seen
should mean, behold, the men which were sent from Cornelius had made
enquiry for Simon's house, and stood before the gate,
18 And called, and asked whether Simon, which was surnamed Peter, were
lodged there.
19 While Peter thought on the vision, the Spirit said unto him, Behold, three
men seek thee.
20 Arise therefore, and get thee down, and go with them, doubting nothing:
for I have sent them.
21 Then Peter went down to the men which were sent unto him from
Cornelius; and said, Behold, I am he whom ye seek: what *is* the cause wherefore
ye are come?
22 And they said, Cornelius the centurion, a just man, and one that feareth
God, and of good report among all the nation of the Jews, was warned from
God by an holy angel to send for thee into his house, and to hear words of thee.
23 Then called he them in, and lodged *them*. And on the morrow Peter went
away with them, and certain brethren from Joppa accompanied him.

Peter Speaks with Cornelius

24 And the morrow after they entered into Caesarea. And Cornelius waited
for them, and had called together his kinsmen and near friends.

25 And as Peter was coming in, Cornelius met him, and fell down at his feet,
and worshipped *him*.
26 But Peter took him up, saying, Stand up; I myself also am a man.
27 And as he talked with him, he went in, and found many that were come
together.
28 And he said unto them, Ye know how that it is an unlawful thing for a man
that is a Jew to keep company, or come unto one of another nation; but God
hath shewed me that I should not call any man common or unclean.
29 Therefore came I *unto you* without gainsaying, as soon as I was sent for:
I ask therefore for what intent ye have sent for me?
30 And Cornelius said, Four days ago I was fasting until this hour; and at the
ninth hour I prayed in my house, and, behold, a man stood before me in bright
clothing,
31 And said, Cornelius, thy prayer is heard, and thine alms are had in remem-
brance in the sight of God.
32 Send therefore to Joppa, and call hither Simon, whose surname is Peter;
he is lodged in the house of *one* Simon a tanner by the sea side: who, when he
cometh, shall speak unto thee.
33 Immediately therefore I sent to thee; and thou hast well done that thou
art come. Now therefore are we all here present before God, to hear all things
that are commanded thee of God.

Peter Understands the Vision

34 Then Peter opened *his* mouth, and said, Of a truth I perceive that God is
no respecter of persons:
35 But in every nation he that feareth him, and worketh righteousness, is
accepted with him.
36 The word which *God* sent unto the children of Israel, preaching peace by
Jesus Christ: (he is Lord of all:)
37 That word, *I say*, ye know, which was published throughout all Judaea,
and began from Galilee, after the baptism which John preached;
38 How God anointed Jesus of Nazareth with the Holy Ghost and with power:
who went about doing good, and healing all that were oppressed of the devil;
for God was with him.
39 And we are witnesses of all things which he did both in the land of the
Jews, and in Jerusalem; whom they slew and hanged on a tree:
40 Him God raised up the third day, and shewed him openly;
41 Not to all the people, but unto witnesses chosen before of God, *even* to us,
who did eat and drink with him after he rose from the dead.
42 And he commanded us to preach unto the people, and to testify that it is
he which was ordained of God *to be* the Judge of quick and dead.
43 To him give all the prophets witness, that through his name whosoever
believeth in him shall receive remission of sins.

The Holy Ghost Descends

44 While Peter yet spake these words, the Holy Ghost fell on all them which
heard the word.
45 And they of the circumcision which believed were astonished, as many
as came with Peter, because that on the Gentiles also was poured out the gift
of the Holy Ghost.
46 For they heard them speak with tongues, and magnify God. Then answered
Peter,
47 Can any man forbid water, that these should not be baptized, which have
received the Holy Ghost as well as we?
48 And he commanded them to be baptized in the name of the Lord. Then
prayed they him to tarry certain days.

Gentiles Can Become Christians

11 And the apostles and brethren that were in Judaea heard that the
Gentiles had also received the word of God.
2 And when Peter was come up to Jerusalem, they that were of the circum-
cision contended with him,
3 Saying, Thou wentest in to men uncircumcised, and didst eat with them.
4 But Peter rehearsed *the matter* from the beginning, and expounded *it* by
order unto them, saying,
5 I was in the city of Joppa praying: and in a trance I saw a vision, A certain
vessel descend, as it had been a great sheet, let down from heaven by four
corners; and it came even to me:
6 Upon the which when I had fastened mine eyes, I considered, and saw
fourfooted beasts of the earth, and wild beasts, and creeping things, and fowls
of the air.
7 And I heard a voice saying unto me, Arise, Peter; slay and eat.
8 But I said, Not so, Lord: for nothing common or unclean hath at any time
entered into my mouth.
9 But the voice answered me again from heaven, What God hath cleansed,
that call not thou common.
10 And this was done three times: and all were drawn up again into heaven.
11 And, behold, immediately there were three men already come unto the
house where I was, sent from Caesarea unto me.
12 And the Spirit bade me go with them, nothing doubting. Moreover these
six brethren accompanied me, and we entered into the man's house:
13 And he shewed us how he had seen an angel in his house, which stood
and said unto him, Send men to Joppa, and call for Simon, whose surname is
Peter;
14 Who shall tell thee words, whereby thou and all thy house shall be saved.
15 And as I began to speak, the Holy Ghost fell on them, as on us at the begin-
ning.
16 Then remembered I the word of the Lord, how that he said, John indeed
baptized with water; but ye shall be baptized with the Holy Ghost.
17 Forasmuch then as God gave them the like gift as *he did* unto us, who
believed on the Lord Jesus Christ; what was I, that I could withstand God?
18 When they heard these things, they held their peace, and glorified God,
saying, Then hath God also to the Gentiles granted repentance unto life.

The Church in Antioch

19 Now they which were scattered abroad upon the persecution that arose
about Stephen travelled as far as Phenice, and Cyprus, and Antioch, preaching
the word to none but unto the Jews only.
20 And some of them were men of Cyprus and Cyrene, which, when they
were come to Antioch, spake unto the Grecians, preaching the Lord Jesus.
21 And the hand of the Lord was with them: and a great number believed,
and turned unto the Lord.
22 Then tidings of these things came unto the ears of the church which was
in Jerusalem: and they sent forth Barnabas, that he should go as far as Antioch.
23 Who, when he came, and had seen the grace of God, was glad, and exhort-
ed them all, that with purpose of heart they would cleave unto the Lord.
24 For he was a good man, and full of the Holy Ghost and of faith: and much
people was added unto the Lord.
25 Then departed Barnabas to Tarsus, for to seek Saul:
26 And when he had found him, he brought him unto Antioch. And it came
to pass, that a whole year they assembled themselves with the church, and
taught much people. And the disciples were called Christians first in Antioch.

Antioch Sends Relief to Judea

27 And in these days came prophets from Jerusalem unto Antioch.
28 And there stood up one of them named Agabus, and signified by the Spirit
that there should be great dearth throughout all the world: which came to
pass in the days of Claudius Caesar.
29 Then the disciples, every man according to his ability, determined to send
relief unto the brethren which dwelt in Judaea:
30 Which also they did, and sent it to the elders by the hands of Barnabas
and Saul.

An Angel Frees Peter from Prison

12 Now about that time Herod the king stretched forth *his* hands to
vex certain of the church.
2 And he killed James the brother of John with the sword.
3 And because he saw it pleased the Jews, he proceeded further to take Peter
also. (Then were the days of unleavened bread.)
4 And when he had apprehended him, he put *him* in prison, and delivered
him to four quaternions of soldiers to keep him; intending after Easter to bring
him forth to the people.
5 Peter therefore was kept in prison: but prayer was made without ceasing
of the church unto God for him.
6 And when Herod would have brought him forth, the same night Peter was
sleeping between two soldiers, bound with two chains: and the keepers before
the door kept the prison.
7 And, behold, the angel of the Lord came upon *him*, and a light shined in
the prison: and he smote Peter on the side, and raised him up, saying, Arise
up quickly. And his chains fell off from *his* hands.
8 And the angel said unto him, Gird thyself, and bind on thy sandals. And so
he did. And he saith unto him, Cast thy garment about thee, and follow me.
9 And he went out, and followed him; and wist not that it was true which
was done by the angel; but thought he saw a vision.
10 When they were past the first and the second ward, they came unto the
iron gate that leadeth unto the city; which opened to them of his own accord:
and they went out, and passed on through one street; and forthwith the angel
departed from him.
11 And when Peter was come to himself, he said, Now I know of a surety, that
the Lord hath sent his angel, and hath delivered me out of the hand of Herod,
and *from* all the expectation of the people of the Jews.
12 And when he had considered *the thing*, he came to the house of Mary the
mother of John, whose surname was Mark; where many were gathered togeth-
er praying.
13 And as Peter knocked at the door of the gate, a damsel came to hearken,
named Rhoda.
14 And when she knew Peter's voice, she opened not the gate for gladness,
but ran in, and told how Peter stood before the gate.
15 And they said unto her, Thou art mad. But she constantly affirmed that it
was even so. Then said they, It is his angel.
16 But Peter continued knocking: and when they had opened *the door*, and
saw him, they were astonished.
17 But he, beckoning unto them with the hand to hold their peace, declared
unto them how the Lord had brought him out of the prison. And he said, Go
shew these things unto James, and to the brethren. And he departed, and went
into another place.
18 Now as soon as it was day, there was no small stir among the soldiers, what
was become of Peter.

19 And when Herod had sought for him, and found him not, he examined
the keepers, and commanded that *they* should be put to death. And he went
down from Judaea to Caesarea, and *there* abode.

Herod's Death

20 And Herod was highly displeased with them of Tyre and Sidon: but they
came with one accord to him, and, having made Blastus the king's chamberlain
their friend, desired peace; because their country was nourished by the king's
country.
21 And upon a set day Herod, arrayed in royal apparel, sat upon his throne,
and made an oration unto them.
22 And the people gave a shout, *saying, It is* the voice of a god, and not of a
man.
23 And immediately the angel of the Lord smote him, because he gave not
God the glory: and he was eaten of worms, and gave up the ghost.
24 But the word of God grew and multiplied.
25 And Barnabas and Saul returned from Jerusalem, when they had fulfilled
their ministry, and took with them John, whose surname was Mark.

Paul and Barnabas Go to Cyprus

13 Now there were in the church that was at Antioch certain prophets
and teachers; as Barnabas, and Simeon that was called Niger, and
Lucius of Cyrene, and Manaen, which had been brought up with Herod
the tetrarch, and Saul.
2 As they ministered to the Lord, and fasted, the Holy Ghost said, Separate
me Barnabas and Saul for the work whereunto I have called them.
3 And when they had fasted and prayed, and laid *their* hands on them, they
sent *them* away.
4 So they, being sent forth by the Holy Ghost, departed unto Seleucia; and
from thence they sailed to Cyprus.
5 And when they were at Salamis, they preached the word of God in the
synagogues of the Jews: and they had also John to *their* minister.
6 And when they had gone through the isle unto Paphos, they found a certain
sorcerer, a false prophet, a Jew, whose name *was* Bar-jesus:
7 Which was with the deputy of the country, Sergius Paulus, a prudent man;
who called for Barnabas and Saul, and desired to hear the word of God.
8 But Elymas the sorcerer (for so is his name by interpretation) withstood
them, seeking to turn away the deputy from the faith.
9 Then Saul, (who also *is called* Paul,) filled with the Holy Ghost, set his eyes
on him,
10 And said, O full of all subtilty and all mischief, *thou* child of the devil, *thou*
enemy of all righteousness, wilt thou not cease to pervert the right ways of the
Lord?
11 And now, behold, the hand of the Lord *is* upon thee, and thou shalt be
blind, not seeing the sun for a season. And immediately there fell on him a
mist and a darkness; and he went about seeking some to lead him by the hand.
12 Then the deputy, when he saw what was done, believed, being astonished
at the doctrine of the Lord.
13 Now when Paul and his company loosed from Paphos, they came to Perga
in Pamphylia: and John departing from them returned to Jerusalem.

Paul and Barnabas Go to Antioch in Pisidia

14 But when they departed from Perga, they came to Antioch in Pisidia, and
went into the synagogue on the sabbath day, and sat down.
15 And after the reading of the law and the prophets the rulers of the syna-
gogue sent unto them, saying, *Ye* men *and* brethren, if ye have any word of
exhortation for the people, say on.

16 Then Paul stood up, and beckoning with *his* hand said, Men of Israel, and
ye that fear God, give audience.
17 The God of this people of Israel chose our fathers, and exalted the people
when they dwelt as strangers in the land of Egypt, and with an high arm
brought he them out of it.
18 And about the time of forty years suffered he their manners in the wil-
derness.
19 And when he had destroyed seven nations in the land of Chanaan, he
divided their land to them by lot.
20 And after that he gave *unto them* judges about the space of four hundred
and fifty years, until Samuel the prophet.
21 And afterward they desired a king: and God gave unto them Saul the son
of Cis, a man of the tribe of Benjamin, by the space of forty years.
22 And when he had removed him, he raised up unto them David to be their
king; to whom also he gave testimony, and said, I have found David the *son* of
Jesse, a man after mine own heart, which shall fulfil all my will.
23 Of this man's seed hath God according to *his* promise raised unto Israel
a Saviour, Jesus:
24 When John had first preached before his coming the baptism of repent-
ance to all the people of Israel.
25 And as John fulfilled his course, he said, Whom think ye that I am? I am
not *he*. But, behold, there cometh one after me, whose shoes of *his* feet I am
not worthy to loose.
26 Men *and* brethren, children of the stock of Abraham, and whosoever
among you feareth God, to you is the word of this salvation sent.
27 For they that dwell at Jerusalem, and their rulers, because they knew him
not, nor yet the voices of the prophets which are read every sabbath day, they
have fulfilled *them* in condemning *him*.
28 And though they found no cause of death *in him*, yet desired they Pilate
that he should be slain.
29 And when they had fulfilled all that was written of him, they took *him*
down from the tree, and laid *him* in a sepulchre.
30 But God raised him from the dead:
31 And he was seen many days of them which came up with him from Galilee
to Jerusalem, who are his witnesses unto the people.
32 And we declare unto you glad tidings, how that the promise which was
made unto the fathers,
33 God hath fulfilled the same unto us their children, in that he hath raised
up Jesus again; as it is also written in the second psalm, Thou art my Son, this
day have I begotten thee.
34 And as concerning that he raised him up from the dead, *now* no more to
return to corruption, he said on this wise, I will give you the sure mercies of
David.
35 Wherefore he saith also in another *psalm*, Thou shalt not suffer thine
Holy One to see corruption.
36 For David, after he had served his own generation by the will of God, fell
on sleep, and was laid unto his fathers, and saw corruption:
37 But he, whom God raised again, saw no corruption.
38 Be it known unto you therefore, men *and* brethren, that through this man
is preached unto you the forgiveness of sins:
39 And by him all that believe are justified from all things, from which ye
could not be justified by the law of Moses.
40 Beware therefore, lest that come upon you, which is spoken of in the
prophets;

41 Behold, ye despisers, and wonder, and perish: for I work a work in your
days, a work which ye shall in no wise believe, though a man declare it unto
you.

Preaching to the Gentiles

42 And when the Jews were gone out of the synagogue, the Gentiles besought
that these words might be preached to them the next sabbath.
43 Now when the congregation was broken up, many of the Jews and reli-
gious proselytes followed Paul and Barnabas: who, speaking to them, persuad-
ed them to continue in the grace of God.
44 And the next sabbath day came almost the whole city together to hear the
word of God.
45 But when the Jews saw the multitudes, they were filled with envy, and
spake against those things which were spoken by Paul, contradicting and
blaspheming.
46 Then Paul and Barnabas waxed bold, and said, It was necessary that the
word of God should first have been spoken to you: but seeing ye put it from
you, and judge yourselves unworthy of everlasting life, lo, we turn to the
Gentiles.
47 For so hath the Lord commanded us, *saying*, I have set thee to be a light
of the Gentiles, that thou shouldest be for salvation unto the ends of the earth.
48 And when the Gentiles heard this, they were glad, and glorified the word
of the Lord: and as many as were ordained to eternal life believed.
49 And the word of the Lord was published throughout all the region.
50 But the Jews stirred up the devout and honourable women, and the chief
men of the city, and raised persecution against Paul and Barnabas, and
expelled them out of their coasts.
51 But they shook off the dust of their feet against them, and came unto
Iconium.
52 And the disciples were filled with joy, and with the Holy Ghost.

Paul and Barnabas in Iconium

14 And it came to pass in Iconium, that they went both together into
the synagogue of the Jews, and so spake, that a great multitude both
of the Jews and also of the Greeks believed.
2 But the unbelieving Jews stirred up the Gentiles, and made their minds
evil affected against the brethren.
3 Long time therefore abode they speaking boldly in the Lord, which gave
testimony unto the word of his grace, and granted signs and wonders to be
done by their hands.
4 But the multitude of the city was divided: and part held with the Jews, and
part with the apostles.
5 And when there was an assault made both of the Gentiles, and also of the
Jews with their rulers, to use *them* despitefully, and to stone them,
6 They were ware of *it*, and fled unto Lystra and Derbe, cities of Lycaonia,
and unto the region that lieth round about:
7 And there they preached the gospel.

Paul and Barnabas in Lystra

8 And there sat a certain man at Lystra, impotent in his feet, being a cripple
from his mother's womb, who never had walked:
9 The same heard Paul speak: who stedfastly beholding him, and perceiving
that he had faith to be healed,
10 Said with a loud voice, Stand upright on thy feet. And he leaped and
walked.
11 And when the people saw what Paul had done, they lifted up their voices,
saying in the speech of Lycaonia, The gods are come down to us in the likeness
of men.

12 And they called Barnabas, Jupiter; and Paul, Mercurius, because he was
the chief speaker.
13 Then the priest of Jupiter, which was before their city, brought oxen and
garlands unto the gates, and would have done sacrifice with the people.
14 *Which* when the apostles, Barnabas and Paul, heard *of*, they rent their
clothes, and ran in among the people, crying out,
15 And saying, Sirs, why do ye these things? We also are men of like passions
with you, and preach unto you that ye should turn from these vanities unto
the living God, which made heaven, and earth, and the sea, and all things that
are therein:
16 Who in times past suffered all nations to walk in their own ways.
17 Nevertheless he left not himself without witness, in that he did good, and
gave us rain from heaven, and fruitful seasons, filling our hearts with food
and gladness.
18 And with these sayings scarce restrained they the people, that they had
not done sacrifice unto them.
19 And there came thither *certain* Jews from Antioch and Iconium, who
persuaded the people, and, having stoned Paul, drew *him* out of the city, sup-
posing he had been dead.
20 Howbeit, as the disciples stood round about him, he rose up, and came
into the city: and the next day he departed with Barnabas to Derbe.

Paul and Barnabas Return to Antioch in Syria

21 And when they had preached the gospel to that city, and had taught many,
they returned again to Lystra, and *to* Iconium, and Antioch,
22 Confirming the souls of the disciples, *and* exhorting them to continue in
the faith, and that we must through much tribulation enter into the kingdom
of God.
23 And when they had ordained them elders in every church, and had prayed
with fasting, they commended them to the Lord, on whom they believed.
24 And after they had passed throughout Pisidia, they came to Pamphylia.
25 And when they had preached the word in Perga, they went down into
Attalia:
26 And thence sailed to Antioch, from whence they had been recommended
to the grace of God for the work which they fulfilled.
27 And when they were come, and had gathered the church together, they
rehearsed all that God had done with them, and how he had opened the door
of faith unto the Gentiles.
28 And there they abode long time with the disciples.

Controversy about Moses' Teachings

15 And certain men which came down from Judaea taught the breth-
ren, *and said*, Except ye be circumcised after the manner of Moses,
ye cannot be saved.
2 When therefore Paul and Barnabas had no small dissension and disputa-
tion with them, they determined that Paul and Barnabas, and certain other
of them, should go up to Jerusalem unto the apostles and elders about this
question.
3 And being brought on their way by the church, they passed through
Phenice and Samaria, declaring the conversion of the Gentiles: and they caused
great joy unto all the brethren.
4 And when they were come to Jerusalem, they were received of the church,
and *of* the apostles and elders, and they declared all things that God had done
with them.
5 But there rose up certain of the sect of the Pharisees which believed, saying,
That it was needful to circumcise them, and to command *them* to keep the
law of Moses.

The Apostles Consult

6 And the apostles and elders came together for to consider of this matter.
7 And when there had been much disputing, Peter rose up, and said unto
them, Men *and* brethren, ye know how that a good while ago God made choice
among us, that the Gentiles by my mouth should hear the word of the gospel,
and believe.
8 And God, which knoweth the hearts, bare them witness, giving them the
Holy Ghost, even as *he did* unto us;
9 And put no difference between us and them, purifying their hearts by faith.
10 Now therefore why tempt ye God, to put a yoke upon the neck of the
disciples, which neither our fathers nor we were able to bear?
11 But we believe that through the grace of the Lord Jesus Christ we shall be
saved, even as they.
12 Then all the multitude kept silence, and gave audience to Barnabas and
Paul, declaring what miracles and wonders God had wrought among the
Gentiles by them.
13 And after they had held their peace, James answered, saying, Men *and*
brethren, hearken unto me:
14 Simeon hath declared how God at the first did visit the Gentiles, to take
out of them a people for his name.
15 And to this agree the words of the prophets; as it is written,
16 After this I will return, and will build again the tabernacle of David, which
is fallen down; and I will build again the ruins thereof, and I will set it up:
17 That the residue of men might seek after the Lord, and all the Gentiles,
upon whom my name is called, saith the Lord, who doeth all these things.
18 Known unto God are all his works from the beginning of the world.
19 Wherefore my sentence is, that we trouble not them, which from among
the Gentiles are turned to God:
20 But that we write unto them, that they abstain from pollutions of idols,
and *from* fornication, and *from* things strangled, and *from* blood.
21 For Moses of old time hath in every city them that preach him, being read
in the synagogues every sabbath day.

The Apostles Send Letters with Their Decision

22 Then pleased it the apostles and elders, with the whole church, to send
chosen men of their own company to Antioch with Paul and Barnabas; *name-
ly*, Judas surnamed Barsabas, and Silas, chief men among the brethren:
23 And they wrote *letters* by them after this manner; The apostles and elders
and brethren *send* greeting unto the brethren which are of the Gentiles in
Antioch and Syria and Cilicia:
24 Forasmuch as we have heard, that certain which went out from us have
troubled you with words, subverting your souls, saying, *Ye must* be circum-
cised, and keep the law: to whom we gave no *such* commandment:
25 It seemed good unto us, being assembled with one accord, to send chosen
men unto you with our beloved Barnabas and Paul,
26 Men that have hazarded their lives for the name of our Lord Jesus Christ.
27 We have sent therefore Judas and Silas, who shall also tell *you* the same
things by mouth.
28 For it seemed good to the Holy Ghost, and to us, to lay upon you no great-
er burden than these necessary things;
29 That ye abstain from meats offered to idols, and from blood, and from
things strangled, and from fornication: from which if ye keep yourselves, ye
shall do well. Fare ye well.
30 So when they were dismissed, they came to Antioch: and when they had
gathered the multitude together, they delivered the epistle:
31 *Which* when they had read, they rejoiced for the consolation.

32 And Judas and Silas, being prophets also themselves, exhorted the breth-
ren with many words, and confirmed *them*.
33 And after they had tarried *there* a space, they were let go in peace from
the brethren unto the apostles.
34 Notwithstanding it pleased Silas to abide there still.
35 Paul also and Barnabas continued in Antioch, teaching and preaching
the word of the Lord, with many others also.

Paul and Barnabas Separate

36 And some days after Paul said unto Barnabas, Let us go again and visit our
brethren in every city where we have preached the word of the Lord, *and see*
how they do.
37 And Barnabas determined to take with them John, whose surname was
Mark.
38 But Paul thought not good to take him with them, who departed from
them from Pamphylia, and went not with them to the work.
39 And the contention was so sharp between them, that they departed asun-
der one from the other: and so Barnabas took Mark, and sailed unto Cyprus;
40 And Paul chose Silas, and departed, being recommended by the brethren
unto the grace of God.
41 And he went through Syria and Cilicia, confirming the churches.

Timothy Joins Paul

16 Then came he to Derbe and Lystra: and, behold, a certain disciple
was there, named Timotheus, the son of a certain woman, which
was a Jewess, and believed; but his father *was* a Greek:
2 Which was well reported of by the brethren that were at Lystra and
Iconium.
3 Him would Paul have to go forth with him; and took and circumcised him
because of the Jews which were in those quarters: for they knew all that his
father was a Greek.
4 And as they went through the cities, they delivered them the decrees for
to keep, that were ordained of the apostles and elders which were at Jerusalem.
5 And so were the churches established in the faith, and increased in number
daily.

The Macedonian Call

6 Now when they had gone throughout Phrygia and the region of Galatia,
and were forbidden of the Holy Ghost to preach the word in Asia,
7 After they were come to Mysia, they assayed to go into Bithynia: but the
Spirit suffered them not.
8 And they passing by Mysia came down to Troas.
9 And a vision appeared to Paul in the night; There stood a man of Macedonia,
and prayed him, saying, Come over into Macedonia, and help us.
10 And after he had seen the vision, immediately we endeavoured to go into
Macedonia, assuredly gathering that the Lord had called us for to preach the
gospel unto them.

Paul and Silas in Philippi

11 Therefore loosing from Troas, we came with a straight course to
Samothracia, and the next *day* to Neapolis;
12 And from thence to Philippi, which is the chief city of that part of
Macedonia, *and* a colony: and we were in that city abiding certain days.
13 And on the sabbath we went out of the city by a river side, where prayer
was wont to be made; and we sat down, and spake unto the women which
resorted *thither*.

14 And a certain woman named Lydia, a seller of purple, of the city of
Thyatira, which worshipped God, heard *us*: whose heart the Lord opened, that
she attended unto the things which were spoken of Paul.
15 And when she was baptized, and her household, she besought *us*, saying,
If ye have judged me to be faithful to the Lord, come into my house, and abide
there. And she constrained us.

Paul Frees a Girl of an Evil Spirit

16 And it came to pass, as we went to prayer, a certain damsel possessed with
a spirit of divination met us, which brought her masters much gain by sooth-
saying:
17 The same followed Paul and us, and cried, saying, These men are the serv-
ants of the most high God, which shew unto us the way of salvation.
18 And this did she many days. But Paul, being grieved, turned and said to
the spirit, I command thee in the name of Jesus Christ to come out of her. And
he came out the same hour.
19 And when her masters saw that the hope of their gains was gone, they
caught Paul and Silas, and drew *them* into the marketplace unto the rulers,
20 And brought them to the magistrates, saying, These men, being Jews, do
exceedingly trouble our city,
21 And teach customs, which are not lawful for us to receive, neither to
observe, being Romans.
22 And the multitude rose up together against them: and the magistrates
rent off their clothes, and commanded to beat *them*.
23 And when they had laid many stripes upon them, they cast *them* into
prison, charging the jailor to keep them safely:
24 Who, having received such a charge, thrust them into the inner prison,
and made their feet fast in the stocks.
25 And at midnight Paul and Silas prayed, and sang praises unto God: and
the prisoners heard them.
26 And suddenly there was a great earthquake, so that the foundations of the
prison were shaken: and immediately all the doors were opened, and every
one's bands were loosed.

The Philippian Jailer Believes

27 And the keeper of the prison awaking out of his sleep, and seeing the
prison doors open, he drew out his sword, and would have killed himself,
supposing that the prisoners had been fled.
28 But Paul cried with a loud voice, saying, Do thyself no harm: for we are all
here.
29 Then he called for a light, and sprang in, and came trembling, and fell
down before Paul and Silas,
30 And brought them out, and said, Sirs, what must I do to be saved?
31 And they said, Believe on the Lord Jesus Christ, and thou shalt be saved,
and thy house.
32 And they spake unto him the word of the Lord, and to all that were in his
house.
33 And he took them the same hour of the night, and washed *their* stripes;
and was baptized, he and all his, straightway.
34 And when he had brought them into his house, he set meat before them,
and rejoiced, believing in God with all his house.
35 And when it was day, the magistrates sent the serjeants, saying, Let those
men go.
36 And the keeper of the prison told this saying to Paul, The magistrates have
sent to let you go: now therefore depart, and go in peace.

37 But Paul said unto them, They have beaten us openly uncondemned, being
Romans, and have cast *us* into prison; and now do they thrust us out privily?
nay verily; but let them come themselves and fetch us out.
38 And the serjeants told these words unto the magistrates: and they feared,
when they heard that they were Romans.
39 And they came and besought them, and brought *them* out, and desired
them to depart out of the city.
40 And they went out of the prison, and entered into *the house of* Lydia: and
when they had seen the brethren, they comforted them, and departed.

Paul Preaches at Thessalonica

17 Now when they had passed through Amphipolis and Apollonia,
they came to Thessalonica, where was a synagogue of the Jews:
2 And Paul, as his manner was, went in unto them, and three sabbath days
reasoned with them out of the scriptures,
3 Opening and alleging, that Christ must needs have suffered, and risen again
from the dead; and that this Jesus, whom I preach unto you, is Christ.
4 And some of them believed, and consorted with Paul and Silas; and of the
devout Greeks a great multitude, and of the chief women not a few.
5 But the Jews which believed not, moved with envy, took unto them certain
lewd fellows of the baser sort, and gathered a company, and set all the city on
an uproar, and assaulted the house of Jason, and sought to bring them out to
the people.
6 And when they found them not, they drew Jason and certain brethren unto
the rulers of the city, crying, These that have turned the world upside down
are come hither also;
7 Whom Jason hath received: and these all do contrary to the decrees of
Caesar, saying that there is another king, *one* Jesus.
8 And they troubled the people and the rulers of the city, when they heard
these things.
9 And when they had taken security of Jason, and of the other, they let them
go.

Paul Preaches at Berea

10 And the brethren immediately sent away Paul and Silas by night unto
Berea: who coming *thither* went into the synagogue of the Jews.
11 These were more noble than those in Thessalonica, in that they received
the word with all readiness of mind, and searched the scriptures daily, wheth-
er those things were so.
12 Therefore many of them believed; also of honourable women which were
Greeks, and of men, not a few.
13 But when the Jews of Thessalonica had knowledge that the word of God
was preached of Paul at Berea, they came thither also, and stirred up the peo-
ple.
14 And then immediately the brethren sent away Paul to go as it were to the
sea: but Silas and Timotheus abode there still.

Paul Preaches in Athens

15 And they that conducted Paul brought him unto Athens: and receiving a
commandment unto Silas and Timotheus for to come to him with all speed,
they departed.
16 Now while Paul waited for them at Athens, his spirit was stirred in him,
when he saw the city wholly given to idolatry.
17 Therefore disputed he in the synagogue with the Jews, and with the devout
persons, and in the market daily with them that met with him.
18 Then certain philosophers of the Epicureans, and of the Stoicks, encoun-
tered him. And some said, What will this babbler say? other some, He seemeth

to be a setter forth of strange gods: because he preached unto them Jesus, and
the resurrection.
19 And they took him, and brought him unto Areopagus, saying, May we
know what this new doctrine, whereof thou speakest, *is*?
20 For thou bringest certain strange things to our ears: we would know there-
fore what these things mean.
21 (For all the Athenians and strangers which were there spent their time in
nothing else, but either to tell, or to hear some new thing.)
22 Then Paul stood in the midst of Mars' hill, and said, *Ye* men of Athens, I
perceive that in all things ye are too superstitious.
23 For as I passed by, and beheld your devotions, I found an altar with this
inscription, TO THE UNKNOWN GOD. Whom therefore ye ignorantly wor-
ship, him declare I unto you.
24 God that made the world and all things therein, seeing that he is Lord of
heaven and earth, dwelleth not in temples made with hands;
25 Neither is worshipped with men's hands, as though he needed any thing,
seeing he giveth to all life, and breath, and all things;
26 And hath made of one blood all nations of men for to dwell on all the face
of the earth, and hath determined the times before appointed, and the bounds
of their habitation;
27 That they should seek the Lord, if haply they might feel after him, and
find him, though he be not far from every one of us:
28 For in him we live, and move, and have our being; as certain also of your
own poets have said, For we are also his offspring.
29 Forasmuch then as we are the offspring of God, we ought not to think that
the Godhead is like unto gold, or silver, or stone, graven by art and man's device.
30 And the times of this ignorance God winked at; but now commandeth all
men every where to repent:
31 Because he hath appointed a day, in the which he will judge the world in
righteousness by *that* man whom he hath ordained; *whereof* he hath given
assurance unto all *men*, in that he hath raised him from the dead.
32 And when they heard of the resurrection of the dead, some mocked: and
others said, We will hear thee again of this *matter*.
33 So Paul departed from among them.
34 Howbeit certain men clave unto him, and believed: among the which *was*
Dionysius the Areopagite, and a woman named Damaris, and others with
them.

Paul in Corinth

18 After these things Paul departed from Athens, and came to Corinth;
2 And found a certain Jew named Aquila, born in Pontus, lately come
from Italy, with his wife Priscilla; (because that Claudius had commanded all
Jews to depart from Rome:) and came unto them.
3 And because he was of the same craft, he abode with them, and wrought:
for by their occupation they were tentmakers.
4 And he reasoned in the synagogue every sabbath, and persuaded the Jews
and the Greeks.
5 And when Silas and Timotheus were come from Macedonia, Paul was
pressed in the spirit, and testified to the Jews *that* Jesus *was* Christ.
6 And when they opposed themselves, and blasphemed, he shook *his* rai-
ment, and said unto them, Your blood *be* upon your own heads; I *am* clean:
from henceforth I will go unto the Gentiles.
7 And he departed thence, and entered into a certain *man's* house, named
Justus, *one* that worshipped God, whose house joined hard to the synagogue.

8 And Crispus, the chief ruler of the synagogue, believed on the Lord with
all his house; and many of the Corinthians hearing believed, and were bap-
tized.
9 Then spake the Lord to Paul in the night by a vision, Be not afraid, but speak,
and hold not thy peace:
10 For I am with thee, and no man shall set on thee to hurt thee: for I have
much people in this city.
11 And he continued *there* a year and six months, teaching the word of God
among them.

The Jews Attack Paul

12 And when Gallio was the deputy of Achaia, the Jews made insurrection
with one accord against Paul, and brought him to the judgment seat,
13 Saying, This *fellow* persuadeth men to worship God contrary to the law.
14 And when Paul was now about to open *his* mouth, Gallio said unto the
Jews, If it were a matter of wrong or wicked lewdness, O *ye* Jews, reason would
that I should bear with you:
15 But if it be a question of words and names, and *of* your law, look ye *to it*;
for I will be no judge of such *matters*.
16 And he drave them from the judgment seat.
17 Then all the Greeks took Sosthenes, the chief ruler of the synagogue, and
beat *him* before the judgment seat. And Gallio cared for none of those things.

Paul's Return to Antioch

18 And Paul *after this* tarried *there* yet a good while, and then took his leave
of the brethren, and sailed thence into Syria, and with him Priscilla and Aquila;
having shorn *his* head in Cenchrea: for he had a vow.
19 And he came to Ephesus, and left them there: but he himself entered into
the synagogue, and reasoned with the Jews.
20 When they desired *him* to tarry longer time with them, he consented not;
21 But bade them farewell, saying, I must by all means keep this feast that
cometh in Jerusalem: but I will return again unto you, if God will. And he
sailed from Ephesus.
22 And when he had landed at Caesarea, and gone up, and saluted the church,
he went down to Antioch.
23 And after he had spent some time *there*, he departed, and went over *all*
the country of Galatia and Phrygia in order, strengthening all the disciples.

Apollos Learns from Priscilla and Aquila

24 And a certain Jew named Apollos, born at Alexandria, an eloquent man,
and mighty in the scriptures, came to Ephesus.
25 This man was instructed in the way of the Lord; and being fervent in the
spirit, he spake and taught diligently the things of the Lord, knowing only the
baptism of John.
26 And he began to speak boldly in the synagogue: whom when Aquila and
Priscilla had heard, they took him unto *them*, and expounded unto him the
way of God more perfectly.
27 And when he was disposed to pass into Achaia, the brethren wrote, exhort-
ing the disciples to receive him: who, when he was come, helped them much
which had believed through grace:
28 For he mightily convinced the Jews, *and that* publickly, shewing by the
scriptures that Jesus was Christ.

Paul in Ephesus

19 And it came to pass, that, while Apollos was at Corinth, Paul having
passed through the upper coasts came to Ephesus: and finding
certain disciples,
2 He said unto them, Have ye received the Holy Ghost since ye believed? And
they said unto him, We have not so much as heard whether there be any Holy
Ghost.

3 And he said unto them, Unto what then were ye baptized? And they said,
Unto John's baptism.
4 Then said Paul, John verily baptized with the baptism of repentance, saying
unto the people, that they should believe on him which should come after
him, that is, on Christ Jesus.
5 When they heard *this*, they were baptized in the name of the Lord Jesus.
6 And when Paul had laid *his* hands upon them, the Holy Ghost came on
them; and they spake with tongues, and prophesied.
7 And all the men were about twelve.

The Jews Reject Paul's Teachings

8 And he went into the synagogue, and spake boldly for the space of three
months, disputing and persuading the things concerning the kingdom of
God.
9 But when divers were hardened, and believed not, but spake evil of that
way before the multitude, he departed from them, and separated the disciples,
disputing daily in the school of one Tyrannus.
10 And this continued by the space of two years; so that all they which dwelt
in Asia heard the word of the Lord Jesus, both Jews and Greeks.
11 And God wrought special miracles by the hands of Paul:
12 So that from his body were brought unto the sick handkerchiefs or aprons,
and the diseases departed from them, and the evil spirits went out of them.

Many in Ephesus Believe

13 Then certain of the vagabond Jews, exorcists, took upon them to call over
them which had evil spirits the name of the Lord Jesus, saying, We adjure you
by Jesus whom Paul preacheth.
14 And there were seven sons of *one* Sceva, a Jew, *and* chief of the priests,
which did so.
15 And the evil spirit answered and said, Jesus I know, and Paul I know; but
who are ye?
16 And the man in whom the evil spirit was leaped on them, and overcame
them, and prevailed against them, so that they fled out of that house naked
and wounded.
17 And this was known to all the Jews and Greeks also dwelling at Ephesus;
and fear fell on them all, and the name of the Lord Jesus was magnified.
18 And many that believed came, and confessed, and shewed their deeds.
19 Many of them also which used curious arts brought their books together,
and burned them before all *men*: and they counted the price of them, and
found *it* fifty thousand *pieces* of silver.
20 So mightily grew the word of God and prevailed.
21 After these things were ended, Paul purposed in the spirit, when he had
passed through Macedonia and Achaia, to go to Jerusalem, saying, After I have
been there, I must also see Rome.
22 So he sent into Macedonia two of them that ministered unto him,
Timotheus and Erastus; but he himself stayed in Asia for a season.

A Riot Erupts

23 And the same time there arose no small stir about that way.
24 For a certain *man* named Demetrius, a silversmith, which made silver
shrines for Diana, brought no small gain unto the craftsmen;
25 Whom he called together with the workmen of like occupation, and said,
Sirs, ye know that by this craft we have our wealth.
26 Moreover ye see and hear, that not alone at Ephesus, but almost through-
out all Asia, this Paul hath persuaded and turned away much people, saying
that they be no gods, which are made with hands:

27 So that not only this our craft is in danger to be set at nought; but also that
the temple of the great goddess Diana should be despised, and her magnifi-
cence should be destroyed, whom all Asia and the world worshippeth.
28 And when they heard *these sayings*, they were full of wrath, and cried out,
saying, Great *is* Diana of the Ephesians.
29 And the whole city was filled with confusion: and having caught Gaius
and Aristarchus, men of Macedonia, Paul's companions in travel, they rushed
with one accord into the theatre.
30 And when Paul would have entered in unto the people, the disciples suf-
fered him not.
31 And certain of the chief of Asia, which were his friends, sent unto him,
desiring *him* that he would not adventure himself into the theatre.
32 Some therefore cried one thing, and some another: for the assembly was
confused; and the more part knew not wherefore they were come together.
33 And they drew Alexander out of the multitude, the Jews putting him for-
ward. And Alexander beckoned with the hand, and would have made his
defence unto the people.
34 But when they knew that he was a Jew, all with one voice about the space
of two hours cried out, Great *is* Diana of the Ephesians.
35 And when the townclerk had appeased the people, he said, *Ye* men of
Ephesus, what man is there that knoweth not how that the city of the Ephesians
is a worshipper of the great goddess Diana, and of the *image* which fell down
from Jupiter?
36 Seeing then that these things cannot be spoken against, ye ought to be
quiet, and to do nothing rashly.
37 For ye have brought hither these men, which are neither robbers of
churches, nor yet blasphemers of your goddess.
38 Wherefore if Demetrius, and the craftsmen which are with him, have a
matter against any man, the law is open, and there are deputies: let them
implead one another.
39 But if ye enquire any thing concerning other matters, it shall be deter-
mined in a lawful assembly.
40 For we are in danger to be called in question for this day's uproar, there
being no cause whereby we may give an account of this concourse.
41 And when he had thus spoken, he dismissed the assembly.

Paul Goes to Macedonia

20 And after the uproar was ceased, Paul called unto *him* the disciples,
and embraced *them*, and departed for to go into Macedonia.
2 And when he had gone over those parts, and had given them much exhor-
tation, he came into Greece,
3 And *there* abode three months. And when the Jews laid wait for him, as he
was about to sail into Syria, he purposed to return through Macedonia.
4 And there accompanied him into Asia Sopater of Berea; and of the
Thessalonians, Aristarchus and Secundus; and Gaius of Derbe, and Timotheus;
and of Asia, Tychicus and Trophimus.
5 These going before tarried for us at Troas.

Paul in Troas

6 And we sailed away from Philippi after the days of unleavened bread, and
came unto them to Troas in five days; where we abode seven days.
7 And upon the first *day* of the week, when the disciples came together to
break bread, Paul preached unto them, ready to depart on the morrow; and
continued his speech until midnight.
8 And there were many lights in the upper chamber, where they were gath-
ered together.

9 And there sat in a window a certain young man named Eutychus, being
fallen into a deep sleep: and as Paul was long preaching, he sunk down with
sleep, and fell down from the third loft, and was taken up dead.
10 And Paul went down, and fell on him, and embracing *him* said, Trouble
not yourselves; for his life is in him.
11 When he therefore was come up again, and had broken bread, and eaten,
and talked a long while, even till break of day, so he departed.
12 And they brought the young man alive, and were not a little comforted.

Paul's Trip to Miletus

13 And we went before to ship, and sailed unto Assos, there intending to take
in Paul: for so had he appointed, minding himself to go afoot.
14 And when he met with us at Assos, we took him in, and came to Mitylene.
15 And we sailed thence, and came the next *day* over against Chios; and the
next *day* we arrived at Samos, and tarried at Trogyllium; and the next *day* we
came to Miletus.
16 For Paul had determined to sail by Ephesus, because he would not spend
the time in Asia: for he hasted, if it were possible for him, to be at Jerusalem
the day of Pentecost.

Paul Meets with the Ephesian Elders

17 And from Miletus he sent to Ephesus, and called the elders of the church.
18 And when they were come to him, he said unto them, Ye know, from the
first day that I came into Asia, after what manner I have been with you at all
seasons,
19 Serving the Lord with all humility of mind, and with many tears, and
temptations, which befell me by the lying in wait of the Jews:
20 *And* how I kept back nothing that was profitable *unto you*, but have
shewed you, and have taught you publickly, and from house to house,
21 Testifying both to the Jews, and also to the Greeks, repentance toward
God, and faith toward our Lord Jesus Christ.
22 And now, behold, I go bound in the spirit unto Jerusalem, not knowing
the things that shall befall me there:
23 Save that the Holy Ghost witnesseth in every city, saying that bonds and
afflictions abide me.
24 But none of these things move me, neither count I my life dear unto myself,
so that I might finish my course with joy, and the ministry, which I have
received of the Lord Jesus, to testify the gospel of the grace of God.
25 And now, behold, I know that ye all, among whom I have gone preaching
the kingdom of God, shall see my face no more.
26 Wherefore I take you to record this day, that I *am* pure from the blood of
all *men*.
27 For I have not shunned to declare unto you all the counsel of God.
28 Take heed therefore unto yourselves, and to all the flock, over the which
the Holy Ghost hath made you overseers, to feed the church of God, which he
hath purchased with his own blood.
29 For I know this, that after my departing shall grievous wolves enter in
among you, not sparing the flock.
30 Also of your own selves shall men arise, speaking perverse things, to draw
away disciples after them.
31 Therefore watch, and remember, that by the space of three years I ceased
not to warn every one night and day with tears.
32 And now, brethren, I commend you to God, and to the word of his grace,
which is able to build you up, and to give you an inheritance among all them
which are sanctified.
33 I have coveted no man's silver, or gold, or apparel.

34 Yea, ye yourselves know, that these hands have ministered unto my neces-
sities, and to them that were with me.
35 I have shewed you all things, how that so labouring ye ought to support
the weak, and to remember the words of the Lord Jesus, how he said, It is more
blessed to give than to receive.
36 And when he had thus spoken, he kneeled down, and prayed with them
all.
37 And they all wept sore, and fell on Paul's neck, and kissed him,
38 Sorrowing most of all for the words which he spake, that they should see
his face no more. And they accompanied him unto the ship.

Paul in Tyre

21 And it came to pass, that after we were gotten from them, and had
launched, we came with a straight course unto Coos, and the *day*
following unto Rhodes, and from thence unto Patara:
2 And finding a ship sailing over unto Phenicia, we went aboard, and set
forth.
3 Now when we had discovered Cyprus, we left it on the left hand, and sailed
into Syria, and landed at Tyre: for there the ship was to unlade her burden.
4 And finding disciples, we tarried there seven days: who said to Paul through
the Spirit, that he should not go up to Jerusalem.
5 And when we had accomplished those days, we departed and went our
way; and they all brought us on our way, with wives and children, till *we were*
out of the city: and we kneeled down on the shore, and prayed.
6 And when we had taken our leave one of another, we took ship; and they
returned home again.
7 And when we had finished *our* course from Tyre, we came to Ptolemais,
and saluted the brethren, and abode with them one day.

Paul in Caesarea

8 And the next *day* we that were of Paul's company departed, and came unto
Caesarea: and we entered into the house of Philip the evangelist, which was
one of the seven; and abode with him.
9 And the same man had four daughters, virgins, which did prophesy.
10 And as we tarried *there* many days, there came down from Judaea a certain
prophet, named Agabus.
11 And when he was come unto us, he took Paul's girdle, and bound his own
hands and feet, and said, Thus saith the Holy Ghost, So shall the Jews at
Jerusalem bind the man that owneth this girdle, and shall deliver *him* into the
hands of the Gentiles.
12 And when we heard these things, both we, and they of that place, besought
him not to go up to Jerusalem.
13 Then Paul answered, What mean ye to weep and to break mine heart? for
I am ready not to be bound only, but also to die at Jerusalem for the name of
the Lord Jesus.
14 And when he would not be persuaded, we ceased, saying, The will of the
Lord be done.

Paul in Jerusalem

15 And after those days we took up our carriages, and went up to Jerusalem.
16 There went with us also *certain* of the disciples of Caesarea, and brought
with them one Mnason of Cyprus, an old disciple, with whom we should lodge.
17 And when we were come to Jerusalem, the brethren received us gladly.
18 And the *day* following Paul went in with us unto James; and all the elders
were present.
19 And when he had saluted them, he declared particularly what things God
had wrought among the Gentiles by his ministry.

20 And when they heard *it*, they glorified the Lord, and said unto him, Thou
seest, brother, how many thousands of Jews there are which believe; and they
are all zealous of the law:
21 And they are informed of thee, that thou teachest all the Jews which are
among the Gentiles to forsake Moses, saying that they ought not to circumcise
their children, neither to walk after the customs.
22 What is it therefore? the multitude must needs come together: for they
will hear that thou art come.
23 Do therefore this that we say to thee: We have four men which have a vow
on them;
24 Them take, and purify thyself with them, and be at charges with them,
that they may shave *their* heads: and all may know that those things, whereof
they were informed concerning thee, are nothing; but *that* thou thyself also
walkest orderly, and keepest the law.
25 As touching the Gentiles which believe, we have written *and* concluded
that they observe no such thing, save only that they keep themselves from
things offered to idols, and from blood, and from strangled, and from forni-
cation.
26 Then Paul took the men, and the next day purifying himself with them
entered into the temple, to signify the accomplishment of the days of purifi-
cation, until that an offering should be offered for every one of them.

Paul Is Arrested

27 And when the seven days were almost ended, the Jews which were of Asia,
when they saw him in the temple, stirred up all the people, and laid hands on
him,
28 Crying out, Men of Israel, help: This is the man, that teacheth all *men* every
where against the people, and the law, and this place: and further brought
Greeks also into the temple, and hath polluted this holy place.
29 (For they had seen before with him in the city Trophimus an Ephesian,
whom they supposed that Paul had brought into the temple.)
30 And all the city was moved, and the people ran together: and they took
Paul, and drew him out of the temple: and forthwith the doors were shut.
31 And as they went about to kill him, tidings came unto the chief captain
of the band, that all Jerusalem was in an uproar.
32 Who immediately took soldiers and centurions, and ran down unto them:
and when they saw the chief captain and the soldiers, they left beating of Paul.
33 Then the chief captain came near, and took him, and commanded *him* to
be bound with two chains; and demanded who he was, and what he had done.
34 And some cried one thing, some another, among the multitude: and when
he could not know the certainty for the tumult, he commanded him to be
carried into the castle.
35 And when he came upon the stairs, so it was, that he was borne of the
soldiers for the violence of the people.
36 For the multitude of the people followed after, crying, Away with him.
37 And as Paul was to be led into the castle, he said unto the chief captain,
May I speak unto thee? Who said, Canst thou speak Greek?
38 Art not thou that Egyptian, which before these days madest an uproar,
and leddest out into the wilderness four thousand men that were murderers?
39 But Paul said, I am a man *which am* a Jew of Tarsus, *a city* in Cilicia, a
citizen of no mean city: and, I beseech thee, suffer me to speak unto the people.
40 And when he had given him licence, Paul stood on the stairs, and beckoned
with the hand unto the people. And when there was made a great silence, he
spake unto *them* in the Hebrew tongue, saying,

Paul Speaks in His Own Defense

22 Men, brethren, and fathers, hear ye my defence *which I make* now unto you.

2 (And when they heard that he spake in the Hebrew tongue to them, they kept the more silence: and he saith,)

3 I am verily a man *which am* a Jew, born in Tarsus, *a city* in Cilicia, yet brought up in this city at the feet of Gamaliel, *and* taught according to the perfect manner of the law of the fathers, and was zealous toward God, as ye all are this day.

4 And I persecuted this way unto the death, binding and delivering into prisons both men and women.

5 As also the high priest doth bear me witness, and all the estate of the elders: from whom also I received letters unto the brethren, and went to Damascus, to bring them which were there bound unto Jerusalem, for to be punished.

6 And it came to pass, that, as I made my journey, and was come nigh unto Damascus about noon, suddenly there shone from heaven a great light round about me.

7 And I fell unto the ground, and heard a voice saying unto me, Saul, Saul, why persecutest thou me?

8 And I answered, Who art thou, Lord? And he said unto me, I am Jesus of Nazareth, whom thou persecutest.

9 And they that were with me saw indeed the light, and were afraid; but they heard not the voice of him that spake to me.

10 And I said, What shall I do, Lord? And the Lord said unto me, Arise, and go into Damascus; and there it shall be told thee of all things which are appointed for thee to do.

11 And when I could not see for the glory of that light, being led by the hand of them that were with me, I came into Damascus.

12 And one Ananias, a devout man according to the law, having a good report of all the Jews which dwelt *there*,

13 Came unto me, and stood, and said unto me, Brother Saul, receive thy sight. And the same hour I looked up upon him.

14 And he said, The God of our fathers hath chosen thee, that thou shouldest know his will, and see that Just One, and shouldest hear the voice of his mouth.

15 For thou shalt be his witness unto all men of what thou hast seen and heard.

16 And now why tarriest thou? arise, and be baptized, and wash away thy sins, calling on the name of the Lord.

17 And it came to pass, that, when I was come again to Jerusalem, even while I prayed in the temple, I was in a trance;

18 And saw him saying unto me, Make haste, and get thee quickly out of Jerusalem: for they will not receive thy testimony concerning me.

19 And I said, Lord, they know that I imprisoned and beat in every synagogue them that believed on thee:

20 And when the blood of thy martyr Stephen was shed, I also was standing by, and consenting unto his death, and kept the raiment of them that slew him.

21 And he said unto me, Depart: for I will send thee far hence unto the Gentiles.

The Jews Denounce Paul

22 And they gave him audience unto this word, and *then* lifted up their voices, and said, Away with such a *fellow* from the earth: for it is not fit that he should live.

23 And as they cried out, and cast off *their* clothes, and threw dust into the air,

24 The chief captain commanded him to be brought into the castle, and bade
that he should be examined by scourging; that he might know wherefore they
cried so against him.
25 And as theybound him with thongs, Paul said unto the centurion that
stood by, Is it lawful for you to scourge a man that is a Roman, and uncon-
demned?
26 When the centurion heard *that*, he went and told the chief captain, saying,
Take heed what thou doest: for this man is a Roman.
27 Then the chief captain came, and said unto him, Tell me, art thou a
Roman? He said, Yea.
28 And the chief captain answered, With a great sum obtained I this freedom.
And Paul said, But I was *free* born.
29 Then straightway they departed from him which should have examined
him: and the chief captain also was afraid, after he knew that he was a Roman,
and because he had bound him.
30 On the morrow, because he would have known the certainty wherefore
he was accused of the Jews, he loosed him from *his* bands, and commanded
the chief priests and all their council to appear, and brought Paul down, and
set him before them.

Paul before the Jewish Council

23 And Paul, earnestly beholding the council, said, Men *and* brethren,
I have lived in all good conscience before God until this day.
2 And the high priest Ananias commanded them that stood by him to smite
him on the mouth.
3 Then said Paul unto him, God shall smite thee, *thou* whited wall: for sittest
thou to judge me after the law, and commandest me to be smitten contrary to
the law?
4 And they that stood by said, Revilest thou God's high priest?
5 Then said Paul, I wist not, brethren, that he was the high priest: for it is
written, Thou shalt not speak evil of the ruler of thy people.
6 But when Paul perceived that the one part were Sadducees, and the other
Pharisees, he cried out in the council, Men *and* brethren, I am a Pharisee, the
son of a Pharisee: of the hope and resurrection of the dead I am called in
question.
7 And when he had so said, there arose a dissension between the Pharisees
and the Sadducees: and the multitude was divided.
8 For the Sadducees say that there is no resurrection, neither angel, nor spir-
it: but the Pharisees confess both.
9 And there arose a great cry: and the scribes *that were* of the Pharisees' part
arose, and strove, saying, We find no evil in this man: but if a spirit or an angel
hath spoken to him, let us not fight against God.
10 And when there arose a great dissension, the chief captain, fearing lest
Paul should have been pulled in pieces of them, commanded the soldiers to
go down, and to take him by force from among them, and to bring *him* into
the castle.
11 And the night following the Lord stood by him, and said, Be of good cheer,
Paul: for as thou hast testified of me in Jerusalem, so must thou bear witness
also at Rome.

Some Jews Plot to Kill Paul

12 And when it was day, certain of the Jews banded together, and bound
themselves under a curse, saying that they would neither eat nor drink till
they had killed Paul.
13 And they were more than forty which had made this conspiracy.
14 And they came to the chief priests and elders, and said, We have bound
ourselves under a great curse, that we will eat nothing until we have slain Paul.

15 Now therefore ye with the council signify to the chief captain that he bring
him down unto you to morrow, as though ye would enquire something more
perfectly concerning him: and we, or ever he come near, are ready to kill him.
16 And when Paul's sister's son heard of their lying in wait, he went and
entered into the castle, and told Paul.
17 Then Paul called one of the centurions unto *him*, and said, Bring this
young man unto the chief captain: for he hath a certain thing to tell him.
18 So he took him, and brought *him* to the chief captain, and said, Paul the
prisoner called me unto *him*, and prayed me to bring this young man unto
thee, who hath something to say unto thee.
19 Then the chief captain took him by the hand, and went *with him* aside
privately, and asked *him*, What is that thou hast to tell me?
20 And he said, The Jews have agreed to desire thee that thou wouldest bring
down Paul to morrow into the council, as though they would enquire some-
what of him more perfectly.
21 But do not thou yield unto them: for there lie in wait for him of them more
than forty men, which have bound themselves with an oath, that they will
neither eat nor drink till they have killed him: and now are they ready, looking
for a promise from thee.
22 So the chief captain *then* let the young man depart, and charged *him*, *See*
thou tell no man that thou hast shewed these things to me.
23 And he called unto *him* two centurions, saying, Make ready two hundred
soldiers to go to Caesarea, and horsemen threescore and ten, and spearmen
two hundred, at the third hour of the night;
24 And provide *them* beasts, that they may set Paul on, and bring *him* safe
unto Felix the governor.
25 And he wrote a letter after this manner:
26 Claudius Lysias unto the most excellent governor Felix *sendeth* greeting.
27 This man was taken of the Jews, and should have been killed of them: then
came I with an army, and rescued him, having understood that he was a
Roman.
28 And when I would have known the cause wherefore they accused him, I
brought him forth into their council:
29 Whom I perceived to be accused of questions of their law, but to have
nothing laid to his charge worthy of death or of bonds.
30 And when it was told me how that the Jews laid wait for the man, I sent
straightway to thee, and gave commandment to his accusers also to say before
thee what *they had* against him. Farewell.
31 Then the soldiers, as it was commanded them, took Paul, and brought
him by night to Antipatris.
32 On the morrow they left the horsemen to go with him, and returned to
the castle:
33 Who, when they came to Caesarea, and delivered the epistle to the gover-
nor, presented Paul also before him.
34 And when the governor had read *the letter*, he asked of what province he
was. And when he understood that *he was* of Cilicia;
35 I will hear thee, said he, when thine accusers are also come. And he com-
manded him to be kept in Herod's judgment hall.

Paul Presents His Case to Felix

24 And after five days Ananias the high priest descended with the
elders, and *with* a certain orator *named* Tertullus, who informed
the governor against Paul.
2 And when he was called forth, Tertullus began to accuse *him*, saying, Seeing
that by thee we enjoy great quietness, and that very worthy deeds are done
unto this nation by thy providence,

3 We accept *it* always, and in all places, most noble Felix, with all thankful-
ness.
4 Notwithstanding, that I be not further tedious unto thee, I pray thee that
thou wouldest hear us of thy clemency a few words.
5 For we have found this man *a* pestilent *fellow*, and a mover of sedition
among all the Jews throughout the world, and a ringleader of the sect of the
Nazarenes:
6 Who also hath gone about to profane the temple: whom we took, and would
have judged according to our law.
7 But the chief captain Lysias came *upon us*, and with great violence took
him away out of our hands,
8 Commanding his accusers to come unto thee: by examining of whom thy-
self mayest take knowledge of all these things, whereof we accuse him.
9 And the Jews also assented, saying that these things were so.
10 Then Paul, after that the governor had beckoned unto him to speak,
answered, Forasmuch as I know that thou hast been of many years a judge
unto this nation, I do the more cheerfully answer for myself:
11 Because that thou mayest understand, that there are yet but twelve days
since I went up to Jerusalem for to worship.
12 And they neither found me in the temple disputing with any man, neither
raising up the people, neither in the synagogues, nor in the city:
13 Neither can they prove the things whereof they now accuse me.
14 But this I confess unto thee, that after the way which they call heresy, so
worship I the God of my fathers, believing all things which are written in the
law and in the prophets:
15 And have hope toward God, which they themselves also allow, that there
shall be a resurrection of the dead, both of the just and unjust.
16 And herein do I exercise myself, to have always a conscience void of offence
toward God, and *toward* men.
17 Now after many years I came to bring alms to my nation, and offerings.
18 Whereupon certain Jews from Asia found me purified in the temple, nei-
ther with multitude, nor with tumult.
19 Who ought to have been here before thee, and object, if they had ought
against me.
20 Or else let these same *here* say, if they have found any evil doing in me,
while I stood before the council,
21 Except it be for this one voice, that I cried standing among them, Touching
the resurrection of the dead I am called in question by you this day.
22 And when Felix heard these things, having more perfect knowledge of
that way, he deferred them, and said, When Lysias the chief captain shall come
down, I will know the uttermost of your matter.
23 And he commanded a centurion to keep Paul, and to let *him* have liberty,
and that he should forbid none of his acquaintance to minister or come unto
him.
24 And after certain days, when Felix came with his wife Drusilla, which was
a Jewess, he sent for Paul, and heard him concerning the faith in Christ.
25 And as he reasoned of righteousness, temperance, and judgment to come,
Felix trembled, and answered, Go thy way for this time; when I have a conve-
nient season, I will call for thee.
26 He hoped also that money should have been given him of Paul, that he
might loose him: wherefore he sent for him the oftener, and communed with
him.
27 But after two years Porcius Festus came into Felix' room: and Felix, willing
to shew the Jews a pleasure, left Paul bound.

Paul Speaks to Festus

25 Now when Festus was come into the province, after three days he
ascended from Caesarea to Jerusalem.
2 Then the high priest and the chief of the Jews informed him against Paul,
and besought him,
3 And desired favour against him, that he would send for him to Jerusalem,
laying wait in the way to kill him.
4 But Festus answered, that Paul should be kept at Caesarea, and that he
himself would depart shortly *thither*.
5 Let them therefore, said he, which among you are able, go down with *me*,
and accuse this man, if there be any wickedness in him.
6 And when he had tarried among them more than ten days, he went down
unto Caesarea; and the next day sitting on the judgment seat commanded
Paul to be brought.
7 And when he was come, the Jews which came down from Jerusalem stood
round about, and laid many and grievous complaints against Paul, which they
could not prove.
8 While he answered for himself, Neither against the law of the Jews, neither
against the temple, nor yet against Caesar, have I offended any thing at all.
9 But Festus, willing to do the Jews a pleasure, answered Paul, and said, Wilt
thou go up to Jerusalem, and there be judged of these things before me?
10 Then said Paul, I stand at Caesar's judgment seat, where I ought to be
judged: to the Jews have I done no wrong, as thou very well knowest.
11 For if I be an offender, or have committed any thing worthy of death, I
refuse not to die: but if there be none of these things whereof these accuse me,
no man may deliver me unto them. I appeal unto Caesar.
12 Then Festus, when he had conferred with the council, answered, Hast
thou appealed unto Caesar? unto Caesar shalt thou go.

King Agrippa Meets Paul

13 And after certain days king Agrippa and Bernice came unto Caesarea to
salute Festus.
14 And when they had been there many days, Festus declared Paul's cause
unto the king, saying, There is a certain man left in bonds by Felix:
15 About whom, when I was at Jerusalem, the chief priests and the elders of
the Jews informed *me*, desiring *to have* judgment against him.
16 To whom I answered, It is not the manner of the Romans to deliver any
man to die, before that he which is accused have the accusers face to face, and
have licence to answer for himself concerning the crime laid against him.
17 Therefore, when they were come hither, without any delay on the morrow
I sat on the judgment seat, and commanded the man to be brought forth.
18 Against whom when the accusers stood up, they brought none accusation
of such things as I supposed:
19 But had certain questions against him of their own superstition, and of
one Jesus, which was dead, whom Paul affirmed to be alive.
20 And because I doubted of such manner of questions, I asked *him* wheth-
er he would go to Jerusalem, and there be judged of these matters.
21 But when Paul had appealed to be reserved unto the hearing of Augustus,
I commanded him to be kept till I might send him to Caesar.
22 Then Agrippa said unto Festus, I would also hear the man myself. To mor-
row, said he, thou shalt hear him.
23 And on the morrow, when Agrippa was come, and Bernice, with great
pomp, and was entered into the place of hearing, with the chief captains, and
principal men of the city, at Festus' commandment Paul was brought forth.
24 And Festus said, King Agrippa, and all men which are here present with
us, ye see this man, about whom all the multitude of the Jews have dealt with

me, both at Jerusalem, and *also* here, crying that he ought not to live any
longer.
25 But when I found that he had committed nothing worthy of death, and
that he himself hath appealed to Augustus, I have determined to send him.
26 Of whom I have no certain thing to write unto my lord. Wherefore I have
brought him forth before you, and specially before thee, O king Agrippa, that,
after examination had, I might have somewhat to write.
27 For it seemeth to me unreasonable to send a prisoner, and not withal to
signify the crimes *laid* against him.

Paul Describes His Life from His Childhood

26 Then Agrippa said unto Paul, Thou art permitted to speak for thy-
self. Then Paul stretched forth the hand, and answered for himself:
2 I think myself happy, king Agrippa, because I shall answer for myself this
day before thee touching all the things whereof I am accused of the Jews:
3 Especially *because I know* thee to be expert in all customs and questions
which are among the Jews: wherefore I beseech thee to hear me patiently.
4 My manner of life from my youth, which was at the first among mine own
nation at Jerusalem, know all the Jews;
5 Which knew me from the beginning, if they would testify, that after the
most straitest sect of our religion I lived a Pharisee.
6 And now I stand and am judged for the hope of the promise made of God
unto our fathers:
7 Unto which *promise* our twelve tribes, instantly serving *God* day and night,
hope to come. For which hope's sake, king Agrippa, I am accused of the Jews.
8 Why should it be thought a thing incredible with you, that God should
raise the dead?
9 I verily thought with myself, that I ought to do many things contrary to the
name of Jesus of Nazareth.
10 Which thing I also did in Jerusalem: and many of the saints did I shut up
in prison, having received authority from the chief priests; and when they
were put to death, I gave my voice against *them*.
11 And I punished them oft in every synagogue, and compelled *them* to blas-
pheme; and being exceedingly mad against them, I persecuted *them* even unto
strange cities.

Paul Describes His Conversion

12 Whereupon as I went to Damascus with authority and commission from
the chief priests,
13 At midday, O king, I saw in the way a light from heaven, above the bright-
ness of the sun, shining round about me and them which journeyed with me.
14 And when we were all fallen to the earth, I heard a voice speaking unto
me, and saying in the Hebrew tongue, Saul, Saul, why persecutest thou me? *it
is* hard for thee to kick against the pricks.
15 And I said, Who art thou, Lord? And he said, I am Jesus whom thou per-
secutest.
16 But rise, and stand upon thy feet: for I have appeared unto thee for this
purpose, to make thee a minister and a witness both of these things which
thou hast seen, and of those things in the which I will appear unto thee;
17 Delivering thee from the people, and *from* the Gentiles, unto whom now
I send thee,
18 To open their eyes, *and* to turn *them* from darkness to light, and *from* the
power of Satan unto God, that they may receive forgiveness of sins, and inher-
itance among them which are sanctified by faith that is in me.
19 Whereupon, O king Agrippa, I was not disobedient unto the heavenly
vision:

20 But shewed first unto them of Damascus, and at Jerusalem, and through-
out all the coasts of Judaea, and *then* to the Gentiles, that they should repent
and turn to God, and do works meet for repentance.
21 For these causes the Jews caught me in the temple, and went about to kill
me.
22 Having therefore obtained help of God, I continue unto this day, witness-
ing both to small and great, saying none other things than those which the
prophets and Moses did say should come:
23 That Christ should suffer, *and* that he should be the first that should rise
from the dead, and should shew light unto the people, and to the Gentiles.

Festus Charges Paul with Insanity

24 And as he thus spake for himself, Festus said with a loud voice, Paul, thou
art beside thyself; much learning doth make thee mad.
25 But he said, I am not mad, most noble Festus; but speak forth the words
of truth and soberness.
26 For the king knoweth of these things, before whom also I speak freely: for
I am persuaded that none of these things are hidden from him; for this thing
was not done in a corner.
27 King Agrippa, believest thou the prophets? I know that thou believest.
28 Then Agrippa said unto Paul, Almost thou persuadest me to be a Christian.
29 And Paul said, I would to God, that not only thou, but also all that hear
me this day, were both almost, and altogether such as I am, except these bonds.
30 And when he had thus spoken, the king rose up, and the governor, and
Bernice, and they that sat with them:
31 And when they were gone aside, they talked between themselves, saying,
This man doeth nothing worthy of death or of bonds.
32 Then said Agrippa unto Festus, This man might have been set at liberty, if
he had not appealed unto Caesar.

Paul Sails for Rome

27 And when it was determined that we should sail into Italy, they
delivered Paul and certain other prisoners unto *one* named Julius,
a centurion of Augustus' band.
2 And entering into a ship of Adramyttium, we launched, meaning to sail by
the coasts of Asia; *one* Aristarchus, a Macedonian of Thessalonica, being with
us.
3 And the next *day* we touched at Sidon. And Julius courteously entreated
Paul, and gave *him* liberty to go unto his friends to refresh himself.
4 And when we had launched from thence, we sailed under Cyprus, because
the winds were contrary.
5 And when we had sailed over the sea of Cilicia and Pamphylia, we came to
Myra, *a city* of Lycia.
6 And there the centurion found a ship of Alexandria sailing into Italy; and
he put us therein.
7 And when we had sailed slowly many days, and scarce were come over
against Cnidus, the wind not suffering us, we sailed under Crete, over against
Salmone;
8 And, hardly passing it, came unto a place which is called The fair havens;
nigh whereunto was the city *of* Lasea.
9 Now when much time was spent, and when sailing was now dangerous,
because the fast was now already past, Paul admonished *them*,
10 And said unto them, Sirs, I perceive that this voyage will be with hurt and
much damage, not only of the lading and ship, but also of our lives.
11 Nevertheless the centurion believed the master and the owner of the ship,
more than those things which were spoken by Paul.

12 And because the haven was not commodious to winter in, the more part
advised to depart thence also, if by any means they might attain to Phenice,
and there to winter; *which is* an haven of Crete, and lieth toward the south
west and north west.
13 And when the south wind blew softly, supposing that they had obtained
their purpose, loosing *thence*, they sailed close by Crete.
14 But not long after there arose against it a tempestuous wind, called
Euroclydon.
15 And when the ship was caught, and could not bear up into the wind, we
let *her* drive.
16 And running under a certain island which is called Clauda, we had much
work to come by the boat:
17 Which when they had taken up, they used helps, undergirding the ship;
and, fearing lest they should fall into the quicksands, strake sail, and so were
driven.
18 And we being exceedingly tossed with a tempest, the next *day* they light-
ened the ship;
19 And the third *day* we cast out with our own hands the tackling of the ship.
20 And when neither sun nor stars in many days appeared, and no small
tempest lay on *us*, all hope that we should be saved was then taken away.
21 But after long abstinence Paul stood forth in the midst of them, and said,
Sirs, ye should have hearkened unto me, and not have loosed from Crete, and
to have gained this harm and loss.
22 And now I exhort you to be of good cheer: for there shall be no loss of *any*
man's life among you, but of the ship.
23 For there stood by me this night the angel of God, whose I am, and whom
I serve,
24 Saying, Fear not, Paul; thou must be brought before Caesar: and, lo, God
hath given thee all them that sail with thee.
25 Wherefore, sirs, be of good cheer: for I believe God, that it shall be even
as it was told me.
26 Howbeit we must be cast upon a certain island.

The Shipwreck

27 But when the fourteenth night was come, as we were driven up and down
in Adria, about midnight the shipmen deemed that they drew near to some
country;
28 And sounded, and found *it* twenty fathoms: and when they had gone a
little further, they sounded again, and found *it* fifteen fathoms.
29 Then fearing lest we should have fallen upon rocks, they cast four anchors
out of the stern, and wished for the day.
30 And as the shipmen were about to flee out of the ship, when they had let
down the boat into the sea, under colour as though they would have cast
anchors out of the foreship,
31 Paul said to the centurion and to the soldiers, Except these abide in the
ship, ye cannot be saved.
32 Then the soldiers cut off the ropes of the boat, and let her fall off.
33 And while the day was coming on, Paul besought *them* all to take meat,
saying, This day is the fourteenth day that ye have tarried and continued fast-
ing, having taken nothing.
34 Wherefore I pray you to take *some* meat: for this is for your health: for
there shall not an hair fall from the head of any of you.
35 And when he had thus spoken, he took bread, and gave thanks to God in
presence of them all: and when he had broken *it*, he began to eat.
36 Then were they all of good cheer, and they also took *some* meat.
37 And we were in all in the ship two hundred threescore and sixteen souls.

38 And when they had eaten enough, they lightened the ship, and cast out
the wheat into the sea.
39 And when it was day, they knew not the land: but they discovered a certain
creek with a shore, into the which they were minded, if it were possible, to
thrust in the ship.
40 And when they had taken up the anchors, they committed *themselves*
unto the sea, and loosed the rudder bands, and hoised up the mainsail to the
wind, and made toward shore.
41 And falling into a place where two seas met, they ran the ship aground;
and the forepart stuck fast, and remained unmoveable, but the hinder part
was broken with the violence of the waves.
42 And the soldiers' counsel was to kill the prisoners, lest any of them should
swim out, and escape.
43 But the centurion, willing to save Paul, kept them from *their* purpose; and
commanded that they which could swim should cast *themselves* first *into the
sea*, and get to land:
44 And the rest, some on boards, and some on *broken pieces* of the ship. And
so it came to pass, that they escaped all safe to land.

Paul on the Island of Malta

28 And when they were escaped, then they knew that the island was
called Melita.
2 And the barbarous people shewed us no little kindness: for they kindled a
fire, and received us every one, because of the present rain, and because of the
cold.
3 And when Paul had gathered a bundle of sticks, and laid *them* on the fire,
there came a viper out of the heat, and fastened on his hand.
4 And when the barbarians saw the *venomous* beast hang on his hand, they
said among themselves, No doubt this man is a murderer, whom, though he
hath escaped the sea, yet vengeance suffereth not to live.
5 And he shook off the beast into the fire, and felt no harm.
6 Howbeit they looked when he should have swollen, or fallen down dead
suddenly: but after they had looked a great while, and saw no harm come to
him, they changed their minds, and said that he was a god.
7 In the same quarters were possessions of the chief man of the island, whose
name was Publius; who received us, and lodged us three days courteously.
8 And it came to pass, that the father of Publius lay sick of a fever and of a
bloody flux: to whom Paul entered in, and prayed, and laid his hands on him,
and healed him.
9 So when this was done, others also, which had diseases in the island, came,
and were healed:
10 Who also honoured us with many honours; and when we departed, they
laded *us* with such things as were necessary.

Paul's Company Departs for Rome

11 And after three months we departed in a ship of Alexandria, which had
wintered in the isle, whose sign was Castor and Pollux.
12 And landing at Syracuse, we tarried *there* three days.
13 And from thence we fetched a compass, and came to Rhegium: and after
one day the south wind blew, and we came the next day to Puteoli:
14 Where we found brethren, and were desired to tarry with them seven
days: and so we went toward Rome.
15 And from thence, when the brethren heard of us, they came to meet us as
far as Appii forum, and The three taverns: whom when Paul saw, he thanked
God, and took courage.

16 And when we came to Rome, the centurion delivered the prisoners to the
captain of the guard: but Paul was suffered to dwell by himself with a soldier
that kept him.

Paul in Rome

17 And it came to pass, that after three days Paul called the chief of the Jews
together: and when they were come together, he said unto them, Men *and*
brethren, though I have committed nothing against the people, or customs
of our fathers, yet was I delivered prisoner from Jerusalem into the hands of
the Romans.
18 Who, when they had examined me, would have let *me* go, because there
was no cause of death in me.
19 But when the Jews spake against *it*, I was constrained to appeal unto
Caesar; not that I had ought to accuse my nation of.
20 For this cause therefore have I called for you, to see *you*, and to speak with
you: because that for the hope of Israel I am bound with this chain.
21 And they said unto him, We neither received letters out of Judaea con-
cerning thee, neither any of the brethren that came shewed or spake any harm
of thee.
22 But we desire to hear of thee what thou thinkest: for as concerning this
sect, we know that every where it is spoken against.
23 And when they had appointed him a day, there came many to him into
his lodging; to whom he expounded and testified the kingdom of God, per-
suading them concerning Jesus, both out of the law of Moses, and *out of* the
prophets, from morning till evening.
24 And some believed the things which were spoken, and some believed not.
25 And when they agreed not among themselves, they departed, after that
Paul had spoken one word, Well spake the Holy Ghost by Esaias the prophet
unto our fathers,
26 Saying, Go unto this people, and say, Hearing ye shall hear, and shall not
understand; and seeing ye shall see, and not perceive:
27 For the heart of this people is waxed gross, and their ears are dull of hear-
ing, and their eyes have they closed; lest they should see with *their* eyes, and
hear with *their* ears, and understand with *their* heart, and should be convert-
ed, and I should heal them.
28 Be it known therefore unto you, that the salvation of God is sent unto the
Gentiles, and *that* they will hear it.
29 And when he had said these words, the Jews departed, and had great rea-
soning among themselves.
30 And Paul dwelt two whole years in his own hired house, and received all
that came in unto him,
31 Preaching the kingdom of God, and teaching those things which concern
the Lord Jesus Christ, with all confidence, no man forbidding him.

Paul's Greeting

1 Paul, a servant of Jesus Christ, called *to be* an apostle, separated unto the
gospel of God,
2 (Which he had promised afore by his prophets in the holy scriptures,)
3 Concerning his Son Jesus Christ our Lord, which was made of the seed of
David according to the flesh;
4 And declared *to be* the Son of God with power, according to the spirit of
holiness, by the resurrection from the dead:
5 By whom we have received grace and apostleship, for obedience to the faith
among all nations, for his name:
6 Among whom are ye also the called of Jesus Christ:
7 To all that be in Rome, beloved of God, called *to be* saints: Grace to you and
peace from God our Father, and the Lord Jesus Christ.

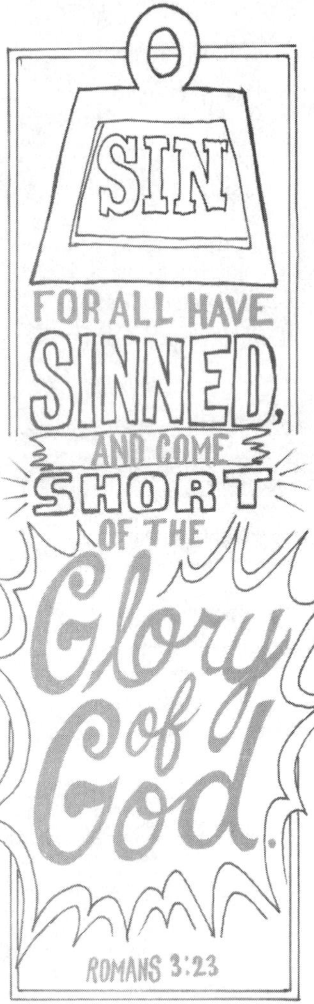

Paul's Desire to Visit Rome

8 First, I thank my God through Jesus Christ for you all, that your faith is
spoken of throughout the whole world.
9 For God is my witness, whom I serve with my spirit in the gospel of his Son,
that without ceasing I make mention of you always in my prayers;
10 Making request, if by any means now at length I might have a prosperous
journey by the will of God to come unto you.
11 For I long to see you, that I may impart unto you some spiritual gift, to the
end ye may be established;
12 That is, that I may be comforted together with you by the mutual faith
both of you and me.
13 Now I would not have you ignorant, brethren, that oftentimes I purposed
to come unto you, (but was let hitherto,) that I might have some fruit among
you also, even as among other Gentiles.
14 I am debtor both to the Greeks, and to the Barbarians; both to the wise,
and to the unwise.
15 So, as much as in me is, I am ready to preach the gospel to you that are at
Rome also.

Not Ashamed of the Gospel

16 For I am not ashamed of the gospel of Christ: for it is the power of God
unto salvation to every one that believeth; to the Jew first, and also to the Greek.
17 For therein is the righteousness of God revealed from faith to faith: as it
is written, The just shall live by faith.

God's Anger at Sinful Humanity

18 For the wrath of God is revealed from heaven against all ungodliness and
unrighteousness of men, who hold the truth in unrighteousness;
19 Because that which may be known of God is manifest in them; for God
hath shewed *it* unto them.
20 For the invisible things of him from the creation of the world are clearly
seen, being understood by the things that are made, *even* his eternal power
and Godhead; so that they are without excuse:
21 Because that, when they knew God, they glorified *him* not as God, neither
were thankful; but became vain in their imaginations, and their foolish heart
was darkened.

22 Professing themselves to be wise, they became fools,
23 And changed the glory of the uncorruptible God into an image made like
to corruptible man, and to birds, and fourfooted beasts, and creeping things.
24 Wherefore God also gave them up to uncleanness through the lusts of
their own hearts, to dishonour their own bodies between themselves:
25 Who changed the truth of God into a lie, and worshipped and served the
creature more than the Creator, who is blessed for ever. Amen.
26 For this cause God gave them up unto vile affections: for even their women
did change the natural use into that which is against nature:
27 And likewise also the men, leaving the natural use of the woman, burned
in their lust one toward another; men with men working that which is
unseemly, and receiving in themselves that recompence of their error which
was meet.
28 And even as they did not like to retain God in *their* knowledge, God gave
them over to a reprobate mind, to do those things which are not convenient;
29 Being filled with all unrighteousness, fornication, wickedness, covetous-
ness, maliciousness; full of envy, murder, debate, deceit, malignity; whisperers,
30 Backbiters, haters of God, despiteful, proud, boasters, inventors of evil
things, disobedient to parents,
31 Without understanding, covenantbreakers, without natural affection,
implacable, unmerciful:
32 Who knowing the judgment of God, that they which commit such things
are worthy of death, not only do the same, but have pleasure in them that do
them.

God Will Judge Everyone

2 Therefore thou art inexcusable, O man, whosoever thou art that judgest:
for wherein thou judgest another, thou condemnest thyself; for thou that
judgest doest the same things.
2 But we are sure that the judgment of God is according to truth against them
which commit such things.
3 And thinkest thou this, O man, that judgest them which do such things,
and doest the same, that thou shalt escape the judgment of God?
4 Or despisest thou the riches of his goodness and forbearance and longsuf-
fering; not knowing that the goodness of God leadeth thee to repentance?
5 But after thy hardness and impenitent heart treasurest up unto thyself
wrath against the day of wrath and revelation of the righteous judgment of
God;
6 Who will render to every man according to his deeds:
7 To them who by patient continuance in well doing seek for glory and hon-
our and immortality, eternal life:
8 But unto them that are contentious, and do not obey the truth, but obey
unrighteousness, indignation and wrath,
9 Tribulation and anguish, upon every soul of man that doeth evil, of the Jew
first, and also of the Gentile;
10 But glory, honour, and peace, to every man that worketh good, to the Jew
first, and also to the Gentile:
11 For there is no respect of persons with God.
12 For as many as have sinned without law shall also perish without law: and
as many as have sinned in the law shall be judged by the law;
13 (For not the hearers of the law *are* just before God, but the doers of the
law shall be justified.
14 For when the Gentiles, which have not the law, do by nature the things
contained in the law, these, having not the law, are a law unto themselves:

15 Which shew the work of the law written in their hearts, their conscience
also bearing witness, and *their* thoughts the mean while accusing or else excus-
ing one another;)
16 In the day when God shall judge the secrets of men by Jesus Christ accord-
ing to my gospel.
17 Behold, thou art called a Jew, and restest in the law, and makest thy boast
of God,
18 And knowest *his* will, and approvest the things that are more excellent,
being instructed out of the law;
19 And art confident that thou thyself art a guide of the blind, a light of them
which are in darkness,
20 An instructor of the foolish, a teacher of babes, which hast the form of
knowledge and of the truth in the law.
21 Thou therefore which teachest another, teachest thou not thyself? thou
that preachest a man should not steal, dost thou steal?
22 Thou that sayest a man should not commit adultery, dost thou commit
adultery? thou that abhorrest idols, dost thou commit sacrilege?
23 Thou that makest thy boast of the law, through breaking the law dishon-
ourest thou God?
24 For the name of God is blasphemed among the Gentiles through you, as
it is written.
25 For circumcision verily profiteth, if thou keep the law: but if thou be a
breaker of the law, thy circumcision is made uncircumcision.
26 Therefore if the uncircumcision keep the righteousness of the law, shall
not his uncircumcision be counted for circumcision?
27 And shall not uncircumcision which is by nature, if it fulfil the law, judge
thee, who by the letter and circumcision dost transgress the law?
28 For he is not a Jew, which is one outwardly; neither *is that* circumcision,
which is outward in the flesh:
29 But he *is* a Jew, which is one inwardly; and circumcision *is that* of the
heart, in the spirit, *and* not in the letter; whose praise *is* not of men, but of
God.

Everyone Is a Sinner

3 What advantage then hath the Jew? or what profit *is there* of circumcision?
2 Much every way: chiefly, because that unto them were committed the
oracles of God.
3 For what if some did not believe? shall their unbelief make the faith of God
without effect?
4 God forbid: yea, let God be true, but every man a liar; as it is written, That
thou mightest be justified in thy sayings, and mightest overcome when thou
art judged.
5 But if our unrighteousness commend the righteousness of God, what shall
we say? *Is* God unrighteous who taketh vengeance? (I speak as a man)
6 God forbid: for then how shall God judge the world?
7 For if the truth of God hath more abounded through my lie unto his glory;
why yet am I also judged as a sinner?
8 And not *rather*, (as we be slanderously reported, and as some affirm that
we say,) Let us do evil, that good may come? whose damnation is just.
9 What then? are we better *than they*? No, in no wise: for we have before
proved both Jews and Gentiles, that they are all under sin;
10 As it is written, There is none righteous, no, not one:
11 There is none that understandeth, there is none that seeketh after God.
12 They are all gone out of the way, they are together become unprofitable;
there is none that doeth good, no, not one.

13 Their throat *is* an open sepulchre; with their tongues they have used
deceit; the poison of asps *is* under their lips:
14 Whose mouth *is* full of cursing and bitterness:
15 Their feet *are* swift to shed blood:
16 Destruction and misery *are* in their ways:
17 And the way of peace have they not known:
18 There is no fear of God before their eyes.
19 Now we know that what things soever the law saith, it saith to them who
are under the law: that every mouth may be stopped, and all the world may
become guilty before God.
20 Therefore by the deeds of the law there shall no flesh be justified in his
sight: for by the law *is* the knowledge of sin.

God's Approval Is a Gift

21 But now the righteousness of God without the law is manifested, being
witnessed by the law and the prophets;
22 Even the righteousness of God *which is* by faith of Jesus Christ unto all
and upon all them that believe: for there is no difference:
23 For all have sinned, and come short of the glory of God;
24 Being justified freely by his grace through the redemption that is in Christ
Jesus:
25 Whom God hath set forth *to be* a propitiation through faith in his blood,
to declare his righteousness for the remission of sins that are past, through
the forbearance of God;
26 To declare, *I say*, at this time his righteousness: that he might be just, and
the justifier of him which believeth in Jesus.
27 Where *is* boasting then? It is excluded. By what law? of works? Nay: but
by the law of faith.
28 Therefore we conclude that a man is justified by faith without the deeds
of the law.
29 *Is he* the God of the Jews only? *is he* not also of the Gentiles? Yes, of the
Gentiles also:
30 Seeing *it is* one God, which shall justify the circumcision by faith, and
uncircumcision through faith.
31 Do we then make void the law through faith? God forbid: yea, we establish
the law.

Abraham's Faith Was Credited to Him for Righteousness

4 What shall we say then that Abraham our father, as pertaining to the flesh,
hath found?
2 For if Abraham were justified by works, he hath *whereof* to glory; but not
before God.
3 For what saith the scripture? Abraham believed God, and it was counted
unto him for righteousness.
4 Now to him that worketh is the reward not reckoned of grace, but of debt.
5 But to him that worketh not, but believeth on him that justifieth the ungod-
ly, his faith is counted for righteousness.
6 Even as David also describeth the blessedness of the man, unto whom God
imputeth righteousness without works,
7 *Saying*, Blessed *are* they whose iniquities are forgiven, and whose sins are
covered.
8 Blessed *is* the man to whom the Lord will not impute sin.
9 *Cometh* this blessedness then upon the circumcision *only*, or upon the
uncircumcision also? for we say that faith was reckoned to Abraham for righ-
teousness.
10 How was it then reckoned? when he was in circumcision, or in uncircum-
cision? Not in circumcision, but in uncircumcision.

11 And he received the sign of circumcision, a seal of the righteousness of
the faith which *he had yet* being uncircumcised: that he might be the father
of all them that believe, though they be not circumcised; that righteousness
might be imputed unto them also:
12 And the father of circumcision to them who are not of the circumcision
only, but who also walk in the steps of that faith of our father Abraham, which
he had being *yet* uncircumcised.
13 For the promise, that he should be the heir of the world, *was* not to
Abraham, or to his seed, through the law, but through the righteousness of
faith.
14 For if they which are of the law *be* heirs, faith is made void, and the promise made of none effect:
15 Because the law worketh wrath: for where no law is, *there is* no transgression.
16 Therefore *it is* of faith, that *it might be* by grace; to the end the promise
might be sure to all the seed; not to that only which is of the law, but to that
also which is of the faith of Abraham; who is the father of us all,
17 (As it is written, I have made thee a father of many nations,) before him
whom he believed, *even* God, who quickeneth the dead, and calleth those
things which be not as though they were.
18 Who against hope believed in hope, that he might become the father of
many nations, according to that which was spoken, So shall thy seed be.
19 And being not weak in faith, he considered not his own body now dead,
when he was about an hundred years old, neither yet the deadness of Sara's
womb:
20 He staggered not at the promise of God through unbelief; but was strong
in faith, giving glory to God;
21 And being fully persuaded that, what he had promised, he was able also
to perform.
22 And therefore it was imputed to him for righteousness.
23 Now it was not written for his sake alone, that it was imputed to him;
24 But for us also, to whom it shall be imputed, if we believe on him that
raised up Jesus our Lord from the dead;
25 Who was delivered for our offences, and was raised again for our justification.

Peace with God

5 Therefore being justified by faith, we have peace with God through our
Lord Jesus Christ:
2 By whom also we have access by faith into this grace wherein we stand, and
rejoice in hope of the glory of God.
3 And not only *so*, but we glory in tribulations also: knowing that tribulation
worketh patience;
4 And patience, experience; and experience, hope:
5 And hope maketh not ashamed; because the love of God is shed abroad in
our hearts by the Holy Ghost which is given unto us.
6 For when we were yet without strength, in due time Christ died for the
ungodly.
7 For scarcely for a righteous man will one die: yet peradventure for a good
man some would even dare to die.
8 But God commendeth his love toward us, in that, while we were yet sinners,
Christ died for us.
9 Much more then, being now justified by his blood, we shall be saved from
wrath through him.
10 For if, when we were enemies, we were reconciled to God by the death of
his Son, much more, being reconciled, we shall be saved by his life.

11 And not only *so*, but we also joy in God through our Lord Jesus Christ, by
whom we have now received the atonement.

A Comparison of Adam and Christ

12 Wherefore, as by one man sin entered into the world, and death by sin;
and so death passed upon all men, for that all have sinned:
13 (For until the law sin was in the world: but sin is not imputed when there
is no law.
14 Nevertheless death reigned from Adam to Moses, even over them that had
not sinned after the similitude of Adam's transgression, who is the figure of
him that was to come.
15 But not as the offence, so also *is* the free gift. For if through the offence of
one many be dead, much more the grace of God, and the gift by grace, *which*
is by one man, Jesus Christ, hath abounded unto many.
16 And not as *it was* by one that sinned, *so is* the gift: for the judgment *was*
by one to condemnation, but the free gift *is* of many offences unto justification.
17 For if by one man's offence death reigned by one; much more they which
receive abundance of grace and of the gift of righteousness shall reign in life
by one, Jesus Christ.)
18 Therefore as by the offence of one *judgment came* upon all men to con-
demnation; even so by the righteousness of one *the free gift came* upon all
men unto justification of life.
19 For as by one man's disobedience many were made sinners, so by the
obedience of one shall many be made righteous.
20 Moreover the law entered, that the offence might abound. But where sin
abounded, grace did much more abound:
21 That as sin hath reigned unto death, even so might grace reign through
righteousness unto eternal life by Jesus Christ our Lord.

No Longer Slaves to Sin

6 What shall we say then? Shall we continue in sin, that grace may abound?
2 God forbid. How shall we, that are dead to sin, live any longer therein?
3 Know ye not, that so many of us as were baptized into Jesus Christ were
baptized into his death?
4 Therefore we are buried with him by baptism into death: that like as Christ
was raised up from the dead by the glory of the Father, even so we also should
walk in newness of life.
5 For if we have been planted together in the likeness of his death, we shall
be also *in the likeness* of *his* resurrection:
6 Knowing this, that our old man is crucified with *him*, that the body of sin
might be destroyed, that henceforth we should not serve sin.
7 For he that is dead is freed from sin.
8 Now if we be dead with Christ, we believe that we shall also live with him:
9 Knowing that Christ being raised from the dead dieth no more; death hath
no more dominion over him.
10 For in that he died, he died unto sin once: but in that he liveth, he liveth
unto God.
11 Likewise reckon ye also yourselves to be dead indeed unto sin, but alive
unto God through Jesus Christ our Lord.
12 Let not sin therefore reign in your mortal body, that ye should obey it in
the lusts thereof.
13 Neither yield ye your members *as* instruments of unrighteousness unto
sin: but yield yourselves unto God, as those that are alive from the dead, and
your members *as* instruments of righteousness unto God.
14 For sin shall not have dominion over you: for ye are not under the law, but
under grace.

15 What then? shall we sin, because we are not under the law, but under grace? God forbid.

16 Know ye not, that to whom ye yield yourselves servants to obey, his servants ye are to whom ye obey; whether of sin unto death, or of obedience unto righteousness?

17 But God be thanked, that ye were the servants of sin, but ye have obeyed from the heart that form of doctrine which was delivered you.

18 Being then made free from sin, ye became the servants of righteousness.

19 I speak after the manner of men because of the infirmity of your flesh: for as ye have yielded your members servants to uncleanness and to iniquity unto iniquity; even so now yield your members servants to righteousness unto holiness.

20 For when ye were the servants of sin, ye were free from righteousness.

21 What fruit had ye then in those things whereof ye are now ashamed? for the end of those things *is* death.

22 But now being made free from sin, and become servants to God, ye have your fruit unto holiness, and the end everlasting life.

23 For the wages of sin *is* death; but the gift of God *is* eternal life through Jesus Christ our Lord.

We Belong to Christ

7 Know ye not, brethren, (for I speak to them that know the law,) how that the law hath dominion over a man as long as he liveth?

2 For the woman which hath an husband is bound by the law to *her* husband so long as he liveth; but if the husband be dead, she is loosed from the law of *her* husband.

3 So then if, while *her* husband liveth, she be married to another man, she shall be called an adulteress: but if her husband be dead, she is free from that law; so that she is no adulteress, though she be married to another man.

4 Wherefore, my brethren, ye also are become dead to the law by the body of Christ; that ye should be married to another, *even* to him who is raised from the dead, that we should bring forth fruit unto God.

5 For when we were in the flesh, the motions of sins, which were by the law, did work in our members to bring forth fruit unto death.

6 But now we are delivered from the law, that being dead wherein we were held; that we should serve in newness of spirit, and not *in* the oldness of the letter.

Moses' Laws Reveal Sin

7 What shall we say then? *Is* the law sin? God forbid. Nay, I had not known sin, but by the law: for I had not known lust, except the law had said, Thou shalt not covet.

8 But sin, taking occasion by the commandment, wrought in me all manner of concupiscence. For without the law sin *was* dead.

9 For I was alive without the law once: but when the commandment came, sin revived, and I died.

10 And the commandment, which *was ordained* to life, I found *to be* unto death.

11 For sin, taking occasion by the commandment, deceived me, and by it slew *me*.

12 Wherefore the law *is* holy, and the commandment holy, and just, and good.

13 Was then that which is good made death unto me? God forbid. But sin, that it might appear sin, working death in me by that which is good; that sin by the commandment might become exceeding sinful.

14 For we know that the law is spiritual: but I am carnal, sold under sin.

15 For that which I do I allow not: for what I would, that do I not; but what I hate, that do I.

16 If then I do that which I would not, I consent unto the law that *it is* good.
17 Now then it is no more I that do it, but sin that dwelleth in me.
18 For I know that in me (that is, in my flesh,) dwelleth no good thing: for to
will is present with me; but *how* to perform that which is good I find not.
19 For the good that I would I do not: but the evil which I would not, that I do.
20 Now if I do that I would not, it is no more I that do it, but sin that dwelleth
in me.
21 I find then a law, that, when I would do good, evil is present with me.
22 For I delight in the law of God after the inward man:
23 But I see another law in my members, warring against the law of my mind,
and bringing me into captivity to the law of sin which is in my members.
24 O wretched man that I am! who shall deliver me from the body of this
death?
25 I thank God through Jesus Christ our Lord. So then with the mind I myself
serve the law of God; but with the flesh the law of sin.

We Are God's Children

8 *There is* therefore now no condemnation to them which are in Christ Jesus,
who walk not after the flesh, but after the Spirit.
2 For the law of the Spirit of life in Christ Jesus hath made me free from the
law of sin and death.
3 For what the law could not do, in that it was weak through the flesh, God
sending his own Son in the likeness of sinful flesh, and for sin, condemned
sin in the flesh:
4 That the righteousness of the law might be fulfilled in us, who walk not
after the flesh, but after the Spirit.
5 For they that are after the flesh do mind the things of the flesh; but they
that are after the Spirit the things of the Spirit.
6 For to be carnally minded *is* death; but to be spiritually minded *is* life and
peace.
7 Because the carnal mind *is* enmity against God: for it is not subject to the
law of God, neither indeed can be.
8 So then they that are in the flesh cannot please God.
9 But ye are not in the flesh, but in the Spirit, if so be that the Spirit of God
dwell in you. Now if any man have not the Spirit of Christ, he is none of his.
10 And if Christ *be* in you, the body *is* dead because of sin; but the Spirit *is*
life because of righteousness.
11 But if the Spirit of him that raised up Jesus from the dead dwell in you, he
that raised up Christ from the dead shall also quicken your mortal bodies by
his Spirit that dwelleth in you.
12 Therefore, brethren, we are debtors, not to the flesh, to live after the flesh.
13 For if ye live after the flesh, ye shall die: but if ye through the Spirit do
mortify the deeds of the body, ye shall live.
14 For as many as are led by the Spirit of God, they are the sons of God.
15 For ye have not received the spirit of bondage again to fear; but ye have
received the Spirit of adoption, whereby we cry, Abba, Father.
16 The Spirit itself beareth witness with our spirit, that we are the children
of God:
17 And if children, then heirs; heirs of God, and joint-heirs with Christ; if so
be that we suffer with *him*, that we may be also glorified together.
18 For I reckon that the sufferings of this present time *are* not worthy *to be
compared* with the glory which shall be revealed in us.
19 For the earnest expectation of the creature waiteth for the manifestation
of the sons of God.
20 For the creature was made subject to vanity, not willingly, but by reason
of him who hath subjected *the same* in hope,

ROMANS 8:28

AND WE KNOW THAT all things work TOGETHER FOR good TO THEM THAT love God, TO THEM WHO are the called according TO HIS PURPOSE.

21 Because the creature itself also shall be delivered from the bondage of
corruption into the glorious liberty of the children of God.
22 For we know that the whole creation groaneth and travaileth in pain
together until now.
23 And not only *they*, but ourselves also, which have the firstfruits of the
Spirit, even we ourselves groan within ourselves, waiting for the adoption, *to*
wit, the redemption of our body.
24 For we are saved by hope: but hope that is seen is not hope: for what a man
seeth, why doth he yet hope for?
25 But if we hope for that we see not, *then* do we with patience wait for *it*.
26 Likewise the Spirit also helpeth our infirmities: for we know not what we
should pray for as we ought: but the Spirit itself maketh intercession for us
with groanings which cannot be uttered.
27 And he that searcheth the hearts knoweth what *is* the mind of the Spirit,
because he maketh intercession for the saints according to *the will of* God.
28 And we know that all things work together for good to them that love God,
to them who are the called according to *his* purpose.

Nothing Can Separate Us from God's Love

29 For whom he did foreknow, he also did predestinate *to be* conformed to
the image of his Son, that he might be the firstborn among many brethren.
30 Moreover whom he did predestinate, them he also called: and whom he
called, them he also justified: and whom he justified, them he also glorified.
31 What shall we then say to these things? If God *be* for us, who *can be* against us?
32 He that spared not his own Son, but delivered him up for us all, how shall
he not with him also freely give us all things?
33 Who shall lay any thing to the charge of God's elect? *It is* God that justifieth.
34 Who *is* he that condemneth? *It is* Christ that died, yea rather, that is risen
again, who is even at the right hand of God, who also maketh intercession for us.
35 Who shall separate us from the love of Christ? *shall* tribulation, or distress,
or persecution, or famine, or nakedness, or peril, or sword?
36 As it is written, For thy sake we are killed all the day long; we are account-
ed as sheep for the slaughter.
37 Nay, in all these things we are more than conquerors through him that
loved us.
38 For I am persuaded, that neither death, nor life, nor angels, nor princi-
palities, nor powers, nor things present, nor things to come,
39 Nor height, nor depth, nor any other creature, shall be able to separate us
from the love of God, which is in Christ Jesus our Lord.

Paul's Concern for the Jews

9 I say the truth in Christ, I lie not, my conscience also bearing me witness in
the Holy Ghost,
2 That I have great heaviness and continual sorrow in my heart.
3 For I could wish that myself were accursed from Christ for my brethren,
my kinsmen according to the flesh:
4 Who are Israelites; to whom *pertaineth* the adoption, and the glory, and
the covenants, and the giving of the law, and the service *of God*, and the prom-
ises;
5 Whose *are* the fathers, and of whom as concerning the flesh Christ *came*,
who is over all, God blessed for ever. Amen.
6 Not as though the word of God hath taken none effect. For they *are* not all
Israel, which are of Israel:
7 Neither, because they are the seed of Abraham, *are they* all children: but,
In Isaac shall thy seed be called.
8 That is, They which are the children of the flesh, these *are* not the children
of God: but the children of the promise are counted for the seed.

9 For this *is* the word of promise, At this time will I come, and Sara shall have
a son.
10 And not only *this*; but when Rebecca also had conceived by one, *even* by
our father Isaac;
11 (For *the children* being not yet born, neither having done any good or evil,
that the purpose of God according to election might stand, not of works, but
of him that calleth;)
12 It was said unto her, The elder shall serve the younger.
13 As it is written, Jacob have I loved, but Esau have I hated.
14 What shall we say then? *Is there* unrighteousness with God? God forbid.
15 For he saith to Moses, I will have mercy on whom I will have mercy, and I
will have compassion on whom I will have compassion.
16 So then *it is* not of him that willeth, nor of him that runneth, but of God
that sheweth mercy.
17 For the scripture saith unto Pharaoh, Even for this same purpose have I
raised thee up, that I might shew my power in thee, and that my name might
be declared throughout all the earth.
18 Therefore hath he mercy on whom he will *have mercy*, and whom he will
he hardeneth.
19 Thou wilt say then unto me, Why doth he yet find fault? For who hath
resisted his will?
20 Nay but, O man, who art thou that repliest against God? Shall the thing
formed say to him that formed *it*, Why hast thou made me thus?
21 Hath not the potter power over the clay, of the same lump to make one
vessel unto honour, and another unto dishonour?
22 *What* if God, willing to shew *his* wrath, and to make his power known,
endured with much longsuffering the vessels of wrath fitted to destruction:
23 And that he might make known the riches of his glory on the vessels of
mercy, which he had afore prepared unto glory,
24 Even us, whom he hath called, not of the Jews only, but also of the Gentiles?

The Calling of the Gentiles

25 As he saith also in Osee, I will call them my people, which were not my
people; and her beloved, which was not beloved.
26 And it shall come to pass, *that* in the place where it was said unto them,
Ye *are* not my people; there shall they be called the children of the living God.
27 Esaias also crieth concerning Israel, Though the number of the children
of Israel be as the sand of the sea, a remnant shall be saved:
28 For he will finish the work, and cut *it* short in righteousness: because a
short work will the Lord make upon the earth.
29 And as Esaias said before, Except the Lord of Sabaoth had left us a seed,
we had been as Sodoma, and been made like unto Gomorrha.
30 What shall we say then? That the Gentiles, which followed not after righ-
teousness, have attained to righteousness, even the righteousness which is of
faith.
31 But Israel, which followed after the law of righteousness, hath not attained
to the law of righteousness.
32 Wherefore? Because *they sought it* not by faith, but as it were by the works
of the law. For they stumbled at that stumblingstone;
33 As it is written, Behold, I lay in Sion a stumblingstone and rock of offence:
and whosoever believeth on him shall not be ashamed.

Those Who Believe Will Be Saved

10 Brethren, my heart's desire and prayer to God for Israel is, that they
might be saved.
2 For I bear them record that they have a zeal of God, but not according to
knowledge.

3 For they being ignorant of God's righteousness, and going about to estab-
lish their own righteousness, have not submitted themselves unto the righ-
teousness of God.
4 For Christ *is* the end of the law for righteousness to every one that believeth.
5 For Moses describeth the righteousness which is of the law, That the man
which doeth those things shall live by them.
6 But the righteousness which is of faith speaketh on this wise, Say not in
thine heart, Who shall ascend into heaven? (that is, to bring Christ down *from
above*:)
7 Or, Who shall descend into the deep? (that is, to bring up Christ again from
the dead.)
8 But what saith it? The word is nigh thee, *even* in thy mouth, and in thy
heart: that is, the word of faith, which we preach;
9 That if thou shalt confess with thy mouth the Lord Jesus, and shalt believe
in thine heart that God hath raised him from the dead, thou shalt be saved.
10 For with the heart man believeth unto righteousness; and with the mouth
confession is made unto salvation.
11 For the scripture saith, Whosoever believeth on him shall not be ashamed.
12 For there is no difference between the Jew and the Greek: for the same
Lord over all is rich unto all that call upon him.
13 For whosoever shall call upon the name of the Lord shall be saved.
14 How then shall they call on him in whom they have not believed? and
how shall they believe in him of whom they have not heard? and how shall
they hear without a preacher?
15 And how shall they preach, except they be sent? as it is written, How beau-
tiful are the feet of them that preach the gospel of peace, and bring glad tidings
of good things!
16 But they have not all obeyed the gospel. For Esaias saith, Lord, who hath
believed our report?
17 So then faith *cometh* by hearing, and hearing by the word of God.
18 But I say, Have they not heard? Yes verily, their sound went into all the
earth, and their words unto the ends of the world.
19 But I say, Did not Israel know? First Moses saith, I will provoke you to
jealousy by *them that are* no people, *and* by a foolish nation I will anger you.
20 But Esaias is very bold, and saith, I was found of them that sought me not;
I was made manifest unto them that asked not after me.
21 But to Israel he saith, All day long I have stretched forth my hands unto a
disobedient and gainsaying people.

God's Love for the Jewish People

11 I say then, Hath God cast away his people? God forbid. For I also am
an Israelite, of the seed of Abraham, *of* the tribe of Benjamin.
2 God hath not cast away his people which he foreknew. Wot ye not what the
scripture saith of Elias? how he maketh intercession to God against Israel,
saying,
3 Lord, they have killed thy prophets, and digged down thine altars; and I
am left alone, and they seek my life.
4 But what saith the answer of God unto him? I have reserved to myself seven
thousand men, who have not bowed the knee to *the image of* Baal.
5 Even so then at this present time also there is a remnant according to the
election of grace.
6 And if by grace, then *is it* no more of works: otherwise grace is no more
grace. But if *it be* of works, then is it no more grace: otherwise work is no more
work.
7 What then? Israel hath not obtained that which he seeketh for; but the
election hath obtained it, and the rest were blinded.

8 (According as it is written, God hath given them the spirit of slumber, eyes
that they should not see, and ears that they should not hear;) unto this day.
9 And David saith, Let their table be made a snare, and a trap, and a stum-
blingblock, and a recompence unto them:
10 Let their eyes be darkened, that they may not see, and bow down their
back alway.
11 I say then, Have they stumbled that they should fall? God forbid: but *rath-
er* through their fall salvation *is come* unto the Gentiles, for to provoke them
to jealousy.
12 Now if the fall of them *be* the riches of the world, and the diminishing of
them the riches of the Gentiles; how much more their fulness?
13 For I speak to you Gentiles, inasmuch as I am the apostle of the Gentiles,
I magnify mine office:
14 If by any means I may provoke to emulation *them which are* my flesh, and
might save some of them.
15 For if the casting away of them *be* the reconciling of the world, what *shall*
the receiving *of them be*, but life from the dead?
16 For if the firstfruit *be* holy, the lump *is* also *holy*: and if the root *be* holy,
so *are* the branches.
17 And if some of the branches be broken off, and thou, being a wild olive
tree, wert graffed in among them, and with them partakest of the root and
fatness of the olive tree;
18 Boast not against the branches. But if thou boast, thou bearest not the
root, but the root thee.
19 Thou wilt say then, The branches were broken off, that I might be graffed in.
20 Well; because of unbelief they were broken off, and thou standest by faith.
Be not highminded, but fear:
21 For if God spared not the natural branches, *take heed* lest he also spare
not thee.
22 Behold therefore the goodness and severity of God: on them which fell,
severity; but toward thee, goodness, if thou continue in *his* goodness: other-
wise thou also shalt be cut off.
23 And they also, if they abide not still in unbelief, shall be graffed in: for God
is able to graff them in again.
24 For if thou wert cut out of the olive tree which is wild by nature, and wert
graffed contrary to nature into a good olive tree: how much more shall these,
which be the natural *branches*, be graffed into their own olive tree?
25 For I would not, brethren, that ye should be ignorant of this mystery, lest
ye should be wise in your own conceits; that blindness in part is happened to
Israel, until the fulness of the Gentiles be come in.
26 And so all Israel shall be saved: as it is written, There shall come out of Sion
the Deliverer, and shall turn away ungodliness from Jacob:
27 For this *is* my covenant unto them, when I shall take away their sins.
28 As concerning the gospel, *they are* enemies for your sakes: but as touching
the election, *they are* beloved for the fathers' sakes.
29 For the gifts and calling of God *are* without repentance.
30 For as ye in times past have not believed God, yet have now obtained mercy
through their unbelief:
31 Even so have these also now not believed, that through your mercy they
also may obtain mercy.
32 For God hath concluded them all in unbelief, that he might have mercy
upon all.

God's Judgments Are Unsearchable

33 O the depth of the riches both of the wisdom and knowledge of God! how
unsearchable *are* his judgments, and his ways past finding out!
34 For who hath known the mind of the Lord? or who hath been his coun-
sellor?

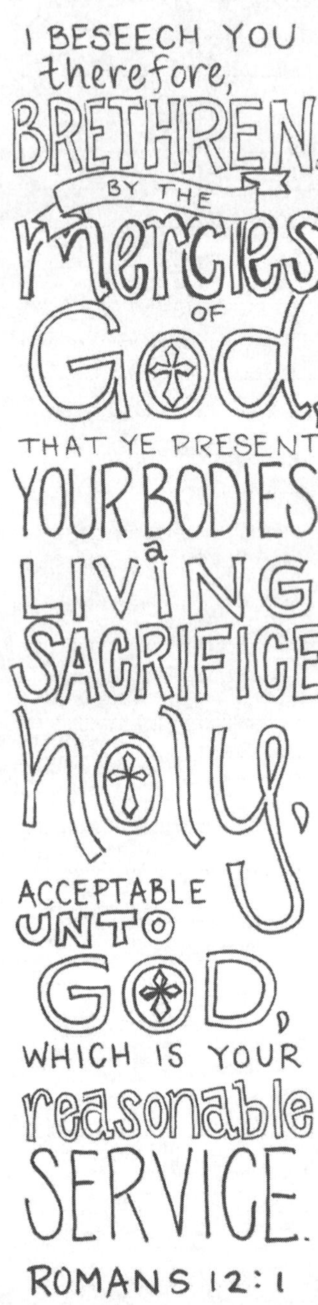

35 Or who hath first given to him, and it shall be recompensed unto him again?

36 For of him, and through him, and to him, *are* all things: to whom *be* glory for ever. Amen.

Dedicate Your Lives to God

12 I beseech you therefore, brethren, by the mercies of God, that ye present your bodies a living sacrifice, holy, acceptable unto God, *which is* your reasonable service.

2 And be not conformed to this world: but be ye transformed by the renewing of your mind, that ye may prove what *is* that good, and acceptable, and perfect, will of God.

3 For I say, through the grace given unto me, to every man that is among you, not to think *of himself* more highly than he ought to think; but to think soberly, according as God hath dealt to every man the measure of faith.

4 For as we have many members in one body, and all members have not the same office:

5 So we, *being* many, are one body in Christ, and every one members one of another.

6 Having then gifts differing according to the grace that is given to us, whether prophecy, *let us prophesy* according to the proportion of faith;

7 Or ministry, *let us wait* on *our* ministering: or he that teacheth, on teaching;

8 Or he that exhorteth, on exhortation: he that giveth, *let him do it* with simplicity; he that ruleth, with diligence; he that sheweth mercy, with cheerfulness.

9 *Let* love be without dissimulation. Abhor that which is evil; cleave to that which is good.

10 *Be* kindly affectioned one to another with brotherly love; in honour preferring one another;

11 Not slothful in business; fervent in spirit; serving the Lord;

12 Rejoicing in hope; patient in tribulation; continuing instant in prayer;

13 Distributing to the necessity of saints; given to hospitality.

14 Bless them which persecute you: bless, and curse not.

15 Rejoice with them that do rejoice, and weep with them that weep.

16 *Be* of the same mind one toward another. Mind not high things, but condescend to men of low estate. Be not wise in your own conceits.

17 Recompense to no man evil for evil. Provide things honest in the sight of all men.

18 If it be possible, as much as lieth in you, live peaceably with all men.

19 Dearly beloved, avenge not yourselves, but *rather* give place unto wrath: for it is written, Vengeance *is* mine; I will repay, saith the Lord.

20 Therefore if thine enemy hunger, feed him; if he thirst, give him drink: for in so doing thou shalt heap coals of fire on his head.

21 Be not overcome of evil, but overcome evil with good.

Obey the Government

13 Let every soul be subject unto the higher powers. For there is no power but of God: the powers that be are ordained of God.

2 Whosoever therefore resisteth the power, resisteth the ordinance of God: and they that resist shall receive to themselves damnation.

3 For rulers are not a terror to good works, but to the evil. Wilt thou then not be afraid of the power? do that which is good, and thou shalt have praise of the same:

4 For he is the minister of God to thee for good. But if thou do that which is evil, be afraid; for he beareth not the sword in vain: for he is the minister of God, a revenger to *execute* wrath upon him that doeth evil.

5 Wherefore *ye* must needs be subject, not only for wrath, but also for conscience sake.

6 For for this cause pay ye tribute also: for they are God's ministers, attending
continually upon this very thing.
7 Render therefore to all their dues: tribute to whom tribute *is due*; custom
to whom custom; fear to whom fear; honour to whom honour.

Love One Another

8 Owe no man any thing, but to love one another: for he that loveth another
hath fulfilled the law.
9 For this, Thou shalt not commit adultery, Thou shalt not kill, Thou shalt
not steal, Thou shalt not bear false witness, Thou shalt not covet; and if *there
be* any other commandment, it is briefly comprehended in this saying, name-
ly, Thou shalt love thy neighbour as thyself.
10 Love worketh no ill to his neighbour: therefore love *is* the fulfilling of the
law.
11 And that, knowing the time, that now *it is* high time to awake out of sleep:
for now *is* our salvation nearer than when we believed.
12 The night is far spent, the day is at hand: let us therefore cast off the works
of darkness, and let us put on the armour of light.
13 Let us walk honestly, as in the day; not in rioting and drunkenness, not in
chambering and wantonness, not in strife and envying.
14 But put ye on the Lord Jesus Christ, and make not provision for the flesh,
to *fulfil* the lusts *thereof*.

The Weaker Believer

14 Him that is weak in the faith receive ye, *but* not to doubtful disputa-
tions.
2 For one believeth that he may eat all things: another, who is weak, eateth
herbs.
3 Let not him that eateth despise him that eateth not; and let not him which
eateth not judge him that eateth: for God hath received him.
4 Who art thou that judgest another man's servant? to his own master he
standeth or falleth. Yea, he shall be holden up: for God is able to make him
stand.
5 One man esteemeth one day above another: another esteemeth every day
alike. Let every man be fully persuaded in his own mind.
6 He that regardeth the day, regardeth *it* unto the Lord; and he that regardeth
not the day, to the Lord he doth not regard *it*. He that eateth, eateth to the
Lord, for he giveth God thanks; and he that eateth not, to the Lord he eateth
not, and giveth God thanks.
7 For none of us liveth to himself, and no man dieth to himself.
8 For whether we live, we live unto the Lord; and whether we die, we die unto
the Lord: whether we live therefore, or die, we are the Lord's.
9 For to this end Christ both died, and rose, and revived, that he might be
Lord both of the dead and living.
10 But why dost thou judge thy brother? or why dost thou set at nought thy
brother? for we shall all stand before the judgment seat of Christ.
11 For it is written, *As* I live, saith the Lord, every knee shall bow to me, and
every tongue shall confess to God.
12 So then every one of us shall give account of himself to God.
13 Let us not therefore judge one another any more: but judge this rather,
that no man put a stumblingblock or an occasion to fall in *his* brother's way.
14 I know, and am persuaded by the Lord Jesus, that *there is* nothing unclean
of itself: but to him that esteemeth any thing to be unclean, to him *it is* unclean.
15 But if thy brother be grieved with *thy* meat, now walkest thou not chari-
tably. Destroy not him with thy meat, for whom Christ died.
16 Let not then your good be evil spoken of:

17 For the kingdom of God is not meat and drink; but righteousness, and
peace, and joy in the Holy Ghost.
18 For he that in these things serveth Christ *is* acceptable to God, and
approved of men.
19 Let us therefore follow after the things which make for peace, and things
wherewith one may edify another.
20 For meat destroy not the work of God. All things indeed *are* pure; but *it*
is evil for that man who eateth with offence.
21 *It is* good neither to eat flesh, nor to drink wine, nor *any thing* whereby
thy brother stumbleth, or is offended, or is made weak.
22 Hast thou faith? have *it* to thyself before God. Happy *is* he that con-
demneth not himself in that thing which he alloweth.
23 And he that doubteth is damned if he eat, because *he eateth* not of faith:
for whatsoever *is* not of faith is sin.

The Strong Must Bear with the Weak

15 We then that are strong ought to bear the infirmities of the weak, and
not to please ourselves.
2 Let every one of us please *his* neighbour for *his* good to edification.
3 For even Christ pleased not himself; but, as it is written, The reproaches of
them that reproached thee fell on me.
4 For whatsoever things were written aforetime were written for our learn-
ing, that we through patience and comfort of the scriptures might have hope.
5 Now the God of patience and consolation grant you to be likeminded one
toward another according to Christ Jesus:
6 That ye may with one mind *and* one mouth glorify God, even the Father
of our Lord Jesus Christ.

God Gives Unity

7 Wherefore receive ye one another, as Christ also received us to the glory
of God.
8 Now I say that Jesus Christ was a minister of the circumcision for the truth
of God, to confirm the promises *made* unto the fathers:
9 And that the Gentiles might glorify God for *his* mercy; as it is written, For
this cause I will confess to thee among the Gentiles, and sing unto thy name.
10 And again he saith, Rejoice, ye Gentiles, with his people.
11 And again, Praise the Lord, all ye Gentiles; and laud him, all ye people.
12 And again, Esaias saith, There shall be a root of Jesse, and he that shall rise
to reign over the Gentiles; in him shall the Gentiles trust.
13 Now the God of hope fill you with all joy and peace in believing, that ye
may abound in hope, through the power of the Holy Ghost.
14 And I myself also am persuaded of you, my brethren, that ye also are full
of goodness, filled with all knowledge, able also to admonish one another.
15 Nevertheless, brethren, I have written the more boldly unto you in some
sort, as putting you in mind, because of the grace that is given to me of God,
16 That I should be the minister of Jesus Christ to the Gentiles, ministering
the gospel of God, that the offering up of the Gentiles might be acceptable,
being sanctified by the Holy Ghost.
17 I have therefore whereof I may glory through Jesus Christ in those things
which pertain to God.
18 For I will not dare to speak of any of those things which Christ hath not
wrought by me, to make the Gentiles obedient, by word and deed,
19 Through mighty signs and wonders, by the power of the Spirit of God; so
that from Jerusalem, and round about unto Illyricum, I have fully preached
the gospel of Christ.
20 Yea, so have I strived to preach the gospel, not where Christ was named,
lest I should build upon another man's foundation:

21 But as it is written, To whom he was not spoken of, they shall see: and they
that have not heard shall understand.
22 For which cause also I have been much hindered from coming to you.
23 But now having no more place in these parts, and having a great desire
these many years to come unto you;
24 Whensoever I take my journey into Spain, I will come to you: for I trust
to see you in my journey, and to be brought on my way thitherward by you, if
first I be somewhat filled with your *company*.
25 But now I go unto Jerusalem to minister unto the saints.
26 For it hath pleased them of Macedonia and Achaia to make a certain con-
tribution for the poor saints which are at Jerusalem.
27 It hath pleased them verily; and their debtors they are. For if the Gentiles
have been made partakers of their spiritual things, their duty is also to min-
ister unto them in carnal things.
28 When therefore I have performed this, and have sealed to them this fruit,
I will come by you into Spain.
29 And I am sure that, when I come unto you, I shall come in the fulness of
the blessing of the gospel of Christ.

Paul Requests Prayer

30 Now I beseech you, brethren, for the Lord Jesus Christ's sake, and for the
love of the Spirit, that ye strive together with me in *your* prayers to God for
me;
31 That I may be delivered from them that do not believe in Judaea; and that
my service which *I have* for Jerusalem may be accepted of the saints;
32 That I may come unto you with joy by the will of God, and may with you
be refreshed.
33 Now the God of peace *be* with you all. Amen.

Paul's Farewell

16 I commend unto you Phebe our sister, which is a servant of the church
which is at Cenchrea:
2 That ye receive her in the Lord, as becometh saints, and that ye assist her
in whatsoever business she hath need of you: for she hath been a succourer
of many, and of myself also.
3 Greet Priscilla and Aquila my helpers in Christ Jesus:
4 Who have for my life laid down their own necks: unto whom not only I
give thanks, but also all the churches of the Gentiles.
5 Likewise *greet* the church that is in their house. Salute my wellbeloved
Epaenetus, who is the firstfruits of Achaia unto Christ.
6 Greet Mary, who bestowed much labour on us.
7 Salute Andronicus and Junia, my kinsmen, and my fellowprisoners, who
are of note among the apostles, who also were in Christ before me.
8 Greet Amplias my beloved in the Lord.
9 Salute Urbane, our helper in Christ, and Stachys my beloved.
10 Salute Apelles approved in Christ. Salute them which are of Aristobulus'
household.
11 Salute Herodion my kinsman. Greet them that be of the *household* of
Narcissus, which are in the Lord.
12 Salute Tryphena and Tryphosa, who labour in the Lord. Salute the beloved
Persis, which laboured much in the Lord.
13 Salute Rufus chosen in the Lord, and his mother and mine.
14 Salute Asyncritus, Phlegon, Hermas, Patrobas, Hermes, and the brethren
which are with them.
15 Salute Philologus, and Julia, Nereus, and his sister, and Olympas, and all
the saints which are with them.
16 Salute one another with an holy kiss. The churches of Christ salute you.

Watch out for Divisions

17 Now I beseech you, brethren, mark them which cause divisions and
offences contrary to the doctrine which ye have learned; and avoid them.
18 For they that are such serve not our Lord Jesus Christ, but their own belly;
and by good words and fair speeches deceive the hearts of the simple.
19 For your obedience is come abroad unto all *men*. I am glad therefore on
your behalf: but yet I would have you wise unto that which is good, and simple
concerning evil.
20 And the God of peace shall bruise Satan under your feet shortly. The grace
of our Lord Jesus Christ *be* with you. Amen.

Praise and Thanks to God

21 Timotheus my workfellow, and Lucius, and Jason, and Sosipater, my kins-
men, salute you.
22 I Tertius, who wrote *this* epistle, salute you in the Lord.
23 Gaius mine host, and of the whole church, saluteth you. Erastus the cham-
berlain of the city saluteth you, and Quartus a brother.
24 The grace of our Lord Jesus Christ *be* with you all. Amen.
25 Now to him that is of power to stablish you according to my gospel, and
the preaching of Jesus Christ, according to the revelation of the mystery, which
was kept secret since the world began,
26 But now is made manifest, and by the scriptures of the prophets, accord-
ing to the commandment of the everlasting God, made known to all nations
for the obedience of faith:
27 To God only wise, *be* glory through Jesus Christ for ever. Amen.

Paul's Greeting

1 Paul, called *to be* an apostle of Jesus Christ through the will of God, and
Sosthenes *our* brother,
2 Unto the church of God which is at Corinth, to them that are sanctified in
Christ Jesus, called *to be* saints, with all that in every place call upon the name
of Jesus Christ our Lord, both theirs and ours:
3 Grace *be* unto you, and peace, from God our Father, and *from* the Lord
Jesus Christ.
4 I thank my God always on your behalf, for the grace of God which is given
you by Jesus Christ;
5 That in every thing ye are enriched by him, in all utterance, and *in* all
knowledge;
6 Even as the testimony of Christ was confirmed in you:
7 So that ye come behind in no gift; waiting for the coming of our Lord Jesus
Christ:
8 Who shall also confirm you unto the end, *that ye may be* blameless in the
day of our Lord Jesus Christ.
9 God *is* faithful, by whom ye were called unto the fellowship of his Son Jesus
Christ our Lord.

Paul Exhorts the Corinthians to Unity

10 Now I beseech you, brethren, by the name of our Lord Jesus Christ, that
ye all speak the same thing, and *that* there be no divisions among you; but
that ye be perfectly joined together in the same mind and in the same judg-
ment.
11 For it hath been declared unto me of you, my brethren, by them *which
are of the house* of Chloe, that there are contentions among you.
12 Now this I say, that every one of you saith, I am of Paul; and I of Apollos;
and I of Cephas; and I of Christ.
13 Is Christ divided? was Paul crucified for you? or were ye baptized in the
name of Paul?
14 I thank God that I baptized none of you, but Crispus and Gaius;
15 Lest any should say that I had baptized in mine own name.
16 And I baptized also the household of Stephanas: besides, I know not
whether I baptized any other.
17 For Christ sent me not to baptize, but to preach the gospel: not with wis-
dom of words, lest the cross of Christ should be made of none effect.
18 For the preaching of the cross is to them that perish foolishness; but unto
us which are saved it is the power of God.
19 For it is written, I will destroy the wisdom of the wise, and will bring to
nothing the understanding of the prudent.
20 Where *is* the wise? where *is* the scribe? where *is* the disputer of this world?
hath not God made foolish the wisdom of this world?
21 For after that in the wisdom of God the world by wisdom knew not God,
it pleased God by the foolishness of preaching to save them that believe.
22 For the Jews require a sign, and the Greeks seek after wisdom:
23 But we preach Christ crucified, unto the Jews a stumblingblock, and unto
the Greeks foolishness;
24 But unto them which are called, both Jews and Greeks, Christ the power
of God, and the wisdom of God.

25 Because the foolishness of God is wiser than men; and the weakness of
God is stronger than men.
26 For ye see your calling, brethren, how that not many wise men after the
flesh, not many mighty, not many noble, *are called*:
27 But God hath chosen the foolish things of the world to confound the wise;
and God hath chosen the weak things of the world to confound the things
which are mighty;
28 And base things of the world, and things which are despised, hath God
chosen, *yea*, and things which are not, to bring to nought things that are:
29 That no flesh should glory in his presence.
30 But of him are ye in Christ Jesus, who of God is made unto us wisdom,
and righteousness, and sanctification, and redemption:
31 That, according as it is written, He that glorieth, let him glory in the Lord.

Paul Preaches Christ Crucified

2 And I, brethren, when I came to you, came not with excellency of speech
or of wisdom, declaring unto you the testimony of God.
2 For I determined not to know any thing among you, save Jesus Christ, and
him crucified.
3 And I was with you in weakness, and in fear, and in much trembling.
4 And my speech and my preaching *was* not with enticing words of man's
wisdom, but in demonstration of the Spirit and of power:
5 That your faith should not stand in the wisdom of men, but in the power
of God.

Maturity in Christ

6 Howbeit we speak wisdom among them that are perfect: yet not the wis-
dom of this world, nor of the princes of this world, that come to nought:
7 But we speak the wisdom of God in a mystery, *even* the hidden *wisdom*,
which God ordained before the world unto our glory:
8 Which none of the princes of this world knew: for had they known *it*, they
would not have crucified the Lord of glory.
9 But as it is written, Eye hath not seen, nor ear heard, neither have entered
into the heart of man, the things which God hath prepared for them that love
him.
10 But God hath revealed *them* unto us by his Spirit: for the Spirit searcheth
all things, yea, the deep things of God.
11 For what man knoweth the things of a man, save the spirit of man which
is in him? even so the things of God knoweth no man, but the Spirit of God.
12 Now we have received, not the spirit of the world, but the spirit which is
of God; that we might know the things that are freely given to us of God.
13 Which things also we speak, not in the words which man's wisdom
teacheth, but which the Holy Ghost teacheth; comparing spiritual things with
spiritual.
14 But the natural man receiveth not the things of the Spirit of God: for they
are foolishness unto him: neither can he know *them*, because they are
spiritually discerned.
15 But he that is spiritual judgeth all things, yet he himself is judged of no
man.
16 For who hath known the mind of the Lord, that he may instruct him? But
we have the mind of Christ.

The Solid Food of Paul's Teaching

3 And I, brethren, could not speak unto you as unto spiritual, but as unto
carnal, *even* as unto babes in Christ.
2 I have fed you with milk, and not with meat: for hitherto ye were not able
to bear it, neither yet now are ye able.
3 For ye are yet carnal: for whereas *there is* among you envying, and strife,
and divisions, are ye not carnal, and walk as men?

4 For while one saith, I am of Paul; and another, I *am* of Apollos; are ye not
carnal?

Paul and Apollos, Fellow Workmen

5 Who then is Paul, and who *is* Apollos, but ministers by whom ye believed,
even as the Lord gave to every man?
6 I have planted, Apollos watered; but God gave the increase.
7 So then neither is he that planteth any thing, neither he that watereth; but
God that giveth the increase.
8 Now he that planteth and he that watereth are one: and every man shall
receive his own reward according to his own labour.
9 For we are labourers together with God: ye are God's husbandry, *ye are*
God's building.
10 According to the grace of God which is given unto me, as a wise master-
builder, I have laid the foundation, and another buildeth thereon. But let every
man take heed how he buildeth thereupon.
11 For other foundation can no man lay than that is laid, which is Jesus
Christ.
12 Now if any man build upon this foundation gold, silver, precious stones,
wood, hay, stubble;
13 Every man's work shall be made manifest: for the day shall declare it,
because it shall be revealed by fire; and the fire shall try every man's work of
what sort it is.
14 If any man's work abide which he hath built thereupon, he shall receive
a reward.
15 If any man's work shall be burned, he shall suffer loss: but he himself shall
be saved; yet so as by fire.

The Temple of God

16 Know ye not that ye are the temple of God, and *that* the Spirit of God
dwelleth in you?
17 If any man defile the temple of God, him shall God destroy; for the temple
of God is holy, which *temple* ye are.
18 Let no man deceive himself. If any man among you seemeth to be wise in
this world, let him become a fool, that he may be wise.
19 For the wisdom of this world is foolishness with God. For it is written, He
taketh the wise in their own craftiness.
20 And again, The Lord knoweth the thoughts of the wise, that they are vain.
21 Therefore let no man glory in men. For all things are yours;
22 Whether Paul, or Apollos, or Cephas, or the world, or life, or death, or
things present, or things to come; all are yours;
23 And ye are Christ's; and Christ *is* God's.

All Ministers Are Servants of Christ

4 Let a man so account of us, as of the ministers of Christ, and stewards of
the mysteries of God.
2 Moreover it is required in stewards, that a man be found faithful.
3 But with me it is a very small thing that I should be judged of you, or of
man's judgment: yea, I judge not mine own self.
4 For I know nothing by myself; yet am I not hereby justified: but he that
judgeth me is the Lord.
5 Therefore judge nothing before the time, until the Lord come, who both
will bring to light the hidden things of darkness, and will make manifest the
counsels of the hearts: and then shall every man have praise of God.
6 And these things, brethren, I have in a figure transferred to myself and *to*
Apollos for your sakes; that ye might learn in us not to think *of men* above that
which is written, that no one of you be puffed up for one against another.

THE Kingdom OF GOD IS NOT IN WORD, BUT IN POWER.
1 CORINTHIANS 4:20

7 For who maketh thee to differ *from another*? and what hast thou that thou
didst not receive? now if thou didst receive *it*, why dost thou glory, as if thou
hadst not received *it*?
8 Now ye are full, now ye are rich, ye have reigned as kings without us: and
I would to God ye did reign, that we also might reign with you.
9 For I think that God hath set forth us the apostles last, as it were appointed
to death: for we are made a spectacle unto the world, and to angels, and to
men.
10 We *are* fools for Christ's sake, but ye *are* wise in Christ; we *are* weak, but
ye *are* strong; ye *are* honourable, but we *are* despised.
11 Even unto this present hour we both hunger, and thirst, and are naked,
and are buffeted, and have no certain dwellingplace;
12 And labour, working with our own hands: being reviled, we bless; being
persecuted, we suffer it:
13 Being defamed, we intreat: we are made as the filth of the world, *and are*
the offscouring of all things unto this day.

Paul as Spiritual Father

14 I write not these things to shame you, but as my beloved sons I warn *you*.
15 For though ye have ten thousand instructors in Christ, yet *have ye* not
many fathers: for in Christ Jesus I have begotten you through the gospel.
16 Wherefore I beseech you, be ye followers of me.
17 For this cause have I sent unto you Timotheus, who is my beloved son, and
faithful in the Lord, who shall bring you into remembrance of my ways which
be in Christ, as I teach every where in every church.
18 Now some are puffed up, as though I would not come to you.
19 But I will come to you shortly, if the Lord will, and will know, not the
speech of them which are puffed up, but the power.
20 For the kingdom of God *is* not in word, but in power.
21 What will ye? shall I come unto you with a rod, or in love, and *in* the
spirit of meekness?

Sexual Sin in the Church

5 It is reported commonly *that there is* fornication among you, and such
fornication as is not so much as named among the Gentiles, that one should
have his father's wife.
2 And ye are puffed up, and have not rather mourned, that he that hath done
this deed might be taken away from among you.
3 For I verily, as absent in body, but present in spirit, have judged already, as
though I were present, *concerning* him that hath so done this deed,
4 In the name of our Lord Jesus Christ, when ye are gathered together, and
my spirit, with the power of our Lord Jesus Christ,
5 To deliver such an one unto Satan for the destruction of the flesh, that the
spirit may be saved in the day of the Lord Jesus.
6 Your glorying *is* not good. Know ye not that a little leaven leaveneth the
whole lump?

The Church Must Be Separate

7 Purge out therefore the old leaven, that ye may be a new lump, as ye are
unleavened. For even Christ our passover is sacrificed for us:
8 Therefore let us keep the feast, not with old leaven, neither with the leaven
of malice and wickedness; but with the unleavened *bread* of sincerity and
truth.
9 I wrote unto you in an epistle not to company with fornicators:
10 Yet not altogether with the fornicators of this world, or with the covetous,
or extortioners, or with idolaters; for then must ye needs go out of the world.

11 But now I have written unto you not to keep company, if any man that is
called a brother be a fornicator, or covetous, or an idolater, or a railer, or a
drunkard, or an extortioner; with such an one no not to eat.
12 For what have I to do to judge them also that are without? do not ye judge
them that are within?
13 But them that are without God judgeth. Therefore put away from among
yourselves that wicked person.

Settling Disputes among Believers

6 Dare any of you, having a matter against another, go to law before the unjust,
and not before the saints?
2 Do ye not know that the saints shall judge the world? and if the world shall
be judged by you, are ye unworthy to judge the smallest matters?
3 Know ye not that we shall judge angels? how much more things that pertain
to this life?
4 If then ye have judgments of things pertaining to this life, set them to judge
who are least esteemed in the church.
5 I speak to your shame. Is it so, that there is not a wise man among you? no,
not one that shall be able to judge between his brethren?
6 But brother goeth to law with brother, and that before the unbelievers.
7 Now therefore there is utterly a fault among you, because ye go to law one
with another. Why do ye not rather take wrong? why do ye not rather *suffer
yourselves to* be defrauded?
8 Nay, ye do wrong, and defraud, and that *your* brethren.

The Wicked Will Not Inherit the Kingdom of God

9 Know ye not that the unrighteous shall not inherit the kingdom of God?
Be not deceived: neither fornicators, nor idolaters, nor adulterers, nor effem-
inate, nor abusers of themselves with mankind,
10 Nor thieves, nor covetous, nor drunkards, nor revilers, nor extortioners,
shall inherit the kingdom of God.
11 And such were some of you: but ye are washed, but ye are sanctified, but
ye are justified in the name of the Lord Jesus, and by the Spirit of our God.

Stay Away from Sexual Sin

12 All things are lawful unto me, but all things are not expedient: all things
are lawful for me, but I will not be brought under the power of any.
13 Meats for the belly, and the belly for meats: but God shall destroy both it
and them. Now the body *is* not for fornication, but for the Lord; and the Lord
for the body.
14 And God hath both raised up the Lord, and will also raise up us by his own
power.
15 Know ye not that your bodies are the members of Christ? shall I then take
the members of Christ, and make *them* the members of an harlot? God forbid.
16 What? know ye not that he which is joined to an harlot is one body? for
two, saith he, shall be one flesh.
17 But he that is joined unto the Lord is one spirit.
18 Flee fornication. Every sin that a man doeth is without the body; but he
that committeth fornication sinneth against his own body.
19 What? know ye not that your body is the temple of the Holy Ghost *which
is* in you, which ye have of God, and ye are not your own?
20 For ye are bought with a price: therefore glorify God in your body, and in
your spirit, which are God's.

Paul Discusses Marriage

7 Now concerning the things whereof ye wrote unto me: *It is* good for a man
not to touch a woman.
2 Nevertheless, *to avoid* fornication, let every man have his own wife, and
let every woman have her own husband.

3 Let the husband render unto the wife due benevolence: and likewise also
the wife unto the husband.
4 The wife hath not power of her own body, but the husband: and likewise
also the husband hath not power of his own body, but the wife.
5 Defraud ye not one the other, except *it be* with consent for a time, that ye
may give yourselves to fasting and prayer; and come together again, that Satan
tempt you not for your incontinency.
6 But I speak this by permission, *and* not of commandment.
7 For I would that all men were even as I myself. But every man hath his
proper gift of God, one after this manner, and another after that.
8 I say therefore to the unmarried and widows, It is good for them if they
abide even as I.
9 But if they cannot contain, let them marry: for it is better to marry than to
burn.

Marriage Vows Are to Be Taken Seriously

10 And unto the married I command, *yet* not I, but the Lord, Let not the wife
depart from *her* husband:
11 But and if she depart, let her remain unmarried, or be reconciled to *her*
husband: and let not the husband put away *his* wife.
12 But to the rest speak I, not the Lord: If any brother hath a wife that believ-
eth not, and she be pleased to dwell with him, let him not put her away.
13 And the woman which hath an husband that believeth not, and if he be
pleased to dwell with her, let her not leave him.
14 For the unbelieving husband is sanctified by the wife, and the unbelieving
wife is sanctified by the husband: else were your children unclean; but now
are they holy.
15 But if the unbelieving depart, let him depart. A brother or a sister is not
under bondage in such *cases*: but God hath called us to peace.
16 For what knowest thou, O wife, whether thou shalt save *thy* husband? or
how knowest thou, O man, whether thou shalt save *thy* wife?
17 But as God hath distributed to every man, as the Lord hath called every
one, so let him walk. And so ordain I in all churches.
18 Is any man called being circumcised? let him not become uncircumcised.
Is any called in uncircumcision? let him not be circumcised.
19 Circumcision is nothing, and uncircumcision is nothing, but the keeping
of the commandments of God.
20 Let every man abide in the same calling wherein he was called.
21 Art thou called *being* a servant? care not for it: but if thou mayest be made
free, use *it* rather.
22 For he that is called in the Lord, *being* a servant, is the Lord's freeman:
likewise also he that is called, *being* free, is Christ's servant.
23 Ye are bought with a price; be not ye the servants of men.
24 Brethren, let every man, wherein he is called, therein abide with God.

Reasons for Marrying or Remaining Single

25 Now concerning virgins I have no commandment of the Lord: yet I give
my judgment, as one that hath obtained mercy of the Lord to be faithful.
26 I suppose therefore that this is good for the present distress, *I say*, that *it*
is good for a man so to be.
27 Art thou bound unto a wife? seek not to be loosed. Art thou loosed from
a wife? seek not a wife.
28 But and if thou marry, thou hast not sinned; and if a virgin marry, she
hath not sinned. Nevertheless such shall have trouble in the flesh: but I spare
you.
29 But this I say, brethren, the time *is* short: it remaineth, that both they that
have wives be as though they had none;

30 And they that weep, as though they wept not; and they that rejoice, as
though they rejoiced not; and they that buy, as though they possessed not;
31 And they that use this world, as not abusing *it*: for the fashion of this world
passeth away.
32 But I would have you without carefulness. He that is unmarried careth
for the things that belong to the Lord, how he may please the Lord:
33 But he that is married careth for the things that are of the world, how he
may please *his* wife.
34 There is difference *also* between a wife and a virgin. The unmarried
woman careth for the things of the Lord, that she may be holy both in body
and in spirit: but she that is married careth for the things of the world, how
she may please *her* husband.
35 And this I speak for your own profit; not that I may cast a snare upon you,
but for that which is comely, and that ye may attend upon the Lord without
distraction.
36 But if any man think that he behaveth himself uncomely toward his virgin,
if she pass the flower of *her* age, and need so require, let him do what he will,
he sinneth not: let them marry.
37 Nevertheless he that standeth stedfast in his heart, having no necessity,
but hath power over his own will, and hath so decreed in his heart that he will
keep his virgin, doeth well.
38 So then he that giveth *her* in marriage doeth well; but he that giveth *her*
not in marriage doeth better.
39 The wife is bound by the law as long as her husband liveth; but if her
husband be dead, she is at liberty to be married to whom she will; only in the
Lord.
40 But she is happier if she so abide, after my judgment: and I think also that
I have the Spirit of God.

Food Offered to Idols

8 Now as touching things offered unto idols, we know that we all have knowl-
edge. Knowledge puffeth up, but charity edifieth.
2 And if any man think that he knoweth any thing, he knoweth nothing yet
as he ought to know.
3 But if any man love God, the same is known of him.
4 As concerning therefore the eating of those things that are offered in sac-
rifice unto idols, we know that an idol *is* nothing in the world, and that *there*
is none other God but one.
5 For though there be that are called gods, whether in heaven or in earth, (as
there be gods many, and lords many,)
6 But to us *there is but* one God, the Father, of whom *are* all things, and we
in him; and one Lord Jesus Christ, by whom *are* all things, and we by him.

Be a Good Example

7 Howbeit *there is* not in every man that knowledge: for some with con-
science of the idol unto this hour eat *it* as a thing offered unto an idol; and
their conscience being weak is defiled.
8 But meat commendeth us not to God: for neither, if we eat, are we the
better; neither, if we eat not, are we the worse.
9 But take heed lest by any means this liberty of yours become a stumbling-
block to them that are weak.
10 For if any man see thee which hast knowledge sit at meat in the idol's
temple, shall not the conscience of him which is weak be emboldened to eat
those things which are offered to idols;
11 And through thy knowledge shall the weak brother perish, for whom
Christ died?

12 But when ye sin so against the brethren, and wound their weak conscience,
ye sin against Christ.
13 Wherefore, if meat make my brother to offend, I will eat no flesh while
the world standeth, lest I make my brother to offend.

Paul Asserts His Rights

9 Am I not an apostle? am I not free? have I not seen Jesus Christ our Lord?
are not ye my work in the Lord?
2 If I be not an apostle unto others, yet doubtless I am to you: for the seal of
mine apostleship are ye in the Lord.
3 Mine answer to them that do examine me is this,
4 Have we not power to eat and to drink?
5 Have we not power to lead about a sister, a wife, as well as other apostles,
and *as* the brethren of the Lord, and Cephas?
6 Or I only and Barnabas, have not we power to forbear working?
7 Who goeth a warfare any time at his own charges? who planteth a vineyard,
and eateth not of the fruit thereof? or who feedeth a flock, and eateth not of
the milk of the flock?
8 Say I these things as a man? or saith not the law the same also?
9 For it is written in the law of Moses, Thou shalt not muzzle the mouth of
the ox that treadeth out the corn. Doth God take care for oxen?
10 Or saith he *it* altogether for our sakes? For our sakes, no doubt, *this* is
written: that he that ploweth should plow in hope; and that he that thresheth
in hope should be partaker of his hope.
11 If we have sown unto you spiritual things, *is it* a great thing if we shall
reap your carnal things?
12 If others be partakers of *this* power over you, *are* not we rather?
Nevertheless we have not used this power; but suffer all things, lest we should
hinder the gospel of Christ.
13 Do ye not know that they which minister about holy things live *of the
things* of the temple? and they which wait at the altar are partakers with the
altar?
14 Even so hath the Lord ordained that they which preach the gospel should
live of the gospel.
15 But I have used none of these things: neither have I written these things,
that it should be so done unto me: for *it were* better for me to die, than that
any man should make my glorying void.
16 For though I preach the gospel, I have nothing to glory of: for necessity is
laid upon me; yea, woe is unto me, if I preach not the gospel!
17 For if I do this thing willingly, I have a reward: but if against my will, a
dispensation *of the gospel* is committed unto me.
18 What is my reward then? *Verily* that, when I preach the gospel, I may make
the gospel of Christ without charge, that I abuse not my power in the gospel.

Paul's Work as an Apostle

19 For though I be free from all *men*, yet have I made myself servant unto all,
that I might gain the more.
20 And unto the Jews I became as a Jew, that I might gain the Jews; to them
that are under the law, as under the law, that I might gain them that are under
the law;
21 To them that are without law, as without law, (being not without law to
God, but under the law to Christ,) that I might gain them that are without law.
22 To the weak became I as weak, that I might gain the weak: I am made all
things to all *men*, that I might by all means save some.
23 And this I do for the gospel's sake, that I might be partaker thereof with
you.

Run the Race

24 Know ye not that they which run in a race run all, but one receiveth the
prize? So run, that ye may obtain.
25 And every man that striveth for the mastery is temperate in all things.
Now they *do it* to obtain a corruptible crown; but we an incorruptible.
26 I therefore so run, not as uncertainly; so fight I, not as one that beateth
the air:
27 But I keep under my body, and bring *it* into subjection: lest that by any
means, when I have preached to others, I myself should be a castaway.

Learn from the Past

10 Moreover, brethren, I would not that ye should be ignorant, how that
all our fathers were under the cloud, and all passed through the sea;
2 And were all baptized unto Moses in the cloud and in the sea;
3 And did all eat the same spiritual meat;
4 And did all drink the same spiritual drink: for they drank of that spiritual
Rock that followed them: and that Rock was Christ.
5 But with many of them God was not well pleased: for they were overthrown
in the wilderness.

Stay Away from Idolatry

6 Now these things were our examples, to the intent we should not lust after
evil things, as they also lusted.
7 Neither be ye idolaters, as *were* some of them; as it is written, The people
sat down to eat and drink, and rose up to play.
8 Neither let us commit fornication, as some of them committed, and fell in
one day three and twenty thousand.
9 Neither let us tempt Christ, as some of them also tempted, and were
destroyed of serpents.
10 Neither murmur ye, as some of them also murmured, and were destroyed
of the destroyer.
11 Now all these things happened unto them for ensamples: and they are
written for our admonition, upon whom the ends of the world are come.
12 Wherefore let him that thinketh he standeth take heed lest he fall.
13 There hath no temptation taken you but such as is common to man: but
God *is* faithful, who will not suffer you to be tempted above that ye are able;
but will with the temptation also make a way to escape, that ye may be able to
bear *it*.
14 Wherefore, my dearly beloved, flee from idolatry.
15 I speak as to wise men; judge ye what I say.
16 The cup of blessing which we bless, is it not the communion of the blood
of Christ? The bread which we break, is it not the communion of the body of
Christ?
17 For we *being* many are one bread, *and* one body: for we are all partakers
of that one bread.
18 Behold Israel after the flesh: are not they which eat of the sacrifices par-
takers of the altar?
19 What say I then? that the idol is any thing, or that which is offered in
sacrifice to idols is any thing?
20 But I *say*, that the things which the Gentiles sacrifice, they sacrifice to
devils, and not to God: and I would not that ye should have fellowship with
devils.
21 Ye cannot drink the cup of the Lord, and the cup of devils: ye cannot be
partakers of the Lord's table, and of the table of devils.
22 Do we provoke the Lord to jealousy? are we stronger than he?
23 All things are lawful for me, but all things are not expedient: all things are
lawful for me, but all things edify not.

1 CORINTHIANS 10:31
WHETHER THEREFORE YE EAT, OR DRINK, OR whatsoever YE DO, do all TO THE glory OF GOD.

24 Let no man seek his own, but every man another's *wealth*.
25 Whatsoever is sold in the shambles, *that* eat, asking no question for con-
science sake:
26 For the earth *is* the Lord's, and the fulness thereof.
27 If any of them that believe not bid you *to a feast*, and ye be disposed to go;
whatsoever is set before you, eat, asking no question for conscience sake.
28 But if any man say unto you, This is offered in sacrifice unto idols, eat not
for his sake that shewed it, and for conscience sake: for the earth *is* the Lord's,
and the fulness thereof:
29 Conscience, I say, not thine own, but of the other: for why is my liberty
judged of another *man's* conscience?
30 For if I by grace be a partaker, why am I evil spoken of for that for which
I give thanks?
31 Whether therefore ye eat, or drink, or whatsoever ye do, do all to the glory
of God.
32 Give none offence, neither to the Jews, nor to the Gentiles, nor to the
church of God:
33 Even as I please all *men* in all *things*, not seeking mine own profit, but the
profit of many, that they may be saved.

Advice about Worship

11 Be ye followers of me, even as I also *am* of Christ.
2 Now I praise you, brethren, that ye remember me in all things, and
keep the ordinances, as I delivered *them* to you.
3 But I would have you know, that the head of every man is Christ; and the
head of the woman *is* the man; and the head of Christ *is* God.
4 Every man praying or prophesying, having *his* head covered, dishonoureth
his head.
5 But every woman that prayeth or prophesieth with *her* head uncovered
dishonoureth her head: for that is even all one as if she were shaven.
6 For if the woman be not covered, let her also be shorn: but if it be a shame
for a woman to be shorn or shaven, let her be covered.
7 For a man indeed ought not to cover *his* head, forasmuch as he is the image
and glory of God: but the woman is the glory of the man.
8 For the man is not of the woman; but the woman of the man.
9 Neither was the man created for the woman; but the woman for the man.
10 For this cause ought the woman to have power on *her* head because of the
angels.
11 Nevertheless neither is the man without the woman, neither the woman
without the man, in the Lord.
12 For as the woman *is* of the man, even so *is* the man also by the woman;
but all things of God.
13 Judge in yourselves: is it comely that a woman pray unto God uncovered?
14 Doth not even nature itself teach you, that, if a man have long hair, it is a
shame unto him?
15 But if a woman have long hair, it is a glory to her: for *her* hair is given her
for a covering.
16 But if any man seem to be contentious, we have no such custom, neither
the churches of God.

Advice about the Lord's Supper

17 Now in this that I declare *unto you* I praise *you* not, that ye come togeth-
er not for the better, but for the worse.
18 For first of all, when ye come together in the church, I hear that there be
divisions among you; and I partly believe it.
19 For there must be also heresies among you, that they which are approved
may be made manifest among you.

20 When ye come together therefore into one place, *this* is not to eat the
Lord's supper.
21 For in eating every one taketh before *other* his own supper: and one is
hungry, and another is drunken.
22 What? have ye not houses to eat and to drink in? or despise ye the church
of God, and shame them that have not? What shall I say to you? shall I praise
you in this? I praise *you* not.
23 For I have received of the Lord that which also I delivered unto you, That
the Lord Jesus the *same* night in which he was betrayed took bread:
24 And when he had given thanks, he brake *it*, and said, Take, eat: this is my
body, which is broken for you: this do in remembrance of me.
25 After the same manner also *he took* the cup, when he had supped, saying,
This cup is the new testament in my blood: this do ye, as oft as ye drink *it*, in
remembrance of me.
26 For as often as ye eat this bread, and drink this cup, ye do shew the Lord's
death till he come.
27 Wherefore whosoever shall eat this bread, and drink *this* cup of the Lord,
unworthily, shall be guilty of the body and blood of the Lord.
28 But let a man examine himself, and so let him eat of *that* bread, and drink
of *that* cup.
29 For he that eateth and drinketh unworthily, eateth and drinketh damna-
tion to himself, not discerning the Lord's body.
30 For this cause many *are* weak and sickly among you, and many sleep.
31 For if we would judge ourselves, we should not be judged.
32 But when we arc judged, we are chastened of the Lord, that we should not
be condemned with the world.
33 Wherefore, my brethren, when ye come together to eat, tarry one for
another.
34 And if any man hunger, let him eat at home; that ye come not together
unto condemnation. And the rest will I set in order when I come.

Spiritual Gifts

12 Now concerning spiritual *gifts*, brethren, I would not have you igno-
rant.
2 Ye know that ye were Gentiles, carried away unto these dumb idols, even
as ye were led.
3 Wherefore I give you to understand, that no man speaking by the Spirit of
God calleth Jesus accursed: and *that* no man can say that Jesus is the Lord, but
by the Holy Ghost.
4 Now there are diversities of gifts, but the same Spirit.
5 And there are differences of administrations, but the same Lord.
6 And there are diversities of operations, but it is the same God which work-
eth all in all.
7 But the manifestation of the Spirit is given to every man to profit withal.
8 For to one is given by the Spirit the word of wisdom; to another the word
of knowledge by the same Spirit;
9 To another faith by the same Spirit; to another the gifts of healing by the
same Spirit;
10 To another the working of miracles; to another prophecy; to another dis-
cerning of spirits; to another *divers* kinds of tongues; to another the interpre-
tation of tongues:
11 But all these worketh that one and the selfsame Spirit, dividing to every
man severally as he will.

The Body and Its Various Members

12 For as the body is one, and hath many members, and all the members of
that one body, being many, are one body: so also *is* Christ.

13 For by one Spirit are we all baptized into one body, whether *we be* Jews or
Gentiles, whether *we be* bond or free; and have been all made to drink into
one Spirit.
14 For the body is not one member, but many.
15 If the foot shall say, Because I am not the hand, I am not of the body; is it
therefore not of the body?
16 And if the ear shall say, Because I am not the eye, I am not of the body; is
it therefore not of the body?
17 If the whole body *were* an eye, where *were* the hearing? If the whole *were*
hearing, where *were* the smelling?
18 But now hath God set the members every one of them in the body, as it
hath pleased him.
19 And if they were all one member, where *were* the body?
20 But now *are they* many members, yet but one body.
21 And the eye cannot say unto the hand, I have no need of thee: nor again
the head to the feet, I have no need of you.
22 Nay, much more those members of the body, which seem to be more
feeble, are necessary:
23 And those *members* of the body, which we think to be less honourable,
upon these we bestow more abundant honour; and our uncomely *parts* have
more abundant comeliness.
24 For our comely *parts* have no need: but God hath tempered the body
together, having given more abundant honour to that *part* which lacked:
25 That there should be no schism in the body; but *that* the members should
have the same care one for another.
26 And whether one member suffer, all the members suffer with it; or one
member be honoured, all the members rejoice with it.

The Church, the Body of Christ
27 Now ye are the body of Christ, and members in particular.
28 And God hath set some in the church, first apostles, secondarily prophets,
thirdly teachers, after that miracles, then gifts of healings, helps, governments,
diversities of tongues.
29 *Are* all apostles? *are* all prophets? *are* all teachers? *are* all workers of mir-
acles?
30 Have all the gifts of healing? do all speak with tongues? do all interpret?
31 But covet earnestly the best gifts: and yet shew I unto you a more excellent
way.

Love Is the Greatest Gift
13 Though I speak with the tongues of men and of angels, and have not
charity, I am become *as* sounding brass, or a tinkling cymbal.
2 And though I have *the gift of* prophecy, and understand all mysteries, and
all knowledge; and though I have all faith, so that I could remove mountains,
and have not charity, I am nothing.
3 And though I bestow all my goods to feed *the poor*, and though I give my
body to be burned, and have not charity, it profiteth me nothing.
4 Charity suffereth long, *and* is kind; charity envieth not; charity vaunteth
not itself, is not puffed up,
5 Doth not behave itself unseemly, seeketh not her own, is not easily pro-
voked, thinketh no evil;
6 Rejoiceth not in iniquity, but rejoiceth in the truth;
7 Beareth all things, believeth all things, hopeth all things, endureth all
things.
8 Charity never faileth: but whether *there be* prophecies, they shall fail;
whether *there be* tongues, they shall cease; whether *there be* knowledge, it shall
vanish away.

9 For we know in part, and we prophesy in part.
10 But when that which is perfect is come, then that which is in part shall be
done away.
11 When I was a child, I spake as a child, I understood as a child, I thought
as a child: but when I became a man, I put away childish things.
12 For now we see through a glass, darkly; but then face to face: now I know
in part; but then shall I know even as also I am known.
13 And now abideth faith, hope, charity, these three; but the greatest of these
is charity.

Speak So as to Be Understood

14 Follow after charity, and desire spiritual *gifts*, but rather that ye may
prophesy.
2 For he that speaketh in an *unknown* tongue speaketh not unto men, but
unto God: for no man understandeth *him*; howbeit in the spirit he speaketh
mysteries.
3 But he that prophesieth speaketh unto men *to* edification, and exhortation,
and comfort.
4 He that speaketh in an *unknown* tongue edifieth himself; but he that proph-
esieth edifieth the church.
5 I would that ye all spake with tongues, but rather that ye prophesied: for
greater *is* he that prophesieth than he that speaketh with tongues, except he
interpret, that the church may receive edifying.

Interpretation Required

6 Now, brethren, if I come unto you speaking with tongues, what shall I
profit you, except I shall speak to you either by revelation, or by knowledge,
or by prophesying, or by doctrine?
7 And even things without life giving sound, whether pipe or harp, except
they give a distinction in the sounds, how shall it be known what is piped or
harped?
8 For if the trumpet give an uncertain sound, who shall prepare himself to
the battle?
9 So likewise ye, except ye utter by the tongue words easy to be understood,
how shall it be known what is spoken? for ye shall speak into the air.
10 There are, it may be, so many kinds of voices in the world, and none of
them *is* without signification.
11 Therefore if I know not the meaning of the voice, I shall be unto him that
speaketh a barbarian, and he that speaketh *shall be* a barbarian unto me.
12 Even so ye, forasmuch as ye are zealous of spiritual *gifts*, seek that ye may
excel to the edifying of the church.
13 Wherefore let him that speaketh in an *unknown* tongue pray that he may
interpret.
14 For if I pray in an *unknown* tongue, my spirit prayeth, but my understand-
ing is unfruitful.
15 What is it then? I will pray with the spirit, and I will pray with the under-
standing also: I will sing with the spirit, and I will sing with the understanding
also.
16 Else when thou shalt bless with the spirit, how shall he that occupieth the
room of the unlearned say Amen at thy giving of thanks, seeing he under-
standeth not what thou sayest?
17 For thou verily givest thanks well, but the other is not edified.
18 I thank my God, I speak with tongues more than ye all:
19 Yet in the church I had rather speak five words with my understanding,
that *by my voice* I might teach others also, than ten thousand words in an
unknown tongue.
20 Brethren, be not children in understanding: howbeit in malice be ye chil-
dren, but in understanding be men.

21 In the law it is written, With *men of* other tongues and other lips will I
speak unto this people; and yet for all that will they not hear me, saith the
Lord.
22 Wherefore tongues are for a sign, not to them that believe, but to them
that believe not: but prophesying *serveth* not for them that believe not, but
for them which believe.
23 If therefore the whole church be come together into one place, and all
speak with tongues, and there come in *those that are* unlearned, or unbeliev-
ers, will they not say that ye are mad?
24 But if all prophesy, and there come in one that believeth not, or *one*
unlearned, he is convinced of all, he is judged of all:
25 And thus are the secrets of his heart made manifest; and so falling down
on *his* face he will worship God, and report that God is in you of a truth.

Do All Things for Edification

26 How is it then, brethren? when ye come together, every one of you hath
a psalm, hath a doctrine, hath a tongue, hath a revelation, hath an interpre-
tation. Let all things be done unto edifying.
27 If any man speak in an *unknown* tongue, *let it be* by two, or at the most *by*
three, and *that* by course; and let one interpret.
28 But if there be no interpreter, let him keep silence in the church; and let
him speak to himself, and to God.
29 Let the prophets speak two or three, and let the other judge.
30 If *any thing* be revealed to another that sitteth by, let the first hold his
peace.
31 For ye may all prophesy one by one, that all may learn, and all may be
comforted.
32 And the spirits of the prophets are subject to the prophets.
33 For God is not *the author* of confusion, but of peace, as in all churches of
the saints.
34 Let your women keep silence in the churches: for it is not permitted unto
them to speak; but *they are commanded* to be under obedience, as also saith
the law.
35 And if they will learn any thing, let them ask their husbands at home: for
it is a shame for women to speak in the church.
36 What? came the word of God out from you? or came it unto you only?
37 If any man think himself to be a prophet, or spiritual, let him acknowledge
that the things that I write unto you are the commandments of the Lord.
38 But if any man be ignorant, let him be ignorant.
39 Wherefore, brethren, covet to prophesy, and forbid not to speak with
tongues.
40 Let all things be done decently and in order.

The Gospel of Christ's Resurrection

15 Moreover, brethren, I declare unto you the gospel which I preached
unto you, which also ye have received, and wherein ye stand;
2 By which also ye are saved, if ye keep in memory what I preached unto you,
unless ye have believed in vain.
3 For I delivered unto you first of all that which I also received, how that
Christ died for our sins according to the scriptures;
4 And that he was buried, and that he rose again the third day according to
the scriptures:
5 And that he was seen of Cephas, then of the twelve:
6 After that, he was seen of above five hundred brethren at once; of whom
the greater part remain unto this present, but some are fallen asleep.
7 After that, he was seen of James; then of all the apostles.
8 And last of all he was seen of me also, as of one born out of due time.

9 For I am the least of the apostles, that am not meet to be called an apostle,
because I persecuted the church of God.
10 But by the grace of God I am what I am: and his grace which *was bestowed*
upon me was not in vain; but I laboured more abundantly than they all: yet
not I, but the grace of God which was with me.
11 Therefore whether *it were* I or they, so we preach, and so ye believed.

The Resurrection of the Dead

12 Now if Christ be preached that he rose from the dead, how say some
among you that there is no resurrection of the dead?
13 But if there be no resurrection of the dead, then is Christ not risen:
14 And if Christ be not risen, then *is* our preaching vain, and your faith *is*
also vain.
15 Yea, and we are found false witnesses of God; because we have testified of
God that he raised up Christ: whom he raised not up, if so be that the dead
rise not.
16 For if the dead rise not, then is not Christ raised:
17 And if Christ be not raised, your faith *is* vain; ye are yet in your sins.
18 Then they also which are fallen asleep in Christ are perished.
19 If in this life only we have hope in Christ, we are of all men most misera-
ble.
20 But now is Christ risen from the dead, *and* become the firstfruits of them
that slept.
21 For since by man *came* death, by man *came* also the resurrection of the
dead.
22 For as in Adam all die, even so in Christ shall all be made alive.
23 But every man in his own order: Christ the firstfruits; afterward they that
are Christ's at his coming.
24 Then *cometh* the end, when he shall have delivered up the kingdom to
God, even the Father; when he shall have put down all rule and all authority
and power.
25 For he must reign, till he hath put all enemies under his feet.
26 The last enemy *that* shall be destroyed *is* death.
27 For he hath put all things under his feet. But when he saith all things are
put under *him, it is* manifest that he is excepted, which did put all things under
him.
28 And when all things shall be subdued unto him, then shall the Son also
himself be subject unto him that put all things under him, that God may be
all in all.
29 Else what shall they do which are baptized for the dead, if the dead rise
not at all? why are they then baptized for the dead?
30 And why stand we in jeopardy every hour?
31 I protest by your rejoicing which I have in Christ Jesus our Lord, I die daily.
32 If after the manner of men I have fought with beasts at Ephesus, what
advantageth it me, if the dead rise not? let us eat and drink; for to morrow we
die.
33 Be not deceived: evil communications corrupt good manners.
34 Awake to righteousness, and sin not; for some have not the knowledge of
God: I speak *this* to your shame.

The Spiritual Body

35 But some *man* will say, How are the dead raised up? and with what body
do they come?
36 *Thou* fool, that which thou sowest is not quickened, except it die:
37 And that which thou sowest, thou sowest not that body that shall be, but
bare grain, it may chance of wheat, or of some other *grain*:

38 But God giveth it a body as it hath pleased him, and to every seed his own
body.
39 All flesh *is* not the same flesh: but *there is* one *kind of* flesh of men, anoth-
er flesh of beasts, another of fishes, *and* another of birds.
40 *There are* also celestial bodies, and bodies terrestrial: but the glory of the
celestial *is* one, and the *glory* of the terrestrial *is* another.
41 *There is* one glory of the sun, and another glory of the moon, and anoth-
er glory of the stars: for *one* star differeth from *another* star in glory.
42 So also *is* the resurrection of the dead. It is sown in corruption; it is raised
in incorruption:
43 It is sown in dishonour; it is raised in glory: it is sown in weakness; it is
raised in power:
44 It is sown a natural body; it is raised a spiritual body. There is a natural
body, and there is a spiritual body.
45 And so it is written, The first man Adam was made a living soul; the last
Adam *was made* a quickening spirit.
46 Howbeit that *was* not first which is spiritual, but that which is natural;
and afterward that which is spiritual.
47 The first man *is* of the earth, earthy: the second man *is* the Lord from
heaven.
48 As *is* the earthy, such *are* they also that are earthy: and as *is* the heavenly,
such *are* they also that are heavenly.
49 And as we have borne the image of the earthy, we shall also bear the image
of the heavenly.
50 Now this I say, brethren, that flesh and blood cannot inherit the kingdom
of God; neither doth corruption inherit incorruption.

Victory over Death

51 Behold, I shew you a mystery; We shall not all sleep, but we shall all be
changed,
52 In a moment, in the twinkling of an eye, at the last trump: for the trumpet
shall sound, and the dead shall be raised incorruptible, and we shall be
changed.
53 For this corruptible must put on incorruption, and this mortal *must* put
on immortality.
54 So when this corruptible shall have put on incorruption, and this mortal
shall have put on immortality, then shall be brought to pass the saying that is
written, Death is swallowed up in victory.
55 O death, where *is* thy sting? O grave, where *is* thy victory?
56 The sting of death *is* sin; and the strength of sin *is* the law.
57 But thanks *be* to God, which giveth us the victory through our Lord Jesus
Christ.
58 Therefore, my beloved brethren, be ye stedfast, unmoveable, always
abounding in the work of the Lord, forasmuch as ye know that your labour is
not in vain in the Lord.

Collection for the Church in Jerusalem

16 Now concerning the collection for the saints, as I have given order to
the churches of Galatia, even so do ye.
2 Upon the first *day* of the week let every one of you lay by him in store, as
God hath prospered him, that there be no gatherings when I come.
3 And when I come, whomsoever ye shall approve by *your* letters, them will
I send to bring your liberality unto Jerusalem.
4 And if it be meet that I go also, they shall go with me.

Paul's Plans

5 Now I will come unto you, when I shall pass through Macedonia: for I do
pass through Macedonia.

6 And it may be that I will abide, yea, and winter with you, that ye may bring
me on my journey whithersoever I go.
7 For I will not see you now by the way; but I trust to tarry a while with you,
if the Lord permit.
8 But I will tarry at Ephesus until Pentecost.
9 For a great door and effectual is opened unto me, and *there are* many adver-
saries.

News about Fellow Believers

10 Now if Timotheus come, see that he may be with you without fear: for he
worketh the work of the Lord, as I also *do*.
11 Let no man therefore despise him: but conduct him forth in peace, that
he may come unto me: for I look for him with the brethren.
12 As touching *our* brother Apollos, I greatly desired him to come unto you
with the brethren: but his will was not at all to come at this time; but he will
come when he shall have convenient time.

Other Greetings

13 Watch ye, stand fast in the faith, quit you like men, be strong.
14 Let all your things be done with charity.
15 I beseech you, brethren, (ye know the house of Stephanas, that it is the
firstfruits of Achaia, and *that* they have addicted themselves to the ministry
of the saints,)
16 That ye submit yourselves unto such, and to every one that helpeth with
us, and laboureth.
17 I am glad of the coming of Stephanas and Fortunatus and Achaicus: for
that which was lacking on your part they have supplied.
18 For they have refreshed my spirit and yours: therefore acknowledge ye
them that are such.
19 The churches of Asia salute you. Aquila and Priscilla salute you much in
the Lord, with the church that is in their house.
20 All the brethren greet you. Greet ye one another with an holy kiss.
21 The salutation of *me* Paul with mine own hand.
22 If any man love not the Lord Jesus Christ, let him be Anathema Maranatha.
23 The grace of our Lord Jesus Christ *be* with you.
24 My love *be* with you all in Christ Jesus. Amen.

2 CORINTHIANS

Paul Comforts the Corinthians

1 Paul, an apostle of Jesus Christ by the will of God, and Timothy *our* brother, unto the church of God which is at Corinth, with all the saints which are in all Achaia:
2 Grace *be* to you and peace from God our Father, and *from* the Lord Jesus Christ.
3 Blessed *be* God, even the Father of our Lord Jesus Christ, the Father of mercies, and the God of all comfort;
4 Who comforteth us in all our tribulation, that we may be able to comfort them which are in any trouble, by the comfort wherewith we ourselves are comforted of God.
5 For as the sufferings of Christ abound in us, so our consolation also aboundeth by Christ.
6 And whether we be afflicted, *it is* for your consolation and salvation, which is effectual in the enduring of the same sufferings which we also suffer: or whether we be comforted, *it is* for your consolation and salvation.
7 And our hope of you *is* stedfast, knowing, that as ye are partakers of the sufferings, so *shall ye be* also of the consolation.
8 For we would not, brethren, have you ignorant of our trouble which came to us in Asia, that we were pressed out of measure, above strength, insomuch that we despaired even of life:
9 But we had the sentence of death in ourselves, that we should not trust in ourselves, but in God which raiseth the dead:
10 Who delivered us from so great a death, and doth deliver: in whom we trust that he will yet deliver *us*;
11 Ye also helping together by prayer for us, that for the gift *bestowed* upon us by the means of many persons thanks may be given by many on our behalf.

The Sincerity of Paul's Preaching

12 For our rejoicing is this, the testimony of our conscience, that in simplicity and godly sincerity, not with fleshly wisdom, but by the grace of God, we have had our conversation in the world, and more abundantly to you-ward.
13 For we write none other things unto you, than what ye read or acknowledge; and I trust ye shall acknowledge even to the end;
14 As also ye have acknowledged us in part, that we are your rejoicing, even as ye also *are* ours in the day of the Lord Jesus.

Why Paul Changed His Plans

15 And in this confidence I was minded to come unto you before, that ye might have a second benefit;
16 And to pass by you into Macedonia, and to come again out of Macedonia unto you, and of you to be brought on my way toward Judaea.
17 When I therefore was thus minded, did I use lightness? or the things that I purpose, do I purpose according to the flesh, that with me there should be yea yea, and nay nay?
18 But *as* God *is* true, our word toward you was not yea and nay.
19 For the Son of God, Jesus Christ, who was preached among you by us, *even* by me and Silvanus and Timotheus, was not yea and nay, but in him was yea.

20 For all the promises of God in him *are* yea, and in him Amen, unto the
glory of God by us.
21 Now he which stablisheth us with you in Christ, and hath anointed us, *is*
God;
22 Who hath also sealed us, and given the earnest of the Spirit in our hearts.
23 Moreover I call God for a record upon my soul, that to spare you I came
not as yet unto Corinth.
24 Not for that we have dominion over your faith, but are helpers of your
joy: for by faith ye stand.

Why Paul Did Not Come

2 But I determined this with myself, that I would not come again to you in
heaviness.
2 For if I make you sorry, who is he then that maketh me glad, but the same
which is made sorry by me?
3 And I wrote this same unto you, lest, when I came, I should have sorrow
from them of whom I ought to rejoice; having confidence in you all, that my
joy is *the joy* of you all.
4 For out of much affliction and anguish of heart I wrote unto you with many
tears; not that ye should be grieved, but that ye might know the love which I
have more abundantly unto you.

Forgive the Repentant Person

5 But if any have caused grief, he hath not grieved me, but in part: that I may
not overcharge you all.
6 Sufficient to such a man *is* this punishment, which *was inflicted* of many.
7 So that contrariwise ye *ought* rather to forgive *him*, and comfort *him*, lest
perhaps such a one should be swallowed up with overmuch sorrow.
8 Wherefore I beseech you that ye would confirm *your* love toward him.
9 For to this end also did I write, that I might know the proof of you, wheth-
er ye be obedient in all things.
10 To whom ye forgive any thing, I *forgive* also: for if I forgave any thing, to
whom I forgave *it*, for your sakes *forgave I it* in the person of Christ;
11 Lest Satan should get an advantage of us: for we are not ignorant of his
devices.

Paul's Mission

12 Furthermore, when I came to Troas to *preach* Christ's gospel, and a door
was opened unto me of the Lord,
13 I had no rest in my spirit, because I found not Titus my brother: but taking
my leave of them, I went from thence into Macedonia.
14 Now thanks *be* unto God, which always causeth us to triumph in Christ,
and maketh manifest the savour of his knowledge by us in every place.
15 For we are unto God a sweet savour of Christ, in them that are saved, and
in them that perish:
16 To the one *we are* the savour of death unto death; and to the other the
savour of life unto life. And who *is* sufficient for these things?
17 For we are not as many, which corrupt the word of God: but as of sincer-
ity, but as of God, in the sight of God speak we in Christ.

The Ministry from Christ

3 Do we begin again to commend ourselves? or need we, as some *others*,
epistles of commendation to you, or *letters* of commendation from you?
2 Ye are our epistle written in our hearts, known and read of all men:
3 *Forasmuch as ye are* manifestly declared to be the epistle of Christ minis-
tered by us, written not with ink, but with the Spirit of the living God; not in
tables of stone, but in fleshy tables of the heart.
4 And such trust have we through Christ to God-ward:

5 Not that we are sufficient of ourselves to think any thing as of ourselves;
but our sufficiency *is* of God;
6 Who also hath made us able ministers of the new testament; not of the
letter, but of the spirit: for the letter killeth, but the spirit giveth life.
7 But if the ministration of death, written *and* engraven in stones, was glo-
rious, so that the children of Israel could not stedfastly behold the face of
Moses for the glory of his countenance; which *glory* was to be done away:
8 How shall not the ministration of the spirit be rather glorious?
9 For if the ministration of condemnation *be* glory, much more doth the
ministration of righteousness exceed in glory.
10 For even that which was made glorious had no glory in this respect, by
reason of the glory that excelleth.
11 For if that which is done away *was* glorious, much more that which
remaineth *is* glorious.

The New Has Supplanted the Old

12 Seeing then that we have such hope, we use great plainness of speech:
13 And not as Moses, *which* put a veil over his face, that the children of Israel
could not stedfastly look to the end of that which is abolished:
14 But their minds were blinded: for until this day remaineth the same veil
untaken away in the reading of the old testament; which *veil* is done away in
Christ.
15 But even unto this day, when Moses is read, the veil is upon their heart.
16 Nevertheless when it shall turn to the Lord, the veil shall be taken away.
17 Now the Lord is that Spirit: and where the Spirit of the Lord *is*, there *is*
liberty.
18 But we all, with open face beholding as in a glass the glory of the Lord, are
changed into the same image from glory to glory, *even* as by the Spirit of the
Lord.

Paul Is Never Discouraged

4 Therefore seeing we have this ministry, as we have received mercy, we faint
not;
2 But have renounced the hidden things of dishonesty, not walking in craft-
iness, nor handling the word of God deceitfully; but by manifestation of the
truth commending ourselves to every man's conscience in the sight of God.
3 But if our gospel be hid, it is hid to them that are lost:
4 In whom the god of this world hath blinded the minds of them which
believe not, lest the light of the glorious gospel of Christ, who is the image of
God, should shine unto them.
5 For we preach not ourselves, but Christ Jesus the Lord; and ourselves your
servants for Jesus' sake.
6 For God, who commanded the light to shine out of darkness, hath shined
in our hearts, to *give* the light of the knowledge of the glory of God in the face
of Jesus Christ.
7 But we have this treasure in earthen vessels, that the excellency of the power
may be of God, and not of us.
8 *We are* troubled on every side, yet not distressed; *we are* perplexed, but not
in despair;
9 Persecuted, but not forsaken; cast down, but not destroyed;
10 Always bearing about in the body the dying of the Lord Jesus, that the life
also of Jesus might be made manifest in our body.
11 For we which live are alway delivered unto death for Jesus' sake, that the
life also of Jesus might be made manifest in our mortal flesh.
12 So then death worketh in us, but life in you.
13 We having the same spirit of faith, according as it is written, I believed,
and therefore have I spoken; we also believe, and therefore speak;

14 Knowing that he which raised up the Lord Jesus shall raise up us also by
Jesus, and shall present *us* with you.
15 For all things *are* for your sakes, that the abundant grace might through
the thanksgiving of many redound to the glory of God.
16 For which cause we faint not; but though our outward man perish, yet
the inward *man* is renewed day by day.
17 For our light affliction, which is but for a moment, worketh for us a far
more exceeding *and* eternal weight of glory;
18 While we look not at the things which are seen, but at the things which
are not seen: for the things which are seen *are* temporal; but the things which
are not seen *are* eternal.

Faith Guides Our Lives

5 For we know that if our earthly house of *this* tabernacle were dissolved, we
have a building of God, an house not made with hands, eternal in the
heavens.
2 For in this we groan, earnestly desiring to be clothed upon with our house
which is from heaven:
3 If so be that being clothed we shall not be found naked.
4 For we that are in *this* tabernacle do groan, being burdened: not for that
we would be unclothed, but clothed upon, that mortality might be swallowed
up of life.
5 Now he that hath wrought us for the selfsame thing *is* God, who also hath
given unto us the earnest of the Spirit.
6 Therefore *we are* always confident, knowing that, whilst we are at home
in the body, we are absent from the Lord:
7 (For we walk by faith, not by sight:)
8 We are confident, *I say*, and willing rather to be absent from the body, and
to be present with the Lord.
9 Wherefore we labour, that, whether present or absent, we may be accepted
of him.
10 For we must all appear before the judgment seat of Christ; that every one
may receive the things *done* in *his* body, according to that he hath done, wheth-
er *it be* good or bad.
11 Knowing therefore the terror of the Lord, we persuade men; but we are made
manifest unto God; and I trust also are made manifest in your consciences.

Christ's Love Guides Us

12 For we commend not ourselves again unto you, but give you occasion to
glory on our behalf, that ye may have somewhat to *answer* them which glory
in appearance, and not in heart.
13 For whether we be beside ourselves, *it is* to God: or whether we be sober,
it is for your cause.
14 For the love of Christ constraineth us; because we thus judge, that if one
died for all, then were all dead:
15 And *that* he died for all, that they which live should not henceforth live
unto themselves, but unto him which died for them, and rose again.
16 Wherefore henceforth know we no man after the flesh: yea, though we
have known Christ after the flesh, yet now henceforth know we *him* no more.
17 Therefore if any man *be* in Christ, *he is* a new creature: old things are
passed away; behold, all things are become new.
18 And all things *are* of God, who hath reconciled us to himself by Jesus
Christ, and hath given to us the ministry of reconciliation;
19 To wit, that God was in Christ, reconciling the world unto himself, not
imputing their trespasses unto them; and hath committed unto us the word
of reconciliation.

20 Now then we are ambassadors for Christ, as though God did beseech *you*
by us: we pray *you* in Christ's stead, be ye reconciled to God.
21 For he hath made him *to be* sin for us, who knew no sin; that we might be
made the righteousness of God in him.

We Are God's Servants

6 We then, *as* workers together *with him*, beseech *you* also that ye receive not
the grace of God in vain.
2 (For he saith, I have heard thee in a time accepted, and in the day of salva-
tion have I succoured thee: behold, now *is* the accepted time; behold, now *is*
the day of salvation.)
3 Giving no offence in any thing, that the ministry be not blamed:
4 But in all *things* approving ourselves as the ministers of God, in much
patience, in afflictions, in necessities, in distresses,
5 In stripes, in imprisonments, in tumults, in labours, in watchings, in fastings;
6 By pureness, by knowledge, by longsuffering, by kindness, by the Holy
Ghost, by love unfeigned,
7 By the word of truth, by the power of God, by the armour of righteousness
on the right hand and on the left,
8 By honour and dishonour, by evil report and good report: as deceivers, and
yet true;
9 As unknown, and *yet* well known; as dying, and, behold, we live; as chas-
tened, and not killed;
10 As sorrowful, yet alway rejoicing; as poor, yet making many rich; as having
nothing, and *yet* possessing all things.

Christians and Their Relationships

11 O *ye* Corinthians, our mouth is open unto you, our heart is enlarged.
12 Ye are not straitened in us, but ye are straitened in your own bowels.
13 Now for a recompence in the same, (I speak as unto *my* children,) be ye
also enlarged.
14 Be ye not unequally yoked together with unbelievers: for what fellowship
hath righteousness with unrighteousness? and what communion hath light
with darkness?
15 And what concord hath Christ with Belial? or what part hath he that
believeth with an infidel?
16 And what agreement hath the temple of God with idols? for ye are the
temple of the living God; as God hath said, I will dwell in them, and walk in
them; and I will be their God, and they shall be my people.
17 Wherefore come out from among them, and be ye separate, saith the Lord,
and touch not the unclean *thing*; and I will receive you,
18 And will be a Father unto you, and ye shall be my sons and daughters, saith
the Lord Almighty.

Paul Was Comforted by the Corinthians

7 Having therefore these promises, dearly beloved, let us cleanse ourselves
from all filthiness of the flesh and spirit, perfecting holiness in the fear of
God.
2 Receive us; we have wronged no man, we have corrupted no man, we have
defrauded no man.
3 I speak not *this* to condemn *you*: for I have said before, that ye are in our
hearts to die and live with *you*.
4 Great *is* my boldness of speech toward you, great *is* my glorying of you: I
am filled with comfort, I am exceeding joyful in all our tribulation.
5 For, when we were come into Macedonia, our flesh had no rest, but we
were troubled on every side; without *were* fightings, within *were* fears.
6 Nevertheless God, that comforteth those that are cast down, comforted us
by the coming of Titus;

7 And not by his coming only, but by the consolation wherewith he was
comforted in you, when he told us your earnest desire, your mourning, your
fervent mind toward me; so that I rejoiced the more.
8 For though I made you sorry with a letter, I do not repent, though I did
repent: for I perceive that the same epistle hath made you sorry, though *it were*
but for a season.
9 Now I rejoice, not that ye were made sorry, but that ye sorrowed to
repentance: for ye were made sorry after a godly manner, that ye might receive
damage by us in nothing.
10 For godly sorrow worketh repentance to salvation not to be repented of:
but the sorrow of the world worketh death.
11 For behold this selfsame thing, that ye sorrowed after a godly sort, what
carefulness it wrought in you, yea, *what* clearing of yourselves, yea, *what* indig-
nation, yea, *what* fear, yea, *what* vehement desire, yea, *what* zeal, yea, *what*
revenge! In all *things* ye have approved yourselves to be clear in this matter.
12 Wherefore, though I wrote unto you, *I did it* not for his cause that had
done the wrong, nor for his cause that suffered wrong, but that our care for
you in the sight of God might appear unto you.
13 Therefore we were comforted in your comfort: yea, and exceedingly the
more joyed we for the joy of Titus, because his spirit was refreshed by you all.
14 For if I have boasted any thing to him of you, I am not ashamed; but as we
spake all things to you in truth, even so our boasting, which *I made* before
Titus, is found a truth.
15 And his inward affection is more abundant toward you, whilst he remem-
bereth the obedience of you all, how with fear and trembling ye received him.
16 I rejoice therefore that I have confidence in you in all *things*.

The Collection for Christians in Jerusalem

8 Moreover, brethren, we do you to wit of the grace of God bestowed on the
churches of Macedonia;
2 How that in a great trial of affliction the abundance of their joy and their
deep poverty abounded unto the riches of their liberality.
3 For to *their* power, I bear record, yea, and beyond *their* power *they were*
willing of themselves;
4 Praying us with much intreaty that we would receive the gift, and *take*
upon us the fellowship of the ministering to the saints.
5 And *this they did*, not as we hoped, but first gave their own selves to the
Lord, and unto us by the will of God.
6 Insomuch that we desired Titus, that as he had begun, so he would also
finish in you the same grace also.

Paul Urges Generosity

7 Therefore, as ye abound in every *thing, in* faith, and utterance, and knowl-
edge, and *in* all diligence, and *in* your love to us, *see* that ye abound in this
grace also.
8 I speak not by commandment, but by occasion of the forwardness of oth-
ers, and to prove the sincerity of your love.
9 For ye know the grace of our Lord Jesus Christ, that, though he was rich,
yet for your sakes he became poor, that ye through his poverty might be rich.
10 And herein I give *my* advice: for this is expedient for you, who have begun
before, not only to do, but also to be forward a year ago.
11 Now therefore perform the doing *of it*; that as *there was* a readiness to
will, so *there may be* a performance also out of that which ye have.
12 For if there be first a willing mind, *it is* accepted according to that a man
hath, *and* not according to that he hath not.
13 For *I mean* not that other men be eased, and ye burdened:

14 But by an equality, *that* now at this time your abundance *may be a supply*
for their want, that their abundance also may be *a supply* for your want: that
there may be equality:
15 As it is written, He that *had gathered* much had nothing over; and he that
had gathered little had no lack.
16 But thanks *be* to God, which put the same earnest care into the heart of
Titus for you.
17 For indeed he accepted the exhortation; but being more forward, of his
own accord he went unto you.
18 And we have sent with him the brother, whose praise *is* in the gospel
throughout all the churches;
19 And not *that* only, but who was also chosen of the churches to travel with
us with this grace, which is administered by us to the glory of the same Lord,
and *declaration of* your ready mind:
20 Avoiding this, that no man should blame us in this abundance which is
administered by us:
21 Providing for honest things, not only in the sight of the Lord, but also in
the sight of men.
22 And we have sent with them our brother, whom we have oftentimes
proved diligent in many things, but now much more diligent, upon the great
confidence which *I have* in you.
23 Whether *any do enquire* of Titus, *he is* my partner and fellowhelper con-
cerning you: or our brethren *be enquired of, they are* the messengers of the
churches, *and* the glory of Christ.
24 Wherefore shew ye to them, and before the churches, the proof of your
love, and of our boasting on your behalf.

The Reason to Give

9 For as touching the ministering to the saints, it is superfluous for me to
write to you:
2 For I know the forwardness of your mind, for which I boast of you to them
of Macedonia, that Achaia was ready a year ago; and your zeal hath provoked
very many.
3 Yet have I sent the brethren, lest our boasting of you should be in vain in
this behalf; that, as I said, ye may be ready:
4 Lest haply if they of Macedonia come with me, and find you unprepared,
we (that we say not, ye) should be ashamed in this same confident boasting.
5 Therefore I thought it necessary to exhort the brethren, that they would
go before unto you, and make up beforehand your bounty, whereof ye had
notice before, that the same might be ready, as *a matter of* bounty, and not as
of covetousness.

Giving Generously and Cheerfully

6 But this *I say*, He which soweth sparingly shall reap also sparingly; and he
which soweth bountifully shall reap also bountifully.
7 Every man according as he purposeth in his heart, *so let him give*; not
grudgingly, or of necessity: for God loveth a cheerful giver.
8 And God *is* able to make all grace abound toward you; that ye, always hav-
ing all sufficiency in all *things*, may abound to every good work:
9 (As it is written, He hath dispersed abroad; he hath given to the poor: his
righteousness remaineth for ever.
10 Now he that ministereth seed to the sower both minister bread for *your*
food, and multiply your seed sown, and increase the fruits of your righteous-
ness;)
11 Being enriched in every thing to all bountifulness, which causeth through
us thanksgiving to God.

12 For the administration of this service not only supplieth the want of the
saints, but is abundant also by many thanksgivings unto God;
13 Whiles by the experiment of this ministration they glorify God for your
professed subjection unto the gospel of Christ, and for *your* liberal distribu-
tion unto them, and unto all *men*;
14 And by their prayer for you, which long after you for the exceeding grace
of God in you.
15 Thanks *be* unto God for his unspeakable gift.

Paul's Authority

10 Now I Paul myself beseech you by the meekness and gentleness of
Christ, who in presence *am* base among you, but being absent am bold
toward you:
2 But I beseech *you*, that I may not be bold when I am present with that
confidence, wherewith I think to be bold against some, which think of us as
if we walked according to the flesh.
3 For though we walk in the flesh, we do not war after the flesh:
4 (For the weapons of our warfare *are* not carnal, but mighty through God
to the pulling down of strong holds;)
5 Casting down imaginations, and every high thing that exalteth itself against
the knowledge of God, and bringing into captivity every thought to the obe-
dience of Christ;
6 And having in a readiness to revenge all disobedience, when your obedience
is fulfilled.
7 Do ye look on things after the outward appearance? If any man trust to
himself that he is Christ's, let him of himself think this again, that, as he *is*
Christ's, even so *are* we Christ's.
8 For though I should boast somewhat more of our authority, which the
Lord hath given us for edification, and not for your destruction, I should not
be ashamed:
9 That I may not seem as if I would terrify you by letters.
10 For *his* letters, say they, *are* weighty and powerful; but *his* bodily presence
is weak, and *his* speech contemptible.
11 Let such an one think this, that, such as we are in word by letters when we
are absent, such *will we be* also in deed when we are present.

Paul's Reason for Boasting

12 For we dare not make ourselves of the number, or compare ourselves with
some that commend themselves: but they measuring themselves by them-
selves, and comparing themselves among themselves, are not wise.
13 But we will not boast of things without *our* measure, but according to the
measure of the rule which God hath distributed to us, a measure to reach even
unto you.
14 For we stretch not ourselves beyond *our measure*, as though we reached
not unto you: for we are come as far as to you also in *preaching* the gospel of
Christ:
15 Not boasting of things without *our* measure, *that is*, of other men's
labours; but having hope, when your faith is increased, that we shall be
enlarged by you according to our rule abundantly,
16 To preach the gospel in the *regions* beyond you, *and* not to boast in anoth-
er man's line of things made ready to our hand.
17 But he that glorieth, let him glory in the Lord.
18 For not he that commendeth himself is approved, but whom the Lord
commendeth.

Paul Contrasts Himself with False Apostles

11 Would to God ye could bear with me a little in *my* folly: and indeed
bear with me.
2 For I am jealous over you with godly jealousy: for I have espoused you to
one husband, that I may present *you as* a chaste virgin to Christ.

3 But I fear, lest by any means, as the serpent beguiled Eve through his sub-
tilty, so your minds should be corrupted from the simplicity that is in Christ.
4 For if he that cometh preacheth another Jesus, whom we have not preached,
or *if* ye receive another spirit, which ye have not received, or another gospel,
which ye have not accepted, ye might well bear with *him*.
5 For I suppose I was not a whit behind the very chiefest apostles.
6 But though *I be* rude in speech, yet not in knowledge; but we have been
throughly made manifest among you in all things.
7 Have I committed an offence in abasing myself that ye might be exalted,
because I have preached to you the gospel of God freely?
8 I robbed other churches, taking wages *of them*, to do you service.
9 And when I was present with you, and wanted, I was chargeable to no man:
for that which was lacking to me the brethren which came from Macedonia
supplied: and in all *things* I have kept myself from being burdensome unto
you, and *so* will I keep *myself*.
10 As the truth of Christ is in me, no man shall stop me of this boasting in
the regions of Achaia.
11 Wherefore? because I love you not? God knoweth.
12 But what I do, that I will do, that I may cut off occasion from them which
desire occasion; that wherein they glory, they may be found even as we.
13 For such *are* false apostles, deceitful workers, transforming themselves
into the apostles of Christ.
14 And no marvel; for Satan himself is transformed into an angel of light.
15 Therefore *it is* no great thing if his ministers also be transformed as the
ministers of righteousness; whose end shall be according to their works.
16 I say again, Let no man think me a fool; if otherwise, yet as a fool receive
me, that I may boast myself a little.
17 That which I speak, I speak *it* not after the Lord, but as it were foolishly,
in this confidence of boasting.
18 Seeing that many glory after the flesh, I will glory also.
19 For ye suffer fools gladly, seeing ye *yourselves* are wise.
20 For ye suffer, if a man bring you into bondage, if a man devour *you*, if a
man take *of you*, if a man exalt himself, if a man smite you on the face.
21 I speak as concerning reproach, as though we had been weak. Howbeit
whereinsoever any is bold, (I speak foolishly,) I am bold also.
22 Are they Hebrews? so *am* I. Are they Israelites? so *am* I. Are they the seed
of Abraham? so *am* I.
23 Are they ministers of Christ? (I speak as a fool) I *am* more; in labours more
abundant, in stripes above measure, in prisons more frequent, in deaths oft.
24 Of the Jews five times received I forty *stripes* save one.
25 Thrice was I beaten with rods, once was I stoned, thrice I suffered ship-
wreck, a night and a day I have been in the deep;
26 *In* journeyings often, *in* perils of waters, *in* perils of robbers, *in* perils by
mine own countrymen, *in* perils by the heathen, *in* perils in the city, *in* perils
in the wilderness, *in* perils in the sea, *in* perils among false brethren;
27 In weariness and painfulness, in watchings often, in hunger and thirst,
in fastings often, in cold and nakedness.
28 Beside those things that are without, that which cometh upon me daily,
the care of all the churches.
29 Who is weak, and I am not weak? who is offended, and I burn not?
30 If I must needs glory, I will glory of the things which concern mine infir-
mities.
31 The God and Father of our Lord Jesus Christ, which is blessed for ever-
more, knoweth that I lie not.
32 In Damascus the governor under Aretas the king kept the city of the
Damascenes with a garrison, desirous to apprehend me:

33 And through a window in a basket was I let down by the wall, and escaped his hands.

Paul's Visions and Revelations

12 It is not expedient for me doubtless to glory. I will come to visions and revelations of the Lord.
2 I knew a man in Christ above fourteen years ago, (whether in the body, I cannot tell; or whether out of the body, I cannot tell: God knoweth;) such an one caught up to the third heaven.
3 And I knew such a man, (whether in the body, or out of the body, I cannot tell: God knoweth;)
4 How that he was caught up into paradise, and heard unspeakable words, which it is not lawful for a man to utter.
5 Of such an one will I glory: yet of myself I will not glory, but in mine infirmities.
6 For though I would desire to glory, I shall not be a fool; for I will say the truth: but *now* I forbear, lest any man should think of me above that which he seeth me *to be*, or *that* he heareth of me.
7 And lest I should be exalted above measure through the abundance of the revelations, there was given to me a thorn in the flesh, the messenger of Satan to buffet me, lest I should be exalted above measure.
8 For this thing I besought the Lord thrice, that it might depart from me.
9 And he said unto me, My grace is sufficient for thee: for my strength is made perfect in weakness. Most gladly therefore will I rather glory in my infirmities, that the power of Christ may rest upon me.
10 Therefore I take pleasure in infirmities, in reproaches, in necessities, in persecutions, in distresses for Christ's sake: for when I am weak, then am I strong.

Paul Was Not a Burden

11 I am become a fool in glorying; ye have compelled me: for I ought to have been commended of you: for in nothing am I behind the very chiefest apostles, though I be nothing.
12 Truly the signs of an apostle were wrought among you in all patience, in signs, and wonders, and mighty deeds.
13 For what is it wherein ye were inferior to other churches, except *it be* that I myself was not burdensome to you? forgive me this wrong.
14 Behold, the third time I am ready to come to you; and I will not be burdensome to you: for I seek not yours, but you: for the children ought not to lay up for the parents, but the parents for the children.
15 And I will very gladly spend and be spent for you; though the more abundantly I love you, the less I be loved.
16 But be it so, I did not burden you: nevertheless, being crafty, I caught you with guile.
17 Did I make a gain of you by any of them whom I sent unto you?
18 I desired Titus, and with *him* I sent a brother. Did Titus make a gain of you? walked we not in the same spirit? *walked we* not in the same steps?
19 Again, think ye that we excuse ourselves unto you? we speak before God in Christ: but *we do* all things, dearly beloved, for your edifying.

Paul's Concern about Their Lifestyles

20 For I fear, lest, when I come, I shall not find you such as I would, and *that* I shall be found unto you such as ye would not: lest *there be* debates, envyings, wraths, strifes, backbitings, whisperings, swellings, tumults:
21 *And* lest, when I come again, my God will humble me among you, and *that* I shall bewail many which have sinned already, and have not repented of the uncleanness and fornication and lasciviousness which they have committed.

Paul Plans to Visit

13 This *is* the third *time* I am coming to you. In the mouth of two or three
witnesses shall every word be established.
2 I told you before, and foretell you, as if I were present, the second time; and
being absent now I write to them which heretofore have sinned, and to all
other, that, if I come again, I will not spare:
3 Since ye seek a proof of Christ speaking in me, which to you-ward is not
weak, but is mighty in you.
4 For though he was crucified through weakness, yet he liveth by the power
of God. For we also are weak in him, but we shall live with him by the power
of God toward you.
5 Examine yourselves, whether ye be in the faith; prove your own selves.
Know ye not your own selves, how that Jesus Christ is in you, except ye be
reprobates?
6 But I trust that ye shall know that we are not reprobates.
7 Now I pray to God that ye do no evil; not that we should appear approved,
but that ye should do that which is honest, though we be as reprobates.
8 For we can do nothing against the truth, but for the truth.
9 For we are glad, when we are weak, and ye are strong: and this also we wish,
even your perfection.
10 Therefore I write these things being absent, lest being present I should
use sharpness, according to the power which the Lord hath given me to
edification, and not to destruction.
11 Finally, brethren, farewell. Be perfect, be of good comfort, be of one mind,
live in peace; and the God of love and peace shall be with you.
12 Greet one another with an holy kiss.
13 All the saints salute you.
14 The grace of the Lord Jesus Christ, and the love of God, and the communion
of the Holy Ghost, *be* with you all. Amen.

Paul's Greeting

1 Paul, an apostle, (not of men, neither by man, but by Jesus Christ, and God
the Father, who raised him from the dead;)
2 And all the brethren which are with me, unto the churches of Galatia:
3 Grace *be* to you and peace from God the Father, and *from* our Lord Jesus
Christ,
4 Who gave himself for our sins, that he might deliver us from this present
evil world, according to the will of God and our Father:
5 To whom *be* glory for ever and ever. Amen.

Follow the Good News We Brought

6 I marvel that ye are so soon removed from him that called you into the
grace of Christ unto another gospel:
7 Which is not another; but there be some that trouble you, and would per-
vert the gospel of Christ.
8 But though we, or an angel from heaven, preach any other gospel unto you
than that which we have preached unto you, let him be accursed.
9 As we said before, so say I now again, If any *man* preach any other gospel
unto you than that ye have received, let him be accursed.
10 For do I now persuade men, or God? or do I seek to please men? for if I
yet pleased men, I should not be the servant of Christ.
11 But I certify you, brethren, that the gospel which was preached of me is
not after man.
12 For I neither received it of man, neither was I taught *it*, but by the revela-
tion of Jesus Christ.
13 For ye have heard of my conversation in time past in the Jews' religion,
how that beyond measure I persecuted the church of God, and wasted it:
14 And profited in the Jews' religion above many my equals in mine own
nation, being more exceedingly zealous of the traditions of my fathers.
15 But when it pleased God, who separated me from my mother's womb,
and called *me* by his grace,
16 To reveal his Son in me, that I might preach him among the heathen;
immediately I conferred not with flesh and blood:
17 Neither went I up to Jerusalem to them which were apostles before me;
but I went into Arabia, and returned again unto Damascus.
18 Then after three years I went up to Jerusalem to see Peter, and abode with
him fifteen days.
19 But other of the apostles saw I none, save James the Lord's brother.
20 Now the things which I write unto you, behold, before God, I lie not.
21 Afterwards I came into the regions of Syria and Cilicia;
22 And was unknown by face unto the churches of Judaea which were in
Christ:
23 But they had heard only, That he which persecuted us in times past now
preacheth the faith which once he destroyed.
24 And they glorified God in me.

Paul Accepted as an Apostle

2 Then fourteen years after I went up again to Jerusalem with Barnabas, and
took Titus with *me* also.
2 And I went up by revelation, and communicated unto them that gospel
which I preach among the Gentiles, but privately to them which were of rep-
utation, lest by any means I should run, or had run, in vain.

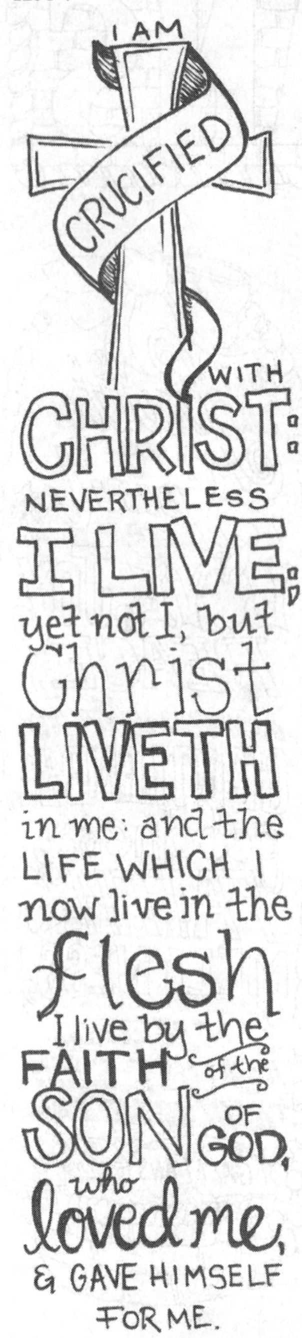

3 But neither Titus, who was with me, being a Greek, was compelled to be
circumcised:
4 And that because of false brethren unawares brought in, who came in
privily to spy out our liberty which we have in Christ Jesus, that they might
bring us into bondage:
5 To whom we gave place by subjection, no, not for an hour; that the truth
of the gospel might continue with you.
6 But of these who seemed to be somewhat, (whatsoever they were, it maketh
no matter to me: God accepteth no man's person:) for they who seemed *to be
somewhat* in conference added nothing to me:
7 But contrariwise, when they saw that the gospel of the uncircumcision was
committed unto me, as *the gospel* of the circumcision *was* unto Peter;
8 (For he that wrought effectually in Peter to the apostleship of the circum-
cision, the same was mighty in me toward the Gentiles:)
9 And when James, Cephas, and John, who seemed to be pillars, perceived
the grace that was given unto me, they gave to me and Barnabas the right hands
of fellowship; that we *should go* unto the heathen, and they unto the circum-
cision.
10 Only *they would* that we should remember the poor; the same which I
also was forward to do.

How Peter Was Wrong

11 But when Peter was come to Antioch, I withstood him to the face, because
he was to be blamed.
12 For before that certain came from James, he did eat with the Gentiles: but
when they were come, he withdrew and separated himself, fearing them which
were of the circumcision.
13 And the other Jews dissembled likewise with him; insomuch that Barnabas
also was carried away with their dissimulation.
14 But when I saw that they walked not uprightly according to the truth of
the gospel, I said unto Peter before *them* all, If thou, being a Jew, livest after
the manner of Gentiles, and not as do the Jews, why compellest thou the
Gentiles to live as do the Jews?
15 We *who are* Jews by nature, and not sinners of the Gentiles,
16 Knowing that a man is not justified by the works of the law, but by the
faith of Jesus Christ, even we have believed in Jesus Christ, that we might be
justified by the faith of Christ, and not by the works of the law: for by the works
of the law shall no flesh be justified.
17 But if, while we seek to be justified by Christ, we ourselves also are found
sinners, *is* therefore Christ the minister of sin? God forbid.
18 For if I build again the things which I destroyed, I make myself a trans-
gressor.
19 For I through the law am dead to the law, that I might live unto God.
20 I am crucified with Christ: nevertheless I live; yet not I, but Christ liveth
in me: and the life which I now live in the flesh I live by the faith of the Son of
God, who loved me, and gave himself for me.
21 I do not frustrate the grace of God: for if righteousness *come* by the law,
then Christ is dead in vain.

God Approves of Those Who Believe

3 O foolish Galatians, who hath bewitched you, that ye should not obey the
truth, before whose eyes Jesus Christ hath been evidently set forth, crucified
among you?
2 This only would I learn of you, Received ye the Spirit by the works of the
law, or by the hearing of faith?
3 Are ye so foolish? having begun in the Spirit, are ye now made perfect by
the flesh?

4 Have ye suffered so many things in vain? if *it be* yet in vain.
5 He therefore that ministereth to you the Spirit, and worketh miracles
among you, *doeth he it* by the works of the law, or by the hearing of faith?

Those Who Believe Are Justified

6 Even as Abraham believed God, and it was accounted to him for righteous-
ness.
7 Know ye therefore that they which are of faith, the same are the children
of Abraham.
8 And the scripture, foreseeing that God would justify the heathen through
faith, preached before the gospel unto Abraham, *saying,* In thee shall all
nations be blessed.
9 So then they which be of faith are blessed with faithful Abraham.
10 For as many as are of the works of the law are under the curse: for it is
written, Cursed *is* every one that continueth not in all things which are writ-
ten in the book of the law to do them.
11 But that no man is justified by the law in the sight of God, *it is* evident:
for, The just shall live by faith.
12 And the law is not of faith: but, The man that doeth them shall live in them.
13 Christ hath redeemed us from the curse of the law, being made a curse
for us: for it is written, Cursed *is* every one that hangeth on a tree:
14 That the blessing of Abraham might come on the Gentiles through Jesus
Christ; that we might receive the promise of the Spirit through faith.
15 Brethren, I speak after the manner of men; Though *it be* but a man's cov-
enant, yet *if it be* confirmed, no man disannulleth, or addeth thereto.
16 Now to Abraham and his seed were the promises made. He saith not, And
to seeds, as of many; but as of one, And to thy seed, which is Christ.
17 And this I say, *that* the covenant, that was confirmed before of God in
Christ, the law, which was four hundred and thirty years after, cannot disan-
nul, that it should make the promise of none effect.
18 For if the inheritance *be* of the law, *it is* no more of promise: but God gave
it to Abraham by promise.
19 Wherefore then *serveth* the law? It was added because of transgressions,
till the seed should come to whom the promise was made; *and it was* ordained
by angels in the hand of a mediator.
20 Now a mediator is not *a mediator* of one, but God is one.
21 *Is* the law then against the promises of God? God forbid: for if there had
been a law given which could have given life, verily righteousness should have
been by the law.
22 But the scripture hath concluded all under sin, that the promise by faith
of Jesus Christ might be given to them that believe.
23 But before faith came, we were kept under the law, shut up unto the faith
which should afterwards be revealed.
24 Wherefore the law was our schoolmaster *to bring us* unto Christ, that we
might be justified by faith.
25 But after that faith is come, we are no longer under a schoolmaster.
26 For ye are all the children of God by faith in Christ Jesus.
27 For as many of you as have been baptized into Christ have put on Christ.
28 There is neither Jew nor Greek, there is neither bond nor free, there is
neither male nor female: for ye are all one in Christ Jesus.
29 And if ye *be* Christ's, then are ye Abraham's seed, and heirs according to
the promise.

We Are God's Children

4 Now I say, *That* the heir, as long as he is a child, differeth nothing from a
servant, though he be lord of all;
2 But is under tutors and governors until the time appointed of the father.
3 Even so we, when we were children, were in bondage under the elements
of the world:

4 But when the fulness of the time was come, God sent forth his Son, made
of a woman, made under the law,
5 To redeem them that were under the law, that we might receive the adop-
tion of sons.
6 And because ye are sons, God hath sent forth the Spirit of his Son into your
hearts, crying, Abba, Father.
7 Wherefore thou art no more a servant, but a son; and if a son, then an heir
of God through Christ.
8 Howbeit then, when ye knew not God, ye did service unto them which by
nature are no gods.
9 But now, after that ye have known God, or rather are known of God, how
turn ye again to the weak and beggarly elements, whereunto ye desire again
to be in bondage?
10 Ye observe days, and months, and times, and years.
11 I am afraid of you, lest I have bestowed upon you labour in vain.
12 Brethren, I beseech you, be as I *am*; for I *am* as ye *are*: ye have not injured
me at all.
13 Ye know how through infirmity of the flesh I preached the gospel unto
you at the first.
14 And my temptation which was in my flesh ye despised not, nor rejected;
but received me as an angel of God, *even* as Christ Jesus.
15 Where is then the blessedness ye spake of? for I bear you record, that, if
it had been possible, ye would have plucked out your own eyes, and have given
them to me.
16 Am I therefore become your enemy, because I tell you the truth?
17 They zealously affect you, *but* not well; yea, they would exclude you, that
ye might affect them.
18 But *it is* good to be zealously affected always in *a* good *thing*, and not only
when I am present with you.
19 My little children, of whom I travail in birth again until Christ be formed
in you,
20 I desire to be present with you now, and to change my voice; for I stand
in doubt of you.
21 Tell me, ye that desire to be under the law, do ye not hear the law?
22 For it is written, that Abraham had two sons, the one by a bondmaid, the
other by a freewoman.
23 But he *who was* of the bondwoman was born after the flesh; but he of the
freewoman *was* by promise.
24 Which things are an allegory: for these are the two covenants; the one
from the mount Sinai, which gendereth to bondage, which is Agar.
25 For this Agar is mount Sinai in Arabia, and answereth to Jerusalem which
now is, and is in bondage with her children.
26 But Jerusalem which is above is free, which is the mother of us all.
27 For it is written, Rejoice, *thou* barren that bearest not; break forth and
cry, thou that travailest not: for the desolate hath many more children than
she which hath an husband.
28 Now we, brethren, as Isaac was, are the children of promise.
29 But as then he that was born after the flesh persecuted him *that was born*
after the Spirit, even so *it is* now.
30 Nevertheless what saith the scripture? Cast out the bondwoman and her
son: for the son of the bondwoman shall not be heir with the son of the free-
woman.
31 So then, brethren, we are not children of the bondwoman, but of the free.

Live in Freedom

5 Stand fast therefore in the liberty wherewith Christ hath made us free, and
be not entangled again with the yoke of bondage.
2 Behold, I Paul say unto you, that if ye be circumcised, Christ shall profit
you nothing.
3 For I testify again to every man that is circumcised, that he is a debtor to
do the whole law.
4 Christ is become of no effect unto you, whosoever of you are justified by
the law; ye are fallen from grace.
5 For we through the Spirit wait for the hope of righteousness by faith.
6 For in Jesus Christ neither circumcision availeth any thing, nor uncircum-
cision; but faith which worketh by love.
7 Ye did run well; who did hinder you that ye should not obey the truth?
8 This persuasion *cometh* not of him that calleth you.
9 A little leaven leaveneth the whole lump.
10 I have confidence in you through the Lord, that ye will be none otherwise
minded: but he that troubleth you shall bear his judgment, whosoever he be.
11 And I, brethren, if I yet preach circumcision, why do I yet suffer persecu-
tion? then is the offence of the cross ceased.
12 I would they were even cut off which trouble you.
13 For, brethren, ye have been called unto liberty; only *use* not liberty for an
occasion to the flesh, but by love serve one another.
14 For all the law is fulfilled in one word, *even* in this; Thou shalt love thy
neighbour as thyself.
15 But if ye bite and devour one another, take heed that ye be not consumed
one of another.
16 *This* I say then, Walk in the Spirit, and ye shall not fulfil the lust of the
flesh.
17 For the flesh lusteth against the Spirit, and the Spirit against the flesh: and
these are contrary the one to the other: so that ye cannot do the things that ye
would.
18 But if ye be led of the Spirit, ye are not under the law.
19 Now the works of the flesh are manifest, which are *these*; Adultery, forni-
cation, uncleanness, lasciviousness,
20 Idolatry, witchcraft, hatred, variance, emulations, wrath, strife, seditions,
heresies,
21 Envyings, murders, drunkenness, revellings, and such like: of the which
I tell you before, as I have also told *you* in time past, that they which do such
things shall not inherit the kingdom of God.
22 But the fruit of the Spirit is love, joy, peace, longsuffering, gentleness,
goodness, faith,
23 Meekness, temperance: against such there is no law.
24 And they that are Christ's have crucified the flesh with the affections and
lusts.
25 If we live in the Spirit, let us also walk in the Spirit.
26 Let us not be desirous of vain glory, provoking one another, envying one
another.

Carry One Another's Burdens

6 Brethren, if a man be overtaken in a fault, ye which are spiritual, restore
such an one in the spirit of meekness; considering thyself, lest thou also be
tempted.
2 Bear ye one another's burdens, and so fulfil the law of Christ.
3 For if a man think himself to be something, when he is nothing, he
deceiveth himself.

Love
Joy
Peace
Longsuffering
Gentleness
Goodness
Faith
Meekness
Temperance
GALATIANS 5:22-23

4 But let every man prove his own work, and then shall he have rejoicing in
himself alone, and not in another.
5 For every man shall bear his own burden.

We Will Reap What We Sow

6 Let him that is taught in the word communicate unto him that teacheth
in all good things.
7 Be not deceived; God is not mocked: for whatsoever a man soweth, that
shall he also reap.
8 For he that soweth to his flesh shall of the flesh reap corruption; but he
that soweth to the Spirit shall of the Spirit reap life everlasting.
9 And let us not be weary in well doing: for in due season we shall reap, if we
faint not.
10 As we have therefore opportunity, let us do good unto all *men*, especially
unto them who are of the household of faith.

Final Teachings

11 Ye see how large a letter I have written unto you with mine own hand.
12 As many as desire to make a fair shew in the flesh, they constrain you to
be circumcised; only lest they should suffer persecution for the cross of Christ.
13 For neither they themselves who are circumcised keep the law; but desire
to have you circumcised, that they may glory in your flesh.
14 But God forbid that I should glory, save in the cross of our Lord Jesus
Christ, by whom the world is crucified unto me, and I unto the world.
15 For in Christ Jesus neither circumcision availeth any thing, nor uncir-
cumcision, but a new creature.
16 And as many as walk according to this rule, peace *be* on them, and mercy,
and upon the Israel of God.
17 From henceforth let no man trouble me: for I bear in my body the marks
of the Lord Jesus.
18 Brethren, the grace of our Lord Jesus Christ *be* with your spirit. Amen.

EPHESIANS

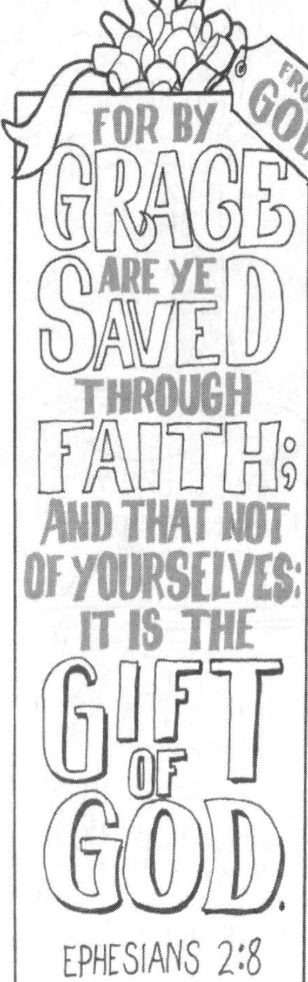

Paul's Greeting

1 Paul, an apostle of Jesus Christ by the will of God, to the saints which are at
Ephesus, and to the faithful in Christ Jesus:
2 Grace *be* to you, and peace, from God our Father, and *from* the Lord Jesus
Christ.

Thanks for Spiritual Blessings

3 Blessed *be* the God and Father of our Lord Jesus Christ, who hath blessed
us with all spiritual blessings in heavenly *places* in Christ:
4 According as he hath chosen us in him before the foundation of the world,
that we should be holy and without blame before him in love:
5 Having predestinated us unto the adoption of children by Jesus Christ to
himself, according to the good pleasure of his will,
6 To the praise of the glory of his grace, wherein he hath made us accepted
in the beloved.
7 In whom we have redemption through his blood, the forgiveness of sins,
according to the riches of his grace;
8 Wherein he hath abounded toward us in all wisdom and prudence;
9 Having made known unto us the mystery of his will, according to his good
pleasure which he hath purposed in himself:
10 That in the dispensation of the fulness of times he might gather together
in one all things in Christ, both which are in heaven, and which are on earth;
even in him:
11 In whom also we have obtained an inheritance, being predestinated
according to the purpose of him who worketh all things after the counsel of
his own will:
12 That we should be to the praise of his glory, who first trusted in Christ.
13 In whom ye also *trusted*, after that ye heard the word of truth, the gospel
of your salvation: in whom also after that ye believed, ye were sealed with that
holy Spirit of promise,
14 Which is the earnest of our inheritance until the redemption of the pur-
chased possession, unto the praise of his glory.

Paul's Prayer for the Ephesians

15 Wherefore I also, after I heard of your faith in the Lord Jesus, and love
unto all the saints,
16 Cease not to give thanks for you, making mention of you in my prayers;
17 That the God of our Lord Jesus Christ, the Father of glory, may give unto
you the spirit of wisdom and revelation in the knowledge of him:
18 The eyes of your understanding being enlightened; that ye may know what
is the hope of his calling, and what the riches of the glory of his inheritance
in the saints,
19 And what *is* the exceeding greatness of his power to us-ward who believe,
according to the working of his mighty power,
20 Which he wrought in Christ, when he raised him from the dead, and set
him at his own right hand in the heavenly *places*,
21 Far above all principality, and power, and might, and dominion, and every
name that is named, not only in this world, but also in that which is to come:

22 And hath put all *things* under his feet, and gave him *to be* the head over all *things* to the church,
23 Which is his body, the fulness of him that filleth all in all.

God's Great Love for Us

2 And you *hath he quickened*, who were dead in trespasses and sins;
2 Wherein in time past ye walked according to the course of this world, according to the prince of the power of the air, the spirit that now worketh in the children of disobedience:
3 Among whom also we all had our conversation in times past in the lusts of our flesh, fulfilling the desires of the flesh and of the mind; and were by nature the children of wrath, even as others.
4 But God, who is rich in mercy, for his great love wherewith he loved us,
5 Even when we were dead in sins, hath quickened us together with Christ, (by grace ye are saved;)
6 And hath raised *us* up together, and made *us* sit together in heavenly *places* in Christ Jesus:
7 That in the ages to come he might shew the exceeding riches of his grace in *his* kindness toward us through Christ Jesus.
8 For by grace are ye saved through faith; and that not of yourselves: *it is* the gift of God:
9 Not of works, lest any man should boast.
10 For we are his workmanship, created in Christ Jesus unto good works, which God hath before ordained that we should walk in them.

Uniting Jews and Non-Jews

11 Wherefore remember, that ye *being* in time past Gentiles in the flesh, who are called Uncircumcision by that which is called the Circumcision in the flesh made by hands;
12 That at that time ye were without Christ, being aliens from the commonwealth of Israel, and strangers from the covenants of promise, having no hope, and without God in the world:
13 But now in Christ Jesus ye who sometimes were far off are made nigh by the blood of Christ.
14 For he is our peace, who hath made both one, and hath broken down the middle wall of partition *between us*;
15 Having abolished in his flesh the enmity, *even* the law of commandments *contained* in ordinances; for to make in himself of twain one new man, *so* making peace;
16 And that he might reconcile both unto God in one body by the cross, having slain the enmity thereby:
17 And came and preached peace to you which were afar off, and to them that were nigh.
18 For through him we both have access by one Spirit unto the Father.
19 Now therefore ye are no more strangers and foreigners, but fellowcitizens with the saints, and of the household of God;
20 And are built upon the foundation of the apostles and prophets, Jesus Christ himself being the chief corner *stone*;
21 In whom all the building fitly framed together groweth unto an holy temple in the Lord:
22 In whom ye also are builded together for an habitation of God through the Spirit.

Paul's Ministry

3 For this cause I Paul, the prisoner of Jesus Christ for you Gentiles,
2 If ye have heard of the dispensation of the grace of God which is given me to you-ward:
3 How that by revelation he made known unto me the mystery; (as I wrote afore in few words,

FOR WE ARE HIS
WORKMANSHIP,
CREATED IN
CHRIST
JESUS
UNTO GOOD WORKS,
WHICH GOD HATH
BEFORE
ORDAINED
THAT WE SHOULD
WALK
IN THEM.

EPHESIANS 2:10

4 Whereby, when ye read, ye may understand my knowledge in the mystery
of Christ)
5 Which in other ages was not made known unto the sons of men, as it is
now revealed unto his holy apostles and prophets by the Spirit;
6 That the Gentiles should be fellow-heirs, and of the same body, and par-
takers of his promise in Christ by the gospel:
7 Whereof I was made a minister, according to the gift of the grace of God
given unto me by the effectual working of his power.
8 Unto me, who am less than the least of all saints, is this grace given, that I
should preach among the Gentiles the unsearchable riches of Christ;
9 And to make all *men* see what *is* the fellowship of the mystery, which from
the beginning of the world hath been hid in God, who created all things by
Jesus Christ:
10 To the intent that now unto the principalities and powers in heavenly
places might be known by the church the manifold wisdom of God,
11 According to the eternal purpose which he purposed in Christ Jesus our
Lord:
12 In whom we have boldness and access with confidence by the faith of him.
13 Wherefore I desire that ye faint not at my tribulations for you, which is
your glory.

Paul's Prayer

14 For this cause I bow my knees unto the Father of our Lord Jesus Christ,
15 Of whom the whole family in heaven and earth is named,
16 That he would grant you, according to the riches of his glory, to be
strengthened with might by his Spirit in the inner man;
17 That Christ may dwell in your hearts by faith; that ye, being rooted and
grounded in love,
18 May be able to comprehend with all saints what *is* the breadth, and length,
and depth, and height;
19 And to know the love of Christ, which passeth knowledge, that ye might
be filled with all the fulness of God.
20 Now unto him that is able to do exceeding abundantly above all that we
ask or think, according to the power that worketh in us,
21 Unto him *be* glory in the church by Christ Jesus throughout all ages, world
without end. Amen.

Christ's Gifts to the Church

4 I therefore, the prisoner of the Lord, beseech you that ye walk worthy of
the vocation wherewith ye are called,
2 With all lowliness and meekness, with longsuffering, forbearing one anoth-
er in love;
3 Endeavouring to keep the unity of the Spirit in the bond of peace.
4 *There is* one body, and one Spirit, even as ye are called in one hope of your
calling;
5 One Lord, one faith, one baptism,
6 One God and Father of all, who *is* above all, and through all, and in you all.
7 But unto every one of us is given grace according to the measure of the gift
of Christ.
8 Wherefore he saith, When he ascended up on high, he led captivity captive,
and gave gifts unto men.
9 (Now that he ascended, what is it but that he also descended first into the
lower parts of the earth?
10 He that descended is the same also that ascended up far above all heavens,
that he might fill all things.)
11 And he gave some, apostles; and some, prophets; and some, evangelists;
and some, pastors and teachers;

12 For the perfecting of the saints, for the work of the ministry, for the edi-
fying of the body of Christ:
13 Till we all come in the unity of the faith, and of the knowledge of the Son
of God, unto a perfect man, unto the measure of the stature of the fulness of
Christ:
14 That we *henceforth* be no more children, tossed to and fro, and carried
about with every wind of doctrine, by the sleight of men, *and* cunning craft-
iness, whereby they lie in wait to deceive;
15 But speaking the truth in love, may grow up into him in all things, which
is the head, *even* Christ:
16 From whom the whole body fitly joined together and compacted by that
which every joint supplieth, according to the effectual working in the measure
of every part, maketh increase of the body unto the edifying of itself in love.

Live as God's People

17 This I say therefore, and testify in the Lord, that ye henceforth walk not
as other Gentiles walk, in the vanity of their mind,
18 Having the understanding darkened, being alienated from the life of God
through the ignorance that is in them, because of the blindness of their heart:
19 Who being past feeling have given themselves over unto lasciviousness,
to work all uncleanness with greediness.
20 But ye have not so learned Christ;
21 If so be that ye have heard him, and have been taught by him, as the truth
is in Jesus:
22 That ye put off concerning the former conversation the old man, which
is corrupt according to the deceitful lusts;
23 And be renewed in the spirit of your mind;
24 And that ye put on the new man, which after God is created in righteous-
ness and true holiness.
25 Wherefore putting away lying, speak every man truth with his neighbour:
for we are members one of another.
26 Be ye angry, and sin not: let not the sun go down upon your wrath:
27 Neither give place to the devil.
28 Let him that stole steal no more: but rather let him labour, working with
his hands the thing which is good, that he may have to give to him that need-
eth.
29 Let no corrupt communication proceed out of your mouth, but that which
is good to the use of edifying, that it may minister grace unto the hearers.
30 And grieve not the holy Spirit of God, whereby ye are sealed unto the day
of redemption.
31 Let all bitterness, and wrath, and anger, and clamour, and evil speaking,
be put away from you, with all malice:
32 And be ye kind one to another, tenderhearted, forgiving one another, even
as God for Christ's sake hath forgiven you.

Imitate God

5 Be ye therefore followers of God, as dear children;
2 And walk in love, as Christ also hath loved us, and hath given himself
for us an offering and a sacrifice to God for a sweetsmelling savour.

Flee Fornication

3 But fornication, and all uncleanness, or covetousness, let it not be once
named among you, as becometh saints;
4 Neither filthiness, nor foolish talking, nor jesting, which are not conven-
ient: but rather giving of thanks.
5 For this ye know, that no whoremonger, nor unclean person, nor covetous
man, who is an idolater, hath any inheritance in the kingdom of Christ and
of God.

6 Let no man deceive you with vain words: for because of these things com-
eth the wrath of God upon the children of disobedience.
7 Be not ye therefore partakers with them.
8 For ye were sometimes darkness, but now *are ye* light in the Lord: walk as
children of light:
9 (For the fruit of the Spirit *is* in all goodness and righteousness and truth;)
10 Proving what is acceptable unto the Lord.
11 And have no fellowship with the unfruitful works of darkness, but rather
reprove *them*.
12 For it is a shame even to speak of those things which are done of them in
secret.
13 But all things that are reproved are made manifest by the light: for what-
soever doth make manifest is light.
14 Wherefore he saith, Awake thou that sleepest, and arise from the dead,
and Christ shall give thee light.
15 See then that ye walk circumspectly, not as fools, but as wise,
16 Redeeming the time, because the days are evil.
17 Wherefore be ye not unwise, but understanding what the will of the Lord *is*.
18 And be not drunk with wine, wherein is excess; but be filled with the Spirit;
19 Speaking to yourselves in psalms and hymns and spiritual songs, singing
and making melody in your heart to the Lord;
20 Giving thanks always for all things unto God and the Father in the name
of our Lord Jesus Christ;

Advice to Wives and Husbands

21 Submitting yourselves one to another in the fear of God.
22 Wives, submit yourselves unto your own husbands, as unto the Lord.
23 For the husband is the head of the wife, even as Christ is the head of the
church: and he is the saviour of the body.
24 Therefore as the church is subject unto Christ, so *let* the wives *be* to their
own husbands in every thing.
25 Husbands, love your wives, even as Christ also loved the church, and gave
himself for it;
26 That he might sanctify and cleanse it with the washing of water by the
word,
27 That he might present it to himself a glorious church, not having spot, or
wrinkle, or any such thing; but that it should be holy and without blemish.
28 So ought men to love their wives as their own bodies. He that loveth his
wife loveth himself.
29 For no man ever yet hated his own flesh; but nourisheth and cherisheth
it, even as the Lord the church:
30 For we are members of his body, of his flesh, and of his bones.
31 For this cause shall a man leave his father and mother, and shall be joined
unto his wife, and they two shall be one flesh.
32 This is a great mystery: but I speak concerning Christ and the church.
33 Nevertheless let every one of you in particular so love his wife even as
himself; and the wife *see* that she reverence *her* husband.

Advice to Children and Parents

6 Children, obey your parents in the Lord: for this is right.
2 Honour thy father and mother; (which is the first commandment with
promise;)
3 That it may be well with thee, and thou mayest live long on the earth.
4 And, ye fathers, provoke not your children to wrath: but bring them up in
the nurture and admonition of the Lord.

Advice to Servants and Masters

5 Servants, be obedient to them that are *your* masters according to the flesh,
with fear and trembling, in singleness of your heart, as unto Christ;
6 Not with eyeservice, as menpleasers; but as the servants of Christ, doing
the will of God from the heart;
7 With good will doing service, as to the Lord, and not to men:
8 Knowing that whatsoever good thing any man doeth, the same shall he
receive of the Lord, whether *he be* bond or free.
9 And, ye masters, do the same things unto them, forbearing threatening:
knowing that your Master also is in heaven; neither is there respect of persons
with him.

Put on the Armor of God

10 Finally, my brethren, be strong in the Lord, and in the power of his might.
11 Put on the whole armour of God, that ye may be able to stand against the
wiles of the devil.
12 For we wrestle not against flesh and blood, but against principalities,
against powers, against the rulers of the darkness of this world, against spir-
itual wickedness in high *places*.
13 Wherefore take unto you the whole armour of God, that ye may be able
to withstand in the evil day, and having done all, to stand.
14 Stand therefore, having your loins girt about with truth, and having on
the breastplate of righteousness;
15 And your feet shod with the preparation of the gospel of peace;
16 Above all, taking the shield of faith, wherewith ye shall be able to quench
all the fiery darts of the wicked.
17 And take the helmet of salvation, and the sword of the Spirit, which is the
word of God:
18 Praying always with all prayer and supplication in the Spirit, and watch-
ing thereunto with all perseverance and supplication for all saints;
19 And for me, that utterance may be given unto me, that I may open my
mouth boldly, to make known the mystery of the gospel,
20 For which I am an ambassador in bonds: that therein I may speak boldly,
as I ought to speak.

Final Greetings

21 But that ye also may know my affairs, *and* how I do, Tychicus, a beloved
brother and faithful minister in the Lord, shall make known to you all things:
22 Whom I have sent unto you for the same purpose, that ye might know our
affairs, and *that* he might comfort your hearts.
23 Peace *be* to the brethren, and love with faith, from God the Father and the
Lord Jesus Christ.
24 Grace *be* with all them that love our Lord Jesus Christ in sincerity. Amen.

FOR WE WRESTLE NOT AGAINST FLESH & BLOOD, BUT AGAINST PRINCIPALITIES, AGAINST POWERS, AGAINST THE RULERS of the DARKNESS OF THIS WORLD, AGAINST SPIRITUAL WICKEDNESS IN HIGH PLACES.

EPHESIANS 6:12

ARMOR OF GOD
Salvation
Righteousness
Faith
Truth
Spirit
Peace
EPHESIANS 6:14-17

Paul's Greeting

1 Paul and Timotheus, the servants of Jesus Christ, to all the saints in Christ
Jesus which are at Philippi, with the bishops and deacons:
2 Grace *be* unto you, and peace, from God our Father, and *from* the Lord
Jesus Christ.

Paul's Prayer for the Philippians

3 I thank my God upon every remembrance of you,
4 Always in every prayer of mine for you all making request with joy,
5 For your fellowship in the gospel from the first day until now;
6 Being confident of this very thing, that he which hath begun a good work
in you will perform *it* until the day of Jesus Christ:
7 Even as it is meet for me to think this of you all, because I have you in my
heart; inasmuch as both in my bonds, and in the defence and confirmation
of the gospel, ye all are partakers of my grace.
8 For God is my record, how greatly I long after you all in the bowels of Jesus
Christ.
9 And this I pray, that your love may abound yet more and more in knowledge
and *in* all judgment;
10 That ye may approve things that are excellent; that ye may be sincere and
without offence till the day of Christ;
11 Being filled with the fruits of righteousness, which are by Jesus Christ,
unto the glory and praise of God.

Paul Advances the Gospel

12 But I would ye should understand, brethren, that the things *which hap-
pened* unto me have fallen out rather unto the furtherance of the gospel;
13 So that my bonds in Christ are manifest in all the palace, and in all other
places;
14 And many of the brethren in the Lord, waxing confident by my bonds,
are much more bold to speak the word without fear.
15 Some indeed preach Christ even of envy and strife; and some also of good
will:
16 The one preach Christ of contention, not sincerely, supposing to add
affliction to my bonds:
17 But the other of love, knowing that I am set for the defence of the gospel.
18 What then? notwithstanding, every way, whether in pretence, or in truth,
Christ is preached; and I therein do rejoice, yea, and will rejoice.
19 For I know that this shall turn to my salvation through your prayer, and
the supply of the Spirit of Jesus Christ,
20 According to my earnest expectation and *my* hope, that in nothing I shall
be ashamed, but *that* with all boldness, as always, *so* now also Christ shall be
magnified in my body, whether *it be* by life, or by death.
21 For to me to live *is* Christ, and to die *is* gain.
22 But if I live in the flesh, this *is* the fruit of my labour: yet what I shall choose
I wot not.
23 For I am in a strait betwixt two, having a desire to depart, and to be with
Christ; which is far better:
24 Nevertheless to abide in the flesh *is* more needful for you.

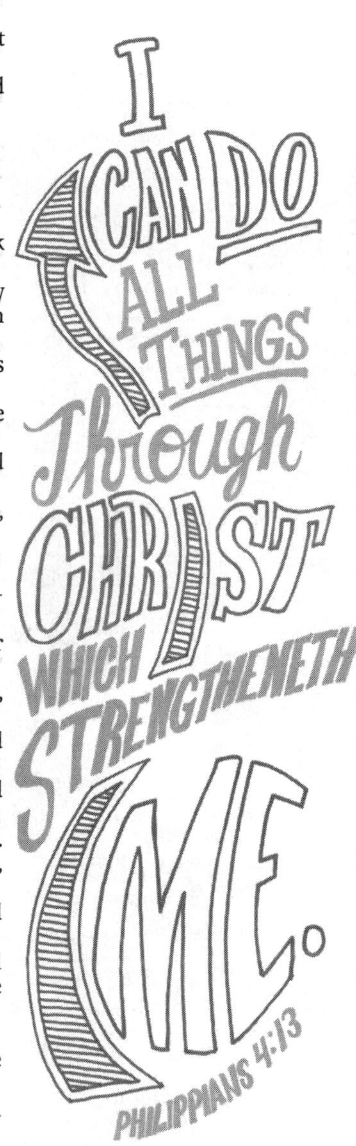

25 And having this confidence, I know that I shall abide and continue with
you all for your furtherance and joy of faith;
26 That your rejoicing may be more abundant in Jesus Christ for me by my
coming to you again.
27 Only let your conversation be as it becometh the gospel of Christ: that
whether I come and see you, or else be absent, I may hear of your affairs, that
ye stand fast in one spirit, with one mind striving together for the faith of the
gospel;
28 And in nothing terrified by your adversaries: which is to them an evident
token of perdition, but to you of salvation, and that of God.
29 For unto you it is given in the behalf of Christ, not only to believe on him,
but also to suffer for his sake;
30 Having the same conflict which ye saw in me, and now hear *to be* in me.

The Attitude of Christ

2 If *there be* therefore any consolation in Christ, if any comfort of love, if any
fellowship of the Spirit, if any bowels and mercies,
2 Fulfil ye my joy, that ye be likeminded, having the same love, *being* of one
accord, of one mind.
3 *Let* nothing *be done* through strife or vainglory; but in lowliness of mind
let each esteem other better than themselves.
4 Look not every man on his own things, but every man also on the things
of others.
5 Let this mind be in you, which was also in Christ Jesus:
6 Who, being in the form of God, thought it not robbery to be equal with
God:
7 But made himself of no reputation, and took upon him the form of a serv-
ant, and was made in the likeness of men:
8 And being found in fashion as a man, he humbled himself, and became
obedient unto death, even the death of the cross.
9 Wherefore God also hath highly exalted him, and given him a name which
is above every name:
10 That at the name of Jesus every knee should bow, of *things* in heaven, and
things in earth, and *things* under the earth;
11 And *that* every tongue should confess that Jesus Christ *is* Lord, to the glory
of God the Father.

A Christian's Obligations

12 Wherefore, my beloved, as ye have always obeyed, not as in my presence
only, but now much more in my absence, work out your own salvation with
fear and trembling.
13 For it is God which worketh in you both to will and to do of *his* good
pleasure.
14 Do all things without murmurings and disputings:
15 That ye may be blameless and harmless, the sons of God, without rebuke,
in the midst of a crooked and perverse nation, among whom ye shine as lights
in the world;
16 Holding forth the word of life; that I may rejoice in the day of Christ, that
I have not run in vain, neither laboured in vain.
17 Yea, and if I be offered upon the sacrifice and service of your faith, I joy,
and rejoice with you all.
18 For the same cause also do ye joy, and rejoice with me.

Timothy and Epaphroditus Will Come

19 But I trust in the Lord Jesus to send Timotheus shortly unto you, that I
also may be of good comfort, when I know your state.
20 For I have no man likeminded, who will naturally care for your state.
21 For all seek their own, not the things which are Jesus Christ's.

22 But ye know the proof of him, that, as a son with the father, he hath served
with me in the gospel.
23 Him therefore I hope to send presently, so soon as I shall see how it will
go with me.
24 But I trust in the Lord that I also myself shall come shortly.
25 Yet I supposed it necessary to send to you Epaphroditus, my brother, and
companion in labour, and fellowsoldier, but your messenger, and he that min-
istered to my wants.
26 For he longed after you all, and was full of heaviness, because that ye had
heard that he had been sick.
27 For indeed he was sick nigh unto death: but God had mercy on him; and
not on him only, but on me also, lest I should have sorrow upon sorrow.
28 I sent him therefore the more carefully, that, when ye see him again, ye
may rejoice, and that I may be the less sorrowful.
29 Receive him therefore in the Lord with all gladness; and hold such in
reputation:
30 Because for the work of Christ he was nigh unto death, not regarding his
life, to supply your lack of service toward me.

Run Straight for the Goal

3 Finally, my brethren, rejoice in the Lord. To write the same things to you,
to me indeed *is* not grievous, but for you *it is* safe.
2 Beware of dogs, beware of evil workers, beware of the concision.
3 For we are the circumcision, which worship God in the spirit, and rejoice
in Christ Jesus, and have no confidence in the flesh.
4 Though I might also have confidence in the flesh. If any other man thinketh
that he hath whereof he might trust in the flesh, I more:
5 Circumcised the eighth day, of the stock of Israel, *of* the tribe of Benjamin,
an Hebrew of the Hebrews; as touching the law, a Pharisee;
6 Concerning zeal, persecuting the church; touching the righteousness
which is in the law, blameless.
7 But what things were gain to me, those I counted loss for Christ.
8 Yea doubtless, and I count all things *but* loss for the excellency of the knowl-
edge of Christ Jesus my Lord: for whom I have suffered the loss of all things,
and do count them *but* dung, that I may win Christ,
9 And be found in him, not having mine own righteousness, which is of the
law, but that which is through the faith of Christ, the righteousness which is
of God by faith:
10 That I may know him, and the power of his resurrection, and the fellow-
ship of his sufferings, being made conformable unto his death;
11 If by any means I might attain unto the resurrection of the dead.
12 Not as though I had already attained, either were already perfect: but I
follow after, if that I may apprehend that for which also I am apprehended of
Christ Jesus.
13 Brethren, I count not myself to have apprehended: but *this* one thing *I
do*, forgetting those things which are behind, and reaching forth unto those
things which are before,
14 I press toward the mark for the prize of the high calling of God in Christ
Jesus.
15 Let us therefore, as many as be perfect, be thus minded: and if in any thing
ye be otherwise minded, God shall reveal even this unto you.
16 Nevertheless, whereto we have already attained, let us walk by the same
rule, let us mind the same thing.

Imitate Paul

17 Brethren, be followers together of me, and mark them which walk so as
ye have us for an ensample.

18 (For many walk, of whom I have told you often, and now tell you even
weeping, *that they are* the enemies of the cross of Christ:
19 Whose end *is* destruction, whose God *is their* belly, and *whose* glory *is* in
their shame, who mind earthly things.)
20 For our conversation is in heaven; from whence also we look for the
Saviour, the Lord Jesus Christ:
21 Who shall change our vile body, that it may be fashioned like unto his
glorious body, according to the working whereby he is able even to subdue all
things unto himself.

Paul's Advice

4 Therefore, my brethren dearly beloved and longed for, my joy and crown,
so stand fast in the Lord, *my* dearly beloved.
2 I beseech Euodias, and beseech Syntyche, that they be of the same mind in
the Lord.
3 And I intreat thee also, true yokefellow, help those women which laboured
with me in the gospel, with Clement also, and *with* other my fellowlabourers,
whose names *are* in the book of life.

Rejoice in the Lord

4 Rejoice in the Lord alway: *and* again I say, Rejoice.
5 Let your moderation be known unto all men. The Lord *is* at hand.
6 Be careful for nothing; but in every thing by prayer and supplication with
thanksgiving let your requests be made known unto God.
7 And the peace of God, which passeth all understanding, shall keep your
hearts and minds through Christ Jesus.
8 Finally, brethren, whatsoever things are true, whatsoever things *are* hon-
est, whatsoever things *are* just, whatsoever things *are* pure, whatsoever things
are lovely, whatsoever things *are* of good report; if *there be* any virtue, and if
there be any praise, think on these things.
9 Those things, which ye have both learned, and received, and heard, and
seen in me, do: and the God of peace shall be with you.

Paul Says Thank You

10 But I rejoiced in the Lord greatly, that now at the last your care of me hath
flourished again; wherein ye were also careful, but ye lacked opportunity.
11 Not that I speak in respect of want: for I have learned, in whatsoever state
I am, *therewith* to be content.
12 I know both how to be abased, and I know how to abound: every where
and in all things I am instructed both to be full and to be hungry, both to
abound and to suffer need.
13 I can do all things through Christ which strengtheneth me.
14 Notwithstanding ye have well done, that ye did communicate with my
affliction.
15 Now ye Philippians know also, that in the beginning of the gospel, when
I departed from Macedonia, no church communicated with me as concerning
giving and receiving, but ye only.
16 For even in Thessalonica ye sent once and again unto my necessity.
17 Not because I desire a gift: but I desire fruit that may abound to your
account.
18 But I have all, and abound: I am full, having received of Epaphroditus the
things *which were sent* from you, an odour of a sweet smell, a sacrifice accept-
able, wellpleasing to God.
19 But my God shall supply all your need according to his riches in glory by
Christ Jesus.
20 Now unto God and our Father *be* glory for ever and ever. Amen.
21 Salute every saint in Christ Jesus. The brethren which are with me greet you.
22 All the saints salute you, chiefly they that are of Caesar's household.
23 The grace of our Lord Jesus Christ *be* with you all. Amen.

True
Honest
Just
Pure
Lovely
Good Report
Virtue
Praise
Philippians 4:8

Paul's Greeting

1 Paul, an apostle of Jesus Christ by the will of God, and Timotheus *our* brother,
2 To the saints and faithful brethren in Christ which are at Colosse: Grace
be unto you, and peace, from God our Father and the Lord Jesus Christ.

Paul's Prayer for the Colossians

3 We give thanks to God and the Father of our Lord Jesus Christ, praying
always for you,
4 Since we heard of your faith in Christ Jesus, and of the love *which ye have*
to all the saints,
5 For the hope which is laid up for you in heaven, whereof ye heard before
in the word of the truth of the gospel;
6 Which is come unto you, as *it is* in all the world; and bringeth forth fruit,
as *it doth* also in you, since the day ye heard *of it*, and knew the grace of God
in truth:
7 As ye also learned of Epaphras our dear fellowservant, who is for you a
faithful minister of Christ;
8 Who also declared unto us your love in the Spirit.
9 For this cause we also, since the day we heard *it*, do not cease to pray for
you, and to desire that ye might be filled with the knowledge of his will in all
wisdom and spiritual understanding;
10 That ye might walk worthy of the Lord unto all pleasing, being fruitful in
every good work, and increasing in the knowledge of God;
11 Strengthened with all might, according to his glorious power, unto all
patience and longsuffering with joyfulness;
12 Giving thanks unto the Father, which hath made us meet to be partakers
of the inheritance of the saints in light:

What Christ Has Done

13 Who hath delivered us from the power of darkness, and hath translated
us into the kingdom of his dear Son:
14 In whom we have redemption through his blood, *even* the forgiveness of
sins:
15 Who is the image of the invisible God, the firstborn of every creature:
16 For by him were all things created, that are in heaven, and that are in earth,
visible and invisible, whether *they be* thrones, or dominions, or principalities,
or powers: all things were created by him, and for him:
17 And he is before all things, and by him all things consist.
18 And he is the head of the body, the church: who is the beginning, the
firstborn from the dead; that in all *things* he might have the preeminence.
19 For it pleased *the Father* that in him should all fulness dwell;
20 And, having made peace through the blood of his cross, by him to recon-
cile all things unto himself; by him, *I say*, whether *they be* things in earth, or
things in heaven.
21 And you, that were sometime alienated and enemies in *your* mind by
wicked works, yet now hath he reconciled
22 In the body of his flesh through death, to present you holy and unblame-
able and unreproveable in his sight:

23 If ye continue in the faith grounded and settled, and *be* not moved away
from the hope of the gospel, which ye have heard, *and* which was preached
to every creature which is under heaven; whereof I Paul am made a minister;
24 Who now rejoice in my sufferings for you, and fill up that which is behind
of the afflictions of Christ in my flesh for his body's sake, which is the church:
25 Whereof I am made a minister, according to the dispensation of God
which is given to me for you, to fulfil the word of God;
26 *Even* the mystery which hath been hid from ages and from generations,
but now is made manifest to his saints:
27 To whom God would make known what *is* the riches of the glory of this
mystery among the Gentiles; which is Christ in you, the hope of glory:
28 Whom we preach, warning every man, and teaching every man in all
wisdom; that we may present every man perfect in Christ Jesus:
29 Whereunto I also labour, striving according to his working, which wor-
keth in me mightily.

Stand Firm in the Faith

2 For I would that ye knew what great conflict I have for you, and *for* them
at Laodicea, and *for* as many as have not seen my face in the flesh;
2 That their hearts might be comforted, being knit together in love, and unto
all riches of the full assurance of understanding, to the acknowledgement of
the mystery of God, and of the Father, and of Christ;
3 In whom are hid all the treasures of wisdom and knowledge.
4 And this I say, lest any man should beguile you with enticing words.
5 For though I be absent in the flesh, yet am I with you in the spirit, joying
and beholding your order, and the stedfastness of your faith in Christ.
6 As ye have therefore received Christ Jesus the Lord, *so* walk ye in him:
7 Rooted and built up in him, and stablished in the faith, as ye have been
taught, abounding therein with thanksgiving.
8 Beware lest any man spoil you through philosophy and vain deceit, after
the tradition of men, after the rudiments of the world, and not after Christ.
9 For in him dwelleth all the fulness of the Godhead bodily.
10 And ye are complete in him, which is the head of all principality and
power:
11 In whom also ye are circumcised with the circumcision made without
hands, in putting off the body of the sins of the flesh by the circumcision of
Christ:
12 Buried with him in baptism, wherein also ye are risen with *him* through
the faith of the operation of God, who hath raised him from the dead.
13 And you, being dead in your sins and the uncircumcision of your flesh,
hath he quickened together with him, having forgiven you all trespasses;
14 Blotting out the handwriting of ordinances that was against us, which
was contrary to us, and took it out of the way, nailing it to his cross;
15 *And* having spoiled principalities and powers, he made a shew of them
openly, triumphing over them in it.
16 Let no man therefore judge you in meat, or in drink, or in respect of an
holyday, or of the new moon, or of the sabbath *days*:
17 Which are a shadow of things to come; but the body *is* of Christ.
18 Let no man beguile you of your reward in a voluntary humility and wor-
shipping of angels, intruding into those things which he hath not seen, vain-
ly puffed up by his fleshly mind,
19 And not holding the Head, from which all the body by joints and bands
having nourishment ministered, and knit together, increaseth with the
increase of God.
20 Wherefore if ye be dead with Christ from the rudiments of the world,
why, as though living in the world, are ye subject to ordinances,

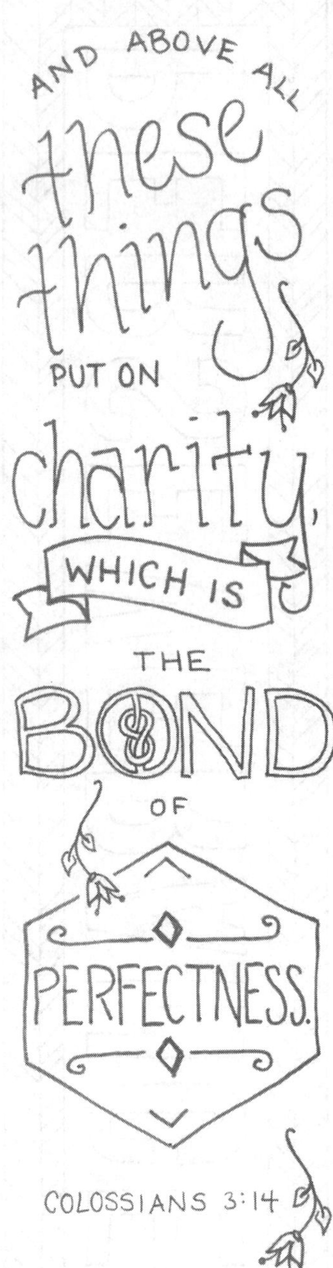

21 (Touch not; taste not; handle not;
22 Which all are to perish with the using;) after the commandments and
doctrines of men?
23 Which things have indeed a shew of wisdom in will worship, and humil-
ity, and neglecting of the body; not in any honour to the satisfying of the flesh.

Live as God's People

3 If ye then be risen with Christ, seek those things which are above, where
Christ sitteth on the right hand of God.
2 Set your affection on things above, not on things on the earth.
3 For ye are dead, and your life is hid with Christ in God.
4 When Christ, *who is* our life, shall appear, then shall ye also appear with
him in glory.
5 Mortify therefore your members which are upon the earth; fornication,
uncleanness, inordinate affection, evil concupiscence, and covetousness,
which is idolatry:
6 For which things' sake the wrath of God cometh on the children of disobe-
dience:
7 In the which ye also walked some time, when ye lived in them.
8 But now ye also put off all these; anger, wrath, malice, blasphemy, filthy
communication out of your mouth.
9 Lie not one to another, seeing that ye have put off the old man with his
deeds;
10 And have put on the new *man*, which is renewed in knowledge after the
image of him that created him:
11 Where there is neither Greek nor Jew, circumcision nor uncircumcision,
Barbarian, Scythian, bond *nor* free: but Christ *is* all, and in all.
12 Put on therefore, as the elect of God, holy and beloved, bowels of mercies,
kindness, humbleness of mind, meekness, longsuffering;
13 Forbearing one another, and forgiving one another, if any man have a
quarrel against any: even as Christ forgave you, so also *do* ye.
14 And above all these things *put on* charity, which is the bond of perfectness.
15 And let the peace of God rule in your hearts, to the which also ye are called
in one body; and be ye thankful.
16 Let the word of Christ dwell in you richly in all wisdom; teaching and
admonishing one another in psalms and hymns and spiritual songs, singing
with grace in your hearts to the Lord.
17 And whatsoever ye do in word or deed, *do* all in the name of the Lord Jesus,
giving thanks to God and the Father by him.
18 Wives, submit yourselves unto your own husbands, as it is fit in the Lord.
19 Husbands, love *your* wives, and be not bitter against them.
20 Children, obey *your* parents in all things: for this is well pleasing unto the
Lord.
21 Fathers, provoke not your children *to anger*, lest they be discouraged.
22 Servants, obey in all things *your* masters according to the flesh; not with
eyeservice, as menpleasers; but in singleness of heart, fearing God:
23 And whatsoever ye do, do *it* heartily, as to the Lord, and not unto men;
24 Knowing that of the Lord ye shall receive the reward of the inheritance:
for ye serve the Lord Christ.
25 But he that doeth wrong shall receive for the wrong which he hath done:
and there is no respect of persons.

Be Fervent in Prayer

4 Masters, give unto *your* servants that which is just and equal; knowing that
ye also have a Master in heaven.
2 Continue in prayer, and watch in the same with thanksgiving;
3 Withal praying also for us, that God would open unto us a door of utter-
ance, to speak the mystery of Christ, for which I am also in bonds:

4 That I may make it manifest, as I ought to speak.
5 Walk in wisdom toward them that are without, redeeming the time.
6 Let your speech *be* alway with grace, seasoned with salt, that ye may know
how ye ought to answer every man.

Final Greetings

7 All my state shall Tychicus declare unto you, *who is* a beloved brother, and
a faithful minister and fellowservant in the Lord:
8 Whom I have sent unto you for the same purpose, that he might know your
estate, and comfort your hearts;
9 With Onesimus, a faithful and beloved brother, who is *one* of you. They
shall make known unto you all things which *are done* here.
10 Aristarchus my fellowprisoner saluteth you, and Marcus, sister's son to
Barnabas, (touching whom ye received commandments: if he come unto you,
receive him;)
11 And Jesus, which is called Justus, who are of the circumcision. These only
are my fellowworkers unto the kingdom of God, which have been a comfort
unto me.
12 Epaphras, who is *one* of you, a servant of Christ, saluteth you, always
labouring fervently for you in prayers, that ye may stand perfect and complete
in all the will of God.
13 For I bear him record, that he hath a great zeal for you, and them *that are*
in Laodicea, and them in Hierapolis.
14 Luke, the beloved physician, and Demas, greet you.
15 Salute the brethren which are in Laodicea, and Nymphas, and the church
which is in his house.
16 And when this epistle is read among you, cause that it be read also in the
church of the Laodiceans; and that ye likewise read the *epistle* from Laodicea.
17 And say to Archippus, Take heed to the ministry which thou hast received
in the Lord, that thou fulfil it.
18 The salutation by the hand of me Paul. Remember my bonds. Grace *be*
with you. Amen.

IN EVERY THING
GIVE
thanks:
FOR THIS IS
THE WILL OF
GOD
IN
Christ Jesus
CONCERNING
YOU.

I THESSALONIANS 5:18

Paul's Greeting

1 Paul, and Silvanus, and Timotheus, unto the church of the Thessalonians
which is in God the Father and *in* the Lord Jesus Christ: Grace *be* unto you,
and peace, from God our Father, and the Lord Jesus Christ.

Paul's Prayer for the Thessalonians

2 We give thanks to God always for you all, making mention of you in our
prayers;
3 Remembering without ceasing your work of faith, and labour of love, and
patience of hope in our Lord Jesus Christ, in the sight of God and our Father;
4 Knowing, brethren beloved, your election of God.
5 For our gospel came not unto you in word only, but also in power, and in
the Holy Ghost, and in much assurance; as ye know what manner of men we
were among you for your sake.
6 And ye became followers of us, and of the Lord, having received the word
in much affliction, with joy of the Holy Ghost:
7 So that ye were ensamples to all that believe in Macedonia and Achaia.
8 For from you sounded out the word of the Lord not only in Macedonia and
Achaia, but also in every place your faith to God-ward is spread abroad; so that
we need not to speak any thing.
9 For they themselves shew of us what manner of entering in we had unto
you, and how ye turned to God from idols to serve the living and true God;
10 And to wait for his Son from heaven, whom he raised from the dead, *even*
Jesus, which delivered us from the wrath to come.

Paul Recalls His Visit

2 For yourselves, brethren, know our entrance in unto you, that it was not in
vain:
2 But even after that we had suffered before, and were shamefully entreated,
as ye know, at Philippi, we were bold in our God to speak unto you the gospel
of God with much contention.
3 For our exhortation *was* not of deceit, nor of uncleanness, nor in guile:
4 But as we were allowed of God to be put in trust with the gospel, even so
we speak; not as pleasing men, but God, which trieth our hearts.
5 For neither at any time used we flattering words, as ye know, nor a cloke
of covetousness; God *is* witness:
6 Nor of men sought we glory, neither of you, nor *yet* of others, when we
might have been burdensome, as the apostles of Christ.
7 But we were gentle among you, even as a nurse cherisheth her children:
8 So being affectionately desirous of you, we were willing to have imparted
unto you, not the gospel of God only, but also our own souls, because ye were
dear unto us.
9 For ye remember, brethren, our labour and travail: for labouring night
and day, because we would not be chargeable unto any of you, we preached
unto you the gospel of God.
10 Ye *are* witnesses, and God *also*, how holily and justly and unblameably we
behaved ourselves among you that believe:
11 As ye know how we exhorted and comforted and charged every one of
you, as a father *doth* his children,

12 That ye would walk worthy of God, who hath called you unto his kingdom
and glory.
13 For this cause also thank we God without ceasing, because, when ye
received the word of God which ye heard of us, ye received *it* not *as* the word
of men, but as it is in truth, the word of God, which effectually worketh also
in you that believe.
14 For ye, brethren, became followers of the churches of God which in Judaea
are in Christ Jesus: for ye also have suffered like things of your own country-
men, even as they *have* of the Jews:
15 Who both killed the Lord Jesus, and their own prophets, and have perse-
cuted us; and they please not God, and are contrary to all men:
16 Forbidding us to speak to the Gentiles that they might be saved, to fill up
their sins alway: for the wrath is come upon them to the uttermost.
17 But we, brethren, being taken from you for a short time in presence, not
in heart, endeavoured the more abundantly to see your face with great desire.
18 Wherefore we would have come unto you, even I Paul, once and again;
but Satan hindered us.
19 For what *is* our hope, or joy, or crown of rejoicing? *Are* not even ye in the
presence of our Lord Jesus Christ at his coming?
20 For ye are our glory and joy.

Timothy's Report to Paul

3 Wherefore when we could no longer forbear, we thought it good to be left
at Athens alone;
2 And sent Timotheus, our brother, and minister of God, and our fellowla-
bourer in the gospel of Christ, to establish you, and to comfort you concerning
your faith:
3 That no man should be moved by these afflictions: for yourselves know
that we are appointed thereunto.
4 For verily, when we were with you, we told you before that we should suffer
tribulation; even as it came to pass, and ye know.
5 For this cause, when I could no longer forbear, I sent to know your faith,
lest by some means the tempter have tempted you, and our labour be in vain.
6 But now when Timotheus came from you unto us, and brought us good
tidings of your faith and charity, and that ye have good remembrance of us
always, desiring greatly to see us, as we also *to see* you:
7 Therefore, brethren, we were comforted over you in all our affliction and
distress by your faith:
8 For now we live, if ye stand fast in the Lord.
9 For what thanks can we render to God again for you, for all the joy where-
with we joy for your sakes before our God;
10 Night and day praying exceedingly that we might see your face, and might
perfect that which is lacking in your faith?
11 Now God himself and our Father, and our Lord Jesus Christ, direct our
way unto you.
12 And the Lord make you to increase and abound in love one toward anoth-
er, and toward all *men*, even as we *do* toward you:
13 To the end he may stablish your hearts unblameable in holiness before
God, even our Father, at the coming of our Lord Jesus Christ with all his saints.

How Christians Should Live

4 Furthermore then we beseech you, brethren, and exhort *you* by the Lord
Jesus, that as ye have received of us how ye ought to walk and to please God,
so ye would abound more and more.
2 For ye know what commandments we gave you by the Lord Jesus.
3 For this is the will of God, *even* your sanctification, that ye should abstain
from fornication:

4 That every one of you should know how to possess his vessel in sanctifica-
tion and honour;
5 Not in the lust of concupiscence, even as the Gentiles which know not God:
6 That no *man* go beyond and defraud his brother in *any* matter: because
that the Lord *is* the avenger of all such, as we also have forewarned you and
testified.
7 For God hath not called us unto uncleanness, but unto holiness.
8 He therefore that despiseth, despiseth not man, but God, who hath also
given unto us his holy Spirit.

Love One Another

9 But as touching brotherly love ye need not that I write unto you: for ye
yourselves are taught of God to love one another.
10 And indeed ye do it toward all the brethren which are in all Macedonia:
but we beseech you, brethren, that ye increase more and more;
11 And that ye study to be quiet, and to do your own business, and to work
with your own hands, as we commanded you;
12 That ye may walk honestly toward them that are without, and *that* ye may
have lack of nothing.

Comfort about Christians Who Have Died

13 But I would not have you to be ignorant, brethren, concerning them which
are asleep, that ye sorrow not, even as others which have no hope.
14 For if we believe that Jesus died and rose again, even so them also which
sleep in Jesus will God bring with him.
15 For this we say unto you by the word of the Lord, that we which are alive
and remain unto the coming of the Lord shall not prevent them which are
asleep.
16 For the Lord himself shall descend from heaven with a shout, with the
voice of the archangel, and with the trump of God: and the dead in Christ shall
rise first:
17 Then we which are alive *and* remain shall be caught up together with
them in the clouds, to meet the Lord in the air: and so shall we ever be with
the Lord.
18 Wherefore comfort one another with these words.

Be Ready for Christ's Return

5 But of the times and the seasons, brethren, ye have no need that I write unto
you.
2 For yourselves know perfectly that the day of the Lord so cometh as a thief
in the night.
3 For when they shall say, Peace and safety; then sudden destruction cometh
upon them, as travail upon a woman with child; and they shall not escape.
4 But ye, brethren, are not in darkness, that that day should overtake you as
a thief.
5 Ye are all the children of light, and the children of the day: we are not of
the night, nor of darkness.
6 Therefore let us not sleep, as *do* others; but let us watch and be sober.
7 For they that sleep sleep in the night; and they that be drunken are drunk-
en in the night.
8 But let us, who are of the day, be sober, putting on the breastplate of faith
and love; and for an helmet, the hope of salvation.
9 For God hath not appointed us to wrath, but to obtain salvation by our
Lord Jesus Christ,
10 Who died for us, that, whether we wake or sleep, we should live together
with him.
11 Wherefore comfort yourselves together, and edify one another, even as
also ye do.

Honor Leaders
12 And we beseech you, brethren, to know them which labour among you,
and are over you in the Lord, and admonish you;
13 And to esteem them very highly in love for their work's sake. *And* be at
peace among yourselves.
14 Now we exhort you, brethren, warn them that are unruly, comfort the
feebleminded, support the weak, be patient toward all *men*.
15 See that none render evil for evil unto any *man*; but ever follow that which
is good, both among yourselves, and to all *men*.

Some Practical Precepts
16 Rejoice evermore.
17 Pray without ceasing.
18 In every thing give thanks: for this is the will of God in Christ Jesus con-
cerning you.
19 Quench not the Spirit.
20 Despise not prophesyings.
21 Prove all things; hold fast that which is good.
22 Abstain from all appearance of evil.

Paul's Farewell
23 And the very God of peace sanctify you wholly; and *I pray God* your whole
spirit and soul and body be preserved blameless unto the coming of our Lord
Jesus Christ.
24 Faithful *is* he that calleth you, who also will do *it*.
25 Brethren, pray for us.
26 Greet all the brethren with an holy kiss.
27 I charge you by the Lord that this epistle be read unto all the holy brethren.
28 The grace of our Lord Jesus Christ *be* with you. Amen.

1 THESSALONIANS 5:16-18
Rejoice evermore.
PRAY without ceasing.
In every thing give thanks:
for this is the WILL of GOD in Christ Jesus concerning you.

2 THESSALONIANS

Paul's Greeting

1 Paul, and Silvanus, and Timotheus, unto the church of the Thessalonians
in God our Father and the Lord Jesus Christ:
2 Grace unto you, and peace, from God our Father and the Lord Jesus Christ.

Paul's Prayer for the Thessalonians

3 We are bound to thank God always for you, brethren, as it is meet, because
that your faith groweth exceedingly, and the charity of every one of you all
toward each other aboundeth;
4 So that we ourselves glory in you in the churches of God for your patience
and faith in all your persecutions and tribulations that ye endure:
5 *Which is* a manifest token of the righteous judgment of God, that ye may
be counted worthy of the kingdom of God, for which ye also suffer:
6 Seeing *it is* a righteous thing with God to recompense tribulation to them
that trouble you;
7 And to you who are troubled rest with us, when the Lord Jesus shall be
revealed from heaven with his mighty angels,
8 In flaming fire taking vengeance on them that know not God, and that
obey not the gospel of our Lord Jesus Christ:
9 Who shall be punished with everlasting destruction from the presence of
the Lord, and from the glory of his power;
10 When he shall come to be glorified in his saints, and to be admired in all
them that believe (because our testimony among you was believed) in that
day.
11 Wherefore also we pray always for you, that our God would count you
worthy of *this* calling, and fulfil all the good pleasure of *his* goodness, and the
work of faith with power:
12 That the name of our Lord Jesus Christ may be glorified in you, and ye in
him, according to the grace of our God and the Lord Jesus Christ.

Do Not Be Deceived

2 Now we beseech you, brethren, by the coming of our Lord Jesus Christ, and
by our gathering together unto him,
2 That ye be not soon shaken in mind, or be troubled, neither by spirit, nor
by word, nor by letter as from us, as that the day of Christ is at hand.
3 Let no man deceive you by any means: for *that day shall not come,* except
there come a falling away first, and that man of sin be revealed, the son of
perdition;
4 Who opposeth and exalteth himself above all that is called God, or that is
worshipped; so that he as God sitteth in the temple of God, shewing himself
that he is God.
5 Remember ye not, that, when I was yet with you, I told you these things?
6 And now ye know what withholdeth that he might be revealed in his time.
7 For the mystery of iniquity doth already work: only he who now letteth
will let, until he be taken out of the way.
8 And then shall that Wicked be revealed, whom the Lord shall consume with
the spirit of his mouth, and shall destroy with the brightness of his coming:
9 *Even him,* whose coming is after the working of Satan with all power and
signs and lying wonders,

10 And with all deceivableness of unrighteousness in them that perish;
because they received not the love of the truth, that they might be saved.
11 And for this cause God shall send them strong delusion, that they should
believe a lie:
12 That they all might be damned who believed not the truth, but had
pleasure in unrighteousness.
13 But we are bound to give thanks alway to God for you, brethren beloved
of the Lord, because God hath from the beginning chosen you to salvation
through sanctification of the Spirit and belief of the truth:
14 Whereunto he called you by our gospel, to the obtaining of the glory of
our Lord Jesus Christ.
15 Therefore, brethren, stand fast, and hold the traditions which ye have
been taught, whether by word, or our epistle.
16 Now our Lord Jesus Christ himself, and God, even our Father, which hath
loved us, and hath given *us* everlasting consolation and good hope through
grace,
17 Comfort your hearts, and stablish you in every good word and work.

Final Instructions

3 Finally, brethren, pray for us, that the word of the Lord may have *free* course,
and be glorified, even as *it is* with you:
2 And that we may be delivered from unreasonable and wicked men: for all
men have not faith.
3 But the Lord is faithful, who shall stablish you, and keep *you* from evil.
4 And we have confidence in the Lord touching you, that ye both do and will
do the things which we command you.
5 And the Lord direct your hearts into the love of God, and into the patient
waiting for Christ.
6 Now we command you, brethren, in the name of our Lord Jesus Christ,
that ye withdraw yourselves from every brother that walketh disorderly, and
not after the tradition which he received of us.
7 For yourselves know how ye ought to follow us: for we behaved not our-
selves disorderly among you;
8 Neither did we eat any man's bread for nought; but wrought with labour
and travail night and day, that we might not be chargeable to any of you:
9 Not because we have not power, but to make ourselves an ensample unto
you to follow us.
10 For even when we were with you, this we commanded you, that if any
would not work, neither should he eat.
11 For we hear that there are some which walk among you disorderly, work-
ing not at all, but are busybodies.
12 Now them that are such we command and exhort by our Lord Jesus Christ,
that with quietness they work, and eat their own bread.
13 But ye, brethren, be not weary in well doing.
14 And if any man obey not our word by this epistle, note that man, and have
no company with him, that he may be ashamed.
15 Yet count *him* not as an enemy, but admonish *him* as a brother.

Paul's Blessing

16 Now the Lord of peace himself give you peace always by all means. The
Lord *be* with you all.
17 The salutation of Paul with mine own hand, which is the token in every
epistle: so I write.
18 The grace of our Lord Jesus Christ *be* with you all. Amen.

1 TIMOTHY

Paul's Greeting

1 Paul, an apostle of Jesus Christ by the commandment of God our Saviour,
and Lord Jesus Christ, *which is* our hope;
2 Unto Timothy, *my* own son in the faith: Grace, mercy, *and* peace, from God
our Father and Jesus Christ our Lord.

Warning about False Teachers

3 As I besought thee to abide still at Ephesus, when I went into Macedonia,
that thou mightest charge some that they teach no other doctrine,
4 Neither give heed to fables and endless genealogies, which minister ques-
tions, rather than godly edifying which is in faith: *so do.*
5 Now the end of the commandment is charity out of a pure heart, and *of* a
good conscience, and *of* faith unfeigned:
6 From which some having swerved have turned aside unto vain jangling;
7 Desiring to be teachers of the law; understanding neither what they say,
nor whereof they affirm.
8 But we know that the law *is* good, if a man use it lawfully;
9 Knowing this, that the law is not made for a righteous man, but for the
lawless and disobedient, for the ungodly and for sinners, for unholy and pro-
fane, for murderers of fathers and murderers of mothers, for manslayers,
10 For whoremongers, for them that defile themselves with mankind, for
menstealers, for liars, for perjured persons, and if there be any other thing
that is contrary to sound doctrine;
11 According to the glorious gospel of the blessed God, which was commit-
ted to my trust.

God's Mercy to Paul

12 And I thank Christ Jesus our Lord, who hath enabled me, for that he count-
ed me faithful, putting me into the ministry;
13 Who was before a blasphemer, and a persecutor, and injurious: but I
obtained mercy, because I did *it* ignorantly in unbelief.
14 And the grace of our Lord was exceeding abundant with faith and love
which is in Christ Jesus.
15 This *is* a faithful saying, and worthy of all acceptation, that Christ Jesus
came into the world to save sinners; of whom I am chief.
16 Howbeit for this cause I obtained mercy, that in me first Jesus Christ might
shew forth all longsuffering, for a pattern to them which should hereafter
believe on him to life everlasting.
17 Now unto the King eternal, immortal, invisible, the only wise God, *be*
honour and glory for ever and ever. Amen.
18 This charge I commit unto thee, son Timothy, according to the prophecies
which went before on thee, that thou by them mightest war a good warfare;
19 Holding faith, and a good conscience; which some having put away con-
cerning faith have made shipwreck;
20 Of whom is Hymenaeus and Alexander; whom I have delivered unto Satan,
that they may learn not to blaspheme.

Guidelines for the Church

2 I exhort therefore, that, first of all, supplications, prayers, intercessions,
and giving of thanks, be made for all men;
2 For kings, and *for* all that are in authority; that we may lead a quiet and
peaceable life in all godliness and honesty.

3 For this *is* good and acceptable in the sight of God our Saviour;
4 Who will have all men to be saved, and to come unto the knowledge of the
truth.
5 For *there is* one God, and one mediator between God and men, the man
Christ Jesus;
6 Who gave himself a ransom for all, to be testified in due time.
7 Whereunto I am ordained a preacher, and an apostle, (I speak the truth in
Christ, *and* lie not;) a teacher of the Gentiles in faith and verity.
8 I will therefore that men pray every where, lifting up holy hands, without
wrath and doubting.

Guidelines for Women

9 In like manner also, that women adorn themselves in modest apparel, with
shamefacedness and sobriety; not with broided hair, or gold, or pearls, or
costly array;
10 But (which becometh women professing godliness) with good works.
11 Let the woman learn in silence with all subjection.
12 But I suffer not a woman to teach, nor to usurp authority over the man,
but to be in silence.
13 For Adam was first formed, then Eve.
14 And Adam was not deceived, but the woman being deceived was in the
transgression.
15 Notwithstanding she shall be saved in childbearing, if they continue in
faith and charity and holiness with sobriety.

Qualifications for Church Leaders

3 This *is* a true saying, If a man desire the office of a bishop, he desireth a good
work.
2 A bishop then must be blameless, the husband of one wife, vigilant, sober,
of good behaviour, given to hospitality, apt to teach;
3 Not given to wine, no striker, not greedy of filthy lucre; but patient, not a
brawler, not covetous;
4 One that ruleth well his own house, having his children in subjection with
all gravity;
5 (For if a man know not how to rule his own house, how shall he take care
of the church of God?)
6 Not a novice, lest being lifted up with pride he fall into the condemnation
of the devil.
7 Moreover he must have a good report of them which are without; lest he
fall into reproach and the snare of the devil.
8 Likewise *must* the deacons *be* grave, not doubletongued, not given to much
wine, not greedy of filthy lucre;
9 Holding the mystery of the faith in a pure conscience.
10 And let these also first be proved; then let them use the office of a deacon,
being *found* blameless.
11 Even so *must their* wives *be* grave, not slanderers, sober, faithful in all
things.
12 Let the deacons be the husbands of one wife, ruling their children and
their own houses well.
13 For they that have used the office of a deacon well purchase to themselves
a good degree, and great boldness in the faith which is in Christ Jesus.

The Purpose of Paul's Writing

14 These things write I unto thee, hoping to come unto thee shortly:
15 But if I tarry long, that thou mayest know how thou oughtest to behave
thyself in the house of God, which is the church of the living God, the pillar
and ground of the truth.

16 And without controversy great is the mystery of godliness: God was man-
ifest in the flesh, justified in the Spirit, seen of angels, preached unto the
Gentiles, believed on in the world, received up into glory.

A Prophecy about the Final Days

4 Now the Spirit speaketh expressly, that in the latter times some shall depart
from the faith, giving heed to seducing spirits, and doctrines of devils;
2 Speaking lies in hypocrisy; having their conscience seared with a hot iron;
3 Forbidding to marry, *and commanding* to abstain from meats, which God
hath created to be received with thanksgiving of them which believe and know
the truth.
4 For every creature of God *is* good, and nothing to be refused, if it be
received with thanksgiving:
5 For it is sanctified by the word of God and prayer.

Guidelines for Serving Christ

6 If thou put the brethren in remembrance of these things, thou shalt be a
good minister of Jesus Christ, nourished up in the words of faith and of good
doctrine, whereunto thou hast attained.
7 But refuse profane and old wives' fables, and exercise thyself *rather* unto
godliness.
8 For bodily exercise profiteth little: but godliness is profitable unto all
things, having promise of the life that now is, and of that which is to come.
9 This *is* a faithful saying and worthy of all acceptation.
10 For therefore we both labour and suffer reproach, because we trust in the
living God, who is the Saviour of all men, specially of those that believe.
11 These things command and teach.
12 Let no man despise thy youth; but be thou an example of the believers, in
word, in conversation, in charity, in spirit, in faith, in purity.
13 Till I come, give attendance to reading, to exhortation, to doctrine.
14 Neglect not the gift that is in thee, which was given thee by prophecy, with
the laying on of the hands of the presbytery.
15 Meditate upon these things; give thyself wholly to them; that thy profiting
may appear to all.
16 Take heed unto thyself, and unto the doctrine; continue in them: for in
doing this thou shalt both save thyself, and them that hear thee.

Guidelines for Dealing with Christians

5 Rebuke not an elder, but intreat *him* as a father; *and* the younger men as
brethren;
2 The elder women as mothers; the younger as sisters, with all purity.
3 Honour widows that are widows indeed.
4 But if any widow have children or nephews, let them learn first to shew
piety at home, and to requite their parents: for that is good and acceptable
before God.
5 Now she that is a widow indeed, and desolate, trusteth in God, and contin-
ueth in supplications and prayers night and day.
6 But she that liveth in pleasure is dead while she liveth.
7 And these things give in charge, that they may be blameless.
8 But if any provide not for his own, and specially for those of his own house,
he hath denied the faith, and is worse than an infidel.
9 Let not a widow be taken into the number under threescore years old,
having been the wife of one man,
10 Well reported of for good works; if she have brought up children, if she
have lodged strangers, if she have washed the saints' feet, if she have relieved
the afflicted, if she have diligently followed every good work.
11 But the younger widows refuse: for when they have begun to wax wanton
against Christ, they will marry;

12 Having damnation, because they have cast off their first faith.
13 And withal they learn *to be* idle, wandering about from house to house;
and not only idle, but tattlers also and busybodies, speaking things which they
ought not.
14 I will therefore that the younger women marry, bear children, guide the
house, give none occasion to the adversary to speak reproachfully.
15 For some are already turned aside after Satan.
16 If any man or woman that believeth have widows, let them relieve them,
and let not the church be charged; that it may relieve them that are widows
indeed.

Guidelines for the Elders

17 Let the elders that rule well be counted worthy of double honour, espe-
cially they who labour in the word and doctrine.
18 For the scripture saith, Thou shalt not muzzle the ox that treadeth out the
corn. And, The labourer *is* worthy of his reward.
19 Against an elder receive not an accusation, but before two or three wit-
nesses.
20 Them that sin rebuke before all, that others also may fear.
21 I charge *thee* before God, and the Lord Jesus Christ, and the elect angels,
that thou observe these things without preferring one before another, doing
nothing by partiality.
22 Lay hands suddenly on no man, neither be partaker of other men's sins:
keep thyself pure.
23 Drink no longer water, but use a little wine for thy stomach's sake and
thine often infirmities.
24 Some men's sins are open beforehand, going before to judgment; and
some *men* they follow after.
25 Likewise also the good works *of some* are manifest beforehand; and they
that are otherwise cannot be hid.

Guidelines for Godly Living

6 Let as many servants as are under the yoke count their own masters worthy
of all honour, that the name of God and *his* doctrine be not blasphemed.
2 And they that have believing masters, let them not despise *them*, because
they are brethren; but rather do *them* service, because they are faithful and
beloved, partakers of the benefit. These things teach and exhort.
3 If any man teach otherwise, and consent not to wholesome words, *even*
the words of our Lord Jesus Christ, and to the doctrine which is according to
godliness;
4 He is proud, knowing nothing, but doting about questions and strifes of
words, whereof cometh envy, strife, railings, evil surmisings,
5 Perverse disputings of men of corrupt minds, and destitute of the truth,
supposing that gain is godliness: from such withdraw thyself.

Godliness Is Great Gain

6 But godliness with contentment is great gain.
7 For we brought nothing into *this* world, *and it is* certain we can carry
nothing out.
8 And having food and raiment let us be therewith content.
9 But they that will be rich fall into temptation and a snare, and *into* many
foolish and hurtful lusts, which drown men in destruction and perdition.
10 For the love of money is the root of all evil: which while some coveted
after, they have erred from the faith, and pierced themselves through with
many sorrows.
11 But thou, O man of God, flee these things; and follow after righteousness,
godliness, faith, love, patience, meekness.

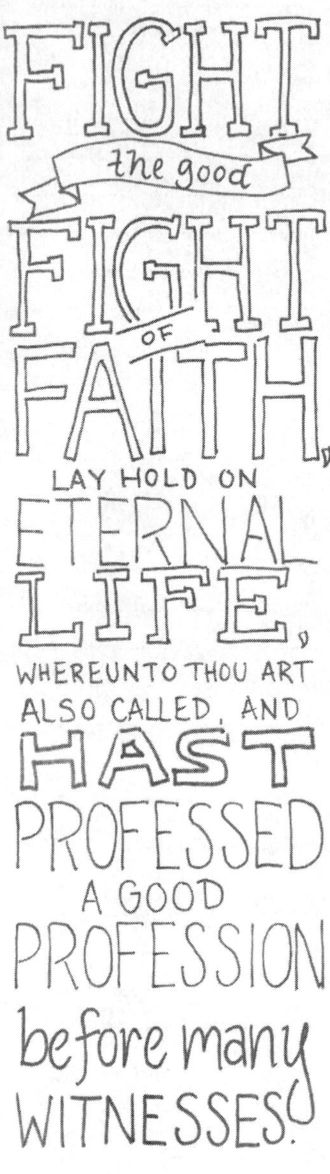

12 Fight the good fight of faith, lay hold on eternal life, whereunto thou art
also called, and hast professed a good profession before many witnesses.
13 I give thee charge in the sight of God, who quickeneth all things, and *before*
Christ Jesus, who before Pontius Pilate witnessed a good confession;
14 That thou keep *this* commandment without spot, unrebukeable, until the
appearing of our Lord Jesus Christ:
15 Which in his times he shall shew, *who is* the blessed and only Potentate,
the King of kings, and Lord of lords;
16 Who only hath immortality, dwelling in the light which no man can
approach unto; whom no man hath seen, nor can see: to whom *be* honour
and power everlasting. Amen.
17 Charge them that are rich in this world, that they be not highminded, nor
trust in uncertain riches, but in the living God, who giveth us richly all things
to enjoy;
18 That they do good, that they be rich in good works, ready to distribute,
willing to communicate;
19 Laying up in store for themselves a good foundation against the time to
come, that they may lay hold on eternal life.
20 O Timothy, keep that which is committed to thy trust, avoiding profane
and vain babblings, and oppositions of science falsely so called:
21 Which some professing have erred concerning the faith. Grace *be* with
thee. Amen.

Paul's Greeting

1 Paul, an apostle of Jesus Christ by the will of God, according to the promise
of life which is in Christ Jesus,
2 To Timothy, *my* dearly beloved son: Grace, mercy, *and* peace, from God the
Father and Christ Jesus our Lord.
3 I thank God, whom I serve from *my* forefathers with pure conscience, that
without ceasing I have remembrance of thee in my prayers night and day;
4 Greatly desiring to see thee, being mindful of thy tears, that I may be filled
with joy;
5 When I call to remembrance the unfeigned faith that is in thee, which
dwelt first in thy grandmother Lois, and thy mother Eunice; and I am per-
suaded that in thee also.

Paul's Advice for Timothy

6 Wherefore I put thee in remembrance that thou stir up the gift of God,
which is in thee by the putting on of my hands.
7 For God hath not given us the spirit of fear; but of power, and of love, and
of a sound mind.
8 Be not thou therefore ashamed of the testimony of our Lord, nor of me his
prisoner: but be thou partaker of the afflictions of the gospel according to the
power of God;
9 Who hath saved us, and called *us* with an holy calling, not according to our
works, but according to his own purpose and grace, which was given us in
Christ Jesus before the world began,
10 But is now made manifest by the appearing of our Saviour Jesus Christ,
who hath abolished death, and hath brought life and immortality to light
through the gospel:
11 Whereunto I am appointed a preacher, and an apostle, and a teacher of
the Gentiles.
12 For the which cause I also suffer these things: nevertheless I am not
ashamed: for I know whom I have believed, and am persuaded that he is able
to keep that which I have committed unto him against that day.
13 Hold fast the form of sound words, which thou hast heard of me, in faith
and love which is in Christ Jesus.
14 That good thing which was committed unto thee keep by the Holy Ghost
which dwelleth in us.

News about Paul's Coworkers

15 This thou knowest, that all they which are in Asia be turned away from
me; of whom are Phygellus and Hermogenes.
16 The Lord give mercy unto the house of Onesiphorus; for he oft refreshed
me, and was not ashamed of my chain:
17 But, when he was in Rome, he sought me out very diligently, and found *me*.
18 The Lord grant unto him that he may find mercy of the Lord in that day:
and in how many things he ministered unto me at Ephesus, thou knowest very
well.

I HAVE FOUGHT A Good FIGHT, I HAVE FINISHED My Course, I HAVE KEPT THE Faith.

2 TIMOTHY 4:7

An Exhortation to Perseverance

2 Thou therefore, my son, be strong in the grace that is in Christ Jesus.
2 And the things that thou hast heard of me among many witnesses, the
same commit thou to faithful men, who shall be able to teach others also.
3 Thou therefore endure hardness, as a good soldier of Jesus Christ.
4 No man that warreth entangleth himself with the affairs of *this* life; that
he may please him who hath chosen him to be a soldier.
5 And if a man also strive for masteries, *yet* is he not crowned, except he strive
lawfully.
6 The husbandman that laboureth must be first partaker of the fruits.
7 Consider what I say; and the Lord give thee understanding in all things.
8 Remember that Jesus Christ of the seed of David was raised from the dead
according to my gospel:
9 Wherein I suffer trouble, as an evil doer, *even* unto bonds; but the word of
God is not bound.
10 Therefore I endure all things for the elect's sakes, that they may also obtain
the salvation which is in Christ Jesus with eternal glory.
11 *It is* a faithful saying: For if we be dead with *him*, we shall also live with
him:
12 If we suffer, we shall also reign with *him*: if we deny *him*, he also will deny us:
13 If we believe not, *yet* he abideth faithful: he cannot deny himself.
14 Of these things put *them* in remembrance, charging *them* before the Lord
that they strive not about words to no profit, *but* to the subverting of the
hearers.
15 Study to shew thyself approved unto God, a workman that needeth not
to be ashamed, rightly dividing the word of truth.
16 But shun profane *and* vain babblings: for they will increase unto more
ungodliness.
17 And their word will eat as doth a canker: of whom is Hymenaeus and
Philetus;
18 Who concerning the truth have erred, saying that the resurrection is past
already; and overthrow the faith of some.

The Foundation of the Lord's Work

19 Nevertheless the foundation of God standeth sure, having this seal, The
Lord knoweth them that are his. And, Let every one that nameth the name of
Christ depart from iniquity.
20 But in a great house there are not only vessels of gold and of silver, but
also of wood and of earth; and some to honour, and some to dishonour.
21 If a man therefore purge himself from these, he shall be a vessel unto
honour, sanctified, and meet for the master's use, *and* prepared unto every
good work.

Guidance for God's Ministers

22 Flee also youthful lusts: but follow righteousness, faith, charity, peace,
with them that call on the Lord out of a pure heart.
23 But foolish and unlearned questions avoid, knowing that they do gender
strifes.
24 And the servant of the Lord must not strive; but be gentle unto all *men*,
apt to teach, patient,
25 In meekness instructing those that oppose themselves; if God peradven-
ture will give them repentance to the acknowledging of the truth;
26 And *that* they may recover themselves out of the snare of the devil, who
are taken captive by him at his will.

Paul Warns of Stressful Times

3 This know also, that in the last days perilous times shall come.

2 For men shall be lovers of their own selves, covetous, boasters, proud, blasphemers, disobedient to parents, unthankful, unholy,

3 Without natural affection, trucebreakers, false accusers, incontinent, fierce, despisers of those that are good,

4 Traitors, heady, highminded, lovers of pleasures more than lovers of God;

5 Having a form of godliness, but denying the power thereof: from such turn away.

6 For of this sort are they which creep into houses, and lead captive silly women laden with sins, led away with divers lusts,

7 Ever learning, and never able to come to the knowledge of the truth.

8 Now as Jannes and Jambres withstood Moses, so do these also resist the truth: men of corrupt minds, reprobate concerning the faith.

9 But they shall proceed no further: for their folly shall be manifest unto all *men*, as theirs also was.

Teach the Truth

10 But thou hast fully known my doctrine, manner of life, purpose, faith, longsuffering, charity, patience,

11 Persecutions, afflictions, which came unto me at Antioch, at Iconium, at Lystra; what persecutions I endured: but out of *them* all the Lord delivered me.

12 Yea, and all that will live godly in Christ Jesus shall suffer persecution.

13 But evil men and seducers shall wax worse and worse, deceiving, and being deceived.

14 But continue thou in the things which thou hast learned and hast been assured of, knowing of whom thou hast learned *them*;

15 And that from a child thou hast known the holy scriptures, which are able to make thee wise unto salvation through faith which is in Christ Jesus.

16 All scripture *is* given by inspiration of God, and *is* profitable for doctrine, for reproof, for correction, for instruction in righteousness:

17 That the man of God may be perfect, throughly furnished unto all good works.

The Duties of a Minister

4 I charge *thee* therefore before God, and the Lord Jesus Christ, who shall judge the quick and the dead at his appearing and his kingdom;

2 Preach the word; be instant in season, out of season; reprove, rebuke, exhort with all longsuffering and doctrine.

3 For the time will come when they will not endure sound doctrine; but after their own lusts shall they heap to themselves teachers, having itching ears;

4 And they shall turn away *their* ears from the truth, and shall be turned unto fables.

5 But watch thou in all things, endure afflictions, do the work of an evangelist, make full proof of thy ministry.

6 For I am now ready to be offered, and the time of my departure is at hand.

7 I have fought a good fight, I have finished *my* course, I have kept the faith:

8 Henceforth there is laid up for me a crown of righteousness, which the Lord, the righteous judge, shall give me at that day: and not to me only, but unto all them also that love his appearing.

9 Do thy diligence to come shortly unto me:

10 For Demas hath forsaken me, having loved this present world, and is departed unto Thessalonica; Crescens to Galatia, Titus unto Dalmatia.

11 Only Luke is with me. Take Mark, and bring him with thee: for he is profitable to me for the ministry.

12 And Tychicus have I sent to Ephesus.

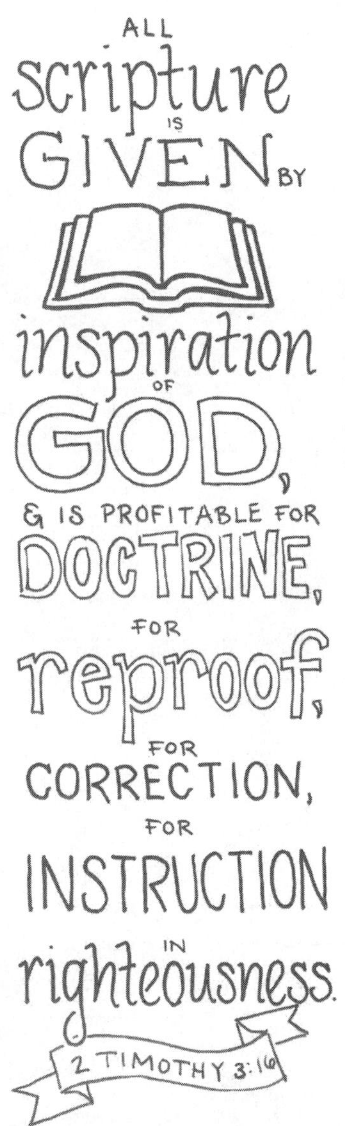

13 The cloke that I left at Troas with Carpus, when thou comest, bring *with*
thee, and the books, *but* especially the parchments.
14 Alexander the coppersmith did me much evil: the Lord reward him
according to his works:
15 Of whom be thou ware also; for he hath greatly withstood our words.
16 At my first answer no man stood with me, but all *men* forsook me: *I pray*
God that it may not be laid to their charge.
17 Notwithstanding the Lord stood with me, and strengthened me; that by
me the preaching might be fully known, and *that* all the Gentiles might hear:
and I was delivered out of the mouth of the lion.
18 And the Lord shall deliver me from every evil work, and will preserve *me*
unto his heavenly kingdom: to whom *be* glory for ever and ever. Amen.
19 Salute Prisca and Aquila, and the household of Onesiphorus.
20 Erastus abode at Corinth: but Trophimus have I left at Miletum sick.
21 Do thy diligence to come before winter. Eubulus greeteth thee, and
Pudens, and Linus, and Claudia, and all the brethren.
22 The Lord Jesus Christ *be* with thy spirit. Grace *be* with you. Amen.

Paul's Greeting

1 Paul, a servant of God, and an apostle of Jesus Christ, according to the faith
of God's elect, and the acknowledging of the truth which is after godliness;
2 In hope of eternal life, which God, that cannot lie, promised before the
world began;
3 But hath in due times manifested his word through preaching, which is
committed unto me according to the commandment of God our Saviour;
4 To Titus, *mine* own son after the common faith: Grace, mercy, *and* peace,
from God the Father and the Lord Jesus Christ our Saviour.
5 For this cause left I thee in Crete, that thou shouldest set in order the things
that are wanting, and ordain elders in every city, as I had appointed thee:

The Qualifications of Ministers

6 If any be blameless, the husband of one wife, having faithful children not
accused of riot or unruly.
7 For a bishop must be blameless, as the steward of God; not selfwilled, not
soon angry, not given to wine, no striker, not given to filthy lucre;
8 But a lover of hospitality, a lover of good men, sober, just, holy, temperate;
9 Holding fast the faithful word as he hath been taught, that he may be able
by sound doctrine both to exhort and to convince the gainsayers.
10 For there are many unruly and vain talkers and deceivers, specially they
of the circumcision:
11 Whose mouths must be stopped, who subvert whole houses, teaching
things which they ought not, for filthy lucre's sake.
12 One of themselves, *even* a prophet of their own, said, The Cretians *are*
alway liars, evil beasts, slow bellies.
13 This witness is true. Wherefore rebuke them sharply, that they may be
sound in the faith;
14 Not giving heed to Jewish fables, and commandments of men, that turn
from the truth.
15 Unto the pure all things *are* pure: but unto them that are defiled and
unbelieving *is* nothing pure; but even their mind and conscience is defiled.
16 They profess that they know God; but in works they deny *him*, being abom-
inable, and disobedient, and unto every good work reprobate.

Guidelines for Christian Living

2 But speak thou the things which become sound doctrine:
2 That the aged men be sober, grave, temperate, sound in faith, in charity,
in patience.
3 The aged women likewise, that *they be* in behaviour as becometh holiness,
not false accusers, not given to much wine, teachers of good things;
4 That they may teach the young women to be sober, to love their husbands,
to love their children,
5 *To be* discreet, chaste, keepers at home, good, obedient to their own hus-
bands, that the word of God be not blasphemed.
6 Young men likewise exhort to be sober minded.
7 In all things shewing thyself a pattern of good works: in doctrine *shewing*
uncorruptness, gravity, sincerity,

8 Sound speech, that cannot be condemned; that he that is of the contrary
part may be ashamed, having no evil thing to say of you.
9 *Exhort* servants to be obedient unto their own masters, *and* to please *them*
well in all *things*; not answering again;
10 Not purloining, but shewing all good fidelity; that they may adorn the
doctrine of God our Saviour in all things.
11 For the grace of God that bringeth salvation hath appeared to all men,
12 Teaching us that, denying ungodliness and worldly lusts, we should live
soberly, righteously, and godly, in this present world;
13 Looking for that blessed hope, and the glorious appearing of the great
God and our Saviour Jesus Christ;
14 Who gave himself for us, that he might redeem us from all iniquity, and
purify unto himself a peculiar people, zealous of good works.
15 These things speak, and exhort, and rebuke with all authority. Let no man
despise thee.

Instructions for Teaching

3 Put them in mind to be subject to principalities and powers, to obey
magistrates, to be ready to every good work,
2 To speak evil of no man, to be no brawlers, *but* gentle, shewing all meekness
unto all men.
3 For we ourselves also were sometimes foolish, disobedient, deceived, serv-
ing divers lusts and pleasures, living in malice and envy, hateful, *and* hating
one another.
4 But after that the kindness and love of God our Saviour toward man
appeared,
5 Not by works of righteousness which we have done, but according to his
mercy he saved us, by the washing of regeneration, and renewing of the Holy
Ghost;
6 Which he shed on us abundantly through Jesus Christ our Saviour;
7 That being justified by his grace, we should be made heirs according to the
hope of eternal life.
8 *This is* a faithful saying, and these things I will that thou affirm constantly,
that they which have believed in God might be careful to maintain good works.
These things are good and profitable unto men.
9 But avoid foolish questions, and genealogies, and contentions, and strivings
about the law; for they are unprofitable and vain.
10 A man that is an heretick after the first and second admonition reject;
11 Knowing that he that is such is subverted, and sinneth, being condemned
of himself.
12 When I shall send Artemas unto thee, or Tychicus, be diligent to come
unto me to Nicopolis: for I have determined there to winter.
13 Bring Zenas the lawyer and Apollos on their journey diligently, that noth-
ing be wanting unto them.
14 And let ours also learn to maintain good works for necessary uses, that
they be not unfruitful.
15 All that are with me salute thee. Greet them that love us in the faith. Grace
be with you all. Amen.

PHILEMON

Paul's Greeting

1 Paul, a prisoner of Jesus Christ, and Timothy *our* brother, unto Philemon
our dearly beloved, and fellowlabourer,
2 And to *our* beloved Apphia, and Archippus our fellowsoldier, and to the
church in thy house:
3 Grace to you, and peace, from God our Father and the Lord Jesus Christ.

Paul's Prayer for Philemon

4 I thank my God, making mention of thee always in my prayers,
5 Hearing of thy love and faith, which thou hast toward the Lord Jesus, and
toward all saints;
6 That the communication of thy faith may become effectual by the acknowl-
edging of every good thing which is in you in Christ Jesus.
7 For we have great joy and consolation in thy love, because the bowels of
the saints are refreshed by thee, brother.

Paul's Advice about Onesimus

8 Wherefore, though I might be much bold in Christ to enjoin thee that
which is convenient,
9 Yet for love's sake I rather beseech *thee*, being such an one as Paul the aged,
and now also a prisoner of Jesus Christ.
10 I beseech thee for my son Onesimus, whom I have begotten in my bonds:
11 Which in time past was to thee unprofitable, but now profitable to thee
and to me:
12 Whom I have sent again: thou therefore receive him, that is, mine own
bowels:
13 Whom I would have retained with me, that in thy stead he might have
ministered unto me in the bonds of the gospel:
14 But without thy mind would I do nothing; that thy benefit should not be
as it were of necessity, but willingly.
15 For perhaps he therefore departed for a season, that thou shouldest receive
him for ever;
16 Not now as a servant, but above a servant, a brother beloved, specially to
me, but how much more unto thee, both in the flesh, and in the Lord?
17 If thou count me therefore a partner, receive him as myself.
18 If he hath wronged thee, or oweth *thee* ought, put that on mine account;
19 I Paul have written *it* with mine own hand, I will repay *it*: albeit I do not
say to thee how thou owest unto me even thine own self besides.
20 Yea, brother, let me have joy of thee in the Lord: refresh my bowels in the
Lord.
21 Having confidence in thy obedience I wrote unto thee, knowing that thou
wilt also do more than I say.
22 But withal prepare me also a lodging: for I trust that through your prayers
I shall be given unto you.
23 There salute thee Epaphras, my fellowprisoner in Christ Jesus;
24 Marcus, Aristarchus, Demas, Lucas, my fellowlabourers.
25 The grace of our Lord Jesus Christ *be* with your spirit. Amen.

HEBREWS

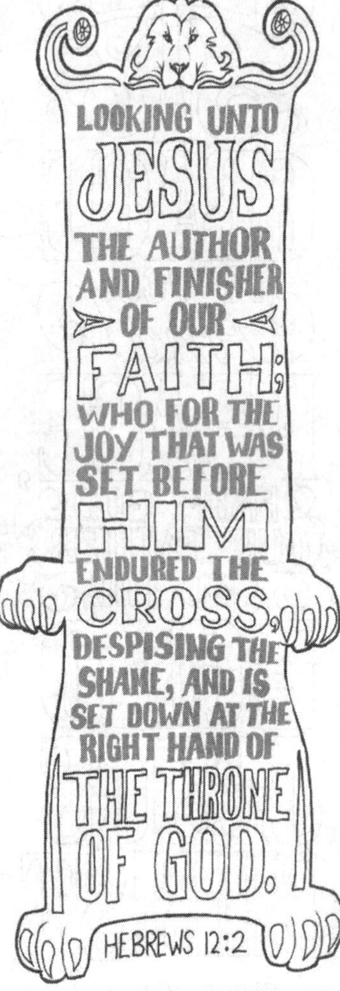

God Has Spoken through His Son

1 God, who at sundry times and in divers manners spake in time past unto
the fathers by the prophets,
2 Hath in these last days spoken unto us by *his* Son, whom he hath appoint-
ed heir of all things, by whom also he made the worlds;
3 Who being the brightness of *his* glory, and the express image of his person,
and upholding all things by the word of his power, when he had by himself
purged our sins, sat down on the right hand of the Majesty on high;

Christ Is Superior to the Angels

4 Being made so much better than the angels, as he hath by inheritance
obtained a more excellent name than they.
5 For unto which of the angels said he at any time, Thou art my Son, this day
have I begotten thee? And again, I will be to him a Father, and he shall be to
me a Son?
6 And again, when he bringeth in the firstbegotten into the world, he saith,
And let all the angels of God worship him.
7 And of the angels he saith, Who maketh his angels spirits, and his ministers
a flame of fire.
8 But unto the Son *he saith*, Thy throne, O God, *is* for ever and ever: a sceptre
of righteousness *is* the sceptre of thy kingdom.
9 Thou hast loved righteousness, and hated iniquity; therefore God, *even* thy
God, hath anointed thee with the oil of gladness above thy fellows.
10 And, Thou, Lord, in the beginning hast laid the foundation of the earth;
and the heavens are the works of thine hands:
11 They shall perish; but thou remainest; and they all shall wax old as doth
a garment;
12 And as a vesture shalt thou fold them up, and they shall be changed: but
thou art the same, and thy years shall not fail.
13 But to which of the angels said he at any time, Sit on my right hand, until
I make thine enemies thy footstool?
14 Are they not all ministering spirits, sent forth to minister for them who
shall be heirs of salvation?

Everything Is under Christ's Control

2 Therefore we ought to give the more earnest heed to the things which we
have heard, lest at any time we should let *them* slip.
2 For if the word spoken by angels was stedfast, and every transgression and
disobedience received a just recompence of reward;
3 How shall we escape, if we neglect so great salvation; which at the first
began to be spoken by the Lord, and was confirmed unto us by them that heard
him;
4 God also bearing *them* witness, both with signs and wonders, and with
divers miracles, and gifts of the Holy Ghost, according to his own will?

God's New Order and His Gifts to Man

5 For unto the angels hath he not put in subjection the world to come, where-
of we speak.
6 But one in a certain place testified, saying, What is man, that thou art mind-
ful of him? or the son of man, that thou visitest him?

7 Thou madest him a little lower than the angels; thou crownedst him with
glory and honour, and didst set him over the works of thy hands:
8 Thou hast put all things in subjection under his feet. For in that he put all
in subjection under him, he left nothing *that is* not put under him. But now
we see not yet all things put under him.
9 But we see Jesus, who was made a little lower than the angels for the suf-
fering of death, crowned with glory and honour; that he by the grace of God
should taste death for every man.
10 For it became him, for whom *are* all things, and by whom *are* all things,
in bringing many sons unto glory, to make the captain of their salvation per-
fect through sufferings.
11 For both he that sanctifieth and they who are sanctified *are* all of one: for
which cause he is not ashamed to call them brethren,
12 Saying, I will declare thy name unto my brethren, in the midst of the
church will I sing praise unto thee.
13 And again, I will put my trust in him. And again, Behold I and the children
which God hath given me.

Christ Shared Man's Mortal Nature

14 Forasmuch then as the children are partakers of flesh and blood, he also
himself likewise took part of the same; that through death he might destroy
him that had the power of death, that is, the devil;
15 And deliver them who through fear of death were all their lifetime subject
to bondage.
16 For verily he took not on *him the nature of* angels; but he took on *him* the
seed of Abraham.
17 Wherefore in all things it behoved him to be made like unto *his* brethren,
that he might be a merciful and faithful high priest in things *pertaining* to
God, to make reconciliation for the sins of the people.
18 For in that he himself hath suffered being tempted, he is able to succour
them that are tempted.

Christ Is Superior to Moses

3 Wherefore, holy brethren, partakers of the heavenly calling, consider the
Apostle and High Priest of our profession, Christ Jesus;
2 Who was faithful to him that appointed him, as also Moses *was faithful* in
all his house.
3 For this *man* was counted worthy of more glory than Moses, inasmuch as
he who hath builded the house hath more honour than the house.
4 For every house is builded by some *man*; but he that built all things *is* God.
5 And Moses verily *was* faithful in all his house, as a servant, for a testimony
of those things which were to be spoken after;
6 But Christ as a son over his own house; whose house are we, if we hold fast
the confidence and the rejoicing of the hope firm unto the end.

Warnings against Unbelief

7 Wherefore (as the Holy Ghost saith, To day if ye will hear his voice,
8 Harden not your hearts, as in the provocation, in the day of temptation in
the wilderness:
9 When your fathers tempted me, proved me, and saw my works forty years.
10 Wherefore I was grieved with that generation, and said, They do alway err
in *their* heart; and they have not known my ways.
11 So I sware in my wrath, They shall not enter into my rest.)
12 Take heed, brethren, lest there be in any of you an evil heart of unbelief,
in departing from the living God.
13 But exhort one another daily, while it is called To day; lest any of you be
hardened through the deceitfulness of sin.

14 For we are made partakers of Christ, if we hold the beginning of our
confidence stedfast unto the end;
15 While it is said, To day if ye will hear his voice, harden not your hearts, as
in the provocation.
16 For some, when they had heard, did provoke: howbeit not all that came
out of Egypt by Moses.
17 But with whom was he grieved forty years? *was it* not with them that had
sinned, whose carcases fell in the wilderness?
18 And to whom sware he that they should not enter into his rest, but to them
that believed not?
19 So we see that they could not enter in because of unbelief.

God's Promise of a Sabbath Rest

4 Let us therefore fear, lest, a promise being left *us* of entering into his rest,
any of you should seem to come short of it.
2 For unto us was the gospel preached, as well as unto them: but the word
preached did not profit them, not being mixed with faith in them that heard *it*.
3 For we which have believed do enter into rest, as he said, As I have sworn
in my wrath, if they shall enter into my rest: although the works were finished
from the foundation of the world.
4 For he spake in a certain place of the seventh *day* on this wise, And God did
rest the seventh day from all his works.
5 And in this *place* again, If they shall enter into my rest.
6 Seeing therefore it remaineth that some must enter therein, and they to
whom it was first preached entered not in because of unbelief:
7 Again, he limiteth a certain day, saying in David, To day, after so long a time;
as it is said, To day if ye will hear his voice, harden not your hearts.
8 For if Jesus had given them rest, then would he not afterward have spoken
of another day.
9 There remaineth therefore a rest to the people of God.
10 For he that is entered into his rest, he also hath ceased from his own works,
as God *did* from his.
11 Let us labour therefore to enter into that rest, lest any man fall after the
same example of unbelief.
12 For the word of God *is* quick, and powerful, and sharper than any
twoedged sword, piercing even to the dividing asunder of soul and spirit, and
of the joints and marrow, and *is* a discerner of the thoughts and intents of the
heart.
13 Neither is there any creature that is not manifest in his sight: but all things
are naked and opened unto the eyes of him with whom we have to do.
14 Seeing then that we have a great high priest, that is passed into the heavens,
Jesus the Son of God, let us hold fast *our* profession.
15 For we have not an high priest which cannot be touched with the feeling
of our infirmities; but was in all points tempted like as *we are, yet* without sin.
16 Let us therefore come boldly unto the throne of grace, that we may obtain
mercy, and find grace to help in time of need.

Christ Is Superior to the Priests

5 For every high priest taken from among men is ordained for men in things
pertaining to God, that he may offer both gifts and sacrifices for sins:
2 Who can have compassion on the ignorant, and on them that are out of
the way; for that he himself also is compassed with infirmity.
3 And by reason hereof he ought, as for the people, so also for himself, to
offer for sins.
4 And no man taketh this honour unto himself, but he that is called of God,
as *was* Aaron.

5 So also Christ glorified not himself to be made an high priest; but he that
said unto him, Thou art my Son, to day have I begotten thee.
6 As he saith also in another *place*, Thou *art* a priest for ever after the order
of Melchisedec.
7 Who in the days of his flesh, when he had offered up prayers and suppli-
cations with strong crying and tears unto him that was able to save him from
death, and was heard in that he feared;
8 Though he were a Son, yet learned he obedience by the things which he
suffered;
9 And being made perfect, he became the author of eternal salvation unto
all them that obey him;
10 Called of God an high priest after the order of Melchisedec.
11 Of whom we have many things to say, and hard to be uttered, seeing ye
are dull of hearing.
12 For when for the time ye ought to be teachers, ye have need that one teach
you again which *be* the first principles of the oracles of God; and are become
such as have need of milk, and not of strong meat.
13 For every one that useth milk *is* unskilful in the word of righteousness:
for he is a babe.
14 But strong meat belongeth to them that are of full age, *even* those who by
reason of use have their senses exercised to discern both good and evil.

Warnings against Backsliding

6 Therefore leaving the principles of the doctrine of Christ, let us go on unto
perfection; not laying again the foundation of repentance from dead works,
and of faith toward God,
2 Of the doctrine of baptisms, and of laying on of hands, and of resurrection
of the dead, and of eternal judgment.
3 And this will we do, if God permit.
4 For *it is* impossible for those who were once enlightened, and have tasted
of the heavenly gift, and were made partakers of the Holy Ghost,
5 And have tasted the good word of God, and the powers of the world to
come,
6 If they shall fall away, to renew them again unto repentance; seeing they
crucify to themselves the Son of God afresh, and put *him* to an open shame.
7 For the earth which drinketh in the rain that cometh oft upon it, and
bringeth forth herbs meet for them by whom it is dressed, receiveth blessing
from God:
8 But that which beareth thorns and briers *is* rejected, and *is* nigh unto curs-
ing; whose end *is* to be burned.

God Will Not Forget You

9 But, beloved, we are persuaded better things of you, and things that accom-
pany salvation, though we thus speak.
10 For God *is* not unrighteous to forget your work and labour of love, which
ye have shewed toward his name, in that ye have ministered to the saints, and
do minister.
11 And we desire that every one of you do shew the same diligence to the full
assurance of hope unto the end:
12 That ye be not slothful, but followers of them who through faith and
patience inherit the promises.
13 For when God made promise to Abraham, because he could swear by no
greater, he sware by himself,
14 Saying, Surely blessing I will bless thee, and multiplying I will multiply
thee.
15 And so, after he had patiently endured, he obtained the promise.

16 For men verily swear by the greater: and an oath for confirmation *is* to
them an end of all strife.
17 Wherein God, willing more abundantly to shew unto the heirs of promise
the immutability of his counsel, confirmed *it* by an oath:
18 That by two immutable things, in which *it was* impossible for God to lie,
we might have a strong consolation, who have fled for refuge to lay hold upon
the hope set before us:
19 Which *hope* we have as an anchor of the soul, both sure and stedfast, and
which entereth into that within the veil;
20 Whither the forerunner is for us entered, *even* Jesus, made an high priest
for ever after the order of Melchisedec.

Christ Is Superior to Melchisedec

7 For this Melchisedec, king of Salem, priest of the most high God, who met
Abraham returning from the slaughter of the kings, and blessed him;
2 To whom also Abraham gave a tenth part of all; first being by interpretation
King of righteousness, and after that also King of Salem, which is, King of
peace;
3 Without father, without mother, without descent, having neither begin-
ning of days, nor end of life; but made like unto the Son of God; abideth a priest
continually.
4 Now consider how great this man *was*, unto whom even the patriarch
Abraham gave the tenth of the spoils.
5 And verily they that are of the sons of Levi, who receive the office of the
priesthood, have a commandment to take tithes of the people according to
the law, that is, of their brethren, though they come out of the loins of
Abraham:
6 But he whose descent is not counted from them received tithes of Abraham,
and blessed him that had the promises.
7 And without all contradiction the less is blessed of the better.
8 And here men that die receive tithes; but there he *receiveth them*, of whom
it is witnessed that he liveth.
9 And as I may so say, Levi also, who receiveth tithes, payed tithes in Abraham.
10 For he was yet in the loins of his father, when Melchisedec met him.

A New Law and a New Priesthood

11 If therefore perfection were by the Levitical priesthood, (for under it the
people received the law,) what further need *was there* that another priest
should rise after the order of Melchisedec, and not be called after the order
of Aaron?
12 For the priesthood being changed, there is made of necessity a change
also of the law.
13 For he of whom these things are spoken pertaineth to another tribe, of
which no man gave attendance at the altar.
14 For *it is* evident that our Lord sprang out of Juda; of which tribe Moses
spake nothing concerning priesthood.
15 And it is yet far more evident: for that after the similitude of Melchisedec
there ariseth another priest,
16 Who is made, not after the law of a carnal commandment, but after the
power of an endless life.
17 For he testifieth, Thou *art* a priest for ever after the order of Melchisedec.
18 For there is verily a disannulling of the commandment going before for
the weakness and unprofitableness thereof.
19 For the law made nothing perfect, but the bringing in of a better hope
did; by the which we draw nigh unto God.
20 And inasmuch as not without an oath *he was made priest*:

21 (For those priests were made without an oath; but this with an oath by
him that said unto him, The Lord sware and will not repent, Thou *art* a priest
for ever after the order of Melchisedec:)
22 By so much was Jesus made a surety of a better testament.
23 And they truly were many priests, because they were not suffered to con-
tinue by reason of death:
24 But this *man*, because he continueth ever, hath an unchangeable priest-
hood.
25 Wherefore he is able also to save them to the uttermost that come unto
God by him, seeing he ever liveth to make intercession for them.
26 For such an high priest became us, *who is* holy, harmless, undefiled, sep-
arate from sinners, and made higher than the heavens;
27 Who needeth not daily, as those high priests, to offer up sacrifice, first for
his own sins, and then for the people's: for this he did once, when he offered
up himself.
28 For the law maketh men high priests which have infirmity; but the word
of the oath, which was since the law, *maketh* the Son, who is consecrated for
evermore.

Christ's Work Is Superior

8 Now of the things which we have spoken *this is* the sum: We have such an
high priest, who is set on the right hand of the throne of the Majesty in the
heavens;
2 A minister of the sanctuary, and of the true tabernacle, which the Lord
pitched, and not man.
3 For every high priest is ordained to offer gifts and sacrifices: wherefore *it*
is of necessity that this man have somewhat also to offer.
4 For if he were on earth, he should not be a priest, seeing that there are
priests that offer gifts according to the law:
5 Who serve unto the example and shadow of heavenly things, as Moses was
admonished of God when he was about to make the tabernacle: for, See, saith
he, *that* thou make all things according to the pattern shewed to thee in the
mount.

The New Covenant Foretold by Jeremiah

6 But now hath he obtained a more excellent ministry, by how much also he
is the mediator of a better covenant, which was established upon better prom-
ises.
7 For if that first *covenant* had been faultless, then should no place have been
sought for the second.
8 For finding fault with them, he saith, Behold, the days come, saith the Lord,
when I will make a new covenant with the house of Israel and with the house
of Judah:
9 Not according to the covenant that I made with their fathers in the day
when I took them by the hand to lead them out of the land of Egypt; because
they continued not in my covenant, and I regarded them not, saith the Lord.
10 For this *is* the covenant that I will make with the house of Israel after those
days, saith the Lord; I will put my laws into their mind, and write them in their
hearts: and I will be to them a God, and they shall be to me a people:
11 And they shall not teach every man his neighbour, and every man his
brother, saying, Know the Lord: for all shall know me, from the least to the
greatest.
12 For I will be merciful to their unrighteousness, and their sins and their
iniquities will I remember no more.
13 In that he saith, A new *covenant*, he hath made the first old. Now that
which decayeth and waxeth old *is* ready to vanish away.

Christ's Sacrifice Is Superior

9 Then verily the first *covenant* had also ordinances of divine service, and a
worldly sanctuary.
2 For there was a tabernacle made; the first, wherein *was* the candlestick,
and the table, and the shewbread; which is called the sanctuary.
3 And after the second veil, the tabernacle which is called the Holiest of all;
4 Which had the golden censer, and the ark of the covenant overlaid round
about with gold, wherein *was* the golden pot that had manna, and Aaron's rod
that budded, and the tables of the covenant;
5 And over it the cherubims of glory shadowing the mercyseat; of which we
cannot now speak particularly.
6 Now when these things were thus ordained, the priests went always into
the first tabernacle, accomplishing the service *of God*.
7 But into the second *went* the high priest alone once every year, not without
blood, which he offered for himself, and *for* the errors of the people:
8 The Holy Ghost this signifying, that the way into the holiest of all was not
yet made manifest, while as the first tabernacle was yet standing:
9 Which *was* a figure for the time then present, in which were offered both
gifts and sacrifices, that could not make him that did the service perfect, as
pertaining to the conscience;
10 *Which stood* only in meats and drinks, and divers washings, and carnal
ordinances, imposed *on them* until the time of reformation.
11 But Christ being come an high priest of good things to come, by a greater
and more perfect tabernacle, not made with hands, that is to say, not of this
building;
12 Neither by the blood of goats and calves, but by his own blood he entered
in once into the holy place, having obtained eternal redemption *for us*.
13 For if the blood of bulls and of goats, and the ashes of an heifer sprinkling
the unclean, sanctifieth to the purifying of the flesh:
14 How much more shall the blood of Christ, who through the eternal Spirit
offered himself without spot to God, purge your conscience from dead works
to serve the living God?

The Promise of the New Covenant

15 And for this cause he is the mediator of the new testament, that by means
of death, for the redemption of the transgressions *that were* under the first
testament, they which are called might receive the promise of eternal inher-
itance.
16 For where a testament *is*, there must also of necessity be the death of the
testator.
17 For a testament *is* of force after men are dead: otherwise it is of no strength
at all while the testator liveth.
18 Whereupon neither the first *testament* was dedicated without blood.
19 For when Moses had spoken every precept to all the people according to
the law, he took the blood of calves and of goats, with water, and scarlet wool,
and hyssop, and sprinkled both the book, and all the people,
20 Saying, This *is* the blood of the testament which God hath enjoined unto
you.
21 Moreover he sprinkled with blood both the tabernacle, and all the vessels
of the ministry.
22 And almost all things are by the law purged with blood; and without shed-
ding of blood is no remission.
23 *It was* therefore necessary that the patterns of things in the heavens should
be purified with these; but the heavenly things themselves with better sacri-
fices than these.

24 For Christ is not entered into the holy places made with hands, *which are*
the figures of the true; but into heaven itself, now to appear in the presence
of God for us:
25 Nor yet that he should offer himself often, as the high priest entereth into
the holy place every year with blood of others;
26 For then must he often have suffered since the foundation of the world:
but now once in the end of the world hath he appeared to put away sin by the
sacrifice of himself.
27 And as it is appointed unto men once to die, but after this the judgment:
28 So Christ was once offered to bear the sins of many; and unto them that
look for him shall he appear the second time without sin unto salvation.

The Weakness of Sacrifices under the Law

10 For the law having a shadow of good things to come, *and* not the
very image of the things, can never with those sacrifices which they
offered year by year continually make the comers thereunto perfect.
2 For then would they not have ceased to be offered? because that the wor-
shippers once purged should have had no more conscience of sins.
3 But in those *sacrifices there is* a remembrance again *made* of sins every
year.
4 For *it is* not possible that the blood of bulls and of goats should take away
sins.
5 Wherefore when he cometh into the world, he saith, Sacrifice and offering
thou wouldest not, but a body hast thou prepared me:
6 In burnt offerings and *sacrifices* for sin thou hast had no pleasure.
7 Then said I, Lo, I come (in the volume of the book it is written of me,) to do
thy will, O God.
8 Above when he said, Sacrifice and offering and burnt offerings and *offering*
for sin thou wouldest not, neither hadst pleasure *therein*; which are offered
by the law;
9 Then said he, Lo, I come to do thy will, O God. He taketh away the first, that
he may establish the second.
10 By the which will we are sanctified through the offering of the body of
Jesus Christ once *for all*.
11 And every priest standeth daily ministering and offering oftentimes the
same sacrifices, which can never take away sins:
12 But this man, after he had offered one sacrifice for sins for ever, sat down
on the right hand of God;
13 From henceforth expecting till his enemies be made his footstool.
14 For by one offering he hath perfected for ever them that are sanctified.
15 *Whereof* the Holy Ghost also is a witness to us: for after that he had said
before,
16 This *is* the covenant that I will make with them after those days, saith the
Lord, I will put my laws into their hearts, and in their minds will I write them;
17 And their sins and iniquities will I remember no more.
18 Now where remission of these *is, there is* no more offering for sin.

We Must Hold Fast to Faith

19 Having therefore, brethren, boldness to enter into the holiest by the blood
of Jesus,
20 By a new and living way, which he hath consecrated for us, through the
veil, that is to say, his flesh;
21 And *having* an high priest over the house of God;
22 Let us draw near with a true heart in full assurance of faith, having our
hearts sprinkled from an evil conscience, and our bodies washed with pure
water.

23 Let us hold fast the profession of *our* faith without wavering; (for he *is*
faithful that promised;)

Encourage Each Other

24 And let us consider one another to provoke unto love and to good works:
25 Not forsaking the assembling of ourselves together, as the manner of some
is; but exhorting *one another*: and so much the more, as ye see the day
approaching.
26 For if we sin wilfully after that we have received the knowledge of the
truth, there remaineth no more sacrifice for sins,
27 But a certain fearful looking for of judgment and fiery indignation, which
shall devour the adversaries.
28 He that despised Moses' law died without mercy under two or three wit-
nesses:
29 Of how much sorer punishment, suppose ye, shall he be thought worthy,
who hath trodden under foot the Son of God, and hath counted the blood of
the covenant, wherewith he was sanctified, an unholy thing, and hath done
despite unto the Spirit of grace?
30 For we know him that hath said, Vengeance *belongeth* unto me, I will
recompense, saith the Lord. And again, The Lord shall judge his people.
31 *It is* a fearful thing to fall into the hands of the living God.
32 But call to remembrance the former days, in which, after ye were illumi-
nated, ye endured a great fight of afflictions;
33 Partly, whilst ye were made a gazingstock both by reproaches and afflic-
tions; and partly, whilst ye became companions of them that were so used.
34 For ye had compassion of me in my bonds, and took joyfully the spoiling
of your goods, knowing in yourselves that ye have in heaven a better and an
enduring substance.
35 Cast not away therefore your confidence, which hath great recompence
of reward.
36 For ye have need of patience, that, after ye have done the will of God, ye
might receive the promise.
37 For yet a little while, and he that shall come will come, and will not tarry.
38 Now the just shall live by faith: but if *any man* draw back, my soul shall
have no pleasure in him.
39 But we are not of them who draw back unto perdition; but of them that
believe to the saving of the soul.

Faith Exemplified

11 Now faith is the substance of things hoped for, the evidence of
things not seen.
2 For by it the elders obtained a good report.
3 Through faith we understand that the worlds were framed by the word of
God, so that things which are seen were not made of things which do appear.
4 By faith Abel offered unto God a more excellent sacrifice than Cain, by
which he obtained witness that he was righteous, God testifying of his gifts:
and by it he being dead yet speaketh.
5 By faith Enoch was translated that he should not see death; and was not
found, because God had translated him: for before his translation he had this
testimony, that he pleased God.
6 But without faith *it is* impossible to please *him*: for he that cometh to God
must believe that he is, and *that* he is a rewarder of them that diligently seek
him.
7 By faith Noah, being warned of God of things not seen as yet, moved with
fear, prepared an ark to the saving of his house; by the which he condemned
the world, and became heir of the righteousness which is by faith.

8 By faith Abraham, when he was called to go out into a place which he should
after receive for an inheritance, obeyed; and he went out, not knowing whither
he went.
9 By faith he sojourned in the land of promise, as *in* a strange country,
dwelling in tabernacles with Isaac and Jacob, the heirs with him of the same
promise:
10 For he looked for a city which hath foundations, whose builder and maker
is God.
11 Through faith also Sara herself received strength to conceive seed, and
was delivered of a child when she was past age, because she judged him faithful
who had promised.
12 Therefore sprang there even of one, and him as good as dead, *so many* as
the stars of the sky in multitude, and as the sand which is by the sea shore
innumerable.
13 These all died in faith, not having received the promises, but having seen
them afar off, and were persuaded of *them*, and embraced *them*, and confessed
that they were strangers and pilgrims on the earth.
14 For they that say such things declare plainly that they seek a country.
15 And truly, if they had been mindful of that *country* from whence they
came out, they might have had opportunity to have returned.
16 But now they desire a better *country*, that is, an heavenly: wherefore God
is not ashamed to be called their God: for he hath prepared for them a city.
17 By faith Abraham, when he was tried, offered up Isaac: and he that had
received the promises offered up his only begotten *son*,
18 Of whom it was said, That in Isaac shall thy seed be called:
19 Accounting that God *was* able to raise *him* up, even from the dead; from
whence also he received him in a figure.
20 By faith Isaac blessed Jacob and Esau concerning things to come.
21 By faith Jacob, when he was a dying, blessed both the sons of Joseph; and
worshipped, *leaning* upon the top of his staff.
22 By faith Joseph, when he died, made mention of the departing of the chil-
dren of Israel; and gave commandment concerning his bones.
23 By faith Moses, when he was born, was hid three months of his parents,
because they saw *he was* a proper child; and they were not afraid of the king's
commandment.
24 By faith Moses, when he was come to years, refused to be called the son
of Pharaoh's daughter;
25 Choosing rather to suffer affliction with the people of God, than to enjoy
the pleasures of sin for a season;
26 Esteeming the reproach of Christ greater riches than the treasures in
Egypt: for he had respect unto the recompence of the reward.
27 By faith he forsook Egypt, not fearing the wrath of the king: for he
endured, as seeing him who is invisible.
28 Through faith he kept the passover, and the sprinkling of blood, lest he
that destroyed the firstborn should touch them.
29 By faith they passed through the Red sea as by dry *land*: which the
Egyptians assaying to do were drowned.
30 By faith the walls of Jericho fell down, after they were compassed about
seven days.
31 By faith the harlot Rahab perished not with them that believed not, when
she had received the spies with peace.
32 And what shall I more say? for the time would fail me to tell of Gedeon,
and *of* Barak, and *of* Samson, and *of* Jephthae; *of* David also, and Samuel, and
of the prophets:
33 Who through faith subdued kingdoms, wrought righteousness, obtained
promises, stopped the mouths of lions,

34 Quenched the violence of fire, escaped the edge of the sword, out of weak-
ness were made strong, waxed valiant in fight, turned to flight the armies of
the aliens.
35 Women received their dead raised to life again: and others were tortured,
not accepting deliverance; that they might obtain a better resurrection:
36 And others had trial of *cruel* mockings and scourgings, yea, moreover of
bonds and imprisonment:
37 They were stoned, they were sawn asunder, were tempted, were slain with
the sword: they wandered about in sheepskins and goatskins; being destitute,
afflicted, tormented;
38 (Of whom the world was not worthy:) they wandered in deserts, and *in*
mountains, and *in* dens and caves of the earth.
39 And these all, having obtained a good report through faith, received not
the promise:
40 God having provided some better thing for us, that they without us should
not be made perfect.

We Must Persevere in Faith

12 Wherefore seeing we also are compassed about with so great a
cloud of witnesses, let us lay aside every weight, and the sin which
doth so easily beset *us*, and let us run with patience the race that is set
before us,
2 Looking unto Jesus the author and finisher of *our* faith; who for the joy
that was set before him endured the cross, despising the shame, and is set
down at the right hand of the throne of God.
3 For consider him that endured such contradiction of sinners against him-
self, lest ye be wearied and faint in your minds.
4 Ye have not yet resisted unto blood, striving against sin.
5 And ye have forgotten the exhortation which speaketh unto you as unto
children, My son, despise not thou the chastening of the Lord, nor faint when
thou art rebuked of him:
6 For whom the Lord loveth he chasteneth, and scourgeth every son whom
he receiveth.
7 If ye endure chastening, God dealeth with you as with sons; for what son
is he whom the father chasteneth not?
8 But if ye be without chastisement, whereof all are partakers, then are ye
bastards, and not sons.
9 Furthermore we have had fathers of our flesh which corrected *us*, and we
gave *them* reverence: shall we not much rather be in subjection unto the Father
of spirits, and live?
10 For they verily for a few days chastened *us* after their own pleasure; but
he for *our* profit, that *we* might be partakers of his holiness.
11 Now no chastening for the present seemeth to be joyous, but grievous:
nevertheless afterward it yieldeth the peaceable fruit of righteousness unto
them which are exercised thereby.
12 Wherefore lift up the hands which hang down, and the feeble knees;
13 And make straight paths for your feet, lest that which is lame be turned
out of the way; but let it rather be healed.
14 Follow peace with all *men*, and holiness, without which no man shall see
the Lord:
15 Looking diligently lest any man fail of the grace of God; lest any root of
bitterness springing up trouble *you*, and thereby many be defiled;
16 Lest there *be* any fornicator, or profane person, as Esau, who for one mor-
sel of meat sold his birthright.

17 For ye know how that afterward, when he would have inherited the bless-
ing, he was rejected: for he found no place of repentance, though he sought
it carefully with tears.
18 For ye are not come unto the mount that might be touched, and that
burned with fire, nor unto blackness, and darkness, and tempest,
19 And the sound of a trumpet, and the voice of words; which *voice* they that
heard intreated that the word should not be spoken to them any more:
20 (For they could not endure that which was commanded, And if so much
as a beast touch the mountain, it shall be stoned, or thrust through with a
dart:
21 And so terrible was the sight, *that* Moses said, I exceedingly fear and
quake:)
22 But ye are come unto mount Sion, and unto the city of the living God, the
heavenly Jerusalem, and to an innumerable company of angels,
23 To the general assembly and church of the firstborn, which are written
in heaven, and to God the Judge of all, and to the spirits of just men made
perfect,
24 And to Jesus the mediator of the new covenant, and to the blood of sprink-
ling, that speaketh better things than *that of* Abel.
25 See that ye refuse not him that speaketh. For if they escaped not who
refused him that spake on earth, much more *shall not* we *escape*, if we turn
away from him that *speaketh* from heaven:
26 Whose voice then shook the earth: but now he hath promised, saying, Yet
once more I shake not the earth only, but also heaven.
27 And this *word*, Yet once more, signifieth the removing of those things that
are shaken, as of things that are made, that those things which cannot be
shaken may remain.
28 Wherefore we receiving a kingdom which cannot be moved, let us have
grace, whereby wc may serve God acceptably with reverence and godly fear:
29 For our God *is* a consuming fire.

The Spirit of Christian Love

13 Let brotherly love continue.
2 Be not forgetful to entertain strangers: for thereby some have enter-
tained angels unawares.
3 Remember them that are in bonds, as bound with them; *and* them which
suffer adversity, as being yourselves also in the body.
4 Marriage *is* honourable in all, and the bed undefiled: but whoremongers
and adulterers God will judge.
5 *Let your* conversation *be* without covetousness; *and be* content with such
things as ye have: for he hath said, I will never leave thee, nor forsake thee.
6 So that we may boldly say, The Lord *is* my helper, and I will not fear what
man shall do unto me.
7 Remember them which have the rule over you, who have spoken unto you
the word of God: whose faith follow, considering the end of *their* conversation.
8 Jesus Christ the same yesterday, and to day, and for ever.
9 Be not carried about with divers and strange doctrines. For *it is* a good
thing that the heart be established with grace; not with meats, which have not
profited them that have been occupied therein.
10 We have an altar, whereof they have no right to eat which serve the tab-
ernacle.
11 For the bodies of those beasts, whose blood is brought into the sanctuary
by the high priest for sin, are burned without the camp.
12 Wherefore Jesus also, that he might sanctify the people with his own
blood, suffered without the gate.
13 Let us go forth therefore unto him without the camp, bearing his reproach.

FOR EVER.
HEBREWS 13:8

14 For here have we no continuing city, but we seek one to come.
15 By him therefore let us offer the sacrifice of praise to God continually,
that is, the fruit of *our* lips giving thanks to his name.
16 But to do good and to communicate forget not: for with such sacrifices
God is well pleased.
17 Obey them that have the rule over you, and submit yourselves: for they
watch for your souls, as they that must give account, that they may do it with
joy, and not with grief: for that *is* unprofitable for you.
18 Pray for us: for we trust we have a good conscience, in all things willing
to live honestly.
19 But I beseech *you* the rather to do this, that I may be restored to you the
sooner.
20 Now the God of peace, that brought again from the dead our Lord Jesus,
that great shepherd of the sheep, through the blood of the everlasting cove-
nant,
21 Make you perfect in every good work to do his will, working in you that
which is wellpleasing in his sight, through Jesus Christ; to whom *be* glory for
ever and ever. Amen.

Farewell

22 And I beseech you, brethren, suffer the word of exhortation: for I have
written a letter unto you in few words.
23 Know ye that *our* brother Timothy is set at liberty; with whom, if he come
shortly, I will see you.
24 Salute all them that have the rule over you, and all the saints. They of Italy
salute you.
25 Grace *be* with you all. Amen.

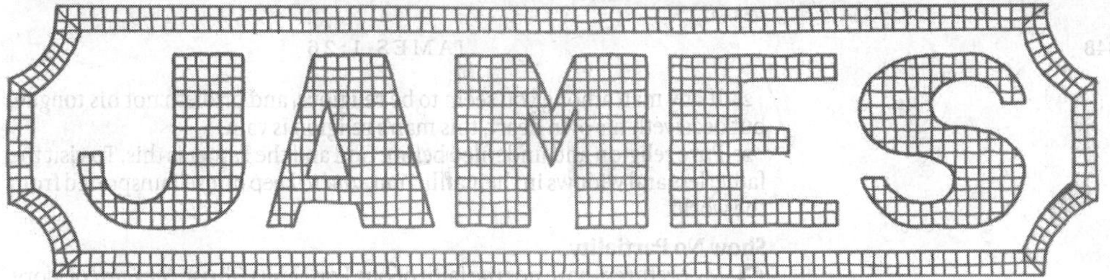

Rejoice under Trials

1 James, a servant of God and of the Lord Jesus Christ, to the twelve tribes
which are scattered abroad, greeting.
2 My brethren, count it all joy when ye fall into divers temptations;
3 Knowing *this*, that the trying of your faith worketh patience.
4 But let patience have *her* perfect work, that ye may be perfect and entire,
wanting nothing.
5 If any of you lack wisdom, let him ask of God, that giveth to all *men* liber-
ally, and upbraideth not; and it shall be given him.
6 But let him ask in faith, nothing wavering. For he that wavereth is like a
wave of the sea driven with the wind and tossed.
7 For let not that man think that he shall receive any thing of the Lord.
8 A double minded man *is* unstable in all his ways.
9 Let the brother of low degree rejoice in that he is exalted:
10 But the rich, in that he is made low: because as the flower of the grass he
shall pass away.
11 For the sun is no sooner risen with a burning heat, but it withereth the
grass, and the flower thereof falleth, and the grace of the fashion of it per-
isheth: so also shall the rich man fade away in his ways.
12 Blessed *is* the man that endureth temptation: for when he is tried, he shall
receive the crown of life, which the Lord hath promised to them that love him.
13 Let no man say when he is tempted, I am tempted of God: for God cannot
be tempted with evil, neither tempteth he any man:
14 But every man is tempted, when he is drawn away of his own lust, and
enticed.
15 Then when lust hath conceived, it bringeth forth sin: and sin, when it is
finished, bringeth forth death.
16 Do not err, my beloved brethren.
17 Every good gift and every perfect gift is from above, and cometh down
from the Father of lights, with whom is no variableness, neither shadow of
turning.
18 Of his own will begat he us with the word of truth, that we should be a
kind of firstfruits of his creatures.
19 Wherefore, my beloved brethren, let every man be swift to hear, slow to
speak, slow to wrath:
20 For the wrath of man worketh not the righteousness of God.
21 Wherefore lay apart all filthiness and superfluity of naughtiness, and
receive with meekness the engrafted word, which is able to save your souls.
22 But be ye doers of the word, and not hearers only, deceiving your own
selves.
23 For if any be a hearer of the word, and not a doer, he is like unto a man
beholding his natural face in a glass:
24 For he beholdeth himself, and goeth his way, and straightway forgetteth
what manner of man he was.
25 But whoso looketh into the perfect law of liberty, and continueth *therein*,
he being not a forgetful hearer, but a doer of the work, this man shall be
blessed in his deed.

Every good GIFT & EVERY PERFECT gift IS FROM ABOVE, & COMETH DOWN FROM THE FATHER of LIGHTS, WITH WHOM IS NO VARIABLENESS, neither SHADOW of turning. JAMES 1:17

26 If any man among you seem to be religious, and bridleth not his tongue,
but deceiveth his own heart, this man's religion *is* vain.
27 Pure religion and undefiled before God and the Father is this, To visit the
fatherless and widows in their affliction, *and* to keep himself unspotted from
the world.

Show No Partiality

2 My brethren, have not the faith of our Lord Jesus Christ, *the Lord* of glory,
with respect of persons.
2 For if there come unto your assembly a man with a gold ring, in goodly
apparel, and there come in also a poor man in vile raiment;
3 And ye have respect to him that weareth the gay clothing, and say unto
him, Sit thou here in a good place; and say to the poor, Stand thou there, or sit
here under my footstool:
4 Are ye not then partial in yourselves, and are become judges of evil
thoughts?
5 Hearken, my beloved brethren, Hath not God chosen the poor of this world
rich in faith, and heirs of the kingdom which he hath promised to them that
love him?
6 But ye have despised the poor. Do not rich men oppress you, and draw you
before the judgment seats?
7 Do not they blaspheme that worthy name by the which ye are called?
8 If ye fulfil the royal law according to the scripture, Thou shalt love thy
neighbour as thyself, ye do well:
9 But if ye have respect to persons, ye commit sin, and are convinced of the
law as transgressors.
10 For whosoever shall keep the whole law, and yet offend in one *point,* he is
guilty of all.
11 For he that said, Do not commit adultery, said also, Do not kill. Now if
thou commit no adultery, yet if thou kill, thou art become a transgressor of
the law.
12 So speak ye, and so do, as they that shall be judged by the law of liberty.
13 For he shall have judgment without mercy, that hath shewed no mercy;
and mercy rejoiceth against judgment.

Faith Is Shown by Deeds

14 What *doth it* profit, my brethren, though a man say he hath faith, and
have not works? can faith save him?
15 If a brother or sister be naked, and destitute of daily food,
16 And one of you say unto them, Depart in peace, be *ye* warmed and filled;
notwithstanding ye give them not those things which are needful to the body;
what *doth it* profit?
17 Even so faith, if it hath not works, is dead, being alone.
18 Yea, a man may say, Thou hast faith, and I have works: shew me thy faith
without thy works, and I will shew thee my faith by my works.
19 Thou believest that there is one God; thou doest well: the devils also
believe, and tremble.
20 But wilt thou know, O vain man, that faith without works is dead?
21 Was not Abraham our father justified by works, when he had offered Isaac
his son upon the altar?
22 Seest thou how faith wrought with his works, and by works was faith made
perfect?
23 And the scripture was fulfilled which saith, Abraham believed God, and
it was imputed unto him for righteousness: and he was called the Friend of
God.
24 Ye see then how that by works a man is justified, and not by faith only.

25 Likewise also was not Rahab the harlot justified by works, when she had
received the messengers, and had sent *them* out another way?
26 For as the body without the spirit is dead, so faith without works is dead
also.

Control the Tongue

3 My brethren, be not many masters, knowing that we shall receive the great-
er condemnation.
2 For in many things we offend all. If any man offend not in word, the same
is a perfect man, *and* able also to bridle the whole body.
3 Behold, we put bits in the horses' mouths, that they may obey us; and we
turn about their whole body.
4 Behold also the ships, which though *they be* so great, and *are* driven of
fierce winds, yet are they turned about with a very small helm, whithersoever
the governor listeth.
5 Even so the tongue is a little member, and boasteth great things. Behold,
how great a matter a little fire kindleth!
6 And the tongue *is* a fire, a world of iniquity: so is the tongue among our
members, that it defileth the whole body, and setteth on fire the course of
nature; and it is set on fire of hell.
7 For every kind of beasts, and of birds, and of serpents, and of things in the
sea, is tamed, and hath been tamed of mankind:
8 But the tongue can no man tame; *it is* an unruly evil, full of deadly poison.
9 Therewith bless we God, even the Father; and therewith curse we men,
which are made after the similitude of God.
10 Out of the same mouth proceedeth blessing and cursing. My brethren,
these things ought not so to be.
11 Doth a fountain send forth at the same place sweet *water* and bitter?
12 Can the fig tree, my brethren, bear olive berries? either a vine, figs? so *can*
no fountain both yield salt water and fresh.

Live Wisely

13 Who *is* a wise man and endued with knowledge among you? let him shew
out of a good conversation his works with meekness of wisdom.
14 But if ye have bitter envying and strife in your hearts, glory not, and lie
not against the truth.
15 This wisdom descendeth not from above, but *is* earthly, sensual, devilish.
16 For where envying and strife *is*, there *is* confusion and every evil work.
17 But the wisdom that is from above is first pure, then peaceable, gentle,
and easy to be intreated, full of mercy and good fruits, without partiality, and
without hypocrisy.
18 And the fruit of righteousness is sown in peace of them that make peace.

Stop Coveting

4 From whence *come* wars and fightings among you? *come they* not hence,
even of your lusts that war in your members?
2 Ye lust, and have not: ye kill, and desire to have, and cannot obtain: ye fight
and war, yet ye have not, because ye ask not.
3 Ye ask, and receive not, because ye ask amiss, that ye may consume *it* upon
your lusts.
4 Ye adulterers and adulteresses, know ye not that the friendship of the world
is enmity with God? whosoever therefore will be a friend of the world is the
enemy of God.
5 Do ye think that the scripture saith in vain, The spirit that dwelleth in us
lusteth to envy?
6 But he giveth more grace. Wherefore he saith, God resisteth the proud, but
giveth grace unto the humble.

7 Submit yourselves therefore to God. Resist the devil, and he will flee from
you.
8 Draw nigh to God, and he will draw nigh to you. Cleanse *your* hands, *ye*
sinners; and purify *your* hearts, *ye* double minded.
9 Be afflicted, and mourn, and weep: let your laughter be turned to mourn-
ing, and *your* joy to heaviness.
10 Humble yourselves in the sight of the Lord, and he shall lift you up.

Stop Slandering

11 Speak not evil one of another, brethren. He that speaketh evil of *his* broth-
er, and judgeth his brother, speaketh evil of the law, and judgeth the law: but
if thou judge the law, thou art not a doer of the law, but a judge.
12 There is one lawgiver, who is able to save and to destroy: who art thou that
judgest another?

Don't Brag about Future Plans

13 Go to now, ye that say, To day or to morrow we will go into such a city, and
continue there a year, and buy and sell, and get gain:
14 Whereas ye know not what *shall be* on the morrow. For what *is* your life?
It is even a vapour, that appeareth for a little time, and then vanisheth away.
15 For that ye *ought* to say, If the Lord will, we shall live, and do this, or that.
16 But now ye rejoice in your boastings: all such rejoicing is evil.
17 Therefore to him that knoweth to do good, and doeth *it* not, to him it is
sin.

Advice to the Rich

5 Go to now, *ye* rich men, weep and howl for your miseries that shall come
upon *you*.
2 Your riches are corrupted, and your garments are motheaten.
3 Your gold and silver is cankered; and the rust of them shall be a witness
against you, and shall eat your flesh as it were fire. Ye have heaped treasure
together for the last days.
4 Behold, the hire of the labourers who have reaped down your fields, which
is of you kept back by fraud, crieth: and the cries of them which have reaped
are entered into the ears of the Lord of sabaoth.
5 Ye have lived in pleasure on the earth, and been wanton; ye have nourished
your hearts, as in a day of slaughter.
6 Ye have condemned *and* killed the just; *and* he doth not resist you.

Be Patient

7 Be patient therefore, brethren, unto the coming of the Lord. Behold, the
husbandman waiteth for the precious fruit of the earth, and hath long
patience for it, until he receive the early and latter rain.
8 Be ye also patient; stablish your hearts: for the coming of the Lord draweth
nigh.
9 Grudge not one against another, brethren, lest ye be condemned: behold,
the judge standeth before the door.
10 Take, my brethren, the prophets, who have spoken in the name of the
Lord, for an example of suffering affliction, and of patience.
11 Behold, we count them happy which endure. Ye have heard of the patience
of Job, and have seen the end of the Lord; that the Lord is very pitiful, and of
tender mercy.

Don't Take Oaths

12 But above all things, my brethren, swear not, neither by heaven, neither
by the earth, neither by any other oath: but let your yea be yea; and *your* nay,
nay; lest ye fall into condemnation.

The Power of Prayer

13 Is any among you afflicted? let him pray. Is any merry? let him sing psalms.
14 Is any sick among you? let him call for the elders of the church; and let
them pray over him, anointing him with oil in the name of the Lord:
15 And the prayer of faith shall save the sick, and the Lord shall raise him up;
and if he have committed sins, they shall be forgiven him.
16 Confess *your* faults one to another, and pray one for another, that ye may
be healed. The effectual fervent prayer of a righteous man availeth much.
17 Elias was a man subject to like passions as we are, and he prayed earnest-
ly that it might not rain: and it rained not on the earth by the space of three
years and six months.
18 And he prayed again, and the heaven gave rain, and the earth brought
forth her fruit.

Help Those Who Wander

19 Brethren, if any of you do err from the truth, and one convert him;
20 Let him know, that he which converteth the sinner from the error of his
way shall save a soul from death, and shall hide a multitude of sins.

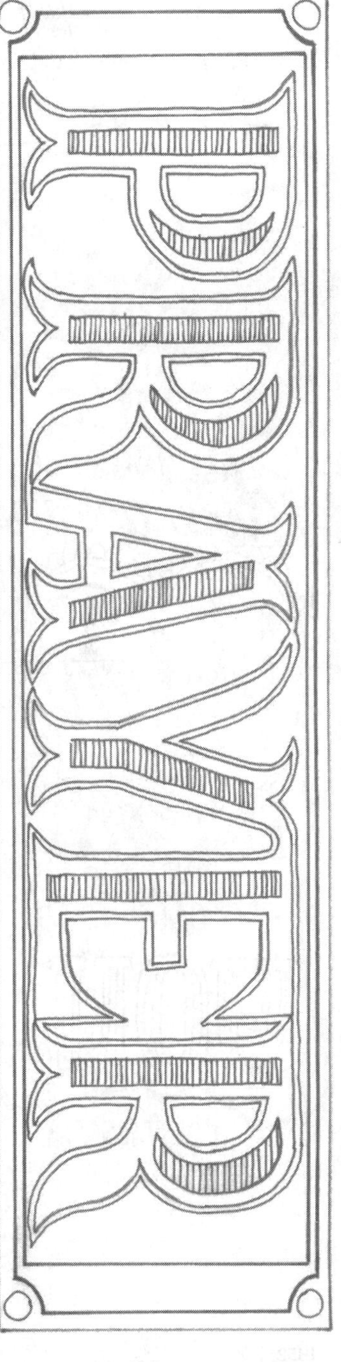

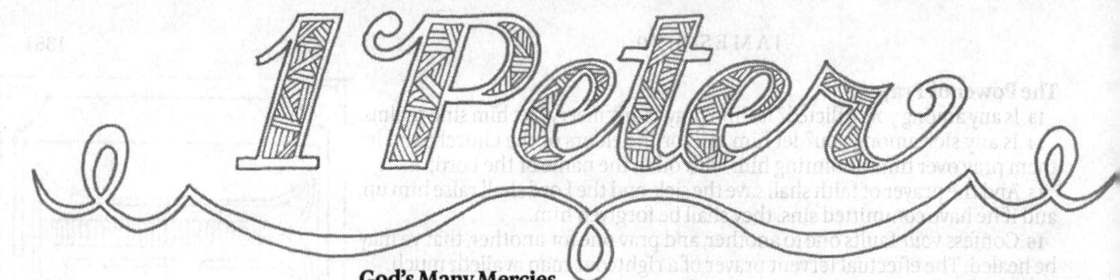

God's Many Mercies

1 Peter, an apostle of Jesus Christ, to the strangers scattered throughout
Pontus, Galatia, Cappadocia, Asia, and Bithynia,
2 Elect according to the foreknowledge of God the Father, through sanctifi-
cation of the Spirit, unto obedience and sprinkling of the blood of Jesus Christ:
Grace unto you, and peace, be multiplied.
3 Blessed *be* the God and Father of our Lord Jesus Christ, which according
to his abundant mercy hath begotten us again unto a lively hope by the resur-
rection of Jesus Christ from the dead,
4 To an inheritance incorruptible, and undefiled, and that fadeth not away,
reserved in heaven for you,
5 Who are kept by the power of God through faith unto salvation ready to
be revealed in the last time.
6 Wherein ye greatly rejoice, though now for a season, if need be, ye are in
heaviness through manifold temptations:
7 That the trial of your faith, being much more precious than of gold that
perisheth, though it be tried with fire, might be found unto praise and honour
and glory at the appearing of Jesus Christ:
8 Whom having not seen, ye love; in whom, though now ye see *him* not, yet
believing, ye rejoice with joy unspeakable and full of glory:
9 Receiving the end of your faith, *even* the salvation of *your* souls.

Salvation Was Prophesied

10 Of which salvation the prophets have enquired and searched diligently,
who prophesied of the grace *that should come* unto you:
11 Searching what, or what manner of time the Spirit of Christ which was
in them did signify, when it testified beforehand the sufferings of Christ, and
the glory that should follow.
12 Unto whom it was revealed, that not unto themselves, but unto us they
did minister the things, which are now reported unto you by them that have
preached the gospel unto you with the Holy Ghost sent down from heaven;
which things the angels desire to look into.

Hope in God's Mercy

13 Wherefore gird up the loins of your mind, be sober, and hope to the end
for the grace that is to be brought unto you at the revelation of Jesus Christ;
14 As obedient children, not fashioning yourselves according to the former
lusts in your ignorance:
15 But as he which hath called you is holy, so be ye holy in all manner of
conversation;
16 Because it is written, Be ye holy; for I am holy.
17 And if ye call on the Father, who without respect of persons judgeth
according to every man's work, pass the time of your sojourning *here* in fear:
18 Forasmuch as ye know that ye were not redeemed with corruptible things,
as silver and gold, from your vain conversation *received* by tradition from
your fathers;
19 But with the precious blood of Christ, as of a lamb without blemish and
without spot:

20 Who verily was foreordained before the foundation of the world, but was
manifest in these last times for you,
21 Who by him do believe in God, that raised him up from the dead, and gave
him glory; that your faith and hope might be in God.

Love Each Other

22 Seeing ye have purified your souls in obeying the truth through the Spirit
unto unfeigned love of the brethren, *see that ye* love one another with a pure
heart fervently:
23 Being born again, not of corruptible seed, but of incorruptible, by the
word of God, which liveth and abideth for ever.
24 For all flesh *is* as grass, and all the glory of man as the flower of grass. The
grass withereth, and the flower thereof falleth away:
25 But the word of the Lord endureth for ever. And this is the word which by
the gospel is preached unto you.

Live as God's Chosen People

2 Wherefore laying aside all malice, and all guile, and hypocrisies, and envies,
and all evil speakings,
2 As newborn babes, desire the sincere milk of the word, that ye may grow
thereby:
3 If so be ye have tasted that the Lord *is* gracious.

Christ Is the Cornerstone

4 To whom coming, *as unto* a living stone, disallowed indeed of men, but
chosen of God, *and* precious,
5 Ye also, as lively stones, are built up a spiritual house, an holy priesthood,
to offer up spiritual sacrifices, acceptable to God by Jesus Christ.
6 Wherefore also it is contained in the scripture, Behold, I lay in Sion a chief
corner stone, elect, precious: and he that believeth on him shall not be con-
founded.
7 Unto you therefore which believe *he is* precious: but unto them which be
disobedient, the stone which the builders disallowed, the same is made the
head of the corner,
8 And a stone of stumbling, and a rock of offence, *even to them* which stum-
ble at the word, being disobedient: whereunto also they were appointed.
9 But ye *are* a chosen generation, a royal priesthood, an holy nation, a pecu-
liar people; that ye should shew forth the praises of him who hath called you
out of darkness into his marvellous light:
10 Which in time past *were* not a people, but *are* now the people of God:
which had not obtained mercy, but now have obtained mercy.
11 Dearly beloved, I beseech *you* as strangers and pilgrims, abstain from
fleshly lusts, which war against the soul;
12 Having your conversation honest among the Gentiles: that, whereas they
speak against you as evildoers, they may by *your* good works, which they shall
behold, glorify God in the day of visitation.

Respect Authority

13 Submit yourselves to every ordinance of man for the Lord's sake: whether
it be to the king, as supreme;
14 Or unto governors, as unto them that are sent by him for the punishment
of evildoers, and for the praise of them that do well.
15 For so is the will of God, that with well doing ye may put to silence the
ignorance of foolish men:
16 As free, and not using *your* liberty for a cloke of maliciousness, but as the
servants of God.
17 Honour all *men*. Love the brotherhood. Fear God. Honour the king.

18 Servants, *be* subject to *your* masters with all fear; not only to the good and
gentle, but also to the froward.
19 For this *is* thankworthy, if a man for conscience toward God endure grief,
suffering wrongfully.
20 For what glory *is it*, if, when ye be buffeted for your faults, ye shall take it
patiently? but if, when ye do well, and suffer *for it*, ye take it patiently, this *is*
acceptable with God.
21 For even hereunto were ye called: because Christ also suffered for us, leav-
ing us an example, that ye should follow his steps:
22 Who did no sin, neither was guile found in his mouth:
23 Who, when he was reviled, reviled not again; when he suffered, he threat-
ened not; but committed *himself* to him that judgeth righteously:
24 Who his own self bare our sins in his own body on the tree, that we, being
dead to sins, should live unto righteousness: by whose stripes ye were healed.
25 For ye were as sheep going astray; but are now returned unto the Shepherd
and Bishop of your souls.

Instructions for Wives and Husbands

3 Likewise, ye wives, *be* in subjection to your own husbands; that, if any obey
not the word, they also may without the word be won by the conversation
of the wives;
2 While they behold your chaste conversation *coupled* with fear.
3 Whose adorning let it not be that outward *adorning* of plaiting the hair,
and of wearing of gold, or of putting on of apparel;
4 But *let it be* the hidden man of the heart, in that which is not corruptible,
even the ornament of a meek and quiet spirit, which is in the sight of God of
great price.
5 For after this manner in the old time the holy women also, who trusted in
God, adorned themselves, being in subjection unto their own husbands:
6 Even as Sara obeyed Abraham, calling him lord: whose daughters ye are,
as long as ye do well, and are not afraid with any amazement.
7 Likewise, ye husbands, dwell with *them* according to knowledge, giving
honour unto the wife, as unto the weaker vessel, and as being heirs together
of the grace of life; that your prayers be not hindered.

Show Brotherly Love

8 Finally, *be ye* all of one mind, having compassion one of another, love as
brethren, *be* pitiful, *be* courteous:
9 Not rendering evil for evil, or railing for railing: but contrariwise blessing;
knowing that ye are thereunto called, that ye should inherit a blessing.
10 For he that will love life, and see good days, let him refrain his tongue from
evil, and his lips that they speak no guile:
11 Let him eschew evil, and do good; let him seek peace, and ensue it.
12 For the eyes of the Lord *are* over the righteous, and his ears *are open* unto
their prayers: but the face of the Lord *is* against them that do evil.
13 And who *is* he that will harm you, if ye be followers of that which is good?
14 But and if ye suffer for righteousness' sake, happy *are ye*: and be not afraid
of their terror, neither be troubled;
15 But sanctify the Lord God in your hearts: and *be* ready always to *give* an
answer to every man that asketh you a reason of the hope that is in you with
meekness and fear:
16 Having a good conscience; that, whereas they speak evil of you, as of evil-
doers, they may be ashamed that falsely accuse your good conversation in
Christ.
17 For *it is* better, if the will of God be so, that ye suffer for well doing, than
for evil doing.

18 For Christ also hath once suffered for sins, the just for the unjust, that he
might bring us to God, being put to death in the flesh, but quickened by the
Spirit:
19 By which also he went and preached unto the spirits in prison;
20 Which sometime were disobedient, when once the longsuffering of God
waited in the days of Noah, while the ark was a preparing, wherein few, that
is, eight souls were saved by water.
21 The like figure whereunto *even* baptism doth also now save us (not the
putting away of the filth of the flesh, but the answer of a good conscience
toward God,) by the resurrection of Jesus Christ:
22 Who is gone into heaven, and is on the right hand of God; angels and
authorities and powers being made subject unto him.

Follow Christ's Example

4 Forasmuch then as Christ hath suffered for us in the flesh, arm yourselves
likewise with the same mind: for he that hath suffered in the flesh hath
ceased from sin;
2 That he no longer should live the rest of *his* time in the flesh to the lusts of
men, but to the will of God.
3 For the time past of *our* life may suffice us to have wrought the will of the
Gentiles, when we walked in lasciviousness, lusts, excess of wine, revellings,
banquetings, and abominable idolatries:
4 Wherein they think it strange that ye run not with *them* to the same excess
of riot, speaking evil of *you*:
5 Who shall give account to him that is ready to judge the quick and the dead.
6 For for this cause was the gospel preached also to them that are dead, that
they might be judged according to men in the flesh, but live according to God
in the spirit.
7 But the end of all things is at hand: be ye therefore sober, and watch unto
prayer.
8 And above all things have fervent charity among yourselves: for charity
shall cover the multitude of sins.
9 Use hospitality one to another without grudging.
10 As every man hath received the gift, *even so* minister the same one to
another, as good stewards of the manifold grace of God.
11 If any man speak, *let him speak* as the oracles of God; if any man minister,
let him do it as of the ability which God giveth: that God in all things may be
glorified through Jesus Christ, to whom be praise and dominion for ever and
ever. Amen.

Share Christ's Sufferings

12 Beloved, think it not strange concerning the fiery trial which is to try you,
as though some strange thing happened unto you:
13 But rejoice, inasmuch as ye are partakers of Christ's sufferings; that, when
his glory shall be revealed, ye may be glad also with exceeding joy.
14 If ye be reproached for the name of Christ, happy *are ye*; for the spirit of
glory and of God resteth upon you: on their part he is evil spoken of, but on
your part he is glorified.
15 But let none of you suffer as a murderer, or *as* a thief, or *as* an evildoer, or
as a busybody in other men's matters.
16 Yet if *any man suffer* as a Christian, let him not be ashamed; but let him
glorify God on this behalf.
17 For the time *is come* that judgment must begin at the house of God: and
if *it* first *begin* at us, what shall the end *be* of them that obey not the gospel of
God?
18 And if the righteous scarcely be saved, where shall the ungodly and the
sinner appear?

19 Wherefore let them that suffer according to the will of God commit the
keeping of their souls *to him* in well doing, as unto a faithful Creator.

Instructions for Spiritual Leaders

5 The elders which are among you I exhort, who am also an elder, and a
witness of the sufferings of Christ, and also a partaker of the glory that shall
be revealed:
2 Feed the flock of God which is among you, taking the oversight *thereof*,
not by constraint, but willingly; not for filthy lucre, but of a ready mind;
3 Neither as being lords over *God's* heritage, but being ensamples to the flock.
4 And when the chief Shepherd shall appear, ye shall receive a crown of glory
that fadeth not away.

Instructions for Believers

5 Likewise, ye younger, submit yourselves unto the elder. Yea, all *of you* be
subject one to another, and be clothed with humility: for God resisteth the
proud, and giveth grace to the humble.
6 Humble yourselves therefore under the mighty hand of God, that he may
exalt you in due time:
7 Casting all your care upon him; for he careth for you.
8 Be sober, be vigilant; because your adversary the devil, as a roaring lion,
walketh about, seeking whom he may devour:
9 Whom resist stedfast in the faith, knowing that the same afflictions are
accomplished in your brethren that are in the world.
10 But the God of all grace, who hath called us unto his eternal glory by Christ
Jesus, after that ye have suffered a while, make you perfect, stablish, strength-
en, settle *you*.
11 To him *be* glory and dominion for ever and ever. Amen.

Farewell

12 By Silvanus, a faithful brother unto you, as I suppose, I have written brief-
ly, exhorting, and testifying that this is the true grace of God wherein ye stand.
13 The *church that is* at Babylon, elected together with *you*, saluteth you; and
so doth Marcus my son.
14 Greet ye one another with a kiss of charity. Peace *be* with you all that are
in Christ Jesus. Amen.

God's Power for Godly Lives

1 Simon Peter, a servant and an apostle of Jesus Christ, to them that have
obtained like precious faith with us through the righteousness of God and
our Saviour Jesus Christ:
2 Grace and peace be multiplied unto you through the knowledge of God,
and of Jesus our Lord,
3 According as his divine power hath given unto us all things that *pertain*
unto life and godliness, through the knowledge of him that hath called us to
glory and virtue:
4 Whereby are given unto us exceeding great and precious promises: that
by these ye might be partakers of the divine nature, having escaped the cor-
ruption that is in the world through lust.
5 And beside this, giving all diligence, add to your faith virtue; and to virtue
knowledge;
6 And to knowledge temperance; and to temperance patience; and to
patience godliness;
7 And to godliness brotherly kindness; and to brotherly kindness charity.
8 For if these things be in you, and abound, they make *you that ye shall*
neither *be* barren nor unfruitful in the knowledge of our Lord Jesus Christ.
9 But he that lacketh these things is blind, and cannot see afar off, and hath
forgotten that he was purged from his old sins.
10 Wherefore the rather, brethren, give diligence to make your calling and
election sure: for if ye do these things, ye shall never fall:
11 For so an entrance shall be ministered unto you abundantly into the ever-
lasting kingdom of our Lord and Saviour Jesus Christ.
12 Wherefore I will not be negligent to put you always in remembrance of
these things, though ye know *them*, and be established in the present truth.
13 Yea, I think it meet, as long as I am in this tabernacle, to stir you up by
putting *you* in remembrance;
14 Knowing that shortly I must put off *this* my tabernacle, even as our Lord
Jesus Christ hath shewed me.
15 Moreover I will endeavour that ye may be able after my decease to have
these things always in remembrance.

Listen to God's Words

16 For we have not followed cunningly devised fables, when we made known
unto you the power and coming of our Lord Jesus Christ, but were eyewit-
nesses of his majesty.
17 For he received from God the Father honour and glory, when there came
such a voice to him from the excellent glory, This is my beloved Son, in whom
I am well pleased.
18 And this voice which came from heaven we heard, when we were with
him in the holy mount.
19 We have also a more sure word of prophecy; whereunto ye do well that ye
take heed, as unto a light that shineth in a dark place, until the day dawn, and
the day star arise in your hearts:
20 Knowing this first, that no prophecy of the scripture is of any private
interpretation.

21 For the prophecy came not in old time by the will of man: but holy men of God spake *as they were* moved by the Holy Ghost.

Warnings about False Teachers

2 But there were false prophets also among the people, even as there shall be false teachers among you, who privily shall bring in damnable heresies, even denying the Lord that bought them, and bring upon themselves swift destruction.

2 And many shall follow their pernicious ways; by reason of whom the way of truth shall be evil spoken of.

3 And through covetousness shall they with feigned words make merchandise of you: whose judgment now of a long time lingereth not, and their damnation slumbereth not.

4 For if God spared not the angels that sinned, but cast *them* down to hell, and delivered *them* into chains of darkness, to be reserved unto judgment;

5 And spared not the old world, but saved Noah the eighth *person*, a preacher of righteousness, bringing in the flood upon the world of the ungodly;

6 And turning the cities of Sodom and Gomorrha into ashes condemned *them* with an overthrow, making *them* an ensample unto those that after should live ungodly;

7 And delivered just Lot, vexed with the filthy conversation of the wicked:

8 (For that righteous man dwelling among them, in seeing and hearing, vexed *his* righteous soul from day to day with *their* unlawful deeds;)

9 The Lord knoweth how to deliver the godly out of temptations, and to reserve the unjust unto the day of judgment to be punished:

10 But chiefly them that walk after the flesh in the lust of uncleanness, and despise government. Presumptuous *are they*, selfwilled, they are not afraid to speak evil of dignities.

11 Whereas angels, which are greater in power and might, bring not railing accusation against them before the Lord.

12 But these, as natural brute beasts, made to be taken and destroyed, speak evil of the things that they understand not; and shall utterly perish in their own corruption;

13 And shall receive the reward of unrighteousness, *as* they that count it pleasure to riot in the day time. Spots *they are* and blemishes, sporting themselves with their own deceivings while they feast with you;

14 Having eyes full of adultery, and that cannot cease from sin; beguiling unstable souls: an heart they have exercised with covetous practices; cursed children:

15 Which have forsaken the right way, and are gone astray, following the way of Balaam *the son* of Bosor, who loved the wages of unrighteousness;

16 But was rebuked for his iniquity: the dumb ass speaking with man's voice forbad the madness of the prophet.

17 These are wells without water, clouds that are carried with a tempest; to whom the mist of darkness is reserved for ever.

18 For when they speak great swelling *words* of vanity, they allure through the lusts of the flesh, *through much* wantonness, those that were clean escaped from them who live in error.

19 While they promise them liberty, they themselves are the servants of corruption: for of whom a man is overcome, of the same is he brought in bondage.

20 For if after they have escaped the pollutions of the world through the knowledge of the Lord and Saviour Jesus Christ, they are again entangled therein, and overcome, the latter end is worse with them than the beginning.

21 For it had been better for them not to have known the way of righteousness, than, after they have known *it*, to turn from the holy commandment delivered unto them.

22 But it is happened unto them according to the true proverb, The dog *is*
turned to his own vomit again; and the sow that was washed to her wallowing
in the mire.

Be Ready for Christ's Return

3 This second epistle, beloved, I now write unto you; in *both* which I stir up
your pure minds by way of remembrance:
2 That ye may be mindful of the words which were spoken before by the holy
prophets, and of the commandment of us the apostles of the Lord and Saviour:
3 Knowing this first, that there shall come in the last days scoffers, walking
after their own lusts,
4 And saying, Where is the promise of his coming? for since the fathers fell
asleep, all things continue as *they were* from the beginning of the creation.
5 For this they willingly are ignorant of, that by the word of God the heavens
were of old, and the earth standing out of the water and in the water:
6 Whereby the world that then was, being overflowed with water, perished:
7 But the heavens and the earth, which are now, by the same word are kept
in store, reserved unto fire against the day of judgment and perdition of
ungodly men.

God's Patience

8 But, beloved, be not ignorant of this one thing, that one day *is* with the
Lord as a thousand years, and a thousand years as one day.
9 The Lord is not slack concerning his promise, as some men count slackness;
but is longsuffering to us-ward, not willing that any should perish, but that
all should come to repentance.
10 But the day of the Lord will come as a thief in the night; in the which the
heavens shall pass away with a great noise, and the elements shall melt with
fervent heat, the earth also and the works that are therein shall be burned up.

Live Holy Lives

11 *Seeing* then *that* all these things shall be dissolved, what manner *of persons*
ought ye to be in *all* holy conversation and godliness,
12 Looking for and hasting unto the coming of the day of God, wherein the
heavens being on fire shall be dissolved, and the elements shall melt with
fervent heat?
13 Nevertheless we, according to his promise, look for new heavens and a
new earth, wherein dwelleth righteousness.
14 Wherefore, beloved, seeing that ye look for such things, be diligent that
ye may be found of him in peace, without spot, and blameless.
15 And account *that* the longsuffering of our Lord *is* salvation; even as our
beloved brother Paul also according to the wisdom given unto him hath writ-
ten unto you;
16 As also in all *his* epistles, speaking in them of these things; in which are
some things hard to be understood, which they that are unlearned and
unstable wrest, as *they do* also the other scriptures, unto their own destruction.
17 Ye therefore, beloved, seeing ye know *these things* before, beware lest ye
also, being led away with the error of the wicked, fall from your own stedfast-
ness.
18 But grow in grace, and *in* the knowledge of our Lord and Saviour Jesus
Christ. To him *be* glory both now and for ever. Amen.

THE Lord IS NOT SLACK CONCERNING HIS PROMISE, AS SOME MEN COUNT SLACKNESS; BUT IS longsuffering to us-ward, NOT WILLING THAT ANY SHOULD perish, BUT THAT ALL should come to REPENTANCE.

2 PETER 3:9

John's Reason for Writing

1 That which was from the beginning, which we have heard, which we have
seen with our eyes, which we have looked upon, and our hands have han-
dled, of the Word of life;
2 (For the life was manifested, and we have seen *it*, and bear witness, and
shew unto you that eternal life, which was with the Father, and was manifest-
ed unto us;)
3 That which we have seen and heard declare we unto you, that ye also may
have fellowship with us: and truly our fellowship *is* with the Father, and with
his Son Jesus Christ.
4 And these things write we unto you, that your joy may be full.

Our Lives Are Living Testimonies

5 This then is the message which we have heard of him, and declare unto
you, that God is light, and in him is no darkness at all.
6 If we say that we have fellowship with him, and walk in darkness, we lie,
and do not the truth:
7 But if we walk in the light, as he is in the light, we have fellowship one with
another, and the blood of Jesus Christ his Son cleanseth us from all sin.
8 If we say that we have no sin, we deceive ourselves, and the truth is not in us.
9 If we confess our sins, he is faithful and just to forgive us *our* sins, and to
cleanse us from all unrighteousness.
10 If we say that we have not sinned, we make him a liar, and his word is not
in us.

Christ Is Our Advocate

2 My little children, these things write I unto you, that ye sin not. And if any
man sin, we have an advocate with the Father, Jesus Christ the righteous:
2 And he is the propitiation for our sins: and not for ours only, but also for
the sins of the whole world.

To Know God Is to Obey

3 And hereby we do know that we know him, if we keep his commandments.
4 He that saith, I know him, and keepeth not his commandments, is a liar,
and the truth is not in him.
5 But whoso keepeth his word, in him verily is the love of God perfected:
hereby know we that we are in him.
6 He that saith he abideth in him ought himself also so to walk, even as he
walked.
7 Brethren, I write no new commandment unto you, but an old command-
ment which ye had from the beginning. The old commandment is the word
which ye have heard from the beginning.
8 Again, a new commandment I write unto you, which thing is true in him
and in you: because the darkness is past, and the true light now shineth.
9 He that saith he is in the light, and hateth his brother, is in darkness even
until now.
10 He that loveth his brother abideth in the light, and there is none occasion
of stumbling in him.

11 But he that hateth his brother is in darkness, and walketh in darkness,
and knoweth not whither he goeth, because that darkness hath blinded his
eyes.
12 I write unto you, little children, because your sins are forgiven you for his
name's sake.
13 I write unto you, fathers, because ye have known him *that is* from the
beginning. I write unto you, young men, because ye have overcome the wick-
ed one. I write unto you, little children, because ye have known the Father.
14 I have written unto you, fathers, because ye have known him *that is* from
the beginning. I have written unto you, young men, because ye are strong, and
the word of God abideth in you, and ye have overcome the wicked one.
15 Love not the world, neither the things *that are* in the world. If any man
love the world, the love of the Father is not in him.
16 For all that *is* in the world, the lust of the flesh, and the lust of the eyes,
and the pride of life, is not of the Father, but is of the world.
17 And the world passeth away, and the lust thereof: but he that doeth the
will of God abideth for ever.

Beware of Seducers

18 Little children, it is the last time: and as ye have heard that antichrist shall
come, even now are there many antichrists; whereby we know that it is the
last time.
19 They went out from us, but they were not of us; for if they had been of us,
they would *no doubt* have continued with us: but *they went out*, that they
might be made manifest that they were not all of us.

Live in Christ

20 But ye have an unction from the Holy One, and ye know all things.
21 I have not written unto you because ye know not the truth, but because
ye know it, and that no lie is of the truth.
22 Who is a liar but he that denieth that Jesus is the Christ? He is antichrist,
that denieth the Father and the Son.
23 Whosoever denieth the Son, the same hath not the Father: *(but) he that
acknowledgeth the Son hath the Father also.*
24 Let that therefore abide in you, which ye have heard from the beginning.
If that which ye have heard from the beginning shall remain in you, ye also
shall continue in the Son, and in the Father.
25 And this is the promise that he hath promised us, *even* eternal life.
26 These *things* have I written unto you concerning them that seduce you.
27 But the anointing which ye have received of him abideth in you, and ye
need not that any man teach you: but as the same anointing teacheth you of
all things, and is truth, and is no lie, and even as it hath taught you, ye shall
abide in him.
28 And now, little children, abide in him; that, when he shall appear, we may
have confidence, and not be ashamed before him at his coming.
29 If ye know that he is righteous, ye know that every one that doeth righ-
teousness is born of him.

We Are God's Children

3 Behold, what manner of love the Father hath bestowed upon us, that we
should be called the sons of God: therefore the world knoweth us not,
because it knew him not.
2 Beloved, now are we the sons of God, and it doth not yet appear what we
shall be: but we know that, when he shall appear, we shall be like him; for we
shall see him as he is.
3 And every man that hath this hope in him purifieth himself, even as he is
pure.

4 Whosoever committeth sin transgresseth also the law: for sin is the trans-
gression of the law.
5 And ye know that he was manifested to take away our sins; and in him is
no sin.
6 Whosoever abideth in him sinneth not: whosoever sinneth hath not seen
him, neither known him.
7 Little children, let no man deceive you: he that doeth righteousness is righ-
teous, even as he is righteous.
8 He that committeth sin is of the devil; for the devil sinneth from the begin-
ning. For this purpose the Son of God was manifested, that he might destroy
the works of the devil.
9 Whosoever is born of God doth not commit sin; for his seed remaineth in
him: and he cannot sin, because he is born of God.
10 In this the children of God are manifest, and the children of the devil:
whosoever doeth not righteousness is not of God, neither he that loveth not
his brother.

Love One Another

11 For this is the message that ye heard from the beginning, that we should
love one another.
12 Not as Cain, *who* was of that wicked one, and slew his brother. And where-
fore slew he him? Because his own works were evil, and his brother's righteous.
13 Marvel not, my brethren, if the world hate you.
14 We know that we have passed from death unto life, because we love the
brethren. He that loveth not *his* brother abideth in death.
15 Whosoever hateth his brother is a murderer: and ye know that no mur-
derer hath eternal life abiding in him.
16 Hereby perceive we the love *of God*, because he laid down his life for us:
and we ought to lay down *our* lives for the brethren.
17 But whoso hath this world's good, and seeth his brother have need, and
shutteth up his bowels *of compassion* from him, how dwelleth the love of God
in him?
18 My little children, let us not love in word, neither in tongue; but in deed
and in truth.
19 And hereby we know that we are of the truth, and shall assure our hearts
before him.
20 For if our heart condemn us, God is greater than our heart, and knoweth
all things.
21 Beloved, if our heart condemn us not, *then* have we confidence toward
God.
22 And whatsoever we ask, we receive of him, because we keep his command-
ments, and do those things that are pleasing in his sight.
23 And this is his commandment, That we should believe on the name of his
Son Jesus Christ, and love one another, as he gave us commandment.
24 And he that keepeth his commandments dwelleth in him, and he in him.
And hereby we know that he abideth in us, by the Spirit which he hath given us.

Test All Teachings

4 Beloved, believe not every spirit, but try the spirits whether they are of God:
because many false prophets are gone out into the world.
2 Hereby know ye the Spirit of God: Every spirit that confesseth that Jesus
Christ is come in the flesh is of God:
3 And every spirit that confesseth not that Jesus Christ is come in the flesh
is not of God: and this is that *spirit* of antichrist, whereof ye have heard that
it should come; and even now already is it in the world.
4 Ye are of God, little children, and have overcome them: because greater is
he that is in you, than he that is in the world.

5 They are of the world: therefore speak they of the world, and the world
heareth them.
6 We are of God: he that knoweth God heareth us; he that is not of God
heareth not us. Hereby know we the spirit of truth, and the spirit of error.

God's Love in His People

7 Beloved, let us love one another: for love is of God; and every one that loveth
is born of God, and knoweth God.
8 He that loveth not knoweth not God; for God is love.
9 In this was manifested the love of God toward us, because that God sent
his only begotten Son into the world, that we might live through him.
10 Herein is love, not that we loved God, but that he loved us, and sent his
Son *to be* the propitiation for our sins.
11 Beloved, if God so loved us, we ought also to love one another.
12 No man hath seen God at any time. If we love one another, God dwelleth
in us, and his love is perfected in us.
13 Hereby know we that we dwell in him, and he in us, because he hath given
us of his Spirit.
14 And we have seen and do testify that the Father sent the Son *to be* the
Saviour of the world.
15 Whosoever shall confess that Jesus is the Son of God, God dwelleth in him,
and he in God.
16 And we have known and believed the love that God hath to us. God is love;
and he that dwelleth in love dwelleth in God, and God in him.
17 Herein is our love made perfect, that we may have boldness in the day of
judgment: because as he is, so are we in this world.
18 There is no fear in love; but perfect love casteth out fear: because fear hath
torment. He that feareth is not made perfect in love.
19 We love him, because he first loved us.
20 If a man say, I love God, and hateth his brother, he is a liar: for he that
loveth not his brother whom he hath seen, how can he love God whom he
hath not seen?
21 And this commandment have we from him, That he who loveth God love
his brother also.

We Are God's Children

5 Whosoever believeth that Jesus is the Christ is born of God: and every one
that loveth him that begat loveth him also that is begotten of him.
2 By this we know that we love the children of God, when we love God, and
keep his commandments.
3 For this is the love of God, that we keep his commandments: and his com-
mandments are not grievous.
4 For whatsoever is born of God overcometh the world: and this is the vic-
tory that overcometh the world, *even* our faith.
5 Who is he that overcometh the world, but he that believeth that Jesus is
the Son of God?
6 This is he that came by water and blood, *even* Jesus Christ; not by water
only, but by water and blood. And it is the Spirit that beareth witness, because
the Spirit is truth.
7 For there are three that bear record in heaven, the Father, the Word, and
the Holy Ghost: and these three are one.
8 And there are three that bear witness in earth, the Spirit, and the water,
and the blood: and these three agree in one.
9 If we receive the witness of men, the witness of God is greater: for this is
the witness of God which he hath testified of his Son.

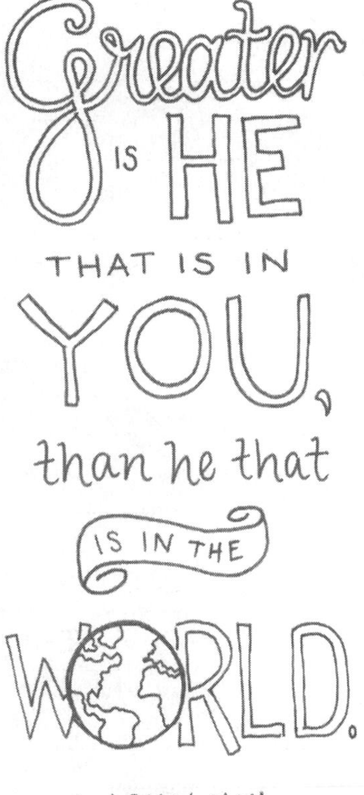

10 He that believeth on the Son of God hath the witness in himself: he that
believeth not God hath made him a liar; because he believeth not the record
that God gave of his Son.
11 And this is the record, that God hath given to us eternal life, and this life
is in his Son.
12 He that hath the Son hath life; *and* he that hath not the Son of God hath
not life.
13 These things have I written unto you that believe on the name of the Son
of God; that ye may know that ye have eternal life, and that ye may believe on
the name of the Son of God.

Our Confidence in Christ

14 And this is the confidence that we have in him, that, if we ask any thing
according to his will, he heareth us:
15 And if we know that he hear us, whatsoever we ask, we know that we have
the petitions that we desired of him.
16 If any man see his brother sin a sin *which is* not unto death, he shall ask,
and he shall give him life for them that sin not unto death. There is a sin unto
death: I do not say that he shall pray for it.
17 All unrighteousness is sin: and there is a sin not unto death.
18 We know that whosoever is born of God sinneth not; but he that is begot-
ten of God keepeth himself, and that wicked one toucheth him not.
19 *And* we know that we are of God, and the whole world lieth in wickedness.
20 And we know that the Son of God is come, and hath given us an under-
standing, that we may know him that is true, and we are in him that is true,
even in his Son Jesus Christ. This is the true God, and eternal life.
21 Little children, keep yourselves from idols. Amen.

Living in the Truth

1 The elder unto the elect lady and her children, whom I love in the truth;
and not I only, but also all they that have known the truth;
2 For the truth's sake, which dwelleth in us, and shall be with us for ever.
3 Grace be with you, mercy, *and* peace, from God the Father, and from the
Lord Jesus Christ, the Son of the Father, in truth and love.
4 I rejoiced greatly that I found of thy children walking in truth, as we have
received a commandment from the Father.
5 And now I beseech thee, lady, not as though I wrote a new commandment
unto thee, but that which we had from the beginning, that we love one another.
6 And this is love, that we walk after his commandments. This is the com-
mandment, That, as ye have heard from the beginning, ye should walk in it.

Reject False Teachers

7 For many deceivers are entered into the world, who confess not that Jesus
Christ is come in the flesh. This is a deceiver and an antichrist.
8 Look to yourselves, that we lose not those things which we have wrought,
but that we receive a full reward.
9 Whosoever transgresseth, and abideth not in the doctrine of Christ, hath
not God. He that abideth in the doctrine of Christ, he hath both the Father
and the Son.
10 If there come any unto you, and bring not this doctrine, receive him not
into *your* house, neither bid him God speed:
11 For he that biddeth him God speed is partaker of his evil deeds.
12 Having many things to write unto you, I would not *write* with paper and
ink: but I trust to come unto you, and speak face to face, that our joy may be
full.
13 The children of thy elect sister greet thee. Amen.

3 JOHN

John Commends Gaius

1 The elder unto the wellbeloved Gaius, whom I love in the truth.
2 Beloved, I wish above all things that thou mayest prosper and be in
health, even as thy soul prospereth.
3 For I rejoiced greatly, when the brethren came and testified of the truth
that is in thee, even as thou walkest in the truth.
4 I have no greater joy than to hear that my children walk in truth.
5 Beloved, thou doest faithfully whatsoever thou doest to the brethren, and
to strangers;
6 Which have borne witness of thy charity before the church: whom if thou
bring forward on their journey after a godly sort, thou shalt do well:
7 Because that for his name's sake they went forth, taking nothing of the
Gentiles.
8 We therefore ought to receive such, that we might be fellowhelpers to the
truth.

John Criticizes Diotrephes

9 I wrote unto the church: but Diotrephes, who loveth to have the preemi-
nence among them, receiveth us not.
10 Wherefore, if I come, I will remember his deeds which he doeth, prating
against us with malicious words: and not content therewith, neither doth he
himself receive the brethren, and forbiddeth them that would, and casteth
them out of the church.
11 Beloved, follow not that which is evil, but that which is good. He that doeth
good is of God: but he that doeth evil hath not seen God.

John Praises Demetrius

12 Demetrius hath good report of all *men*, and of the truth itself: yea, and
we *also* bear record; and ye know that our record is true.
13 I had many things to write, but I will not with ink and pen write unto thee:
14 But I trust I shall shortly see thee, and we shall speak face to face. Peace *be*
to thee. *Our* friends salute thee. Greet the friends by name.

Warnings about False Teachers

1 Jude, the servant of Jesus Christ, and brother of James, to them that are
sanctified by God the Father, and preserved in Jesus Christ, *and* called:
2 Mercy unto you, and peace, and love, be multiplied.
3 Beloved, when I gave all diligence to write unto you of the common salva-
tion, it was needful for me to write unto you, and exhort *you* that ye should
earnestly contend for the faith which was once delivered unto the saints.
4 For there are certain men crept in unawares, who were before of old
ordained to this condemnation, ungodly men, turning the grace of our God
into lasciviousness, and denying the only Lord God, and our Lord Jesus Christ.
5 I will therefore put you in remembrance, though ye once knew this, how
that the Lord, having saved the people out of the land of Egypt, afterward
destroyed them that believed not.
6 And the angels which kept not their first estate, but left their own habita-
tion, he hath reserved in everlasting chains under darkness unto the judgment
of the great day.
7 Even as Sodom and Gomorrha, and the cities about them in like manner,
giving themselves over to fornication, and going after strange flesh, are set
forth for an example, suffering the vengeance of eternal fire.
8 Likewise also these *filthy* dreamers defile the flesh, despise dominion, and
speak evil of dignities.
9 Yet Michael the archangel, when contending with the devil he disputed
about the body of Moses, durst not bring against him a railing accusation, but
said, The Lord rebuke thee.
10 But these speak evil of those things which they know not: but what they
know naturally, as brute beasts, in those things they corrupt themselves.
11 Woe unto them! for they have gone in the way of Cain, and ran greedily
after the error of Balaam for reward, and perished in the gainsaying of Core.
12 These are spots in your feasts of charity, when they feast with you, feeding
themselves without fear: clouds *they are* without water, carried about of winds;
trees whose fruit withereth, without fruit, twice dead, plucked up by the roots;
13 Raging waves of the sea, foaming out their own shame; wandering stars,
to whom is reserved the blackness of darkness for ever.
14 And Enoch also, the seventh from Adam, prophesied of these, saying,
Behold, the Lord cometh with ten thousands of his saints,
15 To execute judgment upon all, and to convince all that are ungodly among
them of all their ungodly deeds which they have ungodly committed, and of
all their hard *speeches* which ungodly sinners have spoken against him.
16 These are murmurers, complainers, walking after their own lusts; and
their mouth speaketh great swelling *words*, having men's persons in admira-
tion because of advantage.
17 But, beloved, remember ye the words which were spoken before of the
apostles of our Lord Jesus Christ;
18 How that they told you there should be mockers in the last time, who
should walk after their own ungodly lusts.
19 These be they who separate themselves, sensual, having not the Spirit.
20 But ye, beloved, building up yourselves on your most holy faith, praying
in the Holy Ghost,

NOW UNTO
Him
THAT IS ABLE
TO KEEP YOU
FROM FALLING,
AND TO PRESENT
You
FAULTLESS BEFORE
THE PRESENCE
OF HIS
Glory
WITH
EXCEEDING JOY,
TO THE ONLY WISE
GOD
our Saviour,
BE GLORY AND
Majesty,
DOMINION AND
Power,
BOTH NOW AND EVER.
Amen.
JUDE 1:24-25

21 Keep yourselves in the love of God, looking for the mercy of our Lord Jesus
Christ unto eternal life.
22 And of some have compassion, making a difference:
23 And others save with fear, pulling *them* out of the fire; hating even the
garment spotted by the flesh.
24 Now unto him that is able to keep you from falling, and to present *you*
faultless before the presence of his glory with exceeding joy,
25 To the only wise God our Saviour, *be* glory and majesty, dominion and
power, both now and ever. Amen.

John Writes His Revelation

1 The Revelation of Jesus Christ, which God gave unto him, to shew unto his servants things which must shortly come to pass; and he sent and signified *it* by his angel unto his servant John:
2 Who bare record of the word of God, and of the testimony of Jesus Christ, and of all things that he saw.
3 Blessed *is* he that readeth, and they that hear the words of this prophecy, and keep those things which are written therein: for the time *is* at hand.
4 John to the seven churches which are in Asia: Grace *be* unto you, and peace, from him which is, and which was, and which is to come; and from the seven Spirits which are before his throne;
5 And from Jesus Christ, *who is* the faithful witness, *and* the first begotten of the dead, and the prince of the kings of the earth. Unto him that loved us, and washed us from our sins in his own blood,
6 And hath made us kings and priests unto God and his Father; to him *be* glory and dominion for ever and ever. Amen.
7 Behold, he cometh with clouds; and every eye shall see him, and they *also* which pierced him: and all kindreds of the earth shall wail because of him. Even so, Amen.
8 I am Alpha and Omega, the beginning and the ending, saith the Lord, which is, and which was, and which is to come, the Almighty.
9 I John, who also am your brother, and companion in tribulation, and in the kingdom and patience of Jesus Christ, was in the isle that is called Patmos, for the word of God, and for the testimony of Jesus Christ.
10 I was in the Spirit on the Lord's day, and heard behind me a great voice, as of a trumpet,
11 Saying, I am Alpha and Omega, the first and the last: and, What thou seest, write in a book, and send *it* unto the seven churches which are in Asia; unto Ephesus, and unto Smyrna, and unto Pergamos, and unto Thyatira, and unto Sardis, and unto Philadelphia, and unto Laodicea.
12 And I turned to see the voice that spake with me. And being turned, I saw seven golden candlesticks;
13 And in the midst of the seven candlesticks *one* like unto the Son of man, clothed with a garment down to the foot, and girt about the paps with a golden girdle.
14 His head and *his* hairs *were* white like wool, as white as snow; and his eyes *were* as a flame of fire;
15 And his feet like unto fine brass, as if they burned in a furnace; and his voice as the sound of many waters.
16 And he had in his right hand seven stars: and out of his mouth went a sharp twoedged sword: and his countenance *was* as the sun shineth in his strength.
17 And when I saw him, I fell at his feet as dead. And he laid his right hand upon me, saying unto me, Fear not; I am the first and the last:
18 I *am* he that liveth, and was dead; and, behold, I am alive for evermore, Amen; and have the keys of hell and of death.
19 Write the things which thou hast seen, and the things which are, and the things which shall be hereafter;

20 The mystery of the seven stars which thou sawest in my right hand, and the seven golden candlesticks. The seven stars are the angels of the seven churches: and the seven candlesticks which thou sawest are the seven churches.

Letter to the Church in Ephesus

2 Unto the angel of the church of Ephesus write; These things saith he that holdeth the seven stars in his right hand, who walketh in the midst of the seven golden candlesticks;

2 I know thy works, and thy labour, and thy patience, and how thou canst not bear them which are evil: and thou hast tried them which say they are apostles, and are not, and hast found them liars:

3 And hast borne, and hast patience, and for my name's sake hast laboured, and hast not fainted.

4 Nevertheless I have *somewhat* against thee, because thou hast left thy first love.

5 Remember therefore from whence thou art fallen, and repent, and do the first works; or else I will come unto thee quickly, and will remove thy candlestick out of his place, except thou repent.

6 But this thou hast, that thou hatest the deeds of the Nicolaitans, which I also hate.

7 He that hath an ear, let him hear what the Spirit saith unto the churches; To him that overcometh will I give to eat of the tree of life, which is in the midst of the paradise of God.

Letter to the Church in Smyrna

8 And unto the angel of the church in Smyrna write; These things saith the first and the last, which was dead, and is alive;

9 I know thy works, and tribulation, and poverty, (but thou art rich) and *I know* the blasphemy of them which say they are Jews, and are not, but *are* the synagogue of Satan.

10 Fear none of those things which thou shalt suffer: behold, the devil shall cast *some* of you into prison, that ye may be tried; and ye shall have tribulation ten days: be thou faithful unto death, and I will give thee a crown of life.

11 He that hath an ear, let him hear what the Spirit saith unto the churches; He that overcometh shall not be hurt of the second death.

Letter to the Church in Pergamos

12 And to the angel of the church in Pergamos write; These things saith he which hath the sharp sword with two edges;

13 I know thy works, and where thou dwellest, *even* where Satan's seat *is*: and thou holdest fast my name, and hast not denied my faith, even in those days wherein Antipas *was* my faithful martyr, who was slain among you, where Satan dwelleth.

14 But I have a few things against thee, because thou hast there them that hold the doctrine of Balaam, who taught Balac to cast a stumblingblock before the children of Israel, to eat things sacrificed unto idols, and to commit fornication.

15 So hast thou also them that hold the doctrine of the Nicolaitans, which thing I hate.

16 Repent; or else I will come unto thee quickly, and will fight against them with the sword of my mouth.

17 He that hath an ear, let him hear what the Spirit saith unto the churches; To him that overcometh will I give to eat of the hidden manna, and will give him a white stone, and in the stone a new name written, which no man knoweth saving he that receiveth *it*.

Letter to the Church in Thyatira

18 And unto the angel of the church in Thyatira write; These things saith the
Son of God, who hath his eyes like unto a flame of fire, and his feet *are* like
fine brass;
19 I know thy works, and charity, and service, and faith, and thy patience,
and thy works; and the last *to be* more than the first.
20 Notwithstanding I have a few things against thee, because thou sufferest
that woman Jezebel, which calleth herself a prophetess, to teach and to seduce
my servants to commit fornication, and to eat things sacrificed unto idols.
21 And I gave her space to repent of her fornication; and she repented not.
22 Behold, I will cast her into a bed, and them that commit adultery with her
into great tribulation, except they repent of their deeds.
23 And I will kill her children with death; and all the churches shall know
that I am he which searcheth the reins and hearts: and I will give unto every
one of you according to your works.
24 But unto you I say, and unto the rest in Thyatira, as many as have not this
doctrine, and which have not known the depths of Satan, as they speak; I will
put upon you none other burden.
25 But that which ye have *already* hold fast till I come.
26 And he that overcometh, and keepeth my works unto the end, to him will
I give power over the nations:
27 And he shall rule them with a rod of iron; as the vessels of a potter shall
they be broken to shivers: even as I received of my Father.
28 And I will give him the morning star.
29 He that hath an ear, let him hear what the Spirit saith unto the churches.

Letter to the Church in Sardis

3 And unto the angel of the church in Sardis write; These things saith he that
hath the seven Spirits of God, and the seven stars; I know thy works, that
thou hast a name that thou livest, and art dead.
2 Be watchful, and strengthen the things which remain, that are ready to
die: for I have not found thy works perfect before God.
3 Remember therefore how thou hast received and heard, and hold fast, and
repent. If therefore thou shalt not watch, I will come on thee as a thief, and
thou shalt not know what hour I will come upon thee.
4 Thou hast a few names even in Sardis which have not defiled their gar-
ments; and they shall walk with me in white: for they are worthy.
5 He that overcometh, the same shall be clothed in white raiment; and I will
not blot out his name out of the book of life, but I will confess his name before
my Father, and before his angels.
6 He that hath an ear, let him hear what the Spirit saith unto the churches.

Letter to the Church in Philadelphia

7 And to the angel of the church in Philadelphia write; These things saith he
that is holy, he that is true, he that hath the key of David, he that openeth, and
no man shutteth; and shutteth, and no man openeth;
8 I know thy works: behold, I have set before thee an open door, and no man
can shut it: for thou hast a little strength, and hast kept my word, and hast not
denied my name.
9 Behold, I will make them of the synagogue of Satan, which say they are
Jews, and are not, but do lie; behold, I will make them to come and worship
before thy feet, and to know that I have loved thee.
10 Because thou hast kept the word of my patience, I also will keep thee from
the hour of temptation, which shall come upon all the world, to try them that
dwell upon the earth.
11 Behold, I come quickly: hold that fast which thou hast, that no man take
thy crown.

12 Him that overcometh will I make a pillar in the temple of my God, and he
shall go no more out: and I will write upon him the name of my God, and the
name of the city of my God, *which is* new Jerusalem, which cometh down out
of heaven from my God: and *I will write upon him* my new name.
13 He that hath an ear, let him hear what the Spirit saith unto the churches.

Letter to the Church in Laodicea

14 And unto the angel of the church of the Laodiceans write; These things
saith the Amen, the faithful and true witness, the beginning of the creation
of God;
15 I know thy works, that thou art neither cold nor hot: I would thou wert
cold or hot.
16 So then because thou art lukewarm, and neither cold nor hot, I will spue
thee out of my mouth.
17 Because thou sayest, I am rich, and increased with goods, and have need
of nothing; and knowest not that thou art wretched, and miserable, and poor,
and blind, and naked:
18 I counsel thee to buy of me gold tried in the fire, that thou mayest be rich;
and white raiment, that thou mayest be clothed, and *that* the shame of thy
nakedness do not appear; and anoint thine eyes with eyesalve, that thou may-
est see.
19 As many as I love, I rebuke and chasten: be zealous therefore, and repent.
20 Behold, I stand at the door, and knock: if any man hear my voice, and open
the door, I will come in to him, and will sup with him, and he with me.
21 To him that overcometh will I grant to sit with me in my throne, even as
I also overcame, and am set down with my Father in his throne.
22 He that hath an ear, let him hear what the Spirit saith unto the churches.

The Throne of God in Heaven

4 After this I looked, and, behold, a door *was* opened in heaven: and the first
voice which I heard *was* as it were of a trumpet talking with me; which said,
Come up hither, and I will shew thee things which must be hereafter.
2 And immediately I was in the spirit: and, behold, a throne was set in heaven,
and *one* sat on the throne.
3 And he that sat was to look upon like a jasper and a sardine stone: and *there*
was a rainbow round about the throne, in sight like unto an emerald.
4 And round about the throne *were* four and twenty seats: and upon the seats
I saw four and twenty elders sitting, clothed in white raiment; and they had
on their heads crowns of gold.
5 And out of the throne proceeded lightnings and thunderings and voices:
and *there were* seven lamps of fire burning before the throne, which are the
seven Spirits of God.
6 And before the throne *there was* a sea of glass like unto crystal: and in the
midst of the throne, and round about the throne, *were* four beasts full of eyes
before and behind.
7 And the first beast *was* like a lion, and the second beast like a calf, and the
third beast had a face as a man, and the fourth beast *was* like a flying eagle.
8 And the four beasts had each of them six wings about *him*; and *they were*
full of eyes within: and they rest not day and night, saying, Holy, holy, holy,
Lord God Almighty, which was, and is, and is to come.
9 And when those beasts give glory and honour and thanks to him that sat
on the throne, who liveth for ever and ever,
10 The four and twenty elders fall down before him that sat on the throne,
and worship him that liveth for ever and ever, and cast their crowns before
the throne, saying,
11 Thou art worthy, O Lord, to receive glory and honour and power: for thou
hast created all things, and for thy pleasure they are and were created.

The Book Sealed with Seven Seals

5 And I saw in the right hand of him that sat on the throne a book written
within and on the backside, sealed with seven seals.
2 And I saw a strong angel proclaiming with a loud voice, Who is worthy to
open the book, and to loose the seals thereof?
3 And no man in heaven, nor in earth, neither under the earth, was able to
open the book, neither to look thereon.
4 And I wept much, because no man was found worthy to open and to read
the book, neither to look thereon.
5 And one of the elders saith unto me, Weep not: behold, the Lion of the tribe
of Juda, the Root of David, hath prevailed to open the book, and to loose the
seven seals thereof.
6 And I beheld, and, lo, in the midst of the throne and of the four beasts, and
in the midst of the elders, stood a Lamb as it had been slain, having seven horns
and seven eyes, which are the seven Spirits of God sent forth into all the earth.
7 And he came and took the book out of the right hand of him that sat upon
the throne.
8 And when he had taken the book, the four beasts and four *and* twenty
elders fell down before the Lamb, having every one of them harps, and golden
vials full of odours, which are the prayers of saints.
9 And they sung a new song, saying, Thou art worthy to take the book, and
to open the seals thereof: for thou wast slain, and hast redeemed us to God by
thy blood out of every kindred, and tongue, and people, and nation;
10 And hast made us unto our God kings and priests: and we shall reign on
the earth.
11 And I beheld, and I heard the voice of many angels round about the throne
and the beasts and the elders: and the number of them was ten thousand times
ten thousand, and thousands of thousands;
12 Saying with a loud voice, Worthy is the Lamb that was slain to receive
power, and riches, and wisdom, and strength, and honour, and glory, and
blessing.
13 And every creature which is in heaven, and on the earth, and under the
earth, and such as are in the sea, and all that are in them, heard I saying,
Blessing, and honour, and glory, and power, *be* unto him that sitteth upon the
throne, and unto the Lamb for ever and ever.
14 And the four beasts said, Amen. And the four *and* twenty elders fell down
and worshipped him that liveth for ever and ever.

The Lamb Opens Six Seals

6 And I saw when the Lamb opened one of the seals, and I heard, as it were
the noise of thunder, one of the four beasts saying, Come and see.
2 And I saw, and behold a white horse: and he that sat on him had a bow; and
a crown was given unto him: and he went forth conquering, and to conquer.
3 And when he had opened the second seal, I heard the second beast say,
Come and see.
4 And there went out another horse *that was* red: and *power* was given to
him that sat thereon to take peace from the earth, and that they should kill
one another: and there was given unto him a great sword.
5 And when he had opened the third seal, I heard the third beast say, Come
and see. And I beheld, and lo a black horse; and he that sat on him had a pair
of balances in his hand.
6 And I heard a voice in the midst of the four beasts say, A measure of wheat
for a penny, and three measures of barley for a penny; and *see* thou hurt not
the oil and the wine.
7 And when he had opened the fourth seal, I heard the voice of the fourth
beast say, Come and see.

8 And I looked, and behold a pale horse: and his name that sat on him was
Death, and Hell followed with him. And power was given unto them over the
fourth part of the earth, to kill with sword, and with hunger, and with death,
and with the beasts of the earth.
9 And when he had opened the fifth seal, I saw under the altar the souls of
them that were slain for the word of God, and for the testimony which they
held:
10 And they cried with a loud voice, saying, How long, O Lord, holy and true,
dost thou not judge and avenge our blood on them that dwell on the earth?
11 And white robes were given unto every one of them; and it was said unto
them, that they should rest yet for a little season, until their fellowservants
also and their brethren, that should be killed as they *were*, should be fulfilled.
12 And I beheld when he had opened the sixth seal, and, lo, there was a great
earthquake; and the sun became black as sackcloth of hair, and the moon
became as blood;
13 And the stars of heaven fell unto the earth, even as a fig tree casteth her
untimely figs, when she is shaken of a mighty wind.
14 And the heaven departed as a scroll when it is rolled together; and every
mountain and island were moved out of their places.
15 And the kings of the earth, and the great men, and the rich men, and the
chief captains, and the mighty men, and every bondman, and every free man,
hid themselves in the dens and in the rocks of the mountains;
16 And said to the mountains and rocks, Fall on us, and hide us from the face
of him that sitteth on the throne, and from the wrath of the Lamb:
17 For the great day of his wrath is come; and who shall be able to stand?

The Mark of God's Servants

7 And after these things I saw four angels standing on the four corners of the
earth, holding the four winds of the earth, that the wind should not blow
on the earth, nor on the sea, nor on any tree.
2 And I saw another angel ascending from the east, having the seal of the
living God: and he cried with a loud voice to the four angels, to whom it was
given to hurt the earth and the sea,
3 Saying, Hurt not the earth, neither the sea, nor the trees, till we have sealed
the servants of our God in their foreheads.
4 And I heard the number of them which were sealed: *and there were* sealed
an hundred *and* forty *and* four thousand of all the tribes of the children of
Israel.
5 Of the tribe of Juda *were* sealed twelve thousand. Of the tribe of Reuben
were sealed twelve thousand. Of the tribe of Gad *were* sealed twelve thousand.
6 Of the tribe of Aser *were* sealed twelve thousand. Of the tribe of Nepthalim
were sealed twelve thousand. Of the tribe of Manasses *were* sealed twelve thou-
sand.
7 Of the tribe of Simeon *were* sealed twelve thousand. Of the tribe of Levi
were sealed twelve thousand. Of the tribe of Issachar *were* sealed twelve thou-
sand.
8 Of the tribe of Zabulon *were* sealed twelve thousand. Of the tribe of Joseph
were sealed twelve thousand. Of the tribe of Benjamin *were* sealed twelve thou-
sand.

God's People at His Throne

9 After this I beheld, and, lo, a great multitude, which no man could number,
of all nations, and kindreds, and people, and tongues, stood before the throne,
and before the Lamb, clothed with white robes, and palms in their hands;
10 And cried with a loud voice, saying, Salvation to our God which sitteth
upon the throne, and unto the Lamb.

11 And all the angels stood round about the throne, and *about* the elders and
the four beasts, and fell before the throne on their faces, and worshipped God,
12 Saying, Amen: Blessing, and glory, and wisdom, and thanksgiving, and hon-
our, and power, and might, *be* unto our God for ever and ever. Amen.
13 And one of the elders answered, saying unto me, What are these which
are arrayed in white robes? and whence came they?
14 And I said unto him, Sir, thou knowest. And he said to me, These are they
which came out of great tribulation, and have washed their robes, and made
them white in the blood of the Lamb.
15 Therefore are they before the throne of God, and serve him day and night
in his temple: and he that sitteth on the throne shall dwell among them.
16 They shall hunger no more, neither thirst any more; neither shall the sun
light on them, nor any heat.
17 For the Lamb which is in the midst of the throne shall feed them, and shall
lead them unto living fountains of waters: and God shall wipe away all tears
from their eyes.

The Lamb Opens the Seventh Seal

8 And when he had opened the seventh seal, there was silence in heaven about
the space of half an hour.
2 And I saw the seven angels which stood before God; and to them were given
seven trumpets.
3 And another angel came and stood at the altar, having a golden censer; and
there was given unto him much incense, that he should offer *it* with the
prayers of all saints upon the golden altar which was before the throne.
4 And the smoke of the incense, *which came* with the prayers of the saints,
ascended up before God out of the angel's hand.
5 And the angel took the censer, and filled it with fire of the altar, and cast *it*
into the earth: and there were voices, and thunderings, and lightnings, and
an earthquake.
6 And the seven angels which had the seven trumpets prepared themselves
to sound.

Four Angels Blow Their Trumpets

7 The first angel sounded, and there followed hail and fire mingled with
blood, and they were cast upon the earth: and the third part of trees was burnt
up, and all green grass was burnt up.
8 And the second angel sounded, and as it were a great mountain burning
with fire was cast into the sea: and the third part of the sea became blood;
9 And the third part of the creatures which were in the sea, and had life, died;
and the third part of the ships were destroyed.
10 And the third angel sounded, and there fell a great star from heaven, burn-
ing as it were a lamp, and it fell upon the third part of the rivers, and upon the
fountains of waters;
11 And the name of the star is called Wormwood: and the third part of the
waters became wormwood; and many men died of the waters, because they
were made bitter.
12 And the fourth angel sounded, and the third part of the sun was smitten,
and the third part of the moon, and the third part of the stars; so as the third
part of them was darkened, and the day shone not for a third part of it, and
the night likewise.
13 And I beheld, and heard an angel flying through the midst of heaven,
saying with a loud voice, Woe, woe, woe, to the inhabiters of the earth by
reason of the other voices of the trumpet of the three angels, which are yet to
sound!

Two More Trumpet Blasts

9 And the fifth angel sounded, and I saw a star fall from heaven unto the earth:
and to him was given the key of the bottomless pit.
2 And he opened the bottomless pit; and there arose a smoke out of the pit,
as the smoke of a great furnace; and the sun and the air were darkened by
reason of the smoke of the pit.
3 And there came out of the smoke locusts upon the earth: and unto them
was given power, as the scorpions of the earth have power.
4 And it was commanded them that they should not hurt the grass of the
earth, neither any green thing, neither any tree; but only those men which
have not the seal of God in their foreheads.
5 And to them it was given that they should not kill them, but that they should
be tormented five months: and their torment *was* as the torment of a scorpion,
when he striketh a man.
6 And in those days shall men seek death, and shall not find it; and shall desire
to die, and death shall flee from them.
7 And the shapes of the locusts *were* like unto horses prepared unto battle;
and on their heads *were* as it were crowns like gold, and their faces *were* as the
faces of men.
8 And they had hair as the hair of women, and their teeth were as *the teeth*
of lions.
9 And they had breastplates, as it were breastplates of iron; and the sound
of their wings *was* as the sound of chariots of many horses running to battle.
10 And they had tails like unto scorpions, and there were stings in their tails:
and their power *was* to hurt men five months.
11 And they had a king over them, *which is* the angel of the bottomless pit,
whose name in the Hebrew tongue *is* Abaddon, but in the Greek tongue hath
his name Apollyon.
12 One woe is past; *and*, behold, there come two woes more hereafter.
13 And the sixth angel sounded, and I heard a voice from the four horns of
the golden altar which is before God,
14 Saying to the sixth angel which had the trumpet, Loose the four angels
which are bound in the great river Euphrates.
15 And the four angels were loosed, which were prepared for an hour, and a
day, and a month, and a year, for to slay the third part of men.
16 And the number of the army of the horsemen *were* two hundred thousand
thousand: and I heard the number of them.
17 And thus I saw the horses in the vision, and them that sat on them, having
breastplates of fire, and of jacinth, and brimstone: and the heads of the hors-
es *were* as the heads of lions; and out of their mouths issued fire and smoke
and brimstone.
18 By these three was the third part of men killed, by the fire, and by the
smoke, and by the brimstone, which issued out of their mouths.
19 For their power is in their mouth, and in their tails: for their tails *were*
like unto serpents, and had heads, and with them they do hurt.
20 And the rest of the men which were not killed by these plagues yet repent-
ed not of the works of their hands, that they should not worship devils, and
idols of gold, and silver, and brass, and stone, and of wood: which neither can
see, nor hear, nor walk:
21 Neither repented they of their murders, nor of their sorceries, nor of their
fornication, nor of their thefts.

John Sees an Angel

10 And I saw another mighty angel come down from heaven, clothed with
a cloud: and a rainbow *was* upon his head, and his face *was* as it were
the sun, and his feet as pillars of fire:

2 And he had in his hand a little book open: and he set his right foot upon
the sea, and *his* left *foot* on the earth,
3 And cried with a loud voice, as *when* a lion roareth: and when he had cried,
seven thunders uttered their voices.
4 And when the seven thunders had uttered their voices, I was about to write:
and I heard a voice from heaven saying unto me, Seal up those things which
the seven thunders uttered, and write them not.
5 And the angel which I saw stand upon the sea and upon the earth lifted up
his hand to heaven,
6 And sware by him that liveth for ever and ever, who created heaven, and
the things that therein are, and the earth, and the things that therein are, and
the sea, and the things which are therein, that there should be time no longer:
7 But in the days of the voice of the seventh angel, when he shall begin to
sound, the mystery of God should be finished, as he hath declared to his serv-
ants the prophets.

John Eats the Book

8 And the voice which I heard from heaven spake unto me again, and said,
Go *and* take the little book which is open in the hand of the angel which
standeth upon the sea and upon the earth.
9 And I went unto the angel, and said unto him, Give me the little book. And
he said unto me, Take *it*, and eat it up; and it shall make thy belly bitter, but it
shall be in thy mouth sweet as honey.
10 And I took the little book out of the angel's hand, and ate it up; and it was
in my mouth sweet as honey: and as soon as I had eaten it, my belly was bitter.
11 And he said unto me, Thou must prophesy again before many peoples,
and nations, and tongues, and kings.

The Lord's Two Witnesses

11 And there was given me a reed like unto a rod: and the angel stood,
saying, Rise, and measure the temple of God, and the altar, and them
that worship therein.
2 But the court which is without the temple leave out, and measure it not;
for it is given unto the Gentiles: and the holy city shall they tread under foot
forty *and* two months.
3 And I will give *power* unto my two witnesses, and they shall prophesy a
thousand two hundred *and* threescore days, clothed in sackcloth.
4 These are the two olive trees, and the two candlesticks standing before the
God of the earth.
5 And if any man will hurt them, fire proceedeth out of their mouth, and
devoureth their enemies: and if any man will hurt them, he must in this man-
ner be killed.
6 These have power to shut heaven, that it rain not in the days of their proph-
ecy: and have power over waters to turn them to blood, and to smite the earth
with all plagues, as often as they will.
7 And when they shall have finished their testimony, the beast that ascendeth
out of the bottomless pit shall make war against them, and shall overcome
them, and kill them.
8 And their dead bodies *shall lie* in the street of the great city, which
spiritually is called Sodom and Egypt, where also our Lord was crucified.
9 And they of the people and kindreds and tongues and nations shall see
their dead bodies three days and an half, and shall not suffer their dead bod-
ies to be put in graves.
10 And they that dwell upon the earth shall rejoice over them, and make
merry, and shall send gifts one to another; because these two prophets tor-
mented them that dwelt on the earth.

11 And after three days and an half the Spirit of life from God entered into
them, and they stood upon their feet; and great fear fell upon them which saw
them.
12 And they heard a great voice from heaven saying unto them, Come up
hither. And they ascended up to heaven in a cloud; and their enemies beheld
them.
13 And the same hour was there a great earthquake, and the tenth part of
the city fell, and in the earthquake were slain of men seven thousand: and the
remnant were affrighted, and gave glory to the God of heaven.

Christ Shall Reign Forever

14 The second woe is past; *and*, behold, the third woe cometh quickly.
15 And the seventh angel sounded; and there were great voices in heaven,
saying, The kingdoms of this world are become *the kingdoms* of our Lord, and
of his Christ; and he shall reign for ever and ever.
16 And the four and twenty elders, which sat before God on their seats, fell
upon their faces, and worshipped God,
17 Saying, We give thee thanks, O Lord God Almighty, which art, and wast,
and art to come; because thou hast taken to thee thy great power, and hast
reigned.
18 And the nations were angry, and thy wrath is come, and the time of the
dead, that they should be judged, and that thou shouldest give reward unto
thy servants the prophets, and to the saints, and them that fear thy name, small
and great; and shouldest destroy them which destroy the earth.
19 And the temple of God was opened in heaven, and there was seen in his
temple the ark of his testament: and there were lightnings, and voices, and
thunderings, and an earthquake, and great hail.

Two Signs

12 And there appeared a great wonder in heaven; a woman clothed with
the sun, and the moon under her feet, and upon her head a crown of
twelve stars:
2 And she being with child cried, travailing in birth, and pained to be deliv-
ered.
3 And there appeared another wonder in heaven; and behold a great red
dragon, having seven heads and ten horns, and seven crowns upon his heads.
4 And his tail drew the third part of the stars of heaven, and did cast them
to the earth: and the dragon stood before the woman which was ready to be
delivered, for to devour her child as soon as it was born.
5 And she brought forth a man child, who was to rule all nations with a rod
of iron: and her child was caught up unto God, and *to* his throne.
6 And the woman fled into the wilderness, where she hath a place prepared
of God, that they should feed her there a thousand two hundred *and* three-
score days.
7 And there was war in heaven: Michael and his angels fought against the
dragon; and the dragon fought and his angels,
8 And prevailed not; neither was their place found any more in heaven.
9 And the great dragon was cast out, that old serpent, called the Devil, and
Satan, which deceiveth the whole world: he was cast out into the earth, and
his angels were cast out with him.
10 And I heard a loud voice saying in heaven, Now is come salvation, and
strength, and the kingdom of our God, and the power of his Christ: for the
accuser of our brethren is cast down, which accused them before our God day
and night.
11 And they overcame him by the blood of the Lamb, and by the word of
their testimony; and they loved not their lives unto the death.

12 Therefore rejoice, *ye* heavens, and ye that dwell in them. Woe to the inhab-
iters of the earth and of the sea! for the devil is come down unto you, having
great wrath, because he knoweth that he hath but a short time.
13 And when the dragon saw that he was cast unto the earth, he persecuted
the woman which brought forth the man *child*.
14 And to the woman were given two wings of a great eagle, that she might
fly into the wilderness, into her place, where she is nourished for a time, and
times, and half a time, from the face of the serpent.
15 And the serpent cast out of his mouth water as a flood after the woman,
that he might cause her to be carried away of the flood.
16 And the earth helped the woman, and the earth opened her mouth, and
swallowed up the flood which the dragon cast out of his mouth.
17 And the dragon was wroth with the woman, and went to make war with
the remnant of her seed, which keep the commandments of God, and have
the testimony of Jesus Christ.

A Beast from the Sea

13 And I stood upon the sand of the sea, and saw a beast rise up out of the
sea, having seven heads and ten horns, and upon his horns ten crowns,
and upon his heads the name of blasphemy.
2 And the beast which I saw was like unto a leopard, and his feet were as *the*
feet of a bear, and his mouth as the mouth of a lion: and the dragon gave him
his power, and his seat, and great authority.
3 And I saw one of his heads as it were wounded to death; and his deadly
wound was healed: and all the world wondered after the beast.
4 And they worshipped the dragon which gave power unto the beast: and
they worshipped the beast, saying, Who *is* like unto the beast? who is able to
make war with him?
5 And there was given unto him a mouth speaking great things and blasphe-
mies; and power was given unto him to continue forty *and* two months.
6 And he opened his mouth in blasphemy against God, to blaspheme his
name, and his tabernacle, and them that dwell in heaven.
7 And it was given unto him to make war with the saints, and to overcome
them: and power was given him over all kindreds, and tongues, and nations.
8 And all that dwell upon the earth shall worship him, whose names are not
written in the book of life of the Lamb slain from the foundation of the world.
9 If any man have an ear, let him hear.
10 He that leadeth into captivity shall go into captivity: he that killeth with
the sword must be killed with the sword. Here is the patience and the faith of
the saints.

A Beast from the Earth

11 And I beheld another beast coming up out of the earth; and he had two
horns like a lamb, and he spake as a dragon.
12 And he exerciseth all the power of the first beast before him, and causeth
the earth and them which dwell therein to worship the first beast, whose
deadly wound was healed.
13 And he doeth great wonders, so that he maketh fire come down from
heaven on the earth in the sight of men,
14 And deceiveth them that dwell on the earth by *the means of* those miracles
which he had power to do in the sight of the beast; saying to them that dwell
on the earth, that they should make an image to the beast, which had the
wound by a sword, and did live.
15 And he had power to give life unto the image of the beast, that the image
of the beast should both speak, and cause that as many as would not worship
the image of the beast should be killed.

16 And he causeth all, both small and great, rich and poor, free and bond, to
receive a mark in their right hand, or in their foreheads:
17 And that no man might buy or sell, save he that had the mark, or the name
of the beast, or the number of his name.
18 Here is wisdom. Let him that hath understanding count the number of
the beast: for it is the number of a man; and his number *is* Six hundred three-
score *and* six.

A New Song

14 And I looked, and, lo, a Lamb stood on the mount Sion, and with him
an hundred forty *and* four thousand, having his Father's name written
in their foreheads.
2 And I heard a voice from heaven, as the voice of many waters, and as the
voice of a great thunder: and I heard the voice of harpers harping with their
harps:
3 And they sung as it were a new song before the throne, and before the four
beasts, and the elders: and no man could learn that song but the hundred *and*
forty *and* four thousand, which were redeemed from the earth.
4 These are they which were not defiled with women; for they are virgins.
These are they which follow the Lamb whithersoever he goeth. These were
redeemed from among men, *being* the firstfruits unto God and to the Lamb.
5 And in their mouth was found no guile: for they are without fault before
the throne of God.

The Harvest of the Earth

6 And I saw another angel fly in the midst of heaven, having the everlasting
gospel to preach unto them that dwell on the earth, and to every nation, and
kindred, and tongue, and people,
7 Saying with a loud voice, Fear God, and give glory to him; for the hour of
his judgment is come: and worship him that made heaven, and earth, and the
sea, and the fountains of waters.
8 And there followed another angel, saying, Babylon is fallen, is fallen, that
great city, because she made all nations drink of the wine of the wrath of her
fornication.
9 And the third angel followed them, saying with a loud voice, If any man
worship the beast and his image, and receive *his* mark in his forehead, or in
his hand,
10 The same shall drink of the wine of the wrath of God, which is poured out
without mixture into the cup of his indignation; and he shall be tormented
with fire and brimstone in the presence of the holy angels, and in the presence
of the Lamb:
11 And the smoke of their torment ascendeth up for ever and ever: and they
have no rest day nor night, who worship the beast and his image, and whoso-
ever receiveth the mark of his name.
12 Here is the patience of the saints: here *are* they that keep the command-
ments of God, and the faith of Jesus.
13 And I heard a voice from heaven saying unto me, Write, Blessed *are* the
dead which die in the Lord from henceforth: Yea, saith the Spirit, that they
may rest from their labours; and their works do follow them.
14 And I looked, and behold a white cloud, and upon the cloud *one* sat like
unto the Son of man, having on his head a golden crown, and in his hand a
sharp sickle.
15 And another angel came out of the temple, crying with a loud voice to him
that sat on the cloud, Thrust in thy sickle, and reap: for the time is come for
thee to reap; for the harvest of the earth is ripe.
16 And he that sat on the cloud thrust in his sickle on the earth; and the earth
was reaped.

17 And another angel came out of the temple which is in heaven, he also
having a sharp sickle.
18 And another angel came out from the altar, which had power over fire;
and cried with a loud cry to him that had the sharp sickle, saying, Thrust in
thy sharp sickle, and gather the clusters of the vine of the earth; for her grapes
are fully ripe.
19 And the angel thrust in his sickle into the earth, and gathered the vine of
the earth, and cast *it* into the great winepress of the wrath of God.
20 And the winepress was trodden without the city, and blood came out of
the winepress, even unto the horse bridles, by the space of a thousand *and* six
hundred furlongs.

Seven Angels with Seven Plagues

15 And I saw another sign in heaven, great and marvellous, seven angels
having the seven last plagues; for in them is filled up the wrath of God.
2 And I saw as it were a sea of glass mingled with fire: and them that had
gotten the victory over the beast, and over his image, and over his mark, *and*
over the number of his name, stand on the sea of glass, having the harps of
God.
3 And they sing the song of Moses the servant of God, and the song of the
Lamb, saying, Great and marvellous *are* thy works, Lord God Almighty; just
and true *are* thy ways, thou King of saints.
4 Who shall not fear thee, O Lord, and glorify thy name? for *thou* only *art*
holy: for all nations shall come and worship before thee; for thy judgments
are made manifest.
5 And after that I looked, and, behold, the temple of the tabernacle of the
testimony in heaven was opened:
6 And the seven angels came out of the temple, having the seven plagues,
clothed in pure and white linen, and having their breasts girded with golden
girdles.
7 And one of the four beasts gave unto the seven angels seven golden vials
full of the wrath of God, who liveth for ever and ever.
8 And the temple was filled with smoke from the glory of God, and from his
power; and no man was able to enter into the temple, till the seven plagues of
the seven angels were fulfilled.

The Angels Pour out Their Bowls

16 And I heard a great voice out of the temple saying to the seven angels,
Go your ways, and pour out the vials of the wrath of God upon the
earth.
2 And the first went, and poured out his vial upon the earth; and there fell a
noisome and grievous sore upon the men which had the mark of the beast,
and *upon* them which worshipped his image.
3 And the second angel poured out his vial upon the sea; and it became as
the blood of a dead *man*: and every living soul died in the sea.
4 And the third angel poured out his vial upon the rivers and fountains of
waters; and they became blood.
5 And I heard the angel of the waters say, Thou art righteous, O Lord, which
art, and wast, and shalt be, because thou hast judged thus.
6 For they have shed the blood of saints and prophets, and thou hast given
them blood to drink; for they are worthy.
7 And I heard another out of the altar say, Even so, Lord God Almighty, true
and righteous *are* thy judgments.
8 And the fourth angel poured out his vial upon the sun; and power was given
unto him to scorch men with fire.
9 And men were scorched with great heat, and blasphemed the name of God,
which hath power over these plagues: and they repented not to give him glory.

10 And the fifth angel poured out his vial upon the seat of the beast; and his
kingdom was full of darkness; and they gnawed their tongues for pain,
11 And blasphemed the God of heaven because of their pains and their sores,
and repented not of their deeds.
12 And the sixth angel poured out his vial upon the great river Euphrates;
and the water thereof was dried up, that the way of the kings of the east might
be prepared.
13 And I saw three unclean spirits like frogs *come* out of the mouth of the
dragon, and out of the mouth of the beast, and out of the mouth of the false
prophet.
14 For they are the spirits of devils, working miracles, *which* go forth unto
the kings of the earth and of the whole world, to gather them to the battle of
that great day of God Almighty.
15 Behold, I come as a thief. Blessed *is* he that watcheth, and keepeth his
garments, lest he walk naked, and they see his shame.
16 And he gathered them together into a place called in the Hebrew tongue
Armageddon.
17 And the seventh angel poured out his vial into the air; and there came a
great voice out of the temple of heaven, from the throne, saying, It is done.
18 And there were voices, and thunders, and lightnings; and there was a great
earthquake, such as was not since men were upon the earth, so mighty an
earthquake, *and* so great.
19 And the great city was divided into three parts, and the cities of the nations
fell: and great Babylon came in remembrance before God, to give unto her the
cup of the wine of the fierceness of his wrath.
20 And every island fled away, and the mountains were not found.
21 And there fell upon men a great hail out of heaven, *every stone* about the
weight of a talent: and men blasphemed God because of the plague of the hail;
for the plague thereof was exceeding great.

Babylon the Great

17 And there came one of the seven angels which had the seven vials, and
talked with me, saying unto me, Come hither; I will shew unto thee
the judgment of the great whore that sitteth upon many waters:
2 With whom the kings of the earth have committed fornication, and the
inhabitants of the earth have been made drunk with the wine of her fornica-
tion.
3 So he carried me away in the spirit into the wilderness: and I saw a woman
sit upon a scarlet coloured beast, full of names of blasphemy, having seven
heads and ten horns.
4 And the woman was arrayed in purple and scarlet colour, and decked with
gold and precious stones and pearls, having a golden cup in her hand full of
abominations and filthiness of her fornication:
5 And upon her forehead *was* a name written, MYSTERY, BABYLON THE
GREAT, THE MOTHER OF HARLOTS AND ABOMINATIONS OF THE EARTH.
6 And I saw the woman drunken with the blood of the saints, and with the
blood of the martyrs of Jesus: and when I saw her, I wondered with great
admiration.
7 And the angel said unto me, Wherefore didst thou marvel? I will tell thee
the mystery of the woman, and of the beast that carrieth her, which hath the
seven heads and ten horns.
8 The beast that thou sawest was, and is not; and shall ascend out of the
bottomless pit, and go into perdition: and they that dwell on the earth shall
wonder, whose names were not written in the book of life from the foundation
of the world, when they behold the beast that was, and is not, and yet is.

9 And here *is* the mind which hath wisdom. The seven heads are seven moun-
tains, on which the woman sitteth.
10 And there are seven kings: five are fallen, and one is, *and* the other is not
yet come; and when he cometh, he must continue a short space.
11 And the beast that was, and is not, even he is the eighth, and is of the seven,
and goeth into perdition.
12 And the ten horns which thou sawest are ten kings, which have received
no kingdom as yet; but receive power as kings one hour with the beast.
13 These have one mind, and shall give their power and strength unto the
beast.

The Victory of the Lamb

14 These shall make war with the Lamb, and the Lamb shall overcome them:
for he is Lord of lords, and King of kings: and they that are with him *are* called,
and chosen, and faithful.
15 And he saith unto me, The waters which thou sawest, where the whore
sitteth, are peoples, and multitudes, and nations, and tongues.
16 And the ten horns which thou sawest upon the beast, these shall hate the
whore, and shall make her desolate and naked, and shall eat her flesh, and
burn her with fire.
17 For God hath put in their hearts to fulfil his will, and to agree, and give
their kingdom unto the beast, until the words of God shall be fulfilled.
18 And the woman which thou sawest is that great city, which reigneth over
the kings of the earth.

Babylon Falls

18 And after these things I saw another angel come down from heaven,
having great power; and the earth was lightened with his glory.
2 And he cried mightily with a strong voice, saying, Babylon the great is
fallen, is fallen, and is become the habitation of devils, and the hold of every
foul spirit, and a cage of every unclean and hateful bird.
3 For all nations have drunk of the wine of the wrath of her fornication, and
the kings of the earth have committed fornication with her, and the merchants
of the earth are waxed rich through the abundance of her delicacies.
4 And I heard another voice from heaven, saying, Come out of her, my peo-
ple, that ye be not partakers of her sins, and that ye receive not of her plagues.
5 For her sins have reached unto heaven, and God hath remembered her
iniquities.
6 Reward her even as she rewarded you, and double unto her double accord-
ing to her works: in the cup which she hath filled fill to her double.
7 How much she hath glorified herself, and lived deliciously, so much tor-
ment and sorrow give her: for she saith in her heart, I sit a queen, and am no
widow, and shall see no sorrow.
8 Therefore shall her plagues come in one day, death, and mourning, and
famine; and she shall be utterly burned with fire: for strong *is* the Lord God
who judgeth her.

Mourning for Babylon

9 And the kings of the earth, who have committed fornication and lived
deliciously with her, shall bewail her, and lament for her, when they shall see
the smoke of her burning,
10 Standing afar off for the fear of her torment, saying, Alas, alas, that great
city Babylon, that mighty city! for in one hour is thy judgment come.
11 And the merchants of the earth shall weep and mourn over her; for no
man buyeth their merchandise any more:
12 The merchandise of gold, and silver, and precious stones, and of pearls,
and fine linen, and purple, and silk, and scarlet, and all thyine wood, and all

manner vessels of ivory, and all manner vessels of most precious wood, and
of brass, and iron, and marble,
13 And cinnamon, and odours, and ointments, and frankincense, and wine,
and oil, and fine flour, and wheat, and beasts, and sheep, and horses, and
chariots, and slaves, and souls of men.
14 And the fruits that thy soul lusted after are departed from thee, and all
things which were dainty and goodly are departed from thee, and thou shalt
find them no more at all.
15 The merchants of these things, which were made rich by her, shall stand
afar off for the fear of her torment, weeping and wailing,
16 And saying, Alas, alas, that great city, that was clothed in fine linen, and
purple, and scarlet, and decked with gold, and precious stones, and pearls!
17 For in one hour so great riches is come to nought. And every shipmaster,
and all the company in ships, and sailors, and as many as trade by sea, stood
afar off,
18 And cried when they saw the smoke of her burning, saying, What *city is*
like unto this great city!
19 And they cast dust on their heads, and cried, weeping and wailing, saying,
Alas, alas, that great city, wherein were made rich all that had ships in the sea
by reason of her costliness! for in one hour is she made desolate.
20 Rejoice over her, *thou* heaven, and *ye* holy apostles and prophets; for God
hath avenged you on her.
21 And a mighty angel took up a stone like a great millstone, and cast *it* into
the sea, saying, Thus with violence shall that great city Babylon be thrown
down, and shall be found no more at all.
22 And the voice of harpers, and musicians, and of pipers, and trumpeters,
shall be heard no more at all in thee; and no craftsman, of whatsoever craft
he be, shall be found any more in thee; and the sound of a millstone shall be
heard no more at all in thee;
23 And the light of a candle shall shine no more at all in thee; and the voice
of the bridegroom and of the bride shall be heard no more at all in thee: for
thy merchants were the great men of the earth; for by thy sorceries were all
nations deceived.
24 And in her was found the blood of prophets, and of saints, and of all that
were slain upon the earth.

The Heavenly Hosts Praise God

19 And after these things I heard a great voice of much people in heaven,
saying, Alleluia; Salvation, and glory, and honour, and power, unto the
Lord our God:
2 For true and righteous *are* his judgments: for he hath judged the great
whore, which did corrupt the earth with her fornication, and hath avenged
the blood of his servants at her hand.
3 And again they said, Alleluia. And her smoke rose up for ever and ever.
4 And the four and twenty elders and the four beasts fell down and wor-
shipped God that sat on the throne, saying, Amen; Alleluia.
5 And a voice came out of the throne, saying, Praise our God, all ye his serv-
ants, and ye that fear him, both small and great.
6 And I heard as it were the voice of a great multitude, and as the voice of
many waters, and as the voice of mighty thunderings, saying, Alleluia: for the
Lord God omnipotent reigneth.
7 Let us be glad and rejoice, and give honour to him: for the marriage of the
Lamb is come, and his wife hath made herself ready.
8 And to her was granted that she should be arrayed in fine linen, clean and
white: for the fine linen is the righteousness of saints.

9 And he saith unto me, Write, Blessed *are* they which are called unto the
marriage supper of the Lamb. And he saith unto me, These are the true sayings
of God.
10 And I fell at his feet to worship him. And he said unto me, See *thou do it*
not: I am thy fellowservant, and of thy brethren that have the testimony of
Jesus: worship God: for the testimony of Jesus is the spirit of prophecy.
11 And I saw heaven opened, and behold a white horse; and he that sat upon
him *was* called Faithful and True, and in righteousness he doth judge and
make war.
12 His eyes *were* as a flame of fire, and on his head *were* many crowns; and
he had a name written, that no man knew, but he himself.
13 And he *was* clothed with a vesture dipped in blood: and his name is called
The Word of God.
14 And the armies *which were* in heaven followed him upon white horses,
clothed in fine linen, white and clean.
15 And out of his mouth goeth a sharp sword, that with it he should smite
the nations: and he shall rule them with a rod of iron: and he treadeth the
winepress of the fierceness and wrath of Almighty God.
16 And he hath on *his* vesture and on his thigh a name written, KING OF
KINGS, AND LORD OF LORDS.
17 And I saw an angel standing in the sun; and he cried with a loud voice,
saying to all the fowls that fly in the midst of heaven, Come and gather your-
selves together unto the supper of the great God;
18 That ye may eat the flesh of kings, and the flesh of captains, and the flesh
of mighty men, and the flesh of horses, and of them that sit on them, and the
flesh of all *men, both* free and bond, both small and great.
19 And I saw the beast, and the kings of the earth, and their armies, gathered
together to make war against him that sat on the horse, and against his army.
20 And the beast was taken, and with him the false prophet that wrought
miracles before him, with which he deceived them that had received the mark
of the beast, and them that worshipped his image. These both were cast alive
into a lake of fire burning with brimstone.
21 And the remnant were slain with the sword of him that sat upon the horse,
which *sword* proceeded out of his mouth: and all the fowls were filled with
their flesh.

Satan Is Bound

20 And I saw an angel come down from heaven, having the key of the
bottomless pit and a great chain in his hand.
2 And he laid hold on the dragon, that old serpent, which is the Devil, and
Satan, and bound him a thousand years,
3 And cast him into the bottomless pit, and shut him up, and set a seal upon
him, that he should deceive the nations no more, till the thousand years should
be fulfilled: and after that he must be loosed a little season.
4 And I saw thrones, and they sat upon them, and judgment was given unto
them: and *I saw* the souls of them that were beheaded for the witness of Jesus,
and for the word of God, and which had not worshipped the beast, neither
his image, neither had received *his* mark upon their foreheads, or in their
hands; and they lived and reigned with Christ a thousand years.
5 But the rest of the dead lived not again until the thousand years were fin-
ished. This *is* the first resurrection.
6 Blessed and holy *is* he that hath part in the first resurrection: on such the
second death hath no power, but they shall be priests of God and of Christ,
and shall reign with him a thousand years.

The Final Judgment
7 And when the thousand years are expired, Satan shall be loosed out of his
prison,
8 And shall go out to deceive the nations which are in the four quarters of
the earth, Gog and Magog, to gather them together to battle: the number of
whom *is* as the sand of the sea.
9 And they went up on the breadth of the earth, and compassed the camp of
the saints about, and the beloved city: and fire came down from God out of
heaven, and devoured them.
10 And the devil that deceived them was cast into the lake of fire and brim-
stone, where the beast and the false prophet *are,* and shall be tormented day
and night for ever and ever.
11 And I saw a great white throne, and him that sat on it, from whose face
the earth and the heaven fled away; and there was found no place for them.
12 And I saw the dead, small and great, stand before God; and the books were
opened: and another book was opened, which is *the book* of life: and the dead
were judged out of those things which were written in the books, according
to their works.
13 And the sea gave up the dead which were in it; and death and hell delivered
up the dead which were in them: and they were judged every man according
to their works.
14 And death and hell were cast into the lake of fire. This is the second death.
15 And whosoever was not found written in the book of life was cast into the
lake of fire.

A New Heaven and a New Earth
21 And I saw a new heaven and a new earth: for the first heaven and the
first earth were passed away; and there was no more sea.
2 And I John saw the holy city, new Jerusalem, coming down from God out
of heaven, prepared as a bride adorned for her husband.
3 And I heard a great voice out of heaven saying, Behold, the tabernacle of
God *is* with men, and he will dwell with them, and they shall be his people,
and God himself shall be with them, *and be* their God.
4 And God shall wipe away all tears from their eyes; and there shall be no
more death, neither sorrow, nor crying, neither shall there be any more pain:
for the former things are passed away.
5 And he that sat upon the throne said, Behold, I make all things new. And
he said unto me, Write: for these words are true and faithful.
6 And he said unto me, It is done. I am Alpha and Omega, the beginning and
the end. I will give unto him that is athirst of the fountain of the water of life
freely.
7 He that overcometh shall inherit all things; and I will be his God, and he
shall be my son.
8 But the fearful, and unbelieving, and the abominable, and murderers, and
whoremongers, and sorcerers, and idolaters, and all liars, shall have their part
in the lake which burneth with fire and brimstone: which is the second death.

The New Jerusalem
9 And there came unto me one of the seven angels which had the seven vials
full of the seven last plagues, and talked with me, saying, Come hither, I will
shew thee the bride, the Lamb's wife.
10 And he carried me away in the spirit to a great and high mountain, and
shewed me that great city, the holy Jerusalem, descending out of heaven from
God,
11 Having the glory of God: and her light *was* like unto a stone most precious,
even like a jasper stone, clear as crystal;

12 And had a wall great and high, *and* had twelve gates, and at the gates twelve
angels, and names written thereon, which are *the names* of the twelve tribes
of the children of Israel:
13 On the east three gates; on the north three gates; on the south three gates;
and on the west three gates.
14 And the wall of the city had twelve foundations, and in them the names
of the twelve apostles of the Lamb.
15 And he that talked with me had a golden reed to measure the city, and the
gates thereof, and the wall thereof.
16 And the city lieth foursquare, and the length is as large as the breadth: and
he measured the city with the reed, twelve thousand furlongs. The length and
the breadth and the height of it are equal.
17 And he measured the wall thereof, an hundred *and* forty *and* four cubits,
according to the measure of a man, that is, of the angel.
18 And the building of the wall of it was *of* jasper: and the city *was* pure gold,
like unto clear glass.
19 And the foundations of the wall of the city *were* garnished with all manner
of precious stones. The first foundation *was* jasper; the second, sapphire; the
third, a chalcedony; the fourth, an emerald;
20 The fifth, sardonyx; the sixth, sardius; the seventh, chrysolite; the eighth,
beryl; the ninth, a topaz; the tenth, a chrysoprasus; the eleventh, a jacinth; the
twelfth, an amethyst.
21 And the twelve gates *were* twelve pearls; every several gate was of one pearl:
and the street of the city *was* pure gold, as it were transparent glass.
22 And I saw no temple therein: for the Lord God Almighty and the Lamb
are the temple of it.
23 And the city had no need of the sun, neither of the moon, to shine in it:
for the glory of God did lighten it, and the Lamb *is* the light thereof.
24 And the nations of them which are saved shall walk in the light of it: and
the kings of the earth do bring their glory and honour into it.
25 And the gates of it shall not be shut at all by day: for there shall be no night
there.
26 And they shall bring the glory and honour of the nations into it.
27 And there shall in no wise enter into it any thing that defileth, neither
whatsoever worketh abomination, or *maketh* a lie: but they which are written
in the Lamb's book of life.

Jesus Is Coming Soon

22 And he shewed me a pure river of water of life, clear as crystal, pro-
ceeding out of the throne of God and of the Lamb.
2 In the midst of the street of it, and on either side of the river, *was there* the
tree of life, which bare twelve *manner of* fruits, *and* yielded her fruit every
month: and the leaves of the tree *were* for the healing of the nations.
3 And there shall be no more curse: but the throne of God and of the Lamb
shall be in it; and his servants shall serve him:
4 And they shall see his face; and his name *shall be* in their foreheads.
5 And there shall be no night there; and they need no candle, neither light
of the sun; for the Lord God giveth them light: and they shall reign for ever
and ever.
6 And he said unto me, These sayings *are* faithful and true: and the Lord God
of the holy prophets sent his angel to shew unto his servants the things which
must shortly be done.
7 Behold, I come quickly: blessed *is* he that keepeth the sayings of the proph-
ecy of this book.

8 And I John saw these things, and heard *them*. And when I had heard and
seen, I fell down to worship before the feet of the angel which shewed me these
things.
9 Then saith he unto me, See *thou do it* not: for I am thy fellowservant, and
of thy brethren the prophets, and of them which keep the sayings of this book:
worship God.
10 And he saith unto me, Seal not the sayings of the prophecy of this book:
for the time is at hand.
11 He that is unjust, let him be unjust still: and he which is filthy, let him be
filthy still: and he that is righteous, let him be righteous still: and he that is
holy, let him be holy still.
12 And, behold, I come quickly; and my reward *is* with me, to give every man
according as his work shall be.
13 I am Alpha and Omega, the beginning and the end, the first and the last.
14 Blessed *are* they that do his commandments, that they may have right to
the tree of life, and may enter in through the gates into the city.
15 For without *are* dogs, and sorcerers, and whoremongers, and murderers,
and idolaters, and whosoever loveth and maketh a lie.
16 I Jesus have sent mine angel to testify unto you these things in the church-
es. I am the root and the offspring of David, *and* the bright and morning star.
17 And the Spirit and the bride say, Come. And let him that heareth say, Come.
And let him that is athirst come. And whosoever will, let him take the water
of life freely.
18 For I testify unto every man that heareth the words of the prophecy of
this book, If any man shall add unto these things, God shall add unto him the
plagues that are written in this book:
19 And if any man shall take away from the words of the book of this proph-
ecy, God shall take away his part out of the book of life, and out of the holy
city, and *from* the things which are written in this book.
20 He which testifieth these things saith, Surely I come quickly. Amen. Even
so, come, Lord Jesus.
21 The grace of our Lord Jesus Christ *be* with you all. Amen.

INDEX of Designed Scripture Verses

The OLD TESTAMENT

GENESIS

1:1 1
1-2 3
2:16-17 4
9:16 11
15:1 16
17:1 18
18:14 19
22:18 25
26:24 32
28:15 35
45:5 59
49:18 64
50:20 65

EXODUS

3:14 69
14:4 83
15:2 85
19:5 90
20 92
20:12 67
23:20 96
34:6 111

LEVITICUS

19:18 148
20:26 150
26:12 158
27:30 122

NUMBERS

6:25-26 162
14:18 184
23:19 198

DEUTERONOMY

6:5 218
4:24 224
6:7 227
7:9 228
8:3 229
10:12 232
13:4 235
28:2 252
31:8 258

JOSHUA

1:9 264
3:5 266
6:16 269
23:14 293
24:15 294

JUDGES

2:1 297
5:31 302
6:12 296
16:28 318

RUTH

1:16 327
2:12 328
4:15 330

1 SAMUEL

2:1 333
3:10 335
7:12 339
12:16 344
12:24 345
16:7 332
17:47 354
30:6 370

2 SAMUEL

6:14 373
7:22 381
22:29 402
22:33 403
23:3 404

1 KINGS

2:3 409
8:23 407
8:27 420
8:56 422
17:24 436
18:39 438
19:12 439

2 KINGS

6:16 454
13:23 465
17:39 471
20:5 447
23:2 479

1 CHRONICLES

4:10 488
16:11 484
16:34 505
17:20 506
22:19 511
28:9 517
29:11 519

2 CHRONICLES

1:7 521
7:14 .... 528, 529
15:7 537
20:15 542
20:17 543
32:8 557

EZRA

3:11 568
7:10 572
10:4 565

NEHEMIAH

4:14 581
8:10 .... 578, 587
9:17 588
13:31 595

ESTHER

4:14 596
8:16 603

JOB

1:21 607
5:8 609
8:21 612
10:12 614
12:10 615
13:15 616
19:25 606
31:1 629
38:4 636
42:2 640

PSALMS

8:1 ... 645
18:2 ... 649
19:1 ... 651
23:1 ... 654
27:1 ... 656
37:4-5 ... 662
46:10 ... 668
51:10 ... 671
96:1 ... 698
118:24 ... 711
119:105 ... 715
135:3 ... 642

PROVERBS

3:5 ... 729
4:23 ... 732
16:3 ... 743
18:10 ... 745
21:2 ... 747
24:3 ... 750
31:25 ... 757
31:30 ... 758

ECCLESIASTES

3:1 ... 761
4:9-10 ... 759
9:10 ... 766
12:13 ... 768

THE SONG OF SOLOMON

2:4 ... 769
6:3 ... 772
8:7 ... 773

ISAIAH

1:18 ... 775
7:14 ... 774
9:6 ... 782
12:2 ... 785
25:1 ... 795
40:31 ... 810
41:10 ... 811
43:1 ... 813
53:5 ... 823

JEREMIAH

10:10 ... 847
15:16 ... 853
17:7 ... 855
20:9 ... 858
20:11 ... 859
32:17 ... 835
33:3 ... 875

LAMENTATIONS

2:19 ... 903
3:24 ... 906
5:21 ... 908

EZEKIEL

1:6 ... 909
11:19 ... 919
22:30 ... 935
36:26 ... 953

DANIEL

3:18 ... 976
4:3 ... 977
6:26 ... 982
6:27 ... 972
7:14 ... 983

HOSEA

2:23 ... 992
12:6 ... 998
10:12 ... 991

JOEL

2:13 ... 1000
2:28 ... 1002

AMOS

4:13 ... 1006
5:14 ... 1007
5:24 ... 1004

OBADIAH

1:15 ... 1012

JONAH

1:17 1014
2:2 1015

MICAH

6:8 1017
7:8 1021
7:19 1022

NAHUM

1:3 1024
1:7 1023

HABAKKUK

2:14 1027
3:19 1026

ZEPHANIAH

2:3 1030
3:17 1029

HAGGAI

1:7 1032
2:9 1033

ZECHARIAH

4:6 .... 1034, 1036
7:9 1038
9:9 1040
13:9 1043

MALACHI

3:6 1047
4:2 1045

The NEW TESTAMENT

SAINT MATTHEW

4:19 1054
5:3-10 1056
5:16 1055
6:9-13 1059
6:33 1060
7:7 1061
10:32 1065
11:28 1051
16:18 1074
19:14 1078
22:37 1084
24:35 1087
28:6 1095
28:19 1096

SAINT MARK

5:36 1104
8:34 1109
9:23 1110
10:9 1112
13:26 1118
15:39 1122
16:15 1097

SAINT LUKE

1:45 1125
2:11 1127
2:14 1128
4:18 1132
6:36 1136
9:23 1124
12:27 1149

SAINT JOHN

3:16 .... 1171, 1175
6:35 1181
8:12 1184
14:1 1194
14:6 1195
16:33 1197

ACTS

2:38 1207
5:29 1211
16:31 1229
17:28 1231
20:35 1236
26:17-18 1205

ROMANS

3:23 1248
5:8 1252
6:23 1254
8:28 1256
10:13 1258
12:1 1260

1 CORINTHIANS

2:9 1266
4:20 1268
6:20 1269
10:31 1274
11:26 1265
15:58 1280

2 CORINTHIANS

4:18 1285
5:17 1282
12:9 1291

GALATIANS

2:20 1294
5:22-23 .... 1293, 1298
6:10 1299

EPHESIANS

2:8 1300
2:10 1301
4:32 1303
6:12 1305
6:14-17 1306

PHILIPPIANS

4:6 1310
4:8 1311
4:13 1307

COLOSSIANS

3:14 1314
3:23 1312

1 THESSALONIANS

5:16-18 1319
5:18 1316

2 THESSALONIANS

3:3 1321
3:16 1320

1 TIMOTHY

2:5 1322
4:12 1324
6:12 1326

2 TIMOTHY

1:7 1328
3:16 1329
4:7 1327

TITUS

2:13 1331
3:5 1332

PHILEMON

1:3 1333

HEBREWS

4:4 1336
4:12 1337
6:19 1338
11:1 1342
12:2 1334
13:8 1345

JAMES

1:17 1348
1:22 1347

1 PETER

3:15 1354
5:7 1352

2 PETER

3:9 1359
3:18 1357

1 JOHN

1:9 1360
3:16 1362
4:4 1363

2 JOHN

1:6 1365

3 JOHN

1:4 1366

JUDE

1:2 1368
1:24-25 1367

REVELATION

1:8 1370
3:20 1369
4:11 1372
5:13 1373

DESIGNED WORD ART

Blessing 172
Courage 276
Cross 1168
Endurance 1273
Faith 24
Forgiven 1154
Grace 1388
Hope 830
Joy 677
Love 871
Mercy 144
Patience 664
Peace 624
Perseverance 1313
Prayer 1351
Provision 86
Purpose 787
Strength 498
Truth 1220
Wisdom 735

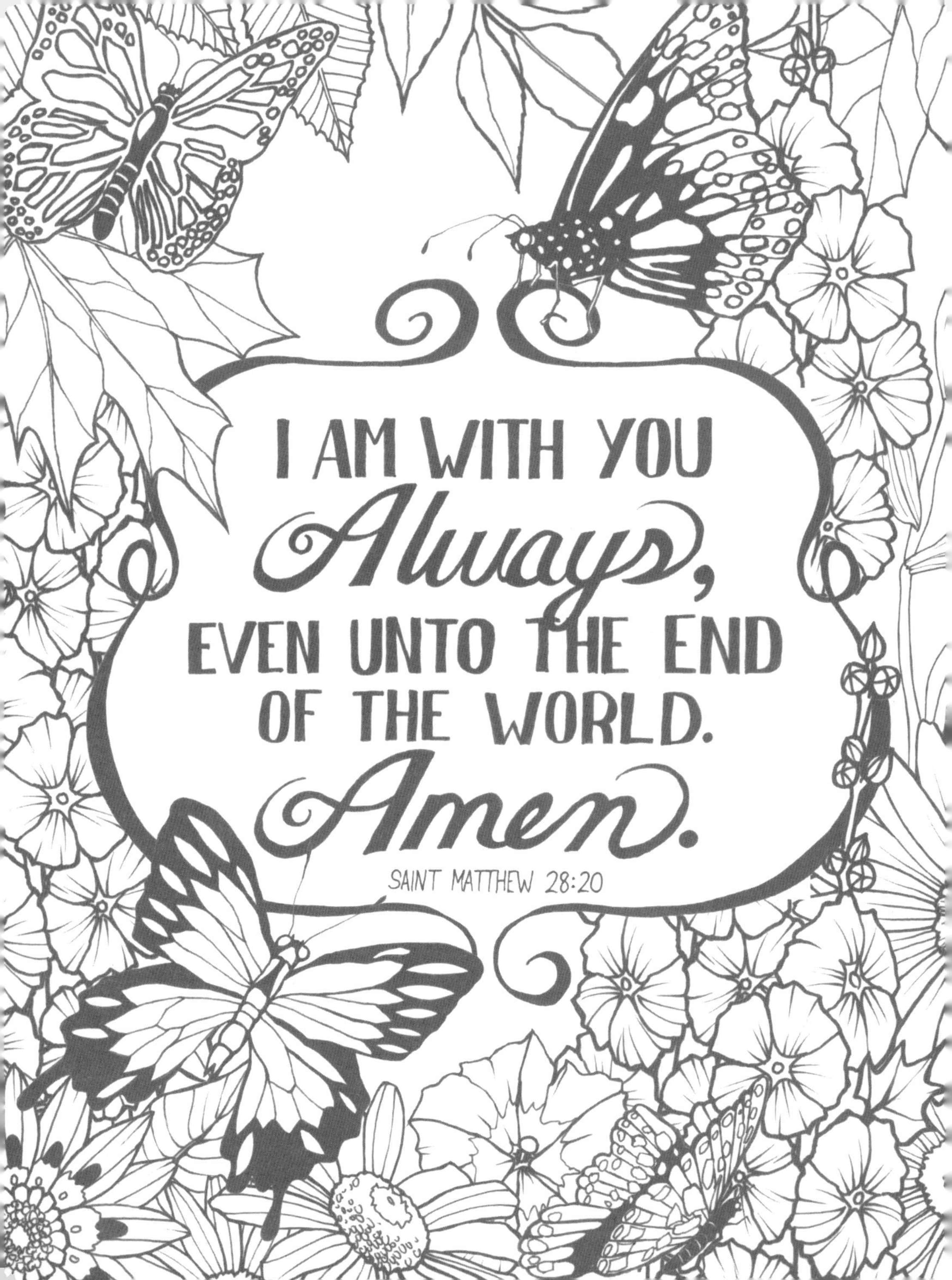
I AM WITH YOU
Always,
EVEN UNTO THE END
OF THE WORLD.
Amen.
SAINT MATTHEW 28:20